D1568673

PHILIP HERSHKOVITZ is curator emeritus, Mammal Division, of the Field Museum of Natural History in Chicago. He has written over 200 scientific articles and is a member of many national and international learned societies.

Living New World Monkeys
(Platyrrhini)

Living New World Monkeys (Platyrrhini)

With an Introduction to Primates
Volume 1

Philip Hershkovitz

The University of Chicago Press
Chicago and London

Philip Hershkovitz is curator emeritus, Mammal
Division, Field Museum of Natural History,
Chicago.

The University of Chicago Press, Chicago 60637
The University of Chicago Press, Ltd., London

Printed in the United States of America

81 80 79 78 77 9 8 7 6 5 4 3 2 1

Library of Congress Cataloging in Publication Data

Hershkovitz, Philip.
Living New World monkeys (Platyrrhini).

Bibliography: p.
Includes index.
1. Callitrichidae. 2. Callimiconidae.
3. Mammals—Latin America. I. Title.
QL737.P92H47 599′.82 75–9059
ISBN 0–226–32788–4

To The Memory of
My Wife—
Anne Marie

Contents

Preface

This volume was begun in 1965 with the stated objective of providing taxonomists and others with a means for making unequivocal identification of all known living callitrichids and callimiconids. It seemed at first that classical taxonomic methods based mainly on skins and skulls would suffice, but it soon became obvious that so simple a treatment would be grossly derelict. The taxonomic revision, while still in midstream, was inundated by an unprecedented flood of publications and republications on callitrichid morphology, odontology, genetics, neurology, pathology, virology, parasitology, behavior, serology, care, and maintenance. The wealth of new taxonomic information riding the wave could not be ignored. Parallel data on other primates and biological subjects borne by the same tide caused radical changes in the scope and tenor of the original research program. To accommodate the new data and new perspectives it was essential to add a broad foundation of primatology and platyrrhine morphology.

While new ideas were being developed for this book, I published a few preliminary papers dealing with old aggravating problems in callitrichid taxonomy and nomenclature. These appear to have satisfied immediate demands for a valid, universally acceptable nomenclature and for a taxonomy in harmony with sophisticated tests devised by biologists and biomedical investigators using callitrichids in research. Several other preliminary papers I published on theoretical subjects, mainly phylogenetic, also passed through critical reviews. They established a background that will permit easier comprehension of the present expanded and revised versions of the original concepts.

Living New World monkeys are more primitively structured than Old World monkeys, living or fossil. They fill the gap between the more monkeylike prosimians and primitive catarrhines and overlap with them. This broad span of evolutionary sequence makes living platyrrhines particularly attractive for studies of critical stages not preserved in lines leading to modern primates. The most primitive platyrrhines are the callitrichids and callimiconids. Except for their advanced visual system and the cranial modifications it entails, they are among the most generalized of living primates.

The book is arranged in three parts. The first includes a brief history and a definition, characterization, and comparison of Primates as a taxonomic unit. Distinctive characters of the major subdivisions of the order are also discussed and compared, with principal emphasis on New World monkeys. Recent advances in the knowledge of earth history and the biological implications of continental drift made it feasible to discuss platyrrhine centers of origin, evolution, and dispersal in other lights than those of Matthewian orthodoxy. The shift in focus hardly brightens the scene, but it helps penetrate the fog of contradictions born of old dogmas.

The second part of the book deals with New World monkeys from comparative anatomical and evolutionary points of view. Whereas representatives of various orders of mammals were compared with primates in part I, the morphological and comparative studies of part II were based on virtually all known genera of living primates.

The most conspicuous and perhaps most important specific primate characters are those that permit individuals to recognize members of their own family and race. They are mainly superficial or display characters of color and pelage patterns, vocalizations and other auditory signals, odor, posture, movement, general behavior, and doubtless other traits unperceived by or meaningless to strange species. These essentially social or bonding characters, the most important for survival of the family group and species, are discussed in detail.

No less attention is paid to cranial morphology and evolution on generic, familial, and subordinal levels.

The importance of dental morphology in phylogenetic studies is reflected in the several chapters devoted to teeth. Dental usage among primates is mentioned, but the mechanics of mastication cannot be confidently inferred from teeth and jaws only. Terms used for most of the forty to fifty dental elements recognized or described here are not new. They were coined through the decades as needed by a variety of workers to supplement the meager and mostly inappropriate terms of the classic Cope-Osborn system.

An interesting by-product of the dental studies was the tabulation of dental and periodontal diseases and aberrations among callitrichids. It appears that these vary independently according to individual and locality.

Primate locomotor patterns are among the most diversified of all mammals and are diagnostic for families, genera, and in many cases for species. Because of limitations of time and space, monographic treatment of the skeletal components of the locomotor system was omitted. Nonetheless, attention is paid in this volume to structure and function of hands and feet. In addition, information on limb ratios, vertebrae, and pelvis and a chapter on locomotion compensate in a small way for absence of a treatise on the postcranial skeleton.

Studies of the central nervous system, a rich and extraordinarily reliable indicator of evolutionary grade and systematic position of primate genera and families, were slighted, mainly for lack of competence and the time to acquire it. Other soft internal systems and organs provided comparatively little information of taxonomic value on the generic and family levels. Actually, internal organs of New World monkeys have been poorly studied. A complete and accurate anatomy of a callitrichid or callimiconid remains to be done. Beattie's (1927) limited dissections of *Callithrix jacchus jacchus* are still the best single sources of reference.

Parasites sometimes cast strong light on ancient faunal histories and relationships only intimated by the fossil record. Unhappily, they prove to be disappointing interpreters of platyrrhine history, mainly because of their own taxonomic disarray. Nothwithstanding, the list of New World monkey parasites compiled for this volume is by far the most comprehensive ever made.

The third, final, and most extensive part of the volume is devoted to the taxonomy and biology of the family Callitrichidae, comprising marmosets and tamarins, and the family Callimiconidae, represented by the callimico only. A fossil record of the families does not exist. The hundreds of bona fide collecting localities and personal sight records, however, made it possible to delineate the present distribution of each recognized kind of callitrichid and callimiconid and to reconstruct with a high degree of acumen the hypothetical centers of origin and dispersal routes of the genera and species.

The scientific management of large stocks of captive callitrichids used in research also resulted in the accumulation of abundant information on reproduction, growth, and development. It is now possible to reconstruct ontogeny among the better-known species from the proverbial glint in the paternal eye to litter production, parental care of young, and step-by-step growth to sexual maturity. Hardly anything is known, however, of embryonic development following placentation.

The information on callitrichid and callimiconid behavior was culled from virtually every published source and combined with much that was heretofore unpublished, including personal observations. Nearly all data were derived from captive animals. So little is known of the animals in the wild that even their sleeping quarters are yet to be discovered and described.

Those who estimate the value of scientific results by the number of mathematical operations used to obtain them may be disappointed with the descriptive methods preferred here for conveying a dynamic concept of animals, their parts, and their functions through time and space. Nevertheless, measurements are essential supports for biological or taxonomic conclusions based on quantitative characters. Most measurements recorded here are of limited or special use, but their value will increase as future compilations of comparable data make possible quantitative comparisons between all primate categories.

A few words are in order regarding the organization of the taxonomic sections. The synonymy preceding the descriptions of each family, genus, species, and subspecies summarizes the published taxonomic and biological history of the named animal or group. The names or name combinations in each synonymy are listed chronologically. The first name properly proposed according to the rules of the International Code of Zoological Nomenclature (1961) is the valid name and the one adopted in scientific work. The junior synonyms and their name combinations follow in chronological order. Misidentifications or invalid uses of names of the taxon in question are listed at the bottom of the synonymy. Records of hybrids, if any, follow. The precise spelling of each name in the literature is shown in the synonymy, together with author, date of publication, bibliographic reference, and annotation of the publication's content. The reader will find practically all the relevant older literature cited in the synonymy or in the text. He is advised to check the index for all page references to the names of animals used in earlier publications, including the pre-Linnaean.

Authors cited in text are listed alphabetically with their bibliographical references in the section Literature Cited. Over 1,500 works are included. These, together with unduplicated bibliographic references in the aforementioned synonymies, make a total of more than 2,500 published sources of information. The few works cited in the synonymies but not available for consultation are so indicated in text.

A gazetteer with essential geographic data for every collecting locality mentioned in the taxonomic accounts is provided at the end of the volume. The name of the collector and the date of collection of every monkey recorded or examined is included with the locality data. Well over seven hundred localities are listed, more than in any previously published gazetteer for neotropical animals.

Conservation is a pressing problem in modern studies of wildlife. I have skirted the subject to avoid becoming involved with complex situations beyond the scope of the book. But much of the information sought for arriving at solutions to the problems is inevitably a part of the present study.

When this monograph was delivered to the University of Chicago Press in June 1973, it was not with the expectation that it could be published the same year. The manuscript was constantly revised and updated nearly to press time in 1975. Coverage of the literature published since 1974, however, became progressively more restricted depending on availability and subject matter.

Some aspects of primate evolution and morphology omitted or inadequately treated here will be included in another volume, in preparation. Extinct platyrrhines, known since the Oligocene, are being monographed separately.

The uneven treatment in depth or breadth given the various subjects is a measure of my interest, knowledge, or competence in the particular fields or the extent to which they contributed to the fulfillment of my two primary objectives. The first of these is investigation into the origin, evolution, dispersal, and interrelationships of New World monkeys. The second is the definition and treatment of primates as wild mammals with no other destiny than living in harmony with nature.

Material and Acknowledgments

This monograph was based primarily on studies of preserved specimens of Primates and other mammals housed in the Field Museum of Natural History. Additional preserved material was studied in or borrowed from the institutions listed below with the abbreviations used for them in the text. The number of callitrichids examined in each institution or made available to me through loans is shown in parentheses. Individuals in charge of the collections in the sister museums are also named as a formal note of appreciation for the courtesies shown me.

- AMNH = American Museum of Natural History (629); Dr. Richard G. Van Gelder, Dr. Sidney Anderson
- BM = British Museum (Natural History) (250); Dr. Gordon Barclay Corbett, John Eric Hill
- CM = Carnegie Museum (27); Dr. J. Kenneth Doutt
- FMNH = Field Museum of Natural History (428)
- GEE = G. E. Erickson Collection (12); Dr. G. E. Erickson, Brown University
- ICN = Instituto de Ciencias Naturales, Universidad Nacional, Bogotá (2); Dr. Jorge Hernández Camacho
- MCNM = Museo de Ciencias Naturales, Madrid (3); Professor Rafael Alvarado, Universidad de Madrid
- MCZ = Museum of Comparative Zoology, Harvard University (6); Dr. Barbara Lawrence
- MNHN = Muséum National d'Histoire Naturelle, Paris (61); Dr. Jean Dorst
- NHMW = Naturhistorisches Museum, Vienna (4)
- RMNH = Rijksmuseum van Natuurlijke Historie, Leiden (71); Dr. A. M. Husson
- SMNH = Natur-Museum und Forschungs-Institut Senckenberg, Frankfurt am Main (39); Dr. Heinz Felten
- UIMNH = University of Illinois Natural History Museum (1); Dr. Donald F. Hoffmeister
- UMMZ = University of Michigan Museum of Zoology (12); Dr. William H. Burt and Dr. Emmet T. Hooper
- USNM = United States National Museum (230); Dr. Charles O. Handley, Jr., Dr. John R. Napier, Dr. Richard W. Thorington, Jr.

The total number of museum-preserved callitrichids examined is over 3,100. The preserved specimens of cebids, catarrhines, prosimians, and other mammals used in the comparisons, diagnoses, and analytical descriptions number in the uncounted thousands. I routinely verified the identification and validity of scientific names of all material examined.

I am also beholden to the following individuals for permission to study a total of approximately 600 living callitrichids and callimiconids maintained in zoos and laboratories:

Dr. Jean Deinhardt and Dr. Friedrich Deinhardt, Rush–Presbyterian–Saint Luke's Medical Center, Chicago, Illinois. Their unstinted cooperation and their contributions of scores of dead specimens from their callitrichid colonies, together with photographs, including X rays, were an enormous boon for which I cannot express adequate thanks.

Dr. Robert W. Cooper, Primate Research Colony, Institute for Comparative Biology, San Diego Zoological Society, San Diego, California.

Dr. Lester Fisher and Saul Kitchener, Lincoln Park Zoo, Chicago, Illinois.

Dr. N. Gengozian, Marmoset Research Center, Medical Division, Oak Ridge Associated Universities, Oak Ridge, Tennessee.

Dr. Clyde A. Hill, Zoological Society, San Diego, California.

Dr. Barnet Levy, Dr. John K. Hampton, Jr., and Dr. Suzanne H. Hampton, Institute of Dental Science, University of Texas, Houston, Texas.

Dr. George Rabb and Dr. W. Peter Crowcroft, Brookfield Zoo, Chicago Zoological Society, Brookfield Illinois.

Dr. Wilhelm Windecker and Miss Uta Hick, Cologne Zoo, Germany.

In addition to the above I have observed thousands of callitrichids (not to mention cebids) in the wild during my eleven years of intensive fieldwork in South America.

The considerable number of fossil primates I used in this study includes the following from tropical America made available by the individuals and institutions mentioned.

Remains of the Colombian La Venta primates of the genera *Cebupithecia, Neosaimiri* and *Stirtonia,* now in the Museum of Paleontology, University of California (Berkeley), were kindly lent to me for study by Dr. Reuben A. Stirton, shortly before his untimely death in 1966, and by Dr. William A. Clemens, who allowed me to keep the material until this monograph was completed. Some fragments of *Homunculus* from the original Ameghino collection, and the type of *Dolichocebus gaimanensis* Kraglievich, were graciously sent to me for examination by authorities of the Museo Argentino de Ciencias Naturales "Bernardino Rivadavia." I am particularly grateful to Dr. Max Birabén, director of the Argentine Museum, Dr. Guillermo del Corro of the Department of Paleontology, and Dr. Jorge A. Crespo of the Department of Mammals. The type of *Homunculus harringtoni* Rusconi (= *Tremacebus harringtoni*), preserved in the Instituto Miguel Lillo in Tucumán, Argentina, was lent for this review through the courtesy of Dr. C. C. Olrog and Dr. José Bonaparte. The authorities of the American Museum of Natural History permitted me to study and photograph the type of *Xenothrix mcgregori* Williams and Koopman, and they contributed a cast of the specimen to the Field Museum. For a cast of *Branisella boliviana* and permission to examine and photograph the collection of *Plesiadapis* remains in the Department of Paleontology, Muséum National d'Histoire Naturelle, Paris, I am indebted to Professor Robert Hoffstetter and Dr. Donald E. Russell.

Preliminary reports on various subjects and data developed for this monograph, with accompanying illustrations, were published in the following:

Evolution 22, no. 3 (1968): 556–78, 13 figures.

Folia Primatologia (Karger) 4, no. 5 (1966): 381–95, 4 figures; 12, no. 1 (1970): 1–37, 4 figures, 12 plates; 13, no. 2–3 (1970): 213–40, 8 figures; 21, no. 1 (1974): 1–35, 14 figures, 2 plates; 22, no. 4 (1974 [1975]): 237–42, 5 figures; 24, no. 2–3: 137–72, 14 figs.

Journal of Mammalogy 52, no. 3 (1971): 607–9, 1 figure.

American Journal of Physical Anthropology (Wistar Institute) 32, no. 3 (1970): 377–94, 5 plates.

Dental Morphology and Evolution, ed. A. A. Dahlberg, pp. 95–150 (Chicago: University of Chicago, Press, 1971), 17 figures.

Evolution, Mammals, and Southern Continents, ed. A. Keast, F. C. Erk, and B. Glass (New York: New York University Press, 1972), pp. 311–431, 16 figures.

The Field Museum staff photographers who made most of the original photographs of skulls and teeth are Homer V. Holdren (retired), Frederic Huysmans, and John Bayalis. Mr. Curtis Bean, graduate student in photography, School of the Art Institute of Chicago, helped complete the collection of original photographs. Most of them are included in the Atlas of Skulls (chapter 29).

Photographs of living animals contributed by individuals and by the New York Zoological Society, the Zoological Society of San Diego, the Jersey Zoological Park, Channel Islands, and the Cologne Zoo are acknowledged in their legends.

Most of the original illustrations were executed by E. John Pfiffner, Marion Pahl, and Field Museum staff artist Samuel Grove, and others. The color and black-and-white portraits, and most of the diagrams and diagrammatic figurines, are the work of Mr. Pfiffner. All artists shared in making the anatomical figures, maps, and so forth, but the talented and patient Mr. Samuel Grove did most of them as well as most of the labeling, alterations, and day-to-day corrections.

This book could not have been completed without the assistance and devoted help of the following people:

Valerie G. Connor, until 1974 my technical assistant, secretary, and stenographer, who learned all the intricacies of the monograph and was most responsible for its clean appearance and orderly march to the publisher.

Barbara Brown, a volunteer, later technical assistant, who faithfully performed through the years many of the time-consuming chores of checking data, helping prepare illustrations for publication, and seeing the manuscript through press.

Dr. Fernando Dias de Avila Pires, Museu Nacional, Rio de Janeiro, for substantial assistance and advice during his short sojourn in the United States.

Jeremy J. C. Mallinson, Jersey Zoological Park, Channel Islands, for information on callitrichid breeding in the Jersey Zoo, and for excellent photographs.

Dr. Federico Medem, Centro de Investigaciones Biológicas, Villavicencio, Colombia, for field data.

Dr. Eustorgio Méndez, Gorgas Memorial Institute of Tropical and Preventive Medicine, Panamá, for drawings reproduced in figure III.29.

Dr. Vernon J. Tipton, formerly chief of the Environmental Health Branch, United States Army Caribbean, Fort Amador, Canal Zone, for field data.

Michael Dode and Mark Alan Hershkovitz, my teenage sons, who grew up with the manuscript and performed nearly every chore connected with it except write plot.

Anne Marie Pierrette Hershkovitz, my wife, without whose assistance this work could not have grown into its present dimensions.

Research was aided by the National Cancer Institute, National Institutes of Health, contract PH 43–65–1040, and National Science Foundation grant GB–30866. The National Library of Medicine, National Institutes of Health, Department of Health, Education and Welfare, grant LM 00563–01, supported final preparation of the manuscript for press and provided financial assistance for publication of this volume.

Corrigenda

P. x, left, line 8 from bottom—after "space" insert: (q.v. Lorenz 1973)
P. 27, left, footnote 1, line 1—before "1965" insert: 1964;
P. 27, left, line 11—after "Manley 1966" insert: ; 1967
P. 37, fig. I.27 and line 1 of caption—for *"Pan"* read: *Chimpansee*
P. 45, right, line 7—before "also" insert: like Martin (1972*b*)
P. 48, line 2 from bottom—for "Carpenter 1973" read: Carpenter 1934
P. 60, left, line 3 from bottom for *"Galago (Euoticus) elegantulus"* read: *Euoticus elegantulus*
P. 60, right, line 12—after "jerboas" insert: (cf. Hatt 1932)
P. 62, right, line 4—after "(1970*a*)" insert: hip and thigh musculature by Uhlmann (1970),
P. 70, line 8 of caption to fig. III.2—after "(Oligocene)" add: The name *Parapithecus grangeri* was introduced by Simons in 1969 and used again in 1971 as a *nomen nudum*. Simons's mention of the name in 1972, however, was accompanied by a valid description according to rules of the International Code of Zoological Nomenclature (1961). A complete and formal description of the species under the name *Parapithecus grangeri* was finally published by Simons in 1974 (Postilla, no. 166). The holotype is the left mandibular ramus with pm_3–m_3, CGM (Cairo Geological Museum) no. 23954. Isolated front teeth that appear in the figure and were used in the reconstruction are among the paratypes.
P. 72, right, line 3 from bottom—for "1927" read: 1937
P. 81, right, line 3 above caption—for "1958" read: 1955
P. 85, left, line 2 from bottom—after "255" add: and see also Beddard (1902)
P. 86, left line 27 from bottom—after "man" insert: although usually denied (cf. Winkelmann 1959, p. 403)
P. 86, right, paragraph 3, line 3—for "Montagna (1962)" read: Montagna (1962; 1972)
P. 90, left, line 19 from bottom—for *"Pan satyrus"* read: *Chimpansee troglodytes*
P. 90, left, lines 6–5 from bottom—for *"Pongo satyrus"* read: *Pongo pygmaeus*
P. 100, left, line 14 from bottom—after "1965" add: also Mainardi, Marsan, and Pasquale)
P. 104, right, line 3—after "263" insert: ; 1922, p. 337)
P. 121, left, line 4—after "chicks," insert: (cf. Massengale and Nussmeier 1930)
P. 127, right, line 29—after "some" insert: colobines (cf. Groves 1970), some
P. 130, left, lines 9 and 5 from bottom—for *"Pan"* read: *Chimpansee*
P. 143, right, last line—after "process" add: (see also Loo 1973).
P. 152, right, line 8—after "see," insert: Ehara 1969; and
P. 166, left, line 4 from bottom—after "gibbons" insert: (see also Edinger and Kitts 1954, with respect to ungulates.
P. 177, fig. IV.65, lower right—for *"Cacajao rubicundus"* read: *Cacajao calvus rubicundus*
P. 183, table 6, line 26 from bottom—for *"Cacajao rubicundus"* read: *Cacajao calvus rubicundus*
P. 184, table 6, last 3 lines—for *"Pan"* read: *Chimpansee*
P. 184, lines 1, 2, and 3 from bottom—for *"Pan"* read: *Chimpansee*
P. 185, fig. IV.72, from heading—delete: "Primate." In "Key," no. 5—for *"goeldi"* read: *goeldii*. In "Key," nos. 21, 23—for *"Pan"* read: *Chimpansee*
P. 187, left, line 14—before "Lay" insert: Hooper (1968) and
P. 296, right, line 19 from bottom—after "1941" insert: ; 1967
P. 318, table 10—for *"Saguinus graellsi"* read: *Saguinus nigricollis graellsi*
P. 346, right, line 20 from bottom—after "383" insert: , 1967
P. 359, right, line 16 from bottom—to end of paragraph add: Compare this with the "progression indices" of Stephan and Andy (1969).
P. 365, right, line 15—for "21" read: about 27
P. 366, left, line 6 to end of paragraph—add: See also Stephan and Andy (1969)
P. 369, right, line 33—after "SV 40" add: [cf. Ushijima, Shininger, and Gardner 1966; Ushijima, Gardner, and Cate 1966]
P. 370, left, line 10 from bottom—for *"Pan"* read: *Chimpansee*
P. 371, left line 28—for "1972" read: 1973
P. 373, line 8 from bottom (footnote 4) after "Trinidad" add: [cf. Downs, Spence, Aitken, and Whitman 1961].
P. 374, right, line 8—for "Mirovic" read: Mirkovic
P. 375, left, line 5—after "1969;" insert: 1970;
P. 375, left, line 7—for "VSU-Indiana" read: VSV-Indiana
P. 375, left, line 10 from bottom—after "1973" add:

; Kawakami, Buckley, Huff, McKain, and Fielding 1973

P. 375, right, line 2—after "Theilen," insert: Gordon,

P. 375, right, line 9—before "F. Deinhardt . . ." insert: Holmes, Wolfe, Rosenblate, and Deinhardt 1969

P. 375, right, line 18—after "Holmes, Capps, and Deinhardt 1965," add: Holmes and Deinhardt 1965;

P. 375, right, line 24—for "(1970)" read: (1969; 1970)

P. 381, right, line 36—change to read: Marinkelle (1966) and Marinkelle and Grose (1968) report

P. 382, left, line 25—after "cf." insert: Warren 1970;

P. 385, left, line 15—after "See" insert: Premvati [1959], and

P. 389, right, line 19—for "Salcedo" read: Rengifo Salcedo

P. 391, right, line 16—after "See" insert: Hull 1970; and

P. 391, right, line 22—after "Kohls" insert: 1944;

P. 403, left, line 15—from bottom before "1913*a*" insert: 1907

P. 419, table 41—for *"Saguinus graellsi"* read: *Saguinus nigricollis graellsi*

P. 501, line 20 from bottom—after "wall." add: Miraglia, Santana Moura, and Santos, 1976, *Acta Anat.* 96(4): 547—histoenzymologic differences between parotid, paramandibular, and submandibular glands.

P. 502, line 20—for "Slick" read: Sick

P. 512, line 9 from bottom—for "18:161" read: 118:161

P. 513, line 8—for "8:28" read 3:28

P. 513, line 10—for "Moura" read: Santana Moura

P. 513, line 11—for "Moura" read: Santana Moura

P. 513, line 13—after glands add: Spatz and Erdmann 1974, *Brain Research* 82:91—striate cortex projections to thalamic nuclei traced by degeneration and autoradiographic methods.

P. 513, line 14—for "Moura" read: Santana Moura

P. 513, line 21—after "amorphous." add: Scheffrahn, 1976, *J. Med. Primat.* (1975), 4(6):383—red cell enzymes and serum proteins (abstract). Miraglia, Sadigursky, and Roters, 1976, *Acta Anat.* 94:237—histochemistry of adrenal glands. Miraglia, Costa Nery, and Costa Guedes, 1976 *Acta Anat.* 96(1):97—histochemistry of volar surfaces (eccrine sweat glands, papillary nerve end organs, Meissner end organs). Miraglia, Santana Moura, and Santos, 1976, *Acta Anat.* 96(4):547—histozygomologic differences between parotid, paramandibular and submandibular glands.

P. 514, line 3 from bottom—for "Keleven" read: Kelemen

P. 621, line 10—for "75:37" read: 73:37

P. 648, line 2—after "6–31 days." add: Gengozian, 1976, *J. Med. Primat.* (1975), 4(6):383—identification of leucocyte antigens by isoimmunization (abstract)

P. 654, line 14—after "pattern" add: Gengozian, 1976, *J. Med. Primat.* (1975), 4(6):383—identification of leucocyte antigens by isoimmunization (abstract)

P. 706, fig. X.46—for "British Guiana" read: Guyana

P. 758, line 25—for "Knouf" read: Knouff

P. 762, line 5—for "Sylvester" read: Silvester

P. 763, line 11—for "Janitsche" read: Janitschke

P. 764, line 15—after "cortex." add: Gengozian, 1976, *J. Med. Primate.* (1975), 4(6):383—identification of leucocyte antigens by isoimmunization (abstract)

P. 764, line 16 from bottom—for "Demoschowski" read: Dmochowski

P. 809, right, last line—for *"L. variegata"* read: *Varecia variegata*

P. 870, right, line 4 from bottom for *"endocallimico"* read: *endocallimici*

P. 921, right—shift line 9 from bottom to precede line 11 from bottom

P. 965, right, between lines 24 and 25 from bottom—enter bibliographic citation: Carpenter, Clarence Ray, and Durham, N. M., 1969. A preliminary description of suspensory behavior in nonhuman primates. *Proc. 2nd Internat. Congr. Primat. (1968)* 2:147–54. 7 figs.

P. 969, right, line 20 from bottom—for "Krantz" read: Kraintz

P. 975, right, between lines 28 and 29—insert: Hampton, J. K., Jr.; Rider, Linda J.; and Parmalee, Marian L. 1971. The significance of "diamine oxidase" and "histaminase" values in New and Old World primates. *Proc. 3rd Internat. Congr. Primate., Zurich, 1970* 2:95–101, 2 figs.

P. 986, left, line 3—for "66(13):1–3" read: 82(5):16, 2 pls.

P. 991, left, line 2 from bottom—for "Salcedo, S. R." read: Rengifo Salcedo, Santiago

P. 996, right—delete lines 8–11 from bottom

P. 998, right, line 26—for "Winkelman" read: Winkelmann

Part I
History and Evolutionary Biology

1 Origin, Evolution, and Definition

Primate Genesis

The earliest known placental mammals are represented by some very small isolated teeth (fig. I.1) more than 100 million years old, found in lower Cretaceous deposits near Forestburg, Texas (Patterson 1956, p. 13). The structure of these teeth indicates that they belonged to tiny shrewlike, insect-eating animals. A suite of three upper molars believed to be of the same species, to which the name *Pappotherium pattersoni* was given, measure about 3.5 mm in combined length (Turnbull 1971, p. 166). This dimension compares with upper molar row lengths of the smaller, but not the smallest, species of living shrews, bats, and mice. Their size and the shape of the reduced third molar indicate that the teeth of *Pappotherium* diverged from a therian stock with substantially smaller, more generalized molars.

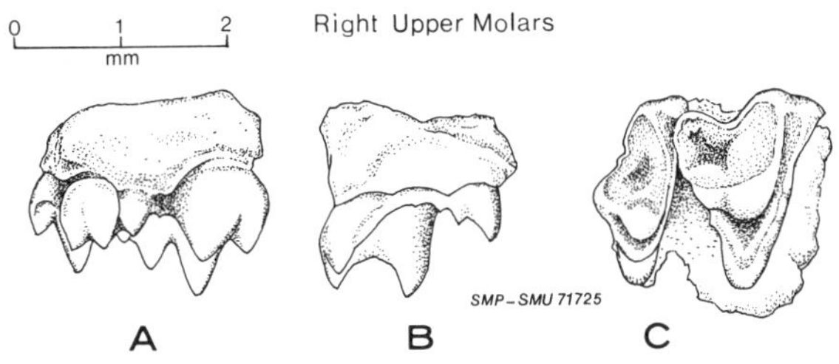

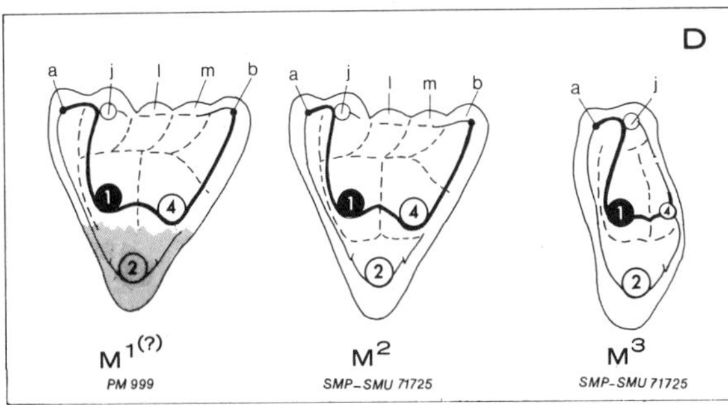

Fig. I.1. *Pappotherium pattersoni* Slaughter, 1965 (Pappotheriidae, Eutheria; Texas Albian, Lower Cretaceous): Right m^{2-3}, holotype (Shuler Museum of Paleontology, Southern Methodist University [SMP-SMU] no. 71725); figures copied from Slaughter 1965, p. 5. A, buccal aspect; B, anterior aspect of m^2; C, occlusal view; D, diagram of occlusal view of molars copied from Turnbull (1971, p. 161) but with his symbols for cusps substituted by those used in this volume. Explanations: PM = Paleontological collection, Field Museum; *1* = eocone (paracone), *2* = protocone, *4* = metacone, *a* = mesiostyle, *b* = distostyle, *j* = stylocone, *l* = ectostyle-*l*, *m* = ectostyle-*m*.

The hypothetical forerunner of *Pappotherium* can be imagined darting furtively from cover to cover along the littered forest floor foraging for tiny insects, itself a prey to larger ground-dwelling nonplacental mammals, reptiles, and possibly even large predatory arthropods. To enable it to survive and ultimately radiate into all favorable niches, the limbs of the primitive mammal were probably nearly equal in length but with the hind pair slightly longer than the front pair. The generalized tail was thinly haired and about equal to combined head and body length. The fur was short and agouti-colored and sensory hairs were thinly scattered over the entire body, with concentrations around the eyes, muzzle, throat, chest, wrists, ankles, and external genitalia. This little ancestral placental must have been solitary except when mating or breeding and was well adapted in a generalized way for running, leaping, climbing, swimming, and digging.

It seems likely that the ancestral therian was essentially nocturnal but that its activities extended well into crepuscular hours. The eyes might have been characterized by a duplex (rod and cone) retina such as occurs in many living nocturnal and diurnal mammals, or perhaps by a retina of generalized cells that could give rise to both rod (nocturnal) and cone (diurnal) types.

As early therians increased in size and variety, interspecific competition and environmental selection would force the smaller insectivorous species into heavier or darker cover, or into new niches such as the fossorial, aquatic, and arboreal. Among those which sought special prey in trees or shrubs or refuge from periodic floods was one that became the forerunner of primates.

The arboreal preprimate could have differentiated during the late Cretaceous, possibly earlier, but probably not later than the early Paleocene. Primitive euthemorphic or primate-type molars (fig. I.2) had already appeared by the late Cretaceous (*Purgatorius,* Van Valen and Sloan 1965), but their possessors may not have been arboreal, and they are less likely to have been primates than nonprimates.

The preprimate had yet to cross a second adaptive threshold. Once entirely or predominantly adapted to arboreal life, it evolved a grasping, opposable great toe

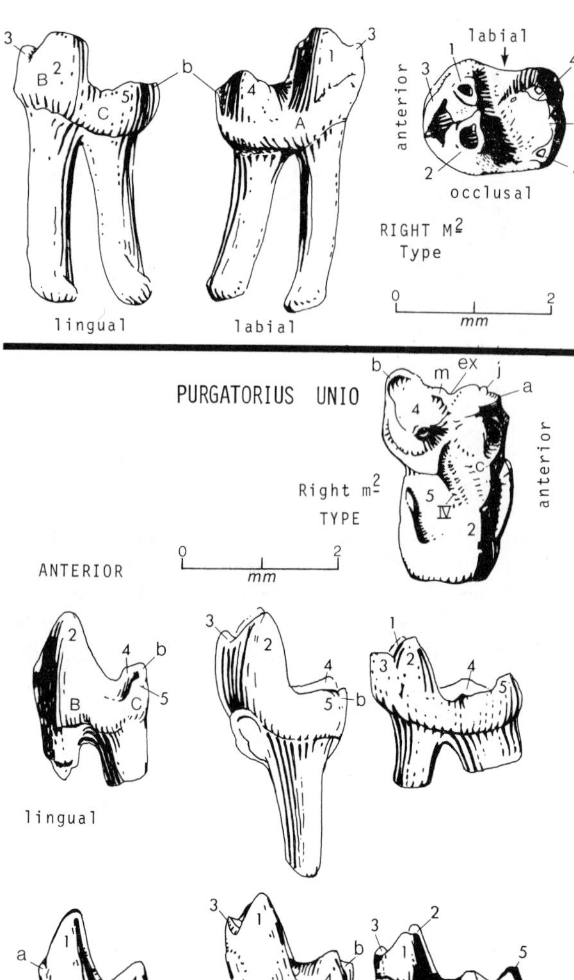

Fig. I.2. *Purgatorius,* known from isolated teeth only. *Purgatorius ceratops* Van Valen and Sloan, right m^2, type and only specimen, from latest Cretaceous, Hell Creek Formation, McCone County, Montana. *Purgatorius unio* Van Valen and Sloan, right m^2 (type) and three lower cheek teeth referred, from early Paleocene, Purgatory Hill local fauna, Tullock Formation, McCone County, Montana. Teeth redrawn from Van Valen and Sloan (1965, p. 744), reoriented and labeled to facilitate comparisons; symbols explained on page 300. *Note:* The type tooth of *P. unio* was wrongly captioned by Hershkovitz (1971, p. 105) as being from Middle Paleocene. New material represented by early Paleocene mandibles of *P. unio* with cheek teeth complete and in place has been described and figured by Clemens (1974).

and thus became the first true primate. In sum, the small body, generalized limb structure and distinctive proportions but with opposable hallux, a broad interorbital region with at least rudiments of a postorbital bar, eutheremorphic molars, and the arboreal habitat were the most important ingredients. There may have been other arboreal mammals with the right combination of characters that did not become primates. They may have tried other means for survival not exploited by preprimates, or they may have veered off into other adaptive zones. Perhaps some became rodents or rodentlike and others lingered for a while then disappeared without issue. Marsupials had already differentiated as such, certainly as forest-floor animals, and only later did some elements evolve into arboreal forms in niches where primates had not preceded them. No placental with a resemblance to any marsupial, including the genera *Marmosa* (Didelphidae) and *Cercartetus* (Phalangeridae) mentioned by Cartmill (1974*a*, p. 76), could be even remotely ancestral to primates.

Specialization of the hallux triggered other modifications in early primates. The grasping foot allowed the forelimb to experiment with a wide range of activities, including new modes of prehension, grooming, and transportation, functions hitherto performed by the front teeth alone. Increasing manual versatility in turn involved alterations in the locomotor system, muzzle reduction, attendant dental modifications, evolution of binocularity, and other profound changes, probably including acceleration of the trend toward greater body size.

Major diversification within the order began with the adaptation of some early crepuscular primates for the nocturnal niche and others for the diurnal—in effect, a double shift that permitted maximum exploitation of the same habitat. Initial divergence in habits must have occurred before the orbital fossa was demarcated from the temporal fossa by a bony bar and long before binocular vision was highly developed. Diurnality accelerated the trend toward separation of the external cranial fossae and evolution of full binocularity, while nocturnality promoted enlargement of the eye and evolution of locomotor

Fig. I.3. The slender loris (*Loris tardigradus*) of Sri Lanka (Ceylon) and southern India, a nocturnal prosimian of ancient lineage and among the most highly specialized of living primates. (Photo courtesy San Diego Zoo).

systems adapted to night travel and foraging. Although nocturnal prosimians appear to be more primitive, they are no less specialized for their milieu (fig. I.3) than modern diurnal monkeys and apes are for theirs.

Primates Defined

Most definitions of the order Primates are no better than diagnostic descriptions of living Old World forms. Wood Jones (1929, p. 69) reviewed some of the older criteria, but his critique concentrated on the often quoted and widely accepted formulation of Mivart (1873, p. 507) which follows:

> Unguiculate claviculate placental mammals, with orbits encircled by bone; three kinds of teeth, at least at one time of life; brain always with a posterior lobe and calcarine fissure; the innermost digits of at least one pair of extremities opposable; hallux with a flat nail or none; a well-developed caecum; penis pendulous; testes scrotal; always two pectoral mammae.

According to Wood Jones (1929, p. 75),

> *there is no single character in this definition which constitutes a peculiarity of the Primates; for a primate animal may only be diagnosed by possessing the aggregate of them all.* The Primates, therefore, constitute a defined group of animals which possess no single distinguishing feature; but they all retain a surprisingly large number of primitive and common mammalian characters collected together in one animal type. The Primate Order is one without distinction but with essentially generalized mammalian features.

Wood Jones's rejection of Mivart's definition because of its composite nature seems out of hand. A few living mammalian orders—the Monotremata, Chiroptera, Cetacea, and Lagomorpha, for example—may indeed be defined by one or two extremely specialized character complexes. On the other hand, fragmentary remains of representatives of these orders may be undeterminable, except perhaps by additional diagnostic but not necessarily unique characters. The nondefinition of Primates substituted by Wood Jones affirms the mammalian nature of Primates but does not in the slightest distinguish this order from any other mammalian order.

The best diagnostic characters in Mivart's definition, "orbits encircled by bones . . . innermost digits of at least one pair of extremities opposable; hallux with a flat nail or none; penis pendulous; testes scrotal," are *specializations* which singly or in combination distinguish most living adult male primates from all other living mammals of the same sex.

The flaws in Mivart's definition are that its usefulness is limited to males of most but not all commonly recognized Primate families and that it is narrowly applicable to only the whole, living animal. Soft parts, including most external features, that clearly distinguish living primates from contemporaries are absent in fossils, and the few hard parts mentioned in the definition may be missing or poorly preserved. Other parts, if well preserved, may not conform to the characterizations based on living models. Orbits, for example, may not have been completely encircled by bone in the earliest primates. Cheek teeth, the only organs of diagnostic value preserved in most early Tertiary primates, were ignored by Mivart and mentioned only cursorily by Wood Jones.

More recently published definitions take all primates into account but show less concern for diagnostic ordinal characters than for evolutionary trends that lead to the aberrant and moribund hominid twiglet. One such definition based on nine trends was proposed by Le Gros Clark (1959, p. 42). It is reproduced below with my critical remarks appended to each of the cited trends.

> Broadly speaking, the order Primates can be defined as a natural group of mammals distinguished by the following prevailing evolutionary trends:
>
> 1. The preservation of a generalized structure of the limbs with a primitive pentadactyly, and the retention of certain elements of the limb skeleton (such as the clavicle) which tend to be reduced or to disappear in some groups of mammals.

Comment: Generalized limb structure has been preserved at least to the same degree in many orders or families of mammals. The real trend among primates (and many other mammals) is toward *diversification* in the relative proportions of limbs, tail, and digits, and in modifications of the angle of limb articulation. Skeletons of callitrichids, gorilla, slow loris and tarsier exemplify the great diversity of primate locomotor skeletons.

> 2. An enhancement of the free mobility of the digits, especially the thumb and big toe (which are used for grasping purposes).

Comment: Enhanced or reduced digital mobility is a specialized, not a generalized, condition. As such it is at variance with Le Gros Clark's first item. The big toe becomes more mobile in most primates; in others, particularly terrestrial primates, it becomes less mobile. Likewise, the thumb becomes more plastic, particularly in *Homo,* but is reduced in many primates, tends to disappear in some, and is lost in spider monkeys and all colobines. The middle finger is highly specialized as an elongate probe in the aye-aye and to a lesser degree in some callitrichids. Second and third toes of the siamang are syndactylous and function as a single digit. Far from unidirectional, the evolutionary trend of the digits has been toward functional diversity in most, degeneration and loss in some.

> 3. The replacement of sharp compressed claws by flattened nails, associated with the development of highly sensitive tactile pads on the digits.

Comment: Sharp claws are retained on all digits but hallux in callitrichids, callimico, tarsiers, and aye-aye among living primates. Compressed but blunt claws prevail on most digits in lemuroids, lorisoids, cebids, and some catarrhines. Claws tend to degenerate into short flattened nails with increase in prehensility of digits and opposability of the first digit. This tendency is correlated with increase in body mass. The larger the animal the greater its need for a secure grasp of supporting branches or tree trunks. Sensitive tactile pads are not peculiar to primates and not necessarily associated with flattened nails in any mammalian order.

4. The progressive abbreviation of the snout or muzzle.

Comment: The same trend characterizes many other arboreal mammals, particularly among Chiroptera, Carnivora, Rodentia, and sloths among the Edentata. The muzzle of pinnipeds and manatees is also greatly reduced. A secondary elongation of the muzzle characterizes many primates, most notably baboons and macaques.

5. The elaboration and perfection of the visual apparatus with the development of varying degrees of binocular vision.

Comment: This item is not separable from number 4. Although the trend among primates is indeed toward binocularity, this form of the visual apparatus is a *specialization.* Binocularity is not necessarily an improvement and not at all a perfection of the primitive system where eyes are lateral in position.

6. Reduction of the apparatus of smell.

Comment: Not separable from number 4. It is interesting to note in this connection that in tupaiids, treated as primates by Le Gros Clark, the trend, particularly in *Urogale,* is toward extreme elongation of the snout.

7. The loss of certain elements of the primitive mammalian dentition, and the preservation of a simple cusp pattern of the molar teeth.

Comment: The trend toward loss of teeth or dental elements is, with few exceptions, universal among mammals. Preservation of a "simple cusp pattern [tritubercular] of the molar teeth" is also true in the vast majority of mammals. The tendency in mammals generally, including primates, is toward progressive elaboration of the "simple cusp pattern" followed by degeneration or secondary simplification.

8. Progressive expansion and elaboration of the brain, affecting predominantly the cerebral cortex and its dependencies.

Comment: This is the universal trend among mammals, even in monotremes.

9. Progressive and increasingly efficient development of those gestational processes concerned with the nourishment of the foetus before birth.

Comment: The primary gestational process here concerned with fetal nourishment is, in a word, placentation. In this respect the trend has been toward increasing complication and all it entails rather than increasing efficiency. The deciduous discoidal placental type in primates also occurs in Insectivora, Chiroptera, and Rodentia. Nevertheless primates, compared body mass for body mass with these and other mammals, need longer periods of gestation to produce fewer and less-developed, albeit usually larger, young requiring longer postnatal care. This increasing *inefficiency* in all gestational processes is compensated for by longer and better postnatal care, presumably lower infant mortality, greater freedom from predation, and other related external factors promoting survival of the young.

Some (1, 7, 8) of the nine "prevailing" evolutionary trends discussed above are simply general mammalian tendencies; others (2, 4, 5, 6) are arboreal adaptations common to many nonprimates and some primates, and one (9) is not a primate character.

The definition of a taxon as ancient and diversified as Primates, with most constituents known only from bits of bone or teeth, must be based essentially on skeletal and dental features. The more there are of such features the more sharply defined the taxon, and the more numerous the fragmentary remains the more certain its ordinal identification.

The following definition of Primates is based on critical examination of living and extinct representatives of the order and comparison with types of other mammalian orders.

Hands and feet, with few living exceptions, pentadactyl, usually palmigrade but always plantigrade; hallux opposable with a short, blunt, degenerate claw, nail, or inunguiculate; manual digits capable of divergence, convergence, and flexions; scaphoid, lunate, triquetrum, centrale, and pisiform bones always present and discrete; tail primitively present and well developed, but secondarily reduced or absent in some species; penis bone present but secondarily lost in a few species; auditory bulla complete or nearly so, the main portions formed by extension of petrosal bone; entotympanic bone absent or rudimentary and not entering into formation of auditory bulla; malleolar orbicular apophysis usually absent, rudimentary when present; perpendicular plate of ethmoid (ossified mesethmoid) present; supraorbital region broad, with edges ridged or overhanging and more or less divergent; orbits large, postorbital process well developed and in all recognized forms continuous with comparably developed orbital process of malar to form a complete ring; pterygoid process of sphenoid bifurcate, the well-developed, often greatly enlarged lateral plate arising anteriorly at the sphenopalatine suture, the medial plate smaller than the lateral, sometimes nearly obsolete; molars euthemorphic, the occlusal surface bunodont to bilophodont.

The foregoing definition admits only animals currently identified as primates. Tupaiids and plesiadapids, treated as primates by some systematists, did not attain primate grade in terms of an opposable hallux with nail, and in both groups the auditory bulla is formed mainly by the entotympanic bone (fig. IV.58), an element absent in primates. The visual system in tupaiids evolved along sciurid lines, and the olfactory, including the elongate muzzle, evolved as in shrews. In *Plesiadapis* (figs. I.4–6), the visual, olfactory, and dental systems seem to have evolved along lines followed by fossorial rodents; the uniquely specialized upper and lower "incisors" are unprimatelike if not certainly nonprimate. One character alone, the narrow constriction of the supraorbital region, separates *Plesiadapis* from all primates and from tupaiids as well. Ordinal affinities of *Plesiadapis* are unknown, but primate type or euthemorphic molars alone do not primates make.

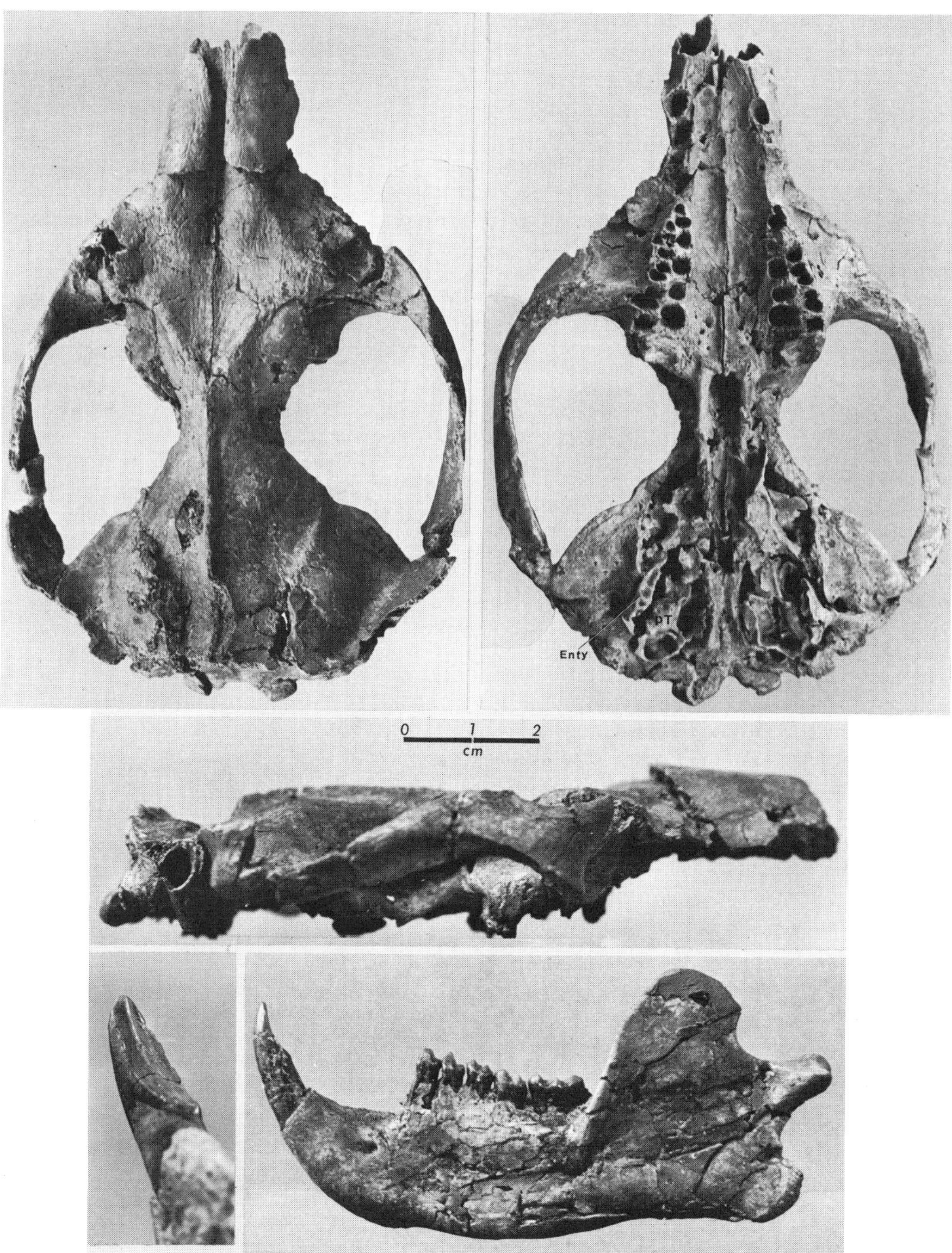

Fig. I.4. *Plesiadapis tricuspidens* Gervais: Cranium (Muséum National d'Histoire Naturelle, Paris, CR 125) dorsal, ventral, and lateral aspects; left mandible and enlargement of incisor tip. Postorbital constrictions and reduced orbits are characters never associated with primates or arboreal mammals, the auditory bulla composed of entotympanic, basioccipital, and alisphenoid bones is nonprimate.

Since the above was written, Cartmill in 1972 and again in 1974 discussed mammalian arboreal characters in general and those diagnostic of primates in particular. He argues with complete justification, as have others before him, that the arboreal theory of mammalian origin as expounded by Wood Jones (1916 [1964]) is both untenable and illogical. Cartmill (1972, p. 121) regards primate arboreality as an adaptation to "nocturnal visually directed predation on insects in the terminal branches of the lower strata of tropical forests." This basal adaptation, says Cartmill (1972, p. 121), "provides an adequate explanation of the origin, persistence, and variable expression of the primate trends toward cheiridial prehensility, periorbital ossification, orbital convergence and approximation, rostral recession, olfactory regression, and neurological integration of the contralateral visual fields." He concludes (Cartmill 1972, p. 121) that a

> monophyletic and adaptively meaningful order Primates may be delimited by taking the petrosal bulla, complete postorbital bar, and divergent hallux or pollex bearing a flattened nail as ordinally diagnostic. Such a diagnosis dictates the removal of the families Plesiadapidae and Microsyopidae to the Insectivora. The Paramomyidae must also be referred to the Insectivora if, as reported by Simons (1967), the still-undescribed skull of *Palaechthon* lacks a postorbital bar. The dental specializations of the carpolestids and

Fig. I.5. *Plesiadapis tricuspidens* (CR 125) enlarged: Right middle ear chamber completely exposed by damaged entotympanic bone (*Enty*); petrous portion (*pT*) of temporal (including cochlear prominence) nearly complete, the suture intact, and not entering into formation of bullar wall.

picrodontids suggest that these families are no more likely to meet these revised criteria of membership in the Primates. By this analysis, no Paleocene prosimians (except perhaps *Berruvius*) are known, and the primate fossil record begins in the Eocene. The five microsyopoid families [Paramomyidae, Microsyopidae, Plesiadapidae, Carpolestidae, Picrodontidae, as arranged by Van Valen, 1969], appear to represent ultimately sterile side branches which diverged from the primate ancestry prior to the crucial shift to visually-directed predation.

Cartmill's taxonomic conclusions appear sweeping, and although his supporting arguments seem sound they are not based on firsthand study of the taxons in question. Cartmill's repeated reference to "ancestral primate" is not always in the same sense. In most instances his "ancestral primate" is less primate than preprimate or of the nonprimate stock from which primates arose. If the ancestral primate was a visually rather than olfactorily directed insect predator it probably was less nocturnal than diurnal in foraging habits. Eyes of all known nocturnal primates are highly specialized and could not give rise to the smaller color-sensitive eyes of diurnal primates which include many small insectivorous species. In similar fashion, eyes of early mammals that might have given rise to primates could not have been "small and degenerate," as described by Cartmill (1974*b*, p. 440). In addition, the postorbital bar of the ancestral primate need not have been completely ossified; and a broadly divergent prehensile hallux (Cartmill 1974*a*, p. 46) rather than a simple divergent pollex (Cartmill 1972) is basic for primates. A divergent thumb may well be a primitive mammalian character, and its mention is not needed in the definition of primates.

Primate molar evolution is paralleled among some marsupials, insectivores (sensu lato), condylarths, ungulates, and rodents. Obviously, the definition of primates cannot be based on dental morphology alone or on any other single character complex. Microsyopoid dentition, particularly the cheek teeth, is primatelike, but the entotympanic bulla, although probably primatelike in

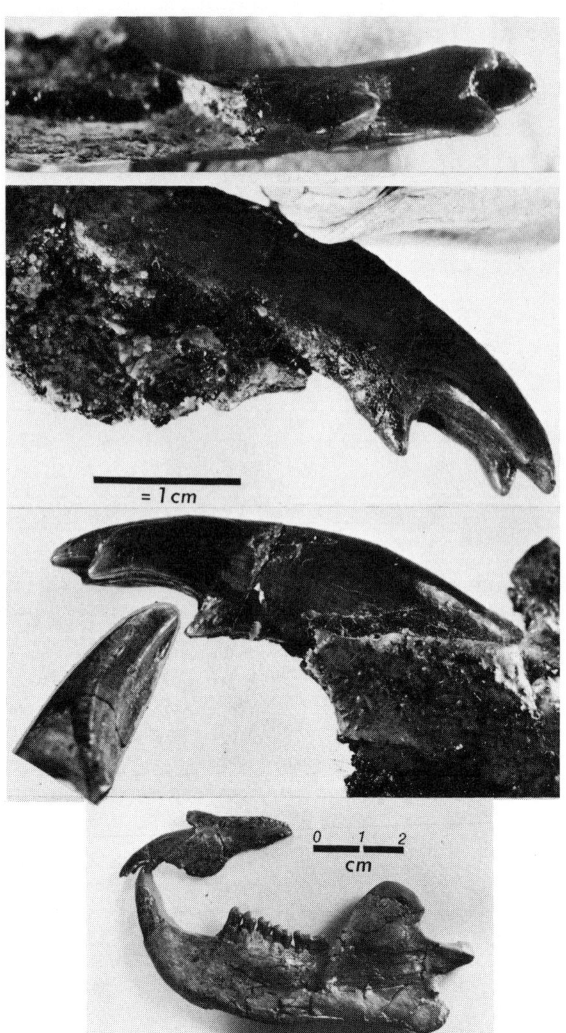

Fig. 1.6. Incisors of *Plesiadapis tricuspidens* and occlusion. Three aspects of left upper incisor (MNHN, CR 404) and lower incisor (CR 424). The correct occlusal position is with outer convex surface of lower incisor tip fitted snuggly against inner concave surface of upper incisor tip.

function, is not primate in morphology and origin (cf. McKenna 1966; Szalay 1969*a,b;* 1972). Bown and Gingerich (1973), who treat microsyopids as primates, argue that evolution of primate molar morphology preceded appearance of the petrosal bulla. This may be true, but Bown and Gingerich also want to believe that the ancestral primate first evolved a complete entotympanic bulla, as in leptictid insectivores and microsyopids, then dismantled the structure and reevolved the adaptively equivalent petrosal bulla, a most improbable event. Further, the claim made by Bown and Gingerich (1973, p. 6) that "earliest primates had molariform [that is, tricuspid with paracone, protocone and metacone] fourth premolars" ignores the fact that fourth upper premolars of many fossil and living simians (cf. chapter 29, and following on dental evolution) are still primitively bicuspid (paracone + protocone) without sign of metacone.

The Paromomyiformes, erected by Szalay (1973) as a new suborder of Primates, is Van Valen's (1969) superfamily Microsyopoidea less the Microsyopidae. The new arrangement still appears to be a composite of nonprimates and dubious primates. Even if primate, nothing resembling a paramomyid, particularly with its dentition, could be ancestral to the Strepsirhini or Haplorhini.

2 Families and Genera of Living Primates and Extinct Platyrrhines
A Reference List

The primary division of Primates into Strepsirhini (lemuroids, lorisoids, doubentonioids) and Haplorhini (tarsioids, platyrrhines, catarrhines) was proposed by Pocock (1918). The greater affinity of *Tarsius* with simians is recognized but the relationships of extinct "tarsioids" are vague and cannot be dealt with in this monograph. *Tarsius* itself is sometimes treated here as a prosimian in grade and at other times is treated as a simian in clade.

Classification of platyrrhines and catarrhines as infraordinal divisions of the Haplorhini reflects the close relationship recognized by all systematists but leaves moot the question whether both groups arose from a common simian or presimian haplorhine ancestor.

Superfamily categories within the Platyrrhini cannot be defensibly defined on the basis of present knowledge. Callitrichids and cebids are the platyrrhine equivalents of and perhaps coordinate with the generally accepted catarrhine superfamilies Hominoidea and Cercopithecoidea. Unlike these Old World groups, there is no fossil record of callitrichids and no known ancestor or surrogate ancestor of any living or fossil cebid group. As for the only living callimiconid, *Callimico goeldii,* most likely it sprang from a common platyrrhine stock. Its stem, however, could not have diverged from the line leading to either callitrichids or cebids. The affinities of the extinct families Xenotrichidae and Homunculidae are unknown. Other extinct taxons and even some living subfamilies now referred to the Cebidae probably belong elsewhere. The systematic position of the oldest known South American primate *Branisella* is problematic. It certainly represents a hitherto undescribed family, but just as certainly it is not a platyrrhine and is too specialized to have given rise to that group.

Order Primates Linnaeus
- I. Suborder Strepsirhini
  - A. Superfamily Lemuroidea
    - 1. Family Lemuridae
      - a. Subfamily Cheirogaleinae
        - *Microcebus* E. Geoffroy, 1828 (Mouse lemurs)
        - *Cheirogaleus* E. Geoffroy, 1812 (Dwarf lemurs)
        - *Allocebus* Petter-Rousseaux and Petter, 1968 (Hairy-ear dwarf lemur)
        - *Phaner* Gray, 1870 (Fork-striped lemur)
      - b. Subfamily Lemurinae
        - *Lepilemur* I. Geoffroy, 1851 (Sportive lemur)
        - *Hapalemur* I. Geoffroy, 1851 (Gentle lemurs)
        - *Lemur* Linnaeus, 1758 (Lemurs)
        - *Varecia* Kerr, 1792 (Ruffed lemur)
    - 2. Family Indriidae
      - *Avahi* Jourdan, 1834 (Avahi)
      - *Propithecus* Bennett, 1832 (Sifakas)
      - *Indri* E. Geoffroy and G. Cuvier, 1795 (Indri)
  - B. Superfamily Lorisoidea
    - 1. Family Galagidae
      - *Galago* E. Geoffroy, 1796 (Galagos)
      - *Euoticus* Gray, 1863 (Needle-claw galago)
    - 2. Family Lorisidae
      - *Loris* E. Geoffroy, 1796 (Slender loris)
      - *Nycticebus* E. Geoffroy, 1812 (Slow lorises)
      - *Arctocebus* Gray, 1863 (Angwantibo)
      - *Perodicticus* Bennett, 1831 (Potto)
  - C. Superfamily Daubentonioidea
    - 1. Family Daubentoniidae
      - *Daubentonia* E. Geoffroy, 1795 (Aye-aye)
- II. Suborder Haplorhini
  - I′. Infraorder Tarsii
    - A. Superfamily Tarsioidea
      - 1. Family Tarsiidae
        - *Tarsius* Storr, 1780 (Tarsiers)
  - II′. Infraorder Platyrrhini—New World Monkeys
    - 1. Family Callitrichidae
      - *Cebuella* Gray, 1866 (Pygmy marmoset)
      - *Callithrix* Erxleben, 1777 (Marmosets)
      - *Saguinus* Hoffmannsegg, 1807 (Tamarins)

Leontopithecus Lesson, 1840
(Lion-tamarin)
2. Family Callimiconidae
Callimico Miranda Ribeiro, 1911
(Callimico)
3. Family †Homunculidae. Upper Oligocene–Lower Miocene
†*Dolichocebus* Kraglievich, 1951
(Long-headed monkey). Upper Oligocene
†*Homunculus* Ameghino, 1891
(Homunculus). Lower Miocene
4. Family Cebidae
a. Subfamily †Tremacebinae. Upper Oligocene
†*Tremacebus* Hershkovitz, 1974
(Sacanana monkey)
b. Subfamily †Stirtoniinae. Upper Miocene
†*Stirtonia* Hershkovitz, 1970
(Stirtonia)
c. Subfamily Saimiriinae. Upper Miocene–Recent
†*Neosaimiri* Stirton, 1951
(La Venta monkey) Upper Miocene
Saimiri Voigt, 1831 (Squirrel monkey)
d. Subfamily Aotinae
Aotus Illiger, 1811 (Night monkey)
e. Subfamily Callicebinae
Callicebus Thomas, 1903 (Titis)
f. Subfamily Alouattinae
Alouatta Lacépède, 1799 (Howlers)
g. Subfamily †Cebupitheciinae. Upper Miocene
†*Cebupithecia* Stirton and Savage, 1951 (False saki)
h. Subfamily Pitheciinae
Pithecia Desmarest, 1804 (Sakis)
Chiropotes Lesson, 1840
(Bearded sakis)
Cacajao Lesson, 1840
(Cacajaos, Uacaris)
i. Subfamily Cebinae
Cebus Erxleben, 1777 (Capuchins)
j. Subfamily Atelinae
Lagothrix E. Geoffroy, 1812
(Woolly monkeys)
Ateles E. Geoffroy, 1806
(Spider monkey)
(†*Montaneia* Ameghino, 1910, a synonym)
Brachyteles Spix, 1823
(Woolly spider monkey)
5. Family †Xenotrichidae. Subrecent
†*Xenothrix* Williams and Koopman, 1952
(Jamaica monkey)

II'. Infraorder Catarrhini—Old World Monkeys, Apes, Man

A. Superfamily Cercopithecoidea
1. Family Cercopithecidae
a. Subfamily Cercopithecinae
Miopithecus I. Geoffroy, 1842
(Talapoin)
Cercopithecus Linnaeus, 1758
(Guenons)
Erythrocebus Trouessart, 1897
(Patas monkey)
Allenopithecus Lang, 1923
(Allen's guenons)
Cercocebus E. Geoffroy, 1812
(Mangabeys)
Macaca Lacépède, 1799
(Macaques; Celebese "ape")
Papio Erxleben, 1777
(Baboons; Drill; Mandrill)
Theropithecus I. Geoffroy, 1843
(Gelada)
b. Subfamily Colobinae
(Guerezas and Langurs)
Presbytis Eschscholtz, 1821
(Langurs)
Pygathrix E. Geoffroy, 1812
(Douc langur)
Rhinopithecus Milne-Edwards, 1872
(Snub-nosed langur; regarded as a subgenus by Groves 1970, p. 562)
Nasalis E. Geoffroy, 1812
(Proboscis monkey)
Simias Miller, 1903
(Pagai Island langur; regarded as congeneric by Groves 1970)
Colobus Illiger, 1811
(Colobus monkeys or Guerezas)

B. Superfamily Hominoidea
1. Family Hylobatidae
Hylobates Illiger, 1811 (Gibbons)
Symphalangus Gloger, 1841
(Siamang)
2. Family Pongidae
Pongo Lacépède, 1799 (Orang)
Chimpansee Voigt, 1831
(*Pan* ["Oken"] Palmer, 1904 [not *Pan* Jardine, 1835, a bird])
(Chimpanzee)
Gorilla I. Geoffroy, 1852 (Gorilla)
3. Family Hominidae
Homo Linnaeus, 1758 (Man)

III. Suborder Incertae Sedis
1. Family †Branisellidae (new)
†*Branisella* Hoffstetter, 1969. Lower Oligocene
2. Family Incertae Sedis
Primate †*Incertae Sedis* (Miller, 1929; Williams and Koopman, 1952). Early Recent.

3 Living Haplorhini and Strepsirhini Compared

a = Haplorhini (Platyrrhini, Catarrhini)
b = Strepsirhini (Lemuroidea, Lorisoidea, Daubentonioidea)
a or *b* = *Tarsius* (Haplorhini)[1]
(Distribution, fig. I.7)

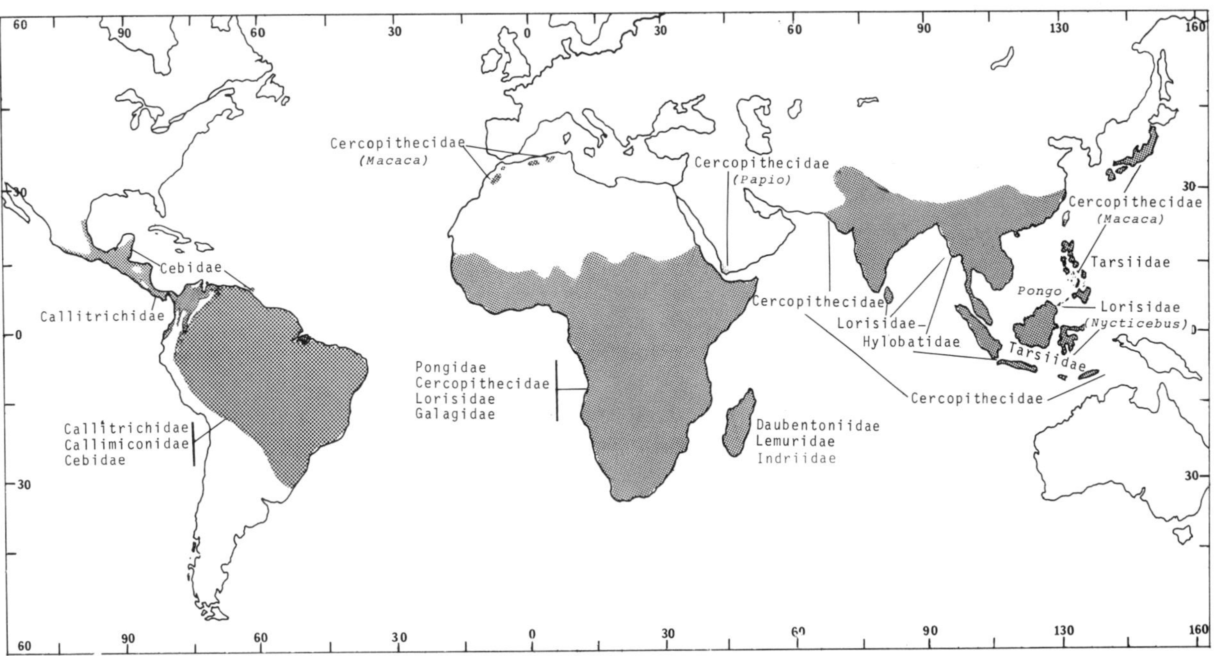

Fig. I.7. Abbreviated world map showing distribution of living nonhuman Primates. Areas (e.g., Gibraltar, northeastern China, Antilles) inhabited by introduced free-ranging colonies of cercopithecids are not shown; see figure XIII.1 for range limits of New World monkey families.

1. *a.* Rhinarium (fig I.9) hairy or naked but not moist or glandular; nostrils completely ringed, without lateral slit; upper lip hairy or bare, primitive groove (philtrum) of median sulcus incomplete, vestigial, or absent (*Tarsius* fits here).
   b. Rhinarium (fig. I.9) naked, glandular, and moist; nostrils with crescentic lateral slit; upper lip hairy except median sulcus marked with conspicuous philtrum.
2. *a.* External ears (fig. III.18) not tubular or leaflike in outline and incapable of more than slight independent movement (including *Tarsius*).
   b. External ears (fig. III.18) variable in form; tubular or leaflike (elliptic, acuminate, ovate) and capable of folding in some species.
3. *a.* Pedal digit II (figs. I.21, 25; II.5; XII.3) provided with claw, clawlike nail, or flat nail like those of pedal digits III–V.

[1] *Tarsius* agrees best with strepsirhines in characters common to primitive primates, including ancestral haplorhines; it differs from both strepsirhines and modern platyrrhines and catarrhines in specialized tarsiid characters.

b. Pedal digit II (figs. I.23, 24), provided with upturned grooming claw conspicuously different from nonprojecting nail or naillike claw of remaining digits (*Tarsius,* with grooming claw on digits II and III [fig. I.22], fits best here, unless a separate category is made for this character complex).

4. *a.* Mammae: 1 pair (pectoral or axillary).
b. Mammae: 1–3, rarely 4–5 pairs, (axillary, pectoral, abdominal, inguinal, according to species or individuals; *Tarsius,* with pectoral and inguinal pairs, fits here).

5. *a.* Facial portion of skull short, the facial angle steep (fig. IV.3) (except in Alouatta [fig. IV.113], *Aotus* [fig. IV.111] and, secondarily, in *Papio* [fig. IV.131], *Theropithecus* [fig. IV.132], and some *Macaca*).
b. Facial portion of skull elongate, the facial angle not steep (fig. IV.3, 87–108) (*Tarsius* [fig. IV.109] fits best here).

6. *a.* Orbits (figs. IV.5, 6, 46–49, 109–144; VI.1) directed forward or more nearly forward than laterally, completely enclosed by bone laterally and separated from temporal fossa posteriorly by a bony plate perforated by the inferior orbital (sphenomaxillary) fissure (*Tarsius* fits here).
b. Orbits (figs. IV.5, 6, 44, 45, 87–108) directed more nearly laterally than forward to slightly more forward than laterally; enclosed by bony bar laterally and completely open posteriorly without partial separation from temporal fossae.

7. *a.* Lacrimal bone entirely or nearly entirely orbital, the fossa (or foramen) orbital (figs. IV.110–44).
b. Lacrimal bone entirely or mostly facial, thc fossa facial or orbital (includcs *Tarsius* [fig. IV.8]) (figs. IV.87–109).

8. *a.* Auditory bulla inflated, cellular or spongiose; tympanic ring (ectotympanic bone) forming external auditory meatus (*Tarsius* fits here) (figs. IV.56–58, 62, 109–44).
b. Auditory bulla inflated, chamber incompletely partitioned or not partitioned; tympanic ring enclosed (lemuriforms) (fig. IV.58) or entering into formations of external auditory meatus (lorisiforms) (figs. 58, 61, 87–108).

9. *a.* Right and left halves of mandible completely ankylosed at symphysis menti to form a single bone without suture in adult (figs. IV.110–44).
b. Right and left halves of mandible unossified at symphysis menti in living forms (*Tarsius* here) (figs. IV. 87–109).

10. *a.* Formula of permanent dentition: $i\frac{2}{2}$, $c\frac{1}{1}$, $pm\frac{2}{2}$ or $\frac{3}{3}$, $m\frac{3}{3}$ or $\frac{2}{2}$ $= 32$ or 36 (*Tarsius* with $i\frac{2}{1}$ is an exception but otherwise fits best here).
b. Formula of permanent dentition variable, total number of teeth ranging from 18 (*Daubentonia*) to 36 (most lemuriforms).

11. *a.* Upper incisors well developed, inner pair in contact at midline or separated by a distance less than one-half the width of either tooth (*Tarsius* fits here) (figs. IV. 109–44).
b. Upper incisors well developed (as in *Daubentonia* with 1 on each side) or degenerate diastema between inner pair more than one-half width of either tooth (figs. IV. 87–106).

12. *a.* Lower incisors well developed, tubular or spatulate in form (*Tarsius* with 1 lower incisor on each side fits best here) (figs. IV. 109–44).
b. Iower incisors of each side paired, elongate, and combining with canine to form a grooming comb (figs. IV. 87–106; V. 1[G]), or incisors absent (*Daubentonia* [fig. IV. 107]).

13. *a.* Lower canine more or less tusklike, never replacing incisors or combining with them as part of a specialized grooming comb (*Tarsius* fits here) (figs. IV. 109–44).
b. Lower canine tusklike and replacing incisors (*Daubentonia* [fig. IV.107]) or lancelike and combining with incisors to form a grooming comb (figs. IV.87–106).

14. *a.* Sublingua (including lytta or stiffening rod) absent or vestigial (cf. plica fimbriata; *Tarsius* fits here) (fig. III. 19).
b. Sublingua with lytta present and well developed (fig. III.19).

15. *a.* Placenta hemochorial, discoidal and deciduate (includes *Tarsius*).
b. Placenta epitheliochorial and diffuse.

4 Some Descriptive, Diagnostic, Quasi-diagnostic, and Primitive Mammalian Characters of Living Primates

A number of morphological traits cited by authors as diagnostic of living primates prove to be primitive mammalian characters present with little modification in most mammals. Others are specializations that also evolved in nonprimate lines. Still others evolved in some primate groups but not in others. Behavioral, physiological, biochemical, and karyological characters are, so far as is known, specialized attributes of individuals, species, or species groups. None of them are diagnostic ordinal characters or otherwise entitled to inclusion in the definition of Primates. Nonetheless, descriptive and quasi-diagnostic characters of Primates are essential complements to the valid diagnostic characters. A selection of these and some of the diagnostic characters used in the definition of Primates (p. 5) are briefly discussed in this chapter. Because of its complexity, primate locomotion is discussed separately in the following chapter.

Size Range

Most living species of mammals are smaller than the North American gray squirrel (*Sciurus carolinensis*), and most living species of primates are larger. Compared with all living mammals, body mass of primates ranges from moderately small to moderately large. The gradient is even, but the number of species involved increases geometrically from the smallest to the middle-sized classes, then decreases sharply toward the largest species. The smallest known primate is *Pseudoloris parvulus* a house-mouse-sized tarsioid of the European Eocene. The mouse lemur, *Microcebus murinus,* one of the three smallest of living primates (cf. p. 466) is about one-third larger. The largest known primate is the giant ape, *Gigantopithecus blacki,* known from lower jaws and isolated teeth of the Asian middle Pleistocene. The massive lower jaw of a full-grown male and type of the species is nearly half again as large as that of a male mountain gorilla (*Gorilla gorilla beringeri*). Simons and Ettel (1970, p. 78) estimate that this huge extinct ape "would have stood about 9 feet tall and may have weighed as much as 600 pounds." The male lowland gorilla, Bushman, who died in 1951 in the Lincoln Park Zoo, Chicago, was 6 feet 2 inches tall and weighed 550 pounds in his prime.

Size, Geography, and Climate

All primates and most, if not all, early mammalian lines originated in warm, humid climates. As is indicated by the fossil record and phylogenetic sequences, earliest mammals were very small (cf. Hopson 1973). Successive species or races became larger and more specialized with the passing of time and changes in ecology. Among mammals, selection for larger size, tantamount to greater strength, begins in the womb, continues in the nest—around the teat, through the "peck order"—and extends into competition for territory and mates. Populations of tropical origin that spread widely in latitude, longitude, or altitude maintain the trend for increasing size, distance traveled being a measure of time.

The exigencies of life in new habitats distant from the geographic center of origin, or in changing climates at the center of origin, usually accelerate the rate of change. Where selective pressure for small size prevails, the natural trend toward larger size may be checked but not reversed. Where the trend seems to have been toward smaller size, more likely it was the smaller and more primitive or older of two or more closely related species or races that survived without prejudice to its own tendency toward aggrandizement. Indeed, the history of organic evolution is in a sense a record of increasing size, climaxed—whether in fact or predictably—by extinction.

Proponents of so-called ecogeographical rules do not consider that the trend toward greater size is universal, not limited to homiotherms. Environmental factors *control the rate* of change. They do not initiate the change. According to Bergmann's rule, as interpreted and developed by Mayr (1963, p. 318), races of warm-blooded species living in cool climates tend to be larger than races of the same species in warm climates. To the extent that cool-climate races are descendants of warm-climate ones, they may be larger, but not smaller. Warm-climate descendants of high-latitude or high-altitude stock also tend to become larger. However, most of the living north temperate races are derived from south temperate or equatorial ones. As animals, particularly mammals, of north temperate or arctic latitudes become better adapted to cold climate, they rarely if ever spread southward, seasonal migrations excepted. Thus a probable preponderance of larger northern races of southern descent obscures the universal trend toward enlargement irrespective of geography or climate.

Available data reveal no well-defined pattern of geographic variation in size among living platyrrhines consistent with any ecogeographical rule. One case among catarrhines has been reported by Fooden (1971). Four allopatric and very closely related species of *Macaca* (*sinica, radiata, assamensis, thibetana*) show a graduated increase in body size correlated with a decrease in tail length from south to north. This variation, Fooden concludes, "conforms to the classic climatomorphologic rules of Bergmann and Allen."

(Wilson [1972, p. 256] presented virtually identical arguments. Evidently, Fooden's paper, published a little earlier, had not reached him. The present text was also completed before Wilson's work came to hand. There is no need to discuss it separately.)

The example of the macaques is interesting because the increase in their body size also conforms to the postulated trend toward accelerated enlargement with dispersal from central to peripheral habitats. The shorter-tailed macaques of colder climates may also enjoy a selective advantage by losing less body heat through the shortened tail.

Fooden's example in support of Bergmann's and Allen's rule seems to be unique among primates. It is more than offset by negative or neutral trends. For example, body size increased and tail length decreased in lines leading to pongids and gibbons without evidence of clinal relationship between morphology and climate or geography. The tail shortened to a bob in the Malagasy indri, African lorisoids, and South American uacaris. Most probably, their body size increased at the same time. Again, a consistent correlation with geography and climate is not apparent. Significant body size and proportional tail length of all other primates associated with the examples did not change in the same directions. Sufficient measurements are not available of the long-tailed langurs (*Presbytis*) associated with macaques that range from hot lowland climates of Ceylon and India to the cold mountain climates of Tibet. It seems however, that unlike macaques, langurs are consistently long tailed. In conclusion, among primates, the Bergmann and Allen rules are hardly "proved" by one exception to the mass of contradictory evidence. And the exception can be explained without recourse to Bergmann or Allen.

Criticisms of Bergmann's rule have centered mainly on tendered explanations of the physiological implications of the consequences of large body mass (cf. McNab 1971), and not, as rightly cautioned by Mayr (1963, p. 319), the "statistical validity of the data on which the [rule] is based."

Other laws or combinations of environmental factors have been invoked to account for morphological differences between closely related taxons. For example, in explaining their hypothesis of *character displacement*, Brown and Wilson (1956, p. 63) contend that "when two species of animals overlap geographically, the differences between them are accentuated in the zone of sympatry and weakened or lost entirely in the parts of their ranges outside this zone. The characters involved in this dual divergence-convergence pattern may be morphological, ecological, behavioral, or physiological." Differences between secondarily sympatric races or sibling species usually include and often are no more than those of size, the invader being the larger. As argued here and elsewhere (Hershkovitz 1962, p. 34; 1963*a*, p. 15; and following discussions of color variation), primary differentiation had already taken place in allopatry. In a situation of secondary sympatry, the main trend among mammals would be toward convergence, whereas the rate of divergence in allopatry would continue. This postulation of mammalian geographic variation is quite the reverse of that of character displacement.

The trend toward greater total mass (Cope's Rule, cf. Stanley 1973) is universal. It begins at the center of origin of the phyletic line and continues in time or space irrespective of the direction or conditions of dispersal. The trend toward greater size begins with competition between littermates, while the rate of increase and limits of size are controlled by many factors besides climate. Internal rhythms, interactions between bodily parts and functions, and intra- or interspecific relationships may each be more important than climate alone. Large size is a specialization, and the larger the animal or its hyper-specialized part, the nearer the animal is to the end of its line. Some organs may also decrease in size, without prejudice to the animal's overall trend toward enlargement. In this case, the organ may become obsolete or disappear before the organism disappears as a whole.

Skull

Gross size of the primate braincase, relative to body mass, may average larger than that of most other mammals of comparable evolutionary grade. But the difference in volume is not impressive and may be nonexistent if only prosimian skulls are compared with skulls of such marine forms as pinnipeds, dolphins, the sea otters *Enhydra* and *Lutra felina*, the more or less arboreal small cats, kinkajou, and the extensively pneumatized braincases of sloths and pangolins, particularly *Smutsia*. In certain Microchiroptera, particularly among chilonycterines, desmodontines, the stenodermine *Centurio* and *Ametrida* (fig. I.8) most emballonurids, and most vespertilionids, braincase size relative to body mass compares favorably with that of higher primates and in many instances probably exceeds it.

Primate orbits are completely ringed by bone. The same is true of many other mammals (cf. p. 131). The interorbital region, sometimes said to be wide in primates, is actually narrow, but interorbital breadth is greatest in the least-evolved lemuroids and smallest in higher forms. In general, the more nearly frontal and concomitantly enlarged the orbits, the smaller the distance between them. In the squirrel monkey (*Saimiri*), many individuals of Old World monkeys, and sometimes in the tarsier, the septum between the orbits is thin and fenestrated. In contrast to the interorbital width, the supraorbital breadth, that is, the distance between the outer superior borders of the orbits, appears to be proportionately greater among higher primates than in other mammals.

Muzzle reduction is an important evolutionary trend in primates and also in felids, manatees, sloths, and many bats, and other mammals.

The tendency toward obsolescence and disappearance of sutures between cranial bones is a mammalian character. The condition in primates departs little from the primitive.

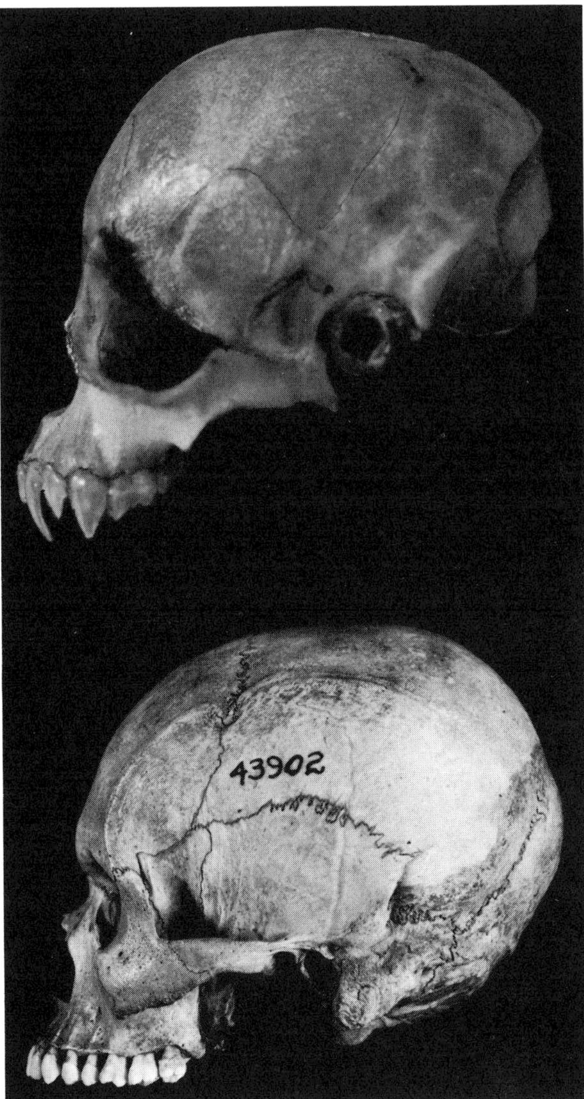

Fig. I.8. Exceptionally inflated foreheads in two mammals. *Above,* Skull of neotropical phyllostomid bat, *Sphaeronycteris toxophyllum; below,* skull of *Homo.*

The position of the primate lacrimal bone is variable. It may be entirely facial, entirely orbital, or divided into facial and orbital portions. Contact between malar (jugal) and lacrimal bones is a character common to many mammals including a number of lemuroid species among primates. The orbital or lateral plate of the ethmoid (os planum) is exposed on the median orbital wall of higher primates, some prosimians, and variably among nonprimates (e.g., domestic cat). It is concealed between the orbits in remaining primates and other mammals. Contact between palatine and lacrimal bones and a long frontopalatine suture are variable characters of prosimians, tupaiids, marsupials, carnivores, and many other mammals.

A supraorbital foramen or notch may be present or absent in primates, as in many mammals with a broad supraorbital region. A malar or jugal foramen of variable diameter is generally present in primates and other mammals. Maximum expansion of the foramen is attained in the nonprimate *Tupaia.*

The auditory bulla is well inflated among prosimians and platyrrhines, but is inflated little or not at all in the highest catarrhines. The same range of variation occurs among mammals generally. Nearly the whole auditory bullar wall of primates is formed by an extension of the petrous bone. The same bone also contributes to formation of the bulla in monotremes, some marsupials, equids, elephants, and a number of other ungulates and other mammals. The entotympanic bone that forms the bullar wall in tupaiids and *Plesiadapis* has not been identified in primates and it is absent or only slightly developed in monotremes, some marsupials, lipotyphlan insectivores, rodents, some carnivores, and most ungulates.

Dentition

No single dental character or combination of dental characters distinguishes all primates from all other mammals. As in most Eutheria, primate teeth are heterodont and diphyodont, with all deciduous teeth replaced. The dental formula of each side of the mouth is variable, but that of the ancestral primate must have been: incisors $\frac{3}{3}$, canine $\frac{1}{1}$, premolars $\frac{4}{4}$, molars $\frac{3}{3} = \frac{11}{11} \times 2$, or 44 total, the same as for primitive placental mammals generally. The abbreviated formula for the permanent set in living primates varies from $\frac{1\text{-}0\text{-}1\text{-}3}{0\text{-}1\text{-}0\text{-}3} = 18$ total in the aye-aye (*Daubentonia madagascariensis*) to $\frac{2\text{-}1\text{-}3\text{-}3}{2\text{-}1\text{-}3\text{-}3} = 36$ total in *Callimico* and all Cebidae. This formula prevails in higher primates, except that the Callitrichidae normally lack third molars for a total of 32 teeth, and all Catarrhini normally lack the first of the three premolars for the same total of 32. The greatest variation in number and kind of teeth occurs among prosimians.

Diversification of individual teeth or dental fields in primates is less than in bats or rodents, but is greater than in living Insectivora, the orders of ungulates, edentates, cetaceans, and the ordinal groups comprising one or a few species. The incisors are most diversified, the canines least. Modification of cheek teeth consists of progressive molarization, with the teeth remaining low crowned with the cusps moderately high and sharp in primitive, mainly insectivorous forms, or high crowned with low cusps in mainly browsing-grazing forms.

The upper premolars vary from unicuspid or tricuspid in the permanent set, and extend to quadricuspid in the deciduous last premolar. Upper molar crowns are triangular to more or less square or rectangular in outline, each with three to five main cusps. The main crest or eocrista connecting the principal outer cusps (eocone [paracone] and metacone) is more or less parallel to the outer border of the tooth. This contour of the eocrista is typical of euthemorphic molars including those of all primates. The tupaiid molars are dilambdomorphic (cf. p. 279). Lower molars, as in eutherians generally, are characterized by the trigonid basin in front defined by the eoconid (protoconid) and metaconid, and by the talonid behind, limited by hypoconid, entoconid, and commonly a fifth cusp, the distostylid (hypoconulid). The primitive anterolingual cusp, the paraconid, present in mandibular cheek teeth of many prosimians, is absent in molars of higher primates but may be present in one or more premolars, more frequently of the deciduous than the permanent series.

Canines of most higher primates deviate little from

the primitive plan. In many species, however, strong control by the premolar field results in molarization of the canine to a bicuspid or tricuspid stage. In prosimians, lower canine modifications are largely controlled by the lower incisor field, but in the aye-aye the entire incisor field is preempted by the canine.

Incisors of primitive primates usually retain the primitive unicuspid or tridentate form. In primates specialized for browsing and grazing, the incisors are molarized to a bicuspid or tricuspid stage. Other adaptive lines show a tendency toward reduction and elimination of upper incisors, or toward the elimination of one of two incisors and hypertrophy of the other into a rodentlike gnawing, cutting, and digging tusk. In still other lines, notably among lemuroids, the lower incisors (with the canine) became long, delicate, comblike grooming teeth. Among higher monkeys, the lower deciduous incisors are modified into spatulate nutritional teeth.

Dental Enamel: Microscopic Patterns

According to Carter (1922), the enamel in living primates, with exception of the aye-eye (*Daubentonia*), is penetrated by a system of microscopic tubules continuous with the dental tubules. Among extinct prosimians he examined, the tubules were present in the teeth of *Hemiacodon* and *Phenacolemur* but absent in *Notharctus* and *Pelycodon*. A similar system of tubules had already been shown to be a consistent feature in marsupials, except *Phascolomys*. They are also present, according to Carter, in the Multituberculata, in some genera of Insectivora, *Tupaia* excluded, in the Hyracoidea, and in jerboa among the Rodentia (Tomes 1914, p. 176). Boyde (1971, p. 81) includes the Chiroptera among mammals with enamel tubules.

Among primates, Carter distinguished two patterns of enamel structure, as follows.

1. Margins of enamel prisms or rods wavy or kinky in outline, the prisms themselves separated by a considerable amount of interprismatic enamel: *Hemiacodon, Tarsius,* Lorisoidea, Platyrrhini.
2. Margins of enamel prisms straight or broadly contoured, the rods separated by a slight amount of interprismatic enamel. *Pelycodus, Notharctus,* Lemuroidea, Daubentonoidea, Catarrhini.

Characters of the enamel pattern outlined by Carter have not been confirmed. Carter evidently examined a considerable number of species, many of which are mentioned and illustrated. Unfortunately, there is no list of specimens examined and no indication of the extent of individual variation. Nevertheless, Carter's findings seem to be important and worthy of reexamination with modern techniques including the scanning electron microscope. Tate Regan (1930) hailed Carter's discoveries as decisive in his proposed classification of primates. Later authors, however, ignored these findings. Carter's article is not mentioned by A. E. W. Miles (1967) and contributors (cf. Poole 1967) to his volume on the structural and chemical organization of teeth, or by Boyde (1971) in his microscopic examination of mammalian tooth enamel.

Nose and Snout

The nostrils or anterior nares are the paired external openings of the organ usually distinguished as a *nose* in haplorhine primates (*Tarsius,* Platyrrhini, Catarrhini) but as a *snout* in strepsirhine primates (prosimians) and other mammals (fig. I.9). The obliquely placed strepsirhine nostrils are shaped like a comma. The oval aperture in front communicates directly with the nasal cavity and usually exposes the lightly pigmented or flesh-colored prominence caused by the internal alar cartilage. The elongate tail or posterior slit of the nostril is a blind cutaneous sac, the *diverticulum nasi.* The *rhinarium,* or the dark, moist, glandular, naked skin surrounding the nostrils of the snout extends in strepsirhines above, to the sides, and between the nostrils, then tapers below across the middle of the upper lip to its inferior border. A deep median cleft, the *philtrum,* extends the length of the rhinarium.

The haplorhine nostril is ovate or elliptical with the posterior slit or diverticulum nasi vestigial or absent. In further contrast with strepsirhines, the skin surrounding the nostrils is undifferentiated from contiguous parts of the nose and upper lip. It is more or less hirsute in platyrrhines, cercopithecids, and hylobatids but is virtually naked although not moist or glandular in pongids and most humans. The philtrum persists as a shallow groove in some primitive haplorhines but appears only as a median dip or depression of the upper lip in most higher primates including man. The degree of development of the primate philtrum is probably directly related to the degree of persistence of sutural definition of the premaxillary (intermaxillary) bones in ontogeny and phylogeny. The cleft lip anomaly of higher primates suggests but almost certainly is not an atavism of the strepsirhine philtrum.

The fleshy internarial septum or columna, measured between the lower median borders of the nostrils, is relatively narrow in catarrhines, but broad in *Tarsius* and platyrrhines. The septum appears to be narrower in howlers (*Alouatta*), spider monkeys (*Ateles, Brachyteles*), and night monkeys (*Aotus*) than in other platyrrhines but is still wider than in catarrhines of comparable body mass.

Similarities between *Tarsius* and higher primates, particularly callitrichids, with respect to structure of the nose, lip, and other characters, convinced Pocock (1918) of the need for a primary division of primates into the Strepsirhini E. Geoffroy and the Haplorhini, a new name he proposed for nonprosimian primates.

External Genitalia

Penis

The copulating organ is pendulous in primates, some insectivores, colugo, most bats, bears, and possibly others, depending on the definition of pendulous and the state of the penis at the time of observation.

Os Penis

The penis bone or baculum is a mammalian character that probably evolved independently in each order where it occurs. It is present in some insectivores (but not tupaiids), bats, carnivores, pinnipeds, rodents, and in all

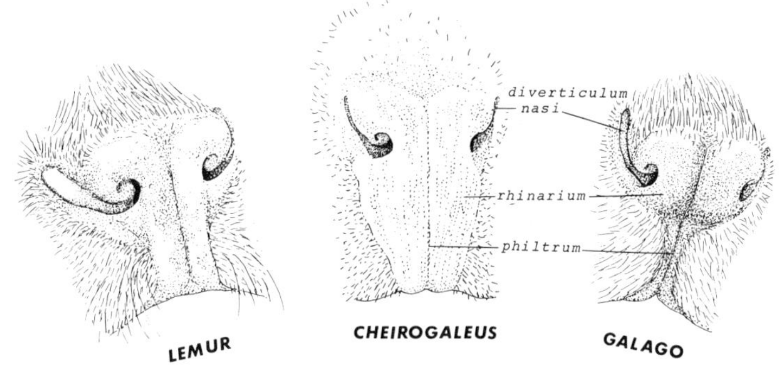

STREPSIRHINI

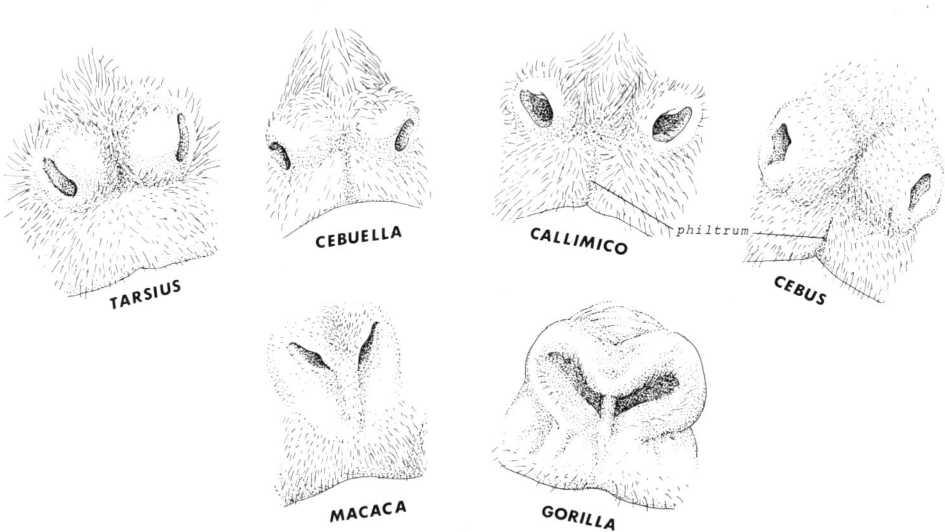

HAPLORHINI

Fig. I.9. Snouts, noses, and nostrils: *Strepsirhine* (lemuroid and lorisoid) snout with true nostril in front produced laterally as a blind slit, the *diverticulum nasi;* entire opening surrounded by the naked, moist, glandular *rhinarium* with median cleft or *philtrum. Haplorhine:* Nose with simple nostrils, no rhinarium, philtrum vestigial or absent; internarial breadth wide in *Tarsius* and all platyrrhines (e.g., *Cebuella, Callimico, Cebus*), comparatively narrow in all catarrhines (e.g., *Macaca, Gorilla*).

primates except man, a few cebids, and the tarsier (cf. p. 117). The os clitoridis is absent in species lacking an os penis, and is not always present or detectable in species with an os penis consistently present.

Scrotum

The testicular pouch evolved to contain the testes during spermatogenesis at a somewhat cooler temperature than usually prevails in the abdominal cavity. In most mammals the scrotum is postpenial. In the majority of primates it is also postpenial, but in lemuroids, callitrichids, and some cebids, it is parapenial. In gibbons and tupaiids, the position of the pouch varies from parapenial to prepenial. In marsupials, the scrotum is consistently prepenial.

Testes

The primitive position of the gonads is abdominal. Descent of the testes through the inguinal canal into a scrotal sac evolved in some mammalian lines but not in others. The testes are inguinal in juvenal or near-term fetal primates and scrotal in adults, but the organs can be retracted into the inguinal region by many, if not most, lemuroids and by all callitrichids. The same pattern obtains in many insectivores, tupaiids, and some rodents, but the withdrawn testes may be lodged in either the abdominal cavity or inguinal canal. Mature testes of other mammalian orders may be consistently abdominal, inguinal, or scrotal (cf. p. 116).

Urethra

Urethra and vagina usually open into a common urogenital sinus. In female primates, as in many other mammals, the sinus is modified into a shallow vulva with the urethra opening at the tip of the clitoris, the vagina at the base. A similar pattern appears in bats, some insectivores (but not tupaiids), many rodents, and the spotted hyena.

Mammae

A single pair of pectoral (or axial) mammae characterizes most primates. Supernumerary or vestigial mammae may occur anywhere along the mammary line extending from axilla to groin. Among lemuroids, however (cf. Schultz 1948), usually one but frequently up to three well-developed mammary pairs are pectoral (including axial), one pair abdominal, and one or two pairs inguinal. The total number, however, rarely exceeds three pairs in any one female. In *Daubentonia*, only a single inguinal pair is present. Reduction of the primitive number of mammae from a score or more with disposition of the remaining ones in specific fields has occurred independently in other mammals. The primate pattern recurs in bats. In sirenians, only a single pectoral pair persists, as in higher primates; and in many ungulates only an inguinal pair remains, thus paralleling the aye-aye.

Internal Organs

Cecum
The blind gut is present in all primates, but its occurrence in other mammals is so variable that systematic importance beyond family grade cannot be attached to the organ.

Liver and Gallbladder
The liver varies considerably in form but is typically lobate in mammals generally. The gallbladder is likewise variable, but its systematic importance lies only in its presence or absence. It persists in all primates and in all members of most orders of mammals. It is consistently absent in the Cetacea, Perissodactyla, and Proboscidea and absent in one or comparatively few species of each of the orders Rodentia, Artiodactyla, Xenarthra, and Sirenia.

Laryngeal Sacs

Laryngeal diverticula or air sacs are present in all primates and many, if not most, placental mammals. Four or five types, depending on the site of the opening relative to the ventricle, are distinguished in primates (figs. I.10, 11). Bartels (1905) reviewed virtually all early literature and classified the laryngeal sacs according to structure in 29 primate species representing 13 genera and 5 families. Starck and Schneider (1960), in their monographic review of primate larynges, compared 64 specimens (including 2 of *Tupaia*) representing 34 species, 25 genera, and 11 families. Hayama (1970) summarized the information and organized primate laryngeal sacs into 5 types on the basis of 458 individuals (including 22 of *Tupaia* and 199 of *Macaca*) representing 64 species, 30 genera, and 9 families. Gautier (1971) made a comparative ontogenetic study of the median superior ventral sac in 79 specimens representing 7 species of Gabonese cercopithecines of all ages and both sexes. The total number of primates listed in the works cited represent 35 genera in 11 families, or all but one or two of the extant primate families. Structure, function, and evolution of the larynx from fish to man has been discussed by Negus (1949).

The arrangement of laryngeal sacs given below is based primarily on the cited works of Bartels, Starck and Schneider, and Hayama. References to laryngeal samples of Callitrichidae and Callimiconidae include the following which I examined: *Cebuella pygmaea,* 1♂/–/1?, *Callithrix jacchus,* 1♂/2♀, *Saguinus midas,* 1/0, *Saguinus mystax,* 1/0, *Saguinus oedipus,* 1/1, *Leontopithecus rosalia rosalia,* 3/2, *Callimico goeldii* 1/0.

1. *Saccus ventriculi laryngis lateralis* (lateral ventricular or Morgani's sac, fig. I.10A)
   Paired sacs, one opening on lateral side of each laryngeal ventricle in all primates. Lateral ventricular sacs directed backward in *Tupaia* and lemuroids are regarded by Hayama (1970) as a type distinct from those directed forward (or in no special direction) in all primates, including lemuroids.
   The paired lateral ventricular sacs attain their greatest extent and complexity in apes.
2. *Saccus medianus superior anterior* (median ventral superior sac, fig. I.10B)
   Unpaired median ventral sac opening between epiglottis and thyroid cartilage superior to ventricle. According to Starck and Schneider (1960) and Hayama (1970) they are present in lemuroids, catarrhine monkeys, and cebids (*Cebus, Ateles, Ateles paniscus paniscus* ♂♀, *A. paniscus geoffroyi* ♂♀, *A. paniscus belzebuth* ♂, *Lagothrix, Alouatta*). There is a suggestion of this sac in the male *Callimico* at hand, but not in callitrichids I examined or in the following platyrrhines examined by Hayama (1970): *Callithrix jacchus jacchus* 2♂♂/♀♀; *C. jacchus penicillata* 2/2; *C. argentata* 1/1; *Cebuella pygmaea* 1/1; *Saguinus tamarin* (=*S. midas niger*) 1/0; *S. oedipus* 6/5; *Leontopithecus rosalia rosalia* 1/1; *Aotus trivirgatus* 3/2; *Saimiri sciureus* 2/2; *Ateles paniscus belzebuth* 0/1. Structure, ontogeny, variation, and function of the median ventral superior sac in cercopithecines are described by Gautier (1971).
3. *Saccus medianus inferior posterior* (median dorsal inferior sac, fig. I.10C)
   Unpaired median dorsal (*posterior* in human anatomy) sac opening below ventricle between cricoid cartilage and first tracheal ring and extending back between trachea and esophagus. Starck and Schneider (1960, figs. 45–47) note the sac in *Indri indri Varecia variegata, Microcebus,* and *Ateles.* Hayama (1970) describes and figures the dorsal sac of an adult male *Ateles* and also records one for *Lagothrix.* The sac was absent in the lemuroids he examined (*Lemur catta* 3/1; *L. mongoz* 1/1; *Loris tardigradus* 2/2; *Nycticebus coucang* 1/1; *Galago senegalensis* 2/1; *G. minutus* 1/1), and in callitrichids and callimicos I examined.
4. *Saccus medianus inferior anterior* (median ventral inferior sac, fig. I.10D).
   Unpaired median ventral sac opening below ventricle between thyroid and cricoid cartilages. According to Starck and Schneider (1960), the sac is rare in primates but well developed in some rodents and in Equidae. Among primates, they note the sac in *Callithrix jacchus* (1/–) and *Leontopithecus rosalia rosalia* (1/1). Hayama records the sac for *Leontopithecus* (1/1) and *Aotus* (3/2).

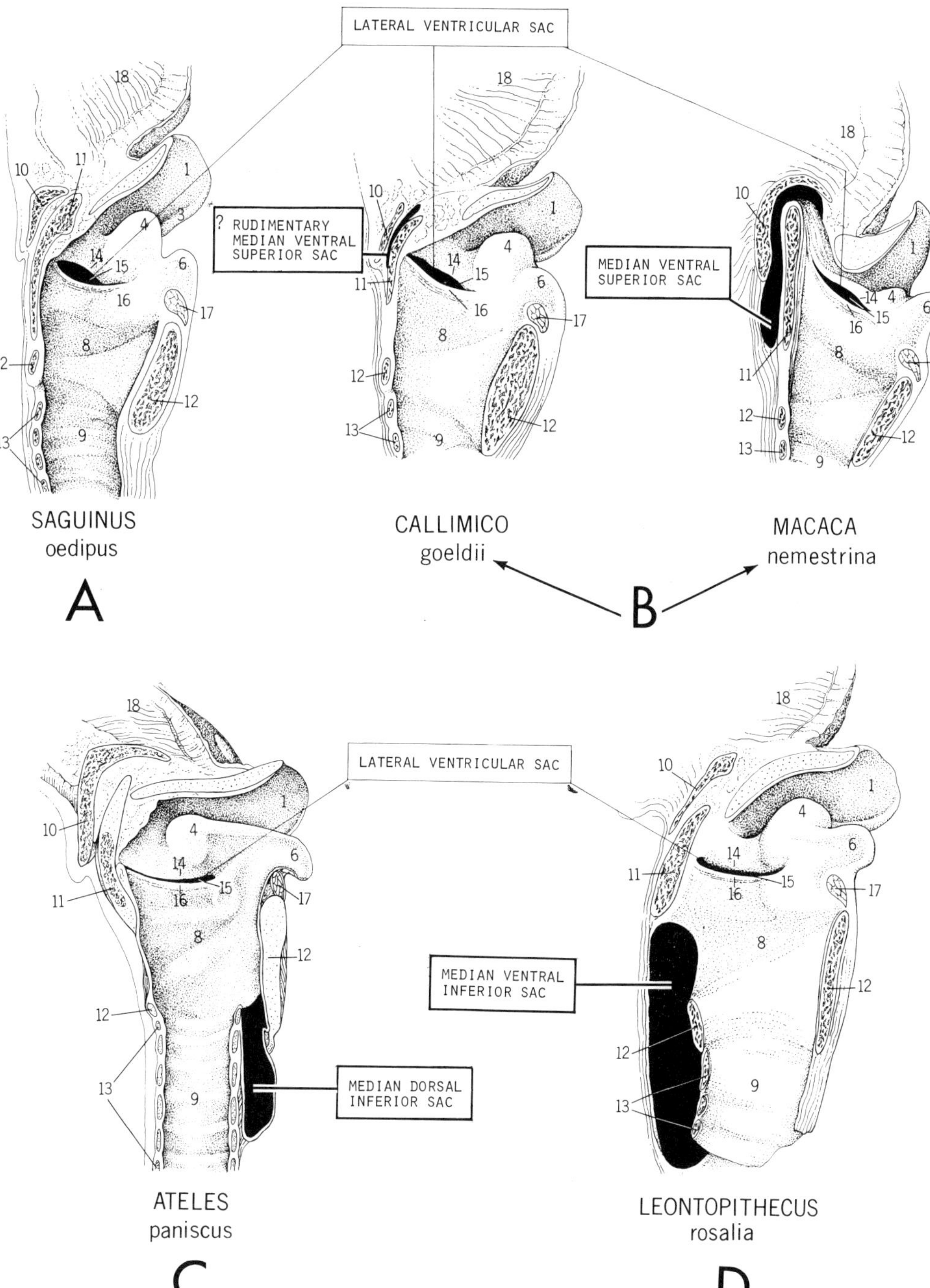

Fig. I.10. Right half of larynges showing air sac types in primates. *A*, Lateral ventricular sac (*saccus ventriculi laryngis lateralis*) in *Saguinus oedipus* and all other living primates; *B*, median ventral superior sac (*saccus medianus superior* anterior) in *Macaca* and many other primates; a rudimentary sac appears to be present in the single sample examined of *Callimico; C*, Median inferior dorsal sac (*saccus medianus inferior posterior*) in *Ateles paniscus* (redrawn from Starck and Schneider, 1960, *Primatologia* 3 (2):499, fig. 46); *D*, median inferior ventral sac (*saccus medianus inferior anterior*) in *Leontopithecus rosalia.* Explanation of symbols: *1,* epiglottis; *2,* aditus larynges; *3,* lateral epiglottic fold (*plica epiglottica lateralis; plica cuneiforme epiglottica*); *4, tuberculum cuneiforme* (Wristberg's cartilage; cuneiform cartilage); *5,* glottis; *6,* plica arytenoides (arytenoidal eminence; arytenoidalwulst; Santorini's cartilage; corniculate cartilage); *7,* esophagus; *8,* laryngeal cavity; *9,* trachea; *10,* hyoid cartilage; *11,* thyroid cartilage; *12,* cricoid cartilage; *13,* tracheal cartilages; *14,* plica ventricularis; *15,* laryngeal ventricle; *16,* plica vocalis; *17,* interarytenoid muscle; *18,* tongue. All samples drawn to approximately the same size.

The median ventral sac was first seen by Cuvier (1805, p. 503) in the lion-tamarin, *Leontopithecus rosalia.* Forbes (1896, p. 138) makes the statement that "these animals are said to possess an air-sac in the throat, at the back of the trachea (or wind pipe) as in *Ateles,"* but fails to give the source of his information. Perhaps Forbes translated the described "posterior" position of the sac into *dorsal* instead of inferior. I found the sac present and well developed in three males of *Leontopithecus,* poorly developed in one

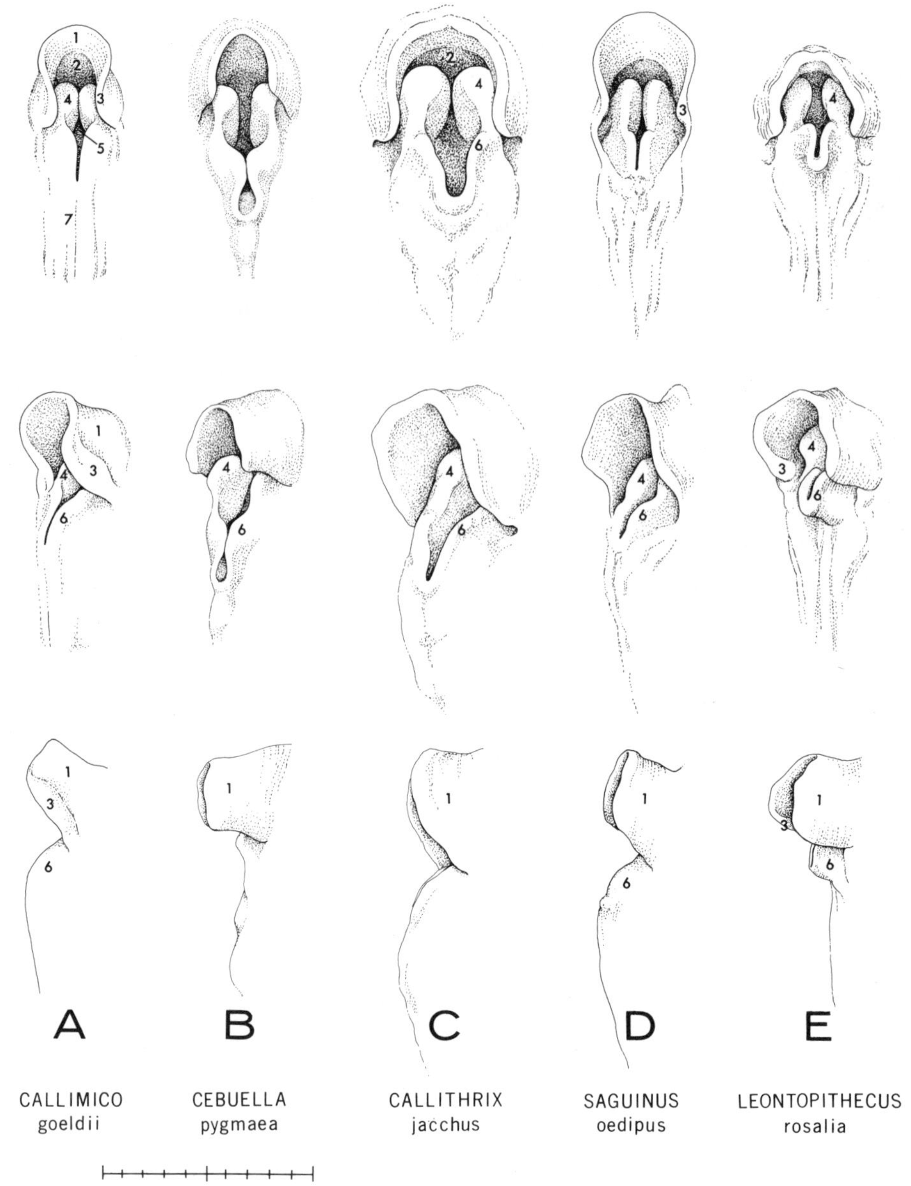

Fig. I.11. Larynx of (*A*) *Callimico;* (*B*) *Cebuella;* (*C*) *Callithrix;* (*D*) *Saguinus;* (*E*) *Leontopithecus.* Surfaces shown are full dorsal (*upper row*), dorsolateral (*middle row*), and right lateral (*lower row*). For explanation of symbols see fig. I.10. The apparent differences between the species in shape, degree of development, and topographical relationships of the pharyngeal parts may vary according to genus, species, or perhaps are individual variables of no taxonomic significance. For number of specimens examined see text page 18.

female, absent in a second, absent in all other callitrichids examined, and absent in *Callimico.*

Remarks. Paired *lateral ventricular* sacs are present in all primates and are probably primitive for the order. The *median ventral superior sac* is present in lemuroids, cebids, and catarrhine monkeys and absent in callitrichids and hominoids. Obviously, neither phylogeny nor body size is a factor in the presence or absence of this sac. Present information indicates that the peculiar *median ventral inferior sac* appears only in the distantly related small platyrrhines *Callithrix jacchus, Leontopithecus rosalia,* and *Aotus trivirgatus.* The equally uncommon *median dorsal inferior sac* is known to occur only in the Malagasy *Varecia variegata* and *Indri indri* on the one hand, and the new World cebid *Ateles paniscus* on the other. All three forms are comparable in size but they differ in most behavioral traits.

Distribution of the various types of laryngeal sacs indicates that each arose independently in one or more lines. The lateral ventricular sacs are universal and the only kind present in hominids. All other primates possess an additional type, and in lemuroids and cebids there is a total of three types.

Variations in type, size, and distribution of the laryngeal sacs is considerable and shows no consistent or plausible correlation with any structural or behavioral trait or evolutionary trend in mammals apart from the obvious relationship to control of air volume and movements. The sacs can, and in many primates do, serve as vocal resonators, modulators, and amplifiers, particularly in adult males, where they attain their fullest development. Keleman (1969) described the role of laryngeal sacs in the vocalization of chimpanzees, and Gautier (1971) detailed and demonstrated experimentally the function of the median ventral superior sac as a sound amplifier in cercopithecines. Hypothetical, often fanciful, nonrespiratory or nonvocal functions attributed to the primate laryngeal sacs were critically reviewed by Starck and Schneider (1960, p. 518). According to these authorities (1960, p. 496), "die Beziehung derartiger Bildung zur Function des Larynx als Stimmorgan kann heute kaum mehr bezweifelt werden, da die Kombination analytisch anatomischer Untersuchung mit Auswertung von Lebenbeobachtungen (Bernstein, [1923], G. and R. Brandes [1938 and 1932, respectively], Hill und Booth [1957], Lampert [1926], und andere, siehe hierzu S. 518) keine andere Deutung zulässt." The observations and experimental evidence of Gautier (1971) add more weight to these conclusions.

The vocal apparatus of catarrhines, according to Bernstein (1923), is more advanced than that of platyrrhines. In the latter, the oral cavity is said to be less differentiated, the larynx more superior in position, the air passages narrower, the vocal chords less flexible, the hyoid bone immobile, the laryngeal muscles weaker, the laryngeal sacs more specialized as resonators, and the entire system tending toward a barking type of vacalization rather than the articular type as in catarrhines. Most of the distinctions drawn by Bernstein are highly questionable (cf. Lampert 1926, p. 652), but the vocal organs and oral cavity of platyrrhines are, as Bernstein implies, less evolved than those of catarrhines. Bernstein's opinions are derived from examination of a single adult of each of the following genera: *Lemur, Nycticebus, Cebus, Lagothrix, Alouatta, Macaca, Hylobates, Pan,* and a juvenal of *Lagothrix* and of *Papio.*

Primate pharyngeal sac evolution cannot be separated from evolution of the hyoid apparatus but seems to be independent of cranial modifications. Nevertheless, a relationship, perhaps incidental, may exist between the median inferior pharyngeal sac in *Leontopithecus* and its complex of sphenoidal sinuses.

As for the hyoid apparatus itself, its intimate morphological relationship with the tongue, mandible, and basicranium is obvious. On the other hand, no close relationship, between the hyoid apparatus and other parts of the body, or body mass, is evident. Judging from his comparative anatomical studies of the hyoid apparatus and skulls of *Callithrix jacchus* (2 specimens), *Saguinus oedipus* (8), *Alouatta villosa* (14), *Cebus capucinus* (3), *Macaca mulatta* (8) and *Papio papio* (8), Hilloowala (1975, p. 380) concluded that "the relative weight of the animals do [*sic*] not have any bearing on the size of the basihyal [or hyoid bone]. The determining factor is the size of the median air sacs." This structure, he continued, "depends on the predominance of herbivorous material in the diet. It is *felt* [italics mine] that the more herbivorous the diet the larger the concavity and size of the [primate] basihyal. This contention is the topic of another paper submitted for publication."

The other paper has not yet come to hand, and the one cited contains no sign of a consistent correlation between size of basihyal and type of diet. A few contradictory notes do appear. For example, howler monkeys (*Alouatta*) are virtually entirely herbivorous, and their basihyal is the largest of all mammals. However, the difference in basihyal size between male and female howlers is enormous, and a comparable size spread exists between the largest basihyal of adult male *Alouatta seniculus* and the smallest of adult male *A. villosa,* but a difference in herbivority does not exist between the sexes or species. Leaf-eating colobines are larger than howlers and no less herbivorous, but the size of the male basihyal is comparable only to that of female *Alouatta villosa,* the species with the smallest basihyal. In contrast, baboons are among the most carnivorous of primates, but the basihyals of the 8 females examined by Hilloowala (1975, p. 368) average larger than those of the 5 female *Alouatta villosa* with which he compared them. It may be added that a consistent correlation between basihyal size and diet type among nonprimates has not been noted. Further, Hilloowala's assertion that "relative weights of the animals do not have any bearing on the size of the basihyal" is itself a contradiction of his thesis. Among land mammals, the more herbivorous the species the greater its body mass as compared with the nearest relatives.

More arguments can be adduced to dispute Hilloowala's contention, but his definitive words on the subject should be awaited.

Cephalic Arterial System

Plans of the primate cephalic arterial system included by Bugge (1972; 1974) in his doctoral dissertation are reproduced here as supplements to my definition (p. 6), classification (p. 9), and cranial description (p. 14) of primates.

Bugge was concerned with the basic or presumed primitive pattern of the internal-external carotid and stapedial arterial systems and their modifications by various anastomoses (fig. I.12) in several orders of mammals. Much of the important literature on the subject appears to have been bypassed. Bugge's efforts at a systematic arrangement of the Primates on the basis of 22 specimens representing 6 primate species and 17 specimens representing 1 tupaiid species derive little from the results of his research. His classification and the specimens he examined follow.

Grade O Subprimates
  Suborder Tupaioidea
    Tupaiidae (17 *Tupaia glis*)
Grade A Strepsirhini
  Suborder Lemuroidea
    Lemuridae (2 *Lemur catta*)
  Suborder Lorisoidea
    Lorisidae (8 *Nycticebus coucang*)
    Galagidae (4 *Galago senegalensis*)
Grade B Haplorhini
  Suborder Tarsioidea
    Tarsiidae (none)
  Suborder Pithecoidea
    Infraorder Platyrrhini
      Cebidae (2 *Aotus trivirgatus*)
      Hapalidae (2 *Saguinus midas*)
    Infraorder Catarrhini
      Cercopithecidae (4 *Macaca mulatta*)
      Pongidae (none)
      Hominidae (none)

The value of the cephalic arterial system in the definition of primates is relative, and the little known of individual and specific variation is subject to conflicting

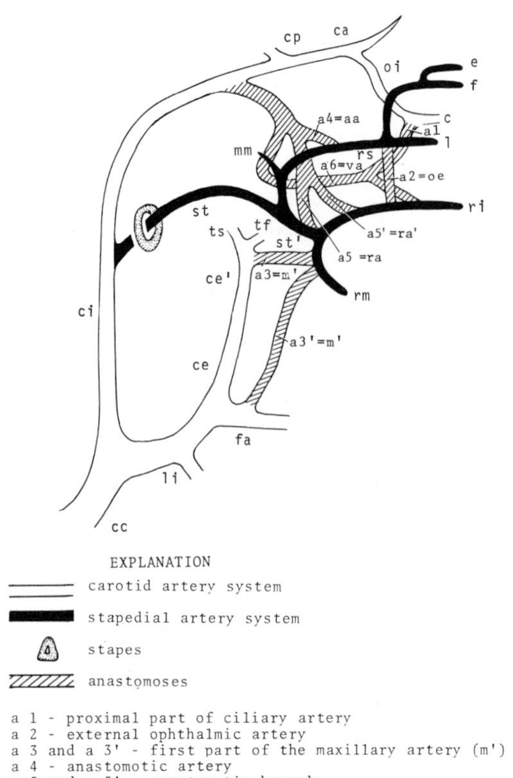

Fig. I.12. Anastomoses of cephalic arterial systems (after Bugge 1974, p. 100). Explanation of abbreviations: *a* = arteria; *aa* = a. anastomotica; *ap* = auricularis posterior; *c* = a. ciliaris; *ca* = circulus arteriosus (arterial circle of Willis); *cc* = a. carotis communis; *ce* = a. carotis externa (proximal part); *ce'* = a. carotis externa (distal part); *ci* = a. carotis interna (= promontory); *ci'* = a. "carotis interna"; *cp* = a. communicans posterior; *e* = a. ethmoidalis; *f* = a. frontalis; *fa* = a. facialis; *l* = a. lacrimalis; *li* = a. lingualis; *m'* = a. maxillaris (first part); *mm* = a. meningea media; *o* = a. ophthalmica; *oe* = a. ophthalmica externa; *oi* = a. ophthalmica interna; *oi'* = a. "internal" ophthalmic artery; *r* = branch; *ra* = anastomotic branch; *ri* = r. infraorbitalis; *rm* = r. mandibularis; *rs* = r. supraorbitalis; *rs'* = r. supraorbitalis (proximal part); *rtm* = rete mirabile; *st* = a. stapedia; *st'* = distal part of stapedial artery stem; *tf* = a. transversa faciei; *ts* = a. temporalis superficialis; *va* = a. canalis pterygoidei = a. Vidii.

interpretations. For example, differences in the cephalic arterial systems of *Lemur catta* and *V. variegata* seem to be of the same kind and degree of those distinguishing *Lemur catta* from *Tupaia glis*. Such specializations of the cephalic arterial system in *Nycticebus coucang* and *Galago senegalensis* as replacement of most of the true internal carotid (= promontory) artery with an independent trunk, absence of anastomosis *a 1*, and development of a unique anastomosis, *a 1'* (figs. I.12, 13) separate at least these two named lorisids from all other primates.

The aberrant and highly specialized *Aotus* is treated by Bugge as a primitive platyrrhine, whereas *Saguinus*, with respect to its cephalic arterial system, is regarded as having attained catarrhine grade. Differences between *Aotus* and *Saguinus* shown by Bugge (1974) are restricted to parts of the stapedial and ophthalmic arterial systems (figs. I.12, 13). Obliteration of the first system is about equal in both genera, but if obliteration progresses distally, as seems most likely, the condition is more advanced in *Aotus*. The ophthalmic arterial supply with anastomosis *X* appears to be a specialization in *Aotus* that is correlated with enlargement and modification of the eye for scotopic vision. It is not, as Bugge may believe, a primitive state. The evidence, supposing it is not made up of individual variables, points to a close relationship between platyrrhines and catarrhines and suggests that the cephalic arterial systems of callitrichids and catarrhines are more primitive than that of *Aotus*.

Anastomoses of Cephalic Arterial System Arrangement Based on Characterizations by Bugge 1974 (figure I.12)

1. All mammals except certain lorisoid Primates (see *a 1'* below)
   - (*a 1*) Between orbital arteries (*l, f, e*) from supraorbital branch (*rs*) and bulbar arteries (*c*) coming off the internal carotid artery (circulus arteriosus); in nonprimates becomes part of ciliary artery (*c*); in primates becomes part of opthalmic artery (*o*); arrangement in *Tupaia* somewhat intermediate.
2. *Varecia variegata* (permanent), *Homo sapiens* (fetus), many nonprimates
   - (*a 2*) External ophthalmic artery (part *oe*); between infraorbital branch (*ri*) and orbital part of supraorbital branch (*l, f, e*).
3. All primates, many nonprimates
   - (*a 3*) In primates, maxillary artery (part *m'*); between distal end of external carotid artery (*ce'*) and proximal part of mandibular branch (*rm*); anastomosis *a 3'* from proximal part of external carotid artery (*ce*); a facial artery (*fa*) sometimes replaces or augments anastomosis *a 3*..
4. Nonprimates and transient in human (and other primate [?] embryos)
   - (*a 4*) Anastomotic artery (*aa*); between distal end of internal carotid artery (*ci*) and orbital end of supraorbital branch (*rs*).
   - (*a 5*) Anastomotic branch (*ra, ra'*); between distal end of internal carotid artery (*ci*) and infraorbital branch (*ri*); also other variable connections.
   - (*a 6*) Pterygoid canal, or Vidian artery (*va*); connects distal end of internal carotid (*ci*) with ciliary artery (*c*) or infraorbital branch (*ri*), or both.
5. Primates: Lorisoidea (*Nycticebus coucang, Galago senegalensis*)
   - (*a 1'*) Between stem of frontal (*f*) and ethmoidal (*e*) arteries and circulus arteriosus (*ca*).
6. Primates: Cebidae (*Aotus trivirgatus*)
   - (*X*) Between ophthalmic artery (*o*) and circulus arteriosus.

Models of Cephalic Arterial Systems: Characterizations According to Bugge 1974 (fig. I.13)

A. *Tupaia glis*
   Internal carotid (= promontory) artery (*ci*) persistent; supplies brain assisted by vertebral artery.

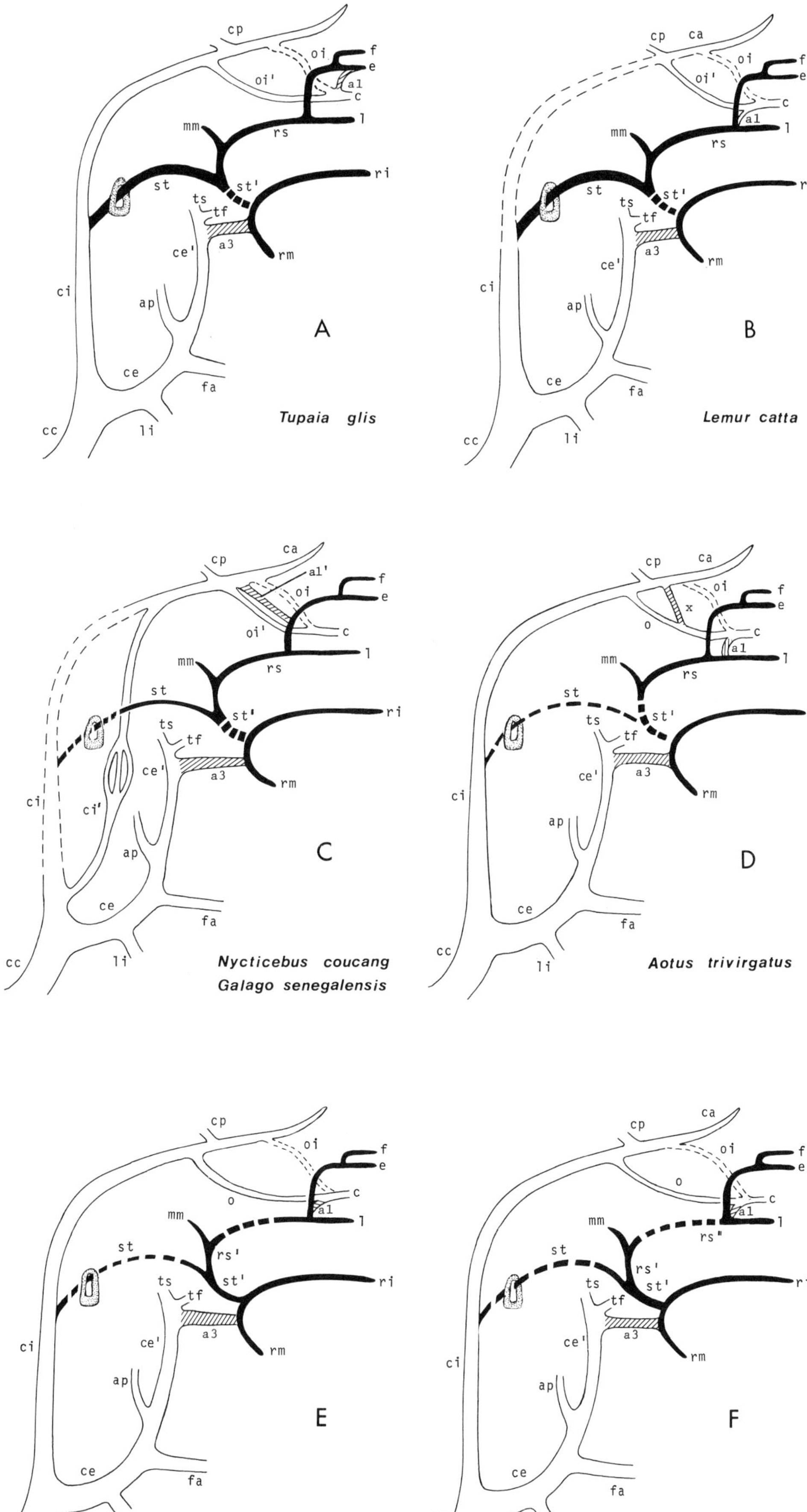

Fig. I.13. Models of cephalic arterial system (after Bugge 1972, 1974). (*A*) *Tupaia glis;* (*B*) *Lemur catta;* (*C*) *Nycticebus coucang* and *Galago senegalensis;* (*D*) *Aotus trivirgatus;* (*E*) *Saguinus midas* and *Macaca mulatta;* (*F*) *Homo sapiens;* see fig. I.12 for explanation of abbreviations.

Stapedial artery stem (*st*) persistent except distal portion; supplies dura and all extrabulbar parts of orbit (*l, f, e*) via supraorbital branch (*rs*); eyeball (*c*) supplied via anastomosis *a 1*.

"Internal" opthalmic artery (*oi'*) given off from distal part of internal carotid (*ci*) proximal to point of origin of posterior communicating artery (*cp*).

External carotid artery (*ce*) supplies upper and lower jaws (*ri, rm*) via anastomosis *a 3*.

Anastomosis *a 1* seems to form proximal part of ciliary artery (*c*) as in nonprimates (Bugge 1974, p. 6).

B. *Lemur catta*

Internal carotid artery (*ci*) obliterated distal to origin of stapedial artery (*st*); brain supplied by vertebral artery alone [Note: In *Varecia variegata*, a weak internal carotid artery distal to departure of stapedial artery is retained, as in *Tupaia* (Bugge 1974, p. 340).]

Stapedial artery stem (*st*) persistent except distally, as in *Tupaia;* supplies dura and most of extrabulbar part of orbit via anastomosis *a 1* as in *Tupaia.*

"Internal" ophthalmic artery (*oi'*) given off from circulus arteriosus (circle of Willis) opposite point of departure of posterior communicating artery (*cp*); supplies eyeball (from vertebral artery).

[Note: In *Varecia variegata,* internal ophthalmic artery given off as in *Tupaia* (Bugge 1974, p. 34).]

External artery supply system via anastomosis *a 3* as in *Tupaia.*

Anastomosis *a 1* becomes part of ophthalmic artery (*o*).

C. *Nycticebus coucang, Galago senegalensis*

Internal carotid (= promontory) artery (*ci*) mostly obliterated, the portion replaced by "internal carotid" artery (*ci'*); communicating internal carotid artery/vertebral artery system (circulus arteriosus) supplies extrabulbar part of orbit and dura via anastomosis *a 1'*.

"Internal carotid" artery (*ci'*) forms rete mirabile (*rtm*), presumed homologous with ascending pharyngeal artery (Bugge 1974, p. 35), and ends in circulus arteriosus (*ca*); supplies brain with assistance of vertebral artery.

Stapedial artery stem (*st*) obliterated proximally; stapedial area of supply annexed by "internal"-external carotid artery system plus vertebral artery.

"Internal" opthalmic artery (*oi'*) arises from circulus arteriosus (*ca*) opposite posterior communicating artery (*cp*) as in *Lemur catta;* supplies eyeball.

External carotid supply system via anastomosis *a 3* as in *Tupaia.*

Anastomosis *a 1* absent.

Anastomosis *a 1'* between common stem of frontal (*f*) and ethmoidal (*e*) arteries and circulus arteriosus (*ca*) is unique to lorisoids.

For more details and explanations of the cephalic arterial system in *Nycticebus* see Krishnamurti (1968), one of many important contributions not cited by Bugge.

D. *Aotus trivirgatus*

Internal carotid (= promontory) artery (*ci*) well developed; supplies brain, assisted by vertebral artery as in *Tupaia.*

Stapedial artery stem entirely obliterated.

Stapedial supply area annexed by internal-external carotid system assisted by vertebral artery.

External carotid artery (*ce*) supplies upper and lower jaws (*ri, rm*) via anastomosis *a 3.*

Ophthalmic artery (*o*) arises from distal part of internal carotid artery (*ci*) but is connected with anterior part of circulus arteriosus (*ca*) via anastomosis *X;* supplies eyeball (*c*); and through anastomosis *a 1* supplies dura (*mm*) and extrabulbar part of orbit (*l, f, e*).

External carotid artery (*ce*) supplies upper and lower jaws via anastomosis *a 3,* as in *Tupaia.*

E. *Saguinus midas, Macaca mulatta* (*Homo* and other catarrhines)

Proximal part of stapedial artery stem (*st*) and mid-part of supraorbital branch (*rs*) obliterated.

External carotid artery (*ce*) supplies upper and lower jaws (*ri, rm*) via anastomosis *a 3* as in *Aotus,* but also most of dura (*mm*) via distal part of stapedial artery system (*st'*) and proximal part of supraorbital branch (*rs'*).

Anastomosis *X* absent.

Other parts of cephalic arterial system as in *Aotus.* For detailed descriptions of the cephalic vascularization of *Callithrix jacchus* see Miraglia and Teixeira (1958; 1960) and de Souza et al. (1962).

Lymphatic System

The lower half of the lymphatic system in all twenty-five representatives of seven platyrrhine genera (*Callithrix, Saguinus, Saimiri, Aotus, Cebus, Alouatta, Ateles*) investigated by Silvester (1912) makes direct and permanent connection with the venous system in the region of the junction of the renal vein with the inferior vena cava. In the sixteen catarrhine monkeys he examined, Silvester found no such lymphaticovenous communication. The platyrrhine upper or thoracic lymphatic region, however, is drained by the anterior jugular-subclavian venous system as in other primates and mammals generally. Beattie (1927, p. 686) tested Silvester's injection methods in *Callithrix jacchus jacchus,* but his results were not conclusive. Ottaviani, Di Dio, and Manfredonia (1958; 1959) did, however, confirm Silvester's findings in the lower half of the lymphatic system of *Callithrix jacchus penicillata.* Job (1918) found a similar condition occurring regularly in embryos of the Norway rat (*Rattus norvegicus*), but in only 40% of the adult rats examined. Direct communication between vena cava and lymphatic collecting vessels was also discovered by Azzali and Di Dio (1965) in the abdominal organs of five specimens of *Bradypus tridactylus.*

The unusual condition of the lymphatic system in such widely separated animals as platyrrhines, Norway rat, and three-toed sloth points to its independent origin in each group. The condition is not necessarily a primitive one, as compared with other mammals. Perhaps it is a fetal condition retained in adults of some species, genera, or families but not in others of closely related groups.

Amino Acids

Urinary amino acids secreted by representatives of ten families of nonhuman primates were analyzed by

Fooden (1961). The study revealed a few relative differences in concentrations between some genera and families but nothing that could readily be translated into characters of phylogenetic or even taxonomic significance. Prosimians, it was shown, were particularly low in urinary glutamine and hydroxyproline. Cebids (*Saimiri, Cebus, Lagothrix, Ateles*) showed high concentrations of all six urinary amino acids analyzed, including a uniquely high concentration of hydroxyproline. Callitrichids (*Callithrix, Saguinus*) tended to be low in serine, glutamine, lysine, and hydroxyline but high in taurine and threonine. Catarrhines tended toward low concentrations of all urinary amino acids except glutamine. As indicated by Fooden (1961, p. 170), no consistent differences in concentrations appeared among the species of any genus. A more representative sampling of the species and genera could conceivably alter significantly, if not erase, all observed differences between the families.

Karyology and Taxonomy

The diploid chromosome number in Primates ranges from 20 to 80. The breakdown by major groups is as follows.

Lemuroidea: 44 (*Lemur macaco*) to 66 (*Microcebus murinus; Cheirogaleus major*).
Lorisoidea: 36 (*Galago senegalensis*) to 62 (*Galago crassicaudatus; Perodicticus; Loris*).
Tarsioidea: 80 (*Tarsius syrichta; T. bancanus*).
Catarrhini: 42 (*Papio*) to 72 (*Cercopithecus mitis*).
Platyrrhini:
- Callitrichidae: 44 (*Cebuella; Callithrix argentata* group) to 46 (*Saguinus; Leontopithecus; Callithrix jacchus* group).
- Cebidae: 20 (*Callicebus torquatus*) to 62 (*Lagothrix lagothricha*).
- Callimiconidae: 48 (*Callimico goeldii*).

In 46 out of approximately 100 valid primate species for which karyotypes are recorded, the diploid chromosome number ranges from 42 to 48. The mean of the extremes (20–80) is 50 chromosomes. These figures suggest that the basic or primary number of chromosomes for living primates lies within the range 42 to 50 (cf. Chu and Bender 1961, p. 1404). Only one chromosome count (2n = 20) is less than 32, and 1 (2n = 80) exceeds 72. Some or most of the gaps between numbers will undoubtedly be filled as more karyotypes become known.

The highest mammalian diploid number recorded to date is 92 for the South American aquatic cricetine rodent *Anotomys leander;* the lowest is 6, for the female of the Indian muntjak, *Muntiacus muntjak.*

The karyotype is a character complex comparable in taxonomic portent to other character complexes of the same organism. The taxonomic significance of any one of them cannot be fully assessed except in terms of the total organism and of the dynamics, ecology, geography, and history of the population to which it belongs. The karyotypes themselves reveal that the similarities between those of different organisms are not reliable criteria for their degree of genetic relationship. Similar-appearing karyotypes are often present in widely separated species, and widely dissimilar karyotypes may appear in sibling species and often in the same species. Not uncommonly, a primitively organized karyotype is preserved in a highly evolved organism and an advanced chromosomal complement resides in a comparatively primitive organism. Although chromosome numbers and structure can be arranged in graded series, the basic or primary chromosome number of any one phyletic line varies independently of those of other lines. The diploid number may increase in some phyletic lines, decrease in others, remain relatively stable in still others, or vary in all directions. Reversal is not precluded in any line. Qualitative changes, some of them undoubtedly correlated with the numerical changes, are irreversible.

In many species with a more-or-less stable number of chromosomes, the gross structure of individual chromosomes may vary without complementarity between the acrocentric and biarmed autosomes. For example, in the North American pocket gopher, *Thomomys bottae,* with 2n = 76, the number of acrocentrics varies from 0 to 38. In the closely related *Thomomys umbrinus,* 2 acrocentrics are present in a population with 76 chromosomes and 10, 10, and 56 acrocentrics are present in three other populations with 78 chromosomes each (Berry and Baker 1971). Perhaps, as suggested by Benirschke, (1969, p. 217), whatever the chromosome number and morphology, "no significant differences exist between the total DNA content of those species possessing a low chromosome number and those with a high number."

The evolutionary trend toward increase or decrease in chromosome number may be inferred, but the essential chronological record to support the inference does not exist. Plausible as it may seem from taxonomic, technical, or mechanical points of view, the karyotype of living species A could not possibly be ancestral to that of living species B. By the same token, there is no proof that the karyotype of species B must have been preceded by a karyotype both quantitatively and qualitatively similar to that of species A.

Differences between the karyotypes and differences between other character complexes involving limbs, eyes, dental systems, pelages, colorations, or genitalia cannot be weighed on the same scales. If genetic origin and content is the criterion, it cannot be demonstrated that similar-appearing chromosomes are, as a whole, homologous. On the other hand, there is usually no question of the homology of similarly formed and oriented organs, tissues, and even the chromosome-containing cells. Visible alterations in chromosomal patterns are often biomechanical in origin and probably reversible. Alterations in other character complexes, however, are genetic expressions and irreversible, except possibly in a quasi manner through hybridization. Changes within the chromosomes of an ostensibly stable karyotype may not be visible. In contrast, the same cryptic chromosomal changes may be expressed as visible, perhaps profound, changes in the phenotype. A karyotype, as usually prepared for study, is an artful arrangement of metaphase chromosomes. The organism, or the combination of all character complexes, is a natural expression of the genome's interaction with the environment.

Taxonomy based on chromosome morphology cannot stand alone. All parts of an organism are completely integrated, but none evolves at the same rate or becomes obsolescent or disappears at the same time as others. Single-character taxonomy lacks perspective. It cannot always separate morphological grades from clades. It often confuses similarities between unrelated systems with similarities between related systems. The several proposed reconstructions of the evolution of karyotypes among various primate groups are essentially phenetic, but they ride the coattails of whatever phyletic arrangement of organisms appears to be ascendant at the time.

Symposia prepared by the following editors supplement the cytogenetic studies cited in text: Barnicot (1963), Benirschke (1969), and Berry and Southern (1970). Important works published since the above was completed in 1972 include de Boer (1973*a*; 1973*b*) on lorisoid karyology, and de Boer (1974) on platyrrhine karyotypes.

Estrus

Data on the primate estrous cycle is available for about 50 species, or one-third the number extant. According to Butler (1974), who compiled most of the recent information, the estrous cycle averages between 39 and 55 days in adult lemurs, between 30 and 47 days in lorisoids (Vincent 1971), 24 days in *Tarsius,* and 21 to 40 days in catarrhine monkeys (72.3± 36.23 days in adolescent female *Cercopithecus aethiops*), 29.8 days in "gibbon," 29 to 32 days in the orangutan, 31 (range 25–35) days in the gorilla, 37 days in the chimpanzee, and 28.32 ± .06 days in humans.

Knowledge of the estrous cycle in platyrrhines is limited. On the basis of variation in sex steroid levels, Preslock, Hampton, and Hampton (1973) determined a mean reproductive cycle of 15.5 ± 1.5 days for *Saguinus oedipus oedipus* and *S. fuscicollis illigeri.* In *Saimiri,* according to Lang (1967), the cycle lasts 12.54 ± 2.01 (6–18) days. Castellanos and McCombs (1968) confirm this with a mean of 12 ± 2.7 (8–16) days. The latest determination at hand, by Travis and Holmes (1974), is 10.9 ± 0.10 (9–13) days. Means calculated by other authors range from 7–8 days (Rosenblum et al. 1967) to 25.2 days (Denniston 1964). The mean and range reported by Castellanos and McCombs (1968) for *Cebus albifrons* is 17.5 ± 1.8 (12–49; greatest frequencies between 23 and 26) days, and for two females of *Lagothrix lagothricha,* 23 and 26 days.

In many species some or most estrous cycles may be anovular.

Vaginal bleeding in the unfertilized female has not been detected in prosimians. Small amounts of blood, hardly enough for discharge, have been noted in *Saguinus, Cebus, Alouatta, Lagothrix,* and *Ateles* but not in *Saimiri.* A menstrual flow lasting 2 to 8 days characterizes catarrhines.

The estrous cycle is repeated throughout the life of wild-living primates. Menopause appears to be unique to humans with life spans extended by cultured environments.

The external genitalia of female prosimians swell slightly during estrus. They swell somewhat more noticeably in callitrichids and cebids and notably in catarrhines except humans. A circumgenital sexual skin is well developed in callitrichids and extraordinarily developed in catarrhines except some species of *Cercopithecus,* chimpanzee, and humans. The brightly colored turgescent genitalia and circumgenital region of estrous monkeys signal the female's receptivity to the male whereas pheromones are the primary attractants in prosimians and callitrichids.

Female receptivity to coitus among prosimians and callitrichids is limited to the period of estrus. The vaginal orifice is widely open during the cycle in dwarf lemurs and galagos and nearly or entirely closed at all other times except during parturition. Cornification of a vaginal epithelium during estrus may be another device for permitting copulation, especially among those species of prosimians and platyrrhines where the penis is spinous and the anestrous vaginal lining is delicate.

Copulation is a social as well as procreative function among most higher primates and perhaps among some of the lower forms. Postpartum estrus among callitrichids, for example, may well be anovulatory, but the copulation it permits reinforces the pair bonds at a time when the dominant male is essential for care of the young. Cebids and catarrhines engage in social copulation outside as well as during the estrous cycle, apparently for establishing and maintaining social ranking. In captivity almost any primate engages in sexual activity, with or without a partner, to relieve boredom.

Reproduction and Development

Placentation

A placental connection between embryo and mother evolved independently in a number of vertebrate lines. Placentation is known among viviparous fish (some sharks and teleosts), reptiles (some lizards), and all mammals except monotremes (platypus and echidnas). Using the classification of Wynn (1968, p. 103) and Van Tienhoven (1968, p. 325), the placenta is epitheliochorial and diffuse in lemuroids and lorisoids, perissodactyls, artiodactyls, pangolins, whales, and some moles among the Insectivora. It is hemochorial, the attachment discoidal or double discoidal in platyrrhines, catarrhines, tarsiers, most insectivores, some bats, dassies, most rodents, xenarthrans, lagomorphs, sirenians, and the spotted hyena. The type in strepsirhines is regarded as the more primitive (cf. Luckett 1974). Numerous transitions between the labyrinthine and villous conditions of the hemochorial type of placenta have been noted, particularly in New World monkeys (Wynn 1968). Placentation in tupaiids, as determined by Martin (1968, p. 426), is typically labyrinthine endotheliochorial, the attachment bidiscoidal. Endotheliochorial placentation which differs from the tupaiid type in attachment or other details is found in elephants, aardvark, most carnivores, bats, and some rodents. Two other placental types, syndesmochorial and hemoendothelial, have been described, but distinction of the first from epitheliochorial and the second from hemoendothelial has been questioned. In any case, variation in placental types cuts across all mammalian orders and many infraordinal groups. Although the distinction between strepsirhine and haplorhine placentations is valid phylogenetic significance cannot be attached to it alone.

Body Mass, Litter Size, and Duration of Gestation

In any given line of living primates, the smaller or more primitive the species, the greater the number of young and the shorter the duration of gestation. Prosimians produce 1 to 3 young each year after a gestation period of 2 to 5 months. *Microcebus murinus,* smallest of prosimians, has the shortest gestation, 59 to 62 days—roughly 2 months—and produces the maximum number of young, usually fraternal twins, rarely triplets (Petter-Rousseaux 1962, p. 36), but according to Bluntschli (in Schultz 1948, p. 5), "mostly 2 to 3, often 4 embryos."

Gestation in the lemurine, *Lemur catta,* according to Evans and Goy (1968), lasts 131 to 136 days, roughly 4.5 months. Petter and Peyrieras (1970*a,* p. 375) report gestation of 140 days, or 4 months and 20 days, for *Hapalemur griseus griseus.* Gestation among lorisoids varies from 4.4 months (131 days) in *Arctocebus* to 6.4 months (193 days) in *Nycticebus,* with one or two young produced (Manley 1966). *Galago minutus (demidovii),* smallest of lorisoids, produces twins after a gestation period of about 4.7 months (140 days). However, Doyle, Pelletier, and Bekker (1967), report a 4-month gestation period in *Galago senegalensis moholi,* usually with twins, rarely with 1 or 3 produced in each of two litters annually. Callitrichids, smallest of platyrrhines, normally beget twins, sometimes triplets, after a gestation period of 4 to 5 months. The tarsier (*Tarsius syrichta*), gives birth to one exceptionally large, well-developed offspring about $\frac{1}{3}$ to $\frac{1}{2}$ the bulk of its mother after an estimated gestation period of 6 months (cf. Ulmer 1963; Le Gros Clark 1924). This species, one of the smallest of living primates, is the largest, most highly specialized end product of a major phyletic line. Almost nothing is known of the reproduction of the Malagasy aye-aye, *Daubentonia madagascariensis,* most aberrant of living primates, and only known member of its line. Petter and Peyrieras (1970*a*) believe the aye-aye produces one young every two or three years with the newborn delivered in a nest during October-November. Cebids and nonhuman catarrhines produce a single young, rarely twins, after a gestation period of 5 to 9 months according to species. The maximum recorded is an estimate of 289 days (9.6 months) for a zoo gorilla (Schaller 1963, p. 288).

The rough correlation between evolutionary grade on the one hand and body mass, litter size, and duration of gestation on the other applies to placentals generally (cf. Asdell 1965 for data). For example, shrews of the family Soricidae, which includes the smallest mammals, produce 2 to 10 young in each litter after a gestation period of 12–16 days in *Cryptotis,* and 17–28 days in larger species (Walker 1968, p. 142). Bats average smaller than insectivores but are much more specialized. Most species including the largest have one young annually, but the smallest species among the most primitive families produce 1 to 4 young, with 2 the average. The largest rodents give birth to one or a few offspring each year. Small species, especially among the more primitive muroids, average 3 to 8 young per litter, with 2 or more litters produced annually.[1] The more specialized species among the largest mammals do or can bring forth a single young each year, and still others, particularly among pinnipeds, sirenians, cetaceans, bears, camels, and elephants, bear only once every two years. Size for size, however, primates produce fewer and larger young after longer periods of gestation than most, if not all other mammals.

Phylogenetic trends alone do not explain the correlation between body mass, litter size, duration of gestation, and evolutionary grade in each lineage. Ecological factors must exert powerful selective pressures on reproductive regulatory mechanisms. As a result, most placentals of the same ecosystem produce young during the same season or seasons irrespective of specific differences in mating seasons and duration of gestation. Delayed fertilization and delayed implantation observed in nonprimates are other controlling factors in the duration of reproductive cycles and synchronization of breeding seasons. The condition or degree of development of the newborn is probably less important for survival than the season in which it is born (cf. Lancaster and Lee 1965; Sadleir 1969, p. 205) and the quality of care it receives.

Riesenfeld (1970) proposed that gravitational stresses related to the upright posture in primates favored reduction of litter size to one young per birth. The hypothesis was tested with surgically produced bipedal laboratory rats. The relevance of this experiment to conditions in nature is dubious. Nearly all nonhuman primates are quadrupedal and all but the most primitive normally produce a single young at a birth. The larger ungulates, pinnipeds, sirenians, and cetaceans also produce one young at a birth. There is not the slightest tendency toward bipedality in the history of any of these mammals.

Hour of Birth

Most primate births, according to records of humans and captive animals compiled by A. Jolly (1972, p. 108), occur during the night, or the most secluded half of the 24-hour day for the particular species. Time of birth among prosimians varies, but seems to coincide in many cases with the normal sleeping hours during daylight hours. In captivity, however, the prosimian circadian rhythm may be partially reversed. Hours of birth among great apes and gibbons seem to be random. Births among New and Old World monkeys, however, are preponderantly nocturnal.

Care of Young

Newborn of the Malagasy cheirogalene lemuroids *Microcebus murinus* and *Cheirogaleus major* are, according to Petter-Rousseaux (1964), born blind, nearly naked, and unable to cling to anything. They are delivered in a nest of leaves or the hollow of a tree where they are nursed until strong enough to accompany their mother on their own power. The eyes open after 2 to 4 days and the helpless young are transported by the mother in her teeth, never riding her back or clinging to her belly or teats. In more advanced lemurines, the eyes are open at birth, but the young of *Lepilemur mustelinus, Hapalemur griseus,* and *Varecia variegata* (Petter-Rousseaux 1964; Petter 1965, p. 312) are delivered in a nest and, like young Cheirogaleinae, are helpless during the first few days and transported orally by their mother. Other lemurines are active at birth, hang on to the mother's hair or wrap themselves around her midriff until strong enough to ride her back. Most lorisoid infant-maternal relationships are similar except that young *Galago minutus, G. senegalensis,* and *G. crassicaudatus* are still transported orally (cf. Davis 1960; Sauer 1967*a, b;* Blackwell 1969). The newborn of a captive tarsier (*Tarsius syrichta*), according to Cuming (1838), was born open-eyed, delivered in a nest, and transported

[1] Asdell (1965) records a maximum of 18 young in a litter of the hamster *Cricetus cricetus,* and a minimum gestation period of 10 days for the golden hamster, *Mesocricetus auratus.* I have not been able to verify Asdell's (1965, p. 282) record of an 11–13-day gestation period for the hamster *Cricetulus migratorius.*

orally like a kitten. Le Gros Clark (1924), who kept Bornean females and young, declares that the infant tarsier clings to the mother's underside. He found no evidence of nest-building in captivity or in the wild. Sprankel (1965) also reports seeing young tarsiers carried ventrally. Schreiber (1968) observed a cage-born young cling to the mother's breast most of the time and occasionally ride its father's back. For information on rearing young in captivity consult Niemitz (1974), and on mating and pregnancy, see Harrisson (1963). Nothing is known of the newborn aye-aye (*Daubentonia madagascariensis*).

Higher primates are usually born open-eyed and instinctively cling to the mother's fur or belly or climb onto her back. All platyrrhine newborn are capable of clinging to adults without assistance. Catarrhine young, however, often require maternal help or hand cradling for several days or even months before they can support themselves on their mother's body. This seeming regression is, on the contrary, a manifestation of progressive evolution in overt maternal care correlated with the longer time required for postnatal development of the infant's increasingly complex nervous system. As an exception among catarrhines, the young of West African *Colobus verus*, according to Booth (1957), is transported orally for the first few weeks after birth. Booth believes the mother resorts to this practice because of the infant's lack of a thumb for grasping, the shortness of the mother's fur, and the maternal propensity for moving through thick cover. None of these reasons, singly or together, seems convincing.

Among platyrrhines and catarrhines, real or surrogate aunts often assist in feeding and transporting the young. Callitrichid and callimiconid fathers are the infant caretakers, except during the maternal nursing periods. The same is true of *Aotus* (Moynihan 1964). According to Mason (1966, p. 27), the titi father (*Callicebus moloch*) is likewise the nearly constant carrier and guardian of the offspring. Paternal care of the young as a casual or special function is widespread. Bernstein (1970), who summarized the data, lists several species of *Macaca, Theropithecus gelada, Papio hamadryas, Cercocebus atys, Cebus albifrons,* and *Alouatta palliata* among the species where paternal care of young has been observed. Males of the prosimians *Tarsius syrichta, Nycticebus coucang,* and *Perodicticus potto* also play a role in caring for the young (Niemitz 1974, p. 271).

The state of blind, helpless, nested, and orally transported young of Cheirogaleinae is comparable to that of the newborn of primitive insectivores, tupaiids, and most rodents. Open-eyed, active, clinging neonates compare with the teat-clinging young of bats, colugos, many kinds of rodents, and certain marsupials. Other marsupial young are pouch borne. Older infants of marsupials (notably the koala), xenarthrous anteaters, and sloths are transported on the mother's back.

Developmental Stages

The period of dependence on parents for food and protection varies from 3 to 4 weeks in *Microcebus* and 5 to 6 weeks in *Callithrix,* to 6 years in primitive man. Adolescence, the period between independence from parental care and sexual maturity, also varies widely, but size for size it is more extended in primates than in other mammals.

Social Relations

Interaction between individual primates bonded in pairs or in social units of family-group size or larger are much too varied and complex for discussion here. The point to be made is that primate social relations are studied and recorded by primates and therefore are better understood by primates than if the social systems and behavioral patterns were studied, recorded, and analyzed by nonprimates. Apart from an inherent bias there is nothing to support the belief that primate societies are better organized, better adapted, or more "perfected" than social groups of other mammals, not to mention other animals such as ants, termites, bees, and wasps. Primate systems of social relations, like those of other animal groups, evolved independently. Different systems are comparable only in terms of survival values and degrees of divergence from a basic system of periodic mating contacts and parent-young relations. Judged by the record of extinctions, primate social systems are no more viable than those of other orders of mammals.

Mother-Infant Relations: Newborn Orientation and Response to Supports

King, Fobes, and Fobes (1974) concluded from experimental data that neonatal behavioral traits strongly related to maternal contact and nursing persist relatively longer through ontogeny among species in which maternal behavior is passive than among species in which mothers manually assist neonatal contact and nursing.

Test subjects of the first type, "which spend most of their time clinging to their parents' backs with little manual support by the mother" (King, Fobes, and Fobes, 1974, p. 106), were neonate twins (♀ ♀) and triplets (♂ ♀ ♀) of cottontop tamarins (*Saguinus oedipus oedipus*), and 3 neonate male squirrel monkeys (*Saimiri sciureus*).

Comparisons were made with published results of tests conducted by others on newborn rhesus macaques to which "mothers lend considerable manual support" (King, Fobes, and Fobes 1974, p. 106) and young *Galago crassicaudatus.* The latter was included with the "maternally supportive species" because "the mother typically supports the neonate in her mouth." The authors (p. 106) acknowledge that newborn galagos spend "most of the remaining time in a nest."

The maternal contact traits used for comparing the species included (1) clasping of a ventrally placed terrycloth cylinder and righting by the subjects for mounting the cylinder, (2) clasping of the cylinder placed dorsally to the subjects and righting as in 1, (3) disappearance of involuntary hand and foot grasping, (4) "orienting up," (5) disappearance of "rooting," that is, nipple searching. Ages, in days, at which the critical neonatal behavioral traits were completely lost are shown in table 1.

The data presented by King, Fobes, and Fobes (1974) are interesting and useful, but they hardly suggest, much less support their hypothesis regarding the correlation between relative persistence of certain neonatal behavioral traits and kind of parental care. Far too few specimens were tested, and only a single species of each of four distantly related primate families were compared. None of the species is, in fact, fairly comparable to any

Table 1. Days of Maturation for Maternally Related Traits

Behavior	*Galago crassicaudatus*[a]	*Saguinus o. oedipus*[b]	*Saimiri sciureus* *1*[a]	*2*[c]	*3*[d]	*Macaca mulatta* *1*[e]	*2*[f]
Clasping 1	17	>68	64	744	45	24	—
Clasping 2	—	>42	>42	—	6	24	—
Righting on clasping 1	—	>48	44	—	—	—	—
Righting on clasping 2	—	46	42	—	—	—	—
Involuntary foot grasping lost	29	26	60	—	69	15	7
Involuntary hand grasping lost	19	26	56	—	48	16	21
Orienting up	21	36	42	50	—	19	—
Rooting	—	12	48	750	—	8	—

SOURCE: Data from King, Fobes, and Fobes (1974); footnotes quoted from King, Fobes, and Fobes (1974, p. 104).
[a] "A. Erlich, unpublished data."
[b] "Present investigation" (i.e., King, Fobes, and Fobes 1974).
[c] "King and King, 1970" (*Dev. Psychobiol.* 2:251–56).
[d] "Schusterman and Sjoberg, 1969" (*Proc. Second Int. Congr. Primatol.* 1:194–203).
[e] "Mowbray and Cadell, 1962" (*J. Comp. Physiol. Psychol.* 55:350–57).
[f] "Hines, 1942" (*Contrib. Embryol. Carnegie Inst. Wash.* 30:153–209).

of the other three within the sense of the experiment, and none is surely typical of the behavioral group to which it is assigned.

Oral support used by the galago is a primitive mammalian method for transporting young and other objects. The galago nest contains the support and shelter that higher primates provide for the neonate on their bodies. Unlike other species of the experiment, the tamarin mother normally produces fraternal twins and supports them only while nursing. The father or other surrogate parent maintains the young on his back the rest of the time. The infant squirrel monkey is also back-supported, but it is the mother's back that is used among cebids. Newborn macaques stay where they feed, on the underside, with some manual support from the mother. Manual support of young catarrhines is a highly evolved primate function that facilitates nursing, insures secure transportation, gives the young a feeling of security and provides a compensatory feedback to the mother.

The relative persistence of behavioral traits regarded by King, Fobes, and Fobes as correlated with maternal support and nursing, if true, more likely reflects a correlation between increasing dependence of the young on more intimate and lasting maternal contact and support on the one hand and a decreasing degree of preadaptation for such support on the other. This correlation lacks the inconsistencies recognized by King, Fobes, and Fobes (1974, p. 107) in their association of galagos with macaques in one mother-infant behavioral category and tamarins and squirrel monkeys in another.

From my point of view, each of the species compared by King, Fobes, and Fobes represents an independent stage in the evolution of newborn adaptations and responses to spatial orientations, or the parental bodies, during and between feedings. The arrangement that follows may suggest but does not certainly answer the question why certain infant behavioral traits related to parental support disappear later in the few captiveborn cottontop tamarins and squirrel monkeys tested by King, Fobes, and Fobes than they do in the few captive rhesus macaques and *Galago crassicaudatus* tested by others under other conditions.

Evolutionary Stages of Newborn Spatial Orientations and Responses to Parental Care

The following stages, with examples, are arranged in sequence from minimal maternal contact and support of a newborn litter through stages of shared parental (or group) contact and support of a reduced litter, or twins, to complete maternal maintenance of a single newborn.

1. Nest for Support and Nursing Litter

Response to gravitational field negative, maternal support unnecessary except for transportation, which, if oral, evokes passive or negative responses. This is the primitive and common mammalian relationship between mother and suckling young.

2. Paternal Dorsum for Support, Transportation; Maternal Ventrum for Nursing Litter

Response to gravitational fields positive with cheiridial clasping and tail embracing usually adequate for insuring stability, at least between feedings. In callitrichids, the paternal dorsum normally used for support of offspring (singletons to triplets) represents, in effect, a secure and mobile litter nest.

3. Maternal Dorsum and Ventrum for Early (1–3) Weeks Support, Transportation, and Nursing Singleton; Thereafter, Paternal Dorsum for Support and Transportation

Behavioral relationships as in 2. In *Callimico goeldii*, *Aotus trivirgatus*, and *Callicebus moloch*, father provides nearly total care between nursings of the single young 2 to 3 weeks after birth.

4. Maternal Dorsum for Support, Transportation, Security; Ventrum for Nursing and Part Early Transportation of Singleton

Response to gravitational field as in 2 and 3; cebids are representative; paternal care, with exceptions noted in 3 (above), minor and begins after young can transfer independently from one parent to the other. Nonprimates include sloth, koala.

5. Maternal Ventrum for Support, Transportation, Security, Display, Nursing Singleton

Response to gravitational field negative; maternal care is constant and manual support an essential supplement to neonatal clasping and embracing. Older and heavier offspring often shift to the positive gravitational field of maternal back for support between feedings. Catarrhines are representative; nonprimates include marsupials with ventral pouch for support of suckling young.

Spatial orientations and responses converge as young of all stages become older and more active.

Binocularity and Sociability

Evolution of binocularity among primates may be correlated with increasing sociability, particularly among diurnal species. As binocularity advanced and the visual field narrowed to the front, the individual presumably became increasingly dependent on conspecifics for sighting enemies outside his own line of vision and for sounding alerts. The survival value of such interdependence would tend to strengthen mating and family bonds. This in turn would provide the basis for the evolution of a complex, enduring society with defense as one of its functions.

Clavicle

This bone, which connects forelimb to axial skeleton and exerts a spoke and strut effect on shoulder movement (Jenkins 1974*a*), is present and well developed in all Primates, Chiroptera, Insectivora (except *Potamogale*), and all Marsupialia (except *Thylacinus* and *Perameles*), Dermoptera, and Tubulidentata. The clavicle is absent or may persist in reduced form or as a tendonous vestige in remaining mammals.

Ischial Tuberosities, Prominences, and Callosities

The posterior (caudal, inferior) border of the ischium, or ischial tuberosity (fig. I.14), of nonprimates and prosimians is hardly or not at all modified from the nearly uniformly narrow condition seen in insectivores (e.g., *Tupaia*) or didelphid marsupials. In adult platyrrhines, the proportions of the posterior ischial surface grade from primitively narrow in lower callitrichids to an expanded club-shaped form in higher cebids. In all platyrrhines, the greatest depth of the ischial tuberosity rarely exceeds one-third its greatest breadth, and its surface is the site of hamstring attachment (cf. Stern 1971 for musculature). The thinly haired skin covering in some callitrichids is glandular and appears swollen when exposed as part of the genital display (fig. I.15). The tegumentary prominence is probably an early-stage homologue of the ischial callosity of Old World monkeys.

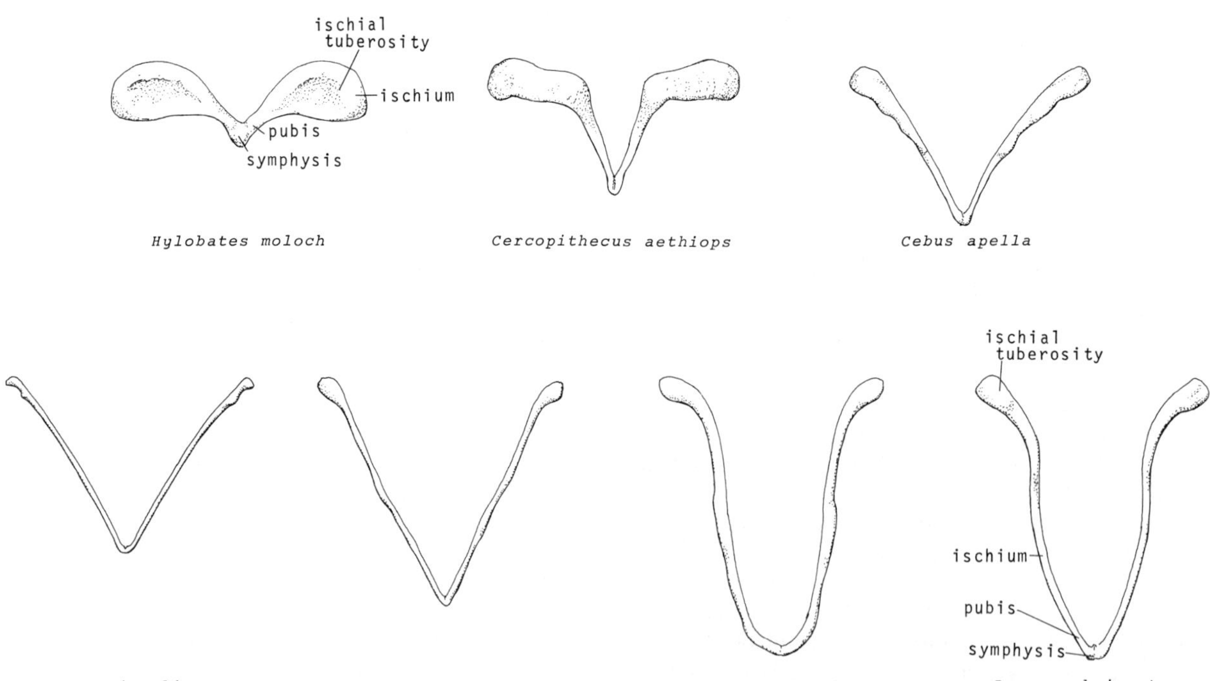

Fig. I.14. Posterior (inferior) aspect of pelvis in representative primates and *Tupaia;* all drawn to same transverse width.

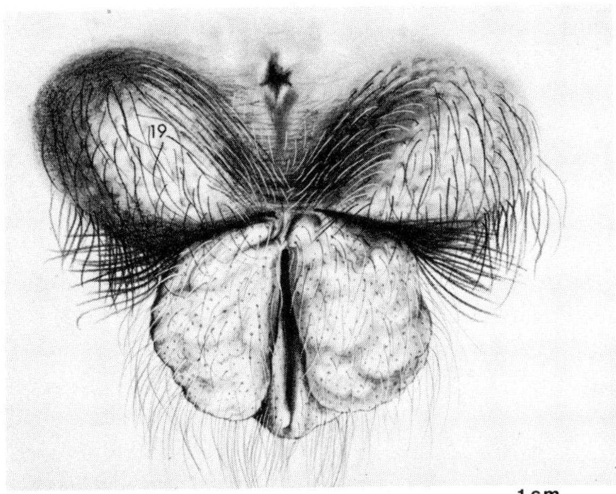

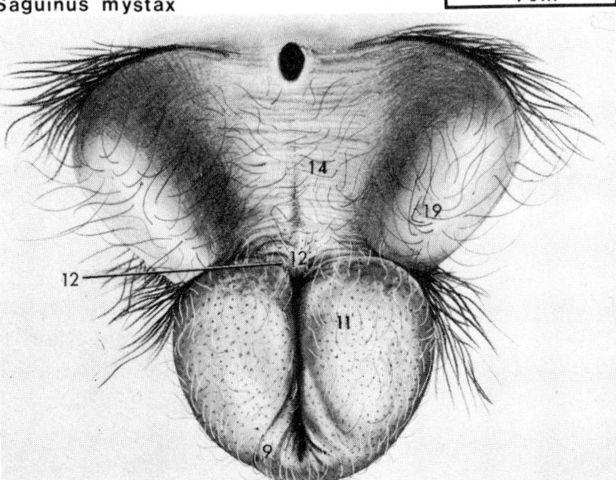

Fig. I.15. Ischial prominences (*19*) and external genitalia in *Saguinus mystax*. Two fluid-preserved samples showing individual variation: *9*, preputial fold; *11*, labium majus; *12* posterior commissure; *14*, perineum; *19*, ischial prominence.

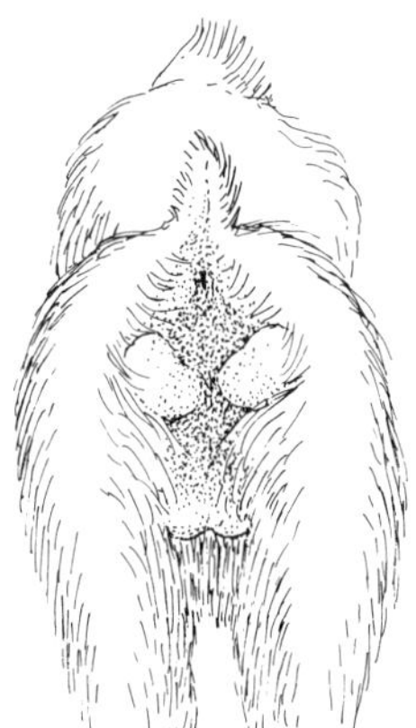

Fig. I.16. Ischial callosities displayed by male drill (*Papio leucophaeus*).

Fig. I.17. Sitting-sleeping posture of hamadryas baboon (*Papio hamadryas*). Callosities cushion the ischia, which support the full weight of head, trunk, and thighs and the wedging pressure exerted by the propped leg or legs. Characteristic cercopithecid sitting posture parallel to branch and tree trunk contrasts with callitrichid transverse perching posture and the suspensory resting posture of pongids and gibbons. Gorillas and chimpanzees also use the cercopithecid branch sitting posture.

The ischial tuberosity of catarrhines (fig. I.14) is flared into a broad, thick, more-or-less ovoid plate with greatest depth usually more than one-third greatest breadth. The tuberose expansion is greatest in cercopithecids and gibbons, proportionately less in pongids, and least in man. The flat surface of the cercopithecid tuberosity serves for attachment of the fibro-fatty callosity. Hamstrings originate on the periphery of the plate.

Ischial tuberosities of some previously zoo-kept cebids, now preserved in the Field Museum, are diseased and enlarged to a size comparable to that of normal cercopithecid tuberosities. Presumably, the longer the cebids sat on concrete or metal supports in captivity, the more advanced the signs of ischial osteitis.

The size and shape of cercopithecid and hylobatid callosities are highly diversified (fig. I.16). Pocock (1925*c*, p. 1530) has demonstrated sexual dimorphism and some generic distinctions. Diagnostic differences between the pads of some species of *Macaca* have also been shown (cf. Büttikofer 1917, pl. 7; Fooden 1969*a;* Wilson 1972, p. 250). Pongid callosities occur only as sporadic vestiges (Schultz 1936), but the tuberosities remain large.

The original function of rudimentary catarrhine ischial callosities may have been display, as in callitrichids. If so, they must have evolved quickly into cushions that provided comfort and stability for branch and rock sitting or sitting-sleeping (fig. I.17). As was noted by Washburn (1957, p. 276) "this is a specialized kind of sitting sleeping posture with feet up, hands near feet and most of the weight on the callosities." In contrast, the callosityless prosimians and New World monkey usually sit with body weight resting on the feet, the ischia held off the support (fig. I.18). Arms and tail also provide considerable suspensory or prop support, and the tail alone may serve as a counterweight. Gibbons and apes with disappearing or lost callosities ease the ischial burden by squatting or by suspending some of their body weight with one or both hands gripping an overhead support (fig. I.19). Prone or nested sleeping postures and quadrupedal or bipedal branch- or ground-feeding stances also tend to suppress the need for cushions. Rose (1974*a;* 1974*b*) has dealt with this subject at greater length.

Fig. I.18. Platyrrhine perching postures with rump not in contact with support. *Above,* balanced transverse perching posture commonly used by cottontop tamarin (*Saguinus oedipus oedipus*) and callitrichids generally for feeding and other activities; arms when free are propped between legs in typical quadrupedal squatting or sitting position. *Below,* parallel tripodal perching posture used by squirrel monkey (*Saimiri sciureus*) and other cebids for propping rump above supporting branch; the prehensile tail in larger cebids helps accomplish the same thing.

Fig. I.19. Suspensory sitting posture of gibbon (*Hylobates lar*), used for support, balance, and thermoregulation (compare with similar posture in *Leontopithecus rosalia,* p. 862).

Cheiridia

Claws and Nails

The long, curved, pointed claws on the digital tips of mammals, birds, reptiles, and amphibians are primitive structures used as tools and weapons. Generalized claws serve for gripping and clinging in climbing; securing purchase for springing; grappling, piercing, and tearing prey or enemy; scratching, scraping, and digging for food, shelter, or sanitation; and grooming. Claws may become specialized for one or a few of the enumerated functions; they may become modified for use in new capacities; or they may degenerate into useless appendages which ultimately disappear.

The technical term for the long, sharp, laterally compressed, transversely convex and protruding claw is *falcula* (fig. I.20). The broad, blunt, and little if at all protruding form of the claw usually described as a nail is called *ungula.* Any evolutionary stage between a distinct claw and a distinct nail is called *tegula* (fig. I.21). The general term for all forms of horny coverings of the terminal phalanx of a digit is *unguis* (plural, *ungues*).

All stages, from claw, or falcula, through tegula and ungula, to the inungulate condition, are evident in living primates. In *Saimiri* alone, stages from claw to nail are present in the same hand or foot (fig. I.21). In callitrichids, with hands and feet least specialized among living primates, each digit of hand and foot, except the opposable hallux, is provided with a claw (fig. I.20) which "shows the closest resemblance [among primates] to the typical mammalian claw" (Le Gros Clark 1936, p. 18). Digits of the prosimian aye-aye (*Daubentonia*) are similarly provided. The thumbnail, present in remaining primates, is lost from some vestigial thumbs of *Ateles* (Hershkovitz 1949, p. 382). Schultz (1941*b,* p. 82) and Tuttle and Rogers (1966) have shown that a majority of orangutans, mostly females, lack both the nail and terminal phalanx of the hallux. Tuttle and Rogers suggest that the evolutionary loss of ungues in *Pongo* is sex-influenced. The phalangeal skeleton is a prime indicator of the evolutionary grade of the ungues (figs. I.26, 27).

It has been said (Gregory 1920, p. 237; 1922, p. 230) that claws of some primates, particularly those of callitrichids, are reverted nails. This statement implies an improbable, and certainly undemonstrable, reversal of the real direction of evolution not only of the claw, but of the entire digit, limb, and even the organism as a whole, to an earlier stage. Notwithstanding, Gregory's unsupported declaration was accepted uncritically by Weber (1928, p. 761) and perhaps through him gained wide currency among anthropologists and even some zoologists. The problem was reviewed by Le Gros Clark (1936; 1959, pp. 174, 205), who demonstrated that primate nails, like those of all other mammals, are degen-

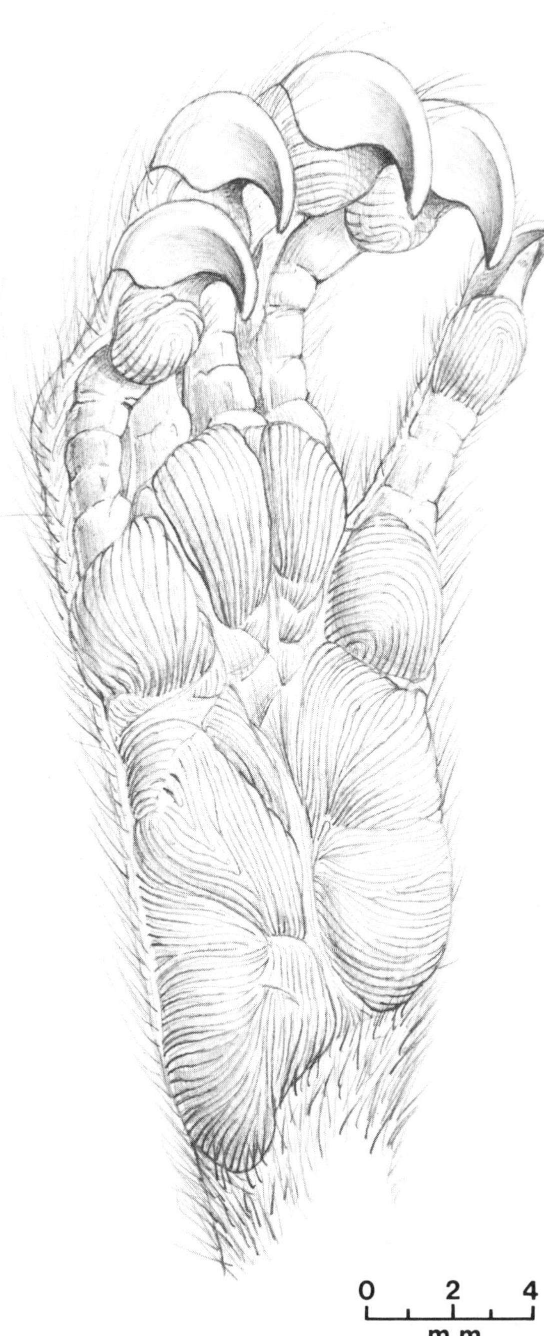

Fig. I.20. Right hand of *Callithrix argentata;* all digits armed with protruding downwardly curved claws specialized for clinging and grappling; the claws preclude opposability.

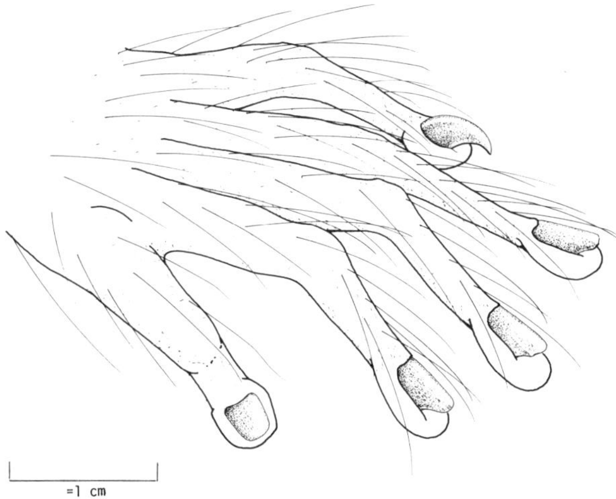

Fig. I.21. Left hand of squirrel monkey, *Saimiri sciureus,* with ungula (nail) on thumb, tegulae on digits *II-IV,* and falcula (claw) on *V.* Pedal ungues are similar. Complete intergradation between claw and nail appears as an individual variable. Opposability evolves with reduction of sharp downwardly curved claw to a harmless nonprotruding nail at least on digit *I.*

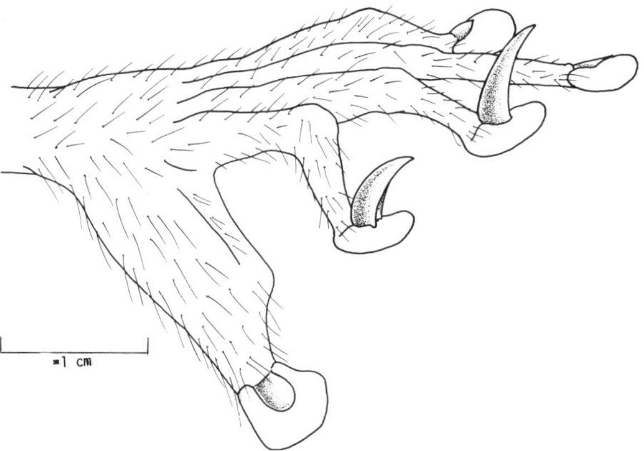

Fig. I.22. Left hind foot of tarsier, *Tarsius syrichta,* with claws of digits *II* and *III* specialized for grooming. Ungues of remaining digits are degenerate claws. The grooming claws project nearly at right angles to the digits, thus avoiding interference with other pedal functions.

erate claws. In turn, clawlessness is the result of a degenerative process often associated with reduction and loss of the terminal phalanx.

In *Tarsius,* extreme hypertrophy of the terminal phalangial touch pads of the hand is associated with a corresponding reduction and modification of the claws into nonfunctional splinters. On the foot, digits II and III are each armed with a short grooming claw of a primitive type which projects nearly at right angles above the touch pads (fig. I.22). The erect position of grooming claws averts interference with other digital functions. Pedal digits IV and V each bear a short pointed, flattened and keeled, nonprojecting tegula. The hallux bears the vestige of a nail or tegula.

In lemurs, hallux and pollex are nailed, and pedal digit II is usually provided with a grooming claw. The remaining ungues are adpressed and nonprotruding tegulae, some flattened, others pointed and keeled; still others, as in *Microcebus* (figs. I.23, 24), may be obsolete. In galagos and lorises, the ungues, except the grooming claw of digit II, are well-defined nails. The unguis of the cebid pollex varies from tegula to nail, all remaining ungues are distinct tegulae except those of the squirrel monkey (*Saimiri*) digits V which persist as short recurved claws. In catarrhine monkeys and gibbons, pollex and hallux are nailed, the remaining digits tegulate, but in some species, particularly the more terrestrial ones, the tegulae are nearly naillike. A nail is present on all digits of man and higher apes except as noted.

Modification of ungues from falculae to tegulae and ungulae, and the ultimate obsolescence and disappearance of the latter are widespread among mammals. An opposable digit, whether in primates, marsupials, or rodents, either bears a nail or is inungulate. A sharp, protruding claw prevents or inhibits opposability. Well-developed digital touch pads in arboreal mammals, including many marsupials and rodents, are characterized

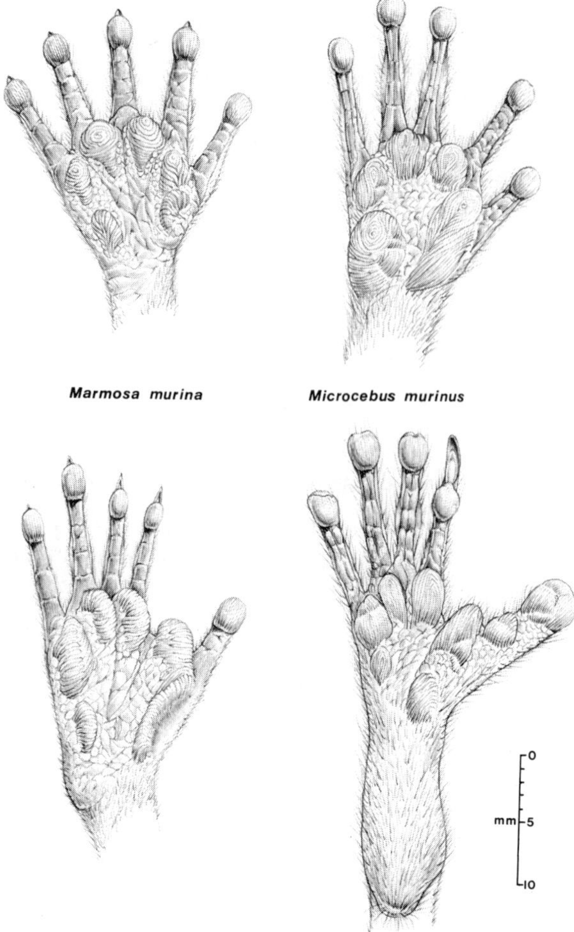

Fig. I.23. Volar surface of right hand (*above*) and right foot (*below*) of *Marmosa murina* (Didelphidae, Marsupialia), and *Microcebus murinus* (Lemuridae, Primates).

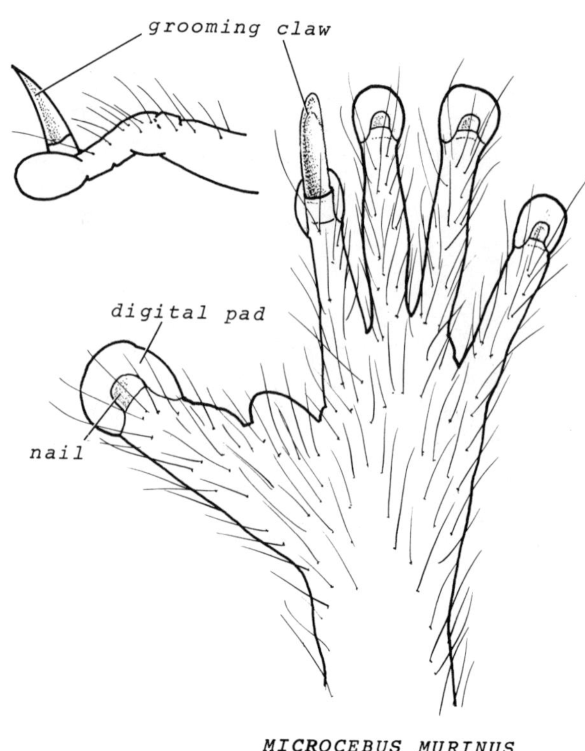

Fig. I.24. Right foot of *Microcebus murinus,* diagram of dorsal surface to show claw of digit *II* specialized for grooming but not effective in climbing, and degenerate ungues of digits *I, III–V* replaced by sensory digital pads.

by comparatively weak claws turned upward so they do not interfere with use of digits for grasping or sensing. As was previously noted, the upturned claws of prosimians and some other mammals, notably among marsupials, for example, *Dromicia,* are secondarily adapted for grooming. Degenerate and lost claws or nails are also common. Examples, in addition to the primates mentioned above, include the nailed or nailless flippers of manatees, the nail of the disappearing thumb of most rodents, the vestigial and lost claws of so-called clawless otters, and the complete loss of ungues in cetaceans.

The hallux of living tupaiids (fig. I.25) and the Paleocene *Plesiadapis* is provided with a well-developed claw. This character alone, although there are other trenchant ones, is evidence enough that neither animal group is Primate.

Opposable Pollex

A more-or-less opposable thumb is present in the vast majority of living primates. In *Ateles, Brachyteles,* and *Colobus,* the thumb is vestigial or absent (fig. II.14). The thumb is well developed but primitively nonopposable and provided with a distinct claw in the tarsier (*Tarsius*), aye-aye (*Daubentonia*), all callitrichids (Callitrichidae), and *Callimico.* The same must have been true of the pollex of the ancestral primate and most, if not all, early Tertiary primates. Evidently opposability was perfected in the great toe before it appeared in the thumb.

Opposability is the capacity of the first digit, pollex or hallux, to seize an object and hold it securely against an opposing digit. The function evolved pari passu with degeneration of the primitively sharp protruding claw into a short nail which disappears in some forms. In primates with thumbs vestigial or lost, opposability is replaced by prehensility between digits II and III. Prehensility between one or more flexed digits and the palm characterizes all primates.

An early stage pollical opposability consists of a movement of adduction combined with digital flexion and some rotation at the carpophalangeal joint of the thumb. This simple form of opposability characterizes cebids. The tarsier's pollex performs the same movements, according to Haines (1958, p. 14), but Napier (1961; also Napier and Napier 1967), regard the tarsier pollex as nonopposable. These conclusions appear to qualify the Day and Napier (1963, p. 132) generalization that "there is a direct relationship between true opposability and the presence of a deep head to flexor pollicis brevis" in the tarsier, all cercopithecoids with thumbs, and the orang and man only (Day and Napier 1963, p. 128) among living hominoids.

In larger primates, increasing specialization of the hand for grasping larger branches is marked by a shift of the thumb from the primitive position of near alignment with the other digits to a more proximal position. The gap or cleft between base of thumb and index finger in most living prosimians allows a wider *power grip,* but no refinement of the *precision grip,* as defined by Napier (1960).

The most advanced form of opposability, occurring in catarrhines, combines the thumb cleft and power grip

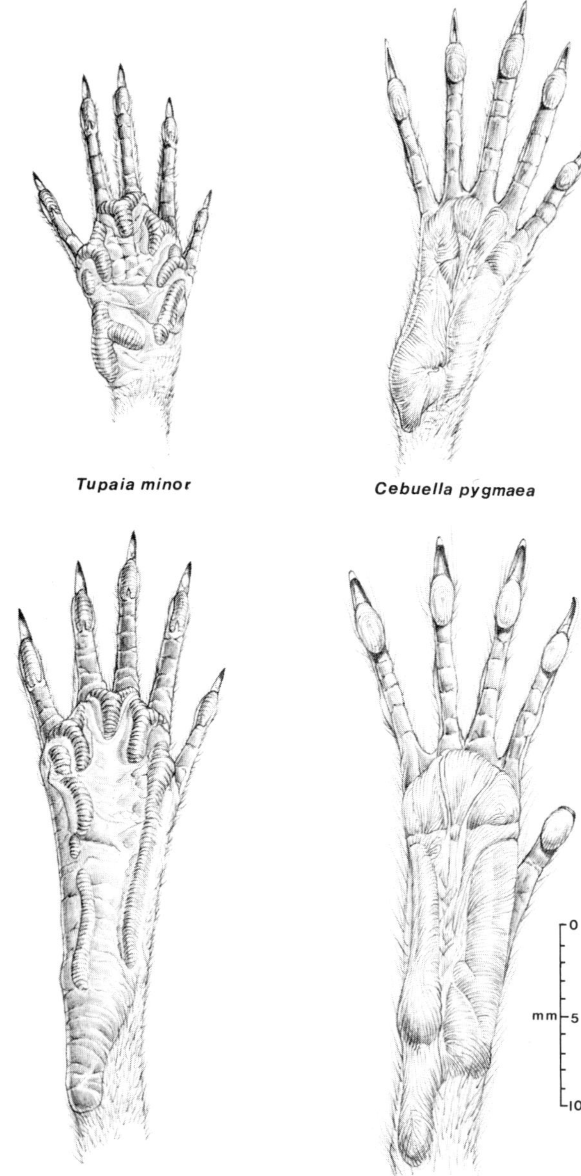

Fig. I.25. Volar surface of right hand (*above*) and right foot (*below*) of *Tupaia minor* (*Insectivora*) and *Cebuella pygmaea* (*Callitrichidae,* Primates).

of prosimians, the carpophalangeal movement of platyrrhines, and a new movement of rotation of the carpometatarsal joint. Catarrhine opposability, according to Napier (1961, pp. 116, 128, fig. 1) is derived from the cebid type. The latter, termed "pseudo opposability" by Napier is a comparatively primitive, or *semiopposable* form as compared with the more *advanced* prosimian type, and the highly evolved or *compound* catarrhine type. The bones alone (figs. I.26–29) hardly reflect the diversity and complexity of hand movements among the different kinds of primates.

Opposable Hallux

An opposable great toe provided with a nail (or inunguiculate) is characteristic of all primates, many marsupials, arboreal rodents, and almost certainly the hypothetical preprimates. Except for *Homo,* animals with nonopposable great toes are not primates. In *Homo* the original opposability of the great toe has been secondarily reduced or lost.

Volar Pads and Papillary Ridges

Cutaneous pads and ridges of palm and sole are modifications of the primitive scaly volar armor. Unmodified, nonimbricated scales or their vestiges are still preserved around the base of the pads in many species.

The primitive number of mammalian volar pads is 11. The plan consists of 5 digital (= phalangeal, terminal, touch, or nail) pads with one on the terminal phalanx of each digit, 4 postdigital (= interdigital or distal) pads, and 2 volar (= thenar and hypothenar) pads. With specialization, individual pads may become suppressed, fuse with a neighboring pad, or subdivide. New or accessory pads also may arise at new points of stress or sensitivity. The skin of the pads may be scaly, warty, pebbled, or ridged. The roughened surface enhances the locomotor, prehensile, and sensory capabilities of the cheiridia.

The primitive primate volar pad system (fig. I.30) is already specialized in its adaptations for arboreal locomotion and prehensile and tactile operations. Compared with those of primitive mammals, the pads are enlarged, more fleshy, highly enervated and vascularized, and distinguished by parallel and concentric cutaneous or papillary ridges arranged in unique patterns of whorls, loops, and arches. Sweat glands are also more profuse and active. The horny scales from which pads and ridges differentiated have virtually disappeared except for the minute warts of incomplete or discontinuous ridges and the scaly pebbling on the central volar area of the more primitive species (figs. I.23, XI.14). The number of pads may increase with specialization, accessory cushions are added to the thenar and hypothenar pads, and new pads appear on phalanges and the central volar surface between the primitive pads.

The tupaiid volar pad pattern (fig. I.25) regarded by Biegert (1963, p. 135) as a model for primitive primate types is essentially a specialized terrestrial type and highly variable. It may have originated from the same basal mammalian pattern that gave rise to primate designs, but it cannot be considered ancestral to them.

Volar pads of some arboreal rodents and marsupials (fig. I.23) may be no less specialized than those of primates. Papillary ridges may also attain as much complexity in some marsupials as in primates. Sensory ridges evolved independently in other mammals as well and are particularly refined in tupaiids, arboreal rodents, arboreal carnivores (especially *Potos* and *Bassaricyon*), some xenarthrans, and pinnipeds. For detailed accounts of mammalian volar pads see Whipple (1904), Kidd (1907), Dankmeijer (1938), Midlo and Cummins (1942), and Biegert (1961).

Digital Formulae

The relative degree of distal projection of each digit of hand and foot tends to be stable in mammals generally. The most projecting digit, however, is usually, but not necessarily, the longest. A long digit with a short metapodial is often less projecting than a shorter digit with a long metapodial (figs. I.26–29).

The following summary (table 2) of digital formulae, arranged by families, is based on the cheiridia described and figured by Biegert (1963), on complete hands and feet (not skeletons) of approximately five hundred museum-preserved callitrichids I examined, and on a rapid survey of the complete cheiridia of representatives of the nearly all other living primates and all tupaiid

Table 2. Formulae of Digital Distal Projection in Primates.

family	manus	pes
Tupaiidae [non-primate]	3–4–2–5–1	3 or 4–2–5–1
Lemuridae	4 or 3–2 or 5–1	4 or 3–2 or 5–1
Indriidae	4–3–5–2–1	3–4–5–2–1
Daubentoniidae	4–3–2–5–1	3 or 4–5–2–1
Galagidae	4–3–2 or 5–1	4–3–5–2–1
Lorisidae	4–3–5–2 or 1	4–3 or 5–2–1
Tarsiidae	3–2–4–5–1	4–3–2 or 5–1
Cebidae	3 or 4–5 or 2–1	3 or 4–2–5–1
Callimiconidae	3–4–2–5–1	4–3–5 or 2–1
Callitrichidae	3 or 4–2–5–1	4 or 3–5 or 2–1
Cercopithecidae		
Cercopithecinae	3 or 4–2–5–1	3–4–2–5–1
Colobinae	4 or 3–2–5–1	3–4–5–2–1
Hylobatidae	3–2–4–5–1	3–2–4–5–1
Pongidae	3–2 or 4–5–1	3–2 or 4–5–1

genera preserved in the Field Museum. The digits are given in the order of most to least projecting. In a hand or foot where either of two digits sometimes projects more than the other, that digit is listed after the first. For example, in the formula 3 or 4–2–5–1, digit 4 is sometimes, but not usually, even with or slightly more projecting than digit 3.

The common digital formula of the hand is 3–4–2–5–1, with a strong tendency for digit 4 to be even with or project slightly beyond digit 3. Deviation from the 2–5–1 portion of the formula occurs in peculiarly specialized hands.

The most widely established digital formula of the foot is (4–3) or (3–4)–5–2–1. In some groups, digit 2 is more projecting than digit 5. As in the hand, most departures from the common formula occur in primates with very special forms of pedal locomotion. There is no correlation between digital length or projection and rate of phalangeal and metatarsal ossification (fig. I.31).

Functional Axes of Cheiridia

The functional axis of the ancestral primate hand (fig. I.32A) probably extended longitudinally between the thenar and hypothenar pads and continued through the middle digit. All digits of this *mesaxonic* hand must have been provided with claws and flexed inwardly against themselves. This type persists in callitrichids, *Callimico*, and the aye-aye, among modern primates.

In a second type of hand, the functional axis extends through the grasping interval between digits 2 and 3. Here, digits 1 and 2 act together in convergence and in a scissorlike adduction with digit 3. Digit 1 has a nail, but its opposability is little more than incipient. This hand type was described by Pocock (1920; 1925*a*) as zygodactylous and shown to occur in the cebids *Cacajao, Chiropotes, Alouatta, Lagothrix, Ateles,* and *Brachyteles*. The term schizodactylous was proposed by Haines

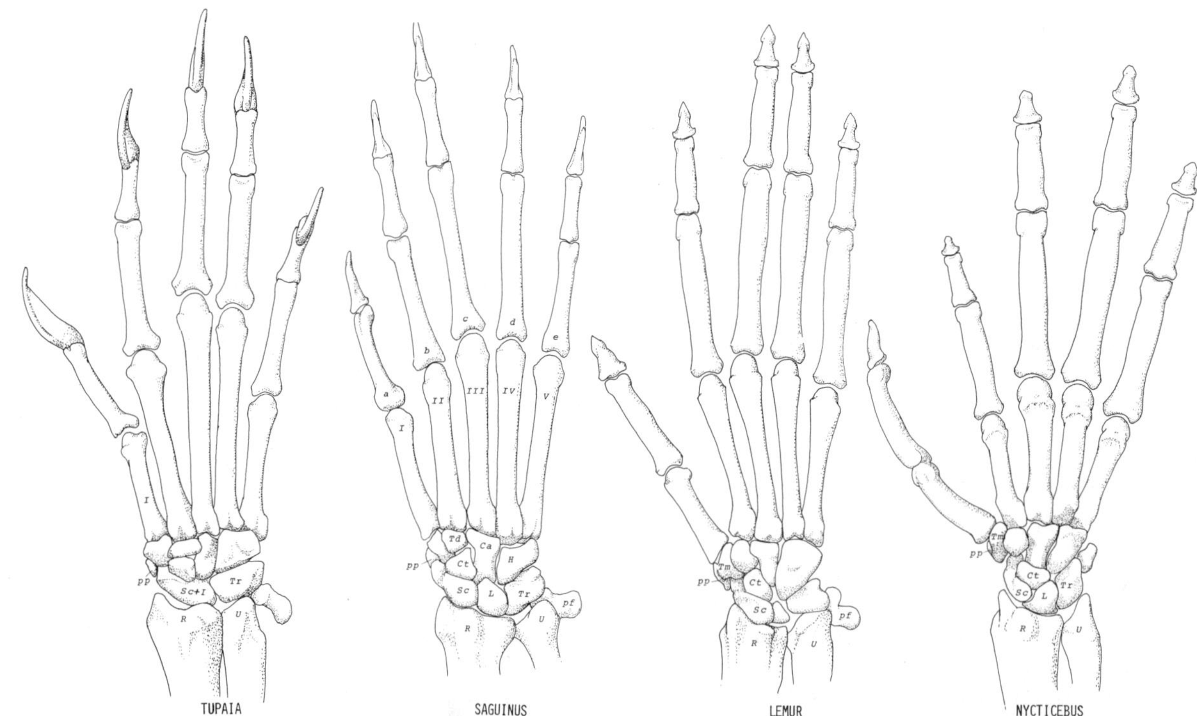

Fig. I.26. Right-hand skeleton of *Tupaia, Saguinus, Lemur,* and *Nycticebus,* all drawn to same size. Shape of terminal phalanx indicates form of its ungues. Forearm bones: *R* = radius, *U* = ulna. Carpal (wrist) bones: *Sc* = scaphoid (scaphoideum, naviculare, navicular, radial); *L* = lunate (lunatum, lunar, semilunar, intermediate); *Sc* + *L* = fused scaphoid and lunate; *Tr* = triquetrum (cuneiform, triangular, pyramidal, cubital, ulnar); *Tm* = trapezium (carpal 1, greater multangular, multangulum majus); *Td* = trapezoid (trapezoideum, carpal 2, lesser multangulum, multangulum minus); *Ca* = capitate (capitatum, carpal 3, magnum); *H* = hamate (hamatum, carpals 4–5, unciform, uncinate); *Ct* = central (os centrale, centrale, multangulum accessorium); *pf* = pisiform (pisiforme, subcarpal accessory, ulnar sesamoid); *pp* = prepollex (praepollex, radial sesamoid). Metacarpal (palmar) bones: *I-V*. Phalangeal (finger, digital) bones: *a–e* = proximal phalanges.

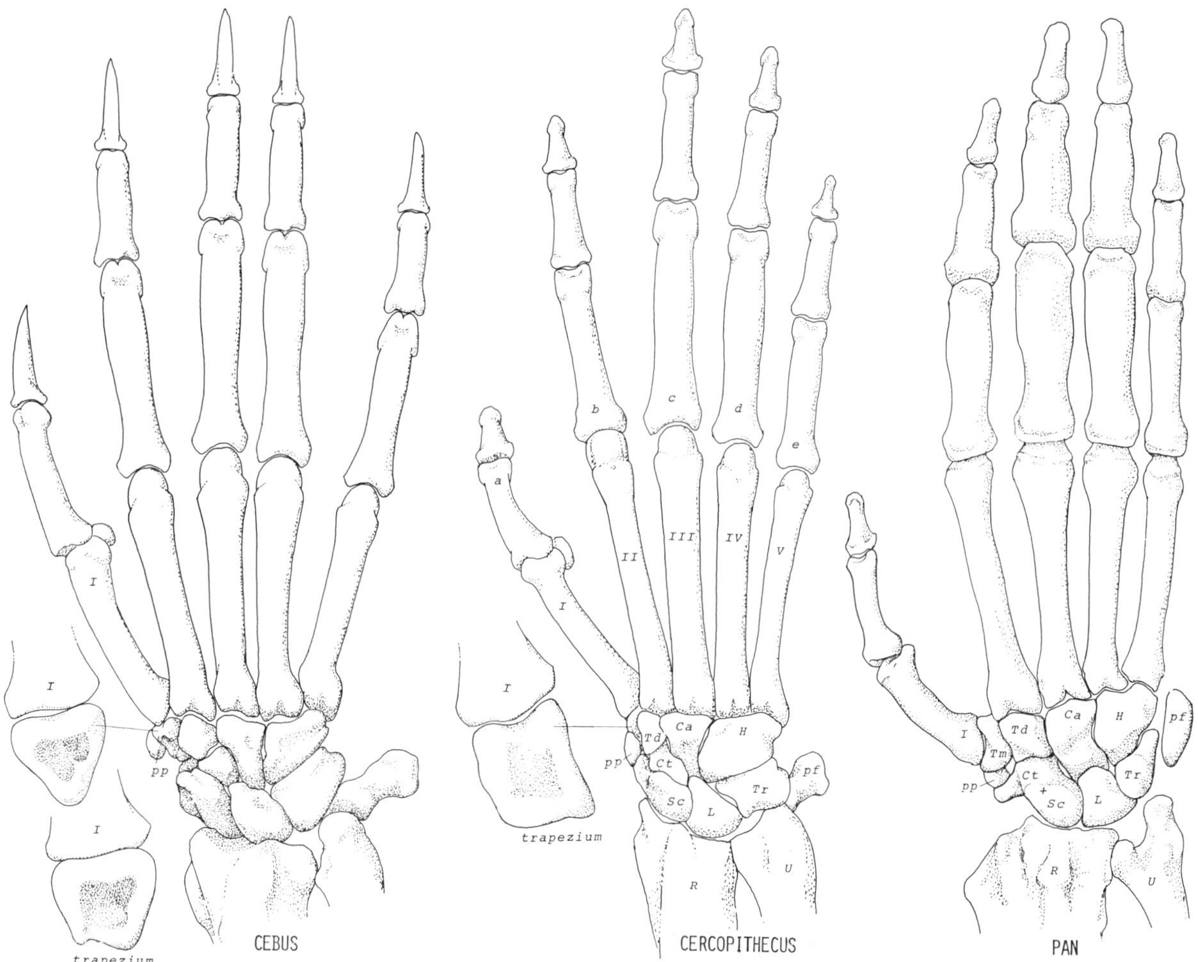

Fig. I.27. **Right-hand skeleton of *Cebus, Cercopithecus,* and *Pan,*** all drawn to same size; shape of terminal phalanges indicates form of its ungues; dorsoproximal aspect of trapezium enlarged to show transition from the triangular shape in platyrrhines (*Cebus*) to the subrectangular shape in catarrhines (*Cercopithecus*). $Ct + Sc =$ fused central and scaphoid bones; for names of all wrist bones see fig. I.26.

(1958), for the same hand. This *schizaxonic* hand (fig. I.33) intergrades morphologically and functionally with the primitive mesaxonic hand.

The schizaxonic hand is functionally interchangeable with the mesaxonic in situations when the latter is of little avail in gaining support on slender branches or vines. Rothe (1972) demonstrated this optional function in the case of *Callithrix jacchus.* Cartmill (1974*b,* p. 75) believes that the schizaxonic or schizodactylous hand is primitive for primates. This hand, however, does not appear as a morphological specialization except in certain higher platyrrhines and prosimians with cheiridia most highly specialized for clutching.

With evolution of pollical opposability, the functional axis of the hand shifted to a line running between interdigital pads 1 and 2 in the grasping interval between digits 1 and 2. This advanced type, the telaxonic hand, is found in the majority of living primates including lorisoids (fig. I.34), where digit 2 tends toward obsolescence. Digit 1 is provided with a nail, digits 2–5 are tegulate or ungulate. The telaxonic type grasp may shift to or combine with a weak schizaxonic grasp.

The functional axis of the primitive mammalian foot was probably mesaxonic. The tupaiid foot is not far removed. With evolution of an opposable hallux in primates, marsupials, and rodents, the axis became telaxonic by shifting to a position between thenar and hypothenar pads proximally and interdigital pads 1 and 2 distally in the grasping interval between digits 1 and 2. In some more-or-less terrestrial primates, the pedal axis may seem to have shifted back toward the middle digit. Thus, Morton (1935, p. 36) depicts the "functional" axis of the pedal skeleton of *Lepilemur* and *Macaca* as running through digit 3. Perhaps he intends to show the morphological rather than the functional axis. In any case, Lessertisseur and Jouffroy (1974, p. 144) define the morphological axes of primate feet as follows:

Mesaxonic: Axis through digit III (pongids).
Ectaxonic: Axis through digit IV (prosimians including *Tarsius,* some platyrrhines—notably *Aotus, Tupaia*).
Entaxonic: Axis through digit II (man only).
Paraxonic: Axis between III and IV (many platyrrhines and cercopithecoids).

Ancestral Primate Cheiridia

A hypothetical model of cheiridia constructed by Biegert (1961, p. 134) from which hands and feet of modern primates could be derived, has the following characters.

1. Digital formula of manus and pes, 3–4–2–5–1.
2. Functional axis, manus and pes, mesaxonic.
3. All digits provided with claws.

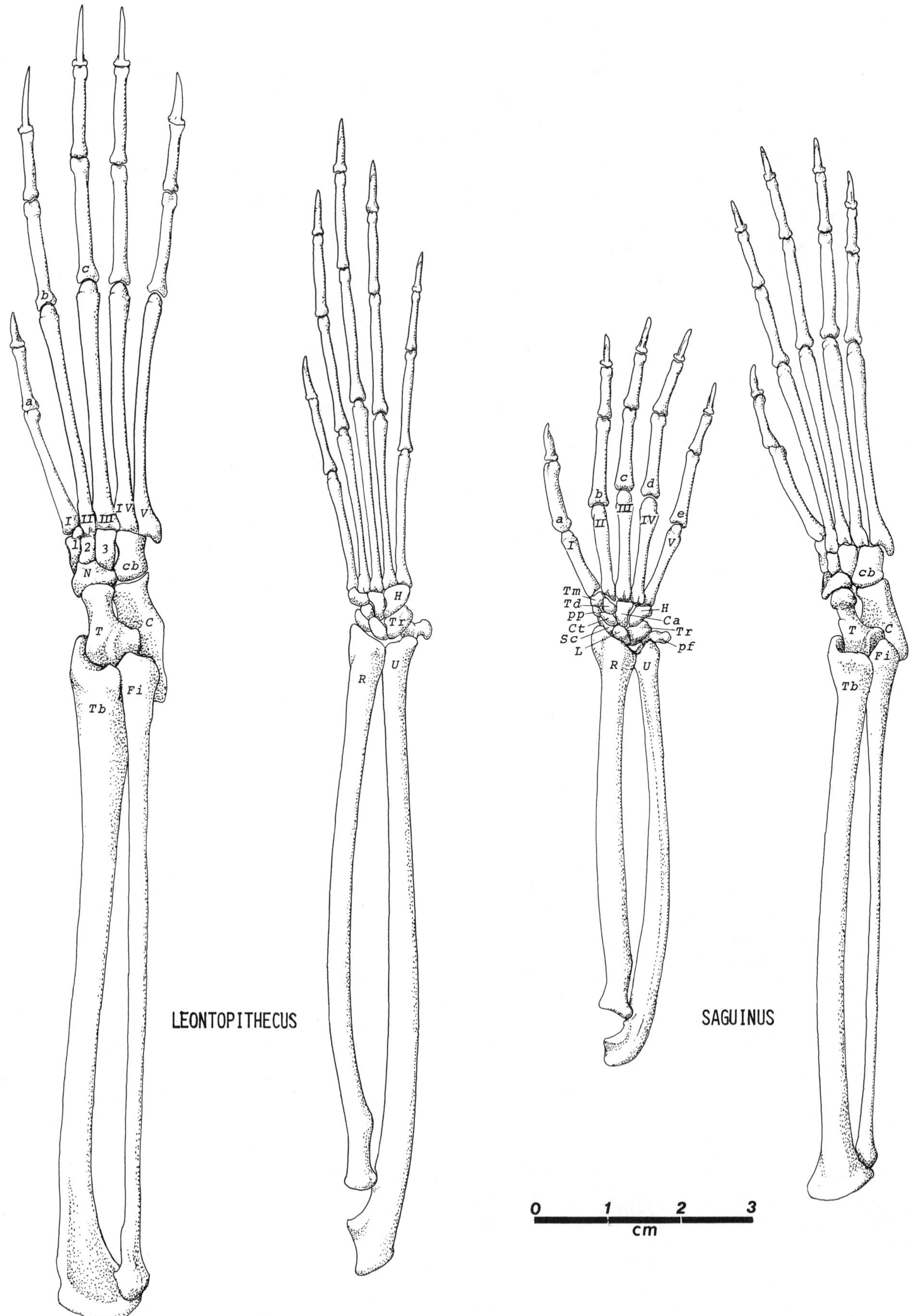

Fig. I.28. Lower right hind limb and lower right forelimb of *Leontopithecus* and *Saguinus*. Shape of terminal phalanx indicates form of its ungues. Arm and leg bones: *Fi* = fibula; *Tb* = tibia; *R* = radius; *U* = ulna. Carpal (wrist) bones: *Sc* = scaphoid (scaphoideum, naviculare, navicular, radial); *L* = lunate (lunatum, lunar, semilunar, intermediate); *Tr* = triquetrum (cuneiform, triangular, pyramidal, cubital, ulnar); *Tm* = trapezium (carpal 1, greater multangular, multan-

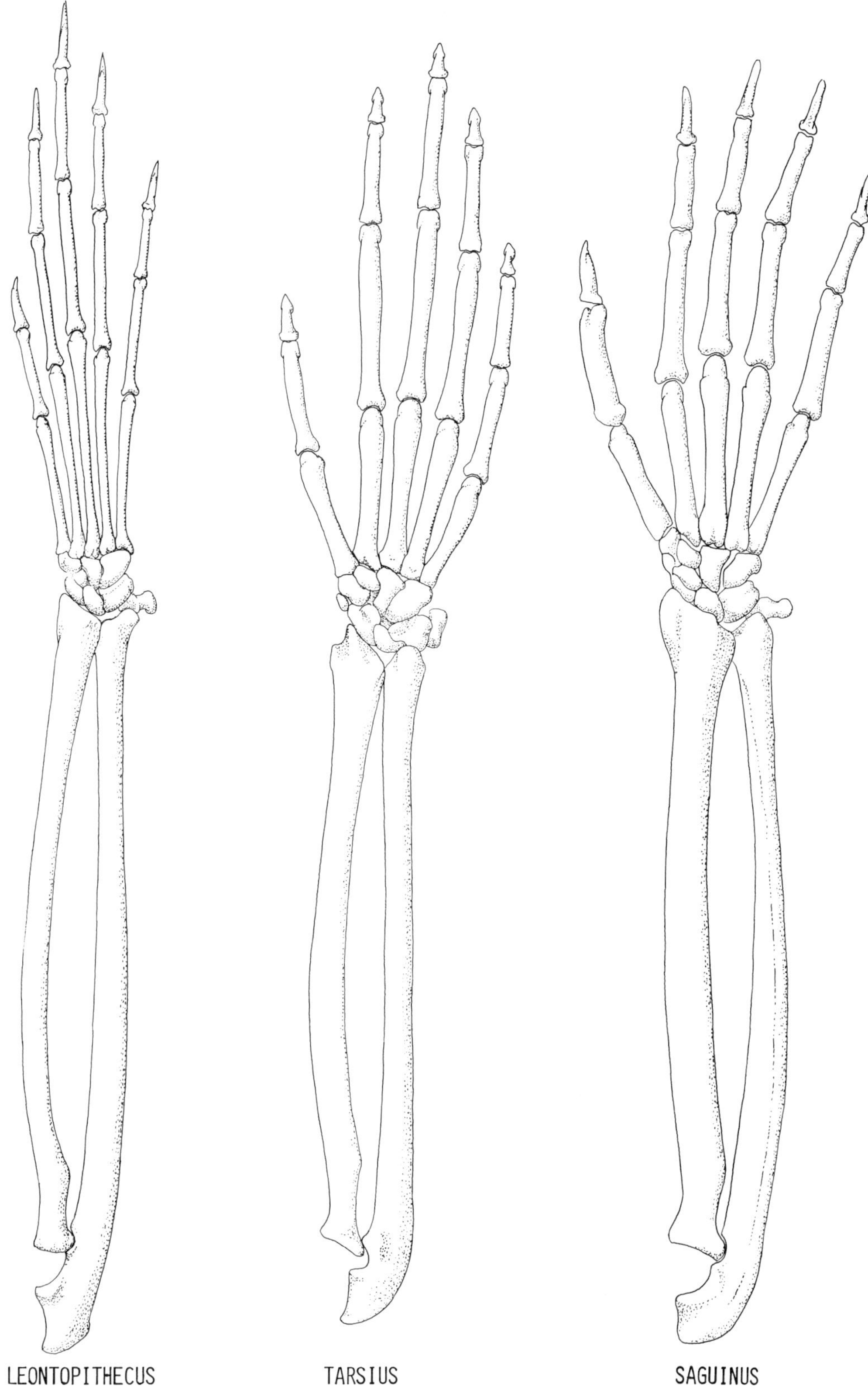

Fig. I.29. Skeleton of right forelimb of *Leontopithecus, Tarsius, Saguinus,* all drawn to approximately same size. Note similarities between *Tarsius* and *Leontopithecus* in certain proportional bone lengths and greater similarities between *Tarsius* and *Saguinus* in proportional bone breadths.

---

gulum majus); *Td* = trapezoid (trapezoideum, carpal 2, lesser multangulum, multangulum minus); *Ca* = capitate (capitatum, carpal 3, magnum); *H* = hamate (hamatum, carpals 4–5, unciform, uncinate); *Ct* = central (os centrale, centrale, multangulum accessorium); *pf* = pisiform (pisiforme, subcarpal accessory, ulnar sesamoid); *pp* = prepollex (pracpollex, radial sesamoid). Tarsal (ankle) bones: *T* = talus; *C* = calcaneum; *N* = navicular; *1* = entocuneiform; *2* = mesocuneiform; *3* = ectocuneiform; *cb* = cuboid. Metacarpal (palm) and metatarsal (sole) bones: *I-V*. Phalangeal (finger and toe) bones: *a-e* = proximal phalanges.

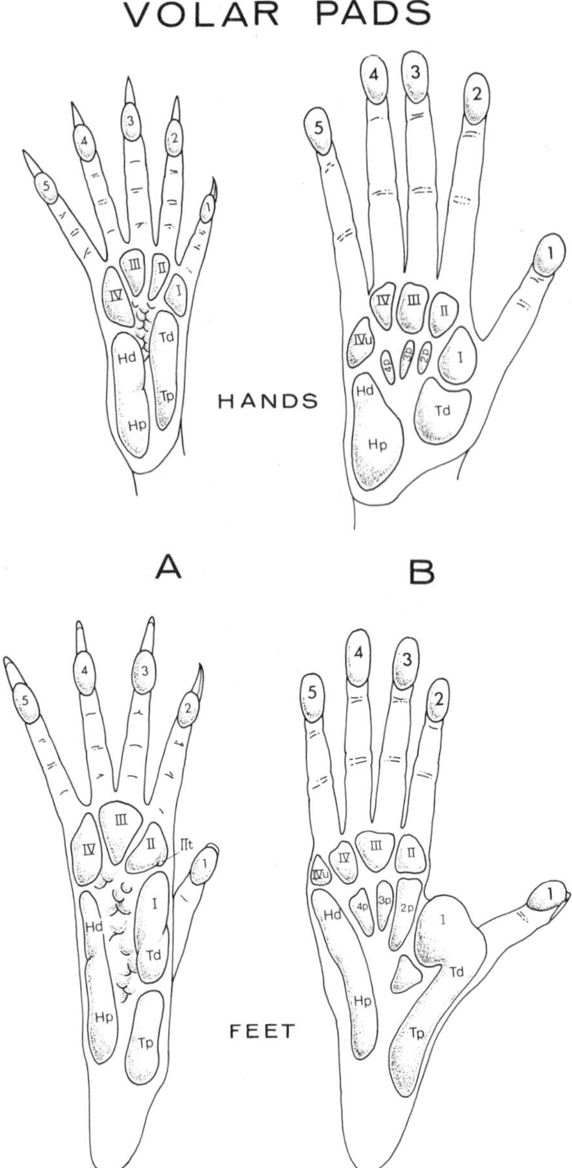

Fig. I.30. Volar pad patterns. *A*, primitive platyrrhine hand and foot pattern based on *Cebuella; B*, complex platyrrhine hand and foot pattern, based on *Aotus*. *1–5* = digital pads; *2p–4p* = central interdigital sensory pads; *I-IV* = postdigital pads; *IIt* = tibial postdigital accessory pad; *IVu* = ulnar postdigital accessory pad; *Hd* = distal hypothenar pad (primary hypothenar of sole); *Hp* = proximal hypothenar pad (primary hypothenar of palm); *Td* = distal thenar (primary thenar of palm); *Tp* = proximal thenar (primary thenar of sole); heel or calcar pad not shown. Terminology of accessory pads based on Cummins and Midlo (1961), Midlo and Cummins (1942), and Biegert (1961).

4. First digits undifferentiated in structure or function from remaining digits.
5. Volar pads with primitive pattern of 5 terminal, 6 primary (4 interdigital, thenar, and hypothenar) pads.
6. Cutaneous ridges restricted to friction skin, insulae primariae restricted to primary pads; ridges formed into proximally opened loops on terminal pads, whorls on palmar and plantar pads.

The model appears to be based on the tupaiid hand. The digital formula of the manus, 3–4–2–5–1, is common among primates and mammals generally. The same formula for the ancestral primate pes, however, is questionable. In fact, item 4 not only flatly contradicts item 1 but is improbable if not nonexistent among mammals of any evolutionary grade. An opposable hallux with nail (cf. items 3, 4) is required by a hypothetical ancestral primate. Any other kind need not be part of an organism leading to modern primates.

As described above, the functional axis of a foot with opposable hallux extends between digits 1 and 2, or the corresponding interdigital pads. The functional axis of a tupaiid or callitrichid hand with nonopposable pollex is mesaxonic. The digital formula of this hand, therefore, is primitively different from that of the grasping foot of the ancestral primate. The digital formula of the most primitively structured primate foot (cf. *Daubentonia*, marmosets) is (3 or 4)–(4 or 3)–5–2–1. The 2–5–1 portion of the formula present in many primates and in Biegert's formula is secondary and unrelated to the similar formula in tupaiids and other nonprimates.

Wrist Bones

The primitive mammalian wrist contains ten discrete bones arranged in two rows (fig. I.26). Bones of the proximal row are scaphoid, lunate, triquetrum, and pisiform. Those of the distal row are trapezium, trapezoid, capitate, hamate, and prepollex. A central bone lies between trapezoid and scaphoid. The pisiform and prepollex are sesamoid bones. Other names used for the same bones are included in the caption to figure I.26.

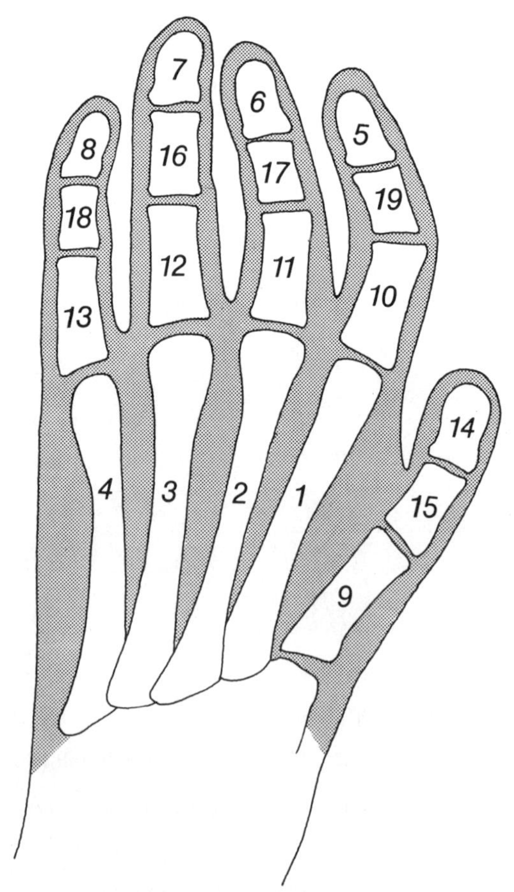

Fig. I.31. Sequence of initiation of ossification, as numbered, in each of 19 foot bones of *Saguinus oedipus oedipus*. The order is based on 8 aborted fetuses, ages not determined. Precise order of ossification within the series *5* to *8* inclusive, *9* to *13* inclusive, and *10* to *13* inclusive is not certainly established. Figure and data from Kraus and Hampton 1969.

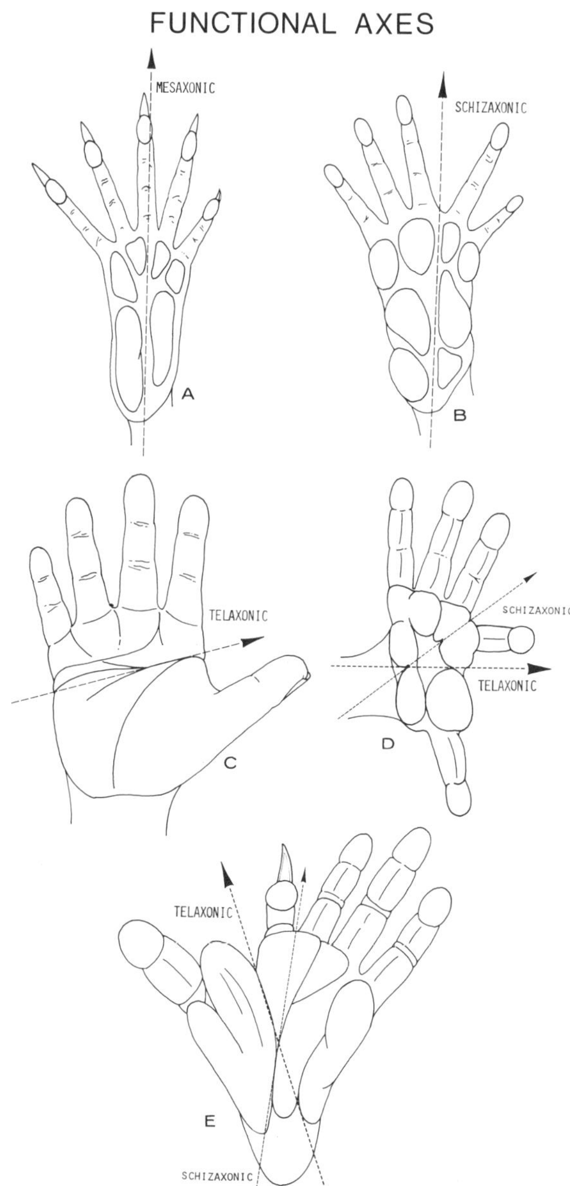

Fig. I.32. Functional axes of primate hands (*A-D*) and foot (*E*). *A,* mesaxonic type based on callitrichids; *B,* schizaxonic type based on *Alouatta; C,* telaxonic type based on *Homo; D,* telaxonic type with weak schizaxonic function, based on *Loris; E,* telaxonic type foot with weak paraxonic function, based on *Loris.*

All adult living primates, with the exceptions noted below, preserve the primitive number and relationships of carpal bones (fig. I.26). Scaphoid and lunate bones articulate with the radius, and the triquetrum articulates with the ulna. In the orang, chimpanzee (fig. I.27), gorilla, and man, however, the triquetrum is separated from the ulna by the articular disk.

The os centrale is present in all primates but is frequently fused with an adjacent bone in chimpanzee, gorilla, some lemuroids, and man. This bone has also disappeared or fused with a neighboring bone in monotremes, marsupials, most insectivores, edentates, pangolins, some histricomorph rodents, carnivores, and most ungulates.

The prepollex between trapezium and scaphoid is absent in a few primates including man.

Most consistent differences in the form of carpal elements occur in the trapezium. The dorsoproximal facet seen in the articulated position is triangular or subtriangular and about as wide as long in lemuroids and platyrrhines; in catarrhines, the facet is nearly trapezoidal or rectangular in outline and usually longer than wide (fig. I.27) The lateral or distolateral surface of the trapezium makes the seat for the first metacarpal in man, gorilla,

Fig. I.33. Schizodactylous hand stance and grip of howler monkey (*Alouatta*). Lower figure based on Grand (1968*b,* p. 116).

Fig. I.34. Slender loris, *Loris tardigradus,* showing the telaxonic hand and foot clasp. (Photo Tierbilder Okapia).

and chimpanzee. The primitive articulation of metacarpal 1 with the distal facet of the trapezium obtains in all other haplorhines. The condition in strepsirhines is variable (fig. I.26).

The scaphoid and lunate, separate and distinct in primates, are the fused scapholunate in treeshrews, genus *Tupaia* (fig. I.26). The same bones are separate in the pen-tail shrew, *Ptilocercus* (Le Gros Clark 1926, p. 1207). The scaphoid and lunate are also fused in monotremes, many marsupials, most insectivores, bats, colugos, rodents, and carnivores.

On the basis of comparisons of hand skeletons of *Tupaia* and *Microcebus,* Altner (1971) distinguished a "spread" and a "prehensile" type of hands. The first, as in *Tupaia,* is adapted for quadrupedal locomotion in shrub and low tree or semiarboreal habitats. The "prehensile" hand, typified by that of *Microcebus murinus,* with at least pseudo-opposition of the thumb, is regarded as requisite for true arboreal life. Altner's distinctions make no provisions for truly arboreal callitrichids, *Callimico,* and many nonprimate mammals with "spread" type hands.

Except as noted, the preceding review is based entirely on skeletal material in the collections of the Field Museum. For a bibliography and account of primate wrist anatomy and evolution, see Lewis (1974).

5 Locomotion

Introduction

Primates have the most versatile locomotion of any mammals except possibly rodents. No primate is a true glider, flyer, or burrower, and none is specialized for aquatic life, although many can swim. Most primates are agile in their natural environment and some are acrobatic, but a few are habitually slow and deliberate walkers or climbers.

The parts of the locomotor skeleton common to all primates depart little from those of a generalized mammalian model, and no single locomotor character or combination of characters distinguishes all primates from other mammals. On the other hand, gross similarities between different primates and between primates and nonprimates in locomotor forms, types, and gaits do not imply corresponding anatomical similarities.

A commonsense definition of primate locomotion is "the voluntary, coordinated movements of limbs and trunk that transfer the body from one point in space to another." *Support* of the body by one or more limbs as a sequence of the gait pattern is considered an integral part of locomotion. *Posture* is also part of the locomotor act. Primate locomotion thus defined involves a complex sequence of moving and stationary bodily parts. The body as a whole may advance, or the bulk of the body may advance while one or more relatively stationary parts complete an episode of posture or support.

Visual observations and motion pictures of the moving animal in its natural habitat are the bases for descriptions and critical discussions of locomotor forms and types most commonly or habitually employed by adult primates. The locomotor *form* may be quadrupedal, bipedal, bimanual, or caudal, with trunk more or less horizontal or vertical. The locomotor *type* may be walking, running, springing, hopping, climbing, leaping, or brachiating. The *gait,* or pattern of limb movements in any locomotor type, is usually opportunistic because of the discontinuous organic substrate. Hildebrand (1967), who made a special study of gaits, found that primates employ virtually every conceivable gait used by arboreal and terrestrial quadrupeds, with no single gait peculiar to them.

Notwithstanding the variety and complexity of movements, adults of all species are distinguishable by their respective locomotor patterns. So marked are these traits that posture alone, where it is a facet of the locomotor pattern, is often sufficient to signal the identity of the species and, to the more discerning observer, the individual as well. Sounds such as footfalls, and the rustle, crack, and crash of vegetation or substrate caused by the moving animal constitute part of the locomotor pattern, and in its own habitat, are likewise species characteristic.

A locomotor cycle consists of these four phases of unequal duration and energy consumption,

1. *Step-off* or *jump-off,* with one or more limbs or the entire body the primary factor of initial movement.
2. *Advance in space* with necessary limb movements and postural adjustments for maintaining equilibrium.
3. *Preparation for landing* with necessary movements and postural adjustments.
4. *Landing,* including shock absorption, braking if necessary, balancing on support, and return to initial position with preparation for next takeoff.

Each phase can be divided and subdivided into its components. Depending on conditions, one phase may flow smoothly and rythmically into the next in sequence, or locomotion may change abruptly, sometimes out of sequence. The complex and interrupted substrate of the arboreal habitat, the flexibility of primate limbs, the versatility of primates' movements, and their resourcefulness and unbounded curiosity combine to make primate locomotion the least regularized among arboreal mammals.

Locomotor forms change with age. Those of infants that differ markedly from those of their parents evolved independently and change abruptly as the individual passes from one age class to the next. Locomotor types, on the other hand, usually increase in number and proficiency as capabilities increase with age. Adults can revert to all juvenal forms of progression, if only by imitation or compulsion.

No attempt is made here to describe musculature or locomotor mechanics. Bones of the primate postcranial skeleton have been adequately monographed by a number of modern workers. References to the more specialized studies of skeletal systems are made in the text. General works on primate locomotion and morphology of postcranial skeletons are mentioned at the close of this section.

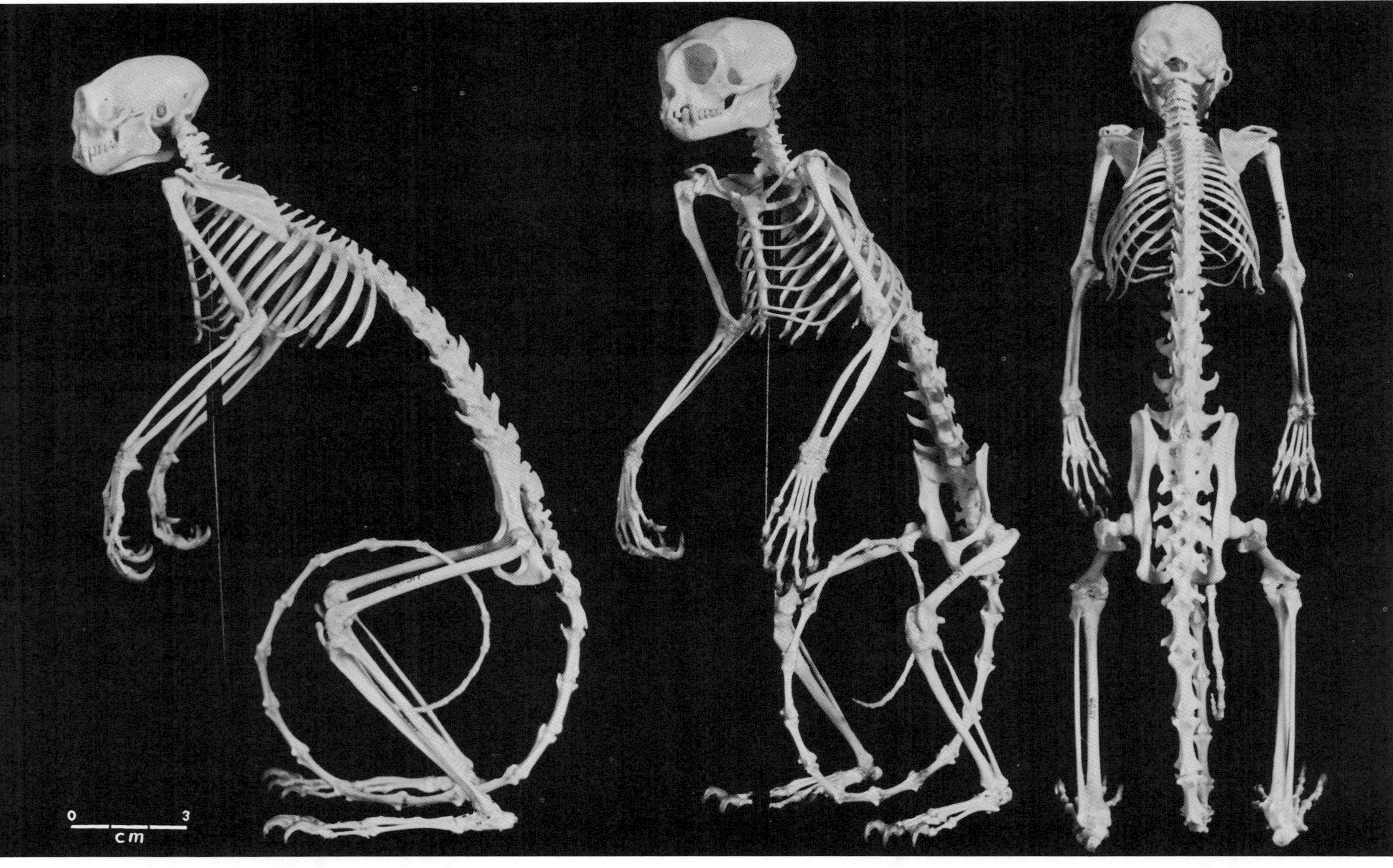

Fig. II.1. Tamarin (*Saguinus*) skeleton with coiled tail used in tripodal support

The Ancestral Locomotor Form

All locomotor types of living primates can be derived from a mouselike quadrupedal horizontal (pronograde) branch running, leaping, and scurrying form with hind limbs slightly longer than forelimbs but shorter than trunk; tibia and fibula separate; carpal and metacarpal bones discrete, the central well developed; hand and foot plantigrade, pentadactyl, hand mesaxonic, pollex non-opposable, hallux opposable; projection of manual digits, 3> 4> 2> 5> 1, pedal digits, 3> 4> 5> 2> 1; phalangeal formula, 2–3–3–3–3; opposable hallux with nail, adapted for grasping; terminal phalanx of each remaining digit of all extremities provided with sharp claw for bark clinging; tail nonprehensile and approximately equal to or longer than combined head and body length; clavicle present and well developed; vertebral formula, as inferred by Schultz and Strauss (1945) from analysis of 1457 skeletons representing all living families, cervicals 7, thoracic 13, lumbar 6, sacral 3, caudal 25, total 54. Other primitive skeletal characters can be inferred from or are correlated with those given above.

According to Napier (1967), Napier and Walker (1967*a, b*), and Napier and Napier (1967), vertical clinging and leaping was the "only known locomotor adaptation of Eocene primates" (Napier and Walker 1967*a*, p. 204). They then concluded (p. 217) that this was possibly "the earliest locomotor specialization of primates and therefore preadaptive to quadrupedalism, brachiation and bipedalism, the principal locomotor categories of living primates."

The expressed view that a specialized vertical clinging and leaping form gave rise to "a more generalized quadrupedal morphology" (Napier and Napier 1967, p. 389) runs counter to accepted evolutionary principles. Generalized primate characters are those common to the greatest number of species and depart least or not at all from primitive mammalian characters. The primitive mammal is a quadruped, and its locomotor form is quadrupedal. All primates except man are quadrupeds, and their common locomotor form aloft or aground is quadrupedal. Napier and Walker (1967*a*, p. 216) concede, unaware of self-contradiction, that vertical clinging and leaping is a specialization that must have evolved from a quadrupedal locomotor form "like that of a treeshrew or possibly a squirrel."

All osteological characters correlated with vertical clingers and leapers are specializations. Among those detailed by Napier and his co-workers are the shortened forelimbs, lengthened hind limbs, greatly enlarged hallux, reduced pedal digits II and III, vertically oriented spinal colunm, and ventrally placed foramen magnum. None of these characters is diagnostic or consistently present in vertical clingers and leapers, and all depart from, rather than lead to corresponding features of primitive quadrupedal branch-walking and running primates.

The trend among vertical clingers and leapers is toward longer and stronger hind limbs for springing, shorter and weaker forelimbs for clinging, and more extreme and habituated saltatorial locomotion on and above ground level. Brachiators also diverged from quadrupedal branch runners and leapers but evolved in opposite directions. The forelimbs became longer and adapted for suspension and swinging, and the hind limbs became relatively shorter and used for bipedal branch and ground walking and running. Hominid bipedalism, still another offshoot from a quadrupedal model, evolved along lines distinct from those of all other primates (cf. Snell and Donhuysen 1968).

The fossil evidence on which Napier and co-workers based their thesis appears to be a skewed record favoring the preservation of environmentally peripheral and, ostensibly, morphologically and locomotorially dead-end forms better described as archaic than primitive. Vertical clinging and leaping practiced by callitrichids are of a primitive grade independently evolved from a locomotor skeleton more generalized than that of any known Eocene prosimian. Conceivably, the callitrichid type of vertical clinging and leaping could give rise to but cannot be derived from any known prosimian type.

Szalay (1972*b*, p. 32), who reviewed the fossil evidence, disputed virtually all claims made by Napier and his associates. Members of each of the living prosimian groups, it appeared to him, attained vertical clinging and leaping independently from nonvertical clinging and leaping ancestors. In a later detailed study of fossil primate foot bones, Decker and Szalay (1974*b*, p. 290) concluded that "in the light of the present knowledge about the adapid pes doubts are raised concerning some alleged correlates of vertical clinging and leaping suggested by Eocene primates." Cartmill (1974, pp. 65–67) also contradicted the inferences drawn by Napier and his associates with the opinion that "the evidence suggests that the vertical clinging and leaping habit is a secondary specialization among Lemuriformes, and that the ancestral Madagascar lemurs were quadrupeds, resembling *Cheirogaleus* or *Microcebus*." Morton (1924, p. 15) who had long anticipated Napier and co-workers in recognizing and describing this and other primate locomotor forms, characterized vertical clinging and leaping as "a distinct divergent specialization . . . associated with elements of the perching or clinging grasp."

Platyrrhine Locomotion

The locomotor skeleton of the squirrellike *Cebuella* and *Callithrix* (Callitrichidae) appears to be more nearly generalized than that of any other living primate (cf. Leutenegger 1970*a, b*, on pelvis). The postcranial skeleton probably departs little from that of the postulated ancestral type except, possibly, for longer, more powerful hind limbs adapted for springing, longer digits, particularly IV–V (p. 36), greater mobility of the manual digits in divergence, convergence, and prehensility, and longer tail. Callitrichids, particularly *Cebuella pygmaea* and *Callithrix jacchus*, still retain the quick start-stop, jerky movements characteristic of a primitive locomotor system. Movements of tamarins (genus *Saguinus*) are similar but more coordinated, and those of *Callimico* possess the fluidity of those of cebids, despite their tamarinlike cheiridia.

Callitrichids, according to Erikson (1963) and personal observations, are essentially quadrupedal branch runners and springers with hind limbs averaging approximately 25% longer than forelimbs (figs. II.1, 2). The long, sharp claws permit vertical clinging on rough tree trunks and branches and the long hind limbs provide the power for springing and, in rudimentary form, the type of vertical leaping most highly evolved in certain prosimians (fig. II.3) (Thorington 1968*a*, p. 97, and below,

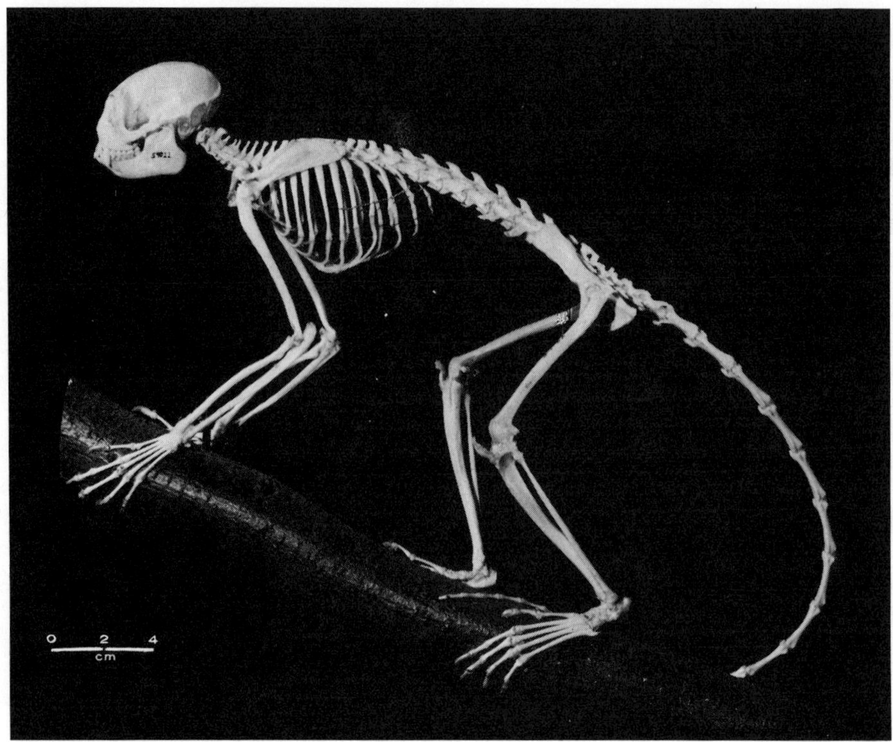

Fig. II.2. Skeleton of *Leontopithecus rosalia* in clinging quadrupedal posture. The position of the tail in this pose is not true to life.

pp. 56, 58). The ability to turn the head 180° (as in vertical clinger and leaper *Tarsius,* and probably other prosimians) allows callitrichids to observe and aim for objects to the rear.

Grounded callitrichids often employ a clumsy quadrupedal bounding gait with all four limbs striking the ground together, or with the front pair alone followed by the hind pair.

Fig. II.3. Vertical clinging pygmy marmoset (*Cebuella pygmaea*); support maintained with the long sharp claws of hands and feet; tail supplies leverage for springing and some support for clinging.

The size gradient from callitrichids to the larger marmosetlike cebids *Callicebus, Aotus* (fig. II.4), and *Saimiri,* is even but crosses the threshold separating generalized from specialized arboreal locomotor types. The crucial change resides in the shift of locomotor dominance from hind limb to forelimb, with the correlated structural modifications. The longer arm and grasping hand with more mobile digits provided with nails or naillike claws convert the forelimb into a suspensory, hoisting, and climbing apparatus as important to cebids as the springing hind limb is to the smaller callitrichids. Rudimentary opposability of the pollex in many platyrrhines, however, is less an adaptation for locomotion than a specialization of the hand for nonlocomotor functions (fig. II.5).

Pithecine cebids, all larger than marmosetlike cebids, are longer-armed and more highly specialized for climbing and to a limited extent—but mainly in *Cacajao* (fig. II.6)—for brachiation. Oxnard (in Stern and Oxnard 1973, p. 12) reports seeing *Cacajao* practice vertical clinging and leaping in a seminatural environment. The opposability of the pithecine thumb is limited, and its effectiveness is greatest when it functions together with the index finger in adducation against the other fingers and palm, especially for grasping vines and thin branches. The howler (*Alouatta*) hand (fig. I.33) is similarly schizodactylous.

A prehensile tail characterizes the next higher stage in the evolution of platyrrhine locomotion. Prehensility is incipient or rudimentary in the newborn of some small platyrrhines, most notably *Saimiri,* but functional prehensility in adults appears only in the larger cebids beginning with capuchins (*Cebus*), smallest of the prehensile-tailed cebids. Capuchins are mainly climbers, their forelimbs nearly as long as the hind limbs. The grasping tip of the completely haired tail supplements the grasping power of hands and feet and provides added security and

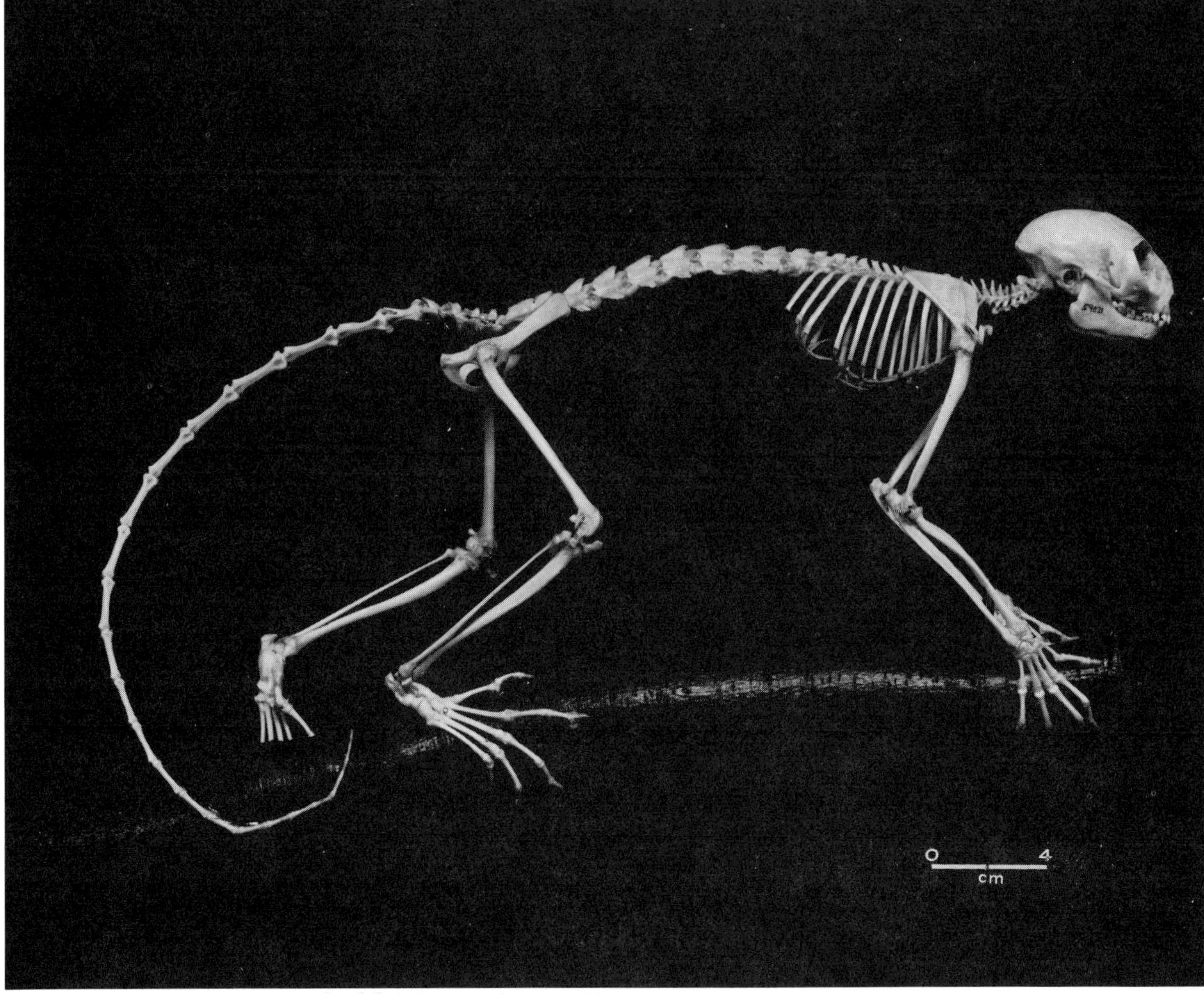

Fig. II.4. Skeleton of *Aotus trivirgatus* in climbing-walking stance

flexibility for displacement of body weight. The tail alone can support the body in suspension, but its main use is as an anchor and stabilizer in climbing and alighting.

The more specialized tail of howlers (*Alouatta*) and atelines (*Lagothrix, Ateles, Brachyteles*), largest of cebids, is more powerful, with distoventral surface bare and tactile. The howler's tail, like that of *Cebus,* is not involved with propulsion. As shown by Ankel (1962, 1963), Knussmann (1967), Carpenter (1934, p. 31), Schon (1968), and Grand (1968*a*), *Alouatta* is a quadrupedal climber and not a brachiator or even a good leaper. Its tail is used primarily for body suspension and as a grasping and supporting organ in climbing. Its structure, compared with the tails of other large cebids, is primitive (Ankel 1962). The ateline tail, in contrast, is both the most highly specialized and the most versatile. It can maneuver independently in takeoff, landing, and rebound, and adds caudal swinging and centrifugal propulsion to the locomotory repertory of spider monkeys (fig. II.7). The differences between *Alouatta* and *Ateles* in tail use and locomotor ability generally correlate with differences in the degree of their respective encephalization.

The prehensile tail is not unique to cebids. A prehensile tail used for grasping or suspension evolved independently among marsupials (most didelphids and phalangerids), edentates (lesser and pygmy anteaters), tree pangolins (*Manis*), rodents (some mice and long-tailed porcupines), and carnivores (kinkajou [*Potos*] and binturong [*Arctictis*]).

In *Saimiri* the transverse processes of the proximal caudal vertebrae form long continuous plates on each side (fig. VII.10). This extreme specialization, unique among primates, was noticed by Wagner (1837, p. 460) and was described more fully by Mivart (1865, p. 566) and Ankel (1967, p. 114, fig. 32). The functional significance of these vertebrae is unknown.

Brachiation, the suspensory hand-over-hand type of arboreal progression, is usually employed by the atelines *Lagothrix, Ateles,* and *Brachyteles.* The forelimbs of these largest of platyrrhines are as long as or longer than the hind limbs, but the prehensile tail is no less powerful an organ for support and propulsion than either limb pair (fig. II.7). *Lagothrix* is more a climber and less a leaper or brachiator than either *Ateles* or *Brachyteles.* For their size, the last two are among the most agile of all living arboreal mammals. Their usual method of rapid progression, especially in flight, displays a bewildering combination of acrobatic leaping, quadrupedal and bipedal running, brachiation, and caudation.

Possibly all New World monkeys can swim, but the few seen doing so in their natural habitat were driven to it. A wounded cotton-top tamarin (*Saguinus oedipus oedipus*) I saw fall into a stream from an overhanging tree branch swam with agility to another tree along the shore and

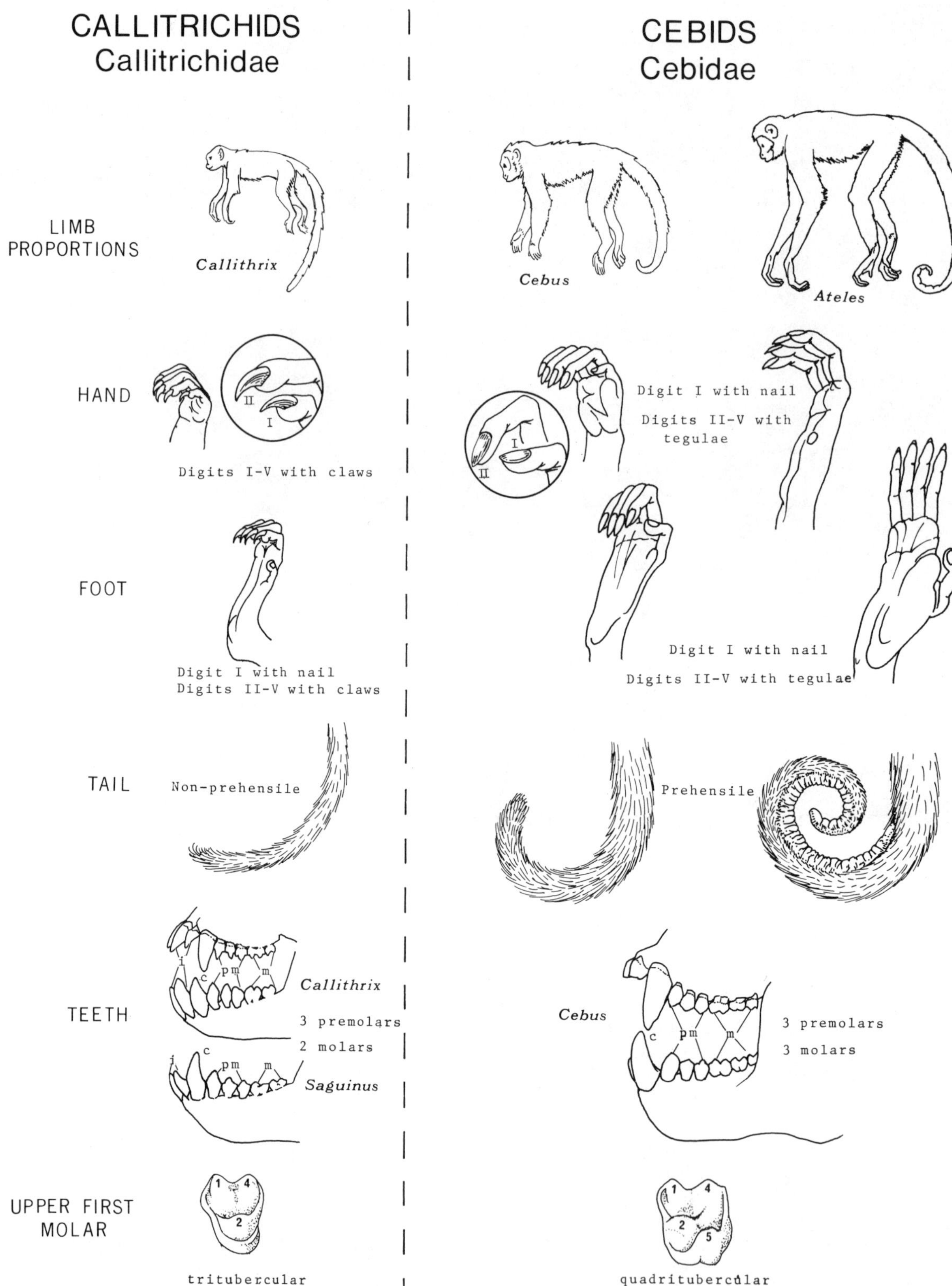

Fig. II.5. Evolutionary changes in platyrrhine body proportions, hands, feet, tail, and teeth correlated with increasing body size in an arboreal habitat. *Callithrix* (marmosets) are the size of the common gray squirrel, *Cebus* (capuchins) compare with terriers in size, and *Ateles* (spider monkeys) equal setters in size but not in bulk. As monkeys became larger, they needed more secure and powerful limbs for grasping and traveling in trees, and larger amounts of readily available and easily secured foods such as fruits and leaves. Because the forest floor is frequently flooded, New World monkeys evolved entirely above ground. Not drawn to scale. Revised from Hershkovitz (1969).

climbed up the trunk. I witnessed a similar incident involving a crested capuchin (*Cebus apella*) in Colombia. A pet squirrel monkey (*Saimiri sciureus*) thrown by its owner into the center of a swimming pool easily swam to the side of the tank and pulled itself out. Carpenter (1934, p. 33) stranded a young female howler monkey (*Alouatta*

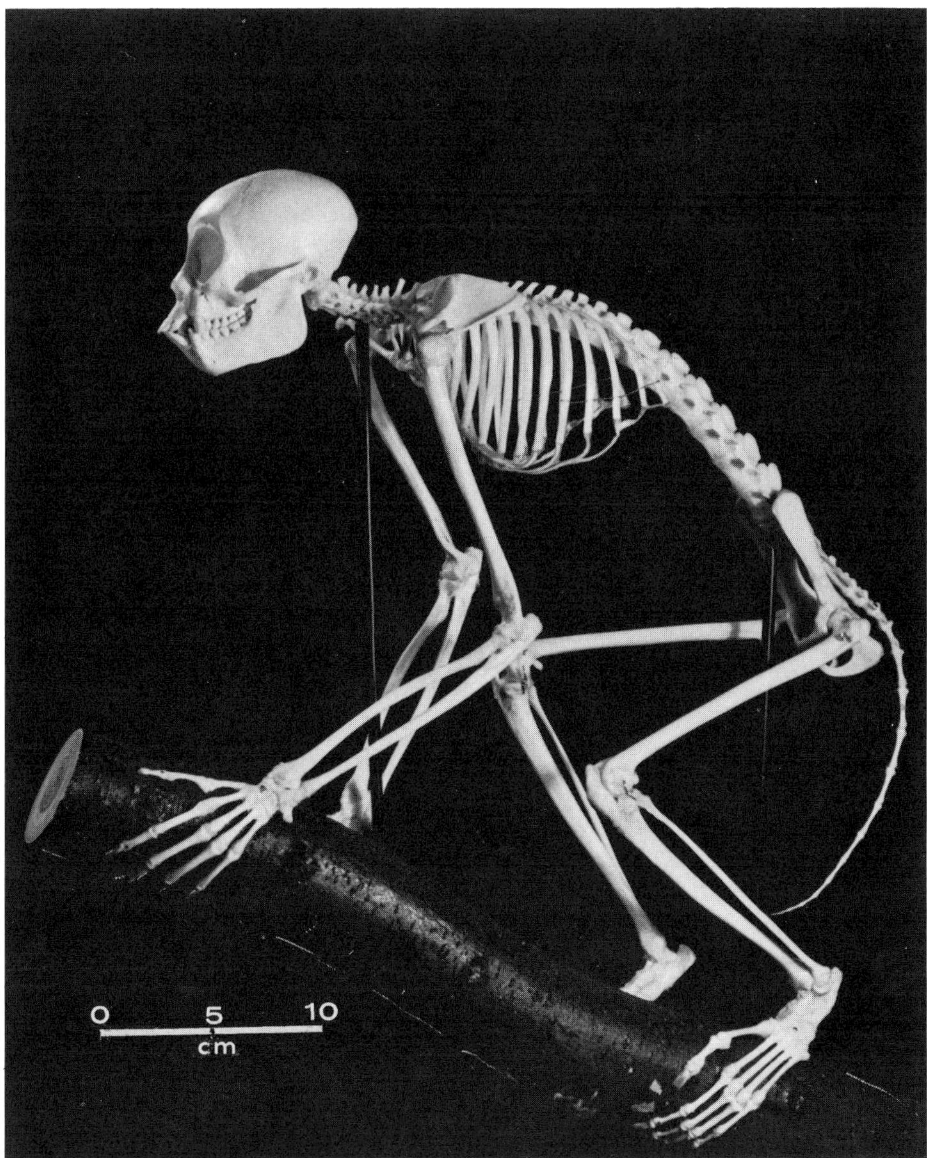

Fig. II.6. *Cacajao calvus rubicundus* skeleton. Uacaris are the only short-tailed platyrrhines.

paliatta) on a small island, from which, he affirms, it escaped by swimming to a larger island. Carpenter also noted reliable reports of howlers crossing rivers using overhand strokes.

Summary of Platyrrhine Locomotor Evolution

Modification of the limbs and their locomotor functions usually correlates with the gradual increase in overall body mass and a corresponding need for more secure purchase and wider displacement of body weight in the discontinuous, unsteady, and multiplanar arboreal substrate (fig. III.4). The forelimb of small springer platyrrhines is shorter than the hind limb. The forelimb of the successively larger, heavier springer-climbers, climbers, climber-brachiators, and brachiators becomes successively longer relative to the hind limb, to absolutely longer than the hind limb. Modifications of the hand itself also correlate with the gradient of increasing body mass. The fingers become more prehensile and abductile, endowing the hand with a firmer grasp. Sharp claws, incompatible with opposable or prehensile digits (cf. p. 32), degenerate into blunt clawlike or flattened nails. As the principal elements of support shift from the grappling and clinging claws of small callitrichids to the grasping, clutching digits of the larger cebids, the whole hand becomes equal to the whole foot as an organ of arboreal support during locomotion. In the most complex or brachiating spider monkey stage of platyrrhine locomotor evolution, the forelimb becomes a principal and virtually independent locomotor organ. The forelimb becomes even longer relative to hind limb or trunk, the palm and last four digits lengthen and curve into a grapplelike tool for hooking branches, and the first digit, now useless in locomotion, becomes obsolete or disappears.

The tail used as a balancing organ and prop in tripodal stance by smaller platyrrhines evolved into a balancing and supporting or buttressing limb in middle-sized cebids. In the largest cebids the tail has become an organ for prehension, suspension, swinging, and propulsion. Prehensility and support is least in *Cebus,* smallest of the prehensile-tailed cebids, and greatest in the largest cebids, the howlers and atelines, in which the ventrodistal portion of the tail is bare and tactile. The howler tail is a powerful grasper and the ateline tail is equal to the arms as a

Fig. II.7. Spider monkey, *Ateles paniscus,* showing long brachiating arms, thumbless telaxonic hand specialized as a hook for grasping and swinging, and the prehensile tail for grasping, support, and locomotion. (Photo courtesy San Diego Zoo).

grappling, swinging, and propulsive locomotor limb. Increasing specialization of the tail, forelimbs, and hind limbs in locomotion appears to have been correlated with increasing specialization of the same organs for other functions.

Evolution from quadrupedal walking and running, as in callitrichids or squirrel monkeys, through the various locomotor types to brachiation, as in spider monkeys, was accompanied pari passu by a gradual shift from a horizontal or pronograde trunk posture to a more or less vertical or orthograde posture.

Bipedalism is not a usual locomotor form among platyrrhines, but all species employ it to some extent. Bipedal capability is least among callitrichids, *Callimico*, and the smallest cebids and most among prehensile-tailed *Cebus* and atelines and the bobbed, nonprehensile-tailed *Cacajao*.

Long fringe hairs on the sides of the trunk of most platyrrhines simulate a patagium and act as a parachute during long spread-eagle leaps.

Platyrrhines rarely descend to the ground in their frequently flooded habitat and they evolved no specialized form of terrestrial locomotion. Prost (1965), in his analysis of *Lagothrix* (and *Macaca*) locomotion, recognized 108 categories of walking and running gaits. A synthesis of gaits habitually employed in common pursuits might well reduce that number to considerably less than half.

Catarrhine Locomotion

Most living catarrhines are larger than platyrrhines, and their arboreal locomotor patterns are correspondingly more advanced. They may be habitual quadrupedal climbers and branch runners, specialized walkers, runners, leapers, brachiators, or bipeds. The digits are provided with nails, and the pollex is opposable but is obsolete or absent in colobines. The fringe of flank hairs is long and well developed in the more arboreal forms and serves as a parachute, especially among such leapers as colobines. The tail, present in most Old World monkeys, is in a strict sense nonprehensile and in short-tailed species is used mainly for display (fig. II.8). In long-tailed forms the tail can be draped around trunks and branches

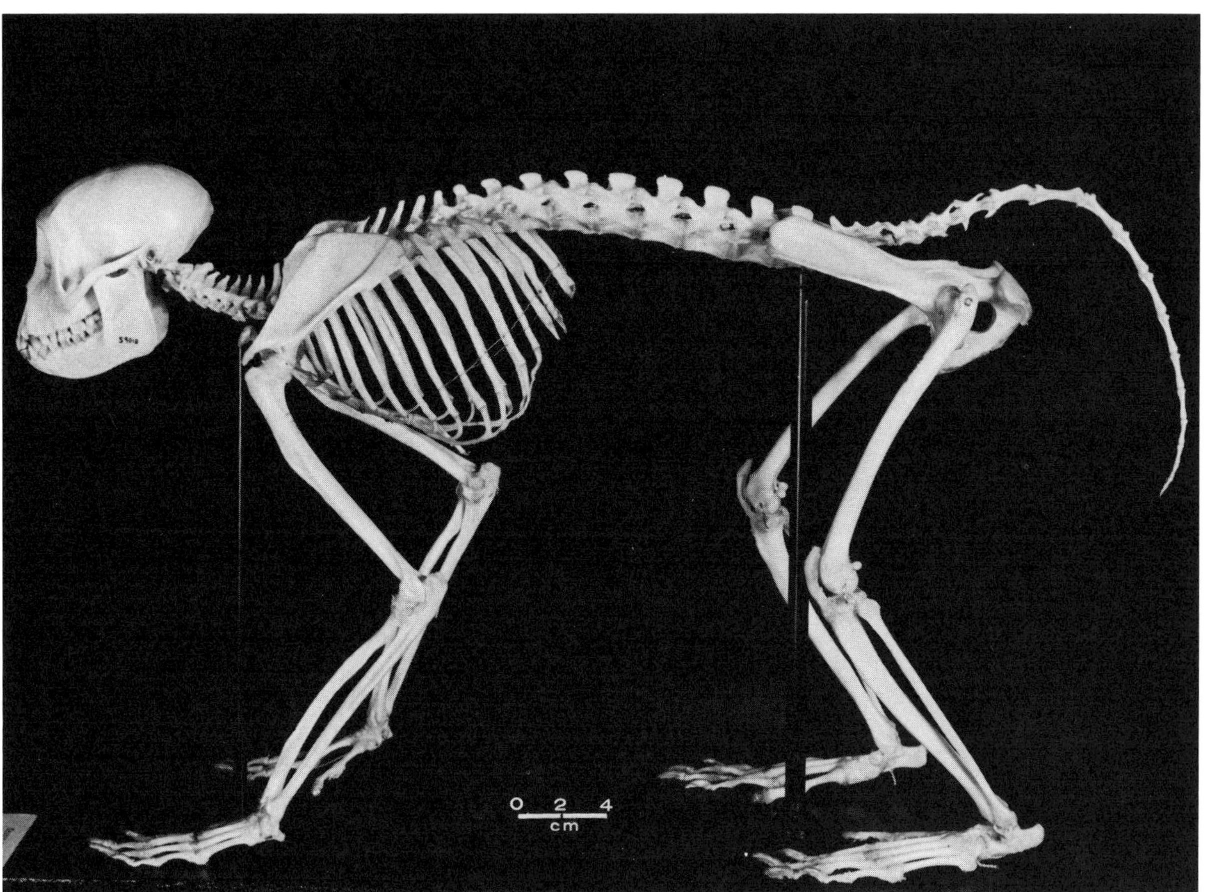

Fig. II.8. Skeleton of *Macaca mulatta* in quadrupedal stance

for support and balance. It may also serve in ricochetal propulsion, perhaps in steering, and sometimes for tripodal standing (fig. II.9).

All catarrhine monkeys (Cercopithecidae) are quadrupedal (fig. II.8, 10). The essentially arboreal langurs (Colobinae) are often classified as brachiators or semibrachiators, but African *Colobus* and Asiatic *Presbytis* are leapers (cf. Davis 1962; Ripley 1967), their powerful hind limbs considerably longer than the forelimbs. The "brachiation" or "semibrachiation" attributed to these genera by Napier (1963) is leaping pure and simple. Remaining langurs (*Pygathrix, Nasalis, Rhinopithecus,* and *Simias*) with forelimbs and hind limbs more nearly equal in length, as in *Nasalis* (Napier and Napier 1967, p. 394), are probably mainly climbers rather than leapers. As was shown by Knussmann (1967), the anterior limb bones of *Colobus, Presbytis,* and *Nasalis* exhibit few characters of brachiators.

Cercopithecines with arms shorter than legs may be almost entirely arboreal (*Miopithecus* [fig. II.11, 12]), *Cercocebus,* and some species of *Cercopithecus* and *Macaca*) or partly terrestrial (other species of *Cercopithecus* and *Macaca*). In mainly terrestrial cercopithecines (*Erythrocebus, Mandrillus, Papio, Theropithecus*), the arms tend to become as long as the legs.

Differences in limb proportions between mainly arboreal and mainly terrestrial monkeys, determined by Gabis (1960), are summarized as follows:

Arboreal (Langurs)	*Terrestrial (Baboons)*
Anterior limbs distinctly shorter than posterior	Anterior limbs nearly as long as posterior limbs
Radius shorter than humerus or tibia	Radius long, tending to equal humerus or tibia in length
Humerus shorter than femur	Humerus and femur nearly equal in length
Thumb short, third finger long	Thumb long, other fingers short
Tarsus short, hallux short, phalanges long	Tarsus long, hallux long, phalanges short

Limb proportions are intermediate in monkeys such as most macaques that are equally at home in trees and on the ground. As a rule, among cercopithecines the larger the species the more terrestrial it is. The same correlation is not evident among colobines.

Fig. II.9. Talapoin (*Miopithecus talapoin*) using tail for tripodal support.

Tuttle (1969*a*, p. 192) suggested that long-tailed species of *Macaca* are more arboreal than species with tails of intermediate length, and that the latter in turn were more arboreal than short-tailed or tailless species. This is confirmed by Wilson's (1972) study of four species of macaques, representing long, medium (fig. II.8), and short tail classes. Tail length, however, is not a reliable indicator of the degree of arboreality or terrestriality among primates generally.

Fig. II.10. Lateral-sequence walk by diana monkey (*Cercopithecus diana,* Cercopithecidae); redrawn from Hildebrand (1967, p. 124).

Brachiation is rarely if ever used by catarrhine monkeys. Jouffroy and Lessertisseur (1960) discussed modifications of the hand among monkeys they considered to be brachiators. However, only simians of the size class of gibbons and spider monkeys are true or habitual brachiators. Evidently brachiation is not an efficient or habitual type of locomotion for primates as large as adult colobines and great apes, and primates smaller than gibbons do well without it.

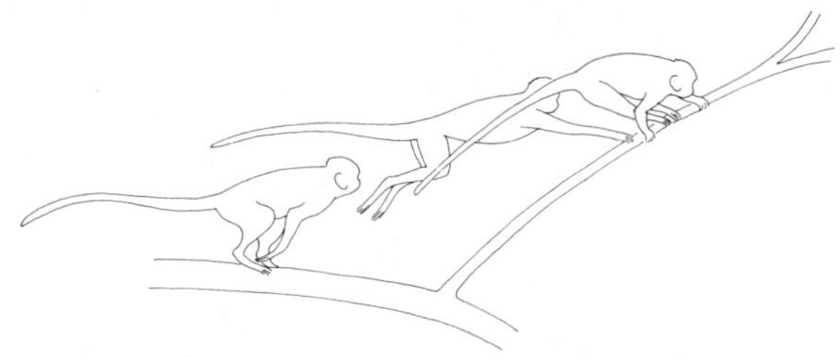

Fig. II.11. Details of talapoin leaping; tamarins use the same paces; from Gautier-Hion (1971, p. 303), based on 16 mm motion-picture film.

Bipedalism in the form of a simple step or hop for a

Fig. II.12. Mixed running walk and gallop used by the talapoin, *Miopithecus talapoin* (Cercopithecidae); gait changing is rapid and often unsymmetrical. Tamarins (*Saguinus,* Callitrichidae) employ the same sequences of mixed gaits. Details after Gautier-Hion (1971, p. 303), from 16 mm motion-picture film.

short distance is practiced by all monkeys whether branch or ground walking.

Apes locomote in trees and on the ground, but each species is better adapted for one or the other substrate. The most exclusively arboreal gibbons (including siamangs) are supreme *brachiators* (figs. II.13, 14), a term

Fig. II.13. Analysis of the pendulumlike brachiation of the siamang, *Symphalangus syndactylus* (Hylobatidae) based on 16 mm motion-picture films of free-ranging and captive animals in Malaysia by John Fleagle (1974). Figure reproduced from *Nature* (1974, no. 5445).

coined by Owen (1859, p. 75). Tuttle (1969*b*) further distinguished the unique hylobatid locomotion in which the forelimbs exert the prime propulsive force as *ricochetal brachiation*. Even when branch or ground walking bipedally, gibbons maintain the erect or semierect posture of brachiators, with arms held aloft, the entire weight supported by feet alone (cf. Carpenter 1964). The dynamics of hylobatid locomotion has been monographed by Tuttle (1972).

The orangutan, nearly as arboreal as gibbons, is mainly a quadrupedal, or quadrumanal, climber because it needs wide displacement for its enormous body weight. Occasionally, however, the orang may brachiate for short distances, or even suspend itself bipedally for resting or eating (Schaller 1961; 1965; Carpenter and Durham 1969). Branch walking by orangs is usually accomplished quadrupedally, often suspended, and sometimes bipedally.

Chimpanzees, insofar as I can infer from Goodall (1962; 1963), with help from other accounts, are as much arboreal as terrestrial. Foraging and nesting are done in trees, and travel between trees is performed on the ground. Treed chimpanzees are quadrupedal or bipedal,

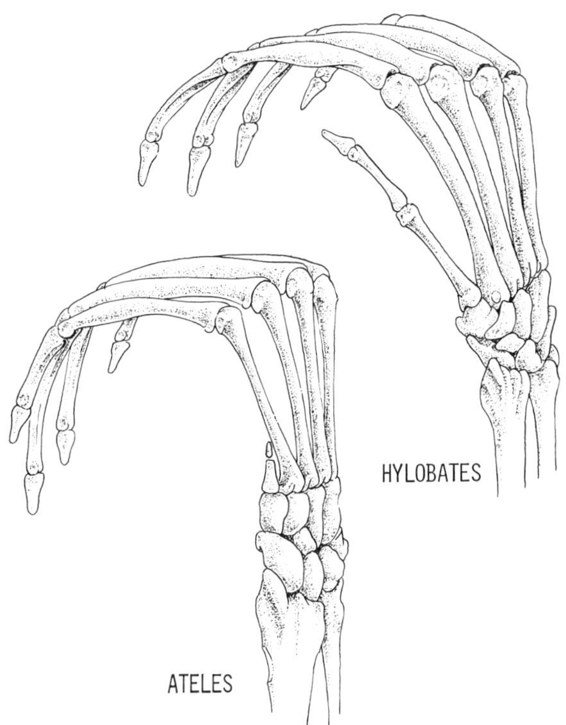

Fig. II.14. Right-hand, medial aspect of spider monkey (*Ateles*) and gibbon (*Hylobates*), modified for brachiation by elongation of digits *II-V* to form hooks. In *Ateles,* digit *I* has virtually disappeared and metacarpal *I* is obsolete, but the carpalia remain well developed. The hylobatid thumb, in contrast, is opposable and specialized primarily for nonlocomotor functions. Evidently the pollex had become an indispensable and well-integrated element of the hand before hylobatid ancestors became specialized for brachiation. Lorenz (1974) explains the thumb's independent adjustment to brachiation. The platyrrhine thumb usually acts in concert with other digits and in a primitive state can lose its functions to more specialized digits.

and are frequent but not habitual brachiators using alternating arm movements (Reynolds and Reynolds 1965; Goodall 1965).

Gorillas, according to Osborn (1963, p. 33) and Schaller (1963, p. 84) are mainly terrestrial but in trees are quadrupedal climbers. They have never been seen to brachiate in the wild. Despite the negative evidence, it has been argued (Napier 1963, p. 185; Oxnard 1968*a*, p. 251) that morphologically gorillas, chimpanzees, and orangutans *can* brachiate and therefore they *are* brachiators. Most primates, *can* swim, but this does not imply that primates are habitual swimmers or aquatic in any sense of the word. For a monographic study and bibliography of ape locomotion see Tuttle (1970).

Grounded catarrhine monkeys and apes, whether long-tailed, short-tailed, or tailless, seem to walk, run, or jump quadrupedally or bipedally on the ground as well as they do in the trees. As was shown by Tuttle (1969*a*), the more terrestrial monkeys may become more digitigrade than others by running higher on the palmar surface of the fingers, but hind foot stance and progression remain plantigrade in all primates. Ground walking gorillas and chimpanzees usually progress with hands held high on the dorsal surface of the middle phalanges of digits II–V in a form called knuckle walking (fig. II.15) (cf. Owen 1859, p. 74). They do not walk palmigrade. New and Old World monkeys also sporadically use a more or less rudimentary form of knuckle walking by

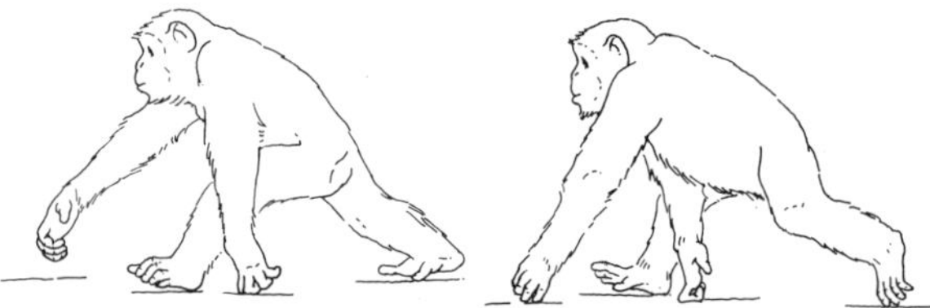

Fig. II.15. Knuckle-walking by gorilla (*Gorilla gorilla,* Pongidae); redrawn from Hildebrand (1967, p. 125).

supporting the body weight on the dorsal surface of flexed terminal phalanges and palms.

The grounded orangutan's walk may be palmigrade or digitigrade with the tread on the back of the flexed terminal or middle phalanges. More commonly, however, the hand is rolled into a fist and only the back of the proximal phalanges—usually with the hypothenar—or the hypothenar alone, making contact with the ground (fig. II.16). Orangs also knuckle walk at times facultatively, according to Susman (1974) and Tuttle (1974). Fist walking as a regular form of progression is restricted to orangs among primates, but a similar form of terrestrial progression is obligate in the greater and lesser anteaters, *Myrmecophaga* and *Tamandua.*

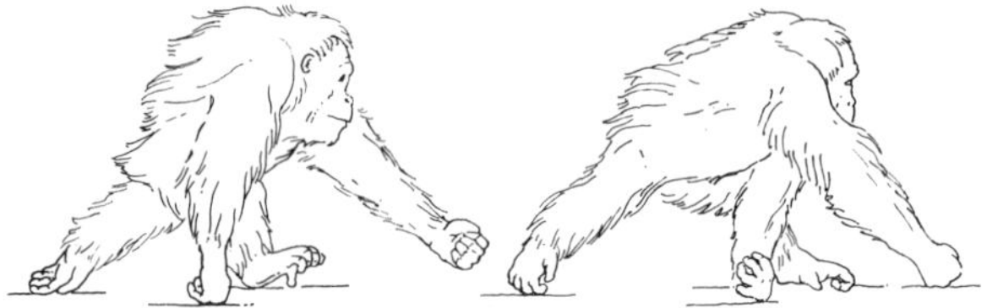

Fig. II.16. Fist-walking by orang (*Pongo satyrus,* Pongidae); redrawn from Hildebrand (1967, p. 125).

Modification of the outer surface of the hand for ground walking, and of the tactile palmar surface for grasping, manipulation, and arboreal progression, is most highly evolved in primates. Fist and knuckle walking in great apes permit rapid progression with maximum stability and shock absorption and minimum exposure or abuse of the more sensitive parts of the hand.

The functional morphology and evolution of ape hands as terrestrial locomotor organs are described in detail by Tuttle (1969*b;* 1969*c;* 1970). He holds that the hypothetically long-fingered arboreal ancestor of African apes utilized flexed-finger posturing or a rudimentary fist walking for moving along branches. As apes became larger and increasingly terrestrial the palm of the locomoting hand became more elevated so that the load rested on the dorsum of the middle phalanges. This posture, together with hyperextension of the proximal phalanges at the metacarpophalangeal joints, firmed the gait and positioned the hand to exert a modicum of propulsive force. It seems to me, rather, that the knuckle walking position of the fingers is actually the same as the grasping position of the flexed fingers. The only difference between the two is that the weight of the body presses against the outer or dorsal surface of the fingers in the one and against the palmar surface in the other. The anteater (*Tamandua*) does the same with claws and digits combined.

Bipedalism is a highly specialized form of locomotion used habitually by man and only infrequently by other primates (fig. II.17). This locomotor form arose independently among a number of vertebrates. Snyder (1962) recognizes four methods of bipedalism which, despite many functional similarities, differ grossly in structure and biomechanics. They are

(1) the reptilian method (thecodonts, dinosaurs, lizards) in which the body is balanced more or less horizontally over the legs and the tail acts as a cantilever; (2) the avian method in which, with obvious exceptions, the body is balanced horizontally over the legs and the center of gravity is directly over the hindlimbs; (3) the primate-human method in which the body is balanced semi-vertically or vertically over the limbs [and the hind legs move with an alternating gait]; and (4) the ricochetal method of saltatorial mammals in which the body is also balanced semi-vertically and the highly modified hind legs are used simultaneously in repetitive jumping. Bipedal locomotion has thus evolved independently at least six times in vertebrate phylogeny; twice in reptiles (thecodont-dinosaur group, lizards), once in birds, and three times in mammals (marsupial ricochet, placental ricochet [including prosimian hoppers, discussed below, p. 60], primate alternating gait).

Short spurts of alternating bipedal progression are frequent among grounded wild gorillas (Schaller 1965) and chimpanzees (Goodall 1965); captive monkeys and apes learn to stand, walk, and run bipedally for minutes at a time (Tuttle 1970). Occupation of hands in food carrying is most commonly associated with bipedal locomotion. Grounded gibbons are unusual in that their posture is consistently orthograde (fig. II.18), their walk alternating (Carpenter 1964; Prost 1967). Bears (Ursidae) and the gerenuk (Bovidae) also use an alternating gait on the infrequent occasions when they take a few steps upright. A bipedal stance or single step is often assumed by terrestrial, quadrupedal mammals while foraging or spying above tall grass or brush. The knee in all mammals except elephants and humans is bent in bipedal or quadrupedal walking, running, or standing.

The principal skeletal modifications of bipedal hominids in normal erect posture are the extended knee which forms a straight angle between leg and thigh bones. (fig. II.19), the rounded and forward-tilted or "bipedal" orientation of the pelvis with wide, flaring ilium turned outward from vertebral midline (fig. II.20), and the ventral convexity or lordosity of the lumbar region. The bipedally postured pongid skeleton is differentiated by the flexed knee which forms a wide angle between thigh and leg bones, retention of the "quadrupedal" femuro-pelvic relationship, less outwardly turned ilia, and the slightly curved or nearly straight lumbar region. Among catarrhines the cercopithecid pelvic region departs least from the primitive condition. For additional information see Schultz (1930); Straus and Cave (1957); Schultz (1961); Straus (1962*a*); Kummer (1965); Snell (1968); Snell and Donhuysen (1968); and Snyder (1967). The evolution of the primate foot and locomotion with particular reference to man is described in detail by Morton 1924, p. 1952).

Many Old World monkeys can and do play or forage in water, and a number have been observed swimming, sometimes across broad streams. Gautier-Hion and Gautier (1971) described the attraction of the talapoin (*Miopithecus talapoin*) and the Brazza monkey (*Cercopithecus neglectus*) to water and their spontaneous diving and swimming on and under water (fig. II.21). The

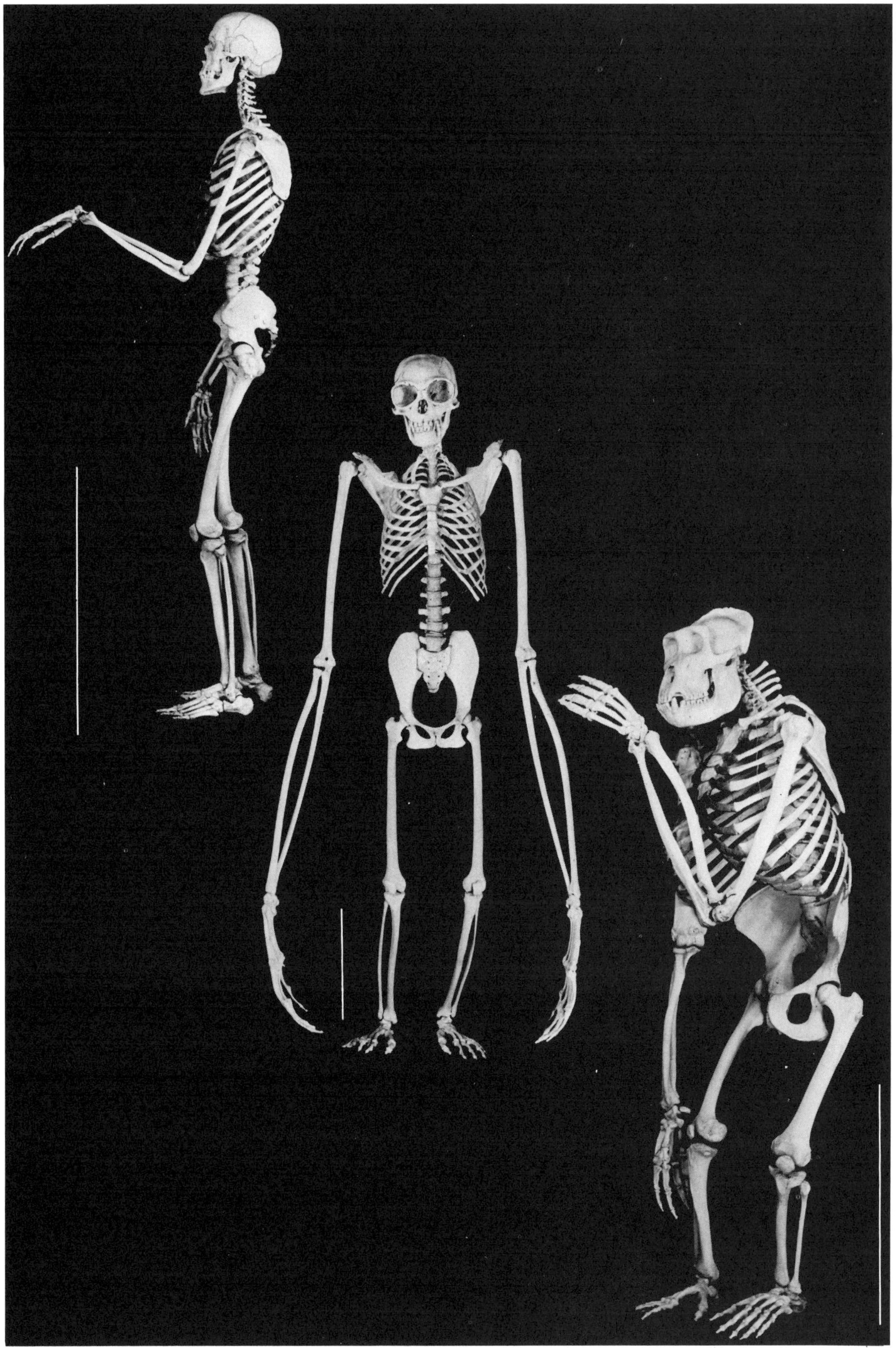

Fig. II.17. Hominoid skeletons in bipedal stance: *from left to right, Homo* (170 cm tall), *Hylobates* (70 cm), *Gorilla* (150 cm); all shown to same height, actual heights given in parentheses; white lines show relative heights drawn to scale.

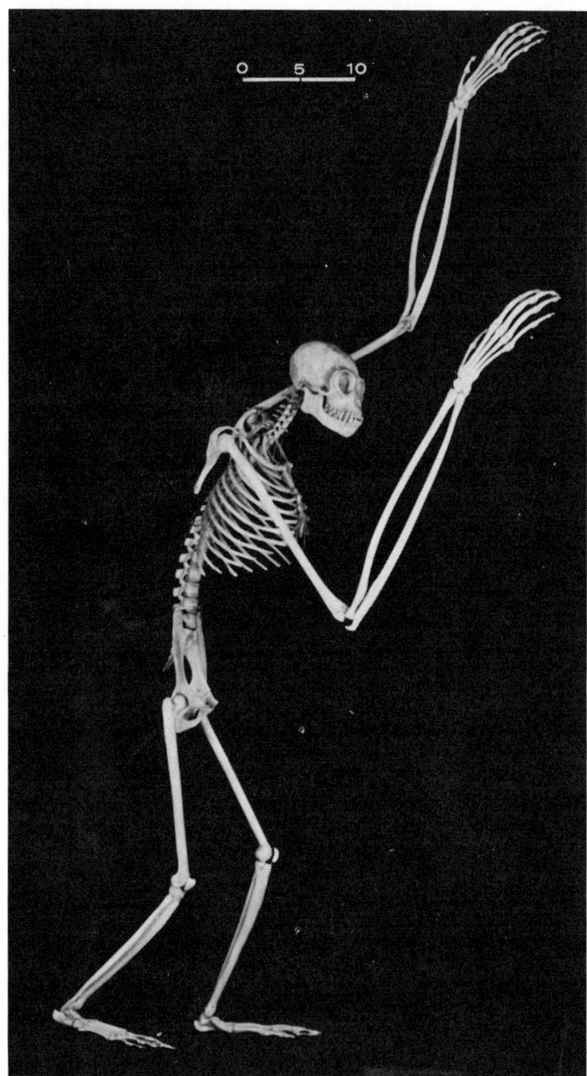

Fig. II.18. Skeleton of *Hylobates* in bipedal walking posture

swimming stroke of the Brazza monkey is said to be comparable to that of the human "crawl," and the talapoin was seen executing a number of swimming maneuvers with the same arm stroke, with the legs kicking at the same time (Gautier-Hion 1973, p. 306). Names of other cercopithecids with swimming predilections compiled from the literature and cited by Gautier-Hion and Gautier (1971) are the Japanese macaque (*Macaca fuscata*), rhesus (*M. mulatta*), crab-eating macaque (*M. fascicularis* [= *irus*]), hamadryas baboon (*Papio hamadryas*), gelada (*Theropithecus gelada*), grivet (*Cercopithecus aethiops*), and the proboscis monkey (*Nasalis larvatus*). The authors mention the South African baboon (*Papio ursinus*) as a poor swimmer and speak of Allen's monkey (*Cercopithecus* [*Allenopithecus*] *nigroviridis*) and the blue monkey (*Cercopithecus mitis*) as occasional swimmers. They conclude that at least for the talapoin and Brazza monkeys swimming serves as a deliberate means of escape from potential predators and sport for the young. Stream crossing by swimming was also discussed as a means of geographic disperal.

Gibbons and apes have never been seen swimming. Carpenter (1964) states that gibbons cannot swim. According to Hooten (1942, p. 124), orangs flounder and drown if thrown into deep water. Schaller (1963, pp. 29, 298) finds that gorillas dislike entering water. If obliged to cross shallow streams they use fallen logs, rocks, or debris for bridges. It is also probable that chimpanzees cannot swim. Van Lawick-Goodall's (1968) sketches of the chimpanzee's aversion to foot wetting are reproduced in figure II.22.

Prosimian (Strepsirhine and Tarsioid) Locomotion

Prosimians are mainly or almost entirely arboreal. Their usual locomotor patterns consist of three principal types. The first, as described by Petter (1965), is a comparatively primitive horizontal quadrupedal form of walking, running, springing, and leaping. The second is a specialized horizontal quadrupedal form of slow climbing. The third is a specialized vertical springing or leaping type, the "tarsi-fulcrumating" leap described by Morton (1924, p. 9). The postcranial skeleton of prosimians (fig. II.23) is for the most part, more specialized than that of catarrhines or platyrrhines.

The first and most generalized prosimian locomotor type, is the horizontal quadrupedal branch walking and running with hands and feet firmly clutching the support.

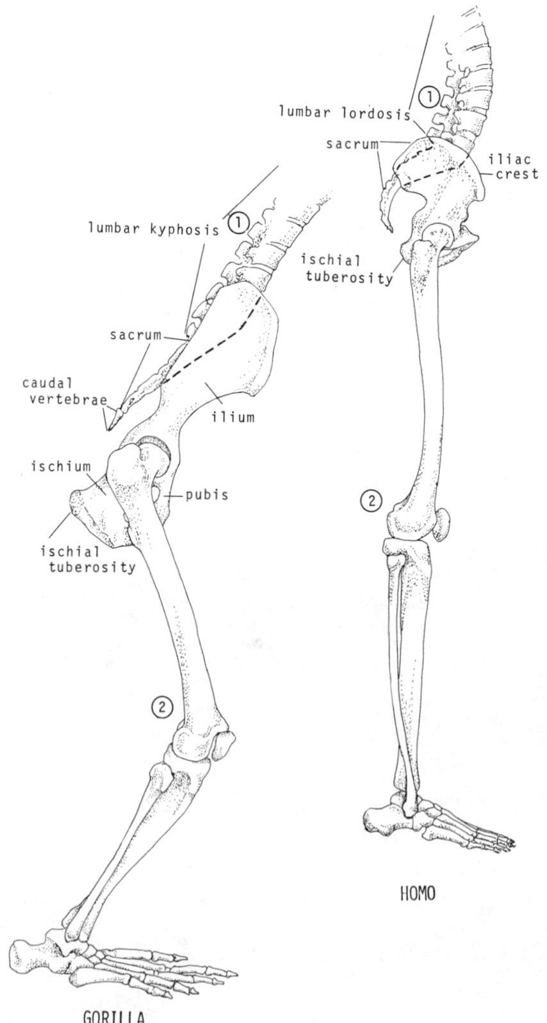

Fig. II.19. Posture and spinal curvature in erect gorilla (*Gorilla*) and man (*Homo*); dotted line across ilium follows curvature of hidden sacrum and adjacent lumbar vertebrae. Principal postural differences are marked: *1*, dorsal contour of lumbar region is convex (kyphotic) in nonhuman primates and mammals generally, but in *Homo* lower dorsal lumbar contour is markedly concave (lordotic); *2*, upper and lower limb bones meet to form angle at knee in nonhuman primates but form a more or less straight line in *Homo*.

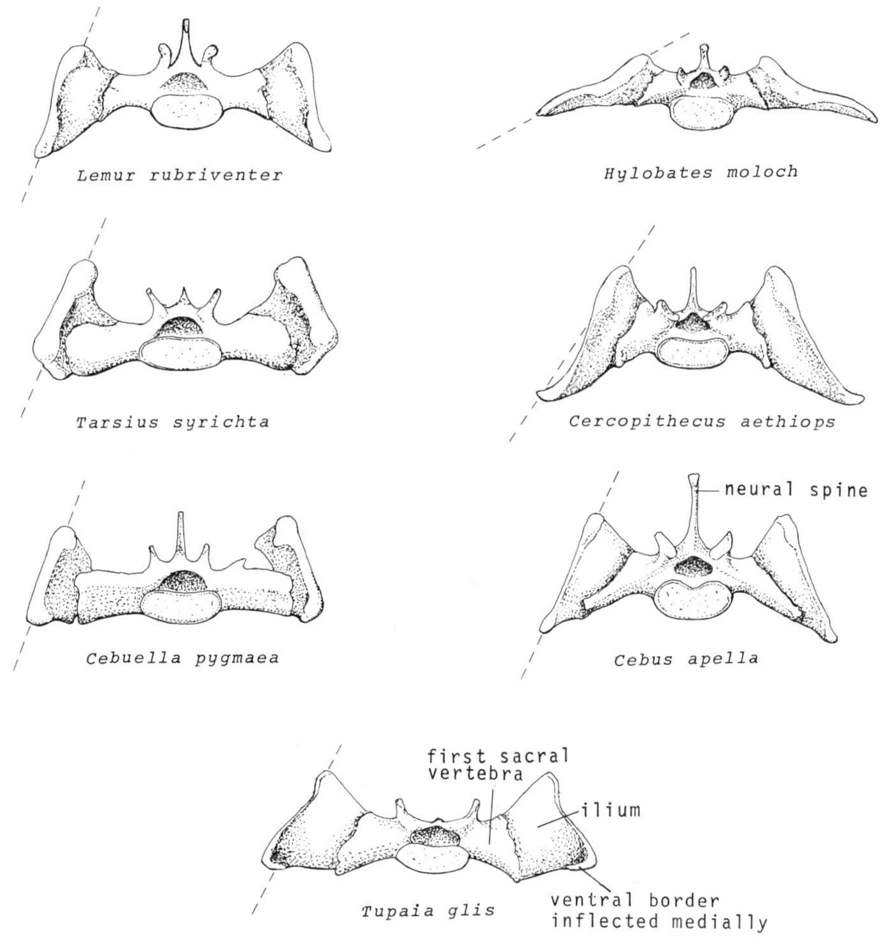

Fig. II.20. Anterior (superior) aspect of pelvis in representative primates and *Tupaia* drawn to same transverse width. In primates, first sacral neural spine is developed and the ventral iliac border is straight or deflected laterally; in *Tupaia*, first sacral neural spine is obsolescent and the ventral iliac border is inflected medially. In gibbons, pongids, and man, ilia are turned outward from vertebral midline; axis or iliac crest is indicated by dotted line.

Fig. II.21. Captive DeBrazza's monkey (*Cercopithecus neglectus*) in enclosed pool, swimming with stroke comparable to human crawl stroke. Diagram redrawn from Gautier-Hion and Gautier (1971), based on 16 mm motion-picture films.

Fig. II.22. Chimpanzee demonstrating three methods for keeping feet dry when crossing stream. Redrawn from van Lawick–Goodall (1968).

It is used (Petter 1962; 1965) by the Cheirogaleinae and most Lemurinae (family Lemuridae). Except for prodigious leaps made between widely separated branches or trees, this locomotor form is similar to that of mouse opossums (*Marmosa,* Didelphidae, Marsupialia) but is more specialized than that of callitrichids. The smaller galagids usually run with fingertips only touching and feet clutching the support (fig. II.24). Quadrupedal tree runners travel without difficulty on the ground, but smaller forms tend to scurry. R. Anthony (1912, p. 317) noted a narrow but well defined white-fringed patagium between elbow and knee in *Microcebus.* Presumably the furred skin fold aids in leaping. In any case, the thick body fur and long tail hairs probably exert a slight braking or parachuting effect during long falling leaps. The tail itself helps steer and balance the body in motion and maintain poise at rest.

The second or horizontal quadrupedal type of slow

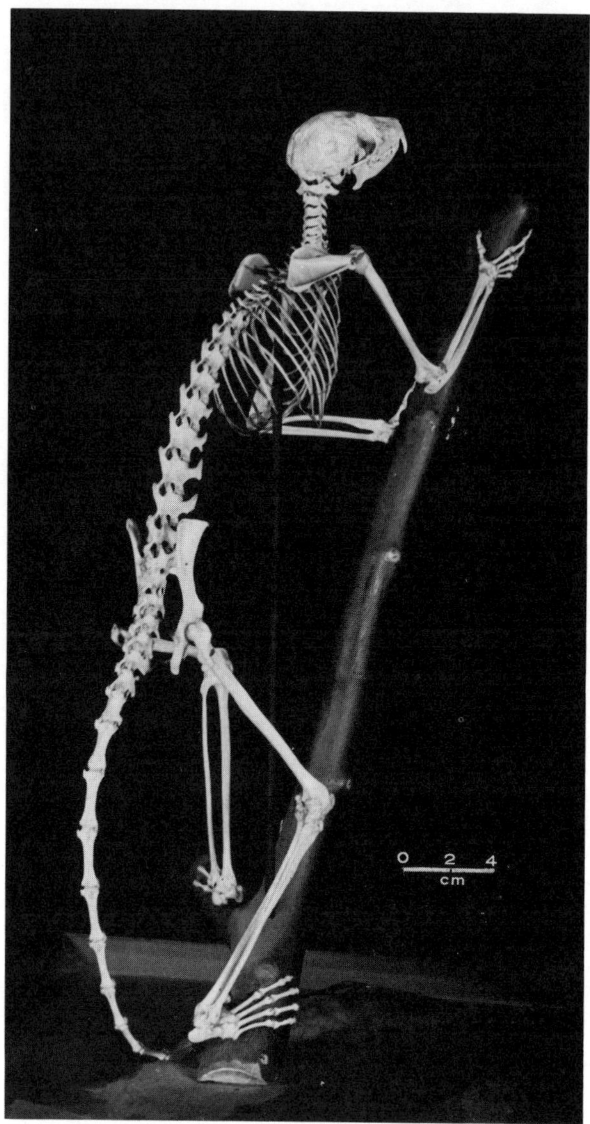

Fig. II.23. Skeleton of *Lemur mongoz* in bipedal supporting posture.

climbing characterizes lorises (*Loris, Nycticebus*), pottos (*Perodicticus*) and angwantibos (*Arctocebus*). These long-limbed practically tailless forms comprising the family Lorisidae depend on the clamping grip of hands and feet for securing support during locomotion (fig. I.32D,E, 34). In certain respects, lorisid locomotion is comparable to that of unrelated edentates of the order Xenarthra. Like sloths, lorisids cannot jump, and their progression is always silent, slow, rythmic, or flowing and usually unperceived by predators (figs. I.3, 34). The body is often suspended by all four limbs or by one or both hind limbs alone (cf. Bishop 1964). The widely expanded ribs and related heavy musculature reinforce the vertebral column during progression and act in returning the bipedally suspended or extended body to the quadrupedal position. The thoracic skeleton of all three living neotropical genera of anteaters, *Tamandua, Myrmecophaga,* and *Cyclopes,* is similar (Jenkins 1970). Lumbothoracic strength and stability combined with a "swivel-jointed" ankle (cf. Grand 1967) allow lorisines to extend their body full length and turn in almost any direction while supported by only one foot clamped to a branch. The little golden anteater, *Cyclopes didactylus,* with a similar "swivel-jointed" ankle, also moves its body freely while anchored to a branch by one foot (personal observation).

The locomotor apparatus characteristic of the slow climbing quadrupedal type distinguishes lorisids from all other primates, whereas characters of no other anatomical system absolutely separate lorisids from the nearest related galagids. Gaits and other details of African lorisid locomotion are described by Charles-Dominique (1971).

Vertical clingers and leapers, representing the third locomotor type among prosimians, jump straight across from vertical support to vertical support. The takeoff is powered by the long hind limbs, the landing insured by the cheiridia with their long flexible digits and expanded touch pads which adhere to nearly any solid surface. Vertical leaping is habitually practiced by the lemuroid

Fig. II.24. Fingertip running by *Galago minutus* (Galagidae); padded fingertips touch the bar while hind feet clutch it between hallux and opposing toes. Diagram after Charles-Dominique (1971, p. 176); based on 16 mm motion-picture film.

Fig. II.25. Vertical leaping by *Lepilemur mustelinus* (Lemuridae) to show backward takeoff, midair twist, and foot-first landing. Details from Charles-Dominique and Hladik (1971, pp. 12–13), with modifications; from photographs taken at 1/1,000 shutter speed.

Lepilemur mustelinus (fig. II.25), the Indriidae (*Indri, Avahi, Propithecus*), galagids (family Galagidae), and the tarsier (*Tarsius*, Tarsiidae). Some mainly horizontal running lemurines, particularly *Hapalemur griseus* and *Lemur catta,* may sometimes use vertical leaping (cf. Petter and Peyrieras, 1970*b*). *Microcebus murinus* also includes this locomotor form in its diversified repertory (Martin 1972*a*).

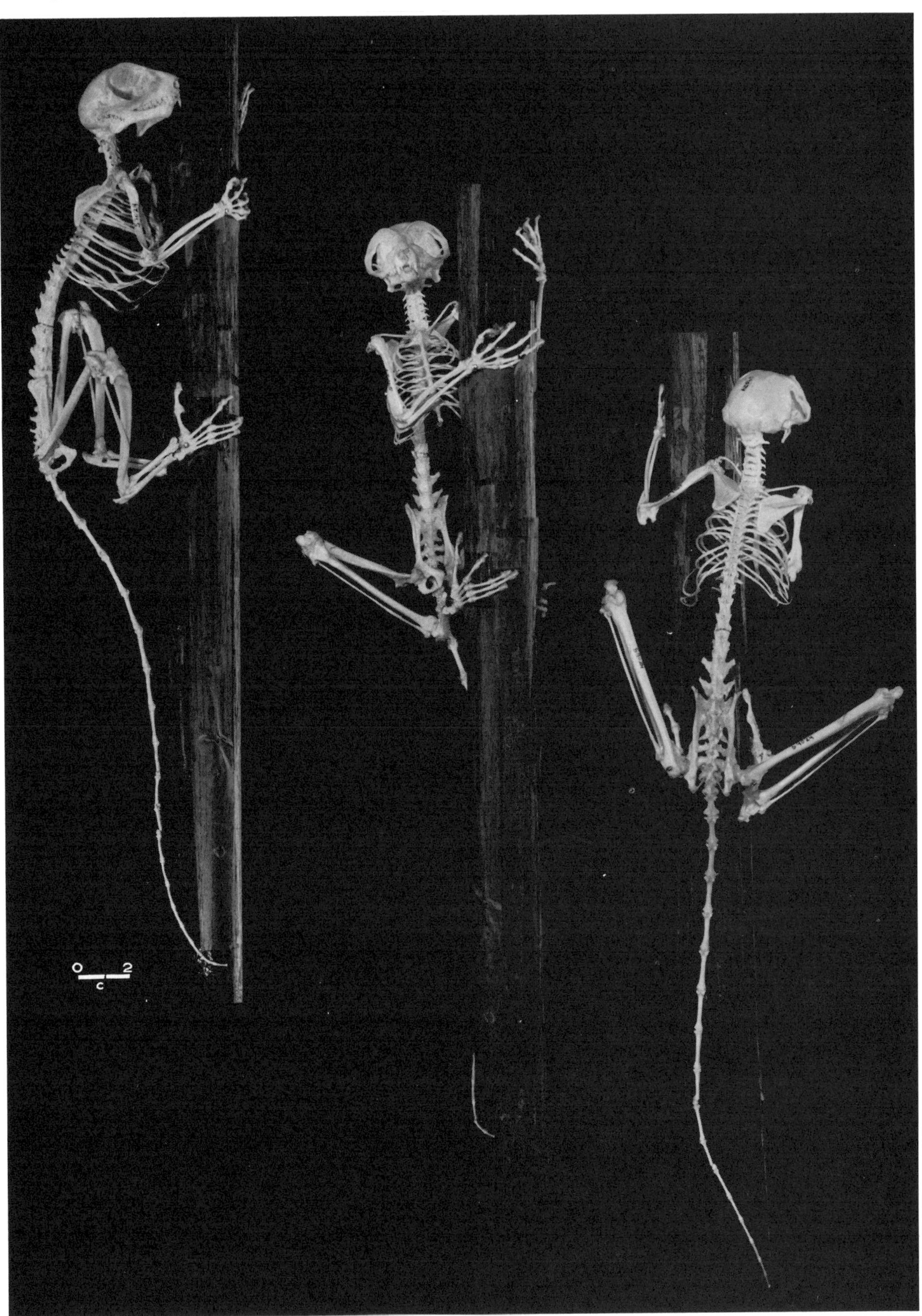

Fig. II.26. *Galago senegalensis* skeleton mounted in vertical clinging posture, lateral, ventral, and dorsal aspects.

Fig. II.27. Vertical leaping by *Galago alleni* (Galagidae) to show rotation around support, midair twist, and hand-first landing. Diagram based on Charles-Dominique (1971, p. 182). For a step-by-step analysis of a jump based on cineradiography, see Jouffroy and Gasc (1974).

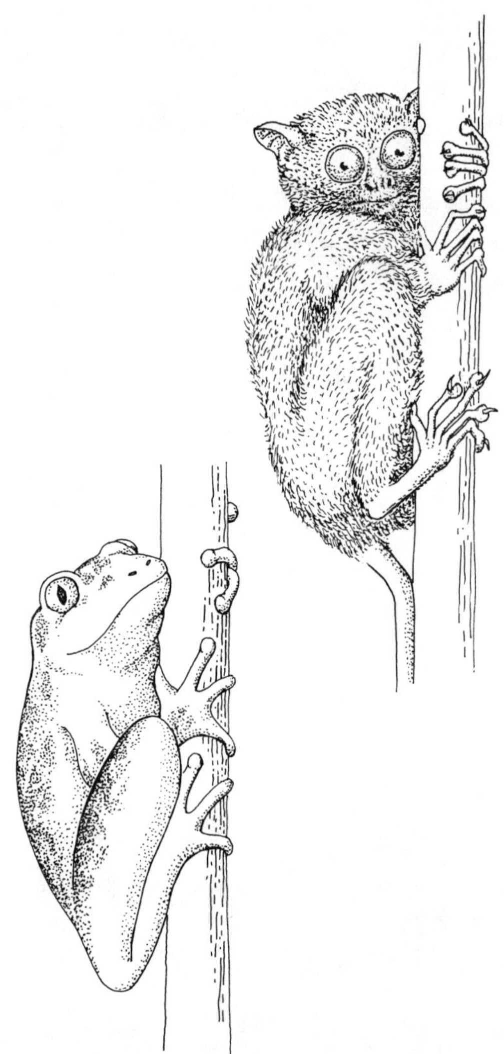

Fig. II.28. Vertical clinging by tarsier (*Tarsius syrichta,* Tarsiidae) and spotted frog (*Hylambates maculatus,* Rhacaphoridae). Long fingers, digital pads, and long hind legs and feet equip both animals for grasping and clinging to smooth vertical surfaces and for vertical leaping.

Vertical leapers usually take off with the trunk in nearly the same sitting or vertical posture used in vertical clinging (fig. II.26). They turn during flight to face the target support for a feet-first landing. Most galagids usually push off with the body extended more or less horizontally, head facing forward and belly up or sidewise. They then twist to a belly-down position and land hands first (fig. II.27). *Galago* (*Euoticus*) *elegantulus,* however, maintains the body vertical rather than horizontal throughout the leap (Charles-Dominique 1971). The tarsier jumps in the lemuroid sitting posture and lands feet first.

Arboreal vertical leaping is a rare form of locomotion that seems to have been observed only in the aforementioned prosimians. The more primitive vertical claw clinging and leaping is practiced by callitrichids. Tree frogs are the only other living arboreal vertebrates adapted to a form of vertical clinging and leaping (fig. II.28).

Grounded vertical clingers and leapers become bipedal hoppers with gaits recalling those of kangaroos, elephant shrews, and jerboas. The tail is not used in leaping except perhaps as a balancing organ. The tarsier's tail, however, is specialized as a prop for vertical clinging and tripodal sitting (fig. II.29). This appendage has received attention from Le Gros Clark (1924), Osman Hill (1953) and Sprankel (1965, p. 153, fig. 7).

Vertical clinging and leaping as a prosimian locomotor form was first described by Morton (1924, pp. 7, 9, 15) on the basis of pedal structure and function. Napier and Walker (1967*a, b*), Napier (1967), and Napier and Napier (1967) developed the concept of vertical clinging and leaping into an elaborate scheme of primate locomotor evolution. It appears, however, that the osteological characters they correlate with this locomotor form are not consistently present, and the historical basis used for support of their argument that vertical clinging and leaping is ancestral is extremely dubious.

Cartmill (1972), who severely criticized Napier and his co-workers, perhaps chose the wrong term in labeling vertical clinging and leaping an "artificial category." This locomotor form, he notes, includes two different kinds of adaptations. One, used by the insectivorous tarsier and small galagos for pouncing on prey, involves tarsal elongation (Morton 1924; Hall-Craggs 1966; Jouffroy and Gasc 1974) and remodeling of hip articulation (Grand and Lorenz 1968). The other, used by herbivorous Malagasy prosimians with long powerful hind limbs but no tarsal or coxal specialization, may serve, Cartmill suggests, for evading predators or perhaps confers an advantage in canopy leaf feeding.

Stern and Oxnard's (1973) separation of the same two kinds of clinging and leaping on the basis of a multivariate analysis of scapular, pelvic, and limb dimensions derives from the circularity of their method. The long tarsus and insectivorous adaptive type, they determined, is less evolved in galagos than in *Tarsius* and is only incipient in *Microcebus* and *Cheirogaleus,* while the long thigh herbivorous adaptive type appears most highly evolved in indriids and is incipient in *Lemur* and *Hapalemur.*

Authors who observed and described vertical clinging

Fig. II.29. Tarsier (*Tarsius syrichta*) using bent tail for tripodal support.

and leaping among prosimians include Rand (1935), Cook (1939), Southwick (1952), Le Gros Clark (1959). J. J. Petter (1962; 1965), A. Jolly (1966), Petter and Peyrieras (1970*b*), Charles-Dominique and Hladik (1971), Jouffroy and Gasc (1974) and Walker (1974). Hall-Craggs (1965) reviewed earlier accounts of vertical clinging and leaping, and he (1966) described the hind limbs and gaits of Galagidae and compared them with those of *Tarsius*. External form and use of the hands are described by Bishop (1964).

The characteristic locomotor patterns of the aye-aye (*Daubentonia*) are unique. The powerful claws of all digits, except hallux, and the attenuate middle finger specialized for probing, feeding, and scratching, impede or limit use of the hand in prehension and quadrupedal locomotion. As described by Petter and Peyrieras (1970*a*), the claws are the main supports for trunk clinging and climbing and for maintaining feeding positions impossible for other prosimians to hold. The hooked claws also serve as supports for upside-down progression and for squirrel-like suspension by feet alone. In quadrupedal branch locomotion, the aye-aye moves more slowly than lemurines and its leaps are shorter, carefully measured, and usually followed by a recovery pause before the next leap. Ground walking is slow, flat-footed and palmigrade but with manual claws and middle digit raised above the substrate. Rapid ground progression is by bounds, with hands and feet landing at the same time. A mounted skeleton of this rare animal is figured (fig. II.30).

The only prosimian that has been observed swimming is the Malagasy gentle lemur (*Hapalemur griseus*). Petter and Peyrieras (1970*b*, p. 362) were informed by native fishermen that the lemur swims dog fashion with only its head above water. Some, including females with young on their backs, were seen swimming across a canal 15 meters wide. No doubt many other kinds of prosimians, including vertical clingers and leapers and those that drop to the ground to escape enemies, could as readily seek refuge by diving into streams or flooded forest banks.

Review of Some Additional Literature on Primate Locomotor System

The classic reference on comparative mammalian locomotion is A. Brazier Howell's 1944 study based on the anatomy, function, and adaptions of the organism. The authoritative reference work on mammalian gaits is still the classic analysis by Muybridge (1887). Among descriptive monographs of the primate postcranial or locomotor skeleton that of Mivart (1865) remains first rank.

A primary source for data on primate limb and trunk proportions and locomotor forms is Mollison (1911). Despite an uneven sampling of the major groups of living primates, too small representation of cebids and prosimians, failure to separate sexes and age groups, and identifications based on antiquated systems, Mollison's work has been the model for statistical analyses of skeletal locomotor parts and definitions of locomotor functions. Mollison distinguished climbers (*Kletterer*) as early offshoots from ancestral springers (*Springer*) typified by *Callithrix* or *Lemur;* brachiators (*Hängeler*) arose from early-stage climbers, and human bipeds (*Gänger*) from incipient brachiators. Runners (*Läufer*), actually cursorial catarrhines such as the mandrill, were conceived as having evolved from advanced climbers. Slow climbing (e.g., *Nycticebus*) is mentioned but not as a first-rank locomotor form. Vertical clinging and leaping, which can hardly be deduced as an extreme locomotor specialization, was unrecognized.

Morton (1924; 1952) was concerned with the evolution and dynamics of primate locomotion and represents a considerable advance over Mollison, particularly in the emphasis placed on functional and theoretical aspects of locomotion. Papers on trunk and limb bones by Schultz (1930; 1961), and another by the same author (1963*b*) on the relative length of foot bones, have already been cited elsewhere. His work on trunk and limb bones of higher primates is a fount of information on number, shape, size, proportions, and evolutionary trends of symmetrically and serially homologous bones. It owes much to Mollison.

Erikson (1963), using membral and intermembral proportions as indicators, divided platyrrhines into the following locomotor types.

1. *Springers: Callithrix, Saguinus, Aotus, Callicebus.* Erikson regarded *Cebuella, Leontopithecus,* and *Callimico as deviant but* included them in this group while excluding their quantitative data.
2. *Climbers: Cebus, Saimiri, Pithecia, Chiropotes, Cacajao.*
3. *Brachiators: Alouatta, Lagothrix, Ateles, Brachyteles.*

Erikson (1963, p. 143) explained that, although the "groups are not sharply defined [they] are useful divisions of a continuum." Much of the large overlap between the groups was attributed to "springer"-like *Saimiri* and "climber"-like *Alouatta.*

The "springer" and "climber" groups are indeed poorly defined, and each of the three groups is heterogenous and largely unnatural in composition. Furthermore, the lumped dimensions of such disparate genera as *Cebuella* and *Aotus* among "springers" and *Saimiri* and *Cacajao* among climbers, to mention only the extremes, conceal more than they reveal. Locomotor patterns of claw-clinging and climbing callitrichids are different from those of the larger finger-gripping *Aotus* and *Callicebus,* all members of the "springer" group. The "climbers," *Saimiri, Cebus,* and pithecines are widely separated in locomotion and phylogenetically as well. Atelines brachiate, but they are not brachiators in the meaning reserved for gibbons.

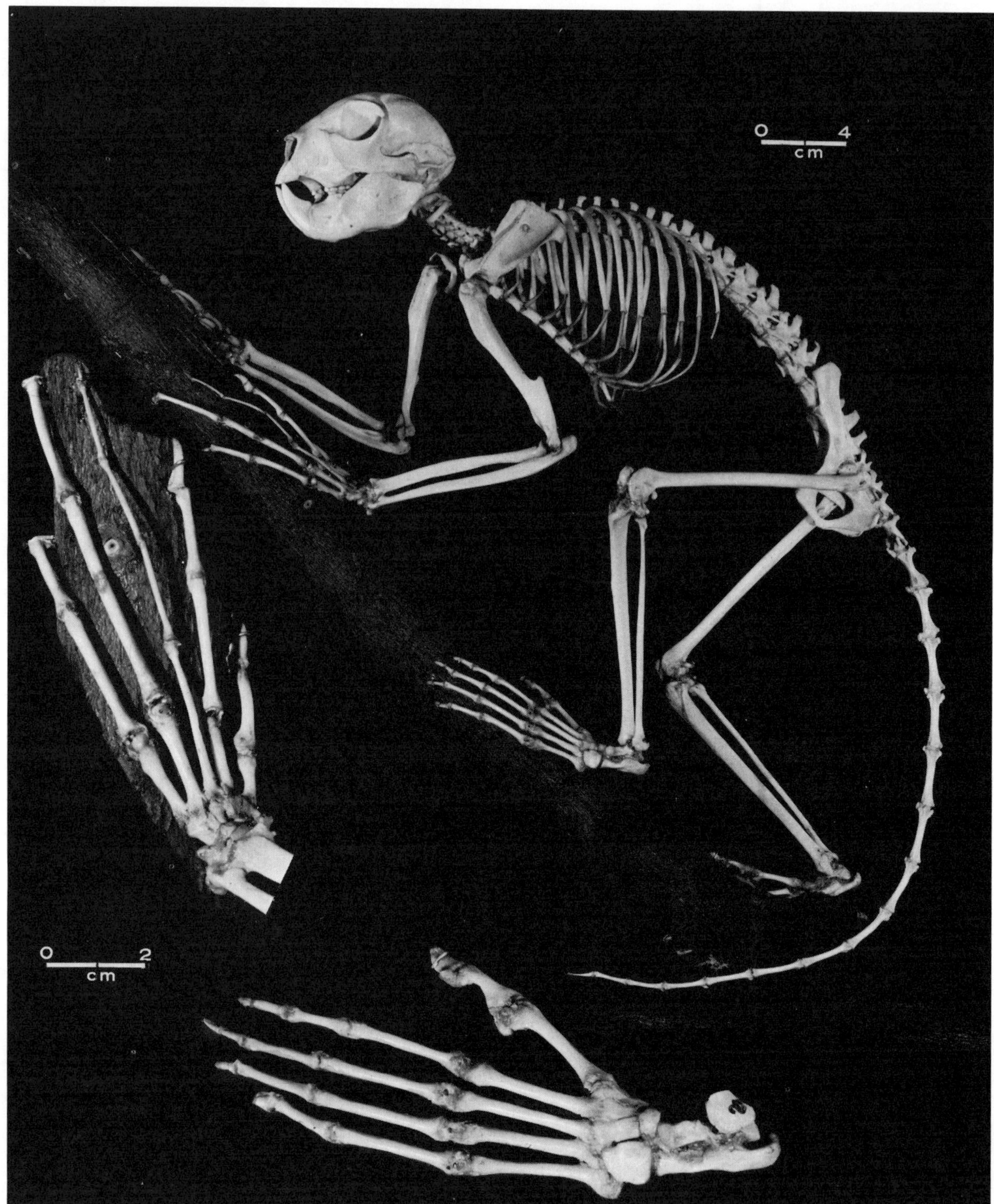

Fig. II.30. Skeleton of aye-aye (*Daubentonia madagascariensis*); insets are enlargements of left hand and foot.

The comparatively short-armed *Alouatta* is not a brachiator in any locomotor sense, and the somewhat longer-armed *Lagothrix* is better characterized as a deliberate climber than a swift brachiator. The unique and unifying quality of Erikson's brachiator group resides not in limb proportions but in use of the highly specialized prehensile tail for suspension and locomotion. Tail dimensions and proportions, however, are not taken into account in Erikson's delineation of locomotor types.

Ankel (1967) described vertebrae, ribs, and sternum of representative living primates. The primate forelimb was monographed by Knussmann (1967), the hand by Wood Jones (1942), Biegert (1961), and Bishop (1964), and Haines (1958) discussed evolution of the mammalian hand from the terrestrial to the arboreal. The pelvis was described by Leutenegger (1970*a*), the tail by Ankel (1962), the foot by Morton (1924; 1935) and Biegert (1961). Simons (1962; 1967) sums up information on the locomotor skeleton of Tertiary primates. Statistical analyses of the scapula by Oxnard and associates are reviewed under the next heading.

Stern (1971) compiled and reviewed published data on cebid locomotion and compared and described cebid hip and thigh musculature. His stated objective was to gain insights into the origin and evolution of human bipedality. Stern and Oxnard (1973) reviewed patterns of vertical clinging and springing. Their several plots of multivariate analyses of skeletal measurements previously recorded in the literature are suggestive of locomotor groupings that have been more accurately defined in purely narrative terms. A second part of their review is devoted to forelimb locomotion.

Several contributors to the symposium volume *Primate Locomotion,* edited by Jenkins (1974*b*), have been cited in text. Others who made original contributions outside the scope of the present monograph include Badoux on biomechanical principles of primate locomotion, and Szalay and Decker (1974) on possible functions of fossil prosimian foot bones.

Canonical Analysis of Scapular Dimensions

In nearly a score of papers published between 1961 (Ashton and Oxnard) and 1969 (Oxnard and Neely), Oxnard attempted to prove that the principal primate locomotor modes and locomotor substrata (i.e., arboreal and terrestrial) may be predicted by means of a multivariate statistical technique, or canonical analysis, of nine selected osteometric features of the scapula (Oxnard 1963; Ashton and Oxnard 1964*b;* Ashton, Healy, Oxnard, and Spence, 1965).

The shoulder musculature of 52 primates representing 22 genera of platyrrhines and catarrhines and 6 prosimian genera were examined by Ashton and Oxnard (1963) for the establishment of a base of reference for correlations with primate locomotor modes. The locomotor modes, in turn, were determined by Ashton and Oxnard (1964*a*) on the basis of information they had uncritically and indiscriminately compiled from several primary and secondary sources. For purposes of their morphological analyses, all data for both sexes were pooled (Ashton and Oxnard 1964*b*, pp. 55–56).

The four principal locomotor modes or forms recognized were brachiators (all apes, and the prosimian "hangers" *Propithecus, Nycticebus,* and *Perodicticus*), semibrachiators (*Alouatta, Lagothrix, Ateles, Colobus*), quadrupeds (most platyrrhines and catarrhines, and *Tupaia, Lemur,* and *Galago* among prosimians). Man, regarded as intermediate between brachiators and quadrupeds, made up the fourth group. Higher primates were arranged in a descending order from extreme arboreality among brachiators to extreme terrestriality in quadrupeds. Prosimians were graded from nonleapers among "hangers" to mainly leapers among quadrupeds. Except for the extreme examples of arboreality and terrestriality (gibbons and baboons, respectively) and a few intermediates, I find Oxnard's groupings and gradings of the individual primates at variance with the well-documented evidence on which the preceding account of locomotion is based.

Correlations between scapular shape and locomotor groupings were next attempted by compounding nine osteometric features into mathematical functions, or canonical variates, best separating the statistical means obtained from individual genera (Ashton, Healy, Oxnard, and Spence, 1965). The first canonical variate served to separate the four locomotor groups, as interpreted by Oxnard from his compilation of locomotor data. Canonical variate 2 supposedly separated the arboreal from the terrestrial primates in each group. How the distinctions were made is not clear. In any case, the second function did not resolve such ambiguities as the classification of the terrestrial, quadrupedal, knuckle-walking gorilla as a brachiator (Oxnard 1968*a*, p. 251). The third canonical variate was used mainly for separating man's locomotor mode from all others. The remaining six functions were said to reveal arrangements similar to those of the first three in primates generally (Ashton, Healy, Oxnard, and Spence 1965, p. 428). However, one or another of them did, in fact, reveal separations among nonarboreal forms not evident in variates 1 and 2 (Oxnard 1968*a,* p. 279).

The preliminary analyses of primate locomotion were followed by Oxnard's (1968*a*) comprehensive application of the multivariate statistical technique on 1,888 specimens representing 194 genera in 8 orders of nonmarine mammals. The scapular features he measured in nonprimates were similar to those chosen in previous studies as having functional significance in relation to shoulder movements in primates. Separations of primate genera achieved by means of canonical variates 1 and 2 (Oxnard 1968*a*, p. 202; for data see Oxnard 1969, p. 322) were plotted. Two double-headed arrows drawn diagonally across the graph were said to represent a summary of the position of the genera with respect to locomotor patterns and relative degrees of arboreality and terrestriality. Other arrows in other directions, however, can be drawn with equal if not greater justification. Other dubious relationships in the bivariate plot are striking. For example, separation by multivariate statistical techniques of so-called terrestrial, low canopy, and high canopy langurs of the genus *Presbytis* implies the detection of specific differences in locomotor morphology, locomotor modes, and habitat preferences which do not, in fact, exist in wild, noncaptive, nonsemidomesticated populations (cf. Jay 1965; Ripley 1967; Oxnard 1967*b,* p. 229). The graph (Oxnard 1968*a*) showing positions of the primate genera omitted tupaiids and prosimians "to avoid confusion." The figures for these forms, given elsewhere in the article (1968*a*, p. 264, table 4), if plotted on the chart in question would indeed reduce the generic separations to a meaningless jumble.

Separation of arboreal from terrestrial marsupials (Oxnard 1968*a,* p. 265) was not obtained in terms of canonical variates 1 and 2, except for a close approximation between the two gliding possums, *Schoinobates* and *Petaurus.* However, variate 8, according to Oxnard (1968*a*, p. 264) showed that terrestrial marsupials are not coplanar with arboreal marsupials and primates. Tree kangaroos of the genus *Dendrolagus* were classified by Oxnard (1968*a,* p. 266) as nonarboreal.

Separation among edentates achieved by canonical analysis conforms more nearly to what is known of the locomotion of these animals than the separations among the preceding groups. Questions do arise regarding the wide spacing on the graph between the locomotorily close *Bradypus* (three-toed sloth), *Choloepus* (two-toed sloth), and *Cyclopes* (silky anteater) and regarding the extremely high degree of arboreality indicated for the mainly terrestrial *Myrmecophaga.*

Results of the multivariate study for reflecting locomotor patterns and substrata of various representatives of the Rodentia are mostly inconclusive, and many are misleading or flatly wrong. For example, the essentially terrestrial ground squirrels (*Citellus* = *Spermophilus*), groundhogs (*Marmota*), Old World porcupines (*Acanthion, Thecurus, Hystrix*), and fossorial mole rats (*Spalax*) were classified as arboreal, while the strictly arboreal caviomorphs *Plagiodontia* and *Thrinacodus* were posted as nonarboreal.

Colugos or flying lemurs, order Dermoptera, were separated canonically into two groups, *Galeopithecus* and *Cynocephalus* (Oxnard 1968*a*, p. 270). The separated plots refer, in fact, to individuals of the same species, *Cynocephalus volans* (= *Galeopithecus volans*).

Application of the multivariate statistical technique to scapular dimensions of the Insectivora represented by 7 genera (Oxnard 1968*a*, tables 12, 13) seems unproductive. The pattern of generic positions, if plotted on the primate chart (fig. 14), would appear nonsensical.

Bat scapular shapes and bat locomotor patterns cannot be confused with those of other animals but Oxnard's (1968*a*, p. 272) plot of canonical axes 1 and 2 confuses them.

The families of Carnivora were analysed in two sections. One graph (p. 274) of canonical variates 1 and 2 shows as arboreal all samples of Procyonidae (5 genera, and the lesser panda, *Ailurus*), Mustelidae (3 genera including the wolverine, *Gulo*), and Viverridae (8 genera). A second graph (p. 275) shows all Ursidae (8 genera including the polar bear, *Thalarctos*) as arboreal, and all Felidae (4 genera) as terrestrial. No convincing explanation was offered for the categorization of all genera of a given family as either arboreal or terrestrial. Relative position of each genus on either graph, irrespective of family, is also subject to question. Had Oxnard plotted all carnivores on the same graph instead of different ones drawn to the same scale, the absurdity of his separations by canonical variates would be even more striking.

Among artiodactyls and perissodactyls, the more nearly related or structurally similar the species, the more similar their locomotor patterns and substratum preferences. However, most separations among the ungulates achieved by canonical variates 1, 2, and 3 (Oxnard 1968*a*, p. 276, table 17), do not reflect these obvious relationships. For example, of 23 ungulate genera analyzed, canonical variate 1 rates goats (*Capra*) nearer the horse, babirussa, llama, camel, pronghorn, blesbok, and gazelles than to sheep (*Ovis*), their nearest relatives. Canonical variate 2 brings them closer, with only gazelles between, but variate 3 lists the horse, bush pig, forest hog, babirussa, pecari, llama, kudu, cattle, bison and gazelle nearer the goat. Variate 3 shows the tapir (*Tapirus*) separated from nearest related horse (*Equus*) by all but 1 of the remaining 21 even-toed and odd-toed ungulates. Similar misalignments can be demonstrated for all other forms listed.

Results of the multivariate statistical techniques used by Oxnard are at best inadequate or distorted reflections of the original biological information and sole basis for the computations (cf. Ripley 1967 for critique). Often they appear to be completely isolated from any rational interpretation of observed facts. No account was taken in the analyses of the plasticity and ready adaptability of the more generalized mammals to either arboreal, terrestrial, or both kinds of life, "so that their habits could not be diagnosed were only fossil material available" (Haines 1958, p. 19). Indeed, the same may be said of living forms with complete skeletons available for comparisons. For example, structural and functional differences between forelimbs of *Tarsius* and the callitrichids *Saguinus* and *Leontopithecus* (fig. I.29) are obvious. In sharp contrast, bone proportions of *Tarsius* are almost exactly intermediate between those of *Leontopithecus* and *Saguinus*, although the two platyrrhine genera are inseparable in all their basic motile functions. The primary locomotor differences between the tarsier and callitrichids reside in the hind limbs.

Not only did Oxnard fail to take into account the effects on locomotion of nonscapular skeletal parts which are present, he also failed to consider parts like the tail or clavicle which might be absent. Further, there is little or no indication in all Oxnard's publications of an awareness that in primates generally "adaptations of the locomotor apparatus to the mode of locomotion are more marked in the distal parts of the extremities than in regions near the trunk" (Leutenegger 1970*b*, p. 332). Even here, function cannot always be determined from the bones alone (Haines 1958, p. 18; Ankel 1962).

The roseate abstracts and considered and balanced summaries and critiques (cf. Oxnard 1968*b*, p. 295) provided by the author (and associates) for each article, fail to reflect the hedgings, negations, and contradictions contained in the substantive portions of the text, particularly the earlier articles. The first assay at statistical analysis based on individual scapular dimensions led Oxnard (1968*a*, p. 261) to conclude that "the results are so complicated and require so much cross referencing from one dimension to another, and from one genus to another, as to complicate rather than clarify the issue. It is already more meaningful to pass directly to the multivariate analysis of the data." Subsequent acknowledgment (Oxnard and Neely 1969) of the errors of omission and commission in the use of specific biological data led to a disillusionment with multivariate or canonical analyses. The well-considered abandonment of this device was followed (Oxnard and Neely 1969) by invention of a third dubbed "neighborhood limited classification." This method gratuitously creates even more problems, none of which are relevant to the present discussion of primate locomotion.

Evidently, the more extensive the mathematical interventions, the more complicated become the statistical analyses and the more sterile, futile, and unrealistic their results. Despite the repeated promises and the numerous published opportunities for fulfillment, Oxnard (1963, pp. 165, 180; 1967*a*, p. 296; 1967*b*, pp. 219–20; 1968*a*, p. 251; 1968*b*, p. 299) failed to prove his principal premise that "by such a method [canonical analysis of scapular dimensions] it would be possible to assess the morphological affinities of an unknown (fossil) primate."

After the above critique was completed, an article by Roberts (1974) on the structure and function of the primate scapula came to hand. The author deals with actual bone and muscle and movements of various types of scapulae and makes direct correlations with locomotor habits. At the close of his account, Roberts (1974, p. 197) observes that "our knowledge of shoulder biomechanics is still far from complete. Furthermore, when it is considered that the shoulder itself is only part of a locomotor system that includes more or less the entire postcranial region of the animal, it will be realized that general conclusions on scapular function must be drawn with great caution."

Part II
Evolutionary and Comparative Morphology of New World Monkeys, Infraorder Platyrrhini

The following discussions and descriptions are based on mammals and primates generally, as in the preceding part of this volume, but with particular reference to platyrrhine-catarrhine relationships and to the families of New World monkeys, especially callitrichids and callimiconids. Each main morphological section, such as External Characters, Skull, Dentition, is followed by a corresponding key to the infraorders Platyrrhini and Catarrhini and to the platyrrhine families Callitrichidae, Callimiconidae, and Cebidae.

6 Geography and Platyrrhine-Catarrhine Relationships

A classification of higher primates based on the divergence of platyrrhines and catarrhines from a common simian or prosimian stock requires a common center of origin. Undoubted monkeys, already well advanced, are known only from Africa and South America since the Oligocene. Only these two continents, therefore, separately or approximated, provide a stage for the common origin. Paradoxically, advocates of this classification, such as Matthew (1915) and his school, point to Asia as the ancestral center of catarrhine origin and to North or Middle America as an independent center of platyrrhine origin.

It was suggested by Simpson (1945, p. 185) that platyrrhines "arose from one of the Paleocene or Eocene prosimian stocks of North America and that their early deployment, or indeed almost all their history, occurred in the more tropical parts of South America, where Tertiary fossils are extremely rare. This is, however, only a hypothesis." Stirton (1951, p. 335) agreed and added that Middle America was the likeliest place of origin and initial radiation. This hypothesis seemed plausible at the time (Hershkovitz 1970*a*, p. 22), but it can now be discounted without prejudice to Middle America as a possible secondary center of platyrrhine radiation and dispersal.

Advocates of a North or Middle American origin of platyrrhines ignore the absence of simians, or eligible ancestral prosimians in the rich North American Tertiary fossil record. Paleocene so-called prosimians of northern continents were already highly specialized and far removed from anything that might give rise to simians. Eocene prosimians are monkeylike, and some, particularly omomyids, seem close to the line leading to higher primates. Nevertheless their evolutionary trends, particularly with respect to the dental system, limb skeleton, visual system and adduced circadian rhythm, are away from, not toward, the primitive simian facies.

Pursuit of the Matthewian hypothesis of a northern origin of most mammals in fixed northern continents surrounded by stable seas (see Hershkovitz 1972 for review) persuaded authors to regard the many obvious signs of close kinship between platyrrhines and catarrhines as products of convergence or parallel evolution. The differences between widely separated phyla evolving along parallel or convergent lines, however, are more numerous, more trenchant, and often more conspicuous than the usually superficial, adaptive similarities. In contrast, no fundamental differences separate New and Old World simians. The relatively minor differences between the fragments of Oligocene parapithecine monkeys from the Egyptian Fayum (cf. Simons 1972, p. 185; Gingerich 1974; Hershkovitz 1975*a*) and some living cebids are no more impressive than characters that separate atelines from pithecines, or alouattines from saimiriines, or cebids generally from callitrichids.

An alternate hypothesis of platyrrhine-catarrhine origin I recently proposed (1972, p. 323) postulates that some unknown prosimians or presimians (i.e., haplorhines) living in rifted South America–Africa, presumably during the Cretaceous, spread across both continents during early drift (fig. III.1). Once isolated, South American and African factions evolved into platyrrhines and catarrhines, respectively. A variant of this hypothesis (Hershkovitz 1972, p. 324) assumes that the unknown haplorhine forerunner of platyrrhines and catarrhines had already evolved to simian grade in rifted but not yet widely drifted South America–Africa. The timing of the geological events may be questioned, but nothing in the fossil record denies the sequence of events outlined here.

A third hypothesis of platyrrhine-catarrhine relationships presented almost simultaneously by Hoffstetter (1972) differs from the preceding mainly in the mechanics and chronology of possible events. According to Hoffstetter, South America was long separated before monkeys were rafted to that continent from Africa at the end or possibly the middle of the Eocene. As in the preceding hypothesis, the colonizing stock is unknown, but the Fayum parapithecids are regarded as related. The resemblances are striking but the relationship is remote. The most primitive monkeys of the Fayum Oligocene are more advanced overall than living callitrichids, callimiconids, and most cebids. Dentally, they are distinctly cercopithecoid. The bilophodont grade of molarization attained by *Parapithecus grangeri* (fig. III.2) is as advanced as that of most modern cercopithecids. This precocious condition combined with the presence of three premolars eliminates parapithecids from lines leading to living forms. On the other hand, the primitive trigon pattern conserved in the upper molars of pongids and hominids suggests a closer relationship to platyrrhines, but the two former groups lack pm2.

The oldest known South American fossil primate,

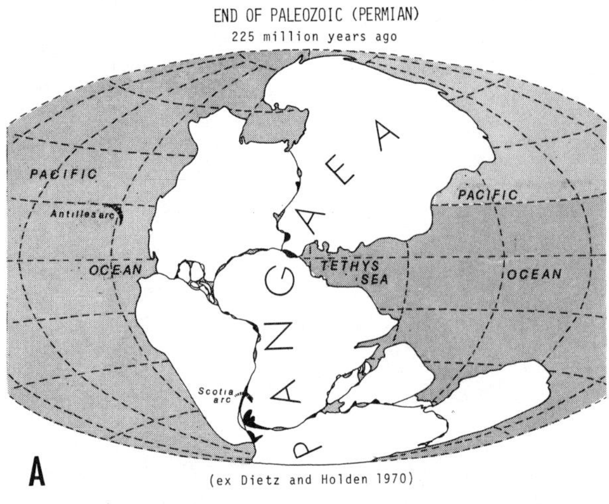

Fig. III.1. Continental drift and possible intercontinental Primate relationships:

A) Pangaea, the universal continent before rift at end of Paleozoic (Permian) 225 million years ago, before mammals had appeared; reconstruction from Dietz and Holden (1970).

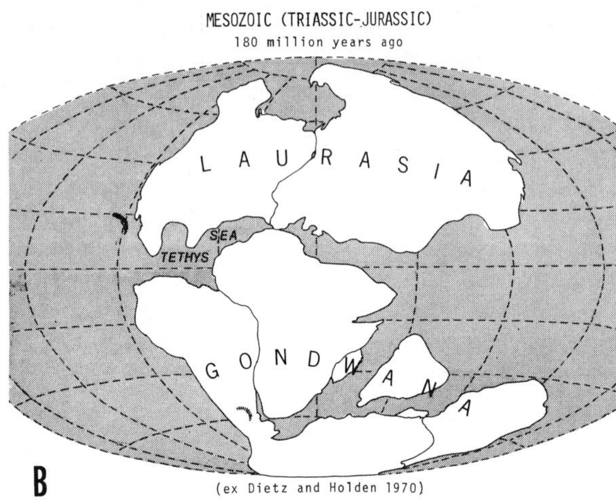

B) Rifted Pangaea at end of Triassic, 180 million years ago, its division into supercontinents Laurasia and Gondwanaland, and drift of major Gondwana components; reconstruction from Dietz and Holden (1970). A rich, noneutherian mammalian fauna evolved during the Triassic and became widely distributed. There is reason to believe, however, that a high degree of endemism existed with a higher proportion in the more isolated or widely drifted land masses.

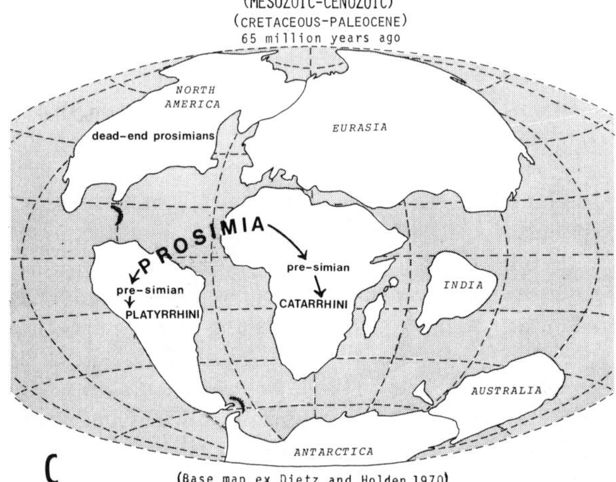

C) Dispersion of continents at end of the Cretaceous, 65 million years ago; reconstruction from Dietz and Holden (1970). Eutherians (marsupials and placentals) evolved and radiated during the period. The placentals were present in Africa, Eurasia, and the Americas, and marsupials appeared in the late Cretaceous in both Americas with spread into Europe. The time of the marsupial advent in Australia, most likely from Antarctica, is unknown. The occurrence of true primates in the latest Cretaceous of North America is uncertain. Isolated primate-type teeth of the genus *Purgatorius* Van Valen and Sloane, 1965, were referred to the Prosimii. The molars with rudimentary hypocones (fig. I.2) were already too specialized to be ancestral to those of living platyrrhines. An ancestor common to platyrrhines and catarrhines in this period would have had to be prosimian but more likely presimian (tarsioid, haplorhine) in grade, and natural to the region of last contact between the drifting Afro-South American continents. The simian grades Platyrrhini and Catarrhini would have evolved independently after complete continental separation. In the reconstruction, South America is seen separated from Antarctica, and the shortest distance between South America and Africa appears to be nearly the same as between South America and North America.

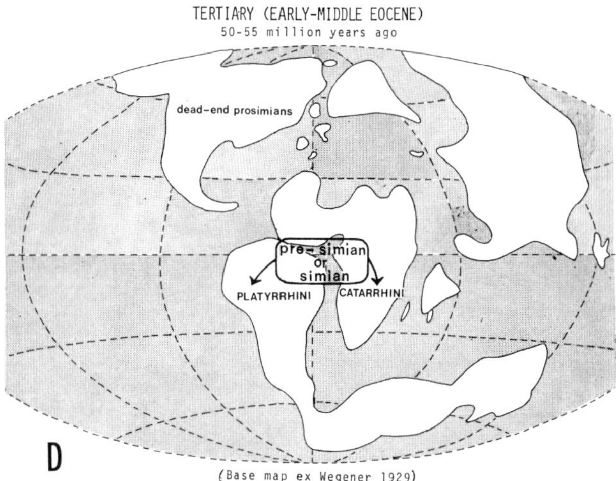

D) Continents during the Eocene; reconstruction from Wegener (1929 [1966]). The Eocene, according to this author (1929, p. 25) began 15 million years ago, but 55–60 million years is the time now generally accepted. A connection between South America and Africa on the east and Antarctica on the south still existed, according to Wegener. If the Wegenerian continental relationship held for the early Eocene (or the late Paleocene as reckoned now), faunal resemblances between Africa and South America would have been much greater and closer than has been conceded. Primates of a common haplorhine stage, perhaps already of simian grade, could have lived in the Afro-South American continents, at least in the region of last contact. After drift, platyrrhines and catarrhines would have evolved independently, the latter from a platyrrhine or preplatyrrhine stock. Nonplatyrrhine simians may have also lived in South America and Africa during the Tertiary. Strepsirhines are unknown in South America unless the nonplatyrrhine Lower Oligocene *Branisella* proves to be one.

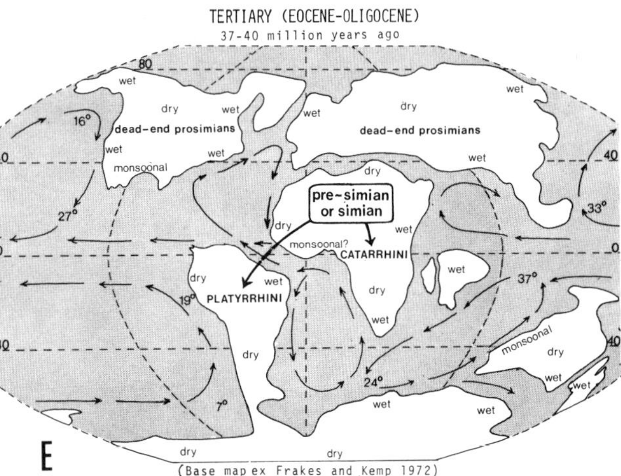

E) Continental relationship and weather patterns in the latter half of the Eocene (40–48 million years ago) and early half of the Oligocene (30–37 million years ago); reconstruction from Frakes and Kemp (1972). This depiction of the earth about the time of divergence between presimians and simians and/or platyrrhines and catarrhines seems to be the best documented and most informative of those currently available. The persistent connection shown between South America and Antarctica is the Scotia arc. Unless primates were already in South America since the early Eocene, or earlier, colonization by rafting of a primate of presimian (tarsioid) or simian grade from Africa must have occurred over the 500 to 600 miles separating the continents' nearest points. The possibility of such rafting from South America to Africa cannot be dismissed absolutely on the basis of present knowledge, but the probability is practically nil. The water gap between South America and North America as shown is nearly three times greater than that between the former and Africa, and the hypothetical prevailing ocean currents did not favor colonization by rafting between the two Americas. Furthermore, known North American prosimians could not have evolved into platyrrhines. Pre-Quaternary North American simians are unknown and likely never existed.

The time of platyrrhine-catarrhine divergence and the degree of relationship between them at this time, assuming a common ancestor, is still speculative. Not speculative, however, is that the resemblances between living South American and African simians are too numerous and close to be products of parallel evolution alone. The same conclusions apply to other Tertiary mammals common to the two continents.

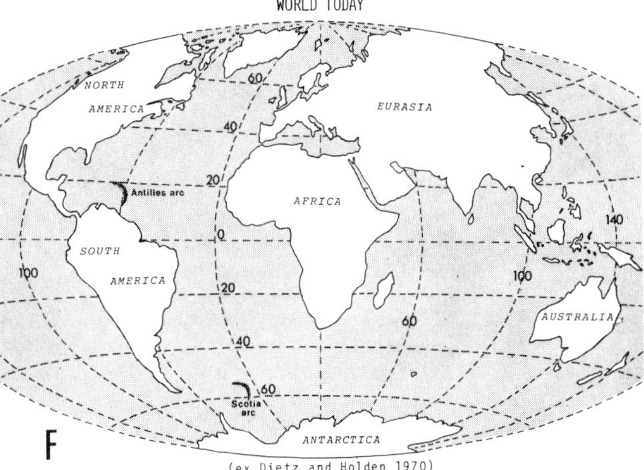

F) World today, showing the extent of continental drift since the Cretaceous. The Antilles and Scotia arcs are markers; redrawn from Dietz and Holden (1970). See fig. I.4 for distribution of the families of living primates.

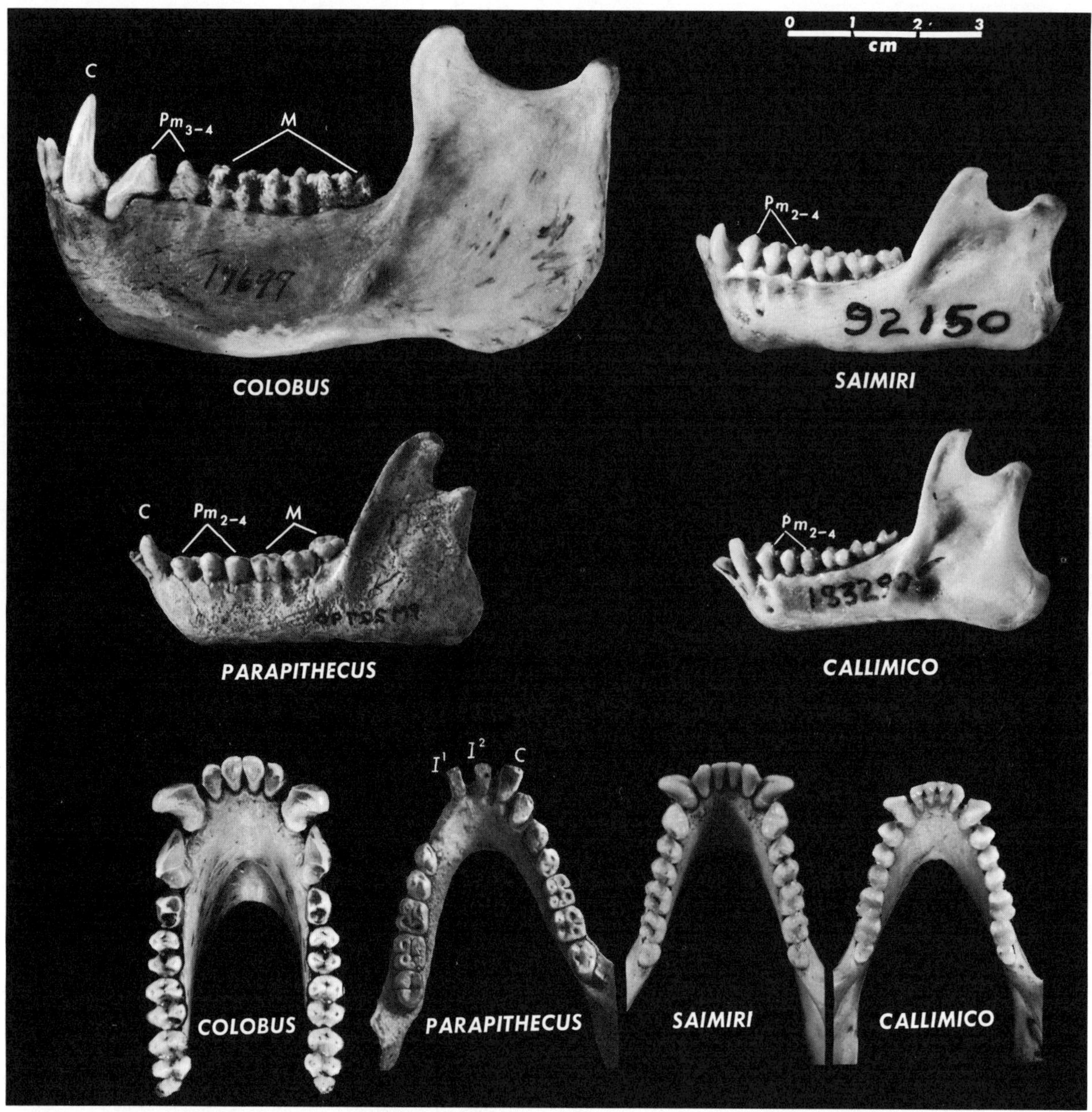

Fig. III.2. Cast of mandible reconstructed from specimens referred to *Parapithecus grangeri* by E. Simons, compared with mandibles of living *Colobus* (Cercopithecidae), *Saimiri* (Cebidae), and *Callimico* (Callimiconidae). Similarities between ascending ramus of *Parapithecus* and those of other available specimens of *Callimico* may be greater or less than shown. Grade of molarization attained by *Parapithecus* is comparable to that of modern cercopithecids. Reconstruction consists of left ramus CGM 26912, *Parapithecus grangeri* Simons right ramus, YPM 23954; symphysis and anterior teeth from other finds, all from Jebel el Quatrani Formation, Fayum, Egypt (Oligocene).

Branisella boliviana Hoffstetter (1969), from the lower Oligocene of the Bolivian Andes, is an extremely important find, but it cannot be identified with certainty as either prosimian, presimian, or platyrrhine. The preserved fragment of its left upper jaw (fig. III.3) shows the dental formula of platyrrhines as well as many prosimians, but the greatly reduced first premolar (pm^2) and a probably well developed third molar suggests an early catarrhine stage of dental evolution. I do not agree with Hoffstetter (1969, p. 4; 1972, p. 338) that the primitively structured premolars of most platyrrhines and the primitive tritubercular molars of callitrichids, or the more advanced tritubercular-quadritubercular molars of *Callimico,* can be derived from a dental system such as that of *Branisella.* Hoffstetter's supposition that the tritubercularity of the upper callitrichid molars is derived by retrogression from the quadritubercular plan of cebids is unfounded. In any case, this view adopted from Gregory (1922, p. 228) does not alter the fact that the dentition of *Branisella* is not platyrrhine.

Differences of opinion regarding the status of *Branisella* do not affect the plausibility of the hypothesis that the stock or stocks which gave rise to modern South American and African monkeys once had a continuous distribution across the separating continents. This second hypothesis (as opposed to the first or Matthewian fixed continent hypothesis) postulates dismemberment of the original stock or stocks at such points, perhaps peninsulas or insular remnants of mainland shores that may have lingered as final intercontinental ties long after drift was in full force. The third, Hoffstetter's, hypothesis assumes rafting of the ancestral platyrrhine stock from Africa to erstwhile primateless South America during the middle or latter part of the Eocene. It seems certain, however, that at that time a floating island of tropical forest would disintegrate long before completing a windblown, wave-swept voyage across the hundreds of miles of ocean separating the continents at their nearest points.

In spite of everything said here, the precise nature of African and South American simian relationships still remains uncertain even within the concept of continental drift. If catarrhines and platyrrhines are monophyletic, as is generally presumed, and each diverged from a common prosimian stock after separation of Africa and South America, each must be treated as an independently evolved suborder of simian grade. If the presumed common ancestor was simian or presimian before drift, the subsequently isolated groups should be treated as divergent lines of a common suborder.

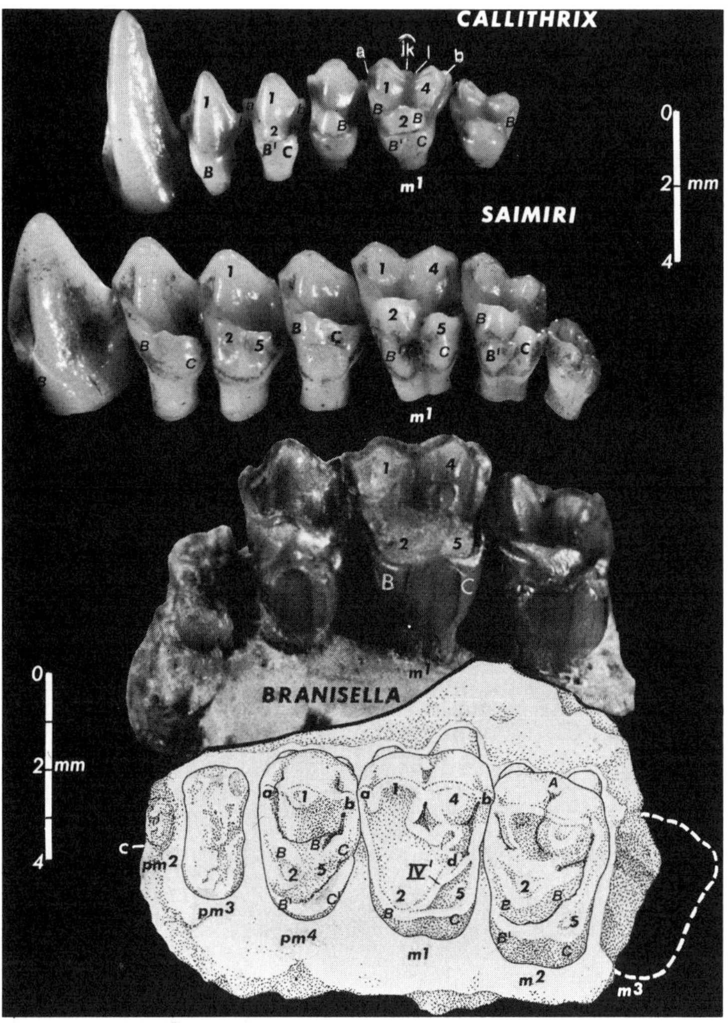

Fig. III.3. *Branisella boliviana* Hoffstetter (type), upper tooth row, compared with upper tooth row of *Saimiri* and *Callithrix*. Diagram of *Branisella* teeth based on Hoffstetter (1969), and on photographs, sketches, and cast of original specimen.

A considerable body of evidence such as the embryonic (Luckett 1974) and the parasitological (Garnham 1973 and others, see chap. 43), in addition to the morphological, points to platyrrhines as monophyletic, but only if living forms are considered. The extinct *Branisella* is not a a platyrrhine and likely did not share a common ancestor. Moreover, there is no reason to believe that other nonplatyrrhine primates did not live in South America during the Tertiary and perhaps earlier. The late Oligocene *Tremacebus* (Hershkovitz 1974) is as highly evolved in most cranial and all dental characters as any progressive cebid yet remains as primitive in other cranial characters as the hypothetical tarsioid or simian primate from which platyrrhines arose. The late Oligocene *Dolichocebus* (Homunculidae) and the subrecent *Xenothrix* (Xenotrichidae) are other South American primates with enigmatic origins. Even the universally recognized subdivisions of the family Cebidae are of dubious affinities. In sum, it is possible that rifted and early drifted South America harbored a diversified primate fauna that gave rise to several independent lineages. It is likely that representatives of more than one of these is now assigned to the Platyrrhini for want of clear evidence to the contrary.

South American–African Mammalian Relationships

A number of South American mammals parallel primates with respect to their tropical American distribution,

African affinities, and absence of ancestral stock among living or extinct North American mammals. The animals (cf. Hershkovitz 1972) include the West Indian zalambdodont insectivores *Solenodon* and *Nesophontes,* both apparently most nearly related to African tenrecoids, American caviomorphs with African phiomorph affinities (cf. Hoffstetter 1972),[1] South American complex penis type cricetines (Sigmodontini), with African complex penis type relatives, as contrasted with the purely simple penis type cricetines (Peromyscini) of North America. To these may be added the tropical American and African vespertilionid, molossid, and emballonurid bats and the pygmy squirrels *Sciurillus* and *Myosciurus.* Manatees, genus *Trichechus,* exist on the African and American sides of the Atlantic; Tertiary dugongs occurred on all coasts. A reconsideration of sirenian origin and dispersal in terms of continental drift is due. Although unknown in Africa, marsupials and freshwater dolphins, family Susuidae (Platanistidae), are additional surviving elements of what must have been a substantial fauna common to South America and one or another of the original Gondwanaland fragments. A number of other families and orders of late Cretaceous–early Tertiary South American mammals seem to have been indigenous.

The full number of South American mammalian taxons with possible or probable African antecedents is difficult to assess now, perhaps because of a reluctance to reject completely the still-influential Matthewian concept of a northern origin of nearly all mammals and the inapposite evolutionary timetable it set. Despite reconstructions mainly by Matthew (1915) and Simpson (1950), and convictions expressed by Patterson and Pascual (1972, pp. 257–60), there is no indisputable proof of the prior occurrence in North America of representatives of Paleogene South American land mammals, including the marsupials, condylarths, xenarthran edentates, platyrrhine primates, bats, rodents, nonperissodactyl and nonartiodactyl ungulates, and the Antillean tenrecoid insectivores still known from the Quaternary only. The affinities of all the nonautocthonous forms are clearly with mammals of the Gondwana continents—definitely Africa (cf. Cooke 1972), and for marsupials, Australia via Antarctica.

Alfred Wegener, father of the reality of continental drift, du Toit, his exponent, and other pioneers anticipated many of the zoogeographic explanations offered by authors during the last quarter century. The controversial history of marsupials and monotremes, for example, was delineated in the light of drift by Wegener (1966 [1929], p. 108), but especially by du Toit (1937, pp. 292, 294, 295, 297), who took into account the entire array of southern faunas and floras.

[1] Since this was written, Wood (1972; 1973) has reported the discovery of a true hystricognathous rodent, *Prolapsus sibilatoris,* from the Eocene of the Texas Big Bend region. Wood (1973, p. 1) notes that "the incisor enamel and the cheek teeth show that *Prolapsus* could not have been a caviomorph." He concludes, nevertheless, that "it seems probable that the Caviomorpha were derived from Middle American [i.e., southern North American] Eocene ancestors of the same general stock as *Prolapsus.* The presence of *Prolapsus* in North America is a weighty argument against late Eocene trans-Atlantic migration of rodents. Unknown but probably related [to *Prolapsus*] forms, from southwest Asia, were presumably ancestral to the African Phiomorpha."

Absolutely nothing in the nature of *Prolapsus,* as described and compared by Wood, (*a*) supports the assumption that this rodent and South American caviomorphs can be derived from a common stock, (*b*) diminishes or excludes the probability of a close relationship between African and South American rodents, or (*c*) throws light on the ancestry of Phiomorpha. If phiomorphs were North American and *Prolapsus* African, it would surely be argued by opponents of the drift theory of faunal relationships that phiomorphs and caviomorphs probably have a common origin and that affinities of *Prolapsus* are problematic at best. There is no need, however, to reverse the geological relationships for a better focus on biological realities. Tertiary colonizations of South America by North American terrestrial mammals could have been accomplished only by rafting. The probability that such colonization occurred or was successful is virtually nil.

7 Size and Evolution

Living New World monkeys vary in bulk from the rat-sized *Cebuella pygmaea,* one of the smallest of living primates, to individuals the size of a setter (fig. III.4). Size gradations among the species or species groups is surprisingly even and correlated with changes in diet, the locomotor system, and to a lesser degree other aspects of primate economy and organization (fig. II.5).

In terms of body mass, the family Callitrichidae comprises the smallest class of living primates. The Lemuridae with its diminutive *Microcebus murinus,* and the Galagidae with *Galago minutus,* include slightly smaller individuals, but the full size range of the members of each family is greater than that of callitrichids.

The small size of callitrichids is correlated with a structure and organization that apart from the advanced architecture of the head, is the most primitive among living primates. Callitrichids resemble treeshrews and tree squirrels in size, form, proportions, color pattern, and general movement. Like the squirrels with which they coexist, callitrichids can support the full weight of their bodies on the tips of the long sharp claws of their hands and feet (fig. I.20). Unlike squirrels, however, the digits of callitrichids are adductible, and the great toe (though not the thumb) is opposable and provided with a nail. These specializations, which permit grasping with both hands and feet, are among the most crucial for separating primitive primates from rodents and other nonprimates such as treeshrews.

Callitrichids are primarily insectivorous. Their small bulk, quick, jerky movements, and sharp claws are eminently suited for effective capture of insects, and their tritubercular molars are efficient tools for cracking the chitinous covering of arthropods. Callitrichids also feed on other animals, including small birds and mammals, nestlings, lizards, and eggs, and they consume fruits, flowers, and resins. The smallest and most primitive species is the pygmy marmoset (*Cebuella pygmaea*) of the upper Amazonian region. Other callitrichids are much larger, but none surpasses in size the largest neotropical squirrels. Callitrichids of the genera *Callithrix* and *Saguinus* are as big as moderately large tree squirrels and occupy roughly similar ecological niches. The lion-tamarin (*Leontopithecus rosalia*), largest member of the family and as large as the largest of New World squirrels, is the most highly specialized. Its long slender arm, narrow palm, and elongate middle fingers are specialized for digging insects and grubs from under loose bark and from cracks or holes in tree trunks and branches (fig. I.28).

The largest callitrichid is twice the body length and four times the bulk of the smallest, but all members of the family possess similar dietary and locomotory systems. In contrast, the size grade between the largest callitrichid and the smallest of the marmosetlike cebids is slight but marks the crossing of a crucial threshold in the form of diet, method of arboreal support, locomotion, and reproduction.

The smaller marmosetlike cebids (*Aotus, Callicebus, Saimiri*), remain essentially quadrupedal but depart from callitrichids in their greater reliance on hands for hoisting and climbing than on hind legs for springing. Pithecines (*Pithecia, Chiropotes, Cacajao*), the next larger group of cebids, possess longer arms and are more proficient climbers. The arms of the larger and prehensile-tailed cebids (*Cebus, Alouatta, Lagothrix, Ateles, Brachyteles*), may be nearly as long as the legs (e.g., *Cebus*) or longer than the legs (e.g., *Ateles*). In all larger cebids, either front or hind limbs alone can support the body in efficient locomotion—the arms in brachiation, the legs in bipedal progression.

Specialization of the hand is also correlated with increasing body size and locomotor specialization. In some of the largest primates, the thumb followed the great toe in becoming more or less opposable and endowing the hand with a locking grip for more effective support of the heavier body. In cebids, most notably the medium-weight pithecines (*Pithecia, Chiropotes, Cacajao*) and the heavyweight howlers (*Alouatta*), the thumb and forefinger move in tandem against or away from the remaining fingers or palm (fig. I.33). As all digits become more powerful adductors and graspers, the claws, like that of the hallux, lose function and degenerate into nails. Thus, the mainstay of arboreal support shifted from the grappling and clinging claws of lightweight callitrichids to the grasping and clutching digits of heavier cebids, and the whole hand became the equal of the whole foot in its adaptation for arboreal progression. In the final stage, represented by the brachiating spider monkeys, the forelimb surpassed the hind limb in locomotory specialization. The palm and last four digits lengthened into an enormous grapnellike organ for hooking branches in the brachiating form of locomotion. The now useless thumb was drastically reduced in size or eliminated entirely (fig II.14).

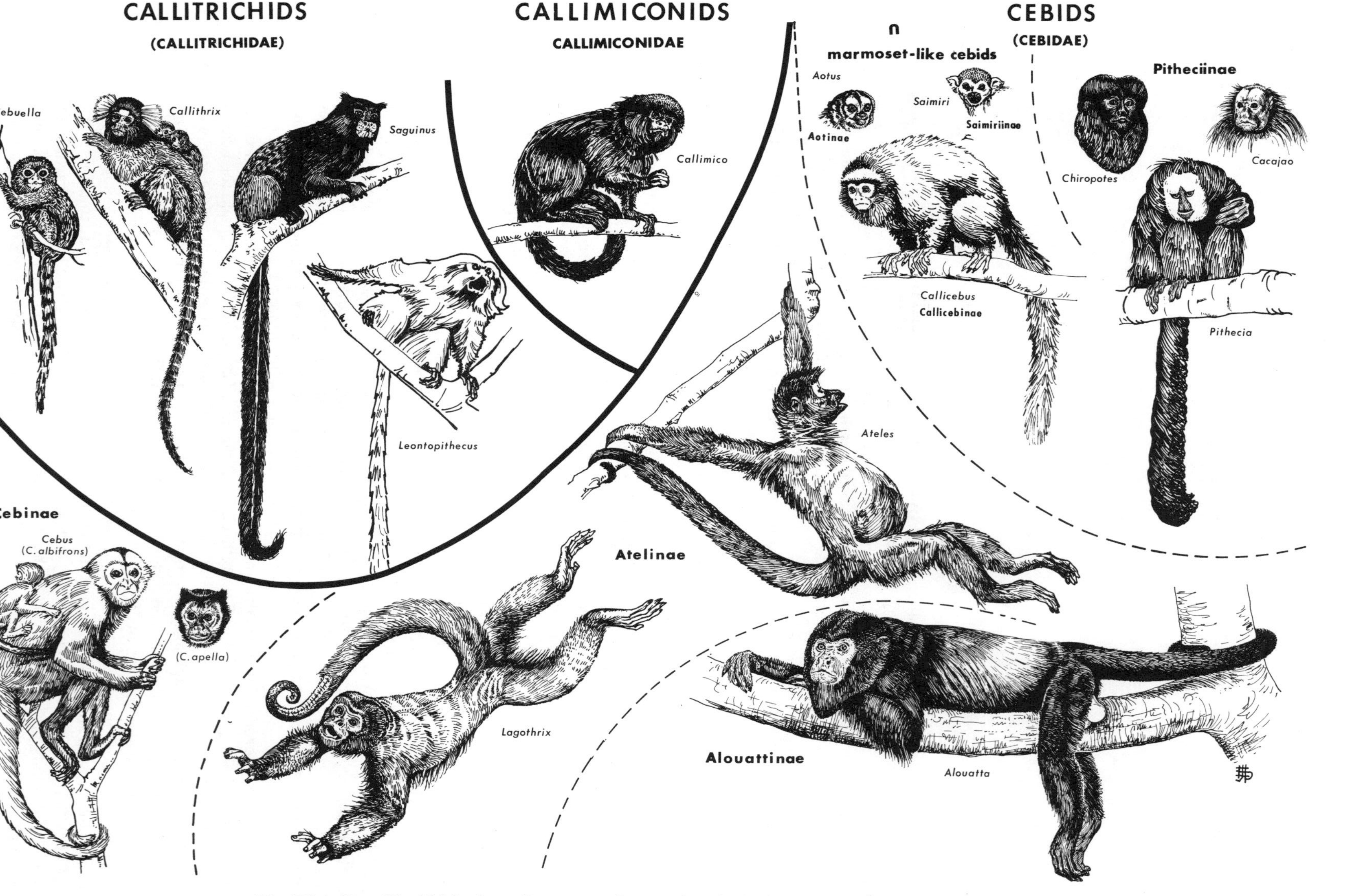

Fig. III.4. New World Monkeys. Representative species of platyrrhines arranged systematically. The size gradient from small to large corresponds with the family and subfamily groupings. A sliding scale is used for size: the larger the individual the smaller the scale of its illustration. (Revised from Hershkovitz 1969.)

Averages of head and body lengths and tail lengths, in centimeters, of 10 or more adults: *Cebuella pygmaea* (pigmy marmoset), 13, 20; *Callithrix jacchus* (common marmoset), 20, 31; *Saguinus* (tamarins), 23, 35; *Leontopithecus rosalia* (golden tamarin) 24, 34; *Callimico goeldii* (callimico), 23, 31; *Aotus trivirgatus* (night monkey), 30, 36; *Saimiri sciureus* (squirrel monkey), 28, 39; *Callicebus* (titis), 32, 42; *Pithecia* (sakis), 41, 41; *Chiropotes* (bearded sakis), 41, 41; *Cacajao* (uacaris), 44, 16; *Cebus* (capuchin monkeys) 40, 43; *Lagothrix lagothricha* (woolly monkey), 43, 61; *Alouatta* (howler monkeys), 50, 65; *Ateles paniscus* (spider monkeys), 48, 75; *Brachyteles arachnoides* (woolly spider monkey, Atelinae, not shown), 58, 72.

The tail also evolved with increasing body mass from a balancing and propping organ in the smallest platyrrhines to a clutching prehensile limb in the largest. Among prehensile-tailed cebids, specialization of the organ is least in *Cebus,* smallest of the group, and greatest in howlers and ateline monkeys, largest of the group. The new caudal function confers upon the larger cebids the equivalent agility, balance, and security in arboreal support and locomotion possessed by the smaller nonprehensile-tailed cebids. Other special caudal functions evolved at the same time independently of increases in body mass.

Evolution of molars and feeding habits are also correlated with increasing body mass and the corresponding need for bulkier and more readily available types of food (fig. III.5). The primitive tritubercular upper molars of callitrichids are specialized for cracking and chopping

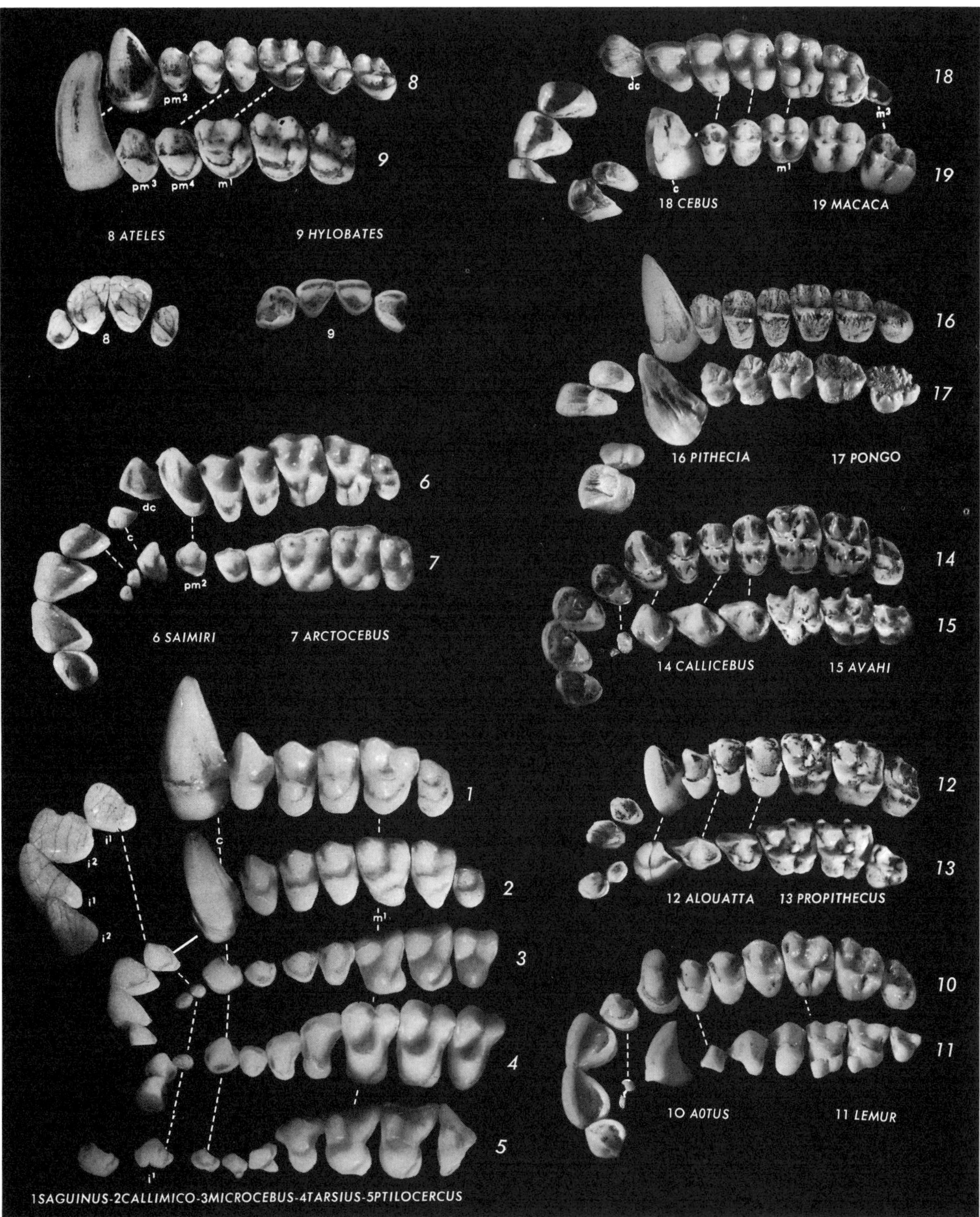

Fig. III.5. Relationships between upper tooth form, body mass, and diet in primates. All tooth rows reduced or enlarged to make length of canines to last molar (c-m) approximately the same, actual measurements tabulated below. Cheek-tooth molarization usually advances as body mass increases, its evolutionary rate and direction, at least in early stages, about the same in all primates irrespective of lineage. Each illustrated grouping or coupling consists of the left upper dental row of 2 or more unrelated species of comparable body size, with one outstanding

chitinous insects but are also used efficiently on a variety of animal and plant foods. Smaller cebids such as the night monkey or douroucouli, *Aotus trivirgatus*, titis, *Callicebus* spp., and squirrel monkey, *Saimiri sciureus*, are still largely insectivorous but more omnivorous, particularly frugivorous. Their quadritubercular molars still retain the primitive form of the callitrichid tritubercular pattern. The larger prehensile-tailed cebids with more highly evolved quadritubercular molars are mainly herbivorous, the howlers, *Alouatta*, being entirely herbivorous and more browsing or leaf-eating than fruit-eating. As the mass of the animal increased, the more specialized hand, foot, and tail assisted the larger body in foraging, perching, and bringing stationary vegetation to the mouth or the mouth to the vegetation. In the absence of negative selective forces, herbivores tend to increase in bulk at an accelerating rate as greater volumes of vegetation with proportionately fewer nutrients are consumed to sustain the enlarging and increasingly complex digestive system.

Reduction in litter size from two or three young per

---

exception; *Pithecia* (16) and *Pongo* (17), with similar cheek teeth and enamel wrinkling, are widely disparate in body mass. Size difference between *Aotus* (19) and *Lemur* (11) are also extreme, but only for the same size class. Smallest species (1–4), with similar molars (tritubercular to early stage quadritubercular) are among the most primitive living primates. Molars of the insectivore *Ptilocercus* (5) of the same size class are comparable in grade.

Nearly all living primates are omnivorous, and cheekteeth alone are unreliable indicators of principal diet or dietary range of single species. Canines, incisors, hands, lips, or tongue often act alone or in various combinations in selection, prehension, or preparation of food for deglutition without the intervention of molar teeth. Incisors, for example, are different in all illustrated samples, with some of the most exaggerated differences exhibited by models with similar molars. Hind teeth are locked in place and their molarization tends toward uniformity. There is more play, more options, and consequently greater diversity in the front part of the mouth and the gut behind. Survival of the organism during long periods of stress, when the common and most easily gathered fare is lacking or scarce, depends heavily on the adaptability of front teeth, highly sensitive parts of the digestive system, and supporting organs for wringing sustenance from unusual, marginal, elusive, or ephemeral foods. Perhaps less frequently but just as effectively, seemingly transitory molar teeth variables also respond positively to extraordinary environmental pressures.

Species No. and Notes	*Species*	FM *Catalog No. and Sex*	*C-M*	*I-M*	*Principal Foods in Wild and Main Bibliographic Source*
1.	*Saguinus oedipus*	69936 ♂	12.0	16.6	Fruit, nuts, insects, resin (Various)
2.	*Callimico goeldii*	57999 ♀	14.5	17.7	Fruit, insects (Various)
3.	*Microcebus murinus*	85863 ♀	11.2	11.9	Fruit (Kay 1975)
4.	*Tarsius syrichta*	56748 ♀	13.3	14.3	Insects (Davis 1962)
5.	*Ptilocercus lowi*	76855 ♂	12.3	16.7	Insects, fruit (Lim 1967)
6.	*Saimiri sciureus*	24201 ♂	16.5	20.0	Fruit, insects (Izawa 1975)
7.	*Arctocebus calabarensis*	99360 ♂	18.9	19.4	Insects (Kay 1975)
8.	*Ateles paniscus*	69580 ♀	33.2	41.5	Fruit, nuts (Kay 1975)
9.	*Hylobates concolor*	46498 ♂	32.3	39.3	Fruit, leaves (Kay 1975)
10.	*Aotus trivirgatus*	55414 ♀	17.5	21.4	Fruit, nuts (Kay 1975)
11.	*Lemur rubriventer*	5651 ♂	36.9	39.1	Leaves, fruit (Kay 1975)
12.	*Alouatta seniculus*	92085 ♂	39.5	47.7	Leaves, fruit, flowers (Fooden 1965; Kay 1975)
13.	*Propithecus verrauxi*	8344 ♂	32.4	37.0	Leaves, flowers, bark (Kay 1975)
14.	*Callicebus moloch*	88859 ♂	17.8	21.8	Insects, leaves, fruit (Izawa 1975)
15.	*Avahi laniger*	170461 ♂	21.7	22.7	Leaves, buds, bark (Kay 1975)
16.	*Pithecia hirsuta*	95507 ♂	22.3	29.3	Leaves, ants (Izawa 1975)
17.	*Pongo pygmaeus*	FM ♂	76.7	98.8	Leaves, fruit
18.	*Cebus apella*	94302 ♂	ca. 29	ca. 36	Fruit, insects (Izawa 1975)
19.	*Macaca fascicularis*	46523 ♂	37.9	58.8	Fruit (Fooden 1969*a*)

Notes

All primates eat ripe fruit and sweet saps, and nearly all plant eaters consume some form of animal food.

Kay (1975) compiled data from many sources. Izawa (1975) observed feeding habits of free-ranging platyrrhines in the Río Caquetá region of upper Amazonian Colombia, and he examined stomachs of 67 wild-caught monkeys representing 8 species. Personal observations of wild-living platyrrhines also entered into listing main diets.

Incisors of some species appear disproportionately large compared with the cheek teeth because they are slightly nearer the camera lens.

6. *Saimiri:* Deciduous canine (*dc*) and tip of permanent canine (*c*) are visible.

11. *Lemur:* Incisors joined at neck by calcium bridge.

12. *Alouatta:* Canine incompletely erupted.

18. *Cebus:* Young individual with unerupted m^3 and deciduous canine (*dc*) selected to show unworn molar bilophodonty for comparison with bilophodont catarrhine molars.

birth among callitrichids to one in cebids is another size correlative. It is generally true of all mammals that the larger the animal the fewer the number of young produced at birth and the longer the period of gestation. This modification is particularly important in species that carry the offspring during their period of helplessness.

The tamarinlike *Callimico* evolved independently at its own pace. It is callitrichidlike with respect to size, nonopposable thumb, and clawed digits, but its more fluid movements are comparable to those of small nonprehensile-tailed cebids. Its molar pattern is transitional from the tritubercular to the quadritubercular, and its diet in the wild is presumably less insectivorous and more frugivorous than that of callitrichids. Retention of the third molar and production of a single young per birth exclude *Callimico* from the callitrichid line.

8 Pelage

Types

The primitive mammalian coat may have consisted of a scaly hide with three melanistic hairs per scale (cf. de Meijere 1894). The hairs were probably bristly, as in many living insectivores such as *Solenodon* or *Tenrec,* and more abundant on upper and outer surfaces of head and body than on throat and under and inner parts of trunk and limbs (fig. III.6). The covering of the tail may have differed little from that of scaly-tailed opossums, insectivores, or rats. The sparse, bristly pelage of primitive mammals was probably wholly *sensory* in function and inherited from their reptilian ancestors.

The primitive tactile hairs or bristles on the outer exposed parts of the body were later modified into various types of sensory *guard hairs* (or monotrichs, sinus hairs, fig. III.7). Those on the probing projections of face, limbs, and sensitive external parts of the genitalia evolved

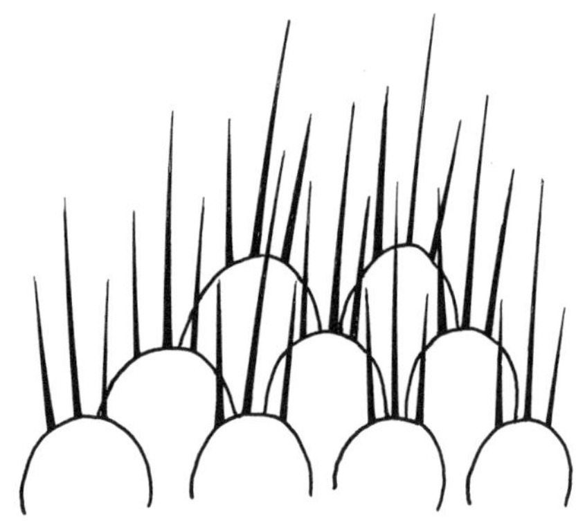

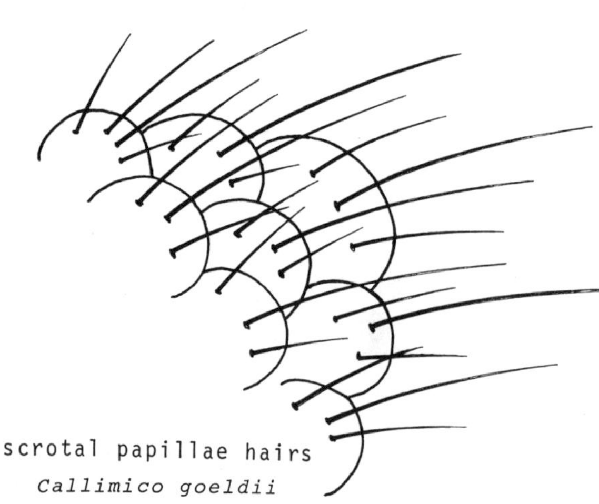

Fig. III.6. Triad hair pattern. Arrangements of vibrissae associated with tail scales in a primitive marsupial, *Marmosa murina* (Didelphidae) and with scrotal papillae in a primitive primate, *Callimico goeldii* (Callimiconidae).

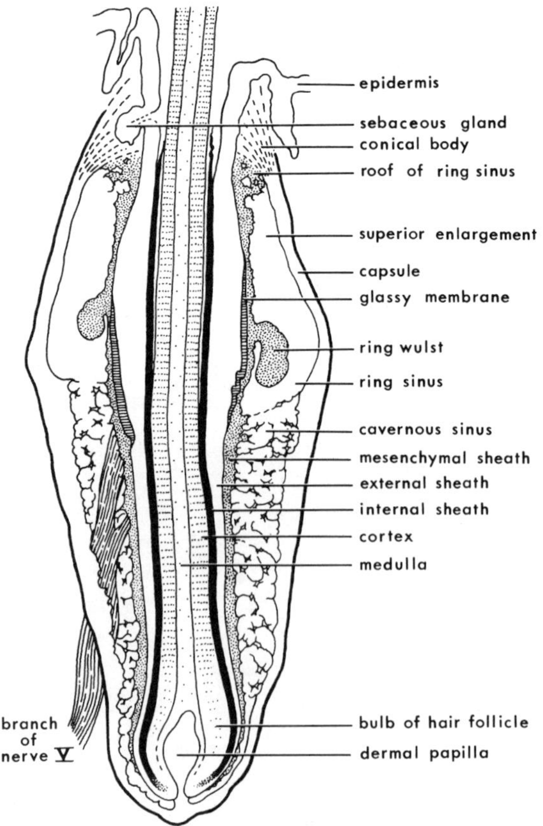

Fig. III.7. Tactile vibrissa and follicle; reconstruction of midsagittal section. Thick portion of glassy membrane is hatched; mesenchymal sheath and derivatives are stippled; arteries opening into lower portion of cavernous sinus omitted. Redrawn from Melargno and Montagna (1953, p. 131, fig. 1).

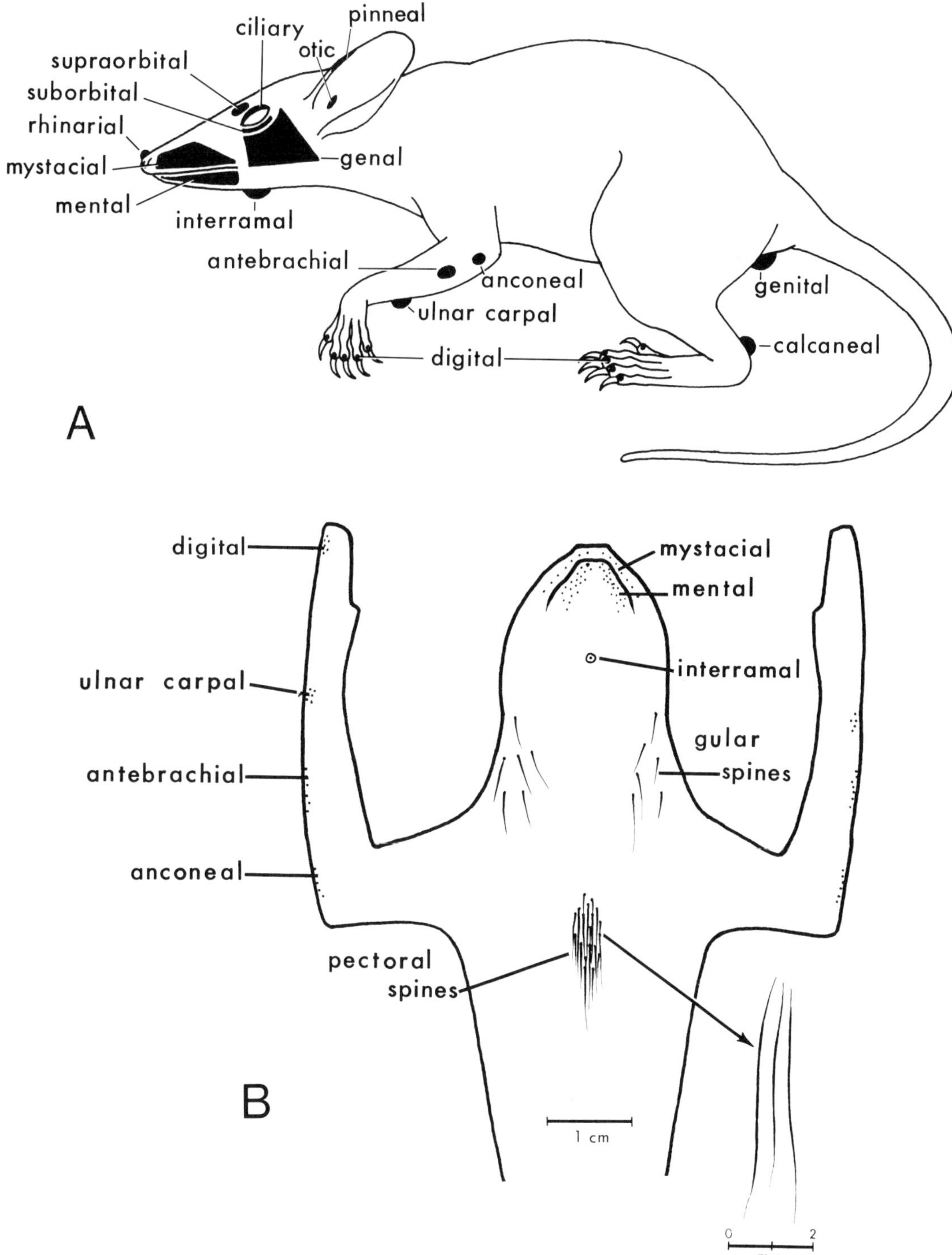

Fig. III.8. Tactile vibrissal fields in mammals: *A*, side of head and body of a primitive mammal showing all vibrissal fields present in primates (although not in all primates); *B*, vibrissal fields on ventral surface and forelimbs of *Cebuella pygmaea*, a primitive primate.

into highly specialized *tactile vibrissae* (p. 84). Other bristles degenerated or disappeared, and some, such as the pectoral and gular spines (fig. III.8), were overgrown and covered. Nevertheless, the triad or numerical relationship between primitive bristles and each scale has persisted, particularly on tail, muzzle, chest, and scrotum. The numerical constancy of each type of tactile vibrissa is significantly high in many species (cf. Danforth 1925), and most vibrissal fields in mammals are homologous and fairly constant.

Meanwhile, with changing environments and increasing mammalian specializations, other types of hairs were evolving from new follicles in species whose survival depended on concealment and reinforcement of their internally controlled thermoregulatory mechanism (fig. III.9). *Cover hairs,* or awls, perhaps the first of the new pelage types to proliferate in early mammals, served both purposes. The heat-conserving *wool hairs,* zigzags or underfur, appeared later in mammalian evolution among species that spread into cool temperate zones. These hairs became secondarily specialized for water repellance. A third strictly mammalian hair type is the fetal lanugo and vellus of the newborn that sometimes persists to puberty.

Each hair type varies considerably in size and structure,

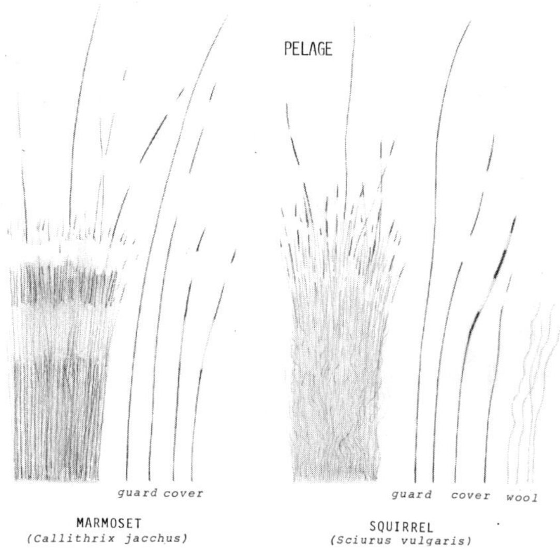

Fig. III.9. Hair types and banding of middorsal pelage in marmoset (*Callithrix jacchus*) and common squirrel (*Sciurus vulgaris*).

and there is wide overlap in form and function between all types. Every type may not be present on every part of the body, and the pelage as a whole varies according to age, season, and wear, and in many species according to sex.

The complete adult pelage of a progressive mammal, including all primates, covers all but narrowly restricted areas of the body. The inner, under, or less-exposed parts, such as throat, axillae, perineum, belly, and inner or auditory surface of external ears, are more thinly furred than the outer. The tail, primitively scaly and sparsely haired, is moderately to thickly pilose in many species. Rhinarium, palms, soles, and eyelids are, with few exceptions, nearly or quite bare, while lips, anus, phallus, and nipples are hairless.

Among certain mammals for which insulating or concealing coats possess little or no survival value, the pelage (and color) may become modified for display. In other species, parts of the body may become bare, exposing vividly colored skin or attractive patterns of bald and hairy areas.

Hair has played an important and progressively more specialized role in primate evolution. All pelage types, namely sensory, insulating or thermoregulatory, concealing or protective, and display, are present and well differentiated in primitive forms of living primates. In higher forms, vibrissal fields are less defined, and the number of their sensory hairs is reduced. Protective or insulating pelage, if present, is simplified and relatively thin. On the other hand, display and bare fields are more extensive and acquire greater importance in the biology of the species. In man, hairlessness dominates. His sensory hairs are reduced to a few facial vibrissae, and effective protective pelage is restricted to the crown. Display hairs of limited distribution appear as a male secondary sexual characteristic.

Depilation, Hypertrichy, and Hair Tracts

Depilation is here defined as the evolutionary process of reduction and elimination of hair in any trichogenetic field. Depilation is therefore a degenerative process. It may proceed evenly along a narrow front, resulting in a localized or patterned baldness, or it may be diffused over some part or over the entire body. Examples of patterned baldness among primates are the relatively bare face, bare crown, ear, or bare rump characteristic of many species (fig. III.10). Man exemplifies patterned depilation on the face and diffuse depilation over most of the rest of the body. Cetaceans, sirenians, elephants, rhinoceroses, hippopotami, naked mole rats (*Heterocephalus glaber*), and the naked bat (*Cheiromeles torquatus*) are examples of extremely diffuse depilation. The sparse pelage of armadillos and pangolins is probably primitive rather than regressive. The primitive facial vibrissae are persistently long in all groups mentioned except man. Well developed guard hairs are also evident in all except whales and man.

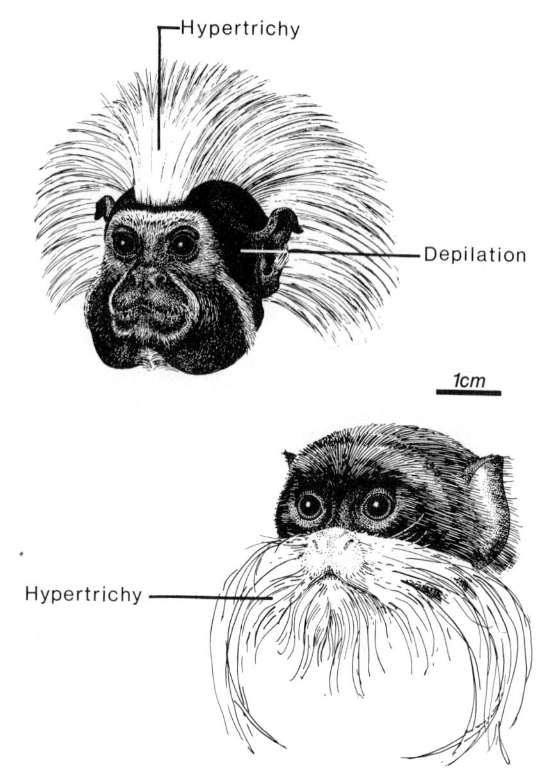

Fig. III.10. The crested tamarin, *Saguinus oedipus oedipus,* exhibits *depilation* in its thinly pilose face and sides of crown, and *hypertrichy* in its flowing white mane. The elongate mustache of *Saguinus imperator* is another example of *hypertrichy*.

Hypertrichy is the evolutionary process of elongation of a primitively short hair. Localized or patterned hypertrichy takes the form of manes, mantles, fringes, switches, crests, tufts, beards, whiskers, and elongate eyelashes (fig. III.10). Winter coat hairs of most living species in northern latitudes are significantly longer than equivalent hairs of the summer pelage. Pelage of high-altitude mammals is almost always longer and denser than that of lowland members of the species living at the same latitude.

Depilation, hypertrichy, or the interplay between both processes, give rise to the distinctive coat patterns of supergeneric groups, most species, and many subspecies.

Hair tracts, or the system of hair slopes or streams, are determined by the angle or direction of hair growth relative to the long axis of the body (fig. III.11). These in turn create the minor patterns of whorls, featherings, and crestings (cf. Kidd 1903).

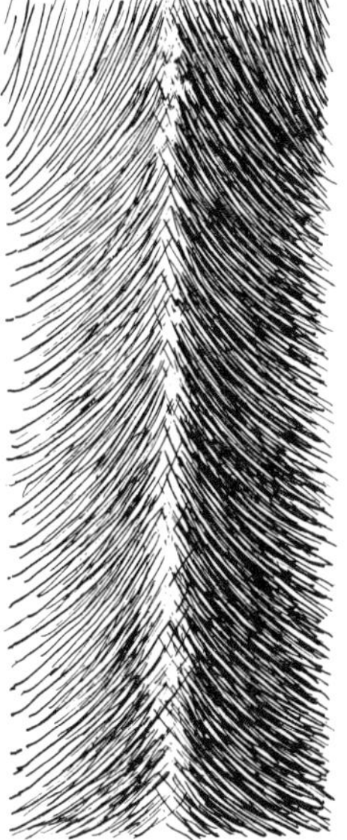

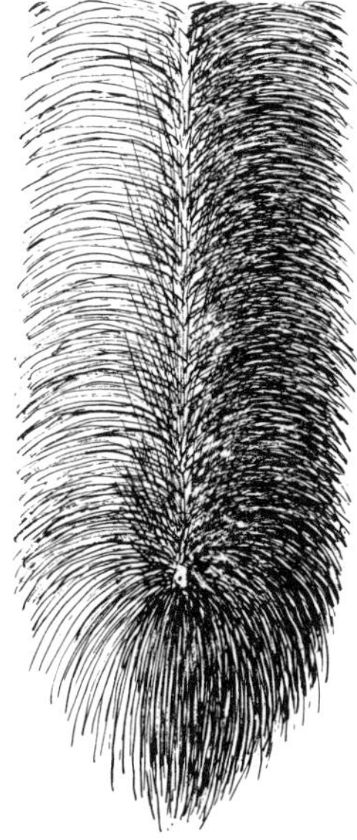

Fig. III.11. Hair patterns. The three shown here represent the principal modifications of main hair streams of head, trunk, tail, and limbs. A *crest* is formed where two bands of hairs growing at opposing angles meet along the axis of a main stream; long-haired crests are usually called manes. Hairs of a *whorl* radiate from a glandular concentration or other centralized modification of skin or underlying tissue. The *feather* or *feathering* is produced by the divergence of hairs from a common axis of a main stream. All special hair patterns resolve into the main stream; the whorl usually feathers before resolution.

Trichogenetic Fields

Any distinctive hair, and each homogenous pilary area with respect to length, density, and slope of the included hairs, represents a separate *trichogenetic field.* Fields of each pelage coat (fetal, juvenal, adult) and each seasonal or molt coat are also independent. Although autonomous locally, all active trichogenetic fields are interrelated and interact to compose the pelage pattern of the individual or species.

The autonomy of trichogenetic fields is clearly demonstrated in experiments conducted by Durward and Rudall (1949, p. 325, pl. 1, fig. 1, pl. 4, fig. 10) on hair growth in the rat and by Johnson (1965, p. 491, figs. 2–4) in the guinea pig. Garn (1951, p. 502, fig. 1) describes and figures the major trichogenetic fields in man.

Trichogenetic and chromogenetic fields (see below) are independently controlled but interrelated. The crown of a tabby cat contains several color fields but only a single trichogenetic field. The crown of a wholly black horse, however, has three trichogenetic fields (it includes forelock and part of mane) and one chromogenetic field. If the forelock were white it would be a separate chromogenetic field coinciding precisely with the corresponding trichogenetic field.

Molt in Mammals

The pattern of hair replacement, or molt, varies from species to species and from place to place. Most mammals, however, molt from fetal to juvenal pelage and from juvenal to adult pelage. Some species have more than two preadult coats and molts. Adult pelage is also replaced. Each molt may be seasonal or cyclical, or individually variable. Replacement may begin in one or more parts of the body and progress in a definite pattern, or it may be diffuse, with each follicle replacing hair independently of other follicles. Each distinct age and seasonal pelage evolved independently.

It has been determined experimentally that the single external factor most important in stimulating the onset of seasonal molt in high-latitude mammals is change in photoperiodicity. Decreasing day length sets off the fall (or winter) molt. Increasing day length signals the onset of spring (or summer) molt. The eyes are the main receptors for the light stimulus (Bissonnette, 1935; Bissonnette and Wilson 1939; Lyman 1943; Rothschild 1944; Bissonnette, Hume, and Bailey 1944; Yeates 1958; Rothschild and Lane 1957; Hewson 1963; Watson 1963; Slee 1965; Ebling and Johnson 1964; Ebling 1965). Nutrition and general physical condition may also control molt in isolated cases, as in domestic animals (Yeates 1958). Although day length at any latitude is the same worldwide, daylight varies significantly from fair to overcast skies, from one mountain slope or valley to another, and from almost any one locality to another. Each species has its own mechanism for hair replacement and each local population has its own biological clock. Molts adjust accordingly. Temperature and endogenous factors, including hormones, probably control the rate of molt once it has started.[1]

Little is known of seasonal molt in adult mammals of tropical latitudes. In any given tropical zone locality, seasonal differences in temperatures and photoperiodicity are minor, and these climatic factors evidently have little or no effect on the organic system or internal mechanisms controlling molt. On the other hand, seasonal differences in rainfall and in quantity and quality of food intake are generally drastic and may well contribute to the control of follicular activity and hair health.

Some tropical zone mammals may molt year round. Others molt from old dry season pelage to prime wet season pelage. They may molt again toward the end of wet and beginning of dry seasons. Terrestrial mammals of north and south temperate zones also molt seasonally, with summer pelage replaced by a longer, thicker winter pelage and old winter pelage replaced by a new short and crisp summer pelage. Molting actually begins in the spring and fall of the year.

New pelage usually differs from the old in length, texture, density, and color. The differences may be ontogenetic, as between fetal, juvenal, and adult pelages. Others are altitudinal, and seasonal or cyclical. At a given time the fur of high mountain populations is longer and thicker than those of the same species living in the warm valleys below. In equatorial American latitudes, for example, lowland mammals are clothed with a "permanent summer" pelage while those of high Andean crests wear a "permanent winter" pelage. Molt in regions of relatively uniform climate is from "summer" to "summer" or from "winter" to "winter" pelages. Differences in pelage and associated color patterns between altitudinally separated populations is often genetic, and sometimes of subspecific grade. Geographic or altitudinal intermediates are usually present. Domestic animals distributed over the same altitudinal gradient respond to the environment in the same way as do wild native species, but their phenotypic differences are purely somatic or niche variables.

Seasonal molt in callitrichids is described under the next heading (p. 83), and in some species accounts.

Pelage in Callitrichidae and *Callimico*

Adult Patterns

All external surfaces except palms, soles, lips, eyelids (except edges), borders of nostrils, nipples, anus, and phallus, are more or less beset with hair. The fur is moderately dense and silky on upper (or outer) parts of head, trunk, and limbs. It consists of a sometimes-present fine underfur, a heavier layer of lax body or cover hairs sparsely superposed by slightly stiffened over hairs or guard hairs (fig. III.9). Cover hairs, which form the bulk of the pelage, average between 2 and 3 centimeters long in mid-dorsal region and nearly a centimeter longer on sides to form a lateral fringe. Underparts, or inner surface, of trunk and limbs are less densely furred than upper or outer parts, and in all species most of skin shows through on axillary, gastric, pubic, pudendal, and perineal regions. Pelage of sexual skin, scrotum, and base of tail behind anus is extremely sparse. Except as noted, tail is thickly clothed but not bushy, its tip tufted. Upper surface of hands and feet is completely covered to tips of phalanges with distal hairs, or digital vibrissae, projecting over claws and nail of hallux. Bristles, guard hairs and cover hair types are usually grouped in triads or clusters, each forming a transverse row of three hairs.[2] This pattern, pointed out in *Callithrix jacchus* and *Leontopithecus rosalia* by de Meijere (1894), appears to be the same in all callitrichids. The primitive pattern of three hairs per scale (cf. antea, p. 78) is still evident on the chest and other bodily parts of callitrichids and is particularly notable on the testicular fold of the scrotum in *Callimico goeldii* (fig. III.6).

Facial hair types include fine short hairs roughly equivalent to human vellus hairs, longer, thicker hairs corresponding to body or cover hairs, and comparatively long and thick sensory vibrissae. Vellus hairs dominate in bare-face tamarins. Facial cover hairs are usually short or absent in bare-face species, thick and long in the hairy-face forms.

Most characteristic expressions of patterned depilation among callitrichids appear in the bare-face tamarins. In *Saguinus oedipus* (fig. III.10), depilation progressed in the form of a wedge from each temple backward, leaving a broad mane or crest on the crown. In *S. bicolor,* hypotrichism proceeded frontally across the entire forehead from front to back. Diffuse depilation occurs on face, ears, underparts of trunk and inner sides of limbs, leaving the skin largely exposed in a number of species.

The patterned hypertrichism among callitrichids is expressed in the forms of mane, crest, mantle, lateral fringe, moustache, and aural, circumaural or caudal tufts. Among hairy-face tamarins, comparatively whiskerless species cannot be confused with long-whiskered species such as *Saguinus mystax* and *S. imperator.* Bare-eared species are clearly separable from hairy-eared species such as *Callithrix humeralifer.* The aural or circumaural tufts of *Callithrix jacchus* and the small bare ears of *C. argentata* are distinctive. The ear-concealing mane of *Cebuella, Leontopithecus,* and *Callimico* sets each genus apart from all others. Facial fringes and gular whorls are pelage specialties of certain callitrichids, particularly members of the *Saguinus oedipus* group. The mantle and lateral fringe of long hairs are characteristic of all callitrichids and *Callimico.*

A patterned depilation is the dominant evolutionary trend among callitrichids, and among primates in general. It is active in at least one field even while hypertrichism may be active in another. Within any one genus, the more advanced the species, the thinner the coat and the larger the bare areas. The most primitive callitrichid, *Cebuella*

[1] The experiment on ermine conducted by Schmidt (1954) and cited by authors as evidence for temperature control of molt was simply a matter of keeping three individuals outdoors in the winter cold and three indoors in a warm room. The first group molted to white, the second retained the summer coat. Unfortunately, the amount and kind of light experienced by each group of animals was not described, measured, or controlled. Herter (1958) showed that a captive kept at a fairly uniform warm temperature indoors molted at appropriate times to summer brown and winter white pelages.

[2] The clusters actually vary from 1 to 5 depending on the number of shed or doubled hairs.

pygmaea, is least denuded. Ouistitis, *Callithrix jacchus,* are well haired, but the most specialized, *C. argentata,* is least hairy, with ears completely exposed. Among tamarins, genus *Saguinus,* the bare-face species are most highly evolved and least covered. The aberrant lion tamarin, *Leontopithecus rosalia,* is the extreme example of hypertrichism. Nevertheless, its mid-frontal "bald spot" is already present in the young and forms an appreciable wedge in adults. The phylogenetically independent *Callimico* also seems to be well covered but pelage of underparts of trunk and inner surfaces of limbs is thin, with axillae, lower belly, and pubic region virtually bare in adults and young.

Callitrichids and *Callimico* do not range far outside warm latitudes, and the marked hypertrichism associated with adaptations to cold climates does not appear among them.

Juvenal Patterns

The newborn is thinly covered with vellus hairs which are quickly shed and replaced by the juvenal pelage. The fully developed juvenal pelage and its color pattern evolved independently of the adult coat and is more primitive in some respects and more advanced in others. Suckling young of *Callithrix jacchus* lack the specialized ear tufts of the parents. The first tufts to appear, during the third month, are soft, lax, dark, and of a generalized type. These are replaced in the half-grown animal by more specialized tufts which gradually assume the shape and color characteristic of adults. The hairy ears of juvenal *Callithrix argentata* become naked with adulthood. The mane of young lion tamarins (*Leontopithecus rosalia*) is little developed, the lateral tufts undifferentiated. With respect to pelage alone, juvenal bare-face tamarins resemble hairy-face tamarins more nearly than adults of their own species. The face of young *Saguinus midas* is also hairier than that of adult members of the species, and its comparatively well-developed side whiskers or "mutton chops" are distinctively white. The elongate whitish whiskers of young *Saguinus fuscicollis* adumbrate the condition in the nearly related but more advanced hairy-face species, *Saguinus mystax.* In all species, juvenal body pelage is shorter and thinner than adult pelage.

Detailed descriptions of pelage and color are given in the species and subspecies accounts.

Seasonal Molt

Seasonal pelage change in callitrichids is known only from studies of *Saguinus oedipus* of Panamá and northwestern Colombia. Correlation between humidity and pelage conditions of samplings of six populations (p. 756) indicate that hair growth is most active during extended rainy periods or seasons and mostly, if not entirely, suppressed during extended dry periods or seasons. Seasonal irregularities in rainfall and a long transition from the active or growing stage of the follicle to the quiescent stage may account for a significant part of the wide range of variation in pelage condition noted in the various populations. The differences, however, are in the degree of wear, aging, and fading of hairs of the same type. There is no molt line and no concerted sloughing of one coat type and synchronized replacement with another type comparable to distinct summer and winter molts of temperate and arctic zone animals.

Pelage differences noted between local callitrichid populations are generally slight. In regions of extremely high rainfall or evergreen forests, pelage appears to be more plush and sleek than in the drier deciduous forests and campos. As a rule, pelage of animals living at higher, cooler elevations is longer and denser than that of animals of lower, warmer sites.

Molt in pregnant and lactating females may or may not be synchronized with that of adult males, but a number of independent endogenous factors are probably involved. Similarly, ontogenetic changes in pelage from birth through infancy to weaning must harmonize with physiological conditions peculiar to the young.

Transient alopecia from artificial irradiation and brusque change in ambient temperature has been observed by Fitzgerald (1935, p. 182), Neill (1829, p. 19, 20), and others. Complete loss of tail hair is noted in both accounts. The details are given in the species account of *Callithrix jacchus* (p. 495).

9 Tactile Vibrissae

One or more tactile or sensory vibrissae are present in all mammals. The hairs may be in a single locus, distributed in a regular pattern, or scattered. Presence or absence and the arrangement and number of vibrissae vary according to the individual, the stock, the population, or the species. The tactile vibrissae or sinus hairs, particularly of the face, are with few exceptions the first hairs to appear in ontogeny (cf. Vincent 1913, p. 16; Noback 1951, p. 481; Lyne 1959, p. 118) and the last to disappear in phylogeny.

Tactile vibrissae of a primitive type (prototriches) were already present in fishes, and hairlike sensory organs occur in amphibians and reptiles (cf. Elias and Bortner 1957). Such organs must have developed independently in many vertebrates but were certainly present in the line leading from mammallike reptiles to mammals. The finer or primarily insulating types of body hairs, including wool hairs and guard hairs, are exclusively mammalian (fig. III.9). Their follicles lack the elaborate blood sinuses, the rich vascularity of the dermal papilla, and the numerous sensory nerves and end organs characteristic of vibrissal follicles (Melargno and Montagna 1953, p. 138).

The vibrissae are distributed within circumscribed bilaterally symmetrical or median unpaired fields of the mammalian skin. The following are present in primates (figs. III.8, 12).

Mystacial. On sides of muzzle and upper lip; number and arrangement of vibrissae variable but usually one, sometimes two, above each nostril, one or two vibrissae beneath on lip and from three to ten or more dispersed laterally in irregular rows to angle of mouth. The paranasal and "rhinal" of authors are included here.

Rhinarial. On distal half of midline of nasals (from tip between nostrils to angle or depression distad of nasion); one to several vibrissae arranged in a single row with two rows sometimes present between nostrils.

The rhinarial field may be an extension of the mystacial. The corresponding vibrissae are present in New and Old World monkeys, absent in the glabrous-muzzled mammals, including lemuroids, insectivores, and marsupials, and absent in apes and man. These are the "vibrissae-dorso-nasale mediane" first noted by De Beaux (1917, p. 96) in *Saguinus oedipus geoffroyi* and *Leontopithecus rosalia rosalia.* The "rhinal" vibrissae of marsupials defined by Lyne (1959, p. 82) are placed high on the side of the muzzle above the nostril and are not homologues of the rhinarial vibrissae described here.

Genal. On cheek from zygoma to corner of mouth medially and angle of jaw laterally; number and arrangement of vibrissae variable and sometimes randomly scattered throughout field, but usually one or a cluster of two or three present behind posterior canthus of eye (the *postorbital* vibrissae of some authors) or below it, and/or below posterior border of ear (includes *postoral* of authors).

Suborbital. Beneath posterior half of eye; vibrissae present or absent in individuals of any population, race, or species; the suborbital field may simply mark the limits of the genal field or be an extension of it.

Postorbital. See *Genal.*

Postoral. See *Genal.*

Supraorbital. From nasion to upper medial third or half of orbital border; number of vibrissae variable, but usually three to six long projecting vibrissae emerge from or flanked by a cluster of shorter vibrissae. These are the *supercilairy* vibrissae of some authors.

Ciliary. On lower border of upper eyelid; ten or more vibrissae evenly distributed in a single row or fringe—the eyelashes.

Mental. On lower jaw on each side of symphysis; vibrissae usually numerous and often arranged in two or three irregular horizontal rows with the greater number of rows nearer angle of gape; posterior median vibrissae often longest and projecting well beyond body hairs. These are the submental vibrissae of Pocock (1914*a*, p. 890).

Interramal. Midway between lower rami from behind symphysis to plane of mandibular angles; one or two, or a cluster of several vibrissae may be present on or near midline about halfway between chin and angle of jaw.

Narial. In vestibule of each nostril; usually numerous and well developed in adult male apes and man; greatly reduced in females; obsolete in monkeys and apparently absent in prosimians.

Otic. In the external auditory meatus.

Pinnal. On upper anterior border of pinna.

Digital. At base of each claw or nail on dorsal surface of each last phalanx; vibrissae poorly developed, clustered and projecting distally for some distance over claws to well beyond.

Ulnar-carpal. Small, slightly raised, glandular pad on

VIBRISSAE—PIGMENTATION

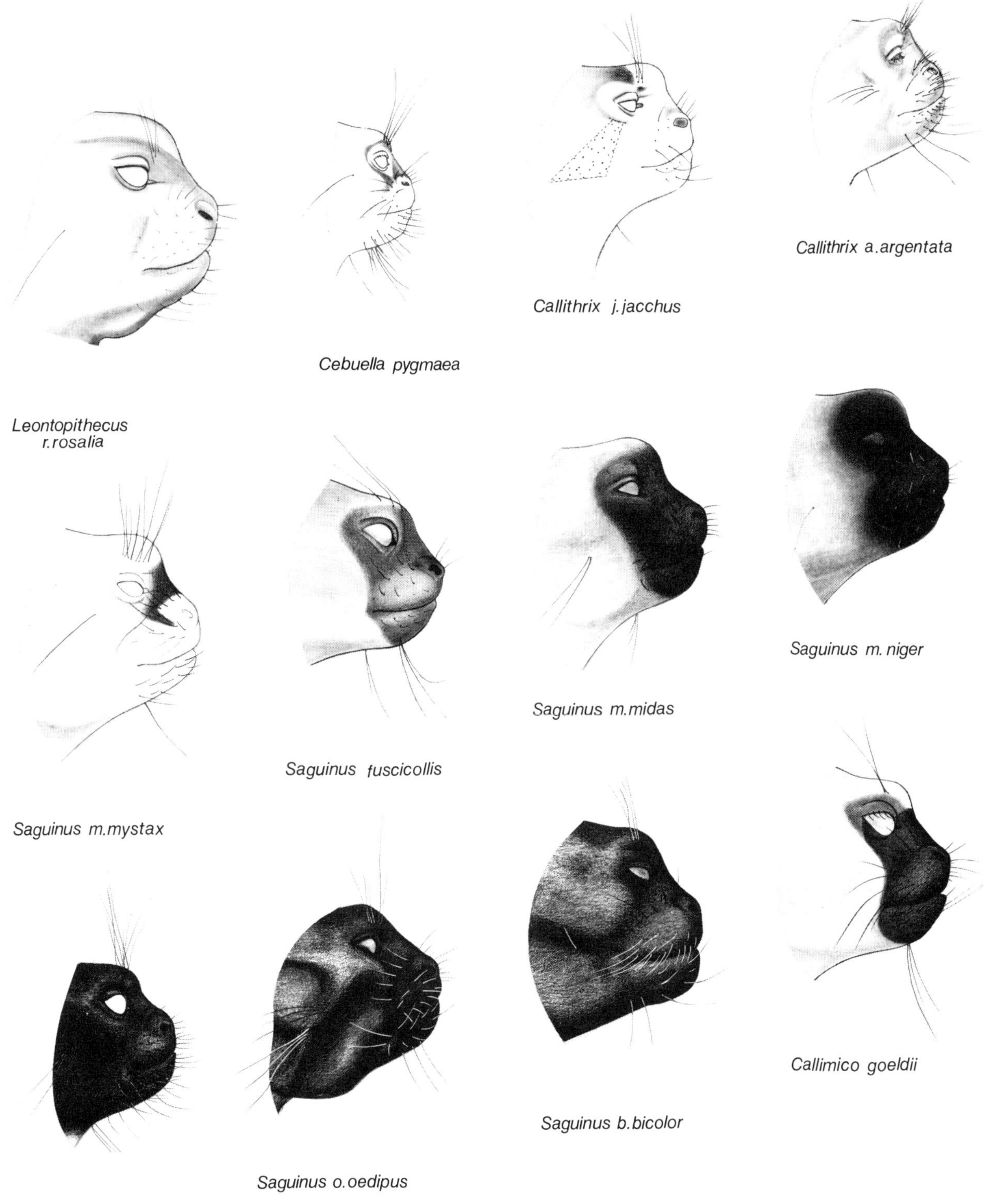

Fig. III.12. Facial vibrissae and pigmentation in Callitrichidae and Callimiconidae (*Callimico*).

inner ulnar surface near wrist; vibrissae usually three to six in number and projected outward well beyond surrounding cover hairs; present in all callitrichids but first noticed in *Callithrix jacchus jacchus* by Frederic (1905, pp. 240, 255).

Genital. On external genitalia, testicular portion of scrotum in male, scrotal fold of labia majora in female. The vibrissae in males are numerous, widely scattered, and not erectile; of females, few in number, surrounding introitus, and erectile. The spines of the penis, present in many species, appear to be homologous.

Other Vibrissae. Brachial and *anconeal* fields are present in prosimians. In callitrichids, they may be represented by the long black vibrissae scattered along the outer side of the forearm in many individuals.

Worthy of special mention are certain spiny or vibrissaelike hairs on throat and sternal region associated with glandular concentrations. Their position and gross structure suggest tactile functions comparable to those of the facial vibrissae. They appear to be related to the rodent tylotrich described by Straile (1960, p. 133). The bristly hairs of certain insectivores (e.g., the tenrec) are similar and may be homologous.

These *gular* and *pectoral* or *sternal* spines are mostly or entirely black with fine tips and constricted bases, adpressed and more or less concealed by the soft body hairs. The gular spines may be few in number and restricted to side of neck or numerous and randomly distributed across the throat. They are present in many callitrichids, some cebids, cercopithecids, insectivores, and other nonprimates. The pectoral or sternal spines are always adpressed, usually in a tuft, and restricted to a narrow median band. They are characteristic of pygmy marmosets, common in marmosets and tamarins, and sporadic in some insectivores.

The glands with which the spines are associated are specialized scent glands. Wislocki and Schultz (1925, p. 242) noted the presence of sternal glands in *Callithrix jacchus penicillata, Saguinus bicolor,* and a large number of other primates including lemurs, cebids, cercopithecids, and apes. A detailed account of the morphology and function of the sternal glands in platyrrhines has been published by Epple and Lorenz (1967). Callitrichid cutaneous glands are reviewed here on page 415.

Remarks. All facial, genital, ulnar-carpal, and digital vibrissae are present in man, most only as nonfunctional individual variables or atavisms.

Ciliary vibrissae have received little if any attention by specialists, although they are present in most mammals, including man. They are comparable to the mystacial but can be as highly developed or as ill-defined as any of the generally recognized facial vibrissae. The rhinarial, narial, otic, and pinnal vibrissae are usually overlooked, particularly in man, where they are always present and sometimes nearly as conspicuous as the ciliary. The trend in primates, however, has been toward the elimination of tactile vibrissae and the accentuation of other sensory faculties.

Vibrissae present in some mammals but not evident in primates include the *calcaneal* (some marsupials) and caudal (marsupials, rodents, and insectivores). The scaly armor of armadillos and pangolins is also provided with vibrissae or vibrissalike bristles.

A systematic study of tactile vibrissae in Primates, including callitrichids and cebids, was first made by Frederic (1905). *Facial vibrissae* in the Mammalia in general were described by Pocock in 1914 (1914*a*, p. 889) and in a series of subsequent papers on particular groups, as follows: Primates (lemurs and tarsiers, 1918, p. 19); Marsupialia 1926*a*, p. 1038); Xenarthra (1924, p. 992 [armadillos], p. 996 [anteaters], p. 1000 [sloths]); Carnivora (Procyonidae, 1921*a*, p. 395; Mustelidae, 1921*b*, p. 811; 1926*b*, p. 1085; Canidae, 1927, p. 307); Rodentia (histrichomorphs, 1922*a*, p. 371; Sciuridae and Castoridae, 1922*b*, p. 1173; Capromyidae, 1926*c*, p. 413); Lagomorpha (1925*b*, p. 674); Artiodactyla (Cervidae, 1923*a*, in text; Hippopotamidae, Cervidae, and Camelidae, 1923*b*, p. 538). A perceptive study of vibrissae in callitrichids was made by De Beaux (1917). Contributions by various authors, particularly Pocock, were reviewed by Huber (1930, p. 180) with additional notes on vibrissae of aquatic mammals and their muscular control.

Economic interest in sheep wool led to considerable basic research on the hair of laboratory mice (*Mus musculus*) and rats (*Rattus rattus*) and, in Australia, on the pelage of Marsupialia and rabbits. The more important modern contributions to knowledge of murine vibrissae were made by Vincent (1913, p. 1), Danforth (1925), and a group of Australian authors including Dun (1958; 1959), Fraser, Nay, and Kindred (1959), and Dun and Fraser (1959). A comprehensive survey of vibrissae in marsupials was conducted by Lyne (1959).

For bibliographies and detailed accounts of the biology of hair and hair follicles, see J. B. Hamilton (1951), Montagna and Ellis (1958*a*), Montagna (1962), and Lyne and Short (1965).

Vibrissae in Callitrichidae

Tactile vibrissae are better developed and more widely distributed in callitrichids (fig. III.12) than in all other supergeneric primate groups except, possibly, some lemuroids. Ciliary, mystacial, rhinarial, mental, and ulnar-carpal vibrissae are consistently present and well developed in all individuals examined, representing all known species and races. Supraorbital, genal, and interramal are present in most species but not necessarily in every race or individual. Digital vibrissae are consistently present but may be obsolete functionally. Genital or perineal vibrissae appear to occur universally in callitrichids.

The number of vibrissae in any one field is variable, and their disposition is often irregular. It may be said, however, that in some fields there are many vibrissae, in others none, one, or a few. These last may be prominent, or weak and difficult to detect. Sexual differences in the kind and number of vibrissae are not evident in the material examined. However, the perineal vibrissae, generally confined to scrotum and labia majora in callitrichids, are usually well developed and erectile in females, usually degenerate and nonerectile in males.

Variation

The greatest diversity and widest distribution of tactile and other sensory hairs occur in the pygmy marmoset, *Cebuella pygmaea,* most primitive of living platyrrhines (figs. III.8, 12). The locomotor vibrissae (ulnar-carpal, brachial, anconeal, digital) are extremely well developed in the pygmy, although the digitals appear to be of no importance in this and all other species of callitrichids. The interramal vibrissae seem to be uncommon, but in the dry skin they may be difficult to detect or confused with (if not functionally replaced by) the exceptionally long lateral mental vibrissae. Gular and pectoral spines are particularly well developed in the pygmy marmoset.

Callithrix jacchus, most primitive member of its genus, has the same complement of sensory hairs as *Cebuella pygmaea.* Its interramals, however, are better defined while the locomotor vibrissae are less developed with only the ulnar-carpal consistently present. Gular and pectoral spines also seem to be less frequent and developed than in *Cebuella pygmaea.* Huber (1931, p. 31) found neither interramals nor genal vibrissae in the specimens he examined.

Tactile hairs in tamarins, genus *Saguinus,* are not as well developed or as widely distributed as in *Cebuella* and *Callithrix.* Mystacial, mental, and ulnar-carpal vibrissae are consistently present and usually well defined in all tamarins. Interramals are present in some or most individuals representing all species of *Saguinus* except the highly specialized bare-face tamarin, *S. bicolor.* Loss of interramals here may be correlated with depilation. Interramals are consistently present in more or less hairy-face *S. inustus* and *S. leucopus* but are absent in most specimens of the bare-face *S. oedipus geoffroyi,* and completely lost in the more advanced *S. oedipus oedipus.*

Genal vibrissae are extremely difficult to detect in tamarins, especially in hairy-face species with black cheek hairs. They appear to be consistently present in *Saguinus nigricollis nigricollis* and *S. n. graellsi* but occur sporadically in the more advanced *S. fuscicollis.* They are well developed in all bare-face species except possibly *S. inustus,* where persistence of long black facial hairs makes detection difficult. Genals are also present in all races but not all individuals of *S. bicolor.* They are small and unpigmented and evidently are becoming obsolete in this species.

Supraorbitals, generally present in all callitrichids, are either obsolete or indistinguishable from contiguous bristles in the black tamarin, *Saguinus midas.* Rhinarials, mystacials, and mentals also tend to be reduced in this species, and in *S. midas niger* they are depigmented as well.

Leontopithecus rosalia is highly specialized and off the main line of callitrichid evolution. Its tactile vibrissae are somewhat less developed than in tamarins in general, its interramals apparently absent, and the genals reduced to one or two inconspicuous hairs.

Vibrissae in the peculiar *Callimico goeldii* are also comparatively poorly developed. Interramals are absent and genals are not evident in present dry or fluid-preserved specimens examined. Ulnar-carpals, however, are well defined in two of four available fluid-preserved specimens.

Tactile vibrissae grow in the same direction as other hairs of the same pilary field. In *Cebuella, Callithrix jacchus, C. humeralifer,* and *Saguinus leucopus,* interramals are directed forward. In *Callithrix argentata* they are directed forward (*melanura*), forward and laterad (*leucippe*), and forward, laterad, and backward (*argentata*). In *Saguinus oedipus geoffroyi* they point forward and sidewise. In all other callitrichids where interramals were detected, the direction of growth is backward.

Degeneration of individual sinus hairs involves depigmentation followed by reduction in size. The vibrissae are best developed in the most primitive species, *Cebuella pygmaea* and *Callithrix jacchus.* They are least developed in the larger, more advanced or specialized species *Leontopithecus rosalia, Saguinus bicolor bicolor,* and *S. midas niger* among callitrichids, and in *Callimico goeldii.* From the foregoing it appears that the more advanced or the larger the species, the fewer the kind and number of its functional tactile vibrissae.

Functions

Vibrissae and hairs in general increase the animal's area and extend the radius of body surface sensibility to tactile stimuli. They transmit impulses *from* and *to* contacted objects or organisms. Contact through vibrissae may also reinforce the stimulating effects of sight or smell. Little is known of the special functions of vibrissae in primates generally. Eyelashes, otics, and narial vibrissae serve as protective screens or filters and, in the case of otics and narials, localize irritating objects. Among frequently observed nonprimates, such as laboratory mice, rats, squirrels, domestic cats, and dogs, facial vibrissae, particularly the mystacial, serve as distance gauges or guides in moving alongside or between solid objects. Vincent (1913, p. 21) concluded from experiments on rats that the facial vibrissae were "intimately connected with equilibrium and that their extreme mobility and sensitivity in rats was a partial compensation for poor vision. . . . The tactile hairs also seemed to assist in determining the exact position of openings or turns and in the discrimination of inequalities of surface." Arm and leg vibrissae may function in the same way. Long and fine vibrissae register air currents and the source of wind-borne odors. They may help the larger predators gauge wind in stalking prey, as suggested by Ismael (1960, p. 213). The exceptionally long, coarse, facial vibrissae of aquatic mammals such as water opossums, water shrews, otters, and pinnipeds respond to currents made by prey or other objects moving through water. Caudal vibrissae may test the security of a support or detect organisms approaching from the rear.

Facial vibrissae in otherwise naked newborn animals may help them find the mammary glands. Dependence on the tactile sense may be vital in a newborn with sight, smell, and possibly other senses latent. Head probing, rubbing, and nuzzling by suckling young in search of a teat has been observed in many mammals including primates. The inability of newborn humans to find the nipple may be correlated with the absence of mystacials. Contact between the facial vibrissae of suckling nonhuman young and the skin surrounding the nipple may also stimulate the mammary glands, or perhaps, soothe the secreting tissue. It is difficult to assign other functions to the tactile vibrissae of newborns, particularly when they are the first hairs to develop.

Vibrissae in adults may be important in stimulating the reproductive organs. Contact between the perineal vibrissae of the receptive female and mystacial vibrissae of the scenting male excites both animals. In the porcupine, according to Po-Chedley and Shadle (1955, p. 91), stimulation of the circumvaginal hairs during precoital play increases sexual arousal. Stimulation of the hairs also orients the female into postures which guide and facilitate entry of the penis into the vagina. Beach (1942, p. 205) has shown experimentally that eliminating any two of the senses of olfaction, vision, or cutaneous sensitivity greatly reduces the probability of copulation in sexually experienced rats and prevents it entirely in inexperienced rats.

Primate scent glands are associated with follicles of certain vibrissae, particularly gular, interramal, sternal, genital, and ulnar-carpal. The vibrissae may stimulate secretions by the glands and, judged by specimens examined, spreading the viscous fluid. The stimulating effect of sniffing by an individual of one sex of markings left by the other is probably heightened when facial vibrissae are brought into play.

The gular and pectoral vibrissalike spines are also associated with cutaneous glands and may function in the same manner as the tactile vibrissae. The spines may possibly guide newborns to the mammae, but where these hairs occur they are equally developed in both sexes.

Functions attributed to primate vibrissae are largely inferential. In many cases, vibrissae are no less developed in the diurnal callitrichids than they are in the nocturnal prosimians, and they are no less developed in aquatic, fossorial, and terrestrial mammals than they are in arboreal mammals. There may be no single or universal explanation for the number, kinds, and disposition of vibrissae in mammals of the same phylogeny but disparate habits or in mammals with similar habits but different origins. It is generally agreed, however, that in mammals generally, as in callitrichids, tactile vibrissae are primitive organs and the more primitive the species, the greater the number and variety and the wider the distribution of its vibrissae.

Survival Value

The survival value of vibrissae was tested in California by Pearson (1962, p. 105) on the harvest mouse, *Reithrodontomys megalotis,* and the meadow mouse, *Microtus californicus.* The mice, all nearly or quite adult, were trapped during August and September and marked with metal tags. Their vibrissae were removed from one or both sides or left intact. The mice were then released at the place of capture. Three to six weeks later, 121 of 243 tagged harvest mice and 70 of 200 tagged meadow mice were recaptured. No significant difference was evident in the number and health of recovered individuals of the groups that were unclipped, clipped on one side, or clipped on both sides. To test predation on the experimental mice, Pearson examined carnivore fecal droppings collected near the trap lines. Six metal tags were recovered from the scats. Five were of unclipped mice and one of a mouse clipped on one side. The investigator concluded that his experiments failed to show the survival value of facial vibrissae.

Whisker clipping inflicts a minor injury from which mice can normally recover completely. Predictably, the temporary mutilation would have little or no effect on movements of animals in their home territory, assuming all other sense organs remained intact and functional. On the other hand, if facial vibrissae are of greatest survival value to suckling and mating individuals, at least in certain species, as described above, their efficiency can be tested in the laboratory.

10 Tegumentary Colors

Functions

The primitive function of tegumentary color in mammals is concealment. It persists as the primary function in most species, particularly those with agouti-patterned pelage. Among progressive mammals relatively free of predation, or adjusted to it as a minor function of their economy, the agouti pattern tends to break down and color becomes less concealing and more attractive or neutral. The pigment is lost first in the less exposed skin and hairs such as those of underparts, axillae, and underfur. In the more socially or physically advanced animals, color loses its primary function of concealment and serves mainly for sexual display or interspecific recognition. With localized loss of hair and increasing exposure of depigmented skin, particularly in primates, hemoglobins show through as secondary display colors. Loss of melanin and ascendance of hemoglobin in mammals mark the beginning of the end of pigmentary color as a significant external character. In man, cosmetics are used to replace, supplement, obscure, or enhance the effects of natural melanins.

Classification

Animal colors are classified as structural or pigmentary. Both kinds are present in mammals, but only those visible at the surface of the body in daylight are listed and briefly described here. For detailed accounts and bibliographies dealing with the biochemistry of animal pigments and the structure and function of pigment-producing cells, see D. L. Fox (1953), Montagna and Ellis (1958*a*), H. M. Fox and Vevers (1960), Billingham and Silvers (1960), Montagna (1962), Lyne and Short (1965), and Wolfe and Coleman (1966).

Structural Colors

Structural colors are caused by *interference, diffraction,* or *scattering* of light by the physical qualities of the tegument. *Interference* colors are iridescent. They appear in the fresh coat, particularly the guard hairs, of many mammals. The colors are usually weak and elusive, and the fur of moles, especially the golden mole (*Chrysochloris*) and the platypus (*Ornithorhynchus*), provides some of the best examples. *Diffraction* colors are rare in animals and may be absent in mammals although the iridescent quality of "eye shine" in nocturnal species may be ascribed to diffraction as much as to interference. The color is reflected by the pigmented tapetum lucidum of the choroid in the back of the eye. Colors produced by *scattered* light, known as *Tyndall scattering,* are not iridescent or altered with the angle of vision. Scattering of the shorter light waves by minute particles, often melanin granules, produces the blue eye color in humans. For the same reason, dark melanin pigments of black hair roots at the base of naked or closely shaven skin appear blue when seen through the epidermis. The brilliant blue of the mandrill's face and buttocks is also due to Tyndall scattering. Purple markings are simply the same blue associated with the red blood in the skin. Whiteness of hair is due to reflection of light from air spaces in the translucent shaft. The apposition of white or unpigmented and black or pigmented areas, as in banded hairs, makes the hairs appear gray.

Pigmentary Colors

Pigmentary colors are synthesized by animals or derived from plant foods. The pigments visible in mammalian teguments are melanins, hemoglobin, possibly carotenoids, and some iron compounds.

Melanins are the blackish-brown pigment granules or *eumelanin* in skin and hair (and feathers) and the reddish brown yellow pigment or *pheomelanin* in hair (and feathers) and the skin of some cetaceans. The intensities of both pigments, or pigmentary tones of each scale, vary from blackish or reddish brown to nearly white. Melanins are synthesized in melanosomes or the cellular organilles within the melanocytes of the skin and the hair bulbs. Melanocytes are differentiated from melanoblasts of neural crest origin.

Eumelanin granules are formed by the enzymatic oxidation of tyrosine or dopa under the catalytic influence of tyrosinase. *Pheomelanin,* according to Prota and Nicolaus (1967, p. 328), is formed by a deviation of the eumelanin pathway involving interaction of cysteine with dopaquinones produced by the enzymatic oxidation of tyrosine.

Two pheomelanins found in hair and feathers and analysed by Prota and Nicolaus (1967) and Prota (1972) are not specifically distinguished in the present account. They are defined as follows.

Gallopheomelanins: Pheomelanic pigments of high molecular weight (2,000–50,000); soluble in alkalies but not acids.

Trichosiderins. Pheomelanin pigments originally believed to contain iron; soluble in dilute acids and alkalies. The red in human hair and the red and violet seen in feathers are artifacts that arise from yellow orange pigments during acid extraction.

Eumelanin and pheomelanin forming melanocytes are present in hair bulbs, but the metabolic pathway of each type is independently controlled in each melanocyte, each hair, each pilary field.

The color or color pattern of hair is determined by deposition of (*a*) one pigmentary type only in varying concentrations, (*b*) both types deposited in alternating cycles or bands, the eumelanin first, to form the agouti pattern, or (*c*) by neither pigment. In the last instance the hair is colorless. Each follicular melanocyte can synthesize both eumelanin and pheomelanin in the production of agouti hairs. According to Silvers (1965, p. 651), the pattern in laboratory mice and rats is determined by the operation of agouti-locus alleles in the hair follicle rather than in the melanocytes.

Differences in skin or hair color depend less on the density of melanocytes than on the production of melanins. Wholly white or unpigmented integument may contain as many melanocytes as, or even more than the melanistic integument of another part of the organism or of a dark race or species. Inability to form melanin is caused by the absence of the enzyme tyrosinase or, as indicated by Chian and Wilgram (1967, p. 198), by the presence of a tyrosinase inhibitor. Graying of hair during senescence results from a gradual loss of tyrosinase activity in the hair bulb.

The distribution of melanotic melanocytes over the general body area in representatives of 48 species of primates studied by Machida and Perkins (1967, p. 50) were arranged in four categories. These groups, slightly reorganized, are listed below. Bare display areas such as genitalia, eyelids, nose, lips, ears, and so forth, are not reckoned with the "general body area."

1. Epidermis only
   - *a.* Heavily pigmented: *Lemur catta, Saguinus oedipus oedipus, Alouatta caraya, Ateles paniscus, Lagothrix lagothricha, Macaca niger, Papio cynocephalus, Presbytis pyrrhus, Pan satyrus, Gorilla gorilla.*
   - *b.* Lightly to moderately pigmented: *Lemur macaco, Saguinus oedipus geoffroyi, Cebus apella, Hylobates hoolock.*
2. Dermis only
   - *a.* Distribution general: *Cacajao calvus rubicundus, Aotus trivirgatus, Saimiri sciureus, Macaca mulatta, Papio sphinx, Papio anubis, Cercopithecus neglectus, C. mona, C. aethiops, C. mitis, Cercocebus atys, C. fuliginosus.*
   - *b.* Restricted to pilosebaceous units: *Lemur mongoz, L. fulvus, Presbytis entellus.*
3. Epidermis and dermis pigmented: *Saguinus nigricollis, Saguinus midas midas, Pithecia monachus, Pongo pygmaeus.*
4. Epidermis and dermis unpigmented: *Tarsius syrichta, Loris tardigradus, Nycticebus coucang, Arctocebus calabarensis, Perodicticus potto, Galago senegalensis, G. crassicaudata, G. minutus, Cebus capucinus, Macaca irus, M. nemistrina, M. speciosa, M. fuscata, M. silenus, Erythrocebus patas.*

Machida and Perkins (1967, p. 57) noted that when the epidermis is pigmented the dermis is usually free of melanin-producing melanocytes, and vice versa. They concluded that there is "a general trend toward greater epidermal pigmentation, largely absent in the lower forms; the number of melanotic melanocytes increases concomitant with phylogenetic ascension."

The contrary is more likely true. Mammals inherited melanin-producing melanocytes through an unbroken line of descent beginning with their chordate ancestors, if not earlier. Mammalian melanins were lost where they are absent and have been retained, not secondarily regained, where they are present. The tarsier and strepsirhines listed in "4" above may be of ancient lineage, but the living species are the end products and among the most highly specialized members of their order. The absence of pigment in their skin is a degenerate and not a primitive character.

Carotenoids, formerly called lipochromes, are the red, orange, and yellow pigments found in plants and in many animals. The pigments are synthesized by plants only. Animals derive their carotenoids from plant food or herbivorous prey. The colors are apparent in yellow flowers and fruits. They also occur in green parts of plants but are masked by chlorophyll. Animal carotenoids appear in egg yolks, red and yellow feathers and bird beaks, various parts of amphibians, fishes, lobsters, crabs, shrimps, and so forth. The yellow coloring of fat, plasma, and sera in mammals is due to carotenoids but the red-yellow tones in hair are melanins, not carotenoids.

Hemoglobin, the coloring matter of blood and flesh, gives a pinkish color to the unpigmented epidermis and shows through the fine naked skin of the newborn. It forms the red in the uacari's face, the baboon's buttocks, the mandrill's muzzle, and the gelada's chest patch, and the pink lips, eyelids, tongue, inner or auditory surface of the ear pinna, external genitalia, and sexual skin of many mammals. The hemoglobin flushing (and blushing) of face, neck, and other exposed parts is often under nervous control.

Inorganic iron compounds produce the brown, red, orange, or yellow color on the labial surface of the incisors in most rodents. Black molars in some rodents (beaver) and the reddish dental crowns of many kinds of shrews also contain iron.

Riboflavin, a yellow substance and a vitamin of the B_2 complex, does not contribute directly to superficial coloration of animals. It is interesting to note, nevertheless, that according to Pirie (1959, p. 985), the yellow tapetum lucidum of the African bushbaby (*Galago crassicaudatus*) is made of crystalline riboflavin. The eye shine or light reflected from the tapetum lucidum in galagos is a brilliant gold.

Agouti Hair and Coat Patterns

The most primitive and stable color pattern of cover hairs is the multibanded or agouti.[1] It is characterized by

[1] This term derives from the vernacular name of a large tropical American harelike caviomorph rodent, the aguti, *Dasyprocta leporina* Linnaeus, 1758 (antedates *aguti* Linnaeus, 1766), with a pronounced "agouti" hair pattern.

a series of alternating blackish (black brown or eumelanin) and reddish (red yellow or pheomelanin) annulations (figs. III.13, 14). The precise number of bands in the primitive pattern is problematic. As a rule, the basal band and the unworn or unbroken tip of fully grown and unmodified agouti hairs are blackish or dark. The number of dark and reddish or pale bands between dark tip and base, however, varies according to species, race, individual, and length and site of the hair. In some races of the aguti animal, for example, the long erectile rump hairs may have as many as 8 dark and 7 pale bands, while shorter, apparently full-grown unbroken hairs of the same trichogenetic field may have as few as 4 dark and 3 pale bands. Typical middorsal hairs in the same samples show 3 dark and 2 pale rings (cf. fig. III.13). In red-rumped agutis of the Guianas, the banding pattern of the most elongate rump hairs is obsolete or obsolescent because of dilution or elimination of the dark annulations. Anteriad,

Fig. III.13. Diagrams of randomly selected hairs plucked from 7 chromogenetic fields of skins representing *Cebuella pygmaea, Callithrix jacchus penicillata, Saguinus fuscicollis, Leontopithecus rosalia,* and *Callimico goeldii.* Hair patterns range from agouti (serially banded) to monochromic. Pheomelanin (red-yellow) hairs or bands are shown stippled to unstippled (white); eumelanin (black-brown) hairs or bands are shown black (black to brown), also stippled (drab to gray), and unstippled (white) but labeled *eu* to distinguish them from similarly stippled unlabeled pheomelanin zones.

on the back and elsewhere, the agouti pattern is clearly defined, with the 3–2 band pattern dominant.

Samples of fully developed unmodified cover hairs from the dorsum of many other kinds of rodents and of other mammals, especially marsupials, insectivores, primates, and carnivores, indicate that the complex 3–2 pattern is widely distributed or typical, but not certainly primitive, in living mammals (fig. III.13). Whether cover hairs evolved with a banded or monochromic pattern will probably never be known. Extraordinary increase in hair length may result in a corresponding increase in the number of contrasting color bands as in the erectile rump hairs of the aguti. As a rule, however, specialization by increase or decrease in hair length, or by increase or decrease in the intensities of pigments, results in a uniformly colored or colorless hair.

The agouti, or "ticked," coat pattern, like the individual hair pattern, appears to be most primitive in living mammals and, in its typical form, most concealing in the greatest variety of habitat types.

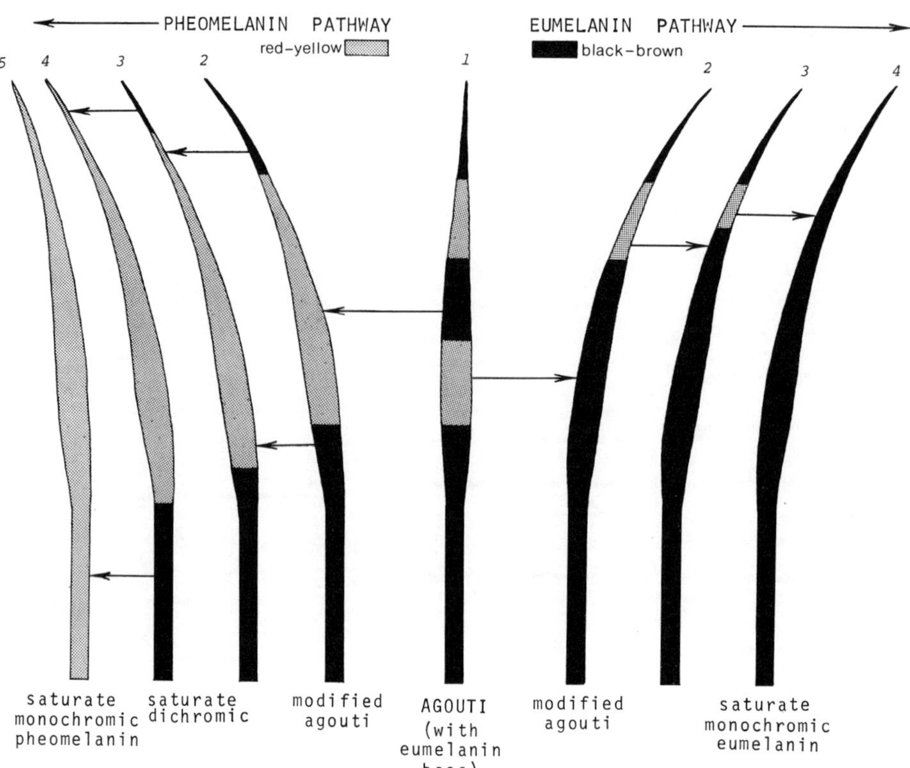

Fig. III.14. Saturation of agouti cover-hair through eumelanin (black-brown) and pheomelanin (red-yellow) pathways. In model shown, only terminal portion of hair is banded and subject to saturation. The basal portion is saturate melanin. Two or three pheomelanin bands separated by eumelanin bands is regarded as the primitive pattern. Saturation may proceed stepwise in either direction as shown here, or may leap from agouti to stage *3, 4,* or *5.* The basal portion of the hair is chromogenetically independent. It is subject to saturation like the terminal portion or, if saturate pheomelanin or saturate eumelanin, it is subject to bleaching. The rate of change is usually uneven, but the direction of change is irreversible. (Adapted from Hershkovitz 1968.)

Chromogenetic Fields

Each distinctively pigmented part of a hair, and each distinctively pigmented area of the coat, is an active chromogenetic field. The color pattern of the mammalian superficies is determined by the arrangement of the color fields of its fur, exposed skin, and iris. The entire coat may make up a single color field, or it may be broken into many fields in the form of bands, stripes, spots, rings, streaks, blazes, stars. Bare areas are frequently brightly or contrastingly colored. All chromogenetic fields are interrelated and respond to the presumed master control system that determines the overall color pattern of the organism of a given sex at any chronological age, physiological condition, season, and locality.

Hair color patterns of individual hairs are determined by the distribution of pigment granules within the hair shaft. The two basic pigmentary colors alternating in three or more bands produce the agouti pattern. Hairs with terminal and basal portions contrastingly colored are *dichromic.* Hairs of one hue with little or no contrast between terminal and basal portions are *monochromic* (fig. III.14).

Cover hairs, (fig. III.9) by virtue of their general distribution, abundance, and wide range of color, are at once the most conspicuous and most concealing features of nearly all mammals. Unless otherwise specified, all descriptions of hair or coat color in the text are based on cover hairs. The projecting guard hairs or sensory hairs are normally inconspicuously monochromic. Shorter hair types concealed by the cover hairs make no contribution to the definitive color pattern.

Coat color patterns are bilaterally symmetrical but with the usual minor irregularities and discrepancies present in other bilaterally symmetrical characters. Gross deviations from symmetry are commonplace in domestic, artificially selected, or confined animals, but unusual in wild or free-ranging individuals. Maximum bilateral asymmetry in domestic or wild stock occurs in the piebald and tortoise patterns and in terminal stages of bleaching. All finally resolve into the uniformity of the achromatic hair or coat.

The number and arrangement of active chromogenetic fields in fresh adult pelage of any individual, race, or species are reflected in the number of visible color bands of the hair and the number and disposition of contrastingly colored areas of the coat. Thus the monochromic hair of a melanistic or an albino fox squirrel exhibits a single chromogenetic field. The entire coat of the melanistic or albino fox squirrel likewise displays a single field. In contrast, the individual agouti hair of the primitive or variegated form of the fox squirrel contains five active chromogenetic fields of three eumelanin and two pheomelanin bands. The coat is also highly diversified. The buffy underparts, sometimes with white spotting, the orange lateral line, pale postauricular patches, black-tipped muzzle, and all other contrastingly colored areas are each a chromogenetic field. Most zebras show only two colors, with each hair a single field of blackish or white. Each stripe of the coat, however, black or white, represents a distinct chromogenetic field. The unstriped ancestral coat was black. In a given coat, pigment normally is lost, not gained.

The arrangement of chromogenetic fields in fresh adult pelage is often diagnostic of the species or species group, as in zebras and almost any other strikingly marked animal. Minor variations in the pattern or color of active chromogenetic fields often distinguish species, races, and populations.

Color and Molt Patterns

Pelage replacement and follicular melanogenesis are interrelated and synchronic. Each distinct pilary coat, however, is independent of the one it succeeds or precedes, and color differences between individual coats are often of the same magnitude as those distinguishing races or species. The differences may be confined to one or a few chromogenetic fields or generally distributed throughout the coat. The juvenal color pattern may be more primitive than that of the adult, as in *Callithrix jacchus* (fig. IX.21), or it may be more advanced in whole or in part. The spotted coat pattern of fawns is metachromically progressive compared with that of adult deer. Among gibbons (*Hylobates* spp.), langurs (*Presbytis*), howlers (*Alouatta caraya*), and sakis (*Pithecia pithecia*), the young of either sex are consistently paler, or more advanced chromatically, than their blackish fathers. Young males of these primates molt again into the dark adult color. The adult condition here is not a regression or reversal of the evolutionary processes. The change is from one discrete coat to another, each with its own evolutionary history and independently controlled color and color pattern.

Molt is sometimes explained as a seasonal change in pelage color. The inert pigment granules in dead hairs of one pelage cannot, of course, change or transmute into the color of the new replacement pelage. In snowshoe hares, for example, the whitish "color" of the winter pelage evolved rapidly because of rigorous selection for concealment in snow-covered terrain. The brownish color of the independently controlled summer pelage also evolves in the same direction, but at a rate so slow that change is practically imperceptible.

Sexual Dichromatism

Primate sexual dichromatism, a product of sexual selection, is a fixed, gross coat color difference between adult males and females of a species or race. Adult sexual dichromatism occurs in *Lemur macaco, Pithecia pithecia, Alouatta caraya,* and the gibbons *Hylobates concolor, H. hoolock,* and *H. pileatus.* In some species cyclical or physiological changes in color may also be sexually dichromatic. Such differences, usually cutaneous, include the normal pigmentary ones enhanced by the addition of hemoglobin red showing through periodically tumescent skin. Secretions of skin glands may also add color.

A second and rare type of cyclical change involves the sexually mature female patas monkey who undergoes striking alterations in pelage color during the reproductive cycle. From mid- to late gestation the dark pelage of nose and temporal and superciliary regions is replaced by a pure white pelage; the facial skin, however, becomes more melanized. In the postpartum molt, the usual adult pattern of blackish nose, blackish supercialiary and temporal regions, and pale brown skin is restored. The pregnancy color pattern signals the female's condition to conspecifics, and incidentally signaled it to Loy (1975), who described this phenomenon for the first time.

In species where sexual dichromatism is fixed, the adult male is dominantly eumelanic, usually with hairs mostly or entirely unbanded, while the adult female is dominantly pheomelanic, with hairs often banded. Young of both sexes resemble the adult female in coloration. Upon approaching maturity, subadult males molt to their dark adult pelage. Subadult females also molt, but the most notable change is in pelage texture rather than color. According to Groves (1972, p. 18), all juvenals of *Hylobates concolor* and *H. hoolock* are pale and molt to a dark pelage the first year. At maturity, females molt to the pale adult pelage of their sex, while males acquire the new black adult coat of their sex.

Few examples of partial or incipient sexual dichromatism come to mind (e.g., *Lemur mongoz, Cebus albifrons* [Hershkovitz 1949, p. 353]), but in none does the primitive agouti pattern separate into more or less saturate eumelanin in adult males and dominantly pheomelanin in adult females, as in the preceding cases. Ontogenetic polychromism in *Presbytis* (cf. Napier and Napier 1967, p. 276), juvenal and adult polychromism in gibbons (Fooden 1969*b;* Groves 1972), and the cyclical molt and change in facial coloration of pregnant patas monkeys suggest evolutionary pathways to fixed sexual dichromatism, possibly through sexual selection.

11 Metachromism
Principle of Evolutionary Change in Tegumentary Colors

The principle of metachromism (Hershkovitz 1968; 1970*e*) holds that evolutionary change in hair, skin, and eye melanins is neither random nor opportunistic but follows an orderly and irreversible sequence of degeneration that ends in loss of pigment or white. Color of individual hairs, pilary fields, or the entire coat changes from the agouti pattern, characterized by alternating blackish brown and reddish bands on the terminal half of the hair to either uniformly blackish brown (eumelanin) or uniformly reddish (pheomelanin) by a process called *saturation*.

Each monochromic hair (or its monochromic terminal half) or pilary field then fades or bleaches, the one along the eumelanin pathway (brown→drab→gray) to white, or colorless, the other along the pheomelanin pathway (reddish→orange→yellow→cream) to white. Each blackish or reddish band of the agouti hair may also bleach independently before, or without intervention of, the saturation process as it affects the entire hair. This dilution and disappearance of pigmentary colors is termed *bleaching*. Color of skin and eye follows the eumelanin pathway, but dilution and disappearance of their pigment is arbitrarily distinguished by the term *depigmentation*.

The bleaching process may switch from the eumelanin to the pheomelanin pathway, and perhaps in some cases both pathways mix. In all events, the direction of change is toward reduction and elimination of pigment. The number of apparent steps from agouti or saturate to white or colorless varies from one to a multitude of intermediate tones in the chromatic run of either pathway.

Metachromism applies to all species of mammals whether terrestrial, arboreal, subterranean, aquatic, or volant, and to all color changes in hair and skin whether ontogenetic, phylogenetic, geographic, seasonal, sexual, or individual. Metachromism also applies to birds and possibly to the melanins of tegumentary structures of other organisms. In feathers, the juxtaposition of eumelanic and pheomelanic barbs and barbules gives an olivaceous effect. This is equivalent to the primitive concealing agouti pattern of hair. Saturation and bleaching follow in feathers as in hairs. The brilliant structural colors (cf. p. 89) of feathers are not to be confused with the pigmentary melanins.

The evolutionary rate of metachromism is controlled by environmental and genetic forces which may accelerate, retard, or terminate metachromic processes or hold them in dynamic equilibrium, but cannot alter, reverse, or deflect them from their course.

All features of metachromism are in accord with what is known of tegumentary structures, melanogenesis, hair growth, and individual and geographic variation in color. Research into controls exerted by endocrine and skin glands on the structure, operation, and multiple effects of "color" genes, and on the side effects of noncolor genes, may throw light on the biochemistry of metachromism. Present ignorance of the biomechanics of metachromic programming, however, does not diminish the value of the phenomenon as a tool for describing mammalian colors, as a base for reconstructing phylogenies and geographic dispersal routes founded on changes in color and color pattern, and for evaluating chromatic changes resulting from experimental matings.

The metabolic pathways described in broad outline above and in the following are deduced from phenotypes and from published information on hair growth and melanization (cf. especially Wright 1917*a, b;* Fitzpatrick, Brunet, and Kukita 1958; Billingham and Silvers 1960; Montagna 1962).

Metachromic Processes

Saturation

This is the process of change from the primitive agouti pattern of a hair, pilary field, or entire coat to a completely blackish (eumelanin) or completely reddish (pheomelanin) color (fig. III.14).

Saturation of an agouti hair to a completely blackish one occurs through switching from deposition of pheomelanin granules to the deposition of eumelanin granules in the growing hair. In a typical agouti hair with 3 dark and 2 pale bands, the proximal (median) pale band is eliminated first. The resulting modified agouti hair pattern of 2 dark bands and 1 pale band produces a pilary field of transverse annulations (as in the banded tails or backs of some animals), or a fine ticking. Elimination of the remaining (subterminal) pale band results in a wholly blackish hair or pilary field. The same phenotypes can also be achieved abruptly by complete failure of pheomel-

BLEACHING PROCESS

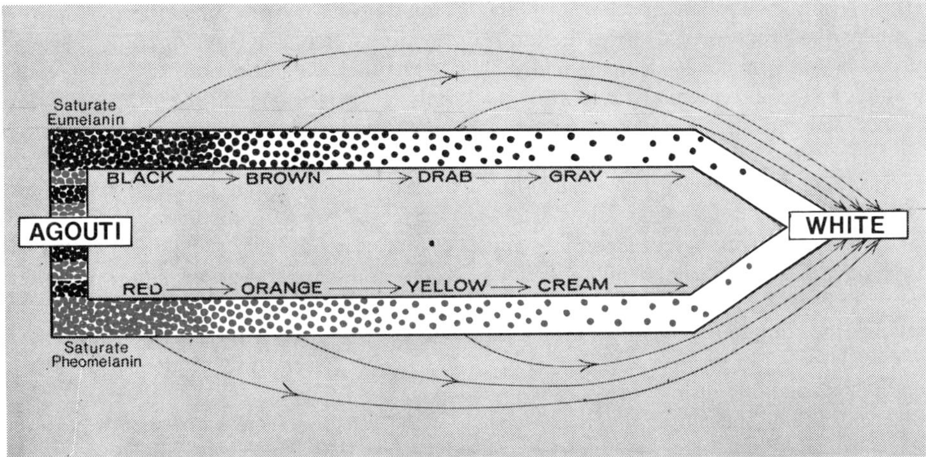

Fig. III.15. Bleaching from saturate eumelanin and saturate pheomelanin fields to white or colorless. Gradual reduction in the amount of pigment deposited in the growing hair results in apparent change from blackish through brown, drab gray to white or colorless in the eumelanin pathway, and from reddish through orange, yellow, cream to white in the pheomelanin pathway. A sudden suppression of pigment production or deposition results in a leap from a pigmented to the unpigmented state (fine curved arrows). Switching from the eumelanin to the pheomelanin pathway occurs in saturation but not in bleaching. (Modified from Hershkovitz 1968.)

anin synthesis or deposition and uninterrupted deposition of eumelanin instead throughout hair growth.[1]

The uniformly reddish or reddish brown cover hair evolves from the agouti hair in the same manner except that pheomelanin granules are deposited in the growing hair. The middle blackish band is usually eliminated first, the basal band next, the dark tip last; or all blackish bands may be eliminated at once by failure of eumelanin deposition by the melanocyte. The *pheomelanotic modified agouti* pattern of 2 dark bands and 1 broad pale band produces a marbled or a transversely striated or banded pattern in the coat.[2] The primitively agouti hairs of the under or inner parts, particularly of the belly, tend to become pheomelanotic rather than eumelanotic.

In the case of failure of either eumelanin or pheomelanin synthesis, a persistent automatic switching mechanism for pigment deposition produces an agouti hair pattern of alternating pigmented and colorless bands. This is not to be confused with saturation, which involves partial or complete failure of the switching mechanism itself.

Bleaching

Bleaching is a process of reduction and elimination of pigment deposition in hair (fig. III.15). Saturate blackish brown (eumelanic) cover hairs (and primitively blackish brown guard hairs) bleach through progressively paler tones of brown, drab, and gray to white. Saturate reddish (pheomelanic) hairs bleach through tones of red,[3] orange, yellow, and cream to white. Bleaching may begin with either the growing terminal or growing basal half of the hair and progress a tone or more before acting on the other growing half of the hair.

Bleaching may also act directly on the unmodified agouti hair and produce a dilute agouti pattern, or it may affect only the saturate portion of a modified agouti hair or pilary field while the remaining portion of the field is still in the process of saturation. Simultaneous bleaching and saturation in adjacent chromogenetic fields produce the interesting and relatively simple zebra, skunk, and guereza patterns, and myriad others of greater or lesser complexity.

Depigmentation

Depigmentation is the dilution and loss of eumelanin in skin and iris of the eye. The exposed skin of primitive and thinly haired mammals was probably well pigmented throughout. Many cetaceans retain the saturate skin but all have lost the pelage except for a few bristles. With increasing hairiness among primarily terrestrial mammals, pigment-producing melanocytes of the skin concentrated in the proliferating hair follicles. As a result, most areas of thickly clothed skin in modern mammals are weakly pigmented or unpigmented. Melanocytes, however, may be as numerous in unpigmented as in pigmented skin, but melanogenesis occurs only in the latter. Galbraith (1964, p. 87) suggested that follicular substrate common to hair growth and melanogenesis is drained into the production of hair.

Nearly or entirely bare and exposed parts such as rhinarium, ears, volar surfaces, claws, tail, and external genitalia usually remain pigmented in the more generalized races or populations of primarily terrestrial mammals. These parts, however, are still subject to depigmentation. In polymorphic species, less densely pigmented populations are derived from more densely pigmented ones, all other things equal.

Depigmentation, like bleaching, may be general, or localized and patterned. General depigmentation is often spotty or blotchy, usually asymmetrical, and sometimes

[1] Bronson and Clark (1966, p. 1349) caused saturation of the coat of prairie field mice, *Peromyscus maniculatus bairdi*, by adrenalectomy.

[2] The "wide-banded" hair pattern of the chinchilla rabbit described and figured by Sawin (1932, p. 46, fig. 29) appears to be a pheomelanotic modified agouti. The character behaves as a typical Mendelian recessive.

[3] Most intense of the pheomelanin series is a brownish or mahogany "red." Primary red is not seen in mammals except as hemochrome in the blood.

vitiligo-like, especially along the field's periphery. In naked mammals such as man and certain cetaceans, hippopotami, and others, the progress of depigmentation is usually general except for completely depigmented display areas such as lips and exposed genitalia, according to species. A patterned depigmentation is characteristic of many species of Delphinidae. In nonhuman primates it may be expressed on face and volar surfaces. Tamarins of the *Saguinus mystax* group, the Zanzibar colobus, *Colobus badius kirki,* and many species of *Presbytis* and *Cercopithecus* exhibit a patterned facial depigmentation. Tail and ears are also frequently patterned. The evenly bicolored scaly tail of the common opossum and relatives and of some rodents (e.g., *Tylomys*) is striking. Other exposed melanotic or amelanotic display organs such as external genitalia and ischial callosities, which contrast sharply with the color of surrounding skin or fur, are additional examples of patterned depigmentation.

Black or dark brown skin is said to be more heat absorbent than white but radiates no more heat (Barnicot 1957; Billingham and Silvers 1960). The same authors have also asserted that the thick stratum corneum, not the deep-lying melanin, is the primary shield against sunburn. Therefore white-skinned mammals or their depigmented parts should be best adapted to hot and exposed habitats and black-skinned mammals or their dark parts to cool situations (but see p. 98). Any such relationship between mammals and their environments, however, appears to be incidental or accidental.

The normal or characteristic color of the skin in general or any portion of it is measured on the protected or nonirradiated surface. Individual variation in the amount of dermal melanization in response to solar (or equivalent) radiation is apparently least in extremely saturate or wholly depigmented areas and greatest in moderately pigmented areas. Darkening of the skin, or tanning, following irradiation may be the effect of either direct oxidation of melanin already present in the skin or increased melanin production.

The normally unpigmented bare skin of primates becomes flushed with blood on exposure to strong sunlight. The bright hemoglobin pigmentation may provide some protection against burning. In many cases, however the red color of the face, as in the uacari (*Cacajao calvus*), or ears and genitalia, as in *Callithrix argentata,* serves for display.

Irreversibility of Metachromic Processes

Metachromic processes involve degeneration and loss of the capacity to produce one or both melanins. Loss of a trait or trait complex in the species is irreversible.

The degenerative nature of color changes is treated at length in Searle's (1968) chapter "Comparative Pathology of Coat Color Mutants." Alleles described as having adverse pleiotropic effects are invariably correlated with dilute to colorless (albino) chromogenetic fields ("spotting"). The more advanced the dilution, the more severe or accumulated the pathological effects. In the heterozygote, fertility and viability are always adversely affected. In the homozygote, the effect of albinism is lethal. To be sure, all genes involved in dilutions are not demonstrably deleterious, but in mammals the end product of bleaching, that is, pure albinism, whatever the cause, is almost universally lethal. This terminal state alone effectively precludes the possibility of reversal in the direction of sequence of color change.

The foregoing does not say that irreversibility operates only toward the end of the chromatic scale. The primitive agouti pattern, once lost in the wild form of the species, is never regained. This applies to the entire coat (cf. human, horse, bears, panda, echidna, moles, elephant, mustelids, beaver, and many others) and to delimited chromogenetic fields (e.g., face, belly, tail, and blazes, spots, and stripes in various parts) in almost all mammals.

Misunderstanding or ignorance of metachromic processes may lead to false interpretations of irreversibility in the direction or sequence of color change. Some examples follow.

a. Transition from a structurally pale-appearing agouti hair to a dark uniformly saturate hair may be mistaken for a reversal of the bleaching process.

b. A structurally pale agouti hair may be (and commonly is) evaluated in the same terms as an apparently equally pale but uniformly colored (saturate) hair despite a real and significant difference in the respective patterns and evolutionary grades of the two hairs.

c. Natural selection may shift mean gene frequency for color intensity in peripheral populations.

d. Simulated regressions of metachromic and related processes may be obtained through hybridization of captive or domestic animals. Among callitrichids studied, cage-bred hybrids or closely related species or subspecies are metachromically intermediate between the parents. Hybrids of more distantly related species are slightly more primitive than either or both parents and resemble one parent more than the other. Offspring of most distantly related species are more primitive or generalized than either parent and resemble neither (cf. p. 444).

The principle of irreversibility is transcendental. There are shifts in gene frequencies expressed particularly, if not exclusively, in highly localized areas, secondary adaptations to habits or habitats once occupied by ancestral forms, and simulated "reversals" caused by the bringing together of two distinct genomes in hybridization. Turning evolution back upon itself, however, is a totally different matter. This feat involves not only the regression or cancellation of a single trait or character complex but also a backward march of the total organism in geological time and space. Evolutionary reversal means the repetition in reverse or unraveling of phylogenetic history. This has never happened. Mammals may revert to the sea as whales but not as fishes.

Geographic and Nonadaptive Variation

Geographic variation in callitrichid pelage color paterns reveals with unusual clarity the unidirection and irreversibility of metachromic processes irrespective of environmental factors.

Races of the upper Amazonian saddleback tamarin, *Saguinus fuscicollis* (pls. III, IV, figs. X.26, 27), exhibit virtually every nuance of mammalian coat colors from primitive agouti to practically colorless, or albinotic. Chromatic variation in a given race begins with agouti in some part, or chromogenetic field, of the pelage (fig. III.13). In successive steps, or races, the agouti color progresses to blackish or brown, or through tones of red, orange, yellow, and cream, to white (figs. III.14, 15). In other chromogenetic fields the sequence may be from agouti to blackish or dark brown as in the first, then through successively paler tones of brown to drab, gray, and white. Ultimately, all color fields fade into a more or less uniformly whitish coat. The chromatic succession is geographic and phylogenetic.

Rivers form the boundaries between each of the thirteen well-differentiated races of *Saguinus fuscicollis* (fig. III.16). Populations of different races within sight and

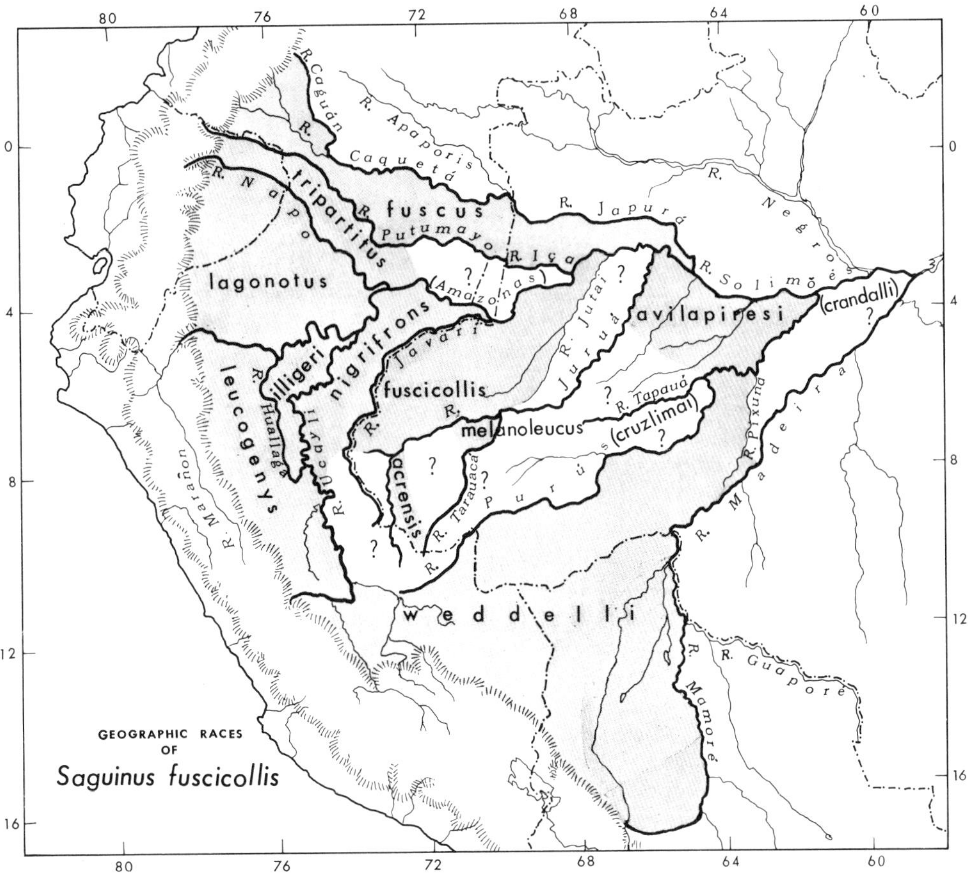

Fig. III.16. Geographic distribution of the subspecies of *Saguinus fuscicollis:* river boundaries between races boldly defined. (From Hershkovitz 1968.)

call of each other on opposite banks of meandering streams (fig. III.17) live within the same wide range of arboreal habitats. They are exposed to the same sun, moon, winds, rains, enemies, diseases, and competition. They consort with the same organisms, use the same kinds of shelters, and eat the same foods available on the same days. Each race, nevertheless, remains sharply defined by color or color pattern throughout a geographic range which may cover thousands of square miles (pl. III).

The moustached tamarin, *Saguinus mystax,* (cf. p. 684, fig. X.37, 38), with only three sharply defined chromatic races also separated by rivers, lives within a territory occupied by at least nine races of *Saguinus fuscicollis.*

Tegumentary differences between races and between related species living in separate parts of the same environment, as in the case of *Saguinus fuscicollis* and *S. mystax,* are apparently nonadaptive. Nevertheless, the same color and pelage characters may seem to be adaptive in other species where geographic variation is correlated with environmental differences.

The common eastern Brazilian marmoset, *Callithrix jacchus,* for example, occupies a greater and more diversified range than any other callitrichid. Differences between the five recognized races (p. 489, figs. IX.5, 7) are expressed in coloration and in the disposition and development of aural and circumaural tufts. Forms of tufts

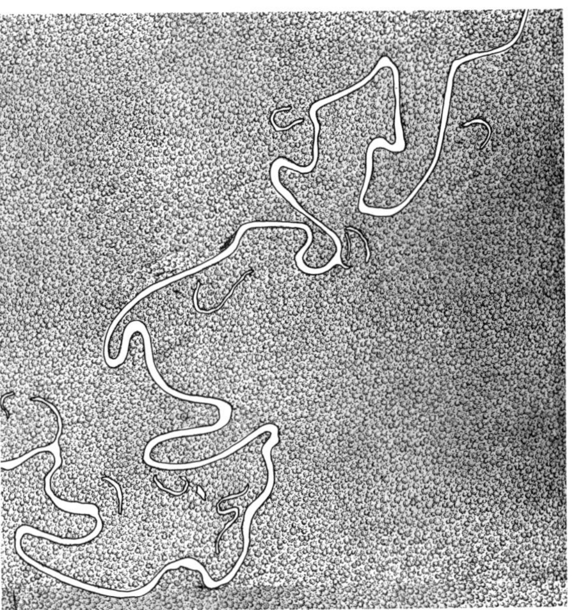

Fig. III.17. A meandering section of Rio Iaco, upper Rio Purús, in the Amazonian selva of Acre, Brazil. Area shown is about 8 kilometers (5 miles) square; adapted from a United States Air Force photograph. River bend cutoffs are mechanisms for passive transfer of arboreal or land-bound animal populations from one river bank to the opposite one.

vary independently of environment. Overall color differences, however, are for the most part clinal and roughly correlated with geographic variation in rainfall. Dark races of *Callithrix jacchus* live in areas of heavy rainfall and pale races in less humid zones, with the nearly white or albinotic populations occupying the driest part of the range.

The sympatric lion-tamarin, *Leontopithecus rosalia* (cf. p. 808, fig. XI.1), is represented by fragments of three races, with the darkest most inland and the less pigmented peripheral. The direction of geographic variation is not entirely coincident with the color gradient in *Callithrix jacchus.*

Geographic variation in the Amazonian *Callithrix argentata* is also clinal, but the relationship of coloration to humidity is precisely the reverse of that in *Callithrix jacchus* (fig. IX.36, 37). The southernmost and darkest race, the brown-furred, black-faced *Callithrix argentata melanura,* occupies the relatively cool, dry scrublands of the Mato Grosso, while the completely albinotic (and black-eyed) *C. a. leucippe* is confined to the hot, humid rain forests in a cul-de-sac above the mouth of the Rio Tapajóz.

The albinotic tamarin *Saguinus fuscicollis melanoleucus* (fig. X.34) sounds still another contradictory note. This and its parental form of the saddleback tamarin, *S. f. acrensis,* live in a small interfluvial basin where humidity and all other environmental factors are the same as in adjacent basins occupied by unmistakably dark races of the same species (fig. III.16).

Common to all five examples cited above is the fact that the greater the geographic separation or longer the reproductive isolation from the more primitive or more saturate-colored form of the species, the greater the loss of tegumentary pigment, irrespective of environment.

Sharing habitats with tamarins are their ecological equivalents among rodents, the so-called giant Amazonian squirrels (*Sciurus igniventris* and *S. spadiceus*). They are approximately the same size, as gaudily colored, live and eat in the same trees, and run and climb very much like tamarins. These squirrels also show the same trends in coloration, but because of their different social structure and greater mobility they exhibit a broader range of individual and local variation.

The primitive pygmy marmoset, *Cebuella pygmaea,* of the upper Amazonian valley, contrasts markedly with sympatric hairy-face tamarins. In addition to its minuscule size, its color is almost uniformly agouti throughout a geographic range occuped by nearly all thirteen races of *Saguinus fuscicollis.* Ecological equivalents of the pygmy marmoset are the primitive pygmy squirrels of the genera *Sciurillus* and *Microsciurus.* They are deceptively similar at first sight, vary as little in their agouti coloration, and inhabit a much more extensive and varied geographic range.

Stability of the agouti color pattern in pygmy marmosets and pygmy squirrels appears to be characteristic of most primitive or generalized species of mammals irrespective of habits or habitats. Breakdown of the agouti pattern of alternating blackish (eumelanin) and reddish or buffy (pheomelanin) bands, and the gradual or abrupt *saturation* of the hair with either of the two contrasting colors in any one chromogenetic field, is a character of progressive mammals generally.

My first assay at interpreting geographic variation in color based on the neotropical squirrel, *Sciurus granatensis* (1947, pp. 9, 31), also described metachromic sequences but without knowledge of the nature of the colors involved or the real direction of chromatic and geographic change. For example (1947, p. 33), it was thought that the smaller high Andean agouti-colored races were derived from the larger, varicolored lowland races when in fact the reverse is true. A re-revision of these squirrels in the light of metachromic processes would yield a more satisfactory and enduring taxonomy.

Depigmentation, or reduction or loss of skin and eye melanins, also varies metachromically irrespective of latitude, whatever may be said of the adaptive or nonadaptive value of the changes.

According to Blum (1961) and Loomis (1967, p. 501), the different skin colors in man regulate the transmission of ultraviolet radiation so that vitamin-D photosynthesis is maintained within physiological limits through the year at all latitudes. Thus, dark skin with its high filtering power prevails at low latitudes, where ultraviolet radiation is greatest, and pale or white skin with its greater absorption prevails at high latitudes where radiation is weak. The correlation between ultraviolet radiation and latitudes perhaps explains the survival of white-skinned northern European man, but it does not explain skin depigmentation per se. As successive waves of nomadic family groups or tribes of dark-skinned men first moved northward from equatorial Africa to the peripheries of Eurasia, isolation and inbreeding accelerated depigmentation and hypertrichy. Broken European topography promoted greater isolation between advancing colonists and an even faster rate of depigmentation through inbreeding. This greater depigmentation correlated with the discontinuous northward dispersal proved to be selectively advantageous (cf. Hulse 1974). Thus the more northern colonists encountered successively less solar radiation, but their advancing depigmentation permitted greater absorption of ultraviolet rays and vitamin-D synthesis.

Northern Asian topography favored a more rapid and continuous northward advance than the European. As a result, gene flow between advancing and settled colonists was almost certainly less disrupted and the depigmentation gradient more evenly progressive than among European races. American Indians are derived from the Asian migrants. The reversed direction of their dispersal from arctic to equatorial latitudes was not marked by an increase in pigmentation or a reversal of metachromism. On the contrary, depigmentation continued apace irrespective of geographic trends. South American Indians are paler than their North American relatives (Steggerda 1950), and lowland equatorial Indians are generally paler than the Andean populations from which many are derived.

The direction of geographic variation in cetacean color and color patterns must likewise be correlated with the trend from saturate to depigmented—this is to say, evolution from the oldest color pattern to the newest, or from patterns nearest the center of origin to those on the peripheries of the geographic range. Assays of analyses of their color patterns may indeed throw considerable light on the little actually known of cetacean evolution and dispersal. Mitchell (1970) derived the pattern of certain forms of *Stenella* and *Delphinus* from one he called "saddled." It appears, however, that this design is too far advanced metachromically to give rise to the supposed derivatives Mitchell described and figured as "striped," "crisscross" and "spotted." Depigmentation of the field anterior to the tail of the "saddled" model, for example, has gone beyond that of all derived patterns. Other chromogenetic fields of the "saddled" pattern are also more depigmented than the corresponding fields of one or more of the supposed derived patterns. In the present exercise, the pattern of the nearest ancestral form must have been eumelanistic except for grayish "flank patch" (quoted terms are Mitchell's), spotted "abdominal field," unpigmented gular field, and some minor markings to allow for individual variation. Dominantly blackish examples of *Lagenorhynchus* and *Cephalorhynchus* figured in the same work by Mitchell (1970) are instructive.

Perrin (1972) also distinguished a basic color pattern and its "component systems" or chromogenetic fields in the coloration of eastern Pacific *Stenella, Tursiops,* and *Delphinus.* He (1972, p. 992) was uncertain about a correlation between the direction of chromatic change and geography, but he indicated an increasing and expanding melanization in *Stenella* cf. *longirostris* and the reverse in *Stenella graffmani, Tursiops truncatus,* and *Delphinus* sp. In an earlier paper, Perrin (1970) regarded ontogenetic variation in the color pattern of *Stenella graffmani* as essentially incremental. He describes, however, a sequence of changing color patterns with overlap between those of successive age classes showing as mosaics. Evidently ontogenetic changes in cetacean skin color parallel ontogenetic pelage changes in furred animals.

Cetacean color or color pattern almost certainly serves primarily for recognition between members of the same species or population and the identification of strangers. Notwithstanding opinions to the contrary (cf. Mitchell 1970; Yablokov 1963) there is no convincing evidence that cetacean coloration is of selective advantage for anything else.

Chromatic adaptability and metachromism have been confused, but the first is never more than an incident of the second. When the right tegumentary color or color pattern evolves at the right time in the right place in the right animal, the color or coloration may be said to be adaptive. Examples of adaptive coloration are legion, especially among lower vertebrates and invertebrates, where structural colors are also brought into play. Examples of white mice in white sand and dark mice in black lava habitats of the Tularosa Basin, New Mexico, were cited by me elsewhere (1968, p. 574) but need not be repeated here.

What is emphasized is that metachromism deals with the evolution of any tegumentary melanin any place any time in any mammalian (or avian) species, whatever the interpretation of the relationship between coat color and ambience. The polar bear (*Ursus maritimus*), for example, evolved in complete isolation, probably from brown bear stock (*Ursus arctos*) (Kurtén 1968, p. 128). Its almost white color, a near end product of metachromic processes accelerated by inbreeding, has no demonstrable adaptive significance, although many of the animals spend most of their lives on ice packs and snowfields. The whitish pelage is not concealing during the long Arctic nights, and the bear cannot conceal the long shadow it casts in sunlight. The coat is always conspicuous on dark rocky shores and varicolored tundra where the bear also hunts and grazes. Prey animals guard against the moving predator, and a predator that cannot conceal its movements, odors, or sounds is not concealed by its color.

An explanation for survival value of a white fur coat in the Arctic offered by Lavigne and Øritsland (1974) seems plausible, but the full documentation had not been published at the time of this writing; however, I quote their observations.

> We recently obtained oblique photographs of polar bears on the tundra south of Churchill, Manitoba, Canada. The low visual contrast of a polar bear on snow is shown by black and white photography in the visible region of the electromagnetic spectrum. Ultraviolet photography, however, resulted in a black image of the polar bear against white snow. . . .
>
> This observation of "black" polar bears seems to have further implications. At present, the biological significance of white coat coloration in animals is not clear. Whiteness in arctic climates obviously provides camouflage for many birds and mammals [whether needed for survival or not—P. H.]. Theoretical analysis and quantitative measurements suggest that some white pelts transfer solar energy more efficiently to the skin than dark pelts. Thus white coloration may also play an important role in thermoregulation for a number of species including the white-coated pups of the harp seal (*Pagophilus groenlandicus*). The older view that dark pelts absorb solar radiation while white pelts reflect it and thus reduce radiation absorption is probably incorrect. Regardless, the fact that some white pelts absorb ultraviolet radiation while others, such as [that of] the arctic hare reflect it, suggests that any discussion of "life's color code" is incomplete without further consideration of the near ultraviolet component in solar radiation.

To the above must be added that it has already been indicated (Woodcock et al. 1955, in Daniels, Post, and Johnson 1972, p. 15) that long white fur may trap heat better than black fur "because solar radiation is converted to heat in or near the skin rather than at the surface of the fur where warming will lead to increased radiation loss."

Snowfields, like certain caves, are peripheral or dead-end habitats occupied by one or a few species of whitish animals. Albinotic animals, however, are metachromic dead ends in themselves and live in a diversity of habitats. Kermode's bear, a white race of black bear (*Ursus americanus*), is isolated in forests of British Columbia. The albinotic dolphins of muddy tropical stream bottoms and the white beluga whales of Arctic seas live in contrasting habitats. White bats, like white callitrichids, shelter and forage in the green canopies of tropical forests. The white mice of temperate-zone white-sand deserts, the white sheep of isolated Holarctic mountain tops, the white goats of the Rocky Mountains, the blond Norsemen, the albinotic San Blas tribesmen of Panamá, and many other dead-end white or whitish animals are all advanced examples of metachromism, whatever the explanations for their survival in habitats simultaneously occupied by other animals of every chromatic grade.

Social Selection

Social selection is the recognition of and preference for the parental (or foster parental) phenotype for social and sexual relations. Its development in the individual is based on an inherited behavior pattern reinforced by impressions, or imprinting, during a critical period of early life. Social selection may be the most important factor in the stabilization of metachromic processes among diurnal social mammals.

Imprinting as a conditioning factor in mate selection has been extensively studied and documented in birds but hardly more than observed in mammals. Much of the literature on birds has been summarized by Sluckin (1965). Beach (1965, p. 128), and Schein and Hale (in Beach 1965, p. 470), questioned or qualified the occurrence of imprinting among mammals, but their concept of the phenomenon seems to be based on sterotyped behavioral patterns of certain birds. Authenticated cases of sexual imprinting in mammals are indeed few and knowledge of them is based solely on experimental or domestic animals. Most of the cases were since compiled by Hinde (1970), Harper (1970), Immelmann (1972), Hess (1973), and Allyn (1974). Additional examples of sexual imprinting including some of particular importance to the idea of social selection, are summarized below.

Hand-reared treeshrews, *Tupaia longipes,* preferred the human hand to their own species in experiments conducted by Sorenson and Conaway (1966). From the time their eyes first opened, about two weeks after birth, hand-reared treeshrews would see the human hands that fed and fondled them. Basic behavior of the imprinted tupaias was the same as that of wild individuals, but they preferred human associations. Few of the tame treeshrews copulated with either tame or wild mates, and those that could would leave a consort during coitus to come to the human hand or chin and rub on it.

The preference of a ram for ewes of its own inbred family herd to introduced ewes willing and able to breed was demonstrated by Hayman (1964, p. 160). The investigator postulated that the selection was based on the ram's inability to recognize the usual olfactory signs of estrus in the introduced ewes. The physiological control was regarded as of genetic origin.

Odor seems to be the dominant factor in conditioning young macrosmatic mammals. In an experiment conducted by Mainardi (1963), female house mice (*Mus musculus domesticus*) reared by their parents showed preference for males of a different strain of the same subspecies but avoided males of a different subspecies (*Mus musculus bactrianus*). In another experiment Mainardi, Scudo, and Barbieri (1965) found that female house mice reared by artificially scented parents preferred similarly perfumed males while control females were repelled by their odor. In this case, all subjects belonged to the same strain. It is significant that in both investigations only the females were influenced in their choice of sexual partners by the traits of their caretaking fathers, whereas both experimental and control males revealed no sexual preference.

Association of odor with form and color is probably critical in successful matings of domestic alpacas (*Lama pacos*) with wild vicuñas (*Vicugna vicugna*). The hybrid is valued for its docility and fine fleece. For siring hybrids, according to Maccagno (1932, p. 15), a young male vicuña is captured and given to a lactating alpaca purposely deprived of her own young. To insure acceptance by the foster mother, the vicuña is wrapped for 8 days with the hide of the alpaca's slaughtered offspring. At 18 months of age, the imprinted male vicuña will breed with female alpacas.

Three geographically isolated but proved interfertile forms of deer mice, *Peromyscus maniculatus blandus, P. polionotus albifrons,* and *P. polionotus leucocephalus,* were variously associated by Blair and Howard (1944) in laboratory tests for sexual isolation. In mixed societies of *leucocephalus* and *blandus,* and of *albifrons* and *blandus,* each nearly always associated with its own kind, and always bred with its own kind. In a mixed society of two laboratory-bred color strains of *blandus,* those of the pale color strain paired more frequently (59 times) with each other than with those of the dark strain (19 times) Imprinting of the experimental animals at an early stage in life is presumed. Actual breeding, however, judged by color of offspring, was controlled, because of the design of the experiment, by male dominance and not by assortative mating. The authors (p. 17) suggest that characters associated with coat color rather than coat color itself were responsible for assortative pairings. Perhaps scent was the primary agent.

In the first of a series of experiments, Levine (1958, p. 21) tested assortative mating with proved fertile black-agouti and white mice. An albino female was caged with a male of each kind. Ten such lots were tested. A total of 76% of the 552 mice produced by the inbred albino females were fathered by the inbred albino males, 12% by the black-agouti males, and 12% were mixed as a result of insemination by both kinds of males. Twice as many albino as black-agouti young made up the mixed litters.

The vast superiority of the albino × albino matings to the albino × black-agouti crosses in confinement suggests that assortative mating might be absolute among free-breeding forms. The experiment also indicates that in certain situations assortative mating may be self-reinforcing by stimulating aggressiveness and higher productivity on the part of the phenotypically similar animals in the presence of phenotypically dissimilar competitors. *Assortative mating based on imprinting is the most important expression of social selection.*

Social selection in mammals has not been studied as such in the wild. Much can be inferred, however, from behavior observed in field and laboratory. Callitrichids are diurnal and depend primarily on vision and color discrimination, smell, sound, and display characters for recognition and social selection. The sexes are superficially similar except in the form and size of their external genitalia and sexual skin. The sexual organs are glandular and figure prominently in both visual and olfactory display. Callitrichids normally produce dizygotic twins at a birth. Both parents attend the newborn, but after the first days the greater burden of care between feedings is assumed by the father (and/or foster parents). Callitrichids are omnivorous but have a predilection for insects. They travel in groups which vary in size from a family of three or four to a troop of twenty or more. These are the essential features of the social organization and habits of callitrichids and the ones most likely to be lastingly impressed on the young.

The developing callitrichid shows preference for, and seeks the security of, its own group, and theoretically the grown individual would prefer to mate with a member of the same group, including either of its parents or a littermate. Under natural conditions, however, low longevity, high mortality, relatively low viability of the family group, and parental rejection of weaned or self-reliant young drastically reduce the opportunities for parent-offspring and brother-sister matings. Notwithstanding, the cohesiveness of the troops and the remarkable uniformity among individuals of each race attest to the action of social selection on a wide scale and its effectiveness in promoting phenotypic homozygosity.

Social selection may operate simultaneously with sexual selection but cannot be confused with it. Social selection brings all members of the group together—the more similar the members, the stronger the bond. Sexual selection determines which males have preference in mating and is operative among solitary as well as naturally social animals.

As conceived by Darwin (1899 [1874], p. 210), "males have acquired their present structure, not from being better fitted to survive in the struggle for existence, but from having gained an advantage over other males and from having transmitted this advantage to their male offspring alone, sexual selection must here have come into action. It was the importance of this distinction which led me to designate this form of selection as Sexual Selection." Thus the trend in sexual selection is toward accentuation of differences between the sexes while the trend in social selection is toward uniformity of appearance between the sexes. Among callitrichids, sexual selection, as determined by the degree of specialization of secondary sexual characters, is weak or incipient. Among howlers, genus *Alouatta*, secondary sexual characters are well defined, with males distinguished from females by larger size, thick beard, greatly inflated hyoid bone, and in *A. caraya*, by distinctive coloration as well. As usual, the secondary sexual characters are best developed in the troop leader (see also Campbell 1972).

Summary

Metachromism is the principle of saturation, bleaching, and elimination of tegumentary pigments, from primitive agouti to colorless, or white, in any given chromogenetic field. Bleaching and loss of skin and eye melanins are also metachromic. Related evolutionary processes are hypertrichy and depilation in their respective trichogenetic fields. Natural selection of whatever kind may accelerate, retard, or terminate metachromic processes but cannot alter, reverse, or deflect them.

Simulated regression of metachromic and related processes may be obtained by shifts in gene frequencies, by secondary adaptations to ancestral type habits or habitats, and by hybridization of captive or domestic animals.

Each of the various pelage types, including prenatal, juvenal, preadult, and seasonal, is independently controlled genetically with respect to its growth pattern and color, and each evolves independently. Primary hair types are the sensory vibrissae and guard hairs, the essentially insulating wool hairs or underfur, and the dominant coat or cover hairs. The form, texture, and color of each hair type, like that of the pelage as a whole, are also separately controlled.

Agouti is the most primitive hair and coat color pattern. A typical agouti hair consists of eumelanin (black-brown) tip and base and two pale intermediate pheomelanin (red-yellow) bands separated from each other by a eumelanin band. The agouti patterned race is nuclear and chromatically most stable. During the course of its existence, however, it may spin off any number of geographically isolated and metachromically advanced issues.

The original function of mammalian tegumentary colors is concealment, and the primitive agouti pattern, is in general the most concealing. Among progressive mammals relatively free of predation, color has become less protective and more attractive or neutral. In more advanced forms, usually among diurnal species, most notably primates, color or color pattern serves mainly for recognition or sexual display. Bald and hypertrichous areas reinforce the display effects. In extreme cases, pigmentary colors are eliminated, or they may be partially replaced or altered by structural colors and hemoglobins. Thus Tyndall scattering of light waves by minute particles, often melanin granules, produces the blue eye color and the blue of the mandrill's face and buttocks. Examples of hemoglobin coloring of the skin are the red lips of the white race of man, the brilliantly contrasting red ears and external genitalia of the white races of the *Callithrix argentata* group (pl. II), the red buttocks of the baboon, and the red chest patch of the gelada. Where tegumentary colors are of no adaptive or social value, the organism expends little or no energy in their production.

Predator selection in an environment favoring concealing coloration tends to eliminate conspicuously colored prey. Shift in mean coloration from agouti toward the saturate or bleached end of the metachromic scale permits establishment of a concealingly dark- or pale-colored prey population. Conspicuously dark-colored colonizers of pale-soil habitats can become concealingly pale, but conspicuously pale-colored or bleached colonizers of dark soils cannot reverse metachromic processes and become concealingly dark.

Social selection is the recognition of and preference for the parental (or foster parental) phenotype in societal grouping and mating. Social selection for color or color pattern through assortative mating tends to stabilize the phenotype within a chromatic range recognized and accepted by free-ranging but chromotypically imprinted members of the social group.

Small reproductively isolated founder colonies inbreed unselectively for survival. Inbreeding relaxes stabilizing forces and stimulates or accelerates metachromic and other degenerative processes.

Growth and spread of a founder colony of a social, diurnal species entails social selection. Effective selection stabilizes the mean chromotype of the colony at a color tone or grade between that of the founders and the amelanism toward which all mammals trend.

The more advanced metachromically each successively isolated breeding colony is, or the farther it moves from the center of origin, the nearer it comes to the end of its chromatic evolution, and the narrower its range of chromatic adaptability. Completion of the degenerative processes of bleaching, depigmentation, or depilation, whether singly or in combination, results in extinction unless the population occupies or evolves into a niche where color and pelage have no survival value. Dead-end, isolated, or peripheral habitats may be occupied by metachromically dead-end populations such as the albinotic callitrichids, white bears, whales, bats, rodents, and ungulates mentioned in the text.

12 External Ear

Characters, Evolution

The auricular lamina (helix, scapha, and antihelix combined) of lemuroids and tarsiers is ovate, membranous, and mobile, and very similar to that of didelphoids, tenrecoids, erinaceids, and macroscelids (fig. III.18). According to Schwalbe (1916, p. 653), the primate ear could easily be derived from one like that of *Erinaceus, Echinosorex,* or *Tenrec.* The involuted portion of the helix in these Insectivora is rudimentary and confined to the anterior (or anterodorsal) and ventral borders of the auricular lamina. In higher forms the auricle is rounded, subquadrate, or suboblong and nearly or quite rigid. The extent of helical involution varies individually and specifically, but as a rule the anterior border of the pinna is always involuted, the dorsal border usually involuted and the posterior border often involuted.

Principal stages in the evolution of the external ear from insectivores and prosimians to higher monkeys, apes, and man resulted in (1) shortening of the long axis of the primitively elliptic or subovate auricular lamina, (2) progressive extension of helical involution of the antihelix, (3) obsolescence of the bursa or postantitragal pouch, (4) increasing rigidity by reinforcement of the cartilaginous support throughout the auricle, (5) concomitant loss of mobility and flexibility by attenuation and atrophy of auricular muscles.

The bursa present in marsupials, insectivores, carnivores, and prosimians (fig. III.18k) is vestigial in higher primates. It is little more than a shallow fossa or sulcus in callitrichids but is better developed in the young, particularly of *Leontopithecus rosalia* (fig. III.18b). The bursa in man is reduced to a weak depression, the posterior auricular sulcus.

Contrary to the opinion of Lasinski (1960, p. 53), the well-rounded tupaiid external ears (1960, fig. 3, p. 45) are more advanced than those of prosimians and differ widely from those of all other Insectivora. Le Gros Clark's (1959, p. 282) use of the term "retrogressive" for describing the evolutionary grade of the tupaiid ear is unfortunate. On the basis of external ear structure alone, tupaiids (fig. III.18) could not be classified as stem primates or even as insectivores.

Although ears appear to be basically the same in all primates and remarkably similar in the specialized forms, Schwalbe (1916, p. 655) believed that those of living platyrrhines evolved independently from those of Old World primates.

Callitrichid and Callimiconid Ears

The callitrichid external ear exhibits all stable features present in higher and lower primates. In general, however, the structure of the auricle is less complex than that of cebids and catarrhines and decidedly more advanced than that of lemuroids and tarsiers (fig. III.18). Evolution in the divergent lines of callitrichids involves (1) modification of the ovate-shaped ear to the round subquadrate, suboblong, or lanceolate shape, (2) decrease in length and density of pelage (depilation) or increase and specialization of pelage to form tufts or tassels (hypertrichism), and (3) progressive depigmentation, usually beginning with the inner (lateral) anterior border and terminating on the posterior border of the helix.

The callitrichid auricular lamina may be leafy in some species and fleshy in others, but the cartilaginous lining is thin. Lamina size varies from the broad, leafy expanse that projects well above and out from the head in the black tamarin (*Saguinus midas*) to the low convoluted, abbreviated, and closely attached ear of the cotton-top tamarin (*Saguinus oedipus oedipus*). The helix is always involuted anteriorly, often anterodorsally, and sometimes posterodorsally, and only in some individuals of *Callimico goeldii* is there a distinct infolding on both dorsal and ventral borders.

External ears of cebids of the genera *Saimiri, Aotus,* and *Callicebus* resemble those of callitrichids more closely than those of prehensile-tailed cebids (*Cebus, Lagothrix, Ateles,* and *Alouatta*).

Individual variation in size and form of the auricle is considerable. In some callitrichids differences between right and left ears are nearly as great as the extremes of variation within the species.

Few comparative studies of the callitrichid external ear have been made. Boas (1912, pp. 205, 206) did not deem significant the differences he noted between external ear and cartilage of a specimen of *Saguinus midas midas* (= *Hapale rufimanus*) and one of *Callithrix jacchus jacchus* (= *Hapale jacchus*). Huber (1931, p. 28) reviewed the literature on ear musculature and declared that "the facial muscles of the species of *Hapale* (*H. jacchus* and *H.*

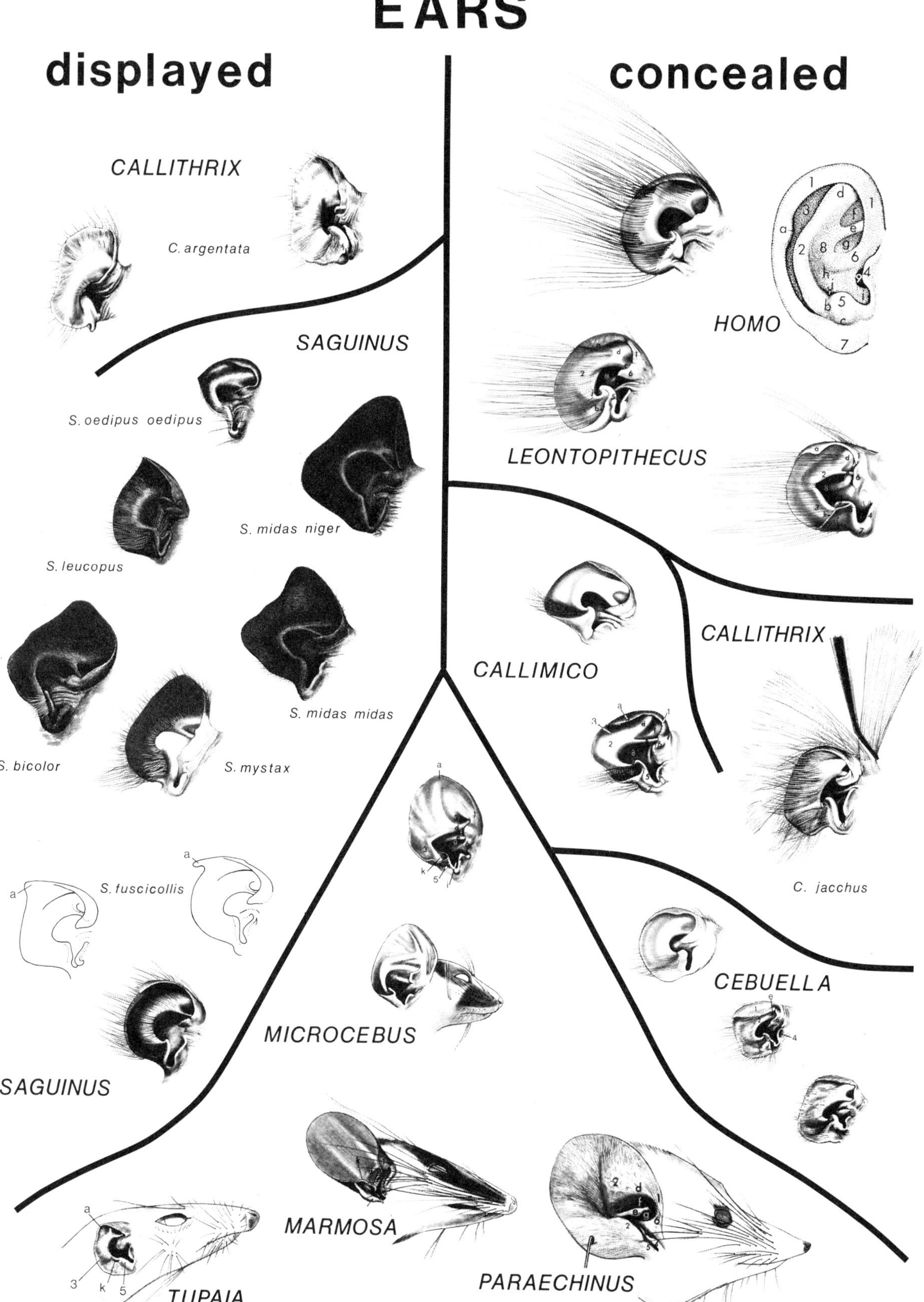

Fig. III.18. External ears, lateral aspect, in nonprimates, callitrichids, man. Primitive mammals: *Marmosa* (Marsupialia); *Tupaia* (Insectivora, *sensu lato*); *Paraechinus* (Insectivora). Primates: *Microcebus murinus* (Lemuridae). *Ears more or less displayed: Saguinus fuscicollis,* showing variation in form; *S. mystax mystax, S. midas midas; S. midas niger, S. bicolor bicolor; S. leucopus, S. oedipus oedipus; Callithrix argentata* with unpigmented ears, the hemoglobin red displayed in life.

Ears almost or totally concealed by headdress: Cebuella pygmaea; Callithrix jacchus jacchus (anteorbital tuft lifted to expose ear); *Callimico goeldii; Leontopithecus rosalia rosalia; Homo*

penicillata) studied by Ruge [1887], Schreiber [1928], Huber [1930], and the various species of *Leontocebus* (*L. mystax, L. rosalia, L. geoffroyi*) studied by Schreiber and Huber, are closely similar. The plan of the facial [including auricular] musculature in the two genera [Huber's *Hapale* = *Callithrix; Leontocebus* = *Leontopithecus* and *Saguinus*] is practically identical. It resembles that of *Tarsius,* if we disregard the specialization in the latter."

Ears of all platyrrhines are indeed basically similar, and those of callitrichids resemble each other very closely. Nevertheless, two specialized callitrichid types are distinguishable. (1) The true marmoset or ouistiti (*Cebuella-Callithrix*) type ear is comparatively small and generally rounded, with all parts distinctly sculptured, helix well involuted, bursa more or less defined, particularly in young, and ears hidden by mane or tufts in all species of the group except *Callithrix argentata.* Ears of *Callimico* and *Leontopithecus* also belong here, but each monkey evolved independently. The ears in both are covered by a mane. (2) The tamarin (*Saguinus*) type ear is conspicuously exposed, large, expanded or laminate, more nearly oblong than ovate or round, with parts, particularly the bursal vestige, less defined; its size ranges from proportionately smallest to largest among callitrichids.

Differences between the marmoset and tamarin type ears are slight but divergent. The evolutionary trend in the first group is toward concealment of the ear, as a result of hypertrichy of the aural area; that of the second is toward greater exposure and display because of depilation of the area. Ears of *Callithrix argentata* belong to the second group.

All exposed ears are deeply pigmented, except those of albinotic races of *Callithrix argentata.* Concealed ears may be pigmented or unpigmented. The human ear, used here for anatomical reference and homologies (fig. III.18), varies from deeply pigmented to completely depigmented. Dark ears in dark-skinned human races are usually exposed. Pale or unpigmented ears in primitive pale or "white" races are usually protected by long tresses from cold, ultraviolet radiation, or both. Man's travels and cultures, however, obscure the pattern. Callitrichid ear types are described herewith.

Cebuella-Callithrix or Marmoset Ear

The external ears of the pygmy marmoset (*Cebuella pygmaea*) and of ouistiti or common marmoset (*Callithrix jacchus*) are similar, but that of the latter is slightly more advanced. Those of other species of *Callithrix* are modifications or specializations of the same type.

The *Cebuella-Callithrix* ear differs from that of tamarins (e.g., *Saguinus nigricollis*) chiefly by a form more quadrate or ovate, cymba concha well defined, tragus and antitragus heavier, inferior laminar fossa (bursa) present and usually well defined, and crus helices clearly differentiated from helix as a structurally and embryologically distinct element (cf. Streeter 1920, p. 263). The ear appears to be less mobile than that of tamarins, and the posterodorsal flap or process characteristics of the latter is absent. Depigmentation to varying degrees is widespread and complete in representatives of two of the four species of this group.

The auricular lamina of *Cebuella pygmaea* is membranous, the entire dorsal border involuted, crus helicis elongate, oblique, and nearly meeting the well-developed tragus to form the incomplete anterior border of the deeply excavated cymba; inferior laminar fossa well defined, scapha defined only between superior crus of antihelix and dorsal border of helix. The outer (medial) side of pinna is usually entirely pigmented, the inner surface varies from fully pigmented to wholly unpigmented. An interesting correlation between depigmented ears and pale underparts has been noted in the description of the species (p. 466). The ear is thinly haired.

The external ear of *Callithrix jacchus* is an elaboration of the *Cebuella* ear. It is more rounded, more thickly cartilaginous, with antihelix sculptured posteriorly, the scapha correspondingly better defined, and helix of dorsal border clearly rolled rather than folded. The ear is thinly to moderately haired in *C. jacchus penicillata* and *C. j. geoffroyi,* while thick tufts emerge from the inner or concave surface of the pinna in *aurita* and *flaviceps.*

The ear of adult *Callithrix argentata* is more specialized, with the auricular lamina and antitragus more fleshy than those of other callitrichids except, possibly, those of *C. humeralifer;* involuted portion of helix confined to anterior border and expanded basally, eliminating most or all of the angle of fusion with crus helicis. Absence of involuted dorsal helical border appears to be secondary and correlated with fleshiness of auricular lamina. The ear of a subadult *C. argentata* is quite like that of *Callithrix jacchus* in all details of form and structure, notably with respect to the membranous auricular lamina, involuted dorsal border, and sharp angle at fusion of helix with crus helicis. Ears of young are hairy, those of adults are thinly haired, virtually naked, and mostly exposed to view. Ears of adult *C. argentata argentata* are entirely depigmented or mottled, mostly on dorsal portion of auricular lamina. Ears of young are generally darker. Ears of whitish *C. a. leucippe* are similar and even more depigmented. The auricular membrane of brownish *C. a. melanura* is pigmented, the concha and anterior peripheral parts more or less unpigmented. The exposed *argentata* ears serve for display, especially the depigmented appendages, which are brilliantly illuminated by the hemoglobin red of the peripheral bloodstream.

Ears in *Callithrix humeralifer,* judged by dry skins,

(Hominidae; slightly pigmented or unpigmented ears usually concealed by tresses in unshorn races, deeply pigmented ears usually exposed in kinky-haired races; pigmented to unpigmented types fully intergrading). Names of numbered parts of pinna given below.

Explanation of symbols: *1,* helix (auricular lamina, part); *2,* antihelix (auricular lamina, part); *3,* scapha (auricular lamina, part); *4,* tragus; *5,* antitragus; *6,* crus helicis; *7,* lobulus; *8,* concha (see *g* and *h*); *9,* auditory meatus.

a, auricular tubercle (Darwin's point); *b,* inferior laminar fossa (posterior auricular sulcus; homologue of *k* below); *c,* antitragic fissure (antitragohelicis fissure); *d,* crus superior antihelicis; *e,* plica principalis (crus inferior antihelicis; "supertragus" of Pocock); *f,* fossa triangularis (fossa articularis superior); *g,* cymba conchae (pars articularis); *h,* cavum conchae; *i,* anterior auricular notch (intertragic notch); *j,* posterior auricular notch; *k,* bursa, homologue of carnivore bursa, lemuroid "pouch" of Pocock (1918, p. 23; see *b* above).

are like those of *C. argentata* in form but have auricular lamina completely covered with long hair and skin mostly pigmented to entirely depigmented.

Leontopithecus Ear

The auricle of the lion-tamarin, *Leontopithecus rosalia* (fig. III.18), is very similar to that of *Callithrix jacchus*, but distinctly rounded, not subquadrate in outline, and more cartilaginous, with anterior and dorsal helical borders more rolled, inferior portion of auricular lamina relatively broader, the crus helicis heavier, longer, and, in fully grown or old adults nearly meeting the correspondingly larger tragus and antitragus. The bursa (fig. III.18 *k*), characteristic of many marsupials, insectivores, prosimians, and carnivores, is marked by a well defined sulcus in old individuals and a narrow, slitlike pocket in young. Pinna is fully pigmented, mottled, or nearly to entirely unpigmented, with inner anterior portion paler than remainder but with sharp contrasts as in some tamarins (*mystax* group) and the pygmy marmoset (*Cebuella*). A thin tuft present on inner (lateral) surface of ear contributes to mane.

Leontopithecus is only remotely related to *Cebuella* and *Callithrix*. The differences between their external ears also point to divergent evolution. On the other hand, the many auricular similarities affirm the basic community of all callitrichids.

Saguinus or Tamarin Ear

Ear form and size varies most among tamarins with those of *Saguinus nigricollis* and *S. mystax* most primitive. The auricular lamina of *Saguinus nigricollis* remains comparatively uncomplicated but reduced in size, more nearly oblong than ovate, thinly haired and fully pigmented, helix not clearly defined from antihelix, anterior border involuted, ventral border rounded and somewhat lobate but not involuted, crus helicis little or not at all defined from helix, scapha rudimentary and confined to angle between superior crus of antihelix and dorsal involution of helix. Judged by dry skins only, the external ear of *Saguinus nigricollis graellsi*, most primitive member of the *nigricollis* group, is indistinguishable from that of *S. nigricollis nigricollis*. Ear of the saddle-back tamarin *S. fuscicollis* (fig. III.18), most advanced species of the *nigricollis* group, also resembles that of *S. nigricollis* except the posterodorsal angle of the auricle is produced into a pronounced flaplike process in most races.

Ears of moustached tamarins of the *Saguinus mystax* group also resemble those of *S. nigricollis* but are hairier, with anterior base and contiguous parts depigmented. Among specific members of the group, the ear of *S. labiatus*, seen in dry skins, appears to be more expansive than that of *S. mystax* or *S. imperator*.

External ears of remaining tamarins can also be derived from the *S. nigricollis* type. The ear of *S. inustus* resembles that of *S. nigricollis* but with posterodorsal angle of auricular lamina hardly or not at all differentiated as a flap, dorsal border more consistently involuted, and inferior half of auricular lamina, particularly ventral margin, comparatively reduced. The ear appears to be more hairy throughout, with hind margin of antitragus tufted.

The external ear of the golden-handed *Saguinus midas midas* is comparatively bare, with a surface area nearly twice that of *S. nigricollis*, entire anterodorsal border of ear more or less involuted, posterodorsal flap often present, involuted, and erectile, posterior border generally concave, posterior half of auricular lamina relatively well expanded, crus helicis well defined.

Ears of *Saguinus bicolor* agree in size and general form with those of *Saguinus midas* but superior border is less involuted, posterior border generally convex.

Reduction in ear surface and hairiness in the *Saguinus oedipus* group follows a geographic cline consonant with the postulated order of dispersal and evolution of its members. Ear of the most primitive *Saguinus leucopus* is least reduced, most hairy and has the antitragal tuft well developed. In the most highly specialized *Saguinus oedipus oedipus* the ear is smallest, with most of ventral portion of auricular lamina deeply emarginate or obsolete. It is also most nearly bare with antitragal tuft least conspicuous. The ear of *S. oedipus geoffroyi* is intermediate in all respects.

Callimiconid or Callimico Ear

The ear of *Callimico* is subquadrate to subovate in outline, dorsal and ventral borders of helix involuted, cartilaginous support slightly heavier than in *Callithrix*, antihelix more prominent, scapha more pronounced, fossa triangularis well excavated, tragus and antitragus no more developed than in *Callithrix* but more so than in *Saguinus*, bursa expanded, crus helicis joined to expanded base of helix without forming angle. Pigmentation is moderate to thin, the outer (medial) surface darker than inner, anterior border ranging from paler than posterior to entirely unpigmented. The pinna is nearly bare and provided with a few long tufts on inner surface.

In general, the ear of *Callimico* is more like that of marmosets than of tamarins.

Callitrichid Ear Movements

The flaplike projection of the posterodorsal angle of the auricular lamina (Darwin's point) in *Saguinus fuscicollis* is usually drooped, but it can be raised by contraction of a slip of the posterior auricular muscle. The posterodorsal angle of the ear of other hairy-face tamarins may also be movable.

Ear musculature of *Callithrix jacchus* has been described by Ruge (1887, text of pl. 1, figs. 1, 2) and others; that of *Saguinus mystax mystax* and *Leontopithecus rosalia rosalia* by Schreiber (1928); and that of *Callithrix jacchus* and *Saguinus oedipus geoffroyi* by Huber (1931, p. 28, fig. 5). According to Huber, callitrichid ear musculature retains the primitive marsupioplacental ground plan. It is less differentiated than in lemuroids and tarsier through degeneration of mm. obliqui and transversi and loss of the m. mandibuloauricularis.

According to Pocock (1917 ,p. 254), the pinna of *Callithrix jacchus jacchus* "is capable of being folded by the forward movement of its posterior half up against its anterior half, so that the central cavity is obliterated and the external meatus closed by the antitragus coming into contact with the tragus." The ears of the Golden Lion-tamarin, *Leontopithecus rosalia rosalia,* continues Pocock, are similar and "fold in the same way." The ear of *Saguinus oedipus oedipus,* he notes, "folds as in the other species. The posterior angular point turning backwards." I have closely observed the ears of species mentioned by Pocock, and those of many others, but have never seen them perform the prosimian type of movements he describes.

Function

Auricular diversity among primates probably evolved through social selection (cf. p. 100). The various types serve for display and recognition among species and probably among races and individuals. Whatever its form, the pinna possibly protects the external auditory meatus and middle ear by acting as a shield or buffer against blows, shocks, and attack or invasion by insects. Pelage could do as much. An auditory function of the external ear, if present, is not obvious. The primate auricle possibly funnels sounds to a limited extent, but the head, not the ear, turns to the source of sound.

A specialized thermoregulatory function cannot be attributed to the primate ear, as it has been in the case of other mammalian ears. The enormous variation in auricular size, form, pilosity, and degree of exposure in primates such as callitrichids which are similar in size, activity, and habitat argues strongly against it.

13 Tongue

Surface Anatomy

The oral portion of the primate tongue (figs. III.19, 20) is spatulate in gross form, ellipsoid in transverse section. Tongues of *Callicebus* and prehensile-tailed species are, according to Sonntag (1921*c*, p. 497 ff.), usually pigmented. Pigment was present on the tongue tip and frenal lamella of specimens of *Callimico goeldii* and *Saguinus midas* I examined and on the upper surface of a tongue of *Leontopithecus rosalia*. The tongue and accessory organs appeared to be entirely flesh-colored in a specimen each of *Saguinus fuscicollis, S. nigricollis, S. oedipus*, and *Cebuella pygmaea* and 2 specimens of *Callithrix jacchus*. The degree of pigmentation may be highly variable, but melanin may be more common in tongues or accessory organs or both of some platyrrhines than in others and possibly never, or rarely, present in *Callithrix* and *Cebuella*. Dummette and Barens (1972), who examined the oral soft tissues of 8 *Saguinus oedipus oedipus*, 1 *S. mystax*, 1 *S. fuscicollis*, 1 *S. leucopus*, and 1 *Callithrix jacchus jacchus*, found some degree of melanin in one or more organs of all specimens except "1 white-faced monkey," meaning, presumably, either *S. mystax* or *S. fuscicollis*. The pigmentation in the 11 specimens ranged from 9% on the tongue to 82% in soft and hard palates, and from 73% on inner to 100% on outer sides of lips.

Weight

Means and extremes of weights of 60 tongues of *Callithrix jacchus jacchus* studied by Ledoux (1963; 1964) are 0.768 g (0.664–0.885).

Histochemistry

Tongue histochemistry of various primate species has been studied by Machida, Perkins, and Giacometti (1967), and that of *Callithrix jacchus* by Ledoux (1963; 1964), and Dreizen, Levy, and Bernick (1970*b*).

Papillae

The upper surface of the tongue of primates and nearly all mammals is characterized by three types of papillae (fig. III.20).

1. Conical

The conical or filiform papillae are smallest and most numerous and cover most of the upper surface, borders, and periphery of the underside of the tongue of mammals. They are tactile and mechanical in function and vary in form from a simple cone to a keratinized fimbriate cylinder. The conical papillae are least complex in platyrrhines, with those of callitrichids the least specialized. The papillae of *Cebuella* appear to be most simple. The conical papillae of *Callithrix jacchus* are larger and appear as wide and deep-mouthed fimbricated cylinders. The papillae of other callitrichids are similar but there is a bewildering amount of individual variation. The average number of filiform papilla counted in 60 tongues of *Callithrix jacchus* by Ledoux (1963; 1964) is 4317 (3834–4920).

2. Fungiform

The fungiform papillae are enlarged conical papillae specialized for gustatory and tactile functions. They are distributed on the dorsal, lateral, and ventral periphery of the oral portion of the tongue. Fungiform papillae are present in all mammals except (*fide* Sonntag 1925, p. 711) Monotremata, Dermoptera, Pholidota, and Myrmecophagidae. They are less numerous, less regularly disposed and less concentrated apically in callitrichids than in cebids. In these respects, therefore, the tongue of the former groups is regarded as more primitive. Kubota and Hayama (1964, p. 476) describe the large fungiform papilla at the tip of the tongue in *Cebuella* and *Callithrix jacchus* as richly innervated and provided with many taste buds "having embryonic characteristics." The fungiform papillae in 60 *Callithrix jacchus* tongues, according to Ledoux (1963; 1964), number 132.4 (99–185).

3. Circumvallate

The circumvallate or vallate papillae are largest in size, fewest in number, and most highly specialized. They occur on the posterior or pharyngeal portion of the tongue and are gustatory in function. Circumvallate papillae are modified fungiform papillae, restricted to mam-

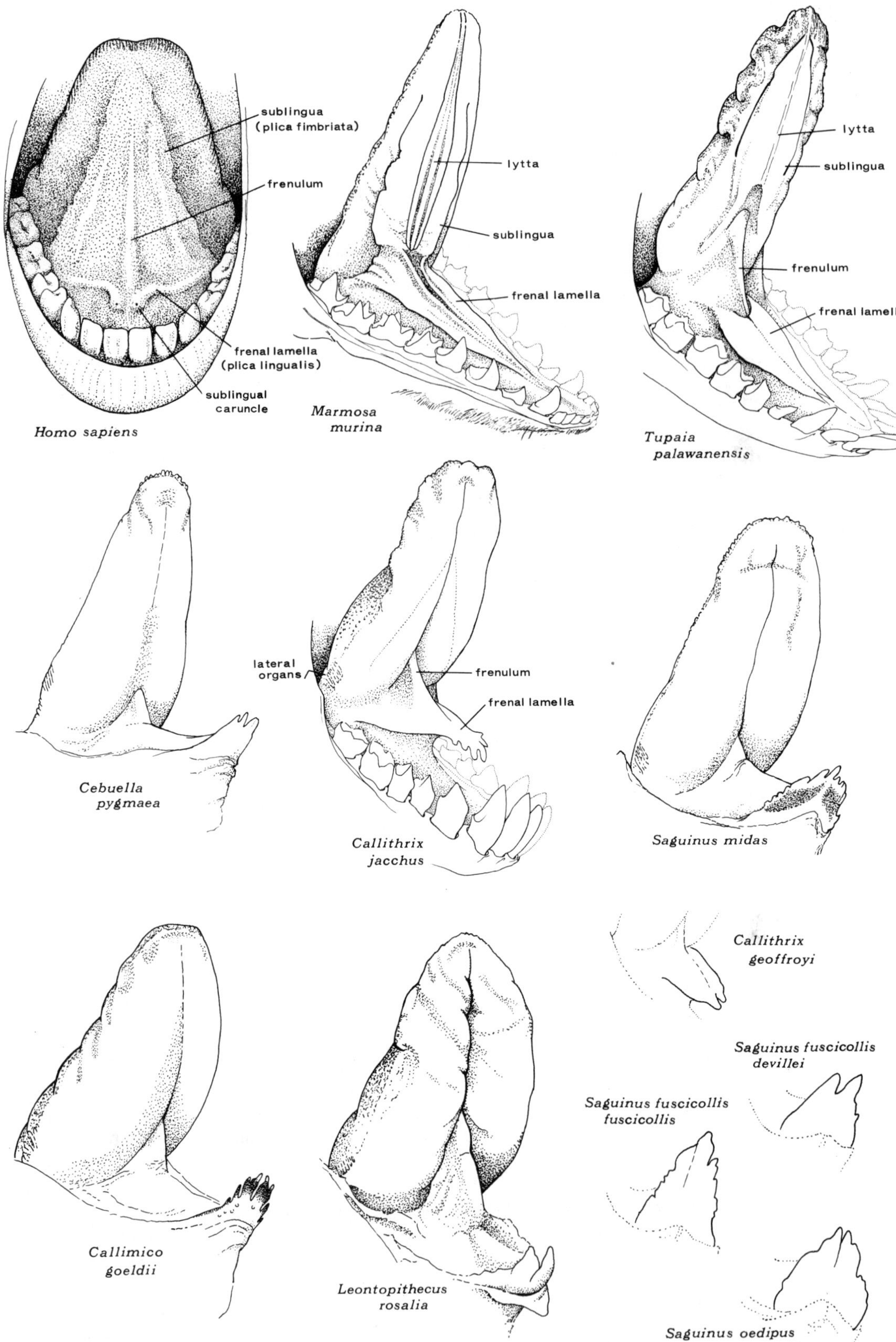

Fig. III.19. Tongues and accessories (enlarged), ventral surface in the marsupial, *Marmosa murina;* insectivore *Tupaia palawanensis;* callitrichids *Cebuella pygmaea, Callithrix jacchus, Saguinus midas, S. fuscicollis, S. oedipus, Leontopithecus rosalia;* callimiconid, *Callimico goeldii;* and hominid, *Homo sapiens.*

mals; but Sonntag (1925, p. 714), notes their absence in "*Hyrax* and some Cetacea and Pinnipedia." The typical or primitive number is 3, arranged in a V form. Other arrangements include Y and T forms.

Platyrrhines normally possess the three papillae in the primitive arrangement as in prosimians. Infrequently, a lateral or the median primary circumvallate papilla may be absent or there may be one or a few extra papillae.

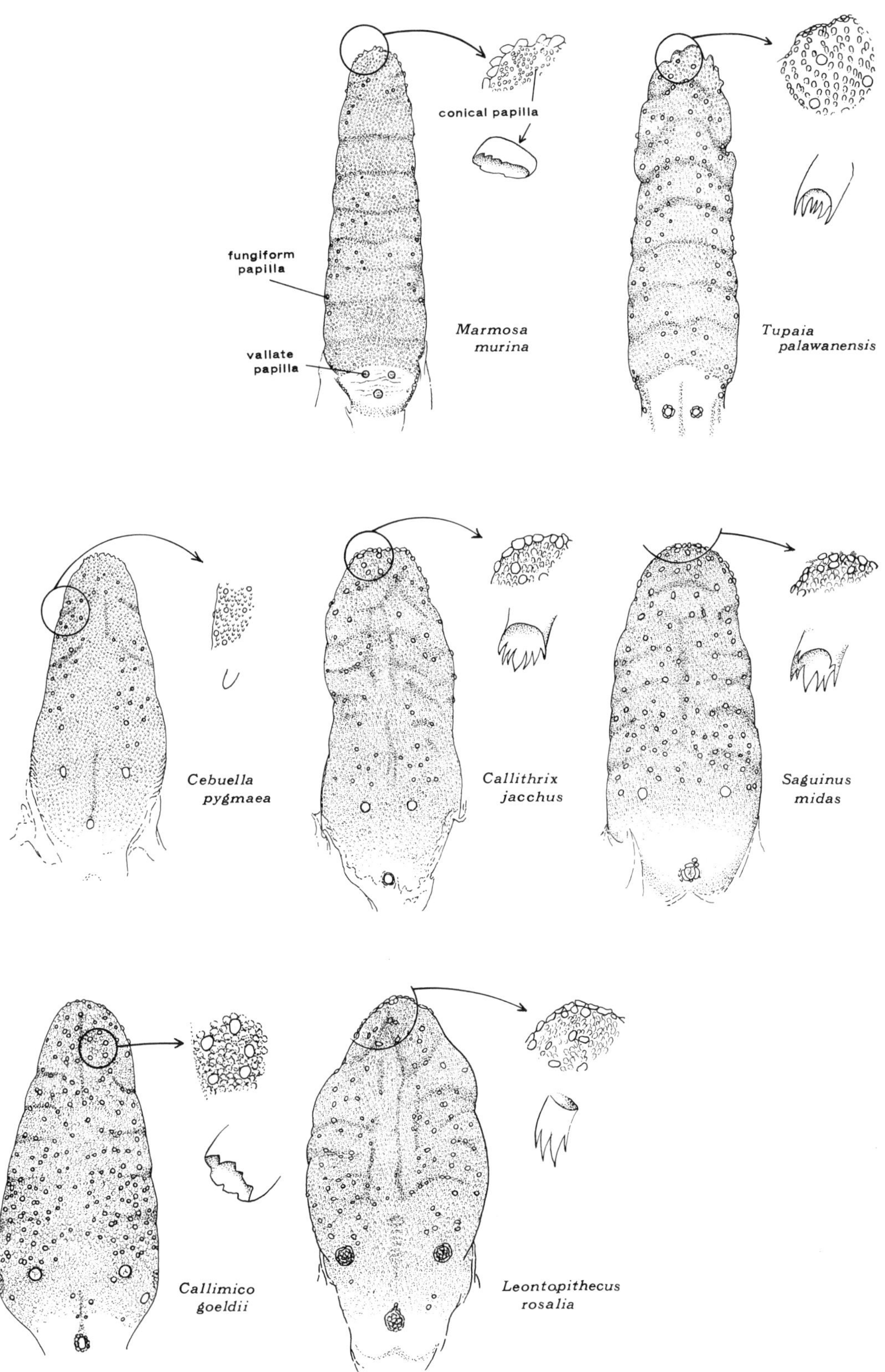

Fig. III.20. Tongues, dorsal surface, showing papillae; same species as shown in fig. III.19 except *Homo.*

The supernumeraries are usually intermediate in form between primary circumvallate papillae and fungiform papillae.

The number of vallate papillae is consistently 3 in tongues of all callitrichids at hand and those reported by most authors. Ledoux (1963; 1964) records 3 papillae in 82% of 60 specimens of *Callithrix jacchus jacchus,* 4 in 16%, and 5 in 2%. The papillae in *Cebuella* and *Callithrix* are least differentiated, those of *Leontopithecus* and *Callimico* most specialized, and those of *Saguinus* intermediate.

The number of vallate papillae in cebids also varies from 3 to 5. Kubota and Hayama (1964, p. 475), who compiled the data from the literature, report 3 to 5 papillae in *Callicebus personatus,* 3 in *Lagothrix.* Machida, Perkins, and Giacometti (1967, p. 265) note 4 papillae in *Lagothrix* but the usual 3 in *Saimiri* and *Alouatta caraya.*

Vallate-papillae in cercopithecids vary from 3 to 5, as in platyrrhines, 6 to 7 in the gorilla, and 9 to 10 in man, according to Machida, Perkins, Giacometti (1967). These authors suggest (1967, p. 266) that the "numbers tend to increase with phylogenetic advance." Their data, however, show only a qualified increase among catarrhines, but monkeys, apes, and man are end products of independent lines. Other data produced by the same authors reveal an increase from prosimians through platyrrhines and catarrhines to hominids in the number of taste buds associated with the vallate papillae.

Organs

The lateral and ventral surfaces of the tongue are marked by three kinds of organs (figs. III.19, 20).

1. Lateral Organs

Lateral organs are the series of vertically disposed laminate or foliate papillae on each lateral posterior border of the tongue, anterior to the attachment of the palatoglossal folds (fig. III.19). The structures are gustatory and are evident in all orders but not all species of mammals. According to Sonntag (1925, p. 714) lateral organs are present in all primates except tarsiers, lorises, galagos, and the aye-aye. Machida, Perkins, and Giacometti (1967) confirm their absence in tarsier, lorises, galagos, and add pottos, but report them present in the mongoose lemur (*Lemur mongoz*). Tupaiids, they note, lack the organs, but they find them particularly well developed in the woolly monkey, *Lagothrix*. The foliate papillae in 60 tongues of *Callithrix jacchus,* according to Ledoux (1963; 1964) numbered 4.4 (2–7) on the right side, 3.6 (2–6) on the left side.

2. Sublingua

The sublingua is a tonguelike structure attached to the underside of the oral portion of the tongue. According to Sonntag (1925), it is present and well developed in adult Marsupialia, Dermoptera, Tupaiidae, "Prosimia," and Gliridae (Rodentia). The organ is vestigial in adult *Homo, Gorilla, Pongo, Pan, Solenodon,* and possibly *Crocidura.* It has been reported in fetal whales and dogs (*fide* Sonntag 1925, p. 775) and may be a fetal character of other mammals. The large sublingua of tupaiids and prosimians is flat and leaf-shaped, with free tip and margins and a supporting median longitudinal rod, the *lytta.* The vestigial sublingua of man is called *plica fimbriata* or sublingual plate. The sublingua is absent in adult catarrhines and platyrrhines, its place being marked by a deep median sulcus and, usually, a pair of low convergent lateral ridges.

3. Frenal Lamella

The *frenal lamella* is a subtriangular body on the floor of the mouth. The large and highly specialized frenal lamella of prosimians is somewhat smaller than the sublingua but it resembles it in shape and the freedom of its margins. The frenal lamella present in all platyrrhines appears to be generalized in structure. It extends along the floor of the mouth from the lingual frenum to the mandibular angle. The dental portion or apex is free and usually, if not always, bifid with each section simple or fimbriate. In the few callitrichid tongues examined, the frenal lamella inflects downward in the open mouth of *Callithrix* and upward in all other genera (fig. III.19).

Notwithstanding statements to the contrary by Sonntag (1925, p. 723),[1] the frenal lamella is present in man as the *plica lingualis* (or sublingual lamella or fold). It is also present in orangs and represented in many, if not all, orders of Mammalia.[2]

The frenal lamella of platyrrhines resembles the sublingua of prosimians but the differences had been adverted. Pocock (1920, p. 104 n., p. 105) observed that the frenal lamella "corresponds to Wharton's papillae of human anatomists, and not to the sublingua of the Lemurs." Sonntag (1920, p. 128; 1925, p. 723), fully aware of the pitfalls, cautioned that the lamella "is not to be confounded with the *sublingua* which is characteristic of the Lemuroidea and represented by the plicae fimbriatae of the Anthropoidea." He (1925, p. 723) reiterated his warning and added that "some authors including Burmeister [1846, p. 106, pl. 6, fig. 2] have made that mistake." Notwithstanding, Beattie (1927, p. 687), who cites both Pocock and Sonntag, refers to the frenal lamella of *Callithrix jacchus* as a sublingua. More recently, Schneider (1958, p. 85, fig. 9) mistook the frenal lamella of *Callicebus*[3] for the sublingua, and his description and figure of a sublingua in *Aotus* (1958, p. 85, fig. 9) are not convincing. These findings induced Schneider (1958, p. 113) to declare that the tongue of the Cebidae most nearly resembles the primitive type as exemplified by that of *Tupaia* and *Tarsius.* Le Gros Clark (1959, p. 288, fig. 137, 290), without allusion to any of the authors cited above, presented a figure of the tongue of *Hapale* [= *Callithrix*] with the denticulated frenal lamella identified as a sublingua. He concluded that "the tongue of the marmoset [*Callithrix jacchus*] (which probably represents the most primitive expression of this organ in the Anthropoidea) is similar in form to that of *Tarsius.*" Kubota

[1] "The frenal lamella is present in all Primates except man and some specimens of Orang. And it is absent in all other Mammalia."

[2] In a spot check of 15 spirit-preserved adults representing 6 mammalian orders, a frenal lamella was found in all as follows: Mouse opossum (*Marmosa,* fig. III.19), musk shrew (*Crocidura*), solenodon (*Solenodon* [vestigial]), long-snouted Philippine "tree" shrew (*Urogale*), tree shrew (*Tupaia,* fig. III.19), African fruit bat (*Rousettus*), neotropical bats (*Phyllostomus, Leptonycteris, Lonchoglossa*), pika (*Ochotona*), Asiatic squirrel (*Callosciurus*), dormouse (*Glis*), gerbil (*Tatera*), polecat (*Vormela*). A yak recently dead in Brookfield Zoo had a frenal lamella but no sublingua. Some recently autopsied mammals which Chicago's Lincoln Park Zoo donated to the Field Museum included a brush-tailed opossum (*Trichosurus vulpecula*) and a tree kangaroo (*Dendrolagus*) with well-developed sublingua but no frenal lamella and a spiny caviomorph rat (*Isothrix*) with neither sublingua nor frenal lamella. Sisson (1910, pp. 335, 411) describes the frenal lamella in the horse and pig.

[3] It is rather curious that the organ misidentified by Beddard (1901, p. 362) as the sublingua in *Callithrix* [*sic* = *Callicebus*] *torquatus* and *C. personatus* was correctly identified as the frenal lamella by Schneider (1958, p. 89). Perhaps Schneider was misled by Beddard's use of the generic name *Callithrix,* for the cebid titis.

and Hayama (1964) also misused the term sublingua for the frenal lamella of *Cebuella* and *Callithrix*. Machida, Perkins, and Giacometti (1967, p. 272) state that a "poorly defined" sublingua is present in *Lagothrix* and *Ateles*, but their figure (1967, p. 267) showing a sectioned "sublingua" with taste buds is certainly a frenal lamella.

Callicebus, according to Hofer (1969*b*), lacks sublingua, plica fimbriata, and caruncula sublingualis. He also reports the absence of a frenulum, which he describes as structurally and functionally independent of the frenal lamella or sublingual fold except for its insertion on the dorsal surface of that body. The organ in *Callicebus* identified by Sonntag (1921*c*) as the frenal lamella is regarded by Hofer (1969*b*, p. 272) as unlike anything in other primates. The *sublingual organ*, the name he proposed for this peculiar structure, lacks muscles but contains salivary glands with their openings in the tentacles at the tip and sides bordered by taste buds.

The structure I have described and figured as a frenal lamella (fig. III.19) is similar to the organ in *Callicebus* as described by Hofer. The "sublingua" in *Lagothrix* figured by Machida, Perkins, and Giacometti (1967, p. 267), and in *Ateles* shown by Saban, Khunson, and Chawaf (1967), are also similar. The "sublingua" in *Cebuella* described and figured by Kubota and Hayama (1964, p. 477, fig. 10) as composed chiefly of the interlaced skeletal muscle and lacking taste buds, may require study of more material. Absence of taste buds, however, may be a primitive character.

The frenal lamella is an extremely variable structure attached to the posteromedian ventral surface of the tongue by a comparably variable frenulum. It appears to me that the frenal lamella and *"sublingua"* of all platyrrhines, including the "sublingual organ" of *Callicebus* and similar organs in marsupials, tupaiids (fig. III.19), and prosimians, are the same organ.

Musculature

The gross anatomy and microanatomy of tongue musculature in *Papio, Ateles,* and *Callithrix* have been described by Saban, Khunson, and Chawaf (1967).

Function

The primate tongue is capable of a greater variety of individual and coordinated movements than any other single independently controlled organ of the body. The highly tactile tongue is the primary seat of taste organs. The tongue is also used for grooming and lapping and assists in more specialized forms of drinking, feeding, mastication, digestion, and B-vitaminization. The tongue is essential for most forms of vocalization and it performs a variety of movements or glossokinetics for the purposes of display or social communication and self-gratification. More information is included in the callitrichid species accounts.

Comparisons

The comparative anatomy of the tongues of platyrrhines and other primates has been extensively treated by several authors including Pocock (1918; 1920), Sonntag (1920; 1921*a*; 1921*b*; 1921*c*; 1925), and Schneider (1958). None found a consistent character or combination of characters for absolutely distinguishing callitrichids from cebids or any one platyrrhine genus or species from all others. No such characters are apparent in present limited material. However, much more material than has already been studied may show that significant differences do exist, particularly in the arrangement and anatomy of the papillae and in the form of the apical portion of the frenal lamella.

Compared with tongues of prosimians, insectivores, and marsupials, those of platyrrhines are simple or, perhaps, simplified. Complete or virtual absence of a sublingua indicates a wide departure from the postulated primitive mammalian condition. On the other hand, the small, comparatively uncomplicated frenal lamella present in all tongues of callitrichids and *Callicebus* is primitive. The lingual papillae and glands of platyrrhines, more particularly of callitrichids, are also less complicated than those of Old World monkeys. These conditions led Sonntag (1925, p. 756) to conclude that the Callitrichidae "are more primitive than all other Anthropoidea in the characters of the tongue."

14 External Genitalia and Accessory Structures

External genitalia are generally used for copulation, excretion, sexual recognition and stimulation, threat, display, and territorial marking. Periodically, the external genitalia and accessory structures of mature individuals, particularly the female of many species, become extraordinarily developed, prominently displayed, and particularly attractive to the senses of sight, smell, touch, and, in many cases, taste of individuals of the opposite sex. Male external genitalia vary more in structure than those of females, and the range of variation between individuals, races, and species is usually broad. Notwithstanding the plasticity and cyclical changeability of most parts, their form may be peculiar to the species or genus. Detailed descriptions of the gross anatomy of genitalia, particularly the organs of taxonomic significance in Callitrichidae and *Callimico,* are given in the respective species accounts. The common features, comparative anatomy, and other aspects of external genitalia are discussed here in terms of mammals and primates generally and callitrichids and *Callimico* particularly.

Homologies of External Organs

All parts of male and female external genitalia identifiable in man are present in platyrrhines (figs. III.21, 22). The same elements, more or less clearly defined, occur in all other primates.

Anatomists of the late eighteenth and nineteenth centuries regarded the labia majora, hymen, and certain accessories of the external genitalia as peculiar to humans. Bischoff (1879), in his attempt to demonstrate anatomical differences between human and nonhuman primates, assumed (p. 240) that prepuce and preputial frenula are derived from the genital fold (i.e., labia minora). This led him to believe that only the labia minora surrounded the genital fissure and glans clitoridis. Paradoxically, his own descriptions and figures of the external genitalia of chimpanzees (pl. 4, figs. 14, 15, labia majora unlabeled), gorilla (pl. 5, fig. 17, labia majora labeled "1"), gorilla (pl. 6, fig. 19, labia majora unlabeled), contradict this interpretation. Bischoff's reproduction of a student's sketch of the genitalia of a gorilla (pl. 6, fig. 21) seems distorted and unclear in some details, but the parts labeled "2," or labia minora, appear to be labia majora.

Presence of labia majora in female nonhuman primates and their homology with the male scrotum were demonstrated by Klaatsch in 1892. He found rudimentary labia majora in a 6-centimeter female embryo of *Callithrix jacchus* (= *Hapale albicollis*) (fig. III.23) and their homologues in the scrotal folds of the male twin (fig. III.24). This enabled Klaatsch to identify labia majora in adult *Callithrix jacchus, Leontopithecus rosalia* (fig. III.21), and *Cebus capucinus* (= *C. hypoleucos*), and a young orang. These findings, he concluded, "korrigieren meine frühere Ansicht, nach welcher ich die Labia majora dem Menschen ausschliesslich zuschrieb."

Bolk (1907, p. 274) confirmed the presence of labia majora in representatives of all major groups of primates as well as their homology with the scrotum. The labia majora, he concluded, are primitive but relatively well developed in man and platyrrhines, less developed in fetal catarrhine monkeys, and in many species disappear during early postnatal life. Bolk also noted the greater resemblance of platyrrhine external genitalia to man than to catarrhine monkeys.

Wislocki's (1930) studies advanced the knowledge of homologies of platyrrhine genital organs, and his work on catarrhines (1936, pp. 321–22) established the presence of labia majora in older postnatal stages than those admitted by Bolk. Some doubts remained, however, with regard to the homologization of external genital folds in Old World monkeys, particularly in a newborn macaque (Wislocki 1936, pp. 322, 329, fig. 18). A subadult *Macaca mulatta* (fig. III.21) at hand, shows clear definitions between discrete organs that become obliterated in the genitalia of older individuals.

The female prepuce, treated by Bischoff as an extension of the labia minora, is in fact the homologue of the hairless reduplication of the male prepuce, or preputial annulus. Its attachment to the glans clitoridis by a frenulum or a pair of frenula preputii, one on each side, leaves no doubt of its derivation from a fold of the major labial swelling. Zuckerman, van Wagenen, and Gardner (1938) arrived at essentially the same conclusions in their study of immature macaques.[1]

[1] Osman Hill (1958, pp. 668–71) also discusses homologies of the external genitalia. He details the overwhelming evidence of the presence of labia majora in platyrrhines, as recognized by Klaatsch, Bolk, and Wislocki, but insists (p. 670), quoting himself for the year 1957, without page reference, that these swellings "are, nevertheless, labia minora." Osman Hill's description of genitalia (1957, pp. 168, 199 ff.) and even the captions (cf. 1958, fig. 29, p. 680) to his figures, are not based on current interpretations of homologies.

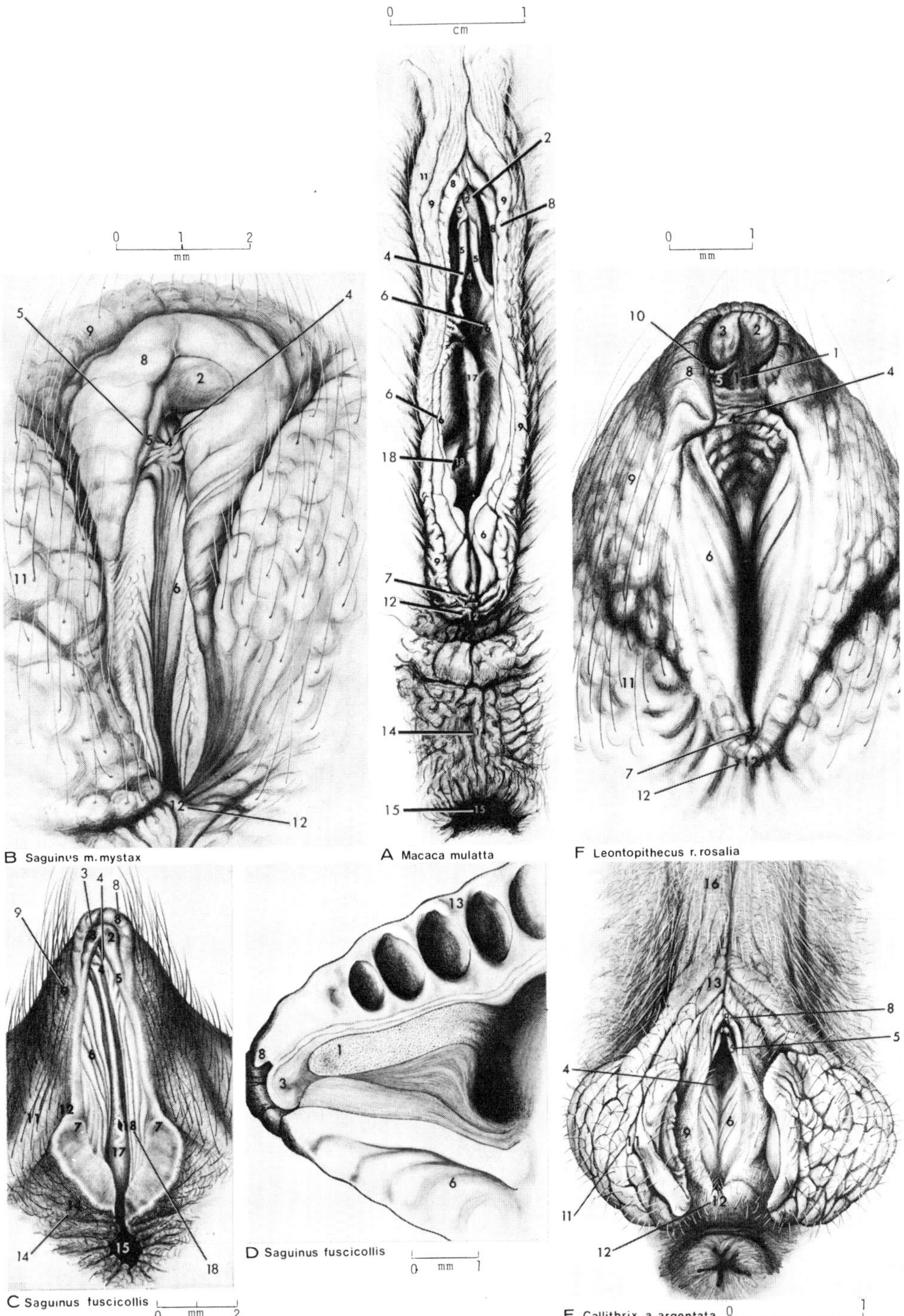

Fig. III.21. Female external genitalia and circumgenital region of Callitrichidae compared with those of a young macaque (Cercopithecidae) to show homologous structures: (*A*) *Macaca mulatta;* (*B*) *Saguinus mystax mystax;* (*C*) *Saguinus fuscicollis;* (*D*) *Saguinus fuscicollis,* sagittal section; (*E*) *Callithrix argentata argentata;* (*F*) *Leontopithecus rosalia rosalia.*

Explanations of Figures of External Genitalia;
Homologous Structures Are Numbered the Same

Female		*Male*	
1. Corpora cavernosa clitoridis	Clitoris and Labium Minus	*1.* Penial shaft	Penis
2. Glans clitoridis, left lobe		*2.* Glans penis, left lobe	
3. Glans clitoridis, right lobe		*3.* Glans penis, right lobe	
4. Urethral groove		*4.* Urinary meatus	
5. Frenulum clitoridis		*5.* Frenulum glandis (6)	
6. Labium minus		*6.* Urethral surface (6)	
7. Frenulum labiorum		*7.* Frenulum urethrae (6)	
8. Preputial fold, annulus	Labium Majus	*8.* Preputial fold, glabrous reduplication	Scrotum and Annexes
9. Preputial fold, hairy pad		*9.* Preputial fold, hairy pad	
10. Frenulum preputii		*10.* Frenulum preputii	
11. Scrotal fold or pad		*11.* Scrotal fold	
12. Posterior commissure		*12.* Scrotal raphe	

(*continued*)

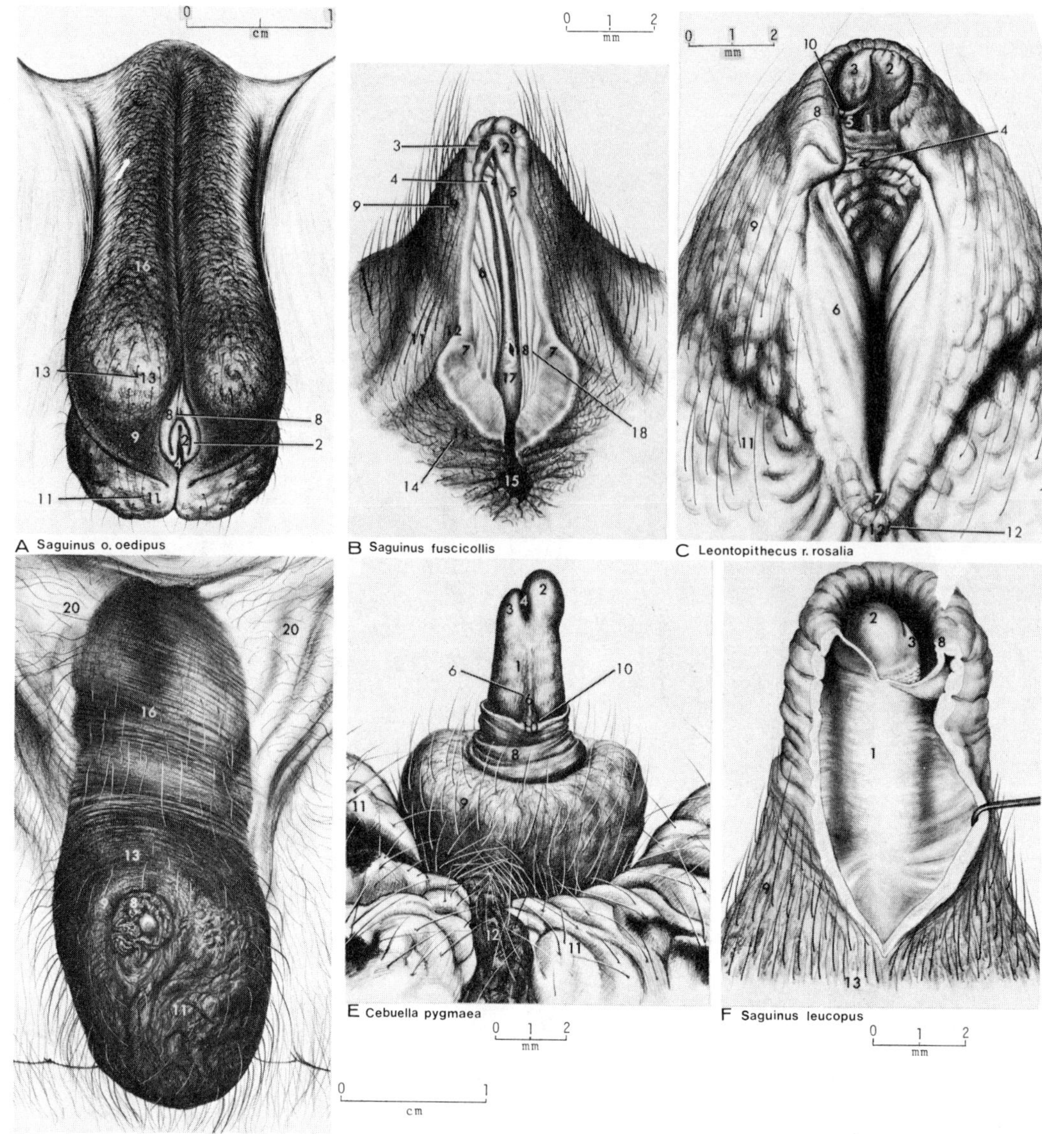

Fig. III.22. Male and female external genitalia and circumgenital regions of Callitrichidae compared to show homologous structures: (*A*) *Saguinus oedipus oedipus;* (*B*) *Saguinus fuscicollis;* (*C*)*Leontopithecus rosalia rosalia;* (*D*) *Saguinus nigricollis nigricollis* (juv.); (*E*) *Cebuella pygmaea;* (*F*) *Saguinus leucopus.* For explanation of symbols, see fig. III.21.

The labia minora in nonhuman primates are described by Wislocki as

> two thin folds of tissue lying medially to the labia majora, hairless, covered by stratified epithelium and containing numerous sebaceous and some sweat glands. They present a moist, reddish appearance, similar to that of a mucous membrane. Each labium divides anteriorly into two lamellae [two subdivided or paired lamellae in callitrichids] which fuse respectively with similar folds of the opposite side to form the frenulum clitoridis and the preputium [this last is a fold of the labia majora, see above]. There is some disagreement, which need not be discussed here, as to whether the labia minora fuse imperceptively with the labia majora to form the posterior commisure of the rima pudendi, or whether they retain their identity as an independent low ridge bordering the posterior wall of the vulva.

The homologies of male and female external genitalia and related areas are summarized in table 3. The parts are shown in figures III.21, 22.

Female	*Male*
13. Mons pubis	*13.* Mons pubis
14. Perineum	*14.* Perineum
15. Anus	*15.* Anus
16. Pubic sexual skin	*16.* Pubic sexual skin
17. Hymen	*17.* —
18. Urethral orifice	*18.* —
19. Ischial prominence	*19.* —
20. Inguinal fold	*20.* Inguinal sac

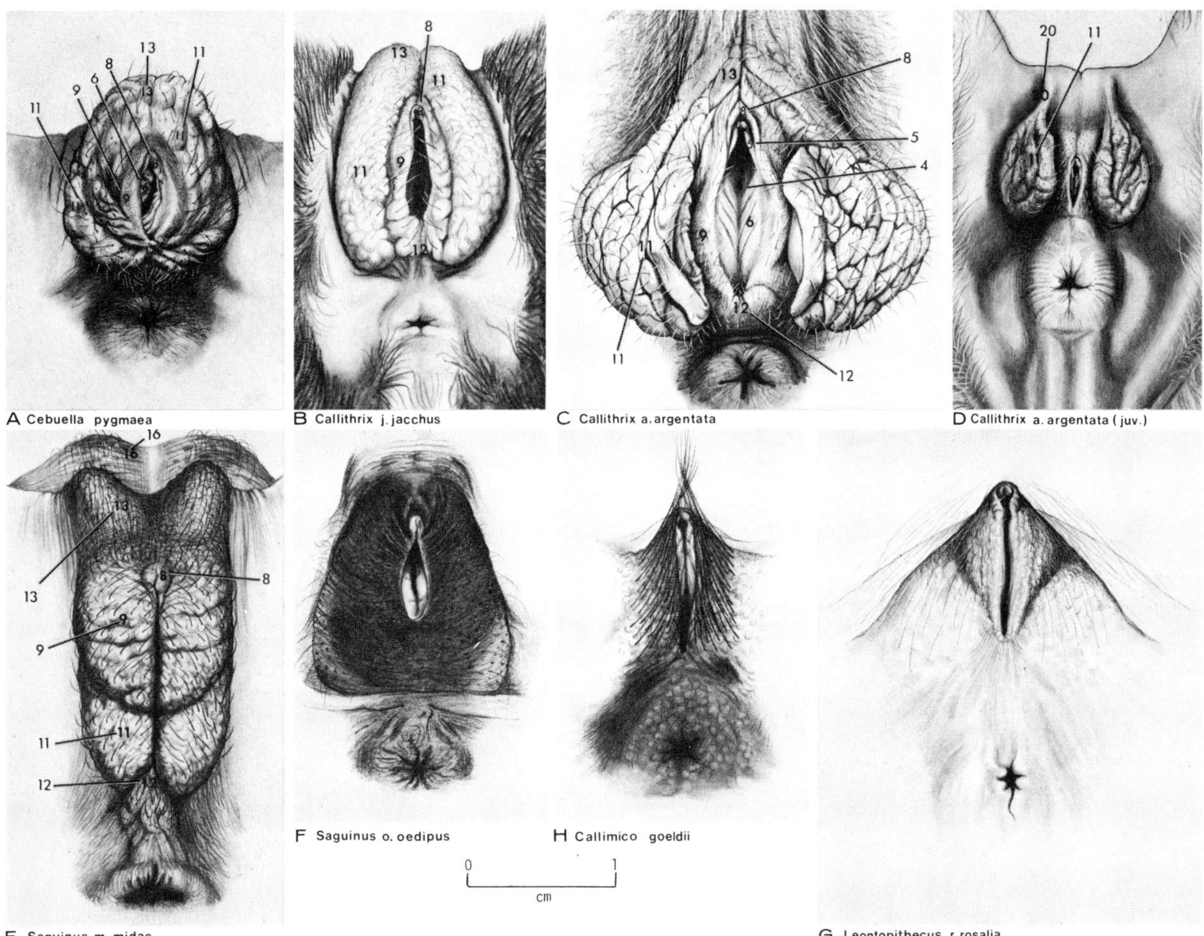

Fig. III.23. External female genitalia of callitrichids and *Callimico* compared for pigmentation and relative size and development of scrotal folds of labia majora (*11*). (*A*) *Cebuella pygmaea;* (*B*) *Callithrix jacchus jacchus;* (*C*) *Callithrix argentata argentata,* adult; (*D*) *Callithrix argentata argentata,* juvenal (note scrotal folds [*11*] and inguinal sacs [*20*]; compare with fig. III.24); (*E*) *Saguinus midas midas,* adult; (*F*) *Saguinus oedipus oedipus,* juvenal; (*G*) *Leontopithecus rosalia rosalia;* (*H*) *Callimico goeldii.*

Table 3. Homologies of External Genitalia and Related Areas

Indifferent Stage	*Female*	*Male*
Phallus	Clitoris	Penis
Phallic shaft	Corpora cavernosa clitoridis	Corpora cavernosa penis
Glans	Glans clitoridis	Glans penis
Urethral groove	Vestibule and urethral groove of clitoris	Urethral orifice; remainder of groove closed by fusion of lips
Urethral or genital folds, or lips of urethral groove	Labia minora (always hairless)	Urethral surface of penis
	Frenulum clitoridis	Frenulum glandis
	Frenulum labii	Frenulum urethrae
Labioscrotal swellings	Labia majora (characteristically hairy)	Scrotum, prepuce, and raphe at closure of labial lips
Posterior fold	Scrotal fold or pad	Scrotal fold
Median fold	Preputial fold or pad	Preputial fold
	Hairy lateral surface	Hairy lateral surface
	Glabrous medial surface	Glabrous medial surface
	Annulus	Annulus
	Frenulum preputii	Frenulum preputii
Anterior fold (median phallic swelling)	Mons pubis	Mons pubis
Pubic swellings	Pubic sexual skin	Pubic sexual skin
Perineum	Perineum	Perineum
Anus	Anus	Anus

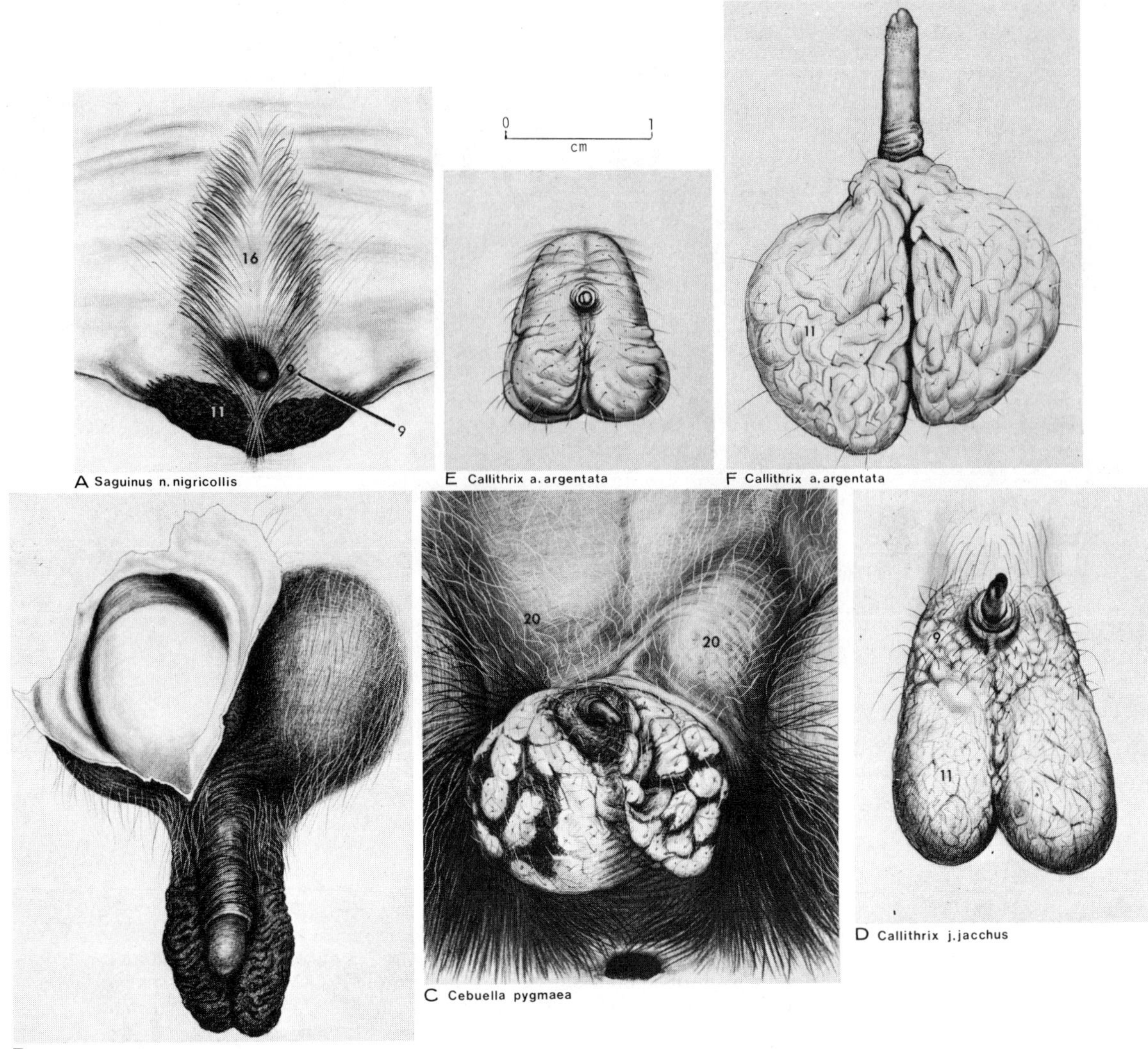

Fig. III.24. Scrota of juvenal and adult callitrichids: (*A*) fused scrotal folds of juvenal *Saguinus nigricollis nigricollis,* testes undescended. (*B*) collapsed scrotal sac of adult *Saguinus oedipus oedipus,* both testes retracted inguinally, the right testicle exposed; (*C*) *Cebuella pygmaea,* with left testicle retracted into inguinal sac (20); (*D*) *Callithrix jacchus jacchus,* adult with testes scrotal; (*E*) *Callithrix argentata argentata,* juvenal, scrotal folds, testes undescended; (*F*) *Callithrix argentata argentata,* adult, testes scrotal.

Scrotal Functions

The primary function of the scrotum is thermoregulation. It stores the testes, whether periodically or permanently, at a temperature slightly cooler than that of the abdominal cavity. As demonstrated by Moore and others (cf. Moore and Oslund 1923; Moore and Quick 1923; Moore and Chase 1923; Moore 1924; 1926; Wislocki 1933*a;* Cowles 1945, p. 160; Ulberg 1958), the cooler scrotal environment permits germ cell production, whereas normal abdominal temperatures (or heat experimentally applied to testes) causes deterioration of the germinal epithelium. In some mammals with comparatively low internal temperature, the testes are permanently and primitively abdominal. These are Monotremata (spiny anteaters and duckbills), some Insectivora (tenrecs, jumping shrews, golden mole), Xenarthra (anteaters, sloths, armadillos), Hyracoidea (dassies), Proboscidea (elephants), Sirenia (sea cows), and Cetacea (whales). They are inguinal, lying just beneath the skin in the Notoryctidae (marsupial mole), Phascolomiidae (wombat), Pholidota (pangolins), Tapiridae (tapirs), Rhinocerotidae (rhinocerus), and Pinnipedia (seals, sea lions).

A secondary but very important scrotal function is display (see below). Size, shape, and color of the mature and fully expanded scrotum combine to offer a conspicuous, often vivid visual signal. The female homologue of the scrotum, the labia majora, also serve for sexual display as well as for marking. These facts might seem to support the thesis presented by Portmann (1952, p. 179) that the scrotum originated primarily for display.

Portmann's proposition is based on some highly specialized primates, a choice of artiodactyls and a few other selected mammals. In rejecting Portmann's views, Ruibal (1957, p. 376) and Cowles (1958, p. 417) noted that the scrotum and the perineal and anal regions of the vast majority of mammals are inconspicuous. Further, the vast majority of scrotumed mammals are nocturnal and rely primarily on smell for sex recognition. It was also emphasized that the body temperature of mammals with testes permanently abdominal is as a rule constantly or periodically well below that of mammals provided with scrota. Finally, each author pointed to certain birds with systems for cooling the testes during the breeding season.

To the above must be added that the scrotum originated merely as the developmental homologue of the female labia majora, which would then be the primary organ. Less likely, the scrotum may have been the primary structure with the labia originating as developmental homologues. In any case, the primitive and comparatively inconspicuous scrotal swellings are capable of lodging the testes without serving as visual signals. The scrotum has no display value in juvenals, and its size in adults is directly related to testicular size. The scrotum shrinks with contraction or retraction of the testes. Any visual display effect attributable to size is evidently incidental. In females, swelling of the labia majora as a manifestation of the estrous cycle is related to increased activity of the specialized labial scent glands. The homologous scrotal skin in callitrichids is also glandular and odoriferous.

All evidence points to the scrotal display function as a relatively newly evolved and highly specialized phenomenon. The primary function of the scrotum remains thermoregulation of the testes during spermatogenesis.

As the homologue of the labia majora, the scrotum also became specialized in some groups, notably callitrichids among primates, for production of olfactory signals. With evolution of the visual sense and degeneration of the olfactory sense in some mammalian groups, scrota (and labia majora) of certain diurnal species tended to become conspicuous and even spectacular.

Baculum

The *baculum* or *os penis* is a mammalian structure without known homologue in other vertebrates. It is normally present in all male callitrichids (figs. III.25, 26,

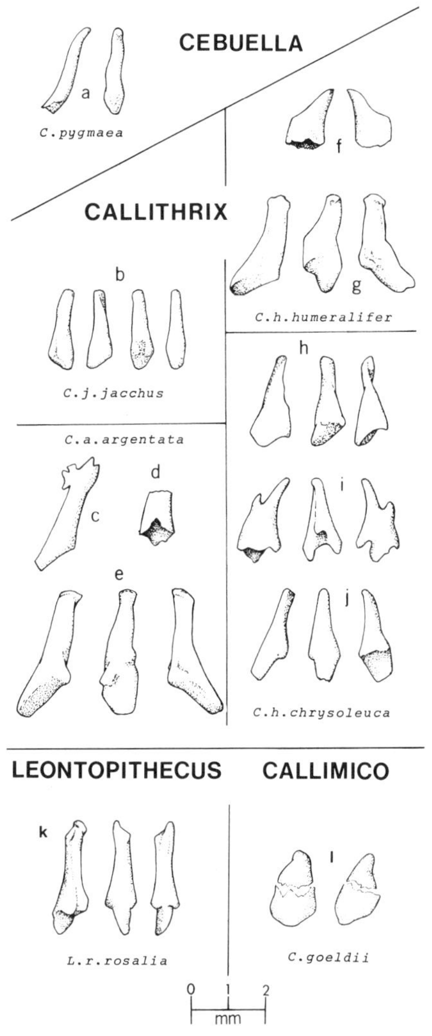

Fig. III.25. Bacula of callitrichids and *Callimico* (concave aspect regarded as right side): *a*, *Cebuella pygmaea*, two aspects of same; *b*, *Callithrix jacchus jacchus*, four aspects of same sample; *c*, *d*, *e*, *Callithrix argentata argentata*, three samples with three aspects of *e*; *f*, *g*, *Callithrix humeralifer humeralifer*, two samples with two aspects of *f*, three of *g*; *h*, *i*, *j*, *Callithrix humeralifer chrysoleuca*, three aspects of each of three samples; *k*, *Leontopithecus rosalia rosalia*, three aspects of same; *l*, *Callimico goeldii*, two aspects of same with severed proximal and distal portions of hollow bone in place.

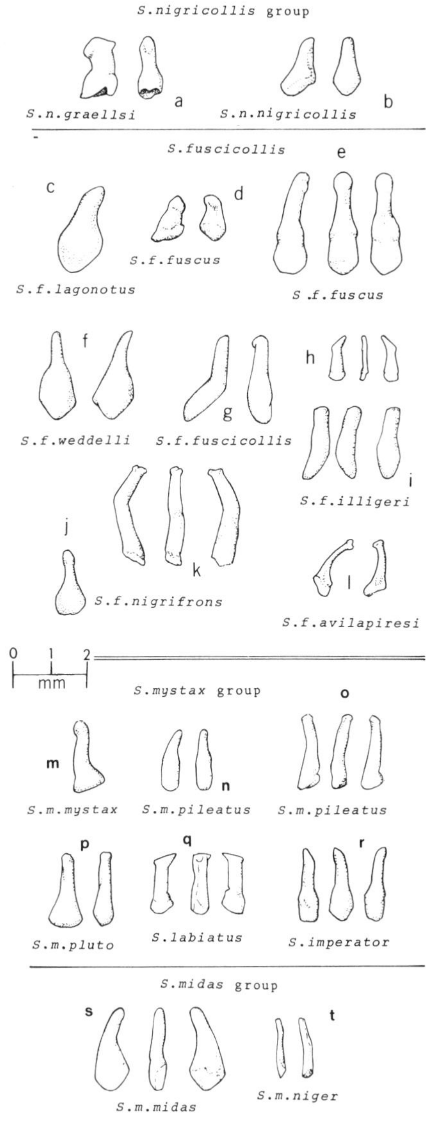

Fig. III.26. Bacula of hairy-face tamarins, *Saguinus* (concave aspect regarded as right side); *a*, *Saguinus nigricollis graellsi*, two aspects; *b*, *Saguinus n. nigricollis*, two aspects; *c*, *Saguinus fuscicollis lagonotus*; *d*, *e*, *Saguinus f. fuscus*, two samples with two aspects of *d*, three of *e*; *f*, *Saguinus f. weddelli*, two aspects; *g*, *Saguinus f. fuscicollis*, two aspects; *h*, *i*, *Saguinus f. illigeri*, two samples, with three aspects of each; *j*, *k*, *Saguinus f. nigrifrons*, two samples with three aspects of *k*; *l*, *Saguinus f. avilapiresi*, two aspects; *m*, *Saguinus mystax mystax*; *n*, *o*, *Saguinus m. pileatus*, two samples with two aspects of *n*, three of *o*; *p*, *Saguinus m. pluto*, two aspects; *q*, *Saguinus labiatus*, three aspects; *r*, *Saguinus imperator*, three aspects; *s*, *Saguinus midas midas*, three aspects; *t*, *Saguinus m. niger*, two aspects.

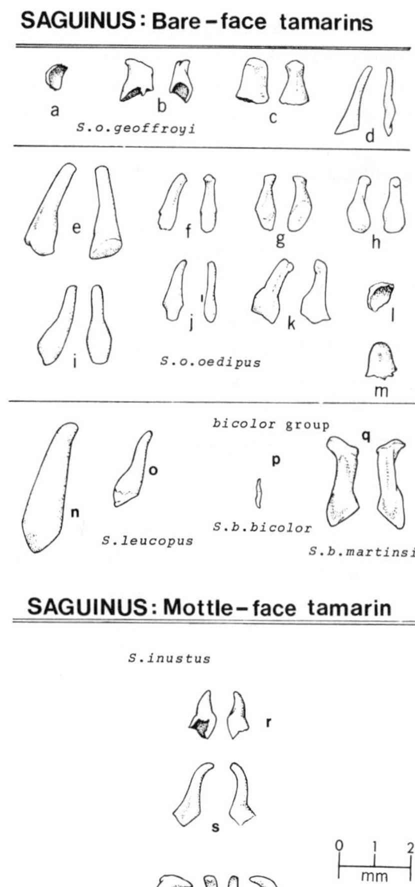

Fig. III.27. Bacula of Bare-face and Mottle-face tamarins, *Saguinus* (concave aspect regarded as right side); *a, b, c, d, Saguinus oedipus geoffroyi,* four samples with two aspects of three; *e* to *m, Saguinus o. oedipus,* nine samples with two aspects each of *e* to *k; n, o, Saguinus leucopus,* two samples; *p, Saguinus bicolor bicolor; q, Saguinus b. martinsi,* two aspects; *r, s, t, Saguinus inustus,* three samples, with two aspects of *r, s,* and four of *t.*

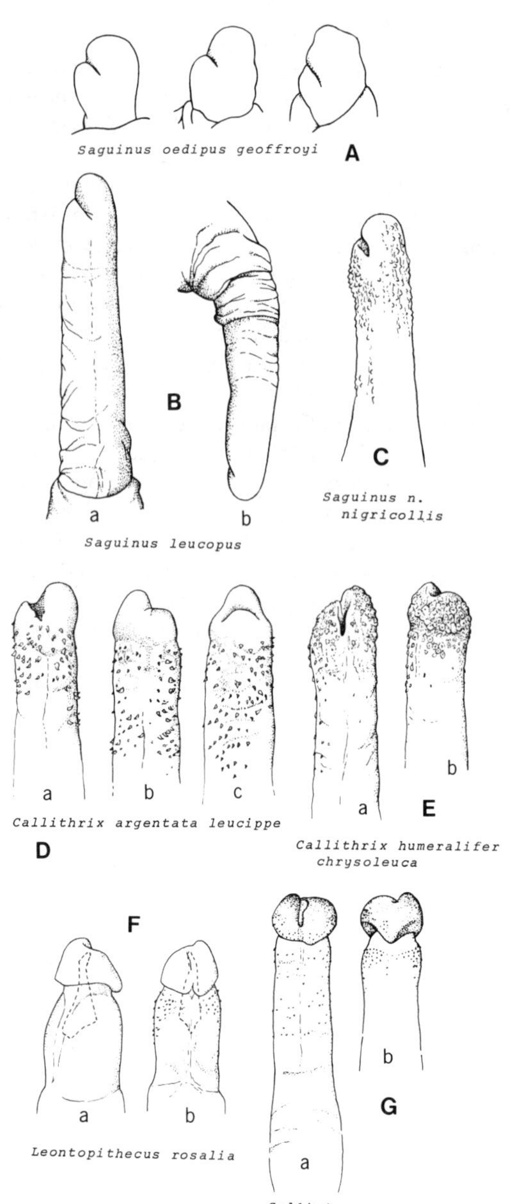

Fig. III.28. Penial staffs and glandes reconstituted with potassium hydroxide from dry genital organs on museum-preserved study skins, except *Saguinus oedipus geoffroyi* (*A*) and shaft with spines of *Callithrix* (*D, E*), and *Callimico* (*G*); see figs. III.22, 24 for size to scale. (*A*) *Saguinus oedipus geoffroyi*—ventral aspect of glans in three freshly killed individuals sketched (September 1959) from life by Dr. Eustorgio Méndez of the Gorgas National Institute of Tropical and Preventive Medicine. (*B*) *Saguinus leucopus—a,* ventral aspect; *b,* right side. (*C*) *Saguinus n. nigricollis*—knobby skin of fluid-swollen specimen. (*D*) *Callithrix argentata leucippe —a,* ventral; *b,* right; *c,* dorsal. (*E*) *Callithrix humeralifer chrysoleuca—a,* ventral; *b,* right. (*F*) *Leontopithecus r. rosalia—a,* right, *b,* ventral; baculum in situ shown by broken lines. (*G*) *Callimico goeldii—a,* ventral; *b,* dorsal.

27) and in nearly all other living primates. Its rudimentary homologue in the female genitalia, the *os clitoridis,* has been observed in most lemuroids, among cercopithecids at least in *Macaca cynomologus* (= *M. fascicularis*) (Pehrsen 1914, p. 165, fig. 3), among platyrrhines in *Cebus capucinus* (Wislocki 1936, p. 316), and in the siamang (*Symphalangus syndactylus*) and chimpanzee (*Pan! satyrus*) by Gerhardt (1909, p. 358, figs. 6*a*, 6*b*). An os clitoridis has not been detected in callitrichids. However, enlargement of the left lobe of the glans clitoridis, as in the baculum-containing left lobe of the glans penis, suggests presence of an os in the fetal or juvenal stage.

The baculum arose independently in a number of mammalian lines. It was almost certainly present in ancestral primate and subprimate stocks. So far as is known, the organ is absent only in atelines (*Lagothrix lagothricha,*[2] *Ateles paniscus,* and *Brachyteles arachnoides*), *Chiropotes satanas,*[3] the tarsier (*Tarsius syrichta sensu lato*) and man (*Homo sapiens*).[4] These forms are the most highly specialized members of their respective groups. Lack of bacula here is clearly secondary or degenerative.

[2] The postcranial skeleton and genitalia of *Lagothrix flavicauda* Humboldt are unknown.

[3] Of four specimens examined, present in two (palpated), absent in two (dissection).

[4] The baculum is present in all other living catarrhines, so far as is known. The belief that the os penis is absent in the so-called Celebese ape (*Macaca nigra,* or *Cynopithecus nigra* of authors) has been shown by Fooden (1969*a*, p. 23) to be mistaken.

Glans Penis, Asymmetry

The urinary meatus in all male callitrichids, *Callimico,* most cebids, most cercopithecids, and some anthropoids (*Hylobates concolor, Gorilla gorilla*) is deflected to the right because of the dorsomedian position of the baculum (figs. III.28, 29). The skewed aperture divides the glans penis into two lobes, with the left lobe, containing the baculum, larger and usually more projecting than the right lobe. In individual callitrichids, some cebids, notably *Aotus,* with the os penis greatly reduced or vestigial, and *Lagothrix* and *Ateles* (cf. Pocock 1925*a,* p. 37, fig. 11), where the bone has been lost, asymmetry of the glans persists. In all asymmetrical glandes, whether of New or Old World primates, the left lobe is always the larger. A comparable asymmetry of the left lobe of the clitoris has been noted in callitrichids.

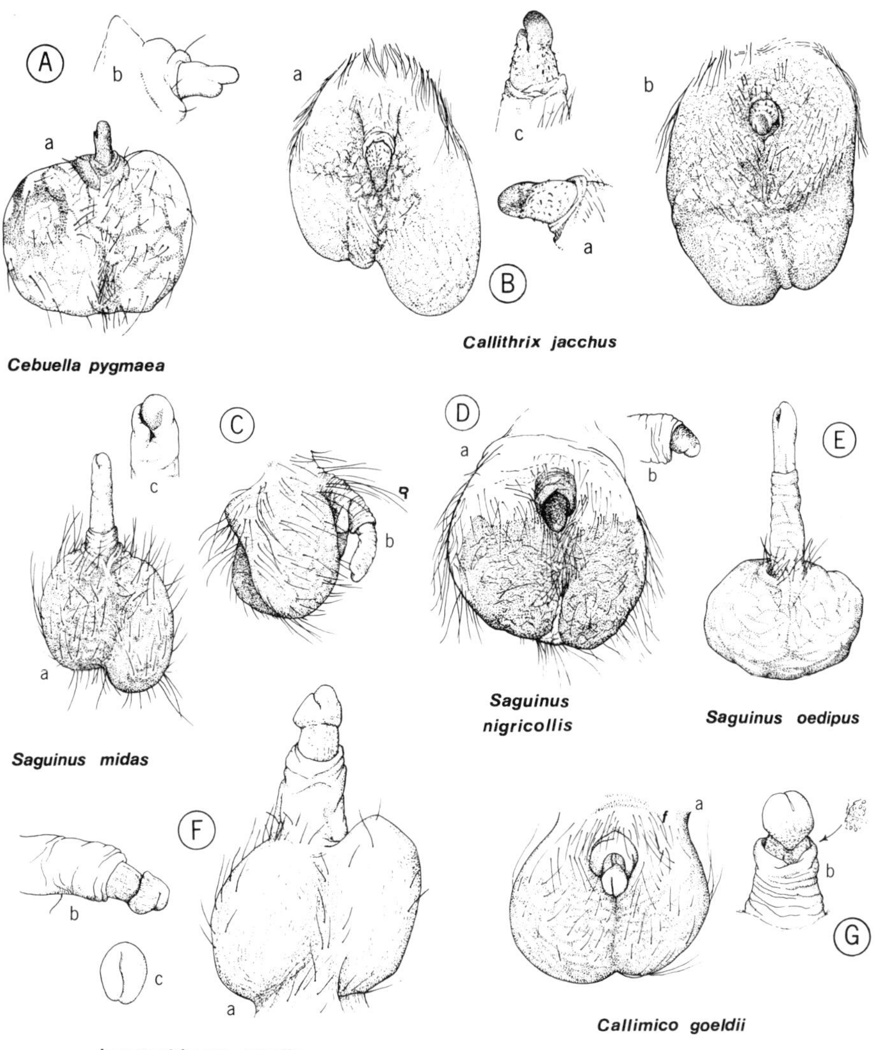

Fig. III.29. Male external genitalia of callitrichids and *Callimico:* (*A*) *Cebuella pygmaea—a,* Ventral aspect of scrotum and penis; *b,* lateral view of penis. (*B*) *Callithrix jacchus jacchus— a,* Ventral aspect of scrotum, dorsal aspect of penis; *b,* another specimen with penis in relaxed position; *c, d,* enlarged views of penis from ventral and left surfaces, respectively. (*C*) *Saguinus midas midas—a,* ventral aspect of scrotum and penis; *b,* right side of same, penis relaxed; *c,* enlarged view of ventral aspect of glans. (*D*) *Saguinus nigricollis—a,* ventral aspect; *b,* right side of penis. (*E*) *Saguinus oedipus geoffroyi*—ventral aspect. (*F*) *Leontopithecus rosalia—a,* ventral aspect; *b,* right side of penis; *c,* frontal view of glans. (*G*) *Callimico goeldii—a,* normal relaxed position; *b,* dorsal view of penis with enlarged section of spines shown in inset. All organs from more or less distorted spirit-preserved specimens. See figs. III.22, 24 for size to scale.

15 Monkey Rickets (Osteomalacia) and Vitamin D

The bone disease osteomalacia, characterized by rapid softening and deformation of the skeleton, has been observed in captive platyrrhines for many years. Ruch (1959) reviewed much of the early literature, but his accounts are almost entirely limited to clinical descriptions of the disease in catarrhines. Lucas, Hume, and Henderson Smith (1927, p. 447), and Lucas, Hume, and Henderson Smith (1937, p. 205), concerned only with the osteomalacia affecting the marmosets, *Callithrix jacchus jacchus*, in their laboratory, treated the diseased animals with artificial ultraviolet radiation. The exposures reversed, cured, and prevented the rickets or cage paralysis, as the disease was called. Supplementary feeding of commercial vitamin D proved ineffective with marmosets, and the use of vitamin D in cod-liver oil was regarded as impractical.

More than a quarter century later, Stare, Andrus, and Portman (1963) discovered that Vitamin D_2, the usual form fed captive animals, did not halt the progress of bone dyscrasia in a captive woolly monkey (*Lagothrix lagothricha*), but that vitamin D_3 reversed bone degeneration and prevented the disease. J. K. Hampton, Jr., (1964, p. 241, footnote) administered 400 IU of vitamin D_3 daily for the cure and prevention of osteomalacia in his colony of callitrichids (*Callithrix jacchus jacchus, Saguinus nigricollis nigricollis* [or *S. fuscicollis* subsp. ?], *S. oedipus, S. leucopus*), and *Callimico*. The amount was later (Hampton, Hampton, and Landwehr 1966, p. 267) increased to 500 IU per day.

Mallinson (1965, p. 139) also demonstrated the effectiveness of vitamin D_3 in reversing, curing, and preventing bone disease and cage paralysis in *Callithrix humeralifer, Saguinus imperator, S. nigricollis,* and *S. oedipus geoffroyi* maintained in the Jersey Zoo, Channel Islands. The treatment was used first on a West African patas monkey, *Erythrocebus patas,* "so immobilized that its head had to be held up so that it could eat. After three weeks of injection of vitamin D_3, the animal recovered completely."

Lehner, Bullock, Clarkson, and Lafland (1966), Bullock and Bowen (1966), and Bullock, Lehner, and Clarkson (1969) reported that bones of squirrel monkeys fed vitamin D_2 demineralized as much as those of monkeys completely deprived of vitamin D. On the other hand, a dose of 1,250 IU/kg diet of D_3 proved adequate to prevent radiologic and histologic signs of rickets or osteomalacia.

In a parallel flurry of articles, Hunt, Garcia, and Hegsted (1966*a*, p. 545; 1966*b*, p. 12; 1967), and Hunt, Garcia, Hegsted and Kaplinsky (1967) also showed experimentally that osteodystrophia fibrosa, as the bone disease was called, appeared in four platyrrhine species maintained on diets containing standard levels of vitamin D_2 (2,000 IU/kg). Substituting D_3 at the same level cured and prevented the disease in the same animals (*Cebus albifrons, Saguinus nigricollis nigricollis* [or *S. fuscicollis* subsp. ?], *S. mystax mystax,* and *S. oedipus oedipus*). Hunt, Garcia, Hegsted and Kaplinsky (1967, p. 943) provided a daily oral supplement of 500 IU of vitamin D_3 and D_2 in experiments with rickets in *Cebus albifrons*. In earlier tests they used up to 2,000 IU of vitamin D_2.

Boulay and Crawford (1968) recorded bone disease in cebids (*Aotus, Saimiri, Cebus, Lagothrix, Ateles* and callitrichids (*Cebuella pygmaea, Callithrix jacchus jacchus, Saguinus* sp., and *Leontopithecus rosalia rosalia*). They showed that catarrhines (*Erythrocebus, Papio, Macaca, Cercopithecus*) as well as platyrrhines developed osteomalacia when placed on a poor-calcium fruit and vegetable diet and that a high protein diet, rich in bone minerals, was essential for recovery in both groups. The protein-rich meat-rice diet consisted of rice cooked in milk mixed with cheese, egg, mince, liver, bread, bone flour, and small supplements of fruit and greens. The vitamin D content was estimated at limits between 50 and 100 IU per day. A curious incidental finding was that of 25 seriously diseased platyrrhines (of a total of 33 cases) all but one were males.

It appears that in catarrhines vitamins D_2 and D_3 may be equally effective in the metabolism of calcium and phosphorus for bone formation. In platyrrhines, however, presumably only vitamin D_3 is effectively utilized in bone metabolism and prevention of osteomalacia. The phylogenetic significance of the physiological difference is apparent.

Barker and Herbert (1972, p. 440) pose the question whether platyrrhines "really do not metabolize vitamin D_2 or whether they require higher levels of the vitamin than the Old World primates." They note in this context that "vitamins D_2 and D_3 show different potency in developing rats and chicks. Vitamin D_3 has equal potency in rats and chicks; vitamin D_2 has equal potency to vitamin D_3 in rats; but vitamin D_2 has only one-tenth the activity of vitamin D_3 in chicks. The relative effectiveness of vitamins D_2 and D_3 has not yet been fully determined for primates."

In nature, animals obtain vitamin D_2 by consuming plants that manufacture it from their own provitamins. Vitamin D_3, on the other hand, is obtained by conversion of provitamins in the skin of the animal through exposure to ultraviolet light from the sun or artificial sources (Hunt, Garcia, and Hegsted 1966*b*, p. 12). This may account for the compulsive need for sunbathing—even in freezing weather—by platyrrhines, particularly callitrichids.

No other vitamin is known to have the natural selective effects on the metabolism of higher categories of primates comparable to those of vitamin D. Chemical synthesis of vitamins D_2 and D_3 and their biological activities are summarized by Lam, Schnoes, and De Luca (1974).

16 External Characters of Living New and Old World Haplorhines Compared

a = Platyrrhini
b = Catarrhini

1. *a.* Nostrils widely separated, least distance between inner margins (across internarial septum) one-half or more greatest distance between outer margins (fig. I.9).
   b. Nostrils approximated, distance between inner margins less than one-half greatest distance between outer margins (fig. I.9).
2. *a.* Nose generally flattened, never conspicuous.
   b. Nose usually raised, sometimes conspicuously.
3. *a.* Cheek pouches absent.
   b. Cheek pouches present (in Cercopithecidae) or absent.
4. *a.* Small, well-developed tonguelike frenal lamella present (fig. III.19).
   b. Frenal lamella vestigial or absent.
5. *a.* Thumb present, vestigial, or absent; when present, nonopposable, or incompletely opposable without rotation at carpometacarpal joint (fig. I.26, 27).
   b. Thumb present, vestigial, or absent; when present, fully opposable with rotation at carpometacarpal joint (fig. I.27).
6. *a.* Manual digits II–V provided with claws or claw-like nails (tegulae), digit I with claw or nail (figs. I.20, 21; II.5; XIII.3).
   b. Manual digits II–V provided with tegulae or nails, digit I with nail (cf. fig. I.27).
7. *a.* Ischial prominences sometimes present (in Callitrichidae [fig. I.15]), pads or callosities absent.
   b. Ischial prominences present and provided with pads or callosities (Cercopithecidae, Hylobatidae [fig. I.16]), or absent.
8. *a.* Ischial tuberosities narrow, unspecialized, greatest depth usually less than one-third greatest breadth (fig. I.14).
   b. Ischial tuberosities wide or flared, specialized for support of ischial callosities, greatest depth usually more than one-third greatest breadth (fig. I.14).
9. *a.* Tail always present, as long as or longer than length of head and body combined (except in *Cacajao* [fig. II.6], where it is much shorter); prehensile in some (*Alouatta, Cebus, Lagothrix, Ateles,* [fig. II.7], *Brachyteles*) (figs. II.5; III.4).
   b. Tail present or absent; where present, ranging from vestigial to more than length of head and body combined; never prehensile.
10. *a.* Eccrine sweat glands absent on hairy parts of body except in larger prehensile-tailed species (atelines, howlers).
    b. Eccrine sweat glands present, distributed over body surface including hairy and friction areas.
11. *a.* Cutaneous scent glands usually present.
    b. Cutaneous scent glands usually absent.
12. *a.* Body weight of sitting animal supported mainly by feet or combination of feet, hands, and/or tail (figs. I.18; III.4).
    b. Body weight of sitting animal supported mainly on rump or ischial callosities (figs. I.17, 19).

17 External Characters of Living Platyrrhine Families Compared

a = Callitrichidae
b = Callimiconidae
c = Cebidae
(Figs. II.5; III.4)

1. *a.* Size and form squirrellike; combined head and body length measured in straight line less than 350 mm, but more than 100 mm (fig. III.4; appendix table 1).
   b. As in *a* but combined head and body length between 200 and 250 mm (fig. III.4; appendix table 1).
   c. Size and form always monkeylike, combined head and body length more than 200 mm but less than 700 mm (fig. III.4).
2. *a.* Hands with 5 more or less evenly spaced, well-developed digits, all with claw; thumb unopposable (figs. I.20, 26, 28; II.5; XII.3).
   b. As in *a.*
   c. Hands with 4 or 5 digits, the thumb with nail, remaining digits with clawlike nails or tegulae; thumb semiopposable or nonopposable (figs. I.21, 27; II.5; XII.3).
3. *a.* Hallux semiopposable, provided with nail or clawlike nail, the digit when turned forward not extending beyond volar pad II, remaining digits with claws (figs. I.25, 28; II.5).
   b. As in *a.*
   c. Hallux opposable, provided with nail, the digit when turned forward extending to base of second digit or beyond; remaining digits of foot and hand with nails, clawlike nails, or claws (figs. II.5, 6).
4. Formula for distal projection of digits:
   a. Hands: 3 or 4–2–5–1; feet: 4 or 3–5–2–1
   b. Hands: 3–4–2–5–1; feet: 4–3–5 or 2–1
   c. Hands: 3 or 4–5 or 2–1; feet: 3 or 4–2–5–1
5. *a.* Tail completely furred, nonprehensile, always longer than combined head and body length, in some species with alternating dark and light bands from base to tip.
   b. As in *a* except alternating dark and light bands, if present, few in number and confined to basal one-third.
   c. Tail completely furred or with ventral surface of terminal one-fifth glabrous, prehensile or nonprehensile, longer to shorter than combined head and body length, and never banded as in *a* or *b* (figs. II.5; III.4).
6. *a.* Color pattern of head and trunk variable; headdress variable, but not as in *b.*
   b. Color of head and trunk dominantly blackish or dark brown with or without irregular grayish streaks or patches on back; headdress a unique pompadour (figs. XII.20, 21).
   c. As in *a.*
7. *a.* Eccrine sweat glands present on palms and soles only.
   b. As in *a.*
   c. Eccrine sweat glands as in *a* in nonprehensile-tailed cebids and in *Cebus,* but present in hairy parts of skin in *Alouatta, Lagothrix, Ateles,* and *Brachyteles.*

18 Skull
1. Introduction and Facial Region

The description of cranial characters and evolutionary processes is based on large series of callitrichids, a representative collection of cebids, samples of the genera of all remaining primate groups, and comparisons with skulls of other mammalian orders. The characters examined here have been selected for their special interest or importance in primate evolution or taxonomy or because they have been considered important in the literature.

Diagnostic characters for separating platyrrhines from catarrhines are keyed in chapter 27, and a key to callitrichid, callimiconid, and cebid characters is given in chapter 28. Figures IV.81–84 show all cranial elements, points, angles, and planes mentioned in the text and used in craniometry.

For convenience of reference, illustrations of a selected number of tupaiid and noncallitrichid primate skulls used in the comparative studies are brought together in chapter 29. The final chapter of this section on comparative cranial morphology includes keys to symbols and abbreviations used in the illustrations.

The cranial characters or character complexes described in this and following chapters are found under the subheadings listed below.

Zygomatic Arch

The zygomatic arch, including the outer orbital margin, seems slender and weak in contrast with the inflated braincase, especially in higher primates. Nevertheless, the arch is strong, and in few orders of mammals is it as universally complete, complex, and prominent as in primates. The malar portion of the zygomatic arch is particularly enlarged and is one of the most salient features of the order (cf. chap. 29).

Nasal Aperture

The opening to the nasal cavity is bounded above by the nasal bones, below by the palatal processes of the premaxillae, and laterally by the nasal processes of the premaxillae (frontal processes of maxillae in human anatomy.

The primitive form of the nasal aperture in primates, and perhaps in mammals generally, is rounded, subovate, or subglobose. The outline of the nasal aperture in primates (fig. IV.1) may be piriform with constricted end up

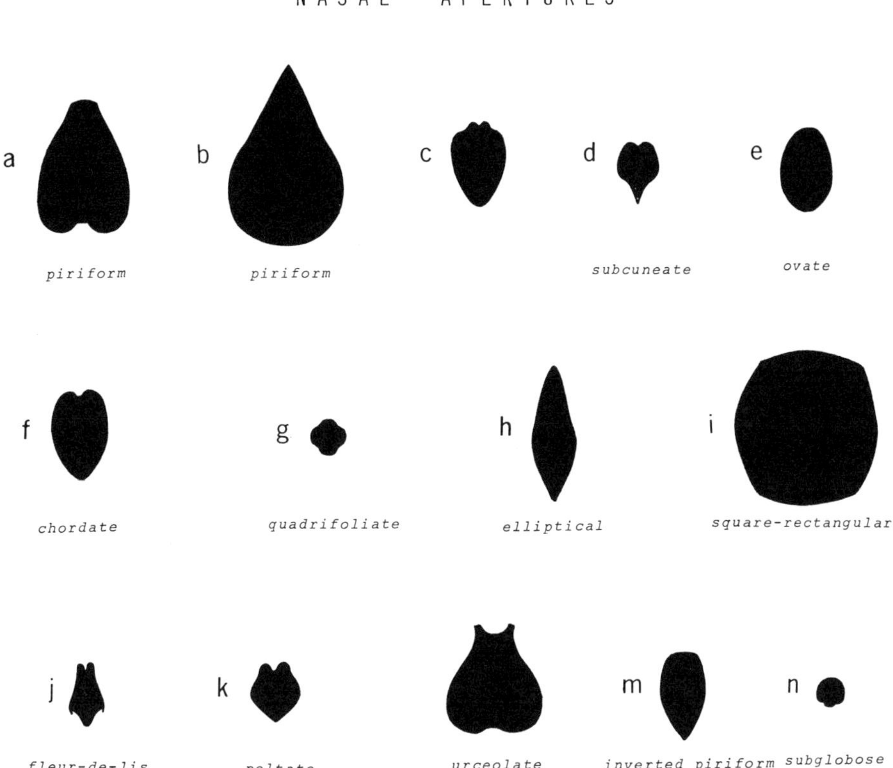

Fig. IV.1. Outlines of nasal apertures based on single specimens more or less representative of their respective genera; *a, b, piriform* with tapered end up as in man and orangs; *c,* piriform with tapered end down as in many New and Old World monkeys; *d, subcuneate* as in many monkeys; *e, ovate* as in many lemuroids; *f, chordate,* many monkeys; *g, quadrifoliate,* most callitrichids, many cebids; *h, elliptical,* most langurs; *i, square* to *rectangular,* some gorillas; *j, fleur-de-lis, Aotus, Callicebus; k, peltate,* gibbon; *l, urceolate,* chimpanzee; *m, inverted piriform* as in many monkeys; *n, subglobose* as in many lemuroids, insectivores, primitive mammals. Outlines drawn to a rough sliding scale.

(*a*) (*b*), as is common in man and orangs, or with constricted end down as in many monkeys including the proboscis (*c*); it may be subcuneate (*d*), ovate (*e*), or chordate (*f*), as in most monkeys, and ovate to nearly round as in many lemuroids, quadrifoliate (*g*) as in most callitrichids and many cebids, elliptical (*h*) as in many langurs, or nearly square or rectangular as in some gorillas. Whatever the shape, it is not restricted to any one group of living primates or correlated with the shape of the nasal bones (fig. IV.2). In general, however, the platyrrhine aperture tends to be wider between premaxillae, shorter between internasal and intermaxillary lines, and nearer the vertical plane, most notably in callitrichids and *Aotus,* than that of catarrhine monkeys (fig. IV.3). Meatal proportions and orientation are about the same in apes as in platyrrhines, and disposition of the human aperture is slightly more or less than vertical as in callitrichids generally.

Many individual variables cross lines between the dominant platyrrhine and catarrhine types. The relatively long, narrow aperture in some specimens of *Aotus* (*j*), or *Callicebus,* for example, resembles that of some individuals of *Cercopithecus.* Conversely, the broad, short aperture of some smaller macaques is like those of larger platyrrhines. Where form and size are not distinctive, structural or developmental details may be. Thus, the platyrrhine interpremaxillary suture of the inferior margin of the aperture usually closes incompletely and only

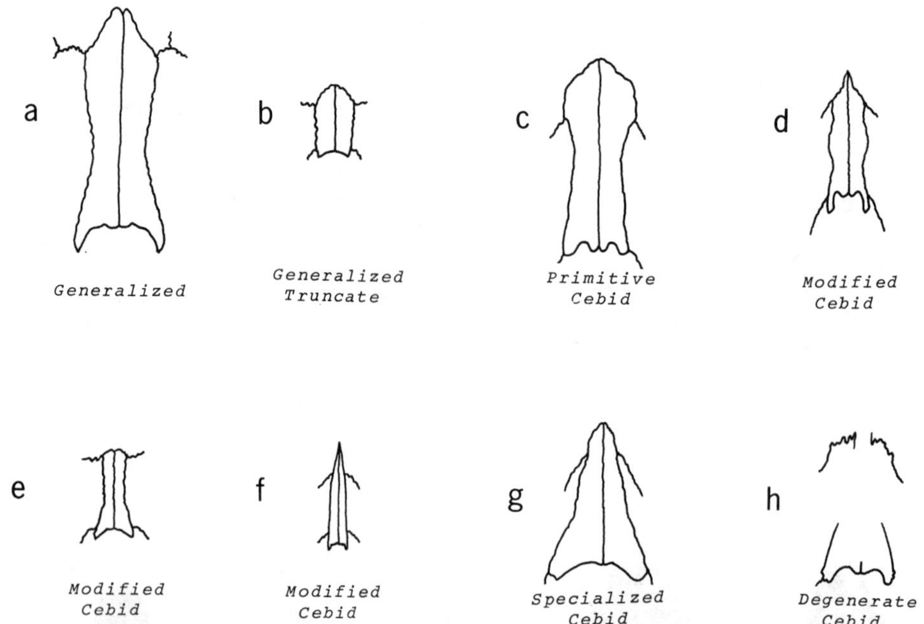

Fig. IV.2. Some nasal bone types in primates, examples for each in parentheses. *a*, generalized (lemur); *b*, generalized truncate (callitrichid); *c*, primitive cebid (*Alouatta*); *d*, modified cebid (*Aotus*); *e*, modified cebid (*Callicebus*); *f*, modified cebid (*Saimiri*); *g*, specialized cebid, trumpet-shaped (*Cacajao*); *h*, degenerate cebid, sutures fused (*Ateles*).

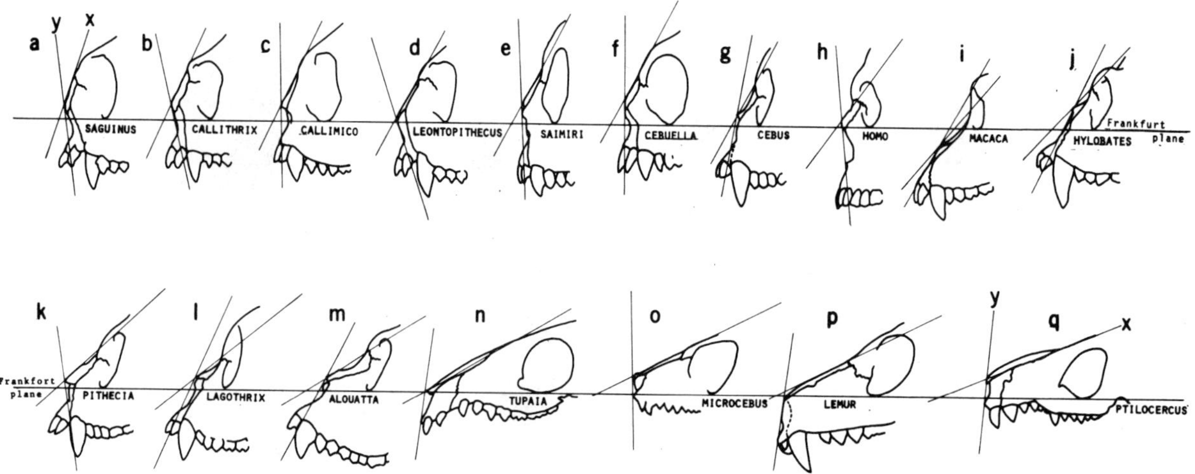

Fig. IV.3. Nasal angle (*x*, nasal tip to frontonasal suture through midline) and angle of nasal aperture (*y*, point between intermaxillaries to tip between nasals) are based on the Frankfort plane (line through top of auditory meatus and bottom of orbit). The nasal angle is slightly steeper than the rostral angle used elsewhere. Nasal angles of the samples are arranged from greatest (*a*) to least (*q*); where nasal angles of two samples are approximately equal, the sample with the steeper nasal aperture takes precedence. Nasal angle is least in tupaiids, lemurs, and howlers (*Alouatta*) among samples shown. Angles in humans (*h*) are not distinctive. Figures are based on individuals more or less representative of their respective genera; all drawings made to same scale.

a, Saguinus; b, Callithrix; c, Callimico; d, Leontopithecus; e, Saimiri; f, Cebuella; g, Cebus; h, Homo; i, Macaca; j, Hylobates; k, Pithecia; l, Lagothrix; m, Alouatta; n, Tupaia; o, Microcebus; p, Lemur; q, Ptilocercus.

after maturity whereas closure in catarrhines is, as a rule, completed at or before maturity (figs. IV.81, 82). On the other hand, the greater part of the maxillopremaxillary suture obliterates early in cebids, as in most apes, but persists well beyond maturity in most catarrhine monkeys. Callitrichids are nearer Old World monkeys in this respect. Finally, the nasal process of the premaxilla which forms the lateral border of the aperture just meets the lateral corner of the nasals in most platyrrhines but extends well between nasal and maxillary in most catarrhine monkeys. There is, however, broad overlap and considerable variation in this character.

According to Vogel (1968; 1969), the shape of the inferior border of the nasal aperture in some catarrhines is determined by root length and divergence of the upper incisors. The long, narrow aperture of Colobinae, as described and figured by Vogel (1968, p. 45; 1969, p. 25), is confined by the long, closely approximated incisor roots, whereas the broad aperture in Cercopithecinae is permitted by the shorter, more widely separated incisor roots. Although it is not specified, Vogel's observations are based on adult skulls with fully erupted permanent incisors. In my material, no consistent relationship is evident between the shape and position of the nasal aperture and the incisor roots. Long, short, divergent, and non-divergent incisor roots occur in every possible combination with broad and narrow apertures. In most if not all species, the nasal aperture attains its definitive shape before the permanent incisors are fully developed or erupted. Development of the incisors, in turn, depends mainly on the growth and ultimate form of the premaxillary bones. As for the nasal aperture, the variety of its shape is a factor of allometric growth of the defining bones, with the more actively or rapidly growing ones exerting selective pressures on the comparatively passive ones.

Nasal Bone

The nasal bone of a generalized placental mammal, as reconstructed from living forms, is long, narrow, one-third or more total skull length, expanded at its proximal half, and slightly tapered distally. Its dorsal outline is plane or slightly convex in sagittal section and evenly convex in transverse section. There is broad sutural contact with the frontal bone behind and the premaxillary in front, but mainly with the maxillary between; all sutures are well defined and persistent.

The nasal bone in lemuriforms generally, and *Lemur* particularly, remains generalized in most respects but deviates in its shorter length, reduction of frontal and intermaxillary boundaries, obliteration of nasopremaxillary suture in some species, and slight contoural distortion associated with pneumatization of the frontal bone (fig. IV.2a). The lorisiform nasal, collectively, is weaker, often widened distally, its dorsal contour usually slightly concave but markedly convex in the potto (*Perodicticus*); sutural contact with frontal and intermaxillary is more reduced than in lemuriforms and inter- and intranasal sutures become more-or-less fused in adults of some species.

The nasal of callitrichids (fig. IV.2b) is truncate in accordance with the short face but otherwise more primitive than that of any living primate. The bone is suboblong in outline, plane or sometimes slightly concave or convex in dorsal contour; sutural contact with frontal and maxillary bones is broad, with premaxillary variable and all inter- and intranasal sutures persistent. The *Callimico* nasal is like that of callitrichids but in most individuals a slight distal expansion is present.

The nasal bone remains short in the marmosetlike cebids but is attenuated proximally, expanded but not flaring distally, and slightly concave in dorsal contour; sutural contact between nasal body and frontal is usually reduced, while union with the premaxilla ranges from none or minimal in *Saimiri* and *Callicebus* to narrow or fairly broad in *Aotus* (fig. IV.2d-f).

The triangular nasal of pithecines (fig. IV.2g), with combined distal width from more than two to over three times greatest width across frontonasal suture, represents an important departure from the nearly parallel-sided bone of callitrichids and marmosetlike cebids; an expanded nasoturbinate is correlated with the widened structure. The nasal bone is evenly and shallowly bowed in dorsal contour and sutures tend to fuse in adults. Extent of contact with neighboring bones is highly variable.

In prehensile-tailed cebids, the sagittal concavity of the nasal bone is deeper, the transverse contour flatter than in other primates. The angularity appears sporadically in *Cebus*, more commonly and more deeply in *Ateles* (fig. IV.2h), and deepest as well as most consistently in *Lagothrix*. Distal expansion of the nasal is less pronounced in prehensile-tailed cebids than in pithecines, but it is more developed in *Cebus* and *Lagothrix* than in *Ateles* and *Alouatta* (fig. IV.2c). Erasure of the nasofrontal and nasointermaxillary boundaries is gradual and terminates with elimination of one or the other in many individuals. Fusion of inter- and intranasal sutures is also more advanced in the larger than the smaller platyrrhines, *Alouatta* excepted. In relative size, shape, and orientation, the nasal bone of prehensile-tailed cebids more nearly resembles that of man than other platyrrhines and catarrhines.

Among catarrhines (cf. chap. 29) the nasal bone of *Cercopithecus* more nearly resembles that of *Cebus* and *Ateles* than that of other platyrrhines or catarrhines. The bone is secondarily elongate in macaques and baboons, including drill and mandrill; in most colobines it is greatly reduced, especially in *Rhinopithecus* (fig. IV.135), where the vestigial nasal may be excluded from contact with the frontal by overlapping premaxillary and maxillary bones. Nasal bone reduction may reach the point of disappearance in some gibbons and the orang (Vogel 1966, p. 192). The sagittal concavity of the nasal bone in man may be more or less than in *Lagothrix* (fig. IV.3).

The internasal suture of catarrhine monkeys (except *Rhinopithecus* and possibly other Colobinae), chimpanzees and gorilla fuses much earlier and more completely than that of platyrrhines. In sharp contrast, the internasal fusion in man, orang, and gibbon is usually delayed until old age.

The dorsal outline of the nasal bone (rhinion-nasion) coincides with the facial angle in many forms, notably callitrichids and primitive mammals generally (fig. IV.3). It varies independently of the facial angle (prosthion-glabella) in higher primates. It also varies independently of the dorsal angle of the nasal aperture (prosthion-rhinion).

Premaxilla

The premaxilla, most anterior bone in mammals, supports all incisors, forms the inferior and lateral margins of the piriform aperture, and helps define the incisive foramen. Premaxillary evolution in primates involved minor reduction in size correlated with changing shape of rostrum and decrease in number and alteration in form and function of incisors. The process of obsolescence and obliteration of inter- and intrapremaxillary sutures appears to be continuous even when no other evolutionary change takes place (figs. IV.81, 82; chap. 29).

The premaxilla of callitrichids and *Callimico* is better developed, its sutures more clearly defined than that of other living primates except *Daubentonia*. In lemuroids, excepting *Daubentonia* with its powerful, specialized incisors, degeneration of upper incisors entailed reduction of the premaxillary palatine process and partial to complete obliteration in adults of all sutures, including the interpremaxillary. Nevertheless, the primitively broad contact with the nasal persists in lemuroids as in callitrichids.

Among higher platyrrhines, reduction of nasopremaxillary abutment and general obliteration of corresponding sutures are progressive processes. In *Callimico,* contact between the bones is not as constant or as broad as in callitrichids. Of the three marmosetlike cebid genera, *Aotus* most nearly resembles callitrichids; *Callicebus* least, with all adult sutures except interpremaxillary obliterated and contact with nasal minimal or absent; *Saimiri* is intermediate. Sutural obsolescence is more advanced in pithecines and most advanced in cebines. In all platyrrhines, sutures usually persist until maturity with the interpremaxillary suture the last to disappear in adults.

In contrast, the catarrhine monkey interpremaxillary suture disappears first, evidently before maturity, while the maxillopremaxillary suture persists well beyond maturity and in some cases into old age. Nasopremaxillary contact is more ample in catarrhine monkeys than in cebids, but there are many individual exceptions. According to Chopra (1957, p. 94) the suture between these bones tends to close sooner and more completely in female *Alouatta* and *Saimiri* and in male *Ateles, Presbytis* and *Macaca* than in the opposite sexes of the same forms. The difference is slight and probably reflects differences in canine tooth eruption.

The maxillopremaxillary suture usually disappears prenatally in man, during infancy in chimpanzees, and mainly during or after maturity in gibbons, gorillas, and orangs. The human interpremaxillary suture, however, persists despite fetal effacement of all other premaxillary sutures, a unique and paradoxical combination.

The present account, based on material in the Field Museum, agrees with results obtained by Ashley-Montague (1935) from his study of the premaxillary bone in 5,277 skulls representing the genus *Lemur,* 2 genera of callitrichids, 9 of cebids (including *Callicebus*), 10 of catarrhine monkeys, and 5 of apes. The same specimens also show that contact between frontal and premaxillary bones, said to be diagnostic of catarrhines (Wood Jones 1929), is practically nonexistent. Finally, the "nasomaxillary bone" seen by Ashley-Montague at the apex of the nasomaxillary process of the premaxilla in a small percentage of catarrhines appears to be an independent ossification of either the premaxilla or the maxilla.

Nasal Spine

The spina nasalis of the upper median margin of the premaxilla is consistently present and eminently developed in man (fig. IV.41). The nasal spine also occurs, usually as a rudiment, in individuals of other primate species (cf. chap. 29). Vogel (1963) found a low, blunt spina nasalis among great apes, and as a rare feature in some catarrhines (*Erythrocebus, Theropithecus*) and platyrrhines (*Alouatta, Callicebus,* and *Pithecia*). This character also appears sporadically in all other platyrrhines, except in specimens I have examined of *Cebuella, Leontopithecus,* and *Aotus.* It is best developed and occurs most frequently in *Callimico* and in *Ateles* but is absent in five available skulls of *Brachyteles.*

Orbital Cavity Volume

Orbital volume relative to body weight was determined by Schultz (1940, p. 389) in 208 nonhuman primates of widely differing ages representing all major taxons. Schultz's measurements show that in diurnal primates, the larger the species the relatively smaller its orbit. Orbital capacity in diurnal forms also proved to be relatively much greater in young than in old individuals, and somewhat greater in females than in males of the same species. The same size and sex relationship holds true for eye volume relative to body weight, according to Schultz. It was also noted that orbital capacity in nocturnal primates was proportionately much greater than in comparable-sized diurnal species. A random sampling of museum-prepared specimens indicates that the relationship between orbital diameter and either total length of skull or combined head and body length is comparable to the relationship between eye volume and body weight as reported by Schultz.

Lacrimal Bone

The primitive mammalian lacrimal bone together with the frontal and jugal bones, contributes to formation of the anterior margin of the orbit. The opening to the lacrimal duct was probably marginal in position and completely surrounded by lacrimal bone.

The primate lacrimal bone and fossa (figs. IV.4, 10) are passive structures, their form and position being determined mainly by the dynamics of the dominant bones and principal organs of a shifting orbit and changing face. Lacrimal bone evolution involved a dwindling in size, often of fossa as well, and the incorporation of these elements into the anterior wall of the orbit. In long-muzzled lemuriforms, lorisiforms, and tarsiforms, however, secondary enlargement of orbits and eyeballs forced the lacrimal duct outward beyond the orbital margin and into anterior contact with the maxillary bone. In the divergent lines leading to short-snouted platyrrhines and catarrhines, the duct or its fossa was more or less overrun by the marginal crest of the orbit; the anterior border of the fossa, however, exposed by the shrinking lacrimal, retained contact with the maxilla.

Pneumatization of the lacrimal extends from the maxillary sinus in all phyletic lines. The lacrimal of the tupaiids (*Ptilocercus* excepted), with its well-developed marginal lingula concealing a secondary foramen within the orbit, has no parallel among known primates (fig. IV.86).

Beyond differences and morphological correlations noted in lower and higher primates, the lacrimal bone and fossa have only a limited and qualified value for distinguishing certain intraplatyrrhine and intracatarrhine groups.

Among callitrichids, a facial portion of the lacrimal is often present, and sutural contact with the nasal bone is frequent in *Cebuella* and *Callithrix,* rare in *Saguinus,* absent in available specimens of *Leontopithecus.* It is individually variable in *Callimico.* In cebids (chap. 29), the frequency of a pars facialis and nasolacrimal contact is nearly 100 percent in *Alouatta,* high in *Ateles* and *Brachyteles,* moderate or low in *Callicebus, Aotus,* and pithecines, and rare in *Saimiri, Cebus,* and *Lagothrix.* In

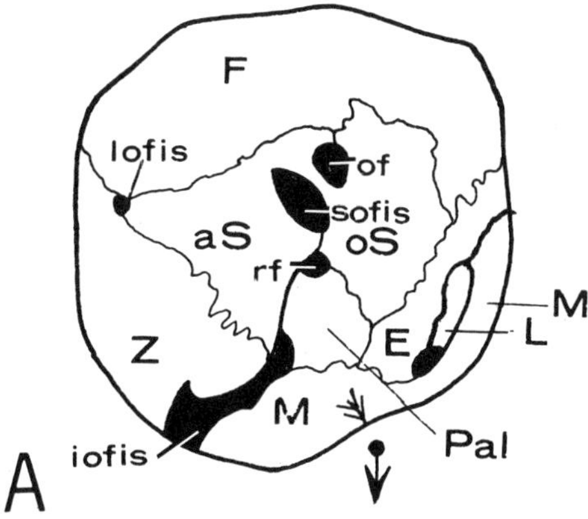

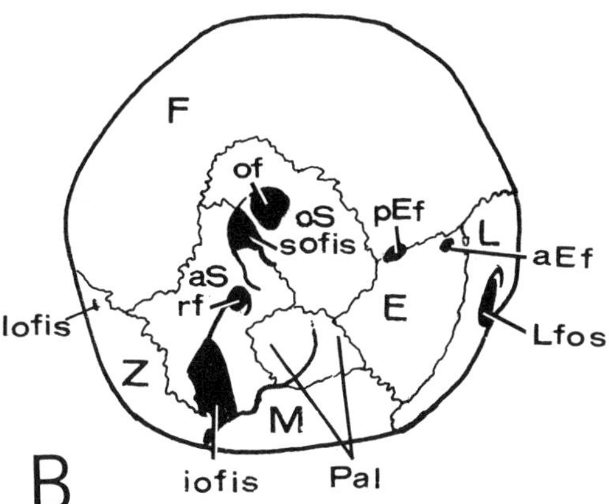

Fig. IV.4. Orbital fissures and foramina. *A*, Callitrichid (*Saguinus*) orbit distorted to show bones and apertures of inner and outer walls on same plane. *B*, Cebid (*Lagothrix*) orbit slightly inclined to show apertures of medial wall. Arrow locates infraorbital foramen; see chapter 31 for key to abbreviations. (Callitrichid orbit from Hershkovitz 1974.)

all cases, the maxillary bone contributes to formation of the lower anterior border of the lacrimal fossa.

In catarrhines, according to Major (1901), lacrimal bone and fossa are usually contained within the orbit and lacrimonasal contact is absent. The lacrimal fossa, however, sometimes extends slightly onto the face in *Nasalis, Papio, Macaca, Cercopithecus,* and *Cercocebus*. According to Vogel (1966), the maxillary bone enters into formation of the lower anterior border of the fossa in Colobinae, Hylobatinae, Ponginae, and Hominiae. Composition of the fossa in Cercopithecinae is variable, with the maxillary bone usually excluded in *Papio* and most cercopithecines, but frequently included in *Macaca*.

Evolution of the lacrimal bone in vertebrates was the subject of a classic study by Gregory (1920).

Malar Foramen

The malar foramen (jugal or zygomatical), appeared independently in a number of mammalian groups in which an enlarging malar bone surrounded the zygomatic nerve and associated vessels. In its most primitive state the foramen may appear as one or a few minute perforations of the malar (jugal or zygomatic) bone. Early specialization or expansion of the foramen, usually to a diameter of ½ mm, is noted in random samplings among marsupials (especially Macropodidae), fruit bats (mainly *Acerodon*, some *Pteropus,* rarely in other genera), bears (some *Ursus arctos*), pinnipeds (a few *Callorhinus*), rabbits (two immature skulls of *Poelagus*). The rudimentary to moderately developed foramen is undoubtedly more widespread than indicated here.

The highest level of foraminal specialization, in terms of size and number of nerves and vessels transmitted, appears in tupaiids and primates, especially among the larger prehensile-tailed cebids. The tupaiid malar foramen, usually a single large elliptical or rounded fenestration, is consistently present and, relative to skull size, larger than in all other mammals. The largest foramina in Bornean *Tupaia glis* are nearly 7 mm in diameter (fig. IV.86).

The malar foramen is almost universally present in primates (fig. IV.82). It is well developed, often with diameter of 1 to 2 or more mm in most lemuriforms (4–7 mm in *Hapalemur*) but is absent in some lemurines and in *Daubentonia*. It is minute or absent on either or both sides of the skull in lorisiforms, absent in *Tarsius*, and consistently present but highly variable in size and numbers in all other living primates (chap. 29).

The malar foramina in higher primates ordinarily perforate the central area of the malar bone. Frequently the dominant aperture, or a similarly large one, occurs high on the frontal process of the malar, sometimes athwart the frontomalar suture.

The principal foramen of the malar group is consistently larger in platyrrhines than in catarrhines of comparable skull size. Its diameter ranges from that of a mere pinprick to more than 2 mm in callitrichids, callimicos, and pithecines, up to 2 and 3 mm in the marmosetlike cebids and *Cebus*, and between 2 and more than 7 mm in the large prehensile-tailed *Ateles, Brachyteles, Lagothrix,* and *Alouatta*.

In most catarrhine monkeys the diameter is usually 1 mm or less, but may surpass 2 mm in baboons. It is usually less than 2 mm in man, somewhat larger in chimpanzees and gorillas, and may exceed 3 mm in gibbons and orangs.

The extremely large malar foramen of *Ateles, Brachyteles, Lagothrix,* and *Alouatta* was examined by J. Anthony (1946*b*, p. 69). Similarity in foraminal size and form, nerves and blood vessels transmitted, and the apparent lack of a sylviointraparietal fissural complex as determined from the modeling on the inner cranial wall of his specimens prompted Anthony to erect the family Atelidae for the genera in question as well as *Aotus* and *Saimiri* (his *Chrysothrix*). Pithecines and *Cebus* were retained in the Cebidae. Present material shows wide overlap in size of malar foramina between the family groups conceived by Anthony and no consistent relationship between size of aperture and pattern of the sylvian and intraparietal cerebral fissures.

The variable distribution of the malar foramen among prosimians points to a late and independent origin of the character in primates generally. Specialization, or enlargement of the primate malar foramen, is not consistently correlated with the evolution of any part of the head, face, or brain.

Presence of a malar foramen in tupaiids, regarded by Saban (1956, p. 53; 1957, p. 95) as evidence of primate affinities, could just as reasonably be interpreted as a mark of kinship with kangaroos.

Infraorbital Foramen

The infraorbital foramen, present in all mammals, is highly variable in size, form, and number of perforations in the different groups. The diagnostic value among primates is limited, but the aperture(s) is described here (fig. IV.82) for comparisons with the phylogenetically more important malar foramen.

The infraorbital foramen in prosimians (cf. chap. 29) is a compressed ovate aperture situated in front of and slightly below the angle of the orbit. The foramen in higher primates is usually divided into a complex of two or more perforations for transmittal of the infraorbital nerve and vessels. The largest of the apertures is usually beneath the lower border of the orbit, and the associated foraminules may be lined to one or both sides or scattered.

Among platyrrhines, the infraorbital foramen is consistently smaller than the malar foramen in *Lagothrix, Ateles, Brachyteles,* and *Alouatta.* It may be smaller or larger than the malar foramen in many individuals or populations of other platyrrhines, but the average size in the relevant species or genus is usually slightly smaller in cebids, slightly larger in callitrichids and callimico.

The catarrhine infraorbital foramen is similar to that of the platyrrhine in size, ramifications, and distribution but is usually larger than the malar foramen, more so in man, gorilla, chimpanzee, and colobines than in the remaining genera.

The number of infraorbital perforations in *Alouatta,* apes, and man was tabulated by Schultz (1954, p. 404). His findings, originally listed by species, are lumped here into their respective genera (mostly monotypic) as follows: *Alouatta,* 1–4 perforations (175 specimens); *Hylobates,* 1–3 (179); *Symphalangus,* 1–3 (27); *Pongo,* 1–6 (75); *Pan,* 1–4 (119); *Gorilla,* 1–3 (479); *Homo,* 1–4 (1038). The average number of perforations, according to Schultz's figures, is fewer than 2 in *Hylobates, Symphalangus, Gorilla,* and *Homo,* fewer than 3 in *Alouatta* and *Pan,* and fewer than 4 in *Pongo.* Intrageneric variation, judged by the same data and by my own samplings, is preponderantly individual and local and is much greater than indicated by Schultz's figures. As a rule, the number of infraorbital perforations in long-muzzled species is greater than in short-faced forms. In *Papio,* for example, there may be 10 infraorbital apertures.

The malar and infraorbital foramina of 7 platyrrhine genera were dissected by Oxnard (1957). This authority noted a close correlation between the caliber of nerves and the foramina through which they emerged. According to his findings, *Aotus* (1 specimen), *Callicebus* (2), and *Pithecia* (1), all with a small zygomatic nerve, are closely related. The caliber of the zygomatic nerve in *Saguinus* (= *Leontocebus,* 4 specimens) and *Callithrix* (10) proved to be variable; hence the genera were regarded as members of a distinct family. Perhaps Oxnard was not impressed by the considerable amount of variation including the bilateral asymmetry in the characters investigated.

Orbital Plane

In primitive primates, the inferior border of the orbit, oriented to the Frankfort horizon, lies below the plane of the jugal point which marks the vertex of the superior angle of the zygomatic arch (fig. IV.81). In living prosimians, the position of the inferior orbital border varies from slightly above to slightly below the level of the jugal point. In nonprimates such as tupaiids, hippopotami, equids, cervids, and cetaceans, with complete or very nearly complete bony orbital ring, the inferior margin remains below the level of the jugal point. The same appears to be true in didelphids, carnivores, many rodents, and other mammals with inferior border of temporal fossa distinguished from the orbital fossa by a short zygomatic (jugal) process.

In living platyrrhines and all catarrhines except hominids, the orbit, in moving to the front, rose above the plane of the jugal point. In hominids as in primative primates the inferior border of the orbit lies below the plane of the jugal point. The hominid condition may be attributed to the relatively small orbits that failed to expand in proportion to the expansion of braincase and face. Pneumatizations of the circumorbital bones fill the extra space between the small orbits and secondarily widened face.

19 Skull
2. Orbits

Orbital Closure

Evolution of the orbit in higher primates involved rotation of the eye to the front, with concomitant separation of orbital and temporal regions by a more or less perforated partition.

First indication of a bony partition between orbital and temporal fossae emerges in the form of a small postorbital process above, followed by a small postorbital jugal process below. This condition must have arisen in the preprimate stage of evolution (fig. IV.5[I]). The strepsirhine or earliest primate stage is marked by the sutural union of postorbital frontal and malar processes to form a single bony bar or ring that defines but does not separate orbital fossa from temporal fossa (fig. IV.5[II]). Although ocular enlargement and orbital rotation forward continued, a bony partition between orbital and temporal cavities did not evolve among strepsirhines.

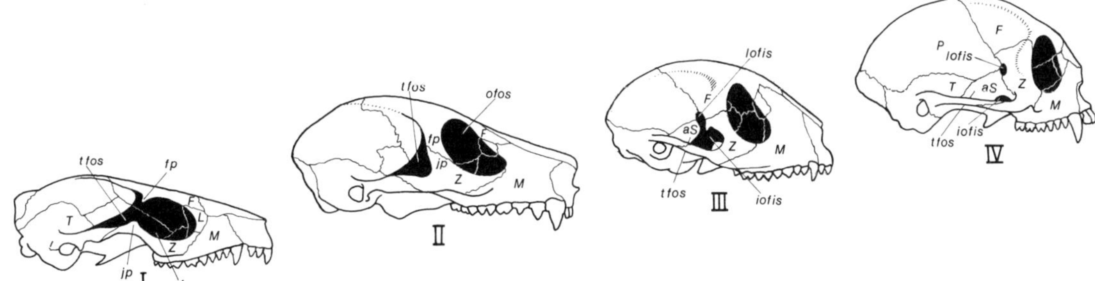

Fig. IV.5. Orbital rotation and closure from preprimate to platyrrhine. *I,* Preprimate stage, orbital fossa (*ofos*) and temporal fossa (*tfos*) partially differentiated by frontal process (*fp*) above and jugal process (*jp*) below. *II,* Prosimian prehaplorine stage, frontal and jugal processes united to provide a bony support for an enlarged, frontolaterally oriented eyeball. *III,* Haplorhine stage, tarsioid grade with incomplete closure of orbit behind and below to support a highly mobile and more frontally oriented eyeball. *IV,* Simian stage, orbital and temporal fossae (*tfos*) almost completely separated by bone; vestiges of orbitotemporal opening are the lateral orbital fissures (*lofis*) persistent in most platyrrhines, and inferior orbital fissure (*iofis*) present in all higher primates. (After Hershkovitz 1974.)

In some groups, however, a short bony flange or two for support of the postorbital membrane arose from the posterior border of the postorbital bar (fig. IV.6B).

A complete bony postorbital bar also appears in a number of nonprimates including tupaiids, artiodactyls (usually incomplete in suids, tagassuids, hippopotamids), equids, and most beaked and toothed whales. A completely ossified postorbital bar occurs as an individual variable among felids, viverrids, procavies, and the African manatee. The Paleocene *Plesiadapis,* generally treated as a primate, not only lacks the most elementary rudiments of a postorbital bar, but its postorbital region is narrowly constricted as in terrestrial quadrupeds, particularly those adapted for aquatic or fossorial habitats.

The tarsioid or earliest grade of the haplorhine stage is characterized by partial closure of the postorbital opening by means of flangelike protrusions of the malar, maxillary, and alisphenoid bones (figs. IV.6–8). Extraordinary expansion of the anterior orbital borders in *Tarsius* is an independent phenomenon.

Primitive platyrrhine and early tarsioid grades of postorbital closure are similar. At higher evolutionary grades, orbital processes of malar and alisphenoid bones united with a downward extension of the frontal bone and an upward salient of the maxillary bone. The resultant partition between orbital and temporal fossae is never complete (figs. IV.5[II], 6). One or two—infrequently three—small vestiges of the primitive orbitotemporal opening, the *lateral orbital fissures,* persist among platyrrhines. They vary from less than 1 mm to 5 mm in diameter among specimens examined and are covered by membrane. Lateral orbital fissures are usually obsolete or

POSTORBITAL CLOSURE

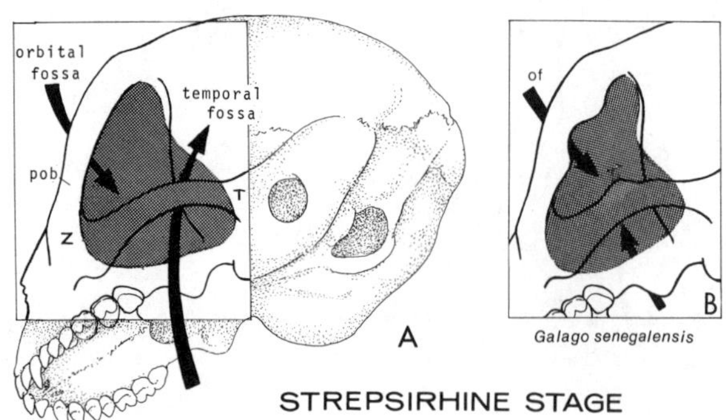

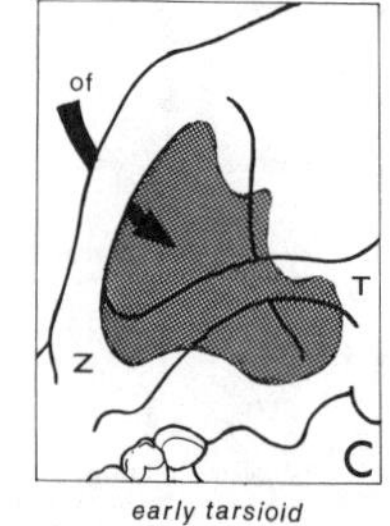

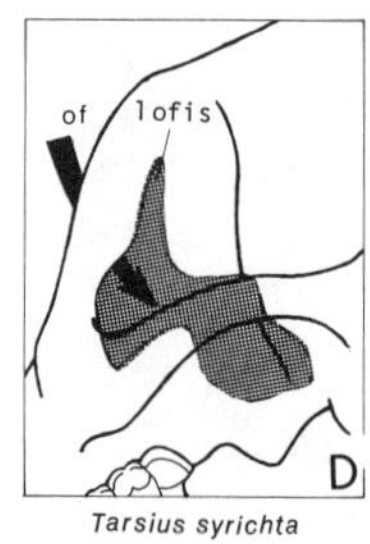

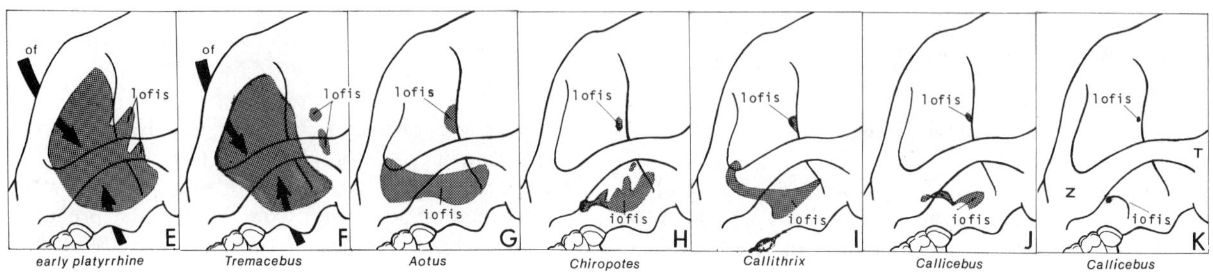

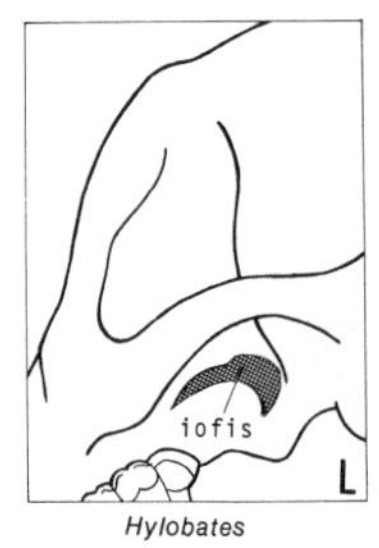

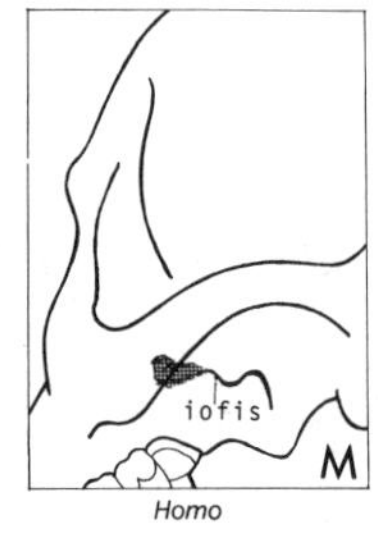

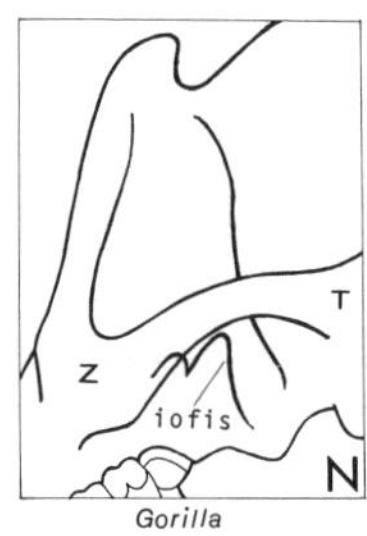

Fig. IV.6. Stages and grades of postorbital closure in primates, a reconstruction based mainly on living forms, seen from posterolateral aspect through temporal fossa and zygomatic arch (*Z, T*), orbitotemporal opening shaded; all figures drawn to same scale. STREPSIRHINE STAGE (lemurs, galagos, lorises), characterized by postorbital bar (*pob*) without separation between orbital and temporal fossae; *A,* Generalized prosimian; *B,* advanced prosimian (*Galago senegalensis*). HAPLORHINE STAGE (tarsioids, platyrrhines, catarrhines characterized by partial to nearly complete separation of orbital from temporal fossa by a bony lamina; *C–D,* tarsioid grade; *E, F,* primitive simian grades; *G–K,* advanced simian grades among living platyrrhines, postorbital closure more than one-half to virtually complete; *L–N,* moderately advanced to highly advanced grades among living catarrhines, postorbital closure moderate to virtually complete; *iofis* = inferior orbital fissure; *lofis* = lateral orbital fissure; *of* = orbital fossa tranversed by arrow; *pob* = postorbital bar; *T* = temporal (squamosal) process of zygomatic arch; *Z* = zygomatic (malar) process of zygomatic arch. (From Hershkovitz 1974.)

absent in living catarrhines but sometimes appear as mere pinpricks.

Largest vestige of the primitive orbitotemporal opening in higher primates is the inferior orbital (sphenomaxillary) fissure. The aperture in platyrrhines varies from approximately one-half the posterior orbital surface in *Tremacebus* and about one-third the surface in *Aotus* to mere slits in many individuals of *Callicebus* (fig. IV.6). This character alone fairly refutes Gregory's (1922, p. 220) assessment that *"Callicebus* seems to be on the whole the most primitive and also the most 'tarsioid' (in a broad sense) of the entire platyrrhine series."

The inferior orbital fissure is never large in living catarrhines but remains fairly extensive in most individuals of man, chimpanzee, orang, gibbons, and many cercopithecids. Seen from within the orbit of most haplorhines, the inferior orbital fissure is larger than the superior orbital (spheno-orbital) fissure and optic foramen combined, and exposes to view part or all of the foramen rotundum. In remaining catarrhines, and in some platyrrhines, notably *Callicebus, Saimiri* and *Alouatta,* with inferior orbital fissures constricted and often smaller than the optic foramen, the foramen rotundum is concealed from anterior orbital view. The postorbital opening allows the superior maxillary division of the 5th nerve to enter the infraorbital groove from the sphenomaxillary fossa.

According to Simons and Russell (1960, p. 13), postorbital closure in *Tarsius* "is chiefly effected by an

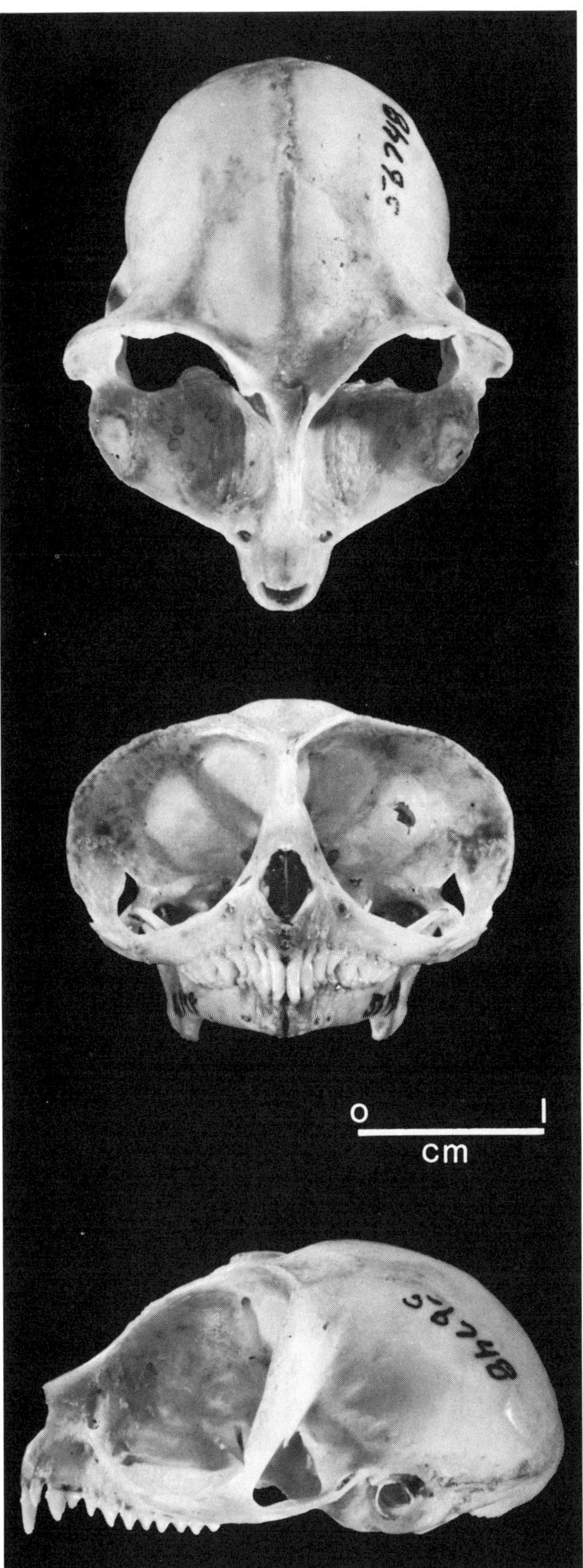

Fig. IV.7. *Tarsius*: Dorsofrontal, frontal, and left lateral aspects of skull.

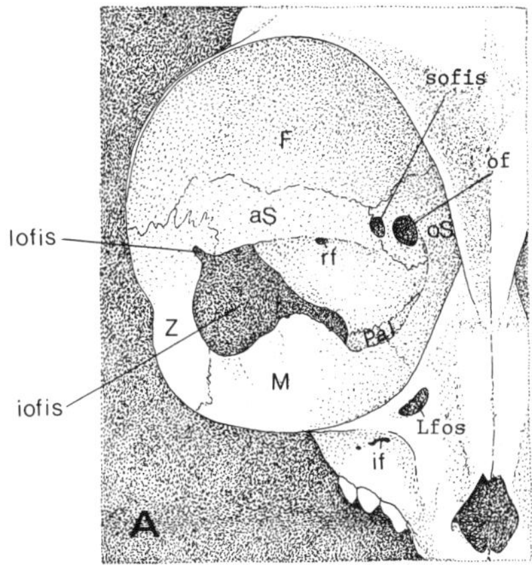

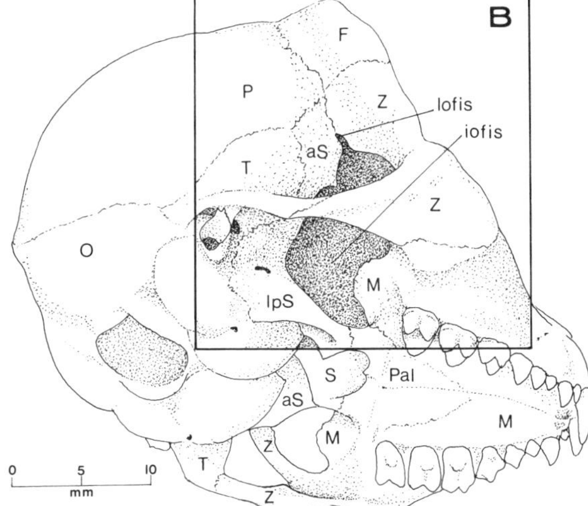

Fig. IV.8. *Tarsius*: Orbital fissures from in front and ventrolaterally, showing bones involved in early haplorhine stage of postorbital closure; see chapter 31 for key to abbreviations (From Hershkovitz 1974.)

outward and downward growth of a flange of the frontal (with relatively little malar expansion) while in higher Primates [platyrrhines and catarrhines] the greater part of the dorsolateral area of enclosure is contributed by the development of an orbital plate of the malar." In our large series of Philippine and Bornean tarsiers (*Tarsius syrichta* and *T. bancanus*), the incomplete dorsolateral closure is produced mainly by a projection of the malar bone anteriorly and an extension of the alisphenoid bone posteriorly; the maxillary bone contributes to ventrolateral closure. Involvement of the frontal bone in lateral closure is minor in most primates. Simons and Russell make no mention of the alisphenoid bone. The sutures of this part of the sphenoid bone in *Tarsius* are faint or indistinguishable and the element itself becomes fused or confused with the frontal bone.

Postorbital closure in higher primates is a continuation of the process that began in early tarsioids. The principal contributors to closure are malar, alisphenoid, maxillary, frontal, and sometimes the parietal, bones (fig. IV.9). Variation in the amount of postorbital surface occupied by each bone is considerable even within the same species or population. In all haplorhines, however, the malar bone contributes most, the parietal least, if anything, to formation of the bony wall between orbital and temporal fossae.

Present evidence shows that a single but highly variable type of ossified postorbital closure occurs among the Haplorhini (tarsioids, platyrrhines, catarrhines). In Strepsirhini, elaboration of bony support for the eyeball did not evolve beyond the postorbital bar stage.

Orbital Fissures and Internal Foramina

Closure of the lateral, inferior, and posterior orbital walls is complete in platyrrhines except for the residual

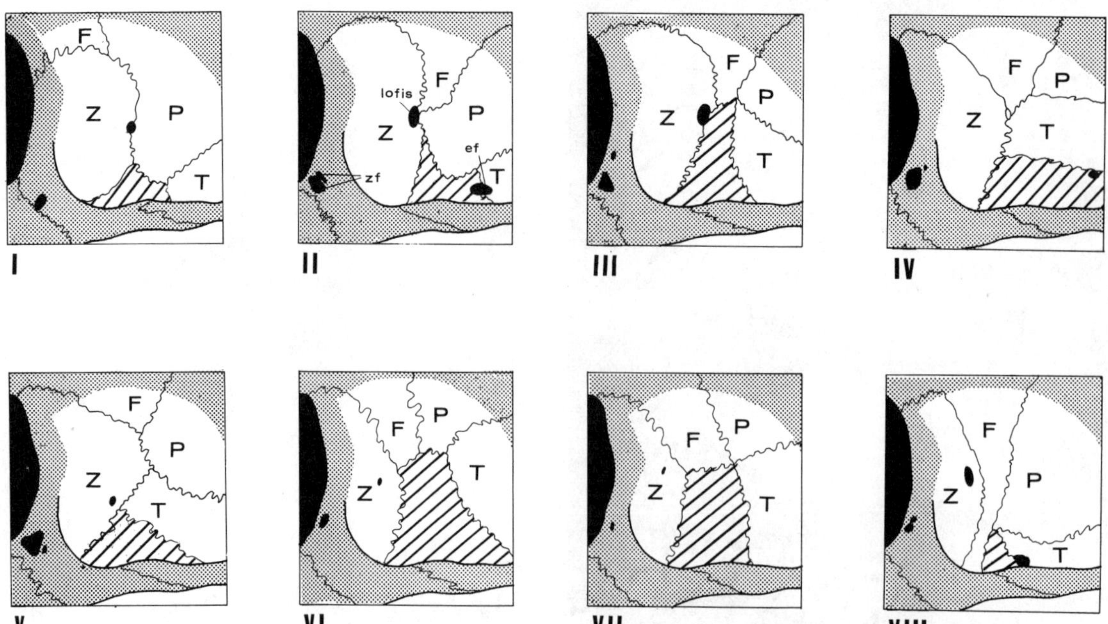

Fig. IV.9. Bone relationships on outer orbital wall, orbit, and foramina shown black, *alisphenoid bone with diagonals;* bone arrangements based on adult individuals which may or may not be representative of their species or superspecific groups; rare patterns (except *VIII*) not shown. *I,* Primitive, with broad contact between frontal (*F*), malar (*Z*), and parietal (*P*) bones (most platyrrhines). *II,* Malar-parietal contact reduced (based on sample of *Ateles;* large emissary foramen (*ef*) through temporal (*T*) or athwart sphenotemporal suture, characterizes *Ateles* and other large platyrrhines). *III,* Malar-parietal contact excluded by alisphenoid (based on sample of *Ateles*). *IV,* Malar-parietal contact excluded by alisphenoid and temporal (squamosal) (based on sample of *Lagothrix;* same bone arrangement characteristic of cercopithecoids, mainly cercopithecines). *V,* Malar-parietal-alisphenoid-temporal contacts broad (based on samples of *Alouatta* and *Brachyteles;* same arrangement present in *Lagothrix* and *Cebus*). *VI,* Malar-parietal contact excluded, alisphenoid-parietal-frontal contacts broad (based on sample of *Alouatta;* same arrangement common in colobines, gibbons, and man). *VII,* Variant of *III* (based on sample of *Alouatta;* arrangement also present in *Presbytis* [*Semnopithecus*], according to Olivier, Liberna, and Fenart [1954, p. 219]). *VIII,* Malar contact with parietal, squamosal, and alisphenoid excluded by frontal (based on sample of *Ateles* [FMNH 89242]), the arrangement is unusual). Apertures shown are ef = emissary foramen; *lofis* = lateral orbital fissure; *Zf* = malar foramen or foramina.

lateral and *inferior orbital fissures* described above (p. 131). Other apertures unrelated to and antedating orbital closure are the *superior orbital fissure,* the universally present *optic foramen,* and the sporadic *ethmoidal foramina* (fig. IV.4).

The *superior orbital fissure* is the archaic orbital fissure that opens just behind and mediad to the orbital foramen in strepsirhines and nonprimate mammals. The fissure communicates with the cranial fossa and transmits a number of cranial nerves and blood vessels. It is known as the *superior* orbital fissure in haplorhines where the residual opening of the neomorphic bony orbitotemporal partition becomes the *inferior orbital fissure.*

The *optic foramen* in callitrichids, *Callimico,* and prosimians is as visible from the middle cranial fossa (figs. IV.44–49) as it is through the orbit. This appears to be the primitive condition. In larger primates of all groups, the outline of the optic foramen is more or less hidden by the overhanging superior border and the body of the sphenoid bone. Together they extend backward as a thick deck with a lateral process, the anterior clinoid process.

Ethmoidal or *ethmofrontal foramina* are uncommon and of sporadic occurrence in platyrrhines (fig. IV.4). They are rare or obsolete in nonprehensile-tailed cebids, obsolete or absent in callitrichids and *Callimico,* and of variable occurrence in catarrhines generally.

Outer Orbital Wall

In platyrrhines, malar (zygomatic) and parietal bones are usually in contact. This is the primitive arrangement. In some individuals of howlers (*Alouatta*), spider monkeys (*Ateles*), woolly spider monkeys (*Brachyteles*), woolly monkeys (*Lagothrix*), and *Cebus,* the alisphenoid separates them. In rare instances the squamosal (temporal) also interposes between the malar and parietal bones (e.g., *Lagothrix lagothricha,* FMNH 31115). In a howler described by Pocock (1925*a*, p. 41) the malar contacts both parietal and squamosal. A similar arrangement appears in a young *Alouatta* and an adult *Brachyteles* at hand. Other combinations of sutural contact are possible (fig. IV.9).

In the vast majority of platyrrhines, the outer orbital bone relationship is more primitive than that of catarrhines. It involves expansion of fewer bones, particularly the orbitosphenoid and squamosal, and less secondary displacement of contiguous ones. Callitrichids, *Callimico,* and smaller cebids do not vary from the primitive pattern; prehensile-tailed cebids sometimes do. The difference is to a large extent allometric. The many forms of sutural contacts between malar, alisphenoid, squamosal, parietal, and frontal are determined by the differential rate of expansion of each bone as the skull enlarges.

In Old World monkeys the outer lateral orbital wall may consist mainly of the malar, or of approximately equal parts of malar and frontal bones in some species, or of variable amounts of frontal and alisphenoid in others. Sutural contact between malar and parietal bones, which occurs in nearly all platyrrhines, is excluded in catarrhines by interposition of the alisphenoid alone or by both alisphenoid and squamosal bones.

Sutural combinations of the temporal region are classified by Olivier, Libersa, and Fenart (1955, p. 218, fig. 135) as jugo (malar)-sphenoparietal, corresponding to pattern I (fig. IV.9), sphenoparietal for pattern VI, frontotemporal (squamosal) for pattern IV, and intermediate type for pattern VII. The arrangement in catarrhines, according to these authorities is either sphenoparietal (VI) or frontotemporal (IV), with one *Colobus* exhibiting the intermediate type (VIII). The proportional distribution of the various sutural patterns in several thousand catarrhine skulls was also calculated by Olivier, Libersa, and Fenart (1955, p. 220).

Orbital Cavity and Inner Medial Wall

The platyrrhine orbital cavity is more or less rounded in outline, with the lower anterior surfaces and floor evenly curved. In the vast majority of catarrhines, the cavity is modified by an inflation of the lower half of the inner anterior surface that forms a notable bulge on the orbital floor and often constricts the inferior orbital fissure.

The primitive arrangement of the primate inner medial orbital surface is based on broad sutural contact between frontal and maxillary bones and unexposed ethmoid, as in *Daubentonia* (fig. IV.10[II]). Partial intervention of the orbital plate of the palatine between frontal and maxillary bones, as in the Malagasy lemur, *Cheirogaleus* (fig. IV.10[III]), is an advanced condition. It leads to complete separation of frontal and maxillary by the palatine bone in most lemuriforms. Other advanced arrangements are exhibited by *Propithecus* (fig. IV.10[IV]), and tupaiids (fig. IV.10[V]).

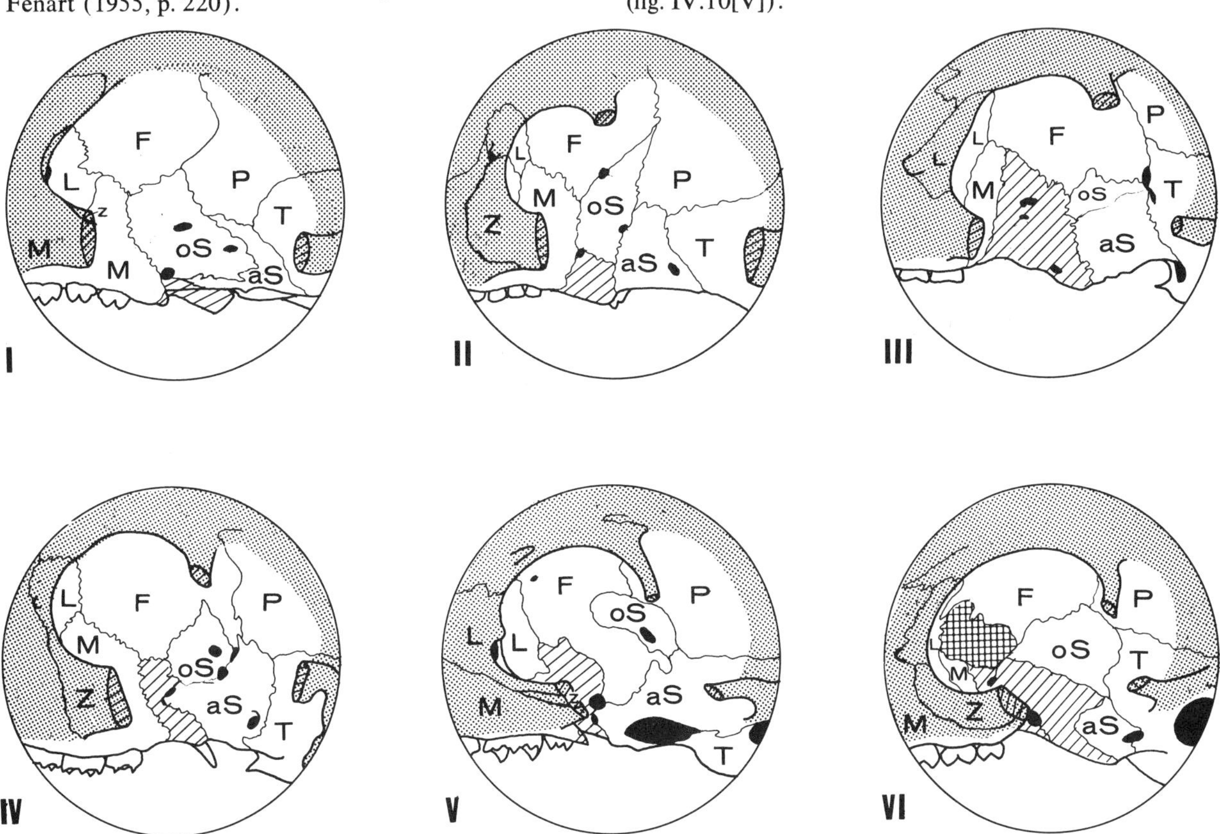

Fig. IV.10. Bone relationships on median and posterior orbital walls; lateral wall including part of zygomatic arch removed, *palatine bone lined diagonally, ethmoid bone cross-hatched. I,* Primitive mammalian pattern, with frontal (*F*) and maxillary (*M*) bones in wide contact, palatine excluded from contact with lacrimal (*L*), ethmoid bone unexposed; arrangement present in some insectivores (e.g., *Echinosorex, Tenrec, Hemiechinus*) and some lemuriforms. *II,* Primitive pattern in *Daubentonia. III,* Advanced pattern with contact between maxillary (*M*) and orbitosphenoid (*oS*) bones excluded by palatine bone, as in *Cheirogaleus* and other lemuriforms, some tupaiids and other insectivores. *IV,* Advanced arrangement as in *Propithecus. V,* Mixed pattern with contact between maxillary and frontal bones excluded by contact between palatine and lacrimal bones as found in *Didelphis, Tupaia, Urogale,* and some lemuriforms. The pattern may be primitive in some mammalian lines but appears to be secondary in primitive primates. *VI,* Complex pattern, ethmoid exposed and excluding palatine and maxillary bones from contact with frontal bone, as in *Microcebus,* lorisiforms, tarsier, platyrrhines, catarrhines. Other bones shown are *aS* = alisphenoid, *P* = parietal, *T* = temporal.

Intervention of both palatine bone and orbital plate of the ethmoid bone between frontal and maxillary bones, as in adult *Microcebus* (fig. IV.10[VI]) and possibly other lemuriforms (cf. Major 1901, p. 131), lorisiforms, tarsiers, and higher primates is the most complex arrangement.

All primate patterns of medial orbital bone articulations, from primitive to complex, are present in lemuriforms. The complex pattern appears regularly in higher primates, including platyrrhines. However, in gorilla and chimpanzee the frontal and maxilla often meet to form a narrow isthmus separating lacrimal from ethmoid. This pattern was found by Schultz (1963*a,* p. 92, fig. 4) in 57% and 50%, respectively, of an unspecified number of specimens. He also records this condition in 14% of pygmy chimpanzees and 3% of an undisclosed number of human skulls (but see Schultz 1962, p. 241).

Evidently, no one arrangement of the bones of the inner orbital wall is diagnostic of any major group of primates.

20 Skull
3. Interorbital Region

Comparative Anatomy and Evolution

The broad interorbital region of lemurs does not differ significantly from that of insectivores and didelphids. The more complicated interorbital region of galagos, with ethmoid exposed, can be derived from the lemuriform type and serves as a model for primitive platyrrhines and catarrhines [fig. IV.11].

A transverse section through the interorbital region of *Galago crassicaudata* below and in front of the brain (fig. IV.12), is roughly m-shaped. The cribriform plate of the ethmoid bone decks the m and most of the outer and middle walls are formed, respectively, by the orbital and perpendicular lamina of the ethmoid bone. The median wall rests on the vomer between its paired alae. The palatine bone floors the entire structure and contributes a base to each lateral wall of the interorbital region.

The area between lateral and median walls of the m is largely filled with the scroll-like turbinated processes of the ethmoid and maxillary bones. These bones are replaced behind by the sphenoid and palatine bones.

As orbits rotated forward in lines leading to platyrrhines and catarrhines the distance between them narrowed. Subsequent orbital enlargement without a compensatory increase in cranial breadth compressed the lateral plates of ethmoid and sphenoid bones toward their respective median plates. Continued expansion of the orbits, actually the eyeballs, at the expense of the interorbital region resulted in fusion of lateral and median bony plates into a thin, translucent, sometimes perforated septum. Examples of extreme interorbital constriction with defective bony septa are found in *Saimiri* (figs. IV.11, 21) among platyrrhines, and individuals of *Cercopithecus* (*C. aethiops* and other species) among catarrhines. The haplorhine *Tarsius* (fig. IV.7) is the only living example among lower primates, and combines lateral with medial orbital expansion for accommodating the enlarging eyeball. Lateral orbital expansion is also characteristic of *Aotus* and, to a lesser degree, *Callimico* and most callitrichids (fig. IV.13).

Progressive neurocranial, actually cerebral, expansion without commensurate orbital enlargement, such as occurred in the lion-tamarin *Leontopithecus* and man (figs. IV.11, 14, 15), entails dilation of the interorbital region. The extra circumorbital expansion is as a rule purely pneumatic. Elements lost or atrophied, such as certain endoturbinals, ectoturbinals, the transverse laminar process of the sphenoid, and parts of the septum, are never restored.

The primitive platyrrhine interorbital region may have been narrow in part but probably not to the extent of being a thin septum. Among living callitrichids the simple marrow-filled interorbital walls of *Callithrix jacchus* or *Cebuella pygmaea* (fig. IV.22) appear to be most primitive. The slightly more pneumatized walls of the larger *Saguinus* (fig. IV.13) are more advanced, and the notably cavitated interorbital and sphenoidal region of the somewhat larger *Leontopithecus* (fig. IV.14, 15) is most specialized. The interorbital region of *Cebuella* appears to be narrower than that of *Callithrix* but in proportion to body or skull size may be no less. In the case of callitrichids, at least, the narrower interorbital septum of the smaller species is due to the relatively larger eyes in smaller heads (fig. IV.11).

Callimico occupies an intermediate position between callitrichids and cebids with respect to interorbital inflation but is nearest *Callicebus* (fig. IV.16) or *Aotus* (fig. IV.17) with respect to orbital expansion.

Among living cebids, the interorbital region of *Callicebus* (fig. IV.16) is distinctly sinusoidal. *Aotus* and *Saimiri* agree with *Callicebus* in size, but their orbits are wider relative to cranial breadth. Major orbital expansion in *Aotus* (fig. IV.11) has been lateral, but median compression is also evident in the narrowness of its interorbital region. In *Saimiri* (fig. IV.18) expansion has been medial and encroachment of the orbits on the interorbital region has resulted in a thin septum with a large central fenestra (fig. IV.21). The orbits of larger cebids are relatively smaller, the interorbital region comparatively broader. In pithecines (fig. IV.31), and *Ateles* (fig. IV.35), the diploe of the frontal and sphenoid bones of the interorbital region is spongiform. In *Cebus* (figs. IV. 19, 20, 33, 36), *Lagothrix* (figs. IV.34), *Brachyteles*, and *Alouatta* (fig. IV.32), it is more or less pneumatized.

A consistent relationship between increasing skull size and increasing interorbital breadth within the various groups of living primates noted by Du Brul (1965, p. 261, abstract), does not seem to hold in the material I have examined. Nor do I find support for his generalization that as primate skulls enlarge the viscerocranial increase outstrips the neurocranial. In hominid evolution, neurocranial increase, mostly in breadth, far outstripped vis-

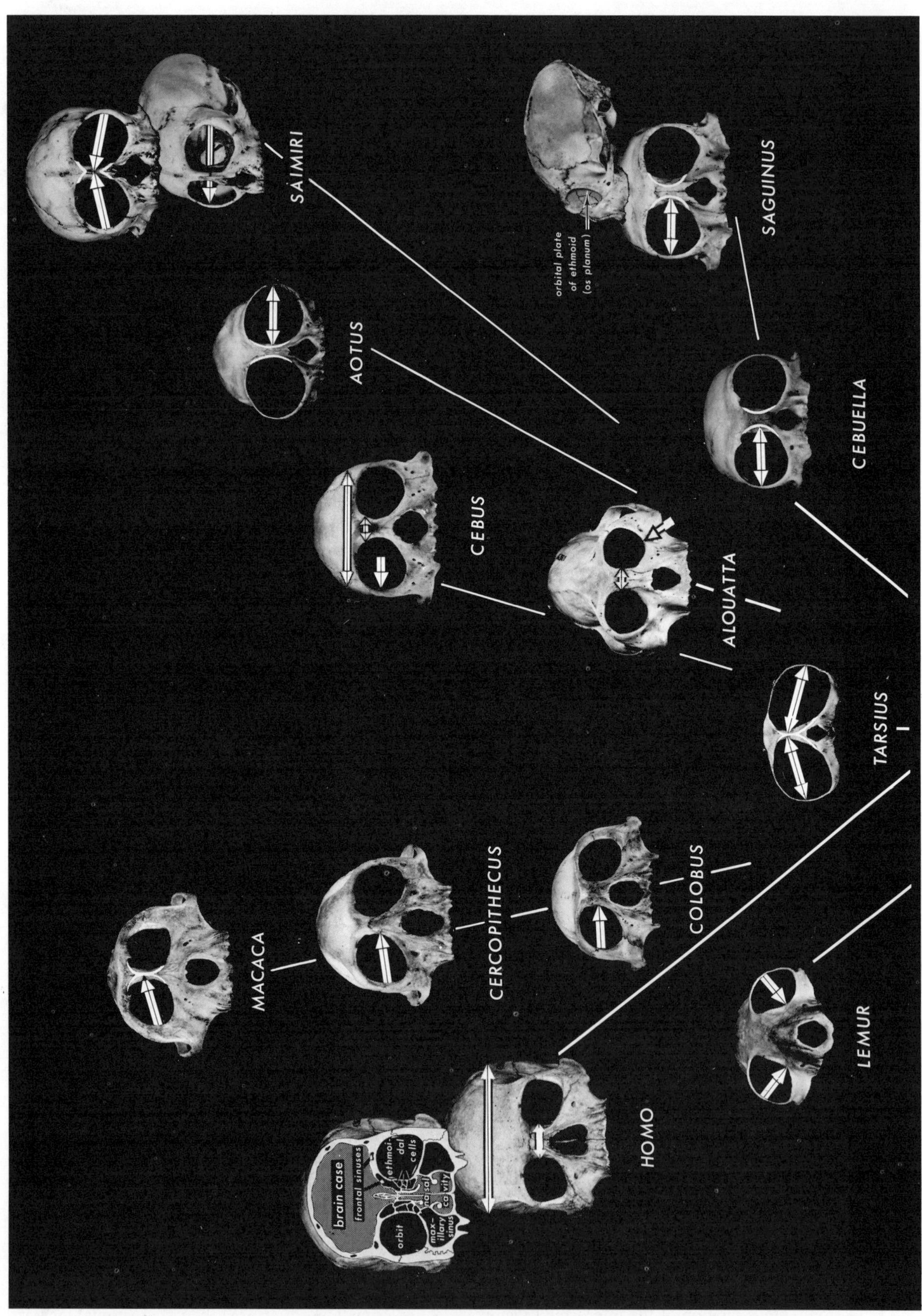

Fig. IV.11. Allometry in cranial evolution. Spatial interrelationships between orbital, interorbital, and frontal regions; not to scale, each figure reduced or enlarged to a uniform width across outer walls of orbits to facilitate comparisons of orbital diameters relative to cranial width. Straight

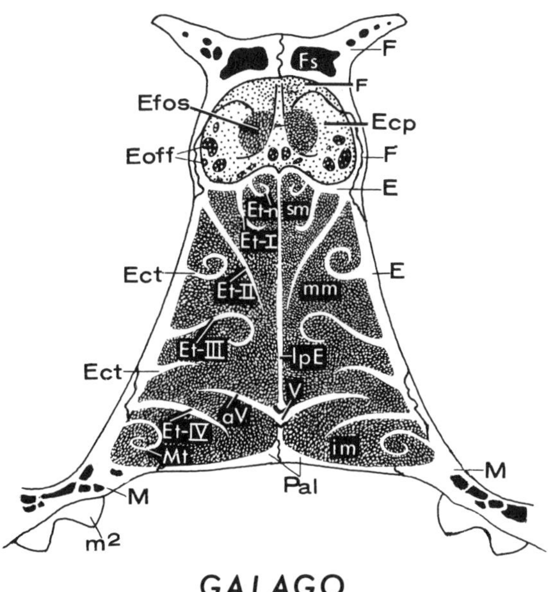

Fig. IV.12. Transverse cranial section, *Galago crassicaudatus;* plane behind m2; greatest skull length, 65 mm, orbital breadth, 42 mm; symbols explained in chapter 31; see also fig. IV.10.

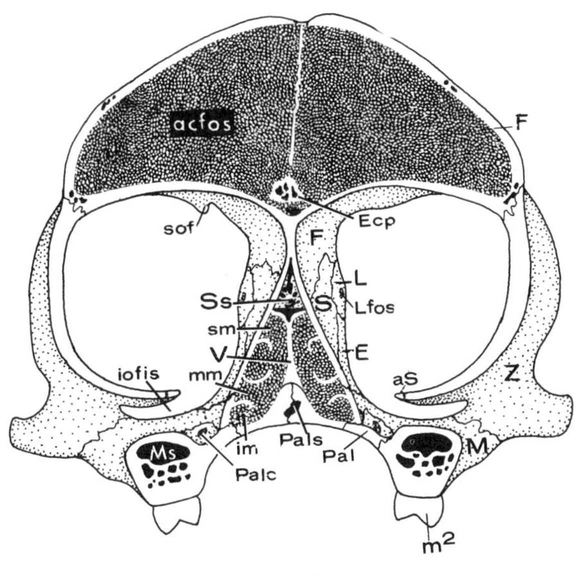

Fig. IV.13. Transverse cranial section, *Saguinus;* anterior plane behind m2; greatest skull length, 52 mm, orbital breadth, 27 mm; symbols explained in chapter 31.

cerocranial increase, and the orbits were forced apart, air cells accounting for the additional space between them (fig. IV.11). The same is true, but to a lesser degree, in a number of other primate phyletic lines. In contrast, facial bone enlargement in baboons and macaques greatly exceeded braincase expansion, while interorbital breadth decreased proportionately. In callitrichids and marmosetlike cebids, neurocranial increase, mainly toward dolichocephaly, was considerably greater than viscerocranial enlargement, but the orbits moved closer, and in *Saimiri* they are virtually tangential. Notwithstanding, small air cells and sinuses form between the septal angles in all lower platyrrhines.

The cebid morphological series arranged by Du Brul (1965, fig. 8) to demonstrate the asserted correlation between increasing interorbital breadth and pneumaticity with increasing skull size makes use of dubious examples. *Saimiri,* the first in Du Brul's sequence is a dead end, with secondarily thin and deficient interorbital septum. *Callicebus* (fig. IV.16), mentioned by Du Brul as a member of the same size group, possesses a comparatively broad and well-pneumatized interorbital region. *Pithecia* (fig. IV.31), with larger skull and perfect interorbital septum, follows *Saimiri* in Du Brul's scheme, but absence of interorbital pneumatization (persistent in *Saimiri*) argues against its placement in the series. *Lagothrix* (fig. IV.34), next in line, is followed by *Cebus* (figs. IV.19, 20). In size, *Lagothrix* considerably exceeds *Cebus* and should follow it, but its skull is less cavitated. *Alouatta* (fig. IV.32) tops Du Brul's platyrrhine sequence for size and

---

lines indicate major primate groupings. Curved white lines on interorbital region of some skulls (*Cebuella, Tarsius, Macaca,* others) show boundaries of orbits in sphenoethmoidal region, where they depart widely from the orbital boundaries on facial surface of nasal bones. Arrows point to main directions of expansion or encroachment of one facial region on another, as follows: *Lemur* (primitive primate)—orbits expanding and converging from side of skull to front; braincase expanding; primitively broad interorbital region in process of reduction. *Cebuella-Saguinus* (callitrichid line)-orbits more nearly frontal, expanding medially by invasion of interorbital region and laterally by distension of free or outer border, braincase expansion nearly commensurate. *Aotus* (marmosetlike cebid)—orbital expansion extreme among platyrrhines, lateral orbital wall distended well beyond borders of more slowly expanding braincase, medial orbital expansion moderate. *Tarsius* (highly specialized prosimian)—orbital expansion extreme among primates, interorbital region compressed to thin septum, outer or free lateral orbital borders distended far beyond borders of slowly expanding braincase. *Saimiri* (marmosetlike cebid)—medial orbital expansion extreme with bony sphenoethmoidal portion of interorbital septum largely fenestrated; braincase expansion mainly anteroposterior, resulting in extreme dolicocephaly. *Alouatta* (primitive cebid)—expanded interorbital and maxillary regions and relatively small orbits, correlated with enlargement of cranial surface for origin of masticatory muscles without commensurate increase in diameter of orbits and braincase; compare with orbits, braincase, and sinuses of *Homo. Cebus* (advanced cebid)—interorbital and maxillary regions (sinuses included) expanded; lateral expansion of orbits associated with lateral expansion of braincase. *Colobus–Cercopithecus–Macaca* (cercopithecid line)—main orbital expansion mediad with compression of sphenoethmoidal portion of interorbital wall into a thin, sometimes perforated septum as in *Macaca* and some species of *Cercopithecus;* lateral expansion of braincase involved complementary thickening of lateral orbital wall. Contrast with lateral orbital wall of *Tarsius. Homo* (specialized hominid)—extreme secondary expansion of braincase and a nearly proportionate increase in width of interorbital region without commensurate orbital expansion, entailed enlargement of frontal, ethmoidal, sphenoidal and maxillary air spaces or sinuses to accommodate the small orbits. Sinuses shown in skull sectioned transversely between plane of first and second molars.

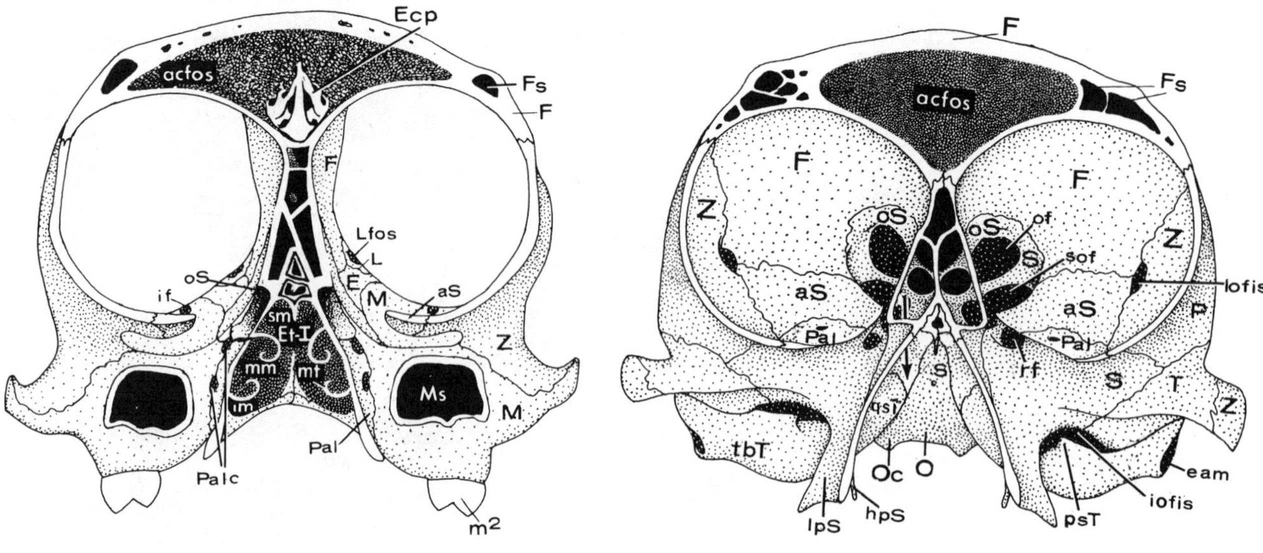

LEONTOPITHECUS (anterior)

Fig. IV.14. Transverse cranial section, *Leontopithecus;* anterior plane behind m^2; greatest skull length, 56 mm, orbital breadth, 29 mm; symbols explained in chapter 31.

LEONTOPITHECUS (posterior)

Fig. IV.15. Transverse cranial section, *Leontopithecus;* posterior plane behind m^2 of skull shown in fig. IV.14; symbols explained in chapter 31.

complexity of paranasal cavities. In this genus, viscerocranial growth exceeded the neurocranial. On the other hand, the comparably large-skulled *Ateles* (fig. IV.35) and *Brachyteles* (fig. IV.123) have large braincases, relatively small faces, and narrow and generally uninflated paranasal and frontal bones, much as in small pithecines. *Leontopithecus* (= *Leontideus*), with its complex sphenoidal sinus system (figs. IV.14, 15, 26), served as springboard for Du Brul's elaboration on the biomechanics of change in the interorbital region. It is not clear, however, that what was said of the sinus system of this callitrichid supports or clarifies the generalizations made about the others.

Cave (1967), focusing on the nasal fossa, traced the evolution of the interorbital region from primitive nonprimates to platyrrhines. Models of primitive primates adopted by Cave are the platyrrhine *Saimiri,* with one of the most specialized interorbital regions among higher primates, and *Tarsius* (fig. IV.7), the most highly specialized terminal twig of an otherwise extinct lineage of

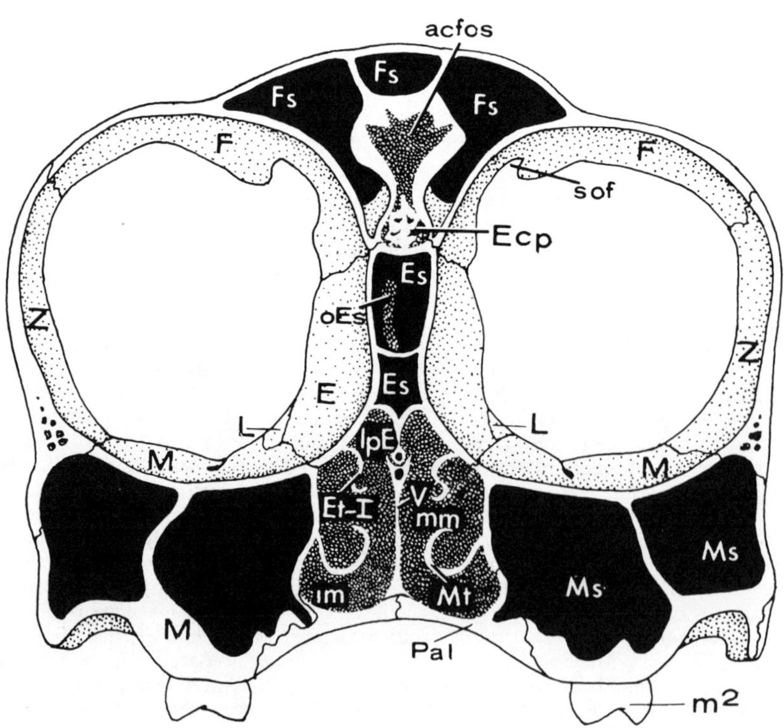

CALLICEBUS

Fig. IV.16. Transverse cranial section, *Callicebus;* plane behind m^2; greatest skull length, 72 mm, orbital breadth, 42 mm; symbols explained in chapter 31.

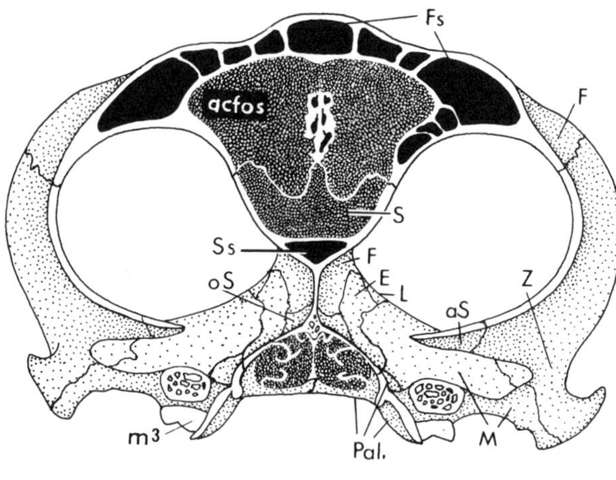

AOTUS

Fig. IV.17. Transverse cranial section, *Aotus;* plane behind hamular process of pterygoid; greatest skull length, 63 mm, orbital breadth, 42; symbols explained in chapter 31.

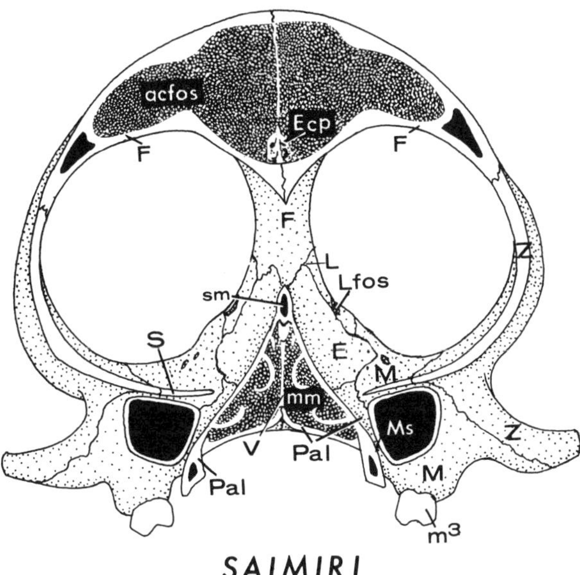

SAIMIRI

Fig. IV.18. Transverse cranial section, *Saimiri;* plane behind m^3; greatest skull length, 69 mm, orbital breadth, 35 mm; symbols explained in chapter 31.

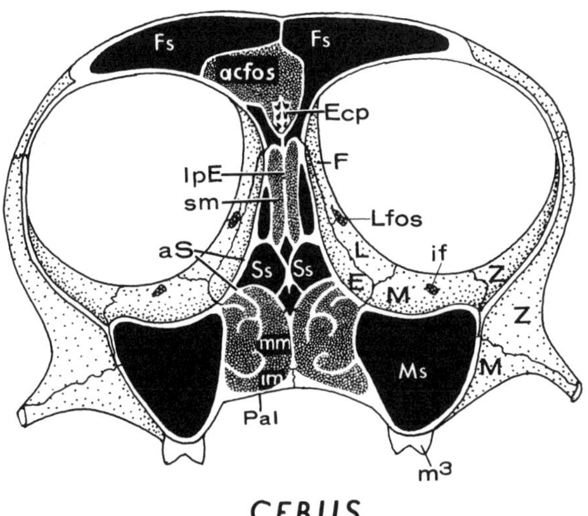

CEBUS

Fig. IV.19. Transverse cranial section, *Cebus nigrivittatus;* plane through anterior portion of pterygoid process; greatest skull length, 102 mm, orbital breadth, 55 mm; symbols explained in chapter 31.

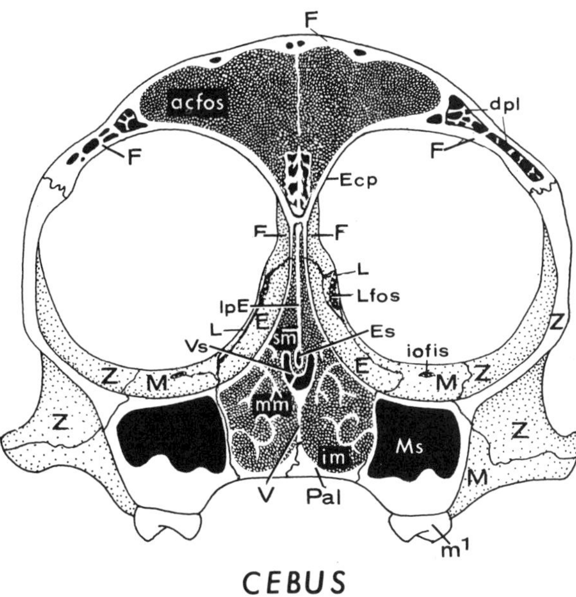

CEBUS

Fig. IV.20. Transverse cranial section, *Cebus nigrivittatus;* plane behind m^1; greatest skull length, 98 mm, orbital breadth, 53 mm; symbols explained in chapter 31.

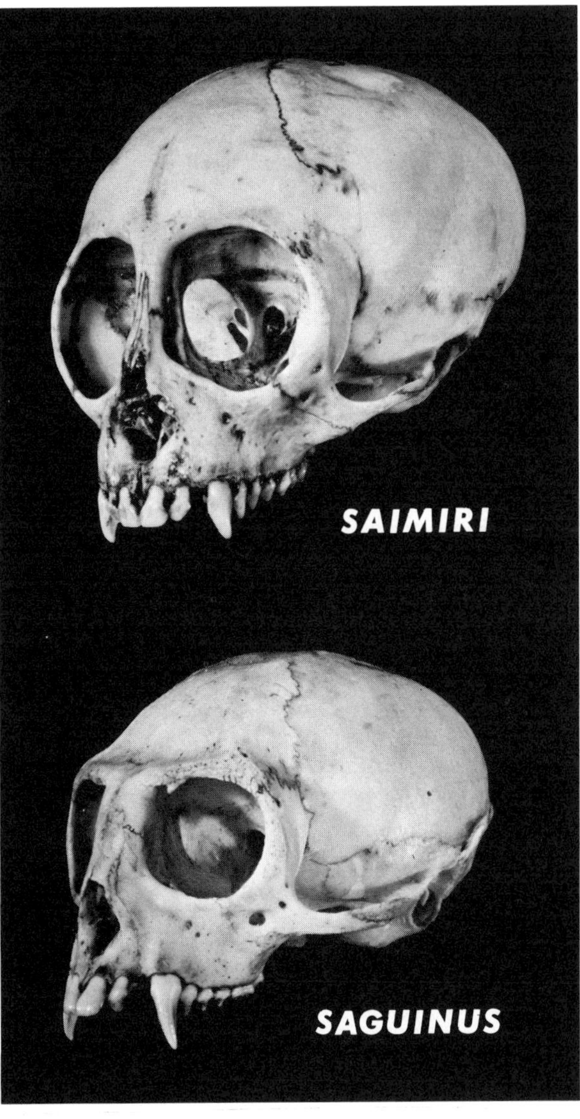

Fig. IV.21. Interorbital septum in *Saimiri* and *Saguinus*. Enlargement of orbits by encroachment on interorbital region resulted in a thin, translucent bony septum in *Saguinus* and fenestration of the septum in *Saimiri*.

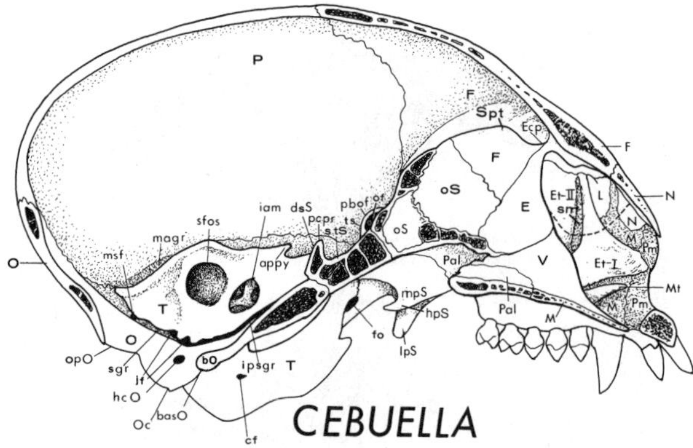

Fig. IV.22. Sagittal section of *Cebuella pygmaea* skull; lateral plate of ethmoid bone removed, its position indicated by dotted line; greatest skull length, 36 mm, orbital breadth, 21 mm; symbols explained in chapter 31.

primitive haplorhine primates. The interorbital region of *Tarsius* retains its primitive orientation relative to the brain, but its constriction is extreme among lower primates and consistently exceeded only by that of *Saimiri* among higher primates. It is even more difficult to understand why Cave (1967, p. 279) dismisses as non-primate the truly primitive type of primate nasal fossa found in *Lemur* and *Galago*. These peculiar views, combined with a rigid concept of the nature of paranasal sinuses, obliged Cave (1967, p. 287) to regard as secondary reacquisitions the very primitive characteristics these lemuroids had never lost in the first place.

Turbinal Bones

The primitive nasoturbinate system, exemplified by that of the marsupial *Didelphis* or the insectivore *Erinaceus,* consists of a highly developed nasoturbinal at the anterior or superior end of the nasal cavity, a larger, more complicated maxilloturbinal at the inferior end, and four endoturbinals, or ethmoturbinal bones, between, in a recess formed by the sphenoid body behind, by the transverse lamina of the same bone below, and largely by the cribriform plate above. The upper or anterior ethmoturbinal (I) is largest, the others (II–IV) follow in order of decreasing size. A second series of turbinals, the ectoturbinals consist of small processes with one or more between each pair of ethmoturbinals, including the nasoturbinal. Presence of more than four ethmoturbinals in highly macrosmatic mammals derives from a bifurcation of one or more basal plates of the primitive ethmoturbinals. Fewer ethmoturbinals, as in microsmatic mammals, including higher primates, result from fusion of

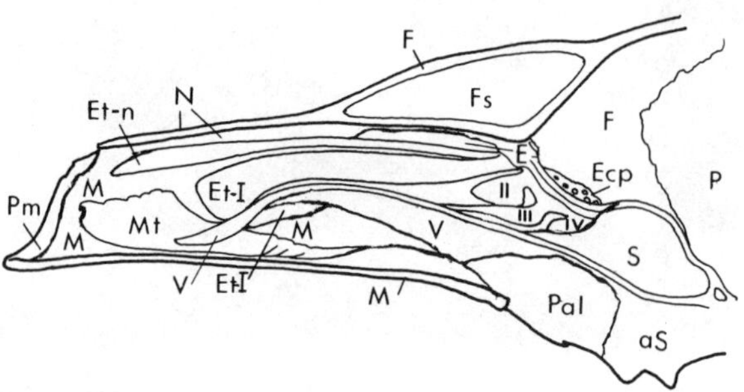

Fig. IV.23. *Lemur*: Sagittal section of skull exposing turbinal system; greatest skull length, 89 mm, orbital breadth, 50 mm; symbols explained in chapter 31.

some turbinals and reduction and loss of others. Ectoturbinals may proliferate in great numbers, especially between nasoturbinal and ethmoturbinal I, in specialized "smell" animals, whereas they tend to disappear in dominantly "sight" animals, as in primates.

The primitive turbinate system, although somewhat reduced, prevails in *Lemur* (fig. IV.23) and *Galago* (fig. IV.12), among strepsirhines. Evolution of the system in

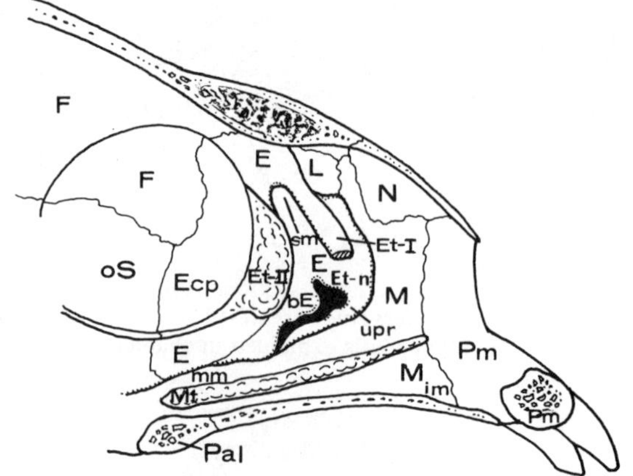

Fig. IV.24. Sagittal section of anterior half of *Cebuella pygmaea* skull with most of ethmoturbinal-I (*Et-I*) removed to expose bones behind; symbols explained in chapter 31.

higher primates is degenerative and involves reduction in size and importance of all turbinals, with obsolescence or loss of ethmoturbinal IV and all but one, or possibly two, ectoturbinals in adults of all species (fig. IV.83). In lemuriforms the dominant turbinals are the naso- and maxilloturbinals (fig. IV.23). In lorisiforms, an expanded ethmoturbinal I overlaps a large maxilloturbinal (fig. IV.12). In higher primates, ethmoturbinal I is usually dominant, the maxilloturbinal reduced but still important, the nasoturbinal usually smaller than ethmoturbinal I and often reduced to a mere ridge or tubercle (figs. IV.22, 25–36).

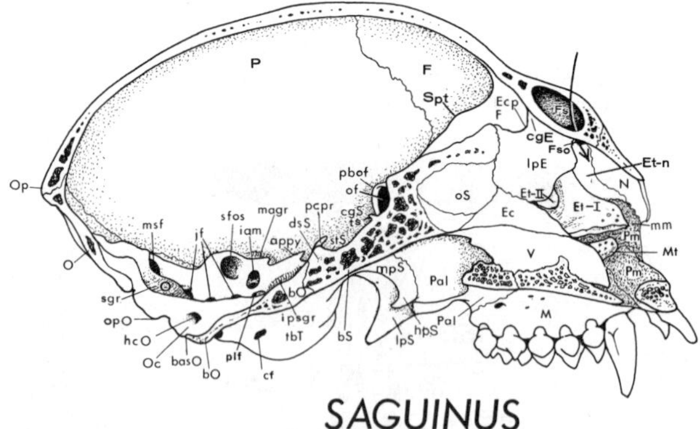

Fig. IV.25. Sagittal section of *Saguinus oedipus* skull; greatest-length of skull, 52 mm, orbital breadth, 27 mm; arrow shows communication between frontal sinus and nasal cavity; symbols explained in chapter 31.

Abbreviation and downward flexure of the muzzle in higher primates entailed a corresponding reduction in size and complexity of all turbinals and a shift in orientation of the long axis of the ethmoturbinals from antero-posterior to nearly vertical. Actual rate of reduction and loss of turbinals relative to change in muzzle length and curvature differs in each phyletic line. The platyrrhine turbinate system, for example, is more primitive than

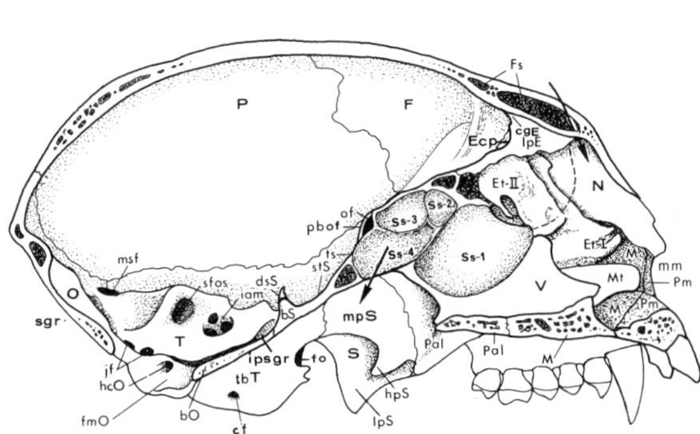

Fig. IV.26. Sagittal section of *Leontopithecusr. rosalia* skull; arrow in midskull shows communication between sphenoidal sinus and pharyngeal cavity; anterior arrow shows communication between frontal sinus and nasal cavity; greatest length of skull 56 mm, orbital breadth, 29 mm; arrow shows communication between frontal sinus and nasal cavity through posterolateral canal (*plc*); symbols explained in chapter 31.

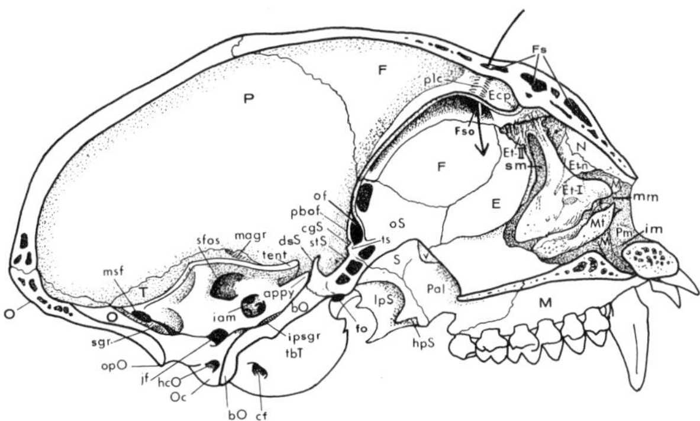

CALLIMICO

Fig. IV.27. Sagittal section of *Callimico goeldii* skull; greatest length of skull 53 mm, orbital breadth, 31 mm; symbols explained in chapter 31.

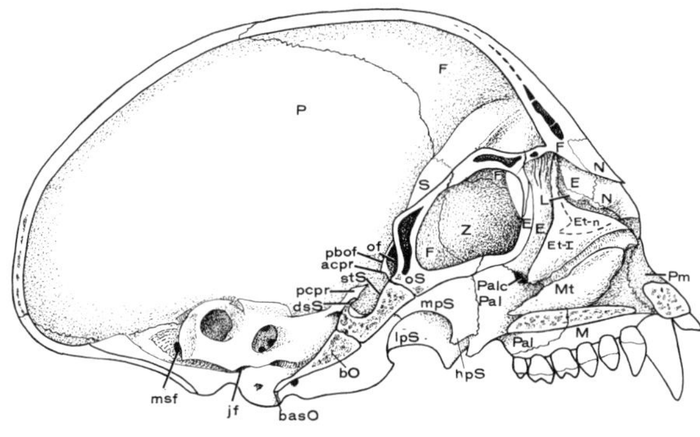

SAIMIRI

Fig. IV.28. Sagittal section of *Saimiri sciureus* skull; lateral orbital bones (*F, Z*) visible through interorbital fenestra; greatest length of skull 69 mm, orbital breadth, 35 mm; symbols explained in chapter 31.

that of catarrhines, a condition already recognized by Seydel (1891, p. 89). Notwithstanding, the muzzle is shorter, the facial angle steeper in the smaller platyrrhines generally than in the Cercopithecidae (cf. fig. IV.3). Comparable disparities in relative evolutionary rates exist between the various families of platyrrhines and catarrhines.

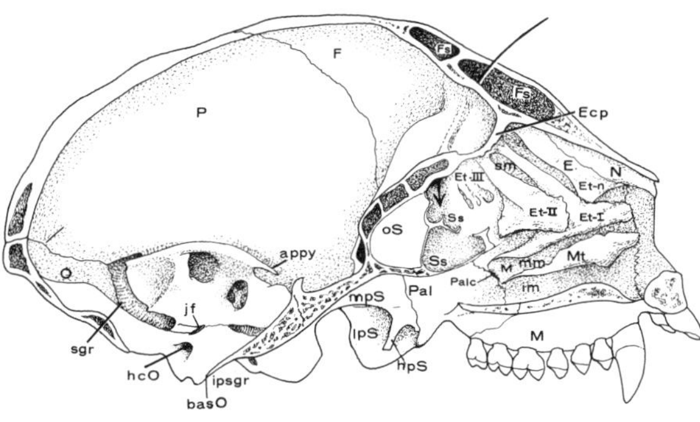

AOTUS

Fig. IV.29. Sagittal section of *Aotus trivirgatus* skull; greatest length of skull, 63 mm, orbital breadth, 42 mm; symbols explained in chapter 31.

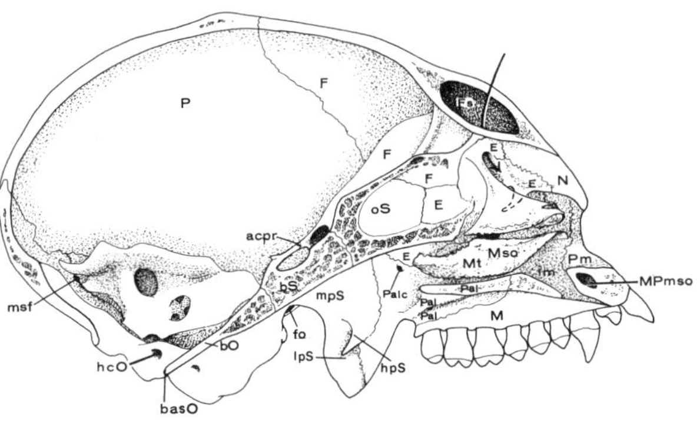

CALLICEBUS

Fig. IV.30. Sagittal section of *Callicebus moloch* skull; greatest length of skull, 65 mm, orbital breadth, 34 mm; arrow shows communication between frontal sinus and nasal cavity; symbols explained in chapter 31.

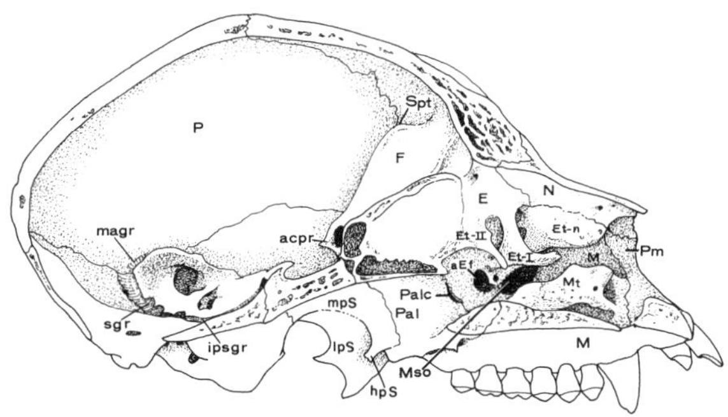

PITHECIA

Fig. IV.31. Sagittal section of *Pithecia monachus* skull; greatest length of skull, 86 mm, orbital breadth, 45 mm; symbols explained in chapter 31.

Among higher primates the nasoturbinal is best developed in platyrrhines, particularly in the prehensile-tailed cebids, but most notably in pithecines. In *Pithecia* (fig. IV.31), for example, the nasoturbinal may even exceed ethmoturbinal I in size. In the ateline *Lagothrix* (fig. IV.34), an expanded nasoturbinal may sometimes fuse with a comparably inflated ethmoturbinal I. The nasoturbinal is greatly reduced or vestigial in catarrhine monkeys, moderately to poorly developed in apes and man, where it may be represented by nothing more than a bony ridge and the uncinate process.

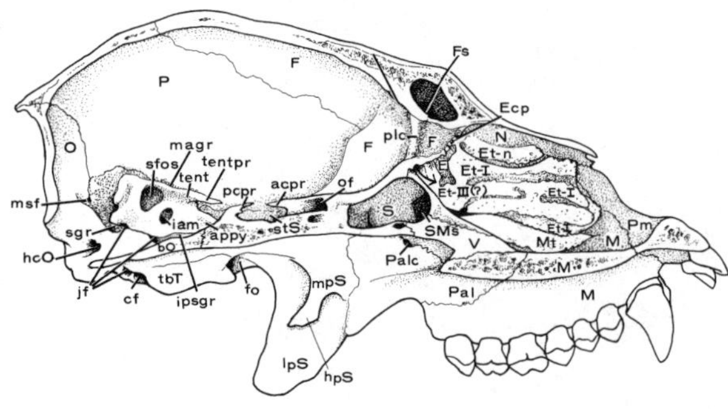

ALOUATTA

Fig. IV.32. Sagittal section of *Alouatta seniculus* skull; greatest length of skull, 123; orbital breadth, 64 mm; arrow shows communication between frontal sinus and nasal cavity; symbols explained in chapter 31.

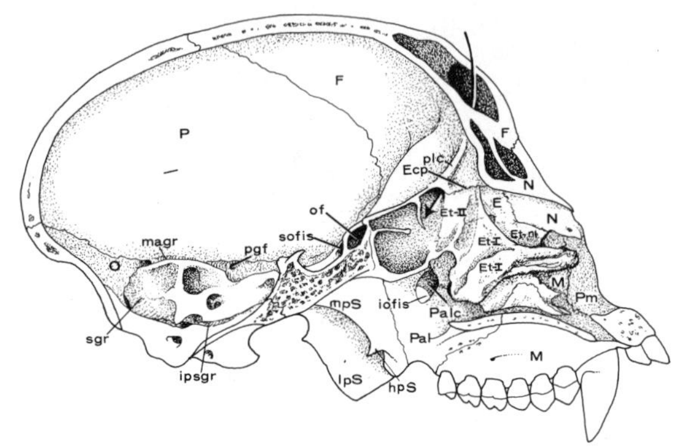

CEBUS APELLA

Fig. IV.33. Sagittal section of *Cebus apella* skull; greatest length of skull, 98 mm, orbital breadth, 53 mm; symbols explained in chapter 31.

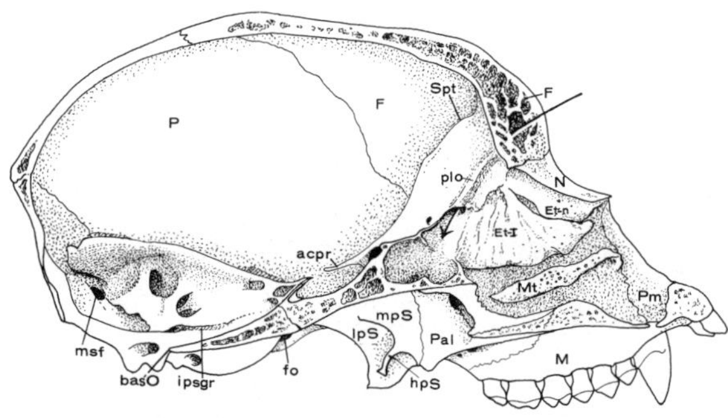

LAGOTHRIX

Fig. IV.34. Sagittal section of *Lagothrix lagothricha* skull; greatest length of skull, 111 mm, orbital breadth, 60 mm; symbols explained in chapter 31.

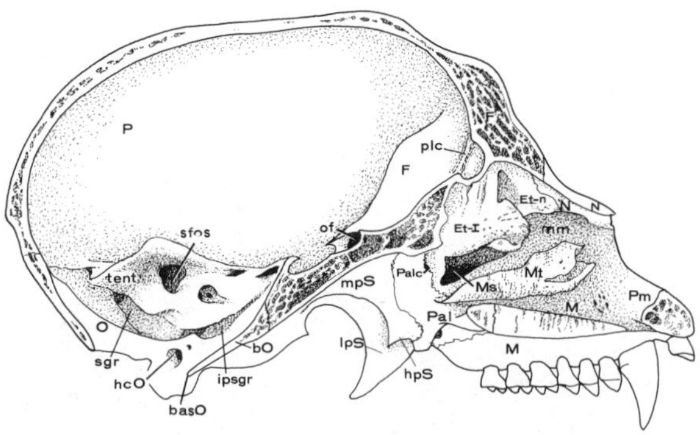

ATELES

Fig. IV.35. Sagittal section of *Ateles paniscus* skull; greatest length of skull, 121 mm, orbital breadth, 67 mm; symbols explained in chapter 31.

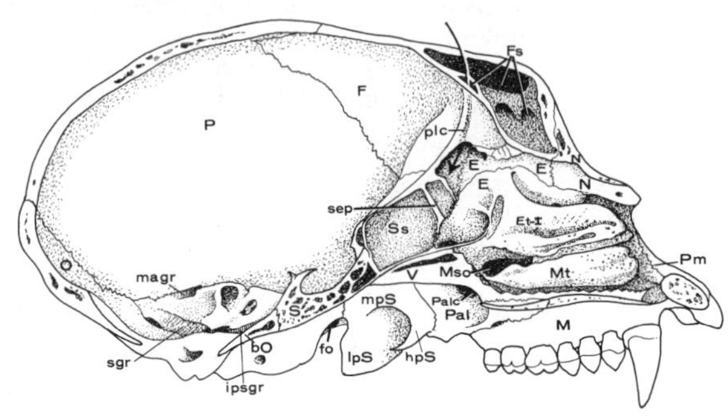

Fig. IV. 36. Sagittal section of *Cebus nigrivittatus* skull; greatest length of skull, 102 mm, orbital breadth, 55 mm; symbols explained in chapter 31.

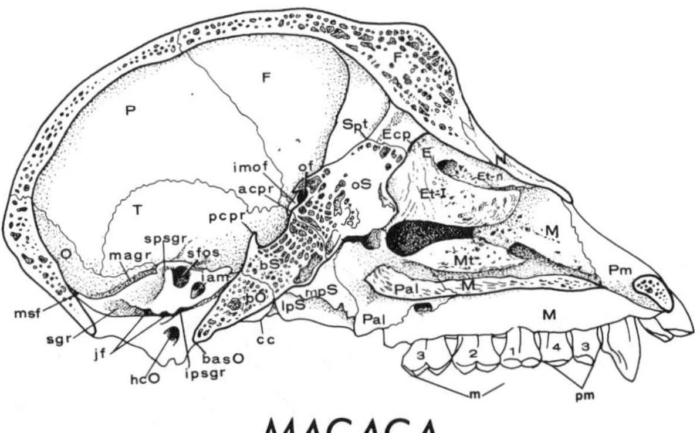

MACACA

Fig. IV.37. *Macaca mulatta,* sagittal section of skull; greatest length of skull, 133 mm, orbital breadth, 76 mm; symbols explained in chapter 31.

The *maxilloturbinal* is present and comparatively well developed in all primates.

Ethmoturbinal I is largest and most complex in platyrrhines and in some species, most notably among atelines (fig. IV.35), is as large as or larger than all other turbinals combined. It is comparatively poorly developed and less rolled in catarrhines (fig. IV.83) and more reduced in monkeys, generally, than in man and apes, where it is known as the *middle concha.*

The platyrrhine *ethmoturbinal II* is a small but constant feature in all callitrichids (fig. IV.24) and in *Callimico* (fig. IV.27). It is well developed to vestigial in the sectioned specimens of pithecines, well developed in *Aotus* (fig. IV.29), but absent or vestigial in *Callicebus* (fig. IV.30) and *Saimiri* (fig. IV.28). Its presence and shape are variable in *Cebus* (figs. IV.33, 36), and it appears to be obsolete or absent in samplings of the larger prehensile-tailed species. In *Alouatta* (fig. IV.32), however, it seems to be either well-developed or confused with a lamina of ethmoturbinal I.

The condition of ethmoturbinal II in catarrhines is obscure. In our samples, the bone is moderately well developed in *Cercocebus* (fig. IV.38), absent in other monkeys, and poorly developed in *Hylobates.* Paulli (1900, p. 544) notes the presence of ethmoturbinal II in the hamadryas baboon and the drill, and of ethmotur-

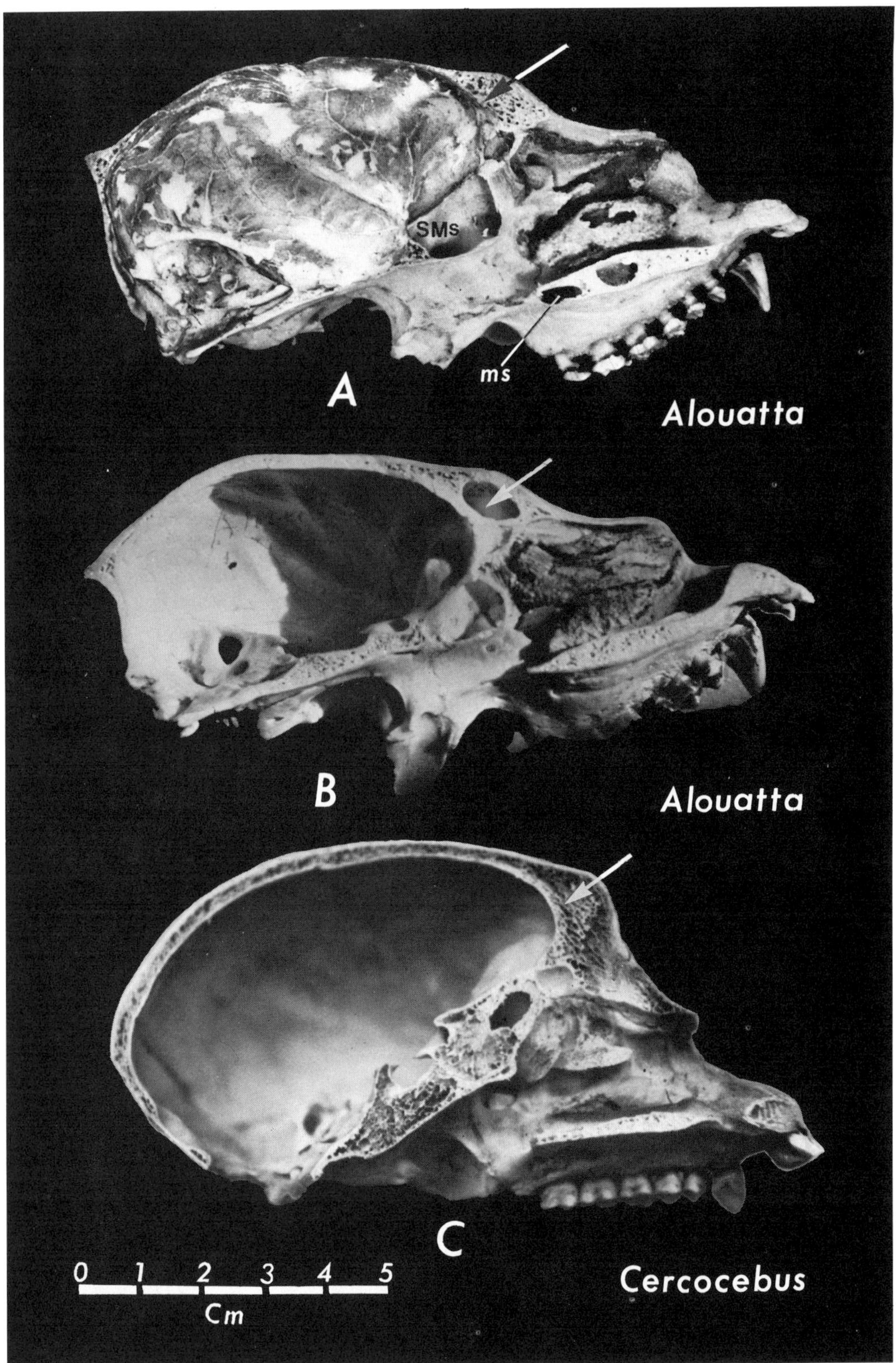

Fig. IV.38. Cranial sinuses in *Alouatta* (Cebidae) and *Cercocebus* (Cercopithecidae). *A, Alouatta seniculus,* with frontal sinusoidal area spongiform (*arrow*), maxillary sinus (*ms*) exposed. *B, Alouatta seniculus* with cavitated frontal sinus. *C, Cercocebus* sp., with expanded diploe but sinusoidal areas spongiform; compare braincase sizes.

binals II and III in the anubis baboon. Cave and Haines (1940) show a well-developed ethmoturbinal II in gibbons, chimpanzees, and gorillas; in man the same element, known as the superior concha, is usually well developed. It is absent in our sample of *Macaca* (fig. IV.37).

Ethmoturbinal III is vestigial or absent in most platyrrhines. A small concha is present in a sample of *Saguinus fuscicollis,* another of *Leontopithecus rosalia,* among the callitrichids examined. It is obsolete or absent in samplings of cebids except for a small process in one *Aotus,* while in one *Alouatta* (FMNH 87794) it is either greatly reduced and fused with a lamina of I or is itself the entire lamina.

Ethmoturbinal IV is not evident in our sectioned specimens of higher primates but a small one, known as the supreme concha, is sometimes present in man.

Ectoturbinals are generally obsolete or absent in most catarrhines, but one often remains as a bony ridge which may be the *bulla ethmoidales* of human anatomy. It is on the upper posterior border of the hiatus semilunaris, opposite the uncinate process, and laterad to and covered by ethmoturbinal I. The bulla ethmoidales is present in platyrrhines (fig. IV.24). Paulli (1900, p. 524) notes a rudimentary ectoturbinal between ethmoturbinals I and II in "*Hapale* sp." which may be the same as the bulla ethmoidalis. A *superior ectoturbinal,* or *ectoturbinal I,* appears to be uncommon, but a well-developed element is present in sectioned skulls of *Pithecia, Aotus, Cebus,* and *Lagothrix.* I see none in three sectioned skulls of *Alouatta* with ethmoturbinals intact, but Cave (1967, p. 284, fig. 6) regards a two-crested bony ridge above ethmoturbinal I as a vestigial ectoturbinal.

21 Skull
4. Paranasal Pneumatizations

Definition

Paranasal pneumatizations may appear in the frontal, sphenoidal, ethmoidal, vomerine, palatine, and maxillary bones of primates. The lacrimal, malar, palatine, pterygoid, temporal, and basioccipital bones are often filled with air spaces in continuity with those of contiguous paranasal bones. Some paranasal pneumatizations are simply enlarged cells of the spongiform tissue. Others are more-or-less well-defined bony fossae or recesses. The paranasal pneumatization classified as a sinus is a chamber of the inner table of a cranial bone lined with mucus derived from epithelium of the nasal cavity with which communication is usually maintained through an ostium.

Clear distinction between a true sinus and other kinds of similarly situated air chambers or honeycombed pockets may not always be possible in the sagittally sectioned dry skulls used in the present study.

Maxillary and sphenoidal sinuses are present in primitive primates. Their absence in many higher primates may be secondary. The loss begins with closure of the ostium in ontogeny and subsequent disappearance of the sinus in phylogeny. The frontal sinus appears to have arisen independently by either or both of two methods in each of the various supergeneric groups (see below). Absence of the frontal sinus may be primitive in some taxons, secondary in others.

Function

Sinuses enlarge the surface area of cranial bones without significant increase in weight or loss of strength and, ostensibly, at no cost to the organism. The cavitated bone gains in insulation, resilience, and resistance to shock. It spans the distance between allometrically small orbits and an enlarged portion of braincase between, as in man (fig. IV.11); and it provides more surface area for muscle attachments, usually in correspondence with an enlarged mandible, as in howlers and titis (fig. IV.16). Likewise, the larger a specialized tooth such as a canine, the more pneumatized the surrounding bone. The internal space filler also modifies the superficial appearance of the head or face and thus acts as a species recognition or display characteristic as in many cercopithecines (e.g., *Macaca* [Fooden 1969*a*]) and platyrrhines (see below).

Maxillary Sinus

Maxillary pneumatizations with exit or ostium opening into the nasal cavity are present in platyrrhines but are highly variable in size, shape, and structure (figs. IV.13–20). The greatest size and complication is attained in howlers (*Alouatta,* figs. IV.32, 38). In this genus, the sinus is usually a large hollowed chamber which may be confined in some species to the alveolar region. In other species, the sinus appears to be nothing more than a shallow recess of the nasal meatus. The ostium also varies considerably in size, shape, and position. In some sectioned skulls of the smaller platyrrhines, the ostium may not be distinguishable.

A maxillary cavitation is not always present in catarrhines. It appears as a true sinus in man (fig. IV.11) and apes (cf. Cave and Haines 1940). In *Macaca,* the sinus is a large depression or recess of the nasal fossa as it is in some platyrrhines. In the mandrill (*Papio sphinx*), the air pocket is completely enclosed except for its opening into the middle meatus of the nasal cavity. The inner table of the maxillary bone is spongiform in the single skull examined of each of the following: *Papio cynocephalus, Cercocebus* (sp.), (fig. IV.38), *Cercopithecus aethiops, Cercopithecus albogularis, Presbytis entellus, Colobus polykomos, Rhinopithecus roxellanae, Nasalis larvatus.*

Sphenoidal Sinus

Pneumatization of the sphenoid is widespread in primitive mammals. The cavitations may not open into the nasal passage in some adult forms—for example, the common opossum (*Didelphis*). In a specimen each of *Lemur catta* and *Galago crassicaudatus,* however, a large sphenoidal sinus communicates with the posterior recess of the nasal cavity. Structure of the sphenoidal sinus in one sample each of *Hylobates concolor* and *H. lar* is essentially the same as in the aforementioned prosimian but much larger. According to Cave and Haines (1940, p. 521) "all anthropoid apes tend to preserve the primitive heritage of paranasal sinus structure, viz. maxillary and sphenoidal only." The human sphenoidal sinus is also well developed and connects with the upper posterior recess of the nasal cavity. The sphenoid in samples of catarrhine monkeys is honeycombed rather than sinusoidal, with the

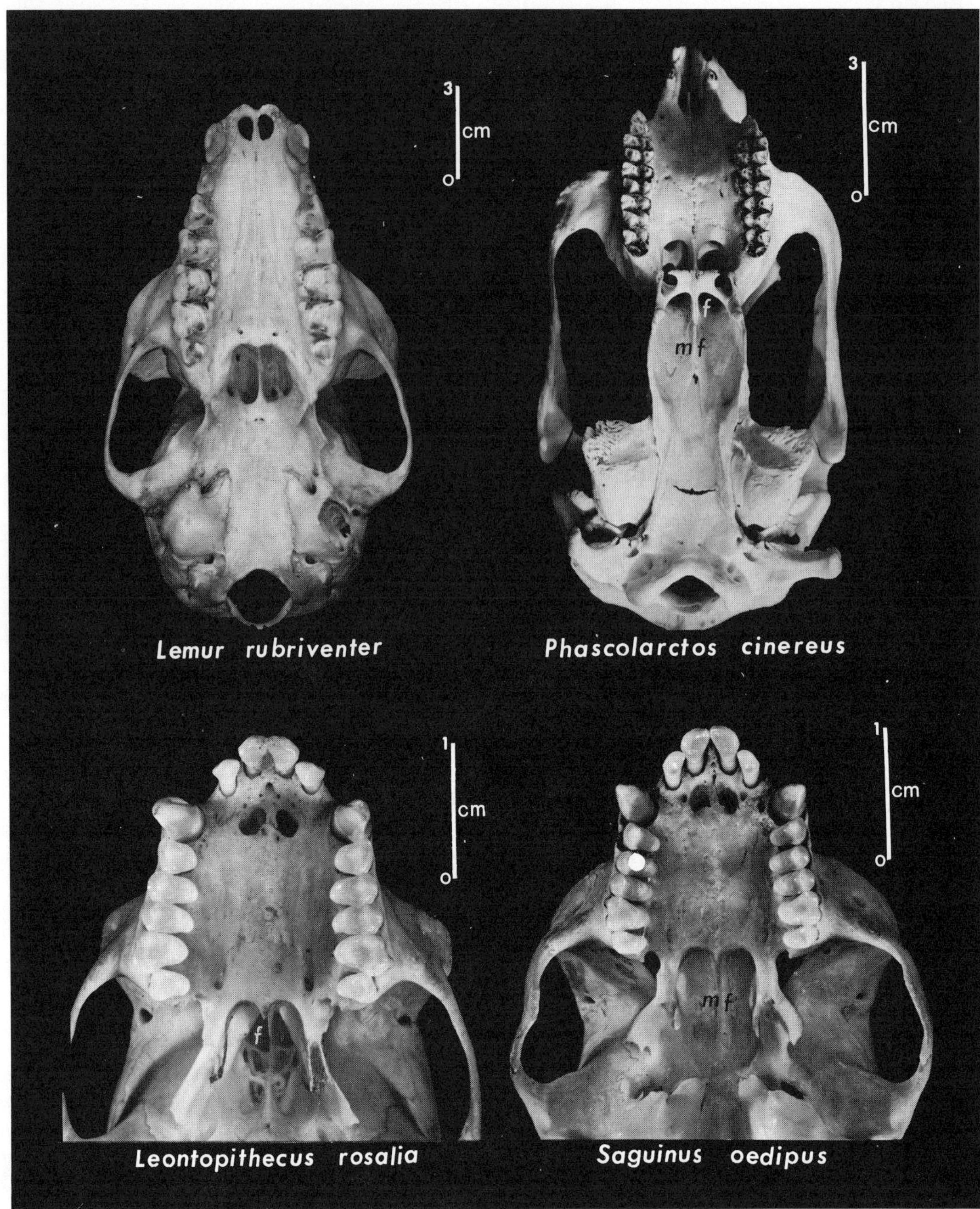

Fig. IV. 39. Mesopterygoid region, showing posterior sphenoidal fossae (*f*) in *A*, lion-tamarin, *Leontopithecus rosalia rosalia; B, Lemur rubriventer* (Lemuridae); *C*, koala, *Phascolarctos cinereus* (Marsupialia). The usual uncavitated condition of the mesopterygoid fossa (*mf*) in platyrrhines, catarrhines, and mammals generally, is shown in *D, Saguinus oedipus.*

largest cells mostly confined to the orbital portion of the bone.

The platyrrhine sphenoid is usually well pneumatized, the cavities often sinusoidal. An ostium leading into the nasal cavity is not always evident. Apparent lack of communication may be a specific character, an individual variable, or an artifact of sectioned skulls with an extremely thin interorbital septum. An ostium of the orbitosphenoid opening into the upper nasal meatus is present in a few longitudinally sectioned callitrichid skulls. Presumably it is present in all Callitrichidae.

The sphenoidal sinus system of the lion-tamarin *Leontopithecus rosalia,* is unique among higher primates (figs. IV.14, 15, 26, 39). It consists of a series of communicating cells (figs. IV.26, Ssl–4) that open behind into a pair of sphenoidal fossae previously noted (Hershkovitz 1949, p. 410). The latter, in turn, communicate through an ostium into the inferior meatus via the nasopharynx, or epipharynx. The posterior fossae (fig. IV.26) (Ss–4), were correctly described by Du Brul (1965) as paranasal sinuses. Cave (1967, p. 277), objected, but without reason or justification. The anteriormost sinus also possesses an ostium. It is very small and opens into the superior nasal meatus, as in man. A functional relationship may exist between the sphenoidal sinus, or at least the posteroinferior sinus (Ss–4), and the well-developed inferior median laryngeal sac in *Leontopithecus* (fig. I.10).

Sphenoidal cells in *Callimico* (fig. IV.27) are larger than those of callitrichids, but they clearly open into the upper nasal chamber.

In *Saimiri* (fig. IV.28), erosion of the interorbital region left isolated air spaces in the upper posterior corner of the orbitosphenoid. Cells of the same bone in *Aotus* (fig. IV.29) and *Callicebus* (fig. IV.30) communicate with the ethmoidal sinus and nasal cavity.

Pneumatization of the sphenoid bone in prehensile-tailed cebids (figs. IV.19, 20, 32–36) is well advanced in four individuals representing *Cebus albifrons, C. nigrivittatus,* and *C. apella* (2). An ostium connecting the large quadrilateral sinus with the middle meatus of the nasal cavity is present in all. Cave (1967, p. 283, figs. 4, 5) does not regard the sphenoidal sinus of *Cebus* as homologous with that of *Homo*. Perhaps the orifice of communication with the nasal cavity in the specimen Cave figures is too wide and too far forward to meet his concept of a sinus. Sphenoidal cavitations in our samples, however, qualify as homologues of their human equivalents by any definition. Weinert (1926) figures 7 skulls of *Cebus* with pneumatization of the sphenoid ranging from spongy through cellular to sinusoidal.

The sphenoidal sinus of *Lagothrix lagothricha* (1 specimen, fig. IV.34) resembles that of *Cebus,* but the opening into the posterior recess of the nasal cavity is wider. On the other hand, the sphenoidal cavities of *Lagothrix* figured by Cave (1967, fig. 8) seem to be completely isolated. The sphenoidal cavity of *Brachyteles,* judged by one sectioned skull, is quite like that of *Lagothrix*. The sphenoidal diploe in two examples of *Ateles* (fig. IV.35) is loosely trabecular, like that of the frontal region. Ostium or chambered recess of the nasal cavity is lacking. The differences between *Ateles* and *Brachyteles,* with well-cavitated paranasal regions, are striking. In these and dental characters as well, *Brachyteles* is nearer to *Lagothrix* than to *Ateles*.

The large sphenoidal cavities in two skulls of *Alouatta seniculus* (fig. IV.38) invade the malar bones of both, the palatine bone of one, and the frontal bone of the other. The frontal extension of the sphenomaxillary sinus in a specimen of *Alouatta villosa* (FMNH 87794), is a narrow blind chamber on each side of the perpendicular plate. It agrees with the pneumatization of the specimen figured by Cave (1967, p. 285) except for absence of connection with the ectoturbinal (lacking in our *Alouatta*) and the nasal chamber. The frontal diverticulum of the sphenoidal sinus is not to be confused with a distinct and independent frontal sinus noted in *Alouatta* and other prehensile-tailed cebids (table 4). Expansion of the facial bones of *Alouatta* through pneumatization provides surface for attachment of the enlarged masticatory muscles of this highly specialized browser-grazer.

Frontal Sinus

Air pockets are normally present in the ciliary region of the frontal bone of some prosimians, African apes, and man. They are said to be lacking in gibbons and virtually all catarrhine monkeys (Weinert 1926). I find only spongiform diploe in a random sampling of adult skulls of *Hylobates, Macaca, Papio, Cercopithecus, Cercocebus* (fig. IV.38), *Presbytis, Rhinopithecus, Nasalis*. Aubert (1929, p. 8, fig. 4) shows a large air space in a skull of "*Cercopithecus Callithrichus*" (= *C. aethiops sabaeus*). The domed skull figured is certainly abnormal, its air space coronal in position rather than ciliary. Osman Hill (1966*a*, pp. 127, 363, pl. IV) mentions this condition and illustrates it in sagittal section, without comment.

Frontal air chambers, whether spongiform or sinusoidal, are present in all platyrrhine species (table 4). Their morphology and their relationship to the nasal cavity support in a broad sense the systematic arrangement of the species and species groups based on other characters.

Diploe of the frontal bone in the pygmy marmoset, *Cebuella pygmaea* (fig. IV.24), is largely trabecular or honeycombed and without evident communication with the nasal cavity. This may be the primitive condition, but obliteration, or simply erasure of the ostium by the saw blade, cannot be ruled out. The frontal cells in *Callithrix* are slightly better defined, and a connection between the cells and the middle meatus of the nasal cavity is present in some individuals (cf. *C. jacchus penicillata* FM 20738). The breakthrough is almost universally established in *Saguinus* (fig. IV.25), where a large ostium connects the well-inflated frontal sinus with the upper recess of the middle meatus of the nasal cavity. The same characters are present in *Leontopithecus rosalia* (fig. IV.26).

The conditions in the marmosetlike cebids, *Callicebus* (fig. IV.30), *Aotus,* and *Saimiri* fill the structural gap between callitrichids and prehensile-tailed cebids. The frontal sinus and ostium of *Callicebus* are like those of *Saguinus,* but with a marked tendency for pneumatization of the roof of the nasal cavity formed by the ethmoid. In *Aotus* (fig. IV.29), communication between nasal cavity and frontal sinus is achieved through a posterolateral canal which is situated behind the plane of the olfactory bulb and connects ethmoidal and frontal cells. The earlier anterior connection, between frontal sinus and middle meatus, persists, nevertheless, in a few individuals (cf. FM 25345). The frontal cells in *Saimiri* lack opening in the several specimens examined, but a posterolateral canal between frontal and ethmoidal cavities is indicated in the form of a rounded ridge.

In prehensile-tailed *Cebus* (figs. IV.33, 36) a large frontal sinus communicates with the upper pneumatized ethmoidal recess of the nasal cavity through the posterolateral canal. The same condition exists in one of two samples of *Alouatta seniculus* (fig. IV.38) (FM 31093). Cave (1967, p. 285) regards the sinuses of this specimen, the same described and figured by Du Brul (1965, p. 269, fig. 8C), as mere intrafrontal offshoots of the maxillary sinus.

Judged by the conditions described in more primitive platyrrhines, including callitrichids and marmosetlike cebids, sphenoidal, maxillary, and possibly frontal sinuses are primitive. Increased pneumatization resulted in confluence of sphenoidal and maxillary sinuses in one sense, sphenoidal and ethmoidal cells in another, and sphenoidal and frontal sinuses in a third. This last union resulted in obsolescence and loss of the primitive passage between frontal sinus and middle meatus.

In *Ateles* (fig. IV.35), *Brachyteles, Lagothrix* (fig. IV.34), and most *Alouatta* (fig. IV.32), the posterolateral canals are little or not at all developed, the frontal diploe coarsely honeycombed or nearly solid, but the broad separation between inner and outer tables persists.

The pithecine (fig. IV.31) frontal cavities are trabecular or finely honeycombed and lack visible outlet. Nevertheless, the short ridge between frontal and nasal cavity may be interpreted as either a rudimentary or a vestigial posterolateral canal.

Table 4. Frontal Pneumatization in Platyrrhini

Taxon	*Number of Specimens*	*Structure*	*Connection with Nasal Cavity*
Callitrichidae			
Cebuella pygmaea	3	cellular	none evident
Callithrix jacchus jacchus	1	cellular	none evident
Callithrix jacchus penicillata	1	cellular	small, anterior[1]
Callithrix argentata argentata	2	cellular	none evident
Callithrix humeralifer chrysoleuca	1	cellular	none evident
Saguinus fuscicollis	1	sinusoidal	large, anterior
Saguinus mystax mystax	1	sinusoidal	large, anterior
Saguinus midas midas	1	sinusoidal	large, anterior
Saguinus leucopus	1	sinusoidal	large, anterior
Saguinus inustus	1	sinusoidal	large, anterior
Saguinus oedipus oedipus	1	sinusoidal	large, anterior
Saguinus bicolor bicolor	1	sinusoidal	large, anterior
Leontopithecus rosalia rosalia	1	sinusoidal	large, anterior
Callimiconidae			
Callimico goeldii	2	sinusoidal	large, posterolateral[2]
Cebidae			
Marmosetlike cebids			
Callicebus moloch	2	sinusoidal	large, anterior, with incipient posterolateral
Aotus trivirgatus	1	sinusoidal	anterior and posterolateral (FM 25945, left side)
Saimiri sciureus	4	sinusoidal	none evident but with posterolateral indication
Alouattines			
Alouatta villosa	1	spongiform	none
Alouatta seniculus	1	spongiform	none
Alouatta seniculus	1	sinusoidal	posterolateral
Pithecines			
Pithecia monachus	2	cellular	not evident, posterolateral connection incipient or vestigial
Chiropotes satanas	1	cellular	same as above
Cacajao rubicundus	2	cellular	same as above
Cebines			
Cebus nigrivittatus	1	sinusoidal	broad, posterolateral
Cebus albifrons	2	sinusoidal	broad, posterolateral
Cebus apella	2	sinusoidal	broad, posterolateral
Atelines			
Lagothrix lagothricha	1	cellular	posterolateral complete left side, incomplete right side
Lagothrix lagothricha	1	cellular	posterolateral channel incomplete
Brachyteles arachnoides	1	cellular	same as above
Ateles paniscus	1	cellular	posterolateral channel complete
Ateles paniscus	1	cellular	posterolateral channel incomplete

[1] Anterior connection with middle meatus through ostium anteriad of cribriform plate.
[2] Posterolateral connection with posterior recess of nasal cavity through bony canal posterolaterad to olfactory bulb.

Callimico (fig. IV.27) resembles *Cebus* with its posterolateral connection between frontal sinus and nasal cavity.

Platyrrhine skulls in the Berlin Museum examined by Weinert (1926) were classified according to presence or absence of frontal sinusoidal cavities. Trabeculated or honeycombed cavities were treated as nonsinusoidal. Communication, if any, between frontal cavity and nasal chamber was not noted. Weinert's findings are summarized below with number of specimens examined shown in parentheses. Where necessary, scientific names used by Weinert are brought up to date.

With sinus
- *Callithrix jacchus jacchus* (1).
- *Callithrix jacchus penicillata* (1).
- *Saguinus midas niger* (2).
- *Callicebus moloch* (3).
- *Aotus trivirgatus* (1).
- *Cebus apella* (11).

Without sinus
- *Chiropotes satanas* (1).
- *Saimiri sciureus* (3), one with spongiosa finely honeycombed.
- *Lagothrix lagothricha* (2), spongiosa finely honeycombed.
- *Brachyteles arachnoides* (1), spongiosa honeycombed.
- *Ateles paniscus* (6), four with spongiosa honeycombed; two finely honeycombed.
- *Alouatta seniculus* (6), two with spongiosa honeycombed; two finely honeycombed, two finely honeycombed to almost solid (compare with fig. IV.38).

Evidently the specimens Weinert examined in the Berlin Museum and those I examined in the Field Museum agree in structure with one exception. A large frontal sinus with anteroposterior length 11.5 mm and dorsoventral depth 6 mm, is present in one of two sectioned skulls at hand of adult male *Alouatta seniculus*. In all other howlers checked, the frontal diploe is a honeycombed spongiosa.

The existence of two types of communication between frontal and nasal cavities raises questions regarding criteria used for establishing homologies. In callitrichids and the cebid *Callicebus*, the frontal sinus opens directly into the middle meatus through the opening anteriad to the cribriform plate of the ethmoid bone. This type appears to be primitive. In *Callimico* and in cebids, except *Callicebus*, communication is through a channel that courses posterolaterad to the plane of the olfactory bulb and opens into the upper posterior recess of the nasal cavity. This arrangement is certainly secondary. It connects with other pneumatizations and may be an extension of the sphenoidal sinus system. Both types of openings, anterior and posterolateral, the first on the right side, the second on the left, have been found in a skull of the marmosetlike cebid, *Aotus trivirgatus*.

A parallel dichotomy occurs in Old World primates. In man and African apes, an anterior ostium of the frontal sinus communicates with the middle meatus, as in callitrichids. In all other catarrhines, the superciliary region is usually spongioform and without opening. Occasionally, as in samples of *Cercopithecus*, *Macaca*, and *Hylobates*, the diploe are honeycombed or trabecular and connected by a posterolateral ridge which may be partially, or rarely entirely, channelized and communicates with the upper posterior recesses of the nasal cavity, as in *Ateles* or *Lagothrix*.

22 Skull
5. Braincase

Crests

Primary cranial crests (figs. IV.40, 82; chap. 29) common to all mammals are the *temporal ridges* extending from behind the orbits to the occipital bone, the *lambdoid crest* traversing the skull between occipital and parietal bones, and the median *occipital crest* or elevation.

Secondary cranial crests include the faint accessory lambdoid crest or *supreme nuchal line,* the *occipital protuberance,* a median excrescence of the lambdoid crest, the *nuchal crests* and *oblique crests* (inferior nuchal line), and a pair of feeble ephemeral accessory temporal ridges or *inferior temporal lines.* Each mastoid process, discussed elsewhere (p. 170), may also form a crest. Facial crests are the independently evolved *orbital ridges* and *maxillary ridges.*

All crests develop with age, starting at the time the permanent teeth erupt (cf. Ashton and Zuckerman 1956, p. 582), and they are usually more pronounced in, if not restricted to, adult males. Crests tend toward obliteration in phylogenetic lines characterized by enlargement of braincase and muzzle reduction.

Temporal ridges, one on each side of the cranium, may be roughly parallel-sided or more-or-less arcuate or may converge and fuse to form a sagittal crest near the front, toward the middle, or farther back, or along most of their length. A sagittal crest characterizes particular individuals (generally males) or species in all primate groups from lemuroids to anthropoids. Among platyrrhines, a low but well-defined sagittal crest appears as an individual variable in callitrichids, and in pithecines, and other cebids. The sagittal crest of male *Cebus apella* (fig. IV.40) is species diagnostic and its development in some old individuals rivals the crests seen in old macaques and great apes. The variably parallel-sided or sagittally fused temporal crests of *Alouatta* also develop strongly.

The lambdoid crest, usually weakly defined or absent, is robust in *Alouatta, Macaca, Gorilla,* and some related forms (cf. chap. 29). Accentuation of the external occipital protuberance is closely related to development of the lambdoid crest. The same is generally true for other occipital crests and processes. The supreme nuchal crest or line appears to be a nascent catarrhine character.

Orbital ridges or beading are absent in lemuriforms, callitrichids, and *Callimico* but are present, though not always well defined, in all other primate groups, preeminently in *Macaca* and *Papio* among catarrhine monkeys and *Gorilla* among apes. Maxillary ridges are present in platyrrhines and catarrhines with long robust canines, especially in males. They are extremely well developed among macaques and baboons. For a detailed discussion of the origin, evolution, and function of the supraorbital crests in Cercopithecinae, Colobinae, Pongidae, and Hominidae, see Ehara and Seiler (1970).

Occipital Region and Foramen Magnum

The plane of the posterior plate of the supraoccipital bone in primitive mammals is inclined slightly rostrad, with the foramen magnum pointing straight back or slightly upward. In most primitive primates the occipital plane is vertical or tilted slightly ventrad, the foramen magnum directed straight back or slightly downward (figs. IV.54, 82). In advanced primates, a bulging of the occiput correlated with expansion of the visual cortex of the brain involved rotation of the foramen magnum ventrad and anteriad (fig. IV.55). The greater the occipital bulge, the more anteroventral the foramen magnum and the more nearly horizontal its plane. No direct relationship between orientation of the foramen magnum and body posture is evident. The foramen magnum lies as far forward and ventral in the quadrupedal squirrel monkey as it does in bipedal man (fig. IV.41).

Progressive expansion with increasing curvature of the occipital region and the corresponding rotation of the foramen magnum can be demonstrated with the smaller species of lemuriforms, lorisoids, tarsiers, nearly all callitrichids, and the smaller cebids. Among larger prosimians, cebids, and all catarrhines except man, expansion of the neurocranium is greater in the parietal and temporal regions. The shift to lateral expansion and brachycephally may displace the foramen magnum slightly ventrad or anteriad. In man, posterior and transverse neurocranial expansion and anteroventral orientation of the foramen magnum are extreme.

Modifications of the viscerocranium of higher primates arise independently. The elongate facial skeleton of baboons and macaques, for example, represents a secondary specialization without alteration of the occipital contour of these highly advanced monkeys. The elongate muzzle of howlers (*Alouatta*), however, is primitive and the

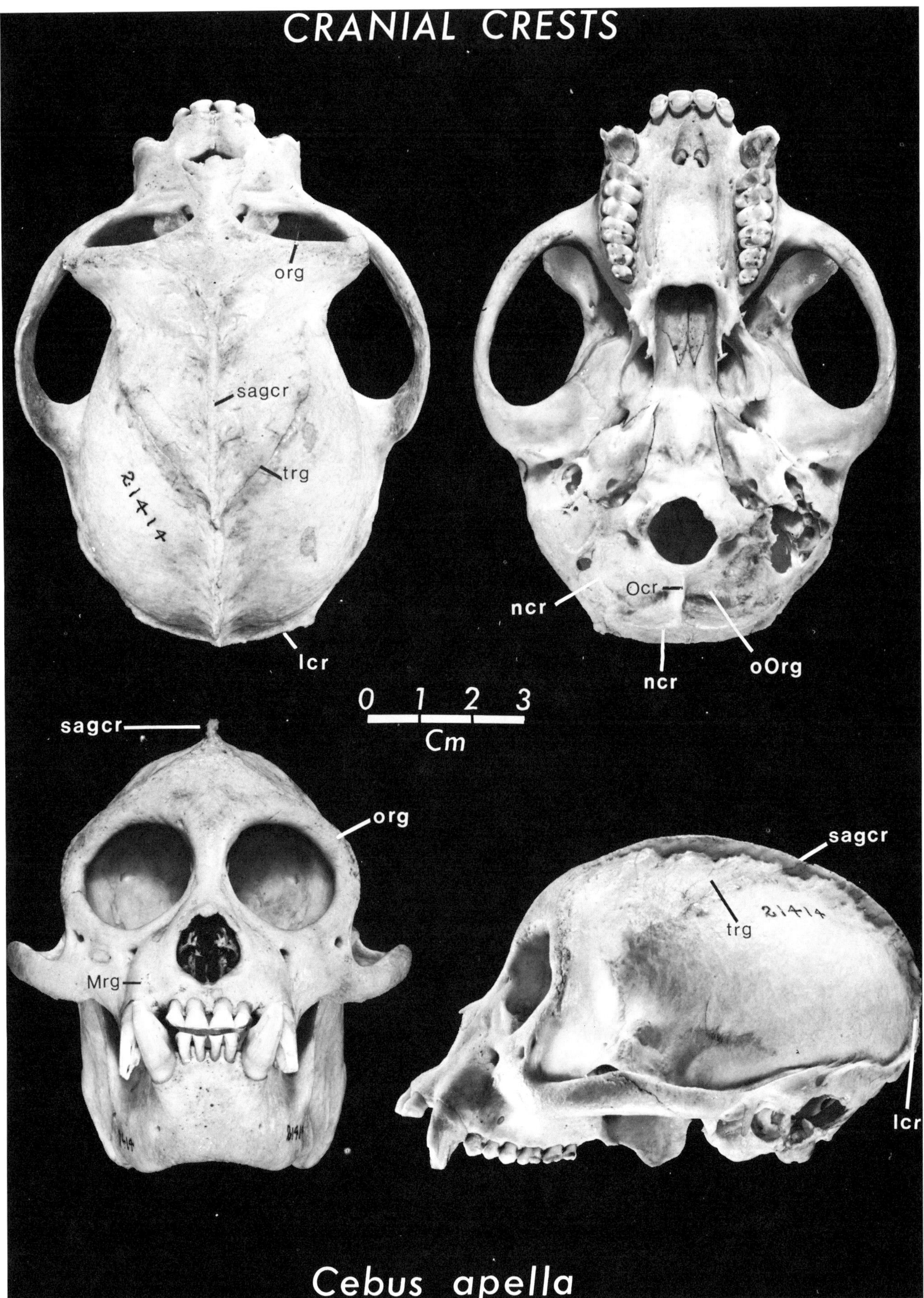

Fig. IV.40. Cranial crests and ridges in *Cebus apella*: *lcr* = lambdoid crest; *ncr* = nuchal crest; *Ocr* = medial occipital crest; *oOrg* = oblique occipital ridge; *org* = orbital ridge or crest; *sagcr* = sagittal crest; *trg* = temporal ridge.

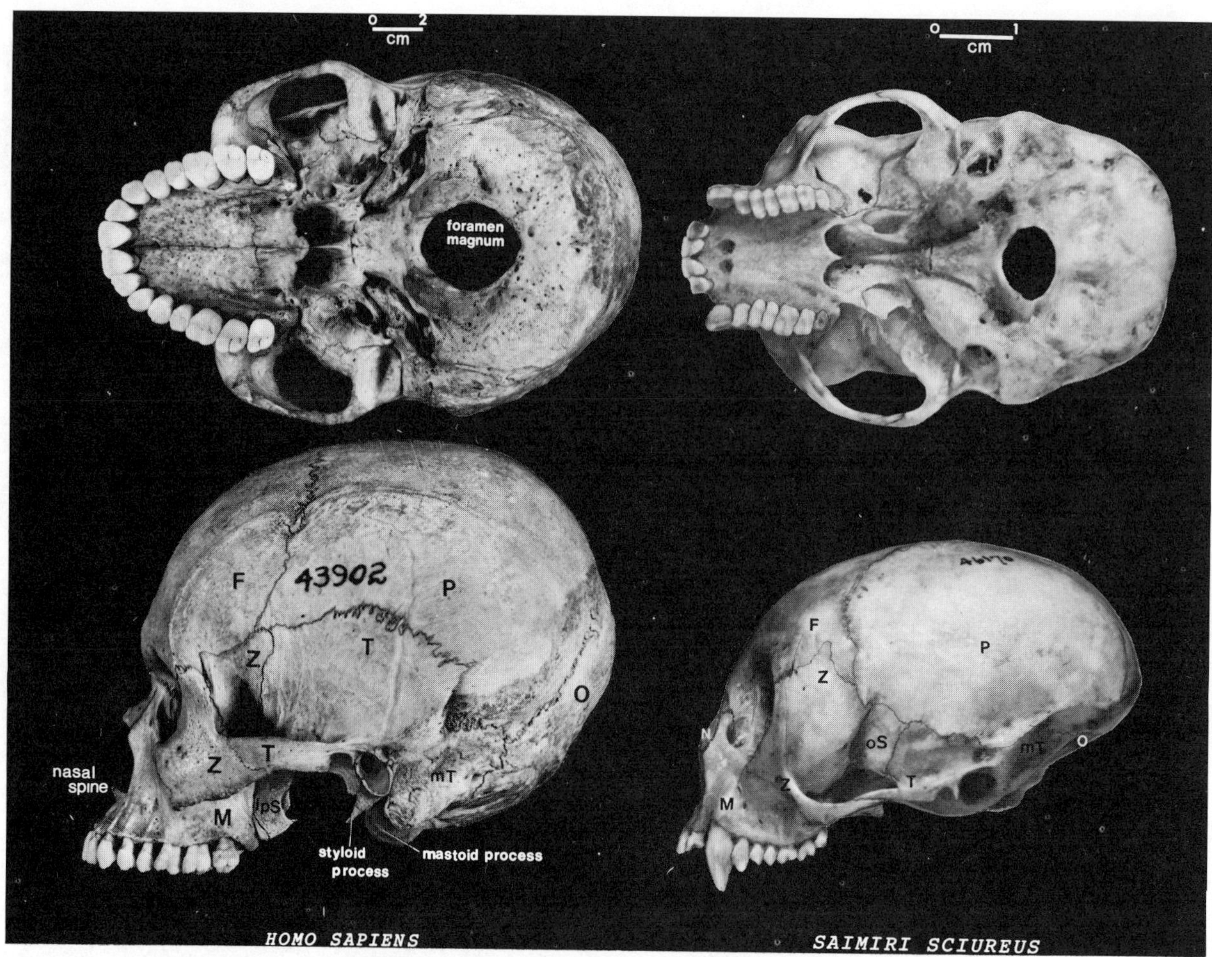

Fig. IV.41. Skull of *Homo* and *Saimiri,* ventral aspect showing similar position of foramen magnum in both; long axis of foramen is variable but usually as appears here; lateral aspect with both skulls aligned to Frankfort plane to show orientation of occipital bone and zygomatic arch. Not to scale.

occipital angle and backward-directed foramen magnum are also primitive.

Ontogenetic shifts in position of the occipital plane were demonstrated by Schultz (1955, p. 97) on the basis of 470 skulls representing juvenal to adult stages in all primate groups.

Interparietal (Inca) Bone

The interparietal bone in vertebrates lies in front of or above the supraoccipital bone (fig. IV.97). Both bones are usually fused into the single occipital bone in adult primates. The interparietal bone is also known as the *postparietal bone* to avoid confusion with sutural or Wormian bones between the parietal bones. The name *Inca* or *incarial bone* has been applied to the interparietal in primates because it appears as a distinct bone in a large percentage of pre-Columbian skulls of Peruvian Inca Indians.

Interparietal and sutural bones were noted in the present study but not recorded. They appear among prosimians, cebids, and catarrhines but were not seen in callitrichids and *Callimico.* Chopra (1957, p. 97), who studied cranial suture closure in 1,500 specimens representing 5 genera of platyrrhines and 57 genera of catarrhine monkeys, discovered Inca bones in *Saimiri* only. He added that of the 62 skulls of *Saimiri* in Professor Schultz's collection (Zürich), the interparietal was present in 10, or 16.1 percent. In the Field Museum collection of 167 skulls collected from throughout the range of the genus, I found 4 skulls (2.4%) with Inca bones (fig. IV.42).

Cribriform Plate and Olfactory Foramina

The extensive, elaborately perforated, and medially crested cribriform plate characteristic of marsupials and insectivores serves as a model for deriving the relatively smaller and less intricately designed plate of lemuriforms and lorisiforms. The cribriform plate of apes and man is considerably smaller and less complex, but the grilled or arabesque design is still retained in many individuals, with the median crest or crista galli attaining maximum size, sometimes with inflation, in *Homo.* The plate is comparatively simple in platyrrhines, considered as a whole, but in cercopithecines it is extremely small, the number of foramina usually reduced to one or two on each side of the median ridge or crest. The apertures in colobines are larger, but a single foramen on each side of the median septum is usual (fig. IV.43).

Specialization of the plate in callitrichids is not correlated with phylogeny or olfactory acuity. The plate seems to be more primitive—that is, larger and more elaborate —in the larger and more highly evolved forms than in

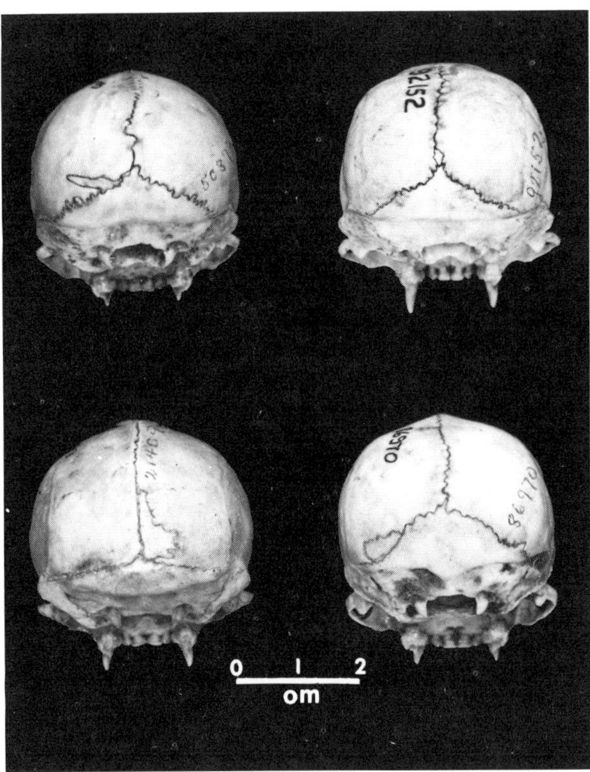

Fig. IV. 42. Inca bones in *Saimiri sciureus* skulls, from the collections of the Field Museum. *Upper left,* FM 50873 ♀, Codajáz, Amazonas, Brazil; *upper right,* FM 92152 ♂, Tapaiuna, Rio Tapajóz, Pará, Brazil; *lower left,* FM 21409 ♀, Buenavista, Santa Cruz, Bolivia; *lower right,* FM 86970 ♀, Santa Rita, Loreto, Peru.

the smaller, more primitive ones. In two adults examined of *Leontopithecus,* largest and most aberrant of callitrichids, the cribriform plate is fully ossified and coarsely grilled, with a well-defined crista galli. In *Saguinus,* next smaller in size, the plate may be ossified or partly to completely cartilagineous, and generally has larger perforations. The most simplified or degenerate types of plates are found in the smaller and more primitive *Callithrix* and *Cebuella.* Here the plate is often entirely cartilaginous with only one or a few large trabeculae.

The plate in *Callimico* is stouter than that of the somewhat larger *Leontopithecus* but is more honeycombed.

In marmosetlike cebids, the plate is usually small, fully ossified, and coarsely grilled, and has in many individuals a well-formed crista galli. The plate is largest in *Aotus* and smallest in *Saimiri* and is marked by several to many foramina, depending on the size of the individual perforations. Cave (1967, p. 282) found only one olfactory foramen in his specimen of *Saimiri.* This condition is unusual and may be aberrant. In any case, *Saimiri* is not a primitive primate, and a single olfactory foramen is not primitive either in primates or in mammals generally.[1]

The cribriform plate in pithecines is fully ossified but apparently is less disintegrated than in the marmosetlike cebids. The plate in prehensile-tailed cebids is likewise ossified but is comparatively large and coarsely grilled in all but *Alouatta,* which conserves the most sievelike or primitive plate among higher monkeys. The crista galli, when present, is best developed in the larger prehensile-tailed forms. In some, particularly *Alouatta,* the crista galli is continuous with an extensive ossification of the anterior portion of the falx cerebri, a specialization first noted in *Alouatta* by Hofer (1955, p. 292). The perpendicular plate of the ethmoid is, in effect, the obverse of the crista galli.

Tentorium Osseum

The tentorium cerebelli, or the transverse partition of dura mater between cerebellum and cerebral hemispheres, is regularly present, according to Klintworth (1968), in birds and mammals but ossifies in mammals only. Well-developed tentorial ossifications occur in marsupials, carnivores, artiodactyls, perissodactyls, sirenians cetaceans, pangolins, aardvark, lemuroids, and platyrrhines (figs. IV.44–49). In many groups, for example felids, virtually the whole tentorium cerebelli becomes ossified. Absence of ossification in some mammalian orders and its irregular or spotty occurrence in others, including catarrhines, indicates independent origin of tentoria ossea at the family or lower group levels.

Tentorial ossification in primates may begin anterolaterally on the crest of the petrous portion of the temporal bone. It may also start posterolaterally on the parietal and progress centripedally. Most extensive ossification in platyrrhines appear in the atelines, *Ateles, Brachyteles,* and *Lagothrix.* In these the tentorium osseum, as seen from above, extends laterally from crest of petrous portion of temporal to angle of the parietal, mastoid, and occipital sutures and projects medially over part of the cerebellar cavity to form a thin canopy with an irregular and sometimes fenestrated margin. A bony process of the petrous crest (processus tentoralis petrosi) continues craniad to bridge the trigeminal impression just behind the apex pyramidis. It may then continue as a lingula above the carotid sulcus to contact the posterior clinoid process of the dorsum sellae.

Tentorial ossification is less extensive, usually only peripheral, in *Callicebus, Aotus,* and pithecines. In *Alouatta* it is variable, and in *Cebus* ossification may be represented by nothing more than the medial lingula of the petrous crest. In *Saimiri,* where the tentorium cerebri is depressed and circumscribed in area, ossification is usually minimal and almost entirely restricted to the crest of the petrosal bone. The bony plate is small but well defined in *Callimico,* and absent or rudimentary in calli-

[1] It is claimed by Cave (1967, p. 282) and others (cf. Osman Hill 1955, p. 211) that one olfactory foramen is characteristic of *Tarsius.* In two transversely sectioned skulls of *Tarsius,* I find a small, trabeculated cribriform plate with about 4 large apertures on each side. The resemblance to most plates found in *Callithrix* and *Cebuella* is striking. The platypus, *Ornithorhynchus anatinus,* seems to be the only mammal regularly conserving the reptilianlike character of a single olfactory foramen on each side of the skull. Turbinals are also lacking. In the two remaining living species of the order Monotremata (*Tachyglossus aculeatus, T. setosus*), a fairly large, completely ossified and well-perforated cribriform plate is present. The single olfactory foramen, or the reduced number of foramina, in primates is the result of secondary reduction or of degeneration.

Findings by Bhatnagar and Kallen (1974) in bats (*Chiroptera*) of correlations and evolutionary trends in size of cribriform plate, perforations, olfactory bulb area, volume, olfactory acuity, and feeding habits do not hold for primates.

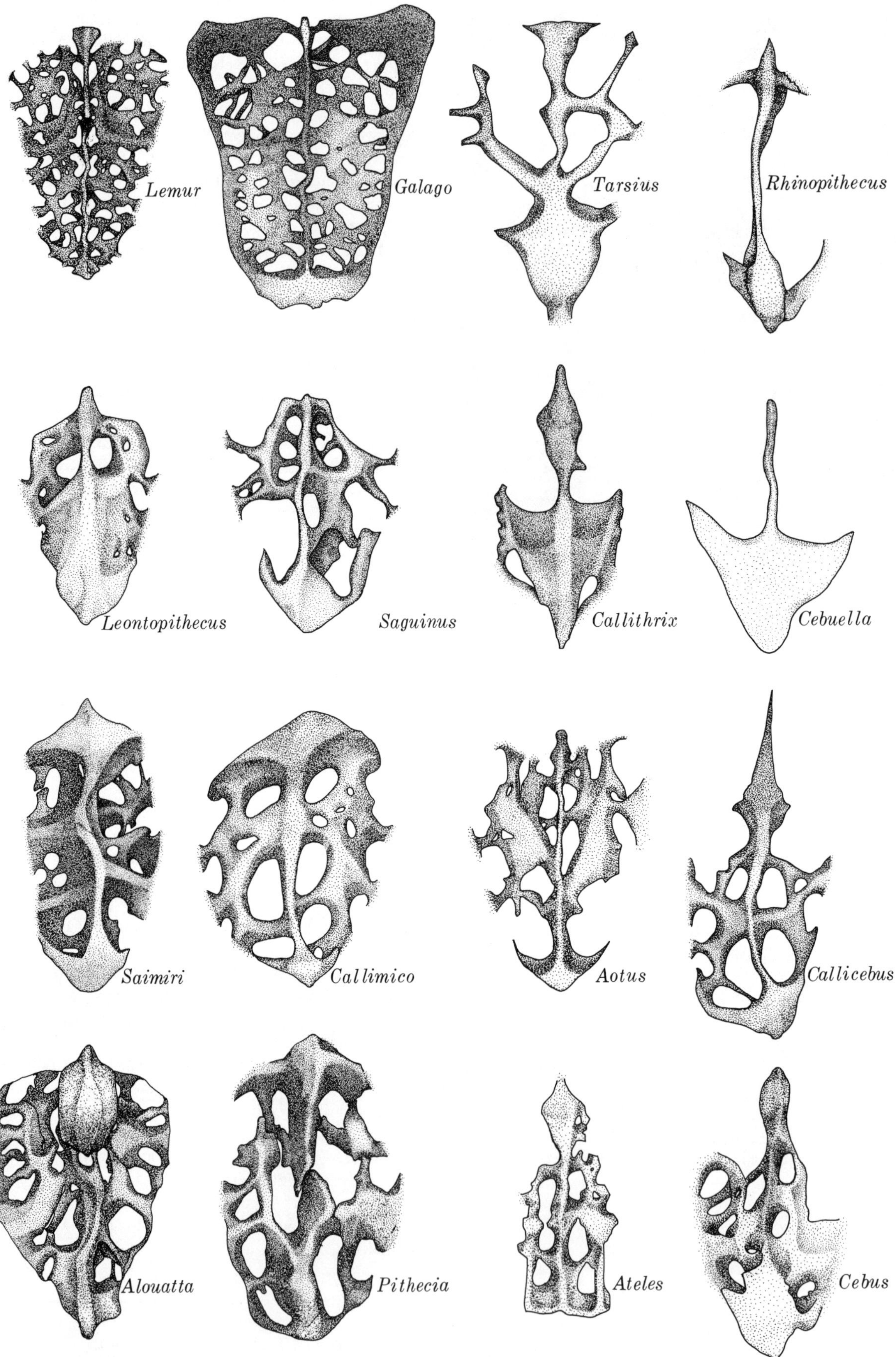

Fig. IV.43. Cribriform plates, superior surface, of specimens not necessarily typical of their respective species; all drawn to approximately same anteroposterior length; absence of distinct frontoethmoidal suture between bones indicated by open borders. *Upper row from left to right,* prosimians and colobine; *second row,* callitrichids; *third row,* marmosetlike cebids and *Callimico; fourth row,* cebids.

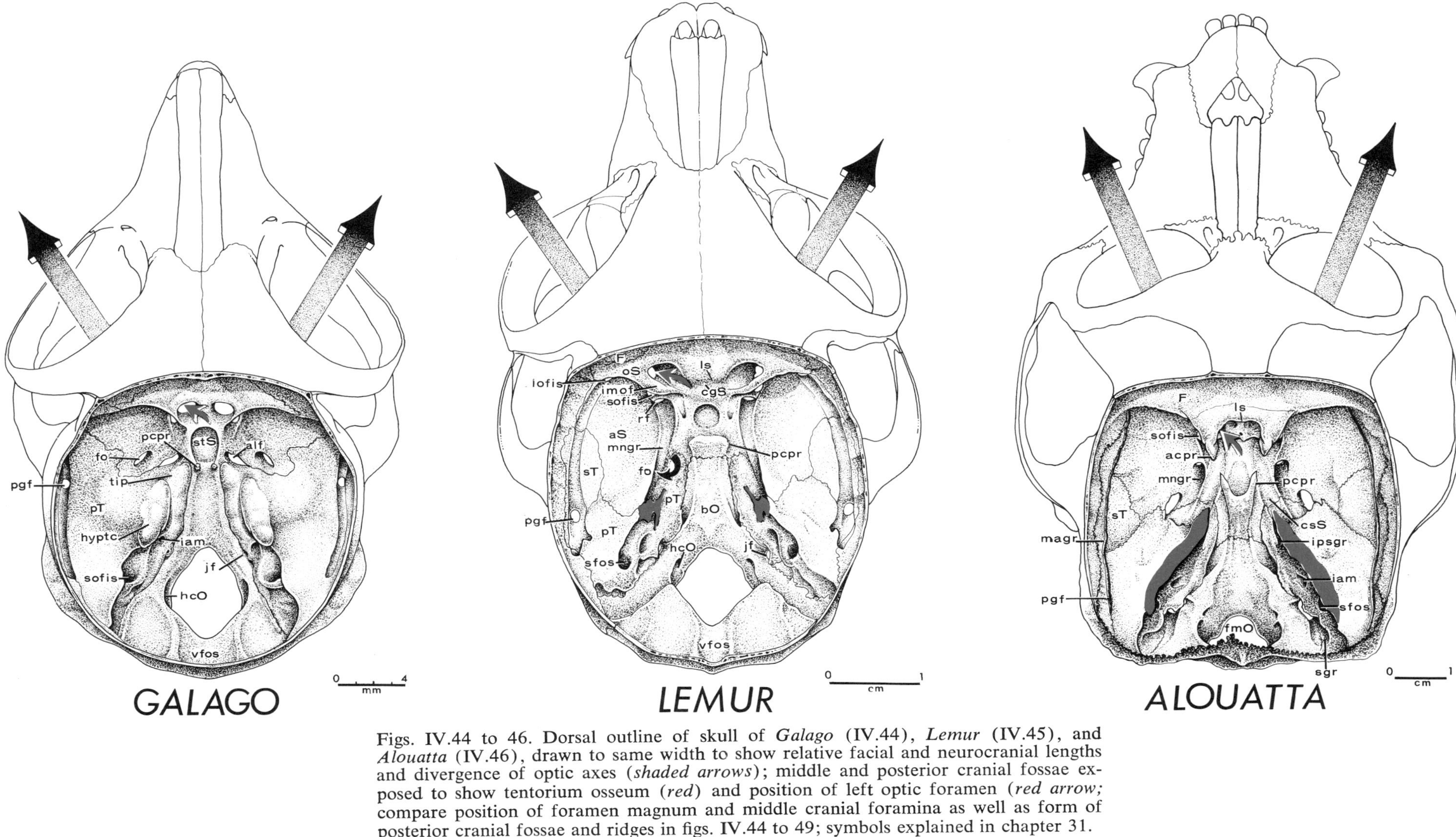

Figs. IV.44 to 46. Dorsal outline of skull of *Galago* (IV.44), *Lemur* (IV.45), and *Alouatta* (IV.46), drawn to same width to show relative facial and neurocranial lengths and divergence of optic axes (*shaded arrows*); middle and posterior cranial fossae exposed to show tentorium osseum (*red*) and position of left optic foramen (*red arrow;* compare position of foramen magnum and middle cranial foramina as well as form of posterior cranial fossae and ridges in figs. IV.44 to 49; symbols explained in chapter 31.

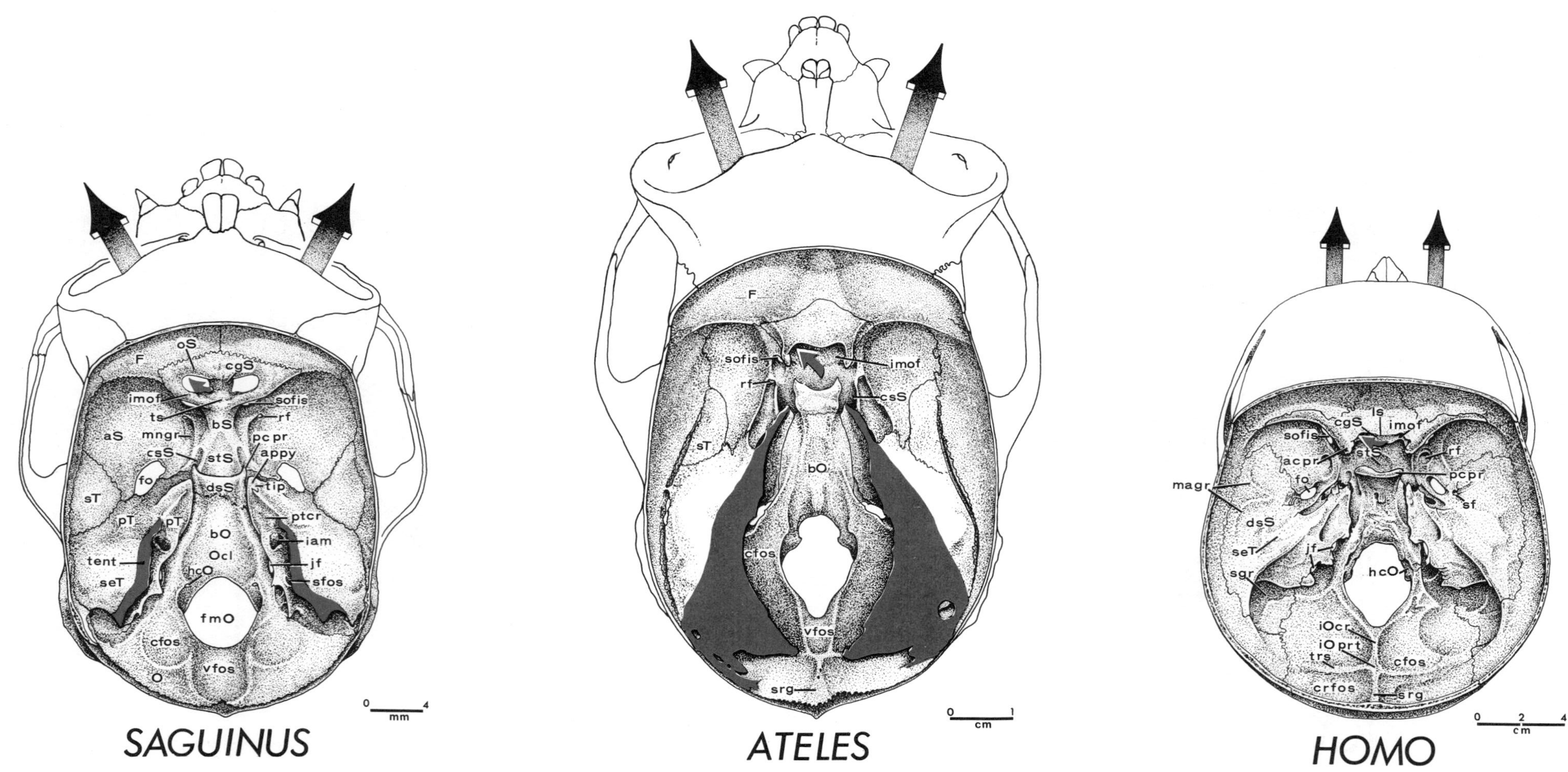

Figs. IV.47 to 49. Dorsal outline of skull of *Saguinus* (IV.47), *Ateles* (IV.48), and *Homo* (IV.49) drawn to same width; for explanation see figs. IV.44 to 49 above.

trichids. In the several catarrhine monkeys I examined the tentorium osseum is absent or rudimentary. However, in very old catarrhine monkeys and apes, according to Hochstetter (1946, p. 90), the fibrous crest may be defined as a weak tentorium osseum.

The tentorium cerebelli supports the occipital lobes of the cerebrum. The advantages of ossification are not clear in specimens examined. The heaviest supratentorial brain elements occur in man, where tentorial ossification is rare or absent. For a discussion of the human tentorium cerebelli, based primarily on radiological studies, see Bull (1969).

23 Skull
6. Basicranium

Bony Palate

The bony palate is formed by the palatine plate of the premaxilla bearing the incisors, the palatine process of the maxilla with canine, premolars and molars, and the horizontal plate of the palatine bone.

The bony palate of primitive mammals and primates is triangular in outline, or V-shaped with the alveolar rows meeting in front to form a narrowly rounded to almost sharp angle. The V-shaped palate persists in the more primitive of living prosimians, notably cheirogaleines, and *Tarsius,* and in lower callitrichids or true marmosets among platyrrhines. A phylogenetic series beginning with the pygmy marmoset, *Cebuella,* and continuing through *Callithrix* and *Saguinus* encompasses nearly the full evolutionary span from a primitive, sharply pointed, V-shaped palate to the curved or square U-shaped palate of most higher monkeys, apes, and man. Adding to the series a cheirogaleine such as *Microcebus* at one end and a cebid such as *Saimiri* or *Cebus* at the other completes the entire evolutionary range in palatal outlines among platyrrhines particularly, and exemplifies it for all primates generally (fig. VII.6).

Transformation of the tapered, projecting, and weakly dentate part of the palate is correlated primarily with changing food habits. In the evolutionary sequence, the acute angle of the upper jaws becomes arcuate, then square, with a stout canine at each outer corner and a slightly bowed or nearly straight line of broad spatulate incisors between. At the same time, the front part of the palatine processes of the maxillae broaden, the cheek teeth become parallel-sided, but often with a slight inward or outward bow.

The peculiarly protruded pithecine premaxillary region with forward projecting incisors is a secondary specialization of the U-shaped palate. The powerful canines and parallel-sided to backwardly convergent molariform rows of these cebids attest to the advanced stage of evolution attained by this group.

The transverse contour of the palatal vault among prosimians is nearly plane or slightly arched, the dental crowns practically on a level with the palatal ceiling. The vaulting is more pronounced in platyrrhines and cercopithecines, and more so in colobines and hominoids in which steep alveolar walls suspend the cheek teeth well below the palatal ceiling (fig. IV.50).

The wide range in shape and degree of palatal vaulting in primates is not matched by any other order of mammals except bats. Palates of the suborder Megachiroptera, or fruit bats, depart little from the primitively flat to slightly curved state. Palates of Microchiroptera, on the other hand, range from flat to steeply vaulted, as in the more specialized platyrrhines and catarrhines. The transverse contour of the arch in bats, however, usually varies from low Roman to high Gothic. The extremely high angular palatal arch of the blood-sucking *Desmodus rotundus* and the less acute one of the fish-eating *Noctilio leporinus* recall the less extremely vaulted palate of *Cebuella* (fig. IV.50). Square vaulting such as occurs in colobines is uncommon among bats. In horses and other ungulates with hypsodont teeth, high crowned molars alone simulate the effect of low crowned molars set in deeply suspended alveoli as in most catarrhines.

The incisive foramina in prosimians extend forward to the base of the weak incisors. In callitrichids, the foramina lie increasingly farther behind as the incisors become larger and stronger, the palate more U-shaped. This relationship is even more advanced in most cebids and catarrhines.

The median posterior border of the palate defining the anterior border of the mesopterygoid fossa is long—that is, it extends posteriad to the plane of the last molars or beyond in primitive mammals including marsupials, insectivores, tupaiids, and some of the smaller lemuriforms such as *Microcebus* and *Cheirogaleus.* The palate recedes to the posterior plane of the last molars in *Tarsius* and some of the larger prosimians. In other prosimians the palate is short, extending only to the posterior plane of the second molar. Among platyrrhines, the palate extends to or slightly beyond the plane of last molars in callitrichids and some cebids, and between the plane of the last and the penultimate molars in remaining cebids and *Callimico* (fig. VII.6). The catarrhine palate is long in large-muzzled monkeys and great apes, long to short in shorter-faced monkeys, gibbons, and man.

Palatal length is determined by the position of the median posterior border relative to the last molar, whether the normal number of molars is two or three. There are two molars in callitrichids, three in all other living primates. A long palate is generally correlated with a long muzzle in catarrhines and with the short-faced callitrichids among platyrrhines.

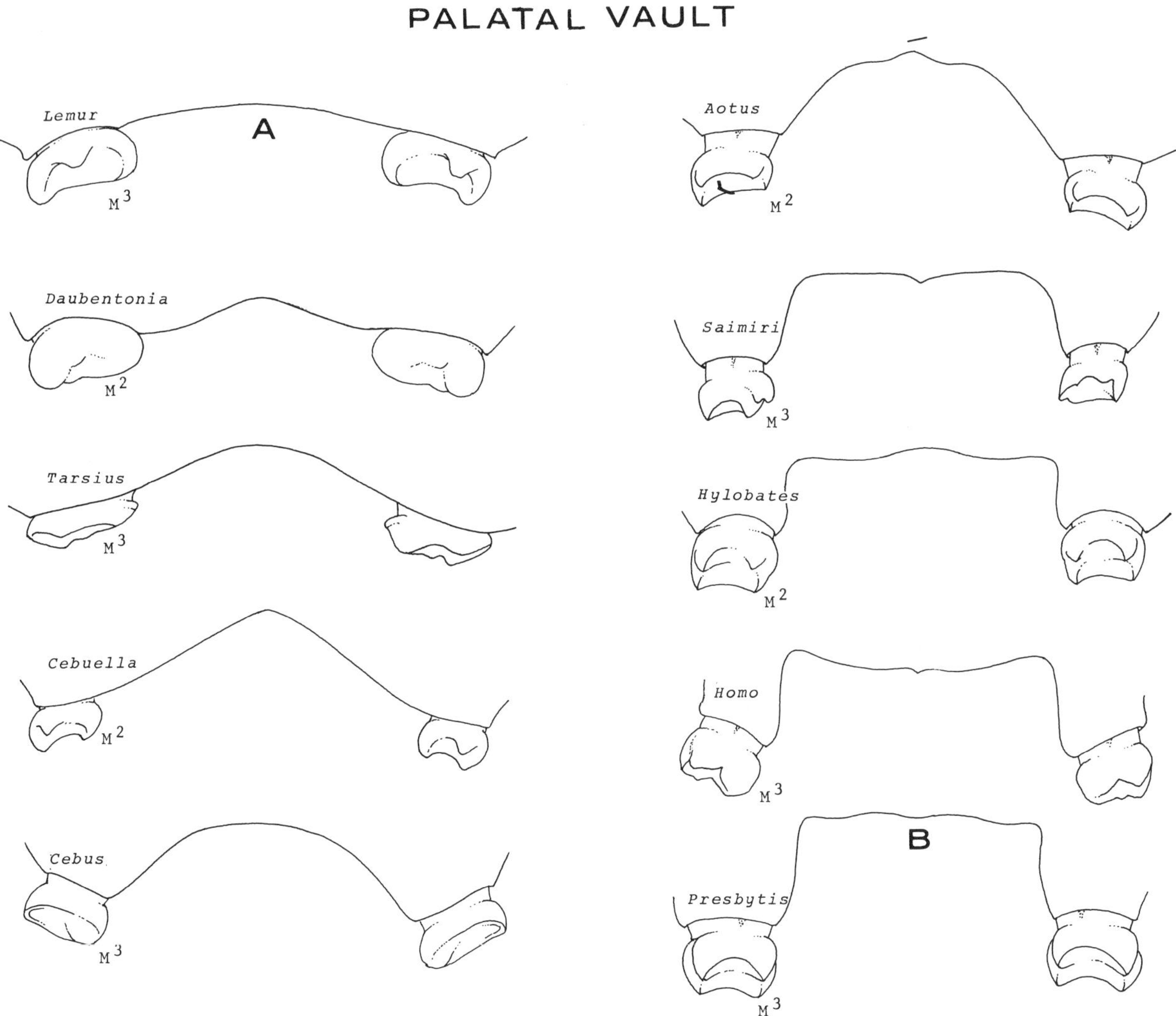

Fig. IV.50. Profiles of palatal vault at level of last molars in representative primates, all drawn to same width. Low palatal vault (*A*) curves evenly from base to base of opposing molar crowns: high U-shaped palatal vault (*B*) with more or less horizontal ceiling and nearly perpendicular walls rising from molar crown bases; low and high palatal vaults intergrade, those of *Cebus* and *Aotus* are intermediate.

Pterygoid Processes

In living primates, each pterygoid process of the sphenoid bone consists of a pair of more or less divergent vertical plates (figs. IV.81, 82). The flaring lateral plate is larger than the medial plate and extends posteriorly from less than one-half the distance between palate and auditory bulla to as far as the outer side of the bulla behind the bullar spine. The medial plate varies in size from slightly more than two-thirds the size of the lateral plate to hardly more than a ridge that usually terminates in a prominent spinous process, the hamulus. The angle or pterygoid fossa between medial and lateral plates may be acute or broad, shallow or deep. The width between roots of right and left processes, measured at the sphenopalatine sutures, is as great or greater than the least width between the auditory bullae measured along the spheno-occipital suture.

Among the more primitive of living mammals, including many marsupials, insectivores, bats, edentates, and some carnivores including dogs, the pterygoid process of each side is a simple platelike ridge continuous with and, except for the suture, hardly distinguishable from the plate of the palatine process (figs. IV.51–53). The plates are parallel-sided or slightly convergent posteriorly and terminate well in front of the anterior plane of the bullae; the valley between the plates, the mesopterygoid fossa, is narrow. With increasing specialization, the pterygoid processes become steeper, longer and extend to or behind the anterior bullar plane. A weak lateral pterygoid plate may arise near the posterior tip of the primitive pterygopalatine plate, as in talpids and some soricids. In tupaiids and many carnivores, the lateral plate originates nearer to the plane of the bulla than to the posterior border of the palate. In most ungulates, the lateral plate is more or less parallel to the medial plate. In pigs, however, the lateral plate is divergent and a deep fossa forms between it and the medial plate.

In primates, as in pigs, a well-developed lateral plate stems from the root of the primitive or medial plate at the sphenopalatine suture near the posterior palatine border. In general, the lateral plate becomes larger as the point of its origin moves anteriad. The plate is canted toward the vertical in some groups, including primates, and toward the horizontal in others. In many rodents, marsupials, edentates, and others the lateral plate becomes extremely enlarged, pneumatized, or fenestrated, or it becomes secondarily simplified or reduced. In primates,

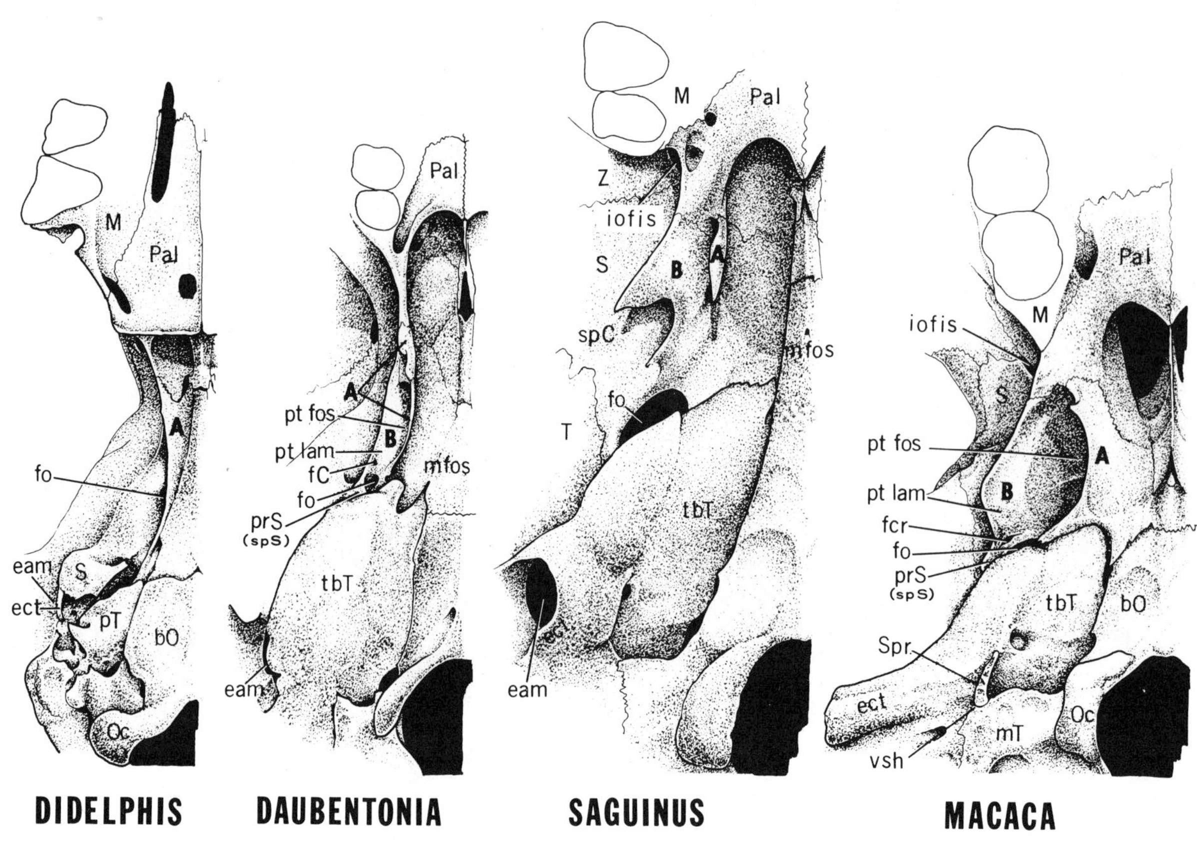

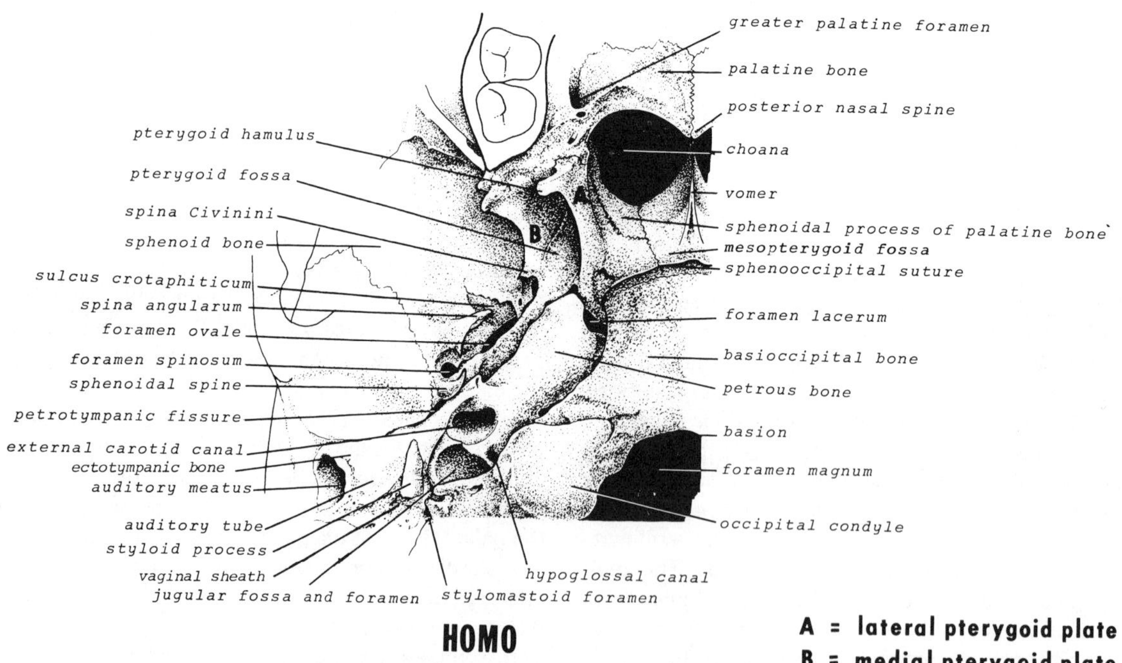

Fig. IV.51. Pterygoid and auditory regions in *Didelphis, Daubentonia, Saguinus, Macaca, Homo,* all drawn to same length. Most symbols used in upper figures are explained in lower; cranial elements labeled are: **A,** medial plate of pterygoid process; **B,** lateral plate of pterygoid process; *M,* maxillary bone; *Pal,* palatine bone; *bO,* basioccipital bone; *Oc,* occipital bone; *S,* sphenoid bone; *T,* temporal bone; *Z,* zygomatic or malar bone; *eam,* external auditory meatus; *ect,* ectotympanic bone or auditory tube; *fC,* foramen Civinini; *fcr,* foramen crotaphiticum; *fo,* foramen ovale; *iofis,* inferior orbital fissure; *prS,* sphenoidal process or spine; *pT,* petrous bone (of temporal); *pt fos,* pterygoid fossa; *pt lam,* pterygospinous lamina; *tbT,* tympanic bulla (of petrous portion of temporal bone). Note: The distal spinous component of the medial pterygoid plane (**A**) is loosely connected in didelphids and missing in the *Didelphis* skull figured.

EVOLUTION OF PTERYGOID SYSTEM

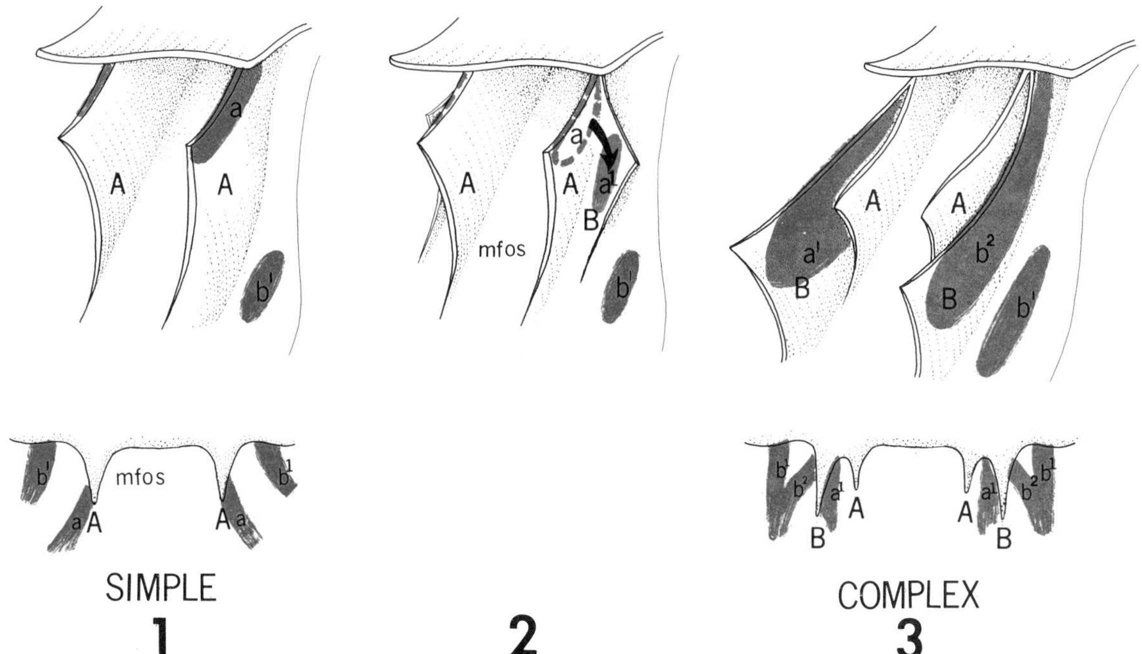

Fig. IV.52. Evolution of simple to complex pterygoid system in mammals seen from ventral surface in top row, and in inverted cross section in bottom row. Explanation of symbols: *A*, primitive pterygoid process or medial plate; *B*, neomorphic lateral plate of pterygoid process which rises from root of medial plate *A* and tends to replace it; *a*, head of internal pterygoid muscle primitively rising from ventrolateral aspect of medial plate (*A*) as shown in *1; a'*, new head of internal pterygoid muscle on medial (ventral) surface of neomorphic lateral plate (*B*). It replaces head *a* of medial plate (*A*) by a shift in site of origin as shown on left lateral plate (*B*) in *2*, and on medial surface of right lateral plate (*B*) in *3*; b^1, primitive head of external pterygoid muscle originating on alisphenoid bone in *1* to *3*; b^2 = neomorphic second head of external pterygoid muscle which rises from lateral (dorsal) surface of lateral plate (B) and reinforces head b^1 in the complex pterygoid system shown in *3*.

the primitive or medial plate becomes relatively smaller as the lateral plate enlarges. At the same time, the pterygoid fossa becomes constricted, the mesopterygoid fossa wider. In many other mammals, the mesopterygoid fossa becomes secondarily narrower.

The lateral or external pterygoid plate in platyrrhines (figs. IV.51, 53) exhibits a wide range of variation. The posteroventral border is usually tapered, directed mainly ventrad, and canted laterad. A small spine, the spina Civinini (cf. Grosse 1893), projects from the middle portion of the posterior border. In most platyrrhines, the plate is short with a wide semilunate space, the incisura Civinini, between it and the anterior border of the auditory bulla. In a few forms, most notably *Aotus*, an ossification of the ligamentum pterygospinosum nearly—sometimes completely—bridges the gap between the spina Civinini and the posteroventral process of the sphenoid bone which abuts against the anterolateral surface of the auditory bulla. An aperture, the foramen Civinini, which is the unossified portion of the closed incisura Civinini, leads into the foramen ovale.

The lateral pterygoid plate in lorisids (fig. IV.53) is as a rule short or incomplete as in most platyrrhines, with the pterygospinal ligament unossified, the deep incisura Civinini well demarcated. In contrast, the lateral plate in the aye aye, lemurids, and galagids is long and greatly expanded, the incisura Civinini completely closed by the lamina pterygospinosum except for the foramen Civinini.

The lateral pterygoid plate in *Tarsius* is long, as in lemurids and galagids, but more widely expanded, more divergent and makes broader contact with the outer wall of the auditory bulla.

The cercopithecoid lateral pterygoid plate is also fully developed. In colobines, the foramen Civinini is usually completely established and serves for passage of vessels including the internal pterygoid nerve. In many cercopithecines ossification of the lamina may be complete and the nerve passes beneath and over the plate. In others, a constricted foramen may be present on the ventral border of the plate. A second perforation, usually with a well-defined sulcus, the foramen and sulcus crotaphiticum, may also appear on the under surface of the plate anterolaterad to the foramen ovale.

The lateral plate in pongids, on the other hand, is short, recalling that of lorisids, its spina Civinini well defined and incisura Civinini well opened, the sphenoidal spine for attachment of the ligamentum pterygospinosum little or only moderately developed.

The posterior portion of the plate in gibbons is intermediate in structure between that of catarrhine monkeys and pongids and suggests progression toward the condition in the former. The resemblance between the pterygoid process (lateral and median plates combined) of hylobatines and the platyrrhine genus *Cebus* is noteworthy (cf. figs. IV.40, 53, 117, 118, 139, 140).

The human lateral plate (figs. IV.51, 53) resembles

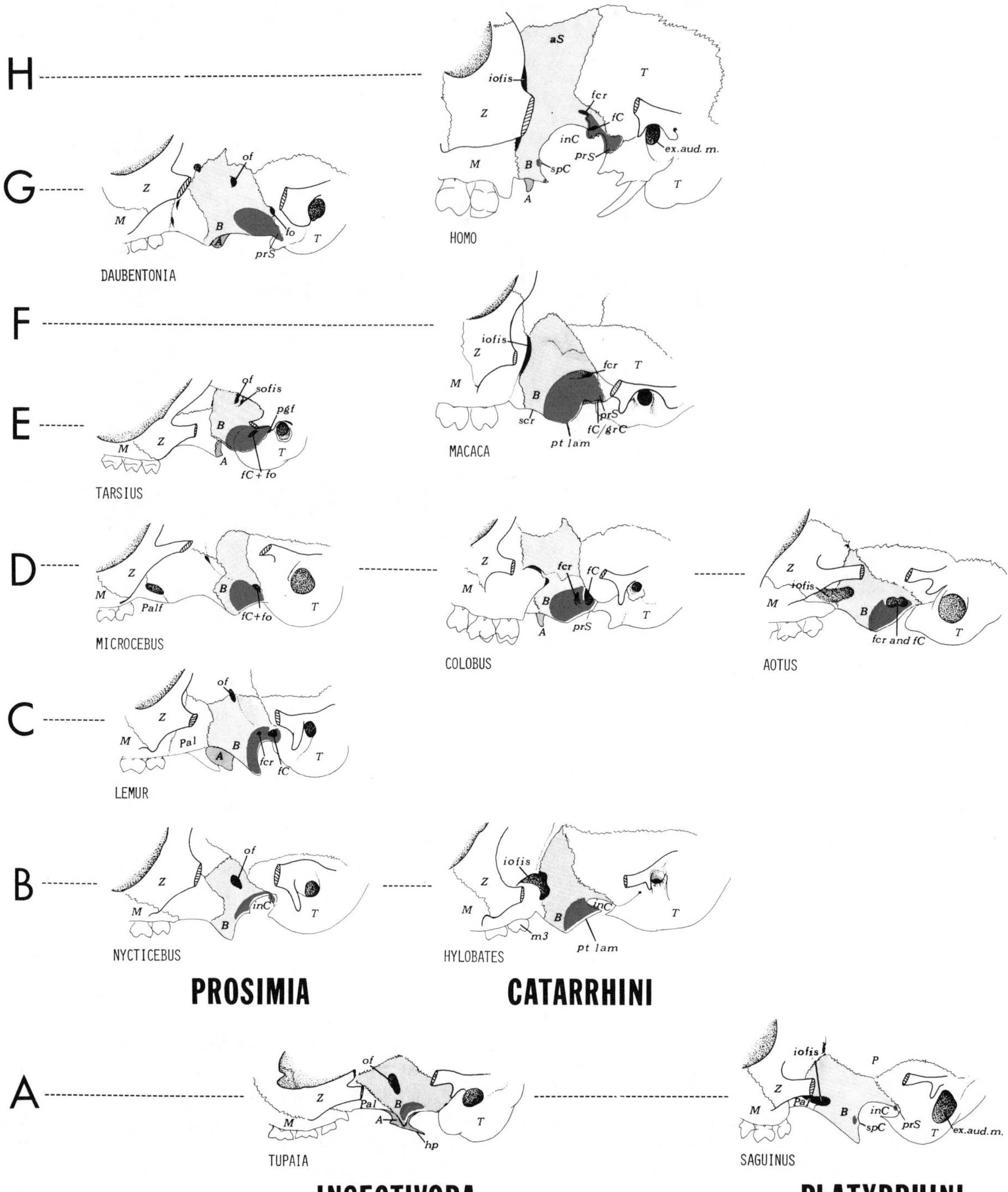

Fig. IV.53. Morphological grades (levels A to H) of lateral plate (*B*) of pterygoid process in prosimians, platyrrhines, and catarrhines. The insectivore *Tupaia* is figured on level A for comparison. All views are of left side of skull with middle portion of zygoma removed to expose alisphenoid portion (*aS*, see in *Homo*, level H), and pterygoid portions (*A, B*) of sphenoid bone (*shaded*); pterygospinous lamina (*pt lam*) is formed by ossification of pterygospinous ligament between the spina Civinini (*spC*) and sphenoidal process or spine (*prS*) shown in red. Level A, relatively primitive grade, the lunulate incisura Civinini (*inC*) nearly fully excised in the platyrrhine callitrichid *Saguinus*, partially closed in the insectivore *Tupaia;* level B, incisura partially closed; level C, incisura closure advanced in *Lemur*, the plate perforated by the foramina Civinini (*fC*) and crotaphiticum (*fcr*), which communicate with the *ff*. ovale and spinosum; level D, fully closed incisura perforated only by f. Civinini or ff. Civinini and crotaphiticum in *Microcebus, Colobus*, and *Aotus;* level E, bony lamina filling incisura Civinini extending posteriad to external auditory meatus in *Tarsius;* level F, incisura fully closed, foramen Civinini on ventral border of plate narrowly constricted or closed, foramen crotaphiticum open or closed in *Macaca;* level G, incisura closed and imperforate; level H, incisura extremely enlarged in *Homo*, presumably secondarily, vestiges of ossifications bounding ff. Civinini and crotaphiticum shown in red; compare with *Saguinus*, level A. Explanation of abbreviations: *A*, medial pterygoid plate, more or less hidden by lateral pterygoid plate; *B*, primitive portion of lateral pterygoid plate; *M*, maxillary bone; *L*, lacrimal bone; *Pal*, palatine bone; *Z*, malar bone; *T*, temporal bone;

that of pongids, but the sphenoidal spine (spina ossis sphenoidalis) is extremely well developed and may be the vestige of a former osseous connection with the spina Civinini rather than the outpost for a bridge or lamina not yet ossified. A groove, the sulcus crotaphiticum (cf. Grosse 1893), leading into the foramen ovale, is partially to completely bridged by the ossification of a ligament which separates the motor from the sensory part of the third branch of the trigeminal nerve. The angular spine and other small or isolated ossifications of the sphenoid laterad of the foramen ovale that define the sulcus or foramen crotaphiticum may be peculiar to *Homo* among living primates. They, together with the large isolated sphenoidal spine, suggest the existence of a former bony pterygospinous lamina that deteriorated as the basicranium of evolving man became wider and relatively shorter.

The primitive, but now medial or internal pterygoid plate of primates is always smaller than the lateral (fig. IV.51). In lemurids and *Daubentonia* it is comparatively well developed, and the pterygoid fossa is capacious. The plate is smaller in galagids and more reduced in lorisids, except for the hamulus. In both phyla, the pterygoid fossa is correspondingly constricted, often to a shallow, narrow recess.

In all platyrrhines except *Cebus* the internal plate is small, generally as in lorisids. In some, notably atelines and the larger callitrichids, the plate is reduced to little more than a small hamular process with the pterygoid fossa nearly or completely suppressed. The pterygoid fossa in *Callimico* (fig. XII.7) is usually better developed than in callitrichids and many cebids.

In *Cebus*, and in all catarrhines (figs. IV.40, 51), the medial pterygoid plate is well developed, the pterygoid fossa correspondingly voluminous. But individual variation is considerable in all forms.

In certain platyrrhines, mostly among callitrichids, but also among insectivores, including tupaiids, marsupials, and other primitive nonprimates, the hamulus is often joined to the petrous spine of the auditory bulla by a thin bony bridge, evidently the ossification of a tendon of the tensor veli palatini. The character appears to be a vestige of the erstwhile dominance of the medial pterygoid plate in pre- or early primates. Subordination and virtual replacement of the medial plate by the neomorphic lateral pterygoid plate in higher primates includes functional replacement of the ossified tendon of the tensor veli palatini by the parallel pterygospinous ligament of the lateral plate.

Remarks. The rate of reduction and obsolescence of the internal plate varies independently of the rate of expansion of the external plate. The medial pterygoid plate and pterygoid fossa retain considerable surface area and vary little in size and shape among catarrhines and prosimians. In platyrrhines, the internal plate and fossa vary from well developed in *Cebus* to greatly reduced or obsolescent in other New World monkeys.

Degeneration of the primitive medial pterygoid plate and rise and dominance of the secondary lateral pterygoid plate depends on modifications of the pterygoid muscles and shifts in their respective origins (fig. IV.52). In primitive mammals such as *Didelphis,* with a simple unbranched pterygoid process, the *internal pterygoid muscle* originates on the ventrolateral surface of the medial plate and contiguous borders of bones. In primates, the muscle takes off mainly from the internal surface of the lateral pterygoid plate and contiguous parts of pterygoid fossa and palatine bone. The *external pterygoid muscle* arises by a single head from the alisphenoid bone in *Didelphis* (fig. IV.51) and other mammals with a simple, primitive pterygoid plate. In mammals such as primates, with the complex bifurcated pterygoid process, a neomorphic second head of the muscle originates on the external (dorsal) surface of the neomorphic external pterygoid plate (figs. IV.51, 52).

The type of variation in pterygoid structure among primates indicates that the relative degree of development of the medial and lateral plates and size or width of fossa are not directly related to special functions of the pterygoid muscles, jaw movements, or dental characters. The unpredictable relationship between apparent form and inferred function of the pterygoid system, when viewed by itself, is demonstrated in models used by Turnbull (1970) in his finely detailed study of mammalian masticatory muscles. *Echinosorex* and *Didelphis,* for example, are treated by Turnbull as representatives of his "Generalized Group." However, *Echinosorex,* with respect to its well-developed horizontally oriented lateral pterygoid plate and two-headed external pterygoid muscle, resembles sciurines which Turnbull includes in his "Specialized Group III." Primates, with their much more specialized pterygoid systems and vertically canted lateral pterygoid plate, are classified by Turnbull (1970, p. 342) as "G[eneralized] basically, some tendency toward S[pecialized]–II or S–III pronounced for many."

Comparative and functional morphologists had failed to recognize the differences between the simple and complex types of pterygoid systems described here. Even the form and function of the two-headed external (lateral) pterygoid muscle were misunderstood or simply treated as a unit. Recently, however, Grant (1973), using heads of rhesus monkeys, human skulls, and the relevant literature, could determine that the "superior head [of the lateral pterygoid muscle] is active during various jaw-closing movements only, while the inferior [neomorphic] head is active during jaw-opening and protrusion only. Functionally, therefore, the lateral pterygoid of man and rhesus macaques appears to be two muscles." McNamara (1973), who monitored 33 rhesus monkeys in 113 electromyographic recording sessions, observed that "the superior head presumably positioned or stabilized the condylar head and disc against the articular eminence during closing movements of the mandible, while the inferior head assisted in the translations of the condylar head

---

aS, alisphenoid bone; *ex. aud. m.,* external auditory meatus; *fC,* foramen Civinini; *fcr,* foramen crotaphiticum; *fC/grC,* foramen or groove Civinini; *fo,* foramen ovale; *inC,* incisura Civinini; *of,* optic foramen; *Palf,* palatine foramen; *iofis,* inferior orbital fissure; *pgf,* postglenoid foramen; *pgpr,* postglenoid process; *prS,* sphenoidal process; *pt lam,* pterygospinous lamina; *sofis,* superior orbital fissure; *spC,* spina Civinini; *spS,* sphenoidal process or spine.

downward, anteriorly and contralaterally during opening movements. Thus, the two heads of the lateral pterygoid can be considered as two functionally distinct muscles."

Foramina Ovale, Spinosum, and Lacerum

The related foramina ovale, spinosum (alisphenoid canal), and anterior foramen lacerum (figs. IV.51, 82) are closely clustered at the posterior margin of the great wing of the sphenoid. All three were probably present in the ancestral primate. They persist in most lemuriforms and, with some exceptions and some coalescences or modifications, in catarrhines.

The *foramen ovale,* anteriormost of the three related basicranial apertures, is present in all primates (and mammals), but not always as a discrete unit. In man, it transmits the mandibular branch of the trigeminal nerve, the small meningeal artery, and sometimes the small petrosal nerve.

The *foramen spinosum,* posteriad, laterad, or posterolaterad to the ovale, gives passage to the middle meningeal artery in man. It is present in lemuriforms, some lorisiforms (*Perodicticus*) and *Tarsius.* In catarrhines, the foramen may be discrete, as in man, or combined with the foramen ovale. The foramen spinosum is defined by the union of a posteroventral process, the spine of Civinini, of the lateral pterygoid plate, with the posterodorsal lingula of the spina ossis sphenoidalis. In man, apes, and many catarrhine monkeys, the lingula alone may complete or partially close the ventral border of the foramen. In other catarrhines, most notably gibbons and many colobines, and in all platyrrhines, the foramina spinosum, ovale, and lacerum merge into a single large aperture.

The *foramen lacerum,* between the apex of the petrous portion of the temporal bone and the body of the sphenoid and basioccipital, gives passage in man to the small nerve of the pterygoid canal and a small meningeal branch from the ascending pharyngeal artery. The foramen is present and well open in such primitive lemuriforms as *Microcebus* and *Cheirogaleus* but is greatly reduced or obsolete in the larger, more specialized forms including *Lemur* and *Daubentonia.* It is present and well developed in all lorisiforms examined, and absent in *Tarsius.* The foramen lacerum appears to be a constant feature of catarrhine monkeys, man, and orang, but it may be present, obsolete, or absent in the remaining apes.

In platyrrhines, a single aperture represents the foramen ovale alone or the union of foramina ovale, spinosum, and lacerum. If the surrounding bone is wholly alisphenoid, the aperture must be regarded as the homologue of the primitive foramen ovale. In most platyrrhine species, however, the median border of the foramen may be either alisphenoid or partly to entirely petrosal. In this case, the foramen could, but need not, be regarded as a combined foramen ovale and foramen lacerum. The presence of a single foramen, the ovale, which provides the services of the primitive foramina ovale, lacerum, and spinosum, is distinctive of platyrrhines generally, and of a small percentage of gibbons. Similarity between platyrrhines and gibbons with respect to structure of the related pterygoid processes has already been noted above.

The *posterior foramen lacerum,* not involved in the present discussion, is usually coalesced with the jugular foramen in higher primates. It is often discrete, however, in callitrichids and other small platyrrhines.

Basicranial Angle, Cranial Kyphosis, and Basis-Angle

The *basicranial angle* is formed by the intersection of palatal axis (prosthion to staphylion) with the basineurocranial axis (basion to sphenoidal point) (fig. IV.84). In primitive mammals, and presumably the ancestral primate, palatal and basineurocranial axes intersect postcranially to form a nearly straight angle. The narrowest angle thus formed in living platyrrhines appears in *Alouatta* with ca. 165° (or ca. 15°), the widest in *Cebuella* with ca. 130° (or ca. 50°). In catarrhines, the minimum and maximum angles are represented, respectively in *Gorilla* with ca. 150° (ca. 30°), and *Papio* with ca. 110° (ca. 70°). The basicranial angle in *Homo* is ca. 143° (ca. 37°), in *Lemur* ca. 147° (ca. 33°).

Judged by the samples cited and others figured (fig. IV.54), the phylogenetic significance of variation in the basicranial angle is not evident. Gross structural changes in the neural part of the skull do, of course, exert mechanical pressures directly on the facial part through the common bones that separate them. The effect of these biomechanical stresses at the point of intersection between basineurocranial and palatal axes is appreciable irrespective of the size of the angle defined by them (table 5).

In the present exercise, it appears that as ontogenetic or phylogenetic structural changes cause the braincase to revolve below the palatal plane, the vertex of the basicranial angle moves forward. Conversely, as the braincase is progressively deflected upward relative to the palatal axis or plane (that is, the face is progressively depressed relative to the basineurocranial axis or plane), the vertex of the basicranial angle moves backward.

In adult male *Gorilla* and adult male *Alouatta,* the braincase lies entirely above the palatal plane, and the vertex of the basicranial angle is postcranial (fig. IV.54). The upward deflection of the *Gorilla* braincase is probably secondary. In *Alouatta,* however, the position of the braincase above the palatal plane is almost certainly primitive. At the opposite extreme, in *Papio* and *Cebuella,* both with braincase prejecting farthest below the palatal plane, the vertex of the basicranial angle is most advanced, or sellary in position. Notwithstanding the respective similarities, the phylogenetic relationship between *Papio* and *Cebuella* is as remote as the relationship between *Gorilla* and *Alouatta.* Likewise, catarrhines *Papio* and *Gorilla,* on the one hand, and platyrrhines *Cebuella* and *Alouatta* on the other, are as widely separated from each other as any two living primates can be within their respective suborders.

The continuous shift of the basicranial angle forward, with increasing projection of the braincase downward below the palatal plane, is indicated in table 5. The data is based on the adult skull for each genus (or species shown in fig. IV.54). Measurements for downward braincase projection are based on photographs of the sectioned skulls, each reduced or enlarged to a uniform anteroposterior length. Table 5 can be read from top down,

Table 5. Proportional Projection of Braincase below Palatal Plane, with Position of Vertex and Divergence of Basicranial Angle above Palatal Plane.

		Basicranial Angle	
	Units of Braincase Projection	*Position of Vertex*	*Divergence*
Gorilla	0	Postcranial	150° (30°)
Alouatta	0	Postcranial	165° (15°)
Lagothrix	3	Basion	159° (21°)
Homo	7	Basioccipital, low	143° (37°)
Cercocebus	7	Basioccipital, low	145° (35°)
Pithecia	8	Basioccipital, low	151° (29°)
Saimiri	8.5	Basioccipital, middle	140° (40°)
Macaca	9	Basioccipital, middle	137° (43°)
Cebus nigrivittatus	9.5	Basioccipital, high	145° (35°)
Hylobates	11	Basioccipital, high	146° (34°)
Callimico	12	Basioccipital, middle	139° (41°)
Presbytis	12	Basioccipital, high	148° (32°)
Aotus	12	Basioccipital, high	142° (38°)
Cebus apella	13	Postsellary	141° (39°)
Leontopithecus	17	Dorsosellary	138° (42°)
[*Tupaia*]	19	Sellary	148° (32°)
Ateles	19	Dorsosellary	140° (40°)
Callicebus	20	Dorsosellary	139° (41°)
Saguinus	20	Dorsosellary	139° (41°)
Lemur	20	Sellary	147° (33°)
Papio	24	Sellary	110° (70°)
Cebuella	33	Sellary	130° (50°)

bottom up, from any intermediate point to either end, or for any selection of species. Irrespective of the arrangement and whatever the biomechanical forces involved in skull modeling and their structural or adaptive effects, the linear correlation between palatal and basineurocranial axes maintains the same positive inclination in all primates.

Cranial kyphosis is the term applied to flexure of the basicranial axis. The degree of kyphosis in primates determined on sectioned heads preserved in spirits by Hofer (1957*a;* 1957*b*), and Hofer and Spatz (1963), is the frontal divergence of the *basis-angle* formed by intersection of the sphenoidal plane (from sphenoidal point to tylion or highest point of limbus sphenoidalis), and the plane of the basioccipital clivus (basion to occipital point of sella). The actual kyphosis is presphenoid (presellary) in most adult nonhuman primates, and basisphenoid (sellary) in most adult humans. Judging by Hofer's (1965; 1969*a*) tabulations, the "basis-angle" of the kyphosis varies from nearly zero to under 10° in primitive insectivores (*Tupaia*) and lower primates (*Daubentonia, Lemur, Cebuella* and *Alouatta*), from 10° to under 30° in platyrrhines (*Saguinus, Saimiri, Cebus, Ateles*), and to less than 50° in catarrhine monkeys (*Macaca* [= *Cynocephalus*], and *Papio*). In apes, the *basis-angle* measures between 25° and 50°, and in man between 40° and 70°.

Sagittal sections of clean dry skulls used in the present study (fig. IV.55) indicate a wider range of variation than suggested by Hofer's data. In the samples measured, neurocranial *basis-angle,* as defined by Hofer (not to be confused with the basicranial angle formed by intersection of basineurocranial and palatal axes), is presellary in lemurs and platyrrhines, suprasellary in *Gorilla, Homo,* and some catarrhine monkeys including *Cercocebus,* and postsellary in the treeshrew, *Tupaia glis.*

The allusion (Hofer 1969*a*) to increasing divergence in the basis-angle from primitive to more advanced primates has little support in our material. Progression from least to greatest divergence of the *basis-angle* in any major primate group is subject to considerable variation, as well as human error in computation, and is not necessarily related to brain shape, volume, flexure, head carriage, or basicranial angle. The most obvious if not the only significant feature of the cranial kyphosis described by Hofer and others is the extreme flexure, or sellary hump, of the human basis neurocranium. An exaggerated sellary hump, however, is not peculiar to man or to hominids. The same tendencies terminating in comparable flexures are notable in some rodents, artiodactyls, proboscideans, and others. According to Hückinghaus (1965*a;* 1965*b*), the basicranium of some wild rabbits (*Oryctolagus*) is strongly kyphosed, while those of the domestic variety of the same species are hardly so. Contrary to Hofer's (1969*a,* p. 15) contention, the human skull with its hump does not represent the final step in vertebrate cranial evolution. The human skull in mammalian evolution is simply the dying end of a minuscule sideline.

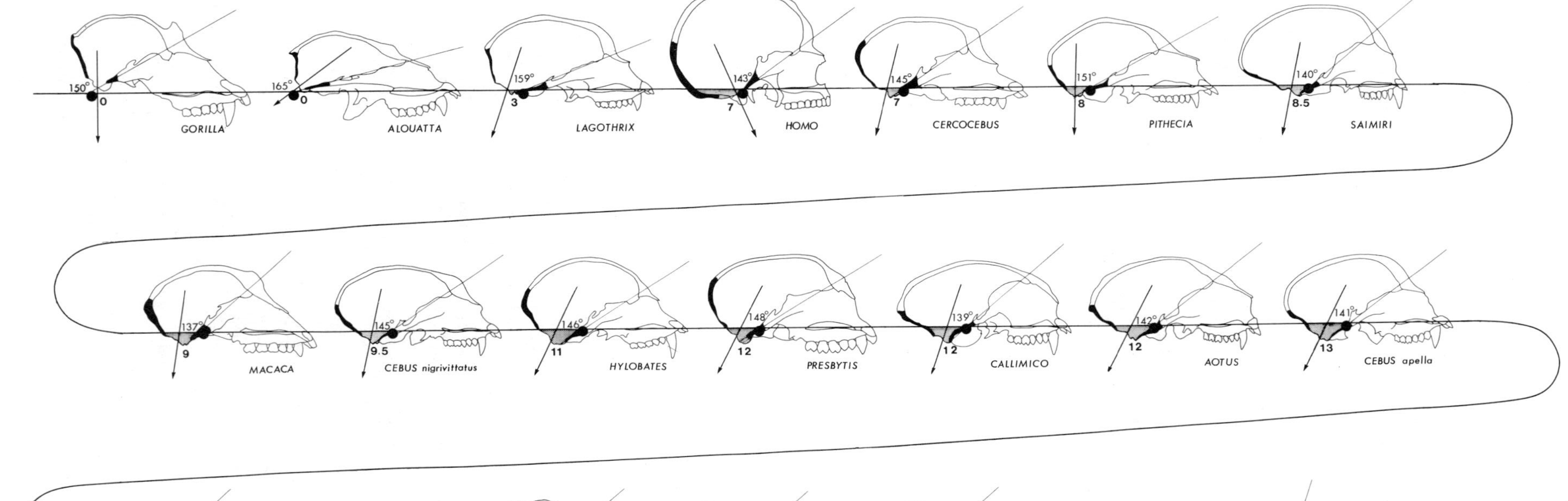

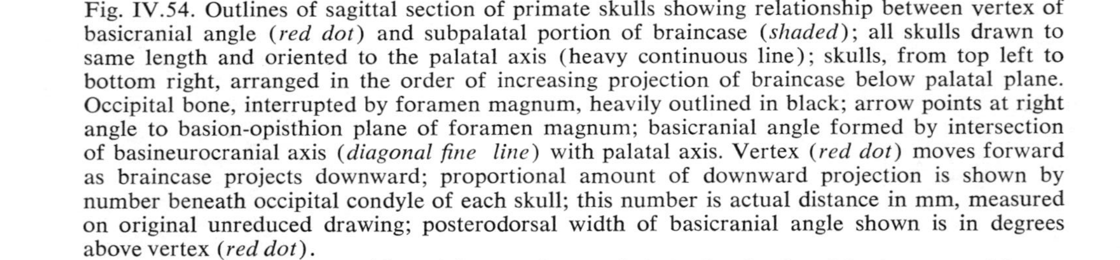

Fig. IV.54. Outlines of sagittal section of primate skulls showing relationship between vertex of basicranial angle (*red dot*) and subpalatal portion of braincase (*shaded*); all skulls drawn to same length and oriented to the palatal axis (heavy continuous line); skulls, from top left to bottom right, arranged in the order of increasing projection of braincase below palatal plane. Occipital bone, interrupted by foramen magnum, heavily outlined in black; arrow points at right angle to basion-opisthion plane of foramen magnum; basicranial angle formed by intersection of basineurocranial axis (*diagonal fine line*) with palatal axis. Vertex (*red dot*) moves forward as braincase projects downward; proportional amount of downward projection is shown by number beneath occipital condyle of each skull; this number is actual distance in mm, measured on original unreduced drawing; posterodorsal width of basicranial angle shown is in degrees above vertex (*red dot*).

Relationship between position of intersection (*red dot*) of palatal and basineurocranial axes and downward projection of braincase expresses the biomechanical relationship between evolving facial and cerebral portions of skull in each species irrespective of its phylogenetic relationship to other species. In other words, no consistent relationship is evident between size of basicranial angle and cranial kyphosis (fig. IV.55), neurocranial volume, amount of downward projection, plane of foramen magnum, or other cranial features distinguishing the species. In *Tupaia* (*skull shaded*), high sellary position of vertex with reference to amount of braincase projection is out of line with that of all primates shown.

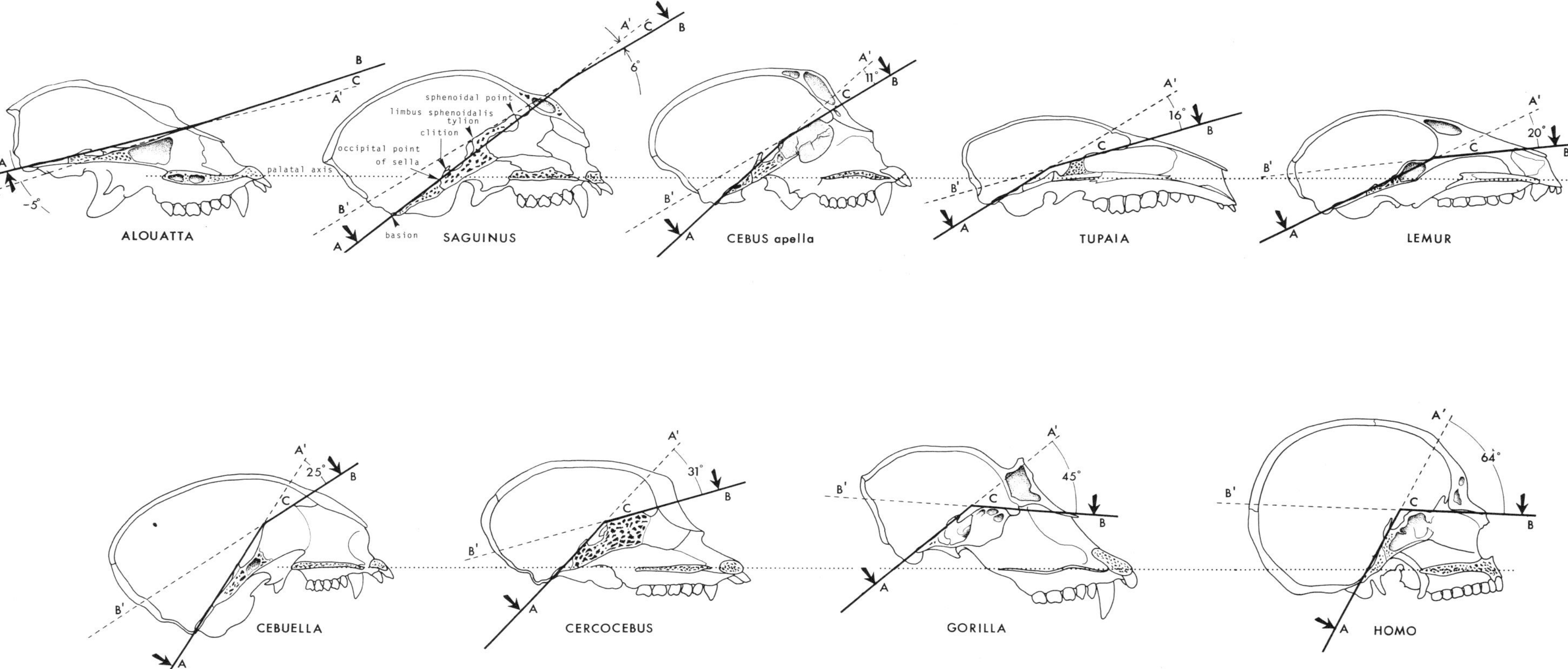

CRANIAL KYPHOSIS

Fig. IV.55. Cranial kyphosis (basicranial flexure) in representative primates. Samples selected from skulls shown in fig. IV.54, oriented to palatal axis (*dotted line*) and arranged from top left to bottom right in the order of increasing kyphosis measured in terms of the degree of divergence of the "basis-angle (*C*)." No correlation between divergence of "basis angle" and phylogeny of samples is apparent or implied. The degree of basicranial flexure of each skull is a grade in the cranial evolution of the phyletic line represented by that skull. Basicranial flexure in *Alouatta* departs little in either direction from the primitively plane basis cranii with approximately zero kyphosis. A slight *upward* flexure of the braincase appears in the sample figured. In remaining samples, *downward* kyphosis of the braincase is consistent, well-marked, and extreme in man. *A–A′, plane of occipital clivus,* determined by line drawn tangent to basion and occipital point of sella; the same plane (*A–A′*) marks the *basis cranii* of the hypothetical ancestral primate. *B–B′, sphenoidal plane,* determined by line drawn tangent to sphenoidal point and tylion. *A–B, basis cranii* of kyphotic skulls. *C, "basis-angle,"* used as a measure of kyphosis or degree of deflection from plane of primitive basis cranii (*A–A′*). "Basis-angle" is not to be confused with the basicranial angle shown in fig. IV.54; for use of terms see Hofer (1965; 1969*a*).

24 Skull
7. Temporal Bone, External Features

Mastoid Process

The mastoid process is not the dominant feature among primates generally as it is in man particularly and in many old individuals of great apes (fig. IV.41; chap. 29). The primitive eminence is usually low and may arise on the lateral or medial border of the mastoid bone. A median mastoid prominence or ridge is usually an extension of the lambdoidal crest or simply an adjunct of a paraoccipital elevation or process. The shifting position and changing form of the mastoid process, prominence, tubercle, ridge, or rugosity indicate that the structure is present in response to demands for special muscle attachments in the individual or its species group.

In lemuriforms the mastoid prominence is hardly more than a slight swelling or tubercle just behind the auditory meatus. The feature assumes minor importance among lorisforms with well-developed lambdoidal crests. The process remains as an inconspicuous swelling behind the meatus in true marmosets but becomes slightly rugose and ridgelike in the larger tamarins. It is a distinct ridge or process in *Leontopithecus,* where it occupies a median position opposite, and often juxtaposed to, the paraoccipital process. A distinct mastoid process is not evident in *Callimico* and in the marmosetlike cebids *Callicebus, Saimiri,* and *Aotus.* The mastoid process is well defined among pithecines, particularly in *Chiropotes* and *Cacajao,* where it is coupled with a pronounced paraoccipital process. The process is prominent in *Alouatta* and *Brachyteles* but highly variable in other prehensile-tailed cebids. The mastoid process becomes prominent in old individuals of *Macaca* and *Papio* and often in the larger colobines.

Styloid Process

The styloid process, like the mastoid process, is exceptionally well developed in man but only moderately developed in African apes. Its development in other primates is irregular, rarely hypertrophic and appears to be controlled less by phylogeny than by ontogenetic processes and individual requirements (figs. IV.51, 82). A styloid process in the form of a cartilaginous or ossified tympanohyal within or projecting from the vaginal sheath, or styloid fossette, is often present in lemuriforms. The vaginal sheath or fossette is not always evident in callitrichids but an ossified process up to 3 mm in length, usually adpressed against or fused with the tympanic bulla, is present in a minority of individuals of all species. The styloid fossette, with or without an ossified process, is also common in *Callimico* and among marmosetlike cebids. The process usually measures a few millimeters, with most or all its length united to the ventral crest of the bulla. Relative size or frequency of occurrence of the styloid process or vaginal sheath is not greater, and the form is no different in the successively larger pithecines and prehensile-tailed cebids. In some individuals, however, the process may be free of the bulla and forward-projecting.

In catarrhines, the styloid fossette is more prominent and the vaginal sheath more projecting than in platyrrhines. On the other hand, ossification of a styloid process appears to be no less sporadic and variable. When present, the process is free of the bulla and usually projects downward and forward.

According to Zuckerman, Ashton, and Pearson (1962, p. 127), a completely ossified styloid process is rare in chimpanzees and gorillas, and neither true styloid process nor styloid pit (i.e., vaginal sheath, or fossette) occurs in monkeys, as represented by *Papio* and *Macaca.* In present material, an ossified styloid process is present, whether inside the fossette or projecting beyond, or was present in life but lost during preparation or preservation of the skull, in each of 15 gorillas, 24 chimpanzees, and 18 orangs examined, and in many of about 150 skulls of *Macaca* and 10 skulls of *Papio* randomly sampled. In these the ossified process varies in length from less than 1 mm within the fossette to 1 cm outside. It is best developed in orangs and least developed in chimpanzees. Evidently the process and/or fossette, often bordered with bony excrescences, may occur in any species on the petrosal bone between the stylomastoid and jugular foramina, as in man. Furthermore, the evidence presented by the cited authorities shows that the protruding portion of the process derives from the stylohyal ligament as in man and gives attachment to the same muscles (m. stylohyoideus, m. stylopharyngeus, m. styloglossus) as in man.

Postglenoid Foramen

The postglenoid foramen, situated posteromediad or posteriad to the glenoid process, is normally present in lemuroids and primitive mammals generally, as well as in others with a more or less developed glenoid process (fig. IV.82; chap. 29). The aperture appears to be absent in man and great apes, and is small, obsolete, or absent in other catarrhines. The foramen in platyrrhines is well developed in some species, vestigial or absent in others. It transmits a vessel to the diploe only in some, or into the brain cavity as well as the diploe, in others. In a random sampling, it was found consistently present, large, and bone-puncturing in *Leontopithecus* and *Cebus*. It is obsolete or absent in *Callicebus,* absent in 7 of 8 skulls at hand of *Callimico,* and present as a shallow pit on the right side only of the remaining skull.

25 Skull
8. Middle Ear Region

The primitive mammalian middle ear consists of a tympanic membrane supported by an incomplete bony ring, the tympanic annulus, and a chain of three ossicles—the malleus, incus, and stapes. The tympano-ossicular system that transforms airborne sounds into fluid vibrations of the inner ear is contained in an open depression or cavity of the temporal region in many species of marsupials, insectivores, bats, edentates, and other primitive mammals. In higher mammals, including all primates, the system is chambered within a nearly entirely closed drum, the auditory bulla, with a simple or specialized external meatus (fig. IV.51).

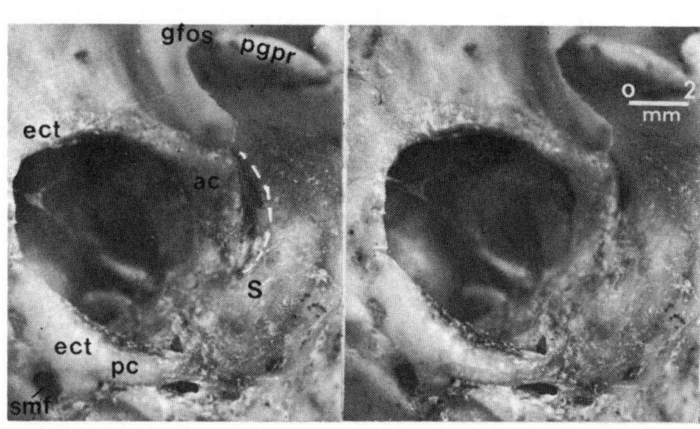

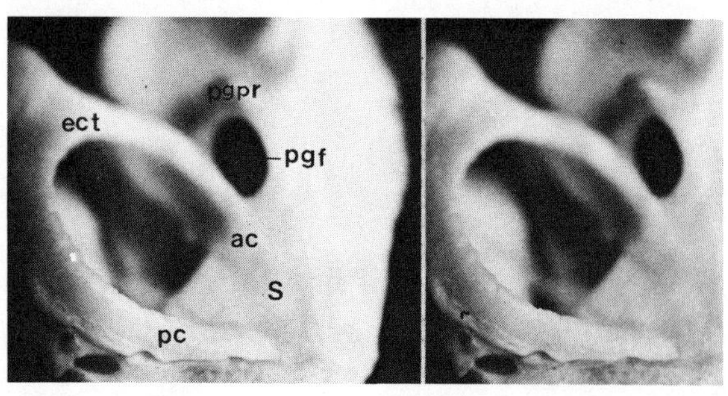

Fig. IV.56. *Top:* Stereophotograph of left middle ear region of *Callicebus moloch* (FMNH 87814). Fused portion of anterior crus (*ac*), with outline of removed unfused portion indicated by dashed line; *gfos*, glenoid fossa; *pgpr*, postglenoid process; *pc*, incompletely fused end of posterior crus; *S*, squamosal bone; *smf*, stylomastoid foramen; *ect*, tympanic annulus.
Bottom: Stereophotograph of left middle ear region of juvenal *Callicebus moloch* (FMNH 24210). Squamous process of posterior crus (*pc*) of tympanic annulus (*ect*) not fused to squamosal bone (*S*); squamous process of anterior crus (*ac*) mostly fused; *pgpr*, postglenoid process; *pgf*, postglenoid foramen. (From Hershkovitz 1975*a*.)

External Auditory Meatus

The external auditory meatus of higher primates is formed by union of the tympanic annulus, that is, the ectotympanic bone, with the squamous portion of the temporal bone (figs. IV.56–58). The platyrrhine bony meatus retains its primitive annular shape and relatively large diameter. The lip is often thickened but never produced distally as a tube. The rim consists of the body of the tympanic annulus and the crural ends which adhere to the squamous portion of the temporal bone. In catarrhines, the annulus is produced into a long tapered tube that extends to or slightly beyond the glenoid process. As in the platyrrhines, the dorsal gap between anterior and posterior cruri of the tympanic annulus is closed by the squamous portion of the temporal bone. The tympanic meatus of *Tarsius* (fig. IV.57) is more nearly catarrhine

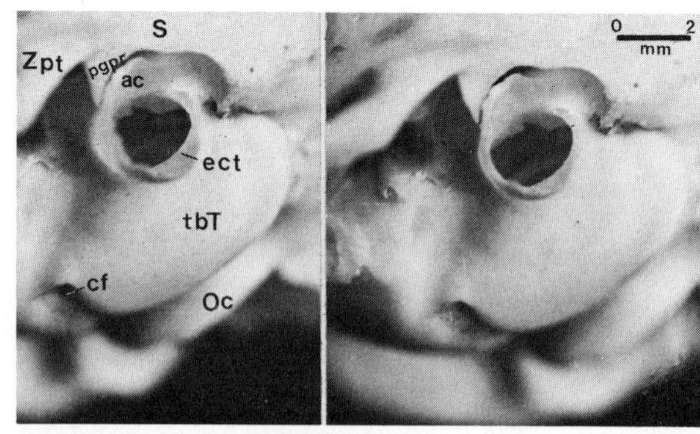

Fig. IV.57. Stereophotograph of left middle ear region of *Tarsius philippensis*. Tubular tympanic annulus (*ect*) retains primitive freedom from squamosal bone (*S*); *tbT*, auditory bulla; *ac*, anterior crus; *cf*, carotid foramen; *pgpr*, postglenoid process; *Oc*, occipital condyle; *Zpt*, squamous process of zygomatic arch. (From Hershkovitz 1975*a*.)

than platyrrhine in the tubular form, but the tympanic annulus is, as a rule, completely separated from the squamosal bone.

The form of the auditory meatus is the most conspicuous and consistent cranial character for distinguishing

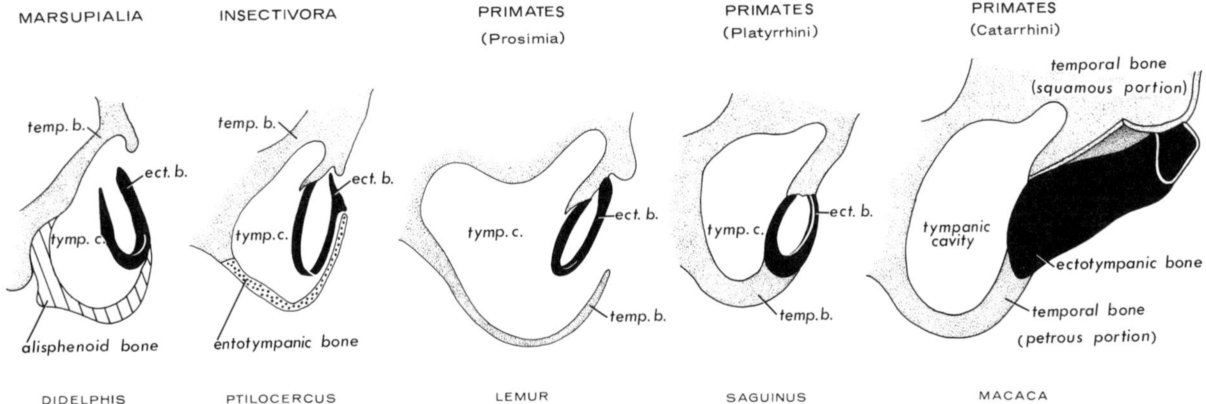

Fig. IV.58. Diagram of cross section of mammalian tympanic bulla and bordering temporal region seen from behind. Tympanic cavity (*tymp. c.*) exposed to show position of tympanic ring or ectotympanic bone (*ect. b.*) in a representative marsupial (*Didelphis*, Didelphidae), tupaiid insectivore (*Ptilocercus*, Tupaiidae), lemurid (*Lemur*, Lemuridae), platyrrhine callitrichid (*Saguinus*, Callitrichidae), catarrhine monkey (*Macaca*, Cercopithecidae). Main bone of auditory bulla (*shaded*) is the alisphenoid in didelphids, entotympanic in tupaiids, and temporal (*temp b*) in all primates.

platyrrhines from catarrhines (fig. IV.58). The bony meatus in lemuriforms is derived from the petrous, or petrous and squamous, portions of the temporal bone. In lorisiforms, the main part of the meatus consists of ectotympanic and squamosal bones. The entrance may be wide and annular as in platyrrhines, or constricted and canopied rather than tubular.

Differences between platyrrhine and catarrhine meati are correlated with responses to changes in braincase form. Increasing brachycephaly in catarrhines was associated with lateral elongation of the meatus in the form of a tube. In platyrrhines with braincases tending toward greater dolichocephaly, the vertical plane of the tympanic ring remains near the lateral surface of the skull and requires no extension tube for union with the cartilaginous auricular meatus. In those platyrrhine neurocrania tending toward brachycephaly, the dorsal border or lip of the meatus slopes outward, scooplike, without contraction or modification into a tube. The subtubular meatus of *Tarsius* may also be correlated with the brachycephalic skull.

Auditory Bulla

The main part of the mammalian osseus bulla, or tympanum, is formed by the ectotympanic bone, the petrous part of the temporal bone, the alisphenoid bone, or from the independently developed and strictly mammalian entotympanic bone (fig. IV.58). Other basicranial bones which may contribute to formation of small parts of the bullar wall or floor are basisphenoid, alisphenoid, basioccipital, exoccipital, and squamous and mastoidal portions of the temporal bone.

The auditory bulla of tupaiids (figs. IV.58, 60) and macroscelidids develops from the entotympanic bone (Major 1899, p. 987; Van Kampen 1905, p. 704; Spatz 1966, p. 26). The same bone (cf. Van Kampen 1905, pp. 363 ff.; Starck 1967, p. 495) forms the main body of the bulla among the Chiroptera, Dermoptera, Pholidota, Xenarthra, some Carnivora, Hyracoidea, some Artiodactyla (*Sus*), some Perissodactyla (*Rhinoceros*), and some Marsupialia; but in didelphids (figs. IV.58, 59), the alisphenoid forms an incomplete drum. The outer bullar wall of the rodentlike *Plesiadapis* (fig. I.4) is formed by the entotympanic.

The primate auditory bulla arises from the petrous portion of the temporal bone. Other basicranial bones may contribute small portions to formation of the bullar wall, but an os entotympanicum is absent (figs. IV.58, 61, 62).

The entotympanic bone was regarded by W. E. Le Gros Clark (1959, p. 134) as an extension of the petrous bone. This view, based on conclusions reached by Saban (1957, p. 93) and others, weighed heavily in Clark's treatment of tupaiids as primates. Saban erred, however, in his identification of an entotympanic bone in primates. He also failed to note that basisphenoid and alisphenoid bones contribute to the bullar wall in many primates. In relating tupaiids to primates, Saban regarded the tupaiid malleolar processus gracilis as reduced, the petrotympanic (Glaserian) fissure closed. In mature skulls of tupaiids I have examined, in all except the single available adult skull of *Anathana* the petrotympanic fissure is open and a well-developed vanelike processus gracilis projects through it to beyond the plane of the auditory meatus. In *Tupaia*, the process is fused to the anterior crus of the tympanic annulus, not to the malleus, as in primates. The structure moves freely in its slot, causing the tympanic ring to move. In life, movement of the processus gracilis is presumably controlled by the sphenomandibular ligament. In the related tupaiid *Urogale*, the process is immovable. In *Ptilocercus* (1 specimen), the process is free of the ring, the posterior half forms part of the roof of the bony meatus, and the anterior half projects outside the bulla. The processus gracilis in adult tupaiids seems to represent a combination of the lamina and anterior process of the malleus of didelphids and primates. For a discussion of the development of the anterior process in mammals see Wassif (1957).

The intrabullar position of the tympanic ring in tupaiids, somewhat as in lemuriforms, was also regarded by Le Gros Clark (1959, p. 139) as evidence of primate affinities. The same character, however, evolved independently in the unrelated American marsupial *Dromiciops* (Microbiotheridae) and in the Australian dasyurid *Dasycercus cristicauda* (Wood Jones and Lambert 1939, p. 72). In the dasyurid anteater, *Myrmecobius fasciatus*,

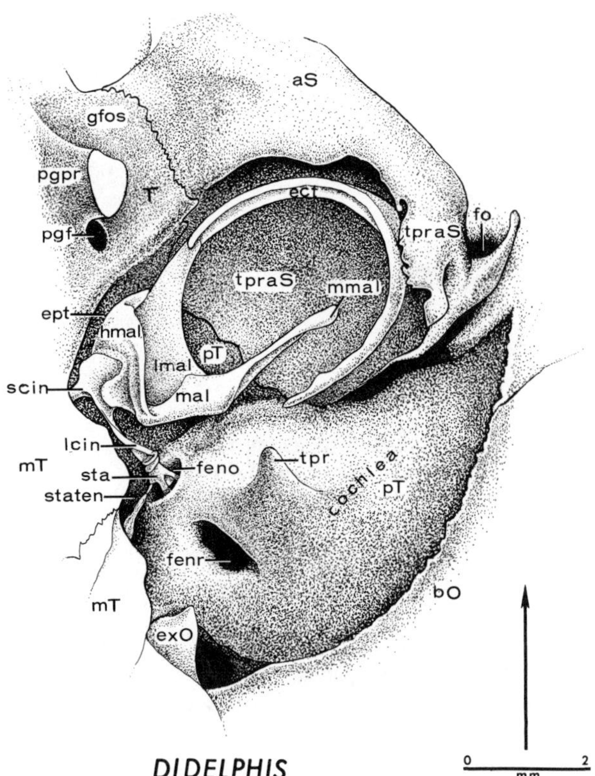

Fig. IV.59. Middle ear region of *Didelphis* (Didelphidae, Marsupialia), incomplete tympanic bulla formed by alisphenoid bone (*aS*), tympanic ring and cochlea completely exposed; arrow point anterior; symbols explained in chapter 31.

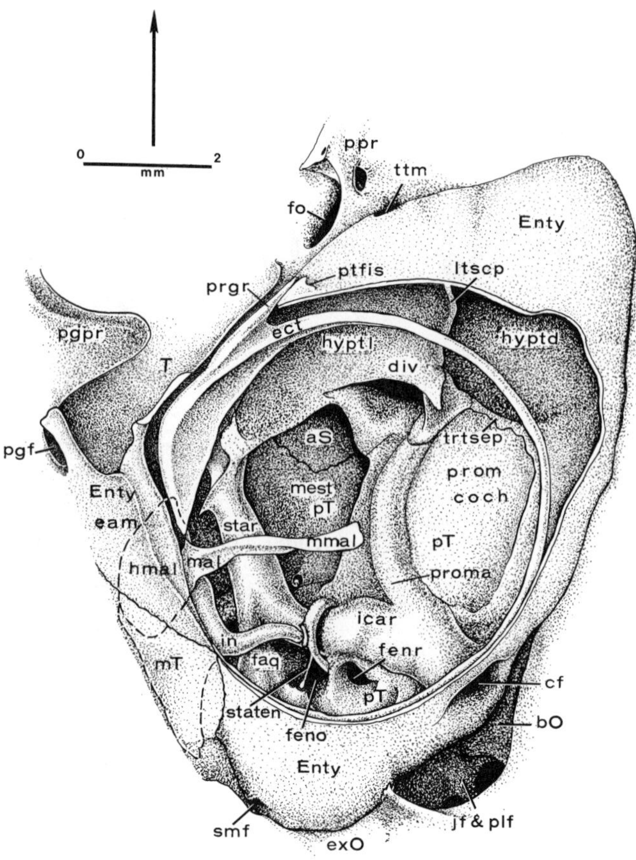

Fig. IV.60. Middle ear region of *Tupaia* (Tupaiidae, Insectivora, *sensu lato*); tympanic bulla, formed by independently evolved entotympanic bone (*Enty*), partially removed to expose tympanic ring, arterial system; petrous bone including cochlear promontorium, and tympanic process of alisphenoid (*aS*); arrow point anterior; symbols explained in chapter 31.

the ectotympanic bone is broad and free, with half the width of the band protruding as an external meatus while the remaining half lies concealed within the bulla. Other evidence from middle ear morphology opposing tupaiid affinities with primates has been presented by Van Valen (1965). The same and more anatomical data have been critically reviewed by Campbell (1974).

Szalay (1972*a*) suggested that the extrabullar ectotympanic seen in all nonlemuriforms was probably the primitive condition in primates. It seems unlikely, however, that a rigidly sutured extrabullar bone would evolve into the suspended intrabullar ectotympanic of lemuriforms (figs. IV.58, 61). It is more likely that the middle-ear cavity was not completely enclosed in the ancestral primate. As the bullar wall expanded among early prosimians the ectotympanic became enclosed in at least one phyletic line and became extrabullar in the others.

Tympanic Cavities and Bullar Size

The primitive primate tympanic bulla consists of three more or less defined communicating cavities (fig. IV.63). The *epitympanic cavity, recess,* or *attic* is smallest and houses the head of the malleus and body of the incus. The recess is little differentiated in primates and mammals generally. In didelphids (fig. IV.59) it is rudimentary, and it is larger and deeper in tupaiids (fig. IV.60) than in primates.

The *mesotympanic cavity,* or tympanic proper, communicates with the mastoid cells behind through the atrium, and opens in front into the auditory or eustachian tube. The cavity ordinarily contains the malleolar manubrium, the long crus of the incus, the stapes, the cochlea with its visible oval and round windows, and the tympanic ring, membrane, and chord. The tympanic ring in lemuriforms is almost entirely free and contained within the cavity. Most of the ring in all other primates is fused with the petrosal bone. The stapedial artery which traverses the stapes between the cruces (fig. I.13) is present in lemuriforms, reduced or absent in lorisiforms, and absent in higher primates. The carotid enters from behind the cochlea in lemuriforms, but along the medial border near the anterior end of the cochlea in lorisiforms and higher primates.

The cochlear promontory and lateral aspect of the bony canal of the carotid artery occupy most of the mesotympanic cavity and are prominently exposed when seen through the auditory meatus, especially in noncatarrhines. In some platyrrhines, the bony canal encasing the facial nerve and stylomastoid artery are likewise visible along the anterior border of the meatus. A peculiar stirrup-shaped process of this canal, the *stapedial process* (fig. IV.64), just laterad to the fenestra rotunda, is often present in some uncrested species of capuchins, genus *Cebus,* but has not been found in other platyrrhines (Hershkovitz 1971*b*).

The tensor tympani muscle behind the malleus lies in the groove which extends from the tympanic or Eustachian tube to just mediad of the malleolar manubrium. The tendon of the muscle, often preserved in the dry,

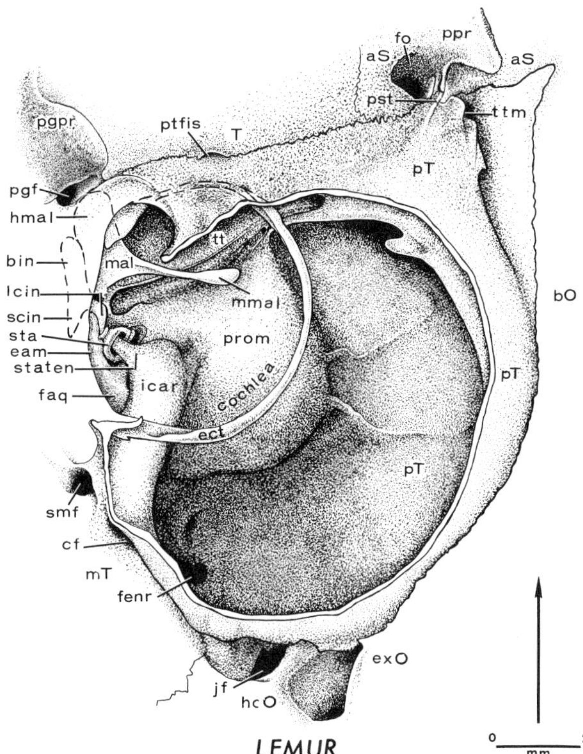

Fig. IV.61. Middle ear region of *Lemur* (Lemuridae), tympanic bulla formed by petrous bone (*pT*) partially removed to expose tympanic ring, internal carotid artery (*icar*) and petrous bone including cochlear promontorium (*prom*); arrow point anterior; symbols explained in chapter 31.

cleaned skull, attaches to the medial surface of the manubrium.

The *hypotympanic cavity* occupies the anterior half of the primate bulla (fig. IV.63). It is more or less subdivided into two large chambers. The lateral, or main, chamber is traversed by the auditory tube and carotid canal which open into the pharynx. The dorsomedial, or quadrilateral, chamber is simple in *Lemur* (fig. IV.61), subdivided or cellular in higher primates and separated from the lateral chamber by an irregular and perforated longitudinal septum. The posterior boundary of the hypotympanic cavity is defined by the cochlea alone in primitive forms and by the cochlea and a more or less pneumatized transverse septum (fig. IV.62) in advanced forms. A more detailed description of primate temporal bone pneumatization is given by Saban (1964).

In lorisiforms and higher primates, an increase in volume of the hypotympanic cavity concomitant with increasing trabeculation and honeycombing results in a relative decrease in size of the other two cavities, but mostly the mesotympanic.

Pneumatization of the mastoid bone is usually correlated with inflation of the hypotympanic cavity, particularly in nocturnal species and the small diurnal ones with well-developed olfactory sense (cf. IV.82; chap. 29). This type of secondary inflation is extreme in lorisoids and, to a lesser extent, in callitrichids and marmosetlike cebids, particularly the night monkey, *Aotus*. The bulla remains prominent in the next-larger-sized pithecines, but the mastoidal swelling is absent.

With progressive increase in body size and importance of the visual sense among diurnal primates, the tympanic bulla and mastoid bone decreased in relative size. In

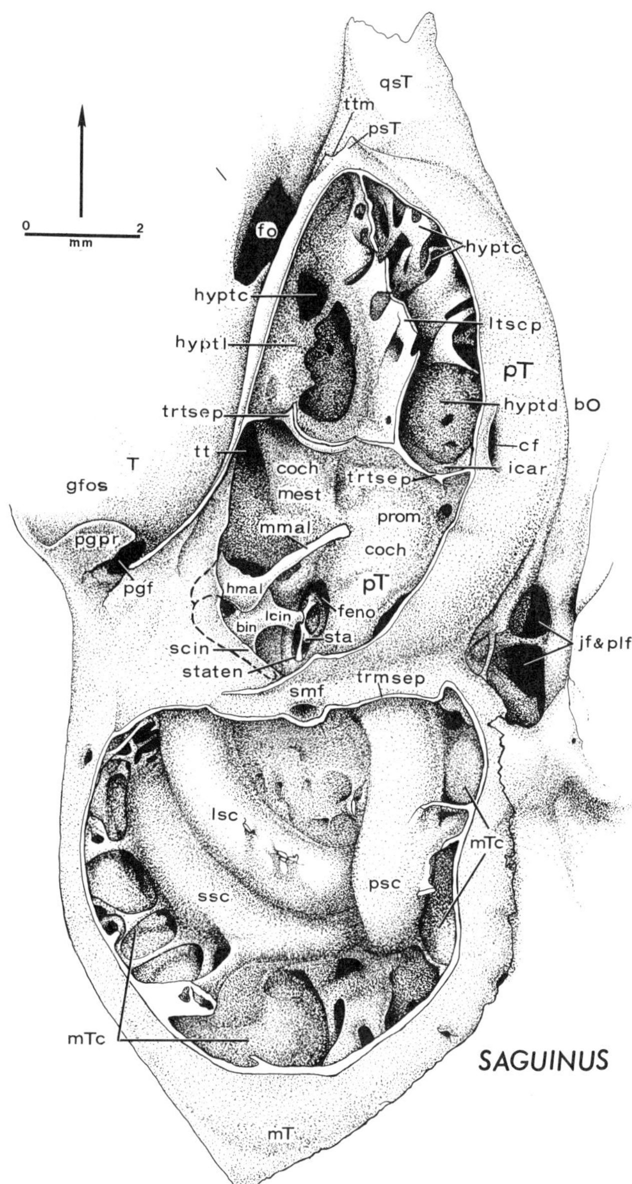

Fig. IV.62. Middle ear region of *Saguinus* (Callitrichidae), tympanic bulla, formed by petrous bone (*pT*) partially removed to expose septa and cells of tympanic cavities; semilunar canals in mastoid region exposed by partial removal of mastoid bone (*mT*); arrow point anterior; symbols explained in chapter 31.

prehensile-tailed cebids, the bulla is large but proportionately less pneumatized than in smaller platyrrhines, and the mastoid region is flattened. The catarrhine auditory bulla is noticeably less inflated, although pneumatization among many smaller species may be approximately as great as in some similar-sized platyrrhines. The bulla of larger cercopithecines, colobines, and gibbons is little inflated and that of baboons hardly or not at all, while the normally pneumatized mastoid is flattened or only slightly convex. In remaining apes and in man, little or virtually no external distention of the auditory bulla or mastoid bone is apparent.

Auditory Ossicles

The three ear bones, malleus, incus, and stapes (figs. IV.64–73), develop precociously and entirely within the

hypotympanic cavity
transverse septum
mesotympanic cavity
malleus
incus
epitympanic cavity

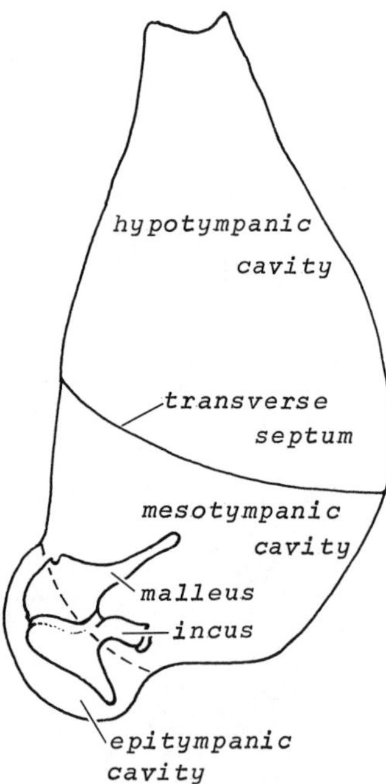

Fig. IV.63. Cavities of auditory bulla; mesotympanic or tympanic cavity and hypotympanic cavity more or less separated by an incomplete transverse septum; malleus and incus included in diagram to show relationship of epitympanic cavity (or recess) to mesotympanic cavity and for orientation of bulla.

sheltered middle ear chamber. Their growth patterns, size, shape, position, and composition are not significantly influenced or modified by movements or stresses generated by the growth or remodeling of unrelated neighboring bones. In effect, ontogeny of the ossicles is virtually a complete and undisturbed expression of the basic controlling genetic factors. Importance of ear bone morphology and ontogeny in phylogenetic reconstructions cannot be underestimated. Differentiation of malleus and incus is the primary criterion for distinguishing the Mammalia from the Reptilia. The shape of the ossicles, particularly the malleus, is characteristic of the order, family, often the genus, sometimes the species, and perhaps only rarely the subspecies (cf. p. 179). The primate ossicles are primitive in their simplicity.

Differentiation of the auditory ossicles in man (cf. Anson and Bast 1946; Hanson, Anson, and Bast 1959; Hanson and Anson 1962) begins at an early stage. The stapes derived from the second branchial (hyoid, Reichert's) arch and the lateral capsular wall appears in the 7 mm fetus. The incus, also derived from the second arch, and the malleus, derived from the first hyoid (Meckel's) bar, are defined as condensed masses of mesenchymal cells in the 10 mm embryo. The ossicles are fully formed in true cartilage in the 28 mm (8 ½ inch) embryo; attain maximum length about the 17th week when ossification has set in, and attain adult pro-

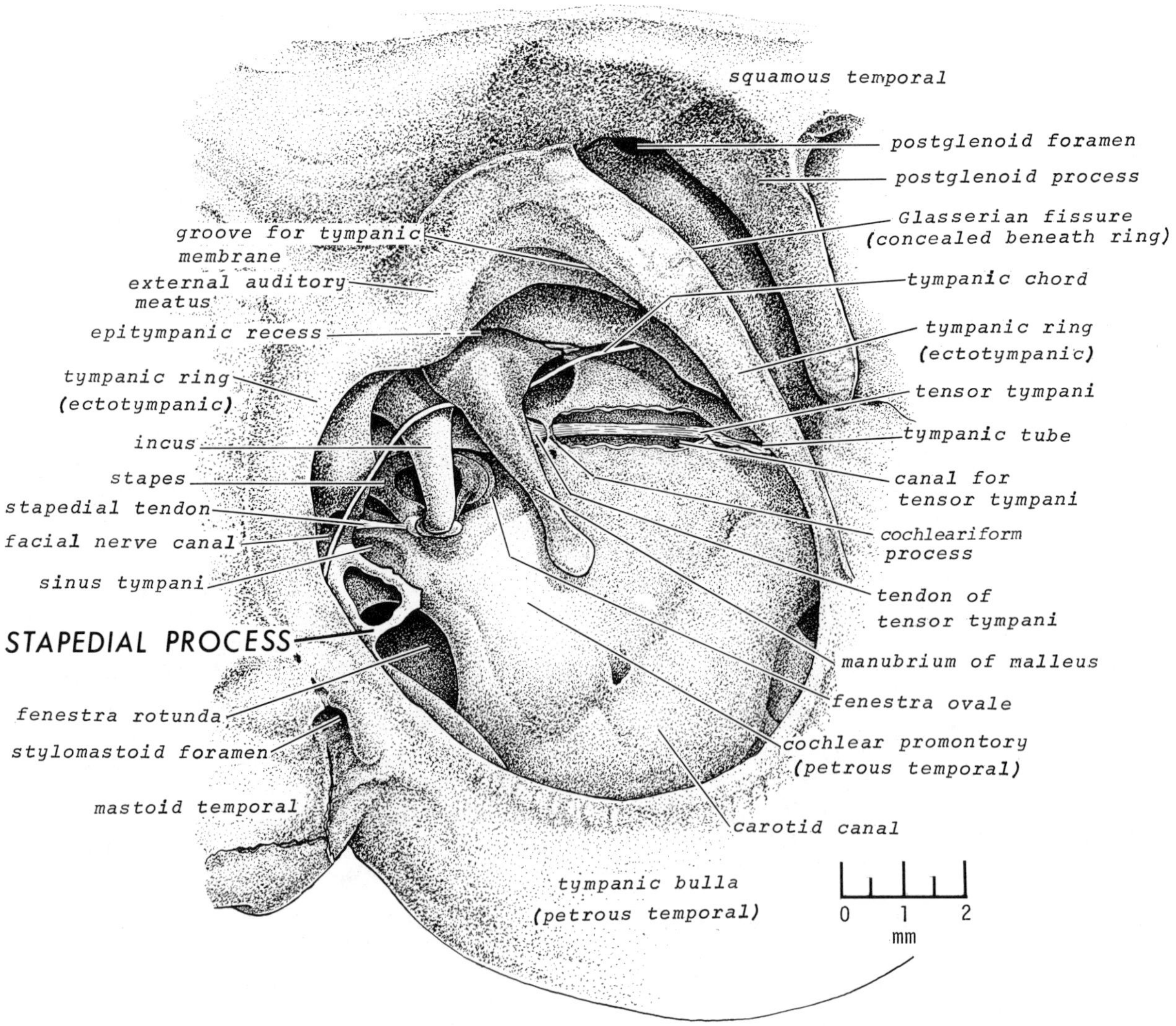

squamous temporal
postglenoid foramen
postglenoid process
Glasserian fissure (concealed beneath ring)
groove for tympanic membrane
external auditory meatus
tympanic chord
epitympanic recess
tympanic ring (ectotympanic)
tympanic ring (ectotympanic)
tensor tympani
incus
tympanic tube
stapes
canal for tensor tympani
stapedial tendon
cochleariform process
facial nerve canal
sinus tympani
tendon of tensor tympani
STAPEDIAL PROCESS
manubrium of malleus
fenestra rotunda
fenestra ovale
stylomastoid foramen
cochlear promontory (petrous temporal)
mastoid temporal
carotid canal
tympanic bulla (petrous temporal)
0 1 2
mm

Fig. IV.64. Right middle ear cavity of *Cebus nigrivittatus* (FMNH 36098) with membranes removed to expose bony parts; tympanic muscle (tensor tympani) and tendon reconstructed. (After Hershkovitz 1971*b*.)

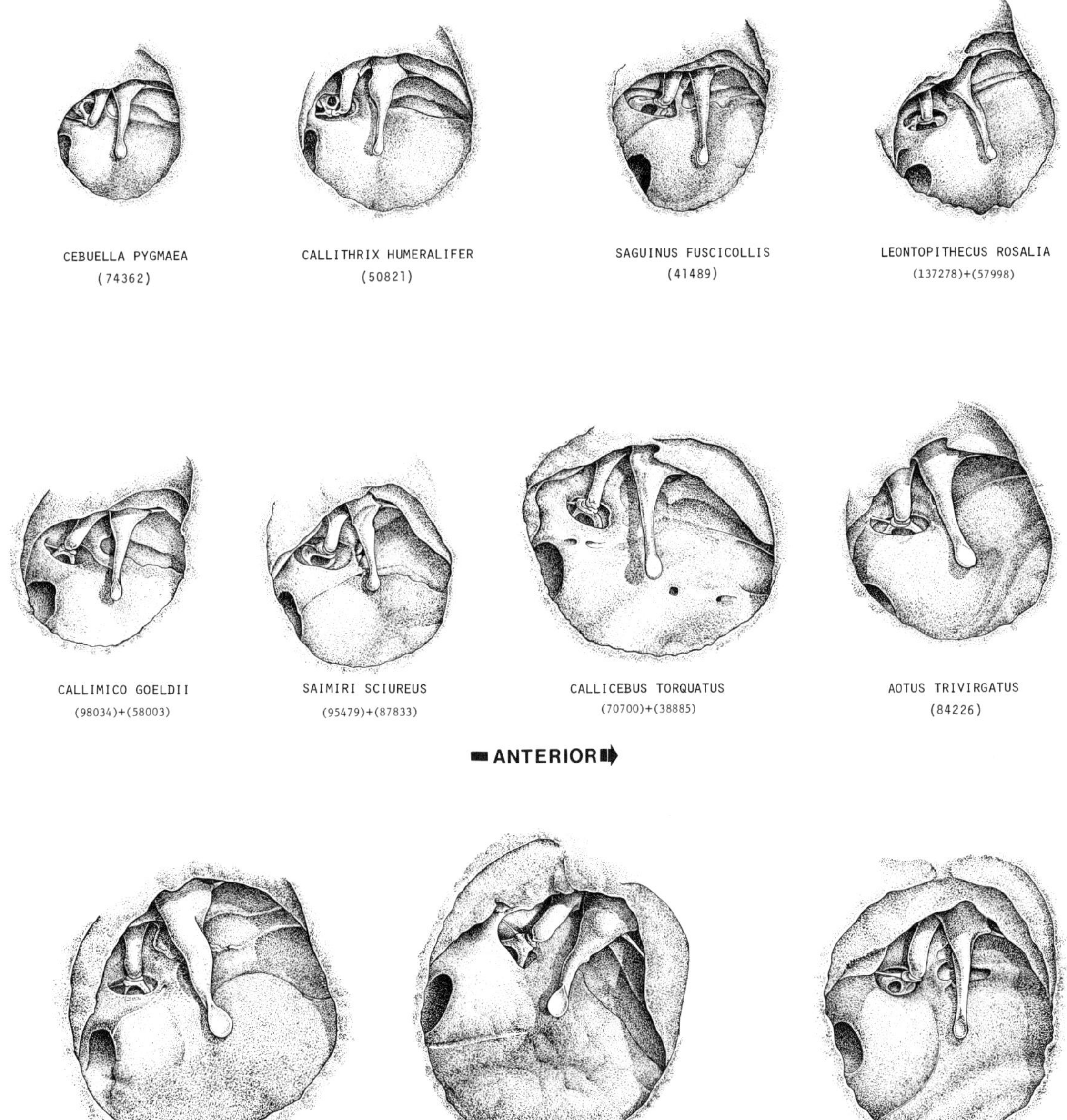

Fig. IV.65. Right middle-ear cavity of representative platyrrhines: *Callitrichids* (*Cebuella, Callithrix, Saguinus, Leontopithecus*); *Callimico;* cebids (*Saimiri, Callicebus, Aotus, Pithecia, Chiropotes, Cacajao*); tympanic and other membranes removed to expose bony structures. Horizontal orientation is to the Frankfort plane; Field Museum catalog numbers of figured specimens are shown; for names of parts see fig. IV.64.

portions in the 20th week. Secondary ossification takes place in the newborn and may continue, in some cases, during adult life. The ossicles lack secondary or epiphyseal centers and do not lengthen once they are fully formed in perichondrial bone.

Auditory ossicles of newborn *Macaca cynomolgus* and *M. mulatta,* studied by Pařizek and Varačka (1967) are fully as large and ossified as those of their respective adults, and those of older juvenals are appreciably heavier. In prosimian and platyrrhine species I examined, the ossicles of all postnatal stages appear to be fully ossified and adult in form.

Malleus

The malleus, so called because it resembles a hammer, is the lateral anterior bone of the ossicular chain. It consists of a head, a handle or manubrium, and in many species a constricted area defined as a neck. A number of outgrowths are also present and mentioned below (figs. IV.70–73).

The *manubrium* is attached to the tympanic membrane. Its lateral or tympanic profile may be nearly straight, as in the primitive condition, to bowed slightly inward, or sigmoid. The lateral surface of the spoon-shaped apex is flat or slightly concave, the medial surface convex. The taut, depressed, central area of the tympanic membrane attached to the malleolar apex or spatula is the *umbo.*

The *neck* is the portion of the manubrium between head and lateral process or orbicular apophysis in malleoli with either or both tubercles. A neck is more or less defined in all catarrhines and some prosimians. It is undefined in remaining prosimians and in all but the few platyrrhines with a well-developed orbicular apophysis.

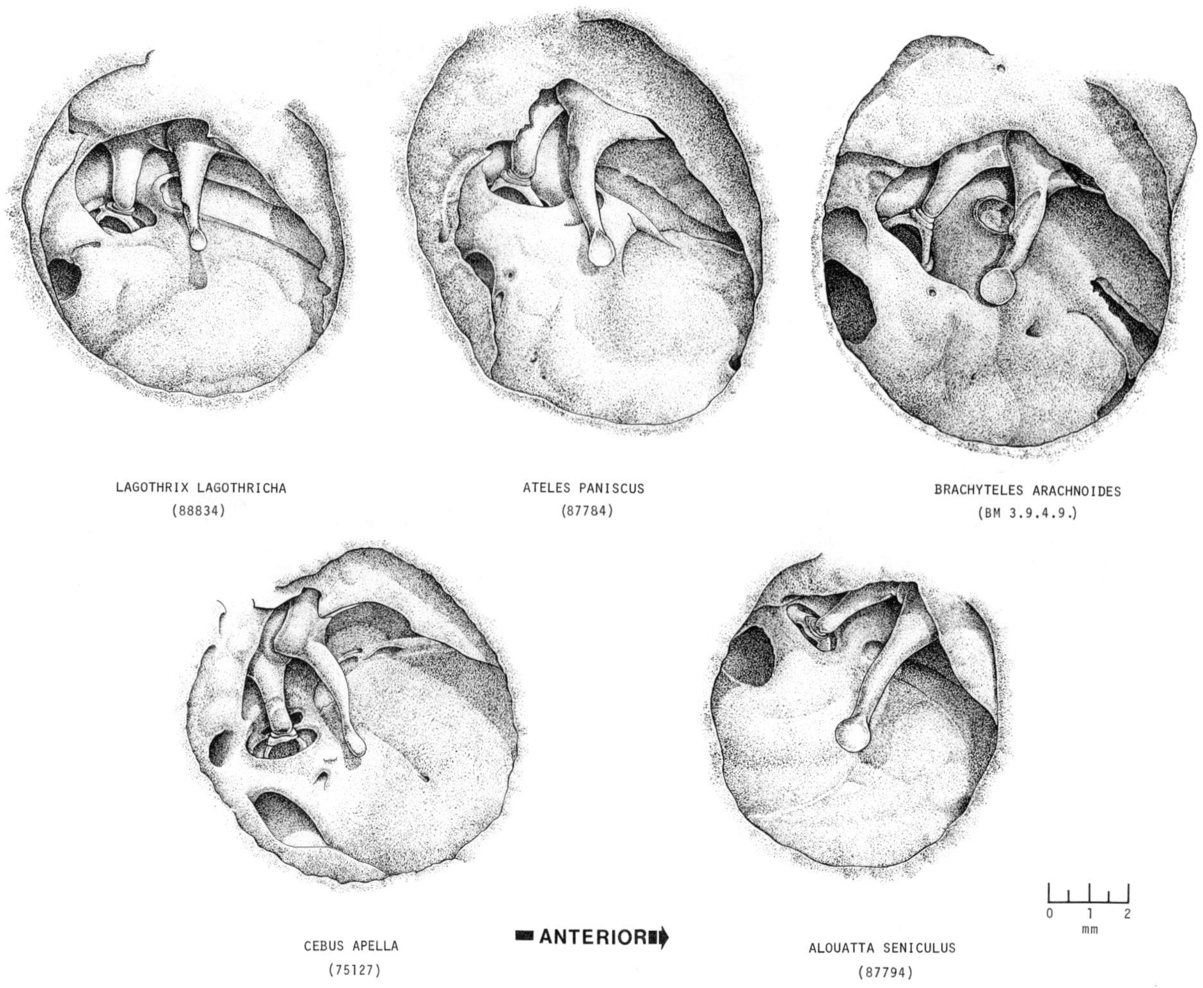

Fig. IV.66. Right middle-ear cavity of cebids: *Lagothrix, Ateles, Brachyteles, Cebus, Alouatta;* tympanic and other membranes removed to expose bony structures. Horizontal orientation is to the Frankfort plane; Field Museum catalog numbers of figured specimens are shown; for names of parts see fig. IV.64.

In many platyrrhine malleoli, the area is the broadened end of a trumpet-shaped manubrium.

The *head* is bulbous, vacuolated, with sides more or less flattened and top rounded or dome-shaped. The anterior aspect of the head may be truncate or, usually, prolonged in the form of one or more tapered ossifications or processes described below. The posterior aspect is broader and articulates with the body of the incus. The articular surface is divided into a pair of concave facets, the lateral separated from the medial by a low ridge. A single broad inferior articular facet is sometimes present. In *Homo,* the facets usually merge into a single concavity with only a faint indication of three primitive subdivisions. The comparative anatomy will be described later.

Osseous malleolar outgrowths consistently present in some or all primate groups are the following:

Anterior (long or *Folian) process,* present in all primates, is certainly a primary character. The element is a long, thin, tapered, friable bony process that extends anteriorly from the inferior angle of the head or the superior angle of the neck or manubrium toward the petrotympanic fissure, where it fuses with the processus gracilis (see p. 173). The latter is a distinct and ancient element with which the anterior process has sometimes been confused (e.g., Doran 1878; Cockerell, Miller, and Printz 1914). The anterior process is most developed in the young individual and tends to atrophy in the old adult. The process usually breaks and is frequently lost when the malleus is extracted from the middle ear cavity.

Cephalic process is a hard spine in some individuals, a delicate friable rod or spicule in others. It originates on the anterodorsal border of the head and is hidden from view in the epitympanic recess. The spine is probably absent more often that it is present.

Bony lamina (lamina ossea) attaches to the roof or wall of the epitympanic chamber and often unites the cephalic and anterior processes. It is extremely variable in form, absent in hominids, and not consistently present in other catarrhines and in platyrrhines. Compared with the specialized vanelike lamina of many rodents and bats the structure, when present in primates, is poorly developed and often shorter than the length of the head. The bony lamina probably originated independently in each line where it occurs, whether as an individual variable or as a specific constant.

Lateral (short) process, where present, projects from the proximal portion of the tympanic surface of the manubrium. It is absent in least specialized forms and becomes increasingly prevalent among more advanced forms, including most prosimians, where it sometimes appears in the form of a crest. The process is well developed in all catarrhines (figs. IV.70, 72), and in some it

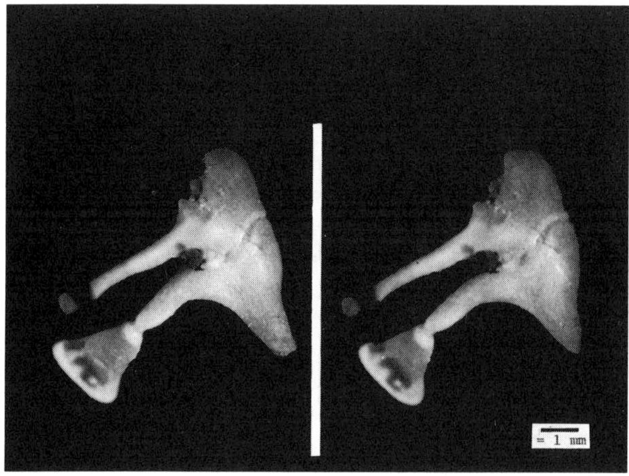

Fig. IV.67. Left auditory ossicles of *Pygathrix nemaeus* (Colobinae, Cercopithecidae), stereoscopic photograph.

produces the malleolar prominence of the tympanic membrane. Its maximum development is attained in hominoids. Absence of the lateral process in platyrrhines indicates absence of the feature in the ancestral primate.

Muscular process for attachment of the tensor tympani muscle is a short tubercle, spine, or low ridge on the medial surface of the manubrium. It is usually found midway along the haft or more distad. In *Pongo* the muscular process appears as a crest on the anterior half of the handle. The process is highly developed in catarrhines, except in hylobatids, where it may be poorly defined or absent, and in man, where it is obsolete or absent. The character is generally well developed in prosimians and moderately to weakly developed or absent in platyrrhines.

The muscular process is widespread among mammals and therefore may be primitive in primates but with a tendency toward disappearance in some specialized species and toward hypertrophy in others.

Orbicular apophysis, a spherical protuberance on the posterior side of the manubrium just below the neck or the inferior articular surface of the head, is rare among primates (fig. IV.71). I found it in each of 18 specimens, with at least one malleus in place, of the albinotic marmoset *Callithrix humeralifer chrysoleuca* from 4 localities. It also appears in 6 of 9 specimens with at least one malleus in place of *Callithrix humeralifer humeralifer* from 2 localities. In the nearly related *Callithrix argentata argentata* the process is present in 4 of 19 specimens from 3 localities, and absent in the 2 specimens checked of *C. a. melanura* and 3 of *C. a. leucippe.* Details are given in tables 77 and 78. The orbicular apophysis is absent in all other available specimens of *Callithrix, Saguinus,* and *Callimico.* The area of the element is swollen in the lion tamarin, *Leontopithecus rosalia,* but without definition of a tubercle. A rudimentary orbicular apophysis appears in some pithecines, but a spot check of other cebids reveals no indication of the protuberance.

The orbicular apophysis is common among marsupials, insectivores, bats, rodents, and carnivores (cf. Doran 1878; Cockerell, Miller, and Printz 1914; Henson 1961). Its function is unknown.

Malleolar Traits

The ovate, least pneumatized *malleolar head* with two, or possibly three, articular facets appears to be most primitive among living primates. The dorsoventral axis of the head may have been continuous with the long axis of the manubrium in the ancestral primate. It retains this shape in a number of platyrrhines, especially in the young.

Subsequent reshaping involves a medial inflection of the head, usually accompanied by a secondary anterior inflection in lorisoids, tarsiids, and catarrhines. Among platyrrhines, the malleolar head is not notably inflected in *Callimico* but is either uninflected or turned anteriad in callitrichids. In cebids, the primary inflection is usually anteriad with a slight secondary medial inflection in many forms. In lemurids, the inflection is usually well marked in either direction. The anterior inflection described here is seen from the medial aspect of the malleus, while the median inflection is appreciated from the anterior surface (figs. IV.68, 69, 72). The difference between platyrrhines and catarrhines with respect to the primary direction of inflection of the malleolar head points to an important dichotomy at an early stage of haplorhine evolution.

Malleolar size or *length* is correlated with size of the total organism. The larger the species, using skull length as indicator, the longer and more specialized the malleus (figs. IV.65, 66, 68, 69). The evolutionary rate of malleolar increment, however, is slow and diminishes as the rate of cranial enlargement increases. In specimens at hand (table 6), the largest skull measured (*Gorilla gorilla,* 310 mm) is 8.7 times longer than the smallest (*Galago minutus* [= *demidovi*], 35.8 mm), but its malleus (9.2 mm) is only 3.4 times longer than the malleus (2.7 mm) of the other.

In ontogeny, the definitive size of the malleus is attained in the fetus. Malleolar length relative to skull length is therefore greatest in the newborn and least in the fully grown adult. The progressive reduction in relative malleolar length is striking in the case of the male baboon (*Papio*), whose muzzle continues to enlarge enormously long after sexual maturity is attained. Sexual dimorphism cannot be demonstrated in the samples studied. Right and left malleoli of the same individual are not always equal in length, but the difference is not significant.

Malleolar orientation with reference to the long axis of the skull or tympanic cavity is nearly horizontal and directed medially in primitive forms, with tympanic ring intrabullar. As the tympanic ring and membrane swing ventrad and laterad, as in lorisoids, the attached malleus moves with them and assumes a more nearly vertical position. In most catarrhines, the tilt of the malleus is still near or on the horizontal plane. In platyrrhines, the tilt is decidedly ventrad or nearly parallel to the sagittal plane of the skull (figs. IV.59–62).

The anterior or posterior deflection of the malleus from the vertical based on the Frankfort plane may range up to 45° (figs. IV.55, 56). Among callitrichids, the malleus may deviate up to 10° in either direction from the vertical in *Cebuella.* In *Callithrix,* most malleoli incline backward and in *Saguinus* the majority are inclined forward. In *Saguinus fuscicollis,* only a few malleoli (2 in 25 sampled) incline slightly backward. In *S. midas,* however, deviation from the vertical in either direction is slight. In 4 samples of *Leontopithecus* with intact tympanic membrane, the malleoli are strongly inclined forward (to about 45°). In one *Callimico,* the inclination is backward, in another the malleus is approximately vertical.

The preceding appreciations are rough estimates based

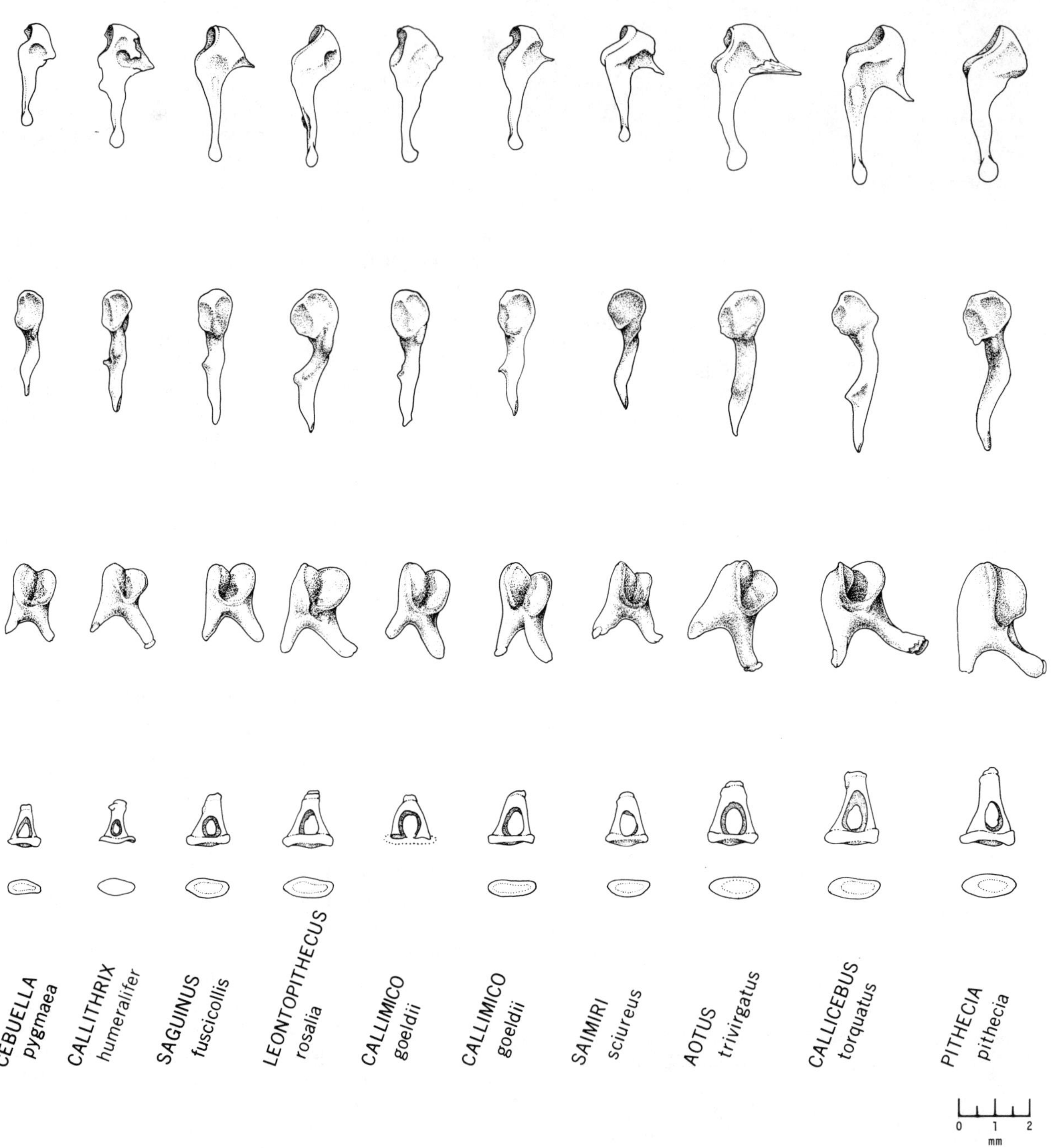

Fig. IV.68. Right auditory ossicles of representative platyrrhines: (Callitrichids, *Callimico*, marmosetlike cebids, saki); bones of each species, from top down, are *malleus*, lateral aspect; *malleus*, posterior aspect; *incus*, anterolateral aspect; *stapes*, ventrolateral aspect; *stapedial base*, outline of surface facing *fenestra ovalis;* drawings of a number of left bones reversed; measurements of malleoli included in table 6.

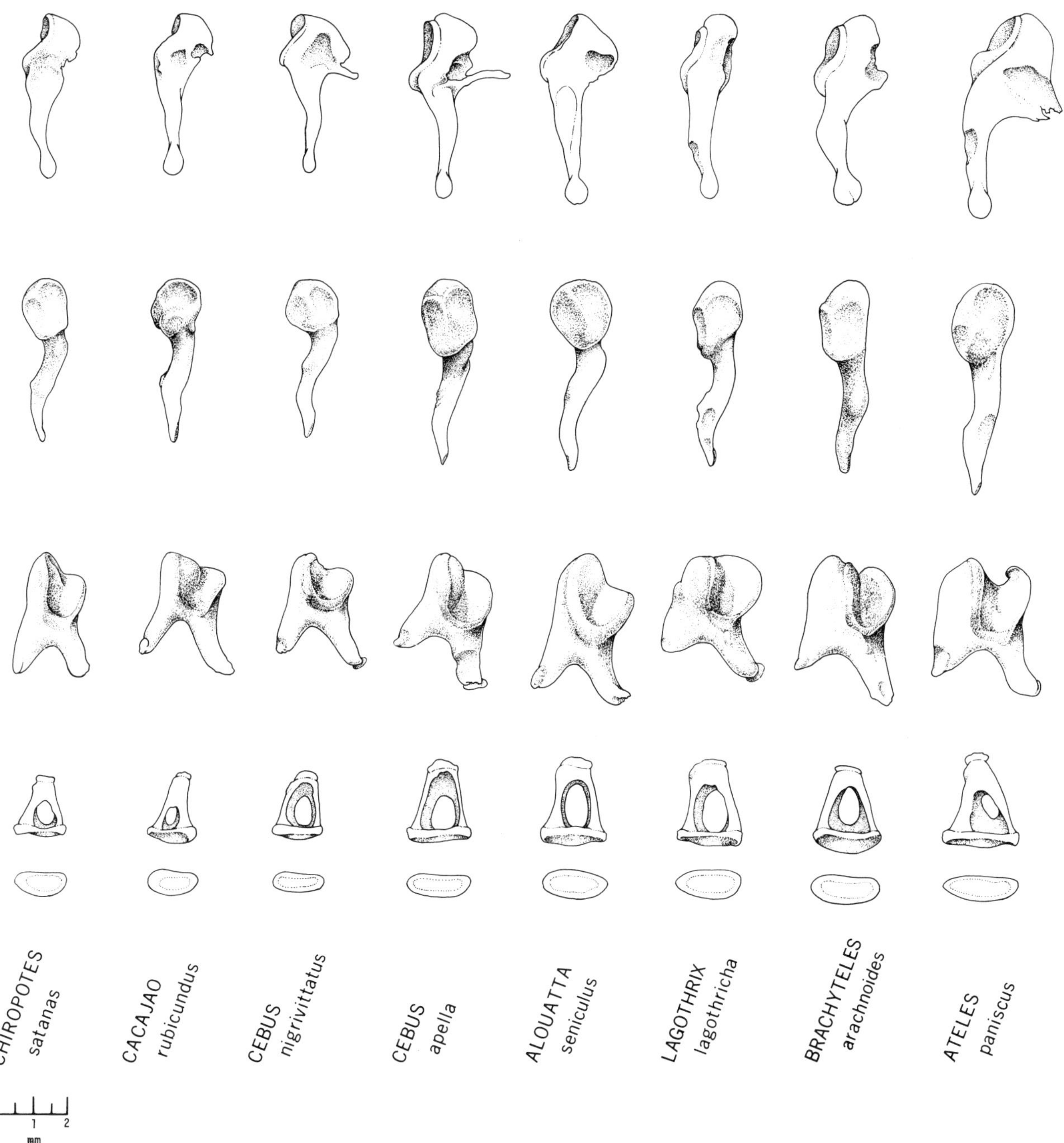

Fig. IV.69. Right auditory ossicles of representative platyrrhines (cebids); explanation given under fig. IV.68.

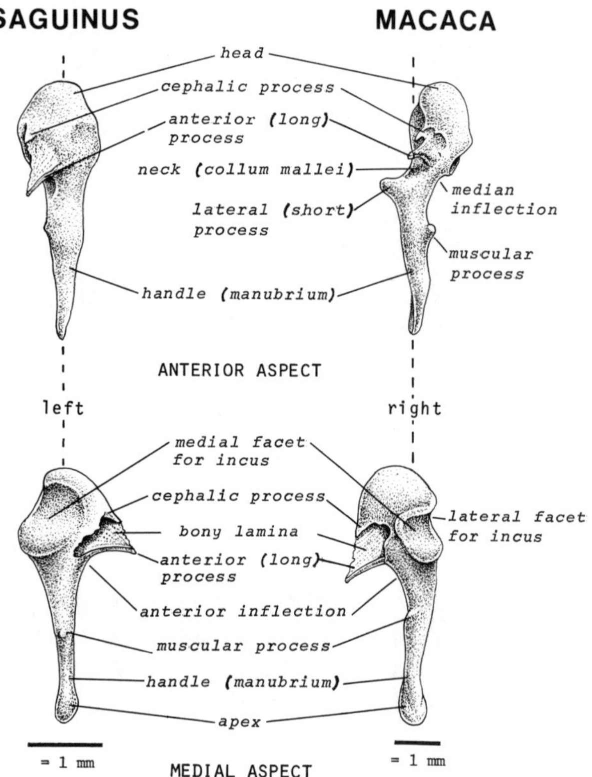

Fig. IV.70. Left malleus of *Saguinus* and right malleus of macaque (*Macaca*). Note anterior inflection common to platyrrhines and catarrhines, median inflection characteristic of catarrhines; lateral (short) process present in all catarrhines is absent in platyrrhines.

on ocular inspection of auditory regions with tympanic membrane intact. In more than 90% of prosimian and platyrrhine skulls examined, the position of the malleus is possibly, and in many cases obviously, altered as a result of postmortem damage to or destruction of the tympanic membrane. Skulls with defective ear regions are not included in the analytical descriptions.

Evolutionary grade of the callitrichid malleus appears to be most primitive among primates, judging by the criteria outlined here. The callimiconid, cebid, and lemuroid malleoli are similar to the callitrichid organ in some respects, slightly more advanced in others. Malleoli of lorisoids, tarsioids, and catarrhines have gone farther and in other directions, those of hominoids being the most specialized. Increasing malleolar specialization is correlated with the overall increase in body size or mass of the entire organism.

Incus and Stapes

Structure of the incus and stapes is less complex than that of the malleus and offers fewer parameters of systematic interest (figs. IV.73, 74). The body of the incus is adapted mainly to the malleolar head and varies accordingly in size and form. A similar relationship exists between the lenticular process (Sylvian apophysis, orbicular tubercle) of the incus and head of the stapes. The latter is the most independent of the ossicular chain. Its base reflects the shape of the fenestra ovale (fenestra

Table 6. Comparative Malleolar Characters

Catalog Number (1)	*Name*	*Malleus Length* (2)	*Skull Length* (3)	*Malleus/Skull* (4)	*Malleolar Head Inflection (5)* (6)	(7)
Tupaiidae (Insectivora)						
76855	*Ptilocercus lowi*	2.7	36.5	7.4	M	S
46642	*Tupaia*	2.9	41.4	7.2	M	S
57329	*Urogale everetti*	2.9	63.8	4.5	M	S
91265	*Anathana ellioti*	2.9	44.0	6.6	M	S
Tarsiidae						
76857	*Tarsius bancanus*	3.2	38.8	8.2	M	S
56749	*Tarsius syrichta*	3.3	39.6	8.3	M	S
Lemuridae						
5651	*Lemur rubriventer*	4.8	83.4	5.7	M	A
8347	*Varecia variegata*	5.2	106.0	4.9	M	A
89766	*Lemur catta*	4.4	83.3	5.3	M	A
5656	*Cheirogaleus major*	3.6	45.3	7.9	M	a
Indriidae						
8349	*Propithecus verreauxi*	4.9	54.5	9.0	M	a
5654	*Avahi laniger*	4.3	—	—	M	A
Lorisidae						
54444	*Galago minutus*	2.7	35.8	7.5	M	S
43732	*Galago elegantulus*	3.1	49.5	6.3	M	S
83627	*Galago senegalensis*	3.6	38.7	9.3	M	S
83616	*Galago crassicaudatus*	4.6	78.5	5.7	M	S
44393	*Perodicticus potto*	4.3	60.0	7.1	M	S
99360	*Arctocebus calabarensis*	3.8	53.4	7.1	M	S
32501	*Nycticebus coucang*	4.0	62.9	6.4	M	S
92861	*Loris tardigradus*	3.4	48.4	7.0	M	S
95027	*Loris tardigradus*	3.3	50.0	6.6	M	S

Table 6. Comparative Malleolar Characters—*continued*

Catalog Number (1)	*Name*	*Malleus Length* (2)	*Skull Length* (3)	*Malleus/Skull* (4)	*Malleolar Head Inflection (5)* (6)	(7)
Callitrichidae						
74362	*Cebuella pygmaea*	2.7	36.2	7.4	S	S
20229	*Callithrix j. jacchus*	3.3	44.0	7.5	S	A
63770	*Callithrix j. penicillata*	3.5	49.0	7.1	S	S
U133694	*Callithrix j. penicillata*	3.2	44.3	7.0	S	A
U133697	*Callithrix j. penicillata*	3.0	43.1	6.9	S	A
U239462	*Callithrix a. argentata*	3.4	46.8	7.3	S	A
A92297	*Callithrix h. chrysoleuca*	3.4	41.2	8.5	S	S
A91837	*Callithrix h. chrysoleuca*	3.7	49.2	7.5	S	S
A50821	*Callithrix h. chrysoleuca*	3.3	47.8	6.9	S	S
A50828	*Callithrix h. chrysoleuca*	3.3	47.2	7.0	S	S
A91835	*Callithrix h. chrysoleuca*	3.3	48.1	6.8	S	A
A50824	*Callithrix h. chrysoleuca*	3.5	49.4	7.1	S	S
A92168	*Callithrix h. humeralifer*	3.2	47.3	6.8	S	S
A78959	*Saguinus fuscicollis*	3.3	46.6	7.1	S	A
U238258	*Saguinus fuscicollis*	3.4	47.7	7.1	S	S
79884	*Saguinus fuscicollis* (juv.)	3.5	38.9	9.0	S	A
41488	*Saguinus fuscicollis*	3.4	49.5	6.9	S	S
69303	*Saguinus oedipus*	3.4	45.2	7.5	S	S
69296	*Saguinus oedipus* (juv.)	3.2	32.0	10.0	S	A
A79415	*Saguinus inustus*	3.8	52.0	7.3	S	A
57839	*Leontopithecus rosalia*	3.8	59.5	6.4	S	A
Callimiconidae						
U183290	*Callimico goeldii*	3.6	51.3	7.0	S	S
98034	*Callimico goeldii*	3.2	53.5	6.0	S	S
Cebidae						
95479	*Saimiri sciureus*	3.1	64.0	5.2	S	A
92150	*Saimiri sciureus*	3.1	64.0	5.2	S	A
70700	*Callicebus torquatus*	4.2	70.1	6.0	m	A
84226	*Aotus trivirgatus*	3.9	63.3	6.2	S	A
95507	*Pithecia pithecia*	4.2	77.2	5.4	S	A
88811	*Cacajao rubicundus*	4.3	98.2	4.4	m	A
95513	*Chiropotes satanas*	4.3	92.4	4.7	m	A
46179	*Chiropotes satanas*	3.9	90.0	4.3	S	S
22246	*Cebus nigrivittatus*	4.2	91.8	4.6	m	A
75127	*Cebus apella*	4.8	107.0	4.7	S	S
95495	*Alouatta seniculus*	5.0	133.0	3.7	m	A
93531	*Lagothrix lagothricha*	5.0	104.8	4.8	S	S
86942	*Lagothrix lagothricha*	4.7	104.0	4.5	S	A
87784	*Ateles paniscus*	5.5	113.0	4.9	S	A
BM 3.9.4.5	*Brachyteles arachnoides*	4.8	117.7	4.0	S	A
Cercopithecidae						
31146	*Rhinopithecus roxellanae*	5.4	102.6	5.2	M	a
15517	*Nasalis larvatus*	5.4	107.8	5.0	M	a
46509	*Pygathrix nemaeus*	5.9	95.0	6.2	M	a
53698	*Presbytis entellus*	5.5	112.0	4.9	M	a
27276	*Colobus polykomos*	6.0	115.3	5.2	M	a
35119	*Colobus polykomos*	5.2	125.8	4.1	M	a
24304	*Colobus badius*	5.2	98.9	5.3	M	a
83632	*Miopithecus talapoin* (juv.)	5.3	85.7	6.2	M	a
38173	*Cercopithecus aethiops*	5.1	96.9	5.3	M	S
38135	*Cercopithecus aethiops*	5.5	117.7	4.7	M	S
38179	*Cercopithecus aethiops*	5.4	99.0	5.5	M	a
51441	*Erythrocebus patas* (juv.)	6.0	104.5	5.7	M	a
93632	*Erythrocebus patas* (juv.)	6.1	118.3	5.1	M	a
57583	*Theropithecus gelada*	6.3	150.0	4.2	M	a
99657	*Macaca fascicularis*	5.1	117.0	4.4	M	a

Table 6. Comparative Malleolar Characters—*continued*

Catalog Number (1)	*Name*	*Malleus Length* (2)	*Skull Length* (3)	*Malleus / Skull* (4)	*Malleolar Head Inflection (5)* (6)	(7)
Cercopithecidae—*continued*						
99642	*Macaca fascicularis*	5.6	133.0	4.2	M	a
99669	*Macaca mulatta*	5.5	119.4	4.6	M	a
35448	*Macaca mulatta*	5.5	138.0	4.0	M	a
27183	*Papio cynocephalus*	6.5	230.0	2.8	M	a
27075	*Papio cynocephalus* (juv.)	6.6	123.0	5.4	M	a
24298	*Cercocebus albigena*	5.7	119.3	4.8	M	a
29813	*Cercocebus torquatus* (juv.)	6.1	133.4	4.6	M	a
Hylobatidae						
43333	*Hylobates klossi*	4.9	71.0	6.9	M	a
8370	*Hylobates concolor*	5.9	112.0	5.3	M	a
44740	*Hylobates* sp.	5.1	102	5.0	M	S
U143577	*Symphalangus syndactylus*	6.0	—	—	M	S
99366	*Symphalangus syndactylus* (juv.)	5.5	121	4.5	M	S
Pongidae						
33535	*Pongo pygmaeus*	9.2	233	3.9	M	a
68673	*Pongo pygmaeus*	8.2	225	3.8	M	a
33536	*Pongo pygmaeus*	8.2	192	4.3	M	S
68611	*Pongo pygmaeus* (juv.)	8.4	138	6.1	M	a
27550	*Gorilla gorilla*	9.6	255	3.8	M	a
26065	*Gorilla gorilla*	9.2	310	2.8	M	S
52429	*Pan troglodytes*	8.3	147	5.6	M	a
47315	*Pan troglodytes*	9.6	181	5.3	M	a
47170	*Pan troglodytes* (juv.)	9.2	154	6.0	M	a

Explanation of Symbols:

(1) All specimens examined are preserved in the Field Museum except numbers preceded by A (= American Museum of Natural History), BM = British Museum (Natural History), or U (= U.S. National Museum).
(2) Greatest length of malleus. No significant difference between right and left ossicle is apparent and each measurement is of either or whichever was available.
(3) Greatest length of skull.
(4) Ratio of malleolar length to cranial length.
(5) Inflection of head relative to long axis of manubrium.
(6) Inflection of head seen from anterior aspect of manubrium.
(7) Inflection of head seen from medial aspect of manubrium.
M Median inflection dominant or primary.
m Median inflection weak or secondary.
A Anterior inflection dominant or primary.
a Anterior inflection weak or secondary.
S No marked inflection, straight or primitive.
(juv.) Juvenal.

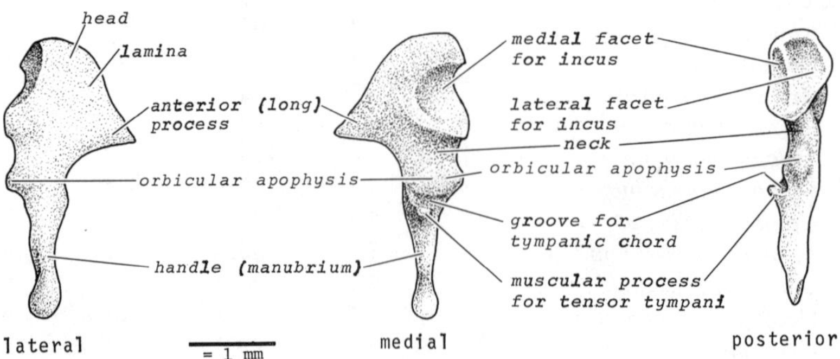

Fig. IV.71. Right malleus of *Callithrix humeralifer chrysoleuca* in lateral, medial, and posterior aspects; orbicular apophysis shown is characteristic of most members of the *Callithrix argentata* group.

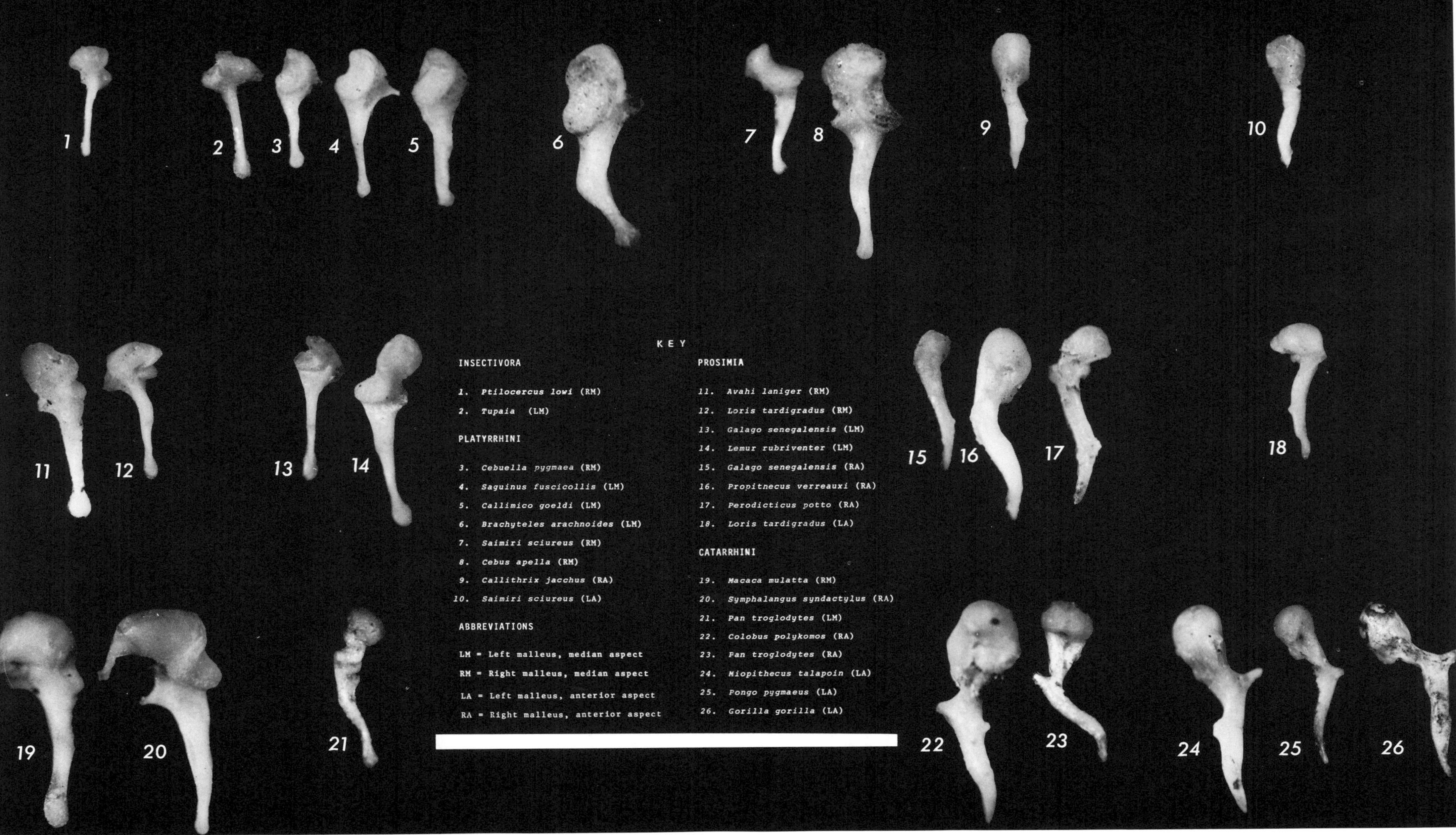

Fig. IV.72. Comparative shapes of malleoli of tupaiids, prosimians, platyrrhines, and catarrhines. Not to scale; measurements are given in table 6.

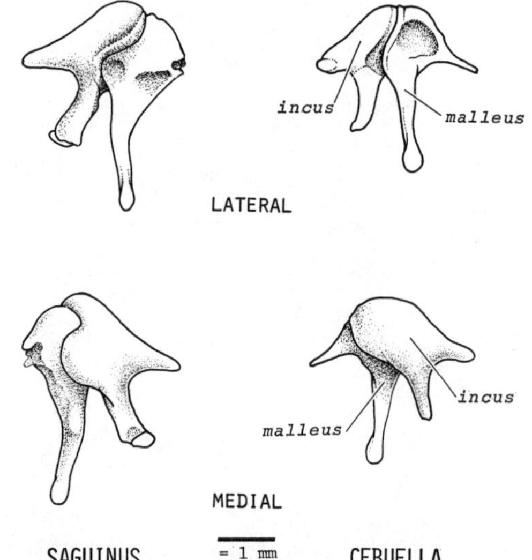

Fig. IV.73. Articulated malleus and incus. Lateral and medial aspects in *Saguinus* and *Cebuella* (Callitrichidae).

vestibuli) (figs. IV.68, 69, 74). The outline of the stapedial or obturator foramen varies independently. The ventral side of the opening formed around the fetal stapedial artery is usually larger than the dorsal, which is sometimes completely filled with bone. Among platyrrhines, the fenestra ovale is more or less tubular, with the lateral opening slightly wider than the medial. The stapedial base rests on the medial rim and only the head or little more than head and neck of the stapes emerges above the outer border of the fenestra ovale (figs. IV.65, 66). The catarrhine fenestra is usually shallower, often no more than a simple opening within a broad fossa that exposes all but the base of the stapes.

Doran (1878, p. 385) placed undue importance on the form of the stapes, particularly the length of the crurae. Resemblance between the stapes of callitrichids and marsupials with respect to the short crurae led him to remark that "in the genus *Hapale* may be found the lowest type of ossicles seen in all the Primates." The callitrichid stapes, and incus as well, varies considerably, but those of *Cebuella, Callithrix,* and *Saguinus* appear to be generalized. The *Callimico* ossicles (including malleus) are more advanced, but those of *Leontopithecus* are even more so. The full range of variation, however, is still unknown.

Hypothetical Middle Ear Functions

The probability that the highly diversified middle ear serves for more than sound transmission alone has been considered by a number of investigators. Recently Beecher (1969) suggested that the middle ear detects such rapid head movements as bobbing or thrusting in locomotion and jerking in feeding. Accordingly, vanelike modifications of malleolar processes such as the lamina ossea or orbicular apophysis impede air currents generated within the tympanic cavity by sudden head movements. The impulses are then transmitted through the ossicular chain to the cochlea, supposedly without hindrance to the virtually continuous auditory functions of the middle ear. Beecher attempts to show that the highest development of motion sense occurs in nocturnal richochetal desert rodents, all with exceptionally large bullae and vanelike manubria. Regarding primates, Beecher notes that head bobbing and thrusting are not characteristic of higher forms, hence, middle-ear motion sense is lacking in them. The sense, however, may be present in prosimians with large bullae and nocturnal habits. The malleolar manubrium in *Galago,* Beecher finds, is vanelike but remains unmodified in *Lemur.*

The hypothesis as described may not hold for primates. The bullae of small platyrrhines are large, particularly those of the night monkey, *Aotus,* and the diurnal callitrichids whose head movements are swift and jerky. Vanelike modifications, specifically the lamina ossea, however, are poorly developed or lacking in platyrrhines, catarrhines, and all prosimians, including *Galago,* I examined.

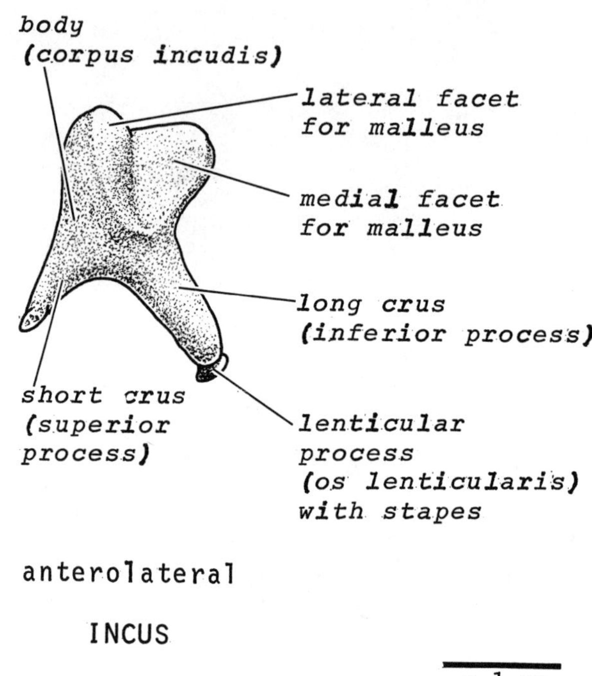

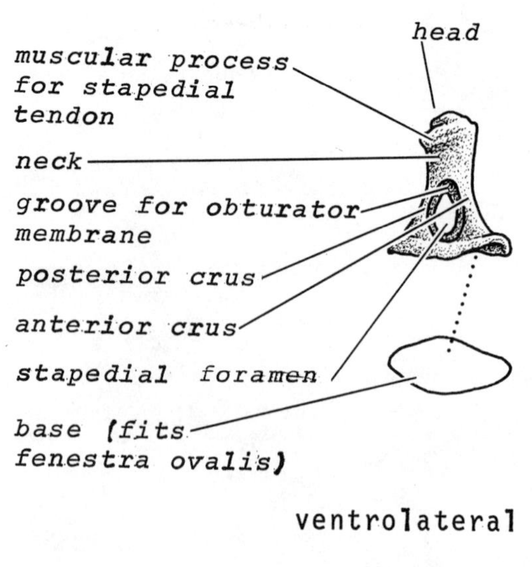

Fig. IV.74. Right incus and stapes of a marmoset (*Callithrix*).

Types of vanelike movements other than those described by Beecher are possible. The anterior "malleolar" process, or the processus gracilis, in *Tupaia,* for example, is fused to the anterior crus of the tympanic ring, its tip freely movable through the petrotympanic fissure. The movement, undoubtedly caused by the sphenomandibular ligament, translates into vanelike movements of the tympanic membrane. The freely suspended tympanic ring of lemuriform primates may also be movable, albeit by other means since the bone lacks the anterior process present in *Tupaia.*

Other functions of the middle ear walls and cavities, mainly in rodents, have been suggested. Most of the propositions are summarized by Lay (1972) and need not be discussed here.

Bibliographic Review

Much has been written about the development and function of the auditory ossicles, but scant use has been made of the bones as taxonomic or phylogenetic indicators. The most comprehensive comparative anatomical study of mammalian auditory ossicles, published by Doran in 1878, is essentially typological but is still the principal reference work. Other texts useful in the present study that stress the evolutionary, anatomic, biomechanic, or bioacoustic are briefly reviewed, or mentioned below.

In his summary of the history of the mammalian middle ear, Hopson (1966) explains the transformation of the reptilian articulare and quadrate bones into the mammalian malleus and incus, respectively. In the same volume, Webster (1966) describes mammalian middle ear structure and the mechanics of transformation of air vibrations by the tympano-ossicular system to fluid vibrations in the inner ear.

An investigation of the development of the auditory ossicles with particular reference to the malleus of insectivores, bats, and mice led Wassif (1957) to conclude that an ossification center is lacking in the cartilage of the developing malleus. Ossification, according to the author "takes place as a nearby membrane bone, the goniale, invades the cartilage of the developing malleus." The goniale, therefore, is regarded as the membraneous center of malleolar ossification. In an adult specimen of *Saguinus inustus* (AMNH 79415) at hand, the inferior facet of the malleolar articular surface in both ears is a separate bone (fig. X.56).

A textbook on the comparative anatomy of middle and inner ear regions by Werner (1960*a*) is monographic in scope. An extract of the section on the primate ear was also published elsewhere by the same author (1960*b*).

Kirikae (1960) deals with the vertebrate middle and inner ear in general but emphasizes function, particularly in man. More restricted and specialized works on the middle ear include those of Cockerell, Miller, and Printz (1914) on the ossicles of American rodents.

Detailed descriptions of the temporal bone, particularly the middle ear region in prosimians, man, and *Plesiadapis,* are provided by Saban (1963).

Three comparative anatomical works by Segall (1969, 1970, 1971) deal respectively with the functional relationship between malleus and incus, the lever ratio (malleolar arm length to incudal lever arm) and other ossicular characters in insectivora and marsupials, and the middle ear cavities and ossicles in gliding mammals.

A symposium volume edited by Busnel (1963) includes contributions by 24 authors on the recording and analysis of sounds produced by insects and vertebrates.

26 Skull
9. Mandible

The mandible of higher primates, that is, platyrrhines and catarrhines, is a single bone, consisting of the fusion at the symphysis of left and right jaw segments of the arcade thus formed (fig. IV.83; chap. 29). Each jaw segment consists of a horizontal body and ascending ramus. The upper surface of each body contains the teeth, which extend in a row from symphysis to anterior angle of the ascending ramus. The teeth of upper and lower jaws are described in chapters 32–38.

Mandibular Arcade

The triangular or V-shaped outline of the primitive mammalian arcade is more precisely delineated by the paired, ankylosed bodies of the mandible than by the upper jaws. The mandibular arcade is longer than the upper, more widely spread behind, narrower in front where it fits into the angle between the upper jaws, its canines less exaggerated or flaring, the remaining teeth narrower. The V-shaped mandibular arcade characterizes most prosimians, many primitive platyrrhines, such as *Cebuella* and *Callithrix* among the living, *Homunculus* among the extinct, and the basal stock of catarrhine lines.

The mandibular arcade of *Homunculus* (fig. IV.75), from the lower Miocene of Patagonia, can serve as a primitive platyrrhine model. (cf. Hershkovitz 1970*a*). Its symphysis is angular, the incisors and canine of each side ranged in echelon. Except for absence of one incisor, one premolar, and diastemas between antemolar teeth, the design of the *Homunculus* mandibular arcade is not very different from that of primitive mammals. Other components of the *Homunculus* mandible, including ascending ramus, symphyseal angle, molar enamel pattern, and curvature of occlusal surface, are evolved to near or quite cebid grade (fig. IV.76).

The V-shaped mandibular arcade of the pygmy marmoset, *Cebuella pygmaea* (fig. IV.77), is most primitive among living platyrrhines. Dental crowding, particularly of incisors, loss of the third molar and hypotrophy of the second, are specializations within, and with little effect on, the primitive mandibular framework. In more advanced callitrichids, *Callithrix jacchus*, the *C. argentata* group, and *Saguinus*, the arcade becomes progressively more arcuate or U-shaped, with the incisor-canine series broadly arced and the horizontal rami less divergent (fig. VII.6).

The cebid mandibular arcade is essentially U-shaped and specializations do not alter the pattern (fig. IV.77). Extreme hypertrophy of the angle in *Callicebus* and *Alouatta*, however, does obscure or skew independent evolutionary trends of other parts of the lower jaw (fig. IV.78).

The U-shaped mandible of living catarrhines is independently derived from V-shaped, or zalambdognathous, types in ancestral catarrhines. Elongation of the muzzle in baboons and macacques secondarily restores to the mandible a false semblance of the primitive V-shape, but the dental arch remains broadly arced with main axis of incisors essentially transverse.

A third mandibular type is V-shaped like the first but with symphyseal region narrowly truncate, the incisor field reduced and compressed transversely between the canines or entirely eliminated. The trend here is toward reduction in size and obsolescence of the incisors as in the extinct platyrrhine *Stirtonia* (fig. IV.75), reduction of the incisors to a single pair as in *Tarsius*, and loss of incisors with their alveolar space occupied by a hypertrophied canine as in *Daubentonia*. Finally, in lemuroids and lorisoids, incisors and canines are modified by compression and elongation into a comblike scraping apparatus. Each type of truncate V-shaped mandibles evolved independently.

All primary modifications of the primitive V-shaped mandibular arcade include (*a*) reduction and elimination of interdental spaces, and (*b*) reduction and ultimate elimination of one or more teeth among incisors, premolars, and molars.

Transformation of the mandibular arcade from triangular or V-shaped to arcuate or U-shaped, involved (*a*) arcing with transverse expansion of the symphyseal region, (*b*) rotation of the primitive anteroposterior axis of the incisors from sagittal to transverse and concomitant expansion of their buccal surfaces, (*c*) increase in mental depth and slope, (*d*) hypertrophy of angular process with reduction or obsolescence of the lunar notch, and (*e*) increase in condylar suspension (see below). All these changes reflect shortening of the face with few notable exceptions, increase in body as well as cranial size, and change in basic diet from insectivorous to omnivorous or herbivorous (figs. IV.75, 77, 78).

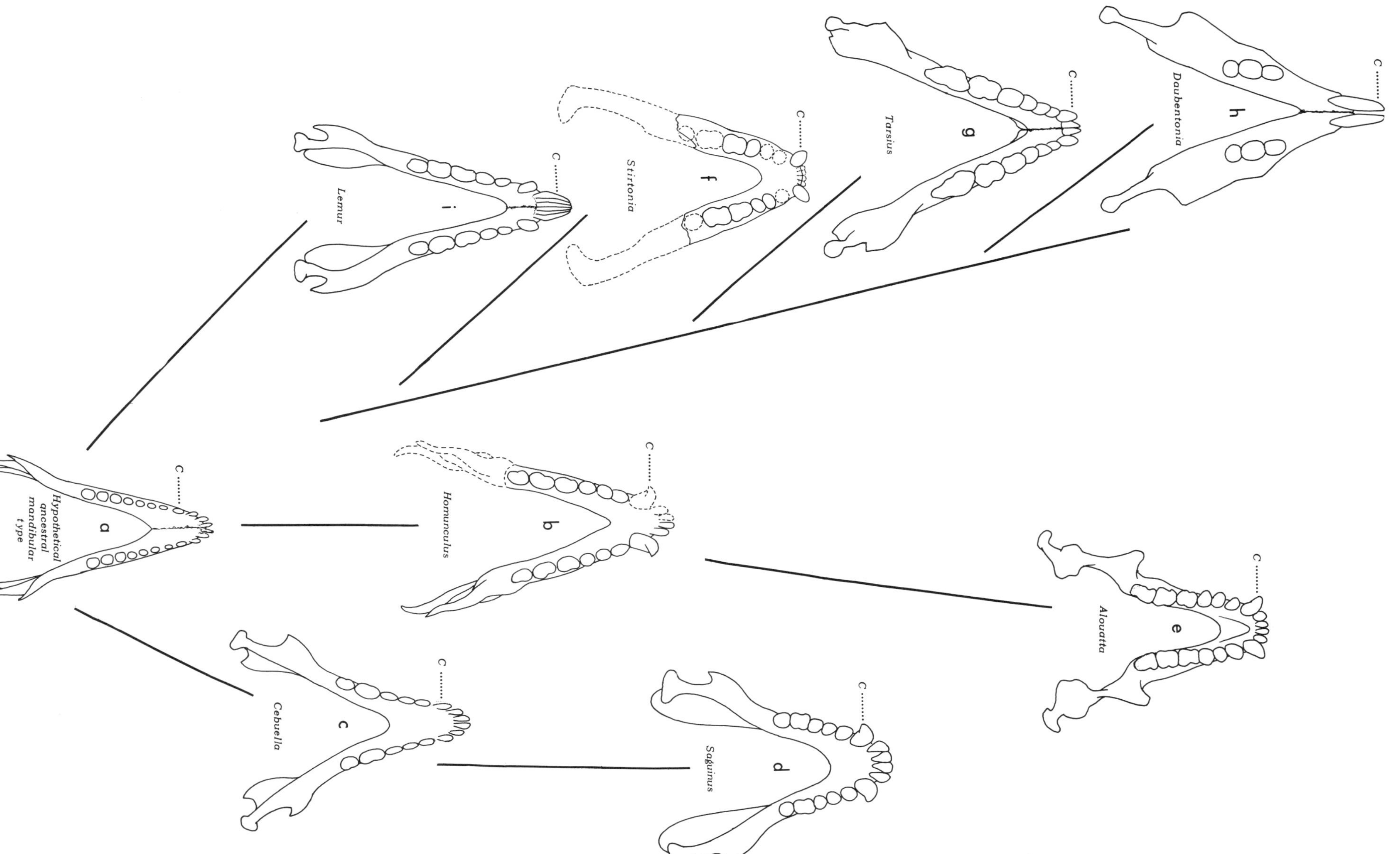

Fig. IV.75. Mandibular forms and types of symphyseal regions; arrangement of morphological series without phylogenetic implications, all samples drawn to same size; *C*, canine. *a*, a primitive type V-shaped mandible, incisors and canines deployed in nearly a straight line; *b*, ***Homunculus***, V-shaped mandible with incisors staggered, the interramal angle broadened, can be derived from type *a*; *c*, ***Cebuella***, V-shaped mandible with incisors staggered, can be derived from type *a*; *d*, *Saguinus*, V to U-shaped mandible with incisor-canine series broadly arced, can be derived from type *c*; *e*, *Alouatta*, U-shaped mandible with incisor-canine series broadly arced, can be derived from type *b* or *c*; *f*, *Stirtonia*, V-shaped mandible with truncate symphyseal region and incisors (indicated by broken lines) crowded transversely between canines, can be derived from type near *a*; *g*, *Tarsius*, V-shaped mandible with truncate symphyseal region and crowded incisors reduced to one on each side, can be derived from type near *a*; *h*, ***Daubentonia*** with V-shaped mandible and incisors crowded out by hypertrophied canines, can be derived from type near *g*; *i*, ***Lemur***, with V-shaped mandible and incisors and canines reduced to a pectinate series between first premolars, can be derived from type *a*. (After Hershkovitz 1970*a*, p. 8.)

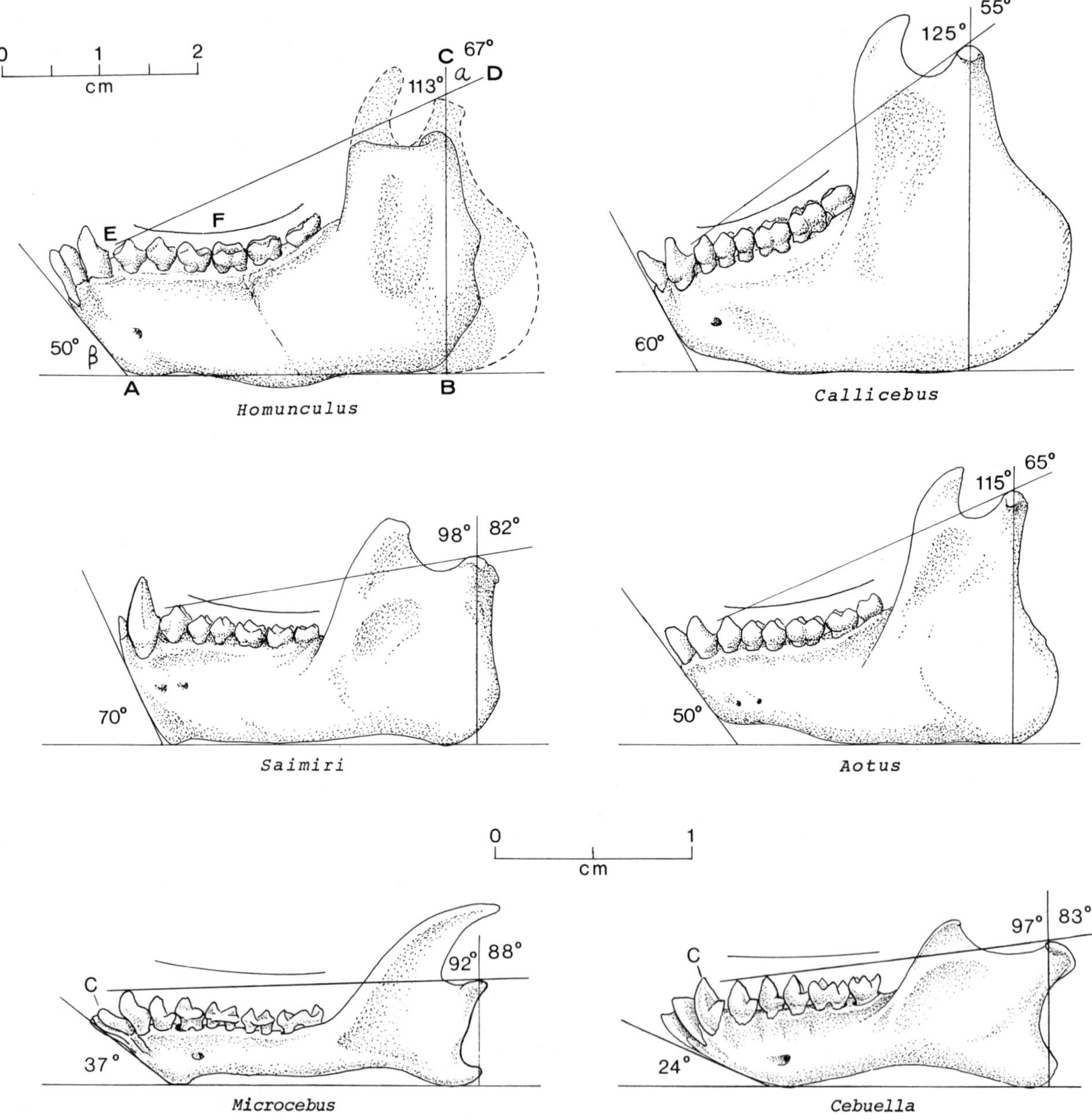

Fig. IV.76. Mandible of *Homunculus patagonicus* (type of *H. ameghinoi* Bluntschli restored), *Callicebus moloch, Saimiri sciureus, Aotus trivirgatus, Microcebus murinus,* and *Cebuella pygmaea. A–B,* basal mandibular plane; *B–C,* condylobasal axis or mandibular suspension (at right angle to *A–B*); *D–E,* condylar-premolar plane; *F* = curve of Spee; α, outer condylar angle, inner condylar angle shown as the supplement; β, symphyseal angle; scales are for figures beneath. (Modified from Hershkovitz 1974, p. 11.)

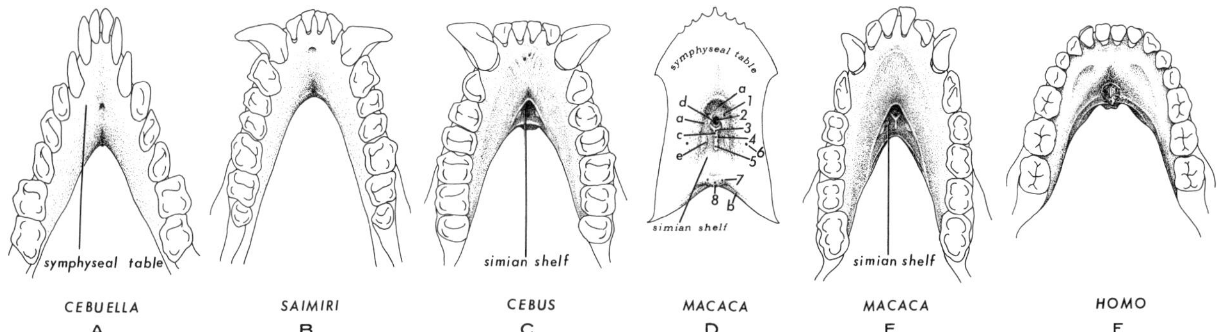

Fig. IV.77. Retromental region in platyrrhines and catarrhines, principal types arranged in a sequence of increasing complexity. *A, Cebuella* (Callitrichidae), primitive type from which all higher types can be derived; symphyseal table broad, genial fossa and digastric grooves rudimentary. *B. Saimiri* (Saimiriinae, Cebidae), with genial fossa, digastric grooves, and retromental foramina more developed, symphyseal table reduced. *C, Cebus* (Cebinae, Cebidae), symphyseal table moderately developed, simian shelf present and well defined. *D*, topography of retromental region in *Macaca* (Cercopithecidae); all parts shown not necessarily present in any one primate. *E. Macaca,* with complex retromental region, symphyseal táble moderately reduced, simian shelf highly developed, genial region depressed in deep fossa. *F, Homo sapiens* (Hominidae), symphyseal table obsolete, simian shelf absent, genial region everted. Compare the V-shaped arch in *Cebuella* with the U-shaped arch in *Homo.*

Explanations of symbols in *D: 1–8,* retromental foramina *(1–5,* genial, *7,* digastric, *8,* interdigastric); *a,* genial fossa; *b,* digastric groove; *c–e,* mental spines (*c,* geniohyoidal, *d,* genioglossal, *e,* paragenial).

Ascending Ramus

The ascending ramus of the primitive mammalian mandible is characterized by three distinct subequal processes. The pointed *coronoid process* juts high above the condylar process, from which it is separated by a deep notch. The *condylar process* projects back, usually with an upward tilt. Its articular surface is level with or higher, rarely lower, than the plane of occlusal surface of the cheek teeth. The hooked, inwardly inflected *angular process* on the inferior border of the ramus is defined from the condylar processes by the broadly incised lunar notch and from the body of the jaw by a shallower indentation. The three-pronged plan is basic in all mammals whatever the form of the mandibular body and diversity of the dentition (figs. IV.78, 79, 83; chap. 29).

The term *condylar suspension* is used to express the distance or drop between the articular surface of the condyle and the occlusal surface of the lower cheek teeth. The suspension is measured in terms of the angle formed by intersection of the condylobasal axis (figs. IV.78, 81) and the condylar-premolar plane. In the primitive mandible, condylar suspension is approximately 90°. The higher the ascending ramus, the greater the condylar angle; in *Alouatta* it may exceed 135°. The condylar angle rarely descends much below 90° in living Primates; in *Daubentonia,* however, it approaches 80°.

Evolution of the primate ascending ramus involves expansion with increase in condylar suspension, and forward rotation of the coronoid and condylar processes with reduction of the gap between them (fig. IV.79). Concurrently, the angular process, with rare exceptions, becomes thicker and more expansive, with its borders rounded. The range of variation is great and reflects evolution of the masticatory system from insectivorous through omnivorous to frugivorous and phytophagous habits. The platyrrhine ascending ramus exhibits most of the evolutionary range and serves as a model not only for all other primates but for marsupials, rodents, and ungulates as well.

Each of the three processes of the ascending ramus in lemuriforms (fig. IV.79) is well defined, but the primitively dominant coronoid process tends to become smaller, the angular portion of the ramus larger, its posterior border rounded, while the condyle rises above the dental plane, most notably in *Propithecus.* Contraction of the coronoid process, with concomitant expansion and rounding of the angle, continues in lorisiforms. In *Tarsius* the coronoid process is reduced to a short hook only slightly raised above the articular surface of the condyle, and the expanded angle constitutes at least one-third the body of the ramus. In the aberrant aye aye (*Daubentonia*), it is the condylar process that hypertrophies, but its articular surface persists on the same or slightly lower plane as that of the lower molar crowns, the angle remaining relatively small and the form of the coronoid process simple.

Among platyrrhines, the ascending ramus (fig. IV.79) of the largely insectivorous pygmy marmoset, *Cebuella,* is most primitive but is definitely advanced over that of typical lemuriforms or lorisiforms and not far removed from the tarsioid form. The position of the articular surface of the *Cebuella* condylar process is on a level with or slightly but distinctly above the dental plane, the coronoid process is reduced, the angle enlarged with its process short and broad. With increasing specialization the callitrichid ramus continuing from *Cebuella* through *Callithrix, Saguinus,* and *Leontopithecus* becomes larger, with the condyle more elevated and the angle more rounded. As the ramus expands and the condylar suspension deepens, condylar and coronoid processes rotate forward and the gap between them narrows to become least in *Leontopithecus.* The *Callimico* ramus most nearly resembles that of *Leontopithecus.*

Evolution of the cebid ascending ramus pursues parallel lines. The ascending ramus of *Saimiri* is near tamarin grade, while that of *Aotus* and *Callicebus* are expanded with greater depth of condylar suspension and closer approximation of condylar and coronoid processes. Evolution of the more specialized pithecine ramus maintains

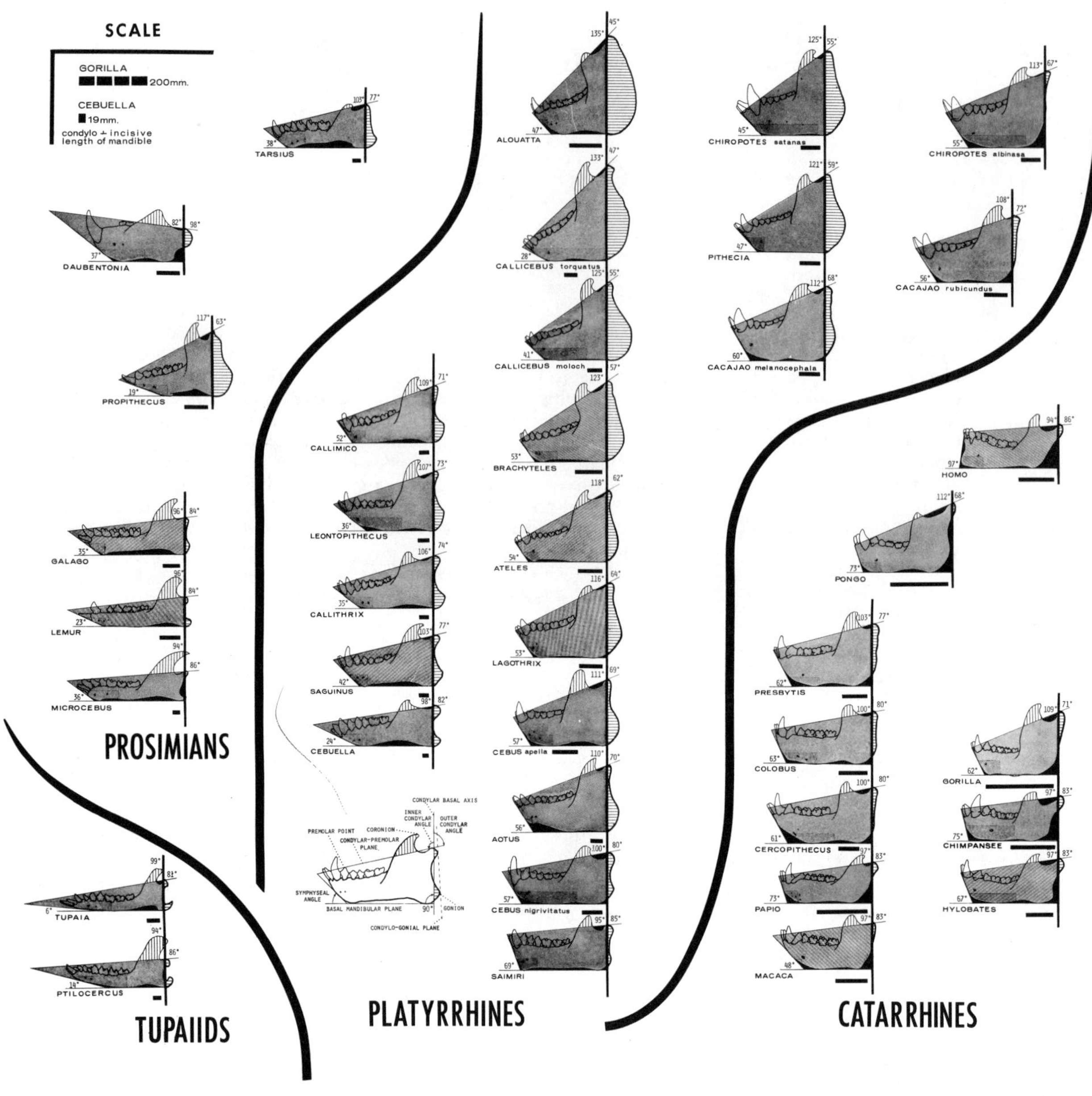

Five. IV.78. Mandibular shape and suspension of randomly selected primate skulls. Not drawn to scale; each figure enlarged or reduced to the same anteroposterior length and arranged in the order of increasing suspensory (condylar) depth (or decreasing condylar angle) in each phyletic line. Parallel line shadings mark portion of coronoid process projecting above condylar-premolar plane and part of angular process extending beyond condylar-basal axis. Measurements are those of specimens figured.

In primitive forms, suspension is shallow, or nearly zero, the condylar angle approximately 90°, the condyle itself nearly on same plane as cheek teeth. As specialization progresses, depth of ascending ramus increases while condylar angle decreases, except in aberrant *Daubentonia* (*upper left*), in which condylar increases slightly above 90°. Low-slung tupaiid mandibles (*lower left*) may be comparable in shape to that of basically insectivorous preprimate or ancestral primate stock. Mandibular suspension, usually shallow in strepsirhines (*left*), is exceptionally deep in the browsing *Propithecus*. The tarsioid mandible (*upper left, center*) is advanced and most specialized for its line. Platyrrhine mandibles (*center*) exhibit greatest diversity and widest range of variation among living primates. They reflect mandibular evolution beginning with mainly insect-eaters (callitrichids) through omnivores (*Cebus*), fruit and leaf-eaters (atelines), to leaf-eaters (*Alouatta*). The principal natural fare of pithecines is unknown. The successive changes in platyrrhine diets entail the depicted increase in suspensory depth and posterior bulge or angular process but often with dissonance (*upper right*) among young adults of the pithecine species shown. Evolution of the platyrrhine ascending ramus from insectivorous to browsing types is paralleled in marsupials, rodents, lagomorphs, ungulates, and other browsing or grazing animals.

Mandibles of the more specialized living catarrhines (*right*) diverge from the prosimian and platyrrhine mandibles by reduction of the angular process and the steeper symphyseal angle. Similarity between the angle of the condylar suspension in catarrhines and primitive primates is secondary owing to the increased depth of the symphysis or chin.

There is no consistent correlation between mandibular body and condylar angle or other features of the ascending ramus.

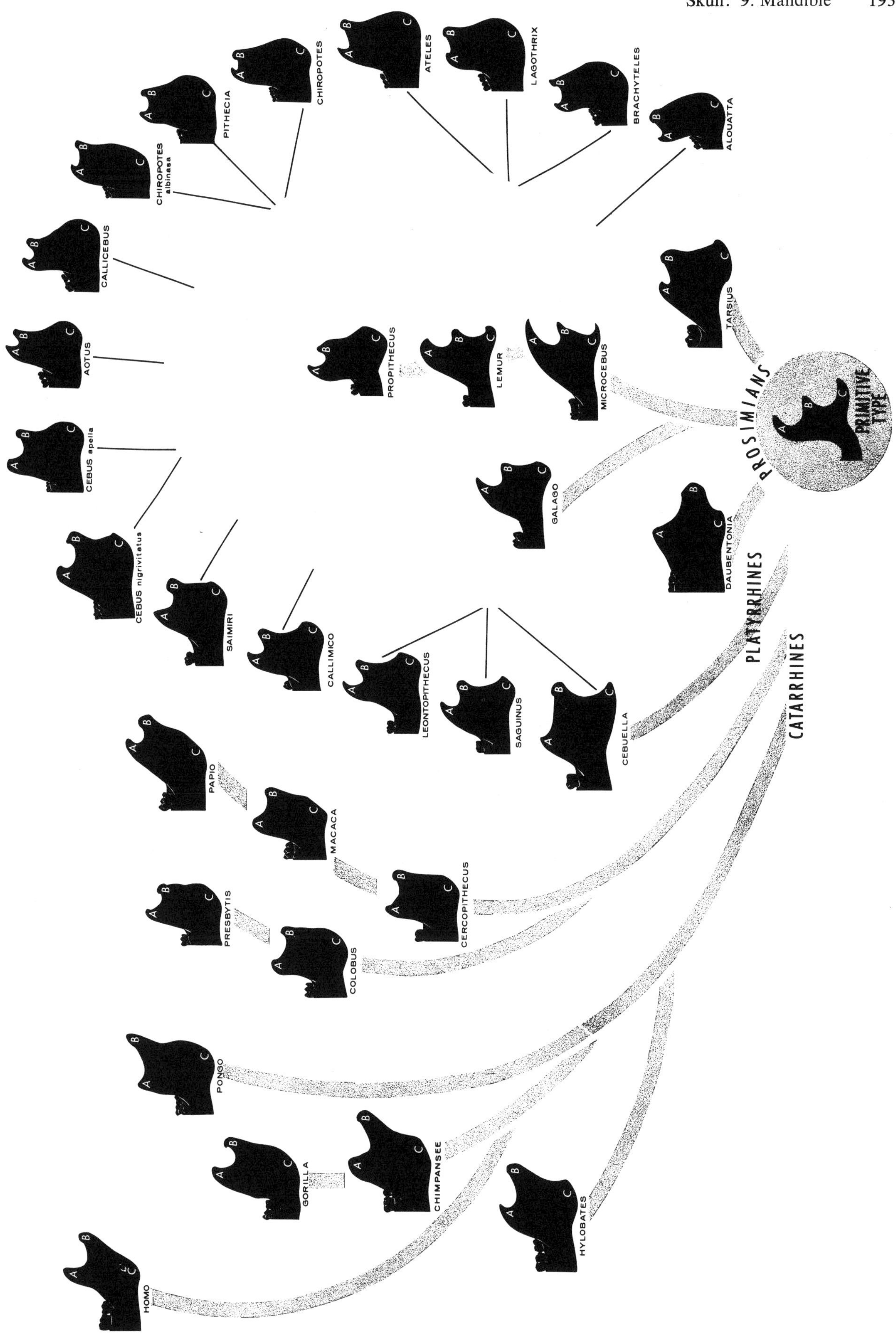

Fig. IV.79. Outlines of ascending mandibular rami of primates oriented to the basal mandibular plane and arranged in morphological and quasi-phylogenetic order. All figures scaled to same height. Compare changing shape, size, and relative position of coronoid process (*A*), condylar process (*B*), and angle (*C*) in all phyletic lines. Platyrrhine rami, arranged in graded series with natural groupings indicated by convergent lines, range nearly as widely in shape as those of all living primates combined, *Daubentonia* and *Tarsius* excluded. Evolution of platyrrhine ascending ramus has parallels in other mammalian lines, most notably among therapsids, marsupials, ungulates, and rodents.

the same trends but with some allometric reduction of the angular process in many individuals. Modification of the ascending ramus in prehensile-tailed cebids begins with *Cebus nigrivittatus* and related species, all near the tamarin or *Seguinus* grade. Deepening suspension, expanding angle, diminishing coronoid process with approximation toward the increasingly higher condylar process progress through *Cebus apella,* and the atelines *Lagothrix, Ateles,* and *Brachyteles* to an extreme in the leaf-eating howlers, genus *Alouatta.*

Variation in the catarrhine ascending ramus parallels that of cebids except that the angular process is inclined backward and reduced, and the lunar notch tends toward obsolescence, as noted in individual pithecines. The gibbon ramus, more primitive than the others, retains a relatively well-developed angular process and lunar notch while condylar suspension remains low. Other parts of the gibbon mandible, dentition included, are more specialized. The condylar process in great apes tends to become dominant, and the suspension in the orang is extremely deep. The lunar notch is more distinct in pongids and *Homo* than in cercopithecoids.

The platyrrhine series of ascending mandibular rami (figs. IV.78, 79) shows direct relationship between increasing condylar depth, increasing herbivority and expanding angular surface for masticatory muscle attachment. On the other hand, a consistent relationship is not obvious between the increasing specialization of the ascending rami and remaining parts of the mandible, including the symphyseal angle, and number, kinds, and forms of teeth. A multitude of ulterior controlling factors including locomotion and extraoral digestion are also involved in modifications of the jaws. For example, a more specialized hand in some species may accomplish functions performed by the front teeth in other species, and certain stages of food processing and digestion accomplished in the mouth of some species may be cycled in a more specialized gut of others.

The above conclusions are in essential agreement with those reached by Moss (1968) regarding the relationship between ascending ramus and mandibular body including the symphysis. On the other hand, the causal relationship between the components of the ascending ramus in each primate phyletic line described and figured in the present study does not support Moss's conclusion (1968, p. 444) that "there is no necessary relationship between size, shape or spatial position of the several ramal components to each other." Most of the examples Moss uses are copies of published figures of mandibles suited to his argument. Juxtaposition of the ramus of a cat and a guinea pig, of a polar bear and an aye aye, or a capybara, shrew, and ground sloth, proves the lack of causal relationship between the components of their respective jaws less than it proves the irrelevance of the comparisons.

Moss's arguments are partly based on prior assumptions regarding aspects of functional craniology. In a paper presented jointly with Young (Moss and Young 1960), repeated emphasis is placed on the "functional independence" of cranial parts. Whether the question is semantic or philosophical, it is axiomatic that no part of an organism is absolutely independent functionally or anatomically of any other part of the same organism. There is no doubt, however, that selective pressures impinging on one point of an organism may be vastly different and even entirely independent of pressures operating on another point of the same organism.

An experiment on the effects of removing masseter and internal pterygoid muscles from the angular process of young laboratory rats also led Avis (1961) to the conclusion that ramal components in primates as in rats vary independently according to function. It is demonstrated here, however, that within a given phyletic line of primates, variation in any one part of the ascending ramus is in harmony with, and often the complement of, variation in other parts of the ramus.

Symphysis Menti

The symphyseal region, or chin, evolved in primates from a low-slung joint, longer than deep (high), into a synostosed chin deeper than long (figs. IV.79, 80). All living prosimians retain the generalized condition of discrete right and left lower jaws bound by ligaments at the symphysis menti. Synostosis of the jaws could have arisen in the prosimian or haplorhine stock from which platyrrhines and catarrhines diverged, or less likely, it may have evolved independently in each line. An ankylosed symphysis menti not only is present in all known platyrrhines and catarrhines but was already present in such specialized extinct prosimians as the Eocene *Caenopithecus* and *Adapis,* and it is of independent origin in Chiroptera, Dermoptera, Proboscidea, Hyracoidea, Perissodactyla, odontocete Cetacea, and sloths among Xenarthra.

The symphyseal angle or slope of the chin in living prosimians is already well pronounced and, in many lorisiforms, quite steep. Among platyrrhines (table 7),

Table 7. Means of Ratios of Mandibular (Coronoidal) Height to Length, and Angle of Symphysis Menti in Callitrichids and Callimico, All Measured from Basal Plane

Species	*Specimens*	*Mean Mandibular Height to Length*	*Mean Symphyseal Angle*
Cebuella	61	45%	28°
Callithrix	80	55%	36°
Saguinus	255	61%	49°
Leontopithecus	7	66%	42°
Callimico	10	64%	55°

NOTE: For measurements of individuals and local series see appendix table 2 and figures IV.78, 83.

the angle in the pygmy marmoset, *Cebuella,* remains low but becomes progressively steeper through *Callithrix jacchus,* the *C. argentata* group, and *Saguinus.* The symphyseal angle of *Leontopithecus* is unexpectedly more recumbent than that of the smaller tamarin, which has a shallower jaw suspension. The angle in *Callimico,* however, is steep. In all forms mentioned, vertical depth of the chin increases with rising slope of the angle. At the same time, the horizontal symphyseal length decreases and the incisors increase in width and decrease in height.

Symphyseal depth in nearly all cebids is already much deeper than long, and the angle is steep. In the deep,

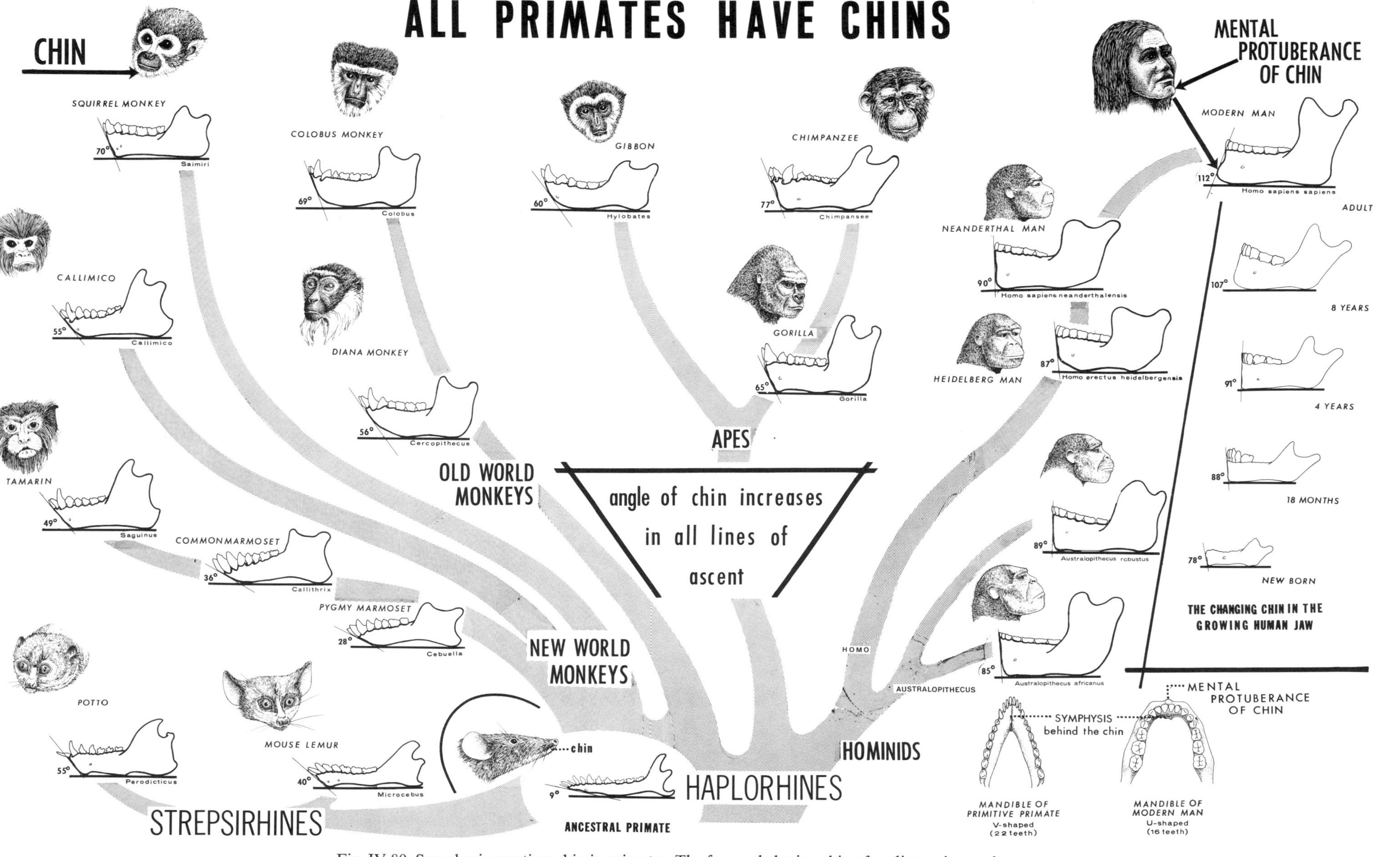

Fig. IV.80. Symphysis menti or chin in primates. The forward-sloping chin of earliest primates became steeper and stronger in all phyletic lines as feeding habits changed from dominantly insectivorous to omnivorous. The receding human chin is secondarily weakened, but the mental protuberance, present only in *Homo sapiens*, makes the chin look stronger. (After Hershkovitz 1970*d*.)

short-chinned *Saimiri* the angle may exceed 70°. The chin in apes is deeper and more nearly upright. In man the angle exceeds 90°, and the inner symphyseal slope had changed from concave, as in nearly all primates, to convex.

The term chin, which by definition applies to the entire symphyseal region of the vertebrate lower jaw, is frequently restricted to the mental protuberance of the human chin. Hence the popular misconception that a "chin" is unique to man. Evolution and possible function of the mental protuberance gave rise to a multitude of improbable hypotheses culminating with the biomechanical explanations proferred by DuBrul and Sicher (1954). The opinions of these authors were critically examined and rejected by Riesenfeld (1969), who based his conclusions on results of tests with rat mandibles. Berger (1969) also confuted the DuBrul and Sicher notions of an "adaptive chin" serving as a brace against the constricting force of the external pterygoid muscles or used for any other mechanical purpose. Apparent lack of mechanical function, however, does not warrant Berger's claim that the mental protuberance (his ambiguous "chin") is possibly an atavism of an earlier sexual dimorphism in some unnamed form, presumably, an earlier race of man. The fossil record indicates that the mental protuberance appeared late in human evolution and only in modern man did it become established as a distinctive trait. *Absence,* not presence, of a mental protuberance would be atavistic in modern man. The human chin is, in fact, a weak, receding structure. The mental protuberance is poor compensation, albeit otherwise directed, for the more powerful symphyseal region present in earlier forms of hominids and in the great apes.

The changing outline of the chin in the various primate lines and origin of the mental protuberance in man were discussed and illustrated in a popular article I wrote earlier (1970*d*). The mental protuberance, I suggested, evolved as a purely cosmetic feature that serves as a "badge of recognition and as a lure and stimulant to mating. In males, particularly, the pointed chin also accentuates gestures of defiance, and in females lends eloquence to expressions of haughtiness or petulence. Natural selection favored rapid spread of the mental protuberance until it became universally established as an ornament unique to modern man."

Retromental Region (Genial and Digastric Depressions: Simian Shelf)

The retromental or genial fossa, for attachment of the genioglossus and geniohyoid muscles, appears as a small shallow depression or pair of pits in the nonsynostosed halves of the prosimian mandible (figs. IV.77, 83). The condition in *Lemur* is representative. The two mandibles of *Daubentonia* at hand lack a fossa, but in *Propithecus* the two parts of the mandible meet in an exceptionally long symphysis, the posterior part of which is deeply excavated, ostensibly for receiving the genial muscles. The floor of the fossa also extends behind as a sloping "simian" shelf. Behind the shelf, on the inferior border of the symphysis, is a long narrow concavity for insertion of the digastric muscle.

The callitrichid genial fossa, like that of typical lemuriforms, lies on the inferior border of the jaw, while the digastric muscle inserts along the vertical edge. The fossa in *Cebuella,* however, is poorly defined or shallow, imperforate and more rudimentary than that of all other living primates. In *Callithrix jacchus* it is usually clearly excavated, often deeply, and pitted. The fossa averages deeper in members of the *Callithrix argentata* group and is often subdivided by a median ridge. In *Saguinus* it varies from shallow and entire to deep, divided, and perforated by vascular canals. The genial region of *Leontopithecus* and *Callimico* is similar. The simian shelf is absent or incipient in individuals of callitrichids.

The retromental region in the marmosetlike cebids, *Callicebus, Aotus,* and *Saimiri,* agrees with that of *Saguinus.* The fossa in pithecines is small, placed well above the ventral border of the jaw, and may be subdivided by a prominent spine. The surface for reception of the digastric muscle in this group is comparatively broad, well defined, and almost entirely posterior in position rather than ventral. The genial fossa in *Ateles, Brachyteles,* and *Lagothrix,* on the other hand, resembles that of *Saguinus.* The fossa of the otherwise extremely modified *Alouatta* mandible remains primitive, with one or a pair of small shallow depressions near the ventral edge of the jaw. Finally, the fossa in *Cebus apella* is larger, more complex and placed higher on the posterior border of the jaw than in all other platyrrhines. A simian shelf is present in *Cebus apella.*

The catarrhine fossa is usually about one-third the distance between lower and upper borders of the symphysis menti. The simian shelf, present in many individuals of all species except man and gibbons, varies with age and sex. As usual, the spiny genial region is depressed or excavated, except in man, where it is usually everted, perhaps in correlation with the forward thrust of the chin. However, an everted genial fossa also appears in some individuals of *Alouatta* and *Callicebus,* rarely in other cebids, where a mental protuberance is absent.

Considerable individual variation occurs in the size and shape of the depressions, separating ridge or spine, if any, and other osseous features along the ventral border of the symphyseal area. In many species, the fossae are fully exposed seen from the ventral surface of the symphysis but completely hidden from dorsal view. In others the reverse is true, and in still others the fossae are only partially visible from either view or, more rarely, both views. In an earlier discussion of the subject (Hershkovitz 1970*a*, pp. 10, 11, fig. 2), I used the phrase "digastric" depression where the expressions *retromental depression* or *genial and digastric depressions or fossae,* should have been used.

The retromental region evolved along parallel pathways in each major prosimian, platyrrhine, and catarrhine group, and the similarities are striking. The simian shelf arises in all major groups and is not restricted to broadly angled symphyseal regions as is implied by Clark (1959, p. 164). Generalizations reached by Inke (1962, pp. 484, 506) regarding the taxonomic significance of differences in the genial region of New and Old World monkeys appear to be based on inadequate sampling.

Mental Foramen

The size, number, and location of mental foramina vary in all primates, but only the larger orifice is used here for orientation (fig. IV.83). In *Cebuella,* the mental foramen is low and usually posteriad to a vertical line drawn between first and second premolars. The mean position of the foramen becomes higher and more anteriad as seen in *Callithrix* through *Saguinus* and *Leontopithecus.* In *Callimico,* the perforation lies between canine and first premolar in the upper tier of the lower half of the jaw. This position holds in the majority of cebids irrespective of species.

Mylohyoid Groove and Mandibular Foramen

Individual variation in the presence or absence of the mylohyoid groove and its relationship to the mandibular foramen is great (fig. IV.83). Straus (1962*b*) determined from a study of 1915 half-mandibles representing 40 primate genera that the groove-foramen relationship was of "very limited taxonomic and phylogenetic significance."

The lingula mandibulae, which usually overlaps the mandibular foramen, is common in man but uncommon in other species, where it appears as an individual variable without evident taxonomic significance.

Remarks

Measurements by Fenart and J. Anthony (1967) of a multitude of planes and angles of platyrrhine mandibles show relative differences between the more specialized genera. The authors' data (table 2), however, do not support their claim that the female mandible is heavier than that of the male. The mandibular measurements are also said to show average differences in each of certain mandibular characters between a majority of platyrrhines and some catarrhine monkeys. Measurements used by Fenart and Anthony are related to but not identical with those used in my discussions. Nevertheless, they point in the same direction or confirm present conclusions.

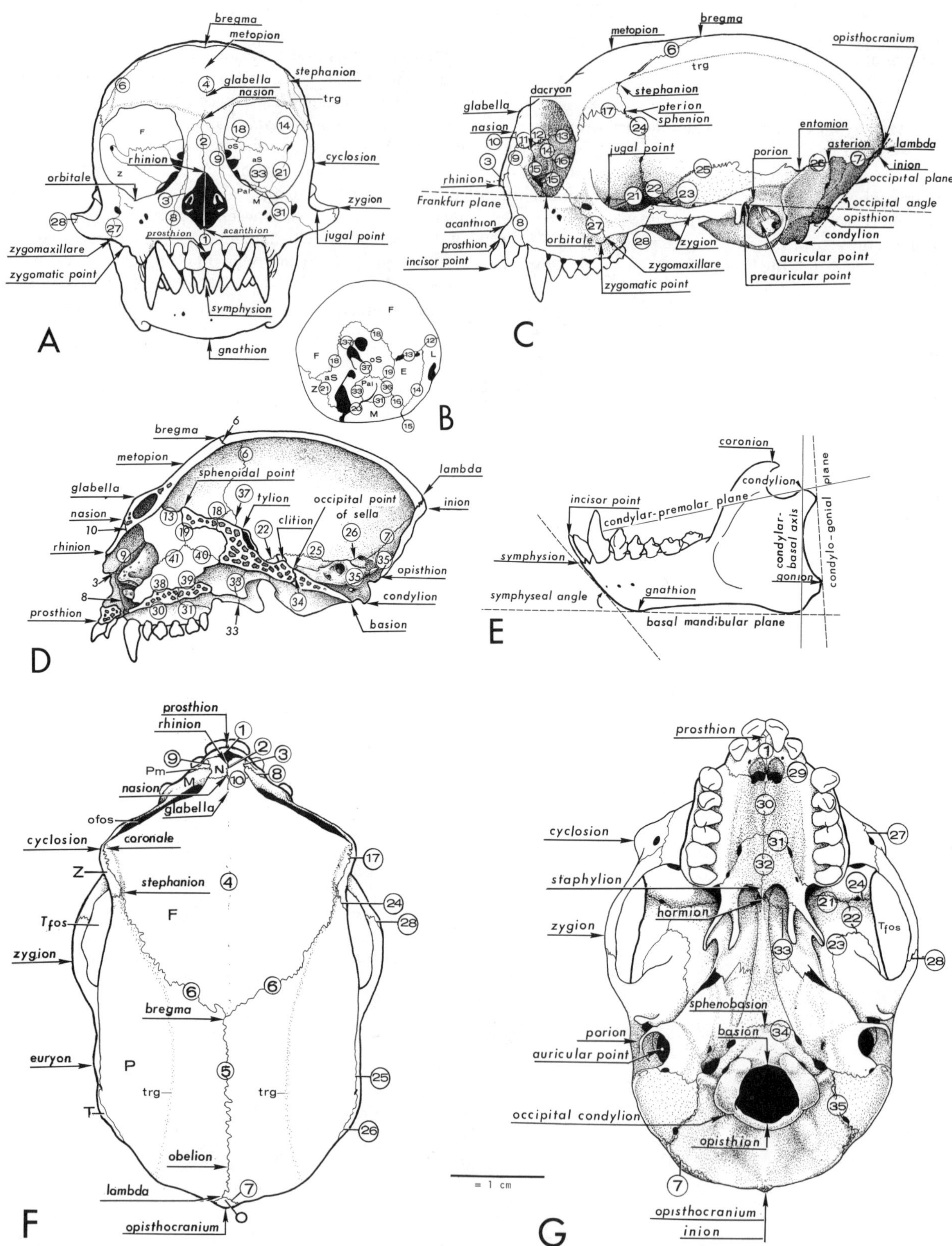

Fig. IV.81. Cranial sutures (numbered) and craniometric points, planes, and axes based on a callitrichid skull. *A*, frontal aspect; *B*, enlarged view of orbit with slight distortion to expose lateral and median sutures; *C*, lateral aspect; *D*, sagittal section; *E*, lateral aspect of mandible; *F*, dorsal aspect of cranium; *G*, ventral aspect of same; symbols and abbreviations explained in chapters 30, 31.

27 Skull
10. New and Old World Haplorhines Compared

a = Platyrrhini
b = Catarrhini
(Figs. IV. 81-84)

1. *a.* External auditory meatus (ectotympanic bone) ring-shaped, lip often thickened but never produced to form a tube (figs. IV.51, 58, 82, 110–24).
   b. Rim of auditory meatus produced to form a long, narrow bony tube extending to or slightly beyond glenoid process (figs. IV.51, 58, 82, 125–44).
2. *a.* Lateral (short) process of malleus absent, muscular process poorly developed or absent; malleolar head uninflected relative to long axis on anterior aspect of manubrium (figs. IV.70, 72).
   b. Lateral process present; muscular process always well developed except in gibbons; malleolar head inflected medially relative to long axis on anterior aspect of manubrium (figs. IV.70, 72).
3. *a.* Lateral pterygoid plate with ventral border usually tapered and directed mainly downward, not extending as process to bullar region (figs. IV.51, 53, 82, 110–24).
   b. Lateral pterygoid plate with posteroventral process (spina sphenoidalis) extending to lateral border of bulla, or with vestige of process in bullar region present as a lingula (figs. IV.51, 53, 82, 125–44).
4. *a.* Medial pterygoid plate greatly reduced (except in *Cebus* [figs. 117, 118], often no more than a hamular process, the pterygoid fossa a narrow, shallow recess, or undefined (figs. IV.50, 51, 53, 82, 83, 110–24).
   b. Medial pterygoid plate usually well developed, basal portion substantially greater than hamular process; pterygoid fossa capacious (figs. IV.50, 51, 53, 82, 83, 125–44).
5. *a.* Foramina lacerum and spinosum absent, foramen ovale only providing passage for meningeal arteries (figs. IV.51, 82, 110–24).
   b. Foramen lacerum present in catarrhine monkeys, man and orangs; foramen spinosum present in most catarrhines (figs. IV. 51, 82, 125–44).
6. *a.* Form of palate and outer border of dental arch subtriangular or V-shaped, to oblong or U-shaped (figs. IV.110–24; VII.6).
   b. Palatal form and dental arch U-shaped (figs. IV. 125–44).
7. *a.* Malar foramen consistently larger than in catarrhines of comparable skull size; greatest diameter from 2 to 7 mm (figs. IV.82, 110–24).
   b. Malar foramen consistently smaller than in comparable platyrrhine skulls; greatest diameter rarely greater than 3 mm (figs. IV.82, 125–44).
8. *a.* Average diameter of infraorbital foramen usually less than that of malar foramen.
   b. Average diameter of infraorbital foramen greater than that of malar foramen.
9. *a.* Nasal process of premaxillary bone hardly meeting lateral corner of nasal bone in cebids, broadly contacting in most callitrichids (figs. IV.82, 110–24).
   b. Nasal process extends well between nasal and maxillary bones in most catarrhines (figs. IV.82, 125–44).
10. *a.* Interpremaxillary suture at inferior margin of nasal aperture usually distinct through life, or incompletely closed after maturity (figs. IV.82, 110–24).
    b. Closure of interpremaxillary suture complete at or before maturity (figs. IV.82, 125–44).
11. *a.* Maxillopremaxillary suture obliterating early usually before maturity in cebids, but often persisting in *Callimico* and callitrichids (fig. IV.82).
    b. Maxillopremaxillary suture usually distinct until middle to old age, or through life (fig. IV.82).
12. *a.* Malar and parietal bones usually in contact on outer orbital wall [except sometimes in individuals of large cebid species with malar-parietal relationship as in 12*b*] (fig. IV.9).
    b. Malar and parietal bones separated by alisphenoid or both alisphenoid and squamosal bones (fig. IV.9).
13. *a.* Lateral orbital fissure consistently present in malar or between malar and adjacent frontal,

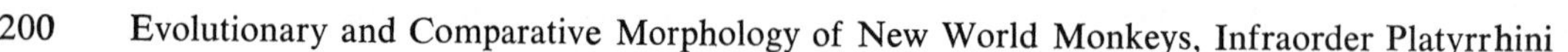

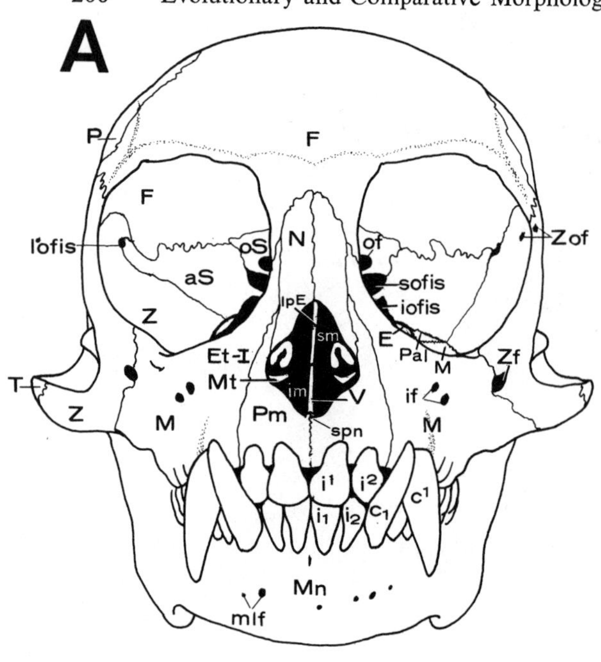

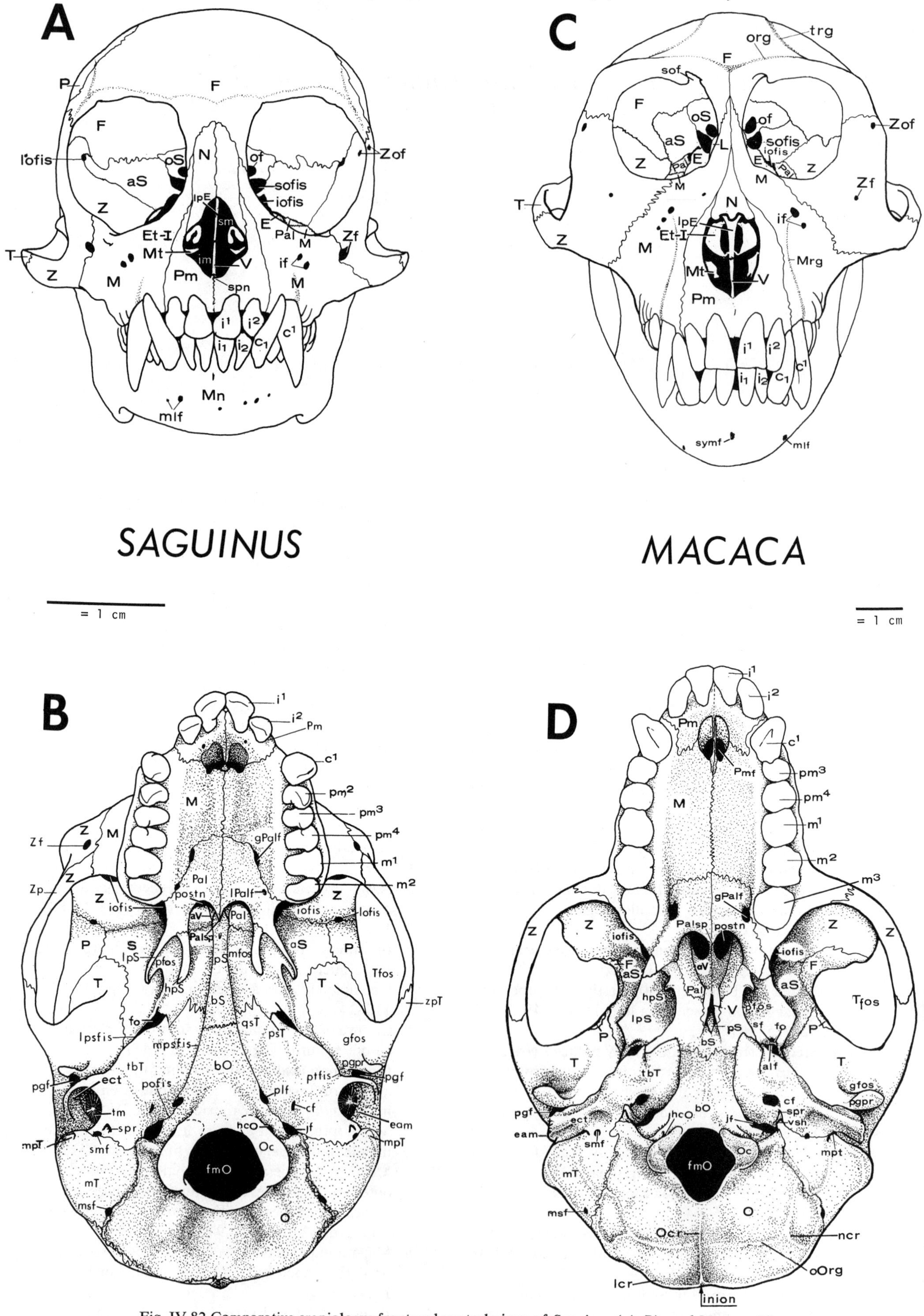

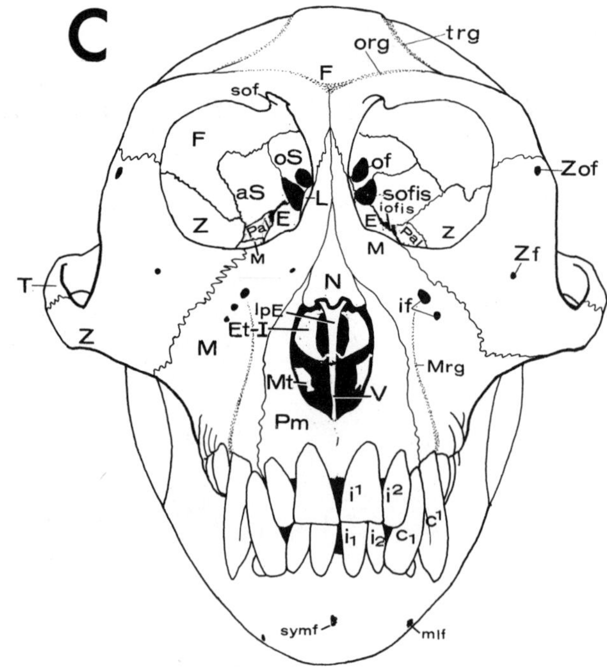

SAGUINUS

MACACA

= 1 cm

= 1 cm

Fig. IV.82 Comparative craniology: front and ventral views of *Saguinus* (*A*, *B*), and *Macaca* (*C*, *D*); symbols explained in chapter 31.

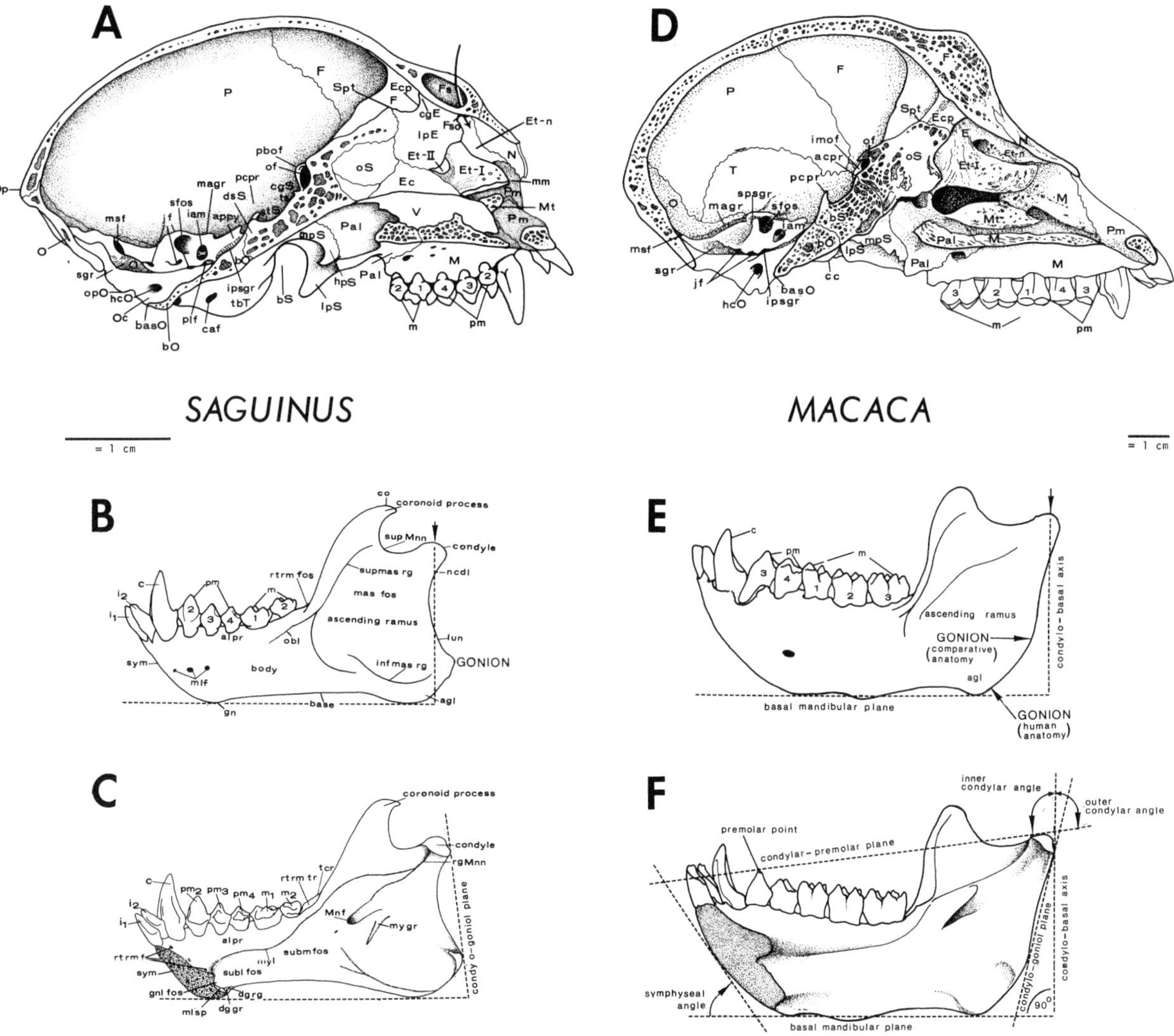

Fig. IV.83. Comparative craniology: sagittal section of cranium, and lateral and medial aspects of mandible of *Saguinus* (*A, B, C*), and *Macaca* (*D, E. F*); symbols explained in chapters 30, 31.

parietal or alisphenoid bones (figs. IV.9, 110–24).

b. Lateral orbital fissure obsolete or absent (figs. IV. 9, 110–24).

14\. *a.* Outer orbital borders usually raised more or less evenly all round, greatest interorbital breadth near or at midline or at frontomalar suture (most notable exception, *Alouatta*) (figs. IV.82, 110–24).

b. Outer orbital borders usually raised superiorly and laterally, flattened inferiorly; greatest interorbital breadth usually well below midline or frontomalar suture (most notable exception, Hylobatidae) (fig. IV.82, 125–44).

15\. *a.* Orbital fossa more or less uniformly rounded, the lower anterior portion evenly concave (figs. IV.82, 110–24).

b. Lower half of anterior portion of orbital fossa usually bulged inward, the inferior orbital fissure often constricted (figs. IV.82, 125–44).

16\. *a.* Nasoturbinal well developed, particularly in pithecines and prehensile-tailed cebids (figs. IV.22, 23–36, 38, 83).

b. Reduced or vestigial in catarrhine monkeys and man (figs. IV.37, 83).

17\. *a.* Ethmoturbinal I largest and most complete of turbinate system.

b. Ethmoturbinal I relatively large but comparatively poorly developed, less rolled (figs. IV.38, 83).

18\. *a.* Maxillary sinus with opening into nasal cavity usually present (figs. IV.13–20, 36).

b. Maxillary sinus absent in most catarrhine monkeys.

19\. *a.* Tentorium osseum often present, in many forms extending from parietal bone to petrous portion of temporal bone (figs. IV.46–48).

b. Tentorium osseum usually absent; when present, restricted to petrosal bone.

20\. *a.* Angular process of mandible well developed with lunar notch usually well incised, except in some pithecines (figs. IV.78, 110–24).

b. Angular process and lunar notch obsolete or absent (figs. IV.78, 125–44).

21\. *a.* Outline of inferior border of mandible V- to U-shaped (figs. IV.110–24; VII.6).

b. Outline of inferior border of mandible U-shaped (IV.125–44).

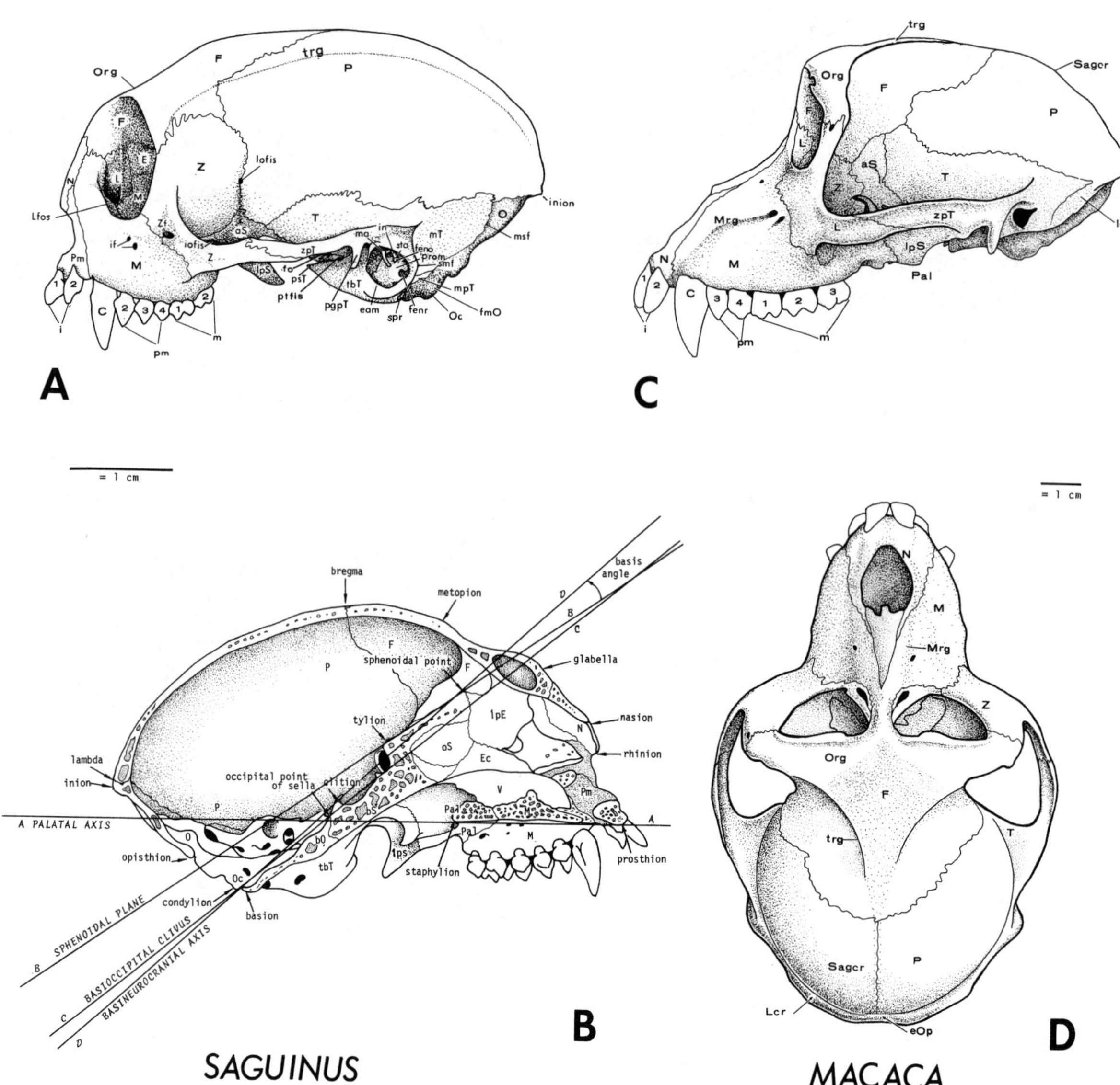

Fig. IV.84. Comparative craniology: bones, craniometric points, and principal planes. *A*, lateral view, and *B*, sagittal section of skull of *Saguinus; C* lateral and *D*, dorsal view of skull of *Macaca*. Symbols explained in chapters 30, 31.

28 Skull
11. Living Platyrrhine Families Compared

a = Callitrichidae
b = Callimiconidae
c = Cebidae

1. *a.* Greatest skull length of fully adult usually less than 65 mm (cf. figs. VII.5, 6; XII.6).
   b. Usually less than 60 mm.
   c. Usually more than 55 mm (figs. IV.110–24).
2. *a.* Occipital angle usually greater than 40° (cf. figs. IV.81; VII.6; XII.6).
   b. Usually less than 40°.
   c. Variable (figs. IV.110–24).
3. *a.* Neurocranial capacity usually less than 15 cc.
   b. Usually less than 13 cc.
   c. Usually more than 15 cc.
4. *a.* Nasal bone comparatively long, suboblong in outline but with proximal ends often rounded or obtusely pointed; dorsal contour plane to slightly concave or convex; sutural contact with premaxillary usually broad; all inter- and intranasal sutures persistent, usually to old age (cf. figs. IV.2; VII.6; XII.6).
   b. Generally as in 4*c* but usually more pointed proximally and slightly expanded distally; sutural contact with premaxillary bone reduced or none; inter- and intranasal sutures persist at least to maturity.
   c. Comparatively short, subtriangular in outline with distal expansion often flaring, dorsal contour moderately concave to deeply bowed; sutural contact with premaxilla from broad to none; inter- and intranasal sutures tending to fuse and disappear after maturity (cf. IV.2, 110–24).
5. *a.* Nasal aperture commonly quadrifoliate in outline; that is, with deep superior, inferior and lateral incisions (cf. figs. IV.1; VII.6; XII.6).
   b. Subcuneate or subchordate.
   c. Cuneate, ovate, chordate, piriform, rarely quadrifoliate (figs. IV.110–24).
6. *a.* Premaxillary bone usually in broad contact with anterolabial surface of nasal (fig. IV.82).
   b. Contact with nasal narrow and infrequent.
   c. Contact with nasal broad, narrow, or absent.
7. *a.* Maxillopremaxillary suture often persistent and well defined past maturity or through life (cf. fig. IV.81).
   b. Persistent.
   c. Usually obliterated before or soon after maturity.
8. *a.* Outline of bony palate and dental arch subtriangular, or V-shaped, to suboblong, or U-shaped (figs. VII.6).
   b. More nearly U-shaped.
   c. U-shaped (figs. IV.110–24).
9. *a.* Median posterior border of bony palate extending to posterior plane of last molars (m^2) or slightly behind (figs. IV.5; VII.6; XII.6).
   b. Extending to plane between posterior margins of first and second molars.
   c. Extending behind from plane of posterior margin of first molars (m^1) to well behind that of last molars (m^3) (figs. IV.110–24; VII.5).
10. *a.* Plane of last molar crown canted outward, its slope more or less in line with transverse arc of palatal ceiling (figs. IV.50; VII.8).
    b. As in *a*.
    c. Plane of last molar crown variable but usually canted inward, its slope forming an angle with transverse arc of palatal ceiling (fig. IV.50).
11. *a.* Lateral pterygoid plate small, medial pterygoid plate consisting of little more than hamular process, pterygoid fossa, a narrow shallow recess (figs. IV.22, 25, 26; IX.1; X.10; XI.7).
    b. As in *a* but with medial plate and pterygoid fossa slightly more developed (figs. IV.27; XII.6).
    c. Lateral pterygoid plate usually well developed, medial plate poorly to moderately developed, pterygoid fossa varying from narrow angular recess to moderately well developed pocket (figs. IV.28–36, 110–24).
12. *a.* Orbit without notable lateral expansion (fig. IV. 11; VII.6).
    b. With notable lateral expansion (fig. XII.6).
    c. Without lateral expansion except in *Aotus* (figs. IV.11, 110–24).
13. *a.* Auditory bulla and mastoid bone always well inflated, cochlea relatively small, inferior portion of mesotympanic cavity large, often cellular (figs. IV.62, 65).
    b. Well inflated, cochlea moderate, mesotympanic cavity large, not cellular (fig. IV.65).
    c. Well to little inflated, cochlea large, filling most

of lower portion of noncellular mesotympanic cavity (figs. IV.64–66).

14. *a.* Frontal sinus present (except in *Cebuella* and many individuals of *Callithrix*) and opening anteriad to olfactory bulb directly into upper recess of middle nasal cavity (figs. IV.22, 24–26).

b. Frontal sinus present, communicating with nasal cavity through pneumatized channel coursing behind and laterad to plane of olfactory bulb (fig. IV.27).

c. Frontal sinus present or absent, when present communicating with nasal cavity as in 13*a* and 13*b*, or with posterolateral channel partially to completely obstructed (figs. IV.28–36, 38).

29 Skull
12. Atlas of Tupaiid and Primate Skulls

Photographs of skulls of representatives of living tupaiids and primates, except callitrichids, are combined in this chapter for convenience of reference and comparisons. The arrangement follows the classification in chapter 2 (p. 9). The specific name of each animal is listed below, with its sex, museum catalog number, and geographic provenance. The following abbreviations are used for the museums where the skulls are stored.

AM = American Museum of Natural History, New York
FM = Field Museum of Natural History, Chicago
MN = Muséum National d'Histoire Naturelle, Paris
US = United States National Museum, Washington, D.C.

IV.85. *Tupaia glis* (FM 76825 ♂) (Tupaiidae, Insectivora). NORTH BORNEO: Sandakan.
IV.86. *Ptilocercus lowi* (FM 76855 ♂) (Tupaiidae, Insectivora). NORTH BORNEO: Sandakan.
IV.87. *Microcebus murinus* (FM 85863 ♀) (Lemuridae). MADAGASCAR: Tulear, Poste Mananteina
IV.88. *Cheirogaleus major* (FM 85145) (Lemuridae). MADAGASCAR.
IV.89. *Phaner furcifer* (AM 100624 ♂) (Lemuridae). MADAGASCAR: Tobiky.
IV.90. *Lepilemur mustelinus* (FM 5658 ♂) (Lemuridae). MADAGASCAR.
IV.91. *Hapalemur griseus* (FM 57631 ♀) (Lemuridae). MADAGASCAR.
IV.92. *Lemur rubriventer* (FM 5651 ♂) (Lemuridae). MADAGASCAR.
IV.93. *Lemur catta* (FM 81543 ♂) (Lemuridae). MADAGASCAR.
IV.94. *Lemur macaco* (FM 8338 ♂) (Lemuridae). MADAGASCAR.
IV.95. *Varecia variegata* (FM 8347 ♂) (Lemuridae). MADAGASCAR.
IV.96. *Avahi laniger* (AM 170461 ♂) (Indriidae). MADAGASCAR: Eminiminy, Fort Dauphin.
IV.97. *Propithecus verreauxi* (FM 8345 ♀) (Indriidae). MADAGASCAR.
IV.98. *Indri indri* (AM 185638 ♂) (Indriidae). MADAGASCAR.
IV.99. *Galago minutus* (FM 54488 ♂) (Galagidae). GOLD COAST.
IV.100. *Galago minutus* (FM 83618 ♂) (Galagidae). ANGOLA: Gabela.
IV.101. *Galago crassicaudatus* (FM 96274 ♂) (Galagidae). NORTHERN RHODESIA: Fort Jameson.
IV.102. *Euoticus elegantulus* (FM 43731 ♀; FM 14046 ♀) (Galagidae). CAMEROON: Sakbayeme (43731); Batuga (14046).
IV.103. *Loris tardigradus* (FM 95024 ♂) (Lorisidae). SRI LANKA: Pindeniya.
IV.104. *Nycticebus pygmaeus* (FM 46829 ♀) (Lorisidae). VIET NAM: Annam.
IV.105. *Arctocebus calabarensis* (FM 99360 ♂) (Lorisidae). AFRICA.
IV.106. *Perodicticus potto* (FM 94239 ♀) (Lorisidae). AFRICA.
IV.107. *Daubentonia madagascariensis* (AM 41334 —) (Daubentoniidae). MADAGASCAR.
IV.108. *Daubentonia madagascariensis* (FM 15529 —) (Daubentoniidae). MADAGASCAR.
IV.109. *Tarsius syrichta* (FM 56748 ♀) (Tarsiidae). PHILIPPINES: Davao Caburan.
IV.110. *Saimiri sciureus* (FM 46170 ♂) (Cebidae). GUYANA: Essequibo, Rockstone.
IV.111. *Aotus trivirgatus* (FM 43219 ♀) (Cebidae). ECUADOR: Napo-Pastaza, Río Pindo Yacu
IV.112. *Callicebus torquatus* (FM 70694 ♀) (Cebidae). COLOMBIA: Putumayo, Río Mecaya.
IV.113. *Alouatta palliata* (FM 13895 ♂) (Cebidae). MEXICO: Veracruz, Achotal.
IV.114. *Pithecia monachus* (FM 86995 ♂) (Cebidae). PERU: Loreto, Santa Luisa.

IV.115. *Chiropotes albinasa* (FM 94926 ♀) (Cebidae).
BRAZIL: Pará, Rio Tapaiuna.

IV.116. *Cacajao calvus rubicundus* (FM 88819 ♀) (Cebidae).
PERU: Loreto, Quebrada Esperanza

IV.117. *Cebus nigrivittatus* (FM 13377 ♂) (Cebidae).
VENEZUELA: Bolívar, Caicara.

IV.118. *Cebus apella* (FM 92121 ♂) (Cebidae).
BRAZIL: Pará, Urucurituba.

IV.119. *Lagothrix flavicauda* (AM 73222 ♂) (Cebidae).
PERU: Amazonas, La Lejía.

IV.120. *Lagothrix flavicauda* (AM 73222 ♂; AM 73223 ♀) (Cebidae).
PERU: Amazonas, La Lejía.

IV.121. *Lagothrix lagothricha* (FM 88829 ♀) (Cebidae).
PERU: Loreto, Río Yaquerana.

IV.122. *Ateles paniscus* (FM 41584 ♂) (Cebidae).
ECUADOR: Esmeraldas, Río Quinindé

IV.123. *Brachyteles arachnoides* (MN 1904–413) (Cebidae).
BRAZIL: Espírito Santa, Engenheiro Reeve.

IV.124. *Brachyteles arachnoides* (US 259474). (Cebidae).
BRAZIL: Rio de Janeiro, Serra Macaé.

IV.125. *Miopithecus talapoin* (FM 83634 ♂) (Cercopithecidae).
ANGOLA: Gabela.

IV.126. *Cercopithecus ascanius* (FM 81597 ♂) (Cercopithecidae).
ANGOLA: Canzelle, Quai Sai River.

IV.127. *Erythrocebus patas* (US 164684 ♂). (Cercopithecidae).
UGANDA: Nimule.

IV.128. *Allenopithecus nigroviridis* (AM 52467) (Cercopithecidae).
DEMOCRATIC REPUBLIC OF THE CONGO: Bolobo.

IV.129. *Cercocebus atys* (FM 48828 ♂) (Cercopithecidae).
AFRICA.

IV.130. *Macaca arctoides* (FM 39160 ♂) (Cercopithecidae).
VIET NAM: Tonkin

IV.131. *Papio anubis* (FM 27192 ♂) (Cercopithecidae).
ETHIOPIA: Amhara.

IV.132. *Theropithecus gelada* (FM 27233 ♂) (Cercopithecidae).
ETHIOPIA: Muger River.

IV.133. *Presbytis phayrei* (FM 99700 ♀) (Cercopithecidae).
THAILAND: Kanchanaburi, Chongkrong.

IV.134. *Pygathrix nemaeus* (FM 46511 ♂) (Cercopithecidae).
NORTH VIETNAM: Annam, Ban Methuot.

IV.135. *Rhinopithecus roxellanae* (FM 31140 ♀) (Cercopithecidae).
CHINA: Szechuan.

IV.136. *Nasalis larvatus* (FM 68682 ♂) (Cercopithecidae).
BORNEO: E. Coast.

IV.137. *Simias concolor* (AM 103362) (Cercopithecidae).
INDONESIA: Mentawai Islands, North Pagai.

IV.138. *Colobus polykomos* (FM 17699 ♂) (Cercopithecidae).
KENYA: Kijabe.

IV.139. *Hylobates lar* (FM 99745 ♀) (Hylobatidae).
THAILAND: Kangchanaburi.

IV.140. *Symphalangus syndactylus* (FM 99366 ♂) (Hylobatidae).
INDONESIA.

IV.141. *Pongo pygmaeus* (FM M44389 ♂) (Pongidae).
BORNEO.

IV.142. *Chimpansee* (or *Pan*) *troglodytes* (FM 18406 ♂)
AFRICA.

IV.143. *Gorilla gorilla* (FM 26065 ♂) (Pongidae).
UGANDA: Volcanos Pass.

IV.144. *Homo sapiens* (FM 43902 ♂; FM 41766 ♂ mandible only) (Hominidae).

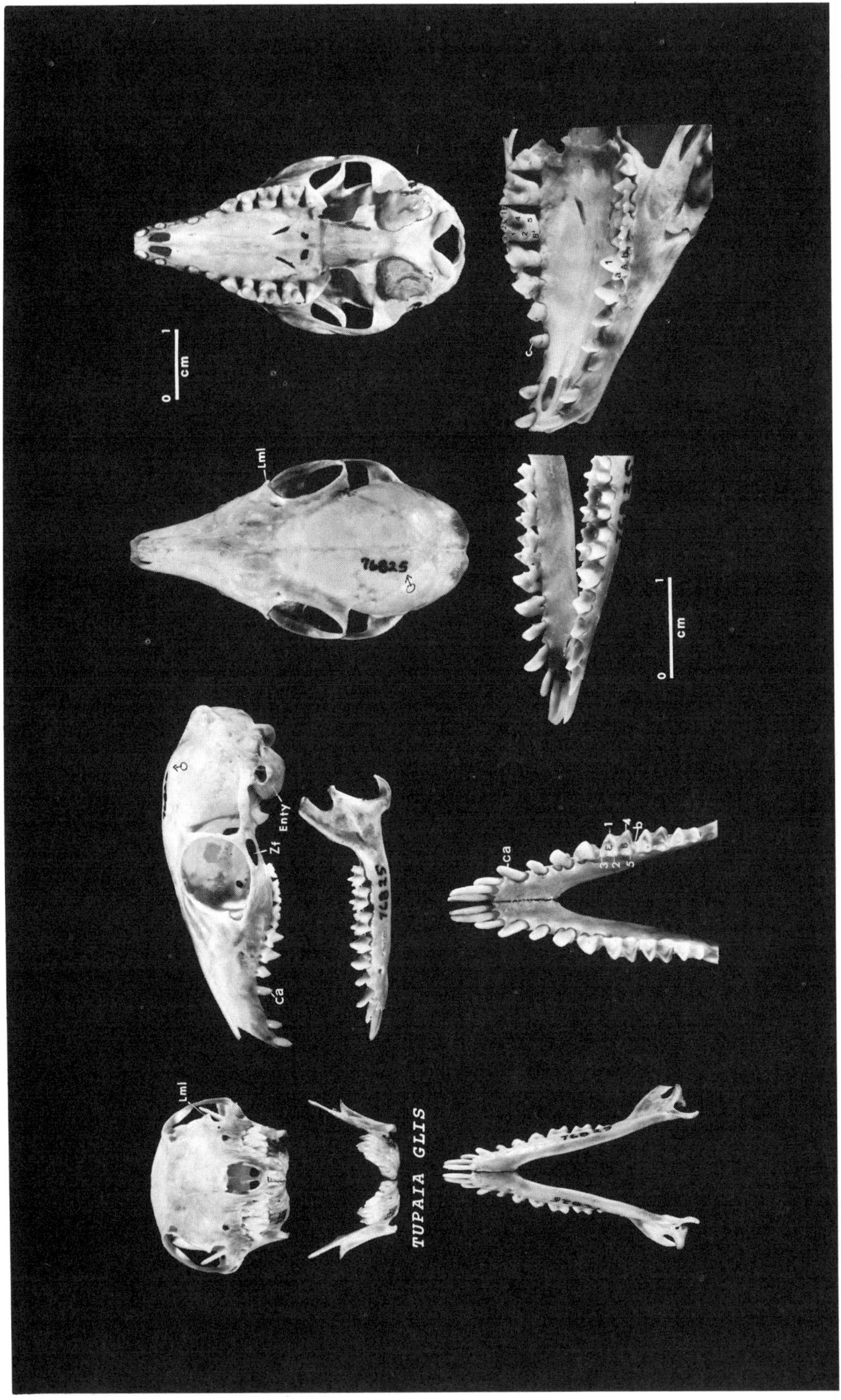

Fig. IV.85. *Tupaia glis* (FM 76825 ♂) Tupaiidae, Insectivora). NORTH BORNEO: Sandakan. Molars primarily dilambdomorphic; rudimentary hypocone present or absent; auditory bulla formed by entotympanic bone (*Enty*).

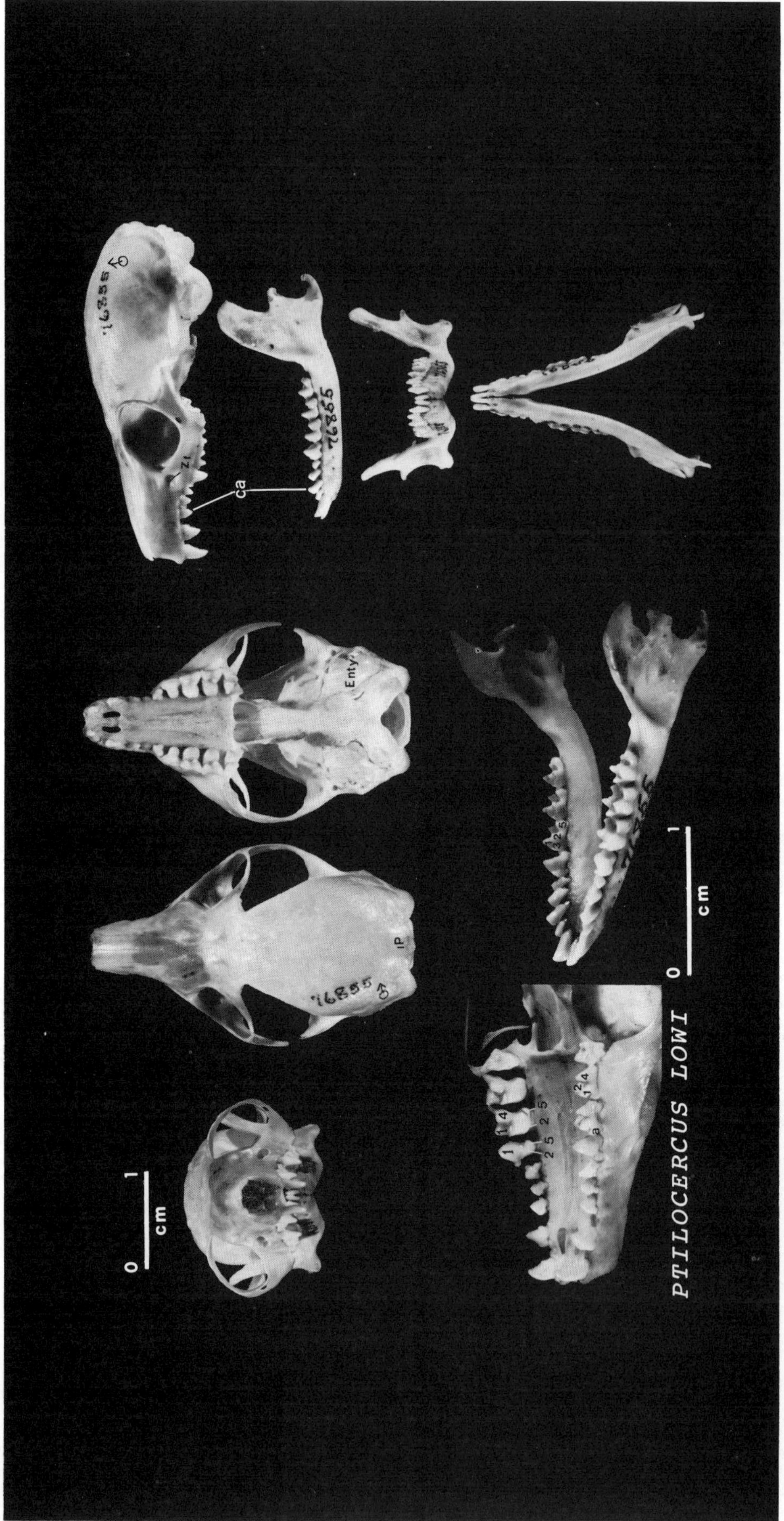

Fig. IV.86. *Ptilocercus lowi* (FM 76855 ♂) (Tupaiidae, Insectivora). NORTH BORNEO: Sandakan. Molars basically euthemorphic as in primates, the first two with low hypocone; auditory bulla formed by entotympanic bone as in all tupaiids.

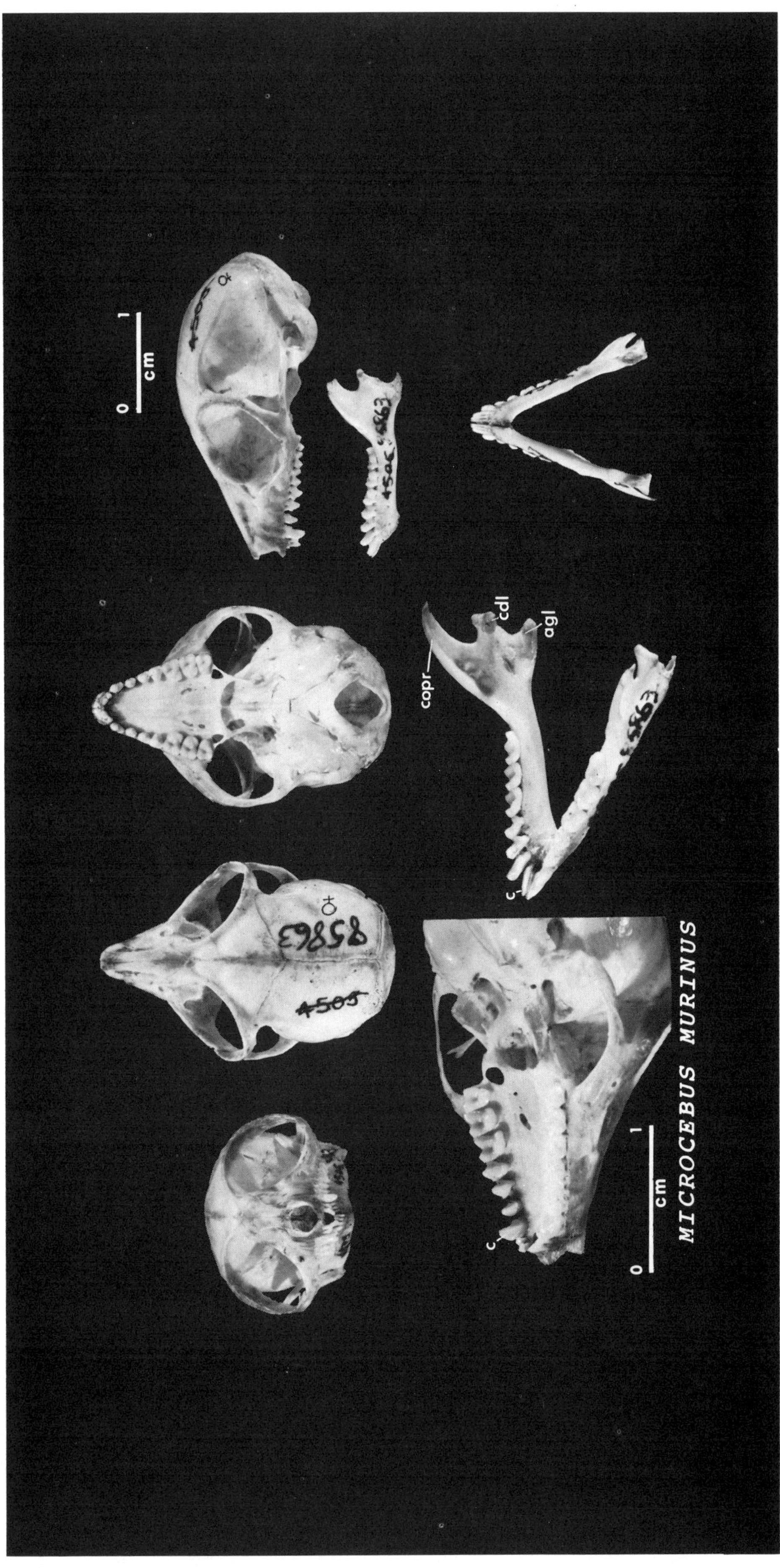

Fig. IV.87. *Microcebus murinus* (FM 85863 ♀) (Lemuridae). MADAGASCAR: Tulear, Poste Manantеina. Cranially and dentally one of most primitive of living strepsirhines.

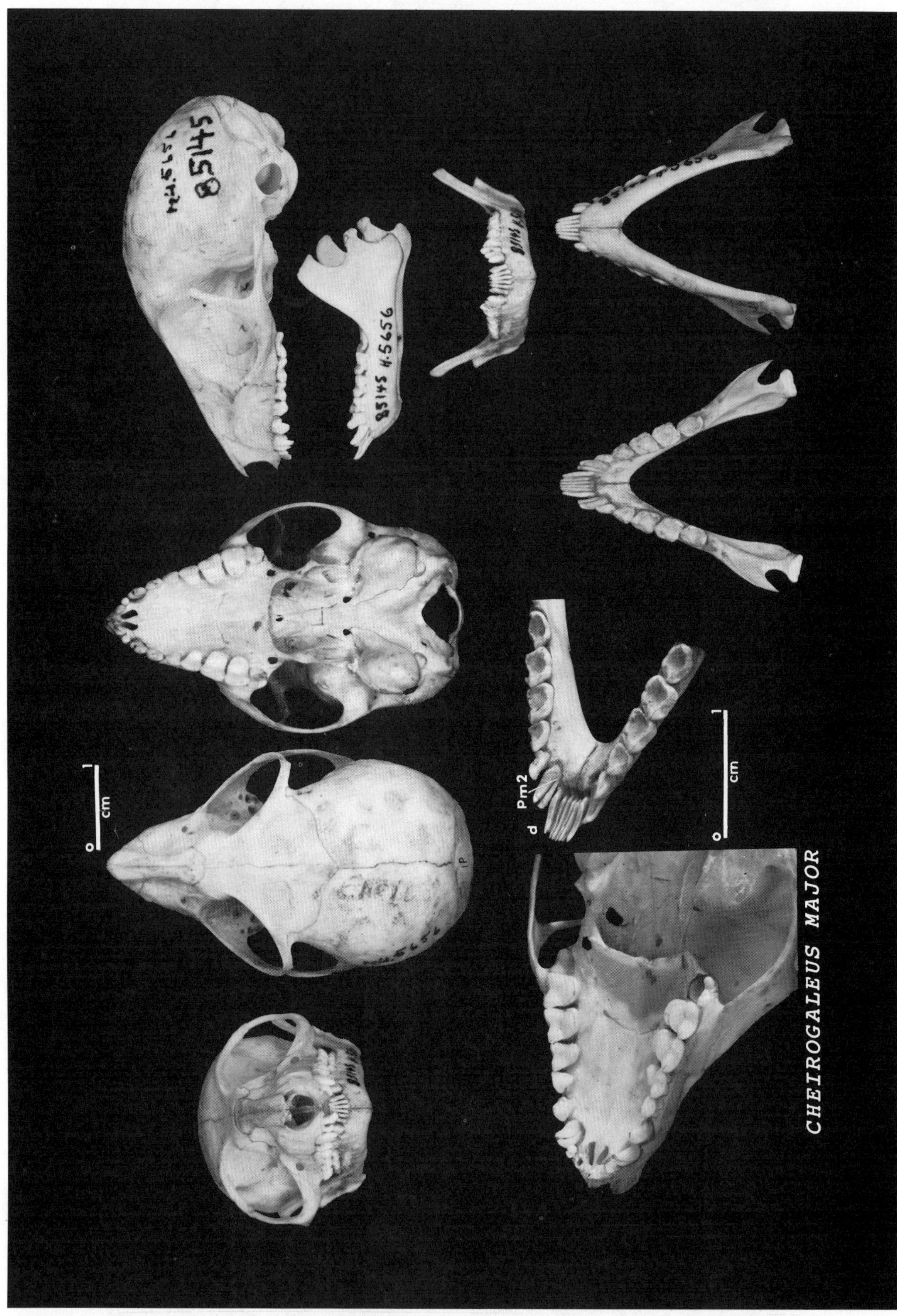

Fig. IV.88. *Cheirogaleus major* (FM 85145) (Lemuridae). MADAGASCAR. Wrinkling of upper and lower cheek-teeth enamel and simplification of enamel pattern of lower cheek teeth are advanced conditions evolved within the primitive tritubercular framework; cracked pm_2 is postmortem damage.

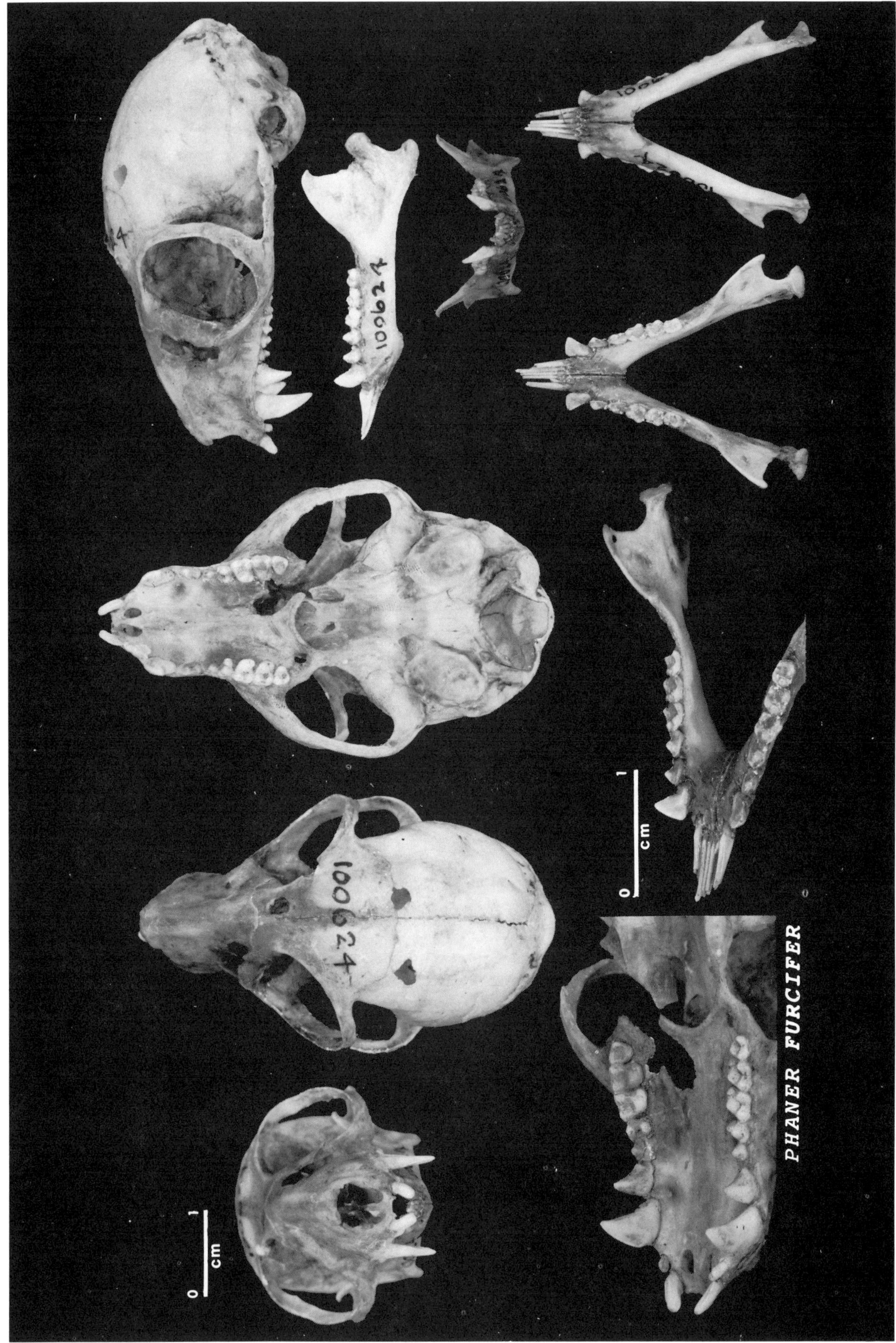

Fig. IV.89. *Phaner furcifer* (AM 100624 ♂) (Lemuridae). MADAGASCAR: Tobiky. Only available skull considerably damaged; tips of lower incisors and canines broken.

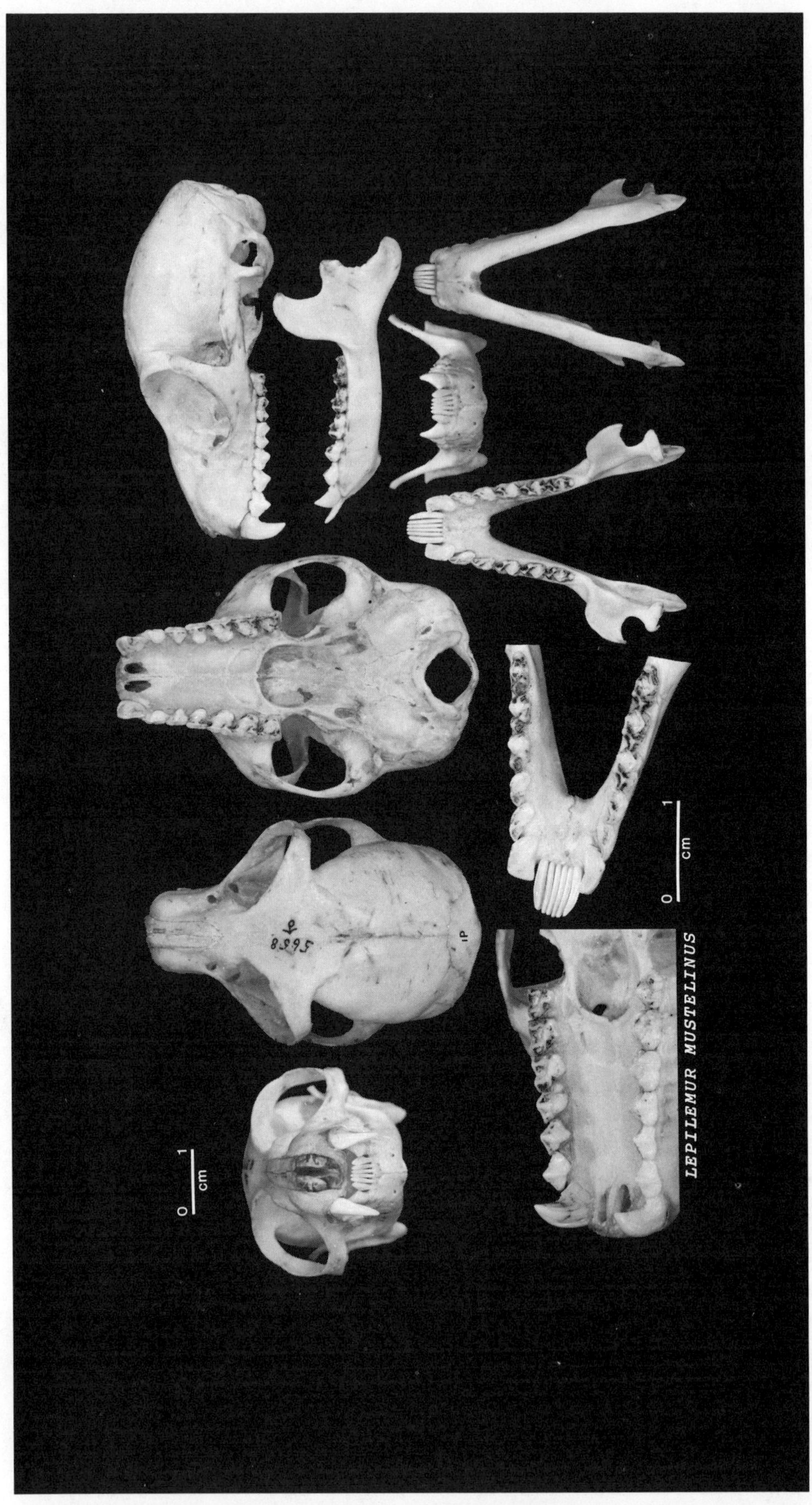

Fig. IV.90. *Lepilemur mustelinus* (FM 5658 ♂) (Lemuridae). MADAGASCAR. Molars essentially tritubercular, but a rudimentary hypocone may be present in some teeth; trend toward secondary dilambdomorphism is apparent.

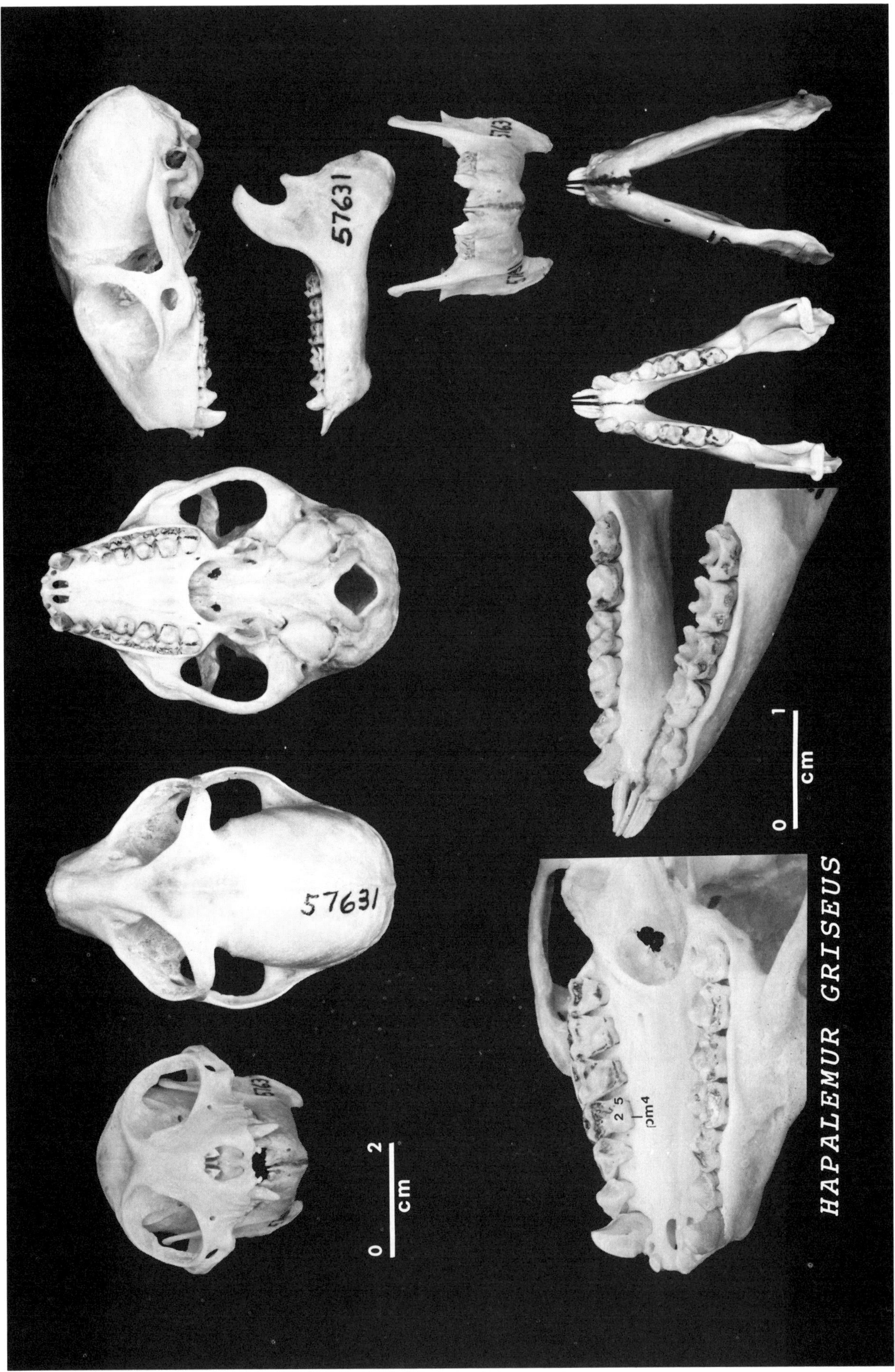

Fig. IV.91. *Hapalemur griseus* (FM 57631 ♀) (Lemuridae). MADAGASCAR. Last upper premolar (pm^4) completely molarized but hypocone (*5*) rudimentary or low in pm^4–m^3.

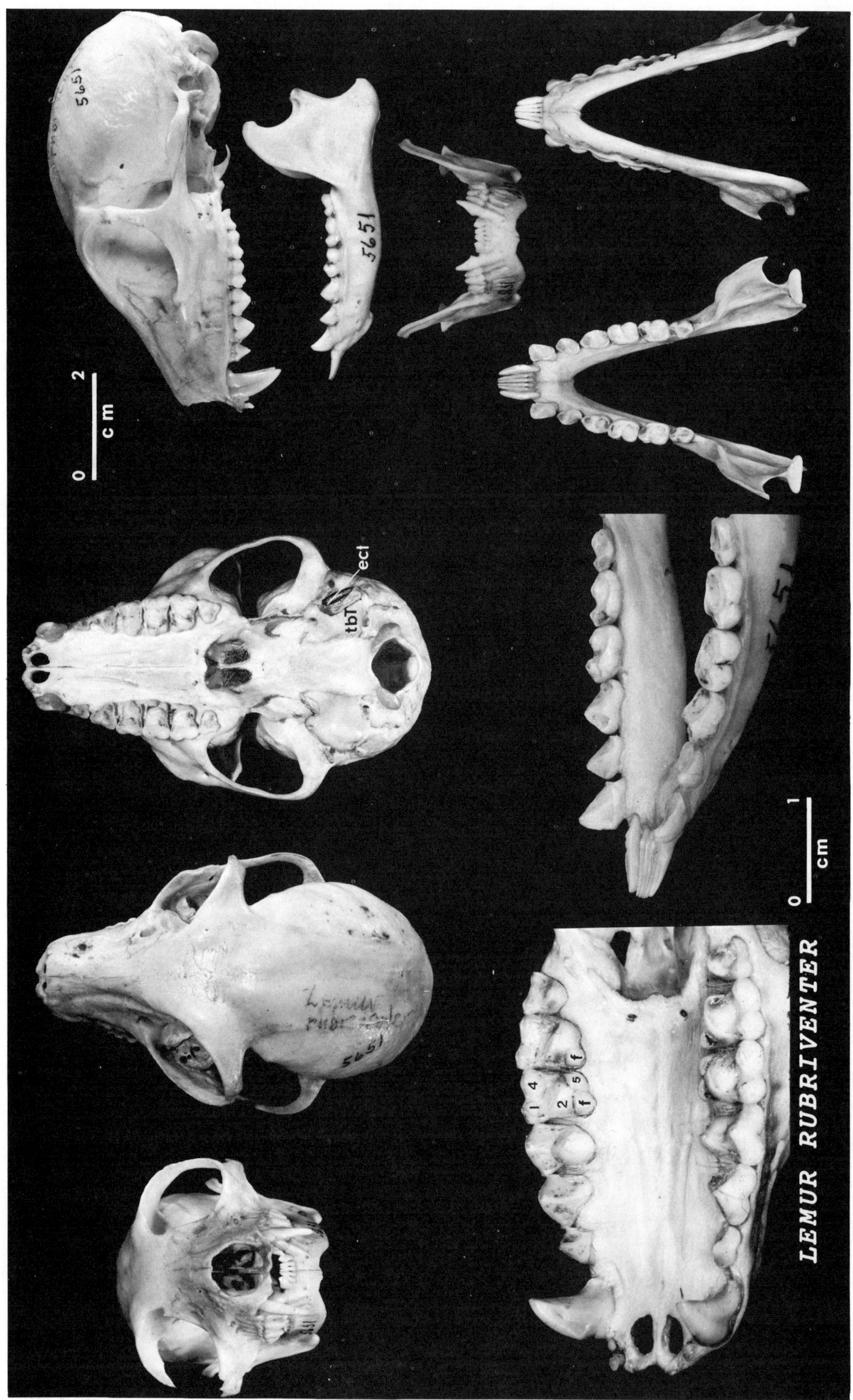

Fig. IV.92. *Lemur rubriventer* (FM 5651 ♂) (Lemuridae). MADAGASCAR. Left tympanic bulla (*tbT*) dissected to expose ectotympanic annulus (*ect*); protostyle (entostyle–*f*) is exceptionally well developed in *Lemur*.

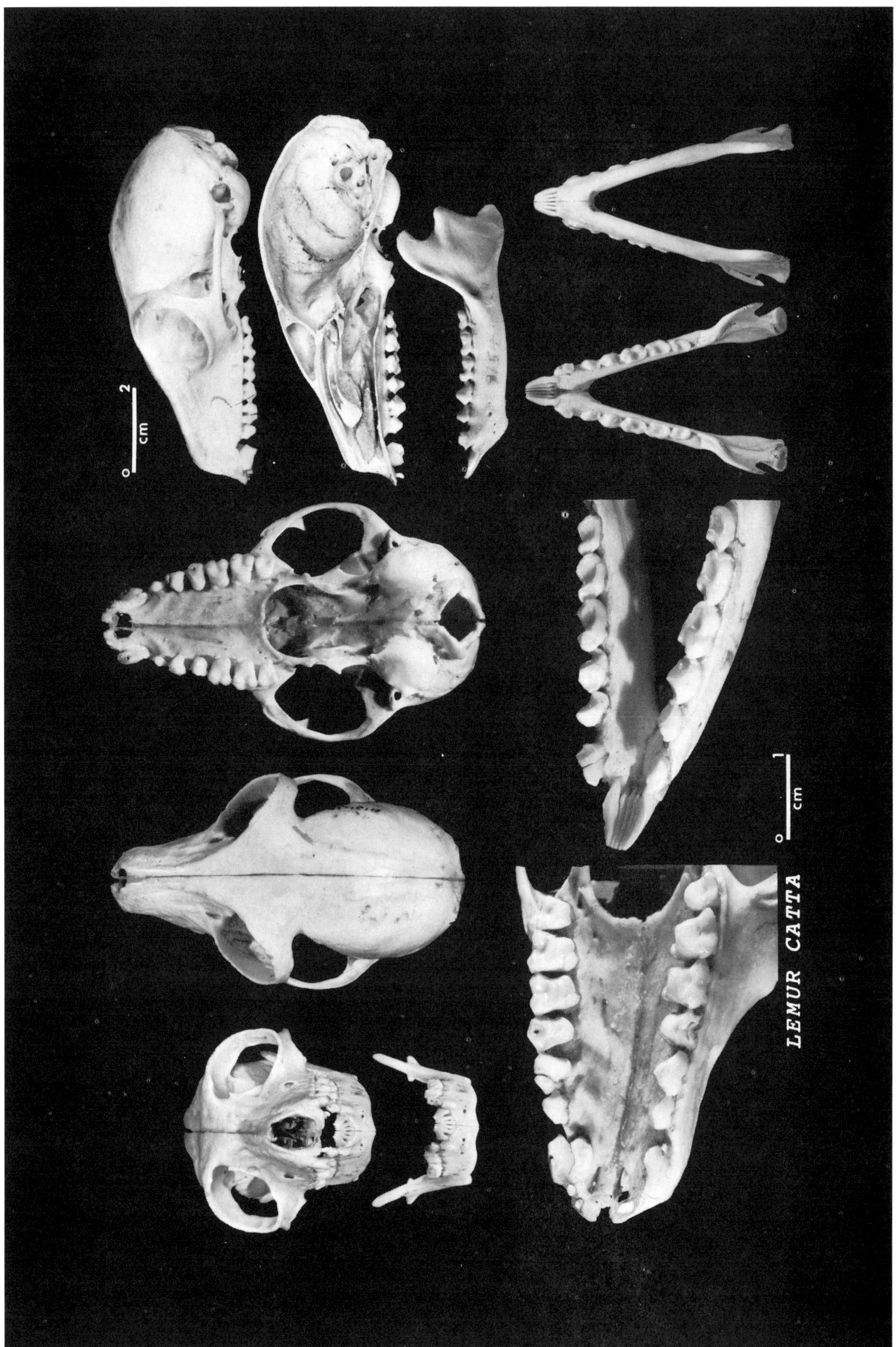

Fig. IV.93. *Lemur catta* (FM 81542 ♂) (Lemuridae). MADAGASCAR. Skull bisected, the halves cemented together for dorsal and ventral aspects; upper canines extremely worn; pm^3 cracked, pm^4 carious; see fig IV.23 for elements exposed in sagittal section.

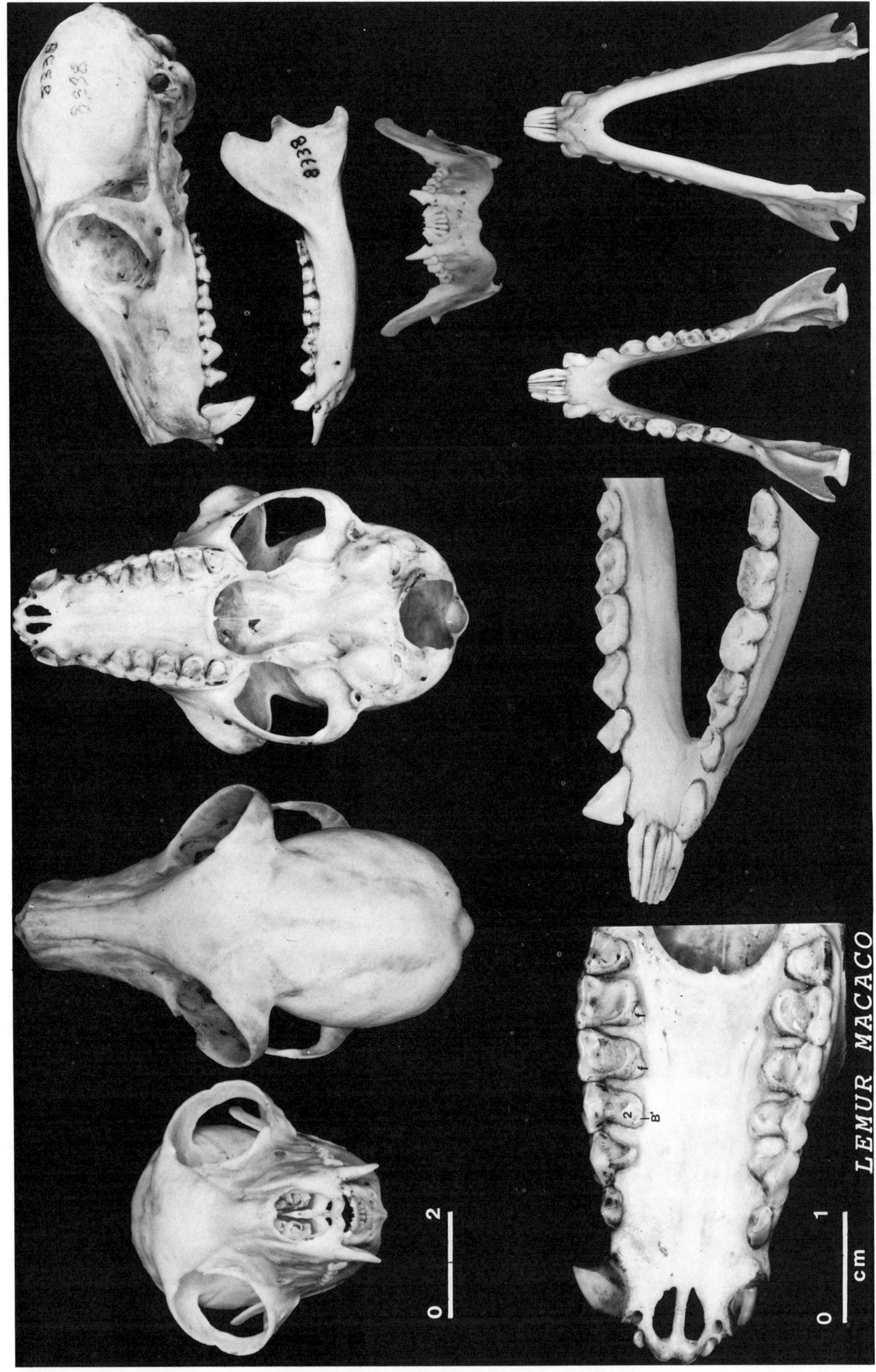

Fig. IV.94. *Lemur macaco* (FM 8338 ♂) (Lemuridae). MADAGASCAR. Molarization of pm^4 well advanced.

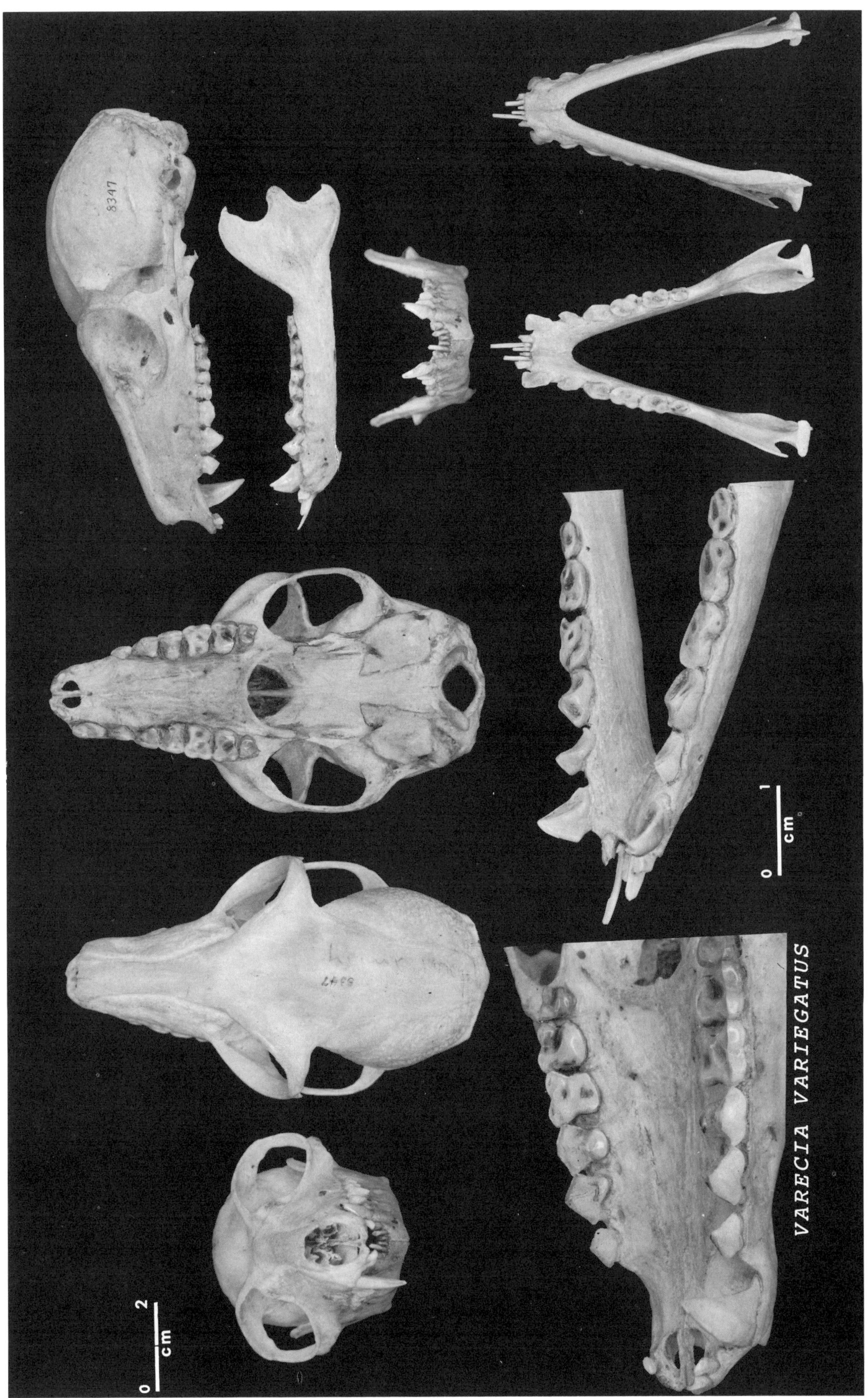

Fig. IV.95. *Varecia variegata* (FM 8347 ♂) (Lemuridae). MADAGASCAR. Upper left canine missing; lower front teeth damaged.

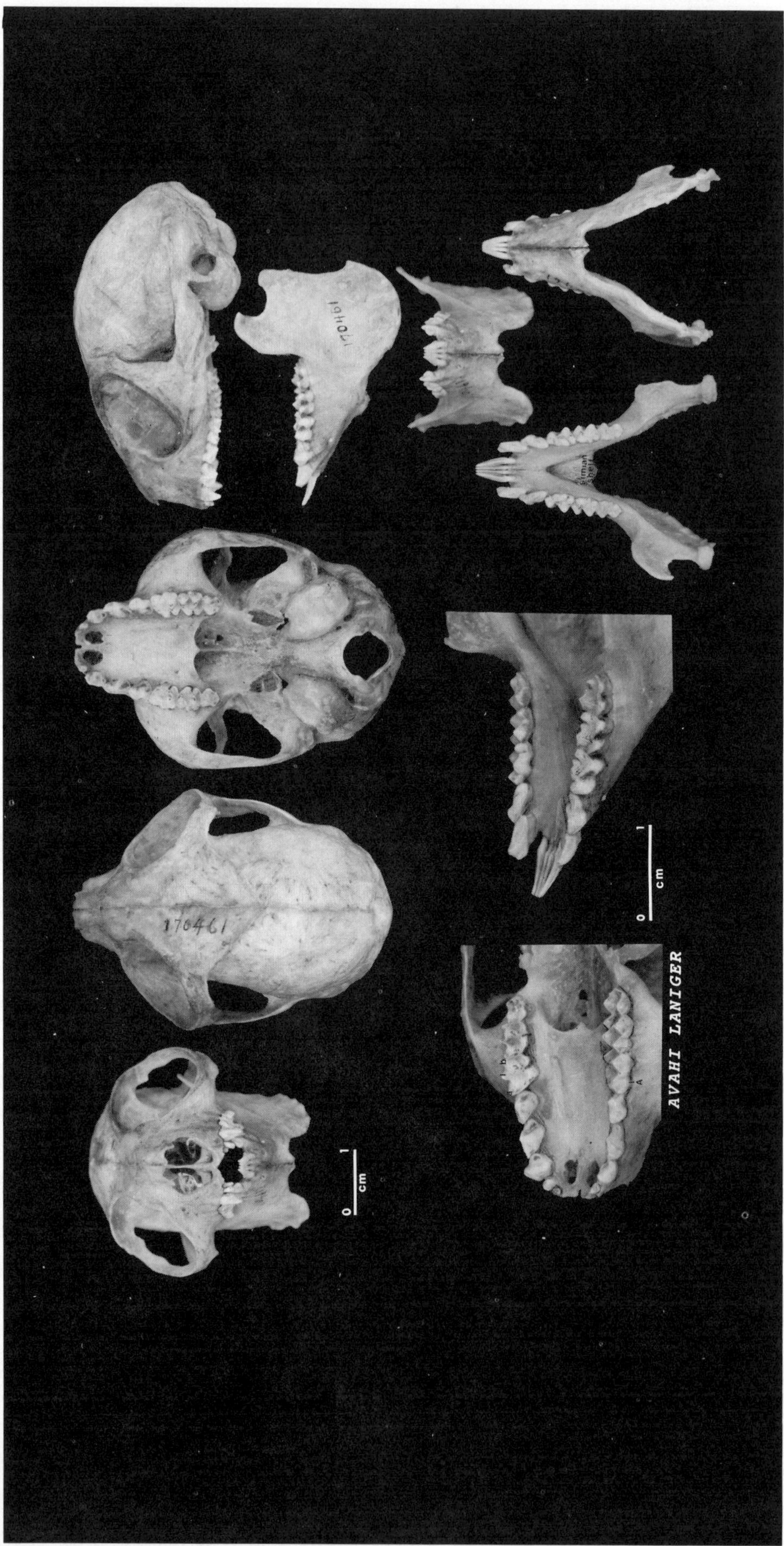

Fig. IV.96. *Avahi laniger* (AM 170461 ♂) (Indriidae). MADAGASCAR. Eminiminy, Fort Dauphin. Secondarily dilambdomorphic upper molars with large buccal shelf (*A*); mesostyle (ectostyle *l*) and simian shelf well developed in the Indriidae.

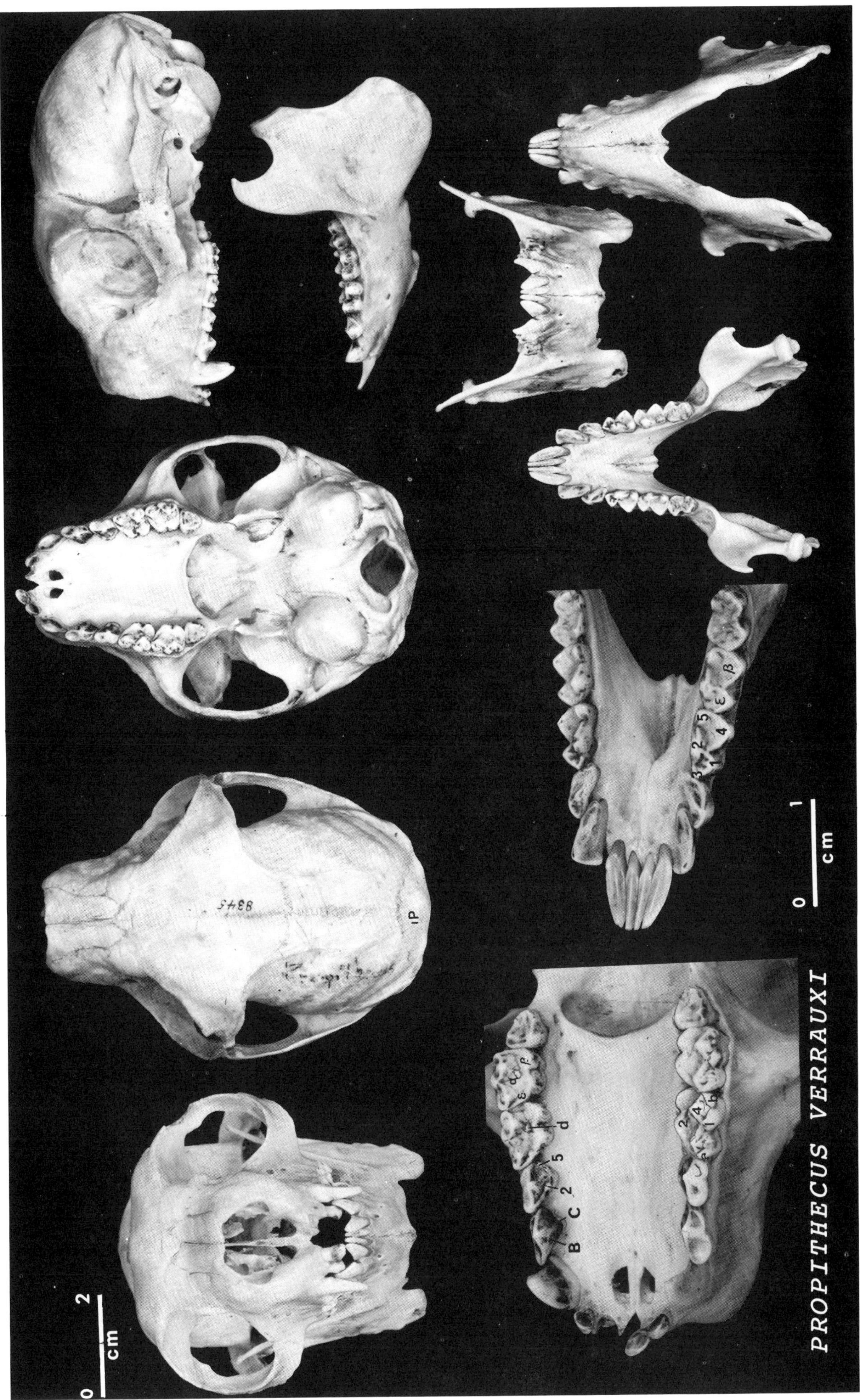

Fig. IV.97. *Propithecus verreauxi* (FM 8345 ♀) (Indriidae). MADAGASCAR. Design of upper molars intermediate between euthemorphic type as in *Microcebus* and secondarily dilambdomorphic type as in *Avahi;* lateral cranial aspect is right side reversed.

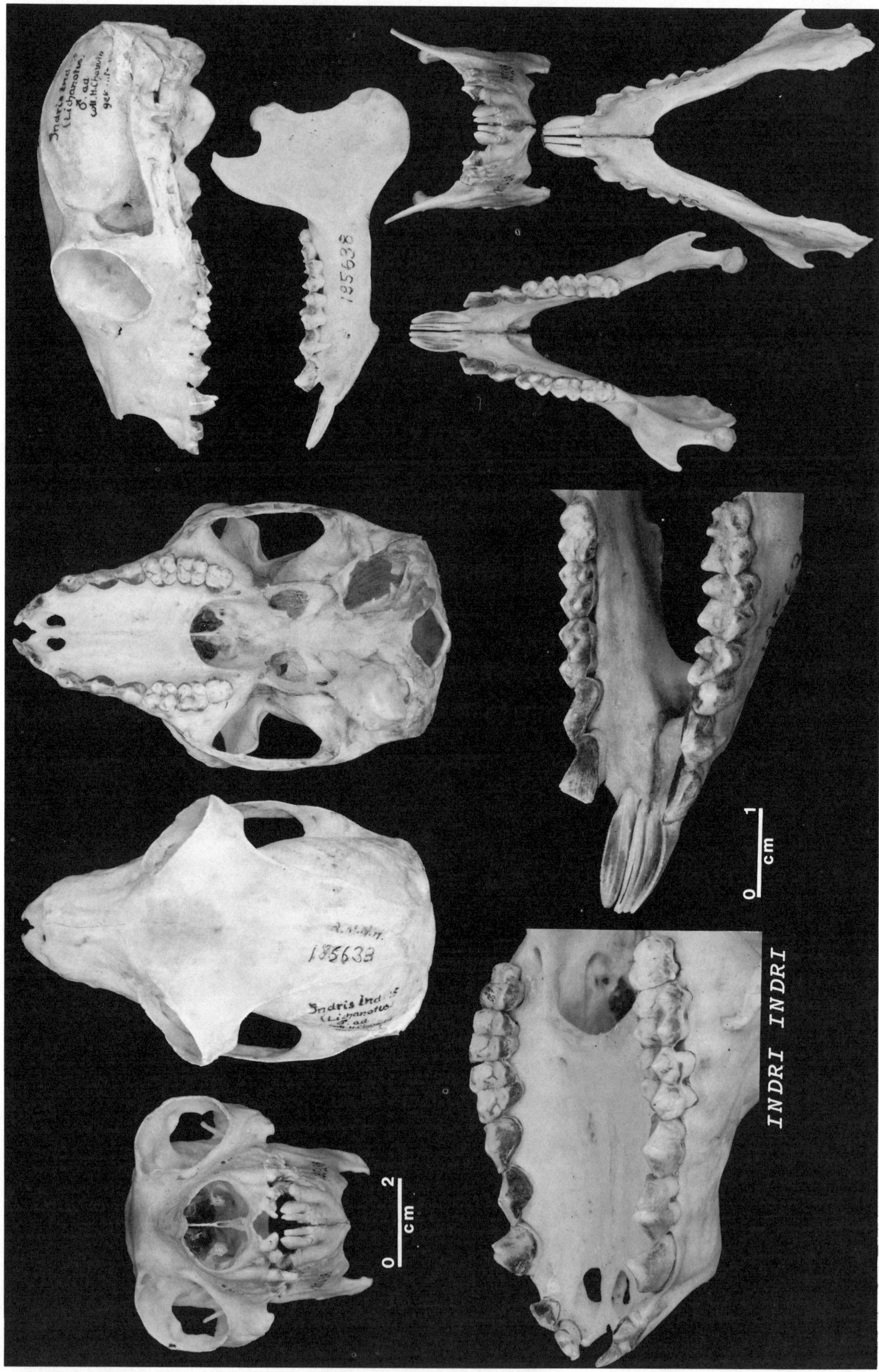

Fig. IV.98. *Indri indri* (AM 185638 ♂) (Indriidae). MADAGASCAR.

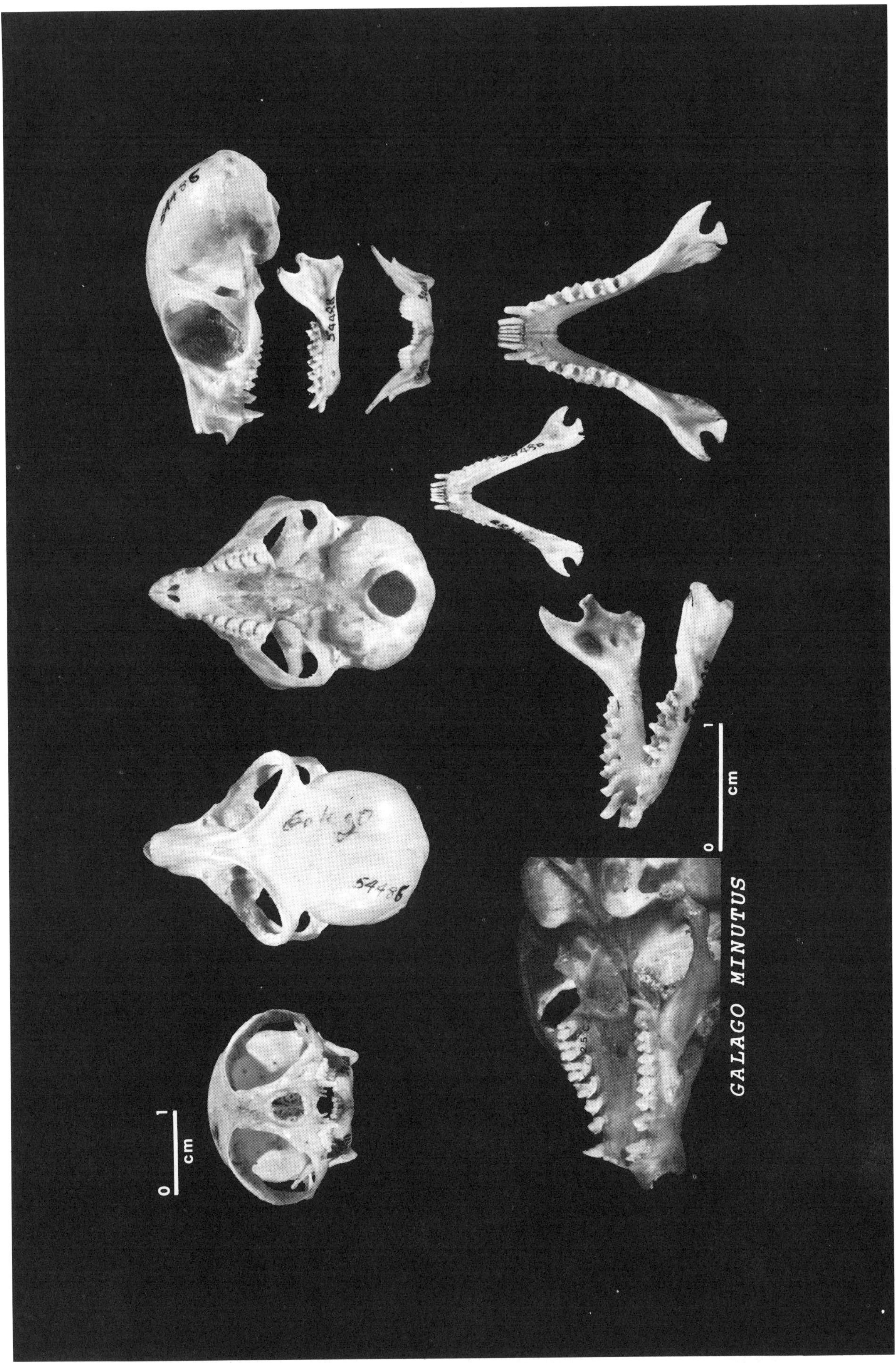

Fig. IV.99. *Galago minutus* (FM 54488 0) (Galagidae). GHANA. Posterolingual cingulum (*C*) of pm^4–m^3 produced as talon in lorisoids.

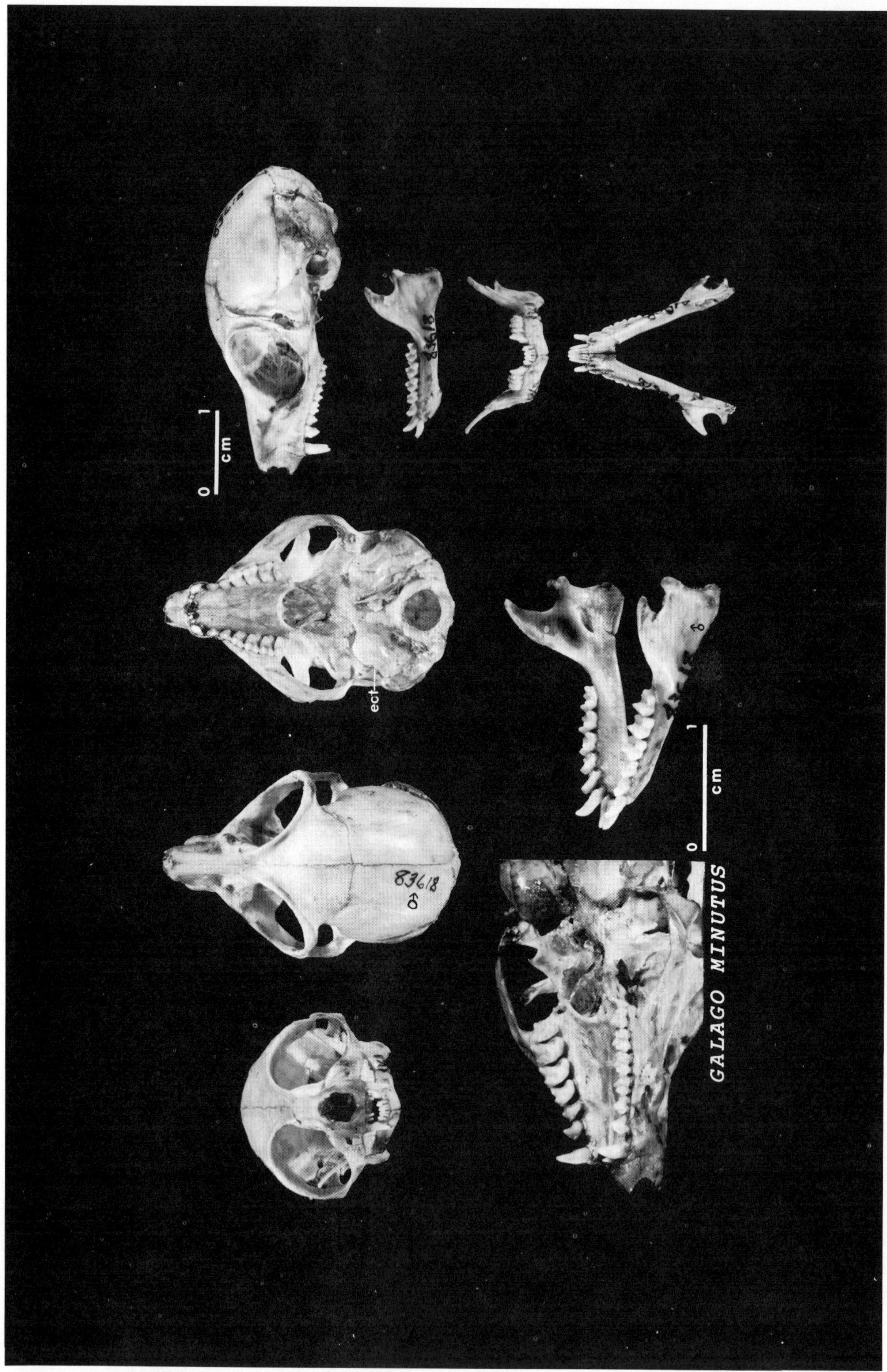

Fig. IV.100. *Galago minutus* (FM 83618 ♂) (Galagidae). ANGOLA: Gabela.

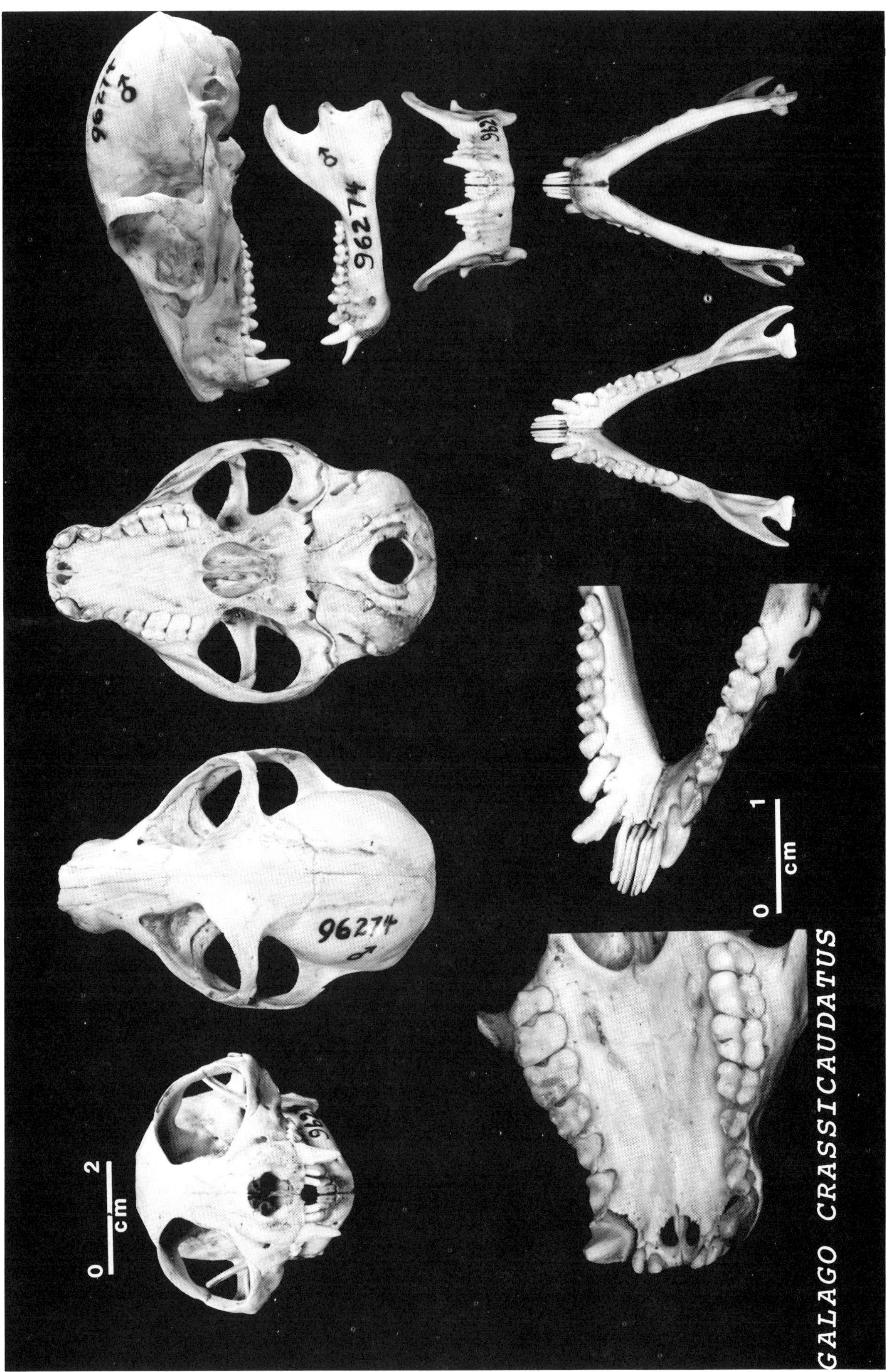

Fig. IV.101. *Galago crassicaudatus* (FM 96274 ♂) (Galagidae). NORTHERN RHODESIA: Fort Jameson.

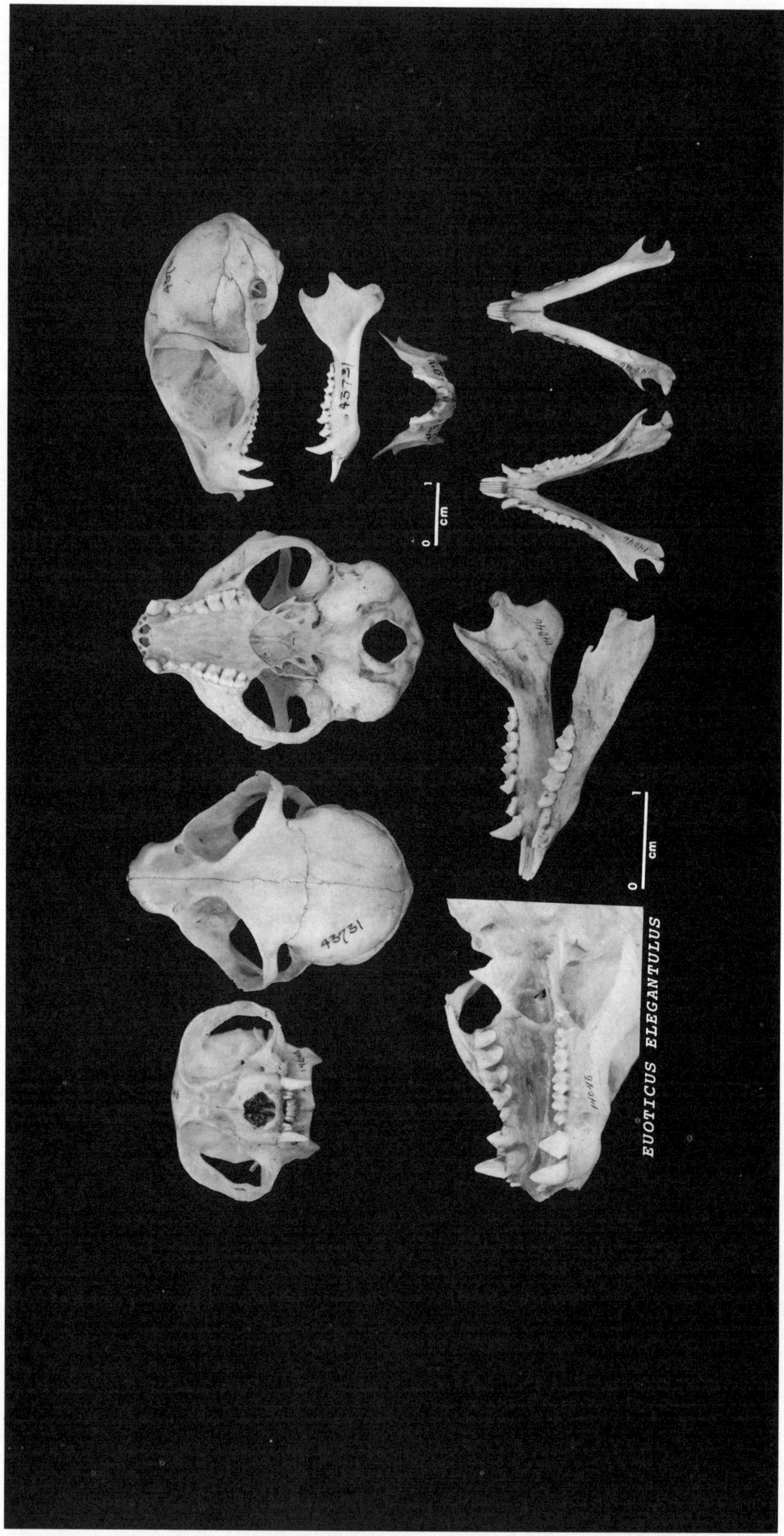

Fig. IV.102. *Euoticus elegantulus* (FM 43731 ♂; FM 14046 ♀) (Galagidae). CAMEROON: Sakbayeme (43731); Batuga (FM 14046). Bones of skull 43731 are complete except for missing process of right lateral pterygoid plate and upper incisors; skull 14046 shows the full dentition.

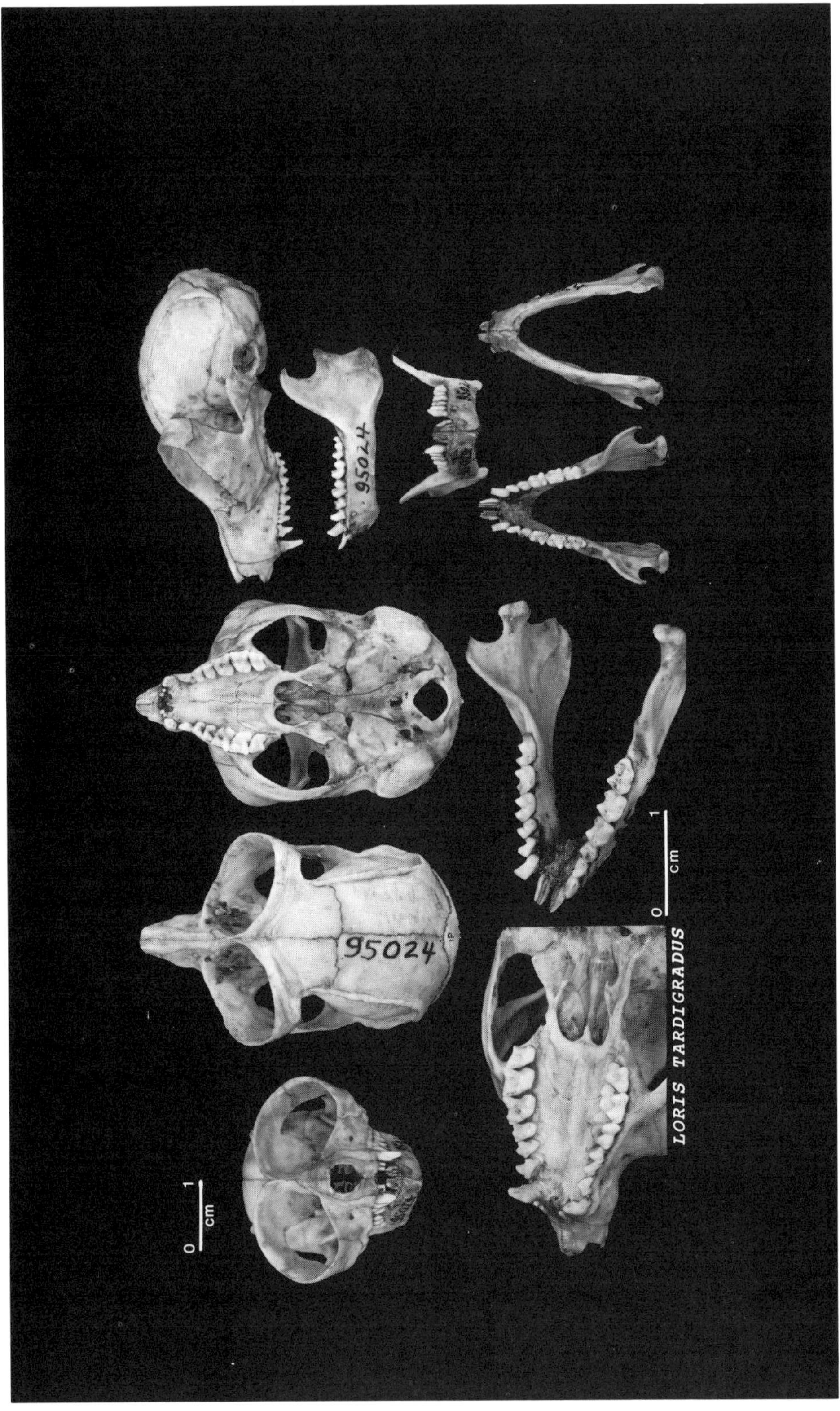

Fig. IV.103. *Loris tardigradus* (FM 95024 ♂) (Lorisidae). SRI LANKA: Pindeniya.

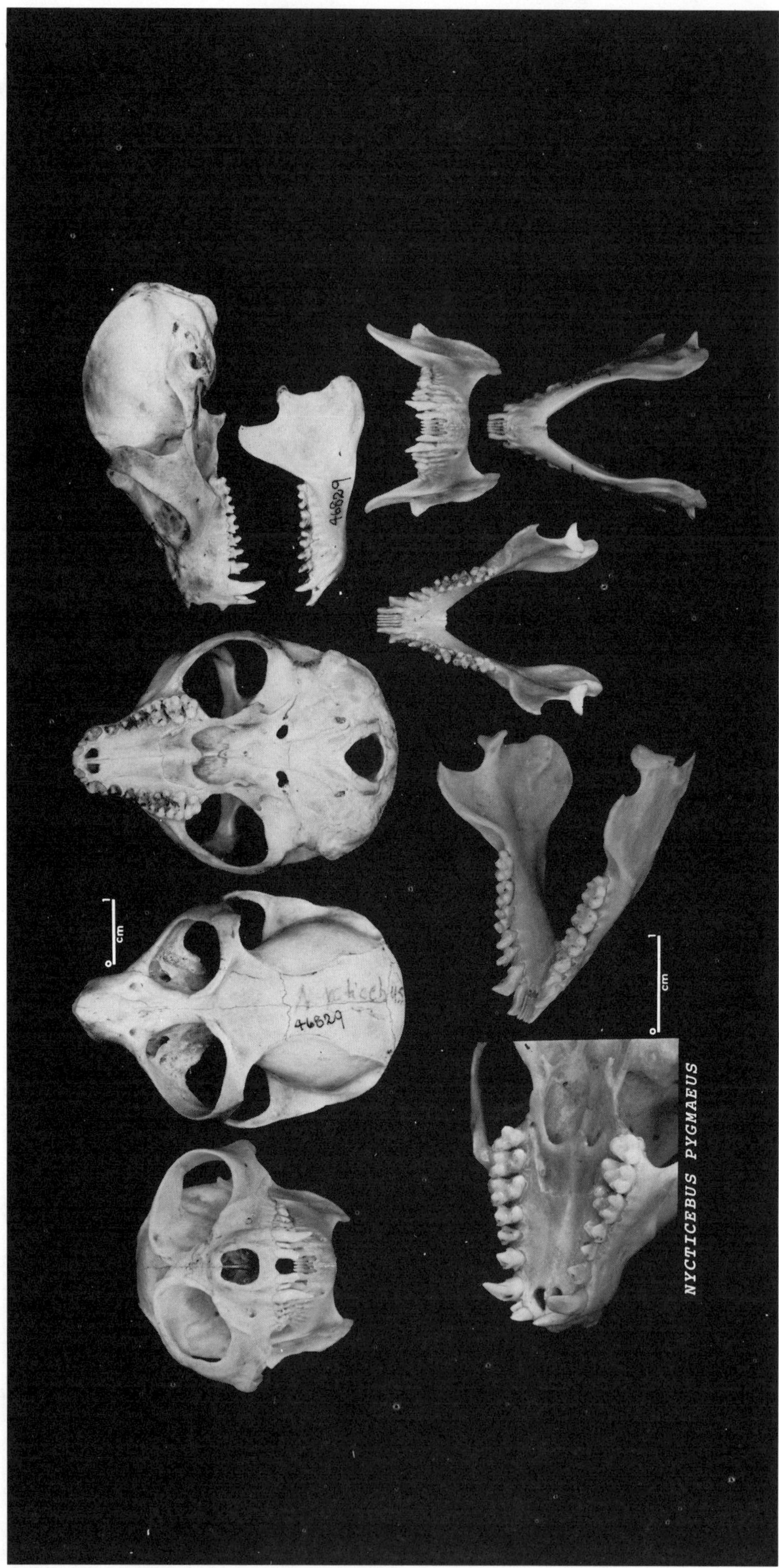

Fig. IV.104. *Nycticebus pygmaeus* (FM 46829 ♀) (Lorisidae). VIET NAM: Annam.

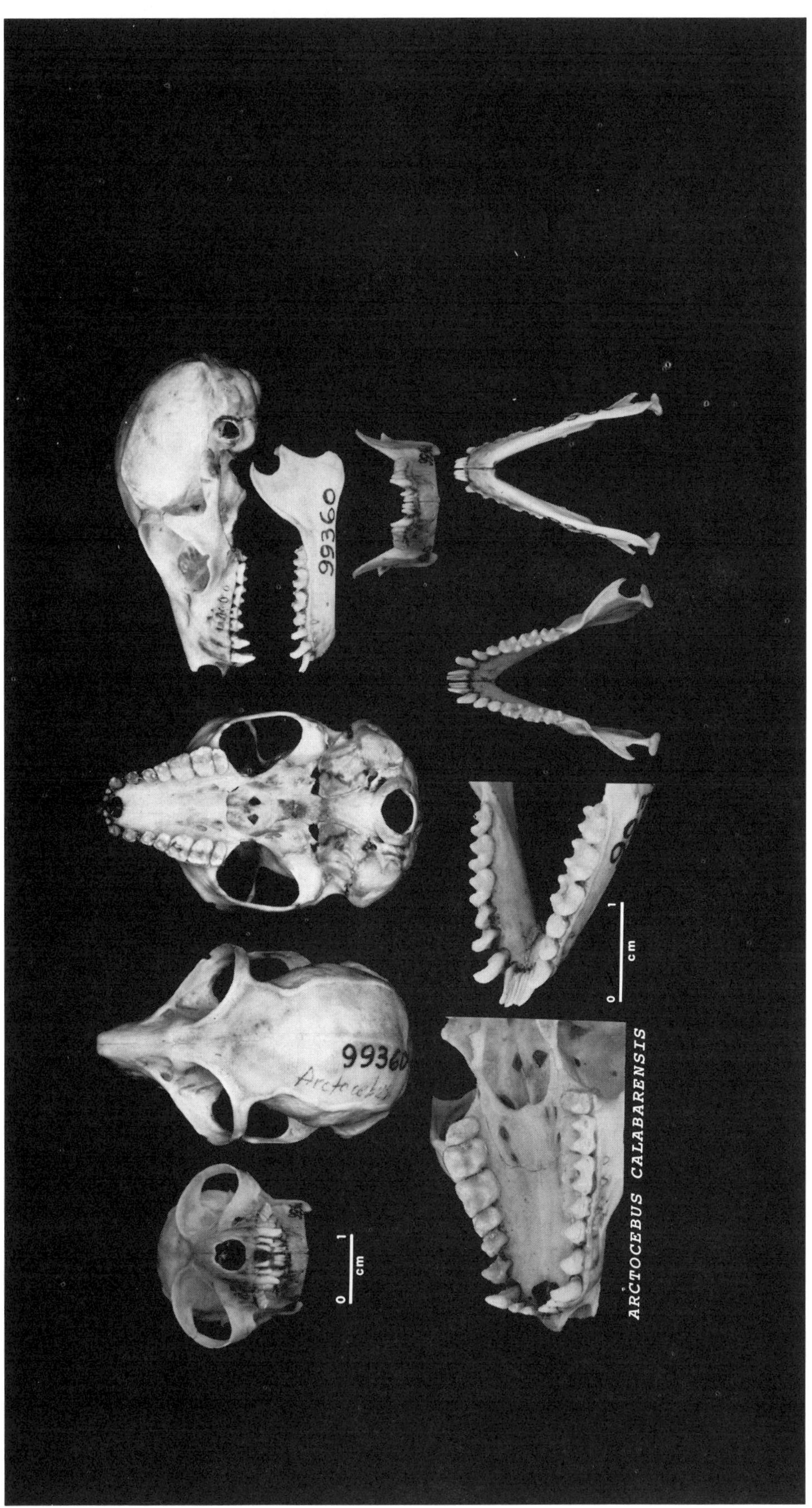

Fig. IV.105. *Arctocebus calabarensis* (FM 99360 ♂) (Lorisidae). AFRICA.

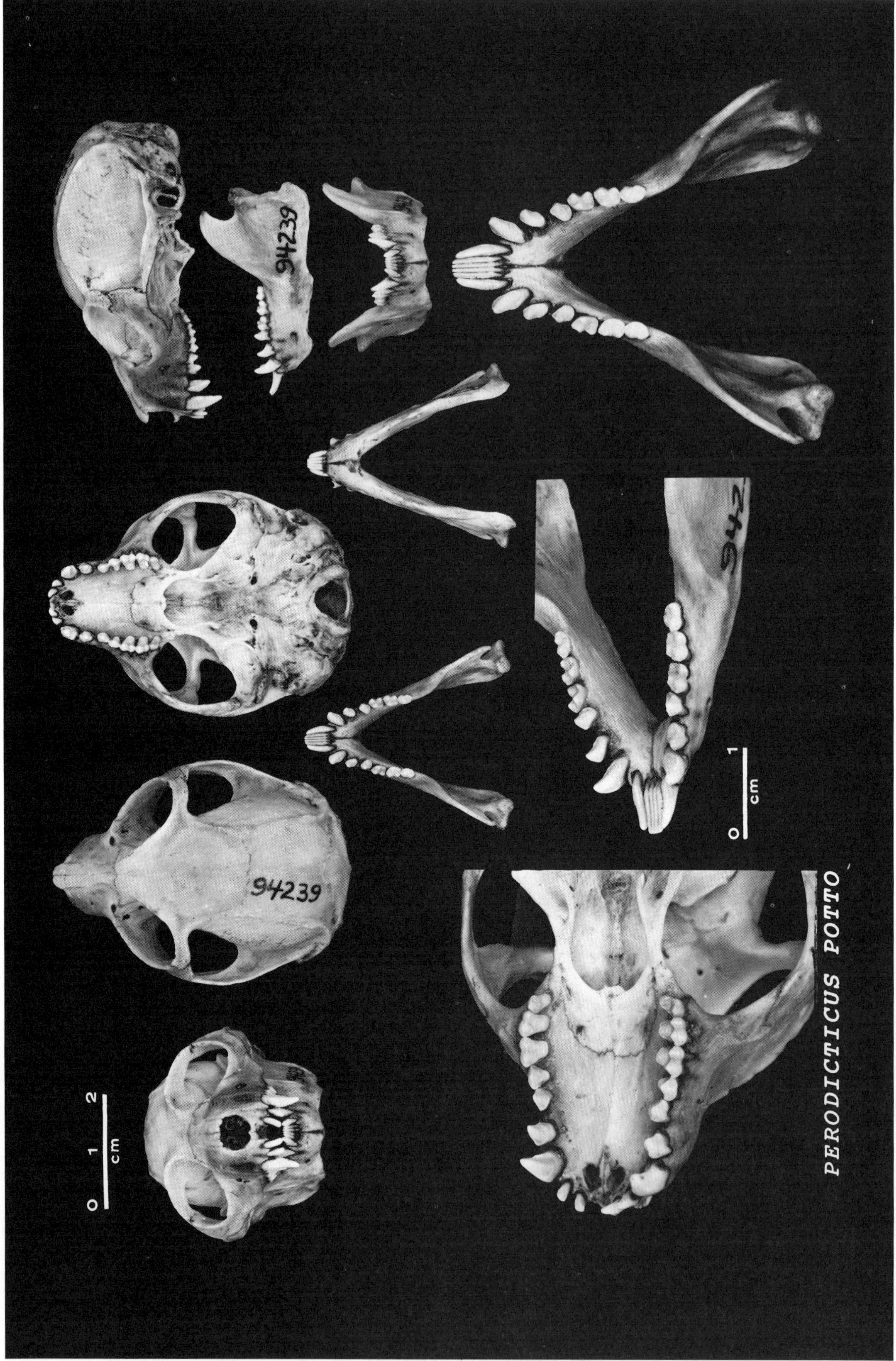

Fig. IV.106. *Perodicticus potto* (FM 94239 ♀) (Lorisidae). AFRICA. Hypocone not always present or well defined; m^3 least molarized among lorisoids.

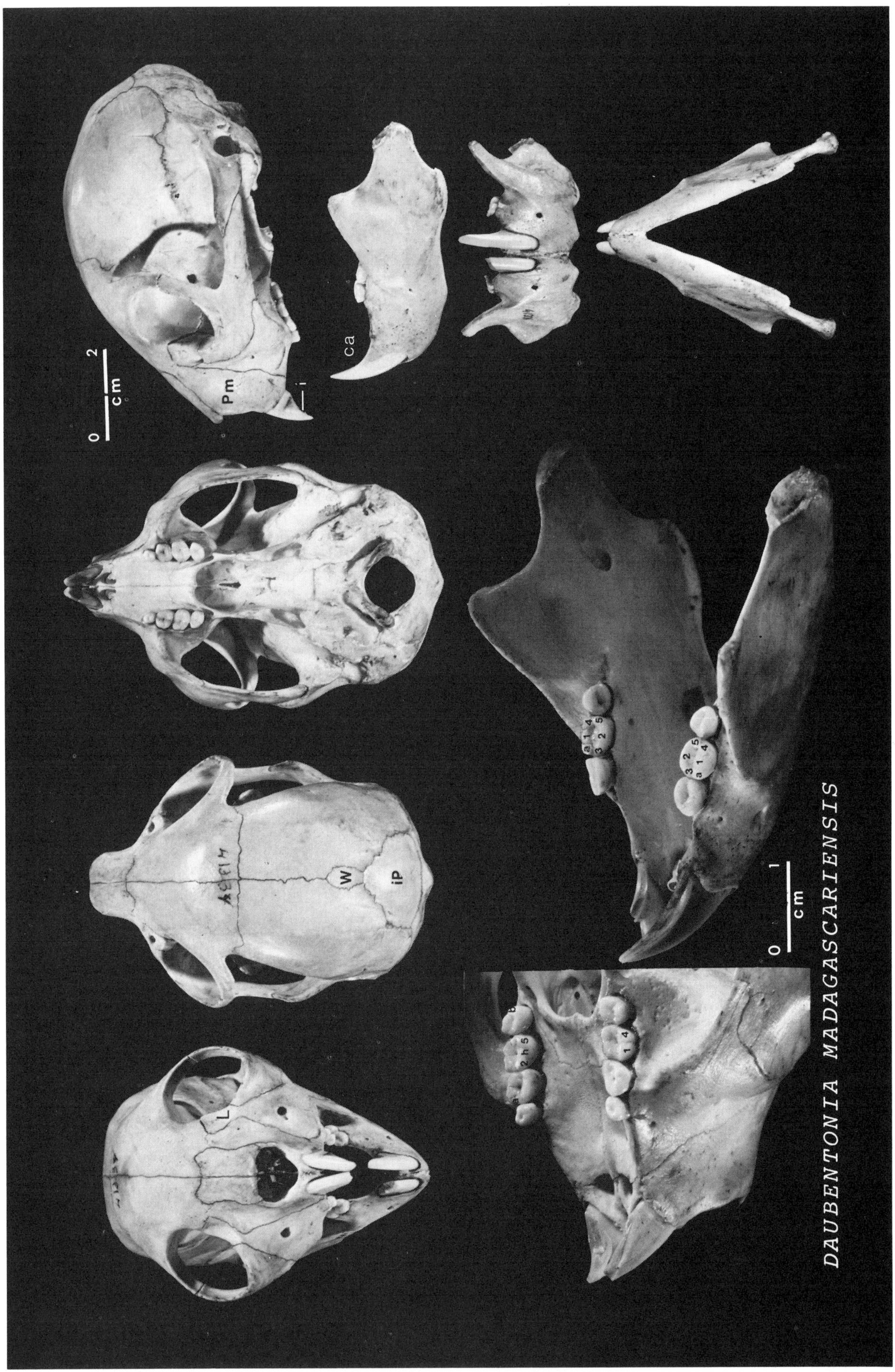

Fig. IV.107. *Daubentonia madagascariensis* (AM 41334 ♀) (Daubentoniidae). MADAGASCAR. The Wormian or sutural bone (*W*) lies anteriad to the interparietal bone (*iP*).

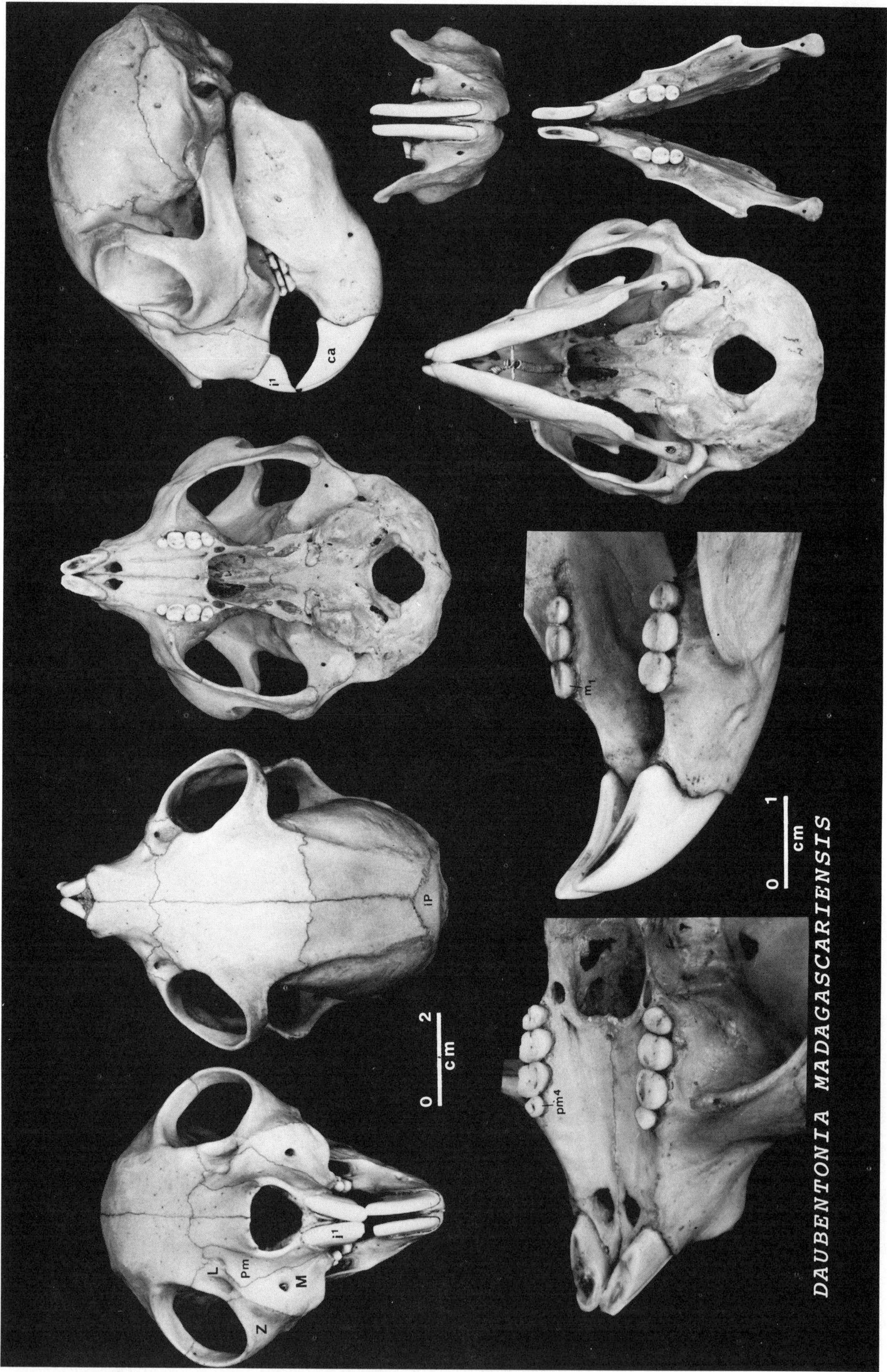

Fig. IV.108. *Daubentonia madagascariensis* (FM 15529 ♀) (Daubentoniidae). MADAGASCAR.

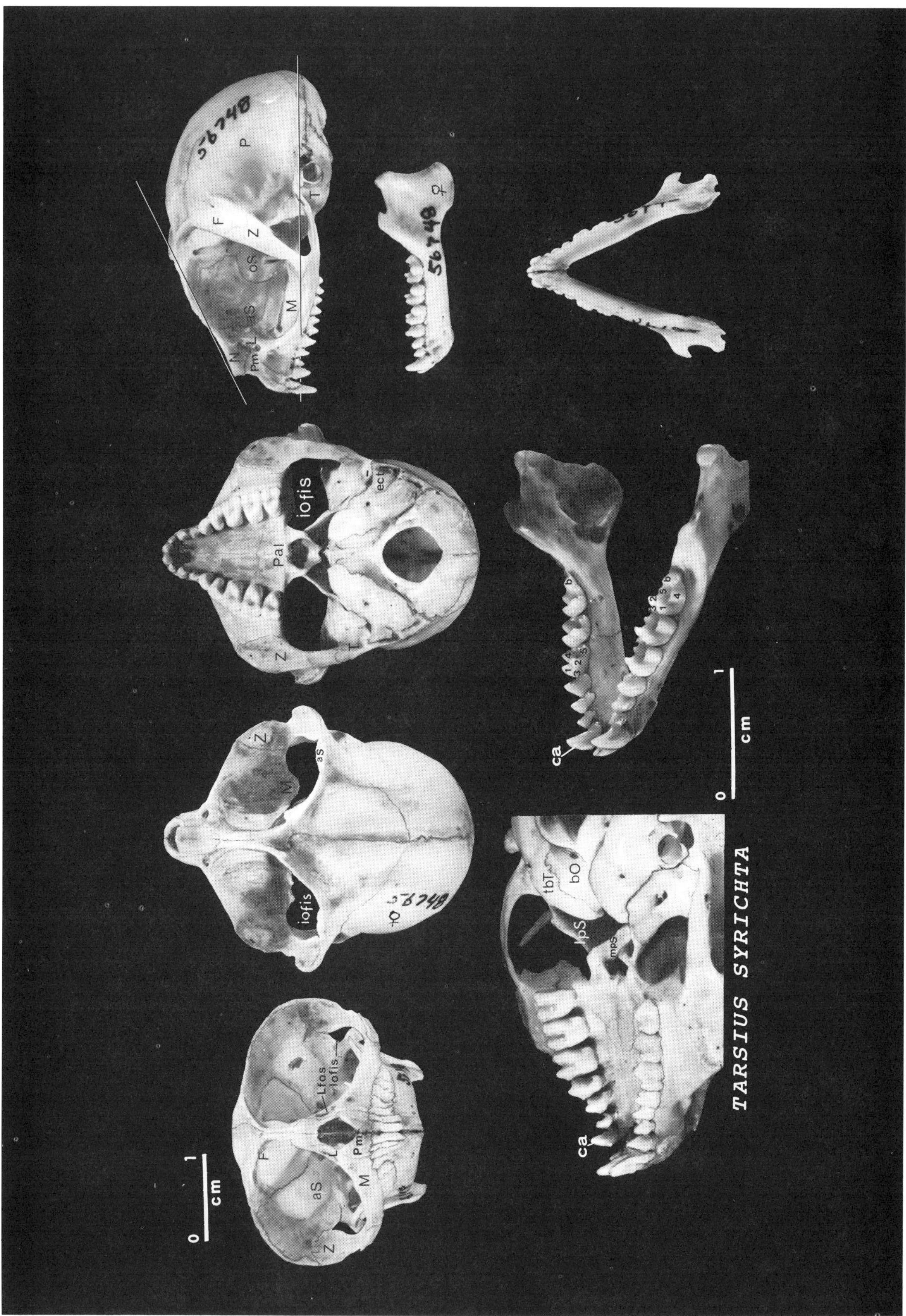

Fig. IV.109. *Tarsius syrichta* (FM 56748 ♀) (Tarsiidae). PHILIPPINES: Davao Caburan. The primitively long muzzle, facial lacrimal fossa (*Lfos*), enlarged orbits, large inferior orbital fissure (*iofis*), tubular external auditory meatus (*ect*), V-shaped jaws, unossified symphysis menti, make *Tarsius* appear galagine. The enumerated characters, except the enlarged orbits, are either those of primitive primates or common to lorisoid strepsirhines and haplorhines. See fig. IV.8. for labeled figure of *Tarsius* skull.

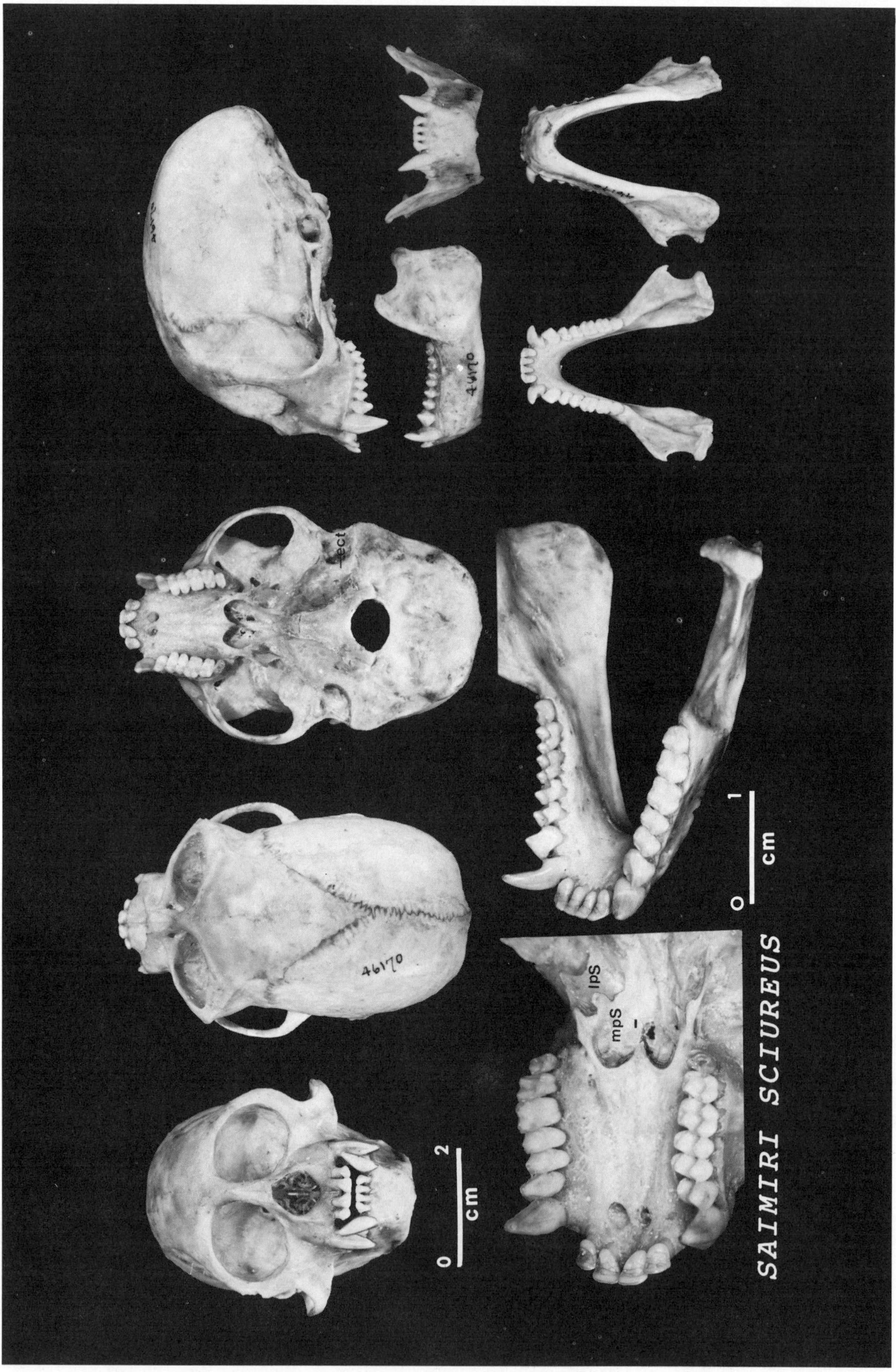

Fig. IV.110. *Saimiri sciureus* (FM 46170 ♂) (Cebidae) (GUYANA: Essequibo, Rockstone. Dorsal aspect not perpendicular to Frankfort plane.

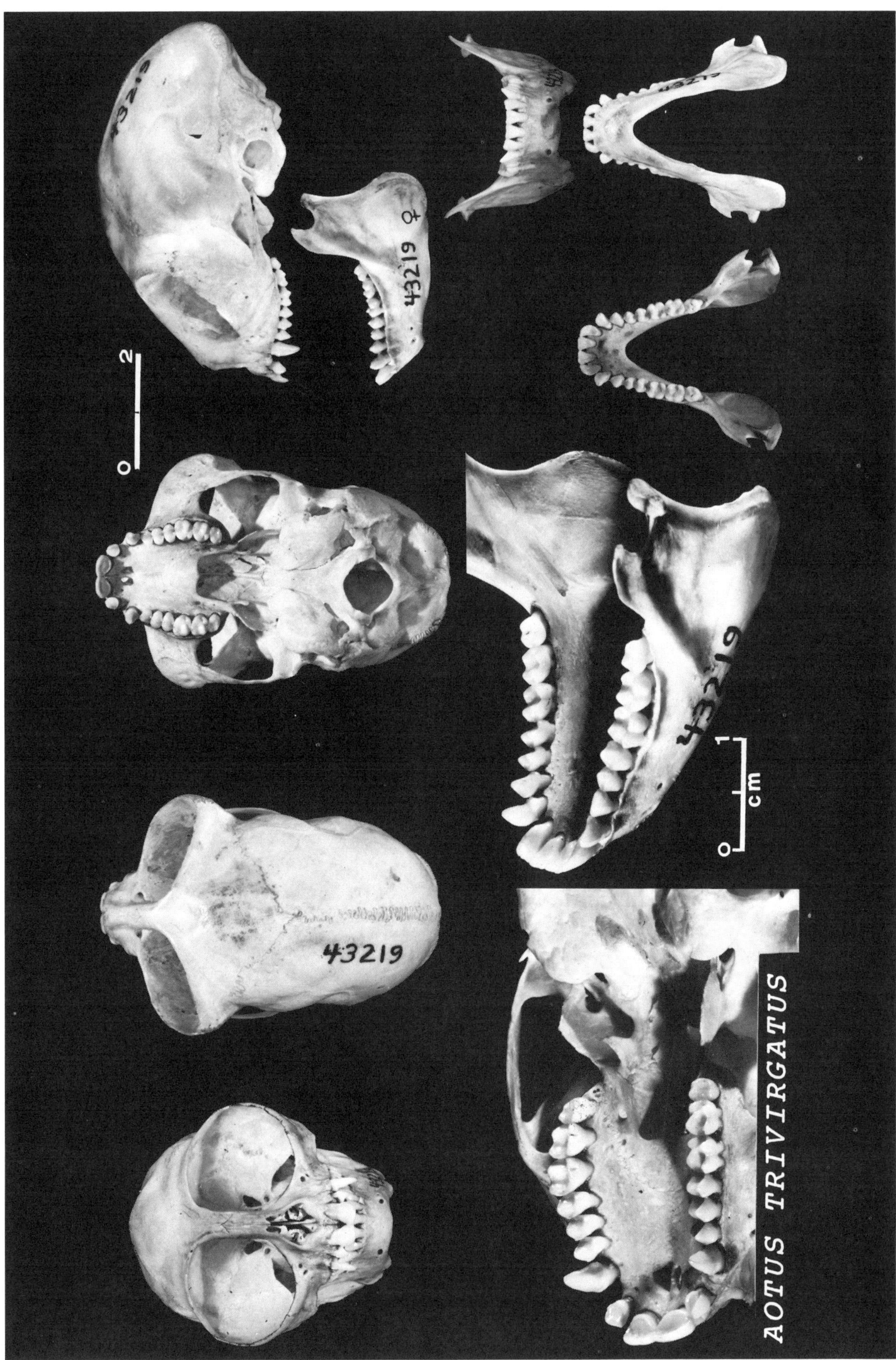

Fig. IV.111. *Aotus trivirgatus* (FM 43219 ♀) (Cebidae). ECUADOR: Napo-Pastazo, Río Pindo Yacu. Dorsal aspect not perpendicular to Frankfort plane; comparatively elongate muzzle comparable to that of *Tarsius* (fig. IV.109) among haplorhines.

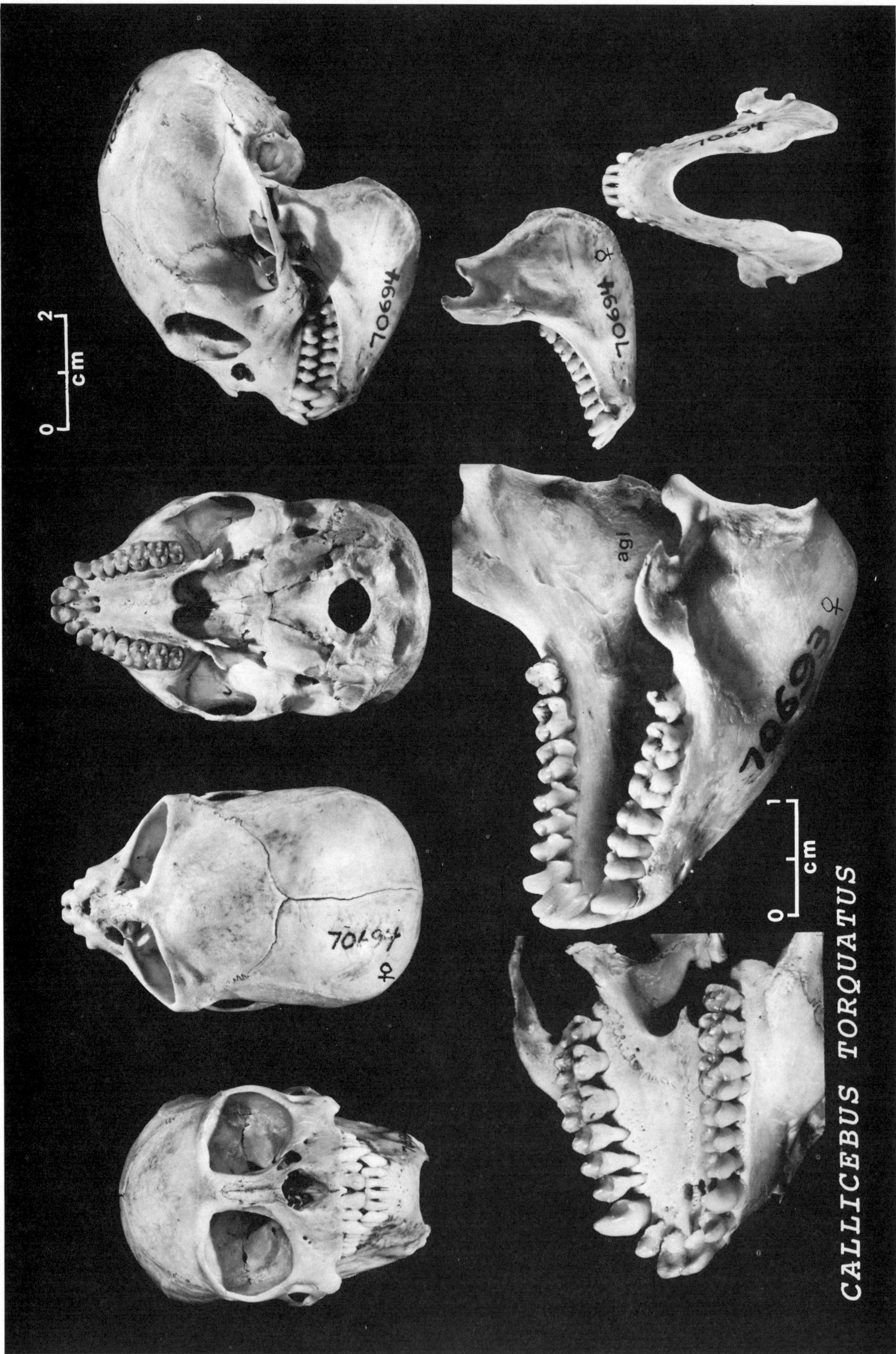

Fig. IV.112. *Callicebus torquatus* (FM 70693 ♀, 70694 ♀) (Cebidae). COLOMBIA: Putumayo, Río Mecaya. Dorsal aspect not perpendicular to Frankfort plane; mandible 70693 substituted in oblique view for 70694 with left ramus damaged.

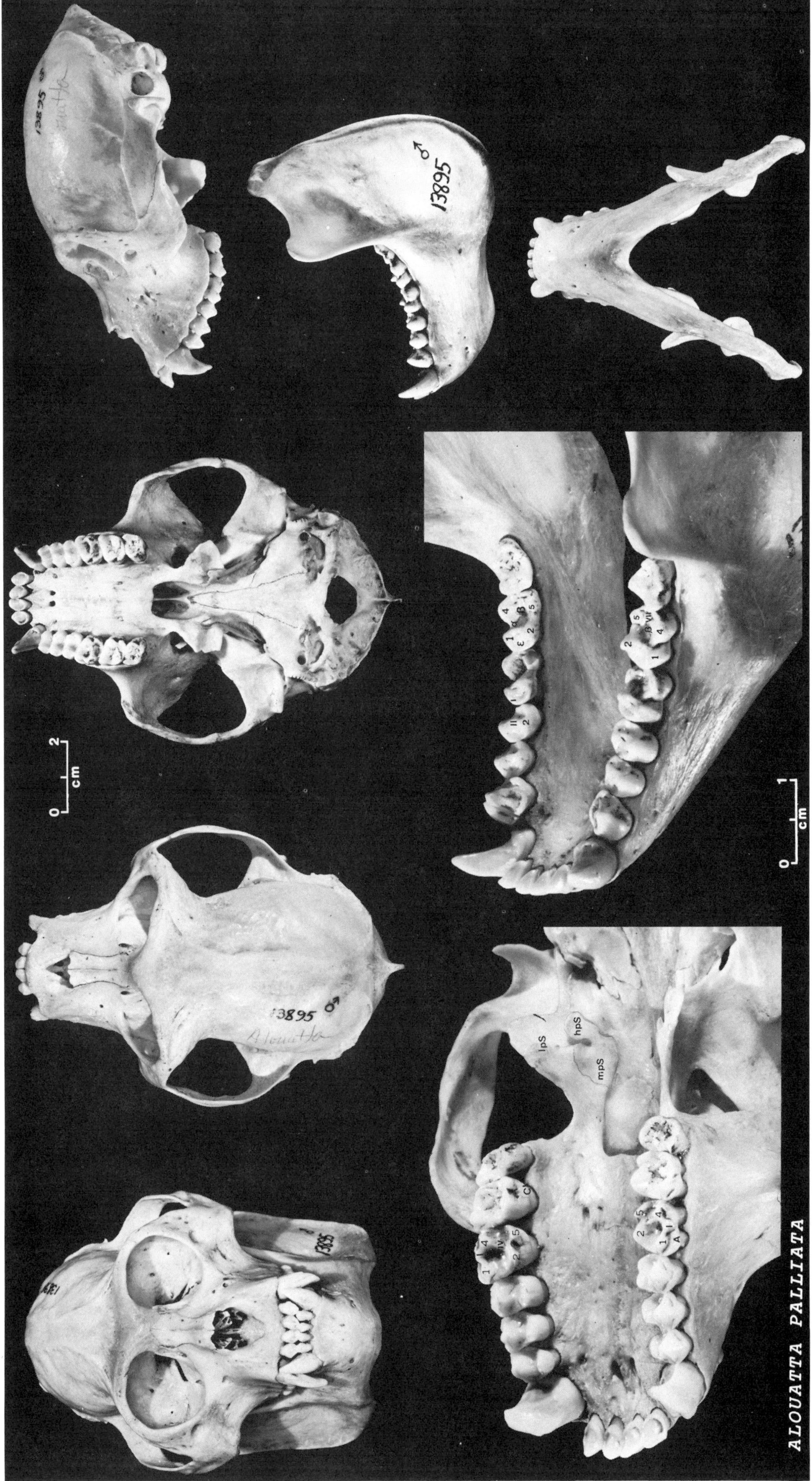

Fig. IV.113. *Alouatta palliata* (FM 13895 ♂) (Cebidae). MEXICO: Veracruz, Achotal. Elongate muzzle is primitive and correlated with the comparatively small, simple brain and nearly horizontal basicranium; mesostyle (or ectostyle—*l*) well developed.

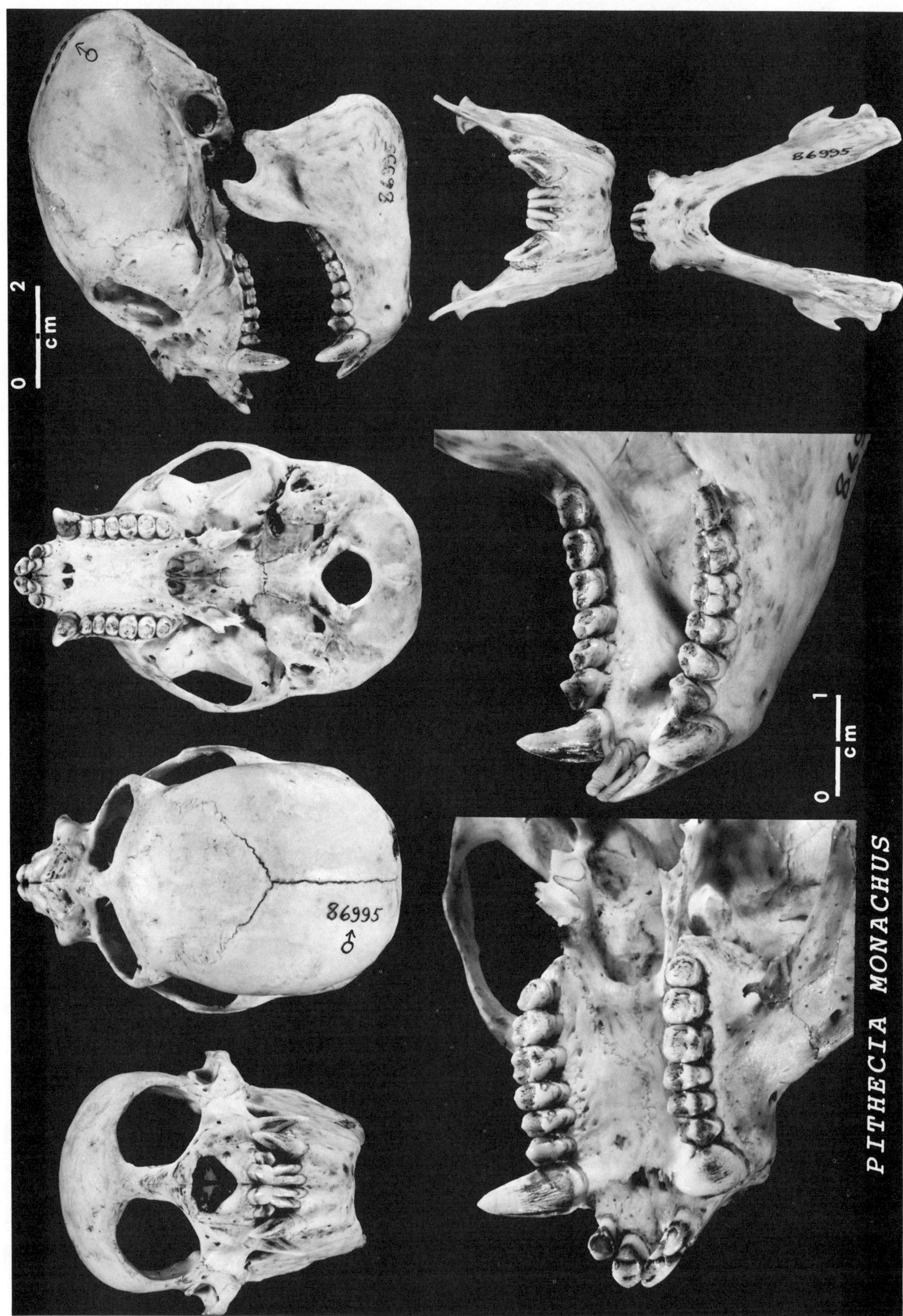

Fig. IV.114. *Pithecia hirsuta* (FM 86995 ♂) (Cebidae). PERU: Loreto, Santa Luisa. Dorsal aspect of skull not perpendicular to Frankfort plane.

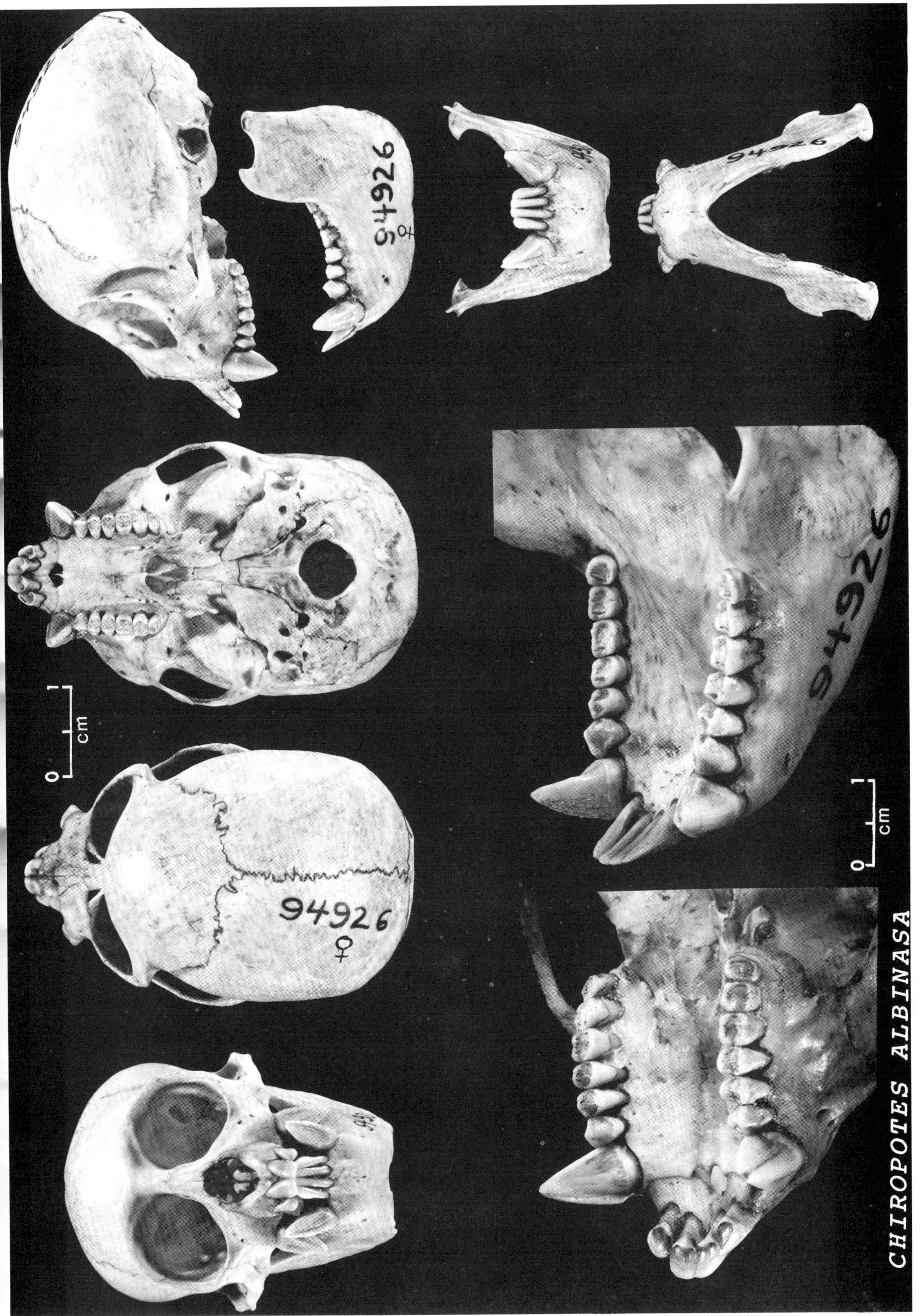

Fig. IV.115. *Chiropotes albinasa* (FM 94926 ♀) (Cebidae). BRAZIL: Pará, Rio Tapaiuna. Dorsal aspect of skull not perpendicular to Frankfort plane.

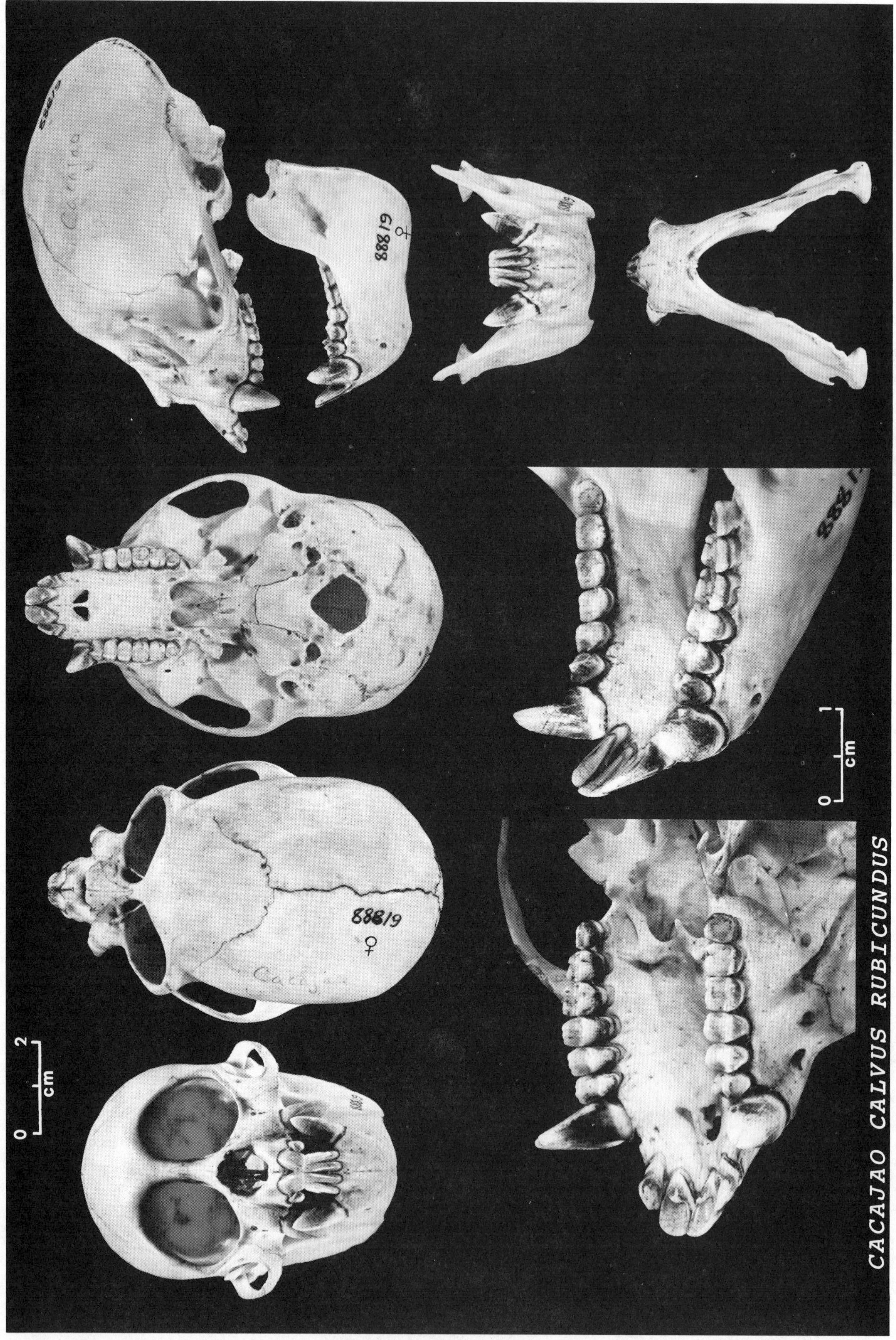

Fig. IV.116. *Cacajao calvus rubicundus* (FM 88819 ♀) (Cebidae). PERU: Loreto, Quebrado Esperanza. Dorsal aspect not perpendicular to Frankfort plane.

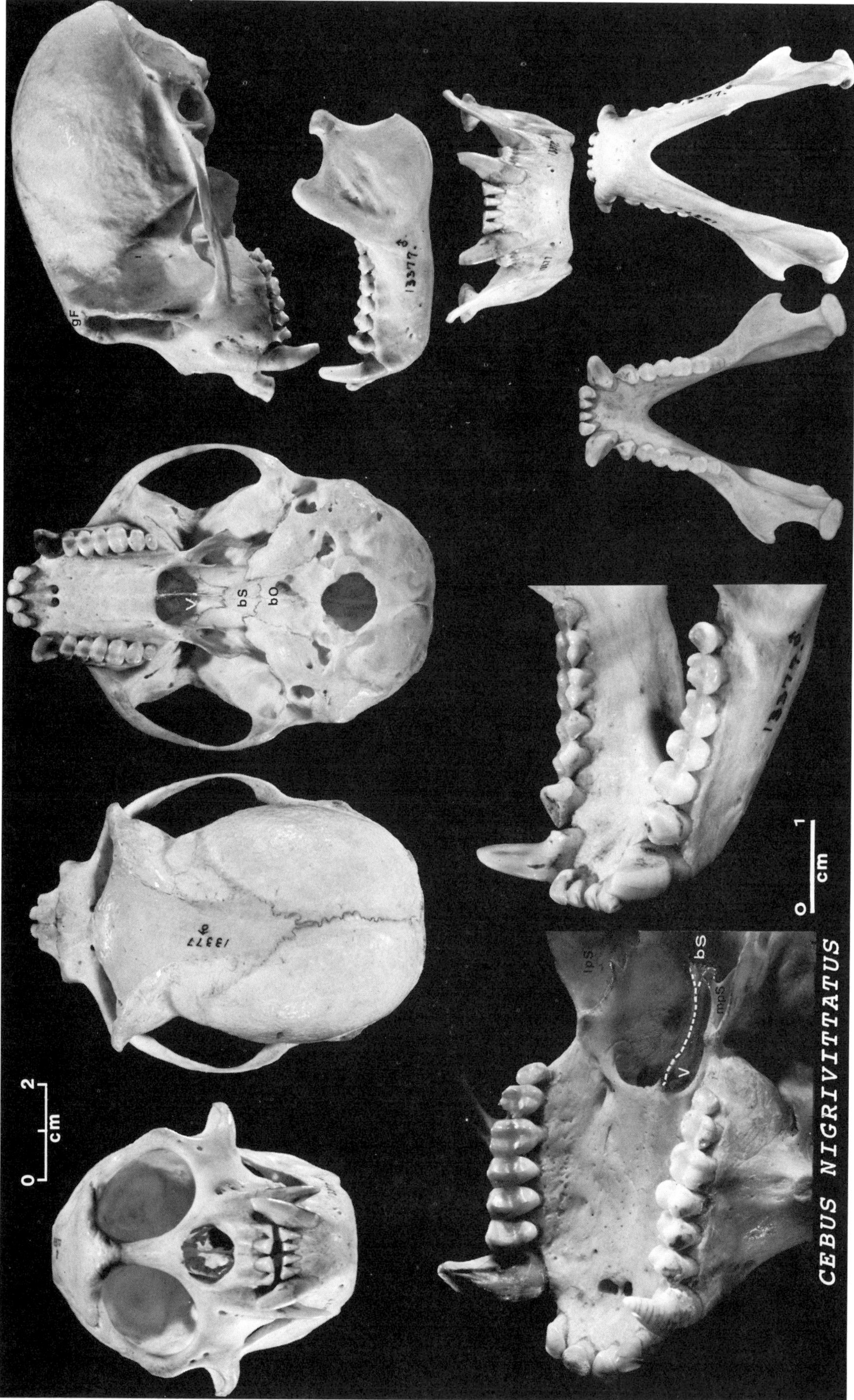

Fig. IV.117. *Cebus nigrivittatus* (FM 13377 ♂) (Cebidae). VENEZUELA: Bolívar, Caicara. Species of the uncrested group (*C. nigrivittatus, C. albifrons, C. capucinus*) differ cranially from crested *C. apella* (fig. IV.118) by uninflated glabella (*Fg*), absence of sagittal crest (*Sagcr*) in males, vertical plate of vomer (*V*) exposed behind posterior border of palate, vomerine wings not or very little separated and not exposing presphenoid bone (*pS*) to view, medial pterygoid plate (*mpS*) and hamular process (*hpS*) parallel-sided or convergent, ascending mandibular ramus comparatively low in males, and other characters not clearly illustrated here (see also figs. IV.19, 20, 36, 82, 83, 84, 130); dashed line in lower left figure marks contour of vomer (*V*).

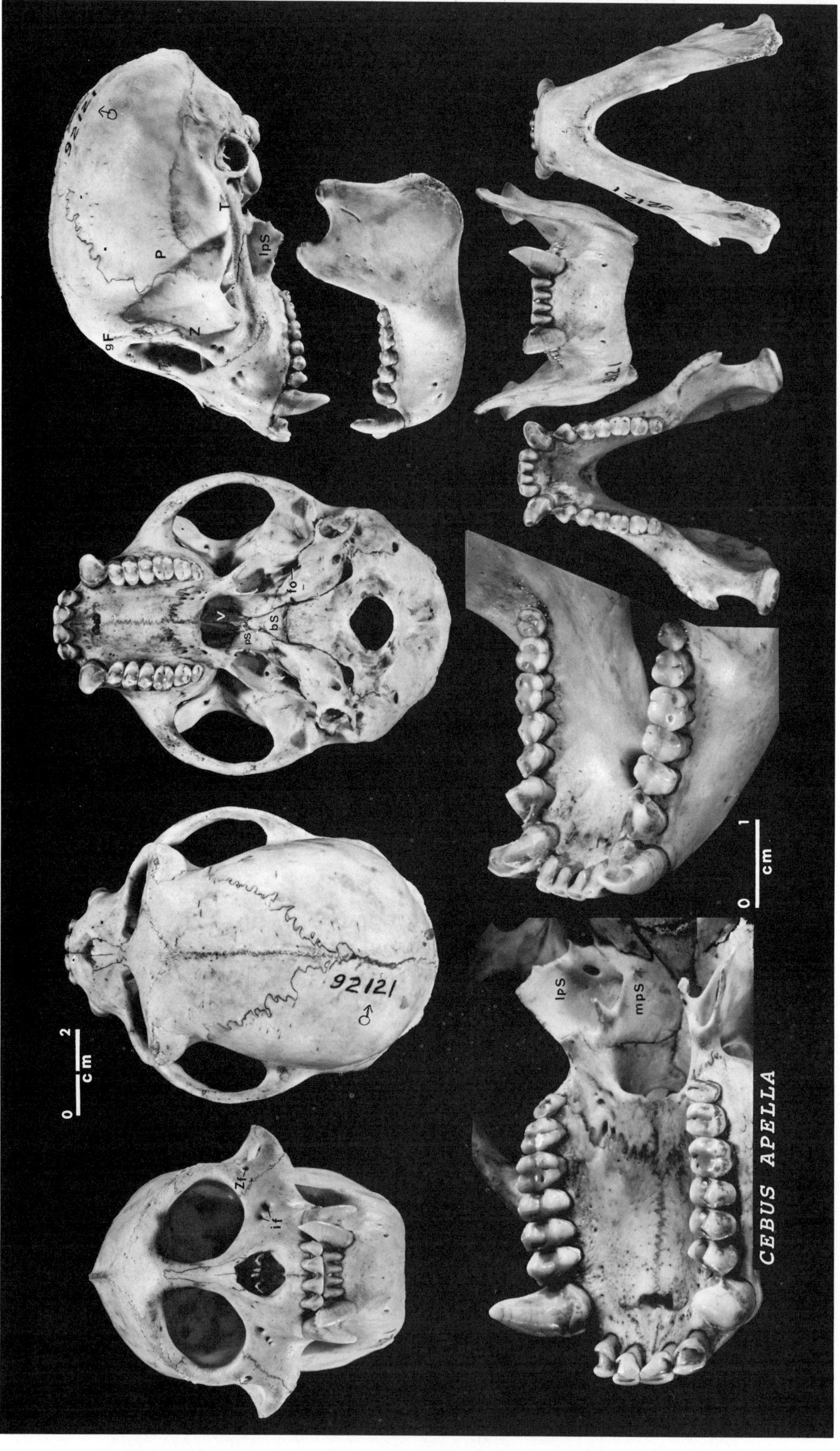

Fig. IV.118. *Cebus apella* (FM 92121 ♂) (Cebidae). BRAZIL: Para, Urucurituba. Parts labeled for convenient comparisons with cercopithecids; see also fig. IV.33.

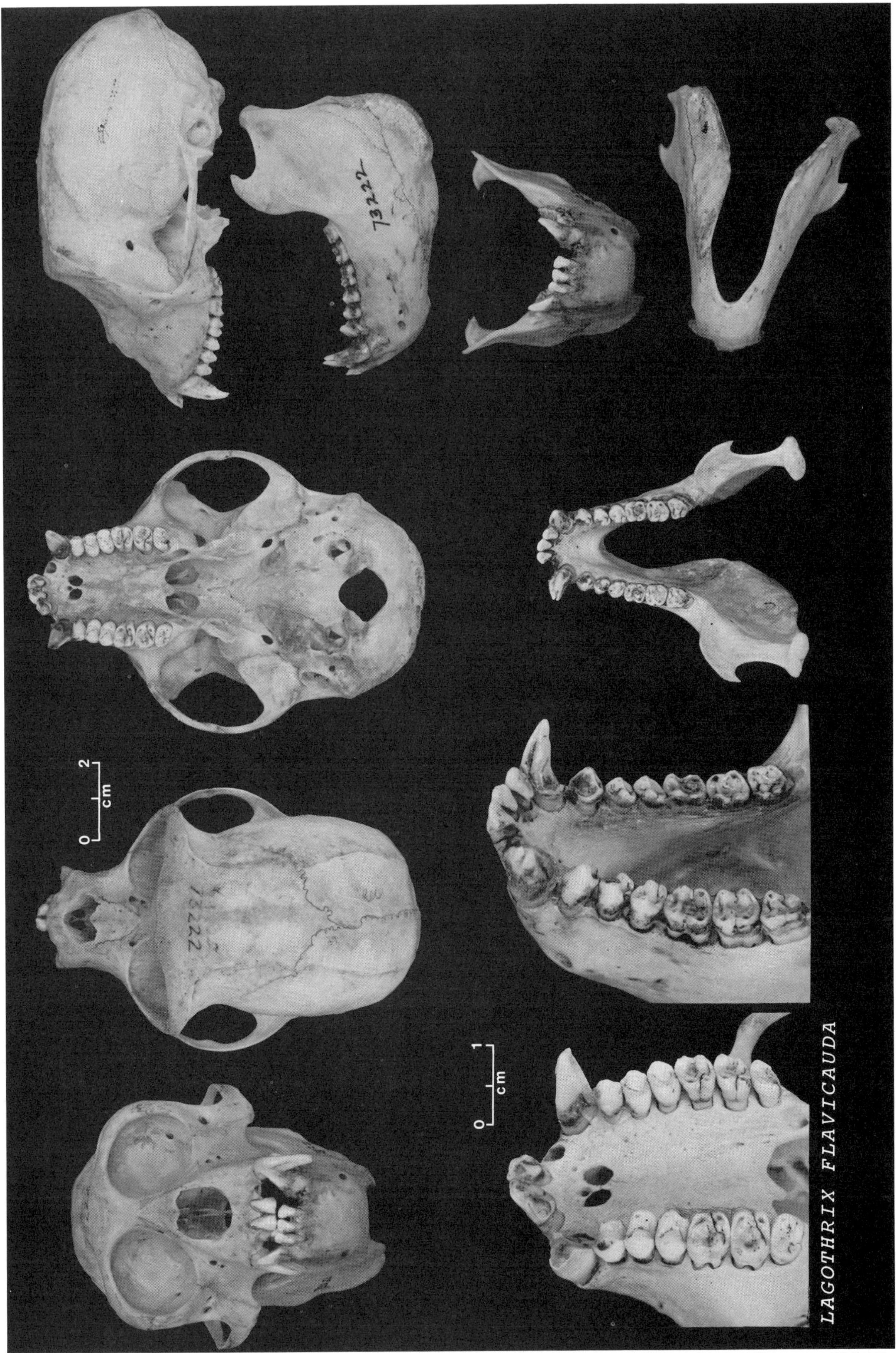

Fig. IV.119. *Lagothrix flavicauda* (AM 73222 ♂) (Cebidae). PERU: Amazonas, La Lejía. Distorted left mandibular ramus result of shotgun wound in early life. Uninjured right side of same skull illustrated in fig. IV.120.

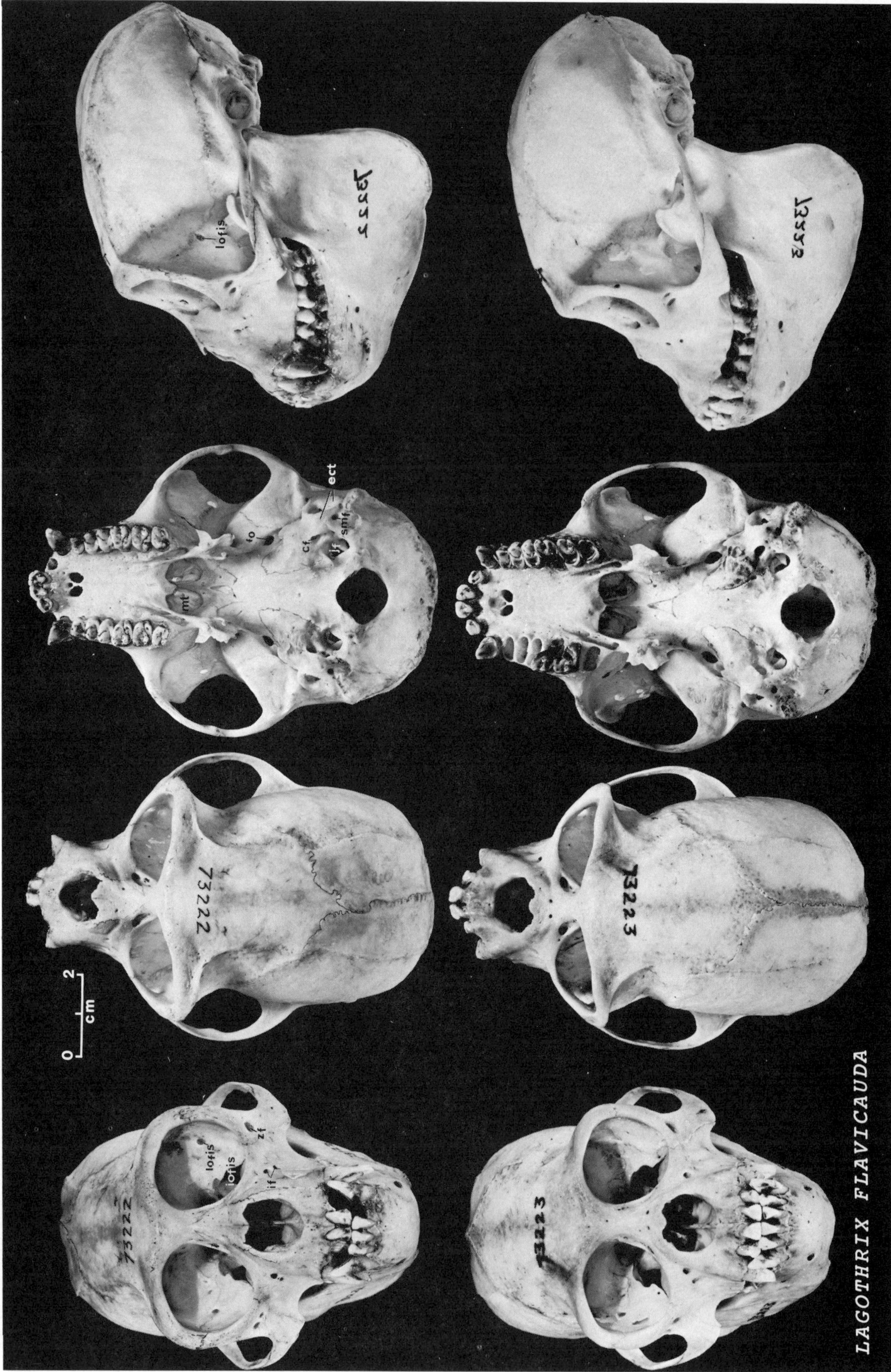

Fig. IV.120. *Lagothrix flavicauda.* (AM 73222 ♂; AM 73223 ♀) (Cebidae). PERU: Amazonas, La Lejía. Lateral aspect of skull is right side reversed; inferior orbital fissure (*iofis*) and lateral orbital fissure (*lofis*) are prominent; malar foramen (*Zf*) is large in all atelines.

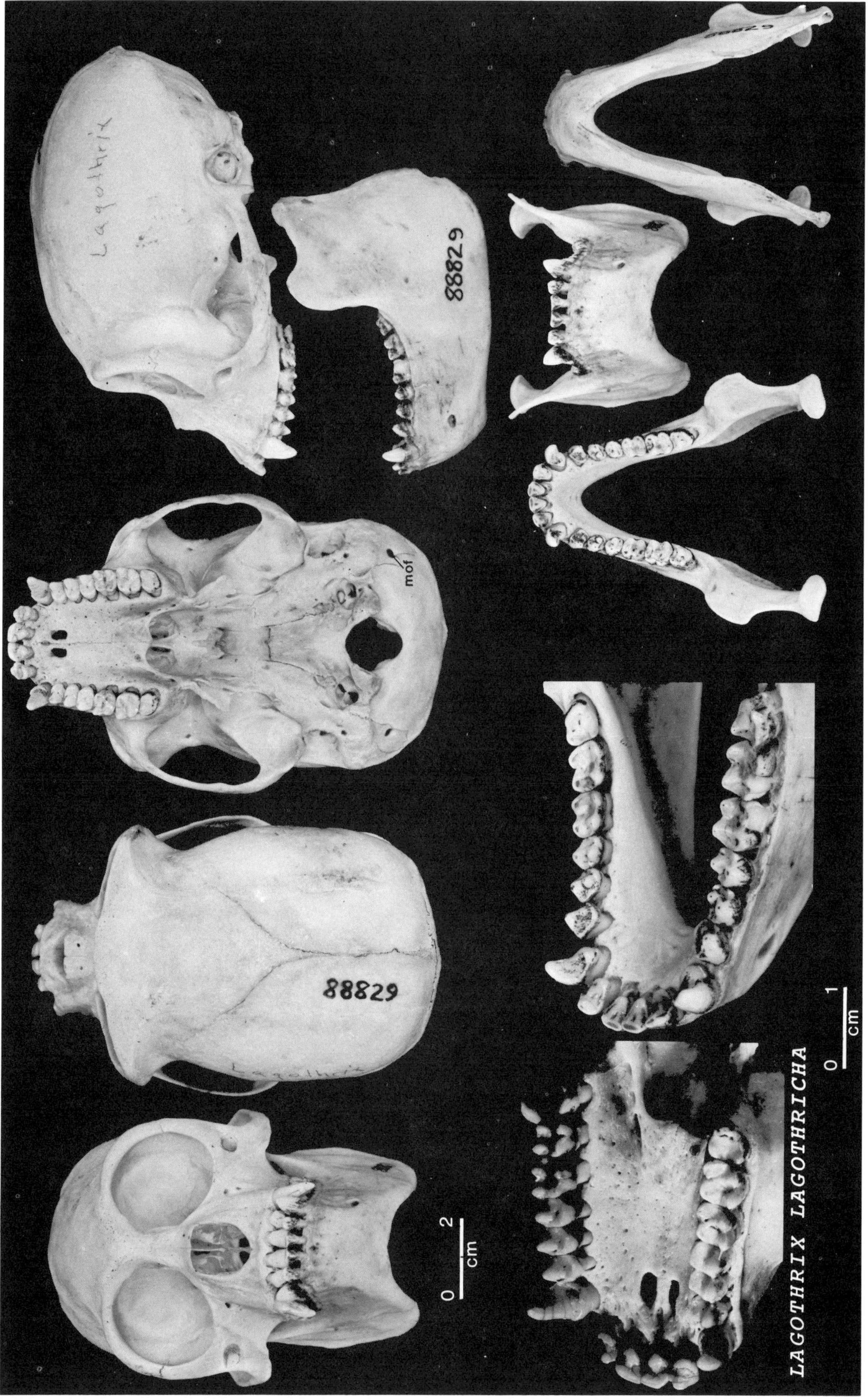

Fig. IV.121. *Lagothrix lagothricha* (FM 88829 ♀) (Cebidae). PERU: Loreto, Río Yaquerana. Prominent mastooccipital fenestrations (*mof*) usually present on each side of skull; the same character may occur in other cebids, mainly the large species.

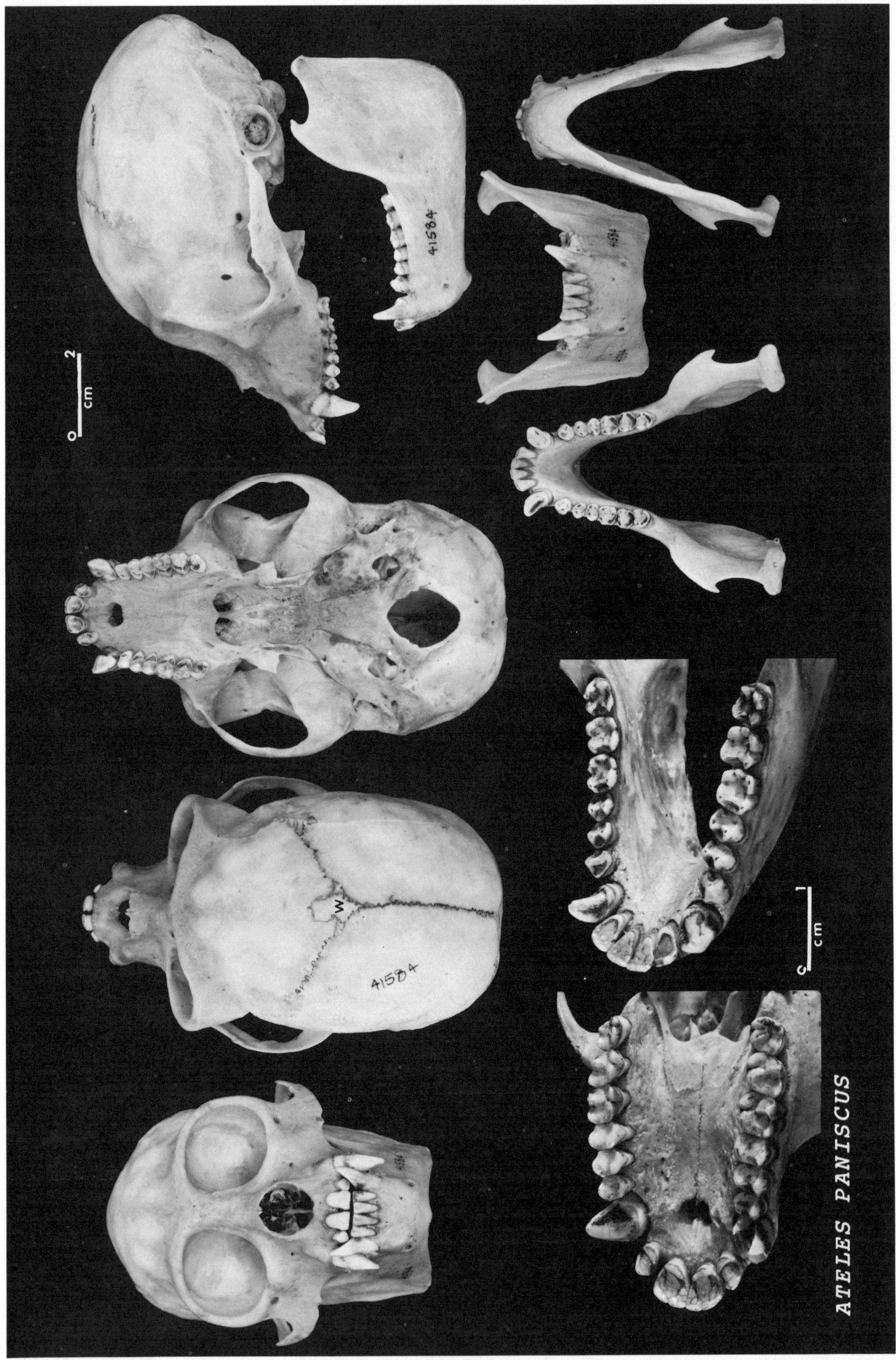

Fig. IV.122. *Ateles paniscus* (FM 41584 ♂, 69580 ♀) (Cebidae). ECUADOR: Esmeraldas, Río Quinindé (41584); COLOMBIA: Antioquia, Villa Arteaga (69580). Frontoparietal Wormian or sutural bone (*W*) most frequent in *Ateles;* shape variable, size from minuscule to nearly as large as parietal or frontal bone.

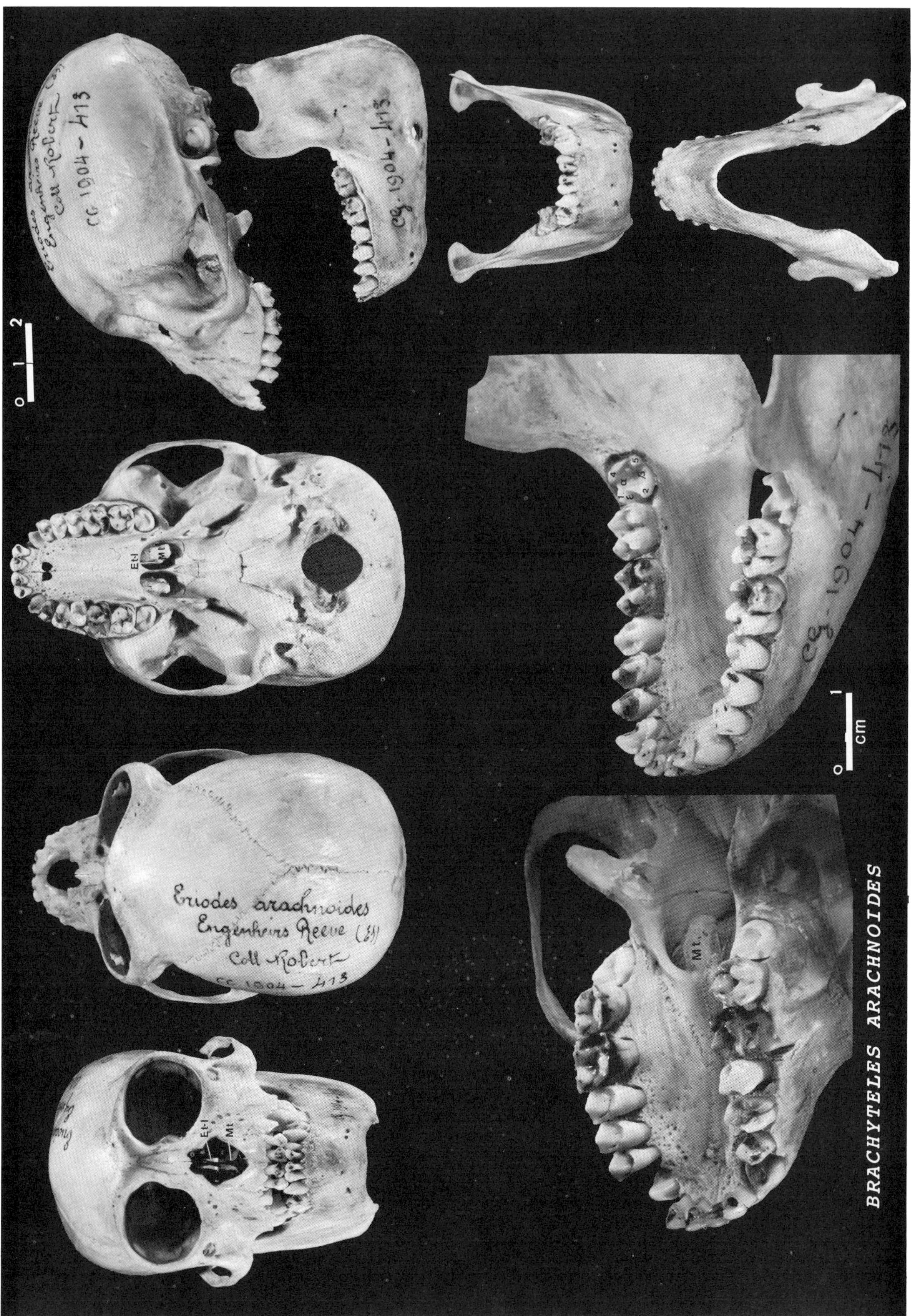

Fig. IV.123. *Brachyteles arachnoides* (MN 1904–413) (Cebidae). BRAZIL: Espírito Santa, Engenheiro Reeve. Upper canines and upper and lower third molars were erupting; they contrast with worn permanent lower incisors and fully erupted and moderately worn lower canines; right m[1] damaged; ethmoturbinals I and maxilloturbinals very large.

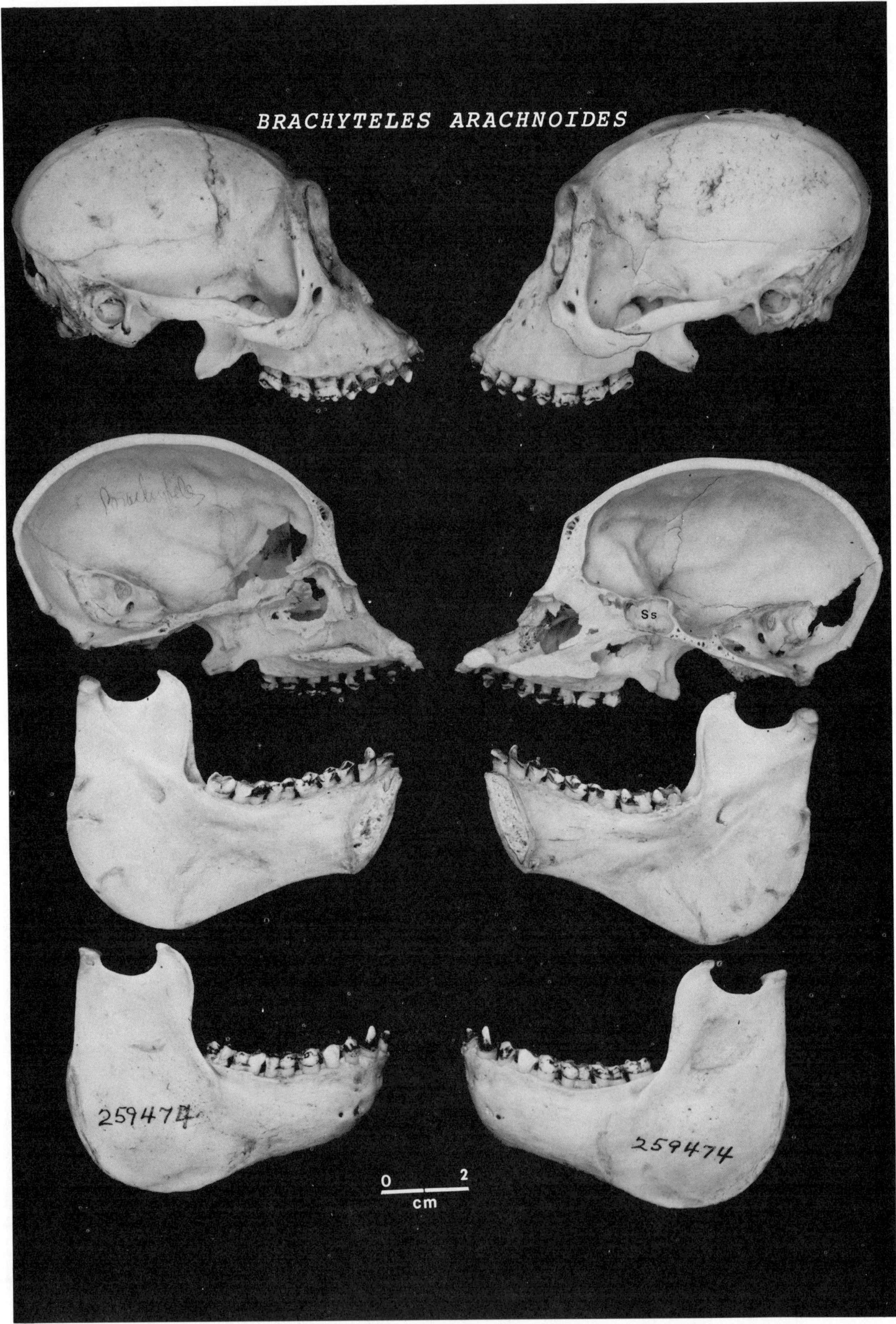

Fig. IV.124. *Brachyteles arachnoides* (US 259474) (Cebidae). BRAZIL: Rio de Janeiro, Serra Macaé. Sphenoidal sinus (*Ss*) large; turbinal bones lost in skull shown.

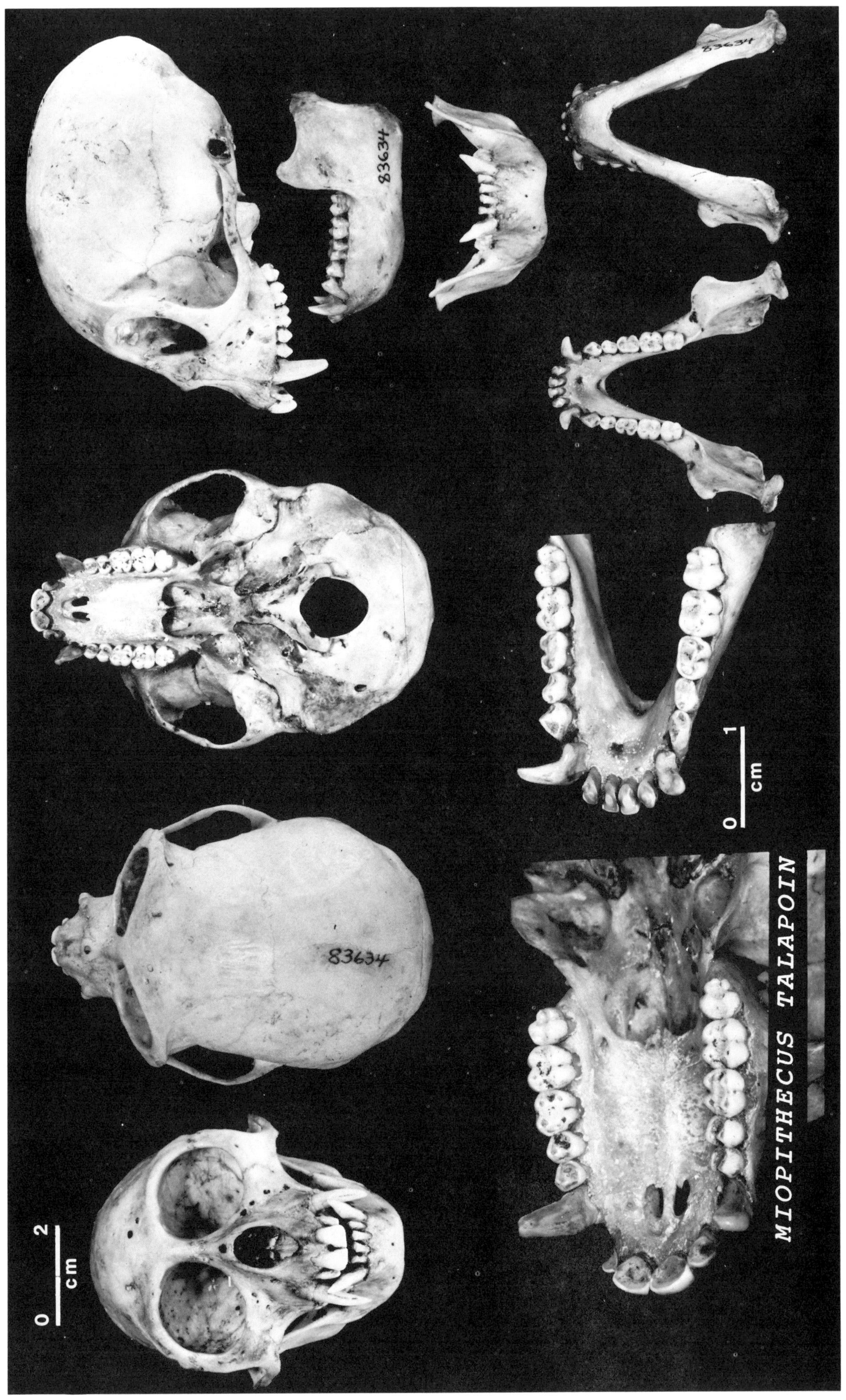

Fig. IV.125. *Miopithecus talapoin* (FM 83634 ♂) (Cercopithecidae). ANGOLA: Gabela. Dorsal aspect not perpendicular to Frankfort plane; skull peppered with shot holes.

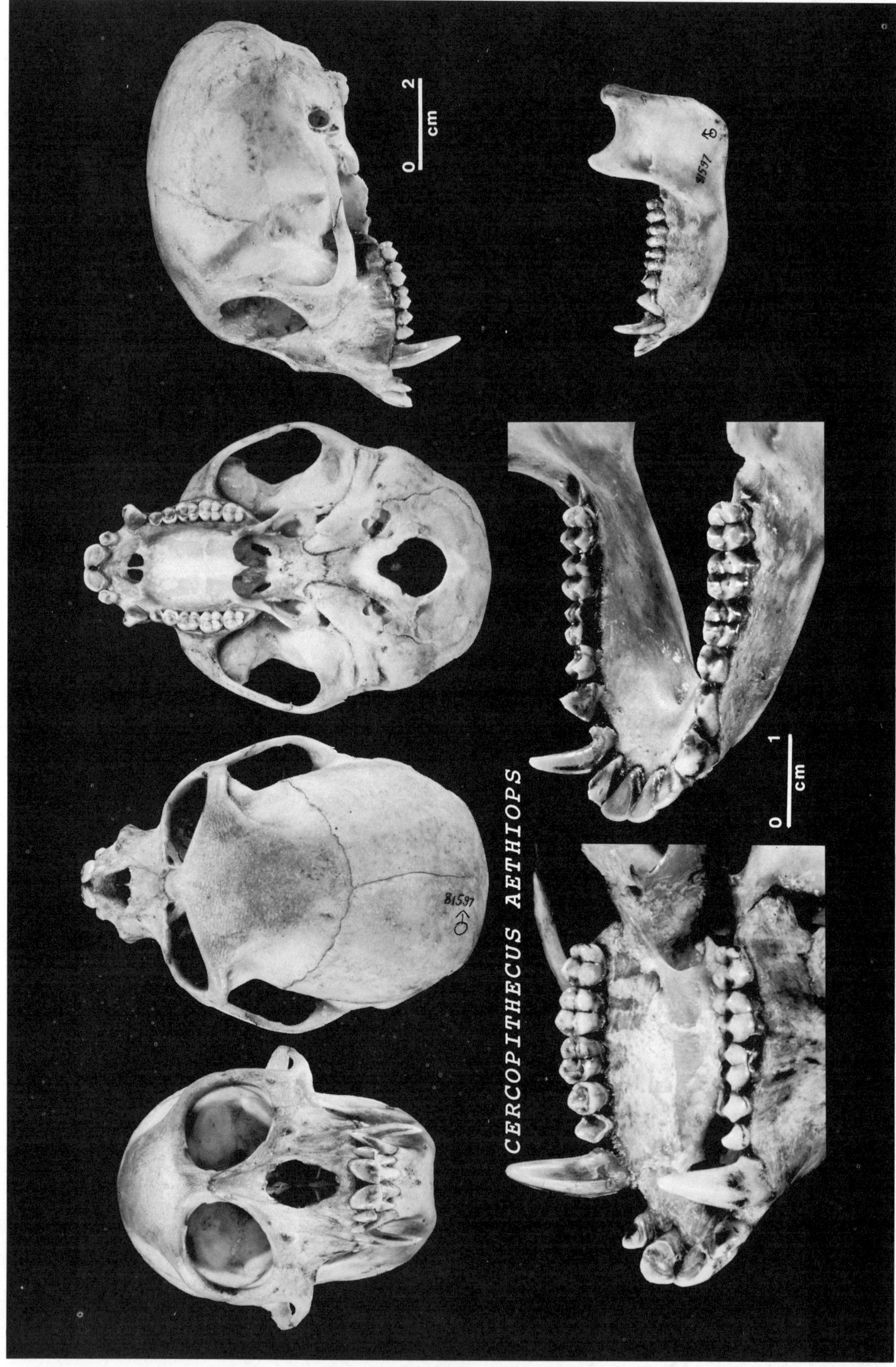

Fig. IV.126. *Cercopithecus ascanius* (FM 81597 ♂) (Cercopithecidae). ANGOLA: Canzelle, Quai Sai River. Dorsal aspect not perpendicular to Frankfort plane.

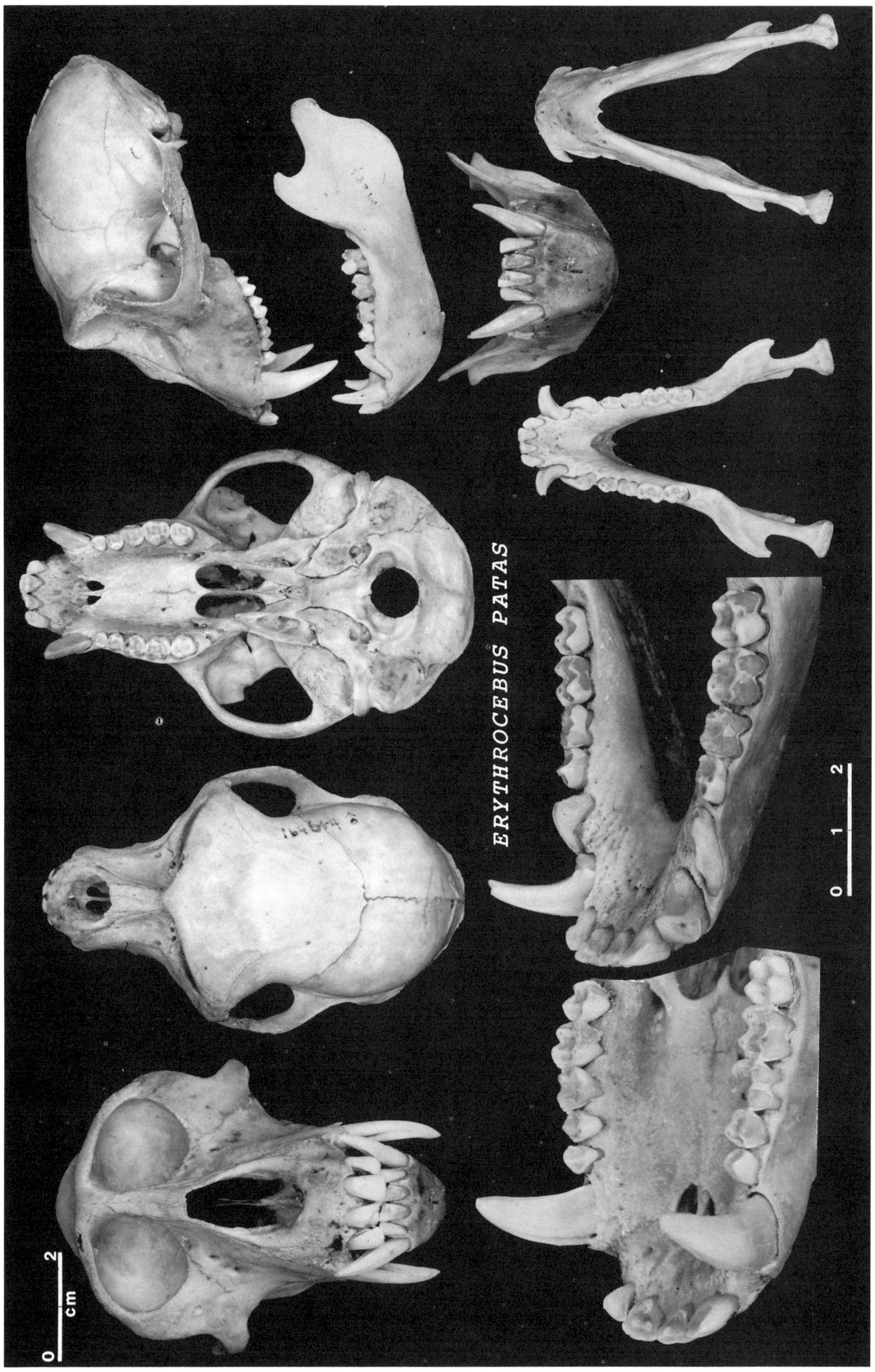

Fig. IV.127. *Erythrocebus patas* (US 164684 ♂) (Cercopithecidae). UGANDA: Nimule. Dental enamel extensively chipped postmortum.

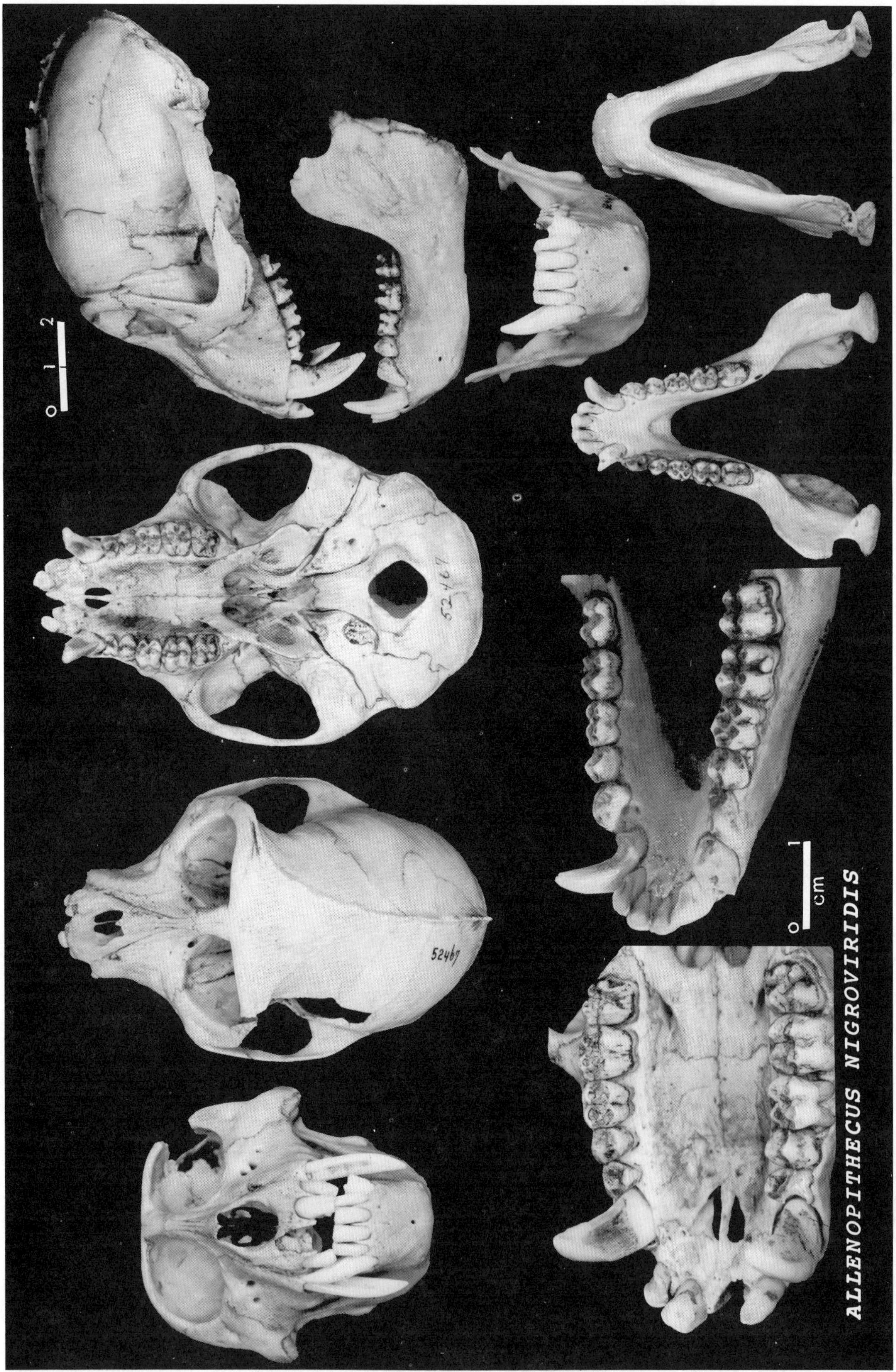

Fig. IV.128. *Allenopithecus nigroviridis* (AM 52467) (Cercopithecidae). DEMOCRATIC REPUBLIC OF THE CONGO: Bolobo. Parietals fractured; lateral aspect is right side reversed.

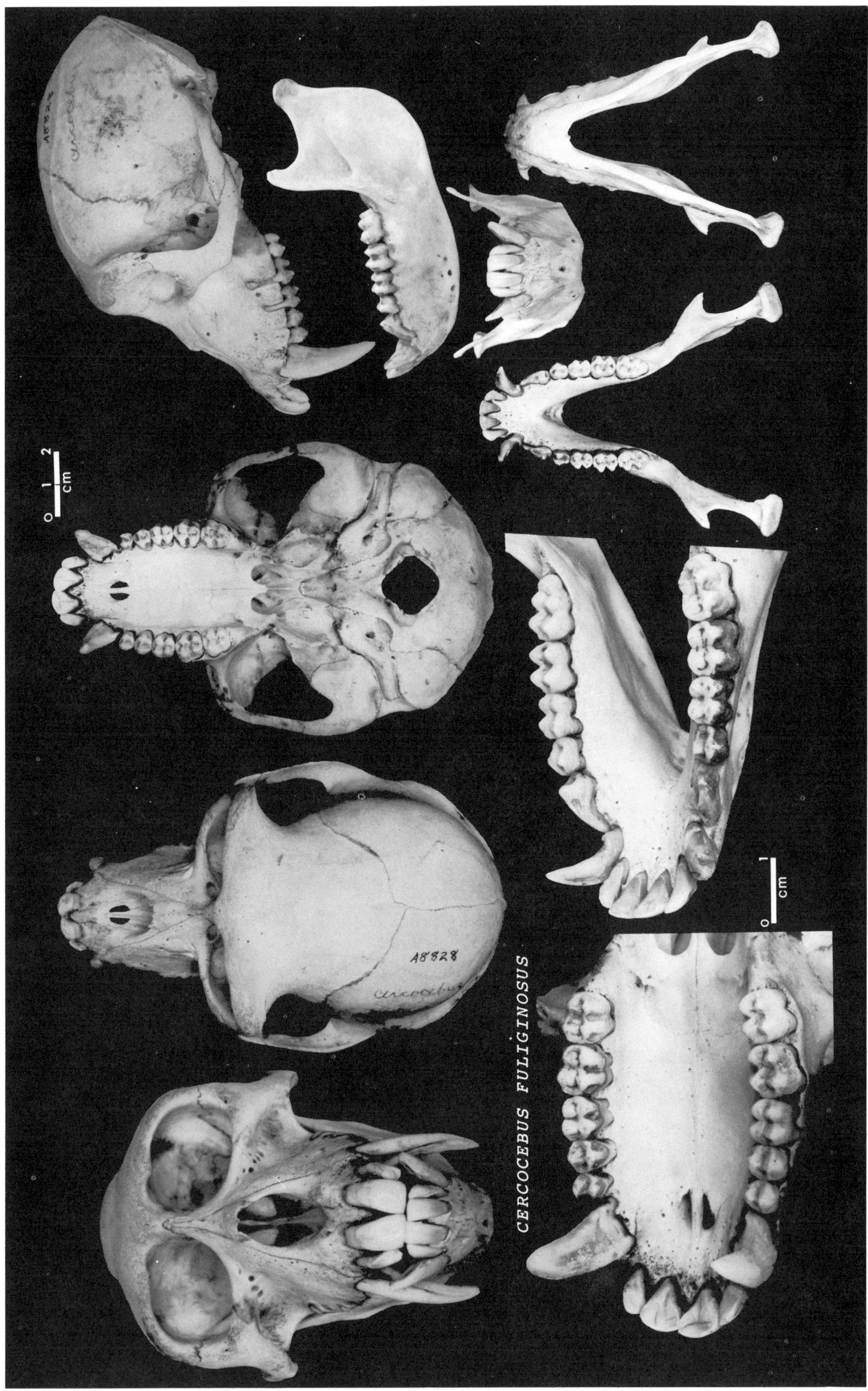

Fig. IV.129. *Cercocebus atys* (FM 48828 ♂) (Cercopithecidae). AFRICA.

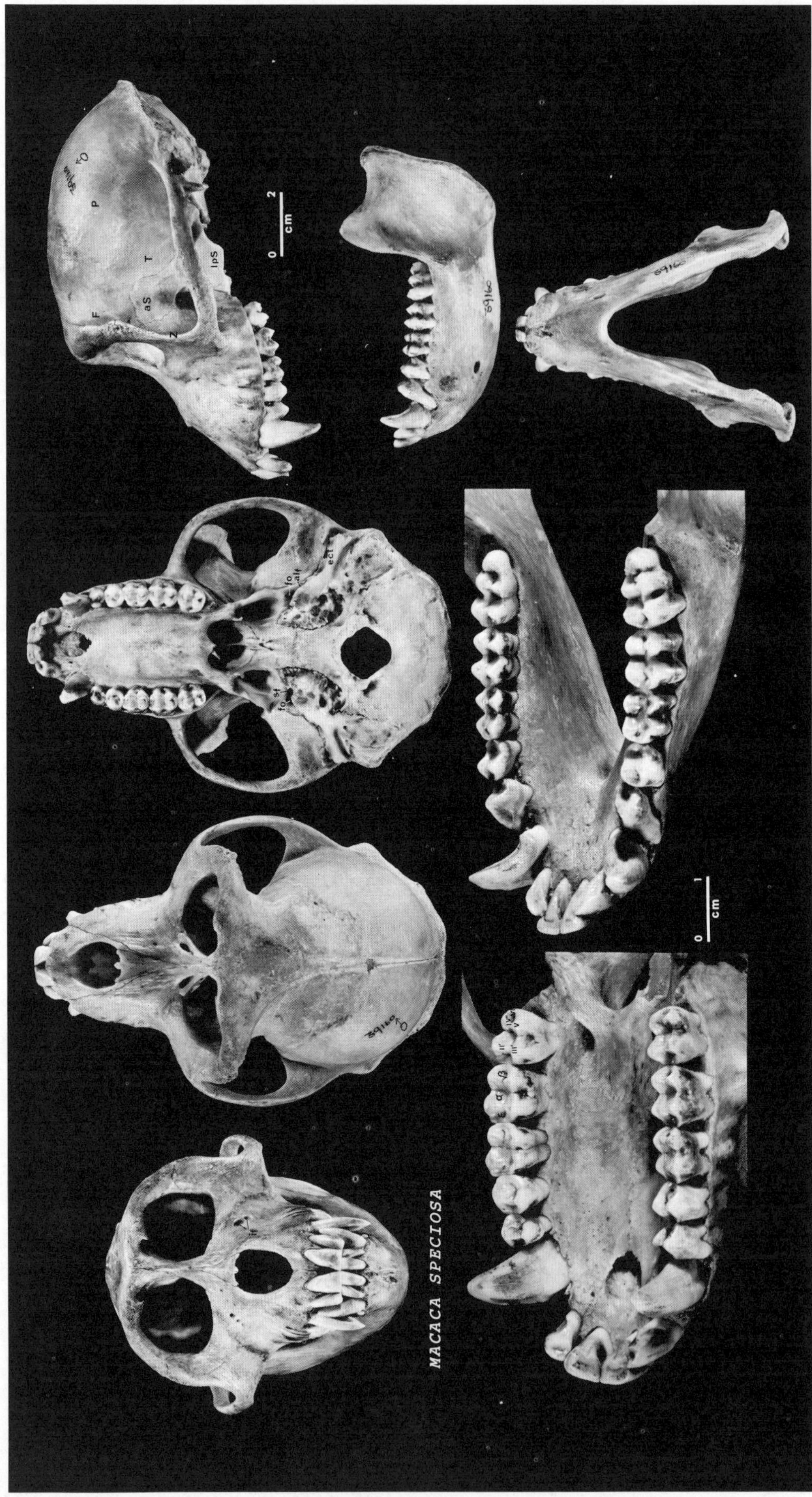

Fig. IV.130. *Macaca arctoides* (FM 39160 ♂) (Cercopithecidae). VIET NAM: Tonkin. Dorsal aspect not perpendicular to Frankfort plane; parts labeled for convenient comparison with cebids; see also figs. IV.37, 82, 83, 84, 117, 118.

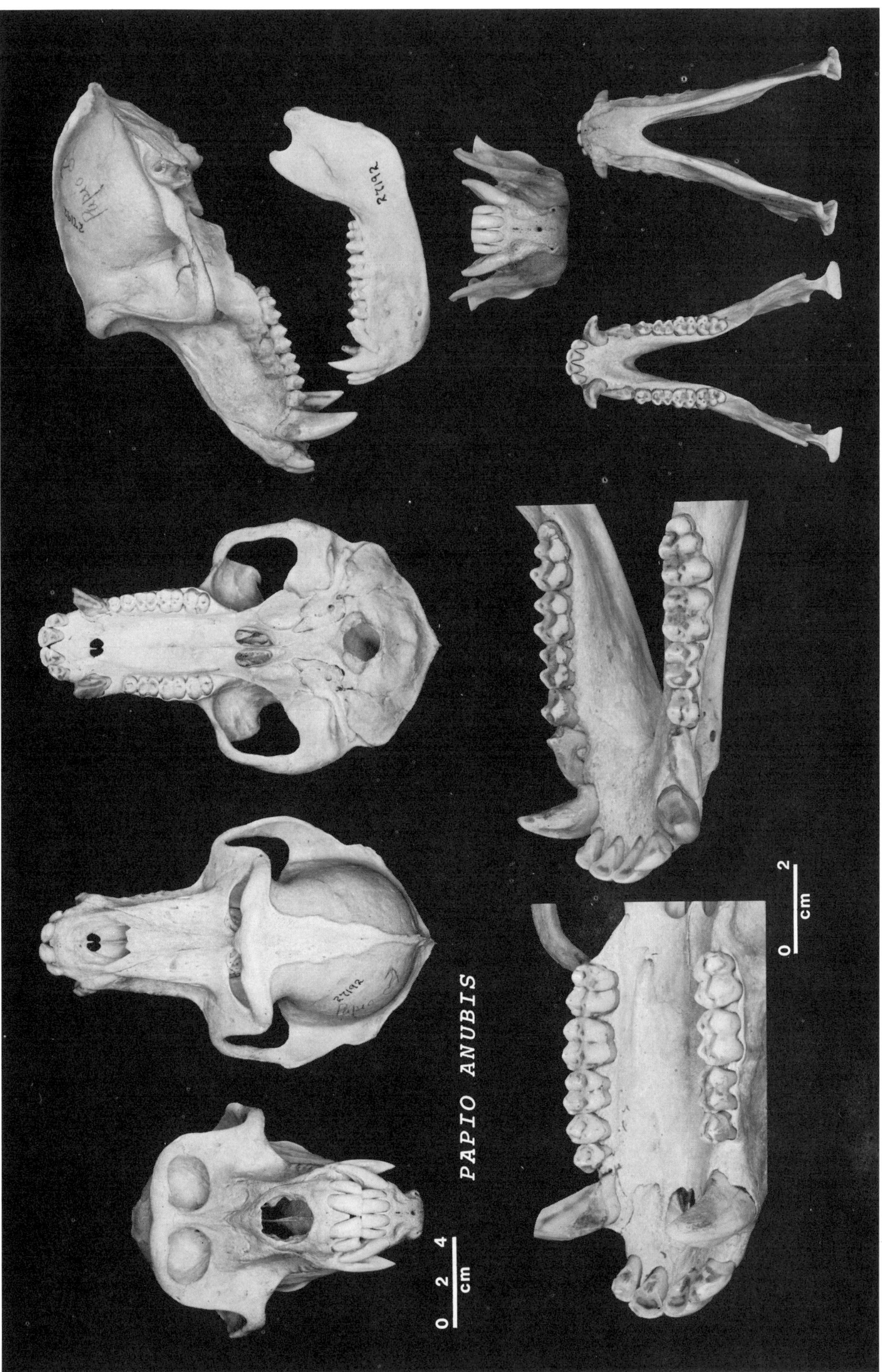

Fig. IV.131. *Papio anubis* (FM 27192 ♂) (Cercopithecidae). ETHIOPIA: Amhara.

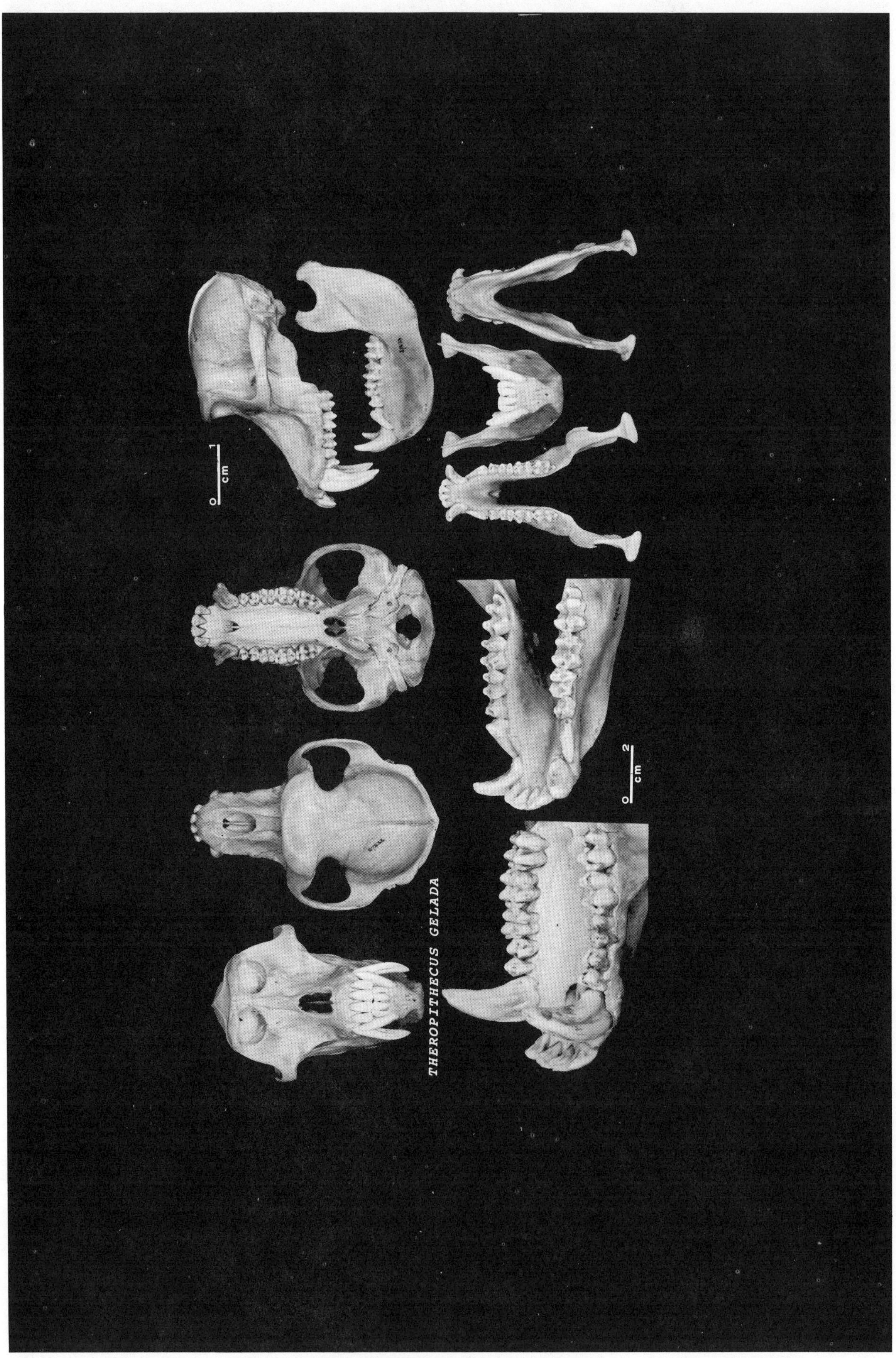

Fig. IV.132. *Theropithecus gelada* (FM 27235 ♂) (Cercopithecidae). ETHIOPIA: Muger River.

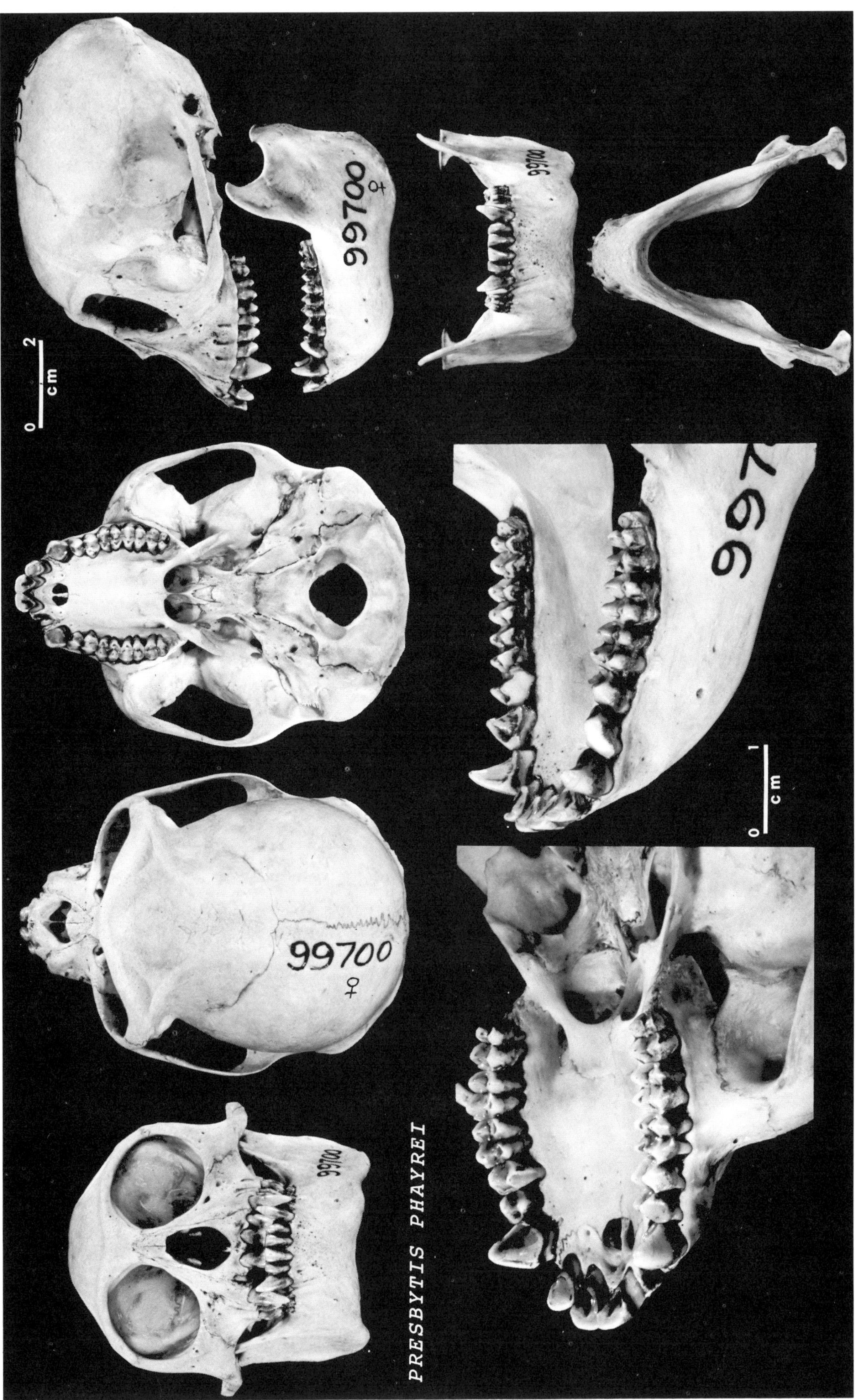

Fig. IV.133. *Presbytis phayrei* (FM 99700 ♀) (Cercopithecidae). THAILAND: Kanchanaburi, Chongkrong. Dorsal aspect not perpendicular to Frankfort plane.

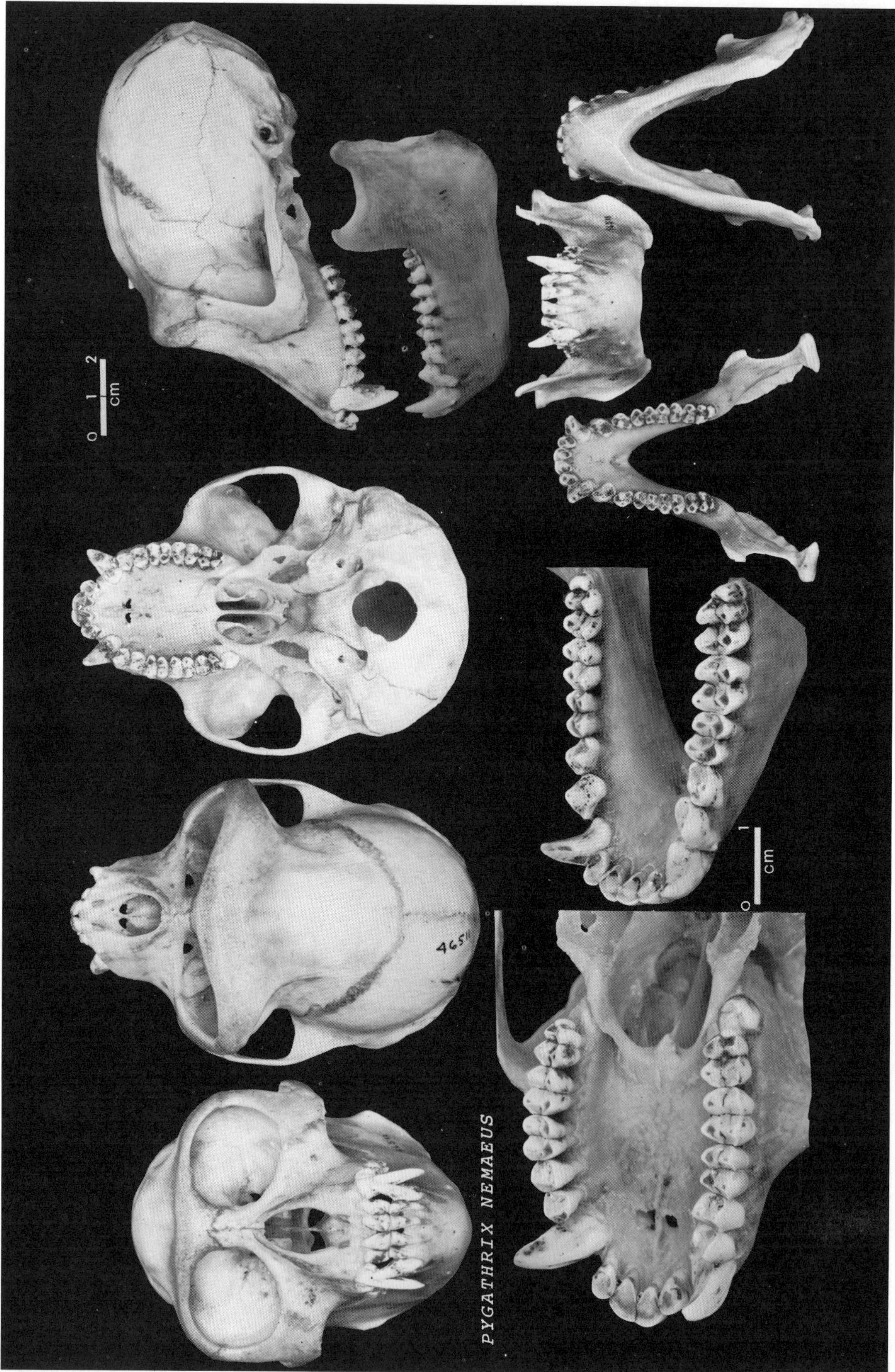

Fig. IV.134. *Pygathrix nemaeus* (FM 46511 ♂) (Cercopithecidae). NORTH VIETNAM: Annam, Ban Methuot. Supernumerary molar (m^4) in right jaw.

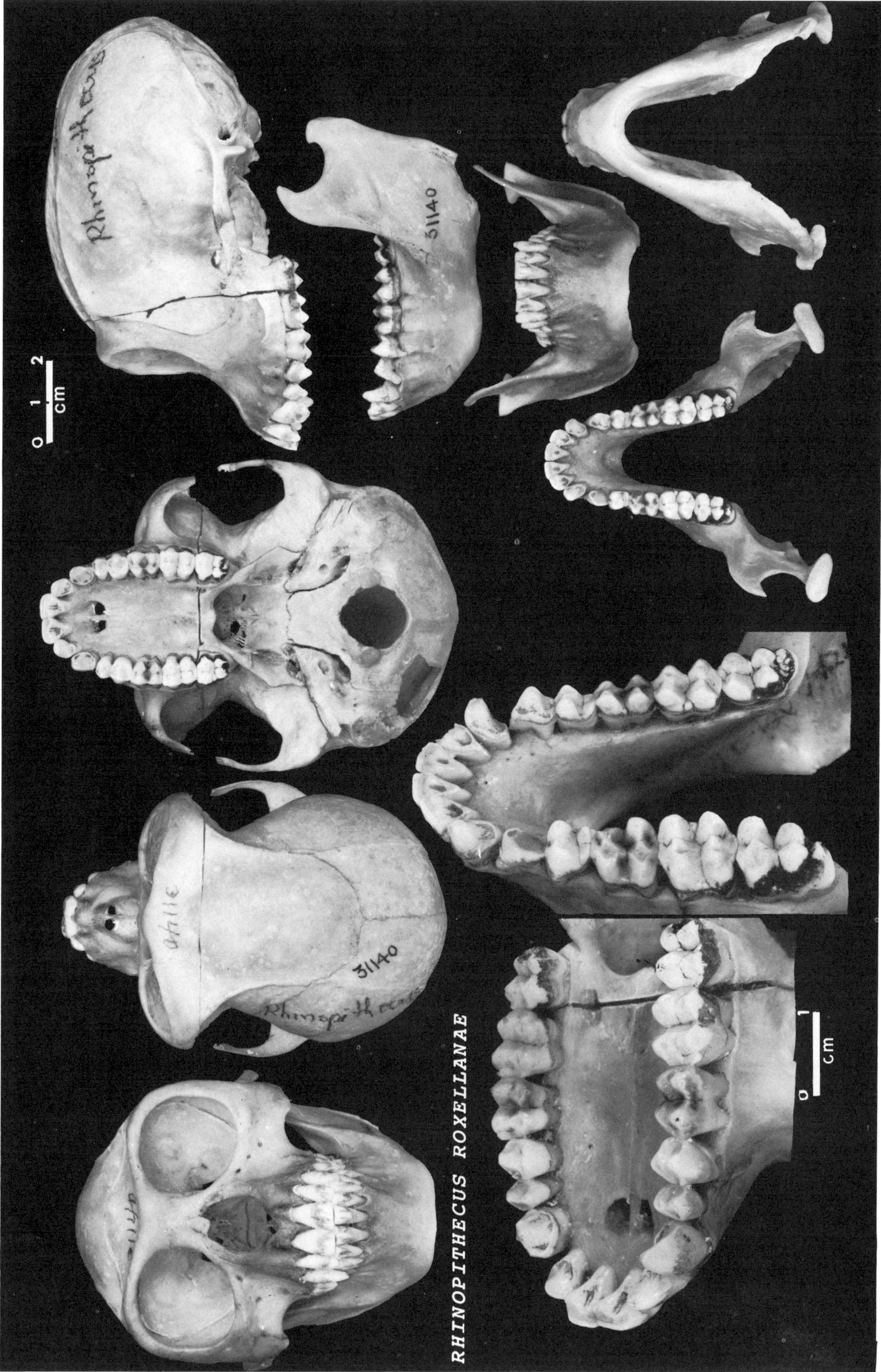

Fig. IV.135. *Rhinopithecus roxellanae* (FM 31140 ♀) (Cercopithecidae) CHINA: Szechuan. Transversely sectioned skull with damaged mandible only available adult specimen with complete and unworn dentition.

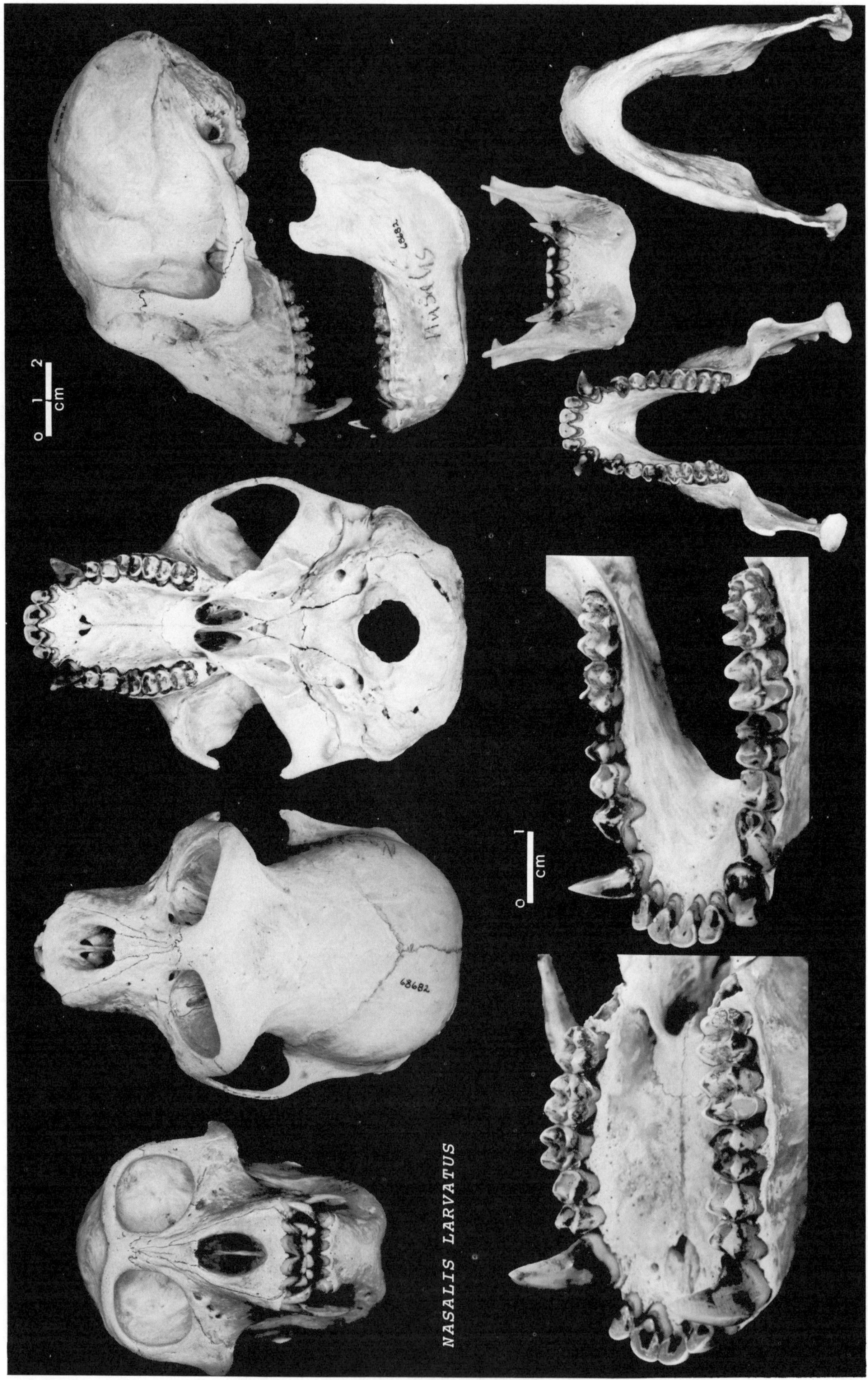

Fig. IV.136. *Nasalis larvatus* (FM 68682 ♂) (Cercopithecidae). BORNEO: East Coast.

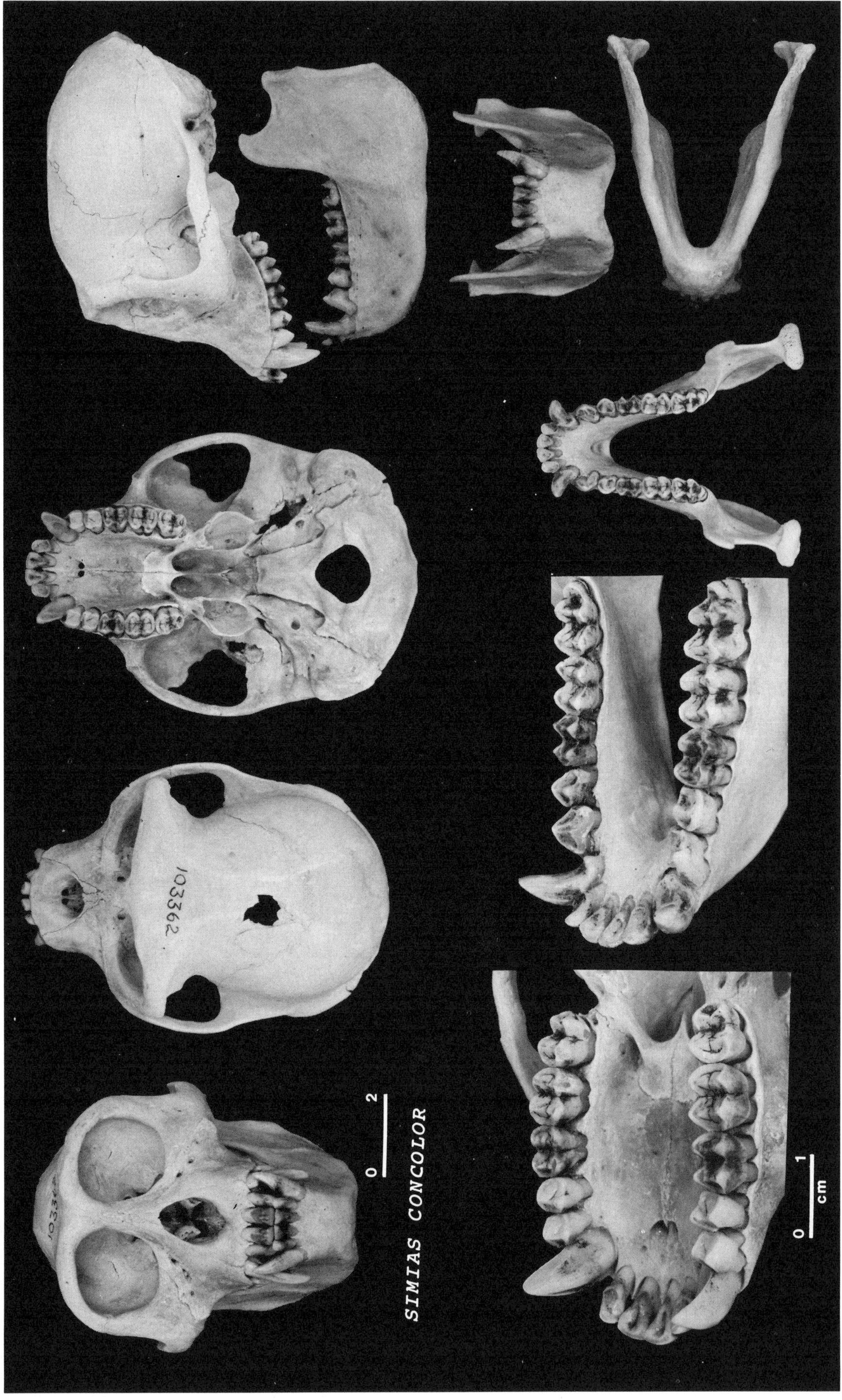

Fig. IV.137. *Simias concolor* (AM 103362) (Cercopithecidae). INDONESIA: Mentawai Islands, North Pagai.

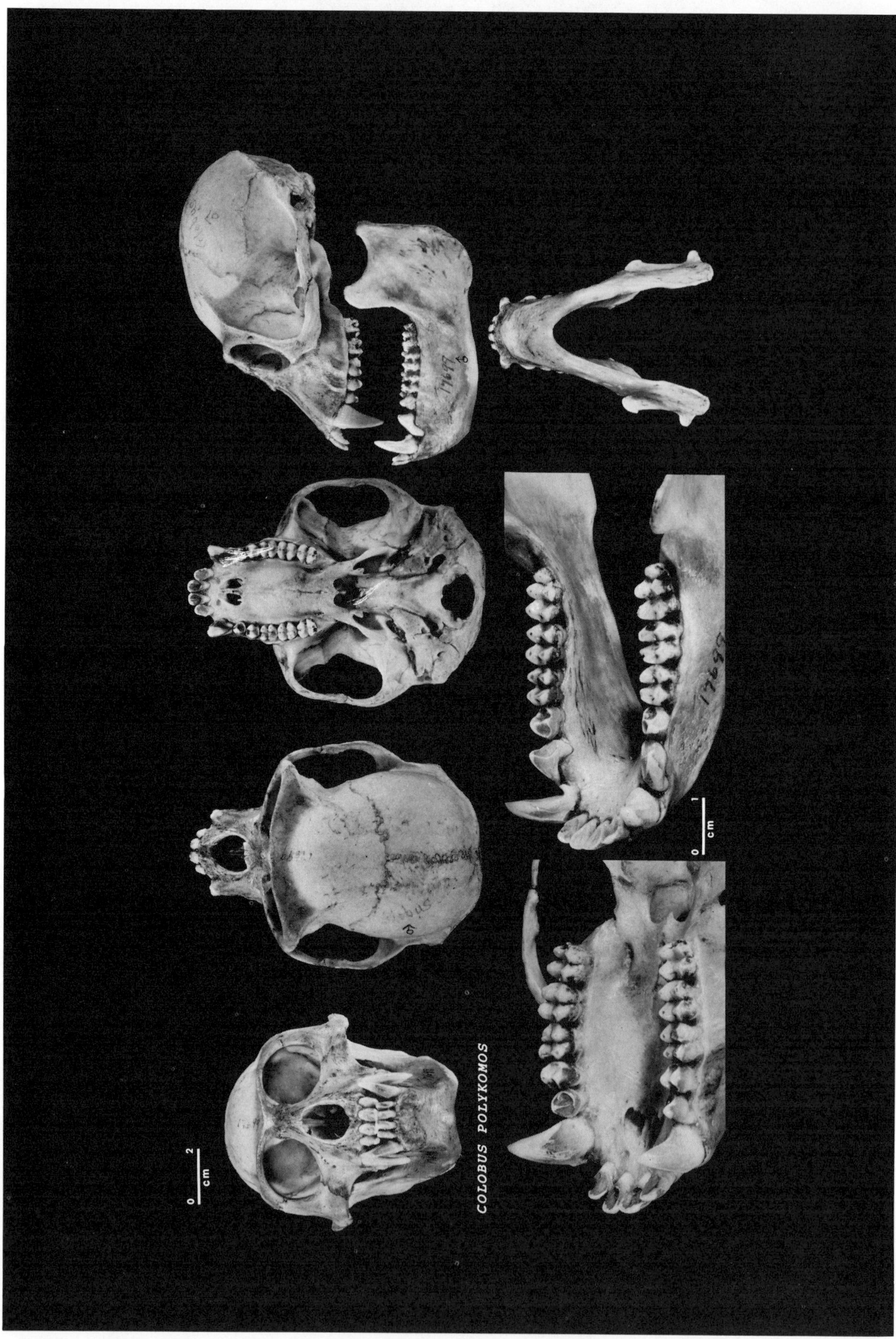

Fig. IV.138. *Colobus polykomos* (FM 17699 ♂) (Cercopithecidae). KENYA: Kijabe. Note underbite in frontal aspect.

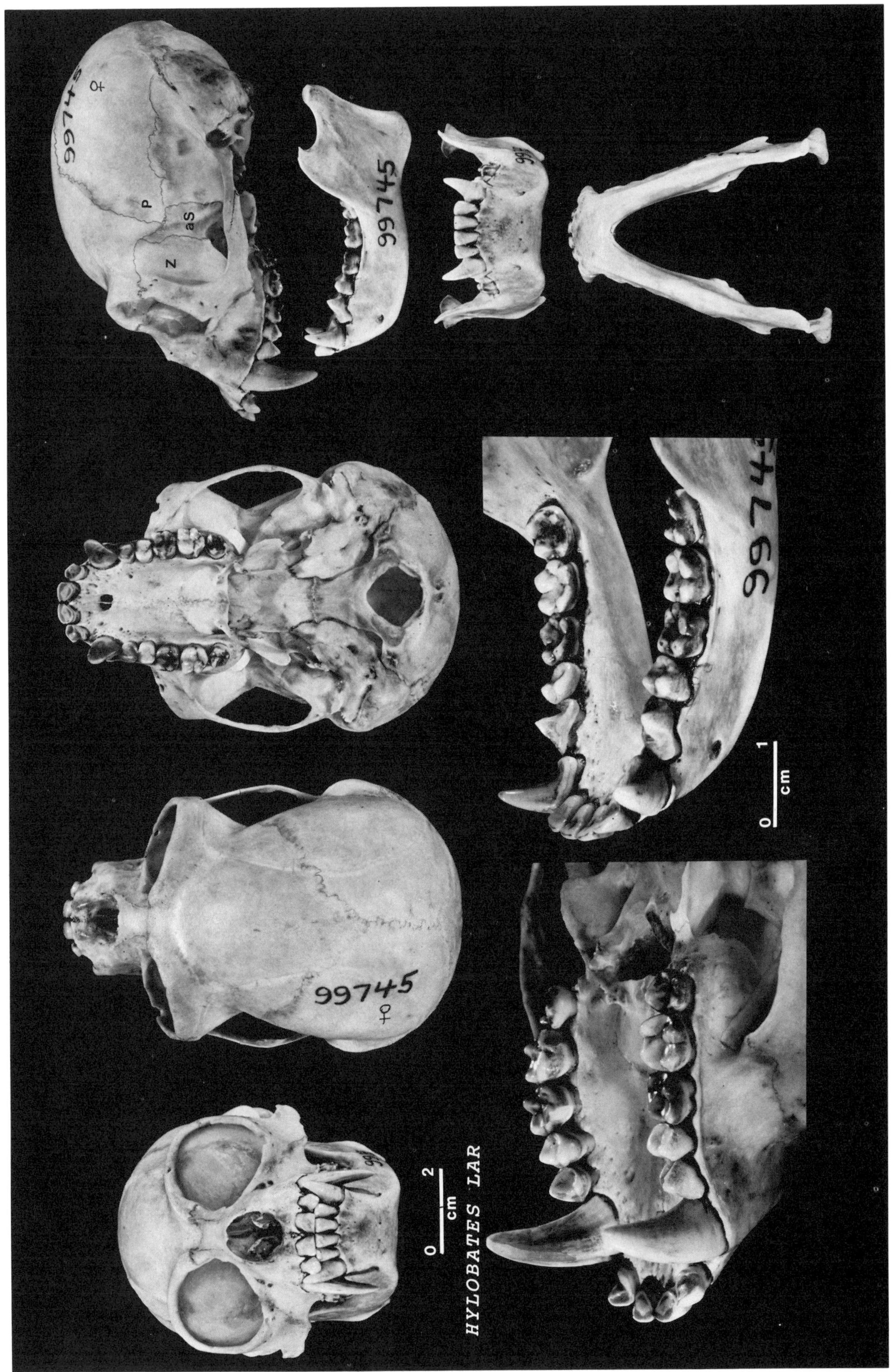

Fig. IV.139. *Hylobates lar* (FM 99745 ♀) (Hylobatidae). THAILAND: Kangchanaburi.

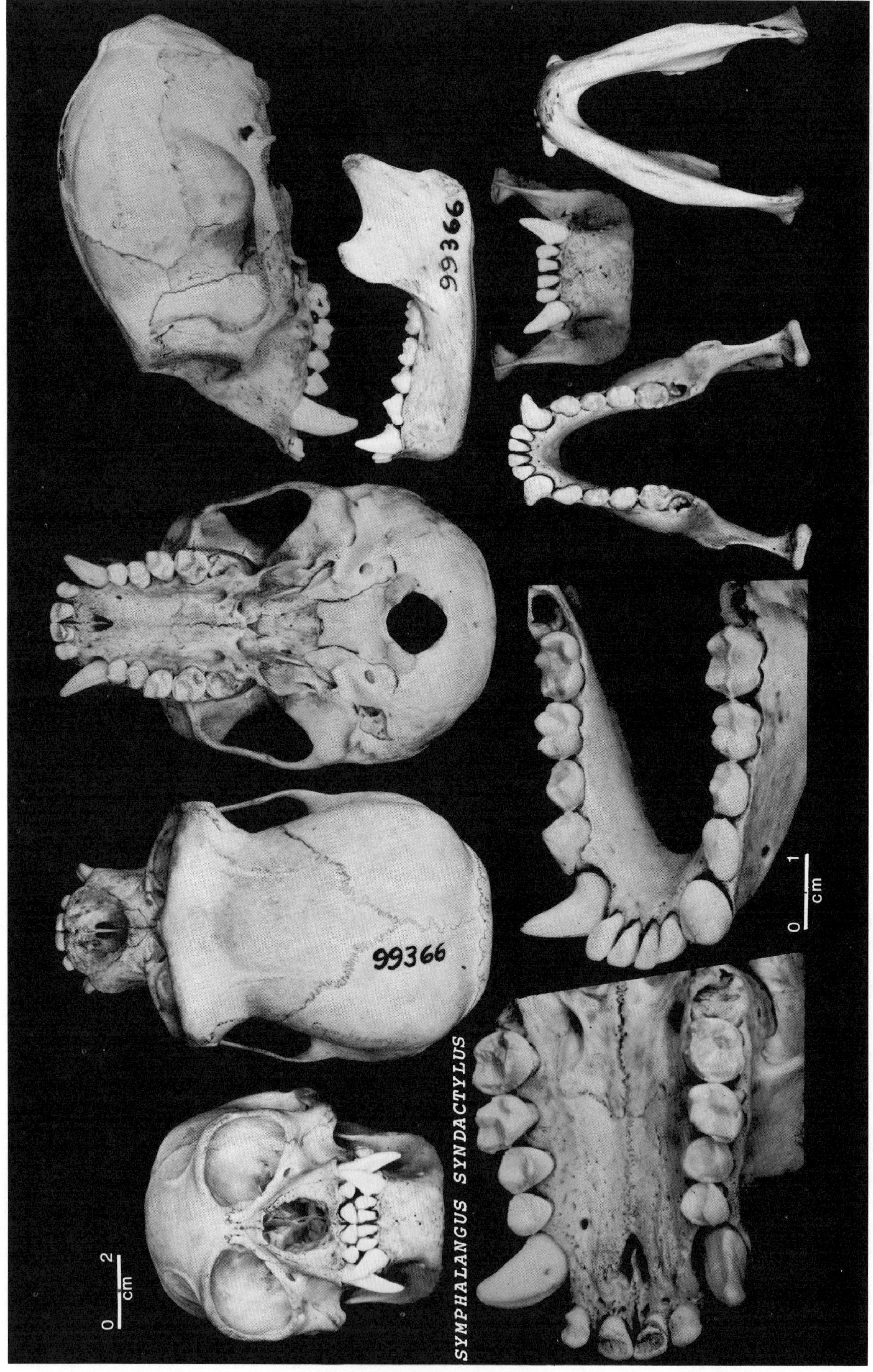

Fig. IV.140. *Symphalangus syndactylus* (FM 99366 ♂) (Hylobatidae). INDONESIA. Main portion of right ectotympanic bone removed; third molars unerupted.

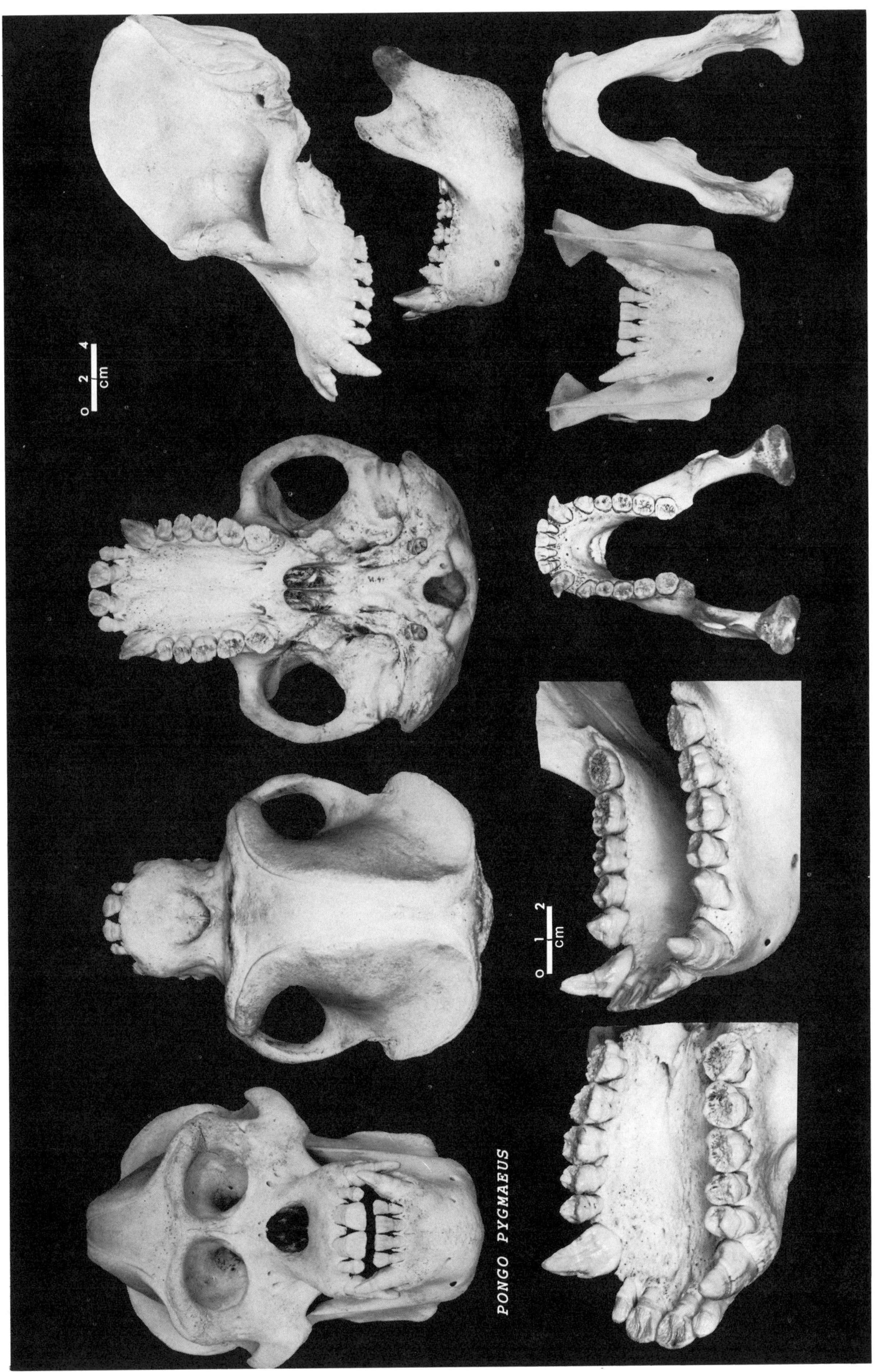

Fig. IV.141. *Pongo pygmaeus* (FM M44389 ♂) (Pongidae). BORNEO.

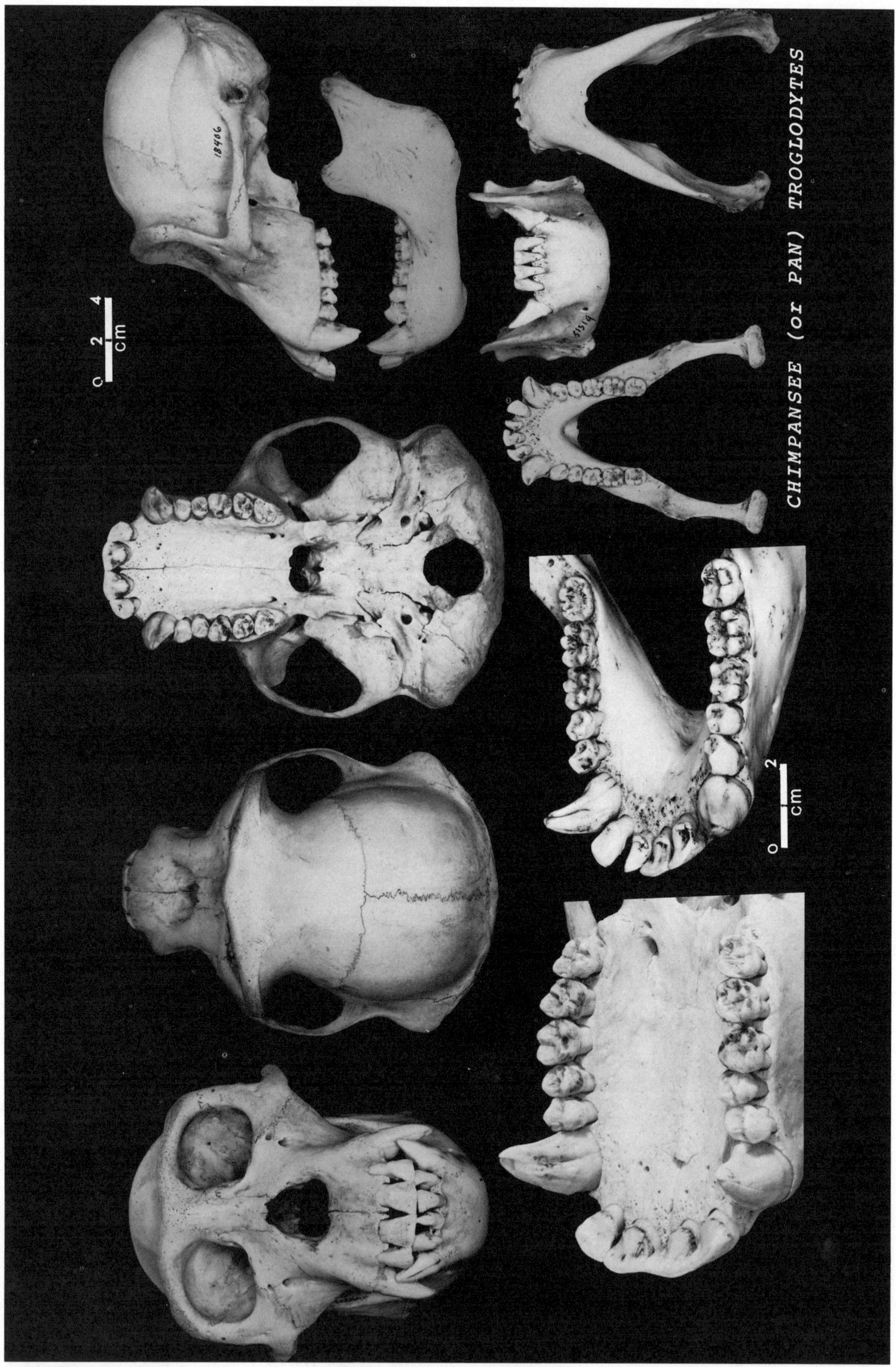

Fig. IV.142. *Chimpansee* (or *Pan*) *troglodytes* (FM 18406 ♂, lower jaw, front FM 51319 ♂) (Pongidae). AFRICA.

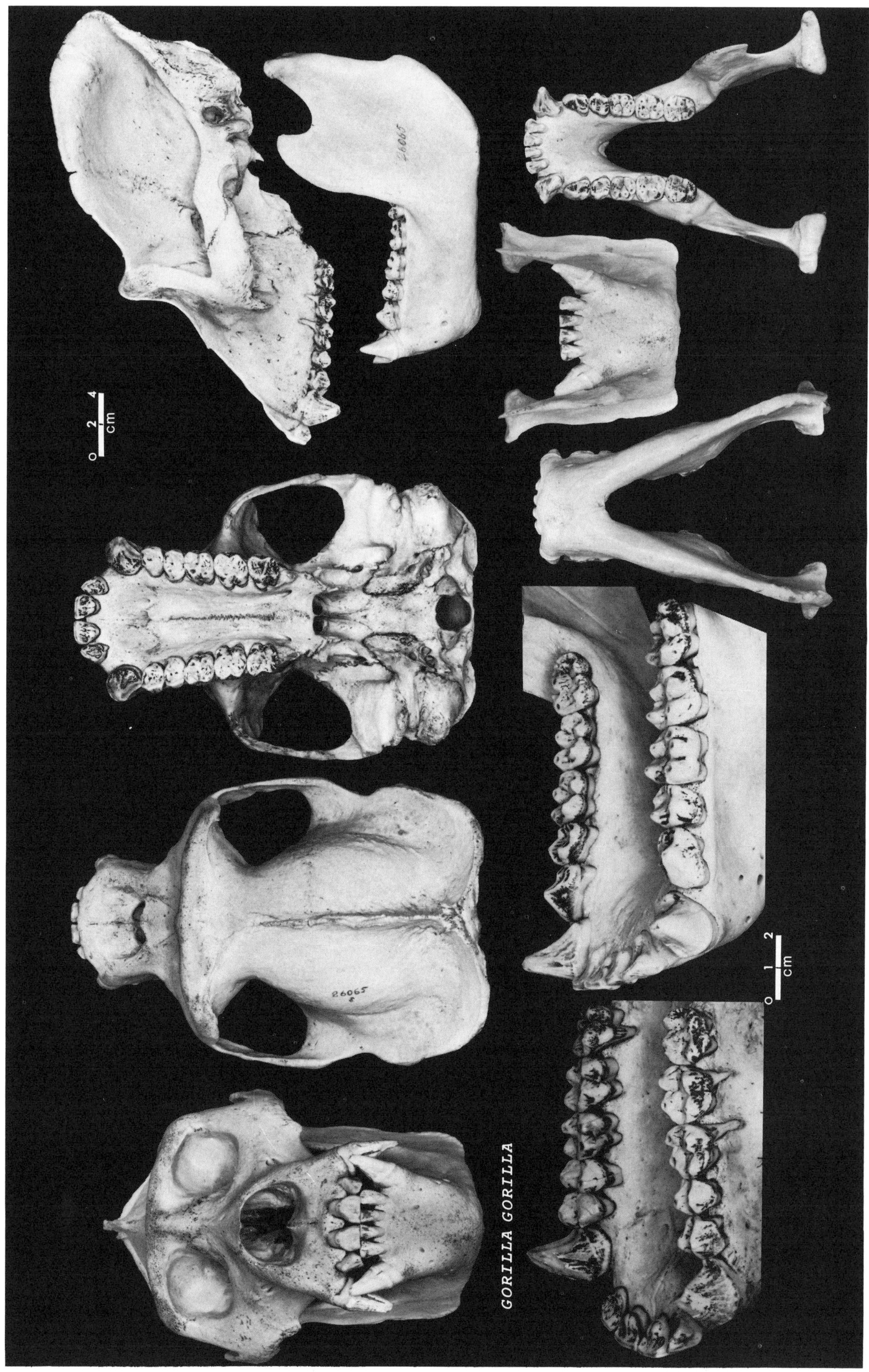

Fig. IV.143. *Gorilla gorilla* (FM 26065 ♂) (Pongidae). UGANDA: Volcanos Pass.

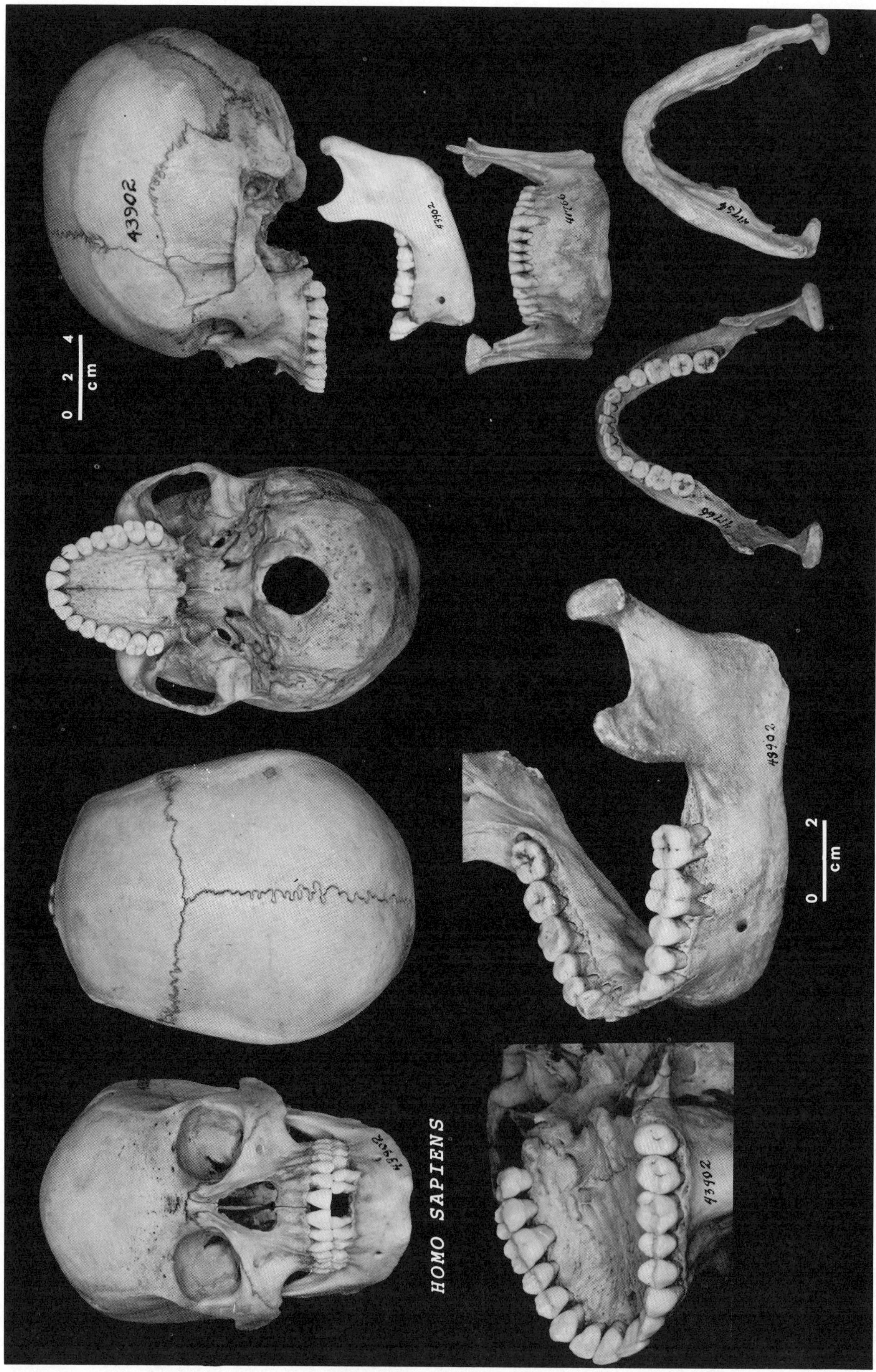

Fig. IV.144. *Homo sapiens* (FM 43902 ♂, FM 41766 mandible only).

30 Skull
13. Cranial Points, Angles, and Planes

(Figs. IV.55, 81, 83, 84)
All transverse planes are drawn perpendicular to the sagittal plane of the skull.

acanthion—Point on median line of skull at base of anterior nasal spine.
alveolar point—See *prosthion.*
antinion—Most distal point on glabella.
asterion—Point where parietal, temporal, and occipital bones meet.
auricular point—Center of external auditory meatus.
basal mandibular plane—Horizon of mandibular base perpendicular to a line through inferior point of mandibular symphysis (gnathion) and inferior point of mandibular angle.
basicranial angle—Angle at intersection of palatal axis with basineurocranial axis.
basicranial axis—See *basineurocranial axis.*
basineurocranial axis—Line through braincase from basion to sphenoidal point.
basioccipital clivus, plane of—Transverse plane through a line connecting basion and occipital point of sella.
basion—Midpoint of anterior (inferior) margin of foramen magnum.
basis angle—Angle at intersection of sphenoidal plane and plane of basioccipital clivus.
bregma—Point where coronal and sagittal sutures meet.
clition—Highest point on midline of dorsum sellae.
condylar angle, inner—Anterosuperior angle at intersection of condylar-premolar plane and condylobasal axis.
condylar-premolar plane—Transverse plane through a line connecting condylion and superior point of anterior premolar (with allowance for excessive attrition).
condylion (mandibular)—Highest point of mandibular condyle.
condylion (occipital)—Most distal point of occipital condyle.
condylobasal axis—Axis of condyle perpendicular to basal mandibular plane.
condylogoniale plane—Transverse plane through a line connecting distal point of mandibular angle and distal point of condyle.
coronale—Point of coronal suture where frontal diameter is greatest.
coronion—Apex of coronoid process of mandible.
cyclosion—Most distal point of outer margin of orbit between zygomaticofrontal suture and angle between horizontal and vertical processes of zygomatic bone.
dacryon—Juncture of frontal, lacrimal, and superior maxillary bones.
dakryon—See *dacryon.*
entomion—Point behind and above auditory meatus where parietal notch of temporal bone meets anterior extension of mastoid angle of parietal bone.
euryon—Point on each side of skull marking greatest transverse diameter of braincase.
Frankfort plane—Transverse plane through a line connecting base of orbit and top of external auditory meatus; also known as the ear-eye (auricle-orbitale or porion-orbitale) plane.
Frankfurt plane—See Frankfort plane.
glabella—Swelling or depression in median line of frontal bone just above nasal root and between superciliary arches.
gnathion—See *mental point.*
gonion—Posterior point of mandibular angle.
hormion—Point on sagittal plane where midline of presphenoid appears between alae of vomer.
incisor point—Distal point of foremost upper or lower incisor.
infradentale—See *symphysion.*
inion—External occipital protuberance; may coincide with opisthocranium or with lambda.
jugal point—Vertex of superior angle between frontal and zygomatic processes of malar.
lambda—Meeting point of sagittal and lambdoid sutures; point at or nearest median line; may coincide with inion, or opisthocranium.
maximum occipital point—See *opisthocranium.*
mental point—lowest point on mandibular symphysis.
metopic point—See *metopion.*
metopion—Point on midline (or metopic suture) between the two frontal eminences.
nasal point—See *nasion.*
nasion—Median point of frontonasal suture.

obelion—In human, point on sagittal suture between the parietal foramina.
occipital angle—Angle at intersection of Frankfurt plane and occipital plane.
occipital condylion—Distal point of occipital condyle.
occipital plane—Transverse plane through a line connecting inion and opisthion.
occipital point—See *opisthocranium*.
ophryon—Midpoint of line drawn across upper margin of orbits.
opisthion—Midpoint of posterior (superior) border of foramen magnum.
opisthocranium—Most distal point of anteroposterior diameter of skull; may coincide with inion and/or lambda.
orbitale—Lowest point on inferior border of orbit.
palatal axis—Axis of bony palate from prosthion to staphylion.
pogonion—In human, anterior projection of chin.
porion—Midpoint of superior margin of external auditory meatus.
preauricular point—Point on inferior margin of posterior border of postglenoid process; point on posterior margin of glenoid fossa in species lacking a postglenoid process.
prosthion—Tip of bone between upper middle incisors.
pterion—Juncture of frontal, parietal, and sphenoid bones; the temporal may also join at this point.
rhinion—Upper median point of anterior nasal opening.
sphenion—Anterior extremity of sphenoparietal suture; may coincide with pterion.
sphenobasion—Midpoint of spheno-occipital (sphenobasilar) suture.
sphenoidal plane—Transverse plane through a line connecting sphenoidal point and tylion or highest point of limbus sphenoidalis.
sphenoidal point—Anterior point of planum sphenoidem of interior surface of sphenoid.
spinal point—See *acanthion*.
staphylion—Distal point of posterior nasal spine.
stephanion—Point of intersection between temporal ridge and coronal suture.
subnasal point—See *spinal point*.
supra-auricular point—Point at root of zygomatic process directly above auricular point.
supranasal point—See *ophryon*.
supraorbital point—See *ophryon*.
symphyseal angle—Angle at intersection of basal mandibular plane and line tangent to external surface or axis of symphysis.
symphysion—Most anterior point on mandibular symphysis, coincides with mandibular alveolar point.
tylion—Point on midline of limbus sphenoidalis (anterior border of optic chiasmatic groove).
vertex—Superior point of skull; may coincide with bregma.
zygion—Most distal point on zygomatic arch.
zygomatic point—Tubercle below inferior angle of root of zygomatic process of maxillary bone; may coincide with *zygomaxillare*.
zygomaxillare—Lowest point on zygomaxillary suture; may coincide with *zygomatic point*.

31 Skull

14. Explanation of Symbols and Abbreviations Used in Illustrations

1 interpremaxillary suture
2 internasal suture
3 nasopremaxillary suture
4 frontal suture (metopic suture; usually obliterated in adults of higher primates)
5 interparietal suture (sagittal suture)
6 coronal suture
7 lambdoidal suture (parieto-occipital suture)
8 maxillopremaxillary suture, vertical
9 maxillonasal suture
10 frontonasal suture
11 frontomaxillary suture
12 frontolacrimal suture
13 frontoethmoid suture
14 ethmolacrimal suture (lacrimoethmoid suture)
15 maxillolacrimal suture (lacrimomaxillary suture)
16 maxilloethmoid suture
17 frontozygomatic suture (frontomalar suture; zygomaticofrontal suture)
18 sphenofrontal suture
19 sphenoethmoid suture
20 sphenomaxillary suture
21 sphenozygomatic suture
22 sphenoparietal suture
23 sphenosquamosal suture (sphenotemporal suture)
24 parietozygomatic suture (zygomaticoparietal suture)
25 parietotemporal suture (squamosal suture)
26 parietomastoid suture
27 zygomaticomaxillary suture
28 zygomaticotemporal suture
29 maxillopremaxillary suture, transverse
30 intermaxillary suture
31 maxillopalatine suture
32 interpalatine suture
33 sphenopalatine suture
34 spheno-occipital suture
35 occipitomastoid suture
36 ethmopalatine suture
37 orbitosphenoid suture
38 intermaxillovomer suture
39 palatovomer suture
40 sphenovomer suture
41 ethmovomer suture

A medial pterygoid plate
a anterior
ac anterior crus
acfos anterior cranial fossa
acpr anterior clinoid process
aEf anterior ethmoidal foramen
agl angle
alf anterior foramen lacerum
alpr alveolar process
appy apex pyramidis
ar artery
aS alisphenoid bone
asng ascending
asngrm ascending ramus
aV ala vomeris
B lateral pterygoid plate
base base of mandible
basO basion
bE bulla ethmoidalis
bin body of incus
bO basioccipital (pars basilaris)
body body of mandible
bS basisphenoid bone
c canal
ca canine tooth
cav cavity
cc carotid canal
cdl condyle
cf carotid foramen
cfos cerebellar fossa
cgE crista galli
cgS chiasmatic groove (optic groove)
co coronion
coch cochlea
copr coronoid process
cr crest
crfos cerebral fossa (occipital fossa)
csS carotid sulcus or groove
dggr digastric groove
dgrg digastric ridge or shelf
div diverticulum
dpl diploe (diploë)
dsng descending
dsS dorsum sella turcica
E ethmoid bone
eam external auditory meatus
Ec cartilaginous plate of ethmoid bone
Ecp cribriform plate (lamina cribrosa)
Ect ectoturbinal bone

ect	ectotympanic (tympanic ring or tympanic annulus)
Ef	ethmoidal foramen
Efos	ethmoidal fossa (houses olfactory lobes)
Enty	entotympanic bone
Eoff	olfactory foramina
eOp	external occipital protuberance (inion)
ept	epitympanic cavity
epT	epitympanum
Es	ethmoidal sinus
Et	ethmoturbinal bones (I-IV)
Et-I	turbinate bone, middle (ethmoturbinal-I; concha nasalis media; middle nasal concha)
Et-II	ethmoturbinal-II (concha nasalis superior; superior nasal concha)
Et-III	ethmoturbinal-III (concha nasalis suprema; supreme nasal concha)
Et-IV	ethmoturbinal IV
Et-n	nasoturbinal (superior turbinate)
exO	exoccipital bone
F	frontal bone
f	foramen
faq	fallopian aqueduct
fC	foramen Civinini
fcr	foramen crotaphiticum
feno	fenestra ovale (fenestra ovalis, fenestra vestibuli)
fenr	fenestra rotundum (fenestra rotunda; fossa fenestra cochleae; round window)
fis	fissure
fmO	foramen magnum
fo	foramen ovale
fos	fossa
Fs	frontal sinus
Fso	frontal sinus, ostium
gfos	glenoid fossa (mandibular fossa)
gn	gnathion
gnlfos	genial fossa
gon	gonion
gPalf	greater palatine foramen (major palatine foramen)
gr	groove
grC	groove Civinini
hcO	condylar foramen (hypoglossal canal or foramen)
hmal	head of malleus
hpS	hamular process of pterygoid (hamulus pterygoideus; hamular process)
hsc	horizontal semicircular canal
hypt	hypotympanum (bulla)
hyptc	hypotympanic cells
hyptd	hypotympanic cavity, dorsomedial
hyptl	hypotympanic cavity, lateral
i	incisor tooth
iam	internal auditory meatus (temporal meatus)
icar	internal carotid artery
if	infraorbital foramen
ifos	foramen lacerum posterius (posterior lacerated foramen)
im	inferior meatus
imof	inferior margin of optic foramen
in	incus
inf	inferior
infmasrg	inferior masseteric ridge
infMn	inferior mandibular notch
inion	inion (external occipital protuberance)
iOcr	internal occipital crest
iof	interorbital foramen
iofis	inferior orbital fissure (sphenomaxillary fissure)
iOprt	internal occipital protuberance
iP	Inca bone
ipsgr	groove for inferior petrosal sinus
jf	jugular foramen and fossa
jfos	jugular fossa (jugular foramen; posterior lacerated foramen)
L	lacrimal bone
l	line
lcin	long crus of incus
lcr	lambdoid crest (superior nuchal line)
Lfos	lacrimal fossa
lig	ligament
lmal	lamina of malleus
Lml	marginal lingula of lacrimal bone
loE	lamina orbitalis (orbital plate of ethmoid; os planum)
lofis	lateral orbital fissure (also situated behind alisphenoid and malar, or between malar and parietal)
lPalf	lesser posterior palatine foramen (minor posterior palatine foramen)
lpE	lamina perpendicularis (perpendicular plate of ethmoid)
lpS	lateral plate of pterygoid process (lamina lateralis processus pterygoidea)
lpsfis	lateral petrosphenoidal fissure
ls	limbus sphenoidalis
lsc	lateral semicircular canal (horizontal semicircular canal)
ltS	transverse lamina
ltscp	longitudinal tympanic septum
lun	lunar notch
M	maxillary bone (superior maxilla, maxilla)
m	molar tooth
ma	malleus
magr	groove or grooves for branches of middle meningeal artery
mal	malleus
masfos	masseteric fossa
mest	mesotympanic cavity (mesotympanum; atrium)
mfos	mesopterygoid fossa
mlf	mental foramen
mlprt	mental protuberance
mlsp	mental spine
mm	middle meatus
mmal	manubrium, of malleus
Mn	mandible
Mnf	mandibular foramen
mngr	groove for maxillary branch of trigeminal nerve
MPmso	maxillopremaxillary sinus, ostium
Mpr	maxillary process of zygomatic arch
mpS	medial pterygoid plate
mpsfis	median petrosphenoidal fissure
mprT	mastoid process
mpT	mastoid process
Mrg	maxillary ridge
Ms	maxillary sinus
msf	mastoid foramen

Mso	maxillary sinus, ostium
Mt	maxilloturbinal bone (inferior turbinate bone)
mT	mastoid bone
mTc	mastoid cells
mTf	mastoid foramen
mygr	mylohyoid groove
myl	mylohyoid line
N	nasal bone
ncdl	neck of condyle
ncr	inferior nuchal line (nuchal crest)
O	occipital bone
obl	oblique line
Oc	occipital condyle
Ocl	clivus of basioccipital
Ocr	external or medial occipital crest (occipital crest)
oEs	ostium, ethmoidal sinus
of	optic foramen
ofos	orbital fossa
oOrg	oblique occipital ridge
op	occipital point
opO	opisthion
org	orbital ridge or crest
oS	orbitosphenoid bone
P	parietal bone
p	post; posterior; postero-
Pal	palatine bone
Palc	palatine canal
Palf	palatine foramen
Pals	palatine sinus
Palsp	posteromedian palatine spine
pbof	posterior border of optic foramen
pcpr	posterior clinoid process
pEf	posterior ethmoidal foramen
pfos	pterygoid fossa
pgf	postglenoid foramen
pgpr	postglenoid process
plc	posterolateral canal
plf	foramen lacerum posterius (posterior lacerated foramen)
pls	planum sphenoideum
Pm	premaxillary bone
pm	premolar tooth
Pmf	incisive foramen
pofis	petro-occipital fissure
pog	pogonion
postn	posterior nares
ppr	pterygoid process
pr	process
prgr	processus gracilis
prom	promontorium (promontorium cochleae)
proma	promontory artery
prt	protuberance
prS	sphenoidal spine, spinous process
pS	presphenoid bone
psc	posterior semicircular canal
psT	petrous spine
pT	petrous part of temporal bone
ptcr	petrous crest
ptfis	glaserian fissure (Glaserian fissure; petrotympanic fissure)
pt lam	pterygospinous lamina
pye	pyramidal eminence
qsT	quadrilateral surface
rf	foramen rotundum
rg	ridge
rgMnn	ridge of mandibular neck
rm	ramus
rtrmf	retromolar foramen
rtrmfos	retromolar fossa
rtrmtr	retromolar triangle
S	sphenoid bone
s	sinus
sagcr	sagittal crest
scin	short crus of incus
scr	sulcus crotaphiticum
sep	septum
seT	subarcuate eminence
sf	foramen spinosum
sfos	subarcuate fossa
sgn	sigmoid notch
sgr	sigmoid groove (lateral groove)
sm	superior meatus
smf	stylomastoid foramen
SMs	sphenomaxillary sinus
sncr	supreme nuchal line
sof	supraorbital foramen or notch
sofis	superior orbital fissure
sp	spine
spC	spina Civinini
spn	spina nasalis
spp	spinous process (sphenoidal spine)
spr	styloid process
spsgr	groove for superior petrosal sinus
Spt	sphenoidal point
srg	sagittal ridge
Ss (1–4)	sphenoidal sinus (1–4)
ssc	superior semicircular canal
sT	squamosal portion of temporal bone
sta	stapes
star	stapedial artery, superior branch
statn	stapedial tendon
stS	sella turcica (hypophyseal fossa)
su	suture
sub	sub-
sublfos	sublingual fossa
submfos	submaxillary fossa
sup	superior
supmasrg	superior masseteric ridge
SupMnn	superior mandibular notch
sym	symphysis
symf	symphyseal foramen
T	temporal bone (squamosal bone)
t	concha (turbinate bone)
tant	tympanic antrum
tbT	tympanic bulla (auditory bulla)
tcav	tympanic cavity
tcr	temporal crest
tdr	tympanic drum
Tfos	temporal fossa
tent	tentorium osseum (tentoralis petrosi)
tentpr	tentoralis petrosi, processus
Tfos	temporal fossa
tip	trigeminal impression
tm	tympanic membrane
tpr	tympanic process of petrous bone
tpraS	tympanic process of alisphenoid bone
tr	transverse
trg	superior temporal line or ridge

trmsep	transverse mastoidal septum
trs	transverse ridge or sulcus
trtsep	transverse tympanic septum
ts	tuberculum sellae
tt	auditory tube (Eustachian tube; tympanic tube; pharyngotympanic tube)
ttm	auditory tube, meatus
upr	uncinate process
V	vomer
vfos	vermiform fossa
Vs	vomerine sinus
vsh	vaginal sheath of styloid process
Z	malar, zygomatic, jugal bone
Zf	malar foramen (zygomaticofacial foramen)
Zof	zygomatico-orbital foramen
Zp	malar process (zygomatic process)
ZpT	squamous portion of zygomatic arch (temporal process of zygomatic arch)

Cranial Terminology with Symbols and Abbreviations

ala vomeris	aV
alisphenoid bone	aS
alveolar process	alpr
angle	agl
anterior	a
anterior clinoid process	acpr
anterior cranial fossa	acfos
anterior crus	ac
anterior ethmoidal foramen	aEf
anterior foramen lacerum	alf
apex pyramidis	appy
artery	ar
ascending	asng
ascending ramus	asngrm
atrium (mesotympanic cavity; mesotympanum)	mest
auditory bulla	tbT
auditory tube (Eustachian tube; tympanic tube; pharyngotympanic tube)	tt
auditory tube, meatus	ttm
base of mandible	base
basioccipital (pars basilaris)	bO
basion	basO
basisphenoid bone	bS
body of incus	bin
body of mandible	body
bulla ethmoidalis	bE
canal	c
canine tooth	ca
carotid canal	cc
carotid foramen	cf
carotid sulcus or groove	csS
cartilaginous plate of ethmoid bone	Ec
cavity	cav
cerebellar fossa	cfos
cerebral fossa (occipital fossa)	crfos
chiasmatic groove (optic groove)	cgS
clivus of basioccipital	Ocl
cochlea	coch
concha (turbinate bone)	t
concha nasalis media	Et-I
concha nasalis superior	Et-II
concha nasalis suprema	Et-III
condylar foramen (hypoglossal canal or foramen)	hcO
condyle	cdl
coronal suture	6
coronion	co
coronoid process	copr
crest	cr
cribriform plate (lamina cribrosa)	Ecp
crista galli	cgE
descending	dsng
digastric groove	dggr
digastric ridge or shelf	dgrg
diploe (diploë)	dpl
diverticulum	div
dorsum sella turcica	dsS
ectoturbinal bone	Ect
ectotympanic (tympanic ring or tympanic annulus)	ect
entotympanic bone	Enty
epitympanic cavity	ept
epitympanum	epT
ethmoid bone	E
ethmoid; cartilaginous portion of septum	Ec
ethmoidal foramen	Ef
ethmoidal fossa (houses olfactory lobes)	Efos
ethmoidal sinus	Es
ethmolacrimal suture (lacrimoethmoid suture	14
ethmopalatine suture	36
ethmoturbinal bones (I-IV)	Et (I-IV)
ethmoturbinal I (turbinate bone; concha nasalis media; middle nasal concha)	Et-I
ethmoturbinal II (concha nasalis superior; superior nasal concha)	Et-II
ethmoturbinal III (concha nasalis suprema; supreme nasal concha)	Et-III
ethmoturbinal IV	Et-IV
ethmovomer suture	41
Eustachian tube	tt
exoccipital bone	exO
external auditory meatus	eam
external occipital protuberance (inion)	eOp
external or medial occipital crest (occipital crest)	Ocr
fallopian aqueduct	faq
fenestra cochleae	fenr
fenestra ovale (fenestra ovalis; fenestra vestibuli)	feno
fenestra rotundum (fenestra rotunda; fossa fenestra cochleae; round window)	fenr
fenestra vestibuli (fenestra ovale, fenestra ovalis)	feno
fissure	fis
foramen	f
foramen Civinini	fC
foramen, condylar	hcO
foramen crotaphiticum	fcr
foramen, hypoglossal (hypoglossal canal or foramen)	hcO
foramen lacerum posterius (posterior lacerated foramen)	ifos, plf
foramen magnum	fmO
foramen ovale	fo
foramen rotundum	rf

foramen spinosum	sf
foramen, stylomastoid	smf
fossa	fos
frontal bone	F
frontal suture (metopic suture)	4
frontal sinus	Fs
frontal sinus, ostium	Fso
frontoethmoid suture	13
frontolacrimal suture	12
frontomalar suture (frontozygomatic suture)	17
frontomaxillary suture	11
frontonasal suture	10
frontozygomatic suture (frontomalar suture)	17
genial fossa	gnlfos
glaserian fissure (Glaserian fissure; petrotympanic fissure)	ptfis
glenoid fossa (mandibular fossa)	gfos
gnathion	gn
gonion	gon
greater palatine foramen (major palatine foramen)	gPalf
groove	gr
groove Civinini	grC
groove for inferior petrosal sinus	ipsgr
groove for maxillary branch of trigeminal nerve	mngr
groove or grooves for branches of middle meningeal artery	magr
groove for superior petrosal sinus	spsgr
hamular process of pterygoid (hamulus pterygoideus; hamular process)	hpS
head of malleus	hmal
horizontal semicircular canal	hsc
hypoglossal canal (condylar foramen)	hcO
hypophyseal fossa (sella turcica)	stS
hypotympanic cavity, dorsomedial	hyptd
hypotympanic cavity, lateral	hyptl
hypotympanic cells	hyptc
hypotympanum (bulla)	hypt
Inca bone	iP
incisive foramen	Pmf
incisor tooth	i
incisura Civinini	iC
incus	in
inferior	inf
inferior mandibular notch	infMn
inferior margin of optic foramen	imof
inferior masseteric ridge	infmasrg
inferior meatus	im
inferior nuchal line (nuchal crest)	ncr
inferior orbital fissure (sphenomaxillary fissure)	iofis
inferior turbinate (maxilloturbinal bone)	Mt
infraorbital foramen	if
inion (external occipital protuberance)	inion
intermaxillary suture	30
intermaxillovomer suture	38
internal auditory meatus (temporal meatus)	iam
internal carotid artery	icar
internal occipital crest	iOcr
internal occipital protuberance	iOprt
internasal suture	2
interorbital foramen	iof
interpalatine suture	32
interparietal bone	iP
interparietal suture (sagittal suture)	5
interpremaxillary suture	1
jugal bone (malar, zygoma)	Z
jugular foramen and fossa	jf
jugular fossa (jugular foramen; posterior lacerated foramen)	jfos
lacerum, anterior foramen	alf
lacrimal bone	L
lacrimal bone, marginal lingula of	Lml
lacrimal fossa	Lfos
lacrimoethmoid suture (ethmolacrimal suture)	14
lacrimomaxillary suture (maxillolacrimal suture)	15
lambdoidal suture (parieto-occipital suture)	7
lambdoid crest (superior nuchal line)	lcr
lamina cribrosa (cribriform plate)	Ecp
lamina lateralis processus pterygoidea	lpS, B
lamina of malleus	lmal
lamina orbitalis of ethmoid (orbital plate of ethmoid; os planum)	loE
lamina perpendicularis (perpendicular plate of ethmoid)	lpE
lateral groove (sigmoid groove)	sgr
lateral orbital fissure (also situated behind alisphenoid and malar, or between malar and parietal)	lofis
lateral petrosphenoidal fissure	lpsfis
lateral plate of pterygoid process (lamina lateralis processus pterygoidea)	lpS
lateral pterygoid plate	B, lpS
lateral semicircular canal (horizontal semicircular canal)	lsc
lesser palatine foramen	lPalf
ligament	lig
limbus sphenoidalis	ls
line	l
long crus of incus	lcin
longitudinal tympanic septum	ltscp
lunar notch	lun
malar, zygoma, jugal bone	Z
malar foramen (zygomaticofacial foramen)	Zf
malar process or zygomatic process	Zp
malleus	ma, mal
mandible	Mn
mandibular base	base
mandibular foramen	Mnf
mandibular fossa (glenoid fossa)	gfos
manubrium, of malleus	mmal
masseteric fossa	masfos
mastoid bone	mT
mastoid cells	mTc
mastoid foramen	msf, mTf
mastoid process	MprT
maxillary bone (superior maxilla, maxilla)	M
maxillary process of zygomatic arch	Mpr
maxillary ridge	Mrg
maxillary sinus	Ms
maxillary sinus, ostium	Mso
maxilloethmoidal suture	16
maxillolacrimal suture (lacrimomaxillary suture)	15
maxillonasal suture	9
maxillopalatine suture	31

maxillopremaxillary sinus, ostium	Mpmso
maxillopremaxillary suture, transverse	29
maxillopremaxillary suture, vertical	8
maxilloturbinal bone (inferior turbinate)	Mt
medial plate of pterygoid process	A, mpS
median petrosphenoidal fissure	mpsfis
mental foramen	mlf
mental protuberance	mlprt
mental spine	mlsp
mesopterygoid fossa	mfos
mesotympanic cavity (mesotympanum; atrium)	mest
mesotympanum (mesotympanic cavity; atrium)	mest
metopic suture (frontal suture)	4
middle concha	Et-I
middle meatus	mm
middle nasal concha	Et-I
molar tooth	m
mylohyoid groove	mygr
mylohyoid line	myl
nasal bone	N
nasopremaxillary suture	3
nasoturbinal (superior turbinate)	Et-n
neck of condyle	ncdl
nuchal crest (inferior nuchal line)	ncr
oblique line	obl
oblique occipital ridge	oOrg
occipital bone	O
occipital condyle	Oc
occipital crest (external or medial occipital crest)	Ocr
occipital fossa (cerebral fossa)	crfos
occipital point	op
occipitomastoid suture	35
olfactory foramina	Eoff
opisthion	opO
optic foramen	of
optic groove (chiasmatic groove)	cgS
orbital fossa	ofos
orbital plate of ethmoid (lamina orbitalis; os planum)	loE
orbital ridge or crest	org
orbitosphenoid bone	oS
orbitosphenoid suture	37
os planum (orbital plate of ethmoid; lamina orbitalis)	loE
ostium, ethmoidal sinus	oEs
ovale, foramen	fo
palatine bone	Pal
palatine canal	Palc
palatine foramen	Palf
palatine foramen, greater (major)	gPalf
palatine foramen, lesser (minor)	lPalf
palatine sinus	Pals
palatovomer suture	39
parietal bone	P
parietomastoid suture	26
parieto-occipital suture (lamboidal suture)	7
parietotemporal suture (squamosal suture)	25
parietozygomatic suture (zygomaticoparietal suture)	24
perpendicular plate of ethmoid (lamina perpendicularis)	lpE
petro-occipital fissure	pofis
petrotympanic fissure (glaserian fissure)	ptfis
petrous crest	ptcr
petrous spine	psT
petrous part of temporal bone	pT
pharyngotympanic tube (Eustachian tube; tympanic tube)	tt
planum sphenoideum	pls
pogonion	pog
post; posterior; postero-	p
posterior border of optic foramen	pbof
posterior clinoid process	pcpr
posterior ethmoidal foramen	pEf
posterior lacerated foramen (foramen lacerum posterius)	plf, ifos
posterior nares	postn
posterior palatine foramen, greater (major)	gPalf
posterior palatine foramen, lesser (minor)	lPalf
posterior semicircular canal	psc
posterolateral canal	plc
posteromedian palatine spine	Palsp
postglenoid foramen	pgf
postglenoid process, postglenoid tubercle	pgpr
premaxillary bone	Pm
premolar tooth	pm
presphenoid bone	pS
process	pr
processus gracilis	prgr
promontorium (promontorium cochleae)	prom
promontory artery	proma
protuberance	prt
pterygoid fossa	pfos
pterygoid process	ppr
pterygospinous lamina	pt lam
pyramidal eminence	pye
quadrilateral surface	qsT
ramus	rm
retromolar foramen	rtrmf
retromolar fossa	rtrmfos
retromolar triangle	rtrmtr
ridge	rg
ridge of mandibular neck	rgMnn
round window (fenestra rotundum; fenestra rotunda; fossa fenestra cochleae)	fenr
sagittal crest	sagcr
sagittal ridge	srg
sagittal suture (interparietal suture)	5
sella turcica (hypophyseal fossa)	stS
septum	sep
short crus of incus	scin
sigmoid groove (lateral groove)	sgr
sigmoid notch	sgn
sinus	s
sphenobasilar suture (spheno-occipital suture)	34
sphenoethmoid suture	19
sphenofrontal suture	18
sphenoidal point	Spt
sphenoidal process	prS
sphenoidal sinus (1–4)	Ss (1–4)
sphenoidal spine, spinous process	prS, spp
sphenoid bone	S
sphenomaxillary fissure (inferior orbital fissure)	iofis
sphenomaxillary sinus	SMs
sphenomaxillary suture	20

spheno-occipital suture (sphenobasilar suture)	34
sphenopalatine suture	33
sphenoparietal suture	22
sphenosquamosal suture (sphenotemporal suture)	23
sphenotemporal suture (sphenosquamosal suture)	23
sphenovomer suture	40
sphenozygomatic suture	21
spina Civinini	spC
spina nasalis	spn
spine	sp
spine, petrous	psT
spinous process (sphenoidal spine)	spp
squamosal bone (temporal bone)	T
squamosal portion of temporal bone	sT
squamosal suture (parietotemporal suture)	25
squamous portion of zygomatic arch (temporal process of zygomatic arch)	ZpT
stapedial artery, superior branch	star
stapedial tendon	statn
stapes	sta
styloid process	spr
stylomastoid foramen	smf
sub-	sub
subarcuate eminence	seT
subarcuate fossa	sfos
sublingual fossa	sublfos
submaxillary fossa	submfos
superior	sup
superior mandibular notch	supMnn
superior masseteric ridge	supmasrg
superior maxilla (maxillary bone; maxilla)	M
superior meatus	sm
superior nasal concha (ethmoturbinal-II; concha nasalis superior)	Et-II
superior nuchal line (lamboid crest)	lcr
superior orbital fissure	sofis
superior semicircular canal	ssc
superior temporal line or ridge	trg
supraorbital foramen or notch	sof
supreme nasal concha (ethmoturbinal-III; concha nasalis suprema)	Et-III
supreme nuchal line	sncr
suture	su
symphyseal foramen	symf
symphysis	sym
temporal bone (squamosal bone)	T
temporal crest	tcr
temporal fossa	Tfos
temporal meatus (internal auditory meatus)	iam
temporal process of zygomatic arch (squamous portion of zygomatic arch)	ZpT
temporal ridge (superior temporal line)	trg
tentoralis petrosi	tent
tentoralis petrosi, processus	tentpr
tentorium osseum	tent
transverse	tr
transverse lamina	ltS
transverse mastoidal septum	trmsep
transverse ridge or sulcus	trs
transverse tympanic septum	trtsep
trigeminal impression	tip
tuberculum sellae	ts
turbinate (turbinal bone; ethnoturbinal bone)	Et
turbinate bone (concha)	t
turbinate bone, inferior (maxilloturbinate bone)	Mt
turbinate bone, middle (ethmoturbinal-I; concha nasalis media; middle nasal concha)	Et-I
turbinate bone, superior (ethmoturbinal-II; concha nasalis superior; superior nasal concha)	Et-II
tympanic annulus (ectotympanic; tympanic ring)	ect
tympanic antrum	tant
tympanic bulla	tbT
tympanic cavity	tcav
tympanic drum	tdr
tympanic membrane	tm
tympanic process of alisphenoid bone	tpraS
tympanic process of petrous bone	tpr
tympanic ring (tympanic annulus; ectotympanic)	ect
tympanic tube (Eustachian tube; auditory tube; pharyngotympanic tube)	tt
uncinate process	upr
vaginal sheath of styloid process	vsh
vermiform fossa	vfos
vomer	V
vomerine sinus	Vs
zygomatic bone (malar bone; jugal bone)	Z
zygomatic process (malar process)	Zp
zygomaticofacial foramen (malar foramen)	Zf
zygomaticofrontal suture (frontozygomatic suture; frontomalar suture)	17
zygomaticomaxillary suture	27
zygomatico-orbital foramen	Zof
zygomaticoparietal suture (parietozygomatic suture)	24
zygomaticotemporal suture	28

32 Teeth
1. Basic Crown Patterns and Cusp Homologies

Introduction

This chapter attempts to establish a scientific basis for tracing homologous dental elements in living placentals and marsupials to their inception in earliest mammals generally and in primates particularly. The text and illustrations are corrected versions of an earlier publication (Hershkovitz 1971*a*).

The much-criticized but widely used Osbornian terminology for dental elements was first devised to serve the aims of this account. Unfortunately the terms, as has been repeatedly shown, are equivocably based and their definitions are obscure when they do not distort or flatly contradict the messages they were designed to convey. One result has been the proliferation of makeshift terminologies, all cast in the Osbornian mold but with some modifications or additions to fit special problems. Another consequence has been the corruption of dental evolutionary thought through use of similar terms for nonhomologous upper and lower dental elements, and dissimilar terms for the homologous elements.

A radical departure from the traditional school is the system of dental terminology proposed in 1961 by Vandebroek. The scheme is founded on the primitive pattern of crests and cusps common to all postincisor teeth of eutherian (marsupial and placental) grade, and to most teeth of subeutherian grade, specifically Triconodonta, Docodonta, Symmetrodonta, and Pantotheria.

Reaction to Vandebroek's thesis has been for the most part reserved and sometimes hostile. General acceptance of his important contributions to knowledge of mammalian dental evolution was probably hindered by minor flaws in arguments, some controversial statements, use of strange terms for familiar dental elements, and perhaps more than anything else, by his assaults on cherished dogmas. Notwithstanding, my independent investigations of dental evolution and homologies based on large series of teeth of living species, mostly primates, insectivores, and marsupials, led to conclusions reached by Vandebroek. It appears to be necessary, therefore, to adopt some names proposed by this authority for dental elements not previously described in formal terms, and use others as replacements or alternates for a few Osbornian terms which more perniciously than others deprive dental descriptions of evolutionary significance. Otherwise, the familiar Osbornian terminology and the essentials of its system have been conserved as an expedient means of communication for detailing revised concepts and explaining new ones. Interpretations of dental homologies and evolution presented here and not anticipated by Vandebroek, or by Cope, Osborn, Gregory, Simpson, Butler, Remane, Patterson, and others cited in the text are derived as much from data and discussions presented by these authorities as from the specimens I studied.

Tridentate Tooth

The primitive mammalian tooth, or its reptilian prototype (fig. V.1A), is single- or double-rooted, sagittate in outline, subovate in cross section, with main cusp, the eocone (-id, or paracone-protoconid) rising to a conical peak; a small tubercle, the mesiostyle (-id) is usually present at the anterior base of the cusp, and another, the distostyle (-id), is present at the posterior base of the cusp. The crest of the eocone (-id) from tubercle to tubercle is the eocrista (-id). The axis of the eocrista from end to end of the three cusps is the primary or eocone (-id) axis. Either or both tubercles or styles (-ids), may become specialized, usually by hypertrophy, or either element, most often the mesiostyle (-id), may disappear. The ledge at the base of the crown which supports each style (-id) may disappear with it, or it may spread horizontally as a narrow band, the *cingulum (-id)*, along the buccal or the lingual, or on both sides to engirdle the base of the crown. This primitive, tricuspidate tooth, dominated by the comparatively enormous eocone (-id), is often called tritubercular, and sometimes triconodont. The equivalent term *tridentate* (fig. V.1A), proposed here for the primitive mammalian tooth, avoids confusion with the homonomous term tritubercular, and avoids the taxonomic connotation of the term triconodont.

Primary Evolutionary Processes

Specialization of the tridentate tooth is achieved through the evolutionary processes of (*a*) *caninization,* (*b*) *nutricialization,* (*c*) *molarization* or complication, and (*d*) *degeneration* or secondary simplification through reduction and elimination of dental elements.

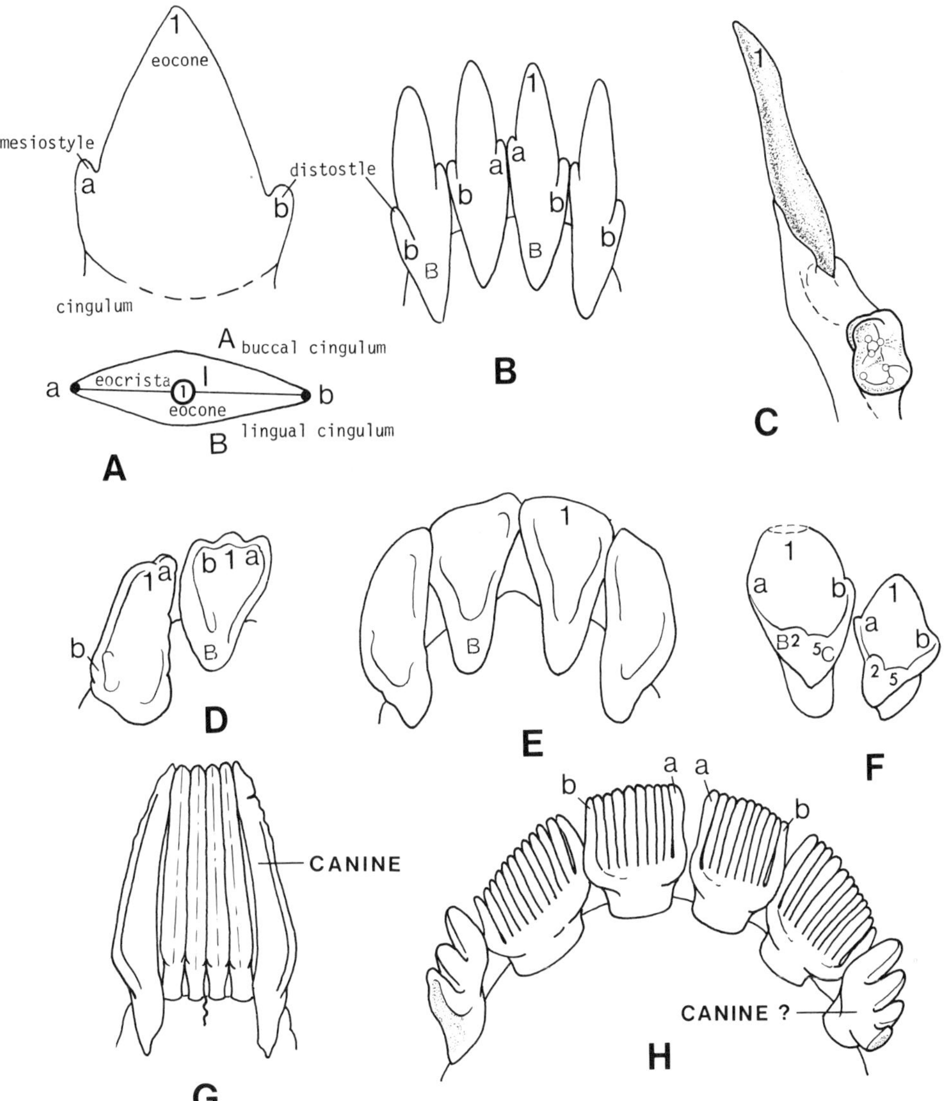

Fig. V.1. Primitive mammalian tooth (*A*) and variously specialized front teeth, buccal and occlusal views of left upper or right lower; *B*, tridentate lower incisors in pygmy marmoset, *Cebuella pygmaea* (Primates, Callitrichidae); *C*, caninized lower right incisor in the extinct *Phenacolemur pagei* (Primates, Phenacolemuridae, U. Paleocene), redrawn from Simpson (1955, pl. 32); absence of terminal stylids (*a*, *b*) and cingulum is a degenerative character; *D*, nutricial lower left incisors in cotton-top tamarin, *Saguinus oedipus oedipus* (Primates, Callitrichidae)—compare with following; *E*, adult lower incisors in cotton-top tamarin, example of caninization by expansion of main cusp (*1*) and fusion with terminal stylids (*a*, *b*); *F*, left upper tritubercular incisors of *Callicebus torquatus*, example of molarization with addition of cusp *2*, *5*; *G*, comblike lower incisors and canines in the ringtail lemur (*Lemur catta*), an example of caninization with secondary simplification or degeneration through loss of terminal stylids; *H*, comblike lower incisors (and canines?) in the colugo, *Cynocephalus volans*, an example of pectinization through complication or molarization, with each process (or crenule) of the morphogenetic field of the main cusp developing into an independent cuspulid. See page 300 and fig. V.21 for complete list of symbols and their respective conventional names. (Modified from Hershkovitz 1971*a*.)

Caninization

Caninization is the specialization, usually through hypertrophy, of the main cusp and of either or both primary cuspules of the tridentate tooth. Caninization may act on any primitive tooth, but it never transgresses the tridentate stage in dental complication.

The true canine, for all its exaggeration in many mammals, often as a sexual character of adult males, departs least from the tridentate model. The primitive canine, like primitive incisors and premolars, is a simple tridentate tooth. Specialization by hypertrophy and curvature or hooking of the main cone and cuspules are results of caninization. Formation of the lingual bulge, or torus, and vertical grooves, and addition of cusps or talon (-id), are manifestations of molarization. Obsolescence or loss of cingulum and primitive mesial and distal tubercles are consequences of degeneration.

The primitive or caninized anterior premolar is in effect a second and smaller canine. It still retains the form and function of a secondary canine in the superior arcade of prosimians, notably in *Euoticus elegantulus*, lorisids, and most callitrichids (fig. V.22), as well as in most primitive mammals. Some expansion or caninization of the main cusp of the second premolar (pm^3) is also common among species with three premolars (fig. V.4). In primates, extreme enlargement occurs in pm_4

of some early Tertiary "prosimians" (e.g., Carpolestidae). Additions to the caninized or tridentate model are products of molarization.

Incisors, like the lower central of *Cebuella,* may remain tridentate or primitively caniniform (fig. V.1B). In many "prosimians," especially early Tertiary Omomyidae and Paramomyidae, the lower incisors (or canines?) are caninized into thick elongate procumbent tusks (fig. V.1C). A more common and more successful form of incisor caninization results in expansion or spatulation of the main cusp, including fusion with one or both tubercles. In callitrichids, and indeed in most higher mammals, the mesial tubercle, or mesiostylid, loses its identity first, as in i_{1-2} of *Callithrix* (fig. V.26), then mesial and distal tubercles disappear from all incisors as in *Saguinus* (fig. V.26). In most higher primates, however, the distal tubercle, or distostylid, persists on the lateral incisor.

Lower incisors of living strepsirhines are narrow, subcylindrical, elongate, and rake- or comblike (fig. V.1H). The hypertrophy may well be the result of caninization, but loss of tubercles is degenerative. The upper strepsirhine incisors degenerated into peglike structures, perhaps directly from the primitive tridentate stage.

Incisivization, as conceived by Butler (1939*a,* p. 3), refers to differentiation of the incisor field. Incisors per se, however, are highly diversified. They may be primitively tridentate or simplified tusks, premolarlike, or peculiarly structured. Whatever their forms, the evolutionary processes leading to them are *caninization, molarization* (fig. V.1F) including nutricialization (fig. V.1D and below), and pectinization or formation of comblike complications as in Dermoptera (fig. V.1H), and, finally, *degeneration.*

Nutricialization

Nutricialization is the specialization of the newborn's milk incisors, particularly the lower, for teat gripping and ingestion of premasticated food. Nutricialization usually involves the splaying of procumbent deciduous tridentate incisors into volar-shaped feeding implements. During expansion, the eoconid fuses with the mesiostylid and often the distostylid as well. The shallow spoon-shaped depression, formed at least on the superior portion of the lingual aspect of each incisor, is possibly homologous with the trigonid basin of cheek teeth. The lower milk canine also appears to be somewhat nutricialized in some species and may perform a subsidiary or peripheral nutricial function. Milk incisors erode rapidly as solid food becomes a regular part of the juvenal diet.

Nutricial incisors are present in some species of newborn callitrichids (figs. V.1D, 2). They are also common among cebids (e.g., *Saimiri,* atelines) and Old World monkeys (e.g., colobines). Only those of callitrichids have been studied in detail or from an evolutionary point of view.

The least-specialized nutricial incisors among callitrichids are the deciduous lateral pair in *Cebuella.* The single worn tooth at hand appears to be caninized as much as nutricialized, but the impression is probably heightened by the fact that the canine is partly nutricialized. The lateral incisor in *Callithrix* is similar, with eoconid remaining dominant, the mesiostylid fused with it, the distostylid, metaconid, and "trigonid" basin distinct. Culmination of nutricialization is attained in the

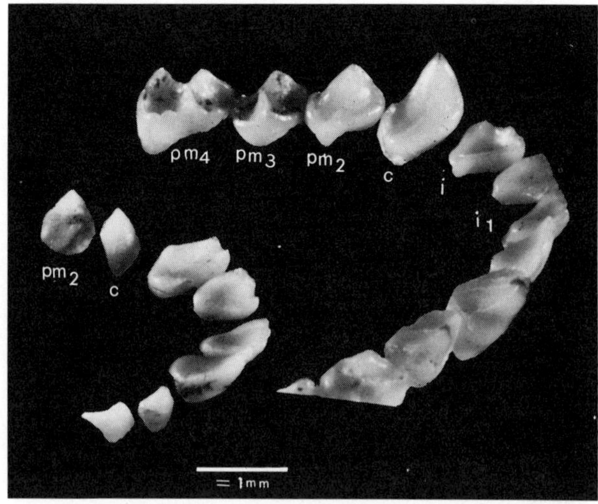

Fig. V.2. Nutricial lower incisors and canines of *Saguinus oedipus;* individual with pm_4 fully erupted is about 6 weeks old; individual with pm_2 erupted is less than 1 week old.

splayed lower lateral incisor of *Saguinus oedipus* with main cusp, the two primary tubercles, and metaconid subequal and surrounding the "trigonid" depression (fig. V.2). The more symmetrical central incisor of *oedipus* is expanded distally, the cutting edge trifid as in the spatulate permanent central incisors.

Striking similarities in form, and perhaps secondarily in function, are noted between callitrichid nutricial incisors and the simplified upper molariform teeth of Megachiroptera and such soft-fruit-eating phyllostomid bats as *Vampyrops.* Mention might also be made of the first upper and lower molars of the Paleocene picrodontids, as illustrated and described by Szalay (1968, p. 49; p. 53, fig. 21). In living forms, mushy foods, particularly soft fruits, are dietary mainstays.

Degeneration

Degeneration is the process of simplification through *reduction, obsolescence,* and *loss* of a tooth or its parts. Reduction often results in distortions of the original proportions and relationships of parts. As a rule, parts diminish and disappear inversely to the order in which they appeared in phylogeny. Some exceptions to the rule, however, may be more apparent than real. Older dental elements such as the paraconid may have disappeared or have been in the process of disappearing before later elements arose in the same tooth. Small size as a characteristic can be the primitive size and not the result of secondary reduction. Many styles and crenulations are plastic and often transient. Their absence in an individual or a population may be followed by full or partial reappearance in another individual or population of a succeeding generation.

Molarization

Molarization is the process of complication of the primitive tridentate crown (fig. I.A) by addition of secondary cusps, crests, cingula or shelves, and other dental elements. Molarization usually progresses from canine to incisors and from canine to molars. In some eutherians, the gradient of increasing complexity is from incisors to molars. Attendant modifications in size, form, and functional relations of teeth and their components are also phenomena of molarization. The end product of molarization is the true molar with a multiple root system and the persistent eocone (-id) forming part of a complex crown pattern. The crown of the mammalian lower molar, a "trigonid" with or without talonid (fig. V.7), conforms to the single basic type described below (p. 281). All therian upper molar crowns conform to one of three basic enamel patterns defined as follows.

Basic Upper Molar Crown Patterns

1. *Zalambdomorphic* (figs. V.3.B; 4.C,D; 6.B–K, 8, 20). A single cone, the eocone (paracone), present; true metacone absent; eocrista V- to nearly U-shaped relative to buccal edge of crown; buccal cingulum (*A*) expanded laterally into a broad shelf supporting mesiostyle, distostyle, and two to five or more ectostyles; lingual shelf (*B*), protocone or hypocone, or both, undifferentiated, rudimentary, or not more than moderately developed.

2. *Euthermorphic* (figs. V.3E,F; 5C; 6N–W; 9, 20). Two cones, the eocone and true metacone (*4*), always present, the second often as well developed as the first; eocrista roughly parallel to buccal edge of crown, the portion between eocone and metacone more-or-less straight or folded into a weak angle; mesiostyle and distostyle present, ectostyles, if present, variable in size and number but usually not exceeding six; lingual cingulum expanded into a prominent shelf, triangular to nearly square in outline and supporting a protocone or hypocone or both, and frequently one or more entostyles.

3. *Dilambdomorphic* (figs. V.3D; 4A,B; 20). Metacone always present, often larger than eocone; eocrista W-shaped relative to buccal edge; buccal cingulum always expanded into a broad shelf subdivided by a distinctive notch or fold into parastylar and metastylar areas with one to three or four ectostyles; lingual shelf produced into a triangular base supporting a distinct protocone; posterolingual cingulum (*C*) if present, with or without hypocone; one or more minute lingual styles, or entostyles, sometimes present.

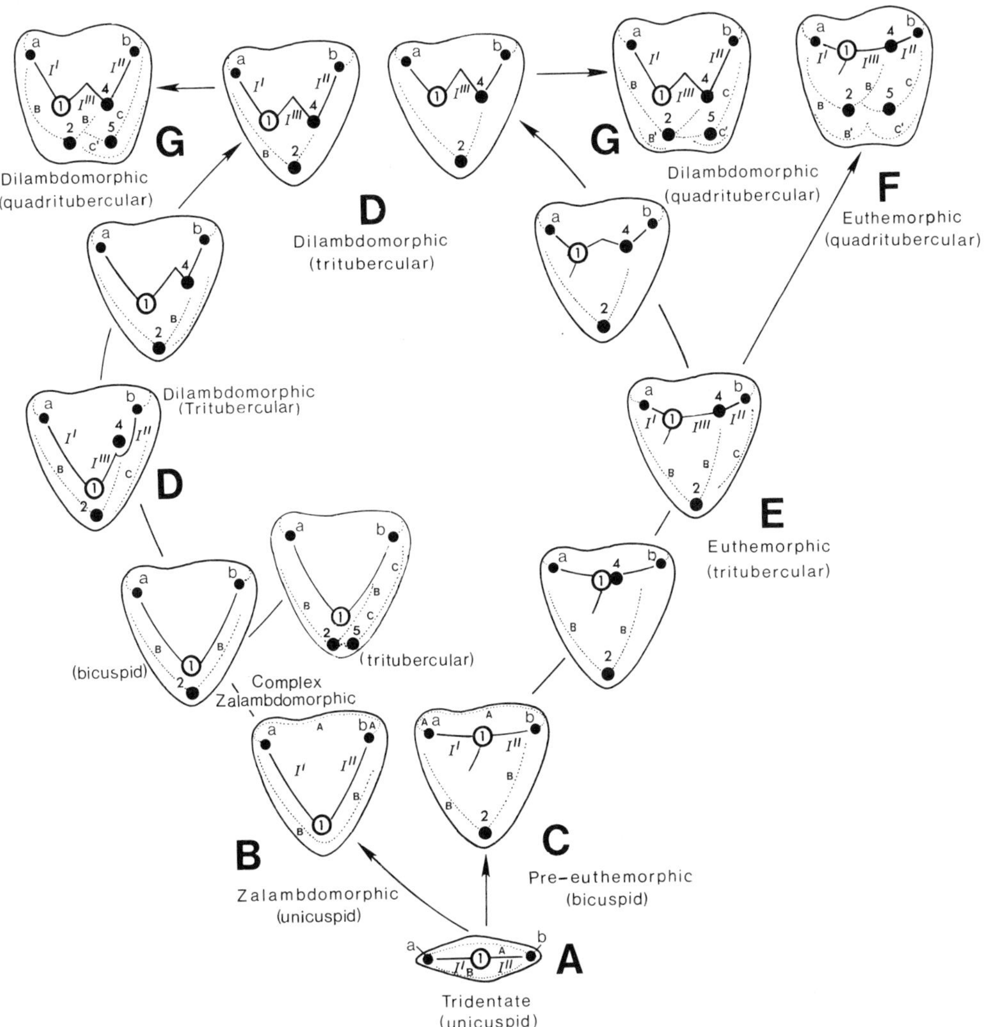

Fig. V.3. Two evolutionary pathways to dilambdomorphic upper molar crown pattern **D** from primitive tridentate **A** through (1) zalambdomorphic **B,** or (2) euthemorphic **C.** The euthemorphic line also progresses from tritubercular **E** to euthemorphic quadritubercular grade **F.** The tritubercular dilambdomorphic grade **D** may also evolve to the dilambdomorphic quadritubercular grade **G.** Note mechanics of differentiation of metacone (*4*) and eocone (*1*), in each morphological series. Cingula *B* and *C* from which cones *2* and *5* arise are shown as dotted lines. Secondary or neocingular *B′* and *C′* are similarly indicated. Buccal cingulum *A* is shown in diagrams labeled **A, B,** and **C,** and omitted in the others except the terminal portions at styles *a* and *b*. Each of the paired dilambdomorphic tritubercular and quadritubercular (**D** + **G**) teeth represents the end of a convergent phyletic line. (Modified from Hershkovitz 1971*a*.)

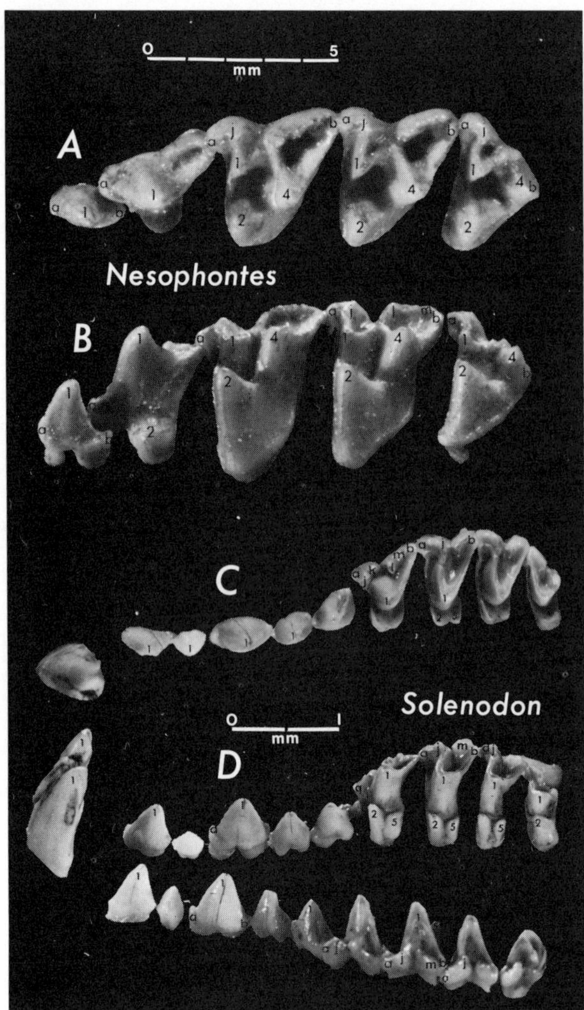

Fig. V.4. *A, B, Nesophontes edithae* (AMNH 17109), left pm^{3-4}, m^{1-3}, occlusal, and lingual aspects. Compare m^1 with fig. V.6*M; C, D, Solenodon paradoxus* (FMNH 18505), left I^1–m^3, occlusal, and left and right oblique views. Compare m^1 with fig. V.6*J*. (Modified from Hershkovitz 1971*a*.)

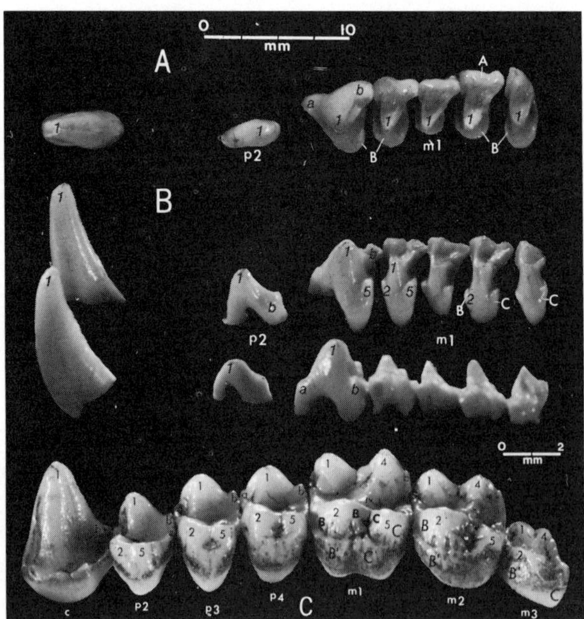

Fig. V.5. *A, B, Tenrec ecaudatus* (FMNH 85515), left c–m^3 occlusal, and left and right oblique views. Compare p^4 with fig. V.6*K; C, Callicebus torquatus* (FMNH 70700), left c–m^3, oblique view from lingual aspect. Compare m^1 with fig. V.6 *W*. (Modified from Hershkovitz 1971*a*.)

Discussion. The *euthemorphic* molar (figs. V.3E,F; 5C) could have evolved directly from the primitive tridentate tooth by differentiation of metacone from eocrista, and formation of buccal and lingual cingula, or shelves, with their respective complement of styles, conules, and cones. This molar type characterizes most orders of mammals including primates, rodents, ungulates, and carnivores. It is the tritubercular molar of Butler's arrangement (1939*a*, p. 8). Retention of the more-or-less straight eocrista and persistence of high-domed or conical cusps are the most primitive characteristics of euthemorphic molars.

The *zalambdomorphic* or V-shaped molar (figs. V.3, 6B) is a tridentate tooth with an extensive buccal stylar shelf. A high conical eocone on a low crown appears to have been retained by the Pantotheria and Symmetrodonta. In living zalambdodont insectivores, such as most tenrecoids and *Chrysochloris*, the buccal aspect of the eocone is triangular in outline, tilted about 45° to nearly horizontal, and serves as the main occlusal surface.

Advanced complications of the zalambdomorphic tooth include rise of the plesioconule and eoconule on the eocrista, expansion of anterolingual and posterolingual cingula which may or may not unite into a common lingual shelf, and differentiation of protocone, hypocone, and frequently, a second-generation lingual cingulum (e.g., m^2 in *Tenrec*, figs. V.5A,B; 6K). The first sign of indentation or infolding of the distal enamel border of the eocone marks the appearance of a true metacone (*4*) and transition from a zalambdomorphic to a dilambdomorphic pattern (fig. V.3D).

The *dilambdomorphic* or W-shaped molar crown can be derived from both a primitive euthemorphic molar and from an advanced zalambdomorphic molar. In the first instance the W-shaped crown in the E–D (fig. V.3) series results from a mediad tilting of the buccal aspect of the eocone and metacone accompanied by a flexure of the portion of eocrista (the centrocrista, *I'''*) between eocone and metacone. In the second instance (figs. V.3B–D), a V-shaped metacone (*4*) is differentiated through flexure of the distal border of the V-shaped eocone. The product in either case is the double V-, or W-shaped dilambdomorphic crown. For example, in the first molar of *Potamogale* (figs. V.6L, 8), the first indication of the metacone is a wedgelike indentation of the distal enamel border of the triangular eocone. The deeper and broader the wedge, the larger the metacone, and the more evenly subdivided or W-shaped the molar crown. The metacone continues to increase in size at the expense of the eocone. Ultimately, as in *Nesophontes* (figs. V.4A,B; 6M), it may become the larger of the two cones in all molars except the last.

So nearly complete is convergence of the two independently evolved W-shaped molars, the one from the euthemorphic molar, the other from the zalambdomorphic molar, that only a dilambdomorphic molar is recognized without distinction of origin (fig. V.3).

According to Butler (1941, p. 437), the zalambdodont molar, as typified by *Potamogale* and *Tenrec*, could give rise to the dilambdodont molar, as typified by *Didelphis* and *Tupaia*. The tritubercular (i.e., euthemorphic), he believes, could evolve from the dilambdodont. Transition from zalambdodont, or zalambdomorphic, to dilambdomorphic can indeed be demonstrated, notably through the several species of *Potamogale* (cf. fig. V.8). On the other hand, the idea that the dilambdomorphic molar pattern of *Didelphis* and *Tupaia* (fig. V.3E–D) derives from the euthemorphic as typified by the Forestburg molars (fig. V.6N), may be entertained. In this event, at least insofar as marsupials are concerned, it would be necessary to demonstrate that the zalambdomorphic molars of the South American Miocene *Necrolestes,* and those of the extant Australian *Notoryctes,* are secondarily simplified, or degenerate, or that the animals themselves are not marsupials. As for Butler's tritubercular (i.e., euthemorphic) molar, it is certain that the generalized form of the tooth could give rise to, but cannot be derived from, a dilambdomorphic pattern (fig. V.3).

Crown Types: Buccal, Lingual

All elements of the eoconal axis of the tridentate tooth, namely, eocone (-id), mesiostyle (-id), distostyle (-id), plesioconule (-id), eoconule (-id), metacone (hypoconid), and connecting eocrista (-id), are strictly homologous wherever they occur in upper and lower teeth, whether incisors, canines, premolars, or molars. Elements resulting from molarization of either the buccal or lingual side of the eoconal axis are also homologous with corresponding elements of the same side of other teeth, upper or lower. Conversely, no element of the buccal side of the eoconal axis is homologous with any element of the lingual side of the axis (figs. V.12, 19, 20, 27). The crown types described below serve to keep the morphological distinctions in focus, whatever the crown patterns derived from them.

1. Buccal or Archaic Upper Crown

The essentially buccal crown is characterized by expansion of the buccal cingulum into a stylar shelf supporting two or more cuspules or styles, frequently with one, sometimes two, comparable to the eocone in size. The buccal crown is the primary "trigon" of Gregory (1922, pp. 105–6) and the earliest known form of the molarized tridentate tooth. It is virtually the entire molar crown of Triconodonta, Symmetrodonta, and Pantotheria, and nearly the whole of most zalambdomorphic or tenrecoid molar crowns (figs. V.4, 5, 6B–G).

2. Buccal Lower Crown

The buccal side of the eoconal axis is unmodified or marked by a complete or interrupted cingulum bearing one or a few small styles. At best, the buccal crown of lower teeth remains relatively uncomplicated and comparatively unimportant (fig. V.7).

3. Buccolingual Upper Crown

a. Dominantly Archaic. Most of crown buccal, stylar shelf elaborate; lingual shelf with anterior or posterior cingula or both, rudimentary protocone or hypocone or both; metacone absent, pattern zalambdomorphic (figs. V.3B; 6H–K).

b. Dominantly Tritubercular. Approximately half of crown buccal, stylar shelf complex; lingual shelf with protocone the dominant if not sole cusp; metacone present but derivation from eocrista identifies it as a cusp of eoconal axis; pattern euthemorphic or dilambdomorphic (fig. V.6L–P; V.8).

4. Buccolingual Lower Crown

Dominantly lingual, the buccal shelf uncomplicated (fig. V.7).

5. Lingual or Tritubercular Upper Crown

The predominantly lingual upper crown is distinguished by usually well-defined axial elements, that is, eocone, mesiostyle, distostyle, and eocrista, and, in addition, the protocone, which rises from the anterolingual shelf, and either hypocone, which originates on the posterolingual shelf, or metacone, derived from the distal slope of the eocone or eocrista. The three cones, whichever the combination, are the tritubercular elements of the lingual crown of the euthemorphic tooth (figs. V.6L–P,R,T,U). When all four cones are present, the quadritubercular stage of molarization is achieved, but the coronal type remains tritubercular (figs. V.6S,V,W; fig. V.12C).

6. Lingual Lower Crown

Molarization of the lower teeth, with its proliferations and hypertrophy of secondary cusps, cingula, and crests, occurs nearly or quite entirely on the lingual side of the eoconid axis. The lingual lower molar crown, characterized by a metaconid, occludes with all quadritubercular upper molar types (figs. V.7, 12). The lower molar homologue of the archaic or primary trigon of Gregory (1922, p. 105) lacks the metaconid.

The conservative nature of the lower molar crown is determined partly by the narrowly limited transverse dimensions of the alveolar space, but mainly by mandibular mobility which permits a set of generalized lower teeth to function effectively against a variety of specialized sets of upper teeth. Upper molar crown evolution is more likely geared to mandibular movements than to possible modifications per se in lower molar form. In some mammalian lines, including all higher primates, the one most important modification in the lower molars, after they attain their highest grade of complexity, has been the obsolescence and disappearance of the paraconid.

Remarks. Failure to understand or recognize the several coronal types described here and their applicability to *all* teeth, not molars alone, has resulted in confusion of buccal crown elements with analogous lingual crown elements, particularly in comparing upper and lower teeth. The Cope-Osborn system of dental terminology, discussed later, reflects this confusion.

Molarization Stages

Evolution from the tridentate to the zalambdomorphic, euthemorphic, and dilambdomorphic tooth is sketched herewith in terms of stages, each significantly more advanced or complex than the preceding. The stages cut across phylogenetic lines and morphogenetic fields. The examples are individual teeth. The taxa they represent range from Mesozoic subeutherians to modern primates. For conciseness, however, only selected stages of a limited variety of teeth are used as models for the diagrams in figure V.9. Dental elements are identified by the conventional terms adopted here and by their respective symbols (cf. p. 300 and fig. V.21).

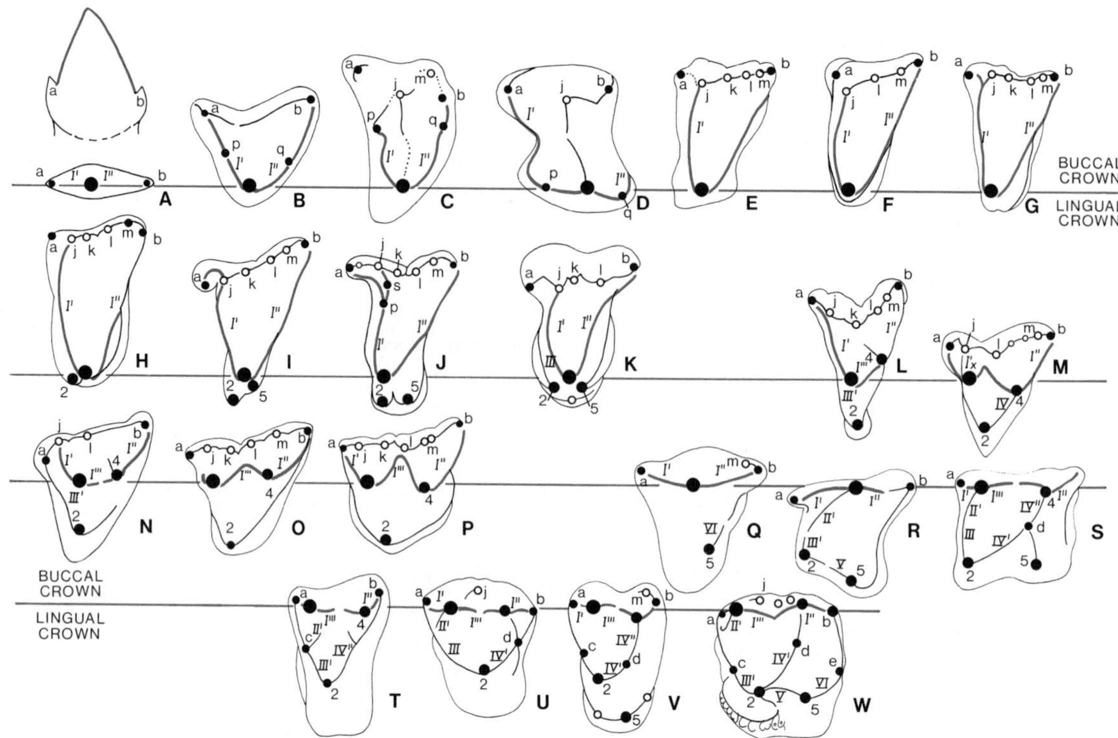

Fig. V.6. Basic crown types and patterns of upper cheek teeth. Models are arranged in independent and increasingly complex morphological series. Identical symbols are used for homologous upper and lower dental elements. Red line passing through eocones arbitrarily divides crowns into buccal (*upper*) and lingual (*lower*) portions; only the eocrista (*I′–I‴*) actually separates true buccal from true lingual crown elements. Medium-sized black dots are secondary main cones, small black dots are terminal styles (*a, b,*) and conules, open circles are ectostyles and entostyles, not always labeled. See figs. V.13, 21 and page 300 for orientation and terminology of dental elements. (Modified from Hershkovitz 1971*a*.)

Ancestral Mammalian

A, Primitive tridentate tooth pattern, buccal and occlusal views.

Simple Zalambdomorphic; Crown Buccal or Archaic

B, Peralestes (Symmetrodonta, Spalacotheriidae, U. Jurassic); molar from Butler 1939*b*, p. 342).

C, Melanodon oweni Simpson (Pantotheria, Dryolestidae, U. Jurassic); m^2 from Simpson (1929, p. 76); see also Patterson (1956, p. 37); dotted lines added on basis of *Melanodon goodrichi* Simpson, Yale Peabody Museum 13748 (cf. Simpson, 1929, p. 77).

D, Docodon (Docodonta; Docodontidae, U. Jurassic); molar composite from Butler (1939*b*, p. 331), and Vandebroek (1961, pls. 1, 6, 7, 9); see also Patterson (1956, p. 69) and Jenkins 1969, p. 6).

Complex Zalambdomorphic; Crown dominantly Buccal, Lingual Shelf Present

E, Nesogale talazaci (Insectivora [Zalambdodonta], Tenrecidae, Madagascar); m^1 FMNH 99800.

F, Echinops telfairi (Insectivora [Zalambdodonta], Tenrecidae, Madagascar); pm^4, FMNH 33948.

G, Setifer setosus (Insectivora [Zalambdodonta], Tenrecidae, Madagascar); m^1 FMNH 85513.

Complex Zalambdomorphic with Lingual Cusps and Styles

H, Echinops telfairi (Insectivora [Zalambdodonta], Tenrecidae, Madagascar); m^1, FMNH 33948.

I, Oryzoryctes hova (Insectivora [Zalambdodonta], Tenrecidae, Madagascar); m^1, FMNH 5641.

J, Solenodon paradoxus (Insectivora [Zalambdodonta], Solenodontidae, Dominican Republic, Hispaniola); m^1, FMNH 18505 (lingual style present in m^2, as in *K.*) Compare with McDowell (1958, p. 150, fig. 13).

K, Tenrec (= Centetes) ecaudatus (Insectivora [Zalambdodonta], Tenrecidae, Madagascar); pm^4, FMNH 85514.

Zalambdomorphic-Dilambdomorphic; Crown Buccolingual

L, Potamogale velox (Insectivora [Zalambdodonta], Tenrecidae, [Potamogalidae], Congo); m^1, FMNH 25973.

M, Nesophontes edithae (Insectivora [Zalambdodonta (dilambdomorphic)], Solenodontidae, Pleistocene, Puerto Rico); m^1, AMNH 17109. Compare with McDowell (1958, p. 150, fig. 13).

Euthemorphic-Dilambomorphic; Crown Buccolingual

N, Therian molar (Subclass Eutheria; E. Cretaceous); molars PM-FMNH nos. 884 and 999 from Patterson (1956, p. 17), the figure reversed, specimens also examined. For discussion and analysis of structure, see Turnbull (1971).

Fig. V.6 caption continued on page 284.

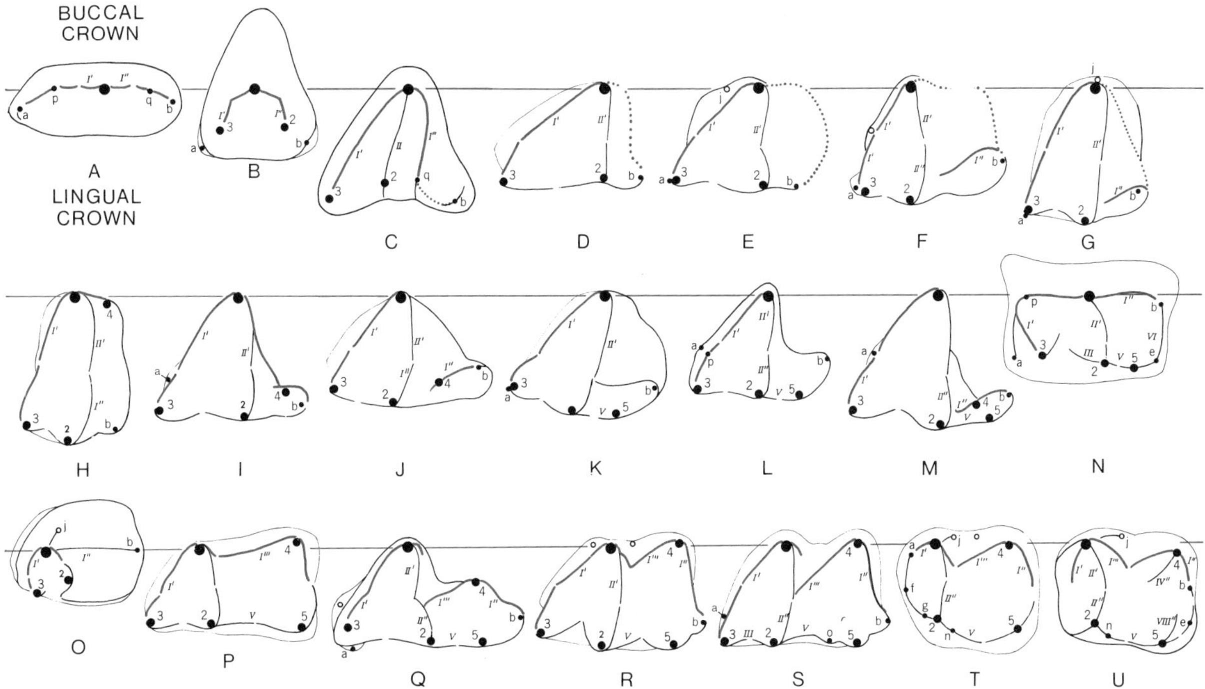

Fig. V.7. Basic crown types and patterns of lower cheek teeth. Models are arranged in independent and increasingly complex morphological series. Identical symbols are used for homologous upper and lower dental elements. Red line passing through eoconids arbitrarily separates buccal (*upper*) from lingual (*lower*) portions of crowns; only the eocristid (*I′-I‴*) actually separates true buccal from true lingual crown elements. Medium-sized black dots are secondary main conids, small black dots are terminal stylids (*a, b*) and conulids, open circles are ectostylids and entostylids, not always labeled. See figs. V.13, 21, and page 300 for orientation and terminology of dental elements. (Modified from Hershkovitz 1971*a*.)

Primitive Mammalian

A, Triconodon (Triconodonta; Triconodontidae, U. Jurassic); molar from Butler (1939*b*, p. 352).

Crown Buccolingual

B, Spalacotherium (Symmetrodonta, Spalacotheriidae, U. Jurassic); molar, from Butler (1939*b*, p. 352).

Crown Dominantly Lingual, Primitive Talonid Rudimentary

C, Laolestes (Pantotheria, Dryolestidae, U. Jurassic); molar from Vandebroek (1961, p. 260).

D, Nesogale talazaci (Insectivora [Zalambdodonta], Tenrecidae, Madagascar); m_1, FMNH 99800.

E, Tenrec ecaudatus (Insectivora [Zalambdodonta], Tenrecidae, Madagascar); m_1, FMNH 85514.

F, Potamogale velox (Insectivora [Zalambdodonta], Tenrecidae [Potamogalidae], Congo); m_2, FMNH 25973.

G, Echinops telfairi (Insectivora [Zalambdodonta], Tenrecidae, Madagascar); m_1, FMNH 33948.

Crown Dominantly Lingual, Primitive Talonid Simple to Complex

H, Setifer setosus (Insectivora [Zalambdodonta], Tenrecidae, Madagascar); m_1, FMNH 85513.

I, Oryzoryctes hova (Insectivora [Zalambdodonta], Tenrecidae, Madagascar); m_1, FMNH 5461.

J, Nesogale talazaci (Insectivora [Zalambdodonta], Tenrecidae, Madagascar); m_3, FMNH 99800.

K, Solenodon paradoxus (Insectivora [Zalambdodonta], Solenodontidae, Dominican Republic, Hispaniola), m_1, FMNH 18505.

L, Oryzoryctes hova (Insectivora [Zalambdodonta], Tenrecidae, Madagascar); pm_4, FMNH 5641.

M, Oryzoryctes hova (Insectivora [Zalambdodonta], Tenrecidae, Madagascar); m_3, FMNH 5641.

N, Docodon (Docodonta, Docodontidae, U. Jurassic); molar after Butler (1939*b*, p. 352); and Vandebroek (1960, pl. 8); see also Jenkins (1969, p. 6).

Crown Dominantly Lingual, Progressive Talonid Simple

O, Echinosorex gymnurus (Insectivora, Erinaceidae, Sarawak); pm_4, FMNH 88323.

Crown Dominantly Lingual, Progressive Talonid Simple to Complex

P, Echinosorex gymnurus (Insectivora, Erinaceidae, Sarawak); m_1, FMNH 88323.

Q, Therian (Subclass Eutheria); molar PM-FMNH 965, diagram based on Patterson (1956, p. 22) only, but specimens also examined. For discussion and complete analysis of structure, see Turnbull (1971).

R, Marmosa cinerea (Marsupialia, Didelphidae, Ecuador); m_1, FMNH 53351.

S, Tupaia glis (Insectivora, Tupaiidae); m_1, FMNH 76825, 76826.

T, Cebuella pygmaea (Primates, Callitrichidae, Peru); m_1, FMNH 88998–99.

U, Callicebus torquatus (Primates, Cebidae, Colombia); m_1, FMNH 70700 (also *C. torquatus,* 70694, Colombia, and *moloch,* FMNH 87810, Colombia).

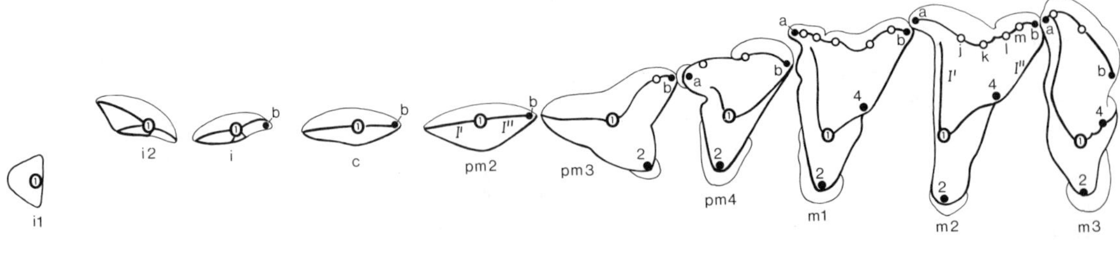

Fig. V.8. *Potamogale velox,* occlusal view of upper left tooth row; dental elements labeled in m2, also compare with fig. V.6*L;* see fig. V.21 and page 300 for orientation and terminology. (Modified from Hershkovitz 1971*a.*)

Upper Teeth (Fig. V.9)

A. *Unicuspid or Tridentate Stage (Eocone and Axial Conules).* Eocone (1) generally large; mesiostyle (*a*), distostyle (*b*), and anterolingual cingulum (*B*) usually present; bulge or torus (crista *II*) usually occurs on slope of eocone in system leading to the euthemorphic (tritubercular-quadritubercular) pattern.

Examples: Incisors and canines of most mammals, including many primates, one or more anterior premolars of many eutherians including *Didelphis,* most tenrecoids and all teeth of *Nesogale* except m^3 and variables of m^{1-2} with rudimentary protocone. Most, if not all, teeth of Symmetrodonta, Pantotheria, and perhaps Triconodonta belong here (fig. V.6).

B. *Bicuspid Stage (Eocone and either Protocone [Type 1], Hypocone [Type 2], or Metacone [Type 3])* (fig V.9 B1–3).

Type 1: Protocone (*2*) appears on anterolingual cingulum (*B*): anterior border of cingulum hypertrophies at this stage or next (Stage C) into crista *III'* (protoloph); protoconule (*c*) usually undifferentiated.

Examples: Incisors and canines of many placental mammals including many primates; one or more premolars in all primates; one or more molars in some Insectivora (cf. *Microgale, Echinops, Nesogale, Setifer, Chrysochloris*[1]—(fig. V.6).

[1] Van Valen (1967) includes tenrecoids and chrysochlorids in his Deltatheridia, a new order which, as he points out (1966, p. 109 n) should have been called Zalambdodonta Gill, as redefined by Vandebroek (1961, p. 308).

Type 2: Hypocone (*5*) arises from apex of posterolingual cingulum; protocone, metacone absent.

Example: Tenrec (penultimate premolar (fig. V.5B). The phylogenetic significance of the difference between types 1 and 2 are evident.

Type 3: Metacone (*4*) defined by enamel fold on distal slope of eocone; protocone, hypocone absent.

Examples: Macroscelididae (the canine in all species, and one or two premolars in many species [fig. V.10)).

The eocone-metacone bicuspid of macroscelidids is not a primary combination. Extensive palatal fenestration has led to degeneration with transverse contraction and apparent loss of lingual shelf including protocone in the canine and premolars of many species. Degeneration of the lingual shelf can be traced through the various described forms of *Elephantulus.*

C. *Tritubercular or Trigon Stage (Eocone, Protocone, and Either Metacone [Type 1], or Hypocone [Type 2])* (fig. V.9C1, 2).

Type 1: Metacone (*4*) differentiates from distal slope of eocone (*1*); borders of anterolingual cingulum now cristae *III'* and *IV* enclose trigon basin (α); hypocone absent.

Examples: Last deciduous premolar of many living primates; molars of tritubercular primates (notably callitrichids), insectivores, marsupials, bats—the tritubercular and dilambdodont molar described by authors (figs. V.6, 8).

Type 2: Hypocone (*5*) rises from apex of posterolingual cingulum; eocone and protocone present, meta-

Fig. V.6 continued.

O, Marmosa cinerea (Marsupialia, Didelphidae, Ecuador); m², FMNH 53351.

P, Tupaia glis (Insectivora, Tupaiidae); m¹, FMNH 76826. Molars of other tupaiids (cf. *Tupaia palawanensis, Ptilocercus lowi*) are quadritubercular. The dilambdomorphic molars exclude tupaiids from Primates, whose molars are characteristically euthemorphic.

Simple Euthemorphic; Crown Dominantly Lingual

Q, Tenrec ecaudatus (Insectivora [Zalambdodonta], Tenrecidae, Madagascar); pm³, FMNH 85514.

R, Podogymnura truei (Insectivora, Erinaceidae, Philippines); pm⁴, FMNH 74852.

S, Podogymnura truei (Insectivora, Erinaceidae, Philippines); m¹, FMNH 74852.

Progressive Euthemorphic; Crown Dominantly Lingual

T, Purgatorius (Primates [?], Middle Paleocene); m², from Van Valen and Sloan (1965, p. 744), the figure reversed.

U, Cebuella (Primates, Callitrichidae, Peru); m¹, FMNH 88998.

V, Callimico (Primates, Callimiconidae, Colombia); m¹, Instituto de Ciencias Naturales, Bogotá, 084.

W, Callicebus torquatus (Primates, Cebidae, Colombia); m¹, FMNH 70700. Note the densely crenulated secondary or neoanterolingual cingulum.

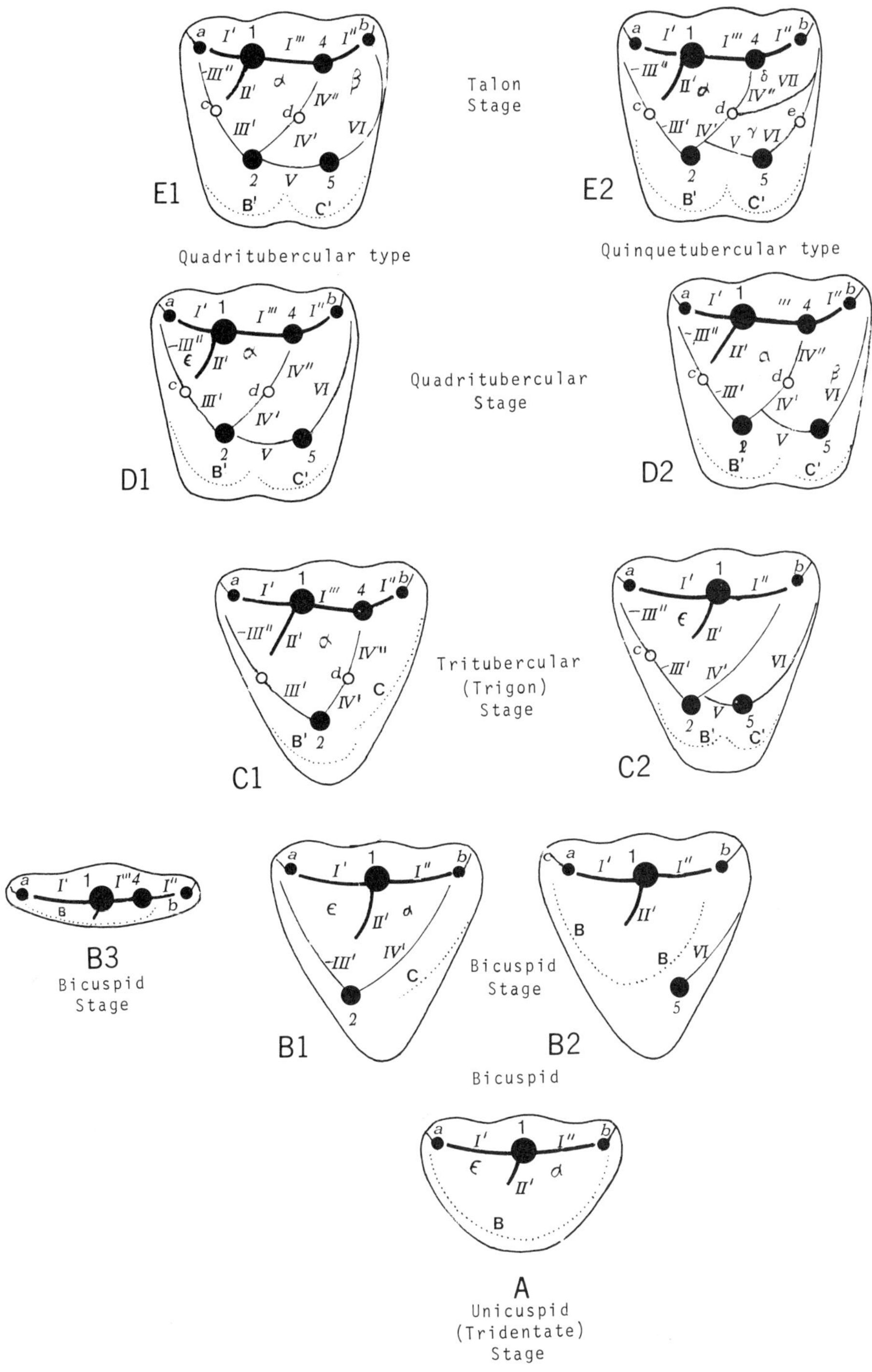

Fig. V.9. Molarization of euthemorphic upper cheek teeth; **A,** unicuspid or tridentate stage; **B** (**B1–B3**), three types of biscuspid stage; **C** (**C1–C2**), two types of tritubercular stage; **D** (**D1–D2**), two types of quadritubercular stage; **E1,** quadritubercular talon stage, **E2,** quinquetubercular talon stage. Primitive anterolingual cingulum (*B*) and posterolingual cingulum (*C*) dotted, derived cristae (*III, IV, V, VI*) shown as fine lines; secondary or neolingual cingula (*B′*, *C′*) dotted. (Modified from Hershkovitz 1971*a*.)

cone absent; neolingual cingula present or absent.

Examples: Premolars and often the incisors of Callicebus (fig. V.5C), premolars of *Alouatta* (variable). In Tupaiidae, last premolar of *Ptilocercus;* in tenrecoids, last premolars and molars of *Solenodon* (fig. V.4C,D) and *Oryzoryctes;* first molar of *Tenrec* ((fig. V.5A,B) variable).

D. *Quadritubercular Stage (Eocone, Protocone, and Either Metacone Followed Chronologically by Hypocone [Type 1], or Hypocone Followed Chronologically by Metacone [Type 2]*—fig. V.9D1,2); neolingual cingula present or absent.

Type 1: Eocone, protocone, and metacone present, as in stage C, type 1; hypocone differentiates from angle of posterolingual cingulum; mesial crista (*V*) of hypocone may contact protocone or crista *IV′;* neolingual cingula (*B′*, *C′*) present or absent.

Examples: Molars of most higher mammals including most primates.

Type 2: Eocone, protocone, and hypocone present as

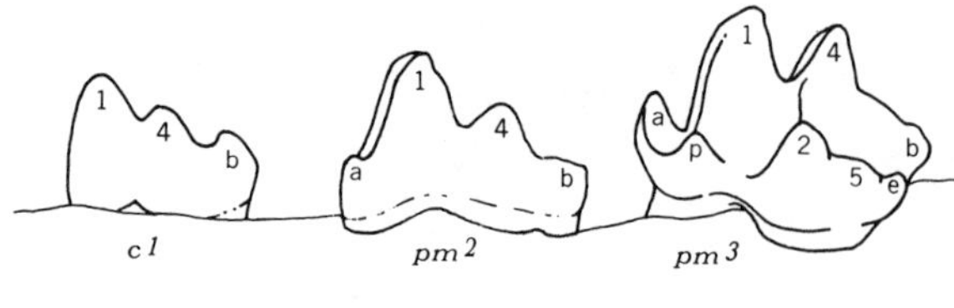

Fig. V.10. *Nasilio brachyrhynchus* (Insectivora, Macroscelididae, Kenya), upper canine and anterior premolars; absence of protocone (*2*) in biscuspid c^1 and pm^2 is regarded as a secondary loss. Note differentiation of metacone (*4*) from eocone (*1*). (Modified from Hershkovitz 1971*a*.)

in stage C, type 2; metacone appears fully differentiated; neolingual cingula often present.

Examples: Molars of Echinosoricinae and Erinaceinae among Insectivora; some *Callicebus* among platyrrhine Primates (fig. V.6).

E. *Talon Stage (With Four or Five Permanent Molar Cones).*

1. Quadritubercular: Modification of posterior border of posterolingual cingulum into broad shelf, often with margin elevated into crista (*VI*) enclosing shallow talon basin (β) (fig. V.9E1).

Examples: Quadritubercular molars of many mammals including those of many primates.

2. Quinquetubercular: Appearance or hypertrophy of postentoconule (*e*); crista *VI* well defined; oblique crista

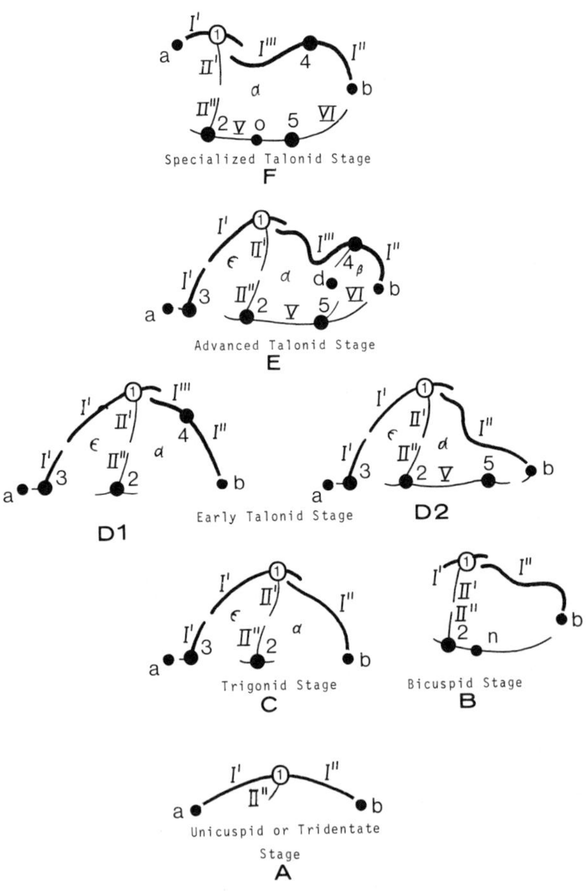

Fig. V.11. Molarization of lower cheek teeth; **A,** unicuspid or tridentate stage with eoconid (*1*); **B,** bicuspid stage with metaconid (*2*); **C,** trigonid stage with paraconid (*3*); **D1,** early talonid stage, with hypoconid (*4*); **D2,** early talonid stage with entoconid (*5*); **E,** advanced talonid stage; **F,** specialized talonid stage. (Modified from Hershkovitz 1971*a*.). See addendum p. 286.

(*VII*) between metaconule and distostyle often present and bisecting talon basin (β) into subbasins (γ) and (δ) (fig. V.9E2).

Examples: molars of many individuals of *Saimiri* and *Callicebus.*

Lower Teeth (fig. V.11)

A. *Unicuspid or Tridentate Stage (Eoconid and Axial Stylids).* Eoconid (1) dominant, mesiostylid (*a*) usually, and distostylid (*b*) always present; pronounced bulge or torus, often with sharp crest (*II*) frequently present on lingual slope of eoconid (fig. V.11A).

Examples: Molars of Triconodonta, canines and anterior premolars of most other mammals.

B. *Bicuspid Stage (Eoconid, Metaconid).* In euthemorphic dental systems with paraconid obsolete or absent; metaconid (2) rises from anterolingual cingulum, its lateral crest (*II″*) uniting with the epicristid (*II′*) on lingual slope of eoconid (fig. V.11B).

Examples: Bicuspid carnassials; premolars, usually pm_2, often pm_3, rarely pm_4, of higher mammals; molars of many Megachiroptera (e.g., *Acerodon*).

Note: The bicuspid stage, as described here, is a degenerate "trigonid" stage basically indistinguishable from type 2 below. Phylogenetically, it would follow stage C, D, or E, with loss of paraconid.

C. *"Trigonid" Stage (Eoconid and Metaconid with Well-Developed Paraconid* [*Type 1*], *or with Paraconid Obsolete or Absent* [*Type 2*]).

Type 1 (fig. V.11C): Paraconid (*3*), probably originates on eocrista of anterior slope of eoconid of premolar, moves linguad on molars, enlarging meanwhile; metaconid arises nearly simultaneously from anterolingual cingulum; resultant "trigonid" encloses basin (ϵ); distostylid usually well developed, small low talonid basin (β) sometimes indicated.

Examples: Molars of Symmetrodonta, Pantotheria, posterior premolars of zalambdomorphic systems.

Type 2: Like type 1, but with paraconid obsolete or absent, "trigonid" basin open anteriorly, or more or less enclosed by raised anteriolingual cingulum.

Examples: Posterior premolars of most mammals with euthemorphic dental system.

D. *Early Talonid Stage ("Trigonid," Plus the Talonid, Distostylid and either Entoconid or Hypoconid)* (fig. V.11D). "Trigonid" cones and basin elevated and well defined; talonid with low distostylid (*b*) and either weak hypoconid (*4*) rising from eocristid or small entoconid (*5*) originating on posterolingual cingulid; short shallow talonid basin (α) usually defined.

Examples: Molars of zalambdomorphic dental system, such as those of *Solenodon* and *Potamogale* (distostylid and entoconid in m_1), *Nesogale* (distostylid and hypoconid in m_3), *Echinops* (distostylid and hypoconid in m_1).

E. *Advanced Talonid Stage ("Trigonid" as in C, Plus the Talonid, Distostylid, Hypoconid, and Entoconid)* (fig. V.11E; V.12). "Trigonid" elevated above talonid, distostylid as in D, hypoconid completely differentiated by upward thrust and infolding of eocristid (*I‴*); conulids and stylids often present on talonid rim; transverse extension of inner torus of entoconid or hypoconid or both sometimes differentiated as cristid; plagioconulid (*d*) present or absent.

Examples: Molars of early euthemorphic and dilamb-

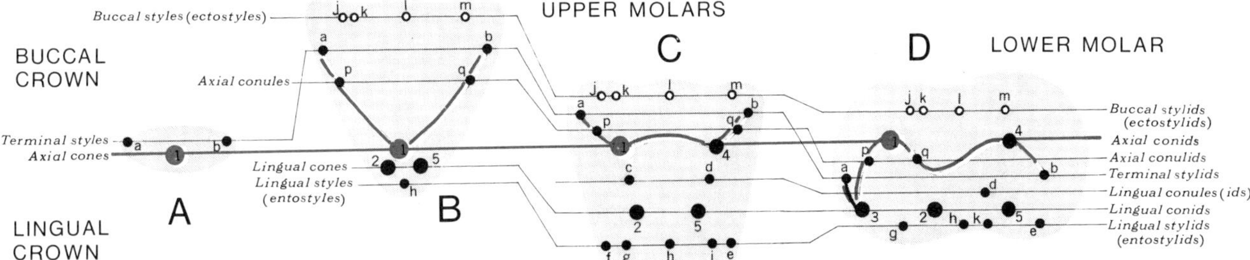

Fig. V.12. Cusp homologies: *A*, primitive tridentate upper crown; *B*, dominantly buccal zalambdomorphic upper crown; *C*, dominantly lingual euthemorphic upper crown; *D*, common lower crown. Red line passing through red eocones and eoconid divides crown into buccal (*upper*) and lingual (*lower*) portions; only the eocrista (eocristid) or eocone (-id) axis shown by heavy line with cones and conules in place, separates true buccal from true lingual crown elements; fine lines connect cusps of similar grade including homologues. (Modified from Hershkovitz 1971*a*.)

domorphic dental systems. The Trinity Sands therian lower molar (fig. V.7Q) (Patterson 1956, fig. 7 [FMNH no. 965]) belongs here.

F. *Specialized Talonid Stage ("Trigonid" and Talonid as in E but with Paraconid Reduced, Obsolete, or Absent)* (fig. V.11F).

Examples: Molars of advanced euthemorphic systems such as those of platyrrhines and catarrhines, rodents, most ungulates.

Notes on Individual Dental Elements

Cingula

A dental cingulum is a masticatory surface that arises as a narrow band, shelf, or ridge from the base of a cusp. Primary cingula form at the buccal and lingual bases of the eocone (-id) or eocrista (-id). Secondary cingula originate along the base of the principal or internal cones derived from the primary lingual cingula.

The primitive primary buccal cingulum (*A*, fig. V.21) became a broad stylar shelf in zalambdomorphic molars and serves as the main portion of the puncturing and crushing crown surface (figs. V.6, 13). Complications of the buccal cingulum are described under the next heading.

In both zalambdomorphic and euthemorphic molars (fig. V.3), the primitive anterior portion of the primary lingual cingulum (*B*) expanded into a triangular or crescentic crushing surface and gave rise at or near its apex to a large puncturing cusp, the protocone (metaconid). The anterior border of the cingulum became a sharp shearing ridge, the protocrista (-id, *III*) and the posterior border became the shearing plagiocrista (*IV'*). A plagiocristid appears to be absent, but its functional equivalent is the epicristid (*II"*).

With advancing molarization the posterior portion of the primary lingual cingulum (*C*), actually an independent outgrowth of the posterolingual base of the eocone-metacone, or amphicone (eoconid-hypoconid), expanded and gave rise to one or a few tubercles or styles (-ids). In complex zalambdomorphic molars (figs. V.3, 6) and in advanced euthemorphic molars (fig. V.9) the first of the tubercles enlarged into the functional hypocone (entoconid). The anterior border of the hypertrophied cingulum became the shearing entocrista (-id, *V*). The entocrista (-id) retains its primitive connection with the anterolingual cingulum at the posterior base of the

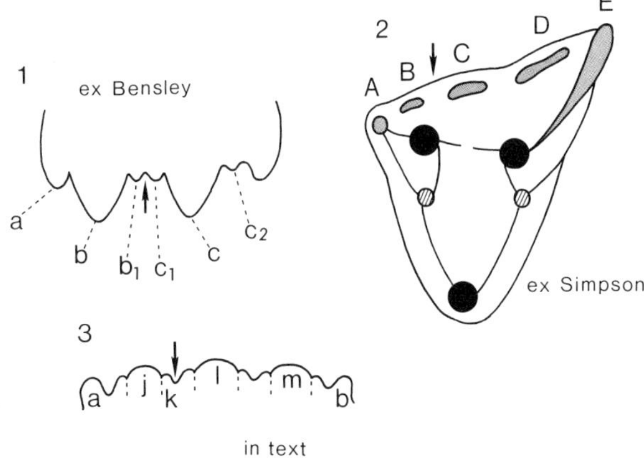

Fig. V.13. Stylar cusps, ectostyles, and terminal styles. The arrow has been added to reproductions 1 and 2 for showing usual position of main enamel fold (ectoflexus).
1. Buccal view, from Bensley (1906, p. 6); anterior terminal cusp (*a*), and three stylar fields ($b + b_1$, $c + c_1$, c_2 + unlabeled cusp), posterior terminal style absent.
2. Occlusal view, from Simpson (1929, p. 119), showing terminal styles (*A*, *E*) and three main stylar fields (*B* [= stylocone], *C*, *D*).
3. Occlusal view of system and symbols used in text showing terminal styles (*a*, *b*) and three main stylar cusps (*j* [=stylocone], *l*, *m*) with potential subsidiary cuspules indicated by broken lines (*k*, shown, is most frequently differentiated and helps define position of ectoflexus). (Modified from Hershkovitz 1971*a*.)

protocone (metaconid) or with the plagiocrista (*IV'*) in upper molars and epicristid (*II'*) in the lower molars. In some phyletic lines, the posterolingual cingulum appears about the same time as its anterolingual counterpart and may unite with it; and in other lines it appears earlier. In many premolars the posterolingual cingulum with its hypocone is the first and only addition to the lingual base of the amphicone.

Establishment of the expanded anterolingual cingulum with its complement of cones (-ids) and cristae (-ids) as stable masticatory elements of the dental crown surface is often followed by the rise of a second-generation cingulum (*B'*) at the base of the protocone (metaconid). A neocingulum (*C'*) may also appear at the base of the enlarged posterolingual cingulum (fig. V.14). The two neophyte cingula meet in the angle or entoflexus (*en*) between protocone (metaconid) and hypocone (entoconid) and often produce one to several styles (-ids).

The foregoing outline of the evolution of successive lingual cingula makes little mention of the considerable

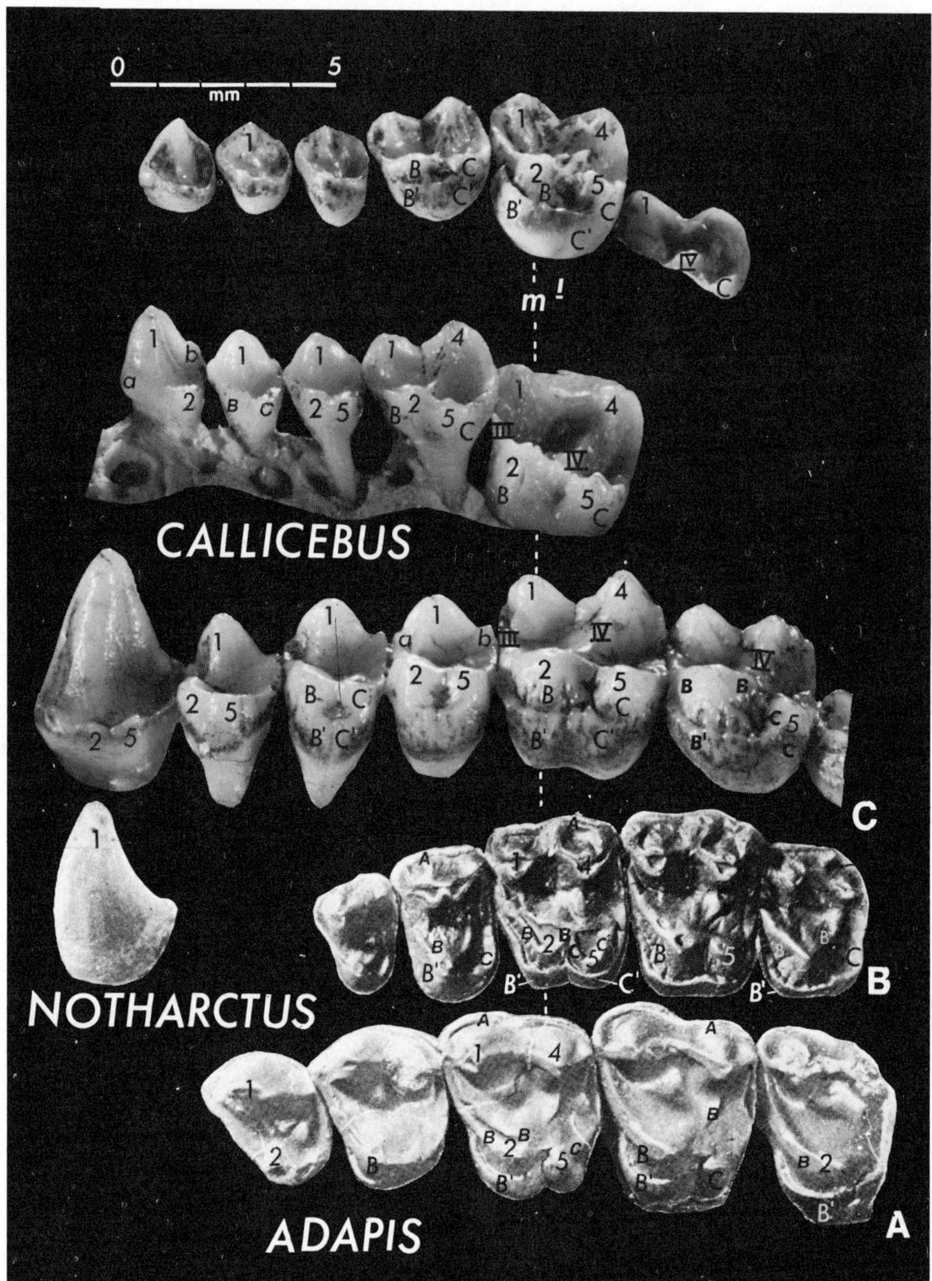

Fig. V.14. Maxillary tooth rows of Eocene prosimians and living *Callicebus* aligned to m¹ for comparison of main cusps and primary and secondary cingula.

A, *Adapis magnus* (Eocene, France; AMNH 10511) with primary cingula *A, B, C* and secondary cingulum *B′* in pm⁴–m³. (Based on photograph from Gregory 1922, p. 136.)

B, *Notharctus crassus* (middle Eocene, Wyoming; AMNH 11982) with primary cingula *A, B, C,* and secondary cingulum *B′* in pm⁴–m³, and secondary cingulum *C′* in m¹⁻³; hypocone incipient in m³. (Based on photograph from Gregory 1922, p. 136.)

C, *Callicebus torquatus* (Río Mecaya, Colombia; FMNH 70700) with primary cingula in all teeth shown, secondary cingulum B′ in pm³–m², secondary cingulum C′ in pm³–m¹, but hardly rudimentary in m². Lingual cingular differences between m¹ and m² are comparable to cingular differences between molars of *Adapis* and *Notharctus.*

D, *Callicebus torquatus* (Río Mecaya, Colombia; FM 70697) with deciduous canine and premolars, and erupting first molar; secondary cingula absent. Dental series **D** and **C** represent individuals of the same natural population with variable cingula.

E, *Callicebus moloch* (La Macarena, Colombia; FMNH 87812) with deciduous canine and premolars, first molar erupted but unworn, second molar unerupted; molars with primary and secondary cingula as in *Callicebus torquatus* shown in **C** but not **D.**

Explanation of symbols: *A,* buccal or external cingulum; *B,* primary anterolingual cingulum; *C,* posterolingual cingulum; *B′,* secondary anterolingual (neoanterolingual) cingulum; *C′,* secondary posterolingual (neoposterolingual) cingulum; *1,* eocone; *2,* protocone; *4,* metacone; *5,* hypocone or the pseudonymous *pseudohypocone* of authors in molars with secondary posterolingual cingulum (*C′*) absent; III, protoloph (anterior crest of *B*); IV = plagiocrista (posterior crest of *B*).

variation in form, relative time of appearance, evolutionary rates, juncture points, and derivatives in the form of cristae, cones, conules, styles, crenulations, and their mandibular homologues.

A detailed but still largely exploratory analysis by Kinzey (1973) of cingular components in 17 platyrrhine species representing 12 genera provides a considerable amount of data of diagnostic value. Kinzey was aware of the difference between primary and secondary cingula, but in some cases he failed to sort them completely.

The cingula with which Kinzey is mainly concerned are the continuous buccal cingulum (*A*) and components, and the "lingual cingulum" consisting of fused "anterior cingulum" (= secondary anterolingual cingulum *B'*) and "posterior cingulum" (= posterolingual cingulum *C* or *C* plus the secondary posterolingual cingulum C').

The premises adopted by Kinzey regarding platyrrhine origin presuppose that all platyrrhines shared a common prosimian ancestor and that a more or less continuous cingulum was established in each cheek tooth of the ancestral species. It also assumes that platyrrhine cingular evolution was one of disintegration into "remnant" styles and ledges which ultimately disappeared in more advanced forms.

Regarding the first point, there is no evidence that platyrrhines as such diverged directly from prosimians or that New World monkeys are monophyletic. The ancestral platyrrhine stock, more likely simian than prosimian, may have consisted of two or more species widely disparate in important features of dental morphology. As for cingula in particular, cingulum *A* or buccal cingulum was already present in the earliest mammalian type tooth, essentially the eocone. Cingulum *B* or primitive lingual cingulum is present in earliest known mammalian teeth. As Kinzey notes, cingulum *A* in the platyrrhine or euthemorphic (but not zalambdomorphic or dilambdomorphic) tooth tends to disintegrate into one or a few small component styles, most persistently the *a*. On the other hand, evolution of the euthemorphic lingual cingula is progressive. They tend to expand and become complicated with increasing herbivority and not, as Kinzey seems to think, degenerate into a few remnants before complete dissipation. Evidently Kinzey views the uncomplicated cingulum as one dental element and its localized hypertrophies such as cones and cristae as different elements that replace it. Whatever the terminology or focus, the Kinzey opus goes far toward restoring cingula to their rightful status as primary structures in dental anatomy and evolution.

Buccal Stylar Shelf and Modifications

The buccal shelf is the enlarged buccal cingulum. In most zalambdomorphic teeth, buccal styles are differentiated from thickened anterior and posterior areas of the cingulum. In euthemorphic cheek teeth, buccal styles rise from anterior, median, and posterior cingular swellings. The three stylar areas (fig. V.13) represented by stylar cusps *B, C,* and *D* described by Simpson (1929, p. 119) are the ectostyles *-j* (and *-k*), *-l*, and *-m,* respectively, described in this volume. The principal division or ectoflexus of the stylar shelf lies between ectostyle *-j* (and *-k*) and ectostyle *-l*. Ectostyle *-j* (stylocone of authors) is often enlarged. Ectostyle *-l* or *-m,* however, is sometimes as large or larger.

Any one or more of the primary buccal styles may divide into two or three stylules. The most frequent and important stylule is *k* derived from *j*. Other stylules are unlabeled and their homologues must be determined separately. Stylar cusps labeled *A* and *E* in Simpson's system are mesiostyle (*a*) and distostyle (*b*), respectively, in the present terminology.

Eocrista, Paracrista (Preparacrista), Stylocrista

The eocrista (*I*) extends from mesiostyle (*a*) through eocone (*1*) to the distostyle (*b*), the styles themselves excluded (fig. V.6). The plesioconule (*p*) between eocone and mesiostyle and the eoconule (*q*) between eocone and distostyle rise from the eocrista. The portion of the eocrista between eocone and mesiostyle, the *paracrista* (*I'*) is frequently complicated, particularly in zalambdomorphic and dilambdomorphic cheek teeth (fig. V.21). The paracrista may course directly from eocone to mesiostyle through the plesioconule, if present. It is labeled *I'z*. In some forms the crest is diverted to an enlarged styloconule (*s*), then continues to the mesiostyle. This stretch of paracrista is shown as *I'y*. Finally, the portion of the paracrista extending to the styloconule (*s*) may continue to the stylocone (*j*), paralleling the stylocrista (*IX*), hence to the mesiostyle. This route, *I'x,* is well developed in the Trinity (Albian) therians described by Turnbull (1971, p. 161).

The term *preparacrista,* proposed by Szalay (1969*a*), is a synonym of the earlier name paracrista (Van Valen 1966). To avoid ambiguity, only the latter term is used here. Its symbols are *I'*, or *I'x, I'y, I'z,* according to topographic position.

The stylocrista (*IX*) from eocone (*1*) to stylocone (*j*) may be present, absent, or vestigial. It may parallel the paracrista (*I'*), and it may become fused or confused with it when the latter passes through the stylocone. One or two conules, or *styloconules,* may rise from the stylocrista, or straddle stylocrista and paracrista should the two run together (fig. V.21).

An analogous case of crista diversion and capture resulting in new alignments can be demonstrated in the transition from the triangular platyrrhine molar pattern to the bilophodont catarrhine pattern as it appears in cercopithecines (fig. V.15). Butler (1956, p. 51–54) discusses the formation and instability of cristae in general with a hypothesis based on ontogenetic processes to account for variation.

Protocone versus Paracone in Buccal and Lingual Type Crowns

The main cusps of the buccal or archaic subeutherian crown labeled *protocone* by authors is not homologous with the protocone of the eutherian (includes Marsupialia) lingual or tritubercular crown (cf. p. 284). The lingual cusp in the buccal crown type molar of the subeutherian *Melanodon* (Pantotheria—fig. V.6C), identified as protocone by Simpson (1929, p. 7, fig. *e*), is the

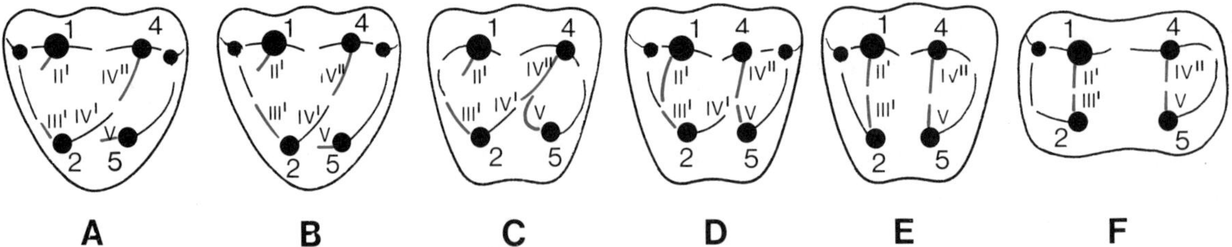

Fig. V.15. Mechanics of crista capture and conversion of platyrrhine triangular molar crown pattern to catarrhine bilophodont pattern. *A-E,* diagrams showing diversion of crista *III'* and capture of crista *II'* (*D-E*) connecting cones *1* and *2,* and diversion of crista *V* to capture crista *IV''* connecting cones *4* and *5.* Diagram *A,* based on molars of *Callicebus* (with unerupted m^3; *B, Lagothrix; C-D, Cebus; E-F, Macaca.* Stages between *B* and *E* are demonstrable in selected specimens of *Cebus.* A similar but hypothetical plan for explaining cercopithecoid bilophodonty was devised by Kälin (1962, p. 35). (Modified from Hershkovitz 1971*a.*)

paracone (= eocone) according to Butler (1939*b,* p. 336). In turn, the lingual cusp of the subeutherian *Docodon* (fig. V.6D), determined as protocone by Butler (1939*b,* p. 331), shows a crest running buccally to the cusp he labels "paracone." In the primitive lingual or tritubercular crown, a crest of the protocone extends to the mesiostyle, another to the true metacone, but none to the paracone, that is, the eocone. Probably the *Docodon* molar belongs to the buccal type and its "protocone," like that of pantotheres and symmetrodonts, is actually an eocone. The larger cusp in midcrown labeled "paracone" must then be, as in other subeutherians, a hypertrophied stylar cusp, most likely the stylocone. Patterson (1956, p. 67) doubts that any cusp of the lingual or tritubercular crown save paracone and protoconid (= eocone and eoconid) can be considered homologous with any in tricodont, docodont, and multitubercular teeth.

Paraconid and Conulid-t (Pseudoparaconid)

The paraconid in primitive eutherian teeth is nearly as well developed as the metaconid and appears almost simultaneously with it in the molarization progression from anterior premolar to molars. A maxillary homologue of the paraconid is not demonstrable. The "anterior accessory cusp," regarded by Butler (1939*b,* pp. 324, 351, fig. 7 *aac*) as the homologue of the paraconid, is probably the plesioconule, an outgrowth of the eocrista. The mandibular homologue of the plesioconule is the plesioconulid, an element sometimes seen on the eocristid between eoconid and paraconid (figs. V.7; V.21).

The paraconid disappears in most primates (and many other mammals) often pari passu with advance and increasing specialization of the quadritubercular molar. Among living haplorhines, a well developed paraconid remains in *Tarsius.* A reduced or vestigial paraconid, if not confused with the mesiostylid (*a*), may persist in living platyrrhines and catarrhines, but mainly as an uncommon individual variable, usually in premolars and more frequently in the deciduous than in the permanent series. It appears to be a consistent feature, however, in pm_{3-4} of the Miocene cebid, *Stirtonia tatacoensis* (fig. V.16). Butler (1939*a,* p. 31) notes a paraconid in dpm_4 of *Brachyteles* and dpm_3 of other genera of Cebidae. He adds that in catarrhines ("platyrrhines" by mistake) the element is present only in dpm_3. I failed to identify this cusp in a random sampling of one or two juvenals of most species.

Conulid-*t,* of sporadic occurrence in platyrrhines (and other mammals), springs from the anterior portion of the protolophid (*III*) or anterolingual cingulum *B.* It can be confused with the epiconulid (*c*) of the same cristid and it may sometimes be confused with stylid-*f,* an outgrowth of the secondary anterolingual cingulum (*B'*). However, both conulid-*t* and stylid-*f* may never appear together in the same tooth or the same species. The lower secondary cingulum *B'* is absent in many forms including callitrichids.

Conulid-*t* is best developed and occurs most frequently in dpm_{3-4}. It may also appear in either or both of the last two permanent premolars and the first, sometimes second molars (figs. V.17C, 18). The element resembles a reduced paraconid and possibly functions as one notably in callitrichids which lack the hypocone. Because of

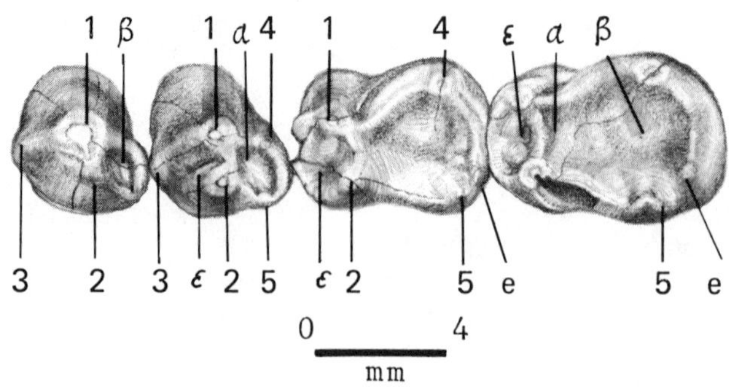

Fig. V.16. *Stirtonia tatacoensis,* right pm_{3-4}, m_{1-2}; note paraconid (*3*) in premolars; for explanation of symbols see fig. V.21. (Modified from Hershkovitz 1970*a.*)

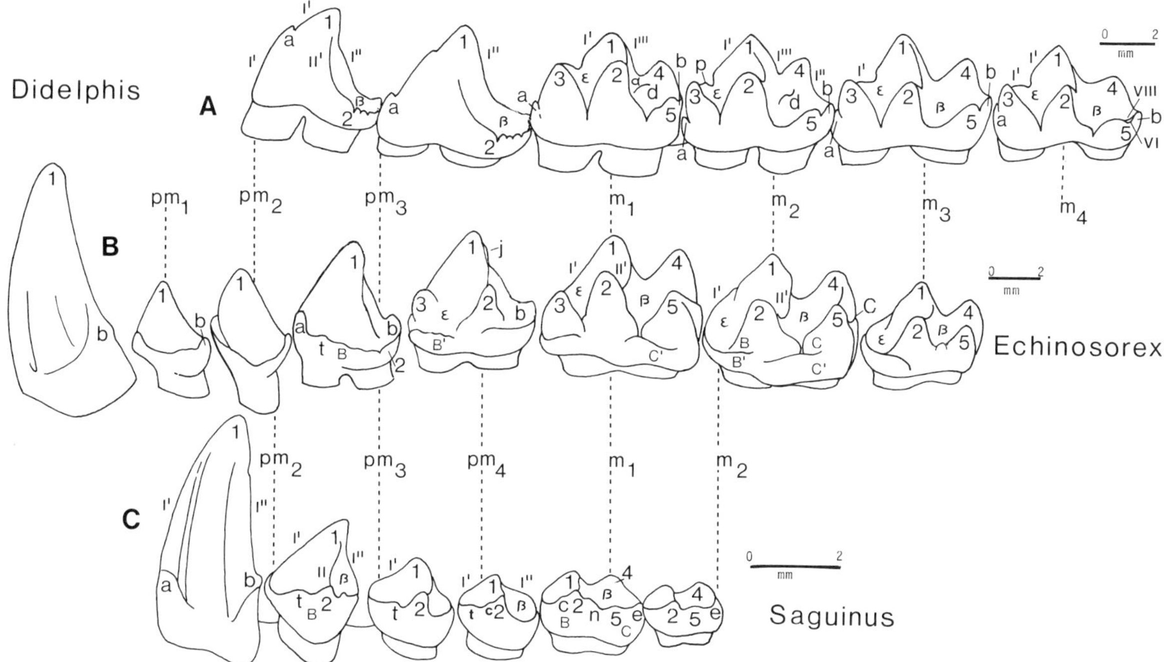

Fig. V.17. The paraconid-eoconid, and pseudoparaconid-metaconid relationships in lower tooth rows of *Didelphis, Echinosorex,* and *Saguinus.* The paraconid (*3*) originates on the eocristid (*I′*), the pseudoparaconid or conulid-*t* springs from the anterolingual cingulum (*B*) or protolophid (*III*) from which the metaconid (*2*) also rises.

A, pm$_2$–m$_4$ of *Didelphis marsupialis;* plesioconulid (*p*) often present in molariform dpm$_3$ (not shown); plagioconulid (*d*), with indications of plagiocristid (*IV′*), often present in one or more unworn molars; cristids *VI* and *VIII* enclose basin γ (not labeled).

B, c–m$_3$ of *Echinosorex gymnurus;* paraconid (*3*) rudimentary in pm$_4$, well developed in m$_1$, absent in remaining cheek teeth; large styloconid (*j*) frequently evident from lingual aspect, as shown in pm$_4$.

C, c–m$_2$ of *Saguinus oedipus,* conulid-*t* (pseudoparaconid), and epiconulid (protoconulid, *c*) are present as individual variables; eocristid (*I′*) approximates the anterolingual cingulum (*B*) in all cheek teeth with eoconid the only cuspid. Not all parts of each tooth are labeled, to avoid clutter. See fig. V.21 and page 300 for terminology. (After Hershkovitz 1971*a*.)

the similarities, conulid-*t* is alternatively termed *pseudoparaconid.*

Metacone (-id) versus Eoconule (-id)

The cusp of the subeutherian archaic or buccal type molar crown, labeled metacone by authors including Butler (1939*b*), Patterson (1956), Kermack, Kermack, and Mussett (1968), and as distocone by Vandebroek (1961), cannot be homologous with the same-named cusp of the eutherian tritubercular, or lingual type, crown. This cusp, the eoconule (-id [*q*]) (cusp *c* of Patterson 1956, p. 69; and Jenkins 1969, p. 5), rises as a protrusion or excrescence of the eocrista between eocone (-id) and true metacone (hypoconid) of the tritubercular crown. An analogous cusp, the plesioconule or conule *p* (fig. V.21) (cusp *a* of Patterson, 1956, p. 69), rises from the mesial slope of the eocrista in the archaic crown, and is sometimes present, usually vestigial, in the tritubercular crown. In contrast, the true tritubercular metacone appears comparatively late in eutherian dental evolution and in molars with lingual portion of the crown well developed. The cusp originates independently in euthemorphic dental systems, and in most advanced eutherian zalambdomorphic systems (cf. *Potamogale*). As a rule, the metacone follows the protocone, sometimes the hypocone, in phylogenetic and ontogenetic sequence of origin and development. The true metacone, like lingual protocone and hypocone, may have its analogue, but evidently no homologue in the archaic or buccal type molar crown of subeutherians.

The eoconule of the buccal type molar crown of late Triassic (Rhaetic) *Kuehneotherium* was correctly identified by McKenna (1969, fig. 2, and p. 219) as a "metacone-like cusp," which together with paracone (eocone) and stylocone (or plesioconule?) formed a triangle. However, McKenna (1969, p. 224) is ambiguous in his insinuation that this "metacone-like cusp," ostensibly the analogue and not the anlage of the metacone of later mammals, became the homologue of the metacone in such Cretaceous eutherians (includes metatherians) as *Holoclemensia* and *Pappotherium.* His footnote (McKenna 1969, p. 225, no. 14) states that the "metacone-like cusp" tended to disappear in dryolestids but in later protocone-bearing zalambdodonts, it is the metacone which "was finally lost as paracone height increased and the protocone decreased." McKenna fails to show a lineal relationship between the subeutherian "metacone-like cusp" and the eutherian metacone, and his detailed sequence of molarization is quite the reverse of what appears to have actually occurred in eutherians.

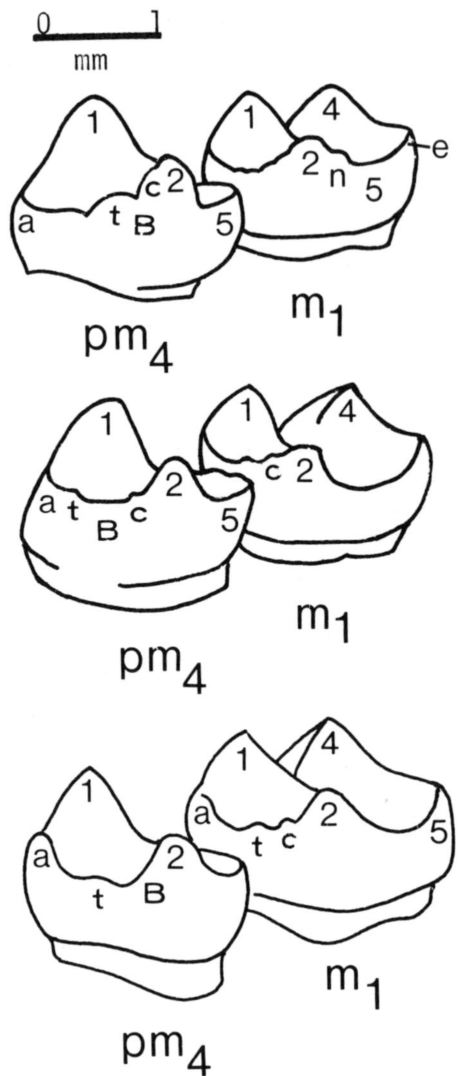

Fig. V.18. Lingual cusp variation in lower molariform teeth of *Cebuella pygmaea*: *Top row,* right pm_4–m_1 (FMNH 74361); *middle row,* right pm_4–m_1 (FMNH 88998); lower row, left pm_4–m_1 (FMNH 88998). *B,* anterolingual cingulum; *a,* mesiostylid; *c,* epiconulid; *t,* conulid-*t* (pseudoparaconid).

Hypoconid

The hypoconid (*4*), like the metacone (*4*), differentiates on the distal slope of the eocristid between eoconid (or eoconulid (*q*), if present) and distostylid (*b*). The two cusps, hypoconid and metacone, therefore, are regarded as serially homologous (figs. V.12, 19). The hypoconid, however, appears even later in phylogeny and ontogeny than the metacone, and out of phase with it. It is interesting that Butler (1941, p. 446) finds no maxillary homologue (i.e., metacone) for the hypoconid in noneutherian teeth. Thus, of the three cusps of the archaic crown, identified by Butler (1939*b;* 1941, p. 446) as paracone, "metacone," and "anterior accessory cusp," only the paracone, the acknowledged *main* cusp or eocone, is strictly homologous with the like-named cusp of the lingual or tritubercular upper crown. As I suggested above, Butler's "metacone" is the eoconule, and his "anterior accessory cusp" is the plesioconule, of the lingual crown.

Hypocone and Pseudohypocone

The hypocone (*5*) rises from the posterolingual cingulum (*C*) and ultimately incorporates it. The time of appearance of the hypocone relative to protocone and metacone varies. In teeth, most notably premolars, of some lineages, it originates before protocone and metacone (fig. V.9B2). More commonly, the hypocone appears later than the protocone but earlier than the metacone (cf. *Callicebus* $pm^{2\text{-}3}$, fig. V.5C). In most primate phyletic lines, however, the hypocone is the last of the four major cusps to differentiate (figs. V.3, 6, 9C2). The order of appearance of the cusps in ontogeny may well reflect the sequence in phylogeny.

The hypocone evolved independently in platyrrhines and catarrhines and in all other lineages in which the tritubercular cheek teeth of the ancestral form lack the hypocone. In the quadritubercular teeth of cebids and hominoids the anterior crest or entocrista (*V*) of the hypocone contacts either the lingual border of the protocone or the protoconal portion of the plagiocrista (*IV′*). In molars of living cercopithecids, crista *V* is transverse and meets the buccal or metaconal portion of the plagiocrista (*V″*) (fig. V.15), and gives rise to the bilophodont molar crown pattern characteristic of Old World monkeys.

Theories regarding the nature of the hypocone and evolution of bilophodonty in catarrhine monkeys were reviewed by Voruz (1970). His conclusions are critically summarized as follows. (1) The posterointernal cusp of the quadritubercular upper molar is a true hypocone. (2) Bilophodonty in lower molars began with fusion of hypoconulid (*b*) and entoconid (*5*) (an assumption with which I do not agree). (3) Evolution of bilophodonty in upper molars has not yet been satisfactorily explained (but see text above and my fig. V.15 with explanations). (4) Evolution of the cercopithecoid bilophodont pattern was not completed by the beginning of the Pliocene (but in the Oligocene *Parapithecus* bilophodonty is already well advanced [fig. III.2]).

Origin of the hypocone from the lingual (i.e., posterolingual cingulum (*C*) seems to be universally recognized. It is not universally recognized, however, that a secondary or neoposterolingual cingulum (*C′*) may arise from the base of the hypertrophied primary posterolingual cingulum (*C*) which is a complex of hypocone and cristas *V* and *VI.* Stehlin (1916, p. 1535) correctly described the hypocone in the molars of the European Eocene *Adapis* as a cingular derivative. On the other hand, presence of a neoposterolingual cingulum at the base of the same posterointernal cusp of the molars of the North American Eocene *Notharctus* implied to Stehlin that the cusp could not have sprung from a cingulum and therefore must have split off from the protocone. Accordingly, he distinguished the element as a "Pseudypoconus" or pseudohypocone.

Gregory (1920, p. 141; 1922, pp. 130, 135, 220) likewise confused secondary with primary cingula. Thus, the neolingual cingulum Gregory (1922, p. 130) saw in the molars of *Notharctus* was interpreted as the primary "internal cingulum, which in other mammals gives rise

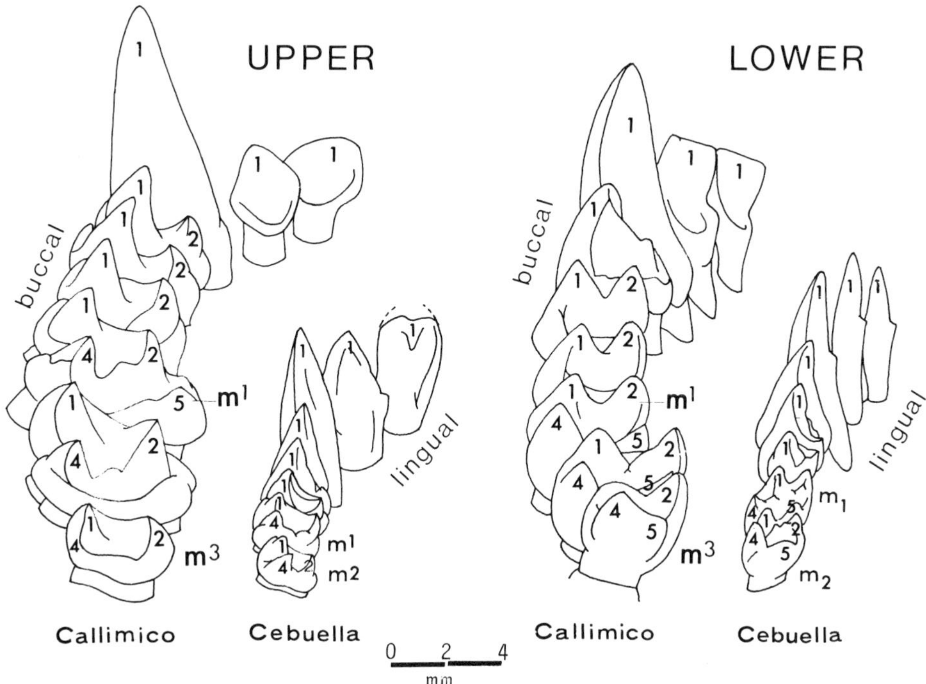

Fig. V.19. Right upper and left lower tooth rows of *Callimico goeldii* and *Cebuella pygmaea*: Occlusal surface seen from behind forward; buccal and lingual upper cusps are homologous with respective buccal and lingual lower cusps. (After Hershkovitz 1971*a*.)

to the hypocone, remains distinct [in *Notharchus*] and fails to produce a normal hypocone. *The budding off* [from protocone] *of the posterointernal cusp or pseudohypocone in the Notharctidae has probably been conditioned by the attrition of the upgrowing entoconid of the lower molar.*" Gregory's illustration (1922, p. 136) to show the difference between the molars of *Notharctus* with a "pseudohypocone" and those of *Adapis* with true hypocone is reproduced here (fig. V.14D, E).

In his revision of the Necrolemuridae, Hürzeler (1948, pp. 19, 44) identified Stehlin's pseudohypocone as a true hypocone. He explained that the "*Nannopithex* Falte" (= entocrista, *V*)[1] that connects hypocone with protocone gives the impression that the posterior internal cusp splits off from the anterior internal cusp. Simpson (1955, p. 435) rejected the discrimination of pseudohypocone from hypocone as a "distinction without a difference." In his discussion of the hypocone, Butler (1956, p. 49) concluded that the "variety of conformations which are observed on the completed teeth may largely be attributed to variations in the time of appearance of the lingual cusps during ontogeny." Returning later to the same subject he (1963, pp. 11–12) referred to the pseudohypocone as without legitimate distinction from the hypocone.

Remane (1960, p. 685) reviewed the conflicting opinions and admitted the possibility of the existence of two hypocones, namely the "euhypocone" that arose from the lingual cingulum and a pseudohypocone that split off from the posterior border of the protocone. In practice, however, he found that the hypocone originated from the lingual cingulum only and its connection with the protocone was secondary. Wood (1962, p. 8) observed that differences between the hypocone and what might be construed as a pseudohypocone in the molars of early Tertiary paramyid rodents are individual variations of the same fundamental structure. My (1971, p. 128) studies of large series of mammalian molars and premolars of all geologic ages and stages of development revealed no evidence of the origin of a hypocone or "pseudohypocone" elsewhere than from the primary posterolingual cingulum.

All previous authors focused on two "kinds" of hypocones without a difference. None seemed to be aware of two kinds of lingual cingula, primary and secondary, with a difference. No student of odontology has ever regarded a protocone with a neocingulum at its base as a pseudoprotocone, although the reasoning for it would be the same as for the pseudohypocone. Probably, the widely held dogma that the protocone is the primitive cone, hence not of cingular origin, led to the conviction that the neoanterolingual cingulum (*B'*) at the base of the cusp is the primary cingulum and that the adjacent neoposterolingual cingulum (*C'*) is a continuation of the same element from which a true hypocone arises.

Hypoconule (Distostyle)

The hypoconule (-id) or conule *b* (fig. V.21) is certainly identical with the Osbornian metastyle (hypoconulid). Historically, the cusp is coeval with the mammalian main cone and is so indicated (1*b*, p. 297). In the tritubercular crown, however, the cusp may appear late in ontogeny, if it is not wholly suppressed in phylogeny, especially where crowded by an adjacent tooth.

Cope-Osborn Tritubercular Theory

Recognition of a common plan in dental morphology based on homologous cusps dates from the discovery by

[1] The crest called *Nannopithex* Falte was used correctly in the text of my earlier report (Hershkovitz 1971, p. 129) but was inadvertently misidentified with the plagiocrista (*IV'*) in the glossary of the same report (1971, p. 143).

Cope (1883, pp. 407–8) of a basic tritubercular pattern in the crowns of upper molars in Eocene mammals. The theory of molar evolution predicated on this primitive pattern was developed in later works by Cope (cf. 1887, p. 359; 1896, pp. 135, 331), and more extensively and independently by Osborn (1888*a,b;* 1897; 1907). The theory was critically reviewed by numerous authors, including Woodward (1896), Gidley (1906), Gregory (1916; 1922; 1934), Simpson (1936), Butler (1941), Patterson (1956), Vandebroek (1961), Romer (1966), and Osborn himself (1897; 1907). Several rival theories of dental evolution and systems of molar cusp terminology had also been proposed and were reviewed by many authorities, including those cited above. The proposals had little acceptance, are mostly forgotten, and need not be considered here. On the other hand, concepts of cusp homologies derived from the generally adopted Cope-Osborn tritubercular theory call for reexamination in the light of the foregoing discussions of dental evolutionary process and descriptions of crown types and patterns.

In his definitive work on trituberculy, Osborn (1907, pp. 2–7) presented the main tenets of the Cope-Osborn theory of molar evolution in the form of four principles from which I quote or abstract the essence.

I. *First Principle: The Primitive Tritubercular Type.* The tritubercular type was ancestral to many if not all higher types of molar teeth.

II. *Second Principle: The Origin of the Tritubercular Type from the Single Reptilian Cone.* The tritubercular type sprang from a single conical type by addition of lateral denticles.

III. *Third Principle: Cusp Addition or Differentiation.* New dentules, cuspules, or smaller cones on the sides of the original reptilian cone [are added by] budding or outgrowth [not by concrescence of discrete elements].

IV. *Fourth Principle: Reversed Upper and Lower Teeth.* In the lower molars the reptilian cone is external and the two denticles internal, while in the upper molars the reverse is true, namely, the reptilian cone is internal and the denticles are external. This principle, if a true one, enables us to establish a kind of [reversed] serial homology between the *main primary cone* and *secondary denticles* or *cusps* of the upper and lower teeth respectively. Osborn expressed the homologies in his system of nomenclature (protocone, paracone, metacone, etc.).

In the same work, Osborn (p. 9) warned that the

> four great principles of molar evolution *do not stand or fall together.* The first or primitive trituberculy principle is now almost undeniable for the majority of mammals; entirely apart from the disputed question of the original homology of the cusps of the upper and lower teeth, there is no question whatsoever as to the beautiful and almost incredible homologies between the cusps of the molar teeth in the most diverse orders of mammals.

The first principle is indeed generally accepted, but it is ambiguous. Only the trigon of euthemorphic upper molars is consistently tritubercular—that is, defined by three main cusps, here the eocone, metacone, and protocone. Upper molars of many zalambdodonts, and the subeutherian pantotheres, symmetrodonts, triconodonts, and multituberculates, are not tritubercular. The "trigonid" on the other hand, is nearly universally tritubercular, although only two of the three cusps are homologues of trigon cusps.

Simpson (1936, p. 5) suggested that the first principle "alone and without prejudice to the other three principles," be called the Cope-Osborn theory. At the same time he coined (1936, p. 8) the single term *tribosphenic* for replacing the somewhat awkward Cope-Osbornian "tritubercular" and "tuberculo-sectorial," used respectively for the essentially euthemorphic upper and lower molars.

The second principle of tritubercular origin, as shown by Gidley (1906), Simpson (1936, p. 16) and others, lacks firm support. The cheek teeth of earliest known mammals and their probable ancestors among mammal-like reptiles are not haplodont, and the eutherian tritubercular cheek tooth need not be derived from a triconodont (s.s.) tooth. Even the apparently haplodont or conical canines and incisors, present in many eutherians, are secondary simplications of tridentate teeth.

The third principle, to the effect that new crown elements originate by budding or outgrowth, is basically correct, as is demonstrated by embryological studies. It fails to allow, however, for proliferation of elements by infolding or subdivision, or by crenulation. Nevertheless, the principle as enunciated is an essential part, if not the only valid part, of the restricted Cope-Osborn theory, and contradicts the next, or fourth, principle.

The fourth principle of reversed upper and lower triangles is equivocal and gave rise to controversies regarding interpretations of cusp homologies and cusp terminologies based on such interpretations. Osborn (1907, p. 227) recognized but failed to resolve serious conflicts between his ideas regarding origin and position of cones forming the trigon (-id), and competing, often conflicting ideas based on evidence from paleontology, embryology, and serial homology.

The hypothesis of cusp rotation, migration, or circumduction as an explanation for seemingly reversed upper and lower triangles is usually attributed to Cope (1884, p. 239). This authority, however, only suggested that "shifting of the two subordinate cusps to the inner sides of the principal one will give a tritubercular [lower] molar." Osborn (1888*c*, p. 1073) concurred but noted that "it has been *assumed* [italics mine] by Cope and the writer [Osborn 1888*a*, p. 243] that the para- and metaconid were first formed upon the anterior and posterior slopes of the protoconid and then rotated inwards, *but it is also possible that they were originally formed upon the inner slopes* [italics mine]." Unfortunately, Osborn did not elect the alternative. In his diagram (1895, fig. 8; 1907, fig. 4) illustrating origin and evolution of primitive molars, the rotation of supposed homologous upper and lower cusps to occupy vertices of upper and lower reversed triangles, respectively, is explicit.

It is evident that Osborn's concepts of cusp terminology and homology disregard historical changes in the form of the molar crown. His topographical system of cusp determination and terminology is ambiguous and subject to more than one interpretation, as is shown in the accompanying comparisons and fig. V.20. The numbers in the last three columns represent my terminology (cf. p. 300).

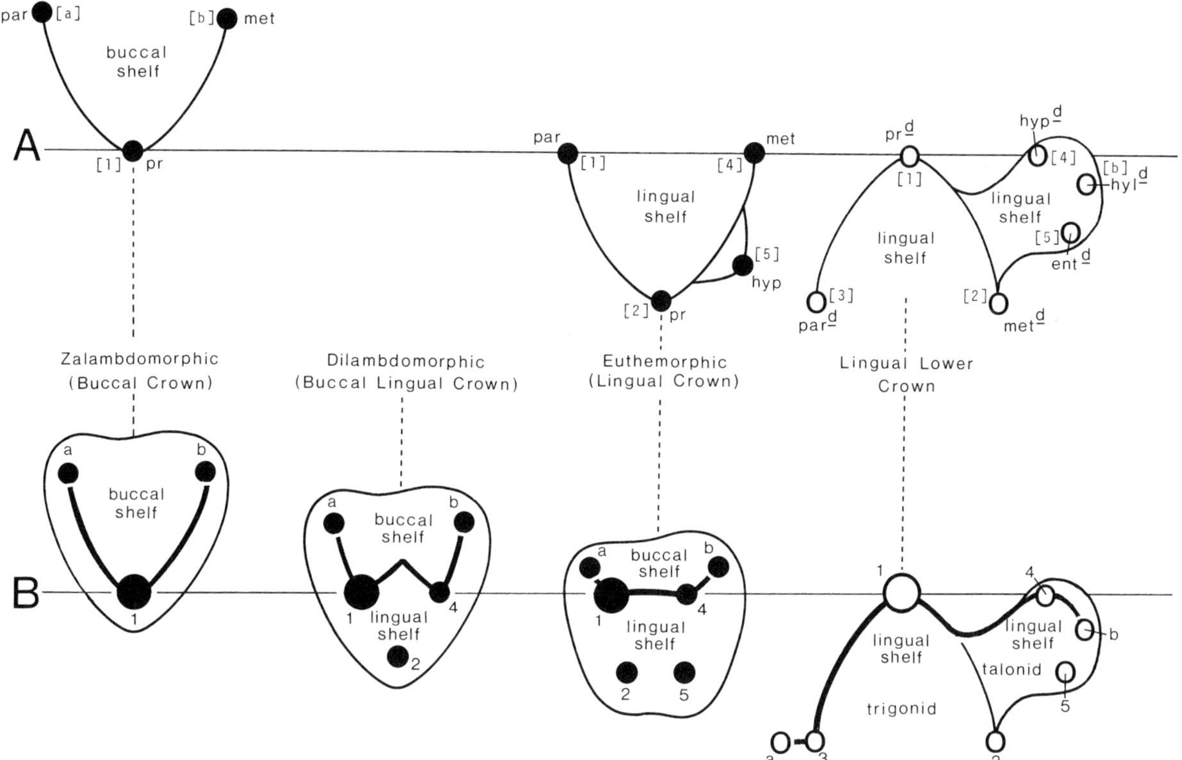

Fig. V.20. Diagrams of molars showing cusp terminologies according to *A*, Osborn (1907, p. 61), but with the homologous elements shown by symbols in brackets; *B*, present system based on homology (figs. V.12, 21). The main cusps (eocone, eoconid) in both systems are oriented to the eocone (-id) axis (horizontal line at *A* and *B*). Osborn may not have appreciated the stability of the main cusps in contrast with the shifting design of the upper molar crown from predominantly buccal in extent to predominantly lingual in extent. Osborn's main cone, his protocone, was always the inner anterior cusp in upper molars and the outer anterior cusp in lower molars. Thus, in an upper molar with a predominantly buccal crown, the true main cusp or eocone was called protocone but in a predominantly lingual crown, a newly evolved cingular element became the protocone because it was, by definition, the inner anterior cusp. In the same vein, Osborn's paracone (*par*) and metacone (*met*) of the buccal (zalambdomorphic) crown are true styles (*a, b,*) and not homologues of the same-named cones of the lingual (euthemorphic) crown. The lower molar, by virtue of being in a movable jaw, retains a stable lingual crown. The lower-upper cusp homologies in Osborn's terminology and symbols used in *B* shown in brackets, follow: Protoconid = paracone [*1*]; metaconid = protocone [*2*]; paraconid [*3*]—no upper homologue; hypoconid = metacone [*4*]; entoconid = hypocone [*5*]; hypoconulid = metastyle [*b*]. Osborn's cristae are also incorrect, but I use his design for the convenience of comparing lower molars.

Cusp	*Term*	*Present System (figs. V.3, 20,21)* Zalambdomorphic Crown	Dilambdomorphic Crown	Euthemorphic Crown
UPPER MOLARS (Osborn 1907, p. 41.)				
Antero-internal	.... Protocone (pr)	1	2	2
Postero-internal	.... Hypocone (hyp)	–	4 or 5	5
Antero-external	.... Paracone (par)	a	a or 1	1
Postero-external	.... Metacone (met)	b	4 or b	4
LOWER MOLARS				
Antero-external	.... Protoconid (pr^d)			1
Postero-external	.... Hypoconid (hyp^d)			4
Antero-internal, or 5th cusp	...... Paraconid (par^d)			3
Intermediate, or antero-internal cusp in quadritubercular molars	. Metaconid (met^d)			2
Postero-internal	.... Entoconid (ent^d)			5
[Postero-median]	... Hypoconulid (hyl^d)			*b*

These comparisons show clearly that the anterointernal cusp, Osborn's protocone, is one derived from the anterolingual cingulum or shelf in the dilambdomorphic or euthemorphic molar crown but is the primitive eocone in the zalambdomorphic molar crown. Osborn's anteroexternal cusp or paracone cannot be consistently identified with the same cusp in most zalambdomorphic or dilambdomorphic teeth. The mesiostyle (*a*), stylocone (*j*), and ectostyle (*k*), all derived from the buccal shelf (cf. fig. V.13) are candidates for the "anteroexternal" post depending on which are present and largest. In the euthemorphic molar crown, the anteroexternal cusp is certainly the primitive eocone (*1*). Regarding lower molar cusps, not one is homologous with the like-named cusp of the upper molar crowns. Osborn failed to see the change in the principal portion of the crown from the archaic buccal shelf to a new lingual shelf with its suite of new cusps that functionally replaced the old. Osborn believed, instead, that the old elements merely shifted, rotated or migrated to occupy their respective predesignated topographic positions in a totally new or radically altered portion of crown.

Evidence for Cusp Homologies

The Fossil Record

Paleontological evidence, as deduced by Winge (1882), Scott (1893), Wortman (1902, p. 41; 1903, p. 365; 1921, p. 178), Gregory (1922, pp. 103, 153), Simpson (1928, p. 172), Butler (1937; 1939*a*) and others show that the main cusp of all upper and lower cheek teeth is the *anteroexternal* (mesiobuccal) cone, the paracone and protoconid, respectively, of the Cope-Osborn terminology, and the eocone (-id) of this paper, following Vandebroek (1961; 1967). The same evidence also reveals that all so-called primary cones originating on the lingual and buccal cingula evolved independently, and that rotation of such cusps from buccal to lingual or from lingual to buccal positions relative to the main cone or axis never occurred.

Support by Crompton and Jenkins (1968) of the Cope-Osborn concept of rotating cusps and reversed triangles is based on new material and old explanations but with emphasis on the role of occlusion in molar evolution. The authors (1968, pp. 447, 453) speak of a trigon in the upper molars of Triconodonta, Docodonta, Symmetrodonta, and Pantotheria, where the eocone is the only cusp of the eutherian trigon. Likewise, their "trigonid" in Triconodonta consists of only the eoconid. Paraconid and metaconid, however, are present and complete the "trigonid" in molars of the remaining subeutherians. These conids are not to be misconstrued as errant homologues of cusps that originated on the buccal cingulum of the upper molars. External or labiad flexure of the eocone axis with its subsidiary cusps, and internal or linguad flexure of the eoconid with homologous subsidiary cusps have also been construed by Crompton and Jenkins as rotation in the sense of a continuous migration of the subsidiary cusps from buccal to lingual zone, or vice versa. The flexures, however, began on a primitively longitudinal axis and curved away from each other in opposite directions, buccally in the upper molars, lingually in the lower. The relative position of the pivotal eocone (-id) remains fixed. In molars of Triconodonta, with comparatively narrow external and internal shelves and a nearly longitudinal axis, the eocone (-id) is central relative to the entire crown surface. As the external shelf enlarged, the locus of the main cone became more lingual relative to the total occlusal surface. With expansion of the lingual shelf and contraction of the buccal, the pole became more buccal. Changes in relative size and importance of occluding buccal and lingual shelves involve no migration of the eocone (-id), no rotation of cusps, and no inversion of triangles.

It was also suggested (Crompton and Jenkins 1968, p. 451) that acquisition of transverse movements of the lower jaw during mastication was coupled with cusp rotation. It seems to me, rather, that the transverse jaw movement is correlated with hypertrophy of the internal shelf and consequent differentiation of metacone and lingual protocone in the upper molars, and lingual metaconid and paraconid in the lower. This in turn reflects the progressive increase in palatal breadth and spread between mandibular rami.

Serial Arrangement

Serial arrangement from the primitive or tridentate tooth to the complex molar of higher mammals involves a progressive accumulation of homologous elements. This is reflected in the gradient of increasing complexity which in most eutherians begins with the canine and advances forward to incisors and backward to molars. In other eutherians the gradient is from incisors to molars. The resulting molar pattern is well defined and permits the identification of each part of a tooth in any part of the dental system (fig. IV.19).

The serial arrangement of similar parts is a clear expression of serial homology. It is not a recapitulation of molar evolution. Rather, it presents a morphological gradient from which phylogeny may be inferred. Serial homology is the basis for the so-called *premolar analogy theory* developed by Scott (1893) and Wortman (1902, p. 41; 1903, p. 365; 1921, p. 178), and strongly supported by Gregory (1922, p. 103), Simpson (1933, pp. 265, 269–70), Butler (1937; 1941), Van Valen (1966, p. 2), and others. In the light of present interpretations, it may be more appropriate to refer to the premolar analogy theory as the Scott-Wortman theory of serial homology.

Ontogeny

Ontogeny reflects phylogeny with respect to the place and sequence of molar cusp origins, and verifies homologies inferred from the serial arrangement of cusps in the tooth row. The first cone of the euthemorphic system to develop and calcify in ontogeny is invariably the eocone (*1*) in the upper teeth and the eoconid in the lower. The second cone to develop in the upper teeth, usually the cheek teeth, is the protocone (*2*), doubtfully the metacone (*4*), which is usually third; the hypocone (*5*) is usually fourth in the quadritubercular tooth but it is sometimes third in the tritubercular premolar and molar. Lower cones of the euthemorphic molar system usually develop in the same sequence and in the same loci as the uppers relative to each other. Thus, the protoconid (*1*) is followed by the metaconid (*2*) or the paraconid (*3*), if present; the entoconid (*5*) is followed, sometimes preceded by, the hypoconid (*4*) in the increasingly complex tooth. The hypoconule (*b*) and hypoconulid (*b*) are emergent cones and are last to develop in the more highly complex upper and lower molars, respectively. The order of cone development in *zalambdomorphic* and *dilambdomorphic* systems of some species may deviate from the *euthemorphic*. In the premolars of *Tenrec*, for example, the eocone and hypocone are often the only principal cones present (fig. V.5).

The ontogenetic sequence of cusp development and calcification outlined above has been demonstrated in man (Röse 1892*a;* Kraus 1963; Kraus and Jordan 1965; Butler 1956; and others), rhesus monkey, *Macaca mulatta* (Swindler and McCoy 1964; 1965), opossum, *Didelphis marsupialis* (Röse 1892), insectivores, *Erinaceus, Gymnura, Sorex, Tenrec* (= *Centetes*), *Setifer* (= *Ericulus*), *Talpa* (Woodward 1896), dog, *Canis familiaris* (Tims 1896), cat, *Felis catus* (Gaunt 1959), mink, *Mustela vison* (Aulerich and Swindler 1968), ungulates *Equus, Sus, Hyemoschus, Cervus, Capreolus, Capra, Bos* (Taeker, in Röse 1892; and Osborn 1893), rodents, including *Rattus rattus* (Glasstone 1967), mouse, *Mus musculus,* and golden hamster, *Mesocricetus auratus* (Gaunt 1955, 1961).

Summary of Cusp Homologies and Terminologies

Evidence from phylogeny, ontogeny, and the serial arrangement of cusps establishes the homologies between upper and lower dental elements. Cristae (ridges and lophs) and cristids connecting serially homologous cusps are likewise homologous. Minor conules (-ids) and styles (-ids) appearing regularly in similar positions are also homologous. Where the chronological sequence of appearance in either archaic (buccal) or tritubercular (lingual) crown appears to deviate, place of origin and position relative to other cusps, particularly the eocone (-id) are crucial for determination of cusp homologies.

In the accompanying list, the same number is used for homologous upper and lower cusps. The number in parentheses refers to the usual order of appearance of each cusp in ontogeny and in most, if not all, cases, phylogeny. Cusp names are from Osborn (1888*b*, p. 927), the synonyms in brackets are from Vandebroek (1961).

Upper Cusps

1 (1*a*) Paracone [eocone]
2 (2) Protocone [epicone] (see note p. 289)
3 —
4 (4) Metacone [distocone] (rarely precedes protocone) (see note p. 291)
5 (5) Hypocone [endocone] (usually precedes metacone in a few forms, including *Callicebus* pm^{3-4}, *Solenodon* pm-m) (see note p. 292)
6 (1*b*) Hypoconule [distostyle] (see note p. 293)

Lower Cusps

1 (1*a*) Protoconid [eoconid]
2 (2) Metaconid [epiconid]
3 (3) Paraconid [mesioconid] (see note p. 290)
4 (5) Hypoconid [teleconid] (see note p. 292)
5 (4) Entoconid [endoconid]
6 (1*b*) Hypoconulid [distostylid]

Homologies: Criteria and Generalizations

Most of the foregoing discussion on dental evolution and bases for the determination of dental homologies can be summarized as follows:

1. All teeth of mammalian dental systems are serially homologous. Deciduous and permanent dental systems evolve independently. Permanent molars are persistent milk molars without successors.

2. Serially homologous cusps of upper or lower tooth rows are aligned in a gradient of increasing complexity from canine to incisors and canine to molars, or incisors to molars, with main cone always conspicuous, if not always largest, and most persistent throughout.

3. Each upper tooth is grossly homologous with the corresponding lower tooth. For example, the first upper molar is homologous with the first lower molar even if one or more elements of one tooth have no homologues in the other.

4. Serially homologous (or equivalent) cusps usually originate, develop, and calcify in approximately the same sequence and the same relative positions in upper and lower teeth.

5. Eocone (paracone) and eoconid (protoconid) are the primary, or reptilian cones, respectively, of all mammalian upper and lower teeth. As such, they are strictly homologous and the common base of reference for all cusp homologies. The same cones are also referred to as main cusps or main cones.

6. Each upper cusp is, as a rule, serially homologous with the lower cusp of same general form and same position relative to other cusps, but particularly the main one (figs. V.19, 21).

7. Primary cingula (-ids) and cristae (-ids) connecting homologous cusps (cuspids) are homologous; conversely, cusps arising in the same position in the same sequence on homologous cingula and cristae are serially homologous. The same applies to mandibular elements. Primitive crest patterns, however, may be disrupted through capture of parts by new crests arising from rapidly expanding peripheral cones, particularly stylocone and hypocone.

8. The eocone (-id) axis, that is, the principal axis, is the structural base for all mammalian teeth. The axial elements, *eocone* (-id), *mesiostyle* (-id), (parastyle [-id]), *distostyle* (-id), (metastyle [hypoconulid]), *plesioconule* (-id), *eoconule* (-id), and connecting *eocrista* (-id), are strictly homologous wherever they occur in upper and lower teeth, whether incisors, canines, premolars, or molars, deciduous or permanent. All cusps and crests of teeth of Triconodonta are axial elements.

9. Buccal side or lingual side, *relative to the primary axis* of each upper tooth is homologous with respective buccal side or lingual side of the corresponding lower tooth (fig. V.19), never the reverse, as suggested by Butler (1937, p. 130).

10. The *archaic* or *buccal crown* (primary trigon of Gregory 1922, pp. 105–6) evolved by expansion of *buccal* side of eocone axis, usually with addition and

complication of buccal cingulum or shelf. The buccal or archaic crown is the only type present in upper teeth of Symmetrodonta and Pantotheria. The upper crown overhangs the lower on the buccal side.

11. The *lingual or tritubercular* crown evolved by expansion of the lingual side of the eocone axis and includes the neomorphic metacone derived from the eocrista, and protocone derived from lingual shelf.

12. Except for the primitive eocone axial elements common to both types, no cusp of the lingual or tritubercular portion of the crown is homologous with any cusps of the buccal or archaic portion of the crown.

13. The primitive "trigonid" consists of primary protoconid, that is, eoconid, on the buccal side, and secondary paraconid and metaconid on the lingual side. The two lingual cusps originated in situ; neither is homologous with the Osbornian like-named cusps of the trigon.

14. Trigon cusps of either archaic or tritubercular crown types are not inverted in position with respect to homologous "trigonid" cusps; only the Osbornian cusp names are transposed.

15. Osbornian-named homologous cusps of the trigon-"trigonid" are paracone-protoconid (= eocone-eoconid), protocone-metaconid. Paraconid without homologue shears with protocone or occludes with hypocone, by which it ultimately may be replaced as a functional unit. Metacone, with allochronic hypoconid as homologue, shears with protoconid.

16. Talon and talonid are specializations of the distal region of the tritubercular crown. They extend into or across the embrasure between adjacent teeth and overlap in occlusion with adjacent opposing teeth. The talonid evolved in an early stage tritubercular lower molar (cf. Pantotheria) to permit limited grinding; the talon appears later in the quadritubercular upper molar of specialized herbivores.

Dental Symbols and Terminology

The Dual System

The equivocal homologies implicit in the Osbornian terminology were recognized early by critics of the tritubercular theory. Nevertheless, the terms have become established and students of dental evolution continue to use them. Others avoid, evade, or change them. In dentistry, purely locational terms for cusps are generally used. Butler (1937, p. 116), in one of a series of papers on dental evolutionary theory, avoided embarrassment by using Osbornian terms for the lower molars only. Vandebroek (1961), guided by true homologies, rejected compromise and proposed an entirely new terminology based on strict homology but patterned on Osborn's system. Those who counteracted by defending the classical system rejected Vandebroek's nomenclature as well as his valid bases for it. Paradoxically, some went on to coin new terms for elements already named by Vandebroek and other workers, including Osborn.

A dual system of symbols and Osbornian-type names is employed here (fig. V.21). The symbols are used in illustrations and the terms in the text, but frequently with their symbols shown in brackets.

In the symbol system, Arabic numerals are used for *cones* (= principal cusps), small letters for *conules* and *styles* (minor cusps), Roman numerals for *cristae* (ridges, lophs), capital letters for *cingula* (peripheral bands or shelves), and Greek letters for *basins* (fossae).

The same symbol is used for serially homologous or equivalent coronal elements of upper and lower teeth. Where confusion might arise, symbols for elements of upper teeth may be underlined, those for mandibular teeth overlined.

The adopted Osbornian terminology is based on a system of prefixes and suffixes which signify type, position, and relationships of the dental elements. The suffix *-cone* or *-conid* is employed for the established or principal cusps of trigon (-id) and talon (-id); *-conule (-id)* is used for diminutive cusps or cuspules rising from cristas (-ids); *-style (-id)* identifies tubercles or "pillars" rising from the cingula or cingulids; *-loph (-id)* refers to any ridge or crest, but the modern term *-crista (-id)* is preferred. In Osborn's terminology, such prefixes as *proto-, para-, meta-, meso-, hypo-, ecto-,* and *-ento-* referred to the supposed primitive position or order of development of the dental element. Like *proto-* in protocone, however, Osborn's prefixes are not consistently valid indicators of phylogenetic or ontogenetic sequences, or of positions. Nevertheless, many do serve as topographic guides, and the more solidly entrenched Osbornian terms are retained here. The Osbornian terms *trigon (-id)*, *talon (-id)*, and the suffix *-id,* for distinguishing mandibular elements, are universally recognized.

The Osbornian system of prefixes and suffixes was also intended to imply evolutionary processes and tendencies. In practice, however, the system is typological. It makes no allowance for change in evolutionary grade of a dental element, and as new terms are introduced, the system becomes more confused and contradictory. The Osbornian hypocone, for example, is typed as a *cone* despite the fact that it begins as a tiny excrescence on the posterolingual cingulum. The hypoconid cannot have evolved from a hypoconulid because that name is used for something entirely different which also began as a stylid. Even such Osbornian terms as paracone and paraconid, used for supposedly homologous upper and lower dental elements, actually refer to unrelated structures. Revised nomenclatures such as Van Valen's (1966) and the totally new one of Vandebroek (1961) are more precise but are no less typological. The open-ended symbol system introduced here has the flexibility others lack but does not solve all problems. It provides one sign for each dental element and its homologue, from anlage to the highest evolutionary grade it attains in the mammalian tooth. As new elements appear or previously unused ones need recognition, new letters, numbers, and superscripts can be assigned to them.

A list of the symbols appears on pages 300, 301.

Names and Symbols for Homologous Crown Elements (fig. V.21)

Approximately forty-four terms are used for elements of upper teeth and about the same number for those of the lower dental series. The dental terms were coined by authors ranging in time from Osborn (1888*a*, 1907) to Vandebroek (1961), Van Valen (1966), Szalay (1968, 1969*a*), and Hershkovitz (1971*a*). In many cases it was necessary to elect one of two or more synonymous terms. All terms used here, their synonyms, and many other names for dental elements, are listed in a glossary to my 1971 publication on teeth. In most cases, the authority for

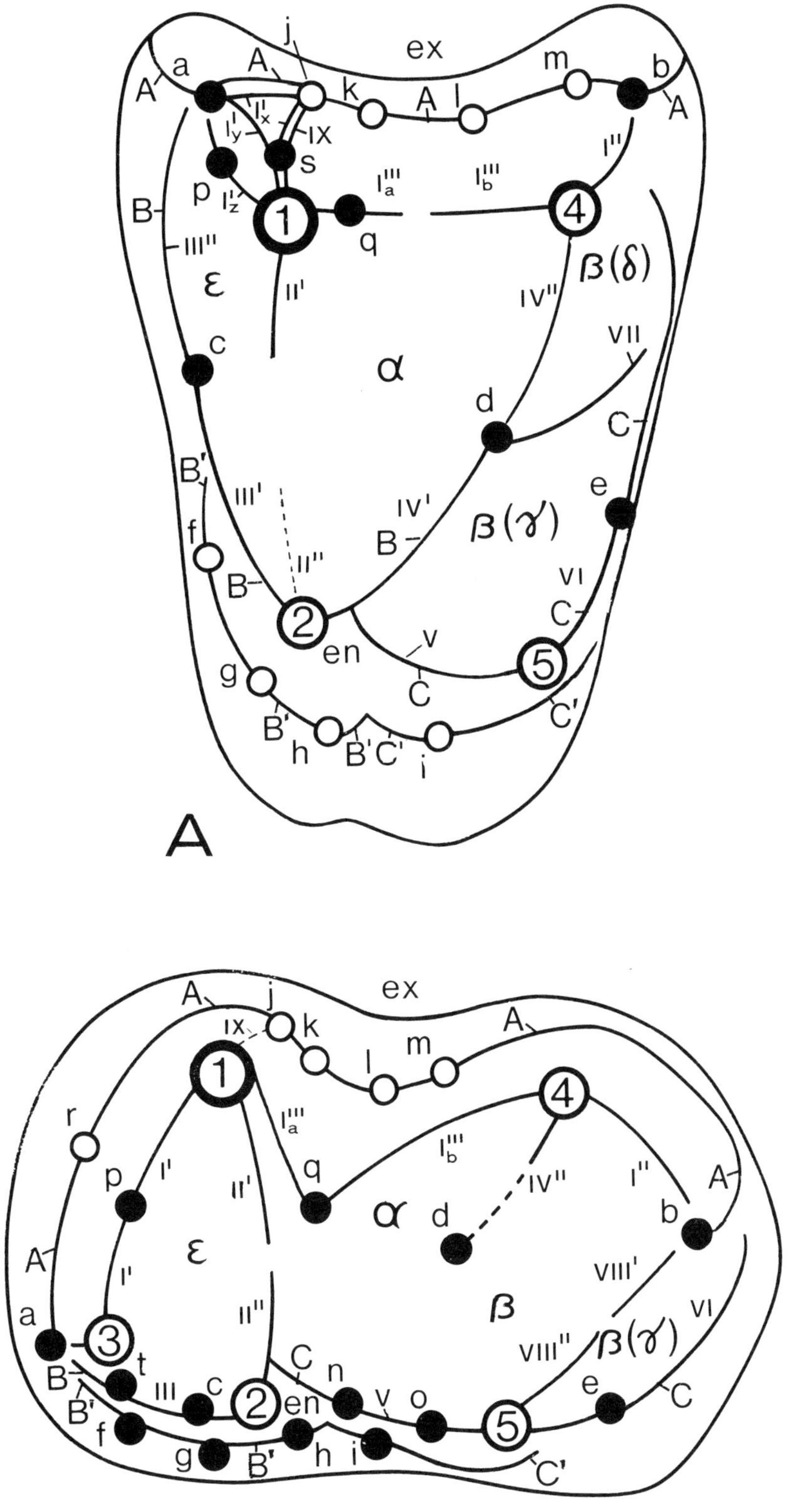

Fig. V.21. Master plan of coronal pattern of upper and lower euthemorphic molars. All dental elements present in primitive and early therian mammals are shown: *A*, left upper molar crown; *B*, right lower crown. (Modified from Hershkovitz 1971*a*.)

the dental term is cited. With few exceptions, the old and familiar Osbornian terms are used for promotion of the new system of dental evolution and homologization.

The letter or number used as a symbol for each dental crown element is followed by the name or names used in the text. The same symbol is used for homologous upper and lower features in all teeth in all toothed mammals. If symbols are used exclusively for dental crown elements, those for the upper crown should be underlined, and those for the lower crown should be overlined.

UPPER TEETH

Cones[3]

1 eocone (paracone)
2 protocone
3 —
4 metacone
5 hypocone

Conules and Styles[4]

a mesiostyle (parastyle)
b distostyle (metastyle; hypoconule)
c epiconule (protoconule)
d plagioconule (metaconule)
e postentoconule
f entostyle-*f* (protostyle)
g entostyle-*g* (pericone, Carabelli's cusp)
h entostyle-*h* (pericone)
i entostyle-*i*
j ectostyle-*j* (stylocone)
k ectostyle-*k*
l ectostyle-*l* (mesostyle)
m ectostyle-*m*
n —
o —
p plesioconule
q eoconule
r —
s styloconule
—

Cristae[5]

(Cristae extend from-to or between cusps shown in brackets; reference cusps in parentheses are not elements of the indicated crista)

I eocrista [(*a*)-(*j*)-*p*-*1*-*q*-*4*-(*b*)]
I' paracrista [*1*-(*a*)] or alternate routes or portions
  I'x [*1*-(*j*)-(*a*)]
  I'y [*1*-(*s*)-(*a*)-]
  I'z [*1*-*p*-(*a*)]
I'' postmetacrista [*1*-(*b*) in absence of *4* or *4*-(*b*)]
I''' centrocrista [*1*-*q*-*4*]
  I'''a postparacrista
  I'''b premetacrista
II epicrista [*1*-(*2*)]
  II' [*1*-median line]
  II'' [(*2*)-median line]
III protoloph (protocrista) [*2*-(*a*) crested portion of cingulum *B*]
  III' [*2*-*c*]
  III'' [*c*-(*a*)]
IV plagiocrista (metaloph) [*2*-(*4*)]
  IV' [*2*-*d*]
  IV'' [(*4*)-*d*]
V entocrista [(*2*)-*5*]
VI distrocrista [*5*-*e*-]
VII transcrista [*d*-]
VIII —
IX stylocrista [*1*-*j*]

LOWER TEETH

Cones

1 eoconid (protoconid)
2 metaconid
3 paraconid
4 hypoconid
5 entoconid

Conulids and Stylids

a mesiostylid (parastylid)
b distostylid (hypoconulid)
c epiconulid (protoconulid)
d plagioconulid
e postentoconulid
f entostylid-*f*
g entostylid-*g*
h entostylid-*h*
i entostylid-*i*
j ectostylid-*j* (styloconid)
k ectostylid-*k*
l ectostylid-*l*
m ectostylid-*m*
n postmetaconulid
o entoconulid
p plesioconulid
q eoconulid
r stylid-*r*
s (not identified in specimens examined)
t conulid-*t* (pseudoparaconid)

Cristids

Cristids extend from-to between cuspids shown in brackets; reference cuspids in parentheses are not elements of the indicated cristid)

I eocristid [(*a*)-*3*-*p*-*1*-*q*-*4*-(*b*)]
I' paracristid [*1*-*p*-*3*-(*a*)]
I'' postmetacristid [*4*-(*b*)]
I''' centrocristid [*1*-*q*-*4*]
  I'''a postparacristid [*1*-*q*]
  I'''b premetacristid [*q*-*4*]
II epicristid [*1*-(*2*)]
  II' [*1*-median line]
  II'' [(*2*)-median line]
III protolophid (protocristid) [*2*-(*3*) or *2*-(*a*), crested portion of cingulid *B*]
IV plagiocristid [incomplete or obsolete]
  IV' [absent in present material]
  IV'' [(*4*)-*d*]
V entocristid [*2*-*n*-*o*-*5*]
VI distocristid [*5*-*e*-]
VII —
VIII postentocristid [in two segments; *5*-(*b*) anteriad to *VI*, but rarely well defined]
IX stylocristid [*1*-*j*; frequently obsolete or absent]

[3] Most cones are numbered in the order of their origin and development.

[4] Most conules and styles are listed in the order of their position from buccal to lingual and anterior to posterior. Rarer or more variable elements of the tritubercular trigon are listed opportunistically toward the end. Supernumeraries or gemini of established cusps are not distinguished.

[5] Most cristae (-ids) are numbered in the order of their appearance or development in phylogeny, others are numbered opportunistically; all cristae (-ids) except *I*-*I'''* inclusive, are modified parts of cingula (ids); homologies of the talonid cristids are not certain in every case and the present arrangement is tentative.

UPPER TEETH

Basins or Fossae

ϵ pretrigon basin or fossa
α trigon basin or fossa
β talon basin or fossa
    γ post-talon basin or fossa
    δ pretalon basin or fossa

LOWER TEETH

Basins or Fossids

ϵ "trigonid" basin or fossid
α talonid basin or fossid
β talonid basin or fossid
    γ post-talonid basin or fossid

UPPER AND LOWER TEETH

Cingula and Cingulids[6]

Primary

A buccal or external (buccal shelf)
B anterolingual or anterior (primary lingual shelf)
C posterolingual or posterior

Secondary

B′ neoanterolingual
C′ neoposterolingual

Main Enamel Folds

ex ectoflexus (between 1–4)
en entoflexus (between 2–5)

[6] Cingulum (id) *B* gives rise to cone (id) *2*, cristae *III′*, *IV′*, and cristids *III*, *II″*; cingulum (id) *C* gives rise to *5*, *V* and *VI*.

33 Teeth
2. Platyrrhine Dental Evolution

Dental and Cranial Morphology

The insectivore stock from which primates were derived must have depended mainly on smell for detecting prey and on front teeth for seizing and killing it. Primitive primates inaugurated the evolution from hunting by smell and killing by bite to detecting food by sight and gathering by hand. All adaptations of primates for arboreal life, such as binocularity, olfactory brain reduction and cerebral expansion, basicranial flexure, shortening and rounding of palate, manual specialization with digital opposition, correlated with the transformation in feeding habits.

Modifications of teeth and jaws are manifestations of the modification of the long narrow V-shaped arcade of primitive primates with unfused mandibular symphysis to the relatively short, broad U-shaped structure of higher primates with fused mandibular symphysis. The changes, in turn, are correlated with progressive increase in body size and changes in diet from basically insectivorous to carnivorous, herbivorous, or omnivorous.

The interrelationship between primary dental and cranial modifications leading to the platyrrhine (and catarrhine) dental systems are summarized herewith and explained in other sections. One or another of the evolutionary processes began or terminated before or after the others but all were broadly overlapping.

1. Shortening of palate, fusion of mandibular symphysis, and constriction of alveolar space with resultant:
   a. Crowding, staggering, reduction, and loss of one or more teeth.
   b. Hypertrophy of some teeth with displacement of others.
   c. Change of primitive dental formula of each jaw from: 3 incisors, 1 canine, 4 premolars, 3 molars = 11 teeth, to 2i, 1c, 3pm, 3m = 9 in Cebidae and Callimiconidae, or 2i, 1c, 3pm, 2m = 8 in Callitrichidae and Xenotrichidae, or 2i, 1c, 2pm, 3m = 8 in Catarrhini.
2. Differentiation of seven dental fields of special functions, but only the functions related to display, food ingestion, and processing are detailed here.
   a. Deciduous labial, caniniform, incisive, or nutricial field lodged in arch of dental arcade; teeth specialized for attachment and feeding during suckling stage.
   b. Permanent labial caniniform or incisive field; teeth specialized for seizing, gnawing, peeling, cutting, scraping and sometimes for display.
   c. Deciduous canine field; tooth essentially unmodified (tridentate) or modified to function as accessory incisor or premolar during suckling and transitional juvenal stage.
   d. Permanent canine field; tooth specialized for puncturing or puncture-crushing, gnawing and, often, for display.
   e. Deciduous premolar field; teeth specialized mainly for puncturing, puncture-crushing, or puncture-shearing and for grinding soft food.
   f. Permanent premolar field; teeth specialized mainly for puncturing or puncture-shearing, cracking crushing, and grinding.
   g. Molar field; teeth specialized mainly for crushing and grinding.
3. Change of main axis of incisors from anteroposterior in the primitive V-shaped jaw to transverse in the U-shaped jaw.
4. Simplification of labial teeth by absorption, fusion, or degeneration of minor elements, or complication by molarization.
5. Continued molarization of cheek teeth by addition of lingual and distal cusps, conules, cingula and cristae; ancestral "trigonid" raised high above talonid, paraconid well developed.
6. Secondary simplification of dental system by degeneration and elimination of dental elements, including reduction of "trigonid," disappearance of paraconid, and loss of individual teeth.

Form and Function

Introduction

Teeth are specialized tools or passive instruments put to a multitude of uses by jaw, neck, lip, and tongue movements. Many types of uses are species-specific and many kinds of uses are not indicated in dental structure or wear. Dental display, for example, must be seen to be appreciated. Use of teeth as weapons, for carrying infants, for gathering or transporting objects such as food and building material, and for grooming, combing, digging, cutting, browsing—including leaf-stripping—bark biting, suckling, and tactile sensing is more often classified as ethological than as odontological.

Finally, all dental structures are not evidently useful, or responses to their use or disuse. Elements such as adventitious conules, crenulations, and sporadic enamel folds are not directly related to bodily function and are not primary products of natural selection. Form, size or proportions, and alignments of teeth are likely results of biomechanical stresses generated by evolutionary modifications of the skull, particularly the splanchnocranium. For example, basicranial flexure and palatal shortening with consequent constriction or loss of alveolar space involves a corresponding reduction in size or number of teeth. Then again, expansion of the roots of one tooth such as an incisor or canine is often at the expense of the alveolar space of adjacent teeth.

Mastication and Molar Wear

Two general types of cheek tooth wear patterns are recognized and described from functional and evolutionary points of view by Butler (1972, 1973). *Wear facets,* as restricted by Butler (1973, p. 3), are wear surfaces of cusps or crests caused by the shearing action of occlusion. Striae formed on the facets run parallel to the direction of the movement of the opposing lower tooth. *Abrasion*—Butler calls it food abrasion—is caused by direct contact between the tooth and food or any object other than the opposing tooth. Abrasion results in cusp and crest wear, crown flattening, and cratering of areas of exposed dentine; scratches on worn surfaces are randomly distributed.

The molar wear facets distinguished by Butler (1973, pp. 9, 15) are the *buccal phase facets* produced by a single upward and medial (lingual) movement of the lower jaw called the "power stroke," and *lingual phase facets* caused by a jaw movement "approximately perpendicular to the protocone-paraconule crest [III'] and parallel to the oblique crest of the upper and lower molars. [The stroke] thus makes an angle of 45° or more with the direction of buccal phase movement." The two movements intersect in the centric position. The function of the lingual phase movement, according to Butler (1973, p. 23), is "essentially one of grinding, including the breaking up of seeds and insects. It would not be an integral component of the chewing cycle. . . . The lingual phase would be a second form of chewing that could be called in as occasion required."

Altogether, 7 buccal phase and 2 lingual phase facets were found in the cheek teeth of 122 specimens representing the 7 Paleocene and Eocene families listed below with the number of representative genera in each shown in parentheses.

Microsyopidae (1)	Paramomyidae (3)
Plesiadapidae (2)	Anaptomorphidae (5)
Carpolestidae (3)	Omomyidae (4)
Notharctidae (3)	

The phylogenetic or taxonomic significance of the two kinds of facets is not clear. Of the 21 genera examined (above) probably all the Paleocene and 1 or more of the Eocene genera are nonprimates, but all are characterized by primatelike, or euthemorphic, molars. Regarding wear facets, Butler (1973, p. 7) notes that "the group as a whole presented a remarkably uniform picture." A survey of other Tertiary mammals made at the same time indicated absence of lingual phase facets in unspecified numbers and species of 5 insectivore families, 3 creodont families, fissipeds, and the Picrodontidae a family of supposed primates. On the other hand, lingual phase facets were seen in representatives of the insectivore family Mixodectidae, Rodentia, Condylartha, Perissodactyla, Litopterna, Pantodonta (*Coryphodon*), Artiodactyla, and Marsupialia (some recent phalangers).

Lingual phase facets, judged by Butler's analysis, are not peculiar to primates or any other mammalian order. They characterize euthemorphic molars of some species studied and not of others; and they are said to be absent in the zalambdomorphic and dilambdomorphic molars examined.

Hiiemäe and Kay (1972; 1973) and Kay and Hiiemäe (1974) made use of cinefluorography and occlusal analysis in their examination of primate masticatory movement and the production of molar crown wear facets. Their study material included at least 4 prepared skulls and a single living representative each of the nonprimate *Tupaia glis,* the lorisoid *Galago crassicaudatus,* and cebids *Saimiri sciureus* and *Ateles paniscus* (*belzebuth*). In addition, they examined upper and corresponding lower molars of the Paleocene *Palenoctha minor* (m1), the Eocene *Pelycodus* (m2), and the Oligocene *Aegyptopithecus zeuxis* (m1).

The authors distinguished molar *abrasion* produced by the *puncture-crushing* cycle during which there is tooth-to-food-to-tooth but not tooth-to-tooth contact, and molar *attrition* (Butler's wear facets) produced by the *chewing* cycle during which tooth-to-tooth contact may occur. Both masticatory cycles as seen on cinefluorographic film, begin with an upstroke, or *preparatory* stroke, at the point of widest opening between the jaws, followed by the two-phased trituration or *power stroke* and completed by a downward or *recovery stroke.* The puncture-crushing cycles pulp the food until it is sufficiently broken and softened for the series of chewing cycles that follow and end, in turn, when the bolus is swallowed.

Phase I of the power stroke of the chewing cycle as described by Hiiemäe and Kay (and Kay and Hiiemäe) is equivalent to Butler's buccal phase movement. It begins with tooth-to-food-to-tooth, or tooth-to-tooth contact when the laterally veered lower jaw moves upward and anteromedially to centric occlusion (protocone in talonid basin). In Phase II, the same as Butler's lingual phase movement, the lower jaw swings anteromedially and downward, carrying the lower molars out of occlusal contact on the active side.

The cinefluorographic film shows a smooth and continuous movement through Phase I and Phase II and does not support Butler's suggestion, based on facet wear alone, that buccal and lingual phase movements represent independent chewing modes. The two lingual phase wear facets (nos. 5 and 10 in Butler's system, 10 and 9 respectively, in Hiiemäe and Kay's system) which Butler saw only in the primatelike or euthemorphic molars are demonstrated by Kay and Hiiemäe (1974, pp. 234, 235) in the dilambdomorphic second molars of *Gypsonictops* (Insectivora, Paleocene) and *Tupaia.* A hypocone is absent in the former, present in the latter.

The accumulated evidence led Hiiemäe and Kay (1972, 1973) and Kay and Hiiemäe (1974) to conclude that basic differences in jaw structure, dental arcade form, and molar tooth design have not involved significant changes in the mode of mastication as expressed in jaw movements, cycle types, and cycle duration. Variation seen in the experimental individuals of *Tupaia, Galago, Saimiri,* and *Ateles* "is not likely to be greater than could have occurred had the results been obtained from four animals of the same species" (Hiiemäe and Kay 1973, p. 50). This was restated in broader perspective by Kay and Hiiemäe (1974, p. 255), as follows, "if the results of the present study can be widely applied to primates . . . the variation that occurs within dentitions [meaning molars and molariform premolars] is an optimization of the effects of tooth-food-tooth interaction. In other words given a basic framework, the food consistency–molar form relationship is important and changes in the general form of the jaw apparatus such as fusion of the symphysis, elevation of the condyle above the occlusal plane and so on, make little difference save as they enhance the occlusal relationship."

The foregoing inference brings into sharper focus what has been known for a long time and was most recently demonstrated by Hiiemäe and Crompton (1971), Butler (1972, 1973), Hiiemäe and Kay (1972, 1973), Kay and Hiiemäe (1974), and others cited by the authors named. This is that *cheek teeth of extinct eutherians respond in the same way to the same forces of attrition and abrasion as those of living forms, and that mastication, as distinct from ingestion, is a mammalian character that evolved with the tribosphenic molar.*

Molar Design and Feeding Habits

Primates evolved in tropical rain forests where suitable plant and animal food has usually been in good supply. Their upper molars evolved from the primitive tridentate form into the euthemorphic type. Molars of associated mammals evolved into either the euthemorphic or dilambdomorphic type (fig. V.9). Whichever the initial direction of upper molar evolution, there was no reversal. Both basic molar types contained the potential if not at first the capacity for a variety of uses. The tritubercular molars of insectivorous marmosets, the quadritubercular molars of herbivorous howler monkeys, the bilophodont molars of omnivorous macaques and the molars of all other primates are euthemorphic. An even greater range of variation in dental morphology and diets occurs among bats, which evolved concurrently with primates. The molars of some bats are euthemorphic and those of others are dilambdomorphic.

It has been suggested by Kay and Hiiemäe (1974, p. 255), that changes in primate cheek tooth design are mainly adaptations to major long-range shifts in the relative amounts of different kinds of diets. For example, a shift from a relatively greater supply of insects to a greater quantity and variety of edible plants would favor a cheek tooth designed for more efficient plant food processing. The likelihood is, however, that the relative quantities of tropical rain forest food plants and insects available to primates remained fairly stable throughout the Cenozoic. Seasonal fluctuations in supply can affect the size of primate populations and the growth of individuals. They may also affect the rate of primate dental wear and even the rate of dental evolution, but they cannot control the direction of molar evolution. As Hiiemäe and Kay, and Kay and Hiiemäe (1974, p. 255) have taken pains to show, "two different animals given the same food will handle it in the same way irrespective of differences in tooth form . . . [and] a single animal will show greater variation in the way it handles two different types of food than occurs between animals of different species."

The principal diet of a primate species is determined less by the relative quantities of different foods than by the organic requirements of the individual. The overall evolutionary trend in body size is toward bigness (cf. p. 13). As primates become larger they become less insectivorous and more herbivorous. The larger animal with a comparatively low energy budget is adapted to the high-bulk, low-protein content of stationary and usually abundant canopy plant food, while the smaller species with higher metabolic rate requires the higher protein yield of mobile and often elusive animal foods. In competition for food niches, the larger, more powerful species better adapted for plant-food gathering over large areas of high forest would force the smaller, less herbivorous, more insectivorous species into lower, thicker growths that provide a stable year-round supply of insects as well as a haven from large predators.

Food Preparation

Food preparation has been equated with mastication (Hiiemäe and Kay, 1973, p. 29). Food preparation, however, does not always involve mastication or any other form of dental use. In its fullest sense food preparation is a combination of physicochemical processes for converting plants or animals into assimilable form. Preparation begins with prehension (or gathering) and terminates with digestion. Preparation of milk by a newborn requires only prehension of the teat, ingestion by suckling, swallowing, and digestion. Alcohol may be assimilated without digestion. In the case of solids, prey may be swallowed whole or piecemeal with no mastication. Many kinds of plant foods undergo some form of preingestive preparation, then are gulped without mastication. Certain kinds of preingestive or ingestive forms of food preparation involving use of hands, fingers, claws, lips, or protractile tongue are characteristic of or peculiar to specific animal groups.

Progressive and Regressive Evolution

Callitrichid dental morphology is more primitive than that of all other known platyrrhines and more generalized than that of any living primate. Save for loss of the third molar and compensatory enlargement of the first molar, the callitrichid dental system is one from which those of higher primates can be derived. Cebid dentition, characterized by 6 cheek teeth and fully quadritubercular upper molars, is a structural extension and radiation of the callitrichid plan except that presence of a third molar excludes cebids from the callitrichid line. The catarrhine dental system, with the same number of teeth as that of callitrichids but with one premolar less and one molar more, includes the most advanced stages of premolar molarization and molar lophodonty among living primates.

Callitrichid dental evolution, reconstructed from graded series of living animals, begins with the smallest, mainly insectivorous, species and attains ever-higher levels of specialization as increasing body mass increases the demand for greater quantities of more easily garnered vegetable food. As callitrichids become larger, their incisors change from the primitive long, sharp, tridenticulate weapon designed primarily for insect snagging to the spatulate nipping, biting, scraping, and slicing tool common to all higher primates with omnivorous or mainly herbivorous feeding habits. The callitrichid upper canine is a long projecting tooth sharply defined from the other teeth. The lower canine, in contrast, runs the evolutionary gamut from a primitive tridentate tooth hardly differentiated from the adjacent teeth in the smallest species to the powerful, salient tusk of the largest callitrichids. Resemblance between lower incisors and canines of *Cebuella* and *Callithrix*, sometimes interpreted as due to incisivization, is in fact the result of incisor teeth caninization. In higher callitrichids and primates generally, incisors and canines are very specialized, the former having become expanded or spatulate, the latter elongate or scimitarlike. The upper premolars, both milk and permanent, exhibit a greater evolutionary range than the dental series of other morphogenetic fields. The compass begins with the caniniform unicuspid first premolar of the smallest species and ends with the tritubercular or incipient quadritubercular deciduous last premolar of the largest species.

Permanent callitrichid molars, all tritubercular, are linear extensions and serial homologues of the deciduous premolar series. Their evolution, however, is not necessarily progressive and in the case of the last molar may be degenerative. The hypocone, sometimes present in the last deciduous premolar, does not appear in the molars, except rarely as a rudiment. Cebids with full quadritubercular upper molars must have diverged from a precallitrichid ancestor with the three molars intact, the upper tritubercular. Precebid molars then progressed from tritubercular to quadritubercular in monkeys of a size class well above the highest grade attained by callitrichids now or at the time of molar cusp transition.

Loss of upper cheek teeth in higher primates is a sequel of cranial modification rather than desuetude. In the case of callitrichids disappearance of the third upper molar is a consequence of suppressed development of the posterior alveolar portion of the maxillary bone. The reduced number of molars persuaded Gregory (1922, p. 228) to believe that callitrichids must be derived from cebid ancestors of unrelated *Aotus* or *Callicebus* stock. This quantitative and phylogenetically unrealistic frame of reference forced Gregory to treat the truly primitive tritubercular molars of callitrichids, and all the obviously primitive dental, skeletal, and external characters, he enumerates, as "retrogressive," "secondary," or of a kind "which no morphologist could safely regard as primitive." These judgments were based on examination of a few skulls of tamarins (*Saguinus*) and not on the more primitive *Callithrix jacchus* or *Cebuella pygmaea*, whose characters conform in most crucial respects to Gregory's own concept of an ancestral platyrrhine (cf. p. 404).

Remane (1960, p. 832), in line with Gregory, argues that absence of the hypocone in the callitrichid molar is the result of a reversal of the evolutionary process. That is to say, evolution of a primitive tritubercular molar from the derived quadritubercular type. Evolution of the canine-incisor relationship also evolved regressively, according to Remane (1960), from the advanced dental system of *Saimiri*, regarded as primitive, through that of *Callimico* to the primitive system of callitrichids regarded as specialized. The available evidence indicates rather that the dental characters of these taxa, whether assessed independently or in the light of all other related characters of phylogenetic significance, yields a natural, graded sequence that begins with the Callitrichidae and grades through *Callimico* to *Saimiri*. This simple arrangement demands no extraordinary or distorted explanations. The obvious had long since been anticipated by Thomas (1913, pp. 132–33), who described the evolutionary gradient as beginning with "(1) the marmosets [i.e., callitrichids], which have no trace of hypocone, through (2) *Callimico*, which has a slight rise in the cingulum that might be called a potential hypocone, to (3) *Saimiri*, which has small and simple hypocones, and is itself again separated from (4) *Callicebus* and other monkeys which have complicated square molars with large hypocones and connecting commissures [fig. V.22]."

Comparative and Functional Morphology with Particular Reference to Callitrichids and Callimiconids

Deciduous and Permanent Teeth

The deciduous suite includes the same number of incisors, canines, and premolars as the corresponding series of replacement teeth. They erupt in sequence from foremost incisor to last premolar. Eruption of the persistent molars of primitive and many higher primates follows in the same order of first to last. The molar series is ontogenetically and phylogenetically an extension of the deciduous premolar series. The first molar is slightly more or less molarized than the last deciduous premolar and replaces it functionally.

The deciduous dental arcade is much smaller than that of the permanent suite, and each tooth is correspondingly smaller. In *Saguinus oedipus oedipus*, the greatest length and width of the arcade, measured from incisor to fully formed but unerupted first molar, are 7.5 and 11.0 mm, respectively, in the smallest juvenal at hand. This compares with 16.5 and 16.3, respectively in an average-sized adult. With exception of the canines, the deciduous teeth are as a rule no less specialized and often more molarized than their replacements.

Upper and lower deciduous incisors in callitrichids and callimiconids are erupted and functional at birth; premolars begin to erupt from the first day, with the last of the series usually appearing within the first week. Milk teeth evolve independently and more rapidly than the replacements. Their functions include teat seizure and ingestion of liquid and premasticated foods. As solid foods enter the diet and chewing patterns begin to take form, milk teeth abrade rapidly and shed.

Incisors

Permanent incisors of the ancestral primate were almost certainly subcylindrical and tridentate, with three widely spaced teeth on each upper and unfused lower jaw aligned in V-formation. Ankylosis of the mandibular rami must have evolved as the long, pointed, angular dental arcades began to transform into the short, rounded, U-shaped arcades with incisors realigned nearly

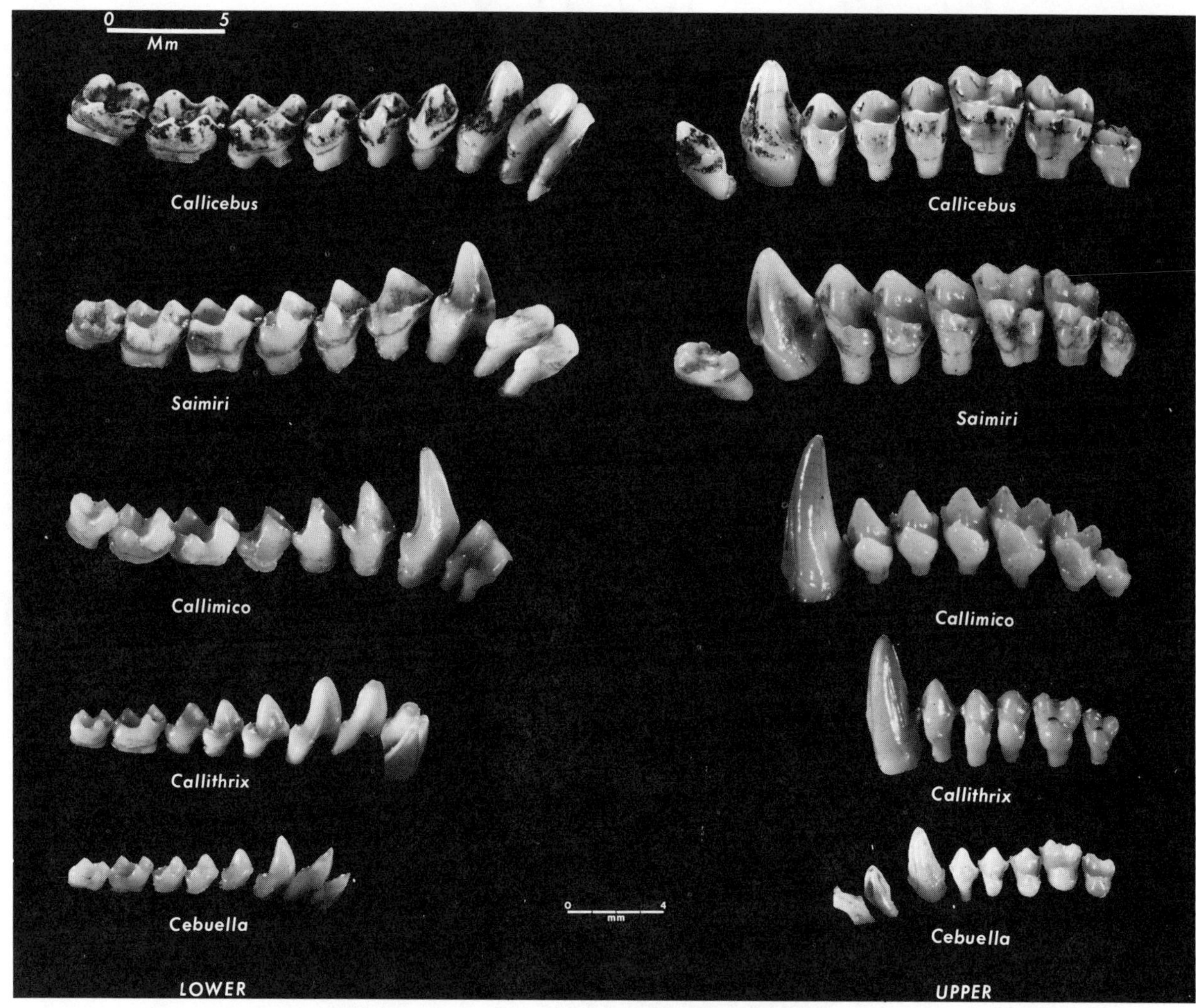

Fig. V.22. Dental gradient of increasing molarization in upper and lower cheek teeth, from bottom to top, *Cebuella* (FMNH 88998), *Callithrix jacchus* (FMNH 20739), *Callimico goeldi* (ICN 084), *Saimiri sciureus* (FMNH 70645), *Callicebus moloch* (FMNH 87810).

transversely in each arch (fig. IV.77). Loss of at least one member of each incisor series in higher primates may be attributed to frontal crowding combined with changing forms and functions and enlargement of the remaining more advantageously placed incisors.

The two pairs of upper and lower incisors in platyrrhines (fig. V.23) are more diversified than those of other major groups of living primates. Most primitive are the primarily insect-capturing incisors of the pygmy marmoset, *Cebuella pygmaea.* Its falciform tridentate lower incisors are adapted for seizing and impaling hard-shelled and agile prey brought to the mouth by hand. The triangular, spearlike upper lateral incisor is also designed for insect feeding. The broader upper central incisor retains the chitin-cracking denticules but serves also for biting and comminuting fruits, berries, and the like. A secondary specialization of the incisors, particularly the lower, in combination with the canines in *Cebuella, Callithrix,* and other callitrichids, is the removal or scraping of bark to permit feeding on the sweet exudates of trees, and for drilling holes in wood (for larvae?) (fig. IX.33, 34).

Continued rounding, then squaring of the dental arch, combined with simultaneous deepening of the symphysis menti in higher callitrichids and platyrrhines generally, involved further change and greater specialization of the incisors. The permanent pairs lost their tubercles and evolved into chisel-shaped cutters with short, wide biting edges meeting on a more or less even plane (fig. V.23). The chisel-shaped or spatulate incisors characteristic of tamarins, genus *Saguinus,* serve for reducing fruits and other yielding organic matter. The more advanced, thicker-crowned incisors of many cebids, particularly leaf-eaters, are specially designed for bruising and tearing leaves and harsh vegetation. Pithecine incisors are modified in still another direction. The teeth are elongate, narrow, and forward-projecting, their crowded tips offer a single convex cutting edge, and seem to be adapted for rodentlike nipping, nibbling, gnawing, and scraping and, perhaps, for sap and blossom feeding and special forms of grooming.

Catarrhine incisors are spatulate like those of most cebids, but generally broader with comparatively little diversification.

The deciduous upper incisors of *Cebuella pygmaea* are more advanced than their replacements with respect to reduction or loss of tubercles and expansion or spatulation of crown (figs. V.23, 24, 28). Spatulation of the upper milk incisors of *Callithrix* attained a grade more nearly comparable to that of the hominidlike permanent incisors of *Saguinus.* On the other hand, the deciduous lower lateral incisors of *Callithrix* and *Saguinus* adum-

UPPER INCISORS

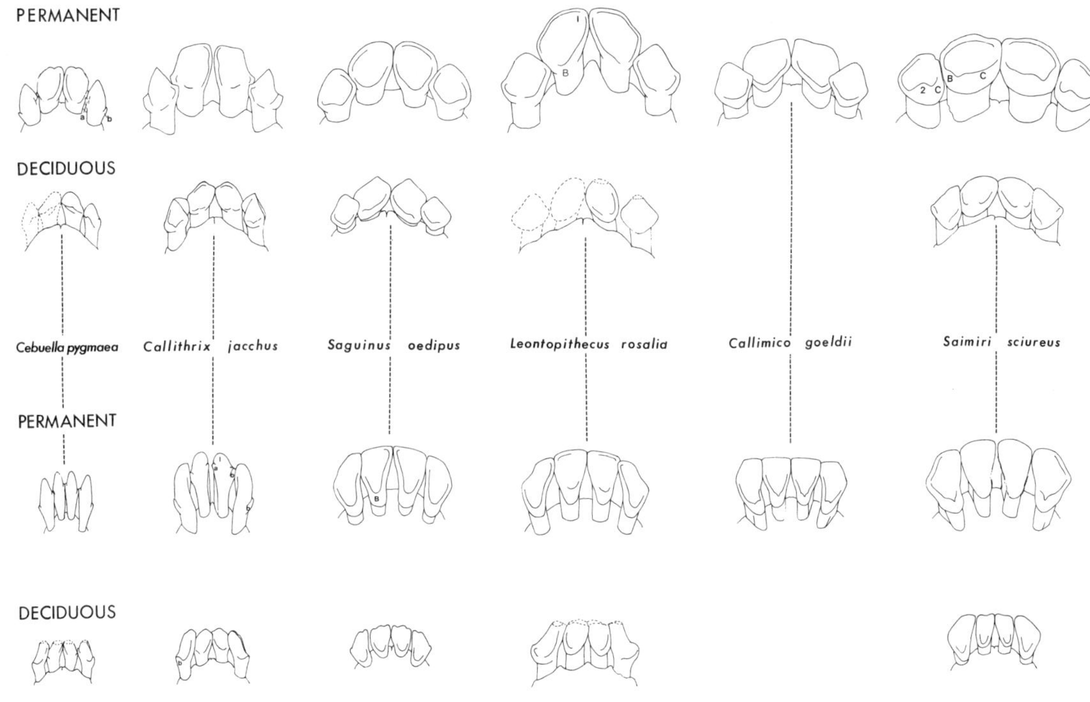

LOWER INCISORS

Fig. V.23. Permanent and deciduous incisors from lingual aspect in callitrichids, *Callimico*, and *Saimiri;* figures enlarged but not all to exactly the same scale—general size relationships, however, are maintained.

brate the molarization incipient in their own canines and already present in their cheek teeth.

The lower milk incisors of callitrichids function from birth as reinforcements of the lips in suckling and for ingesting premasticated food (fig. V.2). These are the nutricial teeth described above (p. 278). They are present in many, if not most, higher primates but deteriorate rapidly once solid food becomes a substantial part of the diet. There is little relationship between the functions of the independently evolved milk and replacement incisors. Nevertheless, any number of advances or innovations present in the deciduous incisors of one generation of primates may be ultimately modified and incorporated into the design and function of the permanent incisors of later generations.

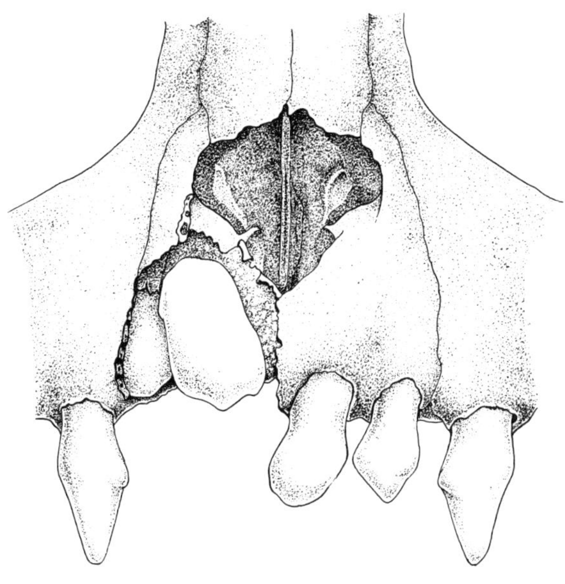

Cebuella pygmaea

= 1 mm

Fig. V.24. Deciduous upper incisors and canines of juvenal *Cebuella pygmaea*: Unerupted permanent incisors of right side exposed by removal of bone.

Canines

The primitive mammalian canine is conceived as one of a series of single-rooted, conical tridentate teeth. The foremost or labial set of the primitive series was differentiated into instruments for the prehension and dispatch of insects, worms, and grubs, and the hindmost for cracking, slicing, and comminuting the same prey. The intermediate tooth, destined to become the canine of progressive mammals, remained virtually undifferentiated and in time evolved independently.

The primitive *upper permanent canine* of primate grade is a slightly recurved and salient tusk, possibly subovate in cross section, with external cingulum and mesial and distal tubercles. The primary function of the upper canine as a puncturing instrument increased with the appearance of a sharp mesial ridge defined by a narrow vertical groove. With continued specialization the tooth became longer, heavier, outwardly deflected, scimitarlike in outline, subtriangular in cross-section and with anterior and posterior cingula joined by a continuous ledge along the lingual border.

In progressive forms, the anterior tubercle or mesiostyle (*a*), of the canine interfered with occlusion and degenerated or disappeared. The posterior tubercle, or distostyle (*b*), and the cingulum remained but with a deep occlusal groove or depression for accommodating the slicing, or gripping and pounding, lower anterior premolar. In certain early primates where a hypertrophied incisor became the principal tool for stabbing, slashing, ripping, digging, or gnawing, the hitherto little-differentiated upper canine disappeared.

The platyrrhine upper permanent canine is usually a pointed tusk projecting below and laterad to the other teeth. The tooth in *Cebuella* (figs. V.25, 27) conserves more nearly the primitive cylindrical form. In all other living platyrrhines, the canine tooth is subtriangular in cross-section with sharp mesial and distal edges, anterior and posterior cingula always present, and distal and/or mesial tubercles often preserved. The canine in the marmosetlike cebids *Aotus* and *Callicebus* and the ateline *Brachyteles,* however, is only moderately elongate, perhaps secondarily reduced in length, its emplacement in line with adjacent teeth. The condition of the human canine is comparable. The extremely large pithecine canine is most specialized among platyrrhines.

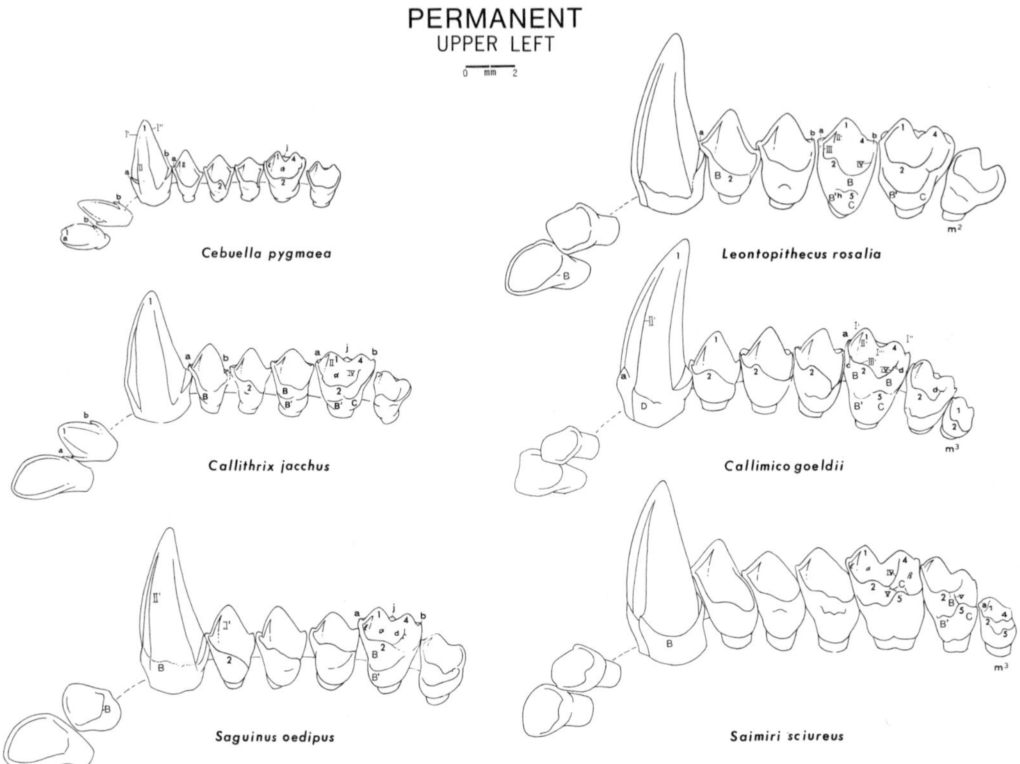

Fig. V.25. Upper left permanent tooth rows from lingual aspect in callitrichids, *Callimico,* and *Saimiri*: Figures simplified to emphasize crests and cusps; position of incisors distorted to show full lingual surface.

The *lower permanent canine* in the majority of primates became a powerful tusk like its maxillary counterpart. In other species it evolved into a highly specialized accessory incisor. In still others it was assimilated into the premolar field. In some species the canine combined its peculiar specialities with functions of incisors and/or premolar. In others, where the incisor hypertrophied, the lower canine disappeared, usually along with the upper. In still others, the lower canines atrophied and dropped out while the upper hypertrophied. In the peculiar aye-aye (*Daubentonia*), the lower canine hypertrophied into a rodentlike tusk, displacing the incisors.

The permanent lower canine of the callitrichid *Cebuella* (figs. V.26, 27) serves as a model from which all higher primate lower canines can be derived. The tooth is falcate, mesiodistally oriented with a slight forward inclination, with rudimentary anterolingual cingulum (*B*) sometimes present and a well-developed posterolingual cingulum (*C*) always present. It resembles the lateral incisor but is somewhat higher and heavier and acts with it in piercing and impaling prey, and, secondarily, in scraping or gnawing away bark for sap feeding. This type of canine is commonly described as incisiform, but it is more appropriate to regard the incisors of *Cebuella* (and *Callithrix*) as caniniform, more accurately, tridentate.

As primitive platyrrhines increased in size and the mainly insectivorous diet was replaced by a basically omnivorous or predominantly herbivorous one, the *Cebuella* type of lower canine evolved into a longer recurved tooth adapted for grappling, piercing, slashing, and ripping in coordination with the upper canine. The "caninization" of the lower canine marks a milestone in primate dental evolution. The fully caninized grade of canine is attained in tamarins (*Saguinus*), lion-tamarins (*Leontopithecus*) and *Callimico.* Lower canines of the species of *Callithrix* exhibit a graded morphological series linking the primitive *Cebuella* type to the specialized *Saguinus* type (figs. V.27; VII.6). The lower canine in most cebids is similarly specialized. In others, particularly

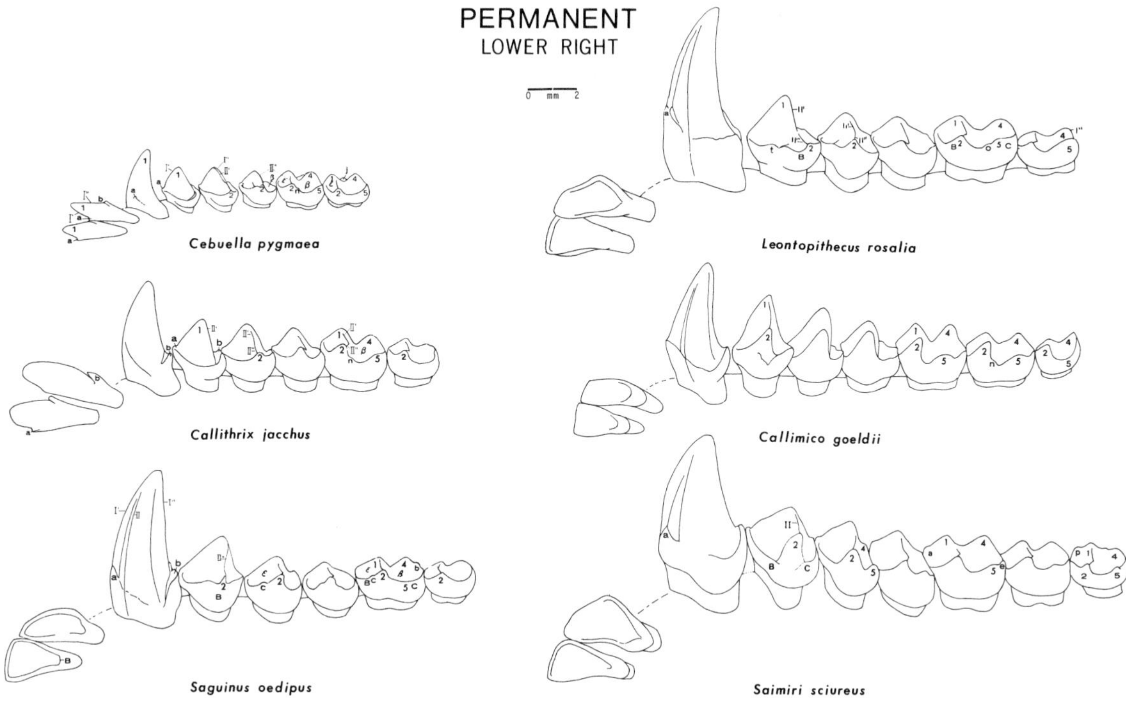

Fig. V.26. Lower right permanent tooth rows from lingual aspect in callitrichids, *Callimico,* and *Saimiri*: Figures simplified to show outline of main crests and cusps; position of incisors distorted to show full lingual surface.

Callicebus and *Lagothrix,* the lower canine resembles the lateral incisor in general form and function, but it is more nearly of the cutting type in the former, and of the tearing and crushing type in the latter. The long, heavy, subpyramidal, laterally deflected pithecine lower canines are, like the upper canines, the most highly specialized among platyrrhines.

In occlusion, the lower permanent canine fits between

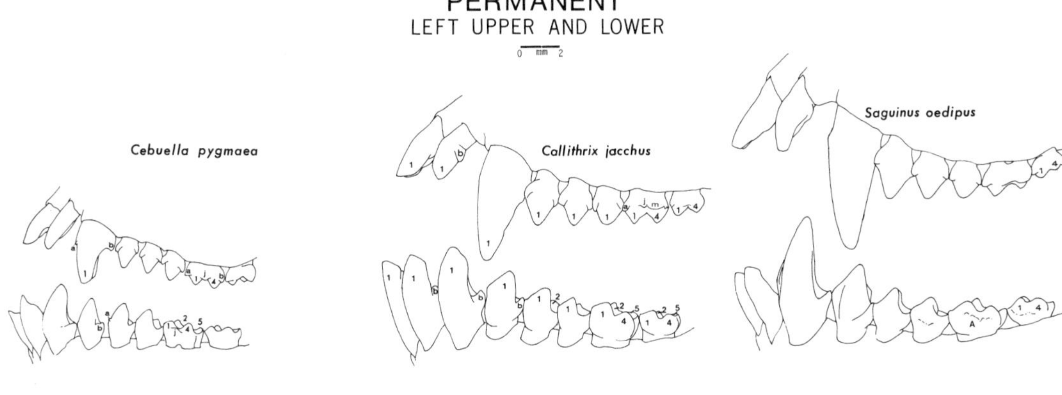

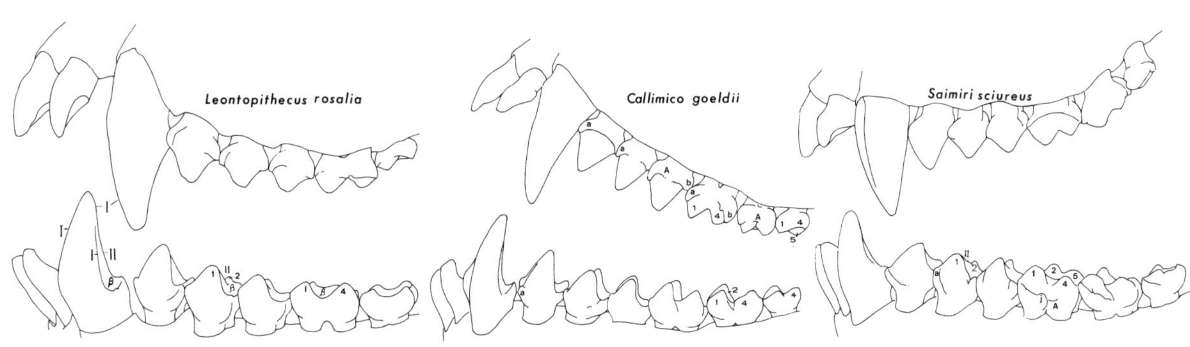

Fig. V.27. Upper left and lower permanent teeth from buccal aspect in callitrichids, *Callimico,* and *Saimiri.*

outer sides of upper canine and lateral incisor and the permanent upper canine normally fits between outer sides of the lower canine and anterior premolar. As a rule, upper and lower canines, usually in coordination with the anterior premolar, are significantly larger in adult males than in females in platyrrhines and catarrhines except callitrichids, *Callimico, Callicebus, Aotus, Brachyteles,* and *Homo.* A small diastema between upper canine and lateral incisor is usually present in all primates except *Aotus, Callicebus, Homo,* and many strepsirhines. Canine sexual dimorphism in lemuroids is restricted to the upper tooth. The sexes of tarsioids and daubentonoids are undifferentiated dentally.

The *deciduous upper canine* in platyrrhines is sagittate, with mesial and distal tubercles present and cingulum continuous along lingual margin. The tooth is slightly larger and notably higher than the adjacent deciduous premolar, and intermediate in form between it and the deciduous lateral incisor. Greater size of the canine may be correlated with the greater alveolar space already provided for its growing replacement. Judged by wear patterns, the deciduous upper canines of *Cebuella* and

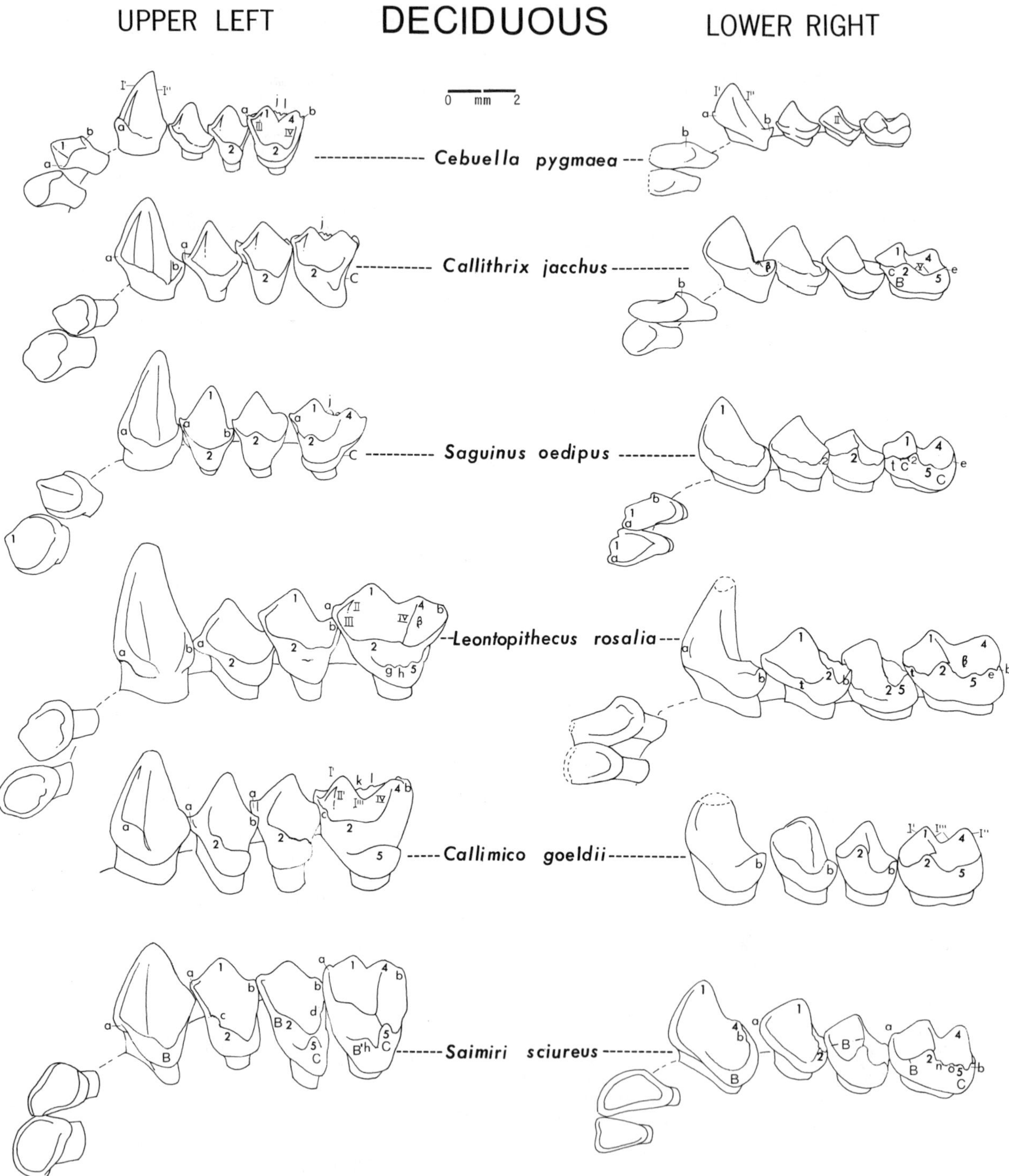

Fig. V.28. Upper left and lower right deciduous teeth, from lingual aspect, of callitrichids, *Callimico,* and *Saimiri*: Figures simplified to show outline of main crests and cusps; position of incisors distorted to show full lingual surface. Teeth, considerably worn in *Leontopithecus* and *Callimico,* the deciduous incisors shed in the latter.

Callithrix (fig. V.28) work with the lateral permanent incisor and anterior premolar in stabbing, slashing, and cutting. The larger upper deciduous canines of more advanced callitrichids more nearly resemble their replacements in form and function.

The *deciduous lower canine* is more diversified than the upper. In *Cebuella* (fig. V.26) it resembles the falcate deciduous lateral incisor in general form, but is larger and more molarized. The eoconid (protoconid) remains dominant, but the mesial tubercle and low sloping heel, or talonid, with well-developed hypoconulid (*b*), are like the corresponding elements of the anterior premolar.

The more sculptured deciduous lower canine of *Callithrix jacchus* is virtually a rudimentary molar. Low but well-defined tubercles that are certainly homologous with hypoconid, metaconid, and entoconid of true molars appear on the low rim bounding a shallow talonid basin. The primitive distal ridge joining eoconid and metaconid is the epicristid (*II*). Its axis in cheek teeth gradually shifts mediad as crowns widen.

The deciduous lower canine of *Callithrix argentata* is less molarized than that of *C. jacchus* (fig. V.28) and more nearly resembles its own deciduous lateral incisor. This is surprising in view of the more advanced grade of its lower permanent canine as compared with that of *jacchus*.

The newly erupted or unworn deciduous lower canine of *Saguinus* is no less a caninized premolar than it is a premolarized canine (fig. V.28). The hypertrophied eoconid is typically tusklike. On the other hand, the well-defined talonid and incipient "trigonid" are characteristically molariform. The molariform traits of the worn tooth, however, are largely eroded by a deep occlusal groove across the talonid.

The deciduous lower canine of the lion-tamarin, *Leontopithecus rosalia* (fig. V.28), is considerably worn in the only young individual available. Nevertheless, its tusklike eoconid and prominent talonid appear to be at least as well developed as in *Saguinus*. In one young individual of *Callimico* (fig. V.28), the tusklike eoconid predominates while the talonid is a cingular shelf with a wide occlusal groove.

The deciduous lower canine in most cebids is relatively lower than the permanent canine and more molariform than incisiform. In general, the tooth more nearly resembles its replacement than it does either of its neighboring deciduous teeth. The deep groove for occlusion with the protocone of the upper canine evidently results from an oblique movement of the mandible in suckling. The condition appears to be more pronounced in cebids and *Callimico* than in callitrichids. Pithecine deciduous canines and incisors are smaller than their permanent counterparts but otherwise are similar.

Human Canines

The relatively small size of human canines is regarded by some authorities as a primitive character and by others as a specialized or degenerate trait. Kinzey (1971) argues for small canines as the primitive state in the line leading to man. However, the comparably small canines of *Callicebus* used as paradigms by Kinzey, have no bearing on canine size in hominids. Moreover, *Callicebus* is not the primitive platyrrhine Kinzey believes it to be on the authority of Gregory (1922, p. 220). The small maxillary canines Kinzey imputes to the Miocene *Homunculus* and Oligocene *Dolichocebus* as evidence that both animals are primitive is likewise unfounded and irrelevant. Upper canines of all known fossil platyrrhines are large by any standard of comparison, and no platyrrhine serves as a model for human ancestry. Tertiary catarrhines invoked by Kinzey are nearer man but offer no support to his thesis. Small canines in critical catarrhines known from fossil mandibles only are no indicators of comparably small maxillary canines. Wide disparities in size and function between lower and upper canines are too numerous to be ignored.

The concept of small canines as a primitive character in human ancestry is reflected in the phylogenetic chart used by Kinzey (1974, p. 195) for illustrating the evolution of V- to U-shaped mandibles in platyrrhines and hominoids. The figure of the hypothetical ancestral mandible with its diminutive and crowded incisors, canines, and first premolars followed by comparatively enormous cheek teeth is, if plausible, more specialized than the mandibles supposedly derived from it.

Fossil evidence proves nothing regarding the relative size of the ancestral hominoid upper and lower canines. It does appear to be true that canines are the most stereotyped teeth of the dental complement. They become larger or smaller or remain relatively unchanged in size with fewer resulting modifications in form than other teeth. Canines may also disappear.

Permanent Maxillary Premolars

The evolutionary sequence from caniniform to molariform premolars is less complex in the maxillary than in the mandibular series. The resemblance between evolutionary grades in callitrichid premolars (figs. V.25, 27) and ontogenetic stages in human molars is as remarkably close in the upper as it is in the lower teeth (cf. Kraus and Jordan 1965, pp. 69 ff.). Molarization of the permanent upper premolars in *Cebuella* is well advanced inasmuch as the primary cusp or eocone of pm^2 has already progressed from the scimitar-shaped fang to the triangular or deltoid form. Nevertheless, the tooth remains caniniform and unicuspid. Appearance of a low but well-formed lingual cusp, the misnamed protocone (*2*) in the middle premolar (pm^3), identifies the biscuspid premolar precursor of the tritubercular tooth. The occlusal surface of the tooth, however, is still deltoid, with the eocone predominating. An enlarged protocone makes the last premolar (pm^4) more evenly bicuspid with occlusal surface more nearly rectangular. The bulk of the protocone in pm^4, however, is still one-half or less that of the sharply pointed eocone. Primitive premolar accessories such as cingula and styles persist without notable modification in the permanent upper premolars of *Cebuella*.

Premolar evolution progresses significantly among the larger, more highly evolved species of *Callithrix*. A protocone tends to develop in the essentially caniniform first premolar and becomes a definitive but small cusp in pm^3. $Pm^{2\text{-}3}$ thus are less triangular, or more nearly rectangular, in *Callithrix* than in *Cebuella*.

Completion of basic premolar molarization in callitrichids is marked by the consistent presence of a well-developed protocone in pm^2 of *Saguinus*, and of an incipient metacone and a rudimentary hypocone in either or both of the last two premolars of the larger *Leontopithecus*. Further molarization of established bicuspid upper premolars in primates leads to approximate equality of size between inner and outer main cones.

Deciduous Maxillary Premolars

Molarization of the deciduous upper premolars in callitrichids (fig. V.28) encompasses a greater range of change than appears in the permanent or deciduous series of other living primates. The first premolar in *Cebuella* is a low but effective canine, and the last premolar is a fully tritubercular molar. In *Saguinus*, trituberculy is often faintly indicated by an incipient metacone in dpm^3, and unmistakable quadrituberculy is manifested sporadically in dpm^4 by a rudimentary fourth cusp, or hypocone (*5*). Deciduous premolar molarization in *Leontopithecus* is more extensive. The dpm^2 is less molarized than pm^2, but dpm^3 often anticipates true molar trituberculy with the appearance of a low but well-formed metacone on the distal crest of the eocone. Dpm^4, with its emergent hypocone and rudimentary talon basin, represents the highest grade of molarization in callitrichids and adumbrates the fully evolved quadritubercular molar of higher platyrrhines. The structure of the *Leontopithecus* fourth premolar is, in fact, intermediate between the tritubercular molar of typical callitrichids and the quadritubercular first molar of the marmosetlike cebid, *Saimiri sciureus*.

Molarization of the maxillary deciduous premolars in *Callimico* attains approximately the same grade as in *Leontopithecus*, but occlusion of the teeth is different.

Permanent Mandibular Premolars

Evolution of platyrrhine lower premolars from tridentate or unicuspid to a fully molarized "trigonid"-talonid type of tooth can be reconstructed from callitrichid dental patterns (figs. V.26, 27). Premolar evolution in catarrhines must have been similar. Parallelism between premolar differentiation in callitrichids and ontogeny of human mandibular molars, as described by Kraus and Jordan (1965, pp. 39 ff., and particularly figs. 14, 17, 18), could just as readily be interpreted as an example of recapitulation. However, it is not phylogeny but the molarization process that is being repeated.

The *Cebuella* first lower premolar (pm_2) is a literally compressed blade practically indistinguishable from the canine except for its full cingulum and lower height. In pm_3, the epicristid (*II*) differentiates from the distal crest of eoconid and separates "trigonid" from talonid by extending the lingual margin of combined cingula *B* and *C*. With eoconid (*1*) of pm_3 nearly as high as that of pm_2, the tooth appears caniniform, but emergence of a rudimentary metaconid (*2*) transforms it from unicuspid to a bicuspid. Pm_4 is also characterized by a lower, heavier, but still salient caniniform eoconid and oblique epicristid. Otherwise the tooth is molariform with metaconid conspicuous but still puny compared to eoconid, pseudoparaconid (*t*) often present and well defined; talonid small, incipient hypoconid (*4*) and entoconid (*5*) present, the deep basin enclosed.

Premolar molarization in *Callithrix* shows significant advances. The first two premolars are essentially caniniform, but the eoconid is deltoid and comparatively smaller than in *Cebuella*. The epicristid is oblique in pm_2 but nearly transverse in pm_4. The talonid is larger relative to the "trigonid," and talonid cusps are present in the last premolar at least. Absence or obsolescence of pseudoparaconid and some trigonid accessories is probably secondary.

Culmination of callitrichid lower premolar molarization is attained in *Saguinus*. The eoconid is salient and deltoid in pm_2, rounded and hardly higher than metaconid in pm_4; the epicristid ranges from oblique to nearly transverse in pm_2, to quite transverse in pm_4; talonid and "trigonid" basins are well developed in pm_{3-4} and sometimes in pm_2; hypoconid and entoconid, however, are never well developed and are not always present. The well-molarized but still dominantly caniniform pm_2 and the fully molarized pm_4 in many individuals of *Saguinus* encompass the full range of molarization in living primates. Further premolar evolution is expressed by specializations or elaborations, and by degeneration and loss of elements already present in the tamarin premolars. *Leontopithecus* premolars are similar but with talonid basin of pm_4 often larger than "trigonid" basin.

The *Callimico* epicristid is consistently more nearly transverse than that of callitrichids, the metaconid of pm_{3-4} is nearly or quite as high as the opposing eoconid. The cebid metaconid is also high and often higher than the eoconid.

Deciduous Mandibular Premolars

The callitrichid deciduous lower premolars (fig. V.28) display a wider range of molarization than the replacement series. In *Cebuella*, the first two premolars are primitively unicuspid and caniniform with eoconid scimitar-shaped, and long axis of dpm_2 parallel to the main line of the mandibular ramus. The last premolar, in contrast, is fully molarized and often nearly as large as the first two combined. The wide gap in morphological grade between last and penultimate premolars suggests suppression of a structurally and topographically intermediate tooth, whether in early ontogeny or in phylogeny. Lower premolars in *Callithrix* are more evenly molarized, with the talonid basin appearing in dpm_{2-3}. In *Saguinus*, the eoconid of unicuspid dpm_2 is deltoid, and molarization, including differentiation of postentoconulid, is complete in many samples of dpm_4. All conids and conulids appear to be as well defined in the worn premolars of the single available juvenal of *Leontopithecus* as in *Saguinus*. Molarization is more advanced in *Callimico*, with dpm_3 almost fully molarized, dpm_4 completely so, and the metaconids of both teeth extremely high.

Premolar Size and Shape

The permanent upper premolars in the more primitive callitrichid species become, from first to last, successively lower, longer, wider, less triangular and more rectangular. In advanced species, they become, from front to back, progressively more nearly uniform in height, general form, and bulk. In the upper deciduous series of all species, premolar size increases from first to last.

The permanent mandibular premolars decrease in height from front to back. The first premolar, sometimes the last, is largest. The middle premolar is often smallest. In the deciduous series, the last premolar is largest, and the first and second are very nearly equal to each other. The talonid basin is always depressed below the "trigonid" basin.

Premolar Sexual Dimorphism

Significant difference in size or shape of premolars is not apparent between the sexes in callitrichids and *Callimico*. The first premolar (pm2), usually the lower, is distinctly larger in males of many cebids and most catarrhines with sexually dimorphic canines.

Molars

Molarization of callitrichid upper molars has not passed beyond the tritubercular stage or tricuspid stage, except where the merest rudiment of a hypocone makes a rare or transient appearance. An emergent and more stable hypocone marks the beginning of quadritubercularity (fig. V.28) in the last deciduous upper premolar of some higher callitrichids (cf. *Saguinus* and *Leontopithecus*).

Molar tritubercularity in callitrichids and molar quadritubercularity in cebids is bridged by the first molar of *Callimico*, where a well-formed cingular (*C*) conule, unmistakably a young hypocone (*5*), appears, often with a short entocrista (*V*) directed toward the plagiocrista (*IV*). The tubercle becomes a prominent cingular cone in the marmosetlike cebid *Saimiri* (V.25). In *Callicebus* it grades from the cingular or so called "pseudohypocone" stage to the coronal stage in molars with cingulum *C′* (fig. V.14). In higher cebids the hypocone is usually a fully integrated coronal cusp coordinate in size and function with the three primary cusps.

Modifications of callitrichid molars are confined to the tritubercular pattern. Most obvious changes are progressive hypertrophy of the first molar and degenerative reduction of the second molar in whole or part. Disappearance of the third molar was a precallitrichid event. Other alterations of a progressive nature more subtle than the preceding affect the shape, size, and relationships of primitive molar elements.

A secondary anterolingual cingulum (*B′*) is not usually evident in the upper molars of *Cebuella*, but the posterolingual cingulum (*C*) is well developed. Both cingula are present in *Callithrix* and unite to form a continuous but not necessarily squared shelf around the inner border of the teeth. The shelf is wider, often excavated in *Saguinus*, and as wide or wider in the larger *Leontopithecus*. *Callimico*, with a hypocone, presents a more specialized subcebid lingual cingular shelf.

Remaining modifications are almost entirely confined to the mandibular row. The talonid basin, hardly if at all larger than the "trigonid" basin in premolars, is as large or larger in the *Cebuella* molars, and becomes progressively larger in the molars of higher callitrichids. Each increase in size of the talonid basin entails a corresponding decrease in size of the "trigonid" basin. As proportions change, each basin becomes more nearly ovate, the transverse width increasing over the length. At the same time, the hypoconid becomes as large or larger, but not higher, than other coronal cones. The archaic mesiostylid, distostylid, and pseudoparaconid are usually obsolete or absent.

The primitive superior height of the eocone (*1*) and metacone (*4*) persists in callitrichids throughout the toothrow from canine to last molar. The same is true in the mandibular teeth of *Cebuella* and *Callithrix*. In *Saguinus*, however, the principal inner cusps of m_1, the metaconid (*2*) and entoconid (*5*) become as high as or slightly higher but not larger than, the outer, and those of m_2 are consistently higher. In *Callimico*, the superior height of the inner cusps of the molars extends to pm_3 (fig. V.19). The shift in occlusal plane and relative cusp heights is correlated with the gradual change from the V-shape mandibular arch in *Cebuella* and *Callithrix* to the U-shape arch in *Saguinus* and, with few exceptions, in all higher primates.

The last lower callitrichid molar is normally rhomboidal with the distolingual cusp or corner always produced farther behind than the distobuccal portion. The same disposition, but less pronounced, is usually true of the lower first molar. The lower last molar of *Callimico* is also rhomboidal, but the distobuccal, rather than the distolingual corner, is produced farther behind (fig. V.22; XII.15). The distinction as a diagnostic character does not hold for other primates.

Change from the elongate V-shaped arch to the short and broad U-shaped arch shifted the center of greatest molar activity to the last premolar-first molar fields. The first molar became larger. The last deciduous premolar, equal to the entire molar field in the young animal, also enlarged to become the most complex tooth of the entire maxillary series.

Body size appears to be the primary controlling factor in platyrrhine molar evolution. The most advanced condition in callitrichids is the rudimentary quadritubercularity of the last milk premolar of *Leontopithecus*, largest of callitrichids. Permanent molars of equal or greater complexity appear in the nearly equal and next larger size groups represented by *Callimico* and the marmosetlike platyrrhines, respectively.

Absence of the third permanent molar and reduction of the second molar may be the crucial factors for maintaining body size of callitrichids adjusted to their present basically insectivorous diet.

34 Teeth
3. Formulas

The primitive primate dental formula, reconstructed from all known living and fossil forms, for each upper and lower jaw, is i $\frac{1\text{-}2\text{-}3}{1\text{-}2\text{-}3}$, c $\frac{1}{1}$, pm $\frac{1\text{-}2\text{-}3\text{-}4}{1\text{-}2\text{-}3\text{-}4}$, m $\frac{1\text{-}2\text{-}3}{1\text{-}2\text{-}3} = \frac{11}{11} \times 2 = 44$ teeth. The universal evolutionary trend has been toward reduction in the number of teeth. The fewest number of teeth in living primates occurs in the aye-aye, *Daubentonia madagascariensis.* Its dental formula for each upper and lower jaw is $\frac{1\text{-}0\text{-}1\text{-}3}{0\text{-}1\text{-}0\text{-}3} = \frac{5}{4} = 18$.

Note: The long, curved, persistently open-rooted anterior tooth of *Daubentonia madagascariensis* is an incisor because it grows from the premaxillary bone (fig. IV. 107). It compares in all respects and is homologous with a typical rodent upper incisor. Tattersall and Schwartz (1974, pp. 152–53) argue, however, that the tooth is the canine because it differs from the incisors of other prosimians, its root extends back to above m^3, and "if this tooth is in fact an incisor the point of root growth would have to penetrate the premaxillary-maxillary junction during development." They add that the tooth is "large and compressed laterally, characteristics of prosimian canine rather than incisors." The comparison with prosimian canines is irrelevant. Every character of the upper anterior tooth of *Daubentonia* detailed by Tattersall and Schwartz is also present in rodent upper incisors. Not only is the rodent incisor mesiodistally compressed as in *Daubentonia,* it also penetrates the maxillary field. Incisors including tusks of the wombat, hyrax, narwhal, and elephant grow from the premaxillary bone. The front tooth of *Daubentonia* is no exception. *Daubentonia* is certainly a primate but is not like the "prosimians" with which Tattersall and Schwartz compare it or a member of the group (Indriiformes) to which they assign it.

The platyrrhine dental formulae, in abbreviated form, are $\frac{2\text{-}1\text{-}3\text{-}3}{2\text{-}1\text{-}3\text{-}3} = 36$, in Homunculidae, Callimiconidae, and Cebidae, and $\frac{2\text{-}1\text{-}3\text{-}2}{2\text{-}1\text{-}3\text{-}2} = 32$, in Callitrichidae and Xenotrichidae.

The above formulae compare with $\frac{2\text{-}1\text{-}2\text{-}3}{2\text{-}1\text{-}2\text{-}3} = 32$, in all known Catarrhini, except a few Oligocene monkeys with the more primitive formula, $\frac{2\text{-}1\text{-}3\text{-}3}{2\text{-}1\text{-}3\text{-}3} = 36$, as in platyrrhines with three molars.

The primitive platyrrhine dental system cannot be derived with certainty from any known prosimian stock. The dental formula of the Eocene Northarctidae, $\frac{2\text{-}1\text{-}4\text{-}3}{2\text{-}1\text{-}4\text{-}3} = 40$, is more primitive numerically, but presence of a rudimentary to well-defined molar hypocone is a specialization. The dental formula of the Eocene, Oligocene, and Miocene Omomyidae, $\frac{2\text{-}1\text{-}3\text{-}3}{2\text{-}1\text{-}3\text{-}3}$, is basically platyrrhine, but, again, presence of a rudimentary molar hypocone eliminates any known member of this family from callitrichid ancestry. Perhaps an undiscovered early Eocene or late Paleocene omomyid, or possibly pre-omomyid, possessed the primitive tritubercular molars from which all platyrrhine dental systems can be derived. In any case, there is no clear indication that all South American primates evolved from the same prosimian or even the same simian stock.

The missing molar in Callitrichidae and Xenotrichidae is clearly the third or last in place. Identity of the missing platyrrhine incisor and premolar, however, is not obvious. It is certain, nevertheless, that loss of teeth in the playrrhine system results from biomechanical loss of alveolar space and from interdental competition for the remaining space in the changing form of the dental arch.

Crowns

Incisors

The primitive number of incisors in placental mammals is three in each premaxillary bone and anterior portion of each mandibular body. In lemurs, indriids, galagos, and lorises, the first, or anteriormost upper incisor, disappeared leaving a gap which accommodates the procumbent lower incisors in occlusion. The alveolar scar of the missing first upper incisor, or perhaps its predecessor, often persists. In one specimen of *Lemur* with the usual pair of spatulate upper incisors (FMNH 81543), a minute peglike tooth, apparently a persistent di^1 (Schwarz 1930, p. 38) is planted on each premaxillary bone where the first incisor would normally occur. At the other extreme, all permanent upper incisors are absent in *Lepilemur.* Hypertrophy of the lower canine, and one upper incisor in the aye-aye (*Daubentonia madagascariensis*) preempted alveolar space of all lower incisors and remaining upper incisors (cf. Gregory 1922, p. 146). Loss of two lower incisors in *Tarsius* appears to be due to muzzle truncation and contraction of alveolar space.

In higher primates, the diastema between upper lateral incisor and canine may have been the seat of the missing, or third, incisor. Suppression of the tooth could be correlated with additional occlusal and alveolar space needed for expanding canines and incisors in a muzzle becoming progressively shorter. Elsewhere, an expanding canine can be accommodated by elongation of the muzzle.

The serial homology of missing lower incisors has not been satisfactorily established. In lemuroids with a dental "comb" the third incisiform tooth is regarded by some investigators as an incisiform canine, by others as possibly a true incisor (Simpson 1967, p. 43). Most recently, Schwartz (1974), using generally accepted criteria, adjudged the lateral tooth a canine. He also suggests that decrease in number of incisors during primate evolution was most likely i1 to i2 to i3. It is clear, however, that whichever teeth are lost and whatever the order of their disappearance, the form, function and interrelationships of upper teeth are not the same as those of the lower teeth, and each tooth need not occupy the same numerical position as its serial homologue, if present, of the opposing jaw.

Canines

Upper and lower canines are present and well defined in all platyrrhines. Loss of the upper canine pari passu with hypertrophy of one of the incisors, in early Tertiary Paramomyidae, Plesiadapidae and Anaptomorphidae, are specializations without parallel or sign in platyrrhines.

Premolars

Loss of the first of the primitive four premolars may have been completed as a result of displacement or degeneration of the tooth in primate stock that gave rise to platyrrhines and catarrhines. Loss of the second premolar in catarrhines may also have been caused by either process concomitant with muzzle reduction or kyphosis. Premolars of *Branisella,* from the lower Oligocene of Bolivia, are particularly interesting in that the second premolar, represented by its posterior alveolar margin in the fragmentary jaw, must have been much smaller than the already greatly reduced pm^3 and is apparently well along toward vanishing.

The question of which tooth of the platyrrhine and catarrhine premolar series was the first to disappear has never been unequivocably answered. That the tooth was the first (pm 1) of the series rather than the last (pm 4) is highly probable. Enlargement of the canine with consequent encroachment on neighboring alveolar space might well result in reduction or elimination of the anterior premolar. It could also be argued that hypertrophy and early eruption of the first molar in a jaw of fixed or progressively decreasing length would also result in displacement or suppression of a small and as yet unerupted permanent last premolar (pm 4). In like manner, the hypertrophied tritubercular or quadritubercular fourth deciduous premolar might preempt the space formerly occupied by a small bicuspid premolar. Other combinations of dominant and subordinate teeth competing for decreasing space can be predicated. In the absence of absolute proof to the contrary, however, it is advisable to retain the conventional formula that implies loss of the first tooth in an otherwise complete upper and lower premolar series.

Molars

Three molars in each jaw is primitive for placental mammals. This number is present in all living primates except callitrichids and subrecent xenotrichids, which have two. Disappearance of the last molar may be related to loss of alveolar space as a result of muzzle contraction and basicranial flexure or kyphosis (cf. p. 166) with concomitant shortening of palate and dental arch. In callitrichids, incomplete development or truncation of the maxillary bone and hypertrophy of the first upper molar forced the third molar out and brought the second to the brink. Continued expansion and usurpation of alveolar space and molar function by the first molar probably contributed significantly to subsequent reduction of the second molar. As already noted above, palatal contraction, molar expansion, or both may have caused loss of one of the original four premolars. In *Callimico* the dental arch appears to have been little affected by palatal shortening and the full molar complement persists. In cebids, where size of postcanine teeth are more evenly graduated than in callitrichids and the palatal portion of the maxillary bone is less reduced, no molars and only one premolar were permanently lost. A small and degenerate third molar, however, is characteristic of many cebid species and its failure to erupt is a frequent individual variable (cf. Schultz 1926, p. 292, footnote; 1935, p. 546). Catarrhines have the same reduced number of teeth as callitrichids, but they have one premolar less and one molar more.

Biomechanical factors involved in the elimination of the callitrichid upper third molar either are absent or do not operate in the same way in the lower jaw. Ample alveolar space for a third molar and often the tooth bud itself are present in the mandible. The third molar, however, with rare exceptions, fails to develop and its alveolus usually fills with bone. Evidently, in callitrichids incomplete development of the posterior alveolar portion of the maxillary bone, with consequent loss of m^3, entails suppression of the corresponding mandibular tooth.

Roots

In the permanent cheek tooth series, fewest roots occur in platyrrhines, most in living prosimians. The milk premolar root formula of callitrichids, however, agrees with that of the permanent premolar series of prosimians. Milk and permanent premolars evolve independently and their respective root formulae vary accordingly (table 8).

Incisors and canines in nearly all living primates are single-rooted. The lower canine is occasionally double-rooted in man (over 5% according to Alexandersen 1963). Double-rooted canines have also been recorded in living prosimians and catarrhines (cf. Alexandersen 1963). An exhaustive search may reveal a small proportion of double-rooted canines in platyrrhines.

The more simple mandibular premolars and generally reduced third molars are supported by a single root, the more complex premolars and lower molars by two roots, one for the entire "trigonid" and one for the entire talonid. A comparable relationship holds for the upper cheek teeth with one or two roots supporting the simpler, two to three roots supporting the more complex. The maximum number of roots in the upper cheek teeth of wild living

Table 8. Callitrichid and *Callimico* Premolar-Molar Root Formulae of Randomly Selected Specimens in the Field Museum of Natural History

Group	*pm2*	*pm3*	*pm4*	*m1*	*m2*	*m3*
Permanent						
Cebuella	$\frac{1}{1}$	$\frac{1}{1}$	$\frac{2-3}{1}$	$\frac{3}{2}$	$\frac{3}{1-2}$	
Callithrix	$\frac{1}{1}$	$\frac{1}{1}$	$\frac{1-3}{1}$	$\frac{3-2}{2}$	$\frac{2-3}{1-2}$	
Saguinus	$\frac{1}{1}$	$\frac{1-2}{1}$	$\frac{1-2}{1}$	$\frac{3-2}{2}$	$\frac{2-1}{1-2}$	
Leontopithecus	$\frac{1}{1}$	$\frac{1-2}{1}$	$\frac{2}{1}$	$\frac{3}{2}$	$\frac{2-3}{1-2}$	
Callimico	$\frac{1}{1}$	$\frac{1-2}{1}$	$\frac{1}{1}$	$\frac{3}{2}$	$\frac{2-3}{2}$	$\frac{2-1}{1}$
Deciduous						
Cebuella	$\frac{1}{1}$	$\frac{2-3}{1}$	$\frac{3}{2}$			
Callithrix	$\frac{1}{1}$	$\frac{2-3}{1}$	$\frac{3}{2}$			
Saguinus	$\frac{1}{1}$	$\frac{2-3}{1}$	$\frac{3}{2}$			
Leontopithecus	$\frac{1}{1}$	$\frac{2}{1}$	$\frac{3}{2}$			
Callimico	$\frac{1}{1}$	$\frac{2}{1}$	$\frac{3}{2}$			

primates is normally three, and the maximum in the lower cheek teeth is normally two, rarely three.

Butler (1956, p. 56) found no constant relationship between the molar cusps and roots. His studies, however, embraced the topographical and morphological as well as the numerical relationships between roots and cusps. No separate tabulation of cusp and root numbers was made and the recorded observations refer to mammals generally, but mainly insectivores. The relationship between number of roots and cusps is probably not always random. The pattern may be clearer in some mammalian orders, Primates for example, than in others such as Insectivora.

Upper and lower premolar-molar root formulae for New and Old World Primates are compared in table 9 in order of increasing complexity. Formulae for catarrhines and living prosimians were compiled by Remane (1960, p. 800). Examination of more specimens of Cercopithecidae and prosimians may show greater variation than appears to be the case now.

Table 9. Primate Premolar-Molar Root Formulae Unusual Root Numbers Shown in Parenthesis

Group	*Pm2*	*Pm3*	*Pm4*	*M1*	*M2*	*M3*
Permanent						
Callitrichidae	$\frac{1}{1}$	$\frac{1-2}{1}$	$\frac{1-3}{1}$	$\frac{2-3}{2}$	$\frac{2-3}{2}$	
Callimico	$\frac{1}{1}$	$\frac{1-2}{1}$	$\frac{1}{1}$	$\frac{3}{2}$	$\frac{2-3}{2}$	$\frac{2-1}{1}$
Cebidae	$\frac{1(2)}{1}$	$\frac{2}{1}$	$\frac{2}{1}$	$\frac{(2)-3}{(1)-2}$	$\frac{2-3}{(1)2}$	$\frac{2-1}{1}$
Hominidae		$\frac{1-2(3)}{1-2}$	$\frac{1-2(3)}{1(-2)}$	$\frac{3(-2)}{2(-3)}$	$\frac{3-2}{2}$	$\frac{2(3-1)}{2-1}$
Chimpansee		$\frac{3-2}{2-1}$	$\frac{3-1}{2-1}$	$\frac{3}{2}$	$\frac{3}{2}$	$\frac{3}{2}$
Hylobatidae, *Gorilla*, *Pongo*		$\frac{3}{2}$	$\frac{3}{2}$	$\frac{3}{2}$	$\frac{3}{2}$	$\frac{2}{2}$
Cercopithecidae		$\frac{3}{2}$	$\frac{3}{2}$	$\frac{3}{2}$	$\frac{3}{2}$	$\frac{3}{2(-3)}$
Prosimians	$\frac{1-2}{1}$	$\frac{3}{1}$	$\frac{3}{1-2}$	$\frac{3}{2(1)}$	$\frac{3}{2}$	$\frac{3}{2}$
Deciduous						
Callitrichidae	$\frac{1}{1}$	$\frac{2-3}{1}$	$\frac{3}{2}$			
Callimiconidae	$\frac{1}{1}$	$\frac{2}{1}$	$\frac{3}{2}$			
Cebidae	$\frac{1-3}{1-2}$	$\frac{1-3}{1-2}$	$\frac{1-3}{2}$			

SOURCE: Data for Old World Primates mostly from Remane (1960, p. 800).

The molar root formula for the cebid genus *Pithecia*, $\frac{1-1-1}{2-1-1}$, given by Bennejeant (1936, p. 158) and copied by Remane is more likely an error than an anomaly. The molar root formula for all pithecines I examined is $\frac{3-2-1}{2-(1-2)-1}$.

Development of bifurcation in multirooted teeth of the eastern Brazilian marmoset, *Callithrix jacchus*, has been described by Bernick and Levy (1968*a*).

35 Teeth
4. Dental Succession

Deciduous teeth normally erupt in serial order from first incisor to last premolar in upper and lower jaws. As a rule, mandibular teeth erupt earlier than their homologues of the upper jaw.

In the permanent dentition, molars and incisors usually erupt before the premolars. The first molar erupts first, the canine or third molar last. Upper and lower teeth nearly always appear in the same sequence, the active mandibular usually slightly ahead of the passive premaxillary-maxillary series. The sequence and chronology of eruption of upper and lower premolars is the most variable of the entire dental system.

The usual order of succession in callitrichids and *Callimico,* determined from skulls, follows.

Cebuella, Callithrix: m1-(m2-i1)-(p4-i2)-p3-p2-c
Saguinus, Leontopithecus: m1-i1-(m2-i2)-p4-p3-p2-c
Callimico: m1-i1-(m2-i2)-p4-p3-p2-(c-m3)

Dental sequences shown enclosed in parenthesis are in the most frequent order, but the arrangement is sometimes or often reversed. Differences between the generic groups with respect to their molar and incisive fields, however, are significant (table 10). The usual m1-m2 order of succession in *Cebuella* and *Callithrix* is similar to that of the more primitive species of prosimians and the marmosetlike cebids *Saimiri* and *Aotus* (cf. Della Serra 1952). The prevailing m1-i1 order of succession in remaining callitrichids and *Callimico* accords with that of the bulk of cebids, including the marmosetlike *Callicebus* (cf. Hershkovitz 1963) and catarrhines generally.

The chronological sequence of dental eruption and succession was determined for the cotton-ear marmoset, *Callithrix jacchus jacchus,* by Johnston, Dreizen, and Levy (1970), and for the black mantle tamarin, *Saguinus nigricollis nigricollis,* by Chase and Cooper (1969). Their findings are tabulated below (tables 11 and 12). Published data from other sources on dental eruption in various callitrichids (table 13) are also summarized here and mentioned in the biological accounts of the pertinent species.

The criterion for dental eruption in living mammals used by Chase and Cooper (1969) is full exposure above gingiva of both crowns of the teeth of a pair, upper or lower. The lag from first cutting to complete emergence of the pair ranges, according to Chase and Cooper, from two weeks to two months, and more. Other investigators including Johnston, Dreizen, and Levy (1970) define eruption as initial gingival penetration of a tooth. A third criterion marks the beginning of the eruptive phase, when the root begins to develop, and its end when the tooth is in occlusion.

Sequence of dental eruption based on emergence through alveolar tissue in the prepared skull is more exact and is verifiable by the status of other teeth visible in the jaws. It does not follow, however, that the same teeth would cut through the gums in the same sequence or after proportionately similar time intervals. Variation is great (cf. Garn and Koski 1957; Garn and Lewis 1963) and determinations based on the various methods, although comparable, should not be combined.

Available data on elapsed time for eruption of the full suite of deciduous and permanent teeth indicate that, in general, the smaller the primate species in a given phyletic line, the earlier the dental eruption and the more rapid the completion of its dental arch complement, whether deciduous or permanent. Stated another way, the larger the primate, the greater its longevity, and the slower the fulfillment of specified individual life processes. Table 14 summarizes chronological data for completion of dental eruption among living platyrrhines and catarrhines arranged in order of increasing size.[1]

Differences between the sexes in the sequence and duration of dental eruption are not evident in callitrichids. In macaques, canines are larger and erupt later in males than in females (Hurme and Van Wagenen 1961).

[1] According to Malinow, Pope, Depaoli and Katz (1968, p. 228, and fig. 1), eruption of the permanent suite of teeth in the howler *Alouatta caraya,* one of the largest of platyrrhines, was completed in two males 18–19 months of age, or less than half grown. The estimated ages and the time intervals shown between successively erupting teeth are grossly out of line with weights given by the authors for the specimens in question, and statistical data provided by others in the same monograph (cf. Malinow, Pope, Depaoli, and Katz, pp. 56–73).

Table 10. Stages of Eruption: Dental Succession in Callitrichidae and Callimiconidae, determined from Museum-Preserved Skulls

	Stages of Eruption							
Species	*I*	*II*	*III*	*IV*	*V*	*VI*	*VII*	*VIII*
Cebuella pygmaea	m1 (6)	m2 (6)	i1 (6), p4 (2)	p4 (6), i2 (4)	i2 (3), p4 (1), p3 (1), p2 (1)	p3 (1), p2 (1)	i2 (1), p3 (1)	c (1)
Callithrix jacchus	m1 (15)	m2 (9), p4 (1)	i1 (3), m2 (2), p4 (1)	i1 (2), i2 (1), p3 (1)	i1 (1)	p3 (1)	p2 (1)	c (1)
Callithrix humeralifer	m1 (1)	m2 (1)	—	—	—	—	—	—
Callithrix argentata	m1 (6)	m2 (3), i1 (1)	i1 (1), i2 (1)	i2 (1), p4 (1)	i2 (1), p4 (1), p2 (1)	i2 (1), p3 (2)	p2 (2), p4 (1)	c (3)
Saguinus graellsi	m1 (3)	m2 (2), i1 (1)	m2 (1)	i2 (1)	p4 (1)	—	—	—
Saguinus fuscicollis	m1 (10), i1 (1)	i1 (4), m1 (1)	i2 (5), i2 (5)/m2 (2)	m2 (3), m2 (2)/i2 (2)	p4 (4)	p2 (3), p3 (1)	p2 (1), p3 (1)	c (1)
Saguinus oedipus	m1 (10), i1 (2)	i1 (6), m2 (2)	m2 (3), i2 (1)	i2 (2), m2 (1)	p2 (2)	p4 (1), p3 (1)	p4 (1)	c (5)
Saguinus midas	m1 (2)	i1 (1)	—	—	—	p3 (1)	p2 (1)	c (4)
Saguinus midas × *oedipus*	m1 (1)	i1 (1)	—	—	—	—	—	—
Saguinus bicolor	m1 (1)	i1 (2)	m2 (1)	—	—	—	—	—
Leontopithecus rosalia	m1 (2)	—	—	—	—	—	—	—
Callimico goeldii	m1 (1)	i1 (1)	i2 (1)/m2 (1)	m2 (1)/i2 (1)	—	—	—	—

NOTE: Order of eruption is based on appearance of teeth in mandibular and maxillary alveoli. Number of specimens is shown in parentheses. Where order of eruption between two teeth is not certain, both teeth are shown in the same column with a slash separating them, the probably more advanced given first. The same combination, inverted, is shown in the succeeding column.

Table 11. Chronological Sequence of Dental Eruption and Succession in *Callithrix jacchus jacchus*, determined from Gross and Radiographic Examination of Wet-Preserved Colony-Born Individuals (all time in days unless otherwise noted)

Deciduous (21 ♂♂, 19 ♀♀), upper and lower combined.

	Days	*Weeks*
i1	2.5 (2–9)	0.35 (0.29–1.3)
i2	9.3 (9–15)	1.3 (1.3–2.1)
c	21 (20–22)	3.0 (2.8–3.1)
p2	21 (20–22)	3.0 (2.8–3.1)
p3	21 (20–22)	3.0 (2.8–3.1)
p4	27.5 (20–30)	3.9 (2.8–4.3)

Permanent (21 ♂♂, 19 ♀♀), upper and lower combined.

						Crown Calcification[1]		*Root Formations*[1]	
	Days[1]	*Weeks*[2]	*Days*[3]	*Weeks*[2]	*Months*[1]	*Begin*	*Complete*	*Begin*	*Complete*
m1	112	16.0	(112–98)	(16.0–28.2)	3–4	12	37	37	152
m2	138	19.7	(136–245)	(19.4–35.0)	4–6	44	112	112	244
i1[4]	160	22.8	(158–245)	(22.6–35.0)	7–8	22	112	112	348
i2[5]	244	34.9	(244–98)	(34.9–42.6)	7–8	37	116	116	377
pm4	244	34.9	(244–87)	(34.9–41.8)	7–8	52	136	136	370
pm3	288	41.1	(288–98)	(41.1–42.6)	8–11	44	138	138	370
pm2	340	48.6	(298–348)	(42.6–49.7)	8–11	37	138	138	390
c	340	48.6	(298–370)	(42.6–52.8)	11–12	37	244	244	390

SOURCE: Data from Johnston, Dreizen, and Levy (1970).

[1] From text of Johnston, Dreizen, and Levy (1970).

[2] Computed.

[3] Adapted from table 1 of Johnston, Dreizen and Levy (1970).

[4] Sometimes precedes m2.

[5] Unerupted in a 348 day ♂.

Additional observations:

1. Tooth considered erupted when any part of crown pierces gingiva.
2. Differences between sexes not significant.
3. At birth, calcified crowns of deciduous teeth and crypts of m1–2 present in jaws.
4. Permanent molars erupt before deciduous teeth are replaced.
5. Stage of mixed (deciduous and permanent) dentition lasted from 112–340 days.
6. Time for complete development ranged from 140 days for m1 to 353 days for c and pm2.

Table 12. Chronological Sequence of Dental Eruption and Succession in *Saguinus nigricollis nigricollis*.

Mandibular		*Age in Weeks*	*Samples*	*Upper*		*Age in Weeks*	*Samples*
Deciduous				*Deciduous*			
i1	—	birth	5	i1	—	birth	5
i2	—	birth	5	i2	—	birth	5
c	—	birth	5	c	—	birth	5
p2	—	0.6 (birth–1)	5	p2	—	1.2 (birth–2)	5
p3	—	2.6 (1–4)	5	p3	—	2.6 (1–4)	5
p4	—	6.2 (4–8)	5	p4	—	7.3 (5–8)	5
Permanent				*Permanent*			
m1	—	16 (14–18)	6	m1	—	17.4 (16–19)	7
i1	—	19.7 (18–23)	9	i1	—	21.2 (19–23)	9
i2	—	22.5 (21–26)	10	i2	—	26.4 (24–28)	10
m2	—	25.6 (25–27)	10	m2	—	28.0 (27–29)	10
p4	—	28.7 (27–32)	9	p4	—	28.9 (26–33)	9
p2	—	31.5 (27–34)	10	p3	—	30.6 (28–34)	8
p3	—	33.5 (30–39)	8	p2	—	32.6 (30–35)	9
c	—	39.6 (39–40)	5	c	—	40.0 (39–41)	5

SOURCE: Chase and Cooper 1969.

NOTE: Additional observations on dental succession in *Saguinus nigricollis* (Chase and Cooper 1967).

1. Deciduous teeth completely erupted at 8 weeks of age.
2. Permanent teeth completely erupted at 41 weeks of age.
3. All mandibular teeth preceded their maxillary counterparts in eruption except p^3 preceded p_2, and p^2 preceded p_3.
4. Canines attained full length at 11 or 12 months of age.

Table 13. Chronology of Eruption of Deciduous Teeth in Callitrichids and *Callimico*

Callithrix jacchus (Marik 1931)

1–3 days	— deciduous teeth erupting
6th week	— deciduous teeth complete
18th week	— deciduous teeth shedding
20th week	— deciduous teeth completely replaced

Callithrix jacchus (Wettstein 1963, p. 260)

Birth	— $i\frac{1\text{-}2}{1\text{-}2}$, $c_{1\text{-}1}$ (1 specimen)
0–7 days	— no teeth visible (1 specimen)
7.5 weeks	— deciduous suite complete

Callithrix argentata argentata (Zukowsky 1940)

2d day	— di, present
9th day	— $di\frac{1\text{-}2}{1\text{-}2}\,dc\frac{1}{1}$, present
15th day	— $di\frac{1\text{-}2}{1\text{-}2}\,dc\frac{1}{1}\,dp_{2\text{-}3\text{-}4}$, present
32d day	— $di\frac{1\text{-}2}{1\text{-}2}\,dc\frac{1}{1}\,dp\frac{2\text{-}3}{2\text{-}3\text{-}4}$, present
46th day	— all deciduous teeth in place postmortem

Saguinus midas × *S. bicolor* (Immendorf 1961)

3 June 1959, born
17 December (29th week, permanent incisors present)
2 April (44th week), permanent dentition complete

Callimico goeldii (Lorenz and Heinemann 1967)

Birth	— $di\frac{1\text{-}2}{1\text{-}2}$ possibly $c\frac{1}{1}$ (in several fetuses)
6th week	— $di\frac{1\text{-}2}{1\text{-}2}\,dc\frac{1}{1}\,dp_{2\text{-}3}$ (1 specimen)
9th month	— $i\frac{1\text{-}2}{1\text{-}2}\,dc\frac{1}{1}$

Table 14. Ages at Emergence of Complete Deciduous and Complete Permanent Dentition in Living Platyrrhines and Catarrhines (in years)

Species	*Deciduous*	*Permanent Canine*	*Permanent 3d Molar*	*Source*
Platyrrhini				
Callithrix jacchus jacchus	0.05–0.08 (40)	0.82–1.01 (40)	—	Johnston, Dreizen, and Levy 1970
Callithrix jacchus jacchus	0.11–0.14 (2)	0.38 (1)	—	Marik 1931; Wettstein 1963
Callithrix argentata argentata	0.09 (1)	—	—	Zukowsky 1940
Saguinus nigricollis nigricollis	0.08–0.15 (10)	0.75–0.79 (10)	—	Chase and Cooper 1969
Saguinus m. midas × *S. b. bicolor*	—	0.84	—	Immendorf 1961
Callimico goeldii	0.12 (1)	0.74+ (1)[1]	—	Lorenz and Heinemann 1967
Aotus trivirgatus	0.19 (1)	—	—	English 1934
Lagothrix lagothricha	—		4.5 (1 ♂)	Fooden 1963
Catarrhini				
Cercopithecus aethiops	—	3.0–3.33 (?)	3.50–4.00 (?)	Hurme and Van Wagenen 1961
Macaca mulatta	0.35–0.49 (41)	—	—	Gavan 1967
Macaca mulatta	0.33–0.58 (49 ♂♂)	—	—	Hurme and Van Wagenen 1953
Macaca mulatta	0.30–0.55 (50 ♀♀)	—	—	Hurme and Van Wagenen 1953
Macaca mulatta	—	3.60–4.61 (14 ♂♂)	4.94–6.93 (12 ♂♂)	Hurme and Van Wagenen 1961
Macaca mulatta	—	2.51–5.12 (39 ♀♀)	4.88–10.87 (34 ♀♀)	Hurme and Van Wagenen 1961
Macaca irus	0.41–0.62 (10)	—	—	Berkson 1968
Chimpansee troglodytes	0.65–0.97 (17)	—	—	Gavan 1967
Chimpansee troglodytes	—	7.86–9.94 (8 ♂♂)	8.88–13.39 (8 ♂♂)	Nissen and Riesen 1964
Chimpansee troglodytes	—	7.48–9.94 (7 ♀♀)	8.88–12.63 (7 ♀♀)	Nissen and Riesen 1964
Gorilla gorilla	1.04–1.41 (3)	—	—	Lang 1966
Homo sapiens	2.0–2.5	12–15	18–25	Wheeler 1968

NOTE: Species of each group are listed in order of increasing body size; number of specimens examined is shown in parentheses. Unless otherwise indicated, ages given are for both sexes combined. Ages at emergence of canines in catarrhines are included for equitable comparisons with callitrichids, in which canines emerge last, the 3d molar being absent. Some age extremes may represent abnormal individuals.

[1] With permanent incisors and deciduous canine. Either c or m3 erupts last in *Callimico*.

36 Teeth
5. *Dental and Periodontal Diseases and Abnormalities in Callitrichidae*

The statistical analysis of callitrichid dental diseases and abnormalities is based on 904 opportunely available skulls and wild-caught callitrichids, table 15. The number includes specimens in the collection of the Field Museum and others at hand from the several institutions listed below (p. 331). This is less than half the total number of callitrichid skulls used in the taxonomic revision of the family. The material examined for the dental study represents 3 genera comprising 14 species or 36 species and subspecies from 207 localities in Middle and South America. The genera *Cebuella, Callithrix,* and *Saguinus* with their species and subspecies are shown in table 15. Detailed information on each diseased individual, including its locality data, is given in the Reference List in this chapter. Data for the few available wild-caught lion-tamarins, *Leontopithecus rosalia,* are deficient and omitted. Too little is known of *Callimico* for useful comparisons and the genus is not discussed here, except to record a supernumerary molar (fig. V.32A) and a geminate upper incisor, the only aberrations noted in 11 skulls at hand.

The text of this chapter is a revised version of the preliminary report I published in 1970. That account included the first published statistical analysis of oral diseases and abnormalities in a random sampling of many species and races of a single family of monkeys from known localities. It showed that diseases and abnormal teeth and jaws are not rare among platyrrhines and that their incidence in any one locality is not representative of populations of the same race or species from other localities. The report also emphasized that nothing is known of the relationship between dental diseases and natural environments, including foods, and heredity.

Diseases

Oral diseases in the form of (*a*) missing teeth, (*b*) caries, and (*c*) alveolar infections including perforations were noted in the dentition of 91 skulls, or 10% of the total examined (table 16) and 20.5% of all individuals collected in the same localities (table 15). The number of diseased or missing teeth and diseased alveoli is 286, or nearly 1% of the total number of teeth (904 × 32 = 28,928, table 17) and 1.6% of the total in the infected series (546 × 32 = 17,472).

Abnormalities such as supernumeraries, "glassy" teeth, congenital dental arch asymmetries and postpartum injuries, dental rotations, and geminous teeth, occur in 21 additional skulls. They are combined in table 15 with the other 91 for a grand total of 112 diseased and abnormal individuals. The affected individuals are distributed in 79 of the 198 localities, or 40% of the total, and constitute nearly 21% of the 546 specimens taken at those sites.

The three categories of dental diseases in the 91 infected skulls are listed, tooth by tooth, in table 16 and the data are summarized and compared in tables 17 and 18. These may be compared with summaries of comparable conditions in New and Old World apes and monkeys presented by Schultz (table 19).

The difference between the proportion of diseased upper teeth (1.07%) and diseased lower teeth (0.90%), shown in table 17, is not significant. A few additional skulls with a high concentration of dental and periodontal disease in either sets of jaws can alter the proportion by as much or more. Other differences, however, are noteworthy. There is the indication (table 18) that the lower the proportion of diseased antepremolar teeth, the higher the proportion of diseased postcanine teeth, and vice versa. The inverse relationship is most strikingly exemplified in *Cebuella.* It also appears that the antepremolar series is in general more diseased than the postcanine series. The higher proportion is mainly due to the large number of diseased canines. The extremes are in *Saguinus,* with 28% of the upper canines infected, and in *Callithrix,* with 18% of the lower canines infected. Healthiest canines are in *Cebuella,* with no disease in the 20 upper and 20 lower canines of the 10 skulls with arcades otherwise diseased.

The incidence of disease is practically nil in juvenals, little more in subadults, low in young adults, and rises rapidly in late maturity and old age. This age gradient has already been demonstrated by Schultz (1935, p. 569), on the basis of 2,394 young, adult, and old wild specimens representing all families of monkeys and apes. His comparison of the wild lot with 514 captive individuals of the same age classes shows no significant difference. Schultz's tables are reproduced here (tables 19, 20, 21). Dental disease in the present material is confined to fully adult callitrichids only cursorially sorted into age groups. The callitrichid life span in the wild is short, perhaps rarely

Table 15. Systematic List of Skulls of Wild-Caught, Museum-Preserved Callitrichids Examined for Oral Diseases and Abnormalities.

Species	*A*[1]	*B*	*C*	*D*
Cebuella pygmaea	72 (10)	10 (3)	55	18%
Callithrix jacchus penicillata	19 (6)	0 (—)	—	—
Callithrix jacchus jacchus	9 (5)	2 (2)	4	50%
Callithrix jacchus flaviceps	3 (1)	1 (1)	3	33%
Callithrix argentata melanura	16 (6)	1 (1)	4	25%
Callithrix argentata argentata	44 (12)	3 (3)	14	21%
Callithrix argentata leucippe	8 (4)	2 (1)	3	67%
Callithrix humeralifer humeralifer	27 (8)	0 (—)	—	—
Callithrix humeralifer chrysoleuca	24 (5)	3 (2)	17	18%
Saguinus nigricollis graellsi	54 (9)	2 (2)	17	12%
Saguinus nigricollis nigricollis	17 (2)	1 (1)	15	7%
Saguinus fuscicollis fuscus	18 (4)	2 (2)	11	18%
Saguinus fuscicollis avilapiresi	4 (2)	0 (—)	—	—
Saguinus fuscicollis fuscicollis	3 (2)	0 (—)	—	—
Saguinus fuscicollis nigrifrons	21 (5)	0 (—)	—	—
Saguinus fuscicollis illigeri	18 (4)	0 (—)	—	—
Saguinus fuscicollis leucogenys	19 (10)	3 (3)	9	33%
Saguinus fuscicollis lagonotus	51 (10)	3 (3)	22	14%
Saguinus fuscicollis tripartitus	23 (4)	0 (—)	—	—
Saguinus fuscicollis weddelli	27 (3)	5 (3)	12	42%
Saguinus fuscicollis melanoleucus	1 (1)	0 (—)	—	—
Saguinus labiatus thomasi	1 (1)	0 (—)	—	—
Saguinus labiatus labiatus	8 (3)	2 (2)	6	33%
Saguinus mystax mystax	37 (7)	5 (3)	30	17%
Saguinus mystax pileatus	3 (1)	1 (1)	3	33%
Saguinus mystax pluto	3 (2)	1 (1)	8	13%
Saguinus imperator	8 (3)	4 (2)	5	80%
Saguinus midas midas	21 (12)	3 (3)	4	75%
Saguinus midas niger	101 (4)	14 (6)	80	18%
Saguinus inustus	12 (5)	3 (3)	10	33%
Saguinus bicolor bicolor	2 (2)	0 (—)	—	—
Saguinus bicolor ochraceus	15 (3)	2 (2)	6	33%
Saguinus bicolor martinsi	10 (3)	1 (1)	2	50%
Saguinus leucopus	6 (2)	0 (—)	—	—
Saguinus oedipus geoffroyi	124 (29)	26 (20)	132	20%
Saguinus oedipus oedipus	75 (8)	12 (8)	74	16%
Totals	904 (198)	112 (79)	546	20.5%

SOURCE: Hershkovitz (1970*c*), corrected and revised.
[1] Explanation of column heads:
A—Number of individuals examined, followed in parentheses by number of collecting localities represented.
B—Number of diseased and abnormal individuals, followed in parentheses by number of collecting localities represented.
C—Total number of specimens from localities listed in column B.
D—Percentage of affected individuals of each taxon from localities listed in column B.

more than 5 years, with aging controlled by myriad environmental factors, most of them unknown.

The data compiled in table 15 suggest that populations of certain localities may be more prone to dental diseases than others. Individuals with diseased or abnormal dental arcades were found in 79 (column B) of the 198 localities (column A) represented by specimens examined. In other terms, 20.5% (column D) of the samples from 79 localities showed oral problems compared with 0 orally diseased or abnormal individuals from the remaining 118 localities. Certain species also seem to be more susceptible to disease than others. The differences between species or subspecies may reflect local differences in the types, abundance, availability, and tastes of foods. Populations inhabiting areas greatly modified by man may show a different, possibly higher, rate of oral disease than their relatives in comparatively undisturbed areas. Schultz (1935, p. 568) points to significant differences in the incidence of caries between two populations of Middle American *Ateles* and to differences between cercopithecine and colobine monkeys and between higher and lower primates generally. He suspects that heredity is the principal factor involved. In any case, the influence of local environmental factors may be at least as strong. In every case, ignorance of the precise habitat and feeding habits is too profound to permit more than idle speculation regarding the true causes of differences in the incidence of oral diseases among wild living primates.

Table 16. Distribution of Certain Types of Diseased Teeth in Callitrichids

Diseased Specimens		Upper Teeth									Lower Teeth									Grand
		i^1	i^2	c	p^2	p^3	p^4	m^1	m^2	*Total*	i_1	i_2	c	p_2	p_3	p_4	m_1	m_2	*Total*	*Total*
10 *Cebuella pygmaea*	a	2	2	—	2	1	2	1	—	10	—	—	—	4	3	3	3	4	17	27
	b	—	—	—	—	—	—	1	—	1	—	—	—	—	—	—	1	—	1	2
	c	—	—	—	—	—	—	1	—	1	—	—	—	3	3	1	2	1	10	11
2 *Callithrix jacchus*	a	2	1	—	—	—	—	—	—	3	2	2	2	1	1	—	1	—	9	12
	b	—	—	—	—	—	—	—	—	0	—	—	—	—	—	1	—	—	1	1
	c	—	—	—	—	—	—	—	—	0	—	—	—	—	1	—	—	—	1	1
6 *Callithrix argentata*	a	3	2	1	—	1	1	—	—	8	—	—	—	1	—	—	—	1	2	10
	b	—	—	—	—	—	—	—	—	0	—	—	1	—	—	1	—	—	2	2
	c	—	1	—	—	—	—	—	—	1	—	—	1	—	—	1	—	—	2	3
3 *Callithrix humeralifer*	a	2	2	—	1	1	—	—	—	6	—	—	—	—	1	—	1	—	2	8
	c	—	—	—	—	—	—	—	—	0	—	—	—	—	1	—	—	—	1	1
3 *Saguinus nigricollis*	a	—	1	—	—	—	—	—	1	2	—	1	—	—	—	—	—	—	1	3
13 *Saguinus fuscicollis*	a	2	2	2	1	—	1	—	1	9	2	2	2	—	—	1	3	3	13	22
	b	3	2	5	—	—	—	—	—	10	—	—	6	—	—	1	—	—	7	17
	c	2	2	—	—	—	—	—	—	4	—	—	—	—	—	1	1	—	2	6
10 *Saguinus midas*	a	1	—	—	—	—	—	2	5	8	—	1	1	—	—	2	2	1	7	15
	b	2	2	—	1	—	1	2	1	9	—	—	1	—	—	—	—	—	1	10
	c	—	—	—	—	—	—	—	—	0	2	2	1	—	—	—	—	—	5	5

3 *Saguinus bicolor*	a	1	—	1	—	—	—	—	—	2	—	—	—	—	—	—	—	—	0	2
	c	—	—	—	—	—	—	—	—	0	—	—	1	—	—	2	—	—	3	3
3 *Saguinus inustus*	a	1	—	1	—	1	1	—	—	4	—	—	—	—	1	—	—	2	3	7
	b	—	—	1	—	—	—	—	—	1	—	—	—	—	—	—	—	—	0	1
	c	—	—	—	—	1	1	—	—	2	—	—	—	—	—	—	—	—	0	2
10 *Saguinus o. oedipus*	a	—	1	—	1	2	—	1	—	5	—	—	—	—	—	—	—	—	0	5
	b	—	—	8	—	—	—	2	—	10	—	—	2	—	1	—	1	1	5	15
	c	—	—	—	—	1	—	—	—	1	—	—	—	—	—	—	—	—	0	1
21 *Saguinus o. geoffroyi*	a	2	4	3	1	1	2	—	—	13	2	1	—	2	—	—	—	—	5	18
	b	3	—	12	—	—	—	—	—	15	—	1	5	1	1	—	1	—	9	24
	c	—	—	1	—	—	1	1	—	3	—	—	1	1	1	2	—	—	5	8
1 *Saguinus labiatus*	b	—	2	2	1	1	—	2	1	9	2	2	1	—	—	1	2	2	10	19
4 *Saguinus mystax*	a	—	—	—	—	1	1	1	1	4	—	—	—	—	—	—	—	—	0	4
	b	—	—	1	1	1	1	2	1	7	—	—	1	1	1	1	1	1	6	13
	c	—	—	—	—	—	—	—	2	2	—	—	—	—	—	—	—	—	0	2
2 *Saguinus imperator*	a	—	—	—	1	—	—	—	1	2	—	—	—	—	—	—	—	1	1	3
	b	—	—	2	—	—	—	—	—	2	—	—	—	—	—	—	—	—	0	2
	c	—	—	—	—	—	—	1	—	1	—	—	—	—	—	—	—	—	0	1
91 Total		26	24	40	10	12	12	17	14	155	10	12	26	14	15	18	19	17	131	286

NOTE: a—lost
b—carious
c—abscessed or perforated alveoli

Table 17. Incidence of Dental Disease among Callitrichids

Genus	*Individuals Examined (all ages)* (N)	*Individuals with Diseased Teeth* (%)	*Diseased Upper Teeth* (N = *16*) (%)	*Diseased Lower Teeth* (N = *16*) (%)	*Total Diseased Teeth* (N = *32*) (%)
Cebuella	72	14	1.04	2.43	1.74
Callithrix	150	7	0.75	0.83	0.79
Saguinus	682	10	1.14	0.76	0.95
Total	904	10%	1.07%	0.90%	0.99%

Table 18. Incidence of Diseased Teeth in Each Dental Field and in All Fields Combined

Diseased Teeth	*Cebuella* (N = *10*) *Number of Teeth*	*Percentage of Total*		*Callithrix* (N = *11*) *Number of Teeth*	*Percentage of Total*		*Saguinus* (N = *70*) *Number of Teeth*	*Percentage of Total*		*Totals* (N = *91*) *Number of Teeth*	*Percentage of Total*	
Incisors												
Upper	4	10.0%	= 5%	13	29.5%	= 19.3%	33	11.8%	= 9.1%	50	13.7%	= 9.9%
Lower	0	0%		4	9.1%		18	6.4%		22	6.0%	
Canines												
Upper	0	0%	= 0%	1	4.5%	= 11.4%	39	27.8%	= 21.8%	40	22.0%	= 18.1%
Lower	0	0%		4	18.2%		22	15.7%		26	14.3%	
Premolars												
Upper	5	8.3%	= 18.3%	4	6.1%	= 10.0%	25	5.9%	= 5.5%	34	5.8%	= 7.4%
Lower	17	28.0%		9	13.7%		21	5.0%		47	8.6%	
Molars												
Upper	3	7.5%	= 17.5%	0	0%	= 3.4%	28	10.0%	= 8.9%	31	6.8%	= 9.2%
Lower	11	27.0%		3	6.8%		22	7.9%		36	9.9%	
Total teeth												
Upper	12	7.5%	= 12.5%	18	10.2%	= 10.7%	125	11.2%	= 8.2%	155	10.6%	= 8.9%
Lower	28	17.5%		20	11.3%		76	6.8%		131	9.0%	

NOTE: The dental formulae for each field, for both sides, above and below, are incisors $\frac{2+2}{2+2}$, canines $\frac{1+1}{1+1}$, premolars $\frac{3+3}{3+3}$, molars $\frac{2+2}{2+2} = \frac{16}{16} = 32$. The total number of teeth in a given field is the formula number for that field multiplied by the number of diseased individuals.

Table 19. Percentage of Wild Primates with Diseased or Antemortem Missing Teeth

Wild Primates (all ages)	*Specimens* (N)	*Percentage of Specimens with* *Caries*	*Abscesses*	*Closed Alveoli*
Large apes and gibbons	744	5.2	20.2	6.7
Cercopithecinae	504	4.6	9.5	4.6
Colobinae	451	0.4	7.1	2.2
Platyrrhini, except *Alouatta*	413	9.0	8.2	2.9
Alouatta (howlers)	282	0.3	7.4	3.5

SOURCE: Data from Schultz (1935, p. 569, table 26).

NOTE: Platyrrhines are represented by the single Middle American species of each of the genera *Cebus, Ateles, Alouatta, Saimiri,* and *Saguinus.*

Bilateral Symmetry in Carious Teeth

Caries in callitrichids does not, as a rule, affect to the same degree homologous teeth of both sides of the arcade. Canines may be an exception, but only because they happen to be much more frequently diseased than other teeth. The incidence of bilateral symmetry in dental diseases among primates generally was determined by Schultz (1935, p. 570) as 56%.

Missing and Supernumerary Teeth

Congenitally missing or supernumerary teeth are rare in callitrichids. The specimens examined had no congenitally missing teeth, but an extra tooth was noted in each of six individuals, and two extra teeth were present in a seventh (table 22). Johnston, Dreizen, and Levy

Table 20. Relation of Age to Frequency of Diseased and Antemortem Missing Teeth in Preserved Skulls

	Wild Specimens			*Captive Specimens*		
Abnormality	*Young* (N = *587*)	*Adult* (N = *1,172*)	*Old* (N = *635*)	*Young* (N = *395*)	*Adult* (N = *78*)	*Old* (N = *41*)
Caries:	0.2%	2.9%	10.5%	1.0%	7.7%	24.4%
Abscesses	0.5%	6.2%	32.9%	0.5%	7.9%	21.9%
Closed alveoli	0%	2.6%	11.7%	0%	2.6%	12.2%

SOURCE: Data from Schultz (1935, p. 569, table 27).
NOTE: Specimens were wild and captive individuals representing all families of monkeys and apes (see table 19 above).

(1970, p. 45) noted a third molar in 1 of 200 laboratory individuals of *Callithrix jacchus jacchus*. Schultz (1935) found no numerical deviation in the teeth of 35 skulls of *Saguinus oedipus geoffroyi* examined by him. Extra teeth were not present in the 247 callitrichid skulls checked by Colyer (1936), but a congenitally missing right m^2 was noted in a specimen of *Saguinus midas midas* (his *Mystax midas*).

Among cebids, the proportion of missing last molars exceeds that of all other absentees combined and is greater than that of all catarrhines excluding *Homo* (cf. Schultz 1935, p. 546; Colyer 1936, p. 1). Tabulations by Schultz and Colyer of extra and missing teeth in platyrrhines are reproduced here (tables 23, 24).

The probable hereditary nature of congenitally missing teeth in cebids was suggested by Schultz (1935, p. 550). He notes as evidence that in 82 skulls of *Ateles* from Chiriquí, Panamá, 3.5% lack one or more of the last molars, while in 89 specimens from one locality in eastern Nicaragua, 15.4% lack a last molar. Specimens examined were from the A. H. Schultz collection (cf. Schultz 1926, p. 287; 1937, p. 492, for number of skulls).

Fig. V.29. Crazing of dental enamel: *A, B,* upper and lower i–m1 (part) of the collared titi, *Callicebus torquatus* (FMNH 70694); *C,* upper incisors and left canine and premolar of the cotton-top tamarin, *Saguinus oedipus oedipus* (FMNH 69942); *D,* left lower tooth row of same cotton-top. Scales, in mm, are rough approximations. (After Hershkovitz 1970*c*.)

Crazing

The fine-line, amber to brown colored fracture patterns of the dental enamel of many mammals resemble the crazing of glazed ware; hence my use of the term here.

Among platyrrhines, crazing is most evident on the lingual surface of the incisors, and is more frequent or dense on the upper than on the lower teeth. Canines are less affected and the molariform teeth least, and then mainly on the occlusal surface (fig. V.29). The status of crazing in fully erupted, permanent teeth of callitrichids and *Callimico* is shown in table 25.

Crazing also occurs on the incisors, canines, and occlusal surface of the molariform teeth of the marmosetlike cebids *Saimiri, Aotus,* and *Callicebus*. The phenomenon is widespread but not universal among other cebids, and among catarrhines, including man. It is rare or absent among prosimians and may be universally absent in rodents. A random sampling of the Carnivora indicates that crazing is uncommon among felines and canines but well-developed in the more omnivorous forms, particularly ripe fruit-eaters such as the coati (*Nasua*) and kinkajou (*Potos*). The most affected teeth in bears and tapirs are the lower canines. The incisors, particularly the outer enamel covering, are crazed in pigs and peccaries. The teeth of Megachiroptera are crazed, but those of Microchiroptera are hardly marked. Teeth of largely insectivorous animals, including representatives of the Insectivora and tupaiids are generally free of crazing. The condition also seems to be restricted or absent in a limited sampling of marsupials.

Brown longitudinal "cracks," an aspect of crazing, have been observed on the buccal enamel of human upper incisors by Brabant and Klees (1957) and Brabant (1960). These authors point out fundamental differences between dental lamellae and brown "cracks" and distinguish the superficial white cracks from the deeper brown ones. The latter, they found, penetrate the dentine and are constantly being "mended" by it. Brown cracks were noted mainly in adults at least 40 years old and, according to Brabant and Klees, are probable channels for caries development. Comparison of my tables 16 and 17 shows no relationship between caries and crazing in callitrichids. Nevertheless, correlations between crazing and specific teeth or dental fields may occur in certain species. Causes for brown cracks in human teeth are said to be mechanical and thermal.

Table 21. Relation of Age to Frequency of Diseased and Antemortem Missing Teeth in Wild Platyrrhines

	Ateles		Cebus		Alouatta		Saimiri		Saguinus	
Abnormality	*Adult* (N = *93*)	*Old* (N = *63*)	*Adult* (N = *70*)	*Old* (N = *16*)	*Adult* (N = *132*)	*Old* (N = *77*)	*Adult* (N = *39*)	*Old* (N = *8*)	*Adult* (N = *28*)	*Old* (N = *5*)
Caries										
% of specimens	3.2%	14.3%	11.4%	25.0%	0%	1.3%	10.2%	50.0%	14.3%	20.0%
Average no. of teeth	2.3	1.7	2.0	1.7	0	1.0	1.0	1.2	2.0	1.0
Abscess										
% of specimens	3.2%	28.6%	5.7%	12.5%	3.0%	22.1%	5.1%	25.0%	3.6%	40.0%
Average no. of teeth	1.7	1.2	2.2	2.5	1.2	2.0	1.0	2.0	2.0	1.0
Tooth missing, alveolus closed										
% of specimens	0%	7.9%	5.7%	0%	0.8%	11.7%	5.1%	12.5%	0%	0%
Average no. of teeth	0	2.2	5.0	0	1.0	2.6	1.0	1.0	0	0

SOURCE: Data from Schultz (1935, p. 547, table 21).
NOTE: Genera listed are represented, perhaps with a few exceptions, by the single species of each occurring in Middle America.

Table 22. Supernumerary Teeth in Wild Callitrichids and *Callimico*

Group	*Museum Number*	*Supernumeraries*
Callithrix jacchus aurita	♂ BM 3.9.4.26	L m^3
Saguinus oedipus geoffroyi	♂ USNM 302337	L pm^4
Saguinus oedipus geoffroyi	♂ FMNH 69964	L pm^4
Saguinus oedipus oedipus	♀ FMNH 69937	R m_3
Saguinus midas niger	♂ AMNH 96500	L m^2, R m^2
Saguinus mystax mystax	♂ FMNH 86952	R m^2
Saguinus mystax mystax	♂ FMNH 86956	R2i^2
Callimico goeldii	♂ USNM 303322	L m^4

NOTE: L = left; R = right. Approximately 1,000 specimens of callitrichids and 10 specimens of *Callimico* were examined.

Table 23. Supernumary, Vestigial, and Antemortem Missing Teeth in Wild Adult Platyrrhines

	Fourth Molars	m^3 *Vestigial*	m^3 *Missing*	*Premolar Missing*	i_1 *Missing*
Ateles (N = 158)	1.3%	6.3%	7.6%	0.6%	—
Cebus (N = 105)	—	24.7%	4.8%	—	1.0%
Alouatta (N = 210)	—	0.5%	—	1.0%	3.8%
Saimiri (N = 48)	—	8.3%	—	—	—
Saguinus oedipus (N = 35)	—	—	—	—	—

SOURCE: Data from Schultz (1935, p. 547, table 21).
NOTE: Genera listed are represented, perhaps with a few exceptions, by the single species of each occurring in Middle America.

Table 24. Supernumerary and Antemortem Missing Teeth in Platyrrhines

		Extra Teeth				*Missing Teeth*			
Group	*Number of Skulls*	*i*	*pm*	*m*	*%*	*i*	*pm*	*m*	*%*
Cebus	651	—	—	4	0.6%	1	3	16	3.1%
Lagothrix	94	—	—	1	1.1%	—	—	1	1.1%
Brachyteles	25	—	1	—	4.0%	1	—	1	8.0%
Ateles	232	2	2	7	4.7%	—	—	8	3.4%
Alouatta	787	4	—	3	0.9%	—	—	3	0.4%
Pithecia	155	—	—	—	—	1	—	2	1.9%
Callicebus	122	—	1	—	0.8%	—	—	—	0.0%
Saimiri	100	—	—	1	1.0%	—	—	—	0.0%
Aotus	10	—	—	—	0.0%	—	—	—	0.0%
Cacajao	23	—	—	—	0.0%	—	—	—	0.0%
Callitrichidae	247	—	—	—	0.0%	—	—	1[1]	0.4%

SOURCE: Data from Colyer (1936, pp. 33, 61) based on skulls in European and American museums.
[1] Right m^2 missing in *Saguinus midas midas*.

The present study suggests that crazing may be attributed in large part to repeated and forceful striking of lower teeth against the upper in biting. Thermal causes, at least in nonhuman primates and wild animals generally, may not exist. Crazing is most extensive in older individuals of larger species with strong jaws and varied diets. It is less widespread, rare, or absent in smaller species with weaker jaws and more restricted diets. Crazing is absent in the deciduous dentition and the newly erupted teeth of callitrichids and all other mammals sampled. The bite of such teeth is weak. Enamel thickness, curvature and angle of teeth, particularly of incisors and canines, form of occlusion, diet, and oral chemistry must be other factors involved in crazing, or lack of it, in particular teeth.

The considerable variation in the distribution and

Table 25. Dental Crazing of Permanent Teeth of Wild Callitrichidae and *Callimico*

Species	$i^{1\text{-}2}$	$i_{1\text{-}2}$	c^1	c_1
Cebuella pygmaea	0	0	0	0
Callithrix jacchus	—	0	—	0
Callithrix argentata group	=	—	=	=
Saguinus spp.	x	x	x	x
Leontopithecus rosalia	x	x	x	x
Callimico goeldii	x	x	x	x

NOTE: 0 = absent
— = sometimes present
= = frequently present
x = usually or consistently present

patterns of crazing may reflect corresponding differences in the prismatic structure of the enamel. Differences in presence or absence of crazing, as, for example, in callitrichids (table 24) or Chiroptera, seem to be taxonomically significant. Differences in pattern, such as the vertical "cracks" in human teeth, the crisscrossing in platyrrhines, the horizontally concentric lines in dog species, and the vertical or oblique concentric lines, like the lines of Retzius, in some Megachiroptera, almost certainly develop along fracture pathways predetermined by specific differences in the primitive structure of the enamel of each tooth, or the teeth of each morphogenetic field.

Literature Review

Previously published information on oral pathology and abnormalities in callitrichids is meager. Reference has already been made to Schultz (1935) and Colyer (1936), who made use of museum-preserved skulls. They found few signs of disease in the comparatively small number of specimens examined. Their main findings in other primates, however, are invaluable for comparisons with oral diseases and abnormalities in callitrichids. Other authors, reviewed below, have explored dental conditions in captive animals maintained on standard diets which include processed foods.

Shaw and Auskaps (1954) reported on 34 living *Callithrix jacchus jacchus*, most of which were young or adolescent. Gross or histologic evidence of caries was not found. Periodontal disease, however, appeared in a "large majority" of their animals. Missing teeth in seven adults, therefore, were regarded as lost because of bone disease rather than caries. Deposits of calculus were heavy in ten specimens, and in eleven, teeth were darkly pigmented. "Many" samples of malocclusion and abnormal crowding of teeth were also noted.

Chase and Cooper (1968) observed uncalcified and calcified masses on the teeth of 52 captive callitrichids representing *Callithrix jacchus, Saguinus fuscicollis, Saguinus nigricollis,* and *Saguinus oedipus.* Recurrence of deposits were frequent after removal at intervals averaging 41 days. The upper teeth, particularly canines and first premolars, were more frequently and extensively involved than the mandibular teeth.

Periodontal and dental anatomy, development, and diseases in laboratory-bred marmosets (*Callithrix jacchus*) are being investigated at the University of Texas, Dental Science Institute, Houston, by Dr. Barnet M. Levy and associates. The development and histology of normal periodontal tissues in the newborn and young marmoset and the process of root bifurcation have been described by Bernick and Levy (1968*a, b*) and Levy and Bernick (1968*a, b*). Arteriosclerotic changes in the periodontal arteries of adult callitrichids were noted by Bernick, Levy, and Patek (1969); the effects of vitamin deficiency by Dreizen, Levy, and Bernick (1970); bone changes resulting from osteomalacia and hyperparathyroidism by Dreizen, Levy, Bernick, Hampton, and Krantz (1967); the effects of excessive amounts of parathyroid hormones in fluoridated and nonfluoridated alveolar bone by Levy, Dreizen, Bernick, and Hampton (1970); the prevalence of gingivitis (96%) and calculus (100%) in the laboratory colony of callitrichids by Friedman, Levy, and Ennever (1972). Data on dental development, eruption, and sequence in *Callithrix jacchus,* published by Johnston, Dreizen, and Levy (1970) has been incorporated into chapter 35 (p. 319). Additional information on biology of callitrichid periodontium is given and the aims and accomplishments of the research program on this animal and their application to other primates, particularly man, are reviewed by Levy (1971), and by Levy, Dreizen, Hampton, Taylor, and Hampton (1971). Then again in 1972, Levy, Dreizen, and Bernick recapitulated previous work on the dental biology of captive *Callithrix jacchus.* More information and references to other contributions by the same group of investigators will be found in the works cited.

Normal and diseased teeth, periodontium, and gingiva of 120 living animals and 40 skulls of wild-caught, laboratory-maintained cotton-top tamarins, *Saguinus oedipus oedipus,* were described by Ammons, Schectman, and Page (1972). Mild localized and transient gingivitis appears to have been the principal pathological condition. Caries was noted in 28 teeth of 18 individuals out of the 160 studied. This compares with 25 carious teeth in 10 individuals of a total of 75 *Saguinus oedipus* I examined (tables 15, 16). Prevalence of spontaneous chronic progressive periodontal disease was "exceptionally low, if it occurs at all [p. 141]." This finding contrasts with mine and those of others.

Reference List of Observed Dental Diseases and Abnormalities in Callitrichids and *Callimico*

The following list of observed dental diseases and abnormalities forms the basis for the preceding account. It is arranged by species (and subspecies) and collecting locality. The locality for each individual is followed by the total number of specimens examined (in parenthesis) from the same locality. Each diseased or abnormal individual is identified by museum number and sex. Diseases and abnormalities recorded include teeth missing, carious, glassy, injured, abnormally eroded, displaced, rotated, geminated, or otherwise deformed or aberrant, supernumeraries, asymmetries, and eroded or abscessed alveoli. Excessive or abnormal attrition is here regarded as caused by caries. Missing teeth with alveoli closed are simply listed as such. Unless expressly indicated otherwise, the loss is assumed to have been caused by caries or periodontal disease.

The specimens listed are from the following institutions.

AMNH = American Museum of Natural History
BM = British Museum (Natural History)
CM = Carnegie Museum
FMNH = Field Museum of Natural History
RMNH = Rijksmuseum Van Natuurlijke Historie
UMMZ = University of Michigan Museum of Zoology
USNM = United States National Museum

Cebuella pygmaea

Tabatinga, Amazonas, Brazil (37)

USNM 336315 ♀, L i^{1-2} missing; corresponding lower present but less worn than R i_{1-2}.

USNM 336317 ♀, R i^1 missing; R pm_3 roots exposed.

USNM 337320 ♂, R m_2 with inner margin of alveolus eroded; dorsobuccal perforation between alveoli of m_{1-2}; upper teeth normal.

USNM 336321 ♂, L m_2 missing, upper normal.

USNM 337323 ♂, L pm_2 missing; L m_1 half-destroyed, alveolus with large sinus and buccal perforation; R m_1 missing, alveolus filled; corresponding upper teeth normal.

USNM 336325 ♂, R pm_{2-4} missing, buccal surface of alveoli destroyed.

USNM 337329 ♀, pm_{2-2} missing, R m_3 missing, alveoli open buccally; upper premolar normal.

USNM 337330 ♀, L pm^2 missing, m^1 with roots exposed, corresponding lower teeth normal.

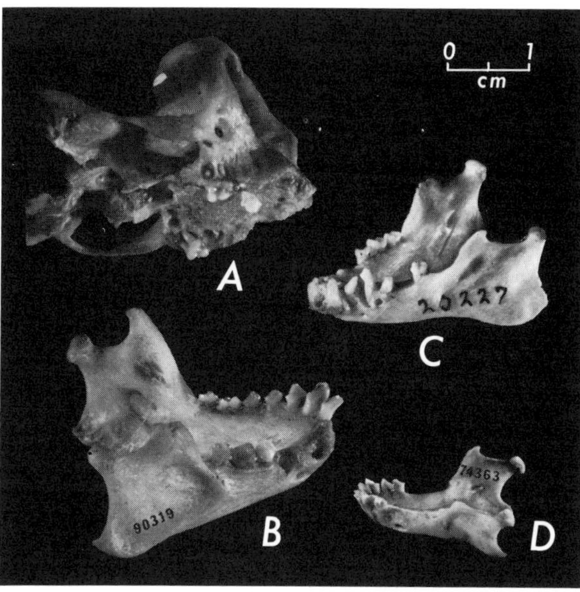

Fig. V.30. Lost, diseased and abnormally worn teeth: *A, B, Saguinus oedipus geoffroyi* (FMNH 90319), very old ♂ (Baudó, Chocó, Colombia). *Missing*—all upper teeth except very worn R pm^3, RL m^{1-2} (second molar lost post mortem); L i_1, R i_{1-2}, Rpm_{2-3}; abscessed ramus excavated with perforation through alveolus of pm_3; carious: L i_2, L c_1.

C, Callithrix jacchus jacchus (FMNH 20227), ad. ♀ (Juá, Ceará, Brazil): Missing—R i_{1-2} with alveoli filled, L i_{1-2} with alveolus of first filled, R c with alveolus enlarged, the bone perforated buccally, R pm_{2-3} with alveoli filled; L c glassy, abnormally worn; L pm_{2-4} snaggled, sockets abscessed, jaw perforated between pm $_{3-4}$; L m_1 missing, alveolus filled. Upper jaw (not shown) with dentition complete, L i^1 abnormally elongate; canines abnormally worn on mesial surface; R pm ^{1} and R m^1 separated by wide (0.8 mm) gap.

D, Cebuella pygmaea (FMNH 74363), old ♂ (Loreto, Peru). *Missing*—all molars, L pm_{3-4}, R pm_4 with alveoli partially filled; remaining teeth considerably worn. (After Hershkovitz 1970*c*.)

Apayacu, Loreto, Peru (11)

FMNH 74363 ♂ (fig. V.30D), R i^2 missing, alveolus filled; L pm^4, m^1 missing, alveoli partially filled; L pm_{3-4}, m_{1-2} missing; R pm_4, m_{1-2} missing, alveoli partially filled; remaining teeth very much worn.

Río Curaray, Loreto, Peru (7)

FMNH 72037 ♀, L pm^{2-4} missing, alveoli partially filled; L m_2 missing, alveolus completely filled.

Callithrix jacchus jacchus

Itaparica Id., Bahia, Brazil (1)

BM 6.6.3.1 ♂, L i^1 and R i^{1-2} missing, alveoli filled; all lower incisors present, the right higher; right upper and lower cheek teeth more worn than left.

Cerro Juá, Brazil (3)

FMNH 20227 ♀ (fig. V.30C), L i^1 abnormally elongate; R pm^4 and R m^1 separated by wide (.8 mm) gap; R L canines abnormally eroded on mesial surface; R i_{1-2}, R c_1, pm_{2-3} missing; alveoli of incisors, canines, premolars filled; R pm_4 eroded and carious; L i_{1-2} missing, L c_1 glassy, abnormally eroded, L pm_{3-4} snaggled, sockets abscessed, jaw perforated between L pm_3 and pm_4; m_1 missing, alveolus filled.

FMNH 20228 ♂, L pm^3 rotated 90° with lingual border anteriad, pm^2 displaced mesiad.

Callithrix jacchus flaviceps

Engenheiro Reeve, Minas Gerais, Brazil (3)

BM 3.9.4.26 ♂, m^{2-2} 3 rooted; supernumerary L m^3 represented by fully formed single-rooted alveolus, tooth lost during skull preparation; no evidence of R m^3 or R m_{3-3}.

Callithrix argentata argentata

Cametá, Tocantins, Pará, Brazil (2)

FMNH 50841 ♂, L c^1 and alveolus absent, whether from injury in early life, or congenitally.

Tapaiuna, Rio Tapajóz, Pará, Brazil (4)

FMNH 92177 ♂, R pm_2 missing, alveolus filled; L m_2 missing, alveolus half-filled.

FMNH 92179 ♀, R i^1 incompletely geminate.

Tapará, Pará, Brazil (8)

AMNH 95918 ♀, L c_1 carious, terminalf half lost; R c_1 with abscessed alveolus.

Callithrix argentata leucippe

Fordlandia, Rio Tapajóz, Brazil (3)

AMNH 133712 ♂, R i^1 missing, alveolus filled.

AMNH 133709 ♂, L pm^4 missing, alveolus filled.

Callithrix argentata melanura

Río Mapaiso, Río Grande, Bolivia (4)

CM 1963, Pm^3 missing, alveolus filled, $i^{1-1, 2-2}$ missing, alveoli filled except of L i^2 with alveolus enlarged, perforated buccally; L pm_2 less worn than R; pm_4 peglike, alveolus perforated buccally, root exposed.

Callithrix humeralifer chrysoleuca

Amarin (Igarapé), Rio Tapajóz, Pará, Brazil (4)

AMNH 91838 ♀, R m_1 missing, alveolus partly filled.

Lago do Baptista, Amazonas, Brazil (13)

RMNH 50824 °, R i^2, L i^{1-2}, R pm^2 missing, alveoli filled, L pm^3 missing, alveolus enlarged.

FMNH 50833 ♂, R i^2 missing, alveolus enlarged; R pm_3 missing, lateral wall of alveolus with large perforation.
FMNH 50827 ♂, L c^1 carious.
Auará Igarapé, Amazonas, Brazil (4)
FMNH 91837 ♂, R c_1 geminate.

Saguinus nigricollis graellsi
San Francisco, Río Napo, Napo-Pastaza, Ecuador (3)
UMMZ 82843 °, R i_2 missing, alveolus filled.
Río Curaray, Loreto, Peru (14)
AMNH 72048 ♂, R m^2 missing.

Saguinus nigricollis nigricollis
Apayacu, Río Amazonas, Loreto, Peru (15)
AMNH 74404 ♂, L i^2 missing, alveolus filled.

Saguinus fuscicollis weddelli
Sandia, Pampa Grande, Puno, Peru (7)
FMNH 79878 ♀, L c^1 missing, alveolus filled; remaining upper teeth eroded nearly to roots; $c_{1\text{-}1}$ and L pm_4 eroded to gums; all lower incisors missing, alveoli nearly filled; all lower molars missing, alveoli filled.
FMNH 79882 ♂, R c^1 carious.
FMNH 79881 ♂, $c^{1\text{-}1}$ carious.
Itahuania, Madre de Dios, Puno, Peru (3)
FMNH 84231 ♂, L i^1 carious.
San Ignacio, Puno, Peru (2)
FMNH 78460 °, R i^2 missing, alveolus filled; $c_{1\text{-}1}$ carious; R pm_4 alveolus abscessed.

Saguinus fuscicollis fuscus
Tres Troncos, Río Caquetá, Colombia (10)
FMNH 71004 ♂, R i^2 missing, alveolus filled.
Tonantins, Amazonas, Brazil (1)
BM 34.6.14.8 °, L m_1 and R pm_4 missing, alveoli filled; R m_1 loose, alveolus perforated buccally; upper cheek teeth normal.

Saguinus fuscicollis lagonotus
Santa Rita, Loreto, Peru (3)
FMNH 86963 ♀, R pm^4 missing, alveolus filled; L m_2 missing, alveolus filled.
Boca Río Curaray, Napo-Pastaza, Ecuador (14)
FMNH 73402 ♂, R pm^2 missing, alveolus closed.
Copotaza, Napo-Pastaza, Ecuador (5)
BM 80.5.6.21 ♀, $c^{1\text{-}1}$ carious and worn to level of pm^1.

Saguinus fuscicollis leucogenys
Moyobamba, San Martín, Peru (1)
BM 24.12.12.1 °, $i^{1\text{-}1}$, crowns missing (injury?); $c_{1\text{-}1}$ eroded at gum line.
Tingo María, Huánuco, Peru (6)
BM 27.11.1.25 ♀, R $c\frac{1}{1}$ and L c_1 missing, alveoli filled.
Yarinacocha, Río Ucayali, Loreto, Peru (2)
FMNH 62701 ♂, All upper incisors eroded to gum line, alveoli abscessed; all other teeth greatly worn. Skull size below average.

Saguinus midas midas
Cayenne, French Guiana (2)
FMNH 21731 ♂, R m^2 and L m^1 glassy.
Dunoon, Guyana (2)
UMMZ 46418 ♂, All uppers more-or-less glassy.
Guyana (captive)
USNM 344916 ♀, (mother of hybrids, *S. midas* × *S. oedipus*) $I^{1\text{-}1}$, $c^{1\text{-}1}$, R pm^2, R m^2 carious; L $m^{1\text{-}2}$ missing, alveoli filled; lower incisors and R c_1 abscessed, with large lateral perforation exposing root; R pm_4, R m_1 missing, alveoli filled.

Saguinus midas niger
Benevides, Pará, Brazil (1)
FMNH 19512 ♂, All upper molars and premolars glassy.
Cametá, Rio Tocantins, Pará, Brazil (3)
FMNH 50852 ♀, L m_2 empty undivided alveolus more than twice normal size, could have contained one abnormally large molar or a normal second molar, and a vestigial third (cf. *Saguinus imperator*, FMNH 50855).

Saguinus midas niger
Cametá, Pará, Brazil (48)
AMNH 96500 ♂, supernumerary labiad to normal, R m^2; another labiad to L m^2; lower dentition normal.
AMNH 96501 ♀, L pm_4 missing, alveolus filled.
AMNH 96523 ♂, L m^2 missing, alveolar space without scar; lower teeth normal.
AMNH 96524 ♂, same as preceding.
AMNH 96529 ♂, L m^2 hypotrophied, diameter 1.3 mm; R m^2 = 2.4 mm; L m^1 = 3.15 mm, crown broader than base, tritubercular pattern distorted; L c_1 with anterior cingulum extending upward and overlying crown.
Baião, Rio Tocantins, Pará, Brazil (14)
AMNH 96541 ♂, L $m^{1\text{-}2}$ missing, L i_2 missing, alveolus filled; remaining teeth normal.
AMNH 96542 ♂, L c_1 carious.
AMNH 96545 ♂, R i^1 missing, alveolus filled; L m_2 missing, alveolar space available, total area as on normal opposite side.
Mocajuba, Rio Tocantins, Pará, Brazil (8)
AMNH 96537 ♂, L m_1, R c_1 missing, alveoli not completely filled; upper dentition normal.
AMNH 96538 ♂, R m^2 missing; R m^1 a small worn buccal remnant. R pm^4 with buccal half degenerate; lowers normal except for uneven wear on L pm_4, $m_{1\text{-}2}$.
AMNH 96540 ♀, R m^1 with metaconal area destroyed by caries, alveolus twice normal size, tooth evidently on way out; left upper and all lower teeth normal.
Recreio, Rio Majary, Pará, Brazil (6)
AMNH 96895 ♀, L m^1 split longitudinally, protocone with separate root; lower dentition normal.

Saguinus inustus
Tabocal, Rio Negro, Amazonas, Brazil (7)
AMNH 79414 ♀, R c^1 missing, alveolus filled, R pm_3 missing, alveolus filled.
Caño Grande, Vaupés, Colombia (1)
FMNH 88252°, R m_2 missing, alveolus filled.
Rio Vaupés, opposite Tahuapunta, Vaupés, Colombia (2)
AMNH 78597 ♀, L m_2 missing, alveolus filled; L i^1 missing, alveolus filled. L c^1 carious, worn to gum line; R $pm^{3\text{-}4}$ absent, alveoli enlarged, confluent; remaining teeth greatly worn.

Saguinus bicolor ochraceus

Castanhal, Rio Yamundá, Brazil (4)

AMNH 94103 ♂, R c^1 missing, alveolus filled; L i^1 missing except for splinter in alveolus, remainder of alveolus filled; all cheek teeth glassy.

Serra do Espelho, Rio Amazonas, Brazil (2)

AMNH 94093 ♀, L c_1, L pm_4 with abscessed alveoli perforated laterally.

Saguinus bicolor martinsi

São Jose, Rio Jamundá, Brazil (2)

AMNH 94088 ♂, R pm_4 with abscessed alveolus perforated laterally.

Saguinus oedipus geoffroyi

Chiva Chiva, Canal Zone, Panamá (4)

USNM 302471 ♂, R $i_{1\text{-}2}$, L i_2 stubs, probably accidentally broken after fully erupted and polished through attrition; upper incisors hardly affected.

Casita Camp, Tacarcuna, Panamá (5)

USNM 310345 ♀, L c^1 missing, alveolus nearly completely filled; lower c normal.

Village Camp, Panamá (6)

USNM 310351 ♀, R c^1 carious, root exposed labially; L c_1 normal; L c^1 carious, alveolus intact; R c_1 half worn.

Quebrada Venado, Armila, Panamá (12)

USNM 335459 ♀, L pm_2 missing.

Río Chucunaque, Panamá (4)

USNM ♀, pm_2 missing, alveolus filled.

Río Paya, mouth, Panamá (8)

USNM 306841 ♂, L pm^4 missing, alveolus filled.

Gamboa, Canal Zone, Panamá (11)

USNM 301390 ♂, R c^1 eroded to gingiva; L c^1 half-destroyed from caries and worn smooth.

Coco Plantation, Canal Zone, Panamá (3)

USNM 301655 ♂, R c^1 destroyed and worn to base; L c_1 wear pattern abnormal.

Pedro Miguel, Canal Zone, Panamá (6)

USNM 301395 ♂, R c^1 carious.

Paraíso, Canal Zone, Panamá (2)

USNM 301396 ♀, asymmetrical arch; L upper c-m2 displaced forward; L c_1 occluding distolingually to L c^1; diastema between L c^1 i^2 unoccupied during occlusion; R c occlusion normal; diastema between R c^1 i^2 occupied by R c_1 in occlusion.

USNM 301397 ♀, L c_1 destroyed to root by caries.

Cocoli, Canal Zone, Panamá (9)

USNM 301649 ♀, L c^1 destroyed to root by caries.

USNM 301650 ♂, $i^{1\text{-}1}$ reduced to stubs by caries; $i_{1\text{-}1}$ worn but not carious.

USNM 301658 ♀, (fig. V.31) asymmetrical arch; R upper c-m2 displaced forward; R c_1 occluding distolingually to R c^1; left canine with occlusion normal.

Summit Road, Canal Zone, Panamá (3)

USNM 302337 ♂ (fig. V.32C), Cusplike supernumerary with independent root coalesced to distolingual border of L pm^4; L c^1 eroded half down, mostly on mesiobuccal surface; remaining canines normal.

Armila, Quebrada Venado, San Blas, Panamá (10)

USNM 335462 ♂ (adult) (fig. V.33). Posterior portions of left upper and lower jaw missing, possibly shot away in infancy but now completely healed; pm^4, $m^{1\text{-}2}$ lost, teeth of lower jaw intact but superior portion of ramus including entire coronoid process lost, functional condylar process with makeshift condyle present, right upper and lower jaws and teeth normal.

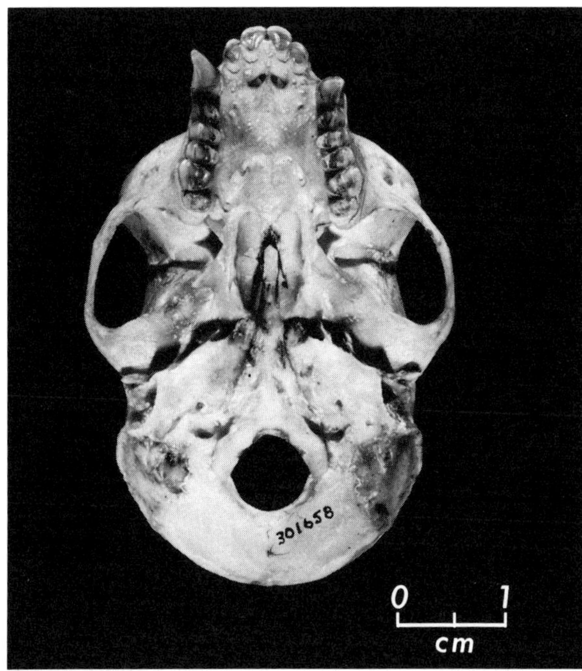

Fig. V.31. *Saguinus oedipus geoffroyi* (USNM 301658) adult ♀ (Canal Zone, Panamá): Arch asymmetrical, right toothrow displaced forward, the lower right canine occluding distolingually to right of upper canine; left canines with normal occlusion. (After Hershkovitz 1970*c*.)

Albrook Air Force Base, Canal Zone, Panamá (3)

FMNH 91373 ♂, R i^1 carious, broken at gum line.

Nuevo Emperador, Panamá (3)

USNM 302472 °, R c^1 reduced to stub by caries; R c_1 normal.

Madden Dam, Panamá (12)

USNM 301644 ♂, R m_1 outer posterior corner destroyed by caries but evidently healed.

USNM 301647 ♂, pm^4 and m^1 with bone between alveoli and outer wall destroyed, roots exposed; $m_{1\text{-}1}$ with outer posterior corner of each destroyed by caries.

USNM 301648 ♀, $i^{2\text{-}2}$ absent; R c^1 reduced to stub by caries.

USNM 302344 ♂, L c_1 reduced to stub by caries.

Fort Kobbe, Panamá (1)

USNM 297888 ♀, L c^1 half destroyed by caries; L c_1 equally worn but without sign of disease.

Unguía, Chocó, Colombia (13)

FMNH 69964 ♂, L pm^4 rotated about 40° forward exposing aveolus for small supernumerary lost during skull preparation; lower dentition normal.

Unguía, Chocó, Colombia (13)

FMNH 69959 ♂, L c_1 carious, alveolus abscessed, with large lateral perforation exposing root; R c^1 carious, worn to gum line; R c^1 carious, half-eroded on lingual surface.

Baudó, Chocó, Colombia (4)

FMNH 90319 ♂ very old (fig. V.30A,B), all upper teeth missing except very worn R pm^3 and RL $m^{1\text{-}2}$, alveoli not completely filled; R $i_{1\text{-}2}$ missing,

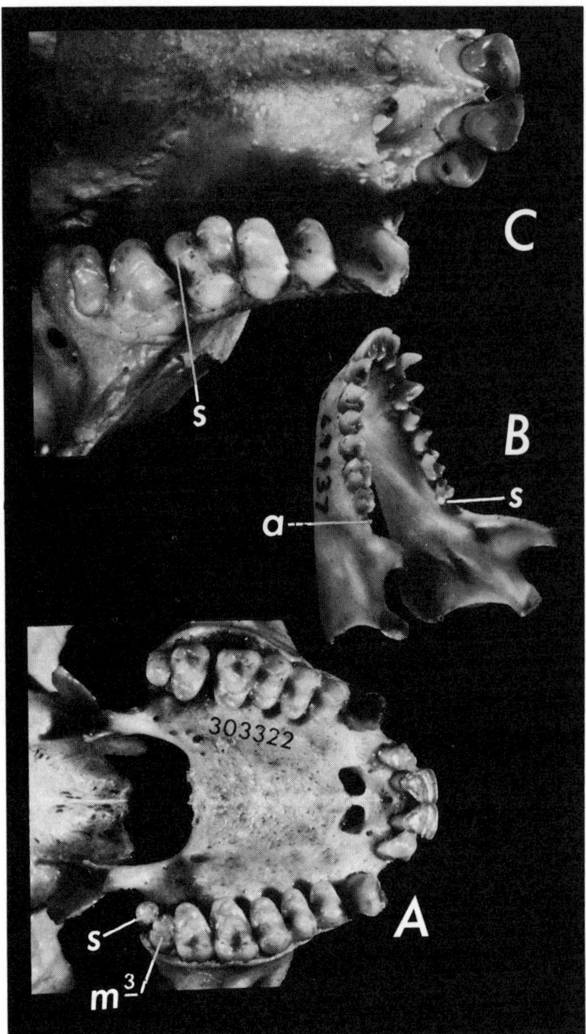

Fig. V.32. Supernumerary teeth (*s*), *A, Callimico goeldii* (USNM 303322) adult ♂ (no locality data): Supernumerary L m^4.

B, Saguinus oedipus oedipus (FMNH 69937), adult (Urabá, Antioquia, Colombia): Peglike supernumerary (or atavistic m^3) projecting from distolingual border of alveolus of R m_2; normal position of alveolus for m_3 shown by *a*.

C, Saguinus oedipus geoffroyi (USNM 302337), adult ♂ (Canal Zone, Panamá). Cusplike supernumerary with independent root coalesced to distolingual border of L pm^4; left canine half eroded, mostly on mesiobuccal surface; remaining teeth normal. (After Hershkovitz 1970*c*.)

alveoli filled; R $pm_{2\text{-}3}$ destroyed by caries; abscessed ramus excavated with perforation through alveolus of pm_3; L i_1 missing, alveolus filled; L i_2 and L c_1 carious; remaining teeth excessively worn.

Saguinus oedipus oedipus

Jaraquiel, Córdoba, Colombia (13)

CM 3615 ♂, $c^{1\text{-}1}$ carious; L $pm^{2\text{-}3}$ missing, alveoli filled; R pm^2 excessively worn; R pm^3 missing, alveolus destroyed; R m^1 missing, alveolus filled; L pm_3 carious; all lower teeth present, extremely worn, and widely spaced.

CM 3619 ♂, R c^1 destroyed to root by caries; R m^1 hollowed by caries; L m^1 carious, only outer shell present; L m_2 carious; L m_1 with cavity between hypoconid and metaconid.

San Juan Nepomuceno, Bolívar, Colombia (11)

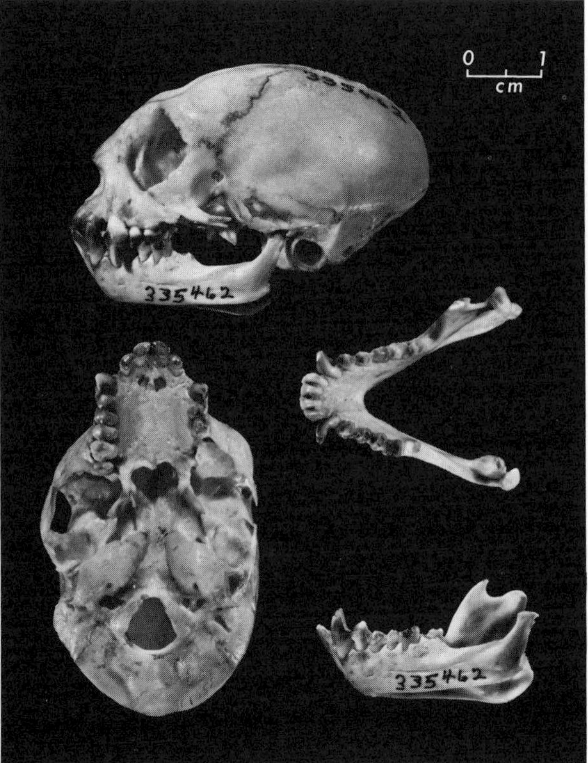

Fig. V.33. *Saguinus oedipus geoffroyi* (USNM 335462), adult ♂ (San Blas, Panamá): Missing bone of left upper and lower jaws possibly destroyed during infancy by gunshot, but now completely healed; pm^4, $m^{1\text{-}2}$ also lost, lower teeth intact but superior portion of left ramus including entire coronoid process lost, functional condylar process with makeshift condyle; right upper and lower jaws and teeth normal. (After Hershkovitz 1970*c*.)

FMNH 69271 ♂, L i^2 lost, alveolus completely filled; lower incisors normal; all teeth glassy.

Catival, Río San Jorge, Bolívar, Colombia (12)

FMNH 69302 ♂, L c^1 carious, terminal half lost.

FMNH 69306 ♀, R c^1 carious, tip lost.

Las Campanas, Colosó, Bolívar, Colombia (7)

FMNH 69294 ♀, R c^1 carious, tip lost.

Villa Arteaga, Urabá, Antioquia, Colombia (9)

FMNH 69937 ♀ (fig. V.32B). Peglike supernumerary (or atavistic) m_3 projecting from distolingual border of alveolus of R m_2 and reaching just below occlusal surface of m_2.

FMNH 69938 ♀, R c^1 carious, tip missing.

FMNH 69939 ♂, L c^1 carious, tip lost; palate and alveolar portion of maxillaries, particularly the left, distorted; all teeth out of line.

Socorré, Córdoba, Colombia (15)

FMNH 69286 ♀, R c_1 carious, tip missing.

Urabá, Río Curulao, Antioquia, Colombia (6)

FMNH 69943 ♀, R c_1 carious, tip missing.

No locality data (1)

FMNH 21866 ♂, R i^1, $pm^{4\text{-}4}$, $m^{1\text{-}2}$, glassy.

Saguinus labiatus labiatus

Rosarinho, Rio Madeira, Amazonas, Brazil (4)

AMNH 92779 ♀, Most upper and lower teeth abnormally worn, evidently eroded from disease; most affected: $i^{2\text{-}2}$, $c^{1\text{-}1}$, R $pm^{2\text{-}3}$, $m^{1\text{-}1}$, R m^2, $i_{1\text{-}1,\,2\text{-}2}$, R c_1 R pm_4, $m_{1\text{-}1,\,2\text{-}2}$.

Lago Miguel, Rosarinho, Rio Madeira, Amazonas, Brazil (2)

AMNH 92780 ♀, Upper cheek teeth glassy.

Saguinus mystax pileatus

Lago Tefé, Rio Amazonas, Brazil (3)

FMNH 78955 ♂, R m^2 missing, alveolus overfilled with spongy bone; R m^1 with outer cusps lost, alveolus enlarged.

Saguinus mystax mystax

Orosa, Loreto, Peru (13)

AMNH 74050 ♀, L m^2 with rudimentary hypocone.

Santa Cecilia, Loreto, Peru (14)

FMNH 86952 ♂, simple conelike supernumerary in lingual angle between R $m^{1\text{-}2}$ and coalesced with m^2; lower molars normal.

FMNH 86956 ♂, R i^2 geminate, inner member lost, probably during cleaning process, alveolar portion intact, smaller than outer alveolar portion; length of inner member may have been normal, judging by length and wear of lower incisors.

FMNH 86960 ♀, R m^1 missing, alveolus partly filled; $pm^{3\text{-}4}$ missing, alveoli filled; corresponding lower cheek teeth slightly less worn than remaining lowers.

Rio Yavarí Mirim, Loreto, Peru (3)

FMNH 88870 ♀, L c $\frac{1}{1}$ reduced to stubs by caries; L upper and lower cheek teeth eroded to gum lines, perhaps by caries; right tooth rows normal.

Saguinus mystax pluto

Ayapuá, Rio Purús, Brazil (8)

BM 27.8.11.1 ♂, m^1 normal but with buccal alveolar border perforated; $m^{2\text{-}2}$ roots exposed buccally.

Saguinus imperator

San Antonio, Rio Juruá, Brazil (3)

FMNH 50855 ♀, L m^2 glassy. Mandible with $m_{2\text{-}2}$ lost in preparation; respective alveoli extremely large and deep, the right 3.8 mm and left 3.9 mm, compared with range of 2.2–2.7 in 10 specimens at hand of same species and 2.7 in m_1 of same mandible. Last molar is normally double-rooted but with alveolus often undivided. Unless alveolus of each side is abnormally expanded, each contained a second molar at least half again larger than first, a unique condition; more likely, each alveolus housed two single-rooted molars, including vestigial m_3.

FMNH 50856 ♀, R pm^2 missing, alveolus filled; R m^1 abscessed; L m_2 missing, alveolus filled.

FMNH 50857 ♂, arch asymmetrical; R $pm^{3\text{-}3}$ displaced lingually; L pm^2 displaced bucally.

Madre de Dios, Río Manú, Altamira, Peru (2)

FMNH 98036 ♂, $c^{1\text{-}1}$ carious, tips destroyed; upper cheek teeth excessively worn and glassy.

Leontopithecus rosalia

No locality data (9)

AMNH 137279 °, L m^2 carious between paracone and metacone.

No locality data

FMNH 48356 ♀, L $pm^{2\text{-}3}$ missing, alveoli filled; L pm^4 diseased and nearly completely destroyed; L $m^{1\text{-}2}$ pitted; R m^2 pitted.

Callimico goeldii

No locality data

USNM 303322 ♂ (fig. V.32A), molariform supernumerary L m^4 on distolingual border of m^3, round crown differentiated from cervix but topography of occlusal surface poorly defined.

No locality data

USNM 303323 ♂, R pm_2 missing, superior surface of alveolus filled, lateral surface with large perforation; large maxillary vacuity behind each third molar, may be alveolus of undeveloped supernumerary molar.

No locality data

AMNH 183290 ♀, L c^1 tip carious; R m_2 missing, alveolus filled.

37 Teeth
6. Living New and Old World Haplorhines Compared

a = Platyrrhini
b = Catarrhini

1. *a.* Three premolars normally present in each jaw; last two upper premolars with occlusal surface ovate to rectangular (figs. IV.110–24; V.22).
   b. Two premolars normally present in each jaw; occlusal surface of last upper more or less round or square (figs. IV.125–44).
2. *a.* Upper premolars usually with 1 root, sometimes 2, rarely 3; lower premolars usually single-rooted, the first unspecialized (figs. IV.110–24).
   b. Upper premolars, except in *Homo,* usually with 3 roots, lower premolars usually with 2; in *Homo,* all premolars usually single-rooted; first lower premolar except in *Homo* sloped backward and specialized for honing upper canine (figs. IV.125–44).
3. *a.* Upper molars tritubercular (Callitrichidae [fig. V.22]), quadritubercular (Cebidae [figs. IV.110–124; V.22]), or intermediate (Callimiconidae [figs. V.19, 22]); major crest pattern basically triangular with protoloph (III′ + III″) and plagiocrista (IV′ + IV″) diverging from protocone (2) to mesiostyle (a) and metacone (4), respectively (figs. V.9, 21).
   b. Upper molars quadritubercular; crown pattern basically triangular as in 3*a* (Hylobatidae, Pongidae, Hominidae), or bilophodont with major crests more or less parallel, epicrista (II′) captured by diverted protoloph (III′) and extending from eocone (1) to protocone (2) and plagiocrista (IV″) captured by diverted entocrista (V) and extending from metacone (4) to hypocone (5) (Cercopithecidae) (figs. IV.125–38; V.15).
4. *a.* First molar larger to slightly smaller than second in upper or lower jaws.
   b. First upper molar larger or smaller than second, lower first molar subequal to or, usually, smaller than second.
5. *a.* Length of complete mandibular tooth row less than 60 mm.
   b. Length of complete mandibular tooth row more than 25 mm.
6. *a.* Lower third molar, if present, shorter than second (except in most individuals of *Alouatta*) (fig. IV.110–24).
   b. Lower third molar usually as long or longer than second (figs. IV.125–44).
7. *a.* Distostylid (hypoconulid, *b*) poorly developed, or undefined from hypoconid (*4*), postentoconulid (*e*) usually present (figs. IV.110–24; V.21).
   b. Distostylid (hypoconulid) generally well differentiated, often as large as hypoconid; postentoconulid present or absent (figs. IV.125–44, V.21).
8. *a.* Plagiocristid (IV″), if present, not more than rudimentary, entirely independent of posterior postentocristid (VIII″) and not dividing talonid into two basins (fig. V.21).
   b. Plagiocristid (IV″) always present in third molar, often in second, sometimes in first; normally contacting postentocristid (VIII″) and, in cercopithecines, dividing talonid into two basins (figs. IV.125–38; V.21).

38 Teeth
7. Living Platyrrhine Families Compared

a = Callitrichidae
b = Callimiconidae
c = Cebidae

1. *a*. Third molar normally absent in upper and lower jaws (fig. III.5).
   b. As in *c* below.
   c. Third molar normally present in upper and lower jaws.
2. *a*. First molar larger than second in upper and lower jaws (fig. III.5).
   b. As in *a* above.
   c. First upper and lower molars larger or smaller than second (figs. IV.110–24; V.22).
3. *a*. Upper molars tricuspid, hypocone (*5*) lacking.
   b. First upper molar, often second, quadricuspid, the hypocone a well-developed conule (fig. V.25).
   c. Upper molars quadricuspid, the hypocone a well developed cingular conule (*Saimiri*) or a fully developed coronal cusp coordinate in form and function with the primary cusps (figs. IV.110–24; V.14, 25).
4. *a*. Entoconid (*5*) of last molar (m_2) extending farther behind than hypoconid (*4*) (fig. V.26).
   b. Hypoconid (*4*) of last molar (m_3) extending farther behind than entoconid (*5*) (figs. V.26; XII.15).
   c. Posterior moiety of third molar (m_3) variable but never clearly or consistently as in *a* or *b*.
5. *a*. First upper premolar (pm^2) unicuspid (*1*) or bicuspid (*1* + *2*), its eocone (*1*, paracone) markedly higher than eocone of pm^4, and usually higher than eocone of pm^3 (figs. V.25, 27).
   b. First upper premolar bicuspid, its eocone relatively about as high or higher than eocone of pm^4 (figs. IV.25, 27).
   c. First upper premolar bicuspid, the eocone relatively as high as eocone of pm^4, never markedly higher (except in *Saimiri*), and often lower (figs. IV.110–24; V.25).
6. *a*. Unworn upper canine about twice as high as incisors and uniformly developed in males and females; lower canine like incisors, or conspicuously enlarged, like upper (figs. V.27; VII.5, 6).
   b. Upper canines as in *a* above, lower canine enlarged more or less like upper (figs. VII.5, 6).
   c. Canines enlarged, never like incisors, and often much larger in males than in females (figs. IV.110–24; V.27).
7. *a*. Lower incisors either spatulate with distal margin of lateral incisor obliquely truncate, distostylid (*b*) absent, or falciform with cuspule on distal margin (fig. V.23).
   b. Lower incisors spatulate with distal margin of lateral incisor obliquely truncate, distostylid (*b*) absent (fig. V. 23).
   c. Lower incisors as in *b* or with lateral incisor more or less entire, distostylid absent (figs. IV.110–24; V.23).
8. *a*. Metaconid (*2*) of $pm_{3\text{-}4}$ lower than protoconid (*1*) opposite (figs. V.19, 26, 27).
   b. Metaconid of $pm_{3\text{-}4}$ as high as or higher than protoconid opposite (figs. V.19, 26, 27).
   c. As in *a* or *b*.

Central Nervous System

Selected aspects of sense organs and topography of cerebral hemispheres are briefly treated here in terms of evolutionary trends, taxonomy and behavior. Most of the section was composed during the height of controversy over the systematic position of treeshrews. A large and convincing body of evidence for regarding tupaiids as aberrant insectivores and not primitive primates was adduced from studies of their visual and auditory systems. It seems that apart from basic adaptations to arboreal exercises common to most sylvan mammals, there is no basis for assuming that tupaiids evolved from the stem that gave rise to primates.

39 Vision

Binocularity

Orbits of the earliest primates must have been more nearly lateral than frontal in position with a correspondingly narrow range of binocularity, perhaps less than that of most tree squirrels. Frontolateral orientation of the orbits still persists in living lemuroids, but the trend toward full frontality, or binocularity, is well advanced in Old World monkeys and apes and fully achieved in man (figs. VI.1, 2). Frontality is particularly noteworthy among the more predatory forms of Carnivora. In the cat, for example, the binocular field is 130° in a total visual field of 287°. This compares with 140° and 180°, respectively, in man (Walls 1942).

Fovea Centralis

Visual acuity is sharpened by the fovea centralis, a depression of the central area of the retina present in the tarsier, platyrrhines (except *Aotus*) and catarrhines (fig. VI.3). The ocular fundus of lemuriforms, lorisiforms, and *Aotus* shows a poorly defined central area, but macula and fovea are absent in these (cf. Jones 1965) and all other mammals. A fovea, however, is present in teleost fishes, some snakes, and birds. Vision in these animals is superior to that of primates (cf. Walls 1942).

Macula Lutea

The macula lutea, or yellow spot, which extends across the fovea (fig. VI.3) and functions as an intraocular filter, seems to be peculiar to the Haplorhini (*Tarsius*, Platyrrhini [except *Aotus*] and Catarrhini). Distinct types of intraocular filters are present in other vertebrates.

Tapetum Lucidum

A tapetum lucidum is present in all nocturnal primates except *Aotus* (Rohen 1962, pp. 131, 141). The eyes of *Aotus* do not reflect light shone on them in the dark (personal experiments).

Retinal Rods and Cones

Earliest mammals are believed to have been nocturnal and, by implication, characterized by a pure rod retina comparable to that of living nocturnal mammals (cf. Polyak 1957, p. 869). It may be more realistic, however, to regard ancestral placentals as having been as much crepuscular as nocturnal. In this event, the retina could have been duplex (rod and cone) or, more likely, characterized by a generalized visual cell type that could evolve into the dominantly or pure rod retina of nocturnal mammals, the dominantly or pure cone retina of strictly diurnal mammals, or the duplex retina of mainly diurnal mammals (fig. VI.4). A duplex retina characterizes all diurnal primates, while a pure rod retina occurs in the crepuscular and nocturnal prosimians. The retina of *Aotus,* the only nocturnal form of higher primate, is duplex (Hamasaki 1967; Murray, Jones, and Murray 1973). Presumably, the ancestral haplorhine possessed the duplex retina that persists in platyrrhines and catarrhines. The ratio of one cone to one rod near the zona ciliaris of *Callithrix jacchus* (Marback and Costa 1962) may represent the ancestral platyrrhine pattern.

The *Tupaia* retina, examined histologically by Ordy and Keefe (1965, p. 394), reveals "a single row of cones distributed uniformly throughout." That of the crepuscular pen-tailed treeshrew (*Ptilocercus*) is composed entirely of rods (Clark 1959, p. 274). A pure cone retina is also present in diurnal squirrels, but other rodents, including the American flying squirrel, *Glaucomys volans,* possess a pure rod retina.

Retinal Centralization

Retinal centralization, as demonstrated by Rohen and Castenholz (1967), is greater in higher than in lower primates. In nocturnal prosimians lacking fovea centralis, there is little or no centralization—that is, transmission of nervous impulses through fewer, more individualized ganglionic cell elements in the central area rather than the peripheral. The retina of crepuscular and diurnal prosimians is more highly centralized, and the foveal region of diurnal platyrrhines and catarrhines shows the highest degree of centralization. Retina of the nocturnal

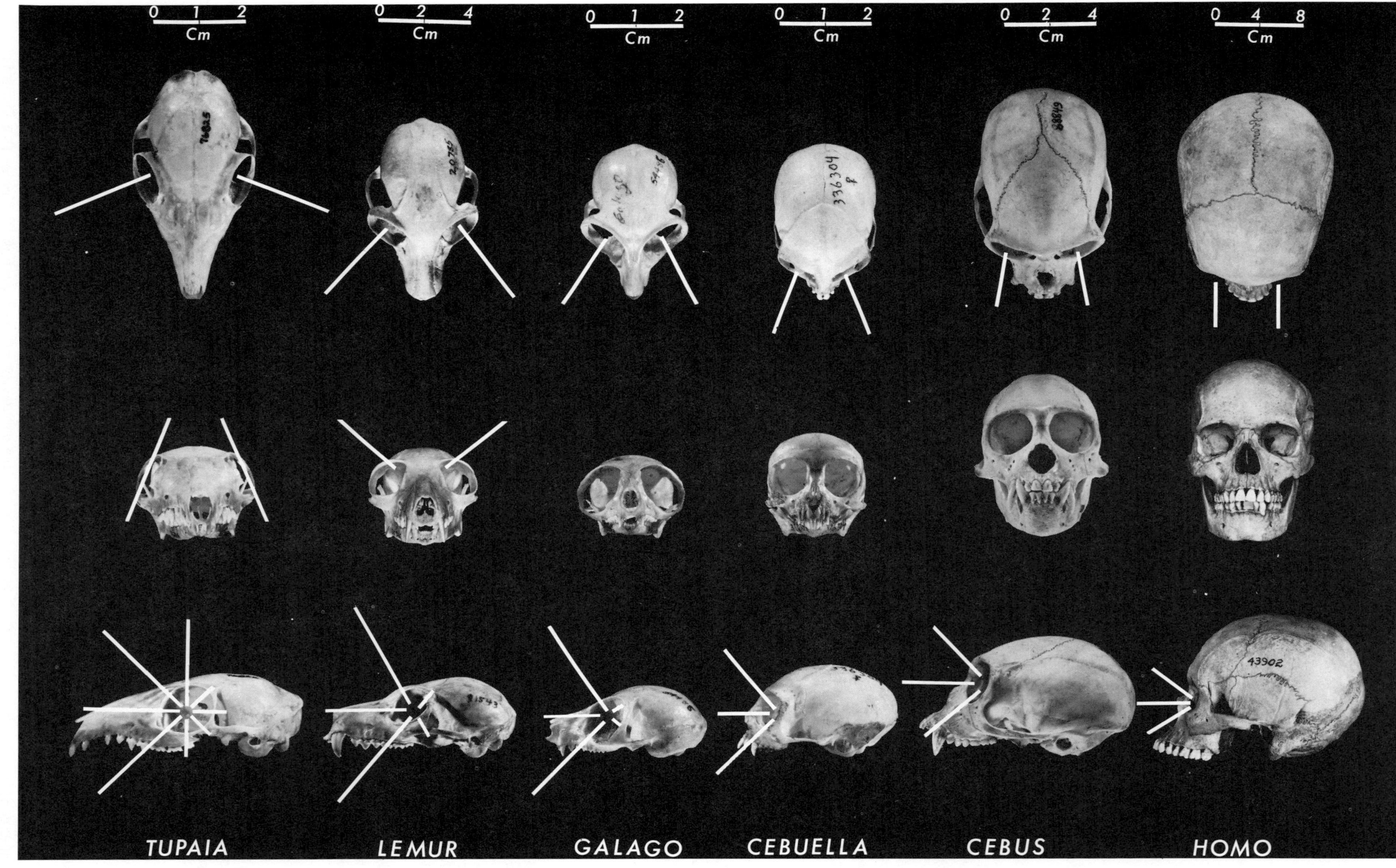

Fig. VI.1. Orbital positions with visual fields, a morphological series grading from the nearly lateral orbits combined with periscopic vision in *Tupaia* to the frontal position with binocular vision in *Homo*. Intermediate stages are represented by prosimians *Lemur, Galago,* and platyrrhines *Cebuella, Cebus.*

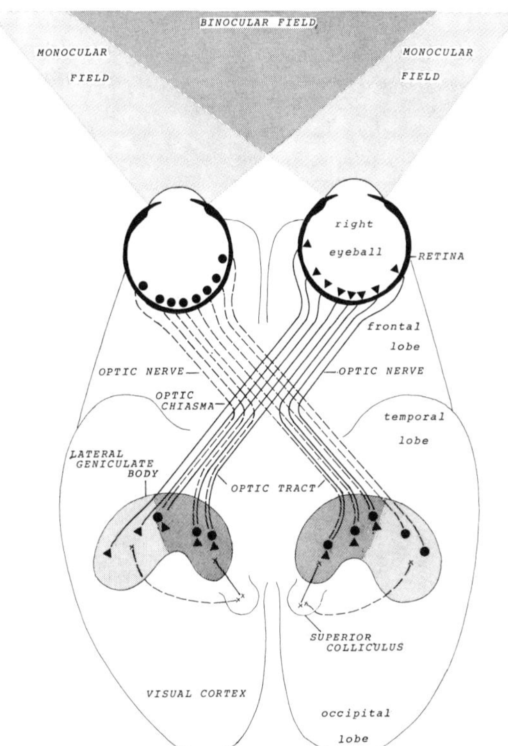

Fig. VI.2. Optic pathways in human shown in simplified form against an outline of the base of the cerebrum. The visual field of each eye is shown by shading; distribution in the brain of the light stimuli carried by nerve fibers from each eye is indicated by black dots and triangles. (Arranged from various sources.)

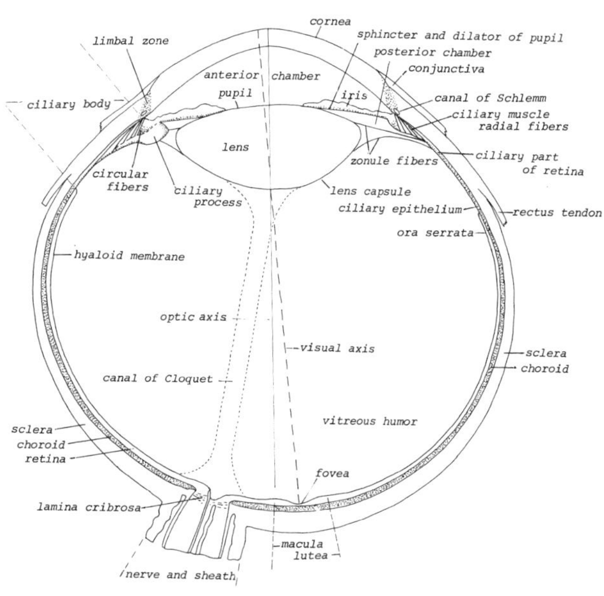

Fig. VI.3. Horizontal section of right human eye. (After Walls 1942.)

prosimian *Tarsius* is exceptional in possessing a well-developed fovea centralis but having a degree of centralization intermediate between that of nocturnal lemuroids and diurnal catarrhines. Retinal centralization in the nocturnal platyrrhine *Aotus* is like that of nocturnal prosimians. In tupaiids, the arealike region is in the temporal retina. According to Rohen and Castenholz (1967, p. 144) it "corresponds to the (probably small)

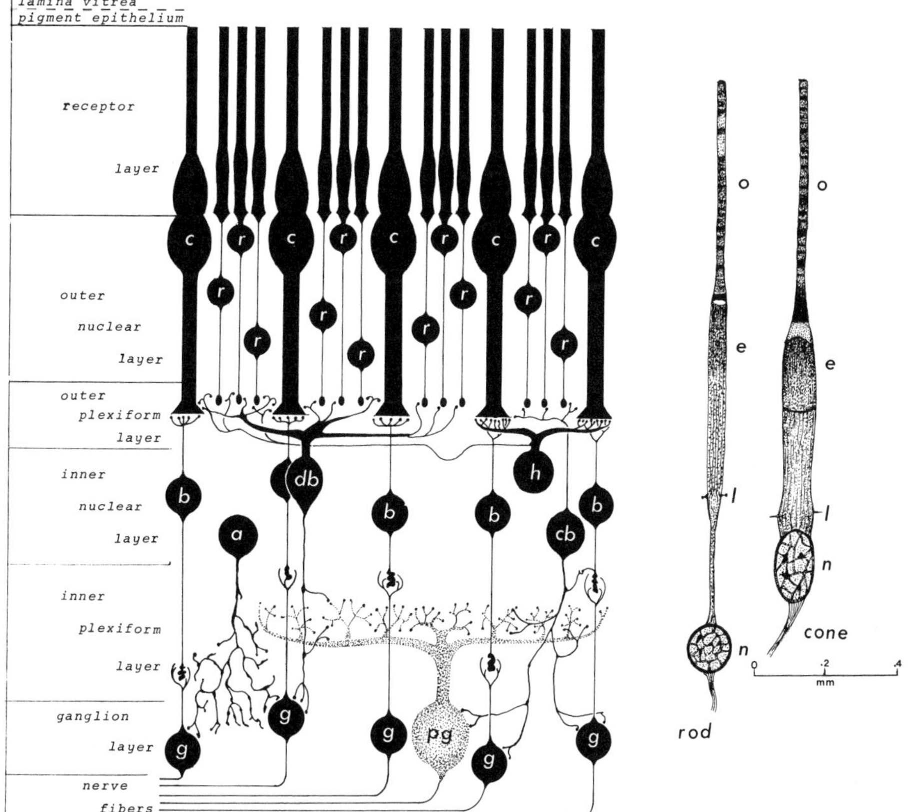

Fig. VI.4. "Wiring diagram" of human retina shows samples of principal elements revealed in section impregnated with silver by the Golgi method (from Walls 1932, based on Polyak; cf. Polyak 1957). Scale shown applies only to human rod and cone figured at right. Explanation of symbols: *a*, amacrine cell (diffuse type); *b*, bipolar cells (ordinary "midget" type); *c*, cone; *cb*, centrifugal bipolar cells; *db*, diffuse bipolar cells; *e*, ellipsoid; *g*, ganglion cells (ordinary "midget" type); *h*, horizontal cell; *l*, external limiting membrane; *m*, myoid; *n*, nucleus; *o*, outer segment; *pg*, parasol ganglion cell; *r*, rod.

Table 26. Optic Tract Fiber Supply to Laminae of Lateral Geniculate Nucleus

Species	*Laminae Receiving Contralateral Retinal Impulses*	*Laminae Receiving Ipsilateral Retinal Impulses*
Prosimians (*Tarsius*)	(1, 5)?	(2, 3)?
Prosimians (Lemuriforms and Lorisiforms)	1, 5	2, 4
Platyrrhines (*Callithrix*, *Aotus* [Jones 1966], *Saimiri* [apud Hassler 1966, p. 431])	1, 4	2, 3
Platyrrhines (cebids, including *Saimiri* [apud Doty, Glickstein, and Calvin 1966])	1, 4, 6	2, 3, 5
Catarrhines	1, 4, 6	2, 3, 5
Tupaiids (*Tupaia, Urogale;* fiber connections of laminae 3, 6, not clearly determined [cf. Glickstein 1967])	2, 4	1, 5

field of binocular vision, i.e., relatively far to the side, and cannot be compared with the central area region of the prosimiae." Wolin and Massopust (1967, p. 693) who examined the treeshrew eye by means of fundus photography, regard it as "certainly unlike that of any other primate we have observed."

Dorsal Lateral Geniculate Body

The cells of the dorsal geniculate body are disposed in 4 laminae in *Tarsius;* 4 in Callitrichidae (*Callithrix*), the marmosetlike cebid *Aotus,* and doubtfully in *Saimiri;* and 5 or 6 laminae in prosimians, Cebidae, and catarrhines (cf. Hassler 1966, p. 431). The lateral geniculate body is also laminated in Tupaia (5 or 6 laminae), seal (*Phoca*), porpoise (*Phocoena*), cat (*Felis*), dog (*Canis*), and possibly other mammals (cf. Campbell 1966). Laminae are absent in the Insectivora except *Tupaia* and *Elephantulus,* according to Hassler (1966, p. 431), who treats tupaiids as "subprimates."

In primates, nerve cells of the first two superficial laminae (1, 2) of the lateral geniculate nucleus are larger than those of the inner (3, 4) layers. In *Tupaia,* the cells of the two superficial layers do not differ significantly in size from those of the inner layers.

Optic-tract fiber supply to the laminae of the lateral geniculate body of primates and tupaiids follows distinct patterns (table 26). Each lamina is numbered according to its position from front or outermost (1) to last or deepest (5 or 6) (fig. VI.5). Sources of data include Campbell 1966; Glickstein, Calvin, and Doty 1966; Glickstein 1969; Hassler 1966; Noback and Moskowitz 1963. Agreement among the authorities is not complete. Table 26 reflects the consensus.

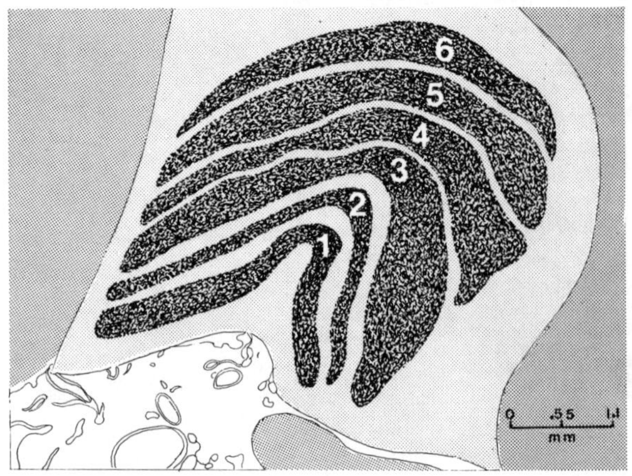

Fig. VI.5. Lateral geniculate nucleus of *Macaca mulatta;* diagrammatic representation of the six cellular layers. Each layer contains an independent map of one-half the visual fields. (After Glickstein 1969.)

Intergeniculate Nucleus

The primate intergeniculate nucleus bordering the lateral intergeniculate body is consistently present and composed of two parts, one with fiber bundles, the other without. Structure of the intergeniculate nucleus is uniform in *Tupaia* and *Urogale* (Hassler 1966, p. 419).

Pulvinar

The pulvinar as a caudodorsal outgrowth of the diencephalon is typical of primates. The structure is absent in tupaiids, but a lateral pulvinar may be present (Hassler 1966, p. 419).

Color Vision

Color vision, or reaction to spectral colors, characterizes all primates with diurnal, or mixed rod and cone, retina. The long-held view, expressed by Walls (1942, p. 688), that the cone of placental mammals "has no consequential capacity for color vision except in primates" is not tenable. Positive reaction to hues has been demonstrated in representatives of most orders of mammals (cf. Dücker 1965 for examples and bibliography). They include hedgehog (*Erinaceus europaeus*), treeshrews (Shriver and Noback 1967), many rodents, most notably ground squirrels (Crescitelli and Pollack 1965; Michael 1966), rabbits, many carnivores including the house cat, and many ungulates. Friedman (1967, p. 836), who found color vision in the nocturnal North American opossum (*Didelphis virginiana*), concluded that the capacity for color perception is a primitive mammalian character.

Nocturnal primates with rod retina and *Aotus* with duplex retina probably lack color perception (cf. Ehrlich and Calvin 1967). Crepuscular and diurnal forms of prosimians without macula and fovea may have some color sense. Mervis (1974) demonstrated trichromatic vision in the diurnal *Lemur catta.* Diurnal platyrrhines react to spectral hues and most may have a two-color visual system of the red-blind type (Easter and Nichols 1951; Miles 1958*a;* Dücker 1965; DeValois and Jacobs 1968), others may be trichromatic (Jacobs 1963, in Shriver and Noback 1967, p. 168). Catarrhines are more advanced, many with trichromatic vision as in man (Tigges 1963; Dücker 1965, p. 586; De Valois and Jacobs 1961). For additional information on color vision, see De Valois (1966) and de Rouk and Knight (1965).

Evolution of color vision could have provided the greatest impetus toward subordination of the olfactory system to the visual system.

Corticospinal Tract

The main corticospinal (pyramidal) tract in all primates occupies the *lateral* funiculus of the spinal cord and extends throughout its entire length. The tract in tupaiids (*Tupaia, Urogale*) is in the *dorsal* funiculus and extends to the midthoracic cord only; the tract in other Insectivora studied is in the *ventral* funiculus. Regarding the position of the corticospinal tract, Jane, Campbell, and Yashon (1965, p. 153) conclude that it may vary from order to order but "no instance of variation in position of the major crossed pyramidal tract has yet been described within the same order." (See also Campbell 1966; Verhaart 1966; Noback and Shriver 1966, p. 321.)

Axonal degeneration studied by the Nauta method in five specimens of *Saguinus oedipus oedipus,* by Shriver and Matzke (1965), was summarized as follows.

> In the spinal cord two pathways of degeneration occurred (large crossed lateral and small uncrossed lateral). The former tract extended throughout the length of the spinal cord, whereas the latter terminated at cervical levels. In this primitive monkey, descending cortical fibers influence the motor nuclei of the cranial and spinal nerves primarily, via internuncial neurons located in the brain stem reticular formation and in the base of the dorsal horn and zone intermedia of the spinal cord. The phylogenetically older "indirect" projections, characteristic of subprimate mammals, are supplemented very little by the phylogenetically newer "direct" projections to the motor nuclei, observed in higher monkeys, apes, and man.

Glabrous Skin Nerve Endings

Sensory nerve endings in the glabrous skin are distinguished as bulb or encapsulated and as Meissner or mucocutaneous (Winkelmann 1963; 1965). Encapsulated nerve endings of the surface dermis (lips, conjunctiva, palms, soles, digits, external genitalia, perineum) have been found in nonprimate mammals and only in the fulvous lemur (*Lemur macaco*) among primates. More deeply encapsulated endings in the panniculus, surrounding fascia, and along nerve trunks, known as Vater-Pacini corpuscles, occur in all mammals including primates. Meissner corpuscles have been found only in primates, and in the marsupial opossum (*Didelphis*) and kangaroo (*Megaleia*). The fulvous lemur appears to be the only animal with both Meissner and encapsulated nerve endings. Treeshrews, according to Winkelman (1963; 1965), lack Meissner corpuscles.

Platyrrhini and Catarrhini Compared

The platyrrhine visual apparatus resembles the catarrhine but is less highly evolved. The cells of the lateral geniculate nucleus in *Callithrix,* at least, among callitrichids and *Aotus,* at least, among cebids retain the primitive pattern of four laminae. Whether the mixed rod-cone retina without apparent fovea in the nocturnal *Aotus* is primitive or secondary has not yet been satisfactorily determined. The evidence suggests that it may be secondary. Absence of a tapetum lucidum in *Aotus* supports this view. The fovea in the diurnal *Callithrix jacchus* is imperfectly developed (Woollard 1926, p. 84), and probably structurally intermediate between the condition in ancestral and higher platyrrhines. Ostensibly, visual acuity and color perception may not be as well developed in callitrichids as in cebids, but the observed activity and visual acumen of the former do not support the assumption.

Experiments conducted by Spatz and Tigges (1972) by means of thermal lesions of the cortical visual field confirmed previous discoveries that in *Saimiri* a striate projection involved a single area of the ipsilateral prestriate belt; but in *Macaca* the striate projection extended onto two areas of the prestriate belt. The authors concluded that the organization of the visual system at the cortical level probably evolved independently in platyrrhines and catarrhines. The gross morphology of the optical and cortical visual areas in *Saimiri,* however, are peculiar, and their microscopical organization need not be representative of those of other platyrrhines.

40 Olfaction and Taste

Olfactory System

The olfactory system, designed for receiving and transmitting taste and smell signals, consists of two structurally and functionally separated but synergistic complexes. Receptors of the primary olfactory complex are located in the epithelial lining of the superior nasal chamber. Those of the accessory olfactory complex reside in paired blind tubes, the vomeronasal (Jacobson's) organs, one on each side of the septum in the ventral portion of the nasal cavity. The open end of each organ communicates with the oral cavity through the incisive (nasopalatine or Stenson's) canals.

Odors perceived in the upper nasal chamber are transmitted through synaptic connections to the olfactory bulb. Fibers from the olfactory bulb project to the lateral olfactory tract, their distribution limited to the anterior olfactory nucleus, piriform cortex, anterolateral part of the olfactory tubercle, and anterolateral part of the cortical amygdaloid nucleus (cf. Girgis 1970).

The small accessory olfactory bulb on the dorsomedian surface of the olfactory bulb receives the vomeronasal nerve from the vomeronasal organ and projects to the medial and cortical amygdaloid nuclei. Fibers from these lead to the anterior and medial hypothalamus and the ventromedial nucleus (Winans and Scalia 1970).

Accessory olfactory bulb and vomeronasal organ are present in all vertebrates, but they may be secondarily lost in some. Estes (1972, p. 316) hypothesized that the "mammalian vomeronasal organ functions primarily as a specialized chemoreceptor of excreted sex hormones and/or their breakdown products likely contained in urine. As such the organ is involved in the detection of estrus and in the release, control and coordination of sexual activity." Power and Winans (1975) demonstrated that in 10 of 26 male hamsters severing the vomeronasal nerves caused loss or severe curtailment of sexual behavior; but deafferentation of both the vomeronasal and olfactory complexes abolished sexual behavior in all test animals. The vomeronasal organ undoubtedly plays a similarly critical role in mediating the sexual behavior of all mammals with a functional accessory olfactory complex.

Dominance of the olfactory organs over other sense organs prevailed in primitive mammals and persists in most living forms including all primarily terrestrial species. Such animals are generally classified as "smell," or macrosmatic. Cetaceans and bats with reduced to obsolete olfactory organs are microsmatic or anosmatic. In these the auditory sense, used for self-orientation and location of objects, predominates over other senses. Sirenians and some pinnipeds are also microsmatic, but the functional relationships of their sense organs are not well understood.

Primates are moderately macrosmatic to microsmatic. The olfactory organs of long-muzzled mainly nocturnal or crepuscular strepsirhines are usually better developed than those of short-faced diurnal platyrrhines and catarrhines. However, the numerous and highly specialized cutaneous scent glands associated with marking in all prosimians and especially callitrichids among higher primates, indicate a well-developed olfactory sense in these forms.

The olfactory bulb of callitrichids is much smaller than that of prosimians but it still projects appreciably beyond the anterior plane of the frontal lobe of the cerebrum. The olfactory bulb is, as a rule, relatively as large or even larger in the nocturnal *Aotus;* it is reduced in larger cebids, and hardly or not at all visible from the dorsal surface of the hemispheres in *Lagothrix, Ateles,* and *Brachyteles.*

The accessory olfactory bulb according to Stephan (1965, p. 239; 1966, p. 383), is well developed in prosimians except *Indri,* present and usually well developed in platyrrhines, and nearly obsolete or absent in catarrhines. The vomeronasal organ is correspondingly vestigial or absent in all catarrhines including man.

Olfaction is clearly related to reproductive functions and thus to hypothalamic activity (Adey 1970). The sex-related olfactory signals are transmitted by cutaneous, genital and circumgenital glands and internal glandular products and wastes mixed with urine and vaginal secretions. Odors associated with sweat and feces are also important elements in social communication. Volatile odors are aspired into the upper nasal chamber. Lips, tongue, and digits carry odors of liquids and solids including secretions and excreta of the urogenital system into the oral cavity, whence they may be transmitted both to the uper nasal cavity and the vomeronasal organ. The aromatized tongue tip pressed against the openings of the incisive canals (fig. VII.14) may insure passage of odors to Jacobson's organ.

Odors are usually classified indifferently or arbitrarily according to the objects or organisms with which they are usually associated or the responses they stimulate. Odors known as pheromones used in social communication are discussed under the next heading.

Pheromones

Odors emitted by the organism serve for identification, spatial orientation, social organization, attraction, repulsion, arousal, and inhibition. Many odors become imprinted on receptors (cf. p. 100). The chemical substance or vapor released as an olfactory or taste signal by members of a group for reception and response by other members of the same group is a *pheromone*. A releaser pheromone stimulates an immediate and usually visible response. A primer pheromone triggers a series of events with the end result delayed and, in most cases, not directly connected to the prime stimulus. Any pheromone can act as either primer or releaser. The intensity of the signal and kind of response depends on the age, sex, genetic relationship, and social position of sender and receiver. Not all odors received or transmitted by an individual are pheromones, and a pheromone is not a pheromone when received by a different animal species.

Olfaction in primates is sometimes regarded as inferior to vision, at least for purposes of communication. This evaluation is based mainly on comparisons of the enormously expanded primate neopallium with the comparatively small extent of olfactory cortex, and the reduced area of olfactory epithelium. The short distance at which primates perceive pheromones, usually no more than one or two arms' length, compared with the long distances at which objects are visible and sounds audible, also contributes to the impression of the relative inferiority of the sense of smell. Odors, however, are pervasive, and many kinds persist and spread, albeit with loss of intensity, long after emission. In addition, perception, discrimination, and analysis of odors by the recipient depends more on the meaning of the message than on its chemical quality or intensity. In any case, a given sense can only be compared with the same sense in other individuals or species.

Marking

Marking is an instinctive or stereotyped form of olfactory signal broadcasting performed compusively by virtually all mammals with a well-developed sense of smell. The random dropping of feces and urine is the most elementary and highly effective form of marking. The same dropped in selected spots is more specialized, if not more elegant. Mixing the feces or urine with secretions of cutaneous glands or saliva is marking of a higher order. In the most advanced state, secretions of specialized glands alone are systematically dropped, daubed, or rubbed on trailways, special places, and objects.

Marking is used for the general purposes already mentioned in the discussion on pheromones. More specifically, it is used for spatial orientation, including identification of trails and territory, identification of self, group members, and objects within the home range, imprinting, and sexual arousing. The pervading or critical odor in an area, usually that of the dominant individual, attracts, orients, and binds members of the resident group and warns, possibly disorients, intimidates, or repels alien conspecifics. The prosimian and callitrichid method of marking by pressing and rubbing scent glands against branches, other objects, and individuals including self necessarily evolved in the arboreal niche, where feces, urine, and casually released scent droplets that might serve as signals are largely lost to the force of gravity.

Olfactory signals of any kind used by primates may also be used by predatory enemies.

The use of urine, feces, and secretions of cutaneous glands by prosimians and catarrhine monkeys and apes for marking and self-anointing has been described by Ilse (1955), J. J. Petter (1965), Marler (1965), A. Jolly (1966), Doyle, Pelletier, and Bekker (1967). Epple (1974) has reviewed the subject with particular reference to callitrichids. Details are given in the following family and species accounts.

Olfactory Testing

Olfactory signals indicating sexual and social status are tested by sniffing and tasting. Adult male monkeys and apes habitually sniff and lick female genitalia and often insert a finger into the vagina for collecting vaginal odors for self-stimulation. Testing has been observed in catarrhine monkeys (cf. Hall, Boelkins, and Goswell 1965; Rahaman and Parthasurathy (1969), chimpanzees (Lawick-Goodall 1968), and platyrrhines (personal observations, and others).

Sexual attraction of male primates by females through olfaction was tested by Michael and Keverne (1968, p. 746) with experimentally anosmic male rhesus monkeys. The animals showed no interest in estrogenated females until their olfaction was restored. The same authors (1970, p. 84) then discovered to their satisfaction what male monkeys and other mammals had long demonstrated to all and sundry, that the sex attractant pheromone was of vaginal origin. Finally, with Bonsell (1971, p. 964), they analyzed the chemical substances responsible for stimulating the males as short-chain aliphatic acids. The same findings were reported again under the recombined and augmented authorship of Curtis, Ballantine, Keverne, Bonsell, and Michael (1971).

Taste

Basic taste stimuli are defined as bitter (quinine-hydrochloride), sour (acetic acid), sweet (sucrose), and salty (sodium chloride). The continuous spectrum between these qualities provides for a multitude of taste sensations. Tastes are perceived by mammals through taste buds found primarily in the foliate, circumvallate, and fungiform papillae of the tongue. Taste buds also occur on the soft palate and posterior surface of the epiglottis.

Gustatory sensations of the anterior two-thirds of the tongue are carried through nerve fibers of the chorda tympani of the seventh cranial nerve. Those from the

Table 27. Values of Taste Thresholds in Mol/1 among Primates and *Tupaia*.

Species	*Sweet*	*Salt*	*Bitter*	*Sour*
Tupaia glis	1/60	1/4	1/2,560	1/240
Loris tardigradus	1/20	1/3	1/1,280	1/60
Nycticebus coucang	1/3	1/3	1/2,560	1/160
Galago senegalensis	1/15	1/60	1/2,560	1/240
Cebuella pygmaea (= *Callithrix pygmaea*)	1/30	1/30	1/1,280	1/160
Saguinus midas niger (= *Saguinus tamarin*)	1/15	1/15	1/20,480	1/240
Saimiri sciureus	1/160	1/15	1/1,280	1/120
Macaca mulatta	—	—	1/1,588	—
Chimpansee troglodytes	—	—	1/6,402	—
Homo sapiens	1/91	1/100	1/1,030,928	1/1,250

SOURCE: Glaser (1972, p. 272).

posterior portion of the tongue are transmitted through the glossopharyngeal nerve, and taste buds of the epiglottis are enervated by fibers of the vagus nerve.

Experiments for determining taste thresholds in primates led Glaser (1968; 1970*a, b;* 1972) to the presumption that stimulation of gustatory cells was triggered by mass effects of the substance rather than molecular effects as in some olfactory systems. Taste-organ capacities, Glasser concluded, were without phylogenetic significance (table 27).

41 Cerebral Hemispheres in Platyrrhines

Introduction

Enlargement of the cerebrum and its complication by fissuration is an outstanding characteristic of highest primates, most particularly prehensile-tailed cebids (except *Alouatta*) among platyrrhines, catarrhines generally, and apes and man signally. Gross cerebral morphology of cetaceans, however, surpasses that of highest primates, and that of tupaiids and primitive species of monotremes, marsupials, insectivores, colugos, edentates, and rodents compares with that of least-advanced species among living primates.

The rhinal sulcus of the temporal lobe is displaced inferiorly in most living primates. A comparable position of the rhinal sulcus obtains in tupaiids, echidna (Monotremata), many marsupials, some rodents and lagomorphs, and others (cf. Campbell 1966). The implied resemblance, however, may be misleading. The position of the primate rhinal sulcus reflects the allometric expansion of the neopallial cortex. Shifting of the rhinal sulcus in nonprimates obeys structural changes and accommodations not necessarily involved with reduction or subordination of olfactory cortex.

Expansion of the occipital lobe in higher primates, with overlap of the corpora quadrigemina and part to all of the cerebellum, is not matched in other phyletic lines. Nevertheless, a condition comparable to that of most prosimians and the more primitive platyrrhines occurs in tupaiids, some marsupials, carnivores, pinnipeds, rodents, cetaceans, and others.

Significant cerebral differences between primates and other mammals are less likely to appear in form and mass than in fine structural details, chemical composition, and function. Differences in fissural (and gyral) patterns, for example, appear to be quantitative to a certain point in mammals generally. Thereafter, each ordinal group is characterized by new fissures and complications of or new relationships between old fissures.

Cytoarchitecture

Cytoarchitectural studies of the common marmoset (*Callithrix jacchus*) brain (fig. VI.6) were made by Brodman (1909), Mott, Schuster, and Halliburton (1909), and by Peden and von Bonin (1947). It appeared to the latter that "differentiation in the cortex of Hapale [*Callithrix jacchus*] has proceeded farther than the habits and behavior of the animal would suggest." Peden and Von Bonin (1947, p. 56) summarized the broader results of their studies in the following terms.

1. The occipital region shows as high a differentiation as is generally found in primates. The striate area, too, shows the same laminar pattern as in higher primates.
2. An acoustic koniocortex on the supratemporal plane can be be recognized, but the para-acoustic cortex could not be identified.
3. The somesthetic cortex is poorly differentiated.
4. The precentral motor cortex consists of a motor and premotor area and resembles in its cytoarchitecture the homologous areas in other primates.
5. The fronto-parietal operculum bears 2 distinct areas, the anterior of which is considered as the homologon of Broca's area in man.
6. The prefrontal region is poorly differentiated, only a large-celled area on the lateral side and a distinctive orbital formation can be separated from the rest of the frontal cortex.
7. The parietal and temporal regions show an areal differentiation somewhat simpler than that found in higher primates, but conforming in their topography to the general primate type.
8. In the limbic region there is a large posterior limbic area. The anterior limbic area is comparatively small and the retrosplenial formation restricted.

Study of Endocasts

Cerebral fissural patterns or sulcal patterns, as determined from plastic endocranial casts, add an important dimension to taxonomic and phylogenetic studies. Neurocranial endocasts produced by synthetic rubber materials provide finely detailed replicas of the surface configuration of the undisturbed brain (fig. VI.7). The ease and simplicity of endocasting permit neurological investigations of virtually every vertebrate, living or extinct, for which a skull or neurocranial fragment is available.

In the present study, the cerebral fissural pattern as reproduced on endocasts is determined for one or more species of each living platyrrhine genus. The arrangement

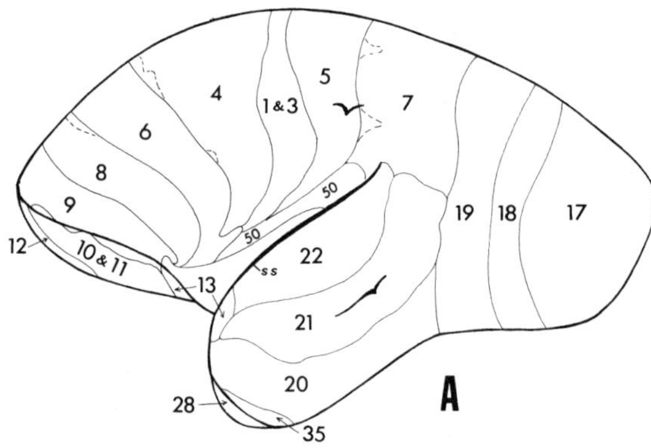

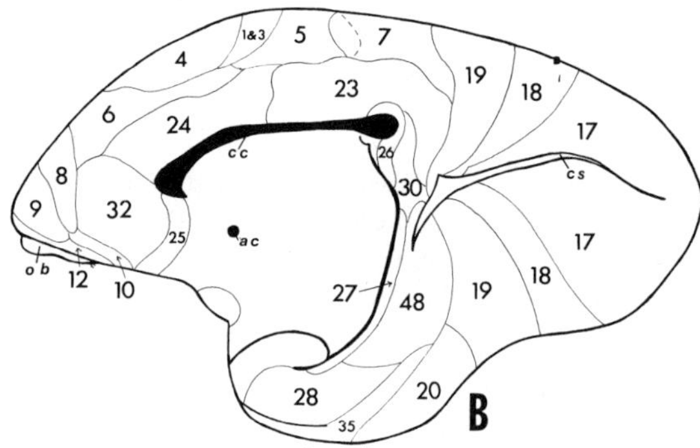

Fig. VI.6. Cytoarchitectural pattern of the cerebral cortex of the common marmoset (*Callithrix jacchus*) according to Brodman (1909, p. 161). *A*, lateral view of left hemisphere; *B*, medial view of right hemisphere; names of CORTICAL REGIONS capitalized, cortical areas numbered; numbers in brackets [ ] are of areas undefined in the marmoset but defined in *Cercopithecus* or *Homo;* broken lines delimit overlap between areas.

POSTCENTRALIS

- *1–3*. Postcentralis
  [*Cercopithecus*: postcentralis intermedia, *1;* postcentralis caudalis, *2;* postcentralis oralis, *3*]

PRECENTRALIS

- *4*. Gigantopyramidalis
- *6*. Frontalis agranularis

FRONTALIS

- *8*. Frontalis intermedia
- *9*. Frontalis granularis
- *10*. Orbitalis externa
- [*11*. Orbitalis interna (*Cercopithecus*)]
- *12*. Frontopolaris

PARIETALIS

- *5*. Preparietalis
- *7*. Parietalis
- [*39*. Angularis (*Homo*)]
- [*40*. Supramarginalis (*Homo*)]

TEMPORALIS

- *20*. Temporalis inferior
- *21*. Temporalis media
- *22*. Temporalis superior
- [*36*. Ectorhinalis (*Homo*)]
- [*37*. Occipitotemporalis (*Homo*)]
- [*38*. Temporopolaris (*Homo*)]
- [*41*. Temporalis transversa interna (anterior) (*Homo*)]
- [*42*. Temporalis transversa externa (posterior) (*Homo*)]
- [*52*. Parainsularis (*Homo*)]

OCCIPITALIS

- *17*. Striata
- *18*. Occipitalis
- *19*. Preoccipitalis

CINGULARIS

- *23*. Cingularis posterior
- *24*. Cingularis anterior
- *25*. Subgenualis
- *32*. Area (the following are not homologues)
- [*32*. Prelimbica (*Cercopithecus*)]
- [*32*. Cingularis anterior dorsalis (*Homo*)]
- [*33*. Pregenualis (*Homo*)]

RETROSPLENIALIS

- *26*. Ectosplenialis
- *30*. Retrolimbica granularis
- [*29*. Retrolimbica granularis (*Lemur*)]

HIPPOCAMPICA

- *27*. Presubicularis
- *28*. Entorhinalis
- [*34*. Entorhinalis dorsalis (*Homo*)]
- *35*. Perirhinalis
- [*48*. Retrosubicularis (*Homo*)]

ABBREVIATIONS

ac = anterior commissure
cc = corpus callosum
cs = calcarine sulcus
ob = olfactory bulb
ss = Sylvian fissure

of the species in the order of increasing fissural complexity relates to the present systematic arrangement of platyrrhines based mainly on other morphological characters and confirms the validity of the generally accepted generic or subfamilial groupings. For the rest, cerebral characters clearly separate certain suspected parallel but sometimes confused lineages and help resolve difficult or controversial issues.

Methods

Casts were made of silicone rubber (Dow Corning Silastic RTV). The prepared liquid rubber is simply poured into the braincase of a hemisected skull with foramina previously plugged from the outside. Parting agents are unnecessary except perhaps for the inner ear apertures and the tentorium. The material sets within a few hours at room temperature and the hardened cast can then be released intact without damage to the skull. The impressions of cerebral fissures, gyri, and blood vessels of the inner surface of the braincase reproduce at least as clearly on the cast as they appear in most spirit-preserved brains. Powdered lampblack or rouge rubbed into depressions helps bring out relief (fig. VI.7). Repeated rinsing, blacking, and rubbing is recommended where fine discrimination is required. The hardened cast must be sprayed with transparent liquid plastic to prevent smudging or erasure of details delineated by the pigment. A label may be pressed into the open or outer side of the cast as it sets in the mold.

A method for endocasting the clean intact skull by pouring liquid latex through the foramen magnum and withdrawing the cured product through the same orifice is described by Radinsky (1968).

Material

This study is based on 60 endocranial hemicasts representing all genera and most species of recent New World monkeys of the suborder Platyrrhini. The specimens are

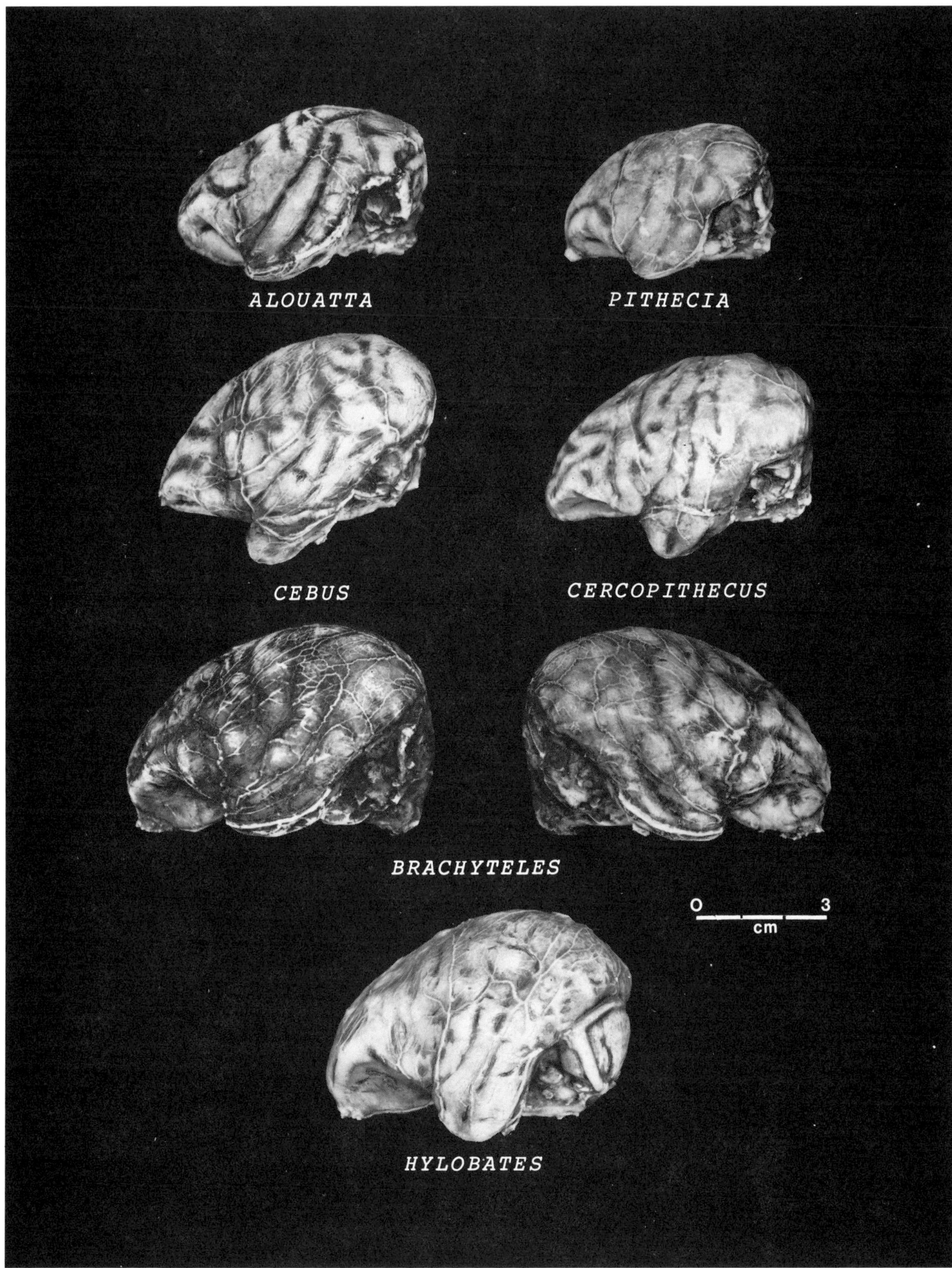

Fig. VI.7. Silicone rubber endocranial casts stained with lampblack to bring out relief. From top to bottom, right to left: *Alouatta seniculus* (FM 48007), *Pithecia monachus* (FM 25321), *Cebus nigrivittatus* (FM 95460), *Cercopithecus kolbi* (FM 17709), *Brachyteles arachnoides*, both halves (BM 3.9.4.4), *Hylobates moloch* (FM 46500). All natural size. Note small size of *Alouatta* hemisphere compared with that of smaller bodied *Cebus* (same cast was mislabeled *Callicebus moloch* by Hershkovitz 1970*b*, p. 214). The similarity between *Hylobates* and ateline endocasts is striking.

listed below. Hemicasts and holocasts representing all genera of living catarrhines and some prosimians were also prepared or were available for comparisons. In addition, a few spirit-preserved brains were examined, and published descriptions and illustrations of many more were used for reference. Platyrrhine endocasts and cra-

List of Platyrrhine Endocranial Hemicasts

Callitrichidae

54290	♀	*Cebuella pygmaea* [Ecuador: Napo-Pastaza, Río Copataza]
337321	♂	*Cebuella pygmaea* (2) USNM [Brazil: Amazonas, Tabatinga]
20419	♀	*Callithrix jacchus jacchus* (2) [Brazil: Bahia]
20738	♂	*Callithrix jacchus penicillata* [Brazil: Minas Gerais, Rio das Velhas]
92178	♀	*Callithrix argentata argentata* [Brazil: Pará, Rio Tapajóz]
50825	♂	*Callithrix humeralifer chrysoleuca* (2) [Brazil: Amazonas, Lago do Baptista]
73392	♂	*Saguinus fuscicollis lagonotus* (2) AMNH [Ecuador: Napo-Pastaza, Boca Río Curaray]
41487	♂	*Saguinus fuscicollis lagonotus* (2) [Ecuador: Napo-Pastaza, Montalvo, Río Bobonaza]
65670	♂	*Saguinus fuscicollis weddelli* (2) [Peru: Cusco, Hacienda Cadena]
86951	♂	*Saguinus mystax mystax* (2) [Peru: Loreto, Santa Cecilia, Río Manití]
86962	♂	*Saguinus mystax mystax* (2) [Peru: Loreto, Santa Cecilia, Río Manití]
50856	♀	*Saguinus imperator* (2) [Brazil: Amazonas, Santo Antonio Rio Eirú]
46190	♂	*Saguinus midas midas* [Guyana: Essequibo, Essequibo River]
79419	♂	*Saguinus inustus* AMNH [Brazil: Amazonas, Río Javanari]
94105	♂	*Saguinus bicolor ochraceus* AMNH [Brazil: Amazonas, Castanhal, Rio Yamundá]
69932	♀	*Saguinus leucopus* [Colombia: Antioquia, Purí]
69308	♀	*Saguinus oedipus oedipus* [Colombia: Córdoba, Catival, upper Río San Jorge]
69314	♂	*Saguinus oedipus oedipus* [Colombia: Córdoba, Catival, upper Río San Jorge]
137273		*Leontopithecus rosalia rosalia* (2) AMNH [no locality data]

Callimiconidae

98034	♂	*Callimico goeldii* (2) [Peru: Madre de Dios, Altamira, 400 meters]
98281	♀	*Callimico goeldii* (2) AMNH [Peru: Loreto, Río Tapiche]

Cebidae

25345	♂	*Aotus trivirgatus* [Peru: Huánuco, Tingo María]
84228	♂	*Aotus trivirgatus* (2) [Peru: Cusco, Cosñipata]
25338	♂	*Callicebus moloch* [Peru: Huánuco, Tingo María]
25339	♂	*Callicebus moloch* (2) [Peru: Huánuco, Tingo María]
50878	♂	*Saimiri sciureus* [Brazil: Amazonas, Lago Grande, Rio Juruá]
70659	♂	*Saimiri sciureus* [Colombia: Caquetá, Tres Troncos, Río Caquetá]
93240	♂	*Saimiri sciureus* [Suriname: Kaiserberg Airstrip]
25321	♂	*Pithecia monachus* [Peru: Huánuco, Río Pachitea]
87002	♂	*Pithecia monachus* [Peru: Loreto, Santa Cecilia, Río Manití]
46178	♀	*Chiropotes satanas* (2) [Guyana: Essequibo, Essequibo River]
88815	♂	*Cacajao rubicundus* [Peru: Loreto, Quebrada Esperanza]
88816	♂	*Cacajao rubicundus* [Peru: Loreto, Quebrada Esperanza]
31093	♂	*Alouatta seniculus* [Peru: Loreto, lower Río Napo]
87794	♂	*Alouatta seniculus* [Colombia: Meta, Los Micos]
48007	♂	*Alouatta palliata* [Honduras: Lago Ticamayo, near San Pedro]
22195	♂	*Cebus albifrons* [Venezuela: Perijá, Río Cogollo]
95460	♂	*Cebus nigrivittatus* [Suriname: Nickerie, West River]
34354	♂	*Cebus apella* [Bolivia: Santa Cruz, Buenavista]
87851	♂	*Cebus apella* [Colombia: Meta, Río Guapaya]
41496	♀	*Lagothrix lagothricha* [Ecuador: Napo-Pastaza, Montalvo, Río Bobonaza]
49343	♀	*Ateles paniscus* [No locality data]
68820	♂	*Ateles paniscus* [Colombia: Córdoba, Catival, upper Río San Jorge]
3.9.4.4	♂	*Brachyteles arachnoides* (2) BM [Brazil: Espírito Santo, Engenheiro Reeve]

nial and external body measurements are from specimens in the collections of the Field Museum of Natural History, except as noted.

Each item listed represents one cerebral hemisphere, usually the left. Where both hemispheres are represented, the figure 2, in parentheses, follows the name of the specimen. The provenance of each specimen is shown in brackets.

Fissural Terminology

Fissures, or sulci, of the lateral and dorsal surfaces of the platyrrhine cerebral hemispheres are identified by number and by name. The number corresponds to the phylogenetic order in which each fissure is believed to appear at the surface. Names used for fissures are taken, with slight modifications, from Elliot Smith (1902), Papez (1929), and Connolly (1950). Reference is also made to Kreiner (1968), who assayed a homologization of the fissural and gyral patterns of the cerebra of the dog (*Canis familiaris*), and "monkeys *Macacus cynomulgus* [?*Papio*] and *Macaca mulatta*." Terms used by these authors are indicated by the initials S, P, C, and K. Numbers used for fissures by Papez (P) and Kreiner (K), are included.

In plotting fissural patterns, the presence of a sulcus of high order in the cerebrum presupposes the existence of all sulci of lower orders. With few exceptions, it is possible to detect in endocasts all superficial fissures predictably present in the cerebral hemispheres. The phylogenetic order in which fissures 1 to 26 appear on the outer and upper surfaces of platyrrhine hemispheres are listed below. Fissures 27 to 29 are present in *Macaca* and other catarrhines, but their precise sequence following fissure 26 has not been verified.

1. Posterior rhinal (S; P93), incisura temporalis of human anatomy; (K1).
2. Orbital (P17; K6), presylvian (S). Perhaps should follow rather than precede the sylvian.
3. Sylvian complex (S; P75; K28, 20).
4. Parallel, postsylvian, superior temporal (S; P69; K23, 24).
5. Rectus, inferior frontal (P7), rostral (S), principalis (K30, 32).
6. Intraparietal (P41; K50, 52), lateral (S).
7. Central (P1; K42), Rolando's (S).
8. Arcuate (S), inferior precentral (P3); (?K31 or 33).
9. Fronto-orbital (?K8).
10. Simian (S), Affenspalte (S, P65), lunate (C; K62).
11. Middle temporal (P71; K81, part), inferior temporal (S).
12. Middle occipital, lateral occipital (S), lateral calcarine (C); (?K60, part).
13. Inferior occipital (S; P77?; K59) [validity and ordinal position questionable].
14. Parieto-occipital (S), postlateral (S), transverse occipital (S); (P67); (?K60, part).
15. Superior occipital, parieto-occipital (P59); (?K58, part).
16. Superior precentral (S; P5); (K38, part, posterior portion).
17. Superior postcentral (P39; K49).
18. Middle frontal (P13); (K37, part, see also 25 below).
19. Superior frontal (S; P9); (K38, part; anterior portion).
20. Inferior temporal (P73); (?K81).
21. Paraoccipital (P55); (?K55); prelunate (C).
22. Angular (P49); (?K23, medial portion).
23. Transverse occipital (P67); (?K58).
24. Inferior postcentral (P37); (?K46).
25. Horizontal branch of arcuate, horizontal branch of precentral (C); (K37).
26. Superior subcentral (C); (?K33, see 8 above).
27. Subcentral anterior (C; *Macaca*).
28. Temporalis medius (K82; *Macaca*).
29. "Cryptosulcus on the ridge of the gyrus parietalis" (K22; *Macaca*).

Evolutionary Sequence and Serial Homology of Cerebral Fissures

Each outer side of the platyrrhine cerebral hemisphere exhibits 4 to 20-odd sulci, according to species. An arrangement of the brains by species (or genera) in the order of increasing size (table 28) reveals a corresponding increase in complexity, or fissuration. More significant, each successively more complex cerebrum exhibits all the fissures or sulci of the preceding cerebrum in addition to one or two others. Moving from the smallest and most simple platyrrhine brain, that of *Cebuella*, with only four fissures evident on the outer surface of each cerebral hemisphere, to the largest and most complex of the suborder (table 28), it is evident that each fissure arises in the same locus in the same sequence in all species. No fissure drops out, none is replaced, and a new or younger fissure does not appear on the surface of the brain before older ones of the series are established. The evolutionary grade of fissuration and, by implication, of corticalization, can be determined for each species by the number of its basic cerebral fissures and the extent of their respective branchings.

The first or oldest cerebral fissure, the rhinal (1), and possibly the second, or orbital (2), were already present in primitive mammals. The ancestral primate certainly possessed at least an indication of the Sylvian fissure (3). The prosimian fissural pattern progressed from the sylvian through all succeeding sulci to the fronto-orbital (9) and possibly as far as the parieto-occipital (14), if this sulcus and the topographically similar one of higher primates are homologous, as was suggested by Elliot Smith (1902, p. 369). The first 14 fissures, therefore, may be provisionally regarded as primary and homologous in all primates. Extra or secondary fissures are present in the largest prosimians, but these appear to be peculiar to the particular species or its phyletic line.

Complication of the platyrrhine cerebrum most likely began at the third or Sylvian fissure level and progressed through all succeeding sulci (4–14) and beyond, to the inferior temporal (20). Additional fissures, from 21 to 26, and possibly one or two more undetected in present material, appear to be complications characteristic of most prehensile-tailed cebids. The fissures are listed on this page in the apparent phylogenetic order of appearance on upper and outer surfaces of the cerebral hemispheres.

Brains of living catarrhines, compared with those of platyrrhines, are larger and more complicated. The fissural pattern of the most simple cerebrum, whether cercopithecine or colobine, includes all features of the *Cebus* or ateline brain plus those characteristic of a more advanced grade. Whatever the size and complexity of the catarrhine brain, its organization (fig. VI.12) is basically indistinguishable from that established by primitive prosimians and elaborated by platyrrhines.

Fissures of the median surface, absent in endocranial casts and not serially homologized in this study, include the calcarine, present in all primates, *Tupaia,* many if not most marsupials, and all higher orders of mammals (Elliot Smith 1902). The retrocalcarine or the postcalcarine sulcus of Elliot Smith (1902), a branch of the calcarine, is present in cebids, catarrhines (fig. VI.12), some carnivores, and pinnipeds. It appears to be absent in the more primitive living primates such as *Microcebus,* the smaller galagos, marmosets (*Cebuella, Callithrix* (fig. VI.6), and also the insectivore *Tupaia* (Le Gros Clark 1959, p. 242).

Fissural Homologization

Noback (1959, p. 24) argues that cerebral fissures that evolve independently in phyletic lines derived from comparatively smooth-brained ancestors cannot be homologous. It is recognized, nevertheless, that all chordate brains are homologous, and those of primitive mammals

Table 28. Lateral Cerebral Fissures in Platyrrhini, as Determined from Endocranial casts

Species	*Number of Specimens*	*Fissures Present by Number*	*Remarks*
Callitrichidae			
Cebuella pygmaea	3	1 2 3 4	
Callithrix jacchus	1	1 2 3 4	From literature
Callithrix jacchus	1	1 2 3 4 5	
Callithrix jacchus	1	1 2 3 4 5 6	
Callithrix argentata	1	1 2 3 4 5	
Callithrix humeralifer	2	1 2 3 4 5 6 7	= *C. humeralifer chrysoleuca*
Saguinus midas	1	1 2 3 4 5	
Saguinus imperator	2	1 2 3 4 5	
Saguinus mystax	2	1 2 3 4 5	
Saguinus mystax	2	1 2 3 4 5	
Saguinus inustus	1	1 2 3 4 5	
Saguinus leucopus	2	1 2 3 4 5	
Saguinus oedipus	1	1 2 3 4 5	
Saguinus bicolor	1	1 2 3 4 5	
Saguinus fuscicollis	1	1 2 3 4	= *S. f. lagonotus,* right hemisphere
Saguinus fuscicollis	1	1 2 3 4 5	= *S. f. lagonotus,* left hemisphere
Saguinus fuscicollis	2	1 2 3 4 5 6 7	= *S. f. weddelli*
Saguinus fuscicollis	2	1 2 3 4 5 6 7 8	= *S. f. lagonotus*
Leontopithecus rosalia	2	1 2 3 4 ?	
Callimiconidae			
Callimico goeldii	4	1 2 3 4 5 6	
Cebidae			
Aotus trivirgatus	3	1 2 3 4 5 6 7 8 9 10 11	
Callicebus moloch	3	1 2 3 4 5 6 7 8 9 10 11 12 13	
Saimiri sciureus	3	1 2 3 4 5 6 7 8 9 10 11 12 13 14	
Alouatta seniculus	2	1 2 3 4 5 6 7 8 9 10 11 12 — 14 15 16 17	
Alouatta palliata	1	1 2 3 4 5 6 7 8 9 10 11 12 — 14 15 16 17	
Pithecia monachus	1	1 2 3 4 5 6 7 8 9 (young adult)	
Pithecia monachus	1	1 2 3 4 5 6 7 8 9 10 11 12 13 14 15 16 17 18 (old adult)	
Cacajao rubicundus	2	1 2 3 4 5 6 7 8 9 10 11 12 13 14 — 16 17 18	
Chiropotes satanas	1	1 2 3 4 5 6 7 8 9 10 11 12 13 14 15 16 — —	
Chiropotes satanas	1	1 2 3 4 5 6 7 8 9 10 11 12 13 14 — — 17 18	
Cebus albifrons	1	1 2 3 4 5 6 7 8 9 10 11 12 13 14 15 16 17 18 19 — 21 22 23 24 25 26	
Cebus apella	2	1 2 3 4 5 6 7 8 9 10 11 12 13 14 15 16 17 18 — 20 21 22 — 24 25 26	
Cebus nigrivittatus	1	1 2 3 4 5 6 7 8 9 10 11 12 13 14 15 16 17 18 — — 21 — — — 25	
Lagothrix lagothricha	1	1 2 3 4 5 6 7 8 9 10 11 12 13 14 15 16 17 18 19 20	
Brachyteles arachnoides	2	1 2 3 4 5 6 7 8 9 10 11 12 13 14 15 16 17 18 19 20 21 22 — — 25 26	
Ateles paniscus	2	1 2 3 4 5 6 7 8 9 10 11 12 13 14 15 16 17 18 19 20 21 22 — — 25 26	

NOTE: Fissures are identified by numbers; see p. 353 for names. A dash indicates fissure presumed present but not certainly visible in cast.

have inherited the capacity to change in the same direction—that is, homologously. Similar structural modifications arising in the same loci, albeit in brains of mammalian orders evolving independently, are here regarded as serially homologous. When the same basic changes occur within closely related phyletic lines of Primates, the question is not one of homology but rather one of the evolutionary grade attained by the organism in which the homologous changes occurred.

Homologies of the more advanced fissures in platyrrhine and catarrhine cerebra are not always clear. Some confusion arises from use of the same or similar names for different fissures or different parts of the same fissures, particularly those of the arcuate (8) complex. As was mentioned above, there is also the probability that an advanced fissure (15 or higher) noted in one or more platyrrhine species is not homologous with a similar-appearing fissure in catarrhines, and vice versa. Indeed, there is every reason to expect that once all basic sulci and gyri are established in a given species further cerebral specialization may be expressed by the differentiation of one or more peculiar sulci and their corresponding gyri. The human brain is most complex, and use of this organ as a reference base has obscured not only the homologies but also the orderly sequence of fissuration in primates generally.

Cerebral Complexity and Mass

Greater cerebral complexity or fissuration is directly related to greater brain size and greater body mass in each phyletic line. The smallest of living primates, with smallest neurocranial capacities, are the lemuriform *Microcebus murinus,* the lorisoid *Galago minutus* G. Cuvier 1798 (= *G. demidovii* G. Fischer, 1808), the tarsier,

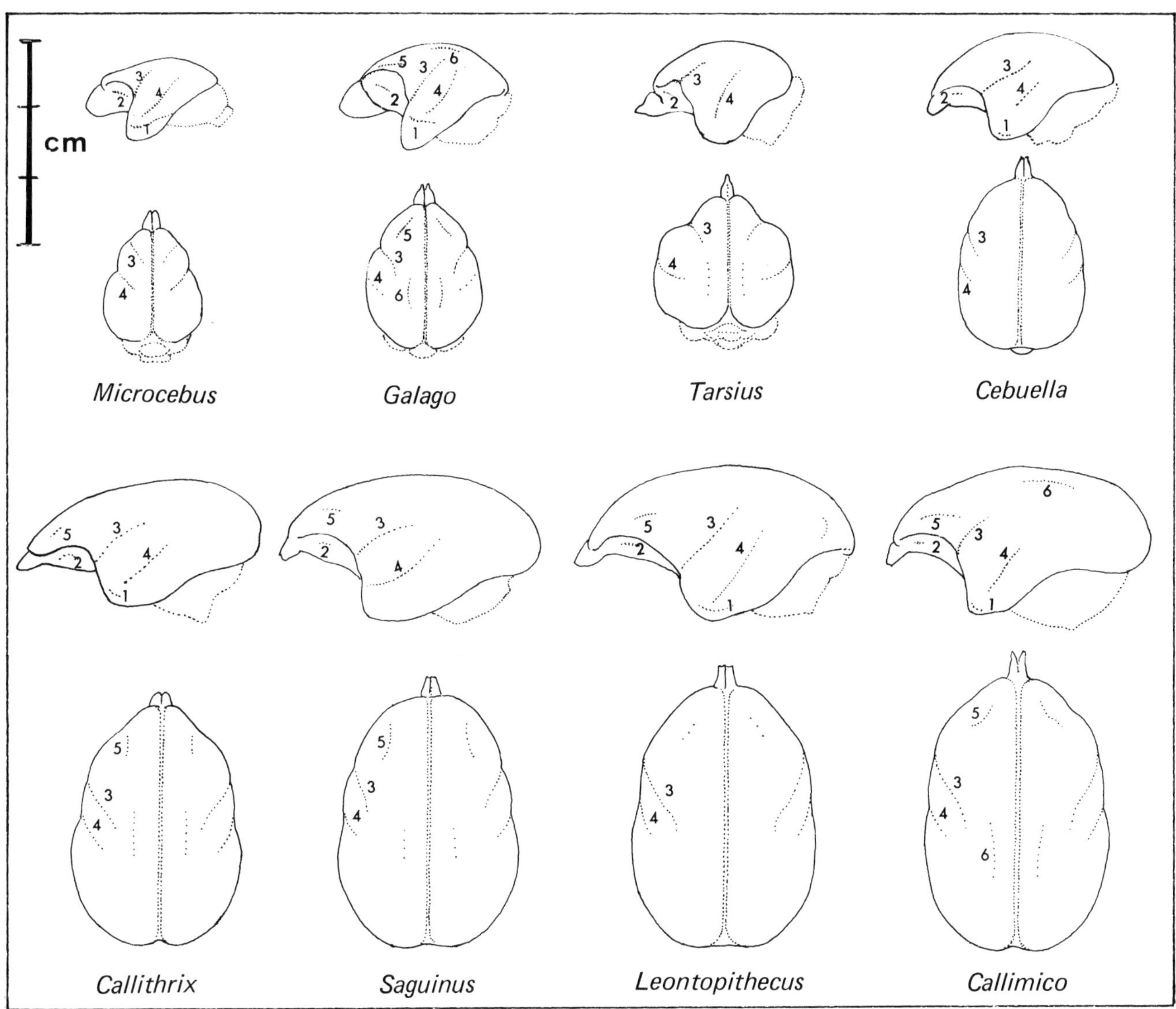

Fig. VI.8. Endocranial cerebral impressions (left and dorsal aspects) of smallest living prosimians (*Microcebus, Galago, Tarsius*), compared with endocranial cerebral casts of callitrichids (*Cebuella, Callithrix, Saguinus, Leontopithecus*) and *Callimico;* names of fissures on page 353. (After Hershkovitz 1970*b*.)

Tarsius syrichta, and the platyrrhine *Cebuella pygmaea.* Despite the disparity of their respective origins, their cerebra are astonishingly similar in form and, for their respective lineages, most simple in design (fig. VI.8, table 29).

The smallest and most primitive brain of living primates belongs to the mouse lemur, *Microcebus murinus* (fig. VI.8). The olfactory bulb of its oval-shaped cerebrum projects well beyond the frontal lobe and contributes considerably to brain (and neurocranial) length. The piriform portion of the temporal lobe is large and prominently exposed laterally, its upper border demarcated by a well-defined rhinal sulcus (1). The Sylvian fissure complex (3) is deep, but the postsylvian or parallel sulcus (4) is weakly defined. The frontal lobe is comparatively small. The occipital lobe is moderately enlarged, overlaps the midbrain, and extends to the anterior surface of the cerebellum. The olfactory bulb of larger lemuriform species is relatively smaller, the olfactory cortical area reduced and less exposed laterally, and the neopallial cortex more fissured and convoluted.

The tarsier cerebrum is considerably expanded, most notably in breadth, and is rounded in outline. The visual area of the occipital lobe is greatly enlarged and partially overlaps the cerebellum, while the frontal lobe rides the hind part of the olfactory bulb. The cerebral surface is nearly as smooth as that of *Microcebus,* but the Sylvian fissure (3) is better defined, and the parallel or postsylvian (4) is a shallow depression. For all its apparent simplicity, the tarsier brain is highly specialized and as advanced as any of its lineage.

The brain of the pygmy bush baby, *Galago minutus,* smallest of lorisoids, is significantly smaller than that of *Tarsius,* but slightly larger than that of *Microcebus* and about equal in mass to that of *Cebuella.* Nevertheless, its cerebral hemisphere, with 6 fissures, is more complex. The greater fissuration points less to a higher evolutionary grade, as compared with unrelated primates, than to a longer evolutionary history beginning with a considerably smaller ancestor with correspondingly smaller and less convoluted cerebrum.

The brain of the pygmy marmoset, *Cebuella pygmaea* (figs. VI.8, 9), is like that of *Galago minutus* in size but more similar to that of *Microcebus murinus* in organiza-

Table 29. Comparison of Body Size, Cranial Size, Brain Volume, and Fissuration

Species	*Head and Body Length*	*Greatest Skull Length*	*Braincase Length*	*Braincase Width*	*Braincase Volume* (cm^3)	*Lateral Cerebral Fissures*
Microcebus murinus	118	32.5	22.5	17.1	2	3–4
Galago minutus	129(121–37)7	36.2(35.4–37.3)7	26.9(25.9–27.8)6	19.0(17.9–19.7)7	2.7(2.4–3.0)6	6
Tarsius syrichta	103; 125	39.1; 39.6	32.0; 33.0	22.4; 24.5	3.5; 4.5	3–4
Cebuella pygmaea	137(120–52)42	35.8(33.7–38.9)61	30.9(28.3–32.8)62	21.1(20.0–22.9)61	4.8(4.0–5.0)19	4
Callithrix (spp.)	217(180–300)130	47.4(41.1–51.8)118	39.7(36.4–45.5)110	25.6(23.9–29.9)109	8.4(7.5–10.5)57	4–7
Saguinus (spp.)	243(200–300)336	50.4(45.1–55.7)548	43.5(38.2–49.3)494	27.0(24.3–30.1)533	10.0(8.0–12.0)102	4–8
Leontopithecus rosalia	261(200–336)17	56.5(53.6–59.8)13	47.3(46.3–49.4)10	28.4(27.5–29.3)13	12.8(12.0–15.0)12	4
Callimico goeldii	225(213–34)12	53.3(50.5–55.5)10	45.8(44.6–49.8)11	29.8(29.0–32.2)10	11.5(11.0–12.2)6	6

NOTE: The smallest living prosimians, *Microcebus, Galago,* and *Tarsius,* are compared with callitrichids (*Cebuella, Callithrix, Saguinus, Leontopithecus*), and *Callimico*. *Cebuella, Leontopithecus,* and *Callimico* are monotypic; measurements given for *Callithrix* and *Saguinus* represent all included species.
See text following table 30 for further explanation.

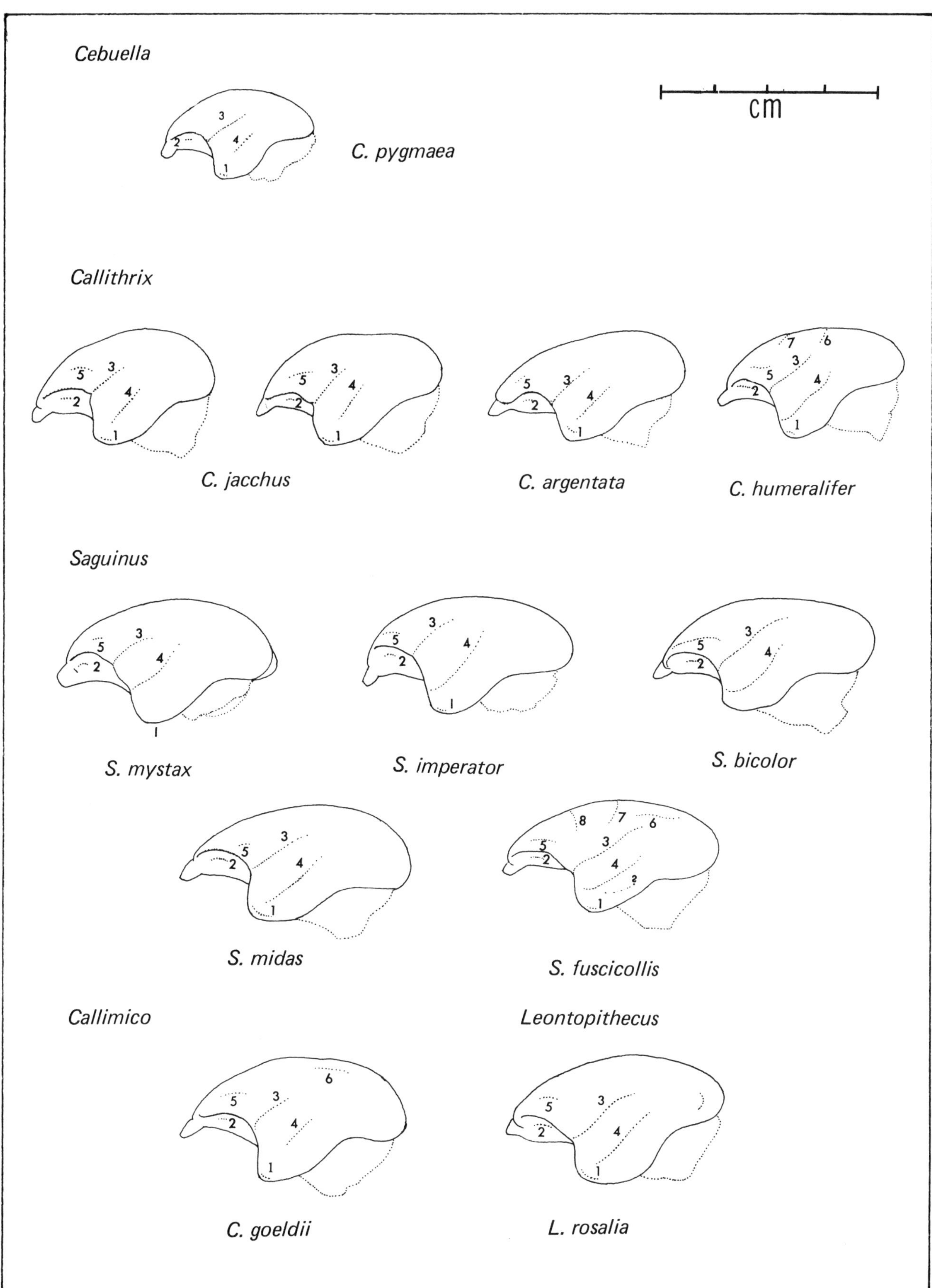

Fig. VI.9. Endocranial cerebral impressions (lateral aspects) of callitrichids and *Callimico;* names of fissures on page 353. (After Hershkovitz 1970*b*.)

tion. The ancestral platyrrhine brain may indeed have resembled the *Microcebus* brain in mass, form, and surface configuration. The *Cebuella* brain, however, is twice the bulk, with olfactory bulb and piriform lobe relatively smaller and less exposed superficially and the rhinal sulcus less defined. Progressive cerebral characters

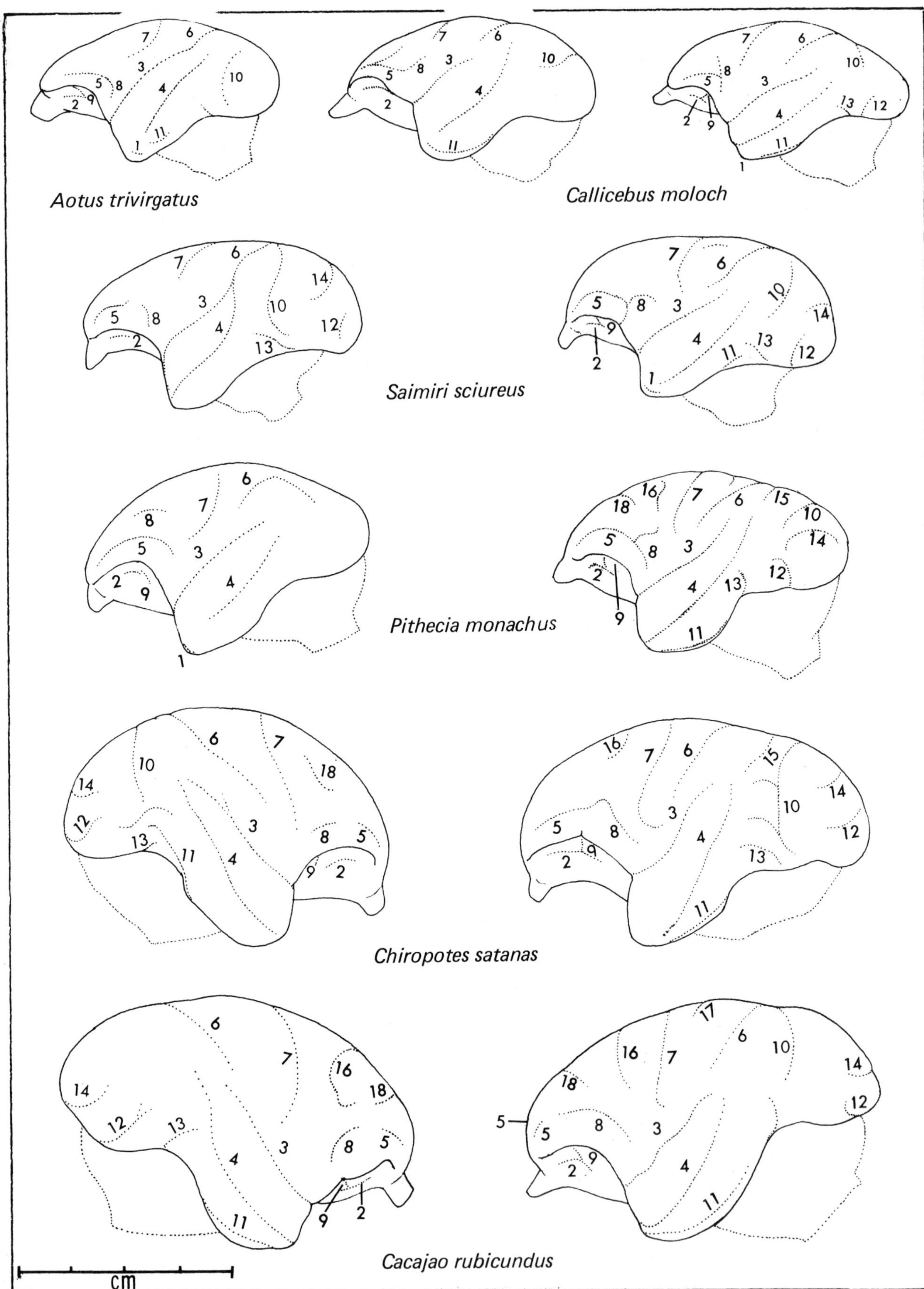

Fig. VI.10. Endocranial cerebral impressions (lateral aspects) of marmosetlike cebids (*Aotus, Callicebus, Saimiri*) and pithecines (*Pithecia, Chiropotes, Cacajao*); names of fissures on page 353. (After Hershkovitz 1970*b*.)

include a larger frontal lobe and the proportionally more expanded occipital lobe, with greater overlap of the dorsal cerebellar surface. As in *Microcebus,* and certainly in the hypothetical ancestral platyrrhine, the parallel sulcus (4) emerges as a weak cortical depression.

The typical marmoset or *Callithrix* brain (figs. VI.8, 9)

is considerably larger than that of *Cebuella* but only slightly more complicated. The parallel sulcus (4) is usually well defined, the rectus (5) and intraparietal (6) are present as shallow depressions in some individuals, and the central (7) is present in the single sample studied of *C. humeralifer chrysoleuca.* The olfactory and piriform lobes in all examples of *Callithrix* are more reduced than in *Cebuella,* and the frontal and occipital lobes are larger with the latter more overlapping posteriorly.

The surface of the tamarin, or *Saguinus* cerebrum (figs. VI.8, 9), ranges from comparatively uncomplicated, like that of any *Callithrix* with 4 or 5 sulci, to nearly as complex as those of the marmosetlike cebids. The cerebrum of *Saguinus oedipus,* often figured and described in texts as "the marmoset" brain, is fairly smooth with only the posterior rhinal (1), orbital (2), and Sylvian (3) distinct, the parallel (4) a shallow depression, and the rectus (5) no more than an indentation, if discernible at all. The fissural patterns of one left hemisphere of *S. inustus* and two of *leucopus,* both of the *S. oedipus* group, are similar. The same fissures are present but much better defined in a left hemisphere of *Saguinus fuscicollis lagonotus.* In other members of the same species, distinct furrows representing the intraparietal (6), central (7), and arcuate (8) are also present (table 28).

Leontopithecus rosalia (figs. VI.8, 9) is, overall, the most highly specialized callitrichid, but its cerebrum appears to be among the least specialized. Only 4 sulci are evident on each hemisphere of a single individual. The fissural pattern itself is no better defined than that of most *Callithrix* brains. The right hemisphere of *Leontopithecus* figured by Anthony (1946*a*, p. 8, fig. 2), shows a very small intraparietal (6) in addition to the Sylvian (3) and parallel (4) fissures. There is no indication or mention of the rectus (5). The left hemisphere of a second specimen figured by the same author (1948*a*) shows only the Sylvian fissure and a depression representing the parallel fissure.

The brain of *Callimico* (figs. VI.8, 9) averages larger than that of all callitrichids except *Leontopithecus,* but its cerebrum, with 6 fissures, seems to be more advanced than that of *Saguinus.*

Cerebra of the three genera of marmosetlike cebids (fig. VI.10) are comparatively uncomplicated, with olfactory areas well exposed. The cerebrum of *Aotus,* judged by two left hemispheres and one right, is least complicated and most callitrichid with respect to the extent of fissuration. The distinctly cebid lunate or simian (10) and middle temporal (11) fissures present in *Aotus,* however, mark the most significant advance over the callitrichid fissural pattern. The sulci are also deeper, and the occipital lobe is produced further behind than in most callitrichids, but the olfactory bulbs remain well developed.

The *Callicebus* cerebrum resembles that of *Aotus* but is slightly more complicated by the addition of occipital fissures 12 and 13.

The *Saimiri* brain, largest of the marmosetlike cebid group, is characterized by an occipital lobe which completely overlaps the cerebellum and is proportionately more extensive than that of any other primate except man. The cerebrum nevertheless remains surprisingly conservative with respect to its sulcal pattern. Only one small fissure, the parieto-occipital (14), appears as an addition to the others of its size class. Despite hypertrophy of the visual cortex, the *Saimiri* olfactory region remains well developed, with olfactory bulbs projecting anteriorly and piriform lobes exposed laterally.

Pithecines are widely separated from callitrichids and marmosetlike cebids, their brains (fig. VI.10) being considerably more massive and complicated. The fissural pattern varies from a nearly callitrichid simplicity, at least in young adults, to a nearly ateline complexity in mature animals. In one young adult of *Pithecia monachus* only 9 primary fissures are evident; in an old adult of the same species there are 18. Up to 18 fissures are also present in the remaining pithecine genera *Cacajao* and *Chiropotes.*

Prehensile-tailed cebids are collectively more advanced in cerebral organization (fig. VI.11) than the smaller platyrrhines (fig. VI.11). Howlers, genus *Alouatta,* most massive of prehensile-tailed cebids, are characterized by the smallest and least complicated brains, a trait already noted by Flower (1864, p. 335). Cerebral fissuration in the remaining prehensile-tailed cebids (*Cebus, Lagothrix, Ateles,* and *Brachyteles*) is approximately twice that of the marmosetlike cebids and up to nearly one-third more than in pithecines. The fissures are consistently deeper or better defined than in nonprehensile-tailed cebids, the olfactory lobe more reduced and nearly or quite entirely hidden by the expanded frontal lobe in *Lagothrix, Ateles,* and *Brachyteles,* and the piriform lobe and rhinal sulcus completely displaced ventrad by the expanded temporal lobe and hidden from the lateral aspect of the cerebrum. Progressively, from *Alouatta* through *Cebus* and *Lagothrix* to *Ateles* and *Brachyteles,* the cerebral orbital cavity becomes more deeply excavated, its medial surface expanded and more sharply defined from the superior surface, while the orbital fissure becomes correspondingly deeper and more complex.

In summary, the fronto-orbital (9), the lunate or simian (10), and following fissures are absent in our samples of callitrichids, but present in all cebids. The marmosetlike cebids attain 14 fissures, pithecines at least 18. The prehensile-tailed *Cebus* and atelines have 20 or more sulci with the largest, most highly developed and most fissurated brain belonging to the long-limbed, brachiating, prehensile-tailed spider monkeys *Ateles* and *Brachyteles.* Howlers are unique among prehensile-tailed cebids in the comparatively small size and simplicity of their brains, with fewer than 20 fissures in the 3 specimens examined.

Fissural patterns of the lateral and medial surfaces of platyrrhine hemispheres grade into those of catarrhines (fig. VI.12).

Sylvian and Intraparietal Fissural Patterns

In most primates, the Sylvian (3), parallel (4), and intraparietal (6) fissures are each distinct and separate, at least superficially. This relationship may be indicated by the formula *s-i-p* (fig. VI.13a). In others, Sylvian and parallel meet and the intraparietal is free, the formula here being *sp-i* (fig. VI.13b). In still others, Sylvian and intraparietal fissures are superficially confluent and the parallel remains distinct. This pattern, the sylviointraparietal complex of Elliot Smith (1902) is represented by the formula *si-p* (fig. VI.13c). Finally, all three fissures may be confluent and indicated by *sip* (fig.

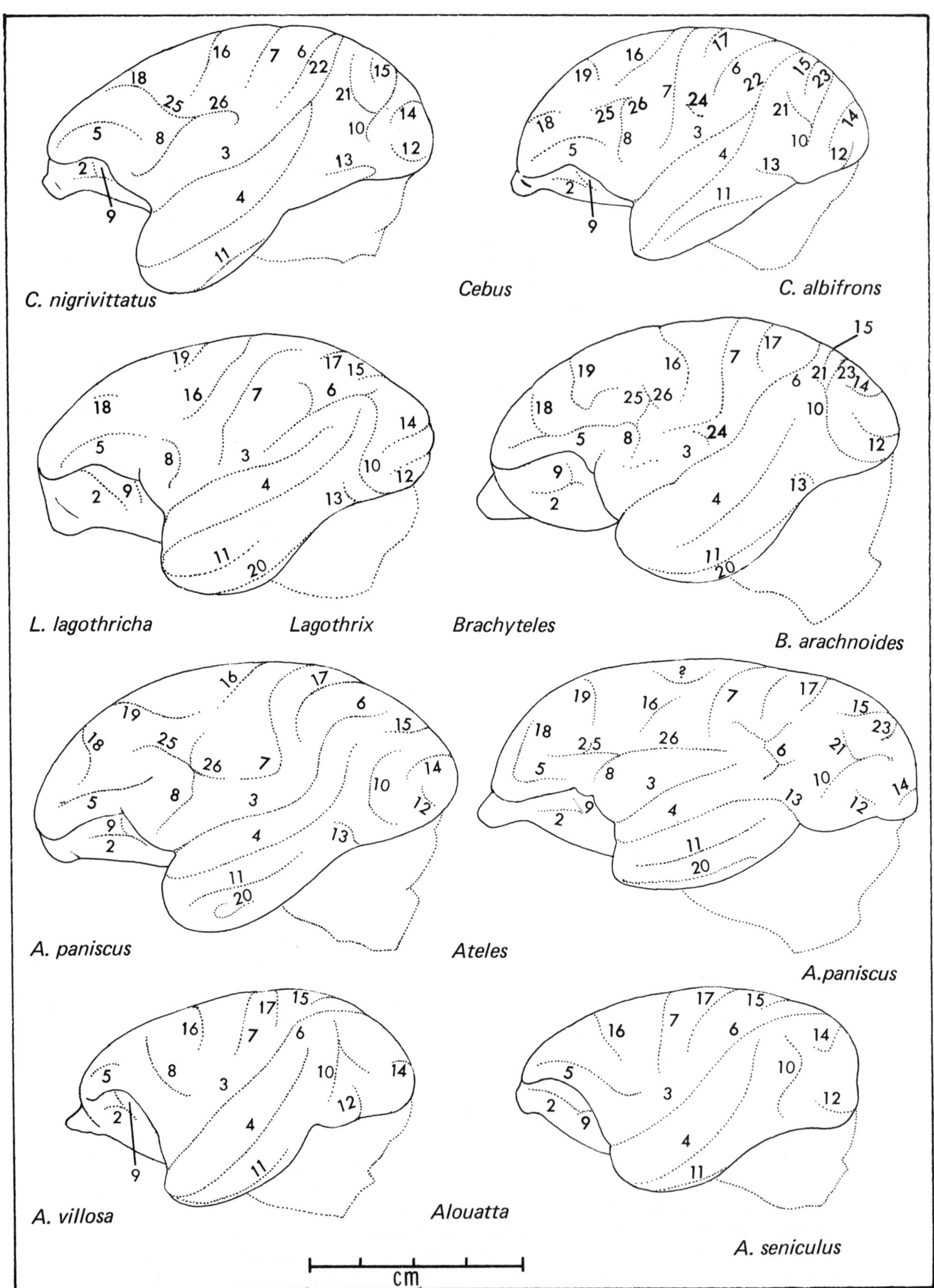

Fig. VI.11. Endocranial cerebral impressions (lateral aspects) of prehensile-tailed cebids (*Cebus, Lagothrix, Brachyteles, Ateles, Alouatta*); names of fissures on page 353. (After Hershkovitz 1970*b*.)

VI.13d). Whichever the pattern, any one of the three component fissures may enter into an independent relationship with another fissure.

The distribution and intraspecific variation of each fissural combination is not fully known. Judged by endocranial casts at hand, and cerebra described and figured

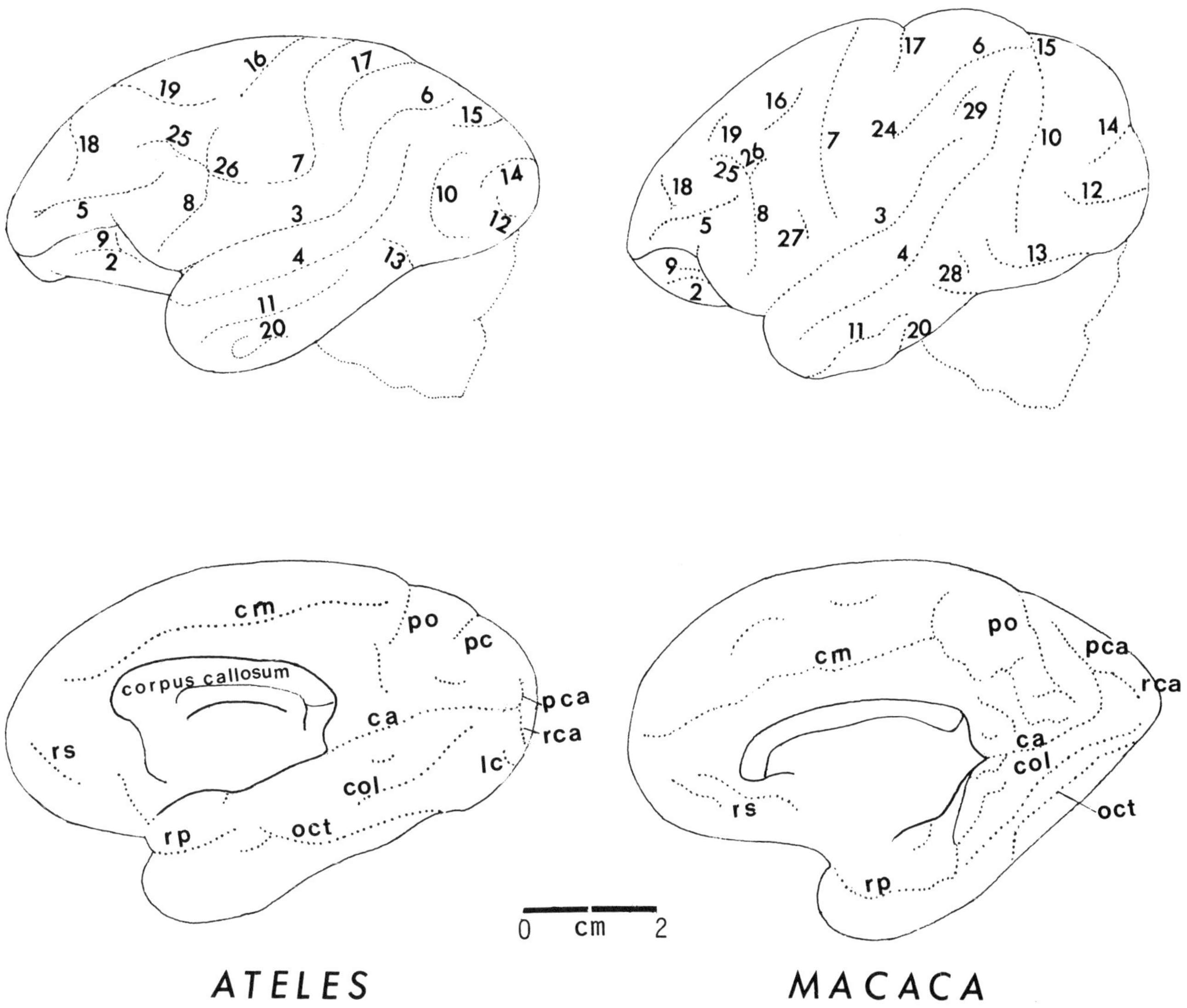

Fig. VI.12. Cerebral hemisphere of *Ateles* and *Macaca*, lateral aspect (*upper figures*) and medial aspect (*lower figures*); numbers used for fissures (sulci) explained on page 353; medial fissures as follows: *ca*, calcarine; *cm*, callosomarginal; *col*, collateral; *lc*, lateral calcarine (cf. no. 12); *oct*, occipitotemporal collateral (cf. 20); *pca*, paracalcarine (superior fork of postcalcarine); *po*, parieto-occipital or superior occipital (cf. 15); *rca*, retrocalcarine (inferior fork of postcalcarine); *rp*, rhinal posterior; *rs*, rostral. Diagram of *Ateles* hemisphere based mainly on Connolly (1950) and that of *Macaca* on Kreiner (1968).

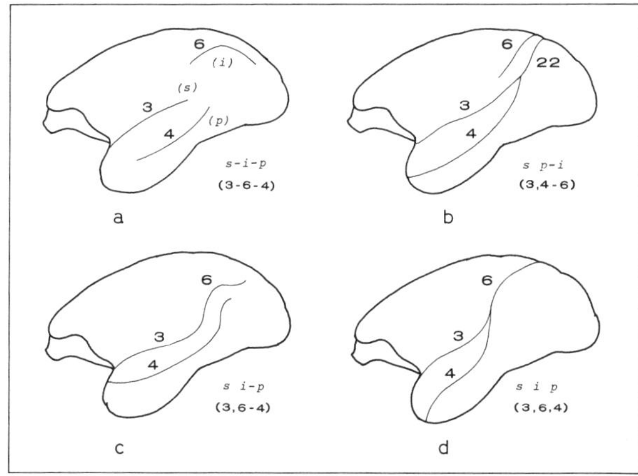

Fig. VI.13. Interrelationships of Sylvian (*3*), intraparietal (*6*), and parallel (*4*) fissures in monkeys. *a*, primitive, *s-i-p* (*3–6–4*); *b*, sylvioparallel, *sp-i* (*3, 4–6*); *c*, sylviointraparietal *si-p* (*3, 6–4*); *d*, anastomotic, *sip* (*3, 6, 4*). (After Hershkovitz 1970*b*.)

in the literature, the combination *s-i-p* prevails among lemuriforms. In lorisiforms, there is the *s-i-p*, or *Perodicticus potto* pattern, and the *si-p*, or *Nycticebus coucang* pattern (Elliot Smith 1902, pp. 378–79). In catarrhines, Sylvian and intraparietal are separate, perhaps consistently, while Sylvian and parallel may be separate or confluent. The catarrhine patterns, therefore, are *s-i-p* and *sp-i*.

Every combination of Sylvian, intraparietal, and parallel fissure relationship occurs in platyrrhines. The patterns, as revealed by endocranial casts, are distributed as follows.

1. Sylvian, intraparietal, and parallel separate (*s-i-p*). **Callitrichidae:** All species of *Callithrix, Saguinus, Leontopithecus,* with intraparietal (6) present. **Callimiconidae:** *Callimico.* **Cebidae:** *Saimiri sciureus* (2 of 3 specimens); *Callicebus moloch* (3); *Pithecia monachus* (2), *Chiropotes satanas* (2), *Cacajao rubicundus* (2); *Lagothrix lagothricha* (1), *Ateles paniscus* (1 [of 2], the parallel uniting with inferior occipital or fissure 13).

2. Sylvian and parallel confluent, intraparietal separate

Table 30. Brain Volume, Cranial Dimensions, and Body Size of Representative Species of Cebidae

Species	*Locality*	*Sex*	*Fissures*	*Braincase Volume*
Aotus trivirgatus	Colombia: Río Caquetá	♂ ♂ ♀ ♀	11	18.2(16–19)10
Callicebus moloch	Peru: Tingo María	♂ ♂ ♀ ♀	13	18.4(17–21)5
Saimiri sciureus	Colombia: Río Caquetá	♂ ♂ ♀ ♀	14	28(23–33)10
Saimiri sciureus	Suriname: Zuid River	♂ ♂	14	28(26–30)4
Alouatta palliata	México, Honduras, Panamá, Colombia, Ecuador	♂ ♂	17	57(52–63)5
Alouatta seniculus	Colombia: Río Caquetá	♂ ♂	17	59(56–62)3
Pithecia monachus	Peru: Río Saimiria	♂ ♂ ♀ ♀	(9)–18	38(35–42)5
Chiropotes satanas	Suriname: Tapahoni River; Kaiserberg	♀ ♀	(16)–18	59(55–63)4
Chiropotes satanas	Suriname: Tapahoni River; Wilhelmina; Saramaca River	♀ ♀	(16)–18	60(55–66)4
Cacajao rubicundus	Peru: Quebrada Esperanza	♂ ♂	18	74.3(65–88)9
Cacajao rubicundus	Peru: Quebrada Esperanza	♂ ♂	18	77.7(74–85)6
Cebus nigrivittatus	Suriname: Nickerie	♂ ♂	25	82; 82
Cebus albifrons	Colombia: Arauca	♂ ♂	26	68(60–75)4
Cebus apella	Colombia: La Macarena	♂ ♂	26	71.3(67–78)4
Lagothrix lagothricha	Colombia: Río Caquetá	♂ ♂	20	95(88–102)6
Lagothrix lagothricha	Colombia: Río Caquetá	♂ ♂	20	98(93–101)3
Brachyteles arachnoides	Brazil: Engenheiro Reeve	♂ ♂	26	110; 115
Brachyteles arachnoides	Brazil: Engenheiro Reeve	♀ ♀	26	115; 120
Ateles paniscus	Suriname: West River	♂ ♂	26	119(116–23)5
Ateles paniscus	Colombia: Río San Jorge	♂ ♂	26	119(115–22)3

NOTE: Species are arranged in order of increasing cerebral complexity within natural supergeneric groups. Measurements given for three or more specimens are means, extremes (in parentheses), and number of samples. For explanation of measurements, see p. 353.

(*sp-i*). **Cebidae:** *Cebus albifrons* (1), *C. apella* (2); *C. nigrivittatus* (1).

3. Sylvian and intraparietal confluent, parallel separate (*si-p*). **Cebidae:** *Aotus trivirgatus* (3); *Alouatta palliata* (1); *Alouatta seniculus* (1); *Ateles paniscus* (1 of 2); *Brachyteles arachnoides* (2).

4. Sylvian, intraparietal, and parallel united (*sip*). **Cebidae:** *Saimiri sciureus* (1 of 3).

The relationship between Sylvian, intraparietal, and parallel fissures is complex and must be even more variable than is indicated here. Nevertheless, the *s-i-p* pattern is more primitive and more prevalent than the others. Its basic modifications (*si-p, sp-i, sip*) arose independently in each major primate group, as was noted by J. Anthony (1946*a*, p. 131), and originated as individual variables among platyrrhines.

Sylvian, Intraparietal, Fissural Pattern in Platyrrhine Classification

An arrangement of noncallitrichid platyrrhines into two families distinguished by the sylviointraparietal relationship was assayed by J. Anthony (1946*a*, p. 131). Genera with the two fissures separate (*s-i*) were assigned to the Cebidae, and those with the fissures confluent (*si*) were classified as Atelidae. Anthony's arrangement is summarized as follows.

Cebidae (*s-i*): *Callicebus* (*Callithrix* of J. Anthony), *Pithecia* (*Chiropotes* included), *Cebus*. The genus *Cacajao* (= *Brachyurus*) was not classified by Anthony, but as figured by him (1946*a*, p. 21), it belongs here.

Atelidae (*si*): *Aotus, Saimiri, Alouatta, Lagothrix, Ateles, Brachyteles* (= *Eriodes*).

Except for *Cebus* in the Cebidae, and the closely knit atelines, *Lagothrix, Ateles,* and *Brachyteles* in the Atelidae, the above groupings appear to be unnatural with respect to all other characters, and except for pithecines, untenable by Anthony's own criteria. Of three examples of *Saimiri* at hand, only one, with fissural pattern *si,* could be referred to Anthony's Atelidae. The other two, with pattern *s-i*, agree with his Cebidae (fig. VI.10). Our lone endocranial cast of *Lagothrix* (fig. VI.11) clearly shows the *s-i* combination instead of the *si* ascribed to it in Anthony's arrangement. The specimen is not unique. The cerebrum of *Lagothrix* figured by Papez (1929, p. 38), and another by Anthony (1946*a*, pp. 29, 34) show the same *s-i* pattern. The type genus of the family Atelidae is likewise subject to individual variation. One of two *Ateles* at hand is characterized by pattern *si,* the other by *s-i* (fig. VI.11). The cerebrum of an *Ateles geoffroyi* figured by Anthony (1946*a*, p. 38) exhibits combination *si* on the left hemisphere and *s-i* on the right. Separation of intraparietal from sylvian in *Ateles* was also noted by Connolly (1950, p. 64) in "some specimens." He (1950, pp. 25, 64) also observed that where the fissures are confluent, intraparietal is actually separated from sylvian by a submerged gyrus at the dorsal bend of the furrow.

As reinforcement for his classification, Anthony (1946*a*, p. 138) characterized the brains of his Cebidae as "globuleux" and those of his Atelidae as "allonges." Adult platyrrhine brains are never globular, only more or less ovate. Individual variation in brain shape, most notably among the species of *Cebus* or *Callicebus,* deprive even this vague distinction of taxonomic signifi-

Table 30. *Continued*

Skull (greatest length)	*Braincase Length*	*Braincase Width*	*Head and Body Length*
62.6(59.3–65.2)10	51.8(49.5–55.2)10	34.1(32.7–35.5)10	315(285–389)6
65.6(64.9–67.1)5	52.5(51.5–53.3)5	34.8(33.3–36.1)5	320(290–350)5
66.4(62.0–68.0)10	54.8(51.3–57.0)10	36.5(34.5–38.6)10	289(249–340)10
66.8(64.9–69.1)4	55.3(53.0–56.9)4	36.6(36.0–37.2)4	289(268–345)4
117.6(114.5–121.5)5	79.9(77.9–81.6)5	51.2(49.3–53.1)5	535(465–605)7[1]
129.5(123–36)3	80.6(76.2–86.0)3	52.1(49.4–54.3)3	602(576–804)3
84.6(82.9–83.9)5	60.3(58.6–63.9)5	43.5(41.8–45.5)5	407(363–434)5
89.9(87.1–92.8)4	65.0(61.7–69.6)4	49.7(48.2–52.2)4	396(370–410)4
88.8(86.7–91.2)4	66.4(64.9–68.9)4	50.7(49.4–53.3)4	409(394–423)4
100.0(97.3–102.0)9	72.0(69.2–74.8)9	52.8(50.3–56.7)9	429(405–17)9
106.5(103.3–108.9)6	75.3(72.4–78.5)6	53.1(52.3–55.3)6	462(455–65)6
102.6; 107.7	80.4; 84.4	54.1; 52.3	450; 425
94.1(90.9–98.0)4	75.9(72.8–78.1)4	52.8(50.4–54.8)4	409(385–426)4
99.5(95.7–101.8)4	74.8(72.2–76.0)4	52.1(50.7–55.0)4	428(395–448)4
102.9(97.7–106.8)6	81.0(79.6–83.0)6	59.0(52.1–60.4)6	440(434–448)5
107.0(105.9–108.4)3	83.9(77.5–84.7)3	59.2(58.4–60.3)3	453(451–58)3
118.0; 118.8	85.5; 83.7	60.9; 62.7	610; 580
117.9; 117.8	86.2; 83.6	65.0; 62.0	565; —
117(114.5–119.6)5	87.2(83.7–89.8)5	62.7(59.8–65.0)5	460(425–505)5
120.8(119.5–122.0)5	91.4(89.4–92.6)3	62.0(60.3–60.7)3	498(488–509)3

[1] External measurements from Lawrence (1933, p. 343), of 7 specimens from Boquete, Panamá; collected by J. H. Batty.

cance. Elsewhere, Anthony (1946*b*) believed that a large malar foramen was associated with his atelid, or *si*, fissural pattern. The character of the foramen, however, proves to be inconsistent and limited in application (cf. p. 129). The mooted concepts involved in the classification of platyrrhines were first introduced by Anthony in 1942 and reviewed by him in 1947. His arrangement of cebids has been cited by Radinsky (1972, p. 179) as an example of the taxonomic value of sulcal patterns.

The Brain in Platyrrhine Taxonomy

Increase in body size from *Cebuella* through *Callithrix* and tamarins of the genus *Saguinus* is correlated with a proportional increase in brain size and complexity (table 29). On the other hand, *Leontopithecus,* largest of callitrichids, has a correspondingly larger but considerably less complicated brain than that of tamarins.

Goeldi's monkey, *Callimico goeldii,* compares with large tamarins in body size and brain mass (table 29). It has been regarded by some authorities as a callitrichid, by others as a cebid. The opinions were usually based on a single character or character complex. Judged by the totality of characters examined, *Callimico* is neither. The developed third molars and incipient quadrituberculy excludes *Callimico* from the marmoset line which begins with absence or obsolescence of the third molar and persistence of trituberculy in the remaining two. That Goeldi's monkey may be a primitive cebid is a possibility. *Callimico,* however, is regarded as sole survivor, if not lone representative, of a line that diverged from a primitive platyrrhine stock characterized by three molars, the upper with the primitive tritubercular pattern. Resemblance of *Callimico* to tamarins in body size, general form and cerebral complexity but with significantly larger brain, indicates parallel evolution of closely related lineages in the same ambience.

Brains of the three unrelated genera of the similar-sized marmosetlike cebids *Aotus, Callicebus,* and *Saimiri* are comparable to each other in mass and complexity (table 30). *Saimiri* is usually classified with *Cebus* in the subfamily Cebinae. Its smaller size, weakly fissured brain, primitive cebid dentition, and perhaps some superficial resemblance suggest an early cebine type. Hypertrophy of the *Saimiri* occipital lobe, however, goes far beyond

Explanation of measurements in tables 29 and 30

Linear measurements in both tables are straight line, in millimeters; volume is given in cubic centimeters. Measurements were taken as follows: *Head and body length:* Tip of head, or muzzle, to base of tail; the dimension is routinely calculated by subtracting tail length from greatest length (tip of head, or muzzle, to tip of last tail vertebra). Only original collectors' measurements of animals in the flesh are used here. *Skull length:* Greatest sagittal length, occipital crests included. *Braincase length:* Nasofrontal suture (nasion) to posteriormost point of occiput. *Braincase width:* Greatest transverse width. *Braincase volume:* Millet seed used for cebid-sized braincase, no. 12 lead shot for callitrichid-sized braincase.

Measurements given are of adults. Those of table 30 are, where possible, of the same sex and from the same locality as the specimen or specimens from which endocasts were made. Unfortunately, adequate samplings of the right kind from the right place, with undamaged skulls and collectors' measurements of body size, were not always available. Sexual dimorphism, at least of parts measured, is absent in callitrichids and smaller cebids. In larger cebids, the male is usually more massive. When species are represented by the endocast of a female, separate measurements are given for females and males to permit comparisons.

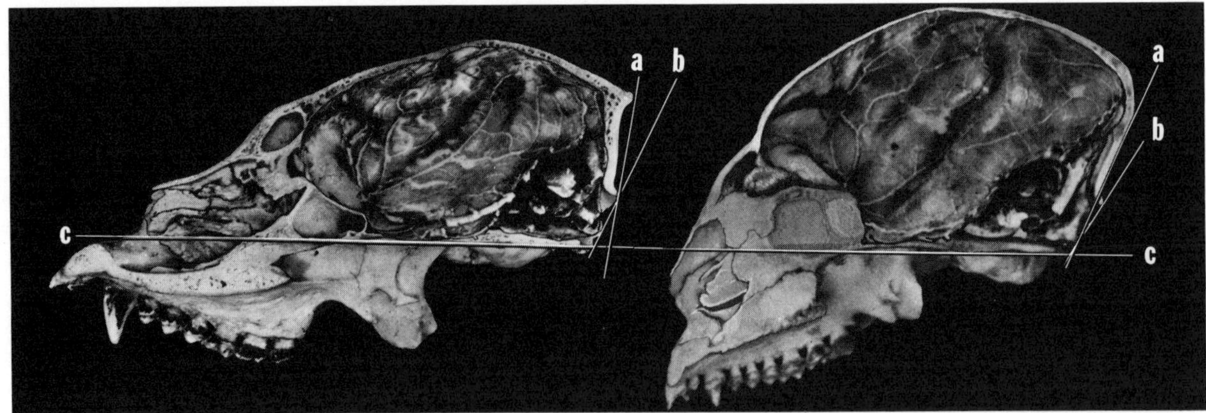

Fig. VI.14. Sectioned skulls with silicone rubber endocranial casts in place. *Left*: Adult howler, *Alouatta seniculus; right*: adult titi, *Callicebus moloch,* enlarged to same size as left (see fig. VI.15 for scale and actual size relationships); skulls horizontal to the basicranial axis. Note comparatively small brain, long muzzle, and complex turbinal bone system in *Alouatta*. Explanations of symbols: *a,* occipital angle (inion-opisthion); *b,* foramen magnum angle (basion-opisthion); *c,* basicranial axis (basioccipital-sphenoid). (After Hershkovitz 1970*b*.)

anything known among other platyrrhines. This specialization, or any one of several skeletal peculiarities such as the extensive interorbital vacuity and flattened caudal vertebrae, separate *Saimiri* widely from all relatives, whether larger or smaller in body size. Its status as representative of a distinct subfamily, the Saimirinae, coordinate with Aotinae and Callicebinae, is strongly indicated.

Pithecines, subfamily Pitheciinae, make up a cohesive group which in body size, brain mass, and fissuration (table 30) stands between marmosetlike and prehensile-tailed cebids, howler monkeys excluded. Sakis, genus *Pithecia,* least specialized of the group, are smallest, and the nearly related *Chiropotes* is larger. The short-tailed uacaris, genus *Cacajao,* are the largest of pithecines and the most specialized.

Fullest expression of platyrrhine cerebral complexity is attained in the prehensile-tailed *Cebus,* subfamily Cebinae, and in the three genera of Atelinae, namely *Lagothrix, Ateles,* and *Brachyteles.* In these, brain size corresponds roughly to body size, with that of *Cebus* significantly smaller than those of atelines (tables 30). Woolly monkeys, genus *Lagothrix,* with the least complicated cerebrum, are the most primitive of atelines.

Howler monkeys, genus *Alouatta,* of the cebid subfamily Alouattinae, approximate woolly and spider monkeys in body mass and cranial bulk (table 30). They deviate widely, however, from all prehensile-tailed cebids, including the much smaller *Cebus* and even some of the smaller, nonprehensile-tailed pithecines, by their less massive, more simple brain (figs. VI.7, 11, 14). The skull of *Alouatta,* with backward-directed foramen magnum and elongate muzzle, is correspondingly more primitive in design than that of all other known platyrrhines (figs. IV.3, 32, 38, 55; VI.15). As was shown by Schultz (1955), the backward position of the occipital condyles

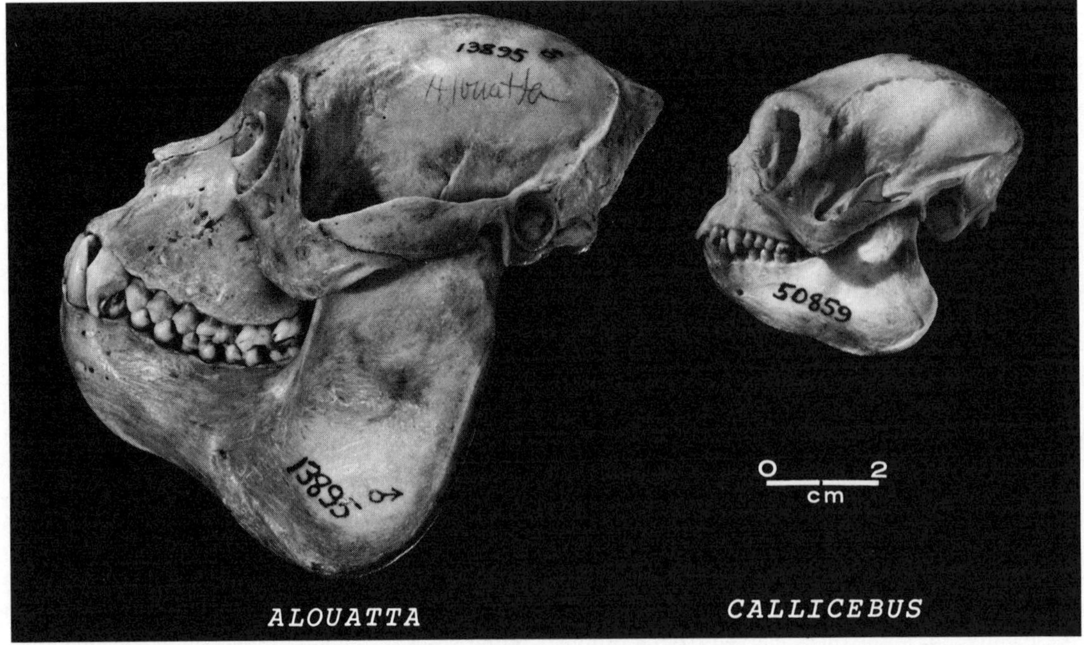

Fig. VI.15. Skull of adult howler, *Alouatta palliata* and adult titi, *Callicebus moloch* aligned horizontal to the Frankfort plane; compare mandibles, facial and occipital angles.

and extended position of the prosthion is extreme in this genus.[1]

It has been suggested (Gregory 1922, p. 217; Biegert 1963, p. 129, fig. 4) that the distinctive cranial characters of *Alouatta* are distortions arising from hypertrophy of the hyoid apparatus and consequent expansion of the mandibular rami housing it. Mandibular expansion in howlers, however, must have preceded hyoidal hypertrophy. The hyoid is enormously inflated in the red howler, *Alouatta seniculus,* the most highly specialized member of the genus, but only moderately inflated in the most primitive species, *Alouatta palliata* (Hershkovitz 1949, pl. XVII, figs. 56, 57). Size and form of mandible and neurocranium are nevertheless strictly comparable in both species. The mandible of titis, genus *Callicebus,* is also similar in form and often larger in proportion (fig. VI.15). Their hyoid apparatus, in contrast, is not comparably expanded. Furthermore, the *Callicebus* neurocranial axis is markedly flexed, the foramen magnum directed more nearly downward than backward, and the face short, not doglike as in howlers. Common to *Callicebus* (cf. fig. IV.16) and all species of *Alouatta* are the pneumatized facial bones and well-developed cranial crests which provide greater surface for attachment of the large mandibular muscles.

Howlers, it appears, evolved into specialized browsers and ready grazers. As in such herbivores generally, body mass, jaws, and teeth enlarged at an accelerating rate as more food bulk, mainly leaves, was consumed to sustain an enlarging body.[2] Meanwhile, evolution of the brain progressed at its own deliberate pace. The resulting inordinate disparity between brain size and complexity relative to what seems to be a proportionately oversized body, may account for the more sedentary habits and sluggish movements of howlers as compared with all other platyrrhines.

Fissuration, Brain Mass, and Body Mass

The relationship between grade of cerebral complexity (or fissuration), neurocranial volume (or brain weight), and body size (or weight), is shown in tables 28, 29, and 30. Each factor used alone or in combination with any of the others, yields very nearly the same phyletic assessment of the species within a given phylum as all three factors combined. In other words, in one lineage each factor is a good index of the others taken singly or in combination. A parallel correlation, determined by Elias and Schwartz (1971) on an assortment of mammals including man, is the strict relationship between surface area of the cerebral cortex, length of superficially exposed gyri, and cerebral volume. Chemical composition, a fourth factor of encephalization, is of equal importance but requires special study.

An index of encephalization, based only on body weight relative to brain weight in insectivores and prosimians, was devised by Bauchot and Stephan (1965; 1966) and then applied (1969) to higher primates, including 21 platyrrhine species. The body and brain weights used in their calculations are equivalent to the neurocranial capacities and the linear skull and body measurements used in mine. It is no surprise, therefore, that our respective estimates of platyrrhine grades of encephalization agree in the main, as well as in most details.[3]

Alouatta and *Callimico* are outstanding deviates in both arrangements. *Alouatta,* according to the Bauchot and Stephan (1969, p. 263) body/brain weight index of encephalization, rates lowest among platyrrhines and catarrhines. When cerebral complexity or grade of fissuration is taken into account, however, *Alouatta* ranks between pithecines and marmosetlike cebids (table 30). Schultz (1941), who used the ratio of cranial capacity to body weight as an indicator for 6 platyrrhine species, also ranged *Alouatta* next above marmosetlike cebids. *Callimico,* in Bauchot and Stephan's groupings, ranks above *Alouatta* and below callitrichids. Weights given for *Callimico,* however, are obviously those of an immature individual. Actually, *Callimico* belongs neither with callitrichids nor with cebids, but stands between them with respect to almost all characters, belonging with callitrichids with respect to cerebral organization alone.

A recomputation of the Bauchot and Stephan measurements were made by Hemmer (1971) using another allometric equation. His indices for callitrichids ranged from 2.1–3.7, with those for *Callithrix jacchus* and *C. penicillata* closely approximated (2.2, 2.1, respectively); highest was *Leontopithecus rosalia. Callimico,* with 2.3, ranked below tamarins (2.5–2.7). The squirrel monkey, *Saimiri* (4.9, 5.4) placed nearer *Pithecia* (5.4, 6.5) than to the marmosetlike cebids *Callicebus* and *Aotus* (3.3–3.5), and far below *Cebus* (11.2, 11.6). The latter, in turn, was graded only slightly below highest-ranked *Ateles* and

[1] Schultz's (1955, p. 101) observations are based on his condylar ($= \frac{\textit{nasion-condylion}}{\textit{nasion-opisthion}} \times 100$) index, projected on the nasion-basion line. The same techniques show the occipital condyles of some adult colobines and mandrills more aboral than in howlers. Using either the eye-ear, that is, Frankfort horizon, or the basicranial axis, the condyles appear to be more aboral in *Alouatta* than in all other simians. This assessment confirms the one derived from a visual comparison of crania. Facial projection of the mandrill is extreme by Schultz's prosthion index (1955, p. 115), or any other criterion. The specialization is certainly secondary in the mandril, as it must be in baboons generally, and other "dog-faced" cercopithecines, and oddly, the adult male orang. On the other hand, facial projection in adult *Alouatta,* second only to that of adult male *Papio sphinx,* is actually primitive.

[2] Leaf-eating colobines, largest of Old World monkeys, but with "normal"-sized mandibles, evolved a sacculated stomach for processing harsh fibrous food. The parallelisms between colobines and ruminants on the one hand and between alouattines and simple-stomach horses, with similarly shaped and powerful mandibles, on the other are striking.

[3] Minor discrepancies can be attributed to faulty data. The body weights of many platyrrhines published by Bauchot and Stephan (1964) were culled uncritically from secondary sources. A high percentage of them appear to be of immature individuals (compare, for example, on p. 252, *Callithrix penicillata* and *C. jacchus,* which should weigh the same; and *Callimico,* adults of which weigh as much as adult tamarins of the genus *Saguinus*). In any case, body weight is highly variable locally, seasonally, and individually in all age brackets. Brain weight relative to body weight in primates is much higher at birth than in adults. The brain then increases rapidly to subadulthood and stabilizes shortly thereafter (Schultz 1941, figs. 1–3). Body weight, however, continues to fluctuate normally up to 40% or more (cf. *Callimico goeldii,* p. 901). The amount of fissuration continuing after cerebral maturity is not certainly reflected in either brain or body weight, but cannot be discounted.

Lagothrix (13.3–14.1); the howler, *Alouatta* sp., with 6.8, ranked between pithecines and *Cebus*. In all, the Hemmer formula, as compared with the cephalization index of Bauchot and Stephan, gives a nearer approximation to the primate classification indicated by cerebral fissural patterns alone.

Brain Complexity, Behavior, and Miniaturization

Attempts to link the gross index of encephalization with specialized behavior in primates, or mammals generally, have been futile. The relationship of body to brain weight appears to be just that. As increase in brain size and complexity keeps pace with increase in bodily size and complexity, the organism remains correspondingly alert and responsive. If increase in brain volume and complexity lags, movements and reactions become sluggish. On the other hand, if brain complication outpaces bodily growth, movements and reflexes quicken or become more complex. Callitrichids, squirrel monkeys, *Cebus,* and atelines, with highest indices among platyrrhines, are quick. Howlers, with the lower indices, are slow. Continuing with the Bauchot and Stephan indices of encephalization for catarrhines, gorillas, and leaf-eating colobines, which are the ecological equivalents of howlers, are slow. Man, chimpanzees, and the talapoin, which is the cercopithecine counterpart of *Saimiri,* are quick.

Bauchot and Stephan (1969, p. 267) believe that the extremely high indices of encephalization in *Cebus* and the talapoin are results of "miniaturization" or dwarfism. Allometric growth, however, explains extreme disparities between body and brain weights. This is apart from the fact that each monkey represents an independent evolutionary line. *Saimiri,* quite unrelated to *Cebus,* is not demonstrably a miniaturized product of anything. Among living species of *Cebus,* the most advanced *Cebus apella* is the largest.

Relationships between brain size and complexity, body size, and behavioral tempos reveal little, if anything, of the actual behavioral patterns of the animals in question. In size and appearance, brains of the comparably small-bodied mouse lemur (*Microcebus murinus*), pygmy bush baby (*Galago minutus*), tarsier (*Tarsius syrichta*), and pygmy marmoset (*Cebuella pygmaea*) are very similar (cf. fig. VI.8 and table 29). In all other respects, including behavior, the animals are widely disparate.

In the same vein, brains of the most specialized members of primate or other mammalian phyletic lines, tend to converge in size and complexity. The brain of the Australian spiny anteater, or echidna (*Tachyglossus,* Monotremata), is as complicated as any primate brain of equal size or weight. The outstanding feature of this terminal and probably most highly evolved product of the most archaic line of living mammals is, in the words of G. Elliot Smith (1902, p. 145),

> the relatively enormous development of the cerebral hemispheres, which are much larger, both actually and relatively, than those of the Platypus. In addition the extent of the cortex is very considerably increased by numerous deep sulci. The meaning of this large neopallium is quite incomprehensible. The factors which the study of other mammalian brains has shown to be the determinants of the extent of the cortex, fail completely to explain how it is that a small animal of the lowliest status in the mammalian series comes to possess this large cortical apparatus. In other small, terrestrial, insect-eating mammals such as the Pangolins, and Anteaters, and in the fossorial Bandicoots, Hedgehogs, and Armadillos, we find highly macrosmatic brains with small neopallia: and yet in *Tachyglossus,* whose mode of life is not dissimilar to many of these mammals, we find, alongside the large olfactory bulb and great pyriform lobe of the highly macrosmatic brain a huge complicated neopallium.

The gross appearance of the brain hardly reflects the total organization of the animal or its specializations for particular ways of life, or the survival value of the species. The human brain viewed through the eye of the American opossum could be assessed as teratological, with the complex anterior or olfactory half degenerated to a vestige and the remainder so abnormally inflated that only a grossly misshapen skull can contain it.

Synopsis

Primate cerebral sulci or fissures, as determined from endocranial hemicasts of silicone rubber, are serially homologous. All the fissures emerge on the brain surface in the same order. Approximately 15 to possibly 20 such sequential fissures appear to be primary in platyrrhines and catarrhines. Additional sulci represent branchings, or novelties peculiar to individual species or genera. Each primate or other mammalian lineage begins with a comparatively small and simple brain. Brain mass and complexity increase with increasing body size. In any given phylogenetic line, rate of increase from the smaller and more primitive to the larger, more complicated brain is fairly constant for all included taxa. In parallel lines, the evolutionary rate may be about the same but the base for brain size, complexity, or body size can be different in each line. A significant change in evolutionary rate of brain growth, cerebral complexity, or body increment marks a divergence from the main line or other lines of ascent. Most notable aberrants among platyrrhines are the golden lion-tamarin, *Leontopithecus rosalia,* family Callitrichidae, and howler monkeys, genus *Alouatta,* family Cebidae. In both, the index of encephalization is low compared with other monkeys of their respective size classes. Primates with low indices are classified as comparatively slow with reference to movements and response to stimuli. Those with high indices are comparatively quick. Beyond this, nothing in gross brain morphology is correlated with distinctive behavioral traits or patterns of the species.

42 Comparative Cerebral Characters: Living New and Old World Monkeys Compared

a = Platyrrhini
b = Catarrhini

1. *a.* Brain extremely small to moderately large; cerebral fissural pattern from simple to complex, with 3 to 20 primary sulci in fully adults (figs. VI.9–11).
   b. Brain moderately large to large, fissural pattern complex, with at least 19 or 20 primary sulci in fully adults (figs. VI.7, 12).
2. *a.* Cells of lateral geniculate body arranged in 4 to 6 laminae (cf. fig. VI.5).
   b. Cells of lateral geniculate body arranged in 6 laminae only (fig. VI.5).
3. *a.* Olfactory bulb moderately well developed, often projecting beyond anterior plan of cerebral hemispheres (figs. VI.9–11).
   b. Olfactory bulb poorly developed, never projecting (fig. VI.12).
4. *a.* Accessory olfactory bulb present but not always well developed.
   b. Accessory olfactory bulb obsolete or absent.

Living Platyrrhine Families Compared

a = Callitrichidae and Callimiconidae
b = Cebidae

1. *a.* Brain small, comparatively smooth, usually with 8 or less (to 3) primary cerebral fissures (fig. VI.9).
   b. Brain larger, cerebrum more convoluted, usually with more than 10 primary cerebral fissures in fully adult (figs. VI.10, 11).
2. *a.* Olfactory bulb well developed, always projecting beyond anterior plane of cerebrum (figs. VI.8, 9).
   b. Olfactory bulb well developed to reduced and not always projecting beyond anterior plane of cerebrum (figs. VI.10, 11).
3. *a.* Postcalcarine (retrocalcarine) fissure present or absent (fig. VI.6).
   b. Postcalcarine fissure always present (fig. VI.12).
4. *a.* Sylvian (*s*), intraparietal (*i*) and parallel (*p*), cerebral fissures always separate (formula *s-i-p*) (fig. VI.13).
   b. Sylvian, intraparietal, and parallel cerebral fissures separate or variously combined (*s-i-p; sp-i* or *sip*) (fig. VI.13).
5. *a.* Dorsal lateral geniculate body arranged in 4 laminae (in *Callithrix;* structure in other callitrichids and in *Callimico* unknown).
   b. Dorsal lateral geniculate body arranged in 4–6 laminae (cf. VI.5).

43 New World Monkey Parasites

Introduction

The records of obligatory parasites of platyrrhines in this chapter were compiled from sources cited in the text. In most cases only the primary reference or the latest compilation, revision, or monograph is given as authority for the record of infection. The lists are not exhaustive but they are more complete than any yet published. Most records of parasitism are based on examinations of captive hosts. Natural infection is presumed where the evidence does not indicate otherwise and in cases where the same parasite/host relationship is consistent. Experimental and obviously accidental infections have been discounted or noted as such by enclosing the parasite name in brackets.

The platyrrhine hosts of any one parasite are listed in systematic order. The systematic arrangement of the parasites used here is a compromise between several published classifications, including obsolete ones with familiar and still current names for ordinal or supraordinal categories. Host names are the current ones and the classification is modern. A complete synonymy of callitrichid names is included in the taxonomic section of this volume. With few exceptions, cebid names used in the original parasitological literature are treated as binomials according to modern usage. For example, *Cebus fatuellus, C. libidinosus,* and *C. azarae,* are listed as *Cebus apella.* All spider monkey records are assigned to *Ateles paniscus.* The following cebid host names are used.

Saimiri sciureus (genus monotypic)
Aotus trivirgatus (genus monotypic)
Callicebus moloch
Callicebus torquatus
Callicebus personatus
Alouatta palliata or *villosa*
Alouatta fuscus
Alouatta belzebul
Alouatta seniculus
Alouatta caraya
Chiropotes satanas
Chiropotes albinasa
Pithecia monachus
Pithecia pithecia
Cacajao calvus (includes *rubicundus* as a subspecies)
Cebus capucinus
Cebus nigrivittatus
Cebus albifrons
Cebus apella
Lagothrix lagothricha
Ateles paniscus (genus monotypic)
Brachyteles arachnoides (genus monotypic)

The parasite/host lists were assembled with the hope of finding clues to unresolved or obscure points in primate phylogeny. It seems, however, that the parasitological problems per se are far more important, numerous, and complex and demand prior solutions.

The following symbols are used to indicate parasite host distribution in the Trematoda, Cestoda, Nematoda, and Acanthocephala.

Letters
A = Amphibia
B = Aves
F = Pisces
R = Reptilia
Superscripts
a = Catarrhini
b = Prosimii (sensu lato)
c = Nonprimate mammals

Present knowledge of viruses and their wild platyrrhine hosts is meager and highly specialized. Very likely, contemplation of the virus/host lists will not provide insights leading to immediate solutions of problems in nonhuman primatology. The challenge, nevertheless, is there.

Bacteria are better known, but few nonpathogenic forms have been studied in nonhuman primates, and fewer still have been investigated in platyrrhines. They have been accorded light treatment.

No investigations have been made of the relationships of fungi to wild living platyrrhines, and very little has been learned from captive monkeys or their skins preserved as museum specimens. The available data does not lead one to believe that mycotic infections in primates are essential to the life of any species of fungus.

Many pathogenic protozoans have been well studied by fieldworkers. It appears that virtually all cebids except *Aotus* may be naturally infected with strains of malarial parasites very nearly related to those of hominids. No callitrichids or other New World mammals are naturally infected. Two wild *Saguinus* and one *Aotus* were reported infected with *Leishmania,* but other platyrrhines seem to be immune to the parasite in the wild. Many other New World mammals and catarrhines, including New World humans, however, are susceptible.

Acanthocephalans or thornyhead worms are very poorly represented among primates.

Flukes (Trematoda) are uncommon among primates. A large number of them are shared with birds. The best known flukes, those of the genus *Schistosoma,* are naturally parasitic in some wild nonprimate mammals and possibly in some cercopithecines, but none have been reported from wild platyrrhines.

Cestodes or tapeworms are better represented among primates, with some species restricted to platyrrhines, others to catarrhines, but the extent of host specificity is not well understood. Distribution of the forms of the parasite infecting a primate species largely depends on the distribution of the invertebrate host included in the parasite's life cycle.

The nematode species parasitic in primates outnumber those of other comparable parasitic groups. Available information on nematodes, their complicated life cycles, and the habits of their platyrrhine hosts is inadequate for the formulation of any but the most tentative hypotheses regarding the phylogenetic or zoogeographic implications of parasite/host relationships. The oft-cited case of the oxyurid *Trypanoxyuris* is discussed in the text.

Tongue worms (Pentastomida) of the genus *Porocephalus,* seem to specialize on the smaller platyrrhines, but the same genus and *Armillifer* infect the full range of Old World primates.

There are few obligatory external parasites of primates among arthropods. No doubt the habit of social grooming among primates restricts their ectoparasites to a very tenacious few among mites, ticks, lice, and botfly larvae. Fleas (Siphonaptera) evidently are not addicted to wild primates of any kind. The larger cebids, man, chimpanzee, and gibbons are infested by sucking lice of the genus *Pediculus* (Anoplura). Callitrichids and the remaining catarrhines are each parasitized by different genera.

Mites infecting the respiratory system and hair follicles are probably better classified as endoparasites. In any event, they are more specialized and host specific than relatives attached to the outer surface of the skin.

Parasitological and epidemological aspects of primate parasitology are discussed by Ruch (1959) and Faust and Russell (1965); zoonoses are taken up by Fiennes (1967); and relationships of parasites and vertebrate hosts generally, but not primates particularly, are discussed in the "First Symposium on Host Specificity among Parasites of Vertebrates" (1957, Institut de Zoologie, Université de Neuchâtel).

Viruses

Introduction and Classification

Use of platyrrhines in experimental studies of human diseases has brought virology close to the attention of primate systematists and behaviorists. The aim of current virological research, however, is not to throw light on nonhuman primate biology, interrelationships, and phylogeny, and few rays have strayed in those directions. It does appear, nevertheless, that as more primates are tested for susceptibilities, less viruses appear to be host specific, at least experimentally.

The purpose of this section is to list the indigenous viruses isolated from New World monkeys and mention some of the better-known viruses infecting captive platyrrhines or inoculated into them for inducing human or humanlike diseases. As information accumulates, it may be possible to shift focus from experimental and pathological conditions to the normal relationships between viruses and their natural nonhuman primate hosts.

The following arrangement of viruses is based on Hull (1968), Wilner (1969), Hsiung (1969, p. 483), Kalter (1972*a*, pp. 386; 1972*b*: 457–62; 1973), Melnick (1973), Fraenkel-Conrat and Wagner (1974), and others cited in the text. Animal viruses are classified according to chemical characteristics and biological properties. The primary division is based on their DNA or RNA content, and groups within each division are distinguished by the structure of the nucleic acid genome and the size, shape, structure, and mode of replication of the virus particle. The following list of viral groups includes mention of principal hosts and some of the more important viral diseases. Groups with representatives naturally infecting platyrrhine monkeys are indicated by an asterisk (*).

DNA-Containing Viruses

Parvovirus (Picodnovirus) Group

Several human and simian infecting viruses; also in mice, rats, domestic artiodactyls, and birds.

Papovavirus Group

Papillomavirus (papillomata or wart viruses in human and other mammals.

Polyomavirus (includes simian SV40 and rabbit vacuolating viruses).

* Adenovirus Group

31 human, 27 simian, other mammalian and avian infecting viruses.

* Herpesvirus Group

Section A (several human, 7 simian, other mammalian, avian, reptilian and amphibian viruses).

Section B (cytomegaloviruses, varicella-zoster viral complex, other human, simian, and other mammalian viruses).

* Poxvirus Group

The following subgroupings are used by Fraenkel-Conrat and Wagner (1974)

1. Variola-related viruses (monkeypox, cowpox, and other mammalian poxes, variola, vaccinia, alastrim).
2. Orf-related viruses (orf, paravaccinia bovine papular stomatitis).
3. Bovine pox viruses.
4. Avian poxes.
5. Myxoma-related viruses (affecting rodents and lagomorphs).
6. Unclassified pox viruses (horsepox, camelpox, molluscum contagiosum).

RNA-Containing Viruses

* Arbovirus Group

This is an ecological assemblage to which have been referred some 300 arthropod-borne viruses transmitted to vertebrate hosts. Subgroups A and B arboviruses have been placed in the new Togavirus

Group (see below). For present purposes, however, they are tabulated with the arboviruses (table 32).

* Togavirus Group

Alphavirus (includes subgroup A arboviruses in table 32, also encephalitis and rubella viruses).

Flavivirus (includes subgroup B arboviruses in table 32, also yellow fever and simian hemorrhagic fever viruses).

Picornavirus Group

Enterovirus (nearly 150 human polioviruses, coxsackie viruses and echoviruses).

Rhinovirus (more than 90 human rhinoviruses and many bovine disease viruses including foot and mouth disease virus).

* Diplornavirus (Reovirus) Group

Reovirus (human, simian, and other mammalian infecting viruses).

Orbivirus (viruses of bluetongue and African horsesickness, Colorado tick fever, epizootic deer disease, and other mammalian, insect and plant diseases.

Orthomyxovirus Group

Influenza viruses of man, horse, swine, chicken, duck.

Paramyxovirus Group

Viruses of human mumps, parainfluenza, measles; also simian measles, distemper, and rinderpest of other mammals, Newcastle disease of birds.

Metamyxovirus Group

Pneumonia virus of mice.

* Rhabdovirus Group

Arboviruses of vesicular stomatitis in cattle, rabies, Marburg, and diseases of bats, birds, fishes, insects, plants.

* Oncornavirus (Leukovirus: RNA Tumor Virus) Group

Leukemia and sarcoma viruses of monkeys, mice, cats; avian Rous sarcoma virus.

Arenavirus Group

Many rodent arboviruses (Machupo, Tacaribe, Junín, Lassa, etc.); lymphocytic choriomeningitis virus.

Coronavirus Group

Includes murine, swine, and avian infecting viruses.

Unclassified Viruses

Hepatitis Viruses

Viral hepatitis type A (infectious hepatitis)

Viral hepatitis type B (serum hepatitis)

* Foamy Viruses

7 serotypes are known

Adenovirus Group

Twenty-seven serotypes have been isolated in the laboratory from *Cercopithecus, Macaca, Papio, Pan, Saimiri* and *Cebus.* Adenovirus infection in the wild is unknown. According to Heberling (1972, p. 572), "a single virus serotype may occur naturally in more than one nonhuman primate. Therefore, these viruses readily pass from one simian species to another and possibly to man."

The squirrel monkey adenoviruses SqM-1 and SqM-2 appear to be serologically distinct and the common cause of infection in several kinds of platyrrhines (Heberling and Kalter 1971, p. 648) including "marmoset" (= *Saguinus*?), *Aotus trivirgatus* (Kalter, 1972*a*, p. 461) *Cebus capucinus, C. albifrons, Alouatta palliata,* and *Ateles paniscus* (Heberling 1972, p. 576).

An adenoviruslike isolate from *Cebus apella* was reported by Meléndez, Daniel, and Fraser (1969) and mentioned again by Meléndez, Daniel, Hunt, García, Fraser, Jones, and Mitus (1971).

Adenovirus antibodies to the adenovirus group antigen have not been found in New World monkeys (Kalter 1972*b*, p. 472).

Herpesvirus Group

(See Barahona, Meléndez, and Melnick 1974 for a compendium of the pathogenecity, serological relationships, cultural, and other characteristics mentioned cursorily or not at all in the following.)

Herpesvirus simplex (H. hominis). This common Old World type virus infects the night monkey, *Aotus trivirgatus,* experimentally and naturally. It also infects tamarins experimentally. (Meléndez, España, Hunt, Daniel, and García 1969.)

*Herpesvirus simiae (Herpes-*B*).* Morphologically indistinguishable from *Herpesvirus simplex,* it is naturally occurring and mildly infectious in catarrhine monkeys but usually lethal in man. It has not been isolated in platyrrhines.

Herpesvirus tamarinus. Isolation of the virus in tamarins was first reported in 1963 by Holmes, Dedmon, and F. Deinhardt and was characterized in 1964 by Holmes, Caldwell, Dedmon, and Deinhardt with the name *Herpesvirus tamarinus.* The identical virus was independently isolated from *Saguinus nigricollis* (or *fuscicollis*?) and characterized by Melnick, Midulla, Wimberly, Barrera Oro, and Levy the same year (1964).

Herpesvirus tamarinus infection of *Saguinus nigricollis, S. fuscicollis,* and *S. oedipus* proved fatal in 90 to 95% of the cases. The effect was similar in the night monkey, *Aotus trivirgatus* (Hunt and Meléndez 1966). As shown by Meléndez, Hunt, García, and Trum (1966), Holmes, Devine, Nowalkowski, and F. Deinhardt (1966), and F. Deinhardt and J. Deinhardt (1966), the natural reservoir host of the virus is *Saimiri sciureus.* The virus also infects *Cebus albifrons* and *Ateles paniscus.* Because of its wide distribution in nature, the cited authors felt constrained to rename the virus *Herpesvirus platyrrhinae.* It has also been recorded as Herpesvirus T.

Additional records of infection, summarized by Kalter and Heberling (1972), include *Callithrix, Lagothrix,* and *Aotus.*

Herpesvirus saguinus. The virus was isolated by Meléndez and Daniel (1971) from a 22-day-old kidney culture obtained from *Saguinus oedipus.*

Herpesvirus aotus 1. The viral agents of spontaneous cell layer alteration were obtained from kidney cultures of the night monkey, *Aotus trivirgatus,* by Meléndez and Daniel (1971).

Herpesvirus aotus 2. Meléndez et al. (1971) isolated this virus from *Aotus* kidney cultures. The discovery was announced or described in a number of publications under various author combinations (cf. Barahona, Meléndez, King, Daniel, Fraser, and Preville [1972, 1973]).

Herpesvirus aotus 3. Named by Meléndez, Daniel,

Barahona, Fraser, Hunt, and García (1971), and described by Daniel, Meléndez, King, Barahona, Fraser, García, and Silva (1973).

Herpesvirus aotus (cytomegalovirus, owl monkey 175H). Isolated from anal and oral orifices of *Aotus* by Ablashi, Chopra, and Armstrong (1972, p. 190). Of 21 owl monkeys tested, 15 (71%) had antibodies to the isolate.

This is said to be the first recorded isolation of a cytomegalovirus from platyrrhines.

Herpesvirus saimiri 1. The virus was isolated by Meléndez, Daniel, Hunt, and García (1968) from primary kidney tissue cultures obtained from squirrel monkeys. It was named *Herpesvirus saimiri* by Hunt and Meléndez (1969) and recharacterized by Meléndez and Daniel (1971). The virus is latent in *Saimiri* but fatal to *Aotus trivirgatus* and *Saguinus oedipus* (Meléndez, Daniel, García, Fraser, Hunt, and King 1969; Meléndez, Hunt, Daniel, García, and Fraser 1969), to *Saguinus nigricollis, S. fuscicollis, Cebus albifrons* (cf. F. Deinhardt, Falk, Marczynska, Shramek, and Wolfe 1972) and to *Ateles* and *Cercopithecus* (Hunt, Meléndez, King, and García 1972).

Herpesvirus saimiri 2. The virus was isolated from squirrel monkey heart cell cultures by Meléndez and Daniel (1971).

Herpesvirus saimiri (HVS-11). Isolated by Falk, Wolfe, and Deinhardt (1972) from squirrel monkey blood samples by cocultivation of lymphocytes or whole blood with vero cells. Falk, Nigida, Deinhardt, Wolfe, Cooper, and Hernández-Camacho (1974) report reactions to HVS-11 of the following wild-caught monkeys: *Ateles paniscus hybridus,* none positive in 4 individuals; *A. p. belzebuth,* positive in 2 of 3 individuals; *A. p. robustus* 9/17; *Ateles paniscus* (captive) 0/5; *Lagothrix lagothricha* (captive) 4/4; *Aotus trivirgatus* 1/10; *Cebus albifrons unicolor* 0/6; *Cebus albifrons pleei* 0/4; *Cebus apella* 0/10. The virus induced malignant *lymphomas* in *Saguinus oedipus, S. nigricollis,* and *S. fuscicollis.*

The properties and cytopathogenicity of *Herpesvirus saimiri* are described and comparisons with *Herpesvirus ateles* made by Meléndez, Hunt, Daniel, Fraser, Barahona, King, and García (1972). Among primates listed, *Herpesvirus saimiri* is pathogenic in *Callithrix jacchus, Saguinus nigricollis, Saguinus oedipus, Aotus trivirgatus, Cebus albifrons,* and *Cercopithecus aethiops. Herpesvirus saimiri* also induces malignant lymphoma in *Ateles,* but *Herpesvirus ateles* is not oncogenic in *Saimiri.*

The biology and etiology of *Herpesvirus saimiri* has also been reviewed by Deinhardt (1973); and a collection of studies with particular reference to *Aotus trivirgatus* as experimental host for *Herpesvirus saimiri* has been published under the editorship of Rabin (1974).

Herpesvirus ateles 1 (SMVH). The virus was isolated by Lennette (in Hunt and Meléndez 1969) from the brain of a 5-month-old female spider monkey, *Ateles paniscus geoffroyi,* in the Roeding Park Zoo, California, where the animal was born and died; then characterized by Hull (1968, p. 22) and Hull et al. (1972). Although the disease induced by the virus killed its young host, spider monkeys appear to be the natural reservoir.

The properties of *Herpesvirus ateles* 1 to 3 have been described and comparisons with *Herpesvirus saimiri* made by Meléndez, Hunt, Daniel, Fraser, Barahona, King, García (1972). Among the animals tested, *Herpesvirus ateles* proved cytopathogenic in *Aotus* and *Saguinus oedipus* but not in *Saimiri sciureus.*

Herpesvirus ateles 2 (SMI 810). Isolated from a kidney culture of a spider monkey *(Ateles paniscus geoffroyi)* imported from Guatemala and said to differ from types 1 and 3 by its cytopathogenicity (Meléndez, Daniel, Barahona, Fraser, Hunt, and García 1971; Meléndez, Castellanos, Barahona, Daniel, Hunt, Fraser, García, and King 1972).

Herpesvirus ateles 3 (AT-46). Isolated from *Ateles* kidney culture and said to differ from types 1 and 2 by the degree of cytopathogenicity (Meléndez, Daniel, Barahona, Fraser, Hunt, and García 1971; Meléndez, Castellanos, Barahona, Daniel, Hunt, Fraser, García, and King 1972).

Herpesvirus ateles (HVA-73, -87, -93, -94). The four viruses from *Ateles paniscus hybridus* and *A. p. robustus* imported from Barranquilla, Colombia, were isolated in early passage night monkey (*Aotus trivirgatus*) kidney cell cultures (Deinhardt, Falk, and Wolfe 1973; Falk, Nigida, Deinhardt, Wolfe, Cooper, and Hernández-Camacho 1974; Falk 1974). They appear antigenically similar if not identical to one another and they seem to share cross-reacting antigens with both *Herpesvirus saimiri* and *Herpesvirus ateles*-810. Their failure to grow in rabbit and human embryonic kidney cell cultures distinguishes them from HVA-810.

Wild-caught monkeys infected with HVA-73 and their reactions were: *Ateles paniscus hybridus,* 2 positive out of 4 individuals; *A. p. belzebuth* 2/3; *A. p. robustus* 10/17; *A. paniscus* (captive) 0/5; *Lagothrix lagothricha* (captive) 4/4; *Saimiri sciureus* 18/20; *Aotus trivirgatus* 1/10; *Cebus albifrons unicolor* 0/6; *Cebus albifrons pleei* 0/4; *Cebus apella* 0/10. The virus induced malignant *lymphomas* in *Saguinus oedipus, S. nigricollis,* and *S. fuscicollis.*

Herpesvirus cebus (AP 18). Isolated from brain of *Cebus apella* by Lewis et al. (1974).

Herpesvirus cebus (AL 5). Isolated from spleen of *Cebus albifrons* by Lewis et al. (1974).

Epstein-Barr Virus. This is a human virus causing infectious mononucleosis. It has also been implicated as the agent of Burkitt's lymphoma and nasopharyngeal carcinoma. The virus is listed here because of its similarities to *Herpesvirus saimiri* and *Herpesvirus ateles.* It can transform in vitro peripheral lymphocytes of *Hylobates lar, Saguinus, Saimiri, Cebus,* and *Aotus. Saguinus nigricollis* (and/or *S. fuscicollis*) and *S. oedipus oedipus* respond immunologically after inoculation (Falk, Wolfe, Deinhardt, Paciga, Dombos, Klein, Henle, and Henle 1974; Deinhardt, Falk, and Wolfe 1974).

Poxvirus Group

Poxvirus antibody in New World monkeys reported by Kalter and Heberling (1972) and Kalter, Heberling, and Cooper (1974) is shown in table 31.

Arboviruses (Including Subgroups A and B Togaviruses)

Arthropod-borne or arboviruses are transmitted to warm-blooded animals by arthropod vectors such as mosquitos, flies, bugs, mites, ticks, and crustaceans, which

Table 31. Poxvirus Antibody in Platyrrhine Monkeys

Species	*Antigen*		*Reference*
	Vaccinia	*Monkeypox*	
"Marmosets"	2/43[1]	6/43	K & H 1972
Saguinus o. oedipus	2/20	4/20	K, H, C 1974
Saimiri sciureus	20/63	20/63	K & H 1972
Saimiri sciureus	10/22	17/22	K, H, C 1974
Aotus trivirgatus	0/8	0/8	K & H 1972
Cebus capucinus	0/8	1/8	K & H 1972
Alouatta sp.	——	14/24	K & H 1972
Lagothrix lagothricha	2/7	2/6	K & H 1972
Ateles paniscus	3/7	3/7	K & H 1972

SOURCE: Data from Kalter and Heberling (1972) and Kalter, Heberling, and Cooper (1974) as shown in column 4.
[1] No. specimens with antibodies/No. specimens tested.

may also serve as reservoirs. More than 300 arboviruses are known. They had been classified on the basis of antigenic relationships into subgroups A, B, and C, and according to the locality name where the first of the kind was discovered under natural conditions. Subgroups A and B are now included with the Togavirus group. The classification has been summarized by Melnick (1973). A major source of information on arboviruses is the account of the Rockefeller Virus Programs 1951–70, by Theiler and Downs (1973), and the "Workshop—Symposium on Venezuelan Encephalitis Virus (1972)."

Many simian arboviruses have been detected by means of sentinel monkeys. The animals are placed in cages on platforms set at different levels from ground to canopy in tropical and subtropical forests, where they are exposed to biting arthropods. Simian viruses isolated from sentinel monkeys, laboratory mice, wild mammals, and man in Belém, Brazil, and in Trinidad, are listed in table 32.

Serologic evidence of arboviral infections in platyrrhines obtained by Kalter and Heberling (1972) from animals maintained in laboratories in Chicago, Illinois (Rush–Presbyterian–St. Luke's Hospital), San Diego, California (Primate Research Colony, San Diego Zoo), San Antonio, Texas (Southwest Foundation for Research

Table 32. Arboviruses Isolated in the Belém Area, Pará, Brazil, and in Trinidad

Virus	*Reference*	*Locality*	*Group*	*Man*	*Sentinels*[1]		*Wild Animals*	*Mosquitos*
					Monkeys	*Mus*		
Mucambo[2]	(1)(2)(7)	Belém	A	X	X	X	X	X
EEE[3]	(1)(7)	Belém	A	X	X	X	X	X
Mayaro	(1)(7)	Belém	A	X	X	—	—	X
Yellow Fever	(1)(7)	Belém	B	X	X[4]	—	—	X
Ilhéus	(1)(7)	Belém	B	X	X[5]	—	—	X
Bussuquara	(1)(7)	Belém	B	X	X[6]	—	X	X
Oriboca	(1)(7)	Belém	C[10]	X	X	X	X	X
Marituba	(1)(7)	Belém	C	X	X	X	—	—
Apeu	(1)(7)	Belém	C	X	X	X	—	X
Murutucu	(1)(7)	Belém	C	X	X	X	X	X
Caraparu	(1)(7)	Belém	C	X	X	X	X	X
Itaqui	(3)(7)	Belém	C	X	X	X	X	X
Guamá	(1)(7)	Belém	Guamá[10]	X	X	X	X	X
Catú	(1)(7)	Belém	Guamá	X	X	X	X	X
Maguari	(7)	Belém	Bunyamwera[10]	X	X[4]	—	—	X
Mirim	(7)	Belém	Bunyamwera	X	X	X	X	X
Kairi	(1)(7)	Belém	Bunyamwera	X	X[7]	—	—	X
Kairi	(4)(7)	Trinidad	Bunyamwera	X	X[8]	—	—	X
Melao	(7)	Trinidad	Bunyamwera	—	X[9]	—	—	X
Manzanilla	(5)(7)	Trinidad	Simbu[10]	—	X[11]	—	—	—
Oropouche	(6)(7)	Trinidad	Simbu[10]	X	X[4]	—	—	—
Tacaiuma	(1)(7)	Belém	Anopheles A	X	X	—	X	X

NOTE: References:
(1) Causey, Causey, Maroja, and Macedo 1961.
(2) Shope, Causey, Paes de Andrade, and Theiler 1964.
(3) Shope, Causey, and Causey 1961.
(4) Anderson, Aitken, Spence, and Downs 1960.
(5) Anderson, Spence, Downs, and Aitken 1960.
(6) Anderson, Spence, Downs, and Aitken 1961.
(7) Theiler and Downs 1973.

1. Unless otherwise indicated, is a race of *Cebus apella*.
2. Originally confused and later treated as a subtype of Venezuelan equine encephalitis (VEE or VE).
3. Eastern equine encephalomyelitis.
4. Wild-living *Alouatta seniculus* (Trinidad) and *Cebus apella* (Belém).
5. Also from *Callithrix jacchus* and *C. j. penicillata* (Koprowski and Hughes 1946).
6. Sentinel *Alouatta belzebul*.
7. *Saimiri sciureus* (Belém) and *Cebus apella* (Belém).
8. *Cebus* and *Alouatta* in experimental neutralization test.
9. *Saimiri sciureus* (Belém), sentinel *Cebus apella* (Belém) (cf. Theiler and Downes 1973, p. 254).
10. Bunyamwera supergroup.
11. Wild-living *Cebus albifrons* and *Alouatta seniculus*.

Table 33. Arbovirus Antibody in Platyrrhine Monkeys

Antigen	*"Marmosets"*	Saimiri sciureus	*"Howler"* (Alouatta *sp.)*
Uganda	2/44[1]	1/25	6/50
Dengue 2	0/44	0/25	1/50
La Crosse	18/44	2/25	4/50
Trivittatus	5/44	1/25	0/50
Sindbis	1/44	2/25	2/50
Chicangunya	4/44	3/25	1/50
Semliki Forest	4/44	3/25	2/50
Buttonwillow	2/44	0/25	1/50
Turlock	1/44	2/25	2/50
Keystone	14/24	——	——
California encephalitis	11/24	——	——
Tahyna	2/24	——	——

SOURCE: Data from Kalter and Heberling (1972).
[1] No. specimens with antibodies/No. specimens tested.

and Education), Panama City, Panamá (Gorgas Memorial Hospital), Caracas, Venezuela (Instituto de Higiene), is listed in table 33. In all, 6 species were tested for antibodies for 18 viruses. Only those with positive reactions are shown in the table. Tests were negative in *Cebus capucinus* (3 specimens), *Lagothrix lagothricha* (1) and *Ateles paniscus* (9). No representatives of the 6 species tested proved positive to Eastern, Western, or St. Louis encephalitis, Colorado tick, dengue 1, or Bunyawera.

Togavirus Group

Alphavirus

Rubella antibodies are recorded by Kalter and Heberling (1972) from a number of platyrrhine monkeys in captivity (table 34).

Table 34. Antibody to Rubella and Lymphocytic Choriomeningitis Viruses in Platyrrhine Monkeys

	Antigen	
Species	*Rubella*	*Lymphocytic Choriomeningitis*
"Marmosets"	7/73[1]	1/66
Saimiri sciureus	18/60	0/40
Aotus trivirgatus	1/4	——
Alouatta sp.	6/25	0/3
Cebus capucinus	0/4	——
Lagothrix lagothricha	4/4	0/1
Ateles paniscus	1/7	0/1

SOURCE: Data from Kalter and Heberling (1972).
[1] No. specimens with antibodies/No. specimens tested.

Flavivirus

Yellow Fever Virus (Group B). The virus is transmitted from forest mosquitos, usually species of *Haemagogus,* to monkeys, where it lives in the bloodstream. The transmissible stage in platyrrhines varies from 2 to 6 days, occasionally longer. Resistance to disease among platyrrhines varies, and in some cases the infection results in death, sometimes wiping out entire populations. The mosquito is unharmed and the virus remains with it for life.

Yellow fever, also known as jungle or sylvatic fever, is comparatively new in tropical America. The virus was imported from Africa with its natural mosquito reservoir, the *Aëdes aegypti.* This arthropod lives in a domestic state and transmits the so-called urban yellow fever directly from man to man.

For additional information and bibliographic references, see Laemmert, Castro Ferreira, and Taylor (1946), Clark (1952), Vargas-Méndez and Elton (1953), D. I. H. Simpson (1969, p. 19), Fiennes (1972*a,* p. 166), Kalter (1972*b,* p. 474), Felsenfeld (1972, p. 523), and Galindo (1973).

Picornavirus Group

The known polio, coxsackie, echo- and rhinoviruses are human, but the following information on experimental results with platyrrhines may be of special interest here.

"Marmoset" (= *Saguinus*?) tested for antibodies proved negative to all known polio and coxsackie and to all but 1 of 13 echo-type viruses. In the latter, only 1 individual of 46 animals tested is listed as positive to type 11 (Kalter 1972*b*). However, Hsiung, Black, and Henderson (1964, p. 5) report (from the literature, not immediately available to me) the susceptibility of *Cebus capucinus* to polio virus type 1, *Ateles* to polio virus types 1 and 2, *Alouatta palliata* to polio virus, probably type 1, and *Callithrix jacchus* not susceptible to polio virus, possibly type 2. Virus susceptibility of primary tamarin kidney cell cultures to polio Brunhilde, polio 1 Chat, polio 2 and polio 3 Fox with cytopathic effect was reported by F. Deinhardt and Deinhardt (1966).

In another report, belatedly come to hand, Kalter and Heberling (1972) give a list of Picornavirus antibody found in the 3 platyrrhine "species" shown in table 35. The same serologic tests were negative in *Saimiri sciureus* (40–70 specimens), *Cebus capucinus* (22–50 specimens),

Table 35. Picornavirus Antibody in Platyrrhine Monkeys

Antigen	*"Marmoset"*	*Howler* (Alouatta *sp.)*	Ateles
Coxsackie A9	2/83[1]	——	——
Coxsackie A20	2/21[2]	0/34	0/36
Echo 3	0/83	3/34	0/36
Echo 4	——	——	——
Echo 6	——	0/41	2/49
Echo 7	1/87	0/56	0/68
Echo 9	——	0/39	0/49
Echo 11	2/83	0/34	0/36
Echo 12	1/87	0/56	0/90
Echo 13	1/82	2/34	0/36
SV 4	0/4	——	——
SV 16	——	0/47	7/13
SV 19	5/80	——	——
SV 45	1/67	0/32	0/31

SOURCE: Data from Kalter and Heberling (1972).
[1] No. specimens with antibodies/No. specimens tested.
[2] From *Saguinus oedipus oedipus* of the Primate Research Colony, San Diego Zoo. Reported by Kalter, Heberling, and Cooper (1974). The same authors report positive serologic tests in the same species for echoviruses 7, 11, 12, 13, SV 16, SV 45.

Lagothrix lagothricha (1 and 7) and *Aotus trivirgatus* (10, 12).

Diplornavirus (Reovirus) Group

Tamarins, genus *Saguinus,* received in a shipment from South America were infected with reovirus type 3 (SA 3) (F. Deinhardt, Holmes, Devine, J. Deinhardt 1967). Kalter (1972*b,* p. 485) lists "marmosets" (= *Saguinus*?) with antibodies positive for types 1 and 3. Kalter and Heberling (1972) present the data on reovirus infection in platyrrhines summarized in table 36. Serological data, according to Heberling (1972, p. 520) "suggest all primates are susceptible to at least one type."

Table 36. Reovirus Antibody in Platyrrhhine Monkeys

	Antigen			
Species	*1*	2	3	*SV 12*
"Marmoset"	3/93[2]	0/93	29/83	0/38
Saguinus oedipus oedipus[1]	1/24	0/24	19/24	0/24
Saimiri sciureus	23/62	26/62	11/61	12/22
Saimiri sciureus[1]	8/22	3/22	1/22	12/22
Aotus trivirgatus	1/8	2/8	5/10	——
Alouatta sp.	0/81	0/81	14/59	0/57
Cebus capucinus	0/42	0/42	21/42	0/37
Lagothrix lagothricha	2/6	2/6	5/7	0/1
Ateles paniscus	3/78	2/78	20/45	15/73

SOURCE: Kalter and Heberling (1972).
[1] Specimens from the Primate Research Colony, San Diego Zoo, reported by Kalter, Heberling, and Cooper (1974).
[2] No. specimens with antibodies/No. specimens tested.

Myxoviruses (Orthomyxovirus and Paramyxovirus Groups)

Tamarins, genus *Saguinus,* contracted influenza virus type A2 (Asian) from humans during shipment to laboratory; other viruses isolated from the shipment include parainfluenza types 2 and 3. (Deinhardt, Holmes, Devine, and Deinhardt 1967, p. 61). Antibodies for myxoviruses found by Kalter and Heberling (1972) are shown in table 37. According to Kalter, Heberling, and Cooper (1974) *Saguinus oedipus oedipus* of the Primate Research Colony, San Diego Zoo, was infected with influenza virus A2 and B and the mumps and parainfluenza 2 viruses. Squirrel monkeys (*Saimiri sciureus*) of the same colony showed antibodies for influenza viruses A and A2 in addition to viruses for measles, mumps, and parainfluenza 3.

Levy and Mirovic (1971) report a measles epizootic that resulted in the death of 326 callitrichids of a colony in the University of Texas Dental Science Institute, Houston. The epizootic that lasted from January into June 1966 affected *Callithrix jacchus jacchus, Saguinus oedipus oedipus,* and *Saguinus fuscicollis* subspp. Clinical aspects of the disease were described in detail, but, curiously, the authors fail to mention either in lump sums or by species the actual number of animals exposed to infection, the percentage infected, and the percentage that survived the disease.

Rhabdovirus Group

Rabies. Rabies is an acute infectious viral disease of the central nervous system in warm-blooded animals. The virus persists in nature as a salivary gland infection and is usually transmitted by biting.

Nothing is known of monkey rabies in the wild. Persons receiving treatment in 1967 for bites inflicted by rabid captive platyrrhines numbered 2 in Brazil, 3 in Uruguay, and 32 in Argentina. It is doubtful that this information reflects a reasonable approximation to the true extent of rabies among primates held as pets or in zoos in the countries mentioned. It does indicate, nevertheless, that wild simians are susceptible to rabies virus, and possibly become infected at times, most likely through the bite of rabid bats. The vampire bat, *Desmodus rotundus,* may be an asymptomatic carrier.

In the United States between 1939 and 1966, 7 cases of platyrrhine rabies were reported. A *Saimiri* and a *Cebus* were identified among these.

Records cited here are from Fiennes (1972*b*).

Vesicular Stomatitis Virus—Indiana Serotype. Vesicular stomatitis virus—Indiana, and arbovirus, naturally infects many mammalian species including the Panamanian primates *Saguinus oedipus geoffroyi, Aotus trivirgatus, Cebus capucinus, Alouatta palliata, Ateles*

Table 37. Myxoviruses (Orthomyxovirus and Paramyxovirus) Antibody in Platyrrhine Monkeys

Antigen	*"Marmosets"*	Saimiri	Cebus capucinus	Lagothrix lagothricha	Alouatta *sp.*	Ateles paniscus
PR 8	0/65[1]	3/59	0/14	0/2	0/7	1/21
FM 1	0/65	4/59	1/14	0/2	0/7	0/21
Jap-2 (influenza)	28/65	41/59	4/14	1/2	1/7	3/21
Lee	18/63	10/59	3/14	1/2	0/7	0/21
Measles	0/75	16/58	0/41	0/3	0/57	0/76
Mumps	23/63	7/53	0/16	0/2	2/6	5/20
Parainfluenza 1	0/75	1/59	0/14	0/3	0/7	0/21
Parainfluenza 2	0/75	0/59	0/14	0/3	0/7	0/21
Parainfluenza 3	4/75	21/59	4/14	1/3	1/7	7/21
Respiratory syncytial	0/50	0/29	0/2	1/6	0/3	0/7
SV 5	10/53	0/49	0/5	——	——	0/7
SV 41	0/15	0/49	0/5	——	——	0/7

SOURCE: Data from Kalter and Heberling (1972).
[1] No. specimens with antibodies/No. specimens tested.

paniscus, and man (Srihongse 1969). Evidence of virus multiplication in, and bite by, experimentally infected sand flies, particularly *Lutzomyia trapidoi*, suggests that these insects may be vectors of the virus (Peralta and Shelokov 1966; Tesh, Peralta, and Johnson 1969; Tesh, Chaniotis, and Johnson 1970).

VSU-Indiana can be transmitted transovarially through two consecutive generations of *Lutzomyia trapidoi*. Thus, the progeny of infected females can transmit the virus by bite to a susceptible animal (Tesh, Chaniotis, and Johnson 1972). Still unknown is where sand flies acquire VSU-Indiana in nature. "Experimental studies indicate that although a variety of animals are susceptible to VSU-Indiana infection, they do not develop sufficient viremia to infect a biting arthropod. This raises the possibility that many or most wild vertebrates may actually be 'dead-end' hosts in the natural cycle of VSU-Indiana" (Tesh, Chaniotis, and Johnson 1970, p. 494).

Oncornavirus (Leukovirus) Group

The oncogenic RNA virus or leukoviruses (Kalter 1972*a*, p. 460) have been reviewed by Wolfe and Deinhardt (1972) under the name oncornaviruses. None are known to be indigenous to platyrrhines.

Rous sarcoma virus. The Schmidt-Ruppin strain of the avian Rous sarcoma virus (RSV-SR) induced invasive metastasizing tumors in newborn *Saguinus fuscicollis* and *S. nigricollis* (F. Deinhardt 1966, p. 443; 1967, p. 183). The same strain induced fibrosarcomas, rhabdomyosarcomas and osteosarcomas in *Callithrix jacchus jacchus, C. j. penicillata, Saguinus fuscicollis*, and *S. oedipus oedipus.* Rous sarcoma virus had not been known to produce osteogenic tumors in any other animal (Levy, Taylor, S. H. Hampton, Thoma 1969).

Other primates susceptible to RSV include *Saimiri sciureus, Cercopithecus, Galago crassicaudatus,* (Wolfe, Marczynska, Rabin, R. Smith, Tischendorf, Gavitt, and Deinhardt, 1971, p. 676), *Macaca, Myopithecus,* and *Papio hamadryas* (Rabin 1971).

The degree of viral susceptibility, according to Wolfe and Deinhardt (1972), ranged in descending order from *Saguinus* spp., *Saimiri, Callithrix,* and catarrhine monkeys to galagos.

Simian sarcoma C-Type Virus (Lagothrix) SSV-1. A C-type simian sarcoma virus type 1 was isolated from tumor and bone marrow tissue of a wooly monkey with spontaneous fibrosarcoma and replicated in vitro in muscle cell cultures of the same species (Theilen, Gould, Fowler, and Dungworth 1971). The virus induced tumors in *Saguinus nigricollis* and *S. fuscicollis* (Wolfe, Deinhardt, Theilen, Rabin, Kawakami, and Bustad 1971), and in *Saguinus mystax* and *Saimiri sciureus* (Rabin 1971, p. 1042; Theilen, Wolfe, Rabin, Deinhardt, Dungworth, Fowler, Gould, and Cooper 1973).

Feline Fibrosarcoma Virus. Two strains of feline fibrosarcoma virus, Snyder-Theilen (ST-FeSV) and Gardner-Arnstein (GA-FeSV) consistently induced sarcomas or fiibrosarcomas in *Saguinus nigricollis, S. fuscicollis,* and *S. oedipus* (Wolfe, Smith, Hoekstra, Marczynska, Smith, McDonald, Northrop, and Deinhardt 1972; and by Deinhardt, Wolfe, Northrop, Marczynska, Ogden, McDonald, Falk, Shramek, Smith, and Deinhardt 1972). The oncogenicity of ST-FeSV in nonhuman primates (*Saguinus fuscicollis*) was first reported by Deinhardt, Wolfe, Theilen, and Snyder (1970), or perhaps Wolfe, McDonald, and Deinhardt (1970).

Other primates susceptible to FeSV include *Saimiri sciureus* and *Macaca* spp. (Wolfe and Deinhardt 1972).

Arenovirus Group

Lymphocytic Choriomeningitis Virus. The viral disease is rare or accidental among platyrrhines. Kalter and Heberling (1972) found antigens in 1 of 66 "marmosets" examined and none in 6 species of cebids (table 34).

Unclassified Viruses

Viral Hepatitis type A (infectious hepatitis). Tamarins of the *Saguinus nigricollis* group, also *S. oedipus* and *S. mystax,* are experimentally susceptible to human or a humanlike hepatitis produced or activated by inoculation with serum from humans infected with acute hepatitis. The disease is serially transferable from tamarin to tamarin (Holmes, Capps, and Deinhardt 1965; F. Deinhardt and Holmes 1966; F. Deinhardt, Holmes, Capps, and Popper 1967). However, the claim of direct involvement of the human viral agent in the production of hepatitis in tamarins is not yet entirely accepted. Parks and Melnick (1969), Parks et al. (1969), and Melnick and Parks (1970), suggest that the cause of tamarin hepatitis may be a latent tamarin virus activated by inoculation with human materials. They also mention cases of spontaneous hepatitis in laboratory *Saguinus oedipus.* Their arguments, however, seem to have been fairly well rebutted (F. Deinhardt, Holmes, Wolfe, and Junge 1970), but the real identity of the hepatitis agent in tamarins remains unknown. Investigations continue and new light has been cast on the subject as this manuscript was about to go to press by Bradley, Krushak, and Maynard (1974) and by Dodd (1974).

Whatever the outcome of further research with tamarin hepatitis, the virus involved appears to be active and serially transmissible only in species of the genus *Saguinus* and questionably in *Callithrix jacchus* among nonhuman primates. The serum has not been tested in other platyrrhines. The reaction in baboons (*Papio*) proved negative and in no other catarrhine except the chimpanzee has the disease been serially transmissible (cf. F. Deinhardt 1970*a;* Holmes, Wolfe, and Deinhardt 1972). The susceptibility of tamarins and possibly other callitrichids to human or a humanlike viral hepatitis and the serial transmissibilities of the disease in tamarins may be tentatively regarded as a unique callitrichid trait.

Foamy Viruses

Simian foamy virus type 4. Saimiri sciureus (isolated by Johnston 1969 and cited by Hsiung and Swack 1972, p. 565).

Simian foamy virus (spider monkey). Ateles paniscus (synctium-forming virus isolated by Hooks et al. 1973 from brain culture grown in vitro).

Simian foamy virus (red uakari). Cacajao calvus rubicundus (unpublished description of a lymphocyte associated virus was mentioned by Barahona et al. in 1975 and an abstract was published by Barahona et al. in 1976.

Bacteria (Schizomycetes)

Bacteria are pervasive, and I have no intention here of dealing with more than selected samples probably pathogenic for platyrrhines.

Eubacteriales (Spherical or Rod-Shaped Bacteria)

Enteric bacteria are cosmopolitan. Only two recent sources for infestation in callitrichids are cited here. Host species examined by F. Deinhardt, Holmes, Devine, and Deinhardt (1967) are the tamarins *Saguinus fuscicollis nigrifrons, S. f. lagonotus* (*S. f. illigeri* misnamed), *S. f. illigeri* (= *S. f. devillei*), all members of the *S. nigricollis* group, and the cotton-top *Saguinus oedipus oedipus*. The authors list the number of individual animals infested but without sorting them to kind. Perhaps both species are equally hospitable to the bacteria listed. Animals examined by Murphy et al. (1972) were identified as *Saguinus nigricollis* (possibly includes individuals of *S. fuscicollis*), and *S. mystax*. Bacteria found in each species is given, as listed below. Only the generic names of the bacteria are given. Those recorded by F. Deinhardt et al. are identified by (D) and those by Murphy et al. by (M).

Pseudomonadaceae
Pseudomonas Migula, 1894 (D; M)
Saguinus nigricollis group
Saguinus mystax
Spirillum Ehrenberg, 1830
Rat-bite fever caused by *S. minus* was seen in catarrhines but not in platyrrhines (cf. Pinkerton 1972).

Micrococcaceae
Micrococcus Cohn, 1872 (D)
Staphylococcus Rosenbach, 1884 (D)
Listed as a synonym of *Micrococcus* by Breed, Murray, and Hitchens (1948, p. 235).

Neisseriaceae
Neisseria Trevisan, 1885 (D)

Lactobacteriaceae
Streptococcus Rosenbach, 1884 (D)
Enterococcus Thiercelin and Jouhaud, 1903 (D)
E. proteiformis Thiercelin and Jouhaud is listed as a synonym of *Streptococcus faecalis* by Breed, Murray, and Hitchens (1948, p. 325).

Achromobacteriaceae
Alcaligenes Castellani and Chalmers, 1919 (D)

Enterobacteriaceae
Escherichia Castellani and Chalmers, 1919 (D; M)
Saguinus nigricollis group
Saguinus mystax
Citrobacter Werkman and Gillen, 1932 (M)
According to Breed, Murray, and Hitchens (1948, p. 448), all nominal species of *Citrobacter* = *Escherichia freundii.*
Aerobacter Beijerinck, 1900 (M)
Saguinus nigricollis group
Saguinus mystax
Klebsiella Trevisan, 1885 (D; M)
Saguinus nigricollis group
Saguinus mystax
Serratia Bizio, 1823 (D)
Proteus Hausser, 1885 (D; M)
Saguinus nigricollis group
Saguinus mystax
Salmonella Lignieres, 1900 (D; M)
Saguinus nigricollis group
Shigella Castellani and Chalmers, 1919 (D; M)
Saguinus nigricollis group
Saguinus mystax

Bacillaceae
Bacillus Cohn, 1872 (D)
Clostridium Prazmowski, 1880 (D)

Actinomycetales (Filamentous or Rod-Shaped Bacteria)

Mycobacteriaceae
Mycobacterium Lehmann and Newmann, 1896
Mycobacterium tuberculosis
Three strains of the acid-fast tuberculosis-causing bacillus *Mycobacterium tuberculosis* recognized are the human, bovine, and avian. All orders of mammals may be infected but primates appear to be the most susceptible.

It is generally agreed that New World monkeys are highly resistant to tuberculosis. Moreland (1970), who collected the published data, concluded that tuberculosis is indeed unusual among wild living platyrrhines but may be contracted in captivity by exposure to diseased catarrhines including humans. The disease has been identified in laboratory or zoo representatives of *Saimiri sciureus, Ateles paniscus, Cebus apella, Aotus trivirgatus, Callithrix jacchus jacchus,* and *C. j. penicillata.* It was fatal to some.

The death rates of various primate groups from an epidemic of *human-type* tuberculosis in the London Zoo between 1946 and 1955 are compared in table 38 with data from Fiennes (1972, p. 317). By 1965, according to Fiennes, no new cases of human-type tuberculosis were encountered. Since then, however, sporadic cases of the *bovine type* of the disease occurred, all in Old World monkeys or apes.

A case of the third and least common strain of tuberculosis, the *avian,* was recorded by Fiennes (1972*c*) for the common marmoset, *Callithrix jacchus.* The source of infection was believed to be raw eggs.

Mycobacterium abscessus
Aotus trivirgatus
(See Karlson, Seibold, and Wolf 1970)

Spirochetales (Spiral Bacteria)

Treponemataceae
Borrelia Swellengrebel, 1907
(Faust and Russell 1965, pp. 758, 801; Pinkerton 1972.) *Borrelia* spp.

Relapsing fever caused by spirochetes of the genus *Borrelia* appears in New and Old World monkeys. The

Table 38. Nonhuman Primate Death Rates from Human-type Tuberculosis

Primate Group	*Total Autopsies*	*Number of Deaths from Tuberculosis*	*Percentage of Deaths from Tuberculosis*
Colobinae	19	1	5.0
Platyrrhini	238	14	5.9
Prosimians and treeshrews	120	9	7.5
Apes	80	11	14.0
Cercopithecus spp.	85	30	35.3
Macaca, Papio, Mandrillus, Cercocebus, Miopithecus, Erythrocebus	208	129	62.0

human body louse, *Pediculus corporis,* serves as chief vector in Europe and Asia. Ticks of the genus *Ornithodoros* (Argasidae) disseminate the disease in central and south Africa, Israel, Iran, and North and South America. The spirochetes transmitted to African and American monkeys are like those found in human cases of relapsing fever. In the New World, monkeys, certain marsupials, rodents, armadillos, and carnivores are evidently among the vertebrate reservoirs from which outbreaks in man originate (Clark, Dunn, and Benevides 1931). Natural infection with *Borrelia* (*Spirochaeta*) *venezuelensis* (= *S. neotropicalis*) was found in *Saguinus oedipus geoffroyi.* Vectors are the ticks *Ornithodoros rudis* (= *venezuelensis*), and *O. talaje.* The same spirochete was transmitted to man, *Aotus trivirgatus, Cebus capucinus,* and *Ateles paniscus* (Clark, Dunn, and Benevides 1931; Dunn and Clark 1933; see also Nouvel 1954).

Leptospira Noguchi, 1917

Leptospira spp.

Leptospirosis (Stuttgart disease, Weil's disease, canicola fever), caused by *Leptospira,* does not appear to be natural to platyrrhines. Serological tests with simians conducted by Minette (1966) exposed histories of natural cases of leptospirosis in individuals representing 11 of 22 catarrhine species and only 1 (*Saguinus oedipus oedipus*) of 11 (12 listed) platyrrhine species. The pathogen in the case of the bare-face tamarin was identified as *Leptospira ballum.* The transmitting agent is not known, but rodents, bats, and other mammals are suspect.

Rickettsiales (Rickettsia organisms)

Rickettsiaceae

Rickettsia da Rocha Luna, 1916 (see Bertram 1962)

Rickettsia burneti (*Coxiella burneti*)

Antibodies to the tick-borne agent of Q-fever have been found in 1 of 13 squirrel monkeys (*Saimiri sciureus*) and 6 of 15 tamarins (*Saguinus oedipus oedipus*) in the Primate Research Colony, San Diego Zoo (Kalter, Heberling, and Cooper 1974).

Fungi

Fungal infections specific to primates are unknown. General infections of nonhuman primates are briefly reviewed by Al-Doory (1972) and need not be treated here. However, among the tegumentary mycoses, the fungi causing piedras are particularly interesting. The pathological conditions of these hair infections are sometimes confused with natural structures or pigments.

Black piedra caused by ascomycetes of the genus *Piedraia* is a common infection of hair in humid tropical regions. It has been found in nearly all primate groups. White piedra, rarely found outside temperate zones of the world, is caused by an imperfect yeastlike fungus, *Trichosporon cutaneum.* It infects man and other mammals. The only nonhuman primate known to have been infected is a "monkey" "imported from Latin America" (Kaplan, Georg, and Ajello 1958).

As described by Kaplan (1959, p. 113), black piedra "invades beneath the hair cuticle, proliferates and eventually breaks out to surround the shaft, forming a discrete brown to black hard nodule." The infection is not spread from animal to animal but can be picked up from the substrate. White fur heavily infected with black piedra appears gray. One or two black nodules on individual hairs may give the illusion of an agouti pattern.

Kaplan (1959) examined 438 prepared skins of primates preserved in the American Museum of Natural History. Thirty-six genera and nearly all families from throughout the geographic range of the order were represented. Of the total, 195, or 44.5%, were infected with black piedra. Among the 67 skins of prosimians alone (lemuroids, daubentonoids, lorisoids), only 1 was infected. Of 33 skins of various primates that had lived in the New York Zoological Garden, only 2 were infected.

It was noted that infected hairs frequently broke at the site of nodule formation. Animals that had lost or shed infected hair rarely became reinfected in environments, such as the New York Zoo, unfavorable for black piedra development.

Van Uden, Barros Machado, and Castelo Branco (1963) reported finding black piedra infection in 53 (64.6%) of 82 central African mammals. Among the 56 primates, 40 colobines and cercopithecines, or 71.4%, were infected, but only 1 of the 11 galagos was infected. No explanation has been offered for the low incidence of infection among prosimians. The tail was the principal site of infection in mammals generally. The same holds true for the callitrichids used in the present study and skins of other mammals in the Field Museum examined at random.

Protozoa

Parasitic protozoans are separable into those inhabiting bloodstream and tissues and those occupying the intestinal tract and genitalia. Most studies have been made on the blood parasites of the genera *Plasmodium, Toxoplasma, Leishmania,* and *Trypanosoma.* The remaining protozoans listed here have been found in the intestinal tract of platyrrhines. In most cases the hosts were captives and exposed to accidental infection.

Records compiled by Kessel (1928), Stiles and Hassall (1929), Stiles and Nolan (1929), Hegner (1935), Dunn (1968), Marinkelle (1969) for *Isospora* (Sporozoa), Wellde et al. (1971) for *Aotus,* Kuntz and Myers (1972), Burrows (1972), and Hoare (1972), are included in the following lists of parasites and hosts. The records for *Saguinus* are mainly from Deinhardt, Holmes, Devine, and Deinhardt (1967).

The major subdivisions of the phylum Protozoa are controversial, but the family and superfamily categories adopted here are generally recognized in one form or another.

Mastigophora (Flagellates)
- Chilomastigidae
  - *Chilomastix* Alexeieff, 1910
    - *Chilomastix mesnili*
      - *Alouatta villosa*
      - *Cebus apella*
    - *Chilomastix* sp.
      - *Aotus trivirgatus*
- Bonoidae
  - *Embadomonas* Mackinnon, 1911
    - *Embadomonas intestinalis*
      - *Alouatta caraya*
      - *Cebus apella*
- Hexamitidae
  - *Giardia* Kuenstler, 1822
    - *Giardia intestinalis* (= *lambia*)
      - *Saguinus nigricollis* group
      - *Saguinus oedipus*
      - *Callimico goeldii* (Lorenz 1972)
      - *Aotus trivirgatus*
      - *Alouatta villosa*
      - *Alouatta caraya*
      - *Cebus apella*
      - *Cebus capucinus*
      - *Ateles paniscus geoffroyi*
- Trichomonadidae
  - *Trichomonas* Dujardin, 1841
    - *Trichomonas hominis*
      - *Saguinus oedipus geoffroyi*
      - *Callimico goeldii* (Lorenz 1972)
      - *Saimiri sciureus*
      - *Aotus trivirgatus*
      - *Alouatta villosa*
      - *Alouatta caraya*
      - *Cebus capucinus*
      - *Ateles paniscus*

    (Levine [1970] recognizes the combination *Pentatrichomonas hominis* and includes *Callicebus* sp. and *Lagothrix lagothricha* among platyrrhine hosts.)
- Trypanosomatidae
  - *Leishmania* Ross, 1903

Leishmania, a parasite of the bloodstream and tissues, causes several types of disease among animals throughout the warmer parts of the world. The species infecting man in the New World is *L. braziliensis.* The first described Old World form, *L. donovani,* causes kala-azar. A form of *Leishmania* resembling *L. braziliensis* was found in 1 of 29 bare-face tamarins, *Saguinus oedipus geoffroyi,* from Panamá (Baker 1972, p. 32). Since then, Herrer, Christensen, and Beumer (1973) demonstrated *Leishmania braziliensis* in wild-caught Panamanian *Aotus* (1 of 64 individuals) and *Saguinus oedipus geoffroyi* (1/87). No parasites were found in 3 *Alouatta palliata,* 10 *Cebus capucinus,* and 5 *Ateles paniscus.* An *Alouatta* from British Honduras examined by Disney (1968) was negative for *Leishmania.*

In addition to primates, *L. braziliensis* is known to infect two- and three-toed sloths. Other Middle American species of *Leishmania* are *L. mexicana* and *L. hertigi,* the latter specific to the prehensile-tailed porcupine, *Coendou rothschildi.* Other reservoir hosts of neotropical forms of *Leishmania* included marsupials, shrews, bats, rodents, and carnivores.

Insect vectors of *Leishmania* are blood-sucking sand flies of the subfamily Phlebotominae (Psychodidae, Diptera). Three species of the genus *Lutzomyia* were incriminated by Christensen and Herrer (1973) as vectors of *Leishmania braziliensis* in Panamá.

Trypanosoma Gruby, 1843

Species of *Trypanosoma* parasitic in mammals are arranged by Hoare (1972, p. 69) in two sections:

Section STERCORARIA: Developmental cycle in the insect vector completed in feces; transmittal to mammalian host by contamination.

Stercorarians are phylogentically most primitive and heterogenous. They are parasitic in virtually all mammalian orders, the most commonly infected being the ungulates and bats. Only stercorarian parasites naturally infect platyrrhines, a few prosimians, guenons (*Cercopithecus*), and macaques (*Macaca*). Few are pathogenic, the most important being *T. cruzi,* the agent of Chagas's disease or trypanosomiasis.

Section SALIVARIA: Developmental cycle in the hematophagous insect-vector completed in the salivary medium; transmittal to mammalian host by inoculation or "biting." The parasites are mainly Old World in distribution with very few infecting primates. The most important pathogenic species, all of the subgenus *Trypanozoon,* include *T. gambiense* and *T. rhodesiense,* agents of sleeping sickness in man.

The following classification of stercorarian trypanosomes follows Hoare for subgenera. The systematic arrangement of the species and list of hosts is based on the review of the genus by Dunn, Lambrecht, and du Plessis (1963), field investigations in Colombia and in Panamá by Sousa, Rossan and Baerg (1974), by Marinkelle (1966), host records compiled by Ribeiro Albuquerque and Perreira Barretto (1970), Baker (1972), and Hoare (1972). Tabulation of host-parasites reveals no particular pattern of infection. Evidently, the kind and number of trypanosomes infecting platyrrhines is controlled by environmental or geographic factors rather than by differ-

Table 39. Platyrrhine hosts of the Neotropical Species of *Trypanosoma*

	cruzi	minasense	rangeli	lambrechti	saimirii	*Species?*
Cebuella pygmaea		X				
Callithrix jacchus penicillata	X	X				
Callithrix jucchus geoffroyi		X				
Callithrix jacchus jacchus	X	X				
Callithrix argentata melanura	X					
Saguinus fuscicollis	X					
Saguinus nigricollis	X					
Saguinus midas midas		X				
Saguinus midas niger		X				
Saguinus leucopus	X					
Saguinus oedipus geoffroyi	X	X	X			
Saimiri sciureus	X	X			X	
Callicebus moloch		X				X
Callicebus torquatus				X		
Callicebus personatus	X					
Aotus trivirgatus	X	X				X
Pithecia pithecia				X		
Chiropotes satanas				X		
Cacajao calvus	X					
Alouatta villosa		X				
Alouatta fusca		X				
Alouatta caraya		X				
Alouatta belzebul		X				
Alouatta seniculus	X	X		X		
Cebus capucinus	X	X	X			
Cebus albifrons	X	X	X	X		
Cebus apella	X	X	X		X	
Lagothrix lagothricha		X				
Ateles paniscus	X	X				

NOTE: Parasite taxonomy following Dunn, Lambrecht, and du Plessis (1963).

ences in host susceptibility to the parasites. Baker believes that all trypanosomes infecting platyrrhines, except *T. lambrechti,* are possibly geographic races of one species for which the oldest name is *Trypanosoma minasense* Chagas, 1909.

Subgenus *Megatrypanum* Hoare, 1964

Regarded by Hoare as most primitive. It comprises a heterogenous group of large trypanosomes parasitic in nearly all mammalian orders but mostly in artiodactyls and bats. Primate hosts are mostly platyrrhines (table 39), but a few lemuroids and cercopithecines are also infected. Megatrypanosomes are nonpathogenic.

Trypanosoma minasense

According to Dunn, Lambrecht, and du Plessis (1963), *T. minasense* is "*rangeli*like" and the following are conspecific or "*minasense*like," *manguinhense* (*Alouatta*), *florestali* (*Alouatta*), *mycetae* (*Alouatta*), *brimonti* (*Alouatta*), *escomeli* (man), *devei* (*Saguinus*). Hoare (1972) classifies most of these as "*rangeli*like" in his subgenus *Herpetosoma* (q.v.). Deane, Silva, and Loures (1974) describe circadian rhythm in parasite density levels in *Callithrix jacchus.*

Trypanosoma sp.

Lambrecht (1965) reports a trypanosome in Colombian "*Cebus griseus*" (= *C. apella*?) similar to *T. conorhini* commonly found in domestic rats and mice (*Rattus, Mus*). Renjifo, Sanmartín, and Zulueta (1952, p. 318), list *Callicebus moloch ornatus* as infected with *Trypanosoma.* Sousa, Rossan, and Baerg (1974) report a *rangeli*like species in 55 (2.3%) individuals of a total of 2,392 wild-caught *Aotus trivirgatus.*

Subgenus *Herpetosoma* Doflein, 1901

Old World intermediate hosts are mainly fleas, those of Central and South America are triatomine bugs and bedbugs (Hemiptera). Most herpetosomes are parasitic in rodents and a few are known from lagomorphs and primates including *T. perodictici* from the African potto and Demidov's galago, and *T. primatum* from hominoids.

Trypanosoma rangeli

Includes *cebus* (*Cebus*), *ariarii* (man), *guatemalense* (man), according to Dunn et al. (1963) and Hoare (1972). The latter also includes *escomeli* (man).

Trypanosoma mycetae

Hoare (1972, p. 318), recognizes this as a valid species with synonyms *forestali* (*Alouatta*), *manguinhense* (*Alouatta*), ? *brimonti* (*Alouatta*). Dunn et al. (1963) include *mycetae* and synonyms in *minasense.*

Trypanosoma advieri
This parasite of *Ateles* is regarded as *lewisi*-type by Hoare (1972, p. 286) and *minasense*like by Dunn et al. (1963, p. 531).
Trypanosoma saimirii
Dunn et al. (1963, p. 529) and Hoare (1972, p. 317) treat this form as *rangeli*like.
Trypanosoma diasi
Dunn et al. (1963, p. 529) believes this form from *Cebus apella* may be conspecific with *T. saimirii;* Hoare (1972, p. 316) argues it may be a valid species.
Subgenus *Schizotrypanum* Chagas, 1909

Occurs in New World edentates, lagomorphs, rodents, carnivores, primates, and bats, including a few cosmopolitan species. The parasite is transmitted by reduviid bugs (Hemiptera) and occasionally, in the case of *T. cruzi,* cause of Chagas's disease, by the common bedbug (*Cimex*). Bafort and Kageruka (1974) demonstrated *T. cruzi* infection in *Aotus trivirgatus.*

Trypanosoma cruzi
Synonyms or "*cruzi*like" include *lesourdi* (*Ateles*), *sanmartini* (*Saimiri*), *prowazeki* (*Cacajao*).

Sarcodina (Amebas)
Entamoebidae
Endolimax Kuenen and Swellengrebel, 1917
Endolimax nana
Cebus apella
Endolimax sp.
Aotus trivirgatus
Entamoeba Casagrandi and Barbagallo, 1897
Entamoeba histolytica
(Produces amebiasis or amebic dysentery in man.)
Saguinus nigricollis group
Saguinus oedipus oedipus
Callimico goeldii
(Lorenz 1972)
Saimiri sciureus
Alouatta villosa
Alouatta caraya
Lagothrix lagothricha
Ateles paniscus
The parasite may not be native to platyrrhines according to Dunn (1968, p. 42.) Flynn (1973, p. 43) includes "capuchins" among the hosts. See also Vickers (1969, p. 665).
Entamoeba coli
Callimico goeldii
(R. Lorenz 1972)
Entamoeba (?) *coli*
Saguinus nigricollis group
Entamoeba sp.
Aotus trivirgatus
Iodamoeba Dobell, 1919
Iodamoeba butschlii
Callimico goeldii
(Lorenz 1972)
Alouatta
Cebus
Ateles paniscus
Iodamoeba sp.
Aotus trivirgatus

Sporozoa (Nonlocomotory protozoans)
Eimeriidae
Eimeria Schneider, 1875
Eimeria viride
Cebus capucinus
Eimeria sp
Saguinus nigricollis group
(F. Deinhardt, Holmes, Devine, and Deinhardt 1967).
Isospora Schneider, 1881
Isospora arctopitheci
Callithrix jacchus penicillata
The same species was also reported by Marinkelle (1969)
Saguinus oedipus geoffroyi
Cebus capucinus
Hendricks (1974) reports the natural infection of the *Cebus* and *Saguinus* in their natural range in Panamá.
Isospora scorzai
Cacajao calvus rubicundus (natural type host)
Cebus nigrivittatus (experimental host)
Isospora cebi
Cebus albifrons
Isospora endocallimici
Callimico goeldii
(See Duszynski and File 1974)
Toxoplasmidae
Toxoplasma Nicolle and Manceaux, 1909
Toxoplasma gondii
The single known toxoplasmid species is a widespread parasite of birds and mammals transmitted through feces. Toxoplasmosis has been experimentally induced in New and Old World primates, but records of natural infection other than in man are few. Nery-Guimarães, Franken, and Chagas (1971) and Baker (1972) observed the parasite in wild-caught individuals of 3 species of prosimians, 5 species of catarrhines, and the following platyrrhines, with addition of records for *Aotus* and *Callicebus* by Seibold and Wolf (1971)
Callithrix jacchus jacchus
Saguinus fuscicollis illigeri
Saguinus oedipus oedipus
Leontopithecus rosalia rosalia
Saimiri sciureus
Callicebus moloch
Aotus trivirgatus
Pithecia monachus
Cacajao calvus rubicundus
Alouatta seniculus
Cebus capucinus
Cebus apella
Lagothrix lagothricha
Ateles paniscus
Sarcocystidae
Sarcocystis Lankester, 1882
Sarcocystis sp.
(See Nelson, Cosgrove, and Gengozian 1966;

Cosgrove, Nelson, and Gengozian 1968; Flynn 1973)

Callithrix sp.

Saguinus nigricollis

Saguinus fuscicollis

Callimico goeldii

Saimiri sciureus

Lagothrix lagothricha

(See Henderson and Bullock 1968)

Ateles paniscus

Karr and Wong (1975) in recording *Saimiri sciureus* as a newly discovered and first known cebid host evidently overlooked previous records.

Plasmodiidae

Plasmodium Marchiafava and Celli, 1885

Plasmodium brasilianum

(See Dunn and Lambrecht 1963*b*;[1] Deane 1969; Deane et al. 1969; Deane, D'Andretta, and Kameyama 1970; Coatney, Collins, Warren, and Contacos 1971; Deane 1972; Ferreira Neto, Deane, and Almeida 1972; Ferreira Neto and Deane 1973).

Saimiri sciureus

Callicebus moloch

Callicebus personatus

Chiropotes satanas

Cacajao calvus calvus

Cacajao calvus rubicundus

Alouatta villosa

Alouatta fusca

Alouatta seniculus

Alouatta caraya

Cebus capucinus

Cebus albifrons

Cebus apella

Lagothrix lagothricha

Ateles paniscus

Brachyteles arachnoides

Plasmodium simium

(See Fonseca 1951; Deane 1969, 1972; Deane et al. 1969; Coatney, Collins, Warren, and Contacos 1971)

Alouatta fusca

Brachyteles arachnoides

Plasmodium Parasite-Host Relationships

Malarial infection of callitrichids in the wild is unproved. In sharp contrast, all cebid genera except *Aotus* and *Pithecia* are natural hosts of *Plasmodium brasilianum*. The excepted genera live where malaria is endemic and absence of records of infection cannot be explained for lack of tests. *Aotus* is widely separated phylogenetically from all other known platyrrhines, but *Pithecia* is nearly related to *Chiropotes* and *Cacajao*, both natural malarial hosts. It is possible, therefore, that more intensive field sampling may reveal natural infection in *Pithecia*. *Aotus*, on the other hand, stands apart. It has proved to be the most useful experimental animal in studies of human malarias, but experimental infection of this animal with *Plasmodium brasilianum* is not transmissible to mosquitos, although it has been suggested that its experimental infection with *Plasmodium simium* might be (Collins, Contacos, Guinn, and Skinner 1973).

Natural infection of callitrichids by a malarial parasite was unknown until Baerg (1971, p. 8) reported a case of an adult male *Saguinus oedipus geoffroyi* with *Plasmodium brasilianum*. The tamarin was captured near Pacora, Panamá. As Baerg notes, blood smears were negative in the other 566 individuals of *geoffroyi* from the same area, and in the combined (1,015 + 749) total of 1,764 previously wild-caught individuals of the same race received from 1931 to 1968 at the Gorgas Memorial Laboratory in Panamá (cf. Porter, Johnson, and De Sousa 1966). It seems that the natural infection of malaria in 1 specimen of *Saguinus oedipus geoffroyi* out of a total of 2,331 in a land where the disease is endemic is exceptional indeed.

All wild-caught callitrichids sampled from 1964 to July 1968 in Brazil by Deane et al. (1969; Deane and Ferreira Neto, 1969) were free of disease. They include the following numbers.

59 *Callithrix jacchus* (includes *penicillata, aurita, geoffroyi*).

53 *Saguinus midas niger*

1 *Saguinus midas midas*

12 *Saguinus bicolor bicolor*

Dunn and Lambrecht (1963) record negative results in 9 *Cebuella pygmaea*, 27 *Saguinus nigricollis*, and 5 *Saguinus oedipus oedipus*, all wild-caught in Peru or Colombia.

Marinkelle (1966) also reports no infection in 3 wild-caught *Saguinus leucopus* and 12 *Saguinus oedipus* from Colombia.

With the single exception noted, representatives of most species groups of all callitrichid genera except *Leontopithecus* have been tested for malarial infection and all proved negative.

The blood of *Callimico*, lone genus of the remaining living platyrrhine family, has not been examined.

In addition to the natural monkey hosts, infection of the malarial *Plasmodium brasilianum* has been induced experimentally in *Callithrix jacchus* (Deane et al. 1969), and *Saguinus oedipus geoffroyi* (Taliaferro and Taliaferro 1934; also see Coatney et al. 1971). A caged Amazonian *Alouatta belzebul*, exposed to *Anopheles cruzi* in a São Paulo forest, was infected with *Plasmodium simium* and later with *P. brasilianum* (Deane, Deane, Ferreira Neto, and Almeida 1971). Infection of *Aotus trivirgatus* by bite of *Anopheles freeborni* experimentally infected with *Plasmodium simium* was positive (Collins, Contacos, Guinn, and Skinner 1973). Infection by inoculation of *Plasmodium simium* was also positive in *Aotus* (Collins et al. 1973) and in splenectomized *Saimiri, Ateles, Lagothrix*, and *Callithrix jacchus* (Deane, Ferreira Neto, Kumura, and Ferreira 1969). The Annual Report of the Gorgas Memorial Laboratory for fiscal year 1973 (1974 U.S. GPO, Washington, D.C., p. 14) informs that all "species of Panamanian nonhuman primates [*Saguinus oedipus, Saimiri sciureus. Aotus trivirgatus,*

[1] Renjifo, Sanmartín, and Zulueta (1952, p. 163) state that in seven eastern Colombian cebid species examined, they noted *Plasmodium* only in "*Saimiri sciureus* which had been found previously infected with *P. brasilianum*." The same authors are cited by Dunn and Lambrecht (1963 *b*, p. 318), evidently incorrectly, for occurrence of *Plasmodium brasilianum* in all the Colombian monkeys examined, namely *Aotus trivirgatus, Alouatta seniculus, Ateles belzebuth, Cebus fatuellus, Lagothrix lagothricha, Callicebus ornatus*, as well as *Saimiri sciureus*.

Alouatta palliata, Cebus capucinus, Ateles paniscus] have been shown to be susceptible to *Plasmodium simium*." Platyrrhine (*Aotus* included) infection with the human malarial parasites *Plasmodium malariae, P. vivax*, or *P. falciparum*, and human infection with the simian malarial parasites has also been induced experimentally (cf. Deane, Deane, and Ferreira Neto 1966; Porter and Young 1967, 1970; Contacos and Collins 1969; Baerg, Porter, and Young 1969; Young 1970; Fitch 1970; Coatney et al. 1971).

Coatney et al. (1971, pp. 223, 242) list 10 species of the mosquito genus *Anopheles* as experimentally infected or infectible with *Plasmodium brasilianum*, and (1971, p. 151) 6 species as acceptable hosts for *P. simium*. The mosquito most susceptible to infection by both malarial parasites was *Anopheles freeborni*. In the summary of their fieldwork, Deane et al. (1969; 1971) conclude that *Anopheles* (*Kerteszia*) *cruzi* is the likely vector of simian malaria in eastern and southern Brazil, and *Anopheles* (*Kerteszia*) *neivai* is the suspected vector in the Amazonian region where *A. cruzi* does not occur. Transmission of both simian malarias by *Anopheles cruzi* was later confirmed experimentally by Deane, Ferreira Neto, Deane, and Silveira (1970).

According to a number of authorities (cf. Coatney, Collins, Warren, and Contacos 1971 for review) primate malarias arrived in the New World with Europeans and their West African slaves during the sixteenth century. Arguments favoring pre-Columbian invasion or origin of malaria in America are weak and have been convincingly denied (cf. Dunn 1965; Coatney et al. 1971). The parasites currently identified as *Plasmodium brasilianum* and *P. simium* when found in platyrrhines are, according to Dunn (1965), strains of Old World *P. malariae* and *P. vivax* respectively, both parasitic in man.

It appears that within fifty years after Columbus discovered America, two imported Old World malarial species found ready hosts in members of nearly every genus of the family Cebidae. Perhaps more impressive is the fact that the Callitrichidae remained virtually untouched despite their intimate ecological association with the Cebidae and all possible anopheline vectors of malaria. The difference in susceptibility indicates a serological difference between cebids and callitrichids perhaps more significant than might be guessed from chemical analyses alone. On the other hand, the similarity of their response to plasmodial infection suggests as close an ecological resemblance between cebids (*Aotus* excepted) and catarrhines as their morphological characters indicate. No New World mammals other than cebids and man are naturally infected by malarial parasites of any kind. Curiously parallel is that among all New World animals only man and cebids are naturally infected by the Old World louse *Pediculus* (q.v., p. 393). Wood (1975), whose paper just came to hand, offers the expected serological evidence in support of the thesis of a post-Columbian introduction of malaria into the Americas. She shows that the distribution of the ABO blood type among natives implies that a force such as malaria selecting for the presence of blood groups A or B was absent until quite recently.

Malaria and Continental Drift

The distribution of malarial parasites prompted Garnham (1973, p. 393) to suggest that "if the theory of a human origin of simian malaria in Latin America is correct, the absence of indigenous *Plasmodium* (and of *Hepatocystis*) could be ascribed to the early separation of the New World monkeys from the main primate line at a date prior to the evolution of malarial parasites in the latter, or in other words to the early date of colonization of the New World by monkeys before malaria had appeared in the Old World." Garnham reinforces this view with the argument that

> If one accepts the theory that malaria did not appear in [Old World] monkeys until *after* the branching off of the New World families, the absence of this infection should be even more apparent in those families which had separated still earlier. Such families are to be found in the prosimians which are widely distributed today in the Old World tropics. The galagos, tarsiers, tree-shrews, slow loris, lemurs and pottos have been extensively examined, and, with a single exception, they are all apparently free of both *Plasmodium* and *Hepatocystis*. . . . The presence of two species of malaria parasites of the subgenus *Vinckeia* in lemurs is interesting, because *Vinckeia* does not occur in other primates, but is essentially a parasite of the lower mammals. The isolation of Madagascar together with the great degree of speciation and the number of families of the lemurs ought to have been accompanied by a similar proliferation of the haemosporidiids. This has not occurred, however.

The if and when of the geographic separation of New World monkeys from possible African ancestors is still largely hypothetical. On the other hand, the phylogenetic separation between cebids susceptible to natural malarial infection and callitrichids and *Aotus* with natural immunities is real and demonstrable.

Nosemidae
- *Nosema* Naegeli 1857
  - *Nosema cuniculi*
    - (Brown, Hinckle, Trevethan, Kupper, and McKee 1973)
    - *Saimiri sciureus*

Ciliata (Ciliated protozoans)

Balantidiidae
- *Balantidium* Claparède and Lachmann, 1858
  - *Balantidium coli*
    - (Produces balantidiasis in man.)
    - *Alouatta caraya*
    - *Cebus apella*
    - *Ateles paniscus*

Pycnothricidae
- *Taliaferria* Hegner and Rees, 1933
  - *Taliaferria clarki*
    - *Ateles paniscus*

Trematoda (Flukes)

The classification of Brazilian trematodes proposed by Travassos, Teixeira de Freitas, and Kohn (1969) is followed here. Other authors consulted in the preparation of the platyrrhine host-trematode parasite list include Yamaguti (1958), Yamashita (1963), Cosgrove (1966), Thatcher and Porter (1968), Cosgrove, Nelson, and Gengozian (1968), Kuntz (1972), and others cited below.

In the list, the superscript [a] signifies that one or more genera or species, or the same species of the marked taxon, infect catarrhines. The superscript [b] means that one or more genera or species of the marked taxon infect prosimians. Superscript [c] indicates that nonprimate mammals are also infected. Other vertebrate hosts are indicated by A (amphibians), B (birds), F (fish), R (reptiles).

Schistosomatiformes
Schistosomatidae (B)
Schistosoma[ac] Weinland, 1858
Schistosoma mansoni[ac]
Aotus trivirgatus
Saimiri sciureus
Cebus apella
Human schistosomiasis has been experimentally induced in *Saimiri* and *Cebus*. The parasite may occur naturally in some catarrhines (*Papio, Macaca, Cercopithecus, Cercocebus*). It also occurs in many New and Old World murid rodents and in the opossum (*Didelphis*). Experiments conducted by Warren and Simões (1966) indicate that *Callithrix jacchus* is resistant to *Schistosoma mansoni*.

Cebus apella and *Saimiri sciureus* have been experimentally infected with *Schistosoma haematobium* (Kuntz, Myers, Huang, and Moore, 1971). *Aotus trivirgatus* is also susceptible to infection by *S. haematobium* and by *S. japonicum*, the third species of the genus pathogenic to man (Erickson, et al. 1971).

Strigiformes
Diplostomidae (B)
Neodiplostomum Railliet, 1919 (B)
Neodiplostomum tamarini
Cebuella pygmaea
Saguinus fuscicollis
Saguinus nigricollis
Leontopithecus rosalia rosalia
"Diplostomid mesocercariae" (Kuntz 1972, p. 110).
Callicebus
(*Papio*)

Plagiorchiiformes
Dicrocoeliidae[ab] (A, R, B)
Conspicuum Bhalerao, 1936 (B)
Conspicuum conspicuum (B)
Includes *Platynosomum amazonensis* Kingston and Cosgrove, 1967; and *P. marmoseti* Kingston and Cosgrove, 1967
Callithrix jacchus
Saguinus fuscicollis
Saguinus nigricollis
Saguinus mystax
Callimico goeldii
The principal hosts of *Conspicuum conspicuum* are birds. A second species, *Conspicuum pulchrum*, infects the terrestrial cricetine rodent *Oxymycterus quaestor*. The forms described by Kingston and Cosgrove were found in 35 of 441 specimens of *Saguinus nigricollis* (or *fuscicollis*) and 9 of 20 individuals of *Callimico goeldii*. Both groups originated in the same "indefinite localities in the upper Amazon Basin" and were maintained in the laboratories of the Oak Ridge Associated Universities, Tennessee.
Zonorchis[c] Travassos, 1944 (B)
Zonorchis goliath[c]
Saguinus oedipus geoffroyi
Aotus trivirgatus
The hosts are Panamanian. Travassos et al. (1969, p. 165) list the opossum (*Didelphis*) as the only known Brazilian host.
Controrchis Price, 1929
Controrchis biliophilus
Alouatta villosa
Ateles paniscus geoffroyi
Athesmia Looss, 1899 (B)
(See Ewing, Helland, Anthony, and Leipold 1968)
Athesmia heterolecithodes[c] (B)
(Includes *Athesmia foxi*) (B)
Saguinus fuscicollis
Saguinus nigricollis
Saguinus oedipus oedipus
Saguinus oedipus geoffroyi
Saimiri sciureus
Callicebus moloch
Aotus trivirgatus
Chiropotes albinasa
Cebus capucinus
Cebus albifrons
Cebus apella
The species has also been recorded from a number of predatory birds and mammals
Athesmia sp.
Callimico goeldii
(Lorenz 1972)
Lecithodendriidae (F, A, R, B)
Phaneropsolus[ab] Looss, 1899 (B)
Phaneropsolus orbicularis
Saguinus fuscicollis
Saguinus mystax
Saimiri sciureus
Aotus trivirgatus
Cebus sp.

Fascioliformes
Echinostomatidae (F, R, B)
Echinostoma[a] Rudolphi, 1809 (R, B)
Echinostoma aphylactum
Saguinus oedipus geoffroyi

Cestoda (Tapeworms)

Cestodes infecting primates belong to the orders Cyclophyllidea and Pseudophyllidea. Adults of the first occur in reptiles, birds, and mammals. Their life cycle includes a bladder larval stage which may occur in vertebrate or invertebrate intermediate hosts. Adults of Pseudophyllidea parasitize fish, amphibians, reptiles, birds, and mammals. Their procercoid and plerocercoid larval stage is passed in crustaceans and their larval stage in vertebrates.

Data for the following list of parasites and platyrrhine hosts were compiled from Yamaguti (1959), Dunn

(1963), Yamashita (1963), Myers (1972), and Porter (1972). For a review of the embroiled taxonomy of the Anoplocephalidae and Davaineidae, see Stunkard (1965*a, b*).

For explanation of symbols used in the lists of parasites, see page 383.

Cyclophyllidea (R, B)
Anoplocephalidae[abc] (R, B)
(Oribatid mites are intermediate hosts.)
Oochoristica[c] Lühe, 1898 (R)
Oochoristica megastoma
(See Della Santa 1956; includes *Atriotaenia megastoma; Mathevotaenia megastoma*)
Callithrix argentata melanura
Saguinus fuscicollis
Saguinus nigricollis
Saguinus midas niger
Saguinus bicolor bicolor
Saimiri sciureus
Callicebus moloch
Callicebus torquatus
Callicebus personatus
Cebus albifrons
Cebus apella
Alouatta belzebul
Alouatta caraya
Ateles paniscus
Brachyteles arachnoides
Mathevotaenia[c] Akhumian, 1946
Mathevotaenia brasiliensis
(See Kugi and Sawada 1970)
Saimiri sciureus
Bertiella[ac] Stiles and Hassall, 1902
Bertiella fallax (? = part *Oochoristica megastoma*)
Cebus capucinus
Probably accidental infection of captive in the Egyptian Zoo.
Bertiella mucronata
Saguinus leucopus
Callicebus personatus nigrifrons
Cebus apella
Alouatta caraya
Moniezia[c] Blanchard, 1891
Moniezia rugosa
Alouatta caraya
Alouatta sp.
Cebus apella
Ateles paniscus
Brachyteles arachnoides
Davaineidae (B)
Raillietina[b] Furmann, 1920 (B)
Raillietina alouattae
Alouatta seniculus
Raillietina demerariensis[ac]
Alouatta villosa
Alouatta seniculus
Raillietina trinitatae
Callicebus moloch
Raillietina (Fuhrmannetta) sp.
Saguinus sp.
Paratriotaenia Stunkard 1965*a*
Paratriotaenia oedipomidatis
Saguinus oedipus
Paratriotaenia sp.
(Cosgrove, Nelson, and Gengozian 1968; Porter 1972)
Saguinus fuscicollis
Saguinus nigricollis
Saguinus leucopus
Saguinus oedipus
Callimico goeldii
Hymenolepidae (B)
Hymenolepis[ac] Weinland, 1858
Hymenolepis cebidarum
Callicebus personatus nigrifrons
Saguinus nigricollis
Saguinus fuscicollis
Hymenolepis sp.
Saimiri sciureus
[*Hymenolepis nana*]
(See Flynn 1973, p. 184)
Saimiri sciureus
Vampirolepis sp.
Callithrix sp.

Pseudophyllidea (F, A, R, B)
Diphyllobothriidae (R, B)
Spirometra[ac] Mueller, 1937 (R) (= Spargana)
Spirometra reptans
Callithrix argentata melanura
Saguinus fuscicollis
Saimiri sciureus
Spirometra mansonoides[c]
(*S. erinaceieuropaei;* cf. Yamashita 1963, p. 47)
Saguinus oedipus geoffroyi
(Cf. Thatcher and Porter 1968, p. 190; also recorded from *Macaca mulatta.*)
Spirometra sp. (Larvae)
Saguinus fuscicollis
Saguinus nigricollis
Saguinus mystax
Saguinus oedipus oedipus
Callimico goeldii
Diphyllobothrium Cobbold, 1858
Diphyllobothrium erinacei
(See *Spirometra* spp. above. Flynn [1973, p. 196] lists *Diphyllobothrium erinacei* for *Saimiri* and *Saguinus* and (p. 568) discusses nomenclature.)

Nematoda (Roundworms)

Records of nematode parasites of primates listed below have been compiled from Stiles and Hassall (1929), Stiles and Nolan (1929), Yamaguti (1961), Yamashita (1963), Dunn (1968), Porter (1972), Kuntz and Myers (1972), and others cited in text. The arrangement of orders, families, and genera follows Chitwood (1969). The *Introduction to nematology* by B. G. Chitwood and M. B. Chitwood (Baltimore: University Park Press, 1974), gives revised classification, but came to hand too late to be of use here. It mentions no additional platyrrhine hosts.

Names of parasite taxons accidentally infecting platyrrhines are enclosed in brackets. The superscript [a] signifies that one or more genera, species, or the same species of the taxon so marked infects catarrhines; superscript [b] means that one or more genera or species of the marked taxon infects prosimians; and superscript [c] indicates that the parasite also infects nonprimate mammals. Parasitization of vertebrates other than mammals is indicated by F (fish), A (amphibians), R (reptiles), and B (birds). The nonprimate host data are mainly from Yamaguti (1961). Life histories of biomedically important nematode groups and species are summarized by Ruch (1959), Yamaguti (1961), and Orihel and Siebold (1972).

Rhabditida (A, R, B)
Strongyloididae (A, R, B)
Strongyloides[a] Grassi, 1879 (A, R, B)
Strongyloides cebus
(See Little [1966] for discussion of genus and species.)
Saguinus sp.
Saimiri sciureus
Cebus capucinus
Cebus apella
Lagothrix lagothricha
Ateles paniscus geoffroyi
[*Strongyloides stercoralis*[a]]
Cebuella pygmaea
Saguinus midas niger
(See Christen 1974, p. 10)
Ateles paniscus geoffroyi
Homo sapiens
[*Strongyloides* sp.]
(See Cosgrove, Nelson, and Gengozian 1968)
Saguinus fuscicollis

Strongylida
[Ancylostomatidae[abc]]
[*Ancylostoma*[a] Dubini, 1843]
(See Dunn 1968, p. 52.)
[*Ancylostoma mycetis*]
Alouatta caraya
[*Ancylostoma* sp.]
Saimiri sciureus
[Uncinariidae]
[*Necator*[ac] Stiles, 1903]
[*Necator americanus*[ac]]
Ateles paniscus
Lagothrix lagothricha
[Strongylidae[a] (R, B)]
[*Characostomum*[a] Railliet, 1902]
[*Characostomum asimilium*[a]]
Aotus trivirgatus
(Probably accidental infection.)
[*Strongylus*[c] Mueller, 1780 (R)]
[*Strongylus hemicolor*]
(See Cobbold [1876], ex Stiles and Nolan [1929, p. 453].)
Pithecia pithecia
Lagothrix lagothricha
[Oesophagostomidae (R)]
[*Oesophagostomum*[a] Molin, 1861]
[*Oesophagostomum aculeatum*]
Cebus capucinus
Trichostrongylidae[ab] (A, R, B)
Trichostrongylus[a] Looss, 1905 (B)
Trichostrongylus cesticillus
Cebus apella
Trichostrongylus sp.
Callimico goeldii
(Lorenz, 1972)
Pithecostrongylus[a] Lubimov, 1930
Pithecostrongylus alatus[a]
Cebuella pygmaea
Molineus[ab] Cameron, 1923
Molineus elegans
Saimiri sciureus
Cebus capucinus
Molineus torulosus
(See Menschel and Stroh, 1963)
Saguinus oedipus
Saimiri sciureus
Aotus trivirgatus
Pithecia pithecia
Cebus capucinus
Cebus apella
(According to Brack, Myers, and Kuntz [1973], the "capuchin" may be an unnatural host.)
Molineus vexillarius
Saguinus nigricollis
Saguinus fuscicollis
Saguinus leucopus
Saguinus oedipus oedipus
Molineus sp.
Ateles paniscus
(See Webster 1968, p. 28)
Graphidioides[c] Cameron, 1923
Graphidioides berlai
Brachyteles arachnoides
Heligmosomatidae
Longistriata[c] Schultze, 1926
Longistriata dubia
Saguinus nigricollis
Saguinus fuscicollis
Saimiri sciureus
Alouatta caraya
Longistriata sp.
(See Cosgrove, Nelson, and Gengozian 1968.)
Saguinus fuscicollis
Metastrongylidae
Metastrongylus Molin 1861
? *Metastrongylus*
Callimico goeldii
(Lorenz, 1972)
Filaroididae[c]
(See Dunn 1968, p. 52.)
Filariopsis van Thiel, 1926
Filariopsis arator
Cebus sp.
Filariopsis aspera
Alouatta seniculus
Filaroides[c] van Beneden, 1858
(See Gebauer, 1933)
Filaroides barretoi
Callithrix jacchus jacchus
Filaroides gordius
Saimiri sciureus
Filaroides cebuellae
Cebuella pygmaea
(Liu 1965, p. 225).
Filaroides cebus
Cebus apella
(Gebauer [1933]; Brack, Boncyk, and Kalter [1974].)

Filaroides sp.
Saguinus fuscicollis
Lagothrix lagothricha

Ascarida (F, A, R, B)
Ascaridae (F, A, R, B)
Ascaris[ac] Linnaeus, 1758
Ascaris cebi
Cebus capucinus
Ascaris elongata
Alouatta
Ascarid (Thatcher and Porter 1968)
Saguinus oedipus geoffroyi
Aotus trivirgatus
Cebus capucinus
Ateles paniscus
Oxyuridae[abc] (F, A, R, B)
[*Enterobius*[abc] Leach, 1853]
[*Enterobius vermicularis*[a]]
Hylobates sp.
Pan troglodytes
Homo sapiens
Cebuella pygmaea
Leontopithecus rosalia rosalia
Ateles paniscus
Paraoxyuronema Artigas, 1937
Paraoxyuronema brachytelesi
Brachyteles arachnoides
Genus *Trypanoxyuris*
(See Inglis, 1961)
Subgenus *Trypanoxyuris* Vevers, 1923
T. trypanuris Vevers, 1923
"Pithecia monacha"—Guyana
(The Guyanan saki is *Pithecia pithecia.*)
Chiropotes satanas chiropotes—Venezuela (Inglis and Díaz-Ungría 1959, p. 182)
Ateles paniscus geoffroyi—Panamá (Thatcher and Porter 1968)
T. atelis Cameron, 1929
Ateles paniscus subspp.—London Zoo; Venezuela (Inglis and Díaz-Ungría 1959); Panamá (Kreis 1932; Thatcher and Porter 1968); Philadelphia Zoo
T. duplicidens Buckley, 1931
Lagothrix lagothricha—London Zoo
T. lagothricis Buckley, 1931
Lagothrix lagothricha—London Zoo; eastern Peru (Inglis and Dunn 1964)
T. interlabiata Sandosham, 1950
Aotus trivirgatus—London; eastern Peru (Inglis and Dunn 1964); Panamá (Thatcher and Porter 1968)
Cebus nigrivittatus—Venezuela (Inglis and Díaz-Ungría 1959)
Chiropotes satanas—Venezuela (Inglis and Díaz-Ungría 1959)
T. minutus Schneider 1866
Saguinus oedipus oedipus—20 imports died of acanthocephalan infection (Menschel and Stroh 1963)
"Alouatta seniculus"—Ipanema, Brazil (The howler of this region is *A. fusca.*)
Alouatta seniculus—Venezuela (Inglis and Díaz-Ungría 1959; 1960; Díaz-Ungría 1965); Colombia (Hugghins 1969); Suriname.
Alouatta caraya—Brazil (Travassos 1925); Argentina (Pope 1966)
Alouatta villosa (= *palliata*)—Panamá (Thatcher and Porter 1968)
Ateles paniscus—Brazil (Cameron [1929, p. 178] argues that the pinworm of the spider monkey included by Schneider with his *T. minutus* from the howler (*Alouatta*) should be assigned instead to *T. atelis* because "each genus of monkey has its own particular species of parasite.")
T. sceleratus Travassos, 1925
Saimiri sciureus—Brazil; Colombia and eastern Peru (Inglis and Dunn 1964); Central America (Cameron 1929)
T. microon von Linstow, 1907
Aotus trivirgatus—Brazil (Travassos 1925)
Subgenus *Hapaloxyuris* Inglis and Cosgrove 1965
T. tamarini Inglis and Dunn 1964
Saguinus nigricollis—eastern Peru
Saguinus fuscicollis—captive (F. Deinhardt, Holmes, Devine, and Deinhardt 1967; Cosgrove, Nelson, and Gengozian 1968)
T. oedipus Inglis and Cosgrove, 1965
Saguinus oedipus—captive
T. callithricis Solomon, 1933
Callithrix jacchus jacchus—captive
Saguinus oedipus geoffroyi—London Zoo; Panamá (Thatcher and Porter 1968)
T. goeldii Inglis and Cosgrove, 1965
Callimico goeldii—captive
Trypanoxyuris (*Hapaloxyuris*) sp. (Porter 1972)
Saguinus fuscicollis
Saguinus oedipus
Callithrix jacchus

Trypanoxyuris includes the nominate subgenus with seven species restricted to cebid hosts, and an eighth found in cebids and a callitrichid (*Saguinus oedipus oedipus*). Subgenus *Hapaloxyuris* Inglis and Cosgrove, 1965, is known only from callitrichids and *Callimico*. The very closely related, if not congeneric, *Paraoxyuronema* Artigas, 1937, with type species *P. brachytelesi* Artigas, 1937, is based on the female only from a wild-caught *Brachyteles arachnoides*. It has been regarded as a subgenus of *Trypanoxyuris* or virtually equivalent to *Hapaloxyuris* but is now treated as *incertae sedis* by Inglis and Cosgrove (1965).

Currently recognized species and respective hosts of *Trypanoxyuris* are listed above. For a complete synonymy see the works cited. The statement of geographic origin distinguishes natural from captive and possibly accidentally infected hosts. The data presented are compiled from Cameron (1929), Sandosham (1950), Inglis and Díaz-Ungría (1959), Inglis (1961), Inglis and Dunn (1964), Thatcher and Porter (1968), and others cited in text. Flynn's (1973, pp. 264, 281–82) listings are not up to date.

In his review of Old and New World pinworms assigned to the then inclusive name *Enterobius*, Cameron (1929, p. 180) noted that:

The genus *Enterobius* is a peculiar one among the parasites of primates in that its life history tends to make it a parasite of the individual. Its eggs do not tend to be broadcast as do those of the other helminths and consequently there must be a tendency for any one species of parasite to restrict itself to the same species of host. The examination of the forms described in this paper suggests that one species restricts itself to one genus of host rather than to one species; in other words the evolution of the parasite is slower than that of the primate. It would seem legitimate to assume, to some extent at least, that the parasite has evolved with the host. If one assumes the existence of a pre-Enterobius form in the pre-simian host, then the modifications of the parasite should accompany the generic differences of the host. One would expect to find forms most closely related to the human parasite in apes, while those in old world monkeys would be closer than [*sic* = to] *E. vermicularis* than [to] those in new world monkeys and the lories [*sic* = lorises] but not so close as [to those] in apes. This actually does seem to be the case although many species are inadequately described and many other species of monkeys have to be examined before the series will be sufficiently extensive to justify any results of value to anthropology.

Studies of 4 pinworm species infecting wild-caught Venezuelan monkeys (cf. Inglis and Díaz-Ungría 1959) impressed Inglis (1961) with the possible usefulness of the "Cameron Hypothesis." With more material at hand, Inglis and Cosgrove (1965, p. 735) summarized the knowledge of pinworm-host relationships as follows:

> It has already been suggested (Inglis and Dunn, 1964) that because the pin-worms grouped in the subgenus *Hapaloxyuris* can be considered more primitive than those grouped in *Trypanoxyuris* the hosts in the Hapalidae (= Callitrichidae) are more primitive than those in the Cebidae. The two new species [*T. oedipus*, *T. goeldii*] described above confirm this suggestion. Further, the relationship of the peculiar monkey *Callimico goeldii* are uncertain. Simpson (1945), for example, follows one school of thought and refers it to the family Cebidae while Hill (1957) after first referring it to a distinct family, Callimiconidae, later agrees that it should be referred to the family Hapalidae (see Hill's preface). The parasites certainly support the reference to the Hapalidae.

These conclusions were hailed by Dunn (1968, p. 63) as "an instance of host-parasite parallelism more striking" than any likely to emerge, and (1970, p. 387) "the most renowned and fully documented example of phylogenetic labeling involving primates."

Considering the state of knowledge of host-parasite relationships, it may be pointless to question Dunn's assessment. Nevertheless, the case is interesting. Separation of New World pinworms of the genus *Trypanoxyuris* from Old World *Enterobius* appears to be valid. Restriction of the subgenus *Trypanoxyuris* to cebids and subgenus *Hapaloxyuris* to callitrichids and *Callimico* does not seem to be true on the basis of the incomplete and not wholly satisfactory data now available. Even if it is true, extensive parasite-host lists show better parallels, but there is no insistance that they point to closer phylogenetic ties between the hosts than can be adduced from the more obvious characters of the hosts alone.

The "Cameron Hypothesis," as described, consists of two parts or principles. First, one parasite species is said to be restricted to one host genus. In agreement with Sandosham (1950), I find the first assumption was not supported by the information available then and has been wholly refuted by evidence accumulated since. Inglis (1961) himself was aware of discrepancies. He noted that *Enterobius vermicularis* infected *Homo, Pan, Hylobates,* and the lion-tamarin, *Leontopithecus rosalia.* Also, *T. trypanus* infected the two genera *Chiropotes* and *Pithecia,* and *T. interlabiata* was hosted by *Cebus* and *Aotus.* All typical records, Inglis (1961, p. 115) observed, are from hosts in captivity but the " 'Cameron Hypothesis'—one species of parasite:one host genus—is a good general guide to the conditions which are likely to be found in the wild." The pinworms from the wild, however, are stubbornly unmindful of the guide. Among the 12 described New World pinworm species, each of 8 is restricted to a single host genus, 1 occurs in 2 host callitrichid genera, 2 in 3 host cebid genera, and 1 in 1 callitrichid and 2 cebid host genera. Possibly a higher frequency of multiple host genera per parasite species will be recorded as platyrrhine parasites become better known.

The second principle, that the phylogeny of the parasite parallels that of the host, is already compromised by breakdown of the first principle. The only pinworm parasite/host relationship with some claim to validity is between parasite-genus and host-suborder (*Enterobius*/*Prosimia,* and Catarrhini; *Trypanoxyuris*/Platyrrhini). On the other hand, the still broad parasite-subgenus to host-family relationship (*Trypanoxyuris*/Cebidae; *Hapaloxyuris*/Callitrichidae and Callimiconidae) does not hold on the basis of present evidence.

The "Cameron Hypothesis" also stipulates narrow parallel evolution between parasite-species and host-genera. No such relationship is indicated. For example, differences between *Aotus, Cebus,* and *Chiropotes* are as great as any among cebids; yet all three are infected by *Trypanoxyuris* (*T.*) *interlabiata.* Four callitrichid species are known hosts of subgenus *Hapaloxyuris,* but only the most distantly related *Callithrix jacchus* and *Saguinus oedipus* share the pinworm species *Trypanoxyuris* (*Hapaloxyuris*) *callithricis.* Ostensibly, the hosts diverged while the parasite remained the same. In contrast, the woolly monkey, *Lagothrix lagothricha,* is infected by two different pinworm species (*T. duplicidens, T. lagothrix*). Other cases of 1 host species with 2 or more parasite species include *Ateles paniscus, Chiropotes satanas, Aotus trivirgatus,* and *Saguinus oedipus.* In these cases, the hosts seemingly were stable while their parasites differentiated. The most ecumenical host is *Saguinus oedipus,* which houses *Trypanoxyuris* (*Trypanoxyuris*) *minuta, T.* (*Hapaloxyuris*) *oedipus,* and *T.* (*H.*) *callithricis,* or representatives of the two supposedly host-segregated subgenera of pinworms.

The significance of the infection of *Callimico* by a pinworm of the subgenus *Hapaloxyuris* is not as clear and simple as believed by Inglis, Dunn, or Cosgrove. The only known host specimen was a captive. Nothing of its history was given and perhaps nothing particular was known. It is reasonable to assume, nevertheless, that the callimico in question, like all callimicos known to me, was closely associated with tamarins at some time between capture in the wild and maintenance in a zoo or laboratory (cf. p. 870). Accidental infection by pinworms was not mentioned as a possibility by Inglis and Cosgrove (1965). Perhaps the possibility was ruled out because the callimico pinworm was regarded as specifically different from the three other known species of *Hapaloxyuris*. Nor was account taken of the fact that pinworms of many more callitrichid species, including those of *Cebuella* and *Leontopithecus,* have not yet been isolated. Furthermore, nothing is known of the wild living parasites of *Callimico* and only eight parasite species have been retrieved from captives to date (1972).

Present knowledge of pinworm distribution and ecology among platyrrhines is too fragmentary to permit judgments on the parallel phylogenetic relationships between parasite species and host genera. It seems to me that only the following can be inferred.

Divergence of African *Enterobius* and South American *Trypanoxyuris* may have occurred during late Mesozoic when the continents began to separate. The association of *Enterobius* with catarrhines, prosimians, lion tamarin (*Leontopithecus*), rat (*Rattus*), and squirrels (*Sciureus*) on the one hand (cf. Sandosham, 1950, p. 203) and the association of *Trypanoxyuris* with platyrrhines and squirrels (*Sciurus*) on the other can be attributed to ecological factors (cf. Inglis 1961, p. 114). Divergence of the platyrrhine infecting subgenera *Trypanoxyuris* and *Hapaloxyuris* may have originated in spatial isolation between ancestral hosts. This is to say that certain cebids evolved in geographic isolation from callitrichids and *Callimico*. As for relationships between *Callimico* and callitrichids the former infected with *Hapaloxyuris* can no more be judged a member of the latter group on this evidence alone than squirrels or *Saguinus oedipus* can be deemed cebids on the basis of the same kind of evidence. If the more primitive pinworm is associated with the more primitive primate, it can be said that callitrichids and *Callimico* are primitive platyrrhines. If all morphological data and their implications are weighed with inferences drawn from parasite/host relationship, then it may be said that *Callimico* probably represents a group coordinate with Callitrichidae and Cebidae. By the same token, Catarrhini and Prosimia all infected with *Enterobius* may also be regarded as distinct but coordinate groups.

Subuluridae[abc] (See Inglis 1958)
- *Primasubulura*[ac] Inglis, 1958
  - *Primasubulura jacchis*
    - *Callitrichidae*
      - (See Porter 1972)
      - *Cebuella pygmaea*
      - *Callithrix jacchus penicillata*
      - *Callithrix jacchus jacchus*
      - *Callithrix jacchus aurita* (? = *jacchus* misnamed?)
      - *Callithrix jacchus aurita* (= *C. aurita coelestis,* Magalhaes Pinto, 1970)
      - *Callithrix argentata argentata*
      - *Callithrix argentata melanura*
      - *Callithrix humeralifer chrysoleuca*
      - *Saguinus nigricollis*
      - *Saguinus fuscicollis*
      - *Saguinus mystax mystax*
      - *Saguinus bicolor bicolor*
      - *Saguinus leucopus*
      - *Saguinus oedipus oedipus*
      - *Saguinus oedipus geoffroyi*
    - *Cebidae*
      - *Callicebus moloch* (= *cupreus*)

Cruziidae
- *Cruzia* Travassos, 1917
  - *Cruzia* sp.
    - *Callimico goeldii*
      - (Lorenz 1972)

Spirurida (F, A, R, B)
- Spiruridae[a] (F, A, R, B)
  - *Protospirura*[a] Seurat, 1914
    - *Protospirura guianensis*
      - (Includes *Spirura tamarini* Cosgrove, Nelson, and Jones, 1963, *apud* Thatcher and Porter 1968.)
      - Monkie-monkie—Suriname (type host = *Saimiri sciureus*)
      - *Saguinus nigricollis*
      - *Saguinus fuscicollis*
      - *Saguinus oedipus geoffroyi*
    - *Protospirura muricola*
      - *Saguinus fuscicollis*
      - *Aotus trivirgatus*
      - *Cebus capucinus*
      - *Ateles paniscus*
    - *Protospirura muriei*
      - (*Spiroptera muriei* Cobbold, 1876, cited in Stiles and Hassall 1929, p. 465.)
      - *Pithecia pithecia*
    - *Protospirura* sp.
      - *Cebuella pygmaea*
        - (See Cristen 1974, p. 10.)
- Habronematidae (R, B)
  - *Parabronema*[c] Baylis, 1921
    - *Parabronema bonnei*
      - (See Díaz-Ungría 1965, p. 394.)
      - *Alouatta villosa*
      - *Alouatta seniculus*
- Thelaziidae[abc] (A, R, B)
  - (See Smith and Chitwood 1967; Orihel and Siebold 1971.)
  - *Trichospirura* Smith and Chitwood, 1967
    - *Trichospirura leptostoma*
      - Callitrichidae
        - *Callithrix jacchus jacchus*
        - *Saguinus oedipus oedipus*
        - *Saguinus fuscicollis*
      - Callimiconidae
        - *Callimico goeldii*
      - Cebidae
        - *Saimiri sciureus*
        - *Callicebus moloch*
        - *Aotus trivirgatus*
- Rictulariidae (R, B)
  - *Rictularia*[abc] Froelich, 1802
    - *Rictularia alphi*[a]
      - *Callithrix jacchus jacchus*
      - *Leontopithecus rosalia rosalia*
      - *Cebus capucinus*
      - *Cebus apella*
- Gongylonematidae
  - *Gongylonema*[a] Molin, 1857 (B)
    - *Gongylonema capucini*
      - *Cebus capucinus*

Gongylonema macrogubernaculum[a]
Cebus capucinus
Cebus apella
Gongylonema pulchrum[a]
Cebus capucinus
Ateles sp.
Gongylonema saimirisi
Saimiri sciureus
Physalopteridae (F, A, R, B)
Physaloptera[abc] Rudolphi, 1819 (A, R, B)
Physaloptera cebi
Cebus apella
Physaloptera dilatata[a]
Callithrix jacchus jacchus
Callicebus moloch
Chiropotes satanas
Alouatta seniculus
(See Hugghins 1969.)
Cebus apella
Lagothrix lagothricha
Physaloptera lagothricis
Lagothrix lagothricha
Physaloptera sp.
Saguinus oedipus geoffroyi
Filariidae (R, B)
Filaria[ac] Mueller, 1787
(The following New World forms are listed in Stiles and Hassall 1929, p. 461; they are probably referrable to other filarial genera.)
Filaria annulata Molin, 1858, p. 386, pl. 1, figs. 5–7
(Syn. *simiae-macaco barrigae*)
Lagothrix lagothricha
Filaria cebi-carayae Molin, 1858, p. 418
(Syn. *simiae-belzebul*)
Alouatta caraya
Filaria cebi-trivirgatae Molin, 1858, p. 418
(Syn. *simiae*)
Aotus trivirgatus
Filaria jacchichrysopygi hepatica Molin, 1858, p. 419
(Syn. *simiae*)
Leontopithecus rosalia chrysopygus
(*"Mystax chrysopygus"*)
Filaria intercostalis Molin, 1858, p. 418
(Syn. *simiae*)
Saimiri sciureus
Filaria nodosa Molin, 1858, p. 380, pl. 1, fig. 3
Callithrix argentata melanura
Callicebus personatus
Filaria torta Molin, 1858, p. 390, pl. 2, figs. 1–4
Lagothrix lagothricha
Filaria sp.
Saguinus midas niger
(See Cristen 1974, p. 10)

Rodríguez López-Neyra (1957) and Yamashita (1963, pp. 41–42) list the following larvae of filaroid nematodes (with respective bibliographic references); more recent references have been added.

Microfilaria marchouxi Mesnil and Brimont, 1910
Callithrix jacchus jacchus
Saguinus midas midas
Saguinus midas niger
Microfilaria midae Mesnil and Brimont, 1909
Saguinus midas midas
Microfilaria paronai, Romaña, 1932
Alouatta caraya
Microfilaria sp.
Callithrix jacchus jacchus (Carini and Marcel 1917; Grieder 1938)
Callithrix jacchus penicillata (Dios, Zuccarini, and Werngren 1925. The authors give Paraguay as host locality, but marmosets do not occur there naturally.)
Saguinus midas midas (Leger 1918)
Saguinus oedipus oedipus (Plimmer 1912; Microfilaria B, D, Chalifoux et al. 1973)
"S. tamarinus" (= "white lipped tamarin," Microfilaria K, Chalifoux et al. 1973)
Leontopithecus rosalia rosalia (Plimmer 1912; Grieder 1938)
Saimiri sciureus (Salcedo 1950; Chalifoux et al. 1973; Ayala, D'Alessandro, Mackensie, Angel 1973)
Aotus trivirgatus (Salcedo 1950)
Callicebus moloch (Ayala, D'Alessandro, Mackensie, Angel 1973)
Alouatta seniculus (Carini and Marcel 1917)
Alouatta fusca (Carini and Marcel 1917)
Alouatta caraya (Romaña 1932)
Cebus albifrons (Plimmer 1912)
Cebus apella (Carini and Marcel 1917; Microfilaria D, Chalifoux et al. 1973; Ayala, D'Alessandro, Mackensie and Angel 1973)
Lagothrix lagothricha (Salcedo 1950)
Ateles paniscus (Plimmer 1912; Leger 1918)
Microfilaria spp. *B, C, D*
Saimiri sciureus (Hawking, 1973)
Microfilaria spp. *F, G, H*
Cacajao calvus rubicundus (Hawking, 1973)
[Dirofilariidae]
Loa[a] Stiles, 1905
Loa loa[a]
Ateles paniscus
Dipetalonematidae[ab] (R, B)
(For review, see McCoy 1936; Webber and Hawking 1955; Rodríguez López-Neyra 1956; Dunn and Lambrecht 1963*a;* Dunn 1968, p. 54. Esslinger and Gardiner 1974.)
Dipetalonema[a] Diesing, 1861
(*Tetrapetalonema* Faust, 1935, and *Parlitomosa* Nagaty, 1935 are regarded as congeneric with *Dipetalonema* by Esslinger and Gardiner 1974. See Sousa, Rosa, and Baerg 1974 for Panamanian records.)
Dipetalonema[a] *caudispina*
(See Stiles and Hassall 1929; Yamaguti 1961, p. 657; Yamashita 1963, p. 38. *D. caudispina* and *D. gracile* are regarded as conspecific by some authorities and distinct by others.)
Callithrix argentata melanura
Saguinus nigricollis group
(See F. Deinhardt, Holmes, Devine, and Deinhardt 1967.)
Saguinus "tamarinus" (= "white-lipped")
Saguinus midas midas
Saguinus bicolor bicolor
Leontopithecus rosalia rosalia

Saimiri sciureus
Callicebus moloch
Callicebus personatus
Aotus trivirgatus
Pithecia monachus
Alouatta seniculus
Alouatta caraya
Cebus albifrons
Cebus apella
Lagothrix lagothricha
Ateles paniscus
Brachyteles arachnoides
Dipetalonema gracile
(See comments under *D. caudispina.*)
Callithrix jacchus jacchus
Callithrix argentata melanura
Saguinus fuscicollis
(*S. nigricollis* of some authors)
Saguinus midas midas
Saguinus mystax mystax
Saguinus bicolor bicolor
Saguinus bicolor
Leontopithecus rosalia
Saimiri sciureus
Aotus trivirgatus
Callicebus personatus
Callicebus moloch
Pithecia monachus
Chiropotes satanas
Alouatta seniculus
Alouatta caraya
Cebus capucinus
Cebus albifrons
Cebus apella
Lagothrix lagothricha
Ateles paniscus
Brachyteles arachnoides
"*Tetrapetalonema* Group"
(See Esslinger, 1966; Esslinger and Gardiner, 1974)
Dipetalonema marmosetae
(Includes *Microfilaria panamensis* McCoy, 1936.)
Saguinus fuscicollis
Saguinus midas niger
Saguinus oedipus geoffroyi
Saguinus oedipus oedipus
(See Tiken 1970.)
"*S. tamarinus*" (= ?, Chalifoux, Hunt, García, Sehgal, and Comiskey 1973)
Saimiri sciureus
Aotus trivirgatus
Alouatta villosa
Cebus capucinus
Ateles paniscus
Dipetalonema tamarinae
Saguinus "nigricollis" (The host range, "southwest from Pebas and Iquitos, parallel to the Ucayali River in eastern Peru" [Dunn and Lambrecht 1963*a*, p. 270] points to *Saguinus fuscicollis,* not *S. nigricollis* with which the first has often been confused.)
"*S. tamarinus*" (= "white lipped tamarin," Chalifoux, Hunt, García, Sehgal, and Comiskey 1973)
Tetrapetalonema dunni described by Mullins and Orihel (1972), from southeast Asian *Tupaia glis* and *T. tana,* is said to be most nearly related to *Dipetalonema marmosetae* and *D. tamarinae.*
Dipetalonema obtusa
(See Esslinger 1966, p. 498.)
Saimiri sciureus
Cebus capucinus
Cebus albifrons
Dipetalonema tenue
Cebus apella
(Cf. Mazza 1930.)
Dipetalonema atelensis
Alouatta caraya
Ateles paniscus
Dipetalonema nicollei
Aotus trivirgatus
Cebus apella
Dipetalonema zakii
Saguinus "tamarinus" (= "white lipped tamarins")
Saguinus oedipus
Leontopithecus rosalia rosalia
Aotus trivirgatus
Saimiri sciureus
Ateles paniscus geoffroyi
(See Chalifoux, Hunt, García, Sehgal, and Comiskey 1973.)
Dipetalonema barbascalensis
Aotus trivirgatus
(Esslinger and Gardiner 1974)
Dipetalonema parvum
Saimiri sciureus oerstedi (Panamá)
Cebus capucinus
Tetrapetalonema sp.
Saguinus oedipus oedipus
Saimiri sciureus
Cebus apella
(See Dunn and Lambrecht 1963*a,* p. 262.)
Cebus albifrons
"Cebus griseus" [= sp?]
(See Dunn and Lambrecht 1963*a,* p. 262.)
Tetrapetalonema "panamensis"
(See Chalifoux, Hunt, García, Sehgal, and Comiskey 1973.)
Saguinus sp.
Saimiri sciureus
Aotus trivirgatus
Cebus sp.

[Trichinellida] (F, A, R, B)]
[Trichuridae (F, A, R, B)]
[*Trichurus*[a] Roederer, 1761]
[*Trichurus* sp.]
Lagothrix lagothricha
[Capillariidae]
[*Capillaria* Zeder, 1800 (F, A, R, B)]
[*Capillaria hepatica*[a]]
Cebus capucinus
Ateles paniscus
Homo sapiens

Acanthocephala (Thornyhead Worms)

About 600 species of Acanthocephala are known. Their larvae live in crustaceans and insects, and the adults live in fish, amphibians, reptiles, birds, and mammals.

Natural infection of primates by acanthocephalans appears to be restricted mainly to platyrrhines. *Prosthenorchis,* indigenous to New World monkeys, causes high mortality, often wiping out entire stocks among accidentally infected zoo, laboratory, and supply house catarrhines and prosimians (cf. Schmidt 1972). *Moniliformes moniliformis,* a natural parasite of *Rattus,* may also accidentally infect captive primates, with dire results. *Nephiriacanthus kamerunensis,* the only other acanthocephalan recorded from primates, infects the African talapoin (*Miopithecus talapoin*), but other species of this genus occur in pangolins.

Captive primates are parasitized through ingestion of cockroaches infected with the acanthocephalan larva or cystacanth. The intermediate hosts in nature are unknown but most likely are insect prey of callitrichids and the more-or-less insectivorous cebids. The herbivorous howlers (*Alouatta*) and pithecines are not known to harbor acanthocephalans.

The data presented here were compiled mainly from Machado Filho (1950), Dunn (1963; 1968), Yamashita (1963), Yamaguti (1963), Stunkard (1965*b*), Kuntz and Myers (1972), Schmidt (1972), and Porter (1972). Yamaguti's classification is used. Machado Filho recognized 10 species of *Prosthenorchis,* since reduced to 3, but his host list is the most representative.

See page 383 for explanation of symbols

Gigantorhynchidea (A, R, B)
- Oligacanthorhynchidae (B)
  - *Prosthenorchis*[bc] Travassos, 1915 (B)
    - *Prosthenorchis elegans*
      - *Cebuella pygmaea*
      - *Callithrix jacchus jacchus*
      - *Callithrix jacchus geoffroyi*
      - *Callithrix humeralifer chrysoleuca*
      - *Saguinus fuscicollis*
      - *Saguinus nigricollis*
      - *Saguinus mystax*
      - *Saguinus midas midas*
      - *Saguinus midas niger*
      - *Saguinus leucopus*
      - *Saguinus oedipus oedipus*
      - *Saguinus oedipus geoffroyi*
      - *Leontopithecus rosalia rosalia*
      - *Saimiri sciureus*
      - *Callicebus moloch*
      - *Aotus trivirgatus*
      - *Alouatta villosa*
      - *Cebus albifrons* (Garner, Hemrick, and Rudiger 1966, p. 310)
      - *Cebus apella*
      - *Lagothrix lagothricha*
      - *Ateles paniscus*
    - *Prosthenorchis spirula*
      (Includes *P. sigmoides* Meyer, 1931)
      - *Cebuella pygmaea*
      - *Callithrix jacchus jacchus*
      - *Saguinus oedipus oedipus*
      - *Leontopithecus rosalia rosalia*
      - *Saimiri sciureus*
      - *Cebus apella*
    - *Prosthenorchis lenti*
      (See Thatcher and Porter 1968, p. 193)
      - *Callithrix jacchus geoffroyi*
      - *Saguinus oedipus geoffroyi*
  - *Prosthenorchis* sp.
    - *Callithrix jacchus*
    - *Saguinus fuscicollis*
    - *Saguinus mystax*
    - *Saguinus oedipus*
  - Acanthocephalan larvae
    - *Callithrix jacchus*
    - *Saguinus fuscicollis*
    - *Saguinus oedipus*
    - *Callimico goeldii*

Acarina (Arachnida, Mites, and Ticks)

Parasitiformes

Laelapoidea
- Halarachnidae (Lung mites)
  (See Innes and Hull 1972.)
  - *Pneumonyssoides* Banks, 1901
    - *Pneumonyssoides stammeri*
      - *Alouatta caraya*
      - *Lagothrix lagothricha*

Ixodoidea (Ticks)
(See Nuttall et al. 1908–26; Cooley and Kohls 1945; Hoogstraal 1956; and Fairchild, Kohls, and Tipton 1966; Jones, Carlton, Clifford, Kierans, and Kohls 1972.)
- Argasidae (Soft ticks)
  - *Ornithodoros* Koch, 1844 (Soft ticks)
    (Ticks of this genus have been incriminated as transmitters of spirochetal relapsing fever Dunn and Clark 1933.)
    - *Ornithodoros rudis* (Includes *venezuelensis*)
      - *Saguinus oedipus geoffroyi*
        (See Clark, Dunn, and Benevides 1931; Dunn and Clark 1933.)
    - *Ornithodoros talaje*
      - *Saguinus oedipus geoffroyi*
        (See Dunn and Clark 1933.)
      - *Saimiri sciureus orstedi*
      - *Alouatta palliata*
      - *Cebus capucinus*
      - "white-faced monkey"
        (= *Cebus capucinus*?)
- Ixodidae (Hard ticks)
  - *Ixodes* Latreille, 1795
    - *Ixodes loricatus*
      - *Ateles paniscus*
        (See Nuttall and Warburton 1911, p. 266.)
  - *Amblyomma* Koch, 1844
    - *Amblyomma cajennense*
      - *Alouatta seniculus*
    - *Amblyomma quasicyprium*
      - *Ateles paniscus*
        (See Nuttall, Warburton, and Robinson 1926, p. 237.)
    - *Amblyomma* sp.
      - *Saguinus oedipus geoffroyi* (larvae)
      - *Aotus trivirgatus* (larvae)
      - *Callicebus torquatus*
      - *Pithecia pithecia*
      - *Chiropotes satanas*
      - *Alouatta villosa* (larvae)

Alouatta seniculus
Cebus nigrivittatus
Cebus capucinus (larvae)
Haemaphysalis Koch, 1844
Haemaphysalis juxtakochi
Cebus nigrivittatus
[*Rhipicephalus* Koch, 1844]
(Some species transmit protozoan and rickettsia diseases.)
[*Rhipicephalus sanguineus*]
Saguinus oedipus geoffroyi
(The tick is cosmopolitan, with Africa its center of dispersal; cf. Hoogstraal 1956, p. 686.)

Acariformes

Cheyletoidea (Follicular mites)
Demodicidae
Demodex Owen, 1843
(See Lebel and Nutting 1973)
Demodex saimiri
Saimiri sciureus
Demodex sp.
Saimiri sciureus
Lagothrix lagothricha
Ateles sp.

Trombidoidea (Red mites, chiggers)
Trombiculidae (Chiggers)
(See Brennan and Yunker 1966)
Eutrombicula Ewing, 1938 (skin chiggers)
Eutrombicula alfreddugesi
Saguinus oedipus geoffroyi
Aotus trivirgatus
Eutrombicula goeldii
Saguinus oedipus geoffroyi
Aotus trivirgatus
Pseudoschoengastia Lipovsky, 1951
Pseudoschoengastia bulbifera
Saguinus oedipus geoffroyi

Listrophoroidea
Listrophoridae (Hair-clasping mites)
(See Fain 1967)
Listrocarpus Fain, 1967
Listrocarpus cosgrovei
Callimico goeldii
Listrocarpus hapalei
Callithrix jacchus
Listrocarpus lagothrix
Lagothrix lagothricha
Listrocarpus saimiri
Saimiri sciureus
Rhyncoptidae (Follicular mites)
Rhyncoptes Lawrence, 1956
(Includes *Rhyncoptoides* Fain, 1962.)
Rhyncoptes anastosi
Saguinus oedipus oedipus
Rhyncoptes cebi
Cebus albifrons

Other species of *Rhyncoptes* are *R. recurvidens,* from the African porcupine, *Hystrix africaeaustralis,* and *R. cercopitheci* from the West African mona monkey, *Cercopithecus mona campbelli.* Fain (1965) remarks that "the finding in two so widely separated groups of mammals (Primates and Hystrichomorpha) of so closely related and at the same time so highly specialized mites is at first surprising. It may suggest the existence of some relationships between these groups. This opinion is reinforced by the fact that these hosts are also parasitized by two other very evolved mite genera belonging to the Trombidiformes and the Mesostigmata."

The examples of the latter are *Psorengatis* (subgenus *Psorobia*) in *Hystrix* and *Cercopithecus* (also in sheep, ox), and *Rhinophaga* in cercopithecines, *Hystrix,* and *Atherurus.* Fain suggests that the host relationship may be based on a chemical environment suited to the parasites.

Psoroptoidea
Audycoptidae (follicle mites)
(See Lavoipierre 1964*a.*)
Audycoptes Lavoipierre, 1964
Audycoptes greeri
Saimiri sciureus
Audycoptes lawrenci
Saimiri sciureus
Saimirioptes Fain, 1968
(See Fain 1968*a*)
Saimirioptes paradoxus
Saimiri sciureus
Lemurnyssidae (nasal mites)
(See Fain 1959, 1964*b* for details)
Mortelmansia Fain, 1959
Mortelmansia brevis
Saimiri sciureus
Mortelmansia duboisi
Callithrix jacchus jacchus
Mortelmansia longus
Saimiri sciureus
Psoroptidae (Follicular mites)
(See Fain 1963*a*; 1963*b*; 1964*a*; 1965; 1966; Lavoipierre 1964*b*; Flatt 1969)
Alouattalges Fain, 1963
(Includes *Rosalialges* Lavoipierre, 1964*b*)
Alouattalges corbeti
(Includes *Rosalialges cruciformes* Lavoipierre, 1964*b*)
Aotus trivirgatus
Alouatta seniculus macconelli (= *A. s. stramineus*)
Cebalges Fain, 1962
Cebalges gaudi
Cebus capucinus
Cebalgoides Fain, 1963
Cebalgoides cebi
Saguinus oedipus oedipus
Cebus albifrons
Cebus apella
Fonsecalges Fain, 1962
(Includes *Dunnalges* Lavoipierre, 1964*b.*)
Fonsecalges johnjadini
Callithrix jacchus jacchus
Callithrix jacchus geoffroyi
Fonsecalges saimiri
(Includes *Dunnalges lambrechti* Lavoipierre, 1964*b.*)

Saguinus nigricollis nigricollis (= *S. fuscicollis*?)
Saimiri sciureus
Procebalges Fain, 1963
Procebalges pitheciae
Pithecia monachus
Schizopodalges Fain, 1963
Schizopodalges lagothricola
Lagothrix lagothricha
Sarcoptidae (lice mites)
(See Fain 1968*b*.)
Prosarcoptes Lavoipierre, 1960
Prosarcoptes pitheci
Cebus capucinus (captive)

Insecta

Phthiraptera (Lice)

Anoplura (Sucking lice)

The parasite-host records have been compiled mainly from Stiles and Hassall (1929), Ferris (1935), Ewing (1938), Hopkins (1949), Ferris and Stojanovich (1951), and Wenzel and Johnson (1966). For distribution of the Phthiraptera, see Hopkins (1957).

Pediculidae
Pediculus Linnaeus, 1758
Pediculus lobatus
(Includes as conspecifics, races, varieties, or strains, [?]*quadrumanus* Murray, 1877; [?] *consobrinus* Piaget, 1880; *affinis* Mjöberg, 1910; *lobatus* Fehrenholz, 1916; *mjöbergi* Ferris, 1916; *atelophilus* Ferris, 1926; *chapini* Ferris, 1926; *pseudohumanus* Ewing, 1938.)
[*Saguinus fuscicollis weddelli*]
("*Leontocebus nigricollis*," "collected by Dr. W. M. Mann, at Tumu Pasa, Bolivia" contaminated from infected *Ateles* [Ewing 1938, p. 30].)
Pithecia monachus
Cacajao calvus rubicundus
Alouatta villosa (accidental?)
Alouatta fusca
Alouatta seniculus
Alouatta belzebul (accidental?)
Alouatta caraya
Cebus capucinus
Ateles paniscus

Type host of each named form except *pseudohumanus*, was a captive spider monkey (*Ateles paniscus* subsp.). The type host of *Pediculus pseudohumanus* was a captive saki, *Pithecia monachus*.

The taxonomy and nomenclature of the named forms is complex, and the present arrangement, following Hopkins (1949, p. 437, but see also Ferris and Stojanovich 1951, p. 267), is a simple device for presenting the data without involvement with the issues.

It is generally believed that *Pediculus lobatus* of cebids was acquired from pre-Columbian man. According to Kuhn (1968, p. 191), the louse made ready transfer to the larger cebids because no anoplurid occupied the New World primate niche before the arrival of man. *Pediculus* infects man, chimpanzee, gibbons, and cebids and is replaced by *Pedicinus* on catarrhine monkeys. *Pthiris* is the gorilla louse and, together with *Pediculus*, also infects man and chimpanzee.

Mallophaga (Amblycera, biting or chewing lice)
(See Wernick 1948–50; Emerson and Price 1975)
[Trimenoponidae]
[*Harrisonia* Ferris, 1922]
[*Harrisonia uncinata*]
Callithrix humeralifer humeralifer
(= *Hapale santaremensis*, accidental contamination, Werneck 1948, p. 34.)
Gyropidae
[*Gliricola* Mjöberg, 1910]
[*Gliricola pintoi*]
Callithrix humeralifer humeralifer
(= *Hapale santaremensis*, accidental infection from rodent, Werneck 1935, p. 373.)
Aotiella Eichler, 1949 (p. 11)
Aotiella aotophilus
(*Tetragyropus aotophilus* Ewing, 1924; *Gyropus aotophilus*, Werner, 1948)
Aotus trivirgatus
? *Pithecia monachus*

Werneck (1948, p. 52) recognizes 23 species of *Gyropus*. In addition to *G. aotophilus* consistently found on night monkeys, one species (*G. hispidus* Burmeister, 1838) is known only from the type specimen said to have been hosted by a three-toed sloth (*Bradypus tridactylus*), but Werneck (1948, p. 72) believes it may have been something other than a sloth. The remaining 21 species are from terrestrial rodents, mainly echimyids (Caviomorpha).

Trichodectidae (Bird lice)
Cebidicola Bedford, 1936
Cebidicola armatus
Cebus apella
Brachyteles arachnoides
Cebidicola semiarmatus
Alouatta fusca
Alouatta belzebul
Alouatta seniculus
Alouatta caraya

Primate-infecting Mallophaga are known from a few cebids, a catarrhine monkey, a lemuroid, and a lorisoid, but not from man or apes.

Diptera (Flies)
Cuterebridae (Botflies)
Alouattamyia Townsend, 1931
Alouattamyia baeri
Alouatta villosa
Alouatta seniculus
Alouatta belzebul
Aotus trivirgatus

In the last two of his reviews, Guimarães (1967; 1971) recognizes 10 species representing 6 genera of neotropical cuterebrid botflies. The monotypic *Alouattamyia baeri* infects howlers and night monkeys as shown above. The remaining cuterebrids parasitize didelphids, cricetines, and squirrels, and one (*Rogenhofera* sp.) is found on the house rat, *Rattus norvegicus*. The type host and type locality of *A. baeri* Shannon and Greene, 1925, are *Alouatta seniculus,* Kartabo, Guyana (formerly British Guiana). Guimarães (1971) incorrectly cites *Alouatta palliata inconsonans,* Panamá, as type host and locality.

[Siphonaptera (Fleas)]

(Johnson 1957 lists no primates other than man among South American flea hosts. Infection, when it occurs, is evidently accidental.)

[Pulicidae]

[*Ctenocephalides* Stiles and Collins, 1930]

[*Ctenocephalides felis felis*]

Callithrix jacchus penicillata

(Costa Lima and Hathaway 1946, p. 357)

Saguinus oedipus geoffroyi

(Hopkins and Rothschild 1953, p. 153)

Cebus albifrons

(Tipton and Machado-Allison 1972, p. 3)

[*Pulex* Linnaeus, 1758]

[*Pulex irritans*]

Cebus apella

(Hopkins and Rothschild 1953, p. 153.)

Pentastomida (Tongue Worms)

This class of soft, wormlike segmented parasites of vertebrate tissues is divided into two orders. Members of the Cephalobaenida, without intermediate hosts, infect snakes, gulls, and terns. Members of the second order, the Porocephalida, parasitize mainly snakes as definitive hosts, and mammals, including some primates, as secondary hosts. The pathology of pentastomid infection is described by Cosgrove, Nelson, and Self (1970), Self and Cosgrove (1972), and Fox, Diaz, and Barth (1972). The list of platyrrhine hosts was compiled from the cited accounts.

Porocephalida

Porocephalidae

Porocephalus Humboldt, 1809

Porocephalus clavatus

Callithrix jacchus

(Porter 1972)

Saguinus fuscicollis

Saguinus nigricollis

Saguinus mystax

(Porter 1972)

Callimico goeldii

Saimiri sciureus

Porocephalus sp.

Saimiri sciureus

(Flynn 1973, p. 497, fig. 16.6, ex Fain, unpublished.)

[*Armillifer* Sambon, 1922]

[*Armillifer armillatus*]

Cebus apella

(The parasite naturally infects catarrhine monkeys and prosimians.)

[*Linguatula* Froelich, 1789]

[*"Linguatula serrata"*]

(Stiles and Hassall 1929, p. 479.)

Callicebus moloch

["Linguatulid"]

(Nelson, Cosgrove, and Gengozian 1966)

Saguinus nigricollis

(Accidental infection)

Part III
Systematics, Evolution, and Biology of the Families Callitrichidae and Callimiconidae

44 Family Callitrichidae Thomas Marmosets and Tamarins *1. History and Systematic Position*

Synonymic History

Quadrumana Illiger, 1811, *Prodr. Syst. Mamm. Avium,* pp. 60, 67—part, *Hapale* [= *Callithrix*] only; family of suborder Pollicatorum Illiger.

Arctopitheci E. Geoffroy St.-Hilaire, 1812, *Ann. Mus. Hist. Nat.* 19:118—subdivision of group Platyrrhini of subordinal group "Les Singes"; genera: *Jacchus* [= *Callithrix*], *Midas* [= *Saguinus, Leontopithecus*]; characters; comparisons.

Harpalidae Gray, 1821, *London Med. Reposit.* 15:298—sole family of order Gampstonychae; genus, *Harpale* Illiger [*sic* = *Hapale* Illiger = *Callithrix* Erxleben].

Trichuri Spix, 1823, *Sim. Vesp. Brasil.*, table of contents, p. 5, 27—part, nonprehensile section of platyrrhines, genera: *Midas* [= *Saguinus*], *Jacchus* or *Iacchus* [*Callithrix, Cebuella*]; characters.

Sariguidae Gray, 1825, *Ann. Philos.* 10:338—part, subfamilies Harpalina (q.v.) and Saguininae (part, q.v.); family name possibly *lapsus* for Saguinidae based on the Sagouin and subfamily Saguinina Gray with *"Saguinus"* Lacépède (= *Sagouin* Lacépède) type by tautonomy.

Saguinina Gray, 1825, *Ann. Philos.* 10:338—part, *"Saguinus"* Lacépède, *lapsus* for *Sagouin* Lacépède [= *Callithrix*] type by tautonomy.

Harpalina Gray, 1825, *Ann. Philos.* 10:338—tribe of family Sariguidae; genera: *Jacchus* E. Geoffroy [= *Callithrix*], *Midas* E. Geoffroy [= *Saguinus, Leontopithecus*].

Titidæ Burnett, 1828, *Quart. J. Sci. Lit. Art* 1828 (Oct.-Dec.), pp. 305, 306, 307—"kind" (= family) of "race" Arctopithecatæ, "type" (= order) Manupeda; genera *Ouistitis* Burnett [= *Callithrix* Erxleben], *Midas* E. Geoffroy [= *Saguinus, Leontopithecus*]; classification.

Ouistidæ Burnett, 1828, *Quart. J. Sci. Lit. Art* 1828 (Oct.-Dec.), p. 305—alternate name for Titidæ Burnett (see above); misspelling of Ouistitidæ Burnett (see below).

Ouistitidæ Burnett, 1828, *Quart. J. Sci. Lit. Art* 1828 (Oct.-Dec.), p. 306—alternate name for Titidæ Burnett (see above).

Hapalina Bonaparte, 1831, *Sagg. Distr. Metod. Anim. Vertebr.*, p. 14—subfamily of family Simidæ, "tribe" (= suborder) Quadrumana, order Primates; genera: *Jacchus* [= *Callithrix*], *Mydas* [*sic* = *Saguinus, Leontopithecus*]. Gray, 1870, *Cat. Monkeys, Lemurs, Fruit-eating Bats Brit. Mus.*, pp. vi, 36, 62, 131—tribe of section Trichiura, family Cebidae, suborder Quadrumana; genera: *Hapale* [= *Callithrix*], *Jacchus* [= *Callithrix*] *Cebuella, Mico* [= *Callithrix*], *Micoella* [= *Callithrix*], *Leontopithecus, Oedipus* [= *Saguinus*], *Midas* [= *Saguinus*], *Seniocebus* [= *Saguinus*]; classification of primates in British Museum; characters.

Cebidæ Swainson, 1835, *Nat. Hist. Class. Quadr.*, pp. vii, 76, 350, part, only *Hapales* [*sic* = *Callithrix, Saguinus, Leontopithecus*]; family of order Quadrumana. Gray, 1843, *List. Spec. Mamm. Brit. Mus.*, p. xvii—part, *Jacchus* [with subgenera *Hapale, Mico, Arctopithecus, Callithrix, Midas, Oedipus, Leontopithecus, Marikina*].

Hapalineæ Lesson, 1840, *Species mammifères, bimanes, et quadrumanes,* p. 184; tribe of family Simiadae, order Quadrumana; genera: *Hapale* [= *Callithrix*], *Mico* [=*Callithrix*], *Midas* [= *Saguinus*], *Oedipus* [= *Saguinus*], *Leontopithecus.*

Hapalidae Wagner, 1840, *Schreber's Säugth.*, suppl. 1 : ix, 238—subgroup of Simiae Platyrrhinae; genera: *Jacchus* [= *Callithrix*], *Liocephalus* [= part *Callithrix,* part *Saguinus*] *Leontocebus* [= part Leontopithecus, part *Saguinus*]. Schinz, 1844, *Syst. Verzeich. Säuget.*, 1:89, 571—"subfamily" of Simiae; genus: *Hapale* [all callitrichids assigned to the single genus]. Wagner, 1855, *Schreber's Säugth.*, suppl. 5:xi, 124—family of group Aneturae, order Simiae; genera: *Jacchus* [= *Callithrix, Cebuella,* part *Saguinus*], *Midas* [part *Saguinus*], *Leontocebus* [= *Leontopithecus,* part *Saguinus*]. Flower and Lydekker, 1891, *Introduction to the study of mammals,* p. 709—genera: *Hapale* Illiger [= *Callithrix, Cebuella*], *Midas* E. Geoffroy [= *Saguinus, Leontopithecus*]; characters; a family of suborder Anthropoidea. Trouessart, 1897, *Cat. Mamm.*, p. 49—family of order Primates; genera: *Hapale* [=*Callithrix, Cebuella*], *Midas* (subgenera *Marikina* Reichenbach [= *Leontopithecus*], *Oedipomidas* [= *Saguinus*], *Seniocebus* [= *Saguinus*]). Weber, 1904, *Die Säugetiere,* pp. xi, 784—characters; family of suborder Platyrrhina; genera: *Hapale* [= *Callithrix, Cebuella*], *Midas* [= *Saguinus, Leontopithecus*]. Osborn, 1910, *Age of mammals,* p. 544—family of Platyrrhine group, suborder Anthropoidea; genera: *Midas* [= *Saguinus*], *Hapale* [= *Callithrix*]. Pocock, 1917, *Ann. Mag. Nat. Hist.* 8th ser. 20:247—external characters; genera: *Leontocebus* Wagner [= *Leontopithecus*], *Œdipomidas* [= *Saguinus*], *Mystax* [= *Saguinus*], *Hapale* [= *Callithrix* and *Cebuella*]. Pocock, 1920, *Proc. Zool. Soc. London,* 1920:91—external characters; comparisons with cebids; *Callimico* regarded as a callitrichid. Pocock, 1925, *Proc. Zool. Soc. London* 1925:38—regarded as a "specialized derivative group that branched off at an early stage from the monkey stock." Weber, 1928, *Die Säugetiere,* 2d ed., 2:783—family of superfamily Platyrrhina, suborder Anthropoidea; genera: *Hapale* [= *Callithrix, Cebuella*], *Midas* [= *Saguinus, Leontopithecus*]; characters. Wood Jones, 1929, *Man's place among the mammals,* p. 177—part, subfamily Hapalinae; classification, characters; comparisons. Cabrera and Yepes, 1940, *Mamíferos Sud-Americanos, Hist. Nat. Ediar,* p. 110—part, subfamily Hapalinae; genera: *Hapale* [= *Callithrix, Cebuella*], *Mystax* [= *Saguinus*], *Leontocebus* [= *Leontopithecus*]; characters; distribution; natural history. Vallois, 1955, in Grassé, *Traité de Zoologie* 17(2): 1967, 1969—part, subfamily Hapalinae only; infraorder Platyrrhina; characters; genera: *Hapale* [= *Callithrix*], *Leontocebus* (subgenera: *Leontopithecus, Oedipomidas* [= *Saguinus*] *Seniocebus* [= *Saguinus*]). Osman Hill, 1957, *Primates,* 3:115—family of Ceboidea, infraorder Platyrrhini; genera: *Tamarin* [= *Saguinus*], *Tamarinus* [*Saguinus*], *Marikina* [= *Saguinus*], *Oedipomidas* [= *Saguinus*], *Leontocebus* [= *Leontopithecus*], *Mico* [= *Callithrix*], *Hapale* [= *Callithrix*], *Cebuella,* † *Dolichocebus* [= a genus of Homunculidae]. Osman Hill, 1959, *Trans. Amer. Philos. Soc.* 49(5):111—subfamilies: Callimiconinae [= Callimiconidae], Leontocebinae (*Tamarin, Tamarinus, Marikina, Oedipomidas, Leontocebus*), Hapalinae, (*Hapale, Mico, Cebuella*); origin; evolution.

Hapalidæ Mivart, 1865, *Proc. Zool. Soc. London* 1865: 547, 587—family of suborder of Anthropoidea; axial skeleton. Flower, 1883, *Proc. Zool. Soc. London* 1883:183, 186—regarded as lowest of suborder Anthropoidea. Forbes, 1894, *Handbook to the Primates,* 1:xi—family of suborder Anthropoidea; genera: *Hapale* [= *Callithrix, Cebuella*], *Midas* [= *Saguinus, Leontopithecus*]. Sonntag, 1921, *Proc. Zool. Soc. London* 1921:497, 517, 757—*Hapale* [= *Callithrix, Cebuella*], *Leontocebus* [= *Leontopithecus*], *Mystax* [= *Saguinus*], *Oedipomidas* [= *Saguinus*]; comparative tongue anatomy. Gregory, 1922, *Origin and evolution of the human dentition,* 114 ff.—family of Platyrrhinae, suborder Anthropoidea; characters; origin; evolution; regarded as dwarfed or degenerate cebids.

Jacchina Gray, 1849, *Proc. Zool. Soc. London* 1849:10—subfamily of unspecified family; genera: *Jachus* (*sic*) [= *Callithrix*], type by autonomy, *Midas* [= *Saguinus, Leontopithecus*]; mandibular characters.

Arctopithecae Dahlbom, 1856, *Stud. Zool.*, p. 45 (table VI), p. 182—family of Platyrrhinae, a subdivision of subordinal series Simiae; genera: *Hapale* [= *Callithrix*], *Midas* [= *Saguinus, Leontopithecus*]; characters; comparisons.

Arctopithecini Huxley, 1864, *Medical Times and Gazette,* 23:124 (work not seen, cited as quoted in Gill 1872, *Smith. Misc. Coll.* 230:38). Huxley, 1872, *Anatomy of vertebrated animals,* p. 392—"family" of "family" [= suborder] Simiadae of order Primates; genera: only *Hapale* [= *Callithrix*] mentioned, tamarins implied in characterizations.

Mididae Gill, 1872, *Smith. Misc. Coll.* 230:2, 54—substitute name for Arctopithecini Huxley, 1864; family of suborder Anthropoidea; genera: *Saguinus* (*sic*) [= *Callithrix, Cebuella*], *Midas* [= *Saguinus, Leontopithecus*], *Jacchus* [= *Callithrix*], *Mico* [= *Callithrix*], *Oedipus* [= *Saguinus*], *Seniocebus* [= *Saguinus*].

Hapalinæ Mivart, 1874, *Man and apes,* pp. 60, 83—subfamily of Cebidae, suborder Anthropoidea; genus *Hapale* [= *Callithrix, Leontopithecus*].

Hapalini Winge, 1895, *E. Mus. Lundii* 2(2):12, 23—subfamily of Cebidae, superfamily or infraorder Ceboidei; genera: *Hapale* [= *Callithrix*], *Midas* [= *Saguinus, Leontopithecus*]; characters; classification. Winge, 1941, *Interrelationships of the mammalian genera* (trans. from original Danish by E. Deichmann, G. M. Allen) 2:294—tribe of Cebidae, infraorder Ceboidei (= Anthropoidei); genera: *Midas* [= *Saguinus, Leontopithecus*] *Hapale* [= *Cebuella, Callithrix*].

Callitrichidæ Thomas, 1903, *Ann. Mag. Nat. Hist.* 7th ser. 12:457—family name based on *Callithrix* Erxleben, antedates Hapalidae based on *Hapale* Illiger. Palmer, 1904, *Index Gen. Mamm., North Amer. Fauna,* no. 23, p. 890—family of order Primates; list of family-group and genus-group names with etymologies and bibliographic references. Thomas, 1913, *Ann. Mag. Nat. Hist.* 8th ser., 11:132—classification; key characters. Elliot, 1913, *A review of the Primates* 1:xlix, 179—family of suborder Anthropoidea; genera: *Seniocebus* Gray [= *Saguinus*], *Cercopithecus* Gronovius [nonbinomial, = *Saguinus*], *Leontocebus* Wagner with subgenera *Tamarinus* Trouessart, [= *Saguinus*], *Marikina* Reichenbach not Wagner [= *Leontopithecus*], *Oedipomidas* Reichenbach [= *Saguinus*], *Callithrix* Erxleben [= *Callithrix*, part, *Cebuella, Callithrix goeldi* (*sic*) = *Callimico,* a genus of Callimiconidae], *Callicebus* [= a genus of Cebidae]; taxonomic review.

Callitrichidae Trouessart, 1904, *Suppl. Cat. Mamm.,* p. 28—genera: *Callithrix, Midas* [= *Saguinus*], *Leontopithecus, Oedipomidas* [= *Saguinus*], *Tamarinus* [nom. nov. for *Midas,* part = *Saguinus*], *Midas* [= *Saguinus*]. Tate, 1939, *Bull. Amer. Mus. Nat. Hist.* 76:207—Guianan forms; genera: *Tamarin* Gray ([= *Saguinus*] with subgenus *Oedipomidas*), *Leontocebus* [= *Leontopithecus*]; taxonomic history; nomenclature. Cruz Lima, 1945, *Mammals of Amazonia,* pp. 54, 203—genera: *Marikina* Lesson [= *Saguinus*], *Tamarin* Gray [= *Saguinus*], *Callithrix* Erxleben, *Cebuella* Gray; taxonomic and natural history of Amazonian forms. Napier and Napier, 1967, *Handbook of living primates,* p. 4—genera: *Callithrix, Cebuella, Saguinus, Leontideus* [= *Leontopithecus*], *Callimico* [= Callimiconidae]; generic profiles.

Callithricidae Simpson, 1945, *Bull. Amer. Mus. Nat. Hist.* 85:65, 184—family of suborder Anthropoidea; superfamily Ceboidea; genera: *Callithrix* [= *Callithrix, Cebuella*], *Leontocebus* [= *Saguinus, Leontopithecus*]. Fiedler, 1956, *Primatologia* 1:156—genera: *Callithrix* [includes *Cebuella*], *Leontocebus* (with subgenera *Leontocebus* [= *Leontopithecus*], *Tamarinus* [= *Saguinus*], *Oedipomidas* [= *Saguinus*]); taxonomy; distribution. Hall and Kelson, 1959, *Mammals of North America,* p. 230—family of superfamily Ceboidea, suborder Anthropoidea. Hershkovitz, 1970, *Folia Primat.* 13:213—genera: *Cebuella, Callithrix, Saguinus, Leontopithecus;* cerebral fissural patterns. Hershkovitz, 1970, *Folia Primat.* 13:318—origin; mandibular evolution. Hershkovitz, 1972, *Internat. Zoo Yearb.* 12:5—family in suborder Platyrrhini. De Boer, 1974, *Genen Phaenen* 17:12—karyology; cytotaxonomy.

Callithrichidae Hershkovitz, 1949, *Proc. U.S. Nat. Mus.* 98:408—genera: *Cebuella, Callithrix* (*Mico* a synonym), *Marikina* ([= *Saguinus*], with subgenera *Tamarin, Marikina, Oedipomidas*); taxonomic review of tamarins. Cabrera, 1957, *Rev. Mus. argentino Cienc. Nat. "Bernardino Rivadavia," Zool.* 4:184—genera: *Callithrix, Cebuella, Leontocebus* ([= *Saguinus*] with subgenera *Leontocebus, Oedipomidas, Marikina*), *Leontideus* [= *Leontopithecus*]; classification; synonymy.

Leontocebinae Osman Hill, 1959, *Trans. Amer. Philos. Soc.* 49(5):111—subfamily of Hapalidae; genera: *Tamarin* [= *Saguinus*], *Tamarinus* [= *Saguinus*], *Oedipomidas* [= *Saguinus*], *Leontocebus* [= *Leontopithecus*].

Callithricinae Simpson, 1969, in Fittkaw, Illies, Klinge, Schwabe, and Sioli, *Biogeography and ecology in South America,* p. 885—subfamily of Cebidae, superfamily Ceboidea.

Type Genus. Callithrix Erxleben.

Included Genera. Cebuella Gray, *Callithrix* Erxleben, *Saguinus* Hoffmannsegg, *Leontopithecus* Lesson.

Distribution (figs. VII.1, 2; XIII.1, 2)

Tropical and subtropical wooded areas of tropical America from about 9° N (Panamá and southeastern Costa Rica), to about 24° S (Brazil, Bolivia); altitudinal range from sea level to about 1,400 meters above in the Brazilian highlands and 1,500 meters above in the Colombian Andes.

Callitrichids are absent in suitable habitats of the following areas within the described geographic limits.

Middle America

Invasion of Panamá and extreme southeastern Costa Rica by the Colombian *Saguinus oedipus geoffroyi* is recent. There is reason to believe that the tamarin continues to spread into optimum habitats in both countries, but evidently no pressures exist to force it into peripheral habitats in the dry Azuero Peninsula and northeast coast of Panamá.

Colombia

Eventual dispersal south of the coastal Chocó is predictable on the basis of present conditions. Meanwhile, transecting rivers such as the Río San Juan are barriers. Spread into the Andes is limited by unsuitable environments at altitudes above 1,500 meters. Callitrichids, abundant in the lowlands on the west bank of the Río Magdalena, are entirely absent in identical habitats on the east bank, also the Sierra Nevada de Santa Marta, the Cordillera Oriental, eastward in the Lake Maracaibo and the Río Orinoco basins north of the tributary Río Guaviare. The present hiatus in distribution between Amazonian and northern Colombian callitrichids cannot be explained on the basis of existing environmental conditions or of known or presumed Pleistocene climatic events.

Venezuela

Complete absence from Venezuela (and much of eastern Colombia) may be a factor of time. Callitrichids that

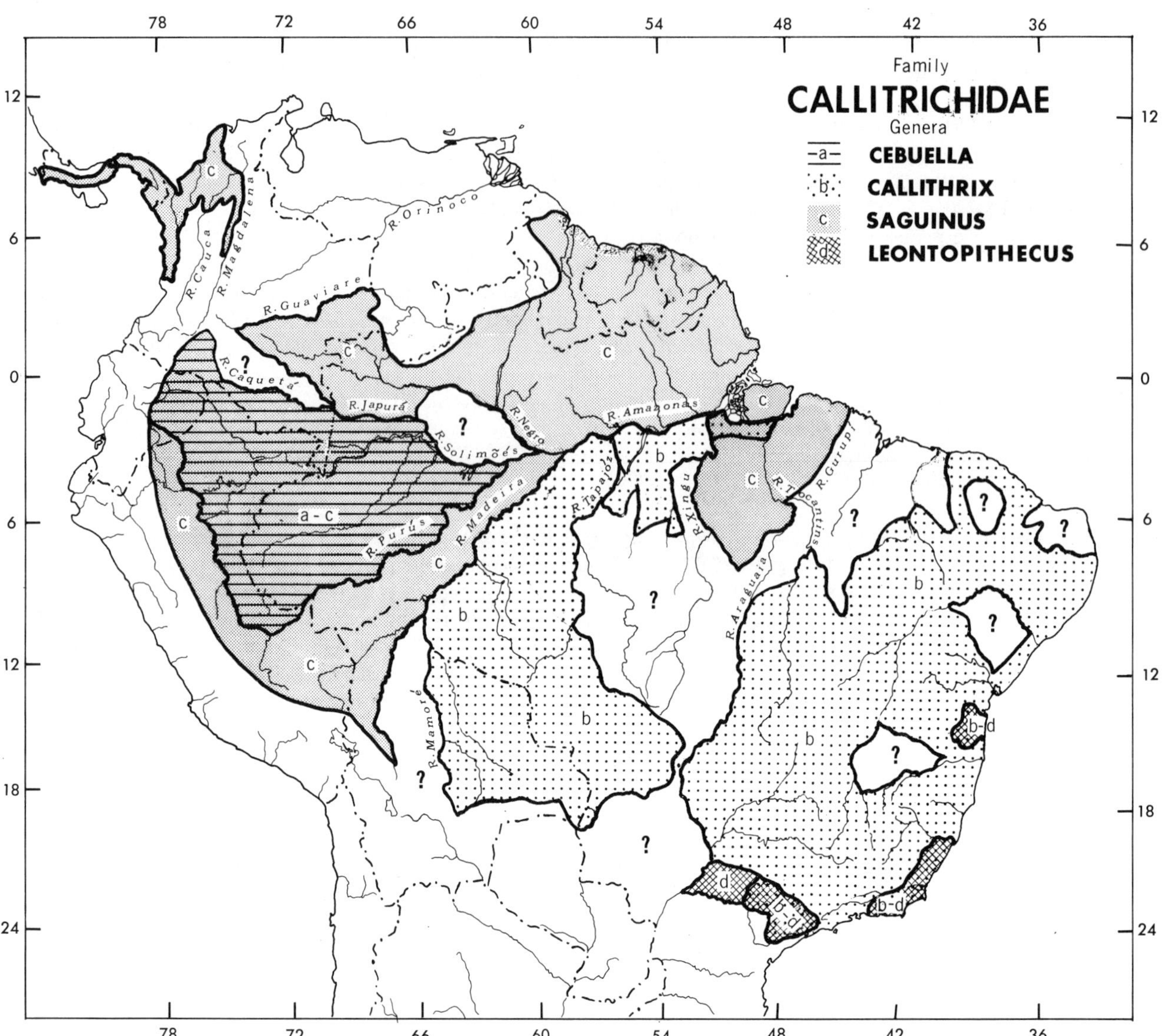

Fig. VII.1. Distribution of the genera of callitrichids, family Callitrichidae (see fig. XIII.2 for locality records mentioned in text).

gained the north bank of the Amazon spread widely, but broad west-east flowing rivers and extensive savannas are deterrents.

Guianas

Absence of callitrichids from some parts of the coast of Guyana and Suriname cannot be explained on the basis of present conditions. Perhaps the native golden-handed tamarin cannot compete with the larger, more aggressive, and very numerous squirrel monkey in dispersed second-growth woodlands.

Ecuador, Peru, Bolivia

Callitrichids are confined to the warm Amazonian basin. There are no topographical barriers to the spread of callitrichids into the cooler forested slopes of the Andes drained by Amazonian streams. Perhaps pressures for exploitation of peripheral habitats are missing.

Brazil

Distributional records are inadequate. Nothing is known of callitrichids, if present, in much of central Brazil and in large, heavily forested tracts north and south of the Rio Amazonas. Much of the land in central Brazil is savanna, or scrubland, but wooded banks of larger streams may support small platyrrhines. Callitrichids (*Saguinus*) are present on the Ilha de Marajó.

Nomenclature

Callitrichidae Thomas, 1903, based on *Callithrix* Erxleben, 1777, is the valid family name and the correct form of spelling according to rules and recommendations of the International Code of Zoological Nomenclature (1961, Art. 23d (i), 29, 40; and p. 135, example no. 24). Because of the difference in spelling, Callitrichidae Thomas, 1903, is not a homonym of Callitricidae Gray, 1821, based on *Callitrix* (*sic*) E. Geoffroy, 1812 (= *Callicebus* Thomas, 1903, a cebid).

The family name Callitrichidae replaces Hapalidae Wagner, 1840, with type genus *Hapale* Illiger, 1811, and all other family group names based on junior synonyms of *Callithrix* Erxleben, 1777.

The vernacular term "callitrichid" is used here for the family and its members in general. The common generic

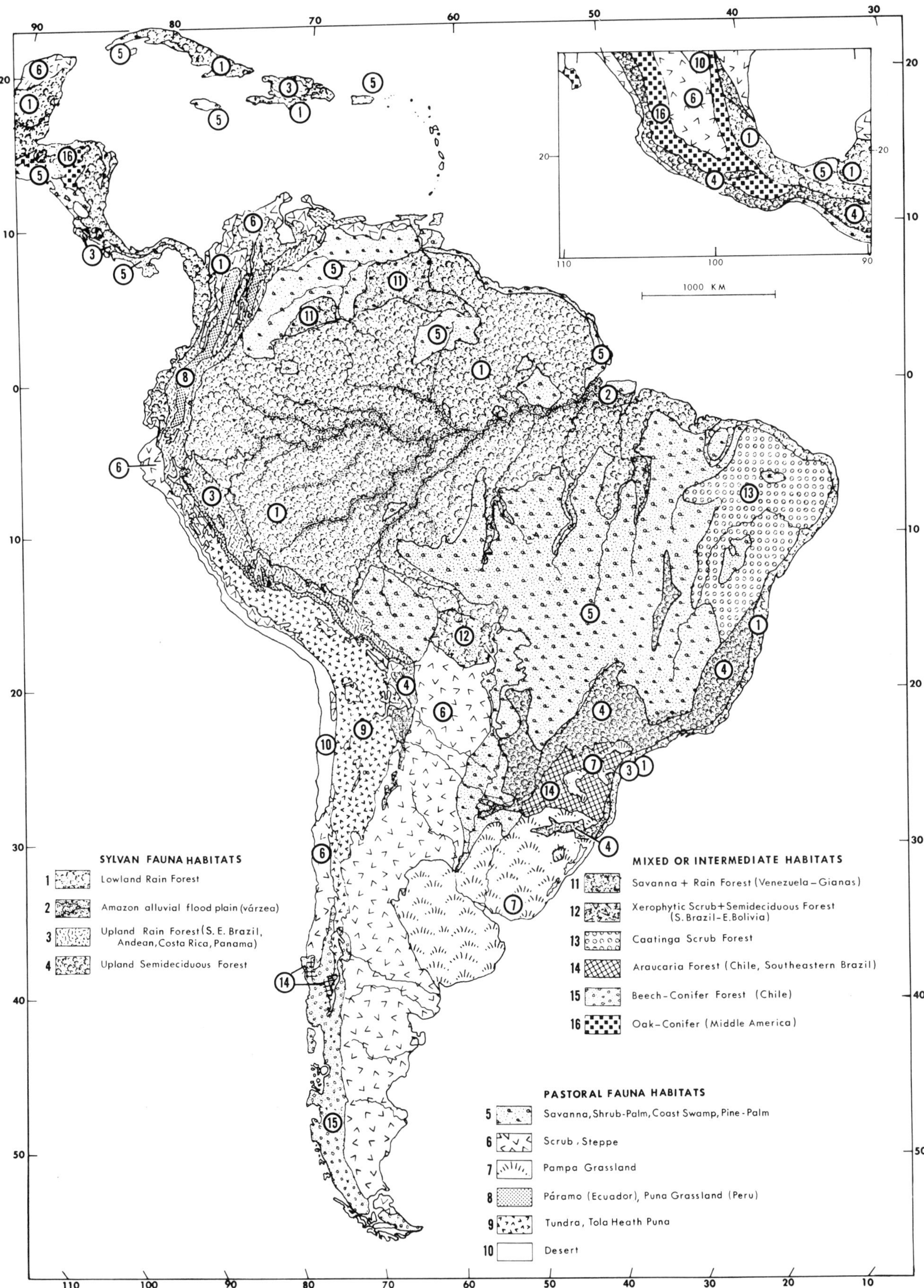

Fig. VII.2. Neotropical region showing major vegetation zones; (After Hershkovitz 1972, adapted from Sauer 1950 and Leopold 1959.)

term "marmoset" is reserved for *Cebuella* and *Callithrix*, or callitrichids with elongate, cylindrical lower incisors. Callitrichids with relatively short, spatulate lower incisors are "tamarins" of the genus *Saguinus* and "lion-tamarins" of the genus *Leontopithecus*. A suggested English vernacular name for each callitrichid species and subspecies will be found on p. 436. The vernacular name may satisfy a need in some quarters but it should never be used without the scientific name.

Taxonomic History

Callitrichids have been known to Europeans since the first half of the sixteenth century. Holbein depicted the common marmoset, *Callithrix jacchus,* cradled in the arms of the four-year-old English prince Edward Tudor in 1541. Gesner, one of the earliest of the encyclopedist-naturalists, described and figured the same species in 1551. Brazilian callitrichids described by Marcgraf in 1648 were classified in 1693 by John Ray, the great English systematist and forerunner of Linnaeus. Ray's arrangement of primates was followed by Pre-Linnaean authors and adopted by the master systematist himself.

Classifications of primates during the late seventeenth, eighteenth, and early nineteenth centuries were customarily based on a few highly visible key characters. Man was separated from all other organisms as sole representative of the order or class Bimana. Nonhuman primates, order Quadrumana, were sorted into simians (or apes and monkeys) and lemurs. Simians (*Simia*) were grouped by their diagnostic external characters as follows.

Tail Absent—Apes and tailless monkeys
Tail Present—
  Cheek pouches and ischial callosities present—
    Old World Monkeys
      Muzzle long—Baboons and some macaques.
      Muzzle short—guenons, langurs, and other macaques.
  Cheek pouches and ischial callosities absent—
    New World Monkeys
      Tail prehensile—
        Tail bare beneath—howlers and atelines
        Tail all furred—capuchins
      Tail nonprehensile—pithecines; callitrichids

Early systematists who relied on diagnostic key characters like the preceding were seemingly indifferent to the fact that some traits cut across phylogenetic lines, and as a result they grossly misplaced some species. Linnaeus, who used the key character device for the arrangement of mammals in all editions of his *Systema naturae,* was followed by such often-cited students of mammals as Schreber (1774), Erxleben (1777), Zimmermann (1780), Boddaert (1784), Kerr (1792), G. Cuvier (1798, 1817), and Desmarest (1820).

The ordinal term Primates for man, apes, monkeys, and lemurs appears in the 10th edition of Linnaeus's *Systema naturae,* published in 1758, the starting date for modern zoological nomenclature. Linnaeus also included bats and the colugo, or flying lemur, in Primates, because the key diagnostic characters did not exclude them. The generic name *Homo* was applied to man, and *Simia* was used for apes and monkeys, *Lemur* for prosimians and the colugo, and *Vespertilio* for bats.

Linnaeus recognized five species of callitrichids. Three of them, *Simia jacchus, S. oedipus,* and *S. midas,* were named in the 10th (1758) edition of the *Systema; Simia rosalia* appears in the 12th (1766) edition, and *Simia argentata* in the *Mantissa* (1771). All are currently known from tropical American coasts and banks of the lower Amazon River, but the manner in which Linnaeus lists them gives few clues to their genetic or geographic relationships.

Buffon, most distinguished of eighteenth-century naturalist-encyclopedists, was the first to separate New World from Old World primates on the basis of anatomical characters. He also perceived the platyrrhine-catarrhine dichotomy and the genetic distance between the two assemblages. New World monkeys, he (1767, p. 14) observed, "different donc des guenons, non-seulement par l'èspece, mais même par le genre, puisqu'ils n'ont aucun des caracteres généraux qui leur sont communs à toutes; et cette différence dans le genre en suppose nécessairement de bien plus grandes dans les espèces, et démontre qu'elles sont très-eloignées." Buffon further distinguished prehensile-tailed "sapajous" (= Cebidae) with nails on all digits, from lax-tailed "sagoins" (= Callitrichidae) with claws on all digits except the hallux. In the first group he included howlers, spider monkeys, capuchins, and squirrel monkeys with tail only "demiprenante" (1767, p. 69). The sagoins comprised *ouistitis* or common marmosets, *mico* or silver marmoset, golden-handed tamarin, *pince* or cotton-top, and *marikina* or lion-tamarin. The saki (*Pithecia pithecia*), known to Buffon from skins only, was regarded as largest of the sagoins. Also, and most significantly, Buffon noted 32 teeth in each jaw of the ouistiti and the long cylindriform lower incisors. These were compared with the 36 teeth, including an additional molar in the cheek tooth complement, and the spatulate lower incisors of the cebid squirrel monkey. Buffon lacked skulls of other species of sapajous and sagoins and so his platyrrhine taxonomy did not go beyond the family and species stage.

The binomial system for Buffon's arrangement of the primates was applied in 1777 by Erxleben, earliest of post-Linnaean specialists in mammalian classification. Erxleben restricted the Linnaean generic name *Simia* to Buffon's "singe," or apes. The genus *Papio* was erected for the "babouins," *Cercopithecus* for the "guenons," *Cebus* for sapajous, and *Callithrix* for sagoins, the saki included. The classification showed *Callithrix* listed next above *Lemur* and preceded by *Cebus.* Notwithstanding the improved diagnoses and taxonomic advances, Erxleben's *Systema* is essentially a catalog in the classical Linnaean mold.

Illiger's (1811), preliminary system of the Mammalia is no more than an incompletely updated abstract of Erxleben's classification. The definitive treatise was never published. His section on New World monkeys is most remembered for the invalid replacement of Erxleben's *Callithrix* by the new name *Hapale* to contain the Linnaean species *Simia rosalia, S. midas,* and *S. jacchus.*

The significance of Buffon's studies and arrangement of primates found fullest expression in the classic *Tableau des quadrumanes* published in 1812 by Etienne Geoffroy St.-Hilaire. Old World primates with "cloison des narines étroite, & ces mêmes narines ouvertes au-dessous du nez comme celles de l'homme," and other characters enumerated by Buffon (1767, p. 14) and repeated by Geoffroy (1812, p. 86), formed the Catarrhini. Buffon's New World sapajous and sagoins with "la cloison des narines fort épaisse, les narines ouvertes sur les côtés du nez," etc., constituted the Platyrrhini. The name Strepsirhini, or slit-nose monkeys, was used for prosimians.

E. Geoffroy's classification of New World primates was based on the collections in the Paris Museum, which then comprised more samples and named forms than had ever been assembled before. Included were the residue of Buffon's material and the Brazilian species collected by Alexandre Rodrigues Ferreira (1756–1815). Mounted specimens of the latter, originally contained in the Museu d'Ajuda in Lisbon, Portugal, had been confiscated as trophies of the Napoleonic conquests and transferred to the Paris Museum. Included were the following five, possibly six, new forms described by E. Geoffroy: *Callithrix jacchus leucocephalus* (= *geoffroyi* Humboldt), *C. j. aurita*, *C. j. penicillata* (?), *C. humeralifer humeralifer*, and *C. argentata melanura*.

The *Tableau of platyrrhini* devised by E. Geoffroy (1812) is summarized as follows.

Heliopitheci
The prehensile-tailed sapajous of Buffon (*Ateles*, *Lagothrix*, *Stentor* [= *Alouatta*], *Cebus*).

Geopitheci
Lax-tailed pithecines (*Pithecia* [= *Pithecia*, *Chiropotes*, *Cacajao*]), the squirrel monkey and titis, assigned to *Callithrix* (*sensu* Illiger 1811) and the douroucouli or night monkey, *Aotus*. The Geopitheci were equated with Buffon's sagoins (sagouins) but include only the saki (*Pithecia pithecia*) of the original group.

Arctopitheci
The sagoins of Buffon or all callitrichids then known, subdivided into true marmosets with new generic name *Jacchus* (for *Hapale* Illiger) and tamarins designated *Midas*.

E. Geoffroy's introduction of the generic name *Jacchus* for marmosets and transfer of the prior name *Callithrix* Erxleben to squirrel monkeys and titis was, like Illiger's action before him, invalid by all recognized rules of zoological nomenclature. Nevertheless, the misuse of names survived until 1903 when Thomas restored *Callithrix* Erxleben, 1777, to marmosets along with the corresponding family name Callitrichidae, replacing the current *Hapale* and Hapalidae.

Arbitrary use of the name *Callithrix* and its variant spelling *Callitrix* remains a source of confusion, particularly to those consulting the older literature. During virtually the whole of the last century, *Callithrix* was restricted to titis, now *Callicebus*. Gray (1821) used Callitricidae as the family name for cebids, and later (1825) as a tribal or subfamilial name, Callitrichina, for *Cebus* alone. Elliot (1913*a*) confused nomenclature with zoology and classified *Callicebus* as a callitrichid because it had been called *Callithrix*. Miranda Ribeiro (1941, p. 800) added another twist in the wrong direction by replacing the name *Pithecia* with *Callithrix*.

Following E. Geoffroy's opus of 1812, contributions to the taxonomy of callitrichids consisted mainly of the erection of new species, the renaming of many more, and a multiplication of superspecific names. The nadir of typological taxonomy and embroiled nomenclature was reached in 1913 with the publication of Elliot's *A Review of the Primates*. The stagnation in primatology that ensued persisted for more than a quarter century. Works by Thomas (1922) and Hershkovitz (1949) resulted in some advances, while Cruz Lima's (1945) atlas of Amazonian monkeys is a milestone in accurate pictorial differentiation of the species despite the faulty, sometimes conflicting taxonomy and confused nomenclature inherited by the author.

The monumental *Primates: Comparative anatomy and taxonomy: A monograph* by Osman Hill began with the first volume on Strepsirhini published in 1953 and is still incomplete with publication of volume 8 in 1970 and volume 7 in 1974, both on Old World monkeys. Most of volume 3 (1957) is devoted to callitrichids, and volumes 4 and 5 (1960, 1962) belong to cebids. The three volumes were reviewed elsewhere (cf. Hershkovitz 1963*b*) and some of their subject matter is examined here. Hill's arrangement of callitrichids (his hapalids) is essentially a compromise of those of earlier authors but with 5 genera of tamarins and 3 of marmosets recognized. For his taxonomy Osman Hill (1957, p. 192) admits to having been influenced by Sanderson (1950), whose concepts of callitrichid characteristics and interrelationships appeared in the popular *Zoo Life* magazine, published by the Zoological Society of London. In this article, Sanderson plays more hob with callitrichid taxonomy, nomenclature, and distribution in 4 pages than Elliot (1913) does in the 79 plus he devoted to the same animals. Sanderson's story was but a prelude to his *Living mammals of the world* (1956, but book not dated), where the account of callitrichids is even more muddled.

Fiedler's (1956) taxonomic review does not stray outside the bounds of previously published information. The data is well organized and attractively presented, and the arrangement of callitrichids is the best for its time.

The use of nonhuman primates in highly sophisticated biomedical and behavioral studies increased dramatically during the fifth decade of this century. Widespread interest in the biology of the animals evoked correspondingly high-level demands for the precise and authoritative taxonomic, nomenclatorial, zoogeographic, and evolutionary data that simply did not exist, despite appearances to the contrary. Results of ensuing research filled some of the gaps in knowledge. Advances during the years between publication of the reviews of Fiedler and by Osman Hill and 1966 are incorporated in the critical, dependable, and widely used *Handbook of living Primates* by Napier and Napier (1967).

In the present account, virtually all contributions to callitrichid biology to 1974 and many dated 1975 are cited either in the pertinent synonymic lists of the family, genera, species, and subspecies or in the descriptions or discussions.

Systematic Position

The primitive organization of callitrichids was recognized since the time of Buffon (1767). Virtually all systematists placed the group at the very bottom of the simians and next above lemurs. Most authorities ranked callitrichids (or hapalids) as a family group coordinate with cebids and cercopithecids. A few, notably Swainson (1835), Mivart (1874), and Winge (1895), treated them as a subordinate group of cebids. Winge coupled his Hapalini with Mycetini (howlers) as the most primitive tribes of Cebidae, the only platyrrhine family he recognized. The Mycetini, however, were believed to be the more primitive of the two because they possessed the full complement of 3 molars in each jaw and retained true nails, not claws, on all digits. The hapaline claws, argued Winge (1895, trans. 1941, p. 315), make it appear "as if they were more primitive in this respect than any known lemurs and monkeys but the case is undoubtedly similar to that of *Chiromys* [*Daubentonia madagascariensis*]. They have readapted the nails for holding on to the branches too thick to be grasped by hand or foot and the nails have therefore reverted to the claw shape." Actually, all primates constantly cope with tree trunks and branches "too thick to be grasped by hand or foot."

Pocock (1917) reiterated Winge's tooth and nail arguments in full but omitted reference to the Danish mammalogist. Both men, however, were strongly doctrinaire in their belief that nail-bearing digits and 3 quadritubercular molars in each jaw were invariably coupled in primitive anthropoid primates. Thus Pocock (1917, p. 252), like Winge before him, argued that

> It might be held that the small hallux and the claw-tipped digits of the Hapalidae are primitive features derived direct from an unguiculate arboreal ancestor, probably of a lemuroid type, but preceding in those particulars modern lemurs, which have a hallux of great length and thickness and digits tipped with flat or flattish nails.

But, Pocock debated,

> in my opinion, the Hapalidae may be best regarded as derived from typical Platyrrhine monkeys, from which they have departed in the numerical reduction of the teeth and in the appendicular particulars above-mentioned. The only Platyrrhine Primate outside the limits of the Hapalidae which has the hallux small and the digits claw-tipped, as in the marmosets, is *Callimico,* Thos. [cf. Winge's aye-aye analog]; and it is to be remembered that both in *Callimico* and the Hapalidae these characteristics of the hands and feet are associated with smallness in size and lightness in build. These little monkeys, indeed, are the most diminutive of all the true Primates, and, owing to the small size and narrow transverse span of the hands and feet, they are unable to grasp branches of any width. Nevertheless, since they are extraordinarily active and jump with great power, they require special means of maintaining a hold on the branches they traverse or alight on. In this need may be found, I think, the modification of the nails into claws and the concomitant reduction of the hallux which, while depriving the hands and feet of the peculiar prehensile capacity seen in other primates, have converted them into extremities resembling functionally those of squirrels in their power of hooking on to the roughnesses of bark, of thick branches, and tree-trunks.

In short, in Pocock's mind the ancestral callitrichid had attained cebid size and organization only to revert to tamarin size, lose digital prehensibility, and restore claws previously modified into nails all for the purpose of relearning to climb where it had climbed successfully before.

Gregory (1922) worked the same trail but without mention of his predecessors. His thesis, like that of Winge and Pocock, begins with recognition of primitive platyrrhine traits and concludes with denials of their retention in callitrichids except in perverted or reverted form. The primitive platyrrhine cranial and dental characters constructed by Gregory (1922, p. 226) are enumerated herewith in that author's terms but with quotation marks omitted and my interpolations bracketed.

1. Face short
2. Braincase expanded
3. Orbits relatively small [i.e., smaller than in *Tarsius*]
4. Lacrymal [bone] mostly within orbits
5. Nose wide, flat [not a cranial character]
6. Auditory bullae expanded [i.e., inflated]
7. Tympanic bones large, ring-like
8. Lower jaw short, deep [not a primitive primate character]
9. No bony chin [i.e., mental protuberance absent]
10. Zygomatic arches short, pitching sharply downward in front
11. Dental formula: I $\frac{2}{2}$, c $\frac{1}{1}$, p $\frac{3}{3}$, m $\frac{3}{3}$
12. Front teeth not rodent-like, but normal [like what?]
13. Dental arches pointed [i.e., V-shaped]
14. Canines small
15. Three upper premolars bicuspid [not entirely primitive]
16. Upper molars tritubercular [in basic plan but] with small hypocone [hence quadritubercular and not primitive]
17. Protoconule and metaconule reduced
18. Lower molars with "trigonid" but little elevated above talonid
19. Talonid large, but not excessively widened
20. Paraconids reduced or absent
21. Hypoconulids present.

The following additions to the list are mentioned elsewhere by Gregory (1922, p. 120) as platyrrhine ancestral characters.

22. Quite small animals, even smaller than the existing tree shrews
23. Of primitive insectivorous habits
24. Arboricolous.

The postulated platyrrhine ancestral characters 1–7, 9, 10, 12(?), 13, and 17–24, are still found in primitive state among callitrichids, particularly in *Cebuella.* Characters 8 and 9 are not compatible. The primitive lower jaw is comparatively longer, lower, and shallower at the symphysis than any jaw derived from it. The low-slung jaw of *Cebuella* is primitive by any standard and more primitive than that of any known platyrrhine or catarrhine. Character 14 presumably applies to upper and lower canines, but the upper, even if "short," is always longer than the lower. Least differentiated canines among platyrrhines are those of *Cebuella* and *Callithrix jacchus.* Although the marmoset lower canine is habitually described as "incisiform," it is the incisors that are still caniniform. Characters 15 and 16, with respect to upper premolar and molar structure, respectively, are more primitive in callitrichids than in the ancestral form conceived by Gregory. The first premolar in *Cebuella* is still unicuspid and primitively trident, and the molars are truly tritubercular without sign of hypocone. Nevertheless, Gregory (1922, p. 230) believed the hypocone had been lost in callitrichids.

The remaining one of the 24 postulated ancestral characters and the most crucial from Gregory's (and Pocock's) point of view, is number 11, the dental formula. The primitive number of molars in upper and lower jaws of all placentals is 3. This number is retained in cebids, callimiconids, and catarrhines. In all callitrichids, the 3d upper and lower molars are lost, the 2d reduced in size.

The 2-molar series of callitrichids, according to Gregory (1922, pp. 228–29), and virtually all contemporaries, must be derived from the 3-quadritubercular molar series of a cebid such as *Aotus* or *Callicebus,* both highly specialized. No one had made the logical assumption that callitrichids might have arisen from a noncebid platyrrhine, preplatyrrhine, or tarsioid with 3 tritubercular molars and that their dental modifications may have begun at a more primtive level and proceeded in a different direction than that of cebids.

Loss of the callitrichid 3d molar might well have been a mechanical sequel to rapid braincase inflation. The ensuing extreme basicranial flexure or kyphosis (cf. fig. IV.55) and constriction of the posterior alveolar portion of the maxillary bone evidently suppressed development of the 3d molar. Ample alveolar space persists in the mandible, but the 3d molar, with nothing to do, rarely develops to the tooth bud stage. In catarrhines, where the basicranial flexure was more anteriad, a premolar yielded to palatal constriction. Similar modifications of the cephalic arterial system in the tamarin *Saguinus midas* (2 specimens) and rhesus macaque, *Macaca mulatta* (4 specimens) and *Homo sapiens* (literature) noted by Bugge (1972) may, if consistent for the respective families, be correlated with the extreme kyphosis that presumably led to the reduced number of cheek teeth.

Comparable cranial modifications in cebids, but with slighter braincase inflation and basicranial flexure, apparently evolved at a more deliberate pace with less displacement of bones and no loss of cheek teeth, and at least in *Aotus trivirgatus* (2 specimens) it is correlated with fewer modifications of the cephalic arterial system (Bugge 1972) than in simians with 5 cheek teeth.

Other callitrichid characters were regarded by Gregory in the same skewed light as the cranial and dental. Small body size, upheld by Gregory (1922, pp. 120, 235) as indicative of a primitive state in primates and mammals generally, was construed, in the case of callitrichids, as a condition of dwarfism. In all logic, the body size of the ancestral callitrichid may well have been considerably less than that of the pygmy marmoset, smallest of its modern descendants.

The sharply pointed, downwardly curved callitrichid claws, the most primitive ungues among primates, were dismissed by Gregory (1922, p. 229) as merely "bent up nails."

In a detailed comparative study of claws and nails, Le Gros Clark (1936) proved conclusively, and almost unnecessarily, that callitrichid and aye-aye claws are actually the primitive structures they appear to be and not the degenerate nails Gregory and others thought they were. Biegert (1961, p. 173), who examined the external morphology of all living primates, described the hands of *Callithrix* as follows:

> All fingers of this genus bear uniformly, very ovate, narrow and proximally round bordered nail balls. They are uniformly on the volar surface covered with the primary sinus and on the dorsal surface with relatively long, curved, sharp and laterally compressed claws. The skin of the middle and basal joints of the fingers are transected by many folds beset with few cutaneous ridges. The extraordinary slender form of the fingers and the aforementioned combination of characters has an extraordinary resemblance to the condition in Tupaiidae and appears to be primitive.

The callitrichid lack of pollical opposability, a trait it never had, was explained as "a degenerate and secondary character."

The callitrichid fibula, Gregory (1922, p. 230) went on, "shows a tendency to be immovably joined or partly coalesced with the tibia at the lower end, a condition which no morphologist could safely regard as primitive." It would be unsafe indeed to regard the partial fusion of tibia and fibula in platyrrhines as anything but an anomalous or diseased condition, as it proved to be in the case of the callitrichid leg bones examined by Gregory.

The opinion, shared by Pocock and Gregory, that callitrichid limbs are products of regressive evolution has been refuted by competent authorities. Beattie (1927, p. 709), monographer of marmoset anatomy, concluded that

> it is more likely that *Hapale* [= *Callithrix jacchus*] is more primitive than has been thought, and there has not been any specialisation in the forelimb in the direction of the typical Primate manus. It is hard to conceive that *Hapale* specialized in the direction of flattened nails and expanded terminal phalanges, and then dropped these undoubtedly specialised features to return to a condition which approximates closely to that seen in some of the most primitive of the Insectivores, animals which have so many affinities to the Metatheria. It is more likely that *Hapale* derived the present sharp clinging claw at a very early stage in its history from claws similar to those of an animal like *Ptilocercus.*

Spinal column and pelvis were seen by Gregory (1922, p. 420) as "more or less intermediate in form between those of the primitive Eocene Notharctidae, on the one hand, and the larger Cebidae on the other, a fact indicating the essentially primate character of their whole locomotor apparatus, and strengthening the conclusion that the clawed condition of their digits is entirely secondary." Gregory evidently implied that callitrichid claws could not be more primitive in structure than the naillike ungues of notharctids, their supposed ancestors. As for the vertebrae, Beattie (1927, p. 708) finds those of callitrichids more primitive than those of *Aotus,* regarded by Gregory (1922, p. 235) as the more primtive form.

It must be noted that in all his deliberations, Gregory (1922, pp. 121–221), (*a*) seriously entertained the notion of platyrrhine descent from a large, specialized Eocene notharctid with 3 quadritubercular upper molars; (*b*) was unable or unwilling to recognize an animal with 2 tritubercular upper molars as otherwise more primitive than a distantly related one with 3 quadritubercular upper molars; (*c*) assessed callitrichids on the basis of a few skulls of tamarins, genus *Saguinus,* and the diseased tamarin skeleton mentioned above; and (*d*) (1922, pp. 227, 231, 233, 236, 467) felt compelled to disprove Bolk's (1916) contention that the pattern of callitrichid dentition represents a stage in human evolution.

Wood Jones (1929, p. 212), who reviewed the conflicting opinions of Gregory and Beattie, concluded that "by

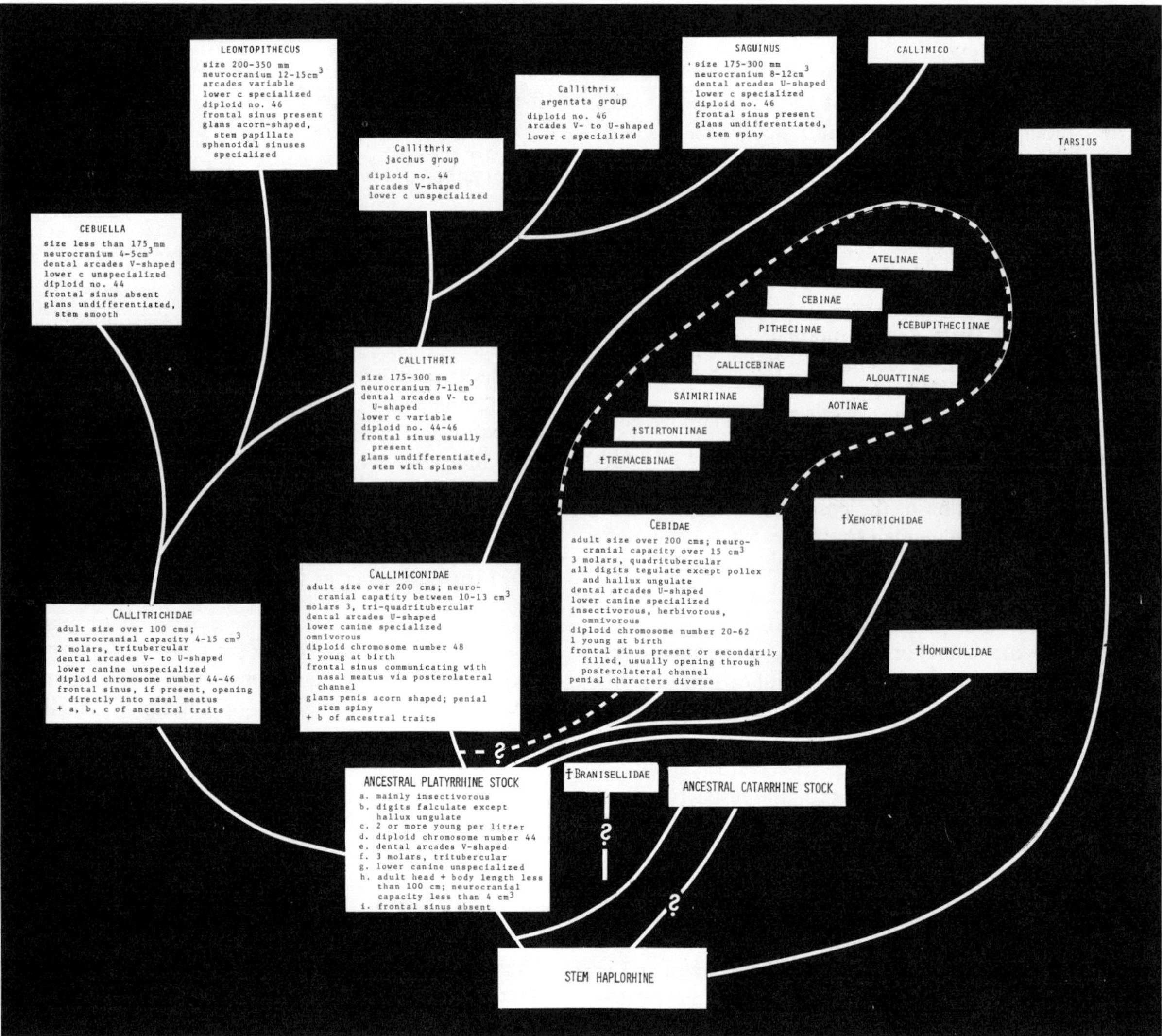

Fig. VII.3. Origin, evolution, and relationships of the Callitrichidae and Callimiconidae. Principal divergent characters among living platyrrhine families and callitrichid genera are enumerated under each taxon. Stepped arrangement with Recent genera at top implies a corresponding evolutionary grade within an unspecified time sequence. Relationships between the subfamilies currently referred to the composite family Cebidae are not clear, and no definite arrangement is offered. For distinctions between platyrrhines and catarrhines and between haplorhines and strepsirhines, see keys (pp. 11, 122, 198, 336, 367).

every criterion of comparative anatomy, the Hapalidae must be judged as having arisen from an early Tarsioid. They must also be recognized as primitive platyrrhines and as generalized forms from which the remaining New World monkeys have radiated in the several directions."

Other contemporary authorities also regarded callitrichids as lowly primates. Elliot Smith (1924, p. 141) considered *Callithrix* (Hapale) as the "most primitive surviving primate." Wislocki (1930, p. 481) observed that "the finding of complex genital glands in marmosets is in keeping with the belief that the organization of these animals is primitive, and that they represent the lowest order of the Simiae." Strauss (1949) was of the same opinion. Le Gros Clark (1959) generally compared callitrichids with tarsiers and tupaiids. Osman Hill (1957, pp. xii, 76, 114, 115) placed the Callitrichidae (his Hapalidae) at the foot of his suborder Pithecoidea (= Platyrrhini and Catarrhini; Anthropoidea of authors) but his discussion of their systematic position and arrangement of the genera was equivocal.

Simpson (1945) followed Pocock by placing the Callitrichidae after the Cebidae, but with marmosets preceding tamarins. Later, Simpson (1969, p. 885) saw fit to reduce the family Callitrichidae (his "Callithricidae") to a subfamily "Callithricinae" of the family Cebidae. "The supposed family differences," he declared, "are not great or consistent and are partly negated by fossil forms." With all due respect for what Simpson may have had in mind, I fail to find in his extensive writings a statement setting forth taxonomic differences between any kinds of platyrrhine monkeys, or mention of a specimen examined for the purpose, or even the citation of a bibliographic reference to a primary source in support of his sweeping conclusion.

In contrast with authors who combine callitrichids with cebids in the Platyrrhini or equivalent Ceboidea, Beattie (1927, p. 713) opined that

> if *Tarsius* is regarded as "standing at the base of the Primate stem" and reaching "forth to the Simian forms" [quotation from Woollard 1925, p. 1182, but see Gregory 1922, pp. 234–35] then *Hapale* is but a

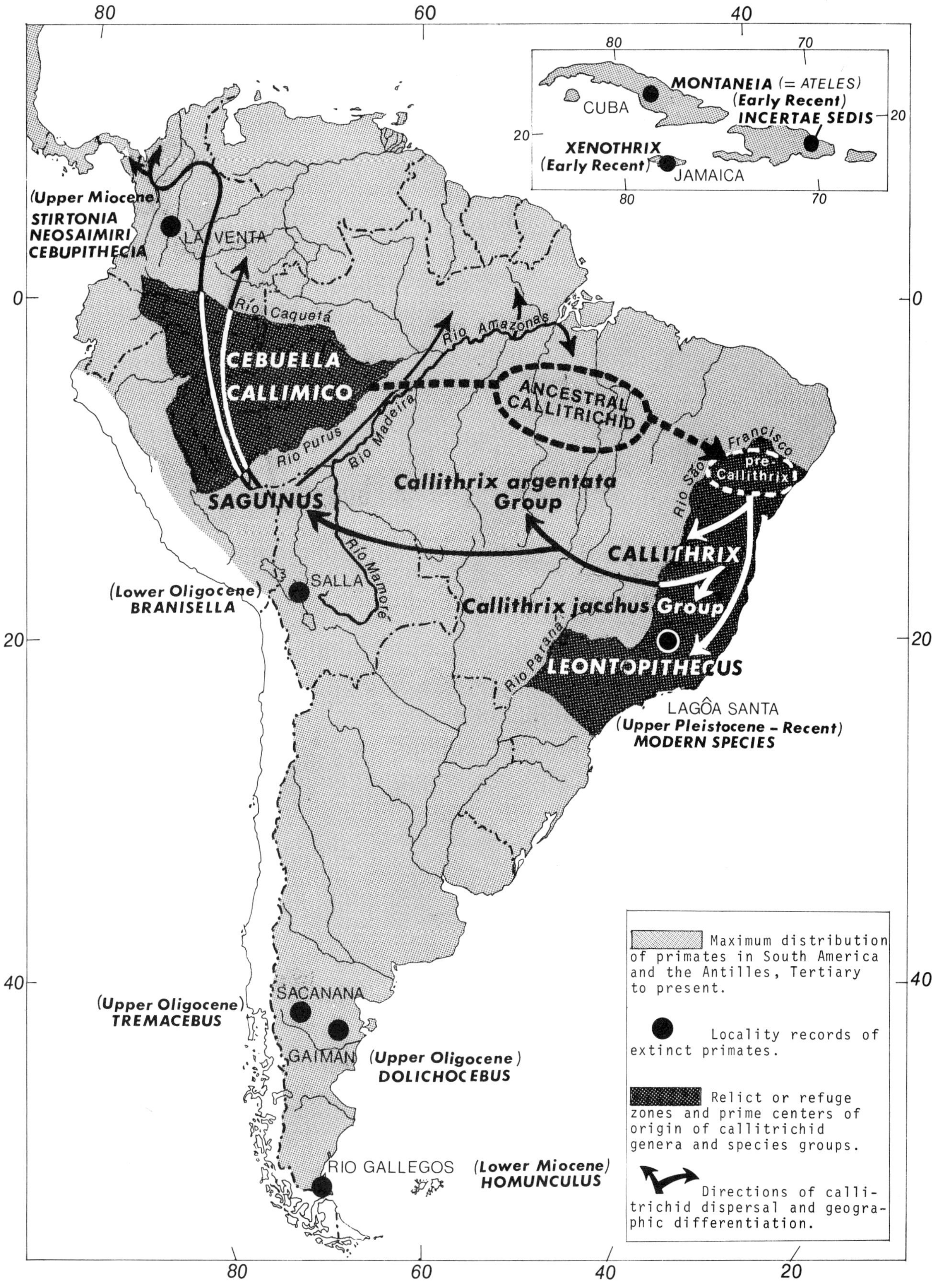

Fig. VII.4. Hypothetical limits of nonhuman primate dispersal in South America and Antilles (*shaded*) throughout the Cenozoic, and directions of callitrichid dispersal and geographic differentiation (*arrows*). Range limits based on fossil records (*dots*) and known distribution of living forms. Callitrichids probably occupied a larger part of the shaded portion than they do now (cf. fig. VII.1). The ancestral callitrichid zone shown encircled by a broken line symbolizes the contraction and disappearance of the Tertiary range that hypothetically extended over much if not most of the shaded area. Solid black areas are early- or pre-Quaternary relict zones and possible centers of origin of modern callitrichid genera and *Callimico*. Relationship between *Callimico* and callitrichids is depicted in fig. VII. 3 and discussed in text. Solid lines and arrows indicate phylogenetic branching leading to modern callitrichid species groups and directions of dispersal where major waterways form boundaries between genera and species groups.

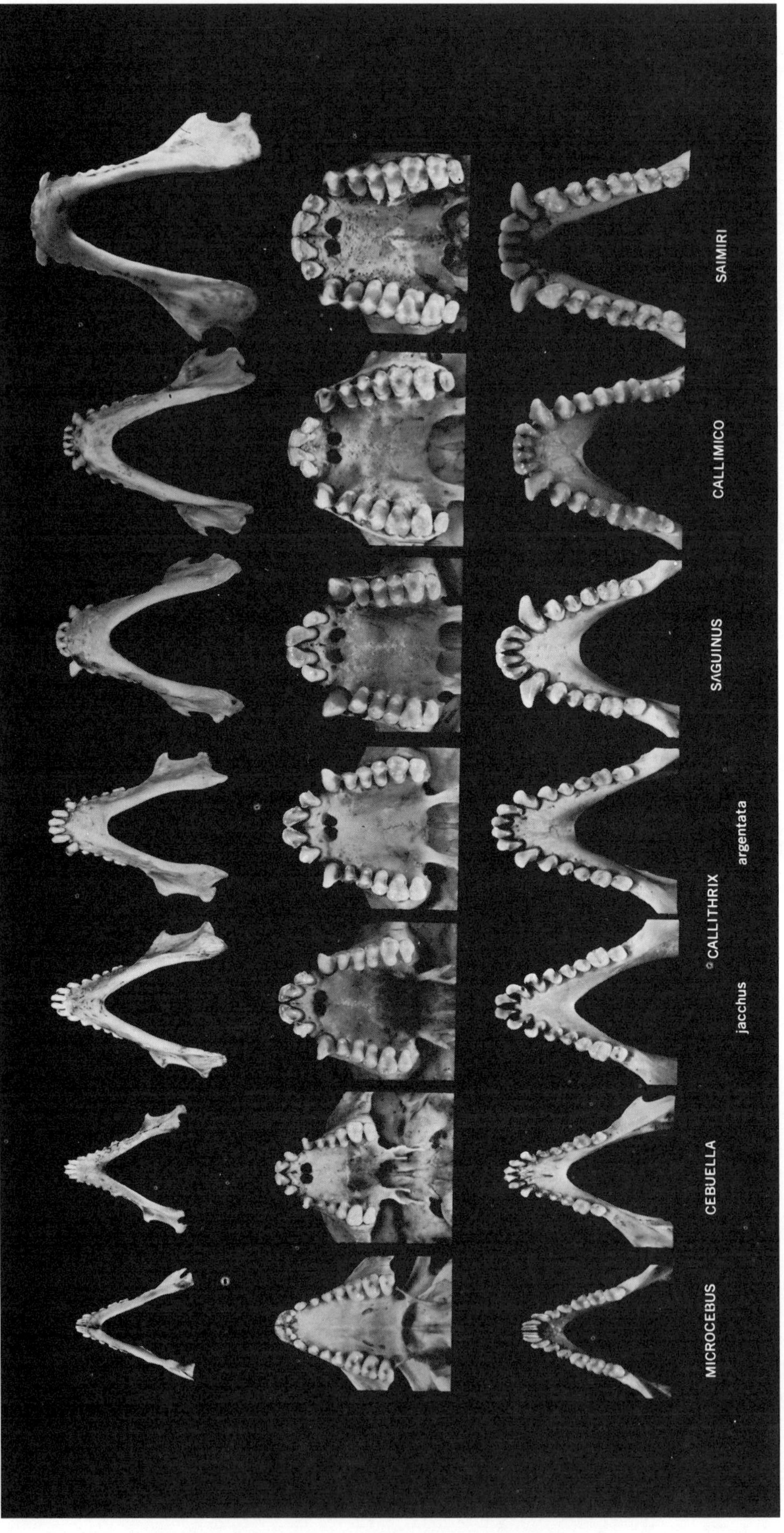
MICROCEBUS
CEBUELLA
jacchus
CALLITHRIX
argentata
SAGUINUS
CALLIMICO
SAIMIRI

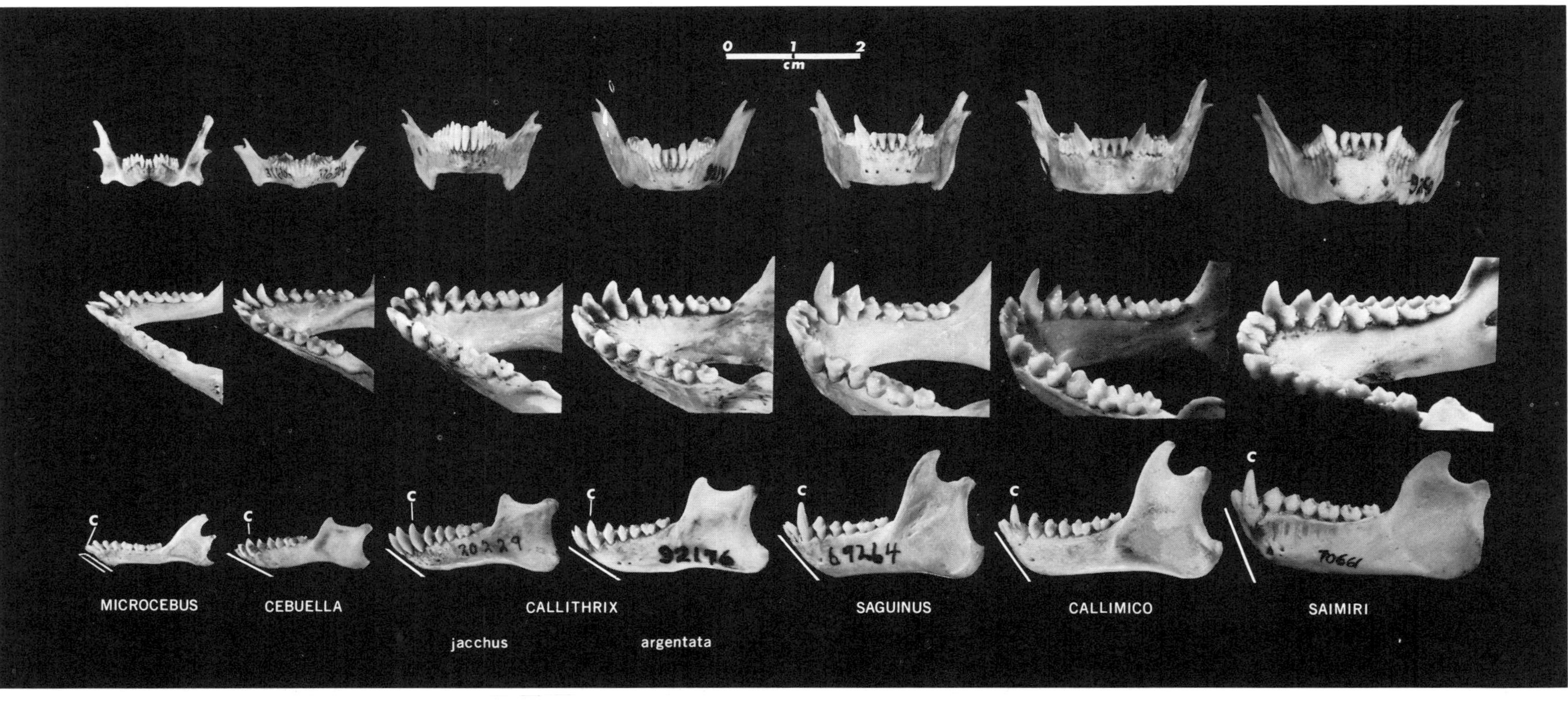

Fig. VII.5. Skulls—palatal aspects and mandibles—of callitrichids compared with those of *Microcebus* (Lemuridae), *Callimico* (Callimiconidae), and Saimiri (Cebidae).

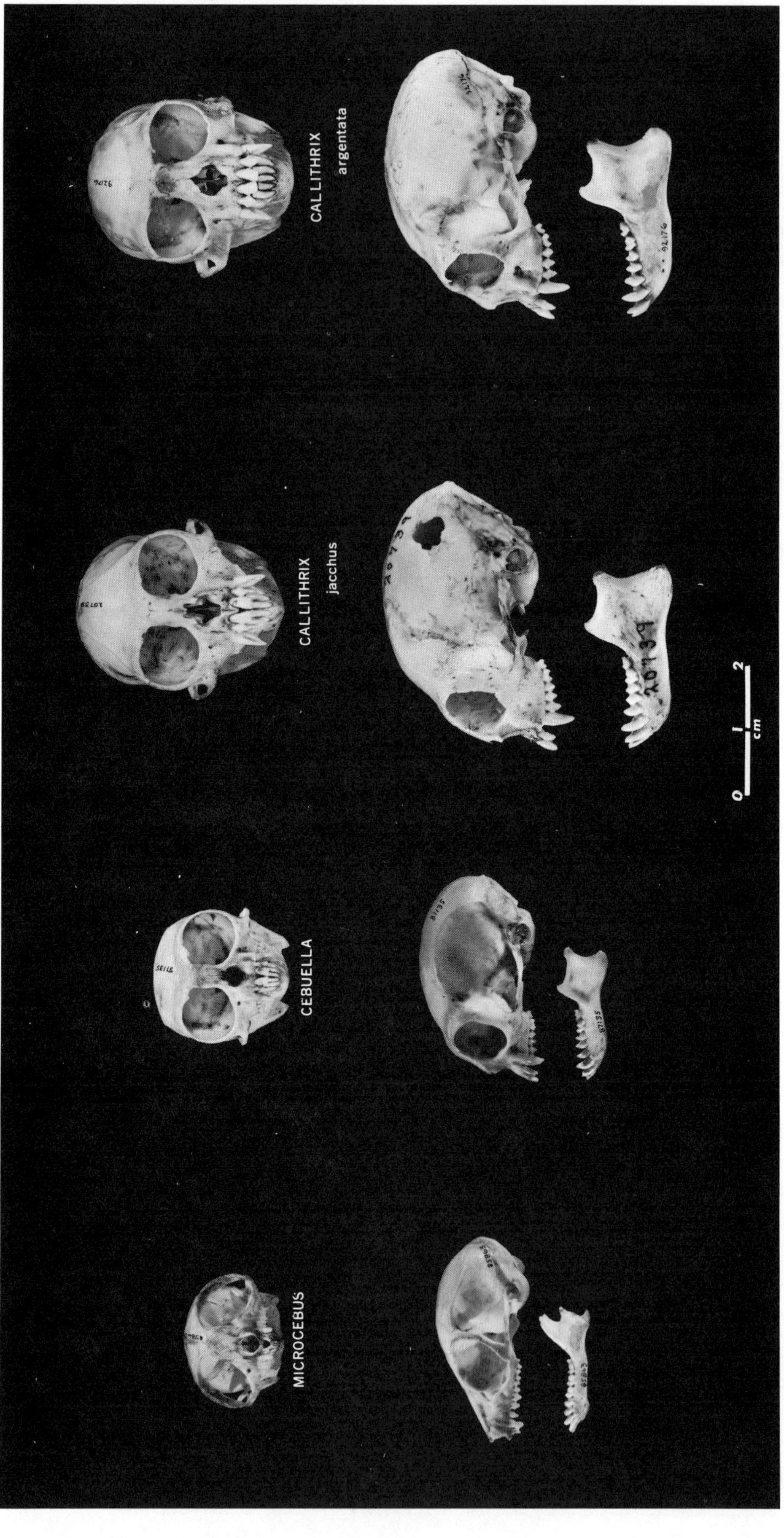
MICROCEBUS
CEBUELLA
CALLITHRIX
jacchus
CALLITHRIX
argentata
0
1
2
cm

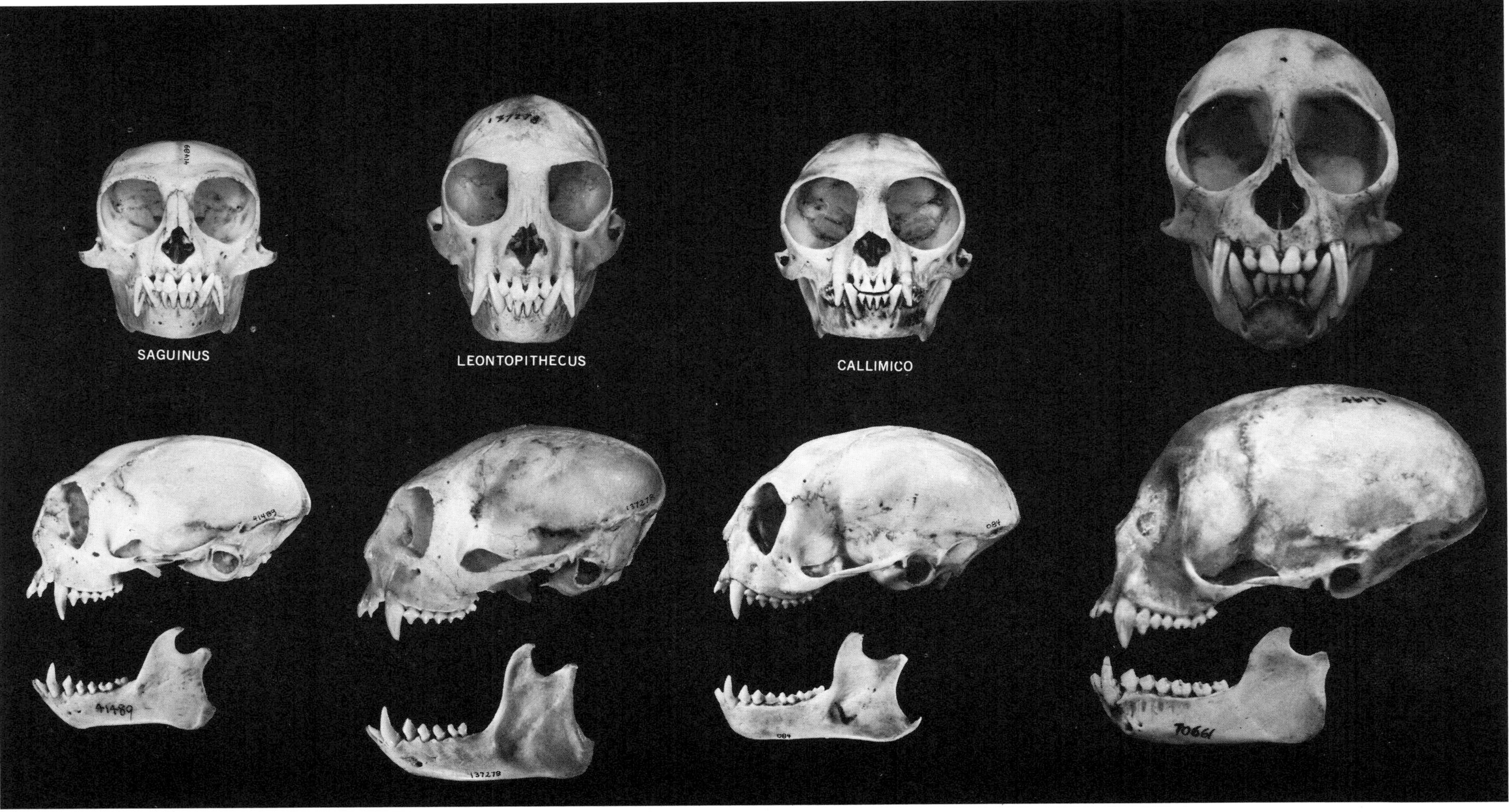

Fig. VII.6. Skulls—front and side views—of callitrichids *Cebuella, Callithrix, Saguinus,* and *Leontopithecus* compared with those of *Microcebus* (Lemuridae), *Callimico* (Callimiconidae) and *Saimiri* (Cebidae).

modification of the Tarsioid ancestor leading upwards toward the Platyrrhinæ and is itself the most primitive and tarsioid of these forms. When the fossil record of the Platyrrhinæ becomes better known, it will connect up the Eocene Tarsioids with the recent Platyrrhinæ, and it is possible that one of the stages in the phylogeny of the group will closely resemble the living Hapalidae. . . . There is little doubt that there is every reason for separating off the Hapalidae from the Platyrrhinæ as Huxley [1872] did, and for regarding them as the most primitive of all living monkeys.

Callitrichids may have arisen independently from tarsioid stock, as Beattie suggested. It is also likely that they differentiated from a post-tarsioid, simian, or platyrrhine stock that gave rise to all other South American monkeys. Whatever the origin, no primate with the advanced cranial architecture and dental formula of callitrichids could be a link between tarsioids and platyrrhines, as presupposed by Beattie. By the same token, callitrichids could not give rise to cebids or any other platyrrhine family with the primitive molar formula or a derived reduced formula. Conversely, no cebid or type of any other known platyrrhine family possesses the generalized organization of the stock from which callitrichids sprang (fig. VII.3).

Differences between the three main groups of existing platyrrhines are few but trenchant, whereas most of their simliarities are common to all primates, including catarrhines, of simian grade. In their adaptations to a common arboreal habitat, callitrichids stand at the lowest or most primitive of the simian or haplorhine stations. *Callimico* evolved to tamarin grade with respect to its general facies, but forged ahead into the lower marmosetlike cebid class with respect to trophic and reproductive adaptations. Larger cebids broke through the restricted size perimeter of lightweight, high protein consumers and radiated into the food-plant rich arboreal niches never fully exploited by other New World herbivorous vertebrates.

Callitrichids are the most primitive and highly stabilized of platyrrhines, and cebids are highly specialized and the most diversified of primates. *Callimico,* known from a single species, is intermediate in grade but not clade between callitrichids and cebids. Its continuing evolutionary trend is toward a more cebidlike facies.

Callitrichids and cebids, sometimes combined in a single family, represent two divergent families of ancient lineages, widely separated in time, and probably in ancestry. The degree of relationship between the two assemblages is neither a simple nor a single measurement. The extremely narrow adaptive zone in which both groups evolved implies that they possess a common store of parallel and convergent traits. Nonsimian adaptive resemblances between the two groups, however, are few. Callitrichids can be closely compared only on the basis of size with such cebids as squirrel monkeys, titis, or night monkeys. Even so, resemblance between a true marmoset and a night monkey, or a uakari, capuchin, woolly, or other cebid type is less than the resemblance between a capuchin or ateline and an African guenon or Asiatic colobine. Cranial and dental resemblances between cebids and the cercopithecidlike *Parapithecus* of the Early Oligocene Fayum are even greater than between the living representatives of the Cebidae and Cercopithecidae.

Origin

Nothing is known of the antecedents of callitrichids beyond what can be inferred from living representatives and the fragmentary fossil record of other South American primates (fig. VII.4).

The eight or nine extinct species of suborder Platyrrhini known to date (cf. Hershkovitz 1970*a;* 1972, p. 323; 1974) represent nearly as many genera referrable to the families Homunculidae (*Homunculus, Dolichocebus*), Xenotrichidae (*Xenothrix*), Cebidae (*Stirtonia, Cebupithecia, Neosaimiri, Tremacebus*). An additional and unassigned species, oldest of all, is *Branisella boliviana* (fig. III.3), from the lower Oligocene of the Bolivian Andes. All attained cebid grade with respect to size and cranial or dental specializations. All disappeared without issue and their remains provide no better clues to their respective ancestors than the morphology of the living pygmy marmoset, *Cebuella pygmaea,* gives to its own history.

The precallitrichid line, perhaps indistinguishable from the basic platyrrhine stock, must have begun with a small mouse- or pygmy squirrel-like monkey almost certainly smaller than *Cebuella* and characterized by a clinging-running-springing locomotor system, skull with frontolaterally oriented orbits, orbitotemporal fenestra large, interorbital separation broad, foramen magnum directed more nearly backward than downward, dental arches V-shaped, mandibular symphysis low slung, angular process unexpanded, condylar suspension low, three tritubercular-sectorial molars with hypocone absent, paraconid probably present in last premolar and first two molars, thumb nonopposable, hallux semiopposable and provided with nail, remaining digits including thumb clawed, brain lissocephalic, cerebral hemispheres with no more than 4, probably only 3, fissures, production of litters of 2 or 3 young, and other primitive primate traits not essential to the present definition. *Cebuella pygmaea* fits the model except for the advanced architecture of its rounded head, absence of third molars and absence of paraconids.

Evolution

The evolution of callitrichids from a hypothetical premarmoset platyrrhine must have involved an accelerated forward rotation of the orbits, postorbital closure, correlative brain case expansion, and relative muzzle reduction. The allometric growths imposed a strong biomechanical flexure or kyphosis on the basicranial axis with resultant contraction of the posterior end of the bony palate and concomitant suppression of alveolar space required for growth of the third molar (fig. IV.55). *When the last molar of the premarmoset platyrrhine disappeared, the first true marmoset appeared.* In a basically insect-eating economy, mechanical loss of the third molar, even with reduction of the second, is not critical for survival if the predatory adaptations, compensatorily enlarged first molar, and generalized gut remain as they do in living callitrichids.

As the body enlarged to tamarin grade and omnivority increased, the dental arcade became U-shaped, the chin more nearly erect, and the ascending ramus broad and high (figs. VII.5, 6). Callitrichids of tamarin grade, however, never became mainly herbivorous. Their body never attained dimensions or weight that would demand a more specialized grip for arboreal suspension than provided by clinging claws, grasping digits, and clasping hallux.

The callitrichid molds for size, body proportions, arboreal and feeding adaptations, and locomotor systems were probably established early and changed little in an equatorial habitat that in all likelihood remained relatively stable throughout most of the Cenozoic. With attainment of a habitus and social system that insured adequate defense against predation, evolutionary processes concentrated on display and other socially significant characters. All callitrichids are highly visible and easily distinguished by size, color, and pelage patterns, external genitalia, pheromones, vocalizations, postures, and gaits. Descriptions of these characters are given in appropriate sections of the text.

Callitrichids form a closely knit group. *Cebuella* is the most primitive member as well as the most primitive of known platyrrhines. *Callithrix* differs grossly by its absolutely greater size. Allometry alone can account for most remaining differences between the genera but discrepancies point to a long separation. The difference in lower incisor-canine size-shape relationship between *Callithrix jacchus* and tamarins of the genus *Saguinus* is almost entirely erased by members of the *Callithrix argentata* group. *Leontopithecus,* the largest and most highly specialized callitrichid, is tamarinlike in grade.

Dispersal and Generic Differentiation

It can be assumed that the tiny ancestral callitrichid was widely distributed throughout much of what are now the tropical parts of the Amazonian basin and the Brazilian highlands (fig. VII.4). Destruction of forest habitats by protracted floods or droughts may have eradicated all but a few relict populations in the Brazilian highlands and along the Andean foothills. *Cebuella* of the upper Amazonian region may well be a descendant of one such relict population. Another isolated relict in the Brazilian highlands must have given rise to *Callithrix jacchus.* Members of the *Callithrix argentata* group can be derived from an offshoot of the primary *Callithrix jacchus* stock. *Leontopithecus* probably evolved independently from another isolate in the Brazilian highlands.

The Rios Amazonas, Madeira, and upper Paraná system define, respectively, the northern, western, and southwestern geographic limits of *Callithrix.* Within, the Rios São Francisco and Paraná circumscribe the range of *Leontopithecus.* There is no probable geographic link between *Leontopithecus* and *Saguinus* now, and there seems to have been none in the past, or directly or indirectly through a common ancestor.

Tamarins of the genus *Saguinus* must have evolved directly from a colony of prototypes of the *Callithrix argentata* group that breached the Rio Madeira barrier and established itself on the west bank. Rapid evolution and dispersal ensued in the virgin territory. Waifing across barrier rivers or passive translation by operation of a river bend cutoff (fig. III.17) may be occasional phenomena. The establishment of a founder colony, its multiplication, subdivision, spread, and long-term occupation of a territory, however, must be extremely rare. Today only *Saguinus* occurs on the west bank of the Rio Madeira, and *Callithrix* is confined to the east bank (fig. VII.1).

The time scale for dispersal and generic differentiation is speculative. The total organization of all callitrichids is more primitive than known Oligocene homunculids and later cebids. The basic stock from which *Callithrix* and *Leontopithecus* arose was probably extant during the late Oligocene or early Miocene. *Leontopithecus rosalia* is the lone survivor of its line. In contrast, the *Callithrix* stem gave origin to the sequentially advanced *C. jacchus,* the *C. argentata* group, and *Saguinus.* Consistent with what is known of the evolution of modern mammalian genera with good fossil records, generic differentiation of *Saguinus* was most likely completed during the Pliocene.

The spread of earliest tamarins along the Andean foothills could have been unimpeded and rapid. Invasion of the Amazonian basin during the Pleistocene must have been opportunistic. Levee or gallery forests facilitated dispersal, and barrier rivers controlled it. Isolated founder colonies initiated speciation. The longer and more effective the isolation, the greater the differentiation.

It has been suggested (Haffer 1969) that fluctuating climatic events, with repeated contractions and expansions of Amazonian forests and savannas, were a major cause of Quaternary faunal speciation. No doubt, periodic isolation in some forest refugia and extinctions in others accelerated speciation among mammals as among the birds that formed the basis for Haffer's exposition. Barrier rivers, however, appear to be the primary isolating factor in the case of callitrichids. Shifting of river courses, and to a minor degree, waifing, where unoccupied territory was involved, was probably more effective in promoting speciation among Amazonian callitrichids during any one climatic regime than shifting climates during the entire Pleistocene.

45 Family Callitrichidae
2. Diagnostic Characters

The diagnostic characters given below are for the most part abstracts of subjects described in detail elsewhere in the text. Some of the more important characters, however, including a number not dealt with in other parts of the volume, are discussed at greater length. Comparisons are made here with *Callimico,* the tamarinlike representative of the family Callimiconidae. Additional comparisons between platyrrhines are found in chapters 17, 28, 36, 41.

External Characters

Size

The Callitrichidae comprise all but two or three of the smallest living primates. Their bulk ranges from that of a moderate-sized mouse to that of a moderate-sized squirrel. The largest callitrichid, *Leontopithecus rosalia,* is smaller than the smallest known members of the platyrrhine families Cebidae, Homunculidae, and Xenotrichidae, and the smallest living species of Catarrhini. The smallest callitrichid, *Cebuella pygmaea,* is smaller than all prosimians except the mouse lemur, *Microcebus murinus* (family Lemuridae), and Demidoff's galago, *Galago minutus* (family Galagidae). The size range of all species of the prosimian families in question, however, far exceeds that of the Callitrichidae.

Other small living primates, lone survivors of their phyletic lines, are comparable only as individual species. The nearly related platyrrhine callimico, *Callimico goeldii* (Callimiconidae) is the size of a large tamarin, genus *Saguinus,* and averages less than lion-tamarins, *Leontopithecus rosalia.* The distant tarsier, *Tarsius* (infraorder Tarsioidea), is larger than the pygmy marmoset but smaller than all other callitrichids. Fossil tarsioids are even smaller and include the smallest known primates, but extinct callitrichids, none of which are known, must also have numbered species smaller than those living now.

Integument

All tegumentary structures are highly variable and none appears to be unique to or particularly characteristic of callitrichids in general. The pelage tends to be finer, longer, more silky and lax than that of other monkeys and lacks entirely the dense woolly or kinky texture of many prosimians. All species are characterized by some erectile hirsute adornment such as mane, crests, tufts, or fringes; color patterns of skin or pelage are usually conspicuous and nearly always marked by one or more vividly contrasted recognition or display features; sensory vibrissae are more highly developed and distributed over more parts of the body than in other platyrrhines, or catarrhines (see below). Associated apocrine scent glands are better developed, more active, and concentrated in greater numbers in more strategic parts of the body than in other higher primates and many prosimians. Eccrine sweat glands are restricted to palms and soles.

For anatomy and histochemistry of callitrichid skin see Perkins (1966, *Saguinus fuscicollis;* 1968, *Cebuella pygmaea;* 1969*a*, *Saguinus oedipus;* 1969*c*, *Callithrix argentata argentata*). Perkins (1969*b*) also examined the skin of *Callimico.*

Vibrissae

Vibrissae or tactile (sinus) hairs are more widely distributed and better developed in callitrichids than in all other comparable primate groups except, possibly, some lemuroids (fig. III.8). The vibrissae consistently present are the mystacial, rhinarial, genal, suborbital, supraorbital, ciliary, mental, interramal, gular, pectoral, digital, ulnar-carpal, brachial, and anconeal. The more advanced the species, the fewer the kind and number of its functional tactile vibrissae. Vibrissae are best developed in the smaller, most primitive *Cebuella* and *Callithrix jacchus,* less developed in the larger *Saguinus,* and least de-

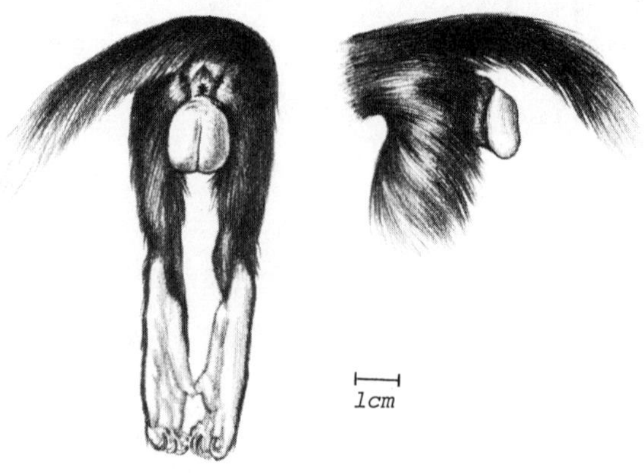

Fig. VII.7. Female external genitalia of *Callithrix humeralifer humeralifer.* The "display" of the preserved individual is lifelike. Note ischial prominences alongside anus. (From Russell and Zuckerman 1935, p. 357.)

Fig. VII.8. Profiles of palatal vaults at level of last molars in selected platyrrhines; dotted line shows cant of last molar crowns. See fig. IV.50 for more samples.

veloped in the largest, most specialized *Leontopithecus rosalia.* They are comparatively poorly developed in *Callimico.*

Cutaneous Glands

Apocrine glands in platyrrhines are distributed over most of the furred surface of the body, usually one gland to each hair group. They are also present in the bare skin of the external genitalia, perineum, and areola. *Eccrine sweat glands* are restricted to the palms and soles of the smaller platyrrhines but occur on both the bare and hairy skin of the large prehensile-tailed atelines and howlers. Insofar as is known, apocrine glands perform little or no function in the hairy skin of primates. Their histochemistry in primates has been reviewed by Solange de Castro Faria and Miraglia (1971). *Sebaceous glands* are most numerous and best developed in facial and anogenital regions of primates and often occur in aggregations with apocrine glands. The oily or waxy secretions of the anogenital region are usually mixed with urine for use in grooming and marking. Labial sebaceous glands, present in most primates, are extremely well developed in *Tarsius* (Montagna and Machida 1966). The secretions, mixed with saliva, are also used for grooming and marking (Sprankel 1971; Niemitz 1974). The glands are probably best developed in *Cebuella* among higher monkeys and may function, but perhaps only to a limited extent, as in *Tarsius.* The histochemistry of labial glands in platyrrhines have been described by Perkins (1966, 1968, 1969*a, b*); those of *Callithrix jacchus* by dos Santos, Miraglia and Costa Guedes (1974).

Apocrine scent glands of particular importance in social communication among platyrrhines are concentrated in one or more of the interramal, gular, sternal, abdominal, genital, circumgenital, including perineal, and ulnar regions. The odoriferous secretions are deposited by pressing and rubbing or by brushing or daubing with the associated stiff hairs. Vibrissae associated with the glands have been described in preceding sections, and glandular areas of the genital and circumgenital areas are discussed elsewhere (p. 86, 421, 423).

Glandular concentrations of the midventral region from throat to navel were investigated by Epple and Lorenz (1967) under the equivocal title of "Sternaldrüse." According to these authorities, they are already present in the advanced fetus and attain maximum development in the adult .They are larger in males than in females and better developed in higher- than in lower-ranking individuals. Among the lowest, the glands may be minuscule or practically absent. In some cases none of the glands may be evident on gross inspection (cf. Wislocki and Schultz 1925).

Distribution of the glandular concentrations or fields among callitrichids is uneven. In some species, only the gular field is highly specialized and macroscopically distinguishable. In others, gular and sternal, or gular and epigastric fields are recognizable. In still other species, the three fields are combined into a single complex. The interramal glands may also be involved by coalescence and confusion with the gular field. The latter situation appears to be the case in *Leontopithecus* and is common among cebids (cf. Epple and Lorenz 1967, figs. 2, 4, 6, 7, 10). In *Callimico,* the interramal glands may seem to be isolated (cf. Epple and Lorenz 1967, fig. 9, labeled IIIa), but glandular skin and well-defined openings connects the interramal with the gular glands in specimens at hand.

The full complement of anteromidventral glands in callitrichids is characterized by the following features, according to Epple and Lorenz (1967).

A. Rhombic glandular area in interramal-gular field (*Leontopithecus* only).
B. Hemispheric glandular area in sternal or gular-sternal field (*Cebuella, Callithrix, Saguinus*).
C. Tuft of sensory hairs of the pectoral region caudad to B (*Cebuella, Callithrix, Saguinus*).
D. Narrow midventral band of nearly bare glandular skin in epigastric field (*Callithrix, Saguinus*).

Table 40. Distribution of Glandular Concentrations of Anteromid-ventral Glandular Complex in Callitrichidae and *Callimico*

Species	N	A	B	C	D
Cebuella pygmaea	5	—	4	4	—
Callithrix jacchus flaviceps	1	—	—	—	1
Callithrix jacchus geoffroyi	2	—	1	—	—
Callithrix jacchus jacchus	25	—	24,1?	—	17
Callithrix jacchus penicillata	7	—	4	1	7
Callithrix argentata argentata	4	—	1	—	4
Callithrix argentata melanura	2	—	1	—	1
Callithrix humeralifer chrysoleuca	1	—	1	—	1
Callithrix humeralifer humeralifer	3	—	3	—	1
Saguinus nigricollis graellsi	4	—	4	4	—
Saguinus nigricollis nigricollis	1	—	1	1	1?
Saguinus fuscicollis fuscicollis	1	—	1	—	—
Saguinus fuscicollis illigeri	3	—	2,1?	1	—
Saguinus fuscicollis lagonotus	4	—	4	2	1
Saguinus fuscicollis leucogenys	7	—	7	4	1,4?
Saguinus fuscicollis tripartitus	2	—	2	2	1?
Saguinus fuscicollis weddelli	4	—	4	4	2?
Saguinus mystax mystax	5	—	5	1	2
Saguinus mystax pileatus	3	—	2,1?	—	—
Saguinus mystax pluto	3	—	3	2	1?
Saguinus labiatus labiatus	1	—	1	—	—
Saguinus labiatus thomasi	2	—	2	1	—
Saguinus midas midas	7	—	7	6	—
Saguinus midas niger	4	—	4	2	—
Saguinus oedipus geoffroyi	2	—	—	—	1,1?
Saguinus oedipus oedipus	3	—	2	—	2
Leontopithecus rosalia chrysomelas	2	2[1]	—	—	—
Leontopithecus rosalia rosalia	10	9[1]	—	—	—
Callimico goeldii	15	4[2]	10,5?	12,3?	12,3?

SOURCE: All data from Epple and Lorenz 1967.
NOTE: N = number of specimens tabulated according to age and sex by Epple and Lorenz (1967); A = interramal-gular or gular field; B = gular-sternal or sternal field; C = glandular area of pectoral tuft; D = epigastric field.
[1] Interramal-gular.
[2] Interramal, the IIIa of Epple and Lorenz (1967, fig. 9), but interramal-gular in specimens at hand.

The glandular concentrations in *Leontopithecus* are most distinctive among callitrichids (and platyrrhines). Those of *Cebuella* are least specialized. The sternal or gular-sternal field is least differentiated in *Calithrix* and the tufted poststernal field is least developed in *Saguinus*. The data on the distribution of glandular concentrations originally tabulated by Epple and Lorenz (1967, p. 101) is reproduced here (table 40) in modified form with revised nomenclature. Significant differences in glandular concentration between sexes and age classes are not evident in the data presented by the authors cited. Accordingly, only the total number of specimens of each taxon examined by them is shown in column 1 (N) of table 40.

Facial Musculature and Expression

Facial muscles of *Callithrix jacchus jacchus* and *C. j. penicillata* studied by Ruge (1887), and Huber (1931) and those of *Saguinus mystax, Saguinus oedipus geoffroyi,* and *Leontopithecus rosalia rosalia* described by Schreiber (1928) and, with the addition of *Saguinus oedipus geoffroyi,* by Huber (1931), are very similar. The facial musculature appears to be more primitive in design and organization than in other higher primates and, in many respects, no more complex than that of prosimians and tarsioids. Facial expressions in callitrichids, according to Huber (1931, p. 31), are "still on a very primitive level. Indeed these lowly representatives of the Simiae, like the Prosimiae, have little facial expression."

Callitrichids may not form the fine facial expressions seen in higher primates, but they do exhibit such basic expressions as grimacing, muzzle wrinkling, teeth baring, brow beetling, and ear twitching. These are supplemented by gaping, lip smacking, tonguing, and piloerection, all controlled by muscles other than those derived from the primitive platysma or sphincter colli profundus. Head cocking, flicking, and turning add another dimension to callitrichid facial expressions.

Elaboration or specialization of facial expressions in primates is often correlated with a corresponding degree of degeneration or obsolescence of older mammalian display characters such as genital presentation, piloerection, posturing, and tail and ear movements. In contrast, vocal expressions increase in variety and complexity with increasing flexibility and versatility of facial expressions.

Philtral Groove

A shallow median groove represented by the line of fusion of the two sides of the upper lip persists in *Cebuella, Callithrix jacchus,* and *Saguinus.* A vestige of this philtral groove appears to be restricted to the lower border of the lip in *Callithrix argentata,* but no sign is present in the available wet specimens of *Leontopithecus.* The groove is well marked on the lower half of the lip in one of 4 spirit-preserved specimens of *Callimico* but is poorly defined in the others. The philtrum is hairy in hairy-face tamarins and *Callithrix jacchus,* and sparsely set with short bristles in remaining callitrichids (fig. I.9).

External Ear

Structure of the auditory aurical is more advanced than that of prosimians but less complex than that of cebids and catarrhines (fig. III.18). Shape is subquadrate, suboblong or lanceolate, with auricular lamina leafy to fleshy, the rim extended or convoluted; skin is pigmented to entirely depigmented, nearly bare to completely hidden by its fur; mobility, if any, is insignificant.

Metamerism

Transverse banding of the lumbar region, and the alternating dark and pale banding of the tail in some callitrichids, closely coincides with the underlying lumbar and caudal vertebrae. The condition is well defined in *Callithrix jacchus* and *C. humeralifer,* faint in *Leontopithecus rosalia.*

Ischial Prominences

In some callitrichids, if not all, but notably in females of *Saguinus mystax* (fig. I.15), *Callithrix humeralifer* (fig. VII.7) and to a lesser extent *Callithrix jacchus,* ischial tuberosities are covered with glandular skin and appear as swellings analogous to the scrotal folds on the labia majora. They feature prominently in the presenting female.

Ischial prominences in callitrichids are probably early-stage homologues of catarrhine swellings and callosities (cf. p. 30). In callitrichids, however, the prominences act in sexual display and marking.

Sexual Dimorphism

This trait is not readily apparent except for usual differences in behavior, form and function of reproductive organs and relatively higher ischiopubic index in females (Leutenegger 1970*a*); also, adult females of some species are slightly heavier and larger in linear dimensions than males of comparable age. A greater extension of bare area in axillary region noted in many adult females compared with males may be a transient condition caused by contact with suckling young. Old males are often more "jowly" than comparable females because of the relatively greater development of their jaw muscles.

Age Polymorphism

Juvenal pelage and coat color pattern are distinctive in all species except *Cebuella,* where color pattern is hardly, if at all, differentiated from that of adults. In all other respects the usual mammalian patterns of growth and development appear in all young callitrichids.

Mammae

Two nipples are present, one in each pectoral region below the axilla. The wide spread between the mammae allows the mother to nurse two infants simultaneously.

External Genitalia and Circumgenital Regions

Male Genitalia

Abstract of Description

Male external genitalia vary in structure from comparatively generalized to highly specialized (figs. III.28, 29). The penis in *Cebuella, Callithrix,* and *Saguinus* is simple and cylindrical, tapering slightly to a rounded, asymmetrical, but otherwise undifferentiated glans with no sulcus retroglandis; in *Leontopithecus* the acorn-shaped glans is differentiated by the sulcus retroglandis, as in many higher primates including *Callimico* and *Homo.* The penial skin is weakly papillate in *Cebuella* and *Saguinus,* spiny in *Callithrix,* and minutely denticulate in *Leontopithecus;* a baculum is always present—primitively structured in *Cebuella,* more elaborate in *Callithrix* and *Saguinus,* and highly specialized in *Leontopithecus* and *Callimico.* Testes are scrotal or inguinal, their position controlled at will; the scrotum is sessile in young, more or less pedunculate or pendulous in adults; the testicular fold is glandular, the preputial fold parapenial.

Female external genitalia are more primitive or generalized in structure than the corresponding male genitalia (fig. III.22).

A specialized pubic sexual skin is present in both sexes. The secretion is used for marking.

Form and Size

The overall appearance of mature external genitalia with descended testes is largely determined by size, shape, and color of scrotal and preputial folds (fig. III.29). Size of callitrichid and callimiconid external genitalia relative to body size is neither impressively large nor particularly small, but the organs are usually well displayed seen from behind, below, or the side. Individual variation in size depends largely on age, degree of sexual stimulation, and position and tumescence of testes. Absolute size differences between species, however, cannot be reliably demonstrated in present fluid-preserved material. Among callitrichids, for example, the greatest scrotal diameter of 19 mm in an individual of the extremely small *Cebuella pygmaea* compares with 18 mm in an adult of the extremely large *Leontopithecus rosalia.* Maximum diameters measured are 28 mm and 29 mm in the moderate-sized *Callithrix argentata.*

Penis

The organ in *Cebuella, Callithrix,* and *Saguinus* is cylindrical, with slight taper and rounded apex. The penis of *Leontopithecus* and *Callimico* is characterized by a prominent acorn-shaped glans, with corona and sulcus retroglandis well defined and the proximal half to the whole of the flaccid penis ensheathed by retractile inner glabrous surface of preputial duplicature (fig. III.28). In juvenals and adults of some tamarin species, the flaccid penis is completely ensheathed by hairy outer and glabrous inner surfaces or preputial folds, the latter attached to the penial stem at base of glans; preputial frenulum is contiguous with preputial and scrotal raphes. The penial integument is smooth or weakly papillate in *Callimico,* invested with horny spicules and recurved spines in *Callithrix,* and minutely denticulate in *Leontopithecus* and the young of at least some species of *Saguinus.*

The virtually smooth, unadorned penis of *Cebuella* or *Saguinus* (figs. III.22, 24, 28) could serve as a prototype from which the phallus of all other male primates may be derived. The baculum (figs. III.25, 26, 27), presumed to have been present in the glans penis of the hypothetical ancestral primate and subprimate stocks, helps provide the rigidity needed for intromission and effective ejaculation. The callitrichid baculum is small and, with exceptions noted, usually simple. That of *Cebuella* is most primitive. Specialization of the glans penis involving enlargement and demarcation from the penial stem by the sulcus retroglandularis, formation of a free overhanging margin, the corona, and development of independent erectile tissue arose among callitrichids only in *Leontopithecus.* The highly specialized glans of *Callimico* (figs. III.28, 29) may, as in man, ultimately dispense with its small, fragile, hollow, egg-shaped baculum. On the other hand (figs. III.28, 29) the helmet-shaped glans penis of *Leontopithecus* (figs. III.28, 29) reinforces the role played by its well ossified and distinctly shaped baculum (fig. III.25). Further specialization correlated with degeneration or loss of baculum may give rise to greater elasticity of the glans and usually a corrugation of its outer covering. This provides for a second stage inflation of the glans during turgescence in coitus and prevents withdrawal before ejaculation.[1]

Recurved spines and spicules investing the penial stalk and proximal portion of the glans are other increments in the genital armament. The spines are keratinizations of the papillae that occur on the penises of some tamarins (fig. III.28). The backwardly curved spines may promote maximum penetration of the tumescent penis by making withdrawal difficult for the male and painful for the female.

The primary function of the penis is to deposit sperm in the female genital tract. The act can be performed by the simplest of organs capable of erection. Fulfillment of this chore alone, however, is no guarantee of fertilization. Specialization of the phallus, therefore, may be the result of selections that are correlated with structural or functional modifications of the female genital tract on the one hand and that maintain a high rate of reproductive success on the other. This implies a "lock and key" relationship between the genitalia of the two sexes, or the need for some such compatability in their reproductive and related systems. There is no evidence that successful mating takes place between female callitrichids and males of any species except those of the same genus with reciprocating or coordinated phalli.

Baculum

The os penis of all male callitrichids and *Callimico* is spongy or nearly to quite hollow. The element is contained in the left and larger, usually more projecting, lobe of the glans penis (figs. III.25, 26, 27). The spongy bone of the golden tamarin, *Leontopithecus,* with its olecranonlike proximal process, and the hollow, egg-shaped penis bone of *Callimico* are at once distinguished from each other and from those of all other platyrrhines. The baculum of *Cebuella,* the most simple and rodlike of all callitrichids, appears to be most primitive.

A diversity of bacula occurs in the species of *Callithrix* and *Saguinus.* The bacula of *Callithrix* are generally subconical or pyramidal with a triangular base. In *Saguinus,* flattened, gourd-shaped bacula with ovoid, sometimes truncate, bases are usual. Boomerang-shaped bones are present in *S. inustus* and *S. fuscicollis nigrifrons,* but the most distinctive bacula among tamarins appear in *Saguinus bicolor martinsi* and *S. labiatus.*

Size and degree of ossification of the baculum do not seem to be correlated with age after sexual maturity is attained. A well-developed bone may be present in a comparatively young adult and only a vestige (or rudiment?) in an older one of the same species (table 41).

In penises cleared and stained in KOH and alizarin, the baculum is seen with its longitudinally concave side canted to the right. Either surface may be straight for most its length in some species, but in all the tip is inflected ventrally with a cant to the right. These orientations may not hold in every individual and, possibly, may be reversed in some. Nevertheless, the bacula in figures (figs. III.25–27) are shown uniformly oriented with the concave aspect regarded as the right side.

The baculum of *Saguinus fuscicollis leucogenys* (AMNH 76597) and *S. inustus* (AMNH 88252), removed from penises previously cleared in 2% KOH and alizarin solutions, failed to take the red dye. Bacula of other callitrichids including members of the aforementioned species stained in the same solutions.

Scrotum

The scrotum (fig. III.29) in callitrichids and *Callimico* is sessile in young and more or less pendulous or somewhat pedunculous in adults; its shape is globose, pyriform, or chordate, the whole divided into asymmetrical halves by a longitudinal raphe; integument of distal scrotal (testicular) fold is more or less glandular, sometimes wrinkled or furrowed, but most frequently corrugated, papillate, or both, each papilla or corresponding section of skin set with one to several stiff hairs or vibrissae. The proximal, or preputial, fold is parapenial and usually redoubled with outer surface of fold variously differentiated from scrotal fold by a poorly defined furrow to a deep sulcus, the integument wrinkled, corrugated or somewhat papillate and more or less hairy; the inner, thin-skinned surface of fold, or preputial sheath, is glabrous forming a duplicature, with soft, smooth to finely corrugated inner surface united to distal portion of penis, the opposing surface similar and usually moist.

The scrotal folds in newborn callitrichids appear as a pair of independent, often pigmented swellings, one on each side of the median line behind the penis (fig. III.24). The preputial swellings or folds develop later around the penis itself. The scrotal folds first fuse along the midline and then coalesce with the preputial swellings to form the double-chambered scrotum. The scrotal sacs enlarge until puberty, when they receive the growing testes, lodged since or shortly after partus in their respective subcutaneous inguinal sheaths.

The mature scrotum with testes enclosed varies in

[1] The glans penis of *Lagothrix* may be an example. In *Ateles,* the skin of the glans is extremely tough and corrugated and evidently completely replaces the need for a supporting bone. The same is true of the peculiar glans of *Chiropotes.*

Table 41. Measurements of Callitrichid Bacula (in mm)

Catalog Number	*Name*	*Baculum Length × Width*	*Condylobasal Length of Skull*	*Remarks*
88997	*Cebuella pygmaea*	2.7 × 0.7	28.6	
57438	*Callithrix jacchus jacchus*	2.0 × 0.7	—	Adult in spirits
50839	*Callithrix argentata argentata*	1.0 × 0.8	38.5	
51888	*Callithrix argentata argentata*	3.3 × 1.5	38.9	
92167	*Callithrix humeralifer humeralifer*	2.6 × 1.6	36.0	
92171	*Callithrix humeralifer humeralifer*	1.6 × 1.0	38.5	
50827	*Callithrix humeralifer chrysoleuca*	2.5 × 1.0	38.5	
50831	*Callithrix humeralifer chrysoleuca*	2.4 × 0.9	39.5	
50833	*Callithrix humeralifer chrysoleuca*	2.3 × 1.3	38.5	
A76597	*Saguinus fuscicollis*	1.1 × 0.3	37.2	Young adult
71004	*Saguinus fuscicollis*	1.2 × 0.6	38.2	
A73389	*Saguinus fuscicollis*	2.3 × 1.2	37.4	
87145	*Saguinus fuscicollis*	2.7 × 1.0	37.8	
65670	*Saguinus fuscicollis weddelli*	2.4 × 1.0	37.4	
31112	*Saguinus graellsi*	1.6 × 0.8	38.0	
A92294	*Saguinus labiatus labiatus*	1.7 × 0.7	40.1	
93239	*Saguinus midas midas*	2.2 × 0.7	—	Complete
A78956	*Saguinus mystax pileatus*	1.6 × 0.5	41.0	
69933	*Saguinus leucopus*	3.5 × 0.9	42.2	
69935	*Saguinus leucopus*	2.0 × 0.7	42.0	
A79412	*Saguinus inustus*	1.7 × 0.6	39.8	
A 79418	*Saguinus inustus*	1.4 × 0.5	41.1	
88252	*Saguinus inustus*	1.3 × 0.6	41.6	
A78965	*Saguinus bicolor bicolor*	0.8 × 0.1	38.2	Immature
A94087	*Saguinus bicolor martinsi*	2.4 × 0.7	41.0	Cartilaginous
69950	*Saguinus oedipus geoffroyi*	1.1 × 0.8	41.5	
69951	*Saguinus oedipus geoffroyi*	Vestige	39.9	
69963	*Saguinus oedipus geoffroyi*	0.7 × 0.5	40.6	
69968	*Saguinus oedipus geoffroyi*	1.8 × 0.9	37.0	Immature
69265	*Saguinus oedipus oedipus*	1.5 × 0.7	39.9	
69274	*Saguinus oedipus oedipus*	1.7 × 0.6	42.4	
69278	*Saguinus oedipus oedipus*	1.8 × 0.5	41.3	
69279	*Saguinus oedipus oedipus*	2.1 × 0.7	40.3	
69285	*Saguinus oedipus oedipus*	0.9 × 0.8	40.0	Vestigial
69287	*Saguinus oedipus oedipus*	1.7 × 0.5	39.1	
69310	*Saguinus oedipus oedipus*	0.8 × 0.5	39.8	Vestigial
69313	*Saguinus oedipus oedipus*	1.7 × 0.8	40.1	
69936	*Saguinus oedipus oedipus*	2.5 × 1.0	39.5	
96084	*Leontopithecus rosalia rosalia*	3.0 × 0.9	—	
U303323	*Callimico goeldii*	1.8 × 1.0	39.0	

NOTE: All specimens are adults in the Field Museum of Natural History except as noted by the catalog number prefix (A = American Museum of Natural History; U = U.S. National Museum).

outline from subovate or globose in *Cebuella, Saguinus,* and *Callimico* to pyriform in *Saguinus* and *Leontopithecus* or chordate in *Callithrix,* with either left or right sac longer or fuller than the other. A relaxed scrotum with enlarged testes may be pendulous, while the same contracted and with testes retracted inguinally may appear pedunculate or sessile.

Testes

Before or shortly after birth the testes descend through the very short and ventrally located inguinal canals and lodge just above the pubic symphysis beneath the skin of the inguinal region, one testis on each side (fig. III.24). The inguinal testes grow to several times their original size while the scrotum completes its development and enlarges to receive them. A similar pattern of incomplete descent and growth of inguinal testes in certain insectivores and rodents was outlined by Backhouse (1959, p. 415). After complete descent, the testes, individually or collectively, can be moved back and forth between scrotum and inguinal pouch or sheath. The movement may be voluntary or hormonally controlled. Scrotal sojourn of the testes is usually brief, and as a rule, occurs in response to sexual arousal, anger, or similarly strong stimuli.

The position of each testis in 53 spirit-preserved specimens is shown in table 42. In the tabulation, testes inguinal in position in adults are marked retracted; in juvenals and subadults they are marked incompletely descended. The empty scrotum of subadults is laterally compressed, that of adults may be collapsed on one side or both depending on the number of retracted testes. Either left or right testis may be entirely or partially scrotal or inguinal. Position of the testes and condition of

Table 42. Position of Testes in Spirit Preserved Callitrichids and Callimicos

Species	*Position of Testes*[1]			
	0	*1*	*1½*	*2*
Cebuella pygmaea	1 adult; 1 juvenal	—	2 adult	—
Callithrix jacchus jacchus	—	—	—	1 adult
Callithrix jacchus geoffroyi	—	—	—	1 adult
Callithrix argentata	2 adult	—	—	1 adult; 1 subadult
Saguinus nigricollis	6 adult; 6 subadult	1 subadult (½)	—	1 adult; 2 subadult
Saguinus fuscicollis	1 adult; 4 subadult	1 adult	—	2 adult
Saguinus mystax	1 juvenal	—	—	2 adult
Saguinus midas	—	—	—	1 adult
Saguinus leucopus	1 subadult	—	—	—
Saguinus oedipus oedipus	2 adult, 1 juvenal	1 adult	—	2 adult, 1 juvenal
Saguinus bicolor	—	—	—	1 adult
Leontopithecus rosalia rosalia	1 adult, 1 subadult	—	1 adult	2 adult
Callimico goeldii	—	—	—	2 adult
Subtotals	13 adult, 12 subadult 3 juvenal	2 adult, 1 subadult	3 adult	16 adult, 3 subadult, 1 juvenal
Totals	28	3	3	20

[1] 0 = Undescended in juvenal and subadults; retracted in adults.
1 = Single testis, right or left, in scrotum, second testis retracted in adult.
1½ = One testis fully descended, other partially retracted in adult.
2 = Both testes descended.

scrotum at a given moment in a wild living troop would be virtually impossible to ascertain.

The large number of very young individuals with both testes contained in very small but fully formed scrota suggests the condition described by Wislocki (1933*b*, p. 234) for the rhesus, *Macaca mulatta,* in which the scrotum during fetal life and at birth "is swollen and as a rule contains descended testes. Shortly after birth the testes ascend into the inguinal canal, and the scrotum retrogresses to become the above-mentioned transverse fold of skin characteristic of the juvenile period. As explained above, descensus occurs again at puberty." Whether or not this form of descent and retraction occurs in small platyrrhines cannot be ascertained in present material. In any case, the empty callitrichid scrotum normally contracts into a longitudinal and not a lateral fold as in macaques. Furthermore, the inguinal canals themselves in callitrichids and *Callimico,* are little more than narrow apertures and apparently are incapable of containing the enlarged testes of weaned young. The same may be true for macaques, rodents, and insectivores with subcutaneous inguinal testes.

Size or weight of testes varies primarily according to age and sexual stimulus or drive. A considerable amount of individual and local variation is also present irrespective of mating conditions. Data on size of testes (with epididymides) relative to head and body length of callitrichids from known localities are available only for *Saguinus oedipus geoffroyi* (table 43). No definite conclusions can be adduced from the data. The mating season for the species is limited, but mature males may be sexually active or stimulated throughout most or all of the year, whether mating or not. Measurements in table 44 of the testes of a few adults selected from available spirit-preserved laboratory specimens representing 6 species of callitrichids suggest that individual variation exceeds the probable mean differences between species. Schultz (1938, p. 387) provides a table of actual and relative body and testes weights for 82 simians including a single example of *Saguinus oedipus geoffroyi.* His data permit some interesting inferences regarding relative weights of testes among major groups of primates.

Gonadal development in both sexes of *Callithrix jacchus jacchus* and *Saguinus oedipus* was studied by S. H. Hampton and Taylor (1971). The material was supplemented by gonads of *Cebuella pygmaea, Callithrix jacchus penicillata, Callithrix argentata,* and *Saguinus fuscicollis.* No differences were seen between the species. According to the investigators, the developmental pattern from early fetal stage through maturity closely resembled the normal sequence observed in other primates.

Female Genitalia

The external appearance of mature female genitalia is determined, as in males, almost entirely by size, shape, and color of scrotal and preputial folds of the labia majora (figs. III.21, 22, 23). Color of perineal and anal regions, and color and size of pubic sexual skin of females contribute more than in males to the overall effect of genital display. Size and shape of labia majora vary according to age, stage of estrous cycle, and species or genus. Conditions of the preputial annulus, clitoris, labia minora, and vestibule in general are considerably altered in the primiparous and further scarred and mutilated in the multiparous female. Labia majora are smallest in *Cebuella* (8–14 mm, 3 specimens), *Leontopithecus* (10–12 mm, 3 specimens), largest in *Callithrix* (15–25 mm, 10 specimens), and intermediate in *Saguinus* (17–18 mm, 18 specimens); greatest diameter of labia may be transverse or longitudinal as in male scrota of same species. Labia majora of *Leontopithecus* and *Callimico* are least differentiated; those of *Cebuella* and *Callithrix* are more complex and resemble each other most, and those of *Saguinus* are most distinctive.

Table 43. *Saguinus oedipus geoffroyi:* Size of Adult Testes Listed by Locality and According to Combined Head and Body Length

Catalog Number	*Date*	*Head and Body Length*	*Weight (lbs.)*	*Testes Length × Width*
Armila, San Blas				
335461	23 Feb. 1963	255	1.1	19 × 7
335453	26 Feb. 1963	250	1.5	18 × 10
335460	23 Feb. 1963	250	1.2	15 × 10
335457	16 March 1963	230	1.2	17 × 11
335462	23 Feb. 1963	228	0.9	15 × 6
Chucunaque, Darién, Panamá				
306836	15 Feb. 1958	230	—	12 × 8
Tacarcuna, Darién, Panamá				
310342	13 Feb. 1959	263	—	10 × 6
310347	13 Feb. 1959	254	—	13 × 8
310343	23 Jan. 1959	250	—	16 × 10
310353	10 March 1959	240	—	15 × 10
310342	20 Jan. 1959	234	—	16 × 8
310348	13 Feb. 1959	233	—	14 × 8
310346	23 Feb. 1959	226	—	16 × 9
310344	23 Feb. 1959	226	—	15 × 17
310350	13 Feb. 1959	210	—	10 × 6

NOTE: All specimens in U.S. National Museum, collected and measured by Charles O. Handley, Jr.

The labia majora are the large paired hairy, glandular cushions, one on each side of the genital fissure or rima pudendi. Each labium consists of two, sometimes three, more or less distinct swellings or folds. The posterior, outer, or scrotal, fold of the labium is differentiated from the anterior, inner, or preputial, fold by a shallow furrow or deep sulcus. Scrotal folds are pigmented, mottled, or unpigmented, and unite behind angle of genital fissure in a low commissure; the integument may be convoluted, finely to coarsely corrugated, papillate, or dissected into asymmetrical polyhedrons, each section of skin having one, or sometimes two, three, or more stiff hairs. Preputial folds are usually smaller than scrotal folds when flaccid, often larger when tumescent, and meet anteriorly to form a rounded or angular hairy mons; lateral surface of preputial folds is usually less sculptured, the hairs shorter and finer than those of scrotal folds; inner anterior surface or annulus is glabrous and meets above glans clitoridis to form a horseshoe-shaped fold. Frenula preputii are usually attached to glans clitoridis one on each side near the frenula clitoridis, median or pudendal walls of labia majora merging with inner posterior lamina of urethral fold, or labium minus, of corresponding side; concave surface of urethral groove convoluted; lateral borders of urethral folds, usually defined as frenula clitoridis distally, are enlarged or swollen proximally to form the labia minora; lamina of labia minora are variable in size, shape, and orientation, but usually two pairs on each side form the anterolateral walls of vestibule; externally visible glans clitoridis is bilobed, with left lobe usually larger than right and often projecting slightly distad; glans is often hidden in the tissue of swollen labia minora or fused with inner borders of prepuce, the urethral groove sometimes persisting only as a pseudourinary meatus on distal surface; rim of genital fissure is formed by preputial fold anteriorly, scrotal fold posteriorly, except in *Cebuella* and *Callithrix* where scrotal fold is excluded except sometimes at the posterior angle or commissure. A hymen is present, often well defined in young but indeterminable in parous and not exposed to external view.

Table 44. Adult Testes of Fluid-Preserved Specimens without Locality Data

Species	*Testes Length × Width*
Cebuella pygmaea	11 × 10
Callithrix argentata argentata	14 × 11
Saguinus nigricollis	16 × 9
Saguinus nigricollis	26 × 10
Saguinus oedipus oedipus	9.5 × 7
Saguinus oedipus oedipus	10 × 8
Saguinus oedipus oedipus	13 × 7.5
Saguinus oedipus oedipus	14 × 9
Saguinus midas midas	15 × 10.5
Leontopithecus rosalia rosalia	10 × 9
Leontopithecus rosalia rosalia	15.5 × 11

Pubic Sexual Skin

A sexual skin or specialized glandular pubic area, the periinguinal gland of some authors, is present but not always well defined in all mature callitrichids and *Callimico* (fig. III.22). It is more developed and extensive in females than in males, and in older individuals than in younger ones. The sexual skin is continuous with the anterior border of the preputial folds or the mons and modified into a system of sebaceous scent glands. It appears as a pair of swellings, one on each side of the median line, in *Cebuella, Callithrix, Saguinus oedipus, S. midas, Leontopithecus rosalia* and perhaps others, or as a single broad median pubic band, often with an incomplete and trenchant median line, as in *Saguinus nigricollis, S. mystax,* and *S. bicolor*. The rounded or bifurcated shape of the mons accords with that of the sexual skin. The latter may be unpigmented as in *Cebuella, Callithrix,* and *Leontopithecus,* where it is usually poorly defined from surrounding integument, or mottled or pigmented as in *Saguinus* and *Callimico.* The glandular area may be restricted to little more than the mons pubis, as appears to be the case in available specimens of *Callimico* and some of *Callithrix jacchus,* or extensive as in most tamarins, genus *Saguinus.*

Individual and cyclical variation in the form and function of the sexual skin is even greater than that of other external sex organs, glands and tissues. The size and prominence of the sexual skin in females of *Saguinus oedipus,* for example, varies from macroscopically undifferentiated in the sexually mature virgin to one of the animal's most conspicuous external characters.

Secretions of the sexual skin mark the nest, perches, other familiar objects, the offspring, and members of the group. The pubic sexual skin is of little or no importance in display.

Color of Genital Area

The color of the external genitalia and surrounding glandular areas ranges from wholly black to colorless or white in the dead or prepared animal, or flesh-colored in the living animal. Bright hues, except for a pinkish glans penis in some *Callithrix,* are absent. In most species some parts, for example the scrotum or labia majora, may be more or less melanistic while other parts, such as the glans, may be unpigmented, or vice versa. Individual variation in color is great and is further complicated by age differences in the presence or concentration of melanin. External genitalia of juvenals may be like those of adults or may be distinctly less pigmented to completely unpigmented; or they may retain the primitive pigmentation lost in the adult. Among mature tamarins, genus *Saguinus,* scrotum and labia majora are as a rule entirely or dominantly black in species *nigricollis, fuscicollis, midas, oedipus, leucopus,* and *bicolor.* The same parts are dominantly white or flesh-colored in *Saguinus mystax, imperator, graellsi,* and *inustus,* and also in all species of *Cebuella, Callithrix,* and *Leontopithecus.* In *Callimico* the scrotum and labia are lightly to moderately pigmented.

The penial staff and glans are more or less pigmented in *Saguinus* and *Callimico* and unpigmented in *Callithrix* and *Leontopithecus.* The glans is pink in *Callithrix jacchus jacchus* and dark in *C. j. geoffroyi.* The penial staff in *Cebuella* is mottled, the glans flesh-colored. Pigmentation of the glans clitoridis in the various species generally parallels that of the glans penis.

The color of sexual skin mainly conforms to that of the scrotum or labia majora; perineal and anal regions are lightly pigmented to unpigmented in *Cebuella, Saguinus,* and *Callimico,* unpigmented in *Callithrix* and *Leontopithecus.* They are most heavily pigmented in *Saguinus oedipus* as determined from spirit-preserved specimens.

There is some relationship between the skin color of external genitalia and contiguous glandular areas and pelage color. In general, dark hairs on pigmented genital organs and pale or white hairs on unpigmented parts accent the form of the genitalia. Pelage framing the genitalia may be of the same color, thus creating an illusion of greater size or enhancing visibility. Contrastingly colored pelage surrounding the genitalia may have the effect of focusing attention on the organs themselves. In every case, the display effect is in the eyes of a conspecific of the opposite sex ready for mating.

Genital Display

Transition of primates from primarily scent to dominantly vision animals is evident in the distinctive shapes and color patterns of the genital region, and the use of external genital organs for sexual display. Other types of visual signals related to sexual play, such as grimacing, tonguing, face-rubbing, and piloerection, are discussed under the species headings.

The external genitalia of most species are prominent. When fully tumescent, they become the most conspicuous feature of the body, especially if the pubic sexual skin is included. The genitalia and surrounding sexual areas of female callitrichids are equal in size to those of many Old World monkeys, but hardly approach those of macaques and baboons.

Hypertrophy of the female external genitalia appears to be correlated with enlargement and increased productivity of the scent-secreting sebaceous glands. With degeneration of olfaction and refinement of binocular vision, the external genitalia and surrounding areas enhance their visibility by cyclical increase in size and exaggeration of colors, particularly in Old World forms.

Among primitive platyrrhines, the most elaborate labia majora occur in *Saguinus, Callithrix,* and *Cebuella.* The most simple labia are found in *Leontopithecus* and *Callimico,* where they are nearly concealed. In contrast, the male genitalia of these last two monotypic genera are more elaborate than those of any of the first three genera. Display efforts by *Leontopithecus* and *Callimico* have not been recorded in detail, but males have more to show than females. The reverse obtains in *Saguinus, Callithrix,* and *Cebuella.*

Female callitrichids display or present their genitalia to males. Male callitrichids display to other males, or to other species. I have not seen them display to females of their own species. The exhibition is an assertion of dominance within the social group and a warning threat to others. In the San Diego breeding colony, a 20-month-old hand-raised virgin *Saguinus oedipus oedipus* presented to a wild-caught experienced adult male the second day after he was introduced into her cage. The male responded by the usual erection. Unfortunately, I could not await developments. A very excited female *Callithrix jacchus jacchus* of the same colony exhausted herself and her entire repertory of sexual play in a vain attempt to arouse her cage mate. She presented, embraced, nuzzled, and marked him and everything else in the cage, to no avail.

I first observed display by a male *Callithrix jacchus jacchus* in the Houston colony. The animal's cage was at eye level for observation. When the marmoset saw me for the first time, he leaped to the perch, crouched on all fours, and presented, in all its boldness, his gleaming white scrotum. In the next instant, the scrotum expanded to twice its size to accommodate the bulging testes that descended into the sac. Hardly a second later, the testes retreated and the scrotum collapsed. Thereupon, the animal faced about and stared me in the eye.

The tumescent labia majora of *Callithrix humeralifer humeralifer*, described and figured by Russell and Zuckerman (1935, p. 356, fig. 1, pl. 1, fig. 2), and reproduced here (fig. VII.7), are quite like the inflated scrotal sacs of males of the *C. argentata* group.

Scent Glands and Olfactory Communication

Sebaceous scent glands are located on the labia majora and scrotum, prepuce, mons pubis, perineal and anal regions, and pubic sexual skin (peri-inguinal gland). The glands of the labia, mons, and sexual skin are particularly large and in tamarins (*Saguinus*) become comparatively gigantic during estrus. Apocrine glands generally distributed over the body are also odor-producing when enlarged and concentrated in numbers as in the gular, sternal, epigastric (pectoral), and ulnar-carpal regions (cf. pp. 79, 86).

The scent glands of the genital areas are most extensive in tamarins, particularly *Saguinus oedipus* and *S. mystax*, followed, in descending order, by *Callithrix argentata* and *humeralifer*, *C. jacchus*, *Cebuella*, *Leontopithecus*, and *Callimico*. The glands occur in both sexes but are more developed and extensive in females.

The circumgenital glands in male and female *Callithrix jacchus* were seen by Cuvier (1819) as a naked area covered with small tubercles which appeared to be components of a glandular complex. The microscopic structure of the genital glands has been described in detail for *Saguinus oedipus geoffroyi*, *Callithrix jacchus jacchus*, and *C. j. penicillata* by Wislocki (1930; 1936), for *Callithrix humeralifer* by Russell and Zuckerman (1935), for *Saguinus fuscicollis* (not *Tamarin nigricollis*, as labeled) by Perkins (1966), and for *Cebuella* by Starck (1969).

The odor of the sebaceous genital glands is musky and clinging. It persisted in a number of our specimens months after preservation in embalming fluid, alcohol, or formaldehyde. It even clung for hours to objects contacted, including my fingers, despite washing with soap. The yellow or orange secretion of the genitals and sexual skin of the silver marmoset (*Callithrix argentata*) stains but washes off readily. Benirschke and Richart (1963, p. 75) detected the vulvar odor emanating from the sebaceous glands of live individuals of *Saguinus oedipus oedipus*, *S. mystax mystax*, *Leontopithecus rosalia rosalia* and *Callithrix jacchus jacchus*. The odor is, in fact, present in all callitrichids and pervades their accommodations in laboratory colonies. Surprisingly, J. K. Hampton, Hampton, and Landwehr (1966, p. 279) perceived no odor on objects marked by *Saguinus oedipus*.

Secretions of the scent glands are used for marking territory and pathways, sexual attraction, registration of social status, individual recognition, threat, mating, social contacts, imprinting, and in general for reinforcement of visual cues or signals.

The circumgenital glands are pressed against the object and rubbed. A few drops of urine are added to the glandular secretions. The pubic (suprapubic) glands release their oils when the sexual skin is dragged across the substrate or rubbed against objects embraced by the animal. Sternal glands are rubbed or pressed against the target for marking. Stiff hairs or vibrissae associated with the glands retain and daub the oily secretions. The most active, persistent, and aggressive role in olfactory communication seems to be played by the alpha male and female. The young are passively imprinted with the odors of their parents, family, or social group. Among caged callitrichids, the sexually mature and stimulated female marks everything, including cage walls and floor, perches, food, food dishes, and the bodies of cage mates irrespective of sex. Some of this activity may be masturbatory, but the odor is there. The female marks the mature male who interests her. If stimulated, the male reciprocates by examining, smelling, nuzzling and licking the genitalia, vibrissae, excreta, urine, and everything else impregnated with the female's odor. Both sexes mark before and after copulating.

Urine, feces, saliva, and sweat used separately or mixed with secretions of cutaneous scent glands and sex hormones also serve as chemical messengers. Epple (1970*b*, 1971, 1972, 1974*a*, *b*) has shown experimentally that callitrichids can differentiate between familiar and strange conspecifics, discriminate between the sexes, assess reproductive condition, and recognize social status of known and unknown conspecifics by odor alone.

The variety, complexity, and extensiveness of natural means of olfactory communication implies a corresponding development of the olfactory brain. This is apparent in the olfactory bulbs, which are proportionately larger in callitrichids than in cebids and catarrhines and in the retention of a functional vomeronasal (Jacobson's) organ which receives through the incisive canals olfactory stimuli related to sexual behavior. In these respects, callitrichids occupy a position between the microsmatic higher primates and the macrosmatic or large smell-brain prosimians.

Unusual and Aberrant Sexual Behavior

Much has been learned of sexual behavior from observations of wild-caught caged animals and their laboratory-bred offspring. The so-called abnormal, unnatural, or aberrant sexual behavior of wild-caught animals living in confinement would probably be regarded as normal if seen performed in the natural environment. Possibly the only real difference between the sexual behavior of wild-caught caged and free-living animals is in the frequency and intensity of each act.

Masturbation by captive tamarins of the *Saguinus nigricollis* group reported by Shadle, Mirand, and Grace (1965, p. 8) is nothing more than the usual marking by rubbing of genital scent glands on cage, food, food dishes, perches, and so on, by members of both sexes. Homosexual acts reported by the same team include mounting of females by other females. The active females performed male copulatory movements with their genitalia rubbing against the rump of the passive females or against the floor of the cage (see also pp. 532, 669, 769).

J. K. Hampton, Hampton, and Landwehr (1966, p. 279) observed a lone female cotton-top (*Saguinus oedipus oedipus*), kept as a house pet, make the hip movements of a copulating male against the edge of a chair cushion. This was accompanied by the tongue movements characteristic of copulating males. "When she stopped, she appeared trance-like for a few seconds," as if experiencing an orgasm.

The practice of holding the tail between the legs in the form of a tightly rolled coil is common to many, if not all, callitrichids. However, I have not seen the golden lion tamarin, *Leontopithecus rosalia rosalia,* carry the tail in this manner. The tail may be coiled two or three times on itself—the tigher the coil, the smaller its diameter. The animal often rests or sleeps squatting and even moves short distances with the tail thus coiled and pressed against the underparts, including the genitalia. Females often stroke the coiled tail across the perineal region for self-stimulation. The frication is usually performed haphazardly and at irregular intervals. One captive callimico, however, was observed using her tail repeatedly in masturbation (cf. p. 906).

Cranial Characters

Skull Size and Shape (figs. VII.5, 6)

Greatest cranial length usually less than 65 mm; face short (orthognathous); braincase strongly dolichocephalic to subbrachycephalic, cephalic index (braincase length to width) 60–76; frontal profile rounded, vaulted, or flattened.

Ridges (figs. IV.81–84)

Temporal ridges present and usually well defined, sometimes elaborated into an interparietal plate or merging to form a sagittal crest; lambdoid crest often well developed; other occipital crests and processes usually weak.

Face

Nasal aperture commonly quadrifoliate in outline, that is, with deep superior, inferior, and lateral incisions (fig. IV.1); nasal bone (fig. IV.2) suboblong in outline, the posterior margin truncate, rounded, or obtusely pointed but never attenuated, anterior portion often slightly narrower than posterior, sometimes slightly expanded but never flared, dorsal profile plane to slightly convex or slightly concave but never deeply bowed or indented; all sutures with and between nasals persistent (fig. IV.82); premaxillary bone well developed, consistently and usually broadly in contact with nasal bone, sutures usually defined into old age; malar (zygomatic) and parietal bones in contact (fig. IV.9).

Orbits

Orbits not markedly enlarged; lacrymal bone with facial process often present and contacting nasal bone (fig. IV.82); lateral orbital fissure present on outer orbital wall of malar, or between malar and adjacent alisphenoid and/or parietal bones (figs. IV.5, 6); inferior (sphenomaxillary) fissure visible within orbit, and usually larger than superior orbital fissure and orbital foramen combined.

Interorbital Region and Pneumatizations (figs. IV.13–15, 22, 24, 26)

Interorbital region often pneumatized or sinusoidal, the septum thin, translucent, but usually imperforate; maxillary sinus and ostium present; sphenoid pneumatized, apparently without opening into nasal cavity, except in *Leontopithecus* with intersphenoidal sinus opening into superior nasal meatus and paired posterior sphenoidal fossae opening into inferior meatus through epipharynx; frontal diploe above orbits pneumatized, a well-developed frontal sinus present except in *Cebuella* and some *Callithrix* and opening directly into middle meatus of nasal cavity; cribriform plate (fig. IV.43) generally small, perforations large and comparatively few in number.

Basicranium

Dental arcade V- to U-shaped (fig. VII.5); median posterior border of palate extending to plane of posterior border of last molars or slightly behind; palate notably vaulted with transverse arc of palatal ceiling more or less continuous with transverse cant of molar crowns (fig. VII.8); mastoid and paroccipital processes little developed or underdeveloped; small styloid process sometimes present and adpressed against or fused with auditory bulla (fig. IV.82); foramen spinosum and foramen lacerum absent, the foramen ovale alone giving passage to meningeal arteries (fig. IV.51); medial pterygoid plate a thin partition often consisting of little more than hamulus; hamular process frequently elongate, often with a bony bridge connecting it to petrous spine of auditory bulla (fig. IV.53); pterygoid fossa never more than a narrow, shallow recess; foramen magnum with longitudinal and transverse diameters subequal, axis pointing down and back, never straight down or straight back (fig. IV.54).

Middle Ear (figs. IV.51, 62, 65, 68, 73, 74)

Auditory bulla well inflated, lower portion of mesotympanic cavity large, with cochlear eminence relatively small; auditory ossicles comparatively simple.

Mandible (figs. IV.75–80; VII.5)

Ascending ramus of mandible square to elongate, condylar, coronoid, and angular process well defined; outline of ventral border of mandible V- to U-shaped, the retromental border angular or rounded; mental foramen usually placed directly below first premolar or slightly anteriad to posteriad; angle of outer slope of symphysis menti about 20° to 60° measured from the basal horizontal mandibular plane.

Remarks. The callitrichid skull is characterized by a large braincase and comparatively short orthognathous face. The particularly globoid, nearly smooth neurocranium of the smallest species suggests the fetal state of cebids. This condition, however, is an archaic primate character correlated with movement of the orbits to the front and their separation from the temporal fossa by a bony partition. The most primitive primates are small and comparatively round-headed. Subsequent elongation of the neurocranium in any lineage is a factor of increasing size correlated with expansion of the occipital lobes of the cerebrum. Beyond a certain magnitude in some cebid and catarrhine lines, neurocrania tend to become globose again following expansion of the temporal and frontal regions of the cerebral hemispheres. In callitrichids, the most globoid neurocranium belongs to the primitive pygmy marmoset, *Cebuella.* The skull is notably less globose in the larger, more advanced *Callithrix*, distinctly ovoid in the still larger *Saguinus*, and most elongate or dolichocephalic in the extremely large and specialized *Leontopithecus*.

Orthognathy (fig. IV.3), one of the most striking characters of the callitrichid skull (or head), also evolved independently in *Callimico, Callicebus Rhinopithecus*, and to a lesser degree in hominoids, but exceptionally in *Homo*. Most remarkable is the fact that extreme orthognathy evolved in two extremes of higher primates, one among the smallest including the most primitive, the other the largest and most specialized.

The specializations and wide range of variation do not obscure the primitive design of the callitrichid skull. Sutures tend to remain open for longer periods of life than in other platyrrhines and in catarrhines. Communication between frontal sinus, if present, and middle nasal cavity through an opening anteriad to the cribriform plate is primitive. The frontal sinus itself, however, is a specialization primitively absent in lowest callitrichids, secondarily occluded in most catarrhines. The orthognathous callitrichid face supports a short nasal bone, but the shape is decidedly primitive and quite unlike the saddle-shaped bone of other higher primate groups. Auditory ossicles are, with an isolated exception, least differentiated among higher primates. The mandible of *Cebuella* is most primitive among higher primates and one of the least modified among primates generally.

Increasing size among callitrichids entailed modifications in diet with concomitant changes in dental structure and osseous support. The shift from mainly insectivorous to increasingly omnivorous food habits is seen in the gradual change from the primitive V-shaped dental arch to the advanced U-shaped, from low and subquadrate ascending mandibular ramus to high and suboblong ascending ramus, and from recumbent to nearly upright symphyseal region (figs. IV.78; VII.5, 6).

Head Rotation

Callitrichids, like tarsiers and perhaps a few other primates, rotate the head about 180° in either direction from front to back. A structural difference between callitrichids and primates with less cervical flexibility is not readily apparent in the occipital condyle, the atlas, or the axis. The functional difference is probably distributed throughout the soft and hard tissues of the entire cervical region.

Cervical mobility is particularly advantageous to small vertical clinging and vertical leaping primates. While they cannot be seen from the far side of their support, callitrichids (and tarsiers) can turn the head around and watch for movements and escape routes to the rear.

Vertebral Column and Thorax

The main body of data presented here was collected by Schultz and Straus (1945) and repeated with additions by Schultz (1961), cited below. The callitrichids he used included 14 specimens of *Callithrix* and 75 of *Saguinus* (= *Leontocebus*). Where necessary, supplementary information from other sources, including specimens at hand, is given (figs. II.1, 2).

Cervical Vertebrae

Usual number in mammals, 7. Variation absent in callitrichids examined, but Schultz noted 1 vertebra more or less in a few prosimians and catarrhines.

Thoracic Vertebrae

12 to 13 in callitrichids seen by Schultz. In cebids 12–16, average between 13 and 14; in catarrhine monkeys 11–13, average slightly more than 12; in apes and man, average between 12 and 13.

Thoracic vertebrae are rib-bearing, but the first or last, sometimes both, may lack the rib on one side. The callitrichid, hominoid (and lemuroid) number of 12–13, appears to be primitive. The number in lorisoids, 13–17½ (rib on one side only) is extreme for all primates; the number in cebids (12–16) is highest among platyrrhines or catarrhines.

Lumbar Vertebrae

5–7 in callitrichids, mean between 6 and 7; in cebids 4–8, mean near 6; in catarrhine monkeys 6–9, mean between 6.5 and 7; in hylobatids, pongids, and man 3–6; in Malagasy prosimians 5–10, mean about 7; in lorisoids 4–8, mean between 6 and 7.

The primitive or mean number appears in callitrichids. In cebids, thoracic and lumbar vertebrae combined average about 19 thoracolumbar vertebrae, or the same as in callitrichids and catarrhine monkeys.

Sacral Vertebrae (fig. VII.9)

2–4 in callitrichids, average 2.9; 4 sacrals in one of four *Leontopithecus rosalia* at hand; in cebids 2–5, average between 3 and 4; Old World monkeys 2–4, average slightly over 3; in hylobatids 3–6, average between 4 and 5; in pongids and *Homo*, average between 5 and 6.

Caudal Vertebrae

Means, extremes (in parentheses), followed by number of samples in *Callithrix*, 27(25–30)7. Wettstein (1963, p. 227) gives 28.8(26–31)30 for *Callithrix jacchus*. In *Saguinus* (= *Leontocebus*), according to Schultz (1961), 31.6(28–34)34.

The greatest number of caudal vertebrae among primates occurs in tamarins (*Saguinus*). The number in *Callithrix* averages greater than in all other kinds of primates except *Saimiri* (28.3[25–31]14) and *Ateles* (31.1[28–35]22).

The structure of the five proximal caudal vertebrae is complex and most nearly like those of the sacrum (fig. VII.9). The more distal vertebrae are simple, with the morphological change abrupt at the 6th vertebra.

Sternal Ribs

Means, extremes, and number of samples in *Callithrix* is 7.7(7–9)6; in *Saguinus* 7.7(7–8)40; in cebids, except *Alouatta*, 8.0–8.8(8–9)68; in *Alouatta* 7.4(7–8)12; in catarrhine monkeys 7.0–8.0(7–9)200; in hylobatids, pongids, and hominids, 6.5–7.1(6–8)781.

Remarks. The hypothetical primitive number of primate vertebrae, according to Schultz and Straus (1945, p. 623), are 13 thoracic, 6 lumbar, or 19 thoracolumbar,

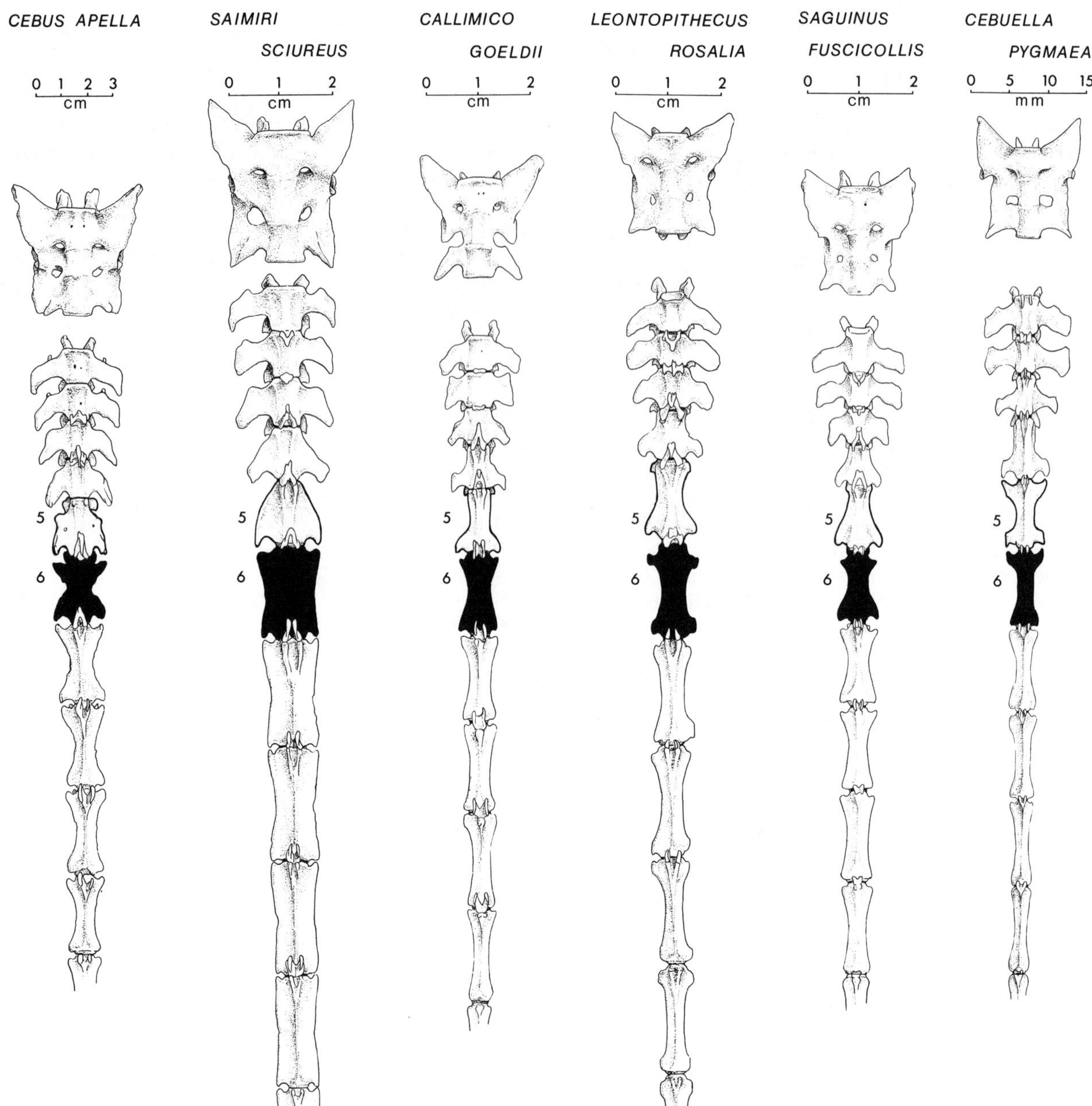

Fig. VII.9. Ventral aspect of sacrum and first 10 caudal vertebrae of *Cebus apella* (♂) *Saimiri sciureus* (♀), *Callimico goeldii* (♂), *Leontopithecus rosalia* (♀), *Saguinus fuscicollis* (♀), and *Cebuella pygmaea* (♀). Sacra are highly variable individually, and apparent differences between the examples are not to be regarded as significant. Caudal vertebral morphology is more specific, particularly in the transition from the last vertebra (5th, boldly outlined) of the complex series to the first (6th, in black) of the simple series. Caudal vertebral series of *Saimiri sciureus* appears to differ most from that of other species.

3 sacral and 25 caudal. In 67% of 75 specimens of *Saguinus* examined by Schultz (1961, p. 22), the following numbers are found: 12 thoracic, 7 lumbar, 3 sacral, and 27 caudal.

Pelvis

The callitrichid pelvis is the most generalized among higher primates (figs. VII.10, 11). This state is reflected in the primitive relationship of the ilia to the sacrum (fig. II.20) and absence of specialized ischial tuberosities (fig. I.14). The significantly greater diameter of the female pelvis for easing passage of characteristically very large-headed newborns is a specialization evidently restricted to higher primates including callitrichids. The wider pubic diameter of females was demonstrated in catarrhines by Washburn (1948) and Schultz (1949*b*). Investigations by Leutenegger (1970*a,* p. 68) also showed sexual dimorphism in platyrrhines with the pelvic difference most pronounced in *Saimiri,* least in *Alouatta.* Among callitrichids the larger female pelvis has been demonstrated in *Callithrix jacchus* (Wettstein 1963), *Saguinus midas* (Leutenegger 1970*a*), *Saguinus nigricollis* (Black 1970), and *Saguinus oedipus* (table 45). According to Leutenegger (1973), sexual dimorphism is absent in lorises and other prosimians which produce comparatively small young.

Table 45. Pelvic Measurements of *Saguinus oedipus*

Measurement	*69286*[1] ♀	*69948* ♀	*69952* ♀	*69290* ♂	*69953* ♂	*69946* ♂
Head and body	247	264	255	234	287	259
Weight	—	560	—	462	504	—
Skull, greatest length	53.8	54.1	55.1	50.4	52.7	54.5
Femur, length[2]	70.1	72.5	71.4	66.7	67.6	69.0
Ischium, length[3]	16.2	17.4	18.0	15.5	16.2	17.4
Pubis, length[3]	12.2	13.4	14.9	12.7	12.4	12.8
Ischium-pubis index	**73**	**77**	**83**	**82**	**76**	**73**
Superior transverse pelvic diameter	25.3	26.8	28.9	24.3	25.4	27.5
Inferior transverse pelvic diameter	23.3	25.0	26.1	18.3	19.4	21.8
Pelvic diameter index	**92**	**93**	**90**	**75**	**76**	**79**
	♀	♀	♀	♂	♂	♂

NOTE: See figs. VII.10, 11. First four measurements are indicators of individual body size.
[1] FM number.
[2] Mean of right and left.
[3] Left.

The ischium-pubis index used by Schultz (1930, p. 346; 1949*b*, p. 407) for demonstrating pelvic sexual dimorphism does not seem to be critical for all species. Nevertheless, the absolute and relatively greater diameter of the female pelvic outlet is obvious in all articulated haplorhine pelvi examined (fig. VII.10). The ratio of inferior to superior pelvic diameters expresses the difference (table 45).

Limbs

Hands and Feet (figs. I.25, 26, 28)

Callitrichid cheiridia are most primitive of known primates. Both extremes are pentadactylous with hand distinctly shorter than foot; pollex nonopposable; all digits except hallux provided with sharp, recurved, laterally compressed claws.

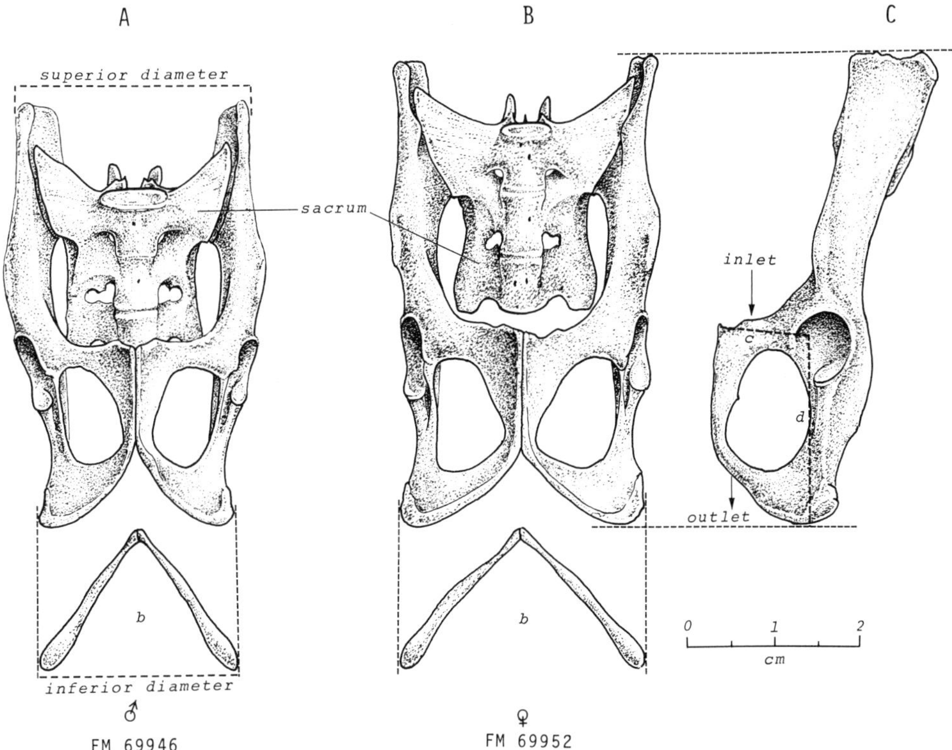

Fig. VII.10. Pelvis of *Saguinus oedipus*, ventral aspect of *A*, adult male; *B*, adult female; *C*, left hipbone (os innominatum), lateral aspect; *b*, posterior aspect of ischium-pubis; greater width of female pelvis, especially at outlet, is shown by relative widths of superior and inferior diameters; *c* (in C) pubic length, *d*, ischial length, measured from acetabulum at point of union of pelvic bones, are used for calculating pubis-ischium index of Schultz (1930, p. 346).

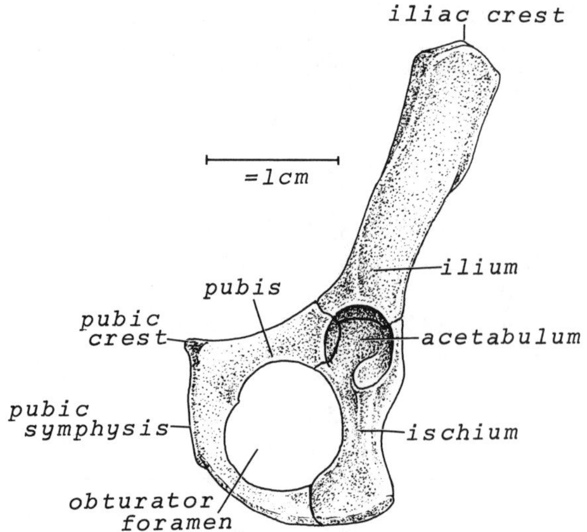

Fig. VII.11. Hip bone (os innominatum) lateral aspect, of subadult *Cebuella pygmaea,* showing primitive form, with unfused ilium, ischium, and pubis.

Digital lengths in terms of distal projection are:

Manus: 3–4–2–5–1, with digit 4 sometimes even with or slightly more projecting than digit 3. This compares with a formula of 3 or 4–5–2–1 in cebids.

Pes: 4–3–5–2–1, with digit 3 sometimes even with or slightly more projecting than digit 4. This compares with a formula of 3 or 4–2–5–1 in cebids. Note that the cebid formulae for hands and feet are the same as those for feet and hands, respectively, in callitrichids.

(Digital projection is an index of combined length of digits and their respective metapodials. A long digit with short metapodial may be less projecting than a shorter digit with longer metapodial.)

Primary volar tubercles or pads (fig. I.30) are represented by 1 touch pad on the terminal phalanx of each of the 5 digits, 4 postdigital or interdigital pads, and the thenar and hypothenar, for a total of 11. Each primary pad is covered with cutaneous or papillary ridges.

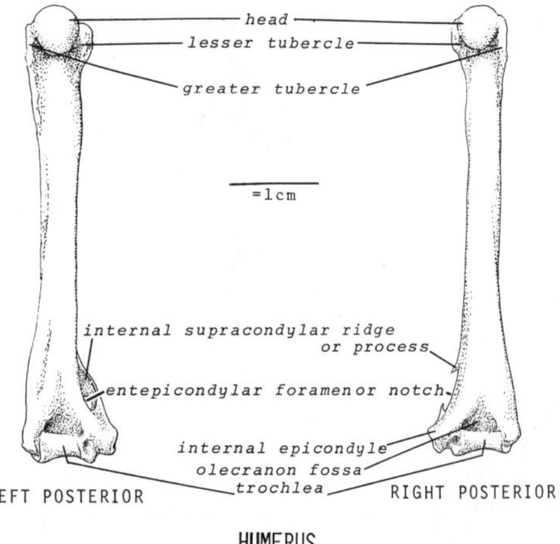

Fig. VII.12. Humerus, two sides, of *Saguinus oedipus oedipus.* The entepicondylar foramen or notch is usually well defined in tamarins (*Saguinus, Leontopithecus*), rare or absent in marmosets (*Callithrix, Cebuella*). The internal supracondylar ridge, shown in humerus at left, is incompletely developed and represented by a pair of spines or processes in humerus at right. The lesser tubercle of the humerus is more prominent than the greater tubercle.

Entepicondylar Foramen (fig. VII.12)

The entepicondylar (supracondylar) foramen of the humerus, generally regarded as a primitive feature, is common in platyrrhines, including tamarins (*Saguinus*) and lion-tamarins (*Leontopithecus*) among callitrichids. It appears to be rare or absent in the more primitive pygmy and common marmosets (*Cebuella, Callithrix*).

Third Trochanter (fig. VII.13)

A weakly developed third trochanter of the femur is often present in callitrichids, as in lower primates generally, but is absent or poorly defined in cebids.

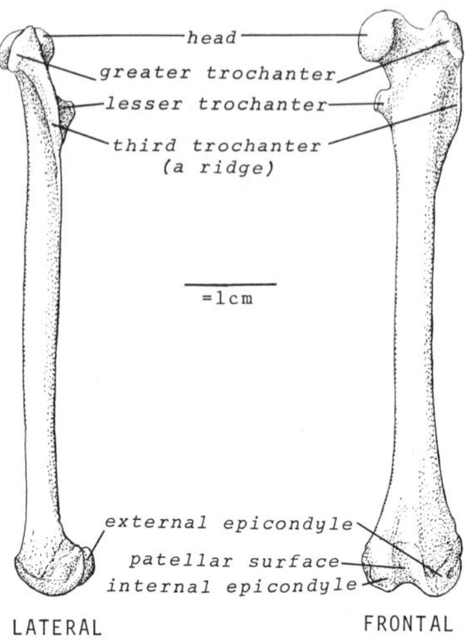

Fig. VII.13. Femur of *Saguinus oedipus oedipus;* third trochanter, usually present as ridge in callitrichids, is poorly defined or absent in cebids.

Foot Bone Ossification (fig. I.31)

The order of commencement of ossification of each of the 19 pedal bones is shown by Kraus and Hampton (1969) in cleared and alizarin-stained feet of 8 fetuses of *Saguinus oedipus.* The sequence, they found, was almost totally different from that of man. The widest divergence in the order of ossification appeared in the distal phalanx of the hallux, 14th in the tamarin, 1st (or 6th) in man.

Kraus and Hampton suggest that the order of initial ossification may be species specific, but so far the differences demonstrated are between widely separated subordinal groups. Additional comparisons should be made with feet, and hands too, of other platyrrhines, representative catarrhines, prosimians, and other arboreal mammals, including selected didelphids and tupaiids.

Limb Ratios and Locomotor Types

New World monkeys are arranged in three locomotor types by Erikson (1963) on the basis of long-bone lengths and proportions (table 46). *Callithrix* and *Saguinus* and the small marmosetlike cebids *Aotus* and *Callicebus* are grouped as "springers." The mostly larger and more specialized *Saimiri, Cebus, Pithecia, Chiropotes* and *Cacajao* are "climbers," and the still larger, prehensile-tailed *Alouatta, Lagothrix, Ateles,* and *Brachyteles,* with highest membral and intermembral ratios, are "brachiators."

The composite figures for "springers" given by Erikson (1963, p. 142) and reproduced here in table 47, are

Table 46. Locomotor Types According to Erikson (1963) Based on Skeletal Proportions Computed by the Same Author

Locomotor Types	*Springer Group (Callithrix, Saguinus, Aotus, Callicebus)*	*Climber Group (Cebus, Saimiri, Pithecia, Chiropotes, Cacajao)*	*Brachiator Group (Alouatta, Lagothrix, Brachyteles, Ateles)*
Humerus + Radius / Trunk			
Group mean	67	84	123
Generic means	63–72	73–90	91–150
Individual extremes	60–77	72–97	85–166
Samples	88	45	39
Humerus + Radius / Femur + Tibia			
Group mean	75	80	101
Generic means	73–77	76–84	98–105
Individual extremes	67–82	73–85	92–110
Samples	117	62	79
Radius / Humerus			
Group mean	89	90	94
Generic means	84–92	85–95	89–102
Individual extremes	86–98	82–102	84–108
Samples	119	69	82

broken down to those of the representative genera with *Cebuella, Leontopithecus,* and *Callimico* added. The data were supplied by Erikson (pers. comm.) from the pool used in determining the three locomotor types.

The ratios provided by Erikson for all locomotor types (table 46) are broadly overlapping in nearly all dimensions, and his figures for "springers" (table 47) show no clear separation between the genera. *Callithrix* and *Saguinus* are indeed similar in their squirrellike forms of locomotion in trees and on the ground. *Cebuella,* however, is more nearly mouselike in its manner of branch running and leaping and more specialized than other callitrichids for vertical clinging and leaping (fig. II.3). Limb ratios of *Leontopithecus* indicate a locomotor type less "springer" than one intermediate between "climber" and "brachiator." The ambiguity arises from the disproportionately long forelimbs of *Leontopithecus,* which are specialized for seeking insects and grubs hidden under loose bark or living in deep holes and not at all for a special type of locomotion. Limb proportions of *Callimico* agree with those of *Callithrix* and *Saguinus* but the tail averages shorter than that of any callitrichid (table 110; appendix table 1). How the tail affects locomotor patterns in this animal is problematic, but callimico locomotion is visibly different from that of callitrichids. *Saimiri* is a "climber" in Erikson's scheme, but its limb proportions indicate "springer." Locomotorily, *Saimiri* is not identifiable with either callitrichids among "springers" or *Cebus* or pithecines among "leapers." *Callicebus* is probably nearer callitrichids than other cebids in locomotor patterns, but *Aotus,* Erikson's model for "springer," stands well apart from all other platyrrhines.

The distinctive locomotor trait of callitrichids is their use of claws for trunk and large branch climbing, upside-down branch running, and rudimentary forms of vertical leaping. Their small bodies and more nearly generalized

Table 47. Membral and Intermembral Ratios in "Springers" (Callitrichids, *Callimico,* and the Marmosetlike Cebids, *Aotus, Callicebus*) and "Climber" *Saimiri*

Genus	*Radius / Humerus*	*Humerus + Radius / Femur + Tibia*	*Humerus + Radius / Trunk Length*	*Femur + Tibia / Trunk Length*
Cebuella	88(84–92)7[1]	82(81–83)6	76(74–79)5	94(92–95)5
Callithrix	88(85–91)31	74(72–76)23	67(60–75)12	89(79–99)16
Saguinus	91(85–97)79	75(72–81)77	69(61–79)59	92(85–102)59
Leontopithecus	99(95–101)7	87(83–90)7	84(80–88)5	95(93–103)4
Callimico	89(87–94)5	71(70–71)5	70(68–75)5	100(96–105)6
Aotus	91(85–99)16	74(72–75)14	66(62–72)12	90(83–98)13
Callicebus	84(81–87)13	74(70–75)12	63(60–67)9	86(81–90)8
Saimiri	92(85–96)29	78(76–80)24	72(69–77)19	93(89–98)20

SOURCE: Data from George Erikson (pers. comm.).
[1] Means and extremes in parentheses followed by sample number.

limb proportions combine with claws to make callitrichid locomotion the most primitive among living primates.

The sudden start and stop movements of trunk, limbs, and tail usually associated with the more primitive forms of terrestrial quadrupedal locomotion are more pronounced in *Cebuella,* smallest of callitrichids, than in other primates I have observed. The movements become more flowing with increasing size, beginning with *Callithrix jacchus* and continuing through *C. argentata* and the representatives of *Saguinus* and *Leontopithecus* I have seen. Bodily movements of *Callimico* seem to be even more coordinated and fluid than those of tamarins.

The *Cebuella* tail, insofar as I have observed it, appears to be least mobile and expressive among callitrichids. The frequent arching, waving, curving, curling, and coiling characteristic of tamarin tail movements are comparatively rudimentary or lacking in the caudal repertory of pygmy marmosets. I have never seen the tail tip of this animal coil on itself, and I find no mention or figure of it in the literature on *Cebuella. Callithrix* tail movements are clearly more complicated than those of *Cebuella,* but tail coiling may be poorly or not developed in *Callithrix jacchus,* whereas it is manifested in the more advanced *C. argentata.* The tamarin tail combines a high degree of expression with the usual locomotor and postural functions. Tail movements of the representative *Saguinus oedipus* are described elsewhere (p. 804). Caudal function may be even more versatile in *Callimico* than in tamarins.

Dentition

Dental Formula $i\frac{2}{2}$, $c\frac{1}{1}$, $pm\frac{3}{3}$, $m\frac{2}{2} = 32$.

The formula is unique among living primates; the tritubercular upper molars are most primitive among known primates; general absence of hypocone as a primary character and loss of molar paraconid as a secondary character are a combination unique to callitrichids among living primates (figs. V.22, 25, 26).

Dental Arches

Upper and lower dental arcades are V- to U-shaped (fig. VII.6).

Upper Incisors (figs. V.23–27)

The teeth are lanceolate, trapeziform, or spatulate in shape, cuspule (*b*) present or absent on distal margins; upper lateral incisor implanted either obliquely and slightly behind central incisor, or nearly in line.

Lower Incisors (figs. V.23–27)

Shape is either falciform and laterally compressed, or spatulate, unworn biting edges pointed and separated, or spatulate and often touching.

Upper Canine (figs. V.22, 25, 27)

The tooth is elongate, sharply pointed, slightly recurved, about twice as high as long, and at least half again higher than adjacent incisor or premolar, a lingual tubercle often present.

Lower Canine (figs. V.22, 26, 27)

The tooth is either falciform like lateral incisor but slightly heavier, or fully caniniform like upper canine, rudimentary talonid basin present or absent.

Upper Premolars (figs. V.22, 25, 27)

The occlusal surface is triangular to subovate or subrectangular; upper first premolar (pm^2) caniniform, unicuspid, or weakly bicuspid, consistently single rooted; pm^3 usually and pm^4 always bicuspid, and with one, sometimes two, roots.

Lower Premolars (figs. V.22, 26, 27)

All teeth are single-rooted; *first premolar* unicuspid or bicuspid, metalophid (epicristid, *II*) and rudimentary talonid basin (β) present; pm_3 with or without paraconid (*3*), hypoconid (*4*), or entoconid (*5*); pm_4 with well-defined "trigonid" basin.

Upper Molars (figs. V.22, 25, 27)

Enamel pattern of crown is simple, tritubercular, the hypocone (*5*) absent; trigon basin (α) deeply conical; protoloph (protocrista, *III*), and metaloph (plagiocrista, *IV*) well developed and converging on protocone (*2*); posterolingual cingulum (*C*) usually distinct, neoanterolingual cingulum (B^1) distinct or absent, *upper first molar* markedly larger than last premolar and last molar, three-rooted, sometimes two-rooted, occlusal surface triangular; *upper second molar* usually with two, often three, roots; molar crowns facing inward.

Lower Molars (figs. V.22, 26, 27)

Shape is quadrate, "trigonid" basin (ϵ) elevated and forward sloping, talonid basin (β) larger; *lower first molar* two-rooted, notably larger than last premolar and last molar; *lower second molar* one or two rooted, distolingual cusp produced more posteriad than distobuccal cusp.

Soft Parts

Palatine Ridges (fig. VII.14)

The fleshy, transverse ridges, rugae, or plicae of the lining of the mammalian hard palate are usually paired with one on each side of the midline, or fused into a single transverse ridge. Each member of a pair may also be branched or broken into a series of small elevations.

The number of transverse palatine ridges in 4 specimens of *Saguinus* examined by Schultz (1949*a;* 1958), is 5 on each side. The same number appears in 4 tamarins (*S. fuscicollis, S. nigricollis*) at hand. Schultz (1949*a;* 1958) records 5–6 rugae in 6 specimens of *Callithrix jacchus.* Means and extremes of rugae in 50 *Callithrix jacchus* examined by Ledoux, Dos Santos, and Santana Moura (1967) are 6.12 (6–7). Two specimens at hand of *C. jacchus* show 6 palatal ridges, with the anteriormost originating on each side of the incisive papillae. These anterior ridges are absent or poorly developed in all other callitrichids examined, and their rudiments, if present, may be counted as papillae rather than transverse ridges. In 3 specimens of *Cebuella pygmaea,* 5 transverse ridges were noted, and the same number appears in 2 specimens of *Leontopithecus rosalia rosalia.* The callitrichid range, as now known, appears to be 5–7 transverse ridges.

Rugae in each of two individuals of *Callimico* at hand

is 6. Osman Hill (1959, p. 64) also shows 6 in one specimen of *Callimico.*

According to Schultz (1958) the fewest number of rugae among cebids is 7 in *Aotus* and *Saimiri;* fewest among prosimians occur in *Perodicticus* with mean and extremes 6.4 (5–8) in 7 specimens; fewest in all primates are found in *Homo* with mean and extremes 4.2 (2–8) in 804 samples. The greatest number of palatine ridges listed by Schultz is 15 in the chimpanzee (9.4 [5–15] in 46 samples).

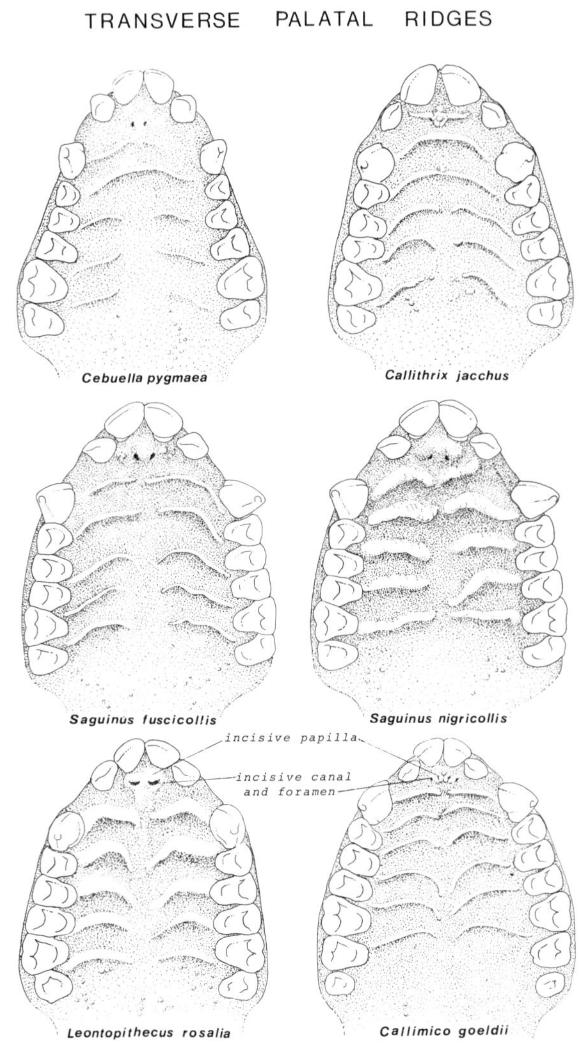

TRANSVERSE PALATAL RIDGES

Cebuella pygmaea

Callithrix jacchus

Saguinus fuscicollis

Saguinus nigricollis

incisive papilla

incisive canal and foramen

Leontopithecus rosalia

Callimico goeldii

Fig. VII.14. Transverse palatal ridges in callitrichids and *Callimico;* incisive canals conduct to Jacobson's organ; all palates drawn to same length.

In adult callitrichids, the rugae extend from the incisive papillae or just behind to the level of the first molars. This span compares with one to m^3 or just behind in prosimians; m^2 in *Callimico;* $m^{2\text{-}3}$ in cebids and catarrhines; m^2 in gibbons and orang; m^1 in chimpanzee and gorilla; pm^2 in man. Wettstein (1963, p. 261, fig. 19), confirms Schultz's findings for *Callithrix jacchus.*

The form and arrangement of the callitrichid rugae appear to be primitive. Loss of the hindmost rugae may well be correlated with reduction in palatal length and concomitant loss of m^3 and reduction of m^2. In anthropoids and man (Schultz 1958, fig. 3) variation in number of ridges seems to be the result of specialization and fragmentation of the anterior ridges, combined with a tendency toward reduction and obsolescence of the posterior ones without regard to palatal length.

Laryngeal Sacs (fig. I.10)

All callitrichids possess a lateral ventricular laryngeal sac. A median ventral superior sac is absent; and the median ventral inferior sac is known to occur only in *Leontopithecus* and *Callithrix jacchus* among callitrichids, and in *Aotus* among cebids.

Trunk and Limb Muscles

According to Beattie (1927, p. 712), "*Hapale* [= *Callithrix*] demonstrates an exceedingly primitive type of musculature more primitive in many ways than that of *Tarsius* [a highly specialized haplorhine], but similar to that animal in so far as they both approach the primitive insectivore condition."

Organs of Thoracic and Abdominal Cavities

Few comparative studies have been made with internal organs of the callitrichid thoracic and abdominal cavities. Spot checks of specimens and reviews of the literature suggest that gross structure of soft parts of the gut, reproductive tract, respiratory, and circulatory systems are more generalized in callitrichids than in cebids and catarrhines. According to Beattie (1927, p. 712), "the arrangement [in *Callithrix*] of the lungs, the tendency to simplification of the lobes and the vascular connections, are more advanced than that seen in *Tarsius.* The digestive system, in many ways primitive, is more like that in some of the Cebidae than in the Lemurs. On the other hand, the form of the liver is still lemurine." No more information of phylogenetic significance can be gleaned, however, from published studies and superficial dissections made here. In contrast, the peripheral soft organs of internal systems, such as larynx, tongue, palatal ridges, and external genitalia, all lodged outside the thoracic or abdominal cavity, reveal a wealth of taxonomic information. Obviously, the more exposed the organ the more liable it is to modification through external selective forces.

Kidneys

The callitrichid kidneys, as described by Straus (1935, p. 93) and Straus and Arcadi (1958, p. 507), are cylindrical with rounded ends, the upper poles broader than the lower, left kidney slightly more caudal than right, at same level, or slightly more anteriad; gross structure simple, unipyramidal, and undivided papilla present on pelvic surface. These kidneys, the same type as those of most primates, are regarded by the authors cited as more primitive than the complex or multiple papillate type in *Homo* and, strangely, some individuals of *Ateles.*

Central Nervous System

The callitrichid brain is actually among the smallest of living primate brains; relative to body mass, however, it is among the largest of mammalian brains. The cerebral hemispheres are comparatively smooth and one of the least fissurated among primates, the olfactory bulb least degenerate among higher primates (figs. VI.8, 9), excepting *Callimico* and possibly *Aotus* and *Callicebus,* and always projecting beyond the anterior plane of the hemispheres; the accessory olfactory bulb is present and well developed, retrocalcarine (postcalcarine) fissure absent

Table 48. Chromosomes in Callitrichidae and Callimiconidae

♂♂	♀♀	∘∘	Name	2n	BiA	M	SM	A	X	Y	References
			Callitrichidae								
5	—	—	*Cebuella pygmaea*	44	32	—	—	10	SM	A	Hsu and Benirschke (1967, fol. 47)
—	—	4	*Cebuella pygmaea*	44	—	—	—	—	M	A	Wohnus and Benirschke (1966, p. 94)
2	—	—	*Cebuella pygmaea*	44	32	4	28	10	SM	A	Benirschke and Brownhill (1962, p. 245)
7	—	—	*Cebuella pygmaea*	44	32	4	28	10	SM	A	Egozcue, Chiarelli, and Sarti-Chiarelli (1968, p. 50)
1	—	—	*Callithrix jacchus jacchus*	46	30	4	26	14	M	M	de Boer (1974)[7]
—	—	5	*Callithrix jacchus jacchus*	46	—	—	—	—	—	—	Wohnus and Benirschke (1966, p. 4)
4	—	—	*Callithrix jacchus jacchus*	46	32	[4]	[28]	12	M	A	Benirschke and Brownhill (1962, p. 245)
2	6	—	*Callithrix jacchus jacchus*	46	30	—	—	14	SM	ST, M	Hsu and Benirschke (1967, fol. 46)
1	1	—	*Callithrix jacchus penicillata*	46	30	4	26	14	SM	M	Hsu and Hampton (1970, p. 184)
1	2	—	*Callithrix "chrysoleucos"*[1]	46	34	4	30	10	SM	M	Bender and Mettler (1960, p. 400; Bender and Chu 1963, p. 285)
			"Callithrix chrysoleuca"[2]	46	34	4	26	14	SM	SM	Egozcue (1969, p. 370)
1	—	—	*Callithrix humeralifer humeralifer*[3]	44	32	4	28	10	SM	A	Egozcue, Perkins, and Hagemenas (1968, p. 82)
1	1	—	*Callithrix humeralifer humeralifer*	44	32	4	28	10	SM	A	Hsu and Benirschke (1970, fol. 196)
1	1	—	*Callithrix argentata argentata*	44	28	4	24	14	SM	M	Hsu and Hampton (1970, p. 184)
1	1	—	*Callithrix argentata argentata*	44	28	—	—	14	SM	A	Hsu and Benirschke (1970, fol. 195)
—	1	—	*Callithrix argentata argentata*	44	32	12	20	10	SM	—	de Boer (1974)[7]
2	—	—	*Callithrix argentata argentata*	44	32	4	28	10	SM	M	Egozcue, Perkins, and Hagemenas (1968, p. 81)
2	—	—	*Saguinus "nigricollis"*	46	30	4	26	14	SM	M	Benirschke and Brownhill (1962, p. 245)
2	—	—	*Saguinus "nigricollis"*	46	32	—	—	12	M	M	Wohnus and Benirschke (1966, p. 94)
1	1	—	*Saguinus "nigricollis"*	46	30	—	—	14	SM	M	Hsu and Benirschke (1968, fol. 100)
1	—	—	*Saguinus "nigricollis"*	46	34	4	30	10	SM	—	Anderson, Lewis, Passovoy, and Trobough (1967)
2	2	—	*Saguinus fuscicollis "illigeri"*[4]	46	34	4	30	10	SM	M	Bender and Mettler (1960); Bender and Chu (1963, p. 285)
1	1	—	*Saguinus fuscicollis "illigeri"*[4]	46	30	—	—	14	SM	M	Egozcue, Perkins, and Hagemenas (1969, p. 155)
1	1	—	*Saguinus fuscicollis "illigeri"*[4]	46	30	4	26	14	SM	M	Hsu and Benirschke (1970, fol. 197)
1	—	—	*Saguinus mystax mystax*	46	30	4	26	14	SM	A	Benirschke and Brownhill (1963); Wohnus and Benirschke (1966)
2	2	—	*Saguinus mystax mystax*	46	30	—	—	14	SM	A	Hsu and Benirschke (1968, fol. 99)
2	1	—	*Saguinus mystax mystax*	46	34	4	30	10	SM	A	Anderson, Lewis, Passovoy, and Trobough (1967)
—	1	—	*Saguinus midas niger*[5]	46	—	—	—	—	—	—	Benirschke and Brownhill (1963, p. 338)
1	—	—	*Saguinus leucopus*	46	—	—	—	—	—	—	Benirschke and Brownhill (1963, p. 338)
1	1	—	*Saguinus leucopus*	46	30	4	26	14	SM	M	Hsu and Hampton (1970, p. 184)
1	4	—	*Saguinus oedipus oedipus*	46	30	4	26	14	SM	M	Benirschke and Brownhill (1962, p. 245)
3	2	—	*Saguinus oedipus oedipus*	46	30	4	26	14	SM	M	Egozcue, Perkins, and Hagemenas (1968, p. 81)
2	—	—	*Saguinus oedipus oedipus*	46	30	8	22	14	M	M	de Boer (1974)[7]
1	1	—	*Saguinus oedipus oedipus*	46	30	—	—	14	M	A	Hsu and Benirschke (1970, fol. 198)
1	1	—	*Saguinus oedipus oedipus*	46	34	4	30	10	M	SM	Anderson, Lewis, Passovoy, and Trobough (1967)
1	1	—	*Leontopithecus rosalia rosalia*	46	42	—	—	2	SM	M	Hsu and Benirschke (1971, fol. 245)
1	—	—	*Leontopithecus rosalia rosalia*	46	32	4	28	12	SM	M	Hsu and Hampton (1970, p. 188)

—	1[6]	—	*Leontopithecus rosalia rosalia*	46	32	4	28	12	SM	M	Benirschke and Brownhill (1962, p. 245); Benirschke, Anderson, and Brownhill (1962, p. 513)
			Callimiconidae								
—	1	—	*Callimico goeldii*	48	32	2	30	16	—	—	Bender and Mettler (1960); Bender and Chu (1963, p. 285)
—	1	—	*Callimico goeldii*	48	26	8	16	22	SM	SM	Boer (1974, p. 25)[7]
2	1	—	*Callimico goeldii*	48	28	4	24	18	SM	A	Egozcue, Perkins, and Hagemenas (1968, p. 81)
—	1	—	*Callimico goeldii*	48	30	2	28	16	SM	A	Hsu and Hampton (1970, p. 187, fig. 4 ♀)
1	—	—	*Callimico goeldii*	47	30	2	28	16	SM	—	Hsu and Hampton (1970, p. 187, fig. 4 ♂, Houston Stock)
6	—	—	*Callimico goeldii*	47	—	—	—	—	SM	—	Hsu and Hampton (1970, Houston Stock)
3	—	—	*Callimico goeldii*	47	31	4	27	15	SM	—	Hsu and Hampton (1970, figs. 8, 9, Oak Ridge Stock)

NOTE: Explanation of symbols:

2n = Diploid number of chromosomes
BiA = Total number of biarmed chromosomes (M + SM)
M = Metacentric chromosomes
SM = Submetacentric chromosomes (includes subtelocentric elements)
A = Acrocentric chromosomes
X = Female sex chromosome
Y = Male sex chromosome

1 Certainly a misidentification of possibly an albinotic *Callithrix jacchus jacchus* or *Saguinus* (e.g., *S. fuscicollis melanoleucus*).

2 Reinterpretation of Bender and Mettler's published karyotype.

3 Misidentified "*Callithrix aurita.*"

4 "Red-mantled tamarin," Bender and Mettler (1960, p. 401) = *Saguinus fuscicollis lagonotus.*

5 *Saguinus tamarin* of authors (not Link 1795).

6 Chimeric.

7 Criterion for metacentric (arm ratio 1.0–1.6 inclusive) is de Boer's (1974, p. 8); his submetacentric and subtelocentric chromosomes are combined here for uniformity.

in the more primitive *Cebuella* and *Callithrix* and often present in *Saguinus* and *Leontopithecus* (fig. VI.12); dorsal lateral geniculate body arranged in four lamina (fig. VI.5).

Karyology

Karyotypes of approximately 98 individual callitrichids have been recorded through early 1974 (table 48). They represent the 4 recognized genera, 11 of the 14 species, but only 12 (excluding the challenged identification of "*Callithrix chrysoleucos*") of the 43 included species and subspecies. The lesser-known callimiconid *Callimico goeldii* is represented by karyotypes of 16 individuals, more than for any other platyrrhine.

All published karyotypes of callitrichids (and callimiconids) are of captive animals. None of the karyotypes have been associated with or related to any other character of the individual organism, and none bear essential geographic data.

For all the deficiencies, callitrichid karyotypes appear to be remarkably uniform (or stable?) after allowances are made for variation in metrical methods used by the various authors and the differences in their interpretations of structural differences. Only two karyotypic complements are distinguishable in present material. One with 46 chromosomes is represented by *Leontopithecus, Saguinus,* and *Callithrix jacchus*. The second, with 44 chromosomes, includes *Cebuella* and two species of the *Callithrix argentata* group, or *C. argentata* and *C. humeralifer*. The quantitative difference cuts straight through the intimate phylogenetic relationship between all species of *Callithrix,* and between species of the genus *Saguinus* and those of the most nearly related *Callithrix argentata* group. The karyotypes fail to show the isolated position of *Leontopithecus* and they align *Cebuella* with the more distantly related of the two branches of *Callithrix*.

De Boer (1974, pp. 23–24), who most recently examined the data, observes that inasmuch as

> only single rearrangements are concerned in the differences between the karyotypes, it is definitely possible that these occurred more than once and independently. In view of the taxonomic position of *Leontopithecus* and *Cebuella,* it is even more plausible that these genera evolved independently of the karyological changes within *Callithrix*. It can hardly be imagined that a rearrangement, causing possible intraspecific variation in *Callithrix jacchus,* at the same time gave rise to such a distinct genus as *Leontopithecus*. Comparably, *Cebuella,* which is often considered as being the most primitive form of the family . . . cannot be believed to have separated from *Callithrix* only after the present speciation in the latter started, even though *Callithrix* and *Cebuella* are sometimes considered as being congeneric. . . . In our opinion, the fusion separating *Cebuella* from a common 2n = 46 stock, may have occurred at a much earlier date than that within *Callithrix* (the more so since it is not altogether clear, whether or not exactly the same acrocentrics were involved in both fusions). Since more important karyotype changes are often not accompanied by marked phylogenetical divergence, the occurrence of a single fusion in *Cebuella* is not in contradiction with the preservation of primitive characters in the genus.

Chimerism

Chimerism is a normal phenomenon in callitrichids where polyzygosity, usually dizygosity, is the rule (table 49). Chimerism is readily detected in heterosexual twins or litters by the presence of both male and female sex cells in the tissues, usually the hemopoietic and gonadal, of each progeny. Male and female sex cells have also been discovered in the testes of about half the number of wild-caught adult male tamarins and marmosets examined by S. H. Hampton (1973). The interchange of cells is permitted by anastomoses of placental circulation between the developing fetuses (Wislocki 1939).

Benirschke and Layton (1969) regard blood chimerism as a permanent condition of callitrichids, at least in all species actually studied. Gengozian, Batson, Greene, and Gosslee (1969), and Gengozian and Porter (1971), using tamarins, found chimerism consistent in heterosexual twins, in a small percentage (3/47) of unisexual twins, and in 3 of 19 singletons. Gengozian suggests three possible pathways to account for chimerism in singletons: (1) Exchange of cells between fetuses followed by death and resorption of one fetus; (2) transplacental passage of hemopoietic cells from maternal to fetal system; or (3) early aggregation of blastomeres of heterosexual twins culminating in a single-born chimeric young. A tendency

Table 49. Chimerism in Heterosexual Callitrichid Twins

Name	*Tissue*	*Reference*
Cebuella pygmaea	Marrow	Benirschke and Brownhill (1962, p. 1963)
Callithrix j. jacchus	Marrow	Benirschke, Anderson, and Brownhill (1962)
	Testis	Benirschke and Brownhill (1963)
Callithrix h. humeralifer	Blood, testis	Egozcue, Perkins, and Hagemenas (1968)
Saguinus "nigricollis"	Marrow	Benirschke and Brownhill (1962)
Saguinus "nigricollis"	Lymph nodes, spleen, neutrophils, bone marrow	Gengozian, Batson, and Eide (1964)
Saguinus fuscicollis subspp.	Hemopoietic tissues; drumstick bearing neutrophils	Gengozian et al. (1969)
Saguinus f. illigeri	Blood, testis	Egozcue, Perkins, and Hagemenas (1969)
Saguinus m. mystax	Marrow, testis	Benirschke and Brownhill (1963)
Saguinus oedipus	Marrow	Benirschke and Brownhill (1962)

for a slightly higher count of male cells than female cells in chimerics has been noted (Gengozian 1971). Unilateral ovariectomy, as demonstrated by Gengozian and Merritt (1970), does not reduce twinning or the incidence of chimerism.

Experiments conducted by Porter and Gengozian (1969), Gengozian (1971), and Gengozian and Porter (1971) show that chimerism endows each callitrichid with two sets of transplantation antigens and a decrease in antigenic incompatibility. Immunity to transplants between co-twins appears to be nearly or quite complete, and survival time for nonfraternal intraspecific grafts proves "significantly longer than those among other mammalian and primate species" (Gengozian and Porter 1971, pp. 173–74). Indeed, the complete success of co-twin skin grafts in unisexual twins (4 male pairs) of *Callithrix jacchus* was regarded as a clear criterion of chimerism by Mahouy (1972).

Freemartinism, a teratogenetic form of chimerism characterized by deformation of reproductive organs and sterility in the female of heterosexual twins, has been observed in domestic ungulates (cattle, pigs, goat, sheep) but is unknown in callitrichids (Wislocki 1939) and other primates. According to Ryan, Benirschke, and Smith (1961), freemartinism in fraternal twin pregnancies may be due to an "androgen" produced by the male twin. Such "androgen" might not persist or accumulate in the presence of an effective aromatizing enzyme system such as exists in the human placenta and, as was demonstrated by Ryan et al., in the callitrichid (*Leontopithecus*) placenta. Freemartinism probably does not occur in nature and would be strongly selected against among wild animals that normally produce two or more young at a birth.

For additional information on callitrichid chimerism, see Wislocki (1939); Benirschke, Anderson, and Brownhill (1962); Benirschke and Brownhill (1962); Gengozian, Batson, and Eide (1964); van Tienhoven (1968); Gengozian and Batson (1975); and other works cited in table 49 and the synonymies.

46 Family Callitrichidae
3. Classification and Keys

Classification of the Genera, Species, and Subspecies

Genus *Cebuella* Gray, 1866—Pygmy Marmosets
Cebuella pygmaea Spix, 1823 (Pygmy Marmosets)

Genus *Callithrix* Erxleben, 1777—true marmosets or ouistitis
Callithrix jacchus group
Callithrix jacchus Linnaeus, 1758—Tufted-ear Marmosets or Ouistitis
C. j. penicillata E. Geoffroy, 1812 (Black-tufted-ear Marmoset)
C. j. geoffroyi Humboldt, 1812 (Geoffroy's Tufted-ear Marmoset)
C. j. jacchus Linnaeus, 1758 (White-tufted-ear Marmoset)
C. j. aurita E. Geoffroy, 1812 (Buff-tufted-ear Marmoset)
C. j. flaviceps Thomas, 1903 (Buffy-headed Marmoset)
Callithrix argentata group
Callithrix argentata Linnaeus, 1771—Bare-ear Marmosets
C. a. melanura E. Geoffroy, 1812 (Black-tail Marmoset)
C. a. argentata Linnaeus, 1771 (Silvery Marmoset)
C. a. leucippe Thomas, 1922 (Golden-white Bare-ear Marmoset)
Callithrix humeralifer E. Geoffroy, 1812—Tassel-ear Marmosets
C. h. humeralifer E. Geoffroy, 1812 (Black and White Tassel-ear Marmoset)
C. h. intermedius Hershkovitz, 1977 (Black and Gold Tassel-ear Marmoset)
C. h. chrysoleuca Wagner, 1842 (Golden-white Tassel-ear Marmoset)

Genus *Saguinus* Hoffmannsegg, 1807—Tamarins
Hairy-face Tamarin Section
Saguinus nigricollis group—White-mouth Tamarin Group
Saguinus nigricollis Spix, 1823—Black-mantle Tamarins
S. n. graellsi Jiménez de la Espada, 1870 (Graell's Black-mantle Tamarin)
S. n. nigricollis Spix, 1823 (Spix's Black-mantle Tamarin)
Saguinus fuscicollis Spix, 1823—Saddle-back Tamarins
S. f. fuscus Lesson, 1840 (Lesson's Saddle-back Tamarin)
S. f. avilapiresi Hershkovitz, 1966 (Avila Pires's Saddle-back Tamarin)
S. f. fuscicollis Spix, 1823 (Spix's Saddle-back Tamarin)
S. f. nigrifrons I. Geoffroy, 1850 (Geoffroy's Saddle-back Tamarin)
S. f. illigeri Pucheran, 1845 (Illiger's Saddle-back Tamarin)
S. f. leucogenys Gray, 1866 (Andean Saddle-back Tamarin)
S. f. lagonotus Jiménez de la Espada, 1870 (Red-mantle Saddle-back Tamarin)
S. f. tripartitus Milne-Edwards, 1878 (Golden-mantle Saddle-back Tamarin)
S. f. weddelli Deville, 1849 (Weddell's Saddle-back Tamarin)
S. f. cruzlimai Hershkovitz, 1966 (Cruz Lima's Saddle-back Tamarin)
S. f. crandalli Hershkovitz, 1966 (Crandall's Saddle-back Tamarin)
S. f. acrensis, Carvalho, 1957 (Acre Saddle-back Tamarin)
S. f. melanoleucus Miranda Ribeiro, 1912 (White Saddle-back Tamarin)
Saguinus mystax group—Moustached Tamarin Group
Saguinus labiatus E. Geoffroy, 1812 (Red-chested Moustached Tamarins)
S. l. labiatus E. Geoffroy, 1812 (Geoffroy's Moustached Tamarin)
S. l. thomasi Goeldi, 1907 (Thomas' Moustached Tamarin)
Saguinus mystax Spix, 1823 (Black-chested Moustached Tamarin)
S. m. mystax Spix, 1823 (Spix's Moustached Tamarin)
S. m. pileatus I. Geoffroy and Deville, 1848 (Red-cap Moustached Tamarin)
S. m. pluto Lönnberg, 1926 (White-rump Moustached Tamarin)
Saguinus imperator Goeldi, 1907 (Emperor Moustached Tamarin)

Saguinus midas group—Midas Tamarin Group
Saguinus midas Linnaeus, 1758 (Midas Tamarins)
S. m. midas Linnaeus, 1758 (Golden-handed Tamarin)
S. m. niger E. Geoffroy, 1803 (Black-handed Tamarin)
Mottled-face Tamarin Section
Saguinus inustus Schwarz, 1951 (Mottled-face Tamarin)
Bare-face Tamarin Section
Saguinus bicolor group (Brazilian Bare-face Tamarins)
Saguinus bicolor Spix, 1823 (Brazilian Bare-face Tamarins)
S. b. bicolor Spix, 1823 (Pied Bare-face Tamarin)
S. b. martinsi Thomas, 1912 (Martin's Bare-face Tamarin)
S. b. ochraceus Hershkovitz, 1966 (Ochraceous Bare-face Tamarin)
Saguinus oedipus group (Colombian and Panamanian Bare-face Tamarins)
Saguinus leucopus Günther, 1877 (Silvery-brown Bare-face Tamarin)
Saguinus oedipus Linnaeus, 1758—Crested Bare-face Tamarins
S. o. geoffroyi Pucheran, 1845 (Red-crested Bare-face Tamarin)
S. o. oedipus Linnaeus, 1758 (Cotton-top or White-plumed Bare-face Tamarin)

Genus *Leontopithecus* Lesson, 1840—Lion-tamarins
Leontopithecus rosalia Linnaeus, 1766 (Lion-tamarins)
L. r. chrysopygus Mikan, 1823 (Golden-rump Lion-tamarin)
L. r. chrysomelas Kuhl, 1820 (Gold and Black Lion-tamarin)
L. r. rosalia Linnaeus, 1766 (Golden Lion-tamarin)

Key to Genera and Sections of Callitrichidae and *Callimico,* Based on External Characters

1\. Adult mouse- to squirrel-sized; prominent preauricular tufts present or absent; pinna bare or tasseled and either exposed and unpigmented or more-or-less concealed by fanlike tuft or tawny mane; tail entirely black, golden, yellowish, silvery, white, or symmetrically banded with alternating dark and pale bars; hands and feet not elongate, length of middle digit (with claw) less than twice width of palm (figs. I.20, 28); lower jaw as seen through opened mouth more or less V-shaped (fig. VII.5); lower canines like adjacent incisors in shape and size (fig. V.27); lower incisors conical, the central pair smaller than the lateral ones (fig. V.23); habitat upper Amazonia or south of the Rio Amazonas and east of the Rio Madeira (true marmosets) 2

1′. Adult squirrel-sized; ear tufts absent; pinna bare or thinly haired, exposed and fully pigmented, or concealed by a blackish, brown, reddish or golden mane (fig. III.18); upper surface of terminal half of tail black, brownish, reddish, golden, or white, never distinctly or symmetrically annulated or symmetrically barred with alternating dark and pale bands; hands and feet normal or elongate, length of middle digit (with claw) approximately twice width of palm (fig. I.28); lower jaw as seen through opened mouth more or less V- to U-shaped (fig. VII.5); lower canines well differentiated from incisors and half again as high, or higher (fig. V.27); lower incisors conical (*Callithrix*), spade-shaped or spatulate, the middle pair larger or smaller (*Callithrix*) than the lateral ones (fig. V.23); habitat, Panamá, Costa Rica (*Saguinus*) and tropical South America; (*Saguinus, Leontopithecus, Callimico,* part *Callithrix argentata*) 3

2\. Size mouselike, adult length of head and trunk combined less than 175 mm (7 in), of tail less than 250 mm (10 in); ears thinly haired and almost entirely concealed by tawny mane of head; tail banded dorsally .... *Cebuella* (pygmy marmoset, p. 450)

2′. Size squirrellike, adult length of head and trunk combined more than 175 mm (7 in), of tail more than 250 mm (10 in); ears thickly tufted, or nearly bare with pinna fully exposed, or more-or-less concealed by tassel- or fanlike pre- or circumauricular tufts; tail more-or-less uniformly colored or completely annulated with alternating dark and light bands .... *Callithrix* (part, p. 488)

3\. Hand elongate, palm narrow, digits long, length of middle finger (with claw) more than twice width of palm; general body coloration whitish, golden (i.e., yellow to coppery), or gold to reddish and black, rarely if ever entirely black; mane golden, gold and black, or entirely black and concealing ears; cheeks and space between eyes thinly haired or bare .... *Leontopithecus* (Lion-tamarins, p. 807)

3′. Hand normal, palm broad, length of middle digit (with claw) less than twice width of palm; general coloration varied or blackish; sides of crown, cheeks, and space between eyes completely covered with hair or nearly bare, the ears exposed (*Saguinus,* part *Callithrix*), or more or less concealed (*Callimico*) 4

4\. Cheeks and sides of face from brow to ears covered with hair nearly like hair of forehead and crown 6

4′. Cheeks and sides of face from brow to ear naked or sparsely haired in sharp contrast with dense pelage of crown behind anterior plane of ears .... *Saguinus* (part) 5

5\. Pelage of head, body, and limbs blackish or dark brown .... Mottled-face Tamarins (p. 732)

5′. Pelage of head, body or limbs not blackish or dark brown .... Bare-face Tamarins (p. 735)

6\. Forehead and crown to level of ears covered with long hairs not markedly shorter or thinner than hairs of crown between ears; hind feet variously colored or, if whitish or buffy, without well-defined brown patch or spotting on ankle and metatarsus, hairs of throat and neck directed forward or straight back 7

6′. Forehead and crown to level of ears covered with short silvery hairs in marked contrast with long brown hairs of crown between ears; upper surface of hind feet whitish or buffy with brown patch or spotting on ankle and metatarsus; hairs of angle between throat and neck forming a complete whorl .... Bare-face Tamarin (*Saguinus leucopus,* p. 748)

7. Dorsal surface of trunk variously colored but not silvery or whitish, posterior portion striated, marbled, or spotted, or uniformly dark brown or blackish like anterior portion; whitish hip patches absent; tail blackish to drab but not whitish; ears exposed or more or less concealed by mane 8

7′. Dorsal surface of trunk brownish, silvery, or whitish, the posterior portion not striated, marbled, or spotted; whitish hip patches present or absent; tail blackish or whitish; ears exposed 9

8. Head, trunk, and either limbs or hands and feet variously or contrastingly colored; lower back marbled or striated black with gray, buffy, or reddish; mane, if present, never thickly developed, the ears well exposed to view; hairs surrounding mouth white or black, hairs of throat directed backward .... *Saguinus* (Hairy-face Tamarins, p. 600)

8′. Head, trunk, limbs, dark brown or black, sometimes variegated with white or buffy; feet black; lower back uniformly blackish or with brown marbling or striations; hairs of head forming thick bobbed mane, nearly or entirely concealing ears; hairs surrounding mouth dominantly or wholly black; hairs of throat directed forward .... *Callimico* (callimico, p. 875)

9. Pelage of head, trunk, limbs, tail whitish 10

9′. Pelage of head, trunk, limbs brownish or silvery, tail black .... *Callithrix argentata* (part, p. 581)

10. Skin of face, ears, palms, soles black in sharp contrast with whitish fur .... *Saguinus* (part, *S. fuscicollis melanoleucus,* p. 664)

10′. Skin of face, ears, palms, soles with little or no pigment (carmine red in living animal) .... *Callithrix argentata* (part, *C. a. leucippe,* p. 588)

Key to Genera of Callitrichidae and Callimiconidae Based on Male External Genitalia

1. Glans penis not sharply differentiated from penial stem, sulcus retroglandis absent (figs. III.28, 29).
   a. Penial stem with small spines .... *Callithrix*
   b. Penial stem without spines
      (*a*) Scrotum globose, papillate; sessile, pendunculate; mottled to entirely unpigmented .... *Cebuella*
      (*b*) Scrotum variously shaped, papillate or corrugated; pedunculate or pendulous; mottled to entirely pigmented .... *Saguinus*
2. Glans penis acorn-shaped, well differentiated from penial stem by sulcus retroglandis (figs. III.28, 29).
   a. Penial stem with spines, scrotum globose, usually wider than long .... *Callimico*
   b. Penial stem papillate but not spiny; scrotum elongate .... *Leontopithecus*

Detailed descriptions of the male external genitalia and related areas are given on pages 112 and 417 and in the separate generic and species accounts.

Key to Genera of Callitrichidae and Callimiconidae Based on Female External Genitalia

Variation in size, form, and color of the mature female genitalia is great in the Callitrichidae and *Callimico,* and the full range of variation can only be suspected. It would be impractical at this time, therefore, to use genitalia alone for distinguishing the genera and species. It seems, nevertheless, that a tentative key to genera and some species can be made on the basis of the form of the mature labia majora.

1. Labia majora well developed, mostly to entirely unpigmented; hairy pad of each preputial fold mediad to scrotal fold or pad (fig. III.23).
   a. Cebuella pygmaea.—Distinguished from following by absolutely smaller size.
   b. Callithrix jacchus.—Distinguished from following by papillate, sessile, scrotal folds.
   c. Callithrix argentata.—Distinguished from preceding by opaque white convoluted and pedunculate scrotal folds.
   d. Callithrix humeralifer (fig. VII.7).—no entire female specimens examined but evidently like *C. argentata.*
2. Labia majora well developed, mottled to mostly or entirely pigmented (rarely unpigmented in adults); hairy pad of preputial fold anteriad to scrotal pad or folds .... *Saguinus* (part)
3. Labia majora poorly developed with hairy preputial pad hardly or not defined from scrotal pad or fold.
   a. Callimico.—mostly pigmented.
   b. Leontopithecus.—mostly unpigmented.
   c. Saguinus (part, immature)—pigmented or unpigmented.

Key to Genera Based on Superficial Cranial Characters

(Note: Distinction between *Callithrix* and *Saguinus* is not aways clear on basis of characters used here. The identification of these genera should be confirmed by the dental characters.)

1. Greatest skull length usually less than 40 mm; paired posterior sphenoidal fossae absent; condyloincisive length of mandible less than 24 mm (fig. VII.5) . . . . *Cebuella*
1′. Greatest skull length usually more than 40 mm; paired posterior sphenoidal fossae, seen from mesopterygoid fossa, present or absent; condyloincisive length of mandible more than 24 mm 2
2. Paired posterior sphenoidal fossae present (fig. IV.39) . . . . *Leontopithecus*
2′. Paired sphenoidal fossae absent 3
3. Greatest skull length usually less than 52 mm; symphysial angle usually less than 46°; coronoid process low, extending slightly above condyle; outline of dental arcade V- to nearly U-shaped; outer alveolar distance between canines slightly more or less than alveolar length of c-m² (figs. VII.5, 6) . . . . part *Callithrix*
3′. Greatest skull length usually more than 45 mm; symphysial angle usually more than 39°; coronoid process high, always extending well above condyle; outline of dental arcade more nearly U- than V-shaped, outer alveolar distance between canines more than alveolar length of c-m² (figs. VII.5, 6) . . . . *Saguinus*

Key to Genera Based on Dental Characters

1. Lower canine slightly higher and larger than lateral incisor but hardly differentiated in form (fig. V.24); lower incisors falcate or lanceolate, biting edges narrow and separated (fig. V.26); crown height of lower lateral incisor more than one-half vertical depth of symphysis menti; central incisor smaller and shorter than lateral; upper and lower lateral incisors with distal cuspule; mandibular dental arch V- to U-shaped (fig. VII.5) 3
1′. Lower canine about twice as large and high as adjacent teeth and well differentiated in form; lower incisors spatulate with wide biting edges usually touching, cuspules absent; crown height of lateral incisor less than one-half vertical depth of symphysis menti; central incisor at least as high and large as lateral incisor; upper incisors without cuspules; mandibular dental arch more nearly U-shaped 3
2. Lower tooth row (i_1 to m_2) less than 13.5 mm long; upper lateral incisor with small mesial and distal cuspule; unworn lower incisors with cuspule on mesial and distal margin of each; first upper premolar with or without protocone; lower molars as long as or longer than wide (figs. V.22, 23, 26) . . . . *Cebuella*
2′. Lower tooth row (i_1 to m_2) more than 13.5 mm long; upper lateral incisor with distal cuspule only; unworn lower incisors with cuspule on distal edge only; first upper premolar without protocone; lower premolars wider than long . . . . *Callithrix*
3. First upper molar from nearly two times to three times larger than second; length of m^1 less than 3.0 mm, width less than 3.5; upper tooth row (i^1 to m^2) usually between 13 and 20 mm; hypocone and entostyle usually absent in pm^4; lower incisor forward projecting but not markedly procumbent . . . . *Saguinus*
3′. First upper molar usually less than twice as large as second; length of m^1 more than 3.0 mm, width more than 3.5 mm; upper tooth row (i^1 to m^2) usually between 18 and 22 mm; rudimentary hypocone and entostyle often present in pm^4; lower incisors procumbent . . . . *Leontopithecus*

47. Family Callitrichidae
4. Biology

Reproduction

Abstract

As a rule, fraternal twins are produced; most singletons are probably survivors of dizygotic pregnancies. A small percentage of triplets are produced in captivity.

Duration of gestation averages from 130 to 150 days among the various species.

Mating normally occurs at the beginning of the regular dry season, and breeding coincides with the early part of the rainy season. The estrous cycle averages between 14 and 18 days; most cycles may be anovular and there is little or no detectable vaginal bleeding.

Periodicity

Reproduction is seasonal, with the most effective mating occurring at the beginning of the dry season or end of the rainy season. This corresponds to fall rutting in the north temperate zone. Breeding (giving birth) coincides with the early part of the rainy season after a gestation period of between 4 and 5 months. A postpartum estrus in most captive female callitrichids has been noted, but seasonality is persistent nevertheless. The explanation may lie in delayed fertilization after insemination, delayed implantation after conception, or gestation prolonged beyond the presumed norm of 130 to 140 days, or and perhaps most likely, in one or a succession of several anovular estrous cycles.

Seasonal breeding also occurs among marmosetlike cebids. In the Peruvian squirrel monkey, *Saimiri sciureus,* as reported by Rosenblum (1972), wild females were observed pregnant from October to January, infants with their mothers, from January to March. Gestation in laboratory females lasts 5.5 to 5.7 months, the interbirth interval averages 13.8 months (9.5–18)26 females. As summarized by Michael, Wilson, and Plant (1973), timing of the 3-month mating period shown by captive and free-ranging squirrel monkeys "depends on geographical location: in Peru mating occurs from July to September; in Florida from December to March; in Tennessee from February to March and in New York and Munich from March to July."

Twinning, Implantation, and Placental Membrane

Twinning in *Callithrix jacchus,* as shown by J. P. Hill (1926; 1932), is dizygotic. The two blastocysts lie side by side with poles reversed, their attachment to dorsal and ventral uterine walls, respectively, accomplished at the opposite poles. The contacting blastocyst walls fuse, disappear, and leave both embryos in a single cavity enclosed in a common chorion, each fetus with its own discoidal placenta.

Wislocki (1932), unaware of Hill's contemporaneous publication on marmosets and its abstract published in 1926, observed essentially the same conditions in later-stage twin fetuses of *Saguinus oedipus geoffroyi.* The findings were interpreted as evidence of monozygous twinning. The assumption that monovulation was the primitive condition in primates led Hamlett and Wislocki (1939, p. 94) to surmise that callitrichids may "not represent a step in the evolution from litter production to single embryo, but that the marmosets may have already passed through the monovular condition which is still found in all other Primates and may have evolved a regular process of fraternal twinning as a specialization superimposed upon the typical Primate condition."

Subsequent examination of 19 pregnant uteri of cotton-top tamarins, enabled Wislocki (1939) to confirm Hill's conclusions regarding the biovular origin of twins in callitrichids and to accept this condition as natural. He (1939, p. 468) persisted, however, in the belief that callitrichids represent "a return from a monovulatory state," because of his mistaken assumption that all primates, lemurs included, "bear but a single young." Wislocki also pointed to a second method of implantation in *Saguinus oedipus geoffroyi* whereby the blastocysts lie side by side on the same wall of the uterus, their embryonic poles pointing in the same direction. Formation of a single cavity and chorion is the same in both methods. In addition, Wislocki (1939) demonstrated the normal anastomosis of embryonic vessels without freemartin effects in the developing animals.

Fusion of the chorial membrane and formation of a single cavity was observed in a twin blastocyst of the golden lion-tamarin by Benirschke and Layton (1971). They also reported that the normal and consistent characteristic of chorionic fusion and the attendant blood chimerism appeared to be peculiar to callitrichids.

Jollie (1973) determined that an early gestational stage, the labyrinthine placental membrane of the cotton-top tamarin, *Saguinus oedipus oedipus,* is hemodichorial, but in the near term stage it has changed to hemomonochorial. Although several fine differences at the ultrastructural level were noted, the tamarin placenta appears to be remarkably like that of higher primates including man. Hemodynamically, however, Jollie (1973, p. 311) observes, the tamarin placenta is quite different. "Whereas the architectural pattern of the placenta of higher forms is villous and blood flow is by spurts into the intervillous sinuses . . . the placenta of the marmoset, like that both of other platyrrhine monkeys [*e.g., Alouatta, Ateles*] which have been examined and of several lower vertebrate orders, is labyrinthine, a pattern in which maternal blood flow is more steady and by countercurrent mechanisms."

Attachment of the umbilical cords of twin fetuses of *Saguinus nigricollis nigricollis* to separate discoidal placentae in close anastomosis was reported by Rabb and Rowell (1960).

Poswillo, Hamilton, and Sopher (1972) note that in *Callithrix jacchus* usually one embryo is attached to each of two placental disks. "When triplets are present two embryos and their membranes are attached to one placental disk and one to the other." They add that "the only two singletons observed in more than 100 hysterotomy specimens were attached to one placental disk, but two placental disks were present and connected by large vascular anastomoses. The anastomes are present between the placental disks when both twins and triplets are born."

Leutenegger (1974, p. 290) has added an odd twist to the preconceived if not contrived notion of regressive callitrichid evolution with the speculation that

> If during callithricid [*sic*] evolution adult body size was smaller or the same as that of the living representatives, then multiple births represent the retention of a primitive mammalian character. In other words, a monovular condition never existed. However, this interpretation would not account for the development of those features associated with reproduction, in which the callithricids followed the anthropoid pattern. The only possible interpretation which accounts for both the anthropoid characters and the twinning is based on the concept of evolutionary miniaturization (= evolutionary decrease in adult body size). It is highly likely that early in callithricid evolution a monovular condition had been developed in conjunction with the development of a unicornuate uterus, the reduction in the number of nipples, etc., as general anthropoid characters, but that a trend toward dwarfing resulting in a relatively larger fetal size necessitated the secondary development of twinning. This interpretation is in accordance with Hoffstetter's [1969] findings on fossils that the extreme smallness of the callithricids can be explained best as the result of a trend toward dwarfism.

The cited Hoffstetter's (1969, p. 4) "findings on fossils" are to the effect that callitrichid size is too small, the organization too primitive to allow for descent from the Oligocene *Branisella* or any other previously appointed ancestral type. Hence, following Hoffstetter's reasoning, callitrichids must have evolved regressively from a larger and generally more advanced ancestor. The rationale in Leutenneger's explanation, that when a singleton becomes too large for viable production it is replaced by twins, is too complex to follow and, besides, contradicts his thesis of "miniaturization." In all logic, either the single fetus should become smaller, thus initiating the "miniaturization" process, or the birth canal should become larger. Historically, however, the number of fetuses in a birth tends to become smaller and the individual fetus larger, whereas the adults respond by selective increases in size.

Like Leutenneger, S. H. Hampton (1975), who described implantation in *Saguinus oedipus,* viewed twinning as "the result of specialization rather than a primitive character." She notes that callitrichids are "the only group with a simplex uterus which normally bears more than one young." She adds that "crowding of the simplex uterus of the marmoset is possibly related to the occurrence of placental vascular anastomoses." "It is interesting," she concludes, "that the bidiscoidal placenta is retained even though the number of young is increased." The size of the litter, it seems to me, is usually determined by the number of viable eggs normally produced in an estral period and the number of blastulae that normally implant. Uterine type, on the other hand, is no reliable indicator of the number of fetuses the organ may support. The bicornuate type, for example, occurs among uniparous and pluriparous strepsirhines, the uniparous tarsier and horse, and the pluriparous cat. Controlling factors and mechanisms of reproduction are highly variable (cf. Amoroso, 1969; Martin, 1969) and in all likelihood, specializations of the callitrichid reproductive system evolved independently of other platyrrhine groups. If a reproductive trend is evident among callitrichids, it is toward reduction in litter size as in mammals generally. As a rule, the trend is correlated with increase in body size. Embryonic abortion (cf. Hampton 1975, p. 112, fig. 18) not only indicates the trend but also accounts for many, if not most reductions in number of young produced at a birth among callitrichids.

Nothing in the callitrichid placenta supports the belief in regressive evolution. As results of their studies of *Saguinus fuscicollis* and *S. oedipus,* Wynn, Richards, and Harris (1975, p. 63) conclude that with respect to the labyrinthine rather than free villous condition of their placenta, callitrichids are relatively primitive. They add (1975, p. 68) that "in its paucity of interstitial connective tissue and in the prominent basal lamina that in places appears to be shared by endothelium and trophoblast, the placenta of the marmoset [that is the tamarin, *Saguinus*] resembles the hypothetical primitive endotheliochorial labyrinth of the carnivores. With respect to the fetal membranes, the retention to term of a large vesicular yolk sac may be regarded as another relatively primitive feature."

Duration of Gestation

The duration of gestation averages between 130 and 150 days, average between 140 and 145 days in *Cebuella, Saguinus oedipus* and *Callithrix jacchus,* and about 133 days in *Leontopithecus* (table 50). It is not possible with present data to arrive at a reasonable mean duration for other callitrichids. The period of gestation in *Callimico* is estimated at about 150 days.

Table 50. Duration of Gestation, Range of Estimates for Captive Callitrichids

Species	*Days*
Leontopithecus rosalia	132–37
Cebuella pygmaea	137–42
Callithrix jacchus	117–73
Saguinus fuscicollis illigeri	158 ± 12 (178 births)
Saguinus midas niger	140–68
Saguinus oedipus	122–53

NOTE: See separate species accounts for sample sizes and bases for estimates.

Litters

Fraternal twins are usually produced at a birth, but up to 35% of births recorded in captivity are singletons. Many, if not most or possibly all, are survivors of dizygotic pregnancies in which one twin is aborted or resorbed at an early stage of development. A small proportion of triplets and rarely quadruplets and quintuplets are also born in captivity (table 51).

The largest recorded litters, with an average of 2.2 young, are produced by the common marmoset. (*Callithrix jacchus jacchus*), because of a high ratio of triplet births and a low rate of singleton births. Litters of golden lion-tamarins (*Leontopithecus rosalia rosalia*) are also large, average 2.0, but the sample size is small. In this as well as the case of *Callithrix j. jacchus,* average litter size is calculated from a compilation of records from diverse sources. The figures are not strictly comparable to, but perhaps are more representative than the means based on the continuous productivity of a single breeding colony. Cotton-top tamarins (*Saguinus oedipus geoffroyi*) produced the smallest recorded litters with an average of 1.7 young, and those of pygmy marmosets (*Cebuella pygmaea*), averaging 1.8 young, are intermediate.

In 19 uteri of wild-shot *Saguinus oedipus geoffroyi,* Wislocki (1939, p. 448) found twins exclusively, or 2 per pregnancy including some degenerate or nonviable fetuses. Average litter size for the same pregnancies would certainly be less than 2.

Productivity

Females become sexually mature at 18 months, but successful breeding is expected after the 30th month. The few observations made in the field indicate that young, usually twins, are produced once a year. In laboratory colonies, a single female may produce 1 to 3, rarely 4, young at a birth 1 to 3 times in the same calendar year. A pair of wild-born captive *Callithrix jacchus jacchus* maintained by Lucas, Hume, and Henderson Smith (1937, p. 206) delivered 12 litters, the first on 28 December 1927, the last on 19 November 1934. Three litters arrived in 1932. Another female of the same species, observed by Rothe (1974*a*), produced 11 litters between 1968 when purchased and February 1973, and a second female of the same colony delivered 10 within the same period.

Wolfe, Ogden, Deinhardt, Fisher, and Deinhardt (1972, p. 145) note that 7 of 20 pairs of white-mouth tamarins (*Saguinus nigricollis* group) kept together for 6 to 7 years delivered 10 or more times each. In 1970, half the females of about 100 pairs delivered twice, and 5 delivered 3 times. Ulmer (1961, p. 253) reported 6 deliveries by a golden lion-tamarin, *Leontopithecus rosalia rosalia,* from 8 August 1957 to 20 August 1960 and Hagler (1975) lists 11 births produced from 10 March 1966 to 19 December 1972 by a wild-caught pair. The last 3 litters, apparently full term, were born in 1972. More information on these and other births is given in the species accounts.

In caged groups of adult males and females, reproduction is usually seen only in the dominant female. Apparently, the presence of an alpha female inhibits reproduction in inferior females, including adult daughters, that may have copulated with the dominant male. Once separated from the dominant female, subordinate females become pregnant after mating.

Table 51. Litter Sizes of Callitrichids Born in Captivity

Source	*Name*	*Number of Litters*	*Young Total*	*Percentage Number of Young per Litter* 1	2	3	4	*Average Number of Young per Litter*
A	*Cebuella pygmaea*	19	34	15%	76%	9%	—	1.8
B	*Callithrix jacchus*	144	288	8%	67%	25%	—	2.0
C	*Callithrix jacchus*	56	121	6%	58%	30%	7%	2.2
D	*Saguinus o. oedipus*	137	235	19%	73%	18%	—	1.7
E	*Saguinus o. oedipus*	31	54	15%	85%	—	—	1.74
F	*Saguinus o. oedipus*[1]	14	27	14.3%	78.6%	7.1%	—	2.0
F	*Saguinus n. nigricollis*[1]	42	79	14.3%	83.3%	2.4%	—	1.9
F	*Saguinus f. fuscicollis*[1]	151	274	11%	85%	3%	—	1.8
G	*Leontopithecus r. rosalia*	28	56	2%	93%	5%	—	2.0

SOURCES:
A—In text, table 57, p. 468.
B—J. K. Hampton, Hampton, and Levy (1971, p. 528).
C—In text, table 61, p. 533.
D—In text, table 95, p. 774.
E—Cooper 1964–68, in text, p. 774.
F—Wolfe, Ogden, Deinhardt, Fisher, and Deinhardt (1972).
G—In text, table 106, p. 839.
[1] Includes stillborn, but not aborted, individuals.

Table 52. Birth Time of Callitrichids and Callimicos

Species	*Deliveries and Time*	*Source*
Cebuella pygmaea	7 nocturnal	Christen (1968)
Cebuella pygmaea	3 early morning	Cooper (1964; 1965)
Callithrix jacchus jacchus	25 nocturnal	Lucas et al. (1927; 1937)
Callithrix jacchus jacchus	1 nocturnal, 1 diurnal	Chartin and Petter (1960)
Callithrix jacchus jacchus	1 nocturnal	Grüner and Krause (1963)
Callithrix jacchus jacchus	16 nocturnal	Epple (1970*a*)
Callithrix jacchus jacchus	21 nocturnal, 1 diurnal (abnormal)	Rothe (1973*b*)
Callithrix jacchus jacchus	2 nocturnal	Rothe (1974*a*)
Saguinus nigricollis group	95 "usually" night or early morning	Wolfe, Ogden, Deinhardt, Fisher, and Deinhardt (1972)
Saguinus imperator	1 nocturnal	Crandall (1964)
Saguinus oedipus (including *geoffroyi*)	Of hundreds recorded by various authors, only 2 occurred during daylight	Epple (1970*a*)
Leontopithecus rosalia rosalia	No records	
Callimico goeldii	12 presumably nocturnal	Lorenz and Heinemann 1967; Heinemann 1970; below, p. 899

Hour of Birth

Records of primate births compiled by Jolly (1972) suggest that most primate young are delivered at night or during normal sleeping hours according to habits of the species, or perhaps the individual. Records compiled here (table 52) indicate that callitrichids and *Callimico* are normally born at night.

Visible behavior of pregnant callitrichids living in captivity usually remains unchanged from conception to a few hours before paturition. The probability is, therefore, that births can occur at any time, with approximately one-half of them during daylight hours. No explanation is available for the fact that the preponderance of mammalian births and the virtual totality of callitrichid births occur during normal sleeping hours. The advantages, however, are clear. The parous mother is sheltered and relaxed and, in the case of social animals, amidst a group alert to danger but not awake to a birth where bungling assistance from group members is unwanted.

Sex Ratios

Sex ratios in callitrichid litters produced in captivity are shown in table 53. Deviation from the expected sex ratio of 1:1 results from a small deficit of females. A minuscule part of the deviation may also be attributed to error in sexing and recording, or to a higher death rate among females than males. It has been suggested (Wolfe, Ogden, Deinhardt, Fisher, and Deinhardt 1972, p. 149) that a small percentage of twins are monozygotic. This is probable and might account for some short-term skewing of sex ratios among twins but not among singletons or triplets.

Hybridization

Successful crosses and backcrosses between representatives of species and geographically continuous and disjunct subspecies of callitrichids have been produced in zoos, laboratories, and private homes. Nineteen are listed

Table 53. Sex Ratios in Litters of Callitrichidae

Source	*Name*	*Number of Litters*	*Single* ♂ ♀	*Twins* ♂♂ : ♀♀ : ♂♀	*Triplets* ♂♂♂ : ♂♂♀ : ♂♀♀ : ♀♀♀
A	*Saguinus* spp.[1]	290	—	1:1:1.7	—
B	*Saguinus fuscicollis*	101	—	1:0.6:1.7	—
C	*Callithrix jacchus*	147	1:0.7	1:1:1.8	1:1.2:1.4:0.8
	Expected		1:1	1:1:2	1:1:1:1

SOURCES:
A—Wolfe, Ogden, Deinhardt, Fisher, and Deinhardt (1972, p. 149).
B—Gengozian (1971, p. 927).
C—In text, p. 544.

[1] Includes mostly *Saguinus fuscicollis*, many *S. nigricollis*, hybrids between the two species, and a small number of *S. oedipus oedipus*.

here, including all recorded in literature. The form of scientific name used in listing hybrids is consistent with the adopted classification but not necessarily with the name used in the original reference source. This method avoids ambiguities, besides placing the crosses in proper taxonomic perspective. More detailed descriptions of the hybrids are given in the species accounts under either parental name.

Callithrix jacchus jacchus ♂ × *Callithrix jacchus penicillata* ♀ (Osman Hill 1957, p. 296, footnote). Two month-old young said to be more nearly like father, a member of the more advanced race. Color and pelage in juvenal *C. jacchus* is always distinct from and more primitive than that of adult (cf. fig. IX.21).

Callithrix jacchus jacchus ♀ × *C. j. penicillatus* ♂ (Mallinson 1971, p. 8). Preauricular tufts black, but form more nearly as in *jacchus.*

Callithrix jacchus penicillata × *C. j. jacchus* (J. K. Hampton, Jr., Hampton, and Levy 1971, p. 528, footnote).

Callithrix jacchus geoffroyi ♀ × *C. j. jacchus* ♂ (Coimbra-Filho 1970*c*). Gave birth to two litters of twins, one of triplets; hybrids described as intermediate in color between comparably aged individuals of the parental races.

(*Callithrix j. jacchus* × *C. j. geoffroyi*) ♂ × *Callithrix jacchus penicillata* ♀ (Coimbra-Filho 1971).

(*Callithrix j. jacchus* × *C. j. geoffroyi*) ♂ × *Callithrix j. penicillata* ♀ (Coimbra-Filho 1973).

(*Callithrix jacchus penicillata* × *Callithrix jacchus jacchus*) × (*Callithrix jacchus penicillata* × *Callithrix jacchus jacchus*). Aborted, unsexed; (Mallinson 1971, pers. comm.).

Callithrix jacchus flaviceps ♂ × *Callithrix jacchus geoffroyi* ♀ (A. Ruschi, in Coimbra-Filho 1973).

Callithrix jacchus jacchus × *Callithrix argentata argentata* (English 1932, p. 1079).

Callithrix jacchus jacchus ♀ × *Callithrix argentata argentata* ♂ (Osman Hill 1961, p. 321). The 7-month-old male hybrid was described from color transparencies and said to be most nearly like father, but more hairy, face pigmented, ears slightly furred, circumaural tufts absent, loins faintly banded; generally more primitive than father but some parts more primitive than those of like-aged juvenal of maternal species; parental species most widely separated of genus.

Saguinus nigricollis nigricollis ♀ × *Saguinus fuscicollis lagonotus* ♂ (Primate Research Colony, Zoological Society of San Diego, personal observation, 1966). Living female, about 8 weeks old.

Saguinus fuscicollis illigeri ♀ × *Saguinus fuscicollis lagonotus* ♂ (Primate Research Colony, Zoological Society of San Diego, personal observation, 1966). Living young.

Saguinus fuscicollis illigeri ♀ × *S. f. lagonotus* ♂ (Gengozian 1969, p. 338).

Saguinus fuscicollis leucogenys ♀ × *Saguinus f. lagonotus* ♂ (Roth 1960, p. 166).

Saguinus fuscicollis illigeri ♀ × *S. nigricollis nigricollis* ♂ (Gengozian 1969, p. 359).

Saguinus fuscicollis lagonotus ♀ × *Saguinus nigricollis nigricollis* ♂ (Primate Research Colony, Zoological Society of San Diego, personal observation, 1966). Living male about 8 weeks old.

Saguinus imperator ♀ × *Saguinus mystax mystax* (Cruz Lima 1945, p. 209). Two near-term fetuses of accidentally killed mother; parental species most distantly related members of *S. mystax* group.

Saguinus midas midas ♀ × *Saguinus bicolor bicolor* ♂ (Immendorf 1961, p. 145). Living male hybrid as figured by Immendorf appears to be more nearly like mother, who represents the more primitive species; parental species distantly related but possibly sympatric.

Saguinus midas midas ♀ × (*Saguinus midas midas* × *Saguinus bicolor bicolor*) ♂ (Hick 1961, *Fr. Kölner Zoo* 4(3):63, fig. of father).

Saguinus midas midas ♀ × *Saguinus oedipus oedipus* ♂ (Reed 1965, p. 113, pl. 3). Living male and female twins; female died half grown, male when fully adult, both unlike parents; coloration dominantly agouti, coat pattern primitive; parental species most distantly related of genus and most widely separated geographically.

Saguinus oedipus geoffroyi ♀ × *S. o. oedipus* ♂ (Epple 1970*a*, p. 66).

The salient features of callitrichid cross-matings known to date follow.

1. Hybridization has occurred between captive representatives of geographically disjunct subspecies and species of the same genus. Only *Callithrix* (3 species) and *Saguinus* (10 species), are polytypic. Representatives of these genera and those of the monotypic *Cebuella, Leontopithecus,* and the callimiconid *Callimico* have been caged together but courtship has not been observed and hybrids are unknown. The diploid number of chromosomes in *Cebuella* and *Callithrix argentata* is 44, in *Callithrix jacchus* and *Saguinus* 46, and in *Callimico* 48.

2. Intraspecific hybrids, or crosses between geographically disjunct subspecies, are intermediate in color. No characters other than color distinguish intraspecific categories.

3. Interspecific hybrids differ from parents in superficial characters only and according to the degree of relationship between the parents.

a. Closely related species crosses such as *Saguinus fuscicollis* × *S. nigricollis* are metachromically intermediate.

b. Distantly related species crosses such as *Saguinus midas* × *S. bicolor,* or *Callithrix jacchus* × *C. argentata,* are slightly more primitive than either or both parents but usually more nearly resemble the more primitive parent.

c. Most distantly related species crosses such as *Saguinus midas* × *S. oedipus* are phenotypically more primitive or generalized than both parents; juvenals may resemble juvenals of the more primitive parental species but adults resemble neither parental species.

Hybrids of parents representing widely separated and specialized species seem atavistic. The phenotype of *Saguinus midas midas* × *S. oedipus oedipus* is that of a generalized tamarin from which each of the parental species groups can be derived. The effect of hybridization in this case is reassertion of the primitive agouti pattern over most of the body and return to a comparatively primitive density of epidermal pigmentation. The pelage pattern is also restored to an ancestral or generalized

Table 54. Proportional Weights and Size of Maternal and Newborn Callitrichids and *Callimico*

Genus	*Weight* $\frac{N^1}{A}$	*Head and Body Length* $\frac{N}{A}$	*Tail Length* $\frac{N}{A}$	*T:H & B* $\frac{N}{A}$
Cebuella	$\frac{15}{125} = 12\%$	$\frac{65}{136} = 48\%$	$\frac{90}{202} = 44\%$	$\frac{1.38}{1.48} = 93\%$
Callithrix	$\frac{30}{316} = 9\%$	$\frac{85}{219} = 39\%$	$\frac{90}{332} = 27\%$	$\frac{1.05}{1.52} = 69\%$
Saguinus	$\frac{43}{450} = 9\%$	$\frac{100}{235} = 42\%$	$\frac{130}{364} = 36\%$	$\frac{1.30}{1.55} = 84\%$
Leontopithecus	$\frac{57}{583} = 10\%$	$\frac{120}{261} = 46\%$	$\frac{122}{370} = 33\%$	$\frac{1.01}{1.42} = 71\%$
Callimico	$\frac{60}{481} = 12\%$	$\frac{110}{224} = 49\%$	$\frac{100}{302} = 33\%$	$\frac{.91}{1.35} = 67\%$

SOURCE: Figures are based on or extrapolated from data in the "Growth and Development" sections of the species accounts in text.
[1] N = neonate; A = average adult.

condition from which the patterned hypertrichy and hypotrichy of the parental species and other tamarins can be derived. External ears are intermediate and primitive in size and form as compared with the reduced pinna of *oedipus* and the extremely large pinna of *midas*. Steiner (1966) observed regressions of the same order in hybrid birds of different species of Spermestidae. In cases where the cross between highly specialized and widely divergent species approximates the ancestral type of the genus, it can be assumed that evolution of the parental species may have been rapid, facile, and little affected by environmental selective pressures.

Growth and Development

Young are born with distinctive juvenal pelage and color patterns, except *Cebuella pygmaea*. Eyes open at birth as a rule, but not later than third day.

Weight of newborn is about 10% (± 2%) of mean adult weight; combined head and body length of newborn between 39% and 50% of adult length; tail about 27% to 44% of adult tail length. Proportion of tail length to combined head and body length is most nearly like adult proportions in *Cebuella pygmaea* (93%), least in *Callithrix* (69%); twins are born smaller than singletons, and triplets are smallest, but size differences disappear by maturity.

Duration of maternal care and nursing lasts from about 1 month to 3 months in captivity. Paternal care extends the period of infantile dependence about 1 month more. Young are completely independent of parental care at 3 to 6 months of age, sexually mature at 12–18 months, and fully mature physically at 18–24 months of age.

The figures given here and in tables 54 and 55 are based on information contained in the "Growth and Development" sections of the species accounts in text. The data is spotty and no clear pattern of variation emerges except that *Cebuella*, the smallest platyrrhine, is most precocious developmentally and least differentiated in external appearance from the adult type. In these respects *Cebuella* conforms more nearly than other callitrichids to a concept of the primitive organization of newborn and young among higher primates.

Behavior

Habitat

Callitrichids are tropical-zone arboreal animals equally successful in evergreen lowland rain forests, humid and xerophytic semideciduous forests, and dry scrub or *caatinga*. They are abundant in high forests of the more humid parts of their range but prefer the thick second growths for the exuberant successions of food plants and animal prey, thick cover, and tortuous escapeways impenetrable or intransitable to most of their larger enemies. Callitrichids are said to prefer forest edge, particularly

Table 55. Chronology of Development of Callitrichids and *Callimico*

Genus	*Gestation Duration (mean days)*	*Weaned (days)*	*Deciduous Teeth Complete (weeks)*	*Permanent Teeth Complete (weeks)*	*Sexual Organs Fully Developed (months)*	*Sexual Maturity and Full Growth*
Cebuella	138	27–90	—	—	12	18
Callithrix	137	52–85	6	25	14	18
Saguinus	140	40–70	8	41	18	>24
Leontopithecus	133	49–63	—	—	18	>24
Callimico	150	70	—	—	—	—

SOURCE: Figures are based on or extrapolated from data in the "Growth and Development" sections of the species accounts in text.

on river banks, but this would apply to clearings as well. It is certain that a greater variety and number of animals can be seen more readily and frequently on the forest edge by travelers and hunters. Where not persecuted, they adjust to wooded parts around human habitations, villages, and even large towns.

Callitrichids generally avoid palm, bamboo, and other predominantly monocotyledonous stands. They rarely descend to the ground and they find their limits of dispersal along the borders of subtropical zone forests in southeastern South America.

Hollow trees or tangled vines are used for sleeping.

Territoriality

Callitrichid social units are characteristically territorial. Trailways and resting and sleeping sites are marked and defended from other units of the species. Two or more family units, however, may cross trails and feed together on the same fruiting trees.

The size of a territory is controlled by the available resources. The area may expand or contract, and its boundaries may shift. It may even disappear as the result of a catastrophe. In tall, uninterrupted but internally variable forest, the territory of a group may measure as much as 1 km in greatest diameter. In regions with highly circumscribed habitats and resources as in cultivated or urbanized areas, the territory may be smaller than a hectare, or 100 m square.

Social Structure

The social unit is the family, normally consisting of 2 to 6 individuals. The smallest unit consists of adult male and pregnant or parous female. The larger units include one or two young of the last litter and one or two of the previous litter. The first born usually leave the unit before the second born mature. One adult female is the rule but two adult males in a family group is common. The social organization is essentially matriarchal, the dominant female being monogamous but sometimes polyandrous.

Actual numbers of individuals reported seen together in the wild vary from 2 up to 12 (*Leontopithecus*), 20 (*Cebuella, Saguinus midas*), or 40 (*Callithrix jacchus*). The reports are based on actual counts, sight estimates, or faint recollections. Figures based on actual counts are always smaller, often because the fewer individuals seen, the easier it is to count them.

In captivity, dominant males tolerate subordinate males irrespective of age. In the absence of mature males, dominant females tolerate subordinate females. In the company of adult males, however, caged females may fight, often until only one survives.

Circadian Rhythm

Callitrichids are strictly diurnal. Their daily activity, mostly foraging, begins shortly after sunrise. Grooming and sunbathing are usually performed during midday but other activities also continue during the heat of the day when most other sylvan warm-blooded vertebrates are resting. The majority of callitrichid species retire for the day well before sundown and fall into deep sleep from which they are not easily roused.

Observations of the daily cycle in the wild indicate a 10-hour active day followed by a 14-hour sleep period for *Callithrix* and *Saguinus*, and a 12–12 hourly cycle for *Leontopithecus*.

Parental Care

Both parents rear their offspring; the mother suckles and cleans the young until it is weaned, the father carries and cares for the young at all other times, often from birth, until they can fend for themselves.

Food

Callitrichids are among the most omnivorous or opportunistic feeders of living primates. Their normal diet consists of large amounts of fruit, the seeds usually being rejected, some leaves, buds, blossoms, green shoots, tree sap, and gums chewed from the bark or twigs (see below), and a high percentage of insects and small vertebrates, including eggs. The animals may gorge themselves on vegetable matter alone, or on crickets, a mouse, bird, lizard, frog, or various combinations of anything edible. As predators, callitrichids are bold, aggressive, and adept at killing prey by piercing the head with a swift stab of their long, sharp canines.

The foods consumed by adult callitrichids in captivity indicate high daily average requirements of calories, protein, and calcium (cf. Clark 1974) and the need for vitamin D_3 for avoidance of osteomalacia.

Survival of a population in the wild depends on close synchronization between cyclical nutritional requirements for young and old and the seasonal changes in the quality and quantity of available food.

Sap Feeding

Callitrichids, like many other arboreal animals including birds and insects, relish the sweet sap or gum produced by trees. They will gnaw on the bark, strip it or bite off twigs and chew on them. Apparently the sap and exudates supply a nutritional requirement not always available in other food. Gum feeding has been reported for *Cebuella* by Charles-Dominique (1971) and observed by Kinzey, Rosenberger, and Ramirez (1975). It was also seen in *Callithrix* by Guenther (1931), Coimbra-Filho (1971; 1972*b*), and Clark (1974) and in *Saguinus* by Hladik and Hladik (1969). Many reports have been published of bark and pith being eaten by apes and catarrhine monkeys. Petter and Peyreiras (1970) report observation of the Malagasy aye-aye (*Daubentonia*) feeding on gum produced by trees of the genus *Hintsyma*. Gum feeding by *Galago minutus* (= *demidovii*), *Euoticus elegantulus*, and *Perodicticus potto* is reported by Charles-Dominique (1971). Bark scraping, gnawing, and enlargement of openings with the teeth described by Charles-Dominique is similar to the method observed in marmosets by Coimbra-Filho. Additional gum eaters mentioned by Charles Dominique (1971; 197) are the lemurids *Microcebus murinus* and *Phaner furcifer* and the didelphid (Marsupialia) *Philander*.

During the course of my own fieldwork in the Cordillera Occidental in Antioquia, Colombia, I saw Pucheran's squirrel, *Sciurus pucherani*, and the larger *Sciurus granatensis* feeding on the sweet resin of the *roble* (oak, *Quercus humboldti*). The larger squirrel always drove off the smaller when the latter approached to feed at the same place. Woodpeckers also visited the tree and perhaps fed on the resin welling from their drillings. The squirrels may have also licked the sap that continued to seep into the holes made by the birds. Sweet-toothed kinkajous (*Potos*) and olingos (*Bassaricyon*) visited the same trees during the night.

Drink

Water accumulated on leaves, in flower cups, or in hollows is lapped; dew and moisture from a hand previously dipped in water are licked. Callitrichids do not suck up liquids or hold vessels to the mouth as do most cebids and catarrhines. The faculty of suckling, a specialization of the young, disappears soon after weaning.

Sleep

In captivity sleeping adults are usually crouched in a squatting position with head against chest, belly, or even the perch. On a slender perch the feet grip the support while haunches and the lax or coiled tail hang free as counterweights. On a broad support, the feet rest flat, the haunches remain raised but the tail is either coiled and drawn between the legs to help support the body or is thrown over the head or shoulders, apparently to conserve heat and shield the head from mosquitos. Dependent young cling to the back of one of the parents, usually the father.

Members of a pair or family group usually sleep huddled together. Sleep is profound and lasts from sundown or dusk to sunrise.

Repose

Callitrichids relax during the heat of the day by sprawling lengthwise along a branch, their limbs and tail hanging free for maximum cooling. *Leontopithecus* also favors sitting on its haunches with arms extended outward and fingers loosely gripping a support, legs outstretched and tail hanging limply.

Vocalization

Sounds emitted by callitrichids are high pitched and vary in tone from a weak, barely perceptible monosyllabic hiss or chirp to loud shrill whistles and screeches, and from soft twitters to far-reaching trills and flute- or songbirdlike warblings of great intricacy. Epple (1968, p. 38) regards the adult calls as "relatively stereotyped while those of young [*Callithrix jacchus jacchus*] show greater variability." The calls of *Callimico* appeared to be more complicated and advanced.

Vocal communication between individuals is commonly conducted in sounds with frequencies above the range of human hearing. Mobbing "tsik" calls of excited adult *Callithrix jacchus jacchus* recorded by Epple (1968, p. 11) reached frequencies up to 80,000 cycles. The same frequencies for similar calls were obtained for the golden lion-tamarin, *Leontopithecus rosalia rosalia,* and frequencies above 60,000 were recorded for the cotton-top tamarin, *Saguinus oedipus oedipus.* The majority of callitrichid calls recorded by Epple, however, reached frequencies between 5,000 and 15,000 cycles.

Tembrock (1963, p. 754) places the principal sound frequencies of callitrichids and *Callimico* investigated by him as shown in the accompanying list.

Name	*Principal Frequencies*
Callithrix jacchus jacchus	2,650–4,304; 3,616
Saguinus oedipus oedipus	1,770–4,300
Saguinus oedipus geoffroyi	2,560–3,535; 6,080–8,625
Leontopithecus rosalia rosalia	3,040–3,535
Callimico goeldii	8,608–10,240

The data were obtained from recordings of one or a few specimens. The frequencies were determined with a sound spectrometer with an upper frequency limit of about 10–14 kc/s, and which filters out 36 quarter octaves (from 40 to 17,216 c/s). The numbers in the list are mean values of the filter ranges.

The threshold of auditory sensitivity of *Callithrix jacchus jacchus* measured on both ears by Wever and Vernon (1961, p. 739) was in the frequency range of 25,000–37,000 cycles. The cochlear potential measured on one ear, they found, exceeds 100,000 cycles.

Calls of most callitrichid species are similar in sound, range, and expression. Trills uttered by *Callithrix humeralifer* and *C. argentata* are comparatively weak and sound somewhat rasping or cricketlike. They are made with open mouth, the vibrato formed by the rapidly moving tongue. Hairy-face tamarins also trill with mouth open, but the vibrato is produced by rapid movements of the lower jaw. The same appears to be true of *Cebuella.* In the bare-face tamarin, *Saguinus oedipus,* the vibrato is controlled in the larynx. *Callithrix jacchus* and *Saguinus midas niger* have not been heard to trill. So-called mobbing cries, fear and anger cries, and warning signals are expressed in about the same way by all callitrichids. A monosyllabic close contact call used by callitrichids in the security of the group is uttered with mouth nearly or entirely closed. More detailed descriptions and comparisons of callitrichid vocalizations are given in the species accounts.

Marking

Use of olfactory signals or pheromones is highly developed among callitrichids. Scent glands of the interramal, gular, sternal, abdominal, and inguinal regions mark runway branches; circumgenital glands mark selected objects, including mates; ulnar-carpal glands leave their odor on anything brushed by the arms; and all glands imprint the offspring with the odor of parents, family group, and race. Callitrichids frequently use their urine or saliva mixed with scent gland secretions for self-anointment or deposit in holes bitten into the bark of frequented trees.

Marking is routine for identification of self and offspring and assertion of social status, sexual readiness, and territorial claims. It is used to invite or repel and to countersign the odors of others.

Tail Coiling

The habit of rolling the entire tail into a tight coil is seen in *Callithrix* and *Saguinus* but not in *Cebuella* or *Leontopithecus.* Callitrichid tail coiling is a specialization unrelated to the power grip coiling of prehensile tails. The coiled callitrichid tail drawn between the legs acts as an accessory support in sitting or as a balancing organ. When the need arises coiling is used to abbreviate the tail's radius of exposure. Other uses are discussed in the species accounts.

Genital Presentation

Female callitrichids present to males to signal sexual receptivity and stimulate the males to copulate. Males present to males to threaten or to enforce social dominance. The dominant male also presents to strangers and potential enemies as a sign of aggression. Both sexes of the species of *Cebuella* and *Callithrix* show the tumescent genitalia from behind. In the case of males, only the scrotum with descended testes is exposed. Within moments of presentation the testes are retracted and the show is over. *Saguinus, Leontopithecus,* and *Callimico* have not been observed presenting from the rear.

The male cotton-top tamarin, *Saguinus oedipus oedipus,* has not been observed presenting in the usual manner. The animal assumes a bipedal posture instead, with entire ventral surface and the imposing mane exposed to full view.

Back Arching

Catlike arching of the back with stiff-legged walking is used by males as a defense threat or precopulatory act by *Cebuella, Callithrix,* and *Leontopithecus,* but not by *Saguinus. Callimico* and *Callicebus* (Mason 1971, p. 118) also display back arching.

Tonguing and Lip Smacking

Rhythmic and usually rapid protrusion and retraction of the tongue is displayed in sexual and social contact by all callitrichids, and in the same or other forms by almost all other primates. Lip smacking is also widely practiced, but its significance varies among the different species.

Handedness

Experiments conducted by Stellar (1960) and Rothe (1973*a*) on *Callithrix jacchus* and by Christen (1974) on *Cebuella pygmaea* and *Saguinus midas* indicate that an individual may be mainly right-handed, left-handed, or ambidextrous. The tests were too limited in scope to reveal the real proportion of each hand type among callitrichids. Perhaps, as suggested by Rothe (1973*a*) in the case of *Callithrix jacchus* alone, all callitrichids are basically ambidextrous.

Enemies

Man, birds of prey, small spotted cats, arboreal mustelids, and snakes are principal enemies, but fear of these and other animals or inanimate objects is acquired.

Defense

Defense against predators is a function of the social organization. The lone callitrichid is virtually defenseless against natural enemies. The individual with its limited binocular visual field cooperates with other troop members for sighting potential enemies and sounding alerts.

Aggressive displays or advances made by possible enemies are often met with confrontation, menacing gestures, or grimaces on the part of the troop leader while subordinates engage in distractive flight and shrill vocalizations. Subordinates may also support the leader with attack threats. Flight is, of course, the principal defense of the troop against superior and determined foes.

Individual acts of intimidation in territorial defense or confrontations with rivals include swaying, rocking, tusk baring, mane raising, stiff-legged jumping, back arching, genital presentation, rasping sounds, and hand drumming. Droppings by individuals or troop members on terrestrial intruders can be interpreted as acts of territorial defense or involuntary manifestations of fear, depending on circumstances.

Locomotion

Callitrichids are quadrupedal, plantigrade branch runners and springers, and hand-over-hand, foot-over-foot climbers. Fingers and toes aid locomotion by grasping, the claws by clinging. Callitrichids do not ordinarily descend to the ground, but their terrestrial locomotion is similar to their branch running, bounding, and springing. Descent from a tree is head first, squirrel fashion, with claws digging into bark for support. All callitrichids swim dog fashion with ease.

Callitrichids are not typical springers as compared with ricochetal marsupials, insectivores, rodents, or even certain prosimians. Their size, however, favors this locomotor form in a habitat used in common with larger monkeys. Because of their small size and light weight callitrichids will spring to a perch that larger monkeys can reach by standing, walking, or climbing. Springing, often vertically, is also used by callitrichids in predation or defense in situations that a larger monkey would only regard with curiosity, walk away from, or confront.

Locomotor patterns of comparably small nocturnal or crepuscular prosimians are very different and far advanced beyond the primitive patterns followed by callitrichids. Prosimians may well have attained something like their present grade of locomotor specialization before higher monkeys appeared on the scene.

Ecological Equivalents

Tree squirrels evolved into the same diurnal habitat, size, physical and locomotory forms, food and prey-predator niches as callitrichids where the latter were absent. With their subsequent invasion of callitrichid territory, squirrels evidently surrendered nothing of their ecological preferences, most of which extend well beyond those of callitrichids. They live or forage from ground to treetops, from rain forest to low scrub, open woodland, and plains with scattered trees. Their food includes all vegetable matter consumed by callitrichids as well as seeds, nuts, and greens eschewed by the latter, but squirrels consume fewer and less varied prey. The range of size and body form of neotropical squirrels compares almost precisely with that of callitrichids, species for species. The range in coloration is similar. The locomotor forms of squirrels and callitrichids represent virtually the same grade but they are specialized for rodents and primitive for primates.

Thermoregulation

Mean body temperature of callitrichids probably lies between 37° and 38° C. The daily amplitudes vary from about 3° to 5° C, depending on species and ambient temperatures and are about twice that observed in other primates. The normal high in body temperature is reached during late morning, the low at night following a sharp drop after sunset. A slight dip in body temperature that occurs in the early afternoon during the high heat of day is followed by a recovery in body temperature when the ambient temperature drops later in the afternoon.

Leontopithecus and *Callithrix* endure freezing temperatures at least a few days of the year in the southern extreme of their natural range in Brazil. Captive callitrichids in temperate zones of the northern hemisphere usually withstand exposure to temperatures below freezing without adverse effects. In one documented case, tamarins frozen stiff during a cold night in unheated quarters (outdoor temperature −30° C) revived completely without complications when warmed at body temperature (see p. 682).

Callitrichids grow longer, thicker fur in cold or freezing climates, but under stress they can lower the body temperature. In the case of the frozen tamarins the body temperature was probably no more than a few degrees above 0°. Kraft (1957) recorded a nocturnal body temperature of 18° C in a captive marmoset (*Callithrix jacchus*). The animal was said to be normally active during the day and lethargic at night, but it died of tuberculosis.

High ambient temperatures are less well tolerated. Callitrichids seek relief at temperatures above 30° C. At 35° (95° F) they assume the characteristic heat dissipating sprawl by lying along the length of a perch with limbs and tail dangling over the sides. Prostration and even death may follow protracted exposure to temperatures above 40°.

Internal temperature control for attaining torpor probably evolved independently among small diurnal arboreal mammals in tropical rain forests as a defense against excessive loss of body heat when the animals are soaked by heavy showers during the night. The effectiveness of hair stream patterns for shedding water is limited, and an oily pelage such as characterizes aquatic land mammals would be too insulating for arboreal mammals during the heat of day.

No systematic studies have been made on thermoregulation in New World monkeys, and only a small fraction of the data gathered has been published. Experimental acclimatization and thermoregulation in the squirrel monkey reported by Chaffee et al. (1966) may be relevant to temperature regulation in callitrichids. Available information on callitrichid thermoregulation is summarized in the individual species accounts in following chapters.

Parasitology

Callitrichids are infected by a great variety of internal and external parasites. Most of the parasites have been found on captive individuals, but none are specific to their hosts. On the other hand, certain parasites inhabiting a number of primates, including platyrrhines, rarely or never infect callitrichids in the wild. The cases are noted below. Details are given in chapter 43.

Malarial parasites infect many kinds of Old World primates and New World cebids with the exception of the genus *Aotus*. All platyrrhines, however, seem to be immune to the fluke, *Schistosoma*. The same may be true of the trypanosome *Leishmania*, except that one Panamanian tamarin, *Saguinus oedipus geoffroyi*, was reported infected. Biting lice (Mallophaga) have been found on a lemuroid, a lorisoid, and a catarrhine monkey, and on a few cebids, but not on man, apes, or callitrichids, except as rare accidental contaminants. Finally, the sucking louse *Pediculus* (Anoplura) infects man, chimpanzee, gibbons, and cebids, but not callitrichids.

A remarkable trait among platyrrhines is the susceptibility of *Saguinus*, and possibly *Callithrix*, to human or humanlike viral hepatitis, and the capability of the tamarin, at least, to transmit the disease serially (cf. p. 375).

48 Genus *Cebuella* Gray
Pygmy Marmoset

Synonymic History

Cebuella Gray, 1866, *Proc. Zool. Soc. London* 1865: 734—subgenus of *Hapale*. Gray, 1870, *Cat. monkeys, lemurs and fruit-eating bats, Brit. Mus.*, p. 64—genus. Cabrera, 1917, *Trab. Mus. Cienc. Nat., Madrid, Zool. Ser.*, no. 31, p. 35—genus; dental characters. Thomas, 1922, *Ann. Mag. Nat. Hist.* (9) 9:198—classification; key characters. Cruz Lima, 1945, *Mamíferos da Amazonia, Primates, Contr. Mus. Paraense*, p. 251—characters. Fiedler, 1956, *Primatologia*, 1:161—subgenus of *Callithrix*. Osman Hill, 1957, *Primates*, 3:3, 79, 113, 120, 121, 125, 163, 180, 192, 194, 215, 272, 282, 302—comparative anatomy; taxonomy; history, Osman Hill, 1958, *Primatologia*, 3 (1):167, figs. 11, 12 (lower gut)—gut anatomy. Remane, 1960, *Primatologia* 3 (2):788—incisors. Biegert, 1961, *Primatologia* 2 (1), *Lief.* 3:5, 179, fig. 56, (palmar surface)—plantar and palmar surfaces of cheiridia. Erikson, 1963, *Symp. Zool. Soc. London*, no. 10, p. 143—locomotory type (springer). Stephan, 1965, *Acta Anat.* 62:217—accessory olfactory bulb. Napier and Napier, 1967, *Handbook of living primates*, p. 84—morphology, ecology, behavior, species, classification. Grimwood, 1968, Recommendations on the conservation of wild life and the establishment of national parks and reserves in Peru. Appendix III, British Ministry Overseas Development (mimeographed), pp. 13, 27—PERU: distribution; exploitation; exportation; conservation. Starck, 1969, *Zool. Gart.* 36(6):312—subgenus of *Callithrix;* circumgenital glands. Hershkovitz, 1970, *Folia Primat.* 12:2, fig. 1 (symphyseal angle of mandible)—mandibular characters and comparisons. Hershkovitz, 1970, *Folia Primat.*, 13:215—cerebral fissural patterns.

Type species.—Iacchus pygmaeus Spix by monotypy.

Distribution

Tropical forests of the upper Amazonian region in western Brazil, southeastern Colombia, Ecuador, and eastern Peru (figs. VII.1; VIII.1).

Taxonomic History

Cebuella was proposed by Gray (1866, p. 734) as a subgenus of *Hapale*, then (1870, p. 164) as a genus. Distinction from other callitrichids was based on the relatively naked ears, absence of preauricular tufts, and annulated tail. *Cebuella* was not generally accepted as generically distinct from *Callithrix*, and Elliot (1913*a*, p. 219) categorically dismissed the name as "unnecessary." Cabrera (1917, p. 35), however, noted certain dental characters that he believed justified generic recognition, and Thomas (1922) pointed to some diagnostic cranial characters as well. Authors have since treated *Cebuella* as a genus or subgenus without further inquiry.

Systematic Position

Cebuella is the most primitive of callitrichids. Except for the advanced architecture of its cranium and absence of a third molar, *Cebuella* is also one of the most generalized of all primates. Among living nonplatyrrhine relatives, *Cebuella* can be compared only with *Tarsius* of similar size, grade of encephalization, and structure of alimentary system including the jaws. The tarsier is more primitive mainly in its larger muzzle, larger orbitotemporal aperture, and unossified symphysis menti. Extreme specialization of its visual and locomotor systems, however, obscure fundamental resemblances and complicate comparisons.

Origin, Evolution, and Dispersal

The ancestral form of *Cebuella* must have stemmed from near the very base of the ancestral callitrichid stock (figs. VII.3, 4). The only living representative of the genus, *Cebuella pygmaea*, although the most stable of modern callitrichids, is probably a relic of what might have been a much more widely distributed and variable species.

Diagnostic Characters

Size

Smallest of known platyrrhines and absolutely smaller than all other callitrichids and comparable in size only

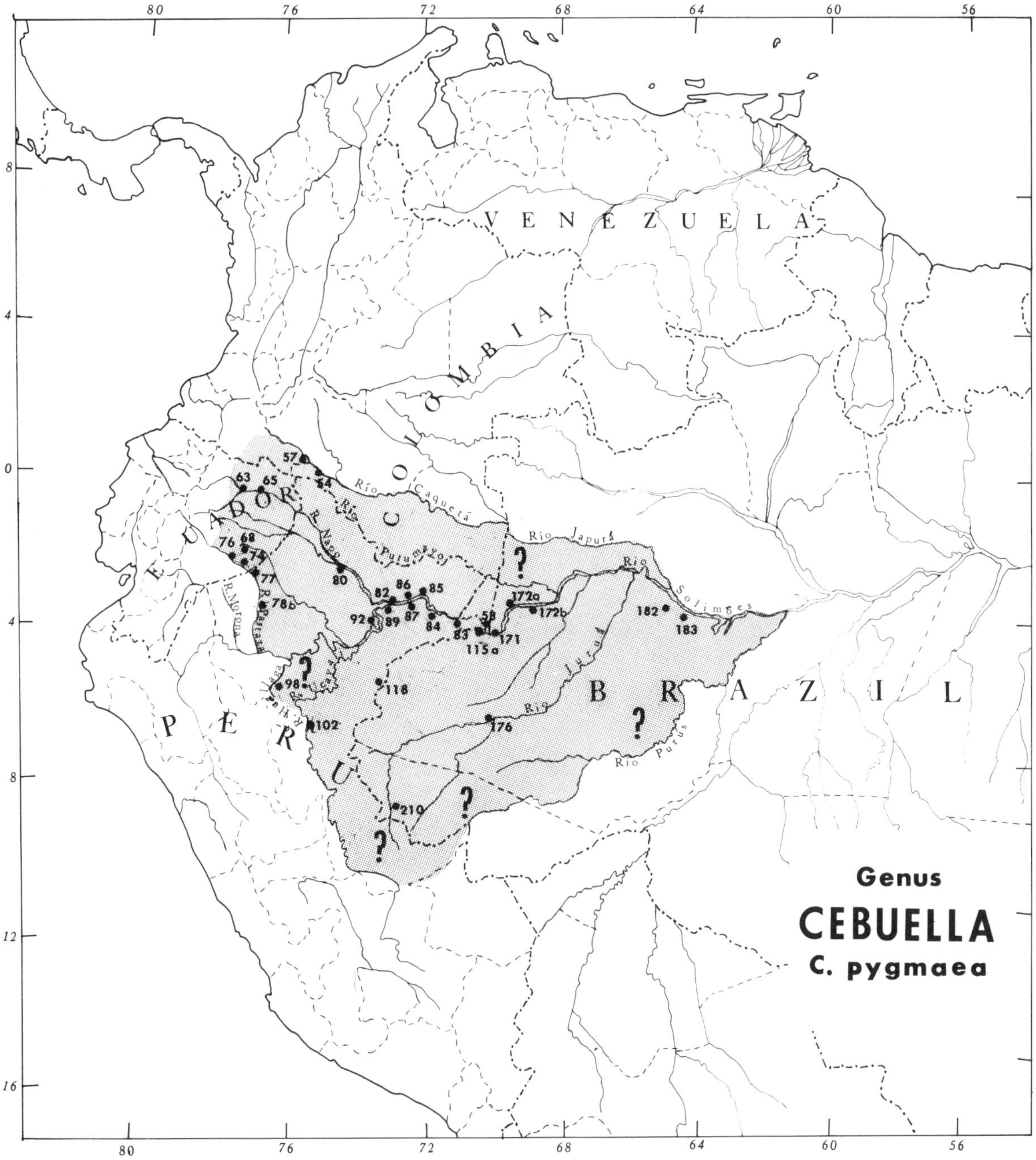

Fig. VIII.1. Distribution of Pygmy Marmosets, *Cebuella pygmaea;* dots show locality records (see gazetteer, for key to collecting and sight localities).

with the still smaller prosimians *Microcebus murinus* and *Galago minutus* (= *demidovii*) (figs. VIII.2–5).

Skull

Most primitively structured of higher primates with particular respect to the consistent V-shaped design of upper and lower dental arcades, architecture of mandibular rami, form of auditory ossicles, comparatively little differentiated incisors, lack of communication between bone diploe and nasal cavity, more frequent persistence of facial portion of lacrimal (figs. VII.5; VIII. 2–7). In contrast, highly specialized characters of the genus include steep, angular palatal vault (figs. IV.50, VII.8) and degenerate or simplified cribiform plate (fig. IV.43). The last, apparently correlated with the short face, has no effect on the olfactory sense, which is better developed in *Cebuella* than in other higher primates.

Dentition

Most primitive of all callitrichids and, except for absence of last molar, and usual absence of paraconids,

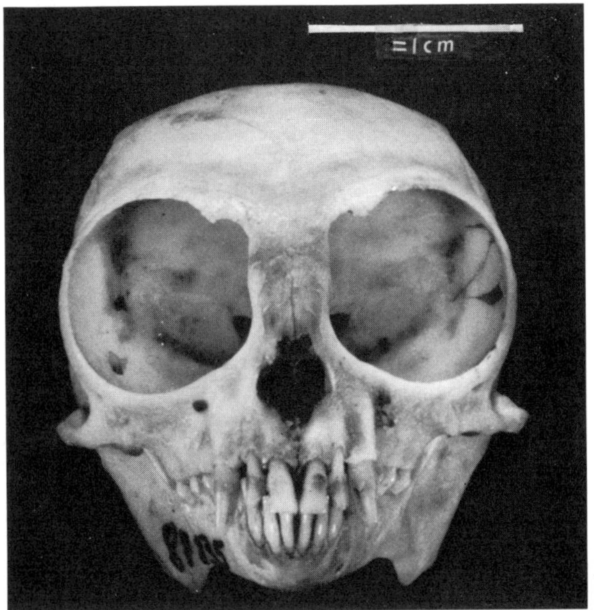

Fig. VIII.2. *Cebuella pygmaea.* Skull, frontal view

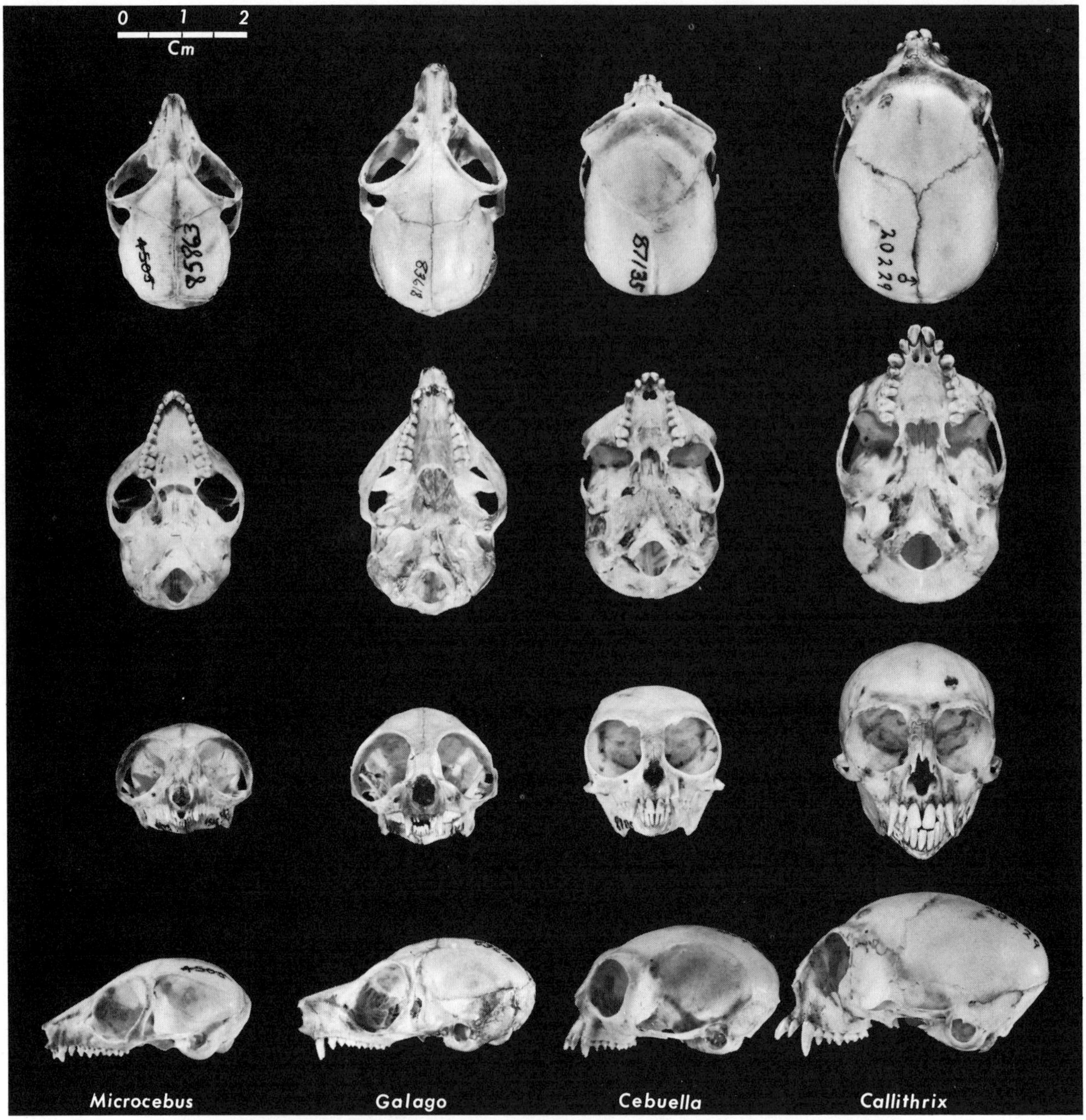

0 1 2
Cm
Microcebus
Galago
Cebuella
Callithrix

Fig. VIII.3. Comparative craniology: Smallest strepsirhines and callitrichids.

0 1 2
Cm
Microcebus
Galago
Cebuella
Callithrix

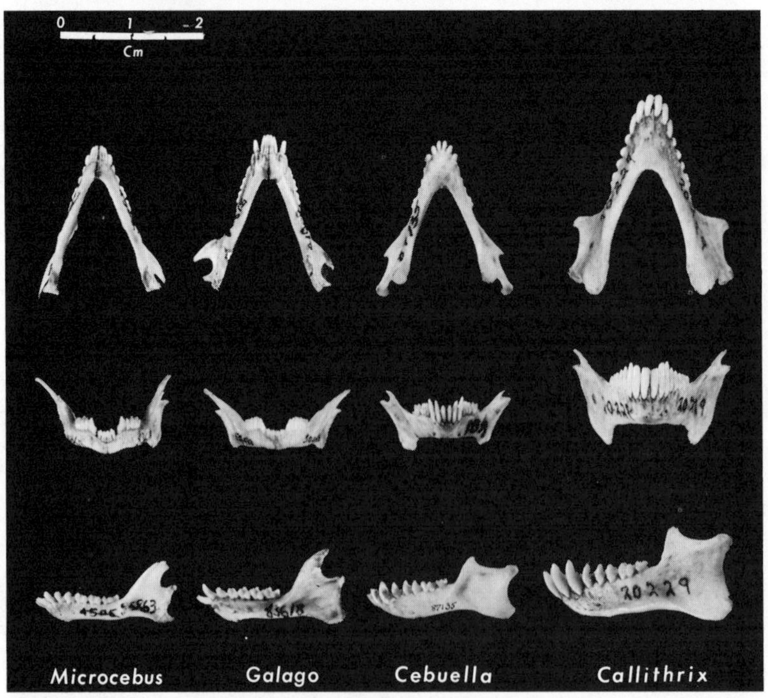

Fig. VIII.4. Comparative craniology: Mandibles, 3 surfaces of those of smallest strepsirhines and callitrichids

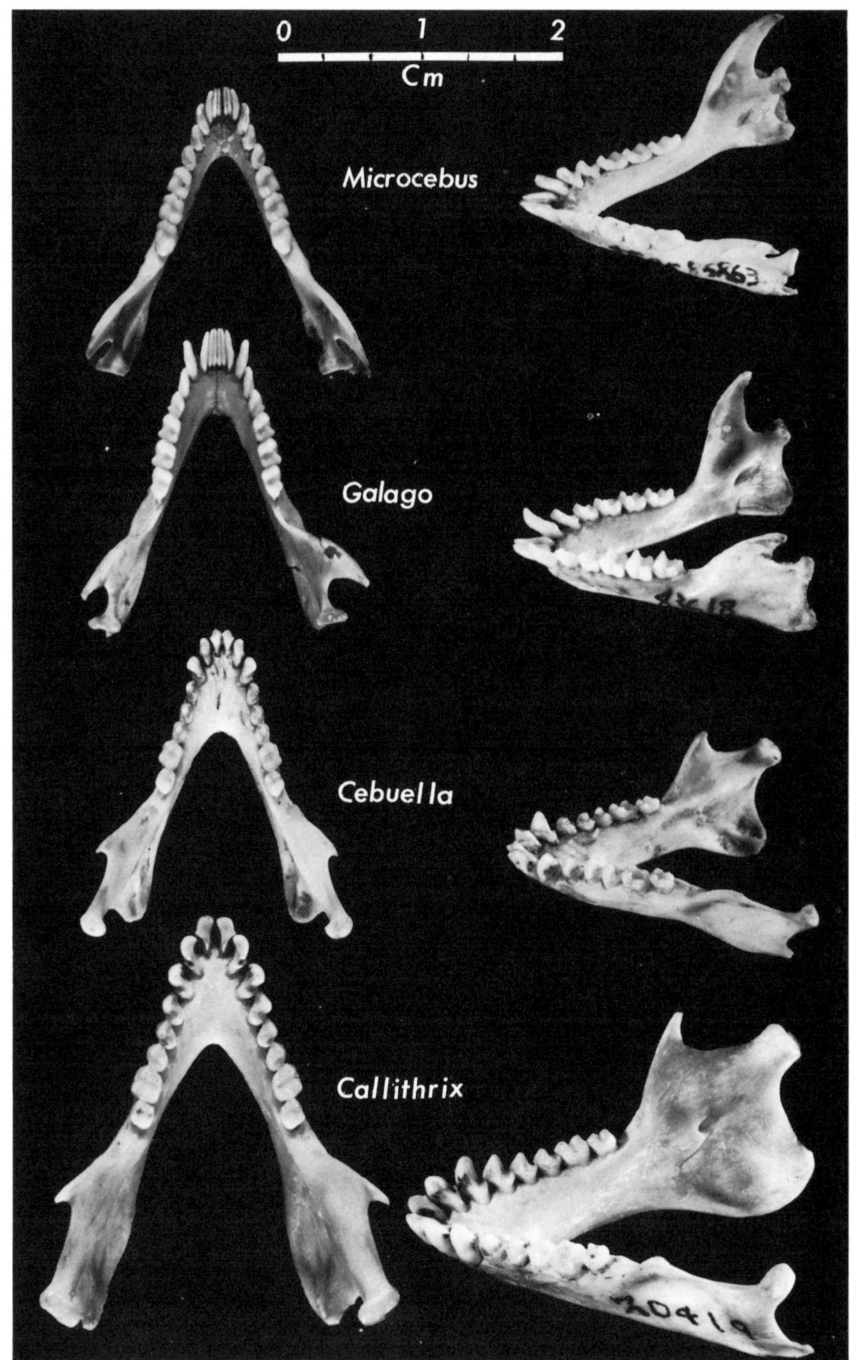

Fig. VIII.5. Comparative craniology: Mandibles, 2 surfaces of those of smallest strepsirhines and callitrichids

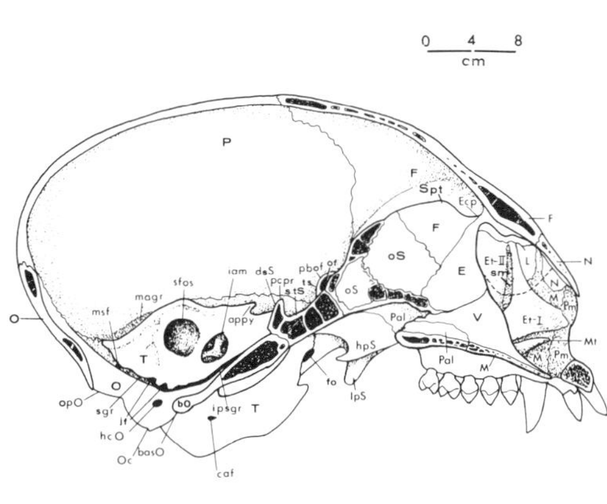

Fig. VIII.6. *Cebuella pygmaea*. Skull, sagittal section

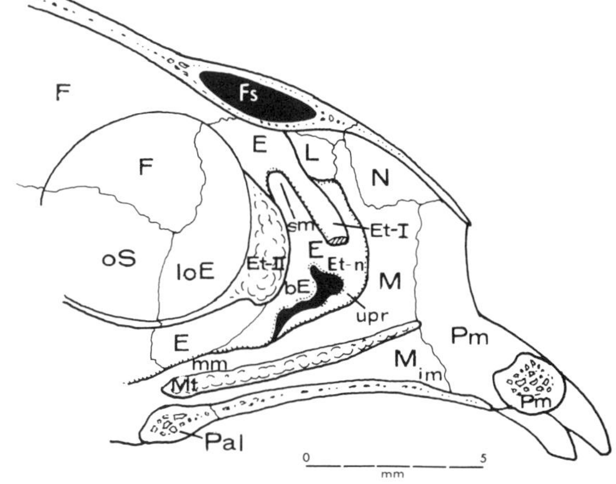

Fig. VIII.7. *Cebuella pygmaea*. Skull, sagittal section through nasal meatus, exposing turbinal system.

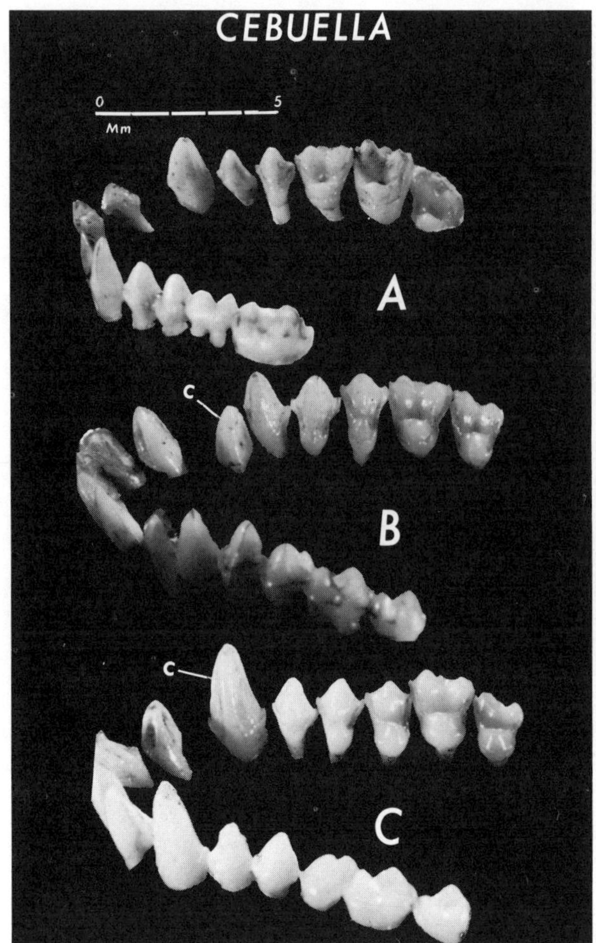

Fig. VIII.8. *Cebuella pygmaea*: Upper teeth; *A,* deciduous teeth and molars; *B,* permanent teeth with canine (*c*) incompletely erupted; *C,* permanent teeth with canine (*c*) fully erupted.

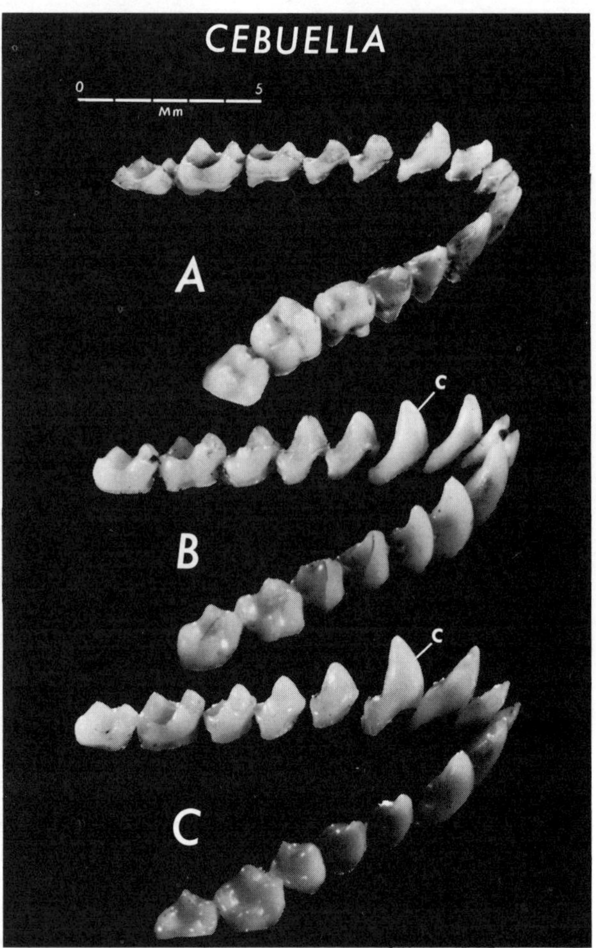

Fig. VIII.9. *Cebuella pygmaea*: Lower teeth of same individuals shown in fig. VIII.8. *A,* deciduous teeth and molars; *B,* permanent teeth with canine (*c*) nearly completely erupted; *C,* permanent teeth with canine (*c*) fully erupted.

most primitive of living platyrrhines (figs. V.1, 6, 7, 18, 19, 22, 25–27; VIII 8–10).

Brain

The surface configuration of the *Cebuella* brain is least complicated of known platyrrhines and catarrhines. The nearly smooth cerebral hemispheres, comparatively large olfactory lobe, and persistent dorsal cerebellar exposure of the *Cebuella* brain fairly fills the morphological gap between the brains of lower prosimians and higher monkeys (figs. VI.8, 9). Size alone is a reliable criterion for cerebral development among primates. As a rule, the smaller the species within a given phyletic line, the smaller and less complicated the surface configuration of its brain.

Integument

Color is more nearly uniformly agouti than that of other platyrrhines (fig. III.13); pelage undistinguished except for ear-concealing mane (fig. VIII.16); sensory hairs more widely distributed, tactile fields more extensive, and cutaneous scent glands more highly specialized and numerous than in other monkeys (figs. III.12; VIII. 11, 12, 13).

External Genitalia

Penis and baculum are least specialized among higher primates; female organs without specializations found in other callitrichids (figs. III.22, 23, 24, 25, 28; VIII.14).

External Ear

Like that of other monkeys, departs widely from primitive mammalian or prosimian type (figs. III.18; VIII.12).

Ischial Prominences

Absent in *Cebuella* but present in higher callitrichids (cf. fig. I.15).

Postcranial Skeleton

Structurally is most primitive of living primates (cf. figs. II.1, 2, 4, 20; VII.9, 10, 12, 13).

Cheiridia

Bones, ungues, volar pads, and papillary ridges are least differentiated among living primates (figs. I.25, 30; cf. I.26, 29).

Tongue

See page 107 and figs. III.19, 20; VIII.15.

Palatal Ridges

See page 431 and fig. VII.14.

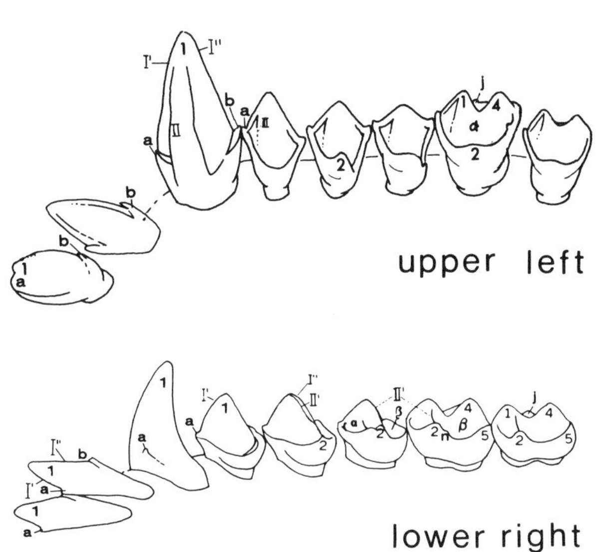

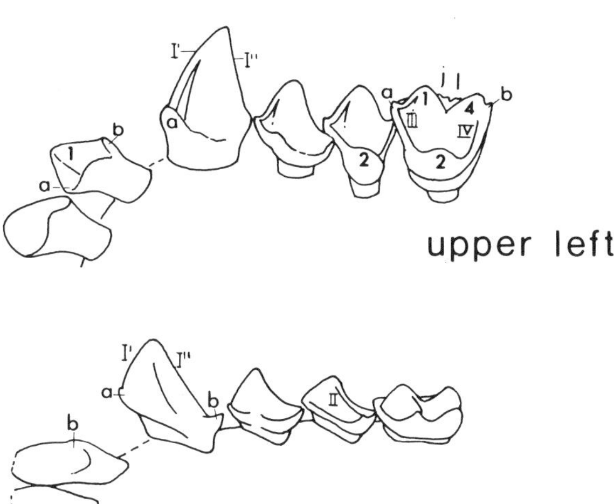

Fig. VIII.10. *Cebuella pygmaea*: Upper and lower tooth rows, permanent and deciduous.

Larynx

See page 18 and fig. I.11.

Dimorphism

Lack of significant differences in pelage and coloration between juvenals and adults is a primitive character distinctive of *Cebuella* among callitrichids. In the species of *Callithrix, Saguinus,* and *Leontopithecus,* differences between young and adult coats are notable and often of a grade comparable to differences between adults of different species.

Fig. VIII.11. *Cebuella pygmaea*: Tactile vibrissal fields of forelimbs and ventral surface of head and trunk.

Absence of sexual dimorphism, except in organs of reproduction and infant feeding, is a primitive mammalian character common to all callitrichids.

Karyotype

The diploid chromosome number 44 in *Cebuella* is lowest among the Callitrichidae but shared with members of the advanced *Callithrix argentata* group. The diploid number in all other callitrichids is 46.

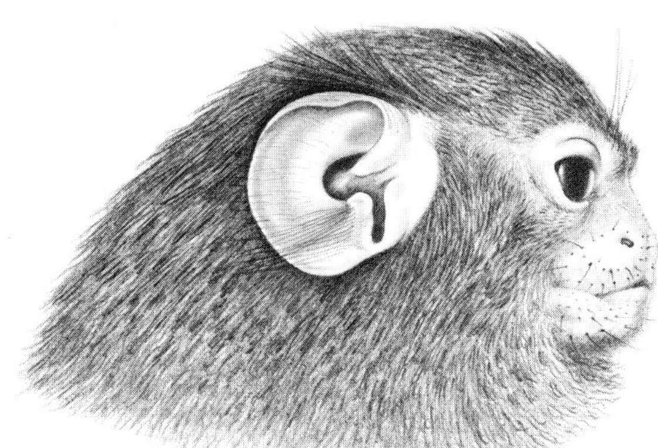

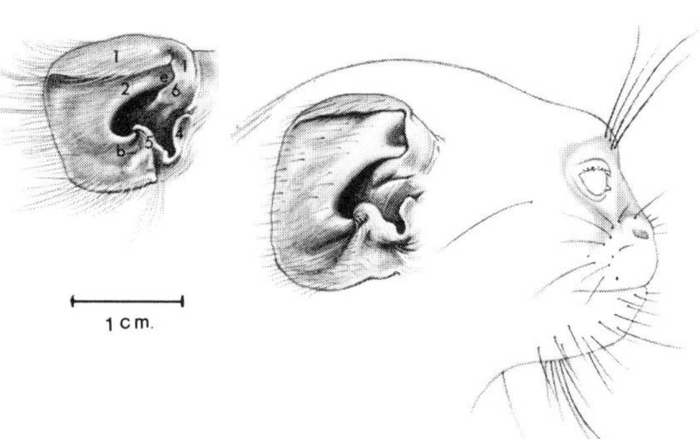

Fig. VIII.12. *Cebuella pygmaea* profile with portion of mane deleted to expose ear; *lower right,* cover hairs omitted to expose ear, vibrissae and facial pigmentation; *lower left,* juvenal ear; *1* = helix, *2* = antihelix, *4* = tragus, *5* = antitragus, *6* = crus helicis, *b* = inferior laminar fossa, *e* = plica principalis; see also fig. III.18.

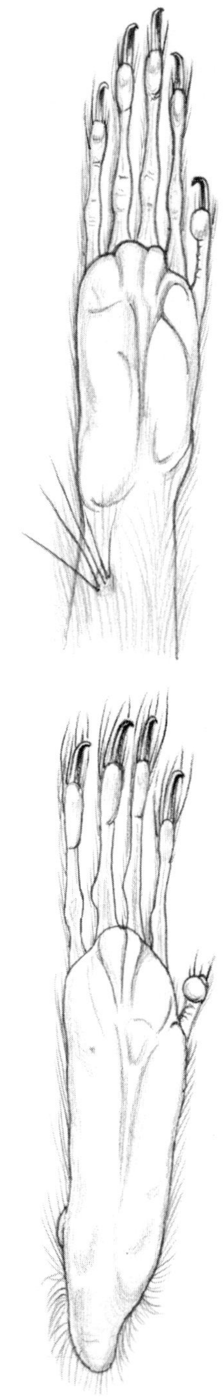

Fig. VIII.13. *Cebuella pygmaea*. Volar surfaces of hand (*upper*) and foot (*lower*) with digital bristles and ulnar-carpal vibrissae visible.

Newborn

Young are proportionately, sometimes actually, heavier at birth, their early development faster, and they become active and are weaned earlier than newborn of other callitrichids. Generally, the smaller, more primitive primates develop more rapidly until weaned than the larger, more advanced species of the same family group.

Additional anatomical characters, more or less diagnostic of the genus, are described and compared under the heading Callitrichidae.

Cranial Characters

Greatest skull length in adults usually between 30 and 40 mm; frontal contour convex but not notably vaulted (figs. VIII.2, 3, 4, 5); weakly defined temporal ridges present and always widely separated on parietals; nasal profile slightly concave; nasofrontal suture from two-thirds to three-fourths distance from nasal tips to glabella (fig. VIII.2); malar foramen rarely more than 1 mm in diameter; infraorbital foramen placed above pm $\underline{3}$ or between pm $\underline{2}$ and canine, its diameter greater than to less than that of malar foramen; orbits more or less rounded in outline; lacrymal bone with facial process sometimes present and articulating with nasal; cribriform plate small, poorly developed or degenerate (fig. IV.43); interorbital septum thin, translucent (figs. VIII.6, 7); paired posterior sphenoidal sinuses or fossae absent; axis of foramen magnum pointing back as much as down (fig. IV.54); auditory bullae well inflated, lower portion of mesotympanic cavity more or less cellular (fig. IV.65); auditory ossicles simple (figs. IV.68, 73); dental arcade subtriangular, or V-shaped, outer alveolar distance between canines less than alveolar length of c-m $\underline{2}$ (figs. VIII.3, 4); palatal vault steep, angular (fig. VII.8); average occipital angle (opisthion - inion) index between 50° and 60°; pterygoid plates small, the medial consisting nearly entirely of long, narrow hamular process, pterygoid fossa rudimentary or virtually absent; postglenoid process comparatively weak (fig. VIII.3); outline of inferior border of mandible V-shaped with symphysial angle acute, the horizontal rami diverging sharply; slope of symphysis menti relative to basal mandibular plane about 28° (20°–40°, 53 specimens); ascending ramus broad, more or less square, average coronoidal height about 45% of condyloincisive length; coronoid process low, the recurved tip extending slightly or not at all above condyle, sigmoid notch broad and shallow; condylar process low, the articular surface nearly on same plane as molar crown surface; inferior border of angular process deflected markedly below basal plane of horizontal ramus (figs. IV.75–79; VIII.4, 5).

Postcranial Skeletal Characters

Vertebral Formula

In two skeletons at hand (FM 71003 juv. ♂; FM 104916 ♀), cervical 7, 7; thoracic 13, 13; lumbar 6, 7; sacral 3, 3; caudal 29, 28.

Entepicondylar Foramen and Third Trochanter

Absent in both skeletons.

Limb Proportions

Those determined by Erikson (pers. comm.) are shown in table 47. They are repeated here for convenience of reference together with those calculated by Christen (1974) and the single mature skeleton at hand. Measurements (cf. Erikson 1963, p. 138) are greatest length of long limb bones and trunk length (combined lengths of thoracic, lumbar and sacral vertebrae); figure groups in the first two lines are means followed by extremes in parentheses and sample number.

	Humerus + radius / *Trunk*	*Femur + tibia* / *Trunk*	*Humerus + radius* / *Femur + tibia*
Erikson	76(74–79)5	94(92–95)5	82(81–83)6
Christen (1974, table 14)	74.2(71–84)?	90(84.9–96.2)?	83(80.7–83.7)?
FM 104916	$\frac{33+30}{90}=70$	$\frac{38+39}{90}=84$	$\frac{63}{77}=83$

Christen forgot to mention sample sizes. Her measurements are based on specimens in Erikson's collection (Christen 1974, p. 75).

Cebuella limb proportions relative to trunk length taken as 100% compare with limb proportions of *Saguinus midas* as follows; data from Christen (1974, p. 46), the sample sizes unspecified.

Humerus + radius: 72 *Cebuella;* 63 *Saguinus*
Femur + tibia: 63 *Cebuella,* 85 *Saguinus*

Dental Characters (figs. V.19, 22–28)

Incisors (figs. V.23, 24; VIII.8, 9, 10)

Permanent upper incisors comparatively high, crowns not markedly differentiated from cervix, the lateral tooth implanted obliquely behind central, often with slight overlap, the incisor pair on both sides combining to form a V-shaped angle or echelon arrangement; unworn *lateral incisor* lanceolate, usually lower, sometimes slightly higher, than central incisor and about one-half to four-fifths its bulk, small mesial (*a*) and distal (*b*) styles present near gingival line; *central incisor* spatulate, forward projecting, and with slight inward inflection, cutting edge weakly trifid in unworn state, rounded in worn, and provided with a minute distostyle (*b*) at base of crown; occlusal groove often present near distal edge of central incisor, sometimes on medial margin of lateral incisor; lingual surface of incisors uncrazed.

Deciduous upper lateral incisor trapeziform, sharply pointed, crown about as high as wide, uncrazed, mesial and distal cutting edges sharp, distostyle probably present

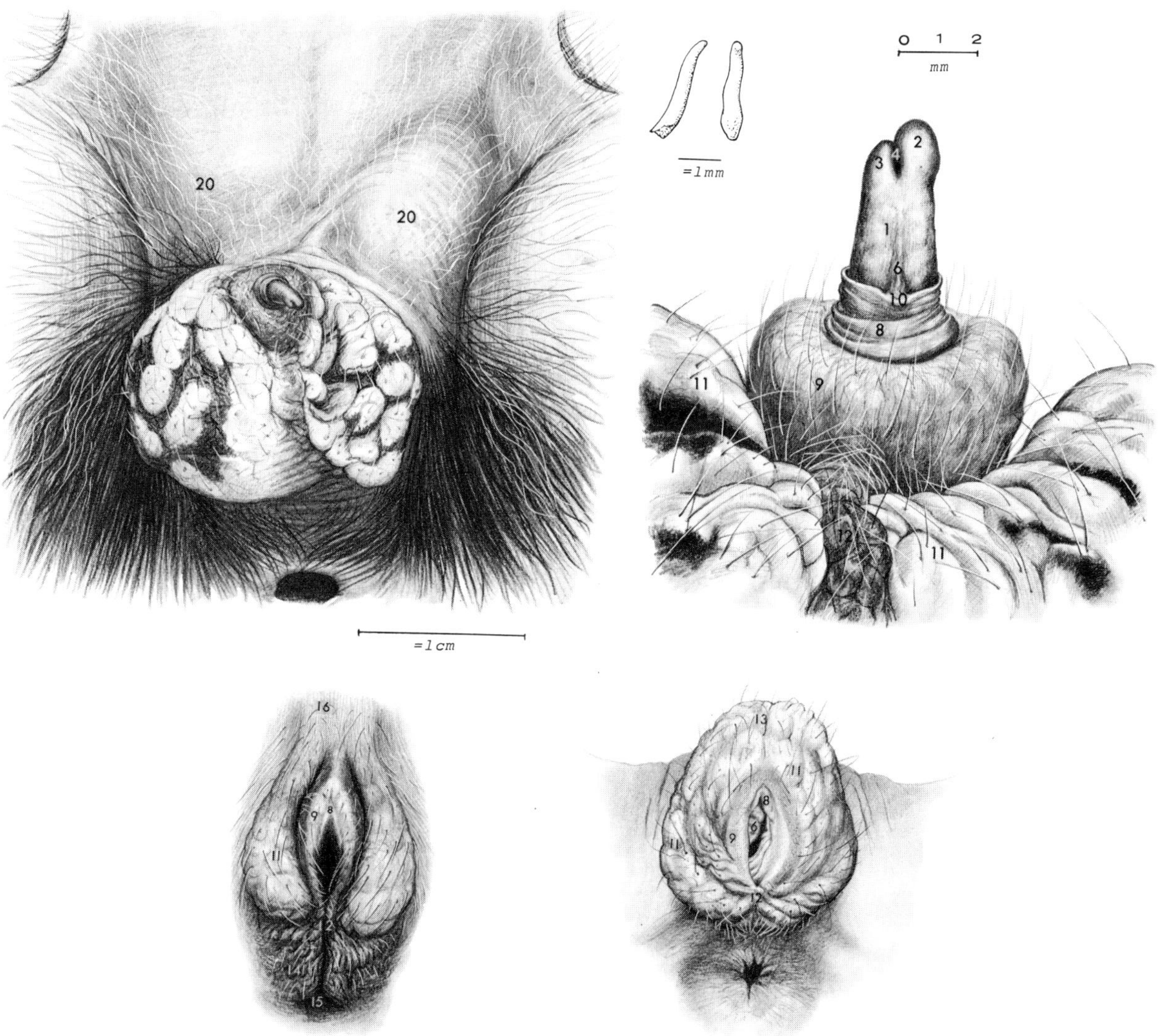

Fig. VIII.14. *Cebuella pygmaea*: External genitalia; *upper left,* male organs with right testicle scrotal, left retracted; *upper right,* penis, and preputial folds (*8, 9*) enlarged; *upper center,* two aspects of baculum; *lower left,* female organs; *lower right,* female organs with left border of labium pulled to one side. See fig. III.21 for names of numbered parts.

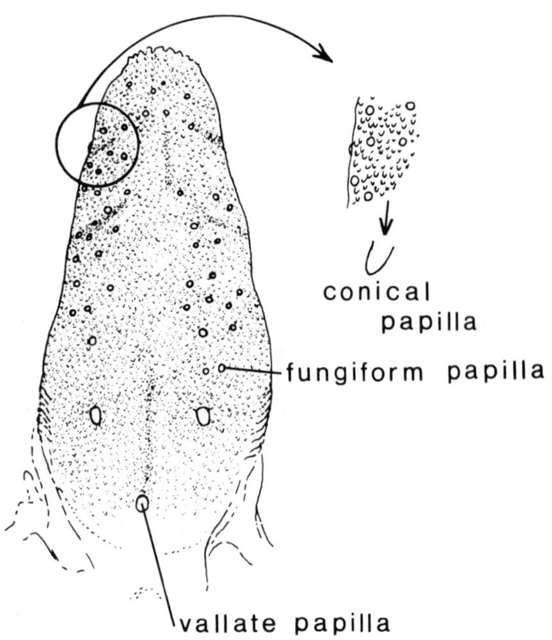

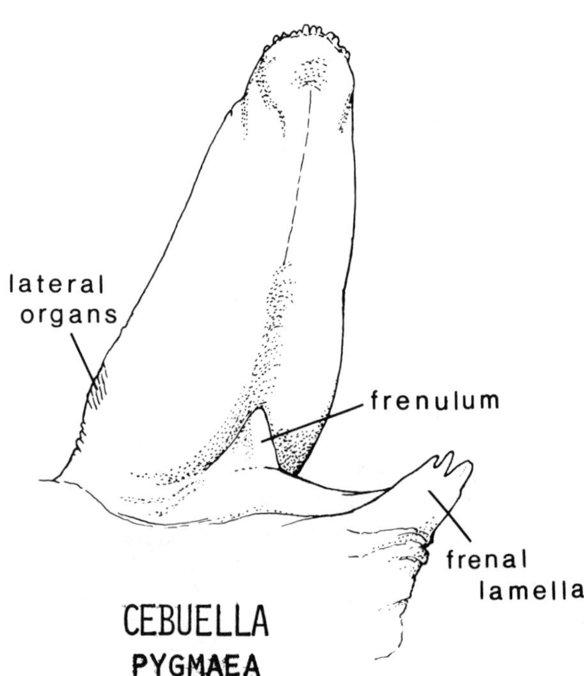

Fig. VIII.15. *Cebuella pygmaea*: Tongue, dorsal and ventral surfaces greatly enlarged.

in unworn tooth, lingual surface with steeply sloping but poorly defined anterolingual and posterolingual facets. *Upper central incisor* excessively worn in material at hand.

Permanent lower incisors laterally compressed, the lateral slightly higher than central, about three times higher than mesiodistal length of labial surface, the teeth falcate or caniniform labially, lanceolate lingually, unworn biting edges sharply pointed and not touching adjacent teeth, lingual surface uncrazed; *lateral incisor* emplaced obliquely behind central, often with slight overlap; the pairs on both sides combining to form a V-shaped arch; incisor height measured on labial surface nearly equal to vertical depth of symphysis menti; mesiostylid present on upper third of mesial margin of unworn crown of lateral incisor, distostylid on lower third or half of distal margin of crown; *central incisor* subcylindriform on outer surface in unworn condition, lanceolate in worn, about two-thirds or less bulk of lateral incisor, coronal outline on lingual surface triangular; minute mesiostylid on upper third of mesial edge, and distostylid on lower distal half of crown.

Deciduous lower lateral incisor scimitar-shaped, about twice as high as long, uncrazed, emplaced laterad to, not staggered behind, half-erupted permanent central incisor; mesial ridge sharp, lingual surface steep; talonid hardly defined, distostylid near base, mesiostylid not evident in worn tooth but possibly present in unworn. *Desiduous lower central incisor* considerably worn in material at hand, but distostylid probably, mesiostylid possibly, present.

Remarks. The deciduous upper lateral incisor is about half the size of its successor, the crown relatively shorter, terminal styles not always well defined and possibly absent in some. Structurally it is more advanced in approaching the specialized spatulate type.

The sharp-edged, scimitar-shaped lower lateral milk incisor differs widely from its replacement. Morphologically, it appears to stand midway between the sharply pointed lanceolate or falcate permanent lateral incisor of *Cebuella* or *Callithrix* and the club-shaped permanent upper outer incisor of *Saguinus*. The more nearly laterad emplacement of the second lower incisor, as compared with the replacement tooth is an advanced condition comparable to that in primates with U-shaped rather than V-shaped dental arches.

Incisor wear is comparatively and relatively greater in *Cebuella* than in other callitrichids. The upper incisors often retain a vestige of the lingual cingulum, but the corresponding lower teeth are usually worn smooth on the lingual surface.

Canines (figs. V.19, 22, 25, 26, 27, 28; VIII.8, 9, 10)

Permanent upper canine elongate, sharply pointed, slightly recurved, at least twice as high as long, about half again higher than adjacent incisor or premolar, subovate in cross-section, buccal surface smooth, convex, lingual surface subtriangular in outline with mesial crest (epicrista *II'*) and groove well developed, minute mesiostyle present, distal edge sharp, short posterior portion of lingual cingulum *B* and distostyle in unworn tooth usually replaced by a broad wear facet in worn; talon absent, enamel uncrazed.

Deciduous upper canine comparatively low, triangular in outline with sharp cutting mesial and distal edges (the eocrista), separated from lateral incisor by wide diastema; general form intermediate between that of permanent lateral incisor and permanent pm^2 but more recurved or scimitar-shaped like incisor; small mesiostyle and sometimes distostyle present, torus of lingual surface with anterior portion of cingulum *B* well developed, distal ridge undefined, but posterior portion of cingulum *B* well developed, talon rudimentary.

Permanent lower canine falciform like lateral incisor but heavier, as high as or slightly higher than and implanted obliquely behind in line with shorter pm_2; about one-third again as high as adjacent premolar; minute mesiostylid and distostylid present in unworn tooth, lingual cingulid poorly defined, distal occlusal groove in worn tooth forming a false talonid basin; enamel usually uncrazed.

Deciduous lower canine (worn) essentially premolariform, heavier but not higher than deciduous lateral incisor, about one-third higher than dpm_2 and well separated from adjacent teeth; mesial and distal edges sharp, mesiostylid poorly defined if present, distostylid exaggerated by deep occlusal groove, lingual shelf deep; enamel uncrazed.

Remarks. The deciduous upper canine is larger than either adjacent tooth but intermediate in grade of molarization. The deciduous lower canine is more molarized than the upper, and differs less in size from neighboring teeth. As in the upper, spatial requirement of the pre-erupted and comparatively small falcate lower permanent canine predetermines the maximum alveolar space available for its deciduous predecessor.

Premolars (figs. V.18, 27; VIII.8, 9, 10)

Permanent upper premolars with pm^2 sagittate on labial aspect and essentially caniniform or unicuspid in general structure with mesial crest slightly convex, distal crest slightly concave, sample height, measured from cingulum, 2.2, length 1.6, width 1.4; lingual cingulum *B* well defined and continuous, small mesiostyle and distostyle present, protocone (*2*) not certainly defined; pm^3 usually bicuspid, larger and heavier but lower than preceding, wider and longer than high, neoanterolingual cingulum *B′* well defined; buccal cingulum (*A*) reduced, mesial and distal styles and low protocone present, minute protoconule (epiconule *c*) sometimes present; pm^4 like preceding but lower, wider, longer, with styles, protocone more fully developed, cingulum *B′* better defined; sample length 1.6, width 2.2.

Deciduous upper premolars with dpm^2 more caniniform than molariform, sample crown height 1.5, length 1.3, width 0.9; dpm^3 bicuspidate, buccal cingulum moderately developed; dpm^4 fully tritubercular, about as large as both anterior premolars combined, eocone (paracone, *1*) tallest and largest cusp, metacone (*4*) slightly lower and generally smaller, protocone (*2*) lowest and smallest, mesiostyle (*a*) and distostyle (*b*) present, the latter not always well developed, ectostyles rudimentary, neolingual cingulum *B′* and posterolingual cingulum (*C*) well developed, buccal cingulum a narrow shelf; minute protoconule (epiconule, *c*) sometimes indicated, sample length 1.7, width 2.0.

Remarks. Molarization of the upper premolars is progressive from front to back but is marked on $pm^{3\text{-}4}$ only. Pm^4 is bicuspid with protocone well developed. The protocone is considerably smaller in pm^3 and practically non-existent in caniniform pm^2.

Molarization of the deciduous series did not affect dpm^2. Dpm^3 is usually more advanced than its successor and dpm^4 is a tritubercular molar.

Permanent lower premolars with Pm_2 falcate, essentially unicuspid, sample crown height, 2.3, length 1.5, width 1.3, main cone (eoconid = protoconid) buccal with mesial edge convex, distal edge rounded and sharp, epicristid (*II*) extending obliquely across molar to rudimentary metaconid (*2*), lingual cingulid (*B*) uniting with epicristid to separate rudimentary "trigonid" basin from talonid basin, mesiostylid (*a*) more or less defined, or obsolete, distostylid (*b*) distinct, paraconid (*3*) and hypoconid (*4*) not defined; pm_3 about same in bulk as preceding but slightly lower and more molarized, eoconid, epicristid and metaconid better developed pseudoparaconid (*t*) indicated, talonid basin broader but hypoconid not indicated, mesiostylid present; pm_4 slightly lower than preceding but approximately equal in bulk and more molarized, "trigonid" with well defined mesiostylid, metaconid and pseudoparaconid when present, low talonid enlarged to about one-third occlusal surface of crown, basin deep, hypoconid barely indicated, entoconid (*5*) low but well defined, sample length 1.3, width 1.3.

Deciduous lower premolars with dpm_2 scimitar-shaped, about two-thirds bulk of successor, sample crown height 1.6, length 1.5, width 0.7, small, narrow talonid basin enclosed by posterolingual cingulid and epicristid (metalophid, *II*), mesiostylid (*a*), distostylid (*b*) and anterolingual cingulid (*B*) weakly defined; dpm_3 slightly lower and larger than preceding, talonid larger, other features not evident in greatly worn tooth but certainly present and no less developed than in preceding tooth; dpm_4 lower than preceding, fully molarized, "trigonid" with high eoconid, (*1*), metaconid (*2*) well defined, paraconid (*3*) indicated in one of three jaws, talonid occupying more than one-half occlusal surface, hypoconid (*4*) well developed, entoconid (*5*) low, stylids and conulids absent, sample length 1.6, width 1.2.

Remarks. All permanent lower premolars are caniniform, with crown dominated by a high bladelike cusp and axis of epicristid more nearly longitudinal or oblique than transverse. As usual, pm_4 is the most molarized tooth of the series. Its "trigonid" with high metaconid and frequent presence of a well-defined pseudoparaconid (*t*) is much larger and more molarized than the talonid.

First and second deciduous premolars are likewise essentially caniniform. Dpm_4, however, is very like m_1, but two-thirds its size and with well-developed metaconid, hypoconid, and entoconid and occasional paraconid.

Molars (figs. V.18, 19, 22, 27; VIII.8, 9, 10)

Upper first molar largest of dental system, from about one-fifth again to nearly twice the size of pm^4 or m^2, occlusal surface subtriangular, trigon basin (*α*) deeply conical, eocone (paracone, *1*) slightly higher and larger than metacone (*4*) and higher than protocone (*2*) but subequal to slightly less in bulk, protoloph (protocrista, *III*) and metaloph (plagiocrista, *IV*) well defined, small metaconule (plagioconule, *d*) often present, epiconule (*c*) rarely present, posterolingual cingulum (*C*) nearly always well defined, neoanterolingual cingulum (*B′*), if differentiated, may fuse with posterolingual cingulum (*C*), mesiostyle (*a*) and distostyle (*b*) minute, large stylocone (*j*) often present; a small style on posterolingual cingulum (*C*) at angle of base of protocone in FMNH 88998, appears to be an incipient hypocone, a similar element appears as one of several styles in pm^4; *second molar* smaller than first with protocone often larger than eocone, metacone smaller, sometimes reduced to one-half size of eocone, distostyle absent, mesiostyle sometimes present, lingual border of tooth usually in line with lingual border of first molar, the buccal border offset; buccal shelf indicated, ectostyle *j* often present and well developed.

Lower molars subrectangular, "trigonid" of anterior third or fourth of crown with elevated, forward-sloping, shallow irregular-shaped basin, multicuspid talonid forming remainder of crown with deeply rounded basin; *first molar* oblong to nearly square, two-thirds to three-fourths again larger than last premolar, eoconid (*1*) connected to slightly lower metaconid (*2*) by high epicristid (*II*) with notched concave crest, plesioconulid (*p*) sometimes indicated on unworn buccal or anterior border of paracristid (*I*), an ectostylid (stylocone-*j*) sometimes present, hypoconid (*4*) more conical and higher than entoconid (*5*), low postentoconulid (*e*) hardly or not differentiated from entoconid, posterior border of talonid with deep median notch; *second molar* like first but about one-fifth to one-fourth less in bulk, distolingual cusp or entoconid extending farther behind than distobuccal cusp or hypoconid.

Sample Measurements of Molars, Buccal Length by Width, in Millimeters:

m^1	m^2	m_1	m_2
1.8 × 2.2	1.6 × 2.0	2.1 × 1.5	1.7 × 1.4
1.9 × 2.2	1.7 × 2.2	2.1 × 1.5	1.9 × 1.3
2.0 × 2.4	1.4 × 1.8	2.0 × 1.6	1.6 × 1.3
2.1 × 2.4	1.7 × 2.2	2.3 × 1.6	1.7 × 1.4

Remarks. The smallest and most primitive platyrrhine molars correspond to the extremely small pygmy marmoset. The hypertrophied upper first molar, largest tooth of the dental system, marks the end of the molarization process in the species. It also interposes a sharp break in the gradient of tooth size beginning with the canine. Size and other structural differences between first molar and last premolar, upper or lower, are nevertheless bridged by the deciduous premolar.

The plane of the superior border of the lower cheek teeth, from peak of first premolar to peak of last molar, is nearly as straight as in primitive prosimians, insectivores, and marsupials.

Significant advances in molarization of m_1, compared with pm_4, are expansion of talonid over more than one-half the crown surface, with corresponding reduction of "trigonid" to one-third or less crown area, hypertrophy of hypoconid to become the dominant cusp, and presence of styloconid. Loss or reduction of mesiostylid and paraconid is a degenerate character.

It has been suggested that the small size of m2 is a case of miniaturization. More likely, it is the retention of primitive dimensions, as compared with the hypertrophied first molar. No part of the second molar is entirely lost and relative proportions of none is reduced except occasionally part of metacone in upper or hypoconid in lower.

The primitive third molar, almost certainly absent in the ancestral callitrichids, is nevertheless often represented in the lower jaw by a vestigial alveolus, sometimes with a bud of the tooth itself. The vestige is often indicated in subadults by one or more perforations of the bone opening into a vacuity which may communicate with the alveolus of the second molar. The alveolar scar which marks the vestige in young adults becomes obliterated in older individuals. A similar trace of the erstwhile upper third molar appears occasionally as a pneumatized extension of the alveolar portion of the maxillary bone behind the second molar. It may contain a tiny aborted tooth bud.

As a rule, the highest cusp of each maxillary and mandibular tooth from incisors through canines and premolars is buccal. The same position is maintained in the molars of *Cebuella,* with eocone higher than protocone and eoconid and hypoconid higher than metaconid and entoconid, respectively.

The combined entoconid and postentoconulid which form the distolingual portion of the heel of the lower first and second molars extend farther behind on the mandibular ramus than the opposing distobuccal cusp, or hypoconid. This condition is due less to the form of the entoconid-postentoconulid complex than to the rhomboidal shape of the entire tooth with mesiobuccal and distolingual corners widest apart. The character, insignificant as it appears, is consistent in the second molar and fairly constant in the first molar of all callitrichids. The distostylid, or hypoconulid (*b*) is usually coalesced with the hypoconid. Its failure to appear as a distinct cusp may be related to the orientation of the molar and emergence of the postentoconulid (*e*).

For an account of diseased teeth, see chapter 36.

External Genitalia

Male (figs. III.22, 24, 25, 29; VIII.14)

Adult. Penis unpigmented, smooth, spineless; glans penis unspecialized, urinary meatus an oblique slit from right, the left lobe, with baculum, larger than right and more projecting; scrotum globose, pedunculate; skin raised into swollen subovate or polygonal papillae each with one to a few black, brown, or white hairs; raphe mottled or entirely brown; prepenial and parapenial portions of scrotum mostly or entirely unpigmented, postpenial portion mottled; prepuce unpigmented or mottled, skin of outer fold like that of scrotum, to which it is attached by a midventral frenulum continuous with scrotal raphe; inner surface of prepuce glabrous, finely wrinkled and with frenular attachment to midventral line of lower half of penial stem; scrotum, with testes, wider than long, greatest diameter 19 mm in one adult; mons glandular and unpigmented; sexual skin not differentiated in present material; perineal and anal regions pigmented or unpigmented; baculum comparatively unmodified.

Juvenal. External genitalia, except annulus of prepuce, unpigmented; penis completely ensheathed by hairy glandular outer preputial fold; scrotal skin contracted into a pattern of crowded subovoid papillae, each papilla with a few long, stiff hairs, raphe pronounced; undescended testes enlarged; skin of perineal and anal regions corrugated, well pigmented, and thinly haired like scrotum.

Remarks. The gross and microscopic anatomy of the male circumgenital glands are described by Starck (1969, p. 312).

Female (figs. III.22, 23; VIII.14)

Adult. Labia majora glandular, hairy, more or less pigmented or mottled, and forming a pair of large thick cushions one on each side of genital fissure; in unswollen labia, preputial fold narrow, crescentic, and usually defined from broad ovate scrotal fold by sulcus; in tumescent labia, preputial folds greatly expanded and usually larger and thicker than scrotal fold; in one of two specimens, scrotal fold furrowed transversely at level of posterior commissure with caudal portion rounded and deeply pigmented like perineal region, anterior portion unpigmented and kidney-shaped; glans clitoridis concealed in labial tissue in one specimen, exposed between annulus of preputial fold in second with tumescent external genitalia; external genitalia longer than wide, greatest diameter 14 mm in tumescent adult, 8 mm in unswollen adult; length of genital fissure 8 mm and 4 mm, respectively; perineal and anal regions unpigmented or pigmented; integument of mons pubis glandular and hairy like outer preputial fold; specialized pubic sexual skin not differentiated in present material.

Cytogenetics

The karyotype of *Cebuella,* with a diploid number of 44, is very similar to those of *Callithrix argentata argentata* and *C. humeralifer humeralifer*. In all, 32 biarmed and 10 acrocentric autosomes are present. It has been suggested (Benirschke and Brownhill 1962; Wohnus and Benirschke 1966) that the karyotype of these marmosets could have arisen from one like that of *Callithrix jacchus* (cf. table 48) through centric fusion of two pairs of small acrocentric chromosomes to form one pair of submetacentric chromosomes. DeBoer (1974, p. 24) suggests that fusion separating *Cebuella* from a common $2n = 46$ stock may have occurred before differentiation of *Callithrix*. It is also possible that the 46 chromosome complement was derived from a $2n = 44$ stock.

A high degree of stability in the form of the meiotic chromosomes of *Cebuella* was noted by Egozcue, Chiarelli, and Sarti-Chiarelli (1968).

49 *Cebuella pygmaea* Spix, Pygmy Marmoset
1. History and Characters

Fig. VIII.16. Pygmy Marmoset, *Cebuella pygmaea* Spix

Synonymic History

Iacchus pygmaeus Spix, 1823, *Sim. et Vesp. Brasil.*, p. 32, pl. 24, fig. 2 (animal).

Jacchus pygmaeus, Wagner, 1833, *Isis von Oken* 10:997—type and only specimen in bad condition; regarded as a juvenal of *Callithrix jacchus*. Wagner, 1840, *Schreber's Säugth., suppl.*, 1:243—perhaps a half-grown *Hapale penicillata*.

J[acchus] pygmaeus, Reichenbach, 1862, *Vollst. Naturg. Affen*, p. 1, pl. 1, fig. 1 (animal)—BRAZIL; COLOMBIA; PERU: *Loreto* (Sarayacu); characters.

Hapale pygmaeus, Schinz, 1825, *Cuvier das Thierreich*, 4:280—characters ex Spix.

Hapale pygmæus, Bates, 1863, *Naturalist on the River Amazons*, 1863, 2:322—BRAZIL: *Amazonas* (near São Paulo de Olivença).

Hapale pygmaea, Wagner, 1848, *Abh. Akad. Wiss. Munich* 5:467—BRAZIL: *Amazonas* (Tabatinga); characters; type an adult and representative of a valid species. Schlegel, 1876, *Les Singes: Simiae*, p. 277—PERU: *Loreto* (Río Yavarí). Jentink, 1887, *Cat. Osteol. Mus. Pays-Bas* 9:51—ECUADOR. Jentink, 1892, *Cat. Syst. Mamm. Mus. Pays-Bas* 11:59—ECUADOR: *Napo-Pastaza* (Río Copataza); PERU: *Loreto* (Río Yavarí). Fiennes, 1964, *Proc. Zool. Soc. London* 143(3):523—cystic bone disease.

H[apale] pygmaea, Wagner, 1855, *Schreber's Säugth., suppl.* 5:126—characters.

Hapale pygmæa, I. Geoffroy, 1855, *Castelnau Expéd. Amérique Sud,* pt. 7, *Zool., Mamm.,* p. 20, pl. 5, figs. 1, 2 (adult and young)—BRAZIL; PERU; characters. Bates, 1863, *Naturalist on the River Amazons,* 2:322; ibid., 2d ed, p. 400—BRAZIL: *Amazonas* (São Paulo de Olivença); MEXICO [!]. Bartlett, 1871, *Proc. Zool. Soc. London,* 1871: 220—PERU: *Loreto* (Santa Cruz, Río Huallaga). Thomas, 1880, *Proc. Zool. Soc. London* 1880: 395—ECUADOR: *Napo-Pastaza* (Río Copataza).

H[apale] pygmæa, I. Geoffroy, 1851, *Cat. Primates,* p. 61—COLOMBIA; PERU: *Loreto* (Sarayacu); BRAZIL: *Amazonas* (Ega). Mitchell, 1911, *Proc. Zool. Soc. London* 1911:433—maximum longevity 5 months in London Zoo.

Midas pygmaeus, Osculati, 1850, *Esplor. Reg. Equator,* p. 134—ECUADOR: *Napo-Pastaza* (upper Río Napo).

Hapale [(Cebuella)] pygmæa, Gray, 1866, *Proc. Zool. Soc. London* 1865:734—characters; type of *Cebuella.*

H[apale] (Cebuella) pygmæa, Cabrera, 1900, *Anal. Soc. Española Hist. Nat.* (2) 9:89—ECUADOR: *Napo-Pastaza* (La Coca, Río Napo); PERU: *Loreto* (Río Cochiquinas); local name, *chichico.*

Cebuella pygmæa, Gray, 1870, *Cat. monkeys, lemurs and fruit-eating bats, Brit. Mus.,* p. 64—characters; classification. Cabrera, 1917, *Trab. Mus. Nac. Cienc. Nat. Madrid, Ser. Zool.* 31:35—ECUADOR: *Napo-Pastaza* (La Coca; Río Cochiquinas); dental characters. Thomas, 1928, *Ann. Mag. Nat. Hist.* (10) 2:257—PERU: *Loreto* (Santa Cruz). Thomas, 1928, *Ann. Mag. Nat. Hist.* (10) 2:287—PERU: *Loreto* (Pebas). Burton, 1962, *Illustr. London News* 241 (6427):523, figs. (animals)—characters. Burton, 1963, *Illustr. London News* 242 (6450):393, figs. (animals)—breeding in captivity.

Cebuella pygmaea, Lönnberg, 1940, *Ark. Zool.* 32A(10):20—BRAZIL: *Amazonas* (João Pessõa, Rio Juruá). W. C. Osman Hill, 1957, *Primates,* 3:191, 308, fig. 36 (distribution), fig. 89 (ear), fig. 90 (dermatoglyphs of hand and foot), figs. 91, 92 (external genitalia), fig. 93 (skull), fig. 94 (dentition), fig. 95 (intestine)—characters; distribution; anatomy. Carvalho, 1957, *Bol. Mus. Paraense Emilio Goeldi, Zool.,* no. 6, p. 8—BRAZIL: *Acre* (Seringal Oriente). Sobell, Mondon, Means, 1960, *Science* 132:415, fig. 1 (animal)—physiology; laboratory care and maintenance. Uible [in Burton], 1962, *Illust. London News* 241(6427):523, fig. (animal)—characters of captive individual. Burton, 1963, *Illust. London News* 242(6450):393, figs. (animal)—breeding in captivity. Benirschke and Brownhill, 1963, *Cytogenetics* 2:331, figs. 2, 3 (karyotype)—2n = 44; chimeric; heterosexual bone marrow cells; XY disruption and loss of Y chromosome in testicular tissue. Kubota and Hayama, 1964, *Anat. Rec.* 150(4): 473, fig. 1 (tongue), pls. 1–4 (microscopic anatomy of tongue)—tongue anatomy. Wohnus and Benirschke, 1966, *Cytogenetics* 5:94—chromosome idiogram; centric fusion between two chromosomes may have occurred during evolution. Egozcue, Chiarelli, and Sarti-Chiarelli, 1968, *Folia Primat.* 8:50, figs. 1–4 (chromosomes)—somatic and meiotic chromosomes; behavior of sex chromosomes during spermatogenesis; 2n = 44. Hershkovitz, 1968, *Evolution,* 22(3):568—comparisons with *Callithrix jacchus.* Uible, 1969, *Animals,* 11 (10[February]):438, fig. (captive animal on banana). C. A. Hill, 1969, *Zoonooz* 42(9):13, plate inside back cover (animal), fig. 14 (father and twins)—characters; behavior; comparisons with *Microcebus murinus.* Hershkovitz, 1970, *Amer. J. Phys. Anthrop.* 32(3):379, pl. 1A (diseased jaw)—dental diseases. Hershkovitz, 1970, *Folia Primat.* 13:215, figs. 2, 3 (endocranial cast)—ECUADOR: *Napo-Pastaza* (Río Copataza); cerebral fissural pattern. Hsu and Hampton, 1970, *Folia Primat.* 13:183—karyotype (2n = 44). Hershkovitz, 1971, in Dahlberg, *Dental morphology and evolution,* pp. 98, 115, fig. 1B (lower incisors), fig. 5U (upper molar pattern), fig. 6T (lower molar pattern)—dental homologies and evolution. Porter, 1972, *Lab. Animal Sci.,* 22(4):503—endoparasites.

Callithrix pygmæa, Elliot, 1913, *Review of the Primates,* 1:232—characters. Schwarz, 1961, *Science* 134:1696—classification; distribution.

Callithrix pygmaeus, Zukowsky, 1937, *Zool. Gart.* 9:64—birth of young in Frankfurt Zoo.

Callithrix pygmaea, Egozcue, Perkins, and Hagemenas, 1968, *Folia Primat.* 9:82, fig. 1 (animal)—karyotype (2n = 44).

Callithrix [Cebuella] pygmaea, Fiedler, 1956, *Primatologia* 1:163—classification.

Callithrix (Cebuella) pygmaea, Osman Hill, 1958, *Primatologia* 3(1):642, 680—external genitalia. Starck, 1969, *Zool. Gart.,* 36(6):312, fig. 1 (animal, ventral aspect), fig. 2, 3 (external genitalia), figs. 4–6 (scrotal sebaceous glands)—genital and circumgenital glands; olfactory signals; comparison with *Perodicticus.*

Cebuella pygmaea pygmaea, Cruz Lima, 1945, *Mamíferos da Amazonia, Primates, Contr. Mus. Paraense,* p. 252, pl. 42 (animal)—PERU: *Loreto* (Iquitos; Chimbote). Ceballos, 1959, *Rev. Univ. Nac. Cusco* 49(117):267—PERU; measurements.

C[ebuella] p[ygmaea] pygmaea, Osman Hill, 1957, *Primates,* 3:309—characters.

Hapale melanotis jeune age? Lesson, 1840, *Species de mammifères: Bimanes et quadrumanes . . . ,* p. 192—*Jacchus pygmaeus* regarded as possibly the young of *Jacchus penicillatus* and renamed *melanotis.*

[?] *Hapale nigra* Schinz, 1844, *Syst. Verz. Säugth.,* 1:95—PERU: Loreto (type locality, Ríos Ucayali and Marañon); based on bibliographic references to "Jacchus niger Pöppig," an unnamed melanistic pygmy marmoset (or immature *Saguinus* species?), recorded by Pöppig (1832, *Frorieps Notizen* 33:100). Lesson, 1848, *Rev. Zool.,* p. 259—characters ex Schinz.

Cebuella pygmaea niveiventris Lönnberg, 1940, *Ark. Zool., Stockholm* 32A (10):21—BRAZIL: *Amazonas* (type locality, Lago do Ipoxona [= Ipixuna], Rio Solimões); cotypes, male and female, skins and skulls, Royal Natural History Museum, Stockholm, collected by João Bezerra de Souza.

C[ebuella] p[ygmaea] niveiventris, Osman Hill, 1957, *Primates,* 3:309—characters.

[?] *Midas leoninus,* Bates (not Humboldt), 1864, *Naturalist on the River Amazons,* 1:98; ibid., 2d ed., p. 59—BRAZIL: "upper Amazons"; habits of household pet.

Type. Skin, mounted, with skull in, Vienna Museum; collected by J. B. von Spix. According to Elliot (1913*a*, p. 233) the "type is in bad condition . . . the fur is discolored and the hair is mostly gone from the tail."

Type Locality. Tabatinga (171), Rio Solimões, Amazonas, Brazil.

Distribution (fig. VIII.1)

Lowland forests of the upper Amazonian region; in Amazonas, Brazil, westward from the left bank of the Rio Purús south of the Solimões and the right bank of the Rio Japurá (Caquetá) north of the Solimões; in Loreto, Peru, west to the right bank of the Río Ucayali, possibly to the upper Juruá and into the lower Río Huallaga drainage; in Peru and Ecuador to the left bank of the Río Pastaza northward through the drainage basin of the Ríos Tigre, Napo, Putumayo into Colombia to the right bank of the Río Caquetá (Japurá).

Specimens recorded from Sarayacu (102), a locality on the left bank of the Río Ucayali and from Huashi or Huachi (78b) on the right bank of the Pastaza, are assumed to have been collected on the opposite sides of the respective rivers. This assumption may be premature or incorrect, should it prove that the species ranges westward to the next major river barriers. The specimen recorded from Santa Cruz, Río Huallaga (98), by Bartlett (1871, p. 220) seems to be the most misplaced geographically. However, Bartlett states unequivocally "I shot only one specimen at Santa Cruz, on the Huallaga River, the only locality in which I have met with it." Bartlett collected along the lower reaches of both the Río Huallaga and the Río Ucayali.

Taxonomy

The type specimen of *pygmaea* was captured by members of the Spix-Martius expedition near Tabatinga on the Rio Solimões and was kept alive for a few weeks. The dead animal was preserved, its skin later mounted with skull in, and exhibited in the Vienna Museum. Wagner (1833, p. 997), who examined all Spix's types, remarked on the poor condition of the specimen and thought it might represent a young individual of the common marmoset, *Callithrix jacchus*. Subsequent examination of the specimen and teeth he had seen before in the mount, together with assurances from Dr. Martius, who had kept a pygmy marmoset alive for a long time, convinced Wagner (1848, p. 467) that Spix's *pygmaea* was actually full-grown and representative of the smallest species of New World primates.

A series of 36 specimens from "near Tabatinga," type locality of *pygmaea*, exhibit approximately the same range of variation in color as all specimens combined from the different localities mentioned below. The Tabatinga specimens were received alive by the National Institutes of Health primate breeding center in San Diego, California. The animals survived only a few weeks, and their bodies, frozen after death, were sent to the United States National Museum where they were prepared as study skins with skulls. According to records at hand, one batch of 24 individuals was captured alive near Tabatinga in January 1963 and succumbed in San Diego from 23 February to 8 April 1963. The underparts in most specimens of this group are buffy, but the color varies individually from nearly white to orange. The second batch of 12 specimens was captured in June or July 1963 and died off in San Diego from 2 August to 16 September 1963. Their underparts are mainly tawny, as in Spix's type, but there are also pale buff and orange-colored underparts. Even with the overlap, the difference in color of underparts between the two batches is striking. In all other series examined, the range of individual variation is narrow and fully intergrading. Probably, the "near Tabatinga" series is made up of specimens from several localities. Most of the January pale-bellied individuals may have originated in a single locality, perhaps on the southern bank of the Amazon. Most of the saturate-bellied June-July specimens appear to be from another locality, likely on the opposite or Tabatinga bank of the Amazonas. The correlation between pale underparts and depigmented ears noted in the Alto Rio Javari and the Santa Cecilia series (see below) is not evident in either batch from Tabatinga.

Hapale nigra is a name applied by Schinz to a small black marmoset mentioned by Poeppig (1832, p. 100) as follows.

> Sonderbar ist es, dass von den niedlichen Jacchus [*sic*] die in Brasilien so zahlreich an Arten sind, hier nur der mit weisser Schnauze vorkömmt. Die Indier kennen keinen andern; er ist ebenfalls sehr gemein, und zieht in Truppen von funfzig und mehr Individuen durch die Wälder. Um Ucayale jedoch, und also wohl auch am Marañon giebt es eine so kleine schwarze Art, dass der letzt Ubrig gebliebene Missionair ein sehr zahmes Geschöpf der Art in der hohlen Hand engeschlossen mit sich zu tragen pflegte.

It seems that Poeppig knew only tamarins which elsewhere (1832, p. 101, footnote), he identified as *Midas labiatus,* but which are certainly a race of *Saguinus fuscicollis.* The missionary's pet, however, is said to be quite different. Its size and color indicates either a eumelanistic adult pygmy marmoset or a juvenal *Saguinus mystax,* the only normally eumelanistic tamarin in the region. A juvenal of the black-mantled *S. nigricollis* is also a possibility. In any case, the description is vague and seems to be based on rumor. *Hapale nigra* is not at all identifiable and is treated here as a synonym of *Cebuella pygmaea* for convenience of reference only.

Cebuella pygmaea niveiventris Lönnberg is based on a male and female from Lago Ipixuna (183), south bank of the Rio Solimões. It was distinguished from 5 specimens collected at João Pessõa (176), upper Rio Juruá, by its sharply defined whitish chest, belly, and inner surface of arms and legs. The upper Juruá series was regarded as representative of true *pygmaea,* although it included specimens with an "irregular and narrow stripe of grayish or even dirty whitish extending some way along the middle of the belly." A specimen from Seringal Oriente (210), higher up the Juruá, and with a white median band on the underside of its body, is also recorded by Carvalho (1957, p. 8). Carvalho adds that the color of the underparts of other specimens in the Belém Museum from Iquitos (92) and Chimbote (83), Peru, and Palmares on the Solimões varies from ochraceous yellow to pure white. Cruz Lima (1945, p. 252), who first recorded the Iquitos and Chimbote specimens, describes them in the same terms. I. Geoffroy notes that the underparts of an unspecified number of young and adults collected by the Castelnau expedition at Sarayacu, Río Ucayali, Peru, and Ega (Tefé, 182), Rio Solimões, Brazil, vary from white to reddish (i.e., buffy to orange or ochraceous tawny). No distinction was made between the pygmy marmosets from the two localities, but presumably underparts of the series from Ega, which is near the type locality of *niveiventris,* vary from whitish to reddish. The underparts of a specimen at hand from Sarayacu are ochraceous.

Two of 3 specimens from Santa Cecilia, Río Manití (89), below Iquitos but on the south side of the Amazon, are like *niveiventris.* One of three specimens from the confluence of the Río Yaquerana and the upper Yavarí is also like *niveiventris,* but the undersurface of the limbs of the second is grayer than that of the first while underparts of the third are dominantly buffy. The ventral surface of the type of *pygmaea* Spix, from Tabatinga, north of the Amazon, is ochraceous. A specimen from Leticia, Colombia (58e), practically a topotype of *pygmaea,* agrees with the type description. Its underparts are ochraceous orange. A series of 12 specimens collected by Olalla higher up the Amazon (Marañon) at Apayacu, Peru (86), also agrees with *pygmaea.* Specimens from the Río Napo (Intillama [65]; Boca Río Curaray [80]), also north of the Amazon, agree with Spix's *pygmaea.* On the other hand, a specimen from the Río Copataza (74) and another from Montalvo, Río Bobonaza (75a), both localities in the upper Pastaza basin, are intermediate, their underparts being grayish and buffy. The specimen, or specimens, from Santa Cruz, Río Huallaga, Peru (98), south of the Amazon, collected by Bartlett are characterized by Thomas (1928*a*, p. 257) as "quite like examples from the typical region [of *pygmaea* Spix] lower down the Amazon," and hence, it is assumed, with underparts also ochraceous.

From the foregoing it appears that color of underparts is individually and locally variable and cannot be used alone to support the subspecific status of *niveiventris.* Significantly, there is remarkably little variation in color of upper and outer parts of head, body, limbs and tail throughout the geographic range of *Cebuella pygmaea.* More material and attention to other characters, including the correlation between bleaching of the ventrum and depigmentation of the ears and volar surfaces (see "Variation," below), may reveal heretofore unappreciated characters or combinations of characters of subspecific grade.

Characters

Diagnostic:

Smallest New World primate, combined head and body length less than 175 mm, general coloration of upper and outer surface of head, body, and limbs tawny agouti, long hairs of cheeks and head forming mane more or less concealing ears, mantle well defined, upper surface of tail barred with black.

Coat (fig. VIII.17):

General coloration of pelage of face, ears, and upper and outer parts of body, limbs, and tail tawny agouti; forehead, crown, mane, and sides of neck agouti, the hairs blackish basally, followed by two or three pale bands, each alternating with a dark band, the medial band orange, subterminal band buffy, tip and intermediate bands blackish; mane, formed by elongate hairs of cheeks, temples, and nape, more or less concealing ears; back behind mane (or mantle) modified agouti, i.e., with cover hairs like those of mantle but with a single and broader middle orange and black band, a narrower subterminal buffy to silvery band, and a fine black tip, long guard hairs black basally and terminally, orange medially, the banding of all hairs disposed to form a quasi-striated dorsal pattern; rump and outer sides of legs slightly darker or paler, more gray than saddle; outer sides of forearms like mantle; upper surface of hands and feet ochraceous, with blackish skin showing through; face comparatively well haired, facial skin lightly to heavily pigmented; circumbuccal area ochraceous to whitish, the hairs at angle of gape usually forming a pale moustache, area around eyes orange to yellowish, midline of muzzle with a thin crest of short ochraceous to whitish hairs; auricle entirely pigmented but often with inner (lateral) side mottled or unpigmented, pelage of pinna thin, often forming tufts but not concealing skin; hairs of interramia forming a low median crest and directed backward or forward; hairs of throat directed backward; throat, ventral surface of neck dominantly agouti with individual hairs entirely pale or with base black, orange, or gray and terminal portion with one to three pale bands each alternating with a dark band; hairs of chest and belly more broadly banded with blackish and orange or gray or dominantly to entirely buffy or white; inner surface of arms and legs varying from modified agouti to dominantly yellowish or white; pudendal tufts mostly or entirely black; exposed genitalia mottled or unpigmented; tail modified agouti with upper surface barred black, under surface with banding shadowy or obsolete, the bands averaging between 25 and 30 in number.

Perkins (1968, p. 353) implies that the skin of the pygmy marmoset has "several specific peculiarities" but lists none that are not shared with other primates, including the tamarins, cebids, and catarrhine monkeys with which comparisons are made.

Vibrissae (figs. III.8; VIII.11, 12, 13). Supraorbitals, suborbitals, mystacials, rhinarials, and mentals well developed, genals present but usually indistinguishable or randomly distributed, interramals directed backward but uncommon, or may be confused with long mentals; locomotor vibrissae well developed in ulnar carpal field and randomly dispersed through brachial and anconeal fields; gular and pectoral spines present and usually well developed in most individuals.

Measurements. See table 56 and appendix table 2.

Comparisons

Extremely small size, with a substantial gap between it and smallest adults of *Callithrix jacchus,* the mane, barred tail, squirrellike hands and feet, and the general agouti coloration of upper and outer surfaces of body distinguish *Cebuella pygmaea* from all other primates. Immature *Callithrix jacchus* with ear tufts undeveloped resemble adult *Cebuella pygmaea.* The definitely nonagouti hairs of head including cheeks, and mantle are sufficient for distinguishing the former from the latter. Other distinctive characters are detailed in the *Callithrix jacchus* accounts (p. 499).

Table 56. Comparative Measurements of Smallest Living Primates

Species	Weights ♂♂	♀♀	♂♂♀♀	Head and Body Length[3]	Tail Length[3]
Galago minutus[1]	63(46–88)54	60(52–79)19	62(46–88)73	123(105–40)66	172(150–205)63
Microcebus murinus[2]	—	—	60(40–100)163	133(120–46)12	138(123–49)12
Cebuella pygmaea	116(107–25)14[4]	133(126–41)17[4]	125(107–41)31[4]	136(117–52)48	202(172–229)49

NOTE: Figures given are means, extremes in parentheses, and number of samples.
[1] Data from Charles-Dominique (1972)
[2] Data from Martin (1972*a*)
[3] Sexual differences not significant, measurements combined.
[4] Wild-caught captives maintained on standard laboratory diet; data from Cooper (1964–65).

Rivals of *Cebuella pygmaea* for the distinction of being the smallest living primate are the Malagasy mouse lemur *Microcebus murinus* and the African Demidoff's bush baby, *Galago minutus.* Head and body length is about the same in all or, at least, broadly overlapping, but the average body mass of caged laboratory pygmy marmosets is much greater than that of field-caught representatives of the African species (table 56). Also, the head (and skull)) of *Cebuella* is larger and more globose (fig. VIII. 3), and the tail is relatively longer.

Variation

Young with permanent teeth erupting are colored like adults. Suckling young, except possibly newborn, presumably are similar. The sexes are alike except for the usual differences in external organs. Hill (1957, p. 308) states that the perineum is bordered by black hairs in females. I find this condition to be true of both sexes and all ages in all specimens examined. Variation in color of underparts from ochraceous to white is discussed in the section on taxonomy. The pigmentation of exposed skin varies individually, but in none are face, ears, external genitalia, and volar surfaces entirely black or dark brown; outer (i.e., medial) surface of pinna is well pigmented in all specimens examined, but color of inner (lateral) surface is correlated with color of underparts; i.e., inner surface of pinna is pale or unpigmented in specimens with pale or whitish chest and belly, pigmented in individuals with wholly ochraceous underparts and mottled where hairs of underparts are ochraceous with grayish median band. In the present material volar surfaces are similarly pale in animals with pale underparts.

Saturation, Bleaching, and Depigmentation

The generalized agouti coloration of *Cebuella pygmaea* is the most primitive among living New World primates and may be near if not quite like the ancestral condition (cf. fig. III.13). Two notable departures from a generalized mammalian color pattern, however, are evident. First, saturation has modified the agouti pattern of the middle and lower back and resulted in black bars on the dorsal surface of the tail in all specimens and a black pencil in some. Saturation or eumelanism is solidly established in the pudental tufts and on adjacent parts of thighs and underside of tail base. Second, saturation on underparts proceeded from the primitive agouti to ochraceous or orange in some populations, and in others only bleaching to buff, gray, and white is evident. On upper parts bleaching or dilution of the subterminal bands of the hairs creates a frosted effect on back and a grayish barring on tail; bleaching of facial area is restricted in most individuals to the circumbuccal region the hairs grading from ochraceous through buff and gray to white. Eyelids and skin surrounding eyes are largely or entirely depigmented. In some localities, the inner (lateral) surfaces of the ears are more or less depigmented in correlation with bleaching of the underparts. The volar surfaces are likewise paler but not wholly depigmented in individuals with pale or whitish underparts.

Specimens Examined

Total: 121. BRAZIL—*Amazonas:* Tabatinga, 36 (USNM); Santa Rita, Rio Solimões, 2 (BM); "upper Amazons," 2 (BM); COLOMBIA—*Amazonas:* Leticia, 1 (FMNH); ECUADOR—*Napo-Pastaza:* Intillama, 2 (UMMZ); Montalvo, Río Bobonazo, 1 (FMNH); Río Copotaza, 3 (BM, 2; FMNH, 1); Río Lipuno, 3 (AMNH); PERU—Loreto: Andoas, Río Pastaza, 1 (AMNH); Apayacu, Río Amazonas, 12 (AMNH); Río Curaray, mouth, 7 (AMNH); Huachi, Río Pastaza, 1 (USNM); Iquitos, 3 (AMNH); Río Napo, 1 (AMNH); Orosa, 4 (AMNH); Pebas, 6 (BM); Santa Cecilia, Río Manití, 3 (FMNH); Santa Cruz, Río Huallaga, 1 (BM); Sarayacu, 5 (AMNH, 4; USNM, 1); Río Yaquerana, mouth, 3 (FMNH); UNKNOWN LOCALITY—24 (USNM, 7; SM, 3; FMNH, 7 [in spirits]; AMNH, 3 [in spirits]; GEE, 4 [in spirits]).

50 *Cebuella pygmaea*
2. *Biology*

REPRODUCTION

The pygmy marmoset is fecund, easy to handle, abundant in the wild, and successfully bred and reared in captivity. The following account, adapted mainly from Christen (1968, 1974), who observed a colony in Zürich of 5 wild-caught and 10 captive-born individuals for 2½ years, is arranged under the following headings.

Courtship	Gestation
Mating	Breeding Season
Copulation	Litters
Pregnancy and Parturition	

Courtship

Christen 1974

The male first marches round the cage stiff-legged, his back arched, hair erected. Then he pursues the female, his tongue darting rhythmically in and out, accompanied by a quivering of the lower jaw. This exercise is repeated with interruptions at frequent intervals for marking.

A receptive female first runs from the pursuing male, then stops to whistle softly and present with tail held high. She may also strut stiff-legged, nuzzle the male, and stroke him with her body. An unreceptive female flees twittering and screaming then crouches submissively to the floor of the cage but without presenting her genitalia to the male.

Mating

Christen 1968, 1974

The 15 pygmy marmosets of the Zürich laboratory colony were separated into mating pairs or natural family groups and housed in small cages. Males were always ready to mate but females were not receptive from the beginning of pregnancy until 3–6 weeks after delivery. Lactating females mated successfully. Sibling matings, however, were unproductive.

Christen may have overlooked the fact that none of the young born in her colony attained the full maturity, usually after 2½ years, necessary for insuring production of full-term, viable young.

Burton 1963, ex litt. Mr. and Mrs. Boswell Miller, Jr.

The female pygmy marmoset was acquired by the Millers in August 1960. She was 2 or 3 years old at the time. Her consort, believed to be about 10 months old, was purchased during the summer of 1961. The pair began mating a few weeks later.

Copulation

Christen 1974

The female is seized from behind by the male, who then mounts with both arms embracing her hindquarters. During coitus, which lasts 4 to 10 seconds, the male tongues, his body quivers, and he may gently bite his partner's nape. The female also tongues during copulation but seldom looks back to her mate. After completion of the act, the male licks his penis, then the genitalia of the female and finally her face, eyes, and head. Grooming in the form of licking and gentle scratching may continue for an hour, when a second copulation may take place. A branch or sitting board in the cage serves for the act.

Pregnancy and Parturition

Christen 1968, 1974

First signs of pregnancy were bleedings that lasted several days, fatigue, somnolence, and failure to participate in experiments being conducted at the time. Conspicuous behaviorial changes occurred during the 13th week of pregnancy, when the female became unsteady, fell frequently, and drank copiously, about 20 times daily. Abdominal swelling became noticeable only during the last month (17th–20th week) of carriage. At the same time the pregnant female's appetite grew, she competed aggressively for food, and mealworms, insects, and meat were taken more eagerly than before. Although her weight increased 22% above normal, fetal movements, mucous secretions, and labor pains were not apparent.

Signs of gestation, often completely overlooked in primiparous females, become increasingly apparent with each successive pregnancy.

One female produced 6 litters, each following a gestation of 19 to 20 weeks, with births occurring at intervals of 22½ to 31 weeks, all at night. No labor pains, mucous secretions, or afterbirth complications were observed in this or two other females, and no placentas were found.

Gestation

Records of 5 full-term births (table 57) show the duration of gestation ranging from 19.5 to 20.3 weeks, for a mean of 19.76 weeks. Interbirth intervals varied from 21½ to 31 weeks. All births occurred at night.

Breeding Season

Christen 1968, 1974

Nothing is known of the reproductive cycle of *Cebuella* in the wild. No regular menstrual period, cyclical genital swellings, or breeding season were noted in captivity (table 57). The 18 litters produced during a 2½-year period of observation reflect no seasonality. One of Christen's breeders produced 6 litters between the end of November 1964 and the beginning of August 1967, or about 2 litters annually with 3 of them produced within a 10-month span from 10 December 1965 to 23 October 1966.

Litters

Records of 22 deliveries compiled from the literature are listed in table 57. The distribution of offspring in 19 litters for which data are available follows:

Young per Litter	*Number of Litters*	*Total Young*
1	6(26%)	6(16%)
2	14(67%)	28(76%)
3	1(5%)	3(8%)
Totals	21	37

Average number per litter is 1.8 young. Most, if not all, singletons are probably lone survivors of early dizygotes. In a single live birth of a 15g male, recorded by Cooper (1965, report no. 10, p. 506), close inspection of the expelled placental membrane "disclosed a small (1.4 cm) mummified fetus in a very early developmental stage. It was tightly enclosed in its amniotic sac and located opposite the single discoid placental attachment of its normally developed twin."

Table 57. *Cebuella pygmaea:* Birth Records Compiled from the Literature

Date Born	*Mother*	*Litter*	*Interbirth Interval (days)*	*Gestation (weeks)*	*Remarks*	*Source*
28 Nov. 1964	C2	♂ ♀	—	—	One partially eaten at birth, other survived 36 hours	Christen 1968; 1974
29 Nov. 1964	C1	♂ ♀	—	—	Born live but bitten to death	Christen 1968; 1974
5 July 1965	C1	♂ ♂	219	20	Live	Christen 1968; 1974
10 Dec. 1965	C1	♂ ♀	158	19½	Live	Christen 1968; 1974
18 May 1966	C1	♂ ♀	160	19½	Live	Christen 1968; 1974
23 Oct. 1966	C1	♂ ♀	158	19½	Live	Christen 1968; 1974
5 Aug. 1967	C1	♂ ♂	286	—	Live	Christen 1968; 1974
15 July 1966	C3	♂ ♂ ♂	—	17	Apparently premature; 2 died after delivery, 1 within 12 hours	Christen 1968; 1974
27 Sept. 1961	—	♀ ♂	—	—	—	Macdonald 1965
21 Feb. 1936	—	o	—	—	Survived 1 day	Zukowsky 1940
12 Aug. 1936	—	o	—	—	Survived 16 days	Zukowsky 1940
16 Feb. 1938	—	o	—	—	Survived 10 weeks	Zukowsky 1940
27 Sept. 1938	—	—	—	20.3	—	C. A. Hill, pers. comm.
May 1939	—	—	—	—	—	C. A. Hill, pers. comm.
14 May 1954	—	—	—	—	—	C. A. Hill, pers. comm.
No date	—	o	—	—	—	Hampton, Hampton, and Levy 1971
No date	—	o o	—	—	—	Hampton, Hampton, and Levy 1971
No date	—	o o	—	—	—	Hampton, Hampton, and Levy 1971
No date	—	o o	—	—	—	Hampton, Hampton, and Levy 1971
No date	—	o o	—	—	—	Burton 1962
Feb. 1962	—	o o	—	—	—	Burton 1963
7 Mar. 1964	—	o o	—	—	Survived 1 day	Cooper 1964 (Rept. 7)
24 Jan. 1965	—	o	—	—	Survived 1 day	Cooper 1964 (Rept. 10)

Fig. VIII.17. Pygmy Marmoset, *Cebuella pygmaea* Spix: Adult with twins. (Photo courtesy of San Diego Zoo.)

GROWTH AND DEVELOPMENT

The available data on growth and development of pygmy marmosets are remarkably similar to those for the ouistiti, *Callithrix jacchus*. It also appears that the two species are much nearer in size at birth than at maturity.

The little known of the growth, development, and care of young is arranged under the following headings.

Chronology of Growth
Sexual Dimorphism
Weights, Measurements, and Allometric Growth
Longevity

Chronology of Growth

The chronology of growth and development of captive-bred *Cebuella pygmaea* is arranged from data recorded by Christen 1968, 1974 (C); Burton 1963, ex Mr. and Mrs. Roswell Miller, Jr. (B); and Macdonald 1965, pp. 33–34, (M); the letter N followed by a figure is the number of samples.

1st day—(C) Body except belly covered with hair; newborn clings to maternal fur, crawls, seeks teat in axilla and begins suckling within first hour; cries, sleeps, and suckles through day; eyes can be opened but usually kept closed.

Average weight, 16 g (N = 13) or about 11% normal weight of mother; head approximately 69% adult size, but relative to body mass, is about twice adult size; limbs, particularly hands and feet, relatively longer than in adults, tail shorter.

(B) "At birth each [of the two males] weighed 20 grams, with a body length of 2½ ins (64 mm) and a tail length of 3½ ins (89 mm) with a rich fur coat but bare stomachs. They had upper and lower rows of tiny pointed teeth and the tongue, palms and soles of the feet were blood red for about 36 hours."

(C) Male survivor of triplets born 3 weeks prematurely (17 weeks gestation) born entirely naked with eyes closed; it "crowed," clutched a bit of its mother's fur, drank a little milk, and died 12 hours after birth.

(Cooper 1965) Male singleton born 24 January in San Diego Zoo Primate Center weighed 15 g exclusive of placenta; "overall length," 14.5 cm.

(M) The surviving twin measured an "astonishingly large six inches over-all [head, body, tail = 152 mm]."

4th day—(C) Begins self-grooming; turns head and gazes in all directions but without awareness of surroundings. Weight about 70 g (N = 3).

7th day—(C) Reacts to light of battery lamp. Weight about 100 g (N = 3).

8th day—(C) Crawls over adults; sits alone on shelf, but legs do not support body above ground. Weight about 115 g (N = 3).

12th day—(C) Beats with hands on partitions between cages; chews and plays with hair tufts and tail of adults; eyes follow moving people and fix on distant objects. Weight about 140 g (N = 3).

16th day—(C) Trills like adult.

17th day—(C) Climbs slowly through branches arrayed in cages; eats from mother's hand; gnaws on everything; begins social grooming. Weight about 145 g (N = 2).

24th day—(C) Frequently left alone by parents; eats from mother's hands.

25th day—(C) Becomes relatively independent.

27th day—(M) Weaned; moves independently but prone to falling from heights.

28th day—(C) Fur thick, tail bushy.

28th day (B) Nearly independent; forced by both parents to strike out on their own. Eat first solid food (strained bananas, custard).

30th day—(C) Eats adult food but not from common food dish; steals tidbits from mother and older siblings but threatens conspecifics who want his food; runs and climbs like adult but seeks safety on parent's back when alarmed.

6 weeks—(B) Eat two mealworms, three times a day.

7 weeks—(B) Eat almost any solid food.

8 weeks—(B) Nursed only every 2 or 3 hours.

2d month—(C) Eats out of common food dish; vocalizes like adult; twins play mostly with each other.

3d month—(C) Suckled briefly about once daily.

4th month—(C) No longer nursed or licked; testes not yet descended, but penis and scrotum fully differentiated.

5th month—(C) Independent but still springs to adult's back when alarmed.

6th month—(C) Scrotal skin more darkly pigmented, glandular field defined.

8th to *10th month*—(C) Testes descended.

10th month—(C) First attempts at mating; penis erectile.

12th month—(C) External sexual characters well developed.

18th month—(C) Female indifferent to courtship.

18th to *24th month*—(C) Sexually mature; females not significantly different from males in size and weight.

23rd month—(C) Female shows vaginal bleeding.

24th month—(C) First litter usually aborted, stillborn, or premature.

36th month—Pregnancy normal, young live at term.

Sexual Dimorphism

No significant difference is noted between the sexes, apart from the organs of reproduction and parturition. As usual in callitrichids, the female is slightly larger in nearly all dimensions. The larger average weight for males computed by Christen (cf. p. 471) is based on 4 males and 4 females of different ages, all excessively fat. Eliminating the heaviest male and lightest female would reverse the weight relationship between the sexes. Weights of the San Diego Zoo pygmy marmosets are probably more nearly representative of those of wild, free-living individuals. In comparing weights of females, allowance must be made for weight of possible fetuses.

Weights, Measurements, and Allometric Growth

Comparative weights and measurements of newborn pygmy marmosets are shown in table 58; table 59 gives weights of known age marmosets; and average weights of wild-caught adult males and females are listed in table 60. Weights of twins from birth to maturity are charted in figure VIII.18, and the diagrams in figure VIII.19 show relative lengths of extremities at newborn, juvenal, and adult stages of development.

In the newborn, according to Christen (1974, p. 26), who does not give individual measurements or mention sample size, the head is 69% of full-grown size, and hind limb length relative to trunk length is about the same (ca. 85%) as in adults. Other bodily proportions are shown in figure VIII.19.

Longevity

Crandall (1964, p. 105) gives the maximum longevity of pygmy marmosets kept in the New York Zoological Society's Gardens as 4 years, 11 months, 14 days.

Jarvis and Morris (1961, p. 289) list 6 individuals in the London Zoo of which 4 died within 12 months; the two survivors lived 12 and 28 months.

Christen (1968), who was most successful in maintaining and breeding marmosets, kept them up to 10 years.

Table 58. Weights (in g) and Measurements (in mm) of Newborn Pygmy Marmosets

Reference	*Weight*	*Head and Body*	*Tail*	*Total*
Christen (1968)	16 (N = 13)	—	—	—
Burton (1963)	20; 20 (♂ ♂)	64	89	153
Cooper (1964)	14.9; 13.2 (♀ ♀)	—	—	—
Cooper (1964)	15 (♂)	—	—	—
Cooper (1965)	15 (♂)	—	—	145
Macdonald (1965)	—	—	—	152

NOTE: Mean weight = 15 g.

Table 59. Mean Weights of Known-Age Male and Female Pygmy Marmosets (in g)

	Age	♂	♀
	1	—	163
	1½	153	—
	1½	145	—
	3½	—	155
	ca. 4	—	100
	ca. 4½	190	—
	7–10	—	145
	10	145	—
Averages		158	136[1]

SOURCE: Christen (1968).
NOTE: Average ♂ ♀ = 147; weight ratio of females to males = 83:100.
[1] Includes 2 females of unknown age.

Table 60. Average Weights of Wild-Caught Adult Males and Females in the Primate Colony, San Diego Zoo

	♂ ♂ *(N)*	♀ ♀ *(N)*	*Report No.*
16 Apr. 1964	107(4)	141(3)	7
8 Aug. 1964	119(3)	124(4)	8
5 Nov. 1964	125(3)	139(4)	9
11 Feb. 1965	117(3)	128(4)	10
12 Aug. 1965	108(1)	138(2)	11/12
Means	116(14)	133(17)	

SOURCE: Cooper (unpublished Quarterly Reports, 1964–65)

BEHAVIOR

The pygmy marmoset appears to be comparatively abundant in the wild but is rarely seen because of its small size and cryptic habits. Its occasional appearance in zoos and laboratories is mainly a by-product of the capture and importation of tamarins native to the upper Amazonian basin where *Cebuella* occurs. Little is known of the behavior of the pygmy marmoset in the wild, and until recently less was known of captive *Cebuella* comportment than of other captive callitrichids. The accumulated data is organized under the following headings. Contributions by Christen (1974), published in German, have been severely edited, paraphrased and annotated.

Habits in the Wild
Social Organization
Daily Rhythm
Threat and Aggression
Defense Behavior
Comparative Behavior: Wild-Caught and Captive-Born Individuals
Group Interaction
Enemies
Care of Young
Grooming
Food and Feeding
Drink
Coprophagy
Elimination and Sanitation
Learning and Color Perception
Mirror Image Response
Fur Doll Response
Handedness
Locomotion
Posture
Repose
Play
Marking
Vocalization
Thermoregulation
Status in the Wild

Habits in the Wild

My limited observations, others by Bates (1863), Izawa (1975) and Kinzey, Rosenberger, and Ramírez (1975) are the only ones available on the habits of pygmy marmosets in the wild or in semicaptivity in their natural habitat.

Cebuella pygmaea prefers low second growth along streams, where cover is thick and protective, visibility good, and insects most abundant. Its small size, light weight, speed, and agility permit it to travel along twigs and vines too delicate to support all but the smallest of scansorial predators.

The pygmy betrays its presence in the wild by a weak, hoarse chirp like the stridulation of a cricket. So nearly alike are the sounds of the two animals that all but practiced ears confuse them. In time, however, the curious listener will try to trace the call to its source. As he bears in, he may become aware of a multitude of hissing chirps coming from behind the foliage or twigs and branches of the thick shrubbery in front of him. A search for the vocalizers is often futile. An overt move too near the sound is met with silence while the little animals melt away unseen into the forest, with only the gentle swaying of a twig here and the dropping of some debris there to mark the springboards of their flight.

I have never seen the pygmy marmoset in association with other monkeys. The very nature of the animal and its habitat make it difficult to espy at close range. It is all the more difficult, if not practically impossible, to

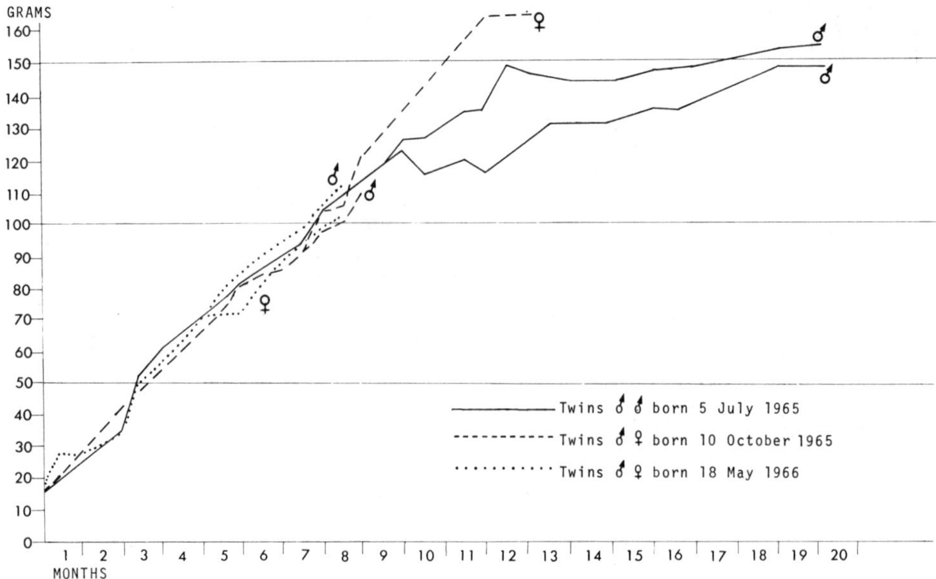

Fig. VIII.18. Weight curves of three twin sets of *Cebuella pygmaea* from birth through 1967. (After Christen 1974, p. 28.)

distinguish the pygmy at the greater distance that larger monkeys hold between themselves and protential enemies on the ground. In any case, it is very likely that the pygmy avoids contact with the carnivorous tamarins and aggressive cebids.

It was during a sultry June afternoon of 1936 in Intillama, an island of the Río Napo in Ecuador, that I first met the pygmy marmoset. I was resting on a fallen log when I heard an insistent chirp, but feeling too listless to raise my head and investigate I shrugged off the sound as that of the ubiquitous crickets. When the chirping became a chorus, however, I looked up suddenly and found myself staring into the face of the tiniest monkey I had ever seen alive. The pygmy was clinging to the terminal twig of a bush no more than an arm's length from my face. Its little eyes were ablaze, tusks bared, and mane bristling, while it hissed, grimaced, and swung menacingly as if to gain momentum for springing upon me. As I watched entranced, the entire shrub came alive with pygmy marmosets. My eyes shifted from the first sprite, no doubt the leader, to the trembling twigs of the bush where the pygmies, perhaps a score in all, were running and leaping back and forth, chirping, hissing, posturing, and grimacing. I was tempted to seize one with my hands, but as I straightened out slowly to do so, the imps simply vanished, leaving only a rear

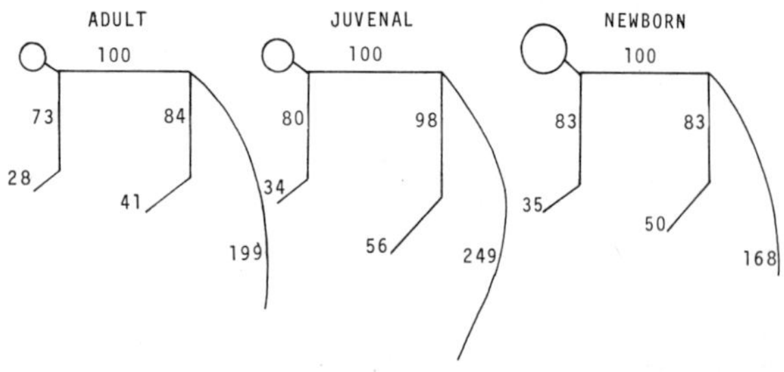

Fig. VIII.19. Bodily proportions of *Cebuella pygmaea* at newborn, juvenal, and adult stages of development; limb and tail proportions (in %) are based on trunk length with a common value of 100. Diagram reproduced from Christen (1974, p. 26), who gives no measurements or other data from which the proportions were calculated.

guard crisscrossing the branches of the trees to confuse pursuit and taunt the enemy with its chirpings.

Pygmy marmosets are known all along the Río Caquetá in southeastern Colombia. I heard them at Tres Troncos, La Tagua, in January 1952, but none showed itself to me. Their local names are *piel roja* (red skin) and *leoncillo* (little lion monkey). I also heard their cricket-like calls at Río Mecaya, higher up the Caquetá, and I caught a glimpse of them but failed to get a specimen. The extreme shyness of this species in captivity was noted by Zukowsky (1940, p. 103). "The little animals sit nervously on the branches when the attendant walks by. They observe his every movement with owl-like movements of the head. Should he come closer they fly into their sleeping box or hide behind branches or foliage."

The monkey identified by Bates (1863, 1:98) as "*Midas leoninus*" may possibly be a pygmy marmoset if not a very young tamarin. Elsewhere, Bates (1863, 2:322) mentions *Hapale pygmaeus* with characters like those of his "*Midas leoninus*," and he clearly distinguishes it from white-mouth tamarins. Bates's (1863, 1:98) account follows.

> On the upper Amazons I once saw a tame individual of the Midas leoninus, a species first described by Humboldt, which was still more playful and intelligent than the one [*Midas ursulus*] just described. This rare and beautiful little monkey is only seven inches in length, exclusive of the tail. It is named leoninus on account of the long brown mane which depends from the neck, and which gives it very much the appearance of a diminutive lion. In the house where it was kept, it was familiar with every one; its greatest pleasure seeming to be to climb about the bodies of different persons who entered. The first time I went in, it ran across the room straightway to the chair on which I had sat down, and climbed up to my shoulder; arrived there, it turned round and looked into my face, showing its little teeth, and chattering, as though it would say, "Well, and how do *you* do?" It showed more affection towards its master than toward strangers, and would climb up to his head a dozen times in the

course of an hour, making a great show every time of searching there for certain animalcula. Isidore Geoffrey St. Hilaire relates of a species of this genus, that it distinguished between different objects depicted on an engraving. M. Audouin showed it the portraits of a cat and a wasp; at these it became much terrified: whereas, at the sight of a figure of a grasshopper or beetle, it precipitated itself on the picture, as if to seize the objects there represented.

Social Organization

Kinzey, Rosenberger, and Ramirez (1975)

The group studied from July to September 1974 in the tropical rain forest along the upper Amazonian Rio Nanay, about 30 km southwest of Iquitos, Peru, consisted of 4 adults, 3 subadults, and 2 infants carried by an adult male, a total of 9.

Christen 1974, p. 47

The senior and usually parous female of a cage group is *alpha*. The senior male is *beta*. In a pair group with female subadult, the adult male is dominant. Older siblings always dominate younger ones. Parents tolerate their own young of one or two generations even after they become adult.

The *alpha* is more active than other cage group members, takes the initiative, eats first and most, including tidbits, threatens and postures often, self-grooms more and social grooms less, presents often, and copulates frequently.

Daily Rhythm

Christen 1974, p. 56

The captive Zürich colony became active at dawn and retired at nightfall. Activity was most pronounced between 10:00 and 18:00 hours with peaks at 11:00, 14:00, and 17:00 (highest), and lulls at 12:00, 15:30 (lowest) and a sudden drop after 18:00. The following activities were measured, the time spent in each expressed as a percentage of total daily activity.

Locomotion	41%	Mostly afternoon
Feeding	26%	Mostly afternoon
Personal care (*Komfortverhalten*), including self-grooming, sanitation	17%	Mostly forenoon
Social, including social grooming	9%	Mostly noon
Aggression, including threat and domination	7%	Mostly during feeding

The large number of pregnant females and hungry young accounts for the large percentage of time spent eating.

Young to about 2½ years old are more than twice as active as adults and maintain their activity, mostly locomotory, all day almost without pause. Adults usually doze for hours and leave their sleeping shelves for little more than feeding or defecating. Males and females are equally active but compared with subordinate females the dominant female devotes more of her energies to eating, drinking, personal care, passive social activities, locomotion, and aggression. The subordinates on the other hand, spend more time grooming her than she spends grooming them.

Kinzey, Rosenberger, and Ramirez (1975)

The wild-living marmosets were normally awake for about 11.5 hr each day from 0615 to 1745. By quantifying frequency and duration of activity patterns for 4 days the authors found that adult animals divided the daily routine in approximately the following proportions.

Feeding, including foraging for insects	48%
Locomotion, excluding movements involved in feeding	12%
Resting, including grooming	40%

During 16 hours observation of feeding behavior, 77% of the adult animals' time was spent clinging to vertical supports of large diameter while feeding on sap.

Threat and Aggression

Christen 1974, p. 48

The threat display of one male to another in an adjoining cage or to strange people, is a frontal confrontation with back arched, fur erect, gait slow and stiff-legged. This is followed by a half-circle turn and presentation of genitalia from the rear with tail raised nearly perpendicularly, head turned back with eyes glaring at his opponent. Adult threat display is practiced only by high-ranking males and females. Young of the same group mimic the adult display in rudimentary form. Genital presentation alone is also used by adults as an expression of superiority over a socially inferior conspecific. It is not an invitation to copulation.

Defensive threat, directed against people, cats, reptiles, and other nonconspecifics, is shown by raised mane, cocked head, and threat cries. Back arching, stiff-legged gait, or presentation are absent, and the act may terminate in flight.

Aggression as seen in competition for food is expressed by piloerection, anger screams, flushing and wrinkling of facial skin. Aggression toward conspecifics in a neighboring cage leads to threat display and fighting. Tonguing as a part of or prelude to threat display was not observed in *Cebuella*.

Defense Behavior

Christen 1974, p. 60

During the first 2 to 3 months of captivity, the pygmy marmoset remains shy and attempts to escape observation by hiding in his sleeping box or behind an upright branch. He urinates frequently when feeling threatened and avoids being seen eating even by the caretaker. The captive-born shows no such fears and defense behavior.

A subordinate individual threatened by a conspecific flattens himself submissively against a branch or cage floor, his fur adpressed, tail drawn between legs, and the corners of his mouth pulled back baring the teeth in a fright grimace. Sexually uninterested females also display this behavior toward sexually aggressive males.

Comparative Behavior: Wild-Caught and Captive-Born Individuals

Christen 1974, p. 38

The 5 wild-caught pygmy marmosets of the Zürich colony, compared with the 10 captive-born offspring, marked and copulated more frequently, were more aggressive, and exhibited escape behavior not seen in the captive-born. They also groomed, played, and ate less but were more fastidious with food than captive-born, and they preferred the higher levels to the floor of the cage. One wild-caught individual was seen scooping up water with his hand, which he then licked, whereas captive-born apparently only lapped water directly from the container, like all the others.

It seems to me that the behavioral traits cited above and one or two more mentioned by Christen are not necessarily the conditionings of wild-caught or captive-born individuals. Differential characteristics attributed to wild-caught can derive from seniority and rank alone while those of their offspring correspond to their youth and subordinate station. In any event, Christen's samples were too small for the kind of analysis she attempted.

Group Interaction

Christen 1974, p. 47

Members of groups occupying adjoining cages for 4 to 8 weeks sniffed, touched, nuzzled, displayed, and threatened. Adults ascertained the sexes of their opposite numbers and seemingly established a social ranking among themselves. When permitted to mingle freely they promptly proceeded to impose previously rehearsed relationships, but with incomplete success. Males who tried to copulate with the females they could only ogle before met with resistance more often than with submission. Dominant adults of the same sex who had previously exchanged courtesies now battled furiously and inflicted deep wounds on their adversaries. Subordinate adults and young watched their elders fight while they themselves cowered in the farthest corners of their own cages.

Enemies

No specific instance of predation on pygmy marmosets has been observed or verified by examination of stomach contents. It is virtually certain, however, that such diurnal predators as snakes, lizards, hawks, and perhaps weasels prey on pygmy marmosets. Tamarins, callimicos, and small cebids, always avid for vertebrate flesh, may also attack and devour pygmy marmosets.

Care of Young

Christen 1968, 1974

Suckling young are carried by father, older silblings, or related adults, often within the first hour of birth. When a caretaker tires of the burden, he brushes the young off his back by rubbing or pressing them against the cage wires or a branch, or he bites them until they leave. The cries of pain usually attract another adult, who rescues the young by lending them an arm for climbing across to his back. The new caretaker then ritually licks the anal region of the transferred young.

The young are returned to their mother at nursing time. Very young twins suckle at the same time for about 13 minutes at half-hour intervals, their lips smacking audibly.

Burton 1963, ex Mr. and Mrs. Roswell Miller, Jr.

For about 4 weeks the father is the chief baby-sitter. The mother nurses the babies about every 1½ hours, but when she decides they have had enough she bites their hands. Thereupon, the father takes them away mounted on his back. Should the father be slow-moving in attending his duties, the mother nips his ear. The babies were evidently due for independence when about 4 weeks old, and both parents bit them into striking out on their own.

Cooper 1964 (Report no. 7).

On the day of birth (7 March 1964), the female twins were "observed to sleep quietly on their mother's back and to nurse on several occasions. The father was never observed to carry either of them. On the morning of 8 March the larger of the twins (14.9 gms) was found dead in the retiring box and several hours later the second twin (13.2 grams) also died."

Cooper 1965 (Report no. 10, p. 4).

"When the caretakers arrived the [male born 24 January 1965] was on the floor of the retiring box, but one of his parents soon retrieved it. A short while later [the newborn] was seen in the possession of the father, first on his back and then cradled ventrally. The cradling observed was evidently a paternal response to a weakened infant as the baby was found cold and dead shortly thereafter at 11 AM the same morning. The umbilical cord had not been severed and the placenta was still intact. The baby weighed 15 grams exclusive of the placenta and was 14.5 centimeters in overall length."

Grooming

Christen 1974

Self-Grooming:
Most individuals groomed themselves after eating or drinking. The fur is scratched with hand or foot in the manner of a cat, and the muzzle is rubbed or scraped on

a branch or other suitable fixture. Feet, toes, fingers, claws, and urogenital region are licked, while the tail is often held by both hands and cleaned with claws and teeth. Wounds, if any, are also licked until healed.

Social Grooming:
The groomee sits at the groomer's foot or lies on back or side. The groomer inspects the groomee's fur with both hands, parts it and picks the scurf with the teeth. Hands, feet, and claws are examined, the mouth is opened with the hands, the teeth picked with fingers and claws.

A dominant female is more often groomed by a subordinate female than vice versa. Otherwise, there appears to be no age, rank, or sex discrimination among groomers and groomees. Solicitation for grooming was not seen in *Cebuella*.

Food and Feeding

General morphology and dentition of the pygmy marmoset indicate that the animal is mainly insectivorous. Like most simians in captivity, however, *Cebuella* eats what it gets, but if given a choice prefers insects, dead or alive, to prepared laboratory food mixes.

Christen 1974

Solid food is taken from the dish with a hand or the teeth and carried to a high branch or the top of the sleeping box, where it is consumed. Seeds and nuts are held in one hand and opened with the teeth. Grasshoppers are stalked and seized with a swift strike of the arm and rapidly consumed head first. Large pieces of food are, perforce, seized with both hands. Branches and boards are frequently chewed and round holes are dug into bark and wood with the teeth. The habit of biting into the bark of trees for the sweet sap appears to be common to all callitrichids and many other primates (cf. p. 446).

Presented with a whole banana, a laboratory-born pygmy circled it with curiosity, sniffed the skin several times, but did not bite. This behavior is surprising, because Christen (1970, p. 9) fed the animals a banana ration of 15 g every afternoon.

Burton 1963, ex Mr. and Mrs. Roswell Miller, Jr.

"At about 4 weeks of age, the young pygmy marmosets were fed strained bananas and baby food custard pudding. At six weeks, Mrs. Miller introduced the marmosets to mealworms. They ate about 2, three times daily. Later on, their diet included shrimp, lobster, ice cream and jelly."

Izawa 1975, p. 305

"[Pygmy marmosets] inhabit with high population density the basin of the River La Tagua, which branches off a little above La Tagua village on the right bank of the middle basin of the River Caquetá. There were five encounters in this area.

"Whenever the author encountered the monkeys, they were clinging to the trunks of large trees. Even with binoculars it was difficult to distinguish what they were doing in such a posture. Examining the trunks after the monkeys left, the author found that the places where they had been were scratched and somewhat moistened. It is supposed from this evidence that they were licking the sap of the trees. On August 29, 1973, a monkey was observed licking sap for 190 seconds, without moving. This was in striking contrast to the feeding behavior shown by the tamarins [*Saguinus fuscicollis*] when eating resin.

"Innumerable stains made by their licking sap appeared on the trunks of the trees which were mainly Lakule (*Vallea stipularis*), Guarango (*Parkia oppositifolia*), and Anun (?). These stains were conspicuous from the part of the tree-trunk near the ground to 6 m above the ground."

Izawa 1975, p. 312

"The stomach of *C. pygmaea* is still smaller than that of *S[aguinus] fuscicollis* and only a very small quantity of pieces of leaves and moss was found in the stomach contents of two individuals. Accordingly, nothing can be concluded from the findings in their stomach contents. Taking into account of a mention (Napier and Napier, 1967) of *C. pygmaea* describing that in the wild the monkeys eat insects, fruits, birds' eggs and birds, the food repertoire of the monkeys is thought to consist of various kinds of foods. However, from the author's observations, the sap can be considered to form the basis of their food habit as resin is the basis of that of *S. fuscicollis,* and in this sense, *C. pygmaea* can be called a sap licker."

Kinzey, Rosenberger, and Ramirez (1975)

"It spends most of its feeding time [in nature] obtaining and eating sap, a behaviour which has also been noted for *Cebuella* in Columbia [*sic*] by Moynihan. In addition, *Cebuella* feeds on insects and berries. Insects and spiders are approached by slow stalking and are frequently captured using a rapid pouncing leap. Most insect foraging occurs in areas of entangled lianas and bushes below the level of the closed canopy (the primary foraging zone). This substrate, in contrast to the canopy, has a relatively high frequency of vertical supports. An individual may spend 85 to 90% of its total waking hours in the primary foraging zone. Berries ('renaco,' *Ficus* sp., and 'caymittillo') are an infrequent source of food and are procured from terminal branches in the canopy (that is, a secondary foraging zone), or from bushes below it.

"In terms of time spent, sap was the most important food resource for *Cebuella* during our study [July–September 1974]. Sap was obtained from lianas and from the trunks of trees of both large and small diameter. *Cebuella* obtained this exudate by using its semiprocumbent lower incisor teeth to scrape fissures into the bark, primarily while clinging to large vertical tree trunks. The trunk diameter of the preferred sap-feeding tree (*Quararibea* sp., Bombacaceae) measured 51 cm at the feeding level. Adult individuals spent an average of 97 min each day preparing, and/or feeding at, sap-holes on this large tree alone. The sap of other large diameter trees, including *Palicourea macrobotrys* (Rubiaceae), was also used for feeding. Throughout these feeding bouts on large tree trunks a variety of clinging postures were used, with the body oriented upright, inclined, or head downward. In the latter posture the lower extremity was rotated laterally. In the upright position the base of the tail was often pressed to the tree trunk: the forelimbs were either abducted and fully extended or adducted at the shoulder and partially flexed at the elbow; the hindlimbs were widely abducted indicating great hip mobility, or closely adducted and flexed beneath the body. In all these postures the claws of *Cebuella* served a particularly important function specific to feeding. During scraping actions of the teeth against the bark, the pedal claws anchored the hind limbs below. The head (and often the shoulders) were fixed on the vertebral column. The forelimbs acted as levers, flexing at the elbow and/or wrist, increasing the mechanical advantage at the mandibular incisors. Most important, during all postural behaviours on large substrates the claws seemed to be firmly embedded in the bark."

The authors conclude that the "semiprocumbent mandibular incisors, small body size and clawed digits are part of an adaptive complex especially related to feeding on sap while clinging to large vertical supports." This is not to say that these characters individually or collectively are specializations for sap feeding. For example, the shape of the lower jaw and incisors of *Cebuella* are as much related to hole drilling for scent marking (cf. *Callithrix jacchus*, p. 556) as for sap feeding, and the virtually identical vertical clinging posture of young *Cebuella* (fig. VIII.17) is totally unrelated to sap feeding. Small arboreal rodents with similar morphological characters and habits are certainly opportunistic sap feeders but are not specially adapted for this behavior. Tamarins are also claw clingers and sap feeders, but their jaws and incisors are markedly different from those of *Cebuella*. Kinzey et al. mention the prosimians *Galago elegantulus, Phaner furcifer*, and *Microcebus coquereli* as convergent vertical clingers (cf. figs. II.26, 27) and sap eaters. However, the ungues (cf. fig. I.23, 24) and lower incisors of these larger animals are very different and not used in the manner described for those of *Cebuella* (figs. I.20, 25; II.3).

Tree sap (including gums or resins) is a general food available even when there is no potable water. It is consumed by many different animals, birds, and other organisms (cf. p. 446). Indeed, almost all arboreal mammals, whatever their postural and climbing equipment, are preadapted for sap feeding. Regarding *Cebuella*, its small size, clawed digits, biting incisors, and concealing agouti coloration permit efficient sap feeding, preferably on broad tree trunks or branches where security is greatest, exposure to danger least, and where there is a haven on the far side of the same support.

It remains to be determined if *Cebuella* feeds mainly on sap throughout the year or if its apparent predilection for the food is seasonal. Judging by its catholic food habits, very likely *Cebuella* can live and reproduce year round without eating sap.

Drink

Christen 1974

Water and food in liquid form are lapped or scooped with a hand which is then licked. Pygmy marmosets of the Zürich colony drank 3 to 6 times daily for an average total volume of 7.5 cc each. Pregnant females drank 2 or 3 times more.

Coprophagy

Christen 1974

Among the 15 pygmy marmosets of the Zürich laboratory colony that were observed over a period of 2½ years only a captive-born female was seen eating feces. Coprophagy among primates appears to be an unnatural and uncommon habit acquired in captivity where the animal is confined with its own excrement. Coprophagy among certain grazing-browsing mammals, notably lagomorphs (rabbits, hares) and many rodents, is a natural process of reingestion comparable to cud-chewing among artiodactyls.

Elimination and Sanitation

Christen 1974

Adults usually urinated in a definite place, but the young clung to the cage mesh and directed their urine to the outside. Feces were dropped to the floor of the cage and the sleeping box was kept clean.

Learning and Color Perception

Christen 1974, p. 66

The animals of the colony learned to get food placed out of reach of their cages by pulling on an accessible string tied to the food pan.

The same marmosets learned to find food in the container with the right color lid because of their ability to distinguish red, blue, green, and yellow from a series of gray tones. They also recognized two-dimensional geometric figures of the same colors and different combinations of colors and figures.

Mirror Image Response

Christen 1974, p. 50

The mirror image of himself seen for the first time provokes the adult male to display threat. He smacks his lips and tongue, tries to seize the image, and searches behind the mirror. Other males may merely show off their genitalia backside toward the image, and females usually display an erected mane. Infants and young touch and sniff their image, cavort around the mirror, and stand up on it, all in clean fun.

Fur Doll Response

Christen 1974, p. 51

A figurine made of pygmy marmoset fur and placed in a cage elicited mixed responses from the occupants. Some reacted aggressively with screams and threat displays. A young, low-ranking female groomed the doll for a few minutes, then nibbled the fur. Another low-ranking but unsocial adult male mounted the dummy with erected penis and went through copulatory motions, tonguing and trembling with ardor. Cat, fox, and lamb fur of the same size and shape did not arouse his passion.

Handedness

Christen 1974

Two adult males and two adult females tested for handedness picked up food or seized prey with either hand and held food in either or both hands. One female and one male removed the lid of a food dish with the left hand only each time in 25 and 13 trials, respectively.

Locomotion

Christen 1974

The pygmy marmoset runs along branches or up and down headfirst like a squirrel or treeshrew. The principal means of support in climbing are the sharp recurved claws. Thin branches, however, are gripped by fingers and toes. A limb may be grasped by all 5 fingers closing from the same side or may be held between digits I and II or between II and III or between II and III + IV. The hallux is extended in running and opposed for grasping small branches. As a rule, 3 or 4 fingers and 4 toes are used for support on the wire mesh of the cages. In leaping, hands and feet land at the same time. The animal can jump a distance of 50 to 70 cm from the wire partition of the cage to a branch. Outside the cage, distances up to 2 m are covered in a jump.

The 5 wild-caught individuals of the colony did not move about the cage floor as much as their 10 captive-born offspring. In this connection, Christen fails to note that the young were almost continuously running and playing during the day.

Macdonald 1965, p. 35

They "execute amazingly long jumps to sixteen feet [4.9 m] from bough to bough."

Hershkovitz (Notes)

The pygmy marmoset can leap from a vertical clinging position. The animal's ability to rotate its head about 180° facilitates targeting and takeoff (cf. fig. VIII.17).

Kinzey, Rosenberger, and Ramirez (1975)

In the wild, *Cebuella* used a wide range of locomotor types "including quadrupedal walking and running along supports as well as leaping between supports. We observed leaps up to 2 m . . . and counted 288 leaps over several days [distributed as follows]"

Vertical to vertical support	38%
Vertical to horizontal	19%
Horizontal to vertical	28%
Horizontal to horizontal	15%

"In *Cebuella,* vertical clinging involves grapsing of slender supports with the hallux but also involves clinging to broad supports with the claws of both hands and feet."

Posture

The usual posture in repose on the cage floor is a crouch with thighs drawn up beside the rump, the arms propping the body in front. The sitting posture is similar to that of a cat, with most of the weight resting on the legs, the forelimbs propping and balancing. In the erect position, the knees remain bent and the tail may help support the body. The branch-sitting posture is squirrel-like with weight resting on legs, the rump held above the branch or extended behind as a counterweight, the tail hanging straight down. The animal frequently hangs from a branch upside down, holding on with the claws. Vertical branch and trunk clinging as a postural sequence in climbing and leaping is common to all callitrichids but is more important to the smaller animal in a habitat used equally by larger ones.

Kinzey, Rosenberger, and Ramirez (1975)

"Vertical positional behavior offers the pygmy marmosets their only (or at least their most efficient) access to sap, an apparently essential food resource [see above, p. 476]. Clinging is a posture not a locomotor adaptation. Failure to distinguish between posture and locomotion may overlook the biological importance of clinging which in *Cebuella* is clearly related to feeding."

These observations and those made on locomotion (see above) "amply justify consideration of *Cebuella pygmaea* as a neotropical vertical clinger and leaper."

There are many clinging postures, but it is doubtful if a valid distinction can be made between those used in repose, feeding, as episodes in locomotion (cf. p. 43), or of young clinging to adults (fig. VIII.17).

Repose

Christen 1974

The animals usually slept or dozed during midday, preferably under the heating lamps. Young often relaxed by hanging head down, supported by the claws of their toes hooked on a branch or the wire of the cage.

Kinzey, Rosenberger, and Ramirez (1975)

"Animals [of the group studied in the wild] spent 57% of their resting time clinging to vertical supports. The longest period during which an adult clung continuously to a vertical support without moving was 96 min.; the longest period that an animal was observed sitting on a horizontal support was 16 min."

Observation time totaled 48 hr during the "July to September" study period. All observations would have been made in daylight and within that portion of the natural habitat where the animals were clearly visible to the observers.

Play

Christen 1974, p. 55

The young but not the adults of the Zürich laboratory colony were seen to play. The young chased each other, wrestled, bit one another lightly, and played hide and seek and ambush. They were attracted by objects made to move, such as a string descending the side of the cage or a pencil pulled across the cage wire. They grabbed and bit them in the manner of kittens at play. Multicolored balls, rings, and other toys placed in the cage evoked no interest.

Marking

Christen 1974, p. 51

Cage partitions, branches, wooden corners, and cage mates are marked by rubbing them with the odoriferous secretions of the cutaneous glands of the urogenital region, abdomen, and sternum. A few drops of urine are usually included in the markings. Adults routinely mark everything in their environment. They are particularly stimulated into marking before and after copulation and at the sight of strange conspecifics of the same sex. Males appear to mark more frequently than females.

Vocalization

The call commonly heard in the wild is a short, reiterated hiss easily confused with a cricket's chirp. I am not sure I can identify this mobbing threat and alarm cry with any described below by Christen.

Christen 1974, p. 60

With the help of a recorder, Christen distinguished and interpreted 10 forms of vocal expression uttered by pygmy marmosets. These are organized below under 8 types.

1. Contact calls

   a. Monosyllabic, soft, high-pitched *pi-pi-pi* uttered with mouth nearly or entirely closed. Sounded when subject is secure, content, and in close physical contact with its group.

   b. Trills made with mouth open widely, lower jaw vibrating; trill begins on a low note, ends on a higher one, frequency 2–4 kHz; sounded in contentment, conspecifics respond with trills of same frequency.

   c. Monosyllabic loud, sustained fear cry uttered in distress with widely opened mouth. Handling by caretaker usually evokes the fear cry.
2. Whistle, high pitched, in sequence of 2 to 5; used when excited or as warning of approach of strangers or at sight of large flying birds; young respond by hiding.
3. Scream of anger or aggressive threat uttered in sequences of short bursts; sound accompanied by piloerection, flushed, tense face; used against conspecifics in competition for food, and assertion of dominance by high-ranking individuals.
4. Mobbing hostility or hate (*Hasslaut*) cry made by the smacking sound of rapid tonguing; used against strange conspecifics, people, dogs, cats, fright-inspiring objects. The cry begun by one individual quickly infects the entire group, which responds by cries, threat displays, and genital presentation. Epple (1968, p. 19) records similar vocal behavior and response by *Callithrix argentata argentata*.
5. Twitter of submission made in a high pitch by subordinate adult and juvenals in protest to unwanted attentions inflicted by superior conspecifics.
6. Juvenal chirps of contentment uttered by healthy young in secure circumstances.
7. Juvenal squall and twitter uttered when abandoned or forced to dismount from back of carrier.
8. Ultrasonic hostility cry uttered with widely opened mouth from which emerges no sound audible to human ears; used against fear-inspiring sights.

Macdonald 1965, p. 35

"Their vocalizations are most extensive, consisting of a wide assortment of shrill, birdlike trillings and Morse-code-like chittering. Many of their sounds are supersonic."

Pola and Snowdon (1975)

This work arrived too late to be incorporated with Christen's analyses. However, the authors find that vocalization and contents of emissions of pygmy marmosets "seem to fit the descriptions of the ten vocalizations that Christen (1974) reported." they also note similarities between calls of *Cebuella* and those of other callitrichids. Thus, "in *C. jacchus* infants there is a combination of calls similar to those of *Cebuella pygmaea* with 'tsik,' 'phee' and squeal components. . . . Nothing like the adult [open-mouth and closed-mouth] trills of *Cebuella* are reported in *Callithrix jacchus* but a trill-like call does appear in *C. argentatus* [*sic*] under conditions similar to those of a *Cebuella* open-mouth trill. The squeals, chatters, and warning calls of *Callithrix jacchus* are virtually identical to those of *Cebuella*. A call physically similar to the 'mobbing call' described for *Callithrix jacchus* and *C. argentatus* [*sic*] was found in *Cebuella* (type A screech [cf. Christen's no. 8, above]). However, *Cebuella* never showed any sign of mobbing behaviour. Each adult acted defensively on its own without any assistance from other group members [but see Christen's no. 4]."

Thermoregulation

In their discussion on the care and maintenance of pygmy marmosets in the laboratory, Sobol, Mondon, and Means (1960, p. 415) emphasized that "it was essential that the temperature be kept uniform and high, and that the humidity should be high. A minimum temperature of 82° F. (27.0° C) was maintained with an automatic heater. The temperature rose above this with the heat of the summer. The air was maintained near water-saturation by means of a steamer." The investigators were evidently attempting to simulate in the laboratory the atmosphere of an upper Amazonian rain forest during the rainy season. They give no longevity figures for their experimental animals but mention that in some animals with the right diet the "serum cholesterol levels rose to a maximum in 4 to 8 months."

The range of temperature tolerance among pygmy marmosets is considerably greater than indicated by Sobol et al. Christen (1968) successfully bred and reared caged pygmy marmosets for more than two years at room temperatures between 24° and 26° C (75° to 78° F). Also, a limited thermoregulatory capability enables callitrichids to survive temperature extremes well beyond the norm. An unrestrained captive adult male and adult female pygmy marmoset kept at 41° C ambient in experiments conducted by Morrison and Middleton (1967), showed deviations of −3° and +3°, respectively, from the neutral diurnal body temperature of 37.9°. In the same experiment at ambient 22°–24°, the daily range was ♀ (34.3°–38.9°) and ♂ (35.0°–39.0°); at ambient 31°–32°, the overall body temperature ranged from 35.9° to 39.0°. The body temperature during diurnal active phase was 37°–38°, as in man and larger apes. Morrison and Middleton's experiments also revealed that the temperature cycle of the two wild-caught pygmy marmosets coincided with the light cycle of equatorial latitudes. Their temperature rose sharply at daybreak (600 hr), maintained highs during midday, and dropped sharply at the beginning of nightfall (1800 hr). This was followed by a gradual loss of body temperature throughout the night, to begin the cycle again at dawn.

Status in the Wild

Distribution of *Cebuella pygmaea* is not precisely known and the territoriality of the species is virtually unknown. The geographic area where it certainly occurs in upper Amazonian Brazil, Peru, Ecuador, and Colombia is vast and no series of localized catastrophes would have long-range adverse effects on the survival of the pygmy marmoset. The animal is not persecuted by man and, it seems, has no other enemies with which it cannot cope. The pygmy is most abundant in thick brush and second growth. Its chances of survival there are optimum compared with those of the larger monkeys which prefer the older or mature types of forest habitats that are being systematically destroyed by man.

Grimwood 1968, p. 27

"*Cebuella pygmaea* (Spix) is the species, of which only the nominate race is found in Peru.

"Judged solely by the number of animals kept as pets, or available on the Iquitos market, this species does not seem to be at all rare within its limited range. Altogether [*sic*] 972 'leoncitos' were recorded as having been exported in 1964 (the only year for which figures are available) and although that total may have included some *Leontocebus* [= *Saguinus*], for the terms 'leoncito' and 'pichico' are to a certain extent inter-changeable, they would be compensated for by *Cebuella* exported amongst the 1,958 'pichicos' which were also despatched. The casualty rate amongst animals of this species in captivity is said to be much lower than in the genus *Leontocebus* [i.e., *Saguinus*]."

51 Genus *Callithrix* Erxleben True Marmosets or Ouistitis

Synonymic History

Callithrix Erxleben, 1777, *Syst. Regn. Anim.*, p. 55—included species: *pithecia* Linnaeus [= *Pithecia pithecia* Linnaeus], *iacchus* Linnaeus [= *C. jacchus jacchus* Linnaeus], *oedipus* Linnaeus [= *Saguinus oedipus oedipus* Linnaeus], *rosalia* Linnaeus [= *Leontopithecus rosalia rosalia* Linnaeus], *argentata* Linnaeus, *midas* [= *Saguinus midas midas* Linnaeus]. E. Geoffroy and G. Cuvier, 1795, *Mag. Encycl.* (Paris), 3:461—part *Callithrix* [*sensu stricto*] of Erxleben only. Thomas, 1903, *Ann. Mag. Nat. Hist.*, ser. 7, 12:457—type, *C. jacchus* Linnaeus; synonyms, *Sagoinus* Kerr, *Sagouin* Lacépède, *Hapale* Illiger, *Jacchus* E. Geoffroy, all with *C. jacchus* designated type. Elliot, 1913, *A review of the Primates* 1:216—synonyms, *Sagoinus* Kerr, *Sagouin* Lacépède, *Hapale* Illiger, *Jacchus* E. Geoffroy, *Sylvanus* Rafinesque [= *Cebus* Erxleben], *Arctopithecus* Virey, *Ouistitis* Burnett, *Liocephalus* Wagner, *Mico* Lesson, *Cebuella* Gray, *Micoella* Gray. Ashley-Montague, 1935, *Quart. Rev. Biol.* 10(2):181—premaxilla. Straus, 1935, *J. Anat.* 69:96—kidneys unipyramidal. Russell and Zuckerman 1935, *J. Anat.* 69:356—sexual skin. Huber, 1939, *Evolution of facial musculature and facial expression,* p. 28, fig. 5 (facial musculature) —facial musculature and expression. Cruz Lima, 1945, Mamíferos da Amazonia, Primates, *Contr. Mus. Paraense,* p. 241—characters; taxonomic history. Hochstetter, 1946, *Denkschr. Akad. Wiss. Wien, Math.-Nat. Kl.* 106:87 —tentorialis ossis petrosi. Schultz, 1948, *Amer. J. Phys. Anthrop.*, n.s. 6:8—twin births is rule. Della Serra, 1952, *Seqüênçia eruptiva dos dentes definitivos nos símios Platyrrhinos* (privately published). Della Serra and Picosse, 1952, *Papeis Avulsos, São Paulo* (10:4):261—cranial sutures. Hofer, 1955, *Gegenbaur's Morph. Jahrb.* 94:290—falx cerebri. W. C. Osman Hill, 1957, *Primates* 3:190, 192, 281, 291—nomenclature; taxonomy. Oxnard, 1957, *Proc. Zool. Soc. London* 128:113—infraorbital and zygomatic branches of maxillary nerve variable in size. Biegert, 1956, *Gegenbaur's Morph. Jarhb.* 97:249—jaw articulation. Straus and Arcadi, 1958, *Primatologia* 3(1): 507—excretory system. Eckstein, 1958, *Primatologia* 3(1):563—reproductive organs. Hill, 1958, *Primatologia* 3(1):143, 149, 160, 201, fig. 2C (stomach), fig. 20 (peritoneal attachments)—gut anatomy. Hanström, 1958, *Primatologia* 3(1):716—hypophysis. Bachmann, 1958, *Primatologia* 3(1):754—suprarenal glands. Frick, 1960, *Primatologia* 3(2):179, figs. 25, 26 (hand), fig. 60 (thoracic cavity)—heart anatomy. Platzer, 1960, *Primatologia* 3(2):282—blood vessels. Starck and Schneider, 1960, *Primatologia* 3(2):423—larynx. Remane, 1960, *Primatologia* 3(2):646, 678, 763, 768, 771, 788, 795, 798, 800, 801, 816, 832, fig. 25 *a* (p^2–m^2), fig. 27 *b, d, e* (m^{1-2}), fig. 55 (p_2–m_2), fig. 118 (upper incisors), fig. 124 (lower incisors), fig. 27 (milk dentition), fig. 137 (dc-dp4). Biegert, 1961, *Primatologia* 2(1), Lief 3:5, 173, fig. 55 (plantar surfaces of cheiridia)—plantar and palmar surfaces of cheiridia. Feremutsch, 1961, *Primatologia* 2(2), Lief. 8:39, 66, figs. 15, 16 (basal ganglion), fig. 38 (corpus striatum), pl. 55 and fig. p. 66 (basal ganglia)—basal ganglion; comparative anatomy and histology. Von Bonin and Bailey, 1961, *Primatologia* 2(2), Lief. 10:24, pl. 1 (cortical map of brain), fig. 17 (parietal cortex, microscopic section). Rohen, 1962, *Primatologia* 2(1), Lief. 6:6, 8, 35, 48, 72, 77, 101, 133, 142, 144, 146, 150, 153, 158, 162, 163, 165, fig. 11 *a, b* (macula), fig. 49 *d* (lens), fig. 61 (facial musculature)—comparative eye anatomy. Feremutsch, 1963, *Primatologia* 2(2), Lief. 6:72, fig. 25 (thalamus)—anatomy of the thalamus. Erikson, 1963, *Symp. Zool. Soc. London* 10:143—locomotory type (springer). Ashton and Oxnard, 1963, *Trans. Zool. Soc. London* 29(7):561, 569, 577, 580, 589, 593—comparative shoulder myology; locomotory grade (quadrupedal). Schultz, 1963, *Folia Primat.* 1:150—relations between foot and trunk skeletal lengths. Stephan and Andy, 1964, *Amer. Zool.* 4(1):59—quantitative brain comparisons (*C. jacchus*). Stephan, 1965, *Acta Anat.* 62:217, fig. 73 (olfactory bulb)—accessory olfactory bulb (*C. jacchus*). Hassler, 1966, in Hassler and Stephan, *Evolution of the forebrain,* p. 419—visual system. Hershkovitz, 1966, *Mammalia* 30:329—composition; ear-tuft characters; synonyms, *Mico* Lesson, *Hapale* Illiger. Rohen and Castenholz, 1967, *Folia Primat.* 5:92, fig. 7 (foveal area)—centralization of retina. Napier and Napier, 1967, *Handbook of living primates,* p. 79—morphology; ecology; behavior; species; classification. Schön and Straus, 1969, *Proc. Nat. Acad. Sci* 63(4):1176—dorsal funicula of first cervical segment of spinal chord; brain weight. Etter, 1974, *Gegenbaur's Morph. Jahrb.* 120(1):163, fig. 18 (carpus)—hand skeleton.

Cercopithecus Blumenbach, 1779, *Handb. Naturg.*, ed. 1, p. 68—included species: *paniscus* [= *Ateles paniscus* Linnaeus], *jacchus* Linnaeus; generic name a homonym of *Cercopithecus* Brünnich, 1772, for a genus of African monkeys. Blumenbach, 1788, *Handb. Naturg.*, ed. 3, p. 68—included species *paniscus* [= *Ateles paniscus paniscus* Linnaeus], *jacchus* Linnaeus.

Callitrix [*sic*], Boddaert, 1784, *Elenchus Anim.* p. 42—misspelling or emendation of *Callithrix* Erxleben, 1777; included species: *pithecia, jacchus* (type), *oedipus, rosalia, argentata, midas.*

Sagoinus Kerr, 1792, *Animal Kingdom* 1:80—subgenus of *Simia;* included species, *pithecia* Schreber [= *Pithecia pithecia* Linnaeus], *jacchus* [type designated by Thomas (1903, *Ann. Mag. Nat. Hist.*, ser. 7, 12:457)] *moschatus* [= *jacchus* Linnaeus], *oedipus* [= *Saguinus oedipus oedipus* Linnaeus], *rosalius* [sic = *Leontopithecus rosalia rosalia* Linnaeus], *argentatus, midas* [= *Saguinus midas midas* Linnaeus].

Sagouin Lacépède, 1799, *Tableau des divisions, sous-divisions, ordres et genres des mammifères,* p. 4—type, *Sagouin jacchus* by monotypy. Lacépède, 1801, Mémoire sur une nouvelle table méthodique des animaux à mamelles, *Mem. Inst. Sci. Arts,* p. 490—classification.

Saguin Fischer, 1803, *National Mus. Naturh., Paris* 2:113—included species, *jacchus* [type now designated] *argentata midas* [= *Saguinus midas midas*], *rosalia* [= *Leontopithecus rosalia rosalia*], *oedipus* [= *Saguinus oedipus oedipus*], *pithecia* [= *Pithecia pithecia*].

Sagoin Desmarest, 1804, *Dict. Hist. Nat.* 25: (Tabl. Meth.), p. 8—invalid spelling of *Sagouin* Lacépède; included species, *midas* [= *Saguinus midas midas*], *niger* [= *Saguinus midas niger*], *oedipus* [= *Saguinus oedipus oedipus*], *morta* [= *Saimiri sciureus sciureus*], *rosalia* [= *Leontopithecus rosalia rosalia*], *iacchus* [= *Callithrix jacchus jacchus* Linnaeus, here designated type], *argentata.* Griffith, 1827, *Animal Kingdom* 1:351—species, *Sagoin iacchus* Linnaeus.

Hapale Illiger, 1811, *Prodr. Syst. Mamm. et Avium,* p. 71—included species: *rosalia* [= *Leontopithecus rosalia rosalia*], *midas* [= *Saguinus midas midas*], *jacchus,* type designated by Thomas, 1903 (*Ann. Mag. Nat. Hist.* (7) 12:457); *"Saguinus* Cuvier, Duméril, Lacépède," (not Hoffmannsegg), a synonym. Kuhl, 1820, *Beiträge Zool.*, p. 46—included species: *jacchus* Illiger, *penicillatus, leucocephalus, auritus, humeralifer, melanurus, argentatus; Jacchus* E. Geoffroy, a synonym. Lesson, 1840, *Species des mamifères: Bimanes et quadrumanes . . . ,* p. 184—subgenus; included species: *leucotis* Lesson [= *Simia jacchus* Linnaeus], *auritus* E. Geoffroy, *vulgaris* E. Geoffroy, *albicollis* Spix, *humeralifer* E. Geoffroy, *melanotis* Lesson [= *Simia penicillata* E. Geoffroy], *penicillatus* E. Geoffroy, *leucocephalus* E. Geoffroy, *pygmaeus* Spix [= *Cebuella pygmaea* Spix]. I. Geoffroy, 1851, *Cat. Primates, Mus. Hist. Nat., Paris,* p. 58—classification; type, *Simia jacchus.* Gray, 1866, *Proc. Zool. Soc. London* 1865: 734—part, subgenera *Hapale* and *Iacchus* only. Oudemans, 1892, *Nat. Berh. Holandsche Maatsch. Wet.*, ser. 3, 5(2):83, pl. 16, fig. 138 (♂ genitalia)—accessory reproductive glands. Major, 1901, *Proc. Zool. Soc. London,* p. 146—lacrymal region of skull (*jacchus, aurita*). Johnson, 1901, *Philos. Trans. Roy. Soc. London,* (B), 194:11, 73, pl. 3, fig. 2 (fundus oculi)—retinal structure. Elliot Smith, 1902, *Cat. Comp. Anat. Roy. Coll. Surgeons, England* (ed. 2) 2:382—brain morphology (*H. penicillata, jacchus*). Thomas, 1914, *Zool. Anzeig.* 44:285—nomen conservandum; type, *Simia jacchus* Linnaeus. Pocock, 1917, *Ann. Mag. Nat. Hist.*, ser. 8, 20:257—nomen conservandum; part, synonyms: *Callithrix* Erxleben, *Sagoinus* Kerr (*jacchus* type), *Arctopithecus* Virey (*jacchus* type), *Ouistitis* Burnett (*jacchus,* type), *Liocephalus* Wagner (*"jacchus,* type" [a species not included in the original genus]), *Mico* Lesson (*argentatus,* type), *Micoella* Gray (*sericeus* = *chrysoleuca,* type). Sontagg, 1921, *Proc. Zool. Soc. London* 1921:517—tongue anatomy; classification. Thomas, 1922, *Ann. Mag. Nat. Hist.*, ser. 9, 9:198—classification. Thomas, 1924, *Proc. Zool. Soc. London* 1924:347—nomen conservandum to replace *Callithrix* Illiger. International Commission on Zoological Nomenclature, 1925, *Opinion 90, Smithsonian Misc. Coll.* 73:34—suspension of Rules for validation of *Hapale* not recommended. Woollard, 1927, *Proc. Zool. Soc. London* 1927:3—retina. Le Gros Clark, 1936, *Proc. Zool. Soc. London* 1936:1, figs. 9, 10, 12, 13—anatomy and homology of claws; regarded as primary *falculae* in marmosets. J. Anthony, 1946, *Ann. Sci. Nat. Zool.*, Paris, ser. 11, 8:7, 50—brain morphology (*H. jacchus, penicillatus*). Shaw and Auskaps, 1954, *Oral Surg.*, 7(6):671, figs. 1–9 (dental arches), figs. 10–14 (dental sections)—dentition (gross anatomy, disease, abnormalities) in *Hapale jacchus.* Osman Hill, 1955, *Primates* 2:27–29, 31, 40, 41, 45, 46, 60, 65, 72, 75, 77, 79, 93, 95, 98, 130, 218—comparative myology; glands; mammae; neurology; gestation; behavior; reproduction; hair. Osman Hill, 1957, *Primates* 3:13, 19, 20, 21, 26, 28, 42–48, 53–55, 62, 63, 70, 85, 89, 91, 95–100, 108, 113, 121–25, 129–32, 137, 140, 143, 145–55, 159, 161–74, 198–202, 247, 253, 255, 257, 263, 266, 272, 274, 277, 280–306, 309, 315, 319—comparative anatomy; taxonomy; history; behavior; distribution. Osman Hill, 1960, *Primates* 4:24, 25, 32, 38, 70, 71, 76, 113, 154, 267, 273, 366, 373, 382—comparisons with Cebidae. Wever and Vernon, 1961, *Proc. Nat. Acad. Sci., Washington* 47(5):739—cochlear potential. Osman Hill, 1962, *Primates* 5:33, 146, 148, 154, 191, 374, 446—anatomical comparison with *Alouatta, Homunculus, Lagothrix, Ateles.* Saban, 1966, *Morph. Jahrb.* 106(4):569, pl. 1 (temporal sinuses)—temporal sinuses. Andy and Stephan, 1966, in Hassler and Stephan, *Evolution of the forebrain,* p. 394—relative size of septum pellucidum. Fenard and Anthony, 1967, *Ann. Paleo.* 53(2):204—comparative osteometry of mandible. Stephan, 1967, *Mitt. Max Planck Gesell.* 2:67—neocortization index. Stephan, 1967, *First Cong. Int. Primat. Soc.*, p. 108—neocortization index.

Saguinus Illiger, 1811, *Prodr. Syst. Mamm. Av.*, p. 71—listed in synonymy of *Hapale;* name preoccupied by *Saguinus* Hoffmannsegg, 1807, a genus of callitrichids, not *Callithrix* Erxleben.

Jacchus E. Geoffroy, in Humboldt, 1812, *Rec. Obs. Zool. Anat. Comp.*, p. 359—included species, *jacchus* Linnaeus [type by absolute tautonomy], *penicillatus* E. Geoffroy, *auritus* E. Geoffroy, *leucocephalus* E. Geoffroy [= *geoffroyi* Humboldt], *humeralifer* E. Geoffroy, *melanurus* E. Geoffroy, *argentatus* Linnaeus. E. Geoffroy, 1812, *Ann. Mus. Nat. Hist. Nat., Paris* 19:118—included species, *jacchus* Linnaeus, *penicillatus* E. Geoffroy, *leucocephalus* E. Geoffroy, *auritus* E. Geoffroy, *humeralifer* E. Geoffroy, *argentatus* Linnaeus. I. Geoffroy, 1827, *Dict. Class.* 12:512—characters; habits; species accounts.

Arctopithecus G. Cuvier, 1817, *Règne Animal* 1:115—generic name listed in synonymy of *Hapale* Illiger based on the *Arctopithèques* of E. Geoffroy; type, *Simia jacchus* Linnaeus, now designated. Virey, 1819, *Nouv. Dict. Hist. Nat.* 31:279—attributed to E. Geoffroy, in synonymy of *Hapale* Illiger. I. Geoffroy, 1851, *Cat. Méth. Coll. Mamm., Paris,* p. 59—generic name derived from the vernacular tribal name *Arctopithèques* of E. Geoffroy, 1812.

Harpale Gray, 1821, *London Medical Repository* 15:298—lapsus for *Hapale;* included species and type by monotypy, *Lemur jacchus* [*sic* = *Simia jacchus* Linnaeus].

Iacchus Spix, 1823, Sim. Vesp. Brasil., p. 32—emendation of *Jacchus* E. Geoffroy; included species, *pygmaeus* Spix [= *Cebuella pygmaea*], *albicollis* Spix, *penicillatus* E. Geoffroy, and in text (p. 34), *auritus, leucocephalus, humeralifer,* "l'Oustiti vulgaire" [= *Simia jacchus* Linnaeus, type by tautonomy]. Gray, 1866, *Proc. Zool. Soc. London* 1865:734—subgenus of *Hapale.*

Ouistitis Burnett, 1828, *Quart. J. Science, Litt. Arts* 26:307—included species, *argentata* Linnaeus, *iacchus* [= *jacchus*] Linnaeus [type by virtual tautonomy designated by Pocock, 1917, *Ann. Mag. Nat. Hist.*, ser. 8, 20:257, footnote].

Hapales F. Cuvier, 1829, *Dict. Sci. Nat.* 59:401—*"les ouistitis"* [= *Simia jacchus*] Linnaeus, type now designated; name a misspelling or emendation of *Hapale* Illiger. Jardine, 1833, *Naturalist's library* 1:227—included species, *vulgaris, penicillatus, leucocephalus, auritus, humeralifer, argentatus, albifrons, melanurus.*

Anthopithecus F. Cuvier, 1829, *Dict. Sci. Nat.* 59:401—*lapsus calami* or typographical error for *Arctopithecus* G. Cuvier, 1817, listed as a synonym of *Hapales* F. Cuvier, 1829 (q.v.).

Mico Lesson, 1840, *Species des mammifères: Bimanes et quadrumanes . . .*, pp. 184, 192—subgenus of *Hapale* Illiger; type by Linnaean tautonomy, *Mico argentatus* [*mico* of Buffon or *Simia argentata* Linnaeus]. Lesson, 1842, *Nouv. Tabl. Reg. Anim., Mamm.*, p. 8—classification. Reichenbach, 1862, *Vollst. Naturg. Affen,* p. 6—included species, *argentatus* (type by Linnaean tautonomy), *chrysoleucus* [sic]. Gray, 1866, *Proc. Zool. Soc. London* 1865:734—classification. Thomas, 1922, *Ann. Mag. Nat. Hist.*, ser. 9, 9:198—included species, *argentatus* (type), *emiliae, leucippe, melanurus.* Osman Hill, 1957, *Primates* 3:121, 124, 137, 160, 163, 178, 180, 187, 188, 192, 197, 202, 215, 240, 253, 272 et seq., 302, 311—comparative anatomy; taxonomy; history; behavior; distribution. Remane, 1960, *Primatologia* 3(2):788—incisors.

Liocephalus Wagner, 1840, *Schreber's Säugth., Suppl.* 1:ix, 244—subgenus of *Hapale* Illiger; included species, *melanura, argentata* [type now designated], *midas* [= *Saguinus midas midas*], *ursula* [= *Saguinus midas niger*], *labiata* [= *Saguinus labiatus*], ?*albifrons* Thunberg [= *Callithrix jacchus* geoffroyi].

Micoella Gray, 1870, *Cat. monkeys, lemurs and fruit-eating bats, Brit. Mus.*, p. 130—included species *chrysoleucos* Wagner, *sericeus* Gray [= *Callithrix humeralifer chrysoleuca*], type designated by Pocock, 1917 (*Ann. Mag. Nat. Hist.*, ser. 8, 20:257, footnote).

Jachus Schlegel, 1876, *Les singes. Simiae,* p. 254, et seq.—emendation of *Jacchus* E. Geoffroy.

Cuistitis Cabrera, 1958, *Rev. Mus. Argentino Cienc. Nat. "Bernardino Rivadavia"* 4(1):185—misprint for *Ouistitis* Burnett in synonymy of *Callithrix* Erxleben.

Middas Cabrera, 1958, *Rev. Mus. Argentino Cienc. Nat. "Bernardino Rivadavia"* 4(1):185—misspelling of *Midas* E. Geoffroy (part), in synonymy of *Callithrix* Erxleben.

Type Species. Callithrix iacchus [*sic*] Linnaeus by Linnaean tautonomy (*callithrix* Pliny cited as a synonym, cf. International Code of Zoological Nomenclature, Art. 68 (*d*) (*i*)).

Included Species. Three. *C. jacchus, humeralifer, argentata.*

Distribution (fig. VII.1)

Suitable habitats in eastern Bolivia and Brazil south of the Rio Amazonas and east of the Rio Madeira.

Taxonomic History

Erxleben (1777, pp. xxxi, 44, 55) appears to have been the first Linnaean systematist to separate New World monkeys from the all inclusive *Simia* Linnaeus, 1758. Erxleben proposed the named *Cebus* for the prehensile-tailed species and squirrel monkey, and *Callithrix* for *pithecia* (a cebid), *iacchus* [*sic*], *oedipus, rosalia, argentata,* and *midas. Callithrix jacchus,* or *iacchus* as Erxleben wrote it, automatically became type of the genus by tautonomy because *Callithrix* Pliny was cited in its synonymy. Obviously, Pliny's *Callithrix,* or any other primate known in his time, was not the *jacchus* of Linnaeus or Erxleben. Notwithstanding, the International Code of Zoological Nomenclature 1961, p. 67 [Art. 68 (d) (i)] leaves no choice by the dictum that: "If, in the synonymy of only one of the species originally included in a nominal genus established before 1931, there is cited a pre-1758 name of one word identical with the new generic name, that nominal species is construed to be the type-species (type by Linnaean tautonomy)."

Several generic names were later proposed to include the various species originally assigned to *Callithrix,* but Erxleben's name remains the first valid and available for primates typified by the common marmoset, *Callithrix jacchus jacchus* Linnaeus. The generic synonyms are discussed below.

Sagoinus Kerr, 1792, the first of three names derived from the Brazilian term *sagüi,* meaning small monkey, is identical in composition with *Callithrix* Erxleben. Its type, *Simia jacchus* Linnaeus, designated by Thomas (1903, p. 457), makes it an objective junior synonym of *Callithrix* Erxleben.

Sagouin Lacépède, 1799, is also a junior objective synonym of *Callithrix.* It contained only *jacchus* Linnaeus, hence its type by monotypy.

Saguin Fischer, 1803, is an emendation of *Sagouin* Lacépède but because of the one letter difference in spelling, is not a homonym. It comprises the same species as *Callithrix.* Its type, *Simia jacchus* Linnaeus, now designated, makes it an objective junior synonym of *Callithrix* Erxleben.

Callitrix Latreille, 1803, is an emendation of *Callithrix* used by French authors of the period for nearly all New World monkeys then known. In effect, *Callitrix* was approximately equal to the *Callithrix* plus *Cebus,* of Erxleben. Because of the one letter difference in spelling, *Callitrix* Latreille is not a homonym of *Callithrix* Erxleben. Its type species, *Simia capucinus* Linnaeus (cf. Hershkovitz 1963*b,* p. 4), however, makes it a junior objective synonym of *Cebus* Erxleben with identical type. *Callitrix* Latreille, in turn, is also a homonym of *Callitrix* Boddaert (1784), a misspelling of *Callithrix* Erxleben, 1777.

Hapale Illiger, 1811, contained *rosalia, midas,* and *jacchus,* the last designated type by Thomas (1903, p. 457). Thus, *Hapale* Illiger is a junior objective synonym of *Callithrix* Erxleben. Strange as it seems, Illiger recognized *Callithrix* Erxleben but used it only for the Linnaean species *capucina* and *sciurea.* In other words, *Callithrix,* as understood and used by Illiger, has as type *Simia capucina* Linnaeus, and thus would be synonymous with *Cebus* Erxleben.

Hapale Illiger was quickly adopted by contemporary German mammalogists and became the most widely used name for callitrichids until the turn of the century, when Thomas (1903), p. 455) revived the prior *Callithrix* Erxleben. Soon after, Thomas (p. 285) repented and requested the International Commission on Zoological Nomenclature to suspend the rules in order to reject *Callithrix* Erxleben, 1777, and conserve *Hapale* Illiger, 1811, as the official name for callitrichids. His argument was that "transfer of the name *Callithrix* [then misused for] Titi monkeys (*Callicebus*) to the Marmosets is highly confusing." His application, signed by six fellow mammalogists, was dismissed by the International Commission on Zoological Nomenclature in Opinion 90 (1925). The predicted confusion resulting from the reshuffling of names never materialized.

Jacchus E. Geoffroy, 1812, with *Simia jacchus* Linnaeus type by absolute tautonomy, is still another junior objective synonym of *Callithrix* Erxleben. In his classic arrangement of primates, E. Geoffroy (1812, p. 112) ignored Erxleben, 1777, and used *Callithrix* for *sciureus* (a *Saimiri*), and the titi monkeys *lugens, amictus, torquatus,* and *moloch,* all unknown to Erxleben. Geoffroy's arrangement was generally accepted and his use of *Callithrix* for titis was followed until 1903, when Thomas (p. 455) restored the name *Callithrix* for marmosets and erected *Callicebus* for titis.

Arctopithecus G. Cuvier, 1817, with type here designated *Simia jacchus* Linnaeus, is identical with *Callithrix* Erxleben. *Arctopithecus* was attributed by Cuvier to E. Geoffroy but the latter (1812, p. 118) used only the vernacular term arctopithèques for callitrichids. *Arctopithecus* Virey, 1819, cited by Pocock (1917, p. 257, footnote), is also based on E. Geoffroy, 1812.

Mico Lesson, 1840, is typified by the silvery marmoset, *Simia argentata* Linnaeus. Mico has had some currency as a generic or subgeneric name for the species in question.

Liocephalus Wagner, 1840, was proposed as a subgenus of *Hapale.* It included two forms of *Callithrix* (*argentata, melanura*), three of *Saguinus* (*midas, ursulus, labiatus*) and *albifrons* Thunberg, a *species inquirenda* at the time. Pocock (1917, p. 257, footnote) designated *jacchus* Linnaeus type but the action is invalid because this species was not included in the original proposal of *Liocephalus.* To make amends, *Simia argentata* Linnaeus, the first species mentioned by Wagner, is here designated type. *Mico* Lesson, published the same year, with the same type, is here regarded as the senior synonym.

Micoella Gray is based on *Mico sericeus* Gray and *Hapale chrysoleucos* Wagner. The first species, actually indistinguishable from the second, was designated type by Pocock (1917, p. 257, footnote). *Micoella* Gray is regarded as a subjective synonym of *Mico* Lesson.

Other names for *Callithrix* Erxleben include a few misspellings and *lapsi.* They are cited and annotated in the synonymy (pp. 480–82).

Systematic Position

The systematic position of *Callithrix* has never been questioned, the name being the first proposed for callitrichids in general. Subdivision of the original composition of *Callithrix* (or *Hapale*) into typical marmosets with short, incisorlike lower canines, for which the name *Callithrix* is retained, and tamarins, now called *Saguinus,* with tusklike lower canines, is generally accepted. Separation of the pygmy marmoset, under the name *Cebuella,* from *Callithrix* was questioned at times but opposition to recognition of the genus was never sustained.

The relationship between *Callithrix, Cebuella,* and *Saguinus* is close, and generic separation between them seems difficult to support on the basis of characters seen in dry skins, skulls, and teeth alone. However, these characters combined with others mentioned below and described in greater detail elsewhere justify separation of

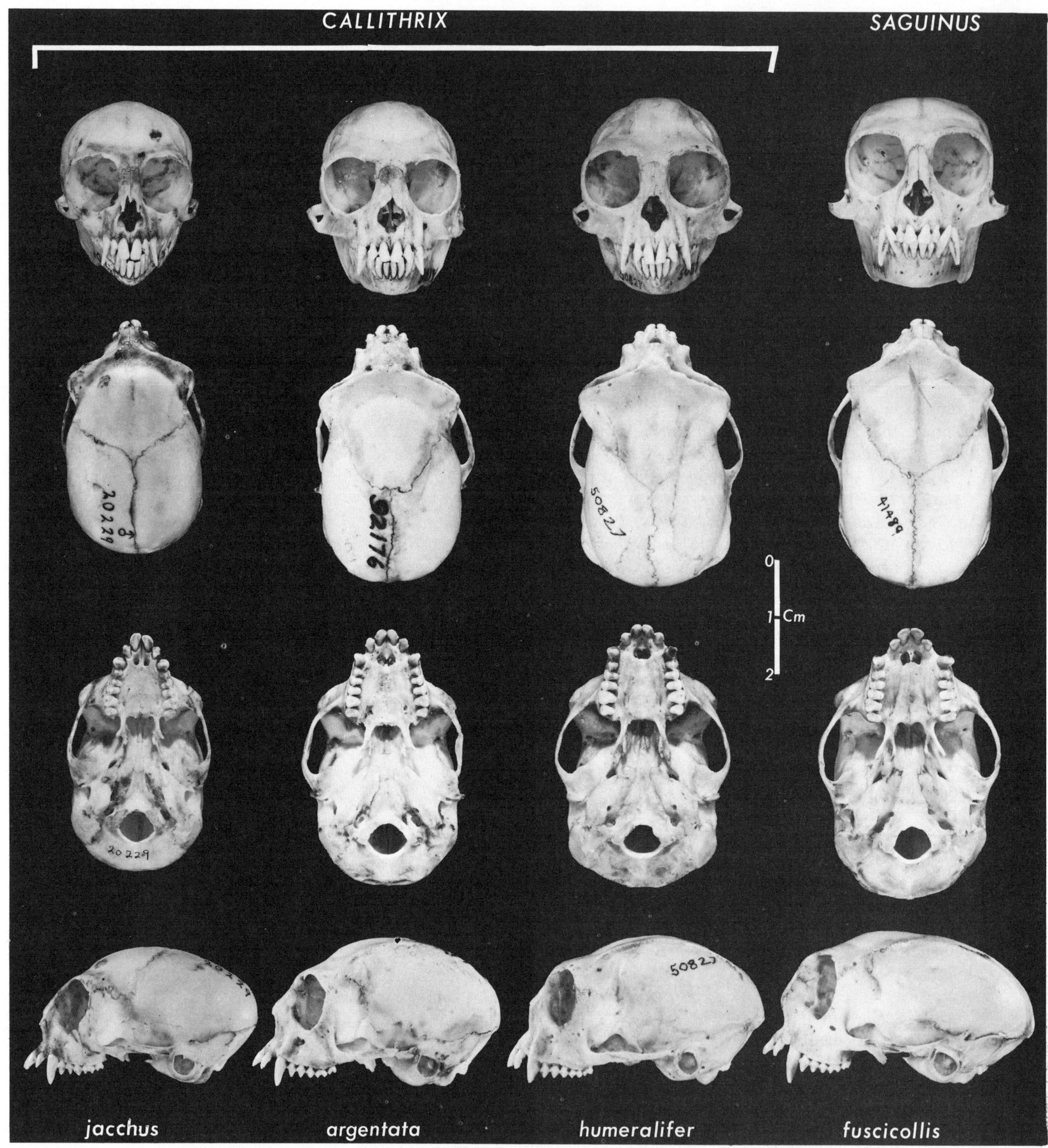

Fig. IX.1. Skulls: *Callithrix jacchus penicillata* (young adult); *Callithrix a. argentata; Callithrix h. humeralifer; Saguinus fuscicollis.* Compare front teeth and dental arcades. Apparent differences in the degree of development of orbital ridges and cranial crests (outline of sagittal plane) are individual variables.

true marmosets, genus *Callithrix,* from *Cebuella* on the one hand and *Saguinus* on the other.

Diagnostic Characters

Size:

All marmosets of the genus *Callithrix* are approximately the same size. They average smaller than tamarins (*Saguinus*) but are absolutely larger than pygmy marmosets (*Cebuella*). Most structural differences between *Callithrix, Saguinus,* and *Cebuella* are correlated with size and effects of allometric growth (appendix table 1).

Skull:

No single cranial character consistently separates *Callithrix* from *Cebuella* or *Saguinus.* Distinction of the *Callithrix* skull lies in its full range of variation from a

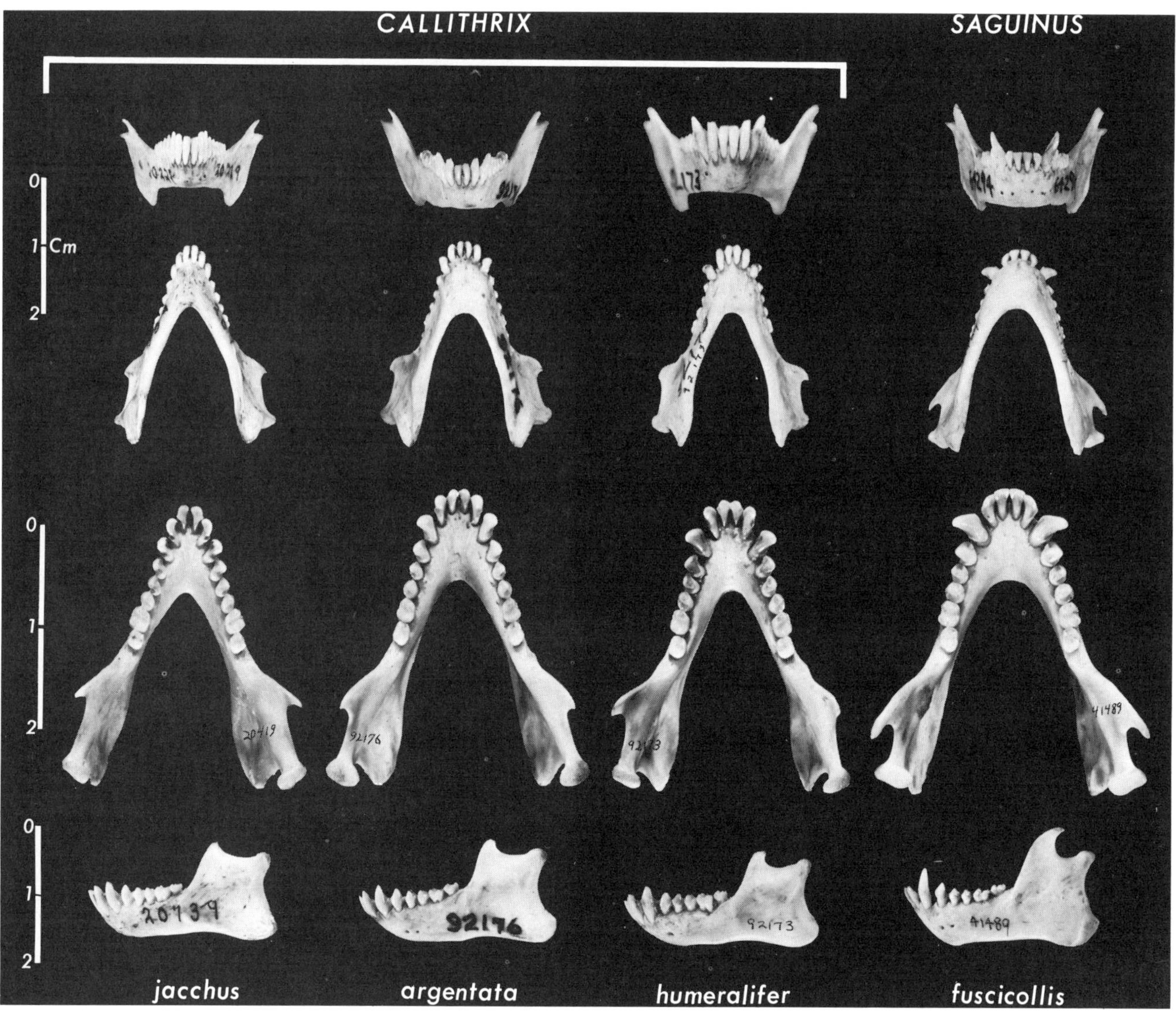

Fig. IX.2. Lower jaws: *Callithrix jacchus penicillata; Callithrix a. argentata; Callithrix h. humeralifer; Saguinus fuscicollis.* Compare front teeth, particularly incisor—canine relationship, dental arcade, ascending ramus, coronoid process, condylar height, symphyseal angle, and incisor height to depth of symphysis.

primitive dental arch V-plan such as characterizes *Cebuella* to the U-plan on which the skull of *Saguinus* and higher primates is constructed (figs. VII.5, IX.1, 2). Cranial characters of the genus are described in greater detail below (p. 487).

Cheiridia: See page 32 and figs. I.20, IX.45.

Dentition (figs. V.21, 22, 23, 25, 26, 27, 28):

Callithrix differs from *Cebuella* mainly by reduction of cuspules of incisors, premolars more nearly rectangular than triangular on occlusal surface, molars larger throughout, contour of lower premolar row more arched anteriorly; from *Saguinus* by retention of distal cuspule on upper incisors, the lateral incisor about as high as and only slightly smaller than central, lower incisors elongate and conical, the crowns not spatulate, the lateral tooth markedly higher and larger than central, its height more than one-half vertical depth of symphysis menti, lower canine incisiform, not conspicuously larger than lateral incisor, and functionally oriented toward incisors.

Second upper molar tends toward secondary reduction, evidently in response to diminishing alveolar space which is gradually being usurped by enlarged first molar; mainly affected is the metacone of m^2, particularly in *Callithrix jacchus,* where the cusp is often deflected distally, sometimes distolingually.

Rotation of the epicristid from oblique in pm_2 to nearly or quite transverse in pm_4 is a significant advance from the caniniform premolars of *Cebuella* toward the well-molarized premolars of *Saguinus.* The sharp-edged eoconid still predominates in $pm_{2\text{-}3}$, but in pm_4 the metaconid shares importance. Absence or obsolescence of stylids and paraconid appears to be a secondary simplification.

In the deciduous suite, the first two premolars are less molarized than their successors. The last deciduous premolar, on the other hand, is fully molarized.

In the sequence of dental eruption, the second molar erupts before the first incisor in *Callithrix* (and *Cebuella*). The reverse is normal in *Saguinus, Leontopithecus, Callimico,* most cebids, and catarrhines generally.

Except for some minor divergences, the dental system of *Callithrix* fills a fair part of the morphological gap between those of *Cebuella* and *Saguinus.* Of the two

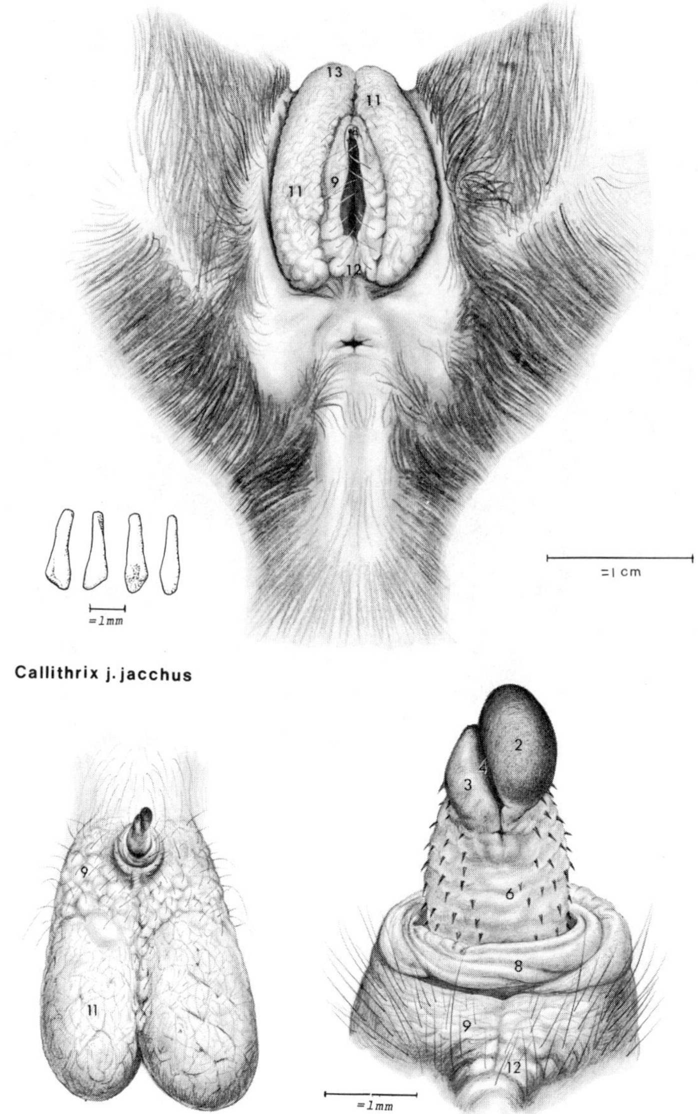

Fig. IX.3. *Callithrix jacchus*: External genitalia, female (*above*), male (*below*), and two aspects of each of two penis bones; for names of parts and explanation of symbols see fig. III.21.

groups of marmosets, the dentition of *C. jacchus* is nearest *Cebuella,* that of the *C. argentata* group nearest *Saguinus.* Detailed descriptions of the teeth of each group is given under the corresponding headings (pp. 496, 574).

Brain:

The generally smooth marmoset brain is not significantly different from tamarin brains of comparable size but, in conformance with skull size, it is considerably larger than that of *Cebuella* with hemispheres slightly more complicated, olfactory and periform lobes more reduced, frontal and occipital lobes larger with the latter more overhanging posteriorly (figs. VI.8, 9).

Integument:

No single tegumentary character consistently separates *Callithrix* from other callitrichids, but two marmoset species are distinguished by conspicuous tufts on, in, or around the external ear. In the third marmoset species, the ear is bare and fully exposed, as in tamarins (figs. III.18, IX.44). The tail is conspicuously annulated in *C. jacchus* and *C. humeralifer humeralifer* by a combination of contrasting color bands (fig. III.13) and disposition of the pelage into a concordant series of flaring tufts; in *C. humeralifer chrysoleuca,* the series of trapezoidal-shaped tufts remains but the tail is more or less uniformly colored.

Sensory hairs in *Callithrix* are nearly as well developed as in the smaller *Cebuella* but better developed than in *Saguinus* and other platyrrhines (figs. III.8, 12).

External Genitalia:

The spiny cylindrical penis, chordate scrotum, distinctive baculum, and mostly unpigmented labia majora, and the position of the female preputial fold relative to the scrotal fold distinguish *Callithrix* from all other primates (figs. III.21, 23, 24, 25, 28, 29). The genitalia are described in greater detail under the family heading.

External Ear:

The somewhat convoluted marmoset external ear is like that of *Cebuella* and quite different from the expanded, leaflike auricle of most tamarins (figs. III.18, IX.8, 44).

Ischial Prominences:

Present and better developed in females than in males (figs. I.15; VII.7).

Tongue: See page 107 and figs. III.19, 20, IX.9.

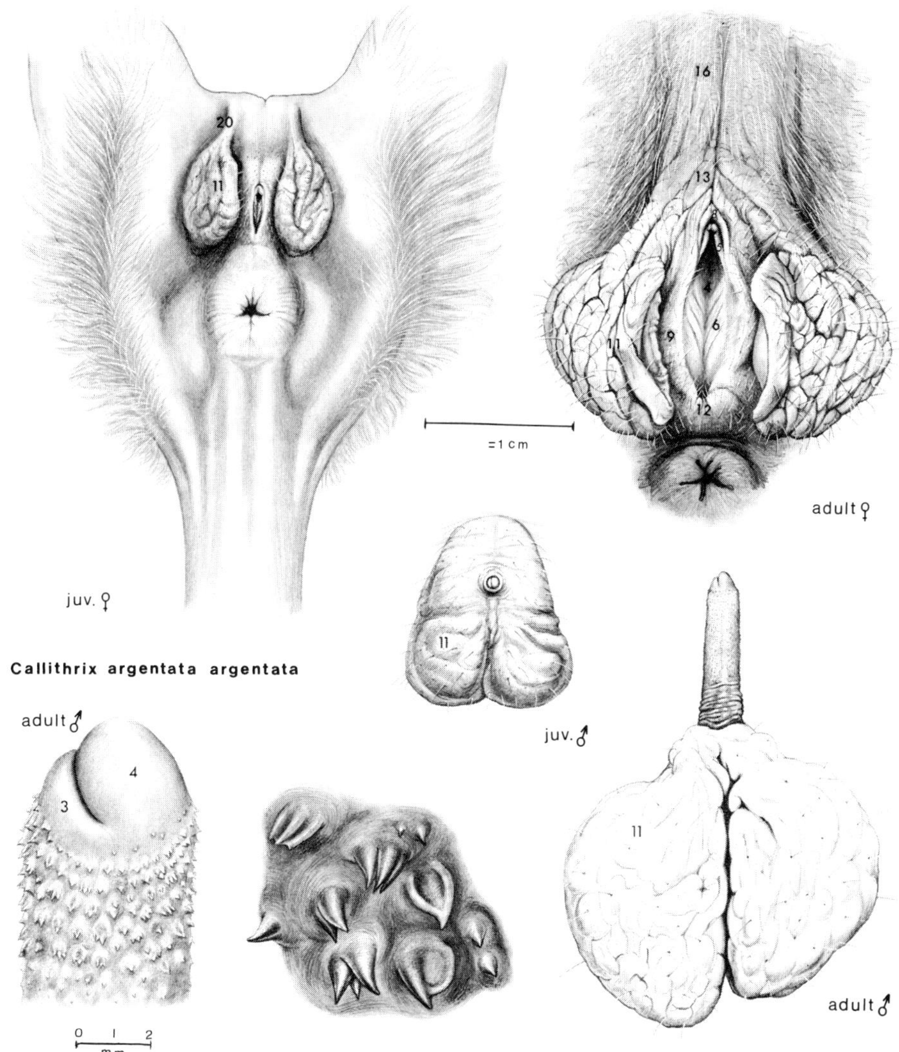

Fig. IX.4. *Callithrix argentata argentata*: External genitalia. *Upper row*: juvenal and adult females; *middle row*: juvenal male with incompletely developed scrotal sac; *bottom row*: adult male genitalia with enlarged anterior aspect of glans and portion of penial shaft, details of spiny shaft magnified; for names of numbered parts see fig. III.21.

Palatal Ridges: See page 431 and fig. VII.14.

Larynx: See page 18 and fig. I.11C.

Dimorphism:

Possession of a distinctive juvenal pelage and coloration distinguishes *Callithrix* from *Cebuella,* but no other platyrrhine.

Karyotype:

The diploid number of chromosomes is 46 in *Callithrix jacchus* and in *Saguinus,* 44 in *Callithrix argentata* and *Callithrix humeralifer,* as in *Cebuella.* In contradiction to their respective karyotypes, morphologically *C. jacchus* is nearer *Cebuella,* and *C. argentata* and *C. humeralifer* are nearer *Saguinus.* The diploid number 46 attributed to *"Callithrix chrysoleucos"* by Bender and Mettler (1960, p. 400) is probably based on incorrectly identified specimens (cf. pp. 598–99).

Cranial Characters

Greatest skull length in adults usually between 40 and 52 mm; frontal contour convex to moderately vaulted; temporal ridges well defined, more or less parallel-sided, sometimes defining an irregular-sided median parietal plate, rarely a sagittal crest (fig. IX.1); nasal profile slightly concave to slightly convex (fig. IV.3); nasofrontal suture more than three-fourths the distance from nasal tip to glabella; malar foramen rarely exceeding 1 mm in diameter; infraorbital foramen placed above pm^2 or between pm^3 and canine, its diameter more frequently greater than less that of malar; orbits more or less rounded in facial outline; lacrymal bone usually confined to orbit but with superior median corner nearly or quite contacting nasal; cribriform plate (fig. IV.43) poorly developed; right and left orbital plates compressed into a thin translucent interorbital septum; posterior sphenoidal fossae or sinuses absent; axis of foramen magnum pointing more nearly down than back; auditory bullae well inflated, lower portion of mesotympanic cavity more or less cellular to noncellular; malleus often with well developed orbicular apophysis (figs. IV.65, 68, 71); incus and stapes simple (fig. IV.74); dental arcade V- to slightly U-shaped, outer alveolar distance between canines slightly more or less than alveolar length of c–m^2 (IX.1); average occipital angle (opisthion-inion index) between 55° and 65°; pterygoid plates small, medial plate consisting of little more than hamular process, pterygoid fossa a shallow, narrow recess; outline of inferior border of mandible V- to slightly U-shaped, the symphyseal angle narrowly rounded, the horizontal rami diverging sharply or with a slight arcing (fig. IX.2); angle of outer slope of symphysis menti relative to basal mandibular plane about 36° (28°–45°, 59 specimens); ascending ramus broad, more or less square to oblong; average coronoidal height about 57% of condyloincisive length of mandible; coronoid process nearly straight to moderately recurved and projecting slightly above condyle; sigmoid notch broad and shallow; articular surface of condylar process hardly higher to about one and one-half times higher than molar crowns measured from base of mandible; inferior border of angular process deflected slightly to markedly below basal mandibular plane of horizontal ramus (figs. IV.78, 80).

Postcranial Skeletal Characters

Vertebral Formula:
See comparative data (p. 425) under family heading.

Sternal Ribs:
See comparative data (p. 425) under family heading.

Arm and Leg Proportions:
Measurements and proportions are of *Callithrix jacchus jacchus* FM 20226 ♂, FM 53734 juv. ♂, FM 53735 sub. ♀, *C. argentata argentata* FM 104805 ♀, respectively.

$$\frac{\text{Humerus } 46, 45, 46, 49}{\text{Radius } 41, 40, 41, 43} = 115\%, 113\%, 112\%, 114\%.$$

$$\frac{\text{Femur } 68, 56, 57, 60}{\text{Tibia } 61, 56, 58, 60} = 111\%, 100\%, 98\%, 100\%.$$

$$\frac{\text{Humerus + radius } 87, 85, 87, 92}{\text{Femur + tibia } 129, 111, 114, 120} = 67\%, 77\%, 76\%, 77\%.$$

$$\frac{\text{Humerus + radius } 87, 85, 87, 92}{\text{Trunk } 130, 105, 122, 128} = 67\%, 81\%, 71\%, 72\%.$$

$$\frac{\text{Femur + tibia } 129, 111, 114, 120}{\text{Trunk } 130, 105, 122, 128} = 99\%, 106\%, 93\%, 94\%.$$

Third Trochanter:
In 11 skeletons examined of *Callithrix jacchus,* absent in 8, weakly developed in 2, present on one femur in 1; absent in one skeleton of *C. argentata.*

Entepicondylar Foramen:
Absent in 11 *Callithrix jacchus* and 1 *C. argentata.*

External Genitalia

Male (figs. IX.3,4)

Adult. Penis cylindrical, tapering slightly distally; penial stem usually unpigmented, undifferentiated glans with or without pigment; exposed portion of penial stem and base of glans with short spines; urinary meatus an oblique slit from right side; left, or bacular, lobe of glans considerably larger and more projecting than right lobe; scrotum semipendulous, pigmented, unpigmented or mottled, and subdivided into asymmetrical right and left sacs; prepuce unpigmented or mottled, outer surface hirsute, inner surface glabrous; pubic region thinly haired like belly, sexual skin glands more or less developed.

Female (figs. IX.3, 4)

Adult. Labia majora thick, hairy, mostly unpigmented, scrotumlike in size and form, and prominently displayed; each labium bilobed with lateral, or scrotal, fold hypertrophied, often convoluted, the integument corrugated or raised into papillae, each studded with from one to a few hairs or vibrissae; median lobe, or preputial fold, distinguished from scrotal fold by sulcus, its skin corrugated, the outer portion hairy, inner portion glabrous with those of each side meeting above glans clitoridis in horseshoe-shaped fold or annulus; glans clitoridis hidden in labial tissue or exposed externally but not projecting beyond plane of rima pudendi; labia minora laminate and merging with inner walls of labia majora; glandular sexual skin in mid pubic region present but often poorly or not at all defined topically; perineal and anal regions glandular and usually unpigmented.

Key to the Species of Callithrix

1. Ear tufts absent, pinna nearly bare and completely exposed; tail more or less uniformly colored (figs. IX. 38, 42, 44) .... *C. argentata*

1′. Ear tufts or tassel present, pinna more or less concealed; tail with alternating dark and light bands or nearly uniformly colored 2

2. Blackish, whitish, or buffy fanlike tufts rising in front, above, below, or from inner (lateral) surface of ear; outer (medial surface of pinna sparsely covered with short hairs; middle or lower back and tail with well-defined alternating dark and pale bands (figs. IX.7, 8, 38) .... *C. jacchus*

2′. Whitish, silvery, or buffy tassellike tufts rising from rim and inner and outer surface of pinna; middle or lower back dominantly blackish or whitish, not banded; tail with alternating dark and light bands or nearly uniformly colored (figs. IX.38, 51, 52) .... *C. humeralifer*

52 *Callithrix Jacchus* Linnaeus Tufted-ear Marmosets or Ouistitis *1. History, Characters, and Subspecies*

Distribution (figs. IX.5, 6)

Eastern Brazil from parts of the state of Maranhão and Ceará south through coastal and upland scrub forests and gallery forests to the Rio Tietê and the angle formed by the upper Rios Paranapanema and Ribeirão do Iguapé in southern São Paulo, west through the state of Goiás to the Rio Araguaia.

Ouistitis visit plantations and gardens in search of food and are, or were, abundant in orchards, gardens, and small farms around villages and even large cities such as São Paulo, Rio de Janeiro, and Salvador.

Taxonomic History

The common Brazilian marmoset, or ouistiti, *Callithrix jacchus jacchus,* had been introduced into Europe as a household pet more than two centuries before Linnaeus named it in 1758. The German painter Hans Holbein portrayed the then 4-year-old Prince Edward Tudor (1537–53) with a marmoset cradled in his right arm.

One of the earliest recognizable descriptions of the species, if not the first, was published by Gesner in 1551 (ed. 1, p. 96, fig. [work not seen]; ed. 2, 1620, p. 869, fig. of animal). Gesner commented on the size of the animal and its food in captivity and he expressed the opinion that the ouistiti might be the offspring of a cross between a small monkey and a weasel. He observed that many kinds of small Brazilian animals interbreed because of the hot climate.

Most ouistitis known to Europeans during the sixteenth century originated in the Brazilian Nordeste, and the Linnaean *jacchus* represents the race of that region. It is certain that ouistitis from other parts of Brazil reached Europe before the nineteenth century. However, it was not until 1812 that the remaining races of *Callithrix jacchus,* namely *penicillata, leucocephalus* or *geoffroyi,* and *aurita,* were made known to science by Etienne Geoffroy St. Hilaire. The new forms, all from unknown locations, were described as full species, and *vulgaris* was proposed as a substitute name for the Linnaean *jacchus.*

The intimate relationship between the Linnaean *jacchus* and the species described by E. Geoffroy was appreciated by early systematists. Spix, who contributed *albicollis* to the list of names applied to ouistitis, expressed the opinion that all species described by E. Geoffroy and even his own *albicollis* "ne sont que des variétés de l'Ouistiti vulgaire." Desmarest (1827, p. 20) also observed that

> tous les ouistitis décrits ci-dessus [*vulgaris* (= *jacchus* s. s.), *penicillatus, leucocephalus, auritus*] ont exactement la même taille, sont pourvus de touffes de poils aux deux côtés de la tête et ont plus ou moins la croupe et la queue rayée ou annelee de couleurs différentes. Ces caracteres existant dans toute leur intégrité dans la première espèce [i.e., *jacchus*] qui a été souvent observée, on sera peu étonné de nous voir conserver quelques doutes sur la distinction de celles qui la suivent, puisqu'elles n'ont été établies que d'après l'observation d'un petit nombre d'individus, et qu'elles ne sont fondées que sur des caractères extérieurs seulement.

John Edward Gray (1866, p. 251) regarded *vulgaris, penicillata, leucocephala,* and *albicollis* as "only slight local accidental varieties" of *jacchus.* These he classified in the genus, or subgenus, *Jacchus.* Gray then commented on the slightly different ear tufts of *aurita* and placed this species apart in the genus, or subgenus, *Hapale.* Finally, Pocock (1917, p. 257, footnote) noted that he had "been able to examine in the fresh state one species—namely, *jacchus,* the common white-eared marmoset, with which the black eared form, quoted as *penicillatus* and given full specific status by Elliot, completely intergrades."

The taxonomies of marmosets by Elliot (1913*a*) and Osman Hill (1957) are hodgepodges. The listing by Cabrera (1958, p. 185) is alphabetical and reveals nothing of the relationships between the eight recognized species of *Callithrix,* including five here treated as subspecies of *C. jacchus.* Napier and Napier (1967, p. 346) follow Cabrera.

The named forms of marmosets regarded as members of a common species by the early nineteenth-century French systematists E. Geoffroy St.-Hilaire and Desmarest were recognized by Hershkovitz in 1966*a* (p. 329) as members of a natural aggregation, the *Callithrix jacchus* group, and in 1968 as subspecies of *Callithrix jacchus.* His arrangement of the races was based on all known distributional records and a demonstration of intergradation in color and pelage from that of the most primitive

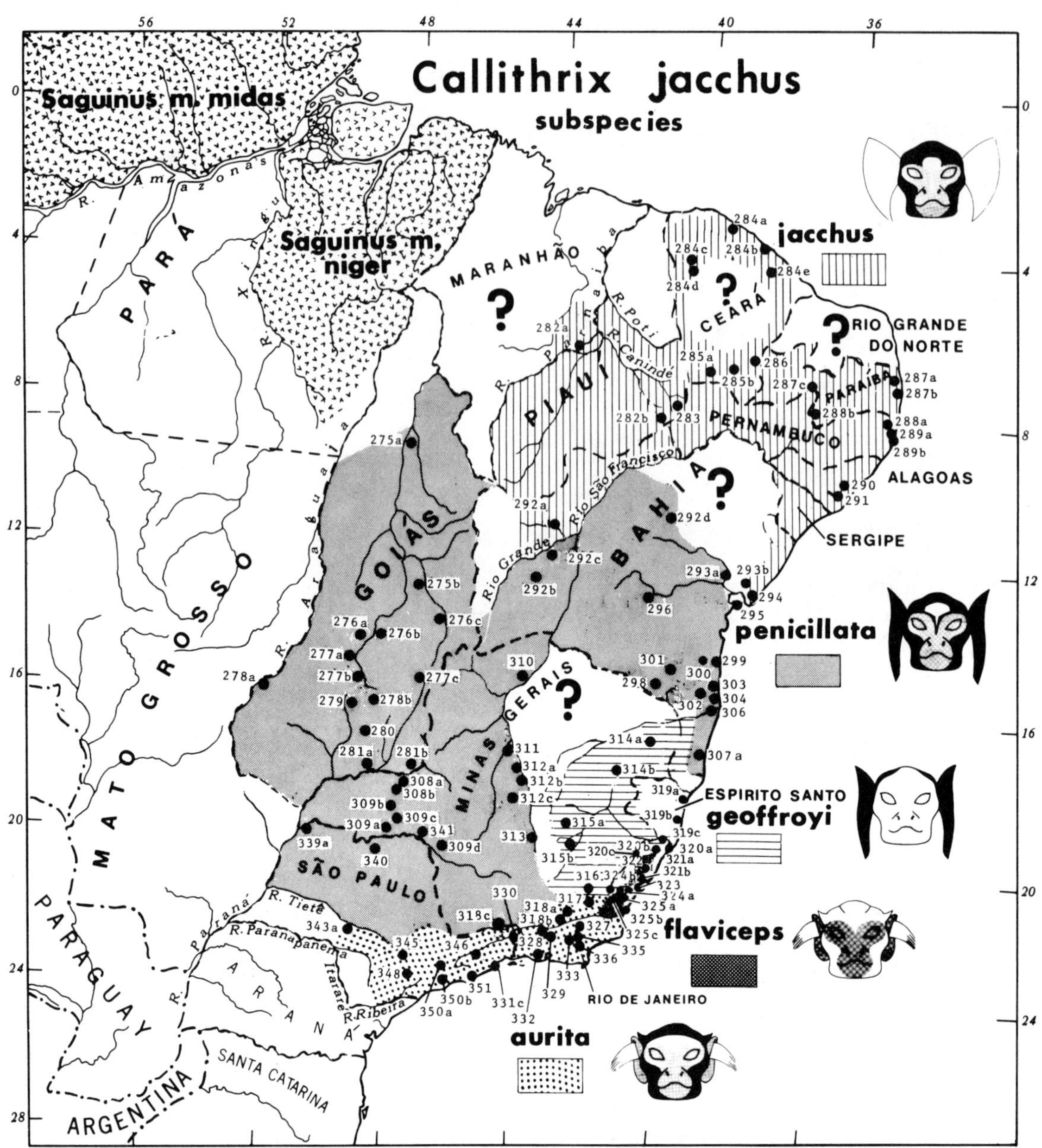

Fig. IX.5. Distribution of the marmoset species, *Callithrix jacchus;* approximate ranges of the subspecies shaded, dots show locality records mentioned in text (see gazetteer, p. 918, for key to collecting and sight localities). *Callithrix jacchus jacchus* was introduced into Guanabara State and has spread into neighboring parts of the State of Rio de Janeiro. Easternmost portion of geographic range of *Saguinus midas* is included to indicate nearest points between natural ranges of tamarins and common marmosets (cf. fig. VII.1).

form at the center of dispersal to the metachromically more advanced at the peripheries of the range.

The taxonomy and zoogeography of the genus *Callithrix* by Avila Pires (1969) is based on the sorting of skins preserved in North American and Brazilian museums. His species and their arrangement are the same as Cabrera's. The review omits generic characterization, inter- and intraspecific comparisons (except for a key), measurements, range maps, and lists of sample sizes. The zoogeography is uncritical and not significantly different from that of Cabrera (1958), who made no attempt to revise the genus.

In their review of the current taxonomy of the genus *Callithrix,* Coimbra-Filho and Mittermeier (1974) recognized the *Callithrix jacchus* group but with *aurita, flaviceps, geoffroyi, jacchus,* and *penicillata* as full species related in alphabetical order. They retain *caelestis* (misspelled *coelestis*) as a subspecies of *Callithrix aurita,* and *jordani* (incorrectly applied) as a subspecies of *penicillata.* This arrangement was based on assertions that evidence exists of sympatry between the nominal species and that natural hybridization is unknown.

Hershkovitz (1975*b*) argued, however, that Coimbra-Filho and Mittermeier failed to show a single case of sympatry between the forms they recognize. He also pointed out that evidence for natural hybridization or geographic intergradation between members of the *Callithrix jacchus* group does in fact exist but that Coimbra-Filho and Mittermeier either chose to ignore it or could not recognize it. He further noted that the portrayal by these authors (1974, figs. 1 and part fig. 2) of a head of each named form to demonstrate "differences in facial

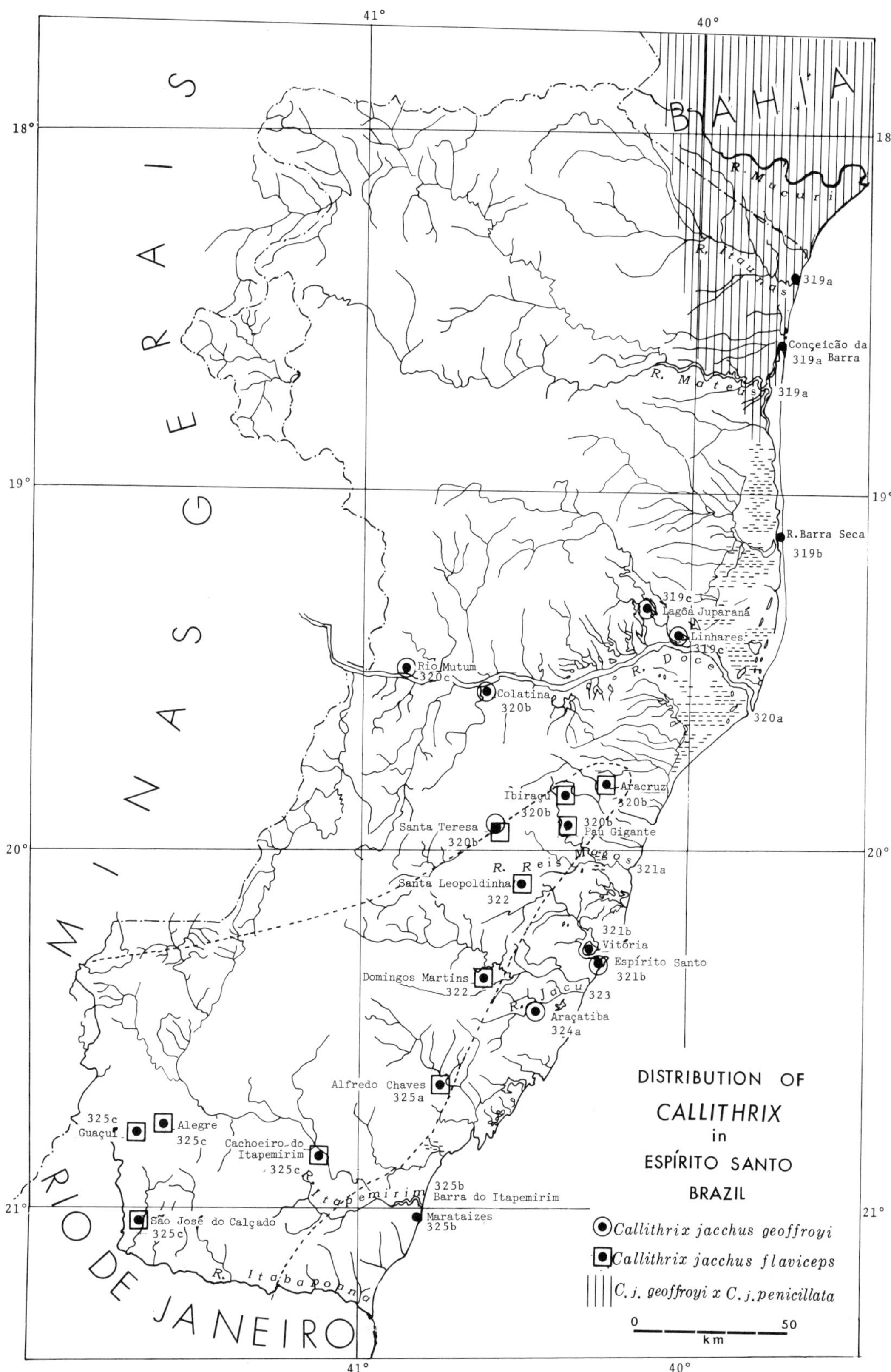

Fig. IX.6. Distributional records for *Callithrix jacchus geoffroyi* (*open circles*) and *C. j. flaviceps* (*open squares*) in Espírito Santo; dotted line indicates the altitudinal segregation between the two forms. Vertical hatching shows area where intergradation between *C. j. geoffroyi* and *C. j. penicillata* probably occurs, western and southern limits unknown. See page 1015 for new data.

color pattern and color and arrangement of ear tufts," presumes the absence of individual variation within the group and dispenses with information regarding the geographic origin of each. Moreover, Hershkovitz observed, the hybrids of captive marmosets depicted on other pages (Coimbra-Filho and Mittermeier 1974, pp. 245, 246, 248) reveal the same kinds of intermediacy between parental types that appear in natural intergrades.

The only valid biological evidence developed by Coimbra-Filho and Mittermeier (actually by the senior author alone in 1970*c*, 1971, 1973) is cases of hybridization in captivity between members of the *Callithrix jacchus* group. Their (Coimbra-Filho and Mittermeier 1974, pp. 253–54) conclusions regarding these are that "hybrids from matings between two different species are fertile and can successfully mate with members of a third species to produce viable (and perhaps also fertile) offspring. This captive hybridization data, viewed alone, suggests that at least in the case of the *C. jacchus* group, we may be dealing with animals that are no more than subspecifically distinct."

Before his collaboration with Mittermeier, Coimbra-Filho (1972*a*, p. 15) had conceded that "the reduction by Hershkovitz, 1968 of *C. penicillata, C. geoffroyi, C. flaviceps* and *C. aurita* to geographical races of *C. jacchus* receives our full support based on the results of our hybridization programme."

Origin, Evolution, and Geographic Variation

Callithrix jacchus is the most primitive of known species of the genus. It probably originated in the Brazilian highlands possibly within or very near the present range of *C. j. penicillata* (fig. IX.5). From this center *Callithrix jacchus* radiated east into the humid coast and northeast into the arid Northeast Region (Grande Região Nordeste). The modern distribution of the species is fragmented. The breakup of erstwhile extensive forests into scattered isolated lots, the discontinuities of gallery and coastal forests, and the cultivation or burning of the wooded savannas, or *campos cerrados,* and scrublands, or *caatingas,* result in many semi-isolated and well-marked populations.

The larger rivers of eastern Brazil may have been effective barriers to distribution at some pre-Recent time when rainfall was more abundant, stream volume and breadth greater, the flow continuous, and the interfluvial forests uninterrupted. Now, most eastern Brazilian streams are narrow or shallow, and large stretches of their beds seasonally dry. The most important factors controlling present marmoset dispersal in eastern Brazil are the extensive deserts or grasslands, much of them man-made, that provide no shelter for monkeys.

The prototype of *Callithrix jacchus* may have been very much like the pygmy marmoset, *Cebuella pygmaea.* Differences between adults of the two species are broadly comparable to differences between adult *Callithrix jacchus* and its own young (fig. IX.7).

The ancestral agouti pattern still persists, though slightly modified, in the crown and dorsum of *C. j. aurita,* and the crown, ear tufts, and mantle of some individuals and highland populations of *Callithrix jacchus penicillata.* The primitive pattern is also discernible in the transverse banding of the back and the caudal annulations of all races (fig. III.13).

A rhomboidal or semilunar frontal blaze probably emerged as an adult character. The unmarked forehead is retained in the juvenal pelage. The blaze is sharply defined in otherwise black-headed populations of *penicillata* and *jacchus.* In coastal populations where the blackish forehead and adjacent parts of crown and sides of head are buffy, the whitish semilunar or rhomboidal blaze remains distinct. As face and crown bleach, the area of the blaze expands. In *geoffroyi* the expanded white of forehead and crown merge into one large field. In *C. j. aurita* and *C. j. flaviceps* the blaze remains distinct in some individuals or confused with the advanced bleaching of the forehead in others. In white tufted-ear *C. j. jacchus,* the blaze persists until the front half of the animal bleaches to white.

Geographic variation in *Callithrix jacchus* is expressed mainly in the auricular and frontal regions. The ancestral auricles were probably moderately hairy and hardly, if at all, adorned by surrounding tresses except for black incipient tufts above and behind the pinna, and from the lateral or auditory surface of the pinna. In the *penicillata-geoffroyi-jacchus* group of living descendents, auricles remain moderately clad, but long black tufts developed in front of, then above and behind the pinna. They are blackish in the nuclear races and white in peripheral *jacchus.* In the *aurita-flaviceps* group, only the intrinsic tufts hypertrophied and bleached to orange, yellow, cream, or white.

The palest race, *Callithrix jacchus jacchus,* inhabits the semi-arid Northeast Region. The most saturate race, *penicillata,* lives in mixed climates, while the dark agouti-colored *aurita* is native to the humid rain forests of the southeastern extreme of the species range. *C. j. geoffroyi* is a somewhat pale peripheral extension of *penicillata,* and *flaviceps* is a pale insular copy of *aurita* except for its slightly more saturate ear tufts. These two chromatically intermediate races occupy the geographically and climatically intermediate coastal strip.

The pale *Callithrix jacchus jacchus* is farthest removed geographically and historically from the postulated center of origin of the species. Its range is most fragmented, its demes scattered and most isolated, its metachromic processes most advanced. Infrequent genetic exchange with bordering representatives of *penicillata* would have the effect of retarding metachromic process in *jacchus,* but not enough to prevent the advance of the geographically most peripheral populations into near albinism. Semi-isolation of *geoffroyi* from *penicillata* had the initial effect of accelerating metachromism. Frequent contact on a broad front, and control by social selection, however, tend to stabilize the phenotype of *geoffroyi* near that of *penicillata.* The same relationship obtains between *aurita* and *flaviceps.*

Isolating factors in the distribution of the races of *Callithrix jacchus* are climatic. These are no less effective as barriers to dispersal than rivers separating races living in identical environments. Whatever the ecology, as each barrier is breached, each successive colonization produces a population a tone or grade nearer the end of its chromatic evolution.

Each of the five named forms recognized here as subspecies of *Callithrix jacchus* is sharply defined except where the ranges meet as in southern Bahia, and in contiguous parts of Espírito Santo, Rio de Janeiro, and Minas Gerais, where the races intergrade. Intermediate or intergrading populations bear names such as *caelestis* Miranda Ribeiro, *jordani* Thomas, *petronius* Miranda Ribeiro, *kuhlii* Wied-Neuwied and *albicollis* Spix. These more or less distinguishable local populations demonstrate the cohesiveness of the currently recognized subdivisions or subspecies of *Callithrix jacchus.* Continued use of the names of local forms would obscure the fact that

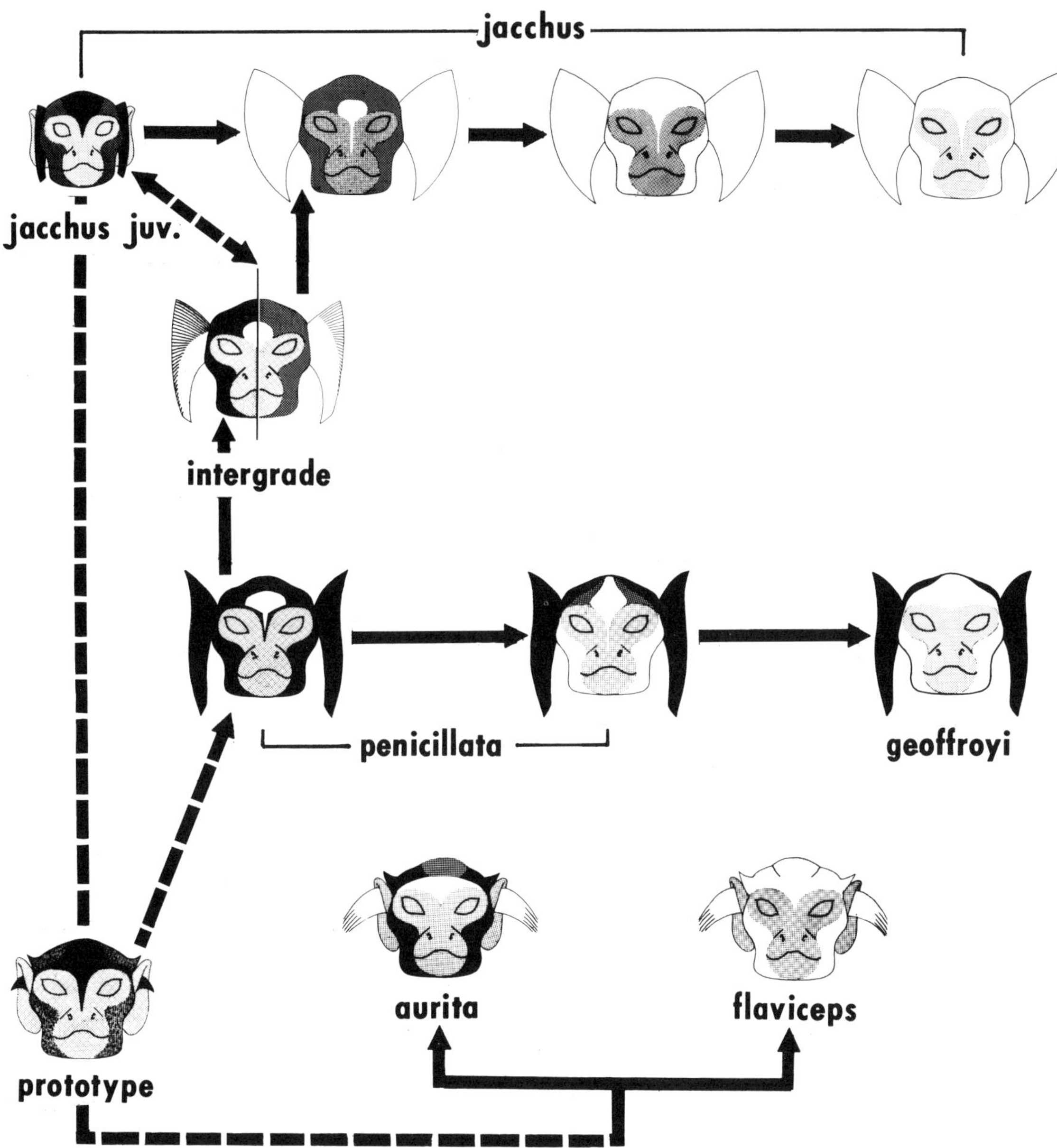

Fig. IX.7. *Callithrix jacchus*: Geographic metachromism and chromatic evolution of the subspecies (cf. fig. IX.5); characters of hypothetical prototype based on those of living juvenal *C. jacchus;* bleaching in northern, central, and southern racial tiers is clinal; ears of northern and central races concealed by large black, white, or mixed preauricular tufts shown as flaps. (From Hershkovitz 1968, p. 569.)

they are minor subdivisions of or links between the major subdivisions of the species.

Diagnostic Characters

General color pattern of body modified agouti; lower half of back blackish and grayish, orange or tawny, the colors usually disposed in alternating transverse bands of blackish and gray with the tawny or orange more or less concealed. Tail from base to tip with alternating broad blackish and narrow pale bands. Long tufts in front and often above and behind base of ears, outer (medial) surface of pinna nearly bare or thinly haired, inner (lateral) surface varies from nearly bare to covered with long projecting whitish or buffy to ochraceous tufts; forehead entirely whitish, yellowish, or buffy to blackish normally with a median whitish semilunar or rhomboidal blaze.

External Characters

Integument. Exposed parts of facial skin pigmented or flesh colored, ears more or less pigmented; muzzle haired or virtually naked but usually with a fine crest of buffy or whitish hairs on median ridge and narial septum; circumbuccal area and chin covered with short, whitish, silvery, or buffy to yellow hairs; a spot, line, or patch of white or buffy hairs beneath each eye; cheeks covered with long hairs; forehead blackish, brown, or buffy to tawny with a well-defined whitish semilunar or rhomboidal blaze, or entirely whitish or yellowish; tufts in front and above ears blackish to whitish or yellowish, medial (outer) surface of pinna nearly bare or thinly haired brown, the helix always exposed, lateral (inner) side thinly to thickly furred, the hairs often elongate and forming a dark brush, or a blackish to yellowish or whitish tuft; crown entirely black to brown, tawny or buffy, or whitish, with lateral borders often contrastingly darker, mantle generally like posterior half of crown; back behind shoulders dominantly blackish brown, tawny, buffy, gray, or rarely whitish, but generally with alternating dark and light transverse bands more sharply defined in lumbar and sacral region than anteriorly, individual hairs of mid back five-banded, with base blackish, median band tawny or orange to buffy, supramedian band blackish, subterminal band grayish to buffy or tawny, fine tip blackish; sides of body and outer sides of arms and legs like back but with striated pattern obscure or absent; chin and throat blackish to white; hairs of chin crested in midline or whorled, of throat cresting in median line, directed straight back or variable; chest blackish or brown, sometimes reddish brown, gray, or whitish, belly hairs usually darker; palms and soles mottled or entirely pigmented; tail with alternating black and grayish or buffy bands; external genitalia unpigmented, the pudendal hairs dark.

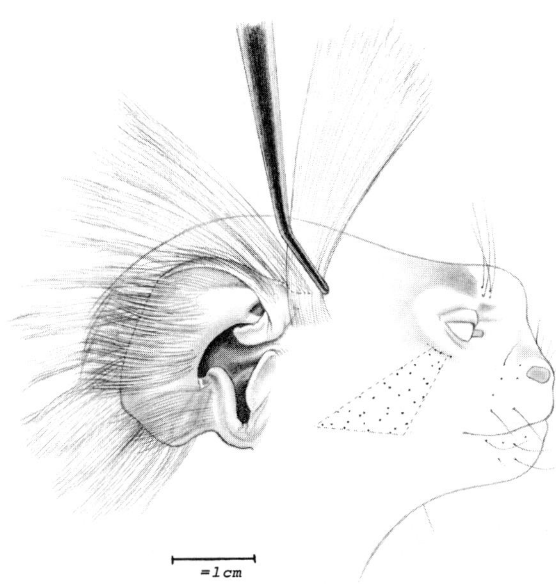

Fig. IX.8. *Callithrix jacchus penicillata*: Profile of head with cover hairs omitted to expose ear, origins of circumaural and auricular tufts, vibrissae, and facial pigmentation.

Ear Tufts (fig. IX.8). Salient tufts present in adults in front, above, behind, or on lateral surface of pinna; their form, color, and position are the most distinctive of racial traits.

In *Callithrix jacchus penicillata,* hair on and surrounding pinna is black, with lock in front and often another immediately above, usually elongate and, when fully developed in some individuals, concealing ear from facial aspect. The inner (medial) surface of pinna is sparsely haired, the outer (lateral) thinly to well covered with hair, sometimes with blackish brush or salient tuft.

In black-tufted *C. j. geoffroyi,* preauricular tuft is more elaborate, the supra-auricular tuft always present and thick, the inner auricular hairs heavier and longer, often salient and tuftlike, a postauricular tuft present and conspicuous; together, the tufts nearly conceal ear seen from front and side. Circumauricular tufts in *C. j. jacchus* are most elaborate and bleached; white in adults (blackish in 3-month-old juvenals, mixed black and white or grayish in subadults), fan-shaped in front and above and, when fully developed, nearly completely concealing ear seen from front, at least; sparsely haired pinna is dark. Salient tufts in *C. j. aurita* and *C. j. flaviceps* project from inner (lateral) aspect of pinna, tawny to whitish in color and nearly completely concealing inner surface of ear; surrounding hairs black in *aurita,* ochraceous in *flaviceps* and usually brushlike without forming salient tufts.

Tufts are individually variable in form but remain within the racial patterns described. Differences between subspecies are based primarily on degree of elongation and/or elaboration of individual wisps composing the tuft complex. Color of tufts remains black (or dark brown) in *penicillata* and *geoffroyi.* In *C. j. jacchus* they are dominantly whitish, but vary ontogenetically from dark through gray to white, and geographically from mixed black and gray or white to pure white. In *C. j. aurita* and *C. j. flaviceps* the salient tufts of the inner (lateral) surface of the pinna vary from tawny to whitish while the circumauricular pelage is black in the first, ochraceous in the second. In effect, form and color of ear tufts in *geoffroyi, jacchus, aurita,* and *flaviceps,* respectively, could be derived from but certainly grade phenotypically into those of *Callithrix jacchus penicillata.*

The circumauricular tufts, particularly the ones in front, are erectile.

Meristic Transverse Banding (fig. IX.38). Dorsal bands most sharply defined on lumbar and sacral regions with approximately 11 paired pale and dark bands present; tawny middle annulations of each hair often showing through as a third transverse color band; tail, excluding pencil, with 18–25 light or dark bands usually well defined in all races but obscure in some individuals.

Each light or dark band of back corresponds in number, and possibly in position, to a lumbar or sacral vertebra. Similarly, each pair of caudal bands corresponds to a caudal vertebra. The bands of the tail are arranged in divergent brushlike whorls with each whorl slightly expanded distally.

Transverse striae across back and around tail are formed by alignment of homologous color bands of the hairs. This suggests that the pattern of the hair follicles themselves may be meristic. Gross examination of the skin, however, reveals no such arrangement.

Vibrissae (figs. III.8; IX.8). Supraorbitals, suborbitals, mystacials, rhinarials, mentals present, forwardly directed interramals not consistently present, genals usually randomly distributed; ulnar carpals present, brachial and anconeal vibrissae present or absent; gular and pectoral spines present or absent.

The ulnar carpal vibrissae seem to have excited more interest than others. They were first recorded for an adult *jacchus* by Frederic (1905, pp. 240, 255). Beattie (1927, p. 602) mentions the presence of a carpal pad with four vibrissae on the ulnar side of each forearm in the same subspecies. Sawaya (1936, p. 146) counted 14 vibrissae on the right arm, 10 on the left of a 3-day-old *jacchus,* and 8 vibrissae on the right, 9 on the left of its father's arms. I find a cluster of 8 ulnar carpal vibrissae on the right and 4 on the left of an immature male *penicillata* (skull 42.7 mm. long). The vibrissae lack basal papillae and are no better differentiated than guard hairs found elsewhere on body and limbs.

Young. See page 540 (Growth and Development)

Molt

Specimens at hand do not lend themselves to a meaningful analysis of seasonal molt. Aspects of the process observed by various authors on caged individuals are quoted below. Included are accounts of hair loss resulting from disease, actually vitamin D_3 deficiency. This phenomenon is not molt in the sense of a normal cyclical process. Ontogenetic changes are described elsewhere (p. 540).

Fitzgerald 1935, p. 182

"As a seasonal occurrence, molting does not take place; but a few stray hairs may be found on the blankets at any time all the year around. An exception to this rule was observed in the case of two marmosets that, when bought, had coats in a terrible condition. Eventually they lost their fur in large patches. The new coats were beautiful and the animals never molted in this unusual way again." No dates are given. The observation was made on caged individuals in New York.

Lucas et al. 1927, p. 448

"The irradiated marmoset remained in perfect health throughout the winter and right up to the present time [in London]. In the first two months after irradiation started, it changed its coat, and again in July and August 1926. It was very noticeable that, whereas most marmosets in captivity sooner or later lose the hair of their tails, which then become partially or quite bald and ratlike, in the present instance the hair was completely regained and the coat came into perfect condition. . . .

"The older control marmoset, after a period of five and a half months, in February 1926, showed loss of appetite, roughness and poverty of the coat and slight loss of activity; the hair of the tail was gradually lost and not regained. As it was not desired to lose him, light treatment was administered as to the other marmoset, with beneficial results; the coat was lost and then fully restored, and the animal has been preserved in health right up to the present time. It would appear that loss of coat and subsequent restoration of it are the usual sequelae in marmosets when light treatment is instituted, as the same process was also observed in the case of the female marmoset. . . ."

Neill 1829, pp. 19, 20

When the ship reached northern latitudes en route to England from Brazil, "the change of temperature affected the monkey very sensibly . . . the hair, especially that on the tail, fell off; and, at the end of the voyage, this organ was almost quite bare and naked. . . .

"From London I brought it with me to Edinburgh last November, and have kept it here till now. During all this time it has thriven perfectly well; it is considerably plumper than it was, and the tail is now completely covered with long darkish hair."

External Genitalia

Male (fig. IX.3, 4)

Adult. Penis cylindrical and slightly tapered; penial staff unpigmented, the free or unsheathed portion papillate, each papilla with a cornified spine, the spines on dorsal (or cranial) and lateral surfaces large and pigmented but becoming smaller, sparser, and depigmented ventrally (caudally); glans pinkish, skin smooth, the left, or bacular, lobe larger, more pigmented and projecting than right; scrotum unpigmented, elongate, and partly subdivided into asymmetrical sacs; proximal half of scrotum and most of raphe densely papillate, each papilla with one or a few long stiff hairs and usually one or more shorter, finer hairs; skin of lower half of scrotum corrugated and usually glabrous; prepuce unpigmented or lightly mottled, inner glabrous fold without externally visible frenular attachment in present material, outer hairy fold with frenular attachment to scrotal fold continuous with raphe; scrotum (with testes) longer than wide, greatest diameter, 14 and 26 mm, in two adults; mons weakly papillate and sparsely haired; perineum and anal region unpigmented.

Remarks. The pubic region is not differentiated superficially into a sexual skin in present material. Wislocki (1930, p. 479) found no special development of an interpubic glandular tissue in a male and a female each of *Callithrix jacchus jacchus* and *C. jacchus penicillata.* Pocock (1920, p. 109), however, observed that in his specimen "the [relatively-P.H.] naked circum-anal integument, the ischial prominences, the scrotum, and the area above the scrotum are studded with white glandular pustules like those of the female [q.v. antea p. 417]."

Beattie (1927, p. 702) saw no hair on the scrotum of his specimen but noted "minute raised whitish areas."

Female (fig. IX.3, 4)

Adult. Labia majora unpigmented, each labium divided into a pair of thick glandular cushions; outer cushion or scrotal fold separated from inner or preputial fold by a sulcus well defined in unswollen state, poorly defined in tumescent condition; integument of outer surface of labia majora densely papillate, each papilla with one or sometimes two or three hairs; clitoris poorly defined superficially or mostly hidden in labial tissue, glabrous inner surface of prepuce surrounding glans clitoridis pigmented, outer surface papillate and hairy like scrotal fold; anterior commissure of labia in deep valley; external genitalia longer than wide, transverse diameter in two adults, 16 and 25 mm; length of genital fissure about 8 mm; sexual skin of pubic region not differentiated topically in specimen examined but reportedly present; perineal and anal regions unpigmented.

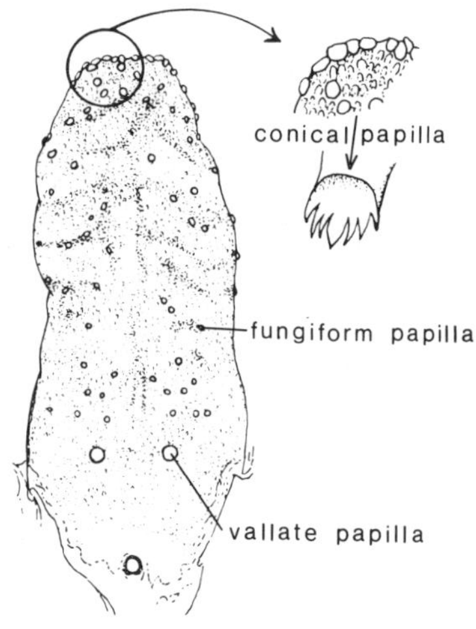

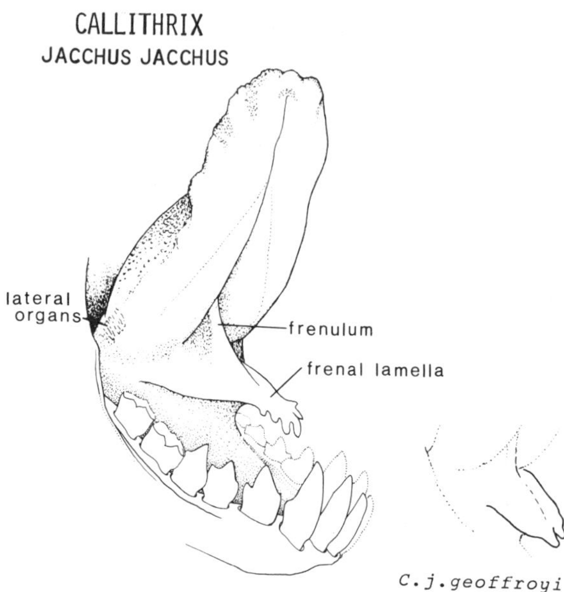

Fig. IX.9. *Callithrix jacchus*: tongue, upper and lower surfaces greatly enlarged.

Remarks. Female external genitalia of *Callithrix jacchus* most nearly resemble those of *Cebuella pygmaea*. As in the latter, cyclical tumescence of the genitalia tends to obliterate the sulcus dividing the preputial fold from the scrotal.

The female external genitalia depicted by Beattie (1927, p. 600, fig. 3) seem normal though lacking in clarity of detail. The folds surrounding the genital fissure, however, are not labia minora, as captioned. They are the inner, or preputial, folds of the labia majora and distinguished from the outer, or scrotal folds by the sulci shown in the cited figure. Osman Hill (1958, p. 680) errs in treating the external pudendal cushions as labia minora and in dismissing the sagittal sulci shown by Beattie as "wholly imaginary." The genitalia of *"Callithrix jacchus"* depicted by Osman Hill (1957, figs. 81–83) are unlike those of any callitrichid known to me.

Beattie (1927, p. 599) describes the perineal region as "studded with numerous nodules closely resembling the condition in the males. Anteriorly they are found as far as the upper level of the body of the pubis [sexual skin?] and posteriorly as far as the root of the tail."

Pocock (1920, p. 107, fig. 10 B, C) notes the presence "of a number of whitish pustules round the anus, on the perineum and on the ischial prominences. These exude under pressure a sebaceous substance which may be odoriferous." Wislocki (1930, p. 479) also records the presence of circumanal glands in *Callithrix jacchus jacchus* and *C. j. penicillata* but found no glandular tissue in the pubic region.

Tongue

See p. 107 and figure IX.9.

Dentition (figs. V.21, 22, 23, 25, 26, 27, 28)

Incisors (fig. V.23)

Permanent upper incisors comparatively high, crowns not markedly differentiated from cervix, uncrazed or with microscopically small fine lines, the lateral tooth implanted obliquely behind central with or without overlap, the incisor pair on both sides combining to form a broad V-shaped angle; mesial and distal edges more or less ridged; unworn *lateral incisor* sagittate, shorter and generally less proodont than central and about one-half its bulk, distostyle present, mesiostyle present or absent; *central incisor* spatulate or shovel-shaped, strongly forward projecting with marked inflection toward midline to meet mesial corner of opposite incisor, unworn cutting edge rounded and entire, distostyle present; horizontal occlusal groove often present near biting edge of central incisor, sometimes on median margin of lateral incisor.

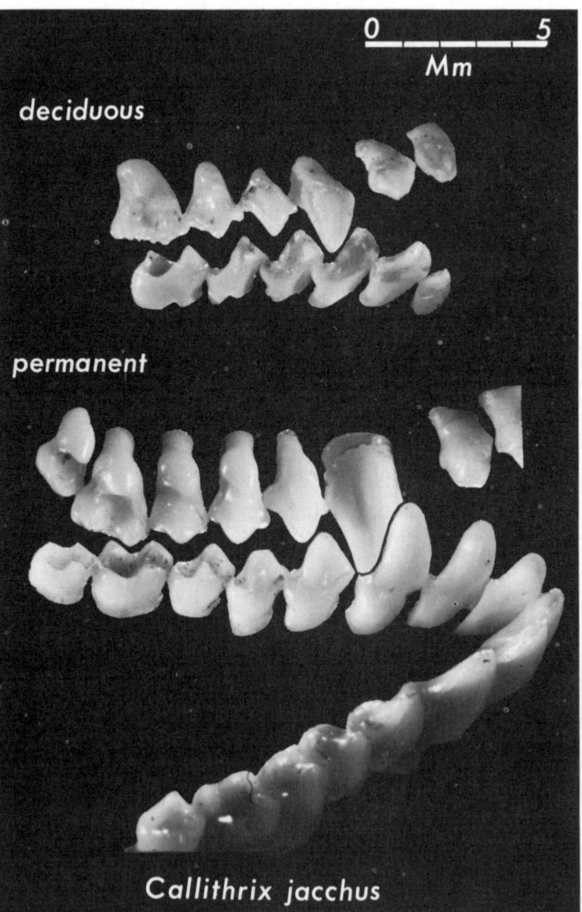

Fig. IX.10. *Callithrix jacchus*: Deciduous and permanent dentition, lingual aspect; upper and lower series shown in near-natural relationship.

Deciduous upper central incisor spatulate, higher than lateral incisor, inflected mesially and touching opposite tooth, crown more or less as wide (1.5) as high, well differentiated from cervix, uncrazed, without stylids, subovate on lateral surface, subtriangular or trapeziform and sloping on lingual surface, cutting edge sharp, rounded; *upper deciduous lateral incisor* implanted obliquely behind central incisor and usually well separated from it and canine, crown triangular, about as wide (1.4) as high from cervix, lingual surface deltoid, lingual cingulum *B* more or less defined; incisor pair of each side uncrazed, markedly less forward projecting than successors and combining to form a V-shaped Gothic arch.

Permanent lower incisors laterally compressed, the lateral incisor higher than central, teeth about two and one-half to three times higher than wide measured on labial surface, falcate or caniniform labially, lanceolate lingually, unworn biting edges obtusely pointed and not touching adjacent teeth, except at level of stylids, lingual cingulum not complete behind; *lateral incisor* emplaced obliquely behind central incisor with very little if any overlap, the pair on both sides combining to form a V-shaped arch, height on labial surface slightly less than depth of symphysis menti, distostylid present on lower half of distal edge; *central incisor* subcylindriform on labial surface, one-half to two-thirds bulk of lateral, lingual surface suboblong, with minute mesiostylid on upper third of mesial edge, distostylid present on distal base of biting surface.

Deciduous lower incisors (unworn) without crazing; outer tooth with mesial edge touching and overlapping distal edge of inner; *central incisor* spatulate, crown slightly higher than wide on labial surface, about as high (1.0) wide (0.9) on lingual, the surface concave, mesiostylids, cingular ridges and heel not defined; *lateral incisor* larger than central, club-shaped or subrectangular, lingual surface of crown longer (1.5) than high (1.2), distostylid present and bounding a more or less well defined lingual basin, mesiostylid absent.

Remarks. The upper deciduous incisors differ from their successors by overall smaller size, relatively broader crown, poor definition of mesial and distal stylids, and more rounded arch with the lateral tooth not staggered behind the central. Resemblance to the upper permanent incisors of *Saguinus* is striking. The lower deciduous incisors also form a rounded arch in most individuals, staggered in some; the central is spatulate, not falcate or lanceolate, the lateral scimitar-shaped with tendency toward development of heel. Again, greatest resemblance is with permanent dentition of *Saguinus*.

Canines

Permanent upper canine slightly recurved, subtriangular in cross section, more than twice as high as long and about twice the height of either adjacent tooth; mesiolingual torus (*II*) defined by a deep groove, distal edge sharp, anterior portion of lingual cingulum (*B*) and mesiostyle poorly defined, distostyle present in unworn, eroded and replaced by shear facet in worn; posterolingual enamel sometimes slightly crazed.

Deciduous upper canine slightly recurved, subtriangular crown about as high as long, the entire tooth at least one-fourth again higher than either adjacent tooth, anterior edge ungrooved, sharply ridged, posterior edge sharp; anterior and posterior portions of lingual cingulum nearly or quite continuous.

Permanent lower canine like lateral incisor but heavier, as high or slightly higher, more recurved, implanted obliquely behind, distostylid better developed, talonid more distinct.

Deciduous lower canine (unworn) premolariform, slightly larger than dpm_2, uncrazed, mesiostylid not evident, median lingual torus present separating incipient "trigonid" basin from talonid, low distostylid present on posterobuccal rim of talonid.

Remarks. The deciduous upper canine, judged by wear patterns, functions like the permanent canine and anterior premolar in stabbing, slashing, and slicing. The molarized deciduous lower canine definitely belongs with the premolar series. In contrast, the permanent lower canine, though somewhat molarized, clearly works in tandem with the lateral incisor.

Premolars

Permanent upper premolars with pm^2 sagittate on buccal aspect and dominantly caniniform in general

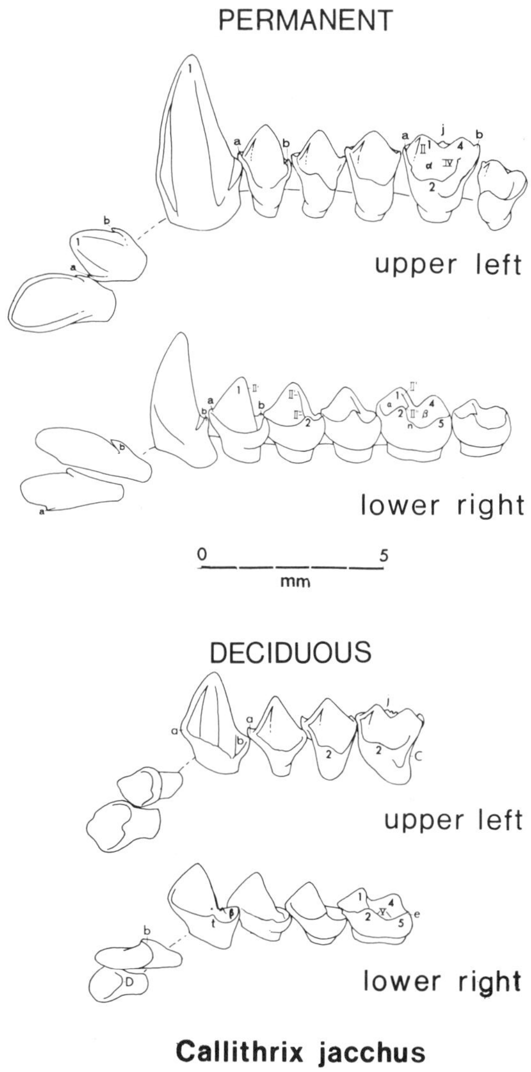

Callithrix jacchus

Fig. IX.11. *Callithrix jacchus*: Deciduous and permanent dentition, lingual aspect (diagrammatic).

structure, sample crown height 2.6, length 1.5, width 2.1; anterior and posterior cingulum *B* is well developed, mesiostyle and distostyle present, protocone from undefined to relatively well developed, the premolar varying from unicuspid to bicuspid; *pm*^{3} bicuspid, slightly larger and somewhat lower than preceding, protocone, mesial, and distal styles well developed, lingual cingulum often raised into a well-developed protoloph (*III*) extending between mesiostyle and protocone; neolingual cingulum (*B'*) indicated or weakly developed, sometimes with weak entostyles; *pm*^{4} usually slightly lower and bulkier than pm^3, protocone larger, mesial and distal styles and cingula no less developed; sample dimensions, 1.8 high, 1.9 long, 2.8 wide.

Deciduous upper premolars with *dpm*^{2} sagittate, dominantly caniniform and unicuspid, higher (2.0), longer (1.6) than wide (1.5), about one-fourth lower than canine and little higher than remaining cheek teeth, cingulum *B* weakly developed, mesiostyle and distostyle present, protocone not indicated; *dpm*^{3} bulkier than preceding, considerably wider (2.0) but slightly lower, mesial and distal styles well developed, protocone weakly to moderately developed; *dpm*^{4} completely molariform with large eocone, somewhat smaller metacone, protocone bulky, mesiostyle, ectostyle, distostyle, ectoloph and protoloph usually well defined; dimensions, 1.6 high, 2.3 long, 2.7 wide.

Remarks. Premolar molarization in *Callithrix* is markedly advanced over that in *Cebuella.* The bicuspid premolar crowns are less triangular, tending to become more rectangular, and the protocone is better developed. Although pm^2 remains essentially caniniform, its lingual shelf is well developed, the protocone often evident and well defined, and the protoloph is distinct in pm$^{3\text{-}4}$.

Dpm^3 retains much of the primitive caniniform character despite its low but well-developed protocone. Dpm^4 is a tritubercular molar and larger than its bicuspid successor.

Permanent lower premolars with *pm*$_2$ falcate, essentially unicuspid, sample crown height 2.8, length 2.4, width 1.7, anterior and posterior lingual cingulids (*B, C*) well defined, but epicristid *II* separating them weakly differentiated, metaconid hardly if at all indicated, mesiostylid poorly defined; *pm*$_3$ approximately equal in bulk to preceding but slightly lower, cingulids well developed, the epicristid present and in conjunction with cingulid *C* enclosing a well-excavated talonid basin; weak metaconid and often an entoconid (*5*) present; *pm*$_4$ lowest of series, the deep forward sloping "trigonid" basin bounded by cingulid *B* and epicristid, metaconid well defined, paraconid not indicated, fully developed talonid basin occupying from about one-third to one-half occlusal surface, entoconid and hypoconid not always evident, mesiostylid but not distostylid evident; sample length 2.1, width 1.8.

Deciduous lower premolar with *dpm*$_2$ like canine but smaller, crown height 2.1, length 2.0, width 1.3, obliquely directed epicristid weakly defined, a small narrow talonid basin enclosed between it and cingulid *C,* cingulid *B* poorly defined, mesiostylid not evident; *dpm*$_3$ slightly lower than preceding with epicristid strong, talonid basin larger, cingulid *B* better demarcated, mesiostylid and distostylid present; *dpm*$_4$ with fully defined "trigonid" and talonid, eoconid and high metaconid joined by nearly horizontal epicristid, paraconid not indicated, talonid nearly twice as large as "trigonid," its deep basin ovate and more than twice as large as "trigonid" basin, hypoconid large but lower than ectoconid; entoconid horizontally expanded; length 2.3, width 1.7.

Remarks. Deciduous pm$_{2\text{-}3}$ are less molarized than their successors but dpm$_4$ is a complete molar and much more advanced than pm$_4$. The epicristid is a well-developed structure but the epicrista is no more than a torus of the eocone.

Molars

Upper first molar half again to nearly twice as large as m^2, one half again to three-quarters again larger than pm^4, occlusal surface subtriangular, trigon basin deeply conical, unworn eocone slightly higher and larger than metacone, higher than protocone but subequal in bulk, protoloph (III) and plagiocrista (IV) or metaloph well defined, plagioconule (metaconule, *d*) often present, epiconule (*c*) rudimentary or absent, secondary lingual cingulum (*B'*) and cingulum *C* usually well defined and often continuous on lingual border, small mesiostyle and distostyle present, buccal cingulum often with one ectostyle, sometimes a cluster of two or three; *second molar* like first but smaller, metacone reduced and often deflected distally, sometimes nearly completely fused to protocone by contracted plagiocrista, epiconule often present and well developed, distostyle and ectostyles obsolete or absent, crown more frequently aligned with lingual than buccal border of first molar.

Lower molars subrectangular, elevated "trigonid" occupying anterior one-third to two-fifths of crown basin, forward-sloping, shallow, and irregular in shape, depressed talonid forming remainder of crown with deeply rounded basin; *first molar* oblong, one-fourth to one-third larger than premolar, eoconid slightly higher than metaconid, crest of transverse epicristid concave or notched, paraconid absent, mesiostylid indicated, ectostylids present or absent, hypoconid lower than eoconid, higher than entoconid, entoconid with convex crest and separated from more elevated metaconid by deep valley, postentoconulid not distinctly differentiated from entoconid, distostylid not evident, posterior border of talonid with median notch or depression; *second molar* like first but one-third to two-fifths smaller, distolingual cusp separated by a broad trough from distobuccal cusp and produced more posteriad.

Sample measurements of molars, buccal length × width:

m^1	m^2	m$_1$	m$_2$
2.3 × 3.0	1.7 × 2.4	2.5 × 2.0	2.2 × 1.8
2.5 × 3.0	2.0 × 2.3	2.6 × 1.8	2.1 × 1.4
2.7 × 3.3	2.0 × 2.6	2.7 × 2.3	2.3 × 1.9

Karyotype

The karyotype of *Callithrix jacchus jacchus* (2n = 46) is grossly similar to those of *Saguinus* (table 48). Hsu and Benirschke (1970) found the karyotype of *C. j. penicillata* like that of *C. j. jacchus* but with the Y chromosome metacentric and larger than the extremely small acrocentric of the other race.

Comparisons

External characters which singly or in combinations distinguish *Callithrix jacchus* from all other callitrichids are ordinary squirrel size, modified agouti color pattern over most of trunk, fully annulated tail, absence of mane and whitish hip patches, presence of long, conspicuous tufts in front of ears or on inner (lateral) surface of pinna, outer (medial) surface of pinna nearly bare to moderately hairy, the skin showing through. Tassel-eared *Callithrix humeralifer humeralifer,* the only other banded-tailed form of *Callithrix,* is similar but with lower dorsum not transversely banded, inner and outer surface of pinna completely clothed by long, thick fur, median frontal region dark and without blaze, and whitish hip patches present (fig. IX.38 and p. 594).

Juvenal *Callithrix jacchus* with undeveloped ear tufts and poorly defined transverse dorsal banding resemble adult pygmy marmosets (*Cebuella pygmaea*) in size and in color and pelage patterns. They are distinguished by throat and mantle unicolor or mottled, not agouti, outline of pinna subquadrilateral as in adult, not rounded, tail broadly annulated as in adult with each black band about twice as wide as pale band and as clearly defined on ventral as on dorsal surface. Obvious juvenal characters such as visage in general, proportionately heavier limbs and digits, silkier, and more lax pelage further differentiate young ouistitis from adult pygmies.

Key to Subspecies of Callithrix jacchus

1. Tufts in front of ears elongate or fanlike and conspicuously displayed; pelage of inner (lateral) surface of ears blackish or brown and not forming a salient tuft 2

1′. Tufts in front of ears not salient or conspicuously displayed; pelage of inner (lateral) surface of ears whitish, buffy, or ochraceous and forming a conspicuous tuft 4

2. Circumauricular tufts dominantly black or brownish 3

2′. Circumauricular tufts dominantly white or grayish .... *C. j. jacchus*

3. Crown, temples blackish .... *C. j. penicillata*

3′. Crown, temples, and sides of face white or creamy .... *C. j. geoffroyi*

4. Sides of head, cheeks, throat black, crown ochraceous, tawny or black, ear tufts whitish .... *C. j. aurita*

4′. Sides of head, cheeks, throat yellowish to ochraceous like crown and ear tufts .... *C. j. flaviceps*

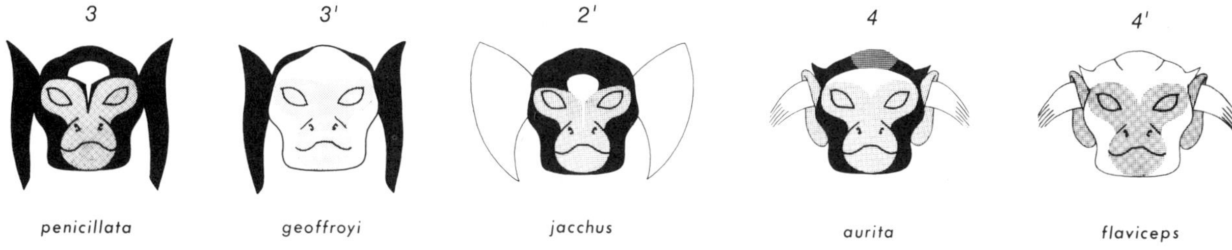

CALLITHRIX JACCHUS PENICILLATA E. GEOFFROY: BLACK-TUFTED-EAR MARMOSET

Fig. IX.12. Black-tufted-ear Marmoset, *Callithrix jacchus penicillata* E. Geoffroy

Synonymic History

Simia penicillata E. Geoffroy in Humboldt, 1812, *Rec. Obs. Zool. Anat. Comp.*, p. 360—"*Jacchus penicillatus,* Geoffroy," in synonymy.

Jacchus penicillatus, E. Geoffroy, 1812, *Ann. Mus. Hist. Nat., Paris* 19:119—BRAZIL: (type locality). Desmarest, 1818, *Nouv. Dict. Hist. Nat.* 24:239—characters. Desmarest, 1820, *Mammalogie,* p. 92—characters. Desmarest, 1827, *Dict. Sci. Nat.* 47:18—characters. I. Geoffroy, 1827, *Dict. Class. Hist. Nat.* 15:517—BRAZIL; characters. Wagner, 1833, *Isis von Oken* 10:997—BRAZIL; characters of specimen collected by Spix. Lund, 1839, *Ann. Sci. Nat.* (1) 11:234—BRAZIL: *Minas Gerais* (Rio das Velhas). Gray, 1843, *List Mamm. Brit. Mus.*, p. 14 —BRAZIL; varieties. Gerrard, 1862, *Cat. bones Brit. Mus.*, p. 29—BRAZIL.

Iacchus penicillatus, Spix, 1823, *Sim. Vesp. Brasil.*, p. 34, pl. 26 (animal)—part, BRAZIL: *Minas Gerais.* Rolle, 1835, *Proc. Zool. Soc. London* 1835:125—BRAZIL: *Bahia;* habits.

J[acchus] penicillatus, Reichenbach, 1862, *Vollst. Naturg. Affen,* p. 4, pl. 1, figs. 11–13 (animal)—BRAZIL; characters.

Hapale penicillata Wagner, 1840, *Schreber's Säugth., Suppl.* 1:242, pl. 33A—characters; distribution. Wagner, 1848, *Abh. Akad. Wiss. Munich* (1847) 5:464—part, BRAZIL: *São Paulo* (Porto do Rio Paraná [Rio Grande]); characters. Burmeister, 1854, *Syst. Uebers. Thiere Brasil.* 1:32—BRAZIL: *Minas Gerais* (Rio das Velhas, behind Santa Lucia); characters; habits. Burmeister, 1869, *Annal. Mus. Publ., Buenos Aires* 1 (6):448, footnote—[!] ARGENTINA: *Salta* (Orán; Esquina Grande); enters occasionally from north. Schlegel, 1876, *Les singes. Simiae,* p. 273—characters; variation; *trigonifer* Reichenbach, a synonym. Burmeister, 1879, *Descr. Phys. Rep. Argentine* 3:61—ARGENTINA: brought captive from Brazil. Pelzeln, 1883, *Verh. K. K. Zool.-Bot. Gesellsch., Wien, Beih.* 33:22—BRAZIL: *São Paulo* (Porto do Rio Paraná [Rio Grande]; *Minas Gerais* (Verissimo); *Bahia.* Jentink, 1887, *Cat. Ostéol. Mus. Pays-Bas,* 9:50—part, BRAZIL: *Bahia.* Jentink, 1892, *Cat. Syst. Mamm. Mus. Pays-Bas* 11:58 —skulls. Winge, 1895, *E Mus. Lundii* 2 (2):5—BRAZIL: *Minas Gerais* (Lagôa Santa). Thomas, 1901, *Ann. Mag. Nat. Hist.*, ser. 7, 8:527—BRAZIL: *Minas Gerais* (Rio Jordão). Weinert, 1926, *Zeitschr. Morph. Anthrop.* 35:282, fig. 95 (paranasal cavities)—frontal sinuses. Cabrera, 1939, *Physis* 16:4—marmosets not natural elements of Argentine fauna. Schultz, 1948, *Amer. J. Phys. Anthrop.*, n.s., 6:8—twins and triplets recorded. Osman Hill, 1957, *Primates* 3:83, 112, 141, 144, 156, 158, 168, 172, 174, 180–82, 184, 185, 239, 251, 286, 288–91, 295–

98, 317, fig. 61 (map, distribution), pl. 25 (animal)—anatomy; taxonomy; distribution; habits; food, reproduction; hybridization with *jacchus.* Day and Napier, 1963, *Folia Primat.* 1:128—deep head of flexor pollicis brevis muscle absent. Krumbiegel, 1966, *Säugetierk Mitt.* 14(2):106—"cryptopaedy," or camouflage of young on mother's back.

H[apale] penicillata, Wagner, 1840, *Schreber's Säugth., Suppl.* 1:242, pl. 33A (animal)—characters; distribution. I. Geoffroy, 1851, *Cat. Primates, Mus. Hist. Nat., Paris,* p. 60—BRAZIL: *Goiás* (collected by St.-Hilaire). Wagner, 1855, *Schreber's Säugth., Suppl.* 5:124—part, not var.*β*.

Hapale penicillatus, Kuhl, 1820, *Beitr. Zool.,* p. 47—BRAZIL: not south of 15° 30′ S. F. Cuvier fils, 1842, in Geoffroy and Cuvier, *Hist. Nat. Mamm.,* 7:table—index.

H[apale] penicillatus, Wied-Neuwied, 1826, *Beitr. Naturg. Brasil.,* p. 142—BRAZIL: *Bahia.*

[Hapale] penicillatus, Pocock, 1917, *Ann. Mag. Nat. Hist.,* ser. 8, 20:257, footnote—"completely intergrades" with *jacchus.*

Hapale jacchus L. var. *penicillata,* De Beaux, 1917, *Giorn. Morph. Uomo, Primati* 1:90, 96—BRAZIL: São Paulo; vibrissae (ulnar carpal; facial).

H[apale] p[enicillata] penicillata, Osman Hill, 1957, *Primates* 3:296—characters; distribution.

[?] *Hapale penicillata penicillata,* Ruschi, 1964, *Bol. Mus. Biol.* "Prof. Mello Leitão." 23A:6—BRAZIL; *Espírito Santo* (coast from Conceição da Barra to Barra do Itapemirim).

Callithrix penicillata, Thomas, 1904, *Ann. Mag. Nat. Hist.,* ser. 7, 14:188—BRAZIL. Elliot, 1913, *A review of the Primates,* 1:226—characters; "type is no longer in the Paris museum." Wislocki, 1930, *J. Mammal.* 11:479—scent glands of pubic region. Laemmert and Ferreira, 1945, *Amer. J. Trop. Med.* 25:231—BRAZIL: *Bahia* (Ilheus); natural host of yellow fever virus. Waddell and Taylor, 1946. *Amer. J. Trop. Med.* 26:455—BRAZIL: *Bahia (Ilheus)*; principal vertebrate host of yellow fever virus. Anthony, Serra, and Serra, 1949, *Bull. Mem. Soc. Anthrop. Paris,* ser. 9, 10:132—palatal surface and cranial capacity. Ottaviani and Manfredonia, 1958, *Anais Fac. Med. Univ. Minas Gerais* 18:173—lymphatics. Di Dio, Manfredonia, and Ottaviani, 1959, *Ateneo Parmense* 30 (Suppl. 4):5—lymphatic system. Werner, 1960, *Primatologia* 2, (1), Lief. 5:11—middle and inner ear. Machado and Di Dio, 1963, *Anat. Anzeiger* 113:45—ampulla of the terminal ileum. Chiarelli, 1963, *Folia Primat.* 1:91—taste sensitivity to phenyl-thiocarbamide. Carvalho, 1965, *Arq. Zool. São Paulo* 12:27—identification of primate "21 a. *Simia jacchus,*" of Alexander Rodriguez Ferreira ,1790. Warren and Simões, 1966, *Amer. J. Trop. Med. Hyg.* 15(2):153—resistant to *Schistosomiasis mansoni.* Marback, 1971, *Fac. Med. Univ. Fed. Bahia (Brazil)* (doctoral thesis)—histochemistry of retina [work not seen]. Miraglia, Moura, and Neves, 1974, *Acta Anat.* 87:334—histochemistry of parotid glands. Costa Guedes, 1974, *Bol. Inst. Biol. Bahia* 31:127—histochemistry of duodenal glands of Brunner. Pedreira and Peixoto, 1975, *J. Human Evol.* 4:293, pl. 1 (karyotype)—karyotypic difference between *penicillata* and *jacchus* regarded as individual variables and taxonomically insignificant. Miraglia, Chavarria Irusta, Castro Filho, Pinto, 1975, *Acta Anat.* 92:385—histochemistry of male kidney activity. Pinto, Miraglia, Santana Moura, 1975, *Acta Anat.* 89:49—aortic wall.

Callithrix penicillatus [*sic*], Rode and Hershkovitz, 1945, *Bull. Mus. Nat. Hist. Nat., Paris,* ser. 2, 17:221—BRAZIL: *Goiás* (specimen collected 1827 by August St.-Hilaire designated "lectotype"). Hershkovitz and Rode, 1947, *J. Mammal.* 28:68—cancellation of improperly designated "lectotype"; Humboldt not E. Geoffroy regarded as author of name. Machado, 1960, *Anais Fac. Med. Univ. Minas Gerais* 20:123 seq., table 1, figs. 7–10 (ileal eminence)—BRAZIL: *Minas Gerais* (Buenópolis); morphology of ileal eminence of large intestine.

C[allithrix] penicillata, Coimbra-Filho, 1971, *Rev. Brasil. Biol.* 31(3):378–79—BRAZIL: *Bahia* (Fazenda Almada).

Callithrix penicillata penicillata, Vieira, 1955, *Arq. Zool., São Paulo* 8:392—BRAZIL: *Bahia* (Vila Nova; Itabuna; Ilhéus; Rio Jucuruçú); *Minas Gerais; Espírito Santo.* Avila Pires, 1969, *Rev. Biol. Bras.* 29(1):60—part, BRAZIL: *Bahia* (Fazenda Pirataquissé, Ilhéus; Rio Jucuruçú).

C[allithrix] p[enicillata] penicillata, Coimbra-Filho, 1971, *Rev. Brasil. Biol.* 31(3):378, fig. 1 (prepared skin)—BRAZIL: distribution. Coimbra-Filho, 1972, *Rev. Brasil. Biol.* 36(4):505, fig. 7 (pits bitten into board)—wood boring and gum eating habits. Coimbra-Filho and Mittermeier, 1974, *Folia Primat.* 20 (1973):243, 260, fig. 1D (animal), fig. 6 (prepared skin)—BRAZIL: character; distribution; hybridization in captivity; alleged sympatry with *geoffroyi* and *flaviceps.*

Hapale jacchus L. var. *penicillata,* De Beaux, 1917, *Giorn. Morph. Uomo, Primati* 1:90, 96—BRAZIL: *São Paulo;* vibrissae (ulnar carpal; facial).

Callithrix jacchus penicillata, Hershkovitz, 1968, *Evolution* 22(3):567, fig. 10 (distribution), fig. 12 (geographic metachromism)—color pattern; comparisons; geographic metachromism. Hershkovitz, 1970, *Amer. J. Phys. Anthrop.* 32(3):379—dental diseases. Hershkovitz, 1970, *Folia Primat.* 13:215—BRAZIL: *Minas Gerais* (Rio das

Velhas); cerebral fissural pattern. S. Hampton and Taylor, 1970, *Proc. 3d Int. Cong. Primat., Zurich* 1:246—gonadal development (resembles pattern in other platyrrhines and catarrhines). Hsu and S. Hampton, 1970, *Folia Primat.* 13:183, fig. 1 (karyotype)—karyotype (2n = 46). J. K. Hampton, Jr., Hampton, and Levy, 1971, in Goldsmith and Moor-Jankowski, *Med. Primat.*, 1970, p. 526—breeding records.

H[apale] penicillatus Kuhlii Wied-Neuwied, 1826, *Beitr. Naturg. Brasilian* 2:142—BRAZIL: *Bahia* (type locality, Rio Belmonte; Serra do Mundo Novo; Rio Pardo; Rio Ilhéus); type, male, Prince Maximilian's collection; collected by Prince Maximilian Wied-Neuwied; distribution (eastern Brazil from 14°–17° S); habits; variation.

Hapale melanotis Lesson, 1840, *Species de mammifères: Bimanes et quadrumanes,* p. 190—part, new name for *Jacchus penicillatus* E. Geoffroy only; characters: Lesson, 1842, *Nouv. Tabl. Reg. Anim., Mamm.*, p. 8—BRAZIL.

J[acchus] trigonifer Reichenbach, 1862, *Vollst. Naturg. Affen,* p. 4, pl. 1, fig. 10 (animal)—BRAZIL: (type locality not specified); type died in captivity, skin [skull?] in the Dresden Museum.

Callithrix penicillata jordani Thomas, 1904, *Ann. Mag. Nat. Hist.*, ser. 7, 14:188—BRAZIL: *Minas Gerais* (type locality, Rio Jordão, altitude, 800 meters); type, female, skin and skull, British Museum (Natural History) no. 1.11.3.9, collected 9 June 1901 by Alphonse Robert. Elliot, 1913, *Review of the Primates,* 1:227—characters ex type. Vieira, 1944, *Papeis Avulsos, São Paulo* 4 (1):6—BRAZIL: *Minas Gerais; São Paulo* (Rio Grande). Hershkovitz and Rode, 1947, *J. Mammal.* 28:68—BRAZIL: *Goiás* (identification of specimen designated "lectotype" of *Jacchus penicillatus* E. Geoffroy, by Rode and Hershkovitz 1945). Vieira, 1951, *Papeis Avulsos* 10 (4):109—BRAZIL: *Goiás* (Goiânia). Vieira, 1955, *Arq. Zool. São Paulo* 8:393—BRAZIL: *Goiás* (Goiânia; Catalão; Ipê Arcado; Canabrava; Jaraguá; Inhumas; Goiabeiras; Rio das Almas); *Minas Gerais* (Pirapoa; Rio São Francisco); *São Paulo* (Barretos, Rio Grande). Slick, 1965, *Arq. Zool., São Paulo* 12:74—BRAZIL: *Goiás* (Cerrados); habitat. Avila Pires, 1969, *Rev. Brasil. Biol.* 29(1):60—part, BRAZIL: *Bahia* (Malhada; Barreiras; Feira de Santana; Riachão das Neves); *Minas Gerais* (Januária; Serra do Itatiaiá; Curvelo; São Joâo do Gloria; Barra do Paraopeba; Lagôa Santa; Araguarí Uberaba; Rio das Velhas; Lassance; Pirapora; Barro Alto, Rio São Francisco); *São Paulo* (Barretos); *Goiás* (Palma; Planaltina, Veadeiros; Anápolis; Ponte Opê Arcado; Jaraguá; Ponte do Paranaíba; Goiânia Cana Brava; Aragarças); *"Rio de Janeiro:* Santa Rita da Floresta (MCZ)"; characters; distributions. Rossoni et al. 1973, *Arch. Oral Biol.* 18, p. 879—autonomic innervation of salivary glands [work not seen].

C[allithrix] p[enicillata] jordani, Coimbra-Filho, 1971, *Rev. Brasil. Biol.* 31(3):378, 380, fig. 1 (prepared skin)—BRAZIL; distribution; comparisons with hybrids. Coimbra-Filho, 1972 *Rev. Brasil. Biol.* 32 (4):505, fig. 5 (animal perforating and marking wood)—wood-boring and gum-eating habits. Deane, Silva, Loures, 1974, *Rev. Inst. Med. Trop., São Paulo* 16:1—BRAZIL: *Minas Gerais* (Lagoa Santa; Curvelo) Trypanosome infection. Coimbra-Filho and Mittermeier, 1974, *Fol. Primat.* 20 (1973):241, 261, fig. 2A (head), fig. 3 (animal)—BRAZIL: distribution; character; hybridization in captivity; "sympatry" with *jacchus.*

H[apale] p[enicillata] jordani, Osman Hill, 1957, *Primates* 3:296—characters.

[*Jacchus vulgaris*] var. 3, Gray, 1870, *Cat. monkeys, lemurs and fruit-eating bats, Brit. Mus.*, p. 63—*penicillatus* a synonym.

Ouistiti à pinceaux, femelle, F. Cuvier, 1832, in Geoffroy and Cuvier, *Hist. Nat. Mamm., livr.* 65 [vol. 7], pl. (animal) and text—characters.

Simia albifrons Thunberg (not Thunberg, 1819, not Humboldt, 1812), 1819, *Handl. Kongl. Vetenskaps Acad. Sweden,* p. 68, pl. 4 (animal)—part, female only [male type = *C. j. geoffroyi*].

Callithrix geoffroyi Avila Pires (part not Humboldt), 1969, *Rev. Brasil. Biol.* 29(1):57—BRAZIL: Bahia (Fazenda Almada, Ilhéus).

Hapale penicillatus ♀ × *Hapale jacchus* ♂, Osman Hill, 1957, *Primates* 3:185—"bred several times in London Zoo from 1950 onwards."

H[apale] penicillata ♂ × *H[apale] jacchus* ♀, Osman Hill, 1961, *Proc. Zool. Soc. London* 137(2):321—hybrid recorded.

Callithrix penicillata ♂ × *Callithrix jacchus* ♀, Mallinson, 1969, *Ann. Rep. Jersey Wildl. Preser. Trust* 6:8, 11, figs. p. 8 (facial pattern of parents and hybrid offspring)—production of viable "hybrids" in Jersey Zoo.

C[allithrix] j[acchus] penicillata × *C[allithrix] j[acchus] jacchus,* J. K. Hampton, Jr., Hampton, and Levy, 1971, in Goldsmith and Moor-Jankowski, *Med. Primat.*, 1970, p. 528—reproduction.

(*Callithrix penicillata* × *Callithrix jacchus*) × (*Callithrix penicillata* × *Callithrix jacchus*), Mallinson, 1971, in personal communication—F_2 hybrids born between 1 and 3 July 1971.

Fig. IX.13. *Simia albifrons* (= *Callithrix jacchus penicillata*). Reproduction of a woodcut from a drawing of a mounted specimen in the museum of the University of Uppsala, Sweden (from Thunberg, 1819, p. 68, pl. 4, female.)

Type. Skin mounted with skull in; collected between 1783–1792 by Alexandre Rodrigues Ferreira during his scientific expedition in Brazil, and shipped to the Museum Royal d'Ajuda, Lisbon, Portugal; acquired in 1808, by the Muséum National d'Histoire Naturelle, Paris; lost or discarded some years after 1812.

Type Locality. Brazil; restricted to Lamarão, Bahia (292d), by Thomas (1904, *Ann. Mag. Nat. Hist.*, ser. 7, 14:188).

When Thomas (1904:188) described *Callithrix penicillata jordani* from Minas Gerais, he regarded specimens from "Lamarão, near Bahia," as true *penicillata* "on geographical grounds." In 1945, Rode and I (p. 68) interpreted Thomas's action as a restriction of the type locality. There are better interpretations and the geographic basis for determining the type locality may not be valid in this case. Geoffroy's specimen originated somewhere within the vast range of *penicillata* as here defined, and only the zoological basis, or direct comparison of specimens of known localities with the type can throw light on the precise type locality. In actual practice, however, any specimen of known locality agreeing closely with the type may be treated by the First Reviser as a topotype unless zoological evidence to the contrary is adduced. Lamarão will, therefore, be regarded as type locality in accordance with the First Reviser principle.

Distribution (fig. IX.5). East central Brazil, from the State of Goiás, south and east into São Paulo north of the Rio Tietê-Piracicaba, thence north into the Rio São Francisco basin of Minas Gerais and, in southern Bahia, from the east bank of the Rio São Francisco–Rio Grande east to the coast; altitudinal range from near sea level to possibly 1,000 meters above.

The coastal strip or panhandle of Bahia and probably adjacent parts of Espírito Santo are zones of intergradation between *penicillata* and *geoffroyi.* Intergradation between *penicillata* and *jacchus* occurs to the north in the Recôncavo da Bahia.

Published references to the natural occurrence of *Callithrix jacchus penicillata* in Argentina are based on incorrect or misleading information. No callitrichid occurs naturally in Argentina or in Paraguay. Occurrence of *penicillata* in Mato Grosso noted by Osman Hill (1957, pp. 296, 297) is probably based on a misreading of the Goiânia, Goiás record by Vieira (1951, p. 109).

The history of some specimens of *penicillata, jacchus,* and *aurita* labeled "Santa Rita" but misinterpreted as "Santa Rita de la Floresta," Rio de Janeiro (Avila Pires 1969) is discussed under the heading of *Callithrix jacchus aurita.*

Taxonomy. In 1826 (p. 142) Wied-Neuwied described *Hapale penicillatus kuhlii* on the basis of a male collected near the mouth of the Rio Belmonte, Bahia (306), in a probable zone of contact between *geoffroyi* and *penicillata.* The type specimen was distinguished from true *penicillata* chiefly by the "weisslich graubraun," crown and whitish cheeks. Wied-Neuwied noted that specimens from Ilhéus (299) also differed from typical *penicillata* by their more buffy cheeks and frontal blaze. Three specimens from the vicinity of Ilhéus I examined agree with Wied-Neuwied's description. Their geographic position, buffy crown, pale cheeks, well-defined white median rostral line, and large frontal blaze extending over the crown mark them as intergrades between *geoffroyi* and *penicillata* (figs. IX.14, 15). Of the three Ilhéus area specimens, one from Fazenda Almada was determined as *Callithrix geoffroyi* by Avila Pires (1969), while a second from Pirataquissé, and the third from Ilhéus were assigned to *penicillata.* Coimbra-Filho (1971, p. 379) objected and referred all marmosets of the Ilhéus region to *penicillata.* These intergrades are found where intergradation is expected. Those from the vincinity of Ilhéus are nearer typical *penicillata,* while those from the Belmonte area, type region of *kuhlii* Wied-Neuwied, are evidently nearer *geoffroyi.* The marmosets in adjoining parts of coastal Espírito Santo probably belong to the same or a similarly mixed stock.

Jacchus trigonifer Reichenbach, 1862, is based on a zoo animal of unknown origin. It was preserved after death as a mounted specimen in the Dresden Museum. The colored figure of the type does not agree with its description in the text. The latter alone indicates an ordinary specimen of *penicillata.*

Callithrix penicillata jordani Thomas, 1904, from Rio Jordão, Minas Gerais (308a), was distinguished from a series of *penicillata* from Lamarão, Bahia (292d), by its more buffy coloration throughout, yellowish rather than blackish belly and inner side of thighs, "dulled whiteness of the nasal septum, the general absence of yellow on the tail-hair, and the long narrow incisors." The differences are trivial and actually less than exists between most series of *penicillata* I have examined. In seven specimens from Agua Suja (309c) in the Paris Museum the mantle ranges from dark brown, slightly ticked, to dark brown agouti, chest varying from brownish as in typical *jordani* to entirely black with the black extending in some specimens over the midventral portion of the belly. The characters of these, in effect, cut across the Rio Jordão series of *jordani* and a series of seven specimens in the British Museum regarded by Thomas (1904, p. 188) as representative of true *penicillata*. Eight specimens in the New York museum, from Annapolis, Goiás (278b), northwest of the type locality, closely agree with the description of *jordani*. On the other hand, 3 specimens from Rio das Velhas, Minas Gerais (313), southeast of Rio Jordão, differ from *jordani* in much the same way *jordani* differs from Lamarão *penicillata*. Surprisingly, two specimens from Lassance, lower down the Rio das Velhas (312a), are more nearly like the geographically distant pale Annapolis series than like the neighboring blackish Rio das Velhas series from upstream. The characters of the middle upper incisors of *jordani* described by Thomas as "longer, narrower, more parallel-sided and less strongly convergent towards each other than in *penicillata*, their breadth in the latter about two thirds their length, while it is about half in the former," lack taxonomic significance.

Diagnostic Characters. Tufts in front and above ears black or dark brown; inner (lateral) surface of pinna more or less covered with hair, sometimes with a brush or elongate tuft; forehead blackish or buffy with a sharply defined whitish median blaze; anterior portion of crown blackish to pale brown (figs. IX.8, 12).

Coloration. Exposed parts of facial skin well pigmented below eyes, less between and above; long hair of cheeks dark brown to buffy, temples darker; forehead dark brown to buffy and marked with a sharply defined whitish or yellowish blaze; crown between ears usually dark brown or paler medially, a whitish or buffy midline sometimes present; blackish preauricular tufts long and comparatively thin, blackish supra-auricular tufts poorly defined or rudimentary without clear differentiation from long hairs of crown and mantle; pinna with black hair, thinly covered medially, more fully covered laterally; back behind shoulders transversely striated more or less as in *jacchus;* upper surface of hands and feet dark brown or black to buffy; throat and neck dark brown or reddish brown to buff often mixed with gray; chest dark brown to orange, the hairs usually tipped with gray, belly like chest but with little or no gray; tail banded as in *jacchus*.

Young. Forehead with dark median sagittal band and a whitish lock on each side, otherwise color pattern and ear tufts more or less as in adult but pelage finer, more lax. With increasing age (eruption of first molars) the whitish lateral bands become dark and merge with me-

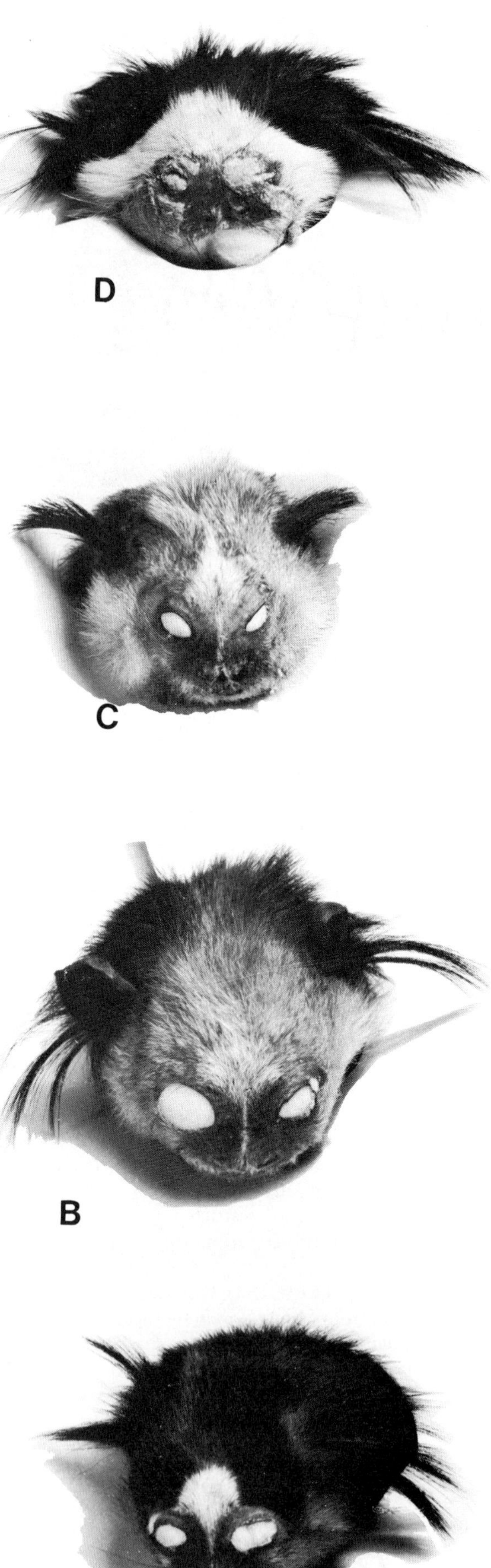

Fig. IX.14. Geographic intergradation between *Callithrix jacchus penicillata* and *C. j. geoffroyi;* heads of stuffed skins preserved in the Field Museum. *A, C. j. penicillata* from Lagoa Santa, Minas Gerais (313); *D*, typical *C. j. geoffroyi* from Espírito Santo, precise locality unknown; *B, C,* intergrades from Ilhéus, Brazil where ranges of *penicillata* and *geoffroyi* meet. In the chromatic cline (cf. fig. IX.7), drab of cheeks in the *penicillata* shown (*A*), extends over frontal and temporal regions in the intergrades and bleaches all the way to white in *geoffroyi*. Captive-born *penicillata* × *geoffroyi* are indistinguishable from natural hybrids. (Based on Hershkovitz, 1975b).

dium band which extends toward crown; frontal blaze emerges with eruption of second molars and first incisors.

Measurements. See Appendix table 2.

Comparisons. Distinguished from *jacchus* by the wholly blackish preauricular tufts, from *geoffroyi* by the generally dark head with comparatively small, sharply defined frontal blaze; from *aurita* and *flaviceps* by the blackish, not pale or brightly colored hairs on inner (lateral) surface of pinna (fig. IX.7).

Ear Tufts. Ear tufts among the races of *Callithrix jacchus* are most variable in *penicillata.* The preauricular tufts may consist of a few strands of black hairs or form a fan-shaped corolla concealing the pinna from in front; in some subadults the tufts are mixed with brown, buffy, or silvery; the inner (lateral) surface of the pinna may be thinly to thickly covered with blackish hairs, sometimes tufted, the hairs up to 20 mm long.

Remarks. Restriction of the type locality of *penicillata* E. Geoffroy to Lamarão (292d) has been generally accepted but not always with awareness of the significance of the action. In his review of the genus *Callithrix,* Avila Pires (1969, p. 60) cites Lamarão as the type locality of *penicillata* but his delineation of the geographic range of *penicillata* (coastal Brazil from Recôncavo da Bahia to Santa Teresa, Espírito Santo [320b]) excludes Lamarão. On the other hand, specimens from the interior of Bahia (Malhada [296] and Barro Alto) which should be referred to typical *penicillata* are assigned, instead, to *"Callithrix penicillata jordani."* Coimbra-Filho (1970*c,* 1971*c,* 1973) and Coimbra-Filho and Mittermeier (1974) follow Avila Pires in applying the name *penicillata* to marmosets that intergrade with *geoffroyi,* and they reserve the name *jordani* for the inland populations.

Coimbra-Filho (1971, p. 380) cites the uncorroborated testimony of Ruschi (1964, p. 6) for the presence of *penicillata* in coastal Espírito Santo "from Conceição da Barra [fig. IX.7, no. 319a] to Barra do Itapemirim [325b]." Coimbra-Filho then suggests that inasmuch as *"C. geoffroyi* and *C. p. penicillata* would now be sympatric, at least in the coastal segment between the Rios Jacu and Itapemirim, it would be well to search there for natural hybrids between the two forms."

Occurrence of *penicillata* in northeastern Espírito Santo is unconfirmed but a local variant or intergrade with *geoffroyi,* the *kuhlii* of Wied-Neuwied, almost certainly ranges southward from bordering Bahia (fig. IX.6). Insofar as known, only *C. j. geoffroyi* inhabits the southern portion of coastal Espírito Santo. The available information dates from Wied-Neuwied (1826, p. 140) who observed the animal in the vicinity of Vitória (321b), the old town of Espírito Santo (321b), the banks of the Rio Jacu (323), Coroaba (324a), and Aracatiba (324a). The coastal range of *geoffroyi* as surmised by Wied-Neuwied extends from Vitória south to the Rio Itapemirim (325c).

A skin preserved in the Museu National, Rio de Janeiro, listed by Avila Pires (1969) as *Callithrix penicillata* is said to be from Santa Teresa, Espírito Santo. Natural occurrence of *penicillata* in the Santa Teresa area is unexpected. However, Avila Pires (1969, p. 60) particularly distinguishes the specimen as having the "dorsal surface including mantle and crown finely punctulated black and white." This description, as far as it goes, suggests a hybrid *geoffroyi* × *flaviceps.*

A specimen of *penicillata* preserved in the Museum of Comparative Zoology, Harvard University, labeled Santa Rita (292a), collected by George Sceva, was recorded by Avila-Pires (1969, p. 61) as *C. penicillata jordani,* its locality given as "Rio de Janeiro: Santa Rita da Floresta [327]." As shown elsewhere (p. 524) the specimen in question agrees best with our material from the upper Rio São Francisco basin and was probably collected in the Lagôa Santa area (313) by George Sceva, a member of Agassiz's Brazilian expedition (1865–66). *Callithrix jacchus penicillata* does not occur naturally in Rio de Janeiro.

A second specimen of *penicillata* in the Museum of Comparative Zoology, collected 26 November 1931 by José Blaser, is labeled Barro Alto, Rio São Francisco. Avila-Pires (1969, p. 61) records it as being from Minas Gerais. Among the several Barro Altos listed by the U.S. Board of Geographic Names, none is in Minas Gerais, but one on the Rio Jacaré, Bahia, (11° 46′ S, 41° 54′ W) lies both within the Rio São Francisco basin and in the geographic range of *penicillata.* The Barro Alto of Bahia

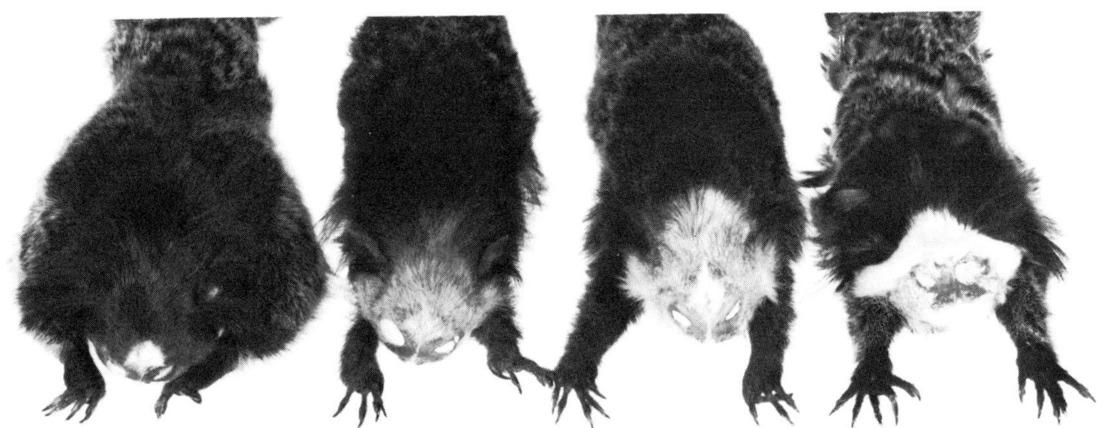

C.j.penicillata intergrades C.j.geoffroyi

Fig. IX.15. Geographic intergradation between *Callithrix jacchus penicillata* and *C. j. geoffroyi;* stuffed skins from dorsal aspect of same specimens shown in fig. IX.14. Metachromism with reduction and elimination of melanin production is seen in color gradient of crown and forehead; dark brown area surrounding white frontal blaze in *penicillata* bleaches to pale brown and drab in intergrades, and to white in *geoffroyi.* Extension of blackish mantle on dorsum is variable. (Based on Hershkovitz, 1975b).

entered in the gazetteer (p. 918) is, I believe, the best guess of the possible place of origin of the specimen in question.

Specimens Examined. 90. BRAZIL—*Bahia:* Ilhéus, 3 (FMNH, 2; MCZ, 1); Lamarão, 300 meters, 7 (BM); *Goías:* Annapolis, 11 (AMNH); Pilar, 1 (MNHN); Rio Araguaia, 2 (BM, 1; MNHN, 1); Fazenda Esperanza, Rio Uru, 1 (BM); Rio Uru, 1 (MNHN); *Minas Gerais:* Agua Suja, 7 (MNHN); Januária, 1 (USNM); Lassance, 2 (AMNH); Barro Alto, Rio São Francisco, 1 (MCZ); Rio Jordão, 7 including type of *jordani* (BM); Rio das Velhas, 4 (FMNH, 3; USNM, 1); *locality unknown:* 42 (AMNH, 9; BM, 3; "Santa Rita," MCZ, 1; MNHN, 3, including type of *penicillata;* RMNH, 19; SM, 7).

CALLITHRIX JACCHUS GEOFFROYI HUMBOLDT: GEOFFROY'S TUFTED-EAR MARMOSET

Fig. IX.16. Geoffroy's Tufted-ear Marmoset, *Callithrix jacchus geoffroyi* Humboldt.

Synonymic History

Simia Geoffroyi Humboldt, 1812, *Rec. Obs. Zool. Anat. Comp.*, p. 360—new name for the manuscript description of *leucocephalus* E. Geoffroy cited in synonymy.

Simia geoffroyi, Cabrera, 1940, *Ciencia (México)* 1:403—antedates *leucocephalus* Geoffroyi 1812.

Callithrix geoffroyi, Cabrera, 1958, *Rev. Mus. Argentino Cienc. Nat. "Bernardino Rivadavia"* 4:187—classification; *leucocephalus* a synonym. Machado, 1960, *Anais Fac. Med. Univ. Minas Gerais* 20:123 seq., table 1, fig. 6 (ileal eminence)—BRAZIL: *Minas Gerais* (Serra do Cipó); morphology of ileal eminence of large intestine. Machado and Di Dio, 1963, *Anat. Anzeiger* 113:45—ampulla of the terminal ileum. Avila Pires, 1969, *Rev. Brasil. Biol.* 29(1):57—part, BRAZIL: *Espírito Santo* ("Espirito Santo"; Colatina; Santa Tereza; Pau Gigante; Vilavelha; Rio Mutum; Lagôa Juparaná; Rio Doce); *Minas Gerais* (Conceição do Mato Dentro; Teofilo Otoni; Fazenda Esperança, São José de Lagôa; Machacalis; Rio Doce near Piracicaba; Visconde do Rio Branco); characters; distribution.

C[allithrix] geoffroyi, Coimbra-Filho, 1971, *Rev. Brasil. Biol.* 31(3):378, fig. 3 (animal)—BRAZIL: distribution. Coimbra-Filho and Mittermeier, 1974, *Fol. Primat.* 20(1973):243, 260, fig. 1A (head), fig. 6G (prepared skin) —BRAZIL: distribution; characters; hybridization in captivity; alleged sympatry with *flaviceps* and *penicillata.* Deane, Silva and Loures, 1974, *Rev. Inst. Med. Trop.* São Paulo, 16:1—BRAZIL: *Minas Gerais* (Araçuí); *Espírito Santo* (Colatina); distribution of *Trypanosoma minasense.*

Callithrix jacchus geoffroyi, Hershkovitz, 1968, *Evolution* 22(3):566, fig. 10 (distribution), fig. 12 (geographic metachromism)—color pattern; comparisons; geographic metachromism.

Jacchus leucocephalus E. Geoffroy, 1812, *Ann. Mus. Nat. Hist. Nat.* 19:119—BRAZIL. Desmarest, 1820, *Mammalogie,* p. 93—characters; *Simia Geoffroyi* Humboldt, a synonym. Desmarest, 1827, *Dict. Sci. Nat.* 47:18—characters. I. Geoffroy, 1827, *Dict. Class. Hist. Nat.* 15:517—BRAZIL: *Minas Gerais.* Lesson, 1834, *Compléments de Buffon* 4:268—characters. Rode, 1938, *Bull. Mus. Nat. Hist. Nat., Paris,* ser. 2, 10:239—type history.

J[acchus] leucocephalus, Reichenbach, 1862, *Vollst. Naturg. Affen,* p. 4, pl. 1, fig. 16 (animal)—characters; *H. melanotis vieillesse* Lesson in synonymy.

Hapale leucocephala, Kuhl, 1820, *Beitr. Zool.,* p. 47—specimen in Prince Maximilian and Paris museums. Schlegel, 1876, *Les singes. Simiae,* p. 274—BRAZIL: *Espírito Santo* (Rio Espírito Santo); characters; variation; synonyms, *leucocephalus* Geoffroy, *vulgaris* var. 4 Gray, *vulgaris* var. 5 Gray, *leucogenys* Gray, *maximiliani* Reichenbach. Jentink, 1892, *Cat. Syst. Mamm. Mus. Pays-Bas* 11:58—BRAZIL: *Espírito Santo* (Rio Espírito Santo, Wied-Neuwied Coll.). Osman Hill, 1957, *Primates* 3:251, 286, 289, 299–301—characters; distribution; *geoffroyi* Humboldt regarded as a junior synonym. Ruschi, 1964, *Bol. Mus. Biol. "Prof. Mello Leito"* 23A:7–8—BRAZIL: *Espirito Santo* (São Mateus; Rio Doce; Reis Magos; Colatina; Linhares Barra Seca; Santa Teresa); characters; habits. Epple, 1967, *Folia Primat.* 7:38—sexual and social behavior in captivity. Epple, 1968, *Folia Primat.* 8:18, figs. 18, 19 (voice recordings)—analysis of vocalizations.

H[apale] leucocephala, Wagner, 1840, *Schreber's Säugth., Suppl.* 1:243, pl. 33B (animal)—characters; regarded as a variant of *penicillata.* Wagner, 1848, *Abh. Akad. Wiss. Munich* (1847) 5:564 (in text)—BRAZIL: *Espírito Santo* (Campos or Villa Vittoria). I. Geoffroy, 1851, *Cat. Primates Mus. Nat. Hist., Paris,* p. 60—BRAZIL: *Minas Gerais* (western part, collected by A. St.-Hilaire); type history. Burmeister, 1869, *Anal. Mus. Publ. Buenos Aires* 1 (6): 448—BRAZIL; *maximiliani* Reichenbach, a synonym. Pelzeln, 1883, *Verh. K. K. Zool.-Bot. Gesellsch., Wien, Beih.* 33:22—BRAZIL: believed to be from "Campos oder Villa Vittoria [Espírito Santo]" received in exchange from Herr Sellow; *Hapale penicillata* var. B. Wagner, 1848, in synonymy.

H[apale] leucocephalus, Wied-Neuwied, 1823, *Abbild. Beitr. Naturg. Brasil.,* Lief 2, pl. 2—BRAZIL: *Espírito Santo* (Araçatiba; Coroaba; Jucú). Wied-Neuwied, 1826, *Beitr. Naturg. Brasil.* 2:135—BRAZIL: *Espírito Santo* (Victoria; Vilha Velha do Espirito Santo; Araçatiba, Rio Jucú; Coroaba, Rio Jucú); characters.

Callithrix leucocephala, Elliot, 1913, *Review of the Primates* 1:229—characters ex type. Vieira, 1955, *Arq. Zool., São Paulo* 8:393—BRAZIL: *Minas Gerais* (Teofilo Otoni; São José de Lagôa, Rio Doce); *Espírito Santo* (Colatina, Rio Doce). Machado, 1960, *Anais Fac. Med. Univ. Minas Gerais* 20:123 seq., table 1, fig. 11 (ileal eminence)—BRAZIL: *Minas Gerais* (Machacales); morphology of ileal eminence of large intestine. Machado and Di Dio, 1963, *Anat. Anzeiger* 113:45—ampulla of terminal ileum.

Simia albifrons Thunberg, 1819, *Handl. Kongl. Vetenskaps Acad., Stockholm* 1819:65, pl. 3 (animals)—BRAZIL: type locality not specified; type, male, mounted skin, Upsala University, presented by the Swedish Consul General, Herr Westins; name preoccupied by *Simia albifrons* Humboldt 1812 (= *Cebus albifrons* Humboldt). Tschudi, 1844, *Fauna Peruana,* p. 53—regarded as a tamarin. Wagner, 1840, *Schreber's Säugth., Suppl.* 1:248, footnote—characters ex Thunberg. Schlegel, 1876, *Les singes. Simiae,* p. 252—description ex Thunberg; a synonym of *Hapale rosalia.* Cabrera, 1940, *Ciencia (México)* 1:403—unidentifiable; name preoccupied.

S[imia] albifrons, Griffith, 1827, *Anim. Kingd.* 5:41—believed to resemble *Leontopithecus rosalia chrysomelas.*

Iacchus albifrons, Desmarest, 1820, *Mammalogie,* p. 534—characters ex original description.

Hapale albifrons, Schinz, 1825, *Cuvier's Das Thierreich* 4:281—characters ex Thunberg.

Jacchus albifrons, Lesson, 1834, *Compl. Buffon* 4:278—characters ex Thunberg.

M[arikina] albifrons, Reichenbach, 1863, *Vollst. Naturg. Affen,* p. 9, pl. 2, fig. 29 (animal)—part, characters ex Thunberg, not fig. 30 (= *Callithrix jacchus penicillatus*).

Hapale melanotis, Lesson (part, not Lesson), 1840; *Species de mammifères: Bimanes et quadrumanes . . . ,* p. 191—part, *Jacchus leucocephalus* in synonymy.

J[acchus] Maximiliani Reichenbach, 1862, *Vollst. Naturg. Affen,* p. 5, pl. 1, fig. 17 (animal *ex* Wied-Neuwied)—BRAZIL: *Espírito Santo* (Rio Jacú, near Vitória, here restricted); type, male, figured and described by Wied-Neuwied (supra cit., 1823; 1826) as *Hapale leucocephalus.*

Jacchus leucogenys Gray, 1870, *Cat. monkeys, lemurs and fruit-eating bats, Brit. Mus.*, p. 63—variety 5 of *Jacchus vulgaris* [= *jacchus*] described without locality or type data; type presumably in the British Museum (Natural History).

[*Hapale penicillata*] var. β Wagner, 1848, *Abh. Akad. Wiss. Munich* (1847) 5:464—BRAZIL: *Espírito Santo* (Villa Victoria or Campos).

[*Jacchus vulgaris*] var. 4 Gray, 1870, *Cat. monkeys, leumurs and fruit-eating bats, Brit. Mus.*, p. 63—*leucocephalus* E. Geoffroy a synonym.

[?] *Hapale flaviceps,* Ruschi (part, not Thomas), 1964, *Bol. Mus. Biol.*, "Prof. Mello Leito" 23A:5—part, BRAZIL: *Espírito Santo* (Calçado; Cachoeira do Itapemirem; Domingos Martins; Ibiraçu; Santa Teresa; Santa Leopoldina).

[?] *Callithrix flaviceps,* Avila Pires (part, not Thomas), 1969, *Rev. Brasil. Biol.* 29(1):56—part, BRAZIL: *Espírito Santo* (Santa Tereza, 700–800 meters).

[?] *Callithrix penicillata penicillata,* Avila Pires (part, not E. Geoffroy), 1969, *Rev. Brasil. Biol.* 29(1)60—BRAZIL: specimen from Santa Tereza only.

[?] *Hapale penicillata penicillata,* Ruschi (not E. Geoffroy), 1964, *Bol. Mus. Biol., "Prof. Mello Leito"* 23A:6—BRAZIL: *Espírito Santo* (Conceiçao da Barra; Barra do Itapemirim).

[?] *Hapale aurita,* Ruschi (not E. Geoffroy), 1964, *Bol. Mus. Biol., "Prof. Mello Leito"* 23A:7—BRAZIL: *Espírito Santo* (Aracruz; Marataizes).

Type. Skin mounted with skull in; collected between 1783 and 1792, by Alexandre Rodrigues Ferreira during his scientific expedition in Brazil, and shipped to the Museum Royal d'Ajuda, Lisbon, Portugal; acquired in 1808 by the Muséum National d'Histoire Naturelle, Paris; catalog no. 607 (599).

Type Locality. Brazil, restricted to near Victoria, between the "Rios Espírito Santo and Jucú," by Cabrera (1958, *Rev. Mus. Argentino Cienc. Nat. "Bernardino Rivadavia"* 4:187) who attributes the action to Wied-Neuwied (1826, *Beitr. Naturg. Brasil.* 2:48 [*sic* = 140]). The latter, however, only recorded and described a specimen from the Rio Jucú or Jacú which is the same as the Rio Espírito Santo.

Distribution (figs. IX.5, 6). East central Brazil west into parts of the coastal drainage basin of Minas Gerais.

Wied-Neuwied (1826, p. 140) provides these important details, translated from the German: "I found it [i.e., *Hapale leucocephalus*] in the State of Espírito Santo; I am unable to determine if it extends north of the Rio Doce or beyond as I could not hunt often in the dark forests of this river because of the Botacudo Indians. I can therefore state that the habitat of this species lies between 20° and 21° South latitude. The animal is common in the forests of the Rio Espírito Santo, especially in the outlying brush and the *mangue* bush (*Conocarpus* and *Avicennis*) bordering the river, as well as the low palm (*Allagoptera pumila* and others) covered sandy coastal districts not far from the mouth of the Espírito Santo, at Çidade de Victoria, Villa Velha do Espírito Santo and in the forests along the Rio Jucú [Jacú], in the Fazendas of Araçatiba, Coroaba, etc."

Ruschi (1964, pp. 7–8) states that *geoffroyi* lives within the drainage basins of the Rios Doce (320a), São Mateus (319a), Barra Seca (319b) and Reis Magos (321a). He names "many municipalities such as Colotina [320b], Linhares [319c], Santa Teresa [320b] and others." Coimbra-Filho and Mittermeier (1974, p. 249) mention the Reserva Biologica de Nova Lombardia near Santa Teresa, and Santa Leopoldinha (322) both in Espírito Santo and give the altitudinal range of *geoffroyi* as sea level to 600–700 m above, occasionally to 800 m. Neither Ruschi nor Coimbra-Filho bases his distributional data on voucher specimens or published records. Upper limits of the range of *geoffroyi* however, may be inferred from a

Fig. IX.17. *Simia albifrons Thunberg* ♂ (= *Callithrix jacchus geoffroyi*). (From Thunberg 1819.)

Santa Teresa (altitude 659 m) specimen in the Rio de Janeiro Museum listed by Avila Pires (1969, p. 57).

C. j. geoffroyi intergrades with *C. j. penicillata* in southeastern Bahia (figs. IX.7, 14, 15; p. 503). Occurrence of marmosets in northern Espírito Santo has not been confirmed but populations intermediate between *geoffroyi* and *penicillata* possibly occur along the coast. Supposed overlap in altitudinal range between the essentially lowland *geoffroyi* and the highland *flaviceps* may actually be a zone of intergradation (see below, also remarks under *Callithrix jacchus flaviceps*).

Taxonomy. Humboldt examined the manuscript or proofs of E. Geoffroy's systematic arrangement of primates and descriptions of New World monkeys and cited much of it in his own work. It so happened by the turn of events that Humboldt's observations were published several months earlier than Geoffroy's System. Nevertheless, E. Geoffroy is usually recognized as author of the original descriptions and the new names clearly attributed to him in Humboldt's book. In the case of the white-headed marmoset, however, Humboldt took the liberty of honoring his colleague by substituting the new name *Simia geoffroyi* for Geoffroy's own *Jacchus leucocephalus.* The former name, therefore, has priority over the latter and is the one adopted here.

Simia albifrons Thunberg 1819 (fig. IX.17) is based on a specimen sent to Upsala by Herr Westins, then Swedish consul general in Rio de Janeiro, Brazil. Judged by the description, the accompanying life-sized woodcut of the clumsily mounted specimen and, particularly, the diagnostic hair and color pattern of head, arms, legs, and lower incisor-canine relationship, *albifrons* is referable to *geoffroyi.* On the other hand, the poorly defined striations of the back and annulations of the tail in *albifrons* are uncharacteristic. The deviations may be individual peculiarities, abnormalities due to rearing in captivity or, possibly, artifacts of the taxidermist. Cabrera (1940, p. 403) believes *albifrons* is unidentifiable. In any case, the name *Simia albifrons* Thunberg, 1819, is preoccupied by *Simia albifrons* Humboldt, 1812, a species of *Cebus,* and cannot be used. A second specimen described and figured by Thunberg as the female of *albifrons* (fig. IX.13) appears to be referrable to *Callithrix jacchus penicillata.*

Fig. IX.18. Geoffroy's Tufted-ear Marmoset (*Calilthrix jacchus geoffroyi*); an excessively fat individual. (Photo courtesy of A. F. Coimbra-Filho.)

Fig. IX.19. Geoffroy's Tufted-ear Marmoset (*Callithrix jacchus geoffroyi*); head of same fat individual shown in fig. IX.18. (Photo courtesy of A. F. Coimbra-Filho.)

Jacchus maximiliani Reichenbach, 1862, is based on the specimen of *Hapale geoffroyi* figured and described by Prince Maximilian Wied-Neuwied. Inasmuch as the type locality of *geoffroyi* and *maximiliani* are identical, the latter is an absolute junior synonym of the former.

Diagnostic Characters. Elongate tufts in front of and above ears black; inner (lateral) surface of pinna moderately hairy and often with a well-developed brush or tuft; forehead to vertex of crown entirely white (figs. IX.7, 16, 17, 18, 19).

Coloration. Exposed parts of facial skin pigmented or flesh colored; cheeks and chin covered with long white whiskers; forehead creamy white to pure white, the color extending onto part of crown or over entire crown as a broad wedge bordered by black on sides and back of head; preauricular and supra-auricular tufts black, the first well developed, the second hardly defined from long hairs of crown and nape; pinna thinly haired black medially, thickly tufted laterally (interiorly); mantle blackish; back behind shoulders striated as in *jacchus* but with orange or tawny middle portions of hairs showing through prominently; upper surface of hands and feet black or dark brown; throat white, hairs of underside of neck entirely white or black terminally and whitish basally; chest like neck or with hairs finely banded buffy to orange subterminally, belly dark brown; tail annulated as in *jacchus.*

Measurements. See Appendix table 2.

Comparisons. Distinguished from equally black tufted *penicillata* by wholly whitish forehead, temples, cheeks and throat (fig. IX.7).

Remarks. Avila Pires (1969) identified one of three specimens from Santa Teresa, Espírito Santo (320b), as *Callithrix geoffroyi,* the second as *Callithrix flaviceps,* and the third as *C. penicillata penicillata.* Natural occurrence of *penicillata* in the Santa Teresa area is unexpected. Avila Pires (1969, p. 60) did not identify the specimen by sex or age, but he particularly distinguished it as "having the entire dorsal surface including mantle and crown finely punctulated black and white." The description, as far as it goes, coupled with the locality, suggests a hybrid *geoffroyi* × *flaviceps.* Occurrence of *flaviceps* in the Santa Teresa area is discussed under the subspecies heading.

Avila Pires (1969, p. 58) thought it odd that Lund (1839) lived and collected for forty years in the Lagoa Santa region of Minas Gerais without having encountered *Callithrix jacchus geoffroyi.* It appears, however, that the marmoset known to and recorded by Lund is *Callithrix jacchus penicillata.* Specimens in the Field Museum from Rio das Velhas, Lagoa Santa (313), confirm Lund's identification. Recent introduction of *geoffroyi* into the region suggested by Avila Pires (1969) and Coimbra-Filho (1971, p. 379) has not been confirmed.

Specimens Examined. 7. BRAZIL—*Espírito Santo:* Rio Doce, 1 (MCZ); *locality unknown:* 6 (BM, 1; FMNH, 1; GEE, 1 in spirits; MNHN, type of *geoffroyi* [*leucocephalus*]; RMNH, 1; SM, 1).

CALLITHRIX JACCHUS JACCHUS LINNAEUS: WHITE-TUFTED-EAR MARMOSET

Fig. IX.20. White Tufted-ear Marmoset, *Callithrix jacchus jacchus* Linnaeus

Synonymic History

Cercopithecus Brasilianus tertius [or] *Sagouin,* Clusius, 1605, *Exoticorum,* p. 372, fig. p. 372 (animal) [work not seen].

Cagui minor, Marcgrave, 1648, *Hist. rerum Nat. Brasil.,* p. 227, fig. (animal).

Sanglin, or *Cagui minor,* Edwards, 1758, *Gleanings of natural history,* p. 15, pl. 218 (animal), pl. opp. p. 16 (animal).

Simia iacchus, Parsons, 1751, *Philos. Trans., Roy. Soc. Lond.* 47:146, pl. 7 [work not seen]. Parsons, 1810, ibid., abridged, 10:171—characters.

Ouistiti, Buffon, 1767, *Hist. Nat.* 15:96, pl. 14 (animal).

Striated monkie, Pennant, 1771, *Syn. Quadr.,* p. 132.

Titi, Azara, 1801, *Essais Hist. Nat. Quad. Paraguay* 2:254—BRAZIL; characters (of a pair in captivity in Buenos Aires).

[*Simia*] *Jacchus* Linnaeus, 1758, *Syst. Nat.,* 10th ed. p. 27. Shaw, 1800, *Gen. Zool.* 1, (1):62, pl. 25 (striated monkey).

Simia Jacchus Schreber, 1775, *Die Säugthiere* 1:126, pl. 33 (*ouistiti* of Buffon); characters; synonymy.

Simia jacchus, Cuvier, 1798, *Tableau élémentaire,* p. 97—*ouistiti* Buffon. Audebert, 1797, *Hist. nat. singes et makis,* fam. 6, sect. 2, p. 5, pl. 4 (animal)—*ouistiti;* breeding in Paris. Humboldt, 1812, *Rec. Obs. Zool. Anat. Comp.*, p. 360—"habite la Guyane française et le Brésil;" part, synonyms, *ouistiti* Buffon, *titi* Azara, *Jacchus vulgaris* Geoffroy. Lichtenstein, 1817, *Abh. Akad. Wiss. Berlin,* 1804–15:211—*çagui* minor Marcgrave. F. Cuvier, 1819, in Geoffroy et Cuvier, *Hist. Nat. Mamm.*, livr. 8 [vol. 1], pl. (male), pl. (juvenal female) and text. F. Cuvier, 1825, *Dents des mammifères,* pp. 24, 248, pl. 9—dental characters. Neil, 1829, *Ann. Mag. Nat. Hist.* 1:18, fig.—BRAZIL: *Bahia;* habits.

S[imia] Sagoinus jacchus, Kerr, 1792, *Animal kingdom,* p. 80—characters.

Simia jaccus [*sic*], Cabrera, 1958, *Rev. Mus. Argentino Cienc. Nat., "Bernardino Rivadavia"* 4 (1):188—misprint in synonymy of *Callithrix jacchus.*

[*Callithrix*] *Iacchus,* Erxleben, 1777, *Syst. Reg. Anim.*, p. 56—classification.

Callithrix jacchus, Thomas, 1910, *Ann. Mag. Nat. Hist.*, ser. 8, 6:500—BRAZIL: *Ceará* (Ipú); variation; *albicollis* Spix, a synonym. Thomas, 1911, *Proc. Zool. Soc. London* 1911:127—BRAZIL: *Pernambuco* (type locality). Pocock, 1911, *Proc. Zool. Soc. London* 1911:856—insect feeding. Silvester, 1912, *Amer. J. Anat.* 12:448—posterior lymphaticovenous communication. Elliot, 1913, *A review of the Primates* 1:228—BRAZIL: distribution, "Island of Marajó [!]." Bresslau, 1927, *Abh. Senchenb. Naturf. Gesellsch.*, 40:226—BRAZIL: *Pernambuco* (Recife; Dois Irmãos). Pohle, 1927, *Abh. Senckenb. Naturf. Gesellsch.* 40:247—BRAZIL: *Pernambuco* (Dois Irmãos); *Paraíba* (Fundão; Penha). Wislocki, 1930, *J. Mammal.* 11:479—scent glands of pubic region. Marik, 1931, *Zool. Garten,* n.f., 4:347—growth and development. Reider, 1936, *Proc. Zool. Soc. London* 1936:533, pl. 3, fig. 8 (colon)—comparative anatomy of colon. Dennler, 1939, *Physis* 16:229—*Titi-ti* in Guaraní. Moojen, 1943, *Bol. Mus. Nac. Rio de Janeiro, Zool.*, no. 5, p. 14—BRAZIL: *Ceará* (Serra do Araripe, Crato). Cruz and Pimenta, 1947, *Mem. Inst. Oswaldo Cruz* 45:119—infection with *Plasmodium knowlesi.* Vieira, 1953, *Arq. Zool., São Paulo* 8:210—BRAZIL: *Pará* [!]; *Alagoas* (Mangabeiras; São Miguel); color variation; *albicollis* a synonym. Vieira, 1955, *Arq. Zool., São Paulo* 8 (11):393—BRAZIL: *Maranhão* [!]; *Pernambuco* (Tapera); *Alagoas* (São Miguel; Mangabeiras). Kraft, 1957, *Säugetierk. Mitteil.* 5:175—torpidity and low body temperature in captive specimen. Cabrera, 1958, *Rev. Mus. Argentino Cienc. Nat. "Bernardino Rivadavia"* 4:187—part synonymy *ex humeralifer* E. Geoffroy; classification. Schneider, 1958, *Primatologia* 3, (1):24—oral region. Starck, 1958, *Primatologia* 3 (1):479, figs. 11 *a-d* (abdominal organs)—organs of abdominal cavity. Osman Hill, 1958, *Primatologia* 3 (1):641, 680, fig. 11c (penis)—external genitalia. Simões, Jr., 1958, *Rev. Técnica (Salvador, Bahia)*, no. 39—compilation of biological data. Miraglia and Teixeira, 1958, *Publ. Univ. Bahia* 7(1):3—eye melanin. Miraglia and Teixeira, 1958, *Publ. Univ. Bahia* 7(2):1–21—anatomy of hypophysis. Miraglia and Teixeira, 1959, *Ciencia e Cultura (Bahia)* 2(3):147—blood supply of hypophysis. Miraglia, Teixeira, 1960, *Biol. Latina (Milano)* 13(2):199—structure and vascularization of hypophysis. Werner, 1960, *Primatologia* 2, (1), Lief 5:12, fig. 5 (cranial angle of malleus), figs. 6, 7 (malleus), fig. 13 (stapes)—middle ear. Machado, 1960, *Anais Fac. Med. Univ. Minas Gerais* 20:123, table 1, figs. 3–5 (ileal eminence)—BRAZIL: *Paraíba* (Mamanguape); *Bahia* (Salvador); morphology of ileal eminence of large intestine. Jones, 1960, *Lab. Primate Newsl.* 1(3): longevity, 5 years, 5 months, (Philadelphia). Fooden, 1961, *Zoologica* 46:167—chromatography and systematics of amino acid excretions. Miraglia, 1961, *Biol. Latina* 14(3): 189—distribution of Periodic Acid Schiff positive. Freitas, Ledoux, and Miraglia, 1961, *Folia Clinica, Biol. (Bahia)* 30:239—Feulgen and Voit plasmal reaction. Marback, Roberto, and Costa, 1962, *Folia Clinica, Biol. (Bahia)* 31:10—structure of retina. Medina, Erlon, and Miraglia, 1962, *Folia Clinica, Biol.* 31:19—neurological structures. Pedreira and Machado, 1962, *Folia Clinica, Biol.* 31:31—microanatomy of oesophagus. Sousa, Teixeira, and Miraglia, 1962, *Folia Clinica, Biol.* 31:104—brain arteries. Torres, Ledoux, and Miraglia, 1962, *Folia Clinica* 31:125—phospate distribution. Wetstein, 1963, *Gegenbaur's Morph. Jahrb.* 104 (2):185—variation with age, sex; pelage; dentition; comparisons; relationships. Miraglia, 1963, *Biol. Latina (Milano)* 16(2):151—microanatomical and chemical structure of teeth. Miraglia, 1963, *Biol. Latina* 16(2):197—mast cell distribution. Gonzalez de Codes, 1963, *Folia Clinica, Biol.* 32:51—pituitary histochemistry of pregnant animals. Machado, 1963, *Anais Fac. Med. Minas Gerais* 20:123 (1960)—eminentia ilealis of large intestine. Machado and Di Dio, 1963, *Anat. Anzeiger* 113:45—ampulla of terminal ileum. Chiarelli, 1963, *Folia Primat.* 1: table pl. 91—taste sensitivity to phenyl-thio-carbamide. Benirschke and Brownhill, 1963, *Cytogenetics* 2:245—karyotype (46 chromosomes); marrow chimerism. Ledoux, 1964, *Folia Clinica, Biol.* 33:23, figs. 1–9 (tongue, microscopic anatomy)—tongue anatomy. Miraglia and Moreira, 1964, *Bol. Hospital Edgard Santos* 10:29—effect of strychnine on adrenals. Miraglia and Neves, 1964, *Rev. Bahiana Odontol.* April–June, p. 27—acid phosphotase in salivary glands. Kubota, Hayama, 1964, *Anat. Rec.* 150(4):473—fig. 1 (dorsal aspect of tongue), pls. 1–4 (microscopic anatomy of tongue)—tongue anatomy. Gomes and Miraglia, 1965, *Biol. Latina* 8(1):37—histochemistry of stomach lining. Pedreira de Oliveira, 1965, *Folia Clinica, Biol.* 34:12—trachea, bronchia, lungs (structure and histochemistry). Santana Moura, 1965, *Rev. Brasil. Odontol. (Guanabara)* 24(138):283—classification of periodontal fibers of insertion. Warren and Simões, 1966, *Amer. J. Trop. Med. Hyg.* 15(2)153—resistant to *Schistosomiasis mansoni.* Hershkovitz, 1966, *Mammalia* 30(2):329—ear tuft characters. Wohnus and Benirschke, 1966, *Cytogenetics* 5:94—chromosome idiogram. Reck, 1966, *Verh. Anat. Ges. Jena* 61:259—frequency of anterior horn cells in spinal cord. Moura, 1966, *Arch. Cent. Estud. Fac. Odont.* 3:61—gingiva [work not seen]. Miraglia, Ledoux, and Castelo Branco, 1967, *Acta Anat.* 68: 459—figs. 1–9 (histology of intestinal tract)—histology and histochemistry of intestinal tract (general structure not different from that of other primates without an appendix vermiformis). Rossi and Moreira, 1967, *Folia*

Clinica Biol. 36:50—liver structure and histochemistry. Ledoux, Dos Santos, and Santana Moura, 1967, *Arq. Centro Estud. Fac. Odontol. Univ. Fed. Minas Gerais* 4(1):73—hard palate (*gross and microscopic anatomy;* histochemistry). Miraglia and Telles Filho, 1967, *Gaz. Med. Bahia* 67(2):99—polysacharids of the ovarian zona pelucida. Dreizen, Levy, Bernick, J. Hampton, and Krainz, 1967, *Israel J. Med. Sci.* 3(5):731—periodontal bone changes in subjects with osteomalacia and hyperparathyroidism. Rocha, da Silva Teles, and Brito, 1968, *Proc. Soc. Exp. Biol.* 129:506—experimental bacteremia and pyelonephritis. Bernick and Levy, 1968, *J. Dental Res.* 47(1):21—figs. 1–15 (histological sections of developing molars), fig. 16 (root bifurcation region of molars)—ontogeny of root bifurcation in molars. Levy and Bernick, 1968, *J. Dental Res.* 47(1):27—figs. 1–16 (histological sections of developing deciduous teeth), fig. 17 (sequential organization of periodontal ligament fibers of deciduous teeth)—development and organization of periodontal ligament of deciduous teeth. Dreizen, Goodrich, and Levy, 1968, *Arch. Oral Biol.* 13(2):229—salivary glands and electrolytes; comparisons with man. Bernick and Levy, 1968, *J. Dental Res.* 47(6):1158—innervation of periodontal ligament. Levy and Bernick, 1968, *J. Dental Res.* 47(6):1166—lymphatic vessels of periodontal ligament. Miraglia, Rossi, and Moreira, 1968, *Acta Anat.* 69: 274—kidney structure and histochemistry. Egozcue, Perkins, and Hagemenas, 1968, *Folia. Primat.* 9:82—karyotype (2n = 46). Chase and Cooper, 1968, *Lab. Animal Care* 18(2):186—dental deposits and control in laboratory animals. Avila Pires, 1969, *Rev. Brasil. Biol.* 29(1):59—BRAZIL: *Piaui* (Deserto; Arara); *Ceará* (Monduby; Pernambuquinho; Mulungu; Crato; Pacoti; São Benedito, Ipú; Serra de Guaramiranga; Baturité; Serra do Castelo; Icarai-Mosquito; Juá; Mamaguape; Coremas); *Pernambuco* (Triunfo; Taperá); *Alagoas* (São Miguel; Mangabeiras; Quebrangulo); *Bahia* (Ilha Madre de Deus; Corupeba, Recôncavo; Santa Rita de Cássia; Santo Amaro); *Maranhão* (no specimens); *Guanabara* (introduced by man: Tijaca; Gavea; Jardim Botanico); *Rio de Janeiro* (introduced by man: Campo Grande; Bom Retiro; Maricá); characters; distribution. Dreizen and Hampton, 1969, *J. Dental Res.* 48(4):579—glandular contribution of selected B vitamins in saliva. Levy, Taylor, S. Hampton, and Thoma, 1969, *Cancer Res.* 29:2237—Rous sarcoma virus produced tumors. Parks, Melnick, Voss, Singer, Rosenberg, Alcott, and Casazza, 1969, *J. Inf. Diseases* 120:(5):548—not susceptible to infection by tamarin hepatitis virus. Giorgi, Matera, Mollaret, and Pestana de Castro, 1969, *Arq. Inst. Biol.* São Paulo 36(2):123—*Yersinia enterocolitica* in liver of São Paulo zoo individual. J. K. Hampton, Jr., and Parmelee, 1969, *Comp. Biochem. Physiol.* 30:367—plasma diamine oxidase (DAO) activity; comparisons with DAO levels in pregnant and nonpregnant humans. Dreizen, Levy, and Bernick, 1969, *J. Period. Res.* 4:274—effect of vitamin C deficiency in periodontium. Bernick, Levy, and Patek, 1969, *J. Period.-Periodontics* 40:49/355—arteriosclerotic changes in periodontal blood vessels. Dreizen and Levy, 1969, *Arch. Oral. Biol.* 14:577—histopathology of experimentally induced nutritional deficiency cheilosis. Miraglia and Moreira, 1969, *Acta Anat.* 72:520—adrenal cortex (anatomy; histochemistry). Miraglia and Ferreira Gomes, 1969; *Acta Anat.* 74:104—meibomian glands (structure; histochemistry). J. Hampton, Levy, and Sweet, 1969, *Endocrinology* 85(1):171—chorionic gonadotropin excretion during pregnancy. Dreizen, Levy, and Bernick, 1970, *J. Dental Res.,* 49(3):616—effect of folic acid deficiency on oral mucosa. Levy, Dreizen, Bernick, and Hampton 1970, *J. Dental Res.* 49:816—effect of parathyroid hormone on fluoridated and nonfluoridated alveolar bone. Dreizen, Levy, Niedermeier, and Griggs, 1970, *Arch. Oral Biol.* 15:179—trace metals in saliva; comparisons with man. Epple, 1970, *Folia Primat.* 12:56—maintenance; breeding; development. Epple, 1970, *Folia Primat.* 13:48—behavior; quantification of scent marking in social groups. J. K. Hampton, Jr., Rider, and Parmelee, 1970, *Proc. 3rd Int. Congr. Primat., Zurich* 2:95—Diamine oxidase and histamine values; comparisons with *Saimiri, Saguinus, Macaca, Pan.* Solange de Castro and Miraglia, 1971, *Acta Anat.* 79(4):466—sweat glands of palms and soles. Coimbra-Filho, 1971, *Publ. Avulsas Mus. Nac. Rio de Janeiro,* no. 57:9—BRAZIL: *Guanabara* (Parque Nacional da Tijuca; introduced from the Noreste; abundant and spreading; destructive to native bird eggs). Coimbra-Filho, 1971, *Rev. Brasil. Biol.* 31:(3): 379—BRAZIL: introduced into Guanabara and spreading into neighboring parts of Rio de Janeiro State. Miraglia and Santos, 1971, *Acta Anat.* 78:295—histochemistry of sebaceous glands of lips. J .K. Hampton, Jr., Parmelee, and Rider, 1971, in *Med. Primat. 1970,* ed. Goldsmith and Moor-Jankowski, p. 245—plasma histaminase and diamine oxidase values. Levy, Dreizen, Hampton, Taylor, and Hampton, 1971, in *Med. Primat. 1970,* ed. Goldsmith and Moor-Jankowski, p. 859—experimental periodontal diseases. Levy, Hampton, Dreizen, and Hampton, 1972, *J. Comp. Path.* 82:99, figs. 2, 3, 7 (thyroid gland, gross, normal, diseased)—chronic thyroiditis in laboratory animals. Levy, Hampton, and Hampton, 1972, *Int. Zoo Yearb.* 12:51—summary of research on periodontium, reproduction, nutrition, metabolism, biochemistry, disease, cytogenetics. Grant, Bernick, Levy, Dreizen, 1972, *J. Periodont.* 43(3):162—periodontal ligament development in premolars, molars (same but chronology different). Rothe, 1972, *Z. Morph. Anthrop.* 64(1):90, figs. 1, 4–6 (climbing), fig. 2 (stance), fig. 3 (hand- and footprints)—cheiridia. Porter, 1972, *Lab. Animal Sci.* 22(4):503—endoparasites. Spatz and Tigges, 1972, *J. Comp. Neurol.* 146(4):451—efferent cortical connections (find "significant [individual] variations in the internal organization of . . . cortical areas"). Werner, 1972, *Gegenbauer's Morph. Jahrb.* 18:161—blood supply system of cerebellum and medulla oblongata; comparisons with macaque, prosimian, insectivores. Rothe, 1972, *Zeitschr. Morph. Anthrop.* 64(1):90—locomotion. Levy, Dreizen, and Bernick, 1972, *J. Oral Path.* 1:61—effect of aging on periodontium. Levy, Nelms, Dreizen, and Bernick, 1972, in *Med. Primat. 1972,* ed. Goldsmith and Moor-Jankowski 3:191—delayed periodontal hypersensitivity reaction. Dreizen, Friedman, Levy, and Bernick, 1972, *J. Periodont.* 43:347—experimentally produced periodontal osteomyelitis [work not seen]. dos Santos, 1972, *Univ. Fed. Bahia* (Brazil)—lip histochemistry [work not seen]. Coimbra-Filho, 1972, *Rev. Brasil. Biol.* 32(4): 505, fig. 3 (animal eating tree gum)—BRAZIL: (Maceió)—wood boring and gum eating habits. de Araujo Sacrimento and Miraglia, 1972, *Acta Anat.* 82 (3):368—polysacharides in salivary glands. Bernaba, 1972, *Rev.*

Fac. Odont. Aracatuba (Brazil) 1:17—temporomandibular articulation [work not seen]. Zerlotti, Bernaba, and Hetem, 1972, *Rev. Fac. Odont. Aracatuba* 1:91—temporomandibular joint, orientation of collagenous fibers of articular disk [work not seen]. Kingston, 1972, in *Med. Primat. 1972* ed. E. D. Goldsmith and J. Moor-Jankowski, 3:68—diseases in captivity. Bernaba, Hetem, Marchi, 1973, *Rev. Fac. Odont. Aracatuba* (Brazil) 2:109—temporomandibular articulation and distribution of elastic fibers. Dreizen, Levy, and Bernick, 1973, *J. Dent. Res.* 52:803—effects of vitamin A deficiency on oral structures. Dreizen, Levy, and Bernick, 1973, *Proc. Soc. Exp. Biol. (N.Y.)*, 143:1218—diet induced atherosclerosis. Pook, 1974, *Primate Eye* 20(2):5—vocalization (abstract). Ingram, 1974, *Primate Eye* 8:28—husbandry [work not seen]. Leutenegger, 1974, *Folia Primat.* 20(4):382—mean maternal and fetal birth weights (262 g/56 g). dos Santos, Miraglia, and Costa Guedes, 1974, *Acta Anat.* 89: 314—histochemistry of sebaceous glands of lips. Pinto, Miraglia, and Moura, 1974, *Acta Anat.* 89:49—histochemistry of aorta. Clark, 1974, *10th Ann. Rept. Jersey Wildl. Preserv. Inst.*, p. 44—daily food requirements in Jersey Zoo. Costa Guedes, 1974, *Bol. Inst. Biol. Bahia* 31:127—histochemistry of duodenal glands of Brunner. Miraglia, Moura, and Neves, 1974, *Acta Anat.* 87:334—histochemistry of parotid glands. Miraglia, Siqueira, Gorini, and Pinto, 1975, *Acta Anat.* 91:57—liver histochemistry. Hilloowala, 1975, *Amer. J. Anat.* 142:367—hyoid aparatus. Pedreira and Peixoto, 1975, *J. Human Evol.* 4:293, pl. 1 (karyotype—karyotypic differences between *jacchus* and *penicillata* regarded as individual variables and taxonomically insignificant. Miraglia, Chavarria Irusta, Castro Filho, and Pinto, 1975, *Acta Anat.* 92:385—male kidney enzyme activity. Pinto, Miraglia, Santana, and Moura, 1975, *Acta Anat.* 89:49—aortic wall. Box, 1975, *Primates* 16(2):155—quantification of captive marmoset behavioral traits (marking, grooming, play, proximity, and huddling). Hobson and Hobbs, 1975, *J. Reprod. Fert.* 44:323—primiparous litter consisted of 3 fetuses including 1 full term, 1 papyraceous, 1 amorphous.

C[allithrix] jacchus, Coimbra-Filho and Mittermeier, 1974, *Folia Primat.* 20(1973):241, 260, fig. 1B, fig. 6F (prepared skin)—BRAZIL: distribution, characters, hybridization in captivity; "sympatry" with *penicillata.* Deane, Silva, and Loures, 1974, *Rev. Inst. Med. Trop.* São Paulo, 16:1—BRAZIL: *Bahia; Sergipe; Alagoas; Ceará;* distribution of *Trypanosoma minasense.*

Callithrix jacchus jacchus, Hershkovitz, 1968, *Evolution* 22(3):568, fig. 10 (distribution), fig. 11 (adult and juvenals), fig. 12 (geographic metachromism)—color patterns; comparisons; habitat; geographic metachromism. Hershkovitz, 1970, *Amer. J. Phys. Anthrop.* 32(3):379, pl. 1D (diseased jaw)—dental diseases. Hershkovitz, 1970, *Folia Primat.* 13:215, fig. 3 (endocranial cast)—BRAZIL: *Bahia* (São Amaro); cerebral fissural pattern. Hsu and S. Hampton, 1970, *Folia Primat.* 13:183—karyotype (2n = 46). S. Hampton and Taylor, 1970, *Proc. 3rd Int. Cong. Primat., Zurich* 1:246—gonadal development (resembles pattern in other platyrrhines and catarrhines). Hampton, Hampton, and Levy, 1971, in *Med. Primat. 1970,* ed. Goldsmith and Moor-Jankowski, 1970, p. 523—breeding records. S. H. Hampton, 1973, *Amer. J. Phys. Anthrop.* 38 (2):265—germ cell chimerism in adult males.

Callithrix [jacchus], Miles and Meyers, 1956, *J. Comp. Phys. Psych.* 49(219)—discrimination learning sets (qualitatively like but quantitatively inferior to rhesus). Miles, 1957, *J. Comp. Phys. Psych.* 50:352—delayed response learning (inferior to rhesus). Miles, 1958, *J. Comp. Phys. Psych.* 51.152—color vision (discrimination based on blue, green, and red combinations).

[Callithrix jacchus], Levy and Mirkovic, 1971, *Lab. Animal Sci.* 21(1):33—epizootic of measles in laboratory colony; pathology.

C[ercopithecus] Jacchus, Blumenbach, 1788, *Handb. Naturg.* ed. 3, p. 68—classification.

Cercopithecus Jacchus, Goldfuss, 1809, *Vergl. Naturbeschr. Säugeth.*, p. 75—classification.

Callitrix jacchus, Latreille, 1804, *Buffon Hist. Nat.*, Sonnini ed., 36:282—classification.

Sagouin Jacchus, Lacépède, 1799, *Tableau des divisions, sous-divisions, ordres et genres des mammifères,* p. 4—type of *Sagouin* Lacépède, by monotypy.

Sagouin jacchus, E. Geoffroy, 1803, *Cat. Mamm. Mus. Hist. Nat., Paris,* p. 10—characters.

Saguin jacchus, Fischer, 1803, *Nationalmus. Naturh., Paris* 2:113—characters.

Sagoin Iacchus, Griffith, 1827, *Animal kingdom* 1:308, 351—habits; classification.

Hapale Iacchus, Olfers, 1818, in Eschwege, *Journal von Brasilian, Weimar* 15(2):203. Kuhl, 1820, *Beitr. Zool.*, p. 46—BRAZIL: (northern part). Wagner, 1840, *Schreber's Säugth., Suppl.* 1:241—*albicollis* Spix, a synonym.

Hapale iacchus, Gray, 1866, *Proc. Zool. Soc. London* 1865:734—variation in color of ear tufts; local or accidental varieties, *vulgaris, albicollis, penicillatus, leucocephalus.* Weinart, 1926, *Zeitschr. Morph. Anthrop.* 35:282, fig. 94 (paranasal cavities)—frontal sinus.

Hapale (Iacchus) iacchus, Gray, 1866, *Proc. Zool. Soc. London* 1865:734—part, synonyms, *vulgaris, albicollis.*

H[apale] jacchus, Wied-Neuwied, 1826, *Beitr. Naturg. Brasil.,* p. 128—BRAZIL: *Bahia* (not seen south of Bahia de Todos os Santos; São Salvador); *Pernambuco* (type from Pernambuco); characters; habits. Wagner, 1840, *Schreber's Säugth., Suppl.* 1:241, pl. 30 (animal)—characters; distribution; *albicollis* Spix a synonym. I. Geoffroy, 1851, *Cat. Primates Mus. Hist. Nat., Paris,* p. 59—BRAZIL; characters. Wagner, 1855, Schreber's Säugth., *Suppl.* 5:124—synonyms, *albicollis, humeralifer.* Cabrera, 1900, *An. Soc. española Hist. Nat.,* ser. 2, 9:89—BRAZIL: *Pernambuco;* variation. Thomas, 1922, *Ann. Mag. Nat. Hist.,* ser. 9, 9:198—type of *Hapale.*

Hapale Jacchus, Rudolphi, 1831, *Abh. K. Akad. Wiss. Berlin* 1828:35, pl. 1 (reproductive organs), pl. 2 (embryo and fetal membranes)—reproduction; fetal membranes.

Hapale jacchus, F. Cuvier, fils, 1842, Geoffroy and Cuvier, *Hist. Nat. Mamm.* 7:table, p. 8—classification. Wagner, 1848, *Abh. Akad. Wiss. Munich,* (1847) 5:464—BRAZIL: (middle coastal area); Guianan records unfounded. Owen, 1853, *Descr. Cat. Osteol. Ser. Roy. Mus. Coll. Surgeons* 2:723—skeleton. Bates, 1863, *Naturalist on the River Amazons,* 1:99; ibid., 2d ed., p. 60—BRAZIL: live pet seen in Pará (Belém) supposedly "captured in the island of Marajó." Giebel, 1865, *Zeitscher. gesammten Naturw., Halle* 26:256—skeleton. Ruge, 1887, *Untersuchungen über die Gesichtmuskulatur der Primaten (Leipzig),* pp. 3 et seq., pl. 1, figs. 1, 2 (facial musculature). Seydel, 1891, *Gegenbaur's Morph. Jahrb.* 17:64, pl. 4, fig. 10 (nasal cavity)—paranasal cavities and turbinals. Seydel, 1892, *Gegenbaur's Morph. Jahrb.* 18:578, fig. 16 (intercostal fibers), pl. 20, fig. 4 (intercostal fibers)—intercostal fibers and metamerism. de Meijere, 1894, *Gegenbaur's Morph. Jahrb.* 21:406—hair grouping and glands. Elliot Smith, 1902, *Cat. Comp. Anat. Roy. Coll. Surgeons* 2d ed. 2:383, fig. 223 (brain)—cerebral fissural pattern. Van Loghem, 1903, Petrus Campus, *Nederl. Bij'd Anat.* 2 (3):350, fig. 24 (gut)—colon. Frédéric, 1905, *Zeitschr. Morph. Anthrop.* 8:240—facial and ulnar vibrissae. De Beaux, 1917, *Giorn. Morph. Uomo, Primati* 1:93, fig. 1–3 (ulnar carpal vibrissae)—ulnar carpal vibrissae. Cabrera, 1917, *Trab. Mus. Nac. Cienc. Nat. Madrid, ser. zool.,* no. 31, p. 34—BRAZIL: *Pernambuco* (Jiménez de la Espada, collector); characters; variation. Pocock, 1917, *Ann. Mag. Nat. Hist.,* ser. 8, 20:249, figs. 1 A, B (hands and feet), fig. 2 A, B (ear)—external characters. Pocock, 1920, *Proc. Zool. Soc. London* 1920:91, 104, 109, fig. 9 *a-b* (tongue), fig. 10 (♀ genitalia), fig. 13 *a-d* (♂ genitalia)—external characters. Lucas, Hume, Henderson, and Smith, 1927, *Proc. Zool. Soc. London,* 1927:447, pls. 1, 2 (animal)—breeding and growth in captivity. Beattie, 1927, *Proc. Zool. Soc. London* 1927:593—anatomy. Pohl, 1928, *Zeitschr. Anat. Entwickl.-Ges.* 18:91, pl. 1, fig. 3 (penis, sagittal section)—characters of penis. Huber, 1931, *Evolution of facial musculature and facial expression* (Baltimore), p. 28, fig. 5 (facial and ear musculature)—origin, evolution and comparison of ear and facial musculature. Fitzgerald, 1935, *J. Mammal.* 16:181, pl. 4 (animal)—life history; breeding and growth in captivity. Zuckerman and Parker, 1935, *J. Anat.* 69:487, pl. 2 (uterus masculinus)—uterus masculinus. Colyer, 1936, *Variation and diseases of the teeth of mammals,* London, p. 299, fig. 37 *b* (upper dentition)—pm^3 rotated. Bennejeant, 1936, *Anomalies et variations dentaires chez les primates,* p. 85, fig. 64 (jaw radiograph), fig. 79 (postcanine differentation)—dental succession. Lucas, Hume, and Henderson Smith, 1937, *Proc. Zool. Soc. London,* ser. A, 107: 205—breeding in captivity. Schultz, 1948, *Amer. J. Phys. Anthrop.,* n.s., 6:8—twins and triplets recorded. J. Anthony, 1946, *Ann. Soc. Nat., Zool., Paris,* ser. 11, 8:7, 50. figs. 2, 29, 30 (brain)—brain morphology. Connolly, 1950, *External morphology of the primate brain,* p. 19, fig. 6 (brain)—brain; fissural pattern. Crandall, 1951, *Animal Kingdom,* 54(6): 179, fig. lower left p. 182—photograph of family group in New York Zoological Gardens. Hill, 1957, *Primates* 3:83, 105, 112, 120, 132, 158, 168, 178, 181–87, 190, 194, 213, 241, 251, 281, et seq., 286–89, 292, 294–98, 302, 319, pl. 32 (animal), fig. 11 (brain), fig. 23 (skull), fig. 25 (dentition), fig. 29 (tongue), fig. 31 (gut), fig. 32 (hypophysis), fig. 33 (arterial system of brain), fig. 34 (brain), fig. 35 (male in sexual posture), fig. 61 (map, distribution), figs. 81–83, (external genitalia), fig. 84 (ear), fig. 85 (palmar surface of hand and plantar surface of foot), fig. 88 (facial hair tracts)—anatomy; taxonomy; history; distribution; behavior; food; reproduction; hybridization with *penicillata* and *argentata.* Shaw and Auskaps, 1954, *Oral Surg., Oral Med., Oral Path.* 7(6):671, figs. 1–9 (dentition), figs. 10–14 (dental sections)—dental abornormalities (calculus; pigmentation; malocclusion; periodontal diseases); no evidence of caries. Osman Hill, 1960, *Primates* 4:61, 67—blood corpuscle count; brain weight to bodyweight. Chartin and Petter, 1960, *Mammalia* 24:153—mating, reproduction, and rearing in captivity. Beath and Benirschke, 1962, *Cytologia* 27(1):1—location of sex chromatin. Benirschke, Anderson, and Brownhill, 1962, *Science* 138 (3539):513, fig. 1 (karyotype)—marrow chimerism. Richart and Benirschke, 1963, *J. Pathol. Bacteriol.* 86 (1):221—causes of death in laboratory colony (*Prosthenorchis elegans* infestation, pneumonia, pancreatitis, bilateral empyema). Benirschke and Brownhill, 1963, *Cytogenetics* 2:331, fig. 1 (karyotype)—heterosexual cells in testes of chimerae. Grüner and Krause, 1963, *Zool. Gart.* 28 (2/3):108, figs. 2–4 (family group)—care; breeding; habits. Brand, 1963, *Proc. Zool. Soc. London* 140 (4):655—seasonal breeding in captivity. Picard, Heremans, and Vandebroek, 1963, *Mammalia* 27:285—immunoelectrophoretic patterns of protein serums; phylogenetic relationships. Dastague, 1963, *Mammalia* 27:265—pronator and supinator muscles. Sandler and Stone, 1963, *Psychol. Rept.* 13:139—laboratory care and treatment. Osman Hill, 1963, *Proc. Zool. Soc. London* 124:305—cleft palate. Fiennes, 1964, *Proc. Zool. Soc. London,* 143(3):523—cystic bone disease. Levy and Artecona, 1964, *Lab. Animal Care* 14(1):20, fig. 3 (animal)—laboratory care. Fain, 1964, *Ann. Soc. Belge Med. Trop.* 44(3):453—parasitic nasal mite (*Mortelsmansia duboisi*). Inglis and Cosgrove, 1965, *Parasitol.* 55:732—pinworm infection (*Trypanoxyuris [Hapaloxyuris] callithricis* Solanen, 1933) from captive. Keleven, 1966, *Acta Oto-laryng.* 61:239, figs. 3, 4 (cochlea)—aural pathology. Berkson and Goodrich, 1966, *Perceptual and motor skills* 23:491—abnormal, sterotyped movements of subjects reared in isolation. Levy, 1966, in *Environmental variables in oral disease,*

Amer. Assoc. Adv. Sci. (Washington, D.C.) p. 231, fig. 5 (jaws), fig. 9 (animal)—use of callitrichids in study of periodontal diseases. Epple and Lorenz, 1967, *Folia Primat.* 7:98, fig. 11 (animal marking)—sternal gland and hair; marking. Epple, 1967, *Folia Primat.* 7:38, figs. 1, 2, 6, 9–11 (animal)—sexual and social behavior. Epple, 1968, *Folia Primat.* 8:4, figs. 1–17 (voice recordings)—vocalization; (ontogeny; comparisons; social significance). F. Deinhardt, 1970, Infections and immuno-suppression in subhuman Primates, ed. Balner and Beveridge (Copenhagen), p. 55—induction of human hepatitis and transmission to other callitrichid species. Schropel, 1972, *Wiss. Z. Humboldt Univ. Berlin* 21:375—recognition of acoustical signals. Werner, Erdman, Just, 1974, *J. Pharmacol,* 5 (suppl. 2):105 (abstract)—distribution of tetrahydrocannabinol C-14.

Lemur jaccus [*sic*], Gray, 1821, London medical Repository, 15:298—lapsus for *Simia jacchus* Linnaeus.

Hapale jachus [*sic*], Schlegel, 1876, *Les singes.* Simiae, p. 271—BRAZIL; characters; synonyms, *humeralifer, albicollis.* Jentink, 1887, *Cat. Osteol. Mus. Pays-Bas* 9:50—skeletons. Jentink, 1892, *Cat. Syst. Mamm. Mus. Pays-Bas* 11:58—mounted specimen.

Hapales [*sic*] *jacchus,* Jardine, 1833, *Nat. Library* 1:193, fig. (dentitition), 194, 222, pl. 24 (animal ex Audebert) —characters; habits.

C[*ebus*] *jacchus,* Blainville, 1839, *Ostéographie* 1 (C):26, 30—dentition; skull.

Saguinus [*sic*] *jacchus,* Hershkovitz, 1968, *Evolution* 22(3):520—generic name lapsus for *Callithrix.*

S[*imia*] (*Sagoinus*) *jacchus moschatus* Kerr, 1792, *Animal kingdom,* p. 80—name based on a composite of animals seen or described in literature, not *le singe musqué* of Brisson (= *Cebus apella*).

Jacchus vulgaris E. Geoffroy, 1812, *Ann. Mus. Hist. Nat., Paris* 19:119—new name for *Simia jacchus* Linnaeus; type locality, said to be La Guyane [= French Guiana]. Desmarest, 1818, *Nouv. Dict. Hist. Nat.* 24:238—synonymy; characters. Desmarest, 1820, *Mammifères,* p. 92, pl. 18, fig. 4 (animal). Desmarest, 1827, *Dict. Sci. Nat.* 47:17—represented in Guido's painting of embarcation of Helen of Troy. I. Geoffroy, 1827, *Dict. Classique Hist. Nat.* 12:516—characters; juvenal coloration; breeding. E. Geoffroy, 1829, *Cours Hist. Nat. Mamm., Leçon* 10, p. 35—color of newborn. Lesson, 1834, *Compléments de Buffon,* 4:263—characters. Gray, 1843, *List Mamm. Brit. Mus.,* p. 14—BRAZIL. Gerrard, 1862, *Cat. bones Brit. Mus.,* p. 28—vertebral formula. Gray, 1870, *Cat. monkeys, lemurs and fruit-eating bats, Brit. Mus.,* p. 63—part, synonyms, *jacchus* (var. 1), *albicollis* (var. 2). Rode, 1938, *Bull. Mus. Nat. Hist. Nat., Paris,* ser. 2, 10:237—history of "type" and two "paratypes."

J[*acchus*] *vulgaris,* Reichenbach, 1862, *Vollst. Naturg. Affen,* p. 2, pl. 1, figs. 3, 4 (juvenals), figs. 5, 6 (adults in new pelage), figs. 7, 8 (adults in old pelage)—characters; habits ex authors.

H[*apale Jacchus*)] *vulgaris,* Voigt, 1831, *Cuvier's das Thierreich* 1.98—classification.

Iacchus albicollis Spix, 1823, *Sim. et Vesp. Brasil.,* p. 33, pl. 25—BRAZIL: *Bahia* (type locality, Bahia [= Salvador]); mounted skin, skull in, Munich Museum, collected by the Spix and Martius expedition.

Jacchus albicollis, Wagner, 1833, *Isis von Oken* 10:997—a pale variety of *Simia Jacchus* Linnaeus.

J[*acchus*] *albicollis,* Fischer, 1829, *Syn. Mamm.,* p. 60—perhaps a variety of *J. vulgaris* (= *jacchus*). Reichenbach, 1862, *Vollst. Naturg. Affen,* p. 4, pl. 1, fig. 9 (animal)—characters.

Hapal[*e*] *albicollis,* Schinz, 1825, *Cuvier Das Thierreich* 4:280—classification; characters.

Hapale albicollis, Osman Hill, 1957, *Primates* 3:83, 158, 163, 183, 286, 301, fig. 28 (peritoneum), fig. 61 (distribution)—BRAZIL: *Bahia* (Itaparica, Bahia de Todos os Santos); characters; distribution; genitalia; peritoneum; intestine.

H[*apale*] *albicollis,* I. Geoffroy, 1851, *Cat. Primates, Mus. Hist. Nat., Paris,* p. 59—characters of two menagerie specimens.

Callithrix albicollis, Elliot, 1913, *A review of the Primates* 1:231—characters "ex specimen in British Museum." N. C. Davis, 1930, *J. Exp. Med.* 52:405—BRAZIL: *Bahia* experimental infection with yellow fever virus.

[*Jacchus vulgaris*] *β rufus,* Fischer, 1829, *Syn. Mamm.,* p. 60—name based on the variety *"A. pelage roux"* of E. Geoffroy (1812, *Ann. Mus. Hist. Nat., Paris* 19:119).

Hapale leucotis Lesson, 1840, *Species de mammifères: Bimanes et quadrumanes,* p. 186—BRAZIL; new name for *Simia jacchus* Linnaeus; synonymy; characters; other synonyms, *vulgaris, albicollis* (= *variété* C), *humeralifer* (= *variété* D).

Hapale communis South, 1845, *Encyclopedia Metropolitana, London* 7:383, pl. 2—new name for the ouistiti or striated monkey.

Jacchus hapale Gray, 1870, *Cat. monkeys, lemurs and fruit-eating bats, Brit. Mus.*, p. 62—evidently a *lapsus* by transposition of *Hapale jacchus*.

Hapale? chrysoleucos, Osman Hill (part, not Wagner), 1957, *Primates* 3:291–92 (in text), pl. 24 (animal)—menagerie specimen purchased in Rio de Janeiro and brought to England via Sierra Leone; characters; may be "a partially albinistic variant (or mutant) of *jacchus* or one of its relatives."

Hapale [sp. ?] H. Matthews, 1952, *Proc. Zool. Soc. London* 121:917—regarded as an undescribed form. Osman Hill, 1952, *Proc. Zool. Soc. London* 121:918—characters.

[?] *Callithrix aurita*, Krieg (not E. Geoffroy?), 1948, *Zwischen Anden und Atlantik*, fig. p. 473 only, not text. Feldman and Harrison, 1971, in *Med. Primat. 1970*, ed. Goldsmith and Moor-Jankowski, p. 336, fig. 8 (superior olivary medius)—form and function of superior olivary complex.

[?] *Hapale aurita*, Bagdon and de Silva (not E. Geoffroy?), 1965, *Toxicol. Appl. Pharmacol* 7:478 (abstract)—as experimental animal in toxicology. F. Deinhardt, 1970, in "Infection and immunosuppression in subhuman Primates," ed. Balner and Beveridge (Copenhagen), p. 55—induction of human hepatitis and transmission to other callitrichids.

H[*apale*] *jacchus* ♂ × *Mico argentatus* ♀, Osman Hill, 1957, *Primates* 3:185—bred in captivity.

Hapale jacchus ♀ × *Mico argentatus* ♂, Osman Hill, 1961, *Proc. Zool. Soc. London* 137, (2):321—characters of hybrid.

Hapale jacchus ♂ × *Mico argentatus* ♀, Osman Hill, 1961, *Proc. Zool. Soc. London* 137 (2):321—hybrid recorded.

Hapale jacchus ♂ × *Hapale penicillatus* ♀, Osman Hill, 1957, *Primates* 3:185—"bred several times in London Zoo from 1950 onward."

H[*apale*] *jacchus* ♂ × *H*[*apale*] *penicillata* [*sic*], Osman Hill, 1961, *Proc. Zool. Soc. London* 137 (2):321—hybrids born in London Zoo.

Callithrix jacchus ♂ × *Callithrix geoffroyi* ♀, Coimbra-Filho, 1970, *Rev. Brasil. Biol.* 30(4):509—3 litters of live-birth twins, Zoological Gardens, Rio de Janeiro; characters; comparisons; behavior.

C[*allithrix*] *jacchus* × *C*[*allithrix*] *geoffroyi*, Coimbra-Filho, 1972, *Rev. Brasil. Biol.* 32(4):505, fig. 2 (animal), fig. 6 (holes bitten into board)—wood boring and gum eating habits. Coimbra-Filho and Mittermeier, 1974, *Folia Primat.* 20(1973), pp. 244, 261—description; offspring (figs. 26D, 3B, C, 4A, B).

(*Callithrix jacchus* × *C. geoffroyi*) ♂ × (*Callithrix penicillata jordani*) ♀, Coimbra-Filho, 1971, *Rev. Brasil. Biol.* 31(3):383, fig. 4 (parents with one double hybrid), fig. 7 (double hybrid), fig. 8 (double hybrid young and adult *jacchus* × *geoffroyi*)—male triplets, Zoological Gardens, Rio de Janeiro, characters; comparisons; behavior. Coimbra-Filho, 1973, *Rev. Brasil. Biol.* 33(1):32, fig. 2 (male hybrid with twin offspring).

(*C*[*allithrix*] *jacchus* × *C. geoffroyi*) × *C*[*allithrix*] *p*[*enicillata*] *jordani*, Coimbra-Filho and Mittermeier, 1974, *Folia Primat.* 20(1973): 244 262—description; double hybrid offspring (figs. 3C, D, 4B)—characters.

Type. None in existence, type restricted to the *Çagui minor* of Marcgrave, by restriction of type locality.

Type Locality. America; restricted to Pernambuco, Brazil, by Thomas (1911, *Proc. Zool. Soc. London,* 1911:127).

Distribution (fig. IX.5). Scrub forests of the Northeast Region of Brazil in Piaui, Ceará, the coastal forests from Paraíba through Pernambuco, Alagoas, and Sergipe to Bahia de Todos os Santos, eastern Bahia, and recorded from western Bahia, west of the Rio São Francisco-Grande; occurrence on the left bank of the Rio Parnaíba, eastern Maranhão, is probable; introduced into Guanabara toward the beginning of the twentieth century, now wild-living in some wooded parts of the state and adjacent parts of the State of Rio de Janeiro where *Callithrix jacchus aurita* might normally occur, but so far as is known, does not.

Callithrix j. jacchus intergrades with *C. j. penicillata* where their ranges meet in the Recôncavo da Bahia (Hershkovitz 1975*b*). The Rio São Francisco-Grande evidently makes sharp separation between the races. Nothing is known of the distribution of *jacchus* between the Rio São Francisco on the west and coastal Bahia and Sergipe on the east.

Present knowledge of the occurrence of *jacchus* in the State of Maranhão is based on two bits of clouded evidence. The first is the report of Avila Pires (1968, p. 159) of two *"penicillata,"* from Maranhão registered in the mammal catalog of the National Museum in Rio de Janeiro. The specimens themselves could not be located, but Avila Pires suggests they probably represent true *jacchus*. The second is a skin only, without field measurements, preserved in the American Museum of Natural History (AMNH 84461), with field number 3, collected in Maranhão, 2 August 1926, by Emil Kaempfer. The gazetteer and maps of Kaempfer's bird collecting stations published by Naumburg (1935) show that the interval from late July through 8 August 1926 was spent collecting birds in the Sierra do Valentim, east central Maranhão. Kaempfer evidently spent most of this time in the village of São João dos Patos except for excursions to Pastos Bons (3 August) and some places along the Riachão, a small stream flowing northeast into the Rio Parnaíba. This Riachão should not be confused with the same name place shown in Naumburg's map. Kaempfer's Maranhão marmoset, whether it was wild caught or a pet introduced from another state, must have been prepared as a study skin during the time the collector was in the Sierra do Valentim region, most likely in São João dos Patos (282a).

Taxonomy. The description of *Simia jacchus* in the 10th edition of Linnaeus's *Systema naturae* (1758, p. 27) is based on references to Clusius (1605, *Exoticorum,* p. 372, fig.), John Ray (1693, *Synopsis methodica animalium quadrupedum et serpentini generis,* pp. 154, 160), Marcgrave de Liebstad (1648, *Historiae rerum naturalium Brasiliae,* p. 227, fig.), Petever (1702, *Gazophylacium naturae et artis,* p. 26, fig. 5) and Klein (1751, *Quadrupedum depositio brevisque historia naturalis,* p. 11, fig. 1). By restricting the type locality of *jacchus* to Pernambuco, Thomas (1911:127) established the Marcgrave account as the primary reference for the description of the species.

Simia (*Sagoinus*) *jacchus moschatus* Kerr is ostensibly based on the *singe musqué* of Brisson (= *Cebus apella*), but the description is obviously that of *Simia jacchus.* In the first part of the description Kerr gives 8 inches for the head and body length of his animal, with the tail "considerably longer than the body." Lower down, in the same paragraph, he notes that the tail is "twice as long as the body and head, which last do not exceed six inches." Evidently, Kerr drew up his account from several sources which need not be traced here. As noted, Brisson's *singe musqué* has nothing to do with Kerr's. It is the *caitaia* of Marcgrave or *Cebus apella.* This, in turn, is the same as *Cercopithecus Brasilianus primus* Clusius (*Supra cit.* 1605, p. 371, text not fig.) and other authors cited by Brisson (*supra cit.* 1756, p. 197). The true *Callithrix jacchus jacchus* described and figured by Clusius is the *Cercopithecus Brasilianus tertius* or *Sagoin.* I have not seen the original by Clusius, but the description and reproductions of his sagoins are available in other pre-Linnaean works at hand (e.g., Jonston 1657, *Hist. Nat. Quadr.,* pl. 78; *Ray, Syn. Meth.,* 1693, p. 160).

Jacchus vulgaris E. Geoffroy, 1812, was proposed as a new combination for *Simia jacchus* Linnaeus to avoid use of the tautonym *Jacchus jacchus.* The *Catalogue* of the types and other specimens of primates of the Paris museum published by I. Geoffroy (1851, p. 59), restores the Linnaean name in the combination *Hapale jacchus* and correctly cites *Jacchus vulgaris* as a junior synonym thereof. Four specimens of *jacchus* in the Paris museum at the time are listed. The first, received from the Lisbon Museum in 1808, may have served E. Geoffroy for his 1812 diagnosis of *vulgaris,* but this specimen is not distinguished as "type" in the *Catalogue.* The remaining specimens were accessioned in 1820 and later. Other skins, however, could have been available to E. Geoffroy (cf. E. Geoffroy 1803, p. 10). In any case, it cannot be presumed that any specimen used in the diagnosis of *Jacchus vulgaris* is a type in a strict sense. Rode's (1938: 38) listing of the original Lisbon Museum specimen as "holotype" and two other specimens as "paratypes," one without date, the other acquired in 1856, has no validity.

Iacchus albicollis Spix, 1823, from Bahia (Salvador) is virtually another name for *Simia jacchus* Linnaeus. Spix met with only two allopatric forms of ouistitis in Brazil. One, Spix's *Iacchus albicollis,* with white auricular tufts, was the first seen in Bahia. The second, his *Iacchus penicillatus,* with black tufts, was observed in Minas Gerais. The difference between the Linnaean *jacchus* and *albicollis,* according to Spix, is that the head is brownish black in the former while the crown as well as nape and neck are whitish in the latter. These differences were regarded as slight, and Spix concluded that all species of ouistitis recognized by Geoffroy, namely, *auritus, leucocephalus, humeralifer,* and his own *albicollis,* are possibly nothing more than varieties of the common species.

Diagnostic Characters. Elongate tufts in front and above ears white, whitish, or buffy, variously mixed or tipped with blackish or dark brown, never dominantly blackish in adult; inner (lateral) surface of pinna nearly bare or thinly covered with hair; forehead blackish or brown with a sharply defined whitish median blaze; temples and anterior portion of crown brownish (figs. IX.7, 20, 21).

Coloration. Exposed parts of facial skin well pigmented below eyes, slightly pigmented between and above; comparatively long hairs of cheeks and throat brown and often mixed with gray, sometimes entirely gray or silvery; forehead dark brown or blackish with a well-defined buffy to pure white blaze; crown, occiput, and mantle brown, or becoming buffy, gray, or whitish; hairs of tufts in front, above, and behind base of ears whitish gray, drab, or yellow with or without black tips or dark bases, the tufts fan-shaped or forming a corolla more or less masking ears when seen from in front and above; pinna thinly haired brown medially, well haired brown laterally (interiorly); back behind shoulders transversely striated with alternating bands of black and gray or buffy, the ochraceous or orange middle portion of hairs more or less concealed; individual hairs blackish on basal third, ochraceous or orange in middle third, followed by a black, gray, or whitish band, tip black; upper surface of hands and feet buffy or gray more or less mixed with brown or nearly entirely brown; throat and underside of neck brown or mixed with gray, sometimes nearly entirely gray or whitish; chest brown or dominantly gray or buffy like belly with the dark brown basal portions of the hairs showing through, rarely underparts nearly entirely whitish; tail with broad black and narrow grayish or buffy annulations, each pair corresponding to a vertebra, individual hairs of basal portion of tail like those of rump, hairs of distal portion with basal band blackish, broad subterminal band whitish or buffy and narrow tip blackish.

Young. Color and pelage of growing captive-born young (fig. IX.21) are described on page 540 (Growth and Development).

Measurements. See appendix table 2.

Comparisons. The dominantly white fanlike tufts in front of, above, and behind ears forming an erectile corolla distinguish *jacchus* from black tufted *penicillata* and *geoffroyi* and all marmosets without circumaural tufts; distinguished from white tufted *aurita* and *flaviceps* by absence of salient aural tufts.

Variation. Callithrix jacchus jacchus is geographically the most peripheral member of the species and the trend toward bleaching is most advanced in this form. Individuals with whitish or grayish brown heads and mantles in troops of otherwise normally colored ouistitis were noted by Wied-Neuwied (1826, pp. 129, 135) in the vicinity of Bahia, or Salvador (294), the type locality of *albicollis*. Thomas in 1910 (p. 500) observed that in 9 marmosets collected by E. Snethlage in Ipú, Ceará, "the color of the nape is . . . very variable, some being gray and others whitish. The latter represents Spix's *albicollis*." The nape—actually mantle is meant here—of still another Snethlage Ipú specimen in the Field Museum is drab or grayish brown. Cabrera (1917, p. 34) examined 7 marmosets from Pernambuco, and remarked that they agreed, in general, with the figures and descriptions of the nominate forms of the species but that the nape of one was considerably mixed with white and in two specimens the mantle was entirely a dirty white quite like the original figure of *albicollis* Spix. Finally, Vieira (1953, p. 210), recorded 14 marmosets from São Miguel (290) and Mangabeiras, Alagoas (291), 5 of them with whitish mantles.

Albinistic *Callithrix j. jacchus* with frontal blaze and striated back and tail obscured or undefined are known, but only one case has been recorded. The live animal, first mentioned by Harrison Matthews (1952, p. 97) and Osman Hill (1952, p. 918), was later described by Osman Hill (1957, pp. 27, 91, and plate opp.) and exhibited in a photograph labeled "white marmoset (*Hapale*? *chrysoleucos*)." According to the authorities cited, the marmoset, a male, was registered 17 October 1951 in the menagerie of the Zoological Society of London. Osman Hill (1957, p. 292) subsequently observed that "the animal was provisionally identified as *H. chrysoleucos*, but with the loss of the golden tinge and development of grey patches this cannot be upheld, and the suggestion naturally arises of its being a partially albinotic variant (or mutant) of *jacchus* or one of its relatives." It is said to "have been brought to England from Sierra Leone whither it had been taken by a seaman who had purchased it in Rio de Janeiro along with six others." The photograph cited above shows a *Callithrix* with the outline of pinna partially obscured by *jacchus*like preauricular tufts. A prepared skin of an albinistic male *Callithrix jacchus jacchus*, number 54.34 in the collection of the British Museum, is undoubtedly the animal in question. It died 9 September 1953, after living two years in the menagerie of the Zoological Society of London. Its skin is unpigmented, pelage white except for a mixture of black in shoulder region, black patch on lower back with an irregular blotch lower down, hairs of chest, inner sides of thighs and midline of underside of tail except terminal one-fifth mixed black and white.

An erythristic individual has been recorded by E.

Fig. IX.21. White Tufted-ear Marmoset, *Callithrix jacchus jacchus* Linnaeus; adult male with mounted twins; circumauricular tufts and frontal blaze are absent in juvenal pelage, about 1½ times natural size. (Photo Gerhard Buddich; courtesy of Tierpark, Berlin.)

Geoffroy (1812, p. 119) but melanistic *jacchus* are unknown.

A specimen in the Field Museum from Santo Amaro, Bahia (293b), with preorbital tufts mixed with black, supraorbital tufts evenly mixed gray and brown and poorly defined from hair of crown is morphologically intermediate with respect to these and other characters, between *Callithrix jacchus jacchus* and *C. j. penicillata* (figs. IX.22, 23). The tendency of the preauricular tufts of the Santa Amaro specimen to be more fan- than pencillike in form inclines me to assign it to *jacchus* rather than to *penicillata.* Santa Amaro is in the Recôncavo da Bahia (Bahia de Todos os Santos) region whence semialbinistic individuals of *jacchus* have been recorded. Marmosets from the nearest localities recorded to the southwest and northwest are referrable to *penicillata;* those to the southeast and north along the coast are true *jacchus.* It appears that Santo Amaro is in a zone of intergradation between the two races in question.

Remarks. Coimbra-Filho and Mittermeier (1974, p. 249) assert that "on the Ilha de Itaparica [295], an island in the Recôncavo da Bahia . . . both *C. jacchus* and *C. penicillata* have been introduced and live sympatrically without apparent hybridizing." Documentation for the alleged introduction is not offered and samples are not mentioned or described. The only marmoset from the Ilha de Itaparica known to me is a skin in the British Museum collected in 1905 by M. J. Nicoll and referred to by Osman Hill (1957, p. 301) under the name *Hapale albicollis* Spix. The specimen and the type of *albicollis* Spix represent albinotic populations of *C. j. jacchus.* In any event, Coimbra-Filho and Mittermeier hedge the claim of sympatry. On page 260 of their work (1974), they declare that the presence of *jacchus* "on the islands in the Recôncavo da Bahia, is *probably* due to introduction by man [italics mine]." Farther on (1974, p. 261) they identify *"Callithrix penicillata penicillata"* and not the supposedly introduced *"C. p. jordani"* as the form inhabiting the Recôncavo da Bahia.

The Recôncavo da Bahia is a zone of secondary contact and integradation between *Callithrix jacchus jacchus* and *C. j. penicillata.* The former has been recorded by Avila Pires (1969, p. 59) from Ilha Madre de Dios (294), Curupeba (294) and Santo Amaro (293b); the latter (under the name *jordani*) from Fiera de Santana (293a). The Santo Amaro intergrade between *jacchus* and *penicillata* is described above (p. 519 figs. IX.22, 23).

Specimens Examined.—52. BRAZIL—*Amazonas*: Tefé, 1 (FMNH); *Bahia*: Itaparica Island, 1 (BM); Macaco Seco, 1 (FMNH); Santo Amaro, 1 (FMNH); *Ceará*: Ipú, 5 (BM, 4; FMNH, 1); Juá, 3 (FMNH); *Pernambuco*: São Lourenço, 7 (BM); *Piauí*: Arara, 1 (FMNH); Deserto, 3 (FMNH, 2; CM, 1); *unknown state*: Pedra Marietta Antonietta, 1 (MNHN); *locality unknown*: 28 (AMNH, 1; BM, 1; FMNH, 11 [6 in spirits]; GEE, 1; MNHN, 7; USNM, 1; SM, 6).

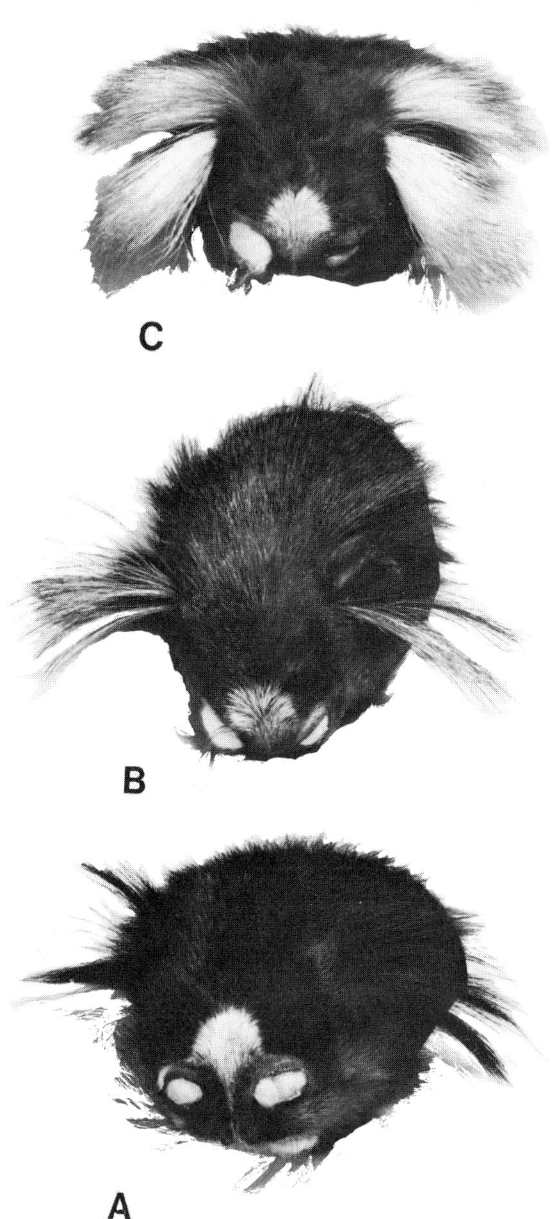

Fig. IX.22. Geographic intergradation between *Callithrix jacchus penicillata* and *C. j. jacchus;* heads of stuffed skins preserved in Field Museum. (*A*) *C. j. penicillata* from Lagoa Santa, Minas Gerais (313), same specimen show in figs. IX.14, 15; (*C*) *C. j. jacchus* from Jua, Ceará (286); (*B*) intergrade from Santo Amaro, Recôncavo da Bahia (293b) where the ranges of *jacchus* and *penicillata* meet. Circumaural tufts of the *penicillata* shown are thin and dark brown, of the *jacchus,* thick, white with pronounced brownish tips, of the intergrade, mixed dark brown and whitish. (Based on Hershkovitz 1975*b*.)

C.j.penicillata   intergrade   C.j.jacchus

Fig. IX.23. Geographic intergradation between *Callithrix jacchus penicillata* and *C. j. jacchus;* dorsal aspect of same specimens shown in fig. IX.22; cape or mantle is blackish brown in the *penicillata,* brown to drab in the *jacchus,* mixed in the intergrade. (Based on Hershkovitz 1975b.)

CALLITHRIX JACCHUS AURITA E. GEOFFROY: BUFFY-TUFTED-EAR MARMOSET

Fig. IX.24. Buffy Tufted-ear Marmoset, *Callithrix jacchus aurita* E. Geoffroy.

Synonymic History

Simia aurita E. Geoffroy in Humboldt, 1812, *Rec. Obs. Zool. Anat. Comp.*, p. 360—"*Jacchus auritus*, Geoffroy," in synonymy.

Jacchus auritus, E. Geoffroy, 1812, *Ann. Mus. Hist. Nat., Paris* 19:119—type locality, "Brésil?" Desmarest, 1820, *Mammifères*, p. 93—characters. Desmarest, 1827, *Dict. Sci. Nat.* 47:19—characters. Gray, 1843, *List Mamm. Brit. Mus.*, p. 14—BRAZIL. Gerrard, 1862, *Cat. bones Brit. Mus.*, p. 29—BRAZIL; vertebral formula. Rode, 1938, *Bull. Mus. Nat. Hist. Nat., Paris*, ser. 2, 10:238—type history.

J[*acchus*] *auritus*, Reichenbach, 1862, *Vollst. Naturg. Affen*, p. 4, pl. 1, fig. 14, 15 (animal)—BRAZIL; characters; synonymy.

Hapale auritus, Kuhl, 1820, *Beitr. Zool.*, p. 48—characters; 3 specimens in Paris museum.

H[*apale*] *aurita*, Wagner, 1840, *Schreber's Säugth., Suppl.* 1:243, pl. 30 C (animal)—characters. I. Geoffroy, 1851, *Cat. Primates Mus. Hist. Nat., Paris*, p. 60—BRAZIL; type history. Burmeister, 1854, *Syst. Uebers. Thiere Brasil.* 1:35—characters. Wagner, 1855, *Schreber's Säugth., Suppl.* 5:125—part, BRAZIL: *São Paulo*.

Hapale aurita, Wagner, 1848, *Abh. Akad. Wiss. Munich* (1847) 5:465—part, BRAZIL: *São Paulo* (Matodentro); characters. Gray, 1866, *Proc. Zool. Soc. London* 1865:734—BRAZIL; characters. Schlegel, 1876, *Les singes. Simiae*, p. 276—BRAZIL: *São Paulo*; characters. Pelzeln, 1883, *Verh. K. K. Zool.-Bot. Gesellsch., Wien, Beih.* 33:21—BRAZIL: *São Paulo* (Matodentro); characters. Jentink, 1887, *Cat. Ostéol. Mus. Pays-Bas* 9:51—BRAZIL. Jentink, 1892, *Cat. Syst. Mamm. Mus. Pays-Bas* 11:59—BRAZIL: *São Paulo* (Matodentro, Natterer collection). Ihering, 1894, *Cat. Mamm. São Paulo*, p. 30—BRAZIL: *São Paulo*. Yepes, 1938, *Gaea* 6:52—not certainly known from Argentina. W. C. Osman Hill, 1957, *Primates* 3:105, 120, 213, 239, 251, 286, 295, 297—characters; comparisons; habits; distribution; taxonomy.

[?] *Hapale aurita*, Ruschi, 1964, *Bol. Mus. Biol. "Prof. Mello Leitao"* 23A:7—Brazil: *Espírito Santo* (coast from Aracruz to Marataizes).

Callithrix aurita, Elliot, 1913, *A review of the Primates* 1:225—characters ex type. Pohle, 1927, *Abh. Senckenb. Naturf. Ges.* 40:247—BRAZIL: *Rio de Janeiro* (Therezópolis). Schirch, 1932, *Bol. Mus. Nac. Rio de Janeiro* 8:78—BRAZIL: *Rio de Janeiro* (Serra dos Orgãos, Therezópolis). Vieira, 1944, Papeis Avulsos, São Paulo, 4 (1):7—BRAZIL: *São Paulo* (Itatiba; São João; Ubatuba); *Rio de Janeiro; "Parana* [!];" type locality restricted to Rio de Janeiro. Waddell and Taylor, 1945, *Amer. J. Trop. Med.* 25:225—BRAZIL: *Rio de Janeiro* (purchased from trapper at Guaratiba); experimental reservoir of yellow fever virus. Krieg, 1948, *Zwischen Anden und Atlantik,* p. 472, text, not fig. p. 473 (animal)—BRAZIL: *São Paulo* (Serra do Mar; São Paulo). Moojen, 1950, *Rev. Brasil. Biol., Rio de Janeiro* 10:501—BRAZIL: *Minas Gerais* (Silveira Lobos designated type locality; Agua Limpa, Além Paraíba); characters; *Hapale petronius* Miranda Ribeiro, a synonym.

Callithrix aurita aurita, Vieira, 1955, *Arq. Zool., São Paulo* 8:392—BRAZIL: *Minas Gerais* (southeastern part); *Rio de Janeiro* (low-lying localities); *Hapale petronius* Miranda Ribeiro, a synonym. Avila-Pires, 1969, *Rev. Brasil. Biol.* 29(1):55—BRAZIL: *Minas Gerais* (Silveira Lôbo; Água Limpa, Além Paraíba; Vargem Grande; Mar de Espanha); *Rio de Janeiro* (Ponto des Flores); characters; distribution.

C[allithrix] a[urita] aurita, Coimbra-Filho, 1971, *Rev. Brasil. Biol.* 31(3):378, fig. 21 (prepared skin)—BRAZIL: distribution; comparisons.

C[allithrix] aurita aurita, Coimbra-Filho and Mittermeier, 1974, *Folia Primat.* 20 (1973):243, 259, fig. 6A (prepared skin)—BRAZIL: distribution.

[Callithrix jacchus] aurita, Hershkovitz, 1968, *Evolution* 22(3):567, 569, fig. 10 (distribution), fig. 12 (geographic metachromism)—color pattern; comparisons; geographic metachromism.

Callithrix jacchus aurita, Hershkovitz, 1970, *Amer. J. Phys. Anthrop.* 32(3):379—supernumerary upper third molar.

[Hapale leucotis] Variété A, Lesson, 1840, *Species de mammiféres: Bimanes et quadrumanes . . . ,* p. 186—*Jacchus auritus* E. Geoffroy regarded as a variety of *leucotis* (new name for *jacchus*); characters.

Hapale caelestis Miranda Ribeiro, 1924, *Bol. Mus. Nac. Rio de Janeiro* 5:212, 214—BRAZIL: Rio de Janeiro (type locality, Therezopolis, Serra dos Orgãos, near Dedo de Deus); 3 cotypes in Museu Nacional de Rio de Janeiro, collected by A. Miranda Ribeiro. Miranda Ribeiro, 1955, *Arq. Mus. Nac., Rio de Janeiro* 42:414—Lectotype, no. 2825; cotypes [= syntypes], nos. 2822, 2815. Avila Pires, 1968, *Arq. Mus. Nac. Rio de Janeiro* 53:171—holotype, a skin and skull; syntypes from type locality, no. 2815 and 2822 collected by Schirch.

C[allithrix] aurita caelestis, Moojen, 1950, *Rev. Brasil. Biol., Rio de Janeiro* 10:502 (in text)—BRAZIL: *Rio de Janeiro* (Teresópolis; Pedra Branca [Paratí]; Itatiaya; Bem Posta; Porto das Flores; Rio Preto); characters.

Callithrix aurita caelestis, Vieira, 1955, *Arq. Zool., São Paulo,* 8:392—BRAZIL: *São Paulo* (Itatiba; Alto da Serra; Ubatuba). Carvalho, 1966, *Rev. Biol. Trop.* 13(2):239—BRAZIL: *São Paulo* (Boraceia Biological Station).

Callithrix aurita coelestis [*sic*], Cabrera, 1958, *Rev. Mus. Argentino Cienc. Nat.* "Bernardino Rivadavia" 4:186—classification. Avila Pires, 1969, *Rev. Biol. Bras.* 29(1):55—BRAZIL: *Rio de Janeiro* (Teresópolis; Bem Posta; Paratí; Itatiaia; "Santa Rita da Floresta"); *São Paulo* (Sertâo do Taquará; Serra do Bocaina; Itatiba; Cantareira; Ubatuba); characters; distribution.

C[allithrix] a[urita] coelestis [*sic*], Coimbra-Filho, 1971, *Rev. Bras. Biol.* 37(3):373, fig. 2 (prepared skin)—BRAZIL: distribution.

C[allithrix] aurita coelestis [*sic*], Coimbra-Filho and Mittermeier, 1974, *Folia Primat.* 20 (1973):241, 259, fig. 6B (prepared skin)—BRAZIL: characters; distribution.

H[apale] coelestis [*sic*], Osman Hill, 1957, *Primates* 3:298—a synonym of *aurita.*

Hapale petronius Miranda Ribeiro, 1924, *Bol. Mus. Nac. Rio de Janeiro* 5:213—BRAZIL: *Minas Gerais* (type locality, Silveira Lobos); 2 cotypes in Museu Nacional, Rio de Janeiro, collected 1922, by Pedro Pinto Peixoto Velho. Miranda Ribeiro, 1955, *Arq. Mus. Nac., Rio de Janeiro* 42:414—lectotype no. 2824; syntype no. 2816. Osman Hill, 1957, *Primates* 3:251, 286, 298—characters ex original description; distribution; possibly merely an extreme melanistic form of *aurita.* Avila Pires, 1968, *Arq. Mus. Nac., Rio de Janeiro* 53:171—holotype a skin and skull.

Hapale caelestis itatiayae Avila Pires, 1959, *Atas Soc. Biol. Rio de Janeiro* 3(4):3—BRAZIL: *Rio de Janeiro* (type locality, Serra de Itatiaia); type, male, skin, Museu Nacional, Rio de Janeiro, no. 2828, collected by Rudolf Pfrimer; validation of a manuscript name attributed to Miranda Ribeiro and regarded as synonymous with *Callithrix caelestis* Miranda Ribeiro. Avila Pires, 1968, *Arq. Mus. Nac., Rio de Janeiro* 53:171—holotype a skin and skull; syntypes, no. 2818, 2819, from type locality, collected by Rudolf Pfrimer.

Hapale chrysopyga, Burmeister (not Mikan), 1854, *Syst. Uebers. Thiere Brasil.* 1:35—BRAZIL: *Rio de Janeiro* (Serra da Macahé); characters of young individual.

Hapale flaviceps, Vieira (not Thomas), 1955, *Arq. Zool., São Paulo* 8:393—BRAZIL: Rio de Janeiro (Serra de Macahé).

[?]*Callithrix flaviceps,* Avila Pires (part, not Thomas), 1969, *Rev. Biol. Brasil.* 29(1):56—part, specimen from Serra de Macaé only.

Type. Skin mounted with skull in Muséum National d'Histoire Naturelle, Paris, no. 615(587); possibly collected by Alexandre Rodrigues Ferreira during his scientific expedition in Brazil, 1783–92; originally deposited in the Muséum Royal d'Ajuda, Lisbon, Portugal; acquired in 1808 by the Paris Museum during the Napoleonic wars.

Type Locality. Brazil, restricted to the vicinity of Rio de Janeiro, Guanabara (332), by Vieira (1944, p. 17). The type locality was redetermined as Silviera Lôbo, Minas Gerais (317) by Moojen (1950, p. 501) on the basis of his identification of a specimen from that locality as typical. The Rio de Janeiro ouistitis were then assigned to *"Callithrix aurita caelestis"* Miranda Ribeiro. It seems, however, that Moojen's concept of *aurita* Geoffroy is based on a rigidly literal interpretation of the brief original diagnosis of the type specimen as being blackish. It now appears that Rio de Janeiro ouistitis are indeed typical whereas the Silveira Lôbo *aurita* is an extremely dark representative of the same form.

Distribution (figs. IX.5, 6). Southeastern Brazil from the Rio Paraíba, northern Rio de Janeiro (or possibly from the southern coast of Espírito Santo), and the Rio Muriaé in bordering Minas Gerais, south through Rio de Janeiro, São Paulo, and lowlands of extreme eastern Minas Gerais to the Rio Ribeira de Iguapé and west between the Rios Tietê and Paranapanema. Avila Pires (1969, p. 55) gives the distribution of his *"Callithrix aurita aurita"* as the woods of low height in southeastern Minas Gerais; and that of *"Callithrix aurita coelestis"* as the highest altitudes in the State of Rio de Janeiro, and the coastal ranges and lowlands in the State of São Paulo.

Callithrix jacchus aurita and *Leontopithecus rosalia chrysopygus* are the southernmost-ranging callitrichids. *Callithrix jacchus jacchus* was introduced into parts of Guanabara and Rio de Janeiro but there is no evidence of contact with *C. j. aurita.* Perhaps the former confines itself to the lowlands, and the latter to the highlands, at least in localities where both occur.

Taxonomy. The original description of *aurita* E. Geoffroy (1812, p. 119) is terse but unequivocably diagnostic. It reads, translated from the French. "Pelage black, tail annulated with black and gray; white spot on forehead; inside of ears covered with very long white hairs." More detailed descriptions of the type specimen were provided later by Desmarest (1820, p. 93) and by I. Geoffroy (1827, p. 518).

A specimen from Brazil, without precise locality, donated to the Munich museum by the Duke of Leuchtenberg, is poorly delineated in color and described by Wagner (1840, p. 244, pl. 33C), as follows, freely translated from the German:

> Differs from the preceding [i.e., *Hapale leucocephalus* (= *C. jacchus geoffroyi*)] by the pale yellowish-white tuft extending across the whole length of the inner side of the ear instead of arising from in front or behind. Color of individual hairs [of body] is shiny black and white with one or two narrow rusty red or rusty yellow bands which appear as an ochraceous wash on black back and outer sides of limbs and as a yellowish wash on nape; middle of crown with a yellowish longitudinal band; the backwardly directed cheek hairs, throat, underside of neck, chest, rump, legs, and an elongate patch on forearm, black; eyes black; upper surface of hands and feet black mixed with rusty red; a three-cornered patch on forehead; face and chin thickly covered with short yellowish white hairs sharply defined from black cheeks; tail black with yellowish or rusty gray bands.

Later, Wagner (1848, p. 465) supplemented this characterization with information on the color of the exposed parts of a male collected by Johann Natterer at Matodentro, São Paulo (346), the first precise locality record for *aurita.* He states, translated from the German: "Iris pale yellowish brown; skin around eyes reddish gray, the eyelids flesh-colored; palms and soles very pale grayish brown; scrotum large, bluish white with a number of flesh-colored papillae, area surrounding penis flesh-colored."

A mounted specimen in the Leiden museum collected by Natterer in the "capitainie de São Paulo," most certainly in Matodentro, the only locality mentioned by Pelzeln (1883, p. 21) was undoubtedly examined by Wagner (vide supra). It agrees with the type specimen in the Paris museum. Three additional specimens of *aurita* without data are preserved in the Leiden museum.

Hapale caelestis Miranda Ribeiro, 1924, from Teresopolis (333), described at the same time as *petronius* (see following), is less black, with more ochraceous. According to Moojen (1950) *caelestis* grades into *aurita* (as represented by *petronius*) but might be recognized as a race of the highlands of Rio de Janeiro and lower altitudes of neighboring parts of São Paulo and possibly Minas Gerais. His redescription of *caelestis* follows, translated from the Portuguese: "Median ventral surface entirely black, internal aspect of hind legs and sides of head yellowish; face, forehead and tufts inside ears yellowish white; band extending across crown to nape varying from ferrugineous yellow in front to brown and black behind; middle zone of hairs of upper surface of body and outer sides of arms and legs black with two broad ochraceous bands, imparting a dominantly blackish-ochraceous aspect to the animal; mantle nearly black, the ochraceous banding of hairs extremely reduced; upper surface of hands and feet mixed black and ochraceous; tail with alternating black and yellowish gray bands. A young individual from Porto das Flores, Rio Preto [Rio de Janeiro] (328), is dominantly blackish on dorsal surface and lacks the median ochraceous band of the head." Nothing in this description indicates a significant difference from the type of *aurita* E. Geoffroy.

Hapale petronius Miranda Ribeiro, 1924, from Silveira Lôbo (317) was described as a melanistic marmoset with auricular tufts white terminally and black basally, but altogether much like *aurita* E. Geoffroy with which it was not compared. Moojen (1950, p. 501) agreed. His description of three cotypes, translated from Portuguese, follows: "Upper and lower surfaces of body black; face, forehead, and internal tuft of ears yellowish white; hands and feet mixed with black, buffy and reddish; tail annulated with alternating black and grayish buffy bands." Moojen also notes that the subterminal bands of some hairs of the back of the paralectotype and the crown of a specimen from Além Paraiba are ochraceous as in *caelestis*.

Moojen's (1950) relocation of the type locality of *aurita* E. Geoffroy to Silveira Lôbo in Minas Gerais involved invalidation of the name *petronius* Miranda Ribeiro and revival of *caelestis* for marmosets natural to Rio de Janeiro. Reinstatement of Rio de Janeiro as type locality of *aurita*, however, sinks *caelestis*, and revives *petronius* as the name for marmosets of extreme southeastern Minas Gerais. In any case, I find nothing in specimens examined or in published descriptions of *petronius* or *caelestis* that warrants separation of either from *aurita*.

The name *Hapale caelestis itatiayae* Avila Pires, 1959, is based on a skin so labeled in the type collection of the National Museum of Rio de Janeiro. In revealing that *itatiayae* was only a manuscript name, Avila Pires (1959, p. 2) took pains to describe the specimen as prodominantly black on dorsal surface and hind legs but not taxonomically distinguishable from *Hapale caelestis* Miranda Ribeiro (= *Callithrix jacchus aurita*). Avila Pires includes the history and museum catalog number of the "type" in the description, thus inadvertently adding another name to the list of synonyms of *aurita*.

Marmosets identified as *Hapale aurita* by Ruschi (1964, p. 7) are said to have been seen in the coastal mangrove swamps, forests, and bordering second growths from Aracruz (320b) to Marataizes (325b). In the absence of specimens, they may not be certainly identifiable as *aurita*. *C. j. geoffroyi* has been recorded from southeastern Espírito Santo, and Ruschi claims that *penicillata* also occurs there. His description and external measurements of "an adult male" of *aurita* agree with those published by Vieira (1944, p. 7) based on São Paulo specimens.

Diagnostic Characters. Hairs of inner (lateral) surface of pinna forming a whitish or buffy salient tuft; pre- and supraauricular tufts comparatively poorly defined; forehead ochraceous to whitish, median anterior portion of crown tawny to pale buff; sides of face and temples black (figs. IX.7, 24).

Coloration. Exposed facial skin more or less pigmented; hairs of face, chin, interramia and forehead white, yellowish, or buffy; cheeks, sides of head black; crown in front buffy to ochraceous becoming tawny on vertex, nape modified agouti, dark brown or blackish; circumauricular tufts blackish, tufts of inner (lateral) surface of pinna whitish to yellowish or golden, the hairs often partially black, some entirely black; mantle like nape or well-defined brown or blackish; back behind shoulders striated as in *jacchus* and more or less overlaid with black guard hairs, the banding poorly or not defined, the orange or tawny subterminal ring of hairs showing through or concealed; upper surface of hands and feet mixed black and ochraceous or gray; underparts entirely black to ochracaeous with middle of belly and posterior portion of chest blackish, tail essentially as in *jacchus*.

Young. Several young are described by Desmarest (1820, p. 93) as follows (freely translated from French). "Rather uniformly dark brown throughout, the hairs dark brown with pale tips; a small yellow patch present at root of nose; tail faintly annulated; crown varying from brown darker than body to tawny gold mixed with black." Pelzeln (1883, p. 22) notes that frontal blaze and ear tufts are absent in young.

Measurements. See Appendix table 2.

Comparisons. Distinguished from *jacchus, penicillata,* and *geoffroyi* by the buffy, salient intraauricular tufts; from *jacchus and flaviceps* by the black sides of face, temples, and black circumauricular tufts (fig. IX.7).

Remarks. Three specimens of *Callithrix jacchus* in the Museum of Comparative Zoology, Harvard University, are labeled "Brazil, Santa Rita, collector Geo. Sceva, Thayer Exp." There is no more information. The original collector's tags, if any, had been replaced by conventional museum tags. One of the specimens, a skull only (MCZ 440) is in fair condition but cannot be identified beyond *Callithrix jacchus*. The second specimen, a skin with skull (MCZ 1824), had been mounted before being prepared as a study skin with skull separate. The skin agrees with those of individuals from the upper Rio São Francisco region heretofore assigned to *jordani* but now regarded as inseparable from *penicillata*. The third specimen (MCZ 1433) was also converted from a mount into a study skin with skull separate. Externally, it nearly resembles such saturate forms as the holotype of *Callithrix jacchus aurita* and a specimen at hand from Itatiba, São Paulo (345) (MCZ 37822).

Judging by their character, it seems certain that neither the skin here identified as *penicillata* nor the one assigned to *aurita* originated in Santa Rita. George Sceva, the collector, was one of several assistants who accompanied Professor Louis Agassiz on his famous geological and ichthyological explorations of Brazil during the years 1865–66. Their itinerary is given by Agassiz (1868, pp. 533–34) in the appendix to his *A journey to Brazil.* Sceva operated in Lagoa Santa, Minas Gerais (313), where he collected "numerous carefully prepared specimens of Brazilian mammalia, which now await mounting in the Museum [of Comparative Zoology, Harvard]. On leaving Lagôa Sancta, Mr. Sceva returned to Rio de Janeiro, taking his collection with him. He paused some days there, in order to repack and put in safety his own specimens as well as those which had been sent back to Rio by other members of the party. He then proceeded to Canta-Gallo, and passed the remainder of the time in collecting and preparing specimens from that part of the country, until he joined me subsequently at Rio just before we returned to the United States" (Agassiz 1868, pp. 534).

Sceva could have collected the specimen of *Callithrix jacchus penicillata* in the Lagoa Santa area, and the specimen of *C. j. aurita* in Rio de Janeiro, perhaps at Canta-Gallo (Cantagalo) (21° 58′ S, 42° 22′ W). There is another Cantagalo (22° 37′ S, 45° 42′ W) in São Paulo, not far from Rio, and within the range of *aurita*.

The locality, Santa Rita (now called Santa Rita de

Cássia, also Ibipetuba, 11° S, 44° 32″ W) on the north bank of the Rio Priêto in the Rio Grande-Rio São Francisco basin, southwestern Bahia, was visited by Orestes St. John, another member of Agassiz's party. According to Agassiz (1868, p. 536), he and Joel A. Allen left Sceva in Lagôa Santa and traveled down the Rio São Francisco to Januária (310). Allen, whose health was failing, struck out for himself to return to the coast with the collections, mostly fish. St. John followed the São Francisco to Villa do Barra, thence to Villa de Santa Rita. Nothing is said of St. John's sojourn there, but the traveler continued on to Belém de Pará, collecting fish, reptiles, birds, and insects along the way.

In his taxonomic review of Brazilian callitrichids Avila Pires (1969) indicated that he had examined the Sceva specimens in the Harvard Museum. For no apparent reason, however, he translated the "Santa Rita" of their labels into Santa Rita de la Floresta (327), a locality in the State of Rio de Janeiro. *"Callithrix penicillata jordani,"* to which Avila Pires assigned one specimen, does not range into Rio de Janeiro, and so far as known, only the pale or *caelestis* form of *aurita,* not the present saturate form, occurs in the Santa Rita de la Floresta region. Other marmosets collected in the Santa Rita (de Cássia) of Bahia State and preserved in the São Paulo museum were identified by Avila Pires (1969, p. 59) as *Callithrix jacchus jacchus.*

Vieira (1944, p. 7) includes the State of Paraná in the range of *aurita* but offers no evidence for this distribution. The Natterer locality, Porto do Rio Paraná (341) (= Rio Grande, see Gazetteer), in São Paulo, is the only "Paraná" that pertains to the known range of *aurita.*

Live ouistitis in North American and European zoos, laboratories, compounds, and pet shops labeled *aurita* are more apt to be *C. j. jacchus.* Until recent years nearly all ouistitis purchased from dealers in Rio de Janeiro were transported from southern Bahia. Free-living individual *jacchus* are now widespread in Guanabara and adjacent parts of Rio de Janeiro.

The animal figured by Krieg (1948, fig. 473) as *"Callithrix aurita"* appears to be a displaced *Callithrix jacchus jacchus.* It was alive and kept as a pet in the town of São Paulo.

Specimens Examined. 9. BRAZIL. *São Paulo:* Itatiba, 1 (MCZ); "Capitanie São Paulo", 1 (RMNH); *Rio de Janeiro:* Campinas, 1 (UIMNH); *unknown locality,* 6 (RMNH, 3; BM, 1; MCZ 1; MNHN, type of *aurita*).

CALLITHRIX JACCHUS FLAVICEPS THOMAS: BUFFY-HEADED MARMOSET

Fig. IX.25. Buffy-headed Marmoset, *Callithrix jacchus flaviceps* Thomas, an excessively fat captive individual. (Photo courtesy of A. F. Coimbra-Filho.)

Synonymic History

Hapale flaviceps Thomas, 1903, *Ann. Mag. Nat. Hist.*, ser. 7, 12:240. Osman Hill, 1957, *Primates* 3:162, 251, 286, 289, fig. 30 (intestine, probably not of *flaviceps* as labeled), fig. 61 (map, distribution), pl. 23 (immature animal [probably not *"Hapale flaviceps"* as labeled])—part, ex original description. Ruschi, 1964, *Bol. Mus. Biol. "Prof. Mello Leitão"* 23A:5—part, BRAZIL: *Espírito Santo* (Alegre; Guaçui; Alfredo Chavez; Calçado; Cachoeiro do Itapemirim; Domingos Martins; Ibiraçu; Santa Teresa; Santa Leopoldinha); characters; food.

Callithrix flaviceps, Elliot, 1913, *Review of the Primates* 1:229—characters ex type. Jones, 1960, *Primate Lab., Newsl.* 1(3):8—longevity, 2 years, 5 months (London Zoo). Avila Pires, 1969, *Rev. Brasil. Biol.* 29(1):—part, Brazil: *Espírito Santo* (Santa Tereza, altitude 700–800 meters).

H[*apale*] *flavescente* [*sic*], Miranda Ribeiro, 1924, *Bol. Mus. Nac. Rio de Janeiro* 5:214—misspelling of *flaviceps* Thomas used in comparisons with *caelestis* Miranda Ribeiro.

Hapale fraviceps [*sic*], Ruschi, 1964, *Bol. Mus. Biol. "Prof. Mello Leito"* 23A:5—misprint for *flaviceps,* in key.

Callithrix jacchus flaviceps, Hershkovitz, 1968, *Evolution* 22(3):569, fig. 10 (distribution), fig. 12 (geographic metachromism)—color pattern; comparisons; geographic metachromism. Hershkovitz, 1970, *Amer. J. Phys. Anthrop.* 32(3):379—dental diseases.

Hapale aurita, Ruschi (not E. Geoffroy), 1965, *Bol. Mus. Biol. "Prof. Mello-Leitao"* 24A:15—BRAZIL: *Espírito Santo* (Domingos Martins; Castellinho).

C[allithrix] flaviceps ♂ × *C[allithrix] geoffroyi* ♀, Coimbra Filho, 1973, *Rev. Brasil. Biol.* 33 (1):33, fig. 3 (father with hybrid twins—BRAZIL: *Espírito Santo* (Santa Teresa): hybridization of wild male with captive female.

Type. Female, skin and skull, British Museum (Natural History) no. 3.9.4.27; collected 11 February 1903 by Alphonse Robert.

Type Locality. Engenheiro Reeve (now Rive [325c]), municipality of Alegre, southwestern Espírito Santo, eastern Brazil; altitude, 500 meters.

Distribution. Highlands of southern Espírito Santo and possibly adjacent parts of Rio de Janeiro and Minas Gerais where intergradation with *aurita* may occur (figs. IX.5, 6).

Diagnostic Characters. Hairs of inner (lateral) surface of pinna forming a salient ochraceous tuft; entire crown, sides of face, temples, and circumauricular pelage thick and dominantly ochraceous.

Coloration. Exposed parts of facial skin well pigmented; forehead and interorbital region pale buff bordered inferiorly with orange, patch beneath eye pale buff, circumbuccal and gular hairs golden, the interramals paler; hairs of side of face and temples forming a thick ochraceous brush, the individual hairs black at roots; crown dominantly ochraceous, the hairs blackish at roots, pale buff subterminally and tipped with dark brown; nape like crown but with basal black more extensive and pale subterminal bands of hairs wider; pinna pigmented, outer (medial) surface thinly covered with hair, inner (lateral) nearly entirely clothed with long projecting tuft, the hairs uniformly ochraceous or with blackish base; elongate, subauricular pelage similar; back a grizzled modified agouti with transverse striations poorly defined anteriorly, better defined posteriorly, the hairs black basally and successively banded orange, black, and buffy with tip black; juxtaposition of the broad orange suprabasal band with succeeding black band defines the transverse dorsal striations; outer surface of thighs like lower back, of arms like shoulders; upper surface of hands and feet ochraceous mixed with yellow, silvery, and black; sides of body and lateral fringe like back with banding of hairs well defined; throat and neck buffy to ochraceous, with blackish base of hairs showing through, median band of chest belly and perineal region black, remainder of underparts yellowish to orange with black bases of hairs showing through; tail distinctly banded.

Measurements. See appendix, table 2.

Comparisons. Distinguished from all members of the *jacchus* group except *aurita* by the salient ochraceous tufts of inner (lateral) surface of pinna, preauricular tufts not salient, circumauricular pelage yellowish or ochraceous, not white as in *jacchus* or black as in *geoffroyi;* from *aurita* by sides of face, throat, temples, and circumauricular region yellowish to ochraceous or orange, not black (fig. IX.7, 25); from all lowland forms by longer, thicker pelage.

Remarks: A skin from Campinas (335), Rio de Janeiro, assigned here to *aurita* as an extremely pale representative of that race, could just as well be treated as a dark individual of *flaviceps* but for its geographic position. However, too little is known of geographic variation and nothing of seasonal changes of pelage with corresponding color changes, if any.

A specimen from Serra de Macaé (336) in the Rio de Janeiro Museum examined by Avila Pires (1969, p. 56) may be intermediate between *aurita* and typical representatives of *flaviceps.*

Coimbra-Filho and Mittermeier (1974, p. 249) assert that there is an altitudinal overlap in the Santa Teresa region (Reserva Biologica de Nova Lombardia) between the ranges of *flaviceps* (700 m upward but occasionally to 400–500 m) and *geoffroyi* (sea level to 600–700 m above, sometimes to 800 m).

The authors do not disclose the source of the geographic data and give no indication that they actually examined Santa Teresa (320b) specimens of *geoffroyi* and *flaviceps,* or that they themselves determined or investigated the zonal distribution of the forms in question. It appears, nevertheless, that the altitudes they give for *flaviceps* may have been taken from Thomas (1904, who gives 500 meters as the altitude of Engenheiro Reeve (325c), type locality of *flaviceps*); Ruschi (1964, p. 5, "altitudes superiores a 500 metros"), and Avila-Pires (1969, p. 57, "Santa Tereza 700 a 800 metros de altitude"). The 400-meter figure found in Coimbra-Filho (1971, p. 378, "altitudes superiores a 400 metros") may be a modification of Ruschi's estimate. The source of the altitudinal range given for *geoffroyi* eludes me. The altitude of Santa Teresa itself is 659 meters.

In the present case a clear distinction must be made between altitudinal overlap and sympatry. Seasonal movements to lower elevations in winter and higher in summer can occur without temporal overlap in range. Catastrophic alterations of habitat usually precipitate local adjustments in altitudinal range without overlap in ecological habitat. Also, considerable altitudinal but not spatial overlap often occurs on mountain slopes where only one of the two forms finds shelter. Any kind of interdigitation between the ranges of adjacent forms is not spatial overlap or sympatry. There is no reason to believe however, that *geoffroyi* and *flaviceps* may not interbreed where their ranges meet.

Specimens identified as *geoffroyi, flaviceps,* and *penicillata* labeled Santa Teresa are preserved in the National Museum in Rio de Janeiro. The *flaviceps,* according to Avila-Pires (1969, p. 57) is a juvenal[1] described as "yellowish chestnut with an olivaceous wash, head yellowish with frontal patch white." The Santa Teresa *penicillata,* age not given, is particularly distinguished by Avila-Pires (1969, p. 60) as having the entire "dorsal surface including mantle and crown, finely punctulated black and white." Natural occurrence of *penicillata* in the Santa Teresa area cannot be explained on the basis of current knowledge of distribution. Description of the skin, however, suggests a hybrid *geoffroyi* × *flaviceps.*

Coimbra-Filho and Mittermeier (1974, p. 249) further

[1] The living juvenal of the London Zoological Society described, figured, and captioned *flaviceps* by Osman Hill (1957, p. 290, pl. 23), is said to have matured into a form that seemed "to be affined to *H[apale] jacchus* rather than to *H. penicillata.*" The young animal could be referrable to either of these two, judging by its photograph. It is definitely not *flaviceps.*

claim that "*C. flaviceps* and *C. geoffroyi* are sympatric near the town of Santa Leopoldinha (322) in Espírito Santo. Twenty years ago *C. flaviceps* was more common, but now *C. geoffroyi* has apparently taken over. This changeover may have resulted from human-induced changes favoring one species over another." A record of the occurrence of *flaviceps* in Santa Leopoldinha was published ten years ago by Ruschi (1964), but I find no documentation of sympatry with *geoffroyi,* and Coimbra-Filho and Mittermeier give none. In any event, Santa Teresa (320b) and Santa Leopoldinha (322) are in the same general region. There is every reason to believe that the altitudinal relationships noted in the first locality obtained in the second before alteration of the ecology.

In 1964, Ruschi recorded *flaviceps* from Domingos Martin (322) and other localities plotted in figure IX.6. A year later, in a formal list of the mammals of Espírito Santo, Ruschi (1965, p. 15) reported *aurita* but not *flaviceps* from Domingos Martins and "Castellinho" (not located). Particulars are wanting and it cannot be established now if the Domingos Martins marmoset called *flaviceps* in 1964 was redetermined as *aurita* in 1965.

Augusto Ruschi, evidently Coimbra-Filho and Mittermeier's principal source of information on the distribution of Espírito Santo marmosets, was associated for many years with the Museu de Biologia "Prof. Mello-Leitão" in Santa Teresa. His fieldwork resulted in the publication of a monograph of the birds in 1951 and a series of papers on the bats in 1954. The 1964 opus on monkeys is said to be based on personal observations, specimens he collected, others he examined in the larger Brazilian museums, and the reviews published by Osman Hill. His key to Espírito Santo callitrichids is confused, its miscouplings and mischaracterizations derived from Osman Hill (1957, p. 286). The descriptions and measurements for each taxon, ostensibly based on a cataloged specimen before him, appear to have been copied or paraphrased from secondary sources, mainly Vieira (1944) and Osman Hill 1957), with the usual compounding of errors of transcription and typography. Some descriptions and measurements of single specimens read like composites of descriptions and measurements taken from two or more publications. Geographic ranges are given in broad terms, but specific distributional records, unless based on literature, mainly Vieira (1955, p. 344), and specimens in the Rio de Janeiro museum (cf. Avila Pires 1969), are presumed to be anecdotal.

Ruschi's vague concepts of platyrrhine taxonomy and destribution reflect the state of knowledge at the time when Osman Hill's monographs (1957, 1960, 1962) were the principal guides. Ruschi could classify and record two or three subspecies of the same species from the same general area in Espírito Santo with his home base in Santa Teresa usually specified. Included were living animals brought from distant places and housed in the museum surroundings in Santa Teresa (cf. p. 531). Shorn of secondary information acknowledged in the bibliography (1964, p. 20), little of the taxonomy or zoogeography that remains in Ruschi's paper is substantive or can be accepted without reservation. Ruschi had no illusion about the quality of his report, and he expressed a hope to expand and revise it later.

Specimens Examined. 3 BRAZIL. *Espírito Santo:* Engenheiro Reeve, 3 (including the type (BM).

53 *Callithrix jacchus*
2. *Biology of the Tufted-ear Marmoset or Ouistiti*

REPRODUCTION

The subject matter in the reports by authors cited below is organized into running accounts under the following subtitles:

Early History	Pregnancy and Parturition
Estrus, Courtship, and Mating	Breeding Seasons
Masturbation	Breeding in Captivity
Homosexuality	Litters
Duration of Gestation	Hybridization

Early History

The common marmoset was introduced into Europe as a household pet from the first decades of the discovery and exploration of Brazil. It may have been bred in captivity during the sixteenth or seventeenth centuries, but the earliest notice I find is in Edward's *Gleanings,* published in 1758 (p. 17). Mr. Edwards, it seems, examined a live *Callithrix jacchus* "at Mr. John Cook's merchant, in London." He adds the information that "Mr. Cook had formerly resided at Lisbon where his lady, for her amusement tried to breed the Sanglin, as they called the little creature, and succeeded so well to produce young ones, the climate being proper for it."

Successful breedings have also been recorded from other European countries in the same century. M. Siret (1778, p. 453) provides the account of a pair bred in France by the Marquis de Néelle, and Pallas (1781, p. 41) chronicles the activities of a breeding colony that thrived in the stark climate of old St. Petersburg in Russia.

Estrus, Courtship, and Mating

Epple 1970*a*, p. 64

"Significant signs of estrus such as conspicuous swellings comparable to the sexual swelling of some old world primates" were not found. There appeared, however, "a slight swelling in *Callithrix jacchus* and *Saguinus geoffroyi* ♀♀ during times of increased sexual activity, but this was too inconspicuous to derive any evidence [of estrus] from it. Reichenbach's [1862] report of menstrual bleeding in *Callithrix jacchus* is unconfirmed."[1]

"The best indication that a female might be in estrus is courtship and mating . . . high sexual activity follows delivery closely. As soon as three days after parturition the male becomes sexually interested in the female. Usually, the female first rejects him but gradually becomes more attentive to the male. First copulations were observed 7–10 days after parturition. A period of increased sexual activity follows, and for about 10 days copulations are observed frequently. After this period sexual activity decreases and mating occurs very infrequently but occasionally copulation occurs even during pregnancy. This behavior indicates that in most captive *Callithrix jacchus* there is one post partum estrus between two pregnancies."

Rothe 1975*a*, p. 260

"Matings with sexual play before or after, such as grooming, tongue-play, face-licking, running towards each other, were limited in all groups to the α-animals and were observed only during estrus . . . and almost exclusively during the postpartum estrus . . . of the α-♀."

Poswillo, Hamilton, and Sopher 1972, p. 460

There is no obvious menstrual cycle in the marmoset as occurs in the macaque.

Hearn and Renfree 1975

Marmosets have a clearly defined ovarian cycle of 16.4 ± 1.7 days. The cyclical stage may be determined by the appearance of prealbumins in vaginal flushings.

[1] Reichenbach (1862:3) actually cites Pallas (1781) for the observations that the female spots blood when in heat, is pregnant three months, and produces twins twice yearly. More from Pallas is cited below.

Phillips 1975, p. 295

Daily smears of vaginal cytology suggest an estrous cycle of 13–15 days. In 2 animals, a sperm find coupled with a retrospective dating of pregnancy indicated an estrous period 9–11 days postpartum.

F. Cuvier 1819

"A pair of these animals were mated [in the Jardin des Plantes] toward the end of September 1818 and copulated without delay. The female produced triplets 27 April 1819 but it was not possible to determine the duration of gestation because marmosets continue to copulate almost to the moment of birth."

Epple 1970*a*, p. 59

"It is noteworthy that in all our groups only the dominant females produced offspring, while inferior females remained without young, though copulations with fertile males occurred."

Rothe 1975*a*, p. 259

In 5 captive artificial groups most hererosexual activity observed was between alpha male and alpha female. In the captive family groups B, C, D, Rothe "observed 688, 823, and 242 heterosexual interactions, respectively, exclusively between the [alpha] parents (with the exception of the three intentional mounting attempts by [group] siblings."

Rothe 1973*b*

In each of the 2 established groups, only the dominant female produced offspring. Since their acquisition in 1968, one of the females delivered 10 litters, the other 9.

Mallinson 1971, p. 8

"A male *jacchus* who had been kept with his sister for 7 yr. 1 mo. 9 days and showed no signs of breeding, copulated almost immediately when mixed with another female, and subsequently proved he was virile at 7 yr. 7 mo. 7 da."

Fitzgerald 1935, p. 184

"Before coming into the author's possession a pair of marmosets had lived with a former owner for about 4 years. Their [marmosets'] eldest daughter was born during this period. Throughout the time that the author observed this group the male was continuously devoted to his mate. If the female moved a few inches he would at once follow and place himself alongside of her. At the time no other male was in this group. Later, when the eldest daughter was about three years old she was very large, well developed and apparently quite mature. At no time was the male seen to pay any sexual attention to her. In another cage nearby were now another male and female, full grown, and still the first male courted no one but his mate. In yet another cage were two particularly fine females. They likewise proved to be no attraction to the first male in spite of the fact that he had the run of the room and could easily have made advances to any of these females, had he wanted to. Since the first male's death, two other males in turn have become leaders of this family group. Although both of them had previously made advances to the eldest daughter each restricted his attentions to the mother when he was promoted to leadership."

Rothe 1975*a*

Attempts by a low-ranking adult male of a family group to mount a sister of equal rank were rebuffed by her "screaming, biting, and hitting, at the same time looking towards her mother, the α-♀ of the group."

Observations by Fitzgerald (1935, p. 184) and Mallinson (1971, p. 8) cited above provide additional evidence for the existence of an incest taboo among marmosets even in the absence of a dominant monogamous breeding pair.

Fitzgerald 1935, p. 184

During courtship "marmosets do not examine each other's genital parts nor are they given to any decided public display of sexual emotion. During love-making, long and intense staring accompanies rapid opening and closing of the mouth with frequent moistening of the lips. At such times no sound is uttered. Mating was not seen. Consequently it must have taken place in the sleeping box or during the author's absence" (fig. IX.26).

[The "moistening of the lips" probably refers to the tonguing display during courtship.]

Pallas 1781, p. 45

"Outside of their nest one never saw them commit any sexual act and the males only rarely displayed their sexual organs" (cf. fig. IX.31).

Zukowsky 1940, p. 101

Copulation takes place only during the night. The male covers the back of the female with his whole body. His legs, however, reach to the ground. Immediately after copulation, the female was observed rubbing her genital region on the branches.

Chartin and Petter 1960, p. 154

Copulation is "of short duration and repeated at frequent intervals. It takes place several times a day throughout the year without any external sign of a female genital cycle noted. The most favorable situation for mating occurs when the female is pursued by the male along a vertical support such as a branch or a pipe where it is difficult for her to avoid his attentions."

Fig. IX.26. *Callithrix jacchus jacchus* female marking male companion with circumgenital glands while backing up into him; in lower view, male sniffs female's genitalia. (Photo courtesy of Gisela Epple.)

Lucas, Hume, and Henderson-Smith, 1927, p. 449

Coitus was observed during three successive days, "then attempts became fewer and less acceptable to the female and finally ceased altogether. During the ensuing months there were no signs of oestrum, and when the young male was at liberty he paid no more attention to the female through the bars of the cage, than he did to the other male."

Langford 1963, p. 300

Copulation is not "confined to the hours of darkness. The 'act' lasts only a matter of seconds, but may be repeated several times during the day. There does not appear to be any sexual foreplay in the accepted sense, but both male and female rub their genitals against a convenient object such as a branch or even the ground, and this apparently forms an important part of their sexual behaviour as they may transfer a sexual odour thereby."

Stellar 1960, p. 4

"Copulation is in the quadrupedal position with the male clasping the female with its hands, but not with its feet which remain on the shelf or floor. The whole pattern involves repeated pursuit by the male with both animals vocalizing frequently, and with abortive mountings followed by brief quiet periods typically occupied by grooming; upon intromission, pelvic thrusts are rapid over a brief period, which is then followed by a long period of quiescence usually involving grooming. The nonreceptive female shakes the male quite effectively with her legs, and even abortive mountings are rare, for she may turn and attack the male aggressively; long periods of mutual grooming usually follow such unsuccessful attempts at mating." [fig. IX.32]

Rothe 1975*a*, pp. 260, 264

The majority of copulations consisted of mounting only, and mounting with pelvic thrusts. Subordinate males never continued with intromission and ejaculation. Likewise, copulation with intromission and ejaculation between alpha male and subordinate females in the 5 artificial groups was not observed.

Copulation with or without intromission and ejaculation lasted an average of 10 seconds (range 2–18 s). Pelvic thrusts averaged 7 (4–11).

Copulations were often disrupted by other male or female members of the caged group irrespective of social rank.

Lucas, Hume, and Henderson-Smith 1937, p. 208

Mating by the female is not resumed until 10 to 20 days after parturition. The "female did not appear to be attractive to the male at all times and unwelcome attentions by the male were rare."

Poswillo, Hamilton, and Sopher 1972, p. 460

"In many cases, soon after parturition or hysterotomy, pregnancy has been confirmed often within two to three weeks, indicating that there is certainly a postpartum oestrus."

Pallas 1781, p. 45–46

"The female spots blood when she is in heat."

"When very tame adult females were stroked, they would press their genitalia against the bars of the cage and emit urine . . . which corrupts everything it touches with a foul smell reeking of musk and ambergris." (The "urine" may also refer to secretions of the genitoanal glands.—P. H.)

Coimbra-Filho 1973, p. 33

"A. Ruschi [of the Museu de Biologia "Prof. Mello-Leitao" in Santa Teresa, Espírito Santo] informed me in 1971 of the attraction of a wild-living male *Callithrix flaviceps* to two females of *C. geoffroyi* caged outdoors in a clearing near the forest's edge. The male was captured and lodged with the females. During the mating period, one of the two females, certainly the dominant one, attacked the other so violently that Ruschi was obliged to separate them. Two live births, twins in both cases, were produced from the cross. The young, unfortunately, died in early infancy."

The wild-living male *flaviceps* of Ruschi's account must have responded first to vocalizations of the probably unseen captive females; or perhaps the females initiated the dialogue by responding to random calls of the male. I have often witnessed such vocal exchanges between captive or pet monkeys leashed in natives' patios and their relatives wandering in the surrounding bush. Once within visual range, the male was attracted close enough to the females so they could sniff one another and become sexually stimulated. There is absolutely no reason to assume that mating would not have occurred if the females had been released from the cage on their first encounter with the male. Were such the case, the evidence of hybridization at hand (Coimbra-Filho, 1973, p. 33, fig. 3, male with hybrid twin) might have been lost.

Hershkovitz (Notes)

The courtship I observed in the primate breeding center of the San Diego Zoo was persistently and energetically performed by the female of a caged pair of *Callithrix j. jacchus*. She repeatedly presented to her mate, embraced him, and marked him, the food, perch, shelf, and cage bars with the secretions from her genitalia. The male responded by behaving as if he weren't there. Otherwise, he acted out his presumed role of dominance and asserted his favored relationship to the female by presenting to other males in adjoining cages, and to me as well.

The change in color, tumescence, and secretions of the glandular skin surrounding the genitoanal region of both sexes are outward signs of heat that have not been adequately studied. The anatomy of the area in callitrichids has been examined grossly by Pocock (1920: 107) and microscopically by Wislocki (1930:479) and Perkins (1966, 1968, 1969*a*, 1969*c*) and is discussed elsewhere in this paper (p. 420). The odoriferous secretions are used for marking, identification, and attraction between the sexes. Cyclical variation in their quantity and chemical composition may exist, but information is lacking.

Masturbation

Rothe 1975*a*, p. 258

"Autosexuality such as licking and chewing the penis, repeated rubbing of the genital region against a branch, were observed in the FG [family groups] B, C and D by dominant and sexually mature male offspring. Ejaculation occurred eight times.

"In the FG, B and C, the high ranking sons experienced erections and spontaneous ejaculations during the mother's estrus (52 instances). . . . This occurred frequently (38 instances) after the sons had sampled the mother's marking spots or had licked up drops of her urine. It is possible that the sons' behaviour was stimulated by pheromones and increased release of estrogen in the urine of the estrus α-♀.

"Autosexual activities and spontaneous ejaculations were observed after at least 2 adults, sexually mature ♂♂ were in the FG (approximately 2.5 years after pairing of the parents)."

Homosexuality

Rothe 1975*a*, p. 258

"Homosexual behaviour, such as mounting and pelvic thrusts was shown by older juveniles and subadults ♂♂ (23 instances) in the FG [family groups] B and C. The majority (17 instances) occurred during play (especially during rough play) and in 18 instances the mounter was dominant over his partner. In the majority (16) of homosexual interactions, the mountee was juvenile, that is, not yet fully integrated into the hierarchy of the group.

"In every instance, the mountee attempted to shake off his mounting brother which led four times to a fight, whereby three times the mounter was subordinate to the mountee."

Duration of Gestation (table 61)

The period of gestation was calculated by Lucas, Hume, and Henderson-Smith (1937, p. 208) as approximately 140 days. The shortest actual period they estimated was 138 days, the longest 170 days (table 61). On the same basis Chartin and Petter (1960, p. 154) record periods of 126 and 150 days. In neither of the minimum periods did the offspring appear to be premature or otherwise abnormal. Judged by these minima, the 102-day period recorded by Grüner and Krause (1963, p. 109) is questionable, but the average period of gestation is probably near 140 days.

Langford (1963, p. 300) observed that it is "difficult to ascertain the exact period of gestation in view of there being no physical signs of menstruation." He believed, however, that gestation is about five months in duration "because I mated a pair of marmosets at the beginning of February 1961. Copulation was first observed on the 22nd February and the female gave birth on the 20th July. . . . Although they performed the act on several occasions during March, the female probably conceived during the latter part of February."

Poswillo, Hamilton, and Sopher 1972, p. 460

"The gestation period is between 120 and 140 days."

Data from eleven pregnancies of five adult, wild-caught females evaluated by Epple (1970*a*, p. 65) showed that the "shortest period between two full term deliveries of the same female was 160 days, the longest period 173 days. In another female (♀ K), imported as a late juvenile or young adult, and apparently breeding for the first time in the laboratory, there were 208 and 255 days between full term deliveries. Her daughter, born in captivity, gave birth to her first pair of twins at the age of 16½ months, and in this animal interbirth intervals were 262 and 184 days (D. v. Holst, personal communication). From these data, a gestation period of 140–50 days is derived [?], which is in accordance with Langford (1963) and Lucas et al. (1937)."

Means and extremes of 6 gestation periods given by Mallinson (1969, p. 8) are 136 (117–56 days). Three interbirths given are 144, 155, 159 days.

J. K. Hampton, Jr., Hampton, and Levy (1971, p. 532) mention "an interbirth interval of 148 days after the female was mated."

Mitchel and Jones (1975, p. 53) calculate a gestation period of 135–140 days from their observations of 36 full-term deliveries. Phillips (1975, p. 298) figures 145–55 days on the basis of 59 full-term pregnancies.

The shortest interbirth intervals from the different sources shown in table 61 are 126, 138, 142, 148, and 160. It may be reasonable to assume that the actual duration of gestation ranges within or between 126 and 160 days or, more likely, between 138 and 148 days.

Rothe 1975*a*, p. 265

Interbirth intervals in days with frequencies in parentheses recorded for 5 females are 150 (2), 151 (3), 152 (5), 153 (7), 154 (2), 155 (3), 156 (1), 160 (1), 163 (1), 184 (1), 190 (1), 267 (1). On the assumption that "conception coincided with the maximal mating frequency, and the day on which the ♀ allows the ♂ to mate and on which copulation with ejaculation is observed to be the beginning of gestation, we have a gestation period of 144–146 days."

Rothe (1975*a*, p. 262) arrives at his estimate of the duration of gestation by this reasoning. "Two to seven days after a birth copulatory activity between the α-♂ and the α-♀ increases, lasting an average of 9–10 days . . . We conclude from the sexual willingness of the α-♀ and the intensive sexual activity of the α-♂ that the ovulation of the α-♀ coincides with the maximum copulatory activity and sexual receptivity, that is, that conception usually occurs during this period."

The wide spread between minimum estimates in the present data suggests a wide range of individual variation, possibly including abnormalities. There is also the possibility that they represent the sum of a number of small differences between natural populations in the wild.

Chemical and physiological tests for detecting pregnancy and following its course are more precise tools for determining the duration of gestation. J. K. Hampton, Jr., Levy, and Sweet (1969) demonstrated that marmosets excrete measurable amounts of gonadotropin during most of gestation. This, it has been reported (Levy, Hampton, and Hampton 1972, p. 54), confirms the previously estimated gestation period of 140–45 days. The same authors acknowledge, however, that gonadotropin may also be excreted by nonpregnant marmosets. It is suspected, in this case that deported residual trophoblastic tissues continue to function in previously pregnant marmosets.

The simpler vaginal mucus spot test (Hardy et al. 1970) was used by Mahoney (1970; 1972) for obtaining dated conceptions within 24 hours of ovulation in *Macaca irus*. Details of the experiments, however, had not been published at the time of this writing.

More recently, Poswillo, Hamilton and Sopher (1972, p. 460) used the human Prepurin agglutination inhibition pregnancy test. They report that using unconcentrated filtered marmoset urine from the 15th day onward "gives a clear, positive result much more reliable and obvious than the same test conducted on concentrated urine of pregnant macaque monkeys." They add that "the Pregnosticon latex pregnancy test does not provide a reliable sign in either species."

Pregnancy detection by abdominal palpation is regarded as most reliable by Phillips (1975, p. 297). He describes uterine variation as follows:

0 days (virgin)—club-shaped, 15 x 4–5 mm
5 days—palpable increase in diameter
15–30 days—more spherical, diameter 6 mm
45 days—uterus softening, diameter 8 mm
70 days—uterus extremely soft, diameter 13 mm
90–100 days—head 8 mm
Preparturition—head 20 mm

Shackleton (1974) finds that the high levels of progesterone and estrogen metabolites excreted by two *Callithrix j. jacchus* in the third trimester of pregnancy were of an order of magnitude comparable to that of man. The plasma sex steroid levels in the marmosets, he reports, are also similar to those of man.

Table 61. Breeding Records of *Callithrix jacchus jacchus* and *C. j. penicillata* in Captivity

Observed Mating	*Birth*	*Estimated Gestation Period*	*Litter*	*Reference*	*Observation*
—	27 Apr. 1819	—	♂ ♀ ♀	Cuvier 1819, p. 1	Parents probably wild born
—	1 Jan. 1835	—	○ ○	Rolle 1835, p. 21	*C. j. penicillata*
—	"about same time as preceding"	—	○ ○	Same as above	*C. jacchus* subsp.?
23/25 March 1926	19/20 Aug. 1926, night	150[b]	♂ ○	Lucas, Hume, and Henderson-Smith, 1927, p. 449	Parents wild born
16 Sept. 1926	4 Feb. 1927, night	142[b]	○ ○	Same as above, 1927, p. 450	Same as above
28 Dec. 1927	11 July 1928, night	—	♀ ♀	Lucas, Hume, and Henderson-Smith, 1937, p. 207.	Parents wild born, Mary Anne and Tittles
8 Oct. 1928	12 March 1929, night	155[c]	♂ ♂	Same as above	Same as above
17/18 June[a] 1929	10 Nov. 1929, night	157[c] 145/6[b]	♂ ♂	Same as above	Same as above
28 Nov.[a] 1929	24 Apr. 1930, night	147[b]	♀	Same as above	Same as above
8 May 1930	23 Nov. 1930, night	138[b]	♀ ♀	Same as above	Same as above
13 Oct. 1930	1 Apr. 1931, night	170[b]	♂ ♀	Same as above	Same as above
—	2 Sept. 1931, night	154[d]	♀	Same as above	Same as above
—	4 Feb. 1932, night	148[d]	♂ ♀	Lucas, Hume, and Henderson-Smith, 1937, p. 207	Parents wild born, Mary Anne and Tittles
—	7 July 1932, night	154[d]	♂ ♀	Same as above	Same as above
—	29 Dec. 1932, night	175[d]	♂ ♀	Same as above	Same as above
—	2 June 1933, night	155[d]	♂ ♂ ♀	Same as above	Same as above
—	19 Nov. 1934, night	535[d]	♂ ♀ ○	Same as above	Same as above
—	—	—	○ ○ ○ ○	Same as above, 1937, p. 210	Parents London born
—	—	—	○ ○ ○	Same as above	Same as above
—	—	—	○ ○ ○	Same as above	Same as above
—	—	—	○ ○ ○ ○	Same as above, 1937, p. 211	Mother wild, father London born
—	10 Aug. 1933, night	—	○ ○	D. Hill in above, 1937, p. 210	Parents London born, Billy and Pip
—	5 Jan. 1934, night	148[d]	♂ ♂	Same as above	Same as above
—	5 June 1934	151[d]	♂ ○ ○	Same as above	Same as above
—	5 Oct. 1934, night	123[d,e]	○ ○ ○	Same as above	Same as above
—	9 March 1935, night	156[d]	♂ ♀	Same as above	Same as above
—	18 Aug. 1927, night	—	♀ ♀	Marik 1931, p. 347	Parents probably wild born
—	3 Aug. 1904	—	○ ○	Stadie 1931	
—	29 May 1892	—	○ ○	Zuckerman 1931, p. 338	*C. j. penicillata*
—	22 March 1832	—	○ ○	Same as above	Same as above
—	6 July 1839	—	○ ○ ○	Same as above	*C. jacchus*
—	14 Sept. 1932, night	—	○ ♀	Fitzgerald 1935 ,p. 181	Parents wild born
—	5 Apr. 1933, night	203[d]	○ ○	Same as above	Same as above

Table 61. *Continued*

Observed Mating	*Birth*	*Estimated Gestation Period*	*Litter*	*Reference*	*Observation*
—	20 Sept. 1933, night	169[d]	○ ○	Same as above	Same as above
—	5 Apr. 1951	—	—	Crandall 1951, p. 182	*C. j. jacchus*
20 Oct. 1956	23 Feb. 1957, 8:00 A.M.	126[b]	♂	Chartin and Petter 1960, p. 153	Parents wild born
—	22 July 1957, night	150[d]	♀	Same as above	Same as above
—	3 May 1958	285[d]	♂ ♀	Same as above	Same as above
14 June 1960	23/24 Sept. 1960, night	102(?)	♀ ♀	Grüner and Krause 1963, p. 108	Parents wild born
—	27 July 1961	306[d]	○ ○	Same as above	Same as above
22 Feb. 1961	20 July 1961	149[b]	○ ○	Langford 1963, p. 300	Bred in South Africa
—	18 Apr. 1962	—	♂ ♀	Epple 1970*a*, p. 62	Mother A
—	6 Aug. 1962	110[d, f]	○ ○	Same as above	Mother A
—	5 June 1963	—	♂ ♀	Same as above	Mother C
—	15 Nov. 1963	163	♀ ♀	Same as above	Mother C
—	7 May 1964	173	?	Same as above	Mother C; young eaten by group
—	9 Nov. 1964	—	♂ ♀	Same as above	Mother J
—	17 Apr. 1965	160	♂ ♀ ○[e]	Same as above	Mother J
—	6 Aug. 1965	111[f]	○	Same as above	Mother J
—	29 Apr. 1965	—	♂ ♀ ♀	Same as above	Mother B
—	9 October 1965	162	♀ ♀ ♀	Same as above	Mother B
—	2 May 1965	—	♂ ♂ ♀	Same as above	Mother N
—	30 Aug. 1965	—	♂ ♀	Same as above	Mother K
—	26 March 1966	208	○ ○	Same as above	Mother K
—	6 Dec. 1966	155	○	Same as above	Mother K
—	11 Jan. 1967	—	♂ ♀	Same as above	Mother Z; born 30 Aug. 1965 (above)
—	30 Sept. 1967	262	♂ ♀	Same as above	Mother Z
—	2 Apr. 1968	184	○	Same as above	Mother Z

[a] Corrected from original, where June and November are accidentally transposed.
[b] Days from first observed mating.
[c] Days from pairing to birth.
[d] Interbirth interval.
[e] Premature.
[f] Abortion.

Pregnancy and Parturition

The placenta is discoidal or bidiscoidal in case of twins (Sawaya 1936, p. 145, fig. 2).

The following case history leading to parturition is given by Lucas, Hume, and Henderson-Smith (1927, pp. 448–49).

16 March—paired with male in cage
23 March—coitus observed
1 April—weight 320 g
15 April—weight 335 g
23 June—weight 405 g
12 July—weight 420 g

"During the last week of July an enlargement of the female breasts was detected and the body was distinctively stouter, but it was impossible to diagnose pregnancy with certainty. Early in August the abdomen became more enlarged and the skin over it became darker-coloured; pregnancy then seemed certain."

19–20 August (night)—twins born.
Period of gestation—150 days.

A female fourteen days before parturition was described by Marik (1931, p. 347) as sleepy and as vomiting several times daily. She refused green food but accepted fish or poultry from the male. The belly was not very much extended and enlargement of the mammae was not observed. She pushed aside a small nesting box in her cage and built a nest of her own with the wood shavings on the floor. Two young were born during the night and Marik found them in the morning on the back of the father. There were a few traces of blood and some remnants of the placenta which the mother had not finished eating.

The 16 parturitions that occurred in Epple's laboratory (1970*a*, pp. 62–63) "took place during the night or early morning hours and [were] never observed."

All births for which the time of day was recorded took place at night, except one. Chartin and Petter (1960, p. 154) report the birth of a male at 8:00 A.M. Delivery lasted one hour. "The female assisted herself using both hands. After licking her young, she subjected him to violent twistings and tuggings before severing the umbilical cord with her teeth. Thereupon the newborn seized hold of his mother's fur and held it fast while the parents

Table 62. History of Five Parturitions by *Callithrix jacchus jacchus* in University of Göttingen Laboratory

	♀ *No. 11*		♀ *No. 12*		♀ *No. 20*[1]
Detail or Stage	*Delivery #9*	*Delivery #10*	*Delivery #8*	*Delivery #9*	*Delivery #9*
Birth date	20 April 1972	Sept. 1972	30 March 1972	30 Aug. 1972	1 July 1968
Birth hour	00:00–03:00	20:30–2:30	20:00–23:00	06:00–07:00	Daylight
Litter young, number	3	3	3	3	1
Interbirth interval, days	152	151	152	153	?
Dilatation, duration, min	15?	75	30?	?	>1
Preliminary labor, contractions	4	3	2	?	>2
Expulsion time, I1, I2, I3, min.	14, 2, 2	17, 2, 5	10, 4, 5	?	36 h
Expulsion interval, min.	I1/I2, 6; I2/I3, 8	I1/I2, 2; I2/I3, 7	I1/I2, 18; I2/I3, 11	?	—
Expulsion contractions	9, 5, 4	3, 3, ?	7, 6, 4	?	>12
Placental stage duration, min	16	0.5	18	?	—
Delivery duration	2 hr, 26 min	40 min	3 hr, 2 min	<1 hr	>26 hr
Presentation I1	Vert., occ., post.	Vert., occ., post.	Vert., occ., post.	?	—
Presentation I2	Vert., ?	Vert., occ., ant.	Vert., occ., ant.	?	—
Presentation I3	Vert., occ., post.	Vert., occ., ant.	Vert., occ., post.	?	—
Nipple contact after min.	I1, 20; I2, 51	I1, 15; I2, 15	I2, 38; I2, 32	?	—
Infant transfer, mother to other after min.	3 hr, 8 min.	1 hr, 34 min.	9 hr, 48 min	<1 hr	—

SOURCE: Data from Rothe (1973*b*).
ABBREVIATIONS: I = newborn; vert. = vertex; occ. = head; post. = posterior; ant. = anterior
[1] Unable to extrude singleton and died of ruptured uterus.

shared in eating of the placenta." Grüner and Krause (1963, p. 108) noted a light flow of blood from a pregnant female on the evening of the night she delivered twins.

Birth, according to Langford (1963, p. 300), who describes breeding in general terms, "is preceded by a slight discharge of blood; the female assists the birth by using a branch or other convenient object above her head to obtain downward pressure by her arms after assuming a squatting posture. The infant is born head first and should there be difficulty the male will assist with his hands. Immediately after the first birth, the male takes the baby, licks off the film of mucus and then hands the baby back to the mother for feeding."

Rothe 1973*b*

The late preparturition period, parturition, and puerperium of 3 females were observed and described in detail (table 62). Females no. 11 and no. 12 were wild-caught and acquired in 1968 when full grown. In captivity, they produced 10 and 9 litters respectively and each was the dominant female of her group. Female no. 20 was purchased from a dealer in 1967. Behavioral changes or signs of parturition were not detected until 1 or 2 hr before birth, when the females became restless and licked and inspected their genitalia. The parturent squats during labor; and extrusion of newborn and placenta proceeds without manual assistance. The young are licked frequently during extrusion and just after expulsion they grip the mother's fur and climb to the nipples unaided. During nocturnal deliveries group members may watch with curiosity but do not assist, and the placenta is eaten by the mother alone.

Rothe 1974

The dominant female of each of the two family groups maintained apart in laboratories of the University of Göttingen delivered young a few days apart. Behavioral or physical signs of pregnancy were not detectable until the beginning of the 3d month, when ♀ no. 11 became listless and her abdomen "enlarged enormously." However, the amount of abdominal enlargement, observed in 30 other cases is no sure sign of the stage of pregnancy.

Both females delivered at night. No. 11 left her group's sleeping box before dilatation, and no. 12 left her group 1 hr, 14 min before the onset of parturition. The females were restless; they ate, drank, and defecated; but the members of their family groups remained quiet.

First visible signs of labor are the sudden halt in locomotion, raising of abdomen and tail, hair ruffling, eye closing, heavy breathing, and flank adduction. At the end of dilatation, the females squat to expel the young. Female no. 11 produced a singleton and no. 12 produced triplets. Details of the deliveries are summarized in table 63.

Delivery of no. 11 was observed without extra light in the housing room. The mother gave birth without assistance or presence of relatives. She retired in the dark and is presumed to have eaten the entire placenta alone. Female no. 12 began delivery when the light in the laboratory was switched on. This aroused the family, and the members approached to watch but did not interfere with delivery until the end. The mother at first paid no attention to the placenta, which was then seized and eaten by other family members. Neither of the two mothers returned to the group sleeping box after parturition.

Table 63. History of Two Parturitions by *Callithrix jacchus jacchus* in University of Göttingen Laboratory.

Detail or Stage	♀ *No. 11*	♀ *No. 12*
Previous deliveries, since 1968	10	9
Present birth date	Feb., 1973	Feb., 1973
Litter young, number	1	3
Time of retirement from group	01:16	19:03
Time dilatation began	02.30	19:41
Dilatation, duration, min	37	91
Contractions during dilatation	6	22
Expulsion time I1/I2/I3, min	21	16/20/10
Expulsion contractions I1/I2/I3	9	16/8/10
Expulsion interval I1/I2/I3/	—	22/1
Presentation of I1	Vertex, occ., post.	Vertex occ., ant.
I2		Vertex, occ., post.
I3		Breech, sacrum post.
Placental stage, duration, min	14	1
Delivery, duration, min	98	161
Nipple contact after min	19	35/21
Gestation period, days	146	?
Interbirth interval, days	155	156

SOURCE: Data from Rothe (1974).
ABBREVIATIONS: I = newborn; occ. = head; post. = posterior; ant. = anterior.

It is suggested that presence of and assistance by family members at parturition of caged females is induced by the full-light method used by previous observers.

Head size of newborn *Callithrix jacchus* purportedly averages larger than the transverse diameter of the female pelvic inlet through which it must pass (Leutenegger 1970*c*, p. 230, fig. 3). Head breadth measurements taken of 4 newborn by Leutenegger average 18 mm. Means and extremes of the transverse diameter of 15 females are 17.2 (15–19) the data having been taken by Leutenegger from Wettstein (1963). The comparisons may not be valid. The newborn measured by Leutenegger are not offspring of or in any way related to the females measured by Wettstein. Furthermore, Wettstein's measurements indicate that the females may average less than full grown. In any event, case histories of the newborn must be known for a valid assessment of the relationship between head size and pelvic inlet. Singletons are usually larger than twins produced by the same mother, and captive born are often larger than wild born. In the present context, it seems that litters of two or more and the mothers would be more viable than singletons and their mothers.

Breeding Seasons

Little is known of how and when *Callithrix jacchus* breeds in the wild. Breslau (1927, p. 226) found no fetuses in six mature female *Callithrix jacchus jacchus* collected by Dr. Pohle from 24–27 May 1914, in Dois Irmãos (289b), Pernambuco, and none in one mature female collected 4 June 1914, in nearby Fundão (289b), Paraiba. These are autumn dates in the southern hemisphere.

Laemmert, Ferreira, and Taylor (1946, p. 42) report that *Callithrix jacchus penicillata* "breed to some extent throughout the year but the greatest number of pregnant females were encountered [in the Ilheus, Bahia region] during the months of September, October and November," or during the winter months. Births, therefore, would be expected in late spring and early summer.

Brand (1963, p. 656) exhibits the half-monthly distribution of 15 births of *Callithrix jacchus* in the National Zoological Gardens of South Africa in the form of a histogram. His percentages are converted into the actual numbers of births as follows.

February (early)—March	4
April (early)	2
May (early)	2
June	0
July (late)	1
August	0
September (early)–October (late)	6
November–January	0

Brand's records of *Callithrix jacchus,* as well as of other mammals, were compiled from zoo registrations dating from 1908 to 1960. The total number of years for any one species is not given and the number of parturitions per female is not recorded. The author states that the "litters varied from one to four with an average of 2.26." The periods of gestation were not recorded, but Brand gives 140–50 days, citing the 1927 work of Lucas, Hume, and Henderson-Smith. He concludes that the data "seems to indicate a protracted breeding season with most of the young born during the spring and autumn" of the southern hemisphere.

My tabulation of the same data shows that approximately 10 births occurred during the spring and summer seasons of the southern hemisphere, the remaining 5 during autumn and winter.

Sawaya (1936, p. 144) records two births by a captive *Callithrix jacchus* in São Paulo. The first occurred 3 October 1935, or spring, the second 12 March 1936, or late summer.

Monthly records of births of *Callithrix jacchus* in the London Zoo for the years 1828 through 1961, compiled by Jarvis and Morris (1961, p. 293), are distributed as follows.

J	F	M	A	M	J	J	A	S	O	N	D
–	–	2	2	4	2	1	–	1	–	2	–

All but 2 of the 14 births listed above occurred during the spring and summer. It is reasonable to assume that each birth was the first of wild parents in an environment lacking the uniformity of breeding laboratories.

The seasonal distribution of 53 cases of full term births in captivity in northern European cities listed in table 61 (excludes the 14 noted above) is summarized as follows.

22 Dec.–21 Mar.	8
22 Mar.–21 June	19
22 June–23 Sept.	15
24 Sept.–21 Dec.	11

The figures show a preponderance of births during spring and summer, or nearly twice as many (34) as in fall and winter (19).

Seventeen births between 1962 and 1968 in the marmoset colony studied by Epple (1970*a*) separate into 1 in winter, 8 in spring, 3 in summer, and 5 in fall, or a total of 11 spring-summer births to 6 fall-winter births, with a preponderance of spring births. The persistence of seasonality in the above cases is the more remarkable for the fact that the record is weighted with births in laboratory-controlled environments where production occurs year round.

On the other hand, the longer the breeding under uniform or controlled conditions and the greater the number of pregnancies after the first conceived in captivity, the less the seasonality. Stated another way, ebb and disappearance of seasonality reflect the degree and duration of disassociation between the organism's internal reproductive rhythms and natural environmental cycles. For example, of 14 laboratory litters born from 1927 to 1937 and recorded by Lucas, Hume, and Henderson-Smith, 4 arrived in winter, 3 in spring, 4 in summer and 3 in autumn. Another example provided by Mallinson (1969, p. 8), is the following monthly distribution of 17 births in the Jersey Zoo, during a 10-year span.

J	F	M	A	M	J	J	A	S	O	N	D
1	1	1	3	1	2	–	2	1	1	1	3

The litters include 5 produced by the same hybrid *Callithrix penicillata* × *C. jacchus* pair, and three litters by a pair of *Callithrix jacchus.* Family histories of the other litters are not given by Mallinson. The birth dates show no significant seasonal differences, but spring births hold a numerical edge.

Rothe 1975*a*, p. 265

Rothe (1975*a*, p. 265, table 3) shows that the 35 litters produced during 1968–73 in his Göttingen laboratory were evenly distributed throughout all months of the year.

Phillips 1975, p. 295

A reversal of seasonal trends noted in some cases is exhibited by the following monthly distribution of births during a 4-year period in laboratories of the Royal College of Surgeons of England, Downe, Orpington.

J	F	M	A	M	J	J	A	S	O	N	D
8	8	6	3	3	3	2	7	7	4	4	4

Roughly, the spring-summer births total 25, the autumn-winter births, 40.

Breeding in Captivity

The difficulty of laboratory breeding and the frequency of aberrant litter sizes are discussed by Lucas, Hume, and Henderson-Smith (1937, p. 210). "The rearing of a second generation has [been] extraordinarily unsuccessful. Full records of all the progeny have not been kept, but the writers have not succeeded in rearing a single young one of the second generation. The males are fertile. A few of the females have failed to become pregnant when mated with males of known fertility, but in the majority of cases the number of foetuses has been three or four instead of the normal two and, as a result, either the babies have been born prematurely and have failed to survive, the mother surviving, or the mother has failed to give birth at term, and she and the young have perished together." The authors then noted the relative success of an associate, Miss Hill, in breeding laboratory-born marmosets. The births are recorded in table 61.

J. K. Hampton, Jr., Hampton, and Levy (1971) also commented on the difficulty of breeding an F_2 generation. Their laboratory colony of 7 callitrichid species and *Callimico goeldii,* maintained from 1961 to 1969, produced 399 offspring from 254 parturitions. Not one of the females born reared offspring, although some were pregnant several times.

Difficulties in breeding are ascribed by Lucas, Hume, and Henderson-Smith (1937, p. 210) "to the general rich feeding particularly with full milk, without which, however, the animals did not thrive." This, in turn, may have increased the fecundity of the mother and the size of the embryos. The added strains of the pregnant mother make labor difficult or lethal. The regular use of ultraviolet light in the laboratory may also have had adverse side effects on fetal development and parturition.

Epple (1970*a,* pp. 72–73) does not seem to agree that rich nutrition is necessarily correlated with overweight in fetuses and adults, excessive fecundity, and difficulties in producing and rearing a second generation of marmosets in captivity. She reports that two females born in her laboratory were successful breeders. One of them reared two pairs of twins and a single offspring without difficulty. Her mate, Epple (1970*a,* p. 65) notes, was wild caught. A colony-born brother and sister pair also bred.

Litters

The distribution of young in the 56 litters listed in table 61 is summarized in table 64.

Litters examined by J. K. Hampton, Jr., Hampton and Levy (1971) were produced under uniformly controlled

Table 64. Litter Sizes of *Callithrix jacchus* Summarized from Table 61.

Young per Litter	*Number of Litters*	*Total Young*
1	7(12.5%)	7(05.8%)
2	35(62.5%)	70(57.8%)
3	12(21.4%)	36(29.7%)
4	2(03.6%)	8(06.6%)
Totals	56(100%)	121(100%)

Average number of young per litter = 2.2.

conditions, and their distribution with respect to number of young in each is probably very nearly ideal. Their figures (1971, p. 529) for *Callithrix jacchus jacchus* and *C. j. penicillata* combined are shown in table 65. Litter

Table 65. Litter Sizes of *Callithrix jacchus* Produced in Laboratories of Tulane University, New Orleans, and University of Texas Dental School, Houston, 1961–69.

Young per Litter	*Number of Litters*	*Total Young*
1	24(16.7%)	24(08%)
2	96(66.7%)	192(67%)
3	24(16.7%)	72(25%)
Totals	144(100%)	288(100%)

Average number of young per litter = 2.

SOURCE: J. K. Hampton, Jr., Hampton, and Levy (1971, p. 528).
NOTE: The total of 144 litters excludes 8 for which the number of young produced is unknown. Of the grand total of 152 litters, 31 (20%) were aborted.

sizes and total number of young recorded by Rothe (1973*b*) are summarized in table 66. All data are combined in table 67.

Table 66. Litter Sizes of *Callithrix jacchus jacchus* Produced in the University of Göttingen Laboratory.

Young per Litter	*Number of Litters*	*Total Young*
1	2(06.2%)	2(02.7%)
2	19(59.4%)	38(51.4%)
3	10(31.3%)	30(40.5%)
4	1(03.1%)	4(05.9%)
Totals	32(100%)	74(100%)

Average number of young per litter = 2.3.

SOURCE: Rothe (1973*b*, p. 260).

The numerical data of deliveries in captivity, summarized in table 67, indicate that litters produced in the wild usually consist of heterozygous twins. Most if not all singletons are survivors of twinnings. The high ratio of triplets suggests that a comparable but perhaps lower proportion of such litters are produced in nature. At least one of the three young must be wasted.

Table 67. Litter Sizes of *Callithrix jacchus* Produced in Captivity

Young per Litter	*Number of Litters*	*Total Young*
1	33(14%)	33(07%)
2	150(65%)	300(62%)
3	46(20%)	138(29%)
4	3(01%)	12(02%)
Totals	232(100%)	483(100%)

Average number of young per litter = 2.09.

SOURCE: Data from tables 64, 65, and 66 combined.

Hybridization

Records of hybridization between captive individuals of the *Callithrix jacchus* group are listed below. The names used are those of the present classification. Name combinations used by the authors cited are given in the synonymies of the subspecies accounts. Additional information on hybridization among callitrichids will be found in chapter 47 and in the accounts of other species (for example, *Callithrix argentata,* p. 590).

Successful crossbreeding and double hybridization of caged members of the *Callithrix jacchus* group prove the intimate genetic relationship between the races. Although the evidence is far from complete, the cases of geographic intergradation between *penicillata* and *geoffroyi, penicillata* and *jacchus, flaviceps* and *geoffroyi,* and, inferentially, *aurita* and *flaviceps* leave no doubt of free gene flow throughout the range of the species. Denials of natural hybridization or geographic intergradation voiced by Coimbra-Filho and Mittermeier (1974) fly in the face of the facts.

Callithrix jacchus jacchus ♂ × *Callithrix jacchus penicillata* ♀ (Osman Hill 1957, pp. 185, 288, 296 and footnote).

"Bred several times in London Zoo from 1950 onward." Parents identified as distinct species.

Interbreeding between *jacchus* and *penicillata* is expected and natural where they meet, whether in the wild or in captivity.

Osman Hill (1957, footnote p. 296) records a "two month old infant closely resembling typical *H. penicillata* but born of a female *H. jacchus,* the father being uncertain, but not likely to have been other than *H. penicillata.*" Hill's description of the animal accords with that of juvenal *jacchus* between 6 and 11 weeks. The external measurements given are, "head and body, 97 mm., tail, 120 mm., hind foot, 32 mm., ear, 18.5 mm."

Callithrix jacchus penicillata ♂ × *Callithrix jacchus jacchus* ♀ (Mallinson 1971, p. 8, 11 figs.) (fig. IX.27).

Parents were observed during daytime copulating on 1 November 1966, February 1967, May 1968, November 1968, January 1969, and July 1969. Five litters were produced. Gestation periods for three observations were estimated at 125, 145, and 146 days. Birth intervals in two cases were 144 and 155 days. The female of one set of hybrids at 13 weeks weighed 120 g, the male 130 g; a female hybrid at 19 weeks, 2 days, weighed 175 g; the

Fig. IX.27. Hybrid bred in captivity: *Above, Callithrix jacchus penicillata* ♂ × *C. j. jacchus* ♀, twins about 12 weeks old in juvenal pelage, born 21 June 1967; *below,* singleton in subadult pelage, 10 months old, born 26 July 1967. (Photos courtesy of J. J. C. Mallinson, Jersey Zoological Park.)

mother weighed 288 g. The weights are normal for the species.

The preauricular tufts of the hybrids were black like those of the father, their shape intermediate but more nearly like those of the mother. The white frontal blaze was intermediate in size between the larger one of the father and the smaller one of the mother. The white suborbital markings present in the hybrids were like those of the mother.

(Callithrix jacchus penicillata × *Callithrix jacchus jacchus)* ♂ × *(Callithrix jacchus penicillata* × *Callithrix jacchus jacchus)* ♀ (Mallinson 1971, personal communication).

Parents of F_2 born of same parents but different litters; ♂ F_1 born 19 August 1968, ♀ F_1 born 25 June 1969.

F_2 hybrid twins, stillborn or aborted between 1 and 3 July 1971.

The F_2 fetuses are deposited in the Field Museum together with one adult ♀ *Callithrix jacchus penicillata* × *Callithrix jacchus jacchus,* born 27 April 1968, died 15 September 1971, in the Jersey Zoological Park, Channel Islands.

J. K. Hampton, Jr., Hampton, and Levy (1971, p. 528, footnotes) recorded matings between two sets of *(Callithrix jacchus penicillata* × *C. j. jacchus)*. There were 4 pregnancies including 3 abortions by the first pair and a full-term parturition by the second.

Callithrix jacchus jacchus ♂ × *Callithrix jacchus geoffroyi* ♀ (Coimbra-Filho 1970*c*) (fig. IX.28).

Twins, live birth, 1 November 1968, Zoological Gardens, Rio de Janeiro, Brazil; sex not recorded. Parents identified as distinct species.

Twins, live birth, 5 April 1969, same parents and place as above; born blind; one died about a month after birth, second died 50 days after birth.

Triplets, live birth, 28 November 1969, same parents and place as above; each blind in left eye; one died within week of birth, second after one month, third transferred to new cage 120 days after birth.

Color and color patterns of hybrids described as intermediate between those of comparably aged individuals of *jacchus* and *geoffroyi.*

Parents of first set of hybrids copulated through wire mesh partition between their respective cages.

Fig. IX.28. Hybrids bred in captivity: *Above,* adult male (*Callithrix jacchus jacchus* × *C. j. geoffroyi*) ♂ × *C. j. penicillata* ♀. *Below,* adult male hybrid *C. j. jacchus* ♂ × *C. j. geoffroyi* carrying twin offspring of mating with *C. j. penicillata* (= "jordani", Coimbra-Filho 1973, p. 32, fig. 2); one of the young matured into the animal shown above. (Photo courtesy of A. F. Coimbra-Filho.)

(*Callithrix jacchus jacchus* × *Callithrix jacchus geoffroyi*) ♂ × *Callithrix jacchus penicillata,* ♀ wild born (Coimbra-Filho 1971) (fig. IX.29).

Triplet males born 1 December 1970 in Zoological Gardens, Rio de Janeiro, Brazil; father was hybrid offspring of first of three matings recorded above (Coimbra-Filho 1970*c*); mother was identified as *Callithrix penicillata jordani;* one young died 7 December 1970, second died 9 December; both deaths attributed to exceptionally high heat (40°C) of day.

Head color patterns of newborn generally like that of *Callithrix jacchus penicillata* (identified as *jordani* by Coimbra-Filho), but forehead of one paler, recalling the pattern of *geoffroyi;* body and tail similar in all three.

Surviving triplet at one month of age resembled *jacchus* of same age; at 100 days like hybrid parent at 170 days; at 6 months more like *penicillata* (*jordani*).

Young of all forms of *Callithrix jacchus* are similar in lacking the diagnostic characters of their respective adult stages. More material than appears to have been available to Coimbra-Filho is needed for critical comparisons of color patterns of juvenal pelages.

(*Callithrix jacchus jacchus* × *Callithrix jacchus geoffroyi*) ♂ × *Callithrix jacchus penicillata* (Coimbra-Filho 1973)

Hybrid father same as in previous mating (Coimbra-Filho 1971); mother purebred captive born identified as *C. penicillata jordani,* by Coimbra-Filho.

♂ ♀ ° born 11 August 1971. Unsexed young died one week after birth. Survivors observed 1 year and still living (1973). Growth, development, and behavior said to be same as that of nonhybrids. Color patterns at 1 year as in FM specimen of adult intergrades between *C. j. penicillata* and *C. j. geoffroyi,* from Ilheus, southeastern Bahia.

Callithrix jacchus flaviceps ♂ × *Callithrix jacchus geoffroyi* ♀ (A. Ruschi in Coimbra-Filho 1973, p. 33, fig. 35 [father with offspring])

Two captive female *Callithrix jacchus geoffroyi* in a cage near the forest edge, in Espírito Santo, Brazil, attracted the wild living male *C. j. flaviceps.* The latter was captured and placed in a cage with the female with which he mated (see above p. 531).

Two litters of twins were produced. Both sets died shortly after birth but no dates or other information are given.

GROWTH AND DEVELOPMENT

The topics covered in this section are as follows.

Chronology of Growth	Birth Sex Ratios
Differential Growth Rates	Sexual Dimorphism
Weights	Longevity
Dental Eruption	

Chronology of Growth

The following chronology of growth and development of captive *Callithrix jacchus jacchus* is a composite of observations made by F. Cuvier (1819), Desmarest (1820), I. Geoffroy (1827), Lucas, Hume, and Henderson-Smith (1927), Marik (1931), Fitzgerald (1935), Lucas, Hume, and Henderson-Smith (1937), Chartin and Petter (1960), Grüner and Krause (1963), Langford (1963), Epple (1970a), and a few others cited in text; weights in grams are from Epple. Particular authorities are cited in specific cases when their respective data are unique or appear to be at variance with those of other authorities. In any case, it may be assumed that minor discrepancies reflect individual variation in rate of growth or development.

Newborn: Head and body length, 60–80 mm; weight about 30 g (1 oz); body seemingly naked (Siret 1778, p. 453) but actually uniformly covered with fine gray or brownish-gray vellus hairs, tail annulated blackish and gray, in some individuals uniformly black for first 4 days (Epple 1970*a*); abdomen, inner sides of limbs nearly naked, palms and soles pinkish; face bare, dark, and framed with white; eyes open, iris and pupil brown or blue-black (Langford 1963, p. 300); in some but not all newborn, eyes remained closed until 4th day; circumorbital region and forehead dark brown, mid-frontal region darker; mane dark brown and covering ears, aural corolla absent, brown stripe between eyes continues through midline of crown back of head and often along spine.

1–3 Days: Born with eyes open, body thinly covered with dark gray hair, tail nearly naked (F. Cuvier 1819). At 40–50 hour young dusky brown, tail with alternating dark and grayish bands, ear tufts absent (Desmarest 1820, p. 92). Head and nape almost entirely black, mid-frontal region blackish and darker than surrounding parts of forehead; tail banded, the terminal portion black; trunk and limbs reddish gray (I. Geoffroy 1827, p. 517).

First milk teeth erupting. Umbilical cord bitten off by parents or, if left long, dries by third day and falls off. Sawaya (1936, p. 146) gives the following measurements: Head and body, 89; tail, 90; ear, 13; hind foot, 20. One-day predelivery female triplets reported by Epple (1970*a*, pp. 70, 73) weighed 27.5, 29.3, 30.0 g; newborn singleton ♀, 34.7 g; two-day-old ♀ survivor of triplets, 21.3 g.

Healthy full-term newborn initiates fur-grasping reflex at touch of mother's fur, grips tightly, and clings unaided within seconds of delivery; begins climbing to mother's nipple within 1–2 min; reaches nipple within 15–40 min. Tail slack at first but tenses after 15–20 min, with distal third coiled and pressed against mother's body. Failure to stimulate maternal response by climbing or vocalizing results in parental neglect, rejection, and often, cannibalization (Rothe 1975*b*, p. 315).

2d Week: Able to crawl unsupported; nursing on 9th day (Grüner and Krause 1963, p. 111).

3d Week: Solid food eaten (Lucas, Hume, and Henderson-Smith 1927, p. 450); suckling continues; leave adult for first time from 17 to 23 days (Epple 1970*a*).

3d to 4th Week: Leave parents voluntarily for short periods; nursed at about half-hour intervals (Grüner and Krause 1963, p. 111); weight of 24-day singleton ♂, 50 g; take first solid food from 26 to 34 days (Epple 1970*a*).

4th Week: Formation of whorl on crown between ears; move about independently though somewhat unsteadily; return to parents when alarmed; continue suckling but also eat portions of insects held in mother's mouth (Grüner and Krause 1963, p. 110) and feed on solids premasticated by the father (Langford 1963, p. 300). Weaning occurs when the offspring begins to eat adult food; young forcibly rejected by mother, but father continues to carry young well into second month (Stellar 1960, p. 4).

5th Week: Lap liquids from dish; ears surrounded by small gray-brown corolla (Epple 1970*a*, p. 67) (compare with 11th week).

6th Week: Head and body length, 120–50 mm; milk dentition complete; weaned and independent (Marik 1931); weaning from 52 to 85 days (Epple 1970*a*); weight of 38-day singleton ♂, 70 g.

6th to 7th Weeks: Face with more whitish hairs; forehead dark; ear tufts absent; sideburns well developed; fur of back below shoulders striated as in adult (Grüner and Krause 1963, pp. 111–12, figs. 2, 3); weight of 48-day singleton ♂, 70 g; of 42-day ♀, 70 g.

7th Week: Physical activities almost of adult type; father refuses to carry young; weight of 52-day singleton ♂, 80 g; of 50-day ♀, 81 g.

"The grasping behaviour of infants after the 5th to 7th week after birth can no longer be distinguished from that of adult animals" (Rothe 1975*c*, p. 384).

8th Week: Head and body length, 140–70 mm; milk teeth shedding; iris paler, the pupil remaining dark and distinct; weight of 60-day singleton ♂, 91 g; of 60-day ♀, 88 g.

9th Week: Weight of 66-day singleton ♂, 97 g.

10th Week: Weight of 74-day singleton ♀, 103 g.

11th Week: Small dark ear tufts appear; skin of face remains dark; fur on back less gray, more yellow (Lucas, Hume, and Henderson-Smith 1927, p. 450); weight of 73-day ♂, 105 g.

12th Week: For all practical purposes, independent of parental care (Coimbra-Filho 1970*c*); but continue sleeping on adult's back from 12th to 17th week (Epple 1970*a*); show adult coloration except for typical facial pattern and white aural corolla (Epple 1970*a*).

13th Week: Face more whitish, ear tufts becoming silvery (Fitzgerald 1935, p. 186, but see below).

13th to 17th Weeks: White frontal blaze appears (Lucas, Hume, and Henderson-Smith 1937, p. 209); in hybrid (*jacchus* × *geoffroyi*), blaze appeared between 21st and 40th week (Coimbra-Filho 1970*c*); weight of 96-day male twins, 120, 145 g; singleton, 119 day ♀, 137 g; of 120-day singleton ♂, 162 g.

18th Week: Milk teeth shedding (Marik 1931); weight of 128-day ♂, ♀ twins 173, 154 g; singleton 130-day ♂, 164 g.

20th Week: No longer seek refuge on adult back; milk teeth replaced (Marik 1931).

21st to 22d Weeks: Circumaural tufts assume adult form; frontal blaze dimly outlined, coronal whorl conspicuous (Fitzgerald 1935, p. 186); weight of 160-day singleton ♂, 179 g.

23d Week: Weight of 153-day singleton ♀, 166 g.

25th Week (approximately): adult pelage color, white ear tufts, triangular frontal blaze; pupil from blue-black to amber; permanent canines become tusklike (Langford 1963).

26th Week: Weight 270 g; iris brown; frontal blaze white and well defined; striations of lumbar region becoming defined; ear tufts sprouting with whitish sheen, but not wholly white (Lucas, Hume, and Henderson-Smith 1927, p. 451); ear tufts acquiring a mixture of white hairs (Lucas, Hume, and Henderson-Smith 1937, p. 209).

28th Week: Weight of 202-day singleton ♀, 174 g.

29th Week: Weight of 205-day singleton ♂, 250 g.

36th Week: Weight of 253-day singleton ♂, 266 g.

37th Week: Weight of 259-day singleton ♀, 201 g.

38th Week: Circumaural tufts completely white (Lucas, Hume, and Henderson-Smith 1937, p. 209); weight of 266-day singleton ♂, 266 g.

43d Week: Weight of 307-day singleton ♀, 215 g.

47th Week: Weight of 329-day singleton ♂, 307 g.

52d Week: Nearly full grown; adult pelage and color pattern achieved.

57th Week: Weight of 400-day singleton ♀, 221 g.

60th Week: Full sexual maturity at approximately 14 months of age (Lucas, Hume, and Henderson-Smith 1937); weight of 426-day singleton ♂, 369 g.

In the female, sexual maturity follows progressive changes in the external genitalia from a small penislike vulva in the immature adult to a turgid organ with collapsing walls in the mature individual. The uterus at maturity has the feel of a pencil 1.5 cm long by 0.5 cm wide (Poswillo, Hamilton, and Sopher 1972).

"Puberty is normally at 13–14 months of age, although we have had 1 female that conceived at 11½ months and delivered a single stillborn offspring at term" (Phillips 1975, p. 297).

Differential Growth Rates

Allometric growth of various extremities relative to trunk length are indicated in measurements taken by Wettstein (1963). His sampling, however, is too small, and his measurements of presumed adults (table 75) suggest that the mean size is that of an animal much less than full grown (cf. appendix table 1). Figures given in table 68 showing relative tail lengths at several growth stages from infancy to maturity are Wettstein's. Additional measurements of tail and combined head and body lengths shown in table 69 are from specimens measured in the field by R. H. Gilmore. Despite the small sample size, trends shown are fairly indicative of the normal pattern of allometric growth. Weights of growing marmosets without correlated linear measurements are supplied by Epple (table 70) and Cooper (table 71).

In general, head and hind foot lengths decrease relative to combined head and body (or trunk) length as body mass increases from birth to maturity; tail length increases relative to overall body mass until late subadulthood then decreases to maturity.

Table 68. Absolute and Relative Lengths of Trunk and Tail in *Callithrix jacchus jacchus,* of Unknown Origin

Age	*Trunk Length*	*Tail Length*	*Tail Length / Trunk Length*
Infant (9 days)	43	94	219
Infant (57 days)	53	124	234
Juvenal	64	168	263
Juvenal	78	234	300
Subadult	96	255	266
Subadult	110	265	241
Adult	125	277	221

SOURCE: Wettstein (1963, p. 199).

Table 69. Absolute and Relative Lengths of Head and Body (H.B.), Tail (T), and Skull of a series of *Callithrix jacchus penicillata* from Anapolis, Goiás, Brazil

	H.B.	*Tail*	*T / H.B.*	*Skull*	*Skull / H.B.*
Young ♂	156	250	160	42.7	27.4
Young ♀	165	260	158	43.4	26.3
Young ♂	170	280	165	44.3	26.0
Adult ♀	190	275	145	46.1	24.3
Adult ♂	200	290	145	—	—
Adult ♀	205	270	132	44.1	21.5
Adult ♀	205	285	140	45.6	22.2
Adult ♂	210	290	138	45.9	21.9

SOURCE: Specimens were collected and measured in 1936 by Raymond H. Gilmore.

Table 70. Weights of Growing Male and Female Marmosets

Days	*Weight in grams* ♂♂	♀♀	*Remarks*
−1	—	27.5, 29.3, 30.0	Fetuses, 1 day before delivery
1	—	34.7	
2	—	21.3	1 (dead) of triplets
4	22.8	—	1 (dead) of triplets
24	50	—	
38	70	—	
42	—	70	
48	70	—	
50	—	81	
52	80	—	
60	91	88	
66	97	—	
73	105	—	
74	—	103	
96	120, 145	—	
119	—	137	
120	162	—	
128	154, 173	—	
130	164	—	
145	195, 204	—	
153	—	166	
160	179	—	
202	—	174	
205	250	—	
253	266	—	
259	—	201	
280	266	—	
307	—	215	
329	307	—	
400	—	221	
426	369	—	
532	377	—	
2 yrs.	—	300	
2¼ yrs.	385	—	Wild-caught singletons
Adults	346, 364 375	375, 387	

SOURCE: Epple (1970*a*).

Table 71. Weights of Growing Marmosets (in grams)

Age *Years, Days*	*9/1/65* ♂♂	*30/5/68* ♂♂	*19/7/65*	*Rep.* *No.*
33	55			10
93		71		22
108			172	13
205			218	14
216	222			11/12
299	263			13
2, 29			174[!]	19
2, 220	349			19
3, 234	339			22

SOURCE: Data compiled from Cooper (1966, reports 10–22).
NOTE: Birth dates are shown for each individual or twin set. Weight given for twin is average of the two siblings.

According to Wettstein (1963), relative growth of arm length in *Callithrix jacchus jacchus* obeys trends similar to those followed by the tail. The same may apply to thorax growth judging by Wettstein's figure 3 (1963, p. 198), but his measurements (1963, p. 202) suggest a progressive decrease relative to trunk size.

Weights

Weight in grams of growing young males and females supplied by Epple (1970*a*) and included in the above chronology are compared separately below (table 70) with those of adults from the same colony. Weights of twins or triplets are grouped.

Tables 70, 72 show newborn (0–4 day) singletons are larger than twins, and twins larger than triplets. Measurements by J. K. Hampton, Jr., Hampton, and Levy (1971, p. 530) of 11 sets of twins and 6 sets of triplets reveal similar size differences between young of the two litter types. Their figures are given below in table 72.

Table 72. Size of *Callithrix jacchus* Newborn to 48 Hours Old

	Combined Head and Body Length	*Hind Foot Length*	*Body Weight Grams*
Twins	84.1(76–89) 11	25.9(22–28) 11	30.3(21–38) 9
Triplets	78.3(72–84) 6	24.8(23–27) 6	23.6(18–27) 4

SOURCE: J. K. Hampton, Jr., Hampton, and Levy 1971.
NOTE: Measurements are means, extremes in parentheses, followed by number of litters.

Average weights of wild-caught males and females in the Primate Colony, San Diego Zoo, recorded by Cooper (1965–68) are shown in table 73. The differences in weight between them and adults listed in table 71 is probably due to fat deposition rather than overall size differences. The females weighed 18 August 1967 may have been pregnant, near term.

Table 73. Weights of Wild-caught Marmosets (*Callithrix jacchus*) in the Primate Colony, San Diego Zoo, 1965–68.

Date	♂♂ (N)	♀♀ (N)	*Report No.*
13 Aug. 1965	303(2)	287(3)	11/12
4 Nov. 1965	323(2)	293(3)	13
10 Feb. 1966	300(2)	277(3)	14
23 Aug. 1966	318(3)	279(3)	16
18 Aug. 1967	305(2)	352(2)	19
– Sept. 1968	314(2)	261(1)	22

SOURCE: Cooper (unpublished Quarterly Reports, 1965–68).

Captive-born marmosets also tend to outweigh their wild-born parents. As noted by Lucas, Hume, and Henderson-Smith (1937, p. 208), "most of the adult Brazilian-born common marmosets that the writers have ever weighed have been less than 400 g. (14 oz.). [Wild caught male] 'Tittles' never weighed more than 350 g., neither did [his wild caught mate] 'Mary Anne' except when pregnant, whereas the young when adult were always palpably much larger, so much so as frequently to excite surprised remarks from strangers. In two cases where weight records were kept, weights of 456 and 617 g. were attained by two non-pregnant [laboratory-born] females."

Dental Eruption

The chronological sequence of dental eruption in *Callithrix jacchus jacchus* was determined by Johnston, Dreizen and Levy (1970). The deciduous teeth erupt, as usual, in serial order from middle incisor (i1), between 2 and 9 days, to last premolar (p4) between 20 and 30 days.

Permanent teeth erupt in the following order: m1, m2, i1, i2, pm4, pm3, pm2, c.

The first permanent tooth (m1) erupts about 112 days (16 weeks) of age; the last permanent tooth (c) erupts at about 340 days (49 weeks).

Full chronologies for dental eruptions, crown calcification, and root formation are given in chapter 35.

Birth Sex Ratios

Sexes of marmoset twin or triplet sets are the same or mixed. The distribution of the sexes in a statistically significant number of litters conforms to the ratios expected in multiple births of multiovular origin.

The distribution of sexes in births listed in table 61, and the combined records for *Callithrix j. jacchus,* and *C. j. penicillata* published by J. K. Hampton, Jr., Hampton, and Levy (1971, p. 529), are shown in table 74.

Sexual Dimorphism

Female *Callithrix jacchus jacchus* averages slightly larger than males in nearly all external and skeletal characters measured by Wettstein (1963, table 6). However, most of the actual size differences (table 75) are hardly,

Table 74. Distribution of Sexes in Three Types of Litters

	Singletons		*Twins*			*Triplets*			
	♂	♀	♂♂	♀♀	♂♀	♂♂♂	♂♂♀	♂♀♀	♀♀♀
Table 61	1	3	3	5	12		2	2	1
Hampton et al.	12	6	21	19	31	5	4	5	3
Totals	13	9	24	24	43	5	6	7	4
Expected ratios	1:1		1:1:2			1:1:1:1			

NOTE: The total number of individuals of each sex is 138 males and 132 females.
SOURCE: Recorded in text, and by J. K. Hampton, Hampton, and Levy.

if at all, significant. Notwithstanding measurements to the contrary, fully mature males *look* bigger than comparably aged females because of their heavier facial musculature, particularly of the jaws, and, in the case of the alpha male, which may be actually larger, their mien. The same kinds and degrees of differences between sexes characterize all callitrichids.

The greater relative lengths of the female ischium and pubis needed to permit passage of the newborn are independent of sex differences in overall body size.

Other differences between sexes, apart from those of body size in general, the reproductive organs, and the enlarged female pelvic inlet, are not evident in present material.

Longevity

Lucas, Hume, and Henderson-Smith 1937, p. 208

"The life span of marmosets is not known. Owing to their usual early death with rickets in this country, there are not records of long survivals. The writers have only heard of one well authenticated case, outside their own colony, where a marmoset survived for ten years in captivity in England.

" 'Tittles' was bought on October 22nd, 1925, probably at the age of a year, and died on May 7th, 1935. He was, therefore about eleven years old. For some months before his death he was becoming enfeebled, without any marked symptoms. At post-mortem the kidneys were found to be small, white, and granular, and showed changes suggestive of advanced old age, the glomeruli being all in an advanced state of fibrosis. He was almost toothless, with only one molar in the upper jaw and two incisors, completely loose, in the lower.

" 'Mary Anne' was bought on Dec. 23rd, 1927. She was certainly more than a year old, so that at the time of writing (Jan. 1937) she must be at least ten years old. Of visible teeth she has only one lower median incisor, which looks loose, and she can eat only soft food, but she is lively and very active and in perfect coat. Her last babies were born on Nov. 19th, 1934, about six months before "Tittles" died. Her reproductive life must therefore have continued for at least seven years. If the loss of teeth is a normal phenomenon, it seems improbable that life would last as long in the wild state as in captivity, for when thus toothless marmosets are defenceless and very limited as to food supply."

Mallinson (1971, p. 9) gives the age of a male marmoset, *Callithrix jacchus,* then living in the Jersey Zoological Gardens as 8 years, 23 days. Mallinson also refers to Jones (1962) for the record of a common marmoset that lived 12 years in the London Zoo. This record does not appear in the work cited. However, Jarvis and Morris (1960, p. 289) list a common marmoset that lived 144 months (12 years) in the London Zoo. Additional "maximum" longevity records include one by Flower (1931, p. 157), who cites a report of a pet female marmoset, *Callithrix jacchus jacchus,* obtained when it was about one year old, and lived in London and other European places until it died at about twelve and one-half years of

Table 75. *Callithrix jacchus jacchus:* Sexual Dimorphism in Size; Means and Extremes of External and Skeletal Measurements of "Adults" (Compare with appendix table 1)

	♀♀	♂♂	♀♀♂♂
Head and body combined	188(158–207)37	185(173–198)44	186.4
Tail	280(247–312)37	274(243–303)44	277.2
Hind foot	56.1(52–64)37	55.3(49–63)44	55.7
Braincase length[1]	37.5(35.0–40.5)15	36.4(33.6–38.5)15	36.9
Braincase width[2]	24.2(22.5–26.0)15	23.9(23.0–25.0)15	24.0
Zygomatic breadth	27.8(26.0–30.5)15	26.6(25.0–28.2)15	27.2
Pubic length	12.1(10.3–13.5)15	10.7(10.0–11.6)15	11.4
Pelvic width	22.8(20.0–26.5)15	20.4(18.5–22.3)15	21.6
Pelvic inlet, transverse diameter	17.2(14.6–19.0)15	15.4(13.9–16.5)15	16.3
Pelvic inlet, sagittal diameter	19.7(17.0–21.8)15	18.0(16.0–21.6)15	18.9

SOURCE: Wettstein (1963, pp. 194, 209, 210).
[1] Schädellänge (cf. Wettstein 1963, p. 190)
[2] Schädelbreite (cf. Wettstein 1963, p. 190)

age. Mitchell (1911, p. 434) also mentions a marmoset kept 16 years by Miss C. Morey. Mallinson's (1971, p. 9) record of 6 years 1 month for *Callithrix j. penicillata* ("black-pencilled marmoset") also cited from Jones, should read 1 year, 6 months.

Breeding continues throughout the sixth, seventh (J. K. Hampton, Jr., Hampton, and Levy 1971) and eighth (Mallinson 1968) years and probably longer among captive females. Mallinson also mentions a fertile male nearly eight years old.

BEHAVIOR

This account is made up of observations published in the primary literature, supplemented by observations of my own based on marmosets living in the breeding colonies of the San Diego Zoological Garden and the University of Texas Dental Science Institute at Houston. I have quoted extensively from older works to emphasize that valid observations are timeless and that observations published within the last decade are often repetitious.

Works cited from German and French authors are freely translated or paraphrased. If not clearly evident from the text, my interpolated observations or comments are identified by the initials P. H. in parenthesis.

Behavioral characteristics are described under the following headings:

Habitat and Relative Abundance	Feeding: Use of Hand or Mouth
Territoriality and Home Range	Predation: Use of Hands and Mouth
Daily Rhythm	Elimination
Social Structure	Sanitation
Associations	Drink
Hierarchy and Dominance	Intelligence and Learning
Competition and Rivalry	Locomotion and Posture
Temperament	Swimming
Threat and Aggression	Play and Concealment
Fear	Sight and Images
Care of Young	Scent and Marking
Grooming	Vocalization
Food	Sleep
Manipulation	Thermoregulation
Handedness	Capture

Mating, breeding, growth and development of young, and related subjects are treated under the headings Reproduction (p. 528) and Growth and Development (p. 540).

Box (1975) devoted himself over a period of 8 months to the tedious task of quantifying data collected on marking, self- and social grooming, social play, physical proximity, and huddling observed in 4 experimental groups housed in a well-described facility presumably in the University of Reading, England. This work reached me too late for incorporation into the text that follows.

Habitat and Relative Abundance

Laemmert, Ferreira, and Taylor 1946, pp. 41, 65 (*penicillata*)

The authors, members of the Serviço de Estudos e Pesquisa sôbre a Febra Amarela (SEPSFA), maintained jointly by the Brazilian Ministry of Education and Health and the International Health Division of the Rockefeller Foundation, found *Callithrix jacchus penicillata* to be the principal host of jungle yellow fever virus in the municipio of Ilhéus, Bahia. The kinds, numbers, and habitats of primates captured in the region between 1943 and 1945 are shown in table 106. Procurement, relative abundance and habitat of *Callithrix jacchus penicillata* are described below.

"The procedure employed in procuring primates, particularly marmosets (*C. penicillata*), does not permit an accurate determination of their relative abundance in different localities. The great majority (83%) was purchased through local agents, and the number captured in any given district depended to a large degree upon the energy and ability of the agent in stimulating the local inhabitants to trap them. In some of the more inaccessible parts it was not feasible to secure satisfactory agents or to arrange for the delivery of the captured animals to the laboratory. Consequently, the sampling was spotty and irregular. There is little doubt however, that this species is widely distributed throughout the region and the number captured in localities where trapping was thorough indicates that they exist in great abundance.

"The largest numbers were trapped in cacao plantations and young forests of limited extent. This may be partially accounted for by more intensive trapping in districts devoted to cacao production and does not necessarily imply that cacao groves constitute a permanent habitat. It is a common observation that marmosets dwelling in a bordering forest enter cacao groves to feed in the early morning hours, and they can be trapped here with greater facility than in the forest. Some may live permanently in the heavily shaded cacao groves where foliage of large trees of other varieties form a more or less contiguous upper canopy.

"The other species of primates [table 106] are much less numerous and were found principally in old extensive forests. Their distribution is therefore limited to areas where this type of vegetation exists."

Territoriality and Home Range

The home range or territory of wild marmosets has not been studied. Even the nest or living quarters in the wild has not been described. The daily cruising range of the wild animal is likewise unknown. It is certain that a small woodlot can support one or a few family groups as relatively permanent residents. The more thickly overgrown the lot, the greater the number and variety of fruits, insects, and small vertebrates, including marmosets, it can maintain.

An old adult *Callithrix jacchus* removed by Heusser (1968) from the zoo in Zürich was allowed complete freedom of movement in the outskirts of town. Its cruising range was confined to an area of 200 × 200 meters. The distances covered in its wanderings totaled about 1 kilometer. At times the animal's excursions extended 300 and 400 meters measured in straight lines. The figures agree in the main with those plotted for the Barro Colorado, Panamá, howler by Chivers (1969). The factors confining the wanderings were inhospitable or hostile territories and the time needed for returning home. Size of the animal itself, as compared with large cebids, is of little consequence. The marmoset maintained regular routes and returned every evening to his sleeping box in Heusser's home.

Daily Rhythm

Laemmert, Ferreira, and Taylor 1946, p. 61 (*penicillata*)

"While the habits of marmosets have not been thoroughly studied, it is common observation that they are more active during the early morning and late evening, and have the custom of resting or napping on the high branches of the trees during the mid-day hours."

Social Structure

Epple 1967*b*, p. 61 (*jacchus*)

"The social structure in Hapalidae [= Callitrichidae] is a family group, with a monogamy-like bond between the α-male and the α-female, from which grown up juveniles are driven by the parent of the same sex."

Epple 1975*b*, p. 205

"In *Callithrix j. jacchus* groups, the dominant male and the dominant female tended to form a stable pair. Although no quantitative data were collected, our observations indicate that the dominant male and the dominant female spent more time in contact with each other than with other group mates. They also engaged in sexual interactions with each other most frequently, though not exclusively. We have repeatedly observed that the dominant male interfered with copulations between the dominant female and another male of the group, threatening the male who immediately withdrew. The dominant female showed a similar behaviour when "her" male engaged in copulation with other females. Thus, *Callithrix j. jacchus,* at least in captivity, shows a strong tendency to establish permanent pair bonds."

Epple 1975*b*, p. 205

"Once the social order was established, aggressive interactions in some groups, but not in all, occurred infrequently. In other groups a high frequency of aggressive interactions both among males and females persisted. Even in groups where no overt aggression was observed for relatively long periods of time (e.g., 1–2 years), serious fights between the dominant male or the dominant female and inferior animals of the same sex suddenly occurred, and in some cases made the removal of the inferior from the group necessary."

Rothe 1975*a*

"Family groups [in captivity] which have grown out of one breeding pair held under the same conditions [as artificial groups] are stable over many years and [may contain] up to 18–20 individuals.

"Group members [of family, and also artificial groups], with the exception of infants and juveniles are integrated into 2 rank orders according to sex. The ♂♂—and the ♀♀—hierarchies are separate and lineal. For the most part disassociative behaviour is seen nearly exclusively by group members of the same sex, although during restructuring of a hierarchy in the FG [family group], fights between brothers and sisters occur occasionally. . . . The rank position held by each member in the group is not dependent on its age or its physical strength.

"The parents in the FG are extremely tolerant and friendly towards their adult sons and daughters. The splitting up of groups or the expulsion of individual members from the group was never brought about by the parents but was due solely to the behaviour of the offspring themselves. We [Rothe] have not seen evidence to confirm the belief that adult sons and daughters are driven from the group by the parents."

Rothe, 1975*a*, p. 266

"The fact that reproduction is carried on only by two members of a *C. jacchus* group is in no way an indication for monogamy. Monogamy does not mean that only two individuals in a society are allowed to breed or interact sexually, rather, that the partner almost always is the same. The limitation of reproduction to the most dominant group member by *C. jacchus* is at best an indication that the possibility for reproductive and sexual interaction is dependent on a certain status"; which, he says, is "a more status-oriented relationship between the animals and not an emotional one."

Perhaps Rothe accepts all marmoset behaviour in captivity as normal, even allowing for differences between the heterogenous artificial captive groups and the imprisoned family groups he studied. In any event, he is right in his statement that monogamy means "the partner almost always is the same." All observers would agree, and Rothe has amply demonstrated that, as defined, monogamy is indeed the type of sexual relationship that prevails among captive and free-living marmoset groups. Monogamy in the captive family group appears to be a bar to incest (cf. Fitzgerald, p. 529, and Rothe, p. 529, above). It also appears that insofar as sexual relations are concerned, an alpha pair does not distinguish between its progeny in a family group and subordinate associates in an artificial group. In the artificial group, however, the monogamous pair is forced to defend its relationship, usually to the death of subordinate rivals and the ultimate establishment of a one-family group. There are no artificial stresses or constraints to complicate normal sexual relationships in nature. There, adult marmosets are free to mate and live the good monogamous life.

Wied-Neuwied 1826, p. 133 (*penicillata*)

In the wild in eastern Brazil, marmosets "live in small groups consisting of one or two families with a total number of 3 to 8 individuals."

Ruschi 1964

Marmosets observed or seen in the State of Espírito Santo are said to live in "colônias" consisting of 8 to 40 individuals.

[Ruschi may be using the term colony for anything ranging from the social unit or family group to the entire population of several social units inhabiting semi-isolated woodlots or parks—P. H.]

Lucas, Hume, and Henderson-Smith 1937, p. 208 (*jacchus*)

"Family life [in captivity] appeared to be happy with little quarreling. Occasionally, with male twins, rough play would develop into a fight. At first, after the parents were left continuously together, the children were removed when a fresh birth was nearly due, but latterly this was not done, and the family might consist of the parents, a pair of senior and a pair of junior twins. When this was the case the senior twins would take their share in carrying the babies, though this did not happen while the babies were still quite tiny."

Epple 1970*a*, p. 59 (*jacchus*)

"Groups could never be housed in adjacent cages, connected by wire mesh. In this case severe fights developed between both groups, and beside injuries, abortions, probably due to social stress, occurred. Hampton et al. (1966) also report a quite significant correlation between aggressive excitement, stress or fright (handling) and abortion in *Saguinus oedipus*. Among 360 tamarins, observed by Shadle et al. (1965) only five pregnancies occured, resulting in one full term delivery. This may be due in part to stress and to the fact that the animals were housed in adjacent cages and could reach each other."

Fitzgerald 1935, p. 184 (*jacchus*)

"The confidence of this animal in the human being is quite subordinate to the tie that binds the family group together. Even to this day the whole group will turn on the writer for any imaginary wrong done to any of its members. A sudden movement in the direction of one animal will bring the others to his defense. The authority of the older members seems to be recognized and respected by all; and obedience is enforced by scolding, cuffing, or by the 'eye command.' They never really bite or attempt to bite except in great anger when fighting.

"No apparent effort is made by the animals to care for their sick, although they may recognize impairment of locomotion and leave a sick animal strictly alone. A cry of pain or distress from an older animal does not bring to him the same assistance as that so quickly given to the babies under the same circumstances.

"The offspring show marked deference to their parents, and though a young one may sometimes 'answer back' when corrected, he never goes so far, under these circumstances, as to lift a paw in self-defense. On the other hand the parents when annoyed often slap and cuff their young. This mild form of discipline seems to have the desired effect.

"The parents seem to recognize the helplessness of the young. A cry of distress from a young one will bring the adults rushing to the scene. As the young grow more independent the parents show less concern; but there is always a strong family 'esprit de corps' and the whole group will come to the help of any member uttering a cry of distress or anger."

Associations

Laemmert, Ferreira, and Taylor 1946, p. 41 (*penicillata*)

Primates collected in the Ilhéus, Bahia, region for studies of yellow fever virology (table 106) included the callitrichids *Callithrix jacchus penicillata* and *Leontopithecus rosalia chrysomelas,* and the cebids *Callicebus personatus melanochir, Alouatta guariba,* and *Cebus apella.*

Hierarchy and Dominance

Epple 1970*a*, p. 59 (*jacchus*)

"One adult male dominates all the other adult group males, but tolerates females and juveniles while one adult female dominates all the other adult females and tolerates males and juveniles (Epple 1967). While aggression against adult, nonrelated group members may be strong, the tolerance against animals born in the group is remarkable. The oldest male born in the colony, remained with his family for 2½ years, and never engaged in aggressive encounters with group males, though he fought male strangers fiercely."

Epple 1975*b*, p. 205

"[In our colony of marmosets] dominance was established by means of overt fighting both between males and between females. In those groups where no fights occurred, the monkeys' behavior indicated the existence of rank relations a few hours after group formation. . . . The direction of aggressive threats as displayed in facial expressions, genital presenting, scent marking and vocalizations . . . and avoidance of the dominant animal by the inferior as well as inferiority calls were indicators of rank in the group."

Rothe 1975*a*, p. 266

"Social stress, under which the subordinate group members, especially the ♀♀, live, has a negative influence on the reproduction and the breeding ability of these ♀♀."

The probability that this type of social stress affects wild-living marmosets is virtually nil except possibly in the case of a large population living in an extremely contracted and isolated habitat.

Lucas, Hume, and Henderson-Smith 1937, p. 208 (*jacchus*)

"The male certainly did not dominate the female; if there was an inequality it was she who dominated him, scolding vigorously and hitting him when he refused to take the babies back after she had done feeding them. . . . Occasionally the father exercised authority over the family, but the offspring were never cowed, and often stole food from the parents which was never resented."

Mallinson 1971, p. 7 (*penicillata*)

"A female *Callithrix penicillata* was kept in a large aviary [in the Jersey Zoo] with a pair of ring-tailed lemurs, *Lemur catta*. These treated the marmoset with guarded respect and would allow it to take choice food from their dish without chasing it away."

Stellar 1960, p. 4 (*jacchus*)

"Large groups, up to four males and four females, may pair off and adapt with little fighting. Typically, however, there is a fairly stable dominance pattern that shows up most clearly in the order of feeding from a single food source. Fighting, leading to injury, occurs when pairs or small groups of adults that have stabilized as separate groups in the laboratory are mixed together in a common cage area. In addition to fighting, part of the pattern of excitement and hyperactivity when strange adults are mixed is for the dominant male to copulate females other than his own mate and even attempt mounting of small submissive males."

Competition and Rivalry

Fitzgerald 1935, p. 183 (*jacchus*)

"As a rule marmosets are not quarrelsome, but in some isolated cases permanent antagonisms have been observed among them. In one instance a mother and her eldest daughter have never been friendly. Scolding outbursts occur quite frequently between them; these, however, have never gone as far as a physical attack. A pair of twins (females) had a quarrel that lasted two days and caused the mother to spend much time stepping in between them to prevent bodily violence. A second example of quarreling was exhibited by two other females (evidently twins) bought from a local dealer. From frequent quarrels the differences led to real fighting. After serious damage had been done, mainly to feet and tails, these two animals had to be separated. Most quarrels between males can be definitely traced to sex problems and desire for supremacy in the family unit. A fight between two animals of opposite sex has never been observed."

Pallas 1781, p. 47 (*jacchus*)

"After a month or 6 weeks, when the young are weaned in captivity, the mother no longer protects them from older offspring. All the young fight among themselves and the weaker one that yields is often attacked and nearly killed by the others."

Rothe 1975*a*, p. 264

"In the FG [family group] over 90% of the copulations of the parents were disrupted by the adult, subadult and even juvenile sons and daughters, inasmuch as these were aware of the copulation. . . . The sons and daughters in the FG [family group] ran towards the parents in display posture, surrounded them, threatened or stood on their hind legs and attempted to separate the father from the mother. Mostly both parents parted in display posture (usually by copulations without intromission) as soon as they were approached by their children. Often, however, especially during the estrus of their mother, they defended themselves by hitting and threatening. The mother was also more aggressive than the father. No serious consequences resulted from such situations, however. Often, all the sons and daughters, with the exception of the infants, followed in display posture the parents after a mating act."

Temperament

F. Cuvier 1819 (*jacchus*)

"They are defiant and threaten to bite everybody without distinguishing between those who feed them and the stranger they see for the first time. They are not affectionate and are always seized with rage; the slightest contradiction irritates them and when overtaken by fear, they utter a short piercing cry and fly into hiding. Sometimes, and without apparent cause, they emit a sharp and extremely prolonged whistle of the same tonal quality as the preceding cry."

Fitzgerald 1935, p. 183 (*jacchus*)

"In temperament, the marmoset is highly nervous and easily startled and frightened; but a disturbed animal soon resumes its normal state and its regular routine in sleeping, eating and grooming. The marmoset is not considered (by this writer) an affectionate pet. Even when tame and easily handled it does not show any pleasure when greeted or any sorrow when left alone."

Neill 1829, pp. 18, 19, 20 (*jacchus*)

"At first it was exceedingly fierce and wild, screeching most vehemently when any one dared to approach it. . . . It was long before it was so reconciled, even to those who fed it, as to allow the slightest liberty in the way of touching or patting its body; and it was almost impossible to do this by surprise, or by the most cautious approach, as the monkey was not steady a moment, but was constantly turning its head round from side to side, eyeing every person with the most suspicious angry look.

". . . For a considerable time there was no evident

change in its habits, as it continued to be nearly as wild as when I first got it, and showed none of the playfulness and vivacity which characterise most of the monkey tribe. . . .

"Though now it is much tamer than it was, it is by no means tractable or docile; it will allow itself to be patted or gently stroked, but all attempts to handle or to play with it are quite unsuccessful. When teased or enraged, it exhibits a most ludicrous physiognomy of passion; the white hairs or whiskers on its cheeks are erected; it grins and shows its teeth; it dilates its nostrils, and the little eyes beam with the most passionate fury; it only wants the power of speech to embody its feelings, to represent most faithfully a true picture of anger. Though it does not possess any of that imitative playfulness which is so amusing in many of the Simiae, there is a something, an air of intelligence, a look of observation, which we search for in vain in those animals lower in the zoological scale."

Stellar 1960, p. 4 (*jacchus*)

"Upon any disturbance, it runs actively about its cage, retreating to the rear and coming forward to look out of its cage, in rapid succession. In addition to the typical mammalian signs of piloerection, pupillary dilation, and rapid breathing, the emotionally disturbed marmoset characteristically licks its nose in quick darts of its long tongue. Also, it chatters and chirps noisily in a characteristic vocal pattern that is different for each strain of marmoset. Upon handling, the marmoset reacts to restraint by vocalizing and struggling wildly, and unlike the rhesus monkey, may continue this emotional display to the point of physical exhaustion."

Hornung 1896, p. 277 (*penicillata*)

"I can recommend the ouistiti as a pet. It is extremely friendly and, if free in the room disports itself without causing any damage to the surroundings. In short, it is a great source of entertainment for its owner."

Hornung 1899, p. 209 (*penicillata*)

"It enjoys human company immensely and wants to have people constantly with it in the kitchen. When left alone it becomes downcast and pleads for the company with a call that is shrill and almost deafening to the ears of those nearby."

Cuvier, in Geoffroy and Cuvier 1819, p. 2 (*jacchus*)

"They are incapable of affection and are of an irritable nature."

Threat and Aggression

Mallinson 1971, p. 6 (*penicillata*)

"When in a threatening posture, they put their circumauricular tufts forward, fluff up their fur as if to make themselves look larger, and make a rapid and continuous vocalization, swaying the body to and fro, before sometimes launching into a heroic attack" (fig. IX.29).

Fig. IX.29. *Callithrix jacchus jacchus,* male, with young, in threat posture. (Photo courtesy of Gisela Epple.)

Epple 1967*b*, p. 62 (*jacchus*)

"Lip smacking and rhythmical protrusion of the tongue are shown in sexual and social contact as well as in aggressive threat.

"Very quick flattening and erection of ears and ear-tufts function as an aggressive threat signal in *Hapale* [= *Callithrix*] *jacchus, Hapale leucocephala* [= *C. jacchus geoffroyi*], and *Mico* [= *Callithrix*] *a. argentatus.*"

Pallas 1781, p. 45 (*jacchus*)

"When very tame adult females were stroked they pressed their genitalia against the bars of the cage and urinated. The males would do the same thing but as an expression of anger especially in the presence of women."

Cuvier, in Geoffroy and Cuvier 1819, p. 2 (*jacchus*)

"They are suspicious of everyone and threaten to bite the people who feed them as well as those they see for the first time."

Fitzgerald 1935, p. 183 (*jacchus*)

"Human strangers are studied from head to foot, and the marmosets are apt to come forward and make grimaces at them by drawing back their ears and raising their faces with puckered lips. They may also turn their posterior extremities towards the visitors. This latter gesture, however, is also used in play with those with whom the animals are familiar. It then invites to a friendly rough house with the hand."

Hornung 1896, p. 275 (*penicillata*)

"When a stranger comes near he shows irritation by arching his back, holding his tail at an angle, making horrible grimaces and by invariably making for the face or hands of the stranger. I feel sorry for anyone he bites. His teeth are very sharp and have drawn blood from a number of people who came too close."

Epple 1967*b*, p. 62 (*jacchus*)

"All species show an arch-posture in defensive threat. Slowly, demonstratively walking in an extremely arched posture functions as a display of dominance . . . [fig. IX.30].

Fig. IX.30. *Callithrix jacchus jacchus* male arching back. (Photo courtesy of Gisela Epple.)

"Presentation of the genitalia . . . does not function as an invitation to mounting or submissive behavior but represents an aggressive threat signal. Often the inferior approaches a presenting dominant, showing submissive behavior, and sniffs the genitalia of the dominant animal intensively."

Epple 1970*b* (*jacchus*)

The frequencies per time unit of scent marking, aggressive threat, and attacking and fighting strange conspecifics were recorded in three test groups. Each consisted of a dominant adult male, a dominant adult female, and one, two, or three subordinate adults and juvenals. The largest group consisted of five individuals, the smallest of four. All groups had existed for at least two months with a stable hierarchy and little or no aggression between group members. It was found that dominant males and dominant females marked more frequently and heavily than their subordinates. Dominant males attacked strange adult males introduced into the cage and dominant females attacked strange females. Increased marking followed aggressive encounters. Perches marked by strange conspecifics also stimulated the dominant individual to more frequent sniffing and marking.

Hershkovitz (*jacchus*)

The genital display by an old male whom I surprised in its cage in the Houston colony ran the following course, observed at eye level. The testes descended completely and the scrotum enlarged to maximum. This operation was completed within a second, and the climax of the spectacle was maintained for about a second. As the testes were withdrawn and the scrotum began to collapse, the animal turned 180° on its perch and confronted me in threat posture, eye to eye (fig. IX.31).

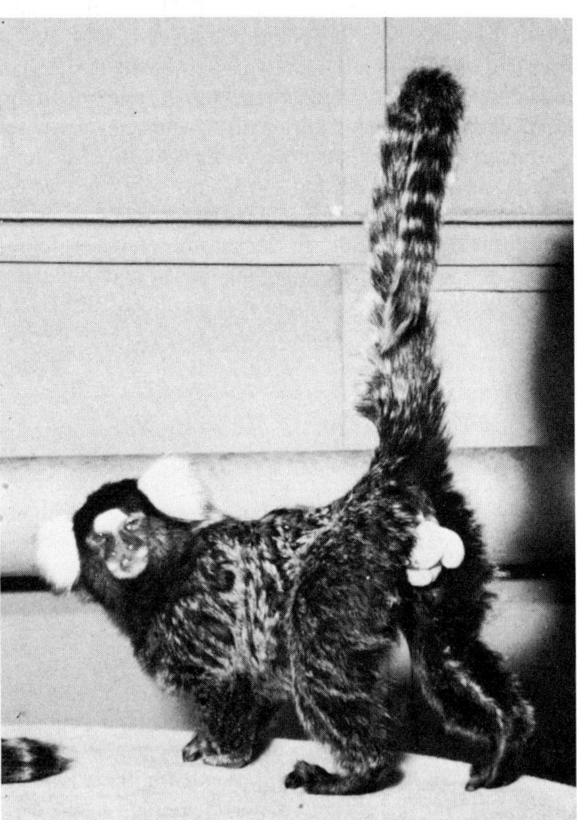

Fig. IX.31. *Callithrix jacchus jacchus* male presenting genitalia. (Photo courtesy of Gisela Epple.)

Mallinson (in litt., 1 October 1968) (*penicillata*)

In the Jersey Zoological Park, Channel Islands, Great Britain, we have "a female *Callithrix penicillata* living with an adult pair of *Lemur catta* in a large outdoor aviary type cage. Although the lemurs will catch and kill sparrows which occasionally find their way into the aviary, they seem to be afraid of the marmoset. The latter had been observed taking a piece of banana from the male lemur."

Rothe 1975*a*, p. 264

In artificial groups, aggressiveness of the estrous alpha female increased toward subordinate females. The alpha male of the groups was indifferent to other males, but he attempted to drive them away from the alpha female. Increase of aggression between the dominant and subordinate females often reached an intensity that abated only after permanent separation of the belligerents.

In family groups, aggressiveness was not seen to increase between the estrous alpha female and her offspring. The mother often allowed genital inspection by all members of the group, but the alpha male usually tried to keep the adults away.

Epple 1970*b;* 1974*a, b* (*jacchus*)

Dominance and threat of aggression are described under Marking (p. 561).

Fear

Hornung 1896, p. 275 (*penicillata*)

"He is afraid of rabbits and runs from them. On the other hand, he lived peacefully in the same cage with a guinea pig. He climbed over it, twisted its ears and groomed its fur with zest. Any stray kitten he might see in the garden, however, would startle him and it would be some time before he calmed down. In contrast, he was not afraid of birds. If one were brought to him he would rush upon it, seize it by the bill and press its body against the floor of his nesting chamber or against the tree trunk in the cage until it was killed. He would play with the feathers but would not eat the flesh."

Heusser 1968, p. 711 (*jacchus*)

Cats and dogs aroused the particular fear of the old male marmoset which roamed freely around Heusser's house in Switzerland. Cats learned the habits of the marmoset and lay in wait for him in the morning outside the door of the house where he lived, and stalked him in the trees. The day the marmoset was surprised by a predator, was the day he changed his route. Dogs were sensed at great distances and their barking frightened him, but the marmoset feared cats more.

Hornung 1896, p. 277 (*penicillata*)

"A dove flying overhead or a falling leaf can frighten him. While I am writing these lines, his loud complaining brings me to him on the run. I find him hiding behind a tree trunk in his cage trembling and chirping ruefully and all the while looking up into the sky. The cause of all this excitement is a kite hovering above the garden; he quieted down only after I covered his cage with a towel."

Hornung 1896, p. 275 (*penicillata*)

"I have a simple device for bringing the little wanderer back to his cage, namely a fur cap. The moment I show it to him he scurries pell mell into his cage. He is terrified by such harmless but unusual objects as a wooden nutcracker with a fur cap covering the wooden head. He is even more frightened by tobacco smoke; when smoke is blown into his face he blinks his eyes shut."

Antonius 1939

Fear of snakes was not noticed among marmosets tested by Antonius in the Vienna Zoo. *Callithrix jacchus jacchus* and *C. j. penicillata* (also *C. humeralifer, Saguinus oedipus, S. midas*) took mealworms from Antonius's hand without paying any attention to a live snake entwined around it.

Fear is also mentioned under the heading of Vocalization.

Care of Young

Siret 1778, p. 453 (*jacchus*)

"Each twin, [born 15 August 1776 in France] when first seen was firmly attached to the back of one of its parents. The mother, however, very often carried both offspring at the same time. The young were fully clothed with hair within one month and were weaned within two. It seemed that the mother cared less for the young than did the father. When seen neglecting her charges the mother was warned by the father with a cry. If this admonition went unheeded, he followed by striking her. After suckling the young, the mother made every effort to rid herself of them. She would free herself by kicking them off or by rolling on her back and tearing them away as they scurried to her underside. Each time the father came to the rescue and invited the twins to mount his back. Once when one of the young fell from a perch and lay stunned below, the Marquis de Néelle, thinking it dead, reached into the cage and picked it up. At this intrusion the father became furious, threw himself upon his lordship and shrieked until the master of the house returned the young to the floor where he found it. The father then picked up his offspring and placed it on his back where it recovered and resumed play, sound as ever."

Pallas 1781, p. 41 (*jacchus*)

"A pair of sagoins belonging to Count Ivan Gregorevitch, vice president of the Admiralty, were kept without particular care in a cage two feet wide in a room [beside a window] which was unheated through spring and autumn [the temperature near freezing most of the time]. The pair had no freedom outside the cage but this did not prevent them from producing three litters during the last two years and raising the young with little effort. Each of the three litters produced were of twins, 'mostly males.' All offspring survived and grew to maturity. "The young which are quite bare in the first few weeks are first carried about by the mother and they cling so tightly and are so well concealed behind the large ears with their long white tufts that only their heads and lively eyes are visible.

When the mother tires of them, she frees herself of her young and throws them onto the male's back and scolds and strikes her mate until he accepts the little ones."

Cuvier (1819) confirms Pallas's observation that the mother attends the young first, then the father takes over. His responsibility for care of the young is complete except during nursing periods. Grüner and Krause (1963, p. 112) affirm, however, that the mother may also carry the young in play, or for relieving the father when he is occupied in eating or performing other tasks. The solicitude of the father for a set of newborn twins, one stillborn, is described by Fitzgerald (1935, p. 185). She found him "hugging and licking the corpse" of the dead twin. He was very attentive to the survivor, licking and cleansing its posterior parts. This anxiety may last for a week or longer before the father begins evading responsibility for the young, then quitting it altogether by the seventh week at the latest.

In actuality, any male or female not a mother but strong enough to carry young may act as "father." Lucas, Hume, and Henderson-Smith (1937, p. 208) describe a situation of this sort. "For the first three or four weeks the babies were always carried exclusively by the parents, nor were they ever set down in that period. Later, when old enough to run about the cages, the small babies, if alarmed always took a leap on the back of the nearest senior, whether parent, brother or sister, and the senior apparently always acquiesced as long as the danger continued. When it was passed the babies were detached again as soon as possible; the adult carrying them would rub them off against the bars of the cage or gently bite their fingers to make them let go. As they grew older they were progressively compelled to be more and more independent, but this was not achieved without great firmness on the part of all the older members of the family."

The female with her single pair of mammae can suckle only two young at once. When the litter consists of three or four young, the male cares for the extra ones until they take their turn at the teat. In the wild, rarely do more than two young in each litter survive to maturity. The mother herself may dispose of the third or fourth member. Cuvier (1819, p. 1) saw triplets born in the menagerie of the Jardin des Plantes "quickly attach themselves to their mother, embracing her and hiding in her fur but before they could suckle, the head of one of them was devoured by the mother."

Babies are suckled every 2–3 hours throughout the day according to Lucas, Hume, and Henderson-Smith (1927, p. 449). They report that the mother "would approach the father and hold out her arm, when the baby would scramble apparently spontaneously, on to her. After the feeding was over, it would pull the baby off and give it to the father." Marik (1931, p. 347) also noted that the young were fed every 2 or 3 hours but with a feeding lasting about 30 minutes. On the other hand Fitzgerald reports that the mother of her young ouistiti fed it "almost every hour for about 10 minutes at a time," while Grüner and Krause (1963, pp. 110–11) observed feeding at an average of 15-minute intervals during the 9th day and an average of 30 minutes on the 25th day. They add that each of the twins they observed were fed in turn, the mother nursing first the one she judged most hungry by smelling the mouths of her young. The same investigators add that the mother always responded promptly to the hunger call of her young. Langford (1963, p. 300) states that "immediately after the first birth, the male takes the baby, licks off the film of mucus and then hands the baby back to the mother for feeding; the same procedure being adopted for the second or third child [of the same litter]. It has happened that a young female giving birth to her first infant is uncertain in which position to hold the baby to her breast and, in consequence, has held it up-side-down until the baby has righted itself. The infant is fed every two or three hours during the first week, and then at ever increasing intervals until it is about a month old when it begins to feed on solids which are pre-masticated by the male."

Rothe 1974*a* (*jacchus*)

The mother licks the newborn shortly after birth while the young immediately grasp her fur with hands and feet and climb to the nipples unaided. A newborn too weak to attach itself to its mother may be licked casually but otherwise ignored and left to die. Group members exhibit great interest and curiosity in the birth and try to sniff and touch the newborn if allowed by the exhausted mother. The babies remain attached to the nipples until daylight, when the mother gets rid of them by permitting an eager and willing relative, usually the father, to take the young. The mother's interest in her offspring evidently does not surpass nursing and licking them at intervals.

Rothe 1975*b*, pp. 316, 317

"Our observations indicate that the firstborn of each litter receives more intensive and more frequent maternal care than the remaining ones, but our data are not sufficient for statistical analysis. As soon as the neonates have reached the nipples or as soon as the mother has eaten the placenta they get no further care for the following 4–6 h with the exception of being transported and fed. Even in critical situations with which the neonates may be confronted after expulsion (e.g. loss of contact to their mother for some moments due to abrupt movement at the moment of expulsion) the neonates—still connected to her by the umbilical cord—succeed unaided in climbing on to their mother, who in the meantime licks littermates or sometimes even leaves the birthplace, dragging the neonate behind.

". . . Neonates who are so severely damaged that they neither move nor vocalize (phi and twitter calls) get no further care by their mothers when once they have been more or less thoroughly cleaned. The same is true for stillborn infants.

"Maternal care becomes more intensive with vocalizing newborns. Two infants, whose births we have observed, lay motionless beside their mothers after delivery, and consequently received only little care. After 13 and 24 min, respectively, they began faintly to vocalize. Both females (one of them was just eating the placenta, the other had already left the birthplace) approached their infants, licked them very intensively and took them with both hands. They held them no longer than a few seconds. Both mothers tried to take their infants 17 and 11 min, respectively, with short interruptions when the neonates did not vocalize. From the moment the babies no longer vocalized, the females showed no further interest in them.

"We played back distress calls of 3-min-old newborns to two mothers who gave birth to two weak infants, and who showed no maternal care after a few minutes. By this experiment we initiated for more than an hour most intensive maternal behaviour without significant satiation over time."

Grooming

Fitzgerald 1935, p. 183 (*jacchus*)

"The grooming of the hair is a very important part of the animal's life. Much time is spent in the process. Grooming consists in separating the hairs (its own or those of another animal) with the fingers and the nails [*sic*], the groomer watching intently for particles of dead cuticle or bits of any foreign substance that may have lodged in the fur. When found, such objects are picked up by the lips, which are kept moistened by the tongue. Much interest and anticipation are shown by the groomer. The request for grooming comes from the "groomee" who approaches the groomer and, facing him, lies down flat in an inviting attitude. The animal that is being groomed relaxes completely, but keeps moving its body so as to present every part of it in turn for inspection. The eyes of the groomed animal may close; his facial expression is always one of ecstatic contentment. No noise of any kind accompanies the operation.

"An experienced groomer sits on his haunches and has perfect freedom and control of his arms; but a novice has to lean on the groomee and has to use only one arm at a time. The marmoset does not sit up with ease until its third year. The older the groomer, the more thorough his work; and a good groomer is in great demand. The process can at times be quite painful; for instance, when a matted bunch of hair must be untangled or removed, I have seen an animal raised off the floor by the groomer's efforts to bite away such a tangle. Some animals welcome a daily finetooth combing. Sometimes the combing is painful, but no sound or effort to escape is ever made. Grooming is extended to the mouth, where the teeth are gone over with particular interest."

Pallas 1781, p. 42 (*jacchus*)

"In warm sunshine they pick each other's lice with front feet and teeth like monkeys."

Hornung 1896, p. 276 (*penicillata*)

"When the weather is good during the day the cage and its occupants are placed outside in the garden. The marmoset enjoys even the weakest ray of sunshine and basks for hours in the warm sun. At the same time, he cleans his fur thoroughly. If I should bring my head within reach he scratches it and tousles my hair with evident pleasure."

Mallinson 1965, p. 138

Grooming by various callitrichids, including representatives of *Callithrix,* in the Jersey Zoological Park, Channel Islands, was performed by "scratching the skin and combing the fur, for the most part with the claws of the hind foot."

Autogrooming movements of the hind limb are usually swift and cat- or doglike. Those of the front limbs are monkey or cebidlike (P. H.).

Rothe 1971, p. 137 (*jacchus*)

"Auto-grooming as well as allo-grooming—the latter one being reciprocal-grooming (Sparks, 1967 [see definitions below])—are a regular part of the marmoset's daily activities. Mutual-grooming (Sparks, 1967) does not occur with *Callithrix;* with *Saguinas tamarin,* however, it is part of the general grooming repertoire. Moreover, Carpenter (cit. Yerkes, 1933 [J. Soc. Psychol. *4*:3–25]) describes a case of heterogrooming (groomer = *Callithrix;* groomee = rat).

"Grooming may either start spontaneously, or be caused by some discomfort of the body or by specific gesture of invitation by any member of the group. (Epple, 1967[*b*]; Fitzgerald, 1935) Non-observance of an invitation gesture is not followed by frustration: the potential groomee starts allo-grooming, less often auto-grooming.

"In adult groups inferior members show higher grooming activity than the high ranking ones do. Low ranking animals groom one another with equal frequency. Among the α-marmosets of the group the male shows a more intense readiness to be groomer than does the female; on the other hand, the female more often acts as groomee. Grooming among animals of the same sex but of different rank could only be observed during the first 6 weeks after establishing an adult group.

"In family groups, allo-grooming is most frequent with the father; the high ranking female displays considerably less allo-grooming activity. It prefers the male of the same rank and its oldest sons, whereas the α-male mainly turns to the oldest among the young ones of the family and within this group prefers the females.

"Allo-grooming occurs about 3–4 times per hour. Duration of grooming per interaction ranges from 7 to 400 sec, with an average of 16 sec. With respect to duration, there is no difference among the members of the group.

"Already 3 to 6 weeks after birth, the first grooming actions are performed by the infants. However, until their subadult age, they stay mainly passive. Active readiness is adressed to the parents rather than to the brothers and sisters.

"During the ovulation phase of the α-female and also in the presence of new borns, allo-grooming activity of the parents increases 1.5–2 times the usual rate [fig. IX.32].

"Eibl-Eibesfeldt (1970, p. 132 [in Liebe und Hass. "Zur Naturgeschichte elementarer Verhaltensweisen (Pi per, München)]) observed that in the same situation grooming became 3 times as frequent as usual among all group members.

"Auto-grooming in adult groups is done more frequently by inferior animals, the activity of which increases during the ovulation period of the α-female.

Fig. IX.32. *Callithrix jacchus jacchus* male engaged in pre-copulatory grooming of female. (Photo courtesy of Gisela Epple.)

Young animals hardly ever auto-groom. With animals kept in social isolation the frequency of auto-grooming is twice as high as with adult group animals.

"During the grooming process the hands are moved alternatively, rather than simultaneously.

"Four different grooming movements could be observed: (1) the groomer draws his hands towards himself in a caudo-lateral direction; at the same time the phalanges are flexed and abducted; (2) the groomer places his pronated hands side by side but about 1–2 cm apart in his partner's fur and draws them synchroneously aside, canting the ulnar part of the hand in a medial direction; the fingers are stretched and completely abducted; (3) both hands are shoved pronated into the fur which is then divided by abducting the stretched fingers; (4) the active marmoset with both hands grips its partner's fur, shoving his arms forward and canting the radial hand towards a lateral position. Depending on the part of the body groomed, the hands are drawn through the fur for 1–3 cm. As concerns the sequence of body parts being groomed, no preference was recorded.

"During grooming, the movements of the hands usually are slow; with displacement grooming, however, they are performed hastily and more in a beating than a drawing fashion. Foreign bodies and dandruff are only taken up with lips and/or teeth. Matted tufts of hair are usually untangled by nibbling at them."

Rothe 1974*b*, p. 544 (abstract) (*jacchus*)

"The allogrooming behaviour of the parents (= α-animals) of three family groups of *Callithrix jacchus* has been studied during 25 days following birth. A total of 22 postpartum periods has been analysed. We recorded significant increase of grooming activity beginning with the 5th day postpartum. Allogrooming initiated by invitation gesture dropped to one-tenth of the total allogrooming frequency within one week, starting from day 5 postpartum. As a rule, allogrooming activity increased abruptly, whereas the decrease was mostly continuous, lasting several days. The maximum of postpartum allogrooming frequency preceded to some extent the maximum of copulatory activity and sexual willingness of the ♀. The ♂ made more attempts to groom the ♀ than vice versa. Up to the 18th day postpartum the ♀♀ ended more grooming sessions than the ♂♂ and then during anoestrus. The ♀♀ refused more invitations to grooming than did the ♂♂. The analysis of postpartum grooming behaviour in *C. jacchus* does not allow for accurate determination of the first and last day of the postpartum oestrus."

Grooming Terminology

Sparks (1967), cited by Rothe (1971) for use of grooming terminology, adopted those of Cullen (1963). The terms are self-explanatory, but the following glossary may be useful:

Autogrooming: Self grooming.
Allogrooming: One individual grooming another.
Mutual grooming: Simultaneous grooming by each of a pair.
Reciprocal grooming: Grooming in alternation of one by the other of a pair.
Heterogrooming: An animal of one species being groomed by an animal of another species.

Food

Fitzgerald 1935, p. 181 (*jacchus*)

"Any food safe for a human seems to be safe for a marmoset. The only exception to this rule made by the writer is that she has never given fish to the animals."

Edwards 1758, p. 17 (*jacchus*)

The ouistiti which "was the property of the good and very obliging Mrs. Kennon, formerly midwife to the Royal Family . . . fed on several sorts of things, as biscuits, fruits, greens, insects, snails, etc. and once when let loose, it suddenly snatched a chinese goldfish out of a bason [*sic*] of water, which it killed and greedily devoured; after which she gave him small live eels which frightened him at first by their twisting round his neck but he soon mastered them, and eat [*sic*] them."

Wied-Neuwied 1826, p. 133 (*penicillata*)

In the wild they "feed on different fruit, especially on the bananas in the plantations, but they also eat many kinds of insects, spiders and the like; it is certainly erroneous that these little animals will eat fish; for even if they did in captivity, it could not be concluded from this that they would do so in their natural habitat."

[Fish are not available in the arborial habitat, but no doubt callitrichids feed on tadpoles hatched in rainwater collected between leaves and in tree hollows.—P. H.].

Heusser 1968, p. 712 (*jacchus*)

"The marmoset fished from the aquarium, snails, tadpoles and once a nearly full-grown frog which he completely devoured except for the limbs. As always, he ate the head first."

Mallinson 1971, p. 6 (*penicillata*)

"Two newly imported female Common marmosets were frequently observed catching and then eating sparrows which had flown into their large aviary [in the Jersey Zoo, Channel Islands]. They would hold the bird by the scruff of the neck, biting at the head first, eating a certain amount but discarding the remainder."

Neill 1829, pp. 19, 20 (*jacchus*)

"As long as the fruit [oranges, bananas, mangoes, corn] which he had on board lasted, it would eat nothing else; but when these failed, we soon discovered a most agreeable substitute which it appeared to relish above every thing. By chance we observed it devouring a large cockroach which he had caught, running along the deck of the vessel; and from this time to nearly the end of the voyage, a space of four or five weeks, it fed almost exclusively on these insects, and contributed most effectually to rid the vessel of them. It frequently eat a score of the largest kind, which are 2 or 2½ inches long, and a very great number of the smaller ones, three or four times in the course of the day. It was quite amusing to see it at its meal. When he had got hold of one of the large cockroaches, he held it in his fore paws, and then invariably nipped the head off first; he then pulled out the viscera and cast them aside, and devoured the rest of the body, rejecting the dry elytra and wings, and also the legs of the insect, which are covered with short stiff bristles. The small cockroaches he eat without such fastidious nicety. In addition to these, we gave him milk, sugar, raisins, and crumbs of bread. . . .

"When I got it on shore, I kept it for some days in a warm room; it gradually recovered its nimbleness, running about the room, and dragging its kennel after it. Even then it would not eat any insects, and its food consisted of milk and crumbs of bread; it was particularly fond of any sweet preserve, as jelly, etc., and of fresh ripe fruit. From London I brought it with me to Edinburgh last November and have kept it here till now."

Hornung 1896, p. 276 (*penicillata*)

"I feed him milk, toast, sweets, fruit (pears, grapes, black currants, preserved whortleberries, fruit juice), dried scraped bacon, spiders with the exception of the cross spider (*Aranea diadema* Linnaeus) which he threw up once and has not touched since, grasshoppers, even larger beetles like dorbeetles [*Geotrupes*] but he dislikes raw meat. His most favorite tidbits are meal worms."

Hornung 1899, p. 208 (*penicillata*)

"He also pursues flies greedily. If one alights on the wire mesh of his cage, he pounces upon it with the speed of lightning and rarely misses. He watches the flies moving outside his cage and tries to catch them with his paw through the mesh."

Burmeister 1854, p. 35 (*aurita*)

Under the name *Hapale chrysopyga* a young individual of *Callithrix jacchus aurita* was observed eating "insects with relish, even dry pinned down specimens. However, it did not touch beetles and specimens preserved in alcohol."

Mallinson 1972, p. 29

"The family of hybrids *C. penicillata* × *C. jacchus* who previously shared the aviary with the Laysan teal had almost completely ignored the ducks until they saw a clutch of eggs starting to hatch. They became sufficiently stimulated towards the usually aggressive duck, and the marmosets as a team mobbed and desecrated the nest, dragging the two partly hatched chicks out of their shells and eating parts of them."

Stellar 1960, p. 2 (*jacchus*)

"These animals require considerable amounts of animal protein, and in the laboratory as well as in the wild, they have a voracious appetite for insects and will eat eggs, newborn birds, and small lizards. A diet of natural foods, high in animal protein, however, is not easy to achieve in the laboratory, for many convenient insects like meal worms and roaches transmit intestinal parasites, and the preference for carbohydrates often outweighs the appetite for other protein sources such as meat and milk. In addition, adult marmosets require steady sources of Vitamin D, and in the past, this has meant the inconvenience of daily sun-lamp treatments."

Epple 1970*a*, pp. 59–60 (*jacchus*)

"A great variety of food appeared to stimulate the animals' activity and since this was desired for our work, no standard diet was used. Since marmosets are carnivorous to a great extent, our animals received a mixed diet of fruit, vegetables, dairy products, cereals, seafish, frogs, mice and also a large amount of insects (mealworms, crickets, locusts, caterpillars). Insects are probably a very important part of the natural diet of these primates.

They do not only provide proteins but also considerable amounts of fat. The large South American cockroaches (e.g. *Blaberus spec.*), well fed crickets and caterpillars have huge intestinal fat bodies. When eating those insects, the monkeys consume at least a part of the fat tissue. For captive marmoset monkeys, such insects, are very palatable. My animals ate as many as 15–20 crickets (the large *Gryllus bipunctata*) or locusts per day without showing satiation while feeding heartily on fruit and cereal as well."

Epple 1970*a*, p. 72 (*jacchus*)

"infants almost entirely depend on the food they actively take away from other group members, and take only minimal amounts from the food dish, these animals literally starved beside the filled dish. The parents, on the other hand, do not actively feed the babies, but leave them only those amounts of food which the infants take from their mouth and hands. In the relatively big enclosures that were available to the monkeys, food competition developed between both infants. The more active and vigorous infant constantly pursued adult group members to take all the food it could get. The other twin made less efforts, thus did not get enough food and became weak and underdeveloped very quickly. Probably this would not have happened in a smaller cage where the adults had less opportunity to withdraw from a begging infant."

Coimbra-Filho 1971, p. 384; 1972, p. 505 (*jacchus*)

"In a small forest preserve in Maceió, Alagoas, I noticed that the bark of the tree *Tapirira guianensis* (Anacardiaceae) was covered with small, more or less evenly spaced perforations. The holes penetrated the bark and cambium layer to the surface of the wood. My local companion informed me that the holes were made by *Callithrix jacchus* and that it was well known to natives that marmosets chew on the tree trunks and branches to get the exuding gums and saps. Later I had an opportunity to observe a marmoset biting a hole into the bark of an *Anacardium occidentale* (Anacardaceae). I also saw a second marmoset licking the gum welling from another part of the same tree trunk. I have since seen *Tapirira* and *Anacardium* with the telltale perforations but none of them were as thoroughly pitted as the Maceió *Tapirira* [fig. IX.33].

"Although the cashews *Tapirira guianensis* and *Anacardium occidentale* seem to be preferred by marmosets, the exudates of *Protium* sp. (Burseraceae), the introduced *Terminalia catappa* (Combretaceae), and those of the exotic palm *Chrysalidocarpus lutescens,* are also eaten. To test the field observations, freshly cut boughs

Fig. IX.33. Cashew tree, *Tapirira guiananis,* in Maceió, Alagoas, with holes bitten into bark by *Callithrix jacchus jacchus.* The bark and underlying vascular layers are excavated and chewed for the exuding gums and saps which are esteemed as food by marmosets (and other animals). Size, shape, and disposition of the perforations recall woodpecker borings. (Photo courtesy of A. F. Coimbra-Filho [1971, p. 385, fig. 5].)

of *Anacardium occidentale* were put into the cages of *Callithrix penicillata, C. geoffroyi, C. flaviceps* and hybrids of various marmoset crosses. The branches were immediately bitten, gnawed, chewed and licked."

Guenther 1931, pp. 41, 174 (*jacchus*)

Marmosets in the Recife (Pernambuco) region were seen nibbling the boughs of cashew trees.

Clark 1974, p. 46 (*jacchus*)

The common marmosets kept in the Jersey Zoological Park (Channel Islands) will strip bark from branches and consume a little. They have also been seen "to bite off a piece of twig and carry it to a safe part of the cage and then chew it for some minutes."

Remarks. The foregoing excerpts and comments suggest that captive marmosets eat almost anything anytime. In the wild, survival of the population depends on close synchronization between its seasonal and cyclical nutritional requirements, and the periodic changes in the kinds and quantities of food available to it.

Manipulation

Pallas 1781, p. 42 (*jacchus*)

"The thumb is not opposable to the fingers as in man and many monkeys. They hold morsels they cannot eat in one mouthful, rather by folding their fingers squirrel-wise against the palm than by the thumb. The great toe of the hind foot, however, is stronger, provided with a rounded claw and is very apt at holding."

Rothe 1975*c*, Summary, p. 384 (*jacchus*)

"The use of the hand of the common marmoset (*Callithrix jacchus* Erxleben, 1777) was analysed on the basis of observation and experiments conducted on 56 animals of all age. . . .

"While gripping the hand adapts to the form of the object. An active variation of the gripping pattern does not occur, so that a differentiation between precision grip and power grip does not appear to be developed, at least as far as the hand form is concerned. The pollex is of little importance for the effectiveness of the grip. It is not opposable, but indicates to a certain extent an individual flexibility, which is independent of the remaining phalanges. The prehensive pattern and the grip forms of *Callithrix jacchus* are essentially more variable in the manipulation of objects than that exhibited in feeding behaviour or in experimental situations. . . .

"During grasping behaviour the nails impede the sensoric control and thus the grasping of the object within the hand region. In any case, they aid the stability of the grip on small objects. . . .

"On the whole, the prehensive pattern of *Callithrix jacchus,* due to the more flexible arm and hand movements, is superior to that of the Prosimii, equal at least to that of *Aotus,* but inferior to that of the other Cebidae."

Handedness

Stellar 1960, p. 5 (*jacchus*)

"When counts were made of which hand the marmoset [*Callithrix j. jacchus*] used to displace the stimulus object from the central food well, a distribution of hand preferences was obtained similar to that found in the rat, cat and rhesus monkey (Table 1 [see table 76 below]). Quite clearly most [i.e., 5 of 8] marmosets are right-handed, a few [2] are left-handed, and a few [1] ambidextrous. These data are based on at least 100 trials and in some cases as many as 500 trials [of 8 animals]. Several cases where handedness was determined again on several occasions showed that the marmoset's preferences are quite consistent in this type of testing situation."

Table 76. Handedness in 8 Marmosets (nos. 2–9) Shown by the Percentage of Times Right and Left Hands Are Used in Displacing an Object Covering Food in a Well

	Animal							
Hand	*2*	*3*	*4*	*5*	*6*	*7*	*8*	*9*
Right	92	60	94	42	3	96	91	0
Left	8	40	6	58	97	4	9	100

SOURCE: Data from Stellar (1960, p. 5).

Rothe 1973*a* (*jacchus*)

Nine male and 12 female *Callithrix j. jacchus* were tested for handedness over a period of 20 months. In spontaneous behavior, 2 marmosets showed preference for the left hand, 6 for the right and the remaining 13 showed no preference. In the tests, however, 5 preferred the left hand in most cases, 14 the right, and 3 used either hand about equally. Lack of consistent handedness and absence of a tendency to increase the use of one hand over the other during the experiments led Rothe to conclude that the common marmoset is basically ambidextrous.

Feeding: Use of Hand or Mouth

Stellar 1960, p. 4 (*jacchus*)

"The usual pattern of *feeding behavior* is to carry food from the food cup to the perch or shelf, and then in squatting position, to feed from the hands. On fairly frequent occasions, however, the marmoset will feed directly from the food cup or the shelf with its mouth and not handle the food."

Rothe 1971, p. 136 (*jacchus*)

"The hand . . . as a grasping organ [for feeding] is rarely used: with all marmosets [30 specimens] use of the mouth was significantly more frequent. ($P<0.001$). All of them handle and shift pieces of food and in taking them up, they sometimes, somewhat accidently, support the bait with their hands. Pulpy food and water are taken up by mouth only, accidental manual contact results in movements expressing disgust: violent shaking of the hand and head, grimaces, closing of the eyes; occasionally saliva is brought out by the tongue. Afterwards, however, the hand is licked clean.

"The relation of frequency between use of the mouth and that of the hand is not influenced by the shape, size, location, and consistency of the object to be seized. Experiments in which marmosets could only use their hands for taking up food did not significantly reinforce the use of the hands under normal conditions."

Hornung 1896, p. 276 (*penicillata*)

"He prefers to take food with his mouth; if a bit of food is placed outside the cage, he grabs it through the wire mesh with one hand and pulls it in with his fingers curved inward."

Rothe 1975*c*, Summary, p. 384 (*jacchus*)

"As a rule, *Callithrix jacchus* reaches for pieces of food with one hand."

Predation: Use of Hands and Mouth

Rothe 1971, p. 137 (*jacchus*)

"Slowly moving insects are more frequently caught with the hands than are fruit pieces. Only 2 out of 30 animals used their hands more often than their mouths.

"Fast running insects—such as crickets or cockroaches—are caught by jumping at them with outstretched and pronated arms and hands and then pressing the insects down to the ground. Then they grasp the prey, by flexing and adducting the fingers and simultaneously turning the radial part of both hands in a lateral direction. The marmosets first quickly bite the insect's head off and then proceed to eat the rest of the insect while holding it with one or, as is usually observed, both hands.

"Insects flying around are not caught while still in motion. The marmosets wait instead until the insects settle down. They sneak up on them from behind with lowered head and slightly slanting body, then get up on their hind legs and with both hands clasp the branch or climbing pole at the point where the prey is believed to be. This seizing operation is performed with great accuracy; quite frequently, however, this grasping was carried out till the very end although the fly or moth had already moved from the spot the marmoset had aimed at. Unsuccessful attempts at seizing are followed by thorough examination of both palms and a final search of the bottom of the cage. Eibl-Eibesfeldt (personal commun., 1969) in his *Callithrix jacchus* group observed free catching of flying insects.

"Towards bigger preys (mice and small birds) the marmosets take up a more cautious attitude. When slowly approaching the animal, with a ruffling of their tail hair and ear tufts and some owl-like turning of the head, they lower the front part of the body and sniff at the prey from a distance of 10–15 cm. Suddenly they run up to it, seizing it with one or both hands and placing the killing bite in the back of the head or the neck; they then start eating, beginning with the head of the prey. While holding it, the nails are deeply pounced into the prey's body. Gnawed cadavers showed obvious punctures near the back, neck, or throat."

Rothe 1975*c*, Summary, p. 384 (*jacchus*)

"A simultaneous use of both forelimbs is prevalent only during the capture of moving prey. The coordination of the arm movements during grasping behaviour is normally well developed. Exact appraisal of distance and direction indicates a precise optical (pre)control of grasping behaviour. Unlike the arm movements, the movements of the hand and, to a greater extent, of the fingers are essentially less variable. Active movements of the individual phalanges, independent of the remaining fingers, do not occur; the grasping is done with the entire hand. Furthermore, the prehensive pattern of *Callithrix jacchus* during fine manipulation activities of the hand does not differ from that during locomotion. The relatively little flexibility of the movement pattern of the fingers has an adverse effect on the grasping accuracy, which is best developed during capture of prey and during the grasping of large bait."

"[Claws] are used to secure larger food objects only during the capture of prey. They prove to be more advantageous and effective when the hand movements are more at hitting and scratching than at sliding and grasping."

Drinking

Pallas 1781, p. 44 (*jacchus*)

"to drink, they sit on all four, with the body stretched out or drawn together, as they either lap like a cat or suck up the water by immersing their lips."

Elimination

Fitzgerald 1935, p. 182 (*jacchus*)

"When the animals are in good health their appetite is very regular and their elimination is sufficient. Elimination takes place very freely and regularly early in the morning when the marmosets first come out of their sleeping quarters where they have remained 13 to 14 hours. They never soil their sleeping quarters or their play room, and they always let their feces fall over the side of cage or perch. They are not interested in the dejections, and they do not repeatedly use a particular place except for convenience. Only one animal, an adult female, has been troubled with constipation. The difficulty has become less since she at last consented to eat vegetables."

Sanitation

Pallas 1781, p. 45 (*jacchus*)

"In the morning they would climb on the sides of the cage and throw the nightly accumulation of urine and of excrement (which is yellowish and mushy) as far as possible, sometimes several feet. They also managed to throw the excreta into the hay of the cage. Their urine defiles everything it touches with a repugnant smell that reeks of foul musk and ambergris; no matter how clean we keep them by changing the hay almost daily and washing the floor of the cage, the ouistitis caused a stink which permeated large rooms and may have been detrimental to health. Their nests, however, stayed dry and clean."

Hornung 1896, pp. 274–75 (*penicillata*)

"He never soils his bed or makes dirt close to a person."

Fitzgerald 1935, p. 181 (*jacchus*)

"The cage is provided with a box play room that hangs inside and with another box that hangs on the open door at night and serves as sleeping quarters. Both boxes are kept lined with clean blankets. These are never soiled by the animals except by foot prints."

Heusser 1968 (*jacchus*)

The pet marmoset never ate in or fouled its sleeping quarters.

F. Cuvier 1819 (*jacchus*)

The adult male and female urinate often, drop by drop, and always in the same place, from a squatting position.

Intelligence and Learning

F. Cuvier 1819, p. 8 (*jacchus*)

"Our adult ouistitis never showed much intelligence. They are so wary and observant of everything happening around them that if one judged by the movement of their large eyes and the liveliness of their glance, he might believe them capable of real understanding. As a matter of fact, they can hardly tell the difference between one person or another."

"Squirrels are not far from being their equal in intelligence."

Miles and Meyers 1956; Miles 1957*a* (*jacchus*)

The capacity to form discrimination-learning sets in the common marmoset and macaque is qualitatively similar. Both solved problems on the basis of symbols or delayed reaction, and general principles. The marmoset, however, learned much more slowly.

Miles 1957*b* (*jacchus*)

The squirrel monkeys proved to be superior to the marmoset, but inferior to the macaque in learning ability.

Mallinson 1965, p. 138

"Marmosets . . . are able to recognize human beings who have been associated with them, even after a considerable period of time and can, moreover, pick them out from a crowd of people."

Mallinson goes on to describe tongue movements with or without vocalizations, as a recognition display in tamarins.

I have seen marmosets and tamarins flicking the tongue when meeting (greeting?) acquaintances or strangers. Similar tongue movements are also used in vocalization.

Stellar 1960, pp. 9–10 (*jacchus*)

"In discrimination learning, marmosets master brightness, form, and multidimensional object problems about as readily as the rhesus monkey. Unlike the rat, they do not appear to be highly "stimulus-bound" and are not disturbed in the performance of form discriminations when the orientation of discriminanda like triangles and squares is randomly changed. In addition, the marmoset shows strong inter-problem transfer, reaching an asymptote of three to five trials for mastery of new problems within 7 to 10 problems. Specific-element transfer is also quite evident, however, for marmosets will remember specific objects across 25 problems and show both positive and negative transfer when the 50 items are recombined into new problems. Particularly striking is the great importance of the positive object, for whether positive or negative transfer is obtained depends almost entirely upon whether the positive stimulus in the new problem was previously positive or negative."

Locomotion and Posture

Postures and movements are treated here not only as acts of transportation but also as physical expressions of the individual or species. The social or temperamental significance of certain attitudes or movements are mentioned under other headings. Forms of locomotion are discussed on p. 43.

Pallas 1781, p. 42 (*jacchus*)

"The Sagoin . . . jumps and climbs very fast when it wants to; but it is not, like many other monkeys in constant state of agitation and motion. It is sluggish when sated, or basking in the sun and it can sit for hours in the company of its playmates, or hang quietly from the wire of its cage. It climbs in all directions, often head down and always rather apathetic. Sometimes it hangs head down holding itself only with the hind feet or it may hang by its hands stretching its body like a lazy man. It can curl its tail in many ways but never rapidly and it does not use the tail as some long tailed monkeys do for supporting itself."

Krieg 1948, p. 174 (*aurita*)

"They ran up the bark of the trees with great agility and glided through the foliage, picking up a leaf here, catching a butterfly there and like squirrels always hiding on the far side of the branches when they fail to find a crack or hole in which to hide."

Wied-Neuwied 1826, p. 134 (*penicillata*)

"In the daytime these animals are in constant motion, at night they sit quietly, bent over each other in sleep their heads covered with their tails. . . . They are very much like squirrels in habits and they are especially agile jumpers and climbers."

F. Cuvier 1819, pp. 2–3 (*jacchus*)

"Their movements are not lively or very agile and they are cautious in climbing up and down their cage. Squirrels which resemble them very much are better climbers and nearly equal in intelligence."

Lucas, Hume, and Henderson-Smith 1927, p. 448 (*jacchus*)

It "was allowed its liberty for a short time each day. At these times it showed itself capable of prodigious leaps; one which was measured proved to be ten feet in length."

Fitzgerald 1935, p. 183 (*jacchus*)

"The tail is used for balancing purposes when the animal is moving about, or as the third leg of the tripod when the animal is sitting on its haunches. The waving of the tail seems to be a signal denoting illness. Very sick or dying animals may continue to wave their tails up and down until relieved or dead."

Hornung 1896, p. 276 (*penicillata*)

"His sitting posture is characteristically squirrel-like but the tail always hangs down. His other postures are also very suggestive of a squirrel and like a squirrel he holds on with the nails of his feet while gliding downward on his belly."

Hershkovitz (Notes)

Movements of the head are swift and jerky. It can be raised about 45° and turned to right or left nearly 180°.

Rothe 1975*c*, Summary, p. 384 (*jacchus*)

"During arboreal locomotion [the] palmar region serves as the main means of support, while the fingers in the locomotor grip also contribute to maintaining balance and support. The greater the need for maintaining balance, for example, during vertikal [*sic*] climbing or in movement along the narrow branches, the more complete the adjustement [*sic*] of the hand form on the surface and the more complete the alignment of the hand on the branch will be. Additional support is supplied by the longitudinal palm furrow, caused by the radio-ulnar adduction of the hand edges and by the clinging properties of the volar pads. The alignment of the hand is most variable on a wider surface and during quick progression, and the adaption [*sic*] of the palm and fingers is incomplete on the running and climbing branches. However, the flexible orientation of the hands during locomotion ensures sufficient safety for the animal, even during limited contact with the surface. . . .

"The claw-like nails do not function as a primary structure for support during arboreal locomotion. They serve [as] additional support in maintaining balance and their effectiveness is dependent upon the situation (speed of locomotion, direction and level, surface qualities) and is to be seen within the framework of a more comprehensive complex of behavioural characteristics."

Rothe's 56 experimental animals of all ages were maintained under wholly artificial conditions, and no distinction was made between wild-born (if any) and captive-born marmosets who learned their lifelong routines under controlled, constricted, and contrived conditions. The thin dowellike supports employed for testing hand use and locomotion are not tree trunks or branches, and the cage environment is not an arboreal one. The artifacts are understood, but Rothe's interpretations of his experiments with them make no allowances for altered relationships and skewed perspectives. Callitrichid hands are the most primitive among living primates. Their claws are primitive claws, not "claw-like nails." They are used as *primary* supports in clinging, grappling, and in moving up, down, or around broad, rough supports such as tree trunks and thick branches. Callitrichid claws are comparable to those of squirrels when used in arboreal support and locomotion and certain other operations including grooming, and comparable to those of cats when used for seizing prey. The hands of other living primates, with the qualified exception of those of the aye-aye, evolved in other directions and function in different ways (cf. p. 32).

Swimming

Mallinson 1971, p. 6 (*jacchus*)

In the Jersey Zoo, "a male Common marmoset, *Callithrix jacchus,* jumped off the island into the water in order to escape being caught up, and it swam in a dog-paddle-like fashion a distance of some nine meters (28 ft.) to the shore. If it had not been for the water-logged state of its coat it would have made good its escape up a tree, but the weight of the water handicapped its usual agility."

Play and Concealment

Fitzgerald 1935, p. 183 (*jacchus*)

"Playing is an important part of the life of the marmoset. It consists mainly in hiding and seeking. The animals slap at each other playfully, attempt to bite each other, and race wildly in all directions. While playing they are apt to misjudge distances and to fall; but generally they land on their feet."

Hornung 1896, p. 275 (*penicillata*)

"As long as some one plays with him he can go on until late at night. He nimbly climbs the wire strung across his cage; he plays with his hairy tail, spins himself around, then stares about and rushes back into his nest. Then again he jumps up to the rope, dives onto the swing and climbs across the roof of his cage."

They are as playful at times as kittens. They like to follow or stalk small moving objects and pounce upon them (P. H.).

Mallinson 1971, p. 6 (*jacchus*)

"When this species wish to conceal themselves, they cling to the opposite side of the branch and lie motionless with their abdomen pressed tightly to it; if they realize that they have been discovered, they move their heads from side to side before jumping or scrambling away from apparent danger."

Sight and Images

Miles 1958*a*, p. 153 (*jacchus*)

Marmosets "readily learned discrimination based upon blue, green, and red color combinations." This indicates that "the marmoset, like other primates, does possess some form of color vision."

Fitzgerald 1935, p. 182 (*jacchus*)

"The sense of sight is very keen and is constantly being stimulated by the innate curiosity of the animals; any change in the position of an object, or any addition to the furnishings of the room is at once investigated. Any figure, however small, representing an animal causes great excitement; a small carved wooden carabao from the Philippine Islands had to be removed from the room as it caused a panic among the marmosets. Pictures, on the contrary, seem not to convey any idea to them. Preferences for special colors have not been observed. The eye is effectively used to 'command.' "

Hornung 1896, p. 275 (*penicillata*)

"When he is shown a book with pictures of spiders and other animals, he attacks the images and tries to grab them with his hands. Finding himself frustrated he finally turns the pages over with his hands and examines them searchingly as if he expected to find something good hidden between the leaves."

Heusser 1868, p. 714 (*jacchus*)

Pictures of snakes frightened Heusser's old male marmoset. Gustatory interest was evinced at the sight of pictures of frogs and insects. Figures of marmosets elicited only transitory interest and those of other mammals were largely ignored.

Scent and Marking

Pallas 1781, p. 111 (*jacchus*)

"Before taking one of her two young for feeding she smelled the mouth of both and selected one. Presumably, the mother recognizes which one was fed last by the smell of the milk and takes the other one first. It must still be determined if the female can distinguish visually between the two young or determine from the sound of their cry which was the hungrier. When the young were carried separately on older marmosets the mother did not smell them."

Fitzgerald 1935, p. 182 (*jacchus*)

"The sense of smell is not highly developed. Food is tested by tasting rather than by smelling."

Epple 1967*b*, p. 62 (*jacchus*) (*geoffroyi*)

"The animals frequently sniff the faces and genitalia of group mates, sex partners and strange animals, introduced into the group. All species [*Callithrix jacchus jacchus, C. j. geoffroyi, Saguinus oedipus geoffroyi, Leontopithecus rosalia, Callimico goeldii*] show scent marking. Dominant ♂♂ and ♀♀ show a much higher marking activity than inferiors. Their activity is markedly increased by sexual encounters, territorial changes and by hostile episodes with group mates or strange animals of the same sex."

Coimbra-Filho 1971; 1972*b* (*jacchus*)

Captive marmosets of the *Callithrix jacchus* group and various hybrids were observed excavating holes with their teeth in the platforms, perches, and other wooden parts of their cages. High-ranking males and females urinated into the pits and also marked by rubbing them with their circumgenital glands. The perforations, about 1 to 2 cm deep, are made in any part of the wood including planed surfaces and the underside of the perches. In the latter case, the animals work hanging upside down (fig. IX.34).

Epple 1970*b* (*jacchus*)

Marmosets establish contact by sniffing each other's genitalia and muzzle. The same activity combined with marking objects and licking the partner's genitalia is a regular part of pre- and post-copulatory courtship [fig. IX.26, 35]. Marking also signals the social and territorial

Fig. IX.34. Pits in wooden plank made by captive *Callithrix jacchus jacchus*. The holes, 1 to 2 cm deep, are excavated with the teeth. The animal then urinates into them and marks the board with glandular secretions. (Photo courtesy of A. F. Coimbra-Filho [1972*b*, p. 508].)

dominance of the individual. Nearly all adults of a group mark but with the frequency and intensity commensurate with his or her rank.

"*Callithrix jacchus* gently rubs the circumgenital area against items of the environment, and rarely against the body of group mates. . . . During scent marking, the secretions of the large apocrine and sebaceous skin glands covering the genitals and the circumgenital area as well as a few drops of urine are applied to the object." Scent marking by means of the sternal gland is infrequent.

Fig. IX.35. *Callithrix jacchus jacchus* female marking wooden platform. (Photo courtesy of Gisela Epple.)

Increased marking follows encounters between cage occupants and strangers. Scent markings of strange conspecifics also stimulated more frequent sniffing and marking.

"The animals also spent a considerable amount of time gnawing at perches. They thus produce deep furrows and holes which are regularly sniffed, licked and scent marked by all members of the group. Their function is not understood."

Epple 1970*b*; 1974*a*, pp. 379; 1974*b*, p. 272 (*jacchus*)

The frequencies per time unit of scent marking, aggressive threat and attacking and fighting strange conspecifics were recorded in three test groups. Each consisted of a dominant adult male, a dominant adult female, and one, two or three subordinate adults and juvenals. The largest group consisted of five individuals, the smallest of four. All groups had existed for at least two months with a stable hierarchy and little or no aggressions between group members. It was found that dominant males and dominant females marked more frequently and heavily than their subordinates. Dominant males attacked strange adult males introduced into the cage and dominant females attacked strange females. Increased marking followed aggressive encounters. Perches marked by strange conspecifics also stimulated the dominant individual to more frequent sniffing and marking (fig. IX.35).

Epple 1974*b*, p. 262 (*jacchus*)

Perches marked with urine of conspecifics presented to 5 males elicited significantly more scent marking response than unmarked perches and perches marked with mouse urine. An equal number of females also sniffed experimental perches but showed no scent marking preference for any of the three kinds. Evidently, males distinguished conspecifics from mice by their odor, but failure of the females to discriminate between the different perches could not be explained.

Hershkovitz (*jacchus*)

The ability of a mammal to distinguish its urine from those of other species by odor alone seems to be a universal trait. Even an inexperienced man can distinguish by odor the urine of his own species from those of domestic animals and commensals such as rats and mice, and in some cases those of wild animals. It would be interesting to compare the reaction of *Callithrix jacchus* to perches marked with urine of other callitrichid species.

More on marking is included in the section on Reproduction (p. 528).

Vocalization

Pallas 1781, p. 42 (*jacchus*)

"They emit a feeble whistling or cooing noise . . . their normal voice is merely a short whistle or coo. When their attention is called, especially to food, they emit a louder call which sounds very nearly like the French name ouistiti. They repeat this several times. When resting after eating, or sunning themselves, the older marmosets would utter, with the mouth wide open, several single whistling sounds which are very penetrating and unpleasant to the ears. They would not stop whistling even when frightened or called. The sight of something strange, especially dogs, crows, etc. would make them chatter like magpies and all the while they twisted the fore part of their bodies round with head outstretched like a man impatiently looking for some particular thing from the precise point of view. The old males emit a rattling and sometimes grunting scolding sound when angry or when shown something from afar which was not given to them. . . . The young born during the summer and already in adult pelage screamed nearly as loud fighting over a dainty morsel; those that would get the smallest portions cried like kittens."

Wied-Neuwied 1826, p. 133 (*penicillata*)

They "constantly emit a small delicate whistling or whirring sound, like a small bird. Buffon says their voice sounds like uistiti! according to which I have named the small animal; however, one needs a vivid imagination to recognize that word in one syllable sound of the Sahuí."

Neill 1829, p. 18 (*jacchus*)

". . . its sense of hearing appeared to be excessively acute, so that the slightest whisper was sure to arouse it. The voice of this little animal was peculiarly sharp and disagreeable consisting of a very quick succession of harsh and shrill sounds (imitated in the name *ouistiti*), so loud, that they might be heard from the remotest part of the ship."

Hornung 1896, pp. 277–78 (*penicillata*)

"He shows anger by making the sound *zick, aa, zick, aa;* a low pleasant *psivivi* means he is at ease. If bored or hungry, he announces it with a loud and prolonged *psiih, psiih;* he expresses fright through a short rapidly executed *zi, a, zi, a.*"

Fitzgerald 1935, p. 182 (*jacchus*)

"The marmoset is not a noisy pet; in fact the usual chatter of contentment is very much like the chirp of a canary; there is a louder cry of alarm, and a scolding sound much resembling a short cough."

Fitzgerald 1935, p. 184 (*jacchus*)

"It is essential not to frighten marmosets with any sudden noise or movements, as either one will throw the group into a panic. Noises practically inaudible to the human ear may have this effect. The distorted state of mind of one animal seems to spread to others through voice contact."

F. Cuvier 1819, p. 2 (*jacchus*)

"When frightened they emit a short, penetrating cry and run for shelter. At other times and for no apparent reason, they let out a high pitched and long sustained whistle."

The ouistiti, like other species of marmosets, often vocalizes with mouth closed and emits sounds inaudible to the human ear but heard and understood by other members of the group (P. H.).

Heusser 1968, p. 713 (*jacchus*)

Nine sounds made by the old, free-living male marmoset kept in Switzerland were identified and transliterated into German, as follows, with the original text abstracted in English.

Zg! zg!—Fright call at sight of objects (teddy bear), certain people, pictures (snakes), animals (dogs).
Zik! z'ik! zi-ke! z'ike!—Intensified higher-pitched fright call.
Kekekeke!—Extreme excitement call combined with threat posture.
Pfiff—Weak, hardly audible fright whistle at sight of birds of prey.
Zu-zu-zu!—Sweet whistle expressing pleasure at sight of sweets and preferred delicacies.
Uisti-uistiti—Sun twitter, when sunning.
Suuuu-suuiii?—Long distance whistle; also on rare occasions uttered in sleep.
Sui? sui?—Middle or short distance contact call.
Sii?—Plaintive call.

Epple 1968 (*jacchus*)

Vocalizations of 40 individuals of all ages of *Callithrix jacchus jacchus* (= *Hapale jacchus*) and 5 of *C. j. geoffroyi* (= *Hapale leucocephala*), were studied, their respective physical structures analyzed and social significance interpreted. The vocal signals of the common marmoset and those of *Callithrix argentata argentata, Saguinus oedipus geoffroyi,* and *Leontopithecus rosalia rosalia* appeared to be relatively stereotyped, whereas those of *Callimico goeldii* were distinguished by a high degree of variability.

Calls of young and adult *Callithrix jacchus* are, according to Epple, essentially the same in quality but differ in social significance to the extent of their differences in age, size, and social rank. In general, infants are usually silent except when distressed. Adults react with sound to visible objects, engage in social signaling, and hold dialogues even when housed in different rooms. They may also indulge in monologues.

In her description of calls, Epple (1968, p. 4) cautions that "since the monkeys were taken out of their usual surroundings and brought to the [professional broadcasting] studio, they did not behave normally, and only some of their calls could be recorded."

It should be added that in captivity, marmosets probably do not vocalize normally even in their "usual" surroundings. Some marmoset calls recorded by Epple may be individual variables or species calls more or less modified by or adapted to conditions in captivity. Certain calls or certain nuances of them uttered in captivity, particularly by cage-born individuals, may be peculiar to the captive state and may become stereotyped. Nevertheless, it is clear that an individual reacts and responds to calls of his own group or species differently than he does to the calls or noise of other groups or species. The specific traits are the main concern here.

Following is an outline of Epple's identifications, definitions and interpretations of the calls of *Callithrix jacchus.*

Epple 1968 (*jacchus*)

Juvenal Calls

1. *Phee:* High-pitched distress call. Response to being dismounted forcibly by adult carrier; a fundamental vocalization that develops into adult contact calls.
2. *Tsik, tsik, tsik:* Sharp loud distress call. Response to extremely rough treatment by mount; develops into adult fright call.
3. *Ngä:* Distress squeal. A contact call; stimulates adults to nursing response.
4. *Twitter:* Rapid sequence of short, high-pitched notes. Serves same purposes as *phee* calls and squeals; number of single notes in twitter vary according to age, as follows:

Babies (2–9 days)	= 2–5 notes
Infants	= 2–12 notes
Adults	= 2–20 notes

Adult Calls

Phonetically identical to juvenal calls but more stereotyped and specific in function. Epple recognizes the following types:

1. Contact calls
   a. Monosyllabic, relatively short *phee* calls. Used when undisturbed and in close visual contact with group members; uttered with mouth closed, the source of sound often difficult to locate by human observers.
   b. Monosyllabic intensified *phee* calls. Used by distressed animal in loose visual contact with group members.
   c. Monosyllabic loud *phee* whistle. Used in isolation or as territorial signal; uttered with mouth widely open; loudest call in repertory; audible to human ear at 200 m; evokes response from group members.
   d. Rhythmical chirp. Faint sound emitted when in close body contact with group members.
   e. Twitter. Uttered when isolated or in loose contact.
2. Submission squeal or *ngä* call. Uttered by adults when approached or threatened by a superior.
3. Aggressive threat *tsee tsee tsee . . .* calls. Uttered by aggressor when threatening an inferior.
4. Defensive threat chatter. A series of short, low-pitched notes.
5. Mobbing *tsik tsik tsik . . .* calls. Contagious call uttered by group members when mobbing stationary or slowly moving potential predator.
   a. Low excitement—single *tsik* calls intermingled with crackles (*egg*) and coughs (*ock*).
   b. High excitement—*tsik tsik* calls.
6. Warning high-pitched whistle. Uttered when surprised by sudden appearance of predator.
7. Fright screams. Uttered when handled, approached by predator, bitten by superior.

In comparison with other callitrichids, *Callithrix jacchus* does not execute trills. I have not seen its tongue vibrate during open-mouthed vocalizations or protrude rhythmically during close-lipped calling (P. H.).

Sleep

Stellar 1960, p. 4 (*jacchus*)

"Around midafternoon, it slows down and is apt to sleep, and it typically sleeps a 14-hr. night. When asleep, the marmoset lies tightly curled with its head tucked into its abdomen and its tail curled around its body. Its sleep is deep, and if aroused, it acts sluggish and drugged like the young child awakened at night, and typically it falls right back to sleep."

Fitzgerald 1935, p. 182 (*jacchus*)

"The sleeping habits are regulated by the clock and not by the sun, the animals sleeping from 13 to 14 hours out of the 24. In addition to their night's rest, marmosets generally take a 'siesta' after their luncheon."

Hornung 1896, p. 274 (*penicillata*)

"In summer he generally goes to bed at 9, in winter at 7. His day begins at 5 in summer and 11 in winter."

Heusser 1968, p. 712 (*jacchus*)

The lone, free-ranging male *Callithrix jacchus jacchus* observed in Zürich slept 11–15 hours. He retired to his sleeping box from 5:00 to 7:00 P.M., according to the season, and arose between 6:00 and 8:00 A.M., later on rainy days. The animal slept soundly. On rare occasions whistling calls were made by the soundly sleeping and possibly dreaming animal.

Hershkovitz (Notes)

Callithrix jacchus I observed in the San Diego Zoo outdoor breeding colony slept sitting on their haunches with tail tightly coiled between the legs and pressed against the belly. In this position the two or three looped tail acts as a prop.

The sleeping family group consists of mother with young on her back and father huddled on top. The colony marmosets retired to their boxes after sundown between 7:00 and 8:00 P.M. in late June and emerged after sunrise. *Callithrix jacchus* retired first and emerged less frequently in response to disturbances (including noises I made deliberately) than the other diurnal species, *Saguinus fuscicollis, S. nigricollis, Callimico* and *Saimiri.*

Thermoregulation

Pallas 1781, p. 46 (*jacchus*)

"Being animals from South America, sagoins have been regarded as much more sensitive to cold than they really are. In the cold days of autumn when they were under my care, they were kept in unheated rooms in cages near the window. Most of the time the thermometer registered a few degrees above freezing, and sometimes as low as 10° F. but the cold did not make them shiver. To be sure, they sought the warmth of the sun or the brazier placed nearby and by which they warmed themselves for hours whilst hanging in the cage. Very surprising is the fact that they showed discomfort at high temperatures. The Baron assured me that he often saw them attacked by epileptic fits on hot summer days but rarely on other occasions. The sound individuals busied themselves with any afflicted one and tried to help it. These facts suggest to us that marmosets may also inhabit the high mountains and cold forests of South America."

Wied-Neuwied 1826, p. 135 (*penicillata*)

"They are very sensitive to the cool sea breezes and the temperature of the temperate zone and even in warm cages most of them died during the ocean crossing."

As the preceding and succeeding accounts prove, exposure to near-freezing temperature would not of itself be the cause of death (P. H.).

Neill 1829, pp. 19–20 (*jacchus*)

"Hitherto the weather was warm [on the voyage from Brazil to England], the thermometer being never below 65° or 60° Fahr.; but as we reached a more northern latitude, and approached England, the change of temperature affected the monkey very sensibly; his appetite failed very considerably, and now he would not even touch the cockroaches when given to him; the hair, especially that on the tail, fell off; and, at the end of the voyage, this organ was almost quite bare and naked. He kept constantly in the kennel, rolling itself up in a piece of flannel, which had been put in for warmth, except when he could reach a sunny part of the deck, where he might bask in the heat. There was a considerable continuance of cold northeasterly winds, the thermometer as low as from 42° to 36° Fahr., and, as the monkey eat little or nothing, and was quite inactive, I hardly expected to have kept it alive."

The animal did survive and after arrival in London was taken by Mr. Neill to Edinburgh in November. It thrived there, became plump and regrew hair on its tail. The symptoms shown by the animal on exposure to cold are similar to those described by Kraft (see below).

Stellar 1960, p. 2 (*jacchus*)

"With the aid of thermostatically controlled electric heaters in the winter and an air conditioner in the summer, the room temperature was typically kept between 75° and 80° F. Perhaps more important, particularly during the dry heat of the winter and especially when animals have respiratory infections, is the humidity. With a humidistat and a spray-type humidifier (Walton Laboratories, N.J.), humidity was always kept above a minimum of 50%."

Fitzgerald 1935, p. 181 (*jacchus*)

"Important considerations in the care of marmosets are temperature, sunlight, food, water and cleanliness. In the experience of the writer the temperatures should never fall below 75° at any time. Higher temperatures do not seem to harm the animals. Direct sunlight is avoided by marmosets except for a few minutes at a time. During the winter, a 75 watt blue electric light bulb was kept lighted in each cage throughout the day. The animals gathered around the bulb with apparent pleasure. A single G.E. sunlight lamp was used to furnish artificial sunlight for a few hours daily except during two summer months when the marmosets were kept in a screened porch in the country."

Krieg 1948, p. 472 (*aurita*)

"They [i.e., *Callithrix jacchus aurita*] occur west of the crest of the Serra do Mar [São Paulo, Brazil] but I am under the impression that during the cold season they move down from the altitudes of night frost into the frost free slopes of the Serra. Some individuals which were kept and even bred in captivity at the German Sportsmen club at São Paulo [probably *Callithrix jacchus jacchus*] did not resist the frost on a cold night. Also, I did not find any marmosets in the outskirts of São Paulo during the cold season (July 1938) although I was assured that they ordinarily occurred there. I had observed before, at the foot of the Bolivian Andes a similar annual migration on the part of *Callicebus pallescens* from the part of their range that was hit by frost."

Mallinson 1972, p. 24

"During the winter of 1970/1971, a family group of hybrids, Black-pencilled Marmoset *Callithrix* (= *Hapale*) *penicillata* × Common Marmoset *Callithrix* (= *Hapale*) *jacchus* had access to a large outdoor aviary [of the Jersey Zoo, Channel Islands) and even when the outdoor temperature fell as low as freezing point, the five specimens maintained their excellent condition. . . . Durrell (in verbis 1971) had a *C. jacchus* which used to enjoy romping through the snow in their garden at Bournemouth (England) keeping in excellent condition throughout its eleven years of life."

The possibility that *Callithrix jacchus* may become lethargic in freezing or near-freezing weather and remain in its habitat unperceived, with perhaps occasional or limited movement during warmer parts of the day, is suggested by the following accounts.

Hornung 1896, p. 277 (*penicillata*)

"Our Pepi is very sensitive to cold and after a frosty morning awoke around noon. If someone should remove his couch on a cold day he will squat in one spot quietly and motionless."

Phillips 1975, p. 303

"Years ago Scholander showed that the marmoset has a very narrow zone of thermal neutrality compared with most animals. We confirmed this: it is only about 4 or 5° C, starting about 1° C above body temperature and going to 3–4° C below body temperature. If you drop below that temperature the marmoset is simply unable to maintain its body temperature. Oxygen consumption will go up, shivering thermogenesis will go up, and the temperature will fall progressively. Marmosets are very sensitive to temperature effects."

Kraft 1957 (*jacchus*)

A ouistiti was brought to Dr. Kraft's (1957, p. 175) attention in February 1955 with the complaint that it had little inclination to eat and spent the time rolled up in a corner. During the following summer when the marmoset was in Dr. Kraft's care, it appeared to be perfectly healthy and behaved normally. With the onset of cold weather in October, however, the marmoset became listless again. It ate poorly and spent the day in a corner with its tail rolled around in the manner previously reported by its owner. Dr. Kraft's records of the animal's last week are summarized as follows.

4 October 1955—took no food.

5 October night cage temperature, 3° C., animal rolled up motionless and cold to touch; responded to warmth of day by becoming active but urinated excessively, drank large quantities of water and ate 5 mealworms; in late afternoon rolled up and relapsed into torpidity; transferred to heated compartment (18° C.) in late afternoon.

6 October lethargic in morning; became active during heat of day.

7 October same as preceding day; morning pulse 41 per minute, respiratory rate 5 per minute (normal summer rate, 55); room temperature night to morning, 15°–18° C., evening pulse, 44, respiratory rate, 5, body cold to touch although covered; rectal temperature, 18° C.

8 October morning room temperature, 17.5°, rectal temperature, 17.5°, respiration, 7, pulse, 46; night (21:15), room temperature, 19.5° C., rectal temperature, 17° C., respiration, 10; reacted to touch by twitching, urinating drop by drop, eyelids opened in a slit, pupils contracted.

9 October morning room temperature 10° C., animal found dead.

An autopsy revealed generalized tuberculosis. Parasites were absent.

Tuberculosis, in the opinion of Dr. Kraft, had nothing to do with the symptoms just described. The animal had been lethargic during the previous winter. It was apparently healthy and normally active during the following summer then became torpid again with cold weather in the fall.

Kraft concludes that this is a case of facultative lethargy in response to cooling. This condition was probably characteristic of generalized mammals with a primitive heat regulation system (cf. Eisentraut 1960, p. 31).

Hibernation or estivation as a regular seasonal function in its natural habitat has not been demonstrated in any South American mammal. The present case and the following, however, suggest that hibernation may occur among some New World mammals of the south temperate zone (cf. Hershkovitz 1962, p. 46).

Brown 1909, p. 90 (*jacchus*)

Minimum-maximum rectal temperature of two males in the Philadelphia Zoo is recorded as 38.5°–39.0°.

Phillips 1975, p. 298

Average rectal temperature was 38.7° C at 24–27° C ambient in the Research Establishment of the Royal College of Surgeons of England.

Morrison and Simões 1962, pp. 167–76 (*jacchus*)

Experiments on body temperature of *Callithrix jacchus* (4 males) and *Aotus trivirgatus* (1 male, 1 female) for comparison were conducted in São Paulo, Brazil. "The daily cycle in the marmosets had an amplitude of 4.3° C, about twice that observed in other primates and higher than seen in any other mammal. The maximum was at 9:30 hours (39.7° ± 0.98°) and the minimum was at 01:30 (35.4° ± 0.4°) . . . *Aotus* maintained its normal body temperature on cold exposure to 8°, while in *Callithrix* the body temperature fell continuously from 38.8 at 31° ambient to 37.3 at 8° ambient." Another peculiarity observed (op. cit., p. 174 was the maintenance "of a high level of temperature for about 10 hours and this active period was clearly divided into two peaks with maxima at 9:30 and 16:30 and an intervening minimum at 14:00, the time of maximum body temperature in other [unspecified] species. This secondary daytime minimum appears shallow compared to the nocturnal low, but it may be noted that its amplitude was almost as large (1.2 vs. 1.40) as the entire daily cycle in *Aotus*. Such bimodal activity or temperature cycles are sometimes seen in crepuscular animals such as bats which are active at dusk and then again at dawn. . . . The maxima seen here appear either too late (9:30) or too early (16:30) to qualify for crepuscularity. But in animals such as the marmosets which characteristically live in the dense rain forest, where light levels are greatly reduced, a mid-day cessation of activity has often been described for animals exposed to heat. This might represent a displacement of dawn and dusk."

Capture

Wied-Neuwied 1826, p. 141 (*penicillata*)

Hunters secure the young by shooting the "parents which carry one or two at their breast or on their back . . . or they trap them in fish creels baited with bananas. The ouistitis crawl in but cannot withdraw through the funnel shaped opening made of pointed canes."

54 *Callithrix argentata* Group, Bare-ear and Tassel-ear Marmosets

Included Species—C. argentata Linnaeus and *C. humeralifer* E. Geoffroy

Distribution (fig. IX.36)

In eastern Brazil south of the Rio Amazonas between the lower Rio Tocantins and Rio Madeira; unknown between the upper tributaries of the Tocantins-Araguaia but common in the upper Madeira (Guaporé and east bank of Mamoré) in Brazil and Bolivia, and across the divide into the upper Rio Paraguai basin in western Mato Grosso, Brazil, and Santa Cruz, Bolivia.

Taxonomic History

From the time it was described in 1812, *Callithrix humeralifer* (= *C. santaremensis* Matschie) was regarded as most nearly related to *Callithrix jacchus* because of the annulated tail and tufted ears. *Callithrix argentata* Linnaeus, on the other hand, was generally treated as an aberrant, albinotic form of the genus. Although the various published classifications placed *humeralifer* and *argentata* in widely separated camps, authors almost consistently regarded the albinotic race of each species, namely, *Callithrix humeralifer chrysoleuca* and *Callithrix argentata leucippe,* as most nearly related to each other. Osman Hill (1957, p. 286) synonymized them and at the same time placed *Callithrix argentata* (with *melanura* and *emiliae*) in the separate genus *Mico.*

The community of characters that unites *C. humeralifer* (with subspecies *humeralifer, chrysoleuca*) and *C. argentata* (with subspecies *melanura, argentata, leucippe*) and collectively distinguishes them from all other primates was recognized by Hershkovitz (1968) in his reconstruction of the evolution of their convergent color patterns. Formal characterization of the *Callithrix argentata* species group, however, was deferred for publication in this monograph.

The idea of close alliance between *humeralifer* and *argentata* was not accepted by Coimbra-Filho and Mittermeier (1974). These author maintained that *C. humeralifer* was more nearly related to *C. jacchus* than to *C. argentata* because (*a*) ears are tufted in the first two but not the third, (*b*) *humeralifer* and *jacchus* are classified as species of the genus *Callithrix* but *argentata* had been placed in the genus *Mico,* and (*c*) a multivariate discriminant analysis of linear cranial measurements of 18 skulls of undisclosed condition and whereabouts representing 5 of 12 nominal forms showed *humeralifer* closer to *jacchus* than to *argentata.*

In a rebuttal that drew information from the manuscript of this monograph, Hershkovitz (1975*b*) showed that (*a*) ear tufts of *humeralifer* differ fundamentally from those of *jacchus* but are basically like those of juvenal *argentata,* (*b*) previous classifications of the species of *Callithrix* adopted by Coimbra-Filho and Mittermeier prove nothing, and (*c*) results of the Coimbra-Filho and Mittermeier multivariate analysis could not possibly be derived from accurate measurements of reasonably comparable adult skulls because significant differences in linear cranial dimensions between the species of *Callithrix* do not exist.

Characters adduced by Hershkovitz (1975*b*) to show the true relationship between the species groups of *Callithrix* are included with those given beyond under the heading Diagnostic Characters and Comparisons.

Origin, Evolution, and Dispersal

The two species of the *Callithrix argentata* group, *C. argentata* and *C. humeralifer,* probably arose from a common ancestor somewhere in the Brazilian highlands where headwaters of the Rio Paraguai interdigitate with tributaries of the Rio Amazonas (figs. VII.4; IX.36). The marmosets spread north, with *C. humeralifer* now confined between the lower Rio Madeira and Rio Tapajóz and *C. argentata* living between the middle and upper Rio Madeira-Mamoré on the west and lower Rio Tocantins and heads of the upper Rio Paraguay on the south. Both species reached the northern limits of their range on the south bank of the Amazonas (fig. IX.36). The range of *C. humeralifer* is restricted to the extreme northwestern corner of the vast territory occupied by the *argentata* group.

The ancestral form of the *Callithrix argentata* group must have been dominantly blackish with pelage of dorsum and tail dark modified agouti, face wholly pigmented, and auricles moderately hairy. Pale hip patches in the darkest race of both species are unique to the group and point to a relatively recent divergence from an

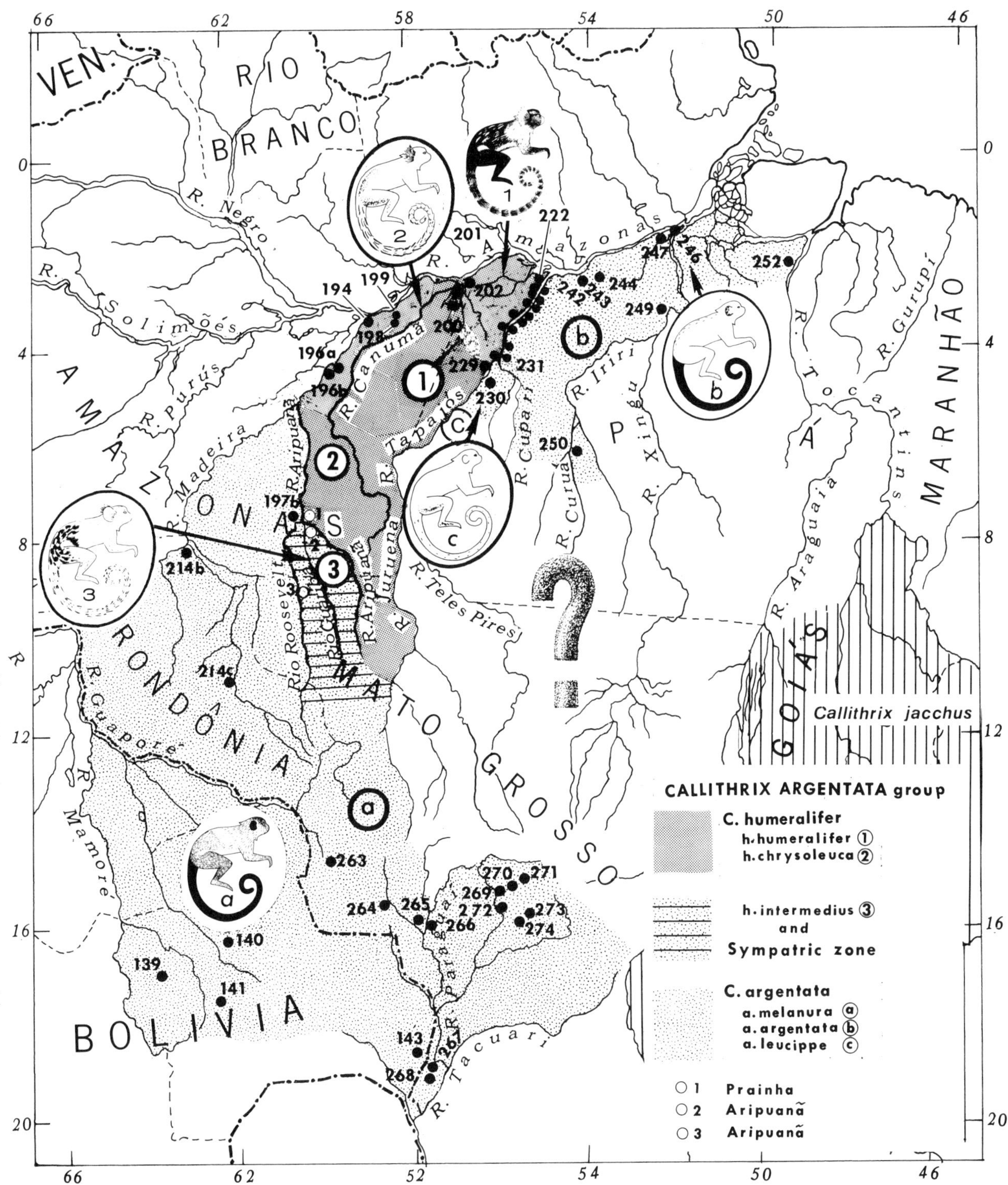

Fig. IX.36. Distribution of the *Callithrix argentata* Group: Bare-ear Marmosets, *Callithrix argentata* (*lightly shaded areas*); Tassel-ear Marmosets (*darkly shaded areas*); range limits of subspecies defined by rivers, but large parts of boundaries are still undetermined. Extreme western portion of range of *Callithrix jacchus* is indicated by vertical hatching.

ancestral form with the same trivial trait. Auricles become nearly bare in *Callithrix argentata* and thickly tufted in *C. humeralifer,* but those of juvenal *argentata* remain moderately hairy as in the hypothetical ancestor (fig. IX.52). The evolutionary processes of saturation, bleaching, depigmentation, and depilation evidently affected the same somatic parts and progressed at more or less the same rates in both species.

The most advanced races of each species, *C. argentata leucippe* and *C. humeralifer chrysoleuca,* stand at the threshold of true albinism. With their nearly pure white coats, amelanic skin, depilated faces, and ears reddened by hemoglobin of the vascular system, they approach complete convergence and, except for the difference in aural covering, simulate identity. Each race is confined to a geographic dead end. Except for the stabilizing or retarding effects of social selection, continued operation of the same evolutionary processes must soon lead to pure albinism and extinction.

Geographic variation in the *Callithrix argentata* group, as in all other callitrichids, is apparently nonadaptive. The dark and albinotic races of *Callithrix*

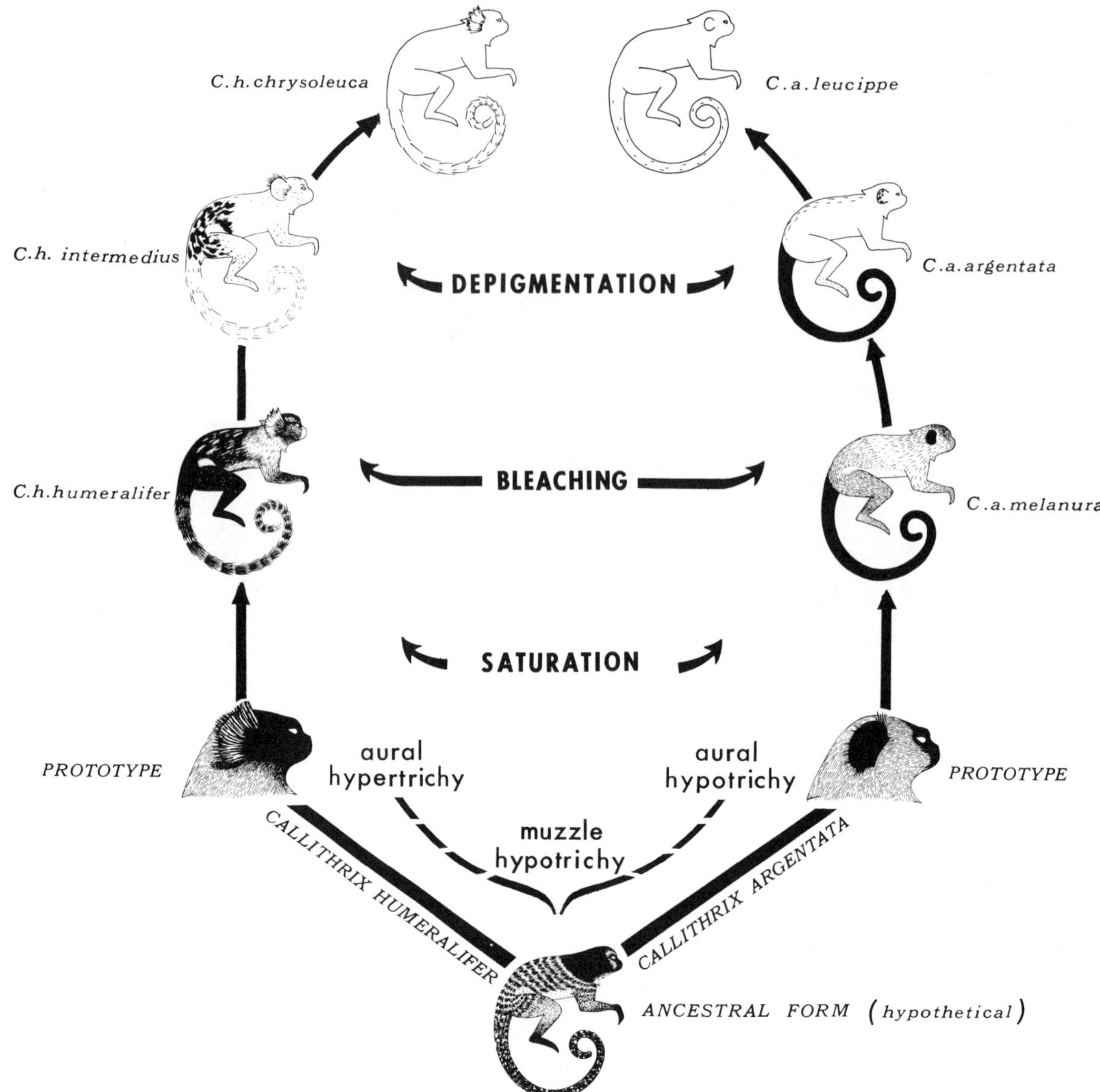

Fig. IX.37. *Callithrix argentata* Group: Geographic metachromism and chromatic evolution of the subspecies of *C. argentata* and *C. humeralifer* after divergence of the hairy-ear and bare-ear species from a hypothetical ancestor with moderately hairy ears. Racial differentiation as a consequence of geographic isolation and inbreeding within the founder colony is manifested by the progressive pilary bleaching and cutaneous depigmentation in the overall and accelerated trend toward albinism. (Based on Hershkovitz 1968.)

humeralifer live in identical rain forest environments with a trivial geographic barrier between them. Eastward, in the same region, only the Rio Tapajóz separates the silvery black-tailed *Callithrix argentata argentata* from albinotic *C. a. leucippe*. In sharp contrast, the most saturate race, *Callithrix a. melanura,* occurs far to the south in the driest and coolest part of the range.

It is generally believed that races occupying the warmer, more humid regions are darker, or tend to become darker, while races of the cooler, drier habitats are pale or become paler. This is true only to the extent that environmental factors may accelerate metachromic processes toward saturation or bleaching, as the case may be. What is generally true, as exemplified by evolution of members of the *argentata* group, is that the more peripheral or isolated a race in time or space, the more it has advanced metachromically, whatever the environmental factors may be.

Diagnostic Characters and Comparisons

The deep-seated cranial and dental characters common to *Callithrix argentata* and *C. humeralifer* mark them as intermediate in most respects between the more primitive *Callithrix jacchus* and the genus *Saguinus*. The superficial characters that distinguish *C. argentata* from *C. humeralifer* indicate relatively recent divergence from a common ancestor. In no instance is a distance between

Plate II. Metachromic evolution of three races of the Bare-ear Marmosets (*Callithrix argentata*). From left to right, *C. à. melanura*, *C. a. argentata* (dark phase), *C. a. argentata* (light phase), *C. a. leucippe*. Original paintings by E. John Pfiffner.

Fig. IX.38. Dorsal aspect of two most distantly related representatives of *Callithrix jacchus* (*C. j. jacchus* and *C. j. aurita*) compared with two specimens of the *Callithrix argentata* group (*C. humeralifer humeralifer* and *C. argentata melanura*). In the *C. jacchus* group, arms and mantle are dark, dorsum transversely striated, the individual hairs banded (agouti), flanks undifferentiated from lower back; in *C. argentata* group, arms and mantle are pale, dorsum unstriated, terminal half of hairs unbanded; contrasting whitish hip patches present (skins from about ½ to ⅓ natural size of animal). (Based on Hershkovitz 1975*b*.)

the two species nearly as great as the distance between either and *Callithrix jacchus* in the broadest sense.

The following characterization of the *Callithrix argentata* group also gives the coordinate characters of *Callithrix jacchus*. Where the characters are related separately, the following symbols are used

a = *Callithrix argentata* Group
b = *Callithrix jacchus* Group

Callithrix argentata Group

Callithrix jacchus Group

C.argentata melanius

C.humeralifer humeralifer

C.j.jacchus

C.j.aurita

Fig. IX.39. Ventral aspect of two representatives of *Callithrix jacchus* (*C. j. jacchus* and *C. j. aurita*) compared with the two specimens of the *C. argentata* group (*C. humeralifer humeralifer* and *C. argentata melanura*); same skins in fig. IX.38 shown in reversed order.

1. *a.* Size about equal to *C. jacchus* in virtually all linear dimensions but proportions of extremities to combined head and body length average slightly greater; *humeralifer* averages slightly larger than *argentata* in most dimensions and proportions hence is more distant from *Callithrix jacchus* and nearer *Saguinus* (appendix table 1).
   b. Size greater than *Cebuella* but significantly smaller than all other callitrichids except *C. argentata* (appendix table 1).

2. *a.* Ear complicated, large (ear:combined head and body length = 14% in *argentata,* 13% in *humeralifer*); pinna completely covered by tassel in *humeralifer,* nearly bald in *argentata,* but both patterns derivable from an ancestral type like that of the moderately hirsute pinna of young *argentata* (figs. IX.44, 47, 49, 52).
   b. Ear comparatively simple and small (ear:combined head and body length = 11%); circum-auricular tufts unique, not outgrowths from outer

or inner surface of pinna; circumaural area and pinna of young untufted (fig. IX.8).

3\. *a.* Tail: combined head and body length = 152 in *argentata,* 157 in *humeralifer;* tail annulated in *humeralifer* the individual hairs banded, tail in *argentata* usually uniformly colored, sometimes irregularly or incompletely banded (fig. IX.38).
b. Tail: combined head and body length = 140, or relatively shorter than in other callitrichids and consistently annulated, the individual hairs banded (fig. IX.38).

4\. *a.* Hind foot: combined head and body length = 29% in *argentata,* 30% in *humeralifer* (appendix table 1).
b. Hind foot: combined head and body length = 27% or relatively shorter than in other callitrichids (appendix table 1).

5\. *a.* Mantle poorly defined or undifferentiated; remainder of back blackish flecked with white or orange or entirely pale brown, gray, silvery, or whitish, never striated; terminal half of dorsal hairs unbanded (nonagouti); conspicuous white hip patches in *humeralifer* extend to thighs in nonalbinotic *argentata* (figs. IX.38, 42).
b. Mantle blackish, well-defined, and present in all nonalbinotic forms; dorsum transversely striated, terminal half of hairs banded (agouti or modified agouti); flanks undifferentiated (fig. IX.38).

6\. *a.* Frontal region dark in nonalbinotic forms, blaze absent, muzzle naked (figs. IX.48, 51).
b. Frontal region with white blaze which tends to spread over entire forehead, crown, and cheeks; muzzle hairy (figs. IX.7, 12, 16, 17, 24).

7\. *a.* Arms pale in nonalbinotic forms (figs. IX.38, 39).
b. Arms dark in nonalbinotic forms (figs. IX.38, 39).

8\. *a.* Median ventral inferior laryngeal sac unknown in *argentata* (fig. I.10).
b. Median ventral inferior laryngeal sac known to be present only in *Callithrix jacchus, Leontopithecus rosalia,* and *Aotus trivirgatus* (fig. I.10).

9\. *a.* External genitalia similar in adults of both species, according to sex, the organs distinctive and highly specialized (figs. IX.4, 46).
b. External genitalia proportionately smaller, less specialized for display, penial spines simple, baculum smaller and more primitive in design (fig. IX.3).

10\. *a.* Chromosome diploid number = 44.
b. Chromosome diploid number = 46.

11\. Cranial characters intermediate in nearly all respects between those of *Callithrix jacchus* and *Saguinus; argentata* and *humeralifer* indistinguishable *inter se* except skull of latter averages slightly larger (figs. VII.5, 6; IX.1, 2; appendix table 1).

12\. *a.* Malleolar orbicular apophysis often present (figs. IV.68; IX.40).
b. Malleolar orbicular apophysis absent in specimens examined.

13\. Dental arcade annectant between V- and U-shapes; dental morphology intermediate between that of *C. jacchus* and *Saguinus,* the incisors shorter, broader, more spatulate, and less forward projecting, canines more specialized and tusklike than in *C. jacchus* (figs. IX.1, 2).

14\. *a.* Trill with tongue.
b. Has not been heard to trill.

15\. Geographic ranges of *argentata* and *humeralifer* contiguous, nonoverlapping and completely isolated from *jacchus.* Small dead-end range of *humeralifer* with that of *argentata* closing southern and eastern borders indicates recent divergence of both species from common ancestor (fig. IX.36).

External Characters

Face sparsely haired with muzzle and circumbuccal region virtually naked, facial skin and pinna depigmented in albinotic forms, sides of face moderately well covered with long, backward-directed hairs; frontal spot or blaze absent in adults, ears bare and exposed or tasselated, extra-auricular fanlike tufts absent; mane absent, mantle, if defined, brownish to silvery or white, never black or agouti, and not sharply demarcated from crown; back black to brown, golden, silvery or white, often irregularly spotted or streaked but never agouti,

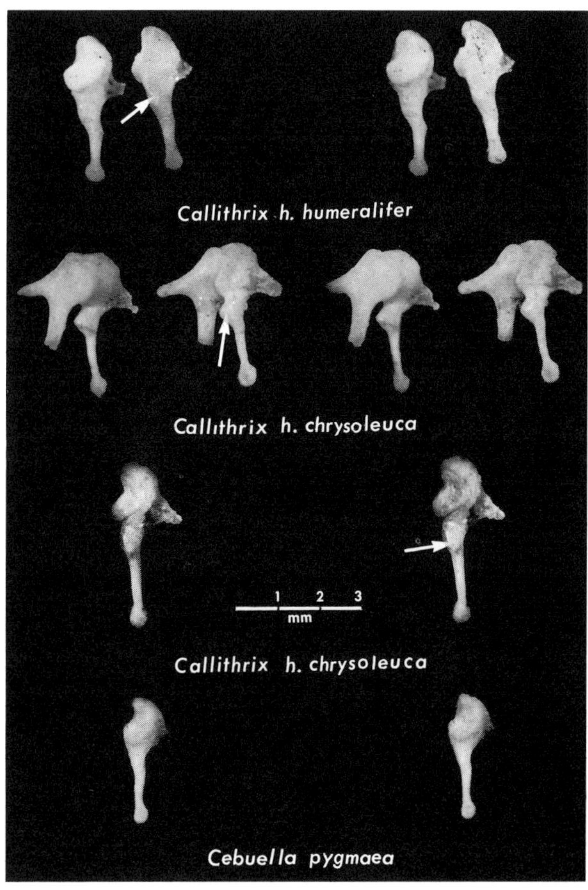

Fig. IX.40. Middle ear bones: *From below to above,* medial surface of malleus in *Cebuella pygmaea, Callithrix humeralifer chrysoleuca;* medial and lateral surfaces of malleus and incus in *Callithrix humeralifer chrysoleuca;* medial and lateral surfaces of malleus in *Callithrix humeralifer humeralifer,* arrow points to orbicular apophysis.

marbled, or transversely striated; whitish hip patches present in nonalbinotic forms; underparts pale brown to golden, silvery or whitish; outer surface of legs like back; tail uniformly colored black, golden, or white or banded black and silvery, the pelage forming a meristic pattern conforming to the serial arrangement of the caudal vertebrae (figs. IX.38, 39); external genitalia mostly or entirely unpigmented; scrotum divided (fig. IX.4).

Skull (figs. VII.5, 6; IX.1, 2, 40)

Cranial characters are given under the generic heading. The previously mentioned malleolar orbicular apophysis (pp. 179, 573 and figs. IV.68, 71; IX.40) appears to be restricted to members of the *argentata* group, mainly *Callithrix humeralifer chrysoleuca,* judged by specimens in the Field Museum collection and a certain number on loan from other museums. Distribution of the element is shown in tables 77 and 78.

Dentition (figs. VII.5; IX.1, 2, 41)

Incisors (cf. fig. V.23)

Permanent upper incisors as in *C. jacchus* but mesial ridge always well developed, distal ridge more or less

Table 77. Distribution of Malleolar Orbicular Apophysis in *Callithrix humeralifer*

Subspecies and Specimen Catalog No.	*Malleolar Orbicular Apophysis*	
	Right	*Left*
Callithrix humeralifer chrysoleuca		
Lago do Baptista (13, FMNH)		
50822 ♂	0	+
50825 ♂	0	0
50827 ♂	+	0
50828 ♂	+	+
50830 ♂	0	0
50831 ♂	+	0
50833 ♂	+	0
50823 ♀	0	+
50824 ♀	*	*
50826 ♀	+	+
50829 ♀	+	+
50832 ♀	0	0
50834 ♀	+	0
Lago Tapayuna (1, FMNH)		
50821	+	0
Borba (5, AMNH)		
91833 ♂	0	0
91834 ♀	+	0
91835 ♀	0	0
92296 ♀	+	0
92297 ♂	+	+
Igarapé Auará (4, AMNH)		
91836 ♂	0	0
91837 ♂	+	+
91838 ♀	+	+
91839 ♂	+	0
Callithrix humeralifer humeralifer		
Urucurituba (5 specimens, FMNH)		
92165 ♂	0	0
92166 ♂	+	+
92167 ♂	—	—
92168 ♀	—	—
92169 ♀	*	*
Arara (4 specimens, FMNH)		
92170 ♂	+	+
92171 ♂	0	+
92172 ♂	+	+
92173 ♂	—	+
Other localities 3 (10, FMNH)		

NOTE: Explanation of symbols and abbreviations: +, present; —, absent; *, poorly to moderately well developed; 0, malleus lost; AMNH, American Museum of Natural History; FMNH, Field Museum of Natural History. Number of specimens examined for orbicular apophysis and institutions where preserved are shown in parentheses.

Table 78. Distribution of Malleolar Orbicular Apophysis in *Callithrix argentata*

Subspecies and Specimen Catalog No.	*Malleolar Orbicular Apophysis*	
	Right	*Left*
Callithrix argentata argentata		
Tapara (8, AMNH)		
95914	+	0
95916	*	*
95919	0	*
95921	+	—
Maica (7 specimens, USNM)		
239458	*	*
Tapauina, Rio Tapajóz (4 specimens, FMNH)		
92179	*	*
Other localities 4 (11, FMNH)		
Unknown localities (4, FMNH)		
Callithrix argentata melanura (2, FMNH)		
Callithrix argentata leucippe (3, FMNH)		

NOTE: Explanation of symbols and abbreviations: Number of specimens examined for orbicular apophysis and institutions where preserved are shown in parentheses. USNM, United States National Museum. Other symbols and abbreviations are explained in the note to table 77.

defined, the two more nearly approximated lingually; *lateral incisor* one-half to three-fourths bulk of central and sometimes as high, distostyle slightly better developed, lingual surface frequently crazed; central incisor as in *C. jacchus* but slightly broader, with more pronounced inward inflection.

Deciduous upper incisors essentially as in *C. jacchus* but with lateral incisor tending toward a trapezoidal rather than triangular form; mesial edges of newly emerged central incisors overlapping.

Permanent lower incisors as in *C. jacchus* but shorter, the lateral emplaced less obliquely or more nearly in line transversely with central incisor, the pair on both sides combining to form a V- to Gothic-shaped arch, height from three-fourths to one-half vertical depth of symphysis menti, distostylid less developed and higher on crown; central incisor with mesial and distal stylids on corners of biting edge, mesial and distal enamel cingular ridges often present and sometimes meeting behind, lingual surface rarely crazed.

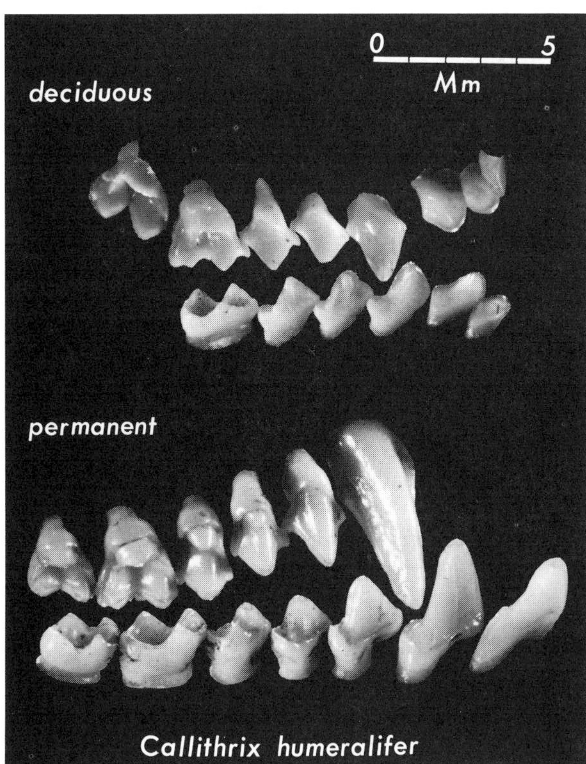

Fig. IX.41. *Callithrix humeralifer*: Deciduous and permanent dentition, the upper and lower series in approximately normal relationships; half-erupted first upper molar present in the deciduous series.

Deciduous lower incisors generally as in *C. jacchus* but central incisors with well-defined mesiostylid, lateral incisors more laterally emplaced and less sharply sculptured, lingual surface less excavated.

Remarks. In size and shape, incisors of the *C. argentata* group show transition from the *jacchus* to the tamarin type. The lower incisors are actually shorter as well as relatively shorter measured against the increasing depth of the symphysis menti. The more lateral emplacement of the lower outer incisor relative to the inner also reflects the greater breadth and depth of the "chin." Frequent crazing of the permanent upper incisors adumbrates the more widespread condition in tamarins. A well-defined and continuous lingual cingulum (*B*) also appears here for the first time. In contrast, the decidouous incisors are less sharply sculptured or molarized than those of *Callithrix jacchus.*

Canines (cf. figs. V.26, 27, 28)

Permanent upper canine slightly recurved, subtriangular in cross section, more than twice as high as wide and about twice as high as adjacent teeth; mesiolingual torus (II) defined by deep mesial groove, mesiostyle projecting above gum line, distal edge defined as a sharp ridge with distostyle at base; enamel sometimes with a few fine lines of crazing on lingual surface.

Deciduous upper canine triangular in outline, slightly recurved and more nearly premolariform than incisiform; about as long as high, twice the size of lateral incisors, slightly longer and about one fourth higher than pm^2; mesial surface ungrooved, mesiolingual torus more or less defined, mesiostyle, distostyle and thin lingual cingulum *B* present; enamel rarely crazed on lingual surface.

Lower permanent canine more caniniform than incisiform, considerably heavier, more recurved, and slightly to notably higher than lateral incisor, about one and one-half times larger and higher than adjacent premolar; mesiolingual torus unridged, cingulids *B* and *C* continuous on lingual surface, the posterior shelf modified as a rudimentary talonid; enamel sometimes finely crazed.

Deciduous lower canine premolariform, only slightly longer than pm_2 or lateral incisor; talonid more or less defined, mesial and distal stylids not evident; crazing absent in present material.

Remarks. The upper canines of the *Callithrix argentata* group are like those of *C. jacchus* in form and function. The same is generally true for the premolariform deciduous lower canine. The permanent lower canine, in contrast, is more recurved, caniniform, and in all other respects, intermediate between the incisiform canine of lower marmosets and the true caniniform tooth of *Saguinus* and other higher platyrrhines.

Premolars (cf. figs. V.25, 26, 27, 28)

Permanent upper premolars are generally as in *C. jacchus* but more molarized, pm^2 usually with distinct protocone, styles well developed, sample crown height 2.6, length 2.1, width 2.0; pm^3 as high as preceding; protocone, protoloph, cingula *B′* and *C*, and other accessories when present, sharply defined; a more or less well defined hypocone sometimes present; pm^4 slightly larger than preceding, mesial and distal styles and lingual cingula *B′* and *C* usually well developed, hypocone sometimes indicated; sample length 2.0, width 2.6.

Deciduous upper premolars with dpm^2 like that of *C. jacchus* but hardly higher than following premolars, sample crown height 2.0, length 1.9, width 1.5; terminal stylids *a* and *b* well developed, anterior and posterior cingula *B′* and *C* poorly defined or absent, protocone indicated; dpm^3 with styles *a* and *b* and cingula *B′* and *C* defined but not strongly developed, low small protocone present; dpm^4 fully molarized or tritubercular, metacone nearly as high but less bulky than eocone, protocone low but full, mesiostyle, distostyle, and one or more ectostyles well defined, minute plagioconule often present, trigon basin large and usually deep; sample length 2.4, width 2.5.

Permanent lower premolars with pm_2 premolariform, sample crown length 2.3, width 2.6, length 1.8, anterior and posterior cingula *B* and *C* well defined, the latter enclosing an incipient talonid, mesiostylid present, distostylid not always defined, metaconid rudimentary, epicristid indicated as slight bulge on lingual surface of eoconid; pm^3 well molarized, small talonid basin enclosed by cingulid *C* and epicristid, large "trigonid" basin with indication of metaconid and often pseudoparaconid, mesiostylid present; pm_4 with high "trigonid" occupying about one-half occlusal surface, eoconid connected to lower metaconid by steep epicristid, paraconid not indicated, talonid low and comparatively shallow, hypoconid, entoconid, and postentoconulid faintly indicated in some specimens; length 2.0, width 1.8.

Deciduous lower premolars are generally as in *jacchus* but somewhat more molarized; paraconid present in one worn dpm_4, sample dpm_2 crown height 1.9, length 2.0, width 1.0, dpm_4 length 2.3, width 1.6.

Remarks. The molarization grade of the premolars, like that of the canines in the *Callithrix argentata* group, is intermediate between that of *C. jacchus* and *Saguinus.* The tendency for development of tritubercular $pm^{3\text{-}4}$ with the emergence of a hypocone rather than a metacone adumbrates the condition in *Callicebus* and *Aotus.*

Molars (cf. figs. V.26, 27)

Upper molars, with *first* generally as in *Callithrix jacchus; second* molar with distostyle greatly reduced or obsolete, ectostyle poorly developed or absent, metacone well formed, rarely deflected distally, and not fused with protocone in material at hand, tooth in line with either lingual or buccal border of first molar, or set off from both borders.

Lower molars as in *Callithrix jacchus* but first molar with crest of entoconid not raised, posterior border of talonid with median trough; second molar like first but smaller, entoconid slightly raised, postentoconulid weakly differentiated from entoconid, posterior border of talonid with distobuccal trough.

Sample measurements of molars, buccal length × width:

M^1	M^2	M_1	M_2
2.4 × 2.9	1.7 × 2.3	2.4 × 1.9	2.3 × 1.6
2.5 × 3.0	2.0 × 2.4	2.5 × 2.0	2.2 × 1.5
2.6 × 2.8	1.7 × 2.2	2.5 × 1.8	2.2 × 1.6

Cytogenetics

The chromosomal pattern in *Callithrix argentata argentata* and *C. humeralifer humeralifer,* with diploid number 44, agrees essentially with that of *Cebuella.* It is presumed that karyotypes of other forms of the *argentata* group (*C. a. melanura, C. a. leucippe,* and *C. h. chrysoleuca*) are similar.

The karyotype with diploid number 46 of 2 females and 1 male identified as *"Callithrix chrysoleucos"* by Bender and Mettler (1960) is more likely that of a different species. According to Egozcue, Perkins, and Hagemenas (1968; 1969) its karyotype appears to be identical with that of *Saguinus oedipus, S. nigricollis, S. mystax,* and *S. fuscicollis.* De Boer (1974, pp. 22, 24) groups the karyotype of Bender and Mettler's *"chrysoleucos"* with that of *Saguinus* and *Callithrix jacchus,* and demurs against my assignment of *chrysoleuca* Wagner, 1842 (not *"chrysoleucos"* Bender and Mettler, 1960) to the *Callithrix argentata* group.

Misidentifications of uncommon callitrichids were frequent at the time Bender and Mettler published their findings. The karyotype of undoubted *chrysoleuca,* although predictably like that of *Callithrix humeralifer humeralifer,* is not certainly known. For further discussion see pages 598–99.

Species of the *Callithrix argentata* Group

(For a key see page 488.)

55 *Callithrix argentata* Linnaeus, Bare-ear Marmosets
1. History, Characters, and Subspecies

Distribution (fig. IX.36)

Central Brazil and extreme eastern Bolivia, from south bank of the Rio Amazonas between the lower Rio Tocantins and Rio Tapajóz, State of Pará, the upper Rio Madeira-Guaporé-Mamoré (right bank) in Brazil and contiguous parts of Bolivia, and upper Rio Paraguay basin in Mato Grosso, Brazil, and Santa Cruz, Bolivia. The species may also occur in parts of the upper Rio Tapajóz basin, but little is known of the mammals of that region.

Taxonomy (color plate II)

Three allopatric races of *Callithrix argentata* are recognized. Available material indicates virtually complete gradation in color from the brownish black-tailed *Callithrix argentata melanura* to the silvery, black-tailed *C. a. argentata*. Gradation from *argentata* to the more blanched and golden-tailed *leucippe* is not as complete in material at hand, but the evidence indicates that all three named forms are color gradients of a single species. As is usual among marmosets, geographic intergradation between wide-ranging neighboring forms is generally demonstrable, but the zoologically extreme and geographically narrowly confined races are as a rule sharply defined.

Callithrix argentata is treated by Osman Hill (1957, p. 272) as the lone species of the genus *Mico,* though with some misgivings. At the same time he regards *leucippe,* the albinotic form of argentata, as inseparable from *Hapale chrysoleuca* (= *Callithrix humeralifer chrysoleuca*).

Evolution and Dispersal

The brownish *Callithrix argentata melanura* is the most primitive race of the species. Its spread northward from Mato Grosso into the Amazonian basin must have been synchronized with establishment of suitable habitats on the rising banks or levees of the tributary streams (fig. IX.36). Dilution of coat color and depigmentation of the skin may have occurred progressively with the northward movement of the species, or these processes may have become operative only after the founder populations were completely isolated from the parental stock (fig. IX.37). Either or both postulates may be true, but the vast unexplored area between the comparatively small known ranges of northern and southern races offers few clues. The dark population (cf. *emiliae*) wedged between the Irirí and its left bank tributary, the Curuá, appears to be a relic of the once continuously distributed species. It is assigned to *C. argentata argentata* on geographic grounds and the fact that even darker individuals appear among otherwise silvery populations of that race. In contrast, the palest of all marmosets, the white-tailed *C. a. leucippe,* occupies an ostensibly isolated enclave (230) across the southwestern border of the range of the black-tailed *argentata.* It must have differentiated in situ after being cut off by the Rio Cupari from the parental *argentata.*

The three races of silvery marmosets, *melanura, argentata,* and *leucippe,* represent three successive grades in the bleaching, depigmentation and, less remarkably, depilation processes (figs. IX.42, 43). In these respects they are more advanced than other callitrichids with albinistic races (cf. *Callithrix humeralifer, C. jacchus, Saguinus fuscicollis,* and *Leontopithecus rosalia*).

Bleaching of the upper, outer parts of the body in *Callithrix argentata melanura* begins with the mantle and hips, whence it spreads along the outer side of the thighs to form the distinctive hip and thigh patch. In one juvenal at hand, bleaching of head begins with a silvery forelock adumbrating the process which culminates in the silvery headed *argentata.* The bleaching process in *melanura* is even more advanced on underparts than on mantle, and the root of the tail has bleached from blackish to brown dorsally and from tawny orange to buff ventrally.

In *C. argentata argentata* the forehead and temporal region are palest, the mantle darker, hip patches merged with pale color of surrounding parts, and tail darker, more black than in *melanura* except underside at root, sometimes to middle region and tip, which are more extensively bleached and vary from tawny to whitish. Atavistically brown individuals of *argentata* are intermediate between this race and *melanura.*

C. a. leucippe occupies an enclave in the southern angle between the Tapajóz and its right-bank tributary,

Fig. IX.42. Subspecies of Bare-ear Marmosets from dorsal aspect: *Callithrix argentata melanura* (FM 44859; Rio Quiser, Bolivia); *C. a. argentata* (FM 50839, Cajiricatuba); *C. a. argentata* (FM 92179, Tapaiuna) less brownish, more silvery than preceding; *C. a. leucippe* (FM 92175, Fordlandia) dark streaking of tail is part pigment, part black piedra fungus; *C. a. leucippe* (FM 92174, Fordlandia) less pigmented throughout than preceding, but some fungus present on tail. Chromogenetic fields susceptible to most rapid bleaching are outer sides of arms, mantle, hips and thighs, rump at tail base; tail is affected least and last; depigmentation of ears and external genitalia is clinal; about ⅓ natural size.

the Rio Cupari. It is nearly uniformly silvery white on dorsal surface of head, back and sides with some yellowish lingering on mid back, neck, chest, and belly. Its tail, rump, and upper surface of arms and legs are golden.

Bleaching of the individual hairs of head and body progresses from base to tip, whereas tail hairs bleach from tip to base.

Depigmentation of the skin of face, ears, and volar surfaces is more advanced in *argentata* than in *melanura* and most advanced in *leucippe*.

Depilation involving baring of the ears and muzzle appears to have been effected early in the history of the adult forms of the species. The face of young, however, is comparatively hairy, the ears (fig. IX.52) notably so, although not nearly comparable to the condition in *Callithrix humeralifer*.

Diagnostic Characters

Ears bare, fully exposed; crown and back brownish, silvery, or whitish, outer sides of limbs similar; tail contrastingly colored blackish to golden (figs. IX.42, 43, 44).

Fig. IX.43. Subspecies of Bare-ear marmosets from ventral aspect: Same specimen shown in fig. IX.42; bleaching of ventral surface pelage is clinal but more rapid than that of dorsal surface; about ⅓ natural size.

External Characters (figs. IX.42, 43, 44)

Coat. Skin of face and ears pigmented, mottled, or unpigmented; iris black; ears entirely naked and completely exposed; area around mouth sparsely covered with long coarse hairs intermixed with shorter finer silvery to blackish hairs; gular area nearly bare anteriorly to thinly haired like chest posteriorly and often with one, rarely more, median papilla bearing an unpigmented vibrissa 1–2 cm long; dorsal surface of head, body, and limbs brownish, silvery gray, golden, yellowish, or whitish; underparts paler and more or less defined from sides of body; hairs of interramia cresting forward, hairs of throat directed backward; tail dominantly or wholly blackish, brown, or golden to pale buff, ventral surface at base paler; external genitalia unpigmented.

Juvenal. Pelage usually darker than in adults, head, notably muzzle and ears distinctly hirsute, usually, the younger the more hairy (fig. IX.52).

Vibrissae (fig. IX.44, 45). Supraorbitals, mystacials, rhinarials (nearly obsolete in *leucippe*) and mentals present, genals randomly distributed or represented by one to three hairs, interramals generally unpigmented and directed forward (*melanura*) or forward, sidewise, and backward (*argentata, leucippe*); ulnar-carpals present; gular and pectoral spines absent. Vibrissae poorly developed and generally unpigmented in *leucippe.*

External Genitalia

Male (figs. IX.4, 46)

Adult. External genitalia and perineal and anal regions unpigmented; penis cylindrical but tapering slightly distally, penial shaft with unsheathed portion unpigmented and papillate, each papilla with a large hollow spine or cluster of two or more single-pointed, two-

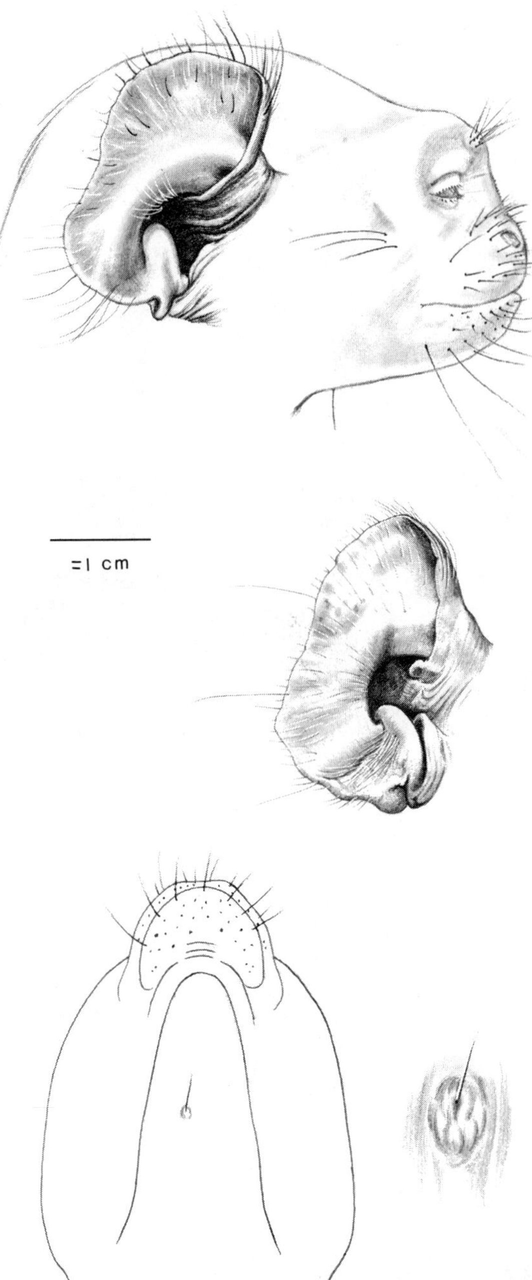

Fig. IX.44. *Callithrix argentata argentata*: *Above,* profile of head, the cover hairs removed to expose ear, vibrissae, and facial pigmentation; *center,* ear of another individual; *below,* gular vibrissa in situ and an enlargement.

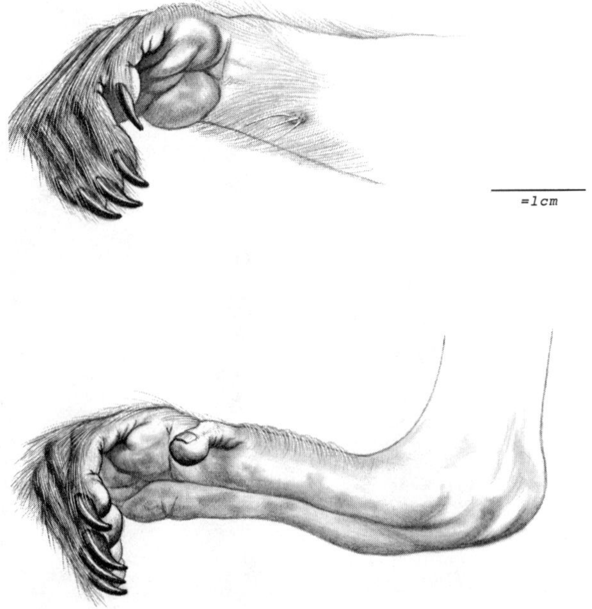

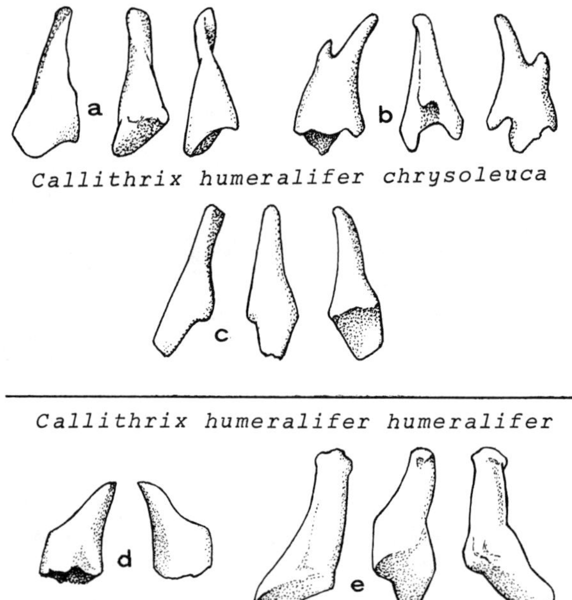

Fig. IX.45. *Callithrix argentata argentata*: Right hand (*above*) and right foot in relaxed position; ulnar-carpal vibrissae shown.

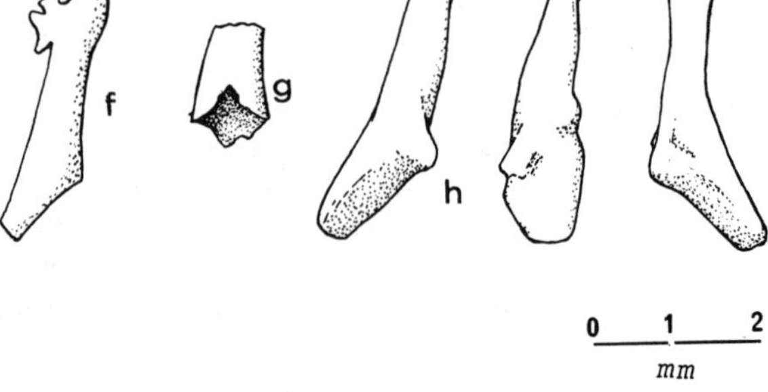

Fig. IX.46. Penis bones of *Callithrix argentata* group: *a, b, c* = *C. humeralifer chrysoleuca,* 3 bones with 3 aspects of each, *b* is abnormal/; *d, e* = *C. humeralifer humeralifer,* 2 aspects of 1 bone, 3 of the other; *f, g, h* = *C. argentata argentata, f* is abnormal, *g* incompletely developed, *h* seen from 3 sides is normal and fully developed.

pointed, recurved, or canalized spines all cornified and translucent; glans penis unpigmented with left, or bacular, lobe larger than right; scrotum white, wider than long with pendulous scrotal folds completely separated by raphe into subequal sacs; scrotal skin convoluted, papillate, and sparsely set with short white hairs; inner preputial fold unpigmented and glabrous, thinly haired outer preputial fold forming low basal sheath in adult; transverse width of scrotum with testes, 28–29 mm; sexual skin apparently undifferentiated.

Juvenal. Genitalia and surrounding area unpigmented, thinly haired scrotum comparatively smooth with few folds or sulci and subdivided by raphe into two distinct sacs; penis unsheathed in outer, or hairy, portion of preputial fold, the glans more or less enclosed by annulus.

Remarks. The external genitalia of *Callithrix argentata* are most elaborate. Large scrotal sebaceous glands, like those of the labia majora, secrete a thick yellowish musky liquid. Perkins (1969*c*) notes nerve end organs and capillary loops inside the hollow penial spines.

Female (fig. IX.4)

Adult. Labia majora unpigmented, scrotal folds extremely enlarged and glandular, the skin convoluted, papillate and sparsely haired white; in old adults, each scrotal fold pedunculate, overhanging preputial fold of same side and extending medially almost to midline; preputial folds conspicuously enlarged and glandular, skin corrugated, the lateral surface thinly haired; clitoris fully exposed below plane of rima pudendi, the frenulae well defined, each labium minus with two pairs of longitudinally grooved lamina; external genitalia wider than long, greatest diameter in two adults, 15, 16 mm, length of genital fissure, 10, 11 mm; glandular sexual skin of pubic region normally unpigmented but stained with yellowish or orange secretion; perineal and anal regions unpigmented.

Juvenals Labia majora pustulated, unpigmented, thinly haired white; scrotal folds convoluted and projecting but not overhanging smaller preputial folds; left lobe of glans clitoridis about three times wider than right lobe.

Remarks. The labia majora, particularly the scrotal folds, are strikingly like their male homologue, the scrotum. These free hanging, probably erectile, folds are used for marking and perhaps clasp the penis during coitus. Labia and sexual skin secrete a bright yellowish or orange musky liquid which stain skin and hair. Ordinary handling of the genitalia of specimens long preserved and hardened in spirits still causes the secretion to ooze from scrotal folds and sexual skin. The odor is musky and persistent.

Comparisons

Distinguished from other species of *Callithrix* by the comparatively bare and exposed ears without tufts in front or above, absence of contrasted whitish frontal blaze, back brownish to silvery or white without marbling or striations, tail black to silvery or white without banding in adult.

Key to the Subspecies of *Callithrix argentata*

1. Tail dominantly pale buff or golden . . . . *leucippe* (p. 588)
1′. Tail black or dark brown 2
2. Forehead, cheeks, sides of crown silvery white; center of crown, back, and outer sides of limbs silvery white, grayish, drab, or brown, whitish hip and thigh patch obsolete or absent; ears unpigmented or mottled. . . . . *argentata* (p. 583)
2′. Forehead, entire crown, back and outer sides of limbs brown; whitish hip and thigh patch sharply defined . . . . *melanura* (p. 581)

1 2 2′

leucippe *argentata* *melanura*

CALLITHRIX ARGENTATA MELANURA E. GEOFFROY: BLACK-TAILED MARMOSET

Synonymic History

Simia melanura E. Geoffroy, in Humboldt, 1812, *Rec. Obs. Zool. Anat. Comp.*, p. 360—"*Jacchus melanurus,* Geoffroy," in synonymy.

Jacchus melanurus E. Geoffroy, 1812, *Ann. Mus. Hist. Nat., Paris* 19:120—"le Brésil;" diagnosis. Desmarest, 1818, *Nouv. Dict. Hist. Nat.* 24:240—characters ex type in Paris Museum. Desmarest, 1820, *Mammalogie,* p. 93—characters. Desmarest, 1827, *Dict. Sci. Nat.* 47:20—characters. I. Geoffroy, 1827, *Dict. Class. Hist. Nat.* 12:518—characters. Gray, 1847, *List Osteol. Spec. Brit. Mus.*, p. 140—BOLIVIA; skin and skull collected by Bridges. Gerrard, 1862, *Cat. bones Brit. Mus.*, p. 29—BOLIVIA; skin and skull, collected by Bridges. Rode, 1938, *Bull. Mus. Nat. Hist. Nat., Paris,* ser. 2, 10:238—type history.

Hapale melanurus, Kuhl, 1820, *Beitr. Zool.*, p. 49—characters; intermediate between *Hapale* and *Midas.*

Hapale melanura, Wagner, 1848, *Abh. Akad. Wiss., Munich* 5:469—BRAZIL: *Mato Grosso* (Cuyabá; Caissara). Sclater, 1876, *Proc. Zool. Soc. London* 1875:419—part (not plate 50); BRAZIL: *Mato Grosso* (Matogrosso, collected by Natterer). Schlegel, 1876, *Les singes.* Simiae, p. 267—BRAZIL: *Mato Grosso* (Cuyabá); BOLIVIA: (Bridges collection); taxonomic history; characters. Pelzeln, 1883, *Verh. K. K. Zool.-Bot. Gesellsch., Wien, Beih.* 33:23—BRAZIL: *Mato Grosso* (Cuyabá; Caiçara; Matogrosso); characters; variations; synonyms, *leukeurin* Natterer (ms.), *Jachus* [*sic*] *leucomeros* Gray. Jentink, 1887, *Cat. Osteol. Mus. Pays-Bas* 9:50—BOLIVIA. Jentink, 1892, *Cat. Syst. Mamm. Mus. Pays-Bas* 12:57—BRAZIL: *Mato Grosso* (Cuyabá); BOLIVIA.

H[*apale*] *melanura,* I. Geoffroy, 1851, *Cat. Primates, Mus. Hist. Nat., Paris,* p. 60—part, type history; BOLIVIA: *Santa Cruz* (Santa Cruz de la Sierra [d'Orbigny, 1834]). Wagner, 1855, *Schreber's Säugth., Suppl.* 5:127, pl. 13 (animal)—BRAZIL: *Mato Grosso* (Cuyabá; Caissara); characters; *Jacchus leucomeros* Gray, a synonym. Miranda Ribeiro, 1914, *Comm. Linhas Telegr., Annexo 5, Zool.,* p. 20, pl. 10 (animals), Appendix p. 2—BRAZIL: *Mato Grosso* (São Luiz de Caceres; Alto Jaurú; Corrego do Cabral, Rio Aricá); characters.

Midas melanurus, E. Geoffroy, 1828, *Cours Hist. Nat. Mamm., Leçon* 10, p. 36—classification.

Midas melanura, De Beaux, 1917, *Giorn. Morph. Uomo, Primati* 1:104—dentally intermediate between *Hapale* [= *Callithrix*] and *Midas* [= *Saguinus*].

H[*apale* (*Liocephalus*)] *melanura,* Wagner, 1840, *Schreber's Säugth., Suppl.* 1:ix, 244—characters; classification.

Hapale [*Mico*] *melanura,* Gray, 1866, *Proc. Zool. Soc. London,* 1865:734—part, BOLIVIA; *Jacchus leucomeros* Gray in synonymy.

Mico melanurus, Gray, 1870, *Cat. monkeys, lemurs and fruit-eating bats, Brit. Mus.,* p. 64—part, BOLIVIA; synonym, *Jacchus leucomeros* Gray.

Callithrix melanura, Thomas, 1904, *Proc. Zool. Soc. London* 1903(2):234—BRAZIL: *Mato Grosso* (Santa Ana de Chapada). Krieg, 1930, *Zeitschrift Morph. Okol. Tiere* 18:761, 778, fig. 1 (skin)—PARAGUAY: (right bank Río Paraguay); BOLIVIA: *Santa Cruz* (near Puerto Suarez); *Chiquitos;* characters; variation in color; limb proportions; habits.

Callithrix argentata melanura, J. A. Allen, 1916, *Bull. Amer. Mus. Nat. Hist.* 35:583—BRAZIL: *Mato Grosso* (type locality, by restriction, Cuyabá; Urucum); characters; taxonomy. L. E. Miller, 1916, *Bull. Amer. Mus. Nat. Hist.* 35:603—habits. Vieira, 1945, Arq. Zool., São Paulo, 4:399—BRAZIL: *Mato Grosso* (Fazenda Aricá; Palmeiras; Santo Antonio, near Cuyabá; Corumbá). Vieira, 1955, *Arq. Zool., São Paulo* 8:294—BOLIVIA: (eastern part); BRAZIL: *Mato Grosso;* distribution. Travassos, 1957, *Publ. Avulsos Mus. Nac. Rio de Janeiro,* no. 20:9—BRAZIL: *Mato Grosso* (Urucum); parasites. Machado, 1960, *Anais Fac. Med. Univ. Minas Gerais,* 20: 123 seq., table 1, fig. 12 (ileal eminence)—BRAZIL: *Rondônia* (Rio Gi-Paraná); morphology of ileal eminence of large intestine. Hershkovitz, 1966, *Mammalia* 32(2):331—characters; taxonomy. Avila Pires, 1969, *Rev. Brasil. Biol.* 29 (1):54—BRAZIL: *Mato Grosso* (Cacéres; Vila de Santo Antonio, Cuiaba; Rio Aricá; Corumbá; Urucum; Rio Paraguai); *Amazonas* (Foz do Rio Castanhas); *Rondônia* (Foz do Rio Urupá, Rio Gi-Paraná); BOLIVIA: *Santa Cruz* (Río Quiser; Santa Cruz; Cercado); characters; distribution. Hershkovitz, 1970, *Amer. J. Phys. Anthrop* 32(3):379—dental diseases. Albuquerque and Barretto, 1970, *Rev. Inst. Med. Trop., São Paulo* 12:121—natural infection with *Trypanosoma cruzi* [work not seen].

M[*ico*] *a*[*rgentatus*] *melanurus,* Osman Hill, 1957, *Primates* 3:107, 251, 278—characters; distribution; variation.

Jacchus leucomerus Gray, 1846, *Ann. Mag. Nat. Hist.,* ser. 1, 18:212—BOLIVIA: (precise type locality not specified); cotypes, British Museum (Natural History), nos. 46.7.28.18 and 46.7.28.19 ♀, collected by Bridges. Gray, 1866, *Proc. Zool. Soc. London* 1865:734—in synonymy of *Hapale melanura.* Osman Hill, 1957, *Primates* 3:273, 278—in synonymy of *Mico argentatus;* name available for Bolivian form.

Iacchus [*sic*] *leucomeros* [*sic*] Gray, 1866, *Proc. Zool. Soc. London* 1865:735—listed as a synonym of *Hapale melanura.*

Callithrix argentata leucomerus, J. A. Allen, 1916, *Bull. Amer. Mus. Nat. Hist.* 35:585—classification.

Callithrix argentata lencomerus [*sic*], Cabrera, 1958, *Rev. Mus. Argentino Cienc. Nat. "Bernardino Rivadavia"* 4:186—misspelling in synonymy of *C. a. leucomerus* (pp. 185–86) erroneously attributed to J. A. Allen, 1916 (supra cit.).

Simia leukeurin Pelzeln, 1883, *Verh. K. K. Zool.-Bot. Gesellsch., Wien, Beih.* 33:23—Natterer manuscript name in synonymy of *Hapale melanura.*

Mico argentatus, Lesson (part, not Linnaeus), 1840, *Species de mammifères: Bimanes et quadrumanes . . . ,* p. 194—variety "Age moyen," only.

Callithrix argentata, Elliot (part, not Linnaeus), 1913, *Review of the Primates* 1:221—description but not plate 8; distribution; synonymy and characters of type of *melanura* E. Geoffroy. Dennler, 1939, *Physis* 16:229—Guaraní name, *titi-hoví.*

Type. Male, mounted, skull in skin, Muséum National d'Histoire Naturelle, Paris, no. 624 (600); collected by Alexandre Rodrigues Ferreira during his scientific expedition in Brazil, 1783–92 (cf. Carvalho 1965, p. 25); originally deposited in the Museum Royal d'Ajuda, Lisbon, Portugal; acquired in 1808 by the Paris Museum during the Napoleonic wars.

Type Locality. Brazil; restricted to Cuyabá [= Cuiabá], Mato Grosso (269), by J. A. Allen, 1916 (*Bull. Amer. Mus. Nat. Hist.* 35:583).

Distribution (fig. IX.36). Upper Rio Madeira-Guaporé-Mamoré (right bank) in Rondônia, Brazil and Beni and Santa Cruz, Bolivia, possibly also in the upper Rio Tapajóz-Juruena in Mato Grosso, then over the divide into the upper Rio Paraguay basin in Bolivia and Brazil. So far as is known, *melanura* does not range south or east of the Rio Taquari in Brazil, or west of the Río Mamoré in Bolivia; most of northern, eastern and central portions of range unexplored.

A description of the habitat is supplied by Krieg (1930, pp. 762–63) as follows, translated from the German:

> We found *Callithrix* [*melanura*] only at the northern border of the Gran Chaco in the region of Chiquitos (142). From the point of view of vegetation this region can be considered as a transition between the low dry forest of the northern Chaco and the humid and tropical Amazonian region. From the point of view of climate, it is distinguished from the Chaco by its heavy rainfall during the rainy season and by the fact that there is better wind protection between the hills of the Serranias de Chiquitos than in the open Chaco plain. Also from a geological point of view this region is clearly distinct from the true pampa Chaco. The Serranias consist of quartz, sandstone, marl and crystalline chalks which cover the primitive gneiss ground and emerge farther north as the Serrania de Parecis. The large intervals between the few hills represent pampa flats which are covered with winter dry brush and *Copernicia* palm. The rivers carry fresh water and some of them dry up during the dry season. The trees are generally more varied in shape and higher than in the Chaco.

Taxonomy. The original description of *melanura* E. Geoffroy is inadequate, the provenance of the type specimen unknown. It was not until 1820 that the distinctive characters were made known by the German anatomist Kuhl, who examined the type in the Paris Museum. Knowledge of the habitat of *melanura* came in 1850 when Wagner recorded specimens collected by Natterer in the vicinity of the Brazilian villages of Cuiabá (269), Caiçara (265), and Matogrosso (263). The type locality was finally restricted to the first by J. A. Allen in 1916.

The intimate relationship between *melanura* and *argentata* was recognized early by authors but I. Geoffroy (1851, p. 61) went too far in treating *argentata* as merely an albino of *melanura.*

Jacchus leucomerus Gray is indistinguishable from *melanura* E. Geoffroy, to which Gray (1866, p. 234) later referred it. Three Bolivian specimens in the British Museum are labeled *leucomeros.* Two are cotypes, both collected by Mr. Bridges. They had been mounted, then "unstuffed 1907." Two additional Bolivian specimens preserved in the American Museum are likewise inseparable from Mato Grosso *melanura.*

Diagnostic Characters. Forehead, crown, and lower back dominantly brown, tail blackish, prominent whitish or pale hip and thigh patch sharply defined from brownish legs and sides of body (fig. IX.42).

Coloration. Face thinly haired dark brown in front with poorly defined blackish superciliary band, cheeks brown to buffy; facial skin and ears deeply pigmented but muzzle or rhinarium often mottled or unpigmented; forehead dark brown, crown brown; poorly to well-defined mantle drab to grayish brown, the hairs buffy or gray to drab basally, drab to pale brown or orange terminally; lower half of back and rump dark brown; hips and outer sides of thighs sharply contrasted whitish or buffy; upper sides of hind legs dark brown, forelimbs paler; underparts well defined from sides, buffy to creamy or pale gray on neck and chest, buffy to ochraceous orange on belly and inner sides of thighs and arms; undersides of legs and ankles brown; upper surface of hands and feet brownish usually mixed with gray or orange; tail dark brown to blackish except for orange to golden brown underside of root.

Young. Generally like adult but crown blackish and forehead with whitish or silvery blaze; body and limbs more uniformly colored with hairs darker basally than terminally the reverse of the pattern in adults, whitish hip and thigh patch not evident.

Measurements. See appendix table 2.

Comparisons. The diagnostic characters given above distinguish *melanura* from all others.

Remarks. Elliot (1913*a*, p. 221) gives the description and distribution of *C. a. melanura* under the heading *Callithrix argentata,* with the following note: "The presumable type of *C. melanura* in the Paris Museum is so faded that it would be useless to attempt a description from it, the various shades of brown having practically become one, the legs alone being somewhat darker than the back, grading into the blackish brown of the feet."

Specimens Examined. 25. BRAZIL—*Mato Grosso:* Serra da Chapada, 2 (BM); Urucum de Corumbá, 5 (AMNH, 4; FMNH, 1); No precise locality, type of ms. name *leukeurin Natterer* (BM); BOLIVIA—*Santa Cruz:* Río Quiser, Chiquitos, 1 (AMNH); Cercado, 1 (FMNH); Palmarito, Río San Julian, 2 (CM); Río Mapaiso, Río Grande, 4 (CM); Río Quiser, N. Chiquitos, 4 (CM); no locality, 2 syntypes of *leucomerus* (BM); UNKNOWN LOCALITY: 3, including type of *melanura* (MNHN).

CALLITHRIX ARGENTATA ARGENTATA LINNAEUS: SILVERY MARMOSET

Fig. IX.47. Silvery Marmoset, *Callithrix argentata argentata* Linnaeus.

Synonymic History

Sahuin, La Condamine, 1745, *Relacion d'un voyage d'Amérique,* p. 165—BRAZIL: *Pará.*

Le petit singe de Para, Brisson, 1756, Reg. Anim., p. 201—"*cercopithecus ex cinereo albus argenteus . . . ;*" BRAZIL: *Pará;* measurements ex type preserved in the Réaumur collection.

Le Mico, Buffon, 1767, *Hist. Nat.* 15:121, pl. 18—BRAZIL.

Simia argentata Linnaeus, 1771, *Mantissa,* 2, Appendix, p. 521. Schreber, 1774, *Säugeth.* 1:131, pl. 36 (animal ex Buffon)—characters. Gmelin, 1788, *Linn. Syst. Nat.,* ed. 13, p. 41—characters. Cuvier, 1798, *Tableau élémentaire,* p. 97—*mico* Buffon. Audebert, 1797, *Hist. Nat. singes et makis,* fasc. 6, sect. 2, pl. 2 (colored *ex* type mounted in Paris Museum)—characters. Shaw, 1800, *Gen. Zool.* 1 (1):66, pl. 26 (fair monkey ex Buffon). Humboldt, 1812, *Rec. Obs. Zool. Anat. Comp.,* p. 360—"habite le Grand Para." J. A. Allen, 1916, *Bull. Amer. Mus. Nat. Hist.* 35:584—taxonomic history.

[*Callithrix*] *argentata,* Erxleben, 1777, *Syst. Reg. Anim.* p. 61—classification.

Callithrix argentata, Thomas, 1912, *Ann. Mag. Nat. Hist.,* ser. 8, 9:85—BRAZIL: *Pará* (Mararú, Rio Tapajóz, near Santarém). Elliot, 1913, *Review of the Primates* 1:221, pl. 8 (animal)—part, colored figure only and corresponding synonymy. J. A. Allen, 1916, *Bull. Amer. Mus. Nat. Hist.* 35:585—BRAZIL: *Pará* (Cametá; Tamacury). Cruz Lima, 1945, *Mamíferos da Amazonia, Primates, Contr. Mus. Paraense,* p. 243, pl. 39, fig. 1 (animal)—BRAZIL: *Pará* (Cametá, Rio Tocantins; Fazenda Vaicajá, Rio Tocantins; Altamira, Rio Xingu; Santarém, Rio Tapajóz; Mararú, Rio Tapajóz); characters; taxonomy. Schneider, 1958, *Primatologia* 3 (1): 90, fig. 12 (tongue)—tongue anatomy. Machado and Di Dio, 1963, *Anat. Anzeiger* 113:45—ampulla of the terminal ileum. Egozcue, Perkins, and Hagemenas, 1968, *Folia Primat.* 9:82, fig. 1 (animal)—karyotype (2n = 44). Levy, S. Hampton, Dreizen, and Hampton, 1972, *J. Comp. Path.* 82:99, fig. 1 (runted juv.)—thyroiditis in normal and runted individuals. Clark, 1974, *10th Ann. Rpt. Jersey Wildl. Preserv. Inst.* p. 44—daily food requirements in Jersey Zoo.

[*Callithrix argentata*], Levy, 1971, *J. Dental Res.* 50 (2), 2:246, fig. 1 (runted and normal individuals), fig. 2 (thyroid)—identification of figured "runted marmoset" in study of periodontal diseases.

Callithrix argentata argentata, Vieira, 1955, *Arq. Zool., São Paulo* 8:394—BRAZIL: *Pará* (Cametá; Santarém; Altamira, Rio Xingu; Maraú [= Mararú?]; Uapoama [= Itapuama]; Aveiro; Caxiricatuba; Piquiatuba, Rio Tapajóz). Cabrera, 1958, *Rev. Mus. Argentino Cienc. Nat. "Bernardino Rivadavia"* 4:185—classification. Hershkovitz, 1966, *Mammalia* 30(2):330, 331—taxonomy. Hershkovitz, 1968 , Evolution 22(3):566, fig. 8 (geographic distribution), fig. 9 (geographic metachromism)—color pattern; geographic metachromism. Avila Pires, 1969, *Rev. Brasil. Biol.* 29(1):52—BRAZIL: *Pará* (Cametá; Fazenda Vaicajá; Santarém; Caxiricatuba; Piquiatuba; Tanarí; Fazenda Maruá; Mararú; Tapaiuna; Aramanaí; Maicá; Tupará; Vilarhino do Monte; Recreio do Rio Majarí; Alatamira [= Altamira]); characters; taxonomy; distribution. Hershkovitz, 1970, *Amer. J. Phys. Anthrop.* 32(3):379—dental diseases. Hershkovitz, 1970, *Folia Primat.* 13:215, fig. 3 (endocranial cerebral impression)—BRAZIL: *Pará* (Rio Tapajóz); cerebral fissural patterns. S. Hampton and Taylor, 1970, *Proc. 3rd Int. Congr. Primat., Zürich* 1:246—gonadal development (resembles pattern in other platyrrhines and catarrhines). Hsu and Hampton, 1970, *Folia Primat.* 13:183, fig. 2 (karyotype)—karyotype (2n = 44).

Callithrix a[rgentata] argentata, Epple, 1970, *Folia Primat.* 12:57—maintenance; breeding; development.

Callithrix (Mico) argentatus, Osman Hill, 1958, *Primatologia* 3 (1):642, fig. 10 (♂ external genitalia)—external genitalia.

Callithrix (Mico) argentata, Perkins, 1969, *Amer. J. Phys. Anthrop.* 30:361, pl. 1 (animal), pl. 2 (penile spines), pls. 3, 4 (Meissner corpuscles), pls. 5–7, 8, fig. 15 (hair follicles), pl. 8, fig. 14 (section toe pad), pl. 9, fig. 16 (section lip), pl. 9, fig. 17 (section scrotum)—skin histology.

Mico argentatus, Lönnberg, 1940, *Ark. Zool., Stockholm* 32A, (10):16—BRAZIL: *Pará* (Rio Tapajóz; Itapoama, Aveiros; Santarém; Cametá, Rio Tocantins); characters. Osman Hill, 1955, *Proc. Roy. Phys. Soc. Edinburgh* 24:50—skull of menagerie specimen. Osman Hill, 1957, *Primates* 3:185, 191, 194, 251, 273–80, 288, 291, fig. 21 (facial hair tracts), fig. 22 (facial hair tracts), fig. 74 (animal), fig. 75 (gular region), fig. 77 (hand and foot), figs. 78, 79 (external genitalia), fig. 80 (intestine), pl. 21 (animal)—anatomy; characters; taxonomy; distribution; reproduction; hybridization; behavior. Osman Hill, 1958, *Primatologia* 3(1):642, fig. 10 (external genitalia)—external genitalia.

Mico argentatus argentatus, Osman Hill, 1957, *Primates* 3:251, 278, pl. 21 (animal)—characters; distribution.

Mico a[rgentatus] argentatus, Epple, 1967, *Folia Primat.* 7:38, fig. 2 (♂ carrying juv. *Callithrix jacchus* twins)—sexual and social behavior. Epple and Lorenz, 1967, *Folia Primat.* 7:99—sternal gland. Epple, 1968, *Folia Primat.* 8:2, 19, figs. 20, 21 (voice records)—vocalizations.

Callitrix argentata, Latreille, 1804, *Buffon Hist. Nat.,* Sonnini ed., 36:281—classification.

Cercopithecus argentatus, Goldfuss, 1809, *Vergl. Naturbeschr. Säugeth.,* p. 76—classification.

S[imia] Sagoinus argentatus, Kerr, 1792, *Animal kingdom,* p. 82—*mico* Buffon.

S[aguin] argentata, Fischer, 1803, *Nationalmus. Naturh. (Paris)* 2:113.

Sagouin argentatus, Lacépède, 1803, *Buffon Hist. Nat.,* Didot ed. (1799) 13:147—*le mico* Buffon. Geoffroy, 1803, *Cat. Mamm. Mus. Hist. Nat., Paris,* p. 14—BRAZIL: *Pará* (type locality); type skinned from spirits and mounted in Paris Museum.

Jacchus argentatus, E. Geoffroy, 1812, *Anal. Mus. Nat. Hist. Nat., Paris* 19:120—classification. Desmarest, 1818, *Nouv. Dict. Hist. Nat., Paris* 24:240—characters; type, "a fait partie de la collection du muséum." Desmarest, 1827, Dict. Sci. Nat., Paris 47:20.

J[acchus] melanurus argentatus, Rode, 1938, *Bull. Mus. Nat. Hist. Nat.,* ser. 2, 10:238—"albino" donated by Count Hoffmannsegg, 1808, said to be from Bolivia [actually collected near Cametá, Pará, Brazil, by Herr Sieber].

Hapale argentatus, Kuhl, 1820, *Beitr. Zool.,* pt. 1:49—part, specimens in Berlin, Temminck (Leiden), Prince Maximilian and Paris museums.

Hapale argentata, Wagner, 1848, *Abh. Akad. Wiss. Munich* 5:471—two specimens in Berlin Museum collected by Sieber. Schlegel, 1876, *Les singes. Simiae,* p. 268—BRAZIL: *Pará* (Cametá, specimens in Berlin and Paris museums collected by Sieber); taxonomic history. Jentink, 1892, *Cat. Syst. Mamm. Mus. Pays-Bas,* p. 58—specimen from Temminck collection without locality. Goeldi and Hagmann, 1904, *Bol. Mus. Paraense* 4:52—BRAZIL: *Pará* (Cametá; Santarém; Monte Alegre [!]). Schultz, 1948, *Amer. J. Phys. Anthrop.,* n.s. 6:8—twin births recorded.

Midas argentatus, E. Geoffroy, 1828, *Cours de l'histoire naturelle des mammifères, leçon* 10, p. 36—classification. Bates, 1863, *Naturalist on the River Amazons* 1:162—BRAZIL: *Pará* (Cametá); characters; habits.

H[apale (Liocephalus)] argentata, Wagner, 1840, *Schreber's Säugth., Suppl.* 1:ix, 245—classification; synonymy.

[Hapale] (Mico) argentatus, Lesson, 1840, *Species de mammiféres: Bimanes et quadrumanes . . . ,* p. 192—part, characters; *vieux male, variété l'âge adulte.* Lesson, 1842, *Nouv. Tabl. Reg. Anim.,* p. 8—BRAZIL: *Pará.*

M[ico] argentatus, Reichenbach, 1862, *Vollst. Naturg. Affen,* p. 6, pl. 2, figs. 21–22 (animal)—taxonomic history; characters; synonyms, *Jacchus melanurus* Geoffroy and *"Cebus canus* Blainv[ille]," regarded as synonyms.

Hapale emiliæ Thomas, 1920, *Ann. Mag. Nat. Hist.,* ser. 9, 6:269—BRAZIL: *Pará* (type locality, Maloca, upper Rio Curuá, upper Rio Iriri, Rio Xingu); type, female, skin and skull, British Museum (Natural History) no. 20.7.14.12, collected 11 November 1914, by Emilia Snethlage.

[*Mico*] *emiliæ,* Thomas, 1922, *Ann. Mag. Nat. Hist.,* ser. 9, 9:198—classification.

Callithrix emiliæ, Cruz Lima, 1945, Mamiferos da Amazonia, *Primates, Contr. Mus. Paraense,* p. 245, pl. 40, fig. 1 (animal)—characters ex topotype; colored plate ex living animal from unknown locality.

M[*ico*] *a*[*rgentatus*] *emiliæ,* Osman Hill, 1957, *Primates* 3:251, 280—characters; distribution.

Callithrix argentata emiliæ, Cabrera, 1958, *Rev. Mus. Argentino Cienc. Nat. "Bernardino Rivadavia"* 4(1):185 —classification.

H[*apale*] *melanura,* I. Geoffroy (part not E. Geoffroy), 1851, *Cat. Primates Mus. Hist. Nat. Paris,* p. 60—BRAZIL: *Pará* (Coll. Castelnau and Deville, 1847); "variété albine . . . donné par M. le Comte de Hoffmannsegg, 1808"; *argentata* Linnaeus an albinistic variety.

Hapale melanura, Sclater (not E. Geoffroy), 1876, *Proc. Zool. Soc. London* 1875:167, pl. 50 (animal)—part, animal figured.

Mico melanurus, Gray (part, not E. Geoffroy), 1870, *Cat. monkeys, lemurs and fruit-eating bats, Brit. Mus.,* p. 64—BRAZIL; synonyms, *argentata* Linnaeus, *"Cebus canus,* Blainv. Ostéogr."

Callithrix argentata melanura, Carvalho (not E. Geoffroy), 1965, *Arq. Zool. São Paulo* 12:25—identification of "18. *Simia* sp." of Alexandre Rodrigues Ferreira, 1790.

Hapale chrysoleucos, Sclater (part, not Wagner), 1870, *Proc. Zool. Soc. London* 1869:593–94—part, *Midas argentatus* Bates (1863, *Naturalist on the River Amazons* 1:162), in synonymy.

Mico argentatus ♀ × *Hapale jacchus* ♂, English, 1932, *Proc. Zool. Soc. London* 1932:1079—notice of exhibition of hybrid (no published description).

Mico argentatus ♂ × *Hapale jacchus* ♀, Osman Hill, 1961, *Proc. Zool. Soc. London* 137 (2):321—characters of hybrid.

Type. Mounted skin, Museum National d'Histoire Naturelle, Paris, old catalog no. XXV, collected 1743 by M. de la Condamine. The original description is based on bibliographic references to Brisson's *le petit singe de Para* and Buffon's *le mico.* These, in turn, are based on M. de La Condamine's description of a living individual presented to him by the Governor of Pará. The marmoset died aboard ship just before reaching France. It was preserved in spirits and donated to M. Réaumur's museum in Paris. Subsequently, it became part of the collection of the Muséum National d'Histoire Naturelle, Paris, where its hide was preserved as a mounted specimen (cf. Audebert 1797; Fischer 1803; and E. Geoffroy 1803, above).

Type Locality. Pará, Brazil; restricted by Carvalho (1965, p. 25) to Cametá (252), left bank of lower Rio Tocantins.

Distribution (fig. IX.36). South bank of the Rio Amazonas in the State of Pará from the left bank of the lower Rio Tocantins, east to the Rio Tapajóz–Cupari; southern limits of range undefined, particularly in the Rios Xingu and Tocantins basins.

Taxonomy. The nominate form of the species was first noticed in 1745, by La Condamine. For more than a century thereafter, the type, which eventually reached the Paris Museum preserved in spirits, was the only known representative of the silvery black-tailed marmoset. The discovery in 1812 of the brown *melanura* E. Geoffroy gave rise to speculation that the original *argentata* was nothing more than an albino of the former. I. Geoffroy (1851, p. 61) actually listed *argentata* in his catalog of the Primates in the Paris Museum as a synonym of *melanura.* Reichenbach (1862, p. 6) agreed, but deferring to the Law of Priority he recognized *argentata* as the valid name with *melanura* the junior synonym. Schlegel (1876, p. 268), however, with much more information than was available to previous authors, showed that *argentata* was consistently albinotic and geographically segregated from *melanura.* Accordingly, each was treated as a valid species.

Hapale emiliae Thomas from Maloca (250), Rio Curuá, upper Rio Xingu, is based on an individual with blackish crown and grayish brown back. All other characters, particularly the whitish face, cheeks, and forehead and absence of a whitish hip patch distinguish *emiliae* from *melanura* and identify it with *argentata.* In fact, *emiliae* is much more like true *argentata* than the *melanura*-like individual of the otherwise typical *argentata* series from Maicá described below. Cruz Lima (1945, p. 245, pl. 40, fig. 1) gives a fairly complete description of a second specimen of the original Maloca series of *emiliae* collected by Emilia Snethlage. The accompanying colored figure of *emiliae* is, according to Cruz Lima (1945, p. 246, footnote 48) "of a living monkey shown to us by a dealer on his way to Europe." The figures agree with the description but none of these expose anything significantly different from the nominate form of *argentata.*

"Cebus canus, De Blainv., ostéogr., 2e fasc., p. 9," is cited by Lesson (1840, p. 193) in his synonymy of *Mico argentatus.* Blainville's (1839, pl. 9) *Cebus canus* applies to a figure of the right upper and lower teeth of a woolly monkey, no doubt *Lagothrix lagothricha cana* E. Geoffroy. Lesson's incorrect reference is repeated by Reichenbach (1862, p. 6), Gray (1870, p. 64), and Cabrera (1958, p. 185).

Diagnostic Characters. Upper parts of head and body typically silvery white to platinum, tail contrastingly colored black; atypical populations or atavistic individuals with dark caps dominantly brownish on upper parts but forehead, cheeks, and sides of crown silvery or whitish (figs. IX.42, 47, 48; Color Pl. II).

Coloration. Face thinly whitish; skin surrounding lips

Fig. IX.48. Silvery Marmoset, *Callithrix argentata argentata* Linnaeus, an excessively fat individual. (Photo courtesy of New York Zoological Society.)

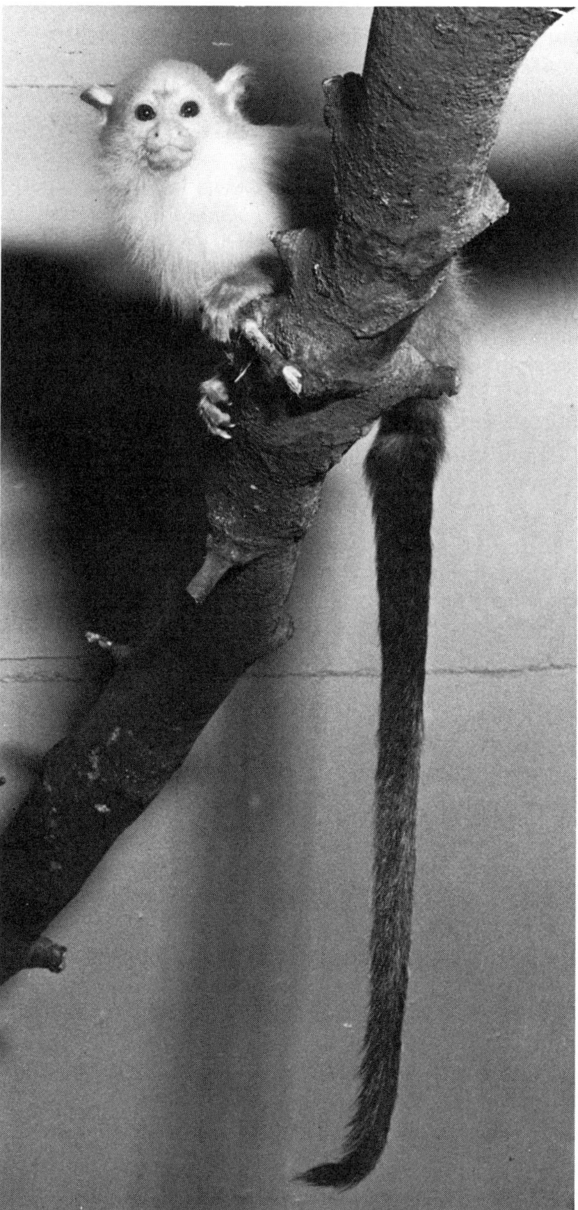

Fig. IX.49. Silvery Marmoset, *Callithrix argentata argentata* Linnaeus, young, approximately 8 months old. The hairy face and hairy ears are characteristic of juvenal *C. argentata;* dark supraorbital band or stripe, one on each side, not present in individual shown, is a common feature of young. (Photo by P. Coffey, courtesy of the Jersey Zoo.)

and nostrils blackish, remainder of facial skin and ears mottled or unpigmented; forehead whitish or silvery with or without a small black V-shaped glabellar patch, remainder of head silvery white, sometimes dark gray or brownish, nape slightly darker, more gray or drab, back silvery gray or platinum, sometimes brown; sides of body paler; outer surface of limbs more or less like sides of body; underparts of body and limbs well-defined yellowish white to buffy or ochraceous; upper surface of hands and feet grayish to brown more or less mixed with ochraceous; tail blackish or dark brown often with a thin scattering of silvery hairs, sometimes with a concentration of them terminally, more rarely in middle region, ventral surface at base tawny through golden brown to silvery or whitish.

Young (fig. IX.49). Generally colored like adult but with long, well-defined black eyebrows, hairs of back faintly punctulated, basal third of tail with faint buffy annulations in one of two specimens. Two-day-old described by Zukowsky (1940, p. 109) as generally blackish throughout except head paler with white spot above each eye, dark eyebrows as above; pelage becoming paler until 18th day, when it is more nearly as in adults.

Measurements. See appendix table 2.

Comparisons. Flesh-colored face, ears, and genitalia, silvery and platinum head and body with sharply contrasted black tail distinguish typical representatives of *argentata* from all other callitrichids; brown atavistic or geographically intermediate *melanura*-like representatives show the distinctive silvery forehead, temple, and cheeks of *argentata.*

Variation. A series of specimens from Maicá (243), below the mouth of the Tapajóz, varies from silvery gray or platinum on upperparts to drab, with one specimen (USNM 239460) dark brown and *melanura*-like. Its forehead, cheeks, and sides of crown are typically silvery and the contrasting hip and thigh patches characteristic of *melanura* are barely indicated, the pale underparts tinged with brown. Color of eight specimens from Tapará (247), Rio Xingu, show the same range of variation except for absence of atavistic brown individuals. Four specimens from Tapaiuna (238), Rio Tapajóz, are extremely pale, with head and mantle silvery white, lower back platinum. Three specimens from Cametá (252), Rio Tocantins, are similar. The middle portion of the tail of a specimen without locality data, received from the Brookfield Zoo, is marked by two broad, irregularly shaped pale bands of mixed grayish and golden hairs. The bands are broadest on underside, the hairs paler basally than terminally.

Remarks. The nearly naked face and ears of living *C. a. argentata* are reddish. La Condamine (1745, p. 165) described these features in the living animal as bright red or vermilion. The color is the hemoglobin of the blood showing through the unpigmented skin. As in bare-faced primates generally, the degree of redness or brownness of naked parts varies according to the density of the dermal pigments, the intensity of sunlight and length of exposure, and the swelling of the capillaries of the skin. Some variation in the amount of pigment can be appreciated in dry skins preserved in museums. The unpigmented parts of the face and ears would be flesh-colored or red in the live animal while the pigmented parts would remain blackish. Bare-faced tamarins of the genus *Saguinus* such as *bicolor* and *oedipus* are black-faced and not visibly affected by sunlight. In contrast, the pale-faced marmosets *C. a. argentata* and *C. humeralifer chrysoleuca* (s.s.) become red faced on protracted exposure to direct sunlight and dilation of their facial blood vessels. The most notable example of red faced monkeys among cebids is the uacari, *Cacajao calvus rubicundus.* The change in its facial color from grayish to bright red has been observed in zoos when the animal is transferred from indoor winter quarters to a sunlit outdoor summer cage.

The figured marmoset misidentified by Sclater (1876, pl. 50) as *Hapale melanura* was copied by Elliot (1913, pl. 8 only, not text) and correctly labeled *Callithrix argentata.*

Goeldi and Hagmann (1904, p. 52) mention specimens in the Pará Museum from Cametá (252), Santarém (242) and Monte Alegro (219). The last is a town on the north bank of the Amazonas where *Callithrix* does not occur. The specimen so labeled could have been taken on the southern bank of the Amazonas opposite Monte Alegre.

Cruz Lima (1945, pp. 244–45) reports that *argentata* "is frequently received alive by the Museu Goeldi and is readily found on sale at the port of Santarém on board the 'gaiolas' (river boats) which ply the lower Amazon, this belying the oft-repeated statement of its rarity."

Specimens Examined. 77. BRAZIL—*Pará:* Aramanai, Rio Tapajóz, 4 (AMNH); Cametá, Rio Tocantins, 12 (AMNH, 9; BM, 1; FMNH, 2); Caxiricatuba, Rio Tapajóz, 4 (AMNH, 3; FMNH, 1); Maica, 7 (USNM); Maloca, Rio Curuá, type of *emiliae* (BM); Mararú, 1 (BM); Piquiatuba, 2 (AMNH, 1; FMNH, 1); Recreio, Rio Majary, 3 (AMNH); Tamarury, 2 (AMNH, 1; FMNH, 1); Tapaiuna, 4 (FMNH); Tapará, 8 (AMNH); Tauary, 9 (AMNH, 8; CM, 1); Vilarhino do Monte, 7 (FMNH); no locality, 2 (FMNH, 1; USNM, 1); UNKNOWN LOCALITY—11 (MNHN, 1; SM, 3; FMNH, in spirits, 7).

CALLITHRIX ARGENTATA LEUCIPPE THOMAS: GOLDEN-WHITE BARE-EAR MARMOSET

Synonymic History

Hapale argentatus, Kuhl, 1820, *Beitr. Zool.* 1:49—part, the white-tailed individual in the Ray Museum, Amsterdam. I. Geoffroy, 1827, *Dict. Class.* 12:518—albinistic form of *melanura?*

Mico leucippe Thomas, 1922, *Ann. Mag. Nat. Hist.,* ser. 9, 9:199.

Callithrix chrysoleuca leucippe, Carvalho, 1959, *Pap. Avulsos, São Paulo* 13:316—BRAZIL: *Pará* (Araipá [Araupé], Rio Tapajóz; Pedreira, Rio Tapajóz; Monte Cristo, Rio Tapajóz); characters; taxonomy.

Callithrix argentata leucippe, Hershkovitz, 1966, *Mammalia* 30:331—characters ex type; classification. Hershkovitz, 1968, *Evolution* 22(3):566, fig. 8 (distribution), fig. 9 (geographic metachromism)—geographic metachromism. Hershkovitz, 1970, *Amer. J. Phys. Anthrop.* 32(3):379—dental diseases. Avila Pires, 1969, *Rev. Brasil. Biol.* 29(1):53—BRAZIL: *Pará* (Pimental; Pedreira; Fordlandia; "Tapajóz")—taxonomy; distribution.

Callithrix sp. Cruz Lima, 1945, Mamíferos da Amazonia, *Primates,* p. 244, footnote 47, pl. 50, fig. 2 (animal)—regarded as an albino of *C. argentata.*

Hapale chrysoleucos, J. A. Allen (not Wagner), 1916, *Bull. Amer. Mus. Nat. Hist.* 35:585—BRAZIL: *Pará* (Pimental, Rio Tapajóz). Osman Hill, 1957, *Primates* 3:290—part, *Mico leucippe* in synonymy.

Callithrix chrysoleucos, Cruz Lima (part, not Wagner), 1945, *Mamíferos da Amazonia, Primates*, pp. 244, footnotes 47, 247—*leucippe* Thomas regarded as a synonym. Vieira, 1955, *Arq. Zool. São Paulo* 8:394—part, BRAZIL: *Pará* (Monte Cristo; Santarém; Rio Tapajóz).

Hapale chrysoleucos, Osman Hill (part, not Wagner), 1957, *Primates* 3:291—*leucippe* Thomas in synonymy and text.

Type. Male, skin and skull, British Museum (Natural History) no. 9.3.9.2; collected 13 November 1908 by E. Snethlage and presented by the Goeldi Museum.

Type Locality. Pimental (230), right bank, Rio Tapajóz, below mouth of Rio Jamanxim, Pará, Brazil.

Distribution (fig. IX.36). In Pará, Brazil, right bank of the Rio Tapajóz between the tributaries Cupari and Jamanxim.

Taxonomy. The white-tailed form of the species was first brought to the attention of mammalogists in 1820 when a specimen in the Ray Museum in Amsterdam was identified by Kuhl (1820, p. 49) as a variety of *Hapale argentata*.

In his review of marmosets, I. Geoffroy (1827, p. 518) opined that typical *argentata* and Kuhl's white-tailed variety might be albinistic varieties of the dark brown *melanura*. Subsequently, he (1851, p. 61) included both animals under *Hapale melanura*. In 1916, J. A. Allen referred to *Hapale chrysoleucus* Wagner a specimen of the series described later by Thomas as *leucippe*. Then, basing judgment on the misidentified specimen, he decided that "*Hapale chrysoleucus* is probably merely a local form of *Callithrix argentata* which is apparently an unstable group, as yet not well understood."

Writing about *Mico leucippe*, Thomas (1922, p. 199) recalled that "this beautiful white marmoset has been supposed to be *Hapale chrysoleuca* but is readily distinguished by its wholly untufted and almost naked ears." Inexplicably, Thomas made no comparisons with the previously described untufted and naked-eared marmosets *argentata* and *melanura*. Later authors also failed to make the association.

Cruz Lima (1945, pp. 247–48) confused naked-eared *leucippe* with tassel-eared *chrysoleuca* Wagner, as most authors did, then figured (pl. 40, fig. 2) a specimen of *leucippe* with the caption "*Callithrix* sp." Osman Hill (1957, p. 286) followed suit, although *leucippe* belongs with his "naked-eared genus" *Mico* (1957, p. 272) and not with his "tuft-eared genus" *Hapale*. Finally, Carvalho (1959, p. 316) correctly identified the "*Callithrix* sp." of Cruz Lima as *leucippe* though still treating this naked-eared form of *Callithrix argentata* as a race of tassel-eared *C. chrysoleuca*.

Diagnostic Characters. Head and body dominantly whitish, tail and feet pale gold; facial skin and ears unpigmented or mottled.

Coloration. Face thinly haired whitish, skin bordering lips and nostrils lightly pigmented or unpigmented, remainder of facial skin and ears unpigmented or faintly mottled, "eyes yellowish brown" (on label of holotype); head and body silvery or creamy white, the hairs uniformly colored or paler basally than terminally; neck, chest, and belly slightly more creamy or buffy than upper parts; forelimbs like trunk or pale golden; hind legs like trunk; upper surface of hands and feet silvery buffy to golden; tail pale gold, the hairs more saturate basally than terminally.

Measurements. See appendix table 2.

Comparisons. *C. a leucippe* is the most nearly completely albinistic callitrichid. It is distinguished from the white tamarin *Saguinus fuscicollis melanoleucus* by greater depigmentation of the integument with exposed parts including face, ears, genitalia, palms, and soles largely or entirely unpigmented.

Remarks. Tail hairs of two specimens from Fordlandia (234) (FMNH, 92175–6) are heavily parasitized with black piedra fungus. Dark nodules of the fungus make the hairs look banded and intermediate in pattern between wholly black-tailed *argentata* and dominantly golden-tailed *leucippe*.

Specimens Examined. 8. BRAZIL—*Pará:* Fordlandia, 6 (AMNH, 3; FMNH, 3); Pimental, 2 (AMNH, 1; BM, type of *leucippe*).

56 *Callithrix argentata*
2. *Biology of the Bare-ear Marmosets*

REPRODUCTION

Hybridization

Hybridization between a male *Callithrix argentata argentata* and a female *C. jacchus* is recorded by Osman Hill (1961, p. 321). The identifications and descriptions of the parents and surviving twin, a seven-month-old male, are based on information and color transparencies supplied by Mrs. Boulter of Singapore. The hybrid resembled the father, but its face was pigmented and it exhibited a "tendency to transverse banding on groin." Osman Hill gives the birth date of the hybrid but fails to mention when the parents were introduced into the same cage. The characters of the nearly full grown hybrid, however, deviated only slightly from those of *C. argentata,* and it is reasonable to assume that its father was a member of that species.

No details accompanied the notice published in the *Proceedings of the London Zoological Society* for 1932 (p. 1079) that Dr. W. L. English, M.B., F.Z.S., exhibited, and made remarks upon, specimens of living hybrid Marmosets (*Hapale jacchus* ♂ × *H. argentata* Linn. ♀).

GROWTH AND DEVELOPMENT

Chronology of Growth

The history of twins of *Callithrix argentata* born in the Frankfurt am Main Zoo in 1939 is recounted by Zukowsky (1940, pp. 106–9). The firstborn was killed by the father at parturition; the second was saved but rejected by its mother and hand reared by the chief keeper. The second day the baby weighed 27 g. "It was hardly the size of a thumb and its face was as long as the nail of the little finger." It slept through the night pressed against the chest of the keeper and during the day its quarters in the zoo were maintained at a uniform temperature of 28° C. The young marmoset was fed milk from a doll's bottle every one and one-half hours. Thanks to the devoted care and excellent treatment received it survived an attack of diarrhea followed by constipation and indigestion. The following outline of its development is summarized from Zukowsky.

1st day (11 Nov. 1939): Rejected by mother
2d day: 27 g, size of "thumb," general color black, head paler.
7th day: 29 g
9th day: Combined head and body length, 55 mm; tail 51 mm; hind foot 25 mm
12th day: 31 g
17th day: 36 g
18th day: Back gray, white frontal spot present
22d day: 41 g
27th day: 46 g
32d day: 50 g
37th day: 54 g
42d day: 58 g
46th day: 26 g, died.

Sequence of eruption of the deciduous dentition was recorded as follows.

2d day: di_1
9th day: $\mathrm{di}\frac{1,2}{1,2}$, $\mathrm{dc}\frac{1}{1}$
15th day: $\mathrm{di}\frac{1,2}{1,2}$, $\mathrm{dc}\frac{1}{1}$, $\mathrm{dpm}_{1,2,3}$
32d day: $\mathrm{di}\frac{1,2}{1,2}$, $\mathrm{dc}\frac{1}{1}$, $\mathrm{dpm}\frac{1,2\,-}{1,2,3}$
46th day: $\mathrm{di}\frac{1,2}{1,2}$, $\mathrm{dc}\frac{1}{1}$, $\mathrm{dpm}\frac{1,2,3}{1,2,3}$

BEHAVIOR

The very little published on the life history of *Callithrix argentata* is summarized under the following headings:

Habitat and Associations	Nesting
Social Structure	Movements
Social Interactions	Display
Care of Young	Marking
Food	Vocalization

Habitat and Associations

Bates 1863, p. 162

Bates observed only two kinds of monkeys during his stay at Cametá, "the Couxio (Pithecia Satanas)—a large species, clothed with long brownish-black hair—and the tiny Midas argentatus. . . . [The latter] is one of the rarest of the American monkeys; indeed, I have not heard of its being found anywhere except near Cameta, where I once saw three individuals, looking like so many white kittens, running along a branch in a cacao grove: in their motions they resembled precisely the Midas ursalus already described. I saw afterwards a pet animal of this species, and heard that there were many so kept, and that they were esteemed as great treasures. The one mentioned was full-grown, although it measured only seven inches in length of body. It was covered with long, white, silky hairs, the tail being blackish, and the face nearly naked and flesh-coloured. It was a most timid and sensitive little thing. The woman who owned it carried it constantly in her bosom, and no money would induce her to part with her pet. She called it Mico. It fed from her mouth and allowed her to fondle it freely, but the nervous little creature would not permit strangers to touch it. If any one attempted to do so it shrank back, the whole body trembling with fear, and its teeth chattered whilst it uttered its tremulous frightened tones. The expression of its features was like that of its more robust brother Midas ursulus; the eyes, which were black, were full of curiosity and mistrust, and were always kept fixed on the person who attempted to advance towards it."

Social Structure

Miller 1916, p. 603

Leo E. Miller, collector of the *Callithrix argentata melanura* recorded by J. A. Allen (1916, p. 585), thought that these marmosets were "exceedingly rare, at least in the region where the present specimens were taken, as only one troop was observed. This consisted of about a dozen adult individuals."

Krieg 1930, p. 763

During his excursions in the Bolivian "Gran Chaco," Krieg "always observed *Callithrix* [*argentata melanura*] in families or related groups of from 3 to 8 individuals."

Social Interactions

Epple 1967*b*

Behavioral traits attributed to *Callithrix argentata argentata* include eyebrow-lowering in threat posture, lip-smacking, and rhythmic tongue protrusion in sexual, social, and aggressive contacts, and arch posture and walk in defensive threat.

Care of Young

Miller 1916, p. 603

"Three adults collected were two males and one female. One of the males was carrying two very small young, one of which was killed, the other living about a week. It took diluted sweetened milk from a spoon, but doubtless the change of diet caused its death. If placed upon a rough surface which afforded a hold for hands and feet, it would run and climb rapidly; but if placed on a smooth surface such as a table it tumbled and was unable to move. The young 'chirped' frequently; but one heard no sound in the forests that could be attributed to the adults of this species."

Food

Krieg 1930, p. 763

"We found remains of insects and vegetable matter in their stomachs. The dentition of all Krallenaffen indicates insect feeding and I have seen various species avidly catching live insects."

Nesting

Krieg 1930, p. 763

"According to the natives of Chiquitos they use nests in tree hollows for sleeping and keeping warm and producing their young."

Movements

Krieg 1930, p. 763

"Their movements reminded us very much of our squirrels; like them they jumped on and off the tree trunks and they preferred to remain on the hidden side of the trunk. At the sight of us they became excited and emitted clear sounds (Geckern) characteristic of Callithricidae. When chased they would withdraw silently with a demonstration of their great jumping ability."

Display (fig. IX. 50)

Hershkovitz (Notes)

The brilliant red external genitalia are routinely presented by the silvery and albinotic races of the species.

Marking

Hershkovitz (Notes)

The effectiveness of scent marking is considerably enhanced by secretions from the giant, multilobular sebaceous glands of the genital and circumgenital area in both sexes.

Vocalization

Epple 1968, p. 19

Vocalizations of 2 captive male *Callithrix argentata argentata* were studied and compared with those of

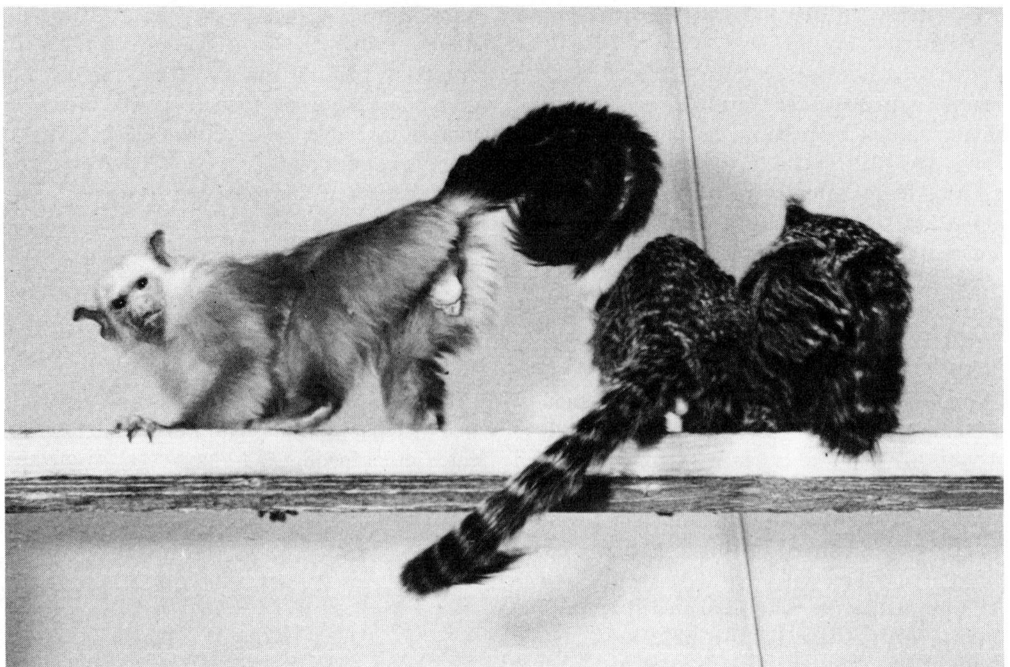

Fig. IX.50. *Callithrix argentata argentata* male presenting to a pair of *C. jacchus jacchus.* (Photo courtesy of Gisela Epple.)

Callithrix jacchus (cf. p. 563). The same types were emitted by *argentata,* and two others not heard from *jacchus.* One of them is an addition to the "mobbing" repertory, the other a trill similar to the trill heard in *Leontopithecus rosalia.* The extra vocal signals are described in the same sequence used for *Callithrix jacchus* (p. 564) but with the extra ones distinguished by bold face type.

5. Mobbing *tsik* calls:
   a. Low-excitement—mingling of *tsik* calls with crackles and coughs, essentially as in *jacchus.*
   b. High-excitement *tsik* . . . calls, essentially as in *C. jacchus.*
   c. High-excitement *tsik* calls: intermingling with **short, low-pitched sounds of noise character produced in sequence of 3 to 8 calls, accompanied by rhythmical protrusion of the tongue.** Epple explains that "tongue protrusions and calls are given simultaneously, the sounds apparently being produced by the tongue [!] as it is vehemently protruded from the mouth." The call is also used as a threat to inferiors.
8. **Trill**—Given when slightly alarmed by predator or human. Similar trill heard in *Leontopithecus rosalia.*

Bates 1863, p. 163

Bates took note of the cry of a frightened silvery marmoset kept as a pet. "Its body trembled . . . teeth chattered whilst it uttered its tremulous frightened tones." Perhaps this is the "trill" described by Epple.

Krieg 1930, p. 763

"Except for the aforementioned cries [*Geckern*] and a few weak chirping sounds I heard no noise from these monkeys, the smallest I encountered on my expedition to the Chaco."

57 *Callithrix humeralifer* E. Geoffroy, Tassel-ear Marmosets *History, Characters, Subspecies, and Biology*

Distribution (fig. IX.36)

South bank of the Rio Amazonas from the west bank of the lower Tapajóz in Pará to the east bank of the lower Madeira in Amazonas.

Taxonomy

Subspecific relationship between *humeralifer* and *chrysoleuca,* the one as an advanced or albinistic form of the other, had not been suspected. Each race had been confused with other similar-appearing callitrichids or with species of an analogous grade of evolution in the bleaching process. The type of *Callithrix humeralifer humeralifer,* because of its banded tail and tufted ears, was often regarded as a member of the *Callithrix jacchus* group. The albinotic *C. h. chrysoleuca,* on the other hand, had been compared with similarly whitish forms of other species, notably *C. argentata leucippe.* Its name had also been incorrectly applied to other whitish marmosets. For example, Osman Hill (1957, pl. xxii) labeled an albinotic *Callithrix jacchus* as "*Hapale? chrysoleucos.*"

Origin, Evolution, and Dispersal

Callithrix humeralifer is represented by three races confined to the southern banks of the Amazon between the lower Rio Tapajóz on the east and the lower Rio Madeira on the west. The comparatively dark eastern race, *C. h. humeralifer,* with silvery forequarters, white-flecked black back, silvery banded black tail, and orange underparts, is well advanced toward albinism. The western race, *C. h. chrysoleuca,* is dominantly whitish, although the yellow, buff, and orange tones, particularly on the extremities, are still very much in evidence. Unless future collecting proves otherwise, it is assumed that the prototype of *C. humeralifer* evolved in Mato Grosso from the same stock which gave rise to *C. argentata.* The latter invaded the Tocantins-Xingu, Xingu-Tapajóz interfluvial basins while *C. humeralifer* expanded into the lower Tapajóz-Madeirá interfluvial basin. At some point in its northward spread the ears of typical *humeralifer* became extremely hairy or tasselated, the tail banded or more or less saturate. Thereafter, the spread of the species along the west bank of the Tapajóz to the Amazon was accompanied by measured advances in the bleaching process. The well-bleached *C. h. intermedius* is an offshoot of ancestral *humeralifer* stock, and albinotic *chrysoleuca* is another derivative (fig. IX.37).

External Characters

Integument. Skin of face and ears pigmented, mottled, or unpigmented; iris black; pinna tasseled with dominantly whitish, silvery or buffy hairs; mid-crown blackish or white, mantle and upper arms dominantly whitish or silvery; back blackish flecked with whitish or entirely whitish to golden; hind limbs blackish or golden; hairs of interramia cresting forward, of throat directed backward; chest and belly ochraceous and brown or whitish to pale gold; tail self-annulated golden, or banded black and silvery or nearly entirely black, the hairs disposed in nodules corresponding to the vertebral series; external genitalia mostly or entirely unpigmented.

Vibrissae. Supraoculars, mystacials, rhinarials, mentals, and anteriorly directed interramals present; genals well defined as one or more randomly dispersed hairs often indistinguishable from cheek hairs; ulnar carpals present; gular spines present in subspecies *humeralifer,* pectorals present or absent.

External Genitalia

Male

Adult. As seen in living animals, wet preserved samples, and in dry skins reconstituted by moistening, scrotum and penis are quite like those of nearest related *Callithrix argentata* (IX.4, 46).

Female

Adult. External (and internal) genitalia (see fig. VII.7) are described by Russell and Zuckerman (1935, p. 356, figs.).[1] They treat the tumescent labia majora as a pedunculated "circumgenital pad," or " 'sexual skin' " but then identify (p. 357) them as "homologues of the labia majora." The "swelling," as described by Russell and Zuckerman, "extends ventrally to overlap the symphysis pubis. Dorsally it terminates in front of the anus. The pedicle is much smaller, both laterally and ventro-dorsally and extends from the lower margin of the symphysis pubis back towards the anus which is on a level with the ischial tuberosities. The ventral two thirds of the swellings are cleft by the urogenital sinus. The swelling is smooth and somewhat tense. The clitoris can be seen at the ventral limit of the cleft."

The size and smooth surface of the labia majora in the animal described by Russell and Zuckerman indicate a turgidity comparable to that of the same organ in *Saguinus oedipus* shown in figure X.68. They differ notably from the less inflated, more convoluted labial surface of our specimens of the most nearly related *Callithrix argentata*. This difference, however, is probably only a matter of the degree of swelling. The "pedunculated" condition and all other characters of *humeralifer* seem to agree with those of *C. argentata* (fig. IX.4).

[1] The authors believed the animal might be a variety of *"Hapale jacchus* . . . which goes by the name of *H. albicollis."* Their figures and photographs of the specimen leave no doubt of its identification with *Callithrix humeralifer humeralifer*.

Comparisons

The silvery or buffy tasselated pinna are unique among primates. Other distinctive characters are mantle buffy, gray, or silvery to white, never agouti or dominantly blackish; back black or golden to creamy white, never agouti or transversely striated; tail meristically tufted or banded; thinly haired face without frontal spot or blaze, salient tufts on, not in front of or above ears.

Bleaching and Depigmentation

Bleaching advances in general from tip to base of the individual hairs. In banded dorsal hairs of *Callithrix humeralifer humeralifer* dilution proceeds from the white median band toward tip and root. The primitive modified agouti pattern of the tail is nearly obsolete and usually not perceptible except under the binoculars in some specimens.

Depigmentation begins in *humeralifer* around the mouth and often the nares and had progressed in *chrysoleuca* to ears and volar surfaces.

Key to the Subspecies of *Callithrix humeralifer*

1. Head and trunk pale gold to whitish, tail golden to orange . . . . *chrysoleuca*

1′. Head and trunk black and silvery, tail annulated black and gray . . . . *humeralifer*

Note: See pages 1019, 1020 for revised key and description of *C. h. intermedius*

CALLITHRIX HUMERALIFER HUMERALIFER E. GEOFFROY: BLACK AND WHITE TASSEL-EAR MARMOSET

Fig. IX.51. Black and White Tassel-ear Marmoset, *Callithrix humeralifer humeralifer* E. Geoffroy.

Synonymic History

Simia humeralifera E. Geoffroy in Humboldt, 1812, *Rec. Obs. Zool. Anat. Comp.*, p. 360—"*Jacchus humeralifer,* Geoffroy," in synonymy.

Jacchus humeralifer, E. Geoffroy, 1812, *Ann. Mus. Hist. Nat., Paris* 19:120. Desmarest, 1818, *Nouv. Dict. Hist. Nat.* 24:240—BRAZIL; characters. Desmarest, 1827, *Dict. Sci. Nat.* 47:19—believed to be doubtfully distinct from *J. vulgaris* [= *jacchus*]. Lesson, 1840, *Species des mammifères: Bimanes et quadrumanes . . . ,* p. 189—Var. D. of *Hapale leucotis* Lesson. Rode, 1938, *Bull. Mus. Nat. Hist. Nat.*, ser. 2, 10:238—BRAZIL; type data.

Jacchus humeralifer, I. Geoffroy, 1827, *Dict. Class. Hist. Nat., Paris* 12:518—characters ex type. Schlegel, 1876, *Les singes. Simiae,* p. 271—characters ex Desmarest (1820, *Mammalogie* 1:93) regarded as a "variété accidentelle du *Hapale jachus.*"

J[*acchus*] *humeralifer,* Reichenbach, 1862, *Vollst. Naturg. Affen,* p. 4, pl. 1, fig. 8 *b* (animal)—BRAZIL; characters.

Hapale humeralifer, Kuhl, 1820, *Beitr. Zool.*, p. 48—characters. Bates, 1863, *Naturalist on the River Amazons,* 2:55—BRAZIL: *Pará* (Rio Tapajóz, near Santarém); habits. Osman Hill, 1957, *Primates,* 3:257, 286, 295, 300, fig. 61 (map)—characters; distribution.

H[*apale*] *humeralifer,* I. Geoffroy, 1851, *Cat. Primates Mus. Hist. Nat., Paris,* p. 60—type history.

Callithrix humeralifer, Elliot, 1913, *Review of the Primates,* 1:230—part, characters ex type only. Hershkovitz, 1966, *Mammalia* 30:330—BRAZIL: *Pará* (Paricatuba, type locality restricted); characters ex type; *santaremensis,* a synonym. Egozcue, Perkins, and Hagemenas, 1968, *Folia Primat.* 9:82, footnote 1, fig. 1, no. 5 (animal captioned *Callithrix aurita*)—name correction for individual misidentified as *Callithrix aurita* in text; karyology. Avila Pires, 1969, *Rev. Brasil. Biol.* 29(1):58—BRAZIL: *Amazonas* (Serra de Parintins; Rio Tupinambarana near Parantins; Urucurituba); *Pará* (Paricatuba; Vila Braga; Boim; Igarapé Brabo; Igarapé Amorim; Arara; Rio Arapiuns); characters; distribution.

Callithrix humeralifer humeralifer, Hershkovitz, 1968, *Evolution* 22(3):565, fig. 8 (distribution), fig. 9 (geographic metachromism)—color pattern; taxonomy; geographic metachromism. Hershkovitz, 1970, *Amer. J. Phys. Anthrop.* 32(3):379—dental diseases.

Hapale santaremensis Matschie, 1893, *Sitzb. Gesellsch. Naturf. Fr. Berlin* 1893(9):227—BRAZIL: *Pará* (type localities, Santarém [!], Rio Tapajóz and Paricatuba, left bank Rio Tapajóz; types, adult male from Paricatuba [here designated lectotype], and female acquired at Santarém where the species does not occur naturally, Berlin Museum, collected by Herr Schultz. Lönnberg, 1940, *Ark Zool., Stockholm* 32A(10):18—BRAZIL: *Pará* (Irocanga; Casa Nova, Rio Arapiuns). Osman Hill, 1957, *Primates,* 3:90, 120, 166, 183, 251, 283–86, 295, 302, fig. 61 (map, distribution), fig. 86 (ear), fig. 87 (plantar surface, hand, foot)—characters; taxonomy; distribution; comparison.

Callithrix santaremensis, Trouessart, 1904, *Suppl. Cat. Mamm.,* p. 28—classification. Thomas, 1912, *Ann. Mag. Nat. Hist.,* ser. 8, 9:85—BRAZIL: *Pará* (Boim, Rio Tapajóz). Elliot, 1913, *Review of the Primates,* 1:224—BRAZIL: *Pará* (type locality, "Santarém," where the species does not occur); type, the male from Paricatuba, Rio Tapajóz; characters ex type. Cruz Lima, 1945, *Mamíferos da Amazonia, Primates, Contr. Mus. Paraense,* p. 246, pl. 49, fig. 2 (animal)—BRAZIL: *Pará* (Boim; Vila Braga); characters; habits. Vieira, 1955, *Arq. Zool., São Paulo* 8:394—BRAZIL: *Pará.*

C[allithrix] santaremensis, Osman Hill, 1958, *Primatologia* 3 (1):641—external genitalia.

Hapale jacchus or *H. albicollis,* Russell and Zuckerman (not Linnaeus or Spix), 1935, *J. Anat.* 69:356, fig. 1 (sexual skin from behind), fig. 2 (genital tract), pl. 1, fig. 1 (animal), pl. 1, fig. 2 (animal from rear), pl. 1, figs. 3–8 (histology of sexual skin)—sexual skin; anatomy and histology of a pedunculated genital swelling in adult ♀.

Hapale jacchus Cabrera, (part, not Linnaeus), 1957, *Rev. Mus. argentino Cienc. Nat. "Bernardino Rivadavia"* 4(1):187—*humeralifera* Humboldt in synonymy; regarded in text (p. 188) as a partial albino.

Callithrix aurita, Egozcue, Perkins, Hagemenas, (not E. Geoffroy), 1968, *Folia Primat.* 9:82, fig. 1 (animal)—karyotype (2n = 44).

Type. Male, mounted with skull in skin, Muséum National d'Histoire Naturelle, Paris, no. 608(589); possibly collected by Alexandre Rodrigues Ferreira during his scientific expedition in Brazil, 1783–92; originally deposited in the Museum Royal d'Ajuda, Lisbon, Portugal; acquired by the Paris Museum in 1808 during the Napoleonic wars.

Type Locality. Brazil, restricted to Paricatuba (222), left bank Rio Tapajóz, near mouth, Pará, Brazil, by Hershkovitz (1966*b*, p. 331).

Distribution (fig. IX.36). In Brazil, south bank of the Rio Amazonas, and left bank of the Rio Tapajóz, from mouth to Vila Braga or not above the cataracts, in the State of Pará, west to the Rio Mamurú and the Lago de Andirá in adjoining parts of the State of Amazonas.

Taxonomy. The type of *humeralifer* E. Geoffroy in the Paris Museum is in poor condition. Hair of face and throat is slipped, the rest of the coat is faded and dirty. The original twelve-word description of *humeralifer* is inadequate. Subsequent descriptions by Desmarest (1820, p. 93; 1827, p. 19; 1828, p. 240) are more informative but equivocal with respect to the ear tufts. There are two on each side, according to Desmarest, with one in front and the other behind each ear. Later, I. Geoffroy (1827, p. 518) supplied a good description of *humeralifer.* He particularly noted that the whitish ear tufts "naissent, non plus comme dans les espèces précédentes [of the *Callithrix jacchus* group], prés de la conque auriculaire, mais bien sur ses faces antérieure et postérieure."

Bates (1863, p. 255) was the first to identify *humeralifer* in its true habitat along the left bank of the lower Rio Tapajóz, in Pará, Brazil. Schlegel (1876, pp. 271–72, in text) questioned Bates's determination and treated *humeralifer* as an aberrant form of *Callithrix jacchus.* Schlegel said he examined the type in Paris, but his judgment may have been influenced by Desmarest's misleading description, which he quotes in its entirety.

Elliot (1913*a*, p. 230) recognized *Callithrix humeralifer* as distinct but he confused Schlegel's (1876, pp. 271–72) account of the type with that author's notes on the distribution of *Hapale jacchus.* As a consequence, Elliot gave the distribution of *humeralifer* as the "vicinity of Bahia, to the Bay of Todos os Santos, Brazil (Wied)." Osman Hill (1957, pp. 300–301) also examined the type of *humeralifer* in the Paris Museum, but his description of the species and incorrect delineation of the geographic range are taken from Elliot's garbled account. Oddly, Hill (1957, p. 286) attributes black ear tufts to *humeralifer,* but the only foundation for this may be a two-century accumulation of soot on the type specimen. (cf. Hershkovitz 1966*b*, p. 300).

The description of *Hapale santaremensis* Matschie is based on an adult and juvenal male, the first from Paricatuba (222), the second said to be from Santarém. The collector, Herr Schultz, notes that he had kept many alive in Santarém (242). The species, however, occurs naturally only on the left bank of the Tapajóz opposite Santarém. Elliot gives Santarém as type locality, but he describes as type the Paricatuba male, giving its total length as 570 mm (or the sum of Matschie's figures of 240 mm for head and body, 330 mm for tail).

Selection of the adult male as type by first reviser, Elliot, automatically makes Paricatuba the type locality. Santarém, on the right side of the Tapajóz, is outside the range of the species and cannot be type locality in any case.

Diagnostic Characters. Ears tasselated with long thick silvery to buffy tufts, the hairs often brownish basally, mantle mixed silvery and black, back black with whitish spots and streaks, hip patches white, tail annulated black and silvery buff (figs. IX.38, 51).

Coloration. Face thinly haired blackish mixed with silvery, dark superciliary band usually present, forehead and temples mixed silvery and blackish; skin of ears and face more or less pigmented except usually around lips; blackish coronal cap bluntly pointed in front and joined with black preauricular region to form a wide circumfacial band; ear tufts silvery, yellowish, or buff; nape and mantle silvery mixed with black, the nuchal hairs black basally, silvery or silvery buff terminally, the scapular hairs often with two dark and two light broad alternating bands, the hairs darker middorsally than laterally; remainder of back and sides of body dominantly blackish, the hairs broadly banded dark brown basally, whitish subterminally, blackish terminally, the whitish banding usually showing through as an irregular spotting or streaking on back, as streaks on sides and as conspicuous patches on hips; rump and outer sides of thighs dark brown to blackish, the hairs uniformly colored on rump, variously banded on thighs but usually with fine hoary or pale buff tips; a silvery buff femoral patch usually present; outer sides of arms like mantle or more saturate; chin brown, throat grayish to buffy, the hairs often brown basally; chest and belly ochraceous orange laterally, dark brown medially; inner sides of thighs ochraceous orange, and of legs brown, inner sides of upper arms orange to brown, forearms darker; upper surface of hands and feet blackish more or less mixed with buffy; tail sometimes faintly annulated or, rarely, entirely black but usually with well-defined broad blackish and narrow gray, silvery, or buffy annulations, the banding effect produced by the meristically disposed silvery tips of the black hairs.

Measurements. See appendix table 2.

Comparisons. Distinguished from *Callithrix jacchus* by presence of thick auricular tufts completely clothing ears, pre-, post-, or supra-auricular tufts absent, diamond-shaped frontal blaze absent, middle and lower back not striated, the subterminal band of hairs whitish, never orange (fig. IX.38).

Specimens Examined. 41. BRAZIL—*Pará:* Arara, 4 (FMNH); Boim, 3 (AMNH, 1; BM, 2); Igarapé Amorim, 1 (AMNH); Igarapé Bravo, 12 (AMNH); Itaituba, 3 (BM); Urucurituba, 5 (FMNH); Vila Braga, 2 (BM, 1; FMNH, 1); *Amazonas:* Rio Andirá, mouth, 1 (AMNH); Lago Andirá, 2 (AMNH); Serra da Parintins, 6 (AMNH); unknown locality, 2 (type of *humeralifer,* MNHN; SM, 1).

CALLITHRIX HUMERALIFER CHRYSOLEUCA WAGNER: GOLDEN-WHITE TASSEL-EAR MARMOSET

Synonymic History

Hapale chrysoleucos Wagner, 1842, *Arch. Naturg.,* ser. 8, 1:357. Wagner, 1843, *Ann. Mag. Nat. Hist.,* ser. 1, 12:42—reprint of original Latin diagnosis. Wagner, 1850, *Abh. Akad. Wiss. Munich* (1847) 5:466—BRAZIL: *Amazonas* (Borba); characters. Sclater, 1870, *Proc. Zool. Soc. London* 1869:592—characters; part, synonyms, *Mico sericeus* Gray, *Hapale argentatus* Sclater, 1868. Sclater, 1871, *Proc. Zool. Soc. London* 1871:229—*Micoella sericeus* Gray, a synonym. Pelzeln, 1883, *Verh. K. K. Zool.-Bot. Gesellsch., Wien* 33:32—BRAZIL: *Amazonas* (Borba); characters; variation; habitat. Osman Hill, 1957, *Primates,* 3:105, 144, 168, 191, 251, 290 (part), 294, 295, fig. 61 (map, distribution)—part, anatomy; taxonomy; habits; distribution; history; not pl. 24 (*"Hapale? chrysoleucos"* [= *Callithrix jacchus,* albino]) *Mico sericeus* a synonym.

H[apale] chrysoleucos, Wagner, 1855, *Schreber's Säugth., Suppl.* 5:125—characters.

Hapale chrysoleuca [*sic*], Schlegel, 1876, *Les singes. Simiae,* p. 277—BRAZIL: *Amazonas* (junction of Rios Madeira and Amazonas [Natterer]; characters. Jentink, 1892, *Cat. Syst. Mamm. Mus. Pays-Bas* 11:59—BRAZIL: *Amazonas* (junction of Rios Madeira and Amazonas [Natterer]). Lönnberg, 1940, *Ark. Zool., Stockholm* 32A, (10):17—BRAZIL: *Amazonas* (Lago do Baptista, Rio Madeira; Lago Tapayuna); measurements.

M[ico] chrysoleucus [*sic*], Reichenbach, 1862, *Vollst. Naturg. Affen,* p. 6, pl. 2, fig. 23 (type, in color)—characters; type in K. K. Hofnaturalien-Cabinet, Vienna.

Micoella chrysoleucos, Gray, 1870, *Cat. monkeys, lemurs, and fruit-eating bats, Brit. Mus.,* p. 131—characters; classification.

Callithrix chrysoleuca, Elliot, 1913, *A review of the Primates,* 1:223—description ex type; *sericeus* Gray, a synonym. Cruz Lima, 1945, Mamíferos da Amazonia, *Contrib. Mus. Paraense, Primates,* p. 247, pl. 41, fig. 1 (animal)—characters. Hershkovitz, 1966, *Mammalia* 30:330—relationship to *C. humeralifer.* Avila Pires, 1969, *Rev. Brasil. Biol.* 29(1):56—BRAZIL: *Amazonas* (Borba; Lago do Baptista; Lago Tapaiuna; Igarapé Auara; baixo Madeira); *Pará* (Fazenda Monte Cristo, Rio Tapajóz); characters; distribution.

Callithrix chrysoleucos [*sic*], Vieira, 1955, *Arq. Zool., São Paulo* 8:394—BRAZIL: part, *Amazonas* (Lago Baptista; lower Rio Madeira); *Pará.* de Boer, 1974, Genen Phaenen, 17 (1/2):5, 6, 17, 22 24—taxonomic status based on karyotype ex Bender and Mettler (1960).

[*Callithrix*] *chrysoleucus* [*sic*], Anthony, 1949, *Bull. Mus. Soc. Anthrop., Paris,* ser. 9, 10:132—palatal surface and cranial capacity.

[?] *Callithrix chrysoleucos* [*sic*], Chiarelli, 1963, *Folia Primat.* 1:91—taste sensitivity to phenylthiocarbamide.

C[allithrix] humeralifer chrysoleuca, Hershkovitz, 1968. *Evolution* 22(3):565, fig. 8 (distribution), fig. 9 (geographic metachromism)—color pattern; geographic metachromism.

Callithrix humeralifer chrysoleuca, Hershkovitz, 1970, *Folia Primat.* 13:215, fig. 3 (endocranial impression)—BRAZIL: *Amazonas* (Lago do Baptista); cerebral pattern. Hershkovitz, 1970, *Amer. J. Phys. Anthrop.* 32(3): 379—dental diseases.

Mico sericeus Gray, 1868, *Proc. Zool. Soc. London* 1868:257, pl. 24 (animal)—type locality unknown, description based on living specimen in gardens of London Zoological Society.

Micoella sericeus, Gray, 1870, *Cat. monkeys, lemurs and fruit-eating bats, Brit. Mus.,* p. 131—characters; type now in British Museum (Natural History).

Hapale argentata, Sclater (not Linnaeus), 1868, *Proc. Zool. Soc. London* 1868:262—misidentification of type specimen of *Mico sericeus.*

Mico melanoleucus Miranda Ribeiro [= Moojen, not Miranda Ribeiro, *fide* Avila Pires, 1968] 1955, *Arq. Mus. Nac. Rio de Janeiro* 42:414—"lectótipo: M. N. no. 2835." Avila Pires, 1968, *Arq. Mus. Nac. Rio de Janeiro* 53:172—lectotype Museo Nacional, Rio de Janeiro no. 2835 designated by Moojen (1955) and identified as a *Callithrix chrysoleuca* Wagner (1842) that had lived in the Rio de Janeiro Zoo.

Type. Seven specimens, including 4 skins in the Vienna Museum, 1 (♀) in the Leiden Museum and 1 in the British Museum (Natural History); collected January and June 1830 by Johann Natterer.

Type Locality. Borba (196b), lower Rio Madeira, Amazonas, Brazil.

Distribution (fig. IX.36). In Amazonas, Brazil, right bank lower Rio Madeira, eastward perhaps to the Rio Canumã; southern limits of range unknown.

Taxonomy. Mico sericeus Gray, as described and figured in color, is absolutely conspecific with *chrysoleuca.* This marmoset has been confused with other albinotic callitrichids such as *Callithrix argentata leucippe* and *Saguinus fuscicollis melanoleucus.*

The callitrichid denominated *"Hapale chrysoleucos"* by Bender and Mettler (1960) with karyotype (2n = 46) is certainly misassigned, Dr. Bender informs me (in litt., November 1972) that the specimens belonged to "some-

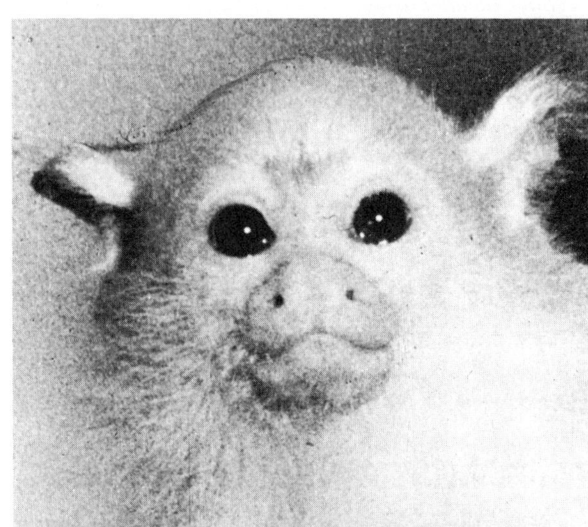

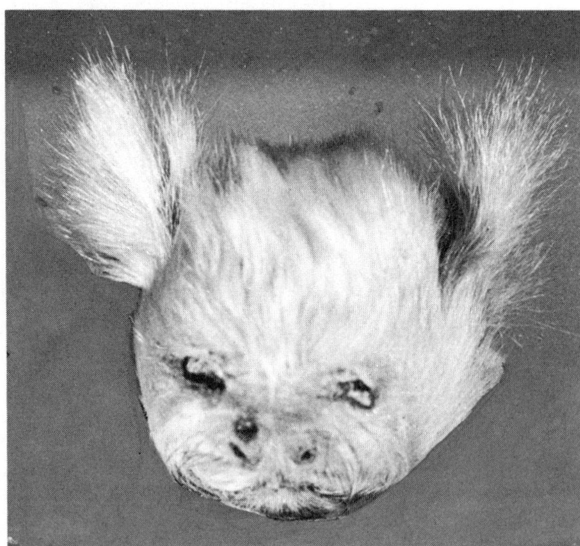

Fig. IX.52. *Top: Callithrix argentata argentata,* juvenal approximately 8 months old, same individual shown in fig. IX.49. (Photo by P. Coffey.) Moderately hirsute pinna of young *C. argentata* suggests ancestral pinna which evolved into the hypotrichous pinna of adult *C. argentata* (fig. IX.47) and the hypertrichous pinna of *C. humeralifer* (*bottom,* and fig. IX.51).

Fig. IX.53. Golden-white Tassel-ear Marmoset, *Callithrix humeralifer chrysoleuca* Wagner. Mounted skin in Field Museum of Natural History.

one else" and were returned to "them" after he and Mettler got their tissue samples. Dr. Bender is "quite certain that we [Bender and Mettler] based our assignment on Osman Hill's monograph [1957]." In the cited work, the photograph of an albinotic *Callithrix jacchus jacchus* (plate 24) is captioned *"Hapale? chrysoleucos,"* and the key characters (p. 286) and description (p. 291 of *"Hapale chrysoleucos"* are of anything but true *chrysoleuca.* The availability of live imported individuals of true *chrysoleuca* at the time in question is also dubious.

Museum-preserved specimens of *Callithrix humeralifer chrysoleuca* and *C. h. humeralifer* were rare until recently, but their numbers are still low and the institutions housing them are few. During the 1960s several live individuals of *C. h. humeralifer* were brought into the United States together with large numbers of live *Callithrix jacchus jacchus* for use in biomedical research. The importation of live *chrysoleuca* into this country, however, has never been recorded or their identifications verified. Irrespective of these other considerations, the karyotype of the *"Callithrix chrysoleucos"* of Bender and Mettler points to *Callithrix jacchus* or, more likely, the albinotic *Saguinus fuscicollis melanoleucus.*

Diagnostic Characters. Near albino, facial skin largely or entirely unpigmented, ears clothed with long thick whitish tufts, head and trunk pale gold to whitish, rump, tail, fore- and hind limbs golden to orange (figs. IX.52, 53).

Coloration. Face nearly bare or sparsely haired whitish; skin of face and ears unpigmented or mottled; head, ear tufts, and anterior third of trunk whitish with a golden tinge, remainder of back and sides of body washed or blotched with gold, rump, fore- and hind limbs pale gold to orange; chest and belly creamy white, buff, gold, or orange; tail golden to orange and self annulated.

Young. Like adult but basal half of tail faintly annulated with blackish in one specimen at hand and in another recorded by Natterer (in Pelzeln 1883, p. 23).

Measurements. See appendix table 2.

Comparisons. Distinguished from the albinistic *C. argentata leucippe* by the tufted, not naked, ears and more golden color throughout; from golden-maned *Leontopithecus rosalia* by smaller size throughout, tufted ears, absence of mane, normal, not elongate, hands and feet and the generic characters detailed elsewhere.

Variation. Appreciable local variation in color is absent. The large series from Lago do Baptista shows the full range of variation as described for the subspecies.

Remarks. The black piedra fungus (*Piedraia*) infecting the medulla of the dorsal hairs of some specimens is conspicuous against the white background.

Specimens Examined. 31. BRAZIL—*Amazonas:* Borba, 7 (AMNH, 5; BM, syntype of *chrysoleuca,* type of *sericeus*); Igarapé Auará, 4 (AMNH); Lago do Baptista, 13 (FMNH); Lago Tapayuna, 1 (FMNH); lower Rio Madeira, 1 (UMMZ); no locality data, 5 (AMNH).

CALLITHRIX HUMERALIFER: BIOLOGY OF TASSEL-EAR MARMOSETS

The categories discussed are:
Behavior
Vocalization
Longevity

Behavior

Bates (1863 [2], pp. 55–56), who was the first author to identify *Callithrix humeralifer humeralifer* in its true habitat, describes the encounter as follows: "I saw in the woods, on one occasion, a small flock of monkeys, and once had an opportunity of watching the movements of a sloth. The monkeys belonged to a very pretty and rare species, a kind of marmoset, I think the Hapale humeralifer described by Geoffroy St. Hilaire. I did not succeed in obtaining a specimen, but saw a living example afterwards in the possession of a shopkeeper at Santarem. It seems to occur nowhere else except in the dry woods bordering the campos in the interior parts of Brazil. The colours of its fur are beautifully varied; the fore part of the body is white, with the hands gray; the hind part black, with the rump and underside reddish-tawny; the tail is banded with gray and black. Its face is partly naked and flesh-coloured, and the ears are fringed with long white hairs. The specimen was not more than eight inches in length, exclusive of the tail. Altogether I thought it the prettiest species of its family I had yet seen. One would mistake it, at first sight, for a kitten, from its small size, varied colours, and the softness of its fur. It was a most timid creature, screaming and biting when any one attempted to handle it; it became familiar, however, with the people of the house a few days after it came into their possession. When hungry or uneasy it uttered a weak querulous cry, a shrill note, which was sometimes prolonged so as to resemble the stridulation of a grasshopper."

Vocalization

A lone *Callithrix humeralifer* in the marmoset colony of the University of Texas Dental Science Institute at Houston reacted to my first appearance by vocalizing with mouth open and tongue vibrating rapidly. The sound was stridulous or cricketlike and lacked the flute-like quality of sounds emitted by *Callithrix jacchus* in adjacent cages. The same sound with mouth closed but tongue vibrating between lips was also made at a lower volume and with less excitement. I have not seen the tongue used for producing a vibrato by other callitrichids (*Cebuella, Leontopithecus, Callithrix jacchus, Saguinus nigricollis, S. fuscicollis, S. mystax, S. oedipus*) and *Callimico.* My observations and Epple's description of the "high excitement" call made by the silvery marmoset with glossokinetics suggest that only members of the *Callithrix argentata* group among callitrichids modify vocal signals with tongue vibrato.

Longevity

An adult purchased 10 July 1954 and donated 10 March 1964 to the Primate Colony of the San Diego Zoo died 10 September 1964, at an estimated age of 12–13 years (Cooper 1964, unpublished Quart. Rep. no. 9).

58 Genus *Saguinus* Hoffmannsegg, Tamarins
1. History, Characters, and Key to Species Groups

Synonymic History

Cercopithecus Gronovius, 1763, *Zoophylacium Gronovianus,* fasc. 1, p. 5—included species, *Edward's little black monkey* [= *Simia midas* Linnaeus, type designated by Elliot, 1911], and Seba's *Cercopithecus minor monkie dictus* [= *Simia morta* Linnaeus = *S. sciurea* Linnaeus]. Elliot, 1911, *Bull. Amer. Mus. Nat. Hist.* 30:341—designated type, *Simia midas* Linnaeus; [zoological names from Gronovius, 1763, Zoophylacium Gronovianum, ruled unavailable for nomenclatural purposes in Opinion 89 (1925), International Commission on Zoological Nomenclature]. Elliot, 1913, *A review of the Primates* 1:xxxi, 190—species, *midas, rufimanus, ursulus.*

Saguinus Hoffmannsegg, 1807, *Mag. Gesellsch. Naturforsch. Freunde, Berlin* 1:102—type by monotypy *Saguinus ursula* Hoffmannsegg. Hershkovitz, 1958, *Proc. Biol. Soc. Washington* 71:53—nomenclature. Hershkovitz, 1958, *Fieldiana: Zool.* 36(6):614—antedates *Marikina* Lesson, 1840 and *Leontocebus* Wagner, 1840. Holmes, Capps, F. Deinhardt, 1965, *J. Lab. Clin. Med.* 66(5):879—inoculation of serum from patients with viral hepatitis. Hershkovitz, 1966, *Folia Primat.* 4:381—nomenclature; species groups; synonyms: *Leontocebus* Wagner (not authors), *Marikina* Lesson, 1840, *Oedipomidas* Reichenbach, 1862, *Tamarinus* Gray, 1870, *Tamarinus* Trouessart, 1904. Holmes, Capps, and Deinhardt, 1967, *J. Clin. Invest.* 46:1072—susceptibility to human viral hepatitis demonstrated. F. Deinhardt, Holmes, and Capps, 1967, *Liver Res.* 23:23—transmittal of human viral hepatitis. Anderson, Lewis, Passovoy, and Trobaugh, 1967, *Lab. Animal Care* 17(1):30—hematology, karyotypes (*oedipus, mystax*). F. Deinhardt, Holmes, Devine, and Deinhardt, 1967, *Lab. Animal Care* 17(1):48—parasitology (bacteria, viruses, invertebrates, flora); diseases; immunities. Wiener, Moor-Jankowski, and Gordon, 1967, *Lab. Animal Care* 17(1):71—blood groups (in *S. oedipus, S. mystax, S. nigricollis, S. fuscicollis*): same blood and saline reactions in all tamarins examined. Hershkovitz, 1968, *Evolution* 22(3):557—metachromism. Dunn, 1968, in *Squirrel monkey,* ed. Rosenblum and Cooper, p. 31—parasites. Egozcue, Perkins, and Hagemenas, 1968, *Folia Primat.* 9(2):81—karyotypes and chromosome evolution. Hershkovitz, 1970, *Folia Primat.* 12:8, 20, 21, figs. 1, 4 (mandible)—lower jaw evolution. Holmes, Wolfe, Deinhardt, and Conrad, 1971, *J. Infect. Diseases* 124(5):520—human hepatitis transmitted to *S. oedipus, S. fuscicollis,* or *S. nigricollis.* J. K. Hampton, Jr., Hampton, and Levy, 1971, in *Medical Primatology 1970,* ed. Goldsmith and Moor-Jankowski, p. 527—reproduction in laboratory colony (*S. leucopus, oedipus, fuscicollis, mystax.*). Thorington, 1972, *Int. Zoo Yearb.* 12:18—importation, exploitation, exhibition, statistics (1967–69). Kuntz and Meyers, 1972, *Int. Zoo Yearb.* 12:61—parasites. Porter and Gengozian, 1973, in *Tissue Culture,* ed. P. F. Kruse, Jr., and M. P. Patterson, p. 93—blood-cell propagation in bone marrow. Etter, 1974, *Gegenbaur's Morph. Jahrb.* 120 (1): 162—hand skeleton, comparisons with *Tupaia, Tarsius.* Cross, Peterson, Deinhardt, and Holmes, 1975, *Amer. Soc. Microbiol., Abstr. Ann. Meet.* 75:S 164—antigen excretion in hepatitis-infected tamarins. Peterson, Cross, Wolfe, and Holmes, 1975, *Amer. Soc. Microbiol., Abstr. Ann. Meet.* 75:S 165—infectivity of feces from human hepatitis. Falk, Schaffer, Wright, Deinhardt, and Benyesh-Melnick, 1975, *Amer. Soc. Microbiol., Abstr. Ann. Meet.* 75:S 237—attenuation of oncogenicity of *Herpesvirus saimiri.* Deinhardt, Peterson, Cross, Wolfe, and Holmes, 1975, *Amer. J. Med. Sci.* 270:73—hepatitis infection.

[*Saguinus*], Holmes, Dedmon, F. Deinhardt, 1963, *Fed. Proc.* 22(2)—isolation of new Herpes-like virus. J. Deinhardt, 1964, *Ill. Soc. Med. Res.,* no. 34:2—care, feeding, breeding as laboratory animal. Schulien, Marczynska, and Deinhardt, 1967, *Fed. Proc.* 26(2)—analysis of Rous sarcoma induced neoplasms. Schaffner, Popper, and Deinhardt, 1967, *Fed. Proc.* 26(2):576—ultrastructural changes in livers induced by human hepatitis serum. Mohr, Holmes, Deinhardt, and Mattenheimer, 1967, *J. Lab. Clin. Med.* 70(5):860—enzyme patterns in marmoset hepatitis. F. Deinhardt and Holmes, 1968, *Perspectives in virology,* p. 89—transmission of human viral hepatitis. Laufs, Holmes, and Deinhardt, 1968, *Clin. Res.* 16(3):460—liver culture for propagation of DNA and RNA viruses. F. Deinhardt, 1968, *Nat. Cancer Inst. Monogr.* 29:327—strains of Rous sarcoma virus oncogenesis. Marczynska, Gavitt, and Deinhardt, 1969, *Fed. Proc.* 28(2)—kidney malignancy induced spontaneously or by Rous sarcoma virus. F. Deinhardt, 1969, *Vox. Sang.* 17:49—investigations of humanlike virus hepatitis. Wolfe, McDonald, and Deinhardt, 1970, *Fed. Proc.* 29:371—transmission of feline fibrosarcoma virus to newborn. McDonald, Wolfe, and Deinhardt, 1971, *Fed. Proc.* 30(2)—in vitro assay for ST-feline fibrosarcoma virus. F. Deinhardt, 1971, *Maryland State Med. J.* 20:59—transmission of human infectious hepatitis; disease caused by inoculum and not by activation of a latent agent. Falk, Wolfe, and Deinhardt, 1971, *Fed. Proc.* 30(2):1781—oncogenesis of *Herpesvirus saimiri* in cotton-top and white-lipped tamarins. R. D. Smith, Wolfe, and Deinhardt, 1971, *Am. J. Path.* 62(84*a*–85*a*):162—pathology of tumors induced with feline fibrosarcoma virus. Essex, Klein, F. Deinhardt, Wolfe, Hardy, Theilen, and Pearson, 1972, *Nature New Biology* 238: 189—induction of feline oncornavirus associated cell membrane analysis. Wolfe, R. K. Smith, and Deinhardt, 1972, *J. Nat. Cancer Inst.* 48(6):1905—induction of fibrosarcoma with simian sarcoma virus Type 1 (*Lagothrix*). Falk, Wolfe, Marczynska, and Deinhardt, 1972, *Bacter. Proc.* 1972:V38—characterization of lymphoid cell lines established from *Herpesvirus saimiri* infection. F. Deinhardt, 1972, *Proc. Symp. viral hepatitis and blood transfusion,* ed. G. N. Vyas et al. (New York: Grune and Stratton)—transmittal of human viral hepatitis; reply to Dr. Melnick.

Saquinus [*sic*], Holmes and Capps, 1966, *Gastroenterology* 50:398—results of human viral hepatitis inoculation. F. Deinhardt, 1967, *Year book of cancer, 1966–1967*—neoplasms induced by Schmidt-Ruppin strain Rous sarcoma virus. R. D. Smith and Deinhardt, 1967, *Fed. Proc.* 26(2):748—ultrastructure of Rous sarcoma virus-induced tumors. Wiener, Moor-Jankowski, and Gordon, 1967, *Lab. Animal Care* 17(1):71—blood groups of *Saguinus oedipus, S. myxtax, S. nigricollis, S. fuscicollis.* R. D. Smith and Deinhardt, 1968, *J. Cell. Biol.* 37 (3):819—cytoplasmic membranes in Rous sarcoma virus-induced tumors. R. D. Smith and Deinhardt, 1968, *Am. J. Path.* 52(6):58a—pathology of Rous sarcoma virus-induced tumors.

Midas E. Geoffroy in Humboldt, 1812, *Rec. Obs. Zool. Anat. Comp.*, p. 361—included species, *rosalia* Linnaeus [= *Leontopithecus rosalia* Linnaeus], *oedipus* Linnaeus, *leoninus* Humboldt, *labiatus* E. Geoffroy, *ursulus* Hoffmannsegg, *midas* Linnaeus [type by tautonomy]; generic name preoccupied by *Midas* Latreille, 1796, a genus of Diptera. E. Geoffroy, 1812, *Ann. Mus. Hist. Nat., Paris* 19:120—included species, *rufimanus* Geoffroy [*Simia midas* Linnaeus in synonymy, hence type by tautonomy], *ursulus* Geoffroy, *labiatus* Geoffroy, *leoninus* Humboldt, *oedipus* Linnaeus, *rosalia* Linnaeus [= *Leontopithecus rosalia* Linnaeus]. Lesson, 1840, *Species des mammifères: Bimanes et quadrumanes . . . ,* p. 184—classification; characters. Boitard, 1845, *Jardin des Plantes, Paris,* p. 65—characters; life histories of some species. I. Geoffroy, 1851, *Cat. Primates, Mus. Hist. Nat., Paris,* p. 61—characters; classification. Gray, 1866, *Proc. Zool. Soc. London* 1865:734—classification. Reichenbach, 1862, *Vollst. Naturg. Affen,* p. 10—characters; classification. Major, 1901, *Proc. Zool. Soc. London* 1901:147, 152—lacrymal region of skull. Thomas, 1903, *Ann. Mag. Nat. Hist.*, ser. 7, 12:457—classification. De Beaux, 1917, *Giorn. Morph. Uomo, Primati* 1:103—included subgenera, *Seniocebus, Tamarinus, Oedipomidas.* Gregory, 1922, *Origin and evolution of human dentition,* p. 228, pls. 12, 13 (skull)—molar and cranial evolution. Ashley-Montagu, 1935, *Quart. Rev. Biol.* 10(2):181—premaxilla. Remane, 1960, *Primatologia* 3(2):754, 762, 788, 800, fig. 84 ($pm_{2\text{-}4}$)—dentition.

Jaccus F. Cuvier, 1829, in *Hist. Nat. Mamm.*, 5 livr. 59, ed. E. Geoffroy and Cuvier—an incorrect subsequent spelling of *Jacchus* E. Geoffroy [= *Callithrix* Erxleben] with sole species, *Jaccus œdipus* [= *Simia oedipus* Linnaeus]; generic name unavailable (cf. Article 33*b* of Code, 1961).

Œdipus Lesson, 1840, *Species des mammifères: Bimanes et quadrumanes, . . . ,* p. 184, 197—subgenus of *Midas;* type by tautonomy, *Oedipus titi* = *Simia oedipus* Linnaeus; generic name preoccupied by *Oedipus* Tschudi, 1838, a genus of Amphibia. Gray, 1870, *Cat. monkeys, lemurs and fruit-eating bats, Brit. Mus.*, p. 65—classification.

Leontocebus Wagner, 1840, *Schreber's Säugth., Suppl.,* 1, Uebersicht, p. ix—subgenus of *Hapale;* included species, *chrysomelas* [a *Leontopithecus*], *chrysopyga* [a *Leontopithecus*], *leonina, rosalia* [a *Leontopithecus*], *bicolor, oedipus.* Miller, 1912, *Bull. U.S. Nat. Mus.* 79:380—type, *Midas leoninus* Geoffroy [= *Simia leonina* Humboldt = *Leontopithecus fuscus* = *Saguinus fuscicollis fuscus* Lesson]. Elliot, 1913, *Review of the Primates* 1:194—part, subgenus *Tamarinus* only. Lampert, 1926, *Morph. Jahrb.* 55:611—larynx of *"Hapale* (*Leontocebus*) *mystax."* Hochstetter, 1946, *Denkschr. Akad. Wiss. Wien, Mat.-Nat. Kl.* 106:86—tentorialis ossis petrosi (*L. labiatus*). Cabrera, 1956, *Neotropica* 2(8):49—type *Simia leonina* Humboldt, identified as a tamarin. Chopra, 1957, *Proc. Zool. Soc. London* 128:67—cranial suture closure; no major species or sex differences noted. Oxnard, 1957, *Proc. Zool. Soc. London* 128:113—infraorbital and zygomatic branches of maxillary nerve variable in size. Straus and Arcadi, 1958, *Primatologia* 3(1):507—excretory system. Frick, 1960, *Primatologia* 3(2):179, 259—heart and body weights. Platzer, 1960, *Primatologia* 3(2):306—blood vessels in *L. oedipus.* Starck and Schneider, 1960, *Primatologia* 3(2):536, fig. 60*a* (larynx)—anatomy of larynx. Schultz, 1961, *Primatologia* 4, Lief 5:1, fig. 5 (sacral vertebrae)—vertebral column. Schultz, 1963, *Folia Primat.* 1:150—foot bone proportions. Dastague, 1963, *Mammalia* 27:266, fig. 24—pronator and supinator muscles. Ashton and Oxnard, 1963,

Trans. Zool. Soc. London 29(7):561, 569, 580, 590—comparative shoulder morphology; locomotory grade (quadrupedal). Stephan and Andy, 1964, *Am. Zool.* 4(1):73—quantitative brain comparisons (*L. oedipus*). Stephan, 1965, *Acta Anat.* 62:217, fig. 74 (olfactory bulb)—accessory olfactory bulb, (*L. oedipus*). Andy and Stephan, 1966, in *Evolution of the forebrain,* ed. Hassler and Stephan, p. 394—relative size of septum pellucidum. Fenard and Anthony, 1967, *Ann Paleo.* 53(2):204—comparative osteometry of mandible. Grimwood, 1968, *Recommendations on the conservation of wild life and the establishment of national parks and reserves in Peru,* Appendix III (British Ministry Overseas Development, mimeographed), pp. 13, 31—PERU: exploitation; exportation; conservation; distribution. Leutenegger, 1970, *Gegenbaur's Morph. Jahrb.* 115(1):1—anatomy of pelvis.

Marikina Lesson, 1840, *Species des mammifères: Bimanes et quadrumanes . . . ,* p. 199—type by monotypy, *Marikina bicolor* [= *Midas bicolor* Spix]. Cruz Lima, 1945, *Mamíferos da Amazonia, Primates, Contr. Mus. Paraense,* p. 203—characters; taxonomy; synonyms, *Oedipus, Oedipomidas, Hapanella, Seniocebus.* Hershkovitz, 1949, *Proc. U. S. Nat. Mus.* 98:410, 418—revision; included species, *bicolor* Spix, *martinsi* Thomas, *leucopus* Günther. Della Serra, 1952, *Sequencia eruptiva dos dentes definitivos nos simios Platyrrhinos,* privately published—sequence of dental eruption. Osman Hill, 1957, *Primates* 3:105, 120, 122, 123, 137, 163, 188, 192, 193, 194, 196, 199, 200, 202, 212, 220—comparative anatomy; taxonomy; history; behavior; distribution. Osman Hill, 1958, *Primatologia* 3 (1):681—female external genitalia. Remane, 1960, *Primatologia* 3 (2):788—incisors. Biegert, 1961, *Primatologia* 2 (1), Lief 3:5, 184, fig. 60 (dermatoglyphes of cheiridia)—plantar and palmar surfaces of cheiridia.

Oedipomidas Reichenbach, 1862, *Vollst. Naturg. Affen,* p. 5 and footnote—included species, *oedipus* Linnaeus, *geoffroyi* Pucheran; new name for *Oedipus* Lesson, preoccupied by *Oedipus* Tschudi, 1838. De Beaux, 1917, *Giorn. Morph. Uomo, Primati* 1:100—subgenus of *Midas;* characters; comparisons. Huber, 1931, *Evolution of facial musculature and facial expression,* p. 28, fig. 5 (facial musculature)—facial musculature and expression. Schultz, 1935, *Am. J. Phys. Anthrop.* 19:512, 545, 565—dental succession; caries. Straus, 1935, *J. Anat.* 69:96—kidneys unpyramidal. Campbell, 1937, *J. Mammal.* 18:66—shoulder anatomy; generic affinities. J. Anthony, 1946, *Ann. Sci. Nat., Paris, Zool.* (11)18:8—brain morphology. Hershkovitz, 1949, *Proc. U.S. Nat. Mus.* 98:411, 414—revision. Connolly, 1950, *External morphology of the primate brain,* p. 19, fig. 6 (brain)—brain; cerebral fissural pattern (*Oedipomidas oedipus*). Biegert, 1956, *Gegenbaur's Morph. Jahrb.* 97:249—jaw articulation. Osman Hill, 1955, *Primates* 2:41, 42, 98—forelimb; musculature; twinning. Osman Hill, 1957, *Primates* 3:9, 27, 81, 90, 95, 98, 107, 119, 121, 122, 137, 141, 150, 159–61, 163, 167, 179, 188, 190–92, 196, 199, 200, 242, 246, 248, 263, 265, 266, 283, 284, 316—comparative anatomy; taxonomy; history; behavior; distribution. Eckstein, 1958, *Primatologia* 3 (1):563—reproductive organs. Schultz, 1958, *Primatologia* 3 (1):130, fig. 2 (palatal rugosities)—palatine ridges. Osman Hill, 1958, *Primatologia* 3 (1):643, 681—external genitalia. Remane, 1960, *Primatologia* 3 (2):788, 832—dentition. Osman Hill, 1960, *Primates* 4:12, 162—comparison with Cebidae. Osman Hill, 1962, *Primates* 5:168, 169—ear. Biegert, 1961, *Primatologia* 2 (1), Lief 3:5, 179, fig. 57, 58 (dermatoglyphs of cheiridia)—plantar and palmar surfaces of cheiridia. Rohen, 1962, *Primatologia* 2 (1), Lief 6:5, 8, 77, 79, 94, 100, 130, 132, 144, 146, 148, 158, fig. 32 (ciliary muscle)—comparative eye anatomy. Cosgrove, 1966, *Lab. Animal Care* 16(1):27—trematode parasites (*Athesmia foxi*).

Œdipomidas Elliot, 1905, *Field Columbian Mus., Zool. Ser.* 6:532—type, *Simia oedipus.* Elliot, 1913, *A review of the Primates* 1:213—characters; species. Elliot, 1914, *Bull. Amer. Mus. Nat. Hist.* 33:643—taxonomy. Pocock, 1917, *Ann. Mag. Nat. Hist.* ser. 8, 20:256—characters; classification. Sonntag, 1921, *Proc. Zool. Soc. London* 1921:523, 757—tongue anatomy; classification. Thomas, 1922, *Ann. Mag. Nat. Hist.* ser. 9, 9:198—classification. J. Anthony, 1946, *Ann. Sci. Nat., Zool.* 8(11):9, fig. 3 (brain)—brain topography.

Leontopithecus Reichenbach (part, not Lesson), 1862, *Vollst. Naturg. Affen,* p. 6—*Simia leonina* Humboldt only.

Hapanella Gray, 1870, *Cat. monkeys, lemurs, and fruit-eating bats, Brit. Mus.* p. 65—subgenus of *Oedipus* Lesson; type species, *Midas geoffroyi,* by monotypy.

Mystax Gray, 1870, *Cat. monkeys, lemurs, and fruit-eating bats, Brit. Mus.,* p. 66—subgenus of *Midas;* included species, *mystax* Spix (type by tautonomy), *labiatus* E. Geoffroy, *rufiventer* Gray, *leucogenys* Gray, *flavifrons* I. Geoffroy, *nigricollis* Spix, *rufoniger* I. Geoffroy, *devillii* I. Geoffroy, *nigrifrons* I. Geoffroy, *illigeri* Pucheran, *fuscicollis* Spix, *weddelli* Deville; generic name preoccupied by *Mystax* Stephens, 1829, a genus of Trichoptera. Cabrera, 1917, *Trab. Mus. Nac. Cienc. Nat., Madrid, ser. zool.* 31:32—subgenus of *Leontocebus* Wagner. Pocock, 1917, *Ann. Mag. Nat. Hist.,* ser. 8, 20:256—nomen conservandum; characters; classification; synonyms, *Cercopithecus, Midas, Tamarin, Seniocebus, Tamarinus.* Sonntag, 1921, *Proc. Zool. Soc. London* 1921:521, 757—classification; tongue anatomy. Thomas, 1922, *Ann. Mag. Nat. Hist.* ser. 9, 9:198—classification; species listed [excl. *chrysopygus,* a *Leontopithecus*].

Tamarin Gray, 1870, *Cat. monkeys, lemurs, and fruit-eating bats, Brit. Mus.,* p. 68—subgenus of *Midas;* type by monotypy, *Midas ursulus* "Geoff." [= *Saguinus ursulus* Hoffmannsegg]. Cabrera, 1917, *Trab. Mus. Nac. Cienc. Nat., Madrid, ser. zool.* 31:32—subgenus of *Leontocebus.* Tate, 1937, *Bull. Amer. Mus. Nat. Hist.* 76:208—oldest valid name for tamarins; *Tamarinus* Trouessart 1904, a synonym. Cruz Lima, 1945, *Mamíferos da Ama-*

zonia, Primates, Contrib. Mus. Paraense, p. 207—genus; characters; taxonomic history; species. Hershkovitz, 1949, *Proc. U.S. Nat. Mus.* 98:410, 411—subgenus of *Marikina;* classification; characters; species: *tamarin, midas, melanoleuca, imperator, subgrisescens, labiata, mystax, pluto, graellsi, pileata, juruana, fuscicollis, weddelli, nigricollis, illigeri.* Osman Hill, 1957, *Primates* 3:53, 90, 94, 102, 105, 112, 120, 121, 124, 125, 129, 137, 138, 140–42, 144–54, 156–58, 161, 163, 172, 175, 176, 180, 187, 188, 190–203, 206–10, 244, 255, 265, 282, 287, 313, 316—comparative anatomy; taxonomy; history; behavior; distribution. Osman Hill, 1958, *Primatologia* 3 (1):642, 681—external genitalia. Osman Hill, 1962, *Primates* 5:28—osteology. Erikson, 1963, *Symp. Zool. Soc. London* 10:fig. 4 (trunk skeleton)—locomotion.

Seniocebus Gray, 1870, *Cat. monkeys, lemurs, and fruit-eating bats, Brit. Mus.,* p. 68—type species, *Seniocebus bicolor* [= *Midas bicolor* Spix], by monotypy. Elliot, 1913, *Review of the Primates* 1:179—genus; characters; included species: *bicolor* Spix, *martinsi* Thomas, *meticulosus* Elliot [= *oedipus* Linnaeus, an *Oedipomidas*]. Thomas, 1922, *Ann. Mag. Nat. Hist.,* ser. 9, 9:198—classification. Gregory, 1922, *Origin and evolution of human dentition,* p. 228, pls. 12, 13 (skull)—molar and cranial evolution.

Tamarinus Trouessart, 1904, *Cat. Mamm., Suppl.,* p. 29—included species, *labiatus, rufiventer, mystax, pileatus lagonotus, weddelli, devillei, nigrifrons, fuscicollis, chrysopygus, nigricollis, illigeri, tripartitus, graellsi.* Elliot, 1913, *Review of the Primates* 1:195—subgenus of *Leontocebus.* Pocock, 1917, *Ann. Mag. Nat. Hist.,* ser. 8, 20:256—*Midas mystax* Spix, designated type. Tate, 1937, *Bull. Amer. Mus. Nat. Hist.* 76:208, footnote 1—designation of *Simia midas* as type [but see Pocock, 1917, above]. Osman Hill, 1957, *Primates* 3:90, 120, 121, 137, 160, 163–66, 180, 187–89, 192, 196, 197, 199, 201, 202, 212 et seq., 244, 246, 262, 270, 271, 275, 287, 313—comparative anatomy; taxonomy; history; behavior; distribution. Osman Hill, 1958, *Primatologia* 3 (1): 643, 681—male external genitalia. Remane, 1960, *Primatologia* 3 (2):646, 788, 800, 832, fig. 27*b* (m^{1-2}) dentition. Cosgrove 1966, *Lab. Animal Care* 16(1):27, 29 (misplaced entry), 33, 38—trematode parasites (*Athesmia foxi, Neodiplostomum* sp., *Phaneropsolus orbicularis, Platynosomum* sp.).

Sanguinus Osman Hill, 1957, *Primates* 3:204—misspelling of *Saguinus* Hoffmannsegg in combination with *S. ursulus* Hoffmannsegg, cited in synonymy of *Tamarin tamarin.*

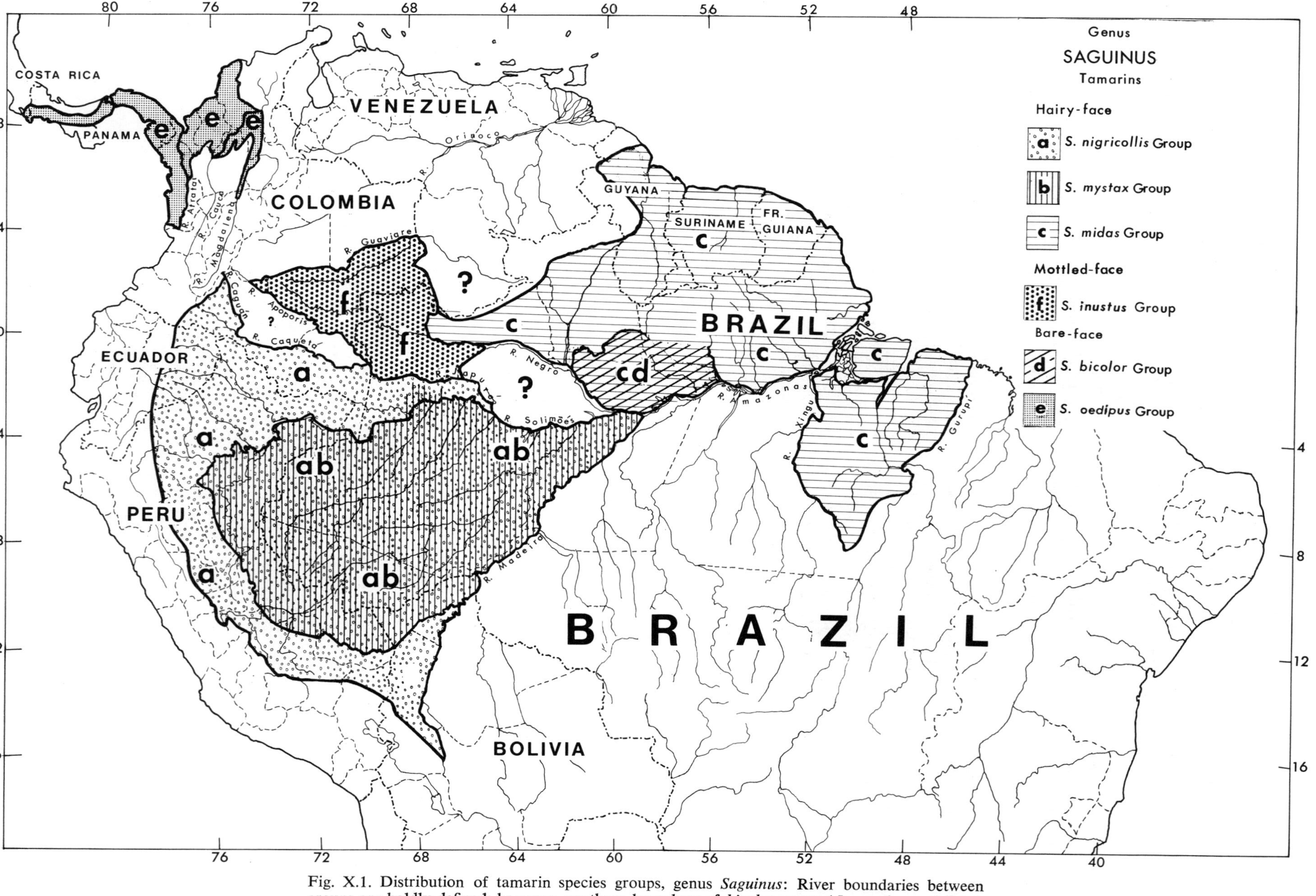

Fig. X.1. Distribution of tamarin species groups, genus *Saguinus*: River boundaries between groups are boldly defined; however, northern boundary of *bicolor* group (*d*) remains undefined, and a representative of the *S. mystax* group lives between the lower Rios Içа and Japurá on north bank of the Solimoes (Amazonas); for distribution of species group components, see figs. X.2, 15, 21, 37, 46.

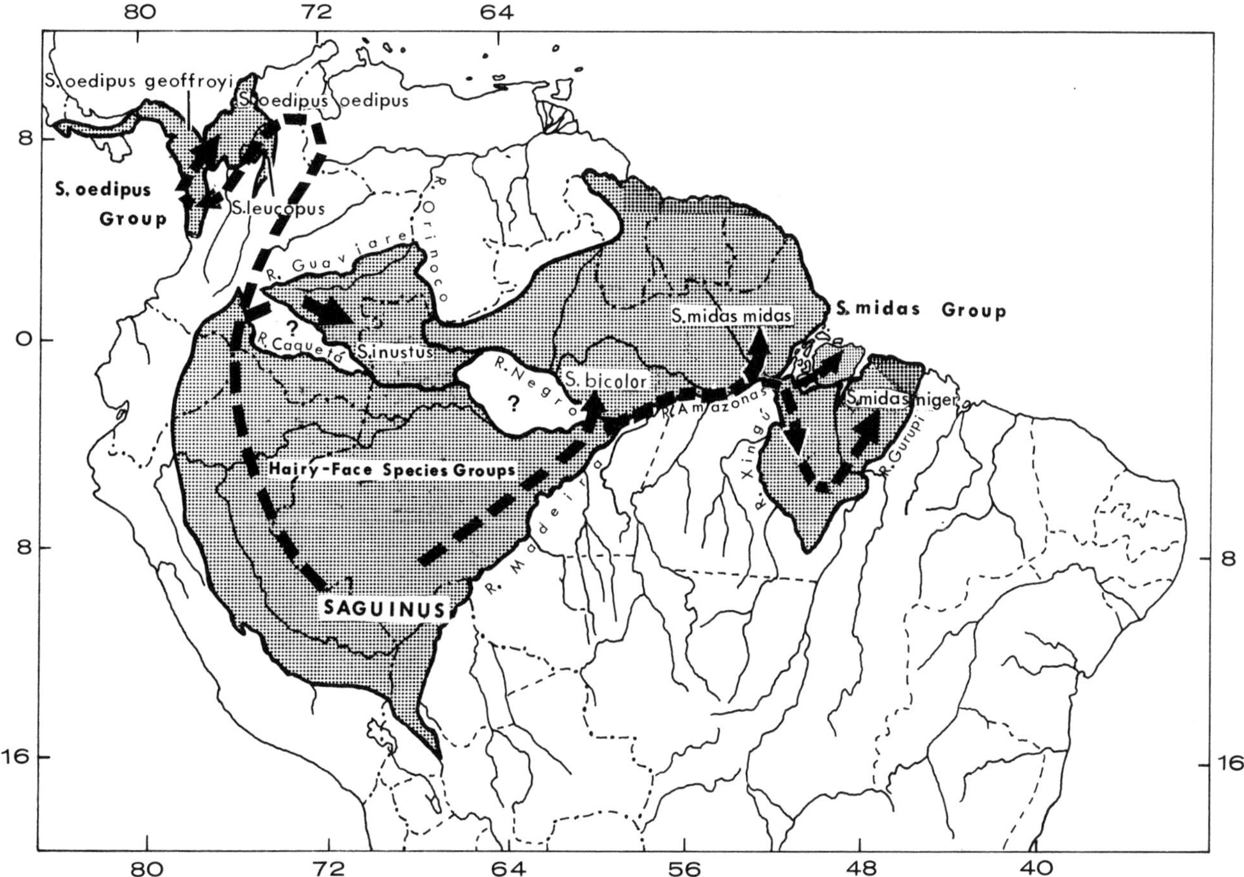

Fig. X.2. Geographic origin of tamarin species, genus *Saguinus,* hypothetically in southwestern section of upper Amazonian region, and possible dispersal routes northward. (Modified from Hershkovitz 1969, 1972.)

Type Species. Saguinus ursula Hoffmannsegg [= *Sagouin niger* E. Geoffroyi = *Saguinus midas niger* E. Geoffroy] by monotypy.

Included Species. 10. *Saguinus nigricollis, fuscicollis, labiatus, mystax, imperator, midas, inustus, leucopus, oedipus, bicolor.*

Distribution (fig. VII.1, 2; X.1).

Forested tropical zones of Panamá and an adjacent part of southeastern Costa Rica, northern and western Colombia west of the Río Magdalena, the Guianas, Amazonian regions of Colombia, Ecuador, Peru, Bolivia; and in Brazil throughout the north bank of the Rio Amazonas, and on the south bank confined to the region west of the Rio Madeira, and the area between the lower Rio Xingu and Gurupí.

Taxonomic History

The long, often confused taxonomic history of tamarins is best elucidated in the chapters dealing with the species groups and species.

Systematic Position

Distinction between the short-tusked marmosets or ouistitis and long-tusked tamarins was first made in 1812 by the celebrated French comparative anatomist, Etienne Geoffroy St. Hilaire. Ouistitis, characterized as having long, narrow, cylindrical, more or less orthodont lower incisors of unequal height, and small lower canines, were assembled in the newly erected genus *Jacchus* (= *Callithrix* Erxleben). Tamarins, distinguished by short, subequal, spatulate, procumbent lower incisors, and well-developed recurved lower canines, were combined into the proposed genus *Midas,* now *Saguinus Hoffmannsegg.* The impressive dental characters that separate tamarins from *ouistitis* or *Callithrix jacchus* are largely bridged by the dental structure of the species of the *Callithrix argentata* group. Nevertheless, the dental characters combined with significant differences in the morphology of the external genitalia and a number of weak characters in other systems support generic distinction of *Saguinus.* Separation of *Saguinus* from *Leontopithecus,* the most highly specialized of callitrichids, is based on peculiarities found in the latter.

Origin, Evolution, and Dispersal

The subject matter is treated elsewhere within the context of callitrichid history (p. 412, figs. VII.3, 4). Discussions of origin, evolution and dispersal of intrageneric categories of tamarins are included under the species or species group headings.

The largest concentration of tamarin species is in the upper Amazonian basin and the most primitive of the species are headquartered along the eastern base of the Cordillera Oriental. The most highly specialized species, on the other hand, are lone outlanders. The bare-face *Saguinus oedipus* is found on the northwestern periphery of the generic range and *S. midas,* most specialized of the hairy-face group, occurs on the northeastern extreme of the range (fig. X.2).

All tamarins can be derived from a prototype of the upper Amazonian *Saguinus nigricollis graellsi.* Differentiation of the species, however, is mostly superficial in character and seemingly could have taken place during late Quaternary. Callitrichids, however, are of an ancient lineage and their present squirrellike form and plasticity are adaptations for survival in changing climates, probably since the Neogene. Success now allows tamarins to indulge in the luxury of specialization primarily for display and social contacts.

Diagnostic Characters

Size:

The size range is narrow, with smaller tamarins overlapping *Callithrix* in size, the larger overlapping *Leontopithecus.* The size range of *Callimico* lies entirely within that of *Saguinus* (cf. p. 945, appendix table 1).

Integument (cf. Chaps. 8–11):

Hair and color patterns are more diversified in *Saguinus* than in other callitrichids, and possibly more so than in any other primate genus. Tamarins display the full metachromic range from agouti to white through eumelanic and pheomelanic pathways. The color pattern may be nearly uniform or arranged in sharply contrasting hues with special markings on face, forehead, crown, nape, and rump. The pelage is also highly varied in length or direction of growth. Conspicuous crests, manes, moustaches, sideburns, and rump tufts contrast sharply in length and often in color with the surrounding fur. Bare, heavily pigmented faces of some species enhance the contrasts. In others, a patterned or a vitiligolike facial depigmentation are display or recognition characters (fig. X.3). Facial pelage in many races of the hairy face species are also colorfully variegated. Ears are always blackish, bare, and exposed to view; circumauricular tufts are absent. The tail may be uniformly colored, bicolor, or with color of terminal or basal portions or both contrasting with that of the intermediate portion.

The usual complement of vibrissae and tegumentary glands are present, but glands of the circumgenital region and belly are extremely well developed.

External Genitalia (cf. chap. 14; figs. III.21, 24, 26–29; X.4):

The tamarin genitalia are distinctive. Those of the male are slightly more specialized than the comparatively generalized organs of *Cebuella* but are visibly different. The female labia majora deviate sharply from those of *Cebuella* and *Callithrix* in size, shape, pigmentation, and position of the preputial fold relative to the scrotal fold. The scent glands of genital and circumgenital areas are among the most highly specialized of higher primates.

Ear (cf. chap. 12; fig. III.18):

The tamarin ear is more varied in shape than that

DEPIGMENTATION AND VITILIGO IN TAMARINS

Saguinus inustus

Saguinus labiatus

Saguinus mystax

Saguinus b.bicolor

Fig. X.3. Facial depigmentation in *Saguinus.* Pigmentation is diffuse in *S. inustus,* patterned in *S. labiatus* and *S. mystax,* vitiligolike (or true vitiligo) in *S. bicolor.*

of other callitrichids and possibly of any other primate genus. The ear evolved to a large leaflike appendage in most species of tamarins and to a truncated, convoluted structure in the others. The skin is usually entirely pigmented and always bare, the entire organ well exposed to view.

Ischial Prominences:

Prominences are well developed in most species but more so in females than in males (fig. I.15; pp. 30, 417).

Postcranial Skeleton:

See chaps. 4, 5; figs. I.26, 28, 29, 31; II.1; VII.9, 10, 12.

Tongue:

See chap. 13; figs. III.19, 20; X.5.

Palatal Ridges:

See p. 431 and fig. VII.14.

Larynx:

See p. 18 and figs. I.10A, 11D.

Skull (chaps. 18–28; figs. VII.5, 6; IX.1, 2)

The tamarin skull is built on the U-shaped dental

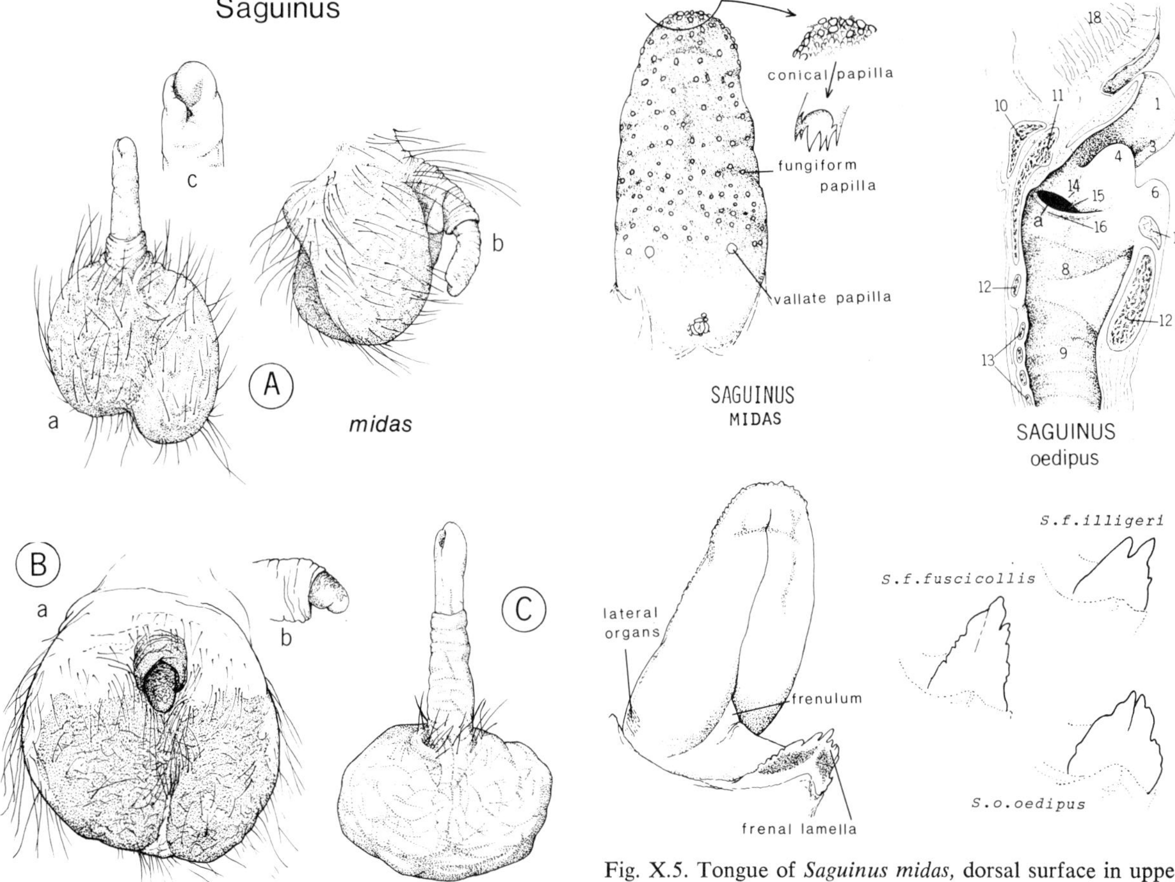

Fig. X.4. Adult male external genitalia of (*A*) *Saguinus midas;* (*B*) *Saguinus nigricollis;* (*C*) *Saguinus oedipus; a,* ventral aspect of scrotum and penis; *b,* penis from right side; *c,* enlarged glans from ventral aspect; all drawings from fluid-preserved specimens.

Fig. X.5. Tongue of *Saguinus midas,* dorsal surface in upper left, ventral surface in lower left; frenal lamella of *S. fuscicollis illigeri, S. f. fuscicollis,* and *S. oedipus oedipus;* larynx of *S. oedipus,* longitudinal section showing left inner surface. Symbols explained on page 19.

arcade plan. Its evolution can be reconstructed without important gaps through skulls of living species of *Cebuella* and *Callithrix.* Each genus, however, attained its position independently of the others. Its comparatively simple system of sphenoidal sinuses readily separates *Saguinus* from *Leontopithecus* (fig. IV.26).

Dentition (chaps. 32–38; figs. V.1, 2, 6, 7, 17, 23, 25–29; 31–33):

Well-developed cingula, styles, and conules are more common among species of *Saguinus* than in other callitrichids; bowing of coronal contour of lower cheek teeth is more pronounced than in *Callithrix,* the incisor crowns wider, upper lateral incisor notably shorter and smaller than central, the lower lateral incisor crown nearly as high but smaller than central, lower canine more complex and about twice as high as adjacent incisor, upper and lower premolars more molarized. Second molar tends toward decrease in size, the metacone greatly reduced to almost obsolete; inner cusps equal to or slightly higher than outer cusps in first lower molar, consistently higher in second lower molar; in marmosets *Cebuella* and *Callithrix,* outer cusps of lower molars are as high as or higher than opposite cusps; lower deciduous incisors are more nutricialized than in *Callithrix,* while deciduous upper and lower *Callithrix* incisors more nearly resemble permanent incisors of *Saguinus* than their own successors.

In all respects, differences between the dentition of *Saguinus* and *Callithrix jacchus* are partially bridged by lesser or fewer differences between the teeth of *Saguinus* and *Callithrix argentata.* The dentition of *Saguinus* and *Leontopithecus* are similar except canines of latter are heavier, more elongate, upper premolars slightly more molarized, lower premolars slightly less molarized, molars larger. Dental differences between tamarins and the larger *Leontopithecus* correlate allometrically with differences in overall size.

The dental system of *Saguinus* is a model for primates above marmoset grade. The chisel-shaped or spatulate type of incisors with biting edges in line is established in nearly all living cebids and catarrhines. Functional and morphological equivalence between upper and lower canines and order of dental succession are also standard in higher primates. These advances in *Saguinus* mark passage through an important threshold in primate dental evolution. Molarization in tamarins is also at a stage where transition from unicuspid to bicuspid and tricuspid premolars, and from tritubercular to incipient quadritubercular molars is demonstrable.

Brain (chap. 41; figs. VI.8, 9):

Judged by external relief, the tamarin brain is most complex among callitrichids, but variation is wide. The simplest tamarin brains are like those of *Callithrix,* and the most complex approach those of marmosetlike cebids.

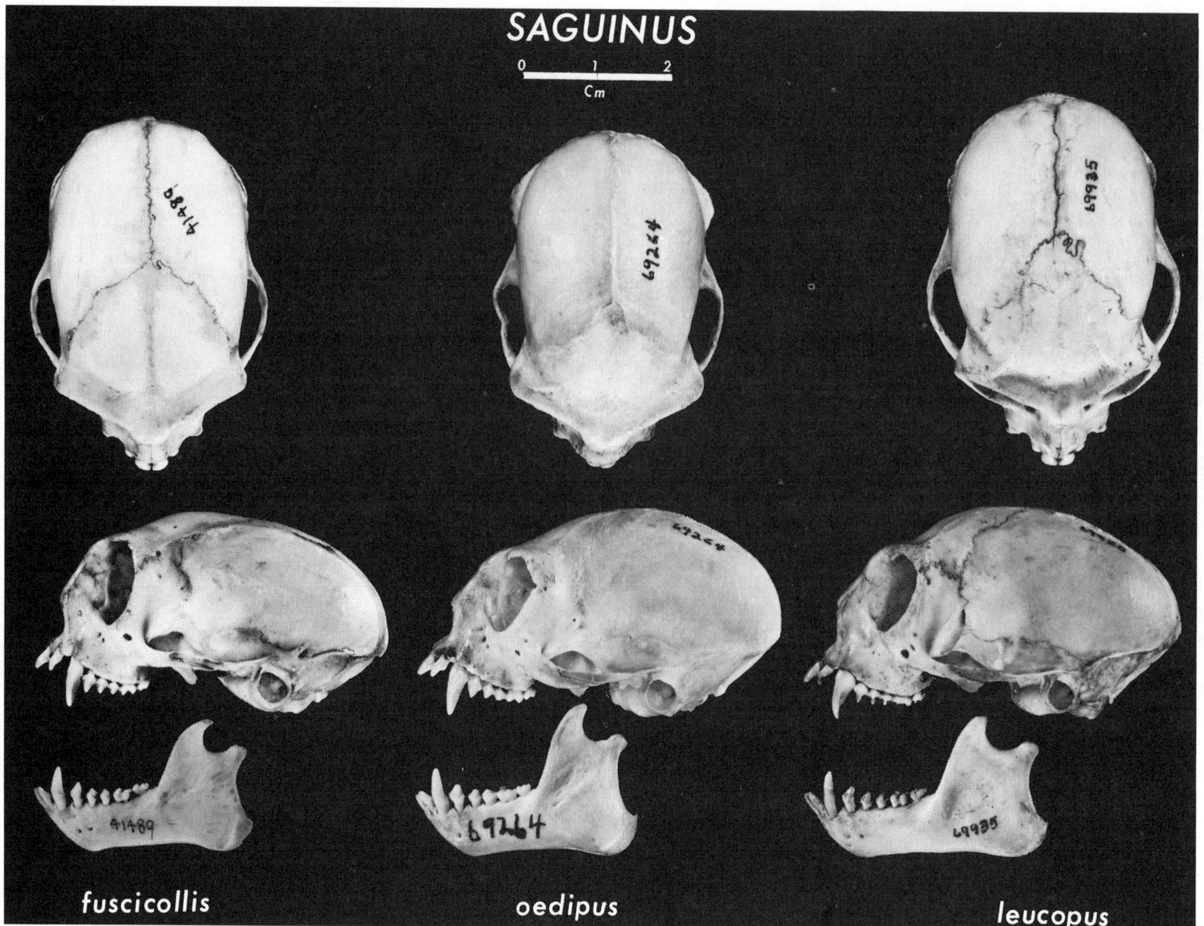

Fig. X.6. Skulls of *Saguinus fuscicollis, S. oedipus,* and *S. leucopus,* dorsal and lateral aspects; apparent differences between the species are mostly individual variables.

Karyotype (p. 432; table 48):

The normal diploid number of chromosomes is 46, but only 6 species of the 10 recognized have been investigated to date. F. Deinhardt (1967), and Marczynska, Trew-Sarnat, and Deinhardt (1970), described some aberrant tumor cell karyotypes of *Saguinus fuscicollis* with diploid chromosome numbers 44, 46, 47, and 49.

Cranial Characters (figs. IV.81–84; X.6–12)

Greatest skull length of adult usually between 44 and 57 mm; frontal contour low to markedly vaulted; temporal ridges nearly parallel-sided to strongly convergent, sometimes uniting on parietal bones to form a sagittal crest; nasal profile concave to plane (fig. IV.3); nasofrontal suture from one-half to four-fifths distance from tip of nasals to glabella; malar foramen minute to nearly ½ cm in diameter; infraorbital foramen situated above and between pm^3 and canine, its diameter variable but not exceeding greatest diameter of malar; orbits more or less square to rounded, lateral inflation absent but horizontal diameter usually slightly greater than vertical; lacrymal bone small to moderately large, rarely extending beyond rim of orbit and not contacting nasal; cribriform plate small (fig. IV.43): right and left orbital plates of ethmoid compressed into a thin translucent, sometimes perforated, interorbital septum (figs. IV.21; X.12); posterior sphenoidal sinuses or fossae absent; axis of foramen magnum pointing more nearly down than back; auditory bullae well inflated, lower portion of mesotympanic cavity large, usually single chambered but sometimes with large cells (fig. IV.62); dental arcade more or less U-shaped, outer alveolar distance between canines more than alveolar length of c-m^2; average occipital angle (opisthion—inion index) between 40° and 60° (fig. IV.81); pterygoid plates moderately developed, medial plate consisting mainly of hamular process, the pterygoid fossa shallow or rudimentary (fig. IV.51, 53); outline of inferior border of mandible V- to U-shaped; the symphysial angle rounded, the horizontal rami diverging in a straight line, or arced; angle of outer slope of symphysis menti relative to basal mandibular plane (fig. IV.78) about 49° (40°–60°, 286 specimens); ascending ramus elongate; average coronoidal height about 63% of condyloincisive length of mandible; coronoid process usually hooked and extending well above condyle; sigmoid notch deep and comparatively narrow; articular surface of condylar process raised well above plane of molar crown surface; inferior border of angular process slightly inflected and in line with basal plane of horizontal ramus or deflected slightly below.

Postcranial Skeletal Characters

Vertebral Formula:

In 4 skeletons of *Saguinus fuscicollis,* 1 of *S. labiatus,* 1 of *S. mystax,* 2 of *S. imperator,* total 15, cervical 7; thoracic 12 in all except 13 in one *imperator* and one

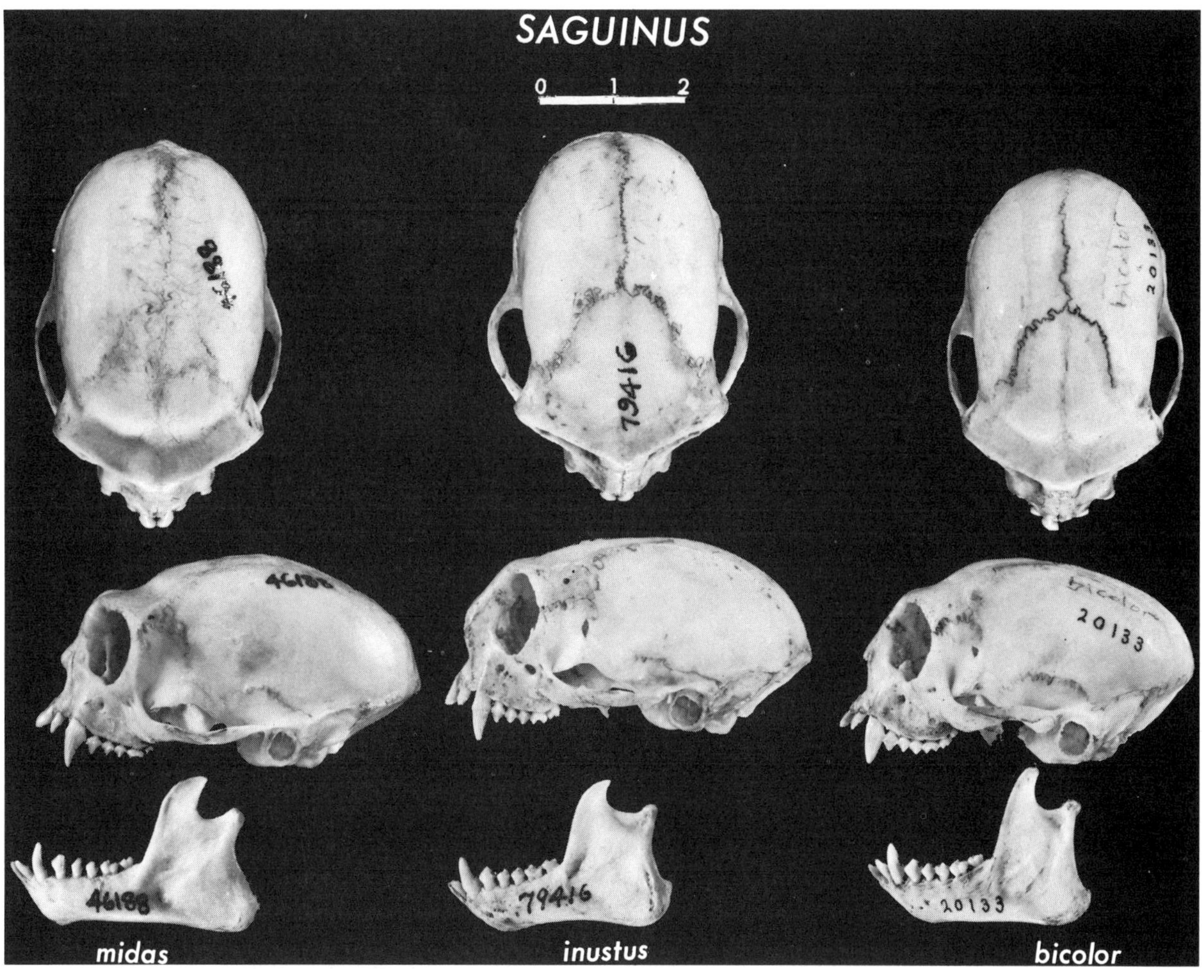

Fig. X.7. Skulls of *Saguinus midas, S. inustus,* and *S. bicolor,* dorsal and lateral aspects; apparent differences between the species are mostly individual variables.

mystax; lumbar 7 in all except 6 in the same *mystax* and *imperator* skeletons; sacral 3; caudal 31(28–34) 13 samples.

The vertebral formulae recorded by Heatherington, Cooper, and Dawson (1975) of a wild-caught pair of *Saguinus nigricollis* and their captive-born twins, are as follows:

	C	T	L	S	C
Male	7	13	6	3	31
Female	7	12	7	3	31
Twin 1	7	12	7	3	20
Twin 2	7	12	7	3	26

Metacarpals 3 and 4 in both hands of twin 2 were fused. The animal was unable to cling most of its time in the cage and it died when 6 days old.

Sternal Ribs:

8 in seven skeletons, 9 in three.

Arm and Leg Proportions:

The samples are arranged by species; limb bone measurements are greatest length; trunk length is combined lengths of articulated thoracic, lumbar and sacral vertebrae.

Saguinus fuscicollis—FM 71011 ♀, FM 71012 ♀, FM 57620 ♀, FM 71004 ♂.

$$\frac{\text{Humerus } 54, 54, 54, 53}{\text{Radius } 51, 51, 50, 47} = 106\%, 106\%, 108\%, 113\%.$$

$$\frac{\text{Femur } 64, 64, 65, 65}{\text{Tibia } 65, 68, 65, 67} = 98\%, 94\%, 100\%, 97\%$$

$$\frac{\text{Humerus + radius } 105, 105, 104, 100}{\text{Femur + tibia } 129, 132, 130, 132} = 81\%, 80\%, 80\%, 76\%.$$

$$\frac{\text{Humerus + radius } 105, 105, 104, 100}{\text{Trunk } 140, 139, 138, 147} = 75\%, 75\%, 75\%, 68\%.$$

$$\frac{\text{Femur + tibia } 129, 132, 130, 132}{\text{Trunk } 140, 139, 138, 147} = 92\%, 95\%, 94\%, 90\%.$$

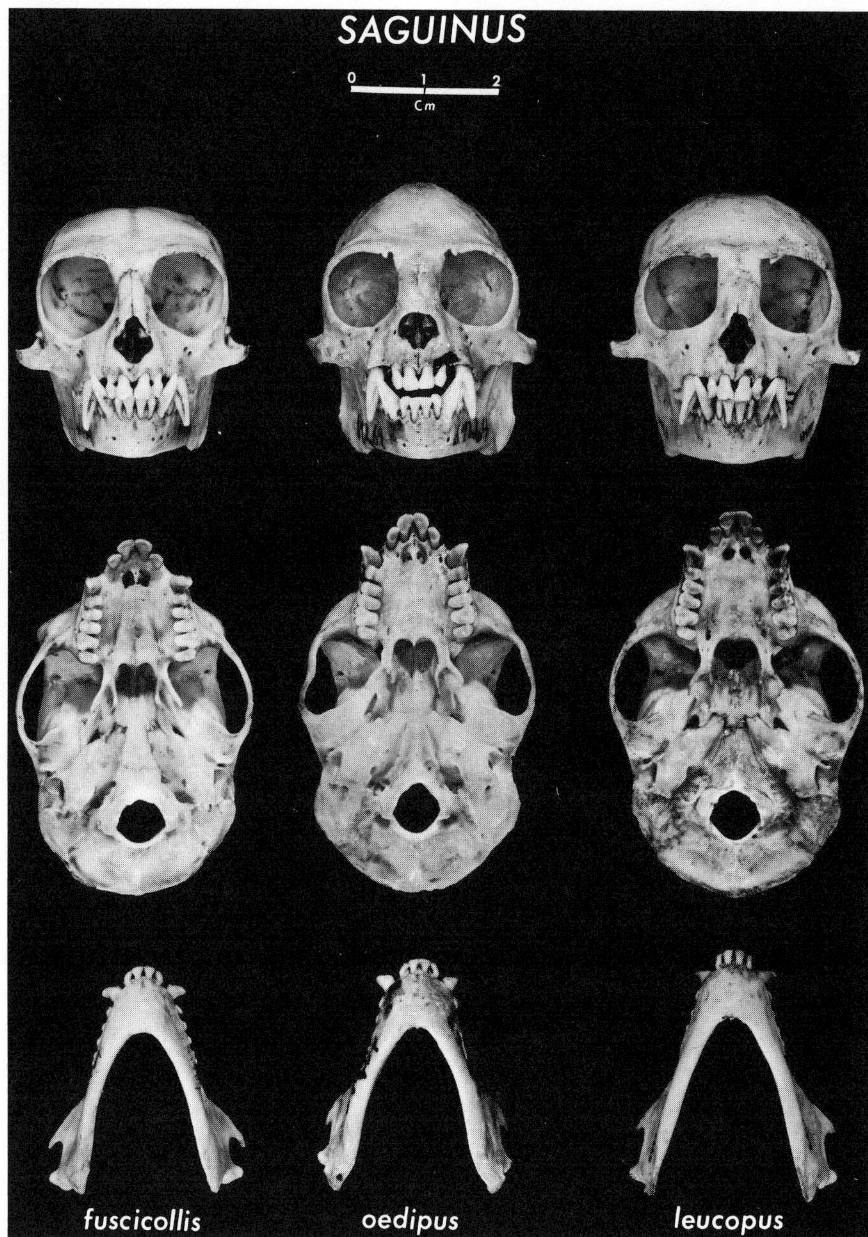

Fig. X.8. Skulls of *Saguinus fuscicollis, S. oedipus,* and *S. leucopus,* frontal and ventral aspects; apparent differences between the species are mostly individual variables.

Saguinus imperator—FM 98035 subadult ♀, FM 98036 subadult ♂.

$$\frac{\text{Humerus } 53, 54}{\text{Radius } 47, 47} = 113\%, 115\%.$$

$$\frac{\text{Femur } 69, 68}{\text{Tibia } 67, 66} = 103\%, 103\%.$$

$$\frac{\text{Humerus + radius } 100, 101}{\text{Femur + tibia } 136, 134} = 73\%, 75\%.$$

$$\frac{\text{Humerus + radius } 100, 101}{\text{Trunk } 143, 154} = 70\%, 66\%.$$

$$\frac{\text{Femur + tibia } 136, 134}{\text{Trunk } 143, 154} = 95\%, 87\%.$$

Saguinus oedipus—FM 69941 ♀, FM 69948 ♀, FM 69952 ♀, FM 69953 ♂, FM 69946 ♂.

$$\frac{\text{Humerus } 51, 58, 58, 55, 53}{\text{Radius } 44, 51, 51, 50, 51} = 116\%, 114\%, 110\%, 104\%.$$

$$\frac{\text{Femur } 64, 73, 72, 68, 68}{\text{Tibia } 65, 77, 73, 70, 73} = 98\%, 95\%, 99\%, 97\%, 93\%.$$

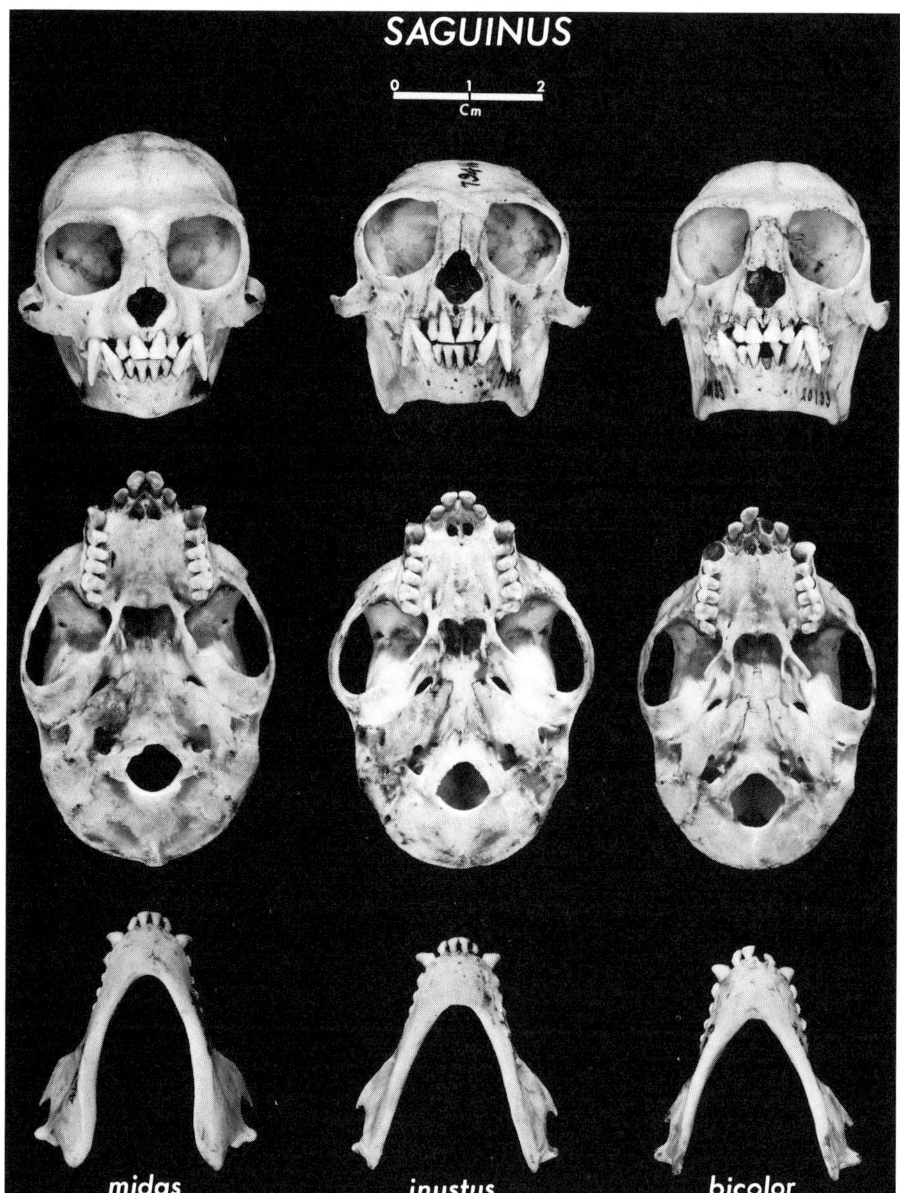

Fig. X.9. Skulls of *Saguinus midas, S. inustus,* and *S. bicolor,* frontal and ventral aspects; apparent differences between the species are mostly individual variables.

$$\frac{\text{Humerus + radius} \quad 95, 109, 109, 105, 104}{\text{Femur + tibia} \quad 129, 150, 145, 138, 141} = 74\%, 73\%, 75\%, 77\%, 74\%.$$

$$\frac{\text{Humerus + radius} \quad 95, 109, 109, 105, 104}{\text{Trunk} \quad 149, 165, 163, 152, 171} = 64\%, 66\%, 67\%, 69\%, 61\%.$$

$$\frac{\text{Femur + tibia} \quad 129, 150, 145, 138, 141}{\text{Trunk} \quad 149, 165, 163, 152, 171} = 87\%, 91\%, 89\%, 91\%, 82\%.$$

Saguinus midas—data from Christen (1974, p. 46), who gives only the means and extremes but no sample size.

$$\frac{\text{Humerus + radius}}{\text{Femur + tibia}} = 72(70\text{–}73)$$

$$\frac{\text{Humerus + radius}}{\text{Trunk}} = 63(62.5\text{–}70.5)$$

$$\frac{\text{Femur + tibia}}{\text{Trunk}} = 85(77\text{–}92)$$

Third Trochanter:

In 4 skeletons of *Saguinus fuscicollis,* 1 of *S. mystax,* 2 of *S. imperator,* 2 of *S. midas,* 7 of *S. oedipus,* 5 of *Saguinus* spp., total 21, present but not well developed in all.

Entepicondylar Foramen:

In same skeletons as above, present in all except in 1 *mystax* and 2 *imperator.*

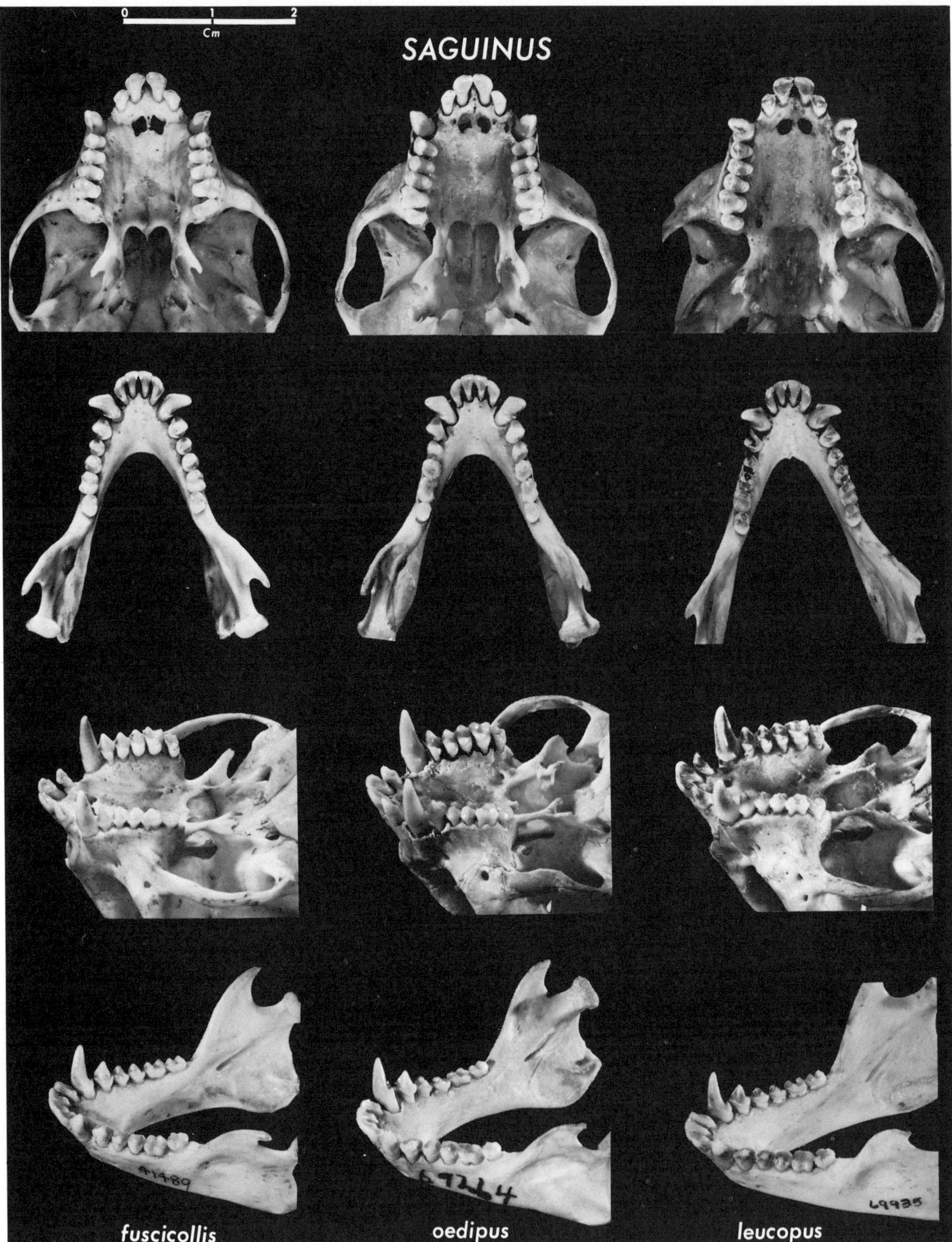

Fig. X.10. Skulls of *Saguinus fuscicollis, S. oedipus,* and *S. leucopus,* palatal and mandibular aspects; apparent differences between the species are mostly individual variables.

Dental Characters (figs. V.1, 17, 23, 25, 26, 27, 28; X.13, 14)

Incisors (figs. V.1, 2, 23)

Permanent upper incisors comparatively low, crowns expanded and well differentiated from cervix, the outer tooth implanted laterad and slightly posteriad to inner, the incisor pair on both sides combining to form a broadly curved or U-shaped arch; trapeziform lateral incisor lower, generally less proodont than central and about three-fourths to one half its bulk; central incisor broadly spatulate, biting edge broad, horizontal, entire, and contacting biting edge of opposite central incisor; mesial and distal cingular ridges (*B*) boldly defined on lateral and central incisors and joined on lingual border

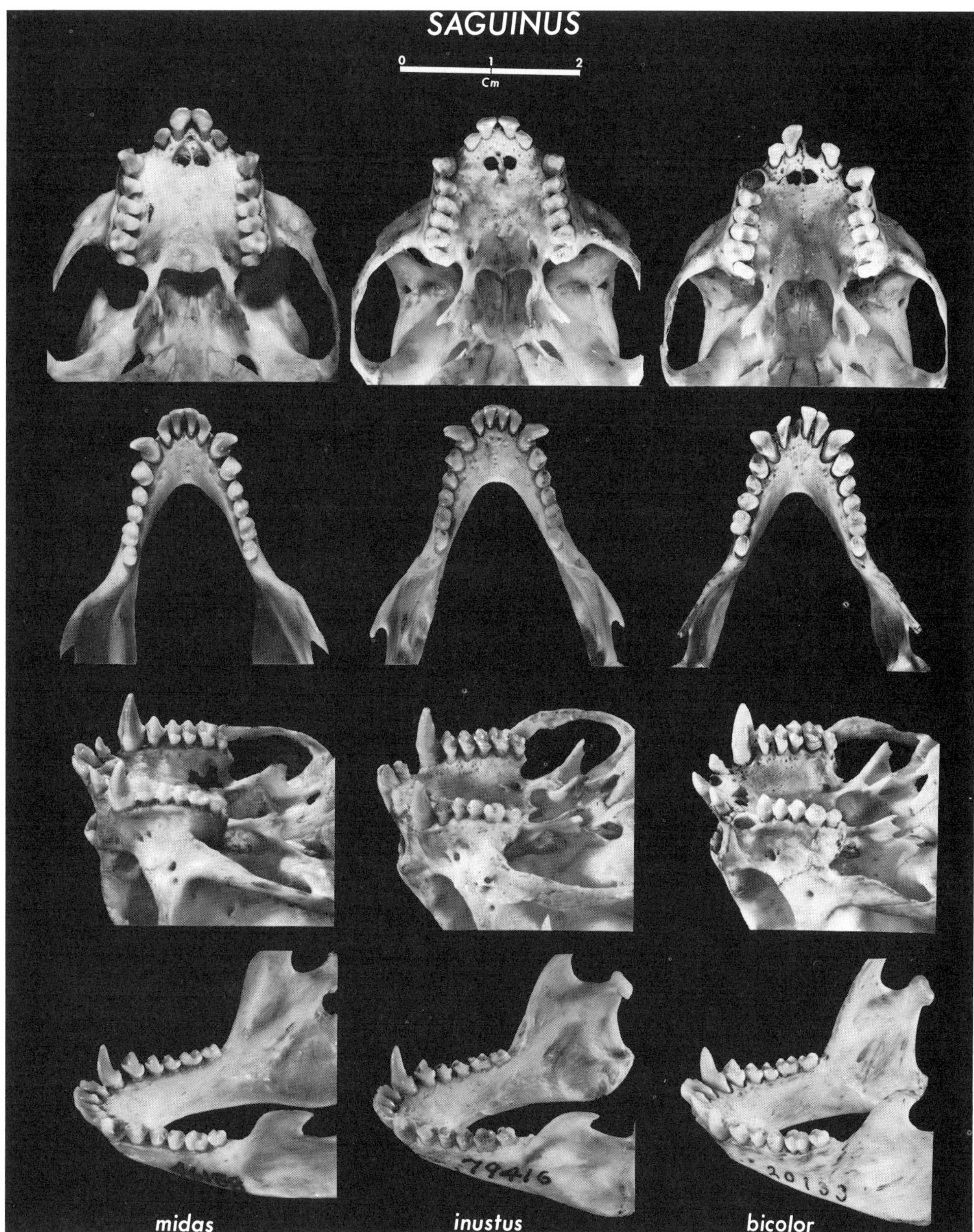

Fig. X.11. Skulls of *Saguinus midas, S. inustus,* and *S. bicolor,* palatal and mandibular aspects; apparent differences between the species are mostly individual variables.

of each tooth; mesial and distal styles absent; occlusal groove usually present about midway across central incisors; lingual surface of incisor pair crazed except in newly erupted teeth.

Deciduous upper incisors (unworn) spatulate and basically similar to unworn permanent teeth but crown proportionately wider; enamel uncrazed, lateral incisor acuneate with apex sharply pointed, mesial and distal cingular ridges joined behind.

Permanent lower incisors with height somewhat more than twice mesiodistal length, crowns broadly expanded transversely, sloping forward in line with symphyseal angle, labial surface plane or slightly convex, biting edges normally touching; inner surface of crowns more or less crazed except in newly erupted teeth; lateral incisors emplaced nearly in line with central, the pairs of both sides combining to form the broad angle or keystone of a U-shaped arch; lateral incisor club-shaped, about equal in bulk to, or slightly larger than spatulate central incisor and as high, horizontal biting edge narrower, one-half

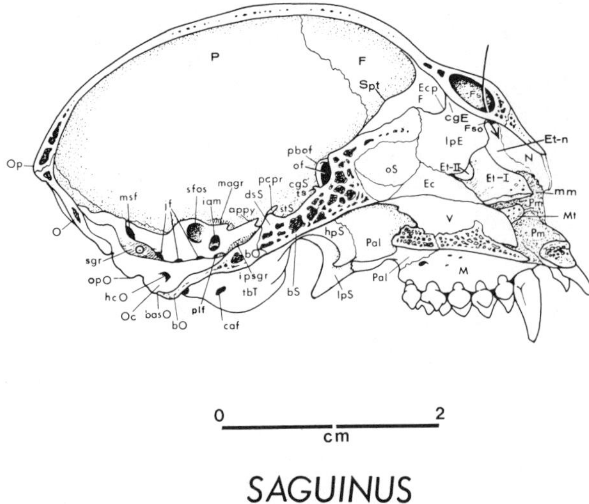

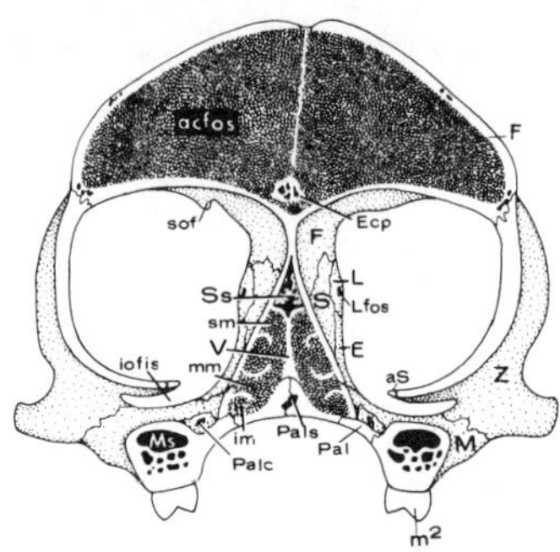

Fig. X.12. Sagittal and transverse sections of a tamarin skull. Symbols explained on p. 269.

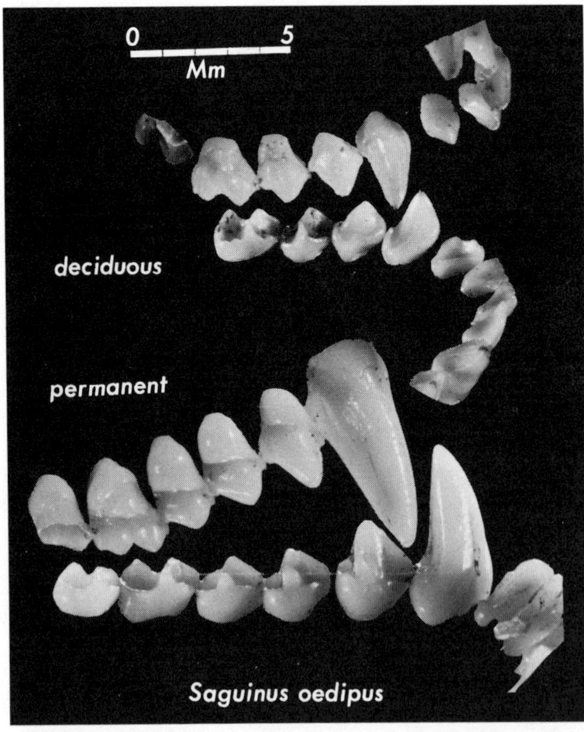

Fig. X.13. Dentition of a tamarin (*Saguinus oedipus*), deciduous and permanent sets from lingual aspect; upper and lower tooth rows of each set arranged in near-natural relationship; permanent upper incisors not in photograph.

its lateral margin obliquely truncate on labial surface, the crown widest basally; labial height of incisors about one-half vertical depth of symphysis menti; mesial and distal stylids absent; mesial and distal cingular ridges more or less defined and framing a broad more or less concave lingual shelf.

Deciduous lower incisors (unworn) without crazing, occlusal surface shorter (mesiodistally) than wide (anteroposteriorly), shelf deeply excavated; *central incisor* with occlusal surface subtriangular, mesial border longest, biting edge more or less evenly tricuspid and more than twice as wide as posterolingual border; *lateral incisor* with the occlusal surface quadrituberculate and subtrapezoidal in outline with mesial border longer than distal, biting edge about one and one-half times longer mesiodistally than that of central incisor; mesiostylid nearly as large and high as eoconid, prominent distostylid near anterior base of tooth, rudiment of metaconid sometimes evident.

Remarks. The upper deciduous incisors are weaker, wider, and spoon-shaped, not chisel-shaped, as compared with the successors and the deciduous incisors of *Calli-*

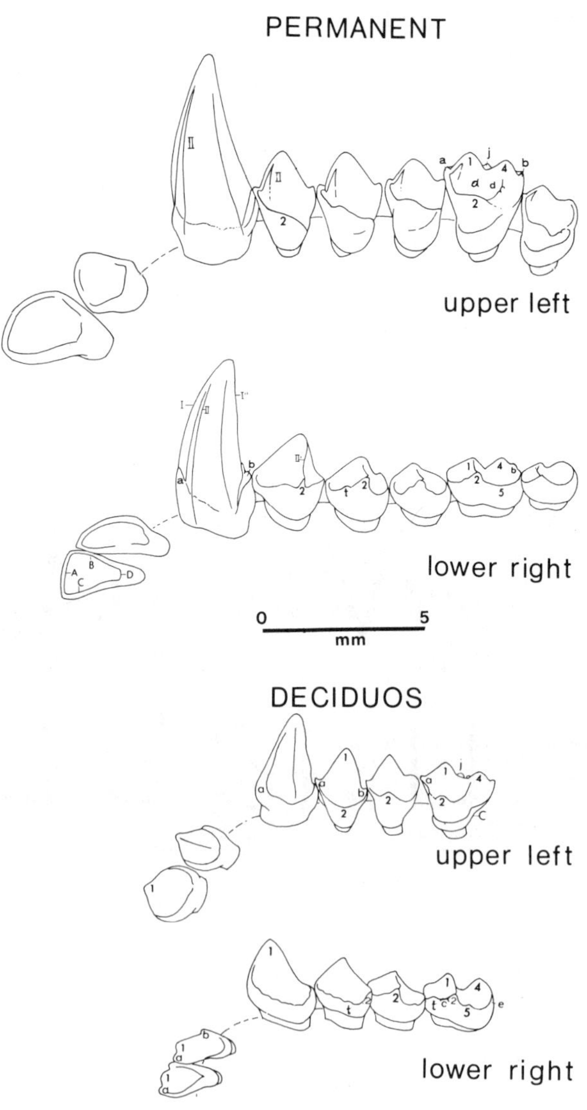

Fig. X.14. Dentition of *Saguinus oedipus;* diagrammatic representation of permanent and deciduous sets from lingual aspect.

thrix. Both teeth seem to adumbrate the ateline and colobine types.

The more precocious lower deciduous incisors resemble those of *Leontopithecus* but, like them, diverged from the marmoset type of permanent dentition. The broadly expanded tricuspid spatulate central incisor and the elongate quadritubercular lateral incisor are most like their respective permanent equivalents in *Saimiri* among small platyrrhines. Their greatest resemblance, however, is to the highly specialized ateline and colobine incisors, although functionally there may be little similarity. Besides reinforcing lip puckering and gripping in suckling, the callitrichid deciduous incisors receive and probably chew lightly on previously masticated solid food deposited in the mouth by the parents. These are the *nutritional* type of lower incisors discussed elsewhere (p. 278).

Canines (cf. p. 307)

Permanent upper canine long, slender, nearly vertical and subtriangular in cross section, more than twice as high as long and about twice as high as adjacent teeth; mesiolingual torus (*II*) defined as deep groove, distal crest (*I″*) sharp, anterior and posterior lingual cingula often connected, weakly defined mesiostyle present or absent; enamel nearly always well crazed.

Deciduous upper canine more nearly caniniform than premolariform, crown much higher than wide and about one-fourth to one-third again higher than pm^2, mesial and distal cingular ridges enclosing shallow depressions; enamel of older teeth sometimes weakly crazed.

Permanent lower canines are characteristically caniniform, more than twice as high as long, about twice as high as adjacent teeth; paracristid (*I″*) of anterior slope joining with anterolingual cingulid in some teeth to enclose a narrow pocket or incipient "trigonid" basin, anterior tubercle or mesiostylid (*a*) more or less defined; cristid *I″* of distal slope in unworn tooth defined by vertical groove which terminates proximally in talonid basin; distostylid more or less indicated in some specimens on posterior rim of talonid; enamel of lingual surface usually crazed.

Deciduous lower canine more nearly premolariform than caniniform, crown about half again as high as long but only about one-fourth again higher than pm_2; occlusal surface of crown trapezoidal and steeply sloping lingually; lingual cingulid *B* bounding a broad shelf, "trigonid" basin hardly or not distinguishable from shallow talonid basin in some, separated by a low faint epicristid in others; mesiostylid and distostylid weakly defined, low but well-marked metaconid often present; crazing not evident.

Remarks. Hypertrophy of the lower permanent canines in tamarins represents a milestone in platyrrhine dental evolution. In *Callithrix* the permanent upper incisors and canines are coupled for prehension and killing of prey and the lower are specialized for biting and scraping. In *Saguinus,* upper and lower canines assume the primary functions of piercing, stabbing, and slashing. The chisel-edged incisors, on the other hand, are preeminently specialized for cutting and scraping.

The upper deciduous canine is more nearly caniniform than premolariform. That is to say, its form is more primitive as compared with the same tooth in *Cebuella* and *Callithrix.* The trend in the lower milk canine, however, is toward increasing molarization. This contrasts with the definitive caninization of its successor.

Premolars

Permanent upper premolars with pm^2 sagittate on buccal surface, bicuspid, higher than third or fourth premolar, sample crown height 2.8, length 2.1, width 2.8, occlusal surface subtriangular in outline, mesial and distal crests (eocrista) of eocone sharply ridged, cingulum *B* well defined, lingual shelf more or less developed, mesial and distal styles (*a, b*) present, protocone full but low; pm^3 like preceding but occlusal surface subtriangular to subrectangular in outline, protocone larger, trigon basin (α) deeper, secondary cingulum *B′* usually present, cingulum *C* often present; pm^4 like preceding but usually larger, less triangular and more molarized, cingula *B′* and *C* indicated to well developed; sample length 2.0, width 3.2.

Deciduous upper premolars with dpm^2 sagittate, dominantly caniniform, unicuspidate to weakly bicuspid, sample crown height 2.2, length 1.9, width 2.1, mesiostyle, distostyle, and cingulum *B* well defined, protocone absent to moderately well developed; dpm^3 wider and slightly shorter than preceding, bicuspid or tricuspid with small metacone; dpm^4 tritubercular, mesiostyle and distostyle present, protoloph (*III*) and plagiocrista (*IV*) well developed, ectostyle, epiconule (*c*) and plagioconule (*d*) present or absent, secondary lingual cingulum *B′* often present, posterolingual cingulum *C* usually present and sometimes with conule (hypocone ?); sample length 2.5, width 3.2.

Remarks. Consistent presence of a well-developed protocone (*2*) in pm^2 completes basic molarization of the permanent bicuspid premolars; the buccal cingulum is obsolete. Dpm^2, in contrast, remains dominantly caniniform, dpm^3 is bicuspid or tritubercular with buccal cingulum present, dpm^4 is completely molarized with buccal cingulum well defined and usually with one or two ectostyles. The frequent presence of a small posterolingual conule in dpm^4 adumbrates the hypocone (*5*) of the established quadritubercular molar.

Permanent lower premolars, with pm_2 well molarized, form deltoid, sample crown height 3.0, length 2.7, width 2.3, mesial and distal ridges well defined and forming deep angle at junction with broad ledged lingual cingulids, respectively, buccal cingulid well defined, sometimes shelflike, oblique to nearly transverse epicristid (*II′*) usually well defined, "trigonid" basin deep or broad, metaconid (*2*) often, pseudoparaconid (*t*) sometimes present, hypoconid and entoconid indicated or poorly defined on posterior rim (*C*) of incipient talonid; pm_3 more molariform and smaller than preceding tooth, "trigonid" separated from talonid by high-ridged epicristid and occupying nearly two-thirds occlusal surface of crown, metaconid nearly as high as eoconid, pseudoparaconid low, talonid basin well rounded, hypoconid and entoconid barely indicated, mesiostylid (a) and distostylid (b) not evident; pm_4 like preceding but slightly larger, lower, and more molarized, "trigonid" equal to about one-half or more occlusal surface of crown, epicristid (*II*) with deeper concavity, metaconid (*2*) and eoconid (*1*) approaching parity, well-defined pseudoparaconid (*t*) often present, hypoconid (*4*) and entoconid (*5*) weakly defined, ectostylid(s) present; sample length 2.0, width 2.1.

Deciduous lower premolars with dpm_2 like molarized canine but much lower, sample crown height 1.7, length 2.1, width 1.2, lingual cingulids *B* and *C* continuous and enclosing a wide, unseparated anterior and posterior shelf or basin, epicristid not defined, metaconid rudimentary, hypoconid and entoconid sometimes indicated; unworn dpm_3 more advanced with "trigonid" and talonid completely separated by high, irregular-edged epicristid, "trigonid" occupying one-third to one-half occlusal surface, metaconid high, pseudoparaconid often indicated, hypoconid and entoconid rudimentary, mesiostylid and distostylid not evident, ectostylids present; dpm_4 molarized, eoconid and metaconid well developed, pseudoparaconid sometimes present, talonid occupying one-half to nearly two-thirds occlusal surface, hypoconid and entoconid flanking deep talonid basin, postentoconulid indicated or absent, sample length 2.5, width 1.7.

Remarks. Molarization of the *Saguinus* pm_{3-4} is more advanced than in other callitrichids. Pm_3, however, may be more caninized in some individuals or species (cf. *S. fuscicollis*) and nearly or quite molarized in others (cf. *S. oedipus*). Pm_4 is completely molarized throughout the genus. Pm_2 remains dominantly caniniform in all living primates. The buccal cingulum is not ledgelike, and ectostyles are present in all premolars.

The deciduous lower premolars follow the same evolutionary trends as their successors. Dpm_4 is completely molarized, dpm_3 may be nearly or quite as complex, but the talonid basin in this tooth is still considerably smaller than the "trigonid" basin.

Molars

Upper molars, with *first molar* largest tooth of dental system, one and one-half to two times larger than second molar and up to nearly twice size of pm^4, occlusal surface subtriangular, trigon basin deeply conical, eocone (*1*) higher than protocone (*2*) but subequal in bulk, metacone (*4*) lower and smaller than eocone (*1*), protoloph (*III*) and plagiocrista (*IV*) strongly developed, epiconule (*c*) and plagioconule (*d*) present or absent, lingual cingula *B'* and *C* forming a broad and continuous shelf, a narrow talon basin (β) sometimes present, mesiostyle (*a*) and distostyle (*b*) present, a small ectostyle often present; *second molar* subrectangular, trapezoidal, or subtriangular, metacone considerably smaller than eocone, often reduced to stylar proportions or near obsolescence, cingula *B'* and *C* and talon basin as in first molar, distostyle and ectostyles not evident, mesiostyle usually present, epiconule weak or undeveloped, plagioconule present or absent, often hypertrophied, giving appearance of a small hypocone, tooth in line with either lingual or buccal border of first molar or set off from both borders.

Lower molars oblong, "trigonid" occupying anterior third of crown with elevated forward-sloping basin, talonid, forming remainder of crown, with deeply rounded basin; *first molar* suboblong, about one and one-fourth to one and one-third larger than last premolar, metaconid (*2*) as high as or higher than eoconid (*1*), crest of transverse epicristid (*II*) concave, often notched medially, paraconid (*3*) and mesiostylid (*a*) absent, a pseudoparaconid (*t*) often present, ledgelike buccal cingulid frequently present, ectostylid(s), usually including styloconid (*j*), more or less developed, hypoconid larger and often as high as eoconid but less elevated above crown base, entoconid (*5*) low, crest flat or slightly rounded, postentoconulid (*e*) hardly or not differentiated from entoconid, posterior border of talonid concave, sometimes notched medially; *second molar* like first but more nearly square, from two-thirds to three-fourths as large, "trigonid" basin often proportionately larger than in m_1, metaconid higher than eoconid, epicristid with deeply notched crest, entoconid usually low, rounded, and as high as and higher than hypoconid, postentoconulid poorly differentiated, ledgelike or rounded buccal cingulid sometimes present, posterior border of talonid often with slight concavity or distobuccal notch, distolingual cusp produced farther behind than distobuccal cusp.

Sample Measurements of Molars, Buccal Length × width

Saguinus oedipus

m^1	m^2	m_1	m_2
2.5 × 3.2	1.3 × 2.1	3.0 × 2.1	2.2 × 1.7
2.5 × 3.2	1.7 × 2.5	2.8 × 1.9	1.9 × 1.8
2.7 × 3.3	1.9 × 2.6	2.8 × 2.0	2.4 × 1.7
2.8 × 3.6	1.6 × 2.7	2.8 × 2.2	2.2 × 1.8
2.8 × 3.3	1.6 × 2.6	2.9 × 2.1	2.0 × 1.8

Saguinus fuscicollis

m^1	m^2	m_1	m_2
2.6 × 2.9	1.5 × 2.5	2.6 × 2.1	2.5 × 1.8
2.8 × 2.9	1.5 × 2.2	2.5 × 2.0	2.3 × 1.6
2.8 × 2.9	1.6 × 2.4	2.5 × 2.0	2.3 × 1.6

Remarks. Well-developed cingula, styles, and conules are more widespread in *Saguinus* than in other callitrichids. The bowing of the contour of the lower cheek teeth (curve of Spee) is more pronounced than in *Callithrix.*

The second molar tends to become secondarily smaller, the metacone being most reduced, sometimes to near obsolescence. In *Cebuella* and *Callithrix,* with primitive V-shaped mandibles, *outer* molar cusps are as high as or higher than the opposing inner cusps. In *Saguinus,* with U-shaped mandible and deep symphysis, *inner* cusps are equal to or slightly higher than outer cusps in the first molar and are consistently higher in the second molar.

External Genitalia

Male (figs. III.21–29; X.4, 18, 19)

Adult. Penis cylindrical, slightly tapered, and more or less pigmented, skin of stem smooth, rugose, corrugated or papillate, but without spines; glans not differentiated from stem, urinary meatus an oblique slit from right, left lobe of glans containing baculum larger and more projecting than right; scrotum subglobose, sessile, pedunculate or pendulous, and partially or not at all subdivided into a pair of testicular sacs; raphe usually pronounced; scrotal, or testicular, fold smooth, corrugated, or papillate, sparsely haired; outer surface of preputial fold usually like scrotal fold but often forming basic sheath, inner surface glabrous and ensheathing part of penial staff to entire penis; one or both testes often retracted in adult; sexual skin usually well developed and modified into a median pubic band or two parallel pubic ridges; perineal and anal regions pigmented, mottled, or unpigmented.

Female (figs. III.21–23; X.20)

Adult. Labia majora pigmented, mottled, or unpigmented and forming hairy glandular papillate cushions surrounding genital fissure; each labium subdivided into a posterior or scrotal fold of one (sometimes two or three) irregularly shaped pads, and an anterior or preputial fold with lateral surface hairy and medial surface glabrous with horse-shoe-shaped annulus attached to glans clitoridis by lateral or dorsal frenulum preputii; shape and relative size of unswollen preputial fold variable, the tumescent fold thick, usually larger than scrotal fold, and in extreme turgidity with rugi and convolutions smoothed out; mons pubis a pair of swellings formed distad to anterior union of preputial folds; glans clitoridis in some samples externally visible on plane of preputial annulus or mons, in others hidden within labial tissue; left lobe of glans separated from smaller right lobe by urethral groove; a frenulum clitoridis extends from each lobe along interior anterior rim of genital fissure; labia minora forming diagonally laminated walls of anterior two-thirds or more of vestibule; hymen distinct in young but not visible from exterior; sexual skin pigmented or unpigmented and defined as a broad band with a more or less continuous median line or furrow, or as two well-defined parallel ridges with deep interpubic valley; perineal and anal regions lightly pigmented or unpigmented.

Remarks. The female external genitalia of each of the recognized species groups of tamarins are distinctive. Present material is too limited in numbers and deficient in quality for evaluation of variation on specific and intraspecific levels. It seems, nevertheless, that selection for form, odor, and presentation of the female external genitalia and accessories plays a very important role in tamarin evolution.

Key to Tamarin Species Sections (figs. X.1, 2)

(Arranged from Key to Genera and Sections of Callitrichidae and Callimiconidae, p. 437)

1. Cheeks and sides of face from brow to ears covered with hair nearly like hair of forehead and crown 3

1′. Cheeks and sides of face from brow to ear naked or sparsely haired in sharp contrast with dense pelage of crown behind anterior plane of ears 2

2. Pelage of head, trunk, and limbs blackish or dark brown, tail uniformly dark, like back . . . . Mottled-face Tamarin (*Saguinus inustus*), p. 732

2′. Pelage of head, trunk, or limbs not blackish or dark brown, tail not uniformly dark . . . . Bare-face Tamarins (*Saguinus bicolor* and *oedipus* Groups), p. 735

3. Forehead and crown to level of ears covered with long hairs not markedly shorter or thinner than hairs of crown between ears; hind feet variously colored or, if whitish or buffy, without well-defined brown patch or spotting on ankle and metatarsus; hairs of throat and neck directed forward or straight back . . . . Hairy-Face Tamarins (*Saguinus nigricollis, mystax,* and *midas* Groups), p. 618

3′. Forehead and crown to level of ears covered with short silvery hairs in marked contrast with long brown hairs of crown between ears; upper surface of hind feet whitish or buffy with brown patch or spotting on ankle and metatarsus; hairs of angle between throat and neck forming a complete whorl . . . . Bare-face Tamarins (*Saguinus leucopus* [*S. oedipus* Group)], p. 748

59 *Saguinus*
2. *Hairy-face Tamarins: Characters, Taxonomy, Key to Species Groups*

Three closely related species groups make up the hairy-face tamarin section of the genus *Saguinus*. The "white-mouth" *Saguinus nigricollis* group with black facial skin is the most primitive. It comprises two species, *S. fuscicollis* and *S. nigricollis*. A subspecies of the latter, *S. n. graellsi,* stands so near the hypothetical ancestral form of the genus that all tamarins, hairy-face or bare-face, can be derived from its hypothetical immediate ancestor. The second or moustached tamarin group, with white-haired, unpigmented circumbuccal skin, is a specialized extension of the *S. nigricollis* group. It contains three species, *S. mystax, S. labiatus,* and *S. imperator*. The third group, with a single species, the black tamarin *S. midas,* is another offshoot of the primitive stock of the *S. nigricollis* group. It retains the black facial pigment but has lost the whitish circumbuccal band of hairs.

Hairy-face tamarins are distributed primarily in upper Amazonia, but the *midas* group is confined to the Guianean and lower Amazonian regions (fig. X.2). The hairy-face character is shared with *Cebuella,* most primitive of callitrichids, and *Callithrix jacchus. Callimico,* sometimes treated as a tamarin, is also hairy faced, but the pelage of the head is unique.

Diagnostic Characters

Pelage of head, body, limbs, and tail variously or contrastingly colored, or more or less uniformly whitish, the entire body never uniformly blackish or brown; skin bordering lips and surrounding or between nostrils entirely blackish, or unpigmented and strongly contrasted with uniformly pigmented skin of remaining parts of face; pelage around mouth inconspicuous or defined as a conspicuous gray to white band or produced into conspicuous white whiskers; temples, forehead, and crown well covered, the shorter hairs in front not markedly different from longer hairs posteriad except, often, in color; cheeks well covered with long hairs; distal half of hairs of posterior portion of back with one or two pheomelanic subterminal bands (agouti or modified agouti), never uniformly colored; tail with rufous base, remainder entirely black to brownish drab, whitish, or reddish, but never with dorsal surface of main portion sharply defined from ventral.

Taxonomy and Nomenclature

Differences between species and groups of hairy-face tamarins are superficial and of low taxonomic grade. The gap between the *nigricollis* group, with grayish circumbuccal band, and the *midas* group, without such a band, is bridged by juvenals of the latter, which retain the distinctive characters of the former. In a similar fashion, a tendency toward depigmentation of the circumbuccal skin in some individuals of the *S. nigricollis* group adumbrates the entirely depigmented condition in the *S. mystax* group. The moustache of the latter is already present in juvenals of the *S. nigricollis* group.

Apart from color and pelage patterns, no single character or combination of characters consistently distinguishes the species of any one group from each other or from species of other tamarin groups.

The redundant generic names proposed for hairy-face tamarins have had tortuous careers. Their complete history is abstracted in the annotated synonymy of the genus *Saguinus* (p. 600). The discussion follows.

Cercopithecus Gronovius, 1763, with originally included species, *the little black monkey* of Edwards (*Simia midas* Linnaeus) and the diagnoses and bibliographic references to *Simia morta* Linnaeus (= *Saimiri sciureus* Linnaeus), was adopted by Elliot (1911, p. 341) for tamarins with *Simia midas* designated type. The system of nomenclature used by Gronovius in his *Zoophylacium Gronovianum,* however, is nonbinomial, and a ruling by the International Commission on Zoological Nomenclature (Opinion 89, 1925) declared that technical names proposed therein are not available in zoological nomenclature.

Saguinus Hoffmannsegg, (Hoffmannsegg 1807, p. 102) is the earliest valid generic name for tamarins. It was proposed in the combination *Saguinus ursula* Hoffmannsegg and cited by all authors but was recognized by none until I did so in 1958. Perhaps previous authors regarded the name *Saguinus* as either a homonym or a junior synonym of *Sagoinus* Kerr, 1792, *Sagouin* Lacépède, 1799, *Sagoin* Desmarest, 1801, or *Saguin* Fischer. The original spelling of all these earlier derivatives of *sagui,* the Brazilian terms for little monkey, are different and therefore none is a homonym of any other. Furthermore, all of them are based on the common marmoset, *Simia jacchus* Linnaeus. Accordingly, all are synonyms of

Callithrix Erxleben, 1777, and none invalidates *Saguinus* Hoffmannsegg as the first properly proposed generic name for a tamarin.

Midas E. Geoffroy (1812), based on *Simia midas* Linnaeus, was the first name explicitly proposed for tamarins and distinguished from ouistitis or true marmosets, the *Jacchus* of E. Geoffroy (= *Callithrix* Erxleben), by their short, spatulate lower incisors and tusklike canines. Tamarins recognized by E. Geoffroy were *Midas rufimanus* E. Geoffroy (a new name for *Simia midas* Linnaeus, type by tautonomy), *M. ursulus* Hoffmannsegg, *M. labiatus* E. Geoffroy, *M. leoninus* Humboldt, and *M. oedipus* Linnaeus. The lion or golden tamarin, *M. rosalia* Linnaeus, also included with the tamarins, was later removed to another genus. *Midas* is antedated by *Saguinus* Hoffmannsegg and is a junior homonym of *Midas* Latreille, 1796, a genus of Diptera.

Tamarin Gray, 1870, with *Midas ursulus* E. Geoffroy (= *Saguinus ursula* Hoffmannsegg) type by monotypy, is a junior objective synonym of *Saguinus* Hoffmannsegg. The name was commonly used for hairy-face tamarins in general, but some authors restricted it to black tamarins only.

Leontocebus Wagner, 1840, originally proposed as a subgenus of *Hapale*, comprised the lion tamarin (*rosalia, chrysomelas, chrysopygus*), two bare-face tamarins (*bicolor, oedipus*), and Humboldt's saddle-back tamarin (*leonina* = *Saguinus fuscicollis fuscus*). Diagnostic characters of the subgenus were not given, but whatever Wagner may have had in mind in 1912 Miller (p. 280) designated *Simia leonina* Humboldt type. This species, long confused with the lion tamarins, was shown by Cabrera (1956, p. 49) and by Hershkovitz (1957, p. 17) to be a saddle-back tamarin. Thus, by virtue of the belated correct identification of its designated type species, *Leontocebus* Wagner falls as a junior subjective synonym of *Saguinus* Hoffmannsegg.

Mystax Gray, 1870, typified by *Midas mystax* Spix and the first name proposed for a moustached tamarin, is preoccupied by *Mystax* Stephens, 1829, a genus of caddis flies (Trichoptera).

Tamarinus Trouessart, 1904, with *Midas mystax* Spix designated type by Pocock in 1917 (p. 256), is valid and available. The name has been used by some authors as a genus or subgenus for all species of hairy-face tamarins and by others for "white-mouth" species only. The name has also been erroneously restricted to black tamarins.

Key to Hairy-face Tamarin Groups

1. Coat entirely whitish or yellowish white, naked parts of face, ears, hands, feet blackish .... *Saguinus nigricollis* group, part the albinotic *S. f. melanoleucus*, p. 664)

1′. Coat variously colored, never entirely whitish or blackish 2

2. White or grayish band encircling mouth; head, mantle, chest, belly, and tail variously colored, whitish frontal band or patch present or absent 3

2′. No white or grayish band encircling mouth; mantle, chest, belly, and tail blackish; whitish frontal band or patch absent .... *Saguinus midas* group (p. 706)

3. Skin around lips and between or around nostrils unpigmented (flesh-colored) and covered with whitish hairs; whiskers of upper lip well defined, often elongated; mantle (long hairs of nape, shoulders, and upper arms) brown or blackish with silvery or buffy ticking or mottling and hardly or not defined from middle back; whitish frontal band or patch absent .... *S. mystax* group, p. 684

3′. Skin around lips and nostrils uniformly black or brown and covered with short grayish hairs; whiskers undefined (except in juvenals); mantle variously colored (black, reddish, orange, yellowish) and more or less defined from middle or lower back; whitish frontal band or patch present or absent ... *Saguinus nigricollis* group, p. 620

60 *Saguinus nigricollis* Group, White-mouth Tamarins: *1. History, Characters, Evolution, and Key to Species*

Included species—nigricollis Spix, *fuscicollis* Spix.

Synonymic History

From about 1957 to about 1966, when the *Saguinus nigricollis* group was formally defined (Hershkovitz 1966*a*), most authors used the blanket name *nigricollis* or simply "marmoset" for "white-lipped" tamarins of the species *Saguinus nigricollis* Spix and *S. fuscicollis* Spix. In some cases the study animals were undoubtedly representative of *Saguinus nigricollis nigricollis;* in others, of one or more races of *S. fuscicollis.* In still other cases, especially in reports on biomedical research, *S. nigricollis, S. fuscicollis,* and *S. oedipus* were lumped under the term "marmoset" or the generic name *Saguinus* alone. Bibliographic references to equivocal identifications are cited below under the generic name or the binomials used by their respective authors. References to study animals unequivocably identified to species or subspecies are listed under the corresponding species or subspecies heading.

Page references to all scientific names and authors cited in the synonymies and text will be found in the corresponding index.

Tamarinus nigricollis, Osman Hill, 1957, *Primates* 3:168, 182, 206, 211–27, 232, 242, fig. 32 (hypophysis), figs. 52, 53 (external genitalia)—PERU: *Loreto* (Pebas); anatomy; characters; taxonomy; distribution; comparisons; not *purillus* Thomas in synonymy. Beath and Benirschke, 1962, *Cytologia* 27(1):1, figs. 1, 10 (sex chromatin)—location of sex chromatin. Gengozian, Batson, and Smith, 1962, *Proc. Int. Symp. Bone Marrow Therapy, Chem., Protection Irradiated Primates,* p. 245—use in laboratory. Sandler and Stone, 1963, *Psychol. Rep.* 13:139—care and treatment in laboratory. Levy, 1963, *Nature* 200:182—induction of fibrosarcoma with 2 methylcholanthrene in 1 of 5 tamarins. Dunn, 1963, *J. Parasit.* 49:718—PERU; helminth parasites (*Prosthenorchis elegans, Hymenolepis* sp.). Dunn and Lambrecht, 1963, *J. Helminth.* 37:261—PERU; filarial parasite (*Tetrapetalonema tamarinae,* new species). Dunn, Lambrecht, and Du Plessis, 1963, *Amer. J. Trop. Med., Hyg.* 12(4):524—PERU; trypanosome infection. Richart and Benirschke, 1963, *J. Pathol. Bacteriol.* 86 (1):221–23—causes of death in laboratory colony (pneumonia; periorbital cellulitis; cystitis; septicemia). Benirschke and Richart, 1963, *Lab. Animal Care* 13(2):73—vulvar odor; reproduction in captivity; care in laboratory. Mirand, Prentice, and Grace, 1964, *Nature* 204(4963):1064—production of and response to erythropoietin (EPF). Levy and Artecona, 1964, *Lab. Animal Care* 14(1):20, fig. 1 (*Saguinus fuscicollis leucogenys*)—laboratory care. Gengozian, Batson, and Eide, 1964, *Cytogenetics* 3:384—hematopoietic chimerism. Holmes, Caldwell, Dedmon, and Deinhardt, 1964, *J. Immunol.* 92(4):602—isolation and description of *Herpesvirus tamarinus.* Inglis and Dunn, 1964, *Z. Parasitenk.* 24(1):83—nematode, *Trypanoxyuris* (*Paraoxyuronema*) [*Hapaloxyuris*] *tamarini* Inglis and Dunn, 1964). Ge*asitology* 55:732—PERU; pinworm infection (*Trypanoxuris tamarini,* new species. Inglis and Cosgrove, 1965, *Par*ngozian, 1966, *Nature* 209:722—isohemagglutinin formation. Gengozian, Lushbaugh, Humason, and Knisely, 1966, *Nature* 209(5024):731—erythroblastosis fetalis. Gengozian, 1966, *Fed. Proc.* 25:435—isohemagglutinin formation. Wohnus and Benirschke, 1966, *Cytogenetics* 5:94—chromosome idiogram. Nelson, Cosgrove, and Gengozian, 1966, *Lab. Animal Care* 16(3):255—infections, diseases of imported individuals (*Prosthenorchis* [Acanthecephala], fungi, sarcocystis; neoplasm suggesting lymphocitic leukemia; probably osteomalasia; peritonitis; pneumonia). Kelemen, 1966, *Acta Oto-laryng.* 61: 239—aural pathology. Stahl and Gummerson, 1966, *Growth* 31:21—analysis and comparisons of relative size-change rates in tamarins, *Saimiri, Cercopithecus, Macaca, Papio.* Hunt, Garcia, and Hegsted, 1966, *Fed. Proc.* 25(2):Abstract—vitamin D requirement.

T[*amarinus*] *nigricollis,* J. K. Hampton, Jr. and Hampton, 1965, *Science* 150:915—breeding seasons, twinning; sex ratios.

Saguinus (*Saguinus*) *nigricollis*, Rabb and Rowell, 1960, *J. Mammal.* 31:401—umbilical cords of twins attached to separate discoidal placentae.

Saguinus nigricollis, Fooden, 1961, *Zoologica* 46:167—chromatography and systematic analyses of urinary amino-acid excretions. J. Deinhardt, Devine, Passovoy, Pohlman, and Deinhardt, 1967, *Lab. Animal Care* 17(1):11—care and pathology of laboratory animals. Anderson, Lewis, Passovoy, and Trobaugh 1967, *Lab. Animal Care* 17(1):37—karyotype (2n = 46); hematology.

Leontocebus nigricollis, Chiarelli, 1963, *Folia Primat.* 1:91—taste sensitivity to phenylthiocarbamide. Mallinson, 1965, *Int. Zoo Yearbk.* 5:139—premature birth of twins, March 1964; tongue display; cage paralysis cured with D_3. Dubois, 1966, *Rev. Suisse Zool.* 75:37—neodipoostome parasite (Trematoda, Diplostomatidae). Dumond, 1967, *Int. Zoo Yearbk.* 7:206—semifree ranging colony in Miami, Florida; habits; habitat.

The following citations refer to species of the *Saguinus nigricollis* group and in some, if not all cases, to *Saguinus oedipus* as well.

Saguinus sp., Holmes and Capps, 1966, *Medicine* 45(6):553—transmission of human viral hepatitis to tamarin and from tamarin to tamarin. Holmes, Devine, Nowakowski, and Deinhardt 1966, *J. Immunol.* 90(4):668—epidemiology of *Herpesvirus tamarinus*. F. Deinhardt, 1966, *Nature* 210:443—induction of neoplasms by Rous sarcoma virus. F. Deinhardt, 1967, *Perspectives in virology* 5:183, figs. 1, 2 (tumor at inoculation site) figs. 3, 4 (section of tumor), figs. 5, 6 (brain tumor), fig. 7 (lung tumor), fig. 8 (karyotype, normal), figs. 9–11 (chromosomal aberrations), fig. 12 (tamarins = *Saguinus fuscicollis*).

[*Saguinus* spp.], Schur and Holmes, 1965, *Proc. Soc. Exp. Biol. Med.* 119:950–52—virus susceptibility of kidney cell cultures. Holmes, Passovoy, and Capps, 1967, *Lab. Animal Care* 17(1):41—blood chemistry; liver structure and function. Holmes, Wolfe, Rosenblate, and Deinhardt, 1969, *Science* 165:816—induction of hepatitis from human volunteers.

Distribution (figs. X.2, 15)

Upper Amazonian region from the Rio Madeira south of the Amazonas and the Rio Japurá (Caquetá) north of the Amazonas in Brazil, west to the eastern slopes of the Andes in Colombia, Ecuador, Peru, and Bolivia; altitudinal range from near sea level to 1,200 meters above.

Saguinus fuscicollis is distributed over most of the range of the *S. nigricollis* Group. *S. nigricollis graellsi* is almost entirely sympatric with *S. fuscicollis lagonotus* in the northwestern portion of the group range. *S. nigricollis nigricollis* seems to be isolated, but *S. fuscicollis tripartitus* or a closely related form may share at least part of its range.

Origin, Evolution, and Dispersal

The color and pelage patterns of *Saguinus nigricollis graellsi* are most primitive for the *nigricollis* group and the genus *Saguinus*. The geographic position of Graell's tamarin and its sympatry with two races of *Saguinus fuscicollis* (*lagonotus* and *tripartitus*) suggest that it may be no more than a slightly differentiated relict of the erstwhile widely distributed ancestral stock from which *S. fuscicollis* and other living tamarins arose.

The ancestral tamarin must have been hairy faced and nearly uniformly agouti-colored throughout, except perhaps for a eumelanized distal portion of the tail and a somewhat extended grizzling about the mouth. It need not have differed significantly in size and proportions from the smallest of living tamarins.

Evolution of modern *Saguinus nigricollis graellsi* from the postulated ancestral tamarin requires only a small increase in size, slight saturation of crown, mantle, upper surface of hands and feet, greater spread of black on tail, expanded blanching of the circumoral region, and a slight bleaching of the temporal region. *Saguinus nigricollis nigricollis* can be easily derived from a *graellsi* prototype by more intensive eumelanization of the forequarters.

Modification of the middorsal agouti of the ancestral tamarin pattern results in the trizonal or saddle-back pattern diagnostic of *S. fuscicollis* (figs. X.16, 17).

Center of origin and dispersal of the progenitor of the *nigricollis* group was perhaps along the eastern Andean base in southern Peru or northern Bolivia. Establishment of suitable habitats progressively from upper to lower reaches of the Amazonian streams permitted spread of the species, while shifting water beds promoted divergence through isolation. Dispersal along the eastern base of the Cordillera Oriental itself may have been spasmodic because of active volcanism and consequent instability of habitats. Numerous locally differentiated populations must have arisen, but connecting forms reside at lower altitudes in the same river basins.

In general, conditions were optimum for rapid and radiating evolution. Four main lines persist today. *Saguinus nigricollis graellsi* is very near the hypothetical ancestral tamarin; *S. n. nigricollis* is a collateral offshoot. *Saguinus fuscicollis*, a second line, is most variable and may be more recent in origin. The third line from the same or a similar ancestral type is that of the sympatric and more highly evolved *S. mystax* group. The fourth line, *Saguinus midas*, is most distant geographically from the ancestral seat and, except for loss of the whitish circumbuccal whiskers and greater expansion of the aural pinna, is very much like *S. fuscicollis*.

Diagnostic Characters

Facial skin, rhinarium, ears, and external genitalia blackish; cheeks, temples, forehead, and crown densely covered with long hairs; broad circumbuccal band thickly haired whitish and not encircling muzzle; long and conspicuous moustache absent in adults; ears thinly haired

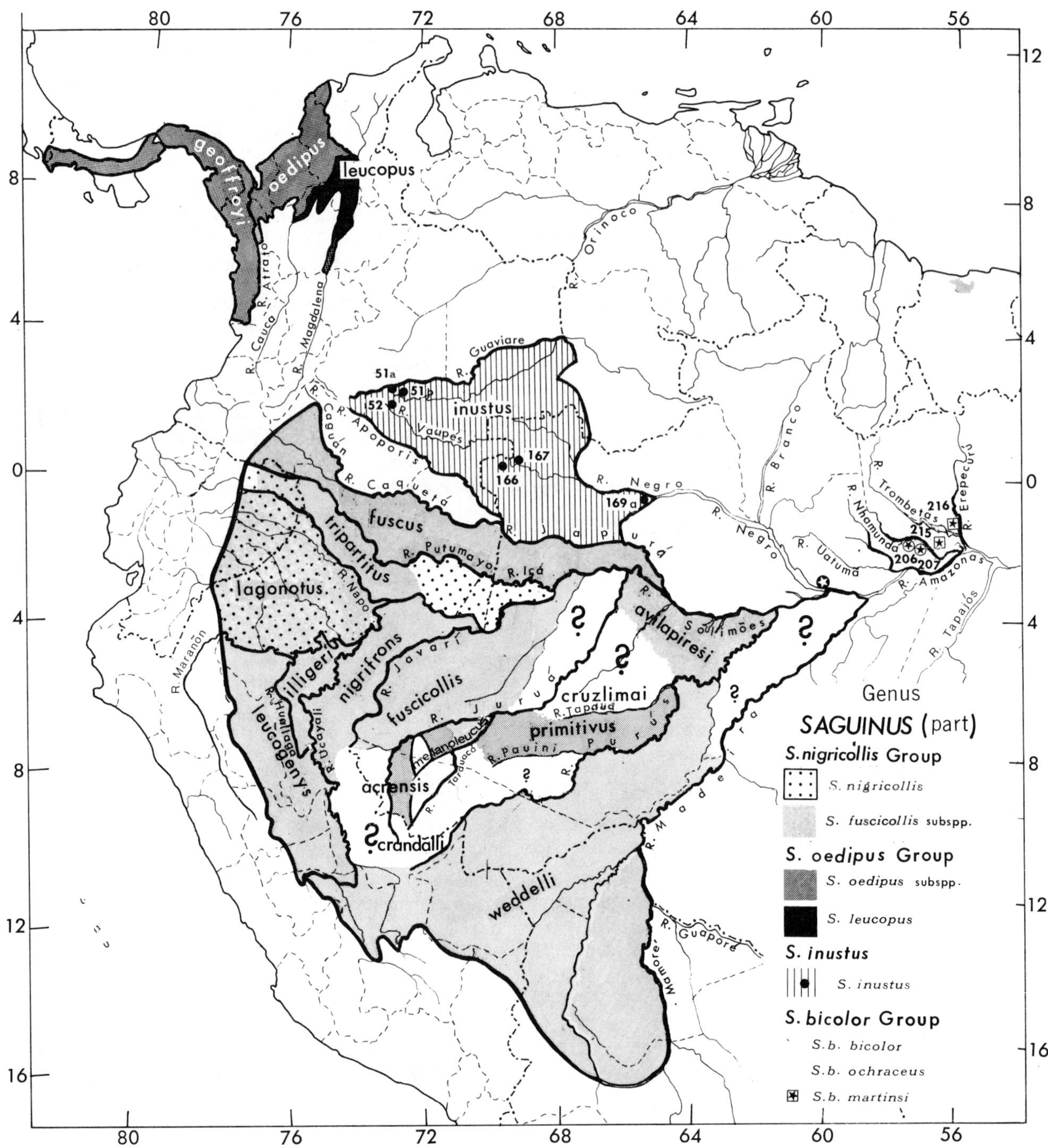

Fig. X.15. Distribution of the subspecies of the Hairy-face Saddle-back Tamarin (*Saguinus fuscicollis*), Bare-face Tamarins of the *S. oedipus* and *S. bicolor* groups, and the Mottled-face Tamarin (*S. inustus*). River boundaries between species and subspecies boldly defined; symbols show locality records for *S. inustus* and *S. bicolor* groups (see maps, fig. XIII.2, 34 and gazetteer, p. 918, for key to numbered and other collecting localities).

and mostly or entirely exposed, not concealed by mane or preauricular tufts; color of middle or lower back more or less well defined from shoulders; terminal half or more of tail uniformly colored, not banded, barred, or with nearly entire dorsal surface sharply defined from ventral.

External Characters (figs. X.16, 17)

Integument.

Facial skin, including circumoral and narial regions, black or brownish; wide band surrounding mouth covered with short grayish hairs, the gray extending dorsad as a patch on each side of nose. Short hairs of dorsal surface of muzzle directed backward without feathering or forming a median crest; hairs of cheeks, temples, forehead, and crown long but not forming a mane; hairs of interramia and throat directed straight back without crests or whorls; contrastingly colored interorbital, superciliary, frontal or temporal bands or patches present or absent; contrastingly colored crown patch normally absent; ears thinly haired and well exposed, not mostly or entirely concealed by a mane; color pattern of dorsal surface from nape to base of tail in all except extremely

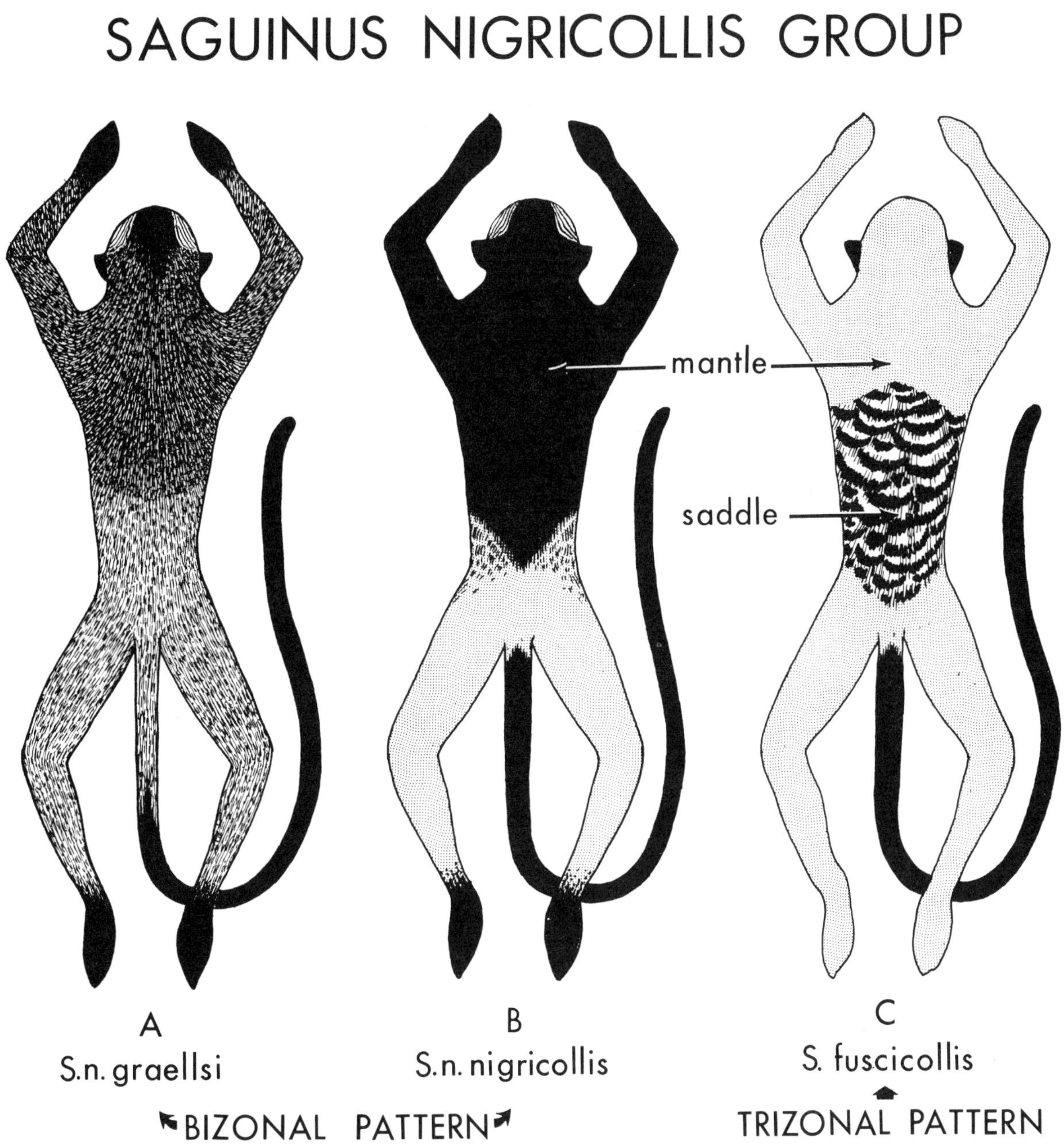

SAGUINUS NIGRICOLLIS GROUP

mantle

saddle

A
S.n. graellsi

B
S.n. nigricollis

C
S. fuscicollis

BIZONAL PATTERN

TRIZONAL PATTERN

Fig. X.16. Dorsal color patterns in *Saguinus nigricollis* group: Bizonal in *S. nigricollis* and trizonal in *S. fuscicollis*. (After Hershkovitz 1966*b*.)

Saguinus nigricollis Group

S. fuscicollis *S. nigricollis*

Fig. X.17. Basic facial color patterns in *Saguinus nigricollis* group. *S. nigricollis* with contrasting pale brown temporal and genal regions; *S. fuscicollis* variable (cf. fig. X.27), but not as in *S. nigricollis*. (After Hershkovitz 1966*b*.)

bleached or albinotic forms of *Saguinus fuscicollis*, either *bizonal*, that is, with forequarters dark and defined from hindquarters, or *trizonal*—with marbled or striated saddle of middle or posterior back more or less distinct from rump and well defined from mantle of nape and shoulders; sides of body generally like back; underparts variable; terminal one-half or more of tail more or less uniformly black, drab, gray, yellowish or white, not banded, barred, or bicolor; external genitalia mostly or entirely pigmented.

Juvenal Coat. See chapter 8 and p. 672.

Vibrissae. See chapter 9.

Ears (Chap. 12). Thinly haired and well exposed, not mostly or entirely concealed by a mane.

External Genitalia

Male (figs. X.4, 18, 19)

Adult. External genitalia mostly or entirely pigmented; penis pigmented, cylindrical, slightly tapered distally, glans undifferentiated from shaft with left, or bacular, lobe larger and more projecting than right, penial integument papillate or corrugated and without spines; scrotum pigmented, sessile or pedunculate without clear separation into testicular sacs, skin corrugated, the scrotal, or testicular, fold sparsely covered with long blackish bristles except for somewhat thicker tufts on raphe; outer surface of preputial fold corrugated and sparsely haired, inner surface, or sheath, glabrous and, in fully adult, forming two corrugated annular folds concealing all but glans of penis; width of scrotum with both testes, 21 mm; sexual skin differentiated as broad, usually pigmented and unctious median pubic band; perineal and anal regions lightly pigmented or unpigmented.

Juvenal and Subadult. External genitalia generally mottled or unpigmented; in newborn, preputial sheath and paired scrotal folds appear as independent pigmented fields or swellings; preputial folds develop after scrotal folds and coalesce with them to form scrotal pouch before initial descent of testes; sexual skin unpigmented in

Saguinus nigricollis nigricollis

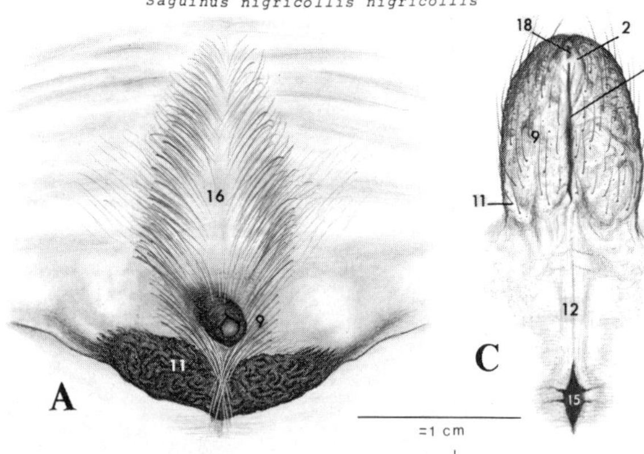

Fig. X.18. External genitalia of *Saguinus nigricollis*. *A*, juvenal scrotum incompletely developed, testes undescended; *B*, adult, right testes retracted, sexual skin (*16*) pigmented; *C*, female circumgenital region, urethral groove (*4*) overgrown by surrounding tissue except for persistence of urethral orifice (*18*) at apex of glans clitoridis (*2*), scrotal fold of labia majora not certainly differentiated from preputial fold. See p. 113 for identification of all external genital parts.

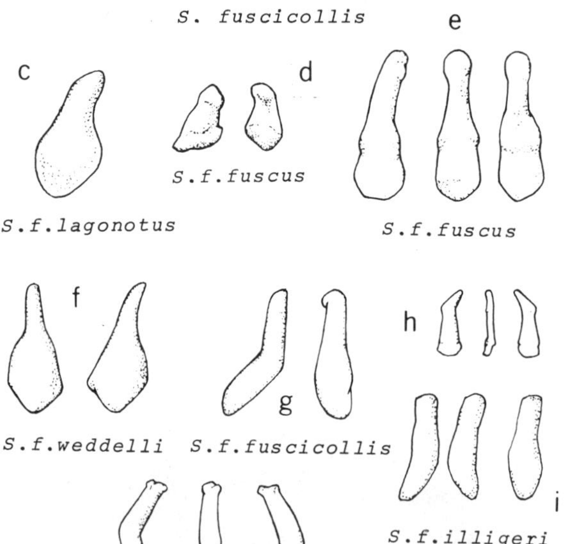

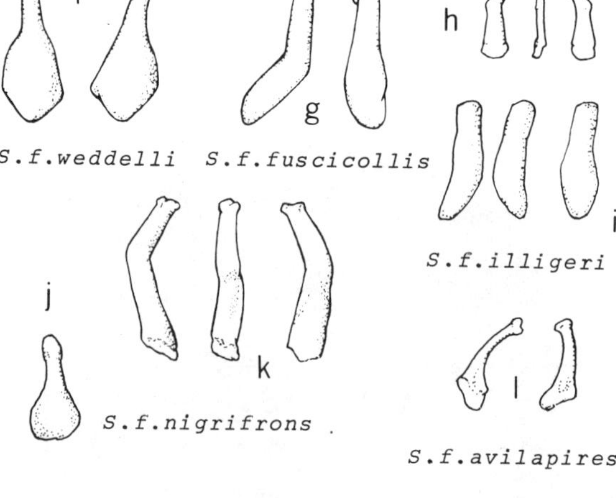

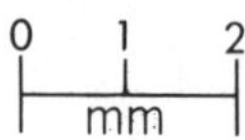

Fig. X.19. *Saguinus nigricollis* group: Bacula of species and most subspecies; each bone labeled with one to three aspects shown of each; differences between samples are individual variables; compare the two bones of *S. f. illigeri* (*h, i*) and those of *S. f. nigrifrons* (*j, k*).

juvenal, its triangular outline defined by inwardly directed brownish hairs.

Remarks. The penis is more completely ensheathed by the preputial folds and one or both testes are more commonly retracted in the *Saguinus nigricollis* group than in other callitrichids; mature external male genitalia with fully retracted testes, completely withdrawn penis, and large preputial annulus resemble the corresponding female organs in tamarins of the *oedipus, mystax,* and *midas* groups.

Female (fig. X.20)

Adult. Labia majora mostly to entirely pigmented, and uniting to form an ovate cushion; skin densely papillate, each papilla with a long stiff black hair and often with a finer hair on each side; scrotal fold in some samples little or not differentiated from preputial fold, in others well defined on posterior half of labium and often subdivided into two or three small pads; posterior labial commissure frequently extended caudally to anus as a thick raphe; preputial folds meeting above clitoris in a well-rounded mons; glans clitoridis may be well defined and visible externally, fused with glabrous annulus of preputial fold, or hidden in labial tissue; urethral groove often overgrown by surrounding tissue except for persistence of small urethral orifice at apex of glans; frenula of clitoris and prepuce usually fused with surrounding tissues; lamina of labia minora not always well marked; external genitalia 12–16 mm long in 6 adults, genital fissure 11–13 mm; pubic sexual skin a long broad pigmented band with median furrow; perineal and anal regions lightly to deeply pigmented, or mottled.

Juvenal. External genitalia unpigmented or slightly mottled in very young, more heavily pigmented in subadults; transverse furrow between scrotal and preputial folds often present and usually well defined; glans clitoridis and frenula usually distinct but often fused with surrounding tissues as in adults.

Cranial Characters (figs. X.6–12)

Frontal contour comparatively low; temporal ridges more or less parallel sided or slightly convergent or divergent but not fusing into a sagittal crest; nasal profile plane to slightly concave; frontal sinuses slightly to moderately inflated; malar foramen from 1 to 2 mm in greatest diameter but usually less than 1 mm; ventral border of mandible more U- than V-shaped. The horizontal rami distended to well arced, the angular process inflected inward and slightly to considerably deflected downward.

Comparisons

Distinguished externally from bare-face species of the genus *Saguinus* by densely hirsute cheeks, temples,

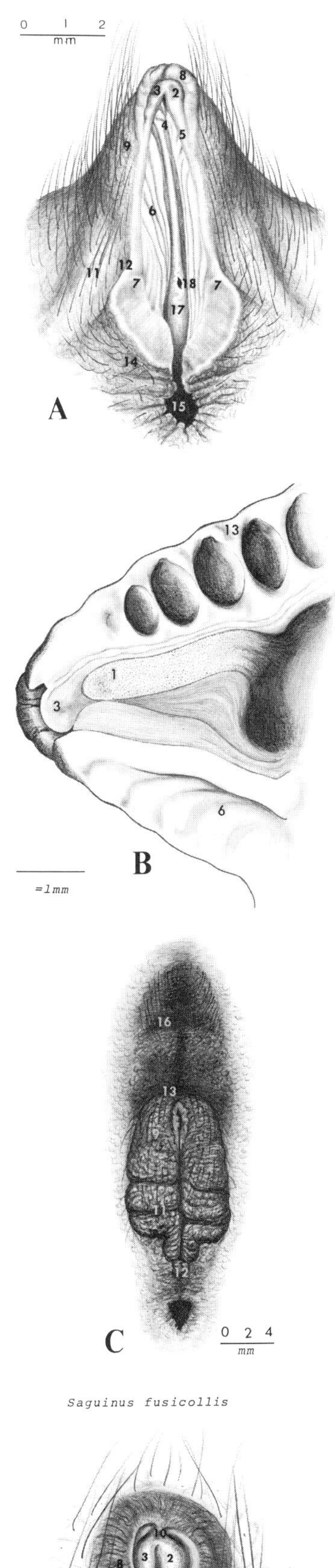

Fig. X.20. External genitalia of female *Saguinus fuscicollis. A,* adult with perineal region sectioned through labial commissure and frenulum labiorum (*7*) to expose hymen (*17*) and urethral orifice (*18*); *B,* juvenal, cross section through vulva to show glandular cells on mons pubis (*13*); *C,* adult with bilobed labia majora (*11*); *D,* juvenal, anterior portion of genitalia; for names of all parts see pp. 113–14.

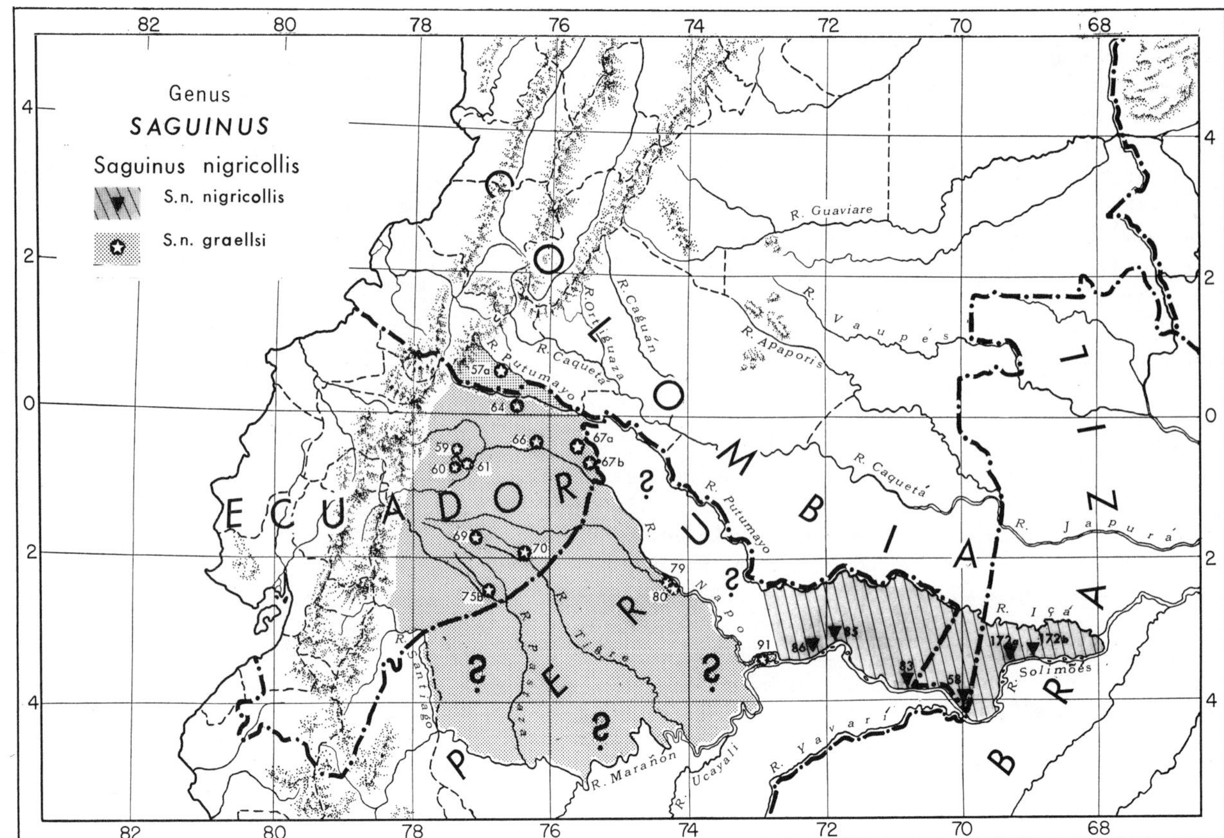

Fig. X.21. Distribution of the subspecies of the Hairy-face Black-mantle Tamarin, *Saguinus nigricollis*: Symbols show locality records (see gazetteer, p. 918, for key to numbers).

and forehead, from the *S. midas* group and *Callimico* by a broad grayish circumbuccal band, from the *Saguinus mystax* group by fully pigmented skin of circumbuccal and narial regions and by more or less well-defined bizonal or trizonal color patterns of dorsum; from larger *Leontopithecus* and the smaller, mouse-sized, pygmy marmoset *Cebuella* by size, fully exposed ears, and absence of well-defined mane; from the various species of *Callithrix* by the combination of blackish skin of face, ears, volar surfaces, and external genitalia, absence of aural and circumaural tufts, tail more or less uniformly colored, at least on terminal half, and other characters detailed above and elsewhere.

Variation

There is no significant difference in size and proportions among the species of the group. Color and color pattern are the only variables of taxonomic value.

Sexual dimorphism, apart from the usual gross differences in the reproductive organs and sexual skin, is not evident. Age variation is described in the species accounts. In general, however, the young show the expected neotonous characters absent in adults of the same species but present in adults of related, more advanced species. Pale or unpigmented facial skin and volar surfaces and long white whiskers or muttonchops are examples of such characters.

Saturation and Bleaching

Eumelanistic saturation is established at least on forehead, terminal three-fourths of tail, and upper surface of hind feet in both species but not all races of the *nigricollis* group. The nearly extreme bleaching, or albinism, around the mouth persists in all living members of the group and was probably not less than incipient in the ancestral form. Bleaching progresses at different rates on other parts of the body through various tones of brown, reddish, orange, yellow, and white. Blanching often appears full bloom as a frontal blaze but progresses gradually on mantle and along tail. Detailed descriptions of saturation and bleaching processes are given in the separate species accounts.

Key to Species of the *Saguinus nigricollis* Group (figs. X.16, 17)

1. Body entirely whitish or yellowish white, naked parts of face, ears, hands, and feet blackish .... *S. fuscicollis* (part, the albinotic *S. f. melanoleucus* (p. 664)

1′. Body variously colored, never entirely whitish or blackish 2

2. Color of dorsum from nape to base of tail two-zoned (fig. X.16); the blackish or buffy to brownish agouti mantle (nape and shoulders) more or less defined from or merging with reddish or brownish hindquarters (lower back, rump, root of tail, outerside of thighs); middle back not forming a color zone or saddle; contrastingly pale brown patch present on each side of forehead (fig. X.17); whitish transverse frontal band or blaze absent .... *S. nigricollis* (p. 628)

2′. Color of dorsum from nape to base of tail three-zoned (fig. X.16), the saddle of middle and lower back marbled, striated, or vermiculated and defined from forequarters (including mantle) and hindquarters (rump, root of tail, outer sides of thighs); contrastingly pale brownish temporal patches absent (fig. X.17); whitish transverse frontal band or blaze present or absent .... *S. fuscicollis* (p. 634)

61 *Saguinus nigricollis* Spix, Black-mantle Tamarins

Distribution (fig. X.21)

The north bank of the Rio Amazonas, from the Rio Içа-Putumayo in Brazil, west to the Río Santiago and foothills of the Cordillera Oriental in Peru, Ecuador, and Colombia.

For information on the biology of the species, see page 667.

Key to the Subspecies of *Saguinus nigricollis*

1. Mantle agouti or melanoagouti and truncate or tapered behind; lower back, rump, thighs, and underparts dominantly olivaceous or buffy brown (fig. X.16) .... *S. n. graellsi* (p. 628)

1′. Mantle uniformly black and tapered behind; lower back, rump, thighs dominantly reddish or mahogany, underparts reddish, more or less mixed with black (fig. X.16) .... *S. n. nigricollis* (p. 628)

SAGUINUS NIGRICOLLIS GRAELLSI JIMENEZ DE LA ESPADA: GRAELL'S BLACK-MANTLE TAMARIN

Fig. X.22. Graell's Black-mantle Tamarin, *Saguinus nigricollis graellsi* Jiménez de la Espada. Photo courtesy of the New York Zoological Society.

Synonymic History

Midas Graellsi Jiménez de la Espada, 1870, *Bol. Rev. Univ. Madrid,* p. 57. Jiménez de la Espada, 1871, *J. Sci. Math. Phys. Nat. Acad. Real Sci. Lisboa* 2:57—PERU: *Loreto* (Río Napo near Tarapoto and Destacamento); local name, *uxpa chichico.* Martínez y Saez, 1898, *Anal. Soc. Española Hist. Nat., Madrid,* ser. 2, 7:215—listed; [account includes biographical sketch of Jiménez de la Espada].

M[idas] Graellsi, Cabrera, 1900, *Anal. Soc. Española Hist. Nat.* ser. 2, 9:90, fig. 2 (skull)—PERU: *Loreto* (*Tarapoto; Destacamento, Río Napo*); local name, *uxpa chichico* (= ashy tamarin).

Midas graellsi, Lönnberg, 1913, *Ark. Zool., Stockholm* 8(16):1—ECUADOR: *Napo-Pastaza* (Río Napo). Lönnberg, 1921, *Ark. Zool., Stockholm* 14(4):9—ECUADOR: *Napo-Pastaza* (Río Napo).

L[eontocebus] graellsi, Cabrera, 1912, *Trab. Mus. Cienc. Nat., Madrid*, no. 11:29—4 cotypes in Madrid Museum; classification.

Leontocebus graellsi, Elliot, 1913, *A review of the Primates* 1:208—characters. Cabrera, 1917, *Trab. Mus. Cienc. Nat., Madrid*, ser. zool., no. 31:32—PERU: *Loreto* (Tarapoto; Destacamento). Cabrera, 1958, *Rev. Mus. Argentino Cienc. Nat. "Bernardino Rivadavia"* 4(1):192—classification.

Tamarin graellsi, Cruz Lima, 1945, *Mamíferos da Amazonia, Primates*, p. 222—characters ex Jiménez de la Espada.

Marikina graellsi, Hershkovitz, 1949, *Proc. U.S. Nat. Mus.* 98:413—key characters; classification.

Mystax graellsi, Crandall, 1951, *Animal Kingdom* 54:179, 184, fig. (animal)—ECUADOR: *Napo-Pastaza* (Río Napo, "left bank").

Tamarinus graellsi, Osman Hill, 1957, *Primates* 3:218, 221, 230, 232, 233, pl. 12 (animal)—characters; distribution; comparisons.

Saguinus graellsi, Hershkovitz, 1966, *Folia Primat.* 4:383, fig. 2A (color pattern), fig. 3A (head)—characters; comparisons; distribution.

Saguinus nigricollis graellsi, Hershkovitz, 1970, *Am. J. Phys. Anthrop.* 32:379—classification; dental disease.

Types. Four cotypes, nos. 643 ♂, 644 ♂, 866 ♂, and 867, originally in the Museo Nacional de Ciencias Naturales, Madrid; collected June and July 1865 by Marcos Jiménez de la Espada, on the Viaje del Pacífico, 1862–65; no. 644, mounted with skull in, is presently in the Mammal Hall of the Madrid Museum; no. 866, skin and skull, was presented to the British Museum (Natural History) and registered as no. 25.7.1.2.

Type Locality. Banks of Río Napo near Tarapoto (79) (cotypes 644, 866, 867), and Destacamento (91), near confluence with the Marañon, Loreto, Peru (no. 643); restricted to Tarapoto by Cabrera (1958, *Rev. Mus. Argentino Cienc. Nat. "Bernardino Rivadavia"* 4:192); here further restricted to right bank Río Napo, opposite Tarapoto and above the mouth of the Río Curaray (80).

Distribution (fig. X.22). Upper Amazonian basin, from the Ríos Putumayo-Guamués, south central Colombia, south through Ecuador and Peru to the Marañon, west to the Río Pastaza, possibly to the Río Santiago and slopes of the Cordillera Oriental; eastern limits of the range between the Ríos Napo and Putumayo in Ecuador and Peru, unknown; altitudinal range between 100 and 1,000 meters above sea level.

The Olallas collected both *S. n. graellsi* and *S. fuscicollis tripartitus* (see p. 658) in January 1926 at Lagarto Cocha, Río Aguarico, and *graellsi* alone higher up at several localities between the Río Napo and its left-bank tributary the Río Coca. This data may have led Cordier (as reported by Crandall 1951, p. 184) to surmise that *graellsi* is restricted to the left bank of the Río Napo. However, abundant material from the Río Tigre (95) and Río Pastaza basins leave no doubt of the presence of *graellsi* on the right bank of the Napo, perhaps as far west as the Cordillera Oriental. Thus, the range of *S. n. graellsi* overlaps that of *S. fuscicollis lagonotus* and part, at least, of the range of *S. fuscicollis tripartitus.*

The presence of *Saguinus nigricollis graellsi* in Colombia on the right bank of the Río Guamués (57a), just above its mouth on the south bank of the Río Putumayo, was communicated to me by Dr. Martin H. Moynihan.

Diagnostic Characters. Dorsal coloration bizonal, head, neck, mantle, forelimbs blackish to blackish brown finely ticked with gray or buffy; temporal patches pale brown; back agouti with rump and thighs undifferentiated from posterior half of back, the whole coarsely mixed buffy and black, but darker anteriorly than posteriorly.

Coloration. Foreparts including head, mantle, forelimbs, throat, neck, and chest brown to blackish, the hairs black, brown or drab basally, blackish or blackish brown terminally except for one or two fine buffy rings; temporal patch light brown the paler color often extending over cheeks; facial skin blackish, hairs around mouth and sides of nostrils gray; middle and lower back evenly ticked blackish and buffy or ochraceous buff, the general effect olivaceous agouti with middle back darker than lower; lateral fringe like back; rump and legs like lower back or more buffy; upper surface of hands and feet black; belly brownish; skin of external genitalia mostly or entirely black; tail black except basal portion like rump or thighs with agouti of ventral surface often extending one-third to one-half length of tail.

Measurements. See appendix table 2.

Vibrissae. Supraorbitals, mystacials, rhinarials, mentals, and posteriorly directed interramals present, genals randomly distributed; ulnar carpals present; gular spines present, pectoral absent.

Young. Unknown.

Comparisons (fig. X.16, 17). The pale brown temporal patches and bizonal dorsal coloration, that is, blackish-brown anterior portion and olivaceous or brownish agouti posterior portion (back, rump, and thighs), separate *graellsi* from the trizonally patterned *S. fuscicollis,* but the dark agouti underparts are very similar to those of *S. fuscicollis avilapiresi;* distinguished from *S. nigricollis nigricollis,* its nearest relative, by softer pelage, finely punctulated mantle and arms, olivaceous or brownish-agouti, not reddish, back and hindquarters, and by the brown agouti pelage of underparts, the hairs with blackish and buffy annulations.

Variation. The dominantly agouti coloration of *S. n. graellsi* and its comparatively small geographic range limit geographic variation to the greater or lesser degree of saturation or eumelanization of the coat, particularly the mantle, and bleaching of the temples and cheeks. The longer, thicker pelage of *graellsi* as compared with that of *nigricollis* may be attributed to its slightly cooler and considerably more humid habitat.

Saturation and Bleaching. Saturation or melanism in *graellsi* is most strongly expressed on the tail, but much of the primitive agouti pattern is still retained on most of its proximal half. In many individuals the basal portions of the otherwise black hairs are agouti throughout most of the tail's length. The blackish crown, mantle, forelimbs, throat, and neck still retain some of the annulations of the primitive agouti pattern.

Bleaching is manifested on the temporal regions as brown patches which often extend onto the cheeks. The general coloration of many individuals also tends to be erythristic or reddish brown agouti as contrasted with the more common olivaceous or olive brown agouti. The tail of a browner than usual immature (FMNH 31111) from "Rio Napo abajo" has a mixture of gray and dark brown hairs, with those of the penciled tip mostly gray. This coloration is not very different from that of albinotic forms such as *S. fuscicollis crandalli.*

Specimens Examined. 84. ECUADOR—*Napo-Pastaza:* Avila, 2 (BM, 1; USNM, 1); Lagarto Cocha, mouth, 1 (AMNH); Río Capihuara, 2 (FMNH, 1; USNM, 1); Río Curaray, mouth, 19 (AMNH); Río Pindo Yacu, 2 (FMNH); Río Suno, below Loreto, 27 (AMNH, 17; BM, 7; FMNH, 3); Río Yana Rumi, 2 (FMNH); San Francisco, Río Napo, 200 meters, 3 (UMMZ); San José, abajo, 14 (AMNH); Santa Rosa de Sucumbíos, 1 (MNHN); Sumaco abajo, 5 (AMNH); Río Pastaza, 2° 5′ S, 1 (BM); PERU—*Loreto:* Río Napo, lower, 1 (FMNH); Tarapoto, Río Napo, 2 (syntype, BM; syntype, MCNM); *locality unknown:* Río Napo, 2 (BM).

SAGUINUS NIGRICOLLIS NIGRICOLLIS SPIX: SPIX'S BLACK-MANTLE TAMARIN

Fig. X.23. Spix's Black-mantle Tamarin, *Saguinus nigricollis nigricollis* Spix.

Synonymic History

Midas nigricollis Spix, 1823, *Sim. et Vesp., Brasil.,* p. 28, pl. 21 (animal). Wagner, 1833, *Isis von Oken* 10:996 —a variety of *M. mystax.* Schlegel, 1876, *Les singes. Simiae,* p. 264—BRAZIL: *Amazonas* (Rios Solimões and Içа).

M[idas] nigricollis, Reichenbach, 1862, *Vollst. Naturg. Affen,* p. 12, pl. 3, fig. 42 (animal)—characters.

H[apale] nigricollis, Wagner, 1855, *Schreber's Säugth., Suppl.* 5:132—characters; *rufoniger* I. Geoffroy, a synonym.

Hapale nigricollis, Jentink, 1892, *Cat. Syst. Mamm. Mus. Pays-Bas* 11:57—BRAZIL: *Amazonas* ("between the Solimões and Içа"); one of the types, mounted in the Leiden Museum.

Leontocebus nigricollis, Elliot, 1913, *A review of the Primates* 1:199—characters ex type; *rufoniger* I. Geoffroy, a synonym. Cabrera, 1958, *Rev. Mus. Argentino Cienc. Nat. "Bernardino Rivadavia"* 4(1):196—classification; part synonymy [not *"Leontocebus (sic) ater"* Lesson, 1840, cited ex Elliot 1913].

Mystax nigricollis, Thomas, 1928, *Ann. Mag. Nat. Hist.* ser. 10, 2:286—PERU: *Loreto* (Pebas).

Tamarin nigricollis, Cruz Lima, 1945, *Mamíferos da Amazonia, Primates,* p. 219, pl. 36, fig. 1 (animal)—PERU: *Loreto* ("Iquitos"; "Chimbote"); characters; *rufoniger* a synonym.

Marikina nigricollis, Hershkovitz, 1949, *Proc. U.S. Nat. Mus.* 98:413—part, key characters; classification; synonym, *rufoniger* Geoffroy and Deville only.

Marikina (Tamarin) nigricollis, Travassos, Teijeira de Freitas, and Kohn, 1969, *Mem. Inst. Oswaldo Cruz* 67:146—trematode, *Conspicuum conspicuum.*

Saguinus nigricollis, Hershkovitz, 1966, *Folia Primat.* 4:383, fig. 2B (color pattern), fig. 3B (head)—characters; comparisons, distribution. F. Deinhardt and Holmes 1966, in *Progress in liver diseases,* ed. Popper and Schaffner, p. 378—epidemiology and etiology of viral hepatitis. F. Deinhardt, Holmes, Capps, and Popper, 1967, *J. Exp. Med.* 125(4):673—susceptible to human hepatitis. J. B. Deinhardt, Devine, Passovoy, Pohlman, and Deinhardt, 1967, *Lab. Animal Care* 17(1):11—care for biomedical laboratory research. Hunt, Garcia, and Hegstead, 1967, *Lab. Animal Care* 17(2):222—reversal of "cage paralysis" by substitution of diet containing vitamin D_2 for one with D_3. Hunt, Garcia, and Hegsted, 1967, *Lab. Animal Care* 17(2):229—vitamin D requirements in osteodystrophia fibrosa. Egozcue, Perkins, Hagemenas, 1968, *Folia Primat.* 9(2):84—karyotype ($2n = 46$). Chase and Cooper, 1968, *Lab. Animal Care* 18(2):186—dental deposits and control. Chase and Cooper, 1969, *Amer. J. Phys. Anthrop.* 30(1):111—physical growth and sequence of dental eruptions. Holmes, Ogden, and Deinhardt, 1969, *Animal models for biomedical research II, Nat. Acad. Sci. Publ.* 1736:11—malignancy induction with Rous sarcoma virus; production of humanlike viral hepatitis. Williamson and Hunt, 1970, *Lab. Animal Care* 20:1139—adinocarcinoma of the thyroid. F. Deinhardt, 1970, in *Infections and immuno-suppression in subhuman Primates,* ed. Balner and Beveridge (Copenhagen), p. 55—induction of "human" hepatitis and transmission to marmoset species. Tischendorf and Wolfe, 1970, *Lab. Animal Care* 20(4):697—extramedullary hematopoiesis following blood loss. Black, 1970, *J. Mammal.* 51(4):794—pelvic sexual dimorphism. Cosgrove, Nelson, and Self, 1970, *Lab. Animal Care* 20(2):354—intermediate host for pentastomid *Porocephalus clavatus;* pathology. Falk, Wolfe, Shramek, and Deinhardt, 1970, *Proc. Central Soc. Clinical Res.* 43:80—induction of fatal disease with *Herpesvirus saimiri.* Tappen and Severson, 1971, *Fol. Primat.* 15:293—correlation between sequence of eruption of permanent teeth and epiphyseal union. Wolfe, Falk, and F. Deinhardt, 1971, *J. Nat. Cancer Inst.* 47:1145—induction of lymphomas or lymphocytic leukemias by *Herpesvirus saimiri.* Gengozian and Porter, 1971, in *Med. Primat. 1970,* ed. Goldsmith and Moor-Jankowski, p. 165—survival time of intraspecies skin grafts (16–160 days). Wolfe, Marczynska, Rabin, Smith, Tischendorf, Gavitt, and Deinhardt, 1971, in *Med. Primat. 1970,* ed. Goldsmith and Moor-Jankowski, p. 671—viral oncogenesis (susceptibilities to human, nonhuman and cultured tumor cells). Holmes, Wolfe, Deinhardt, and Conrad, 1971, *J. Infect. Diseases* 124(5):520—transmission of human hepatitis. Wolfe, Falk, and Deinhardt, 1971, *J. Nat. Cancer Inst.* 47:1145—oncogenicity of *Herpesvirus saimiri.* Wolfe, Deinhardt, Theilen, Rabin, Kawakai, and Bustad, 1971, *J. Nat. Cancer Inst.* 47:1115—induction of tumors by simian sarcoma virus, type 1 (*Lagothrix*). F. Deinhardt, 1971, in *Med. Primat. 1970,* ed. Goldsmith and Moor-Jankowski, p. 918—use in biomedical research. Lehner, 1971, in *Med. Primat. 1970,* ed. Goldsmith and Moor-Jankowski, p. 873—comparative serum lipid levels (low) and aortic atherosclerosis (least extensive). F. Deinhardt et al., 1972, *J. Med. Primat.* 1:29—tumor induction by Rous sarcoma virus, feline sarcoma virus, simian sarcoma virus, *Herpesvirus saimiri.* Murphy, Maynard, Krushak, and Berquist, 1972, *Lab. Animal Sci.* 22(3):339—microbial flora of imported animals (respiratory virus; bacteria) of animal and human origin. Soini, 1972, *Int. Zoo Yearbk.* 12:28—capture; exportation. Falk, Wolfe, Hoekstra, and Deinhardt, 1972, *J. Nat. Cancer Inst.* 48:523—*Herpesvirus saimiri* associated antigens in peripheral lymphocytes. F. Deinhardt, Wolfe, Northrop, Marczynska, Ogden, McDonald, Falk, Shramek, Smith and Deinhardt, 1972, *J. Med. Primat.* 1:29—neoplasm induction with Rous, Feline, Simian viruses, and *Herpesvirus saimiri.* Marczynska, Deinhardt, Schulien, Tischendorf and Smith, 1973, *J. Nat. Cancer Inst.* 51:1255—Rous sarcoma virus–induced tumor.

S[aguinus] nigricollis, Noyes, 1970, *J. Nat. Cancer Inst.* 45(3):579—tumors induced by Carr-Zilber and Schmidt-Ruppin strains of Rous sarcoma virus. F. Deinhardt, Holmes, Wolfe, and Junge, 1970, *Vox. Sang.* 19:261—transmission of viral hepatitis from humans. F. Deinhardt, Holmes, and Wolfe, 1970, *J. Infect. Diseases* 121 (3):351—tamarin hepatitis infection more likely by human agent than activated latent tamarin agent (reply to critique by Park and Melnick, 1969, ibid. 120:539). Möhr, Mattenheimer, Holmes, Deinhardt, and Schmidt,

1971, *Enzyme* 12:99—enzymology of experimental liver disease; comparisons with man, horse, dog, guinea pig, rat, and mouse, ibid., p. 161, close resemblance between enzymal patterns of tamarin experimental hepatitis and human hepatitis. Hershkovitz, 1972, *Int. Zoo Yearbk.* 12:5—classification (*graellsi* regarded as a subspecies). Holmes, Wolfe, and Deinhardt, 1972, in *Pathology of simian primates,* ed. Fiennes, 2:684—transmission and characters of human infectious hepatitis. Falk, Wolfe, and Deinhardt, 1972, *J. Nat. Cancer Inst.* 48(5):1499—experimental infection with *Herpesvirus saimiri* lethal within 18–26 days. Wolfe, Falk, and Deinhardt, 1972, *Lab. Invest.* 26(4):496—induction of lymphoproliferative disease with terminal leukemia by *Herpesvirus saimiri.* Wolfe, Smith, Hoekstra, Marczynska, Smith, McDonald, Northrop, and Deinhardt, 1972, *J. Nat. Cancer Inst.* 49(2):519—oncogenicity of fibrosarcoma viruses. Marczynska, Falk, Wolfe, and Deinhardt, 1973, *J. Nat. Cancer Inst.* 50:331—response to transplanted *Herpesvirus saimiri*-induced tumor tissues. Holmes, Deinhardt, Wolfe, Froesner, Peterson, and Casto, 1973, *Nature* 243:419—specific neutralization of human hepatitis type A. Klein, Pearson, Rabson, Ablashi, Falk, Wolfe, Deinhardt, and Rabin, 1973, *Int. J. Cancer* 12:270—antibody reaction to *Herpesvirus saimiri* induced antigens. Peterson, Wolfe, Deinhardt, Gajdusek and Gibbs, 1974, *Intervirology* 2:14—transmission of kuru and Creutzfeld-Jakob diseases.

[*Saguinus nigricollis*], Falk, Wolfe, Marczynska and Deinhardt, 1972, *Bacteriol. Proc.* 1972 (V38)—cell lines from *Herpesvirus saimiri.*

Saguinus (Tamarinus) nigricollis, Cooper, 1966, *Lab. Animal Dig.* 2(2):10, fig. 1 (animal)—*Herpesvirus tamarinus* infection; epizootiology.

Saguinus nigricollis nigricollis, Hershkovitz, 1970, *Am. J. Phys. Anthrop.* 32:379—classification; dental disease.

Midas rufoniger I. Geoffroy and Deville, 1848, *Comptes Rendus Acad. Sci. Paris* 27:499—PERU: *Loreto* (type locality, Río Marañon); types in Paris Museum collected by MM. Castelnau and Deville. I. Geoffroy, 1855, *Castelnau Expéd. Amérique Sud, pt. 7, Zool., Mamm.,* p. 22, pl. 5, fig. 3 (animal)—description. Bates, 1863, *Naturalist on the river Amazons* 2:321—BRAZIL: *Amazonas;* habits. Rode, 1938, *Bull. Mus. Nat. Hist. Nat., Paris,* ser. 10:239—Cotypes, female (lectotype) and male skins mounted, Muséum National d'Histoire Naturelle, Paris nos. 651 (633) and 650 (632), respectively, received 1847; regarded as a synonym of *Midas nigricollis* Spix.

M[idas] rufoniger, I. Geoffroy, 1851, *Cat. Mus. Hist. Nat., Paris, Primates,* p. 64—PERU: *Loreto* (type locality near Pebas); cotypes, male and female characters. Reichenbach, 1862, *Vollst. Naturg. Affen,* p. 12—characters.

Midas rufo-niger, I. Geoffroy, 1852, *Arch. Mus. Hist. Nat., Paris,* p. 275—characters.

[*Leontopithecus ater* Variété B] *Jeune âge* no. 2, Lesson, 1840, *Species des mammifères: Bimanes et quadrumanes* . . . , p. 205—*Midas nigricollis* Spix regarded as an immature of *ater* [= *Leontopithecus rosalia chrysopygus* Mikan].

Leontocebus fuscicollis, Hershkovitz (not Spix), 1957, *Proc. Biol. Soc. Washington* 70:footnote 1, pl. 18—misidentification of *Tamarin nigricollis* Cruz Lima, 1945, pl. 36, fig. 1.

Types. Originally five (3 adults, 2 young), Munich Natural History Museum; collected by the Spix and Martius expedition; now two, both mounted with skull, in the Munich Museum and 1 mounted specimen of the original series in the Leiden Museum.

Type Locality. North bank of the Solimões, near São Paulo de Olivença (172b), Amazonas, Brazil.

Distribution (fig. X.22). North bank of the Rio Amazonas from the mouth of the Rio Içá (Putumayo) in Amazonas, Brazil, west through the Leticia panhandle of Colombia, to the mouth of the Río Napo, Loreto, Peru; northwestern limits of range between the Ríos Putumayo and Napo in Peru, are unknown.

Taxonomy. Saguinus nigricollis has been confused with members of the *S. fuscicollis* group, notably *leucogenys.* In my first published key (1949, p. 413) to the hairy-faced tamarins, I listed the specific synonyms of *nigricollis* as *rufoniger, devilli* (*sic*), *leucogenys, pacator,* and *micans.* Only the first is identical with *nigricollis,* the others represent *S. fuscicollis* (*cf.* Hershkovitz 1966*a*, p. 384).

Diagnostic Characters. Dorsal coloration bizonal; head, neck, mantle, and forelimbs blackish, the mantle tapered posteriorly, the temporal patches brown; middle of lower back faintly striated reddish and black and hardly or not differentiated from mantle; dusky patch present between hip and knee.

Coloration. Forehead to crown, mantle, forelimbs, throat, and neck blackish brown, the hairs more or less uniformly colored, temporal patch brown; facial skin black, short hairs surrounding mouth and sides of nostrils gray; mantle tapering posteriorly to a point and terminating well behind middle of back; lower back faintly striated blackish and reddish, and merging with black of mantle, the hairs black with reddish orange subterminal band; lateral fringe like back; rump and legs mahogany red, the hairs reddish terminally, black basally, femoral patch blackish; upper surface of hands and feet black; chest comparatively thinly haired blackish brown, fine belly hairs like chest or more reddish; tail black except for short reddish basal portion; external genitalia mostly or entirely pigmented and sparsely covered with brown or reddish hairs.

Measurements. See appendix table 2.

Vibrissae. Supraorbitals, mystacials, rhinarials, mentals and posteriorly directed interramals present; genals randomly distributed; ulnar carpals present; gular spines present, pectoral absent.

Young. See p. 672.

Variation. Individual variation is slight and almost entirely restricted to minor differences in color. Evidence of local variation is absent in available material.

Cruz Lima (1945, p. 219) describes a specimen in the Goeldi Museum with the reddish annulated hairs of lower back "extending up the back to the shoulders and arms." In two other skins he notes "irregular white patches . . . in one of them scattered over all the body."

Comparisons (figs. X.16, 17). Distinguished from *S. fuscicollis* by brown temporal patches, posteriorly tapered black mantle extending to mid-back or beyond, indistinct or incipient saddle, its color merged with mantle anteriorly and reddish of rump posteriorly, glossy pelage stiffer throughout, particularly on head and mantle, with ready exposure of yellowish skin, posterior margin of pinna reduced; distinguished from *S. n. graellsi* by the reddish, not olivaceous or buffy, back and hind limbs and pelage of underparts reddish to blackish without annulations.

Saturation and Bleaching. Eumelanization is more extensive in *nigricollis* than in any other species of the group. The blackish color is fully established on crown, forelimbs, feet, tail and most of the back and dominates the underparts. Bleaching, apart from the grayish circumoral band, is little advanced. The brown temporal patches are one grade or tone removed from the blackish of the head, while the reddish banding of hairs of rump, hind limbs, and tail base is a second step removed from the otherwise saturate forequarters. The thin mixture of brownish to reddish hairs of underparts represent first and second grades of bleaching.

Origin, Evolution, and Dispersal. Saguinus nigricollis nigricollis is so nearly related morphologically and geographically to *graellsi* that it may well have evolved from a troop of the latter fortuitously isolated on the left bank of the lower Río Napo. Both forms share the diagnostic characters of bizonal color pattern and brown temporal patches. The general coloration of *nigricollis,* however, is more advanced. Here, saturation through eumelanization of the forequarters has been completed, while saturation through phaeomelanization is well advanced on the hindquarters. The underparts remain dominantly blackish.

Remarks. The animal described and figured by Cruz Lima (1945, p. 219, pl. 36, fig. 1) as *nigricollis* is unquestionably representative. His locality records, Chimbote and Iquitos, however, are outside the range of the species and possibly represent shipping points.

Specimens Examined. 47. BRAZIL—*Amazonas:* "Forêts entre Solimõens et l'Iça," syntype of *nigricollis* (RMNH); Santa Rita, 3 (BM); COLOMBIA—*Amazonas:* Leticia, 2 (GEE); PERU—*Loreto:* Pebas, 6 (AMNH, 2; BM, 2; MNHN, 2 syntypes of *rufoniger*); Yahuas Territory, near Pebas, 1 (BM); Río Apayacu, 15 (AMNH, 14; FMNH, 1); *locality unknown,* 1 (BM); UNKNOWN LOCALITY—18 (FMNH, 17 in spirits; SM, 1).

62 *Saguinus fuscicollis* Spix, Saddle-back Tamarins

Synonymic History

The bibliographic citations under the following synonymies refer to laboratory animals identified as *Saguinus fuscicollis.* They most likely represent *Saguinus fuscicollis illigeri, S. f. lagonotus, S. f. leucogenys,* and *S. f. nigrifrons,* all from northeastern Peru.

Study animals identified by authors to subspecies are listed under the corresponding subspecies heading.

Saguinus fuscicollis, F. Deinhardt and Holmes, 1966, in Progress in liver disease, ed. Popper and Schaffner, p. 378—epidemiology and etiology of viral hepatitis. Gengozian and Batson, 1966, *Int. J. Rad. Biol.* 11(6):539—effects of whole body radiation; parasitism; bone-marrow grafting attempts after whole-body irradiation. F. Deinhardt and Deinhardt, 1966, *Zool. Soc. London,* symp. no. 17, p. 127—use in virological research; hemotologic and biochemical values. J. Deinhardt, Devine, Passovoy, Pohlman, and Deinhardt, 1967, *Lab. Animal Care* 17(1):11—care for use in biomedical laboratory research. Perkins, 1967, *Amer. J. Phys. Anthrop.* 27:409—correction: *S. nigricollis* Perkins (not Spix) 1966 (*Amer. J. Phys. Anthrop.* 25:41), a misnomer. F. Deinhardt, Holmes, Capps, and Popper, 1967, *J. Exp. Med.* 125(4):673—susceptible to human hepatitis. Dreizen, Levy, Bernick, Hampton, and Krantz, 1967, *Israel J. Med. Sci.* 3(5):731—periodontal bone changes caused by osteomalasia and hyperparathryoidism. F. Deinhardt, Holmes, Devine, and Deinhardt, 1967, *Lab. Animal Care* 17(1):60—parasitology; virology; immunities. Chase and Cooper, 1968, *Lab. Animal Care* 18 (2):186—dental deposits and control in laboratory animals. Cosgrove, Nelson, and Gengozian, 1968, *Lab. Animal Care* 18:654—helminth parasites. Kraus and Garret, 1968, *Cleft Palate Journal* 5:340, figs. 1–5 (sections of cleft palate)—cleft palate in aborted fetus. Porter and Gengozian, *Proc. Soc. Exp. Biol. Med.* 127:860—skin autografts; technique; *S. nigricollis* of previous reports = *S. fuscicollis.* F. Deinhardt, 1969, *Ann. N.Y. Acad. Sci.* 162(1):551—use in virological research. Gengozian, Batson, Greene, and Gosslee, 1969, *Transplantation* 8(5):633—hemopoietic chimerism. Gengozian, 1969, *Ann. N.Y. Acad. Sci.* 162:336—importation; caging; handling; conditioning; feeding diet; diseases; breeding; fraternal twinning; hybridization; parasites; chimerism; radiation. F. Deinhardt, 1969, in *Comp. Leukemia Res., Bibl. Haemat.,* ed. R. M. Butcher, no. 36, p. 401—induction of tumors with feline fibrosarcoma virus. Dreizen and Hampton, 1969, *J. Dental Res.* 48(4):579—glandular contribution of selected B vitamins in saliva. Levy, Taylor, Hampton, and Thoma, 1969, *Cancer Res.* 29:2237—tumors produced by Rous sarcoma virus. J. K. Hampton, Jr., and Parmelee, 1969, *Comp. Biochem., Physiol.* 30:367—plasma diamine oxidase activity. F. Deinhardt, Wolfe, Theilen, and Snyder, 1970, *Science* 167:881—induction of malignancies by feline fiibrosarcoma virus. F. Deinhardt, 1970, in *Infections and immuno-suppression in subhuman Primates,* ed. Balner and Beveridge (Copenhagen), p. 55—induction of "human" hepatitis and transmission to other marmoset species. F. Deinhardt, Holmes, Wolfe, and Junge, 1970, *Vox. Sang.* 19:261—transmission of viral hepatitis from humans. F. Deinhardt, Holmes, and Wolfe, 1970, *J. Infect. Diseases* 121(3):351—tamarin hepatitis infection more likely by human agent than activated latent tamarin agent (reply to critique by Parks and Melnick, 1969, ibid. 120:539). J. K. Hampton, Jr., Rider, and Parmelee, 1970, *Proc. 3rd Int. Cong. Primat., Zurich* 2:95—diamine oxidase and histaminase values. Tischendorf and Wolfe, 1970, *Lab. Animal Care* 20(4):697—extramedullary hematopoiesis following blood loss. Cosgrove, Nelson, and Self, 1970, *Lab. Animal Care* 20(2):354—intermediate host for pentastomid *Porocephalus clavatus;* pathology of infection. Gengozian and Merritt, 1970, *J. Reprod. Fert.* 23:509—effect of unilateral ovariectomy on twinning and chimerism. Falk, Wolfe, Shramek, and F. Deinhardt, 1970, *Proc. Central Soc. Clin. Res.* 43:80—induction of fatal disease with *Herpesvirus saimiri.* Cosgrove, Humason, and Lushbaugh, 1970, *J. Amer. Med. Assoc.* 157(5):696—*Trichospirura leptostoma* (nematode) in pancreatic duct. J. K. Hampton, Jr., Parmelee, and Rider, 1971, in *Med. Primat. 1970,* ed. Goldsmith and Moor-Jankowski, p. 245—plasma histaminase and diamine oxidase values. J. K. Hampton, Jr., Hampton, and Levy, 1971, in *Med. Primat. 1970,* ed. Goldsmith and Moor-Jankowski, p. 527—reproduction in a laboratory colony. Wolfe, Marczynska,

Rabin, Smith, Tischendorf, Gavitt, and Deinhardt, 1971, in *Med. Primat. 1970,* ed. Goldsmith and Moor-Jankowski, p. 671—viral oncogenesis (susceptibility to human, nonhuman and cultured tumor cells). F. Deinhardt, 1971, in *Med. Primat. 1970,* ed. Goldsmith and Moor-Jankowski, p. 918—use in biomedical research. Gengozian, 1971, in *Med. Primat. 1970,* ed. Goldsmith and Moor-Jankowski, p. 926—statistical analysis of chimerism; twinning frequency; newborn sex ratios. Wolfe, Falk, and Deinhardt, 1971, *J. Nat. Cancer Inst.* 47:1145—oncogenicity of *Herpesvirus saimiri.* S. H. Hampton and Taylor, 1971, *Proc. 3rd Int. Cong. Primat. Zürich* 1:246—gonadal development. Levy and Mirkovic, 1971, *Lab. Animal Sci.* 21(1):33—measles epizootic in laboratory colony. Wolfe, F. Deinhardt, Theilen, Rabin, Kawakami, and Bustad, 1971, *J. Nat. Cancer Inst.* 47:1115—induction of tumors by simian sarcoma virus, type 1 (*Lagothrix*). F. Deinhardt, Wolfe, Theilen, and Snyder, 1971, in *Yearbook of Cancer, 1971,* ed. Clark and Cumley—susceptibility to C type RNA virus (Snyder-Theilen [ST]) from a naturally occurring cat fibrosarcoma; susceptibility to Gardner strain of feline fibrosarcoma virus. F. Deinhardt, et al., 1972, *J. Med. Primat.* 1:29—tumor induction by Rous sarcoma virus, feline sarcoma virus, simian sarcoma virus, *Herpesvirus saimiri.* Soini, 1972, *Int. Zoo Yearbk.* 12:28—capture; exportation. Levy, Hampton, Dreizen, and Hampton, 1972, *J. Comp. Pathol.* 82:99—chronic thyroiditis in laboratory animals. Falk, Wolfe, Hoekstra, and Deinhardt, 1972, *J. Nat. Cancer Inst.* 48:523—*Herpesvirus saimiri* associated antigens in peripheral lymphocytes. F. Deinhardt, Wolfe, Junge, and Holmes, 1972, *Canadian Med. Ass. J.* 106:468—susceptibility to acute phase human infectious hepatitis; review of transmittal attempts. Wolfe, Smith, Hoekstra, Marczynska, Smith, McDonald, Northrop, and Deinhardt, 1972, *J. Nat. Cancer Inst.* 49(2):519—oncogenicity of fibrosarcoma viruses. Porter, 1972, *Lab. Animal Sci.* 22(4):503—endoparasites. Deinhardt, Wolfe, Northrop, Marczynska, Ogden, McDonald, Falk, Shramek, Smith, and Deinhardt, 1972, *J. Med. Primat.* 1:29—neoplasm induction with Rous, feline and simian viruses, and *Herpesvirus saimiri.* Cohn, 1972, *Arch. Oral Biol.* 17:261—Sharpey's fibers in alveolar bone. Felsburg, Heberling, Brack and Kalter, 1973, *J. Med. Primat.* 2, (1):50—experimental injection with *Herpesvirus hominis* type 2 fatal. Porter and Gengozian 1973, *Transplantation* 15(2):221—in vitro histocompatability with *S. oedipus.* Schauf, Kruse, and Deinhardt, 1974 *J. Med. Primat.* 3(5):315—response to tuberculosis vaccine (BCG); use in tumor immunotherapy. Preston, Brewen, and Gengozian, 1974, *Radiation Res.* 60:516—persistence of radiation-induced chromosome aberrations; comparisons with man.

S[aguinus] fuscicollis, Möhr, Mattenheimer, Holmes, Deinhardt, and Schmidt, 1971, *Enzyme* 12:99—enzymology of experimental liver disease; comparisons with man, horse, dog, guinea pig, rat, mouse, ibid., p. 161—close resemblances between enzymal patterns of tamarin experimental hepatitis and human hepatitis. Falk, Wolfe, and Deinhardt, 1972, *J. Nat. Cancer Inst.* 48(5):1499—experimental infection with *Herpesvirus saimiri* lethal within 18–26 days. Wolfe, Falk, and Deinhardt, 1972, *Lab. Invest.* 26(4):496—induction of lymphoproliferative disease with terminal leukemia by *Herpesvirus saimiri.* Marczynska, Falk, Wolfe, and Deinhardt, 1973, *J. Nat. Cancer Inst.* 50:331—response to transplanted *Herpesvirus saimiri*-induced tumor tissues. Holmes, Deinhardt, Wolfe, Froesner, Peterson, and Casto, 1973, *Nature* 243:419—specific neutralization of human hepatitis type A. Marczynska, Deinhardt, Schulien, Tischendorf, and Smith, 1973, *J. Nat. Cancer Inst.* 51:1255—Rous sarcoma virus-induced tumor. Peterson, Wolfe, Deinhardt, Gajdusek, and Gibbs, 1974, *Intervirology* 2:14—transmission of kuru and Creutzfeldt-Jakob diseases.

[*Saguinus fuscicollis*], Falk, Wolfe, Marczynska, and Deinhardt, 1972, *Bacteriol. Proc.* 1972 (V 38)—cell lines from *Herpesvirus saimiri.*

Saguinus [*fuscicollis*], Porter and Gengozian, 1973, in *Tissue culture,* ed. P. F. Krause and M. K. Patterson, p. 93—bone marrow culture and propagation of hemopoietic cells in vitro.

Saquinus [*sic*] *fuscicollis,* Klein, Pearson, Rabson, Ablashi, Falk, Wolfe, Deinhardt, and Rabin, 1973, *Int. J. Cancer* 12:270—antibody reactions to *Herpesvirus saimiri* induced antigens. Fischer, Falk, Rytter, Burton, Luecke, and Deinhardt, 1974, *J. Nat. Cancer Inst.* 52, (5):1477—*Herpesvirus saimiri,* attempted transmission through hematophagous insects.

Tamarinus nigricollis (not Spix), Gengozian, Batson, and Smith (not Spix), 1962, *Proc. Int. Symp. Bone Marrow Therapy and Chemical Protection in Irradiated Primates,* p. 245—use as a laboratory research animal; care; health, disease, biochemistry; effects of irradiation. Gengozian, Batson, and Eide, 1964, *Cytogenetics* 3:384—hematopoietic chimerism. Nelson, Cosgrove, and Gengozian, 1966, *Lab. Animal Care* 16(3):255—diseases; mortality; parasites. Gengozian, 1966, *Nature* 209:722—formation of isohaemagglutinins. Gengozian, Lushbaugh, Humason, and Knisely, 1966, *Nature* 209:731—natural occurrence of "erythroblastosis fetalis." Perkins, 1966, *Amer. J. Phys. Anthrop.* 25(1):41, pl. 1 (animal = *Saguinus fuscicollis*), fig. 2 (sternal gland), fig. 3 (peri-inguinal gland), fig. 4 (radial papillae), fig. 5 (ulnar gland and sinus hair), fig. 6 (scalp melanocytes), fig. 7 (lip, arrector pili muscle), fig. 8 (palm, Meissner's corpuscles), fig. 9 (tail apocrine duct), fig. 10 (melanocytes of proximal tail), fig. 11 (lip end organs), fig. 12 (eyelid, meibomian gland), fig. 13 (external genitalia, sebaceous gland), fig. 14–16 (lip, sebaceous acini), fig. 17 (sternal region, apocrine gland), fig. 18 (external genitalia, apocrine secretory tubules and melanocytes), fig. 19 (sternal gland), fig. 20 (palmar sweat gland)—histology of skin.

Leontocebus nigricollis, Mazur and Baldwin, (not Spix), 1968, *Psychol. Rep.* 22(2):441—social behavior in "Monkey Jungle," Miami, Florida.

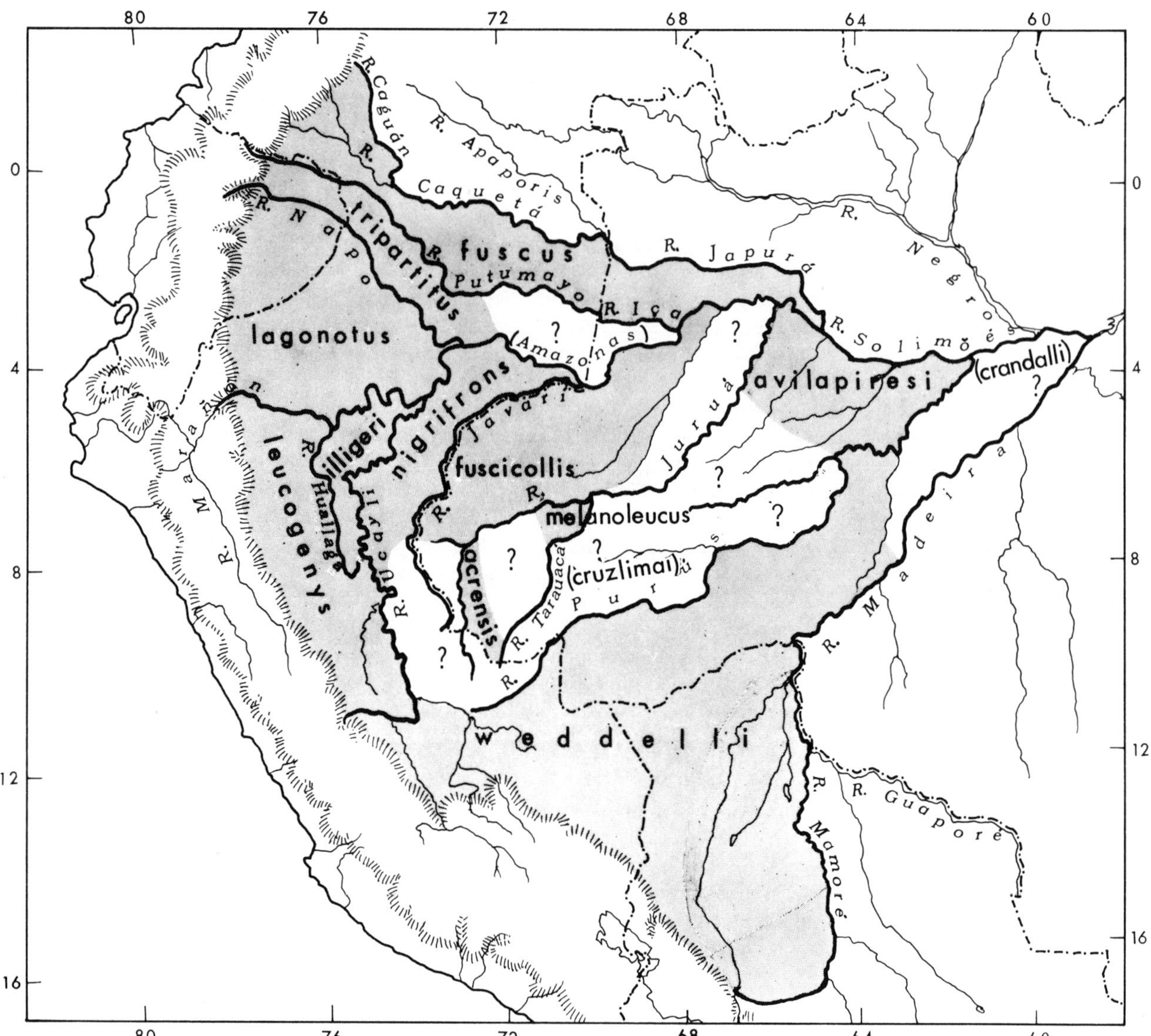

Fig. X.24. Geographic distribution of the subspecies of *Saguinus fuscicollis;* river boundaries between races boldly defined. For names of collecting localities and collectors see gazetteer (p. 918) and maps (figs. XIII.2, 4). (Modified from Hershkovitz 1968.)

Distribution (figs. X.15, 24)

Upper Amazonian region from west bank of the Rio Madeira south of the Rio Amazonas in Brazil, and the south (right) bank of the Japurá-Río Caquetá-Caguán north of the Amazonas in Brazil and Colombia, west to the eastern base of the Cordillera Oriental in Colombia, Ecuador, Peru, and Bolivia.

The great length and breadth of the Rio Madeira has detained spread of the species eastward and beyond the basins fed by streams with sources in the Cordillera Oriental. Occupation of the eastern bank of the Rio Madeira by marmosets of the *Callithrix argentata* group (fig. IX.36) is also an obstacle to successful colonization by alien callitrichids.

In contrast, no evident geographic or ecological factor or the presence of another callitrichid restrains *Saguinus fuscicollis* from invading the forested base of the Cordillera Oriental beyond the northernmost tributary of the Amazon (maps, figs. X.2, 15).

The extrapolated range of *S. fuscicollis* is greater than that of any other species of the genus (cf. X.1). Actually, *S. fuscicollis* is known to occur with certainty in about half of the indicated area. Representatives of the species have not been collected or recorded from the lower inter-Madeira-Purús basin. Nearly the whole of the inter-Purús-Juruá basin in Amazonas, Brazil, and the crucial portion between the upper Ríos Purús and Ucayali in Peru remain unexplored. Much of the lower inter-Javarí-Juruá basin in western Brazil has not been visited by collectors of mammals. Likewise the area between the Iça (lower Putumayo) and Amazonas, except for the Leticia-Tabatinga localities and the enormous zone between the Ríos Putumayo and Caquetá (Japurá) except at the heads and mouths of these streams, are virtually unknown mastozoologically.

Origin, Evolution, and Dispersal

Saguinus fuscicollis can be derived from an agouti-colored ancestor very much like some individuals of

Saguinus nigricollis graellsi but with incipient development of the saddle characteristic of the trizonal dorsal color pattern. The grayish circumbuccal band was already present in the progenitor of the *nigricollis* group. Otherwise, the facial pelage of ancestral *S. fuscicollis* as well as the tail and upper surface of hands and feet may have been dominantly blackish.

The center of origin and dispersal of the basic stock of the *nigricollis* group appears to have been the eastern base of the Cordillera Oriental. The branch giving rise to *S. fuscicollis* then spread throughout the upper Amazonian region as habitats became available during the Pleistocene. Subspeciation of successive founder colonies may have been fairly rapid and must have occurred within the present range of the species. Modern representatives of *S. fuscicollis* nearest the hypothetical ancestral form are the still largely agouti *S. f. fuscus* at the northwestern extreme of the range in the Caquetá-Putumayo region of Colombia and the nearly uniformly agouti albeit saturate *S. f. avilapiresi* at or near the northeastern extreme of the range between the Rios Juruá and Purús in Amazonas, Brazil. Each intervening geographic race evolved in the isolation of an interfluvial basin of the larger Amazonian streams. Together they form a graded series with the differences between them nothing more than the sequences of saturation from agouti to blackish or reddish, and of bleaching to white. The color grades are indicators of the relative length of isolation of each subspecies of *S. fuscicollis*.

Correlation between external environment and coloration is not apparent. Races inhabiting demonstrably identical ecologies on opposite banks of the same river within sight and call of each other may be strikingly different. This is explained by the isolation of founder colonies, obligatory inbreeding with resultant accelerated metachromic evolution or degeneration, population expansion followed by assortative mating, or social selection with consequent establishment of a relatively stable phenotype.

Diagnostic Characters

Dorsal coloration trizonal, that is, with mantle, saddle, and rump more or less well defined except in extremely bleached or albinistic forms (fig. X.16); thighs and forelegs not black.

External Characters

Integument (figs. III.13; X.16, 17, 25). Facial skin, ears, and volar surfaces blackish, short hairs surrounding mouth and sides of nostrils forming a broad, grayish band; forehead agouti to black, gray, or whitish; crown agouti, black, or drab to white; mantle variously colored and sharply defined from marbled or striated or vermiculated saddle; rump and base of tail more uniformly and, usually, more brightly colored than saddle; upper arms like mantle, forearms usually darker; legs like rump proximally and generally becoming darker distally, their color from agouti to reddish orange to white, never black; underparts variable but never wholly black; hairs of chin directed back or sometimes crested medially and

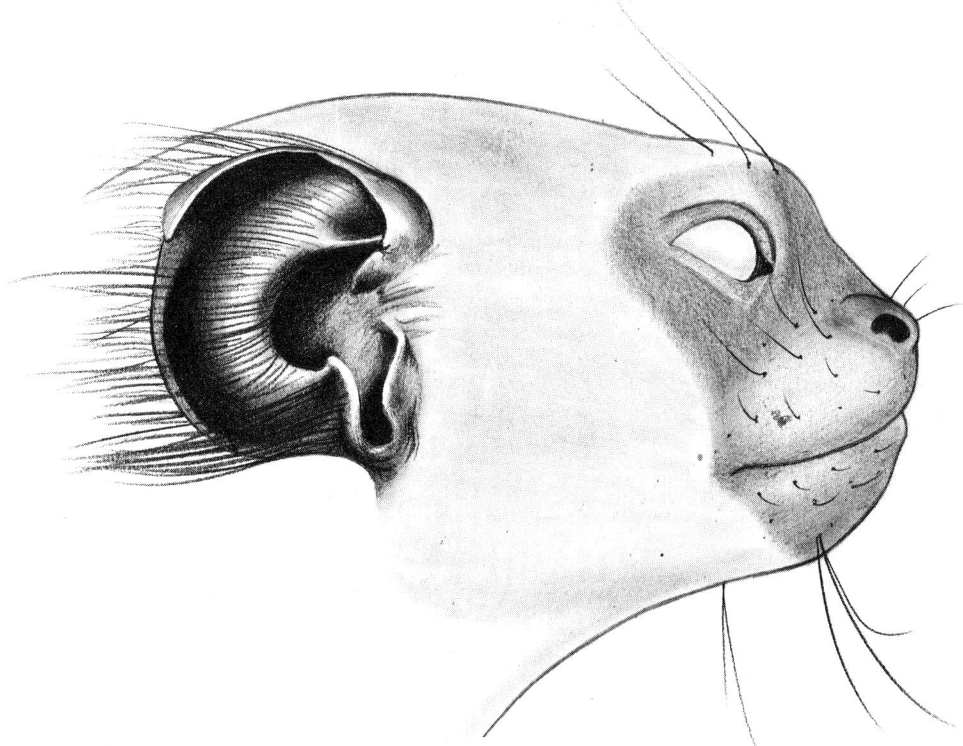

Fig. X.25. *Saguinus fuscicollis lagonotus* profile: Mane and facial hairs omitted to fully expose ear, vibrissae, and facial pigmentation.

directed forward, hairs of throat and underside of neck directed back; upper surface of hands and feet agouti to black, or drab to white; tail in northern and central races and in *weddelli* black at least on terminal one-half, root like rump, remainder of proximal portion of tail black, sometimes irregularly or incompletely annulated with reddish orange or with upper surface black, beneath reddish or orange, tail in southern races varying from blackish or reddish through drab or orange to whitish; external genitalia mostly to entirely pigmented.

Vibrissae (fig. X.25). Supraorbital, mystacial, rhinarial, and mental normally present; interramal backwardly directed but rarely detectable in dry skin; genals sometimes distinguishable in dry skin; ulnar carpals present; gular spines present or absent.

Comparisons

Distinguished from all other callitrichids by hairy face and temples, gray circumbuccal band, large, nearly bare, and fully exposed ears, trizonal color pattern of back, terminal half of tail uniformly colored, thighs and forelegs not black.

Coloration and Color Pattern (fig. III.13; X.26, 27; pls. 3, 4; table 79)

A large representation of independently controlled chromatic fields or zones, and all evolutionary color grades from primitive agouti to terminal white are displayed by the races of *Saguinus fuscicollis*. The chromogenetic fields of taxonomic significance within the species are the following.

1. *Crown:* Agouti or blackish; bleaching proceeds through browns and drab to white, and from basal to terminal portions of hairs.

2. *Forehead:* Agouti or blackish and either undifferentiated from crown or with well-defined grayish superciliary band or with gray lunar or chordate-shaped blaze; albinism of forehead precedes blanching of crown.

3. *Circumbuccal Band:* Short, coarse, grayish to nearly pure white hairs surrounding lips and forming patch on each side of rhinarium; consistently present in all members of the species and the *nigricollis* group, and well defined from surrounding parts in nonalbinotic forms.

4. *Cheeks:* Black with mixture of primitive agouti to entirely blackish; eumelanization progresses to temples and forehead; bleaching progresses approximately pari passu with bleaching of crown.

5. *Throat:* Agouti in forms with undifferentiated underparts; becomes blackish independently; bleaching progresses through brown, reddish, orange, yellow, and white.

6. *Mantle:* Pelage of nape and shoulders combined; always well or sharply defined from saddle, the posterior border truncate or incised; primitive agouti hairs become eumelanized or pheomelanized, then bleach from blackish or brown to drab, or from reddish through orange, drab, or yellow to whitish; color of mantle continuous with that of crown at the agouti or whitish stage, or sharply defined.

7. *Saddle:* Middle of back and contiguous parts of lower back and lateral fringe sharply to well defined from mantle and moderately well defined from rump (see below) and outer sides of thighs; most stable color zone and last to blanch completely; color pattern a modified agouti, that is, hairs blackish except for wide pheomelanic subterminal band, giving overall effect of blackish with reddish, orange, yellow, drab, or gray striae or marbling; the saturate or wholly blackish grade does not occur in known forms of *S. fuscicollis.*

8. *Rump:* Buttocks and tail base more uniformly colored than saddle; color zone may extend to hips and over parts or all of thighs.

9. *Tail:* Dorsal surface, ventral surface, proximal portion, distal portion and, often, penciled tip are quasi-independent color zones or chromogenetic fields, but for present purposes they are treated under one heading; distal three-fourths of blackish bleaching through drab to white; proximal portion agouti, this color pattern extending distally for variable lengths but always more on ventral than dorsal surface, saturation by pheomelanization, bleaching proceeds through reds, orange, drab, or yellow to white, from underside to upper side, and from proximal to distal portions, but penciled tip often more advanced metachromically than remainder of tail.

Saturation, Bleaching, and Geographic Variation (figs. III.13, 14, 15; X.26, 27; pl. 4)

Chromogenetic fields of *Saguinus fuscicollis* most significant in geographic variation or subspeciation are forehead (including brows), crown, nape, and mantle (table 79). The white circumbuccal band, the marbled or striated saddle of modified agouti hairs, the dominantly blackish terminal portion of tail, the blackish upper surface of hands and feet, and the pigmented exposed, or bare, skin are fairly stable throughout most of the geographic range of *S. fuscicollis.* Pigmentation of saddle, tail, and limbs breaks down, however, as the species nears the end of its metachromic run. Other fields such as the throat, chest, belly, midventral band, and rump vary individually or locally in most races but bleach to yellow, cream, or white in terminal races.

The thirteen races of *Saguinus fuscicollis* form three geographic groups (figs. X.26, 27). The northern consists of *S. f. fuscus,* a relict near the ancestral type. It occurs with little individual variation throughout the enormous basin between the Ríos Caquetá-Japurá and Putumayo. It is dominantly agouti with a maximum distribution of agouti on the underside of the basal half of the otherwise blackish tail. Its offshoot, *Saguinus fuscicollis avilapiresi,* was isolated on the south bank of the Amazon as a result either of rafting or, more likely, a river bend cutoff. It is generally more saturate than the parental *fuscus* but retains more of the ancestral agouti on the hind part of the crown.

The six central races, each occupying a separate interfluvial basin, represent as many successively graded steps in the metachromic scale. *S. f. fuscicollis* of the Jurua-Javari basin, with agouti forehead, crown, nape, and mantle, is most primitive but generally more advanced chromatically than the northern *S. f. fuscus.* The agouti of the forehead of *fuscicollis* becomes blackish in *nigrifrons* of adjacent inter-Yavarí-Ucayali basin. Saturation of crown follows in *illigeri* of the basin to the west be-

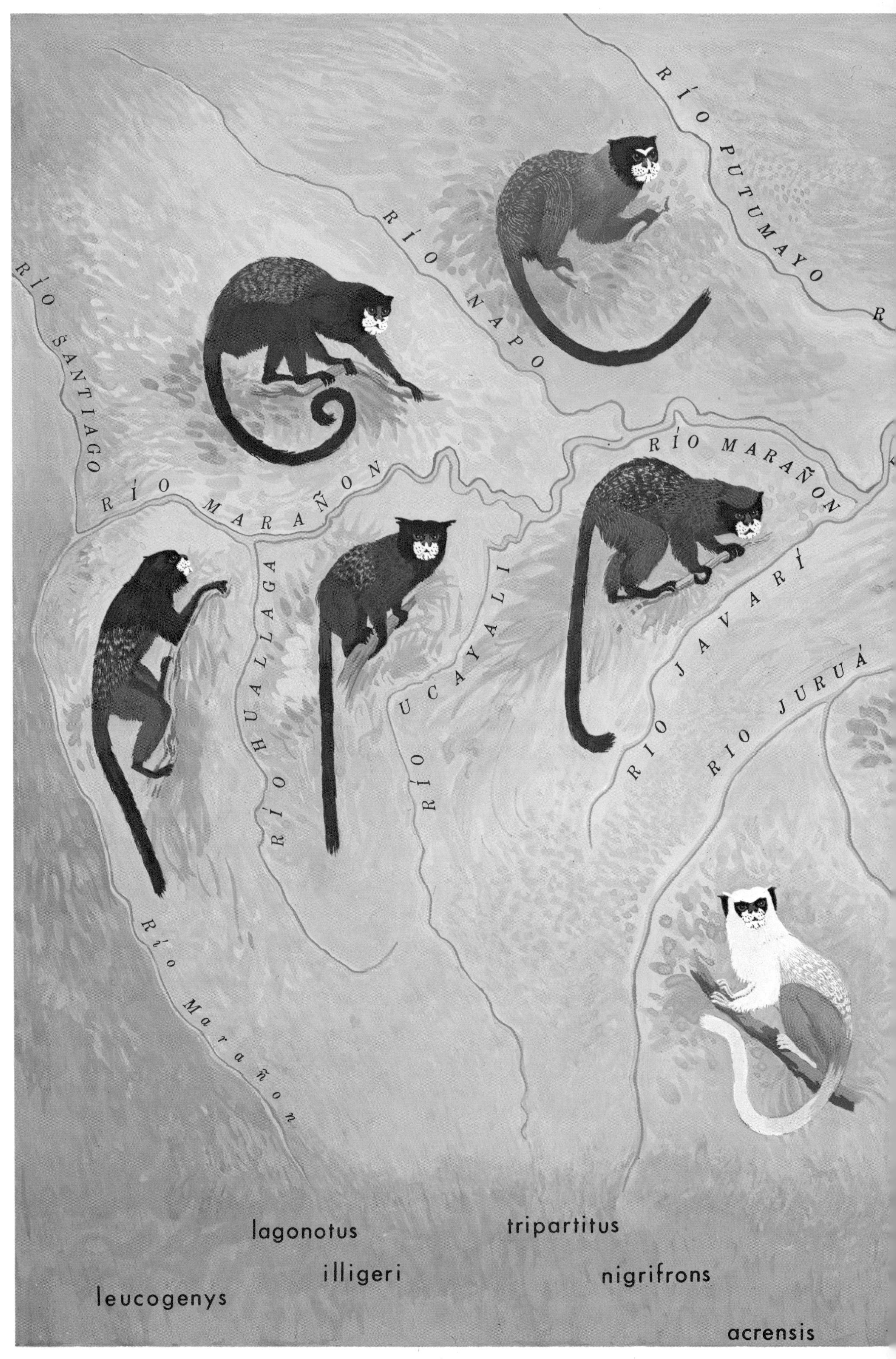

Plate III. Geographic metachromism: Distribution of thirteen races of the Saddle-back Tamarin (*Saguinus fuscicollis*); the habitats of two are presumed and indicated by ?. Discoveries made since this plate went to press suggest that the habitat of *crandalli* lies just south of that of *acrensis,* and that of *cruzlimai* more likely occurs south of the Rio Pauini (not shown) than north of the Rio Tapauá (shown). The newly described

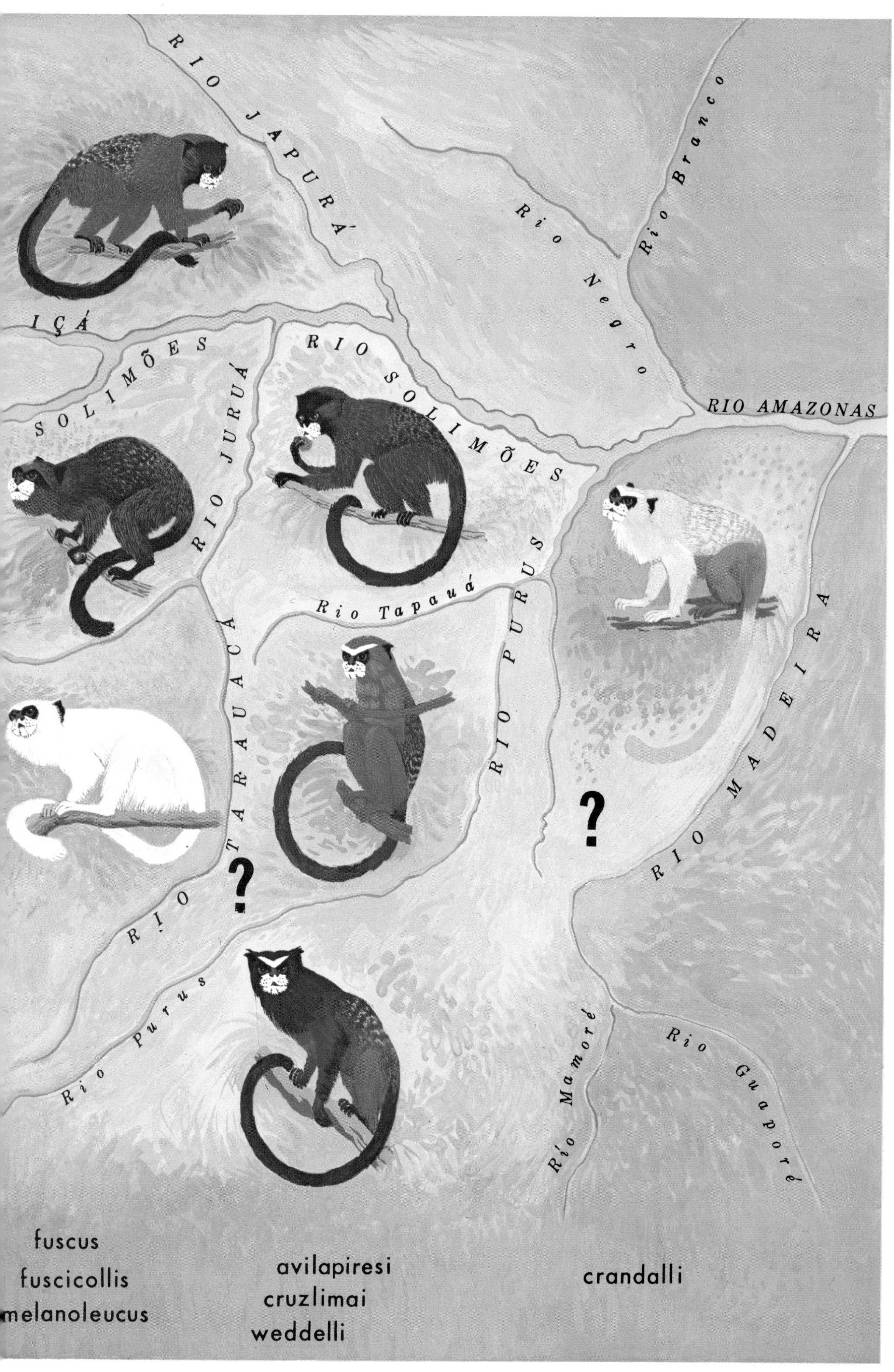

Saguinus fuscicollis primitivus (cf. p. 1022) lives within the area defined by the Rio Purús and tributaries Tapauá to the north and Pauini to the south, as shown in figure X. 15. River courses and distance relationships are distorted to accommodate the figures. Original painting by E. John Pfiffner.

Table 79. Distribution of Coat Colors in the Races of *Saguinus fuscicollis*

	Chromogentic Fields			
Subspecies	*Forehead or blaze*	*Crown*	*Nape-Mantle*	*Tail*
Northern races				
fuscus	blackish	blackish	agouti	agouti-blackish
avilapiresi	blackish	dark agouti	dark agouti	blackish
Central races				
fuscicollis	agouti	agouti	agouti	blackish
nigrifrons	blackish	agouti	agouti	blackish
illigeri	blackish	blackish	agouti	blackish
leucogenys	blackish	blackish	agouti-blackish, blackish	blackish
lagonotus	blackish	blackish	reddish	blackish
tripartitus	white	blackish	orange-yellow	blackish
Southern races				
leucogenys[1]	blackish	blackish	blackish	blackish
weddelli	white	blackish	blackish	blackish
cruzlimai[2]	white	reddish	reddish	blackish-reddish (?)
crandalli	white	drab	drab	drab-orange
acrensis[3]	white	yellow	yellow	orange-yellow
melanoleucus	white	white	white	yellow-white

1. Repeated listing of central *leucogenys* for indicating metachromic continuity with southern races.
2. Distribution of colors based on published descriptions and colored plates (cf. Cruz Lima 1945, p. 229, pl. 38, fig. 3*a;* Hershkovitz 1966, p. 388).
3. Distribution of colors based on original description of 4 specimens and photograph of holotype skin (cf. Carvalho 1957, p. 219, fig. 1).,

tween the Ríos Ucayali and Huallaga. More or less complete saturation of the mantle follows in *leucogenys,* next in westward geographic progression. The race on the north bank of the Amazon west of the Río Napo and opposite the range of the agouti-mantled *illigeri* and black-mantled *leucogenys* is the red-mantled *lagonotus.* An additional distinction found in most individuals of *lagonotus* is the blanched suborbital region. Crossing to the eastern bank of the Río Napo into *tripartitus* territory, the mantle, which is reddish in *lagonotus,* is here bleached to a golden orange, and a small whitish chevron-shaped blaze appears in mid-brow.

The five southern white "eyebrowed" races stem from a saturate form such as *leucogenys* and compose a graded series from blackish *weddelli* to albinotic *melanoleucus.* The forequarters of southernmost *weddelli* are entirely blackish except for the white brows and basal drab of the mantle hairs. As *weddelli* spread northward, founder colonies trapped in a dead end between the Juruá and its tributary, the Taraucá, bleached into the dominantly yellowish *acrensis* at the mouth of the pocket. Others, more effectively isolated at the closed end, degenerated into the almost wholly white-haired *melanoleucus.* The reddish orange *cruzlimai* is metachromically intermediate between *weddelli* and *acrensis,* but its habitat in the upper Rio Purús valley is not precisely known. It is arbitrarily assigned to the pocket between the Purús and Tapauá. The drab *crandalli,* also of unknown provenance, is in every respect a "washed-out" *weddelli.* Its provisional assignment to the area north of the Rio Pixuna between the Purús and Madeira takes account of the fact that *weddelli* inhabits the same major interfluvial basin but is known only from the Pixuna southward.

With the possible exception of some individuals from geographically intermediate areas where integradation might occur between *leucogenys, lagonotus,* and possibly *illigeri,* color differences between adults of neighboring subspecies are as sharply defined as the rivers segregating them. A geographic zone of intergradation is missing. Invaders from opposite shores, if they survive, are absorbed by the resident population. Intermediacy between races is evident, nevertheless, in juvenal pelage and in hidden portions of adult pelage.

Races most nearly like the hypothetical agouti-colored ancestor are oldest and most widely distributed. The albinotic forms at the other extreme are youngest and occupy the very smallest ranges. Absence of racial characters other than color points to relatively recent geographic differentation. The most obvious metachromic racial characters are summarized in table 79.

Immunogenetics and Inheritance of Blood Factors

Studies were conducted by Gengozian (1969; 1972*a*), Gengozian and Porter (1971), and Porter and Gengozian (1969) on tolerance of skin transplants and reactions to isoimmune blood sera within and between subspecies *Saguinus fuscicollis nigrifrons, S. f. illigeri, S. f. leucogenys,* and *S. f. lagonotus.* Other studies by Gengozian and Patton (1972) were made on the inheritance of blood factors in the same subspecies. The findings reaffirm the genetic basis for the present classification. Other subspecies of *S. fuscicollis* were not available to the authors cited.

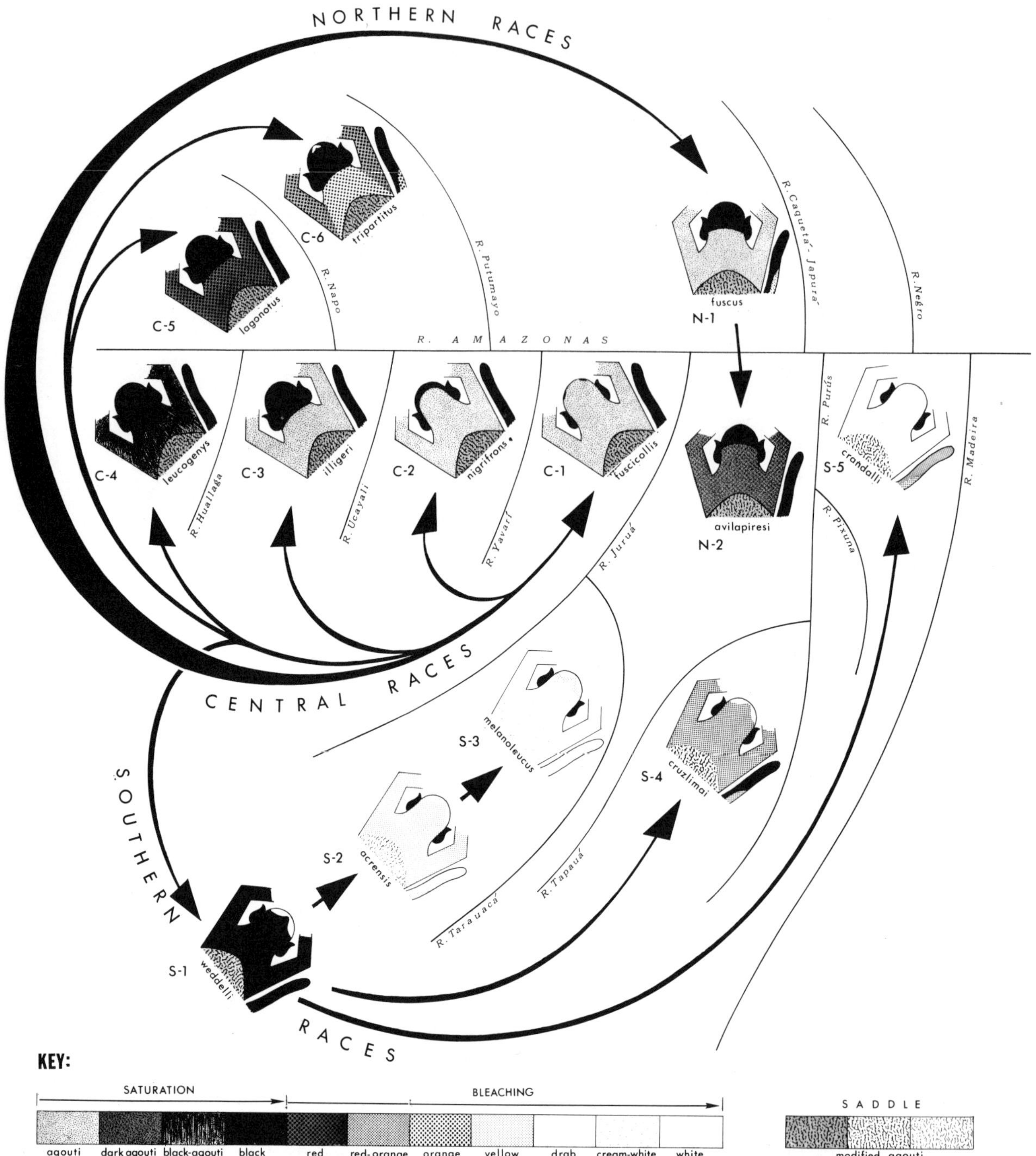

Fig. X.26. Geographic metachromism in *Saguinus fuscicollis* demonstrated by color patterns of frontal and dorsal surface of head, back, and tail. It is presumed that the species originated at the base of the Cordillera Oriental between the Río Huallaga and the Río Pastaza or Río Morona, then spread north and south along the Andes and into forested interfluvial river basins of the upper Rio Amazonas (Marañon and Solimões) system. The llanos to the north in the Río Orinoco system and the great length and breadth of the Rio Madeira are barriers to further spread at present. Each subspecies represents a metachromic grade in the northern, central, or southern series. C4 and S1 connect the central and southern series. The northern series N1,N2 is cladistic. The same may be true of series C1,C2,C3,C4 continuing through C5,C6 or with a branching from C3 to C5,C6. The southern series consists of two or three branches. These are S1–S3, and S1,S4,S5, or S1,S4 and S1,S5. (After Hershkovitz 1968.)

Key to Subspecies of *Saguinus fuscicollis* (figs. X.26, 27; pls. 3, 4)

1. Body from head to tip of tail dominantly whitish or yellowish white . . . . *S. f. melanoleucus* (p. 664)

1′. Body variously colored, saddle vermiculated or marbled blackish with gray or buffy and more or less defined from mantle and rump; tail usually black, sometimes brownish, drab or partly gray 2

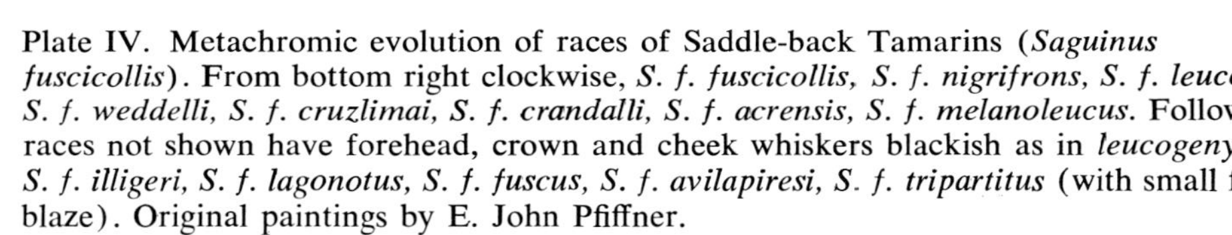

Plate IV. Metachromic evolution of races of Saddle-back Tamarins (*Saguinus fuscicollis*). From bottom right clockwise, *S. f. fuscicollis, S. f. nigrifrons, S. f. leucogenys, S. f. weddelli, S. f. cruzlimai, S. f. crandalli, S. f. acrensis, S. f. melanoleucus.* Following races not shown have forehead, crown and cheek whiskers blackish as in *leucogenys: S. f. illigeri, S. f. lagonotus, S. f. fuscus, S. f. avilapiresi, S. f. tripartitus* (with small frontal blaze). Original paintings by E. John Pfiffner.

SAGUINUS FUSCICOLLIS
GEOGRAPHIC METACHROMISM

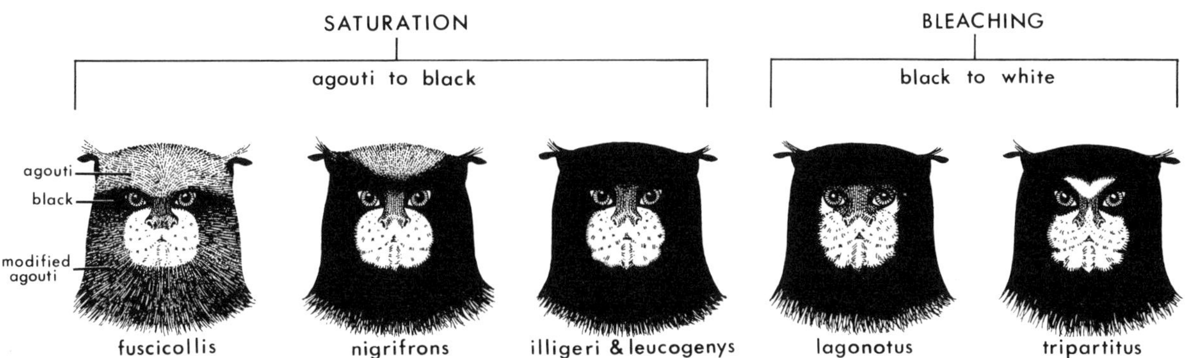

CENTRAL RACES

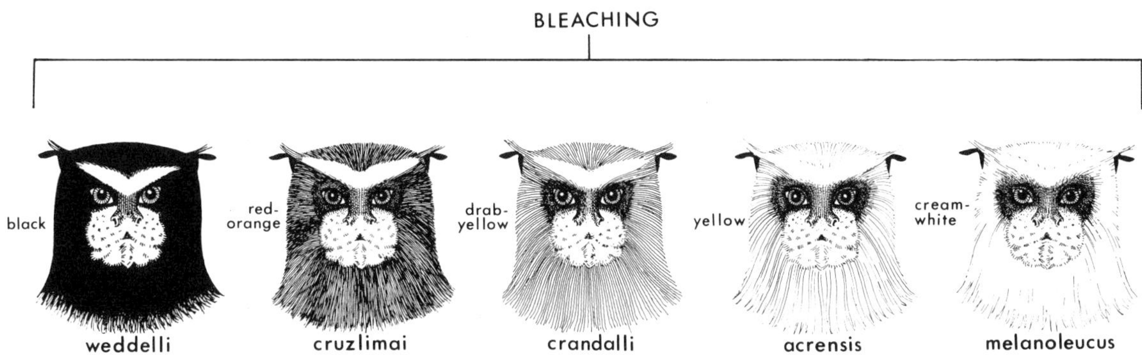

SOUTHERN RACES

Fig. X.27. Geographic metachromism in *Saguinus fuscicollis* demonstrated by the facial color patterns; facial patterns of northern races *fuscus* and *avilapiresi* are indistinguishable from *illigeri* (C3) and not shown. For geographic relationships see fig. X.24, 26 and pls. 3, 4.

2. Crown white, grayish, yellowish, or drab; tail white, yellowish, grayish drab, or brown, except sometimes at base 3

2′. Crown buffy or orange ticked with black (agouti) or dominantly to entirely black; tail black or blackish brown except at base 4

3. Head, mantle, and forelimbs dominantly drab, or pale pinkish brown . . . . *S. f. crandalli* (p. 663)

3′. Head, mantle, and forelimbs dominantly white or yellowish white . . . . *S. f. acrensis* (p. 664)

4. Crown buffy or orange punctulated with black or dark brown (agouti) 5

4′. Crown entirely or dominantly blackish 8

5. Forehead with whitish superciliary band ("eyebrows"); mantle, arms and upper surface of hands orange . . . . *S. f. cruzlimae* (p. 661)

5′. Forehead agouti like crown, or black; mantle agouti to dark brown, arms darker, upper surface of hands black 6

6. Hind legs dark brown or olivaceous, forehead blackish agouti and not defined from crown . . . . *S. f. avilapiresi* (p. 643)

6′. Hind limbs reddish or chestnut, forehead black, sharply defined from crown, or orange agouti not defined from crown 7

7. Forehead and sides of head black, mantle agouti like crown . . . . *S. f. nigrifrons* (p. 645)

7′. Forehead and sides of head buffy or agouti like crown, mantle darker . . . . *S. f. fuscicollis* (p. 644)

8. Mantle blackish, like crown 9

8′. Mantle agouti, reddish, or golden, contrasting with blackish of crown 11

9. Forehead with gray or whitish superciliary band ("eyebrows"); base of mantle hairs brownish or drab . . . . *S. f. weddelli* (p. 660)

9′. Forehead blackish like crown, base of mantle hairs blackish 10

10. General color of body brownish, rump and outer sides of thighs brownish like mantle and not sharply demarcated from saddle . . . . *S. f. avilapiresi* (p. 643)
10′. Body color trizonal, black mantle and reddish rump and thighs well demarcated from striated saddle . . . . *S. f. leucogenys* (p. 650)
11. Mantle golden, sharply defined from black crown and sides of head; grayish midfrontal chevron or patch present . . . . *S. f. tripartitus* (p. 657)
11′. Mantle agouti or reddish, forehead black or grizzled, never with a well-defined grayish chevron or patch . . 12
12. Mantle and outer sides of arms and legs dominantly agouti, upper surface of hands and feet variably mixed with black; throat and neck rufous . . . . *S. f. fuscus* (p. 642)
12′. Mantle and outer sides of arms and legs dominantly reddish or chestnut, upper surface of hands and feet dominantly black; throat reddish brown to black 13
13. Mantle and outer sides of arms and legs uniformly reddish or mahogany, hairs in adults little or not at all annulated or ticked with black . . . . *S. f. lagonotus* (p. 653)
13′. Mantle and outer sides of arms and legs chestnut, the hairs distinctly agouti, that is, terminal portion finely multibanded black and reddish . . . . *S. f. illigeri* (p. 647)

SAGUINUS FUSCICOLLIS FUSCUS LESSON: LESSON'S SADDLE-BACK TAMARIN

Synonymic History

Simia leonina Humboldt, 1805, *Rec. Obs. Zool. Anat. Comp., Paris,* p. 18 (name), p. 28 (description), pl. 5 (animal)—COLOMBIA: *Putumayo* (type locality, "plaines de Mocoa" between the Ríos Putumayo and Caquetá). Humboldt, 1811–12, *Rec. Obs. Zool. Anat. Comp., Paris,* ed. 2, p. 14 (description), p. 16 (name), p. 361 (tableau), pl. 5 (animal). Cabrera, 1940, *Ciencia (México)* 1:404 name preoccupied by *Simia leonina* Shaw, 1800 and replaced by *Leontopithecus fuscus,* 1840. Hershkovitz, 1949, *Proc. U.S. Nat. Mus.* 98:424—treated as a synonym of *Simia rosalia* Linnaeus. Cabrera, 1956, *Neotropica, Buenos Aires* 2 (8):49—a species of *Tamarin.* Hershkovitz, 1957, *Proc. Biol. Soc. Washington* 70:17—systematic position; characters; COLOMBIA: *Putumayo* (between Ríos Caquetá and Putumayo).

Simia leonia [*sic*], Wolf, 1818, *Abbild. Beschreib. merkw. naturg. Gegenst., Nurnberg,* p. 38, pl. 8 (animal)—lapsus for *leonina;* description and figure from Humboldt.

Midas leoninus, E. Geoffroy, 1812, *Ann. Mus. Hist. Nat., Paris* 19:121—characters ex Humboldt. Kuhl, 1820, *Beitr. Zool.,* p. 51—characters ex Humboldt; two specimens seen in Bremen.

[*Callithrix*] *leonina,* Fischer, 1813, *Zoognosia Tab. Syn.* 2:527—characters ex Humboldt; classification.

Jacchus leoninus, Desmarest, 1818, *Nouv. Dict. Hist. Nat.* 24:242—characters ex Humboldt. I. Geoffroy, 1827, *Dict. Sci. Nat.* 47:23—characters ex Humboldt.

H[*apale*] *leonina,* Wagner, 1840, *Schreber's Säugth., Suppl.* 1:249—characters ex Humboldt; specimen without locality data in Frankfurt Museum [?].

L[*eontopithecus*] *leoninus,* Reichenbach, 1863, *Vollst. Naturg. Affen,* p. 6, pl. 2, fig. 24 (animal)—characters ex Humboldt.

Leontocebus leoninus, Elliot, 1913, *A review of the Primates* 1:210—characters ex Humboldt.

L[*eontocebus*] *leoninus,* Osman Hill, 1957, *Primates* 3:262, 269—history; regarded as a synonym of *rosalia.*

[*Midas*] (*Leontopithecus*) *fuscus* Lesson, 1840, *Species des mammifères: Bimanes et quadrumanes . . . ,* p. 184—new name for *Simia leonina* Humboldt. Lesson, 1842, *Nouv. Tableau Reg. Anim.,* p. 9.

Leontocebus fuscus, Cabrera, 1940, *Ciencia (México)* 1:404—next available name for *Simia leonina* Humboldt, preoccupied by *Simia leonina* Shaw, 1800 [a cercopithecid]. Cabrera, 1958, *Rev. Mus. Argentino Cienc. Nat., "Bernardino Rivadavia"* 4:191, 192—classification.

Leontocebus (*Leontocebus*) *fuscus,* Hershkovitz, 1957, *Proc. Biol. Soc. Washington* 70:18—taxonomy.

[*Saguinus fuscicollis*] *fuscus,* Hershkovitz, 1966, *Folia Primat.* 4:385—classification.
S[*aguinus*] *f*[*uscicollis*] *fuscus,* Hershkovitz, 1968, *Evolution* 22(3):560, fig. 4 (diagnostic color pattern)—characters; distribution; metachromism.

Saguinus fuscicollis fuscus, Hershkovitz, 1970, *Am. J. Phys. Anthrop.* 32:379—classification; dental disease.

[?] *Hapale illigeri,* Jentink (part, not Pucheran), 1892, *Mus. Hist. Nat. Pays-Bas* 11:56—COLOMBIA: "Medellín."

Type. None in existence, description of *Simia leonina* Humboldt based on two young caged animals seen in Popayán, Colombia.

Type Locality. "Plaines de Mocoa (55)," that is, lowlands in the Mocoa district, between the Ríos Putumayo and Caquetá, Putumayo, southeastern Colombia.

Distribution (fig. X.24). Southeastern Colombia and northwestern Brazil between the Río Caquetá-Caguán (Japurá) and the Putumayo (Içа); altitudinal range, 50 to possibly 600 meters above sea level. *Saguinus f. fuscus* is the northernmost representative of "white-lipped" hairy-face tamarins.

Taxonomy. Saguinus fuscicollis fuscus was first described as *Simia leonina* by Humboldt in 1805. This name is invalidated by *Simia leonina* Shaw, 1800, an Old World monkey (certainly the langur currently known as *Presbytis johnii* Fischer rather than a macaque as has been suggested). The homonym has since been replaced by *Midas fuscus* Lesson.

The colored plate of *Simia leonina* Humboldt published with the original description was based on Humboldt's field notes by an artist who never saw the animal. The nearly uniformly golden brown figure with flowing leonine mane misled authors into identifying the animal with the eastern Brazilian Golden Lion-tamarin, *Simia rosalia* Linnaeus, or *Leontopithecus rosalia rosalia*. Wagner (1840, pp. iv, v ff) included Humboldt's tamarin in the genus *Leontocebus* he had erected primarily for Brazilian lion-tamarins. Lesson (1840, p. 184) did likewise in proposing the name *Leontopithecus* for the same group. Such was the conviction that Humboldt's tamarin was indeed a geographically misplaced and faultily described representative of the true Golden Lion-tamarin that Reichenbach (1862, p. 6) restricted it to the genus *Leontopithecus* while Miller (1912, p. 380) designated it the type species of *Leontocebus* Wagner. This state of affairs was maintained for well over a century until Cabrera (1956, p. 49) demonstrated conclusively that *Simia leonina* was a white-lipped hairy-face tamarin of the genus *Saguinus*. As I have shown elsewhere (1957, p. 17), specimens of undoubted *S. fuscicollis* collected by me, and subsequently by others, in the type region agree in the main with Humboldt's description of *leonina*. No other form of *Saguinus* occurs in Colombia between the Ríos Putumayo and Caquetá and no other kind of callitrichid can be identified with *leonina*, now *fuscus*.

Diagnostic Characters. Crown black, orange mantle evenly ticked with black, the base of the hairs pale, tufts below and behind ears like mantle, underparts almost uniformly reddish brown.

Coloration. Crown, forehead, cheeks, interorbital space black; gray hairs around mouth and sides of nostrils short; facial skin entirely black; sides of head beneath ears reddish brown to blackish brown; mantle extending over upper third of back, ochraceous orange evenly ticked with black, the hairs drab to whitish at roots; lower back marbled buffy and black; arms, rump, and thighs like mantle; upper surface of hands and feet blackish mixed with orange; throat, chest, belly, inner surface of limb rufous lightly suffused with blackish or dark brown, base of hairs of chest and throat buffy to whitish; tail black with ventral surface of basal third rufous.

Measurements. See appendix table 2.

Comparisons. Resemblance between agouti-mantled *fuscus* and *illigeri* is greater than between either of them and the geographically intermediate red-mantled *lagonotus;* distinguished from *illigeri* by orange throat, the hairs with pale bases, and by extension of orange agouti to one fourth or more of basal portion of tail. *S. f. fuscus* appears to be the only race of *fuscicollis* with the hairs of the agouti-colored mantle consistently paler basally than terminally. In many individuals of *fuscus* the basal portion of hairs of neck and chest is also paler than terminal portion. *S. f. weddelli* resembles *fuscus* with respect to color of basal portion of hairs of mantle, neck and chest but differs markedly by its frontal blaze and black mantle.

Variation. Individual variation is comparatively slight and most noticeable in the mantle, rump, and hind legs, where the pale annulations of the agouti-patterned hairs vary from ochraceous orange to tawny. The series of 9 specimens of *fuscus* from Río Mecaya (57b) and another of 7 from Tres Troncos (54) lower down the Caquetá vary in the same way. One specimen from La Rastra, Río Orteguaza (53), above Mecaya is more saturate (tawny) on mantle than on rump and hind legs (ochraceous orange). Two specimens from Solita (56) on the Caquetá above Mecaya are slightly more saturate throughout than the preceding. Finally, one specimen from Tonantins (173), at the eastern extreme of the range in Brazil, is most saturate, or deeply reddish on mantle and thighs. The difference, nevertheless, is not significant. In all other respects, the Brazilian specimen agrees with Colombian *fuscus* even to the pale bases of the hairs of the mantle, throat and chest.

Specimens Examined. 20. COLOMBIA—*Caquetá:* La Rastra, Río Orteguaza, 1 (AMNH); Tres Troncos, Río Caquetá, 7 (FMNH); *Putumayo:* Río Mecaya, Río Caquetá, 9 (FMNH); Solita, Río Putumayo, 2 (GEE); BRAZIL—*Amazonas:* Rio Tonantins, 1 (BM).

SAGUINUS FUSCICOLLIS AVILAPIRESI HERSHKOVITZ: AVILA PIRES'S SADDLE-BACK TAMARIN

Synonymic History

Midas rufoniger Bates (not I. Geoffroy and Deville), 1863, *Naturalist on the river Amazons* 1:321; ibid., 1864, ed. 2, p. 399—BRAZIL: *Amazonas* (near Ega [= Tefé]).

Saguinus fuscicollis avilapiresi Hershkovitz, 1966, *Folia Primat.* 4:386. Hershkovitz, 1968, *Evolution* 22(3):561, figs. 4, 5 (diagnostic color pattern)—characters; distribution; metachromism.

Type. Adult female, skin and skull, American Museum of Natural History, no. 78959; collected 15 July 1928 by the Olalla Brothers.

Type Locality. Mouth of the Lago de Tefé (182), south bank of the Rio Solimões (Amazonas), Amazonas, Brazil.

Distribution (fig. X.24). South of the Rio Amazonas between the lower Rios Juruá and Purús; southern limits of range unknown.

Diagnostic Characters. Most uniformly and somberly colored race of *S. fuscicollis;* body dominantly dark brown or melano-agouti throughout, rump and thighs like mantle and well defined from but not sharply contrasted with saddle (pl. 3).

Coloration. Foreparts including forehead, crown, mantle, and upper arms blackish brown, finely ticked with orange, the blackish brown hairs generally with two narrow subapical orange bands; lower arms with more black; facial skin black, gray hairs of circumbuccal band paler and longer than usual, and forming a triangular patch on each side of muzzle with apex beneath the eye; saddle (middle of lower back) blackish brown, the long brownish hairs with a broad buffy subterminal band; lateral fringe with more buff than back; rump and outer sides of thighs dark brown like mantle and not sharply contrasted with back, hairs brownish with one or two fine subterminal orange bands, legs darker than thighs; upper surface of hands and feet black; throat, neck, chest, and belly brown finely ticked with orange; inner sides of legs more black; tail black except base like rump.

Measurements. See appendix table 2.

Comparisons. Distinguished from all other races of *fuscicollis* by rump and thighs blackish-brown agouti, not reddish, and by the generally dark brown coloration throughout; from its nearest relative, *Saguinus fuscicollis fuscus* by reduction of the phaeomelanic bands and dominance of the eumelanic of hairs of nape, shoulders, rump, underparts, limbs, and tail base, circumbuccal band more white, moustache longer; from *Saguinus nigricollis graellsi* by definition of saddle from mantle, rump, and thighs, brown temporal patches absent, whitish hairs of circumbuccal band longer, and border of whitish paranarial patches divergent from muzzle, not tending to encircle it; from *Saguinus mystax pluto* which it approaches in overall coloration by smaller size, circumbuccal and circumnarial band of skin darkly pigmented like that of remainder of face, and by pelage of perineum and ventral surface of tail base dark agouti brown not sharply contrasted whitish.

Remarks. Saguinus fuscicollis avilapiresi can be defined as a rapidly melanizing offshoot of the predominantly agouti-colored *S. f. fuscus.* Differences between the two suggest that the first diverged from the second after a river bend cutoff of the Rio Amazonas somewhere between the mouths of the Tefé and Juruá shuttled a breeding population of an earlier grade of *fuscus* from the northern to the southern bank of the great river. The crown of the present form of *fuscus* became more or less uniformly black as contrasted with the melanoagouti crown of *avilapiresi.* In all other respects *fuscus* is metachromically one grade more primitive than *avilapiresi.*

The type series of *avilapiresi* (AMNH nos. 78958–78960), consisting of two males and the female holotype, is remarkably homogenous. A specimen from Ayapuá (184), in the British Museum agrees with the others. First notice of the existence of this race of tamarin was published in 1863 by Henry Walter Bates in his account of the monkeys of the vicinity of Ega, now known as Tefé (182). Bates (1863, p. 321) observed that

> our old friend Midas ursulus [= *Saguinus midas* Linnaeus], of Pará and the lower Amazons, is not found on the Upper river, but in its stead a closely-allied species presents itself, which appears to be the Midas rufoniger of Gervais [another name for *Saguinus nigricollis nigricollis* Spix but actually *S. f. avilapiresi*], whose mouth is bordered with longish white hairs. The habits of this species are the same as those of the M. ursulus, indeed it seems probable that it is a form or race of the same stock, modified to suit the altered local conditions under which it lives.

Specimens Examined. 4. BRAZIL—*Amazonas:* Lago de Tefé, 3 (AMNH); Ayapuá, Rio Purús, 1 (BM).

SAGUINUS FUSCICOLLIS FUSCICOLLIS SPIX: SPIX'S SADDLE-BACK TAMARIN

Synonymic History

Midas fuscicollis Spix, 1823, *Sim. et Vesp. Brasil.*, p. 27, fig. 20 (animal). Wagner, 1833, *Isis von Oken* 10:995—believed to be a variety of *mystax.* Ihering, 1904, *Rev. Mus. Paulista, São Paulo* 6:415—BRAZIL: *Amazonas* (upper Rio Juruá, near São Felipe).

M[idas] fuscicollis, Reichenbach, 1862, *Vollst. Naturg. Affen,* p. 13—characters.

H[apale] fuscicollis, Wagner, 1855, *Schreber's Säugth., Suppl.* 5:131—characters; comparisons; *Midas flavifrons* I. Geoffroy regarded as a synonym.

Hapale fuscicollis, Schlegel, 1876, *Les singes. Simiae,* p. 264—BRAZIL: *Amazonas* (Rio Javarí). Jentink, 1892, *Cat. Syst. Mamm. Pays-Bas* 11:56—BRAZIL: *Amazonas* (Rio Javarí).

Leontocebus fuscicollis, Elliot, 1913, *A review of the Primates* 1:207—description; synonymy (part, not *"Hapale chrysomelas* Schlegel"). Cabrera, 1958, *Rev. Mus. Argentino Cienc. Nat. "Bernardino Rivadavia"* 4(1):191—classification; synonymy (part, not *"Hapale chrysomelas* Schlegel"); part, synonyms, *flavifrons* only.

Mystax fuscicollis, Lönnberg, 1940, *Ark. Zool. Stockholm* 32A(10):10—BRAZIL: *Amazonas* (João Pessôa, Rio Juruá, north side).

Tamarin fuscicollis, Vieira, 1948, *Bol. Mus. Paraense* 10:254—BRAZIL: *Amazonas* (Igarapé, Rio Juruá do Gordão, Rio Juruá).

Marikina fuscicollis, Hershkovitz, 1949, *Proc. U.S. Nat. Mus.* 98:413—part, key characters; synonyms [part, *flavifrons* I. Geoffroy only].

Tamarinus fuscicollis, Osman Hill, 1957, *Primates* 3:218, 222, 224, 226, 227, 229—characters; distribution; geographic variation; taxonomy; part synonymy, *flavifrons* I. Geoffroy only.

[*Saguinus fuscicollis*] *fuscicollis,* Hershkovitz, 1966, *Folia Primat.* 4:385—classification (*flavifrons* I. Geoffroy and Deville, a synonym).

S[*aguinus*] *f*[*uscicollis*] *fuscicollis,* Hershkovitz, 1968, *Evolution* 22(3):560, figs. 4, 5 (diagnostic color pattern)—characters; distribution; metachromism.

Midas flavifrons I. Geoffroy and Deville, 1848, *Comptes Rendus, Acad. Sci., Paris* 27:499—PERU: (type locality, "haut Amazone"; type, mounted with skull in, Muséum National d'Histoire Naturelle, Paris, no. 649 (637, 1847–1690), collected by Castelnau and Deville. I. Geoffroy, 1852, *Arch. Mus. Hist. Nat., Paris* 5:574—characters. Rode, 1938, *Bull. Mus. Nat. Hist. Nat., Paris,* ser. 2, 10:240—type history.

M[*idas*] *flavifrons,* I. Geoffroy, 1851, *Cat. Primates, Mus. Hist. Nat., Paris,* p. 64—types, male and female "Du Brésil, Bas-Amazone, près Pebas, par MM. de Castelnau et Deville, envoi de 1847." I. Geoffroy, 1855, *Castelnau Exped. Amérique Sud,* pt. 7, *Zool., Mamm.,* p. 22, pl. 6, fig. 1 (animal)—"environs de Pebas." Reichenbach, 1862, *Vollst. Naturg. Affen,* p. 13—characters.

"M[*idas*] *ruficollis* Spix," Slack, 1861, *Proc. Acad. Nat. Sci. Philadelphia* 13:464—lapsus for *fuscicollis* Spix, in synonymy of *Midas mystax* Spix.

Midas labiatus, Temminck (part, not E. Geoffroy), 1824, *Monogr. Mammal.* 1:xv—*fuscicollis* Spix regarded as a synonym.

J[*acchus*] *labiatus,* S. Fischer, 1829, *Syn. Mamm.,* p. 64—part *fuscicollis* Spix regarded as a variety.

Midas tamarin, Lesson (part, not Link), 1840, *Species des mammifères: Bimanes et quadrumanes . . . ,* p. 197—*fuscicollis* regarded as the "jeune âge" of *tamarin.*

Type. In the Munich Museum; collected by Spix and Martius.

Type Locality. "It occurs near the district of São Paulo de Olivença in the forests between the Solimões and Iça"; here restricted to the vicinity of São Paulo de Olivença (172b) on the south bank of the Rio Solimões.

Distribution (fig. X.24). Western Brazil, south of the Solimões, between the Rios Juruá and Javarí but with the section between the Juruá and Jutaí unknown; altitudinal range between 75 and 150 meters above sea level.

Taxonomy. Midas flavifrons I. Geoffroy and Deville is hardly, if at all, distinguishable from *fuscicollis.* The colored figure given by Geoffroy (1855, pl. 6, fig. 1) shows the white of the mouth extending across the nostrils. The same artistic liberty was taken in depicting the face of *devillei* (fig. 3) on the same plate. These two tamarins and all other members of the *fuscicollis* group known then were correctly characterized by I. Geoffroy (1851, p. 64) as "espèces à lèvres blanches (mais non à nez blanc)." The type locality of *flavifrons,* "haute Amazone," given in the original description, is vague. Its restriction (later) by I. Geoffroy to the vicinity of Pebas, a locality on the north bank of the Marañon in Loreto, Peru, is incorrect.

Diagnostic Characters. Crown, forehead, and temples dominantly orange-agouti, cheeks black, mantle dark agouti to blackish brown (figs. X.26, 27; pls. 3, 4).

Coloration. Forehead, crown, and sides of head in front of ears orange minutely ticked with black; facial skin black, short hairs surrounding mouth and sides of nostrils gray; sides of face blackish, interorbital space black or with a weakly defined V-shaped buffy to grayish patch; mantle extending little beyond shoulders, blackish or dark brown, sparsely stippled with orange; arms like mantle; middle and lower back marbled black with buffy or orange; rump and thighs reddish; upper surface of hands and feet black; throat, neck, chest dark brown or reddish brown, more or less mixed or washed with black; belly with less black; external genitalia mostly or entirely black; tail black except for short rufous basal portion.

Measurements. See appendix table 2.

Comparisons. Retention of primitive agouti hair pattern on forehead and sides of head separates *fuscicollis* from fully black-cheeked, black-fronted *nigrifrons* of the Peruvian side of the Yavarí as well as all other races of *S. fuscicollis.* The poorly defined pale interorbital patch present in some individuals of *fuscicollis* foreshadows the well-marked chevron-shaped interorbital patch of *tripartitus* and the broad crescentic frontal band of *weddelli, crandalli, acrensis* and *melanoleucus.*

Specimens Examined. 14. BRAZIL—*Amazonas:* Igarapé do Gordão, Rio Juruá, 2 (FMNH); João Pessõa, Rio Juruá, 3 (FMNH); PERU—*Loreto:* "Río Yavarí", 2 (RMNH); UNKNOWN LOCALITY—7 (AMNH, 3; MNHN, type of *flavifrons;* BM, 1; FMNH, 1 in spirits; SM, 1).

SAGUINUS FUSCICOLLIS NIGRIFRONS I. GEOFFROY: GEOFFROY'S SADDLE-BACK TAMARIN

Synonymic History

Hapale nigrifrons I. Geoffroy, 1850, *Comptes Rendus, Acad. Sci., Paris* 31:875—type locality unknown. I. Geoffroy, 1851, *Rev. Mag. Zool.,* p. 25—description repeated. Schlegel, 1876, *Les singes. Simiae,* p. 263—BRAZIL: *Amazonas* (Rio Yavarí). Jentink, 1892, *Cat. Syst. Mamm. Mus. Pays-Bas* 11:56—PERU: *Loreto* (Río Yavarí).

M[idas] nigrifrons, I. Geoffroy, 1851, *Cat. Primates Mus. Hist. Nat., Paris,* p. 64—description repeated; type history. Reichenbach, 1862, *Vollst. Naturg. Affen,* p. 13—characters.

Midas nigrifrons, I. Geoffroy, 1852, *Arch. Mus. Hist. Nat., Paris* 5:572—characters. Rode, 1938, *Bull. Mus. Nat. Hist. Nat., Paris,* ser. 2, 10:240—type history.

Leontocebus nigrifrons, Elliot, 1913, *A review of the Primates* 1:198—characters ex type.

Tamarin nigrifrons nigrifrons, Cruz Lima, 1945, *Mamíferos da Amazonia, Primates,* p. 230, pl. 38, fig. 1 (animal) —characters.

T[amarinus] nigrifrons, Osman Hill, 1957, *Primates* 3:224, 226, 227—characters; taxonomy; "at most . . . can be regarded only as a subspecies of *fuscicollis.*"

[Saguinus fuscicollis] nigrifrons, Hershkovitz, 1966, *Folia Primat.* 4:385—classification (*pebilis* Thomas, a synonym). Hershkovitz, 1968, *Evolution* 22(3):560, figs. 4, 5 (diagnostic color pattern)—characters; distribution; metachromism.

S[aguinus] f[uscicollis] nigrifrons, Gengozian, 1969, *Ann. N.Y. Acad. Sci.* 62:338, fig. 1C (facial characters)—red cell specificity. Gengozian, 1972 *J. Med. Primat.* 1, (3):172—inter- and intrasubspecific red cell immunizations.

Mystax nigrifrons pebilis Thomas, 1928, *Ann. Mag. Nat. Hist.,* ser. 10 2:286—PERU: *Loreto* (type locality, Pebas, Río Marañon, 330 ft.); type, male, skin and skull, British Museum (Natural History) no. 28.7.21.12, collected 6 February 1928 by R. W. Hendee.

T[amarinus] nigrifrons pebilis, Osman Hill, 1957, *Primates* 3:226, 227—characters; regarded as a synonym of *nigrifrons.*

Mystax devillei micans, Thomas (part, not Thomas), 1928, *Ann. Mag. Nat. Hist.,* ser. 10 2:256—PERU: *Loreto* (Cerro Azul, near Contamana).

Marikina fuscicollis, Hershkovitz (part, not Spix), 1949, *Proc. U.S. Nat. Mus.* 98:413—*Hapale nigrifrons* I. Geoffroy and *pebilis* Thomas in synonymy. Cabrera, 1958, *Rev. Mus. Argentino Cienc. Nat. "Bernardino Rivadavia"* 4:191—part, *nigrifrons* and *pebilis* in synonymy.

Leontocebus illigeri, Cabrera (part, not Pucheran), 1958, *Rev. Mus. Argentino Cienc. Nat. "Bernardino Rivadavia"* 4 (1):192—*Tamarin nigrifrons nigrifrons* of Cruz Lima in synonymy.

Type. Male, skin mounted with skull in, Muséum National d'Histoire Naturelle, no. 117 (647[636]); purchased 1850 from M. Verreaux.

Type Locality. Unknown, here restricted to lower Río Yavarí (115a), Loreto, Peru.

Distribution. (fig. X.24). Northeastern Peru south of the Marañon between the lower Ríos Yavarí and Ucayali, at least as far south as Cerro Azul, Department of Loreto.

Taxonomy. The provenance of the type of *nigrifrons* is unknown, but all tamarins of known origin identifiable as *nigrifrons* inhabit the forests between the lower Ríos Yavarí and Ucayali. Present restriction of the type locality to the lower Yavarí confirms the first definite locality record (Schlegel 1876:263) for a black-fronted tamarin.

Mystax nigrifrons pebilis Thomas was compared with a secondary (I. Geoffroy 1851:572) description of *nigrifrons.* The cheeks, throat, neck, and chest in *pebilis* were described as black, while the same parts in *nigrifrons* were interpreted as "grizzled olivaceous or rufous." In present material, forehead with cheeks are black, that is, "front noir, ainsi que le tour de la face," as first described by I. Geoffroy, but underparts from throat to chest vary from black as in *pebilis* to rufous or reddish brown more or less ticked with black as in the type of *nigrifrons.* The type locality of *pebilis,* said to be Pebas (85), an old established, sizeable town on the left bank of the Marañon, is here construed as the forests on the opposite bank of the river.

Diagnostic Characters. Black of forehead and sides of head sharply contrasted with dominantly buffy-orange agouti of crown and mantle (figs. X.26, 27; pls. 3, 4).

Coloration. Forehead and interorbital space, sides of head and neck black; facial skin pigmented, short hairs surrounding mouth and sides of nostrils gray; crown and mantle buffy evenly ticked with black, the terminal halves of hairs with four or five buffy bands each separated by a black band, tips and basal halves of hairs black; outer sides of upper arms more saturate than mantle, forearms and inner sides of arms blackish; saddle well defined, striated or marbled black and grayish or buffy; rump and thighs reddish orange; upper surface of hands and feet black; chest dark brown to black, washed with orange or reddish; belly with less black; tail black except for rufous base; external genitalia mostly or entirely black.

Measurements. See appendix table 2.

Comparisons. The black cheeks, forehead, and temples distinguish *nigrifrons* from *fuscicollis.* The black extends well above and around the ears in some specimens, but in none does it cover the crown as in *S. f. illigeri.* In other respects, *nigrifrons* and *illigeri* are similar except that the mantle of the latter is more red with coarser black ticking, the underparts less black.

Remarks. A series of 15 specimens collected by the Olalla Brothers at "Sarayacu," Río Ucayali, in March, April and August, were certainly taken on the right, or east, bank of the river opposite the village of Sarayacu. The Olallas also secured 17 specimens of *illigeri* in Sarayacu (102), the first dated 13 March, when the first *nigrifrons* was collected. The remaining 16 specimens were taken on 7 dates in April, all different from the *nigrifrons* dates, and in May when no *nigrifrons* were taken.

A specimen from Cerro Azul (103), near Contamana, mentioned by Thomas (1928, p. 256) as doubtfully referable to his *Mystax devillei micans* (= *Saguinus fuscicollis leucogenys*), resembles *illigeri* in the extension of black over the crown. It agrees with *nigrifrons* in all other respects and points to intergradation with black-mantled *weddelli* higher up the Río Ucayali.

Specimens Examined. 47. PERU—*Loreto:* Cerro Azul, 1 (BM); "Marupa," 2 (AMNH); Pebas, 6 (BM, 5 including type of *pebilis;* RMNH, 1); Orosa, 15 (AMNH); Quebrada Esperanza, Río Yavarí, 1 (FMNH); Río Yavarí, 1 (RMNH); San Fernando, Río Yavarí, 1 (FMNH); Santa Cecilia, Río Manití, Iquitos, 3 (FMNH); Sarayacu, opposite, Río Ucayali, 15 (AMNH); *locality unknown:* 2 (type of *nigrifrons,* MNHN; FMNH, 1 in spirits).

SAGUINUS FUSCICOLLIS ILLIGERI PUCHERAN: ILLIGER'S SADDLE-BACK TAMARIN

Fig. X.28. Illiger's Saddle-back Tamarin, *Saguinus fuscicollis illigeri* Pucheran.

Synonymic History

Hapale Illigeri Pucheran, 1845, *Rev. Zool.* 8:336. Rode, 1938, *Bull. Mus. Nat. Hist., Nat.,* ser. 2, 10:240—type history.

Hapale illigeri, Schlegel, 1876, *Les singes. Simiae,* p. 263—PERU. Jentink, 1887, *Cat. Ostéol. Mus. Pays-Bas* 9:49 part, PERU: *Loreto* (Amazonian region). Jentink, 1892, *Cat. Syst. Mamm. Mus. Pays-Bas* 11:56—part, PERU: *Loreto.*

Midas illigeri, I. Geoffroy, 1852, *Arch. Mus. Hist. Nat., Paris* 5:531 (footnote), 580—characters.

M[idas] illigeri, I. Geoffroy, 1851, *Cat. Primates Mus. Hist. Nat., Paris,* p. 65—type history. Reichenbach, 1862, *Vollst. Naturg. Affen,* p. 13—characters.

Leontocebus illigeri, Elliot, 1913, *A review of the Primates,* 1:205—part, characters ex type. Cabrera, 1958, *Rev. Mus. Argentino Cienc. Nat. "Bernardino Rivadavia"* 4 (1):192—part, *illigeri* Pucheran, *devillei* Sclater, 1871, *mounseyi* Thomas, *illigeri* part of Hershkovitz, 1949.

Tamarin illigeri, Cruz Lima, 1945, *Mamíferos da Amazonia, Primates,* p. 235—characters ex Pucheran; taxonomy.

Marikina illigeri, Hershkovitz, 1949, *Proc. U.S. Nat. Mus.* 98:413—part, *bluntschlii* Matschie and *mounseyi* Thomas, in synonymy.

Saguinus illigeri, Porter, 1972, *Lab. Animal Sci.* 22(4):503—endoparasites.

Saguinus fuscicollis illigeri, Hershkovitz, 1966, *Mammalia* 30(2):328—PERU: *Loreto* (type locality redetermined as left bank Río Ucayali, near mouth); characters of holotype; synonyms: *devillei, bluntschlii.* Egozcue, Perkins, and Hagemenas, 1968, *Folia Primat.* 9:82, fig. 1 (animal)—karyotype, (2n = 46). Hsu and Hampton, 1970, *Folia Primat.* 13:183—karyotype (2n = 46). Gengozian and Porter, 1971, in *Med. Primat. 1970,* ed. Goldsmith and Moor-Jankowski, p. 165—survival time of intrasubspecific skin grafts (9–64 days); *illigeri* to *Sagui-*

nus fuscicollis lagonotus, 9–29 days; *lagonotus* to *illigeri,* 7–33 days; *illigeri* to *mystax,* 5–19 days; *mystax* to *illigeri,* 8–32 days; *illigeri* to *oedipus,* 5–days; *oedipus* to *illigeri,* 6–31 days.

[*Saguinus fuscicollis*] *illigeri,* Hershkovitz, 1966, *Folia Primat.* 4:385—classification; synonyms: *devillei* I .Geoffroy; *mounseyi* Thomas; *bluntschlii* Matschie. Hershkovitz, 1968, *Evolution* 22(3):560, figs. 4, 5 (diagnostic color pattern)—characters; distribution; metachromism.

S[*aguinus*] *f*[*uscicollis*] *illigeri,* Gengozian, 1969, *Ann. N.Y. Acad. Sci.* 162:338, fig. 1A (facial characters)—red cell specificity. Porter and Gengozian, 1969, *Transplantation* 8(5):653—survival time of skin allografts, between individuals, 9–64 days; *illigeri* to *lagonotus,* 7–26 days; *lagonotus* to *illigeri,* 7–33; co-twins, long-term acceptance. Gengozian, 1972, *J. Med. Primat.* 1, (3):172—inter- and intrasubspecific red cell immunizations.

S[*aguinus*] *fuscicollis illigeri,* S. H. Hampton, 1973, *Amer. J. Phys. Anthrop.* 38, (2):265—germ cell chimerism in adult males.

Hapale Devilli [*sic*] I. Geoffroy, 1950, *Comptes Rendus Acad. Sci., Paris* 31:875—PERU: (type locality, "rivière des Amazonas"); types in Paris Museum. I. Geoffroy, 1851, *Rev. Zool.,* p. 23—characters. Rode, 1938, *Bull. Mus. Nat. Hist. Nat.,* ser. 2, 10:240—type, male mounted with skull in, Muséum national d'histoire naturelle, Paris, no. 116 (644[635]) received 1847 from MM. Castelnau and Deville.

Hapale devillei, Schlegel, 1876, *Les singes. Simiae,* p. 262—characters; *leucogenys* Gray regarded as a synonym.

M[*idas*] *Devilli* [*sic*] I. Geoffroy, 1851, *Cat. Primates Mus. Hist. Nat., Paris,* p. 64—PERU: *Loreto* (type locality, "mission de Sarayacu," Río Ucayali); syntypes, male and female, collected by Castelnau and Deville, accessioned 1847.

Midas Devilli [*sic*] I. Geoffroy, 1852, *Arch. Mus. Hist. Nat., Paris* 5:570—PERU: *Loreto* (type locality, Sarayacu). I. Geoffroy, 1855, *Castelnau Expéd. Amérique Sud, pt. 7, Zool., Mamm.,* p. 22, pl. 6, fig. 3 (animal)—PERU: *Loreto* (Sarayacu).

M[*idas*] *devillei,* Reichenbach, 1862, *Vollst. Naturg. Affen,* p. 13—characters.

Midas devillii [*sic*] Bartlett, 1871, *Proc. Zool. Soc. London* 1871:220—PERU: *Loreto* (Ríos Huallaga and Ucayali). Sclater, 1871, *Proc. Zool. Soc. London* 1871:220, footnote, pl. 13 (animal)—exhibition of colored figure.

L[*eontocebus*] *devillei,* Hanström, 1958, *Primatologia* 3(1):716, figs. 8–10 (hypophysis)—hypophysis.

[*Mystax*] *devillei,* Thomas, 1922, *Ann. Mag. Nat. Hist.* 9(9):198—classification.

[?] *Mystax devillei,* Thomas, 1927*a*, *Ann. Mag. Nat. Hist.* 9(19):365—part, *mounseyi* a synonym. Colyer, 1936, *Variation and diseases of the teeth of mammals,* p. 297, fig. 373 (mandible), fig. 374 (skull)—irregular position of teeth.

Tamarin devilli devilli [*sic*] Cruz Lima, 1945, *Mamíferos da Amazonia, Primates, Contr. Mus. Paraense,* p. 233, pl. 38, fig. 2 (animal)—part, characters; not *purillus* Thomas in synonymy.

Tamarinus devillei, Osman Hill, 1957, *Primates* 3:182, 223, 224, 225, 228, 229—characters; habits; variation; tentatively treated as a synonym of *nigricollis.*

Mystax bluntschlii Matschie, 1915, *Sitzungsb. Gesellsch. Naturf. Freunde, Berlin,* p. 96—PERU: *Loreto* (type locality, Río Samiria); type, male, skin and skull, Berlin Museum no. A.157,13,272, collected August 1912 by Professor H. Bluntschli.

Tamarin bluntschlii, Cruz Lima, 1945, *Mamíferos da Amazonia, Primates,* p. 232—characters ex Matschie.

Leontocebus mounseyi Thomas, 1920, *Ann. Mag. Nat. Hist.,* ser. 9, 5:144—PERU: Loreto (type locality, Río Pacaya, opposite Sapote, lower Ucayali, altitude, 250 feet); type, male, skin and skull, British Museum (Natural History) no. 20.1.9.1, collected 25 July 1912 by J. J. Mounsey.

Marikina nigricollis, Hershkovitz, (part, not Spix), 1949, *Proc. U.S. Nat. Mus.* 98:413—part, Hapale devilli Geoffroy, in synonymy.

S[*aguinus*] *f*[*uscicollis*] *illigeri* ♀ × *S. f. lagonotus* ♂, Gengozian, 1969, *Ann. N.Y. Acad. Sci.* 162:338, 357, fig. 1D (facial characters)—red cell specificity. Porter and Gengozian, 1969, *Transplantation* 8(5):653—survival of co-twin skin grafts over two years.

Saguinus fuscicollis illigeri ♀ × *S. nigricollis* ♂, Gengozian, 1969, *Ann. N.Y. Acad. Sci.* 162:359—hybridization.

S[*aguinus*] *f*[*uscicollis*] *illigeri* ♀ × *S. nigricollis* ♂, Porter and Gengozian, 1969, *Transplantation* 8(5):653—survival of co-twin skin graft over two years.

Type. Male, mounted with skull in, Muséum National d'Histoire Naturelle, Paris no. 652 (638); accessioned 1843 through the agency of M. Parzudaki. The type had been donated by Engineer M. Courtine to the menagerie of the Paris Museum, where it lived for some time.

Type Locality. Originally believed to be Colombia and accordingly restricted to the Colombian banks of the Rio Solimões by Hershkovitz (1949, *Proc. U.S. Nat. Mus.* 98:413). The type, however, was subsequently examined and found to agree with forms described as *devillei, bluntschlii,* and *mounseyi.* The type locality was, therefore, redetermined, by Hershkovitz (1966*b*, p. 328), as the left bank of the lower Río Ucayali, near its mouth, Loreto, Peru.

Distribution (fig. X.24). In Loreto, eastern Peru, between the lower Ríos Huallaga and Ucayali, from the south bank of the Marañon south to the Río Caxiabatay and, possibly, to the Pisquí.

Taxonomy. The type of the black-crowned, agouti-mantled *illigeri* in the Paris museum was a menagerie animal of uncertain provenance. It is of the kind known to inhabit the basins between the lower Ríos Huallaga and Ucayali in the Department of Loreto, northeastern Peru. The names *"Hapale devilli"* Geoffroy, 1850, *"Mystax bluntschlii"* Matschie, 1915, and *"Leontocebus mounseyi"* Thomas, 1920, proposed for individuals of the same species from the same area are junior synonyms of *Saguinus fuscicollis illigeri.*

The original description of *illigeri* is indifferent and misleadingly suggests the black-crowned, red-mantled tamarin of eastern Ecuador and Peru north of the Marañon and west of the Río Napo. As a result, authors, beginning with Thomas (1880, p. 395), applied the name *illigeri* to the red-mantled tamarin of eastern Ecuador, which is properly *Saguinus fuscicollis lagonotus* Jiménez de la Espada, 1870.

Hapale devilli [*sic*] I. Geoffroy (1850) is an agouti-mantled tamarin. Its name was long used for the saddle-backed tamarins of the inter-lower Huallaga-Ucayali basins as well as for other Peruvian forms.

The original description of *devillei* follows: "Lombes, cuisses, jambes d'un beau roux marron; dos annelé de noir et de gris; partie antérieure du dos et des membres antérieurs noirs, ainsi que les mains et la queue.

"Du Pérou, rivière des Amazonas."

The above characterization could apply to the tamarin now recognized as *Saguinus fuscicollis leucogenys* Gray. Two subsequent descriptions of *devillei* by the same author (1850) merely repeat the first. Finally, in 1851 (p. 64; also 1855, p. 22) I. Geoffroy revealed that the types are two poorly preserved specimens from the "mission de Sarayacu," Río Ucayali, Peru. His expanded description includes the significant details. "Le dessus du cou, les épaules, le devant du dos sont de couleur très foncée aussi, mais tirant sur le roux[1] [footnote as follows, "il se peut que le roux domine chez les individus où le pelage est dans son état parfait"] et un peu tiquetée, parce que les extrémités des poils sont de cette couleur." The accompanying colored plate of what is probably the mounted skin of the holotype is poor and misleading, but the long whiskers indicate a juvenal. In any case, the specimen labeled "type" in the Paris Museum is of a young animal. It agrees with Geoffroy's 1855 description and with specimens at hand from the type locality, Sarayacu (102), on the left bank of the Río Ucayali.

Mystax bluntschlii Matschie from the Río Samiria (96), a small tributary of the Marañon and well within the range of *Saguinus fuscicollis illigeri,* was originally compared with *Saguinus nigricollis* and *S. mystax.* Its description agrees with *illigeri* and our topotypes of *bluntschlii* from Santa Elena (97).

Leontocebus mounseyi Thomas is virtually a topotype of *devillei,* but its author compared its type and only specimen, a juvenal, with the Ecuadorian *apiculatus* (= *lagonotus*), the type of which is is also a juvenal. No mention was made of *devillei* or even *bluntschlii* Matschie from the same district. Thomas (1927*a*, p. 366) confessed later that neither *mounseyi* nor *apiculatus* should have been separated from *devillei,* that is, *illigeri.*

Diagnostic Characters. Forehead and crown black, mantle generally chestnut, the terminal halves of individual hairs with a series of alternating reddish orange and black bands; throat blackish (figs. X.26, 27; pls. 3, 4).

Coloration. Crown, forehead, interorbital spaces, sides of face, and throat black; facial skin black, short hairs surrounding mouth, and sides of nostrils gray; mantle barely extending beyond shoulders reddish orange finely ticked with black, the terminal halves of the hairs with two to four orange bands, each separated by a black band, tips and basal halves of hairs black; outer sides of arms like mantle; back marbled black and gray or buffy to ochraceous; rump and thighs reddish orange; upper surface of hands and feet black and often mixed with reddish; chest, belly, and inner sides of fore- and hind limbs reddish, the base of the hairs black; tail black except for short reddish basal portion; external genitalia mostly or entirely black.

Measurements. See appendix table 2.

Comparisons. The wholly black crown distinguishes *illigeri* from *nigrifrons* and *fuscicollis.* The chestnut-agouti mantle separates *illigeri* from black-mantled *leucogenys* and *weddelli;* the black, not pale, bases at roots of mantle hairs from *weddelli* and *fuscus* and the dominantly blackish, not orange, throat from *fuscus.* The finely annulated or ticked mantle hairs of *illigeri* differ markedly from the nearly uniformly reddish or mahogany colored terminal portion of the mantle hairs of *lagonotus.* Altogether, the mantle and limbs of *lagonotus* are more deeply red and the hands, feet, and ventral surface of body more suffused with black.

Remarks. Differences between *illigeri* and *lagonotus* seem slight and suggest that the latter is merely saturate red-mantled mutant of the former with agouti mantle. It is also probable that the relationship between *illigeri* and *lagonotus* is through *leucogenys,* with which both intergrade.

A blood factor in *S. illigeri* with an isoimmune serum was identified by Gengozian (1972). The blood factor was not detected in limited numbers of other tamarins in the same laboratory colony. These represent *S. fuscicollis lagonotus, S. f. leucogenys, S. f. nigrifrons, S. nigricollis, S. oedipus,* and *S. mystax.* According to Gengozian, the blood factor is inherited as a simple Mendelian dominant and is useful in detecting red blood cell chimerism.

Specimens Examined. 49. PERU—*Loreto:* Cerro Azul, 1 (BM); "Iquitos", 1 (AMNH); "Marupa," 2 (AMNH); Río Pacaya, type of *mounseyi* (BM); Río Ucayali, 2 (BM); Santa Elena, Río Samiria, 3 (FMNH); Sarayacu, Río Ucayali, 18 (AMNH, 17; MNHN, type of *devillei*); UNKNOWN LOCALITY—21 (BM, 1; MNHN, type of *illigeri;* RMNH, 1; FMNH, 18 in spirits).

SAGUINUS FUSCICOLLIS LEUCOGENYS GRAY: ANDEAN SADDLE-BACK TAMARIN

Synonymic History

Midas leucogenys Gray, 1866, *Proc. Zool. Soc. London* 1865:735. Gray, 1870, *Cat. monkeys, lemurs and fruit-eating bats, Brit. Mus.*, p. 67—"BRAZIL."

[*Midas*] *leucogenys,* Thomas, 1914, *Ann. Mag. Nat. Hist.*, ser. 8, 13:346 (in text) and footnote—type a juvenal; characters; regarded as identical with *devillei.* Osman Hill, 1957, *Primates,* 3:224—"a pure synonym of *devillei.*"

Saguinus fuscicollis leucogenys, Hershkovitz, 1966, *Mammalia* 30(2):329—PERU: *Huánuco* (restricted type locality); characters of type; synonyms, *micans, pacator.* Hershkovitz, 1970, *Am. J. Phys. Anthrop.* 32:379—classification; dental diseases. Mallinson, 1971, *Sixth Ann. Rep. Wildl. Preserv. Trust,* pp. 5, 9—longevity in Jersey Zoo, 7 yrs., 2 mo., 28 days, still living.

[*Saguinus fuscicollis*] *leucogenys,* Hershkovitz, 1966, *Folia Primat.* 4:385—classification. Hershkovitz, 1968, *Evolution* 22(3):560, figs. 4, 5 (diagnostic color pattern)—characters; distribution; metachromism.

S[*aguinus*] *f*[*uscicollis*] *leucogenys,* Gengozian, 1969, *Ann. N.Y. Acad. Sci.* 162:357—red cell specificity. Gengozian, 1972, *J. Med. Primat.* 1, (3):172—inter- and intrasubspecific red cell immunizations.

L[*eontocebus*] *pacator* Thomas, 1914, *Ann. Mag. Nat. Hist.*, ser. 8, 13:346—PERU: *Huánuco* (type locality, Río Pachitea, near mouth, altitude, 150 meters); type, female, skin and skull, British Museum (Natural History), no. 4.7.7.5, collected 15 November 1903 by Otto Garlepp.

[*Leontocebus*] *pacator,* Osman Hill, 1957, *Primates* 3:224—"nothing in original description to separate it from *'nigrifrons,* i.e., *fuscicollis.*' "

Mystax pacator, Thomas, 1927, *Ann. Mag. Nat. Hist.,* ser. 9, 20:597—PERU: *Huánuco* (Chinchavita; Tingo María); characters. Colyer, 1936, *Variations and diseases of the teeth of mammals,* p. 299, fig. 377 (upper teeth)—displaced m^2.

Mystax devillei pacator, Thomas, 1928, *Ann. Mag. Nat. Hist.,* ser. 10, 2:256—PERU: *Loreto* (Cumaria, altitude 1,000 feet).

Tamarin devilli [*sic*] *pacator,* Cruz Lima, 1945, *Mamíferos da Amazonia, Primates,* p. 232—characters ex Thomas.

Mystax devillei micans Thomas, 1928, *Ann. Mag. Nat. Hist.,* ser. 10, 2:256—PERU: *San Martín* (type locality, Yurac Yacu, 2,500 feet altitude); *Huánuco* (Tingo María; Chinchavita); type, female, skin, and skull, British Museum (Natural History), no. 27.1.1.28; collected 25 July 1926 by R. W. Hendee.

[*Mystax devillei*] *micans,* Osman Hill, 1957, *Primates* 3:224—characters; probably a synonym of *nigricollis.*

Tamarin devillei micans, Cruz Lima, 1945, *Mamíferos da Amazonia, Primates, Contrib. Mus. Paraense,* p. 234—characters ex Thomas.

[?] *M*[*idas*] *labiatus,* Tschudi (not E. Geoffroy), 1844, *Fauna Peruana,* pp. 9, 53—PERU: local name, pinchecillo.

L[*eontocebus*] *devillei,* Thomas (not I. Geoffroy), 1914, *Ann. Mag. Nat. Hist.,* ser. 8, 13:346—part, PERU: Junín (Río Perené); variation.

Leontocebus devillii [*sic*] Elliot (part, not I. Geoffroy), 1913, *A review of the Primates* 1:203—*leucogenys* Gray in synonymy.

Leontocebus devillei, Cabrera (part, not I. Geoffroy), 1958, *Rev. Mus. Argentino Cienc. Nat. "Bernardino Rivadavia"* 4:190–91—*micans* Thomas and *leucogenys* Gray in synonymy.

Mystax devillei, Thomas (not I. Geoffroy), 1927, *Ann. Mag. Nat. Hist.,* ser. 9, 19:365—PERU: San Martín (Yurae Yacu; Moyobamba).

Marikina nigricollis, Hershkovitz (part not Spix), 1949, *Proc. U.S. Nat. Mus.* 98:413—*leucogenys* Gray *pacator* Thomas, *micans* Thomas in synonymy.

Leontocebus nigricollis, Cabrera (part, not Spix), 1958, *Rev. Mus. Argentino Cienc. Nat. "Bernardino Rivadavia"* 4:196—part, *pacator* in synonymy.

Marikina nigricollis nigricollis, Sanborn (not Spix, 1949), *J. Mammal.* 30:284—PERU: *Loreto* (Yarinacocha, Río Ucayali; Pucallpa, Río Ucayali).

Marikina devillei devillei, Sanborn (not I. Geoffroy), 1949, *J. Mammal.* 30:285—*Huánuco* (Agua Caliente, near mouth Río Pachitea).

[?] *M*[*idas*] *chrysomelas,* Tschudi (not Wied-Neuwied), 1844, *Fauna Peruana,* pp. 9, 53—"nördlich und mittlere Peru bis 140 S. B."

Type. Subadult, skin and skull, British Museum (Natural History) no. 39.7.25.12; purchased of Warwick.

Type Locality. Said to be Brazil, restricted to the Department of Huánuco, Peru, by Hershkovitz (1966, p. 329).

Distribution (fig. X.24). Tropical zones of northcentral Peru from northern San Martín through Huánuco and Pasco to the Río Perené in northern Junín, thence east to the Río Ucayali in Loreto to as far north as the Río Pisquí; the corner of Loreto between the Ríos Huallaga and Marañon may also enter into the range of *leucogenys;* altitudinal distribution between 100 and 1,000 meters.

Taxonomy. *Saguinus fuscicollis leucogenys* Gray and *S. fuscicollis weddelli* are the black-mantled members of the *fuscicollis* group. Neither has been confused with the other, but each has been misidentified with other tamarins. The case of *weddelli* is discussed elsewhere (p. 661). The identification of *leucogenys* as conspecific with *devillei* or as a subspecies of it is substantially correct. On the other hand, my previous (1949, p. 413) confusion of the black-mantled *leucogenys* (*pacator*) with the black-mantled *Saguinus nigricollis* Spix and use of this last name for some members of the *fuscicollis* group was unwarranted.

Leontocebus pacator Thomas, with its nearly wholly black mantle and well-developed blackish femoral patch, is the most saturate form of the species. It is sharply defined from agouti-mantled *illigeri* but can be identified with populations of tamarins from higher up the mountains in Huánuco and San Martín represented by *leucogenys* and *micans*.

Mystax devillei micans from Yurac Yacu, San Martín (119), was distinguished from *pacator* by the fine "olive" ticking of its mantle hairs and by absence of a dark femoral patch. Four specimens of the type series agree with the type of *micans* as well as that of *leucogenys*. On the other hand, the femoral patch is more or less developed in all other specimens here referred to *leucogenys* but is more strongly marked in the southern than the northern localities. The character may be clinal or purely local and is not regarded as crucial. The greater or lesser amount of ticking of the mantle hairs also appears to be a local variable. In nearly all specimens of *leucogenys* examined the nape hairs are black with little or no buffy subterminal banding. In *illigeri,* the nape hairs are, as a rule, distinctly agouti; in *lagonotus* they are, as a rule, dominantly reddish. One year before he described *micans,* Thomas (1927*b*, p. 597) had assigned specimens from Huánuco (Chinchavita (122); Tingo María (121)) to *pacator,* that is, *leucogenys*.

Diagnostic Characters. Head, mantle, forelimbs, and throat dominantly black or blackish brown, exceptionally agouti, front of the thigh usually with dark patch; whitish interorbital frontal patch absent (figs. X.26, 27, pls. 3, 4).

Coloration. Crown, forehead, interorbital space, sides of face, throat, anterior portion of chest, black; facial skin pigmented, short hairs surrounding mouth gray; mantle black or blackish brown often with a scattering of fine orange ticking, sometimes agouti, outer sides of arms like mantle but slightly more ticked; saddle, as usual, marbled buffy and black; rump and thighs orange lined with black; front of legs from hip to knee usually with dark patch; upper surface of hands and feet black; posterior portion of chest, belly, and inner sides of thighs reddish and washed or lined with black; tail black except for short reddish basal portion; external genitalia mostly or entirely black.

Measurements. See appendix table 2.

Comparisons. With exceptions noted below, distinguished from *illigeri* and *lagonotus* by dominantly blackish forequarters with reduction or nearly complete suppression of orange or reddish annulations or agouti pattern of mantle hairs; dark femoral patch usually present in *leucogenys,* weakly indicated in some individuals of *illigeri;* underparts as in *illigeri* but less saturate than in red-mantled *lagonotus*. Superficially similar to black-mantled *weddelli* but differs by black, not drab or bleached, basal portions of mantle hairs and absence of gray frontal band.

Variation. Specimens from localities on the left bank of the Río Ucayali (Yarinacocha (105), Pucallpa (106), Agua Caliente (123a), Santa Rosa (111)) and tributaries Pachitea (San Antonio (123b), Puerto Mairo (123c), Pozuzo (124), type locality of *pacator*) and Perené (125), are predominantly black-mantled. The nuchal hairs are mostly or entirely black, those of the shoulders generally with a scattering of fine orange ticking and, frequently, a concentration of subterminally banded and even agouti-patterned hairs bordering the saddle. These tamarins are quite distinct from the uniformly agouti-mantled *illigeri* lower down the Ucayali. They resemble *weddelli* from higher up the Ucayali basin but shown no tendency toward bleaching of the basal portion of the mantle hairs or development of a frontal blaze.

Material from the Río Huallaga basin includes typically black-mantled representatives of *leucogenys,* others indistinguishable from typically agouti-mantled *illigeri,* and extreme agouti-mantled individuals of *lagonotus*. Still others are intermediate between *illigeri* and the usually red-mantled *lagonotus*. The mantle in the Tingo María (121) series is dominantly black, but in some individuals the shoulder hairs are distinctly agouti but with the black bands dominant. Five specimens from Yurac Yacu (119) (800 meters) are also dominantly black-mantled, but the agouti pattern is more general, the orange annulations of the hairs more conspicuous than in the preceding. Two agouti-mantled specimens from Moyobamba (120) (820 meters) with the orange or ochraceous bands dominating the hairs are absolutely indistinguishable from our Sarayacu series of *illigeri*. Evidently they represent an isolated remnant of the more primitive form of the species. Similar remnants occur in the Andean foothills of Ecuador (Río Copotaza representatives of *illigeri*), and in eastern Colombia the relict agouti-mantled *S. f. fuscus* is the prevailing form.

The dark femoral patch appears as an extension of the black basal portion of the hairs by reduction or suppression of the orange banding of the distal portion. As such, it is present in all examined specimens of Río Ucayali populations, present but not always well developed in the Tingo María series of the Huallaga basin and absent in all other available representatives of the same watershed. In this respect, as in the character of the mantle, the Río Huallaga valley populations of *leucogenys* are more primtive than those of the Río Ucayali.

Remarks. *Saguinus fuscicollis leucogenys* occupies a

geographically intermediate position between agouti-mantled *illigeri* to the east, red-mantled *lagonotus* to the north, and black-mantled and white-browed *weddelli* to the south. It intergrades with all three, and some individuals or isolated populations well within its range may be indistinguishable from true *illigeri* or *illigeri*like *lagonotus*.

The specimens from Yarinacocha (105) and two from Pucallpa (106) recorded by Sanborn (1949, p. 284) as *Marikina nigricollis nigricollis* and a juvenal from Agua Caliente (123a) recorded as *M. devillei devillei,* are indistinguishable. All are referrable to *leucogenys,* the juvenal being very much like the type.

A flat skin of the Bassler collection, remade into a round skin (AMNH 98301) and labeled "Iquitos," is not certainly identifiable. Its dark mantle and femoral patch indicate *leucogenys*. The base of the hairs of head and back are bleached pale brown as in *weddelli* but a frontal blaze is absent. Instead a white tuft is present on the back of the nape and another on the crown above the right ear. The tail is also peculiar in its bleached coloration of brown and reddish brown or mahogany throughout its length.

A second flat skin of the Bassler collection (AMNH 98278), labeled "Iquitos up river Amazonas," is also unidentifiable as to race. The skin appears to be considerably faded. The mantle pelage is agouti-patterned, but the dark brown rather than the fine pale bands are dominant, the tail dark brown above, pale or golden brown beneath; what appears to be a femoral patch may be an artifact. The specimen is best included here. Perhaps more collecting between the Marañon and Huallaga will reveal a population of tamarins like the individual just described.

Specimens Examined. 50. PERU—*Junín:* Perené, 1 (BM); *Huánuco:* Agua Caliente, 1 (FMNH); Chinchavita, 1 (BM); Puerto Mairo, Río Palcazú, 2 (BM); San Antonio, Río Pachitea, 1 (BM); Tingo María, 13 (BM), 9; FMNH, 4); Pozuzo, 6 (FMNH); *Loreto:* Cumaria, 7 (BM); "Iquitos," 1 (AMNH); Pucallpa, 2 (FMNH); Río Pachitea, 2 (BM, type of *pacator;* FMNH, 1); Santa Rosa, alto Río Ucayali, 3 (AMNH); Yarinacocha, 2 (FMNH); *San Martín:* Moyobamba, Río Mayo, 2 (BM); Yurac Yacu, 5 (BM, including type of micans); *locality unknown:* type of *leucogenys* (BM).

SAGUINUS FUSCICOLLIS LAGONOTUS JIMÉNEZ DE LA ESPADA: RED-MANTLE SADDLE-BACK TAMARIN

1 cm

Fig. X.29. Saddle-back Tamarins, *Saguinus fuscicollis cf. lagonotus.* (Photo courtesy of Dr. Friedrich Deinhardt, Rush–Presbyterian–St. Luke's Medical Center, Chicago.)

Synonymic History

Midas lagonotus Jiménez de la Espada, 1870, *Bol. Rev. Univ. Madrid,* pp. 11–16. Jiménez de la Espada, 1871, *J. Sci. Math. Phys. Nat. Acad. R. Sci. Lisboa* 2:57—"Hab. in Ecuador; ad ripas flum. Napo prope la Coca et Tarapoto mensibus Jun. et Jul." Martínez y Saez, 1898, *Anal. Soc. Española Hist. Nat.,* ser. 2, 7:215—listed [article includes biographical sketch of Jiménez de la Espada].

M[idas] lagonotus, Cabrera, 1900, *Anal. Soc. Española Hist. Nat.,* ser. 2, 9:91, fig. 3 (skull)—ECUADOR: *Napo-Pastaza* (La Coca, Río Napo; Humu Yacu, Río Napo); PERU: *Loreto* (Tarapoto, Río Napo); characters; local name, *chichico.*

L[eontocebus] lagonotus, Cabrera, 1912, *Trab. Mus. Cienc. Nat.,* no. 11:29—ECUADOR: *Napo-Pastaza* (La Coca, Río Napo; Humu-Yacu, Rio Napo); PERU: *Loreto* (Tarapoto, Río Napo; Destacamento, Río Napo; 4 specimens, cotypes).

Leontocebus lagonotus, Elliot, 1913, *A review of the Primates,* 1:206. Cabrera, 1917, *Trab. Mus. Nac. Cienc. Nat. Madrid, Ser. Zool.,* no. 31:33—ECUADOR: *Napo-Pastaza* (Río Napo); PERU: *Loreto* (Destacamento; Tarapoto); characters. Cabrera, 1958, *Rev. Mus. Argentino Cienc. Nat. "Bernardino Rivadavia"* 4 (1):194—classification; synonyms, *tripartitus, bluntschlii.*

Mystax lagonotus, Thomas, 1928, *Ann. Mag. Nat. Hist.,* ser. 10, 2:286—PERU: *Loreto* (Iquitos); ECUADOR: *Napo-Pastaza* (type locality, La Coca, Río Napo; Alpayacu, Río Pastaza; Río Copataza).

Tamarin lagonotus, Cruz Lima, 1945, *Mamíferos da Amazonia, Primates, Contrib. Mus. Paraense,* p. 237, pl. 36, fig. 2 (animal)—PERU: *Loreto* (Iquitos; Palmares); characters; comparisons; distribution; *Midas illigeri* of Goeldi (not Pucheran), a synonym.

Tamarinus illigeri lagonotus, Osman Hill, 1957, *Primates* 3:213, 217, 229, fig. 50 (ear), fig. 54 (intestine), pl. 9 (animal)—ECUADOR: *Napo-Pastaza* (Río Pastaza; Río Copataza); characters; distribution.

Saguinus fuscicollis lagonotus, Hershkovitz, 1966, *Mammalia* 30(2):328—*illigeri* of authors, not Pucheran. Lushbaugh and Gengozian, 1969, *Amer. J. Trop. Med. Hyg.* 18, (5):622—intrauterine fetal death from congenital Chagas's disease (trypanosomiasis). Hershkovitz, 1970, *Amer. J. Phys. Anthrop.* 32:379—classification; dental disease. Hershkovitz, 1970, *Folia Primat.* 13:215—fig. 3 (endocranial cast—ECUADOR: *Napo-Pastaza* (Boca Río Curaray; Montalvo, Río Bobonazo); cerebral fissural pattern.

[*Saguinus fuscicollis*] *lagonotus,* Hershkovitz, 1966, *Folia Primat.* 4:385—classification (*apiculatus* Thomas, a synonym). Hershkovitz, 1968, *Evolution* 22(3):560, figs. 4, 5 (diagnostic color pattern)—characters; distribution; metachromism.

S[*aguinus*] *f*[*uscicollis*] *lagonotus,* Gengozian, 1969, *Ann. N.Y. Acad. Sci.* 162:338, fig. 1B (facial characters)—red cell specificity. Porter and Gengozian, 1969, *Transplantation* 8(5):653—survival time of skin allografts: *lagonotus* to *illigeri,* 7–33 days; *illigeri* to *lagonotus,* 7–26 days. Gengozian, 1972, *J. Med. Primat.* 1 (3):172 inter- and intrasubspecific red cell immunizations.

Midas apiculatus Thomas, 1904, *Ann. Mag. Nat. Hist.,* 7, 14:190—ECUADOR: *Napo-Pastaza* (type locality, Río Copataza, upper Pastaza); type, female, skin and skull, British Museum (Natural History) no. 80.5.6.25; collected between December 1877 and February 1878 by Clarence Buckley.

[*Mystax*] *apiculatus,* Thomas, 1927, *Ann. Mag. Nat. Hist.,* ser. 9, 19:365—regarded as a synonym of *devillei.*

Leontocebus apiculatus, Elliot, 1913, *A review of the Primates,* 1:204—description ex type. Rode, 1937, *Bull. Mus. Nat. Hist., Paris,* ser. 2, 9:344—ECUADOR: *Napo-Pastaza* (Siguín, Río Pastaza).

Tamarin apiculatus, Cruz Lima, 1945, *Mamíferos da Amazonia, Primates,* p. 234—characters ex original description.

Midas elegans Cabrera, 1912, *Trab. Mus. Cienc. Nat. Madrid,* no. 3:18—manuscript name cited as a synonym under *Midas lagonotus* Espada.

[?] *Midas leoninus,* Osculati (not Humboldt), 1850, *Esplor. Reg. Equator,* p. 124—ECUADOR—*Napo-Pastaza* (Puerto Napo). Cornalia, 1850, *Esplor. Reg. Equator,* p. 302—ECUADOR.

Midas nigrifrons, Thomas (not I. Geoffroy), 1880, *Proc. Zool. Soc. London* 1880:395—ECUADOR: *Napo-Pastaza* (Río Copataza).

Midas illigeri, Thomas (not Pucheran), 1880, *Proc. Zool. Soc. London* 1880:395—ECUADOR: *Napo-Pastaza* (Río Copotaza). Goeldi, 1907, *Proc. Zool. Soc. London* 1907:99—PERU: *Loreto* ("Iquitos"). Lönnberg, 1921, *Ark. Zool., Stockholm* 14(4):9—ECUADOR: *Napo-Pastaza* Río Curaray, 1,000 feet altitude).

Hapale illigeri, Schlegel (not Pucheran), 1876, *Les singes. Simiae,* p. 263—part. Jentink, 1887, *Cat. Ostéol. Mus. Pays-Bas* 9:49—ECUADOR. Jentink, 1892, *Cat. Syst. Mamm. Mus. Pays-Bas* 11:56—part, ECUADOR: *Napo-Pastaza* (Río Copotaza).

Œdipomidas illigeri, Elliot (not Pucheran), 1906, *Cat. Mamm. Field Columbian Mus., Zool. Ser.* 8:554—ECUADOR.

Leontocebus illigeri, Cabrera (part, not Pucheran), 1958, *Rev. Mus. Argentino Cienc. Nat. "Bernardino Rivadavia"* 4(1):192—*apiculatus* Thomas in synonymy only.

[?] *Leontocebus illigeri,* Fiennes (not Pucheran), 1964, *Proc. Zool. Soc. London* 143(3):523—cystic bone disease.

[*Mystax*] *illigeri,* Thomas (not Pucheran), 1922, *Ann. Mag. Nat. Hist.,* ser. 9, 9:198—classification.

Mystax illigeri, Lönnberg (not Pucheran), 1922, *Ark. Zool., Stockholm* 14(20):6—ECUADOR: *Napo-Pastaza* (Río Napo).

Marikina illigeri, Hershkovitz (part, not Pucheran), 1949, *Proc. U.S. Nat. Mus.* 98:413—part, taxonomy; restriction of type locality; synonyms, *lagonotus* Jiménez de la Espada, *apiculatus* Thomas.

[?]*Saquinis* [*sic*] (*saquinis* [*sic*]) *tuscus* [*sic*] *illigeri,* Wiener, Moor-Jankowski and Gordon, 1965, *Amer. J. Phys. Anthrop.* 22(2):184, footnote 2—typographical (?) error for *Saguinus* (*Saguinus*) *fuscicollis illigeri;* blood groups.

Tamarinus illigeri, Osman Hill (part, not Pucheran), 1957, *Primates* 3:214–22, 227, 232—ECUADOR: *Napo-Pastaza* (Río Pastaza; Río Copotaza); characters; distribution (part); taxonomy.

Tamarinus nigricollis, Layton (not Spix), 1966, *Int. Arch. Allergy* 30:360—white skinned; use in biomedical research (testing with reaginic human sera).

T[*amarin*] *apiculatus* or *lagonotus* ♂ × *T. devillei* ♀, Roth, 1960, *Zool. Gart.* 25:166, pl. 1, fig. 1 (male only), pl. 1, fig. 2 (young animal), pl. 3 (young animals), figs. 4, 6, 7 (male and young only)—captive phenotypes mated producing 2 ♀♀ said to resemble mother [but should be father]; parents regarded as conspecific.

Type. Three males, nos. 645, 646, 864, and one female, no. 865, originally in the Muséo Nacional de Ciéncias Naturales, Madrid; collected by Jiménez de la Espada, June–July 1865 in the "Viaje al Pacífico," 1862–65. Nos. 645 and 646, mounted with skull in, are exhibited in the Mammal Hall of the Madrid Museum; no. 865, a skin, was presented to the British Museum (Natural History) and registered as no. 25.7.1.1.

Type Locality. "In Ecuador; ad ripas flum. Napo prope la Coca et Tarapoto mensibus Jun. et Jul." The syntypes, according to Cabrera (1912, p. 28), were collected, respectively, from La Coca (63), Río Napo, Napo-Pastaza, Ecuador (no. 865, now BM 25.7.1.1), and type locality by restriction (Thomas 1928*b*, p. 286), Humu-Yacu (63), Río Napo, Ecuador (no. 646), Tarapoto (79), Río Napo, Loreto, Peru (no. 864), and Destacamento (91), Río Napo, Peru (no. 645). The actual provenance of each of the specimens must have been the forests on the right bank of the Río Napo opposite the sites named.

Distribution (fig. X.24). In northeastern Peru and eastern Ecuador from the right bank of the Río Napo, north of the Marañon, west to the Río Santiago and the foothills of the Cordillera Oriental; altitudinal range 100 to approximately 1,200 meters above sea level.

Taxonomy. Midas apiculatus Thomas is based on three specimens, including the juvenal holotype, collected by Clarence Buckley on the Río Copotaza (74), a stream well within the range of *lagonotus.* The three types are part of a series of six previously identified by Thomas (1880, p. 395) as *Midas nigrifrons.* Thomas also listed at the same time 21 specimens from the Río Copotaza identified as *Midas illigeri.* These he described as "agree[ing] in having the fur across the shoulders and loins of a rich reddish chestnut-colour, thus differing from the next species [his *Midas nigrifrons*], which has the hair on the same parts annulated with black and yellow."

Six specimens of the original Buckley Copotaza series, including the type of *apiculatus,* are still preserved in the British Museum. The mantle of the type is dark, with the nape hairs agouti and approaching that of *micans* (= *leucogenys*) from Yurac Yacu (119). Two other immatures are paler and resemble agouti-mantled *illigeri.* A third immature and two adults are quite like typical red-mantled *lagonotus.* Five additional specimens of the Buckley Copotaza series are in the Leiden Museum. The mantle in three, all adults, varies from mahogany red to dark chestnut; in two, both young, the mantle is sparsely annulated.

The above accounts for only 11 of the original 27 of Thomas's combined *illigeri* and *nigrifrons* series. Whatever the fate of the others, present material indicates that Thomas identified the red-mantled adults and some young as *illigeri.* The annulated-mantled immatures he called *nigrifrons* were later described as *apiculatus.* The same pattern reappears in a juvenal and two adult topotypes of *apiculatus* at hand. Greatest skull length of the juvenal (FMNH) is 46.8 mm and compares with 45 mm in the type of *apiculatus.* The milk premolars are still in place, the second molar unerupted. The mantle is darker than that of the adults, the terminal portions of the hairs distinctly annulated. In these respects the juvenal shares characters of *lagonotus, illigeri,* and *leucogenys.* The mantle and thighs of the adults are redder, the hairs without subterminal banding, and altogether quite like typical *lagonotus.* More material with precise and authenticated locality data from the base of the eastern Andes of Ecuador is needed for elucidating the true relationships of *apiculatus.*

A breeding pair of tamarins and twin offspring in the Ruhr Zoo were described and figured in color by Roth (1960, p. 166, pls. 1, 2, fig.) as a red-mantled male, blackish-mantled female, and two female red-mantled offspring. The male was regarded as referrable to either *lagonotus* or *apiculatus.* The female was believed to rep-

Fig. X.30. Red-mantle Saddle-Back Tamarin, *Saguinus fuscicollis lagonotus.* Photograph without documentation but apparently of a mounted museum exhibit.

resent *devillei* (i.e., *illigeri*), but the mantle described as "schwärzlich braun, mit vielen einzelnen gelbrötlichbraun endenden Haaren durchsetz" could pertain to *leucogenys* or extremely dark-mantled *lagonotus*. Plate 2, fig. 1 of the work cited shows the reddish hind leg of the female without trace of the dark femoral patch characteristic of most *leucogenys*. In any case, the point is made that red- and black-mantled tamarins interbreed and produce young resembling one of the parents. The same conclusion is derived from study of the Río Copotaza material.

Diagnostic Characters. Crown, forehead, and sides of head uniformly black, mantle reddish to dark mahogany, the hairs generally not at all or only inconspicuously annulated rarely agouti-patterned; rump and outer sides of thighs dark reddish like mantle (figs. X.26, 27, 30; pls. 3, 4).

Coloration. Forehead, crown, sides of head, throat, and neck black; skin of face black, superciliary region and interorbital space sparsely set with short grayish hairs; short hairs around mouth and sides of nostrils gray; mantle reddish to blackish red, extending to middle third of back, the individual hairs orange to mahogany terminally, black basally; outer sides of upper arms darker than mantle, becoming black on lower arms; saddle striated black with buffy; rump, thighs reddish, the terminal halves of the hairs with few or no annulations; upper surface of hands and feet black; chest and inner sides of arms reddish heavily washed with black or nearly entirely black; belly and inner sides of thighs reddish; tail black except for short reddish basal portion. External genitalia mostly or entirely pigmented.

Measurements. See appendix table 2.

Comparisons. Generally distinguished from *leucogenys* by reddish, not black, mantle and absence of a conspicuously developed dark femoral patch; from Colombian *fuscus* by more or less uniformly reddish, not agouti-colored, mantle and outer sides of thighs and hairs of forequarter black basally to roots; from *illigeri* by nonagouti mantle; facial gray more extensive than in other races.

Variation. The three type specimens of *lagonotus,* two in the Madrid and one in the London museums, are red-mantled tamarins sharply defined from all other races of the species. Other specimens from the type region on the right bank of the Río Napo are equally well defined. The usual range of variation here in color of mantle is from bright reddish orange to dark mahogany, with little, if any, subterminal banding of the hairs.

At the western extreme of the range where interbreeding with neighboring races is expected along the foothills of the Cordillera, bright reddish, dark reddish, blackish, and agouti-mantled tamarins mingle and intergrade.

Mantle of the Curaray series varies from bright reddish to nearly blackish mahogany; a similar range of variation in the color of the mantle appears in *lagonotus* from the upper Río Pastaza region. The mantle of some young individuals is darker and more nearly as in *leucogenys* than that of adults. In others, the mantle is markedly punctulated and approaches the agouti type of *fuscus* or *illigeri.* Details of variation in the Río Copotaza series referred to *lagonotus* are given in the discussion on taxonomy.

The face of *lagonotus* (figs. X.29, 30) may be completely grizzled, or only cheeks and circumbuccal band may be gray, with the remainder black. Variation in extent of gray is independent of age, sex, and locality. In some individuals, the gray superciliary region recalls the grayish band in *weddelli.* In other specimens, the gray interorbital patch assumes the V- or chevron shape characteristic of *S. f. tripartitus.*

Remarks. The tendency for the mantle to become nearly black in *lagonotus* and the admixture of reddish in the mantle in many *leucogenys* indicate intergradation between the two races where their geographic ranges meet.

Two specimens of *lagonotus* labeled "Marupa," a locality on the south bank of the Marañon between the mouths of the Ucayali and Yavarí, were certainly taken on the north bank of the Marañon. Another pair of specimens with the same locality data are definitely *nigrifrons,* a race proper to the south bank. The Marupa (88) material was collected by the Olallas and forms part of the Bassler collection in the American Museum of Natural History.

Specimens Examined. 96. ECUADOR—*Napo-Pastaza:* Alpayacu, Río Pastaza, 2 (BM); La Coca, Río Napo, 3 syntypes of *lagonotus* (BM, 1; MCNM, 2); Montalvo, Río Bobonaza, 3 (FMNH); Río Conambo, 1 (AMNH); Río Copotaza, 14 (AMNH, 2; BM, 6 including type of *apiculatus;* RMNH, 5; FMNH, 1); Sarayacu, Río Bobonaza, 6 (MNHN); Shell Mera, 1 (FMNH); "Ambato," 1 (AMNH); *Santiago-Zamora:* Méndez, 3 (MNHN); PERU—*Loreto:* "Iquitos," 9 (AMNH, 6; BM, 3); "Marupa", Río Marañon, 2 (AMNH); Pampa Chica, 2 (FMNH); Puerto Indiana, 16 (AMNH); Río Curaray, 14 (AMNH); Río Mazán 1 (AMNH); lower Río Napo, "north side," 1 (AMNH); Río Tigre, 1 (AMNH); Santa Rita, 3 (FMNH); Siguín, 1 (AMNH); UNKNOWN LOCALITY—12 (RMNH, 3; FMNH, 9 in spirits).

SAGUINUS FUSCICOLLIS TRIPARTITUS MILNE-EDWARDS: GOLDEN-MANTLE SADDLE-BACK TAMARIN

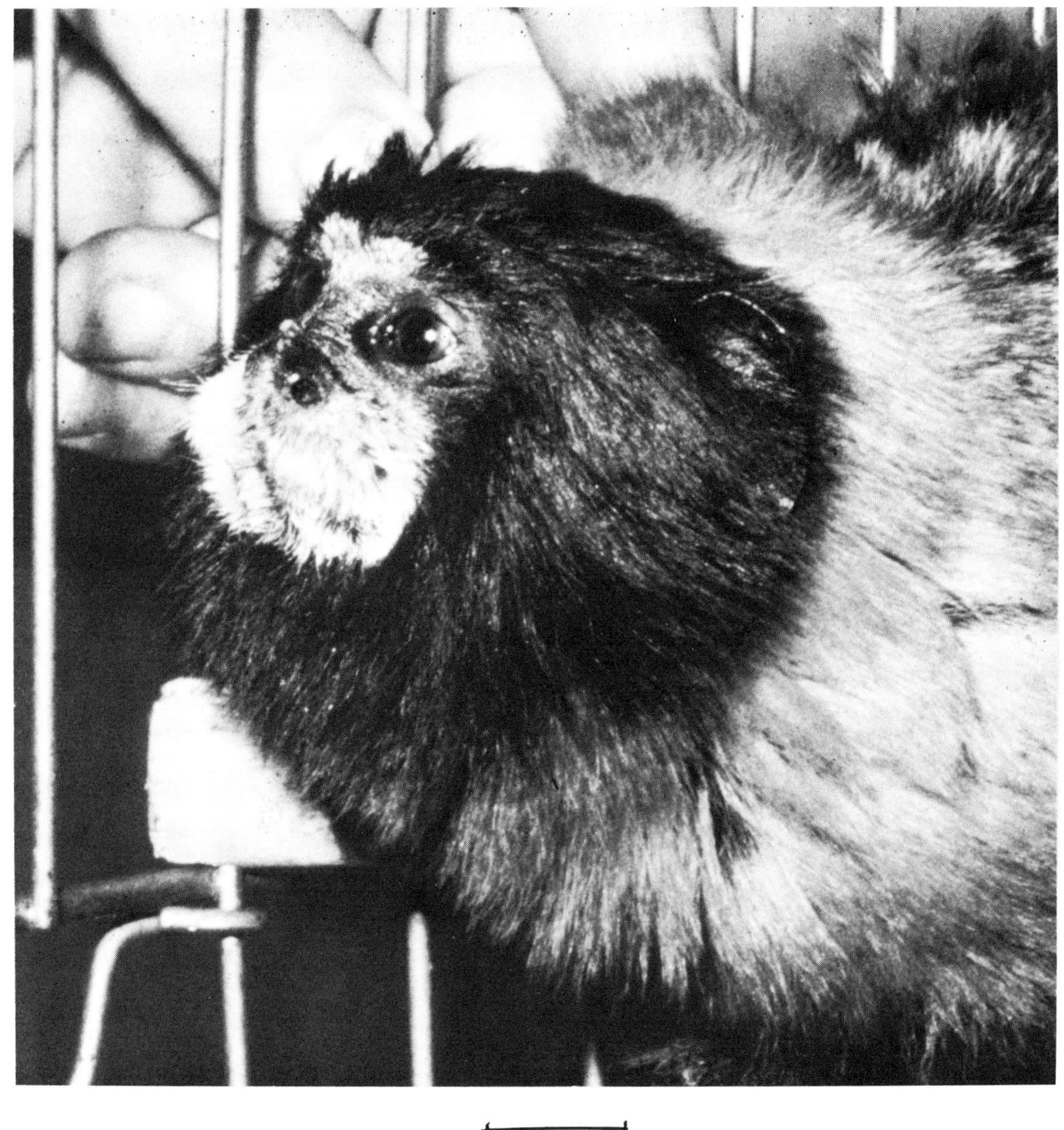

= 1 cm

Fig. X.31. Golden-mantle Saddle-back Tamarin, *Saguinus fuscicollis tripartitus*. Photograph of individual formerly living in Brookfield Zoo, now preserved in Field Museum.

Synonymic History

Midas tripartitus Milne-Edwards, 1878, *Arch. Mus. Hist. Nat., Paris,* ser. 2, 1:161, pl. 3 (animal). Rode, 1938, *Bull. Mus. Nat. Hist. Nat., Paris,* ser. 2, 10:241—type history.

Midas tripartitus, Pelzeln, 1883, *Verh. K. K. Zool.-Bot. Gesellsch., Wien* 32:443—ECUADOR: *Napo-Pastaza* (Río Napo).

M[idas] tripartitus, Pelzeln, 1883, *Verh. K. K. Zool.-Bot. Gesellsch., Wien, Beih.* 33:27, footnote—ECUADOR: *Napo-Pastaza* (Río Napo). Thomas, 1904, *Ann. Mag. Nat. Hist.,* ser. 7, 14:191—comparisons; regarded as probably distinct from *Midas lagonotus* [= *Saguinus fuscicollis illigeri*].

Leontocebus tripartitus, Elliot, 1913, *Review of the Primates* 1:206—characters ex type.

Mystax tripartitus, Thomas, 1928, *Ann. Mag. Nat. Hist.,* ser. 10, 2:410—ECUADOR:*Napo-Pastaza* (Río Napo). Crandall, 1951, *Animal Kingdom* 54:179, fig. p. 183 (animal, lower left)—ECUADOR: *Napo-Pastaza* (Río Napo, right bank).

Tamarin tripartitus, Cruz Lima, 1945, *Mamíferos da Amazonia, Primates,* p. 221—characters ex Elliot 1913.

Tamarinus tripartitus, Osman Hill, 1957, *Primates* 3:218, 222, 228, 230, 232, 234, pl. 10 (animal)—ECUADOR: *Napo-Pastaza* (Río Napo, 3,000 feet); characters; taxonomy; comparisons; distribution.

S[aguinus] tripartitus, Crandall, 1964, *Management of wild animals in captivity,* p. 105—longevity in New York Zoo (5 years, 9 months, 19 days).

Saguinus fuscicollis tripartitus, Hershkovitz, 1966, *Folia Primat.* 4:385—classification. Hershkovitz, 1968, *Evolution* 22(3):560, figs. 4, 5 (diagnostic color pattern)—characters; distribution; metachromism.

M[idas] lagonotus, Cabrera (part, not Jiménez de la Espada), 1900, *Anal. Soc. Española Hist. Nat.,* ser. 2, 9:91—*tripartitus* Milne-Edwards in synonymy.

Leontocebus lagonotus, Cabrera (part, not Jiménez de la Espada), 1958, *Rev. Mus. Argentino Cienc. Nat. "Bernardino Rivadavia"* 4:194—*tripartitus* in synonymy only.

Marikina illigeri, Hershkovitz (part, not Pucheran), 1949, *Proc. U.S. Nat. Mus.* 98:413—*tripartitus* in synonymy.

Type. Female, skin only, Museum National d'Histoire Naturelle, Paris, no. 122 (653 [633A, 1877–562]).

Type Locality. Río Napo, Ecuador.

Distribution (fig. X.24). Between the Ríos Napo and Putumayo, Ecuador and Peru; altitudinal range from 100 to at least 250 meters and possibly over 300 meters above sea level.

Taxonomy. Imprecise locality data led Cabrera (1900, p. 91) to believe that the type of *tripartitus* was an unusually pale individual of *lagonotus.* In the absence of specimens at hand, I (1949, p. 413) followed Cabrera in treating *tripartitus* as a synonym of *lagonotus.* Ample material and reliable locality data now available prove that the two named forms are distinct, their respective ranges separated by the Río Napo in Ecuador.

Bleaching is more advanced in *Saguinus fuscicollis tripartitus* than in other members of the species known to occur north of the Marañon. *S. f. tripartitus* inhabits the upper half of the inter Ríos Napo-Putumayo basin. Perhaps the lower half of the same basin is occupied by even paler forms comparable to the albinistic *cruzlimai-acrensis-melanoleucus* series of the inter Purús-Juruá basin in Brazil.

Diagnostic Characters. Golden mantle sharply defined from black head; prominent gray chevron-shaped midfrontal patch present; underparts of body and limbs orange (figs. 26, 27, 32; pls. 3, 4).

Coloration. Crown, forehead, sides of head, and throat black; facial skin entirely black; midfrontal region with prominent gray chevron-shaped patch; gray hairs around mouth and sides of nostrils moderately long; golden orange to creamy mantle sharply defined from black head and marbled back, the hairs not annulated terminally, basal portions brown becoming drab at roots; arms orange; saddle marbled with gray to golden; thighs grizzled orange; upper surface of hands and feet orange lined with black; chest, belly, and inner surface of limbs orange; tail black with ventral surface of basal one-fourth to one-half reddish orange; external genitalia pigmented.

Measurements. See appendix table 2.

Comparisons. Colors of mantle, limbs and underparts of *S. f. tripartitus* are dilutions of the reds with suppression of the eumelanins found in other members of the *fuscicollis* group, most particularly *lagonotus* and *fuscus.*

Remarks. Crandall's (1951, pp. 179, 183, fig.) account of a golden-mantled marmoset brought to the New York Zoo by Charles Cordier is the first published record of an actual specimen of *tripartitus* since the original description in 1878 and Pelzeln's notice in 1883. Crandall credits Cordier with the observation that *tripartitus* occurs only on the right bank of the Río Napo while *Saguinus nigricollis graellsi* is restricted to the left bank. This is not quite true. *S. fuscicollis tripartitus* inhabits the left or eastern bank of the Río Napo; *S. f. lagonotus* resides on the right bank; and *S. nigricollis graellsi* occupies both banks.

Two specimens labeled "Iquitos" in the collection of the American Museum of Natural History, one collected by Schunke, the other by Arrevalos, were more likely purchased there from dealers or Indians who brought them from afar.

Specimens Examined. 30. ECUADOR—*Napo-Pastaza:* Lagarto Cocha, mouth, Río Aguarico, 2 (AMNH); San Francisco, Río Napo, 2 (UMMZ); near Aguarico, Río Napo, 1 (BM); Río Napo, 2 (BM, 1; MNHN, type of *tripartitus*); PERU—*Loreto:* Puerto Indiana, Río Napo, 7 (AMNH); Río Curaray, mouth, 15 (AMNH, 14; FMNH, 1); "Iquitos", 1 (AMNH).

Fig. X.32. Golden-mantle Saddle-back Tamarin, *Saguinus fuscicollis tripartitus.* (Photo courtesy of New York Zoological Society.)

SAGUINUS FUSCICOLLIS WEDDELLI DEVILLE: WEDDELL'S SADDLE-BACK TARAMIN

Synonymic History

Midas Weddellii Deville, 1849, *Rev. Zool.*, p. 55. Deville in I. Geoffroy, 1852, *Arch. Mus. Hist. Nat.* 5:531 (footnote), 581—characters.

Midas Weddellii, Deville in I. Geoffroy, 1855, *Castelnau Expéd. Amérique Sud, pt. 7, Zool., Mamm.*, p. 23, pl. 6, fig. 2 (animal)—characters; habits. Rode, 1938, *Bull. Mus. Nat. Hist. Nat., Paris,* ser. 2, 10:241—type history. Cruz Lima, 1945, *Mamíferos da Amazonia, Primates,* p. 210—taxonomy.

M[idas] Weddellii, I. Geoffroy, 1851, *Cat. Primates, Mus. Hist. Nat., Paris,* p. 65—type history. Reichenbach, 1862, *Vollst. Naturg. Affen,* p. 13—characters.

M[idas] weddelleri [*sic*], Slack, 1861, *Proc. Acad. Nat. Sci. Philadelphia* 13:464—lapsus for *weddelli* in synonymy of *M. devillii* [*sic*].

Hapale Weddellii, Gervais, 1854, *Hist. Nat., Mamm.* 1:152, fig. (head)—characters. Schlegel, 1876, *Les singes. Simiae,* p. 262—characters.

H[apale] Weddelli, Burmeister, 1869, *Anal. Mus. Publ. Buenos Aires* 1:448—BOLIVIA: *Santa Cruz* ([?] Chiquitos).

Leontocebus weddelli, Osgood, 1916, *Field Mus. Nat. Hist., Zool. Ser.* 10:214—BRAZIL: *Guaporé* (Porto Velho, Rio Madeira). Cabrera, 1958, *Rev. Mus. Argentino Cienc. Nat. "Bernardino Rivadavia"* 4:197—listed.

Marikina weddelli, Hershkovitz, 1949, *Proc. U.S. Nat. Mus.* 98:413—key characters; classification; synonyms, *purillus* Thomas, *imberbis* Lönnberg. Sanborn, 1951, *Publ. Mus. Hist. Nat. "Javier Prado," Lima, (A), Zool.*, no. 6:18—PERU: *Cusco* (Hacienda Cadena). Sanborn, 1953, *Publ. Mus. Hist. Nat. "Javier Prado," Lima, (A), Zool.*, no. 12:5—PERU: *Puno* (San Ignacio; Pampa Grande, Sandía).

Tamarinus weddelli, Osman Hill, 1957, *Primates* 3:218, 220, 221, 225—characters; distribution.

Leontocebus weddeli [*sic*], Elliot, 1913, *A review of the Primates* 1:202—characters ex type.

[*Saguinus fuscicollis*] *weddelli,* Hershkovitz, 1966, *Folia Primat.* 4:385—classification (synonyms: *purillus* Thomas, *imberbis* Lönnberg). Hershkovitz, 1968, *Evolution* 22(3):560, figs. 4, 5 (diagnostic color pattern);—characters; distribution; metachromism.

Saguinus fuscicollis weddelli, Hershkovitz, 1970, *Am. J. Phys. Anthrop.* 32:379—classification; dental diseases. Hershkovitz, 1970, *Folia Primat.* 13:215, fig. 3 (cerebral hemisphere)—PERU: *Cusco* (Hacienda Cadena); cerebral fissural pattern. Mallinson, 1971, *Sixth Ann. Rep. Jersey Wildl. Preserv. Trust,* p. 6, fig. 12(young)—BOLIVIA: *Beni.*

[*Leontocebus*] *purillus* Thomas, 1914, *Ann. Mag. Nat. Hist.* ser. 8, 13:347—BRAZIL: *Acre* (type locality, Rio Xapury, Rio Acre, upper Rio Purús); type, male, skin and skull, British Museum (Natural History) no. 14.2.21.1, received from the Goeldi Museum.

Leontocebus purillus, Thomas, 1920, *Proc. U.S. Nat. Mus.* 58:221—PERU: *Cusco* (Río Cosireni, 3,000 feet; Río San Miguel, 4,500 feet); frontal patch.

Mystax purillus, Thomas, 1928, *Ann. Mag. Nat. Hist.*, ser. 10, 2:257—PERU: *Loreto* (Chicosa, upper Río Ucayali, 1,000 ft.).

Marikina weddelli purillus, Vieira, 1952, *Papeis Avulsos* 11 (2):23—BRAZIL: *Acre* (Iquiri).

Mystax imberbis Lönnberg, 1940, *Ark. Zool., Stockholm* 32A, (10):11—BOLIVIA: *Beni* (type locality, Victoria, Ríos Beni and Madre de Díos); type, male and female, skin and skull, Stockholm Museum, collected 6 October 1937 by A. M. Olalla.

Midas fuscicollis, Goeldi (not Spix), 1905, *Compte Rendu VI International Zool. Congr., Berne, 1904,* p. 544—part, BRAZIL: *Amazonas* (upper Rio Purús), the adult only. Goeldi, 1907, *Proc. Zool. Soc. London* 1907:96—BRAZIL: *Amazonas* (upper Rio Purús); characters.

Tamarin fuscicollis, Cruz Lima (part, not Spix), 1945, *Mamíferos da Amazonia, Primates, Contr. Mus. Paraense,* pp. 214, 229, pl. 38, fig. 3*b* (animal)—part, the animal figured in pl. 3*b* and corresponding description; BRAZIL: *Amazonas* (Rio Purús).

Tamarin devilli devilli [*sic*] Cruz Lima (part, not I. Geoffroy), 1945, *Mamíferos da Amazonia, Primates,* p. 232—*purillus* Thomas in synonymy only.

Tamarinus nigricollis, Osman Hill, 1957, *Primates* 3:222, 223, 225—part (not Spix), *Leontocebus purillus* Thomas in synonymy.

Type. Male, skin mounted, skull in, Muséum National d'Histoire Naturelle, Paris, no. 642 (639); collected 1848, by M. Weddell.

Type Locality. Province of Apolobamba [= Caupolicán (137)], La Paz, Bolivia.

Distribution (fig. X.24). The southwestern Amazonian basin, in Brazil, between the Rios Madeira-Mamoré and Purús in the states of Amazonas, Rondônia, and Acre; in Bolivia, the departments of Pando, northern La Paz, and Beni to the Río Mamoré; in Peru, from the departments of Madre de Díos and Puno into the upper Ucayali basin in Loreto and Cusco; altitudinal range from approximately 100 to 1,000 meters above sea level.

Taxonomy. The type of *weddelli,* with head and body 150 mm long, is immature. The more pigmented or yellowish transverse frontal band and the elongate whiskers are characteristic of juvenals (fig. X.36). Otherwise, the color pattern of young is quite like that of adults. A series of three specimens from Tumupasa (138), north of the type locality in La Paz, Bolivia, includes a juvenal with whiskers and "eyebrows" like those of the type, but the color is buffy not white. A second juvenal from Pampa Grande (133), Puno, is considerably larger (head and body, 136 mm) with typically white "eyebrows" and whiskers.

Leontocebus purillus Thomas is based on a specimen said to be from the upper Rio Purús. The original description, published in 1914, is deficient but the diagnostic frontal band mentioned later by Thomas (1920, p. 221) leaves no doubt of the identity of *purillus* with *weddelli.* The type specimen was received from the Goeldi Museum in Pará. It probably belonged to the series described by Dr. Emilio Goeldi (1905, p. 544; 1907, p. 96) under the name *Tamarin fuscicollis* (cf. discussion p. 000).

Mystax imberbis Lönnberg was compared with the original description and colored plate of the young type specimen of *weddelli.* The trivial differences noted (less developed frontal band and whiskers) are individual or age variables. Nothing was said of *purillus* Thomas. Judged by measurements, the male and female types of *imberbis* are young adults. The collector observed that the female was "gravid with a nearly fully developed foetus."

Diagnostic Characters. Crown, mantle, and arms blackish; forehead with a well defined whitish crescentic transverse band or "eyebrows." (Figs. X.26, 27; pls. 3, 4).

Coloration. Crown, sides of head, throat, neck, chest, and mantle blackish or blackish brown, often with a sprinkling of orange ticking, hairs of mantle and chest becoming paler or drab, often whitish toward roots; forehead with whitish transverse crescentic band or "eyebrows" of variable size and definition; facial skin pigmented, short hairs surrounding mouth gray; interorbital space grizzled; saddle vermiculated or marbled black with ochraceous buff or gray; rump and thighs reddish orange; outer side of arms and upper surface of hands and feet black; inner sides of forearms black, more or less mixed with orange or reddish; inner side of upper arms black to dominantly reddish; belly reddish orange; tail black except for short rufous basal portion; external genitalia mostly or entirely pigmented.

Measurements. See appendix table 2.

Comparisons. Distinguished from *leucogenys* by whitish frontal band, mantle hairs with pale bases, and little if any subterminal banding; and distinguished by black crown, nape, and mantle from other races of *fuscicollis* with whitish frontal band or patch.

Remarks. The geographic range of *weddelli* is more than half that of all other members of the *fuscicollis* group combined. The geographic position of *weddelli* suggests the possibility of intergradation with *acrensis* in Brazil and with *leucogenys, nigrifrons,* and *fuscicollis* in southern Loreto, Peru, where headwater streams do not effectively separate the forms. Nothing is known, however, of the tamarins occupying the vast area between the known limits of the range of *weddelli* and those of the other races mentioned.

The individual figured by Cruz Lima (1945, pl. 38, fig. 3*b*) as *Tamarin fuscicollis,* adult, agrees in every respect with *weddelli* except that inner sides of the forearms appear to be entirely reddish, whereas in those I have examined they are dominantly blackish.

Specimens Examined. 57. BOLIVIA—*La Paz:* Apolobamba, type of *weddelli* (MNHN); Tumapasa, 3 (USNM); BRAZIL—*Acre:* Rio Xapury, type of *purillus* (BM); *Amazonas:* Lago do Mapixi, Rio Purús, 4 (BM, 2; FMNH, 2); *Rondônia:* Porto Velho, 1 (FMNH); *locality unknown:* 1 (UMMZ); PERU—*Cusco:* Hacienda Cadena, Marcapata, 2 (FMNH); Río San Miguel, 2 (BM, 1; USNM, 1); Uvini, Río Cosireni, 4 (USNM); *Loreto:* Chicosa, alto Río Ucayali, 3 (BM); Lagarto, alto Río Ucayali, 12 (AMNH); Río Inuyu, mouth, 3 (AMNH); Río Urubamba, mouth, 6 (AMNH); *Madre de Dios:* Itahuania, 3 (FMNH); *Puno:* Candamo, 1 (FMNH); Pampa Grande, Sandia, 8 (FMNH); San Ignacio, 2 (FMNH).

SAGUINUS FUSCICOLLIS CRUZLIMAI HERSHKOVITZ: CRUZ LIMA'S SADDLE-BACK TAMARIN

Synonymic History

Midas fuscicollis, Goeldi (part, not Spix), 1905, *Comptes Rendus VI Cong. Int. Zool.,* Berne, 1904, p. 544—BRAZIL: *Amazonas* (upper Rio Purús), "young" only. Goeldi, 1907, *Proc. Zool. Soc. London* 1907:96 —part, "young" only.

Tamarin fuscicollis, Cruz Lima (part, not Spix), 1945, *Mamíferos da Amazonia, 1, Primates,* p. 229, pl. 38, fig. 3*a* (animal, "jovem")—part, BRAZIL: *Amazonas* (upper Rio Purús), "young" only, as figured.

Saguinus fuscicollis cruzlimai, Hershkovitz, 1966, *Folia Primat.* 4:388.

S[aguinus fuscicollis] cruzlimai, Hershkovitz, 1968, *Evolution* 22(3):560, figs. 4, 5 (diagnostic color pattern) —distribution; metachromism.

Type. Specimen figured by Cruz Lima (1945; pl. 38, fig. 3*a*) captioned *"Tamarin fuscicollis* jovem" and represented by a skin said to be mounted and preserved in the Museu Paraense Emilio Goeldi de Historia Natural e Etnografía, Belém do Pará, Brazil.

Type Locality. Said to be from the upper Rio Purús region, Amazonas, Brazil.

Distribution (fig. X.24). Unknown but probably on the west bank of the upper Rio Purús and possibly between it and the tributary Rio Tapauá, Amazonas, Brazil.

Diagnostic Characters. Crown, mantle, arms, and upper surface of hands and legs reddish orange; forehead with well-defined whitish transverse band or "eyebrows." (Figs. X.26, 27; pls. 3, 4).

Measurements. See appendix table 2.

Comparisons. Distinguished from *weddelli* and *crandalli* by the reddish orange forequarters, and from all other callitrichids by the combination of diagnostic characters given above and the whitish circumbuccal band, trizonal dorsal pattern, blackish tail, and large, nearly bare and fully exposed ears. The nominate race, *Saguinus fuscicollis fuscicollis* Spix, with which the present form had been confused, is marked by agouti-patterned forehead and crown, melano-agouti or brownish mantle, tawny to mahogany colored limbs and underparts, and blackish hands and feet.

Remarks. The reddish orange tamarin with white "eyebrows" described here and figured by Cruz Lima (1945, pl. 38, fig. 3*a*) as the "young" of *"Tamarin fuscicollis"* agrees more nearly with *crandalli* than with any other known race of *fuscicollis.* The seeming whitish ventral surface of the proximal part of the tail shown in the figure is a highlight used for defining the tail against the black background. Whatever the true age of the purportedly "young" animal, it seems to be about the same size as the other three ostensibly adult tamarins illustrated by Cruz Lima on the same plate. Its color pattern and pelage, as depicted, are adult. The black-mantled, white-eyebrowed tamarin treated by Cruz Lima (pl. 38, fig. 3*b*) as the "adult" form of *fuscicollis* is an unmistakable representative of *Saguinus fuscicollis weddelli* I. Geoffroy and Deville.

Cruz Lima's concept of *fuscicollis* was based on Goeldi's (1907, p. 96) misidentification of eight specimens of the black-mantled *Saguinus fuscicollis weddelli* Deville as *Midas fuscicollis* Spix. The error was compounded by Goeldi's intimation that the young of this *"fuscicollis"* differed significantly in color from the adult. Goeldi failed to describe the young, but he alluded to an unpublished color plate with figures illustrating the juvenal and adult color phases of *"fuscicollis."* The specimens in question, 6 males and 2 females, were said to have been collected in the upper Rio Purús basin for the Goeldi Museum in Pará. The "young" and "adult" figured by Cruz Lima as *"fuscicollis"* may have been part of the same collection described by Goeldi. The age dichromatism, such as described by Goeldi and Cruz Lima, does not exist among callitrichids.

Whatever the names he used, the animals described and faithfully depicted by Cruz Lima are positively identifiable. The holotype of *cruzlimai* is presumed to be preserved as a mounted specimen in the collections of the Museu Goeldi in Pará. Several inquiries addressed to that institution regarding the specimen elicited no response.

Dr. Eladio da Cruz Lima, in whose memory this tamarin is named, was a Justice of the Supreme Court of the State of Pará, an accomplished artist, literary critic, archaeologist and zoologist. His untimely death in 1943 at the age of 43 during the printing of his first volume of the "Mammals of Amazonia" deprived Brazilian mammlogy of one of its most dedicated scholars.

Specimens Examined. None.

SAGUINUS FUSCICOLLIS CRANDALLI HERSHKOVITZ: CRANDALL'S SADDLE-BACK TAMARIN

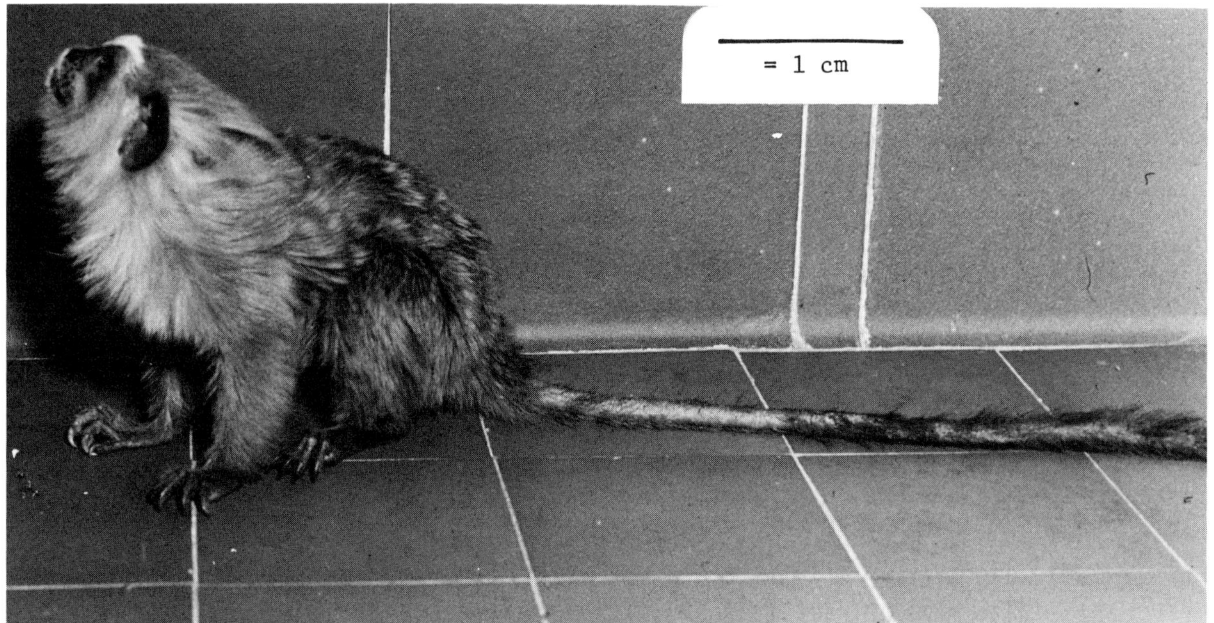

Fig. X.33. Crandall's Saddle-back Tamarin, holotype of *Saguinus fuscicollis crandalli*. Photograph of individual formerly living in New York Zoo but now preserved in the American Museum of Natural History. (Photo courtesy of New York Zoological Society.)

Synonymic History

Mystax fuscicollis, Crandall (not Spix), 1951, *Animal Kingdom* 54:179, fig. (live animal)—characters.

Saguinus fuscicollis crandalli, Hershkovitz, 1966, *Folia Primat.* 4:389.

[*Saguinus fuscicollis*] *crandalli,* Hershkovitz, 1968, *Evolution* 22(3):560, figs. 4, 5 (diagnostic color pattern)—characters; distribution; metachromism.

Type. Adult male, skin and skeleton, American Museum of Natural History no. 165018, received 13 July 1954 from the New York Zoological Society.

Type Locality. Unknown.

Distribution (fig. X.24). Unknown, possibly between the lower Rios Purús and Madeira, Amazonas, Brazil.

Diagnostic Characters. Crown, mantle, and arms drab, rump and thighs orange, tail pale brown; broad white transverse frontal band present and well-defined; throat, neck, and chest buffy to nearly white (figs. X.26, 27; pls. 3, 4).

Coloration. Facial skin pigmented, sparsely haired gray; forehead with broad whitish transverse band or eyebrows; band around mouth extending to sides of nostrils covered with short gray hairs; mantle drab, the basal portions paler to nearly white; outer sides of arms drab like mantle but with wisps of ochraceous orange near shoulders; saddle vermiculated buffy and black; rump, thighs, and legs orange; throat whitish; neck and chest ochraceous buff with a mixture of whitish hairs, belly and underside of hind limbs dominantly orange; upper surface of hands drab, of feet mixed buffy and orange with the dark bases of the hairs showing through; tail dark brown except for orange on ventral surface of proximal fifth; skin of volar surface and external genitalia well pigmented.

Measurements. See appendix table 2.

Comparisons. Color more dilute throughout than in all races of *S. fuscicollis* except semialbinotic *acrensis* Carvalho and albinotic *melanoleucus* Miranda Ribeiro; distinguished from first by generally drab, not yellowish white, head, mantle, limbs and tail; from second by rentention of well-defined trizonal color pattern of dorsal surface characteristic of nonalbinotic forms of *S. fuscicollis.*

Remarks. Saguinus fuscicollis crandalli appears to be intermediate in coloration between the more saturate *S. f. cruzlimai* and the more dilute *S. f. acrensis.*

The type and only known specimen of *crandalli* was received alive by the New York Zoological Society 2 November 1951. It remained on exhibition until its death, 26 June 1954. The preserved skeleton exhibits none of the malformations or decalcifications usually found in animals raised in captivity. The slight wear of the molars indicates that the tamarin was not old when captured. Its overgrown claws are symptoms of confinement. The external measurements, presumably taken in the flesh by the preparator of the deceased specimen, are questionable. Tail length, recorded as 257 mm on the skin label, is disproportionately short for an adult of the species. In the dry skin the tail, with a goodly piece of the terminal portion lost, measures about 260 mm.

The faded appearance of the type skin was virtually the same in the live animal. Shortly after the tamarin's arrival at the Zoological Park, Crandall (1951, p. 183, fig.), for whom this tamarin was named, noted that the "soft beige foreparts have a faint suggestion of pink, and the white forehead is sharply defined."

Specimens Examined. 1. BRAZIL: unknown locality, 1 (AMNH, type of *crandalli*).

SAGUINUS FUSCICOLLIS ACRENSIS CARVALHO: ACRE SADDLE-BACK TAMARIN

Synonymic History

Leontocebus melanoleucus acrensis Carvalho, 1957, *Rev. Brasil. Biol.* 17(2):219, fig. 1 (skin)—BRAZIL: *Acre* (Pedra Preta; Seringal Oriente, 12 km. below Vila Taumaturgo, Rio Juruá). Carvalho, 1957, *Bol. Mus. Paraense Emilio Goeldi, n.s., Zool.,* no. 6, p. 8—BRAZIL: *Acre* (Pedra Preta; Seringal Oriente).

[*Saguinus fuscicollis*] *acrensis,* Hershkovitz, 1966, *Folia Primat.* 4:385—classification. Hershkovitz, 1968, *Evolution* 22(3):560, figs. 4, 5 (diagnostic color pattern)—characters; distribution; metachromism.

Type. Male, skin and skull, Museu Paraense Emilio Goeldi no. 738; collected 6 July 1956 by M. Moreira.

Type Locality. Opposite Pedra Preta (209), about 15 km below Vila Taumaturgo, right bank upper Rio Juruá, Acre, Brazil.

Distribution (fig. X.24). Extreme southwestern Brazil between the upper Juruá and its tributary, the Tarauacá, western Acre; altitudinal range between 100 and 200 meters.

Diagnostic Characters. Crown, mantle, and arms yellowish white; white frontal band present; back marbled drab and ochraceous buff, rump and thighs orange, underparts yellowish (figs. X.26, 27; pls. 3, 4).

Coloration (from original description). Head, mantle, and forelimbs white lightly washed with buffy or yellow; facial skin and ears black, thinly covered with short white hairs; chevron-shaped frontal patch white; middle and lower back marbled drab and ochraceous-buff, hairs whitish basally, becoming dark brown medially, ochraceous-buff subterminally, tips drab; rump and thighs orange; upper surface of hands whitish, of feet yellow; underparts yellowish; tail yellowish, the underside lined with brown.

Measurements. See appendix table 2.

Comparisons. Distinguished from *melanoleucus* by retention of the trizonal color pattern of dorsum including well-defined saddle; from *crandalli* by paler color throughout with mantle yellowish not drab.

Remarks. The coloration of *Saguinus fuscicollis acrensis* is intermediate between that of *crandalli* and *melanoleucus.* The three races, *crandalli, acrensis,* and *melanoleucus* represent, respectively, three preterminal grades in the bleaching process. The last two races are parts of a geographic cline. Whether or not *crandalli* belongs to the same cline is moot.

The original description of *acrensis* is based on the holotype from Pedra Preta and three specimens from Seringal Oriente. The description and diagnostic characters presented here are adapted from the original.

Specimens Examined. None.

SAGUINUS FUSCICOLLIS MELANOLEUCUS MIRANDA RIBEIRO: WHITE SADDLE-BACK TAMARIN

Synonymic History

Mico melanoleucus Miranda Ribeiro, 1912, *Brasilianische Rundschau* 2(1):22, fig. (head). Thomas, 1922, *Ann. Mag. Nat. Hist.,* ser. 9, 9:199—"is a *Mystax* [= *Saguinus*]." Avila Pires, 1968, *Arq. Mus. Nac. Rio de Janeiro* 53:172—cotypes, 1 skin and skull in Museu Nacional Rio de Janeiro, without locality data; second specimen in Museu do Pará; type in British Museum (Natural History); specimen M. N. no. 2835 designated lectotype by Moojen (in Miranda Ribeiro, 1955, *Arq. Mus. Nac. Rio de Janeiro* 42:414), is a *Callithrix chrysoleuca* Wagner.

H[*apale*] *melanoleucos* [*sic*], Thomas, 1920, *Ann. Mag. Nat. Hist.,* ser. 9, 6:269 (in text)—cotype in British Museum (Natural History).

[*Mystax*] *melanoleucus,* Thomas, 1922, *Ann. Mag. Nat. Hist.,* ser. 9, 9:198, 199—classification.

Callithrix melanoleuca, Cruz Lima, 1945, *Mamíferos da Amazonia, Primates, Contr. Mus. Paraense,* p. 248, pl. 41, fig. 2 (animal)—BRAZIL: *Amazonas* ("Manaus," from dealer; Lago Grande, Rio Juruá); *hololeucus* Pinto, a synonym. Vieira, 1948, *Bol. Mus. Paraense* 10:254—BRAZIL: *Amazonas* (Santo Antonio, Rio Eirú, Rio Juruá; Igarapé Grande, Rio Juruá; Santa Cruz, Rio Juruá). Dela Serra, 1950, *Papeis Avulsos* 9 (19):285, pl. 1, fig. 8, pl. 2, fig. 9 (skull), pl. 4, fig. 10 (mandible)—cranial and dental characters; comparisons; a true tamarin; *Leontocebus hololeucus* Pinto, a synonym.

Marikina melanoleuca, Hershkovitz, 1949, *Proc. U.S. Nat. Mus.* 98:412, footnote 11—key characters; classification; *Leontocebus hololeucus* Pinto, a synonym.

[*Tamarin*] *melanoleucus,* Della Serra, 1950, *Papeis Avulsos, São Paulo* 9 (19):294—classification.

Leontocebus melanoleucus, Cabrera, 1958, *Rev. Mus. Argentino Cienc. Nat. "Bernardino Rivadavia"* 4 (1): 194—classification; type locality said to be Pará.

Leontocebus melanoleucus melanoleucus, Carvalho, 1957, *Bol. Mus. Parense Emilio Goeldi, n. s., Zool.,* no. 6:7—BRAZIL: *Acre* (Cruzeiro do Sul, right bank upper Rio Juruá).

Tamarinus melanoleucus, Osman Hill, 1957, *Primates* 3:220, 222, 240, 282, 291—characters; distribution; taxonomy.

S[*aguinus*] *f*[*uscicollis*] *melanoleucus,* Hershkovitz, 1966, *Folia Primate.* 4:384—key characters; classification.

Fig. X.34. White Saddle-back Tamarin, *Saguinus fuscicollis melanoleucus.* (Photo courtesy of New York Zoological Society.)

[*Saguinus fuscicollis*] *melanoleucus,* Hershkovitz, 1968, *Evolution* 22(3):560—figs. 4, 5 (diagnostic color pattern)—characters; distribution; metachromism.

Leontocebus hololeucus Pinto, 1937, *Bol. Biol.* 3 (n.s.), no. 5, p. 3—BRAZIL: *Amazonas* (type locality, Santo Antônio, Rio Eirú); type, male, skin and skull, Museu Paulista, São Paulo, no. 4159, collected 14 October 1936 by A. M. Olalla. Lönnberg, 1940, *Ark. Zool., Stockholm,* 32A, (10):1—BRAZIL: *Amazonas* (Lago Grande, Rio Juruá; Santo Antônio, Rio Eirú, Rio Juruá).

Types. Two syntypes, the first seen live in the Rio de Janeiro Zoological Garden, the second living in the Zoological Garden of the Museu Paraense Emilio Goeldi; only the second individual, a male (here designated lectotype), was preserved 30 July 1913, as skin and skull, and presented by the Museu Goeldi to the British Museum (Natural History) where its registry number is 14.2.21.2.

Type Locality. Amazonas, Brazil; restricted to Santo Antônio, Rio Eirú (180), upper Rio Juruá, Amazonas, by Carvalho (1957, *Rev. Brasil. Biol.* 17 [2]:222).

Distribution (fig. X.24). Southwestern Brazil in the basin between upper Rio Juruá and its tributary the Tarauacá ,southwestern Amazonas and perhaps bordering parts of Acre; altitudinal range in the neighborhood of 100 meters.

Taxonomy. The original description of *melanoleucus* Miranda Ribeiro as a *Callithrix* (i.e., *Mico*) in 1912 was based on the author's cursory examination of a live animal in the Pará Zoo and his recollections of a live individual seen in the Rio de Janeiro Zoological Garden. Thomas (1922, pp. 198, 199) examined one of the two syntypes and classified it as a typical tamarin. *Leontocebus hololeucus* Pinto, described in 1937, proves to be the first recorded specimen of *melanoleucus* with a precise locality label.

Diagnostic Characters. Dominantly whitish throughout with skin of ears, face, and external genitalia blackish; underparts and inner surface of limbs whitish or yellowish to ochraceous (figs. X.26, 27, pls. 3, 4).

Coloration. Pelage of upper and outer parts creamy white often washed or streaked with yellowish, or buffy, hairs whitish, buffy, or drab basally; upper surface of hands and feet mixed silvery and buff; undersides of body and inner sides of limbs white to buffy or ochraceous the hairs uniformly colored; forehead with poorly defined whitish crescentic band; hairs surrounding mouth and sides of nostrils gray; facial skin, ears, palms, and soles black; skin of head, back, sides of body, limbs, external genitalia and tail more or less pigmented, of belly paler or unpigmented.

Measurements. See appendix table 2.

Comparisons. Distinguished from all other tamarins by dominantly creamy white pelage of upper and outer parts; differs from the phenotype equivalent *Callithrix argentata leucippe* by black facial skin and ears, generally well-pigmented hide, hairy circumbuccal band, and frontal blaze (fig. X.34).

Remarks. The quasi-albino *Saguinus fuscicollis melanoleucus* represents the extreme of the bleaching process among tamarins. It is one grade removed from *acrensis* and another from *crandalli.* In the most heavily pigmented specimen of four at hand, basal portions of mantle hairs are nearly as drab as the overall mantle color of *crandalli,* its underparts nearly as orange.

Judged by specimens with precise locality data, those labeled Igarapé Grande (177) must have originated on the right bank of the Rio Juruá.

A made-up study skin of a subadult in the Paris Museum (MNHN 1908–27), without data, is typical except for a pair of *Leontopithecus*like tufts on crown behind ears. The tufts seem artificial but I cannot establish this. The specimen was first labeled *Hapale jacchus* and perhaps the preparator tried to make it look like that species.

Specimens Examined. 6. BRAZIL—*Amazonas:* Santo Antônio, Rio Eirú, 4 (FMNH); UNKNOWN LOCALITY—2 (BM, type of *melanoleucus;* MNHN, 1).

Plate V. White Saddle-back Tamarin (*Saguinus fuscicollis melanoleucus*).
Plate courtesy of the Cologne Zoo.

63 *Saguinus nigricollis* Group
2. Biology of White-mouth Tamarins

REPRODUCTION

Information on breeding compiled from several sources is quoted, paraphrased, or reorganized in the following pages.

Studies by Shadle, Mirand, and Grace (1965, p. 1) of the breeding behavior of a tamarin colony mostly of individuals identified as *"Tamarinus illigeri"* [= *Saguinus fuscicollis ?lagonotus*] and *"T. fuscicollis"* are particularly interesting. The authors note that *"T. mystax"* [= *Saguinus mystax mystax*] and *Oedipomidas oedipus* [= *Saguinus oedipus oedipus*] were also represented in the colony. No particular species is mentioned in their accounts. What is said, however, appears to be applicable to tamarins in general, but particularly to members of the *Saguinus nigricollis* group. The authors were prone to regard nearly every behavioral trait as sexually motivated. In most cases, the activities they describe can be interpreted otherwise. During the 18 months of observation, only 5 pregnancies and 1 live birth occurred in the colony of 360 tamarins. Taxonomic mismatching of breeding pairs could account for most of the reproductive failures.

The data compiled from various sources are organized under the following subtitles; unless otherwise indicated, the information given refers to members of the *Saguinus nigricollis* group:

Mating and Sex Play	Estrus
Copulation	Periodicity
Homosexuality	Reproductive Capacity in Captivity
Interbirth Interval	Hybridization
Parturition	
Litters	

Mating and Sex Play

Epple 1975*b*, p. 209

"In groups containing more males than females, one of the females actively inhibits the other females from establishing a pair bond. In the [2 experimental] groups containing 2 males and 2 females, the animals showed a tendency to establish two permanent pairs. However, in all [4 experimental] groups, 1 female finally eliminated all other females from the group by attacking them so viciously that they had to be removed in order to save their lives."

Shadle, Mirand, and Grace 1965

One or both sexually aroused individuals of a breeding pair stimulate the partner by tonguing, kissing with closed mouth, often alternating with tonguing, yawning, body stretching, scratching, rubbing the white circumoral band against a part of the cage, vigorous rubbing of genitals against cage floor or any object including partner, sniffing and touching genitals of partner, touching, snuggling, crowding, crawling over and around, usually of male by female, seizing, pulling usually of female by male, vocalizing in high-pitched birdlike notes.

The sight or sound of tamarins engaged in sexual play or copulation may arouse sexual activity in other tamarins, more so in the females than the males.

"Female receptivity and sex play vary with the individual and with the stage of oestrus. She may be almost completely passive in her receptivity, may make almost no calls, exhibit no sex play and almost no activity, but she will readily accept the male when he attempts to mount, and sit placidly by when coitus is completed.

"Moderately active females may touch the male, snuggle up to him and crowd against him as he sits on the resting shelf or on the cage floor. She may groom him, examine and test his genitals, crawl around, over and under him, and in various ways may seek to arouse him to sexual activity.

"After they have copulated, strongly sexually aroused females often become so active and insistent in their efforts to arouse the male that he may become annoyed and strike her, but he rarely does more than make a few well directed slaps with a forepaw.

"Good breeding males that are regularly used as studs seem to have a very keen sense of the degree of receptivity of the females offered to them in the breeding cage. If the female is not sexually receptive, an active male may give her a very perfunctory examination; or if he finds her totally uninteresting sexually, he may virtually ignore her presence in the breeding cage, even without any apparent examination. In such a case, no matter how long they are left together in the breeding cage, he will usually continue to ignore her and simply sit beside her on the resting shelf, or sit alone on the floor. When a good active male breeder (which has not been overworked sexually) reacts in this way, it is useless to try that female with any other male at that time."

Hershkovitz (Comments)

With few exceptions, every behavioral trait described by the authors in the account partially abstracted above was interpreted as sexually stimulated or directed. It seems to me, however, that many of the actions are not directly and in many cases not even indirectly sex related. Such acts include grooming, mouth wiping, territorial scent-marking, "group" vocalizations, social, as opposed to sexual, body contact, signs of recognition, social dominance, antagonisms, and signs of boredom. The taxonomic composition of the colony was mixed and there is no doubt that cage groupings were also mixed and unstable.

Benirschke and Richart 1963, p. 80

The mate of a pair of breeding tamarins purchased 21 October 1958 was observed with a penile erection 23 November 1958 "but copulation never took place during sunning. Mating was observed in their sleeping box, only once, during the daytime on March 5, 1959. The same day a small blood spot was present in the towel under which they slept. This must have been vaginal bleeding, since no injuries were seen. Two new blood spots were present on March 7, 1959. A frog-test with 3 ml. of urine taken on March 15, 1959, was negative. . . . The female died May 21, 1959 from an infection."

Epple 1975*b*, p. 208

"In group 1 and group 3 [each consisting of 2 adult males and 1 adult female], we observed both males actively competing for the female at times when she was apparently in estrus. In both groups both males followed the female very closely wherever she went. Both constantly sniffed her body, her genitals, and her scent marks [and] tried to establish contact with her, sit by her side, and groom her. In both groups, the male with whom the female normally associated more closely was frequently successful in replacing the second male by her side. He would simply jump between the female and the second male, pushing him away from her. In one case, male 26 maneuvered the female (female 21) into one corner of the cage and sat in front of her holding onto the wire of the cage so that his arm encircled the female and prevented her from moving away. It was surprising for us that during both of these periods of active competition for the apparently receptive female, we did not observe overt aggression or even an unusually high amount of threats between the two males.

Shadle, Mirand and Grace 1965, p. 7

"On one occasion, a very receptive female was placed in the cage with three males to determine (a) whether the female would accept each of the three males, or (b) whether each of the males would attempt to copulate with her, or (c) whether any antagonism among the three male cage-mates would develop due to (1) the female's presence in their cage, (2) a struggle for the possession of the female and the mating rights, or (3) the close proximity of the two males to a copulating pair.

"When the female was placed in the cage, she was promptly mounted by one male that completed coitus in 8 seconds without any apparent interest in or interference from the other two males. Following the sex act, the male became passive and assumed a sitting position on the cage floor with his tail curled like a watch spring under him.

"The female immediately resumed active sex play, calling insistently, cavorting about the cage, snuggling up to the other two males and trying persistently to sexually arouse them. Ordinarily both males are eager and prompt in their sex reactions to a receptive female, but in this case they showed only slight sexual interest in this receptive female and made no effort to possess her, nor to exhibit sex play. The female was so insistent in her efforts to stimulate the two males to sexual activity that both males became antagonistic and struck and rebuffed her."

Copulation

Wolfe, Ogden, Deinhardt, Fisher, and Deinhardt 1972, p. 151

As confirmed by the presence of spermatozoa in vaginal smears, pregnant females permit copulation even late in the gestation period, and, apparently different from other species of nonhuman primates, heads of spermatozoa were still found in the vaginal smears of tamarins as long as 10–14 days after copulation.

Shadle, Mirand, and Grace 1965, p. 7

"The time element of the individual males in reaching the mounting state of copulation may vary a great deal. Some males are slow, patient and deliberate in reaching the mounting stage, but a strong, vigorous, and aggressive male tamarin will usually mount a sexually receptive female within 3 to 10 seconds after they are brought together in the breeding cage.

"Once a strong vigorous male has seized and mounted a female, he clasps her tightly around the abdomen with his arms and hands and with his hind feet holding firmly to her calves or her thighs, makes sexual contact and begins vigorous pelvic thrusts. The copulatory act usually may be completed in from 6 to 15 seconds, after which he dismounts. Once the male is firmly mounted, it is difficult for the average female to dislodge him until coitus is completed, even though she may rush about the cage and even jump from the resting shelf to the cage floor. We have seen a mounted female twist her hind quarters so violently that the male, still mounted and thrusting, was flopped over to lie upon his right side, then to his left side, and again to his right side and he still maintained his position and contact and completed the copulation. During a recent copulation, the female bent her head down between her hind legs, turned a complete somersault (which involved both animals) and landed on all four feet with the male still in position where he continued and completed the coitus."

Shadle, Mirand, and Grace 1965

The following statistics are based on 400 timed copulations involving 360 tamarins over a period of 18 months in the Roswell Park Memorial Institute, Buffalo, New York.

Shortest copulation—6 seconds.

Longest copulation—335 seconds (5 minutes, 35 seconds; see below).

Most frequent period—8 seconds (21% of total).

Completed within 10 seconds—42%.

Completed within 20 seconds—35%.

1 ♀ accepted 1 ♂ 7 times in 3.5 hours.

1 ♀ accepted 1 ♂ 6 times in 42 minutes.

Preceding ♀ accepted 4 different males in 92 minutes.

Greatest number of copulation by 1 ♀—87 in 5 months.

Periodicity: highest frequency months listed.

May, 78 copulations = 19.5%
June, 68 copulations = 18.0%
July, 81 copulations = 20%
Remaining months = 42.5%

In longest coitus observed (5 minutes, 35 seconds), "the male held the female firmly and maintained continual sexual contact. The act consisted of intermittent periods of rapid, vigorous pelvic thrusting, interspersed by similar periods of inaction during which he held his position and maintained intromission. This is typical of long copulations."

Homosexuality

Shadle, Mirand, and Grace 1965, pp. 8–9

"Receptive females may perform homosexual acts, mounting other females or permitting themselves to be mounted by other females. The mounting female often puts on such a convincing copulatory act in technique, vigor and endurance that checks were made to make sure that a male had not been introduced by mistake into the cage with the female.

"One young female was timed during her homosexual pseudo-copulatory act with a mature oestrous female and once she held a continuous mount for 3 minutes and 33 seconds. In six homosexual mounts made in one morning, she spent 17 minutes and over 20 seconds or approximately an average mount of almost three minutes.

"Another case was a very unusual performance. A female mounted the hips of another female but allowed her hind quarters to lag about 4 inches behind sexual contact with the second female. The mounting female proceeded to make typical pelvic thrusts and because her genitals were in contact with the floor of the cage, they were being stimulated during the pelvic thrusts."

Hershkovitz (Comments)

The homosexual acts quoted above may be interpreted as such in a broad sense, but they were performed by caged heterosexual females deliberately deprived of males during a period of hypersensitivity. In some, if not most cases under the unnatural circumstances, mounting may be primarily a display of dominance by an alpha female. The cited authors also regard simple genital rubbing or marking as a homosexual act. The activity, however, is usually interpreted as scent-marking, a trait not mentioned by Shadle, Mirand, and Grace and probably overlooked. Scent-marking is a normal behavioral trait of all mature callitrichids. It may be practiced more assiduously by sexually aroused than by indifferent individuals but the performance is not one of homosexuality.

Interbirth Interval

Among tamarins bred in the laboratories of the Rush–Presbyterian–St. Luke's Medical Center, Chicago, Wolfe, Ogden, J. Deinhardt, Fisher, and Deinhardt (1972) record intervals ranging from 134 to 505 days between 105 births. The shortest interval, 134 days, between births of hand-reared young, is within the limits of variation of the duration of "normal" pregnancy determined by other methods. The extreme of 505 days between stillborn or aborted young is nearly 4 times as long. It was noted that in cases of hand-rearing, the sooner the young were separated from the mother, the shorter the mean interval between births.

In an updated and revised report on breeding in the same laboratories, Wolfe, Deinhardt, Ogden, Adams, and Fisher (1975, p. 806) record the following means and extremes of interbirth intervals for 284 deliveries of hand-reared and 99 parent-reared White-mouth Tamarins (*Saguinus fuscicollis illigeri, S. f. nigrifrons, S. nigricollis nigricollis, S. fuscicollis* subspp. × *S. n. nigricollis, S. fuscicollis* subspp. × *S. f. subspp.*)

Hand-reared 182 days (146–383) 284 litters
Parent-reared 252 days (168–545) 99 litters

Hand-reared offspring were separated from their parents within 72 hours after birth; parent-reared offspring remained with their parents 2–6 months. The shortest mean intervals for hand-reared and parent-reared were recorded for *Saguinus fuscicollis illigeri* with 170 days (146–383) 61 litters, and 241 days (171–312) 25 litters, respectively. The survival rate for newborn to 30 days of age was about the same for hand-reared (80.1%) and parent-reared (83.8%).

Duration of Gestation

In a single observation by Wolfe, Deinhardt, Ogden, Adams, and Fisher (1975, p. 804), a date-mated *Saguinus fuscicollis illigeri* together for 1 week, produced full-term twins between 145 and 152 days after conception.

External palpation of the uterus was used by Gengozian, Smith, and Gosslee (1974) to determine pregnancy in saddle-back tamarins of the subspecies *Saguinus fuscicollis illigeri*. Earliest sign of gestation was a hard sphere measuring 5 mm between the palpating fingers. Employing a growth curve model relating uterine size to an exponential function of age, the authors predicted 12, or 7%, of 178 delivery dates to the day, and 108 (61%) within 5 days. Actual gestation period was computed at 158.8 ± 12.7 days.

The gestation period of 159 days appears to be too long. The high standard error of 12.7 days probably does not reflect nearly enough the sampling errors and the crude and inconsistent observational methods used. The authors readily admit as much and they concede that 140–50 is acceptable as a minimum gestation period. Interbirth interval or the count between first mating and delivery, both rigidly controlled and properly evaluated, are still the best methods for estimating the duration of gestation in callitrichids.

Parturition

Mallinson 1965, p. 139

"March, 1964, a female black-and-red tamarin, *Leontocebus nigricollis,* gave birth [her first] prematurely to twins. The young were found in the morning and one had been partly eaten. There were practically no signs of blood after parturition and the placenta had been eaten."

Wolfe, Ogden, Deinhardt, Fisher, and Deinhardt 1972, p. 151

In the research laboratories of the Rush–Presbyterian–St. Luke's Medical Center, "parturition usually occurred at night or in the early mornings."

Litters

The number of young per litter and the number of each litter size of laboratory bred tamarins compiled from the literature are summarized in tables 80 and 81.

Estrus

Wolfe, Ogden, Deinhardt, Fisher, and Deinhardt 1972, p. 151

"We have not observed cyclical "swellings" in any of our marmosets, nor has menstrual bleeding been observed, either visually or by vaginal smears. Likewise, the study of vaginal smears collected at short sequential intervals from several marmosets has not helped to define the estrous cycle."

Preslock, Hampton, Hampton 1973

Using levels of progestins and immunoreactive estrogens as index, the estrous cycle of *Saguinus fuscicollis illigeri* was determined as 15.5 ± 1.5 days.

Periodicity

Breeding periodicity is not evident in the full-term parturition dates of the San Diego tamarins listed in table 82.

DuMond (1967, p. 207) reports two births in the "Monkey Jungle," Miami, Florida, of unsexed singletons, one on 10 July 1965 and the other 22 April 1966. Mazur and Baldwin (1968) add birth of twins, 24 October 1966 in the same place.

Roth (1960) reports the birth in the Ruhr Zoo of female twins, 2 April 1955. The pregnant female cotype of *Mystax imberbis* Lönnberg (= *Saguinus fuscicollis weddelli*) collected 6 October 1937, near Victoria, Bolivia (11°S) was near term.

In the tamarin colony of Rush–Presbyterian–St. Luke's Medical Center, the hundreds of births recorded "occurred in all months of the year, with no particular groupings in any month or season" (Wolfe, Ogden, Deinhardt, Fisher, and Deinhardt 1972, p. 151). Breeding in the laboratories was rigidly managed for maximum productivity and viability.

Table 80. Reproductive Record of Wild-Caught White-mouth Tamarins

				Offspring					
				Total Live/Total Produced					
Taxon	*Pairs*	*Total Litters*	*Percent Abortions*	*1st Delivery*	*≧ 2d Delivery*	*Total Live*	*%*	*Live Births Pair/Year*[5]	*Avg. Live Per Litter*
illigeri[1]	23	184	6.5	31/41	269/312	300	85	2.9	1.6
fuscicollis[1]	23	148	13.5	30/42	177/228	207	77	2.6	1.4
nigrifrons[1]	17	31	16.1	20/28	18/23	38	75	1.9	1.2
nigricollis[2]	17	88	13.6	22/31	99/129	121	76	2.2	1.4
Hybrids 1[3]	18	115	12.2	27/34	147/181	174	81	2.5	1.5
Hybrids 2[4]	10	65	10.8	14/17	77/99	91	78	2.3	1.4
Totals	108	631	11.1	144/193	787/972[6]	931	80	2.6[5]	1.5

SOURCE: Wolfe, Deinhardt, Ogden, Adams, Fisher (1975; Rush–Presbyterian–St. Luke's Medical Center, Chicago, Illinois).

[1] Subspecies of *Saguinus fuscicollis.*
[2] Subspecies of *Saguinus nigricollis.*
[3] *Saguinus fuscicollis* subspp. × *Saguinus n. nigricollis.*
[4] Subspecies crosses of *Saguinus fuscicollis.*
[5] Average number of live births produced per female per "animal year" following first delivery.
[6] Average number of live + stillborn young per litter (972–631) = 1.8 (cf. tables 51, 81).

Table 81. Number of Litters and Young per Litter Produced in Captivity

Source	*Taxon*	*Pairs*	*Litters*	*Number of Each Litter Size* 1 (%)	2 (%)	3 (%)	*Total Young*	*Avg. Young Per Litter*
A	*illigeri*[1]	23	184	25 (14%)	149 (81%)	10 (5%)	353	1.9
A	*fuscicollis*[1]	23	148	32 (22%)	110 (74%)	6 (4%)	260	1.8
A	*nigrifrons*[1]	17	31	11 (35%)	20 (64%)	0 (0%)	51	1.6
A	*nigricollis*[2]	17	88	17 (20%)	70 (79%)	1 (1%)	160	1.8
A	Hybrids 1[3]	18	115	18 (16%)	94 (81%)	3 (3%)	215	1.9
A	Hybrids 2[4]	10	65	17 (26%)	45 (69%)	3 (5%)	116	1.8
A	Totals	128	631	120 (19%)	488 (77%)	23 (4%)	1,165	1.8
B	*fuscicollis*[1]	—	51	7 (14%)	41 (80%)	3 (6%)	98	1.9
C	*fuscicollis*[1]	—	152	47 (31%)	101 (66%)	4 (3%)	261	1.7
D	*fuscicollis*[1]	—	44	13 (30%)	31 (70%)	0 (0%)	75	1.7

SOURCE:
A Wolfe, Deinhardt, Ogden, Adams, and Fisher (1975, p. 804; Rush–Presbyterian–St. Luke's Medical Center, Chicago, Illinois.
B Gengozian (1969, p. 350; Oak Ridge Associated Universities, Oak Ridge, Tennessee).
C Gengozian (1971, p. 927; Oak Ridge Associated Universities).
D J. K. Hampton Jr., Hampton, and Levy (1971, p. 528; University of Texas, Dental Science Institute, Houston, Texas).
[1-4] See footnotes, table 80.

Table 82. Birthdates and Chronology of Weights, Primate Colony, San Diego Zoo.

Birth Date	*Litter*	*Weight*	*Rep. No.*
1 February 1964	♂ ♂	—	6
9 February 1964[1]	♂ ♀	—	6
1 June 1964	♀		8
6 August 1964		135 g	8
14 August 1965		431 g	11/12
11 September 1964	♂ ♀		14
5 November 1964		140, 145 g	9
9 February 1965		283, 313 g	10
14 August 1965		430, 454 g	11/12
30 September 1963[2]	○ ○	—	8
7 October, 1964	♀ ♀		9
9 February 1965		212, 220 g	10
14 August 1965		340, — g	11/12
6 November 1964	♂ ♀		9
9 February 1965		153, 162 g	10
14 August 1965		343, 377 g	11/12
7 December 1964[2]	○ ○	—	10

SOURCE: Cooper (unpublished Quarterly Reports, 1964–66).
[1] Stillborn; head misshapen; average weight each, 37 g; total length, 210 mm.
[2] Full-term stillborn.

Reproductive Performance in Captivity

Epple 1975*b*, p. 211

"In all breeding groups (*Callithrix j. jacchus*, *Saguinus oedipus geoffroyi*, and *Saguinus fuscicollis* maintained in our laboratory during the last 10 years (approximately 200 individuals) only the dominant female of each group reproduced. Although inferior females copulated with the alpha male and the other group males, none of them ever became visibly pregnant. Christen (1974), on the other hand, reports that both the dominant and the submissive female in a *Cebuella pygmaea* and in a *Saguinus m. midas* group delivered full-term young. Not one of the females, however, raised her offspring. In our colony, young females, born in the group never reproduced when they remained with their parental group into adulthood (up to 3 years). These females, as well as inferior adult females, however, almost immediately became pregnant when they were removed from their group and paired with an adult male or when the dominant female was removed from the group and the formerly inferior animal gained the alpha position in her group."

Productivity of about 100 breeding pairs of *Saguinus fuscicollis, S. nigricollis nigricollis,* crosses among 3 subspecies of *S. fuscicollis,* and between the subspecies of *S. fuscicollis* and *S. n. nigricollis* maintained in a laboratory colony established in 1963 in the Department of Microbiology, Rush–Presbyterian–St. Luke's Medical Center, Chicago, and about 75 breeding pairs in a supplementary facility started 1966 in the Lincoln Park Zoo, Chicago, is summarized here from data recorded by Wolfe, Deinhardt, Ogden, Adams, and Fisher (1975).

1. Wild-caught *Saguinus fuscicollis illigeri* were more prolific (2.9 live births per pair per year) than wild-caught *S. f. nigrifrons, S. f. fuscicollis,* or *S. nigricollis nigricollis.*

2. A trend toward excess fecundity in aged pairs of wild-caught tamarins was not observed.

3. Twenty-one of 128 wild-caught females have had 10 or more deliveries with largest number 18 produced by a female *S. fuscicollis illigeri* (purchased 1963, first delivery October 1964).

4. First generation captive-born crosses by hybrids (Group A) outbred first generation captive-born *Saguinus fuscicollis illigeri* (Group B). The superiority of the crosses and hybrids was maintained by the combinations of inbred, outbred, hand-reared, or parent-reared pairs. Live births of Group A, excluding first deliveries, was 88% with average 2.7 live births per pair per year. This compares with 81% and 0.8% for Group B (Wolfe, Deinhardt, Ogden, Adams, and Fisher 1975, p. 809, table 5).

5. Performance of first-generation crosses or hybrids with average 2.7 live births per pair per year compared favorably with that of wild-caught pairs of the same taxons (cf. table 80).

6. Mean age at first delivery of Group A was 28 months and that of Group B was 37 months. Mean pairing age for both groups was 10 months.

7. Youngest animal to deliver viable offspring was a 17.5-month-old *Saguinus fuscicollis illigeri.*

8. Spermatozoa and corpora lutea were observed in animals 11 months old.

9. Wild-caught × first-generation laboratory-born males or females, hand-reared or parent-reared, produced as well as wild-caught pairs.

10. Three of 5 *second-generation* laboratory-born pairs of *S. f. illigeri* × *S. n. nigricollis* (parent-reared, 1 outbred, 2 inbred) produced 4 litters (2 twin, 2 single) at 20, 29, and 30 months of age, respectively, at time of first delivery. Only the singletons, produced 176 days apart by the outbred pair, were born alive.

11. About 90% of all pairs reproduced after a mean interval of 1 year between mating and first delivery (range: 5.2–36 months).

12. Mean intervals (in days) between successive live births for wild-caught and laboratory-born pairs were as follows.

		Interbirth Intervals		
Parents	*Offspring*	*Mean*	*Extremes*	*N*
Wild-caught	Parent-reared	252	(168–545)	99
Wild-caught	Hand-reared	182	(146–383)	284
Captive-born, 1st generation	Parent-reared	295	(–)	20
Captive-born, 1st generation	Hand-reared	179	(–)	4
Captive-born, 2d generation	?	176	(–)	2

13. Tamarins are less productive than wild-caught marmosets (*Callithrix jacchus*), at least with respect to triplet production.

Hybridization

A. *Saguinus fuscicollis lagonotus* ♂ × *Saguinus fuscicollis leucogenys* ♀ (Roth 1960, p. 166)

Female twins born 2 April 1955 in the Ruhr Zoo, Gilsen Kirchen, Germany. General color pattern of 12-month-old young like that of father, *S. f. lagonotus.* The author (Roth 1960, p. 167) says, "Kaum noch von der Mutter unterscheiden," but his color plates 2 and 3 clearly show he must have meant "Vater."

B. Hybrids, with parents, in Primate Center of San Diego Zoo, examined by me in June 1966.

1. *Saguinus nigricollis* ♀ × *Saguinus fuscicollis lagonotus* ♂ Hybrid ♀, 8 weeks old; color pattern trizonal, with nape and mantle dominantly reddish as in father.
2. *S. fuscicollis lagonotus* ♀ × *S. nigricollis nigricollis* ♂. Hybrid ♂, 8 weeks old; color pattern trizonal with crown, nape, and mantle blackish as in father.
3. *S. fuscicollis illigeri* ♀ × *S. f. lagonotus* ♂. Trizonal pattern with paternal type black crown and reddish nape and mantle.

C. 1. *Saguinus fuscicollis illigeri* ♀ × *S. f. lagonotus* ♂ (Gengozian 1969, p. 338; Porter and Gengozian 1969, p. 653).

2. *Saguinus fuscicollis illigeri* ♀ × *S. nigricollis* ♂ (Gengozian 1969, p. 359; Porter and Gengozian 1969, p. 653).

In the *illigeri* × *lagonotus* combination, (Gengozian 1969, p. 338, fig. 1D) the whitish circumlabial band is oval in the mother, trapezoidal in the father, with the whitish hairs extending nearly to the outer corners of the eyes; in the hybrid offspring, the shape of the band is intermediate but more nearly like that of the father.

In skin transplants performed by Porter and Gengozian (1969) acceptance of the grafts between the co-twin subspecies and species hybrids listed above was complete for 667–822 days of the duration of an experiment then still in progress. Second and third sets of grafts were likewise accepted between the chimeric hybrid co-twins.

GROWTH AND DEVELOPMENT

The following subjects are treated:

Chronology of Growth	Adult Organ Weights
Allometry	Dental Eruption
Color	Sex Ratios
Adult Body Weights	Longevity

Chronology of Growth

The chronology of growth of *Saguinus nigricollis* from birth to maturity (table 83) by Chase and Cooper (1969) is an important document and a model for comparisons with other species. This is followed by the comparative weights with seasonal fluctuations of adult *S. nigricollis* and *S. fuscicollis.*

Allometry

Chase and Cooper 1969; table 1, p. 113
(reproduced as table 83)

"At birth, a twin weighs approximately 8.5% of the non-pregnant maternal weight, consequently a set of twins is equal to 17% of the mother's weight.

"Linear growth is much more rapid than weight gain and is complete or nearly so at 12 months of age, while weight does not reach a level comparable to wild caught adults until 16 to 17 months of age" (1969, p. 114).

Head and body, and foot growth patterns are nearly identical. "Seventy-five percent of head-body and foot linear growth was realized at 16 weeks of age and growth was complete, or nearly so, at 12 months of age. Body weight reached the level of the wild-caught adults (mean weight 464 gm as determined from 232 observations of 11 individuals with no difference noted between sexes) at 16 to 17 months of age. Forty-four percent of this gain from birth was exhibited at 16 weeks of age and 85% at one year."

Color

The basic color pattern of independently active young is like that of adults. Circumbuccal hairs, however, are longer, with those of angle of gape forming a long tuft or "mutton-chop," the whiskers white instead of gray,

Table 83. Growth and Development of *Saguinus nigricollis* from Birth to Maturity

Age	*N*	*Weight*	*Head and Body*	*Hind Foot*
Birth	7	43(33–57)	102(97–114)	32(28–39)
1 week	5	47(41–61)	103(98–115)	34(30–38)
2 weeks	5	55(50–70)	110(101–27)	37(34–42)
3 weeks	5	65(55–83)	119(114–32)	39(37–43)
4 weeks	5	74(60–100)	125(113–43)	41(39–45)
5 weeks	5	85(68–111)	133(125–53)	43(41–49)
6 weeks	5	96(78–129)	141(131–54)	47(45–52)
7 weeks	5	109(86–144)	145(135–63)	49(47–54)
8 weeks	8	128(97–162)	146(130–65)	51(50–55)
9 weeks	11	137(112–87)	149(135–70)	51(47–57)
10 weeks	5	150(122–200)	161(146–82)	55(52–58)
11 weeks	5	162(135–215)	162(157–71)	57(54–61)
12 weeks	5	175(146–234)	174(163–89)	58(55–62)
13 weeks	12	194(153–247)	173(151–200)	58(50–64)
14 weeks	5	212(189–276)	182(168–97)	63(62–65)
15 weeks	5	217(197–274)	187(178–203)	63(62–66)
16 weeks	5	230(206–88)	193(181–204)	64(62–68)
4 months	12	248(198–289)	191(165–225)	64(52–69)
5 months	12	275(228–328)	194(166–210)	65(60–71)
6 months	13	311(259–375)	208(188–222)	67(55–73)
7 months	11	329(271–373)	209(195–226)	69(64–73)
8 months	9	358(274–422)	215(198–235)	72(69–74)
9 months	11	360(294–436)	219(200–236)	73(69–74)
10 months	11	388(314–464)	216(201–238)	72(68–74)
11 months	9	404(321–454)	221(202–241)	72(69–76)
12 months	7	400(345–475)	222(202–236)	74(69–75)

SOURCE: Chase and Cooper (1969).

NOTE: Measurements given in each vertical column are means with extremes in parentheses. Weights are in grams, lengths are in millimeters. For measuring points and methods, see p. 944.

The data were collected at intervals from 5 or more of a total of 9 ♀♀ and 7 ♂♂, born as twins, and 1 singleton, all born between February 1964 and August 1966. The babies were reared by their parents until well past weaning (between 10 and 13 weeks of age). Youngest separation from parent was at 15 weeks of age, the oldest at 8 months.

The male singleton weighed 57.4 g at birth as compared to 44.4 g for the largest twin birth. He continued to be well advanced until 13 weeks of age, for observations based on 5 samplings. After the 4th month, individuals born and raised as twins nearly equaled and in some observations exceeded the singleton in weight and linear growth.

and often buffy or ochraceous, especially in the younger individuals (fig. X.35). The frontal band, usually present in southern races, is broader transversely than in adults and colored ochraceous, buffy, or white in agreement with the whiskers (fig. X.36).

Body Weight

Additional weights recorded of tamarins in the laboratories of the Rush–Presbyterian–St. Luke's Medical Center (tables 84A, 84B, 85, 86) permit comparisons with animals kept in the Primate Colony of the San Diego Zoo (tables 83, 87).

Updated records of weights of first generation White-mouth Tamarins born in the Rush–Presbyterian–St. Luke's Medical Center facilities are shown in table 84B. Significant differences between males and females were not observed and the data for both are combined. As expected, the larger the litter size, the smaller the mass of the individual.

Table 84A. Mean Birth Weights (in grams) Recorded within 48 Hours, of Young Produced in 357 Litters from 1968 to 1970 in Laboratories of the Microbiology Department, Rush–Presbyterian–St. Luke's Medical Center, Chicago, Illinois

	Mean Birth Weight	*Total Individuals*	*Standard Deviation*
Singleton	46.5	55	5.0
Twin	43.5	580	3.8
Triplet	32.5	36	4.5

SOURCE: Wolfe, Ogden, Deinhardt, Fisher, and Deinhardt (1972, pp. 148–49).

Mean weights of parents of offspring listed in table 84B are as follows (N = 15–36), the data from Wolfe, Deinhardt, Ogden, Adams, and Fisher (1975), p. 807).

Saguinus fuscicollis nigrifrons	359 g
Saguinus fuscicollis fuscicollis	375 g
Saguinus fuscicollis illigeri	314 g
Saguinus nigricollis nigricollis	447 g

Weights (table 87) of adult wild-caught *Saguinus nigricollis* and *S. fuscicollis* in the Institute of Comparative Biology, San Diego Zoological Society, were combined in 1963 and 1964, because the species were not recognized as distinct taxons. Males of the composite, however, averaged larger than the females. Beginning 1965, the two species were separated. The weights show *nigricollis* significantly heavier than *fuscicollis,* in conformity with its larger external and cranial measurements. It also appears that in *nigricollis* the females are heavier than the males while in *fuscicollis* the males are heavier. Linear measurements, however, show no significant differences between the sexes in either species or in callitrichids generally. Female weights, it must be noted, vary with the reproductive cycle.

Differences between mean weights recorded by Cooper (tables 83, 87) and those by Wolfe et al. (tables 84A, 84B, 85, 86) are not significant. It seems that whatever the differences at birth, all growing tamarins, whether colony- or wild-born, parent- or hand-reared, singleton, twin, or triplet, tend to converge in weight and size when living in uniformly controlled scientific laboratory environments. Size variation among adults collected in the wild (appendix table 2) indicates that the same trend occurs in nature.

Fig. X.35. Three-month-old Saddle-back Tamarin, *Saguinus fuscicollis* subspecies. (Photo by Phillip F. Coffey, courtesy of Jersey Zoological Park.)

Adult Organ Weights

Benirschke and Richart 1963

Organ weights in grams of an adult female *Saguinus "nigricollis"* that died 21 May 1959 are given. Her combined head and body length was 210 mm, weight, 340 g on 1 March 1959, and 310 g at death.

Heart, 3.7
Kidney, right, 1.2/ left, 1.4
Adrenal, right, 0.093/ left, 0.11
Spleen,1.5
Liver, 16.4
Uterus (enlarged), 1.0 (0.8 × 0.5 × 0.6 mm)
Ovaries (enlarged, unusually red), 1.1 (1.2 × 0.7 × 0.7)

Dental Eruption

Chase and Cooper 1969, p. 115 (*nigricollis*)

"Teeth present at birth will include [deciduous] incisor and canine and in some instances the first premolars. All deciduous teeth [incisor to last premolar] will be present at eight weeks of age and the first permanent tooth, the first mandibular molar may be present at as early as 14

Table 84B. Birth Weights (in grams) Recorded within 48 Hours, of Young Delivered between 1964 and 1974 in the Laboratories of the Microbiology Department, Rush–Presbyterian–St. Luke's Medical Center, Chicago, Illinois

Taxon	*Singletons* *Mean (Range)* N	*Twins* *Mean (Range)* N	*Triplets* *Mean (Range)* N
illigeri[1]	45.2(40.2–53.8)9	37.9(30.1–46.0)146	38.3(32.3–47.8)11
fuscicollis[1]	45.2(36.0–51.9)9	39.9(34.0–52.7)93	30.6(25.0–35.5)6
nigrifrons[1]	49.8(48.6–51.0)2	42.1(33.2–52.8)26	—
nigricollis[2]	49.3(35.5–56.4)8	43.5(33.8–56.8)72	—
Hybrids 1[3]	50.1(45.4–55.9)3	44.7(37.0–50.1)16	36.4(31.8–44.8)4
Hybrids 2[4]	—	42.4(32.0–54.8)62	—
Hybrids 3[5]	—	38.5(32.0–48.1)16	—
Totals	47.2(35.5–56.4)33	40.4(30.1–56.8)463	35.8(25.0–47.8)29

SOURCE: Wolfe, Deinhardt, Ogden, Adams and Fisher (1975, p. 808).
[1] Subspecies of *Saguinus fuscicollis*
[2] Subspecies of *Saguinus nigricollis*
[3] *Saguinus fuscicollis* ♀ × *S. n. nigricollis* ♂
[4] *Saguinus n. nigricollis* ♀ × *Saguinus fuscicollis*
[5] *S. fuscicollis* subspp. × *S. fuscicollis* subspp.

Fig. X.36. Young Saddle-back Tamarins, *Saguinus fuscicollis*. Left, *fuscicollis* subspecies, probably from the Iquitos area, Peru; right, Weddell's Saddle-back Tamarin, *S. f. weddelli,* from Río Mamoré, Bolivia; left photo courtesy of J. K. Hampton, Jr., Adelphi University, Garden City, Long Island, New York; right photo courtesy of J. J. C. Mallinson, Jersey Zoological Park.

Table 85. Chronology of Body Weights of Randomly Selected Hand-Reared Tamarins, *Saguinus nigricollis* (nos. 1–10) and *S. oedipus oedipus* (no. 11)

Tamarin Number	*Body weights (in grams)*						
	Birth	*7 Days*	*14 Days*	*30 Days*	*2 Months*	*4 Months*	*2 Years*
1	48.4	49.0	53.5	74.0	121.5	225.6	466
2	45.7	46.9	53.1	84.1	131.0	239.5	454
3	35.3	39.9	46.3	76.2	117.5	216.5	526
4	42.6	45.8	50.0	73.0	122.0	217.0	391
5	43.5	45.5	47.8	69.0	116.1	205.5	411
6	44.5	49.0	56.8	84.0	155.5	258.0	442
7	46.5	51.0	58.5	84.0	130.9	221.5	467
8	47.5	52.8	64.8	91.9	150.2	276.9	414
9	43.3	44.8	53.5	83.2	150.0	282.7	455
10[1]	37.5	40.1	45.0	57.0	76.8	173.1	420
11	44.0	46.0	58.0	84.0	101.0	210.0	511
Mean	43.5	46.4	53.4	78.2	124.8	230.0	451
SD	(3.8)	(3.8)	(5.7)	(9.2)	(22.0)	(30.9)	(39.9)

SOURCE: Wolfe, Ogden, Deinhardt, Fisher, and Deinhardt (1972, p. 154).
[1] No. 10 rejected by parents.

Table 86. Comparisons of Mean Body Weights in grams of 10 Hand-Reared and 10 Parent-Reared Tamarins of the *Saguinus nigricollis* Group

Age (Months)	*Hand-reared Mean* (SD)	*Parent-reared Mean* (SD)
6	268 (11)	271 (22)
12	390 (57)	380 (45)
24	448 (40)	400 (55)

SOURCE: Wolfe, Ogden, Deinhardt, Fisher, and Deinhardt (1972, p. 155).

Table 87. Average Weights of the Wild-Caught Adults of the *Saguinus nigricollis* Group in the Primate Colony, San Diego Zoo

Date	♂♂ (N)	♀♀ (N)	*Rep. No.*
Saguinus nigricollis group			
— 1963	419(12)	432(10)	5
6 Feb. 1964	446(8)	438(9)	6
8 May 1964	480(8)	435(9)	7
6 Aug. 1964	491(8)	467(9)	8
5 Nov. 1964	470(9)	436(9)	9
Saguinus nigricollis (species)			
9 Feb. 1965	450(6)	458(6)	10
14 Aug. 1965	482(6)	494(5)	11/12
4 Nov. 1965	472(6)	487(5)	13
4 Feb. 1966	469(5)	505(5)	14
18 Aug. 1966	477(5)	491(4)	16
Saguinus fuscicollis			
9 Feb. 1965	389(5)	370(3)	10
8 July 1965	436(3)	372(2)	11/12
3 Nov. 1965	419(3)	338(2)	13
6 Feb. 1966	415(3)	345(1)	14
18 Aug. 1966	422(3)	429(1)	16

SOURCE: Data recorded by Cooper (upublished Quarterly Reports, 1963–66).

Table 88. Chronology of Dental Eruption in *Saguinus nigricollis*

Deciduous Teeth	*I1*	*I2*	*C*	*P1*	*P2*	*P3*		
Upper								
Mean age (weeks)	birth	birth	birth	1.2	2.6	7.6		
Range	birth	birth	birth	Birth–2	1–4	6–8		
Specimens	7	7	7	5	5	5		
Lower								
Mean age (weeks)	birth	birth	birth	0.4	2.6	6.2		
Range	birth	birth	birth	Birth–1	1–4	4–8		
Specimens	7	7	7	7	5	5		
Permanent Teeth	*I1*	*I2*	*C*	*P1*	*P2*	*P3*	*M1*	*M2*
Upper								
Mean age (weeks)	21.2	26.4	40.0	32.6	30.6	28.9	17.4	28.0
Range	19–23	24–28	39–41	30–35	28–34	26–33	16–19	27–29
Specimens	9	10	5	8	9	9	7	10
Lower								
Mean age (weeks)	19.7	22.5	39.6	31.5	33.5	28.7	16.0	25.6
Range	18–23	21–26	39–40	27–34	30–39	27–32	14–18	25–27
Specimens	9	11	5	10	8	9	6	10

SOURCE: Data from Chase and Cooper 1969, p. 114.

weeks of age. All permanent teeth will probably be erupted by 40 weeks of age." The canine is the last to appear. The timetable for eruption is summarized in table 88.

Sex Ratios

Sex ratios of *Saguinus fuscicollis* twins born 1966–70 in laboratories of Oak Ridge Associated Universities, Oak Ridge, Tennessee, are shown in table 89A.

Table 89A. Sex Ratios of *Saguinus fuscicollis* twins born 1966–70 in Oak Ridge

	♂♂	♀♀	♂♀
Number	50	30	86
Ratio	1 :	0.6 :	1.72
Expected	1 :	1 :	2

SOURCE: Data from Gengozian (1971, p. 927).

The large deficit of first- and second-generation captive-born female White-mouth Tamarins was noted by Wolfe, Deinhardt, Ogden, Adams, and Fisher (1975, p. 806) in twin litters of the same sex (table 89B). A similar disparity was also recorded for *Saguinus oedipus oedipus* (table 101). Comparable deficits among twins of the same sex are reported by Gengozian (1971) for *Saguinus fuscicollis* (table 89A) and by Hampton, Hampton, and Levy (1971) for *Saguinus oedipus geoffroyi* (table 101). The imbalance cannot be explained on the basis of present information, but chimerism may be a factor. In any event, of the 6 classified twin groups listed by Wolfe et al. (table 89B), the female deficit appears only in twin litters of the same sex produced by *illigeri* and *nigrifrons* and hybrids of *S. fuscicollis* and *S. nigricollis*. The small shortage of males among singletons (table 89B) may be purely random.

Sex ratios in litters produced in the facilities of the Microbiology Department, Rush–Presbyterian–St. Luke's Medical Center are shown in table 89B.

Table 89B. Sex Ratios of White-mouth Tamarins Born 1963–74 of Wild-Caught Parents in Facilities of the Rush–Presbyterian–St. Luke's Medical Center, Chicago, Illinois

	Singletons		*Twins*			*Triplets*			
Taxon	♂	♀	♂♂	♀♀	♂♀	♂♂♂	♀♀♀	♂♀♀	♀♀♀
illigeri[1]	11	14	53	25	65	2	3	3	0
fuscicollis[1]	10	17	21	22	48	0	1	1	0
nigrifrons[1]	5	6	7	1	10	0	0	0	0
nigricollis[2]	9	8	15	15	32	0	1	0	0
Hybrids 1[3]	9	4	30	14	44	0	1	1	0
Hybrids 2[4]	7	7	10	9	20	0	1	0	0
Totals	51	56	136	86	219	2	7	5	0
Ratios	1 :	1	1 :	.6 :	1.6	1 :	3.5 :	2.5 :	0
Expected	1 :	1	1 :	1 :	2	1 :	1 :	1 :	1

SOURCE: Wolfe, Deinhardt, Ogden, Adams, and Fisher (1975, p. 806).

[1] Subspecies of *Saguinus fuscicollis.*
[2] Subspecies of *Saguinus nigricollis.*
[3] Subspecies of *S. fuscicollis* × *S. n. nigricollis.*
[4] Subspecies crosses of *S. fuscicollis.*

Longevity

Table 90. Records for Longevity in Zoos

Species	*Years*	*Months*	*Days*	*Reference*
S. nigricollis graellsi	5	9	19	Crandall 1964, p. 105
S. fuscicollis tripartitus	5	9	19	Crandall 1964, p. 105
S. fuscicollis leucogenys	7	2	28	Mallinson 1971, p. 9

BEHAVIOR

The two species of the *nigricollis* group, *Saguinus nigricollis* with 2 subspecies (*nigricollis, graellsi*) and *Saguinus fuscicollis* with 13 recognized subspecies, are among the tamarins most commonly seen in biomedical laboratories, zoos, and museum collections. Notwithstanding, their biology is less known than that of the cotton-top, *Saguinus oedipus,* and the common marmoset, *Callithrix jacchus.* In fact, until recent years, when they were made available in large numbers, no attention was paid to members of the *nigricollis* group as subjects for behavioral studies. All tamarins of the group were confused by investigators as a single bewilderingly variable species and used in research laboratories for little else than living test tubes.

Behavioral traits described under the following headings have been culled from the literature and my personal notes. Unless otherwise indicated, the information given refers to undetermined members of the *Saguinus nigricollis* group:

Habitat	Interspecific Relations
Territoriality	Food
Spatial Orientation	Narcissism
Social Organization	Locomotion
Discrimination	Marking
Dominance	Odor
Threat and Aggression	Vocalization
Mutual Aid	Thermoregulation
Care of Young	Heart Rate
Grooming	Commerce

Habitat

Tamarins of the *Saguinus nigricollis* group are conspicuous elements of the fauna of the upper Amazonian rain forest. They are as much at home in thick second growth as in high virgin or reestablished forest. Like other primates, tamarins follow the fruiting cycle, but they also forage for insects in the brush and tangled thickets ordinarily avoided by cebids.

Territoriality

The territory of a troop in any one season is usually small, perhaps no more than one or a few hectares. It is not staked out or defended. Possibly the sleeping tree is the only base to which the animal regularly returns unless forced to find another.

Troop Size

Most troops of *Saguinus fuscicollis* number 8–20 individuals.

Spatial Orientation

Izawa 1975, p. 304

Saguinus fuscicollis of the Río Caquetá region (Colombia) "utilized a lower layer of the forest and most of the times they were encountered they were in a tree 2 to 10 m above the ground."

Mazur and Baldwin, 1968

In the Miami, Florida, "Monkey Jungle," with canopy reaching to 60 ft, the tamarins were usually seen at 10 to 20 ft high and "occasionally were on the ground."

"On one occasion we came upon some tamarins crossing our path on the ground. Two looked at us and gave their chirp-twitters, but they showed no tendency to coalesce [i.e., close ranks]. We moved toward one, and it gave successive single high-pitched squeak-screams, probably a distress call. Two others came close to this one, and the three coalesced against us, all chirp-twittering."

Hershkovitz (Comment)

After years of tamarin watching I must conclude that the animals travel freely through all forest stories but rarely on the ground. They are most readily observed, of course, where seen by Izawa when resin feeding.

The seemingly casual ground-walking of the tamarins and evident indisposition to seek safety in a tree when surprised by Mazur and Baldwin is odd. However, these animals were not in their natural habitat and the circumstances under which they were reared is undisclosed.

Social Organization

Epple 1975*b*, p. 206

"In our *Saguinus fuscicollis groups,* formed of adult nonrelated animals, dominance interactions were of a more serious nature among females than males. In five out of a total of six groups containing more than 1 adult female, vicious fighting between the females occurred within a maximal period of 13 months after group formation and made the removal of the inferior animal from the group necessary. On the other hand, eight groups, formed from 1 adult female and 2 or more adult males, have been stable over periods up to 2 years and no fighting has occured. Very little aggressive behavior was observed among the males of these groups. The occurrence and direction of mild threats, however, indicated that the males did not hold equal status in the group. Moreover, the single female of the group seemed to associate more closely with one of her male group mates than with the others."

Discrimination

Mallinson 1965, p. 139 (*nigricollis*)

Recognition of people is indicated by protruding the tongue very rapidly between the lips.

Dominance

Epple 1975*b*, p. 208

In an experimental group of 2 adult males and 1 adult female, the heretofore subordinate male 73 "began to associate more closely with the female than he did during the tests. After several weeks of this, both males engaged in a prolonged fight during which they injured each other quite severely. The fight resulted in a reversal of social dominance. During the days following it, the formerly dominant male 72 showed all behavioral patterns and vocalizations of a clearly submissive animal. He was frequently threatened by male 73 who did everything to prevent him from contacting the female. During the hours immediately following the fight, the female repeatedly threatened male 73, the victor of the fight, when he squeezed himself between her and the now submissive male 72. Overt sexual interest in the female was not noticed at that time in either of the males."

Epple 1975*b*, p. 209

"Relationships between males in our groups were quite subtle. Even under the relatively crowded conditions of captivity the males did not direct a high frequency of aggressive behavioral patterns at each other. It seems that in groups of this structure [2 males, 1 female], social dominance among males is mainly expressed as the relative frequency with which a male associates with the female."

Threat and Aggression

Tamarins may intimidate intruders with menacing gestures and grimaces. During a thirteen-month sojourn in the upper Río Napo region I had many confrontations with both *Saguinus nigricollis graellsi* and *S. fuscicollis lagonotus*. In a typical encounter with a troop of either species, each individual flees noisily to his own hiding place where he remains silent. The act of freezing in my tracks and remaining motionless encourages the leader of the troop, always a powerful male, to emerge from hiding and scurry down to the low branches of the tree nearest me for a better appraisal of the situation. At first the leader makes a few passes, darting back and forth and uttering rasping sounds. Meeting with no reaction, he charges suddenly, stops abruptly, retreats a short distance, and again awaits response. My immobility seems to hearten the entire troop, and while the leader continues to engage my attention with bold antics others move stealthily through the branches to positions above my head. The big male continues to hold my attention by leaping, climbing, swaying, and charging repeatedly, each time coming a little closer. Just as he arrives at the end of the limb within a foot of my face and while we glare at each other, as if by signal a shower of feces and urine hits me from above. Caught by surprise I swing round and look up into the angry faces of a bevy of tamarins, one of them so near I could grab it if my hand were swift enough. Frightened by my sudden counterattack the beasts simply dissolve into the shadows of the leaves.

Shadle, Mirand, and Grace 1965, p. 6

"A highly excited female may become very antagonistic, even combative, with female cage mates or with those in contiguous cages. On rare occasions a female may attack a breeding male. Fights through the openings in cage walls develop between excited females that are loose in the breeding room and are circulating among the cages, trying to get to other excited females who resent their close proximity to their cages.

"These inter-cage fights frequently result in injured ears and limbs, particularly forelimbs that have been thrust into a cage to seize an antagonist. These injuries usually occur among females but seldom among the males. Three mature breeding males often may be caged together with little or no animosity shown among them even though they are being used for breeding and returned to their cage."

Shadle, Mirand, and Grace 1965, p. 5

"Only a few times have we seen a male really attack a female, and in one case the attack was so vigorous that he had to be returned to his own cage lest the female be injured. This was a male of one species (*T. illigeri*) and the female of another species (*T. fuscicollis*)."

Mutual Aid

Hershkovitz (Notes)

The solicitude of the group for a distressed member is characteristic of virtually all primates. The parents, particularly the father, will defend their young, sometimes at the cost of their own life. A wounded individual calling for help is answered by the calls of its comrades. I have seen the leader or perhaps the father come to the ground to help the victim climb back into the trees. On occasion, while I was attempting to seize a wounded, screaming individual shot to the ground, the entire band boldly intimidated me with shrill calls and feinted charges that brought them to within a few feet of me.

DuMond 1967, p. 207 (*fuscicollis*)

The white-lipped tamarins in the Miami, Florida, "Monkey Jungle" show strong group ties when one individual is endangered or threatened from outside. "on one occasion a tamarin that had injured itself on a thorn and could not keep up with the group was captured for treatment. It started making cries of terror. The remainder of the group immediately appeared and making threat calls, gave every indication that they would attack me had I not sought cover in a nearby building."

Grooming

Mazur and Baldwin 1968 (*fuscicollis*)

"All observed instances of grooming [in the semi-natural "Monkey Jungle," Miami, Florida] involved two individuals at a time. The groomer and groomee roles would switch every 10 to 30 seconds. The switch usually occurred when the groomer stopped grooming and lay down in front of its partner's face, sometimes jumping over the partner to accomplish this. Grooming is done mainly with the hands, but both mouth and tongue were also used occasionally. Grooming was done all over the body, with the groomee being on its back or front and having whatever was on top groomed. Total grooming episodes have lasted as long as 10 min. . . . If a baby lay down right in front of an adult, the adult would groom it briefly. In one such instance, the adult groomed the baby for about a minute, and then jumped over it and moved away. The baby approached another adult and rolled under its chin, presumably an unsubtle presentation for grooming. But this adult ignored the baby, at least as much as possible."

Care of Young

Epple 1975*c*

Parental and group-member care of newborn to 40-day-old infants was studied in 7 test groups. Each cage group consisted of a mother with her young, the father or a substitute dominant male, and 1 or 2 independent young. It is shown that the alpha male tends to carry the infants longer and more often than does the mother, but there is considerable individual variation. The inferior members of the group also support the infants but to a much lesser degree. Experience gained by the adolescents probably insures development of normal patterns of infant care.

Pook 1975

A 2-day-old infant rejected by its mother was hand-reared to the 46th day, then reintroduced into the parental cage where it was accepted. The author believes that the new-found compatibility between infant and parents was due to the changed relationship between them.

Pook did not consider the possibility that any callitrichid infant of the same or another species might also have been accepted.

Interspecific Relations

Saguinus fuscicollis and *S. nigricollis* are sympatric north of the upper Amazon. Troops of both species cross trails and even feed in the same trees. Their contact with the numerous species of cebids within their respective geographic ranges is likewise casual.

Izawa 1975, p. 269

In a study area of about 10 sq km along the Río Peneya in the angle between the Ríos Caquetá and Caguán in Amazonian Colombia, Izawa identified the following monkey species: *Saguinus fuscicollis Aotus trivirgatus, Saimiri sciureus, Pithecia monachus, Alouatta seniculus, Cebus albifrons, C. apella, Lagothrix lagothricha,* and *Ateles paniscus.*

Hershkovitz (Notes)

In the same region at Tres Troncos (54) above La Tagua, I found *Callicebus torquatus,* in addition to those mentioned above. *Callimico goeldii* may also be present. The saki of the area is *Pithecia hirsuta* Spix rather than *P. monachus* Spix, with which it has been generally confused. *Cebuella pygmaea* occurs on the right but not the left bank of the Río Caquetá, whereas *Saguinus fuscicollis* is common to both sides above the mouth of the Río Caguán. All together, the tamarin, *Saguinus fuscicollis fuscus,* is found in association with 10 or 11 primate species other than man. Nearest callitrichid ecological equivalents, however, are the 5 species of Amazonian squirrels (*Sciurillus,* 1; *Microsciurus,* 1; *Sciurus,* 3). Competition, if any, between tamarins and other arboreal forms is, nevertheless not obvious. Adequate year-round cover and food appears to be available to all.

DuMond 1967, p. 202; 1968, p. 89

New and Old World monkeys were introduced into an artificially controlled tropical forest in Miami, Florida, called the "Monkey Jungle." The facility is located on a 15-acre "hammock" or subtropical hardwood patch with an ecology similar to that of Caribbean and tropical Middle American rain forests.

A colony of about 100 crab-eating macaques are maintained in one section, and a second section of about 4 acres called the "rain forest" is occupied by four semi-free-ranging species of upper Amazonian primates. These are a reproducing group of 7 red uacaris (*Cacajao rubicundus rubicundus*), 5 red howlers (*Alouatta seniculus seniculus*), more than 100 reproducing squirrel monkeys, and a reproducing colony of 8 tamarins (*Saguinus fuscicollis* or *"nigricollis"*) mentioned in the 1968 publication cited above. They represent 6 adult survivors of the original colony of 19, and the young of two single births.

The tamarins were observed associated with squirrel monkey play groups (1968, p. 89).

Food

One day I was surprised by the sight of a saddle-back tamarin (*S. fuscicollis fuscus*) climbing a fruiting *Cecropia* tree just three meters from where I was sitting in my camp in Mecaya, Río Caquetá, Colombia. The animal tested the fruit by pressing a few samples between its fingers. Finding them unripe it departed as nonchalantly as it had arrived.

Izawa 1975, pp. 304, 311

"*S*[*aguinus*] *fuscicollis* is widely distributed in the basin of the River Caquetá and inhabits with high population density both the basin of the River Peneya and the established study areas, Pto. Japon and Pto. Tokio.

"Twice they were observed eating flowers and fruits of some species which grow directly on tree trunks and developed into fruit there. The monkeys were frequently seen eating something while sitting on the end of the branch about 10 m high. However, it was difficult to distinguish whether it was the leaves of the tree, buds of woodvine creeping on the trees, moss, ants, or other insects.

"Apart from these observations, the monkeys were seen clinging to the trunk of a Guamo (*Inga* sp.) tree eating resin which had oozed and hardened on it.

"Their feeding behavior was rather different. After finding their favorite food, monkeys in the Amazon and also in other places have a tendency to be absorbed in eating it. The monkeys of this species, however, were constantly changed their posture nervously. While they were eating resin, for example, they would pick out a piece of resin with their fingers, gnaw it a bit and look around, then move aside to a little and soon move back, and so on.

"In the first observation of November 12, 1973 in Pto. Tokio, one monkey repeated this series of actions 18 times in 4 minutes. In addition, on January 21, 1974, in Pto. Tokio, another monkey was observed taking no less than 7 seconds from eating one bit to beginning the next."

"Various kinds of objects, including fruits, flowers, leaves and insects, were found in their stomach contents. The findings of resin was particularly noticeable. Some small lumps of it were found in seven individuals and many more lumps in three of them.

"It can be said that the food habits of the tamarins show a strong omnivorous tendency like the capuchins and the squirrel monkeys, but the former cannot be regarded in the same light as these three latter species. This is because the tamarins were often observed eating resin. In addition, the fact that they tended to live in the lower levels of the forest and that Guamo (*Inga* sp.) trees, from which the monkeys often ate resin, were common in the forest of the basin of the River Caquetá, makes it possible to conclude that they feed on various kinds of foods but rely on resin for their stable food.

"In this sense, although it eats both fruit and insects by preference, *S. fuscicollis* can be called a resin eater because of resin characterizing its food habit."

Hershkovitz (Note)

It has been generally overlooked by authors and I failed to include elsewhere (p. 446) the observation that callitrichids derive much of their protein at little expense from insects trapped in the resin they eat.

Narcissism

Shadle, Mirand, and Grace 1965, p. 5

"When with a sexually uninteresting female, he will ignore her, sit in a corner and do pushups with his hind legs to rub his back against the sides of the cage corner. He may run actively about the cage grimacing and calling to the females in the other cages if the breeding cage is not covered with the cloth curtain, or he may watch and "court" the reflections in the observation glass. For some males the breeding cage must be turned at an angle so that they cannot see the reflections which divert their sexual interest. Sometimes all lights, except the single bulb beneath the cloth cover of the breeding cage, must be turned off to reduce the reflections, quiet the colony, and bring back the male's attention to the female with him in the breeding cage."

Hershkovitz (Comment)

In the situation described, the aggressive action of males toward other males, including their own images is in response to visual stimuli and not at all a diversion from females who may not have been sexually or otherwise stimulating at the time in question.

Locomotion

Bates 1863, p. 321

"Whilst walking along a forest pathway, [on the upper Amazonas], I saw one of these lively little fellows ["Midas rufoniger," another name for *Saguinus nigricollis,* but actually *Saguinus fuscicollis avilapiresi*] miss his grasp as he was passing from one tree to another along with his troop. He fell head foremost, from a height of at least fifty feet, but managed cleverly to alight on his legs in the pathway; quickly turning round he gave me a good stare for a few moments, and then bounded off gaily to climb another tree."

Marking

Mazur and Baldwin 1968 (*fuscicollis*)

"Four adults in single file began crossing a limb [in the Miami, Florida, "Monkey Jungle"]. The first one straddled it with his hind legs and rubbed his crotch across a few inches of the limb. The second one did the same thing at the same place. The third began this movement at the same spot but did not complete it. The fourth took a round-about way and didn't cross the limb."

(Presumably, the authors were unable to determine the sex and estimate the age of the tamarins—P. H.)

Odor

Epple 1972 (*fuscicollis*)

Scent-marking is performed by gently pressing and rubbing the circumgenital and sternal glands against the object. A few drops of urine are added to the secretions of the circumgenital glands. Marking with the suprapubic glands is accomplished by dragging the region across the substrate. Urine is also added.

Virtually everything in the cage is marked, including

all members of the group. Males and females mark with circumgenital glands before and after copulation. The male sniffs and licks the female's genitalia and her markings; the female reciprocates.

Epple 1975*b*, p. 214

"In hand-raised *Saguinus fuscicollis,* we noticed the typical body odor of adults at a time coinciding with the development of the scent glands, scent marking behavior, and other patterns of adult sexual and social behavior. These observations suggest that the development of the glands and of scent marking behavior are under the control of gonadal hormones."

Epple 1971, p. 166 (*fuscicollis*)

Tests on 4 male and 5 female *Saguinus fuscicollis* indicate that the tamarins discriminate perches marked by strange males from those marked by strange females of the same species. A preference was shown for the male-scented perches, judged by the significantly higher frequency with which the subjects marked them with their own circumgenital, suprapubic, and sternal glands.

Epple 1973; 1974*a*, p. 371; 1974*b*, pp. 263, 267; 1975*a*, p. 142 (*fuscicollis*)

Tests showing the ability of tamarins to distinguish between sexes by scent marks (Epple 1971, above) were followed by others with use of urine-marked wooden perches placed in cages of the experimental animals. The results are as follows:

1. Experimental males and females preferred perches carrying the odor of tamarins with which they had interacted aggressively over those marked by strangers.
2. Adult wild-caught males and females discriminated between perches scent-marked by dominant and submissive males.

Perches were marked with urine, but the substance or pheromone identifying the individual or its social status was not isolated. It may be a component of urine or a substance of the circumgenital glands picked up by the urine. Epple also recognized that the ability to discriminate between odors of dominant and submissive males may depend on the intensity of the smell rather than a distinctive pheromone. Dominant males scent-mark frequently and heavily, while subordinate or submissive males usually mark faintly or not at all.

Benirschke and Richart 1963, p. 75

The vulvar odor is not very strong as compared with that of *Callithrix jacchus, Leontopithecus,* and *Saguinus mystax mystax.*

Vocalization

Members of the group communicate by whistling, chirping, trilling, and rasping. They make a pastime of answering birdcalls and can imitate intricate birdsongs with amazing fidelity. The twittering or trilling is produced in the throat and rapid movement of the lower jaw. The tongue is not vibrated as in *Callithrix humeralifer.*

Shadle, Mirand, and Grace 1965

"Another very important factor in the sexual arousal of the tamarin is the calling of the various individuals of the colony. While the males may indulge in some calling during their courting antics the females usually are more vociferous and at times they call almost incessantly when at the peak of sexual arousal and sexual receptivity. The sexually receptive female's call is a series of very high-pitched birdlike notes which often stimulates the whole colony into a state of excitement, activity, and produces a bedlam of calls as she rushes crazily about the cage."

(The calls and movements suggest contagious fear, hysteria, and panic rather than sexual frenzy—P. H.)

Thermoregulation

Reports of captive callitrichids exposed experimentally or accidentally to ambient temperature extremes indicate great tolerance to near- or below-freezing weather (pp. 448, 565, 806). Dr. James D. Ogden, veterinarian in charge of the monkeys used in biomedical research conducted by Dr. Friedrich Deinhardt and associates of the Rush–Presbyterian–St. Luke's Medical Center in Chicago communicated to me the following account of an experience in 1969.

"Space limitations in our animal-holding facilities in Chicago led me to house about 75 acclimatized white-lipped tamarins (*Saguinus nigricollis* and *S. fuscicollis*) and cotton-top tamarins (*Saguinus oedipus oedipus*) on a farm I was renting near Mundelein, Illinois. The animals were used in a long-term hepatitis experiment and had lived in the same colony from 1 to 3 years. The remodeled poultry house to which they were transferred was 14′ × 12′ × 8′ high, well insulated, and heated by a propane furnace with humidity controlled by a common household console. Ambient conditions were maintained at 80°F and >50% relative humidity. The tamarins, most of them in pairs, were placed in standard rabbit cages. They received the same diet and care given the animals in our main facilities.

"The colony had lived on the farm some 10–11 uneventful months when I checked them at 9:00 PM on or about 29 December 1969. That night the official outside temperature dropped to −22°F.

"The following morning I departed for my duties at the Presbyterian–St. Luke's Hospital without a routine inspection of the animal house. My teen-age children, home for the Christmas vacation, were charged with looking after the animals. Shortly after arriving at the hospital, I received a frantic telephone call from my wife. The furnace of the animal house, she gasped, had gone out during the night. The room was cold and the water in the humidifier tank (about 10″ × 14″ × 20″) was frozen solid. What was to be done? I ordered my wife to move the tamarins to our living room immediately and to report back while I prepared to return home. The next message informed me that the animals had been transported across the snow on a toboggan the 300 feet to the house and were now accommodated in the living room, where the temperature was 72°–74°F. The paired animals had huddled together during the night and managed to stay warm. Seven of the loners, however, were found frozen stiff, clinging to the bars in a crouched position. They could not be removed from the cages until their stiff, clutching fingers were forceably disengaged from the bars. I ordered the "statues," as my wife called them, wrapped in blankets, placed on the heat registers and, as soon as possible, force-fed 2 drops of bourbon each. Whereupon, I left the hospital for the farm.

"During the 40-mile drive home I had visions of performing 75 necropsies. It turned out, however, as I soon learned, that within 10 minutes of receiving the prescribed therapy, the 7 tamarins began climbing drapes, running the stairs, leaping across furniture, and generally reducing the house to a shambles. As a result of the whole incident, only a 10-day-old cotton-top died. The remaining animals survived without a sign of ill effects."

Heart Rate

J. K. Hampton, Jr. 1973

Heart rates (beats/minute) of an adult male and female *Saguinus fuscicollis* maintained in a controlled environment of 27° ± 1° C and a daily cycle of 12 light and 12 dark hours showed an abrupt rise from about 160 at nearly 0600 hours (dark) to about 217 at 0800 hours (light), a difference of about 57 beats per minute. The rate dropped rapidly from nearly 210 at 1800 hours (first dark hour) to about 163 at 2200 hours. The lowest rate during daylight was about 198 between 1400 and 1500 hours.

Heart rate in the experimental pair of *S. fuscicollis* averaged about 35 beats per minute less at all hours than 2 adult males of the larger (by about 100 g) *S. o. oedipus*. Body temperatures or other physiological data that might be correlated with the possibly significant difference between the species were not reported, and whether the experimental animals were captive-born or wild-caught is not stated. In any case, the number of specimens examined was too few to provide conclusive results.

Commerce

Soini 1972, p. 28 (*fuscicollis*)

"This polytypic species makes up the bulk of tamarin exports [from Peru]. Its abundance in the [Iquitos] region is surpassed only by *Saimiri sciureus*. . . .

"The trade in *Saguinus fuscicollis* consists of the following races listed in the order of highest to lowest number of individuals exported: the black-crowned and brown-mantled *S. f. illigeri;* the red-mantled *S. f. lagonotus* and the brown-crowned and mantled *S. f. nigrifrons.* A few specimens of the yellow-mantled *S. f. tripartitus,* and perhaps, the blackish-mantled *S. f. leucogenys* are shipped through Iquitos. No specimens of the southernmost races, *S. f. weddelli,* have been observed captive in Iquitos."

64 *Saguinus mystax* Group, Moustached Tamarins
1. Characters, Evolution, and Key to Species and Subspecies

Included species—labiatus, mystax, imperator.

Distribution (figs. X.1, 37)

Amazonian region of Brazil, Bolivia, and Peru, from the Rio Madeira-Madre de Díos south of the Amazonas in Brazil and Bolivia, west to the Río Huallaga in Peru; north of the Rio Amazonas, between the Rios Japurá and Iça, Brazil.

Origin, Evolution, and Dispersal

Each of the three species of the *Saguinus mystax* group can be derived from a hairy-face, agouti-colored *Saguinus graellsi*-like tamarin with narrow grayish circumbuccal band and densely pigmented facial skin. The ancestral geographic center of origin is postulated as being on

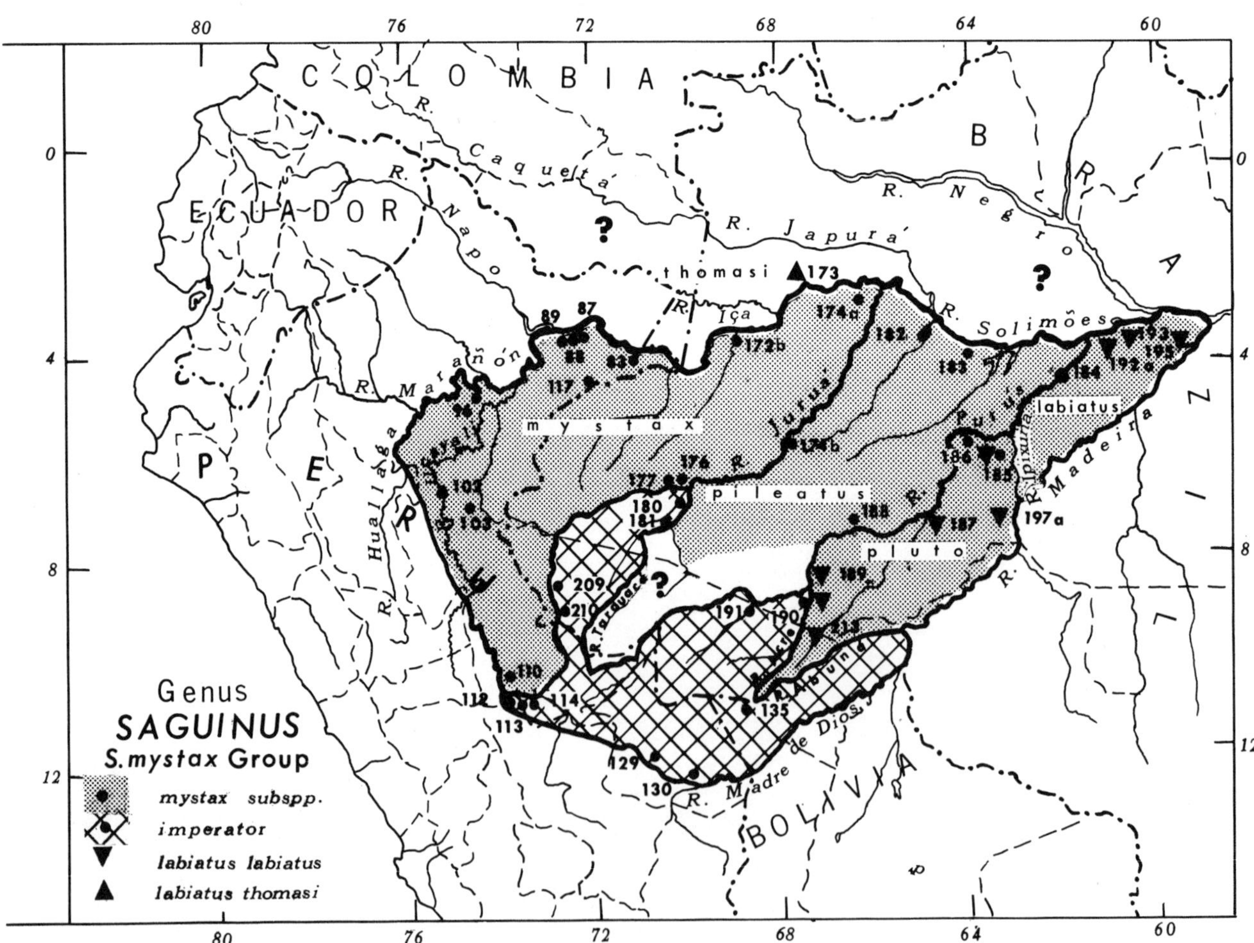

Fig. X.37. Distribution of moustached tamarins of the *Saguinus mystax* group: *Shaded,* subspecies of *S. mystax; triangles,* locality records for *S. labiatus* (*S. mystax* and *S. labiatus labiatus* are sympatric); crosshatch, *S. imperator*. River boundaries between species and subspecies are boldly defined; numbered dots show locality records for *S. mystax* and *S. imperator* (see gazetteer, p. 918, for key to numbers).

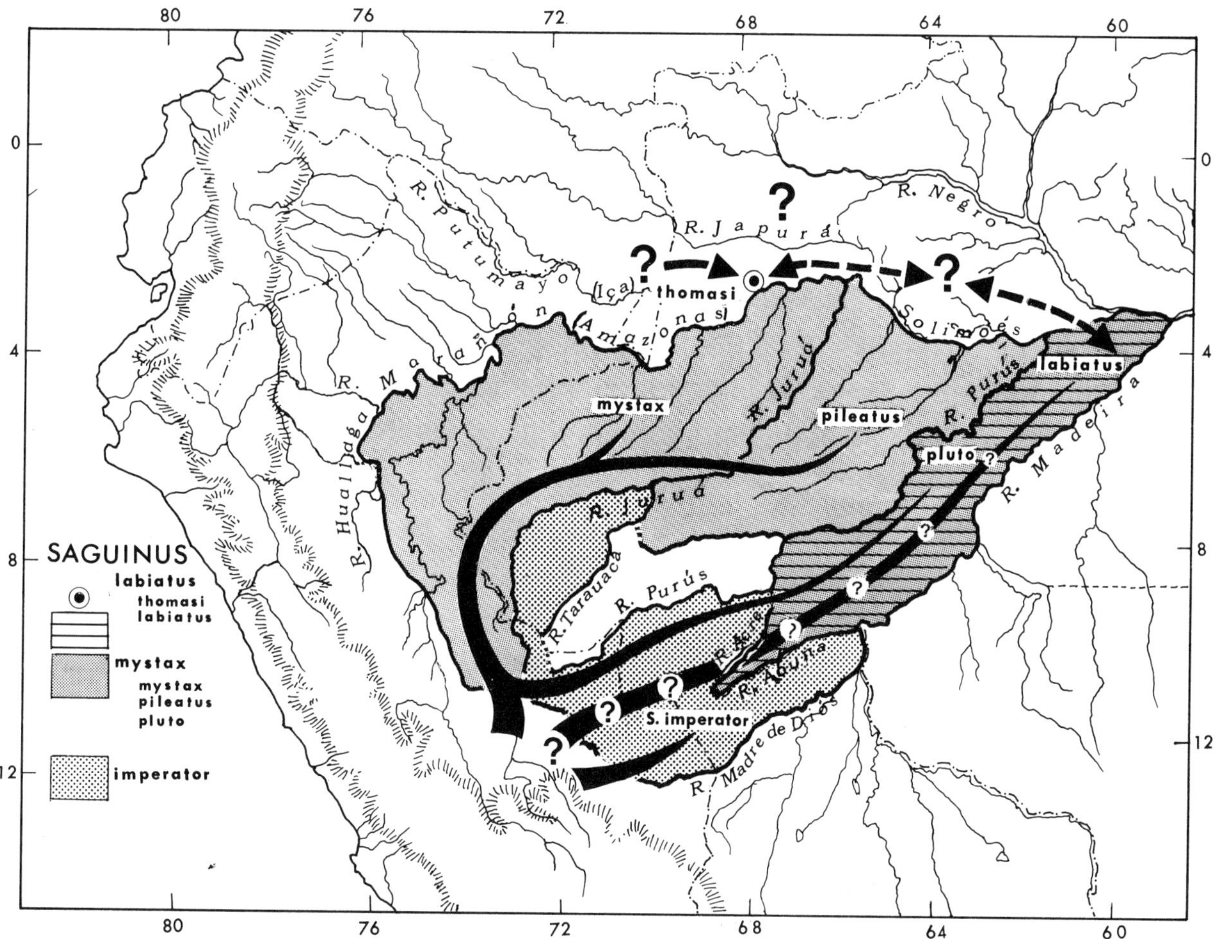

Fig. X.38. *Saguinus mystax* group: Theoretical geographic origin, dispersal and divergence of the species and subspecies. See explanation in text for origin, dispersal and divergence of the races of *S. labiatus.*

the eastern base of the Peruvian Andes. The present distribution of the group is contained within the geographic range of *Saguinus fuscicollis.* As in that species, rivers define the geographic limits of the species or races (fig. X.38.).

Divergences of the members of the *Saguinus mystax* group from the line leading to the *S. nigricollis* group began with depigmentation of the circumbuccal skin. Blanching of the grayish circumbuccal hairs already established in the ancestral stock preceded depigmentation. Bleaching and depigmentation then progressed to the nasal septum as in living *Saguinus labiatus.* Continued blanching and depigmentation over ever-widening areas around mouth and nose, with concommitant thickening and lengthening of the whiskers, mark the evolutionary trend culminating with *S. imperator. S. labiatus* is least differentiated, and *S. mystax* is intermediate (fig. X.39).

The distributional pattern of the group (fig. X.38) suggests an independent origin of each of the three included species. *Saguinus mystax* and *S. imperator* probably stem from a common ancestor. *S. labiatus,* however, appears to be related only through the basic tamarin stock described above. Whatever the history, the three species form a graded morphologic series with respect to facial depigmentation and mystacial hypertrichism. Body pelage patterns are similar in all and their respective color patterns are clearly of a kind.

Saguinus labiatus is the least specialized with respect to facial depigmentation and whisker development. On the other hand, its pileated crown and red underparts are advanced metachromic features as compared with other members of the group. The geographic range of the species *S. labiatus* includes a wide hiatus between the race *S. f. thomasi* of the north bank of the Amazon, between the Rios Iça and Japurá, and the race *S. l. labiatus* on the southern side of the Amazonas between the Rios Purús and Madeira.

Increasing development and availability of habitats along the banks of the larger southern Amazonian tributaries gave scope to the dispersal of the more advanced *Saguinus mystax.* Populations of this species spread successively into the inter Madeira-Purús basin (*S. m. pluto*), the inter Purús-Juruá basin (*S. m. pileatus*), and the inter Juruá-Huallaga basin (*S. m. mystax*). Geographic isolation in each of the interfluvial basins provided the setting for divergence by differential bleaching.

Saguinus imperator, most advanced in facial depigmentation and whisker development, still retains much of the primitive agouti pattern of coloration. This species diverged most and spread least. Its range comprises the hypothetical center of origin of the *Saguinus mystax* group.

Diagnostic Characters

Skin bordering mouth and between or around nostrils unpigmented and covered with white hairs, remainder of

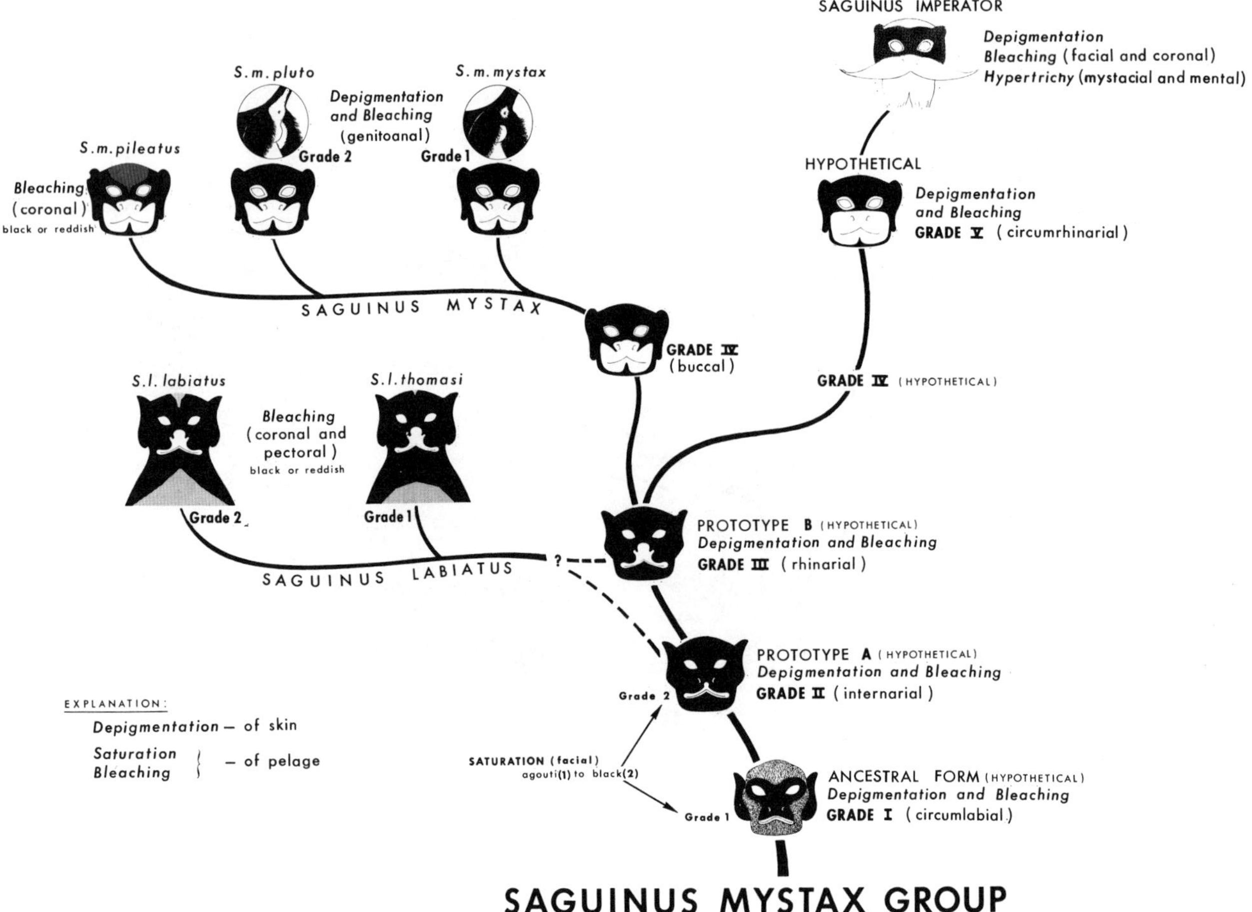

Fig. X.39. *Saguinus mystax* group: Geographic metachromism and speciation. Depigmentation of circumbuccal skin on the one hand and blanching and hypertrichy of corresponding hairs on the other, are directly correlated. Bleaching in other chromogenetic fields is independently controlled. Grade or extent of facial depigmentation is designated by a Roman numeral, the higher the number the more extensive the depigmentation; grades of saturation and bleaching are similarly indicated by Arabic numbers. (After Hershkovitz 1968.)

facial skin pigmented or unpigmented and more or less covered with black hairs; anterior external base of auricle generally unpigmented; white mustache usually well defined; hairs of midline of muzzle crested; dorsum brown or blackish and mixed with silvery or buffy, mantle slightly or not at all defined from lower back; lateral fringe with basal portion of hairs drab to white and always paler than terminal portion; external genitalia mostly or entirely unpigmented.

External Characters

Integument. Skin surrounding mouth (except at symphysis) and between nostrils (*labiatus*) or between and around nostrils unpigmented and clothed with white hairs (figs. X.39, 41); circumbuccal hairs forming poorly to extraordinarily well developed whiskers; hairs surrounding outer borders of nostrils black (*labiatus*), or white and forming a conspicuous trapezoidal patch (*mystax*), or completely fused with circumbuccal band (*imperator*); remainder of facial hairs blackish; hairs of midline of muzzle feathered to form a fine low crest; hairs of cheeks, temples, forehead, and crown long but not forming a mane; hairs of interramia and throat directed straight back, or cresting in midline (*imperator*); forehead black, brown, or reddish (*pileatus*); crown black, brownish, or with silvery, orange, or reddish patch; back from nape to rump dominantly agouti (*imperator*), or blackish streaked or striated with brown, buffy or silvery; rump like back or orange (*imperator*); sides like back with base of hairs of lateral fringe drab to whitish; outer surface of fore and hind limbs like sides of body, upper surface of hands and feet blackish; underparts not markedly different from sides, or sharply defined reddish orange (*labiatus*); tail uniformly black with base like rump; or mixed with reddish orange (*imperator*).

Ears. See chap. 12, fig. III.18.

Vibrissae. See chap. 9, fig. III.12.

Adult and Juvenal Pelage. See chap. 8.

External Genitalia

Male (fig. X.40)

Adult (*S. mystax*). External genitalia variegated or blotched; penis unpigmented or lightly pigmented, the skin corrugated, glans undifferentiated, as usual, with left lobe larger than right; scrotum pedunculate or semipendulous and partially separated into asymmetrical sacs; skin corrugated and thinly haired except for longer,

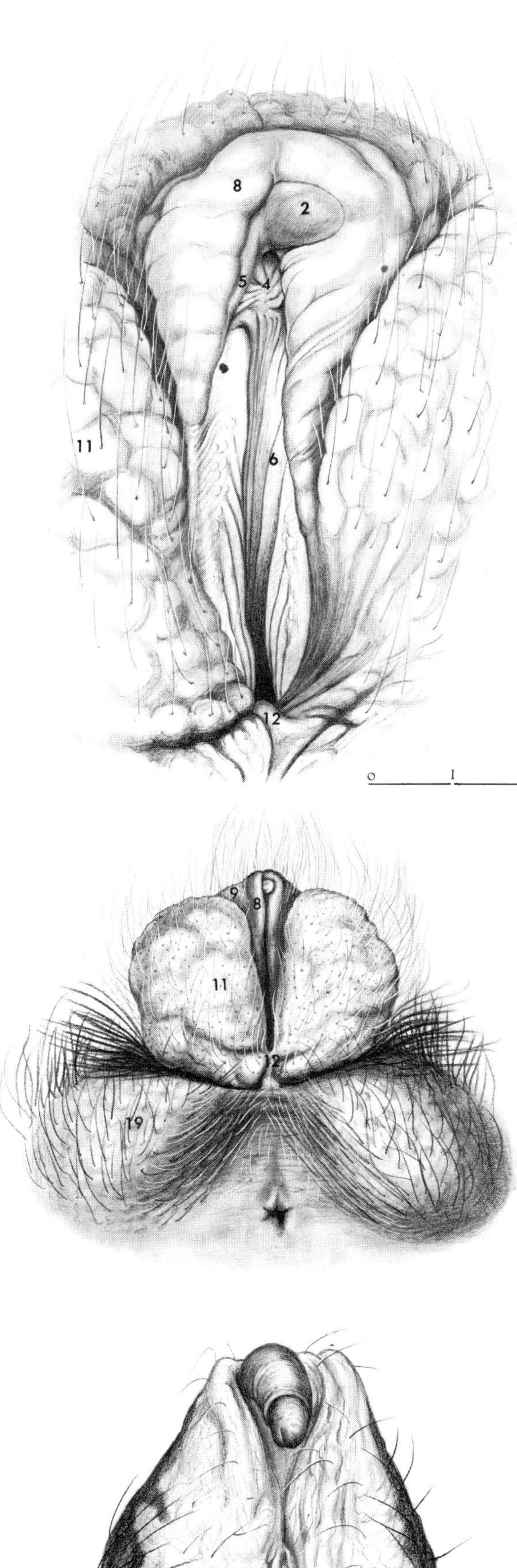

Fig. X.40. External genitalia of *Saguinus mystax;* female vulva enlarged to show details. Symbols explained on pages 113–14.

thicker tufts on raphe; the hair color generally corresponding to that of skin; preputial folds glabrous and unpigmented or lightly mottled; scrotum in one sample longer than wide, sagittal diameter 23 mm, in another sample wider than long, transverse diameter, 25 mm; sexual skin a narrow lightly pigmented median pubic band, skin of perineal and anal regions unpigmented, the hair black.

Female (fig. I.15; X.40)

Adult (*S. mystax*). External genitalia unpigmented; tumescent labia majora approximately as wide as long, extremely thick, and sparsely haired white, integument comparatively smooth and pustulate in one specimen, papillate in second; scrotal folds enormously enlarged and overlying portion of preputial folds forming border of rima pudendi; glans clitoridis concealed in first specimen with surrounding prepuce or annulus comparatively smooth-skinned and more or less compressed by scrotal folds; in second specimen glans exposed with annulus well defined and inflated; sexual skin little differentiated and limited to narrow unpigmented median pubic band; greatest diameter of labia majora about 18 mm, genital fissure, 13, 14 mm; perineal and anal regions slightly or not pigmented; ischial region with prominent glandular prominences (fig. I.15), one on each side roughly similar in size and shape to the scrotal fold; perineal and anal regions unpigmented.

Subadult (*S. mystax*). Labia majora forming a thick rounded cushion slightly longer than wide, comparatively thickly haired and with outer preputial folds hardly differentiated from dominant scrotal folds; glans clitoridis exposed but not well defined; ischial prominences larger than labia majora but not distinctly padded or glandular; length of labia majora in two virgins 10, 12 mm, length of genital fissure 6, 11 mm respectively.

Cranial Characters (cf. fig. X.6–12)

Frontal contour low or moderately rounded in *labiatus* and *mystax,* well rounded to markedly domed in *imperator;* temporal ridges strongly convergent along frontoparietal suture and sometimes fusing into a sagittal crest; nasal profile plane to slightly concave; frontal sinuses slightly to moderately inflated; malar foramen from less than 1 mm to nearly 4 mm in greatest diameter; ventral borders of mandible distinctly U-shaped, the horizontal rami well arced, the angular process from slightly to considerably inflected inward, slightly to moderately deflected downward.

Comparisons

Distinguished from bare-face tamarins by hairy cheeks, temples, forehead, and white-haired circumbuccal band; from hairy-face tamarins by white unpigmented skin of circumbuccal band, nasal septum, and external genitalia and crested hairs of midline of muzzle; from *Leontopithecus* and *Callimico* by well-exposed ears, lack of specialized mane, and other characters mentioned above; from *Cebuella* and one or another species of *Callithrix* by larger size, dark color of back, sides, and limbs with hairs never uniformly colored, ears nearly naked, black, and without conspicuous aural or preauricular tufts, tail not banded and other characters mentioned above.

Saturation and Bleaching (fig. X.39)

The primitive agouti pelage pattern is dominant in *Saguinus imperator*. The melanistic grade dominates in the remaining species of the *mystax* group, but a modified agouti persists on dorsum and sides of body from nape to rump and on outer sides of hind limbs. Evolution of body color from agouti to modified agouti and melanistic was general without clear demarcation zones as occurs in bizonal or trizonal members of the *S. nigricollis* group.

The bleaching process in the *mystax* group is particularly marked on face, perineum, crown, tail, and basal portion of hairs, most notably of nape, shoulders, and lateral fringe. The white circumbuccal area was already present in the ancestral stock, but rhinarial bleaching is characteristic of the *mystax* group.

The perineum of *Saguinus mystax pluto* is grayish with the same color covering the ventral surface of the base of the tail. Otherwise, underparts of all races of *S. mystax* are saturate eumelanic, although fading to brownish. In *S. labiatus* the underparts, except throat, are sharply defined reddish orange or saturate pheomelanic. In *S. imperator,* a modified grayish agouti dominates the ventral surface, but the lower portions tend toward pheomelanism, the tail being dominantly reddish orange or golden, but with basal portion of hairs and terminal tuft black. The black and red hairs covering most of the tail produce a faint, disrupted annular pattern. In *Saguinus mystax,* the tail is entirely black, but the tip is sometimes grayish. The different color patterns in the two species confirm the chromogenetic independence of the terminal tuft of the tail. The same independence exists on the ventral surface of the tail base.

Color modification of crown begins as a reddish patch between ears and spreads to the front where the field constricts to a point or line, and expands to the back as a silvery fan-shaped patch in *labiatus,* or as a reddish orange bilobed patch in *pileatus.*

Bleaching of the individual hairs of back and lateral fringe progresses from base distally. On crown, rump, and tail the process proceeds from distal portion of hair to base. The pale subterminal band of the modified agouti hairs bleaches independently.

Depigmentation and Hypertrichy

Facial depigmentation in the *Saguinus mystax* group is confined to the circumbuccal, narial, and genal regions but sometimes the entire face (figs. X.39, 41). Steps in the process can be traced from the narrow band of depigmentation around the lips and its extension over the internarial septum in *S. labiatus* through the widened band around the mouth and nares in *mystax,* to *imperator* with lower half of face completely depigmented. White facial pelage is confined to the depigmented zones in all members of the group but not all depigmented areas are white-haired.

Except for the usual reduction or obsolescence of pelage of the interorbital region, no tendency toward bare-facedness is evident in the group. It appears rather that the greater the depigmentation of the rostral area, the longer and thicker the whiskers covering it (figs. X.42, 44).

Key to Species and Subspecies of *Saguinus mystax* Group

Skin surrounding mouth and between or around nostrils unpigmented (flesh colored) and covered with whitish hairs; whiskers of upper lip well defined; mantle (long hairs of nape, shoulders, upper arms) brown or blackish, usually with fine silvery or buffy ticking and hardly or not at all defined from middle back; whitish frontal band or patch absent.

1. Skin between and completely around nostrils unpigmented (flesh colored); hairs surrounding mouth forming long white whiskers; crown black, brown, or reddish; chest, belly, inner sides of limbs blackish, brown, or gray-brown 3

1′. Skin of inner borders of nostrils white, of upper and outer borders black; hairs surrounding mouth short, not forming long whiskers; crown with small reddish, orange, or silvery patch or streak; chest, belly, inner sides of limbs sharply defined yellowish, orange, or rusty reddish 2

2. Black crown with reddish line or forked patch in front, a well-defined or diffused silvery patch behind; throat mostly to entirely black, remainder of throat and chest pheomelanic . . . . *Saguinus labiatus labiatus* (p. 691)

2′. Black crown with fine reddish line in front, small pale spot behind; throat and upper part of chest black . . . . *Saguinus labiatus thomasi* (p. 693)

3. Whiskers extremely long, extending to back of head when laid back; tail dominantly reddish; underparts grayish or brownish, the belly often reddish . . . . *Saguinus imperator* (p. 701)

3′. Whiskers shorter, not extending beyond cheeks or front of ears when laid back; tail dominantly or entirely black; underparts blackish . . . . (*Saguinus mystax*) 4

4. Crown and forehead reddish . . . . *Saguinus mystax pileatus* (p. 699)

4′. Crown and forehead black 5

5. Hairs of inguinal, genital, and anal regions and contiguous portions of tail base white; mantle hairs wavy, their bases drab and not showing through at surface . . . . *Saguinus mystax pluto* (p. 700)

5′. Hairs of genitalia often whitish, surrounding hairs of pudendal region and tail base black; mantle hairs straight, bases whitish and usually showing through at surface . . . . *Saguinus mystax mystax* (p. 696)

2

S. l. labiatus

2′

S. l. thomasi

3

S. imperator

4

S. m. pileatus

5

S. m. mystax

5′

S. m. pluto

65 *Saguinus labiatus* E. Geoffroy, Red-chested Moustached Tamarins

Distribution (figs. X.37, 38)

Middle Amazonian region of Brazil; on the south bank of the Rio Solimões (Amazonas), between the Rios Madeira and Purús in the states of Amazonas and Acre (*labiatus*); on the north bank of the Solimões, the Rio Tonantins regions between the Rios Içа and Japurá, Amazonas (*thomasi*).

The apparently unnaturally disrupted distribution of the species on both sides of the Rio Solimoes is discussed below.

Origin, Evolution, and Dispersal (fig. X.38)

Saguinus labiatus appears to be the most primitive species of the *mystax* group, at least with respect to facial depigmentation and whisker development. On the other hand, it is most advanced with respect to the taxonomically less trenchant characters of color grade attained in the metachromic scale. The distinctive characters of *S. labiatus* as a member of the *mystax* group, are differences of grade. That they are cladistic as well is not at all certain.

If *S. labiatus* is indeed a member of the *mystax* group, it could have originated in the southwestern portion of the Amazonian basin and spread northward between the Madeira and Purús rivers to the southern shores of the Rio Amazonas (Solimões). However, the occurrence of *S. l. thomasi* in the Rio Tonantins area on the north bank of the Solimões about 700 kilometers upstream from its nearest relative is equivocal. Introduction by man is a possibility. Whatever the means of transportation, an inbreeding colony, once established, should be more advanced metachromically than the parental stock. This is not the case.

It seems more plausible to assume on the basis of present knowledge that *S. l. thomasi* represents the parental stock and that *S. l. labiatus* is derived from a waifed detachment rafted down the Solimões and shuttled to the southern shore between the Rios Purús and Madeira. The hypothesis of growth and spread of the colony southward between the two rivers is supported by what is known of local variation in color. The northernmost population, *Saguinus labiatus thomasi,* isolated on the north bank of the Solimões, is least differentiated in coloration. The southernmost populations of *S. l. labiatus,* found between the Purús and Madeira south of the Rio Ipixuna, are most advanced metachromically; and the populations north of the Ipixuna are intermediate.

Sympatry between *S. labiatus labiatus, S. mystax pluto,* and possibly *S. imperator* reinforces the probability that *S. labiatus* originated independently from a northern Amazonian white-mouthed *S. nigricollis graellsi*-type of stock related to but independent from the postulated southern branch that gave rise to other members of the *S. mystax* group.

A better knowledge of the true relationships of *Saguinus labiatus* depends on a sampling of the almost completely unknown primate fauna of the vast area between the Rios Negro, Solimões, and Japurá. To this may be added the inter-Japurá-Içа basins where *thomasi* occurs.

Diagnostic Characters

Crown with a golden, reddish, or coppery line, or with a more or less bifurcated patch in front, and a black, gray, or silvery spot or patch behind; skin of circumlabial band and narial septum unpigmented and haired white, outer borders of nostrils black; back black marbled with silvery; tail black except for reddish ventral portion at root; throat and sometimes upper part of chest black, remainder of underparts sharply defined reddish or orange (fig. X.39).

External Characters

Integument. Facial skin black except thin unpigmented circumbuccal band and narial septum with whitish hairs; remainder of face covered with black hairs with those of middle of muzzle forming a thin low crest; white mustache weakly developed; forehead and much of crown black, a coppery or rusty reddish to golden line or forked patch in front; mid-crown mixed silvery and black or with a whitish or buff spot to a well-defined silvery triangular patch; back from nape to rump weakly bizonal, the mantle (hairs of nape and shoulders) blackish with pale skin and drab bases of hairs showing through at surface, the pale drab to silvery subterminal band of hairs extremely fine or obsolete; middle back and rump marbled or vermiculated with silvery, the hairs blackish with broad, silvery subterminal bands; lateral fringe like back but hair bases drab to white; outer sides of hind legs and base of tail like rump; outer sides of upper arms like mantle, of forearms uniformly blackish; upper surface of hands and feet black, the black often extending completely around wrists and ankles; interramia and all or part of throat black; posterior portion or entire chest, belly, perineum, and inner sides of arms and legs sharply defined orange or rusty red; tail black except underside of proximal one-sixth to one-third like perineum; external genitalia more or less pigmented and sparsely clad with orange to reddish hairs.

Vibrissae. Supraorbitals, mystacials, rhinarials, mentals, and backwardly directed interramals normally present, genal not certainly distinguishable in dry skin; ulnar carpals probably present; gular spines present.

Cranial Characters

Malar foramen with diameter from 1 to nearly 4 mm, a range greater than in any other callitrichid examined.

Comparisons

Distinguished from all other members of the *mystax* group and members of the *S. nigricollis* group (*fuscicollis nigricollis*) by thin band of unpigmented skin around mouth and between but not around nostrils, back marbled silvery and black and without clear definition of bizonal or trizonal pattern, crown with silvery to orange or reddish line, patch, or both, and underparts of limbs and trunk sharply defined orange to reddish.

Bleaching and Depigmentation

Eumelanins still dominant on the upper and outer parts of *S. labiatus* are being eliminated from below. The black hairs of the body are silvery subterminally, drab to white basally, the coronal patch is bleaching topically and geographically from a fine reddish line in front to a reddish orange, then golden to a silvery patch behind. Except for the neck and the upper part of the chest in some populations, notably *thomasi,* the hypothetically primitive agouti underparts gave way to the pheomelanic reddish or orange.

The tendency for the tail to become reddish is patent on the ventral surface. The sharp line between the black neck and orange chest of *labiatus* recalls the equally sharp definition between black crown and orange or golden mantle of *S. fuscicollis tripartitus.*

In pigmentation of facial skin, *S. labiatus* stands midway between the *nigricollis* and the *S. mystax* groups. In all other respects, it is more nearly related to the latter.

SAGUINUS LABIATUS LABIATUS E. GEOFFROY: GEOFFROY'S MOUSTACHED TAMARIN

Synonymic History

Simia labiata E. Geoffroy in Humboldt, 1812, *Rec. Obs. Zool. Anat. Comp.,* p. 361—"*Midas labiatus* Geoffroy" in synonymy.

Midas labiatus E. Geoffroy, 1812, *Ann. Mus. Hist. Nat., Paris* 19:121—description of type; type locality, Brazil? Temminck, 1827, *Monogr. Mamm.* 1:xv—*fuscicollis, nigricollis, mystax* regarded as synonyms. Pelzeln, 1883, *Verh. K. K. Zool.-Bot. Gesellsch., Wien, Beih.* 33:24—BRAZIL: *Amazonas* (Luiz, Lago do Joanacan, Rio Solimões); synonyms, *erythrogaster* Natterer (ms.), *elegantulus* Slack, *rufiventer* Gray. Goeldi and Hagmann, 1904, *Bol. Mus. Paraense* 4:53—BRAZIL: *Amazonas; Acre* (Rio Acre). Rode, 1938, *Bull. Mus. Nat. Hist. Nat., Paris,* ser. 2, 10:239—type history.

M[idas] labiatus, I. Geoffroy, 1851, *Cat. Primates, Mus. Hist. Nat., Paris,* p. 63—type history.

Jacchus labiatus, Desmarest, 1818, *Nouv. Dict. Hist. Nat.* 24:242—characters. Desmarest, 1820, *Mammalogie,* p. 95—characters. Desmarest, 1827, *Dict. Sci. Nat.* 47:21—characters. Gray, 1843, *List Mamm. Brit. Mus.,* p. 15—BRAZIL.

H[apale (Midas)] labiatus, Voigt, 1831, *Cuvier's das Thierreich* 1:99—classification.

Leontocebus labiatus, Elliot, 1913, *A review of the Primates,* 1:195—description ex type; synonymy.

Leontocebus labiatus labiatus, Cabrera, 1958, *Rev. Mus. Argentino Cienc. Nat. "Bernardino Rivadavia"* 4(1): 193—classification.

Tamarin labiatus, Cruz Lima, 1945, *Mamíferos da Amazonia, Primates, Contrib. Mus. Paraense,* p. 225, pl. 35, fig. 2 (animal in foreground)—characters ex Elliot.

Marikina labiata, Hershkovitz, 1949, *Proc. U.S. Nat. Mus.* 98:412—key characters; classification; part synonyms, *rufiventer* Gray, *elegantulus* Slack, *erythrogaster* Reichenbach, *griseovertex* Goeldi.

Tamarinus labiatus, Osman Hill, 1957, *Primates,* 3:218 (map), 221, 229, 235—characters; distribution; taxonomy.

T[amarinus] l[abiatus] labiatus, Osman Hill, 1957, *Primates,* 3:236—characters; distribution.

Saguinus labiatus labiatus. Hershkovitz, 1968, *Evolution* 22(3):563, fig. 7 (diagnostic color pattern)—characters; distribution; metachromism (depigmentation); hypertrichy. Hershkovitz, 1970, *Am. J. Phys. Anthrop.* 32: 379—dental disease; supernumerary lower molar.

Jacchus rufiventer Gray, 1843, *Ann. Mag. Nat. Hist.*, ser. 1, 12:398—"MEXICO": (type locality); type male, skin and skull, British Museum (Natural History) no. 43.10.12.6. Gerrard, 1862, *Cat. bones Brit. Mus.*, p. 28—"SOUTH AMERICA"; skull in collection. Gray, 1875, *Zoology of the voyage of H. M. S. Erebus and Terror,* 1 (*Mammalia*): 12a, pl. 18 (animal)—"MEXICO"; characters.

Iacchus rufiventer, Sclater, 1872, *Proc. Zool. Soc. London,* p. 8—species Amazonian, not Mexican.

Midas rufiventer, Gray, 1870, *Cat. monkeys, lemurs and fruit-eating bats, Brit. Mus.*, p. 66—BRAZIL; *elegantulus* Slack, a synonym. Major, 1901, *Proc. Zool. Soc. London,* pp. 147, 152, pl. 12, fig. 5 (lacrymal region)—lacrymal region of skull. Goeldi, 1907, *Proc. Zool. Soc. London* 1907:90, fig. 21 (back of head)—description ex type. Elliot, 1913, *A review of the Primates* 1:196 (in text)—synonym of *labiatus* Geoffroy; characters ex type.

Midas rufoventer [*sic*], Gray, 1866, *Proc. Zool. Soc. London* 1865:735—BRAZIL; characters; *elegantulus* Slack, a synonym.

Midas elegantulus Slack, 1861, *Proc. Acad. Nat. Sci. Philadelphia* 13:463—BRAZIL: *Amazonas* (type locality, Amazonian region); type, male, skin and skull, U.S. National Museum no. $\frac{5132}{37870}$, collected 1851 by W. L. Herndon. Poole and Schantz, 1942, *Bull. U.S. Nat. Mus.* 178:236—type history.

M[*idas*] *erythrogaster* Reichenbach, 1862, *Vollst. Naturg. Affen,* p. 14, pl. 36, fig. 488 (animal)—BRAZIL: (type locality not specified); type mounted in Vienna Museum collected by Johann Natterer.

Hapale erythrogaster, Pelzeln, 1883, *Verh. K. K. Zool.-Bot. Gesellsch., Wien, Beih.* 33:24—BRAZIL: *Amazonas* (Luiz, Lago do Joanacan, Rio Solimões); collected January 1833 by Johann Natterer, original number 150; name listed in synonymy of *Midas labiatus;* one specimen only.

Midas griseovertex Goeldi, 1907, *Proc. Zool. Soc. London,* 1907:92, fig. 22 (back of head)—BRAZIL: (type locality, Rios Purús and Acre regions); seven cotypes, skins and skulls, male and female mounted in the Berne Museum, male, female, and young mounted in the Goeldi Museum, Pará, male and female in British Museum (Natural History), all collected 1903–4 by the Pará Museum expeditions. Carvalho, 1959, *Rev. Brasil. Biol.* 19(4):460—BRAZIL: *Amazonas* (type locality restricted to Bom Lugar, upper Rio Purús); designated lectotype, male, skin only, Museu Goeldi, no. 913, collected July–August 1903 by J. Schönmann. Lönnberg, 1940, *Ark. Zool., Stockholm* 32A(10):5—BRAZIL: *Amazonas* (Labrea, Rio Purús).

Midas griseoventris [*sic*], Elliot, 1913, *A review of the Primates* 1:197, 198—lapsus for *griseovertex* Goeldi in synonymy of *Leontocebus labiatus.*

Marikina labiata griseovertex, Vieira, 1952, *Papeis Avulsos* 11:24—BRAZIL: *Acre* (Iquiri).

Leontocebus labiatus griseovertex, Cabrera, 1958, *Rev. Mus. Argentino Cienc. Nat. "Bernardino Rivadavia"* 4(1): 193—BRAZIL: *Amazonas* (type locality restricted to upper Rio Purús). Carvalho, 1959, *Rev. Brasil. Biol.* 19 (4):460—BRAZIL: *Amazonas* (Bom Lugar, upper Rio Purús, restricted type locality); lectotype designated.

T[*amarinus*] *l*[*abiatus*] *griseovertex,* Osman Hill, 1957, *Primates* 3:237—characters; distribution.

Type. Skin mounted with skull in, Muséum National d'Histoire Naturelle, Paris, no. 630; collected by Alexandre Rodrigues Ferreira during his scientific expedition to Brazil, 1783–92; originally deposited in the Museum Royal d'Ajuda, Lisbon, Portugal; acquired by the Paris Museum in 1808 during the Napoleonic wars. (cf. Carvalho 1965, p. 26).

Type Locality. "Probablement le Brésil"; restricted to Lago do Joanacan (= Janauacá, 193) Amazonas, type locality of *erythrogaster* Reichenbach, by Cabrera (1958, *Rev. Mus. Argentino Cienc. Nat.* "Bernardino Rivadavia" 4(1):194). The greater probability, however, is that the type of *labiatus* originated somewhere between the Rios Purús and Madeira south of the Rio Ipixuna, in the region of *griseovertex* Goeldi.

Distribution (fig. X.37). Western Brazil south of the Rio Amazonas (Solimões) between the Rios Madeira and Purús in the states of Amazonas and Acre. The range of *S. labiatus labiatus* encompasses that of *S. mystax pluto.*

Taxonomy. The type of *Jacchus rufiventer* was described by Gray in 1843 and figured by him in 1875. Revisers regarded *rufiventer* as identical with or representative of a locally differentiated population of *Saguinus labiatus.* It agrees best with our Rozarinho–San Miguel series from the lower Rio Madeira with coronal patch reddish and Y-shaped in front and diffused silvery or silvery buff behind.

Midas elegantulus Slack, 1861, resembles *griseovertex,* judging by my notes on the types of both. This suggests that the type of *elegantulus* originated between the middle Rios Purús and Madeira. The type was mounted but is now preserved as a study skin with skull separate.

The type of *Midas erythrogaster* Reichenbach, 1862, is the specimen collected by Natterer and recorded from Luiz, Lago do Joanacan (= Janauacá), Rio Solimões, by Pelzeln (1883, p. 24) under the name *Midas labiatus.* The animal, figured in color by Reichenbach, is undoubtedly referrable to that species and, like the preceding, appears to agree best with specimens from the south bank of the Solimões and lower reaches of the Madeira. It differs from these and all others, however, by the extension of black from throat to upper part of the chest and across deltoid and axillary regions. Inclusion of the shoulder joint in the black area may be an artifact. I have not seen the type.

Midas griseovertex Goeldi, 1907, with a grayish or silvery coronal patch more strongly defined than the reddish patch in front, agrees best with the type of *labiatus* and our two specimens from Lago Mapixi (185) and one in the British Museum from Humaitá (197*a*). These localities are south of the Rio Ipixuna between the Rios Purús and Madeira and suggest that it may have been wiser to restrict the type locality of the nominate form of the species within this area rather than to the north at the Lago do Januaucá.

Diagnostic Characters. Black crown with well-marked reddish midline or Y-shaped patch in front, well-defined triangular or diffused silvery patch behind; throat mostly to entirely black, remainder of underparts, except sometimes upper part of chest, sharply defined reddish.

Coloration. That of the species except as restricted by the diagnostic characters given above.

Measurements. See appendix table 2.

Comparisons. Distinguished from *thomasi* by prominent coronal patch, darker, more red underparts, and, with a few exceptions, extension of the reddish over entire chest and part of throat.

Variation. The northermost populations, represented by specimens from Lago do Janauacá (*erythrogaster*), Rosarinho (195), and Lago Miguel (195) and by *rufiventer* without locality data, probably range from the Solimões to the Rio Ipixuna. They are characterized by a well-developed rusty red or orange Y-shaped coronal patch and a poorly defined silvery buff patch behind. Specimens from south of the Ipixuna, and the type of *labiatus* from unknown provenance, are marked by a comparatively weakly defined reddish line or small Y-shaped patch in front and a large and solid coronal patch behind. At the southern extreme of the range (Iquiri (213), Acre), the reddish patch gives way to an entirely silvery one (cf. Vieira 1952, p. 24).

From the foregoing, in seems that the color and form of the patch shift gradually from north to south from a dominantly reddish Y-shaped form in front to a silvery subtriangular one behind. Except for the persistence of black on chest and undersurface of shoulder region in the Lago do Janauacá specimen (*erythrogaster*), there appears to be no significant variation in the color of underparts throughout the range of the subspecies.

Specimens Examined. 17. BRAZIL—*Amazonas:* Bom Lugar, 2 (BM, syntypes of *griseovertex*); Canabuoca, Paraná do Jacaré, 1 (BM); Humaitá, Rio Madeira, 1 (BM); Lago do Mapixi, 4 (BM, 2; FMNH, 2); Lago Miguel, 2 (AMNH); Rosarinho, 4 (AMNH); *locality unknown,* 3 (BM, 2, including type of *rufiventer;* MNHN, type of *labiatus*).

SAGUINUS LABIATUS THOMASI GOELDI, THOMAS' MOUSTACHED TAMARIN

Synonymic History

M[*idas*] *rufiventer,* Bates (not Gray), 1863, *Naturalist on the River Amazons* 2:321—BRAZIL: *Amazonas* (Rio Tonantins).

Midas labiatus, Gray (not E. Geoffroy), 1870, *Cat. monkeys, lemurs and fruit-eating bats, Brit. Mus.,* p. 66—BRAZIL: (north side of Amazonas).

Hapale labiata, Schlegel, 1876, *Les singes. Simiae,* p. 266—BRAZIL: *Amazonas* ("Rio Yavari"). Jentink, 1892, *Cat. Syst. Mamm. Mus. Pays-Bas* 11:56—BRAZIL: *Amazonas* ("Rio Yavari").

Marikina labiata, Hershkovitz, 1949, *Proc. U.S. Nat. Mus.* 98:412—part, *thomasi* Goeldi in synonymy only.

Midas thomasi Goeldi, 1907, *Proc. Zool. Soc. London* 1907:89, fig. 20 (rear of head).

Leontocebus thomasi, Elliot, 1913, *A review of the Primates* 1:198—characters ex type.

Tamarin thomasi, Cruz Lima, 1945, *Mamíferos da Amazonia, Primates,* p. 227—characters ex Goeldi.

T[*amarinus*] *l*[*abiatus*] *thomasi,* Hill, 1957, *Primates* 3:237—characters ex literature.

Saguinus labiatus thomasi, Hershkovitz, 1968, *Evolution* 22(3):563, fig. 7 (diagnostic color pattern)—characters; distribution; metachromism (depigmentation).

Type. Male, skin and skull, British Museum (Natural History) no. 57.10.17.5; collected November 1856 by Henry Walter Bates.

Type Locality. Tonantins (173), Rio Tonantins, north bank Rio Amazonas below mouth of Rio Içа, Amazonas, Brazil.

Distribution (figs. X.37, 38). Known from type locality only.

Diagnostic Characters. Black crown with fine reddish midline in front, small pale spot behind, throat and upper part of chest black, remainder of underparts sharply defined orange to reddish orange.

Coloration. That of the species except as restricted by the diagnostic characters given above.

Measurements. See appendix table 2.

Comparisons. Distinguished from *labiatus* by poorly developed coronal line or patch, throat and upper portion of chest black, underparts orange, not reddish.

Remarks. The differences between *thomasi* and *labiatus* of the lower reaches of the Rios Madeira and Purús are not impressive. Differences between some local populations of *labiatus* are as great. Only the complete geographic isolation from *labiatus* combined with the minor color differences noted justify subspecific separation.

The type specimen collected by Bates was recorded by him (1863, p. 321) as follows: "At Tunantins I shot a pair of a very handsome species of Marmoset, the M. rufiventer [i.e., *labiatus*], I believe of zoologists. Its coat was very glossy and smooth; the back deep brown and the underside of the body of rich black and reddish hues." Bates (1863, p. 371) informs that he sojourned in Tunantins (i.e., Tonantins) from 11 to 30 November 1856. The specimen in the British Museum seen by Goeldi (1907, p. 89) and described as type of *thomasi* was labeled *"Midas rufiventer* ♂ 'the red-bellied Tamarin' Upper Amazonia. W. Bates. Exp. 1857a., 'Tunantins, north side of Amazons.' "

The second specimen of the pair mentioned by Bates may be a mounted individual in the Leiden museum acquired in 1864 and described by Schlegel (1876, p. 260) under the name *Hapale labiatus.* It is indistinguishable from *thomasi* but is labeled "Rio Yavari," where the species does not occur. In this connection, it may be relevant to note that the Leiden museum has a specimen of *Saguinus fuscicollis fuscicollis* from the Rio Javarí collected by Bates. It is labeled "acquis, 1858."

Two additional specimens in the British Museum were collected at the Rio Tonantins in 1926 by Wilhelm Ehrhardt.

Saguinus labiatus thomasi and *S. fuscicollis fuscus* are the only callitrichids known to inhabit the north bank of the Amazon between the Rios Japurá and Içа in Brazil. Both gave rise to slightly differentiated subspecies on the south bank of the Amazonas. Callitrichids are unknown farther east on the north bank between the lower Rio Japurá and lower Rio Negro. West, between the Iça and lower Napo, there is *S. nigricollis.*

Specimens Examined. 5. BRAZIL—*Amazonas:* Rio Tonantins, 4 (BM, 3 including type of *thomasi;* SM, 1); UNKNOWN LOCALITY—(labeled "Rio Yavari"), 1 (RMNH).

66 *Saguinus mystax* Spix, Black-chested Moustached Tamarins

Distribution (figs. X.37, 38)

Western Brazil and eastern Peru south of the Rio Amazonas; from the left bank of the Rio Madeira in Amazonas, Brazil, west to the Río Ucayali and the lowlands between the Ucayali and the lower Río Huallaga in Loreto, Peru.

Origin, Evolution, and Dispersal (fig. X.38)

The ancestral form of *Saguinus mystax* may have been dominantly modified agouti on dorsum, sides, and limbs. In living forms of *S. mystax,* the terminal portion of the hairs of these parts is bleaching from brown to drab, the pale subterminal band fading from reddish orange to pale buff or gray.

Saguinus mystax probably originated along the eastern base of the Andes in southeastern Peru. It spread northward confined between the Andean foothills and the Rio Juruá. *S. m. pileatus* appears to be an offshoot that evolved from a founder colony shuttled from the left bank of the Juruá to the right. *S. m. pluto* can also be derived directly from *mystax* or a prototype. It cannot be derived from *pileatus* because it retains the more primitive uniformly black crown. It cannot have given rise to *pileatus* because the latter retains the primitively saturate perineal area. It appears that *pluto* is more widely separated from its nearest relative, *mystax,* than from the more divergent *pileatus* living on the opposite banks of the Purús. Future collecting in the unexplored territories of the headwaters of the Purús and Juruá may fill the geographic gap between the races.

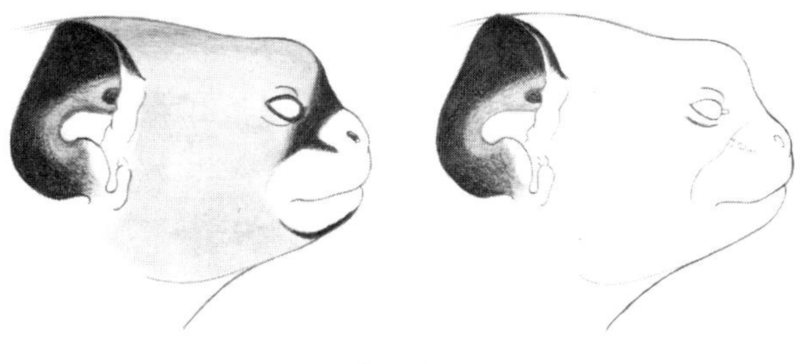

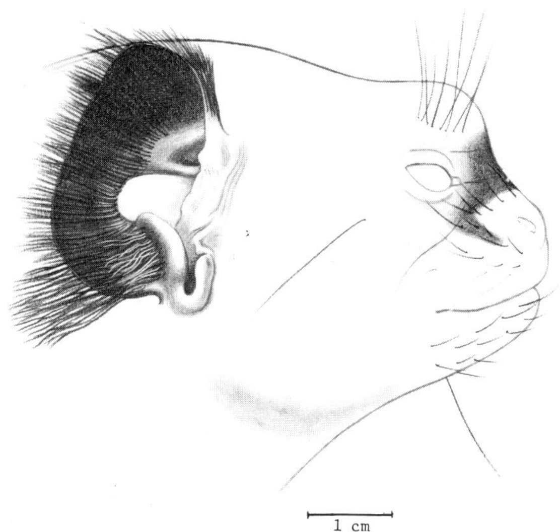

Fig. X.41. *Saguinus mystax mystax*: Profiles of selected individuals with manes removed to expose ears, vibrissae, and facial pigmentation; upper figures show variation in extent of pigmentation of face, crown, and ears.

Diagnostic Characters

Crown entirely black or with reddish patch on forehead and crown; skin of circumbuccal band and circumnarial borders unpigmented and haired white; skin of narial septum pigmented or unpigmented; underparts blackish brown, tail black; whiskers well developed but not remarkably elongate.

External Characters

Integument. Circumbuccal and circumnarial skin unpigmented and covered with white hairs; remainder of facial skin including symphysis of jaw pigmented or unpigmented (fig. X.41); white circumbuccal hairs forming a well-developed mustache; white hairs surrounding nares forming a trapezoidal patch; remainder of facial hairs black; hairs of dorsal surface of muzzle feathered and forming a low thin median crest; forehead and crown entirely blackish or with a large reddish patch; blackish mantle weakly or not at all defined from vermiculated portion of back, the basal portion of the hairs drab, gray or pure white; lateral fringe blackish brown finely ticked with buffy, the basal portion of the hairs drab to whitish; upper surface of hands and feet black; underparts blackish brown. External genitalia mostly or entirely unpigmented; ischial prominence (fig. I.15) usually well developed.

Vibrissae (fig. X.41). Supraorbitals, mystacials, rhinarials, mentals, and backward directed interramals present; genals randomly distributed; ulnar carpals probably present.

Ears. See chap. 9; fig. III.18, X.41.

External genitalia (fig. X.40). See chap. 14.

Comparisons

Distinguished from *S. imperator* mainly by whiskers not exceptionally long, somber coloration with tail entirely black; from *S. labiatus* by underparts black or dark brown, not sharply defined reddish orange.

Bleaching

Continued evolution after differentiation of the living races of *Saguinus mystax* mainly involves progressive bleaching of the long hairs of mantle and lateral fringe from base distally. Hair bases of these areas are drab in *pluto,* or least bleached within the species, paler in *pileatus,* and palest in *mystax.* The distinctive characters of *pileatus* indicate that isolation from the parental *mystax* stock evoked switching of pigment production in crown pelage from black to red, or perhaps pheomelanic saturation of the ancestral agouti hairs. On the other hand, extensive blanching of pubic and perianal hairs is distinctive of *pluto.*

Subspecies. See page 689 for key to subspecies *mystax, pileatus,* and *pluto.*

SAGUINUS MYSTAX MYSTAX SPIX: SPIX'S MOUSTACHED TAMARIN

1 cm

Fig. X.42. Spix's Moustached Tamarin, *Saguinus mystax mystax*

Synonymic History

Midas mystax Spix, 1823, *Sim. et Vesp.,* p. 29, pl. 22 (animal). Wagner, 1833, *Isis von Oken* 10:996—characters. Goeldi and Hagmann, 1904, *Bol. Mus. Paraense* 4:53—BRAZIL: *Amazonas* (Rio Juruá). Ihering, 1904, *Rev. Mus. Paulista, São Paulo* 6:415—BRAZIL: *Amazonas* (Rio Juruá, 7° S). Goeldi, 1907, *Proc. Zool. Soc. London,* p. 98—BRAZIL: *Amazonas* (Rio Juruá).

M[idas] mystax, G. Cuvier, 1829, *Reg. Anim.* 1:106, footnote—perhaps a variety of *labiatus.* I. Geoffroy, 1851, *Cat. Primates Mus. Hist. Nat., Paris,* p. 64—BRAZIL: *Amazonas* (São Paulo de Olivença, Rio Solimões). I. Geoffroy, 1855, *Castelnau Expéd. Amérique Sud, pt. 7, Zool., Mamm.,* pp. 20, 21—BRAZIL: *Amazonas* (São Paulo de Olivença); comparisons. Slack, 1861, *Proc. Acad. Nat. Sci. Philadelphia* 13:464—part, not synonymy. Reichenbach, 1862, *Vollst. Naturg. Affen,* p. 12, pl. 3, fig. 41 (animal)—characters. Cabrera, 1900, *Anal. Soc. Española Hist. Nat.* ser. 2, 9:90—PERU: *Loreto* (Río Napo[!]).

Jacchus mystax, Gerrard, 1862, *Cat. bones Brit. Mus.,* p. 29—BRAZIL.

H[apale] mystax, Wagner, 1855, *Schreber's Säugth., Suppl.* 5:129—characters.

Hapale mystax, Schlegel, 1876, *Les singes. Simiae,* p. 261—BRAZIL: *Amazonas* (São Paulo de Olivença). Jentink, 1887, *Cat. Ostéol. Mus. Pays-Bas* 9:49—BRAZIL: *Amazonas* (São Paulo de Olivença). Jentink, 1892, *Cat. Syst. Mamm. Mus. Pays-Bas* 11:56—BRAZIL: *Amazonas* (cotype from north bank of Rio Solimões; São Paulo de Olivença).

L[eontocebus] mystax, Cabrera, 1912, *Trab. Mus. Cienc. Nat., Madrid,* no. 11:29—PERU: *Loreto* (Río Napo; Jiménez de la Espada, collector).

Leontocebus mystax, Elliot, 1913, *A review of the Primates,* 1:201—characters. Cabrera, 1917, *Trab. Mus. Nac. Cienc. Nat., Madrid, Ser. Zool.* 31:32—PERU: *Loreto* (lower Río Napo [!]). Schreiber, 1928, *Gegenbaur's Morph. Jahrb.* 60:183, fig. 1–6, 53*a*–56*a*, 58*a*, 59*a* (facial musculature)—comparative facial morphology. Carvalho, 1957, *Bol. Mus. Paraense Emilio Goeldi, n.s., Zool.,* no. 6, p. 6—BRAZIL: *Acre* (Seringal Oriente, left bank, upper Rio Juruá).

Hapale (Leontocebus) mystax, Lampert, 1926, *Morph. Jahrb.* 55:611, fig. 1–3 (larynx)—PERU: *Loreto* (Río Samiria); comparative anatomy of larynx.

[Mystax] mystax, Pocock, 1917, *Ann. Mag. Nat. Hist.,* ser. 8, 20:256—classification. Sonntag, 1921, *Proc. Zool. Soc. London* 1921:521, 757—tongue anatomy. Thomas, 1922, *Ann. Mag. Nat. Hist.* ser. 9, 9:198—classification; type of *mystax* Gray.

Mystax mystax, Thomas, 1928, *Ann. Mag. Nat. Hist.,* ser. 10, 2:255—PERU: *Loreto* (Cerro Azul, Contamana, Río Ucayali); variation in light-colored bases of hairs. Lönnberg, 1940, *Ark. Zool., Stockholm* 32A(10):6—BRAZIL: *Amazonas* (João Pessõa, Rio Juruá).

Tamarin mystax Cruz Lima, 1945, *Mamíferos da Amazonia, Primates, Contr. Mus. Paraense,* p. 220, pl. 37, fig. 2 (animal)—BRAZIL: *Amazonas* (Rio Purús [?]; Rio Juruá); PERU: *Loreto* (Chimbote, Río Napo [i.e., Río Marañon below mouth of Río Napo]). Vieira, 1948, *Bol. Mus. Paraense* 10:253—BRAZIL: *Amazonas* (João Pessõa, Rio Juruá; Igarapé Grande, Rio Juruá).

Marikina mystax, Hershkovitz, 1949, *Proc. U.S. Nat. Mus.* 98:412—key characters; classification.

Tamarinus mystax, Osman Hill, 1957, *Primates,* 3:164, 185, 213, 214, 217–22, 231, 233, 239, 241, pl. 11 (head of preserved animal)—BRAZIL: *Amazonas* (Fonteboa); characters; taxonomy; distribution; comparisons. Benirschke and Brownhill, 1963, *Cytogenetics* 2:331, figs. 4–6 (karyotypes)—heterosexual cells in testes of chimerae. Benirschke and Richart, 1963, *Lab. Animal Care* 13(2):73—care in laboratory; vulvar odor. Wohnus and Benirschke, 1966, *Cytogenetics* 5:94—chromosomal idiogram.

Saguinus mystax, Anderson, Lewis, Passovoy, and Trobaugh, 1967, *Lab. Animal Care* 17(1):37, fig. 1 (karyotype)—karyotype (2n = 46); hemotology. F. Deinhardt, Holmes, Devine, and Deinhardt, 1967, *Lab. Animal Care* 17(1):60—parasitology; virology; immunology. Hunt, Garcia, and Hegsted, 1967, *Lab. Animal Care* 17 (2):229—reversal of "cage paralysis" by substitution of diet containing vitamin D_2 for one containing D_3. Egozcue, Perkins, and Hagemenas, 1968, *Folia Primat.* 9(2):84—karyotype (2n = 46). Baer and Lorenz, 1970, *Proc. Soc. Exp. Biol. Med.* 134:410—induced delayed hypersensitivity reactions and antibody response to tuberculin and dinitrofluorobenzene. Lorenz, Barker, Stevens, et al., 1970, *Proc. Soc. Exp. Biol. Med.* 135:348—hepatitis. Gengozian and Porter, 1971, in *Med. Primat. 1970,* ed. Goldsmith and Moor-Jankowski, p. 165—survival time of intraspecific grafts (8–79 days); *S. mystax* versus *S. fuscicollis illigeri* recipient (8–32 days); *S. fuscicollis illigeri* versus *S. mystax* recipient (5–18 days). J. K. Hampton, Jr., Hampton, and Levy, 1971, in *Med. Primat. 1970,* ed. Goldsmith and Moor-Jankowski, p. 527—reproduction in laboratory colony. Murphy, Maynard, Krushak, and Berquist, 1972, *Lab. Animal Science* 22(3):339—microbial flora of imported animals (respiratory viruses; bacteria) of animal and human origin. Porter, 1972, *Lab. Anim. Sci.* 22(4):503—parasites. Anon., 1975, Oryx, 13:132—PERU: Loreto (Rio Maniti; confiscated animal captured for export must be returned to natural habitat [presidential order]).

Saguinus mystax mystax, Hershkovitz, 1968, *Evolution,* 22(3):563, fig. 7 (diagnostic color pattern)—characters; distribution; metachromism (depigmentation; bleaching). Hershkovitz, 1970, *Am. J. Phys. Anthrop.* 32:379—dental disease; supernumerary upper molar and incisor. Hershkovitz, 1970, *Folia Primat.* 13:215, fig. 3 (endocast of cerebral hemisphere)—PERU: *Loreto* (Santa Cecilia, Río Manití); cerebral fissural pattern. Hsu and Hampton, 1970, *Folia Primat.* 13:183—karyotype (2n = 46).

[?] *Jacchus labiatus,* Poeppig (not E. Geoffroy), 1831, *Froriep Not.* 32:148—PERU. Poeppig, 1836, *Reise Chile, Peru, Amazonst.* 2:378—PERU: *Loreto* (Maynas).

H[apale] labiatus, Wagner (not E. Geoffroy), 1840, *Schreber's Säugeth., suppl.* 1:246—part, description; *mystax* Spix in synonymy.

M[idas] labiatus, Reichenbach (not E. Geoffroy), 1862, *Vollst. Naturg. Affen,* p. 11, pl. 3, fig. 39 (animal)—characters.

T[amarin] mystax ♂ × *T[amarin] imperator* ♀, Cruz Lima, 1945, *Mamíferos da Amazonia, Primates,* p. 209—♂ probable but not certain mate in fertile cross-breeding; twin fetuses.

Tamarinus mystax ♂ × *T[amarinus] imperator* ♀, Osman Hill, 1957, *Primates,* 3:185—cited ex Cruz Lima, 1945.

L[eontocebus] mystax ♂ × *L[eontocebus] imperator* ♀, Osman Hill, 1961, *Proc. Zool. Soc. London* 137(2):321—cited ex Cruz Lima, 1945.

Fig. X.43. Spix's Moustached Tamarin, *Saguinus mystax mystax*. (Photo courtesy of J. K. Hampton, Jr.)

Types. One syntype, mounted with skull in the Munich Museum, another in the Leiden Museum; collected by the Spix and Martius expedition.

Type Locality. Near São Paulo de Olivença (172b), south bank Rio Solimões, Amazonas, Brazil.

Distribution (fig. X.37). South of the Amazon in western Brazil and eastern Peru; from the left bank of the Rio Juruá in Brazil to the right bank of the lower Río Huallaga, Peru, thence south along the base of the Andes to the junction of the Urubamba and Ucayali.

Diagnostic Characters (fig. X.43). Crown and tail black; white mustache moderately long, basal portion of mantle hairs white and often showing through at surface; inguinal hairs blackish, phallic hairs whitish.

Coloration. Head blackish or dark brown, skin of circumnarial and circumbuccal area except at symphysis unpigmented and covered with white hairs, the whiskers well developed, remainder of face pigmented or unpigmented and clothed with black hairs; mantle blackish brown lightly ticked with orange, the basal one-fourth to one-half of hairs white and showing through irregularly at surface; arms black; hairs of back, rump, and outer side of thighs blackish with orange or ochraceous orange subterminal band; lateral fringe like back but basal portion of hairs drab or whitish; upper surface of hands and feet black; black hairs of chin directed back or feathered and cresting at midline, hairs of throat directed back; underparts from middle of lower lip to belly and innersides of limbs black to blackish brown; tail black except base like rump, penciled tip sometimes gray; external genitalia mostly or entirely unpigmented and sparsely covered with white hairs.

Measurements. See appendix table 2.

Comparisons. Distinguished from all members of the *mystax* group by the dominantly blackish or dark brown color of head, trunk, and extremities.

Remarks. The type locality of *Saguinus mystax mystax* was originally given by Spix as near São Paulo de Olivença on the south bank of the Solimões. Spix added that his *Midas fuscicollis* and *M. nigricollis* also occurred there. Actually, only *mystax* and *fuscicollis* were secured on the southern bank while *nigricollis* had already been recorded by Spix from the northern bank in his account of this species. For no apparent reason, authors understood Spix to mean that all three species, including *S. mystax,* ranged on the north bank of the Solimões!

The young female collected by Jiménez de la Espada and recorded by Cabrera in 1917 (p. 32) and in earlier works (supra cit.) as being from the Río Napo must have originated on the right (south) bank of the Marañon, perhaps opposite the mouth of the Napo.

In 19 specimens from João Pessôa (176), Rio Juruá, collected by A. M. Olalla, Lönnberg (1940, pp. 6–7) finds the "somewhat shorter hairs along the centre of the back . . . black to their roots," in contradistinction to the conditions described by all other authors. In 2 specimens at hand collected at the same place and the same time by the same collector, and 2 from nearby Igarapé Grande (177), with the same history, the basal portions of the mantle hairs vary from nearly white to drab, those of the back lower down, from drab to brown but always paler than the dark brown middle portion of the hair.

Our four specimens from the upper Rio Juruá agree with Spix's colored figure of *mystax,* particularly with respect to the rufous outer side of the hind limbs and the contrasting black of the feet. Our Peruvian material (Río Yavarí Mirím (117) and Santa Cecilia (89)) is darker throughout with little contrast between the hind feet and limbs.

The mustache is as well developed in juvenals as in adults. Webbing between the fingers is not present in any of the specimens examined. In one *mystax,* Pocock (1920, p. 97) found the third and fourth digits of the right hand webbed between the first phalanges. He rightly held this to be an anomaly.

A fertile crossbreeding between a male *mystax* and female *imperator* was recorded by Cruz Lima (1945) and cited twice by Osman Hill (supra çit.). The case is discussed below (p. 704).

Specimens Examined. 79. BRAZIL—*Amazonas:* "Entre les fleuves Solimões et Iça," syntype of *mystax* (RMNH); Fonteboa, 4 (SM, 1; BM, 3); Igarapé Grande, Rio Juruá, 2 (FMNH); João Pessôa, Rio Juruá, 2 (FMNH); Olivença, 1 (RMNH); Rio Juruá, 1 (BM); *locality unknown:* 1 (BM); PERU—*Loreto:* Cerro Azul, 7 (BM) "Iquitos", 1 (AMNH); Lagarto alto, 8 (FMNH); "Marupa", Río Marañon, 2 (AMNH); Quebrada Esperanza, Río Yavarí Mirím, 3 (FMNH); Orosa, Río Marañon, 13 (AMNH); "Río Huallaga", 2 (AMNH); Santa Cecilia, Río Manití, 14 (FMNH); Río Ucayali, 1 (BM); Sarayacu, Río Ucayali, 13 (AMNH); UNKNOWN LOCALITY—3 (FMNH, in spirits).

SAGUINUS MYSTAX PILEATUS I. GEOFFROY AND DEVILLE, RED-CAP MOUSTACHED TAMARIN

Synonymic History

Midas pileatus I. Geoffroy and Deville, 1848, *Comptes rendus Acad. Sci., Paris* 27:499. I. Geoffroy, 1855, *Castelnau Expéd. Amérique Sud, pt. 7, Zool., Mamm.*, p. 21—BRAZIL: *Amazonas* (près de Pébas"). Goeldi, 1907, *Proc. Zool. Soc. London* 1907:97—BRAZIL: *Amazonas* (upper Rio Purús); *juruanus* Ihering a synonym. Rode, 1938, *Bull. Mus. Nat. Hist.*, ser. 2, 10:239—type history. Lönnberg, 1940, *Ark. Zool., Stockholm* 32A, (10):12, footnote 1—BRAZIL: *Amazonas* (Lago do Ipoxono [Ipixuna?], Rio Solimões, 64° W).

M[idas] pileatus, I. Geoffroy, 1851, *Cat. Primates Mus. Hist. Nat., Paris,* p. 63—BRAZIL: *Amazonas* ("près Pébas"). I. Geoffroy, 1852, *Arch. Mus. Hist. Nat., Paris* 5:569, pl. 31 (animal)—BRAZIL: *Amazonas* (Rio Javarí).

Hapale pileata, Gervais, 1854, *Hist. Nat. Mamm.* 1:152, fig. (head)—characters.

Leontocebus pileatus, Elliot, 1913, *A review of the Primates,* 1:197—description ex type. Cabrera, 1958, *Rev. Mus. Argentino Cienc. Nat., "Bernardino Rivadavia"* 4 (1): 196—classification; *juruanus* Ihering, a synonym.

Tamarin pileatus, Cruz Lima, 1945, *Mamíferos da Amazonia, Primates, Contr. Mus. Paraense,* p. 228—BRAZIL: *Amazonas* (São Luiz do Mamoriá, Rio Purús; Rio Juruá).

Marikina pileata pileata, Hershkovitz, 1949, *Proc. U.S. Nat. Mus.* 98:413—key characters; classification.

Tamarinus pileatus, Osman Hill, 1957, *Primates,* 3:218, 221, 231, 232, 234—characters; distribution.

Saguinus mystax pileatus, Hershkovitz, 1968, *Evolution* 22 (3):563, fig. 7 (diagnostic color pattern)—distribution; characters; metachromism (depigmentation); color pattern; hypertrichy. Hershkovitz, 1970, *Am. J. Phys. Anthrop.* 32:379—dental disease.

Midas pileatus juruanus Ihering, 1904, *Rev. Mus. Paulista, São Paulo* 6:416—BRAZIL: *Amazonas* (type locality, Rio Juruá, about 7° S); type, male, Museu Paulista, São Paulo, no. 1182, collected by E. Garbe; one syntype no. 733, in São Paulo Museum, syntype in British Museum (Natural History). Goeldi, 1907, *Proc. Zool. Soc. London* 1907:98—doubtfully distinct.

Marikina pileata juruana, Hershkovitz, 1949, *Proc. U.S. Nat. Mus.* 98:413—classification.

T[amarinus] p[ileatus] juruanus, Osman Hill, 1957, *Primates,* 3:235—characters; distribution.

Type. Male, skin and skull, Muséum National d'Histoire Naturelle, Paris, no. 641 (631); collected by Castelnau and Deville.

Type Locality. Originally given as the Rio Javarí, Brazil, then said to be near Pebas, Peru. The species does not occur in the general region of either locality. Specimens at hand from Lago de Tefé (i.e., Ega) where collections were made by the Castelnau Expedition, agree in all essentials with the description of *pileatus* and with no other known species. The type locality, therefore, is redetermined as the Lago de Tefé (182) near its mouth at the Rio Solimões, Amazonas, Brazil.

Distribution (fig. X.37). Western Brazil south of the Rio Amazonas (Solimões) between the Rios Juruá and Purús, State of Amazonas.

Taxonomy. The detailed description of *pileatus* published in 1855 is somewhat misleading with respect to coloration of back. The hairs, according to I. Geoffroy are "ainsi qu'on l'observe si souvent chez les Hapaliens . . . roux dans la plus grande partie de leur étendue, annelée de blanchâtre et de noir vers la pointe." As shown by Goeldi (1907, p. 98), who examined the type, I. Geoffroy's choice of the adjective *roux* was poor. In members of the *mystax* group, the hairs of the back are dark brown or blackish, banded buffy subterminally and becoming paler basally, to whitish or drab on the mantle and lateral fringe.

Midas pileatus juruanus Ihering based on three specimens was distinguished from *pileatus* I. Geoffroy by the dark, not "reddish," bases of the hairs of the back. Only the misleading published description of *pileatus* was used for reference. The color of *juruanus* is quite like that of specimens at hand from Lago Tefé, the restricted type locality of *pileatus.*

Diagnostic Characters. Forehead and crown rusty red, tail black; mustache moderately developed; inguinal hairs blackish, phallic hairs whitish.

Coloration. Forehead and crown with broad posteriorly bifurcated reddish orange cap, the color extending forward as a thin line between orbits; superciliary region, cheeks, temples, and interorbital space black; hairs of midline of muzzle forming a low crest, black anteriorly, reddish posteriorly, the color continuous with that of mid-frontal region; skin of circumnarial and circumbuccal areas except at symphysis unpigmented and covered with comparatively long white hairs forming whiskers, remainder of facial skin more or less pigmented and covered with black hair; mantle blackish brown with fine buffy or orange ticking, the basal one-fourth to one-half of the hairs drab to brownish black along midline, paler to white laterally, the pale color showing through at the surface; middle and lower back including rump mixed blackish brown and buffy, the hairs uniformly brown except for buffy subterminal band (i.e., modified agouti); dark brown hairs of lateral fringe faintly or not at all banded subterminally, pale brown, drab, or white basally; outer sides of fore- and hind limbs brown becoming blackish on upper surface of hands and feet; ventral surface from middle of lower lip to belly and inner sides of limbs, blackish brown; tail black, except root like rump; external genitalia mostly or entirely unpigmented and sparsely covered with scattered white hairs.

Measurements. See appendix table 2.

Comparisons. Distinguished from all callitrichids by the sharply defined rusty-red cap extending from ear to ear, over forehead and bifurcating posteriorly, black temples and cheeks, and dark brown underparts except for whitish pudendal hairs.

Remarks. The white of the perineal region in specimens at hand does not extend to the inner side of the thighs as described for the type by I. Geoffroy.

Saguinus mystax pileatus is sympatric with *S. fuscicollis avilapiresi* in the northern part of the range and with no other known species of tamarin.

The color pattern of the head of *pileatus* is inversely similar to that of *Saguinus nigricollis.* In the first species, the temporal region is black, crown and forehead bleached red. In the second, the forehead and crown remain black while the temporal region of each side is bleached brown.

Specimens Examined. 8 BRAZIL—*Amazonas:* Lago de Tefé, mouth, 3 (AMNH); Tefé, 3 (BM); Rio Juruá, type of *juruana* (BM); "Rio Javary," type of *pileatus* (MNHN).

SAGUINUS MYSTAX PLUTO LÖNNBERG, WHITE-RUMP MOUSTACHED TAMARIN

Synonymic History

Mystax pluto Lönnberg, 1926, *Ark. Zool., Stockholm* 18B (9):1. Lönnberg, 1940, *Ark Zool., Stockholm* 32A (10):7—BRAZIL: *Amazonas* (Jaburú, west side Rio Purús).

Tamarin pluto, Cruz Lima, 1945, *Mamíferos da Amazonia, Primates,* p. 238—characters.

Marikina pluto, Hershkovitz, 1949, *Proc. U.S. Nat. Mus.* 98:413—key characters; classification.

Tamarinus pluto, Osman Hill, 1957, *Primates* 3:218, 221, 232—characters; distribution.

Saguinus mystax pluto, Hershkovitz, 1968, *Evolution* 22(3):563, fig. 7 (diagnostic color pattern)—characters; distribution; metachromism; hypertrichy. Hershkovitz, 1970, *Am. J. Phys. Anthrop.* 32:379—dental disease.

Type. Male, skin and skull, Stockholm Natural History Museum; collected 18 October 1925 by C. Lako. A skin and skull labeled type in the British Museum (Natural History) no. 27.8.11.3 is a topotype; it was collected 21 March 1927 by Wilhelm Ehrhardt.

Type Locality. Ayapuá (184) but probably opposite Ayapuá, on the right bank of the Rio Purús, Amazonas, Brazil.

Distribution (fig. X.37). Western Brazil, south of the Rio Amazonas (Solimões) on right bank of the lower Rio Purús; the range probably incorporates the entire basin between the Rios Purús and Madeira from their mouths at the Solimões to at least 6° possibly 8° or farther south. Specimens, including the type, reported from localities on the left bank of the Purús are regarded as having originated on the opposite bank.

Diagnostic Characters. Crown and tail black, mustache moderately developed; basal portion of mantle hairs drab; hairs of perineum and ventral base of tail whitish.

Coloration. Head black, skin of circumnarial and circumbuccal areas except at symphysis unpigmented and covered with white hairs forming prominent whiskers, remainder of face covered with black hairs; mantle black and ticked with buffy, basal portions of hairs drab, sometimes whitish; arms black, rump and outer sides of thighs like mantle but with a more even mixture or vermiculation of blackish and buff, the individual hairs black except for pale subterminal banding; lateral fringe like back but hairs drab to grayish basally; upper surface of hands and feet black; underparts from midline of lower lips to anterior part of belly and inner sides of limbs black to blackish brown; lower belly, inguinal region, and circumanal region whitish; tail black except base like rump above, white below; external genitalia hardly or not pigmented and sparsely covered with white hairs.

Measurements. See appendix table 2.

Comparisons. The whitish genital and circumanal region and underside of tail at root distinguish *pluto* from all other members of the *mystax* group; the black, not reddish, crown further separates *pluto* from *pileatus* its nearest geographic ally; the pink or unpigmented circumbuccal and circumnarial band of skin, whitish perineal region and larger size separate *pluto* from all members of the *Saguinus nigricollis* group, particularly *S. fuscicollis avilapiresi,* which it most nearly resembles in general coloration.

Variation. The axillary hairs, normally black, are whitish in one specimen from opposite Lago do Mapixi (185). The nasal septum, usually unpigmented, is pigmented in a specimen from opposite Ayapuá. The median narial borders, however, are unpigmented as in the species.

Remarks. The type locality Ayapuá is on the left bank of the Rio Purús, Jaburú (186), from which Lönnberg later recorded additional specimens, is also on the left or "western" side of the Purús. Our specimens from Lago do Mapixi are labeled by Mr. Lako, the collector, "eastern of Rio Purús." The lake is on the right bank opposite the settlement of Mapixi. Judging by specimens at hand, *pluto* is restricted to the eastern banks of the Purús, where it is sympatric with *S. labiatus* and in the south with *Saguinus fuscicollis weddelli* as well. The western bank of the Purús is occupied by *S. mystax pileatus* and the remarkably similar-appearing but smaller *S. fuscicollis avilapiresi.*

Specimens Examined. 13. BRAZIL—*Amazonas:* Ayapuá, 10 (BM, 8; SMNH, 2); Lago Mapixi, 3 (AMNH, 1; FMNH, 2).

Plate VI. Emperor Moustached Tamarin (*Saguinus imperator*).
Plate courtesy of the Cologne Zoo.

67 *Saguinus imperator* Goeldi, Emperor Moustached Tamarin

Synonymic History

Midas imperator Goeldi, 1907, *Proc. Zool. Soc. London* 1907:93, fig. 23 (head)—BRAZIL: *Amazonas* (Rio Acre; Rio Purús).

Leontocebus imperator, Elliot, 1913, *A review of the Primates* 1:209—characters. Mallinson, 1965, *Int. Zoo Yearbk.* 5:138—tongue display and vocalization; aggressiveness.

Leontocebus (*Tamarin*) *imperator,* Harms, 1956, *Primatologia* 1:563, fig. 2 (head)—secondary sexual characters.

Mystax imperator, Crandall, 1951, *Animal Kingdom* 54(6):179, 2 figs. p. 182 (animal)—form of mustache.

Tamarinus imperator, Osman Hill, 1957, *Primates* 3:105, 168, 185, 212–14, 216, 222, 232, 237, 240, 321, fig. 51 (hand and feet dermatoglyphs) pl. 13 (animal)—characters; habits; distribution; behavior; taxonomy; comparisons. Epple and Lorenz, 1967, *Folia Primat.* 7:98—sternal gland (form; function).

Saguinus imperator, Hershkovitz, 1966, *Evolution* 22(3):563, fig. 7 (diagnostic color pattern)—characters; distribution; metachromism; hypertrichy. Hershkovitz, 1970, *Am. J. Phys. Anthrop.* 32:379—dental disease. Hershkovitz, 1970, *Folia Primat.* 13:215, fig. 3 (cerebral endocast)—BRAZIL: *Amazonas* (Santo Antônio, Rio Eirú). Mallinson, 1971, *Sixth Ann. Rep. Jersey Wildl. Preserv. Trust,* pp. 5, 9, fig. 10, 12 (animal)—longevity in Jersey Zoo, 8 yr., 6 mo., 21 days, still living.

Tamarin imperator imperator, Cruz Lima, 1945, *Mamíferos da Amazonia, Primates, Contrib. Mus. Paraense,* p. 222, pl. 37, fig. 1 (animal)—BRAZIL: *Amazonas* (Rio Acre, alto Purús); BOLIVIA: *Pando* (Cobija).

T[amarinus] i[mperator] imperator, Osman Hill, 1957, *Primates* 3:23—characters; distribution.

Marikina imperator imperator, Hershkovitz, 1949, *Proc. U.S. Nat. Mus.* 98:412—key characters; classification.

Leontocebus imperator imperator, Cabrera, 1958, *Rev. Mus. Argentino Cienc. Nat. "Bernardino Rivadavia"* 4 (1):192—BRAZIL: *Acre* (Rio Acre, type locality restricted).

Saguinus imperator imperator, Ceballos, 1965, *Rev. Universitaria, Cuzco* (*1916*) 50(120):296—PERU: *Madre de Dios* (Boca Quebrada Juárez, Río Manú); characters.

Mystax imperator subgrisescens Lönnberg, 1940, *Ark. Zool., Stockholm* 32A(10):9—BRAZIL: *Amazonas* (type locality, Santo Antônio, Rio Eirú, upper Rio Juruá); four cotypes, (2 males, 2 females), Stockholm Museum, collected September 1936 by A. M. Olalla.

Tamarin imperator subgrisescens, Cruz Lima, 1945, *Mamíferos da Amazonia, Primates,* p. 224—characters ex Lönnberg. Vieira, 1948, *Bol. Mus. Paraense* 10:252—BRAZIL: *Amazonas* (Rio Juruá; Santo Antônio; Santa Cruz, Rio Eirú).

Marikina imperator subgrisescens, Hershkovitz, 1949, *Proc. U.S. Nat. Mus.* 98:412—key characters; classification.

Leontocebus imperator subgrisescens, Carvalho, 1957, *Bol. Mus. Paraense Emilio Goeldi, n. s., Zool.,* no. 6, p. 6—BRAZIL: *Acre* (Pedra Preta, upper Rio Juruá; Seringal Oriente, upper Rio Juruá).

T[amarinus] i[mperator] subgrisescens, Osman Hill, 1957, *Primates* 3:222, 239—characters; distribution.

T[amarin] mystax ♂ × *T[amarin] imperator* ♀, Cruz Lima, 1945, *Mamíferos da Amazonia. 1. Primates,* p. 209 —♂ probable mate in fertile crossbreeding; twin fetuses.

T[amarinus] imperator ♀ × *T[amarinus] mystax* ♂, Osman Hill, 1957, *Primates* 3:185—cited ex Cruz Lima, 1945.

Leontocebus imperator ♀ × *L[eontocebus] mystax* ♂, Osman Hill, 1961, *Proc. Zool. Soc. London* 137(2):321 —cited ex Cruz Lima, 1945.

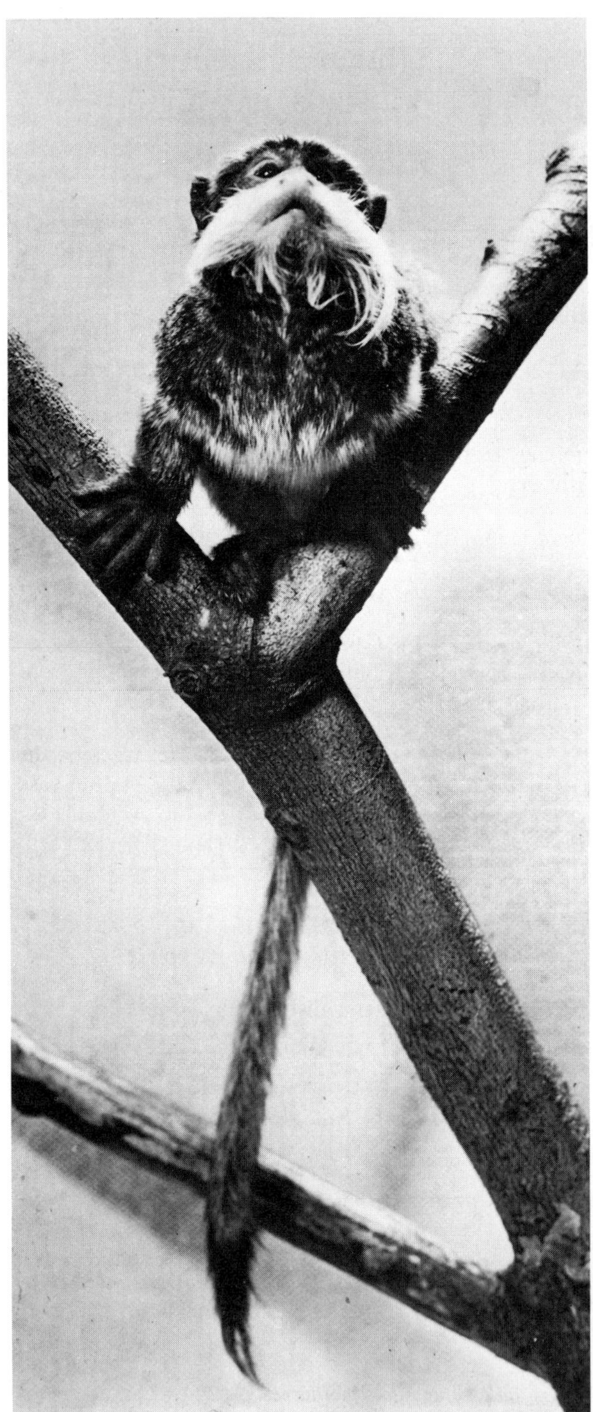

Fig. X.44. Emperor Tamarin, *Saguinus imperator.* (Photo courtesy of New York Zoological Society.)

Types. Five cotypes, as follows: ♂ ♀ and juvenal from Rio Purús in Pará Museum; juvenal ♂ from Rio Acre (190), in Berne Museum; juvenal ♀ from Rio Acre in British Museum; lectotype, selected by Carvalho (1959, *Rev. Brasil. Biol.* 19(4):459), adult female, mounted in Museu Goeldi, no. 914, collected April-May, 1904 by J. de Sá.

Type Locality. Upper Rio Purús "two [cotypes] from the Rio Acre and three from the upper Rio Purús"; lectotype (see above) from the upper Rio Purús, probably from Bom Lugar (189) on the right bank or perhaps from Monte Verde (191) on the left bank (Carvalho, supra cit., p. 460). This restriction, based on a selected lectotype takes precedence over Cabrera's earlier restriction of the locality to the Rio Acre whence only two juvenals were collected and distributed as duplicates, one each to the British and Berne museums.

Distribution (fig. X.37). Extreme southeastern Peru, northwestern Bolivia and southwestern Brazil; from the Department of Madre de Dios and the Río Urubamba in Loreto, Peru, southeast into Pando, Bolivia (Río Madre de Dios) and northeast into Brazil in Acre and the upper Rio Juruá and upper Rio Purús basins of southwestern Amazonas.

Taxonomy. According to Goeldi (1907, p. 96) the underparts of the 5 cotypes of *imperator* are in "marked contrast with that of the dorsal aspect, by having a pronounced tendency towards a rusty red, especially in the younger specimens. This rusty-red shade covers the whole under side, from the throat backward including the inner side of the arms and legs and no small extent of the underside of the tail. The same colour tends to form regions or patches of a deeper shade, one between the arms, covering the chest, and another between the legs, covering the abdomen and surrounding the anus. The chest-patch, especially in the old female, looks as if soiled by dried blood." Elliot (1913, p. 209) found the underparts of the young cotype in the British Museum with "throat black and gray . . . breast, lower part of belly pale vinaceous, cinnamon." The underparts of the three mounted cotypes in the Pará Museum were described by Cruz Lima as "throat and chest with black and white hairs. Lower chest, belly and inner side of the thighs varying from light yellowish to ferruginous, the young in general lighter at these places. In some examples one sees wine-colored patches in the middle of the chest or of the belly."

The underparts of *Mystax imperator subgrisescens* Lönnberg are "dark brown to blackish with long whitish tips, so that the general appearance becomes grizzled grey (instead of 'rusty red' as in the typical form)." Lönnberg's characterization is based on four specimens from Santo Antônio (180), upper Rio Juruá, and the published description of Goeldi's *imperator.* Three topotypes of *grisescens* of the original collector's series are at hand. They agree with Lönnberg's description and grade into our slightly grayer and paler specimens from the base of the Peruvian Andes in the Upper Ríos Madre de Dios and Ucayali basins. From this it appears that the difference between the named forms and other populations of the species are not of taxonomic grade but, rather of a local if not clinal nature.

Diagnostic Characters. Mustache extraordinarily elongate, extending well beyond ears when laid back; crown silvery brown, tail dominantly reddish orange, genital, inguinal, and circumanal hairs reddish orange (fig. X.44).

Coloration. Head glossy brown with forehead and sides of face darker than crown; pelage of crown close-cropped, its silvery brown sheen appearing sometimes as a silvery whitish patch; skin of circumnarial and circumbuccal areas except symphysis forming a continuous unpigmented band covered with white hairs; mustache of upper lip 4–7 cm long and usually curling backward and downward, never backward, downward and upward in handlebar form; chin whiskers 2–4 cm long and directed downward and back; mantle brown ticked with orange (i.e., orange agouti), back like mantle but more coarsely mixed orange and dark brown, the terminal halves of hairs brown ringed with two or three orange bands, basal portions becoming drab to white at roots; lateral fringe like back but base of hairs paler; outer sides of fore- and hind legs like sides but hairs of outer edge of forearm broadly tipped silvery buff and crested; rump reddish orange; upper surface of hands and feet black interspersed with golden hairs; inner side of limbs mixed brown, orange, buffy, or silvery; symphysis and throat brown washed with silvery buff, the hairs of interramia and throat cresting in midline; chest and belly, brown, reddish, or orange with or without a mixture of silvery gray or buff; external genitalia mostly or entirely unpigmented; genital, inguinal, and circumanal hairs reddish orange; tail either black above, orange beneath with terminal portion entirely black, or tail dominantly reddish orange throughout with base like rump and basal portions of hairs and terminal tuft blackish.

Vibrissae. Supraorbitals, mystacials, rhinarials, mentals, and backwardly directed interramals present, genals not detected in dry skins; ulnar carpals not detected; gulars present.

Measurements. See appendix table 2.

Comparisons. The extremely long mustache extending to shoulders when laid back is unique among nonhuman primates, and complete fusion of the depigmented circumbuccal and circumnarial areas is unique among callitrichids. The mainly agouti-colored body with dominantly reddish orange tail also distinguishes *imperator* from all other members of the *mystax* group.

Remarks. Saguinus imperator is distinguished cranially from other members of the *mystax* group by more rounded or domed frontal profile, greater convergence of temporal ridges and small, usually less than 1 mm diameter, size of malar foramina.

Fig. X.45. Emperor Tamarin, *Saguinus imperator,* reproduced from Goeldi (1907). The figure is of an adult male cotype mounted in the Goeldi Museum, Pará, Brazil. The handlebar form of the moustache is an artifact of the taxidermist.

It is more specialized than other members of the group in the extent of facial depigmentation, length of mustache and whiskers, and in grade of bleaching of rump and tail. On the other hand, the dominantly agouti-colored pattern of the body of *imperator* is primitive. Origin and evolution of external characters are discussed in greater detail above (p. 684).

The old male cotype in the Goeldi Museum depicted by Goeldi (1907, p. 94, fig. 23) shows the mustache in the form of handlebars with an elegant upward swing. Goeldi believed that the mustache was better developed in males than in females, and he stated (1907, p. 95) that the collectors informed him that "the moustache is worn in life not straight, but with the modern upward twist." As already indicated by Cruz Lima (1945, p. 223) this is an artifact. The mustache of the specimen mounted in the Goeldi Museum and one sent to the London Museum were waxed to hold the anthropomorphic form (fig. X.45). In life, the mustache droops, usually with an inward curve on each side. Sexual dimorphism with respect to the mustache, or hair and color patterns in general, is not evident in present material.

Specimens Examined. 29. BRAZIL—*Acre:* Rio Acre, syntype of *imperator* (BM); *Amazonas:* Santo Antônio, Rio Eirú, 3 (FMNH); PERU—*Madre de Dios:* Altamira, Río Manú, 2 (FMNH); Zona Boca Amigo, 3 (FMNH); *Loreto:* Río Inuya, mouth, Río Urubamba, 2 (AMNH); Río Tambo, Río Alto Ucayali, 2 (AMNH); Río Ucayali, 1 (AMNH); Río Urubamba, mouth 15 (AMNH).

68 *Saguinus mystax* Group
2. Biology of Moustached Tamarins

The meager information presented here on the biology of members of the *Saguinus mystax* group is based entirely on observations of captive animals. The data are organized under the following headings:

Reproduction	Dominance and Aggression
Hybridization	Food
Weight	Odor
Longevity	Tonguing and Vocalization

Reproduction

J. K. Hampton, Jr., Hampton, and Levy 1971, p. 528

Two full-term pregnancies are recorded for *Saguinus mystax*. One terminated in birth of a male, the other in heterosexual twins. Birth dates or estimate of the duration of gestation were not given.

Wolfe, Deinhardt, Ogden, Adams, and Fisher (1975, p. 805)

"We learned from [D.] Lorenz that 6 of 7 pairs [*Saguinus mystax mystax*] in that laboratory [Bureau of Biologics, Federal Department of Agriculture, Bethesda, Maryland], housed in an environment not designed as a breeding colony, have reproduced. They averaged about 1 live birth per pair per yr over a 3-yr period, suggesting that under more ideal conditions, the reproductive performance of *S mystax* might be as good or better than some of the other [callitrichids]."

Hybridization

Hybridization between a female *imperator* and a male *mystax* is recorded as follows by Cruz Lima (1945, p. 209). "In a large cage there lived for many months a female *T. imperator* together with small monkeys, such as those of *Saimiri* and *Callithrix* and an adult male *T. mystax*. An attendant carelessly allowed the female *T. imperator* to escape from the cage one day and, on being chased, as it leaped from branch to branch, it fell from a great height and died as a consequence of the fall. As it was being prepared, two fetuses in an advanced state of development were found. As this monkey had lived for more than a year in captivity in the zoological garden, the possibility of a previous fecundation is removed. Pregnancy could have been brought only by a specimen of a different species, probably the *mystax* which was its prison companion."

Weight

Cooper 1969 (unpublished report)

Mean weights recorded of adult wild-born *Saguinus mystax* maintained in the San Diego Primate Colony are:

5 ♂♂	639 g
5 ♀♀	633 g

Longevity

A live emperor tamarin in the Jersey Zoo was 8 years, 6 months, and 21 days old at the end of 1969 and still living, according to Mallinson (1971, p. 9). An individual in the New York Zoo, recorded by Crandall (1964, p. 115), lived 7 years, 9 days.

Dominance and Aggression

Managers of laboratory colonies of callitrichids are in agreement that *Saguinus mystax mystax* is too aggressive toward the other tamarins and marmosets and must be kept in separate quarters.

In a mixed group of callitrichids kept in the Jersey Zoo, an old male *Saguinus imperator,* according to Mallinson (1965, p. 138), dominated all the others irrespective of species.

Food

Mallinson 1971, p. 6

White mice added to the diet of the considerable number of callitrichids in the Jersey Zoo were "taken readily by all but the male Emperor Tamarin, *Leontocebus imperator,* which has been in the collection for eight and a half years."

Odor

Benirschke and Richart (1963, p. 75) note that the vulvar odor in *Saguinus mystax mystax* is stronger than in *Callithrix jacchus, Saguinus nigricollis, S. oedipus oedipus,* and *Leontopithecus rosalia.*

Tonguing and Vocalization

Mallinson 1965, p. 138

The Emperor Tamarin in the Jersey Zoo displays recognition of people by vibrating its tongue up and down in a widely opened mouth. The movement "is sometimes accompanied by rapid and continuous vocalization."

Epple 1967*b*, p. 51

A male *Saguinus imperator* tongued at the approach of a sexually interested female. The same ♂ displayed to the ♀ and people known to him, by emitting short, loud, high-pitched calls with mouth open wide while standing on all fours, or erect on his hind legs. At the same time his tongue moved back and forth and up and down, but without being protruded. The head shook to the same rhythm. Loud calling and head shaking were also performed without tonguing.

Remarks. Two distinct uses of the tongue are mentioned here. The rapid protrusion and retraction of the tongue in a sort of lapping movement is used in recognition, or when excited as during copulation. Vibration of the tongue up and down during vocalization produces the trill.

69 *Saguinus Midas* Group, Midas Tamarins. *Saguinus Midas* Linnaeus
1. Characters, History, Evolution, and Subspecies

Distribution (figs. X.1, 2, 46)

Guyana, Suriname, French Guiana, and in Brazil from the north bank of the Rio Amazonas and the left bank of the Rio Negro in the state of Amazonas east to the coast, and in the state of Pará south of the Amazonas, between the Rios Xingu and Gurupi; recorded from the Ilha de Marajó at the mouth of the Amazonas.

Saguinus midas is the only callitrichid in Guyana, French Guiana, Suriname and, in Brazil, the states of Amapá and Rio Branco, north of the Amazonas, and northeastern Pará, and most of Maranhão south of the Amazonas. It occurs in Pará north of the Amazonas including the region between the Rios Erepecurú and Nhamundá inhabited by the bare-face tamarin, *Saguinus bicolor*. There is no information, however, that the two species actually live in the same localities.

Problems of disjunct distribution were noted in Suri-

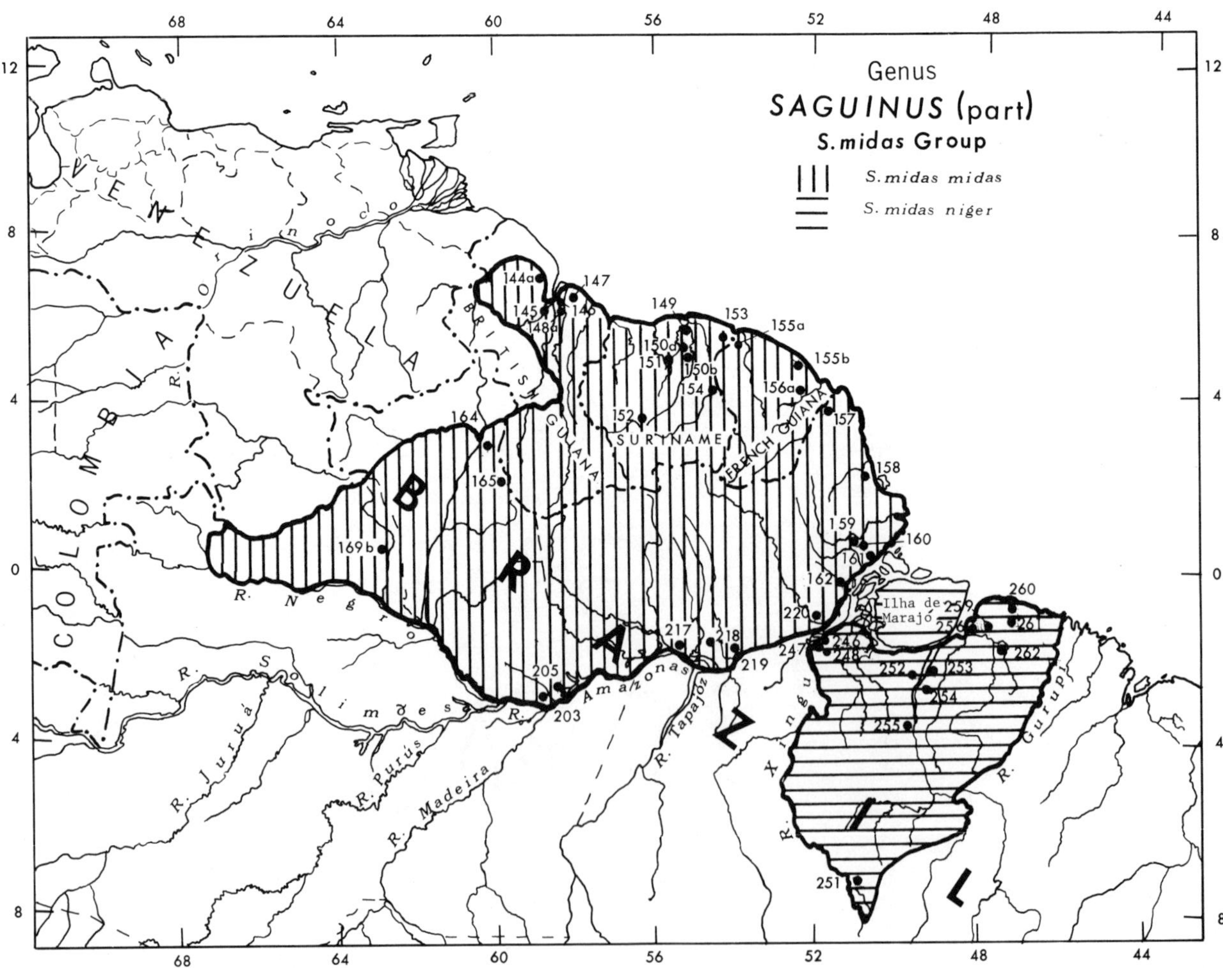

Fig. X.46. Distribution of midas tamarins of the *Saguinus midas* group: *S. midas midas* (*vertical bars*) and *S. m. niger* (*horizontal bars*); numbered dots are the locality records (see gazetteer, p. 918, for key to numbers).

name. The golden-handed tamarin was found in suitable habitats everywhere I traveled except in the La Poule and Dirkshoep regions on the coast (fig. 46 and gazetteer). Both localities are on the south or left bank of the Saramacca River between 30 and 40 kilometers SWW of Paramaribo. La Poule is the seat of a government agricultural station and citrus fruit orchard. A variety of cebids are common here and *Saimiri* was especially abundant in second growth and cultivated fields.

Dirkshoep is the center of another government citrus fruit farm a few kilometers west of La Poule. It is bounded by long-established and extensive swamp forests with a representative cebid fauna, but no callitrichids. Residents of the area unanimously affirmed that callitrichids were absent but abounded on the opposite side of the Saramacca along the coast. This distribution was inexplicable. I had taken tamarins at Loksie Hattie, about 70 km, measured in a straight line, higher up the Saramacca on the same side as La Poule and Dirkshoep. There are no visible geographic, ecological, or social barriers to a continuous distribution of tamarins between these points. Perhaps a catastrophe, possibly disease, exterminated the tamarins in an area of hundreds of square miles between the lower Saramacca and lower Coesewijne Rivers.

Origin, Evolution, and Dispersal (fig. X.2)

Saguinus midas may be derived from the same stock that later gave rise to, or evolved into, the *S. nigricollis* group. The ancestral face was necessarily black and hairy, the body pelage dominantly agouti. This ancestral form may have been distributed throughout the upper and middle Amazonian region but was present at least on the southern banks of the middle Rio Amazonas before giving rise to *Saguinus midas*.

The original breeding colony or troop of the *Saguinus midas* prototype must have become separated from the south bank of the Rio Amazonas by rafting or as the result of a river cutoff or shift in channel. In the isolated environment, forequarters, hind limbs and tail of the inbreeding *midas* prototype became blackish, hands and feet may have remained agouti. The face retained the primitive blackish pigment but tactile vibrissae degenerated while the ears expanded.

After establishment of an insular prototype of *Saguinus midas* as defined, representatives of it could have been carried downstream to the southern shore of the Amazon east of the Rio Xingu while others were shunted to the northern or Guianan shore east of the Rio Negro.

The south bank colonizers spread to and around both sides of the Rio Tocantins. This branch of the species, now differentiated as the black-handed *Saguinus midas niger,* may be nearer the parental stock in color but probably differs by greater enlargement of ears and degeneration of vibrissae. Differences between populations on right and left banks of the Tocantins are slight.

North bank colonizers, now the nominate form of the species, are even larger eared but their vibrissae are less reduced. Most striking divergence from the hypothetical insular parental stock is the saturation of hands and feet to reddish followed by bleaching to golden. Hands may have become reddish first. Cabrera (1917, p. 30) records a *midas* with golden hands and brownish feet supposedly from Pernambuco, where tamarins do not occur naturally. Whatever the real habitat of this individual, its color pattern is significant.

The color of the cheiridia dictates the proffered hypothesis of racial differentiation. The pheomelanic or eumelanic cheiridia can be derived directly from the primitive agouti colored cheiridia (cf. fig. III.14) and either of the saturate patterns can switch to the other. Furthermore, presence of callitrichids on the Ilha de Marajó (fig. X.46) discounts the probability of one race arising from a stock of the other. It remains to be determined if tamarins with agouti cheiridia still persist on any of the innumerable islands of the lower Amazon.

Diagnostic Characters

Skin of face, including rhinarium, ears, and external genitalia blackish; ears nearly naked and fully exposed; hairs of forequarters, thighs, and tail blackish; face of adult sparsely haired and without contrastingly colored whitish circumbuccal band; middle and lower back marbled, striated, or vermiculated buffy to orange or reddish and well defined from blackish mantle.

External Characters (fig. X.47)

Integument. Facial skin including lips and narial region black; muzzle and circumbuccal area nearly naked,

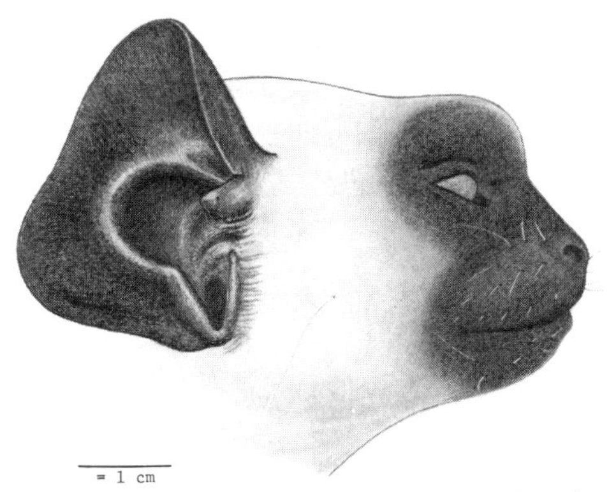

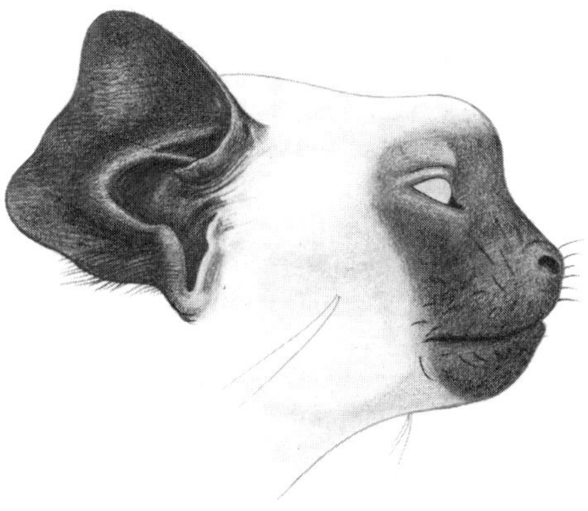

Fig. X.47. *Saguinus midas*: Profile with mane removed to expose ear, vibrissae and facial pigmentation: Upper figure of *S. m. niger;* lower of *S. m. midas.*

minute hairs surrounding mouth black, buffy, or whitish, without defining circumbuccal band in adults, but moderately well-developed and defining whiskers or spotted pattern in juvenals; short hairs of dorsal surface of muzzle black and directed backward without feathering or cresting in midline; forehead and crown uniformly black in adults but a grayish transverse supraorbital band usually present in juvenals; back from nape to rump bizonal or weakly trizonal with uniformly blackish mantle well defined from marbled or striated saddle; rump including base of tail and buttocks like saddle or slightly darker, legs like buttocks or darker to entirely black; arms uniformly blackish; upper surface of hands and feet black or yellowish, orange or reddish; sides of body like back; underparts blackish or dark brown; hairs of throat directed backward with or without cresting in midline; tail uniformly black except base like rump; skin of external genitalia mostly or entirely pigmented.

Vibrissae (figs. III.12; X.47). Supraorbitals undifferentiated, mystacials and mentals present, poorly developed, and mostly unpigmented in *S. m. niger,* rhinarials not always well developed, interramals absent, genals usually indistinguishable (single white vibrissa detected on right side of cheek in one skin of *niger*); ulnar carpals usually indistinguishable in dry skin; gular spines present or absent, pectorals absent, or present as whitish hairs in *midas*.

Ears. See chapter 12, and figs. III.18; X.47.

Tongue. See chap. 13, and figs. III.19, 20; X.5.

Young (fig. X.50). Pelage and color pattern of juvenals are as in adults except face more hairy, side whiskers (mutton chops) buffy to whitish, pale transverse frontal band or blaze present, black mantle with greater admixture of agouti hairs. Transition from juvenal to entirely black adult facial pattern is marked by an irregular pattern of whitish spots on forehead and whiskers.

External Genitalia

Male (fig. X.4)

Adult. External genitalia pigmented; distal half of exposed surface of penial shaft corrugated, proximal half with annular wrinkles; glans as usual with left or bacular lobe dome shaped, larger and more projecting than right; scrotum in the available specimen ovate, longer than wide and pendulous with left testis hanging lower than right; skin of scrotal fold papillate, each papilla with a long stiff hair; outer surface of preputial fold like scrotal fold, inner or reduplicated surface of preputial fold loosely multifolded, wrinkled, and glabrous; greatest diameter (sagittal) of scrotum 17 mm.

Remarks. The fluid-preserved external genitalia described above were removed from an individual shot in the field and prepared as a museum study skin. The pubic sexual skin in dry specimens is pigmented, well developed, and distinctly glandular. The penis of *"Tamarin tamarin"* figured by Osman Hill (1957, p. 199, fig. 39) is the same he labeled *Tamarin midas* (1958, p. 643, fig. 11 A) in his article on primate genitalia. The view of the penis, said to be from the "perineal aspect," is almost certainly from the right side and so distorted as to produce the illusion of a symmetrically cleft glans.

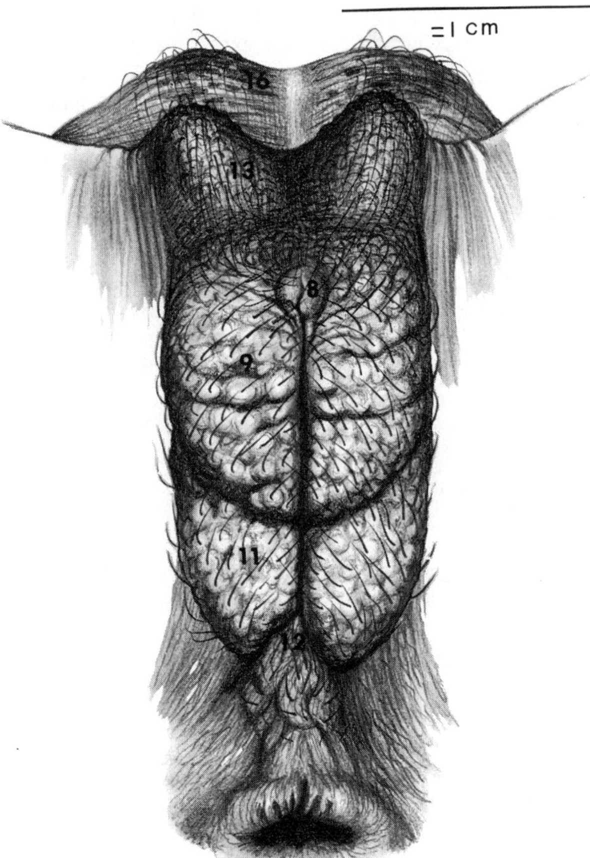

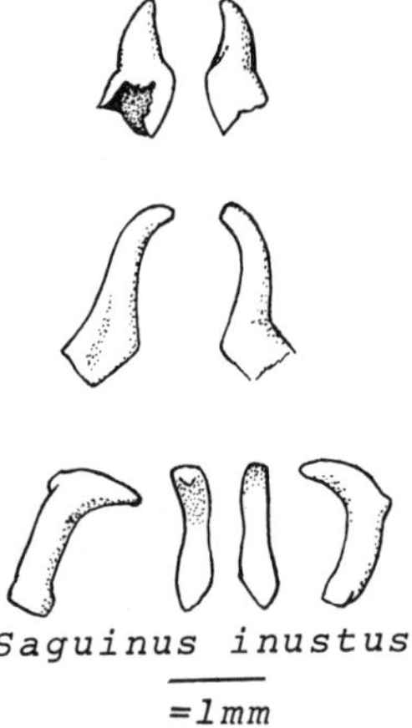

Fig. X.48. Genitalia: Upper figure, external genitalia of female *Saguinus midas midas;* lower figure, three bacula of *Saguinus inustus,* two aspects of two bones and four of one.

Female (fig. X.48)

Adult. External genitalia in one spirit-preserved specimen of *Saguinus midas midas* mottled; tumescent labia majora twice as long as wide, skin papillate, each papilla with a long, stiff black hair; scrotal fold, or cushion, of each side smaller than preputial fold and demarcated from it by a deep sulcus; tumescent mons elevated into a pair of pads; sides of glans clitoridis fused with inner surface of annulus of preputial folds; sexual skin mottled, thinly haired, and raised into a pair of longitudinally swollen folds; length of labia majora 18 mm, of genital fissure 12 mm; perineal and anal regions lightly pigmented.

External genitalia in one spirited-preserved specimen of *S. m. niger* excessively dried and distorted but otherwise apparently similar to those of *midas,* except labia majora wider than long and entirely pigmented blackish, mons more tumescent, elevated, and nearly as large as scrotal fold, perineal and anal regions more deeply pigmented, sexual skin entirely pigmented with lateral longitudinal ridges more sharply defined, median valley deeper; ischial prominences nearly as pronounced as in *Saguinus mystax* (cf. fig. I.15); labia majora 12 mm long x 17 mm wide.

The differences noted between the genitalia of *niger* and *midas* are partly, perhaps mostly, results of dessication and shrinkage of the former. Nevertheless, the differences may be well within the expected range of variation in undistorted specimens.

Cranial Characters (figs. X.7, 9, 11)

Frontal contour nearly flat to moderately rounded; temporal ridges markedly convergent along frontoparietal suture but separated and more or less parallel sided on parietal; a low independent sagittal crest sometimes present; nasal profile plane to notably concave; frontal sinuses well inflated; malar foramen from 1 to 2 mm in greatest diameter but usually less than 1 mm; lacrymal bone often extending quite to rim of orbit and sometimes slightly beyond; ventral border of mandible more nearly U- than V-shaped, the horizontal rami notably arced, the angular process inflected inward with slight to moderate deflection downward.

Comparisons

Distinguished from other hairy-face tamarins, including all members of the *Saguinus nigricollis* and *S. mystax* groups by nearly naked, fully pigmented muzzle and absence of grayish circumbuccal band or whitish whiskers in adults; from bare-face tamarins by long, black hair of forehead, sides of head, and upper throat, arms uniformly blackish and black mantle well defined from marbled or striated middle and lower back; differs from remotely related but comparably blackish *Callimico goeldii* by pelage of head and neck directed straight back and adpressed, not whorled or forming mane, and by marked color contrast between mantle and middle back.

Saturation, Bleaching, Depilation, and Depigmentation

Saguinus midas is at once the most saturate and bare faced of the hairy-face tamarin group. Its face from orbits to chin and interramia is sparsely set with short, fine black hairs in addition to the extremely reduced or degenerate vibrissae. In some individuals the face is nearly as bare as that of true bare-face tamarins. Forehead and sides of head, however, are as well covered with body hairs as they are in hairy-face members of the *S. nigricollis* group. Juvenals are more primitive in retaining the genal whiskers but more advanced in presenting whitish circumbuccal hairs and a whitish supraorbital band.

Bleaching of the dominantly blackish *S. midas* proceeds in some individuals to brown, chestnut, and, rarely, reddish black (fide Cabrera 1900, pp. 89–90) on all parts of the body except the saddle. In most specimens, however, the terminally blackish hairs usually become paler, to drab basally.

Depigmentation of face, ears, and volar surfaces is not evident in present material. However, face and ears of *Edward's little black monkey,* the type of the species, are described and depicted as flesh-colored. The face of Buffon's *le tamarin* is also said to be flesh-colored (cf. infra, p. 713). Both animals were household pets.

The most striking feature of the pelage is the reduction or degeneration of the tactile vibrissae.

Key to the Subspecies of *Saguinus Midas*

No white or grayish band encircling mouth; head, mantle, chest, belly, and tail black.

1. Upper surface of hands and feet black, like arms . . . . *Saguinus midas niger*

1′. Upper surface of hands and feet yellow, orange, or reddish, sharply contrasted with black forearms . . . . *Saguinus midas midas*

SAGUINUS MIDAS MIDAS LINNAEUS, GOLDEN-HANDED TAMARIN

= 1 cm

Fig. X.49. Golden-handed Tamarin, *Saguinus midas midas*

Synonymic History

Little black monkey, Edwards, 1751, *A natural history of birds,* pt. 4, p. 196, pl. 196 (animal).

Tamarin Buffon, 1767, *Hist. Nat.* 15:92, pl. 13 (animal)—FRENCH GUIANA: (Cayenne).

Tamarin nègre Buffon, 1789, *Hist. Nat., Suppl.* 7:116, pl. 32—FRENCH GUIANA: (Cayenne). Audebert, 1797, *Histoire naturelle des singes et makis, Paris,* fam. 6, sec. 2, pl. 5, and text p. 7—FRENCH GUIANA.

Tamarin aux mains rousses, F. Cuvier, 1826, in Geoffroy and Cuvier, *Hist. Nat. Mamm.,* livr. 54 (vol. 5, 1824), pl. and text.

[*Simia*] *Midas* Linnaeus, 1758, *Syst. Nat.,* ed. 10, p. 28. Linnaeus, 1766, *Syst. Nat.,* ed. 12, p. 42. Schreber, 1775, *Säugthiere* 1:132, pl. 37 (animal ex Edwards)—SURINAME: (type locality). Shaw, 1800, *Gen. Zool.* 1, (1):65, pl. 26 (*great eared monkey,* ex Edwards).

Simia Midas, Audebert, 1797, *Histoire naturelle des singes et makis, Paris,* fam. 6, sec. 2, pl. 5 (animal) and text p. 7—FR. GUIANA; characters; *le tamarin* of Buffon a synonym.

S[*imia*] *Sagoinus midas,* Kerr, 1792, *Animal kingdom,* p. 82—SURINAME; *tamarin.*

[*Callithrix*] *Midas,* Erxleben, 1777, *Syst. Reg. Anim.,* p. 62—classification.

Sagouin midas, Lacépède, 1803, *Buffon Hist. Nat.,* Didot ed., 13:147—*tamarin* Buffon. E. Geoffroy, 1803, *Cat. Mamm. Mus. Hist. Nat., Paris,* p. 12—type locality, La Guyane.

Callitrix midas, Latreille, 1804, *Buffon Hist. Nat.,* Sonnini ed., 36:281—characters; classification.

Cercopithecus midas, Goldfuss, 1809, *Vergl. Naturb. Säugth.,* p. 76—GUIANA. Elliot, 1911, *Bull. Amer. Mus. Nat. Hist.* 30:341—nomenclature. Elliot, 1913, *A review of the Primates* 1:190—characters; synonymy.

Jacchus midas, Desmarest, 1818, *Nouv. Dict. Hist. Nat.* 24:241—*Midas rufimanus* Geoffroy, a synonym. Gray, 1843, *List Mamm. Brit. Mus.,* p. 14—BRAZIL.

H[*apale* (*Liocephalus*)] *midas,* Wagner, 1840, Schreber's Säugth., *Suppl.* 1:245—classification.

Hapale midas, Wagner, 1848, *Abh. Akad. Wiss. Munich* 5:472—characters. Schlegel, 1876, *Les singes. Simiae,* p. 266—FRENCH GUIANA: (Cayenne); SURINAME. Gervais, 1854, *Hist. Nat. Mamm.* 1:151—*rufimanus* Geoffroy a synonym. Jentink, 1887, *Cat. Ostéol. Mus. Pays-Bas* 9:49—GUYANA; *Demerara.* Jentink, 1892, *Syst. Nat. Mus. Pays-Bas* 11:57—FRENCH GUIANA: (Cayenne); GUYANA: *Demerara;* SURINAME: (Paramaribo).

Midas midas, Forbes, 1894, *Handbook of Primates* 1:148—SURINAME; classification; characters. Goeldi and Hagmann, 1904, *Bol. Mus. Paraense* 4:54—BRAZIL.

Leontopithecus midas, Thomas, 1911, *Proc. Zool. Soc. London* 1911 (1):128—Linnaean references.

[*Leontocebus midas*] Thomas, 1912, *Ann. Mag. Nat. Hist.* ser. 8, 10:44—BRAZIL: *Rio Branco* ("Moon Mountains" [= Serra da Lua].

Leontocebus (Tamarin) midas, Immendorf, 1961, *Säuget. Mitt.* 9:145—mother of "hybrid" from presumed crossing with cage mate *"Leontocebus (Marikina) bicolor"* or *"Leontocebus (Tamarin) mystax."*

Leontocebus (Tamarin) midas, Osman Hill, 1958, *Primatologia,* 3 (1):149—stomach. Osman Hill, 1960, *Primates* 4:67—brain weight relative to body weight.

Leontocebus midas midas, Cabrera, 1958, *Rev. Mus. Argentino Cienc. Nat. "Bernardino Rivadavia"* 4 (1):195—classification; synonymy. Carvalho, 1962, *Papeis Avulsos, São Paulo* 15:288—BRAZIL: *Amapá* (Vila Velha do Cassiporé, Oiapoque; Rio Amapari, Macapá; Rio Maruanum; prox. Amapá, Amapá; Rio Vila Nova, Mazagão; Macapá); Brazilian name, *macaco mão de ouro.*

Mystax midas, Pocock, 1917, *Ann. Mag. Nat. Hist.* ser. 8, 20:254, 258, fig. 2E (ear)—characters of ears, hands, and feet. Colyer, 1936, *Variation and diseases of the teeth of mammals, London,* p. 61—m_2 absent. Lönnberg, 1940, *Ark. Zool., Stockholm* 32A(10):13—BRAZIL: *Amazonas* (Itacoatiara; Lago do Canasary); *Pará* (Rio Maycuru, Monte Alegre; Lago Cuitêua). Sanderson, 1949, *Proc. Zool. Soc. London* 119(3):767, pl. 1, figs. 3, 4 (♀ genitalia)—SURINAME; pubic glandular pads interpreted as adhesive pads. Crandall, 1951, *Animal Kingdom* 54(6):179, fig. p. 182 (animal)—Guianas. Fiennes, 1964, *Proc. Zool. Soc. London* 143(3):523—cystic bone disease.

Tamarin midas, Anthony, Serra, and Serra, 1949, *Bull. Mem. Soc. Anthrop. Paris,* ser. 9, 10:132—palatal surface and cranial capacity. Osman Hill, 1957, *Primates* 3:87, 150, 152, 157, 166, 168, 171, 183, 193, 197–200, 203, 204, 207, 212–15, 254, 256, 319, fig. 26 (patella with associated muscles), fig. 27 (leg musculature), fig. 37 (hand and foot dermatoglyphs), fig. 41 (tongue), fig. 43 (brain), fig. 44 (distribution), fig. 47 (ear), figs. 48, 49 (external genitalia), pl. 8 (animal with pale supraorbital band)—anatomy; characters; taxonomy; distribution; behavior; reproduction. Osman Hill, 1958, *Primatologia* 3 (1):642, fig. 11*a* (penis), fig. 29 (♀ external genitalia)—external genitalia. Day and Napier, 1963, *Folia Primat.* 1:128—deep head of flexor pollicis brevis of thumb absent.

Tamarin (Tamarin) midas midas, Tate, 1939, *Bull. Amer. Mus. Nat. Hist.* 76:208—GUYANA.

T[*amarin*] *midas midas,* Osman Hill, 1957, *Primates* 3:208—characters; distribution.

Marikina midas, Hershkovitz, 1949, *Proc. U.S. Nat. Mus.* 98:412—key characters; classification; synonyms, *lacepede* Fischer, *rufimanus* Geoffroy, *egens* Thomas.

Marikina (Tamarin) midas midas, Husson, 1957, *Studies on the fauna of Suriname and other Guayanas* 1:37, pl. 7 (skull)—SURINAME: (Moengo Tapoe); type locality "restricted to Dutch Guiana."

Saguinus (Saguinus) midas midas, Hershkovitz, 1958, *Proc. Biol. Soc. Washington* 71:53—nomenclature.

S[*aguinus*] *midas midas* Hershkovitz, 1969, *Quart. Rev. Biol.* 44(1):19, fig. 6 (map)—origin; distribution.

Saguinus midas midas, Hershkovitz, 1970, *Am. J. Phys. Anthrop.* 32:379—classification; dental disease. Hershkovitz, 1970, *Fol. Primat.* 13:215, fig. 3 (cerebral hemisphere)—GUYANA: *Essequibo* (Essequibo River); cerebral fissural pattern.

Saguinus (Saguinus) midas, Avila Pires, 1964, *Bol. Mus. Paraense Emilio Goeldi, n.s., Zool.* 42:8, 13—BRAZIL: *Amazonas* (Igarapé Cuieiras, Rio Negro); GUYANA: (Río Marauni [*sic* = Mazaruni]).

S[*aguinus*] (*S*[*aguinus*]) *midas,* Bauchot and Stephan, 1969, *Mammalia* 33(2):227—degree of encephalization.

Saguinus midas, Thorington, 1968, *Folia Primat.* 9:95—BRAZIL: *Amapá* (Porto Platon, 5 mi W on road to Fazenda Campo Verdi)—habitat; habits; group composition; leaping. Thorington, 1969, *An. Acad. Brasil. Cienc.* 41 (suppl.):257—BRAZIL: *Amapá*—census. Mallinson, 1969, *Sixth Ann. Rep., Jersey Wildl. Preserv. Trust,* pp. 5, 9, fig. p. 12 (animal)—longevity in Jersey Zoo, 5 years, 10 mo. 11 days, still living. Mallinson, 1971, *Eighth Ann. Rep. Jersey Wildl. Preserv. Trust,* p. 19—breeding; rearing; care in captivity. Clark, 1974, *10th Ann. Rpt. Jersey Wildlife Preserv. Trust,* p. 44—daily food requirements in Jersey Zoo.

C[*ebus*] *Tamarin* Link, 1795, *Beitr. Naturg.* 1(2):63—name based solely on *le tamarin nègre* of Buffon.

Midas tamarin, Lesson, 1840, *Species de mammifères: Bimanes et quadrumanes . . . ,* p. 194—*le tamarin ordinaire;* part synonyms, *midas* Linnaeus, *rufimanus* Geoffroy.

Simia lacepedii Fischer, 1806, *Mem. Soc. Imp. Nat. Moscow* 1:24—type locality, America; type, a mounted specimen in the Moscow Natural History Museum.

Callithrix Lacepedii Fischer, 1811, *Mem. Soc. Imp. Nat. Moscow* 2d ed., 1:9—characters ex type.

[*Callithrix*] *Lacepede* [*sic*] Fischer, 1813, *Zoognosia, Tab. Syn.* 2:524—South America.

H[*apale*] *Lacepedii,* Olfers, 1818, in Eschwege, p. 202—classification.

M[*idas*] *lacepedii,* Slack, 1861, *Proc. Acad. Nat. Sci. Philadelphia* 13:464—*rufimanus* Geoffroy, a synonym.

Midas rufimanus E. Geoffroy, 1812, *Ann. Mus. Hist. Nat., Paris* 19:121—new name for *Simia midas* Linnaeus; FRENCH GUIANA: (type locality). Kuhl, 1820, *Beitr. Zool.,* p. 50—synonyms, *tamarin* Audebert, fig. 5, *midas* Schreber (fig. ex Edwards). Pelzeln, 1883, *Verh. K. K. Zool.-Bot. Gesellsch., Wien, Beih.* 33:25—BRAZIL: *Río Branco* (Forte do Rio Branco [= São Joaquim, upper Rio Branco]); SURINAME. Ménégaux, 1902, *Bull. Mus. Nat. Hist. Nat., Paris* 8:297—FRENCH GUIANA (Ouanary River). Cabrera, 1902, *Rev. Chilena Hist. Nat.* 6:231—color variation. Rode, 1938, *Bull. Mus. Nat. Hist. Nat.* ser. 2, 10:241—type history.

M[*idas*] *rufimanus,* Tschudi, 1844, *Fauna Peruana,* pp. 9, 53—erroneously presumed to occur in Peru. Cabanis and Schomburgk, 1848, *Reisen Br. Guiana* 3:772—GUYANA: (coast to 1,500 feet above sea level). I. Geoffroy, 1851, *Cat. Primates Mus. Hist. Nat., Paris,* p. 63—FRENCH GUIANA: (Cayenne, "par M. Poiteau, 1822"). Reichenbach, 1862, *Vollst. Naturg. Affen,* p. 10, pl. 3, figs. 34–36 (animals)—GUIANA. Cabrera, 1900, *An. Soc. Española Hist. Nat.,* ser. 2, 9:89—BRAZIL: *Pernambuco* [!].

Jacchus rufimanus, Desmarest, 1820, *Mammalogie,* p. 94, pl. 19, fig. 3 (animal)—"La Guyane et la Maragnon où il porte le nom de Tamary." Desmarest, 1827, *Dict. Sci. Nat.* 47:21.

H[*apale* (*midas*)] *rufimanus,* Voigt, 1831 *Cuvier's das Thierreich* 1:99—classification.

Hapale rufimanus, F. Cuvier fils, 1842, *Hist. Nat. Mamm., 7, tabl.* p. 2—*tamarin aux mains rousses,* F. Cuvier, 1826. Boas, 1912, *Ohrknorpel und äusseres Ohr der Säugetiere (Kopenhagen),* p. 205, pl. 15, fig. 149 (ear cartilage), pl. 23, fig. 243 (external ear)—anatomy of the external ear; comparisons. Streeter, 1922, *Anat. Rec.* 23:338–39, fig. 13 (external ear)—no text.

Leontocebus rufimanus, Pocock, 1911, *Proc. Zool. Soc. London* 1911:856—insect feeding.

Cercopithecus rufimanus, Elliot, 1913, *A review of the Primates* 1:191—FRENCH GUIANA: (type locality, Ipoussin).

Tamarin rufimanus, Cruz Lima, 1945, *Mamíferos da Amazonia, Primates, Contrib. Mus. Paraense,* p. 217, pl. 35, fig. 1 (animal)—characters.

Leontocebus midas egens Thomas, 1912, *Ann. Mag. Nat. Hist.,* ser. 8, 10:44—BRAZIL: *Pará* (type locality, Óbidos, lower Rio Amazonas); type, female, skin and skull, British Museum (Natural History) no. 12.5.11.5, collected 15 February 1912 by E. Snethlage. Cabrera, 1917, *Trab. Mus. Nac. Cienc. Nat., Ser. Zool.,* no. 31, p. 30—BRAZIL: *Pernambuco* [!]; color variation.

Leontocebus midas egans [*sic*], Hershkovitz, 1949, *Proc. U.S. Nat. Mus.* 98:412—lapsus for *egens* Thomas in synonymy of *midas* Linnaeus.

Tamarin (*Tamarin*) *midas egens,* Tate, 1939, *Bull. Amer. Mus. Nat. Hist.* 76:208—classification.

Tamarin midas egens, Cruz Lima, 1945, *Mammals of Amazonia, Primates,* p. 219—BRAZIL: Pará (island regions between Marajó and mainland; Colonia do Veado; Óbidos; Jary); *Amapá* (Macapá); *Amazonas* (Itaquatiara [*sic* = Itacoatiara]).

T[*amarin*] *midas egens,* Osman Hill, 1957, *Primates* 3:204, 210—characters; distribution.

Cercopithecus midas egens, Elliot, 1913, *A review of the Primates* 3:256—characters ex type.

M[*idas*] *ursulus,* Reichenbach (part, not Hoffmannsegg), 1862, *Vollst. Naturg. Affen,* pl. 3, figs. 37–38 (animals) only.

Midas ursulus, Bates (not Hoffmannsegg), 1863, *Naturalist on the River Amazons,* 1:95, 243; ibid, ed. 2 (1864) 57:151—BRAZIL: *Pará* (Obidos). Savoury, 1960, *J. Br. Guiana Mus., Zoo,* no. 26:54—GUYANA: Rupununi (Aran-tau); reproduction in captivity.

Leontocebus (*Tamarin*) *midas* ♀ × *Leontocebus* (*Marikina*) *bicolor,* Immendorf, 1961, *Säugetierk. Mitt.* 9:145, pl., figs. 1–6 (animal)—growth and development of hybrid in Cologne Zoo.

Leontocebus midas ♀ × *Leontocebus bicolor* ♂, Morris and Jarvis (eds.), 1959, *Int. Zoo Yearb.* 1:140—hybrid bred in Cologne, Germany.

[(*Leontocebus bicolor* × *L. midas*) ♂ × *Leontocebus midas*] ♀, Hick, 1959, *Freunde des Kölner Zoo* 4(3):63, fig. ("Stupps," the father)—twins of backcross born 4 August 1961; parents mated since 1960.

(*L[eontocebus] bicolor* × *L. midas*) × *Leontocebus midas,* Jarvis and Morris (eds.), 1961, *Int. Zoo Yearb.* 3:275 —backcross hybrid, Cologne Zoo; same hybrid as preceding.

Saguinus midas ♀ × *Saguinus oedipus* ♂, Reed, 1965, *Rep. Nat. Zool. Pk., Smithsonian Rep. 1964,* p. 113, pl. 3, right photograph (hybrid twins)—born in National Zoological Park, Washington, D.C.

Saguinus midas midas × *Saguinus oedipus oedipus,* Hershkovitz, 1968, *Evolution* 22(3):572, fig. 13 (hybrid twins and father)—hybrid relationship to parents; same hybrid as preceding.

Type. None in existence, name based primarily on the *little black monkey* of Edwards, 1751 (A natural history of birds, pt. 4, p. 196, pl. 196). It "was brought from the *West Indies,* by the Honourable Commodore Fitzroy Lee, Anno 1747, and presented by him to the Right Honourable the *Countess Dowager of Leichfield,* by whose permission I made a draught of it from Life: It was a female."

Type Locality. "America" as given by Linnaeus; restricted to Suriname by Schreber (1775, *Säugtiere,* 1:132).

Distribution (fig. X.46). Forested parts of Guyana, Suriname, French Guiana, and the Guianan province of Brazil or the territory between the north bank of the Amazonas and the east bank of the Rio Negro; altitudinal range, sea level to approximately 450 meters above.

Taxonomy. Edward's *little black monkey,* basis for the Linnaean *Simia midas,* is characterized by flesh-colored face, flesh-colored, funnel shaped ears, and a harelip. Nothwithstanding the abnormalities, Edward's monkey is positively identifiable with the Guianan golden-handed tamarin.

Buffon described two tamarins, both from Cayenne (155b). The color of the face, ears, soles, and claws of the first, *le tamarin* (1767, p. 94, pl. 13) was said to be brown. The second, *le tamarin nègre* (1789, p. 116, pl. 32) "ne diffère en effet du tamarin de notre *planche XIII, volume XV,* que parce qu'il a la face noire, au lieu que l'autre l'a blanche, et parce qu'il a ainsi le poil beaucoup plus noir; mais au reste, ces deux animaux se ressemblant à tous égards ne paroissent former qu'une variété d'une seule et même espèce."

The respective woodcuts of the *tamarin* and *tamarin nègre* show clearly the color of hands and feet contrasting sharply with the blackish bodies. Authors readily identified Buffon's *tamarin* with the golden-handed *midas* of Linnaeus, but, perhaps because of its name, erroneously associated Buffon's *tamarin nègre* with the black-handed, black-footed Brazilian tamarin, an animal Buffon never saw.

The first binomial proposed for Buffon's *tamarin nègre* appears to be *Cebus tamarin* Link, 1795. Link's complete description was derived from Buffon and reads "unterscheidet sich von *Midas* durch das schwarze Gesicht." This was indeed the only difference. Nevertheless the notion persisted that the name *tamarin nègre* implied an entirely black animal. Gray, in 1843 (p. 14), erroneously used the name *tamarin* Link for the dark-handed Brazilian race with *Saguinus ursula* Hoffmannsegg a synonym. This usage was ignored until 1945 when Cruz Lima (p. 215) adopted Link's *tamarin* for the black-handed and black-footed tamarin and all authors followed suit.

Midas tamarin Lesson was independently proposed as a new name for the golden-handed tamarin, the *midas* of Linnaeus, *rufimanus* of E. Geoffroy, etc. Lesson regarded the black-handed tamarin as a mere variety of the subadult stage of *midas* and he described it under the title *Midas tamarin,* "age moyen." In the synonymy of the latter he included *niger* E. Geoffroy and *ursulus* Hoffmannsegg, both bona fide black-handed tamarins. The golden-handed *tamarin nègre* of Buffon was also listed with the black-handed forms.

Simia lacepedii Fischer, described in 1806, is based on a golden-handed tamarin preserved in the Moscow Museum. It was distinguished from *midas* by its normally black face and unsplit lip.

When E. Geoffroy erected the genus *Midas* in 1812 to contain the hairy-face tamarins, he substituted the name *rufimanus* for the Linnaean *midas* to avoid the tautonymic *Midas midas,* a usage then discountenanced. In other words, *rufimanus* and *midas* are different names for precisely the same type specimen and species. No more precise locality than "La Guyane," i.e., French Guiana, was given as the habitat, but Schreber (see above) had already restricted the type locality of *midas* to Suriname.

Authors followed Geoffroy in using *rufimanus* as a substitute or alternate name for *midas.* In 1913, however, D. G. Elliot formally recognized *Cercopithecus* [*sic*] *rufimanus* E. Geoffroy as a valid species distinguished from *midas* Linnaeus by warmer color of back and some cranial characters. The "type locality" of *rufimanus* was said to be Ipoussin (156a), French Guiana, the "type" itself preserved in the Paris Museum as a mounted specimen with skull in skin. All this about a type, its color, and its cranial characters is patent nonsense. Notwithstanding, Rode (1938, p. 241) lists a "holotype" of *rufimanus* in the Paris Museum, with "provenance: Amérique méridionale." The skull, according to this authority is preserved separately with number A 2. 785. Obviously, Elliot's "type' 'and Rode's "type" of *rufimanus* are not the same, and neither is type of anything described by E. Geoffroy.

Leontocebus midas egens Thomas from Óbidos (217), Pará, Brazil, is said to differ from "true Guianan *midas,*" by the "paler colour of its hands, a difference verified on five examples of *egens* as compared with ten of *midas.*" Other differences were mentioned including "back more strongly suffused with *dark buffy* . . . black of head less deep [italics mine] . . ." and more such trivialities. That the manual character of *egens* was, at best, a local disconformity can be gleaned from Thomas's observation (1912, p. 44) that "curiously enough, two specimens from the Moon Mountain, the nearest locality in Guiana to Obidos, have hands of an even darker tone than those of British Guiana, and resemble in this respect, one from Cayenne which I have always considered to represent Geoffroy's *rufimanus.*" Lönnberg (1940, p. 13), with specimens from several localities along the Rio Amazonas but evidently none from the Guianas, also noted minor local variations but retained *egens* as valid.

Our specimens from the northern half of Suriname,

Fig. X.50. Golden-handed Tamarins, *Saguinus midas midas;* adult female above (photo by Phillip F. Coffey, courtesy of Jersey Zoological Park); twins at 56 days, ♀ left, ♂ right (photo by D. W. Baudains, courtesy of Jersey Zoological Park).

Guyana, and French Guiana vary in the same way and to the same extent as those from along the left bank of the Amazonas in Brazil.

A specimen at hand from Colonia do Veado (217), Obidos, one of the original series collected by Snethlage, agrees with the description of *egens* but is not significantly different from a Cayenne *midas* with slightly redder hands and feet. In contrast, the cheiridia of a specimen from Georgetown (147), Guyana, are even paler. Indeed all color tones of limbs can be mixed and matched from throughout the range of *midas*, where barriers to free and full intergradation do not exist. The only significant racial character is the reddish hands and feet of *midas* in all their color tones as compared with the wholly melanistic ones of *niger*.

Diagnostic Characters. General coloration blackish as for the species (p. 707) with upper surface of hands sharply contrasted golden to reddish orange (fig. X.50).

Coloration. Foreparts including head, mantle, arms, throat, neck, and chest blackish, dark brown, or sometimes chestnut, the hairs blackish or brown terminally becoming paler to drab basally; facial skin black with area around mouth and nostrils sparsely covered with short black hairs; middle and lower back striated black with gray, buff, or orange; rump like saddle or with more black; outer sides of thighs like saddle or rump, legs like thighs but darker or entirely black; lateral fringe like back; upper surface of hands and feet sharply defined yellowish, orange, or reddish orange, the bright color often extending onto wrists and ankles; inner sides of legs and belly blackish; tail black except basal portions above like rump, below black to reddish or orange; external genitalia mostly or entirely pigmented and sparsely covered with dark brown hairs.

Young. See page 724 and fig. X.50.

Measurements. See appendix table 2.

Comparisons. Distinguished from *S. m. tamarin* by the yellowish to reddish orange surface of hands and feet.

Specimens Examined. 69. BRAZIL—*Amazonas:* Itacoatiara, 1 (FMNH); Lago do Canaçary, 1 (FMNH); *Pará:* Colonia do Veado, Óbidos, 4 (AMNH, 1; BM, 2 including type of *egens;* FMNH, 1); Óbidos, 3 (BM); *Roraima:* Serra do Lua, 3 (BM, 2; FMNH, 1; *locality unknown:* 1 (BM); GUYANA—Bonasica, 2 (BM); "coast region," 1 (BM); Colaroo, Demerara River, 1 (BM); Dunoon, 2 (UMMZ); Essequibo River, 5 (FMNH); Georgetown, 1 (FMNH); Kartabo, 2 (AMNH); Mahaienbally Creek, 2 (BM); Monasica Creek, Essequibo River, 1 (BM); Supinaam River, 4 (BM); FRENCH GUIANA—Cayenne, 4 (MNHN, 2; FMNH, 2); Haute Carterenne, 1 (MNHN); Ipoussin, 1 (BM); Saint Laurent, Maroni, 1 (MNHN); Saut Macaque, 2 (MNHN); *locality unknown:* 7, (MNHN, 1; RMNH, 6); SURINAME—"Camp 1," 1 (BM); Carolinakreek, 2 (FMNH); Loksie Hattie, 2 (FMNH); Kaiserberg Airstrip, Zuid River, 4 (FMNH); Paramaribo, 1 (BM); Tapahoni River, 1 (FMNH); Zanderij, 2 (BM); *locality unknown:* 3 (BM); UNKNOWN LOCALITY—3 (SM, 2; FMNH, 1 in spirits).

SAGUINUS MIDAS NIGER E. GEOFFROY, BLACK-HANDED TAMARIN

Synonymic History

Tamarin nègre, Audebert (not Buffon), 1797, *Histoire naturelle des singes et makis,* fam. 6, sec. 2, pl. 6 and text p. 8 (*tamarin variété a*). F. Cuvier, 1819, in Geoffroy and Cuvier, *Hist. Nat. Mamm.,* livr. 9 [vol. 1], pl. (animal) and text.

Sagouin niger E. Geoffroy, 1803, *Cat. Mamm. Mus. Hist. Nat., Paris,* p. 13.

Saguinus midas niger, Hershkovitz, 1970, *Am. J. Phys. Anthrop.* 32:379—classification; dental disease; supernumerary left and right upper molars.

S[aguinus] midas niger, Hershkovitz, 1969, *Quart. Rev. Biol.* 44(1):19, fig. 6 (map)—origin; distribution.

Saguinus Ursula Hoffmannsegg, 1807, *Mag. Gesell. Naturf. Fr., Berlin* 1:102—BRAZIL: *Pará* (type locality, vicinity of Pará, i.e., Belém de Pará); cotypes, a considerable number of specimens of both sexes, young and old collected by Sieber; one cotype, at least, may still be preserved in the Berlin Museum. Gervais, 1854, *Hist. Nat. Mamm.* 1:151, fig. (head)—characters.

Simia Ursula, Humboldt, 1812, *Rec. Obs. Zool. Anat. Comp.,* p. 361—BRAZIL: *Pará.*

Midas ursulus, E. Geoffroy, 1812, *Ann. Mus. Hist. Nat., Paris* 19:121—BRAZIL: *Pará.* Kühl, 1820, *Beitr. Zool.,* p. 50—BRAZIL: *Pará;* synonymy. Bates, 1863, *Naturalist on the River Amazons* 1:95; ibid., 2d ed. (1864):57—BRAZIL: *Pará* (Pará); characters; habits. Pelzeln, 1883, *Verh. K. K. Zool.-Bot. Gesellsch., Wien, Beih.* 33:24—BRAZIL: *Pará* (Pará); *Amazonas* (*"Manaqueri,"* specimen received in exchange [locality incorrect]). Goeldi and Hagmann, 1904, *Bol. Mus. Paraense* 4:54—BRAZIL: *Pará.* Müller, 1914, *Abh. K. bayerisch Akad. Wiss., Munich, Math. Phys. Kl.* 26 (1):8 (1912)—BRAZIL: *Pará* (Peixe-boi, Belém).

M[idas] ursulus, I. Geoffroy, 1851, *Cat. Primates, Mus. Hist. Nat., Paris,* p. 63—two specimens listed. Reichenbach, 1862, *Vollst. Naturg. Affen,* p. 10—part, characters [not figures 37–38, = *M. midas*].

Jacchus ursulus, Desmarest, 1818, *Nouv. Dict. Hist. Nat.* 24:242—characters; part synonymy. Desmarest, 1820, *Mammalogie,* p. 95—characters. Desmarest, 1827, *Dict. Sci. Nat.* 47:21.

H[apale (Midas)] ursula, Voigt, 1831, *Cuvier's das Thierreich* 1:99—classification.

H[apale] ursula, Wagner, 1840, *Schreber's Säugth., Suppl.* 1:246—characters.

Hapale ursula, Wagner, 1848, *Abh. Akad. Wiss. Berlin* 5:471—part, BRAZIL: *Pará.* Schlegel, 1876, *Les singes. Simiae,* p. 265—BRAZIL: *Pará* (near mouth of Rio Tocantins, collected by Sieber). Anderson, 1881, *Cat. Indian Mus., Calcutta,* pt. 1, p. 89—"permanent absence of the last molar on the right side." Jentink, 1887. *Cat. Ostéol. Mamm. Mus. Pays-Bas* 9:49—BRAZIL: *Pará.* Jentink 1892, *Cat. Syst. Mamm. Mus. Pays-Bas* 11:57—BRAZIL: *Pará.* Weinert, 1926, *Zeitschr. Morph. Anthrop.* 35:282, fig. 97 (paranasal cavities)—frontal sinuses.

L[eontocebus] ursulus, Cabrera, 1912, *Trab. Mus. Cienc. Nat., Madrid,* no. 11:29—BRAZIL: *Pará* (lower Rio Amazonas).

Cercopithecus ursulus, Elliot, 1913, *A review of the Primates,* p. 192—characters.

[Mystax] ursulus, Pocock, 1917, *Ann. Mag. Nat. Hist.* ser. 8, 20:256—type of *tamarin* Gray. Sonntag, 1921, *Proc. Zool. Soc. London* 1921:521, 757—tongue anatomy. Osgood, 1921, *J. Mammal.* 2:40—*Saguinus ursula* Hoffmannsegg, 1807, author of name.

Mystax ursulus, Colyer, 1936, Variation and diseases of the teeth of mammals, (London), p. 298, fig. 375 (dentition)—pm^2 rotated. Fiennes, 1964, *Proc. Zool. Soc. London* 143(3):523—cystic bone disease.

Leontocebus ursulus, Weinert, 1926, *Zeitschr. Morph. Anthrop.* 35:282, fig. 96 (paranasal cavities)—frontal sinuses. N. C. Davis, 1930, *J. Exp. Med.* 52:410—experimental infection with yellow fever virus.

[Callithrix] gracilis Fischer, 1813, Zoognosia, Tab. Syn. 2:525—South America (type locality); type, skin and skeleton in Moscow Museum, secured from a traveling menagerie.

H[apale] gracilis, Olfers, 1818, in Eschwege, *Journal von Brasilien, Weimar* 15 (2):202—*lugubris* Erxleben and Zimmermann possibly a synonym.

Mystax ursulus umbratus Thomas, 1922, *Ann. Mag. Nat. Hist.,* ser. 9, 9:265—BRAZIL: *Pará* (type locality, Cametá, Rio Tocantins); type, female, skin and skull, British Museum (Natural History) no. 11.4.28.4, collected 20 January 1911 by E. Snethlage. Lönnberg, 1940, *Ark. Zool., Stockholm* 32A, (10):8—BRAZIL: *Pará* (Cametá); measurements.

Tamarin tamarin umbratus, Cruz Lima, 1945, *Mamíferos da Amazonia, Primates, Contr. Mus. Paraense,* p. 216—characters; doubtfully distinct.

T[amarin] t[amarin] umbratus, Osman Hill, 1957, *Primates* 3:203, 206—characters; distribution.

Marikina tamarin umbrata, Hershkovitz, 1949, *Proc. U.S. Nat. Mus.* 98:412—classification.

Leontocebus tamarin umbratus, Carvalho, 1960, *Arq. Zool., São Paulo* 11 (1958):126—BRAZIL: *Pará* (Gradaús, Rio Fresco); distribution.

Midas tamarin, age moyen, Lesson (not Link), 1840, *Species des mammifères: Bimanes et quadrumanes . . . ,* p. 196—synonyms, *niger* Geoffroy, *ursula* Hoffmannsegg.

M[idas] tamarin, Slack (not Link), 1861, *Proc. Acad. Nat. Sci. Philadelphia* 13:464—*ursula* Geoffroy, a synonym.

Jacchus tamarin, Gray (not Link), 1843, *List. Mamm. Brit. Mus.,* p. 14—BRAZIL. Wallace, 1852, *Proc. Zool. Soc. London* 1852:109—BRAZIL: *Pará* ("found only in the district of Pará").

Marikina tamarin, Hershkovitz (not Link), 1949, *Proc. U.S. Nat. Mus.* 98:412—key characters; classification.

Tamarin tamarin, Osman Hill (not Link), 1957, *Primates* 3:83, 160, 181, 193, 198, 199, 201, 206, 220, 270, figs. 38, 39 (♂ external genitalia), fig. 40 (skull), fig. 42 (intestine), fig. 44 (distribution), fig. 45 (ear), fig. 46 (♀ external genitalia), pl. 7 (animal)—anatomy; characters; distribution; behavior; reproduction; taxonomy. Osman Hill, 1958, *Primatologia* 3(1):642, 681—external genitalia. Dunn, Frederick, and Lambrecht, 1963, *J. Parasitol.* 49(2):316—*Plasmodium* infection. Benirschke and Brownhill, 1973, *Cytogenetics* 2:338—karyotype.

Tamarin tamarin tamarin Cruz Lima (not Link), 1945, *Mamíferos da Amazonia, Primates, Contr. Mus. Paraense,* p. 215, pl. 34, fig. 2—BRAZIL: *Pará* (Belém Conceição, Rio Mojú; Arumatéua, Rio Tocantins); [!] *Amazonas* ("Itaquatiara"); [!] PERU: *Loreto* (Chimbote, occurrence here "seems doubtful"); variation. Osman Hill, 1955, *Proc. Roy. Phys. Soc. Edinburgh* 24:50—BRAZIL: *Pará* (Rio Xingu); mounted specimen purchased from Rowland Ward [locality data dubious].

T[amarin] t[amarin] tamarin, Osman Hill (not Link), 1957, *Primates* 3:203, 207—characters; distribution.

Leontocebus tamarin, Cabrera (not Link), 1958, *Rev. Mus. Argentino Cienc. Nat. "Bernardino Rivadavia,"* 4(1): 197—classification; *umbratus* Thomas, a synonym. Avila Pires, 1958, *Bol. Mus. Paraense Emilio Goeldi, Zool.,* no. 19:6—BRAZIL: *Pará* (Belém de Pará; type locality). Machado, 1960, *Anais Fac. Med. Univ. Minas Gerais* 20:123 seq., table 1—morphology of ileal eminence of large intestine. Chiarelli, 1963, *Folia Primat.* 1:91—taste sensitivity to phenylthiocarbamide. Machado and DiDio, 1963, *Anat. Anzeiger* 113:45—ampulla of terminal ileum. Leutenegger, 1970, *Folia Primat.* 12:224—pelvis (sexual dimorphism).

Saguinus tamarin, Egozcue, Perkins, and Hagemenas (not Link), 1968, *Folia Primat.* 9(2):84—karyotype (2n = 46). Porter, 1972, *Lab. Animal Sci.* 22(4):503—parasites.

Saguinus (Saguinus) tamarin, Bauchot and Stephan (not Link), 1969, *Mammalia* 33(2):227—degree of encephalization.

Saguinus t[amarin] tamarin, Carvalho and Toccheton (not Link), 1969, *Rev. Biol. Trop.* 15(2):219—BRAZIL: *Pará* (Belém [Utinga]; Belém-Brasilia, km 94).

Simia midas v[ariété] A. Audebert, 1797, *Histoire naturelle des singes et makis,* fam. 6, sec. 2, p. 8, pl. 6 (animal) erroneously identified with the tamarin nègre of Buffon [= *midas* Linnaeus].

Type. Skin, presumably mounted, Muséum National d'Histoire Naturelle, Paris, original catalog number 24.

Type Locality. Said to be Cayenne, here restricted to Belém de Pará (256), the type locality of *ursula* Hoffmannsegg, and *tamarin* of authors, not Link (cf. Wallace, 1854, *Proc. Zool. Soc. London* 1852:109; Avila Pires, 1958, *Bol. Mus. Paraense Emilio Goeldi, Zool.,* no. 19, p. 6).

Distribution (fig. X.46). Eastern Brazil in the State of Pará, south of the Amazonas between the Rios Gurupi and the lower Xingu; present on the Ilha de Marajó at the mouth of the Amazonas.

Taxonomy. The description of *Sagouin niger* E. Geoffroy, (1803, p. 13), reproduced below, seems to be based as much on a specimen in the Paris Museum as on the *tamarin nègre* of Audebert cited in the synonymy.

[p. 13 "T[aille], 0^{m}, 21 (7 p[ouces], 9 l[ignes]). Tête arrondie, face jaunâtre, lèvre supérieure echancrée, oreilles très-grandes, membraneuses; pelage entièrement noir, ondoyé de fauve sur le dos; doigts couverts de poils jusqu'-aux ongles.

"Patrie. Cayenne.

"No. XXIV. Individu qui a servi de sujet pour la description précédente."

E. Geoffroy's synonymy also includes a bibliographic reference to the *tamarin nègre* of Buffon which is the golden-handed form (antea, p. 713).

Saguinus ursula Hoffmannsegg, 1807, is based on adequate material with precise and correct locality data "aus der Nachbarschaft der Stadt Para." The binomial itself contains the earliest valid generic name for tamarins in general.

The type of *Mystax ursulus umbratus* Thomas is a specimen from Cametá (252) on the left bank of the lower Tocantins. It is said to differ from those of the right bank of the river, including the vicinity of Belém by darker color throughout, mantle extending farther down the back, and saddle more finely banded with "dull ochraceous instead of coarsely with buffy." The differences in the color and banding of saddle, evident in our material from east and west of the Tocantins, are too slight and broadly overlapping to merit taxonomic recognition.

Cebus tamarin Link, 1795, is based on the golden-handed, golden-footed *tamarin nègre* of Buffon and nothing else. Misuse of *tamarin* Link for the black-handed tamarin started with Gray in 1843 but had no currency until 1945, when Cruz Lima adopted it without explanation. The taxonomic history of *tamarin* Link is given in the account of *Saguinus midas midas* (p. 713).

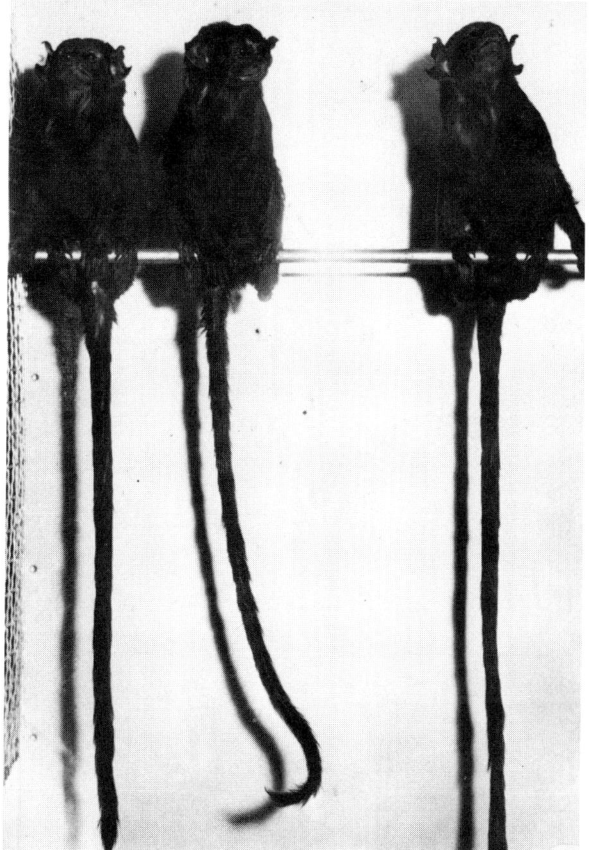

Fig. X.51. Black-handed Tamarins, *Saguinus midas niger.* (Photo courtesy of Kurt Benirschke.)

Diagnostic Characters. Those of the species (p. 707) with upper surface of hands and feet blackish (fig. X.51).

Coloration. Foreparts including head, mantle, forelimbs, throat, neck, and chest blackish or blackish brown, the hairs more or less uniformly blackish or dark brown terminally becoming paler basally; facial skin black; middle and lower back, rump, and outer sides of thighs evenly striated black with buff, orange, or reddish orange, the hairs blackish with a pale subterminal band, legs darker to entirely black; lateral fringe like back; hind legs and upper surface of hands and feet black; inner sides of legs and belly blackish or dark brown; tail black except base like rump; genitalia mostly or entirely pigmented and sparsely covered with blackish or reddish brown hairs.

Measurements. See appendix table 2.

Comparisons. Distinguished from *S. m. midas* by black upper surface of hands and feet.

Remarks. The female sexual skin of the black tamarin was described in 1848 by the Austrian naturalist Johann Natterer (in Wagner, p. 472). The wide flat pad extending from the lips of the vulva to the umbilical region, he observed, appeared to be some kind of musk gland which when squeezed produced an odoriferous oil.

Specimens Examined. 137. BRAZIL—*Pará:* Ananindéua, 1 (FMNH); Arumatéua, 1 (AMNH); Baião, 14 (AMNH); Benevides, 1 (FMNH); Cametá, 57 (AMNH, 52; BM, 2, including type of *umbratus;* FMNH, 3); Mocajuba, 8 (AMNH); Igarapé Assu, 12 (BM, 11; MNHN, 1); Murucutu, 1 (FMNH); Peixe Boi, 2 (AMNH, 1; FMNH, 1); Porto do Moz, 3 (AMNH); Recreio, Rio Majary, 6 (AMNH); Rio Amazonas, 2 (FMNH); Rio Tocantins, 1 (AMNH); Tapará, 1 (AMNH); Vilarinho do Monte, 11 (AMNH); Utinga, 1 (FMNH); *locality unknown:* 13 (BM, 1; MNHN, 1; RMNH, 11; SM, 1; FMNH, 1 in spirits).

70 *Saguinus midas*
2. *Biology of Midas Tamarins*

The activities of the black-handed tamarin (*Saguinus midas niger* [= *Tamarin tamarin* of recent authors, not Link, 1795]) are adapted from studies by Christen (1974) published in German. Notes on the golden-handed tamarin (*Saguinus midas midas*) are compiled from the other sources cited.

REPRODUCTION

The data is presented under the following headings

Mating	Breeding Season
Copulation	Homosexuality
Pregnancy and Parturition	Hybridization
Gestation	

Mating

Christen 1974 (*niger*)

An adult male and 2 adult females, all wild-caught, caged together in the Zürich laboratory did not engage in ritualized courtship. Neither sex seemed to dominate the other and both joined in mock fighting and tonguing before copulation. Both females copulated up to a few hours of giving birth and again two days after or during secondary hemorrhaging.

Copulation

Christen 1974 (*niger*)

The male seized the female around the hips, mounted, and copulated 2 or 3 times in rapid succession while tonguing and nipping the nape and back of his partner. The male often copulated first with one then the other of the two females in his cage. The dominant female, however, was wont to intervene when the male was exchanging favors with the subordinate female.

The sexually engaged female plants herself squarely with hands and feet on floor or branch. She may peep softly, tongue, and look back to her partner.

Pregnancy and Parturition

Mallinson 1972, p. 20 (*midas*)

Signs of pregnancy observed before a female's first and second parturition (BP) in the Jersey Zoo are chronicled as follows:

First Parturition:
- 19 days BP—Female spends more time in nest box during daylight hours
- 11 days BP—Abdomen greatly enlarged
- 24 hours BP—Abdominal movements observed
- 23 March 1970, 09:58 hours—Breach presentation with obstetric complications
- 10:05 hours—Stillborn male, weight 60 g; birth assisted by author; considerable amount of blood discharged, but placenta not evident.

Second Parturition:
- 17 days BP—Definite signs of pregnancy not seen
- 26/27 September 1970—Male and female twins born unassisted

Christen 1974 (*niger*)

Pregnancy was not apparent until one month before parturition, when the dominant female ate and drank considerably more than usual, vomited occasionally and yawned frequently. A few days before delivery less mucus was expelled from her vagina and the base of her tail was less moist and sticky.

The female became more aggressive toward the subordinate female in her cage and toward the male as well but she continued copulating until noon. Later she visited her sleeping box at intervals and finally laid down with eyes closed as if in pain, but abdominal contractions were not apparent.

Birth occurred between 16:35 and 17:55 when an observer was not present. The mother was found swallowing an umbilical cord about 25 cm long; placenta, blood, two short pieces of umbilicus, and 2 dead neonates were on the floor of the cage, one of them decapitated, its brains eaten. The three adult cagemates were twittering excitedly. Apparently all had shared in the cannibalism.

Nineteen days after the event, the subordinate female produced a pair of twins at night. The two survived 46 and 57 days respectively. Overt signs of pregnancy were not seen.

After an interval of 31 weeks the subordinate female produced a second litter of twins. Christen found the young decapitated, their heads evidently eaten by the adults.

The second litter produced by the dominant female was born 39 weeks after the first. Signs of pregnancy were indirect. The damp sticky tail base caused by vaginal secretions appeared several weeks before parturition and an extraordinary appetite for food developed during the last 10 days. The young, born at night, were found dead the next morning, their skulls crushed, the placenta intact. As Christen (1974, p. 11) belatedly discovered, housing more than one adult of the same sex in the same cage is highly inauspicious.

Dominant and subordinate females bleed a few drops daily for about 10 days after parturition. One copulated 2 days after delivery, the other after 7 days.

Gestation

Christen 1974 (*niger*)

Estimated duration of gestation in 4 full-term pregnancies by the 2 females of the Zürich laboratory colony is between 20 and 24 weeks.

Breeding Season

Geijskes 1957, p. 38 (*midas*)

"We are not able to say anything about a breeding season, if one exists."

Savoury 1960, p. 54 (*midas*)

A pair of suckling young captured toward the end of 1958 in Aran-tau, Rupununi District, Guyana, was brought to Georgetown in March 1959 and observed copulating for the first time in May 1959 and on subsequent occasions. A single young was produced 26 April 1960.

Hershkovitz

Breeding or production of young in the wild evidently occurs during the northern hemisphere's spring and possibly early summer. A lactating female was taken May 1961 by Harry A. Beatty of the Field Museum's Suriname Zoological Expedition. Three females (1 subadult) I collected in the same expedition between November 1961 and February 1962 lacked embryos and showed no signs of lactation. The sexual pad of the female taken 28 December measured 15 x 37 mm.

Of a total of 15 births recorded in northern hemisphere zoos and laboratories, 11 occurred during spring and summer months (March to September). If the female

Table 91. Records of Full-Term Births of *Saguinus midas midas* and *Saguinus midas niger*

Birth Date	*Birth Place*	*Litter*	*Mother*	*Interbirth Interval Days*	*Source*
26 April 1960	Guyana	♂	—	—	Savoury 1960
— June 1951	London Zoo	♂	—	—	Mallinson 1972
— May 1952	London Zoo	♂	—	—	Mallinson 1972
23 March 1970	Jersey Zoo	♂	a	—	Mallinson 1972
— September 1970	Jersey Zoo	♂ ♀	a	187	Mallinson 1972
April–May 1961	Suriname[1]	—		—	H. A. Beatty, field notes
8 Nov. 1965	Zurich	♂ ♀	1[2]	—	Christen 1974
20 Aug. 1966	Zurich	♂ ♀	1	285	Christen 1974
26 Nov. 1965	Zurich	♂	2[3]	—	Christen 1974
5 July 1966	Zurich	♂ ♀	2	220	Christen 1974
13 Jan. 1968	Zurich	♂ °	2	—	Glaser in Christen 1974
1 Aug. 1968	Zurich	° °	2	200	Glaser in Christen 1974
18 Feb. 1969	Zurich	° °	2	201	Glaser in Christen 1974
6 Aug. 1969	Zurich	♂ ♀	2	169	Glaser in Christen 1974
21 March 1970	Zurich	° °	2	227	Glaser in Christen 1974

[1] Lactating female, young not captured.
[2] Purchased 9 November 1964.
[3] Purchased 9 November 1964.

no. 2 (table 91), in continuous production nearly 6 years, were excluded from the reckoning, the spring-summer/fall-winter ratio would be 8/2 (November).

Homosexuality

Christen 1974 (*niger*)

Although housed with an adult male with which they copulated regularly, the two females sometimes engaged in sexual play and simulated coitus. They licked each other's faces, mounted and performed copulatory movements. As a rule, the subordinate female assumed the masculine role.

Hybridization

Saguinus midas midas ♀ × *Saguinus bicolor bicolor* ♂
(Immendorf 1961, p. 145)

Of the hybrid twins born 3 June 1959 in the Cologne Zoo, the female was stillborn and the mother died shortly after parturition. The surviving male was hand reared from birth and cared for as if human by Fräulein Magret Immendorf.

The births took place in a cage with three adult tamarins. One adult, the mother, was identified as a red-handed tamarin (*Saguinus midas midas*). The others were said to be a pied tamarin (*Saguinus bicolor*) and a moustached tamarin (*Saguinus mystax*). Until the birth of the young, all three adults were thought to be males. Inasmuch as the surviving twin was discovered clasped to the pied tamarin, the latter was taken to be the father. The published photographs of the young support the assumption but no assurance is given that the mother was not pregnant before being caged with the males.

Three growth stages of the hybrid are illustrated by Immendorf. The 7-day (1961:frontispiece and fig. 1) and 3-month-old (1961, fig. 2) young appears to have the facial hairiness and white whiskers of *S. midas midas.* The large white frontal patch combines the juvenal characters of both *midas* and *bicolor.* The 10-month-old male is shown in four photographs (1961, p. 150, fig. 3–6). The coloration, particularly the seemingly contrastingly pale hands, is *midas*-like. The whiskers appear black, and the forehead remains hairy but with the white frontal patch reduced to a large spot over each eye as in young or subadult *midas.* The animal shown in figure 5 (Immendorf 1961) has the visage of an adult *Saguinus bicolor* but otherwise is identifiable with *S. midas.*

The chronology of growth and development of the hybrid is summarized on page 724.

Saguinus midas midas ♀ × *Saguinus oedipus oedipus* ♂
Reed 1965, pp. 113, 120 (figs. X.52, 53)

The male and female twins of the cross were born 19 February 1964 in the U.S. National Zoological Park, Washington, D.C. The mother died 18 April 1964, and the female hybrid died 26 June 1964, age 128 days, or 4 months, 8 days. Both are preserved as skins and skulls in the U.S. National Museum (nos. 344916 and 344917, respectively). The male hybrid was loaned 17 January 1966 to Dr. Kurt Benirschke for chromosome studies and was sacrified 30 January 1966, age 710 days, or nearly 2 years, weight, 480 g. The body was forwarded to the U.S. National Museum, where it arrived in an advanced state of decomposition. The carcass was immediately fixed in formaldehyde, and it was in this condition that I received it for study. The 2-year-old, fully adult male, together with the preserved half-grown female hybrid and the mother, were also kindly made available to me by Dr. Charles O. Handley, Jr. The vital statistics of the mixed family were supplied by Sybil E. Hamlet of the National Zoological Park.

The *midas* × *oedipus* adult male is a nearly uniformly reddish agouti-colored, hairy-face tamarin with pale hands and feet. It has none of the specializations or diagnostic characters of either parental species or of any other known callitrichid. Externally, it most nearly resembles *Saguinus graellsi,* most primitive of living tamarins, at least in coloration, but is more generalized in the absence of a dark mantle and head markings and more advanced in the bleaching of the upper surface of hands and feet. In both hybrids, pelage of cheiridia is a mosaic of the dominantly golden of *midas* and dominantly whitish of *oedipus.* The external ears are intermediate and altogether primitive in size and form as compared with the reduced pinna of *oedipus* and the extremely large one of *midas.* Coloration of the adult male is more primitive than that of the juvenal female. In all respects, its phenotype is one from which both the *Saguinus midas* and *S. oedipus* groups can be derived. The coat of the adult male and subadult female hybrids are described and compared below with those of the parental types (figs. X.52, 53).

Skin of face, ears, volar surfaces, and genitoanal region densely pigmented as in parents and primitive species of callitrichids. Skin of densely haired parts of head and body weakly pigmented but slightly heavier than in *midas;* skin of unexposed parts of *oedipus* depigmented, blotched, or spotted. Muzzle of hybrids thinly covered, sparse gray circumbuccal hairs short, fine; muzzle of parental species more nearly bare, the hairs black in *midas,* grayish in *oedipus.* Long hairs of cheeks and chin in male hybrid modified agouti, the subterminal band reddish, and in female hybrid, sparsely interspersed with shorter black hairs; entirely black in *midas,* whitish in *oedipus.* Flowing mane as in *oedipus* or well-defined mantle as in *midas* absent in hybrids. Hairs of forehead, crown, nape, shoulders, and back primitive agouti in male, forehead and crown in female a mosaic of entirely black as in *midas,* whitish as in *oedipus,* and black with buffy subterminal band (modified agouti), the mosaic gradually giving way to modified agouti on nape and to agouti on shoulders and back, the hairs with broad median orange band followed distally by narrow black band, a buffy golden subterminal band and fine black tip; in *midas,* forehead, crown and nape well-defined blackish, in *oedipus* sharply defined white and forming flowing mane; shoulder and back dark modified agouti in *midas,* dilute in *oedipus.*

Lateral fringe like back, as in all tamarins. Outer sides of thighs agouti, more or less like rump but banding finer, black guard hairs inconspicuous; in *midas* thighs

Fig. X.52. Hybrid twins, *Saguinus midas midas* × *Saguinus oedipus oedipus,* 4 months old, with father (*S. oedipus oedipus*); inset, Golden-handed Tamarin (*S. midas midas*) represents the maternal species. Animals photographed living in the National Zoological Park, Washington, D.C., where the twins were born. Grayish frontal spots and ruff are characters of juvenal pelages. Female hybrid twin, rear, died at 18 weeks with color pattern shown; male hybrid twin died at 2 years of age in adult pelage with hairs of forehead primitive agouti and hairs of ruff modified agouti. (Photo courtesy of National Zoological Park, Washington, D.C.)

Fig. X.53. Hybrid twins, *Saguinus midas midas* ♀ × *Saguinus oedipus oedipus* ♂, same 4-month-old twins shown in fig. X.52. (Photo courtesy of National Zoological Park, Washington, D.C.)

modified agouti like back and nearly as in hybrid, in *oedipus* reddish dorsally, dilute agouti laterally. Legs like thighs in hybrids, black in *midas,* reddish to orange, creamy or white in *oedipus.* Upper surface of feet of hybrids mixed buffy and white, the hairs tipped with black on metatarsus and most of toes, the distal phalanges in female entirely black; hairs of feet entirely orange in *midas,* reddish to whitish in *oedipus,* hairs often with dark tips. Upper arms of hybrids agouti, lower arms grading to mixed grayish and golden of hands; in *midas,* arms black proximally, changing abruptly to golden distally like upper surface of hands, in *oedipus,* arms white except at shoulders.

Hairs of throat golden and reddish in male hybrid, but in female hybrid gray forming a gular band continuous with gray of cheeks; inflection of hairs not certainly determinable in hybrids; in *midas,* throat hairs black with whitish bases and directed back, in *oedipus* whitish, buff, or orange and directed back or cresting toward midline. Neck and anterior portion of chest of hybrids dominantly reddish or tawny agouti, the hairs with broad median pale band reddish or orange, narrower subterminal band slightly paler, cover hairs of lower part of chest, belly, and inner sides of arms and legs agouti in male, passing progressively to modified agouti and uniformly buffy, except for black tip, in female; in *midas* underparts and inner sides of arms and legs black, in *oedipus* orange to white.

Tail modified reddish agouti for proximal half in male and becoming uniformly black distally; tail in female like that of male but proximal third only dominantly modified agouti, this pattern more extensive on ventral surface than on dorsal in both hybrids; in *midas,* basal portion of tail with reddish orange-banded hairs less extensive, in *oedipus* more extensive, particularly on ventral surface, but hairs not banded and usually bleached.

All facial tactile vibrissae, ulnar carpal vibrissae, and gular and pectoral spines present and well developed; tactile vibrissae and spines not well developed in *midas* with interramals absent, genals obsolete or absent; in *oedipus,* facial vibrissae present except interramals, gular and pectoral spines absent.

Size, proportions, and cranial and dental characters of hybrids as in tamarins in general.

The karyotype of the mature male as shown by Low and Benirschke (1968) and by Benirschke (1969, p. 220) is very similar to that of the paternal form of the species, *Saguinus oedipus oedipus,* and, by inference, to that of *Saguinus midas midas,* the maternal form of the species. A slight but consistent asymmetry in the length of the short arms of the third pair of the hybrid chromosomes was the only disparity noted. Cytological and histological studies by Low and Benirschke of the hybrid's testes demonstrated meiotic arrest, and the animal was presumed to be sterile. Reasons given by the authors for sterility are: (1) mechanisms operative in the hybrid state, (2) abdominal location of the testes, (3) a seasonal spermatogenic cycle, (4) a combination of preceding factors or other reasons unsuspected.

As was pointed out by Low and Benirschke (1968, p. 188), morphological similarities of the parental karyotypes, and fertility of other hybrids of intrageneric crossings, do not suggest the presence of hybrid sterility mechanisms.

It is also essential to note that the abdominal location of testes, regarded by Low and Benirschke as abnormal, is in fact normal in mature males. As shown elsewhere (p. 419), callitrichid testes are more often inguinal (not abdominal) than scrotal in position. With regard to explanation 3 above, meiotic arrest of spermatogenesis may well be cyclical. The breeding season in the wild state is usually carried over into life in captivity, at least for the first or second generation. Individual periodicity in gametogenesis is also a factor. In the majority of cases observed in laboratories, elapsed time between first observed matings and full-term births far exceeds the expected duration of gestation. The delay in fecundity suggests, more than anything else, a temporary sterility on the part of either partner or both partners.

Saguinus midas midas ♀ × (*Saguinus midas midas* × *Saguinus bicolor bicolor*) ♂, (Hick, 1961, *Fr. Kölner Zoo* 4(3):63, fig. of father).

Backcross hybrid twins born 4 September 1961 in the Cologne Zoo. The father, "Stupps," is the original *midas* × *bicolor* cross described by Immendorf (1961); the mother, "Rommy," had lived with "Stupps" since 1960.

GROWTH AND DEVELOPMENT

Chronology of Growth

Published reports on rearing *Saguinus midas* in captivity are here summarized separately. The subject of the account by Christen (1968; 1974) is a Black-handed Tamarin (*S. m. niger*). The second, by Mallinson (1972), is a Golden-handed Tamarin (*S. m. midas*), and the third, by Immendorf (1961), is a hybrid *S. m. midas* × *S. bicolor bicolor*. Relative length of extremities in newborn, juvenal, and adult *Saguinus midas niger* is shown in figure X.54.

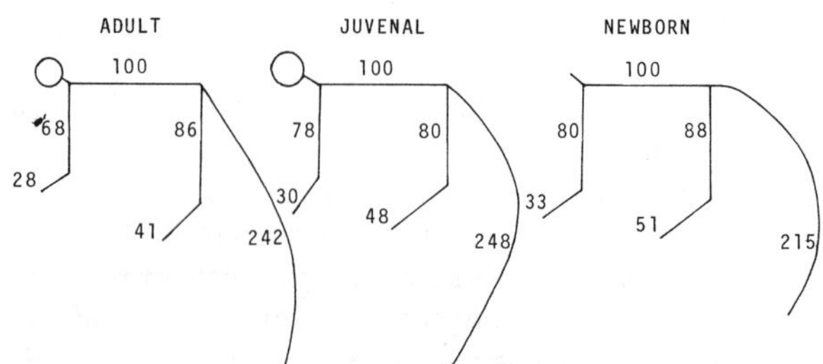

Fig. X.54. Bodily proportions of *Saguinus midas niger* at newborn, juvenal, and adult stages of development; limb and tail proportions (in percent) are based on trunk length with a common value of 100. Diagram reproduced from Christen (1974, p. 26); measurements or other data from which the proportions may have been calculated are not available.

Christen 1968; 1974 (*niger*)

The following chronology is a composite of the following young born in the Zürich laboratory and quartered with their parents (2 wild-caught females and 1 wild-caught male).
Twins ♂ ♀, born 8 November 1965, mother T1.
Twins ♂ ♀, born 20 August 1966, mother T1.
Singleton ♂, born 26 November 1965, mother T2.
Twins ♂ ♀ born 5 July 1966, mother T2.

1st day	Weight at birth 30–55 g or about 1/13 maternal weight; body completely covered with fine lanuga, hairs of head and nape about 7 mm long, of dorsum 5 mm; limbs, underparts thinly haired; tail unbanded; claws fully developed, about 3 mm long; volar surfaces and eyelids unpigmented. Eyes open at birth but kept closed most of time; can climb over mother but mostly remain attached to mother's nape with head buried in fur, tail hanging limply; chirp loudly when hungry; suckle 10 minutes at most, at hourly intervals, the suckling audible.
2d day	Turn heads with eyes open.
5th day	React to light of pocket lamp.
6th day	React to noise.
8th day	Play, beat on partitions between cages.
10th day	Juvenal pelage replacing lanuga; scratch selves
12th day	Scratch selves; sleep most of time.
14th day	Sit on shelf alone for short periods of time.
15th day	Fix attention on people.
16th day	Transfer from one adult to another without aid.
24th day	Engage in social grooming.
26th–33d day	Climb independently for short time on branches.
1st month	Coat color as in adults.
35–45 days	Take food from hand and mouth of adults.
45–60 days	Eat from food dish.
5th–6th month	Independent of adult care.

Age of weaning is not recorded.

Immendorf 1961 (*Saguinus midas* × *S. bicolor bicolor*)

The chronology is abstracted and translated from Immendorf's account of rearing "Stupps" in her home.

3 June 1959	Born.
3d day	Eats fruit, weight 50 g.
4th day	Weight, 50 g.
5th day	Eats more than drinks.
6th day	Indicates necessity to defecate, vacates soiled bed.
8th day	Climbs, observes people and objects.
9th day	Weight, 50 g.
11th day	Pea-sized testicles detected descending.
13th day	Eats little, bites strongly.
15th day	Trained to defecate in author's hand.
16th day	Extends tongue as greeting, also at unusual sights and in mimicry.
20th day	Drinks 4 bottles [contents and volume not stated].
21st day	Eats some banana; weight, 75 g.
25th day	Drinks 8 bottles; weight 80 g.
26th day	Runs on floor; reaches for everything; weight, 90 g.
29th day (2 July)	Shifts from sleeping on author to sleeping alongside; disagreeable to strangers, weight, 92 g.
35th day	Plays with everything.
37th day	Eats everything.
38th day	Eats alone at times; weight 110 g.
41st day	Attempts to drink unaided.
42d day	Interested in visitors but fears them.
43d day	Mounts scales alone; weight 120 g.
51st day	Weight 145 g.
59th day (1 August)	Recognizes mirror for what it is.
70th day	Weight 160 g.
13 Aug.–22 Nov.	Lame during this period.
76th day	Recognizes author's mother after 3-week absence; attracted to her as before.
78th day	Weight 160 g.
83d day	Introduced to a "half-starved" orphaned *Callithrix jacchus,* 6 weeks older but half the size. Hybrid watches newcomer climb floor lamp; both callitrichids placed in same cage for night but bedded separately.
84th day	Awakes and runs for lamp, climbs it for first time; resents roommate and does not play with it.
90th day	*Callithrix jacchus* returned to zoo; hybrid appears to enjoy being alone again; jumping and climbing had improved considerably during week with companion.
96th day (5 Sept.)	Learns to drink from cup without upsetting it.
102d day (11 Nov.)	Refuses milk; otherwise eats well.
114th day	Author notes white frontal band has gradually receded and almost disappeared.
115th day	Sleeps late during cold mornings.
123d day (12 Dec.)	Enjoys first bath given by author.
128th day	Permanent incisors erupt.
235th day (2 April 1960)	Permanent dentition complete; long black hairs covering head as in *S. midas* and concealing short white hairs such as characterize *S. bicolor.*

Mallinson 1972 (*midas*)

The chronology is of the development of male and female twins born 26/27 September 1970 in the Jersey Zoo. They were reared by mother alone when father died three days after birth of his progeny.

Age in Days	
8	One infant on branch by self.
10	Both infants leave mother.
34	One eats banana; ♀ twin much smaller than ♂ twin; crawls on his back and is carried about the branches.
54	500 IU vitamin D_3 given daily to twins.
56	White frontal blaze well developed.
58	Twins eat locusts.
120	Frontal blaze reduced but still evident.
121	♂ marks branches with genitals.
216	Frontal blaze nearly gone.
313	♂ with penile erection.

Savoury 1960, p. 54

The young born in the Georgetown, Guyana Zoo, was observed at two months of age "trying to lap her own milk."

Longevity

Crandall (1964, p. 105) gives 5 years, 10 months, 11 days as the longevity record for the Red-handed Tamarin (*Saguinus m. midas*). A live animal in the Jersey Zoo, according to Mallinson (1971, p. 9), was aged 4 years, 0 months, 14 days by the end of 1969. Christen (1974, pp. 7, 17) lists an adult female *Saguinus midas niger* purchased 9 November 1964 and still alive and productive 21 April 1970, when she must have been at least 7½ years old.

Longevity records based on captive animals more nearly reflect the care received than the capacity of the animal to survive in the wild.

BEHAVIOR

Observations on the following subjects are based on published reports and personal observations.

Habitat	Care of Young
Associations	Grooming
Range and Population Density	Handedness
Troop Size and Organization	Food
Daily Rhythm	Drink
Temperament	Posture
Threat	Locomotion
Defense	Play
Tonguing	Repose
Mirror Image Response	Exploitation
Marking	
Vocalization	

Habitat

Thorington 1968, p. 95 (*midas*)

Tamarins were observed during the course of one week in November 1964, in an area 750 × 400 yards in Porto Platon, Amapá, northeastern Brazil. "The forest in this area consists of low growth to a height of 30 ft. and trees to heights of 50 to 60 ft. The roadside vegetation provided an edge habitat more dense than the low growth within the woods themselves. A few hundred yards to the south the forest is 100 to 120 ft. tall. Near Santana I observed tamarins in a less forested area, where a grove of 10- to 20-foot *Cecropia* trees was bordered by trees 80 to 100 ft. in height.

"The temperature in the habitats of the tamarins ranged from 70° F to 90° F during the day with a relative humidity of 95% to 50%.

"Optimal habitats for these tamarins probably include both secondary forest and forest edge providing good areas for feeding and foraging, and deep forest providing these black animals with refuge from solar radiation."

De la Borde (in Buffon) 1789, p. 116 (*midas*)

They keep to the tall forest in the high grounds while howlers (sapajous) live in the humid lowland forests. They are not afraid of humans and come near their habitations.

Geijskes 1957, p. 38 (*midas*)

They "are quite common in savanna forests and along the banks of the rivers, but also in the bush of the sand ridges in the coastal plains [of Suriname]."

Bates 1863, p. 96 (*niger*)

"It seems to be less afraid of the neighbourhood of man than any other monkey. I sometimes saw it in the woods which border the suburb streets [of Belém de Pará], and once I espied two individuals in a thicket behind the English consul's house at Nazareth [in the vicinity of Belém de Pará]."

Cruz Lima 1945, p. 215 (*niger*)

"It is often found wild even in the suburbs of the cities, including, up to a short time ago, Belém, the capital of the state. In Pará, therefore, it is one of the commonest and best-known monkeys, rivaling *Saimiri sciureus,* the common 'macaquinho de cheiro.' They live in small bands, generally up to four individuals, preferably in open woods and secondary growth."

Hershkovitz (Field Notes) (*midas*)

Tamarins favored the higher bush in Suriname and were not seen in the low second growth where squirrel monkeys abounded.

Associations

Geijskes 1957, p. 38 (*midas*)

In Suriname, "sagoewintjes are sometimes found together with monki monkis [*Saimiri*] and kesi kesis [*Cebus apella*]."

Mallinson 1972, p. 23 (*midas*)

Ram Singh communicates that tamarins were seen mixed in large groups of squirrel monkeys, *Saimiri sciureus*.

Sanderson 1949, p. 761 (*midas*)

"Troops of [the capuchin, *Cebus apella*] are invariably associated with an approximately equal number of the big Tamarins (*Mystax midas*). Native hunters from all coastal districts confirm this habit. The two species feed, travel and even sleep together and only separate temporarily when greatly alarmed. In such instances the Tamarins descend to the lower foliage where they travel individually and much faster. The *Cebus* remain together and go aloft, but the two groups join up again as soon as possible and usually at no great distance."

Hershkovitz (*midas*)

In my frequent encounters with tamarins and capuchins in Suriname, I never saw the two together. This does not mean they may not be found together at times. Callitrichids often cross trails with larger monkeys and sometimes feed with them in the same fruiting trees. However, they do avoid squirrel monkeys, their nearest-sized relatives.

The permanent bond between tamarins and *Cebus* described by Sanderson is based on native hunters' accounts, which seem to have been garbled and elaborated in the writing. *Cebus* and *Saimiri,* however, are often seen together, and Sanderson's use of the term "big Tamarin" suggests the squirrel monkey rather than the smaller true tamarin.

Range and Population Density

Thorington 1968, p. 97 (*midas*)

"In the study area of approximately 750 by 400 yards, I saw 17 different tamarins. Of these, 7 animals spent at least half their time in the study site and were probably there all the time. This is a minimum density of one tamarin per 15 acres with a probable density of one tamarin per 7.5 acres. Utilization of the habitat was not uniform, however. Much of the foraging and feeding of the tamarins took place in the secondary growth along the road, two strips of vegetation 900 yards long and approximately 16 yards wide. The density of tamarins was much lower elsewhere near Porto Platon and Santana."

Hershkovitz

Under ordinary circumstances, tamarins are rather sedentary. Their cruising range in extensive forest is certainly confined to a radius of much less than 1 kilometer from the sleeping tree. Near coastal Lelydorplan, I saw a troop of about 8 tamarins living in a completely isolated and thickly overgrown woodlot about 100 meters square. The group had lived there for three years, I was told.

Estimates of population density are interesting, but in all cases, a population tends to fill the carrying capacity of its range. The factors controlling density, however, are legion. Some of the more important ones are food, fecundity, availability of sleeping and breeding sites, competition, predation, disease, meteorological fluctuations, and barriers to dispersal. Monkeys tend to concentrate where their preferred food is most abundant. It is not certainly known, however, if monkey populations, like those of many other kinds of mammals, most notably mice, undergo regular cycles of highs and lows.

Troop Size and Organization

De La Borde (in Buffon) 1789, p. 116 (*midas*)

"They go about in large troops."

Bates 1863, p. 95 (*niger*)

"The only [monkeys] which I saw frequently [in the vicinity of Belém de Pará] was the little Midas ursulus [= *Saguinus midas niger*] . . . [it] is never seen in large flocks; three or four is the greatest number observed together."

Cruz Lima 1945, p. 215 (*niger*)

"They live in small bands, generally up to four individuals."

Geijskes 1957, p. 38 (*midas*)

In Suriname, it "lives in families of five to twenty individuals."

Thorington 1968, p. 96 (*midas*)

Eight troops (A–H) of 2–6 individuals were distinguished, 4 of them (A–D) with 3–6 individuals in the study site (see "Habitat," above). Troop D, with 6 individuals, traveled as groups of 4 and 2; troop B, with 4 individuals, frequently joined troop C with 3.

"The interactions of group B and C, and of the individuals of group D, suggest intermediate stages in troop formation. The case is weak for troop D in which I only observed that the animals travelled in groups of 4 and 2, each of several times I watched them. However, a stronger case is presented by troops B and C, which occupied adjacent areas separated by a dirt road. The seven tamarins would frequently travel together. However, during interactions between troops A and B, the 3 animals of troop C would retreat to their side of the road while the other 4 animals would remain on the southeast side of the road. They might rejoin, but at other times the two troops travelled separately."

Mallinson 1972, p. 23 (*midas*)

Ram Singh communicates that he has frequently observed groups of from 4 to 15 tamarins in Guyana.

Hershkovitz (Field Notes, November 1961–February 1962)

Tamarins were seen in groups of 4 to about 10 individuals.

During certain fruiting seasons, individual trees may attract two or more troops of the same species. The aggregation might well be counted as a single troop. Some exchange and realignments probably take place during such incidental associations.

Estimates of the size of a large aggregation encountered casually and fleetingly are not always precise. When tamarins are near enough to be seen clearly for a count, they are near enough to know they are seen. The usual response to a possible aggressor is a distractive retreat flight, involving explosive and sustained whistling, leaping, scurrying, climbing, scrambling, tumbling and criss-crossings of trails. The swift movements of the animals, swishing of branches, fluttering of leaves, shaking of vines, falling of debris are dizzying and distracting to the beholder who needs to train his sights on particular individuals. Under these circumstances a head count is apt to be exaggerated. In contrast, seen unobserved or from a safe distance, the orderly procession of a troop making a routine round yields a reasonably accurate count.

Social Relations

Hershkovitz (*midas*)

The bond between family members is strong. The leader, usually the breeding male, looks out for all others. The cries of a wounded member of the family brings response from the other members in the form of vocalizations and distractive maneuvers to confuse the aggressor and turn his attention from the victim.

Christen 1974 (*niger*)

The single cage group maintained in the Zürich laboratory consisted of the dominant male, two incompatible adult females with one dominating the other, and one or two young.

Daily Rhythm

Christen 1974, p. 57 (*niger*)

Daily activity is from dawn to just before dusk, actual hours shifting with the seasons. Greatest activity occurs between 7:00 and 16:30 hours, with peaks at 11:00, 12:00, 14:00 (highest) and 16:30 (lowest); the lows at 11:30, 1:00, 16:00; and a sudden drop after 16:30. The following activities were measured, the time spent in each expressed as a percentage of total daily activity.

Locomotion	42%	mostly late afternoon
Social (including mutual grooming)	19%	mostly midday
Personal care (*Komfortverhalten*)	19%	
Feeding	12%	mostly late afternoon
Aggression	8%	

Adults spend nearly as much time in play (included with locomotion, above) as the young, and 11 times more than adult pygmy marmosets (*Cebuella*) in the same laboratory. The dominant female is more active than subordinate females in locomotion, social behavior, aggression and drinking; less active in personal care and in passive social activities inasmuch as she is groomed by subordinates more often than she grooms them.

Thorington 1968, p. 97 (*midas*)

"The tamarins were most active and most vocal in the morning at temperatures between 70°F and 80°F (85–95% r[elative] (h[umidity]). During the late morning, when the temperature and solar radiation increased, they moved out of the low forest and into the taller trees, which provide a dense canopy. I observed them in the low growth along the road during the early afternoon only on a day that was overcast and not as hot as usual."

Sanderson 1949, p. 767 (*midas*)

The tamarin "in captivity is active at night as well as in the day."

Hershkovitz

The movements observed by Thorington are common to many sylvan, diurnal mammals and birds.

With exception of the night monkey, *Aotus trivirgatus*, platyrrhines are normally inactive during the night whether in the wild or in captivity.

Temperament

Bates 1863, p. 97 (*niger*)

"It is a quick, restless, timid little creature, and has a great share of curiosity, for when a person passes by under the trees along which a flock is running, they always stop for a few moments to have a stare at the intruder. In Pará, Midas ursulus is often seen in a tame state in the houses of the inhabitants. When first taken, or when kept tied up, it is very timid and irritable. It will not allow itself to be approached but keeps retreating backwards when any one attempts to coax it. It is always in a querulous humour, uttering a twittering, complaining noise; its dark, watchful eyes, expressive of distrust, are observant of every movement which takes place near it. When treated kindly, however, as it generally is in the houses of the natives, it becomes very tame and familiar. I once saw one as playful as a kitten, running about the house after the negro children, who fondled it to their heart's content. It acted somewhat different towards strangers, and seemed not to like them to sit in the hammock which was slung in the room, leaping up, trying to bite, and otherwise annoying them. The expression of countenance in these small monkeys is intelligent and pleasing. This is partly owing to the open facial angle, which is given as one of 60°; but the quick movements of the head, and the way they have of inclining it to one side when their curiosity is excited, contribute very much to give them a knowing expression."

Cruz Lima 1945, p. 215 (*niger*)

"Although they do not fear the proximity of man, they are timid and easily frightened, not imitating the audacious imprudence of other Amazon monkeys. . . . not uncommonly, when fleeing from a pursuer, they hide and try to peek from their place of concealment with their bright and expressive little eyes, which give their physiognomy an air of intelligence.

"When recently caught, principally if already adult, they reveal a bad and irritable temper, but become domesticated with relative facility and may even become really interesting pets, although their shrill cries are not very agreeable."

De la Borde (in Buffon) 1787, p. 116 (*midas*)

They tame easily but become more troublesome in captivity than the sagouin (*Pithecia*). They are ill-tempered and bite the hand that tries to touch them. They will, however, climb up to the head or sit on the shoulders of familiar people who treat them gently.

Threat

Christen 1974 (*niger*)

The threat display to conspecifics and humans includes drawing back facial skin, muzzle wrinkling, teeth baring, head shaking and vocalizations. The male does not threaten the females but the dominant female often intimidates the subordinate female.

Defense

Christen 1974, p. 53 (*niger*)

The recently caged wild-caught tamarins reacted to strangers and loud noises by running excitedly about the cage, urinating, defecating, and whistling shrilly. They tame quickly, however, and soon eat from the caretaker's hands.

Tonguing

De la Borde (in Buffon) 1787, p. 116

"Tonguing directed toward people was accompanied by a peculiar movement of the head."

Judged by the text, De la Borde regarded tonguing as an impudent gesture.

Mirror Image Response

Christen 1974, p. 51 (*niger*)

An experimental mirror suspended in their cage excited the tamarins. They gazed at it from a distance, whistled softly and ran about. The dominant male flicked his tongue at his image from a distance of 30 to 40 cm, then charged and grabbed for his reflection. Meanwhile, the other animals rubbed their noses on branches, then moved up closer to the mirror and flicked their tongues at the strangely familiar apparitions.

Marking

Christen 1974, p. 51 (*niger*)

The tamarin marks by rubbing with the anogenital region and urinating. Marking usually accompanies a threat display and precedes and follows copulation. The dominant male marks more frequently than the females.

Vocalization

Christen 1974, p. 60 (*niger*)

The vocal expressions recorded and analyzed are of a single caged group consisting of an adult male, two adult females, and two young. Long distance and intergroup vocal communications are lacking or were not distinguished.

1. Contact calls
   a. Monosyllabic, soft, high pitched, *pi-pi-pi-;* uttered with mouth nearly or entirely closed, used in close contact by self-assured contented individuals of a group. The call with slight variation seems to be common to all callitrichids.
   b. Twitter and warble; used between group individuals separated by short distances. (Tamarins were not heard trilling like congeneric *Saguinus nigricollis, S. fuscicollis, S. oedipus,* or *Callimico goeldi* under similar circumstances).
   c. Monosyllabic intense fear or distress cry; uttered with widely open mouth; used when caught and held securely, or in jeopardy.
2. Two-syllable *di-ah* warning signal; first syllable high and short, second low and longer; uttered with mouth

open widely; used for warning of approach of terrestrial or flying enemies.
3. Hoarse croak; uttered by hungry tamarins in front of full feeding dish; meaning of the froglike nearly toneless croak not clear; not reported for other primates.
4. Aggressive threat or anger scream; uttered in series of short vocalizations each lasting a few seconds and accompanied by head shaking and threat display.
5. Juvenal squall and twitter; uttered when neglected or forced to dismount from back of caretaker.

Care of Young

Savoury 1960, p. 54

One young was produced 26 April 1960 [in Georgetown, Guyana, of wild-caught parents]. When it was first seen by the owner of the pair, the "father at once flew to the side of the cage in a desperate attempt to keep off any danger from the 'babe in arms [of its mother].' That day for the first time was anyone bitten.

"After a few days the mother gave up her charge to the father who then slung her across his back and so cared for and protected her and still does. It is amazing, however, to see how, like humans, this child is handed over to its mother to be nursed, and then returned to its guardian, and the manner in which they not only fondle her but also remonstrate with her when not inclined to go off on a little climbing venture alone."

Mallinson 1972, pp. 22–23

Twins (♂ ♀) born the night of 26/27 September 1970 in the Jersey Zoo were observed for patterns of parental care between the hours of 8:00 and 19:15 from 27–29 September, inclusive.

Out of 49 observations, one infant was seen on each parent 19 times, both infants on father 19 times, and both on mother 11 times.

The father died three days after birth of the young, and the mother successfully reared the twins by herself.

Christen 1974, pp. 19 (*niger*)

Twins born to subordinate female were handled from the first day by the dominant female, whose own young had died 19 days earlier. The young were suckled by both females from the third day after birth, but partial rejection by their mother and competition between the adults caused them suffering and hunger. They weakened and died, one at 46 days, the other at 57.

Grooming

Christen 1974 (*niger*)

Self Grooming. Most individuals groomed themselves mechanically after eating or drinking. They wipe the muzzle against a branch, sneeze, scratch themselves with hand or foot, lick and clean toes, fingers, and anogenital regions.

Social Grooming. An individual solicits grooming by lying down with throat exposed to the muzzle of a prospective groomer, who usually responds favorably. An uninterested animal, however, will scratch and push the soliciting individual away. The adult male shows no preference for either adult female, but the dominant female is more likely to be groomed by a subordinate female than the reverse.

De la Borde (in Buffon), 1787, p. 116

"They like to groom dogs."

Handedness

Christen 1974 (*niger*)

The two females of the group used either hand for taking and holding food but used mostly the left hand for lifting the lid of a food dish. The male used his left hand almost exclusively in all tests for handedness.

Food

Bates 1863, p. 97

"It is generally fed on sweet fruits, such as the banana; but it is also fond of insects, especially soft-bodied spiders and grasshoppers, which it will snap up with eagerness when within reach."

Geijskes 1957, p. 38

It likes "fruit and is very agile in securing insects, on which it chiefly feeds."

Cruz Lima 1945, p. 215

"They do not seem to be particular about their food, which may be vegetable or animal, preferring, however, insects and spiders. They do not seem to be repelled by bloody food, the massacre of small birds frequently being attributed to them."

Fooden 1965, p. 228

Stomachs of three individuals taken in the wild in Suriname contained fruit and seeds only. One of the three was shot in Carolinakreek, the other two on different days in Loksie Hattie, on the Saramacca River.

Hershkovitz (Field Notes, November 1961–March 1962)

In connection with Fooden's studies of the digestive system, it was noted that hard ovate pips about 13 mm long occurred throughout the intestinal tract of one individual. The pips are excreted whole, thus aiding in plant dispersal.

Christen 1974 (*niger*)

Tamarins take bits of food and small objects with one hand and use both hands for large items. A whole banana is peeled before eating. Insects are captured and consumed.

Pocock 1911, p. 816

In a test of feeding English insects to selected birds and mammals in the London Zoo, the Red-handed tamain reacted as shown below. Reactions of the Lion-tamarin (*Leontopithecus rosalia*) are described on page 858. Although the experiment was limited in scope and very uneven in application, it did prove that birds or mammals are not stereotyped in their prey preferences. Two individuals of the same species, and even the same individual, do not always react the same way every time to the same bait.

"Small white butterfly (*Pieris rapae*). Inspected but not touched by one tamarin, eagerly taken and eaten by another.

"Wall butterfly (*Perarge megaoera*). Eagerly seized and eaten by tamarin. A capuchin ate one without apparent liking, but another avidly devoured the butterfly.

"Seven-spotted ladybird (*Coccinella 7-punctata*). One licked but rejected by a tamarin. Another tamarin and a common marmoset (*Callithrix jacchus jacchus*) refused to taste it. Ladybirds were tasted and rejected by a capuchin (*Cebus* sp.). Another offered later to the same capuchin was smelled, tasted, rubbed between the hands and on the cage boards, and finally pulled into little pieces and eaten, bit by bit."

Drink

Christen 1974, p. 9 (*niger*)

Water and liquid food are lapped. Daily water consumption of the five tamarins (1 ♂, 2 ♀, 2 juvenals) in the Zürich colony averaged 12 c^3.

Posture

Christen 1974, p. 46 (*niger*)

The branch-sitter rests catlike with body weight supported on hind legs, slightly raised rump extending back, tail hanging straight down or resting on another branch, arms propped between legs.

An upright posture is often assumed for reaching objects and making inspections. The tail may be used as a prop in this exercise.

Locomotion

Bates 1863, p. 96

"Its mode of progression along the main branches of the lofty trees is like that of the squirrel; it does not ascend to the slender branches, or take those wonderful flying leaps which the Cebidae do, whose prehensile tails and flexible hands fit them for such headlong travelling. It confines itself to the larger boughs and trunks of trees, the long nails being of great assistance to the creature, enabling it to cling securely to the bark; and it is often seen passing rapidly round the perpendicular cylindrical trunks."

Cruz Lima 1945, p. 215

"It is interesting to observe their rapid maneuvers through the branches and their climbing of vertical cylindrical trunks like squirrels with the help of their curved and pointed nails. They leap with astounding agility, especially in a horizontal plane, this not being in agreement with Bates' observations."

Geijskes 1957, p. 38

It "is quite slow, leaping from one tree to another and grasping the smaller twigs with its claws."

Sanderson 1949, p. 767

"An individual leaped from the top of a palm tree to the ground, a distance of 50 ft. and was unharmed." (See also Bates 1863, p. 321, quoted in this volume, p. 681.)

Thorington 1968, p. 97

"The tamarins . . . moved predominantly among smaller branches when foraging. When they were frightened or chasing each other, however, they moved along large branches and trunks of trees. . . . The longest leap I observed was made regularly by the tamarins of group C in crossing the road. This leap measured 25 ft. horizontally. The accompanying vertical drop was approximately 25 ft. Short leaps were frequently made from small branches, but the longest leaps were made from vertical trunks, which provide better launching sites. Near Santana the tamarins regularly moved through a grove of 10- to 20- foot *Cecropia* trees by leaping five to ten feet from one vertical trunk to another, in the manner ascribed to primitive primates by Napier and Walker [1967*a*]."

Christen 1974 (*niger*)

The tamarin is less a branch-runner than a springer. It moves with short bounds from branch to branch, across the wire mesh of the cage or on the floor, the animal's arms and legs leaving and landing at the same time. In leaping from the highest branches to the floor of the cage, a distance of 1.5 m, the arms arrive slightly before the legs.

The head is always directed forward in climbing up or down. Claws are used for support, but thin branches are usually grasped with all five fingers holding from the same side. The big toe may grip from the same side as the other toes or in opposition.

Hershkovitz (Field Notes, November 1961–February 1962)

The red-handed tamarin, like all callitrichids, is a prodigious leaper. In Suriname, along the Saramacca River, I saw the individuals of a troop of 4 leap one by one from the canopy of a mature tree towering at least 100 feet above the side of a logging trail, into the coppice below on the other side. The horizontal distance spanned must have been at least 20 feet, the vertical drop not less than 50.

The rudimentary grade of callitrichid vertical clinging and leaping (see above, p. 730) lacks the froglike characteristic of the takeoffs and landings of the specialized prosimian vertical clinging and leaping.

Play

Christen 1974, p. 55 (*niger*)

Adults (♂ ♀ ♀) and offspring played constantly. They chased each other, wrestled, and engaged in mock fights. A rope hung in the cage was used for climbing and springing, but the play balls and rings in the cage were ignored.

Repose

Christen 1974 (*niger*)

The relaxed animal reclines like a cat on his belly with hind limbs drawn up beneath, trunk propped on elbows, head on outstretched arms. When resting in close contact the animals often pile up one on top of the other. The tamarins were not seen lying on their backs or sides except for grooming.

On days when the sun shone into the cages, the tamarins stretched themselves out in vantage places for basking in the warmth of the rays.

Exploitation

The tamarin is not hunted for food (Geijskes 1957, p. 38). By some it is regarded as unpalatable (De la Borde 1787, p. 117). The few tamarins exported are usually destined for zoos. They are rare and are infrequently used as experimental animals in biomedical laboratories and primate centers.

71 *Saguinus* 3: Mottled-face Tamarin Group *Saguinus inustus* Schwarz

Synonymic History

Jacchus [sp.], Wallace, 1854, *Proc. Zool. Soc. London* 1852:107, 109, 110—BRAZIL: *Amazonas* (upper Rio Negro, south bank); "the new black *Jacchus*."

Leontocebus midas inustus Schwarz, 1951, *Novit. Amer. Mus.* no. 1508:1—BRAZIL: *Amazonas* (Tabocal [= Tabacal?]; Javanari [= Yauanari], Rio Papuri; Rio Vaupés; "frente à Talmapunta [= Tahuapunta])".

Leontooebus [*sic*] *midas inustus,* Cabrera, 1958, *Rev. Mus. Argentino Cienc. Nat. "Bernardino Rivadavia"* 4:195 —listed.

Tamarin inustus, Osman Hill, 1957, *Primates,* 3:196, 204 (footnote), 211—characters; distribution; regarded as "an individual hybrid between *midas* and *nigricollis.*" Hershkovitz, 1963, *Am. J. Phys. Anthrop.* 21 (1):97; Ibid., 1964, 21 (3):396—"member of the bare-faced *marikina* group."

Saguinus inustus, Hershkovitz, 1966, *Folia Primat.,* 4:391—member of *oedipus* group; distribution. Hershkovitz, 1970, *Am. J. Phys. Anthrop.* 32:379—dental disease. Hershkovitz, 1970, *Folia Primat.,* 13:215—BRAZIL: *Amazonas* (Rio Javanari).

Type. Male, skin and skull, American Museum of Natural History no. 79413, collected 15 September 1915 by Olalla Brothers.

Type Locality. Tabocal (168), Rio Negro, Amazonas, Brazil.

Distribution (Map, figs. X.1, 15)

North of the Amazonas between the upper Rios Negro and Japurá (Caquetá) from about 65° W in northwestern Amazonas, Brazil, westward into eastern Colombia between the Ríos Apaporis and Guaviare to the base of the Serranía de la Macarena; eastern limits of range probably along the Ríos Atabapo-Guainia boundary with Venezuela.

Origin, Evolution, and Dispersal (fig. X.2)

The geographic position and morphology of *Saguinus inustus* point to its divergence from the same stock that could have given rise to the *S. oedipus* group. The common ancestor was almost certainly a dark agouti, hairy-face tamarin that may have ranged along the southeastern base of the Colombian Cordillera Oriental. *S. inustus,* the melanistic offshoot, is well on the road toward complete bare-facedness. The fully furred forehead and forepart of crown and the comparatively long hairs on cheeks and temples represent a grade of depilation between that of an extremely bare-faced species such as *S. bicolor* and the hairy-cheeked *S. leucopus.* The pelage pattern, including hair streams of the entire head, throat, and neck, however, is still like that of hairy-face tamarins such as *Saguinus mystax* or *S. midas.* The dominantly blackish brown coloration of *inustus* with no agouti hairs remains unique within the genus *Saguinus.*

The geographic range of *Saguinus inustus* and *Saguinus midas* may meet but there is no evidence that they overlap. Geographic approximation in this case appears to be the result of the spread of each species in the direction of the other rather than derivation of one form from the other. The coat color of *S. midas* with its black mantle and modified agouti lower back, thighs, and tail base cannot be derived from or give rise to the coloration of *S. inustus.* Although more advanced in depigmentation and saturation than *midas,* the skull of *inustus* is very near the primitive model, while that of *midas* is relatively specialized.

Taxonomy

The first notice of the black bare-face tamarin was published by Wallace (1854, pp. 107, 109, 110) in his brilliant exposition of the role of rivers in delimiting the distribution of the monkeys inhabiting the Amazonian basin. Among the twenty-one kinds of primates observed by Wallace in Brazil, three were tamarins identified as *Jacchus* [*sic*] *bicolor, J. tamarin,* and a third "entirely black, with the face of bare white skin [which] inhabits the district of the upper Rio Negro. It appears to be quite new." In describing food habits of tamarins Wallace noted that "the little black *Jacchus* last mentioned was particularly savage."

The formal description of Wallace's "black *Jacchus*" was delayed a century until Schwarz, on the basis of specimens collected by the Olallas in 1915, named it *Leontocebus midas inustus.* There is no close relationship, however, between mottled-face *inustus* and the more hairy-faced *midas* of the Guianan region.

Remarks. Osman Hill (1957) asserts that "there can be no question of *inustus* being an individual hybrid between [*Saguinus*] *midas* and [*Saguinus*] *nigricollis,* for 11 specimens, all alike, are referred to in the original description." I see no logical or biological relationship between the conclusion stated first and the premise that follows. There is also the question of judging the characteristics of 11 unseen specimens by the published description of one. *S. midas* and *S. nigricollis* do not meet in nature and cannot therefore hybridize there. In any event, the characters of *S. inustus* are not intermediate or intergrading between those of *S. nigricollis* and *S. midas.* The uniformity of the samples of *S. inustus* from 6 widely scattered localities, spread over a range of thousands of square miles, precludes the possibility of their derivation through hybridization. The probable origin of *inustus* through geographic isolation from a hairy-face *S. nigricollis*-like stock is highly probable (p. 605).

Diagnostic Characters

Pelage melanistic throughout; facial skin and external genitalia mostly unpigmented; skin of philtrum unpigmented and marked by conspicuous whitish patch; tail uniformly dark (fig. X.55).

External Characters

Integument. Muzzle black with white patch between upper lip and nostrils, remainder of face and sides of head unpigmented except for occasional black spotting and mottling, particularly around eyes and front of cheeks; skin from superciliary region and temples to throat completely exposed beneath sparse black fuzz; minute hairs of muzzle feathered and crested in midline; a more or less well defined black fringe present between corner of eye and base of ears; blackish hairs of forehead

Fig. X.55. Mottled-face Tamarin, *Saguinus inustus.* Two views of same individual combined in one photograph. The tamarin was obtained live by Dr. Lewis L. Klein in San José del Guaviare, Vaupés, Colombia. It appears to differ from typical forms of the species by the whitish hairy cheeks. (Photo courtesy of Lewis L. Klein.)

and front of crown short but dense; long pelage of dorsum from back of head to base of tail blackish anteriorly, becoming dark chestnut posteriorly, the individuals hairs nearly uniformly colored throughout their length; mantle not defined; outer sides of shoulders and fore- and hind limbs blackish, of medial surface of rump and hind limbs chestnut with a fringe of longer golden brown hairs on inner edge of rump; hands and feet black; sides of body and lateral fringe dark brown, chestnut, or golden brown; underparts dominantly blackish with hairs of belly brown, of genitalia whitish; tail uniformly blackish; external genitalia unpigmented.

Vibrissae. Supraorbitals, mystacials, rhinarials, mentals and backward-directed interramals constantly present; genals not detected; ulnar carpals present; gular and pectoral spines absent.

Genitalia (fig. X.48). Judged by their appearance on the dry skin, male and female genitalia are indistinguishable from those of other tamarins. Bacula (fig. X.48) are not distinctive, given the wide range of variation within the genus.

Cranial Characters

Frontal contour low; the postglabellar depression slightly or hardly defined; temporal ridges well defined, usually closely approximated but not fusing; nasal profile plane to slightly convex; frontal sinuses moderately inflated; malar foramen from 1 mm to 2 mm in greatest diameter; lacrymal small and wholly within orbit; ventral border of mandible V- to U-shaped, the horizontal rami hardly or not arced, the angular process slightly or not at all deflected downward.

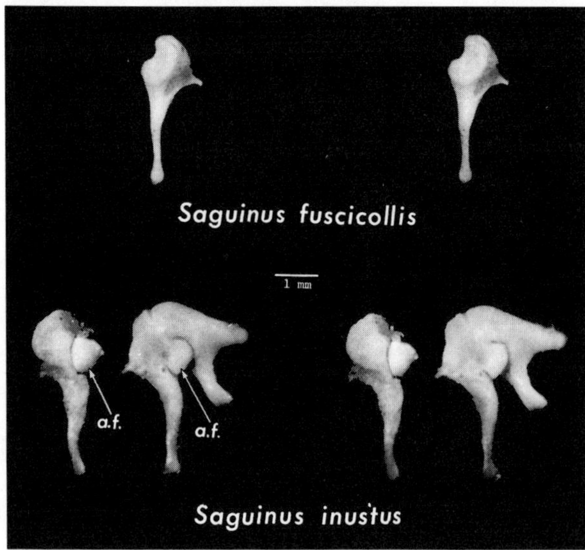

Fig. X.56. Ear bones, stereoscopic views: *S. inustus,* right malleus (median aspect) and left malleus (lateral aspect), with incus in place; right and left malleolar articular facets (*a.f.*) are separate bones. Compare with left malleus (median aspect) of *Saguinus fuscicollis.*

Ossification of the malleus from two centers and their persistence as two separate bones; perhaps as an individual anomaly, is exhibited in figure X.56.

Measurements

See appendix table 2.

Comparisons

Distinguished from all callitrichids by the diagnostic characters given above. The similar sized, dominantly melanistic *Callimico goeldii* is readily distinguished from *S. inustus* by its entirely black and hairy face and peculiar bobbed mane with pompadour in front.

Saturation, Bleaching, Depilation, and Depigmentation

Saguinus inustus is the most nearly completely eumelanistic species of callitrichid. No trace of agouti appears in the specimens examined. Only some forms of *Ateles* and *Alouatta* among cebids are comparably saturate.

The small white philtral patch is the most conspicuous bleached feature of the coat color pattern of specimens examined. However, individuals from the upper Río Guaviare basin, as indicated in figure X.55, are strikingly white-cheeked and probably unusually hairy-cheeked. Bleaching on other parts of the body is little more than incipient except on the pale brown lateral fringe.

Depilation on sides of head, throat, and neck is nearly complete, and the remaining hairs barely outline the pelage pattern of the ancestral hairy-face tamarin.

Depigmentation of the head seems to have progressed evenly from in front of ears toward muzzle and crown. Only the areas around lips, nostrils, and between the eyes remain uniformly pigmented. Scrotum and remainder of body except plantar surfaces and ears are also depigmented.

Facial depigmentation (fig. X.3) is more advanced in *Saguinus inustus* than in other tamarins and in no tamarin are both depigmentation and depilation of the face as advanced as in *inustus.* The nearest parallel occurs in the vitiligolike facial markings of many individuals of bareface *Saguinus bicolor.* Facial depigmentation in *inustus,* however, is distinctly patterned, but that of *bicolor* appears to be random and extends asymmetrically over other parts of the body. The degree of facial depigmentation in the paler races of *Callithrix argentata* is also comparable to that of *Saguinus inustus,* but the face remains hairy. The white philtral patch of *inustus* suggest the incipient stage in the depigmentation and bleaching of the circumbuccal and narial regions in members of the *Saguinus mystax* group, particularly *S. m. labiatus.* Depigmentation of the scrotum also evolved independently in *S. inustus* and members of the *S. mystax* group.

Specimens Examined

Total: 13. BRAZIL—*Amazonas:* Papuri, mouth, 1 (AMNH); Rio Uaupés, opposite Tahuapunta, 2 (AMNH); Tabocal, Rio Negro, 4 (AMNH); Jauanari, 3 (AMNH); COLOMBIA—*Vaupés:* Alto Caño Itillo, 1 (FMNH); Caño Grande, 1 (FMNH); San José del Guaviare, 1 (FMNH, in spirits).

72 *Saguinus* 4: Bare-face Tamarins History, Characters, and Key to Species and Subspecies

Bare-face tamarins include the *Saguinus bicolor* group with one species and the *Saguinus oedipus* group with two species. The two groups are recognized by three independent features. They (1) occur north of the Rio Amazonas, (2) diverged independently from hairy-face tamarins, and (3) attained a grade of facial depilation that distinguishes them collectively or individually from other callitrichids.

Diagnostic Characters

Pelage of head, body, limbs, and tail variously or contrastingly colored, never uniformly whitish or blackish; skin around lips and nostrils, ears and external genitalia blackish, or more or less blotched or mottled, but never mostly or entirely unpigmented; circumbuccal and circumnarial areas bare or sparsely covered with short hair, never with well-developed mustache or band of whitish hairs; temples and sides of crown to level of anterior border of ears nearly bare or thinly covered with short hairs sharply contrasted with long, thick pelage of mid-crown and nape, cheeks nearly bare or covered with long hairs; ears bare and completely exposed; distal half of hairs of middle portion of back with subterminal pale band (modified agouti) or unbanded; color pattern of back never trizonal; tail with dorsal surface blackish, ventral surface reddish, or terminal portion blackish and proximal portion reddish, or tail entirely dark except pale pencil.

Composition

Saguinus bicolor Group:

Bare-face tamarins of Brazil north of the Rio Amazonas between the Rios Negro and Erepecurú represent the single species of the group, *Saguinus bicolor*. The group is most advanced in facial depilation and chromatic dilution. It probably evolved in situ from a founder colony of hairy-face tamarins separated by a river-bend cutoff from the ancestral stock on the south bank of the Amazonas west of the Rio Madeira. Juvenals of *S. bicolor* retain the hairy-face ancestral condition. Three geographic races are recognized. *S. bicolor bicolor* Spix occupies the western end of the range, *S. b. martinsi* Thomas inhabits the eastern end, and *S. b. ochraceus* Hershkovitz is geographically intermediate.

Saguinus oedipus Group:

This line is more diversified than the first. It arose independently from an upper Amazonian stock of hairy-face tamarins, spread northward along the eastern base of the Andes thence west into northern Colombia and Middle America. The most primitive species of the lineage, the northern Colombian *S. leucopus*, is characterized by retention of much of the ancestral pilosity of face and frontal region. The most advanced species, *S. oedipus* (with *geoffroyi*) of northwestern Colombia, Panamá, and Costa Rica, is nearly as bare-faced as *S. bicolor*, but its young retain much of the ancestral facial and frontal hairiness still preserved in adult *S. leucopus*. External ears of the *S. oedipus* group became progressively smaller from *leucopus* through *S. o. geoffroyi* and *S. o. oedipus*.

Taxonomy and Nomenclature

The earliest generic name for a bare-face tamarin, *Marikina* Lesson (1840, p. 199), appeared in the binomial *Marikina bicolor*. This combination, a lapsus for the original *Midas bicolor* Spix, was treated as a synonym of *Oedipus titi* Lesson, a new name for *Saguinus oedipus* Linnaeus. There is nothing in the International Code of Zoological Nomenclature that invalidates this inadvertent erection of a new generic name. *Marikina* gained wide currency in 1945 when Cruz Lima adopted it for all bare-face tamarins. In my (1949, p. 410) first classification of callitrichids, *Marikina* Lesson, 1840, was accepted as the oldest valid generic name for tamarins in general, and particularly, as the subgeneric name for the bare-face tamarins of the *bicolor* group, which then included *Saguinus leucopus*. *Marikina* has since been replaced by the prior name *Saguinus* Hoffmannsegg 1807 (cf. Hershkovitz 1958, p. 53). Other generic or subgeneric names proposed for bare-face tamarins follow.

Seniocebus Gray, 1870, with *Seniocebus bicolor* (= *Midas bicolor* Spix), type by monotypy, is an objective junior synonym of *Marikina* Lesson.

Oedipus Lesson, 1840, with the tautonymic-type, *O.*

titi Lesson (= *Simia oedipus* Linnaeus), is preoccupied by *Oedipus* Tschudi, 1838, a genus of Amphibia, and unavailable.

Oedipomidas Reichenbach, 1862, was proposed as a new name for the preoccupied *Oedipus* Lesson, 1840. The included species were *Simia oedipus* Linnaeus, designated type by Elliot (1905, p. 532), and *Hapale geoffroyi* Pucheran. The name had little or no acceptance until Elliot used it in 1913 (p. 213) and 1914 (p. 643) as the generic name for all bare-face tamarins.

Hapanella Gray, 1870, with monotype *geoffroyi* Pucheran, was proposed as a subgenus of *Oedipus* Lesson. This meant that Gray regarded each of the two races of *Saguinus oedipus* as subgenerically distinct.

The history of the generic names for bare-face tamarins is outlined in the synonymy of the genus *Saguinus* (p. 600). The taxonomic validity of each generic name proposed for tamarins need not be moot. All tamarins can interbreed in captivity, and except for differences in color and pelage patterns, no single character has been adduced for absolutely distinguishing one species of tamarin from all others.

Present treatment of all bare-face tamarins as a unit is simply a convenience of organization. Each of the two natural superspecies, *S. bicolor* and *S. oedipus,* intergrades with hairy-face tamarins, and only through this common bond is each related to the other.

Saturation, Bleaching, Depilation, and Depigmentation

The dorsum of *Saguinus oedipus* (sensu lato) and lower back of *S. bicolor bicolor* retain banded hairs of the modified agouti pattern. The trend toward albinism by bleaching and extension of the pale subterminal band in *S. oedipus geoffroyi* is well advanced. The dorsal coloration in *S. o. oedipus,* however, is more complex, and the trend is toward dilute melanism or drab on midback, and albinism via erythrythism on rump, thighs, and sides of the body and tail. This sequence was evidently completed on crown and nape. In *Saguinus leucopus,* dilute melanism or drab remains on the dorsal surface of head, trunk, and thighs. The hairs of the underparts, including the inner sides of limbs, are pheomelanic terminally, eumelanic basally, with the blackish pigmentation evidently switched to reddish. The albinistic trend is apparent in the silvering of head, body, and tail pelage, and the nearly white arms, legs, and tail tip.

The prototype of the *Saguinus bicolor* group was evidently primitive agouti on upper parts, saturate pheomelanic on underparts. In *S. b. martinsi,* the middorsal stripe from nape to tail tip is saturate eumelanin while limbs became pheomelanic. In *S. b. ochraceus* the agouti is gone, the more or less advanced pheomelanic saturation condition in *martinsi* is dilute in *ochraceus,* the mantle nearing white. If *ochraceus* is derived from *martinsi,* as appears, pheomelanin must have replaced the eumelanin on the middorsal line of the trunk.

In all bare-face tamarins, bleaching began on the head and advanced rapidly from face to forehead and forepart of crown. Depilation followed nearly as rapidly, except in *S. leucopus* where it remains at an early stage. Bleaching followed on nape, shoulder, and forelimb. These parts are already almost entirely white in *S. bicolor bicolor* and *S. oedipus* (*sensu lato*) and well advanced in the other bare-face forms. Blanching of the chest is followed by blanching of the hind legs in the *S. bicolor* group. In the *S. oedipus* group, the legs whiten first. Blanching of the belly follows in *S. bicolor* and *S. leucopus,* but the belly became nearly white in *S. oedipus* along with the other underparts.

The tail is eumelanic dorsally and pheomelanic ventrally in *S. bicolor,* pheomelanic basally and eumelanic terminally in *S. oedipus.* In *S. leucopus,* the tail hairs are dominantly eumelanic but tend to pheomelanism basally, drab to silvery terminally with pencil whitish.

The hypertrichy represented by the white crest of *S. oedipus oedipus* is unique among platyrrhines. An earlier stage of the crest appears in *S. o. geoffroyi,* where the wedge-shaped coronal patch of comparatively short whitish pelage expands and grades into the longer, dominantly reddish nuchal crest behind.

General depigmentation of exposed parts of head and limbs is conspicuous in many individuals of *Saguinus bicolor bicolor.* In some, the piebald skin suggests effects of the disease vitiligo. The possibility that this depigmentation in *bicolor* is morbid rather than natural is worth investigation.

Key to the Species and Subspecies of Bare-Face Tamarins

1. Forehead and crown to level of ears entirely covered with short silvery hairs; sides of face with long silvery tufts; tail dominantly blackish above and below except penciled tips silvery to orange . . . . *S. leucopus* (p. 748)

1′. Forehead and crown to level of ears practically bare or with white median crest; sides of face practically bare and with or without thin fringe of short silvery hairs; tail variously colored 2

2. Forehead and crown to level of ears in adult bare except for fine fuzz not concealing skin, in young more or less covered with short silvery hairs; median frontal crest absent, sides of face without fringe; ears broad, lower posterior lamina of pinna nearly as large as upper anterior lamina; tail entirely orange to reddish orange or brown to blackish above, orange or reddish orange beneath 3

2′. Forehead and crown to level of ears or beyond adorned with a whitish wedge-shaped crest or whitish (rarely reddish or brown) flowing mane; sides of face with silvery fringe; ears narrow, lower posterior lamina of pinna greatly reduced or absent, upper anterior lamina normal; terminal half of tail entirely black 5

3. Arms and chest dominantly or entirely whitish, belly reddish . . . . *S. bicolor bicolor* (p. 741)

3′. Arms ochraceous or orange, crown to shoulders brown to buffy like back, chest orange or ochraceous like belly 4

4. Crown and nape dark brown, hairs of back and sides distinctly punctulated (agouti); hairs of angle between throat and neck orange punctulated with brown . . . . *S. bicolor martinsi* (p. 745)

4′. Crown and nape buffy to cinnamon, hairs of back, at least anteriorly, hardly or not punctulated; hairs of angle between throat and neck buffy to whitish without annulations . . . . *S. bicolor ochraceus* (p. 747)

5. Headdress extending back from forehead over nape as a flowing white mane . . . . . *S. oedipus oedipus* (p. 761)

5′. Headdress a white wedge-shaped crest from forehead to between ears, pelage of nape and shoulders forming a reddish mantle . . . . *S. oedipus geoffroyi* (p. 757)

73 *Saguinus bicolor* Group
Saguinus bicolor Spix, Brazilian Bare-face Tamarins

Distribution (figs. X.1, 15)

In Amazonas, Brazil, north of the Rio Amazonas from the east bank of the lower Rio Negro east to the west bank of the Rio Erepecurú (Paru do Oeste); northern limits of range unknown but almost certainly within Brazil.

Origin, Evolution, and Dispersal (fig. X.2)

The bare-face prototype of *Saguinus bicolor* almost certainly originated in the eastern angle between the Rios Amazonas and Negro and there gave rise to the three known races. No other species has the same pelage pattern of face and scalp and none described is intermediate between *S. bicolor* and living hairy-face tamarins. It is certain, nevertheless, that the ancestral tamarin was hairy faced. Representatives of them were shuttled across the Amazon at the Rios Negro-Madeira ferry and established the colony which was to become *S. bicolor* by progressive thinning, shortening, and loss of facial and coronal pelage. This evolution of bare-face tamarins had already been surmised by Thomas in 1912 (p. 85).

The geographic history of the phyletic line leading to *bicolor* parallels that of *Saguinus midas* and other primates (e.g., *Cebus nigrivittatus, Pithecia pithecia*).

Saguinus bicolor and *S. midas* are the only callitrichids indigenous to the Guianan region. The advanced grade of color dilution in *Saguinus bicolor,* the extent of its geographic diversification, and the absence of bare-face tamarins south of the Amazonas indicate that this species is the older and arrived first in the region. Its present restricted geographic range is considerably smaller than that of *S. midas.* This may be attributed to a geographic accident that forced the species into a cul-de-sac or it may be due to mutual exclusion. So far as known, *bicolor* and *midas* are locally, if not regionally, allopatric. The prototype of *S. midas* evidently spread rapidly into all suitable habitats in the Guinas not then occupied by *S. bicolor.* The presence of this more primitive or generalized species may have contained the spread of *S. bicolor.* The two species have interbred in captivity (cf. p. 721).

Speciation of isolated populations of *S. bicolor* is well advanced, whereas in *midas* it is barely incipient. The brown, faintly agouti *S. b. martinsi* at the eastern extreme of the geographic range appears to be least advanced while the partly albinistic nominate form at the western extreme is most highly specialized. The dilute brown *S. b. ochraceus* is geographically intermediate but is nearest *martinsi,* from which it is separated phenotypically (paler throughout) and geographically by the breadth of the Rio Nhamundá.

Diagnostic Characters

Head from throat to crown in front of ears black and practically bare, tail usually blackish to pale brown above, reddish to orange beneath, sometimes uniformly orange, pencil orange, sometimes black, ears large.

External Characters

Integument. Facial skin entirely black (fig. X.57), sometimes blotched (figs. X.3, 61); muzzle, cheeks, forehead, and crown to front of ears virtually bare except for the vibrissae and often a light fuzz, the whole sharply defined from the long brown, buff, or white hairs of back of head including nape, forepart of back, and shoulders;

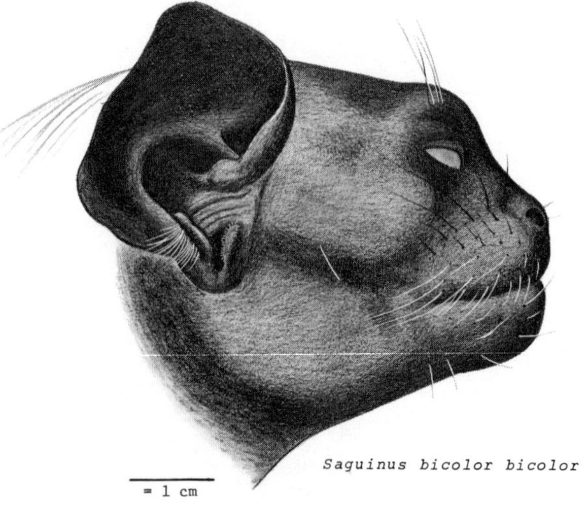

Fig. X.57. *Saguinus bicolor bicolor*: Profile view with mane removed to expose ear, vibrissae, and facial pigmentation.

remainder of back buffy to brown with or without punctulations; upper surface of feet buffy to rufous; belly and innersides of hind limbs ochraceous to reddish; throat and chest like belly or sharply defined white or yellowish, the hairs of throat directed backward; tail blackish to pale brown above, ochraceous orange or reddish beneath, rarely uniformly orange or reddish, penciled tip orange or black.

Vibrissae (figs. III.12; X.57). Supraorbitals, mystacials, rhinarials, mentals present; interramals not detected in dry skins or in two fluid-preserved *S. bicolor bicolor;* genals sometimes present, ulnar carpals present; gular spines present.

Ears. See page 102 and figs. III.18; X.57.

External Genitalia

Male (fig. X.58A,C)

Adult. External genitalia and pubic region mottled, skin leathery; pigmented penis cylindrical, tapered distally, the glans asymmetrical as usual; subglobose scrotum pendulous, wider than long and not clearly subdivided into testicular sacs, the skin broadly wrinkled and somewhat convolute but otherwise smooth and sparsely set with dark hairs; outer portion of preputial folds glabrous like internal portion, or sheath; transverse width of scrotum, with testes, 26 mm; sexual skin extensive and well defined as a median pubic band; perineal and anal regions with slightly mottled skin, pelage orange; baculum in one adult *Saguinus bicolor martinsi* distinct from those of all other callitrichids.

Female (fig. X.58C)

Adult. External genitalia extremely small, labia majora mottled, scrotal folds forming caudal half of labial cushions, the skin densely papillate, each papilla with a long, stiff hair, the pelage extending to inner edge of vestibule and deep broad labial commissure; preputial fold more than twice as large as scrotal fold, integument of hairy portion corrugated but not papillate, glabrous pigmented portion, or annulus surrounding glans clitoridis, approximating in median line to form peaked cupola as seen from ventral surface; clitoris and frenulae mostly hidden in labial tissue; external genitalia wider than long, transverse width 18 mm, genital fissure 7 mm; perineal and anal regions lightly pigmented; sexual skin a pigmented median pubic band; perineal and anal regions lightly pigmented.

Remarks. Labia majora in dry skins of fully mature females may have been substantially like that of the spirit-preserved subadult but probably larger. The sexual skin, however, is definitely more extensive and glandular in adults than in young.

Cranial Characters (figs. X.7, 9, 11)

Frontal contour low to moderately rounded; temporal ridges well separated to closely approximated but not fusing, a weak but independent sagittal crest sometimes present; nasal profile plane to markedly concave; frontal sinuses moderately inflated; greatest diameter of malar foramen usually less than 1 mm; ventral border of mandible V-shaped to U-shaped, the horizontal rami little or not at all arced, the angular process slightly inflected inward and slightly deflected downward.

Comparisons

Distinguished from other bare-face tamarins by larger ears, virtually bare forehead and anterior portion of crown, pelage of crown between ears directed straight back without forming whorls, median crest or plume, and tail usually sharply bicolor throughout except at tip.

Reproduction

Two litters from a pair of captive *Saguinus bicolor bicolor* in the Frankfurt am Main zoological garden, are recorded by Zukowsky (1940, p. 103). One young was produced 10 April 1936, another 20 October 1936. The 194 days between births exceed by far the probable gestation period for the second litter. The history of the parents during the interval is not recorded.

Longevity

Crandall (1964, p. 105) records an individual of *Saguinus bicolor bicolor* that lived 8 years, 2 months, and 10 days in the New York Zoo, and one of *S. b. martinsi* that survived 9 years and 10 months.

Hybrids

The *midas* × *bicolor* cross and back-cross are discussed under the heading of *Saguinus midas.*

Remarks

The only known habitat of *bicolor* is the wooded areas surrounding the then village of Barra do Rio Negro, now the city of Manaus (170). Bates (1863, pp. 343–34) obtained a specimen of *Saguinus bicolor* during his stay in Barra or Manaus, on the Rio Negro "[It] was rather common in the forest; it is the *Midas bicolor* of Spix, a kind I had not before met with, and peculiar, as far as at present known, to the eastern bank of the Rio Negro." Cruz Lima (1945, p. 205) notes that these tamarins "live in small bands in the woods and copses undisturbed by the vicinity of [man] inhabited places." He adds that "they are still common at Flores, suburb of Manaus."

Practically nothing is known of the behavior of *Saguinus bicolor.* Bates (1863) notes that "like its congeners, it keeps together in small troops, and runs along the main boughs of the loftier trees, climbing perpendicular trunks, but never taking flying leaps."

It is surprising that Bates, who spent three months, January to March 1850, in Barra and vicinity failed to surprise the pied tamarin in a flying leap.

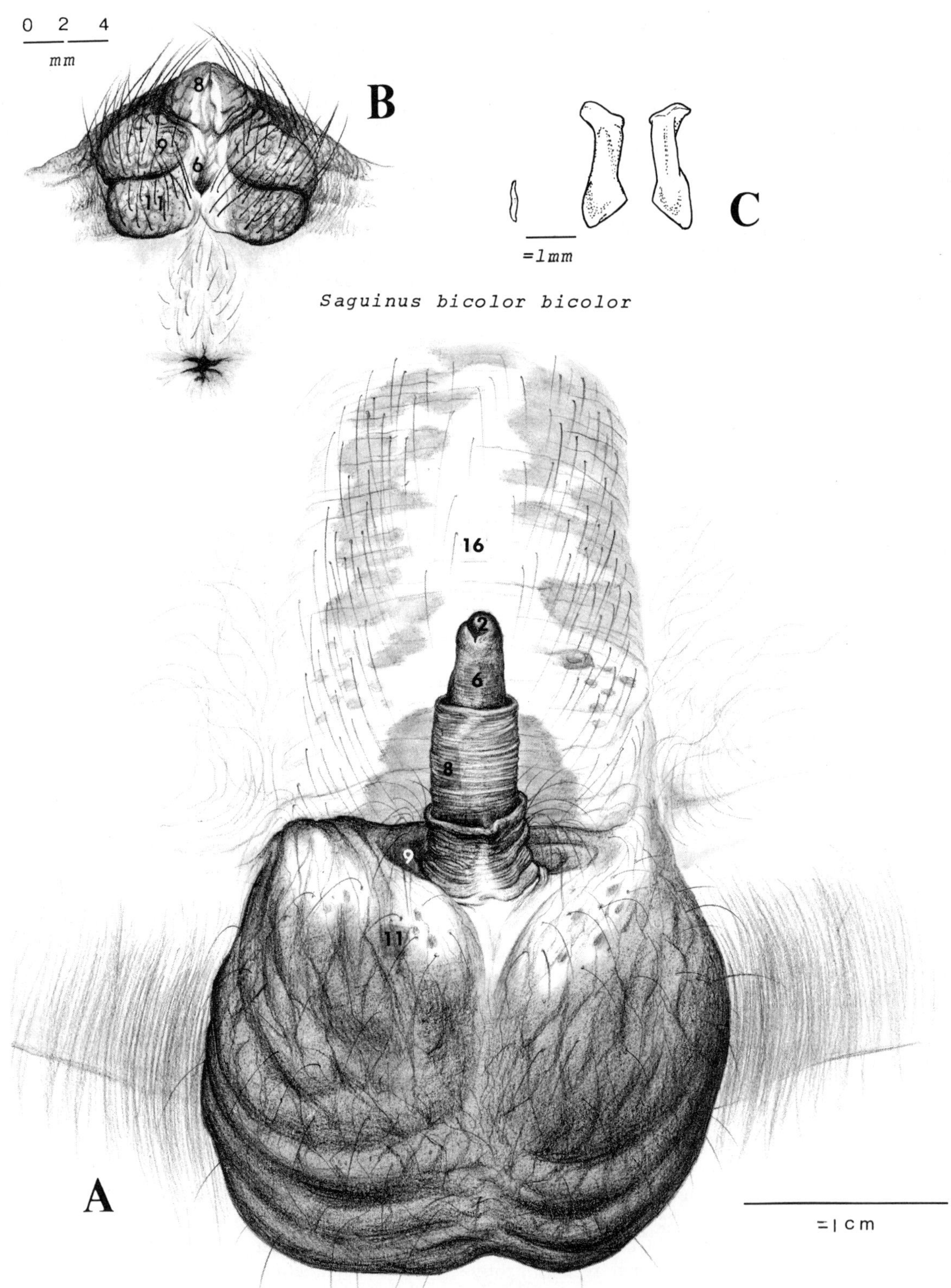

Fig. X.58. *Saguinus bicolor,* external genitalia: *A,* adult male, *S. b. bicolor,* portion of sexual skin shown, penis arranged for better exposure of parts; *B,* underdeveloped baculum of *S. b. bicolor* and two aspects of fully developed baculum of *S. b. martinsi; C,* genitalia of adult female *S. b. bicolor*. Symbols explained on pages 113–14.

SAGUINUS BICOLOR BICOLOR SPIX, PIED BARE-FACE TAMARIN

Fig. X.59. Pied Bare-face Tamarin, *Saguinus bicolor bicolor.*

Synonymic History

Midas bicolor Spix, 1823, *Sim. et Vesp. Brasil.*, p. 30, pl. 24, fig. 1 (animal). Wagner, 1833, *Isis von Oken* 10: 996—may be a variety of *oedipus.* Pelzeln, 1883, *Verh. K. K. Zool.-Bot. Gesellsch., Wien, Beih.* 33:25—BRAZIL: *Amazonas* (Barra do Rio Negro). Goeldi and Hagmann, 1904, *Bol. Mus. Paraense* 4:53—BRAZIL. Zukowsky, 1940, *Zool. Gart.* 12:103, fig. 6 (animal)—birth of young in Frankfurt Zoo.

Mid[as] bicolor, G. Cuvier, 1829, *Reg. Anim.*, 2d ed., p. 106, footnote—perhaps a variety of *Simia oedipus.*

M[idas] bicolor, I. Geoffroy, 1851, *Cat. Primates, Mus. Hist. Nat., Paris,* p. 63—BRAZIL: *Amazonas* (Natterer specimen); "pres Pebas, par MM. de Castelnau et Deville. I. Geoffroy, 1855, *Castelnau Expéd. Amérique Sud, Mammifères,* p. 21—PERU: *Loreto* (Pebas). Reichenbach, 1862, *Vollst. Naturg. Affen,* p. 11, pl. 3, fig. 33 (animal)—characters.

Marikina bicolor, Lesson, 1840, *Species des mammifères: Bimanes et quadrumanes . . . ,* p. 199—in synonymy of *Oedipus titi* Lesson. Elliot, 1913, *A review of the Primates,* 1:187—in synonymy of *Seniocebus bicolor* and incorrectly attributed to Reichenbach. Cruz Lima, 1945, *Mamíferos da Amazonia, Primates, Contr. Mus. Paraense,* p. 204, pl. 33, fig. 1—BRAZIL: *Amazonas* (Flores, suburb, of Manaos); characters. Hershkovitz, 1949, *Proc. U.S. Nat. Mus.* 98:421—revision; BRAZIL: *Amazonas* (Manaus; Campos Salles, Manaus). Hill, 1957, *Primates,* 3:192, 193, 220, 241, 248, 251, fig. 17 (uterus and adnexa), fig. 57 (ear), fig. 58 (hand and foot, plantar surface), fig. 59 (♀ external genitalia), fig. 60 (intestine), pl. 16 (animal)—anatomy; habits; distribution; taxonomy.

H[apale] bicolor, Wagner, 1840, *Schreber's Säugth., Suppl.* 1:251. Wagner, 1855, *Schreber's Säugth., Suppl.* 5:135, pl. 12 (animal)—BRAZIL: *Amazonas* (Barra do Rio Negro).

Hapale bicolor, Wagner, 1848, *Abh. Akad. Wiss. Munich,* 5:473—BRAZIL: *Amazonas* (Barra do Rio Negro). Schlegel, 1876, *Les singes. Simiae,* p. 257—BRAZIL: *Amazonas* (Manaus Natterer collection). Jentink, 1887, *Cat. Syst. Mamm. Mus. Pays-Bas* 11:55—BRAZIL: *Amazonas* (Manaus).

J[acchus] bicolor, Fischer, 1829, *Syn. Mamm.* p. 67—classification. Wallace, 1852, *Proc. Zool. Soc. London* 1852:109, 110—BRAZIL: *Amazonas* (Guiana side of Rio Negro near Barra).

Jacchus bicolor, Gerrard, 1862, *Cat. bones Brit. Mus.* p. 29—BRAZIL: *Amazonas* (Rio Negro).

Seniocebus bicolor, Gray, 1870, *Cat. monkeys, lemurs and fruit-eating bats, British Museum,* p. 68—type of *Seniocebus* Gray; BRAZIL. Elliot, 1913, *A review of the Primates,* 1:186—characters ex type. Lönnberg, 1940, *Ark. Zool. Stockholm* 32A, (10):15—BRAZIL: *Amazonas* (Manaus).

Œdipomidas bicolor, Elliot, 1914, *Bull. Amer. Mus. Nat. Hist.* 33:645—classification.

Oedipomidas bicolor, Schultz, 1948, *Amer. J. Phys. Anthrop., n.s.* 6:8—3 single births recorded.

[Mystax] bicolor, Pocock, 1917, *Ann. Mag. Nat. Hist.* 20(8):256—classification.

Mystax bicolor, Crandall, 1951, *Animal Kingdom* 54(6):179, fig. p. 183 (animal)—BRAZIL.

Tamarin (Oedipomidas) bicolor, Tate, 1939, *Bull. Amer. Mus. Nat. Hist.* 76:208—BRAZIL: *Amazonas* (near Manaus).

Leontocebus bicolor, Cabrera, 1958, *Rev. Mus. Argentino Cienc. Nat. "Bernardino Rivadavia"* 4 (1):199—classification. Chiarelli, 1963, *Folia Primat.* 1:91—taste sensitivity to phenylthiocarbamide.

Leontocebus (Marikina) bicolor, Ortmann, 1958, *Primatologia* 3 (1):367—histology of anus. Immendorf, 1961, *Saüget. Mitt.* 9:145—presumed father of a hybrid form crossing with a "rothand-Tamarin" which died at parturition without further identification [see my discussion under *Saguinus midas midas*].

S[aguinus] bicolor, Crandall, 1964, *Management of wild animals in captivity,* p. 105—longevity in New York Zoo (8 years, 2 months).

Saguinus bicolor bicolor, Hershkovitz, 1966, *Folia Primat.* 4:391—classification; distribution. Hershkovitz, 1972, *Int. Zoo Yearb.* 12:9—geographic range; survival endangered.

Œdipus titi Lesson, 1840, *Species des mammifère: Bimanes et quadrumanes . . . ,* p. 199—part, specimen *âge non adulte* only, with *Marikina bicolor* Spix described as the example.

Leontocebus midas ♀ × *Leontocebus bicolor* ♂, Morris and Jarvis, 1959, *International Zoo Year Book* 1:140—hybrid bred in captivity in Cologne, Germany [the Immendorf record, see above].

(*L[eontocebus] bicolor* × *L. midas*) × *Leontocebus midas,* Jarvis and Morris (eds.), 1961, *Int. Zoo. Yearb.* 3: 257—born in Cologne Zoo.

Type. Juvenal mounted, in the Munich Museum; collected by the Spix and Martius Expedition.

Type Locality. Near the village of Rio Negro (= Manaus, 170), Barra do Rio Negro, Amazonas, Brazil.

Distribution (fig. X.15). Vicinity of Manaus, east bank of Rio Negro near mouth at Rio Amazonas. The range of *bicolor* is probably confined to the angle between the east bank of the Rio Negro and the north bank of the Amazonas. A specimen said to have been taken by Castelnau (cf. I. Geoffroy 1851, p. 63; 1855, p. 21) on the banks of the Marañon near Pebas, Peru, is certainly mislabeled.

Diagnostic Characters. Forequarters (arms, shoulders, mantle, neck, chest) white or yellowish white, sharply defined from the modified agouti of hindquarters and reddish orange of belly and inner sides of hind limbs.

Coloration. Skin of face blackish or mottled, throat, forehead, and crown entirely blackish and bare except for the usual vibrissae and a sparse covering of fine gray or buffy fuzz; crown from line between ears with long white or yellowish hairs, the whitish continuing on mantle, arms, upper surface of hands, throat, chest and tapering to a point on anterior half of belly; saddle and rump a coarse olivaceous or grizzled agouti with a poorly defined dark median dorsal band usually present; outer sides of thighs like rump or slightly warmer; upper surface of feet entirely rufous or mixed with silvery; belly and inner sides of thighs sharply defined reddish orange; tail more or less uniformly ochraceous orange (in type) or black above, sharply defined orange or reddish orange beneath, the hairs entirely orange or black basally; penciled tip black, orange, or mixed; external genitalia black.

Young. Head of newborn and very young like adult except cheeks, forehead, and crown fully clothed with white hairs. With advancing age, pelage of cheeks becomes vestigial, followed by that of forehead and front of crown. In three-quarter-grown individuals, a fine fringe of white hairs persists around muzzle while another encircles the otherwise virtually bare face.

Measurements. See appendix table 2.

Comparisons. The pied coloration is unique among known bare-face tamarins; the bare face and forepart of crown distinguish *bicolor* from similarly pied members of the *Saguinus nigricollis* group.

Variation. Midas bicolor Spix as originally described and figured is a pied tamarin with an orange or reddish tail. The monochromatic tail is described in the Latin diagnosis as *"cauda et abdomine ferruginieis,"* in the formal Latin description as *"cauda rufa,"* and in the vernacular as follows, "les poils du dos et de la queue sont noirs à leur racine, brun-mélangé aux milieux, et roux au bout." The colored figure of the type (pl. 24, fig. 1) shows the tail more or less uniformly ochraceous orange. Spix's measurements for the type, trunk 7", head 1½", tail 9", equal 231 mm for head and body combined and 243 mm for tail, using the old French inch = 27 mm (old German = 26). These dimensions are disproportionate for any callitrichid, but either measurement taken together with the hairy cheeks, forehead, and crown shown in the original figure points to a very young individual. The mounted type, examined by Elliot (1913*a*, p. 187) nearly a century after its description, was "in good condition and . . . well represented in Spix's plate, though the coloring in the specimen is not so bright."

It is curious that the photograph (fig. X.60) of what appears to be a young individual of *Saguinus bicolor* that lived in the New York Zoo more nearly resembles the original colored figure of Spix's *bicolor* than any prepared specimen I have seen. In the photograph, the sides of face, forehead, and chin seem more hairy than in adults, and the tail appears to be uniformly colored throughout.

All other specimens of *bicolor* described in the literature agree with the type except that the tail is black above, orange or reddish orange beneath with the penciled tip black, orange, or a mixture of both colors. The first of these is one of a series of 9 from Barra do Rio Negro (= Manaus) collected in 1830 by Johann Natterer. The tail of the specimen, an immature (head and body 6", tail 9") is described by Wagner (1840, p. 251) as black on

Fig. X.60. Pied Bare-face Tamarin (subadult), *Saguinus bicolor bicolor*. (Photo courtesy of New York Zoological Society.)

upper surface, reddish on underside and tip. Later accounts (Wagner 1848, p. 473; 1855, p. 135, pl. 12; Pelzeln 1883, p. 25) of Natterer's series of young and adults of both sexes confirm the dichromatic pattern of the tail and include the description of an adult male with the penciled tip black. The dorsal surface of the pencil of the specimen in the Field Museum of Natural History is also black. The tail tip of a Natterer specimen in the Leiden Museum, and another in the American Museum is essentially orange. In a pair of specimens preserved in spirits from near Manaus, the pencil is black dorsally in the male, entirely orange in the female.

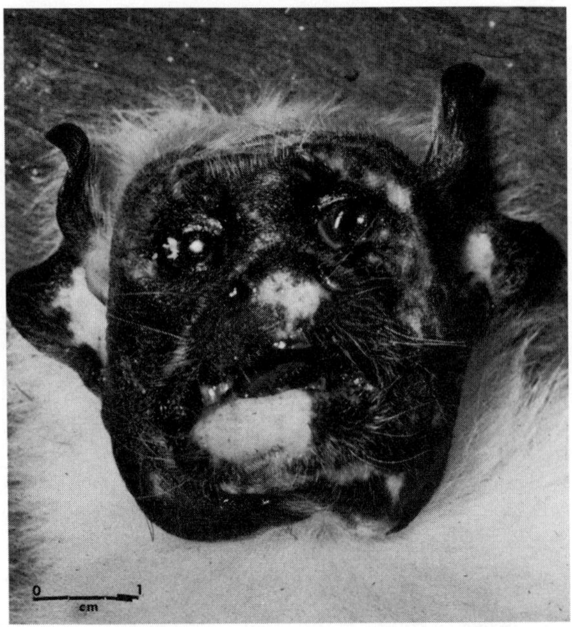

Fig. X.61. *Saguinus bicolor bicolor,* piebald face of wild-caught individual preserved in spirits; the mottled appearance is suggestive of the human skin disease vitiligo. (Photo courtesy of G. E. Erikson.)

The two preserved specimens mentioned above were collected 5 September by G. E. Erikson. In the male, apparently a very old individual, the skin of the body, most notably of the face, is strongly blotched (fig. X.61). The face and other bare parts are uniformly black in the female.

The vitiligolike condition of the male is common, but nowhere among callitrichids, except in *Saguinus inustus,* is it so strongly marked on the face.

Remarks. The range of *Saguinus bicolor bicolor,* so far as known, is one of the smallest among South American mammals. The pied tamarin is poorly represented in museums. The single specimen in the American Museum of Natural History was collected 25 August 1928 by the Olalla Brothers. The specimen in the Field Museum of Natural History was taken 23 April 1913 by R. H. Becker. The type in the Munich Museum was collected by the Spix and Martius Expedition early in the nineteenth century. A skin in the British Museum was "purchased of Stevens" about 1850. Two individuals preserved in spirits were taken September 1966 by G. E. Erikson for his personal collection. All other museum-preserved specimens known to me are those collected in the early part of the nineteenth century by Johann Natterer and now preserved in the Vienna, London, Leiden, and, possibly, the Paris museums.

Specimens Examined. 7. BRAZIL—*Amazonas:* Barra do Rio Negro, 1 (RMNH); Campos Salles, Manaus, 1 (AMNH); Manaus, 1 (FMNH); Rio Negro, 2 (BM); near Manaus, 2 (GEE, in spirits).

SAGUINUS BICOLOR MARTINSI THOMAS, MARTIN'S BARE-FACE TAMARIN

Synonymic History

Leontocebus martinsi Thomas, 1912, *Ann. Mag. Nat. Hist.,* ser. 8, 9:85. Cabrera, 1958, *Rev. Mus. Argentino Cienc. Nat. "Bernardino Rivadavia"* 4(1):200—classification.

Seniocebus martinsi Elliot, 1913, *A review of the Primates* 1:189—description quoted.

Oedipomidas martinsi, Elliot, 1914, *Bull. Amer. Mus. Nat. Hist.* 33:645—synonymy.

[*Mystax*] *martinsi,* Pocock, 1917, *Ann. Mag. Nat. Hist.* ser. 8, 20:256—classification.

[?] *Mystax martinsi,* Crandall, 1951, *Animal Kingdom* 54(6):179, fig. p. 183 (animal).

Tamarin (Oedipomidas) martinsi, Tate, 1939, *Bull. Amer. Mus. Nat. Hist.* 76:209—BRAZIL: *Pará* (Faro).

Marikina martinsi, Cruz Lima, 1945, *Mamíferos da Amazonia, Primates, Contr. Mus. Paraense* p. 205, pl. 33, fig. 2 (animal)—characters; BRAZIL: *Pará* (Rio Jamandú [= Nhamundá]; Rio Erepecurú). Hershkovitz, 1949, *Proc. U.S. Nat. Mus.* 98:422—part, BRAZIL: *Pará* (Rio Yamundá [= Nhamundá]).

[?] *S*[*aguinus*] *martinsi,* Crandall, 1964, *Management of wild animals in captivity* p. 105—longevity in New York Zoo (9 years, 10 months).

S[*aguinus*] *b*[*icolor*] *martinsi,* Hershkovitz, 1966, *Folia Primat.* 4:391—classification; distribution.

Saguinus bicolor martinsi, Hershkovitz, 1970, *Am. J. Phys. Anthrop.* 32:379—dental diseases.

Type. Adult male, skin and skull, British Museum (Natural History), no. 11.12.22.2; collected 27 April 1911 by Oscar Martins.

Type Locality. Faro (215), north side of Rio Amazonas, near mouth of Rio Nhamundá, Pará, Brazil.

Distribution (fig. X.15). Pará, Brazil, north of the Rio Amazonas between the Rios Nhamundá (at Faro) and the Rio Erepecurú.

Diagnostic Characters. Dorsal surface from crown to base of tail dark brown, shoulders and sides of trunk paler, the hairs distinctly punctulated or agouti.

Coloration. Skin of face, throat, forehead, and crown to level of ears blackish and bare except for usual superciliary and circumbuccal vibrissae and a sparse sprinkling of minute buffy or golden fuzz, especially around mouth; crown from between level of ears with long uniformly dark brown hairs usually continuing as a broad middorsal band to base of tail; mantle undefined; shoulders, sides of body, and outer aspect of hind legs cinnamon agouti, the agouti hairs drab basally, annulated terminally with a series of 4 brown rings alternating with buffy rings, the tips brown; lateral fringe interspersed with long, fine wholly white hairs; forearms orange or ochraceous buff, the hairs uniformly colored or lightly punctulated with brown; upper surface of hands and feet ochraceous or golden brown. Underparts from neck to belly, inner side of fore- and hind limbs ochraceous orange, the hairs of neck, chest, and sometimes anterior portion of belly punctulated with brown and not sharply defined from sides; tail black above, orange to reddish orange beneath, the hairs black basally or entirely reddish, underside and penciled tip orange; external genitalia black.

Young. Of a juvenal with head and body length 136 mm, hind foot, 46 mm, (BM 11.12.22.3), trunk and tail as in adults, forehead and front of crown to level of ears thinly covered with silvery gray hair lightly mixed with brown; remainder of crown silvery with dark brown median band merging with dark brown of nape.

Measurements. See appendix table 2.

Comparisons. Bare face and forehead, dark brown middorsal band and pale brown agouti pelage of shoulders and sides of body distinguish *martinsi* from other races of *bicolor* and all species of *Saguinus.*

Remarks. The resemblance between *martinsi* and *bicolor* led Thomas (1912, p. 85) to speculate that the first may have given rise to the second. On second thought, however, Thomas noted that the face and forehead of the juvenals of both forms were clothed with silvery gray hairs. He concluded that the ancestor of both may have been gray-headed.

An individual exhibited in the New York Zoo and identified as *Mystax martinsi* by Crandall (1951, p. 179, 183, fig. lower middle) does not appear to be typical. In the photograph (fig. X.62), upper arms, shoulders, and legs seem to be agouti brown as in *S. bicolor martinsi.* The chest and forearms, however, appear to be sharply contrasted white or whitish as in *S. bicolor bicolor.* In *martinsi,* these parts are a dark orange and only moderately defined from the brown of shoulders and sides of body. If color contrasts are accurately reproduced in the illustration, the subject is intermediate in coloration between *bicolor* and *martinsi* and may represent an undescribed subspecies. The skin was not preserved.

Specimens Examined. 11. BRAZIL—*Pará:* Faro 7 (AMNH, 4; BM, 2 including type of *martinsi;* FMNH, 1); San José, Rio Nhamundá, 2 (AMNH); Yacarana, Rio Nhamundá, 2 (AMNH).

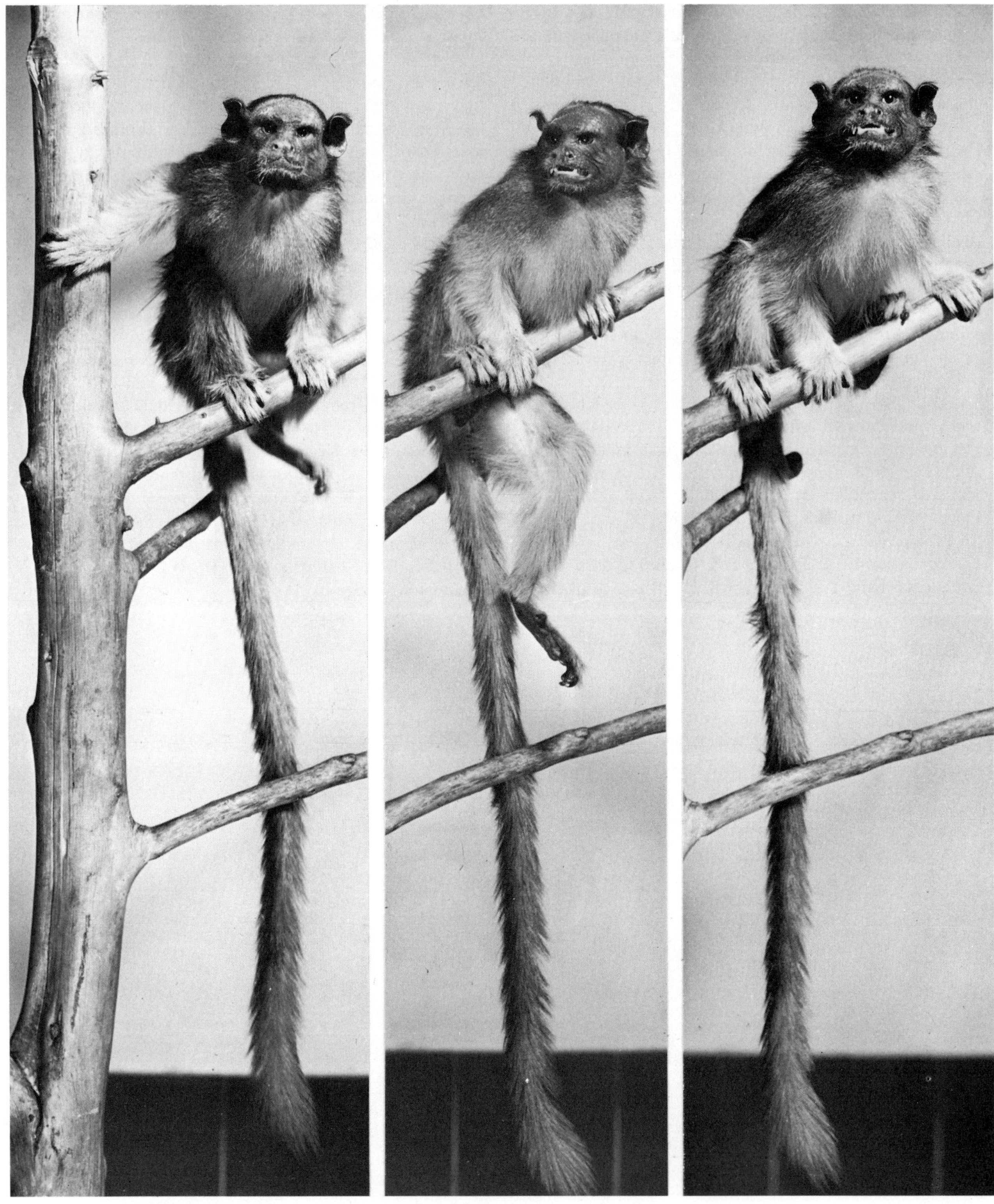

Fig. X.62. Martin's Bare-face Tamarin, *Saguinus bicolor martinsi,* three views of same animal. (Photos courtesy of New York Zoological Society.)

SAGUINUS BICOLOR OCHRACEUS HERSHKOVITZ, OCHRACEOUS BARE-FACE TAMARINS

Synonymic History

Marikina martinsi, Hershkovitz (part, not Thomas), 1949, *Proc. U.S. Nat. Mus.* 98:422—part, BRAZIL: *Amazonas* (Piratucu [= Paratucú]; Serra do Espelho).

Saguinus bicolor ochraceus Hershkovitz, 1966, *Folia Primat.* 4:391. Hershkovitz, 1970, *Am. J. Phys. Anthrop.* 32:379—dental disease. Hershkovitz, 1970, *Folia Primat.* 13:215, fig. 3 (cerebral hemisphere)—BRAZIL: *Amazonas* (Castanhal, Rio Yamundá); cerebral fissural pattern.

Type. Adult female, skin and skull, American Museum of Natural History no. 94097, collected 17 December 1930 by the Olalla Brothers.

Type Locality. Mouth of Rio Paratucú (207), a right-bank tributary of the Nhamundá, Amazonas, Brazil.

Distribution (fig. X.15). Northeastern Amazonas, Brazil, on the right bank of lower Rio Nhamundá; the range may extend west between the Nhamundá and northern bank of the Rio Amazonas to the Rio Uatumã.

Diagnostic Characters. Uniformly palest of bare-face tamarins, upper surface a streaky mixture of buff, olivaceous, and brown with forequarters more dilute or "faded" than hind quarters; multibanded or agouti pattern of hairs shadowy or absent.

Coloration. Skin of face, throat, forehead, and crown to level of ears blackish and exposed beneath sparse silvery or buffy fuzz; long hairs of dorsal surface from crown between level of ears to base of tail, shoulders, and outer sides of thighs cinnamon brown to buffy or drab on terminal portions, more brown on basal portions, the darker color showing through as streaks at surface; hairs of lower back finely punctulated buffy and brown; mantle hardly defined, but area usually more bleached than remainder of dorsal surface; sides of body and lateral fringe like back but hairs more uniformly colored throughout; outer sides of hind legs ochraceous buff to ochraceous orange, the hairs more or less uniformly colored or finely punctulated with pale brown; forelimbs and upper surface of hands and feet ochraceous; chest and belly ochraceous orange to golden brown, neck like chest or finely punctulated with brown, angle between throat and neck more dilute, to buffy or whitish; inner sides of limbs bright orange, the hind more saturate than the fore; tail above uniformly brown or mixed with orange, underside and penciled tip entirely orange; external genitalia blackish.

Measurements. See appendix table 2.

Comparisons. Distinguished from *Saguinus bicolor martinsi* Thomas, its nearest geographic relative, by paler color throughout, hairs of back and sides unbanded or faintly annulated, nape buffy or pale brown like back or paler; ruff (i.e., long hairs between angle of throat and neck) silvery to buffy, upper surface of tail more dilute and usually with a strong mixture of orange. Pale nape and, in most specimens of *ochraceus,* the whitish ruff, adumbrate the entirely whitish forequarters of *Saguinus bicolor* Spix.

Remarks. In my earlier (1949, p. 422) review of the bare-face tamarins, five specimens from Paratucú (207) and one from the Serra do Espelho (207) in the American Museum of Natural History were regarded as representative of true *martinsi* and recorded as such. The type of *martinsi* from Faro, on the opposite side of the Nhamundá had been examined independently several years earlier in the British Museum (Natural History), and a male topotype was seen later in the Field Museum of Natural History. Direct comparisons of the seventeen specimens of *ochraceus* at hand in the present study with seven of *martinsi,* including 5 topotypes, reveal the consistent differences between the bare face tamarins of the opposing banks of the Rio Nhamundá.

The discovery of *ochraceus* partly fills the geographic gap between *martinsi* on the east and *bicolor* on the west. Geographically and morphologically, however, *ochraceus* is nearer *martinsi* and is probably a comparatively recent offshoot from it with the dark brown tones and agouti pattern diluted or bleached out. The photograph published by Crandall (1951, p. 183) and reproduced here (fig. X.62) is of an individual that apparently combines some of the diagnostic characters of *ochraceus, martinsi,* and *bicolor.*

The description of *martinsi* presented by Hill (1957, p. 249) is a paraphrase of my earlier one based on specimen now treated as *ochraceus.* Measurements used by Hill are the means of individual measurements I had given for a male topotype of *martinsi* and three female topotypes of *ochraceus.*

Specimens Examined. 17, all in the collection of the American Museum of Natural History. BRAZIL—*Amazonas:* Castanhal, Rio Nhamundá , 4; Rio Paratucú, mouth, 11 (including holotype); Serra do Espelho, Rio Nhamundá, 2.

74 *Saguinus oedipus* Group
Saguinus leucopus Günther, Silvery Brown Bare-face Tamarin

Fig. X.63. Silvery-brown Bare-face Tamarin, *Saguinus leucopus.*

Synonymic History

Hapale leucopus Günther, 1877, *Proc. Zool. Soc. London* 1876:743, pl. 72. Anderson, 1881, *Cat. Mamm. Indian Museum, Calcutta* pt. 1:87—COLOMBIA: *Antioquia.* Jentink, 1887, *Cat. Ostéol. Mus. Pays-Bas* 9:48—COLOMBIA: *Antioquia* (Medellín); possibly a variety of *Hapale bicolor.* Jentink, 1892, *Cat. Syst. Mamm. Mus. Pays-Bas* 11:55—COLOMBIA: *Antioquia* (Medellín).

Callithrix leucopus, Elliot, 1907, *Publ. Field Columbian Mus., Zool. Ser.* 8:553—COLOMBIA: *Antioquia* (Medellín). Elliot, 1913, *A review of the Primates* 1:222, pl. 27 (skull)—characters; selection of lectotype.

Œdipomidas leucopus, Elliot, 1914, *Bull. Amer. Mus. Nat. Hist.* 33:645—*pegasis* Elliot, a synonym. J. A. Allen, 1916, *Bull. Amer. Mus. Nat. Hist.* 35:228—COLOMBIA: *Antioquia* (Puerto Berrío; Malena; Puerto Valdivia).

Mystax leucopus, Crandall, 1951, *Animal Kingdom* 54(6):179, fig. p. 180 (animal, upper left, name upper right).

[*Mystax*] *leucopus,* Pocock, 1917, *Ann. Mag. Nat. Hist.,* ser. 8, 20:256—classification.

Marikina leucopus, Hershkovitz, 1949, *Proc. U.S. Nat. Mus.* 98:419—revision; COLOMBIA: *Antioquia* (Medellín; Puerto Valdivia; Malena; Simití, 1000 meters); *Bolívar* (Norosí; Río San Pedro, Norosí; opposite Puerto Estrella, Río Magdalena). Marinkelle, 1966, *Trans. Roy. Soc. Trop. Med. Hyg.* 60(1):112—COLOMBIA: *Trypanosoma cruzi* reservoir.

[*Marikina*?] *leucopus,* Hershkovitz, 1964, *Amer. J. Phys. Anthrop.* 21, (3):395—taxonomy.

Tamarinus leucopus, Osman Hill, 1957, *Primates* 3:213, 214, 217–22, 243, 249, fig. 56 (♂ external genitalia), fig. 88 *c* (hair tracts of face), pl. 14 (animals), pl. 15 (head)—anatomy; habits; distribution; taxonomy. Osman Hill, 1958, *Primatologia* 3 (1):643, fig. 11*b* (penis)—external genitalia; classification.

Leontocebus leucopus, Cabrera, 1958, *Rev. Mus. Argentino Cienc. Nat. "Bernardino Rivadavia"* 4(1):200—classification.

Saguinus leucopus, Fooden, 1961, *Zoologica* 46:167—chromatography and systematic analyses of urinary amino-acid excretions. Egozcue, Perkins, and Hagemenas, 1968, *Folia Primat.* 9(2):84—karyotype (2n = 46). Marinkelle, 1968, *Caldasia* 10(47):162—COLOMBIA: *Caldas; Antioquia.* Hershkovitz, 1970, *Am. J. Phys. Anthrop.* 32:379—dental disease. Hershkovitz, 1970, *Folia Primat.* 13:215—COLOMBIA: *Antioquia* (Purí); cerebral fissural pattern. Hsu and Hampton, 1970, *Folia Primat.* 13:183, fig. 3 (karyotype)—karyotype (2n = 46). Hampton, Parmelee, and Rider, 1971, in *Med. Primat. 1970,* ed. Goldsmith and Moor-Jankowski p. 245—plasma histaminase and diamine oxidase values. J. K. Hampton, Hampton, and Levy, 1971, in *Med. Primat. 1970,* ed. Goldsmith and Moor-Jankowski, p. 527—reproduction in laboratory colony. Levy, Hampton, Dreizen, and Hampton, 1972, *J. Comp. Pathol.* 82:99—chronic thyroiditis in laboratory animals. Porter, 1972, *Lab. Animal Sci.* 22(4):503—endoparasites.

S[*aguinus*] *leucopus,* Crandall, 1964, *Management of wild animals in captivity* p. 105—longevity in New York Zoo (5 years, 8 months, 8 days).

Seniocebus pegasis Elliot, 1913, *Bull. Amer. Mus. Nat. Hist.* 32:252—COLOMBIA: *Antioquia* (type locality, Puerto Berrío, Río Magdalena); type, female, skin and skull, American Museum of Natural History no. 34563, collected 29 January 1913, by L. A. Fuertes. Goodwin, 1953, *Bull. Amer. Mus. Nat. Hist.* 102:264—type history.

Type. "Several specimens, identical in coloration, collected by Mr. T. K. Salmon"; all in British Museum (Natural History); lectotype, skin and skull, British Museum no. 75.6.3.1; collected by T. K. Salmon, selected by Elliot (1913, *A review of the Primates,* 1:222); syntypes, both females, skin and skull, British Museum, nos. 75.6.3.2, 76.8.8.2.

Type Locality. Near Medellín (35), Antioquia, Colombia.

Distribution (figs. X.1, 15)

Northern Colombia, between the Ríos Magdalena and Cauca from their confluence in the department of Bolívar south into the department of Antioquia nearly to the latitude of Medellín, and probably continuing southward along the tropical forested slopes of the Cordillera Central into western Caldas; altitudinal range from near sea level to approximately 1,500 meters above.

Origin, Evolution, and Dispersal (fig. X.2)

Saguinus leucopus necessarily arose from a hairy-face tamarin, probably one like *S. nigricollis graellsi.* The geographic position of *graellsi,* between the Ríos Marañon and Putumayo, favors this hypothesis. The prototype of *leucopus* must have spread along the eastern base of the Cordillera Oriental in Colombia and thence through a pass into the Río Magdalena basin. *S. inustus* probably diverged from or near the prototypal stock (see p. 732). Disappearance of connecting forms between present *leucopus* and hypothetical sources of origin in the upper Amazonian region requires explanation.

Remarks. The gular whorl of *Saguinus leucopus* is better defined than in other callitrichids where a similar feature is present. The center and parts of skin covered by the whorl are glandular. The processes of bleaching and depilation in *leucopus* are compared with those in other bare-face species (p. 736).

Taxonomy

The taxonomic shufflings of *Saguinus leucopus* have been many. Günther described it as a species of *Hapale* Illiger, 1811. Trouessart (1882, p. 137) referred it to *Oedipomidas* Reichenbach, 1862, and treated it as a subgenus of *Hapale* but subsequently (1897, p. 49) returned *leucopus* to *Hapale* (sensu stricto). Elliot (1907, p. 553) followed suit but replaced *Hapale* with the senior generic synonym *Callithrix* Erxleben, 1777. He still regarded *leucopus* as a species of *Callithrix* in his 1913 monograph (p. 222) and figured its skull (1913, pl. 27) as the example of his notion of the cranial and dental characters of that genus. In a following publication Elliot (1913*b*, p. 252) described a specimen of *leucopus* as a new species, *Seniocebus pegasis.* Later, Elliot (1914, p. 645) sank *Seniocebus* Gray in the synonymy of the older *Oedipomidas* which contained the bare-face *oedipus* and *geoffroyi.* Pocock (1917, p. 248 and footnote, 256) felt otherwise and treated *Seniocebus* with *leucopus, bicolor,* and *martinsi* as a subgenus of *Mystax* Gray, 1870. *Oedipomidas,* with *oedipus* and *geoffroyi,* was distinguished generically as a specialized, small-eared "offshoot of the bald-faced or so called *Seniocebus* group of *Mystax.*" Thomas (1922, p. 198) also believed *Seniocebus* merited full generic rank. Tate (1939, p. 207), however, sided with Elliot and accepted the union of *Seniocebus* with *Oedipomidas* but as a subgenus of *Tamarin* Gray, 1870. Cruz Lima (1945, p. 203) followed Tate in uniting all members of the bare-face group but used the older generic name *Marikina* Lesson. Hershkovitz (1949, pp. 409, 418) adopted this classification which grouped all Tamarins in the genus *Marikina* Lesson, 1840, but he restored *Tamarin* as a subgeneric name for the hairy-face forms, *Oedipomidas* for the crested bare-face species, and *Marikina* (s.s.) for *leucopus, bicolor,* and *martinsi.* Osman Hill (1957, pp. 212, 241) recognized *Oedipomidas* and *Marikina* (s.s.) as full genera but transferred *leucopus* from the bare-face *Marikina* group to the hairy-face, "white-lip" group of the genus *Tamarinus* Trouessart, 1904. This arrangement obliged Osman Hill (p. 241) to treat *leucopus* as "anomalous" and omit it from his key to the species of *Tamarinus.*

The present study indicates that *Saguinus leucopus* and *S. bicolor* (including *martinsi*) are independent offshoots from related but different stocks or races of hairy-face ancestors. Cranial differences between *leucopus* and *bicolor* are minor but as great as any within the genus. External similarities between the two species, notably in the degree of bleaching and depilation, are similar stages in a parallel evolution such as may occur in any pair of distantly related callitrichids. The hair tracts themselves, particularly the gular and coronal whorls of *leucopus,* are not indicated in *bicolor.* On the other hand, coronal whorls similar to those of *leucopus* appear in such diverse and distantly related species as *Leontopithecus rosalia* and *Callimico goeldii.* This incongruity alone is strong evidence that the ancestry of *leucopus* is independent from that of *bicolor.*

Fig. X.64. Silvery-brown Bare-face Tamarin, *Saguinus leucopus,* male and female. (Photo courtesy of New York Zoological Society.)

Diagnostic Characters

Face, forehead, and crown to level of ears with short adpressed silvery hairs sharply defined from brownish of posterior portion of cheeks and crown; hairs of crown between ears forming a pair of tufts; back buffy brown, arms and legs dominantly whitish, ankles and metatarsus with brown patch or spotting; brown hairs of throat forming a complete whorl; chest and belly reddish orange or brown, tail blackish with contrastingly pale pencil (fig. X.64).

External Characters

Facial skin black and hardly showing through the covering of fine silvery or buffy hairs; fringe of silvery gray hairs extending from above nostrils to each angle of gape; hairs of cheeks long and forming an upward- and outward-projecting fringe or crest; fine hairs of muzzle feathered and sometimes cresting in midline; superciliary fringe usually present and often well defined; forehead and crown to level of front of ears well covered with short adpressed silvery white to silvery brown or ochraceous hairs disposed in two lateral whorls cresting in midline and separating long brown hairs of crown summit into two tufts; brown hairs of back of crown and nape tipped with buffy and often extending onto shoulders as a poorly defined mantle; back dark brown, the hairs dark brown basally, silvery to buffy terminally; outer sides of shoulders and thighs like back of arms and legs, hands and feet whitish to ochraceous buff; ankle with brown patch, metatarsus with brown patch or spots; sides of body and lateral fringe like back; chin evenly haired silvery to buff, throat brown, the hairs grayish to drab at roots, buff or orange at tips and forming a whorl; chest, belly, inner sides of arms and legs reddish brown to reddish orange, the basal portions of the hairs dark brown; tail dominantly dark brown but undersurface with streaks or patches of silvery orange or reddish orange with many of the brown hairs diluted basally, the penciled tip whitish or silvery to golden or orange.

Vibrissae (fig. III.12; X.65). Supraorbitals, rhinarials, mystacials, mentals, genals, and forward-directed interramals consistently present; ulnar carpals present; gular spines present, pectorals absent.

Ears. See text p. 102 and figs. III.18; X.65.

Cranial Characters (figs. X.6, 8, 10)

Frontal contour well rounded to domed; temporal ridges strongly convergent and often fusing into a sagittal crest; nasal profile slightly concave; frontal sinuses well inflated; molar foramen from 1 to 2 mm in greatest diameter; ventral border of mandible more nearly V-shaped than U-shaped; the horizontal rami moderately arced, the

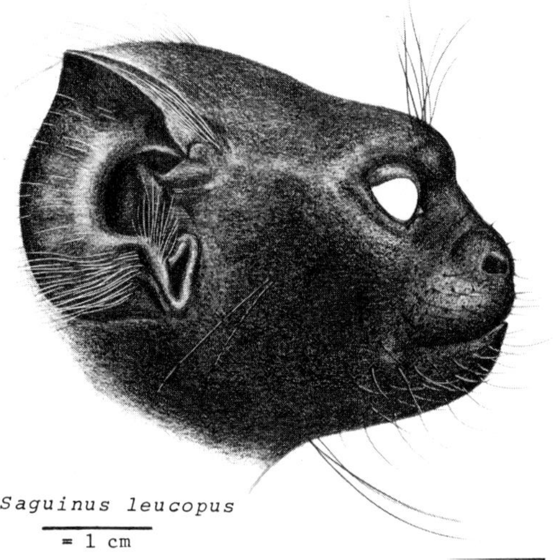

Fig. X.65. *Saguinus leucopus*: Profile view with mane removed to expose ear, vibrissae, and facial pigmentation.

angular process slightly inflected inward but usually well deflected downward.

Measurements

See appendix table 2.

External Genitalia

Male (figs. III.22, 27, 29; X.66A)

Subadult. Penis completely ensheathed in prepuce, skin of shaft, as exposed by dissection of preputial fold, rugose, frenulum preputii near base of asymmetrically cleft glans; scrotum little developed, perineal and anal regions unpigmented.

Adult. External genitalia including sexual skin in dry skins of mature males are as well developed and pigmented as in comparable specimens of *Saguinus oedipus.*

Female (fig. X.66B)

Subadult. Labia majora not conspicuously enlarged, mostly pigmented and papillate, each papilla with one, occasionally two, or three long stiff, orange hairs; scrotal fold not certainly separable from preputial fold; glabrous preputial surface surrounding glans clitoridis lightly pigmented; glans swollen and pigmented, with left lobe larger than right; laminate labia minora well defined; borders of rima pudendi and posterior labial commissure unpigmented; external genitalia wider than long, the greatest width about 12 mm, genital fissure 7 mm; pubic sexual skin not certainly defined topographically in present specimen; perineal and anal regions lightly pigmented.

Remarks. Except for the lighter color the external genitalia and vestibule of the present fluid-preserved subadult agree with those of comparably aged individuals of *Saguinus oedipus.* External genitalia and sexual skin in dry study skins representing all ages show the same range of variation in size, form, definition, and glandular development as in comparable skins of *Saguinus oedipus oedipus* and *S. o. geoffroyi.*

Comparisons

Gular whorl and paired coronal tufts present in *leucopus* are well developed in distantly related *Leontopithecus rosalia* and *Callimico goeldii* but differ in details; a weakly developed gular whorl is present in most nearly related *S. oedipus geoffroyi* but in no other tamarin. The coating of short adpressed silvery hairs on face, forehead, and crown to ears is unlike that of all other adult tamarins of the genus *Saguinus* but agrees with that of the juvenal of bare-face *S. bicolor.* The mutton-chop-like whiskers of *leucopus* are specializations of the smoothly adpressed cheek tufts of the *S. nigricollis* group. The same special-

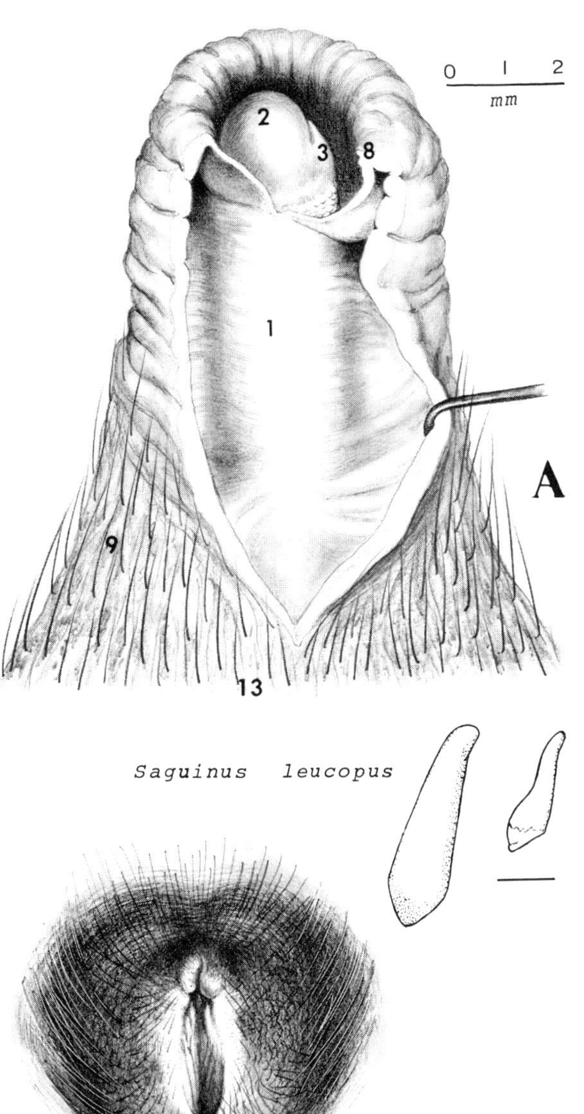

Fig. X.66. *Saguinus leucopus*: External genitalia and bacula of *A*, adult male with dorsal surface of prepuce parted to expose duplicature (*8*); *B*, female genitalia.

ization appears in juvenals of the most nearly related bare-face *S. oedipus*. The brown ankle band and metatarsical patches on whitish feet are not present in other callitrichids. The dominantly blackish tail agrees with that of hairy-face tamarins in general and with its closest bare-face relatives *oedipus* and *geoffroyi* in particular. The skull of *leucopus* is also like that of its nearest geographic allies, *oedipus* and *geoffroyi.*

Habits and Habitat

Saguinus leucopus is a hardy animal and, like most callitrichids, manages to survive and thrive in second growth forests long after persecution by man and destruction of primary forests have caused all other monkeys of the area to disappear. It was fairly abundant and the only remaining native primate species in the sugar cane and corn growing region of Bellavista, Antioquia. The fact that natives do not hunt them for food is an advantage tamarins have over the *Aotus, Cebus, Ateles,* and *Alouatta* that have disappeared from the region.

Tamarins are well adjusted to the low, thick second growth. When alarmed they may climb to the higher branches of the trees, but usually they move off in a horizontal direction. They have been compared with squirrels, and many of their activities are similar, but tamarins are more active and agile and seem to be unable to hold still for more than a few seconds. They sit on their haunches catlike, the tail hanging straight down with tip usually curled inward.

As many as 10 to 15 individuals compose a troop. When alarmed the tamarins usually hide quietly behind tree trunks and branches until the danger is passed. A sudden alarm, however, can cause them to spring in all directions, but with frequent stops to look back, grimace, jump up and down, and engage in other such tactics for confusing the potential enemy and distracting him from pursuing any single member of the troop. At Norosí (49) one large fellow of a group I surprised stared at me menacingly and then repeatedly extended and retracted his tongue in rapid succession.

It is not uncommon for older individuals to come to the aid of comrades. They will respond to the call of an injured individual by vocalizing, and I have seen them descend to the ground and help a wounded companion mount the nearest tree or shrub.

The usual call of *leucopus* is a shrill and somewhat melancholic *tee-tee*. The sound and pitch resemble those of other tamarins. The vocalizations, whether warble, chirp, or trill, are likewise characteristic, whatever differences there may be in nuance between the calls of different species. Although sounds are generally birdlike in quality, I have not heard tamarins "sing" songs. My impression is that the *tee-tee* call is a stereotype for keeping the troop together and for territorial defense. Other calls meet needs for communication between individuals.

The local name for *Saguinus leucopus* is *titi* or some variant of the *tee-tee* call uttered by the animal. In the Bellavista (34), Antioquia area, the animal is called *mico,* a name usually applied to cebids.

Reproduction

Young carried on the backs of adults were observed in Norosí, Bolívar, during the month of June. Judging by the size of two captured samples, the young were born in May.

Specimens Examined

Total: 49. COLOMBIA—*Antioquia:* Bellavista, Río Porce, 3 (FMNH); Malena, 2 (AMNH); Medellín, 3 (BM, including lectotype and 2 syntypes of *leucopus*); Puerto Berrío, 3 (AMNH, including type of *pegasis*); Puerto Valdivia, 1 (AMNH); Purí, 5 (FMNH); Valdivia, 2 (FMNH, 1; BM, 1); *Bolívar:* Norosí, 15 (USNM); Río San Pedro, Norosí, 12 (USNM); UNKOWN LOCALITY—3 (SM, 1; FMNH, 2 in spirits).

75 *Saguinus oedipus* Linnaeus, Crested Tamarins
1. History, Characters, Evolution, and Subspecies

Distribution (figs. X.1, 2, 15; XIII.3)

Tropical forested zones of Colombia, Panamá, and Costa Rica, from the west bank of the lower Río Magdelena-Cauca, northwestern Colombia, west to the Pacific coast, north into Panamá and bordering parts of southeastern Costa Rica.

Origin, Evolution, and Dispersal (fig. X.2)

The crested bare-face *Saguinus oedipus* (sensu lato) is the culmination of an evolutionary line of tamarins that diverged from a hairy-face ancestor of the upper Amazonian region. The divergent stock must have spread northward along the eastern base of the Andes and filtered into the valley between the Cordilleras Oriental and Central. The present occupant of the habitat, *Saguinus leucopus,* is presumed to be a direct descendant of that bare-face prototype. *Saguinus oedipus,* its neighbor to the west, occupies the outermost corner of the range of the Callitrichidae. It cannot be derived from any tamarin other than the form that evolved into modern *S. leucopus.* This last hairy-cheeked quasi-bare-face species still preserves most of the intermediate characters connecting *oedipus* with hairy-face tamarins.

S. oedipus is more conservative than *S. leucopus* in retaining the modified agouti pattern on dorsum. In most other respects including facial depilation, specialization of the pelage of the nape, the greater extension of whitish yellow, particularly on all underparts, dichromatic tail and reduction of pinna, *oedipus* has advanced beyond *leucopus.*

Juvenal pelage of *S. oedipus* points to the morphological progression from hairy-face to bare-face tamarins. The less specialized short adpressed coronal pelage of juvenal *oedipus* is similar to that of adult *leucopus* and the more primitive long projecting whiskers of juvenal *oedipus* are quite like those of adult *leucopus.* Vestiges of the hairy face and cheek whiskers, or mutton-chops, appear in adult *oedipus* in the form of a supraorbital band and as a thin fringe from corner of eye to angle of jaw. A fringe from muzzle to corner of mouth may well be the remains of the upper boundary of the whitish circumbuccal band characteristic of hairy-face tamarins.

Cranially, *oedipus* and *leucopus* are more like each other than either is like any other species. The skull of *oedipus* is generally slightly less specialized, but the mandible, particularly, is more primitive or more nearly V-shaped with less torsion of the ramus and flexion of the angle than that of any other species of *Saguinus.* This comparatively primitive form of the mandible contrasts with its more highly vaulted braincase and greater development of temporal and sagittal crests than occurs in other tamarins. The combination of primitive mandible coupled with a specialized braincase also appears in the lowest forms of callitrichids and in prosimians.

The most primitive form of the species is *Saguinus oedipus geoffroyi* of the Colombian Chocó, Panamá and a bordering part of Costa Rica. As compared with the nominate form of the genus, its ears are more nearly normal in size and shape, the specialized coronal crest is restricted to the frontal region, the white areas are less extensive, the underparts not as uniformly white and, in specimens from the Chocó, have patches of reddish brown as in *Saguinus leucopus.* Cranially it is less advanced, particularly in its more V-shaped mandible.

Initial separation of the *Saguinus oedipus geoffroyi* line from the ancestral *leucopus* stock was accomplished when a founder colony gained the opposite shore of the then marine inlet or strait, now the Río Atrato. This may have occurred during late Pliocene when the lowlands between the lower Ríos Cauca-Magdalena and the lower Río Atrato, were covered by the sea. Descendants of the original isolates probably spread throughout most of the present range of *geoffroyi* during the Pleistocene. Meanwhile, emergence of land along borders of the marine barrier separating *S. o. geoffroyi* from *S. leucopus* and the establishment of suitable habitats thereon provided additional opportunities for colonization by tamarins. This was successfully accomplished from the west, or the present Río Atrato side of the original barrier. This last differentiated race of tamarins, the *Simia oedipus* of Linnaeus, now occupies the tropical lowlands isolated between the Ríos Atrato and Cauca-Magdalena. It evolved hardly more than a grade beyond *geoffroyi* with respect to bleaching and reduction of the auricular pinna. It is also somewhat more advanced cranially, with mandible less rigidly and consistently V-shaped (see also the subspecies accounts).

Diagnostic Characters

Forehead and crown with a wedge-shaped crest of usually white hairs; temples and sides of head to front and inner sides of ears nearly bare; ears small, lamina of lower posterior margin of pinna deeply emarginate or obsolete; dorsum modified agouti, underparts and limbs usually whitish, terminal half or more of tail entirely black.

External Characters

Integument. Skin of face black, temples and sides of head from virtually bare to thinly covered with short adpressed silvery hairs. Face adorned with grayish or whitish supraorbital band, a grayish fringe from corner of eye to angle of jaw, and a grayish fringe across muzzle to each corner of mouth; wedge-shaped midfrontal crest white and either continuous with white of nape as a flowing mane or sharply defined from reddish mantle including nape; back modified agouti, the dominant color black or brown, the pale subterminal bands of the hairs buffy to white; underparts of body, arms, and legs dominantly whitish to yellow or buff, often ochraceous; hairs of throat crested medially or whorled or directed straight back; tail reddish orange proximally, black distally; external genitalia pigmented.

Fig. X.67. *Saguinus oedipus oedipus*: Profile view with mane removed to expose ear, vibrissae, and facial pigmentation.

Vibrissae (fig. X.67). Supraorbitals, mystacials, rhinarials, mentals present, forward- and sidewise-directed interramals often present in *geoffroyi,* absent in *oedipus;* genals present and well defined; ulnar carpals present; gular and pectoral spines absent.

Ears. See text p. 102 and figs. III.18; X.67.

Larynx. See text p. 18 and figs. I.10, 11; X.5.

Tongue. See text p. 107 and figs. III.19; X.5.

Cranial Characters (figs. X.6, 8, 10, 12)

Frontal contour well rounded to steeply domed; temporal ridges convergent on frontal and either divergent on parietal with an independent sagittal crest between or convergent and fusing with median crest; nasal profile concave; frontal sinuses well inflated; malar foramen 2 mm or less in greatest diameter; ventral border of mandible more often V- than U-shaped, the horizontal rami from completely distended to notably arced, the angular process slightly or not inflected inward and slightly to markedly deflected downward.

External Genitalia

Male (figs. III.24, 27, 28, 29; X.68D–G)

Adult. External genitalia deeply pigmented; exposed surface of penial shaft wrinkled, glans mostly to entirely pigmented, with left lobe larger and more projecting than right; scrotum globose, pedunculate, wider than long, skin of scrotal, or testicular, fold corrugated, nearly or entirely hairless on outer surface, except for sparse cover of long hairs on raphe and thin covering at pedunculated base; outer surface of preputial fold corrugated and papillate, each papilla with a long hair, inner or distal surface of preputial sheath glabrous and folded without corrugations or papillae; greatest diameter of scrotum 18 mm; sexual skin in mature individuals sometimes as extensive as in females but not conspicuously swollen or extremely glandular; perineal and anal region moderately or lightly pigmented to unpigmented; baculum undistinguished.

Remarks. The glands of the pubic sexual skin in adult *Saguinus oedipus geoffroyi* are described by Wislocki (1930, p. 477) as smaller than those of the female. Almost no trace of pubic glands were found in three juvenals of the same race. Wislocki (1930, p. 479) notes that in the scrotal area of the adult, "glandular differentiation is wanting, neither glands nor hairs being present whereas in the perineal and anal regions small sebaceous and tubular glands are encountered which do not, however, warrant elevation to the rank of glandular organ." In our material, including more than a dozen spirit-preserved genitalia, all sides of the scrotal base, the scrotal raphe, and the outer surface of the preputial fold are thinly haired, and only the main body of the scrotal or testicular fold may be nearly or quite glabrous; the skin of both scrotal and preputial folds appears to be more or less glandular.

Female (figs. III.22, 23; X.68A–C)

Adult. External genitalia usually longer than wide; labia majora richly glandular, deeply pigmented, swollen scrotal fold or posterior cushion densely papillate, each papilla with one hair, some with two or three; preputial fold or anterior cushion enormously hypertrophied, the outer fold hairy, loosely papillate, and scored, inner horseshoe-shaped annular fold surrounding glans clitoridis glabrous and slightly wrinkled; left lobe of glans clitoridis larger than right, more projecting, its apex pigmented, right lobe lightly pigmented; frenula clitoridorum well defined in present material, the frenula expanding dorsad and caudad into laminated labia minora; greatest length of labia majora 18 mm, length of

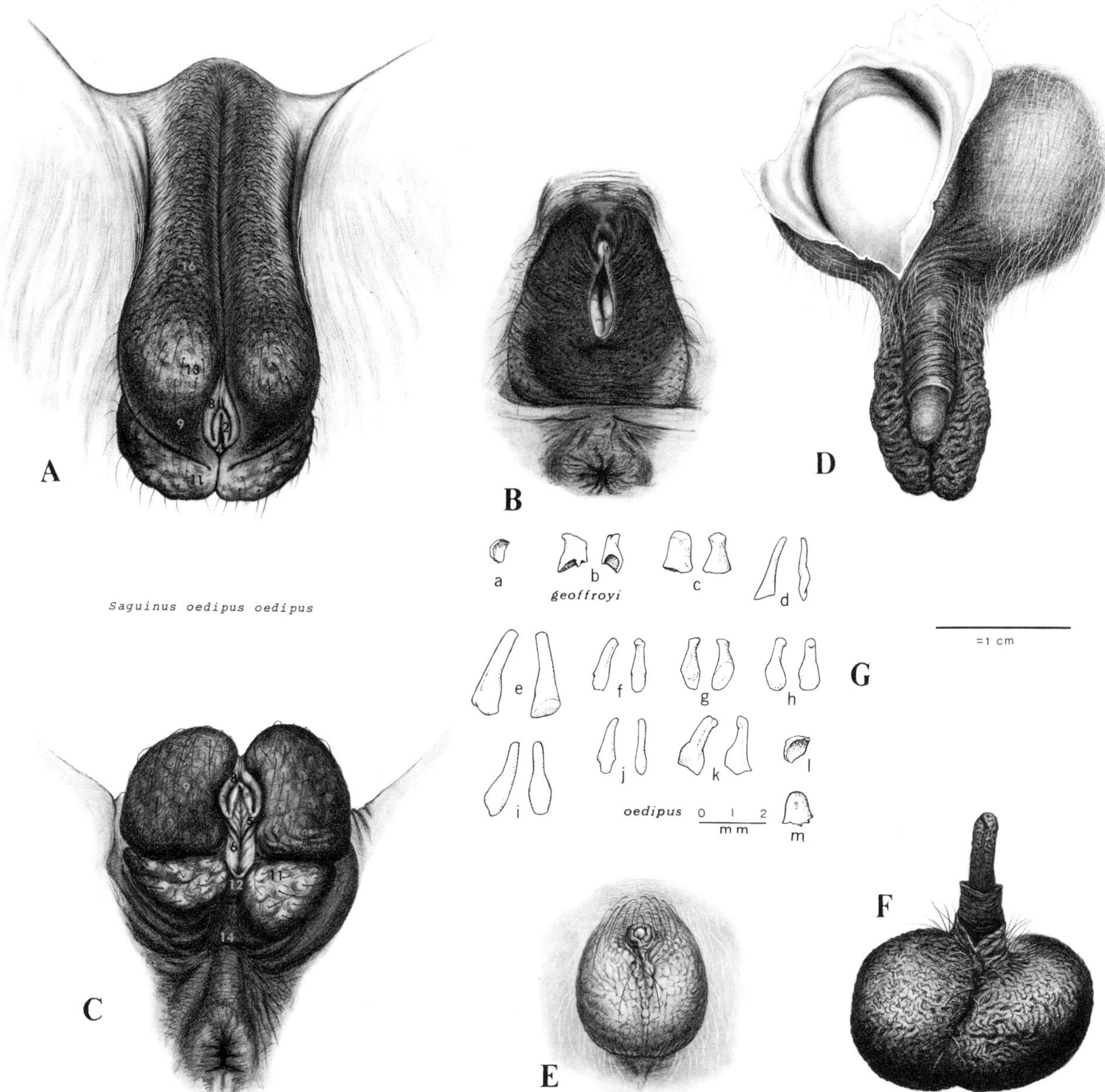

Fig. X.68. *Saguinus oedipus,* external genitalia: *A,* female organs and sexual skin; *B,* vulva distended to expose vestibule; *C,* details of female genital region; *D,* scrotum collapsed, testicles withdrawn, right side in inguinal region opened to expose testicle; *E,* juvenal male; *F,* adult male; *G,* bacula of *S. oedipus oedipus* and *S. o. geoffroyi,* one or two aspects of each baculum. See pp. 113–14 for explanation of symbols.

genital fissure 14 mm; sexual skin a broad band raised into two thick ridges separated by a median longitudinal sulcus, thickly glandular, deeply pigmented, and greatly enlarged in old adults; perineal and anal regions pigmented.

Juvenal. Outer surface of labia majora pigmented, weakly papillate and sparsely set with long stiff hairs as in mature females, but labium of each side forming a simple unpigmented pad, the scrotal and hairy portion of preputial fold undifferentiated; inner or glabrous fold of prepuce not well differentiated from outer fold or from glans clitoridis; glans clitoridis extruded to level of pudendal angle; mons pubis low, sexual skin differentiated but unswollen.

Remarks. The sexual skin attains its maximum development in this species. Wislocki (1930, p. 476, pls. 22–23, 1936, p. 313, fig. 1) gives a detailed account of the gross and microscopic anatomy of the labia majora and sexual skin of both sexes of *Saguinus oedipus geoffroyi.* Pocock (1920, p. 107) found no trace of an anogenital glandular area in the female of *Saguinus oedipus oedipus,* but his specimen must have been sexually immature. In available dry skin and spirit-preserved specimens, the sexual skin is equally well developed in all mature members of the *oedipus* group. However, only a minority of mature individuals of a population attain maximum swelling and pigmentation of external genitalia and sexual skin at the same time.

The parts of the external genitalia of a supposedly menstruating individual described and figured by De Beaux (1917, p. 107, fig. 8) as labia minora are labia majora. The areas he labeled "porz. super. gen." and "porz. inf. gen. est.," are the scrotal and preputial folds, respectively.

Comparisons

The facial and coronal color and pelage patterns of *Saguinus oedipus* are distinctive. The modified agouti dorsum, usually sharply defined whitish or yellow underparts, arms and legs are likewise peculiar; hypotrophy of the posterior lamina of the ear appears to be restricted to this species of callitrichid.

Molt

The series at hand of *Saguinus oedipus* are the only ones suitable for a pilot study of molt in tamarins. Most of the material was collected during a 17-month period and within a fairly homogenous and geographically restricted range.

Saguinus oedipus oedipus

Pelage of 62 specimens I collected in 1949 and 1950 from 6 localities is in all stages of molt from juvenal to adult and from old to new. The data tabulated indicate that molt occurs throughout the year, but the large majoriy of individuals taken during the rainy season are in new or slightly worn pelage while nearly all individuals caught in the dry season are in old, worn, and faded pelage. Old pelage is dry and coarse in texture, lax and wavy in disposition, the individual hairs usually without the black tips of new pelage.

San Juan Nepomuceno (45), *Bolívar.* 12 specimens, 11–25 January 1949, dry season—all in old pelage.

Socorré (40) *upper Río Sinú, Córdoba.* 15 specimens, 6 March–2 April 1949, end of dry season and beginning of rainy season—all in old pelage.

Las Campanas (46), *Colosó, Bolívar.* 12 specimens, 19 May–2 June 1949, rainy season—all in old pelage.

Catival (41), *upper Río San Jorge.* 13 specimens, 6–31 July 1949, rainy season—all pelage conditions from old and worn and faded to completely new and several with molt lines showing across shoulders in one specimen and across midback to hind back in others.

Villa Arteaga (30), *Antioquia.* 4 specimens, 18–29 January 1950, "dry" season, three in old pelage, one in completely new pelage.

This locality is normally more humid than San Juan Nepomuceno, and its 1950 dry season was abnormally wet.

Curulao (29), *Urabá, Antioquia.* 6 specimens, 25 April–2 May 1950, rainy season—moderately worn to new pelage.

Saguinus oedipus geoffroyi

The conditions of the pelage of 31 adults taken during the months of March, July, August, September, and October appears to be individually variable. The breakdown by locality and date is as follows. Weather was recorded in the first locality only.

Unguía (24), *Chocó, Colombia.* 20 specimens, 8–26 March 1960, end of dry season—all conditions evenly distributed from worn to unworn, the wear progressing from front to back.

Barro Colorado (17), *Canal Zone, Panamá.* 1 specimen, 4 July 1929—new pelage on anterior half of body separated from worn posterior half by a distinct molt line.

Allbrook Air Force Base (19), *Canal Zone, Panamá.* 4 specimens, 18 August 1959—all in new pelage; 2 specimens, 29 September 1959—1 in new, 1 in old pelage.

Río Sandó (28), *Chocó, Colombia.* 4 specimens, 8–13 October 1958—2 in new, 2 in old pelage.

The pelage of more than 100 specimens of *Saguinus oedipus geoffroyi* from Panamá, collected by Charles O. Handley, Jr., is difficult to classify, but a rough sorting is possible. Sixty specimens are from 12 localities (Chiva Chiva (20); Cocoli (18); Farfan (18); Fort Kobbe (18); Gamboa (21); La Chorrera (4); Madden Road and Dam (22); Nueva Emperador (18); Paraíso (20); Pedro Miguel (20); Radio Station Hill (22); Summit (22)) in the deciduous forest region of the Pacific coast, most of them in the Canal Zone. The collections were made during the months from April to November. Pelage of the great majority of the specimens is old or moderately worn. Tamarins from the evergreen forest region in northern and southern Panamá represented by 45 specimens from 8 localities (Armila [6d]; Boca de Paya [13b]; Casita [15b]; Fort Gulick [5b]; Mandinga [6c]; Río Chucunaque [7b]; Río Seteganti [12]; Tacarcuna Village [15a]) were taken from January into March. Their pelage is fresh or slightly worn. The months from December to March are not represented in the deciduous forest group, and only the January to March months are represented in the evergreen forest group. There is no reason to believe, therefore, that the pelage conditions of the two groups are strictly comparable.

Remarks. Processes of saturation, bleaching, and depilation in *Saguinus oedipus* are described in the species group section (p. 736). The taxonomic history is given in the following subspecies accounts.

SAGUINUS OEDIPUS GEOFFROYI PUCHERAN, RED-CRESTED BARE-FACE TAMARIN

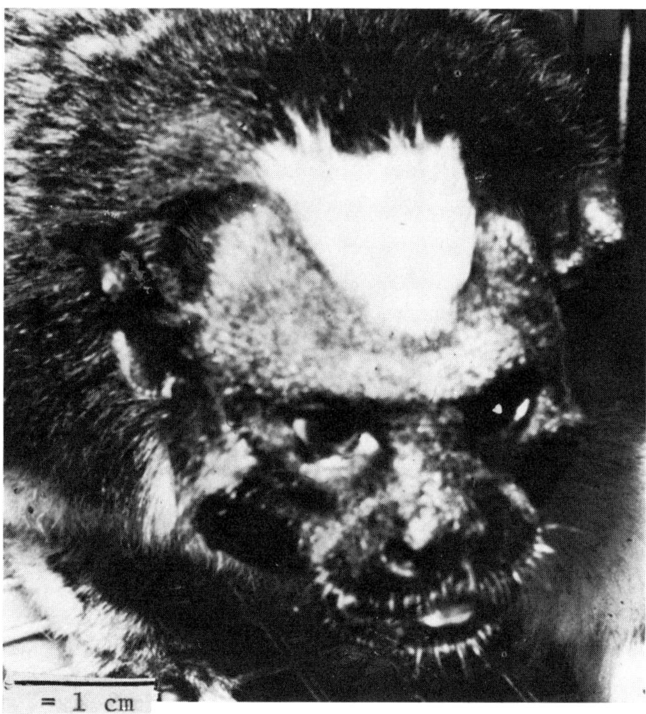

Fig. X.69. Red-crested Bare-face Tamarin, *Saguinus oedipus geoffroyi*

Synonymic History

Midas Œdipus (varietas), Spix (not Linnaeus), 1823, *Sim. et Vesp. Brasil.* p. 30, pl. 23 (animal)—characters; habitat, "vraisemblablement dans la Guiane." Wagner, 1833, *Isis von Oken* 10:996—correctly regarded by Spix as color variety of *oedipus.*

Hapale oedipus, Sclater (not Linnaeus), 1861, *Nat. Hist. Rev.* 1861:509—PANAMA: (Chiriquí).

Hapale Geoffroyi Pucheran, 1845, *Rev. Mag. Zool., Paris* 8:336. Wagner, 1848, *Abh. Akad. Wiss. Munich* 5: 475—Panamá locality questioned. Rode, 1938, *Bull. Mus. Nat. Hist. Nat., Paris,* ser. 2, 10:239—type history.

Hapale geoffroyi, Schlegel, 1876, *Les singes. Simiae,* p. 258—PANAMA. Jentink, 1887, *Cat. Ostéol. Mus. Pays-Bas* 9:48—PANAMA. Jentink, 1892, *Cat. Syst. Mamm. Mus. Pays-Bas* 11:56—PANAMA.

M[idas] Geoffroyi, I. Geoffroy, 1851, *Cat. Primates Mus. Hist. Nat., Paris* p. 63—type history. I. Geoffroy, 1851, *Arch. Mus. Hist. Nat.* 5:531, footnote, 579—PANAMA; characters.

Midas geoffroyi, Alston, 1882, *Biol. Centr.-Amer.* p. 17—COLOMBIA; PANAMA (Chiriquí; Colón). Major, 1901, *Proc. Zool. Soc. London* 1901:147, 152, pl. 12, fig. 2 (orbit)—lacrimal region of skull. Festa, 1903, *Boll. Mus. Zool. Anat. Comp.* 18(435):17—PANAMA: *Darién* (Río Cianati; Laguna de la Pita).

Midas geoffroii [*sic*], Sclater, 1861, *Nat. Hist. Rev.* p. 509. Sclater, 1871, *Proc. Zool. Soc. London* 1871:478, pl. 38 (animal)—COLOMBIA: *Chocó* ("forests of New Granada near the coast"; PANAMA: (Chepó). Sclater, 1872, *Proc. Zool. Soc. London* 1872:8—PANAMA: (Chiriquí; Colón); *Hapale oedipus,* a synonym.

Oe[dipomidas] Geoffroyi, Reichenbach, 1862, *Vollst. Naturg. Affen* p. 5, pl. 1, fig. 2 (animal)—characters.

Œdipomidas geoffroyi Elliot, 1913, *A review of the Primates,* 1:214—characters ex type; *spixi* a synonym. Elliot, 1914, *Bull. Amer. Mus. Nat. Hist.* 33:644—synonymy; distribution.

Oedipomidas geoffroyi, J. A. Allen, 1916, *Bull. Amer. Mus. Nat. Hist.* 35:227—COLOMBIA: Chocó (Río Salaquí). Wislocki, 1913, *J. Mammal.* 11:476—scent glands of pubic areas. De Beaux, 1917, *Giorn. Morph. Uomo, Primati* 1:94, 107, fig. 4 (facial vibrissae), fig. 8 (female genital tract)—PANAMA: *Darién* (Laguna de la Pita); vibrissae; female genitalia in menstrual phase. Wislocki, 1932, *Anat. Rec.* 52:381—placentation; twins regarded as monozygotic. Enders, 1935, *Bull. Mus. Comp. Zool.* 78:439—PANAMA: *Canal Zone* (Barro Colorado); life history. Carpenter, 1935, *J. Mammal.* 16:171—COSTA RICA (Río La Vaca, Coto region). Wislocki, 1936, *Human Biol.* 8:311, 313, fig. 1 (♀ genitalia)—external genitalia. Schultz, 1938, *Anat. Rec.* 72:388—weight of testes to body weight. Wislocki, 1939, *Amer. J. Anat.* 64:445—twinning now regarded as result of biovulation, triplets from three ova. Schultz, 1940, *Amer. J. Phys. Anthrop.* 26:389—relative size of orbit and eye to weight of body. Schultz, 1948, *Amer. J. Phys. Anthrop.*, n.s. 6:8—single birth recorded. Harms, 1956, *Primatologia* 1:577 —relative weight of testes. Schultz, 1956, *Primatologia* 1:877—postembryonic growth changes. Fiennes, 1964, *Proc. Zool. Soc. London* 143(3):523—cystic bone disease. Hershkovitz, 1964, *Amer. J. Phys. Anthrop.* 21(3): 397—*Oedipomidas geoffroyi* Pucheran not a homonym of *Callithrix geoffroyi* Humboldt. Willig and Wendt, 1970, *Säuget. Mitt.* 18(2):117, fig. 1 (young), fig. 2 (facial expressions)—breeding; rearing; facial expressions; reactions to color pictures.

[*Oedipomidas*] *geoffroyi*, Schultz and Straus, 1945, Proc. *Amer. Phil. Soc.* 89:601—vertebral formula.

Oedipus [(*Hapanella*)] *Geoffroyi*, Gray, 1870, *Cat. monkeys, lemurs and fruit-eating bats, Brit. Mus.* p. 65—PANAMA.

Leontocebus geoffroyi, Miller, 1912, *U.S. Nat. Mus.* 79:380—classification. Anthony, 1916, *Bull. Amer. Mus. Nat. Hist.* 35:374—PANAMA: *Darién* (Boca de Cupe; Chepigana; Cituro; Tacarcuna; Tapalisa); *Panamá* (Maxon Ranch). Goldman, 1920, *Smiths. Misc. Coll.* 69:226—PANAMA: *Darién* (Cana) *Panamá* (Río Indio, near Gatún). G. M. Allen, 1923, *Bull. Mus. Comp. Zool.* 65:273—PANAMA: *Darién* (Río Esnape; Río Jesusito). Straus and Arcadi, 1958, *Primatologia* 3(1):507—excretory system. Cabrera, 1958, *Rev. Mus. Argentino Cienc. Nat. "Bernardino Rivadavia"* 4(1):198—classification. Lasinski, 1960, *Primatologia* 2(1), Lief. 5:59, 60—external ear. Mallinson, 1965, *Int. Zoo Yearb.* 5:139—cure of cage paralysis with vitamin D_3.

Leontocebus (*Oedipomidas*) *geoffroyi*, Huber, 1931, *Evolution of facial musculature and facial expression* (Baltimore), p. 28—ear musculature. Osman Hill, 1958, *Primatologia* 3 (1):166—gut anatomy.

Marikina geoffroyi, Hershkovitz, 1949, *Proc. U.S. Nat. Mus.* 98:416—PANAMA (La Chorrera; Agua Blanca [sic = Aguas Buenas]; Alajuela; Las Cascadas; Río Indio, near Gatun; Cana; Chepo); COLOMBIA: *Chocó* (Sautatá, Río Atrato; Río Salaquí; Baudo); revision; nomenclature (*geoffroyi* Pucheran valid, *spixi* Reichenbach a synonym). Hinchcliffe and Pye, 1969, *J. Zool., London* 157:280—PANAMA; middle ear morphology; synovial type of stapedovestibular joint.

Saguinus geoffroyi, Hall and Kelson, 1959, *Mammals of North America* p. 231, fig. 163 (skull)—characters; distribution in North America. Houser, Hartman, Knouf, and McCoy, 1962, *Anat. Rec.* 142(1):44, pl. 1, fig. 8 (adrenal, cross section)—PANAMA; comparative anatomy of adrenal. Porter, Johnson, and De Sousa, 1966, *J. Parasit.* 52(4):669—malaria *Plasmodium brasilianum* absent in 749 specimens examined. Porter and Young, 1966, *Military Med.* 131(9) Suppl.:952—experimental transmission of *Plasmodium vivax* from man. Porter and Young, 1967, *J. Parasit.* 53(4):845—transfer of *Plasmodium falciparum* from man. Schneider, 1967, *J. Parasit.* 53:1135—susceptibility to infection with *Besnoitia* (Protozoa). Chivers, 1968, *Animals* 11(8):355—PANAMA: *Canal Zone* (Barro Colorado). Thatcher and Porter, 1968, *Trans. Amer. Microsc. Soc.* 87(2):186—helminth parasites. A. Hladik and C. M. Hladik, 1969, *La Terre et la Vie* 23:92—PANAMA: *Canal Zone* (Barro Colorado); habits; habitat; food and seed dissemination. Mallinson, 1971, *Sixth Ann. Rep. Jersey Wildl. Preserv. Trust* p. 9—longevity in Jersey Zoo, 8 years, 5 mo., still living. Young, 1970, *Lab. Animal Care* 20(2):363—susceptibility to *Plasmodium vivax* and *P. falciparum* of human origin. Porter, 1970, *Amer. J. Vet. Res.* 31:379 —hematologic values. Epple, 1970, *Folia Primat.* 12:56, fig. 1 (3-day-old ♀), fig. 15 (15-day-old ♀ with parent)—housing; diet; feeding; reproduction; characters and development of young. Moynihan, 1970, *Smiths. Contrib. Zool.*, no. 28, p. 1—characters; distribution; habitat; habits; reproduction; vocalization; visual communication; tail pattern; piloerection. Baerg, 1971, *J. Parasit.* 57(1):8—PANAMA: *Panamá* (Pacora); natural infection with *Plasmodium brasilianum*.

Saguinus oedipus geoffroyi, Hershkovitz, 1969, *Quart. Rev. Biol.* 44(1):19, fig. 6 (map)—origin; distribution. Hershkovitz, 1970, *Am. J. Phys. Anthrop.* 32:379—dental disease. Hsu and Hampton, 1970, *Folia Primat.* 13: 183—karyotype (2n = 46). J. K. Hampton, Jr., Hampton, and Levy, 1971, in *Med. Primat. 1970,* ed. Goldsmith and Moor-Jankowski, p. 527—reproduction in laboratory colony. J. K. Hampton, Jr., Parmelee, and Rider, 1971, in *Med. Primat. 1970,* ed. Goldsmith and Moor-Jankowski, p. 245—plasma histaminase and diamine oxidase values.

S[*aguinus*] *oedipus geoffroyi*, Hull, Dwyer, Holmes, Nowakowski, Deinhardt, Lennette, and Emmons, 1972, *J. Nat. Cancer Inst.* 49(1):225—lethal infection with spider monkey virus.

J[*acchus*] *Spixii* Reichenbach, 1862, *Vollst. Naturg. Affen*, p. 1, pl. 1, fig. 2 (animal)—name based on the description and figure of *Midas Oedipus* Varietas Spix, a female, mounted in the Munich Museum; type locality mistakenly believed to be the Guianas.

Midas spixi, Elliot, 1913, *A review of the Primates* 1:215 (in text)—a synonym of *geoffroyi;* type in Munich Museum.

Oedipomidas Spixi, Cabrera, 1940, *Ciencia, Rev. hispano-americana, México* 1:403—substitute for *Hapale geoffroyi* Pucheran, "preoccupied" by *Simia geoffroyi* Humboldt.

Oedipomidas spixi, Osman Hill, 1957, *Primates* 3:120, 156, 166, 182, 189, 203, 253, 256–260, 262, fig. 44 (map, distribution), fig. 63 (ear), fig. 66 (♀ external genitalia) fig. 67 (intestine), pl. 19 (animal)—anatomy; characters; taxonomy; distribution; *geoffroyi* Pucheran regarded as invalid. Dunn, Lambrecht, 1963, *J. Parasit.* 49

(2):316—*Plasmodium* infection. Epple, 1967, *Folia Primat.* 7:37—sexual and social behavior; reproduction; rearing of young; marking. Epple and Lorenz, 1967, *Folia Primat.* 7:98—sternal gland (form; function). Epple, 1968, *Folia Primat.* 8:1—vocalization. Graetz, 1968, *Sitzungsb. Gesell. Naturg. Fr.* 8:29—PANAMA; behavior in semiwild captivity.

Oe[dipomidas] spixi, Osman Hill, 1958, *Primatologia* 3(1):681—external genitalia.

Œdipomidas salaquiensis Elliot, 1912, *Bull. Amer. Mus. Nat. Hist.* 31:137—COLOMBIA: *Chocó* (type locality, Río Salaquí); type, male, skin and skull, American Museum of Natural History no. 33076, collected 1912 by Mrs. E. L. Kerr. Elliot, 1913, *A review of the Primates* 3:255—description. Goodwin, 1953, *Bull. Amer. Mus. Nat. Hist.* 102:264—type history.

Oedipomidas [sp.], Wislocki, 1930, *Carnegie Inst. Contrib. Embryol.* 22 (133):176—PANAMA; breeding season.

S[aguinus] geoffroyi ♀ × *S[aguinus] oedipus* ♂, Epple, 1970, *Folia Primat.* 12:66, 74—2 pairs produced in captivity.

Type. Female, skin mounted, skull separate, Muséum National d'Histoire Naturelle, Paris, skin no. 112, skull no. 621, originally donated to the menagerie of the Jardin des Plantes where it died 25 August 1845.

Type Locality. "Panamá," restricted to the Canal Zone, by Hershkovitz (1949, *Proc. U.S. Nat. Mus.* 98:417).

Distribution (figs. X.15; XIII.3). Tropical forested zones of Panamá and bordering Coto region of southeastern Costa Rica; in extreme northwestern Colombia, west of the Ríos Atrato and San Juan in the department of Chocó; altitudinal range from sea level to nearly 900 meters above.

Taxonomy. The crested bare-face tamarin was first noticed by Spix in 1823 (p. 30, pl. 23) under the name *"Midas oedipus varietas."* A different individual was described 22 years later by Pucheran, who named it *Hapale geoffroyi* in honor of M. Etienne Geoffroy St.-Hilaire. The specimen known to Spix was the mounted skin of a captive animal of unknown origin. The claws, as shown in the colored plate, are abnormally long and recurved, a consequence of long confinement. Even the hallux supports a claw as long and curved as those of the other digits of the feet.

Spix was aware of the differences between his specimen and the Linnaean *Simia oedipus,* which was based on the figure of Edward's "little lion monkey." The discrepancies, however, were attributed to artifacts of preparation and faulty portrayal. Wagner (1833, p. 995) commented on the characters of Spix's *oedipus* but conceded that the animal may have been correctly treated as only a variety. Later, however, he (1848, p. 475) identified Spix's *Midas oedipus varietas* with Pucheran's *geoffroyi.* On the other hand, Reichenbach (1862, p. 1, pl. 1, fig. 2) thought Spix's animal was different from both *oedipus* and *geoffroyi,* and he renamed it *Jacchus Spixii* for its discoverer.

Oedipomidas salaquiensis Elliot, from Colombia, was distinguished from Panamanian *oedipus* primarily on the basis of its more saturate color and supposedly larger skull. Later, Elliot (1914, p. 644) allowed that "additional material from Colombia seems to show that the characters for distinguishing *O. salaquensis* [*sic*] are not reliable, the yellowishness of the underparts having been produced by staining and the size of the skull is an individual variation." J. A. Allen (1916, p. 227) reiterated the staining hypothesis and pointed to other specimens from Colombia (Baudó) and Panamá with "stained" underparts. The so-called "stain" is the natural yellow grade of the bleaching process and a common character in most mammals with otherwise white or near white underparts.

Nomenclature. The name *Hapale geoffroyi* Pucheran 1845, as originally proposed, is no primary homonym of *Simia geoffroyi* Humboldt 1812 (= *Callithrix jacchus geoffroyi* Humboldt). At no one time were both *geoffroyi* Pucheran and *geoffroyi* Humboldt regarded as congeneric and classified under the same generic name, whether *Hapale, Simia* or any other. This is to say that neither species was ever a secondary homonym of the other. Indeed, Humboldt's *Simia geoffroyi* was almost immediately replaced by E. Geoffroy's *Jacchus leucocephalus* and fell into disuse until 1940 when Cabrera (1940, p. 403) revived it as the senior synonym, this time in the combination *Callithrix geoffroyi* Humboldt. Cabrera erred, however, in assuming that thereby the *Hapale geoffroyi* of Pucheran became a secondary homonym of *Callithrix geoffroyi* simply because *Hapale* and *Callithrix* are synonymous. Although the problem is purely one of nomenclature it must be reemphasized that Geoffroy's bare-face tamarin, *Hapale geoffroyi* Pucheran (= *Saguinus oedipus geoffroyi* Pucheran) and Geoffroy's tufted-eared marmoset, *Simia geoffroyi* Humboldt (= *Callithrix jacchus* Humboldt), are not and never were cogeneric and never was the name of the one used in precisely the same way as that of the other in any revision or scientific publication. In short, a real state of homonymy never existed. Evidently Cabrera (1958, pp. 187, 198) heeded the objections I raised in 1949 (pp. 417–18) and he recognized both *"Callithrix geoffroyi* Humboldt" and *"Leontocebus geoffroyi* Pucheran" in his monumental catalog of South American mammals. Osman Hill's (1957, p. 260) use of *spixi* Reichenbach for *geoffroyi* Pucheran is based on Cabrera's repudiated 1940 opinion.

Diagnostic Characters. White wedge-shaped midfrontal crest sharply defined from reddish mantle; dorsum modified agouti, underparts, forearms, sides of neck dominantly whitish to yellowish or ochraceous and sharply defined from upper parts (fig. X.70).

Coloration. Skin of face, throat, sides of head including temples black and sparsely sprinkled with fine buffy to silvery hairs; muzzle with a fine whitish to buffy fringe extending from above nostrils to each corner of mouth; a heavier fringe of whitish to buffy hairs extending from corner of eye to angle of jaw; grayish superciliary band moderately well defined to nearly obsolete; crown and forehead nearly bare like face except for whitish to buffy wedge-shaped midfrontal crest; hairs of mantle from

Fig. X.70. Red-crested Bare-face Tamarin, *Saguinus oedipus geoffroyi*. (Photo courtesy of New York Zoological Society.)

back of head to interscapular region reddish orange to reddish black, hairs drab to blackish basally, reddish terminally and with or without a blackish subterminal band; remainder of back black coarsely mixed or striated with silvery buffy or ochraceous buff, base and tips of hairs blackish, subterminal band buffy; sides of neck and arms whitish to ochraceous; outer sides of thighs like back of legs with less admixture of black; upper surface of hands and feet gray more or less mixed with buffy, sides of body and lateral fringe like back, the coarse modified agouti fringe extending along outer edge of upper arms for varying distances; under parts of body and lower side of limbs from white to buffy or yellowish, sometimes with brown stains or mottling; proximal one-third to one-fifth of tail black mixed with buffy, orange, or reddish, the paler colors dominant on ventral surfaces; remainder of tail black; external genitalia pigmented.

Cranial Characters. Frontal contour well rounded, temporal ridges convergent on frontal and divergent on parietals or, sometimes, fusing into a sagittal crest; nasal profile concave; frontal sinuses well inflated; malar foramen 2 mm or less in greatest diameter; ventral border of mandible extremely V-shaped, the horizontal rami forming a sharp, widespread angle without arcing, angular process with little inward inflection or downward deflection.

Measurements. See appendix table 2.

Comparisons. Distinguished from *oedipus* primarily by the reddish nuchal and scapular regions, dominantly blackish, not brownish, back with coarse modified agouti pattern extending to rump and outer sides of thighs; from all other callitrichids by the sparsely haired face and sides of head and strongly contrasted wedge-shaped whitish coronal crest and reddish mantle.

Variation. Saguinus oedipus geoffroyi appears to become progressively paler from south to north. The most saturate series is from Sandó (28), Chocó, the the southern extreme of the range. Here the mantle is mahogany, underparts yellowish to ochraceous stained or mottled with reddish brown, recalling the reddish brown underparts of *leucopus*. Canal Zone *geoffroyi* is palest with mantle reddish, the extent of the basal black of the hairs reduced and the underparts more uniformly white than in the more southern series. The larger series from Unguía (24), northern Chocó, is intermediate. In contrast, the face and cheeks of Panamanian *geoffroyi* are more thickly clothed with hair, nearly as in *leucopus*.

Specimens Examined. 220. PANAMA—*Canal Zone:* Agua Buena, 1 (USNM); Albrook Air Force Base, 3 (FMNH); Alajuela, 3 (USNM); Barro Colorado, 1 (UMMZ); Chiva Chiva, 4 (USNM); Chorrera, 2 (USNM); Coco Plantation, 3 (USNM); Cocoli, Río Cocoli, 11 (USNM); Farfan, 5 (USNM); Fort Gulick, 1 (USNM); Fort Kobbe, 2 (USNM); Gamboa, 11 (USNM); Las Cascadas, 1 (USNM); Madden Dam, 12 (USNM); Madden Forest, 3 (FMNH); Pac, 1 (USNM); Paraíso, 2 (USNM); Pedro Miguel, 6 (USNM); Radio Station Hill, 2 (USNM); Río Indio, 8 (USNM); Summit Road, 3 (USNM); *Darién:* Boca de Cupe, 1 (AMNH); Cana, 2 (USNM); Chepigana, 6 (AMNH); Cituro, 4 (AMNH); Río Chucunaque, 4 (USNM); Río Paya, Boca de, 9 (USNM); Río Seteganti, 1 (USNM); Tacarcuna, 12 (AMNH); Tacarcuna, Casita Camp, 5 (USNM); Tacarcuna, Laguna Camp, 1 (USNM); Tacarcuna, Village Camp, 6 (USNM); Tapalisa, 4 (AMNH); Tocumén, 3 (BM); *Panamá:* Arraiján, 2 (USNM); Chepo, 3 (BM, 2; USNM, 1); La Chorrera, 2 (AMNH, 1; USNM, 1); Maxon Ranch, Río Trinidad, 1 (AMNH); Nuevo Emperador, 3 (USNM); *San Blas:* Armila, Quebrada Venado, 12 (USNM); Mandinga, 6 (USNM); locality unknown: 1 (MNHN, type *geoffroyi*); COLOMBIA—*Chocó:* Baudó, 2 (AMNH); Río Salaquí, 1 (AMNH); Río Saudó, 4 (FMNH); Sautatá, 7 (CM); Unguía, 23 (FMNH); *locality unknown:* 10 (AMNH, 6; USNM, 4).

SAGUINUS OEDIPUS OEDIPUS LINNAEUS, COTTON-TOP OR WHITE PLUMED BARE-FACE TAMARIN

Fig. X.71. Cotton-top or White-plumed Bare-face Tamarin, *Saguinus oedipus oedipus.*

Synonymic History

Little lion-monkey, Edwards, 1751, *A natural history of birds,* pt. 4, p. 195, pl. 195 (animal).

Petit singe du Mexique, Brisson, 1756, *Reg. Anim.* p. 210.

Pinche, Buffon, 1767, *Hist. Nat.* 15:114, pl. 17 (animal).

Pinche mâle, F. Cuvier, 1829, in Geoffroy and Cuvier, *Hist. Nat. Mamm.,* livr. 59 (vol. 5), pl. (animal).

[*Simia*] *Œdipus* Linnaeus, 1758, *Syst. Nat.,* ed. 10, p. 28. Linnaeus, 1766, *Syst. Nat.,* ed. 12, p. 41—characters. Audebert, 1797, *Hist. Nat. singes et makis,* fam. 6, sect. 2, p. 1, pl. 1 (animal)—"n'en est pas très-nombreuse dans les environs de Cayenne et de Surinam"; characters. Shaw, 1800, *Gen. Zool.* 1 (1):63, pl. 25 (red-tailed monkey)—characters. Humboldt, 1805, *Rec. Obs. Zool. Anat. Comp., Paris,* p. 9, pl. 8, fig. 1, 2 (larynx)—voice. Humboldt, 1812, *Rec. Obs. Zool. Anat. Comp., Paris,* pp. 8, 332, 337, 361, pl. 3, figs. 1–2 (larynx)—COLOMBIA: *Bolívar* (Cartagena; Turbaco; mouth of Río Sinú); PANAMA: *Darién:* ["Guyane françoise," p. 361, a lapsus]; characters; habits; anatomy of larynx.

Simia Ædipus [*sic*], F. Cuvier, 1829, in Geoffroy and Cuvier, *Hist. Nat. Mamm.,* livr. 59 [vol. 5], pl. (animal)—characters.

S[*imia*] (*Sagoinus*) *Œdipus,* Kerr, 1792, *Anim. Kingd.,* p. 81—characters.

[*Callithrix*] *Œdipus,* Erxleben, 1777, *Syst. Regn. Anim.,* p. 59—classification.

Callitrix oedippus [*sic*], Latreille, 1804, *Buffon Hist. Nat.,* Sonnini ed. 36:281—characters.

Sagouin oedipus, Lacépède, 1803, *Buffon Hist. Nat.,* Didot ed., (1799), 14:147—classification.

Sagouin oedipus, Geoffroy, 1803, *Cat. Mamm. Mus. Hist. Nat. Paris,* p. 11—*le pinche* of Buffon and Daubenton in the museum collection.

Cercopithecus Œdipus, Goldfuss, 1809, *Vergl. Naturb. Säugth.,* p. 75—classification.

Jacchus œdipus, Desmarest, 1818, *Nouv. Dict. Hist. Nat.,* 24:243—classification. Desmarest, 1827, *Dict. Sci. Nat.* 47:23—classification.

Jacchus Œdipus, Gray, 1843, *List. Mamm. Brit. Mus.,* p. 15—"BRAZIL"; *Œdipus titi* Lesson, a synonym.

Jaccus [*sic*] *Ædipus* [*sic*], F. Cuvier, in Geoffroy and Cuvier, 1829, *Hist. Nat., Mamm.,* livr. 59 [vol. 5], pl. (animal)—characters.

C[*ebus*] *Œdipus,* Blainville, 1839, *Ostéographie,* 1, sect. C, pl. 4 (skeleton)—osteology.

H[*apale*] *Oedipus,* Voigt, 1831, *Thierreich,* p. 99—characters. Wagner, 1840, *Schreber's Säugth., Suppl.* 1:251, pl. 34 (animal)—characters.

Hapale Œdipus, Giebel, 1865, *Zeitschr. gesammt. Naturw., Halle* 26:257—skeleton.

[?] *Hapale oedipus,* Zelebor, 1868, *Novarra Exped., Zool., Saugeth.,* p. 9—"NICARAGUA."

Hapale oedipus, Schlegel, 1876, *Les singes. Simiae,* p. 258—COLOMBIA: *Magdalena.* Jentink, 1887, *Cat. Osteol. Mus. Pays-Bas* 9:48—COLOMBIA; "PERU." Jentink, 1892, *Cat. Syst. Mamm. Mus. Pays-Bas* 11:55—COLOMBIA; "PERU."

Midas oedipus, E. Geoffroy, 1812, *Ann. Mus. Hist. Nat., Paris* 19:122—classification. Elliot Smith, 1902, *Cat. Comp. Anat. Roy. Coll. Surgeons, England* (ed. 2) 2:381, fig. 222—cerebral fissural pattern. Sylvester, 1912, *Amer. J. Anat.* 12:448—lymphaticovenous communications.

M[idas] oedipus, I. Geoffroy, 1851, *Cat. Primates, Mus. Nat., Paris,* p. 62—COLOMBIA.

Oe[dipomidas] Oedipus, Reichenbach, 1862, *Vollst. Naturg. Affen,* p. 5—classification; characters.

Œdipomidas oedipus, Elliot, 1905, *Field Col. Mus., Zool. Ser.* 6:532—listed. Elliot, 1913, *A review of the Primates* 1:213—characters. Elliot, 1914, *Bull. Amer. Mus. Nat. Hist.* 33:644—*Seniocebus meticulosus* Elliot, a synonym. J. A. Allen, 1916, *Bull. Amer. Mus. Nat. Hist.* 35:228—COLOMBIA: *Córdoba* (Río San Jorge). Pocock, 1917, *Ann. Mag. Nat. Hist.,* ser. 8, 20:251, 254, fig. 2F (ear)—external characters.

Oe[dipomidas] oedipus, Schultz, 1948, *Amer. J. Phys. Anthrop.,* n.s., 6:8—twin birth recorded. Osman Hill, 1955, *Proc. Roy. Phys. Soc. Edinburgh* 24:51—mounted specimen, no locality. Osman Hill, 1958, *Primatologia* 3(1): 643–81—external genitalia.

Oedipomidas oedipus, Pohl, 1928, *Zeitschr. Anat. Entwickl.-Geschichte* 18:93, pl. 3, fig. 9 (penis bone)—characters of penis. Bates and Roca-Garcia, 1946, *Amer. J. Trop. Med.* 26:492—COLOMBIA: susceptibility to yellow fever infection. Osman Hill, 1957, *Primates,* 3:120, 164, 174, 183, 193, 203, 244, 253–55, 258–62, 319, fig. 44 (map, distribution), fig. 62 (ear), fig. 64 (hand and foot dermatoglyphs), fig. 65 (male external genitalia), pl. 18 (animal)—anatomy; characters; taxonomy; distribution; reproduction; behavior. Osman Hill, 1960, *Primates,* 4:67—brain weight to body weight. Benirschke and Richart, 1960, *Amer. J. Trop. Med. Hyg.* 9(3):269—spontaneous acute toxoplasmosis in imported animal. Beath and Benirschke, 1962, *Cytologia* 27(1):1, figs. 3, 4, 6, 8 (chromatin)—location of sex chromatin. Dunn, Lambrecht, and Du Plessis, 1963, *Amer. J. Trop. Med. Hyg.* 12(4):524—trypanosome infection. Benirschke and Brownhill, 1963, *Cytogenetics* 2:245—karyotype (46 chromosomes); marrow chimerism. Richart and Benirschke, 1963, *J. Path. and Bacteriol.* 86(1):221—causes of death in laboratory colony (toxoplasmosis, pyelonephritis, *Prosthenorchis* infestation). Menschel and Stroh, 1963, *Z. Parasit.* 23:376—helminth parasites. Dunn, 1963, *J. Parasit.* 49:718—COLOMBIA; helminth parasites (*Prosthenorchis elegans*). Benirschke and Richart, 1963, *Lab. Animal Care* 13(2):73, fig. (♂, ♀)—vulvar odor; laboratory care. Levy and Artecona, 1964, *Lab. Animal Care* 14(1):20, fig. 2 (animal)—laboratory care. J. K. Hampton, Jr., 1964, *Amer. J. Phys. Anthrop.* 22(2):239—husbandry; caging; diet (use of vitamin D_3 for prevention and cure of osteomalacia); parasitology; cleaning; behavior in laboratory and wild. Holmes, Caldwell, Dedman, and Deinhardt, 1964, *J. Immunol.* 92:602—isolation of *Herpesvirus tamarinus,* new species; fatal to tamarins. Skougaard, 1964, *Acta Odont. Scand.* 22:693—distribution kinetics of tritiated thymidine. Holmes, Caldwell, J. K. Hampton, Jr., and Hampton, 1965, *Science* 150:915—breeding seasons; twinning; sex ratios. Inglis and Cosgrove, 1965, *Parasitology* 55:732—pinworm infection: *Trypanoxyuris* (*Hapaloxyuris*) *oedipi,* n. sp. Stunkard, 1965, *J. Parasit.* 51(4):544—cestode infection in captive, *Paratriotaenia oedipomidatis,* new genus and species. J. K. Hampton, Jr., Hampton, and Landwehr, 1965, *Lab. Animal Care* 15(2):178—design for special breeding cage. J. K. Hampton, Jr., 1965, *Amer. J. Phys. Anthrop.* (1964) 22 (2):239—laboratory care; parasites. Wiener, Moor-Jankowski, and Gordon, 1965, *Amer. J. Phys. Anthrop.* (1964) 22(2):183—blood factors. Shriver and Marzke, 1965, *Anat. Rec.* 151:416—corticobulbar and corticospinal tracts. J. K. Hampton, Jr., Hampton, and Landwehr, 1966, *Folia Primat.* 4:265, fig. 1 (female carrying twins)—laboratory colony care and behavior; food, reproduction, grooming, play, postures, tranquilizers, diseases, and therapy; parasites. Hunt, Garcia, and Hegsted, 1966, *Fed. Proc.* 25(2):abstract—reversal of osteomalacia and osteodystrophia fibrosa by use of vitamin D_3. Kelemen, 1966, *Acta oto-larync* 61:239, figs. 1, 7 (tympanic membrane), fig. 5 (infected middle ear), fig. 6 (cochlea), fig. 8 (eustachian tube), figs. 9, 11, 12 (labyrinth), fig. 13 (tympanic cavity)—aural pathology. Anderson, Lewis, Passovoy, and Trobaugh, 1967, *Lab. Animal Care* 17(1):37—fig. 2 (karyotype)—karyotype (2n = 46); hemotology. Epple, 1967, *Folia Primat.* 7:37, 44, fig. 4 (tonguing), fig. 5 (back arching), fig. 7 (marking)—sexual and social behavior; reproduction; rearing of young; marking. Epple and Lorenz, 1967, *Folia Primat.* 7:98, fig. 12 (sternal marking)—sternal gland (form; function). Merritt and Hampton, 1967, *Proc. Soc. Exp. Biol. Med.* 124:134—human A-like antigens on red cell. Epple, 1968, *Folia Primat.* 8:1—vocalization. Dunn and Lambrecht, 1968, *J. Helminth* 37(4):261—*filarial* parasites (*Tetrapetalonema marmosetae*). Dunn and Matzke, 1968, *J. Comp. Neur.* 133:429—efferent fiber connections of trigeminal nucleus caudalis. Guraya, 1974, *Acta Anat.* 89:58—histochemistry of interstitial gland tissue in developing ovary.

Iacchus oedipus, Flower, 1863, *Proc. Zool. Soc. London* 1862:333—vertebral formula.

Leontopithecus oedipus, Thomas, 1911, *Proc. Zool. Soc. London* 1911:127—Linnaean references.

Leontocebus oedipus, Pocock, 1911, *Proc. Zool. Soc. London* 1911:856—insect feeding. Cabrera, 1958, *Rev. Mus. Argentino Cienc. Nat. "Bernardino Rivadavia"* 4(1):198—classification. Stephan, 1967, *Mitt. Max Planck Ges.* 2:67—neocorticalization. Stephan, 1967, *1st Cong. Inter. Primat. Soc.,* p. 108—neocorticalization.

Leontocebus (Oedipomidas) oedipus, Wendt, 1964, *Säugetierk. Mitteil.* 12(2/3):49, fig. 1 (young and parents)—reproduction; rearing and behavior of young.

Marikina oedipus, Hershkovitz, 1949, *Proc. U.S. Nat. Mus.* 98:141—COLOMBIA: *Córdoba* (Jaraquiel, Río Sinú; San Jorge); *Antioquia* ("Isthmus of Darien"); characters; taxonomy. Schäuffelen, 1958, *Säugetierk. Mitteil.* 6:159—carnivorous food habits.

Saguinus (Oedipomidas) oedipus, F. Deinhardt and Deinhardt, 1966, *Zool. Soc. London, Symp.,* no. 17:127—hemotologic and biochemical values; virology; use in virological research. F. Deinhardt, Holmes, Devine, and Deinhardt, 1967, *Lab. Animal Care* 17(1):60—parasitology; virology; immunities. S. H. Hampton and Hampton, 1967, *Lab. Animal Care* 17(1):1—breeding from birth by artificial laboratory techniques. Lange, Apodeca, and Kohler, 1968, *Zentralb. Bakter. Parasit. Infectionskr. Hyg.* 208:192—microfilaria; significance in experimentally induced hepatitis. Werner, Janitsche, and Kohler, 1969, *Zbl. Bakt. I. Abt. Orig.* 209:553—oral and intraperitoneal infection by cyst-forming toxoplasma. F. Deinhardt, 1970, in *Infections and immunosuppression in subhuman Primates,* ed. Balner and Beveridge (Copenhagen), p. 55—induction of "human" hepatitis and transmission to other marmoset species. Noyes, 1970, *J. Nat. Cancer Inst.* 45(3):579—tumor induced by Carr-Zilbur and Schmidt-Ruppin strains of Rous sarcoma virus. Holmes, Wolfe, Deinhardt, and Conrad, 1971, *J. Infect. Diseases* 124(5):520—infection with human hepatitis. F. Deinhardt et al., 1972, *J. Med. Primat.* 1:29—tumor induction by Rous sarcoma virus, feline sarcoma virus, simian sarcoma virus, *Herpes-virus saimiri.*

S[aguinus] (Oedipomidas) oedipus, F. Deinhardt, Holmes, and Wolfe, 1970, *J. Infect. Diseases* 121(3):351—tamarin hepatitis infection more likely by human agent than activated latent tamarin agent (reply to critique by Parks and Melnick, 1969, ibid. 120:569).

Saguinus (Oedipomidas) oedipus, Bauchot and Stephan, 1969, *Mammalia* 33(2):227—degree of encephalization.

Saguinus (Oedipus [sic]) oedipomidas [sic], F. Deinhardt, Holmes, Capps, and Popper, 1967, *J. Exp. Med.* 125 (4):673—susceptible to human hepatitis. Parks, Melnick, Voss, Singer, Rosenberg, Alcott, and Casazza, 1969, *J. Inf. Diseases* 120(5):548—marmoset hepatitis virus; serially infectious in marmosets; specific for tamarin marmosets.

S[aguinus] (oedipomidas [sic]) oedipus, Möhr, Mattenheimer, Holmes, Deinhardt, and Schmidt, 1971, *Enzyme* 12:99—enzymology of experimental liver disease; comparisons with man, horse, dog, guinea pig, rat, and mouse, ibid., p. 161, close resemblance between enzymal patterns of tamarin experimental hepatitis and human hepatitis.

Saguinus oedipus, Fooden, 1961, *Zoologica* 46:167—chromatography and systematic analyses of urinary amino acid excretion. Hunt, Garcia, Hegsted, and Kaplinsky, 1967, *Science* 157:943—vitamin D_3 effective in prevention and reversing metabolic bone disease (vitamin D_2 ineffective). S. H. Hampton and Hampton, 1967, *Lab. Animal Care* 17(1):1, fig. 5 (animal)—artificial rearing from birth. Dreizen, Levy, Bernick, Hampton, and Kraintz, 1967, *Israel J. Med. Sci.* 3(5):731, fig. 1–11 (normal and pathological periodontal bone)—periodontal bone changes caused by osteomalacia and hyperparathyroidism. Hunt, Garcia, and Hegsted, 1967, *Lab. Animal Care* 17(2):222—reversal of "cage paralysis" by substitution of vitamin D_2-containing diet for one with vitamin D_3. J. B. Deinhardt, Devine, Passovoy, Pohlman, and Deinhardt, 1967, *Lab. Animal Care* 17(1):11—care for use in biomedical laboratory research. Egozcue, Perkins, and Hagemenas, 1968, *Folia Primat.* 9(2):84—karyotype (2n = 46). Perkins, 1969, *Amer. J. Phys. Anthrop.* 30(1):13, pl. 1 (animal), pl. 2 (location and histology of suprapubic glandular field), pl. 3, fig. 4 (sinus hairs of ulnar tuft), pl. 3, fig. 5 (vascularization of suprapubic gland), fig. 6 (melanocytes of frontal scalp), fig. 7 (scalp hair follicles), fig. 8 (section female suprapubic region), fig. 9 (eccrine sweat glands of finger ball), fig. 10 (capillaries of lower lip)—histology of skin. Kraus and Hampton, 1969, *Amer. J. Phys. Anthrop.* 30:393, fig. 1–3 (ossification of foot bones)—sequence of initiation of ossification of foot bones. Levy, Taylor, Hampton, and Thoma, 1969, *Cancer Res.* 29:2237—tumors produced by Rous sarcoma virus. Hampton, and Parmelee, 1969, *Comp. Biochem. Physiol.* 30:367—plasma diamine oxidase activity. Kraus and Hampton, 1969, *Amer. J. Phys. Anthrop.* 30(3):393, figs. 1–3 (sequence of foot bone ossification—ossification of foot bones; distal phalanx of hallux 14th bone to begin ossification. Dreizen and Hampton, 1969, *J. Dental Res.* 48(4):579—glandular contributions of selected B vitamins in saliva. Holmes, Ogden, and Deinhardt, 1969, Animal models for biomedical research. II, *Nat. Acad. Sci. Publ.* 1736:11—malignancy induction with Rous sarcoma virus; production of humanlike viral hepatitis. Dreizen, Levy, Niedermeier, and Griggs, 1970, *Arch. Oral Biol.* 15:179—trace metals in saliva; comparison with human. Tihen, 1970, *Lab. Animal Care* 20:759—COLOMBIA; filiarial parasite (*Tetrapetalonema marmosetae*). Epple, 1970, *Folia Primat.* 12:56—housing; care; diet; reproduction. Hampton and Taylor, 1970, *Proc. 3rd Inter. Cong. Primat. Zürich* 1:246—gonadal development. Hampton, Rider, and Parmelee, 1970, *Proc. 3rd Int. Cong. Primat., Zürich* 2:95—diamine oxidase and histaminase values. Dreizen, Smith, and Levy, 1970, *Oral Surg., Oral Med., Oral Path.* 30(4):527—microfilarial infection of oral structures. Hunt, Melendez, et al., 1970, *J. Nat. Cancer Inst.* 44:447—induction of malignancy by *Herpesvirus saimiri.* Falk, Wolfe, Shramek, and Deinhardt, 1970, *Proc. Central Soc. Clin. Res.* 43:80—induction of fatal disease with *Herpesvirus saimiri.* Wolfe, Falk, and Deinhardt, 1971, *J. Nat. Cancer Inst.* 47:1145—induction of lymphomas and lymphocytic leukemias by *Herpesvirus saimiri.* Wolfe, Marczynska, Rabin, Smith, Tischendorf, Gavitt, and Deinhardt, 1971, in *Med. Primat. 1970,* ed. Goldsmith and Moor-Jankowski, p. 671—viral oncogenesis (susceptible to human, nonhuman, and cultured tumor cells). Levy and Mirkovic, 1971, *Lab. Animal Sci.* 21(1):33—measles epizootic in laboratory colony. Dreizen, Levy, and Bernick, 1971, *J. Periodont.* 42(4):217, figs. 1–4 (gingivitis in cortisone-treated samples), fig. 5 (calcareous deposits in kidney of cortisone-treated samples), fig. 6 (adrenal cortex)—cortisone-induced periodontal and skeletal changes. Levy, Dreizen, Hampton, Taylor, and Hampton, in *Med. Primat. 1970,* ed. Goldsmith and Moor-Jankowski, p. 859—experimental periodontal diseases. Deinhardt, 1971, in *Med. Primat. 1970,* ed. Goldsmith and Moor-Jankowski, p. 918—use in biomedical research. Falk, Wolfe, and Deinhardt, 1972, *J. Nat. Cancer Inst.* 48(5):1499—experimental infection with *Herpesvirus saimiri* lethal within 18–26 days. King and Melendez, 1972, Lab. Invest. 26(6):682—ultrastructure of *Herpesvirus saimiri*–induced lymphoma. Bueltmann, Karlson, and Edie, 1972, *Archs Oral Biol.* 17:645—quantitative ultrastructure of intradental nerve fibers. Wolfe, Falk, and Deinhardt, 1972, *Lab. Invest.* 26(4):496—induction of lymphoproliferative disease with terminal leukemia by *Herpesvirus saimiri.* Porter, 1972, *Lab. Animal Sci.* 22 (4):503—endoparasites. Guraya, 1974, *Acta Anat.* 89 (1):58—interstitial cell gland development of thecal origin during ovary maturation. Leichnitz and Astruc 1975, *Brain Res.* 84:169—efferent connections of orbitofrontal cortex.

S[aguinus] oedipus, Wolfe, Smith, Hoekstra, Marczynska, Smith, McDonald, Northrop, and Deinhardt, 1972, *J. Nat. Cancer Inst.* 49(2):519—oncogenecity of feline fibrosarcoma viruses (ST-FeSV and GA-FeSV); pathology, virologic, and immunologic findings. F. Deinhardt, Wolfe, Northrop, Marczynska, Ogden, McDonald, Falk, Shramek, Smith, and Deinhardt, 1972, *J. Med. Primat.* 1:29—induction of neoplasms by Rous, Feline, and Simian viruses and *Herpesvirus saimiri.* Holmes, Wolfe, and Deinhardt, 1972, in *Pathology of simian primates,* ed. R. Fiennes, 2:684—transmission of human infectious hepatitis. Hershkovitz, 1972, in *Dental morphology and evolution,* ed. A. Dahlberg, pp. 97, 98, 115, 126, fig. 1D (nutricial lower incisors), fig. 1E (permanent lower incisors), fig. 15C (lower teeth, c-m_2)—cusp homologies. Levy, Hampton, Dreizen, and Hampton, 1972, *J. Comp. Path.* 82:99—chronic thyroiditis in laboratory animals. Kawata, 1972, *Int. Zoo Yearb.* 12:45—exhibition and maintenance in Topeka Zoo. Weber, 1972, *Int. Zoo Yearb.* 12:49—breeding; maintenance in Melbourne Zoo. Jollie, 1972, *Med. Primat. 1972,* ed. E. I. Goldsmith and J. Moor-Jankowski, pt. 1:271—protein transport in placenta. Marczynska, Falk, Wolfe and Deinhardt, 1973, *J. Nat. Cancer Inst.* 50:331—response to transplanted *Herpesvirus saimiri*-induced tumor tissue. Holmes, Deinhardt, Wolfe, Froesner, Peterson and Casto, 1973, *Nature* 243:419—specific neutralization of human hepatitis type A. Porter and Gengozian, 1973, *Transplantation,* 15 (2):221—in vitro histocompatability with *S. fuscicollis.* Dreizen, Levy and Bernick, 1973, *Proc. Soc. Exp. Biol. Med.* 143:1218—diet induced atherosclerosis. Felsburg, Heberling, Brack and Kalter, 1973, *J. Med. Primat.* 2 (1):50 experimental infection with *Herpesvirus hominis* type 2 fatal. Fischer, Falk, Rytter, Burton, Luecke, and Deinhardt, 1974, *J. Nat. Cancer Inst.* 52, (5):1477—*Herpesvirus saimiri,* attempted transmission through hematophagous insects. Meléndez, Hunt, García, Daniel and Fraser, 1974, *J. Med. Primat.* 3 (4):213—oncogenic action of *Herpesvirus saimiri* prevented by simultaneous inoculation with specific antisera. Murphy, Krushak, Maynard and Bradley, 1974, *Lab. Animal Sci.* 24 (1):229—effect of Vitamin C supplement in parainfluenza type III virus infection. Clark, 1974, *10th Ann. Rpt. Jersey Wildl. Preserv. Trust,* p. 44—daily food requirements in Jersey Zoo. Schauf, Kruse and Deinhardt, 1974, *J. Med. Primat.* 3, (5):315—response to tuberculosis vaccine; use in tumor immunotherapy. Peterson, Wolfe, Deinhardt, Gajdusek and Gibbs, 1974, *Intervirology* 2:14—transmission of Kuru and Creutzfeldt-Jakob diseases. Leichnetz and Astruck, 1975, *Brain Res.* 84:169—efferent connections of the orbitofrontal cortex. Hilloowala, 1975, *Amer. J. Anat.* 142:367, figs. 1–3 (hyoid bones), fig. 4 (digastric muscle)—hyoid apparatus, comparative anatomy. Laufs and Steinke, 1975, *Nature* 255:226—prevention of herpesvirus induced malignancy by passive immunization. Seman, Panigel, Demoschowski, 1975, *J. Nat. Cancer Inst.,* 54:251—type C virus particles in placenta.

[*Saguinus oedipus*], Melnick and Parks, 1970, *J. Infect. Diseases* 121(3):353—not host for human viral hepatitis. Skougaard, Levy and Simpson, 1970, *Scand. J. Dental Res.* 78:256—collagen metabolism in skin and periodontal membrane. Falk, Wolfe, Marczynska and Deinhardt, 1972, *Bacteriol. Proc.* 1972, (V38)—cell lines from *Herpesvirus saimiri.*

Sagvinus [*sic*] *oedipus,* Crandall, 1964, *Management of wild animals in captivity,* p. 105—longevity in New York Zoo (7 years, 2 months, 13 days).

Saquinus [*sic*] *oedipus,* Wiener, Moor-Jankowski and Gordon, 1965, *Am. J. Phys. Anthrop.* 22(2):183, footnote 2 (misspelled generic name)—blood types. Macdonald, Cerny, Fraser, Meléndez and Hunt, 1973, *Fed. Proc.* 32:1073 (abstr.)—immune response to *Herpesvirus saimiri,* sheep red blood and tetanus toxoid.

S[aquinus (sic)] oedipus, Fischer, Falk, Rytter, Burton, Luecke and Deinhardt, 1974, *J. Nat. Cancer Inst.* 52(5): 1477—infection through experimental transmission of *Herpesvirus saimiri.*

Sanguinus [*sic*] *oedipus,* Marinkelle, 1966, *Trans. Roy. Soc. Trop. Med. Hyg.* 60, (1):112—trypanosome infection (negative).

S[anguinus (sic)] (Oedipomidas) oedipus, Deinhardt, Holmes, Wolfe and Junge, 1970, *Vox Sang.* 19:261—transmission of viral hepatitis from human.

S[aguinus] oedipus oedipus Hershkovitz, 1969, *Quart. Rev. Biol.* 44, (1)19, fig. 6 (map)—origin, evolution, distributions. Hampton, 1975, *Contemporary Primatology,* 5th Int. Congr. Primatol., Nagoya, 1974, p. 106—placental development.

Saguinus oedipus oedipus, Hershkovitz, 1970, *Am. J. Phys. Anthrop.* 32:379—dental disease; supernumery lower premolar. Hershkovitz, 1970, *Folia Primat.* 13:215—COLOMBIA: *Bolívar* (Catival, upper Río San Jorge); cerebral fissural pattern. Hsu and Hampton, 1970, *Folia Primat.* 13:183—karyotype (2n = 46). J. K. Hampton, Hampton and Levy, 1971, in Goldsmith and Moor-Jankowski (eds.), *Med. Primat.* 1970, p. 527—reproduction in laboratory colony. Hampton, Parmelee and Rider, 1971, in *Med. Primat., 1970,* ed. Goldsmith and Moor-Jankowski, p. 245—plasma histaminase and diamine oxidase values. Gengozian and Porter, 1971, in *Med. Primat., 1970,* ed. Goldsmith and Moor-Jankowski, p. 165—transplantation immunology; survival time of intraspecific grafts, 15–179 days; *oedipus* versus *fuscicollis* recipient, 6–30 days; *fuscicollis* versus *oedipus* recipient, 5–16 days. Hershkovitz, 1972, *Int. Zoo Yearb.* 12:9—geographic range; survival endangered. Hampton, 1973, *Amer. J. Phys. Anthrop.* 38, (2):265—germcell chimerism in adult males.

Hapales doguin Griffith, 1821, *General and particular description of the vertebrated animals . . . class quadrimembria, Order Quadrumana,* p. 100, pl. opposite (animal)—name based on colored figure only of New World primate.

Œdipus titi Lesson, 1840, *Species des mammifères: Bimanes et quadrumanes . . . ,* p. 199—part, the *adulte* only; new name for *oedipus* Linnaeus. Lesson, 1842, *Nouv. Tabl. Regn. Anim., Mamm.,* p. 9—COLOMBIA. Gray, 1870, *Cat. monkeys, lemurs, and fruit-eating bats, Brit. Mus.,* p. 65—"BRAZIL."

Seniocebus meticulosus Elliot, 1912, *Bull. Amer. Mus. Nat. Hist.* 31:31—COLOMBIA: *Córdoba* (type locality, Río San Jorge); type, male, skin and skull, American Museum of Natural History no. 32703, collected 12 December 1911 by Mrs. E. L. Kerr. J. A. Allen, 1912, *Bull. Amer. Mus. Nat. Hist.* 31:95. Elliot, 1913, *A review of the Primates,* 1:188, pl. 1, frontispiece (animal), pl. 22 (skull)—characters. Goodwin, 1953, *Bull. Amer. Mus. Nat. Hist.* 102:264—type history.

C[allithrix] Sciurea, Schott (not Linnaeus), 1861, *Exec. Doc.* 7 (9) 36th Congress, Session 2, Appendix E, Zool., p. 216—COLOMBIA: *Antioquia* ("Isthmus of Darien"); tame individual secured from natives.

Saguinus oedipus ♂ × *Saguinus midas* ♀, Reed, 1965, *Rep. Nat. Zool. Park, Smithsonian Rep.* 1964:113, 120, pl. 3 (hybrid pair)—hybrids born 19 February 1964; most nearly resemble mother. Low and Benirschke, 1968, *Folia Primat.* 8:180, fig. 1 (face of hybrid)—history; karyotype; coloration; comparisons with parent; fertility.

Saguinus oedipus ♂ × *Tamarinus midas* ♀, Benirschke, 1969, *Ann. N.Y. Acad. Sci.* 162(1):220—karyotype of hybrid.

Type. None in existence, name based on the description and colored plate of Edward's *"little lion-monkey,"* a female originally kept as a pet by the Countess of Suffolk.

Type Locality. "America," determined as western Colombia by Humboldt (1812, *Rec. Obs. Zool. Anat. Comp.,* p. 337) and restricted to the lower Río Sinú (38), Córdoba, Colombia, by Hershkovitz (1949), *Proc. U.S. Nat. Mus.* 98, p. 415). According to Edwards (1751, p. 195) "the countess of Suffolk (in whose Possession the above described Animal is) . . . it was brought from *La Vera Cruz, in New Spain* [i.e., Mexico]."

Distribution (fig. X.15). Northwestern Colombia between the Río Atrato and the lower Río Cauca-Magdalena in the departments of Atlántico, Bolívar, Córdoba, northwestern Antioquia, and northeastern Chocó east of the Río Atrato; altitudinal range from near sea level to nearly 1,500 meters above.

Taxonomy. The colored figure, in natural size, of *Edward's little lion-monkey*, is that of a juvenal. The black fringe bordering the front of the white headdress is still present, but the muttonchop whiskers characteristic of the very immature are absent. The *little lion-monkey* was believed to have originated in Mexico. A second specimen, recorded by Brisson as the *petit singe du Mexique,* is also said to have been brought alive from that country. Humboldt (1812:337, 361) was the first to record the animal from its true habitat in Colombia but this authority also included "Darien" in the range, a region in Panamá where only *Saguinus oedipus geoffroyi* occurs. Humboldt's addition of the "Guyane française" to the geographic distribution of the crested bare-faced tamarin may have been a lapsus.

"Hapales doguin" Griffith (1821, p. 100, pl. opposite) is based solely on a colored figure of a bare-face tamarin in a collection of drawings possessed by the author. There is no description except for the figure's caption, "the pug faced monkey. Hapales doguin." It is not clear whether Griffith used the nonitalicized "Hapales doguin" as a scientific or a vernacular name. "Hapales" was one of three major subdivisions of New World Primates recognized by Griffith (1821, p. 73). The term was used coordinately with "Sapajous" and "Sagoins" as a vernacular group name for New World monkeys (cf. footnotes Griffith 1821, pp. 74, 82, 93). On the generic level, Griffith employed *Simia,* italicized, for nearly all monkeys including callitrichids, with the exception noted.

The zoological status of Griffith's pug-faced monkey is also dubious. It agrees with *oedipus* in its whitish mane, arms, and underparts and its tail with basal portion reddish and terminal portion blackish. It differs by its dark hands and feet and by the extension of the white of arms to shoulders. These discrepancies may be more representational than real. The figure differs significantly from *Saguinus bicolor,* the only other species with which comparisons need be made.

Seniocebus meticulosus was described by Elliot in 1912 and in 1914 he relegated it to the synonymy of *oedipus.*

Diagnostic Characters. Crest of long whitish hairs from forehead to nape flowing over shoulders and sharply defined from practically bare black sides of crown and temples; back brown agouti, underparts, arms, and legs whitish to yellow; rump and inner sides of thighs reddish orange, tail reddish orange proximally, blackish terminally (fig. X.72).

Coloration (Adult). Skin of face, throat, sides of head including temples and broad band around ears black and hardly or not at all hidden by a sparse sprinkling of short, fine silvery to buffy hairs or fuzz; superciliary region whitish or gray; a fine whitish fringe extending from each corner of mouth across muzzle, another fringe of whitish to brownish hairs extending from each corner of eye to angle of jaw; hairs of muzzle slightly feathered or directed straight back; mane white or white stained with yellowish or buff and spreading from midsection of forehead across crown and nape and flowing over interscapular region; arms colored like mane; back brownish and punctulated, streaked or striated with buffy, orange, or cinnamon, basal portions of individual hairs dark brown, terminal portions with two to four alternating bands of buffy and brown, tips brown; rump reddish orange, the banded hairs like those of back but with the brown replaced by reddish orange, the unbanded hairs entirely reddish orange except for dark roots; inner sides of thighs like rump, outer sides agouti like sides of body, legs white more or less washed with orange or yellow; upper surface of hand and feet whitish, silvery gray, buffy, or ochraceous; sides of body like back but brown band of hairs bleached to orange, the basal brown to drab; underparts of body and limbs yellowish or white but usually with an uneven mottling of buffy or yellowish; tail dark brown on distal half, reddish on proximal half, the hairs bleaching from tip to base; external genitalia pigmented.

Coloration (Young) head and body 100–115 mm). Face comparatively hairy, cheek with long thick upward and outward-projecting fringe as in adult *leucopus;* grayish superciliary band well developed and bordered behind by fringe of erect hairs, the fringe extending along sides of crown to behind ears; crown between dark lateral fringes thickly covered with silvery or silvery-buff hairs short and adpressed in younger, longer and lax in older individuals; a dark brown median line present in younger; nape like crown but hairs whitish, longer and fringed with black; back dominantly blackish or dark brown, the hairs in older individuals blackish at tips and roots, ochraceous orange between; rump like back but hairs becoming more orange; upper surface of limbs whitish; sides and lateral fringe like back but with orange banding showing through; distal third of tail black, proximal portion reddish orange above with a fine black median line, paler orange, yellow, or whitish beneath, pale color of underside extending more distally than orange of upper.

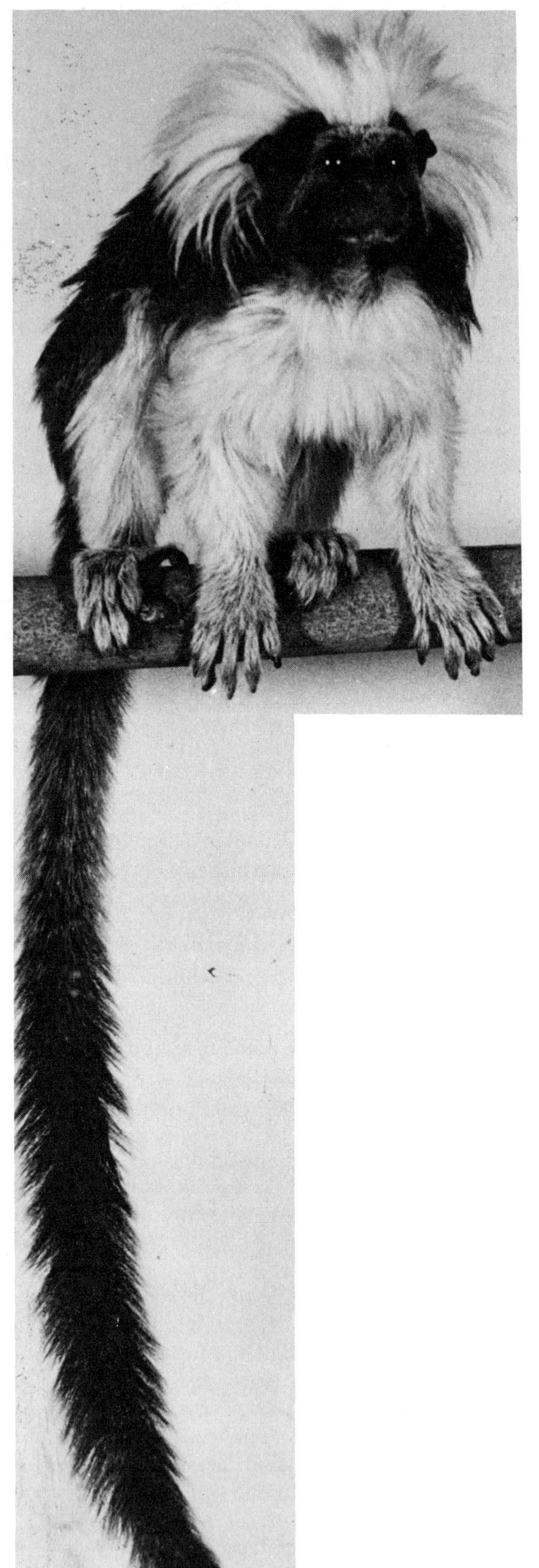

Fig. X.72. Cotton-top or White-plumed Bare-face Tamarin, *Saguinus oedipus oedipus.* (Photo courtesy of New York Zoological Society.)

Newborn with fine fuzz, undersurface nearly bare but with fine hairs appearing days later, grayish anteriorly, orange posteriorly, the skin always showing through; color pattern of 4-day-old (total length 90 mm) as described but with skin showing through hairs of trunk and limbs.

In one-third grown individual (head and body ca. 125 mm, greatest skull length 42.6) all deciduous teeth fully erupted, the hairy face, projecting cheek whiskers, and hairy crown with black frontal and lateral borders persist, whitish mane as in adults but thinner, and pelage of back finer with more black.

For a chronology of growth and development, see page 778.

Cranial Characters. Frontal contour well rounded to steeply domed; temporal ridges strongly convergent on frontal, divergent on parietal, sometimes with an independent sagittal crest between, or converging to fuse with crest; nasal profile concave, frontal sinuses well inflated; malar foramen small, the greatest diameter less than 2 mm; ventral border of mandible more often V-shaped than U-shaped, the horizontal rami from completely distended to notably arced, the angular process slightly to moderately inflected inward and slightly to markedly deflected downward.

Measurements. See appendix table 2.

Comparisons. The whitish, fanlike flowing mane sharply defined from bare black sides of head distinguishes *oedipus* from all other primates.

Variation. Mane, hindlegs, and underparts from pure white to yellow; the usually brown agouti dorsum often divided into patches or portions of more or less uniformly brown hairs, nearly as in *leucopus.* Variation in color of tail is a product of the bleaching process (cf. p. 736). In extremes, the usually black terminal portion of the tail may be generously mixed with drab to silvery hairs, the underside of the usually orange proximal portion may be similarly affected, in one adult from San Juan Nepomuceno it is nearly all silvery.

Age variation is described elsewhere (p. 766). Local variation, apart from seasonal differences in pelage (cf. p. 756), is not evident.

Remarks. Saguinus oedipus oedipus is more highly evolved than *S. o. geoffroyi* and appears to be directly descended from its prototype. Nonetheless, some admixture with *leucopus* stock cannot be ruled out, as evidenced by the *leucopus*-like cheek whiskers in the young of *oedipus,* the *leucopus*-like brown mottling or patches of hair of dorsum in adult, and the tendency for the tail to bleach terminally. As compared with adult *geoffroyi,* facial hair tracts and color are the same. The characteristic flowing white mane of *oedipus* is simply the predictable extension of the whitish crest of *geoffroyi* into a blanched mane. The modified agouti pattern of *geoffroyi* is weaker and more dilute on dorsum of *oedipus* and bleached to reddish on rumph and thighs. The bleaching process of tail in *oedipus* is also conspicuously more advanced on proximal portion and ventral surface. The ears of *geoffroyi* are in the process of reduction while those of *oedipus* are extremely reduced. Juvenals of *oedipus* are intermediate in most external characters and nearer *geoffroyi* in some such as color of back and retention of the black frontal and temporal fringe of hairs. Cranially, adult *oedipus* is also slightly more advanced in the development of the temporal crests and the lesser angularity of the mandible.

Specimens Examined. 100. COLOMBIA—*Bolívar:* Las Campanas, Colosó, 12 (FMNH); Río San Jorge, 1 (AMNH); San Juan Nepomuceno, 12 (FMNH); *Córdoba:* Catival, upper Río San Jorge, 13 (FMNH); Jaraquiel, Río Sinú, 8 (CM); Socorré, upper Río Sinú, 15 (FMNH); *Antioquia:* Río Curulao, Urabá, 6 (FMNH); Villa Arteaga, 4 (FMNH); *locality unknown,* 29 (AMNH, 18; MNHN, 1; SM, 4; FMNH, 6 in spirits).

76 *Saguinus oedipus*
2. *Biology of Crested Bare-face Tamarins*

REPRODUCTION

Information selected from the literature and personal notes is organized under the following headings:

Courtship and Copulation	Parturition
Masturbation	Estrus
Homosexuality	Breeding Seasons
Pregnancies	Litters
Gestation Period and Interbirth Intervals	Hybridization

Courtship and Copulation

Wendt 1964 (*oedipus*)

The male shook his mane, swayed the forepart of his body, danced around the female and tongued her. After a few attempts the pair copulated with the male covering the female and tonguing her face. Coitus lasted only a few seconds. The act was performed repeatedly in the nest box and outside as well, before my eyes.

J. K. Hampton, Jr., Hampton, and Landwehr 1966, p. 278 (*oedipus*)

"No pre-coital play has been conspicuous and usually no post-coital behavior is characteristic. While the female may have subtle, unnoticed means of soliciting attention, we do not observe the 'presenting' which is typical of baboons, rhesus, etc. Some olfactory exploration of the female's genitals is sometimes seen but this, too, does not form a conspicuous part of an otherwise perfunctory interaction. In a couple of instances, reactions by a female, who remained 'in position' following withdrawal and the male's retreat, suggested extensor spasm and may indicate an orgastic response. We do not suggest that this is typical."

Willig and Wendt 1970 (*geoffroyi*)

The male approached the female, with the forepart of his body swaying. He danced around his partner, tongued her, then mounted holding her firmly with both hands. Coitus lasts only a few seconds. After intercourse, they groom each other.

Mating was observed every day, even during pregnancy. Before copulation, the female lay on her belly, tongued the male and emitted a high-pitched whistle.

J. K. Hampton, Jr., Hampton, and Landwehr 1966, p. 278 (*oedipus*)

"Copulation is *a posteriori* and the male may or may not clasp the hind legs or heels of the female with his feet. His hands grasp the female's flanks and intromission is prompt. The act may last from a few seconds to much longer.

"Attempts at copulation while the female was in labor and by a male while carrying its 31 day old young on his back have been observed."

Hershkovitz (Notes)

Copulation is performed at any hour of the day by captive animals.

Moynihan 1970, p. 14 (*geoffroyi*)

Captive adults long separated from mature individuals of the opposite sex may perform many copulations in rapid succession when given access to a suitable and receptive partner (one male copulated 15 times within an hour). This is very different from the usual behavior. Captive animals with close and stable pair bonds, including individuals which bred successfully, do not copulate more than once or twice in a 24-hour period, even at the height of the sexual season. Some apparently well-adjusted pairs may copulate even less frequently.

The male mounts the female from the rear, clasping her tightly around the "waist" with his arms, while continuing to grasp the perch with his feet. Intromission and pelvic thrusts begin almost immediately. These movements are irregular; their number is variable but usually ranges from 3 to 20. Sometimes the male presses his face into the fur of the female's back during coitus. He may also wrinkle his nose, partly close his eyes, perform tongue-protrusions and occasional head-flicks. The behavioral pattern can be considered a type of "Sexual Sniffing." During particularly prolonged and vigorous copulations, the male may climb up the female's back. His tail hangs straight down throughout the performance. The female sits quietly, in a hunched posture, her head brought forward and down as the male mounts, and then kept in that position. If her tail had been raised in Upward Tail-coiling before coitus, she usually lowers and partly uncoils it as copulation progresses.

The whole performance is brief. The male dismounts immediately after the last pelvic thrust. No postcopulatory display follows. Within a few seconds after copulation, the male may scratch or massage his genitals, and/or bends his head in an attempt to lick them.

Sometimes a male mounts and dismounts without copulating. An unwilling female may walk away when a male attempts to mount. Or she may simply sit and turn her head, to look at him over her shoulder.

Masturbation

J. K. Hampton, Jr., Hampton, and Landwehr 1966, p. 279 (*oedipus*)

"While playing a rolling, tumbling 'game' in the seat of a chair [in the authors' home, the hand-tamed female] paused along the edge of the cushion and began the copulatory motions of a male. These persisted for some time, accompanied by the tongue movements described above for copulating males. When she stopped, she appeared trancelike for a few seconds. In this there is a resemblance to the possible orgastic response seen in an adult female following copulation and mentioned above."

Hershkovitz (Notes)

The firmly coiled tail brought forward between the legs and upward to press against the belly (fig. X.83) is frequently rubbed against the sexual skin by males and females for stimulation. In captivity, the otherwise sexually frustrated female may rub the coiled tail vigorously across the external genitalia in a simulation of pelvic thrusts, until satisfied.

Homosexuality

Moynihan 1970, p. 15

Among the caged tamarins in Barro Colorado Island there occurred "homosexual mountings, with pelvic thrusts, among males, in the absence of a female, and among females, in the presence of an adult but sexually inactive male."

Hershkovitz (Notes)

In this and other accounts of homosexuality among tamarins (q.v. page 669) no indication is given of the

Table 92. Chronology of Two Pregnancies of a Tamarin, *Saguinus oedipus oedipus*, Caged with Her Mate; Male Weights also Recorded

Date	♀	♂
14 August 1958	450 g	600 g
15 August 1958[1]	Observed mating	
29 August 1958	Observed mating	
9 September 1958	430 g	545 g
6 October 1958[1]	Fertilization	
13 October 1958	Negative frog test	
21–23 November 1958	Vomiting	
23 November 1958	Observed mating	
7 December 1958	Observed mating	
8 February 1959		650 g
1 March 1959	500 g	600 g
5 March 1959[1]	Stillbirth (54 g)[1]	
6 March 1959	450 g	640 g
12 April 1959	450 g	600 g
22–24 May 1959	Vomiting; diarrhea	
23 May 1959		Vomiting[2]
20 June 1959	425 g; ravenous for worms	
21 June 1959	420 g	
1 July 1959	Abdomen enlarging	
2 July 1959	450 g	580 g
11 July 1959	460 g	
14 July 1959	430; sacrificed while pregnant	530 g

SOURCE: Benirschke and Richart 1963, p. 76.

[1] Interval between date of first observed mating and parturition, 5 March 1959, is 202 days; from date of "fertilization," 150 days. No criterion for "fertilization" was given. For description, see p. 770; for measurements and weights compare table 98.

[2] Possibly sympathetic.

hierarchical status of each of the tamarins. Possibly, the active or mounting partner is the alpha male or female of the group while the mounted partner is simply submitting to social dominance rather than obeying a sexual urge. Then again, the aim of the act may be to provoke a passive partner of the opposite sex into action.

J. K. Hampton, Jr., Hampton, and Levy 1971, pp. 532, 534 (*oedipus*)

"Sexual maturity may be reached in less than two years but successful pregnancies may be expected only during the third year."

Pregnancy

Benirschke and Richart 1963, pp. 75, 77 (*oedipus*)

The history of two pregnancies in a laboratory of the Dartmouth Medical School, Hanover, New Hampshire, follow.

"The first pair of *oedipomidas oedipus* . . . was purchased on June 21, 1958, from a dealer who had kept them in a small cage in her kitchen. Her close care had resulted in two very healthy animals who had given birth twice previously during the two years in captivity [Table 92]. The first twins born in captivity were killed by the parents. When the second pregnancy came to term the pair was separated and a pair of healthy offspring was reared by the mother.

"An interesting phenomenon occurred during the first month of both pregnancies from this pair. The female began to be less eager for food and even insects were no longer taken. Then for three or four weeks marked intermittent vomiting and diarrhea occurred. Marmosets vomit occasionally when fed an excessively large number of mealworms in too short a time. Under those circumstances, however, the animal will vomit into its hand and carefully lick up the brei. During early pregnancy, vomiting was mostly nonproductive except for a minimal amount of mucus and the animal gave the impression of being in distress. The best indication of pregnancy came from periodical weighing, taking into account the time of day because one meal frequently will consist of 20–40 mg. of food. Mating was observed repeatedly during these two pregnancies and was thus not a useful criterion."

The single young was born 5 March 1959 (see below).

"The next pregnancy ensued within two months after this event and again was associated with vomiting, diarrhea and a significant weight gain. In order to gain fresh placental tissue for enzyme studies, this pregnancy was terminated at a stage when it was expected that fetal gonadal differentiation would be active."

Graetz 1968, p. 32

When the female became pregnant, she climbed into a dark high corner of the house on the outskirts of Panama City and ignored the play of the male. She took sugar water again but shunned the light and looked to me for protection from humans. The behavior of the male also changed three days later. He became shy and stopped playing. Both animals deserted the house to nest in a high tree nearby. They were seen only fleetingly a few times a day and when they climbed softly to the window sill to "steal" the sugar water set out for them in a bowl.

Hershkovitz (Notes)

Chemical and physiological tests for the detection of pregnancy have been attempted with limited success. The frog test employed by Benirschke and Richart (1963, pp. 76, 79) on a 4–6-week-pregnant *Saguinus oedipus oedipus* was negative. Diamine oxidase (DAO) values which rise during human pregnancies has been shown by J. K. Hampton, Jr., Rider, and Parmelee (1971) to be unusually high in *Saguinus oedipus, S. fuscicollis,* and *Callithrix jacchus* but about the same in pregnant and nonpregnant females and in normal gonadectomized males and females. Assays of chorionic gonadotropin in the urine performed by J. K. Hampton, Jr., Levy, and Sweet (1969) for detection of pregnancy in *Callithrix jacchus jacchus* are reliable within limits. No such tests have yet been made with *Saguinus oedipus*.

Gestation Period and Interbirth Intervals

Present estimates of the duration of gestation in *Saguinus oedipus oedipus* are based almost entirely on inferences from observed mating activity, manifest signs of pregnancy, and evidence of parturition. Chemical or physiological means for detection of pregnancy such as the frog test, and assays of chorionic gonadotropin excretion and plasma diamine oxidase activity proved negative or of limited value in callitrichids. They are mentioned above and elsewhere (p. 532).

The interval between births produced by the same female with uninterrupted opportunities for mating is sometimes accurate. In the event of a postpartum estrus, which probably occurs regularly in callitrichids, the shortest interbirth interval is a good approximation of the precise duration of gestation for the particular pregnancy, if not for the species.

A more accurate measure of the duration of gestation is the interval between time of first mating and parturition. It is not certain, however, that conception follows every first mating and that implantation is not delayed significantly after conception. In a number of cases it may be possible to record only dates of pairing (not copulation) and parturition.

A method employed by Cooper (1966, report no. 14) for estimating the duration of gestation in *Saguinus oedipus oedipus* is based on measurements of uterine expansion.

"The seven females which reached term this quarter measured 1.0 to 1.5 centimeters in uterine diameter last 3 November. The nongravid uterus of this species is about 0.5 centimeters in diameter and a maximum of 30 days is required for the pregnant uterus to reach 1.0 to 1.5 centimeters in diameter. On this basis, we estimate the gestation period of *Saguinus oedipus* to be 127±5 days or approximately two weeks less than the shortest previous estimate for this species."

The previous estimates are those of J. R. Hampton, Jr., and Hampton (1965). Interbirth intervals for *Saguinus oedipus oedipus* in 21 cases ranged from 187 to 334 days, average 240 days. These figures are patently excessive for a normal pregnancy. The authors (1965, p. 917), however, mention one full-term birth of 153 days after a pairing. In another case under their control, a female had been alone from the 162nd to the 147th day before giving birth. The inference here is that conception occurred either more than 162 days or less than 147 days before parturition. The shorter period is the more likely. The authors concluded from available data on callitrichid reproduction that 140 days is a reasonable estimate for the duration of gestation in *Saguinus oedipus oedipus.*

Wolfe, Ogden, Deinhardt, Fisher, and Deinhardt (1972) made the interesting discovery that in the case of 4 hand-reared cotton-top females (*Saguinus oedipus oedipus*) and 28 white-lip females (*Saguinus nigricollis* and *Saguinus fuscicollis*), the earlier the infants were separated from the mother the shorter the interbirth interval. The shortest period was 134 days but the particular species was not identified. In a subsequent revised and updated report with data restricted to intervals between deliveries of viable offspring, Wolfe, Deinhardt, Ogden, Adams, and Fisher (1975, p. 106) give the mean of 259.1 days (range, 166–523) for 17 hand-reared litters versus a mean interbirth interval of 280 days (191–258) for 17 parent-reared litters. These intervals are longer and less affected by separation (within 48 hr) of offspring than those recorded by the same authorities for white-mouth tamarins (cf. p. 669).

Parturition

Epple 1970*a*, p. 66 (*geoffroyi*)

"In *Saguinus geoffroyi,* the male and two adult daughters intensively licked the genitalia of the breeding female for many minutes during an early abortion. Two of the full term deliveries of this female took place during the day, and I observed the group immediately after one of the deliveries: Thirty minutes before parturition nothing in the behavior of the pregnant female seemed unusual. Half an hour later she had given birth to twins. She and the male were on the floor of the room, licking one infant."

Willig and Wendt 1970 (*geoffroyi*)

The first young was produced 20:30 in the nest box. After licking the newborn the female drank some water, then ran around the cage losing a little blood in the meantime. She returned to the nest box and fifteen minutes later gave birth to the second young. The father watched from outside then entered to consume the afterbirth.

At 21:40 the young attached themselves to the mother, who thereupon uttered a high pitched cry and smacked her lips.

Benirschke and Richart 1963, p. 77 (*oedipus*)

"On March 5, 1959, at feeding time at 7 A.M. the male *Oedipomidas* was holding a baby in his hand, biting its face. The female had overturned the water vessel and was extremely thirsty. Birth must have taken place shortly before (1–2 hours) in their sleeping box, where the towel had one large blood spot. The baby was covered with a slimy mucus and on the placenta, which was still attached, there was some fresh meconium. The baby and placenta (fig. 2) were forcibly taken from the male. There were no signs of a second placenta or fetus. The mother recovered quickly over the next three days, at first being quite weak, seeking warmth and producing an occasional blood spot per vaginam. Lochia and breast-swelling were not observed."

Estrus

Preslock, Hampton, and Hampton 1973, p. 1100

"Using the mean time interval between successive progestin peaks as an index, a mean reproductive cycle of 15.5 ± 1.5 days is demonstrated. . . . If the fluctuations of estrogens and progestins . . . is related to ovulation as in [the rhesus monkey], then it is likely that ovulation occurs sometime between the estrogen and progestin peaks, at a time when the serum estrogens are at maximum levels or decreasing, and the progestins increasing."

Breeding Seasons

In the Wild

Hershkovitz (Field Notes)

All three forms of the *Saguinus oedipus* group were observed during the course of my fieldwork in northern Colombia. Bare-face tamarin habitats were surveyed May and June 1943, January through July 1949, and January through May 1950. Adult females averaged significantly heavier than males during March 1949 and March 1950, and about the same or less in other months. Newborn and suckling young of *Saguinus leucopus* were met May 1943 in the Norosí, Bolívar region, and those of *S. oedipus oedipus* were encountered May 1949, at Las Campanas, Colosó, Bolívar. Obviously young individuals of *S. o. geoffroyi* were not seen. Comparative weights of adult females (table 93) and estimated age of wild-caught museum-preserved specimens of juvenals and subadults taken throughout the year point to a single breeding season in northern Colombia with most if not all births occurring during April and early May.

The rainy season in northern Colombia extends from late March through November. April and May are months of high precipitation in northern Colombia.

Length of fetuses in three pregnant females of *S. o. geoffroyi* collected by Charles O. Handley, Jr. in Tacarcuna, southern Panamá, are as follows: 23 January 1959, 60 mm; 13 February 1959, 55 mm. in second female, and 75 mm in the third female. Assuming full term in April or May after a gestation averaging 145 days, mating

Table 93. Seasonality of Full Term Pregnancies in Wild-Living *Saguinus oedipus* Shown by Mean Body Weights Compared with Mean Body Length and Skull Length of Both Sexes Taken in Different Months at Various Localities

Subspecies	*Locality*	*Date*	*N*	*Head and Body Length*	*Greatest Skull Length*	*Weight*[1]	*Weight Ratio* ♀ : ♂
geoffroyi	Unguía	March 1950	5 ♀♀	247	53	521	107:100
			8 ♂♂	252	53	486	
oedipus	Socorré[2]	March 1949	5 ♀♀	233	52	515	121:100
			8 ♂♂	225	52	427	
oedipus	San Juan	January 1949	4 ♀♀	239	51	375	96:100
	Nepomuceno		6 ♂♂	235	51	390	
oedipus	Colosó	May 1949	3 ♀♀	229	51	425	90:100
			3 ♂♂	237	50.5	471	
oedipus	Catival[2]	July 1949	2 ♀♀	232	51	462	102:100[3]
			8 ♂♂	240	51	453	

[1] Taken in ounces and converted to 1 oz = 28 g.
[2] Localities in same general region.
[3] Mean weight difference between 2 ♀♀ and 8 ♂♂ not significant; individual weights: 17 oz (3 ♂♂; 1 ♀); 16 oz (3 ♂♂; 1 ♀); 15 oz (2 ♂♂).

would have occurred toward the end of the rainy season in October or beginning of the dry in November 1958.

Wislocki (1932, p. 381) reported crown-rump lengths of 44 mm and 47 mm for twin male fetuses of a pregnant female killed 22 April 1931, near Panama City. The differences in size between these twin fetuses and the singleton fetuses mentioned above may be partly due to their younger age. Twin fetuses and newborns are as a rule smaller than singletons, but individual variation in size is great.

Enders 1935, p. 440 (*geoffroyi*)

"There appears to be a fairly well-defined breeding [i.e., mating] season in February, or even earlier. Many specimens taken from that month to June were pregnant. Birth takes place sometime in June to judge from the size of embryos at this time of the year."

Wislocki 1939, p. 448 (*geoffroyi*)

"Regarding a possible breeding season the following considerations are available. Of a total of 19 pregnant uteri secured in various years, 11 uteri containing young embryos were obtained in January or early February. From the same months only 2 advanced gestations are recorded. On the other hand, in the month of June a total of 6 pregnant females was obtained, all in advanced stages of gestation. These observations suggest that in the wild state in Panama the optimum time for mating may lie in January and February."

Moynihan 1970, pp. 13–14 (*geoffroyi*)

A pair of very young infants were "seen in the wild [by a reliable correspondent] on 29 March."

One pregnant female caught in the wild "gave birth to two normal young in late June."

"I observed a very young infant in the wild in July."

"Fewer [wild-caught] infants appear for sale in Panamá in June than in May. Even fewer appear in July, and none appear later in the year."

"Three sets of infants conceived in captivity on Barro Colorado were born in late May and early June."

Captive individuals copulated "more frequently in January than in any other month of the year."

In the light of the foregoing data, Moynihan suggests that "normal or effective breeding [i.e., mating] behavior is 'triggered' by the beginning of the dry season which usually or often occurs during the last week of December or the first week of January in central Panama." This, Moynihan believes, insures "that births will coincide with the beginning of the rainy season which usually occurs around the end of April." [Note: As a rule of thumb, dry and rainy seasons in central Panamá begin, respectively, about a month later than in the departments of Bolívar and Códoba in northern Colombia but not necessarily so each year.—P. H.]

Hershkovitz (Notes)

The various estimates of breeding seasons in the wild are not strictly comparable. With exception of my limited field observations (p. 752, table 93), no two observations are based on populations of the same geographic areas for different years, and none are based on populations of different areas for the same year. Furthermore, the dry or rainy season in any one region may be extraordinarily early, late, or missed completely. How these climatic fluctuations affect mating and breeding has not been studied. Nevertheless, during the many years members of the *Saguinus oedipus* group have been observed in northern Colombia and Panamá, pregnant females and suckling young have never been reported or captured except from January to June. Personal observation and data for 45 Panamanian species of mammals compiled and analysed by Fleming (1973) indicate that reproductive seasonality is a widespread phenomenon in the wild and that births usually occur during the rainy season when food is more abundant.

In Laboratories

Breeding experiments with *Saguinus oedipus* in captivity have not been altogether satisfactory. Some dates recorded by Wendt (1964), Willig and Wendt (1970), and Epple (1970*a*) are of abortions, or for prematures or stillborns, and cannot be used for present purposes, and other birthdates indiscriminately lumped would be misleading because of differences in taxonomic content, geographic locations, and controls. Results obtained with the comparatively large colonies in San Diego and New Orleans, however, provide some insights.

Cooper, in his unpublished report no. 13 (1966) on breeding of cotton-tops, *Saguinus oedipus oedipus,* during 1965, in the outdoor facility of the Institute for Comparative Biology, Zoological Society of San Diego, California, makes the following statement:

"Except for the above three [births, April, July, and October 1965] no further pregnancies were detected this quarter [Aug.–Nov. 1965] until the first week in November. A routine examination at that time disclosed that the remaining 12 [of the 15] adult females were all in early stages of pregnancy. Their uterine measurements were closely estimated to be between 1.0 and 1.5 centimeters in diameter as compared to an 0.5 centimeter diameter for the nongravid uterus in this species. The records of this group last year disclose a very similar incidence of pregnancies during the same period. Such apparent breeding seasonality in marmosets has not been described elsewhere. It is known from previous examinations that few, if any, of the present pregnancies were of greater than one month duration when detected. As a result when all have reached term, we think that for the first time it will be possible to accurately estimate the gestation period for this species."

In his unpublished report no. 16 for the same year, Cooper emphasized that "a very marked reproductive seasonality has appeared in *Saguinus oedipus* this past year. Approximately 78% of the adult females became pregnant in September and October of 1965 [judged by the amount of uterine expansion detected early in November]. Another "secondary" breeding season seemed to occur in February and March, involving only some of the females which, as a result of reproductive failure at some point during the primary reproductive cycle, were not nursing infants."

Given a gestation period between 140 and 150 days, September–October matings or conceptions should result in February–March births. In the case of the San Diego colony, however, very few pregnancies were fulfilled (table 94). Notwithstanding, periodicity in mating, as reported by Cooper, is strongly marked.

Results of breeding in the tamarin colony maintained in the Tulane University School of Medicine, New Orleans, have been detailed by John K. Hampton and Suzanne H. Hampton (1965, p. 915). The colony had been in existence nearly five years, but breeding took place only during the last two and one-half years. Thirty

Table 94. *Saguinus oedipus oedipus:* Birth Records of Primate Research Colony, San Diego Zoo

♀ *Number*	*Parturition*	*Litter*	*Observations*	*Interbirth Interval*	*Quarterly Report*
9	9 Jan. 1964	00	Abortion, 2nd trimester	—	No. 8 (Aug. 1964)
9	6 Dec. 1964	00	Early abortion	—	No. 10 (Feb. 1965)
9	10 June 1965	♂ ♀	Live	—	No. 10 (Feb. 1965)
19	10 Jan. 1964	♂ ♀	Abortion	—	No. 6 (Feb. 1964)
18	4 Feb. 1964	♀	Stillborn	—	No. 6 (Feb. 1964)
18	21 March 1965	0	Live	319	No. 11–12 (Aug. 1965)
6	26 Feb. 1964	♂ ♀	Live	—	No. 7 (May 1964)
6	11 Jan. 1965	00	Stillborn, slightly premature	340	No. 10 (Feb. 1965)
4	7 April 1964	—	Early abortion	—	No. 8 (Aug. 1964)
4	4 Aug. 1964	—	Early abortion	—	No. 8 (Aug. 1964)
7	— July 1964	00	1 stillborn, 1 live	—	No. 8 (Aug. 1964)
7	26 March 1965	00	Stillborn	268	No. 11–12 (Aug. 1965)
11	5 Nov. 1964	0 ♂	Live	—	No. 10 (Feb. 1965)
11	5 June 1965	—	Early abortion	—	No. 11–12 (Aug. 1965)
5	28 Dec. 1964	00	Early abortion	—	No. 10 (Feb. 1965)
5	23 July 1965	00	Live	207	No. 11–12 (Aug. 1965)
12	31 Dec. 1964	♂ ♀	Live	—	No. 10 (Feb. 1965)
12	17 July 1965	♀	Live	198	No. 11–12 (Aug. 1965)
17	5 Jan. 1965	00	Early abortion	—	No. 10 (Feb. 1965)
16	15 Jan. 1965	00	Early abortion	—	No. 10 (Feb. 1965)
8	18 Jan. 1965	0	Stillborn, slightly premature	—	No. 10 (Feb. 1965)
8	14 July 1965	00	Abortion	—	No. 11–12 (Aug. 1965)
15	29 Jan. 1965	♂ ♀	Stillborn	—	No. 10 (Feb. 1965)
15	23 July 1965	00	Early abortion	—	No. 10 (Feb. 1965)
10	7 April 1965	♂ 0	Live	—	No. 11–12 (Aug. 1965)
13	9 April 1965	0	Live	—	No. 11–12 (Aug. 1965)
14	9 Sept. 1965	00	Abortion	—	No. 11–12 (Aug. 1965)

SOURCE: Data from Cooper (Quarterly Reports, 1964–65).

females were pregnant a total of 65 times. Forty-six, or 71%, of the pregnancies came to full term. All but two of the breeding pairs were cotton-tops (*Saguinus oedipus oedipus*). The others, a pair of *S. mystax* accounted for two, or 3%, of the pregnancies, and *S. nigricollis* (sensu lato) accounted for 5, or 7%. The 46 births were distributed by months as follows.

J	F	M	A	M	J	J	A	S	O	N	D
6	5	7	4	4	2	4	0	3	1	5	5

The highest number of births, 5–7, occurred during November through March and averaged 5.6 per month. This compares with 0–4 births, average 2.9, for the remaining 7 months, April through October.

The clustering of birth dates within a five-month period, and their greatest concentration in January through March, coincides with the reported peak September-October mating months in San Diego which, latitudinally, is only some 80 miles north of New Orleans.

Peak mating and breeding seasons in San Diego–New Orleans zone are about 2 months ahead of the corresponding ones maintained by cotton-tops in the wilds of northern Colombia. Perhaps the wide latitudinal and climatic differences account for the difference in rhythm. In any case, the fact remains that reproductive periodicity persists at least for a while among the caged animals despite the traumas of displacement and captivity and the heterogenous character of the breeding stock.

Litters

The number of full-term litters produced by *Saguinus oedipus oedipus* and the number of young in each recorded by J. K. Hampton, Jr., Hampton, and Levy (1971, p. 528) are shown in table 95. The figures are based on records of production from 1961–69 inclusive; first in the laboratory colony of the Tulane University Medical Schools, New Orleans, from 1961–1966, then the product of this colony integrated in 1966 with that of the University of Texas Dental Science Institute in Houston. The output of the Houston facility was further increased as a result of the addition in June 1968 of the stock of 20 male and 21 female cotton-tops transferred from the Institute of Comparative Biology, Zoology Society of San Diego.

In 1965, when the original New Orleans colony had produced only 58 litters, the proportion of singletons, 34%, twins, 64%, triplets, 2%, was virtually the same (J. K. Hampton, Jr. and Hampton 1965.)

Table 95. Full-Term Litters of *Saguinus oedipus oedipus* and Distribution of Young Produced by the New Orleans and Houston Colonies 1961–69 inclusive.

Young per Litter	*Number of Litters*	*Total Young*
1	45(33%)	45(19%)
2	86(63%)	172(73%)
3	6(4%)	18(8%)
Totals	137	235

SOURCE: Data from J. K. Hampton, Hampton, and Levy (1971, p. 528).
NOTE: The average number of young per litter is 1.7. The total of 137 litters excludes 36 pregnancies for which the number of young is unknown. Using the mean litter rate of 1.7, they represent 61 individuals. Thus, of the grand total of 173 litters, and 296 offspring, 21% were aborted.

Breeding results in the Primate Research Colony of the San Diego Zoo differ significantly with respect to the relative number of litter sizes but not in average litter size. In 31 litters recorded by Cooper 1964–68) there were 8 singletons and 23 twins, or 26% and 74%, respectively, of the total. The live-birth litters numbered 14, abortions 9, and 8 litters included stillborns. The actual number of individuals produced was 54, or 1.74 per litter. Three additional litters were early abortions without indication of the number of young in each. Thus, of a grand total of 34 litters, 12, or 35%, were aborted. Birth dates for all litters are scattered throughout the year without definable pattern.

Epple (1970*a*, p. 66) reports that the female *Saguinus oedipus geoffroyi* owned by Graetz (1968) gave birth to at least 3 litters of twins in Panamá, 3 litters of twins and 1 early abortion after joining Epple's colony, and 2 twin births after transfer to another colony. These total at least 8 full-term births. Epple also cites a personal communication from Erler that 7 litters (6 twins, 1 singleton) were produced over a period of 7 years by a pair of *Saguinus oedipus oedipus* in his possession.

Litters produced by *Saguinus oedipus oedipus* and by members of the *Saguinus nigricollis* group (*S. nigricollis, S. fuscicollis,* crosses and hybrids) bred at the same time in facilities of the Rush–Presbyterian–St. Luke's Medical Center, are compared on the basis of data published by Wolfe, Deinhardt, Ogden, Adams, and Fisher (1975, p. 804), as follows.

	Litters	*Abortions*	*First Litter Live/Total %*	*Subsequent Litters %*	*Total Live*	*Live Births Pair/Yr*	*Live per Litter*
S. oedipus	68	13.2%	21/38(55.3%)	69/92(75.0%)	90(69.2%)	1.6	1.32
S. nigricollis group	631	11.1%	144/193(74.6%)	787/972(81.0%)	931(79.9%)	2.6	1.25

Hybridization

A captive-born female *Saguinus oedipus geoffroyi* mated with a captive-born *Saguinus o. oedipus,* gave birth to two litters of twins, according to Epple (1970*a*, p. 66) as reported to her by Wendt.

The *Saguinus m. midas* × *Saguinus o. oedipus* twins are described under the heading of *S. midas* (p. 721).

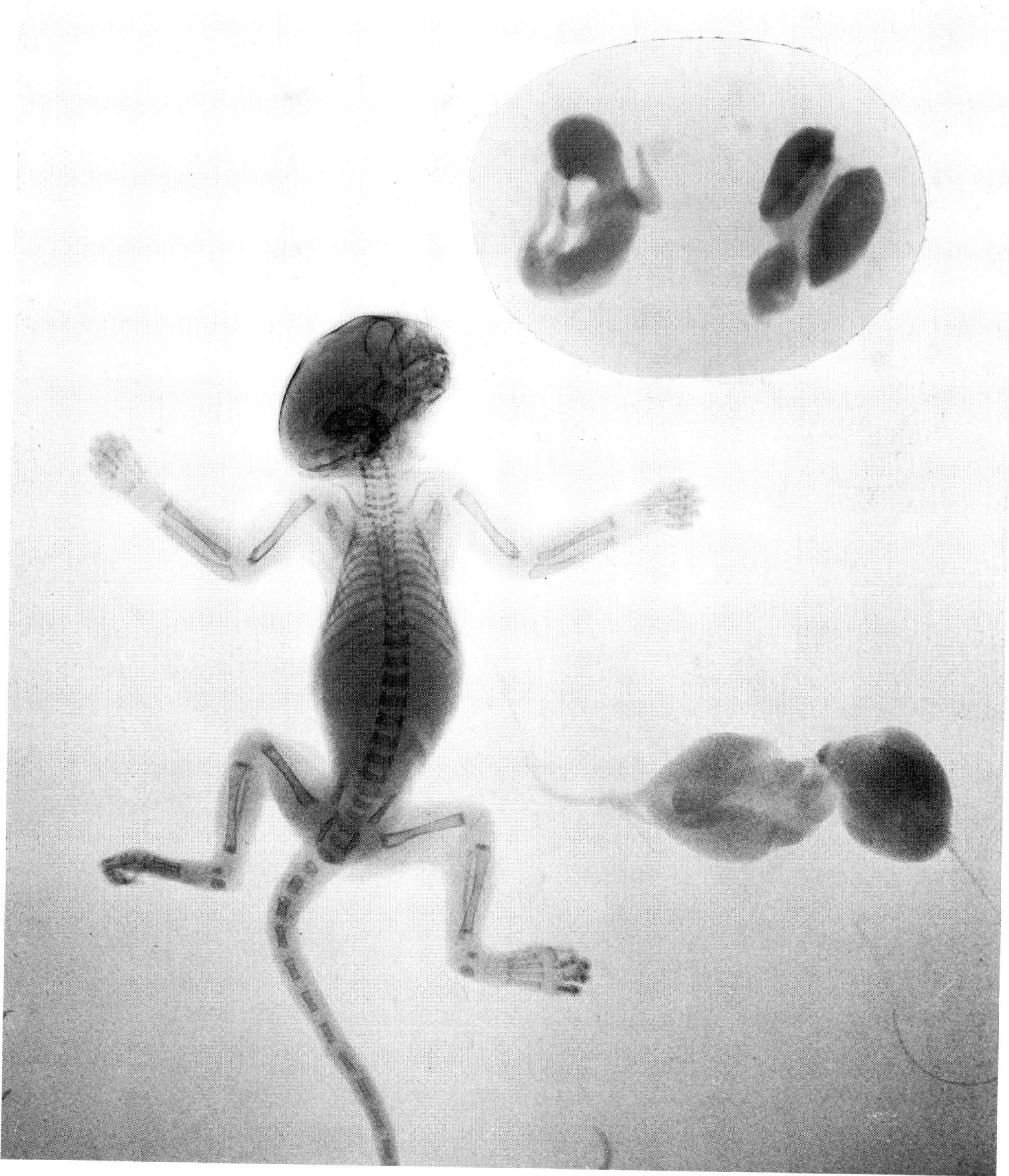

Fig. X.73. *Saguinus oedipus,* X-ray photograph of aborted fetus, approximately 35 mm, and of newborn and fetal membranes. (Photo courtesy of Friedrich and Jean Deinhardt.)

Fig. X.74. Two intermediate developmental stages in tamarins, genus *Saguinus*. *Right*, approximately half-grown individual (skull length 41.5 mm) with deciduous teeth only, first molar in alveolus; *left*, larger individual (skull, 48 mm) with permanent molars erupted, deciduous canines in place, permanent cainines in alveoli. (Photo courtesy Friedrich and Jean Deinhardt.)

Fig. X.75. Adult, age unknown (skull 52 mm) (Photo courtesy Friedrich and Jean Deinhardt.)

GROWTH AND DEVELOPMENT

The data are arranged under the following headings:

Chronology of Growth
Diet and Growth (table)
Weights
Internal Organs: Weights and Measurements
Sex Ratios
Sexual Dimorphism
Longevity

Chronology of Growth

Data for the following chronology of growth and development of captive, including wild-caught, individuals of *Saguinus oedipus oedipus* and *S. o. geoffroyi* from birth to old age has been compiled from sources indicated by the following abbreviations.

BR = Benirschke and Richart 1963 (*oedipus*)
C = Cooper 1964 (*oedipus*)
E = Epple 1970*a* (*geoffroyi*)
G = Graetz 1968 (*geoffroyi*)
HH = S. H. Hampton and Hampton 1967 (*oedipus*)
HHL66 = J. K. Hampton, Jr., Hampton, and Landwehr 1966 (*oedipus*)
HHL71 = J. K. Hampton, Jr., Hampton, and Levy 1971 (*oedipus*)
W = Wendt 1964 (*oedipus*)
KFF = King, Fobes, and Fobes 1974 (*oedipus*)
WW = Willig and Wendt 1970 (*geoffroyi*)

In addition to the chronological arrangement, table 97 shows weight increases of cotton-tops at broad intervals from 7 days to 3½ years. Table 98 gives fiuctuations of captive adults from 1963 through June 1968. The data in both tables are taken from unpublished reports by Cooper of *Saguinus oedipus oedipus* maintained in the San Diego Primate Colony. Table 100 shows the weekly diet and weight change of an artificially reared female cotton-top (*Saguinus oedipus oedipus*) compared with those of a white-mouth male tamarin of the *Saguinus nigricollis* group. The data are from F. Deinhardt (1970). X-ray photographs (X.73, 74, 75) of *Saguinus oedipus oedipus,* contributed by Friedrich and Jean Deinhardt of the Rush–Presbyterian–St. Luke's Medical Center, illustrate three developmental stages.

Newborn *geoffroyi:* Born fully furred; ochraceous triangular crown patch with dark median line; nape reddish as in adults; ears fully exposed; dorsal surface of trunk haired blackish; throat and chest sparsely haired white; belly and inner sides of limbs with scattered ochraceous hairs; tail black except for rufous underside of basal portion; arms ochraceous mixed with white; legs blackish, ankles rufous; hands and feet whitish above; eyes open in some newborns, closed in others; weight, ♀, 41 g (E).

oedipus: Fully furred; incipient white mane or crest present; tail coiled; said to be semiprehensile for attachment to mother during first few days, the prehensibility lost after first weeks. Twins born in December, taken over by father first day and released to mother for suckling only (W).

Singleton born August; taken over completely by mother from birth; turned over to father after several weeks; developed much faster than December twins (W).

Note: As a rule, newborn singletons average larger than twins. These, in turn, average larger than triplets. The advantage in size and rate of development persists for weeks or months. See table 96 for comparative sizes and newborns of the different litter sizes.

oedipus: Weight of Caesarian-delivered singleton 78 g (HH). This is extreme for genus.

oedipus (stillborn, term or near term): Face, crown, body, tail well-haired, underparts bare; head, body and extremities darkly pigmented; clitoris large, tip pigmented; vulva relatively unpigmented; length crown to rump 100 mm, tail 130; hand 20; foot 34; fronto-occipital length 37; biparietal width 20; unsevered, uncoiled umbilical cord 70; body weight 49 g, attached fetal membranes 5, total 54. For weights of adult internal organs, see table 99 (BR).

Fig. X.76. Cotton-top Tamarins, *Saguinus oedipus oedipus,* adult and suckling young a few days of age; from callitrichid breeding colony, Tulane University. (Photo courtesy of J. K. Hampton, Jr., and Suzanne H. Hampton.)

	oedipus: Grasping reflex and hind limbs developed, climb upward on any surface affording hold; vocalize loudly at few hours of age; eyes open at birth in full-term infant but vision not focused; no reaction to sounds (HH).
1 day	*oedipus:* Weight of two infants (of triplets) 30, 31 g; eyes closed (HH).
2 days	*geoffroyi:* attempted climbing on fur of father; unable to lift head (WW).
3 days	*geoffroyi:* Eyes opened (WW).
	oedipus: Eyes follow moving objects (HH).
4 days	*oedipus:* Weight twin, 38 g (HHL66).
5 days	*geoffroyi:* Weight ♀, 57 g (E).
5–7 days	*oedipus:* Reacts to noises (HH).
7 days	*geoffroyi:* Forehead and cheeks develop white down; triangular frontal patch brighter; lifts head for several minutes (WW).
6–9 days	*oedipus:* Caloric intake, 200–300 kilocalories per kilogram in artificially reared young; fed formula 8–9 times daily (HH).
9 days	*oedipus:* Feeding of artificially (hand) reared young reduced to 6–8 times daily (HH).
10 days	*geoffroyi:* Arms white; remains awake nearly all day (WW).
10–14 days	*geoffroyi:* Rump hairs with orange bases; tail base rufous; ochraceous hairs of neck, chest, and arms replaced by white hairs; dark median coronal line absent (E).
12 days	*oedipus:* Disappearance of "rooting" or nipple-searching (KFF).
12–14 days	*oedipus:* Visual orientation to horizontally and vertically moving stimuli (KFF).
14 days	*oedipus:* Crawling, 20 cm within 2 min (KFF).
	oedipus: Weight average, 7 hand-reared young 50 g; legs support body when walking; scratching with hands or feet well coordinated; caloric intake unchanged (HH).
16 days	*geoffroyi:* display tongue protrusion like adults; scratch with foot behind ear without falling (WW).
18 days	*oedipus:* Complete descent of terry-cloth-covered wire mesh cylinder (KFF).
2–3 weeks	*oedipus:* Artificially reared young begin playing; grasp and inspect small objects; caloric intake maintained at 200 kilocalories in artificially reared infants (HH).
20 days	*oedipus:* Formula feeding of artificially reared infants 5 per day, other foods added (HH).
	oedipus: 1 set twins and 1 set triplets consistently walking after 20 days (KFF).

Fig. X.77. Cotton-top Tamarins, *Saguinus oedipus oedipus,* adult and young about 1 week older than infant shown in fig. X.76; from callitrichid breeding colony, Tulane University. (Photo courtesy of J. K. Hampton, Jr., and Suzanne H. Hampton.)

Fig. X.78. Cotton-top Tamarins, *Saguinus oedipus oedipus; below,* young about same age shown in fig. X.77; *above,* older individual (about 4 weeks old) with mane more than half the full adult development; from callitrichid breeding colony, Tulane University. (Photo courtesy of J. K. Hampton, Jr., and Suzanne H. Hampton.)

3 weeks	*geoffroyi:* Leave back of adults first time at 21, 23 days; weight ♂, 68.5 g at 22 days, ♀, 69 g at 27 days (E). Drink water at 24 days (HHL66). Involuntary infantile hand and foot clasping disappeared after 26 days (KFF).
4 weeks	*oedipus:* Average weight, 7 artificially reared infants, 50 g (HH). *geoffroyi:* First solid food at 29 days; weight ♀, 87 g at 30 days (E). *geoffroyi:* First solid food at 35 days (G). *geoffroyi:* Still suckling (WW).
4–5 weeks	*oedipus:* Being weaned from father's back (HH). Leave back of one parent and scramble onto back of other (C). Auditory orientation to clicker after 32 days (KFF).
5 weeks	*geoffroyi:* Observed eating independently (WW). *oedipus:* Twins make first attempt at crawling away from paternal fur (W). [Compare 3 weeks]. Climb cage wire; when alarmed jump immediately to father's back; eat solid food (soaked monkey chow) (C). *oedipus:* A Tinker Toy framework and diaper were imprinted security symbols to artificially reared young (HH).
4–6 weeks	*geoffroyi:* Typical adult coloration developed on body, limbs, and tail; one set twins takes first solid food at 29 days; second set at 40 days (E).
5–6 weeks	*oedipus:* Receives food from hands of adults (HHL66). *oedipus:* Artificially reared infants self-feeding at age 40 days (HH).
6 weeks	*geoffroyi:* Twins weaned; coloration as in adults (WW). *oedipus:* Average weight 7 artificially reared infants 65 g (HH). Occasionally rejected by mother (C).
6–10 weeks	*oedipus:* Frequency of clasping, righting, and sitting astride terry-cloth-covered cylinder diminished from day 18 to 0 between 6 and 10 weeks (KFF).
7 weeks	*oedipus:* August singleton exercises independently (W).
8 weeks	*oedipus:* Suckling, carried, and fed by hand; physical development of August born singleton equal to that of older December-born sister (a twin) at 3 months (W). Average weight 7 artificially reared infants 85 g (HH). One of mother-reared twins weaned at 60 days (HHL66). [Compare 6 weeks].
10 weeks	*geoffroyi:* Weaned at 70 days (G). [Compare 8 weeks]. *oedipus:* Average weight 7 artificially reared infants 130 g (HH).
12 weeks	*oedipus:* At 83 days, mother-reared twin 181 g, hand-reared twin 167 g; average weight 7 artificially reared infants 140 g (HH). *oedipus:* Young independent but share parents' food and seek their protection when alarmed (W). When alarmed fly to father's back, although almost too large and heavy to be carried (C).
14 weeks	*oedipus:* Average weight 7 artificially reared infants 165 g (HH).
14½ weeks	*oedipus:* Facial hairs black with distinct white annulation (HH).
14–36 weeks	*oedipus:* Black facial hairs replaced by dense, more extensive white hairs (HH).
21 weeks	*geoffroyi:* Cease sleeping on adult's back after 5 months (E).
26 weeks	*geoffroyi:* Do not seek parents' fur when alarmed, continue huddling with parents when frightened (WW).
30 weeks	*geoffroyi:* Cease flight to adult's back when alarmed (E).
35–36 weeks	*oedipus:* Adult facial pattern developed, with loss of white hairs (HH).
10 months	*geoffroyi:* ♀ retains appearance and behavior of juvenal; takes food from mouth of 2½-year-old ♂ *oedipus,* examines his genitalia with innocent interest (WW).
15 months	*geoffroyi:* ♀ mated; canines erupted (WW).
1½–3 years	*oedipus:* "We have seven female *S. o. oedipus* born in our colony which have bred. One aborted when she was 23 months old and another at 24 months of age. Full-term births have occurred once when the female was 2 years, 8 months old, and twice at 2 years, 9 months. Two males were 18 months and 20 months old, respectively, when abortions occurred which they had sired. Thus, sexual maturity may be reached in less than two years but successful pregnancies may be expected only during the third year" (HHL71). "We have ascertained that 7 of our 15 cotton-top females have previously given birth. This is quite easy to determine in cotton-tops because a mammary nipple which has *not* been nursed is *non-pigmented* and quite small" (Cooper, unpublished quarterly Report no. 5, 19 Nov. 1963).

Weights

Data for full-term or live births of cotton-tops, presented by J. K. Hampton, Jr., Hampton, and Levy (1971) and reproduced in table 96, reveal that the smaller the litter the larger the newborn.

On the basis of 36 g as average newborn weight and 437 g (table 98) as average adult female weight, mass of the former is 8.2% of the latter.

Appreciably higher weights for newborn (to 48 hr) *Saguinus oedipus oedipus* are recorded by Wolfe, Deinhardt, Ogden, Adams, and Fisher (1975, p. 808), as follows: Singletons, 44g(44,44)2 individuals; twins, 43.2

Table 96. Size of Newborn *Saguinus oedipus oedipus*, Measured within 48 Hours of Birth

Litter Size	Head and Body Length	Hind Foot Length	Weight
Singles	96(94–97)4	30(29–31)4	37(34–40)4
Twins	92(82–103)20	29(24–31)20	36(24–45)20
Triplets	89(87–91)4	28(26–30)4	34(32–40)3

SOURCE: J. K. Hampton, Jr., Hampton, and Levy (1971).
NOTE: Measurements are means, extremes (in parentheses), followed by number of litters.

(35.3–52.0)32; triplets, 36.2(30.0–43.5)8; mean twin weight calculated at 9.7% mean parent weight (447 g).

Mean weights of randomly selected adult *Saguinus oedipus oedipus* in the Rush–Presbyterian–St. Luke's Medical Center facilities are for wild-caught, 447 g(N = 15–36); laboratory-born, parent-reared, 452 (N = 10); laboratory-born, hand-reared, 511(N = 1); data from Wolfe, Deinhardt, Ogden, Adams, and Fisher (1975, p. 807).

Weights of a few growing and mature singletons and twins ranging in age from 7 days to 3 years, 173 days are arranged sequentially in table 97. Fluctuating mean weights of wild-caught adults during 4½ years of captivity are shown in table 98. Weights and proportions of some internal organs are given in table 99.

Diet and Growth

Approximately 160 newborn white-mouth and cotton-top tamarins used for biomedical research by Dr. Friedrich Deinhardt and his group were artificially reared in the laboratories of Rush–Presbyterian–St. Luke's Medical Center, Chicago. Diet and growth of a randomly selected individual of each group is shown in table 100. The species of white-mouth tamarin was not given, but both *S. fuscicollis* and *S. nigricollis* average slightly smaller than *S. oedipus,* with *fuscicollis* the smallest of the three.

The newborn were transferred from the parents within 24 hours of birth and placed in a standard baby incubator. The weekly additions or changes in the diet and weight of the young are represented by Deinhardt (1970) in a growth curve. Table 100 combines information from Deinhardt's text and weight estimates from his curves.

Table. 97. Weights (in grams) of Growing Cotton-Top Tamarins, *Saguinus oedipus oedipus.*

Age (Years, Days)	26/2/64 ♀	26/2/64 ♀	5/11/64 ♀	7/4/65 ♂	17/7/65 ♀	27/10/65 ♂ ♂	28/1/66 ♀ ♀	Report Number
7	—	—	—	—	—	49	—	13
12	—	—	—	—	—	—	50	14
13	—	—	—	—	55	—	—	11/12
71	132	152	—	—	—	—	—	7
96	—	—	186	—	—	—	—	10
105	—	—	—	—	—	163	—	14
109	—	—	—	—	241	—	—	13
114	—	—	—	216	—	—	—	11/12
163	274	301	—	—	—	—	—	8
207	—	—	—	—	281	—	—	14
210	—	—	—	327	—	—	—	13
220	—	—	—	—	—	—	300	16
252	366	380	—	—	—	—	—	9
267	—	—	413	—	—	—	—	11/12
308	—	—	—	374	—	—	—	14
313	—	—	—	—	—	331	—	16
348	372	381	—	—	—	—	—	10
415	—	—	—	—	311	—	—	16
1, 155	450	455	—	—	—	—	—	11/12
3, 173	483	—	—	—	—	—	—	19

SOURCE: Data compiled from Cooper (1966; Quarterly Reports 7–19).
NOTE: Birth dates are shown for each individual or twin set. Weight given for twins is the average of the two siblings.

Sex Ratios

The number and distribution per litter of male and female cotton-tops born alive in the Houston, Texas, and

Table 98. Average Weights of Wild-Caught Male and Female *Saguinus oedipus oedipus* in the Primate Colony, San Diego Zoo.

Date Weighed	♂ ♂ (N)	♀ ♀ (N)	Report Number
— 1963	431(12)	433(15)	5
6 Feb. 1964	434(11)	429(14)	6
7 May 1964	458(12)	447(14)	7
7 Aug. 1964	473(14)	458(14)	8
4 Nov. 1964	470(14)	461(14)	9
9 Feb. 1965	435(15)	431(15)	10
30 July 1965	456(14)	436(15)	11/12
3 Nov. 1965	457(14)	452(15)	13
9 Feb. 1966	443(14)	429(15)	14
15 Sept. 1966	454(18)	412(18)	16
17 Aug. 1967	451(18)	448(17)	19
— June 1968	457(17)	459(17)	22

SOURCE: Cooper, unpublished Quarterly Reports, 1963–68.

Table 99. Measurements, Weights, and Proportions of Internal Organs of 5 Adult Wild-Caught *Saguinus oedipus geoffroyi* and One Laboratory Term or Near-Term Stillborn *Saguinus oedipus oedipus* (in millimeters and grams).

	Specimens[1]					
Size	♂ *#11*	♂ *#13*	♂ *#14*	♀ *#12*	♀ *#15*	♀ *Stillborn*[4]
Total length[2]	640.000	—	630.000	630.000	650.000	230.000
Body weight[3]	510.000	482.000	510.000	453.000	567.000	49.000
Brain weight	10.620	12.390	12.390	8.850	12.390	5.700
Ratio	2.080	2.590	2.430	1.950	2.180	11.630
Heart	3.540	3.540	3.540	3.540	3.540	0.415
Ratio	0.694	0.734	0.694	0.780	0.624	0.847
Lungs	5.310	5.310	3.540	3.540	3.540	1.100
Ratio	1.041	1.102	0.694	0.780	0.624	2.240
Liver and gall	26.550	21.240	19.470	24.780	21.240	2.300
Ratio	5.203	4.407	3.815	5.463	3.746	4.690
Spleen	1.770	1.770	1.770	—	2.650	0.050
Ratio	0.347	0.367	0.347	—	0.467	0.102
Kidneys	3.540	3.540	2.650	3.540	3.540	0.170, 0.160
Ratio	0.694	0.735	0.519	0.780	0.624	0.347, 0.326
Gonads	1.770	0.890	1.770	—	—	—
Ratio	0.347	1.850	3.470	—	—	—

SOURCE: Data for adults from Hrdlička (1925, p. 202); for stillborn from Benirschke and Richart (1963, p. 78).

[1] Adult cotton-tops collected March–April 1924 along Río Chucunaque, Panamá. Weights and measurements taken from the freshly killed animal by John L. Baer, who died of an infection during the course of his fieldwork.

[2] From "point of nose to tip of tail."

[3] Ratios of organ weights based on individual body weight.

[4] For chronology of gestation, see table 92; for additional measurements, see appendix table 2.

predecessor colonies (J. K. Hampton, Jr., and Hampton 1965; J. K. Hampton, Jr., Hampton, and Levy 1971) and in the facilities of the Rush–Presbyterian– St. Luke's Medical Center (Wolfe, Deinhardt, Ogden, Adams, Fisher 1975), are summarized in table 101.

The deficit of females (table 101), like that noted for newborn white-mouth tamarins (table 89B, p. 677), has not been explained. The higher deficit among twins, however, is partly offset by a lower deficit in other litter sizes. In the figures recorded by Hampton et al. the overall and twin sex ratios are 1 : .93 and 1 : .75. Here, deviations from the expected 1 ♂ : 1 ♀ ratio are hardly significant.

Sexual Dimorphism

The faces of old males are heavier and more jowly or pear-shaped than those of females of comparable age or of young adult males. A six-year weight record of 25–36 adults kept in the San Diego Colony (table 98), shows that males average slightly heavier than females.

Figures presented by Schultz (1956, p. 895) show the reverse. In 34 wild-shot *Saguinus oedipus geoffroyi* the proportions of average weight of fully adult females to fully adult males is 104.2. No breakdown of the number of individuals of each sex was given. The actual weight of one specimen given in another connection by Schultz (1956, p. 932) as 660 g, is extreme if not abnormal.

Linear measurements (appendix table 2) reveal no significant differences between the sexes except possibly a slightly longer tail in females of *Saguinus oedipus oedipus* and *S. o. geoffroyi.*

Other differences between the sexes, apart from organs of reproduction and lactation, are not apparent.

Longevity

Life Span, *Saguinus oedipus*

S. o. oedipus, San Diego Zoo, 7 years, 8 months, (Jones 1962).
New York Zoo, 7 years, 2 months (Crandall 1964, p. 105).

S. o geoffroyi, Jersey Zoo, over 13 years, "adult on arrival 6 July, 1961, still living May, 1973", (Mallinson in litt.; also see earlier report, Mallinson 1971,p. 9).

Reproductive Life, *Saguinus oedipus oedipus*

Privately owned pair produced 6 pairs of twins and one singleton, a total of 7 litters in 7 years of captivity. (Epple 1970*a*, p. 65). The age of the pair must have been at least 10 years.

"Longevity of breeders is indicated by our record of 10 females which have been pregnant 7 or 8 times." (J. K.

Table 100. Diet and Growth by Weight of a Male White-Mouth Tamarin and a Female Cotton-Top Tamarin Artificially Reared under Uniform Conditions in the Laboratories of Rush–Presbyterian–St. Luke's Medical Center

		Weights (in grams)		
Week	♂ *White-Mouth Tamarin*	♂	♀	♀ *Cotton-Top Tamarin*
Birth	From mother to incubator within 24 hrs. Liquid formula 0.5 ml with gradual increases	40	—	From mother to incubator within 24 hrs. Liquid formula 0.75 ml with gradual increases
1		45	48	
2		50	60	Add: baby cereal
3	Add: baby cereal	68	70	
4.5	Self-feeding	85	85	
5		90	87	Add: junior baby food; powdered monkey chow pellets; self-feeding
6	Add: junior baby food; powdered monkey chow pellets	105	90	
7	Add: fresh fruit	115	92	Add: fresh fruit
8	Transferred from incubator to rabbit cage; junior baby foods eliminated	135	95	Junior baby foods eliminated
8.5	Foot injury	133	—	
9	Add: whole monkey chow pellets	132	105	
10		135	118	
11		135	130	
12		145	140	Transferred from incubator to rabbit cage. Add: whole monkey chow pellets
15		165	185	
16		162	205	
17	Add: liquid formula to 30 ml	170	210	
18		—	225	
20		—	245	Add: liquid formula to 60 ml
22		—	285	
4–18 months	Add: cow's milk, 60 ml	—	—	Add: cow's milk, 60 ml
1.5 years	Change to adult diet exclusively (commercial monkey chow pellets; fresh fruit, filtered tap water)	—	—	Change to adult diet (commercial monkey chow pellets; fresh fruit; filtered tap water)

SOURCE: Data from F. Deinhardt (1970*b*, text and graphs, pp. 179, 180).

Table 101. Sizes, Distribution of Sexes, and Sex Ratios in 186 litters of *Saguinus oedipus oedipus*

	♂	♀	♂♂	♀♀	♂♀	♂♂♂	♂♂♀	♂♀♀	♀♀♀
A	19	23	24	18	32	1	2	2	1
B	3	2	18	8	30	0	2	1	0
Totals	22	25	32	16	62	1	4	3	1
Ratios	.88 :	1	1 :	.5 :	1.9	.25 :	1 :	.75 :	.25
Expected	1 :	1	1 :	1 :	1	1 :	1 :	1 :	1
Totals of each sex			♂♂ 182	♀♀ 152					
Ratios			1 :	.84					
Expected			1 :	1					

SOURCE:
A Hampton and Hampton (1965); Hampton, Hampton, and Levy (1971)
B Wolfe, Deinhardt, Ogden, Adams, and Fisher (1975)
NOTE: Sexes of 7 sets of twin fetuses of wild?caught Panamanian *Saguinus oedipus geoffroyi* recorded by Wislocki (1939, p. 449) are: ♂♂, 2; ♀♀, 2; ♂♀, 3

Hampton, Jr., Hampton, and Levy 1971, p. 530.) The authors do not state how many, if any, pregnancies were aborted.

BEHAVIOR

The compiled material of this section has been, variously, quoted verbatim, paraphrased, abstracted, or freely translated if in a foreign language and often heavily edited to eliminate all but essential information. The total data were then organized under one or more of the following headings.

- Habitat
- Territoriality
- Social Structure
- Daily Rhythm
- Care of Young
- Rejection of Young
- Intraspecific Relations
- Grooming
- Interspecific Relations
- Food
- Milk Composition
- Food Plant Relations
- Drinking
- Predation
- Predators
- Curiosity
- Image Response
- Locomotion
- Swimming
- Play
- Repose
- Display
  - Facial Expressions
    - Brow Beatling
    - Grimacing
    - Staring
    - Frowning
    - Gaping
    - Lip Smacking
    - Lip Protrusion
    - Tonguing
    - Ear Twitching
    - Ear Flattening
  - Head Movements
    - Head Rotation
    - Head Lowering
    - Head Flicking
  - Body Postures
    - Confrontation
    - Back Arching
    - Bipedal Stance
    - Chest Display
    - Swaying
    - Freezing
    - Play Dead
    - Genital Presentation
- Piloerection
- Marking
- Vocalization
- Tail Movements
- Thermoregulation
- Heart Rate

Habitat

Hershkovitz (Notes)

Tamarins of the *Saguinus oedipus* group seem to be as much at home in tall forest as in low, dense second growth. The second growth, however, supports a larger population over longer periods of time, perhaps because of its greater productivity. Desirable fruits ripen during more times of the year, and edible insects and small vertebrates are certainly more abundant there than in high forest. In any case, tamarins are more conspicuous, whether seen or heard, in well-advanced second growth. In contrast, much of the animal life of the high forest canopy is invisible to the grounded observer.

Goldman 1920, p. 226 (*geoffroyi*)

"In the Canal Zone and at localities visited [1910–12] in eastern Panama, Geoffroy's squirrel monkey [i.e., tamarin] seems to be the most abundant representative of the order, ranging from sea level to at least 2000 feet altitude on the slopes of the mountains."

Enders 1935, p. 439 (*geoffroyi*)

"On [Barro Colorado Island (17)], Squirrel Monkeys [i.e., tamarins] are seen almost everywhere, for second growth is as much frequented as the deeper forest. In fact, the deeper forest does not contain many, for they appear to seek trees of smaller size, often near or about clearings. As Chapman notes (1929 [My tropical air castle], p. 284), 'They travel . . . usually at mid-forest altitudes and sometimes through the lower growth.' Barbour (1923 [in G. M. Allen and Barbour, *Bull. Mus. Comp. Zool.*, vol. 60], p. 273) reports their coming into low bushes along the Sambu River. Similarly, they were frequently observed in the trees on the banks of the many esteros of the Island, as well as in the low growth along the stream from Las Cascadas Plantation. Here numbers were seen in the growth that was impenetrable but not more than fifteen feet high. Numbers were observed in the rather small growth along the Chagres, as well as that surrounding the natural savannas near this river."

Enders 1939, p. 105 (*geoffroyi*)

"Profound changes have occurred [on Barro Colorado Island] in the relative abundance of various species since 1932. The large mammals have diminished in numbers [attributed to poaching] while the smaller ones have increased. The outstanding surprise, next to the decrease in the numbers of large carnivores, was the slight change of population about the laboratory area. . . .

"Carpenter records an increasing population of howling monkeys. His figures are very accurate being based on actual count. . . . The territory occupied by howlers is more extensive as the trees in the forest toward Barbour Point grow taller. The white face monkey holds its own or is increasing while the titi or squirrel monkey [= *Saguinus oedipus geoffroyi*] appears to be increasing."

A. Hladik and Hladik 1969, pp. 26, 92 (*geoffroyi*)

Barro Colorado Island in Lake Gatun is now covered with dense, semideciduous humid forests nearing its climax. The fauna has also been affected by the changes in composition and relative abundance of food trees. Tamarins are becoming progressively fewer in numbers than they were in 1935 when younger second growth forests were more widespread. These animals cannot survive in high forests.

Moynihan 1970, pp. 2–3 (*geoffroyi*)

"In Panama, [*Saguinus oedipus geoffroyi*] seems to be most characteristic of regions of moderate humidity . . . they are also common in forest and scrub which are dense but not very tall. They do not seem to flourish in either high rain forest with little understory vegetation. . . . Tamarins were abundant [on Barro Colorado Island] in the 1920s and early 1930s . . . when most of the island was covered with obviously young second-growth forest. Since then the forest has been allowed to grow up, and large parts of it seem to be approaching maturity, becoming typical monsoon forest . . . During the same period, with gradual change in the vegetation, the tamarins have become increasingly rare."

Moynihan 1970, p. 3 (*geoffroyi*)

They remain in trees or large bushes but come down to the ground to get special foods or when they cannot pass from one bush or tree to another by other means. In the forest, they range from the lower branches to as high as 60–75 feet above the ground. They prefer the vicinity of the forest edge where fruits and insects are most abundant and which at the same time provides cover as well as high visibility.

Territoriality

Moynihan 1970, p. 6 (*geoffroyi*)

Each band, and probably each solitary individual, has its home range or territory which is defended from other bands by a special whistle. The irregularly shaped territory may be as much as a quarter mile in greatest diameter and comparable in size to the territories of bands of other platyrrhines of the area such as *Aotus trivirgatus, Cebus capucinus,* and *Alouatta villosa.* The tamarin band is highly mobile and may move through its range several times during the day in search of plant food and insects. Territorial trespassing is uncommon and usually limited to the fringe and occurs when the resident band is at the far end of its range. Any band, however, may make forays into neighboring nontamarin areas such as gardens or orchards when attracted by ripe cultivated fruits.

Wendt 1964 (*oedipus*)

"In summer, the pair roamed freely in the wooded area of my home in Baden-Baden, Germany. At nightfall, they returned to their quarters in the house entering through the window left open for the purpose. When parturition was imminent, the pair was quartered in the winter garden where the two were free to run among the plants, and go outdoors through an opening to enjoy the sun and fresh air."

Graetz 1968, p. 31 (*geoffroyi*)

After loss of their young, the tamed, captive adults took up residence inside the house but continued to forage in the surrounding bushes. They never wandered out of sight of the house and retreated to it when frightened.

Moynihan 1970, p. 4 (*geoffroyi*)

"Under natural conditions, they move along a great variety of tree trunks and branches of very diverse sizes. They also show a strong preference for dense 'tangles' of vines or lianas. They usually avoid palms and other large monocotyledons such as *Heliconia* and related genera (except when they are searching for a few special foods and/or the leaves of a monocotyledon provide the only convenient 'bridge' between other trees or bushes which are particularly favored)."

Social Structure

Hershkovitz (Field Notes, *oedipus*)

Troops consisted of from two to six individuals with four the usual number. An entire band of cotton-tops taken March 1949, in Socorré (40), upper Río Sinú, Córdoba, was made up of one adult female, two adult males and one young male. A more usual band consists of an adult male and female and one or two young of either or both sexes. These small groups seem to be stable although their composition may differ. Sometimes two or three bands cross trails or congregate in one fruiting tree. When chased or dispersed, by whatever means, each of the original units goes its own way.

J. K. Hampton, Jr. 1964, p. 243 (*oedipus*)

The cotton-top was observed in the wild state in the vicinity of San Juan Nepomuceno (45), northern Colombia, during the dry months of February 1962 and February and March 1963.

The animals appear "to travel only in small family groups consisting, perhaps, of two parents and their juvenile and/or infant offspring. This type of grouping is strongly suggested by our experience with animals in small and large cages. They are most often found very high in large trees and, when pursued, move very rapidly from one tree to the next. They can complete phenomenally large jumps, appearing almost to glide great distances. Other primates in the area, such as the white-faced capuchin and the red howler, move much more slowly and only to a distance slightly removed from any disturbance."

Enders 1935, p. 339 (*geoffroyi*)

"Most of the Squirrel Monkey [i.e., tamarins] seen [on Barro Colorado Island] are in small bands, numbering up to a dozen and more (Chapman, 1929, My tropical air castle, p. 284). Sometimes single individuals are observed and very frequently, two. Whether or not such animals represent pairs was not determined."

A. Hladik and Hladik 1969, p. 92 (*geoffroyi*)

They form stable groups of 6 to 7 individuals on Barro Colorado Island.

Moynihan 1970, pp. 5–6 (*geoffroyi*)

The sizes of social units seen in all environments studied in Panamá are tabulated as follows.

No. of Individuals per Unit	*No. of Units Seen*
1	5
2	6
3	5
4	5
5	2
6	4
9	1

"All total number of units counted was 28. The total number of individuals counted was 95. The average number of individuals per unit was 3.39.

"All the single individuals seen were apparently adult. All the groups of two also were composed of adults, presumably mates in all or most cases. Some groups of three included one individual which was obviously young. And all the larger groups included one or more young."

"Chapman (op. cit.) states that *geoffroyi* individuals occur in groups as large as 12 or more. Various inhabitants of the Canal Zone have reported seeing equally large groups in recent years. I think, however, that many or all of these recent records must be gross overestimates."

J. K. Hampton, Jr., Hampton, and Landwehr 1966, p. 277 (*oedipus*)

A typical group consists of the three age groups; adult pair, late juvenal offspring, and young juvenals or infants, total 4 to 6. By the time a fourth age group is on its way, the oldest juvenals are probably driven off.

Epple 1967*b*, p. 61 (*geoffroyi*)

"The social structure in Hapalidae is a family group, with a monogamy-like bond between α-male and the α-female, from which grown-up juveniles are driven by the parents of the same sex."

J. K. Hampton, Jr., Hampton, and Landwehr 1966, p. 278 (*oedipus*)

"That these animals may be monogamous by choice, in the usual sense, is not supported by our frequent observations of copulation shortly after pairs are placed together. Also, animals in adjacent cages commonly attempt to reach others of opposite sex. In one such instance a swap was carried out. The male copulated with the female in the adjacent cage and then again with its own cage mate as soon as it was returned. A monogamy-like social structure is probably enforced by the fierce competition between females."

J. K. Hampton, Jr., Hampton, and Landwehr 1966, p. 282 (*oedipus*)

"The notable female intolerance of female and the particularly prominent marking behavior of females as contrasted to males point to a possibly unique social structure among primates. We leave to the behaviorist the decision of whether or not it is wise to call it a matriarchal order."

Hershkovitz (Notes)

There is, in fact, reason to believe that female tamarins may be polyandrous. Tolerance between male members of a group is known and this relationship is compatible with a matriarchal society.

Daily Rhythm

A. Hladik and Hladik 1969, p. 92 (*geoffroyi*)

The rhythm of *geoffroyi* differs from that of the other platyrrhine species of Barro Colorado Island by absence of rest or siesta periods during the day. Tamarins become active well after sunrise and retire during the early part of the evening to their sleeping quarters (probably hollow trees).

Moynihan 1970, p. 4 (*geoffroyi*)

"In the wild, they are never seen moving around until at least a quarter of an hour after it has become fully light. In most cases they apparently do not get up until approximately three-quarters of an hour, or more, after full light. . . . After arising, they remain quite active throughout most of the rest of the day. They may rest briefly in the middle of the morning but . . . they usually show little or no tendency to slow down or take a 'siesta' at noon or during the first part of the afternoon, when the heat is greatest. It is only approximately an hour or half hour before sunset that they gradually stop feeding and drift off in the general direction of their sleeping trees."

J. K. Hampton, Jr., Hampton, and Landwehr 1966, p. 268 (*oedipus*)

"Subjectively bright lighting is maintained [in our laboratory] and it is cycled on and off by a timer control to provide a 12 h day. We have noted that marmosets are quite sensitive to various levels of illumination. As the light dims, activity is markedly reduced and 'nesting' or sleeping behavior is initiated. Vocalizations characteristic of active animals are reduced and finally stopped altogether when darkness is approached. These observations have influenced our choice of room illumination, as well as cage design and placement."

F. Cuvier 1829 (Livr. 59, *oedipus*)

"The individuals I saw [in Paris] spent the entire day sleeping in the darkest part of their cage. They didn't even move to defecate. As the sun went down, however, they became very active and ate the food left for them. At the break of day they returned to their hiding place.

When in need of anything, they uttered a short, soft, one-toned whistle."

Hershkovitz (Notes)

The nocturnal habits and call attributed to these monkeys by Cuvier (cited above) suggest *Aotus*. The brief physical description following Cuvier's account and the accompanying color plate, however, belong to the common Cotton-top Tamarin, *Saguinus oedipus oedipus*.

Care of Young

Epple 1970*a*, p. 66 (*geoffroyi*)

"The [newborn] baby was still wet and bloody, it vocalized and made nondirected movements. By holding his arms out to the baby, and pulling it softly, the male directed the infant's movements towards him. However he did not take the baby in his arms. Once its movements were directed toward the male, it mounted him by its own efforts, clinging tightly to his pelage."

Wendt 1964 (*oedipus*)

The single newborn was welcomed, admired, and tongued by his father and older sister of the previous birth. The mother, however, took immediate charge of her offspring and cared for him for several weeks before letting the father take him. Meantime, father and sister watched over mother and child, accompanying them like bodyguards.

Cooper (1964, unpublished *Quarterly Report*, no. 7, p. 6)

"The [twin newborn] babies were rather clumsy and [the mother] was very irritable; soon one baby fell off her back to the floor of the retiring box and it wasn't found until it had become quite chilled. It was taken into the laboratory and warmed in a makeshift incubator. Meanwhile the father was placed back with the mother and he quickly took the remaining baby from her. The baby which had fallen from the mother was weighed (42.5 grams) and then returned to the cage, after being warmed for an hour. The father came to the cage door immediately and pushed the baby onto his back from the hand offering it. He carried both babies for almost 2 hours and then tried to get the mother to take them. She would not accept them willingly at first but by early afternoon she was nursing the babies one at a time for short periods. At one month of age the babies were first noted to leave one parent's back and scramble across the retiring box to the other parent. A few days later the twins began to climb on the wire of the RT cage; when alarmed they jumped immediately on their father's back. Soaked monkey chow was first eaten by the babies at about 5 weeks of age. When they were between the ages of 6 and 7 weeks, the mother was noticed to occasionally reject them when they jumped onto her back. The father still carries the babies without visible signs of protest when they jump on him in alarm, even though they are now nearly 12 weeks old and so large that he can scarcely carry them both. The parents are exceptionally docile cotton-tops but the twins are still extremely shy and nervous."

J. K. Hampton, Jr., Hampton, and Landwehr 1966, pp. 275–76

The young adult female and both males in the same cage "showed extraordinary interest in the twins [born 14 June 1964, to the older female]. The males, especially, persisted in transferring the young between themselves and the mother with such frequency that we were alarmed. The young female's interest occasionally resulted in one of them getting on her back. At this time, she became disturbed and attempted to dislodge it by biting at it and rubbing against the cage wire. Usually its cries brought one of the males to the rescue."

Willig and Wendt 1970 (*geoffroyi*)

From about the time the young was 10 days old, the father began playing the tail-biting game. Every afternoon he bit the tail of one of the young sitting on his back until it climbed off crying with pain. The second offspring was bitten in turn and forced to dismount. Then both tried to return to the father's back as soon as possible.

At first the father allowed the young to scramble back with little delay. After a few days, he jumped aside when they tried to mount and the young had to give chase. When one managed to return too quickly, its tail was bitten and it had to dismount. During the "game," the father would also nip the claws of his offspring. The mother neither paid attention to the outcries nor interfered with their training. She nursed the young and cleaned them, but no more. The father did the rest.

When the second litter of twins was born 23 December 1967, the father took over from the first day and released the young to the mother for suckling only. When the father died a short time later, the mother gave all her attention to the young. She even played the tail-biting game after the twins were about 10 days old. This time the first born sisters were around and took turns carrying the young and quitting an old score by playing the tail-biting game until the mother intervened and took back her squealing young.

The tail-biting game was used to teach independence to the young. It obliged them to forsake the protective fur of the parents and find security on the branches.

Graetz 1968, p. 32 (*geoffroyi*)

The tamarins arrived as usual on the window sill looking for sugar water. This time, however, the male let the female go first. The reason was immediately apparent. Two newborn young were clinging to the mother, one on each shoulder.

While the young were suckling, the father permitted the mother to remove from his hand or mouth the insects he had caught. The young were on the father's back about

80% of the time and the rest was spent being nursed by the mother and carried to and from the nesting tree.

Graetz 1968, p. 34 (*geoffroyi*)

After a very bad storm, the mother was afraid to walk the tangled 40-meter length of telephone wire that connected the sleeping tree with the house where I lived on the outskirts of Panamá City. The male had already crossed and was calling his mate with the usual distress cry, *titiih*. The female answered in kind but after the calls were repeated several times, "the male ran back across the wire and returned to the house with one young on his back. He set it down carefully on a branch, and returned for the second infant. As he started across with the offspring on his back, the female overcame her fear of falling and followed."

Graetz 1968, pp. 34–35 (*geoffroyi*)

The father assumes complete responsibility for the young after they are weaned. Tidbits once given by the father to the mother are now reserved for the young. He also teaches the offspring to distinguish poisonous or unpalatable food by smell.

When the second litter arrived, special food brought by the father was again given to the mother, then to the second-litter young after weaning. Those born first now took care of themselves and their younger siblings until old enough to have young of their own.

Rejection of Young

Graetz 1968, p. 35 (*geoffroyi*)

One of the second-litter twins died as a result of a fall from its father's back to the ground. The parents watched it from the trees above. As they saw no movement and heard no call, they made no attempt to help. The surviving twin, however, missed her sister and for several days made the *titiih* contact call.

S. H. Hampton and Hampton 1967, p. 2 (*oedipus*)

Male and female cotton-tops born in the University of Texas Institute for Dental Science laboratory "were reared by their parents until 18 days of age. At that time the cage containing these animals was transferred to another room. Within two hours of the transfer the parents began biting the infants to dislodge them from their backs and the female refused to nurse them. They were removed to the artificial rearing program at that time."

Epple 1970*a*, p. 66 (*geoffroyi*)

"A second infant [of twins newly born in captivity] was found on the floor of the outdoor enclosure. It was unattended by the parents, cold, wet and immobile. The baby was fully developed but born with a hare's lip. It probably had been dragged along the ground, since the skin of the right side of the head was badly scratched. Handling caused the baby to breathe, move and vocalize faintly. It was placed close to the parents, who licked it. When the infant did not respond and soon ceased to move and vocalize, they lost all interest and left it on the ground. These observations indicate that infantile movements and especially vocalizations probably are the most essential stimuli for the parental responses. An attempt to rear this infant artificially was unsuccessful."

S. H. Hampton, and Hampton, 1967, p. 1 (*oedipus*)

"Infant marmosets weighing approximately 40 grams at birth, are often lost due to rejection by their parents. This may occur even when several days old and is often associated with factors which cause any upset in the normal care regime."

Hershkovitz (Notes)

The maternal response to her dependent young is less solicitous than the paternal. Neither parent, however, shows an attachment to their own dead or unresponsive infants such as has been observed in squirrel monkeys (Kaplan 1973) and other higher primates.

Intraspecific Relations

J. K. Hampton, Jr., Hampton, and Landwehr 1966, pp. 268–69 (*oedipus*)

In housing strange individuals, "only pairs of opposite sex can be caged together due to almost invariable fighting between animals of the same sex."

J. K. Hampton, Jr., Hampton, and Landwehr 1966, p. 275 (*oedipus*)

The group, consisting of 2 adult males and 3 adult females (A, B, C) and one (D) of two original juvenals, was received December 1962 as part of a shipment that occupied one compartment. The animals seemed generally compatible. Late in April 1963 this group was placed in a cage in the author's backyard in New Orleans.

June 19—Adult females A and B fought with resultant death of B (in early pregnancy).

July 31—Females A and C fought, C badly injured and removed from cage; large mutilated placenta found in nest box, but no evidence of fetuses.

Both males remained peaceful throughout. Juvenal female, probably 9–11 months old in July, behaved as subordinate young, receiving food from all adults.

Moynihan 1970, pp. 12–13 (*geoffroyi*)

"Overt attacks are relatively *very* rare among Rufous-Naped Tamarins in the wild. . . . The only observed attack performances by tamarins under natural conditions were brief rushes of or chases with or without rasping vocalizations. . . . I never saw actual physical combat, serious wrestling and biting in the wild. This rarity is interesting in view of the obvious aggressiveness of tamarins in captivity . . . Individuals of the same group usually have plenty of room to retreat from one another in the wild. And individuals of different groups usually do not approach one another closely enough to permit fighting. . . . The escape behavior . . . is more or less rapid retreat."

Moynihan 1970, p. 16 (*geoffroyi*)

"When two previously unacquainted [captive] *geoffroyi* individuals encounter one another for the first time, they may sniff one another nose to nose, or one may sniff at the genito-anal region of the other, or (most frequently) the two individuals may place themselves in a mutual "nose to tail" position and sniff one another's genito-anal region simultaneously."

Hershkovitz (Notes)

Fighting usually takes place between strange adults of the same sex. Caged individuals of the opposite sex are mutually tolerant and become acquainted by ritualistic sniffing of genitalia, marking, and other forms of sensing.

Moynihan 1970, p. 6 (*geoffroyi*)

"The captive individuals tended to form definite pair bonds. When several males and females were kept together, each individual tended to select an individual of the opposite sex as its 'mate.' Mates tended to associate more closely with one another than with the other individuals in the same cage, to perform all or most of their copulatory behavior together, and to fight with one another less frequently than with other individuals. . . . Some of the pair bonds between captives were not only strong but long sustained, enduring for at least four years (as long as my observations continued in any given case). . . . It seems overwhelmingly probable that the groups of only two adults (alone or with young) observed in the wild also were pairs of mates. Perhaps the members of larger groups in the wild are equally likely to form semipermanent sexual attachments among themselves. If so, their pair bonds may not be conspicuous, to a human observer, simply because mates do not stick particularly close together during the daily search for food. (I might add that I never saw copulations in the wild; i.e., I did not see the reactions which should reveal the existence of pair bonds most clearly.)"

Graetz 1968, p. 31 (*geoffroyi*)

When I brought the female with her two young to my home on the outskirts of Panama City, I turned the male out of the bird cage which hung under a lemon tree in front of the house and I put her in. The cage and its new occupants were visited by the male every day. The encounter resulted in angry cries and a battle between the bars of the cage as each adult tried to bite and scratch the other. Five weeks later mother and young were given their freedom and the quarreling ended. The male became the female's consort and both took care of the young. Unfortunately, one infant died soon after and the other disappeared a little later (see following).

Graetz 1968, pp. 35–36 (*geoffroyi*)

While the family was adjusting to the large bird cage, the daughter strayed and hid herself in a large mango tree on the other side of the street on the outskirts of Panama City. She remained in contact with her parents, nevertheless, by means of the *titiih* call. When she finally made her way back to the cage, the parents refused to accept her. The mother at first tried marking her estranged daughter to restore the family odor. But the foreign scents she had picked up in exile were too strong and provoked the parents into attacking their daughter, breaking her hip bone, and pursuing the bleeding animal to a hole in the ground where she sought asylum.

Graetz saved the wounded animal and put her in a small cage by herself. Everytime he brought her into the vicinity of her parents' cage she called *titiih* and kept this up for weeks. The parents, however, responded by trying to scratch and bite their offspring through the mesh.

During the transatlantic voyage when parents and daughter were being transported in separate cages from Panama to Germany, the sense of hierarchy vanished. After that, daughter and parents lived together peacefully in Germany.

In the first instance described by Graetz, invasion of the familiar environment by a strange element was violently rejected. In the second instance, discovery of a familiar element in a strange environment was warmly accepted. It is understood, of course, that the circumstances described here would not exist except through human contrivance.

Grooming (fig. X.79)

J. K. Hampton, Jr., Hampton, and Landwehr 1966, pp. 279–80 (*oedipus*)

"Mutual and self grooming occupy a considerable portion of the time of our animals. To the best of our knowledge each sex is equally responsive as a groomer. While the groomer may occasionally initiate the activity, it is more usual that the groomee 'invites' the other by placing itself before the groomer in postures similar to that observed in rhesus monkeys. Grooming sessions may be long and thorough. The general impression of this act differs in no way from other more familiar primates except in one way. This is a peculiar mouth grooming in which the mouth is pulled widely open and its interior given attention by the long tongue of the groomer. This behavior pattern has been observed often and we have observed a female groom the mouth of her young at an age of 61 days.

"Self grooming is not neglected. It is directed primarily at the tail and legs. The tail is frequently scratched vigorously as well as inspected and groomed slowly. It is drawn forward between the legs or grasped and brought

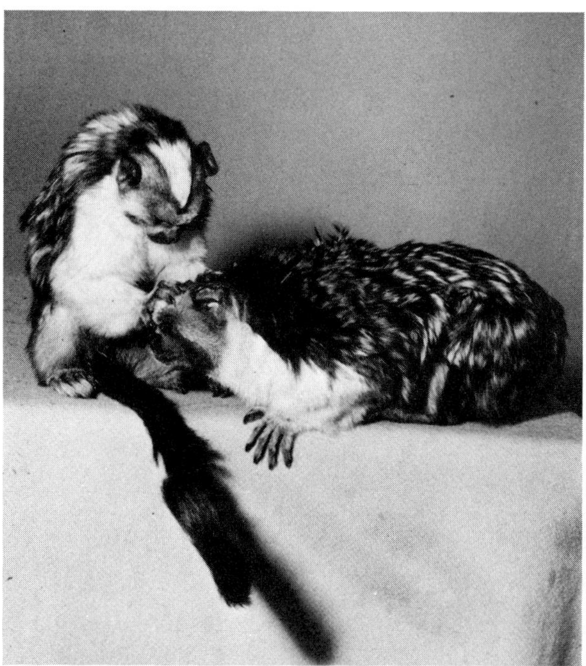

Fig. X.79. Grooming: Two adults, *Saguinus oedipus geoffroyi*. (Photo courtesy of Gisela Epple.)

up from under a perch. Both hands are used in the rapid motions, directing the claws opposite to the direction of the hair. The rear feet, despite claws, are skillfully used in slow 'digging' at the ears. The claws of the hands are cleaned by the mouth with careful visual inspection repeatedly given."

Moynihan 1970, pp. 15–16 (*geoffroyi*)

Groomer and groomee are usually of opposite sexes. Their roles may change once or repeatedly during the grooming session. As a rule, subordinates groom dominants more frequently or for longer periods of time than the reverse. Allogrooming is more frequent during the breeding season than at other times of the year. In the majority of observations, however, grooming was not a prelude or sequel to copulation. When allogrooming does precede mating, the male is always the groomer. On two [of number?] occasions, the precopulatory grooming was interrupted by wrestling.

A would-be groomee usually invites grooming by sitting or lying before the prospective groomer. The acquiescent groomer pays particular attention to certain parts of the fur and ignores others. The allogroomer employs hands and teeth. The self groomer does little more than scratch with hands or feet. Bright sunlight strongly stimulates grooming.

Willig and Wendt 1970 (*geoffroyi*)

After copulation the female combed the male's fur to remove the scales, which were eaten. During the operation, the male turned from time to time to present all parts of his coat. Finally, the male groomed the female.

Interspecific Relations

Enders 1935, p. 339 (*geoffroyi*)

"The name of Squirrel Monkey [for *Saguinus oedipus geoffroyi*] is very fitting for, when they are seen far up in a large tree, or running along vines, or leaping, their color and tail, as well as size, give them a marked resemblance to the squirrel. In fact, the only specimen of this species collected on the Island was shot as a squirrel, the mistake not becoming evident until too late. These animals are lacking in the characteristics that make the other monkeys of such great interest. The voice is weak, their size small, and they lack the dashing activity of the White-face, and the gentleness of the Night Monkey."

Hershkovitz (Notes)

Callitrichids share habitats with squirrels and resemble one or another of the sympatric species in size, form, and conspicuous coloration. They climb and leap like squirrels and even flip their tails and turn their head with similar jerky movements. The nervous twitching of the alarmed or suspicious tamarin's hand compares with the finger drumming of squirrels, and the vibrating or fluttering tongue of the excited tamarin recalls the incisor clicking of scolding squarrels.

A. Hladik and Hladik 1969, p. 93 (*geoffroyi*)

To the extent that the tamarin does not search the dead trees and branches where insects hide, they use resources partially different from those utilized by *Cebus*.

The two species seem to be strongly antagonistic if judgment may be based on the intensity of the warning calls of tamarins set into motion by the approach of a troop of *Cebus*. Other species of monkeys generally ignore each other.

Hershkovitz (Notes)

Under the heading "Relations with Other Species," Moynihan (1970, pp. 7–11) names the five other Panamanian monkey species, a number of non–Central American monkey species, a squirrel, and some flycatchers with which *Saguinus oedipus geoffroyi* does *not* associate regularly if at all, or with which it does *not* compete because it does *not* live where they do, or is *not* active when they are, or they simply avoid each other. This segregation, Moynihan points out (p. 9) "is highly advantageous in the Panamanian environment." The ability of tamarins to adjust their activities to those of flycatchers and other potential competitors (p. 10) "may help explain why *Saguinus* is the only genus of tamarin or marmoset which has been able to invade Central America."

It may be more to the point to mention that *Saguinus oedipus geoffroyi* is the only callitrichid known to have originated in the region that includes Panamá in its faunal zone or biotic province.

Fig. X.80. Geoffroy's Bare-face Tamarin, *Saguinus oedipus geoffroyi,* eating locust; male arrived Jersey Zoological Park 6 July 1961, still living May 1973. (Photo by Phillip F. Coffey, courtesy of Jersey Zoological Park.)

The economic or ecological effects of the nonrelationship between tamarins and the few Panamanian species mentioned by Moynihan is impossible to assess. My guess is they are insignificant. Tamarins persist in suitable, including grossly modified, habitats long after all other monkey species have disappeared or where some or all of them never occurred. The same species of squirrels and flycatchers may or may not disappear from the same places but they are just as numerous where *Saguinus oedipus* or other callitrichids do not occur. Where they are sympatric it cannot be said which of the species was there first or which was obliged to adjust or accommodate to the other. At any rate, there appears to be enough food and cover in the wild for all, if not in one tree or bush, then in another. Each population adjusts to the carrying capacity of its range.

There are myriads of organisms, exclusive of plants and man, with which tamarins have real and vital relationships and many of them can visibly alter the status of the animal in the wild. Among these, predators and parasites are in the front ranks. Equally important are the animals on which tamarins prey. They are discussed in other sections.

Foods (figs. X.80, 81)

Enders 1935, p. 440 (*geoffroyi*)

"A wide range of food, both vegetable and animal, is eaten. The only stomach examined contained some unidentified seeds. Star-apples and figs are eaten as well as a variety of flowers. A band visited the balsa tree blooming near the laboratory with great frequency, as well as blooming cecropia trees. These visits may have been to drink the water that accumulates in the blossoms, to eat the flower, or to search for the insects found there. Some termites are secured by pulling apart dead leaf stems. Captive animals were very fond of insects, chiefly grasshoppers.

"It is doubtful if this monkey is carnivorous, in spite of its insectivorous habit. They will eat cooked meat, but were never observed to more than sniff at it in the raw state. Mr. Zetek handed one captive specimen a bat (probably *Myotis nigricans*) which it took between its paws, turning it over and over to examine it, but making no attempt to molest it until the bat nipped a finger. With great rapidity, the monkey bit the bat's head, crushing the

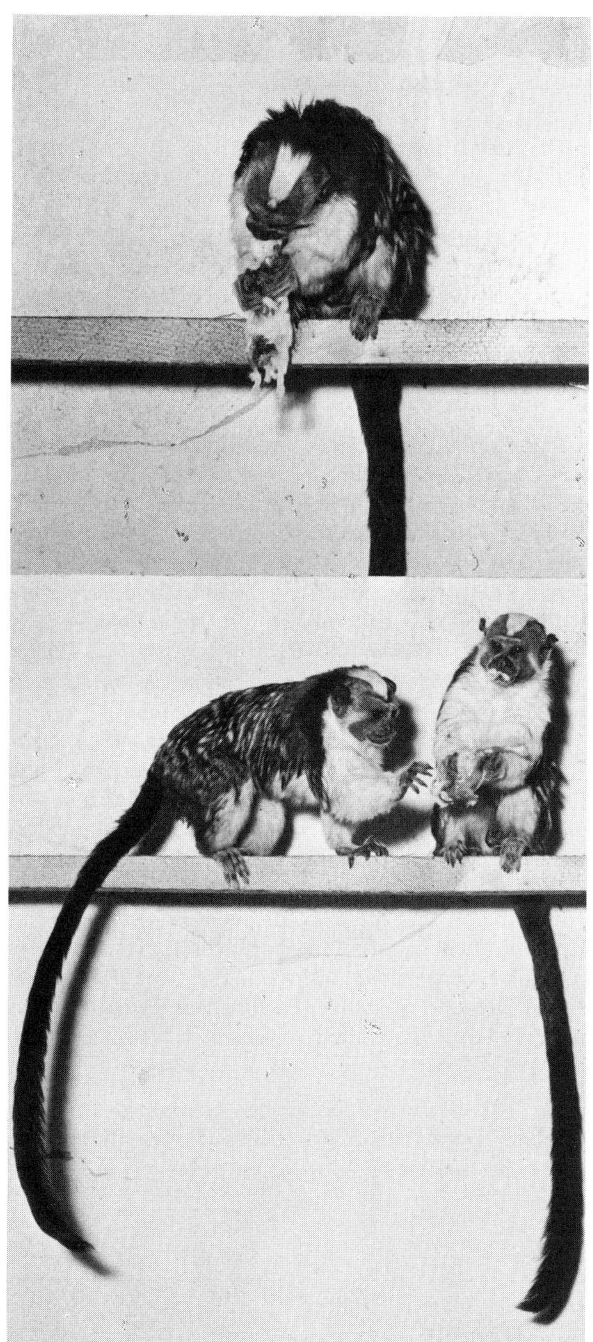

Fig. X.81. Eating mouse head first; *above,* male *Saguinus oedipus geoffroyi;* below same male with young female daughter begging. (Photos courtesy of Gisela Epple.)

skull, and then tossed the dead body away, taking no more interest in it. When sloths were confined in their cage, the marmosets would hunt insects in the long hair of the non-resistant sloths."

Moynihan 1970, p. 4 (*geoffroyi*)

"Captive animals [on Barro Colorado Island] show a definite preference for insects. . . . They also catch and devour small lizards of the genera *Anolis* and *Mabuya* . . . and will eat freshly killed bats and small birds. . . . During my own observations, most of the food seen to be taken were vegetable, including a wide assortment of fruits and buds. Insects are probably less abundant, or less immediately available, than fruits and buds in many of the environments inhabited by the species, at least at certain times of the day or periods of the year."

J. K. Hampton, Jr., Hampton, and Landwehr 1966, p. 266 (*oedipus*)

"In the few we have collected in their habitat [in northwestern Colombia], all have had insect remains in their stomachs, but, also, berries and the bulk of various seed pods and seeds were present."

Epple 1970*a,* p. 60 (*oedipus*)

"The diet should contain some indigestible material, such as feathers or hair. When our *Leontideus rosalia* and *Saguinus geoffroyi* produced soft feces, these became solid as soon as the animals received a bird or a mouse. *Saguinus geoffroyi* regularly skinned a mouse (fig. X.81), and at first consumed a rather large amount of the pelage before eating any meat. This was done only when the animals had not received birds or mice for one or two weeks. When birds or mice were supplied regularly, the monkeys discarded most of the pelage. When eating birds, small amounts of plumage sticking to the meat are consumed, while most of the feathers are removed with the teeth."

Wendt 1964 (*oedipus*)

Tamarins depend mainly on animal food. Their diet in captivity included grasshoppers, cockroaches, caterpillars, moths, and wood bugs. The latter seemed to stimulate the males sexually. In winter, meal bettles and mealworms were fed, supplemented with small pieces of raw liver, heart, or other red meat, and fresh herring. Insects, fish, and meat were fed by hand to each animal to be sure each had its share. They were also fed bananas, dates, figs, plums, grapes, and fresh green vegetables.

Graetz 1968, pp. 30–31 (*geoffroyi*)

The captive tamarins did not eat cockroaches and other blattids, although there is a surplus of these animals in every household [in Panama City]. The male, kept temporarily in a bird cage, accepted scrambled eggs in lieu of his accustomed spiders and insects. He soon tired of eggs, however, and became very particular, refusing to eat the same food more than two days running. I gave him beef, chicken, very ripe bananas, mangos, and grapes. He disdained canned milk because I didn't sweeten it for him the first time. After he returned to a semifree life in the surroundings of my house, he retained one last tie with his former residence by partaking of a sugar syrup set out in a bowl on the window sill.

Willig and Wendt 1970 (*geoffroyi*)

The monkeys were very fastidious and bad tempered when it came to food. What they ate with greed one day, they might disdain the next day. The diet, therefore, had to be of a very changeable nature. The animals received a daily mess or pudding that consisted of cornflakes, water, dextrose, and Kalzan D, Sanasol, and milk sugar. They had bananas in season, apples, plums, grapes, raisins, carrots, lettuce, earthnuts, coconuts, insects, cooked and raw eggs, mice, cooked chicken, sometimes with bones, and fresh lean beef. There are no limits to the variety of food eaten. Everything fresh and edible for children is consumed by them. This includes cake, cheese, cooked vegetables, and noodles.

J. K. Hampton, Jr., Hampton, and Landwehr 1966, p. 268 (*oedipus*)

"The amount given each feeding [in the New Orleans colony] is 25 g per animal and represents (when doubled) a daily availability of 98 cal. Estimates indicate that the average actual intake is about 200 cl/kg/day."

Clark (1974, p. 46)

"[The] Cotton-Headed Tamarins will strip bark from the branches and will occasionally consume a little."

A. Hladik and Hladik 1969, pp. 27, 92 (*geoffroyi*)

The authors studied the relationship between the vegetation of Barro Colorado Island and the five species of native primates from November 1966 to January 1968. They list 82 trees, shrubs, vines and palms visited by the monkeys, the parts eaten, and the months of productivity. Capuchins (*Cebus capucinus*) were observed feeding on 59 of the plants; howlers (*Alouatta palliata*) on 35; spider monkeys (*Ateles paniscus*) on 32; night monkeys (*Aotus trivirgatus*) on 1, and tamarins (*Saguinus oedipus geoffroyi*) on 8. The plants visited by *Saguinus* are listed in table 105.

Determination of the kinds of food taken by the tamarins was based on the identification of stomach contents of an unspecified number of individuals taken during May, June, August, October, and November 1967 in Miraflores and on a hill above Balboa in the Canal Zone. The following proportions of food were found in the stomachs.

Green vegetation	10%
Fruit	60%
Insects and other prey	30%

The prey consisted mostly of Orthoptera, Coleoptera, a small number of Lepidoptera, and a large tarantula.

Fruit is often sought near the ground. The large number of seeds of *Cardulovica palmata* in the stomach of tamarins proves this, although the authors never saw the animals descend to the shrubs. The fruit of the low-growing *Piper carriloanum* was also sought. *Cecropia* and perhaps *Almedia* are visited often. Their fruits, produced nearly the year round, are important in the tamarin's diet.

The resin of certain trees, most notably *Enterolobium cyclocarpum*, is consumed, possibly in large amounts. Seeds in pulpy fruits are ordinarily rejected with a flip of the head. The small seeds of the fruit of *Genipa americana*, however, adhere to the fibers and are swallowed whole. Resin-sweetened water accumulated in the corolla of the large flower of the balsa (*Ochroma limonensis*) is drunk by the tamarin as well as by *Cebus* (cf. Hladik and Hladik 1969, p. 95). Insects trapped in the solution may also be consumed.

The quality of food ingested by *Saguinus oedipus geoffroyi, Cebus capucinus, Ateles paniscus geoffroyi,* and *Alouatta palliata* on Barro Colorado Island, Panama, was analyzed and the quantity estimated in a second publication by Hladik and Hladik in collaboration with Bousset, Valdebouze, Viroben, and Delort-Laval (1971). The authors regret that the data for tamarins were not complete and their comparisons with cebids, presented here in tabular form (tables 102, 103, 104), are provisional.

The analyses of native Panamanian plant nutrients made by the authors cited are detailed. Nothing is said,

Table 102. Gross Food Types Consumed by Four Monkey Species on Barro Colorado Island, Panamá

	Food Types (percentages)		
Species	*Leaves, Shoots*	*Fruit*	*Animal*
Saguinus oedipus geoffroyi	10	60	30
Cebus capucinus	15	65	20
Ateles paniscus	20	80	0
Alouatta palliata	40	60	0

SOURCE: Data from C. M. Hladik et al. (1971).

Table 103. Diversity of Food Plants, Mainly Trees, used by Four Monkey Species on Barro Colorado Island, Panamá

	Number of Food Plant Species Utilized		
	1	*2*	*3*
Species	*Number Seen Used for Food*	*Number Analyzed for Nutritive Substances*	*Percentage Edible Bulk Supplied by 2*
Saguinus oedipus geoffroyi	8	6	?
Cebus capucinus	59	36	60
Ateles paniscus	32	18	80
Alouatta palliata	35	12	80

SOURCE: Data from A. Hladik and Hladik (1969) and Hladik et al. (1971).

Table 104. Analysis of Food Properties Consumed by Four Monkey Species on Barro Colorado Island, Panamá

	Chemical Composition of Food (percentages)					
	Proteins			*Reducing*		
Species	*Animal*	*Plant*	*Lipids*	*Glucides*	*Cellulose*	*Indigestible*[1]
Saguinus oedipus geoffroyi	16.0	4.6	9.1	29.0	7.3	34.0
Cebus capucinus	8.8	5.6	15.8	26.3	7.6	36.0
Ateles paniscus	0.1	7.4	4.9	33.7	11.0	43.0
Alouatta palliata	0.5[2]	9.1	3.2	21.7	13.6	51.9

SOURCE: Data from C. M. Hladik et al. (1971).

[1] "Fraction complémentaire," consisting of mineral salts, all glucides not included with the reducing glucides, and cellulose. It is directly proportional to the "coefficient d'encumbrement intestinal," or indigestible bulk.

[2] Accidentally swallowed with fruit.

however, about the number of monkeys observed feeding, the conditions under which they were observed, and the methods employed for determining the quantity and quality of food eaten by each species. The figures supplied, however, seem reasonable.

The dietary requirements of Panamanian *Aotus trivirgatus* and *Saimiri sciureus* were estimated as intermediate between those of *Saguinus* and *Cebus*. Little mention is made of resins utilized by all species.

The year-round availability of leaves and unripe fruits such as figs [*Ficus*], which are consumed in large quantities by *Alouatta*, accounts for the comparatively sedentary habits of that monkey. *Ateles* is basically a fruit eater and fills out its dietary needs with leaves, buds, and shoots, especially palm shoots. *Cebus* indulges in the greatest variety of foods, visits the largest number of food trees, and rejects more of the undersirable, albeit edible, parts of plants than the other cebids mentioned. *Saguinus* is mainly insectivorous, its food altogether more nutritious, with unassimilable or indigestible bulk reduced to a minimum. The activity of these small predaceous animals is much greater than that of the predominantly grazing and browsing monkeys.

Nelson 1975

A study of the order of feeding behavior by members of a free-ranging social group was made between April and July 1973 at Rodman Naval Ammunition Depot, Panama Canal Zone. Data was collected from a ground-level blind 30–40 feet distant from a tree which supported a feeding station at a height of 25 feet. The station was provisioned with 4–8 ripe mangoes or bananas at the beginning of each of the 19 observation days. The order in which the 4 marked animals entered and left the

Table 105. Food-Producing Trees and Shrubs Utilized by the Tamarin, *Saguinus oedipus geoffroyi*, on Barro Colorado Island

Food Plant	*Part Eaten*	*Months Edible*	*Remarks*
Apocynaceae			
Lacmellea edulis	Pulp of fruits rich in white latex	March	Seeds not eaten; also eaten by *Alouatta*
Bombacaceae			
Ochroma limonensis, "balsa"	Sweet water accumulated in corolla		Also drunk by *Cebus*
Cyclanthaceae			
Cardulovica palmata	Fruit grouped in red spike	May, June	Eaten with seeds
Leguminosae			
Enterolobium cyclocarpum	Resin on branches	All year	
Moraceae			
Cecropia longipes	Fruit	July, Aug. Sept.	Entire fruit eaten; also visited by *Cebus*, *Ateles*, and *Alouatta*
Olmedia aspera	Fruit	Most of year	Seeds probably also eaten; also visited by *Cebus*
Piperaceae			
Piper carriloanum	Fruit catkins	Jan., Feb.	Seeds also eaten
Rubiaceae			
Genipa americana	Large odoriferous fruit	May, June	Entire fruit eaten

SOURCE: Data from A. Hladik and Hladik (1969, pp. 28–35).

feeding station appeared to be nonrandom. The 2 marked juvenals tended to feed most often during the early segments of the total number of visits to the station by all group members. The marked adult male fed more or less evenly throughout the visitations, whereas the adult female fed most during the last segment. Records of an unmarked juvenal and adult of the 6-member group were not included in the account.

Experiments of the sort described here are best conducted under controlled conditions in a laboratory. It would have been at least as interesting to record the hours of feeding under natural conditions, but perhaps the author intends to publish this data, if collected, as a separate article. Quantification of the amount eaten by each group member might be the subject of a third article.

Milk Composition (*oedipus*)

Glass and Jenness 1971

Weight percentage of fatty acids of milk fats from milk of 3 captive *Saguinus oedipus oedipus* is analyzed as follows (the indication for carbon atoms is followed by number of double bands, if any).

$C_{8:0}$ 2.4%; $C_{10:0}$ 14.7; $C_{12:0}$ 15.7; $C_{14:0}$ 12.1; $C_{16:0}$ 21.5; $C_{16:1}$ 2.2; $C_{18:0}$ 3.4; $C_{18:1}$ 19.6; $C_{18:2}$ 8.0.

For general information on primate milk see Buss (1971).

Food Plant Relations

A. Hladik and Hladik 1969, p. 95 (*geoffroyi*)

Tamarins play a role in disseminating seeds of plants passed through their alimentary tract. This role takes on significance only where they are abundant, as in second growths in Panamá outside Barro Colorado Island. Such early-stage trees as *Cecropia,* whose fruit is eaten year round by tamarins, depend on animal propogators for maintaining their range and expanding into newly formed openings in high forest.

Hershkovitz (Notes)

It is unlikely that tamarins or platyrrhines generally contribute significantly to plant propagation. Fruit is eaten in situ and the animal remains long enough in the general area to defecate where the plants are already established. Areas where such early seral stage fruit plants as *Cecropia* are absent would not be visited by monkeys. Fruit-eating birds and bats offer better possibilities for plant propagation.

Drinking

Graetz 1968, pp. 30, 31 (*geoffroyi*)

Tamarins are dew drinkers and do not descend to the ground in search of water.

Captives were never seen drying their lips with their fingers or hand. Instead, they wiped their mouths on the edge of a table or chair.

Hershkovitz (Notes)

Drinking is by lapping and licking.

Predation

Schäuffelen 1958, p. 159 (*oedipus*)

The male and two females in the Augsburg Zoo are excited by the sight of live spiders, and all other small moving animals. When a live bird is placed in the cage, only one of the tamarins stalks it while the others watch carefully. Once the bird is caught with the hands it is seized quickly by the neck and bitten in the head. Death is almost always instantaneous. The beak is then bitten off and thrown away with a toss of the head. Even when given a dead bird, the tamarin still removes the beak first. Holding the body with the hands, the tamarin eats the head first, beginning at the root of the beak. The skull bones are picked off with the teeth and the brain is consumed with relish. The monkey then proceeds to other parts of the body, first plucking the feathers with its teeth. Heart, lung, and liver are devoured, but the intestinal tract is never pulled out or eaten.

Mice are captured and killed the same way. A well-aimed bite on the head dispatches them, and the prey is consumed brain first. Sometimes the head is removed and only the brain is eaten. More often the tamarin also removes front and hind limbs at the shoulder and hip; then, holding them in hand, it eats bones and all to the phalanges. A headless, limbless torso and tail are all that remain.

Small frogs are killed by the same swift technique and almost completely consumed. Large full-grown frogs are noticed by the tamarins but usually left alone. Lizards are taken but the bite to the head fails to kill immediately. Instead, the wound stimulates involuntary movements of the victim, making the prey more difficult to hold and immobilize. After one experience with the lizard's sharp claws, the tamarin is likely to leave the reptile alone.

Cockroaches, mealworms, and other small invertebrates are seized by the head and eaten forthwith, the head bite being superfluous.

Robinson 1966, p. 587

Caged *Saguinus oedipus geoffroyi* spied concealingly colored insects quickly even on camouflaging backgrounds. The same tamarins, however, failed to find stick-mimicking insects on a contrasting background. It was also observed that the rocking movements resembling passive wind-induced movements, made by walking-sticks, attracted less response than linear movements. Robinson concluded that the predator may very well have seen the phasmids but had been conditioned to regard them as inedible sticks.

Predators

Moynihan 1970, p. 4 (*oedipus*)

It was reliably reported that a tayra (*Eira barbora,* Mustelidae) was seen carrying a dead tamarin in its mouth. "Extreme alarm reactions to snakes by captive tamarins" have been observed by a correspondent. "In my experience, they keep a weather eye out for possible aerial predators much more consistently than for any other kind of danger. And their reactions to the actual appearance of a hawk usually are quite unmistakable."

J. K. Hampton, Jr., Hampton, and Landwehr 1966, p. 282 (*oedipus*)

"One of the conditions most likely to produce extreme excitement [in the New Orleans colony] is a swift bird overflying the cage or even the shadow of an airplane flicking past. This stimulus seems to never lose its force with time and suggests that significant predators in the wild may be birds of prey."

Graetz 1968, p. 31 (*geoffroyi*)

The shadow of large birds, such as pelicans and vultures [in Panamá] made them run for cover, usually into the dense foliage.

Moynihan 1970, p. 13 (*geoffroyi*)

"*Saguinus geoffroyi* individuals [on Barro Colorado Island] alarmed by a bird flying overhead may roll under a branch (M. H. Robinson, personal communication), but they seldom or never dodge and hide behind a branch when a potential predator is approaching on the ground.

"One distinctive form of escape or partial escape behavior is a common reaction to 'potential predators,' such as man, gradually approaching from a distance (on the ground). When the members of a band of tamarins first become aware of the alarming stimulus, all the individuals usually begin to vocalize. . . . They are very conspicuous at this time. As the source of the alarm comes closer, however, one individual after another will fall silent. Each individual also begins to run away as soon as it shuts up. Finally, in many cases, only a single individual is left vocalizing. Then it too falls silent and runs away. This behavior is obviously adaptive. The initial outburst calling, and then the change from conspicuous vocalization to silence, may be confusing. And the last remaining individual certainly helps to 'cover' the retreat of its companions. It concentrates the attention of the potential predator upon itself while the other individuals disappear unobserved. The whole performance also is comparable to the 'distraction displays,' or even 'mobbing' of many birds."

G. M. Allen and Barbour 1923, p. 273 (*geoffroyi*)

"Their flesh is very delicate."

Hershkovitz (Notes)

There is virtually no factual information about predation on callitrichids. I have never seen a tamarin in the clutch, mouth, or stomach of a predator. Though its flesh is esteemed by Indians, it is not economical to hunt. There is no doubt, however, that tamarins live under constant threat of attack during the day by raptorial birds, felids, mustelids, and probably snakes. My impression is, however, that such diurnal predation is opportunistic rather than routine. The group cooperation, coordination, signaling system, alertness, speed, and agility of callitrichids provide ample protection. Nocturnal predation, on the other hand, may be more effective. Small felids and arboreal snakes are the probable enemies of consequence. Their approach could be perceived only through smell. Small cats pounce from above or below. Snakes search the canopies and dangle from branches like hanging vines while inspecting the perches and pathways below. As others have noted, callitrichids seem to become torpid during deep sleep. Although a lowered metabolic rate may reduce their sensitivity to danger signals from the outside, it may also reduce the amount of predator-attracting signals released from the inside.

Curiosity

J. K. Hampton, Jr. 1964, p. 243 (*oedipus*)

"A few animals that appeared to have been somewhat tamed in their country of origin have been received. Observations of such animals reveal curiosity about their environment and prominent play behavior not seen in untamed animals. Those that do not fear their environment are very manipulative, inquisitive, and will carry on extensive play with various objects."

Image Response

Willig and Wendt 1970 (*geoffroyi*)

Our breeding pair of tamarins became very excited at first sight of a colored picture of butterflies and caterpillars. They showed no fear and tried to seize the insects they recognized as prey. Colored pictures of nesting birds, bird eggs, and mice excited them in the same manner, but photographs of reptiles and fish in color and prey in black and white photographs brought no reaction. A colored picture from a magazine showing a leopard and baboons he killed threw the tamarins into a fit. They screamed like never before and tried to hide in the darkest corner. They trembled while staring at the picture. When we removed the picture, they screamed again, and continued to stare in the same direction for half an hour before calming down. The experiments with colored pictures were repeated several times at two-day intervals. The tamarins always gave the same responses.

Epple 1967*a*, p. 51, fig. 4 (*geoffroyi*)

A male regularly threatened its own mirror image by tonguing.

Locomotion

Hershkovitz (Field Notes, *oedipus*)

Actively engaged tamarins surprised by the sudden appearance or sound of a potential enemy were never seen to "freeze" in the manner of squirrels. They either take flight or, more often, return the intruder's attention with a greater attention of their own. They peek inquisitively at the observer from every angle while flitting and leaping from vantage point to vantage point. They never seem to be at rest and are very difficult to follow with the eye alone. Even when seated on a perch just looking, they sway from side to side (fig. X.70). Only when at ease and gamboling with each other do their running and bounding slacken and take on some characteristics of a kitten's play. A forcibly or accidentally grounded tamarin panics. Its gait becomes an awkward bounding punctuated with flying leaps and vertical springs as the frenzied animal tries to select from a strange horizon the once familiar stem or trunk that leads to safety.

Enders 1935, p. 439 (*geoffroyi*)

"This monkey is by no means as well adapted to the arboreal life as the White-face [*Cebus capucinus*] or Spider [*Ateles paniscus*] and probably not as well adapted as the Howler [*Alouatta*]. The toes, with the exception of the great toe, end in claws which, while useful in certain types of climbing, do not give the animal the purchase upon a limb so necessary for a truly arboreal type of primate life. Even in leaping, the feet and tail are disposed as much after the manner of squirrels as primates. In moving along a small limb the weight is carried on the foot which is placed at right angles to the limb, the claws pointing outward, the feet being advanced alternately. As a limb becomes more nearly perpendicular the angle is reduced until, in climbing, the claws take much of the weight. However, if the limb is large and not too much inclined, they gallop along, putting down the forefeet together, reaching forward with the hind feet together, and repeating. They do not give the impression of speed. No leaps were measured, but several were observed leaping from tree to tree across narrow *esteros* [i.e., inlets]."

Hershkovitz (Notes, *geoffroyi*)

Enders (1935, p. 439) errs in attempting to equate the locomotory requirements of tamarins with those of much larger, prehensile-tailed cebids. For their size and habitat preferences, tamarins, or callitrichids in general, are no less well-adapted for arboreal life than cebids are for their size class and niche. What Enders probably means is that callitrichids are less specialized, i.e., more generalized for arboreal life—not less adapted—than other living primates.

Swimming

Hershkovitz (Field Notes, *geoffroyi*)

Tamarins are good swimmers. A badly wounded *geoffroyi* that fell into a quiet pool of the Río Unguía near my camp swam in circles dog fashion for quite some time until it found a low jutting branch of an overhanging tree. Seizing it, the animal pulled its body out of the water and quickly climbed to the upper story of the plant.

Enders 1935, p. 339 (*geoffroyi*)

"Sylvestri [Enders's assistant on the Barro Colorado Island] says that they can swim well."

Play

J. K. Hampton, Jr., Hampton, and Landwehr 1966, p. 280 (*oedipus*)

"Play between older adults is not uncommon. However, young animals seem never to get enough. Play is often solitary with the animal racing about its cage, usually in some repeated pattern. Also, examination and fondling of objects while hanging by the feet from some seemingly inappropriate point is another common method. Play between animals usually is in the form of rough and tumble attacks. Feinting approaches and withdrawals and 'follow the leader' chases are other common patterns of play. Very young animals have a great fondness for carrying things in their mouths. Smooth stones or bits of string are suitable subjects. This type of preoccupation is not observed in adults."

Graetz 1968, p. 32 (*geoffroyi*)

Most of the day in the house was occupied by the adult pair in play. They enjoyed "hide and seek" and liked to fight for and defend the highest place on the easy chair. A favorite game was "surprise attack." The male would spring on my bare shoulders, nip me on the nape and jump away before I could react. The bite was light and not intended to hurt. My shepherd dog was also attacked and bitten the same way.

Repose

J. K. Hampton, Jr., Hampton, and Landwehr 1966, p. 280–81 (*oedipus*)

"The common resting position is perpendicular to a perch with the feet outside the placement of the hands. Sleeping is characterized by a curled-up position in which the head is brought between the arms and the face is almost in contact with the abdomen. In such a position the top of the head rests upon the surface with the hands and feet. The tail is brought between the legs and rolled tightly into a coil underneath, a common placement of the tail even while resting in the sitting position. It is interesting that in the sleeping posture almost none of the abundant white of the coat shows. Also the hairless surfaces of the face and head are nicely covered which may afford some protection from insects. A remarkable observation is the extreme somnolence of animals which are ordinarily so alert. When asleep in this position they often can be prodded with considerable force before arousal. Then some time elapses as the bewildered animal reaches a state of full wakefulness."

J. K. Hampton, Jr. 1964, pp. 242, 281 (*oedipus*), and other Authors

The characteristic posture of lassitude in warm weather is the belly sprawl, with fore- and hind limbs hanging loosely from both sides of the perch. This is a state of complete relaxation that involves no muscle tone.

J. K. Hampton, Jr., Hampton, and Landwehr 1966, p. 282 (*oedipus*)

"Their obvious fondness for a nest box plus the fact that it is the only part of their environment which they protect from excreta suggest that they are hole dwellers in nature. . . . Yet, on warm nights, the ones in our yard do not hesitate to sleep outside. Their extreme depth of sleep also could be taken as a response to a situation usually considered safe."

Moynihan 1970, p. 4 (*geoffroyi*)

"Captive individuals always spend the night in boxes or holes in tree trunks, whenever these are available."

Hershkovitz (Notes)

No one knows how tamarins spend the night in the forest. From their behavior in captivity, it can be inferred that the family group or troop sleep huddled whether side by side or draped over each other, depending on the number of young and nature of the perch. In tall forest, tamarins may use tree holes, but the greater possibility is that the larger tree cavities would be preempted by *Aotus* or other nocturnal animals whose hours conflict with those of the early-to-bed and late-to-rise tamarins. The ecologically equivalent diurnal tree squirrels generally build nests on branches, but some species may use tree holes. Again, no one knows.

Primates carry their suckling young with them. They are not, therefore, bound to a particular sleeping site or to a stable nest. On the other hand, tamarins are habituated to a territorial routine that includes preferred sleeping, resting, and sunning sites. In second growth, where tree hollows of suitable size are virtually nonexistent, tamarins probably shelter among brambles, epiphytes, tangles of vines, and in the forks and on branches of the large trees.

Display

The expressions described here, and many more, can be seen any day in any laboratory colony composed of a dozen or more healthy, active bare-faced tamarins. Some experimentation, however, may be necessary to evoke certain traits.

Most of the observed acts are typically "monkey," many of them purely mammalian in a general sense. Others are characteristically callitrichid, a few peculiar to *Saguinus oedipus*. Some, peculiar to other callitrichid species, are mentioned, nevertheless, for comparison. Each act is part of a complex behavioral pattern. The meaning of an isolated act of piloerection, for example, may be interpreted one way, but the correlated posture, facial expression, vocalization, external stimulus, or a combination of these may point to an entirely different explanation. Again, the act in question may be accidental or incidental with no behavioral significance.

All observed traits are modified by life in captivity. Certain acts, including some performed ritualistically, possibly originated or at least became specialized in captivity. In many, if not most, cases, it is not the display but the stimulus that requires prime attention. Then again, mimicry, itself a typical monkey trait, involves displays related to the act and not the actor.

Display characters described here are divided into three categories, (1) facial expressions, (2) head movements, and (3) body postures. Coloration and pelage, both important in display, are primarily structural rather than behavioral characters, and except for incidental mention here are treated elsewhere in the text.

Facial Expressions

Brow Beetling or Lowering. "Eyebrow lowering [is] an important response in Ceboidea. We have even observed this in very young marmosets and it can be elicited by a like action on the part of the experimenter or another marmoset. The brows are lowered to such a marked degree that the eyes are almost obscured. It is a slow movement and is maintained for some time while the animal fixes its gaze. It does not resemble the rapid up and down movements of the brows seen in some other primates" (J. K. Hampton, Jr., Hampton, and Landwehr 1966, p. 281).

Grimacing. Drawing back corners of the closed or half-closed mouth. This feature is sometimes described as a grin (Andrew 1963), or as a laugh, and even misinterpreted as such (cf. Willig and Wendt 1970). The grimace is usually a hostile signal. The friendly grin or smile displayed in the form of a grimace by humans is likewise seen as a hostile sign by most, if not virtually all, wild animals.

Staring. Usually associated with an aggressive or threat posture.

Frowning. As used by authors, refers to some form of brow-beetling, grimacing, or both combined.

Gaping. Wide opening of the mouth as in yawning without drawing back the lips or vocalizing is a common mammalian act. In *Saguinus oedipus,* exposure of the fleshy pink tongue and buccal cavity contrasts with the black face. This display could, in certain circumstances, signal a desire for mouth grooming. Yawning itself, an involuntary stretching of the circumoral muscles, *reflects* boredom or fatigue.

"Rapid movements of the lower jaw without actual closure of the mouth is a variation always accompanied by a staccato cry given in an excited state" (J. K. Hampton, Jr., Hampton, and Landwehr 1966, p. 281).

Lip Smacking. The trait was observed by Epple (1967*b*, p. 51) in males of *Callithrix jacchus* and *C. argentata* when approaching conspecifics as friend or foe; not seen in *Saguinus oedipus.*

Lip Protrusion. Epple (1967*b,* pp. 49, 62) observed this trait used with lowering of the brows, in aggressive threat. Moynihan (1970, p. 58) says he did not notice this display in his animals.

Tonguing. Rhythmic protrusion and retraction of the tongue is common among callitrichids. The trait has been studied by Epple (1967*b,* pp. 50–51), J. K. Hampton, Jr., Hampton, and Landwehr (1966, p. 278) and Moynihan (1970, p. 56) in *Saguinus oedipus.*

Tonguing, according to the authors cited, is usually performed as a sign of recognition or greeting of conspecifics and others, including humans. It is also used by the male to show anger or curiosity, as a threat to conspecifics including mirror images of the subject himself, in courtship, and before, during, and after coitus. Adults of either sex may sometimes tongue each other's face or the face of their young, perhaps as a display of affection or care.

Intensive tonguing is often accompanied by head flicks. Moynihan (1970, p. 56) attempted to distinguish between tongue flicking correlated with feeding and vocalizing and the more deliberate form of tongue protrusions used in display. He conceded, however, that the two types are intergrading. The male, according to Moynihan, tongues more frequently than the female. J. K. Hampton, Jr., Hampton, and Landwehr (1966, p. 281) compare the use of tonguing with genital display for assertion of social and sexual status.

Display tonguing has been observed in many other primates, including lemurs, cebids, cercopithecids, and hylobatids.

Ear Twitching. Ear movements are greatly reduced in tamarins and possibly more so in *Saguinus oedipus* than in other callitrichids. The ear of *S. oedipus* is completely exposed, and its form alone has considerable display (and corresponding taxonomic) significance (cf. p. 102). Using movement as well, the ear could be a formidable communicator. Perkins (1969*a,* p. 13) observed that "when distressed or angered . . . alternate external ear muscles relax and contract causing the ears to elevate and depress asynchronously, gliding back and forth like the antennae of a cockroach."

Ear Flattening. Tamarin ears are incapable of flattening. Epple (1967*b*) mentions quick flattening and erection of ears as an aggressive threat signal in *Callithrix jacchus jacchus, C. j. geoffroyi* (= *leucocephala*), and *Callithrix argentata argentata.* In her English summary, Epple (1967*b,* p. 62, paragraph 3 from bottom) includes *Oedipomidas spixi* (= *Saguinus oedipus geoffroyi*) and *oedipus* among callitrichids who "flatten ears and ear-tufts" in defensive threat. This is clearly a lapsus (cf. 1967*b,* pp. 52, 62, last paragraph).

Head Movements

Rotation. The callitrichid head can turn nearly 180° in either direction from the front. The maneuver increases visual and auditory fields but, so far as is known, serves no display purpose.

Lowering. This is the "head down" of Moynihan (1970, p. 38). It may be performed in submission, one of the many probabilities or possibilities mentioned by Moynihan.

Flicking. Two or three swift movements to either side of the head and back, or from one side then to the other in alternation, is a feat performed by many kinds of mammals. As described by Moynihan (1970, p. 41) it is performed by tamarins mainly during interspecific and intraspecific encounters as a response to hostile activity. Other situations are mentioned. I have seen tamarins use head flicking for spitting out fruit seeds or foreign particles.

Body Postures

Confrontation. An aggressive stance in front of a potential enemy or stranger is a restricted definition of the term confrontation. The posture is assumed with four limbs firmly planted, body erect or half-crouched, face forward, eyes fixed on the intruder (cf. fig. X.72). According to J. K. Hampton, Jr., Hampton, and Landwehr (1966, p. 281), confrontation may be accompanied by a movement of head and body from side to side in quick jerks. With incdeasing excitement, the animal may stand on hind legs while the side-to-side shifting continues. Moynihan (1970, p. 36) elaborates on the same.

Back Arching. Back arching is a quadrupedal stance commonly associated with frightened cats. Its display by callitrichids, usually combined with stiff-legged walking, is as a defense threat. Epple (1967*b*) observed the posture in all species studied (*Callithrix jacchus jacchus, C. j. geoffroyi, C. argentata argentata,* and *Callimico goeldii*) but not in *Saguinus oedipus oedipus* or *S. o. geoffroyi.* Absence of the trait in the bare-face species has since been confirmed by Moynihan (1970, p. 40) and Willig and Wendt (1970). The former argues, however, that back arching became the bipedal stance in *Saguinus oedipus.*

Bipedal Stance (fig. X.82). The posture varies from a crouch to a nearly upright position and is usually accompanied by swaying. The bipedal stance displays hostility, aggressive intentions, or assertion of dominance. It may follow a confrontation, climax an attack of intimidation, or signal a leap. In the absence of aggressive situations, it may be a form of progression or used to increase the reach or enlarge the field of observation. It can also be a posture for more facile pivoting and defense of flanks and rear.

Moynihan (1970, pp. 40–41) studied stand-up postures executed by an aggressive male and believes the display has little significance. He suggests that some stand-up postures "probably are secondarily simplified or dedifferentiated [*sic*] remnants of the more elaborate [back] Arch [posture]. Such a process of simplification may be called 'de-ritualization.' "

In matter of fact, the bipedal stance is a specialization peculiar to *Saguinus oedipus* among callitrichids. There is nothing about it to suggest that it evolved from a back-arching posture or that it is a simplification, "dedifferentiation," or "de-ritualization" of anything characteristic of ancestral tamarins or platyrrhines, of whose behavior nothing is known.

Chest Display. Maximum exposure of the white chest is achieved by turning the elbows out and assuming the bipedal stance. The display is supposed to mean threat or intimidation. Epple (1967*b,* p. 54) questions whether it does have display function. Moynihan (1970, p. 59) believes, however, that when the underparts of *Saguinus*

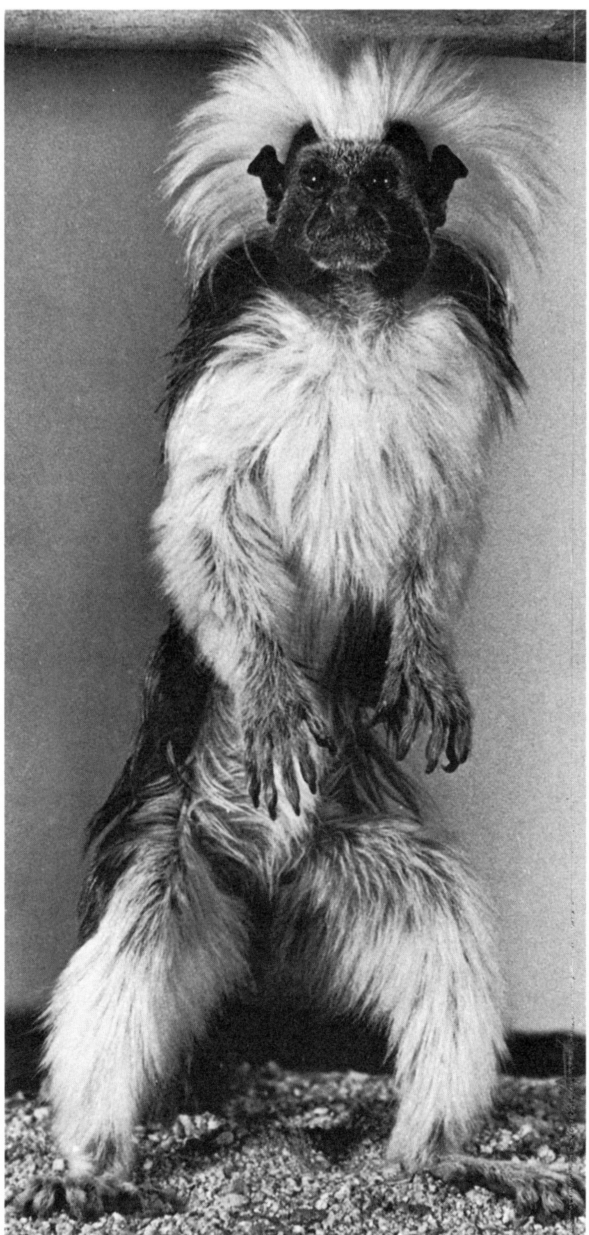

Fig. X.82. Cotton-top or White-plumed Bare-face *Saguinus oedipus oedipus,* in typical bipedal posture. (Photo courtesy of San Diego Zoo.)

oedipus geoffroyi became white, the animal evolved the bipedal stance to better display its new aggressive sign. Moynihan (1970, p. 40, and see above) had already mentioned that the white-fronted stance replaced the neutral colored arch. As he (1970, p. 59) explains, "one can easily imagine that such a behavioral pattern [the presumed ancestral arch] would become much less effective as soon as white coloration became intimidating and was concentrated on parts of the body which the pattern did not emphasize." Moynihan continues with the statement that "selection probably did not favor development of white on the back, because it would render individuals too nearly continually conspicuous, and therefore vulnerable, to predators, especially flying birds of prey."

It can easily be overlooked by students with insufficient material that the underparts of *Saguinus oedipus* are not consistently white. They range from white to yellowish in Panama, and yellowish to ochraceous mottled or patched with reddish brown in Colombia. The underparts of *Saguinus leucopus,* a member of the *oedipus* group, are entirely reddish brown. Insofar as known, its habits are like those of *S. oedipus,* but it has not been recorded whether it prefers the bipedal stance to the quadrupedal arch. Regarding coloration of the back, or upper parts generally, the trend appears to be toward white in all callitrichid lines. In the species *Saguinus oedipus,* the red nape of *S. o. geoffroyi* gives way in *S. o. oedipus* to a white crest that extends over the shoulders. The frontal half of *Saguinus bicolor bicolor* is as white dorsally as ventrally. Tendencies in the same direction are apparent in the other two races of *S. bicolor.* The heads and backs of *Saguinus fuscicollis melanoleucus, Callithrix argentata leucippe,* and *C. humeralifer chrysoleuca* are entirely white. The backs of other callitrichid species are also approaching the blanched state. In the black-backed members of the *Saguinus mystax* group, for example, the basal half of the hairs are already white or nearly so.

Colored upper parts in callitrichids are either concealing or more or less conspicuous, never neutral. Underparts, on the other hand, tend to be neutral in quadrupeds inasmuch as they are not ordinarily visible from above or below. Selection for preservation of color on underparts is therefore weak or nil, and the pigments tend to disappear much more rapidly than those of the upperparts. In the case of *Saguinus oedipus,* the white or yellowish chest could be regarded as display, but only because of its strong contrast with the black skin of face and ears. The display character of the bipedal stance and the arch depends primarily on the posture, reinforced by associated gestures and, possibly a supercharged release of pheromones. If coloration plays any part in bipedal postural display, it must be in the enhancement of visibility and sharpening of focus. For all the apparent correlation between display posture and coloration in some cases, each characteristic evolved independently, in most cases without correlation.

Swaying. A moderately slow side-to-side movement of the body is often performed during confrontation and the bipedal stance. The movement probably signals that the enemy has been seen and that the tamarin is prepared to leap to either side if attacked.

Freezing. This initial fright response to an alarming situation in a cage or trap from which flight is impossible has been observed in *Saguinus oedipus geoffroyi* by Moynihan (1970, p. 36). The objective of freezing is concealment through immobility. In the wild, monkeys usually hide by withdrawing from sight.

Playing Dead. This is the "lie-back" described by Moynihan (1970, p. 39). It was seen performed by a captive individual so harassed and beaten by its cage mate that its only escape lay in rolling over on its back and playing dead. With the opponent thrown off guard, the victim would spring up and start the chase anew. This display is improbable in the wild, where avenues of escape are open on all sides. Moynihan knows of no such behavior among other platyrrhines. I have never seen it among nonhuman primates but "playing possum" is a favored defense trait among mammals generally.

Genital Presentation. A 20-month-old, hand-raised female cotton-top in the San Diego monkey breeding facility presented her genitalia to a wild-caught experienced adult male the second day he was introduced into her cage.

As a rule, female callitrichids present their genitals to males as a signal of sexual receptivity and for sexual stimulation. Males of *Callithrix* and *Cebuella* present to males or their surrogates routinely for the purpose of intimidation. Perhaps male cotton-tops accomplish the intent or effect of genital presentation by confrontation or bipedal stance.

Piloerection

Piloerection of one or more areas of the hairy coat is a response to excitement. The stronger and more sudden the stimulus, the more extensive the erection is likely to be. Head and tail tip are the most sensitive fields and respond first. Hairs of the back are next, followed by those of the outer sides of limbs. Hairs of ventral or inner surfaces are hardly, if at all, affected.

Certain objects, for example, food or sexual odors, stimulate to the degree that the subject needs them. Others like the sudden appearance of a feared predator evoke a violent reaction from a healthy subject. A mild stimulus may involve only hairs of crown or tail tip. Stronger stimuli also involve nape, entire mantle, entire tail, the entire dorsal surface, and so on.

Moynihan (1970, p. 52) recognized several localized patterns of piloerection and suggests meanings for each. His terminology is borrowed from the ornithological literature, and perhaps his behavioral interpretations as well. The types follow.

General Ruffle:
Entire pelage raised as a threat, often in conjunction with threat postures and vocalizations.

Crown Raising:
Erection of wedge of white hairs on forepart of head and reddish nape or mantle behind; less hostile display than general ruffle.

Crown Smoothing:
Smoothing down or flattening of white coronal hairs while rufous nape hairs and remaining pelage of body remain normal; the inverse of crown raising; performed in retreat, escape, or defensive movements and as appeasement display.

[Note: Crown smoothing as described by Moynihan implies the mediation of depressor muscles the existence of which have not been demonstrated. The arrectores pilorum muscles attached to the hair follicles, are responsible for the erections—P. H.]

Rufous Ruffle:
Raising of reddish nape hairs only; display of friendliness, sexual interest, or appeasement.

Tail Ruffling:
Raising of hairs of distal portion of tail; used in reaction to awareness of potential predator and as retreat or escape signals; one of most common displays, often used in combination with twittering.

Tail Fluffing:
Variant of tail ruffling.

Tail Smoothing:
Probably another display.

Marking

Epple 1967*b*, p. 55 (*oedipus, geoffroyi*)

All species observed (*Callithrix jacchus, C. argentata, Saguinus oedipus,* and *Callimico goeldii*) mark all objects regularly and often by pressing the circumgenital glands against them and rubbing back and forth. Even the fur of cage mates is marked. *Saguinus oedipus* also marks with suprapubic and sternal glands, especially when excited. That females mark more frequently than males could not be verified, but higher-ranking members of each sex mark more than the lower ranks.

Self-anointing or perfuming for the purpose of seducing or imprinting a sexual partner is practiced by the female. Epple (1967*b*, p. 62) relates that [her English translation] "the female curls up her tail and saturates it with urine and the secretion of the circumgenital scent glands. The male sniffs the female's tail intensively."

Mallinson 1965, p. 139

"The branches in the cages are changed fairly frequently when they become too dirty, and they are then re-arranged. The marmosets and tamarins spend a considerable amount of time marking out their territories in these branches by rubbing their genitalia on certain portions of the bark. The males appear to do this more often than the females. The fairly frequent changing of the branches is consequently a form of occupational therapy for, as soon as fresh branches are put in, all the inmates of the cage remark their territories."

J. K. Hampton, Jr., Hampton, and Landwehr 1966, pp. 278–89 (*oedipus*)

A hand-raised young female given freedom of the Hampton's house and yard "showed an increase in a 'marking' behavior wherein the genitals are rubbed over objects and surfaces and, frequently, cage mates. Although glandular secretions, from the moist surface of this tissue, may be the primary substance deposited, we were able clearly to observe a drop or two of urine being presented just before an object was to be marked. Perhaps the urine acted as an extender.

"Marked objects carry no odor which we could readily detect although this may vary among different species. In no instance has any behavior resembling foot marking been observed.

We have noticed that marking by females is the rule. Males may mark occasionally but in no way with the persistence and frequency seen with females. . . . Marking may serve primarily as a territorial signal rather than a sexual one."

Benirschke and Richart 1963, p. 75 (*oedipus*)

The vulvar odor emanating from the very large number of sebaceous glands in *Saguinus oedipus* is perceptible to man but not as strongly as the odor from *Saguinus mystax* or *Callithrix jacchus* and *Leontopithecus rosalia.*

Moynihan 1970, p. 18 (*geoffroyi*)

"Rubbing [of genitoanal glands] is produced by hostile motivation. Probably, it is produced by simultaneous activation of both attack and escape tendencies." [It is altogether possible that the animals were not in the least so motivated (cf. fig. X.83)—P. H.]

Vocalizations

Enders 1935, p. 440 (*geoffroyi*)

"Many times attention is drawn to these groups [of tamarins in the wild] by the chatter of the animals as they scold, and the noise made as they scurry from limb to limb apparently attempting to secure a better view. Even when not disturbed, the larger bands do considerable calling in a very high pitched, squeaky tone, possibly to maintain communication with the others of the party. Such bands are composed of animals of both sexes."

Hershkovitz (Field Notes)

All callitrichids have a wide repertory of shrill calls, and flute like notes, and some trill or warble like canaries. They often vocalize with closed mouth, and many of their sounds are inaudible to the human ear.

Saguinus oedipus also vocalizes with mouth closed, but the sounds thus produced are weak. Trills are made with mouth open, the vibrato being produced in the throat and not by the tongue as in *Callithrix humeralifer* or with the lower jaw as in *Saguinus fuscicollis* and *S. nigricollis*.

Graetz 1968, p. 34 (*geoffroyi*)

The cry *titiih* is used by animals separated from each other. Lost or abandoned individuals sometimes cry for hours. The call is rarely used between animals in a group.

Edwards 1751, p. 195 (*oedipus*)

"What is very wonderful in this little animal is, that it hath a soft, whistling note, something resembling the singing of a canary-bird."

Andrew 1963, pp. 45–46

"The main type of vocalisation in all these genera [*Cebuella, Callithrix, Saguinus, Leontopithecus, Callimico*] is the twitter. At low intensity these [*sic*] are given singly; at higher intensities in rapid bouts, which join together at their end into a long squeak with steady pitch (e.g. *Oedipomidas oedipus, Leontideus rosalia*). In the highest intensity vocalisation of all, the fundamental broadens into a wide band of sound producing a very high rasping screech (*Leontideus rosalia, Cebuella pygmaea, Oedipomidas oedipus, O. spixi*). Such screeches are given when threatened or attacked by a superior, but they are also given when approaching a fellow, for example to share food which he is eating, or when trying to pass a barrier in order to groom a human friend."

Andrew 1963, p. 47 (*geoffroyi*)

"*a.* Twitters. Series of steeply descending squeaks (F[undamental]: typically 12 to 9 Kc. (c. 0.02 sec.). Later ones may be lower and have a final prolongation at 4 Kc. N[oise]: 0]." [These calls are identical with Moynihan's "twitters."]

"*b.* Rasping screech. This develops out of a squeak by the quite sudden broadening of the fundamental. Both this and twitters are accompanied by marked grins while attempting to reach a human friend to groom him." [This is Moynihan's "Long Rasp."]

Epple 1968, pp. 25, 30 (*oedipus, geoffroyi*)

Juvenal Contact Calls

Te, similar to *phee* call of *Callithrix jacchus* (q.v., p. 564) but shorter, louder; used in response to discomfort of low intensity.

Tsik, used in same situations as above but of higher intensities.

Adult Calls

1. Contact Calls
    - *a. Monosyllabic Calls Given in Close Visual Contact:* Short high-pitched *te* calls; used between undisturbed group members in close contact.
    - *b. Monosyllabic Calls in Loose Visual Contact:* High pitched *te* calls varying in intensity, duration, and frequency modulation (25–40 kilocycles); used in loose visual contact when disturbed or slightly frightened.
    - *c. Monosyllabic Calls Given in Isolation:* Notes singly and in series of 2–3 with rising intensity; lower frequency modulation (1.5–2.5 kc) than loose visual contact calls; used in visual isolation with intensity increasing as isolation and excitement increase, the frequencies ranging to 24 kc.
2. *Trills Given in High Excitement.* Sequences of 2–25 loud notes like rolling canary trill; frequencies to 52 kc; very contagious; used as contact, mobbing, and alarm call in response to potential danger.

    [Trills are not produced by *Callithrix jacchus.*]
3. *Squeals Given in Submission.* Similar to juvenal and adult squeals of *jacchus* (q.v., p. 564); used by subordinate when approached or threatened by superior.
4. *Chatters Given When Angry.* Series of short, low-pitched notes similar to "defensive threat chatter" of *jacchus* (q.v., p. 564).
5. *Mobbing Calls. Tsik* calls intermingled with trills; used when mobbing a predator; intensity directly related to level of excitement; frequency range 2–60 or more kc.

6. *Warning Calls.* High-pitched whistle as in *jacchus;* used in response to sudden appearance of flying birds or other predators.

Moynihan 1970, pp. 21, 62, 70 (*geoffroyi*)

Adult calls of *Saguinus oedipus geoffroyi* are arranged in three groups. The calls of each are considered intergrading components of a single complex pattern. Calls described by Epple (1968, and outlined above) are included [in brackets] under the heading of the equivalent vocalization according to Moynihan's homologizations.

1. Plaintive Notes
   a. *Long whistles.* Loud, plaintive, prolonged sound uttered singly or in series of 2–4 notes; used as long distance signal by individuals separated from group and in response to separated individual, in territorial defense, confrontations with invaders.

      ["Monosyllabic calls given in isolation," Epple 1968, p. 26.]

   b. *Twitters.* Moderately soft, short, high-pitched notes uttered in series of 4–10 notes; the single note uttered as short whine has plaintive quality of long whistle; used in low intensity reaction to potential predators, intraspecies disputes as alarms, greeting among captive animals.

      ["Monosyllabic calls in loose visual contact," Epple 1968, p. 26.]

2. Sharp Notes
   a. *Trills.* Moderately loud series of 7–12 rapidly sounded short notes; include loud ultrasonic components up to at least 24 kc; used in reaction to potential predators and other hostile situations.

      ["Trills given in high excitement," Epple 1968, p. 27.]

   b. *Loud Sharp Notes.* Variable series of *tsit* sounds or single loud, sharp notes but louder and with higher ultrasonic components; extremely contagious; used in reactions to potential predators, intraspecific disputes, escape movements.

      [? "Mobbing calls," Epple 1968, p. 29.]
      [? "Warning calls," Epple 1968, p. 30.]

   c. *Soft Sharp Notes.* Single or short variable series of *tsit* notes basically identical with loud sharp notes or individual trill notes; includes ultrasonic components up to 44 kc; use not certainly known, heard infrequently in captivity, too soft to be heard in wild.
   d. *Sneezing Sharp Notes.* Single note sneezelike or *tschuck* sound. "It seems likely that both Sneezing and Soft Sharp Notes subserve much the same range(s) of functions," but Moynihan does not say what the functions are in either case.

3. Rasping
   a. *Long Rasps.* Loud, harsh, prolonged screech; used in violent intraspecific bodily clashes, hostile chases, and capture.
   b. *Broken Rasps.* Rapid series of short, harsh notes like segments of long rasp; used rarely in same situations as long rasps.

      ["Chatters given when angry," Epple 1968, p. 29.]

Young may utter all adult calls when motivated by the same stimuli. However, the following two are typical juvenal vocalizations.

1. *Squeaks.* Single notes usually uttered in short series of monotones; used in situations of distress or discomfort such as hunger, thirst.
2. *Rasp.* Loud, harsh rasp like adult long rasp with notes shorter, pitch more uniform; used in same situations as squeaks but with stimuli more intense.

   ["Squeals given in submission," Epple 1968, p. 28.]

Juvenal calls are retained longer and voiced more frequently by captive-born tamarins than by wild-living conspecifics. Moynihan labels these *persistent juvenal calls.*

Hershkovitz (Notes)

Moynihan is critical of Epple's (1968) account of callitrichid vocalizations, particularly her section on *Saguinus oedipus geoffroyi* (Epple's *Oedipomidas spixi*). One aspect of Epple's interpretations that may have presented difficulties is, as Moynihan (1970, p. 70) points out, her extrapolations from the vocalization pattern of *Callithrix jacchus.* The described calls of this species, however, formed the basis for comparative studies of vocalizations superior to any yet offered for platyrrhines.

Real difficulties and misunderstandings can easily arise from the fact that (1) the science and art of describing vocalizations of nonhuman primates are crude, (2) the subjects studied by Moynihan and Epple were caged animals maintained in radically different environments, the first in large outdoor pens in the Barro Colorado Island forest, the second in indoor-outdoor cages of the Zoological Institute of the Museum of Frankfurt am Main, Germany, (3) hypothetical studies by a third party of calls uttered by a third set of tamarins, in a third environment, would result in a third set of variables and probably a number of calls not previously heard or recognized.

Tail Movements

Hershkovitz (Field Notes)

When the wild, free animal sits on a branch its tail hangs limply straight down, often with tip curved, or is draped over a branch. When the animal runs or climbs, the tail may be whipped or swished around, or it just seems to follow the rest of the body. At Curulao (29) I observed a captive cotton-top at rest. At times, its tail was brought forward and wrapped around the shoulder. At other times the tail was tightly coiled into three rings and held alongside the thigh.

In a female cotton-top a few days old kept in my camp in Las Campanas (46), the tail would coil to form a half loop or coil into three rings. There was no grip or spring in the coiled part of the tail and during the few days the animal lived the tip of the tail was not seen to curl around objects.

J. K. Hampton, Jr. 1964, p. 242 (*oedipus*)

There "is a characteristic procedure for rolling the tail when seated. The tail is brought forward, rolled, and brought under one leg so that it is in midline and is held in this tight roll for sitting (fig. X.83). While not truly prehensile, the tip sometimes rolls around a cage bar or other small object."

Epple 1967*b*, p. 45

Tail used only for contact holding and balance. Prehensibility does not occur in the postembryonic development.

Moynihan 1970, pp. 45–52 (*geoffroyi*)

"The tail probably is the most 'expressive' organ of *S. geoffroyi*. It can be held and moved in many ways, to convey different messages."

The positions of the tail and their significance as interpreted by Moynihan, are abstracted below, with comments added.

1. *Tail extending horizontally straight out* or S-shaped with subject running or leaping.

Comment: No display significance is attached to this tail position.

2. *Tail hanging straight down* with subject standing or sitting. Indicates "individual is not alarmed but is not prepared to relax."

Comment: The totally relaxed state of the tail more likely suggests that the subject is relaxed. In any case, a hanging tail serves for dissipation of body heat on a warm, humid day.

3. *Tail looped forward and upward* between legs or alongside body. The position indicates subject is prepared to rest or sleep. It is also "a means of concealing a potentially dangerous sign stimulus from individuals of other species."

Comment: I have seen tail looping performed by individuals not prepared to rest or sleep. The animal covers itself with the tail for warmth and possibly for the feeling of security conveyed by the embrace of its own tail or that of a mate alongside.

Tail concealment as an object of looping is extremely doubtful. The tail did not become the longest and most conspicuous extremity of the body for the purpose of being concealed.

4. *Tail forward.* It is "performed by an individual while sitting, standing, or walking. The tail hangs downward, but is inclined forward and more or less curved at the tip. The actual angle of inclination and degree of curving differ in different circumstances." The tail positions indicate alarm.

Comment: My impression of this varying tail position, after having watched hundreds of subjects, hundreds of times, is that it is mostly related to maintaining the animal's equilibrium. It would be impossible to determine which, if any, "tail-forward" movements are designed to display the fears or frustrations in the life of a tamarin.

5. *Tip coiling.* Like tail-forward, but the distal one-fourth to one-half of the tail is coiled on itself; performed by subjects "unmistakably alarmed"; said to be rare in the wild but common in captivity where individuals are crowded.

Fig. X.83. Cotton-top tamarin, *Saguinus oedipus oedipus,* with coiled tail pressed against glandular sexual skin; the annointed tail is used for marking.

Comment: I have sat motionless watching at close range up to 6 tamarins sitting side by side on a bare tree limb in the large alligator enclosure in Chicago's Lincoln Park Zoo. All stared at me intently as one. Collectively they executed the entire repertory of sitting tail movements. Yet, in no two were the tails held or moved in the same way or at the same time except by chance.

6. *Upward tail-coiling* (fig. X.83). Entire tail is coiled tightly, brought forward between legs, and pressed against belly. Upward tail coiling is performed by both sexes, most frequently by females, particularly the sexually unsatisfied or frustrated. The performance of tail-coiling is said to be attractive to males, but the completed act of "sitting with tail coiled underneath the body may indicate receptivity and nothing else [Moynihan 1970, p. 49]." Moynihan had previously remarked (p. 48) that "the tail becomes very inconspicuous indeed as soon as it is passed underneath the body, even less conspicuous than when it is looped."

Comment: The practice of holding the coiled tail between the legs and pressed against the genitalia and lower half of the belly is common to callitrichids and *Callimico*. I have observed it in young and old of both sexes in many species of all genera except *Leontopithecus*. The tail may be coiled into a single large or small loop or into two or three loose or tight coils. The tail is not kept coiled for long, but is relaxed and recoiled repeatedly. The animal may rest, sleep, or travel short distances with the coiled tail projecting behind, hanging down or brought forward and pressed against the underparts. The tail in this position is conveniently disposed for an animal resting or sleeping in crowded quarters, for grooming, and, very commonly, for tripodal support.

The upward-coiled tail of adults indicates at certain times sexual arousal, as suggested by Moynihan, but the posture is not always an invitation to copulation, if needed it serves that purpose. I have seen females, and less often males, intermittently brush the glandular genital and sexual skin with a few light up and down strokes of the coiled tail. The anointed tail can serve for marking. It is also probable that the presumed titillation caused by the caressing and stroking could prime and maintain sexual motivation and reinforce sexual satisfaction during coitus. The action occurs at any time of the day among caged animals with nothing else to do. Under certain conditions of strong external stimuli during sexual deprivation, the female in estrus may actually employ the coiled tail in masturbation. The hand is also used for the same purpose.

Whatever the specialization, the primary or primitive function of the callitrichid tail, as in all long, nonprehensile-tailed mammals, is maintaining equilibirum.

Thermoregulation

Internal control of tamarin body temperature has not been investigated. All that can be reported here is the tolerance of the captive animal to environmental temperatures in the United States and western Europe. The mean daily extremes year round in the natural habitat of tamarins (genus *Saguinus*) are about the same (roughly 55°–95° F) as those of summer temperatures near sea level in the middle latitudes north of the equator.

J. K. Hampton, Jr., Hampton, and Landwehr 1966

"[We] kept a large cage in the backyard of [our] home [in New Orleans] during the entire year. The only protection given was a tarpaulin about the cage as a windbreak plus a 60 W light bulb beneath a wooden nest box and a 250 W infra-red reflector placed to shine along a perch. These measures were provided only when the temperature dropped to about 45° F. The coldest weather experienced was approximately 18° F. The animals developed a fuller, richer pelage and, despite obvious dislike of the cold, maintained excellent health. . . . This experience does not indicate that low temperatures are desirable or even tolerable in the crowded conditions of an indoor colony. Respiratory difficulties are more frequent at temperatures below 80° F. Below 70° F huddling and other subjective signs of reduced activity and increased discomfort are apparent among animals in small cages. Likewise, without the freedom of movement of a large cage, higher temperatures are not well tolerated. We have observed a great number of animals kept in small holding cages in an outdoor shaded compound. Whenever the temperature reached 98°–102° F prostration and sometimes death ensued. Even the animals in our large outdoor cage seek shade when the temperature is around 85° F and when it is around 95° F they spend most of their time in a characteristic sprawling posture along the axes of perches."

J. K. Hampton, Jr. 1973

Diurnal body temperatures of a cotton-top (*Saguinus oedipus oedipus*) were measured with a sensor placed at the tympanic membrane in a controlled environment with temperature 27° ± 1° C and daily cycle of 12 light and 12 dark hours. The results were "altogether similar to that [*sic*] reported by Morrison and Simões [see this volume, p. 566] for *Callithrix jacchus*. A change of about 4° C was characteristic and showed the distinct biphase form during daytime with a low point near noon." Actual body temperatures were not recorded in this paper.

Wendt 1964 (*oedipus*)

The family of cotton-tops kept in my home in Baden-Baden, Germany lived indoors at "normal" room temperatures but also enjoyed being outdoors during the winter on sunny days.

Fox 1925, p. 534

Minimum-maximum rectal temperatures of one individual in the Philadelphia Zoo is recorded as 38.6°–39.6°.

Heart Rate

J. K. Hampton, Jr. 1973

Heart rates (beats/minute) of two adult male *Saguinus oedipus oedipus* maintained in a controlled environment of 27° ± 1° C and a daily cycle of 12 light and 12 dark hours showed an abrupt rise from near 200 between 0500 and 0600 hours (dark) to over 250 between 0800 and 0900 hours (light), a difference of about 55 beats/minute. The rate dropped rapidly between 1700 and 1800 (light) from about 235 beats to about 200 beats at 2300 hours. The figures are estimated from the chart prepared by Hampton (1973, p. 341).

It is interesting that the heart rate of *S. o. oedipus* averaged about 35 beats faster than that of the smaller (by about 100 g) *S. fuscicollis* used in the same experiment (cf. p. 683).

77 Genus *Leontopithecus* Lesson, Lion-tamarins

Synonymic History

Leontopithecus Lesson, 1840, *Species des mammifères: Bimanes et quadrumanes . . .* , pp. 184, 200—subgenus of *Midas;* included species *marikina* Lesson [= *Simia rosalia* Linnaeus], *fuscus* Lesson [new name for *Simia leonina* Humboldt (preoccupied) = *Saguinus fuscicollis fuscus* Lesson], *ater* Lesson [new name for *Jacchus chrysopygus* Mikan], *ater* Var. A [= *Midas chrysomelas* Kuhl], *ater* Var. B [= *Midas chrysomelas* Kuhl], *ater* Jeune age 1 [= *Midas mystax* Spix, a *Saguinus*], *ater* Jeune age 2 [= *Midas nigricollis* Spix, a *Saguinus*]. Gray, 1870, *Cat. monkeys, lemurs, and fruit-eating bats, Brit. Mus.,* p. 64—characters; included species, *rosalia, chrysomelas.* Pocock, 1917, *Ann. Mag. Nat. Hist.* 20(8):255—type, *marikina* Lesson = *rosalia* Linnaeus; genus listed in synonymy of *Leontocebus* Wagner for lion-maned marmosets. De Beaux, 1917, *Giorn. Morph. Uomo, Primati* 1:100—genus; characters; comparisons; included species, *rosalia.* Hershkovitz, 1970, *Amer. J. Phys. Anthrop.* 32(3):378, footnote 1—*Leontopithecus* Lesson 1840, earliest available generic name for lion-tamarins. Hershkovitz, 1972, *Int. Zoo Yearb.* 12:4—classification. Warland, 1972, *Int. Zoo Yearb.* 12:17—conservation; proposal for establishment of semicaptive breeding center in Brazil. Coimbra-Filho and Mittermeier, 1972, in *Saving the lion marmoset,* ed. D. D. Bridgewater Wild Animal Propagation Trust Golden Lion marmoset Conference p. 7—taxonomic review. Coimbra-Filho and Mittermeier, 1973, *Primates* 14(1):47—distribution; ecology; behavior; reproduction.

Marikina Gray, 1843, *List. Spec. Mamm. Coll. Brit. Mus.,* pp. xviii, 15—subgenus of *Jacchus* E. Geoffroy; generic name attributed to Mikan probably a lapsus for Lesson cited (p. 15) in combination *"Leontopithecus Marikina* Lesson, [= *L. rosalia rosalia* Linnaeus]," type by tautonomy; generic name preoccupied by *Marikina* Lesson, 1840, for bare-face tamarins [= *Saguinus*]. Reichenbach, 1862, *Die vollständigste Naturgeschichte der Affen,* p. 7—included species: *rosalia, chrysomelas, albifrons* [a *Callithrix*], *chrysopygus*; type species *Simia rosalia* Linnaeus, selected by Pocock, 1917 (*Ann. Mag. Nat. Hist.* 20[8]: 255). Elliot, 1913, *A review of the Primates,* 1:209—part, subgenus of *Leontocebus.*

Leontocebus Elliot (part, not Wagner), 1913, *A review of the Primates* 1:xxxv, 194—*Hapale chrysomelas* Wied Neuwied designated type [but see prior designation of *Simia leonina* [= *Saguinus fuscicollis fuscus*] by Miller, 1912]. Pocock, 1917, *Ann. Mag. Nat. Hist.* 20(8):255—classification; included species: *rosalia, chrysomelas, leoninus* [= *Saguinus fuscicollis fuscus* Lesson]; characters. Cabrera, 1917, *Trab. Mus. Nac. Cienc. Nat. Madrid, Ser. Zool.,* no. 31, p. 32—*L. chrysomelas* Wied-Neuwied designated type; characters. Pocock, 1920, *Proc. Zool. London* 1920:92—external characters; comparisons. Thomas, 1922, *Ann. Mag. Nat. Hist.* 9(9):198—review. Sonntag, 1921, *Proc. Zool. Soc. London,* pp. 520, 757—anatomy of tongue; classification. J. Anthony, 1946, *Ann. Sci. Nat., Paris, Zool.* ser. 11, 8:8—brain morphology. Hershkovitz, 1949, *Proc. U.S. Nat. Mus.* 98:410, 423—classification; characters. Della Serra, 1951, *Papeis Avulsos Rio de Janeiro* 10:147, 7 figs. (dentition)—characters of incisors; systematics (subgeneric separation of *L. chrysomelas* indicated). W. C. Osman Hill, 1955, *Primates* 2:38, 40, 41, 45—musculature. Osman Hill, 1957, *Primates* 3:25, 53, 81, 95, 98, 102, 108, 119, 120–22, 126, 129, 136, 137, 140–42, 144, 146–49, 151–61, 163, 166–68, 172, 175, 187–93, 195–200, 212, 214, 248, 253, 309, 315, 316, 322—anatomy; taxonomy; distribution; reproduction; development; behavior. Osman Hill, 1958, *Primatologia* 3(1):644, 681—external genitalia Platzer, 1960, *Primatologia* 3(2):306—blood vessels. Starck and Schneider, 1960, *Primatologia* 3(2):423, figs. 42, 61 *h* (larynx)—anatomy of larynx. Remane, 1960, *Primatologia* 3(2):208, 816, 832, fig. 27 *a, c* ($m^{1\text{-}2}$)—dentition. Lasinski, 1960, *Primatologia* 2(1), Lief. 5:59, 60—external ear. Biegert, 1961, *Primatologia* 2(1), Lief. 3:5, 185, fig. 39 (dermatoglyphs of hand, feet)—palmar and plantar surfaces of cheiridia. Rohen, 1962, *Primatologia* 2(1), Lief. 6:8, 77, 79, 99, 116, 130, 142, 146, 150, 158, fig. 19 (optic nerve), fig. 25 (iris), fig. 31*d* (ciliary processes)—comparative eye anatomy.

Leontideus Cabrera, 1956, *Neotropica, Buenos Aires* 2(8):52—new name for *Leontocebus* of authors not Wagner. Osman Hill, 1960, *Primates,* 4:6, 44, 67, 149, 248, 256, 350—anatomical comparisons with Cebidae. Erikson, 1963, *Symp. Zool. Soc. London* 10:143—locomotory type (springer). Napier and Napier, 1967, *Handbook of living primates,* p. 197—morphology; ecology; behavior; species; classification; bibliography. Coimbra-Filho, 1969, *An. Acad. Brasil. Cienc.* 41(suppl.):29—review (characters, distribution, taxonomy). Coimbra-Filho, 1970, *Rev. Brasil. Biol.* 30(2):249—characters; distribution; habits; taxonomy. Kuntz and Meyers, 1972, *Int. Zoo Yearb.* 12:61—parasites.

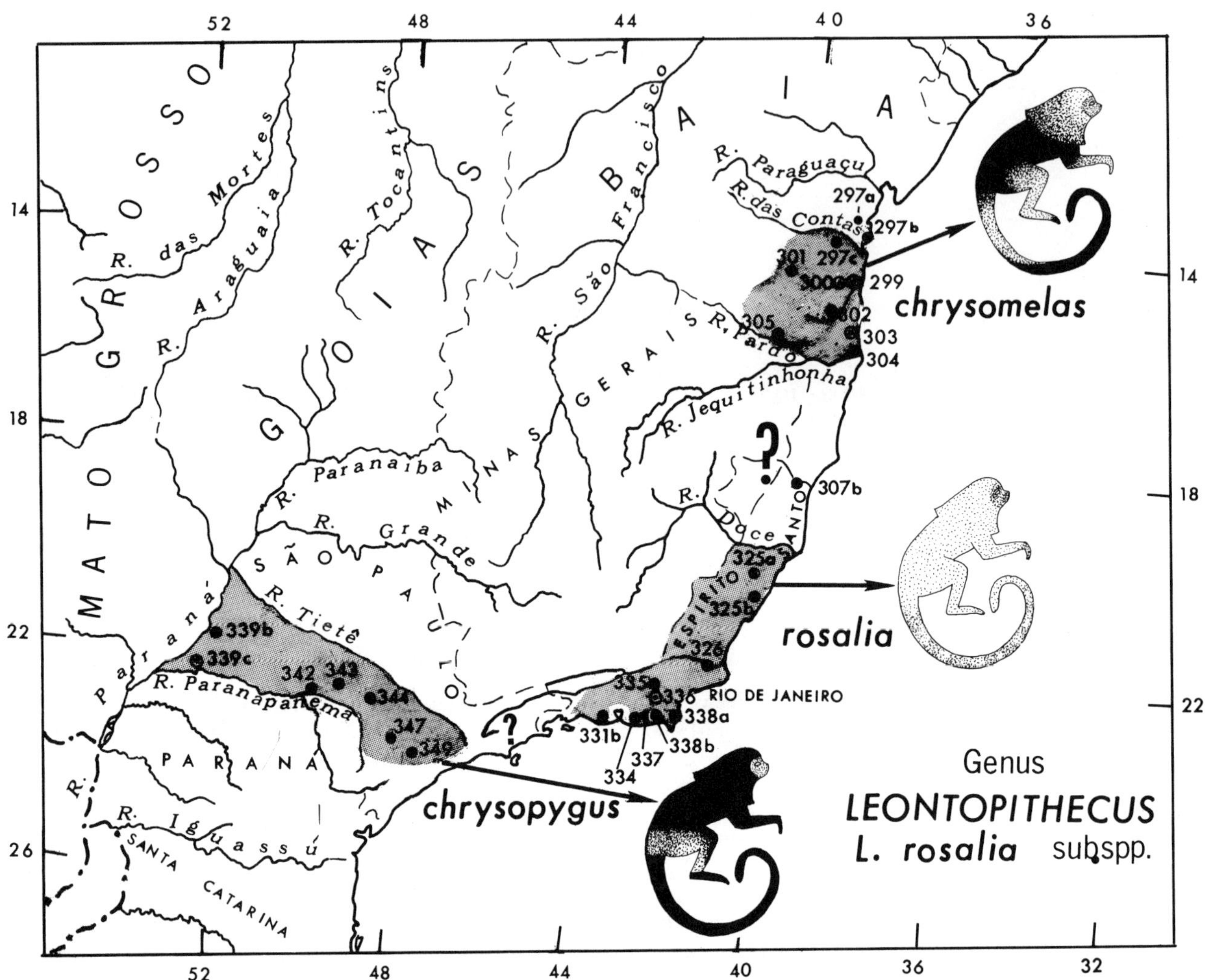

Fig. XI.1. Fragmented range (*shaded*) of *Leontopithecus rosalia.* Shaded areas include localities (*numbered dots*) where each of the three recognized races is known to have occurred within the last two centuries. Circled dots are the localities where representatives of each race are still extant. Color pattern of *chrysomelas, rosalia,* and *chrysopygus* shown diagrammatically. Numbers explained in gazetteer (p. 918).

Type and Only Species. Leontopithecus marikina Lesson = *Simia rosalia* Linnaeus, subsequent designation by Pocock (1917, *Ann. Mag. Nat. Hist.* ser. 20, vol. 8, p. 255).

Distribution (figs. VII.1; XI.1)

In historic times, the lowland rain forests of eastern Brazil in the States of Bahia, Espírito Santo, Guanabara, Rio de Janeiro, and São Paulo; now extinct in Espírito Santo and Guanabara but reintroduced in Guanabara for breeding (cf. p. 828).

Taxonomic History

Leontopithecus Lesson, 1840, proposed as a subgenus of *Midas,* was distinguished by its "Pelage très long sur le cou et le dos, formant crinière longue; favoris et barbe épais; oreilles cachées sous les poils: *Marikina, Leontopithecus.*" The name, description, and use of the vernacular term marikina apply only to lion-tamarins. The originally included species were *L. marikina* [new name for *rosalia* Linnaeus], *fuscus* [new name for *leonina* Humboldt], *ater* [new name for *chrysopygus* Mikan] *ater* variété A and *ater* variété B [= *Hapale chrysomelas* Kuhl , *Midas mystax* Spix and *Midas nigricollis* Spix. The type specimens of the last two were mistakenly regarded as immature lion-tamarins with "crinière non developpée."

The original composition of *Leontopithecus* Lesson was very much like that of *Leontocebus* Wagner, and the concept of the type of each genus was probably the same, but no type species was designated at the time for either. Both names were published in 1840, but only *Leontocebus* gained wide acceptance.

In 1862, Reichenbach (p. 6) restricted *Leontopithecus* to *leonina* Humboldt (= *fuscus* Lesson) but this action in itself does not constitute a type designation (*International Code of Zoological Nomenclature* [1961, 1964: Art. 67, (c), Art. 69]). Gray (1870, pp. 64–65), on the other hand, used *Leontopithecus* solely for the lion-tamarins *rosalia* and *chrysomelas,* but he too failed to specify a type in the strict meaning of the Code. Finally, Pocock (1917, p. 255) in his classification of callitrichids treated *Leontopithecus* Lesson as a junior synonym of *Leontocebus,* with "type *Marikina* Less[on] = *rosalia* Linn[aeus]." Since my short note (1970) on the availability of *Leontopithecus* for lion-tamarins, the name has returned to general usage. The status of each of other generic names proposed or used for lion-tamarins is summarized below.

Leontocebus Wagner, 1840, with type *Simia leonina* Humboldt (= *Saguinus fuscicollis fuscus* Lesson) designated by Miller (1912, p. 280), is a junior synonym of *Saguinus* Hoffmannsegg, 1807. Miller's prior designation of the type species invalidates selection of the lion-tamarin by Elliot (1913*a,* p. 194) and use in that sense by Pocock (1917).

Marikina Reichenbach, 1862, proposed for lion-tamarins, is a junior homonym of *Marikina* Lesson, 1840, for the bare-faced tamarin, *Saguinus bicolor* Spix.

Leontocebus of Elliot, 1913, and later authors (not Wagner, 1840 = *Saguinus* Hoffmannsegg, 1807) was widely used for lion-tamarins and tamarins in general by some authors, and for lion-tamarins in particular by others. I have already noted (above) that *Leontocebus* of authors, not Wagner, must be replaced by *Leontopithecus* Lesson.

Leontideus Cabrera, 1956, with type *Simia rosalia* Linnaeus, was proposed as a substitute for *Leontocebus* of authors, not Wagner, hence is a junior synonym of *Leontopithecus.* Cabrera (1956, p. 49) showed that *Simia leonina* Humboldt, subsequently designated type of *Leontocebus* Wagner, was the saddle-back tamarin, *Saguinus fuscicollis fuscus* Lesson, and not a lion-tamarin as was generally supposed. In rejecting *Leontocebus,* Cabrera wrongly threw out *Leontopithecus* with it because, he erroneously believed, it had the same type species. The name *Leontideus* Cabrera for lion-tamarins has had little currency.

Systematic Position

Leontopithecus has no near relatives within the Callitrichidae. It needs no comparisons with *Cebuella* and *Callithrix,* and its greater resemblances to *Saguinus* appear to be parallelisms associated with the size class to which both belong. The unrelated *Callimico* is even nearer in size, and resemblances in some respects are even greater. The prominent, ear-concealing mane, more complex external genitalia, and more advanced molarization of the cheek teeth are examples in point. On the other hand, the cerebral hemispheres of *Leontopithecus* have not advanced beyond *Callithrix* grade, whereas those of *Callimico* are tamarinlike in complexity.

The disparate assortment of resemblances and differences at varying evolutionary levels emphasizes the independent origin of each of the groups under discussion. Presumably, *Leontopithecus* diverged early from the ancestral callitrichid stock. Its evolution then proceeded along lines parallel to that of tamarins but at different rates for the various parts that make lion-tamarins unique.

Diagnostic Characters

Size:

Lion-tamarins are the largest and most highly specialized callitrichids.

Integument:

The whorled mane of *Leontopithecus* and its developmental pattern are distinctive (figs. XI.2, 18, 24, 28).

External Genitalia:

The acorn-shaped glans penis, without parallel among callitrichids, most nearly resembles that of *Homo* or *Callimico* (figs. III.28, 29; XI.11). The baculum (fig. III.25) is correspondingly distinct. Form of the female external genitalia also follows suit in its greater resemblance to those of *Homo* and *Callimico* than to those of related callitrichids (figs. III.21–23; XI.12).

Ear:

External ear hidden by mane in adult, exposed in juvenal, auricle rounded in outline, more cartilagenous than in other callitrichids, the borders more rolled, bursa usually better developed. For details see chapter 12, figs. III.18; XI.17.

Larnyx:

The unpaired median ventral laryngeal air sac with opening between thyroid and cricoid cartilages is said to occur in *Callithrix* as well as in *Leontopithecus* among callitrichids. The sac, however, is consistently present in males, at least, and better developed in the lion-tamarin than in other primates (see p. 18, figs. I.10D, 11E; XI.3, 4).

Tongue:

See chapter 13; figs. III.19, 20; XI.3, 4.

Palatal Ridges:

See p. 431, fig. VII.14.

Brain:

The comparatively simple brain of *Leontopithecus* argues for an origin from an older, more primitive stem than one giving rise to the smaller *Callithrix* and *Saguinus* with slightly more complex brains (figs. VI.8, 9; XI.3).

Skull:

The system of sinuses in *Leontopithecus,* with four communicating sphenoidal cavitations opening behind in a pair of large sphenoidal fossae (fig. XI.5, 8), has no counterpart among higher primates, but similar fossae occur in some lemurs (*Lemur rubriventer, L. variegata*)

Fig. XI.2. Golden Lion-tamarin, *Leontopithecus rosalia rosalia*: Group consisting of 3 adults, 1 subadult with mounted young, and 1 pale juvenal (right); visible juvenal characters include underdeveloped mane, the pelage of crown not parted into two whorls, ears exposed, midcoronal streak.

(fig. IV.39). A comparable sphenoidal sinus system exists in the marsupial koala (*Phascolarctus cinereus*), and possibly in other mammals, too. Interorbital sinuses like those in *Leontopithecus* are common among primates. These interorbital air spaces arise in response to the need for more interorbital breadth in skulls where braincases expand without proportional increase in orbital breadth (fig. IV.11).

Consistent presence of a well-developed postglenoid foramen (fig. XI.5) is nearer the primitive condition than in other callitrichids. The shallower and more sloping mandibular symphysis of *Leontopithecus,* as compared with the smaller tamarins, genus *Saguinus* (fig. XI.6, 7), points to the independent origin of the former. In primates of the same lineage, the larger the mandible the higher and more nearly vertical its symphysis.

Dentition:

Dental evolution likewise proceeded along independent lines in *Leontopithecus*. As compared with other callitrichids (figs. V.23, 25–28), the teeth are relatively larger, the canines are better developed, molarization of the premolars is more advanced, and the tendency toward development of a hypocone in the last premolar is more pronounced. These, taken together with the extremely large, highly molarized deciduous pm^4, mark a shift of the functional center of mastication from first molar as in callitrichids generally to last premolar as in *Leontopithecus* particularly.

Limbs:

The slender, elongate arm, hand, and partially syndactylous middle fingers designed for probing, discovering, and snagging or spearing concealed grubs and insects are unique among higher primates (figs. I.28, 29: XI. 13–15). The specialized forelimb can nevertheless be derived directly from that of a typical marmoset. The primate foot, normally much longer and relatively narrower than the hand, is more nearly equal to the hand in *Leontopithecus*. Altogether, fore- and hind limbs of lion-tamarins are more nearly equal in length than those of other callitrichids (fig. I.28; XI.13).

Cranial Characters (figs. IV.3, 14, 15, 26, 39, 43, 54, 65, 68, 78, 79; XI.5–8)

Greatest skull length in adults usually between 50 and 62 mm; frontal contour low, not vaulted; temporal ridges sharply convergent but not meeting on frontal, more or less parallel-sided on parietal (fig. XI.5); nasal profile slightly concave (figs. IV.3; XI.6); nasofrontal suture usually more than three-fourths distance from nasal tip to glabella; diameter of malar foramen usually less than 1 mm; infraorbital foramen placed directly above pm^3 or between roots of pm^3 and pm^4, its diameter usually greater than that of malar; orbits comparatively small and somewhat square in outline; lacrymal bone extremely small and entirely contained within border of orbit; interorbital region comparatively wide and pneumatized; cribriform plate comparatively well developed, crista galli often present (fig. IV.43); left and right orbital plates of ethmoid separated by median cellular spaces and perpendicular plate of ethmoid (fig. XI.8); intersphenoidal sinus present with ostium opening into superior nasal meatus; posterior pair of large ovate sphenoidal sinuses or fossae present and communicating posteroventrally with inferior nasal meatus via epipharynx; mesopterygoid fossa steeply arched exposing posterior sphenoidal fossae (figs. IV.39; XI.3, 8); axis of foramen magnum pointed back as much as or slightly more than down (fig. IV.54); auditory bullae well inflated, lower portion of mesotympanic cavity extremely cellular (cf. fig. IV.62); dental arcade Gothic, that is, between V- and U-shaped, outer alveolar distance between canines more than alveolar length of c-m^2; occipital angle (opisthion-inion index) 64° in one specimen (cf. IV.81); pterygoid fossa rudimentary or represented only by angle between hamular process and external pterygoid plate; outline of inferior border of mandible V-shaped with symphysial angle slightly rounded, the horizontal rami arced (fig. XI.6); angle of outer slope of symphysis menti relative to basal mandibular plane (fig. IV.78) about 43° (38°–51°, 5 specimens); ascending ramus elongate, average coronoidal height 66% of condyloincisive length of mandible; coronoid process hooked and extending well above condyle, sigmoid notch deep and narrow; articular surface of condyle raised well above plane of molar crown surface; inferior border of angular process deflected slightly below basal plane of horizontal ramus (fig. IV.79).

Postcranial Skeletal Characters

Vertebral Formula:

In 5 skeletons, cervical 7; thoracic 12; lumbar 7; sacral 3(in 3), 4(1); caudal 22 +, 23 +, 24, 25, 28.

Sternal Ribs:

See comparative data (p. 425) under family heading.

Arm and Leg Proportions:

Linear measurements and proportions are of specimens FM 46165 °, 57152 ♀, FM 57988 ♀, FM 57839 ♂, AM 137279 °, respectively.

$$\frac{\text{Humerus}\ \ 64, 62, 63, 63, 61}{\text{Radius}\ \ 65, 60, 63, 64, 62} = 98\%, 103\%, 100\%, 98\%, 98\%.$$

$$\frac{\text{Femur}\ \ 72, 68, 71, 72, 70}{\text{Tibia}\ \ 76, 72, 70, 77, 72} = 95\%, 94\%, 101\%, 94\%, 97\%.$$

$$\frac{\text{Humerus + radius}\ \ 129, 122, 126, 127, 123}{\text{Femur + tibia}\ \ 148, 140, 140, 145, 142} = 87\%, 87\%, 90\%, 88\%, 87\%.$$

$$\frac{\text{Humerus + radius}\ \ 129, 122, 126, 127, 123}{\text{Trunk}\ \ 160, 151, 170, 166, 160} = 81\%, 81\%, 74\%, 77\%, 77\%.$$

$$\frac{\text{Femur + tibia}\ \ 148, 140, 140, 145, 142}{\text{Trunk}\ \ 160, 151, 170, 166, 160} = 93\%, 93\%, 82\%, 87\%, 89\%.$$

Third Trochanter:

Present but poorly defined in 7 specimens examined.

Entepicondylar Foramen:

In the 7 skeletons examined, present in 2 and in 1 humerus of a 3d, absent in the others.

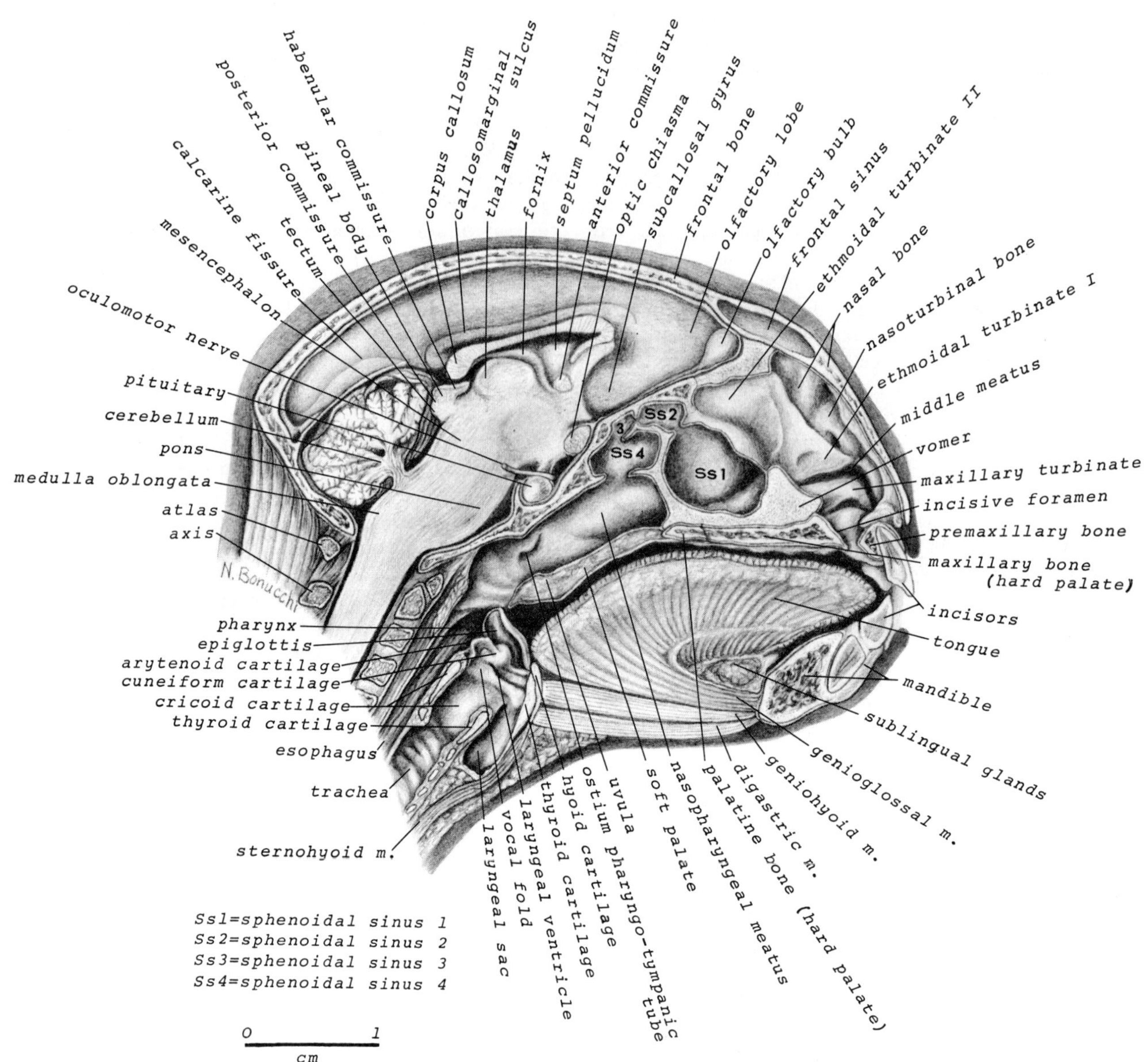

Fig. XI.3. *Leontopithecus rosalia*: Sagittal section of head and upper part of neck.

Dental Characters (figs. V.23, 25, 26, 27, 28; XI.9, 10)

Incisors (fig. V.23)

Permanent upper incisors comparatively low, crowns expanded and markedly differentiated from cervix, outer tooth implanted obliquely and posteriad to the inner incisor pair of both sides combining to form a Gothic arch, that is, between V- and U-shaped; *lateral incisor* trapeziform, lower than central about three-fourths its bulk and about as proodont; *central incisor* spatulate, biting edge entire, its mesial half horizontal or convex and touching opposite tooth, the distal half oblique; lateral and central incisors with mesial and distal cingular crests well defined and joined behind; mesial and distal styles absent, occlusal groove not strongly marked in present material; worn lingual surface of incisor pair crazed.

Deciduous upper incisors (worn) generally like their successors; central incisor ovate, higher than wide, lateral incisor more triangular; enamel uncrazed.

Permanent lower incisors slightly more or less than twice as high as mesiodistal length, crowns transversely expanded, markedly procumbent, their labial surface nearly plane or slightly recurved, biting edges normally touching, lingual surface of worn crowns crazed; lateral incisor emplaced behind plane of central, the pairs of both sides combining to form the broad angle of a Gothic to U-shaped arch; lateral incisor club-shaped, larger in bulk than spatulate central incisor and on a plane with or projecting slightly above, as seen from the front, horizontal biting edge narrower, one-half or more lateral margin on labial surface obliquely truncate, the crown wider basally; labial height of incisor little more or less than one-third vertical depth of symphysis menti; mesial and distal stylids absent; mesial and distal cingular ridges poorly defined on central incisor, well developed on lateral incisor and meeting behind.

Deciduous lower incisors (worn) without crazing, occlusal surface higher than wide, slightly excavated, lingual cingulum well developed; central incisor with occlusal surface more nearly triangular than obovate, mesial border longest, worn labial biting edge at least one and

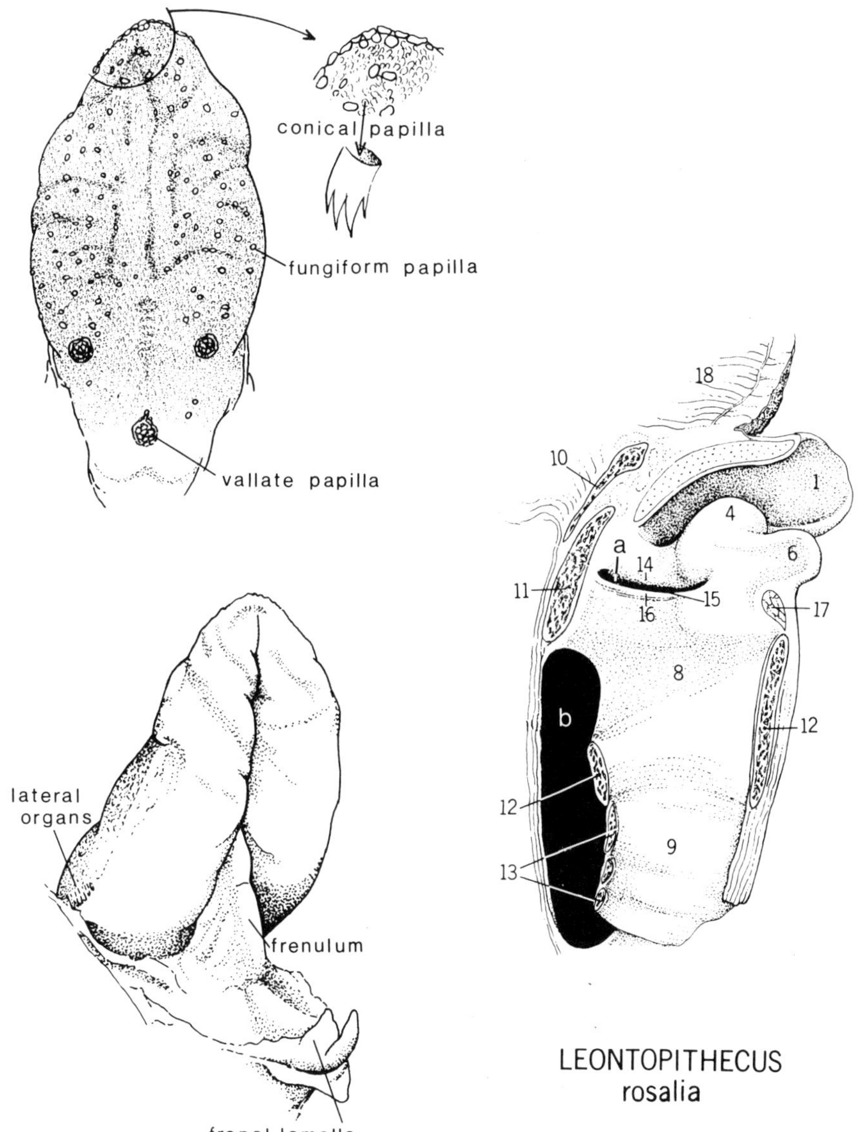

Fig. XI.4. *Leontopithecus rosalia*: Tongue, dorsal and ventral surfaces; larynx, inner surace of left half. Symbols explained on p. 19.

one-half times wider than posterolingual margin; lateral incisor with occlusal surface quadrituberculate, subtrapezoidal in outline, superior labial border of crown narrower than lingual border, middle anterior cone (eoconid) well developed, mesiostylid (*a*) present, distostylid (*b*) and metaconid (*2*) enclosing an open-ended basin.

Remarks. The lower deciduous incisors of the single juvenal of *Leontopithecus* at hand are considerably worn. It is apparent, nevertheless, that like those of *Saguinus,* they are specialized as spoon-shaped tools or receptacles for ingestion of food during the lactating stage.

According to Della Serra (1951), *chrysomelas* differs from *rosalia* by crown of upper central incisor ovate (in *rosalia* trapezoidal), height greater than width (approximately equal), lingual fossa deep (shallow), lingual tubercle larger, pointed, and inclined medially (rudimentary, rounded and continuous with posterior cingulum [= *B*]), posterior cingulum (*B*) well defined (poorly defined). All definitions enclosed in parentheses apply to *rosalia,* according to Della Serra.

Except for the so-called lingual (= mesiolingual), tubercle or mesiostyle, all characters attributed above either to *chrysomelas* or to *rosalia,* are present in our *rosalia.* The mesiolingual tubercle, if present, would appear strange in upper incisors such as those of *Leontopithecus.*

Canines

Permanent upper canine saberlike, subtriangular in cross section, more than twice as high as long, and usually more than twice as high as adjacent teeth; mesial anterolingual crest of torus defined by deep, broad groove on mesial aspect of unworn tooth, distal ridge (I″) defined by narrow groove on posterolingual aspect of unworn tooth, anterior and posterior portion of lingual cingulum (*B*) continuous; mesiostyle not evident, distostyle not always defined; an incipient mesiolingual tubercle (protocone *2*) on lingual cingulum often present; enamel of worn tooth more or less crazed.

Deciduous upper canine partially premolarized, higher than long, and half again as high as dpm²; mesial and

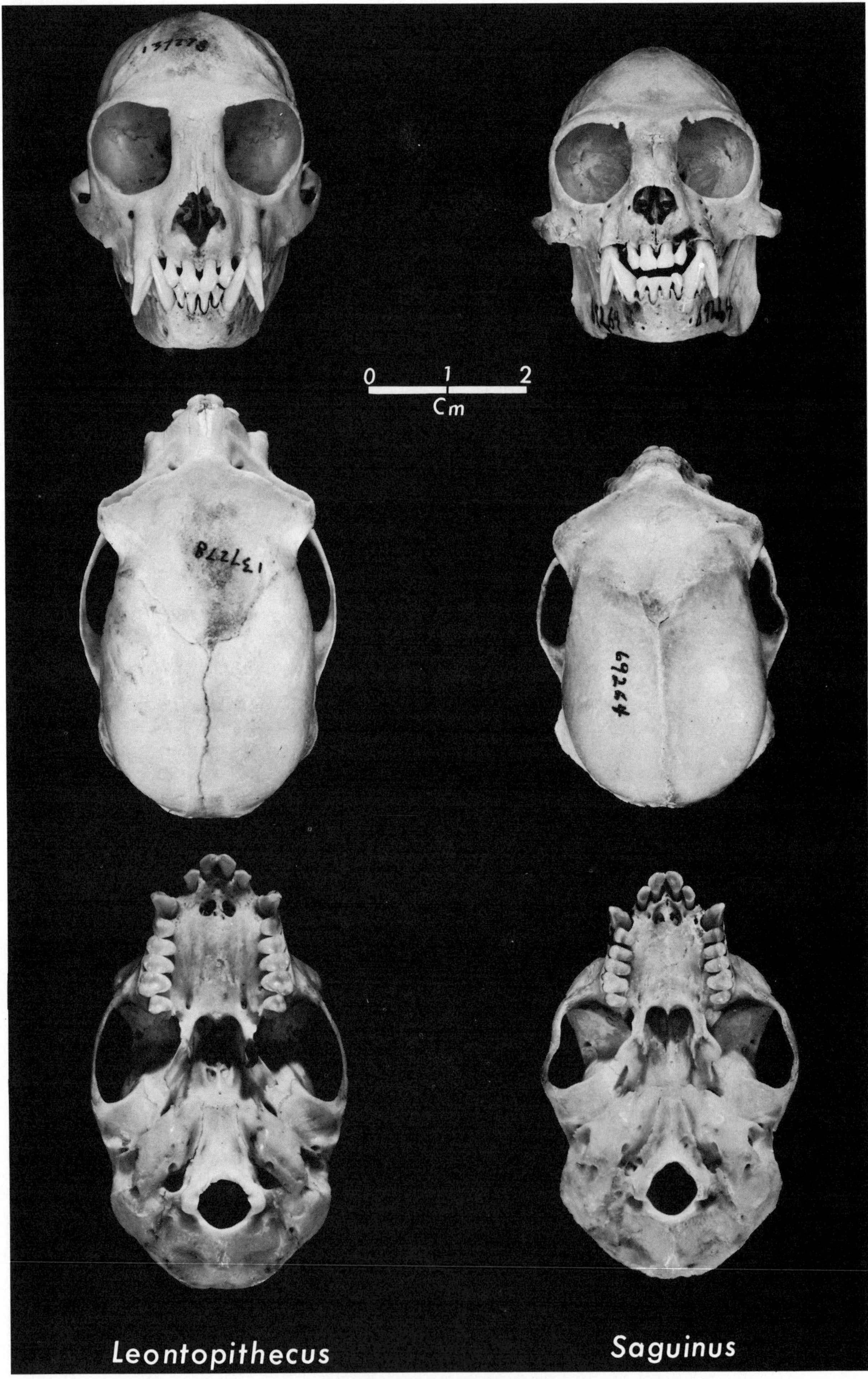

Fig. XI.5. *Leontopithecus rosalia*: Skull—front, dorsal, and ventral aspects—compared with skull of *Saguinus oedipus*.

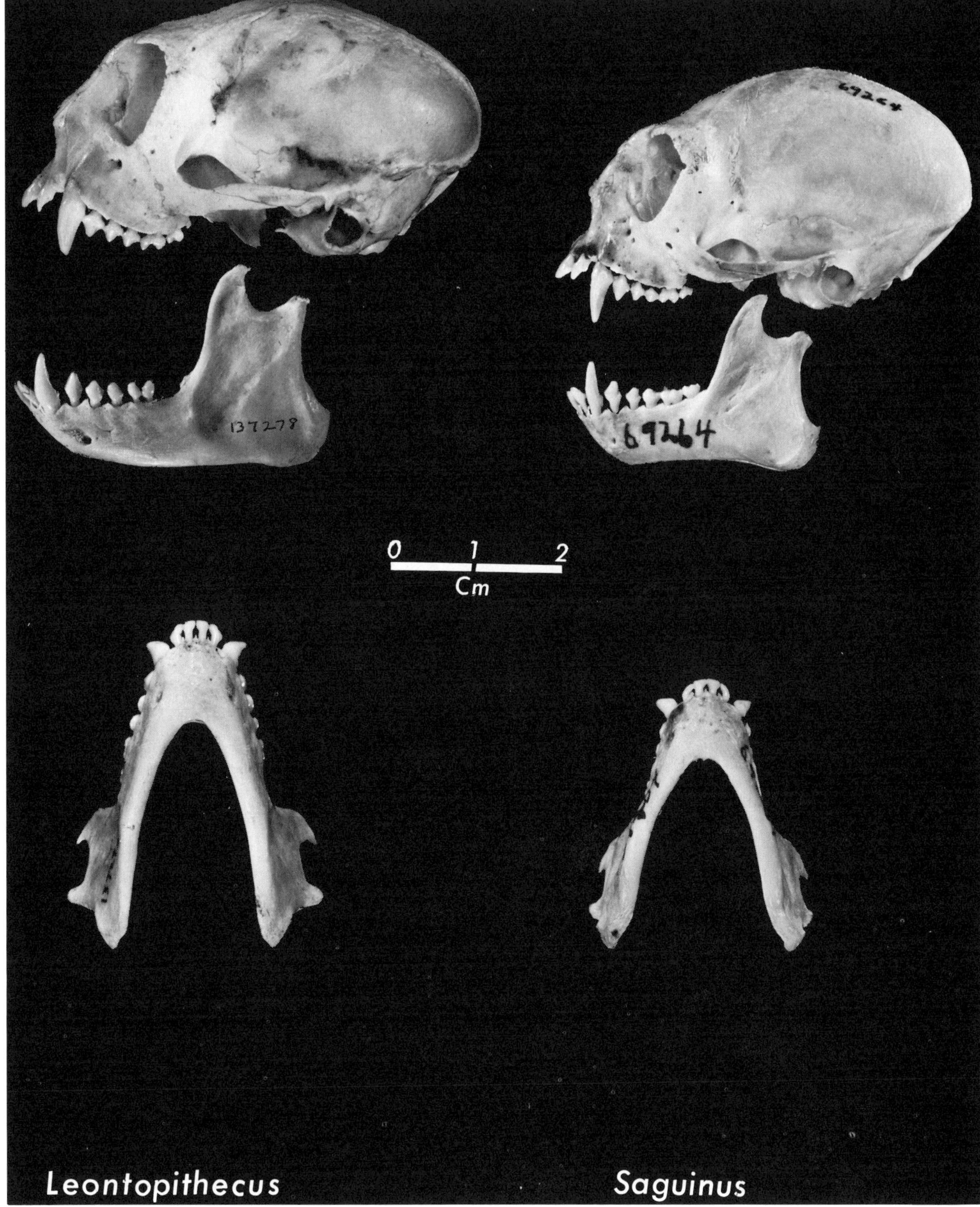

Fig. XI.6. *Leontopithecus rosalia*: Skull—mandible, lateral, and ventral aspects—compared with skull of *Saguinus oedipus*.

distal ridges each defined by longitudinal groove; anterior and posterior portions of lingual cingulum continuous and partially enclosing a concavity; mesiostyle and distostyle well developed; enamel crazing not apparent.

Permanent lower canine distinctly caniniform, more than twice as high as long, and somewhat less than twice as high as pm_2; mesial cristid (*I'*) separated from lingual torus (*II*) by shallow groove, mesiostylid and distostylid present; distal cristid (*I''*) more or less defined, lingual cingulid *B* not strongly developed, posterior portion enclosing a narrow talonid basin; enamel crazed in moderately worn tooth.

Deciduous lower canine (worn) partly premolarized, about one-third again higher than long, main cusp half again as high as that of pm_2; mesial cristid and anterolingual cingulid indistinct or eroded, distal cristid (*I''*)

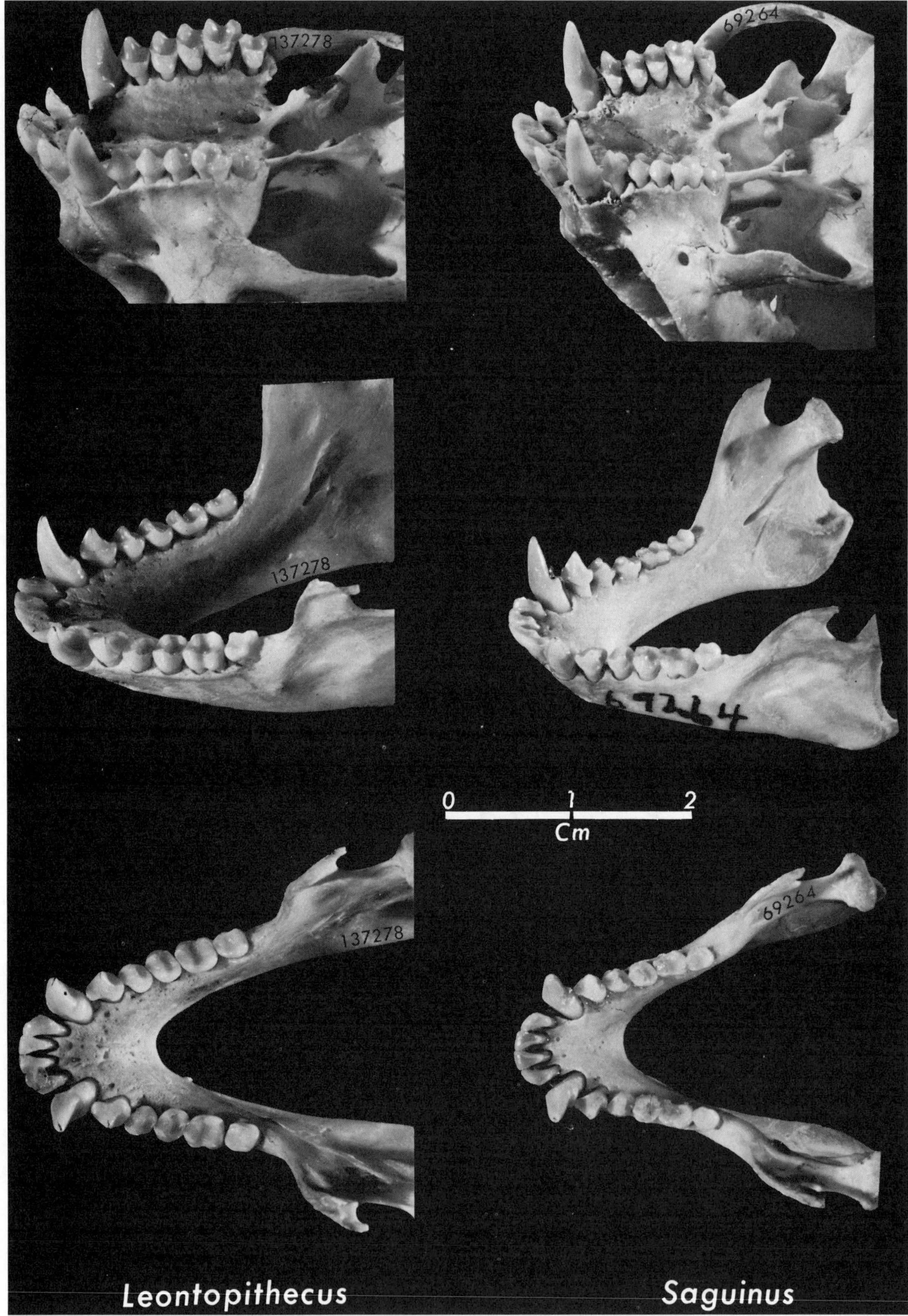

Fig. XI.7. *Leontopithecus rosalia*: Skull—upper and lower jaws from dental aspects—compared with jaws of *Saguinus oedipus*.

undefined; talonid about half total tooth length, sculpturing worn and nearly smooth, distostylid (hypoconid?) barely indicated; enamel uncrazed.

Remarks. The lower permanent canines are definitive tusks performing independently functions which in true marmosets may be shared with the pointed incisors. Upper and lower deciduous canines are also more tusk-like than those of *Cebuella* and *Callithrix*.

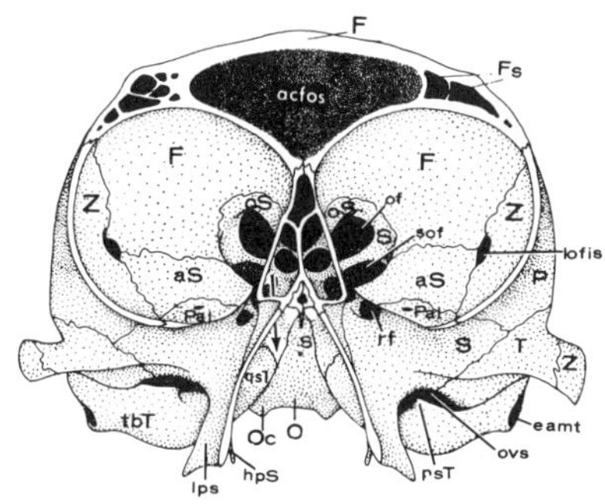

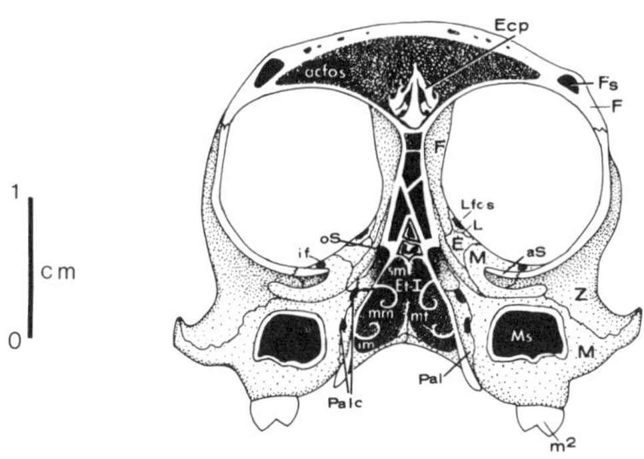

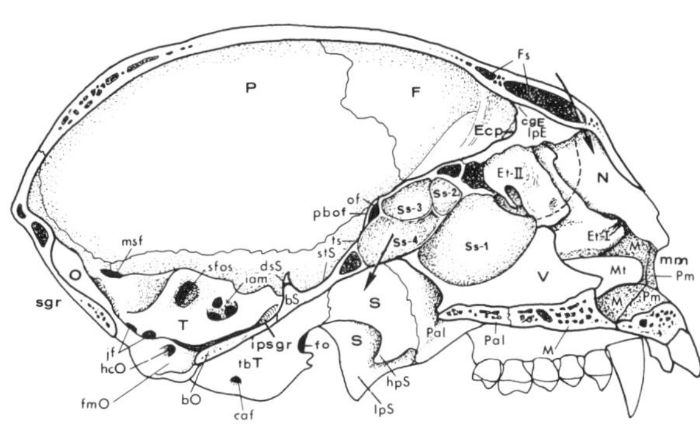

LEONTOPITHECUS

Fig. XI.8. *Leontopithecus rosalia*: Skull, sagittal and transverse sections.

Premolars

Permanent upper premolars with pm^2 bicuspid, occlusal surface subtriangular in outline, about half as high as canine and slightly higher than adjacent premolar, sample crown height 3.0, length 3.0, width 3.3, anterolingual cingulum (*B*) well developed, buccal cingulum (*A*) poorly defined, mesiostyle (*a*) and distostyle (*b*) present but not raised (worn?), protocone (*2*) well defined; pm^3 subtriangular in outline, slightly lower, shorter, and wider than preceding, buccal cingulum more or less defined, mesial and distal styles poorly defined, rudimentary metacone (*4*) on distal crest of eocone (*1*) sometimes present, small secondary posterolingual cingulum (*C′*) well marked, usually with weak style; pm^4 like preceding but wider, eocone and protocone larger, metacone, if present, rudimentary as in preceding, posterolingual cingulum (*C*) more extensive and sometimes with a rudimentary hypocone, a neoanterolingual cingulum (*B′*) sometimes present; sample length 2.5, width 4.2.

Deciduous upper premolars (worn) with dpm^2 premolariform and weakly bicuspid, sample crown height, 2.4, length 2.4, width 2.5, lingual cingulum (*B*) well defined in worn tooth, protocone (2) indicated, mesiostyle not certainly identifiable in worn specimen, distostyle present; dpm^3 longer and wider than preceding, trigon basin deep, low metacone clearly defined, protocone moderately developed, plagioconule (*d*) not distinct, buccal cingulum well indicated, but styles not certainly identifiable; dpm^4 half again as large as preceding and fully molarized, plagiocrista (*IV*) well developed, plagioconule (*d*) present, metacone smaller than eocone, protocone well developed, lingual cingulum *C* prominent, rudimentary hypocone present, neoanterolingual cingulum (*B′*) with two entostyles; sample length 3.2, width 3.2.

Remarks. Molarization of upper premolars is more advanced, particularly in the erstwhile caniniform pm^2, than in other callitrichids. All permanent upper premolars are distinctly bicuspid, with an incipient metacone often present in either or both of the last two premolars. The posterolingual cingulum, usually present and often ledgelike in pm^4 and frequently present in pm^3, bears clear indication, in some specimens, of hypocone, and the neoanterolingual cingulum may have one or two entostyles.

Dpm^2 appears to be somewhat less molarized than its successor but tritubercular dpm^4 is, as usual, fully molarized. Dpm^3 is intermediate with its small low metacone. As in *Saguinus,* a minute posterolingual conule in dpm^4 must be interpreted as an incipient hypocone.

Permanent lower premolars with pm$_2$ comparatively well molarized, sample crown height 3.4, length 2.9, width 2.5, epicristid (*II*) defining trigonid from talonid basins frequently present, metaconid (*2*) incipient, mesial and distal stylids obsolete or absent; pm$_3$ with steeply sloping trigonid basin completely separated from talonid basin by epicristid, its area subequal to or less than that of talonid basin, metaconid low but usually well defined, low pseudoparaconid (*t*) sometimes present, talonid basin deep, hypoconid (*4*) and entoconid (*5*) low and often well defined in unworn tooth; buccal cingulid absent, mesiostylid and distostylid not defined; pm$_4$ like preceding but metaconid high, talonid basin deep, hypoconid (*4*), postentoconulid (*e*) and entoconid (*5*) weakly differentiated in unworn tooth; sample length 2.5, width 3.0.

Deciduous lower premolars (worn) with dpm$_2$ considerably eroded but sculpturing of main elements preserved, crown height 2.4, length 2.4, width 1.5, epicristid (*II*) elevated, metaconid distinct, anterolingual and posterolingual cingulids well defined; pm$_3$ with sloping trigonid, metaconid well formed, anterolingual cingulid ledgelike, talonid basin deep, hypoconid and entoconid indicated; pm$_4$ half again as large as preceding, trigonid area about one-third occlusal surface of crown, metaconid (*2*) full but slightly lower than eoconid (*1*), pseudoparaconid (*t*) and mesiostylid (*a*) present, talonid nearly square, basin deep, metaconid (*2*), entoconid (*5*) and postentoconulid (*e*) prominent, conids 2 and 5 separated by a deep cleft; sample length 3.0, width 2.1.

Remarks. Molarization of pm$_{3\text{-}4}$ is more advanced than in *Callithrix* but less than in *Saguinus*. Metaconids are low, stylids obsolete or absent, talonid cusps weak, buccal cingulum and protolophid absent. There is no indication of a

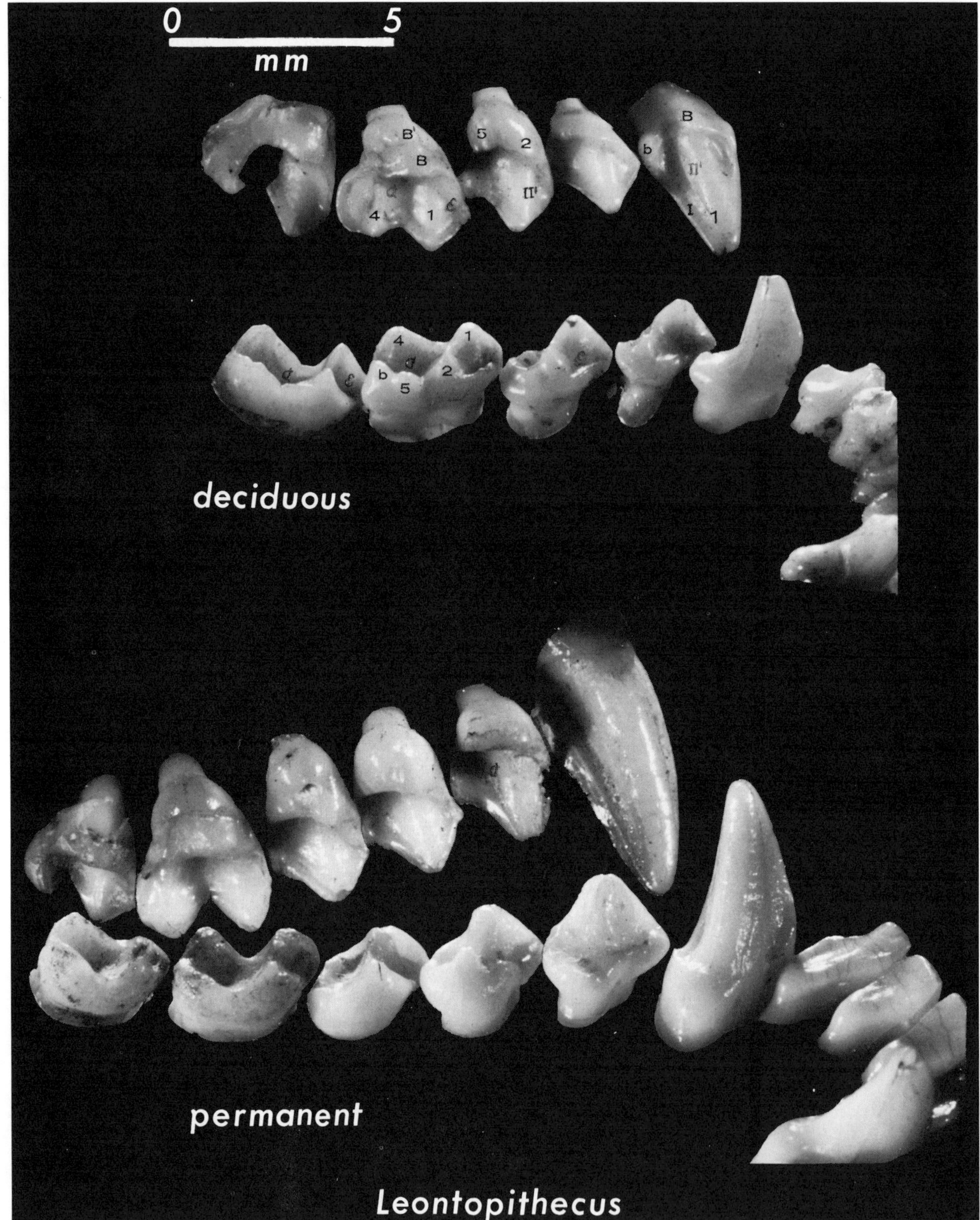

Fig. XI.9. *Leontopithecus rosalia*: Upper and lower permanent and deciduous teeth; first molar newly erupted appears in deciduous series; upper incisors not shown.

paraconid, but present material is not entirely satisfactory for detailed study.

The deciduous premolars show the same evolutionary trends, but pm_4 is completely molarized, the three main talonid cusps conspicuous, pseudoparaconid small but well defined, at least in $pm_{3\text{-}4}$.

Molars

Upper first molar, one-half to two-thirds again larger than second molar, about one-third to one-fifth again larger than pm^4, occlusal surface subtriangular, trigon basin deeply concave, eocone higher than protocone but

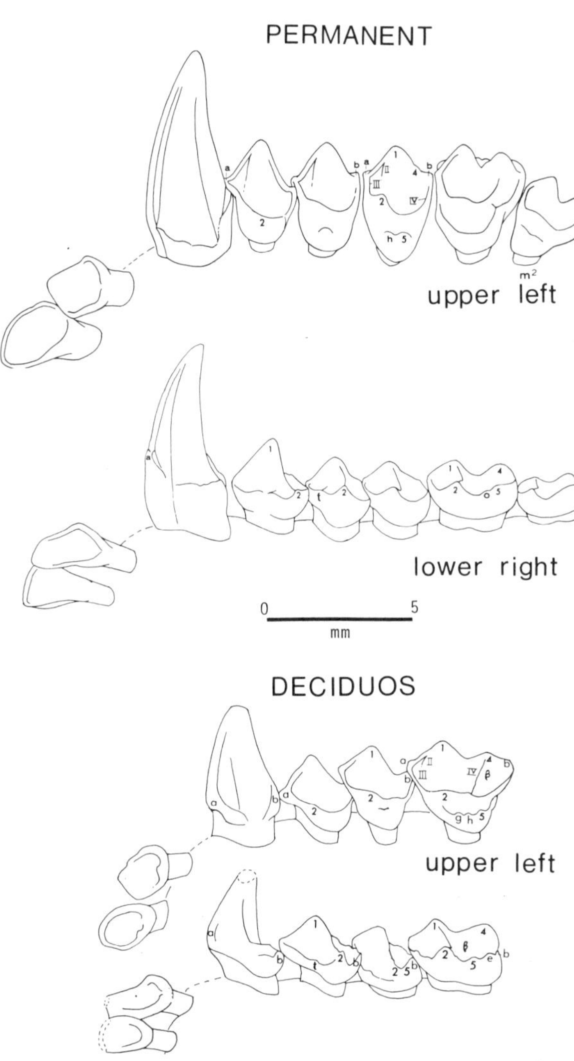

Fig. XI.10. *Leontopithecus rosalia*: Diagrams of upper and lower permanent and deciduous teeth; newly erupted first molar appears in deciduous series.

approximately equal or slightly less in bulk, metacone usually slightly lower than eocone, subequal or somewhat smaller in bulk, protoloph and plagiocrista (*IV*) well developed, epiconule (*c*) rudimentary or absent, plagioconule (*d*) absent or rudimentary, lingual cingula *B′* and *C* forming a broad and continuous shelf, distostyle (*b*) frequently and mesiostyle (*a*) sometimes present, ectostyles rudimentary or absent; *second molar* generally like first but smaller, occlusal surface triangular, eocone highest, protocone subequal or larger, metacone nearly as large as eocone, rudimentary epiconule (*c*) sometimes present, plagioconule (*d*) not evident, cingulum *C* well developed, cingulum *B′* poorly developed, the two cingula just meeting, mesial and distal styles not evident, ectostyles usually absent.

Lower molars quadrate, elevated trigonid occupying anterior one-third or less of crown with forward-sloping basin, talonid forming remainder of crown, with deeply rounded basin; *first molar* suboblong, about one and one-fourth to one and one-third larger than last premolar, metaconid (*2*) slightly lower than eoconid (*1*), epicristid (II) with deep notch separating segments II′ and II″, mesiostylid (*a*) absent, buccal and secondary lingual cingulids and stylids not evident, hypoconid (*4*) larger and deeper than eoconid but slightly less elevated above crown base, entoconid (*5*) low with crest plane or slightly rounded, postentoconulid (*e*) seen differentiated from entoconid (*5*) in unworn but not in worn crown, posterior border of talonid concave, or deeply notched in unworn crown and showing separation between cristids I″ and VI; *second molar* like first but from three-fifths to three-fourths as large, talonid distinctly wider than trigonid, metaconid and entoconid slightly higher than eoconid and hypoconid respectively, epicristid (*II*) and posterior border of talonid deeply notched, postentoconulid (*e*) not differentiated in specimens at hand, distolingual cusp (*5*) produced slightly more posteriad than distobuccal cusp (*4*).

Sample measurements of Molars, Buccal Length × Width (in millimeters)

m^1	m^2	m_1	m_2
3.3 × 4.1	2.5 × 3.1	3.4 × 2.9	2.9 × 2.3
3.4 × 4.2	2.7 × 3.3	3.2 × 2.7	3.0 × 2.4
3.5 × 4.0	2.7 × 3.3	3.4 × 2.6	2.9 × 2.2
3.5 × 4.1	2.6 × 3.3	3.5 × 2.8	3.1 × 2.3
3.6 × 4.2	2.8 × 3.3	3.3 × 2.8	3.0 × 2.3
3.6 × 4.3	2.6 × 3.3	3.4 × 2.7	3.1 × 2.4

Remarks. Molars of *Leontopithecus* are larger than those of all other callitrichids and of *Callimico.* The upper row is supplied with well-developed accessories, the lower is extremely simplified. The contour of the lower cheektooth row, however, is not quite as bowed as in *Saguinus.* The second molar, with metacone well developed, also appears to average larger relative to the first than in other callitrichids. As compared with *Saguinus,* the talonid of lower molars is more expanded, the trigonid correspondingly smaller and more regularly ovate, with transverse diameter greater than sagittal.

The more distal of two or more well-developed conules arising from the posteriorlingual cingulum (*C*) of the last upper premolar, here interpreted as a rudimentary hypocone, has no equivalent structure on either of the two upper molars.

Relative cusp heights of opposing sides of the crown are not easily determined in present material consisting of captive individuals with possibly abnormal cusp wear. In the newly erupted m_1 of one individual the buccal cusps are slightly higher than the respectively opposite lingual cusps. In the remaining samples, all with worn teeth, the lingual cusps of $m_{1\text{-}2}$ are as high as or higher than the opposing buccal cusps. In every case, however, the inner cusps are slightly to moderately worn, the outer considerably to excessively worn. Ostensibly, the animals exercised the outer more than inner sides of their teeth in chewing. In any event, the *Leontopithecus* mandible is intermediate between the V-shaped *Callithrix* type and the U-shaped *Saguinus* type. The occlusal plane of the molars may well be intermediate as well.

As in callitrichids generally, the distolingual cusp of the rhomboidal second molar projects farther behind than the distobuccal. The first molar, however, is more nearly square and the plane of its posterior border is more nearly straight across than in other callitrichids.

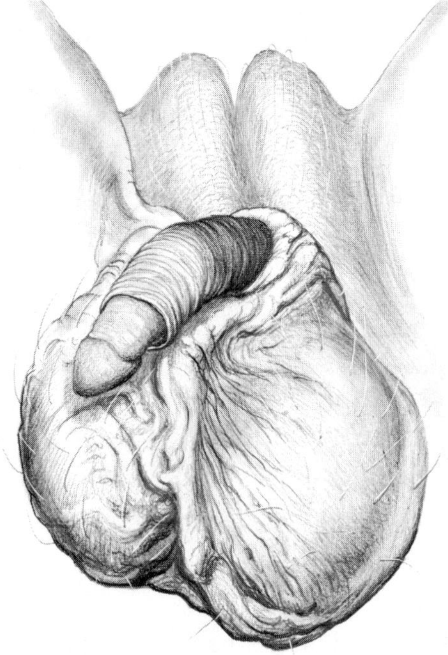

Leontopithicus rosalia

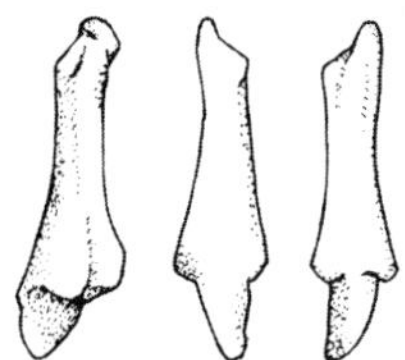

Fig. XI.11. *Leontopithecus rosalia rosalia*: Male external genitalia and pubic region; three aspects of a baculum.

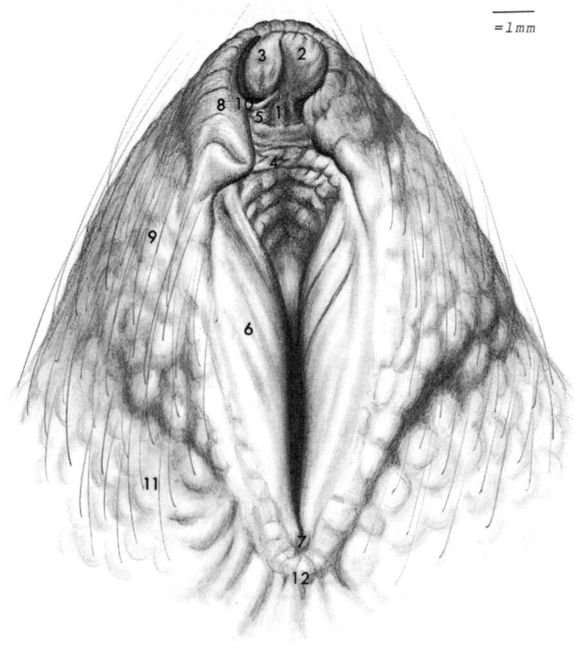

Leontopithicus rosalia

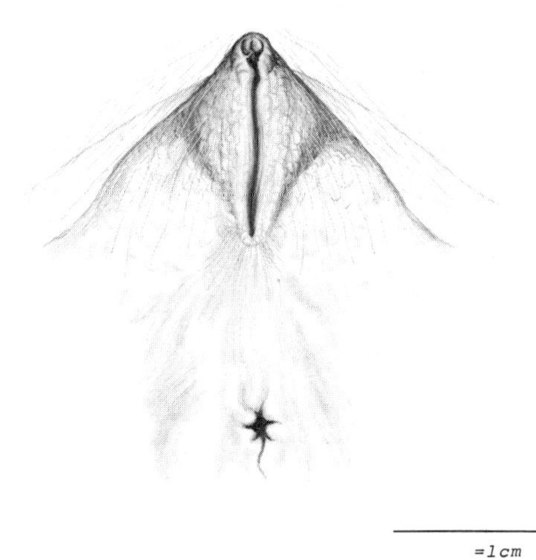

Fig. XI.12. *Leontopithecus rosalia rosalia*: Adult female (upper) and juvenal (lower) external genitalia and circumgenital area: for explanation of symbols, see p. 113.

External Genitalia

Male (figs. III.25, 28, 29; XI.11)

Adult. External genitalia mostly to entirely unpigmented; penis well exposed, lightly pigmented or unpigmented, with stem and well-differentiated, acorn-shaped glans thickly set with small colorless denticles; urinary meatus apical and vertical but, as usual, demarcating the larger left, or bacular, lobe from the smaller right lobe; pedunculate, unpigmented scrotum comparatively small, laterally compressed and much longer than wide, the skin wrinkled, sparsely haired white; outer preputial fold not clearly differentiated from scrotal fold, inner preputial fold, or sheath, glabrous with proximal half pigmented or unpigmented; length of scrotum with testes 17 mm in one, 18 mm in another; pubic sexual skin modified in one old individual into two unpigmented parallel ridges; perineal and anal regions unpigmented.

Juvenal. Testes incompletely developed and inguinal in specimen at hand, the scrotum represented by a pair of longitudinal folds with raphe depressed in midline like a urogenital fissure. In contrast, the scrotum of juvenal tamarins (*nigricollis* group) develops as a pair of small ovate swellings on each side of the raised raphe.

Remarks. External genitalia of adult lion-tamarins, with exposed penis and acorn-shaped glans coronis, resemble those of man. A similarly expanded glans penis occurs in *Callimico,* but the latter is less acorn-shaped than helmet- or toadstool-shaped. Also, in *Callimico,* the penis, including glans, is papillate, without spines, the scrotum globose, pigmented, and papillate. In *Leontopithecus* the genital pelage is sparse, the hairs unpigmented and irregularly dispersed as contrasted with the pigmented and fairly evenly distributed genital hairs of *Callimico.*

Female (figs. III.21–23; XI.12)

Adult. External genitalia comparatively simple, unpigmented; labia majora longer than wide and not forming a thick cushion in specimen examined, the integument papillate, each papilla with a single long, stiff, unpigmented hair; hairy or outer portion of preputial fold (fig. XI.12 (*9*) defined from scrotal fold (*11*) by sulcus and uniting in front of glans clitoridis to form a low mons,

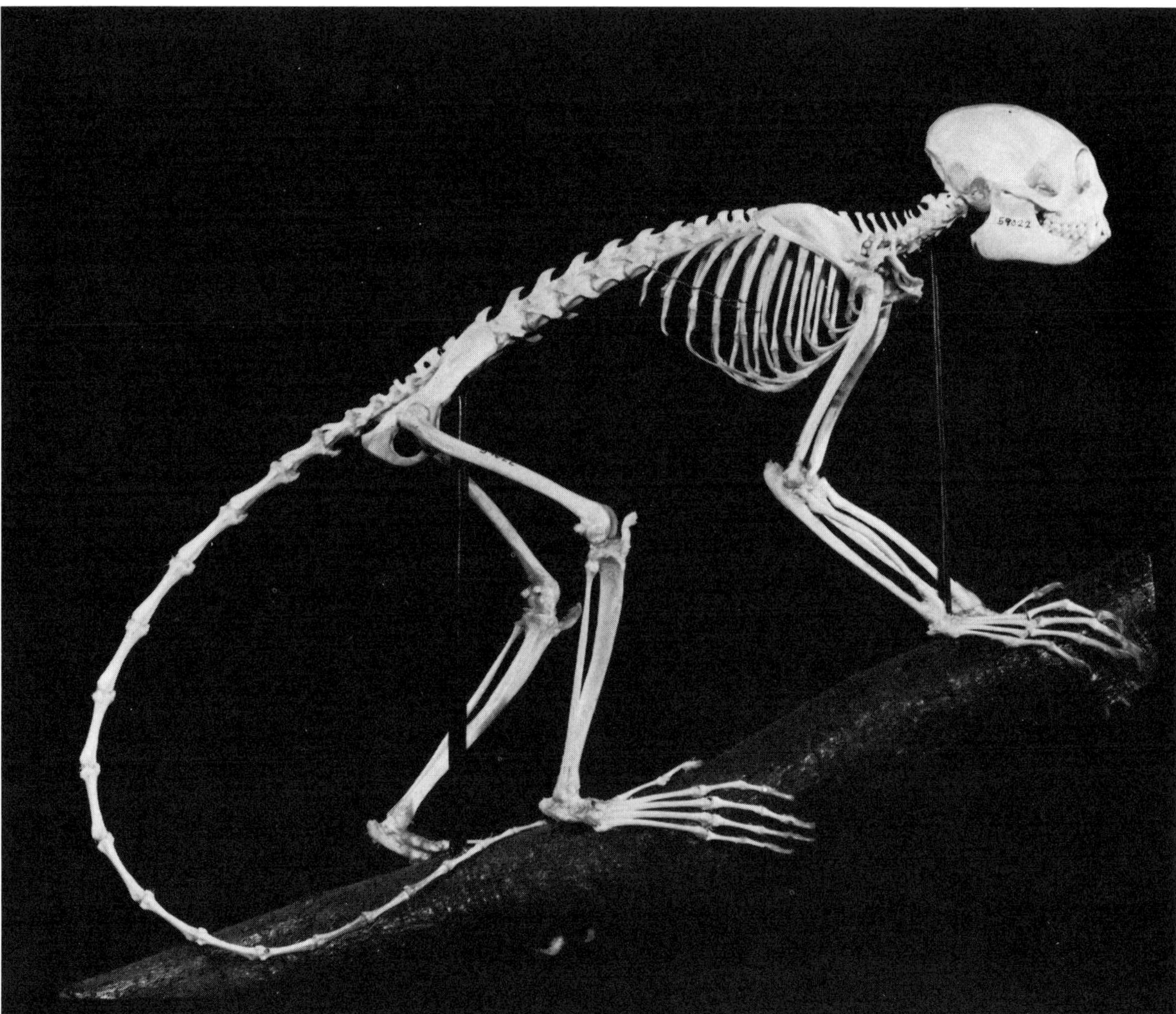

Fig. XI.13. *Leontopithecus rosalia rosalia*: Skeleton

glabrous inner, or annular, portion of preputial fold (*8*) attached medially to left lobe of glans clitoridis (*2*) by frenulum preputiae (*10*); clitoris well defined and extrusible, the glans expanded with left and right lobes unequal; outer walls of labia minora extended as lamina from sides of urogenital groove to form anterior half of vaginal vestibule; length of genital fissure about 9 mm. Sexual skin poorly defined in specimen examined; perineal and anal regions unpigmented.

Remarks. The resemblance between the female external genitalia of lion-tamarins and humans is striking. Also the female external genitalia of *Callimico* are similar. It is significant that in both *Leontopithecus* and *Callimico* the glans penis is acorn- or helmet-shaped, as in man. In none of the specimens examined, including dry skins, do the labia majora appear swollen as in receptive females of *Cebuella, Callithrix,* or *Saguinus.*

Bolk (1907, p. 275, fig. 9) describes the female genitalia of *Leontopithecus rosalia* in detail but incorrectly identifies the prepuce together with the connecting folds surrounding the rima pudendi as part of the labia minora. Osman Hill (1957, p. 265, fig. 71) recognizes the integument surrounding the vulva as labia majora but also notes that the clitoris is completely enclosed by the labia minora and therefore not extrusible. The latter condition, like the genitalia figured by Osman Hill, is unnatural.

Hands and Feet (figs. I.28, 29; XI.13–15)

The elongate feet of the lion-tamarin, according to Pocock (1917, p. 20), imply "leaping powers surpassing those of *Hapale jacchus* and it seems probable that the elongation of the palm and fingers of the hand and the tying together [by a membrane at base] of the second, third and fourth fingers are characters functionally correlated with the increasing activity and serve the purpose of giving at the same time a longer span and a safer grip on a branch when the animal alights from a long distance spring."

The lion-tamarin is undoubtedly a more powerful jumper than *Callithrix jacchus,* but it is also larger and stronger. Contrary to Pocock's supposition, the longer and more slender hand is not designed for ensuring a firmer grip. The "excess" finger length of the resting lion-tamarin is not ordinarily used for gripping the perch, especially when the animal is resting most of its weight on palms or soles. The fingers simply project outward or dangle freely (figs. XI.2, 29, 31). The same is true of the toes. The "extra" toe length may, however, ensure a better hold on thick tree trunks or branches, thus freeing the hands for other functions such as probing for and seizing prey.

The elongate hand and fingers, particularly the middle

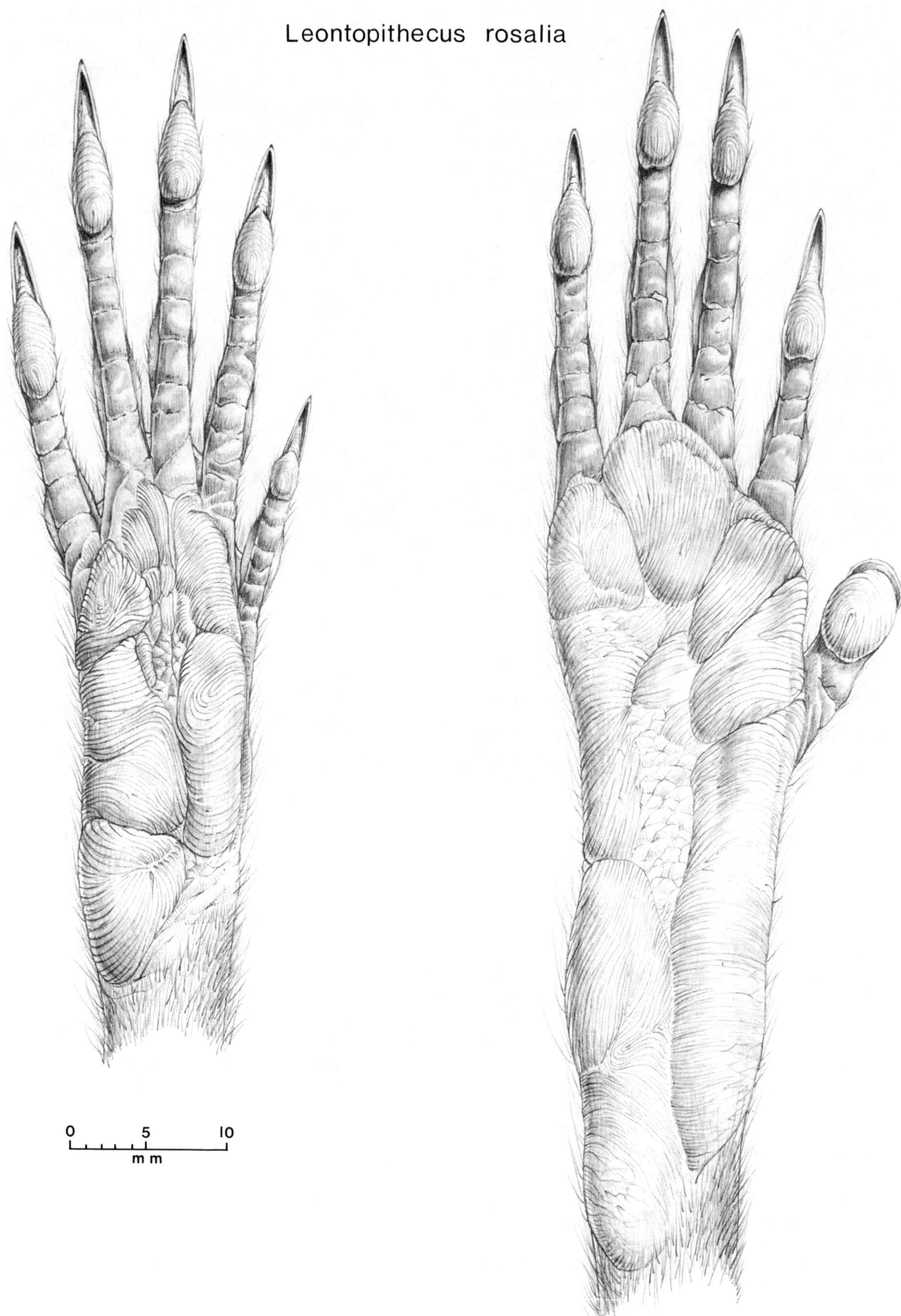

Fig. XI.14. *Leontopithecus rosalia rosalia*: Volar surfaces of right hand and foot

finger, of lion-tamarins are adapted for probing and extracting insects from crevices, holes, and under loose bark. I observed this activity in the fall of 1963 in Mr. Murray Hill's farm near Burlington, Wisconsin. At my request, one of several lion-tamarins on the farm was put into a large cage containing part of a tree trunk with

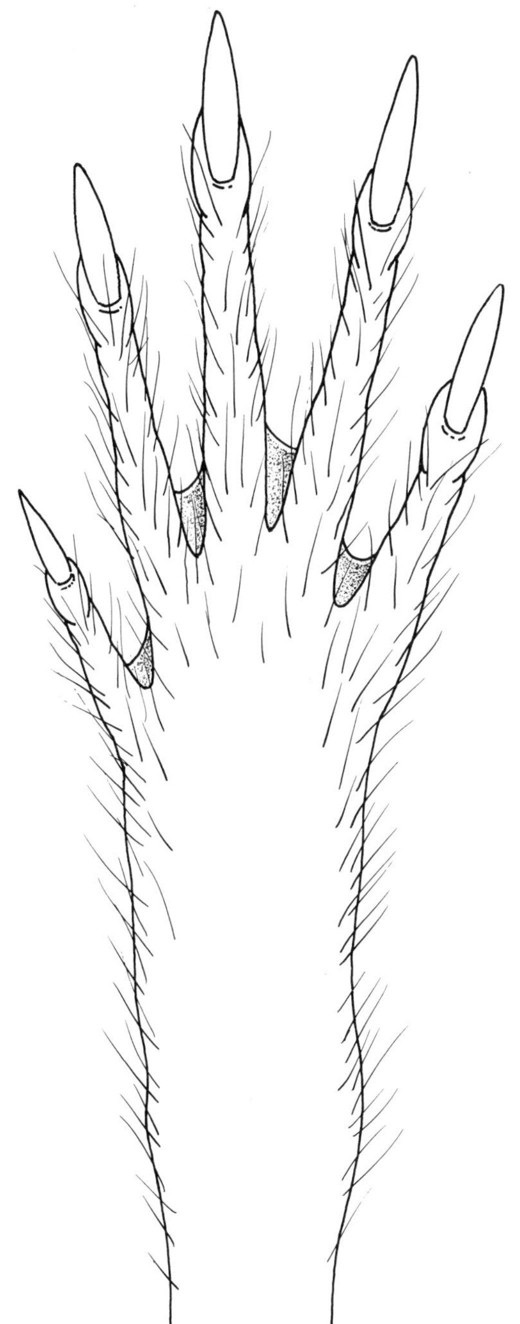

Fig. XI.15. *Leontopithecus rosalia rosalia*: Dorsal surface of right hand with the fingers spread to show interdigital membranes.

some branches. One of the first reactions of the animal to the new quarters was a quick and systematic finger probing of the loose bark of the tree trunk. The purpose of this activity was evident, but I tested it by dropping a grasshopper into the empty handle socket of a large push broom on the floor of the cage, in full view of the lion-tamarin. The animal immediately leaped to the broom, extracted the grasshopper from the hole with the claws of its middle fingers, bit off the head of its prey, leaped back to its perch, and devoured the remains. The entire performance happened in what seemed to be the blink of an eye. A common marmoset, *Callithrix jacchus,* placed in the same cage, accepted grasshoppers from my hand and ate them greedily. It showned no interest in snagging insects out of the broom socket although it saw the lion-tamarin do so several times.

Two lion-tamarins of the farm zoo were tested the following week with a specially constructed wooden block with holes of different diameters through its length. The block was sectioned lengthwise through the holes and the cut side of a section was covered with plexiglass. A grasshopper was pressed into the bottom of the 1-inch bore and the block with the insect visible through the plexiglass was shown to a common marmoset, *Callithrix jacchus jacchus.* The marmoset attempted to seize the grasshopper through the plastic but gave up after several trials. The apparatus with a grasshopper in the ½-inch bore was then held up to the cage of the Golden Lion-tamarin. After one attempt to seize the insect through the transparent plexiglass the animal plunged its arm unerringly through the mouth of the hole, hooked the grasshopper at the other end with its long fingers, and extracted the prey forthwith (fig. XI.16). The experiment was successfully repeated several times. Struggling grasshoppers were torn by the claws and removed in bits.

The manner in which the lion-tamarin probes for and extracts insects with its narrow hands and long fingers is swift, sure, and precise. The membrane between the middle fingers binds the narrow digits together into a stronger and more efficient grappling tool. The webbing serves no evident purpose in climbing or jumping.

The similar structure of the elongate tarsus and toes may be partly, if not entirely, pleiotropic effects of factors controlling growth of the hands. No special function can be attributed to the pedal pecularities. Toe tips of the perched animal seem to flop awkwardly.

A hand so obviously specialized for probing for and extracting insects appears in no other living primate except the Malagasy aye-aye (*Daubentonia*). Specialization here is extreme.

Hands and fingers of a New Guinea marsupial, the striped phalanger, *Dactylopsila,* are similar to those of *Leontopithecus* and used in a similar way (cf. Rand 1937). Both the aye-aye and the striped phalanger evolved rodentlike front teeth for gnawing into wood for grubs, but the lion-tamarin shows no trend in that direction. Its long canines, however, are well adapted for stripping bark and biting into wood.

Cytogenetics

The karyotype of a Golden Lion-tamarin *Leontopithecus rosalia rosalia* (2n = 46) examined by Benirschke, Anderson, and Brownhill (1962, p. 513, fig. 2), and the same reexamined by Benirschke and Brownhill (1962, p. 245, fig. 1), but with the chromosomes rematched and regrouped, resembles those of tamarins, genus *Saguinus.* It has, however, one additional biarmed pair (32 versus 30) and one less acrocentric pair (12 versus 14). Egozcue, Perkins, and Hagemenas (1968) believe that a chromosomal pattern like that of *Leontopithecus* can be derived from a *Saguinus* type by a translocation from any biarmed pair to one of the acrocentrics, or by pericentric inversion.

Hsu and Benirschke (1971, fol. 245) demonstrate male and female karyotypes of Golden Lion-tamarins with the usual 2n = 46, but with only 2 acrocentric autosomes in each.

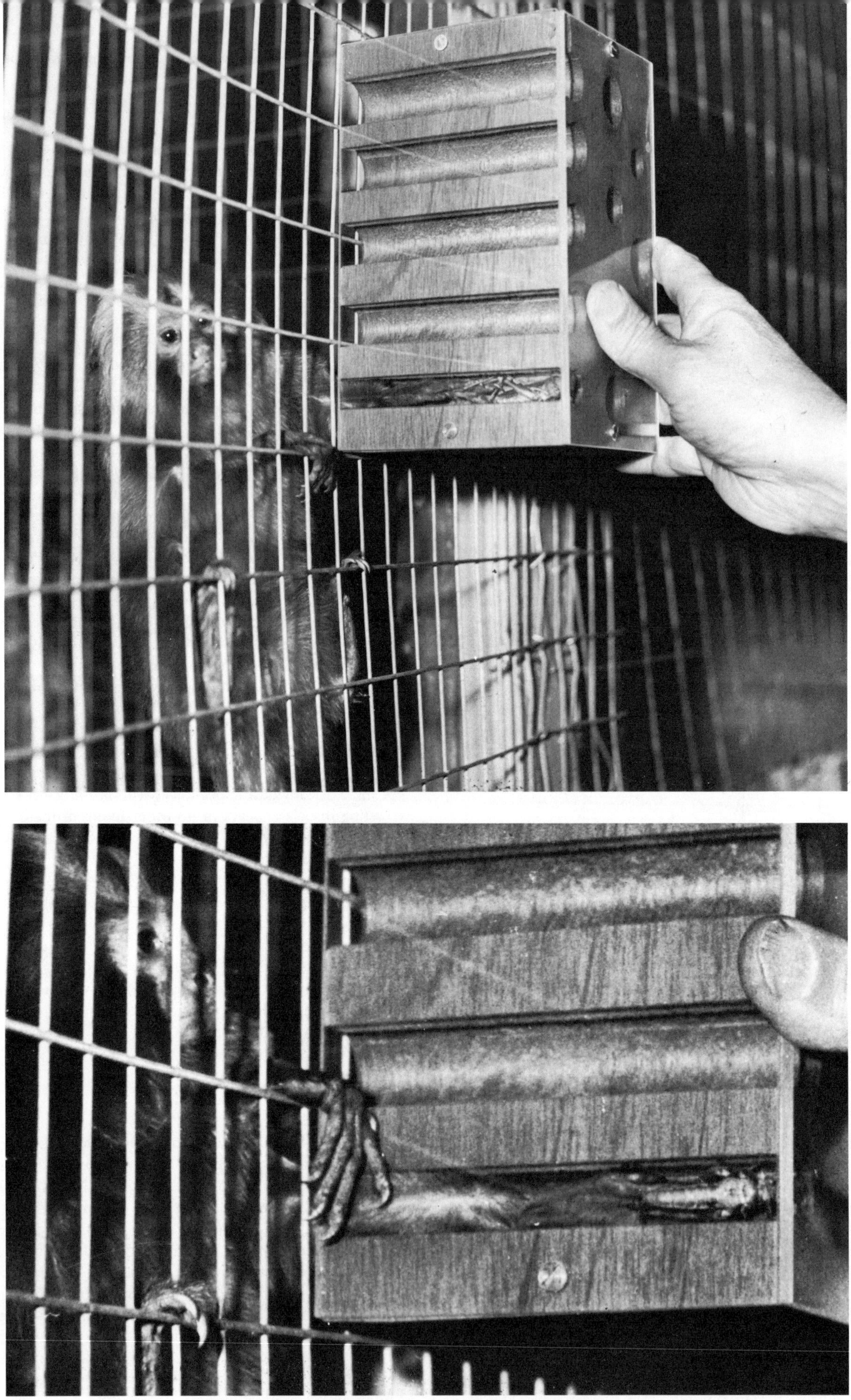

Fig. XI.16. Golden Lion-tamarin, *Leontopithecus rosalia rosalia*: The long thin arms and elongate fingers are used for probing in holes and crevices and under loose bark and debris for arthropods, which are snagged with the sharp claws of digits III and IV. Shown is a perforated wooden block with grasshopper bait used for testing callitrichid hand use. The probing hand is visible through the plexiglass cover. The long, sharp-clawed fingers are seen in the enlarged lower figure.

Plate VII. Lion-Tamarins (*Leontopithecus rosalia*)

Golden rump Lion-Tamarin
(*Leontopithecus rosalia chrysopygus*).
(Plate courtesy of the Cologne Zoo).

Gold and Black Lion-Tamarin
(*Leontopithecus rosalia chrysomelas*).
(Plate courtesy of the Cologne Zoo).

Golden Lion-Tamarin
(*Leontopithecus rosalia rosalia*).
(Photo courtesy of the Brookfield Zoo).

78 *Leontopithecus rosalia* Linnaeus, Lion-tamarins
1. History, Characters, Evolution, and Subspecies

Distribution (fig. XI.1)

In historic times, eastern Brazil in southeastern Bahia, southern Espírito Santo, Guanabara, coastal Rio de Janeiro, and southern São Paulo from the Rio Paraná between the Rios Tietê and Paranapanema to the coastal ranges. The range before the advent of Europeans in Brazil, was certainly more extensive but not necessarily continuous and may have included suitable habitats in Minas Gerais.

Origin and Evolution

The ancestral form may have been nearly or entirely black, the mane uncomplicated, or no more so than in the living young of *Leontopithecus,* or as in adult *Cebuella.* Elongation of the mane with hypertrophy of the hairs of cheek, neck, and ear tufts and evolution of lateral coronal whorls and shortening of midfrontal hairs must have occurred before racial divergence. This ancestral lion-tamarin probably occupied suitable habitats throughout eastern Brazil from the Rio das Contas, Bahia, south to the Rio Paranapanema in São Paulo, and from the intervening coastal area inland to the Rio São Francisco and the Rio Grande-Paraná in Bahia, Minas Gerais, and São Paulo. Differentiation of modern forms probably began with extinction of the western and central populations because of a contraction of rain forests and isolation of peripheral populations in three relict forests during a dry interval of the Pleistocene.

The primary evolutionary strategy exercised by each of the three isolated lion-tamarin groups with respect to coat color appears to have been a switch from eumelanin to pheomelanin production, first in chromogenetic fields with high display value and finally overall.

Surviving populations of the southern extreme of the range in São Paulo appear to be nearest the ancestral form in their entirely black coat, now broken only by the flashing golden-reddish rump and thighs. Modern descendants of the isolated populations of the northern forest refuge of southeastern Bahia are still dominantly blackish but display brilliant gold and reddish forequarters, hind limbs, and caudal patches. The relict southern coastal populations, on the other hand, became dominantly golden with only a residuum of coppery and black and an overall trend toward dilution and loss of all pigment. The flash of the golden coat is considerably enhanced by the sheen of the long silky pelage.

Taxonomy

The three described forms of *Leontopithecus—rosalia, chrysomelas,* and *chrysopygus*—represent color grades of an otherwise morphologically uniform species. Complete chromatic integration in color is not evident in present material but can be extrapolated from what is known of adult and juvenal variation within each color grade. Color pattern, despite the range of color variation from black through the reds to white, remains similar throughout the species as here recognized. The pelage, which is more characteristic of the species than color or color pattern, also remains remarkably uniform, particularly with respect to such diagnostic details as texture, mane, ear tufts, and whorls in adults and in juvenals.

Della Serra (1951) called attention to differences between the incisors of *chrysomelas, chrysopygus,* and *rosalia.* Our material, inadequate as it is, does not bear out the distinctions made. Everything else known of all named forms of *Leontopithecus* point to their conspecificity.

The *Midas chrysomelas* recorded from Peru by Tschudi (1844, p. 54–55) must be something else, possibly the black-mantled *Saguinus fuscicollis leucogenys.*

Characters

Diagnostic. Largest of callitrichids; dominant color pale golden to orange, reddish, or black, individual hairs unbanded; long hairs of crown, cheeks, and sides of neck forming erectile mane concealing ears; hairs of interramia and throat cresting to midline and directed forward, hairs of underside of neck directed back; palmar and plantar surfaces narrow, digits elongate with length of middle finger (with claw) more than twice palmar width, digits 3 and 4 partially united by interdigital web.

Integument. Face nearly bare, the skin pigmented or unpigmented (fig. XI.17), hair of forehead short, adpressed, coming to a point between eyes and prolonged

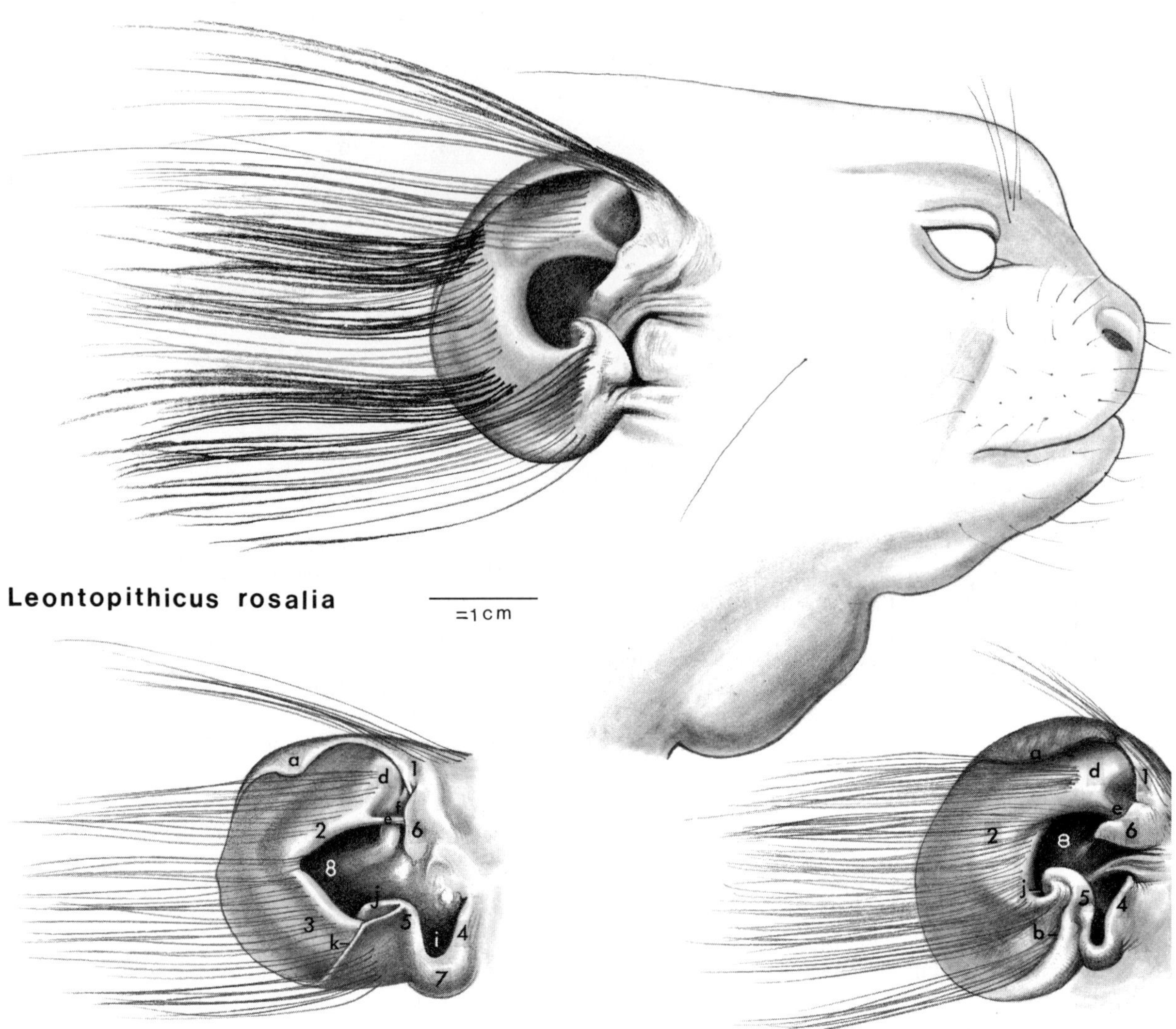

Fig. XI.17. *Leontopithecus rosalia rosalia*: Profile of head with mane and cover hairs removed to expose ear, vibrissae, facial pigmentation, and inflated laryngeal sac; *lower left,* ear of subadult; *lower right,* ear of juvenal. Symbols explained on page 104–5.

backward along midline of frontal; hair of cheeks, crown, throat, and sides of neck forming a long mane concealing ears; hairs of crown usually parted in center; thick intraramal tuft directed forward in the form of a goatee (figs. XI.18, 24, 28, 29); hairs of throat directed back; ears rounded, pigmented or unpigmented like face, the inner (lateral) surface with long tufts; general coloration from golden orange or reddish to straw color or whitish in some individuals or populations, to dominantly black in others, individual hairs uniformly colored or slightly darker or paler basally than terminally but not annulated; tail nearly uniformly colored, bicolor or particolor, sometimes with golden or reddish annulations, terminal tuft usually thickened; genitalia little pigmented or unpigmented.

Vibrissae (fig. XI.17). Supraorbitals, rhinarials, mystacials, and mentals moderately well defined; genals of *L. rosalia rosalia* distinguishable in fluid specimens as black hairs slightly longer and stiffer than golden facial hairs of cheek, genals not evident in black-faced *chrysomelas,* interramals not evident; ulnar carpals usually detectable; gular and pectoral spines absent.

Molt. A distinct molt pattern is not evident in present material. It appears, however, that in *L. rosalia rosalia* the older pelage fades progressively. It has been noted (I. Geoffroy 1827, p. 520, and see below, p. 846) that the pelage of wild-caught individuals is often replaced in captivity by a paler one.

Young (fig. XI.2). Generally like adult in color pattern and pelage but mane little developed, long frontal hairs extending straight back from forehead without forming two lateral tufts; ears not fully concealed.

For additional information, see Growth and Development, below (p. 851), and subspecies accounts.

Comparisons

Large size, long, slender hands, feet, and digits, the proximal phalanges of middle fingers connected by a membrane, thickly haired forehead, long side whiskers, ear-concealing erectile mane and normal absence of agouti-patterned hairs are some of the more obvious external characters which singly or in combination separate lion tamarins from all others. The long cheek hairs are the muttonchops of *Saguinus leucopus* and *Callimico goeldii.* In *Leontopithecus,* however, they are longer and contribute to formation of the mane. The lateral coronal whorls are the principal components of the dorsal aspect of the mane, but similar whorls in *Callimico* and *Saguinus leucopus* are located between and behind the ears, not in front as in *Leontopithecus*. The ears are also concealed by the headdress in *Callimico* but not in *Saguinus*. The goatee of the lion-tamarin is suggested in *S. leucopus* but in no other callitrichid. *Callimico* and the larger tamarins average nearly as large as the lion-tamarin. In coloration, *Leontopithecus rosalia chrysopygus* is nearest darkest representatives of *Saguinus nigricollis*. Some of the paler or straw-colored individuals of *L. r. rosalia* may be matched with specimens of *Callithrix humeralifer chrysoleuca* or *Callithrix argentata*, particularly *C. a. leucippe*.

Saturation and Bleaching (fig. XI.1)

Saturation of the postulated general agouti color pattern of the stock from which lion-tamarins sprang must have been to eumelanin. Significant diversification in coat color and pattern in the ancestral lion-tamarin is manifested only by a progressive switching from eumelanin to pheomelanin production in certain chromogenetic fields. The switching process begins with the expression of reddish orange on rump and thighs of the dominantly black *Leotopithecus rosalia chrysopygus*. Switching advances to the forequarters and parts of the tail of *L. r. chrysomelas* and becomes generalized in the dominantly golden *L. r. rosalia*.

Further color change in *Leontopithecus rosalia rosalia* can occur only through bleaching along the pheomelanin pathway. The trunk is most affected, the crown least, with the short-haired midfrontal wedge between coronal tufts darkest, often with some hairs retaining the eumelanin pigment. The tail may also conserve a pattern of eumelanin, usually in the form of annulations, as in *Callithrix jacchus*.

The effects of domestication or captivity complicate or distort the natural evolutionary bleaching process in *rosalia*. Some caged individuals bleach through a series of molts and may become nearly or completely whitish, others variegated with white.

Coimbra-Filho (1965, p. 109), then Director of the National Zoological Park in Rio de Janeiro, states that bleaching "frequently observed in the animals [i.e., captive *Leontopithecus rosalia rosalia*] can be avoided by feeding them eggs and carrots, both rich in carotenoids." The bright color of the caged Golden Lion-tamarin, he affirmed later (1969, p. 46; 1970a, p. 252) is lost after several months of nourishment deficient in protein and carotenoids, mainly those found in certain arthropods. A properly balanced diet, he concluded, restores life and brilliance to the color of the animal.

Perhaps the conditions described by Coimbra-Filho are the normal molt cycle from the shedding of old, worn, and faded pelage to its replacement by a sleek, brightly colored new pelage, with growth accelerated and health possibly enhanced by the rich diet. So far as is known, carotenoids are not present in hair or hair follicles, and diets cannot restore pigments and pristine sheen to old and dead pelage.

Exposure for long daily periods to direct sunlight in the outdoor cages in the Rio de Janeiro Zoo, may alone have contributed to the bleaching and loss of pelage observed by Coimbra-Filho. Benirschke and Richart (1963, p. 72) report that the Golden Lion-tamarins in their laboratory colony received direct ultraviolet irradiation daily from a General Electric sunlamp placed about 1 foot from the cage. The dilute pigmentation of the animals' fur caused some alopecia and necessitated reduction of sunning. Benirschke and Richart suggested replacing ultraviolet light treatment with vitamin supplements in the diet.

Depilation and Depigmentation

The face of *Leontopithecus rosalia* is sparsely haired, the frontal patch with short, pale, adpressed hairs penetrating the crown as a wedge. The seeming "bald spot" recalls the "bare" frontal region of *Saguinus leucopus* and the frontal blaze of *Callithrix jacchus*.

The facial skin and ears of *chrysopygus* are blackish, judged from the literature. In *chrysomelas,* they are described as fully pigmented in adults, and they are unpigmented in a juvenal at hand. Face and ears vary from unpigmented to completely pigmented in *rosalia.*

Coloration

Coimbra-Filho (1970, p. 255) suggests that the dominantly golden color of *Leontopithecus rosalia rosalia* may be protective or concealing and not just a more or less stabilized product of social selection as I have defined it here (p. 100) and elsewhere. (1968). A predator, Coimbra-Filho feels, may confuse the color of the Golden Lion-tamarin with scattered patches of light filtering through the forest canopy (cf. fig. XI.20). He also believes that the blackish and golden colors of *chrysomelas* and *chrysopygus* produce the effects of light and shadow. Such color patterns, he avers, are examples of "obliterative coloration" as defined by Cott (1940, p. 35).

This interesting and imaginative hypothesis lacks consistency. It is unlikely that a coloration that varies from almost completely black through black with increasing amounts of reddish or golden, and from almost completely golden to yellowish or almost all white would be equally concealing under similar conditions. Should one color pattern be more "obliterative" than another, the concealment afforded would benefit only the happy animal with the right pattern stationed in precisely the right place on a bright day with sun high and a light breeze gently stirring the canopy leaves. At this hour, however, warm-blooded vertebrates, whether prey or predator, are usually retired or inactive. Coimbra-Filho specifies only a hawk (*Spizaetus*) as a probable predator. Most important callitrichid enemies, apart from man, are the nocturnal felids and snakes, which do not distinguish colors, at least at night.

The coloration of lion-tamarins, by human criteria, is conspicuous. A color pattern attractive to primates cannot be concealing to predatory birds that depend mainly on sight for localizing prey. Routine activities and vocalizations make lion-tamarins even more conspicuous, often at great distances, and even out of sight. Visibility, in terms of sound, movement, and color, not concealment, is the primary factor in callitrichid security. Shrill cries of alarm alert all members of the group. The swift scattering of individuals frustrates, and the conspicuous coloration distracts the predator as bounding, leaping monkeys crisscross the flight path of the target prey.

Emphasis on the protective value of coloration is often misplaced. An experienced predator zeros in on his intended victim with the full power of all his senses. A resting monkey may be detected by sound, by smell, by body heat, or by sight alone, and the fleeing primate is not concealed by its color. In the absence of a ready haven, escape for the target prey lies in evasive action and distractive sorties by other members of the group. The instinct for mutual protection among callitrichids is strong. Coimbra-Filho notes that the flight of lion-tamarins he came upon appeared to be disorganized. Very likely, at sight of the observer, the alarmed tamarins took to distractive flight, leaving the beholder disorganized.

Conspicuous or attractive coloration like that of most callitrichids is not concealing, but for that reason is not less protective. Coimbra-Filho concedes that the lion-tamarin color pattern may be largely controlled by social selection, but still only partly. He (1970, p. 255) maintains that predator selection is also an important factor. I find it difficult to conceive in this particular case that selection for coloration could be controlled by such diverse if not entirely antithetical selective factors.

Conservation

The status of *Leontopithecus rosalia* in eastern Brazil has been examined by the Brazilian zoologist Adelmar Faria Coimbra-Filho. His survey, published in 1969, shows the geographic range of the golden race *L. rosalia rosalia,* which formerly extended over thousands of square kilometers, shrunken to an area of 900 square kilometers in the lower Rio São João Valley in the State of Rio de Janeiro. Dr. Coimbra-Filho notes that the remnants of suitable habitat in this circumscribed range are disappearing as a result of lumbering, farming, road building, and urbanization. The Golden Lion-tamarin population of the area, according to Coimbra-Filho, had then been reduced to about 600 individuals. The estimate in 1971 was 400.

In view of the urgent need for protection and conservation, Coimbra-Filho recommended the establishment of controlled breeding centers in seminatural and artificial habitats, including zoological parks, use of natural refuges (see Perry 1971), and public parks such as the Parque Nacional da Tijuca in Guanabara State (cf. Coimbra-Filho and Aldrighi 1971; Magnanini and Coimbra-Filho 1972; S. Hampton 1972). The *chrysomelas* population in 1971 was an estimated 200–300, that of *chrysopygus* 100–500 (Magnanini, Coimbra-Filho, Mittermeier, and Aldrighi, 1975).

Survival of the northern race of the lion-tamarin, *Leontopithecus rosalia chrysomelas,* is similarly endangered by the shrinkage and fragmentation of its range and by human predation. The southern race, *L. r. chrysopygus,* which seemed to have disappeared, at least in the eastern part of southern São Paulo, was rediscovered (Coimbra-Filho 1970) in good condition and occupying a substantial area in and around the Floresta Estadual da Morro du Diablo (339c), a forest reserve in extreme western São Paulo.

Considerable progress has already been made toward conservation of *Leontopithecus.* The Brazilian government now prohibits exportation of the animal and provides protection in some national reserves. North American and European institutions have banned importation, and special breeding centers in the United States (cf. C. A. Hill 1970) are attempting to conserve and propagate lion-tamarins in captivity (cf. p. 00).

The number of lion-tamarins used in biomedical and taxonomic research, behavioral studies, and museum and zoo exhibits has been insignificant compared with the total of other monkeys, or even other kinds of callitrichids, used for the same purposes (cf. Thorington 1972). Conservation of the species in guarded preserves would enormously enhance the value of the animal for scientific study. This is in addition to the essential role the lion-tamarin performs in nature's economy and the animal's aesthetic appeal to man. Aroused biologists and conservationists have already taken steps toward positive action.

A conference sponsored by the Wild Animal Propagation Trust for conservation of the lion-tamarin was held February 1972 in Washington, D.C. The published proceedings edited by Donald D. Bridgewater, contain a large body of information on the taxonomy, present and past distribution, behavior, reproduction, and the care and maintenance in captivity of the lion-tamarin. Of special interest are the articles by Magnanini and Coimbra-Filho (1972) on the establishment in Brazil of a captive breeding program and wildlife-research center for the lion-tamarin, the account by Du Mond (1972) of a basic husbandry program for the lion-tamarin, and the recommendations by Kleiman (1972) for research priorities and conservation measures. Lion-tamarin conservation and breeding are discussed in greater detail below (p. 847).

Key to the Subspecies of *Leontopithecus Rosalia*

1. Mane and trunk blackish, outer side of thighs contrastingly colored golden to reddish *L. r. chrysopygus* (p. 829)

1′. Mane, at least in front, mostly or entirely golden, reddish or coppery, trunk blackish, reddish, golden or buffy, thighs not contrastingly colored 2

2. Trunk blackish . . . . *L. r. chrysomelas* (p. 835)

2′. Trunk reddish, orange, golden, or buffy to nearly white . . . . *L. r. rosalia* (p. 841)

LEONTOPITHECUS ROSALIA CHRYSOPYGUS MIKAN, GOLDEN-RUMP LION-TAMARIN

Fig. XI.18. *Leontopithecus rosalia chrysopygus,* adult male (natural size). (Photo courtesy of A. F. Coimbra-Filho.)

Synonymic History

Jacchus chrysopygus Mikan, 1823, *Delectus florae et faunae Brasiliensis, Vienna,* fasc. 3, pl. (animal, skull, front teeth). Lesson, 1827, *Bull. Sci. Nat. Geol., Ferussac* 11:385—abstract of original description. Lesson, 1834, *Compl. Buffon* 4:285—characters.

Jacchus [Midas] chrysopygus, I. Geoffroy, 1827, *Dict. Class. Hist. Nat.* 12:520—characters ex Mikan.

Midas chrysopygus, Schinz, 1825, *Cuvier's das Thierreich,* 4:284—characters. Pelzeln, 1883, *Verh. K. K. Zool.-Bot. Gesellsch., Wien, Beih.* 33:26—BRAZIL: *São Paulo* (Varge grande [= Vargem Grande]; Ypanema). Ihering, 1894, *Cat. Mamm. São Paulo,* p. 30—BRAZIL: *São Paulo.*

H[apale (Midas)] chrysopyga Voigt, 1831, *Cuvier's das Thierreich,* 1:100—classification.

H[apale (Leontocebus)] chrysopygus, Wagner, 1840, *Schreber's Säugth., Suppl.* 1:ix, 249, 314—BRAZIL: *São Paulo* (Ipanema); characters.

Hapale chrysopyga, Wagner, 1848, *Abh. Akad. Wiss. Munich* 5:476—BRAZIL: *São Paulo.* Schlegel, 1876, *Les singes. Simiae,* p. 254—BRAZIL: *São Paulo* (Ipanema, male and female cotypes); characters. Jentink, 1892, *Cat. Syst. Mamm. Mus. Pays-Bas* 11:55—BRAZIL: *São Paulo* (Ipanema, male and female cotypes).

H[apale (Midas)] chrysopygus, Wagner, 1855, *Schreber's Säugth., Suppl.* 5:138—classification.

M[arikina] chrysopygus, Reichenbach, 1862, *Vollst. Naturg. Affen,* p. 9, pl. 2, fig. 31 (animal)—characters.

Leontocebus [(Tamarinus)] chrysopygus, Elliot, 1913, *A review of the Primates,* 1:201—characters ex cotype in Leiden museum.

Leontocebus chrysopygus, Vieira, 1944, *Papeis Avulsos, São Paulo* 4:4—BRAZIL: *São Paulo* (Vitoria, Botucatú; Baurú). Krieg, 1948, Zwischen Anden und Atlantik (Munich), p. 475—BRAZIL: *São Paulo* (Rio Paranapanema, right bank); a relict becoming extinct. Della Serra, 1951, *Pap. Avulsos, Dept. Zool., São Paulo* 10(8):149, figs. 6*a*, 7, 8 (incisors)—morphology of incisors; comparisons. Vieira, 1955, *Arq. Zool., São Paulo* 8:398—BRAZIL: São Paulo (Ipanema; Botucatú; Baurú); local names, *saguí, sauim.* Osman Hill, 1957, *Primates,* 3:203, 262, 268, 271, fig. 44 (map, distribution)—characters; taxonomy; distribution.

L[eontocebus] chrysopygus, Hershkovitz, 1949, *Proc. U.S. Nat. Mus.* 98:423—classification; characters.

[Mystax] chrysopygus, Thomas, 1922, *Ann. Mag. Nat. Hist.* 9(9):198—classification.

Leontideus chrysopygus, Cabrera, 1958, *Rev. Mus. Argentino Cienc. Nat. "Bernardino Rivadavia"* 4(1):201—classification. Coimbra-Filho, 1970, *Rev. Brasil. Biol.* 30(2):249, 261, figs. 8, 9 (skin), figs. 10–13 (skull)—BRAZIL: *São Paulo* (Vitória, Botucatú; Baurú; Floresta Estadual do Morro do Diabo near Teodoro Sampaio; Presidente Epitácio; Presidente Wenceslau); characters; distribution; habits; habitat; common names (mico-leão prêto; sagüi prêto; sauí prêto; sauim prêto; probably extinct. Coimbra-Filho, 1970, *Rev. Brasil. Biol.* 30(4):609, figs. 1–4 (animals); BRAZIL: *São Paulo* (Floresta Estadual do Morro do Diabo; Frazenda Kitayama, Presidente Wenceslau; Presidente Epitacio); rediscovery of living animals; characters; distribution; habitat.

L[eontideus] chrysopigus [*sic*], Melo Carvalho, 1971, *Biol. Conserv.* 4(1):66—BRAZIL: *São Paulo* (western end of state); conservation.

L[eontopithecus] r[osalia] chrysopygus, Hershkovitz, 1972, *Int. Zoo Yearb.* 12:5, 9—classification; distribution; survival endangered.

Leontopithecus rosalia chrysopygus, Coimbra-Filho and Mittermeier, 1972, *Saving the lion marmoset* (Bridgewater, ed.), p. 11, fig. 3 (skull), fig. 6 (skin), fig. 7 (photo of original color plate of type specimen) fig. 8 (color pattern)—characters; distribution; taxonomy. Coimbra-Filho and Mittermeier, 1973, *Primates* 14(1):50, fig. 5 (mounted specimen)—BRAZIL: *São Paulo* (Morro do Diabo State Forest); ecology; distribution; habitat; habits. Silva, 1975, Zeitschr. Kölner Zoo, 18(4):113, pl. (animal color)—BRAZIL: *São Paulo* (ranged reduced to a 20,000 ha unprotected nature reserve); collection of 3 breeding pairs for Tijuca bank; reproduction; conservation.

L[eontopithecus] r[osalia] chrysopygus, Coimbra-Filho and Magnanini, 1972, *Saving the lion marmoset* (Beveridge, ed.), p. 59—conservation.

Midas [(*Leontopithecus*)] *ater*, Lesson, 1840, *Species des mammifères: Bimanes et quadrumanes . . .*, p. 203—new name for *Jacchus chrysopygus* Mikan.

[*Hapale*] (*Leontopithecus*) *ater*, Lesson, 1842, *Nouv. Tabl. Reg. Anim., Mamm.*, p. 9—classification.

Types. At least 6 cotypes, as follows: 2 males and 2 females, Vienna Museum, collected 19 March 1822 by Johann Natterer; a male and a female both mounted, in Leiden Museum, collected June 1822 by Johann Natterer; animal in the Vienna Museum figured by Mikan is selected as lectotype.

Type Locality. Ipanema (347) [= Varnhagen or Bacaetava], São Paulo, Brazil.

Distribution (fig. XI.1). In historic times, the tropical rain forests of São Paulo, Brazil; the highlands between the upper Rio Paranapanema-Itararé and upper Rio Tietê; unknown from the coast and coastal hills; altitudinal range, according to Coimbra-Filho (1970*a*, p. 265), 300 to 700 meters above sea level. The present range appears to be restricted to the Floresta Estadual do Morro do Diabo, and possibly a few other remnants of suitable habitat in the municipios of Presidente Wenceslau and Presidente Epitacio in southwestern São Paulo State.

Environment. Mean annual rainfall along the Rio Paraná in western São Paulo where a few relict stands of primary forest provided haven for Golden-rump Lion-tamarins varies from 1,000 to 1,300 mm. The dry season extends from May through September. Rainfall along the Rio Paranapanema to its mouth at the Rio Paraná varies from 1,100 to 1,700 mm, the precipitation increasing from west to east. The dry season begins later than along the Paraná and the rainiest months are January and February. The mean temperature of the coldest month is less than 18° C. and that of the warmest month is over 22° C. Elevation along the banks of the Paraná and the Paranapanema ranges from about 300 to 450 meters above sea level.

Taxonomy. In his description of *chrysopygus* Mikan pointed to *rosalia* as most nearly related. Authors agreed until Forbes (1894, p. 144) listed the species between two tamarins genus *Saguinus*. Elliot (1913*a*, p. 200) followed suit and Thomas (1922, p. 198) included it in his genus *Mystax* [= *Saguinus*] while *rosalia* was referred to the then-restricted genus *Leontocebus*. The Golden-rump Lion-tamarin was since regrouped with *rosalia* and *chrysomelas* (cf. Vieira 1944, p. 4; Hershkovitz 1949, p. 423).

Diagnostic Characters. Trunk, mane, and forelimbs black.

Coloration (fig. XI.18, 19, pl. VII). The following is based on the original description and color plate of the type (Mikan, 1823), of the type series (1 male, 2 females) in the Vienna Museum, and a subadult male and female of the original Natterer series in the Leiden Museum.

> Facial skin darkly pigmented, hairs of forehead in adult type (fide Mikan) short, golden, adpressed, coming to a point between eyes and prolonged as a wedge along midfrontal line, in Leiden specimens, hairs of forehead black, long, directed back and entering into composition of mane; hairs of cheeks and crown forming a long, blackish erectile mane concealing ears; nape, shoulders, arms, back, sides of body, chin to belly black; inner sides of thighs reddish gold mixed with black, outer sides with more black, knee patch black; rump golden or reddish more or less mixed with blackish hairs; base of tail like rump, remainder of tail and feet, black; scrotum "grayish" (Pelzeln 1883, p. 26).

Schlegel's (1876, p. 254) diagnosis of the aforementioned male and female follows, translated from the French: "Black; rump, basal portion of tail, thighs and legs reddish; hairs in front of forehead and base of nose of ordinary length [i.e., not short as in *rosalia* and *chrysomelas*]." Elliot (1913*a*, p. 201) mentions "a few white hairs above eyes" of type in the Vienna Museum.

The description that follows quoted from Coimbra-Filho and Mittermeier (1972, p. 17) is based on 4 skins in the São Paulo Museum, the two mounted specimens from Presidente Wenceslau, and what the senior author could have glimpsed of three fleeing individuals in the Morro do Diabo State Forest in western São Paulo.

> "*L. chrysopygus* has even less of the golden-yellow color pattern than *L. chrysomelas*. Glossy black predominates except on the rump, base of the tail and inner and outer parts of the legs. The hairs on the head are black except for a small yellowish patch on the forehead and some reddish-brown hairs at the edges of the mane. The outer surfaces of the legs are reddish or yellowish-brown, tending more towards red in the males and yellow in the females in the few speci-

Fig. XI.19. *Leontopithecus rosalia chrysopygus,* young adult male eating a banana; same captive shown in fig. XI.18.

mens observed. A black patch in the knee region varies in extent from individual to individual. Inner surfaces of the legs are also reddish or yellowish-brown. The reddish tones on the legs become darker towards the feet, while the feet themselves are black.

"The extent of light color on the rump and base of the tail is variable. The four specimens in the São Paulo Museum and three live individuals observed in the Morro do Diabo State Forest have the golden-yellow color restricted to a small area at the base of the tail. Surrounding parts of the rump are dark reddish-brown in color. The female of a pair collected in Presidente Wenceslau, W. São Paulo, has a much larger patch of light yellowish-brown on the lower back and roughly the first 80 mm. of the tail. In the male of this pair, the rump and base of the tail are reddish-brown. In both of these animals, the yellowish or reddish-brown coloration on the rump, outer parts of the legs and base of the tail is lighter and more extensive than in the other specimens observed. Natterer's description (in Pelzeln, 1883) of the type series agrees most with the male from Presidente Wenceslau."

Measurements. See appendix table 2.

Comparisons. Distinguished from *rosalia* by blackish mane, trunk, and forearms; from *chrysomelas* by wholly black mane, forelimbs, and tail except for reddish base.

Occurence and Survival. Nothing more was known of the Golden-rump Lion-tamarin until its rediscovery in western São Paulo State by Coimbra-Filho (1970*a,* p. 267; 1970*b*). Evidence of the existence of *chrysopygus* was gotten from a taxidermist who had mounted two skins of individuals shot in the Fazenda Kitayama, an estate in the municipio of Presidente Wenceslau. It proved, however, that the woodlot where the "sauis-pretos" lived had been destroyed. Continued search of remaining forest stands in the municipio led to the sighting at about 4:00 P.M., 14 May 1970, of three "sauis-pretos" running through the trees in the Floresta Estadual do Morro do Diabo. It appeared that the three *chrysopygus* were the

Fig. XI.20. Scene in the Reserva Florestal do Morro do Diabo (1970). View of the very place where living *Leontopithecus rosalia chrysopygus* were seen 14 May 1970 by Coimbra-Filho (1970*b*, p. 614, fig. 6). In the caption to this photograph Coimbra-Filho (p. 614) observes that the interlacing branches and vines and contrasting lights and shadows are possibly protective or concealing for the lion-tamarins. These light effects, however, seem to be flitting and fleeting. Coimbra-Filho did distinguish three lion-tamarins here, and it is not likely that the discernment of sharp-eyed hawks and nocturnal predators would be less. (Photo courtesy of A. F. Coimbra-Filho.)

Fig. XI.21. Forest habitat of *Leontopithecus rosalia chrysopygus* in the Morro do Diabo; tree in foreground is an "adro-rosa" (*Adrela*). (Photo courtesy of A. F. Coimbra-Filho.)

Fig. XI.22. Highway to Morro do Diabo bulldozed through forest of the Municipio of Presidente Wenceslau. *L. r. chrysopygus* occurs here. (Photo courtesy of A. F. Coimbra-Filho.)

Fig. XI.23. Scene of highway and destroyed portions of state forest in Municipio of Presidente Wenceslau; Morro do Diabo or Devil's Mount in background. (Photo courtesy of A. F. Coimbra-Filho.)

rear guard of a band in flight. When first encountered, the animals were no more than 15 meters away and at a height of 6 to 10 meters (fig. XI.20).

The 37,156 hectare Floresta Estadual (State Forest) do Morro do Diabo may be the last refuge of *Leontopithecus rosalia chrysopygus* (figs. XI.20–23). The forest was revisited in July 1971 by Coimbra-Filho (Coimbra-Filho and Mittermeier 1973, p. 52). Lion-tamarins were not encountered on this occasion, but the warden had seen groups "at least 20 times in the past year." The same warden had heard rumors of a callitrichid in Barranca do Rio Paraná, about 120 km from Morro do Diabo. Coimbra-Filho and Mittermeier (1973, p. 62) question whether the animal "is actually *L. r. chrysopygus* or the more abundant *Callithrix aurita.*" Another rumor heard by Coimbra-Filho (1970*b*, p. 613) was of a *chrysopygus*like callitrichid said to inhabit the wooded right bank of the Rio Ivinheima near Pôrto Guarani in Mato Grosso. As yet, only *Callithrix argentata melanura* is known from the State of Mato Grosso (cf. map, fig. IX.36).

The present number of wild-living Golden-rump Lion-tamarins according to Coimbra-Filho (1970*b*, p. 613), is less than 100, with most in the Morro do Diabo Reserve, and the remaining in neighboring stands of primary forest, all in southwestern São Paulo.

Remarks. According to Pelzeln (1883, p. 26) the original series of *chrysopygus,* collected by Johann Natterer, consisted of 8 specimens. He lists and describes an adult male and female from Ipanema, an adult female from Vargen Grande (349), and a young female without data but presumably from one of the two mentioned localities. These are in the Vienna National Museum. Two mounted specimens, a male and a female from Ipanema, are in the Leiden Museum. This accounts for 6 of the 8 Natterer specimens.

Regarding the Leiden material, Schlegel (1876, p. 251) notes that the hairs of midfrontal region are not short as in adult *rosalia* but elongate as in juvenal *rosalia.* This I have confirmed, but the mounted specimen appears to be less than fully adult. The same pattern obtains in comparably aged and mounted specimens of *rosalia* and *chrysomelas* in the Leiden Museum. The pelage of the forehead shown in the colored plate of the type of *chrysopygus* appear to be short and golden as in *rosalia.* Mikan (1823) specifically states, freely translated from the Latin, "the forehead is covered with bright yellow adpressed hairs which extend midfrontally as a wedge dividing the mane."

Study Material Extant. In addition to the original series of 8 specimens collected by Natterer, *Leontopithecus rosalia chrysopygus* is known from 4 specimens in the São Paulo Museum, recorded by Vieira (1944, p. 4). The latter were collected in 1902 (Victória and Botucatú) and 1905 (Baurú). Several skins of *chrysopygus* shot on the right bank of the Rio Paranapanema were presented in 1938 by Dr. Hempel of São Paulo to Professor Krieg (1948, p. 475). Krieg remarked on the restricted range of the race, its scarcity and absence from the Serra do Mar, and the probability of imminent extinction. Pressumably, the skins were deposited in a German institution. The two mounted individuals shot in Presidente Wenceslau, which stimulated search for the living animals in the same municipio, are now preserved in the Museu da Fauna, Rio de Janeiro.

Specimens Examined. 6. BRAZIL—*São Paulo*: Ipanema, 5 syntypes of *chrysopygus* (RMNH, 2; NHMW, 3); Vargem Grande, 1 (NHMW).

LEONTOPITHCUS ROSALIA CHRYSOMELAS KUHL, GOLD AND BLACK LION-TAMARIN

Fig. XI.24. *Leontopithecus rosalia chrysomelas,* adult female captured in Itabuna, Bahia, now in Instituto da Conservação da Natureza (about one-half natural size). (Photo courtesy of A. F. Coimbra-Filho.)

Synonymic History

Midas chrysomelas Kuhl, 1820, *Beitr. Zool.,* p. 51. Avila Pires, 1965, *Amer. Mus. Novit.* no. 2209, p. 11—type history.

M[idas] chrysomelas, I. Geoffroy, 1851, *Cat. Primates,* p. 62—male cotype in Paris Museum, accessioned 1820.

[?] *M[idas] chrysomelas,* Tschudi, 1844, *Arch. Naturg. Jahrg.* ser. 10, 1:246—PERU [certainly a misidentification, for the species does not occur naturally in Peru; it is cited here only for convenience of reference].

Nidas [*sic*] *chrysomelas,* Avila Pires, 1965, *Amer. Mus. Novit.,* no. 2209, p. 16—misprint for *Midas.*

Jacchus [(*Midas*)] *chrysomelas,* Desmarest, 1820, *Mammalogie* p. 95—characters. Desmarest, 1827, *Dict. Sci. Nat.* 47:22—characters; species not seen. I. Geoffroy, 1827, *Dict. Class. Hist. Nat.* 12:520—characters; *"chrysurus"* [nomen vanum?] attributed to Wied-Neuwied and regarded as possibly a synonym.

Hapale chrysomelas, Wied-Neuwied, 1821, *Reise nach Brasilien* 2:137, footnote—BRAZIL: *Bahia* (type locality, Ribeirão das Minhocas "am Reise von S. Pedro d'Alcantara durch die Urwälder"); description. Wied-Neuwied, 1822, Abbild. *Beitr. Naturg. Brasil.,* Lief 2, pl. 3 (animal) and text—BRAZIL: *Bahia* (Ilhéos; Rio Pardo); characters; local names, *Sahuim preto, pakakang.* Wagner, 1848, *Abh. Akad. Wiss. Munich* 5:476—diagnosis. Sclater, 1869, *Proc. Zool. Soc. London* 1869:407—BRAZIL: believed to be first live individual exhibited in society's collection. Schlegel, 1876, *Les singes. Simiae, Mus. Pays-Bas,* p. 254—BRAZIL: *Bahia* (Sertam d'Ilhéus); female cotype; characters. Jentink, 1892, *Cat. Syst. Mamm. Mus. Pays-Bas* 11:55—BRAZIL: *Bahia* (Sertam d'Ilhéos); adult female cotype mounted in Leiden Museum.

H[apale] chrysomelas, Wied-Neuwied, 1826, *Beitr. Naturg. Brasil.,* p. 153—BRAZIL: *Bahia* (Rio Ilhéos; Rio Pardo; Barra da Vareda; north of Rio Belmonte); characters; habits. Burmeister, 1854, *Syst. Uebers. Thiere Brasil.* 1:35 —BRAZIL: *Bahia* (Rio Ilhéus; Rio Pardo); characters.

H[apale (*Leontocebus*)] *chrysomelas,* Wagner, 1840, *Schreber's Säugth., Suppl.* 1:ix, 248—characters.

H[apale (Midas)] chrysomelas, Wagner, 1855, *Schreber's Säugth., Suppl.* 5:139—classification.

M[arikina] chrysomelas, Reichenbach, 1862, *Vollst. Naturg. Affen,* p. 8, pl. 2, fig. 28 (animal)—characters.

Leontopithecus chrysomelas, Gray, 1870, *Cat. monkeys, lemurs and fruit-eating bats, Brit. Mus.,* p. 65—BRAZIL.

L[eontopithecus] rosalia chrysomelas, Hershkovitz, 1972, *Int. Zoo Yearb.* 12:5, 9—classification; distribution; survival endangered.

L[eontopithecus] r[osalia] chrysomelas, Coimbra-Filho and Magnanini, 1972, *Saving the lion marmoset* (Bridgewater, ed.), p. 59—conservation.

Leontopithecus rosalia chrysomelas, Coimbra-Filho and Mittermeier, 1972, *Saving the lion marmoset* (Bridgewater, ed.), p. 10, fig. 3 (skull), fig. 5 (photo of original color plate of type specimen), fig. 8 (color pattern)—characters; distribution; taxonomy. Coimbra-Filho and Mittermeier, 1973, *Primates* 14 (1):50, figs. 3, 4 (animal)—BRAZIL: *Bahia* (Ilhéus; Una; Buerarema; Itabuna); *Espírito Santo* (Rio Mucurí, 15 km from coast); distribution; ecology; habitat; habits. Silva, 1975, Zeitschr. Kölner Zoo, 18(4):112, pl. (animal in color)—BRAZIL: Characters; conservation; breeding in Tijuca bank.

L[eontopithecus] r[osalia] chrysomelas, Coimbra-Filho and Magnanini, 1972, *Saving the lion marmoset* (Beveridge, ed.), p. 59—conservation.

Leontocebus chrysomelas, Elliot, 1913, *A review of the Primates,* 1:211—characters; male cotype in American Museum of Natural History. Laemmert, Ferreira and Taylor, 1946, *Amer. J. Trop. Med.* 26:31, 41—BRAZIL: Bahia (Almada; Fortuna; Pirataquissé; Urucutuca); yellow fever zoonosis. Della Serra, 1951, *Pap. Avulsos, Dept. Zool., São Paulo* 10(8):149, figs. 1–5, 6b (incisors)—incisor morphology and comparisons. Vieira, 1955, *Arq. Zool. São Paulo* 8:398—BRAZIL: *Bahia* (Ilhéus; Rio Pardo; Rio Gongogi); local name, *sauim-una.* Osman Hill, 1957, *Primates* 3:190, 193, 203, 262, 268, 270, fig. 44 (map, distribution); characters; distribution.

L[eontocebus] chrysomelas, Cabrera, 1917, *Trab. Mus. Nac. Cienc. Nat., Madrid,* ser. zool., no. 31:32—type of *Leontocebus* Wagner by selection. Hershkovitz, 1949, *Proc. U.S. Nat. Mus.* 98:423—classification; characters.

Leontideus chrysomelas, Cabrera, 1958, *Rev. Mus. Argentino Cienc. Nat. "Bernardino Rivadavia"* 4(1):200—classification. Coimbra-Filho, 1970, *Rev. Bras. Biol.* 30(2):249 figs. 1–4 (skull), fig. 5 (animal)—BRAZIL: *Bahia* (Estação da Mata do Cacau, Riberão da Fortuna; Fazenda São José, Rio do Braço, Pontal, Ilhéus; Poçoes; Una; Itabuna; Camamu; Maraú; Uruçuca); characters; comparisons; evolution; distribution; habits; habitat; common names (*mico-leão de cara dourada; mico leão prêto; sauí; sauí prêto; sauim; sauim do sertão; sauim-prêto; sauim-una; pakakang; grifado*).

L[eontideus] chrysomelas, Melo Carvalho, 1971, *Biol. Conserv.* 4(1):66—BRAZIL: *Bahia* (Una region); conservation.

[Jacchus] Chrysurus I. Geoffroy, 1827, *Dict. Class. Hist. Nat.* 12:520—name attributed to Maximilian Wied-Neuwied and cited under *Jacchus chrysomelas.*

Hapale chrysurus, Lesson, 1840, *Species des mammifères: Bimanes et quadrumanes . . . ,* p. 204—lapsus for *chrysomelas* Wied-Neuwied; type of *Midas (Leontopithecus) ater* Variété A.

[Midas (Leontopithecus) ater] Variété A, Lesson, 1840, *Species des mammifères: Bimanes et Quadrumanes . . . ,* p. 204—*"Chrysurus"* [= *Hapale chrysomelas*] Wied-Neuwied regarded as a variety of *ater* Lesson [= *chrysopygus* Mikan].

[Midas (Leontopithecus) ater] Variété B, Lesson, 1840, *Species de mammifères: Bimanes et Quadrumanes . . . ,* p. 205—*Hapale chrysomelas* Kuhl regarded as a variety of *ater* Lesson [= *chrysopygus* Mikan].

Types. Mounted specimens, said to have been preserved in the Berlin, Temminck (Leiden), and Maximilian Museums. A male of the original series was acquired by the Paris Museum and another male by the American Museum of Natural History; all collected about 1820 by Prince Maximilian Wied-Neuwied; syntype in Leiden Museum, no. 17961 (see Avila Pires, 1965, *American Mus. Novit.,* no. 2209, p. 11).

Type Locality. Ribeirão das Minhocas (302), left bank upper Rio dos Ilhéus (299), southern Bahia, Brazil (Wieud-Neuwied 1821, p. 137.).

Distribution (fig. XI.1). Tropical rain forests of coastal Bahia, eastern Brazil, formerly from the south bank of the Rio Contas to the north bank of the Rio Belmonte (or Jequitinhonha), between 14° and 16° south latitude, but now not farther than the north bank of the Rio Pardo (15° 40′ S). Much of the original forest has been replaced by cacao plantations with high shade trees where callitrichids and other monkeys may find shelter; altitudinal range, sea level to about 100 meters above along the coast and somewhat higher inland.

Small populations of *chrysomelas* may still be found, according to Coimbra-Filho (1970*a*, p. 258), in the vicinities of Ilhéus (299), Buerarema (299), Uruçuca (299), Itabuna (300), Una (303), Camamu (297a) and Maraú (297b). The municipios of Camamu and Maraú, however, lie north of the Rio das Contas, recognized by all authorities, including Coimbra-Filho (1970*a* p. 257), as the northern limit of the range of lion-tamarins. In a subsequent report on lion-tamarins, Coimbra-Filho and

Mittermeier (1973, p. 50) mention only Ilhéus, Buerarema, Itabuna, and Una as the areas in Bahia where *chrysomelas* may still be found. They add, however, that "a previously unknown population was discovered on the border between the states of Espírito Santo and Bahia (Ruschi, pers. comm.). This population is in a 5,000 hectare tract of virgin forest a few km south of the Rio Mucurí and 15–20 km from the coast. The discovery of this population extends the range of the subspecies approximately 3° farther south," or to approximately 18° S.

Coimbra-Filho has recently informed me (in a letter) that his personal investigations and those of reliable observers in the area convince him that there is absolutely no foundation for Ruschi's report of lion-tamarins in northern Espírito Santo. It appears therefore that in the absence of voucher specimens or reliable spot records, the present range of *chrysomelas* does not extend beyond the boundaries of the Rio das Contas in the north and the Rio Belmonte in the south as determined in 1821 by Maximilian Wied-Neuwied on the basis of his collections, observations, and the testimony of native hunters. Confirmed records and eyewitness reports accumulated to date fall within these boundaries.

Habitat and Environment. By all accounts the present range of the Gold and Black Lion-tamarin is reduced to a few isolated patches of forest and cacao plantations within an area extending about one degree north, one degree south and one degree west of *Ilhéus.* The ecology of the general region and habitats of its monkey fauna are described by Taylor and Fonseca (1946, p. 8) in a report on investigations of endemic yellow fever in the Ilhéus region of eastern Brazil. Their ecological data are mainly from Veloso (1946). His phytogeographic chart, used by Taylor and Fonseca, is reproduced here (fig. XI. 25) with some additions.

> "Bordering the sea is a flat strip of sandy soil varying in depth from a few hundred meters to several kilometers. This flat strip of sandy soil gives way to undulating hills, interlaced with small rapidly flowing rock-bed streams. As the hills are approached the soil changes from sandy marine type to a dark reddish clay enriched by the decompostion of gneiss which appears in outcroppings on the sides of hills and the eroded banks of the streams. Geologically it belongs to the archaic formation of the Serra do Mar. Near the sea the hills are low and gently rolling, rarely exceeding a height of 100 meters, but further inland the terrain becomes more broken and the elevation gradually increases to join the central plateau.
>
> "The *climate* varies with the distance from the coast. Along the seaboard and inland for a depth of 50 kilometers or more, depending upon the altitude, it may be described as a humid tropical climate. The mean annual temperature is slightly above 22° C. and the monthly mean temperature never falls below 18° C., nor does it vary more than 6° C. from month to month.
>
> "The *annual precipitation* usually exceeds 1,900 mm. and during the period (1924–1935) averaged 2,115.5 mm. The rainfall is fairly evenly distributed throughout the year but is commonly somewhat greater during the months of March, April and July, and again in November and December. A great part of the precipitation occurs in the form of thunder showers, and a day without some sunshine is infrequent. The heaviest and most equally dispersed rainfall occurs near the coast. Inland it tends to diminish and becomes more seasonal in character until the semiarid plateau region with its scanty and highly seasonal rainfall is reached.
>
> "The *predominant wind* from November to March is east by northeast, and during the remainder of the year it is east by southeast. The mean monthly wind velocity varies from 2 to 4 meters per second. It is usually somewhat stronger during the months of April, July and August. Except near the coast, where there is commonly a light to moderate breeze, there is little consistent air movement except preceding and during thunder storms, when it may for a limited period attain considerable velocity.
>
> "The character of the *vegetation* varies with the nature of the soil, rainfall, elevation and the distance from the coast. Bordering the sea and extending inland according to the width of the sandy soil, is a strip of halophilous vegetation among which planted coconut palms occur. Next comes the xerophilous zone which may be described as a transition between the halophilous and hygrophilous vegetation, and is characterized by the presence of cultivated piassava palms (*Attalea junifera*), scraggly forests or even patches of savanna. This zone, which is indefinite in extent, blends into the massive hygrophilous humid to semihumid forests that commence a few kilometers from the coast and extend inland for 40 kilometers or more. The hygrophilous belt has two characteristics. The semihumid mesothermal vegetation which covers the tops of hills is peculiar to the Ilheus region and can be clearly differentiated from the type which covers the tops of the Serra do Mar Mountains to the south. The humid megathermal vegetation covers the slopes of hills and lowlands and is essentially Amazonian in character; many of the same botanical species are found in both regions. At intervals along the coast, where the formation of sandbars or silt in the mouths of streams has obstructed the outflow of water, swamps covered with mangrove and other types of swamp vegetation have developed.
>
> "As the altitude and the distance from the coast increases and the rainfall diminishes and becomes more seasonal in distribution, the forests change from the humid and semihumid to the semiarid type. On the central plateau, where rainfall is scarce, the vegetation is xerophilous, consisting of stunted bushes, Cactaceae and Bromeliaceae. This general vegetational pattern extends from the Rio das Contas in the State of Bahia southward along the coast to the Rio Doce basin in the State of Espirito Santo.
>
> The most characteristic feature, and the one which is of particular interest, is the broad band of humid forest with its dense upper canopy that lies between the coast and the elevated central plateau. This type of forest and the accompanying climatic conditions are encountered only here and in portions of the Amazon basin and, it would appear, constitutes an environment peculiarly adapted to harboring the virus of jungle yellow fever.
>
> "The area chosen for more intensive study forms roughly a rectangle approximately 30 by 50 kilometers, bounded on the north by the Almada River which flows just south of Castelo Novo, on the west by Ita-

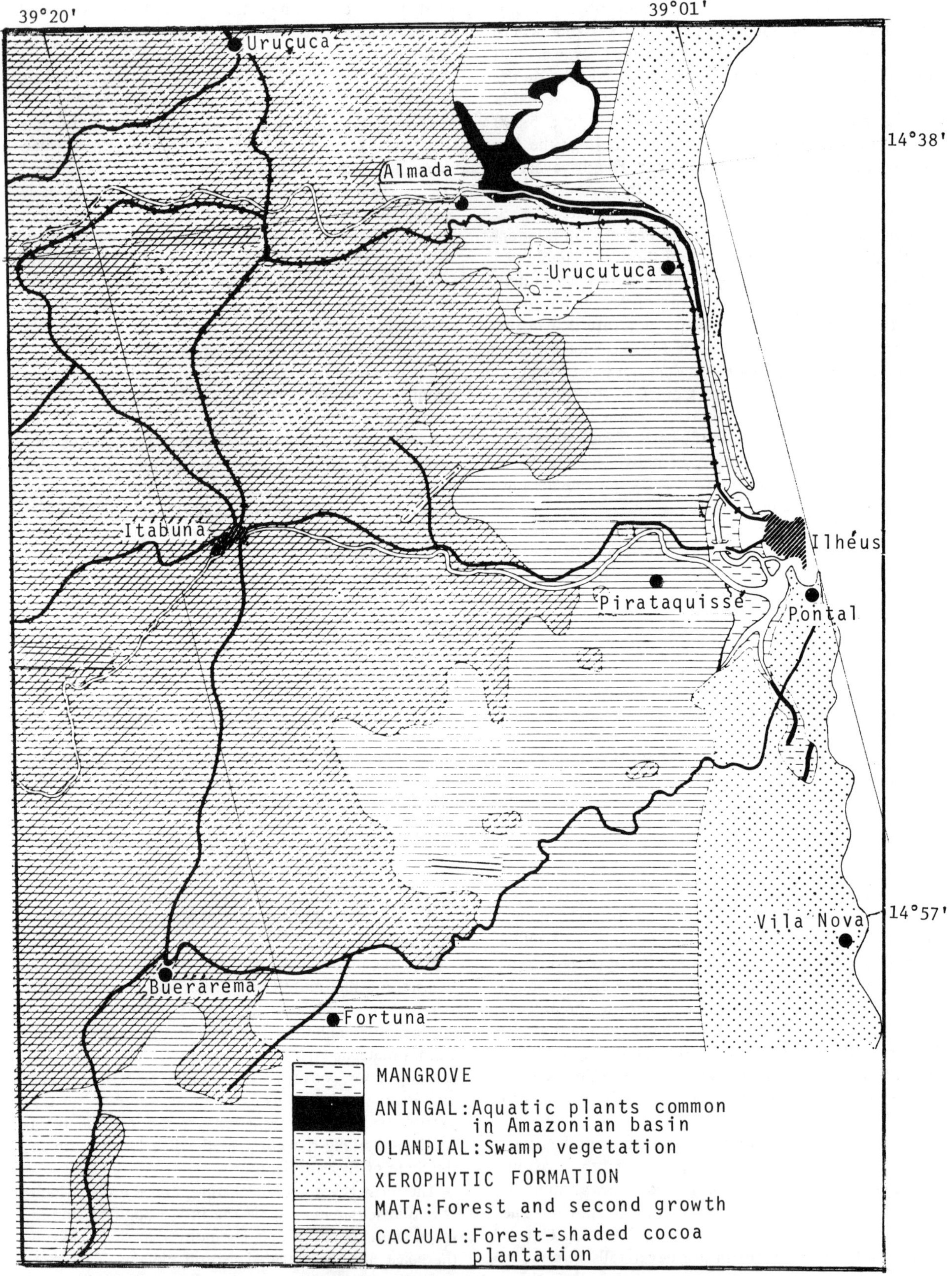

Fig. XI.25. Phytogeographic map of the part of the Ilhéus region investigated by the Serviço do Estudos e Pesquisa sôbre Febra Amarela (SEPSFA) conducted jointly by the Ministry of Health of Brazil and the International Health Division of the Rockefeller Foundation. Lion-tamarin collecting localities are plotted (see gazetter). (Map from Veloso 1946, with additions and translation of Portuguese legend.)

buna, on the south by Buerarema, and on the east by the sea. This will be referred to subsequently as the *Study Area*. The more extensive and older forests extend along the east near the coast and to the south (map 3) [map, fig. XI.25]. In the strict definition of the term there remains only a very limited amount of virgin forest in the area. From most of the forest indicated on the map [fig. XI.25] either selected timber has been cut or the land was at one time more or less completely cleared but has since returned to forest. There is also within this forested zone a rather extensive swamp lying between Aritagua and Castelo Novo. The western portion of the area is largely devoted to the cultivation of cacao.

"The zones, as shown on map 3 [fig. XI.25] represent the predominant type of vegetation only. In reality there are small cultivated areas, principally of mandioca and some cacao, and patches of pasture land within the more extensive forested region. Likewise there are clumps of trees, usually second-growth, or partially lumbered forests on the hilltops and along the streams in the cacao zone, as well as some open grasslands for pasturing pack-mules and a few cattle. The cacao is grown under partial shade afforded by tall trees that spread their branches 5 to 10 meters above the dense foliage of the smaller cacao trees. Thus, there are two distinct canopies, the less homogenous one above, through which filters some sunshine, and the lower canopy formed by the cacao trees which virtually prevents all direct rays of the sun from reaching the ground. The floor of the old and well-developed groves is open and free of surface vegetation. These shaded plantations, with the interspersed patches of forest, constitute a not unfavorable habitat for certain species of arboreal animals, such as marmosets. There are two methods of establishing the cacao. The first and more common procedure is to clear the forest floor but to leave enough trees standing to furnish the required shade. The second method is to clear the forest completely and to plant the young trees in corn or mandioca which furnish temporary shade until the fast growing tree of the genus *Erythrina* that is planted at the same time attains sufficient height to give permanent coverage."

The zoological collections made between 1943 and 1945 by the Serviço do Estudos e Pesquisas sôbre a Febre Amarela (SEPSFA) of the Ministry of Health in Brazil, in cooperation with the International Health Division of the Rockefeller Foundation, are described and analyzed by Laemmert, Ferreira, and Taylor (1946). Most of the study material came from four stations in the Ilhéus region. *Fortuna,* at the southern boundry of the Study Area, is in rolling hill country covered by old and mostly primary forest with relatively few openings for pasture and cultivated plots of mandioca and cacao. The nearby *Pirataquissé* (Pirataquicé) station is in a fazenda surrounded by the same type of old forest, but the more even topography of the region is more extensively cultivated. *Urucutuca* is in swampland that becomes innundated during the height of the rainy season. Patches of forest surrounding the swamp are mostly second growth whereas those on islands are climax. The *Almada* station is in a region almost entirely devoted to cultivation of cacao. Remaining tree cover is represented by stands of thinned-out forests and second growth on hilltops, along streams and in swamps.

The habitats of vertebrates collected at the *Pirataquissé* and *Fortuna* stations are treated as "Old-type forest" and those of *Almada* and *Urucutuca* as "Young-type forest" or "Swamp forest."

Nearly all the 1851 primates examined representing 6 species were purchased through local agents. The number captured in any one station or district depended largely on the influence of the agents, the interest of local hunters and the ease and security with which the largest number of monkeys of any kind could be secured in the shortest possible time. Hence, the number of each species delivered to SEPSFA is not a reliable indicator of habitat preferences population size, or relative number in the wild.

Black Tufted-ear Marmosets, *Callithrix jacchus penicillata,* made up 99% of the catch (1829 specimens). Only 14, or less than 0.8%, were *Leontopithecus rosalia chrysomelas.* Seven of them were taken in "Old-type forest." The same habitat yielded 155 marmosets, 3 howlers (*Alouatta guariba*), and 2 tufted capuchins (*Cebus apella xanthosternus*). The "Young-type forest" catch consisted of 1 lion-tamarin and 590 marmosets. Trapping in "Swamp forest" produced 1 lion-tamarin, 15 marmosets, and 1 titi (*Callicebus personatus melanochir*). Cacao plantations yielded 936 marmosets. In contrast, not one lion-tamarin was recorded from cacao, banana, or coconut plantations or groves. Habitat of the remaining 5 lion-tamarins was not specified (table 106).

At least 6 of the 14 *chrysomelas* collected by the Serviço do Estudos e Pesquisa sôbre a Febra Amarela (SEPSFA) are deposited in the Museu Nacional in Rio

Table 106. Kinds, Numbers, and Collecting Localities of Primates Captured in the Ilhéus, Bahia Region by the Serviço do Estudos e Pesquisa sôbre a Febra Amarela (SEPSFA).

Vegetation Type	*Bahia: Ilhéus Collecting Station*	*Leontopithecus rosalia chrysomelas*	*Callithrix jacchus penicillata*	*Callicebus personatus melanochir*	*Alouatta guariba*	*Cebus apella xanthosternus*	*Total*
Old-type forest	Pirataquissé and Fortuna[1]	7	155		3	2	167
Young-type forest	Almada	1	590				591
Swamp forest	Urucutuca[2]	1	15	1			17
Cacao plantation			936				936
Banana patch			26				26
Coconut grove			62				62
Not specified		5	45	1		1	52
Totals		14	1,829	2	3	3	1,851

SOURCE: Laemmert, Ferreira and Taylor (1946, p. 41)

[1] Includes some specimens from bordering cacao plantations

[2] Includes some specimens from "Young-type forest"

de Janeiro (Coimbra-Filho 1970*a*, p. 258). These include a specimen from the Fazenda São José, Pontal, Ilhéus, dated December 1944, and another from Fazenda São Luis, Rio do Braço (Pontal), Ilhéus, dated January 1945, captured in cacao groves (*roça de cacau*). A Field Museum specimen, one of the original 14 SEPSFA specimens, collected April 1945 in the Fazenda Borrachuda, Fortuna, Ilhéus, is labeled as having been taken in "Cacao."

Diagnostic Characters. Trunk entirely blackish; front of mane and forearms dominantly golden or reddish.

Coloration (figs. XI.24, 26, 27, pl. VII). Facial skin pigmented or unpigmented; pelage of cheeks and front of crown forming a resplendent golden to golden orange erectile mane parted in front and directed back, concealing ears; long hairs encircling face golden yellow to golden orange, distally becoming darker, crown black or silvery; ears rounded, inner (lateral) surface with black or dark brown tufts; nape, shoulder, and dorsum black thinly interspersed with reddish or coppery hairs, midportion of rump golden; sides of body like back or with a greater admixture of reddish hairs; chin and throat golden, orange, or coppery, chest and belly black, coppery, reddish, golden, or a combination of two or more of these colors; arms and hands golden yellow to golden orange; legs orange or reddish to black, feet similar or contrastingly colored golden orange or black; tail particolored, basal one-third golden or reddish, the bright color continuous with that of rump and prolonged distally for a variable distance as an attenuated band on upper surface of otherwise entirely black distal portion of tail.

Fig. XI.26. *Leontopithecus rosalia chrysomelas,* adult female, same shown in fig. XI.24. (Photo courtesy of A. F. Coimbra-Filho.)

Measurements. See appendix table 2.

Comparisons. Distinguished from black-bodied *chrysopygus* by golden anterior portion of mane, orange throat and forelimbs.

Fig. XI.27. *Leontopithecus rosalia chrysomelas,* adult male (*left*) and same female shown in fig. XI.24. (Photo courtesy of A. F. Coimbra-Filho.)

Variation. A color pattern such as that of *chrysomelas* is susceptible to considerable individual variation. This is evident from the above description based on a juvenal topotype at hand, a syntype in the Leiden Museum, two specimens without data in the British Museum, and the original description and colored plate of the type.

In the juvenal topotype at hand the hair of the midfrontal region is elongate and lacks the median patch characteristic of the adult headdress. In adult *chrysomelas, chrysopygus,* and *rosalia,* the hair of the midfrontal region is short and forms a wedge-shaped divide between the flowing lateral frontal tufts. The headdress of the colored figure of the type of *chrysomelas* agrees in general with that of the Field Museum juvenal specimen but appears to be exceptionally erect, forming a rufflike mane encircling the face. The facial skin of the type is shown black, whereas that of our topotype is almost entirely unpigmented. Schlegel (1876, p. 251) had already noted the similarity in the coiffures of young *chrysomelas, chrysopygus,* and *rosalia.*

I. Geoffroy (1851, p. 62) records a young individual said to be like one of the cotypes of *chrysomelas* in the Paris Museum except for its almost wholly black tail.

Study Material Extant. All together, 16 museum-preserved specimens of *Leontopithecus rosalia chrysomelas* are known. In addition to the type specimen in the American Museum of Natural History (see above) and the 4 specimens listed below, Coimbra-Filho (1970, p. 258) records 11 specimens with locality data (10 with external measurements) now preserved in the Museu Nacional de Rio de Janeiro.

Specimens Examined. 4. BRAZIL. *Bahia:* Sertam d'Ilhéus, syntype of *chrysomelas* (RMNH); Fazenda Borrachudo, Itabuna, 1 (FMNH); unknown locality: 2 (BM).

LEONTOPITHECUS ROSALIA ROSALIA LINNAEUS, GOLDEN LION-TAMARIN

Fig. XI.28. Golden Lion-tamarin, *Leontopithecus rosalia rosalia,* portrait.

Synonymic History

"Le petit singe-lion," Brisson, 1756, *Reg. Anim.,* p. 200—cercopithecus ex albo flavicans . . . BRAZIL.

"Le marikina," Buffon, 1767, *Hist. Nat.* 15:108, pl. 16 (animal). F. Cuvier, 1818, in *Hist. Nat., Mamm., Paris,* ed. Cuvier and Geoffroy, 1:pl. (animal)—characters; habits of animal in captivity.

"Silky monkie," Pennant, 1771, *Synopsis of quadrupeds,* p. 133, pl. 15 (animal)—GUIANA [!].

[*Simia*] *Rosalia* Linnaeus, 1766, *Syst. Nat.,* ed. 12, 1:41.

Simia Rosalia, Audebert, 1797, *Hist. nat. singes et makis,* fam. 6, sect. 2, p. 4, pl. 3 (animal)—"le marikina"; specimen in the Paris Museum. Cuvier, 1798, *Tabl. Element. Hist. Nat.,* p. 97—"le marikina ou singe léon". Shaw, 1800, *Gen. Zool.* 1(1):64, pl. 25 (silky monkey)—characters. Humboldt, 1812, *Rec. Obs. Zool. Anat. Comp.,* p. 361—BRAZIL. Paulus Schrank, 1819, *Annal. Wetter. Gesellsch. f. d. ges. Naturk.* 4(n.f. vol. 1):325–28—observations on a pair of lion tamarins [work not seen].

Simia Roralia [*sic*], F. Cuvier, 1818, in *Hist. Nat. Mamm., Paris,* ed. Cuvier and Geoffroy, 1:text p. 4—misprint.

S[imia] Sagoinus rosalius, Kerr, 1792, *Anim. Kingd.,* p. 82—characters ex Brisson and others.

Callithrix Rosalia, Erxleben, 1777, *Syst. Reg. Anim.,* p. 60—classification; synonymy.

Sagouin rosalia, Lacépède, 1803, *Buffon Hist. Nat.,* Didot ed., 13:147—classification.

Callitrix rosalia, Latreille, 1804, *Buffon Hist. Nat.,* Sonnini ed., 36:282—classification.

Cercopithecus Rosalia, Goldfuss, 1809, *Vergl. Naturb. Säugeth.,* p. 76—classification.

Jacchus rosalia, Desmarest, 1818, *Nouv. Dict. Hist. Nat.* 24:243—characters. Gerrard, 1862, *Cat. bones Brit. Mus.,* p. 29—skeleton listed.

Jacchus [(Midas)] rosalia, Desmarest, 1820, *Mammifères,* p. 95, pl. 19, fig. 1 (animal)—characters. Desmarest, 1827, *Dict. Sci. Nat.* 47:22—characters. I. Geoffroy, 1827, *Dict. Class. Hist. Nat.* 12:520—characters; bleaching with age.

Midas rosalia, E. Geoffroy, 1812, *Ann. Mus. Hist. Nat., Paris* 19:121—BRAZIL; var. *à* said to be from Fr. Guiana. Pelzeln, 1883, *Verh. K. K. Zool.-Bot. Gesellsch., Wien* 33:26—BRAZIL: *Rio de Janeiro* (Sapitiba); characters. Forbes, 1894, *Handbook of the Primates,* 1:138—characters; part distribution. De Meijere, 1894, *Gegenbaur's Morph. Jahrb.* 21:320, 407, fig. 4 (hair groups)—hair grouping.

M[idas] Rosalia, I. Geoffroy, 1851, *Cat. Primates,* p. 62—BRAZIL: (male received 1808 from the Ajuda Museum in Portugal); two menagerie males 1818–24, bleached during captivity. Mitchell, 1911, *Proc. Zool. Soc. London* 1911:433, 434—maximum longevity 9 years in London zoo.

H[apale] Rosalia, Wied-Neuwied, 1826, *Beitr. Naturg. Brasil.* 2:148—BRAZIL: *Rio de Janeiro* (Cabo Frio; Serra de Inuá; São João da Barra; Ponta Negro; Gurapina); characters; distribution habits; local name, "sahuim vermelho."

Hapale Rosalia, Wagner, 1837, *Abh. Akad. Wiss. München* 2:452, pl. 2, fig. 6 (skull)—osteological characters. Burmeister, 1854, *Syst. Uebers. Thiere Brasil.* 1:34—BRAZIL: *Rio de Janeiro* (Cabo Frio; Serra da Macahé; Neu Freiburg); characters.

Hapale rosalia, Giebel, 1865, *Zeitschr. gesammt. Naturw. Halle* 26:257—skeleton. Schlegel, 1876, *Les singes. Simiae, Mus. Hist. Nat. Pays-Bas* 7:250—BRAZIL: *Rio de Janeiro* (Rio Parahyba do Sul). Jentink, 1887, *Cat. Osteol. Mus. Pays-Bas* 9:47—BRAZIL: *Rio de Janeiro* (north bank Rio Parahyba do Sul); Lidth de Jeude collection. Jentink, 1892, *Cat. Syst. Mamm. Mus. Pays-Bas* 11:54—BRAZIL: *Rio de Janeiro* (north bank Rio Parahyba do Sul); "Amazonie."

Hapale [(Leontocebus)] Rosalia, Wagner, 1840, *Schreber's Säugth., Suppl.* 1:ix, 250—characters; synonymy.

Hapale (Midas) Rosalia, Wagner 1848, *Abh. Akad. Wiss. München* 5:477—BRAZIL: east coast, Guianan records of authors based on specimen in transit from Rio de Janeiro. Burmeister, 1854, *Syst. Uebers. Thiere Brasil.* 1:34—BRAZIL: *Rio de Janeiro.*

H[apale (Midas)] Rosalia, Wagner, 1855, *Schreber's Säugth., Suppl.* 5:138—classification.

M[arikina] Rosalia, Reichenbach, 1863, *Vollstand. Naturg. Affen,* p. 7, pl. 2, figs. 25–27 (animals)—characters; distribution; habits.

Leontopithecus Rosalia, Gray, 1870, *Cat. monkeys, lemurs and fruit-eating bats, Brit. Mus.,* p. 65—BRAZIL; color variation.

Leontopithecus rosalia, De Beaux, 1917, *Giorn. Morph. Uomo, Primati* 1:95, fig. 5 (facial vibrissae), figs. 6, 7 (hand, foot)—characters; comparisons; vibrissae. Hershkovitz, 1969, *Quart. Rev. Biol.* 44(1):38, fig. 11 (animal)—pharyngeal sac; specialization of long hand for hunting insects. Hershkovitz, 1970, *Folia Primat.* 13:218, 224, 229, figs. 2, 3 (endocast of cerebral hemisphere)—cerebral size, fissures and fissural patterns; cerebral evolutionary grade. C. A. Hill, 1970, *Lab. Primat. Newsl.* 9(2):4—BRAZIL: *Rio de Janeiro* and *Guanabara* (coastal rain forest; sea level to 1,500 feet above); export and import controls; conservation, preservation in captivity (construction of breeding center in San Diego Zoo). Coimbra-Filho, 1972, *Inter. Zoo Yearb.* 12:15—reproduction; cannibalism. Epple, 1972, *Int. Zoo. Yearbk.* 12:36—scent glands; scent marking.

[Leontopithecus] rosalia, Hershkovitz, 1970, *Amer. J. Phys. Anthrop.* 32(3):378—footnote (type of *Leontopithecus* Lesson; *L. marikina* Lesson, a synonym.).

L[eontopithecus] r[osalia] rosalia, Hershkovitz, 1972, *Int. Zoo Yearb.* 12:5, 9—classification; distribution; survival endangered.

Leontopithecus rosalia rosalia, Coimbra-Filho and Mittermeier, 1972 *Saving the lion marmoset* (Bridgewater, ed.), p. 10, fig. 8 (color pattern)—characters; distribution; taxonomy. Coimbra-Filho and Mittermeier, 1973, *Primates*

14 (1):47, fig. 2 (animal), fig. 6 (tree routes), fig. 10 (habitat)—BRAZIL: *Rio de Janeiro* (Rio São Jaõa basin); *Guanabara* (now extinct); *Espírito Santo* (now extinct)—distribution; ecology; habitat; habits. Silva, 1975, Zeitschr. Kölner Zoo, 18(4):111, pl. (animal in color), fig. (caged pair)—BRAZIL: *Rio de Janeiro* (Poços das Antas Reserve; characters; conservation.

L[eontopithecus] r[osalia] rosalia, Coimbra-Filho and Magnanini, 1972, *Saving the lion marmoset* (Beveridge, ed.), p. 59—conservation; nutrition and housing in captivity; pigmentation; reproduction.

Leontopithecus r[osalia] rosalia Coimbra-Filho, 1972, *Rev. Brasil. Biol.* 32 (4):511—bark-stripping and eating in captivity.

Leontocebus rosalia, Pocock, 1911, *Proc. Zool. Soc. London* 1911:856—insect feeding. Elliot, 1913, *A Review of the Primates,* 1:209, pl. 25 (skull)—characters. Pocock, 1917, *Ann. Mag. Nat. Hist.* 20(8):251, fig. 1, *c, d* (hand and foot), fig. 2 *c* (ear)—external characters of ears, hands, and feet. Pocock, 1920, *Proc. Zool. Soc. London* 1920:91, fig. 1 *a* (nostrils), fig. 9 *c, d* (tongue), fig. 10 *a* (♀ genitalia), fig. 13 *e, f* (♂ genitalia)—external genitalia. Schreiber, 1928, *Gegenbaur's Morph. Jahrb.* 60:183, figs. 53b, 59n (facial musculature)—comparative facial myology. Zuckerman, 1931, *Proc. Zool. Soc. London* 1931:339—young born 13/11/1872 in London Zoo. Bigalke, 1936, *Zool. Gart.* 8:169—twins born in South African museum. Zukowsky, 1937, *Zool. Gart.* 9:64—birth and growth of twins in Frankfurt Zoo. Dennler, 1939, *Physis* 16:229—name in Guaraní = titi pihtá. Zukowsky, 1940, *Zool. Gart.* 12:101—birth and development of young. J. Anthony, 1946, *Ann. Sci. Nat. Zool., Paris,* ser. 11, 8:8, fig. 2 (cerebrum)—brain morphology. Schultz, 1948, *Amer. J. Phys. Anthrop.* 6:8—twin births recorded. Hershkovitz, 1949, *Proc. U.S. Nat. Mus.* 98:423—characters. Vieira, 1955, *Arq. Zool., São Paulo* 8:398—BRAZIL: *Espírito Santo* to *Rio de Janeiro;* local names, *sauim-piranga, mico-leão.* Osman Hill, 1955, *Primates* 2:93—gestation. Osman Hill, 1957, *Primates* 3:83, 183, 203, 259, 262, 265–69, fig. 44 (map, distribution), fig. 68 (ear), fig. 69 (hand and foot dematoglyphs), fig. 71 (♀ external genitalia), fig. 72 (skull), fig. 88 (facial hair tracts)—anatomy; characters; taxonomy; distribution; behavior. Schneider, 1958, *Primatologia* 3(1):90—tongue anatomy. Hanström, 1958, *Primatologia* 3(1):716—hypophysis. Ryan, Benirschke, and Smith, 1961, *Endocrinology* 69(3):613, fig. 1 (twin placenta and fetuses)—placental conversion of androstenedione–4–C^{14} to estrone. Ulmer, 1961, *J. Mammal.* 42:253—litter size; period of gestation. Benirschke, Anderson, and Brownhill, 1962, *Science* 138(3539):513, fig. 2 (karyotype)—marrow chimerism. Beath and Benirschke, 1962, *Cytologia* 27(1):1, fig. 2 (chromatin)—location of sex chromatin. Benirschke and Brownhill, 1963, *Cytogenetica* 2:245—karyotype (46 chromosomes); marrow chimerism. Fiennes, 1964, *Proc. Zool. Soc. London* 143(3):523—cystic bone disease. Ruschi, 1964, *Bol. Mus. Biol. Prof. Mello Leitão,* no. 23A:3, 4—BRAZIL: *Espírito Santo* (Iconha; Anchieta; Itapemirim); characters; habits. Epple, 1967, *Folia Primat.* 7:38, fig. 3 (animal sniffing toy dog rear)—behavior in captivity. Epple and Lorenz, 1967, *Folia Primat.* 7:99, fig. 2 (sternal gland) fig. 13 (animal marking with sternal gland)—sternal gland. Benirschke and Layton, 1969, *Folia Primat.* 10 (1/2):131—presomite twin blastocyst with chorial membranes fused forming single cavity; blood chimerism permanent in all marmoset twins; freemartinism absent. Hsu and S. Hampton, 1970, *Folia Primat.* 13:183—karyotype (2n = 46).

Leontideus rosalia, Cabrera, 1958, *Rev. Mus. argentino Cienc. Nat. "Bernardino Rivadavia"* 4(1):201—classification; synonymy exclusive of *Simia leonina* Shaw (a macaque). Rabb and Rowell, 1960, *J. Mammal.* 41:401—gestation 134 days. Du Brul, 1965, *Am. J. Phys. Anthrop.* 23:261, fig. 1–6 (skull), fig. 7 (pterygoid muscles), fig. 9 (skull)—cranial characters (sphenoidal sinusus). Carvalho, 1965, *Arq. Zool., São Paulo* 12:22—BRAZIL: *Rio de Janeiro* (restriction of type locality to right bank, Rio São João); identification of the "Macaco leão" of Alexandre Rodrigues Ferreira, 1790, manuscript name and description. Coimbra-Filho, 1965, *Int. Zoo. Yearb.* 5:109—maintenance and breeding in Rio de Janeiro. Anonymous, 1966, *Zoonooz* 39 (1):cover color plate (animals)—captive animals in San Diego, California Zoo. Egozcue, Perkins, and Hagemenas, 1968, *Folia Primat.* 9(2):84—karyotype (2n = 46). Coimbra-Filho, 1969, *An. Acad. Brasil. Cienc.* 41 (suppl.):29, figs. 1, 2 (skull), figs. 3, 4 (animal), fig. 5 (map, past and present distribution), fig. 6, 7 (habitat), fig. 8, 9 (karyotype)—BRAZIL: *Espírito Santo* (Iconha; Anchieta; Itapemirim); *Rio de Janeiro* (Rio São João basin; Araruama, Silva Jardim; São Pedro de Aldea; Cabo Frio; Casimiro de Abreu; Mangaratiba; Nova Iguaçu; Nilopolis; São João de Meriti; Duque de Caxias; Magé; São Gonçalo; Niteroi; Itaboraí; Estanislau, Silva Jardim; Presidente, Silva Jardim; Maricá; Saquarema; Barro Blanco; Marica; Fazenda Rio Vermelho; Guapi; Juturnaíba; Poço d'Anta; Gaviões; Bananeiras; Correntezas; Rio Aldea Velha; Sobara; Rio Bonito; Cachoeiras de Macaçu; Macaé; Conceição de Macabu; Campos; São João da Barra); characters; past and present distribution; habitat; habits; reproduction; care and feeding in wild and captivity; karyotype; local names (sauí; mico leão; sagüi-amarelo; sagüi-piranga; sauim-piranga; saui-vermelho; sagüi-dourado; and all other combinations with same nouns and adjectives); conservation. Perry, 1971, *Oryx* 11(1):22, fig. (animal)—BRAZIL: *Rio de Janeiro* (gallery forests along Rio São João); conservation; habitat threatened; need for preservation and propagation in zoos. Coimbra-Filho, 1970, *Rev. Brasil. Biol.* 30(2):249—characters; comparisons; habits.

L[eontideus] rosalia, Melo Carvalho, 1971, *Biol. Conserv.* 4(1):66—BRAZIL: *Rio de Janeiro* (Rio São João, counties of Rio Bonito and Silva Jardim); conservation.

[Jacchus Rosalia] Guyannensis, Fischer, 1829, *Syn. Mamm.,* p. 65—FRENCH GUIANA: (type locality [but certainly

an eastern Brazilian individual transshipped from Cayenne to France]); name based on *Midas rosalia* var. à Geoffroy, 1812 (*Ann. Mus. Hist. Nat., Paris* 19:121).

[*Jacchus Rosalia*] *Brasiliensis* Fischer, 1829, *Syn. Mamm.*, p. 65—BRAZIL: (type locality not specified); name based on a specimen in the Paris Museum (the Brazilian variety of E. Geoffroy [1812, *Ann. Mus. Hist. Nat., Paris* 19:121]).

[*Midas*] *Leontopithecus marikina* Lesson, 1840, *Species des mammifères: Bimanes et quadrumanes . . .* , p. 200 —new name for *rosalia* Linnaeus; classification.

[*Hapale*] (*Leontopithecus*) *marikina,* Lesson, 1842, *Nouv. Tabl. Reg. Anim.*, p. 9—classification.

Leontocebus pithecus marikina, Elliot, 1913, *A Review of the Primates,* 1:209—in synonymy of *Leontocebus rosalia;* name combination a lapsus for *Midas* (*Leontopithecus*) *marikina* Lesson, 1840.

L[*eontopithecus*] *aurora* Elliot, 1913, *A review of the Primates,* 1:182(in text)—lapsus for *L. marikina* Lesson (1840) "= *L. rosalia.*"

Leontocebus leoninus, Pocock (not Humboldt), 1914, *Proc. Zool. Soc. London* 1914:898, fig. 6 *b* (facial vibrissae) —facial vibrissae.

Simia leonina, Cabrera (not Shaw or Humboldt), 1958, *Rev. Mus. Argentino Cienc. Nat. "Bernardino Rivadavia"* 4(1):201—name attributed to Shaw in synonymy of *Leontideus rosalia* Linnaeus [n.b., Shaw's *leonina* is a macaque, Humboldt's a tamarin].

Leontopithecus leoninus [*sic*], Hershkovitz, 1970, *Evolution* 24(3):646—possible occurrence of nonmelanic reddish pigment in pelage; name *leoninus* a lapsus for *rosalia.*

Leontopithecus leoninus leoninus [*sic*], Hershkovitz, 1970, *Folia Primat.* 13:215—name listed a lapsus for *L. rosalia rosalia.*

Type. Not known to be in existence; name based on *Le petit singe-lion, Cercopithecus ex albido flavicans . . .*, of Brisson; brought from Brazil to Paris in 1754 for Madame la Marquise de Pompadour in whose home it was living as a pet when described.

Type Locality. Brazil, restricted to the coast between 22° and 23° south by Wied-Neuwied (1826, *Beitr. Naturg.* 2:(148), further restricted to right bank, Rio São João, Rio de Janeiro by Carvalho (1965, *Arq. Zool., São Paulo* 12:22).

Distribution (fig. XI.1). Formerly, the tropical rain forests of the coast and low coastal ranges of eastern Brazil, from the Rio Doce, Espírito Santo, south into Rio de Janeiro and Guanabara; altitudinal range below 300 m. The range is now reduced, according to Coimbra-Filho (1969) and Coimbra-Filho and Mittermeier (1973), to an area of approximately 900 km^2 in the Rio São Jaõa basin (336) in Rio de Janeiro.

There is a rough guess (Coimbra-Filho in Perry 1971, p. 22) that fewer than 400 individuals survive in the wild, but attempts are being made to reestablish and breed the Golden Lion-tamarin in the Parque Nacional da Tijuca, Guanabara, and the Poço das Antas Biological Reserve, Rio de Janeiro (Magnanini and Coimbra-Filho 1972; Magnanini, Coimbra-Filho, Mittermeier, and Aldrighi 1975).

Taxonomy. The type of *Leontopithecus rosalia* is the *petit singe-lion* of Brisson. It was a pet in the household of Madame de Pompadour where Brisson must have seen it. Buffon (and Daubenton 1767, p. 108, pl. 16) also described a lion-tamarin under the name marikina, a word formed from Marignon, the French name for the Río Marañon, the region of which was supposed to have been the natural habitat of the animal. Buffon treated the Guianan *acarima* of Barrère (1741, p. 141) as another form of the same species, but this animal is not certainly identifiable with *rosalia* or any other known primate. Nevertheless, early Linnaean authors accepted the determination and included French Guiana in the range of *Leontopithecus rosalia.* E. Geoffroy (1812, pp. 121–22) even distinguished two varieties of Golden Lion-tamarins, one French Guianan with tail variegated blackish and reddish, the other Brazilian with tail bright reddish. Fischer (1829, p. 65) never saw the animals but formalized Geoffroy's concept of the two kinds by naming the first *Jacchus rosalia guyannensis,* the second *Jacchus rosalia brasiliensis.*

Diagnostic Characters. Trunk dominantly golden reddish, orange, or pale buff, sometimes white, mane usually of same color, rarely mostly or entirely black; forearms golden to reddish.

Coloration (fig. XI.17, 28, 29). Facial skin usually pigmented, darkest around lips and nostrils, palest on muzzle and around eyes; muzzle and upper lips bare except for thin vibrissae; forehead with short yellowish to reddish orange or blackish adpressed hairs directed backward as a wedge across midfrontal regions and forming a distinct boundary between lateral tufts of mane; pelage of sides of forehead, cheeks, and crown forming a uniformly or particolored buffy, golden, or reddish mane, the individual hairs unbanded; long fine cheek tufts usually divided, with part directed upward and back and part curving downward; front of crown above each eye with a long buff, reddish, or blackish erectile tuft that extends straight back or whorled, concealing ear; ear rounded, outer (median) side naked, inner side with long tufts colored like mane or contrastingly darker; nape like crown but without tufts or whorls, shoulders like back, the unbanded hairs not forming a mantle, buffy or pale golden to orange or tawny, but usually slightly paler terminally (faded?) than basally; sides of body like back; chin, throat, and chest more saturate than sides of body,

Fig. XI.29. Golden Lion-tamarin, *Leontopithecus rosalia rosalia*: Adult male and female in defensive pose. (Photo courtesy of San Diego Zoo.)

belly like chest or paler; forearms and legs like sides of body but usually darker in individuals with pale bodies; hands and feet from whitish or buffy to golden, orange, reddish, dark brown, or black, or with a mixture of pale and dark hairs, the hands, particularly the fingers, often darker than feet; tail sometimes nearly uniformly colored whitish to golden orange, reddish, dark brown, or black, but more often bleached, streaked, particolored or more or less distinctly annulated, tip usually darker or paler than proximal portion, individual tail hairs darker or lighter terminally than basally but not banded; external genitalia mostly to entirely unpigmented.

Measurements. See appendix table 2.

Comparisons. Distinguished from golden-maned *chrysomelas* by its golden reddish orange or buffy body.

Variation. The body pelage of adults is generally long,

silky, and pale golden to reddish golden, the individual hairs never banded or agouti. Some individuals are golden yellow with white mottling, a few are almost entirely white. I. Geoffroy (1827, p. 520) noted that the pelage of specimens newly arrived in the Paris menagerie was golden but that by the time the animals died their fur was pale buff. The same author (1851, p. 62) later identified the specimens as two males which lived in the zoological garden from 1818 to 1824. The thighs and lower back of one had become white. According to Dr. Barnard Levy (personal communication), the pelage of some individuals of his callitrichid colony in Houston, Texas, becomes more saturate outdoors while that of others fades indoors. The facial skin of specimens taken outdoors also becomes darkly pigmented the same day. The faces of animals kept in indoor cages are notably paler.

Gray (1870, p. 65) records a specimen in the British Museum with head, feet, hand, and end of tail blackish. In one specimen at hand (AMNH 70316) the terminal three-fourths of the tail is black, but the bases of the hairs are orange or reddish. Tails in specimens I have examined are more varicolored than other parts of the body. Tails may range from nearly entirely black through the tones of red, orange, and so forth, to almost entirely white. The tail may be annulated with alternating black and reddish bands throughout its length or on the terminal portion only, or it may be bicolor with dorsal surface sharply paler—white in one (AMNH 60647)—than ventral surface.

Remarks. All specimens preserved in American museums and most of those in European institutions were imported alive and died in captivity. Alteration in coat color during captivity has been noted above. Use of ultraviolet irradiation on laboratory specimens also has deleterious effects on the pelage. Benirschke and Richard (1963, p. 72) observed that "the relative lack of pigmentation in golden marmosets (*Leontocebus rosalia*) caused some alopecia and necessitated a reduction of sunning [i.e., ultraviolet irradiation] of these animals."

The animal identified by Bates (1864, ed. 2, p. 59) as *Midas leoninus* Humboldt does not belong here, but Elliot (1913*a*, p. 210) and Forbes (1894, p. 139) questionably include it in the synonymy of *rosalia.* This animal, a household pet seen alive in the "upper Amazons," is described by Bates (1864, ed. 2, p. 59) as "only seven inches in length exclusive of the tail. It is named *leoninus* on account of the long brown mane which depends from the neck, and gives it very much the appearance of a diminutive lion." The animal is not certainly identifiable from this description. It may be a pygmy marmoset (*Cebuella pygmaea*) judged by its size and brown mane, or a juvenal tamarin, possibly *Saguinus fuscicollis,* which includes Humboldt's leonine tamarin. Bates then mentions another "species of this genus" which could distinguish objects depicted on an engraving. Bates refers to I. Geoffroy as the source of his information but cites no bibliographic reference. Forbes and Elliot mention the same anecdote and likewise credit I. Geoffroy without documentation. Elliott, however, identified Geoffroy's callitrichid with *rosalia.* The subject of I. Geoffroy (1827, p. 514), however, is not a *Leontopithecus.* It is the common marmoset, the *Jacchus vulgaris* of his classification and *Callithrix jacchus jacchus* of the present system.

Specimens Examined. 37. BRAZIL—precise locality unknown, 7 (AMNH); 10 (FMNH); 10 (RMNH); 1 (BM); 4 (SM); 5 (in spirits, FMNH).

79 *Leontopithecus rosalia*
2. *Biology of Lion-tamarins*

REPRODUCTION

The data on reproduction in *Leontopithecus rosalia rosalia,* collected from the literature, have been organized under the following headings:

Conservation; Breeding in Captivity	Gestation
Courtship, Mating, and Copulation	Breeding Seasons
Pregnancy	Litters

Conservation; Breeding in Captivity
Leontopithecus rosalia roslia

S. Hampton 1972, p. 86

"Only limited success has been obtained with breeding the golden lion marmoset in captivity. There are about 130 in captivity, with 70 of these in the United States. These 70 animals are housed in 13 institutions, 11 of which have breeding potential. However, evidence suggests that reproduction will occur only when one or both parents were wild-caught. True breeding in second-generation-captive marmosets has never occurred. Because the last wild marmosets were imported in 1968, and they have a life-span of approximately 10 years, the wild-caught stock now in captivity will become negligible within the next 3 to 5 years. Unless consistent second-generation breeding is achieved soon, the future of this species in captivity is bleak."

Studbook 1973

A studbook for Golden Lion-tamarins is maintained under the auspices of the American Association of Zoological Parks and Aquariums. The first official studbook keeper, Dr. Marvin L. Jones, was succeeded in 1975 by Dr. Devra Kleiman of the National Zoological Park, Washington, D.C. The first edition of the studbook contains a register of 378 animals imported or captive-born since 1958 in the 39 cooperating parks and laboratories throughout the world, and a register of the 68 Golden Lion-tamarins alive 1 April 1973.

Census 1973

The census of rare animals in captivity published in the 1974 *International Zoo Yearbook* (vol. 14, p. 413) lists 71 individuals, including 46 males, 23 females, 2 unsexed, in 10 American, 2 Japanese (Inuyama; Tokyo), 1 English (London) and 1 Brazilian (São Leopoldo) zoos.

"The Golden-headed Lion Marmoset [*Leontopithecus rosalia chrysomelas*] has never been exhibited in the U.S. and only once outside of Brazil (in London in 1869). Presently, there are five captive specimens in Rio de Janeiro. The Golden-rumped Lion Marmoset [*L. r. chrysopygus*] has never been kept in captivity (Mittermeier and Douglass 1973).

Census 1974

Dr. Theodore H. Reed, director of the National Zoological Park, Washington, D.C., informs me in a letter dated 11 September 1974 that a census conducted from his office shows a total of 72 individuals (40/28/4) alive on 10 August 1974, in 12 zoos in the United States. The total includes about 10 second-generation animals, most of which were born in 1974, but "there have been some serious losses in older animals. Next year there should be some births at Brookfield, Los Angeles, Oklahoma City and Washington. The following year Oklahoma should have some. It is still a very iffy proposition whether we can maintain the species in captivity but I think this cooperative effort is going to pay off."

In 1975, Roney (1975) of the San Antonio Zoo reported the birth on 31 March of third-generation captive twins but one of the young was killed by its mother.

Census 1975

Kleiman 1976

The summary and tabulation by sex (♂/♀/?) of Golden Lion-tamarins (*Leontopithecus rosalia rosalia*) in zoos prepared and circulated by Dr. Debra G. Kleiman, reproduction zoologist, National Zoological Park, Smithsonian Institution, Washington, D.C. 20009, USA, and official stud book keeper, is reproduced in table 106A.

Table 106A. Summary and Tabulation by Sex (♂/♀/?) of Golden Lion-tamarins, *Leontopithecus rosalia rosalia* in Zoological Garden Breeding Centers

Location	*Total 1974*	*Births*	*Deaths*	*Transferred*		*Total 1975*
				To	*From*	
Brookfield, U.S.A.	2.3	3.0.2	2.0			3.3.2
Fort Worth, U.S.A.	1.1	4.0	3.0			2.1
Fukuoka, Japan*	1.1					1.1
Houston, U.S.A.	1.1		1.0			0.1
Japan Monkey Centre	2.1		2.0			0.1
London ZSL, G.B.	1.0					1.0
Los Angeles, U.S.A.	4.3	4.1.3	5.1.3		2.0 San Diego	5.3
Miami-Goulds, U.S.A.	9.1	3.0.1	4.0.1	2.0 Washington	1.0 Washington	7.1
Oklahoma, U.S.A.	7.8	1.0	4.1			4.7
Omaha, U.S.A.	1.1				1.0 San Diego	2.1
Pretoria, S. Afr.	4.5	0.0.1				4.5.1
Roskilly, U.S.A.	1.0					1.0
San Antonio, U.S.A.	1.1	2.0	1.0			2.1
San Diego, U.S.A.	3.0			2.0 Los Angeles 1.0 Omaha		0.0
Tokyo Ueno, Japan	1.0					1.0
Washington, U.S.A.	11.10	6.7.2	6.7.2	1.0 Miami-Goulds	2.0 Miami-Goulds	12.10
Total	50.36	23.8.9	28.9.6	6.0	6.0	45.35.3

SOURCE: Dr. Debra G. Kleiman, National Zoological Park, Smithsonian Institution, Washington, D.C.

* No reply to communication

"The Register for 1975 shows a decrease in the overall population from 86 to 85 specimens. Forty young were born, but this was offset by the loss of 41 specimens. Of the 16 collections maintaining *Leontopithecus* [*rosalia*] *rosalia,* 8 had births during 1975. The sex ratio continues to be skewed in favor of males."

Conservation in Brazil

Magnanini, Coimbra-Filho, Mittermeier, and Aldrighi 1975

A plan for establishment of the 3,000 hectares Federal Biological Reserve of Poço das Antas in the municipality of Silva Jardim, Rio de Janeiro, for preservation of the extant wild-living *Leontopithecus rosalia rosalia,* was submitted to the Minister of Agriculture for approval.

Leontopithecus rosalia chrysopygus is supposedly protected in the Morro do Diabo Forest Reserve (figs. XI.20–23), all that remains of the former range of the subspecies. The fate of *L. r. chrysomelas* is uncertain. "Several areas in the southern part of the state of Bahia, most notably some forest patches in the municipality of Una, are potential reserves. Magnanini and Coimbra-Filho have already indicated an area of approximately 4,000 ha to CEPLAC (Executive Commission for Planning and Rural-Economic Recuperation of the Cocoa Plantation) as a possible site for a reserve."

The Tijuca Bank

Mittermeier and Douglass 1973

"In Brazil, a special breeding project, known as the Tijuca Bank of Lion Marmosets and headed by Dr. Coimbra-Filho and Dr. Alceo Magnanini, is underway at the Conservation Institute in Tijuca National Park. Tijuca is located near the city of Rio de Janeiro and was once part of the natural habitat of the Golden Lion Marmoset. The world's entire captive population of Golden-headed Lion Marmosets is kept in the Tijuca Bank, along with about 10 Golden Lion Marmosets.

"The goal of the Tijuca Bank is to breed Lion Marmosets for later reintroduction into reserves (for which plans are now underway) and to hold marmosets from areas where habitat destruction is inevitable.

"This project is partially financed by the World Wildlife Fund. However, additional funds are urgently needed for the construction of more breeding cages and for finding and translocating animals from habitats destined for destruction."

Magnanini, Coimbra-Filho, Mittermeier, and Aldrighi 1975

"In May 1971 [Brazilian Forestry Development Institute] gave official instructions for the establishment of the Tijuca Bank in the valley of the Rio dos Macacos (River of Monkeys) in the 3300 ha Tijuca National Park in Rio de Janeiro. The area ranges from 80–1024 m in altitude and is covered with dense forest. It has a year round supply of fresh water and is naturally protected by its topography from cold southeastern winds. The surrounding forest of Tijuca National Park was once part of the natural habitat of *L. r. rosalia* and carefully planned and monitored reintroduction of this form will take place in the near future."

With funds contributed by the IBDF and the U.S. National Appeal of the World Wildlife Federation, "it was possible to complete the 22 breeding cages, facilities for researchers and the barbed wire fences surrounding the bank by January 1974. The Brazilian Academy of Sciences provided funds for defraying costs of hiring two animal keepers for 1974.

"At the present time [1973], the bank contains six *L. r. rosalia,* six *L. r. chrysomelas* and six *L. r. chrysopygus.*"

Kleiman 1976

"As of December 1975, the Tijuca Bank contained 39 *L. r. rosalia,* 8 *L. r. chrysomelas,* and 14 *L. r. chrysopygus.*"

Courtship and Mating

Benirschke and Richart 1963, p. 30

"The pair of *Leontocebus* [= *Leontopithecus*] *rosalia* . . . was obtained two days after the arrival of a large shipment (approximately 30) of these monkeys of which we were able to pick out the healthy specimens. The pair accepted each other from the day of purchase (August, 1959) and it appeared the female was older and more experienced than the male. She (#27) often attempted to gain the attention of the cotton-top male (#1 [*Saguinus oedipus*]) but, despite periods of obvious sex play together, mating with the cotton-top did not occur. . . . In this pair [i.e., the original, male and female lion-tamarins] mating was not observed but the steady increase of the weight of the female and the later marked abdominal protuberance indicated pregnancy." The authors noticed that the vulvar odor of the lion-tamarin was particularly strong.

Snyder 1972, pp. 42, 43 (*rosalia*)

"Observation of behavior following parturition was made in two successful breeding pairs of *L. rosalia* consisting of a feral male × feral female and a feral female × captive born male in March 1971. In both cases the male began paying attention to the female two days following the birth, sniffing the female's genitalia and the neonates. More time was spent near the female and the frequency of grooming increased markedly over previous observations (particularly in the feral × feral mating). Copulatory behavior was observed on the second and third day following parturition in the feral × captive pair; but was not in the feral × feral pair. Copulatory behavior was also observed one week after an unsuccessful parturition in another feral × captive pair. None of the attempts were successful."

"The possibility that copulatory behavior in *L. rosalia* is occurring in the animals' sleeping quarters also exists [DuMond, pers. comm., 1971], in that in this primate species the male and female sleep together at night."

"The male mounts the female from the rear, sitting behind and partly on top of her. He clasps her tightly around the waist with his arms and grasps the perch with his feet. It appears that the penis is inserted almost immediately and pelvic thrusts begin. The number of insertions varies, and with less insertions it becomes more difficult to observe the behavior. After a successful copulation, the male may be seen to lick his genitalia."

Coimbra-Filho 1969 (*rosalia*)

A mating ceremony performed by a female in the Rio de Janeiro Zoo consisted of a walk with back steeply arched, tail raised perpendicularly. After a short while, the male approached and copulated.

Ulmer 1961, p. 253 (*rosalia*)

Copulation takes place immediately after parturition.

Frantz 1963 (*rosalia*)

Parents of suckling twins were observed copulating 9:15 A.M. on 7th day, and noon on 22d day, after birth of young.

Pregnancy

Pregnancy in callitrichids is not externally visible until well advanced. Body weight alone, measured at regular intervals, is an indicator, but the quantity of fat gained or lost during pregnancy may exceed the weight of the embryo. Weights of an adult female that became pregnant during captivity from 19 August 1959 to 14 February 1960, when she was sacrificed, follow. The data are from Benirschke and Richart (1963, p. 81). Mating was not observed.

19 August 1959	paired with adult ♂
13 August 1959	530 g
27 August 1959	580 g
4 October 1959	600 g
18 October 1959	620 g
— November 1959	vomiting "on several occasions"; "relatively obese"; breasts enlarged.
14 February 1960	700 g

Two fetuses removed by laparotomy; combined weight 53 g, plus placenta 17.8 g, total 71 g. Taking 133 days as average duration of gestation, and considering that embryos were near term, conception must have occurred during the first week of October when mother weighed approximately 600 g, or 100 g less than terminal weight. With allowance for embryonic fluid and tissue weight not accounted for by Benirschke and Richart, maternal weight increase from conception to termination of pregnancy is nearly all of fetal origin.

Gestation

In 9 records of interbirth intervals (table 107), 5 range from 132 to 136 days. The remaining 4 intervals, ranging from 221 to 303 days, evidently embrace more than a single gestation period. Each of the two longest intervals (302, 303 days) spans at least the equivalent of two normal gestation periods, whether or not pregnancies were involved. Coimbra-Filho (1969) had estimated 146 days for the duration of gestation, but the evidence points to a period between 132 and 137 days, average about 133.5.

Table 107. Breeding Records for *Leontopithecus rosalia rosalia.*

Date of Birth	*Offspring*	*Interbirth Interval*	*Place of Birth*	*Reference*	*Remarks*
13 Nov. 1872	○	—	London Zoo	Zuckerman 1931, p. 339	
26 Apr. 1933	♂ ♀	—	New York	Ditmars 1933, p. 175; Crandall 1964, p. 101	
22 Feb. 1934	○ ○	302	New York	Crandall 1964, p. 101	Same parents as preceding
7 July 1934	○ ○	136	New York	Crandall 1964, p. 101	Same parents as preceding
27 Mar. 1936	○ ○	—	Frankfurt	Zukowsky 1940, p. 101	
7 Aug. 1936	♂ ♀	132	Frankfurt	Zukowsky 1940, p. 101	Same parents as preceding
— June 1938	○ ○	—	Frankfurt	Zukowsky 1940, p. 101	Same parents as preceding
—	○ ○	—	Brookfield	Rabb and Rowell 1960, p. 401	
12 Feb. 1951	○ ○	—	Brookfield	Rabb and Rowell 1960, p. 401	Same parents as preceding
25 June 1951	○ ○	133	Brookfield	Rabb and Rowell 1960, p. 401	Same parents as preceding
8 Aug. 1957	○ ○	—	Philadelphia	Ulmer 1961, p. 253	
7 June 1958	○ ○	303	Philadelphia	Ulmer 1961, p. 253	Same parents as preceding
22 Apr. 1959	○ ○	319	Philadelphia	Ulmer 1961, p. 253	Same parents as preceding
1 Sept. 1959	○ ○ ○	132	Philadelphia	Ulmer 1961, p. 253	Same parents as preceding
9 Apr. 1960	○ ○	221	Philadelphia	Ulmer 1961, p. 253	Same parents as preceding
20 Aug. 1960	○ ○	133	Philadelphia	Ulmer 1961, p. 253	Same parents as preceding
2 May 1957	♂ ♀	—	Frankfurt	Frantz 1963, p. 115	
28 Jan. 1934	○ ○	—	Pretoria	Bigalke 1936, p. 169	
— Nov. —	○ ○	—	Rio de Janeiro	Coimbra-Filho 1965, p. 109	
— Nov. —	○ ○	—	Rio de Janeiro	Coimbra-Filho 1965, p. 109	
— Sept. —	○ ○	—	Rio de Janeiro	Coimbra-Filho 1965, p. 109	
— Sept. —	○ ○	—	Rio de Janeiro	Coimbra-Filho 1965, p. 109	
— Jan —	○ ○	—	Rio de Janeiro	Coimbra-Filho 1965, p. 109	
1 Sept. 1968	♂ ♂	—	Rio de Janeiro	Coimbra-Filho 1969, p. 43	
14 Sept. 1970	○ ○	—	Rio de Janeiro	Coimbra-Filho and Magnanini 1972 p. 66	
8 Sept. 1970	♂ ♂	—	Rio de Janeiro	Coimbra-Filho and Magnanini 1972 p. 66	
11 Feb. 1971	♂ ♂	—	Rio de Janeiro	Coimbra-Filho and Magnanini 1972 p. 66	
15 Feb. 1971	○ ○	—	Rio de Janeiro	Coimbra-Filho and Magnanini 1972 p. 66	

The report by Hagler (1975) on Golden Lion-tamarin births in the Oklahoma City Zoo came to hand opportunely. The zoo's wild-caught breeding pair acquired in 1964 produced 11 litters from 1966 through 1972. The published data for sequential and presumably full-term litters, that is, those with living young, are tabulated in table 107A. Birth date of the last stillborn litter serves as base date.

Breeding Seasons

The vast majority of dated births (14 to 16 recorded) occur during the spring and summer of the northern hemisphere. The same periodicity prevails within the natural range of the species in the southern hemisphere. Coimbra-Filho (1965, p. 109), who bred the nominate form of the race in Rio de Janeiro, reports "one of four

Table 107A. Golden-Lion tamarin (*Leontopithecus rosalia rosalia*) births in the Oklahoma City Zoo

Birth Date	*Litter*	*Interbirth Interval*
3 February 1971	Singleton (stillborn)	—
16 June 1971	Twins (2 live)	134
31 October 1971	Twins (1 live)	137
16 March 1972	Triplets (1 live)	137
6 August 1972	Triplets (1 live)	143
19 December 1972	Twins (1 live)	135

SOURCE: Hagler (1975).

pairs of *L. rosalia* has reared litters of two young for three consecutive years; another pair has reared young for the first time this year. The young have been born on two occasions in November, on two occasions in September and on one occasion in January. Thus it would seem that the breeding season corresponds with the warmer rainy months of the Brizilian spring and summer." In a second report (Coimbra-Filho and Magnanini 1972) 2 births are recorded for the winter-spring dry month of September and 2 for the warm moist summer month of February.

The seasonal distribution of 16 births in captivity in American and European Zoos (northern hemisphere), and 11 births in South African and southern Brazilian Zoos (southern hemisphere) are shown in table 108.

Table 108. Seasonal Distribution of Recorded Births of Captive Golden Lion-tamarins, *Leontopithecus rosalia rosalia*

Season	*Northern Hemisphere*	*Southern Hemisphere*
22 December–21 March	2 (winter)	4 (summer)
22 March–21 June	7 (spring)	—
22 June–23 September	6 (summer)	3 (winter)
23 September–21 December	1 (fall)	4 (spring)
Totals: Spring, 11; Summer, 10; Fall, 1; Winter, 5		

Litters

Records of 28 deliveries are given in table 106. Distribution of the offspring per litter is shown in table 109.

Table 109. Young per Litter Produced by *Leontopithecus rosalia rosalia*

Young per Litter	*Number of Litters*	*Total Young*
1	1 (3.5%)	1 (2%)
2	26 (93%)	52 (93%)
3	1 (3.5%)	3 (5%)
Totals	28	56

NOTE: Average size per litter is 2.0.
SOURCE: Table 107, p. 850.

GROWTH AND DEVELOMENT

The topics are divided as follows:

Chronology of Growth
Weight
Sexual Dimorphism
Longevity

Chronology of Growth

The following chronology of growth and development is based on twins observed by Ditmars (1933) in the New York Zoological Gardens and Frantz (1963) in the Frankfurt am Main Zoo, and on a singleton observed by Altmann-Schönberner (1965) in the Berlin Zoo. All individuals are *Leontopithecus rosalia rosalia*.

1st Day. Eyes open, head and body length about 75 mm (Ditmars), 122 mm (Altmann-Schönberner); clings to mother by grasping fur with hands and feet, and crawls to breast for suckling. Head and upper surface of trunks well haired yellowish or golden, arms, legs, and tail nearly bare; head with or without blackish frontoparietal band; pelage of front of head long like crown and nape, not short and adpressed as in adults; hair surrounding face golden or blackish.

Measurements of dead male a few hours old: weight 57 g; afterbirth tissues 9 g; combined head and body length 122 mm; tail 120 mm; ear, lateral ("innen") surface 13 mm; ear, median ("aussen") surface 6 mm; upper arm 28 mm; lower arm 31 mm; hand 24 mm; thigh 26 mm; lower leg 31 mm; foot 30 mm (Altmann-Schönberner).

2d Day. Twins carried by father and adults other than mother when not suckling. Suckled every 30–40 minutes for first three weeks (Altmann-Schönberner).

3d Day. Supports itself, walks, climbs, and jumps about 8 cm; copulation between parents of singleton observed (Altmann-Schönberner).

4th Day. Singleton carried by father for first time (Altmann-Schönberner). Black wedge of hair appears on occiput where "bald" spot develops later (but not before fifth week, Zukowski 1940, p. 102); look about but eyes stare into space (Frantz).

7th Day. Singleton makes first clumsy movements; grooms by scratching with leg (Altmann-Schönberner). Ear tufts agouti; parents of twins observed copulating (Frantz).

8th Day. Singleton observes surroundings (Altmann-Schönberner).

9th Day. Singleton attached to father most of time between feedings; active and restless, movements jerky; calls mother when hungry by emitting high-pitched rhythmical cries with mouth wide open; fed every 40 minutes, suckles intermittently for 2–8 minutes (Altmann-Schönberner).

13th Day. Singleton moves rapidly but clumsily; yawning first observed; often clings to parents with hind legs only, seizing branch with hands; cared for by father exclusively except during nursing periods (Altmann-Schönberner). Twins acquire jerky "owllike" head movements characteristic of adults; develop interest in surroundings and grooming, commence fighting (Frantz).

14th Day. First seen yawning; copulation between parents of singleton observed twice during second week (Altmann-Schönberner). Dark coronal patch formed (fig. XI. 2); twins rejected by mother 16 times in day (Frantz).

18th Day. Twins attempt climbing (Frantz).

19th Day. Twins take first solid food (banana and milk) from keeper (Frantz).

21st Day. Mother of singleton shows signs of rejection; young vocalizes and eats more; during first three weeks fed every 30–40 minutes; intermittent suckling lasts from ½ minute to 1 hour.

22d Day. Parents of twins observed copulating (Frantz).

31st Day. Singleton forced by father to make first independent movements on branch (Altmann-Schönberner).

4th Week. Singleton fairly independent but always seeks parents' backs for safety; one leap to father's back measured 30 cm; takes solid food from parents' mouth and hand, or from common feeding pan; mother no longer responsive to hunger calls, young seeks mother for suckling and triturated food (Altmann-Schönberner). Young very active (Frantz).

5th Week. Singleton adjusts to adult activity pattern; most active in morning, retires early evening, takes short rest breaks between.

6th Week. Pelage markedly longer, thicker, and darker; leaps to cover 20–30 cm (Altmann-Schönberner). Female born in Los Angeles Zoo 12 February 1975, weaned after death of mother from measles; fed liquids, soft food mixtures, fruits, live crickets and mealworms (Crotty 1975).

7th Week. Singleton rejected by both parents but still accepted by mother for occasional nursing (Altmann-Schönberner). Twins acquire reddish color of parents, limbs and tail fully furred; volar surfaces pigmented and padded, iris brown; eat everything, including grasshoppers and cockroaches (Frantz).

8th Week. Leave father's back voluntarily for short periods (Ditmars); parents of singleton terminate grooming and licking of young's anogenital region. Twins weaned after 57 days (Frantz).

9th Week. Singleton completely weaned.

11th Week. Twins independent (Frantz).

3d Month. Eat soft food from hands of father and taste solid food in feeding trays (Ditmars).

4th Month. Twins nearly independent of parents (Ditmars; Frantz); singleton engages in sportive tilts with father.

5th Month. Locomotion of singleton lacks adult agility, leaps do not cover over 1 meter (Altmann-Schönberner); "twins half grown and leaping as nimbly about the cage as their parents" (Ditmars).

6th Month. Singleton appears to be completely independent in all activities; prefers company of father to that of mother (Altmann-Schönberner).

8th Month. Twins three-quarters grown, pelage as long and silky as parents' (Ditmars).

14th Month. Singleton seen mounting mother's back, 30 March 1965; copulation between parents observed (Altmann-Schönberner).

15th Month. Singleton seen mounting mother's back, 13 April 1964; copulation between parents observed again (Altmann-Schönberner).

18th Month. Singleton signals parents for attention and begs for food but without response (Altmann-Schönberner).

39 Month. Female born 11 August 1970 in the Oklahoma City Zoo produced twins 23 November when 39 months, 12 days old. The twins were alive 20 February 1976 (Ernest Hagler, personal communication).

Weight

Altmann-Schönberner (1965, p. 231) gives the following weight and external measurements of an adult male Golden Lion-tamarin: weight, 560 g; (length, head and body combined, 279 mm; tail 355; hind foot 82). Weights of two wild-caught females recorded by Epple (1970, p. 71) are 540, 623.

Benirschke and Richart (1963, p. 81) compared weights at different periods of a captive adult pair, as follows:

	♂	♀	
19 August 1959	—	—	Purchased
13 September 1959	430	530	
27 September 1959	460	580	
4 October 1959	—	600	Twins conceived probably 1st week of October
18 October 1959	—	620	Pregnant
14 November 1959	—	700	Pregnancy terminated

Weights of a pair of Golden Lion-tamarins maintained in the Primate Colony, San Diego Zoo, recorded by Cooper (unpublished Quarterly Reports, 1963–64), follow.

Date	♂	♀	*Report Number*
29 August 1963	437	545.5	5
14 November 1963	609	636.5	5
6 February 1964	614	635	6
2 May 1964	612	601	7
8 August 1964	627	633	8
21 October 1964	—	654	9

The following weights of adult Golden Lion-tamarins in the Rio de Janeiro Zoo are given by Coimbra-Filho (1969, p. 36).

Heaviest male = 710 g (approximately 4 years old)
Heaviest female = 665 g
Lightest female = 361 g
One female = 520 g (approximately 5 years old)
One female = 530 g (approximately 5 years old)
Mean of 38 individuals = 499 g (includes recorded weights of 11 specimens preserved in the Museu Nacional de Rio de Janeiro)

Sexual Dimorphism

Material at hand is insufficient for analysis of size relationship between the sexes. The usual anatomical and behavioral differences distinguishing the sexes are present. In addition, the median ventral laryngeal sac is notably enlarged in male lion-tamarins, greatly reduced or absent in females.

Longevity

Crandall (1964, p. 105) records a Golden Lion-tamarin that lived 10 years, 4 months, 18 days in the New York Zoo.

BEHAVIOR

Published information on behavior has been quoted or translated, paraphrased, edited, abstracted, annotated, and organized under headings listed below; subspecific names of the animals discussed are given in the subheadings:

Habitat	Hand Use
Habits in the Wild	Drink
Daily Rhythm	Predators
Social Organization	Locomotion
Association	Play
Dominance and Aggression	Exercise
Care of Young	Repose
Cannabalism (Neonatophagy)	Display
Grooming	Scent Markings
Food and Feeding	Vocalization
Milk Composition	Thermoregulation

Habitat

Coimbra-Filho 1969, p. 39 (*rosalia*)

The Golden Lion-tamarin lives in bottomland and upland forests with mean annual rainfall about 1570 mm and alternating dry and rain seasons. The animal prefers the life zone between upper and middle canopies, where interlacing branches, vines, and epiphytes provide optimum shelter and an abundance of insect and small vertebrate prey.

Coimbra-Filho 1970*a*, p. 260–261 (*chrysomelas*)

The Gold and Black Lion-tamarin lives in the canopy level like the Golden Lion-tamarin except that the forests are higher and mightier than the lowland woods of Rio de Janeiro. Also, *chrysomelas* shelters in the branches immediately above the main forks that support bromeliads notable for their great size. These plants are valued for cover and the small vertebrate and animal prey they harbor.

Coimbra-Filho and Magnanini 1972, p. 69 (*rosalia*)

"Our experimental cages have an earthen floor with a narrow canal of running water. We also leave on the ground several pieces of semi-decomposed branches which are pitted by Coleoptera larvae. All this is done with the purpose of providing the animals with a diversified environment. In these cages, the marmosets spend much of the day scrutinizing things. In spite of the fact that the floors of some of these cages have not been cleaned for long periods of time, no problems with infections, diseases or parasites have occurred. The remnants that are left on the earthen floor, especially the banana peels, are quite agreeable to the marmosets who search among them for small arthropods."

Magnanini, Coimbra-Filho, Mittermeier, and Aldrighi 1975

"The cages [for the Lion-tamarins in the Tijuca Bank, Rio de Janeiro] vary in size from 4 x 3 x 2.5 m to 9 x 3 x 2.5 m and all are supplied with wooden nestboxes and wooden horizontal perches. The natural dirt floors and wooden fixtures of these cages are never washed, since the constant washing and sterilization procedures used by many laboratories remove biologically important olfactory signals important for the psychological well being of Callithricidae. Cages are constructed with a cement base, two adjacent cement walls and slanting roofs of translucent, heavyduty corrugated plastic. The cages are arranged so that the two cement walls of one cage always face the open wire walls of adjacent cages, blocking from view monkeys in neighbouring cages and reducing tension resulting from the constant visual presence of many conspecifics—an important consideration for the highly aggressive *Leontopithecus*. . . . As a protection from excessive heat in summer, the cages are sprayed daily with a hose between 1100 and 1500 hours."

Territoriality

Coimbra-Filho 1969, p. 41 (*rosalia*)

Lion-tamarins may be regarded as sedentary. Their travels are largely restricted to foraging, and they rarely wander more than a few kilometers from their usual sleeping quarters. They live, in general, in shrunken habitats that offer limited possibilities for dispersal.

Snyder 1972, p. 30 (*rosalia*)

"DuMond (pers. comm., 1971) reports that territorial ranges in a simulated rain forest environment [Monkey Jungle, Miami] were quite extensive, being four or more acres per social unit in *L. rosalia, S. fuscicollis, S. oedipus,* and *C. geoffroyi.* He also noted that these marmosets were observed to forage in trees at heights no greater than twenty feet above the ground."

Habits in the Wild

Lion-tamarins are among the most visible of New World monkeys. Most of their natural range lies within areas more densely populated by humans than others of comparable size in South America. Notwithstanding, recorded observations of wild-living lion-tamarins are few and far between. The first notice, by Prince Maximilian Wied-Neuwied, was published in 1826, the second by Ruschi in 1964, and a third, fourth, and fifth by Coimbra-Filho in 1969 and 1970. The accounts by Wied-Neuwied have been freely translated and edited but kept intact. They include observations on social organization, associations, movements, food, and care of young.

Wied-Neuwied 1826, p. 151–52 (*rosalia*)

The *sahuim vermelho* [*Leontopithecus rosalia rosalia*] is nowhere abundant; we saw only single individuals or family groups, particularly in the Serra da Inuá (334), the forests of São João, and in the hilly forests surrounding Ponta Negra (338b) and Gurapina (337). The animal lives just as well on bushy sandy plains as in the high mountain forests. It feeds on fruits and insects and hides from strangers by disappearing into the leafy treetops. One or two young are produced at a birth. The female carries the offspring on her back or at her breast until they are strong enough to follow her on their own. . . . Any excitement causes them to erect the long hair surrounding their faces. In general, however, their habits are similar to those of other sahuis.

"Where I travelled these animals are generally known as *sahuim vermelho* (red tamarins). The tails of some individuals are marked with black while others are uniformly colored. Authors have erroneously regarded the first as Guianan and the second as restricted to Brazil."

Wied-Neuwied, 1826, pp. 159–162 (*chrysomelas*)

"The *sahuim preto* [*Leontopithecus rosalia chrysomelas*] lives only in the great forests of the Sertam de Ilhéos (299), four or five days' travel from the coast. The Botacudos assured me they were also found in the high forests of the Rio Pardo which is as far as these Indians roam. The area within which I have seen the animals lies between 14° and 15½° S. I did not meet with this *sahui* on the Rio Belmonte. But trustworthy natives assure me that this little monkey which they call *pakakang* does live in the deep forests north of Rio Belmonte. It would be impossible for these tamarins to live near the seashore; they are unable to cross swift flowing rivers and are therefore confined to the headwaters of the Rio da Cachoeira where streams are narrow and do not act as barriers. My hunters found the first of these *sahuis* about 4 days' travel upstream on the Rio Ilhéos. From there on we met them rather frequently in bands of from 4 to 12 individuals, and sometimes alone or in pairs. Like all of their kind, they climb swiftly and leap nimbly. They are curious but not particularly shy. On seeing a stranger they jump behind the thicker branches and show only their little faces. Their heads are in constant motion. Their food consists of fruit and insects. One or two young are produced at a birth. The mother carries them on her back or at her breast. Often one mother will have a large, half grown individual on her back and a suckling young at her breast. Lion-tamarins born in Europe are carried by the father but I have never seen this here.

"This *sahui* often associates with the white fronted tufted marmoset, *Hapale penicillatus*. The remarkably erect collar-like mane of the former gives the animal a strange appearance. Its mane seems to be directed more forward than that of the red *sahui* [*L. rosalia rosalia*]. It is fascinating to watch these animals fleeing from danger with each one leaping after the other from tree to tree. Once a band is met it is fairly easy to shoot down several individuals; they die quickly but the mane of those that fall wounded remains remarkably erect. During our travels through the forests of the Rio do Ilhéos and the Rio da Cachoeira hunger obliged us to live for several days on the flesh of these squirrel-like animals.

"The beautiful black pelt of this *sahui* has sometimes been made into caps. The animal is called *sahuim preto* (black *sahui*) or *sahuim de Sertão* in the region of the Rio Ilhéos and Barra da Vareda. The same name is used for *Hapale penicillatus* in Minas Gerais."

Daily Rhythm

Frantz 1963 (*rosalia*)

Golden lion-tamarins kept in the Frankfurt am Main Zoo became active early in the morning, took short naps at irregular intervals during the day, and retired for the night between 5:00 and 5:30 P.M. The routine was observed during the spring and early summer.

Coimbra-Filho 1969 (*rosalia*)

Lion-tamarins in the Rio de Janeiro Zoo retired at sundown, slept with tail thrown over head and shoulders, and arose with the sun.

Social Organization

Wied-Neuwied 1826, p. 151, p. 159 (*chrysomelas*)

We saw only single individuals or family groups. . . . My hunters found the first of these *sahuis* about 4 days' travel upstream on the Rio Ilhéos. From there on we met them rather frequently in bands of from 4 to 12 individuals, and sometimes alone or in pairs.

Ruschi 1964, p. 4 (*rosalia*)

In Espírito Santo, the bands of lion-tamarins consisted of 4 to 8 individuals.

Coimbra-Filho 1969, pp. 41, 42 (*rosalia*)

Wild-living Golden Lion-tamarins live in groups of 2 to 8. The usual aggregation is the family consisting of adult male and female with young. Hunters, however, say they have seen bands of a dozen or more individuals.

Associations

Wied-Neuwied 1826 (*chrysomelas*)

Often associates with *Hapale penicillatus*.

Coimbra-Filho 1970, p. 255 (*chrysomelas*)

Leontopithecus rosalia chrysomelas often travels in the company of other monkeys, most notably *Callithrix penicillata*. Where seen together the latter far outnumbers the former.

Laemmert, Ferreira, and Taylor 1946, p. 41

Platyrrhines collected in the Ilhéus region for virological studies of yellow fever (table 106) included *Leontopithecus rosalia chrysomelas, Callithrix jacchus penicillata, Callicebus personatus melanochir, Alouatta guariba,* and *Cebus apella xanthosternus*.

[It may be assumed that at times lion-tamarins occupy the same tree at the same time as one or more other kinds of monkeys. The information supplied, however, gives no information that lion-tamarins habitually associate with or purposefully avoid the company of other primates (but see Wied-Neuwied's account, p. 854).—P. H.].

Dominance and Aggression

Snyder 1972, p. 28 (*rosalia*)

"Observations of three family units of *L. rosalia* indicate that although the units were separated from each other physically, a dominance relationship between the groups appears to exist. The most dominant pair appeared to be a successful feral born breeding pair with one juvenile female offspring and a pair of younger twin male offspring. This pair showed a more complete repertoire of social and sexual behaviors and vocalizations as compared to the other two less successful breeding pairs. They were also older than the other two pairs of animals. The next most dominant pair was a captive born male, whose parents are the above mentioned most dominant family unit, and a feral born female mate. These animals performed a less complete repertoire of social and sexual behaviors and vocalizations. Their behavior patterns were interrupted more frequently by the presence of human beings than were those of the more dominant pair. The least dominant pair was a feral born male and the captive born female offspring of the dominant pair. They had not successfully bred as had the above mentioned pairs and behaved less like the above two pairs sexually and socially and therefore are considered the most subordinate pair. The female in this pair was also quite tame and interacted with human beings frequently."

Snyder 1972, pp. 26–27 (*rosalia*)

"In six month old *L. rosalia* juveniles, the larger of the two male twins, in two instances, appeared to be dominant over the smaller. This dominance was especially serious during feeding and play periods. . . . A fifteen month old juvenile female *L. rosalia* assumed a subordinate position to the six month old male juveniles as she became less tolerated within the family unit."

Snyder 1972, p. 25 (*rosalia*)

"Just before and after parturition in *L. rosalia* the female assumes a more dominant position within the family unit. She displays more aggressive patterns of behavior and directs them toward other members of the family. Immediately following parturition, for one or two days, the male is not allowed near the female and infants. Any attempts made by the male to approach the female result in attacks and growls made by the female directed toward the male. The female becomes particularly aggressive during feeding periods, vocalizing in a disturbed manner and attacking other family members who appear to want to eat mealworms or crickets. The other family members tolerate her behavior and never retaliate."

Snyder 1972, p. 30 (*rosalia*)

"A juvenile female, *L. rosalia,* was observed to have aggressive interactions with *Macaca fascicularis* and *C. geoffroyi*. . . . These interactions, although infrequent, consisted of piloerection, disturbed vocalizations and actual attack of the other species, when either was walking on the roof of the cage or in the adjacent cage."

Valerie Conner, April 1973 (*rosalia;* pers. comm.)

The pair of Golden Lion-tamarins Keith and I observed in the Brookfield Zoo were housed in a small cage provided with a cross branch for perching. Both my head and Keith's, like those of the little monkeys that stared back at us, are adorned with thick golden shocks of hair. As we peered closer, smiling broadly, the male focused on Keith's exposed teeth and turned furious. Jumping to his perch, he planted himself firmly, raised his mane, and grimaced, baring long tusks. His body rocked and swayed while his hands beat a rapid tattoo on the branch. The female meanwhile had retreated to a corner of the cage to watch the proceedings and reinforce her mate's threats with measured shrieks.

Coimbra-Filho 1969, p. 42 (*rosalia*)

The angered lion-tamarin whistles shrilly, shrieks, and shows its fangs with wide-open mouth (fig. XI.31).

Coimbra-Filho 1969 (*rosalia*)

In the Rio de Janeiro Zoo, the alpha male invariably attacked newcomers introduced into his cage. Subordinate males and females of the established group were also attacked by the dominant male, and some were bitten to death. Each assault was swift, with several slashes inflicted in rapid succession with the long canines. Males are fearless in defense of females with young. At one time, a male Golden Lion-tamarin was seen attacking two female wooly monkeys (*Lagothrix lagothricha*) despite the wire partition separating their cages.

Hershkovitz (*rosalia*)

The ferocity and audacity of lion-tamarins was also brought to my attention on a visit to Mr. Murray Hill's countryside animal show near Burlington, Wisconsin. To facilitate my observations, Mr. Hill transferred a mating pair of lion-tamarins from a small box enclosure to a large floor-to-ceiling cage alongside another inhabited by a powerful macaque. When the lion-tamarins entered their cage, the curious macaque sprang high onto the wire-mesh partition for a better view. In a flash, the male lion-tamarin lunged at the macaque with teeth bared and voice shrilling (fig. XI.31). The astounded monkey fell back to the floor but recovered quickly and hurtled against the lion-tamarin, who was gripping the wire and pushing and pulling on it as if to tear his way through. The smaller animal evaded the macaque's thrust by springing aside, then rebounding to the attack, this time

Fig. XI.30. Golden Lion-tamarin, *Leontopithecus rosalia rosalia*: Albinotic individual in threat posture. (Photo courtesy of New York Zoo.)

Fig. XI.31. Golden Lion-tamarin, *Leontopithecus rosalia rosalia*: Caged male fearlessly attacking adult crab-eating macaque, *Macaca fascicularis*. (Photo courtesy of Mr. Murray Hill.)

making several quick passes with his fangs. Realizing the futility of it all, both withdrew from the wire partition to observe a sullen, hostile truce.

Care of Young

Ditmars 1933 (*rosalia*)

Uninformed of the paternal role in callitrichid infant care, Ditmars watched closely and noted that the father transferred young from the mother at regular intervals. This developed into a systematic process, whereby the father took them from the female after short periods of nursing.

"The practice was regularly established within two or three days and from this period the father took over entire care of the young, carrying them at all times, even during the night, except when they were nursing. The young appeared to comprehend the process of transference. At approximate periods of two to two and one-half hours, the parents, otherwise nimbly leaping about the cage, would settle together. The female would raise her arms and the male push and shove at the infants, until they had crawled upon the mother, when they immediately started nursing. If they were hesitant about the transfer, the male would bend downward and nip them with enough vigor to induce squeaks of protest, but the disciplinary measure was, as a rule, immediately effective. Nursing periods were approximately a quarter of an hour, when the transference process was reversed. During the periods the male was carrying the young marmosets, the mother paid no attention to them.

". . . As they grew heavier, the father was literally borne down with his burden, and grew noticeably thinner from the task he assumed. The burden had greatly decreased his opportunity for exercise and frequent picking over food to obtain variety, which is a marmoset characteristic.

". . . Day by day, inclination developed for the twins to leave the father for longer periods, but to remain close by and leap upon him at [the] slightest disturbance. He was not well rid of carrying them the greater part of the time until they were close to four months old, and even after that time there were periods of hours when they would roost upon his back, grasping his long hair with tightly clenched hands. The inclination of the male was to savagely rush at strangers who too closely approached the cage. The mother evinced no such disposition."

As the young learned to eat everything consumed by the parents, the mother continued to seize and immediately devour all food offered. The father also rushed for insect food, decapitated the grasshoppers, then permitted the young to take them until each had its share.

Frantz 1963 (*rosalia*)

Nearly all active care was provided by the father. The mother tolerated the young only for suckling or when they were in repose or asleep. She also groomed them, but otherwise she showed little interest in her offspring.

All the lion-tamarins slept huddled together. This custom not only saved energy by decreasing the surface loss of heat but provided an opportunity for the young to suckle. When active the mother rid herself of the twins by a more or less fixed procedure. She pulled them off by hand and, when necessary, forced them to release their grip by biting, punching, pushing or kicking them. Once the mother chewed their tail tips. The wounds healed, but one twin lost about a centimeter of its tail. The maltreated young always disengaged themselves, but their crying brought the father, who promptly took them into his care. On May 16, I saw the mother reject her [2-week-old] young 16 times. . . .

The mother developed a characteristic suckling posture with arms outspread, pelvis pushed slightly forward and tail curved. . . .

On June 5, the father, after supporting the young for 34 days, died suddenly from an intestinal abscess. The mother took over his duties, but not with the same energy and devotion. Nevertheless, she became more protective as well as aggressive in caring for the twins and defending them.

Altmann-Schönberner 1965 (*rosalia*)

The first week or so after the birth of a single young was marked by quarrels and jealousy between the parents, until a system of give and take was established. The mother's posture while nursing is on her haunches, with back erect. The young feeds from either nipple indiscriminately. Frequent licking of the young's anogenital region by the parents was noted.

Coimbra-Filho 1969 (*rosalia*)

Young in the Rio de Janeiro Zoo took food from the hands and mouths of the parents with impunity.

Snyder 1972, p. 27 (*rosalia*)

"Five days after infants were born to a *L. rosalia* breeding pair, the nine month old juvenile female in the family unit carried one of the infants. It appeared that the infant crawled from the female accidently. The adult female chased the juvenile until she retrieved her infant. The same juvenile female reportedly began sharing in the responsibility of caring for the infants approximately sixteen days after parturition (the juvenile assumed duties in carrying the infants at that time) (DuMond, pers. comm., 1972)."

Snyder, 1972, p. 25 (*rosalia*)

"A successful breeding female (*L. rosalia*) carried her infants for approximately seven days after parturition before she allowed the male to carry them. Then she allowed the male to carry them for only a few hours a day until about the ninth day after parturition when the male carried the infants almost continuously except for nursing periods. In another instances, an *L. rosalia* female allowed the male to carry the infants only two days after parturition. This breeding pair was a newly formed pair and this birth episode was their first together."

Snyder 1972, p. 42 (*rosalia*)

"First transfer of infants to the male occurred on the third day in the first pair and on the seventh day in the second pair."

Snyder 1972, p. 26 (*rosalia*)

"In two breeding pairs of *L. rosalia,* it was noted that the male played with and groomed the juvenile animals more frequently than the female. This occurred in one instance when the juveniles were both males and two male twins and a single older female in another instance."

Cannibalism (Neonatophagy)

Eating of their newborn by primiparous mothers or inexperienced fathers has been observed among animals in captivity. In rare cases, the second litter is also consumed. The critical period in neonatophagy is between parturition and migration of the newborn to the nipples when a mother instinctively eats the afterbirth tissues. The following case of overt cannibalism by a naive father occurred in the Rio de Janeiro Zoo.

Coimbra-Filho 1972, p. 15 (*rosalia*)

Twins born of an 8-year-old wild-caught female and a captive-born male were killed by the father, their tail tips and hind limbs eaten. Twins produced by the same pair a year later were carried dorsally by the mother for the first five days when the father should have been in charge. On the sixth day, one of the young transferred to the back of its father was killed by him, its head partially eaten. Five days later, the sire accepted the surviving young without incident, returning it to its mother only for nursing.

Grooming

Snyder 1972, pp. 31–32 (*rosalia*)

"Adult males and females frequently groom not only each other, but also their young infants and juveniles. An increase in the frequency of mutual grooming with the male or juvenile as the groomer occurred immediately before and after the female gave birth in two separate instances. In order to be groomed, the juvenile usually will initiate the episode by approaching the male or female adult, begin to part the parent's fur with its hands and lying on its back presents its belly to the parent."

Snyder 1972, p. 31 (*rosalia*)

"[Fitzgerald, 1935] also mentions that grooming is extended to the mouth of the groomee, where the teeth are gone over. This type of ritualization and grooming has been observed to occur in *L. rosalia*."

Food and Feeding

Natterer, in Pelzeln 1883, p. 26 (*chrysopygus*)

Stomach contents of wild-caught *Leontopithecus rosalia rosalia* consisted of insects and fruit seeds; those of *L. r. chrysopygus* included insects and berries.

Pocock 1911, p. 816

In an experiment of feeding English insects to selected birds and mammals in the menagerie of the London Zoological Society, the golden lion-tamarin, *Leontopithecus rosalia rosalia,* reacted as follows:

Large white butterfly (*Pieris brassicae*): Taken from hand and eaten at once.

Red admiral butterfly (*Pyrameis atalanta*): Same history.

Meadow brown butterfly (*Epinephele jurtinax janira*): Same history.

Sumatran stick insect (*Lonchodes* sp.): Same history.

Telephorid beetle (?*Rhagonyche fulva*): One offered "was taken in hand, smelt and promptly dropped. Marmoset then descended from perch, picked it up again, smelt it and dropped it. The beetle crawled away unhurt." Pocock adds that the same insect was rejected by a meerkat without being tasted. "Four offered to four capuchins [*Cebus*] were eaten, two readily and without examination, two after a good deal of tasting and examination between tastes. Two offered to two capuchins were taken into the mouth, tasted, then taken out, wiped on the bars [of the cage] and left. One refused by Ceylonese macaque after being smelt. One eaten by mona monkey after a great deal of tasting, smelling and pulling about." Most birds rejected the beetle.

Humble bee (*Bombus agrorum*): Refused untouched. The tamarin was busy catching houseflies and bluebottles at the time. It didn't hesitate to accept and eat a red admiral butterfly offered a moment later.

Saw fly (*Allantus arenatus*): Refused.

Ruschi 1964, p. 4 (*rosalia*)

The golden lion-tamarins in Espírito Santo were observed eating certain kinds of beetles, butterflies, grasshoppers and other insects, wild fruit, tree leaves, and bananas ripening in the fields bordering their forest habitat They were also seen stealing eggs from nests of the red-bellied thrush (*Turdus rufiventris*) and preying on the young of smaller birds.

Coimbra-Filho 1969 (*rosalia*)

The lion-tamarins in the Rio de Janeiro Zoo eat constantly, mostly insects, and defecate frequently. They relish Blattariae, Orthoptera, Homoptera, Lepidoptera, and Coleoptera, including the larvae of certain forms. Large beetles, grasshoppers, and crickets are furiously fought over. Spiders are devoured and mollusks are relished. A lion-tamarin was seen running down a tree trunk after a lizard, which it seized and devoured. The entire episode happened too quickly to identify the victim. Birds, eggs, and young mice are also eaten.

A variety of plant food, mainly soft fruits, is consumed. Large hard seeds are either swallowed whole or ejected. Leaves are not eaten. The favorite food in captivity is bananas. The lion-tamarin can live for years on bananas alone with an occasional supplement of raw eggs.

It seemed to Coimbra-Filho that certain insects rejected in the wild are sometimes eaten in captivity. In the case of a homoptera, the *saui* that ate it sniffed it, then sneezed and rubbed its mouth several times against its perch. Vividly or warningly colored larvae are always rejected because of their disagreeable odor.

Captive-borne individuals, Coimbra-Filho believes, are afraid of or feel inhibited from seizing prey normally captured in the wild. This trait is particularly true of lion-tamarins born or raised in narrow quarters. They may even show fear of large grasshoppers which in the wild are seized quickly and consumed with gusto.

Coimbra-Filho was impressed with the benevolent and tolerant attitude of lion-tamarins toward their young, who took the food out of their parents' hands and mouth without being punished.

Ditmars 1933 (*rosalia*)

"A varied diet was provided [in the New York Zoo], as in the wild state marmosets have been noted to feed on fruits, small reptiles and insects—in fact, they are definitely insectivorous and the chitinous covering of insects appears to be a necessary part of the diet. Small lizards were also regularly supplied to the marmosets. They devoured them ravenously.

"As the young began feeding upon practically all items consumed by the parents, the feeding habits of the female remained the same. She would greedily rush to the cage front, seize and immediately devour all special foods to be offered. The feeding habits of the male, however, were greatly modified. He would also rush for insect food, decapitate a grasshopper, then hold it until it had been taken by one of the young. This continued until both young had received their share. Any interference with such action by the female, was savagely resented."

Coimbra-Filho 1972, p. 511 (*rosalia*)

One lion-tamarin in the Rio de Janeiro zoo stripped and chewed bits of bark from freshly cut branches placed in its cage.

Epple 1970, p. 60 (*rosalia*)

Diets of laboratory lion-tamarins should include such undigestible material as feathers and hairs. "When our *Leontideus rosalia* and *Saguinus geoffroyi* produced soft feces, these became solid as soon as the animal received a bird or a mouse."

Coimbra-Filho 1969, p. 46 (*rosalia*)

A diet deficient in insects results in loss of pelage pigment. The coats of freshly caught lion-tamarins are a bright reddish orange that contrasts markedly with the dull faded pelage of captive individuals that have been maintained for a long time on a poor diet. The lion-tamarins in the Rio de Janeiro Zoo keep their natural colors for years when fed on an experimental diet that includes insects. The natural color is attributed to various carotenoids, particularly those found in arthropods [but see discussion on p. 827].

Coimbra-Filho and Magnanini 1972, p. 63 (*rosalia*)

"We have successfully corrected cases of serious alopecia and improved the coat color of marmosets donated by persons who had kept them inadequately for a long time. This has been done by supplementing their diets with "Ravitan" (F. Hoffman/La Roche & Cia. S.A.) (This is highly palatable because of its cocoa contents) and vitamins A and E mixed in a daily ration of 5–10 g of ground raw meat, or diluted in milk and Ovaltine (Swiss type). Medications and nutritional supplements, which are quite often of low palatability, must be offered by stratagems. Marmosets, when in captivity, may refuse to eat many food forms, especially when they have been recently captured. Conversion to strange foods may take a long time. We have successfully used products such as Ovaltine dissolved in milk as vehicles for vitamins, mineral salts, and medications. We have been satisfied with the results obtained through the use of certain dietetic products made for human use, such as 'Gevral Protein with Autrinic' (Lederle Lab.). The latter, mixed with Ovaltine dissolved in milk has been extremely well accepted by all species of *Callithricidae* we tested. This morning ration is highly palatable and of high nutritional value. Its deficiency in certain amino acids can be corrected by the addition of raw meat, raw egg yolk, cheese, or small live animals, especially arthropods. As to fruit, the banana assumes an important place and should be offered whole so that the animals must peel them with their hands and teeth. Other fruits are given to our marmosets, including some dried fruit, but none is as important as bananas to the marmosets. Ovaltine as a vehicle for dietary supplements is given in the morning at 7:00 A.M. At 11:00 A.M. the leftovers must be removed and fruit supplied. In the afternoon, at 4:00 P.M., insects or small vertebrates are offered. The marmosets have a marked preference for small lizards, which are, however, quite difficult to obtain regularly. Desirable foods should always be given in the afternoon (e.g., live food, fruit). If live food is supplied in the morning, the marmosets become conditioned to this and will wait for more, abandoning, at least partially, the morning ration, which is important because of the nutrient supplements and medications they provide. This can be detrimental to a balanced diet. We feel that marmosets should be fed parsimoniously, but more frequently; preferably about three times a day. At 6:00 P.M., all leftovers should be removed."

Magnanini, Coimbra-Filho, Mittermeier, and Aldrighi 1975

"The daily diet [of the Lion-tamarins in the Tijuca Bank, Rio de Janeiro] consists of whole wheat bread soaked in milk fortified with vitamins, minerals and various amino acids in the morning; bananas, pears, apples and grapes and other seasonally available fruits in the afternoon; water is given twice daily; one quail egg each every fourth day and one grasshopper each every third day."

Milk Composition

Buss 1975

A single sample of milk taken from a Golden Lion-tamarin 3 days postpartum and 1 day after the infant had died from dystocia consisted of the following:

Major constituents (g/100 ml): lipids 5.8; protein (N × 6.38) 5.7; lactose 6.9; ash 0.78.

Major minerals (mg/100 ml): sodium 47; potassium 30; calcium 170; phosphorus 120.

Fatty acids (wt. %): $C_{8:0}$ 2.2; $C_{10:0}$ 22.2; $C_{12:0}$ 17.5; $C_{14:0}$ 9.9; $C_{16:0}$ 14.7; $C_{18:0}$ 2.0; $C_{18:1}$ 15.5; $C_{18:2}$ 15.9.

[Fatty acid designation indicates number of carbon atoms followed by number of double bands, if any].

"The sample . . . was very white and rich looking and was rich in protein and ash compared with other simian milks (Buss 1971) but the high calcium and phosphorus and low sodium levels suggest that the sample was not colostrum. Lactose was essentially the only carbohydrate present, as shown by paper chromotography. The very high levels of medium chain fatty acids are similar to those found in milk from *Saguinus oedipus* (Glass and Jenness, 1971)."

"Milk from *Leontopithecus rosalia rosalia* thus appears similar to milks from other New World monkeys which have been investigated, and similar methods of hand raising should prove appropriate."

Hand Use

Coimbra-Filho 1970, p. 255 (*rosalia*)

The elongate hands and feet of lion-tamarins appear to be adaptations for swift and sure movements through their tangled habitat, and the claws permit them to travel through the trees with the facility of squirrels. The hands have poor power of prehension because they lack opposability in the thumb. Nevertheless, I have seen them use their fingers and claws for exploring cracks and fissures in the bark and branches of trees and extracting the small animals hidden there. The prey is torn in the process of capture and the pieces are brought to the mouth. The mouth is also used at times for seizing prey but usually after the victim has been secured by hand. Fingers and claws are also used for grooming including combing, removing ectoparasites, and fondling.

Hershkovitz (Notes)

The long slender arm, narrow palms, and elongate fingers of the lion-tamarins are specialized for probing and for snagging insects and grubs that live under loose bark and in cracks, crevices, and holes in tree trunks and branches. The specialization is described in detail above (p. 00, fig. XI.16). My investigations of hand use by the lion-tamarin had already been remarked upon by DuBrul (1965, p. 272) and C. A. Hill (1970, p. 15).

Drink

Frantz 1963 (*rosalia*)

They drink water by lapping like cats but dip their noses in the liquid.

Predators

Snyder 1972, p. 29 (*rosalia*)

"Often a hawk or buzzard would fly over the cages of three pairs of *L. rosalia,* the initial results being moving down from higher elevations in the trees, crouching and emitting no vocalizations."

Locomotion

Coimbra-Filho 1969, p. 42 (*rosalia*)

Their flight is extraordinarily swift and disorganized, with some individuals leaping on the branches, others climbing and springing from treetop to treetop.

Coimbra-Filho 1970*a,* p. 254 (*chrysopygus*)

The "saui-preto" (*L. r. chrysopygus*) like the "mico-leao-vermelho" (*L. r. rosalia*) prefers traveling along a more or less horizontal pathway, and leaping rather than climbing up or down, which they do with less agility.

Coimbra-Filho 1970*a* (*chrysomelas*)

Habits of *chrysomelas* are similar to those of *rosalia,* but it seems that the former prefers running to leaping and climbing.

Coimbra-Filho and Magnanini 1972, p. 65

"After observing different species of marmosets in their natural environments, we have reached the conclusion that their movements always have a tendency to be horizontal. They move about by running along branches, jumping from one tree to another, only climbing up or down when in search of food."

Coimbra-Filho 1969, p. 42

A Golden Lion-tamarin escaping from the Rio de Janeiro Zoo descended a tree trunk head first, squirrel fashion, its claws digging into the bark for support, the tail held straight behind.

Hershkovitz (Notes)

The seemingly "disorganized" or helter-skelter flight of lion-tamarins is the well-organized *distractive* flight practiced by callitrichids and many other kinds of small usually diurnal animals that live in small social groups. Animals that live in herds, pods, or schools usually take flight in a body.

Travel by horizontal movements in the trees or on the ground is most efficient for covering the greatest distance in the shortest time. Vertical movements and leaping are resorted to for changing levels or for detouring impassable stretches in the same level. Climbing and leaping, however, demand more of the resources of quadrupedal ground- or branch-running mammals than does horizontal progression.

Play

Frantz 1963 (*rosalia*)

The young liked to play hide-and-seek; they hid from each other and from the adults and then slowly peeped from out of their place of concealment. In the "catapult" game they repeatedly threw down twigs they broke from branches by bending their weight against them. Their favorite game when they were older was the double attack on their aunt. In this they displayed remarkable cooperation.

Snyder, 1972, p. 40 (*rosalia*)

"Play consisted of much chasing through the trees [of the Monkey Jungle, Miami] with little wrestling, whereas *C.* [*sic* = *S*(*aguinus*)] *geoffroyi* displayed more wrestling on the ground and less chasing through the trees."

Exercise

Hershkovitz (Notes)

Back arching and stiff-legged walking performed by caged callitrichids are often merely exercises for stretching and tensing muscles, tendons, and ligaments little used in confinement. The Golden Lion-tamarin and other callitrichids may arch the back by standing erect, gripping the roof bars with their hands, and pulling hard while leaning backward. This exercise may be reversed by gripping the overhead bars with the feet and pushing against the floor of the cage with the hands. These and other calisthenics, when performed for relieving the apathy of the limbs or the boredom of confinement, have no social significance or psychological connotations. They are executed when the animal is completely alone or in the company of cagemates who couldn't care less.

Repose

Coimbra-Filho 1969, p. 41 (*rosalia*)

They retire about 17:30 to hollow trees or thick tangles of epiphytes and sleep in a crouched position with tail thrown over head and body. Lion-tamarins in the Rio de Janeiro Zoo also retire about the same time according to the season. They awake at dawn to bask in the first rays of the sun, especially on cold mornings after a long rain.

Display

Common monkey traits exhibited by Golden Lion-tamarins studied by Epple (1967) include scent marking, genital sniffing, brow beetling, ear flattening, mane raising, and back arching.

Snyder 1972, p. 35 (*rosalia*)

"When *L. rosalia* juveniles or adults are startled by either a human being or another animal, they display their teeth, raise their eyebrows, squint, pull the corners of their mouths back, and jerk back their heads."

Snyder 1972, p. 32 (*rosalia*)

"Scent marking activity was observed to occur after arched back and piloerection display of one male mate in a successful breeding pair of *L. rosalia.* This arched back and piloerection appeared to be in some instances either non-directive or directed at the observer."

Scent Marking

Use of the sternal gland for territorial marking was noted by Epple and Lorenz (1967), and scent marking with circumgenital and suprapubic glands was described by Epple (1970*b;* 1972) (figs. XI.32, 33).

Snyder 1972, p. 34 (*rosalia*)

"Sternal scent marking is displayed more frequently than circumgenital scent marking in *L. rosalia* by the adult male in the family unit. Sternal scent marking can be conspicuously observed continuously throughout the year. The possibility exists that circumgenital scent marking may be important in social-sexual communication between groups and within the family unit in *L. rosalia.* . . . Scent marking, both sternal and circumgenital, occurred less frequently in the purportedly dominant, successful breeding cage of *L. rosalia,* than in either of the other two cages."

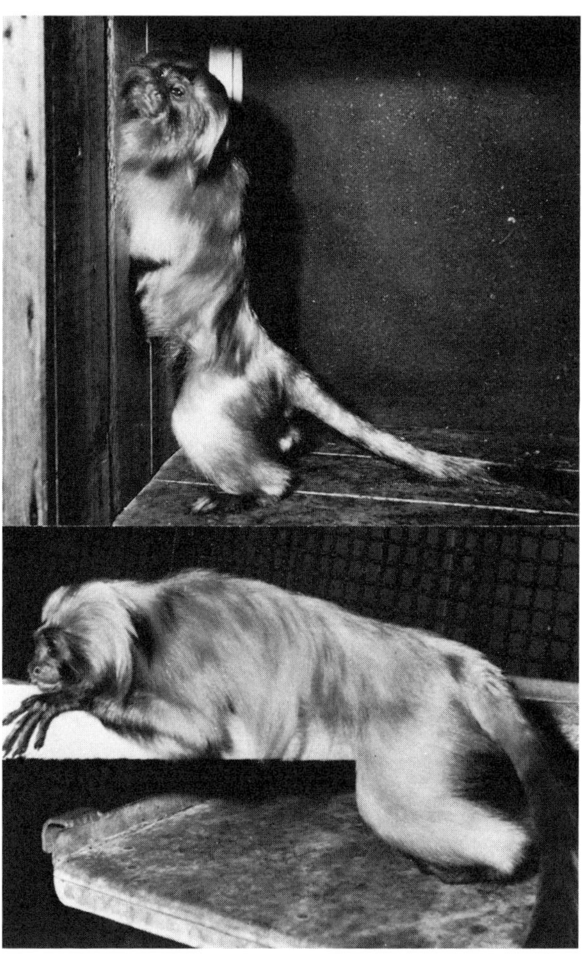

Fig. XI.32. *Leontopithecus rosalia rosalia,* caged female sternal marking. (Photo courtesy of Gisela Epple.)

Fig. XI.33. *Leontopithecus rosalia rosalia,* caged male, marking with circumgenital glands. (Photo courtesy of Gisela Epple.)

Snyder 1972, p. 33 (*rosalia*)

"Usually after a heavy rainfall, *L. rosalia, C. geoffroyi* and *C. goeldii* were observed to rescent mark an area previously marked. . . . DuMond (pers. comm., 1971) noted that when *L. rosalia, C. geoffroyi* and *C. goeldii* were placed in new, large cages they began scent marking their new territory and that after a period of time the frequency of scent marking decreased significantly."

Vocalization

Epple 1968, p. 20

Calls of 2 male and 2 female Golden Lion-tamarins

were compared with those of *Callithrix jacchus* and other callitrichids and described and classified in the same terms and in the same order (cf. p. 000). The following abstract of Epple's account includes data that may be useful for distinguishing calls of *Leontopithecus*. There is no convincing evidence, however, that certain calls are anything more than individual or group variables, some cultured, others acquired in captivity.

1. Contact calls
   a. Monosyllabic *pe* calls, as uttered by *jacchus,* but slightly shorter and louder.
   b. Monosyllabic *phee* calls of *jacchus* sound like *whee.*
   d. Rhythmical heterotypical sound sequences rather than single sounds as in species of *Callithrix.* These are followed during great excitement by loud, short, high-pitched *pii, pii, pii,* calls.
2. Squeals in submission, as in *jacchus.*
3. Screams when angry. Chatters emitted by all other callitrichids replaced by screams in the same situation.
4. Mobbing *tsik* as in species of *Callithrix,* but frequency modulation higher.
5. Trills, as in *Callithrix argentata;* sounded when slightly alarmed, angry, or threatening; action of tongue not mentioned. Trills were not registered for *Callithrix jacchus.*
6. Warning calls as in *jacchus* but seem to sound louder and lower pitched.
7. Monosyllabic food rejection calls; short high-pitched notes uttered when smelling or tasting food; call may be made while corners of mouth are drawn back.

Andrew 1963, pp. 46–47 (*rosalia*)

His analysis of recorded calls follow.

"a. *Twitters.* [F(undamental): steeply ascending or descending c. 7 Kc. to c. 4Kc. (0.03 sec.) or short ascent and long descent, inflected at 6–7 Kc. N(oise): inflection prolonged horizontally. E(nergy distribution): 4–14 Kc.] Bouts of twitters tend all to have the inflection point at the same pitch. They may be given when threatening a human stranger at a distance, when the mouth is opened wide for each bout, and threatening forward leaps occur. Twitters are also given when approaching a fellow to share his food, or, in the case of an infant, to seek bodily contact.

"b. *Wavering squeak.* [F: c. 8 Kc., level, made up of series of almost continuous calls (.15 sec. initially to 0.5–0.7) sec]. This call replaced twitters at high intensity and clearly corresponded to a twitter bout in which only the inflection points were present.

"c. *Screech.* This is given, as in other marmosets, when approaching very close to a superior, or approached by one."

Coimbra-Filho 1969, p. 42 (*rosalia*)

Calls heard in the Rio de Janeiro Zoo included short, high-pitched whistles, sonorous sustained notes, and bird-like trills and warbles. A clicking sound made with the teeth was also noted.

Coimbra-Filho 1970*a,* p. 255

Their most characteristic sounds when observed in their natural habitat are a shrill whistle and a chirp or chirring.

Fig. XI.34. Thermoregulatory spreadeagle posture of Golden Lion-tamarin (*Leontopithecus rosalia rosalia*). Drawing from photograph of individual in callitrichid colony, University of Texas Dental Science Institute, Houston, Texas. Compare with gibbon suspensory sitting posture (fig. I.19).

Benirschke and Richart 1963, p. 80–81 (*rosalia*)

"Their peculiar keening noise was quite distinct from all others [of the colony (*Saguinus oedipus oedipus, S. "nigricollis", S. mystax mystax, Callithrix jacchus jacchus, Callicebus moloch cupreus*)] noted by us and indicated fear or anger."

Thermoregulation

Hershkovitz (Notes)

Golden Lion-tamarins I observed in the Houston laboratory colony often relaxed and cooled their bodies by sitting with back resting against the far corner of the cage, legs spread and outstretched, arms crooked at the elbow and held above the head, the fingers grasping the ceiling bars. The posture was gibbonlike, and the thin long limbs and spread-eagled posture of the animals enhanced the resemblance (fig. XI.34).

The relaxed or thermoregulatory position with belly down and extremities dangling, also assumed by Golden Lion-tamarins, is common to all callitrichids and many other diurnal arboreal mammals.

Coimbra-Filho 1969, p. 42 (*rosalia*)

On cold days in Rio de Janeiro, the Golden Lion-tamarins sun themselves while grooming in relaxed positions on a branch.

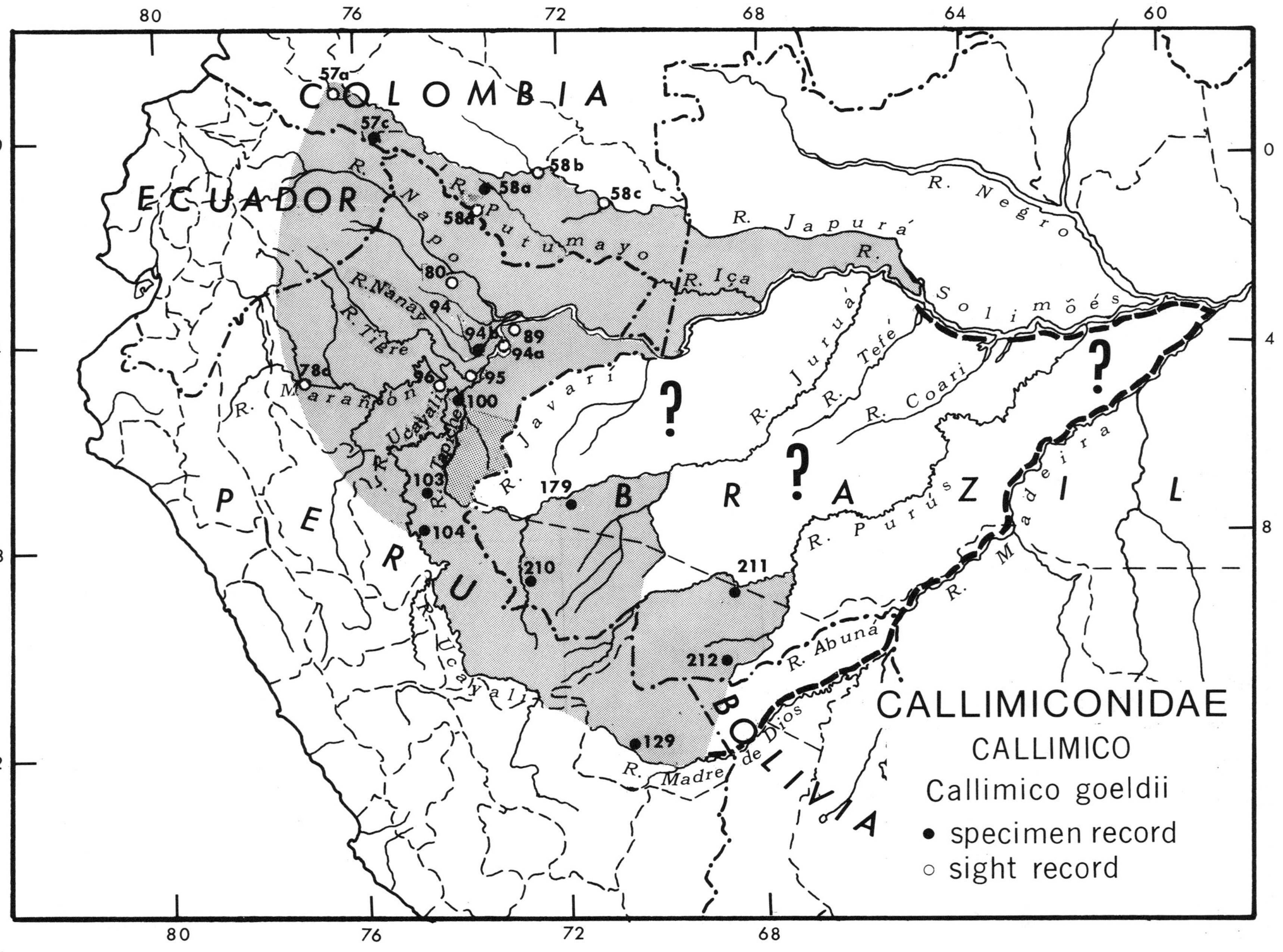

Fig. XII.1. Distribution of callimicos, *Callimico goeldii;* dots show collecting localities and sight records (see gazetteer, p. 918 for key to symbols).

80 Family Callimiconidae Dollman, Callimico *History, Systematic Position, and Characters*

Synonymic History

Callimiconinae Thomas, 1913, *Ann. Mag. Nat. Hist.*, ser. 8, 11:131—subfamily of Cebidae. Thomas, 1913, *Proc. Zool. Soc. London* 1913:3—subfamily of Cebidae. Elliot, 1913, *A review of the Primates,* 3:261—subfamily of Cebidae. Pocock, 1920, *Proc. Zool. Soc. London* 1920:113—subfamily of Hapalidae. Pocock, 1925, *Proc. Zool. Soc. London* 1925:38—subfamily of Hapalidae. Thomas, 1928, *Ann. Mag. Nat. Hist.*, ser. 10, 2:255—a primitive marmoset. Weber, 1928, *Die Säugetiere,* ed. 2, pp. 788, 796—subfamily of Cebidae. Simpson, 1945, *Bull. Amer. Mus. Nat. Hist.* 85:65, 185—subfamily of Cebidae. Vallois, 1955, *Primates,* in *Traité de Zoologie,* ed. Grassé, vol. 17, ser. 2:1970—subfamily of Hapalidae. Fiedler, 1956, *Primatologia* 1:155—subfamily of Cebidae. Osman Hill, 1957, *Primates,* 3:viii—primitive tamarin, family Hapalidae. Osman Hill, 1959, *Trans. Amer. Philos. Soc.*, n.s. 49, 5:111—primitive marmoset, subfamily of Hapalidae. Napier and Napier, 1967, *Handbook of living Primates,* p. 347—subfamily of Callitrichidae. Thenius, 1969, *Zeitschr. Zool. Syst. Evol.* 7(3):169—subfamily of Callitrichidae.

Callimiconidae Dollman, 1931, in *The Standard Natural History,* ed. Pycraft, p. 908—family of Anthropoidea. Dollman, 1937, *Proc. Zool. Soc. London,* ser. C, 107:64—review and classification. Osman Hill, 1957, *Primates,* 3:311—review. Hershkovitz, 1970, *Amer. J. Phys. Anthrop.* 32(3):377—dental formula. Hershkovitz, 1970, *Folia Primat.* 12:3—similarities to cebids and callitrichids attributed to parallelisms. Hershkovitz, 1970, *Folia Primat.* 13:216, 237—organization of brain, intermediate between callitrichids and cebids. De Boer, 1974, *Genen Phaenen* 17:6, 25, 84, 89, 91—karyology; phylogeny (independent evolution).

Type and Only Known Genus. Callimico Miranda Ribeiro.

Distribution (figs. VII.1, 4; XII.1; XIII.1)

The same as for the only known species, *Callimico goeldii* Thomas (q.v.).

Taxonomic History

The first callimico known to science is represented by a hide described by Oldfield Thomas in 1904 under the name *Hapale goeldii.* In 1912, Miranda Ribeiro recognized an individual living in the zoological gardens of the Belém, Pará (Goeldi) Museum as unique and gave it the new name *Callimico snethlageri.* The generic name was in allusion to the resemblance of the animal to a cross between *Callicebus,* a marmosetlike cebid, and *Mico* (= *Callithrix*), a true marmoset.

When the peculiar monkey died, it was prepared as a study skin and skull and forwarded to the British Museum (Natural History) for examination by Oldfield Thomas (1913, p. 131). Comparison with the previously described *Hapale goeldii* revealed that the animals were the same species. The additional specimen however, confirmed the uniqueness of *Callimico* as a genus intermediate in grade in most respects between cebids and callitrichids.

Externally, particularly in body size, limb proportions, and characters of hands and feet, the animal appeared to be a callitrichid. Cranially it seemed positioned between *Saimiri* and *Callithrix.* The dental formula, with 6 cheek teeth, was cebid, but molar structure was more nearly callitrichid. Although Thomas (1913, p. 132) adjudged *Callimico* "exactly intermediate between the otherwise well-defined families, Cebidae and Callitrichidae," he gave greater weight to the dental formula and assigned *Callimico* to the Cebidae as type of a special subfamily, the Callimiconinae.

Pocock (1920, p. 113), reexamined the same two specimens and doubtless a third that had been exhibited in the London Zoo (Flower 1929, p. 50). He attached greater systematic importance to the cheiridia than to the teeth and transferred the Callimiconinae to the Callitrichidae (= Hapalidae). In Pocock's mind, callitrichids (and *Callimico*) were dwarfed cebids, their claws converted nails, their squirrellike hands and feet degenerate or enfeebled derivatives of the clutching cebid cheiridia.

Again, in 1925, Pocock (1925*a*, p. 38) reasserted his

stand regarding *Callimico* as a primitive callitrichid, and his concept of callitrichids as "a specialized derivative group that branched off at an early stage from the monkey stock." Thomas (1928, p. 255), now toward the end of his career, accepted Pocock's views without comment.

Dollman (1937) saw the problem in a different light. The three specimens then preserved in the British Museum (Natural History), convinced him of the need for separating *Callimico* from callitrichids because of the difference in dental formulae, and from cebids because of differences in form of molars and cheiridia. The status of *Callimico* was then resolved by raising it to the rank of family, the Callimiconidae.

In a long discourse on platyrrhine interrelationships, Miranda Ribeiro (1941, p. 828) reiterated earlier opinions to the effect that "marmosets are degenerate Cebidae and *Callimico* renders untenable to high division as family-ranks [for cebids and callitrichids]." He (1941, p. 849) then arbitrarily rearranged living platyrrhines in a phylogenetic sequence that began with *Callicebus,* said to be most primitive with "lemuroid skull," and ended with *Callithrix* (*Hapale*), regarded as most evolved or degenerate. Intermediate taxa were pithecines (his "callitriches"), followed by howlers (his *Cebus*), *Ateles, Brachyteles, Saimiri, Cebus* (his *Pseudocebus*), *Lagothrix, Callimico,* and *Leontocebus* (= *Saguinus* and *Leontopithecus*). All were included in a single unnamed family, but certainly the Cebidae was intended. It is not clear how many or which subfamilies were recognized by Miranda Ribeiro, but Callimiconinae appears to be one of them.

Regarding *Callimico,* Miranda Ribeiro's detailed descriptions and comparisons, led him (1941, p. 786) to conclude that it is "a Primate with the skull of a *Callicebus* the mandible and feet of a marmoset and the tail and teeth of *Pseudocebus* [= *Cebus*] that is to say: it is a generalized form." If so, perhaps Miranda Ribeiro did not really mean to attribute to *Callimico* the prehensile tail and quadritubercular and nearly bilophodont molars of *Cebus,* and the highly pneumatized skull of the leaf-eating *Callicebus.*

Osman Hill (1957, pp. 79, 114, 311) preferred Dollman's (1937) family ranking for *Callimico,* but his description of the animal inclines toward callitrichid relationships. Indeed, Osman Hill recanted while the volume containing his classification was still in press. In a brief statement added to the preface of the opus in question (1957, p. viii) he declared that the study of fresh material now led him to believe that *Callimico* is a primitive tamarin and "should form no more than a subfamily, Callimiconinae, of the Hapalidae."

In a following monographic study of the anatomy of a freshly preserved callimico, Osman Hill (1959, p. 109) aligned *Callimico* with callitrichids on the basis of 19 characters which are so highly qualified that none can be taken as diagnostic of either callitrichids or *Callimico.* Some of the 19 characters actually appear to be of dubious validity, and a few are illusory. The callimico that served Osman Hill for his studies, judging by the photograph of the live animal, was normal. Its description in the text and the anatomical illustrations, however, suggest a monstrosity. The callitrichids ostensibly used for comparisons were vaguely identified (1959, p. 3) as "several hapalid Primates."

The list of 19 characters is followed by another of 24 "tarsioid or prosimian characters" said to be present in *Callimico.* These traits are also heavily qualified. Some are not true (e.g., no. 1), others are individually variable (e.g., no. 2), and none are diagnostic of prosimians or *Callimico,* separately or collectively. A third list of 16 characters, apart from the dental formula, is intended to indicate affinities between *Callimico* and cebids. These characters are also conditional but, on the whole, more apposite.

In sum, Osman Hill's exercise lacks phylogenetic content. The arguments for his disposition of *Callimico* are based on Gregory's (1922) philosophy of regressive or reversible evolution, with the highly specialized *Callicebus* used as a model for primitive platyrrhine organization.

The reconstruction in the form of a dendrogram of New World monkey evolution proposed by Osman Hill (1959) shows a primary dichotomy between callitrichids and cebids, with *Callimico* near the base of the main stem. Three molars are assigned to the unknown callitrichids at this evolutionary grade. The main stem terminates with two-molar tamarins (*Saguinus*), while true marmosets or ouistitis (*Cebuella, Callithrix*) branch off to one side near the top. No characters other than number of molars and form of "lower incisors" are shown in the dendrogram of callimico-callitrichid relationships.

Later examination of a newborn callimico said to be the survivor of a twin birth, confirmed Hill (1966*b*) in his opinion regarding the callitrichid affinities of the animal and sustained his belief in the regressive evolution of callitrichid claws from the cebid type of nails.

Basing his opinion on published data, Remane (1956, p. 339) aligned *Callimico* with the subfamily Cebinae. Later, in his great work on primate dentition, he (1960, p. 832) accepted current thinking that allowed evolutionary reversals from an advanced cebid state to the "secondarily" primitive callitrichid state. His example of dental reversal or regression from *Saimiri* with 3 quadritubercular molars to callitrichids with two tritubercular molars makes *Callimico* the central figure. Neither in this nor in his (1961) discussion of problems in primate classification does Remane actually clarify the systematic status of *Callimico,* specimens of which he evidently had not seen.

Results of cytotaxonomic studies of *Callimico* have been equivocably interpreted. Bender and Mettler (1960) regarded the karyotype of a female *Callimico goeldii* with diploid number 48 as "markedly different from the marmoset karyotype." They observed that "of the cebid karyotypes available for comparison, that of *Callimico* most closely resembles that of *Callicebus* [*cupreus*]. The karyoytpe of *Callimico* is, however, no closer to those of the Cebidae studied [*Callicebus, Saimiri, Cebus, Ateles*] than it is to that of the marmosets." Although their conclusions cannot be reconciled with the evidence, Bender and Mettler (1960, p. 403) and Chu and Bender (1961, p. 1405) decided in virtually identical terms that the "chromosomal evidence is in agreement with the idea, expressed by [Osman] Hill, that the Callithricidae are a specialized, rather than a primitive group, and that *Callimico* is more primitive (and unspecialized) and is hence probably closer to the ancestral cebid stem." Egozcue, Perkins, and Hagemenas (1968, p. 90) suggested that "from a chromosomal point of view, *C*[*allimico*] *goeldii* is more [nearly] related to *Saguinus* and consequently

Callithrix and *Leontideus* [= *Leontopithecus*] than to any other ceboid studied." In a later review of primate karyology, Egozcue (1969, pp. 369–70) observed that *Callimico* with *Saimiri* constituted "two clear links between the Cebidae and the Callithricidae." The "chromosomal similarities," he continued, "are such that a continuity between the Cebidae, the Callimiconidae, and the Callithricidae is clear. . . . Nevertheless, not all Cebidae are chromosomally related to the Callithricidae, or at least there is no evidence for such a relationship."

De Boer (1974, p. 92), who considered all available information, concluded that

> "in view of the structural characters by which *Callimico* is distinguished from the *Callithricidae* (e.g., retention of third molars which were lost in the callithricids), it seems more likely that its karyotype evolved largely independently. Possibly, the ancestral lineage leading to the *Callimiconidae* at first followed the common reduction [of chromosome number] in the *Callithricidae,* but it must have separated from the latter at quite an early stage; in any case before the typical *Callithricidae* characters evolved. Cytologically, there are no starting-points from which to trace the possibility that the Callimiconidae initially originated from the oldest ancestral *Cebidae* line."

The karyotype of *Callimico* is not intermediate between cebids and callitrichids. It simply falls, as do those of many other primates, within the numerical zone (2n = 44–48) from which hypothetically all platyrrhine (and primate diploid chromosome numbers can be derived by rearrangement of the chromosomal material. Furthermore, chromosome form and number alone do not serve as reliable criteria of phylogenetic relationships. The karyotype of *Callimico* was regarded by Bender and Mettler (1960) as nearest that of *"Callicebus,"* meaning *Callicebus cupreus* (cf. Bender and Mettler 1958, p. 187) with 46 chromosomes. Diploid number of the sibling species *Callicebus torquatus,* with karyotype then unknown, is 20 (Egozcue 1969, p. 365), the lowest recorded for primates.

Systematic Position

Callimico is a relatively primitive platyrrhine, but it is not a callitrichid or a cebid or a link between the two. The diagnostic characters *Callimico* shares with callitrichids are not the diagnostic characters it shares with cebids, and those of its characters that appear to be intermediate between callitrichid and cebid grades appear to have been independently evolved. The more important diagnostic traits are discussed under the following heading and in the generic account.

Origin, Evolution, and Dispersal

The ancestral stock of the first callimiconid remains to be discovered among primitive platyrrhines. Known fossil cebids were already highly specialized and left no modern descendants. Extinct homunculids were also highly evolved and without living issue. No primate having three molars like *Callimico* could evolve from a callitrichid, and no primate with a quadritubercular molar could evolve into a callitrichid.

The distinctive anatomical traits *Callimico* shares with tamarins (or callitrichids sensu lato) and marmosetlike cebids are parallelisms correlated with size or body mass. As a rule, members of each size class of higher primate phyletic lines, Old or New World, evolving in the same arboreal environment or similar ones subject to the same or similar selective pressures tend to evolve along similar lines. *Callimico* fills part of the morphological gap between callitrichids and cebids because its line is predictably evolving from "tamarin" grade to "marmosetlike cebid" grade in a common environment. It is not evolving as a tamarin to become a cebid or, as some authorities would have it, as a cebid to become a tamarin.

Callitrichids, callimiconids, and cebids must have diverged from primitive platyrrhine stock long before anything near *Callimico* or even *Cebuella* size or grade existed. No evidence exists that the three living platyrrhine families differentiated at the same time or within the same epoch, but each must have arisen during the Tertiary. *Callimico* is the lone and comparatively little differentiated survivor of a line of primitive platyrrhines (fig. VII.3).

Callimico almost certainly originated within its present geographic range (fig. XII.1), perhaps during the upfolding of the Cordillera Oriental and long before differentiation of the Amazonian fluvial system as it appears today. Rate and extent of callimiconid dispersal in the upper Amazonian region was controlled by the speed of suitable habitat formation in the neogene Amazonian basin and the time and circumstances of colonization. It is virtually certain that coexistence of *Callimico* and pygmy marmosets, genus *Cebuella,* began long before the appearance of *Saguinus* (fig. VII.4).

Additional information relevant to callimiconid history is included in chapter 44, p. 397, and other sections (see index).

Diagnostic Characters

The diagnostic characters of callimiconids listed below are selected and abstracted from those described in greater detail in other chapters. Many more characters are mentioned in chapter 45 on the Callitrichidae and in the separate chapters on callitrichid genera.

Size (fig. III.4):

Average larger than tamarins (*Saguinus*) and smaller than *Leontopithecus;* absolutely smaller than all cebids.

Integument:

See chapters 8–11 and figs. III.6, 12, 13; XII.2.

Cheiridia (fig. XII.3):

Relative to body size, larger and heavier than in callitrichids.

Claws (fig. XII.3):

Present on all digits except hallux as in callitrichids but less falcate or more tegulate. Long, curved and pointed claws may become adapted to secondary functions, disappear, or degenerate into nails that shield sensitive digital tips. Nails are modified claws. They do not evolve into or revert to claws.

Hill (1966*b*) noted that the ungues of a 4-day-old callimico "are decidedly less falcate than in typical tamarins and marmosets. This strongly suggests," he felt, "that the claw-like nails of adult tamarins and marmosets are a relatively late secondary evolutionary reversal in adaptation to the squirrel-like activities, where hook-like clinging to roughness of the substrate is advantageous." I fail to see the purported relationship between the ungues of newborn callimico and those of adult callitrichids. Those of newborn callitrichids (fig. XII.3) are true claws but not developed to the point where they would interfere with the fur-clutching function of the digits. The less falcate ungues of newborn callimico are likewise functionless but in form are nearer the cebid grade toward which those of their parents are probably evolving.

Thumb:

Nonopposable as in callitrichids. The callitrichid type of thumb is primitive; it cannot be derived from any cebid type of thumb but conceivably could evolve into a *Saimiri* or *Cebus* type (figs. I.26, 27).

Ear (XII.2):

As in ouistitis (true marmosets) but relatively smaller as in many cebids, and incompletely concealed by mane (see chap. 12 and figs. III.18; XII.2).

External Genitalia (figs. III.23, 25, 28, 29; XII.18, 19):

Those of female are more primitive or generalized than those of callitrichids; of male, superficially similar to those of *Leontopithecus* but more specialized than in callitrichids.

Tongue:

See chapter 13, figs. III.19, 20; XII.4.

Palatal Ridges:

See page 431 and fig. VII.14.

Larynx (figs. I.10, 11; XII.4):

Cebid type; vocalization not certainly callitrichid.

Cerebral Hemispheres (figs. VI.8, 9):

Fissuration of low tamarin grade (see chap. 20).

Interorbital Septum:

As in *Callicebus* or *Aotus* (see chap. 20).

Frontal Sinus (figs. IV.27; XII.5):

Connection with nasal cavity through posterolateral channel is as in cebids (see chap. 21).

Tentorium Cerebelli:

Ossification well developed. This is an independently acquired character evidently not related to body or head size. Ossification is also present in a number of cebids but is absent or no more than incipient in callitrichids (see chap. 22).

Cribriform Plate (fig. IV.43):

Apparently cebid in morphology and evolutionary grade.

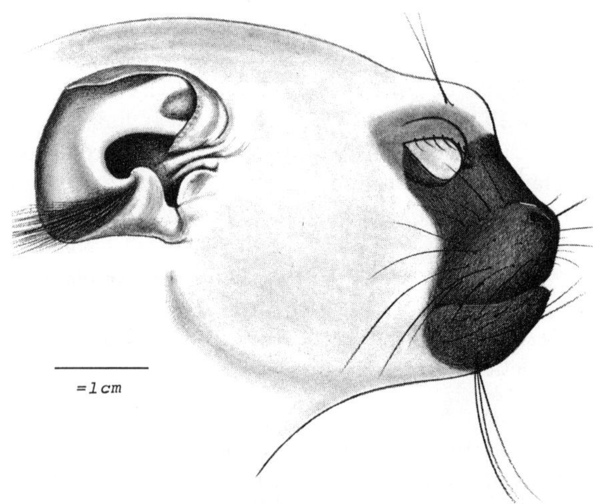

Fig. XII. 2. *Callimico goeldii*: Profile of head with mane and facial hairs removed to expose ear, vibrissae, and facial pigmentation.

Mandible (figs. IV.78–80; XII.7, 8, 10, 11):

Well advanced but not particularly specialized; nearly U-shaped form, intermediate between those of *Callithrix* and *Saguinus,* or like that of ancestral catarrhines. All primate U-shaped jaws are derived from primitive V-shaped (zalambdognathous) jaws (see chap. 26).

Additional Cranial Characters (figs. XII.5–11):

See comparisons with cebids and callitrichids (chap. 28).

Dental Formula (chap. 34):

Cebid or primitive catarrhine $= \frac{2}{2}, \frac{1}{1}, \frac{3}{3}, \frac{3}{3} = 36$ (cf. Fayum Oligocene *Parapithecus,* fig. II.2).

Dental Succession:

As in the larger callitrichids (*Saguinus, Leontopithecus*), most cebids and catarrhines (see chap. 35; table 10).

Premolars:

Divergences from callitrichid and cebid patterns are detailed in the dental description in the generic section (p. 881, also chap. 33).

Molars (figs. V.19, 25–28; XII.13–15):

Three molars in each jaw distinguish *Callimico* from all callitrichids; combination of tritubercular tuberculosectorial molars with a weak hypocone regularly present in m^1 only, and absence of external cingulum in lower molars, distinguishes *Callimico* from all living cebids; cusps more hypsodont than in all known platyrrhines; incipient hypocone sometimes present in m^2 is the criterion for a grade of molarization beyond that attained in callitrichids and approaching that of cebids.

A disproportionately small m3 as in callimiconids is a common phenomenon among primates (chap. 33, p. 302). In most cases, the small size of the tooth is the result of reduction or degeneration. In *Callimico* the third upper and lower molars are premolariform and apparently in a state of arrested or comparatively retarded molarization. Absence of the paraconid in permanent molars is common in living platyrrhines and catarrhines.

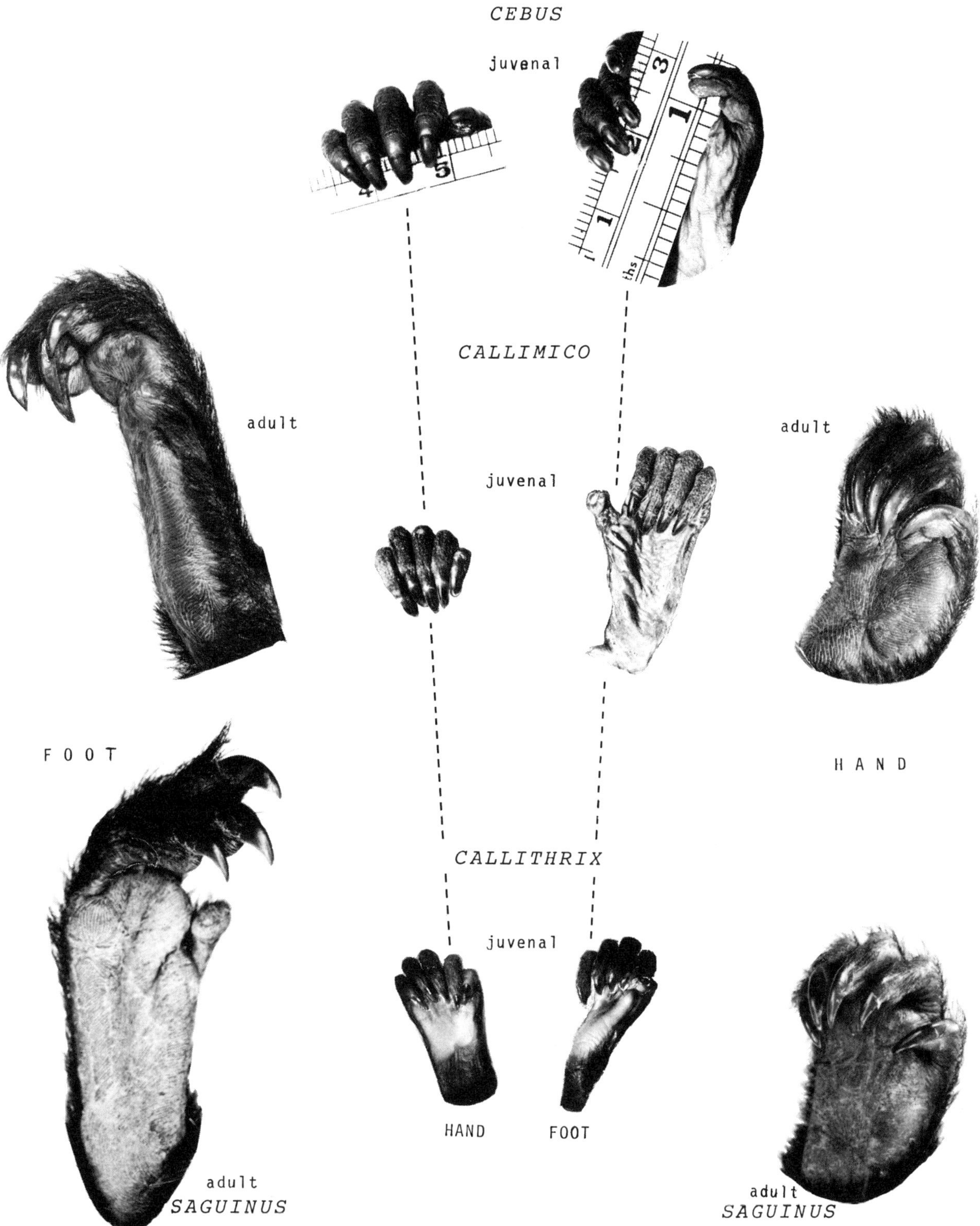

Fig. XII.3. Ungues of hand and foot each of a newborn and adult *Callimico goeldii,* an adult *Saguinus nigricollis,* a newborn *Callithrix jacchus,* and a newborn *Cebus apella;* all to scale shown.

Note: The paraconid is a primitive mammalian cusp that once lost is never regained. The hypocone is a comparatively new mammalian cusp differentiated by progressive molarization in an anteroposterior direction in the dpm^4–m^3 series, as in *Callimico.* The hypocone, once gained, has not been lost except in the last molar, when that tooth, whichever of the original three it is, becomes obsolescent. A vestige of the hypocone, slight as it might be, usually persists as long as the tooth remains.

Karyotype:

The diploid chromosome number of 48 (or 47 in cases with a translocated Y chromosome) lies within the hypothetical basic or primary zone of 44–48 chromosomes for all primates studied. The diploid number in callitrichids is 44–46, in cebids 20–62. Cebids with diploid chromosome numbers within 44–48 range are *Saimiri sciureus* and *Alouatta seniculus* with 44, and *Callicebus moloch, Cacajao rubicundus,* and *Pithecia pithecia* with 46. Ex-

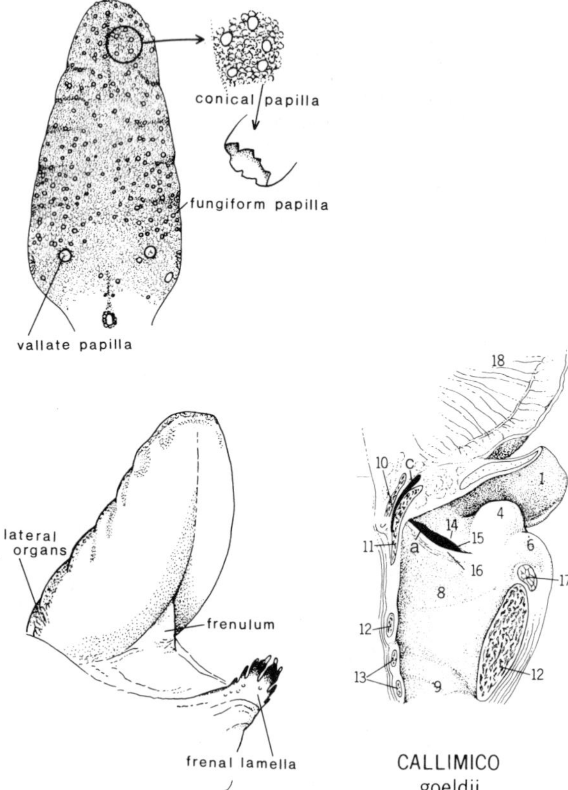

Fig. XII.4. *Callimico goeldii*: Tongue, dorsal and ventral surfaces, a section of conical papilla shown enlarged; larynx, inner surface of left half; symbols explained on page 19.

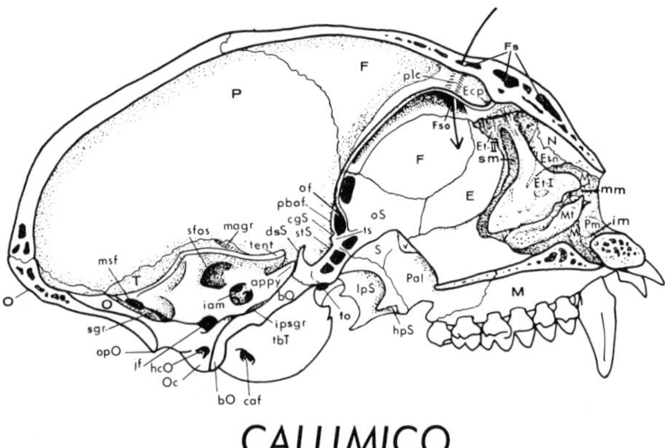

Fig. XII.5. *Callimico goeldii*: Medial aspect of sagittal section of skull; symbols explained on page 269.

cept for *Cacajao* and *Pithecia,* none of the cebids are closely related to each other, and none are related to *Callimico.* Published karyotypes of other species of the same genera are grossly different.

Reproduction:
A single young is produced at a birth as in cebids. A multiple-birth litter as in callitrichids is primitive for platyrrhines.

Gestation:
The average duration is approximately 150 days or intermediate between the shorter period in callitrichids and the longer one in cebids.

Pregnancy:
The abdominal swelling, enlarged breasts and nipples, behavioral and other signs become noticeable the second month and conspicuous during the last six weeks. External signs of pregnancy are not apparent in callitrichids until two or three weeks before parturition.

Care of Young:
By mother alone as in cebids for first 2 to 4 weeks, thereafter, by father alone, except for nursing; maternal transportation of young dorsal or ventral.

Paternal care of young from day of birth is a callitrichid specialty. Paternal behavior as guardian of and "nest" for the young is likewise specialization of callimiconids but begins at a later ontogenetic stage. In most cebids, the young are even more advanced when the father assumes a relatively minor role in infant care. In this and other aspects of breeding and rearing, *Callimico* is nearer cebid than callitrichid grade (see p. 29).

Habits:
Observations of the animal in semifree habitat and in captivity indicate that *Callimico* may be crepuscular to part nocturnal, prefers the lower forest story, and commonly frequents the ground. It may be the most carnivorous or predatory of all platyrrhines.

Parasites

The recorded parasites of *Callimico* are one species of ectoparasitic mite and seventeen endoparasites listed below. They were recovered from different individuals maintained in laboratory primate colonies. The same kinds of parasites were found in associated captive callitrichids and small cebids. More information on platyrrhine parasites is given in chapter 43.

Giardia intestinalis (Hexamatidae, Mastigophora, Protozoa)
The genus is parasitic in vertebrates and invertebrates; species is widely distributed among primates, including man.

Trichomonas hominis (Trichomonadidae, Mastigophora, Protozoa)
The flagellate genus and species are widely distributed parasites of primates.

Entamoeba coli (Entamoebidae, Sarcodina, Protozoa)
The genus is parasitic in vertebrates and invertebrates. *E. coli* is widely distributed among mammals, including man and other primates.

Entamoeba histolytica
This intestinal parasite is the causative agent of human amebic dysentery or amebiasis. It is widely distributed among primates.

Iodamoeba butschlii (Entamoebidae, Sarcodina, Protozoa)
The species infects man and other primates; a second species is parasitic in pigs.

Isospora endocallimico (Eimeriidae, Sporozoa, Protozoa)
Oocytes found in feces of 5 individuals maintained in the Delta Regional Primate Research Center were described by Duszynski and File (1974). The genus is

parasitic in amphibians, reptiles, birds, and mammals. Two species are known to infect man, and one each has been described from *Callithrix, Cacajao,* and *Cebus.* One of the human parasites (*Isospora hominis*) has been found in a dog and chimpanzee, and the marmoset parasite (*I. arctopitheci*) has been reported from *Galago senegalensis.*

Sarcocystis sp. (Sarcocystidae, Sporozoa, Protozoa)
The genus is one of the most widely distributed vertebrate parasites, and there appears to be no host specificity among the species.

Conspicuum conspicuum (Dicrocoeliidae, Trematoda)
This common bird parasite also occurs in captive *Callithrix* and *Saguinus. Platysomum amazonensis* Kingston and Cosgrove (1967) is a synonym.

Athesmia sp. (Dicrocoeliidae, Strigiformes, Trematoda)
The genus is known from birds and mammals; and *A. heterolecithodes* is parasitic in platyrrhines.

Paratriotaenia sp. (Davaineidae, Cestoda)
The genus, described by Stunkard in 1965, is now known from *Callimico* and several species of *Saguinus.* The type host of *Paratriotaenia oedipomidatis* was a specimen of *Saguinus oedipus oedipus,* from the Tulane University laboratory colony. The cestodes of *Callimico* and other tamarins were found in autopsied individuals of the Miami laboratory colony.

Spirometra sp. (larvae) (Diphylobothriidae, Cestoda)
Also found in several species of *Saguinus.* The species of *Spirometra* (*reptans, mansonoides*) in platyrrhines (cf. p. 384) are natural parasites of felids and probably canids, and accidental in monkeys.

Trichostrongylus sp. (Trichostrongilidae, Strongilida, Nematoda)
The genus is parasitic in birds and mammals. *T. cesticillus,* parasitic in *Cebus apella,* is the only species as yet known from platyrrhines.

?*Metastrongylus* sp. (Metastrongilidae, Strongilida, Nematoda)
Listed by Lorenz (1972, p. 101) as parasitic in *Callimico* without particulars except for the addition of *Filaroides* in parentheses, presumably as an alternative identification.

Trypanoxyuris (*Hapaloxyuris*) *goeldii* (Oxyuridae, Nematoda)
Known from *Callimico* only. Three other species of the subgenus *Hapaloxyuris* infect callitrichids. Species of the nominate subgenus, *Trypanoxyuris,* infect cebids and a callitrichid. The host/parasite relationships are discussed on page 387.

Cruzia sp. (Ascarida, Cruziidae, Nematoda)
The genus is parasitic in New World turtles and marsupials. The record for *Callimico* (Lorenz 1972) may be the first for platyrrhines.

Trichospirura leptosoma (Thelaziidae, Nematoda)
This species has also been found in captive *Callithrix, Saguinus, Saimiri, Callicebus, Aotus. T. leptosoma* was originally believed to be a callitrichid parasite, but a high incidence of infection among small platyrrhines was subsequently found in the Tulane University primate colony. Orihel and Seibold (1971, p. 1368) note that the "parasite infection can be transmitted in the laboratory probably through an arthropod intermediate host."

Acanthocephala (Larvae)
In all probability, the parasite is one of two or three species of *Prosthenorchis* common among platyrrhines and captive primates generally .

Listrocarpus cosgrovei (Listrophoridae, Acarina)
The hair-clasping mites from a single specimen of *Callimico* were found together with others on several unnamed tamarins (*Saguinus*) maintained in the Oak Ridge Laboratory. Other species of *Listrocarpus* occur in *Callithrix, Saimiri,* and *Lagothrix* (Fain 1967).

In his report on trematodes of laboratory primates, Cosgrove (1966, p. 29) inadvertantly listed *Callimico* and *Tamarinus* (= *Saguinus*) as hosts of *Leipertrema.* They should have been listed under his *Platynosomum* (= *Conspicuum*), as he shows on pages 36 and 38 of the work cited.

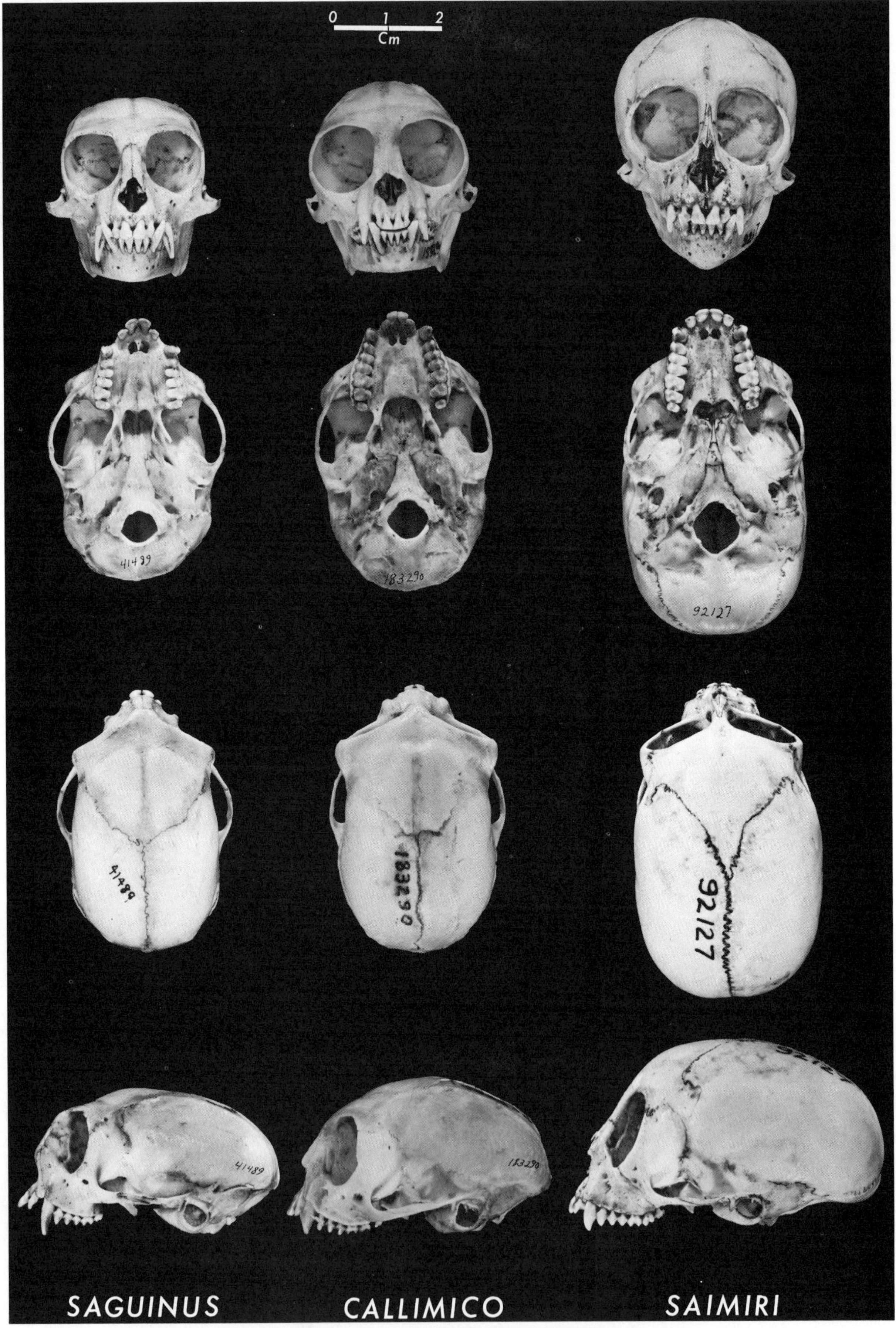

Fig. XII.6. *Callimico* skull: frontal, basicranial, dorsal and lateral aspects compared with same views of *Saguinus* (Callitrichidae) and *Saimiri* (Cebidae) skulls.

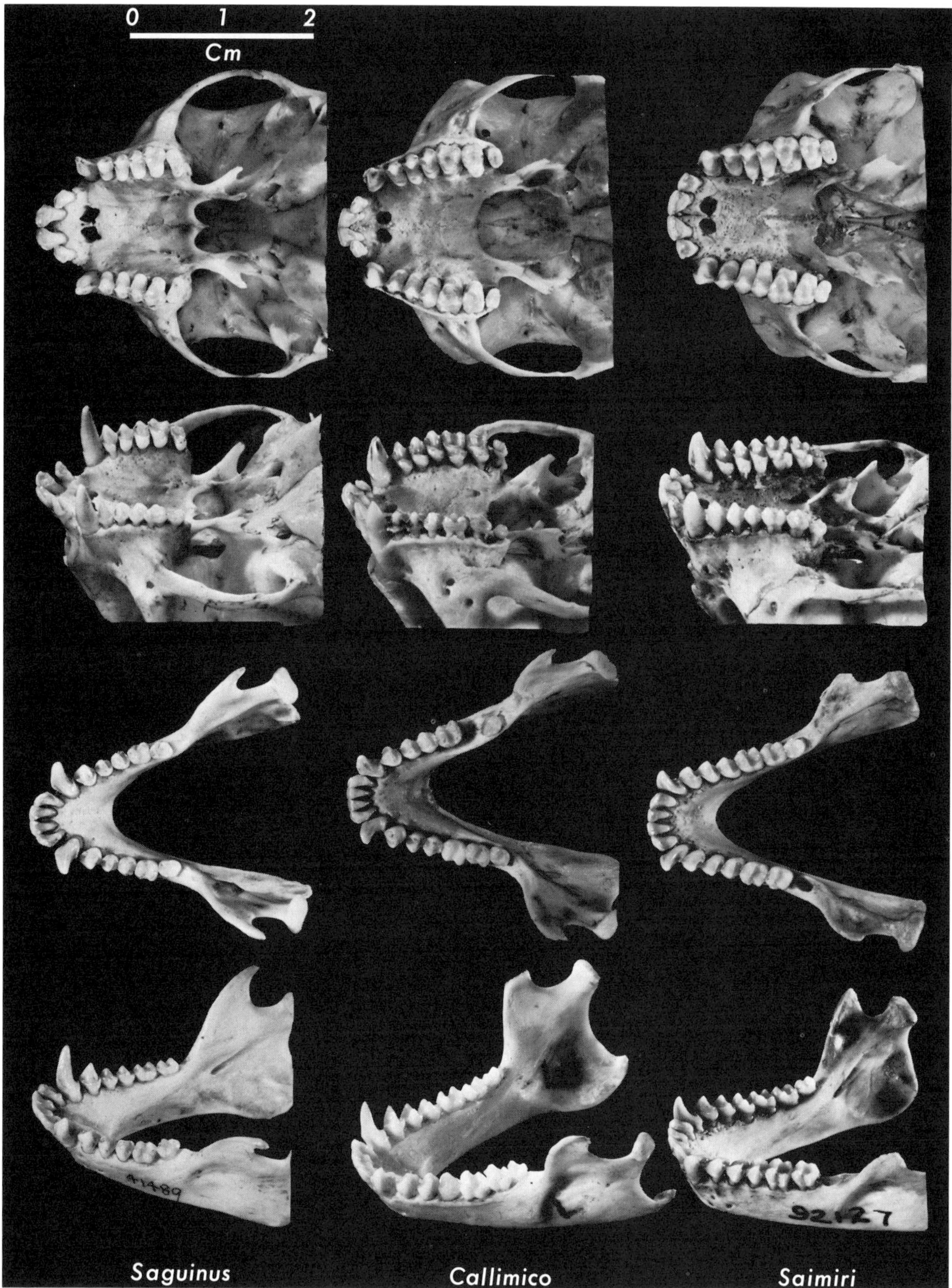

Fig. XII.7. *Callimico* upper and lower jaws compared with those of *Saguinus* (Callitrichidae and *Saimiri* (Cebidae).

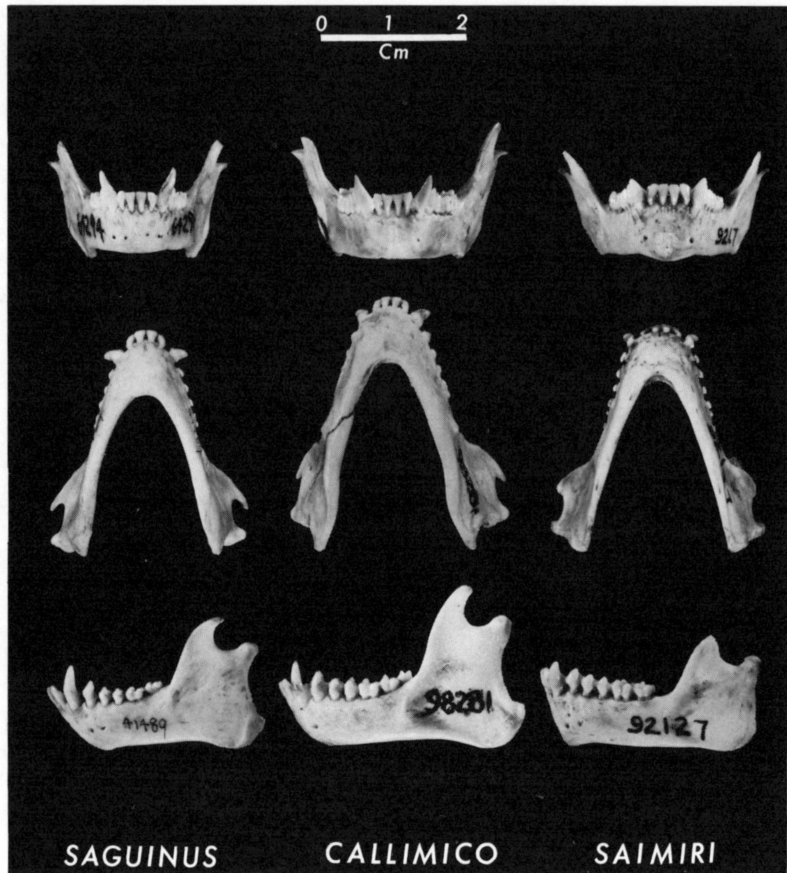

Fig. XII.8. *Callimico* mandible: lateral and ventral aspects compared with same views of *Saguinus* (Callitrichidae) and *Saimiri* (Cebidae) mandibles.

81 Genus *Callimico* Miranda Ribeiro, Callimico

Synonymic History

Callimico Miranda Ribeiro, 1912, *Brasilianische Rundschau* (1911) 2:21. Thomas, 1913, *Ann. Mag. Nat. Hist.*, ser. 8, 11:131—type of subfamily Callimiconinae (Cebidae); characters. Thomas, 1913, *Proc. Zool. Soc London* 1913:4—type of subfamily Callimiconinae (Cebidae). Elliot, 1913, *A review of the Primates* 3:261—reclassification as cebid, fide Thomas, 1913. Pocock, 1920, *Proc. Zool. Soc. London* 1920:92, 113—external characters; regarded as a callitrichid. Pocock, 1925, *Proc. Zool. Soc London* 1925:38—a primitive callitrichid. Thomas, 1928, *Ann. Mag. Nat. Hist.*, ser. 10, 2:255—a primitive callitrichid. Flower, 1929, *List of vertebrated animals exhibited in the gardens of the Zoological Society of London, 1828–1927,* p. 50—BOLIVIA (deposited 14 April 1915). W. E. Le Gros Clark, 1936, *Proc. Zool. Soc. London* 1936:1—anatomy and homology of claws. Miranda Ribeiro, 1940, *Mem. Inst. Oswaldo Cruz* 35:780—characters; relationships; taxonomic history. Cruz Lima, 1945, *Mamiferos da Amazonia, Primates, Contr. Mus. Paraense,* p. 199—characters; taxonomy; family Cebidae. Simpson, 1945, *Bull. Amer. Mus. Nat. Hist.* 85:65, 185—Callimiconinae (Cebidae). Williams and Koopman, 1952, *Amer. Mus. Novit.*, no. 1546, p. 11—comparison with *Xenothrix*. Remane, 1956, *Primatologia* 1:339—relationships. Osman Hill, 1957, *Primates* 3:viii, 46, 79, 81, 89, 114, 211, 282, 307, 311, 322—comparative anatomy; behavior; taxonomy; regarded as type of family Callimiconidae, but later (p. viii) treated as a callitrichid, subfamily Callimiconinae (Hapalidae). Osman Hill, 1958, *Primatologia* 3 (1):142, fig. 1 *g* (soft palate)—no text reference. Osman Hill, 1958, *Primatologia* 3 (1):644, fig. 12 (♂ external genitalia). Osman Hill, 1959, *Trans. Amer. Philos. Soc.*, n.s., 49 (5):1–116—anatomy; measurements; taxonomic history; interrelationships; regarded as a primitive callitrichid, subfamily Callimiconinae (Hapalidae). Remane, 1960, *Primatologia* 3 (2):788, 832—dentition, incisors. Biegert, 1961, *Primatologia* 2 (1), Lief 3:5, 185, fig. 61 (plantar and palmar surfaces)—palmar and plantar surfaces of cheiridia. Schultz, 1961, *Primtologia* 4 Lief 5:1—vertebral column. Remane, 1961, *Zeitschr. Wiss. Zool.* 165(1–2):20—systematic position. Erikson, 1963, *Symp. Zool. Soc. London* 10:143—locomotory type (springer). Cosgrove, 1966, *Lab. Animal Care* 16(1):29 (entry misplaced!), 36—trematode parasites (*Platynosomum* sp.). Osman Hill, 1966, *Proc. Roy. Soc. Edinburgh* 69(3/4):331—regarded as "essentially a tamarin," family Hapalidae. Fenard and Anthony, 1967, *Ann. Paleo.* 53(2):204—comparative osteometry of mandible. Napier and Napier, 1967, *Handbook of living Primates,* p. 76—morphology, ecology, behavior, species, classification, bibliography. Uhlmann, 1967, *1st Cong. Int. Primat. Soc.*, p. 174—hind limb muculature; locomotion. Thenius, 1969, *Zeitschr. Zool. Syst. Evol.* 7(3):169—regarded as a callitrichid of cebid origin. Bauchot and Stephan, 1969, *Mammalia* 33(2): 227, 231, brain weights; classified between Alouattinae and Callithrichinae on basis of index of encephalization. Hershkovitz, 1970, *Folia Primat.*, 12:3—regarded as representative of platyrrhine family Callimiconidae. Hershkovitz, 1970, *Folia Primat.* 13:237—brain weights used by Bauchot and Stephan are of juvenal; regarded as neither cebid nor marmoset.

Callimidas Miranda Ribeiro, 1912, *Brasilianische Rundschau* 2:23—lapsus for *Callimico* in the combination *Callimidas Snethlageri.*

Gallimico Cabrera, 1958, *Rev. Mus. Argentino Cienc. Nat. "Bernardino Rivadavia"* 4(1):184—misprint for *Callimico* in synonymy of *Callimico* Miranda Ribeiro.

Type Species. Callimico snethlageri Miranda Ribeiro [= *Callimico goeldii* Thomas], by monotypy.

Distribution (fig. XII.1; XIII.1)

Tropical forest of upper Amazonian region between 1° N and 13° S in Colombia, Ecuador, Peru, and Bolivia and contiguous parts of Brazil to the west bank of the Rio Madeira south of the Rio Amazonas, and the Rio Japurá north of the Rio Amazonas.

Cranial Characters (figs. IV.3, 27, 43, 54, 56, 68, 72, 78–80; XII.5–11)

Skull length in adult, usually between 49 and 56 mm; face short; cephalic index (braincase width to length)

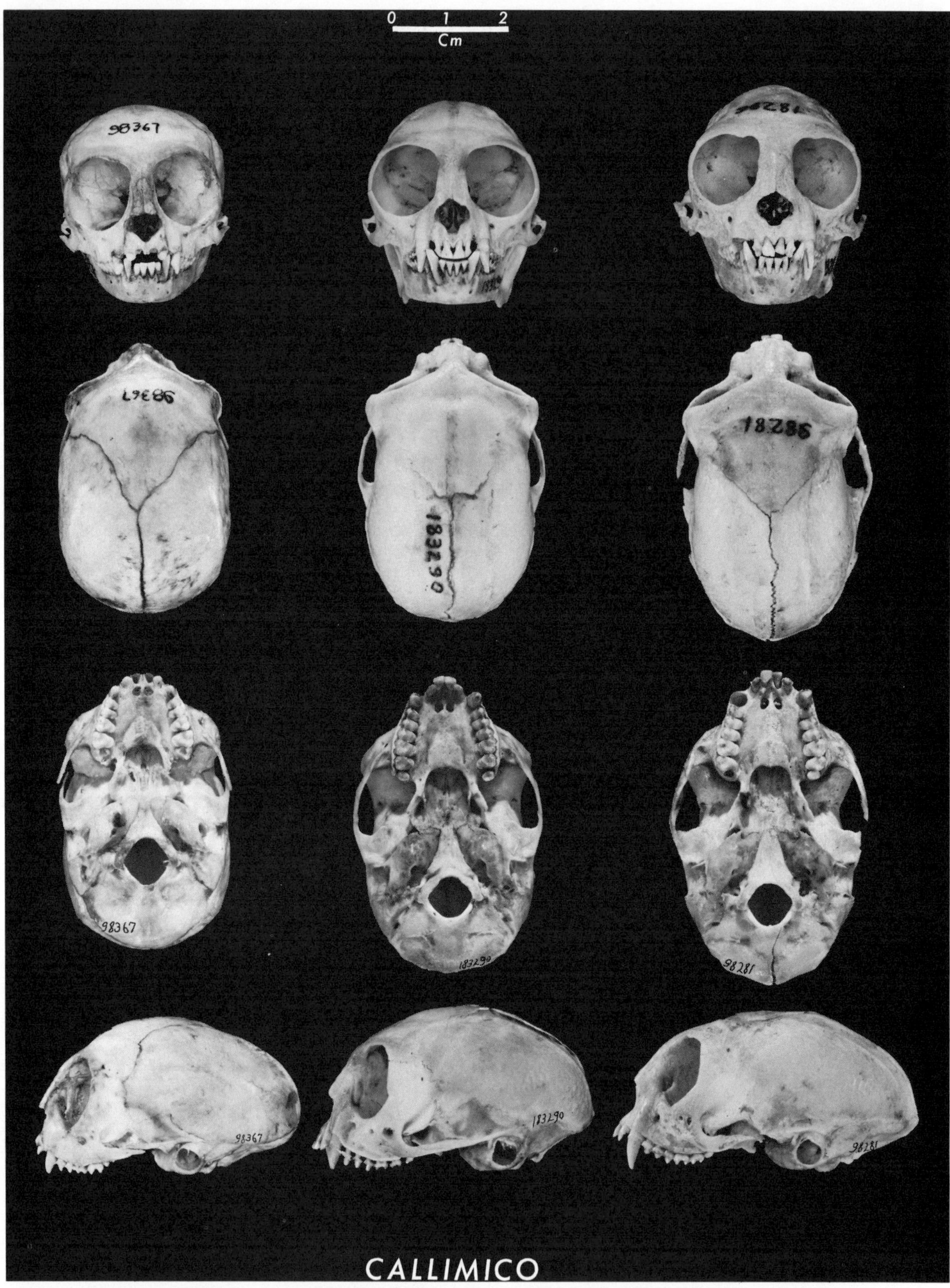

Fig. XII.9. Skulls of *Callimico goeldii*: Frontal, dorsal, basicranial, and lateral aspects of juvenal (*left*), young adult (*center*), and old adult (*right*).

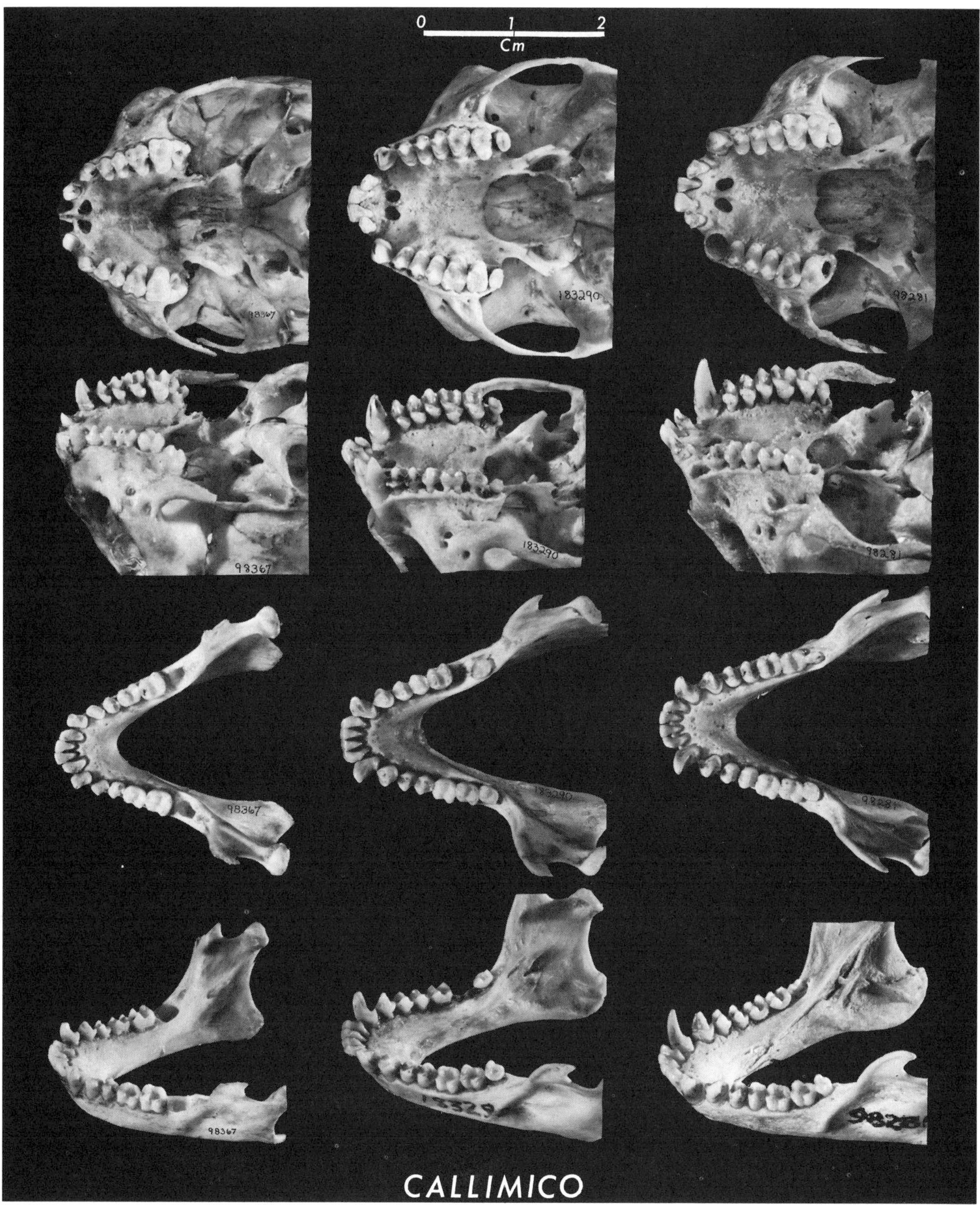

Fig. XII.10. Skulls of *Callimico goeldii*: Palate and mandible of juvenal (*left*), young adult (*center*), old adult (*right*).

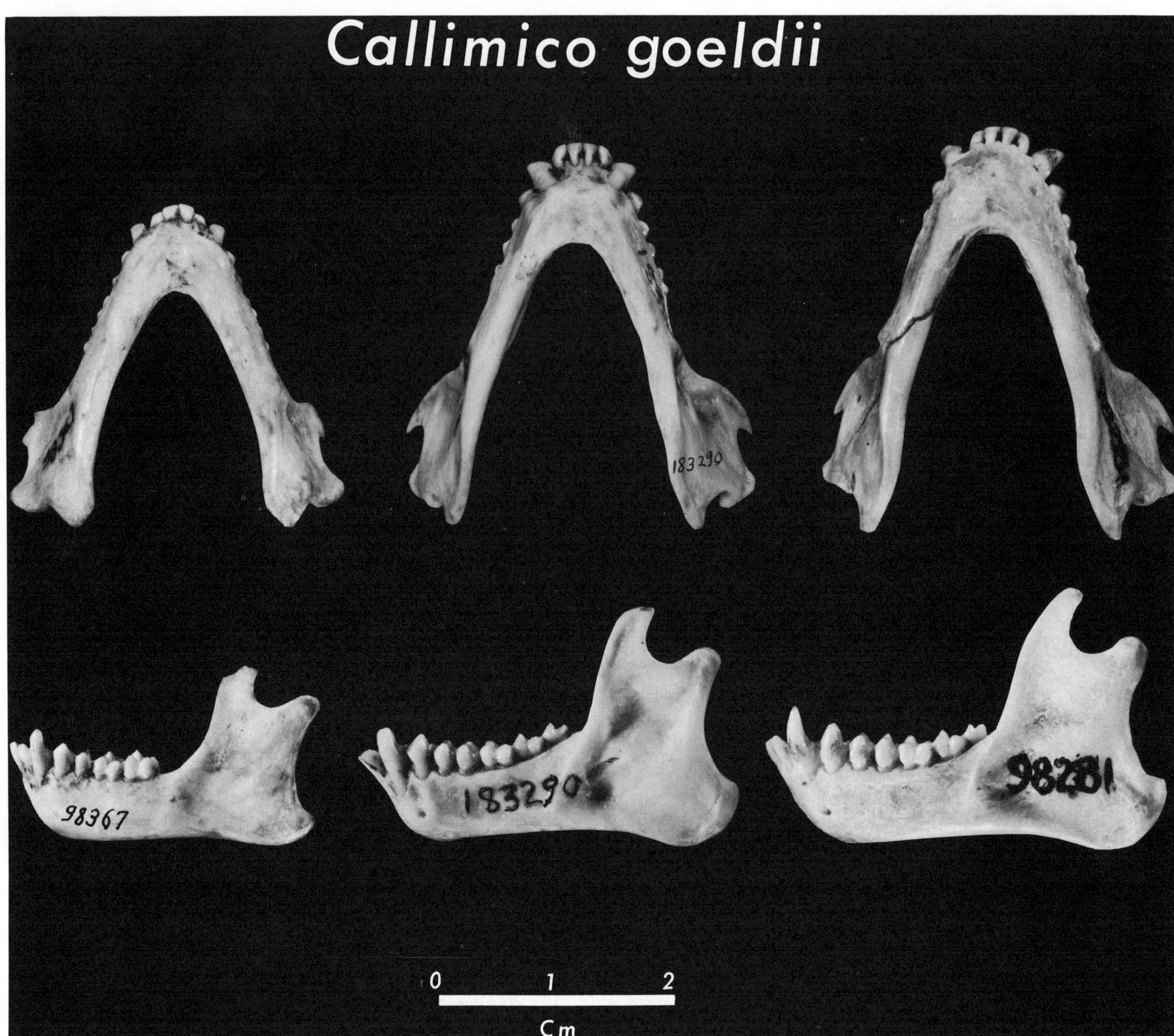

Fig. XII.11. Skulls of *Calimico goeldii*: Mandible of juvenal (*left*), young adult (*center*), old adult (*right*).

about 64; frontal profile usually flattened in superciliary region, slightly vaulted behind; temporal ridges well defined, bowed on frontal bones, parallel-sided on parietal bones; occipital processes and crests weak; foramen magnum more or less circular in outline; axis pointing almost straight down; average occipital angle (opisthion-inion index) between 28° and 35°; auditory bullae well inflated, lower portion of mesotympanic cavity large, noncellular; nasal aperture commonly subcuneate or subchordate in outline; nasal bone nearly parallel-sided except for slight distal expansion, and obtuse point proximally, dorsal profile plane to slightly concave; nasofrontal suture from one-half to three-fourths distance between tip of nasal and glabella; premaxillary bone well defined, sutures remaining open into old age, contact with nasal narrow or absent; malar (zygomatic) and parietal bone always in sutural contact; orbits enlarged, rounded with notable lateral expansion; lacrymal bone large, sometimes with pars facialis extending to nasals; lateral orbital fissure in malar or between malar and parietal bones; malar foramen large, diameter about 1 to 2 mm; infraorbital foramen placed directly above pm^2, its diameter subequal to that of malar foramen; inferior (sphenomaxillary) orbital fissure often constricted; interorbital region sinusoidal, septum thin, imperforate, translucent; maxillary sinus and ostium present; sphenoid pneumatized or sinusoidal with complicated or obstructed communication with nasal cavity; posterior sphenoidal sinuses or fossae absent; frontal cavitation honeycombed or sinusoidal, communicating with pneumatized upper recess of nasal cavity from behind and laterad of plane of olfactory bulb, as in *Cebus;* cribriform plate usually robust and elaborate; dental arcade more nearly U- than V-shaped, outer alveolar distance between upper canines

Table 110. Comparative Size of Orbits in *Callimico* and Callitrichids.

Species	*1 Orbital Breadth*	*2 Braincase Width*	*3 Orbital Breadth / Braincase Width*	*4 Greatest Skull Length*	*5 Orbital Breadth / Skull Length*
Callimico	30.7(29.8–32.6)11	29.8(29.0–32.2)10	103	53.3(50.5–55.5)10	58
Cebuella	20.6(19.0–22.0)53	21.1(20.0–22.9)61	98	35.8(33.7–38.0)61	58
Callithrix	26.1(23.1–27.9)113	25.7(23.9–29.9)113	102	47.0(41.1–50.8)142	56
Saguinus	27.7(20.4–30.6)470	27.1(24.0–30.1)600	102	50.6(44.3–55.7)626	55
Leontopithecus	28.8(27.5–30.6)12	28.4(27.5–29.3)13	101	56.5(53.6–59.8)13	51

NOTE: Comparisons are based on greatest distance across both orbits (1) relative to greatest width of braincase (2), and greatest length of skull (4). The two ratios (3, 5) are required to offset the variance in the relatively shorter-wider skull of *Cebuella* and the relatively longer-narrower skull of *Leontopithecus*. Measurements given are means, extremes in parentheses, followed by number of samples. See appendix table 2 for basic data.

slightly more or less than alveolar length of c–m², as in tamarin marmosets (*Saguinus*), but less than length of c–m³; median posterior border of palate extending back to plane of posterior border of first or second molar; auditory bulla well inflated; mastoid and paraoccipital processes poorly or not developed; styloid fossette present and well developed; foramen spinosum and foramen lacerum absent, the foramen ovale alone providing passage for meningeal arteries; pterygoid plates small, the medial consisting mainly of short hamular process defining narrow, shallow pterygoid fossa or recess; inferior border of mandible more nearly V- than U-shaped in outline; retromental border narrowly rounded, the horizontal rami slightly arced; vertical plane of mental foramen between roots of canine and first premolar; ascending ramus elongate, or suboblong; average coronoidal height about 64% of condyloincisive length of mandible; coronoid process hooked, projecting above condyle; sigmoid notch deep, narrow; articular surface of condylar process about twice height of molar crowns measured from base of mandible; inferior border of angular process in line with or deflected slightly below basal plane of horizontal ramus; angle of outer slope of symphysis menti about 52° (49°–55°, 5 specimens) relative to basal mandibular plane.

Comparisons (figs. VII.5, 6, 8; XII.5–8)

Compared with that of callitrichids, the braincase of *Callimico* is more nearly brachycephalic than that of *Saguinus* and *Leontopithecus*, less globose than that of *Cebuella*, perhaps nearest that of *Callithrix;* axis of foramen magnum pointing more nearly straight down; occipital index (opisthion–inion to Frankfort line) less; outline of nasal aperture less callitrichid than cebid; contact between premaxillary bone and anterolateral surface of nasal bone narrower and much less frequent; orbits relatively larger and laterally expanded; sphenoidal cavitations more inflated and complicated; communication of frontal sinus with nasal cavity through posterolateral channel, not medially through midfrontal ostium; bony palate shorter, that is, with median posterior border not extending to posterior plane of last molars; auditory ossicles slightly more specialized.

Callimico approaches cebids in most of those characters which distinguish it from callitrichids. Some of this is due to the size factor, some to greater variation among cebids, and some to the universal primate tendency toward convergence where habitats and selective pressures are similar. The rounded occipital region and nearly vertical axis of the foramen magnum in *Callimico* is nearest the condition in the squirrel monkey (*Saimiri*), but the character represents an evolutionary grade acquired independently by each of these animals as well as by other primates including man. The outline of the *Callimico* nasal aperture appears to be more cebid than callitrichid, but the relationship between premaxillary and nasal bones in *Callimico* is distinctly cebid. The character is a specialization unrelated to size or any other obvious growth or behavior pattern. Lateral expansion of orbits in *Callimico* is considerably less than in the cebid night monkey *Aotus* but notably more than in other cebids, and only slightly more than in callitrichids (table 110). The short palate of *Callimico* finds similarities not only among short-faced cebids but among catarrhines as well. The *Callimico* communication system between frontal sinus and nasal cavity is definitely noncallitrichid. It appears to be the more primitive state of the particular system that became complex then degenerate in cebids and vestigial in catarrhine monkeys.

Postcranial Skeletal Characters (figs. VII.9; XII.12)

Vertebral Formula:

In 4 skeletons (3 at hand, 1 analyzed by Schultz 1961, and listed last), cervical 7, 7, 7, 7; thoracic 13, 13, 12, 12; lumbar 6, 6, 7, 7; sacral 3, 3, 3, 3; caudal 25 (+ 1?), 26 (+ 1?), 25 (+ 1?), 28.

Sternal Ribs:

8, 9, 9,7.

Arm and Leg Proportions:

(Linear measurements [averages of the paired bones] and the proportions are of specimens FM 57999 ♂, FM 98034 ♂, and FM 58003 ♂, respectively; Limb bone measurements [in mm] are of greatest length; trunk length is combined lengths of articulated thoracic, lumbar, and sacral vertebrae.)

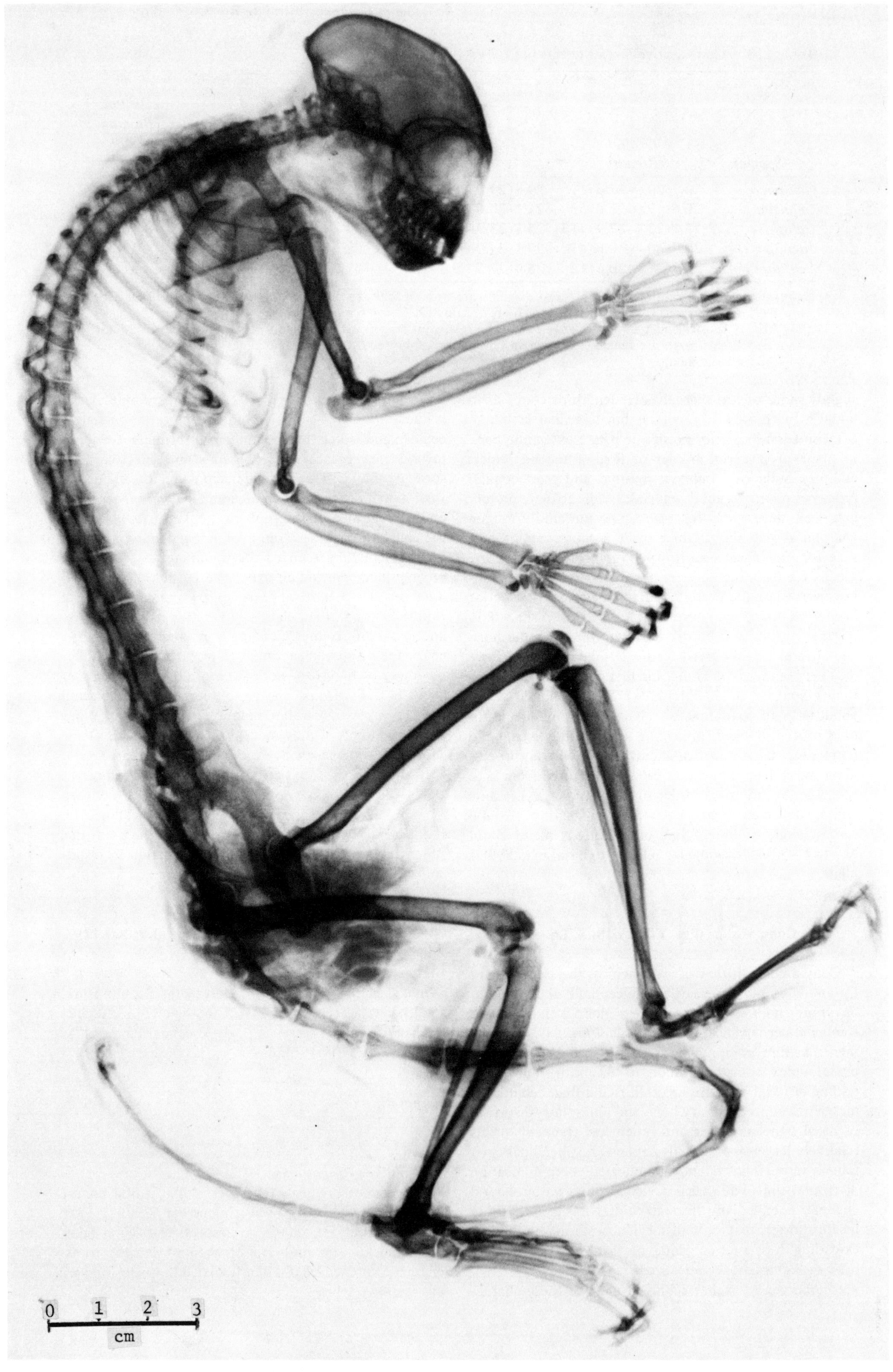
0 1 2 3
cm

$$\frac{\text{Humerus } 54, 53, 54}{\text{Radius } 50\ 49\ 51} = 108\%, 108\%, 106\%.$$

$$\frac{\text{Femur } 73, 73, 75}{\text{Tibia } 75\ 75\ 77} = 97\%, 97\%, 97\%.$$

$$\frac{\text{Humerus + radius } 103, 102, 104}{\text{Femur + tibia } 149, 148, 151} = 69\%, 69\%, 69\%.$$

$$\frac{\text{Humerus + radius } 103, 102, 104}{\text{Trunk } 145, 145, 135} = 71\%, 70\%, 77\%.$$

$$\frac{\text{Femur + tibia } 149, 148, 151}{\text{Trunk } 145, 145, 135} = 103\%, 102\%, 112\%.$$

Third Trochanter:

Present in the 3 skeletons examined. The feature is often present in callitrichids, absent or poorly defined in cebids.

Entepicondylar Foramen:

Present in the 3 skeletons examined but absent in right humerus of FM 57999; among callitrichids, the trait is often present in *Saguinus* and *Leontopithecus,* and rare or absent in *Cebuella* and *Callithrix.*

Digital Length Formulae:

Manus 3–4–2–5–1; pes 4–3–5–2–1; the same in callitrichids.

Remarks. Limb proportions of *Callimico* are comparable to those of the springer group (callitrichids and marmosetlike cebids) as defined by Erikson (1963). My measurements of three callimicos agree with those of Erikson (shown in table 47). Vertebral formula and other postcranial skeletal characters are primitive for primates. The callimico tail is shorter than that of callitrichids and the number of caudal vertebrae may average one or two less, or nearer the postulated primitive number of 25 (Schultz 1961, p. 22).

Dental Characters (figs. V.19, 22, 25–28; XII.13–17)

Incisors (fig. V.23)

Permanent upper incisors comparatively low, crowns expanded and well differentiated from cervix; outer tooth implanted obliquely and posteriad to central with considerable overlap, the pair on each side combining to form a gothic to U-shaped arch; lateral incisor trapeziform, less forward projecting than central and about two-thirds to three-fourths its bulk; central incisor spatulate, horizontal biting edge entire with mesial corner touching opposite tooth; both incisors with mesial and distal cingular ridges well defined (except in well worn) and continuous behind; mesial and distal styles absent; occlusal groove not strongly marked in specimens at hand; lingual surface crazed in worn teeth.

Deciduous upper incisors not represented in present material.

Permanent lower incisors slightly more than twice as high as wide, crowns transversely expanded, forward projecting but not procumbent, labial surface plane to slightly convex but not recurved, biting edges normally touching, lingual surface of crowns crazed except in newly erupted teeth; lateral incisor emplaced nearly in line with central, the pairs of both sides combining to form the broad angle or keystone of a U-shaped arch; lateral incisor spatulate except for oblique truncation of lateral one-fourth to one-third of biting edge, the crown correspondingly wider basally than apically; central incisor spatulate as high as lateral but smaller; labial height of incisors about one-third vertical depth of symphysis menti, stylids absent, mesial and distal cingular ridges weakly developed on lateral incisor, obsolete or absent on central; enamel crazed on lingual surface of well-worn teeth.

Deciduous lower incisors not represented in present material.

Canines

Permanent upper canine is distinctly caniniform, about twice or slightly less than twice as high as long and about twice as high as adjacent pm; distal portion of eocrista (I″) sharp, epicrista (II) defined by deep groove, mesiostyle weak, cingulum *B* weak to moderately well developed but with posterior portion ill defined or obliterated by occlusal groove; enamel crazed in worn tooth.

Deciduous upper canine is more nearly caniniform than premolariform, crown trapezoidal and well differentiated from cervix; tooth about as high as long and about half again as high as dpm²; mesial ridge poorly delineated by shallow groove, distal edge sharp; anterior portion of cingulum *B* indicated, posterior portion eroded in specimen examined.

Permanent lower canine is distinctly caniniform, more than twice as high as long but somewhat less than twice as high as adjacent premolar; mesiobuccal (*I′*) and mesiolingual (II) crests separated by wide shallow groove or primitive trigonid basin; mesiostlid (*a*) poorly defined or obsolete, distostylid well developed; lingual cingulids *B* and *C* joined, talonid basin narrow; enamel crazed in well-worn tooth.

Deciduous lower canine is partially molarized, probably about one-half again higher than long, and about one-fourth again higher than pm²; mesial and distal edges rounded from wear; talonid nearly half total length of tooth, metaconid, cingulid, and mesiostylid not evident in worn teeth of specimen examined.

Remarks. Upper and lower permanent canines are tamarinlike tusks. The deciduous canines of a single individual with worn teeth are partially molarized quite like those of tamarins. The lower deciduous canine, however, is more nearly cebid than callitrichid in form.

Premolars

Permanent upper premolars with *pm²* distinctly premolariform and bicuspid, triangular or subtriangular in outline, sample crown height 2.5, length 2.5, width 3.0, eocrista sharp, cingulum (*B*) broad-ledged and enclosing a deep trigon basin, secondary internal cingulum poorly defined or absent, buccal cingulum (*A*) present and often forming a broad ledge, protocone (*2*) fully developed,

Fig. XII.12. Radiograph of adult male *Callimico goeldii* (natural size) (AMNH 183291). Photo courtesy Jean and Friedrich Deinhardt, Rush–Presbyterian–St. Luke's Medical Center.

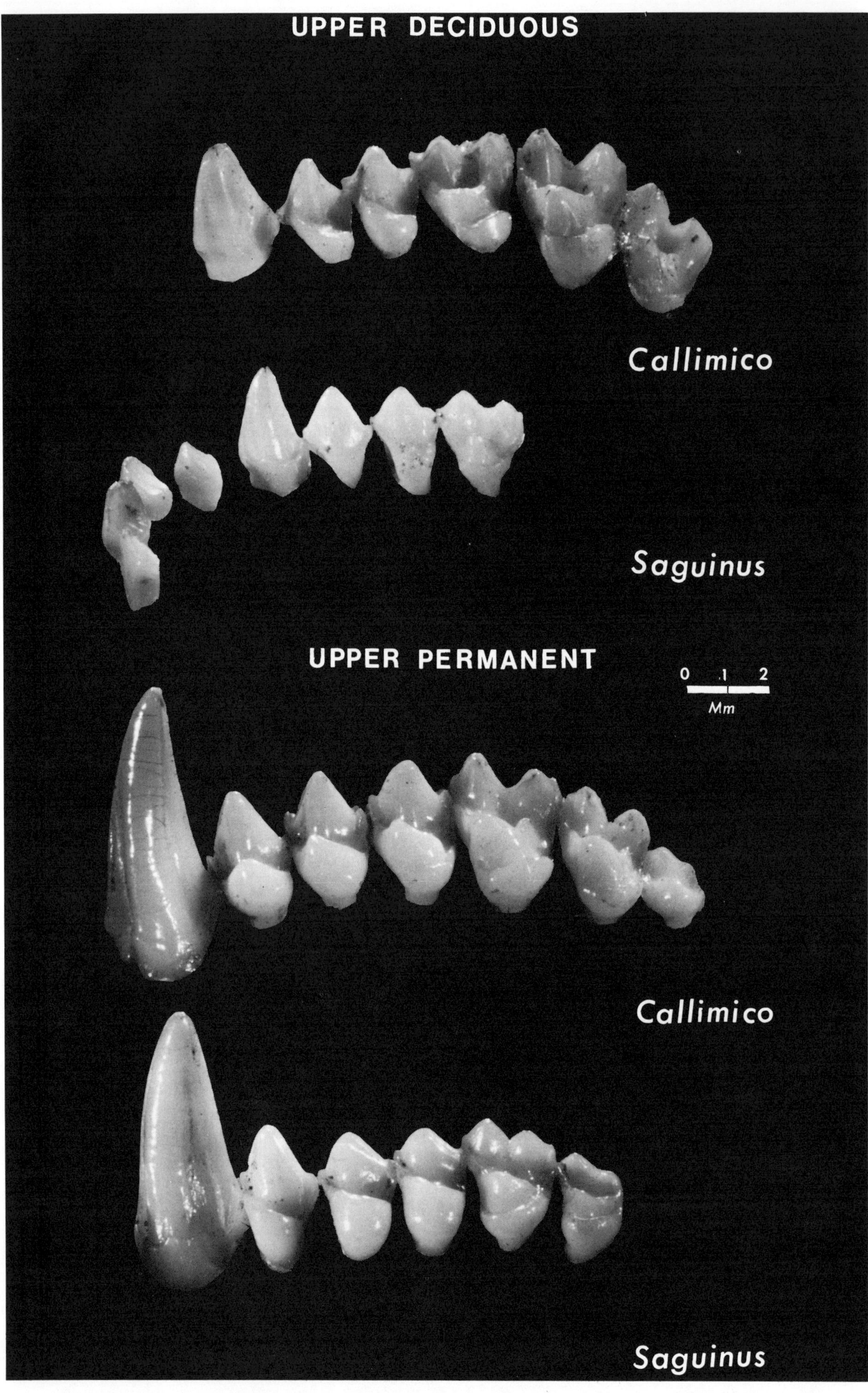

Fig. XII.13. Left upper deciduous and permanent teeth of *Callimico* and *Saguinus,* occlusal and lingual surfaces; deciduous series of *Callimico* followed by first two (of three) molars; incisors not shown.

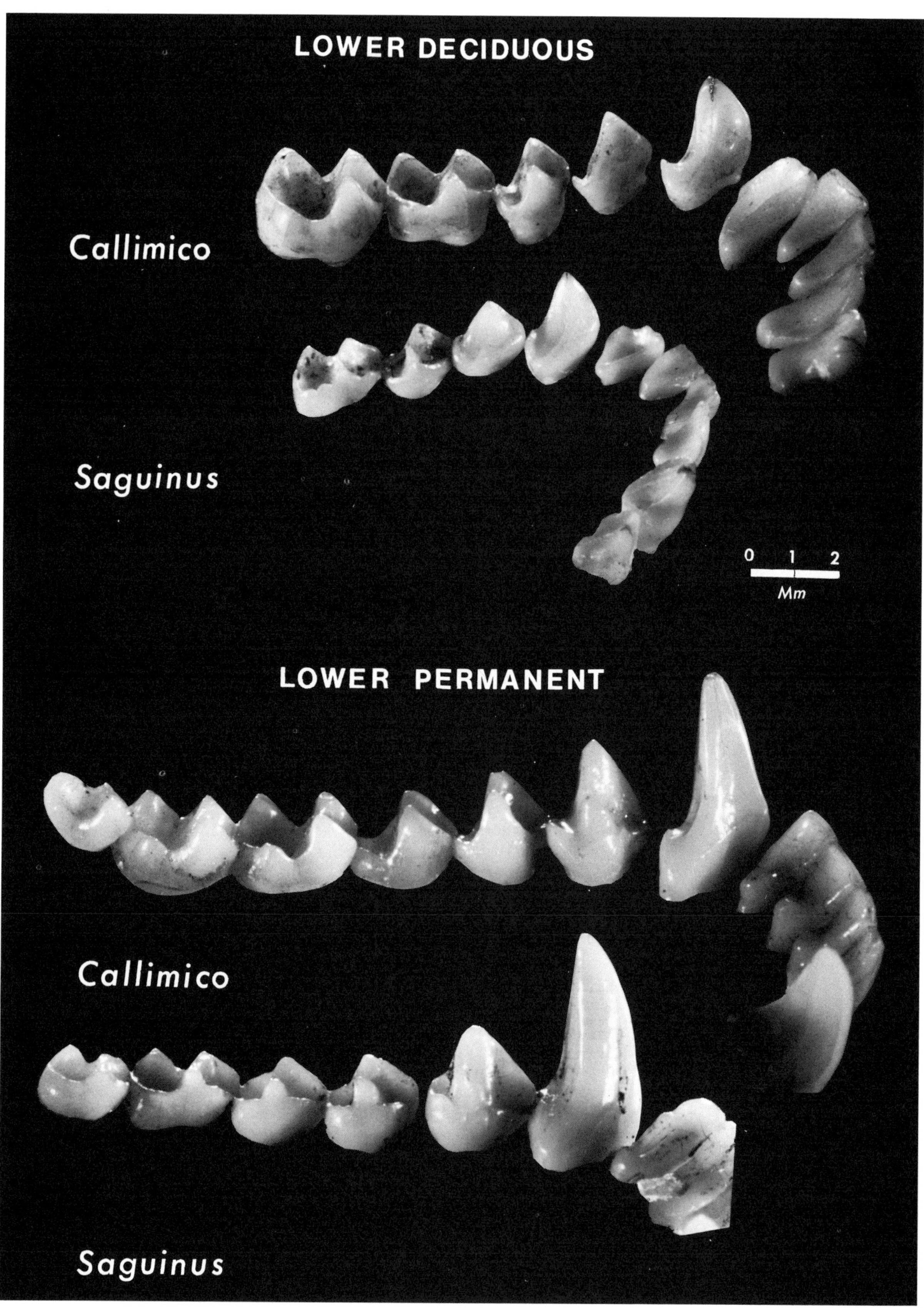

Fig. XII.14. Left lower deciduous and permanent teeth of *Callimico* and *Saguinus,* occlusal and lingual surfaces; deciduous series of *Callimico* followed by first (of three) molars.

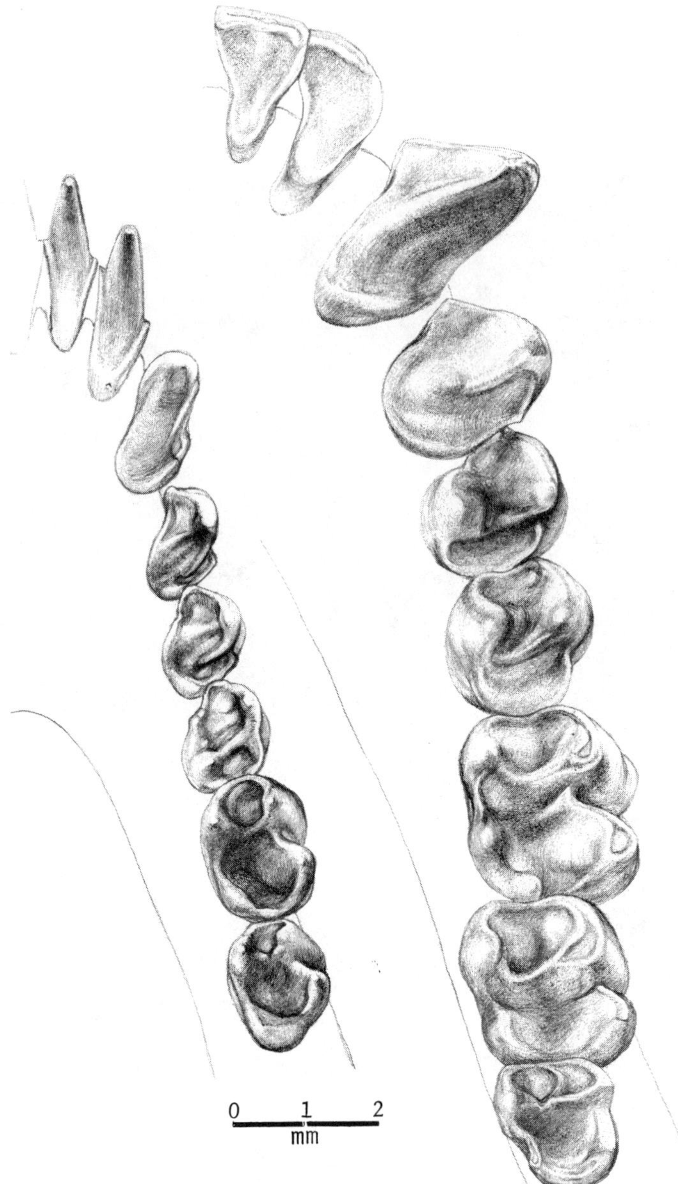

Fig. XII.15. Right lower tooth row of *Callimico goeldii*, occlusal surface, compared with that of *Cebuella pygmaea*.

about half as high as eocone (*1*) measured from base of crown, mesiostyle (*a*) and distostyle (*b*) low; *pm*³ like preceding but occlusal surface more nearly triangular in outline, cingulum *B* broader, cingulum B′ better developed, protocone fuller; *pm*⁴ like preceding but slightly wider, more rectangular and heavier, with cingulur shelves more expanded, trigon basin less steep, sample length 2.2, width 3.4.

Deciduous upper premolars (worn) with *dpm*² premolariform, sample crown height 2.5, length 2.3, width 2.4, mesiostyle and distostyle flaring, cingulum *B* poorly defined but with indication of epiconule (protoconule *c*), protocone (*2*) undefined in worn tooth; *dpm*³ like preceding but shorter and wider, protocone slightly raised, hypocone (*5*) indicated on cingular shelf *C; dpm*⁴ tritubercular, about twice as large as preceding tooth, metacone (*4*) slightly smaller and nearly as high as eocone (*1*), low protocone well developed, protoloph (*III*) with epiconule (*c*), plagiocrista (metaloph, *IV*) well defined, plagioconule (*d*) may be present in unworn tooth, posterolingual cingulum broad and sloping mesiad, with faint indication of small worn conule or hypocone, mesiostyle (*a*), minute ectostyle, and distostyle (*b*), present, trigon basin deeply conical; sample length 2.8, width 3.9.

Remarks. Upper premolar molarization is more advanced in *Callimico* than in tamarins with respect to the protocone and trigon basin but not so with respect to cingulum *B′*. The completely bicuspid permanent premolars with high pointed protocone are characteristic. The buccal cingulum is often ledge-like and usually present in all premolars. The secondary cingulum B′ and posterolingual cingulum C are weak or absent on $pm^{2\text{-}3}$ and no more than moderately developed on pm^4.

As usual, dpm^2 appears to be slightly less molarized than its successor, while dpm^4 is a molar in fact.

Permanent lower premolars with pm_2 about two-thirds as high as canine, sample crown height 3.0, length 2.7, width 2.5, crown deltoid or conical when well worn, with epicristid (*II*) nearly transverse and defining, sometimes completely separating, incipient or well-defined trigonid basin from talonid basin, metaconid (*2*) frequently indicated but never well developed, cingulids B′ and C well developed and forming a continuous band, mesiostylid (*a*) and distostylid (*b*) small, entoconid (*5*) often present, hypoconid (*4*) not evident; *pm*$_3$ smaller and considerably lower than preceding, trigonid smaller than talonid or subequal, metaconid as high but slightly smaller than eoconid, hypoconid and entoconid absent or weakly developed, distostylid extremely small; *pm*$_4$ with trigonid smaller than talonid or subequal, the basins comparatively shallow, metaconid and eoconid subequal, hypoconid, entoconid and distostylid indicated, pseudoparaconid (*t*), secondary lingual and buccal cingulids not defined; sample length 2.3, width 2.7.

Deciduous lower premolars with *dpm*$_2$ like molariform canine, higher than third and fourth premolars, sample crown height 2.1, length 2.1, width 2.4, steep epicristid weakly defined, metaconid not evident, talonid with deep occlusal groove; *dpm*$_3$ molarized with trigonid and talonid subequal, metaconid nearly as large as eoconid, low talonid with deep buccal occlusal groove, stylids absent; *dpm*$_4$ fully molarized, nearly as large as first two premolars combined but lower than either, trigonid equal to about two-fifths occlusal surface of crown, metaconid slightly smaller but higher than eoconid (1 specimen), hypoconid well developed, entoconid indicated, paraconid, stylids, and buccal cingulid absent; sample length 2.6, width 2.3.

Remarks. Molarization of pm$_{3\text{-}4}$ is no less advanced in *Callimico* than in *Saguinus* but has progressed in a slightly different direction. Hypertrophy of the metaconid to nearly or quite the size and height of the opposing eoconid surpasses anything known in callitrichids. These characters, combined with the deep notch of the interconnecting epicristid (*II*) form a unique specialization. The epicristid of pm$_2$ is also more nearly transverse than in callitrichids. The pseudoparaconid, often present in one or more lower premolars of *Saguinus* and other callitrichids, is not evident in the short, narrowly constricted *Callimico* trigonid. Lower premolars of the marmosetlike cebid *Saimiri sciureus* are similar, but with epicristid more oblique and its occlusal border evenly concave rather than notched.

Deciduous premolars in the single specimen available are considerably worn and have a deep, steep transverse wear facet separating trigonid from talonid. Dpm$_{2\text{-}3}$ are like their successors but about one-fourth smaller. Dpm$_4$, however, is slightly larger than pm$_4$ and like m$_1$ in all but very minor structural details.

Molars

Upper molars, with *first molar* about one-fifth to one-third again larger than second, about one-third to one-half again larger than last premolar, occlusal surface trapezoidal, trigon basin deeply conical, eocone (*1*) higher than protocone (*2*), metacone (*4*) slightly smaller and lower, incipient or rudimentary to low but well defined hypocone (*5*) present, an entostyle often present, protoloph (*III*) and plagiocrista (metaloph, *IV*) strong, epiconule (*c*) and plagioconule (*d*) moderately defined to absent, cingula *B′* and *C* broad each enclosing a basin, mesiostyle (*a*), distostyle (*b*), and one or more ectostyles present, entostyles present or absent; *second molar* like first but smaller, occlusal surface triangular, metacone well developed but reduced, rudimentary hypocone present or absent, epiconule (*c*) absent or weakly defined, plagioconule (*d*) rudimentary or absent, mesiostyle (*a*) present, distostyle (*b*) reduced or absent, ectostyles and entostyles present or absent; *third molar* with occlusal surface rectangular, one-half or less bulk of second molar, eocone higher and larger than protocone, metacone small or vestigial, conules and styles absent or poorly defined in unworn tooth, cingula B′ and C weak, slightly raised, but sometimes forming shelves or meeting on lingual border.

Lower molar form quadrate, trigonid of anterior two-fifths to nearly one-half of crown with elevated deep oblong forward-sloping basin, talonid or remainder of crown with deep rounded subquadrate basin, conids hypsodont, metaconid (*2*) higher than eoconid (*1*), hypoconid (*4*) of first two molars as high as eoconid but smaller, of third molar less well differentiated and usually lower, entoconid low, posterior border of molars concave or notched; *first molar* subsquare, about one-third again larger than last premolar, trigonid basin ovate with transverse axis longer, epicristid (*II*) reduced on steep inner slopes of eoconid (*1*) and metaconid (*2*) and deeply notched to nearly suppressed medially, postentoconulid (*e*) absent, rudimentary, or rarely present as a well-differentiated and independent cusp; a weak mesiostylid (*a*) sometimes present, distostylid (*b*) and ectostylids usually absent or poorly defined; *second molar* like first but smaller, postentoconulid (*e*) absent, stylids absent except a weak mesiostylid (*a*) in one tooth; *third molar* like preceding but much smaller, about one-half size of first molar and two-thirds size of second molar, postentoconulid and stylids absent, distobuccal cusp, or hypoconid (*4*), projecting more posteriad than distolingual cusp, or entoconid (*5*).

Sample Measurements of Molars, Buccal Length × Width (in millimeters)

M^1	M^2	M^3	M$_1$	M$_2$	M$_3$
2.8 × 4.1	2.7 × 3.5	1.8 × 2.1	3.1 × 2.7	3.0 × 2.4	2.4 × 2.1
2.9 × 4.0	2.4 × 3.6	2.0 × 2.1	3.1 × 2.7	3.0 × 2.6	2.1 × 2.1
2.9 × 4.0	2.6 × 3.1	1.7 × 2.2	2.9 × 2.8	3.1 × 2.4	2.4 × 2.1
3.0 × 4.4	2.5 × 3.7	1.6 × 2.3	3.2 × 2.8	2.7 × 2.4	2.3 × 1.8
3.3 × 4.1	2.7 × 3.7	1.6 × 2.3	3.1 × 2.8	3.1 × 2.6	2.1 × 2.1
3.1 × 4.2	2.6 × 3.5	1.8 × 2.1	3.1 × 2.8	2.9 × 2.4	2.1 × 1.9

Remarks. Three molars in each jaw distinguish *Callimico* from all callitrichids. The combination of tritubercular molars with a more or less developed and consistently present hypocone in m^1, a rudiment in some m^2, and the usual absence of external cingulids and stylids in lower molars, distinguishes *Callimico* from all cebids.

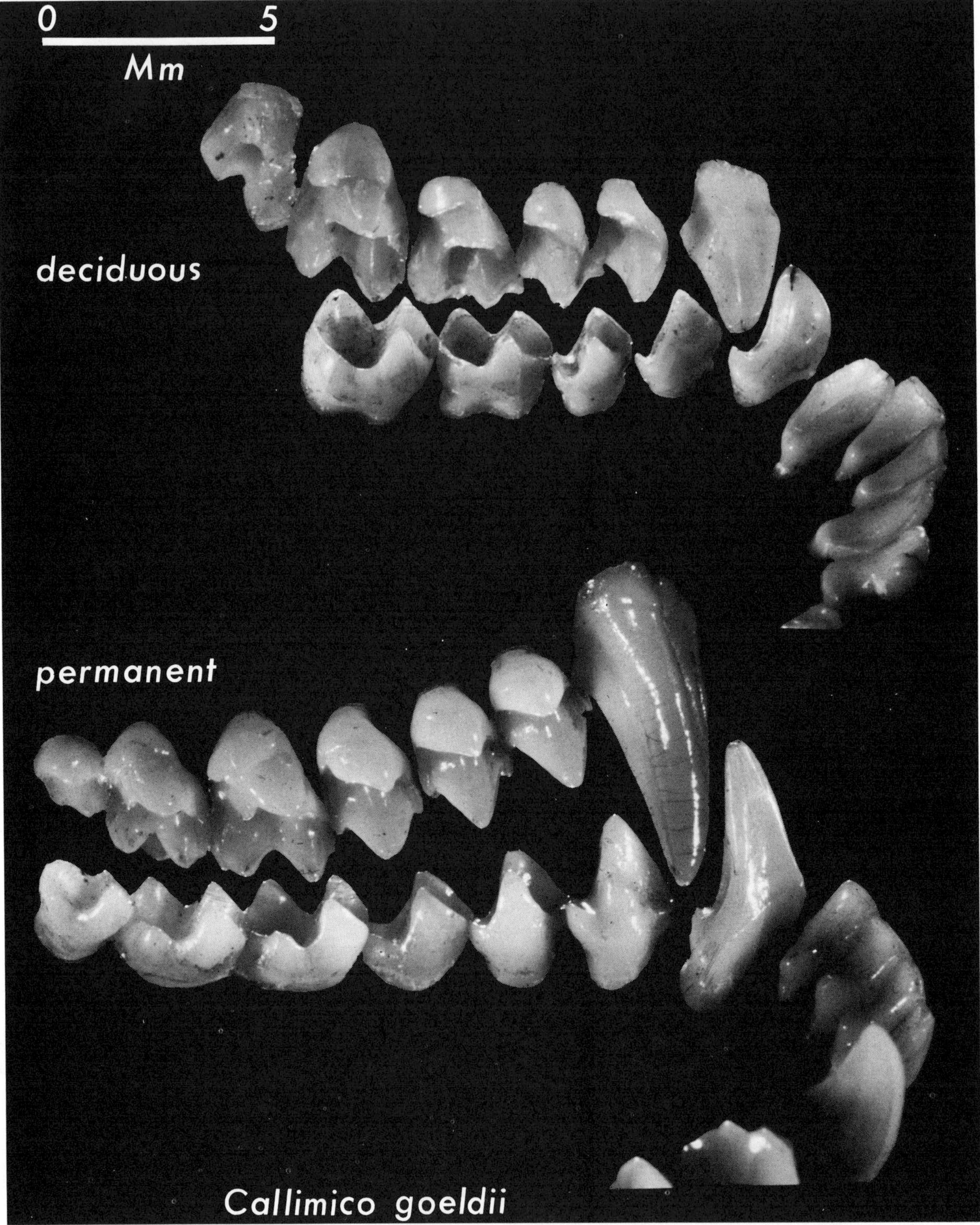

Fig. XII.16. *Callimico goeldii*: Left upper and lower permanent and deciduous teeth in simulated occlusal position; deciduous series followed by first two upper and first lower molars (second lower missing, third erupting); upper incisors not shown.

The second upper molar is typically tricuspid, although an incipient hypocone is sometimes present. The small bicuspid third upper molar may be primitive or, as usual in most primates, secondarily reduced and degenerate. The second mandibular molar is hardly smaller than the first, and the third, though small, is well developed. The latter is rhomboidal as in callitrichids, but with the disto-buccal, not the distolingual, cusp produced farther behind.

As in *Saguinus,* inner cusps of all lower molars are higher than their opposite numbers on the buccal side. The same height relationship, however, continues anteriad in *Callimico* to pm_3. The first premolar (pm_2) remains caniniform, as in most primates.

Unworn cusps of all lower cheek teeth are more hypsodont in *Callimico* than in platyrrhines generally, and the contour of the molariform row appears to be slightly more bowed than in *Saguinus.*

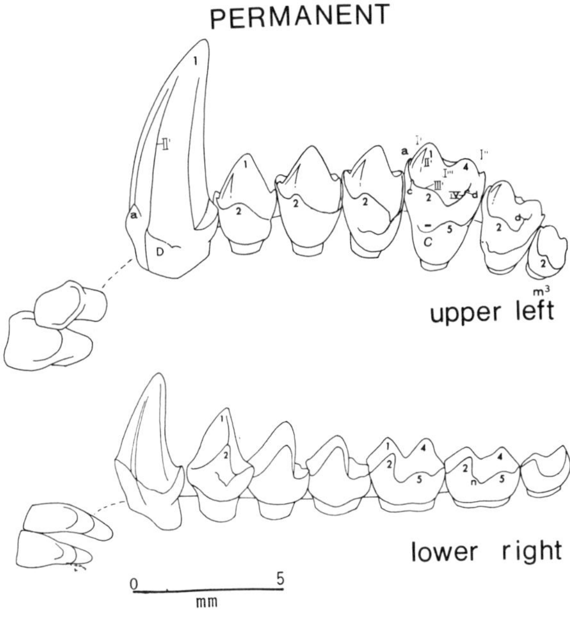

DECIDUOS

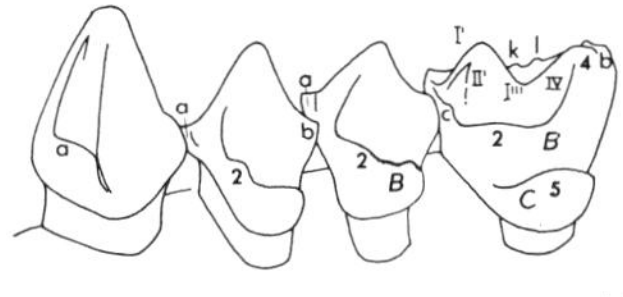

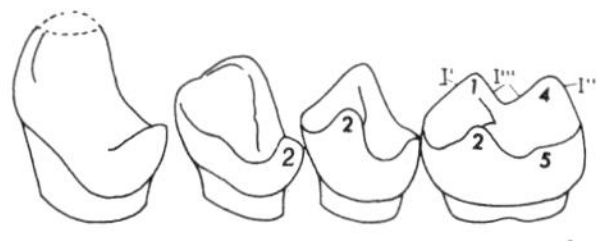

Callimico goeldii

Fig. XII.17. *Callimico goeldii*: Upper and lower permanent and deciduous teeth shown diagrammatically.

The ovate trigonid basin is deep and extremely wide transversely, the larger talonid basin more nearly rounded than in other platyrrhines.

Dental formula, molar orientation, and cusp morphology remove *Callimico* from the callitrichid line of dental evolution. Among cebids, dentition of the marmosetlike *Saimiri* is most similar but is more advanced in most respects, though more primitive in others. In *Saimiri*, the upper last molar is larger and more molarized. Buccal to lingual cusp height relationships in molars are as in *Callimico*, but in the *Saimiri* premolars the outer cusps retain their primitive superiority in height. Presence of a buccal cingulid, better definition of the distostylid (hypoconulid), and better developed hypocone in the *Saimiri* molars are indications of a higher evolutionary grade and not necessarily expressions of phyletic divergence from other platyrrhines such as *Callimico*. On the other hand, strengthening of the epicristid between eoconid and metaconid in *Saimiri* and its deterioration in *Callimico* point to a significant divergence at an early stage in platyrrhine evolution. The condition in *Saimiri* suggests an early stage of molar bilophodonty while the trend in *Callimico* is toward greater elevation of opposing cusps and deeper separation between them. The *Callimico* dental system, intermediate as it may appear to be between callitrichids and cebids, remains unique in many respects.

External Genitalia

Male (figs. III.25, 28, 29; XII.18)

Adult. Penis pigmented and with well-differentiated, acorn-shaped glans; papillae of penial stem crowded and conical, of glans vallate and glandular; glans corona differentiated from stem by deeply incised sulcus retroglandis, urinary meatus apical but, as usual, dividing glans into a larger left bacular lobe and smaller right lobe; scrotum globose, pedunculate, lightly to moderately pigmented, raphe well marked, expanded posteriorly and clearly defining the testicular sacs; skin of scrotal fold papillate, each papilla with one to a few black hairs but generally a triad with middle hair usually longer and thicker than outer ones; outer preputial fold furrowed or corrugated and sparsely covered with hair, the triad pattern infrequent or absent; inner preputial fold or sheath glabrous and lightly pigmented; scrotum with testes wider than long, width, in two specimens, 18 and 21 mm; sexual skin weakly defined and lightly pigmented in two fluid-preserved specimens examined; perineal and anal regions unpigmented.

Remarks. Osman Hill (1959, p. 17, figs. 5, 6) asserts that the penis of *Callimico* lacks frenulum preputii, baculum, and spines. These features are clearly present in all specimens I examined. Osman Hill also denies *Callimico* a scrotum and takes Pocock (without bibliographic reference but should be 1920, p. 109, fig. 12 *g*) to task for depicting "a small globose scrotum similar to that of the tamarins of the genus *Tamarinus* [= *Saguinus*] and presumably containing the testes." Osman Hill reinforces his remonstration by figuring the external genitalia of *Callimico* without a scrotum (1959, fig. 5, p. 15). He adds that "in the mature animal here studied, there is no apparent scrotal sac whatever. The scrotal sac is occupied by a somewhat raised hairless and thickened area of integument extending. . . ." His photograph of the genitalia of this animal (1959, fig. 6), however, shows a well-developed hairy scrotum. In the following paragraph, Osman Hill states, "In the older male [of the two spirit specimens at hand] the testes are scrotal in position. Here the scrotum forms a distinct bilobed subpendulous sac depending some 21.8 mm. and a dorsoventral diameter of 19 mm. The sac closely resembles a human scrotum in general shape."

Female (fig. III.23; XII.19)

Adult. External genitalia moderately pigmented; combined labia majora in one sample longer than wide, not conspicuously enlarged, and well defined from unpigmented thighs, the skin papillate, each papilla with one hair; hairy portion of preputial fold not well defined from scrotal fold, glabrous inner, or annular, portion deeply pigmented and finely textured; glans clitoridis with left lobe larger than right and projecting slightly beyond,

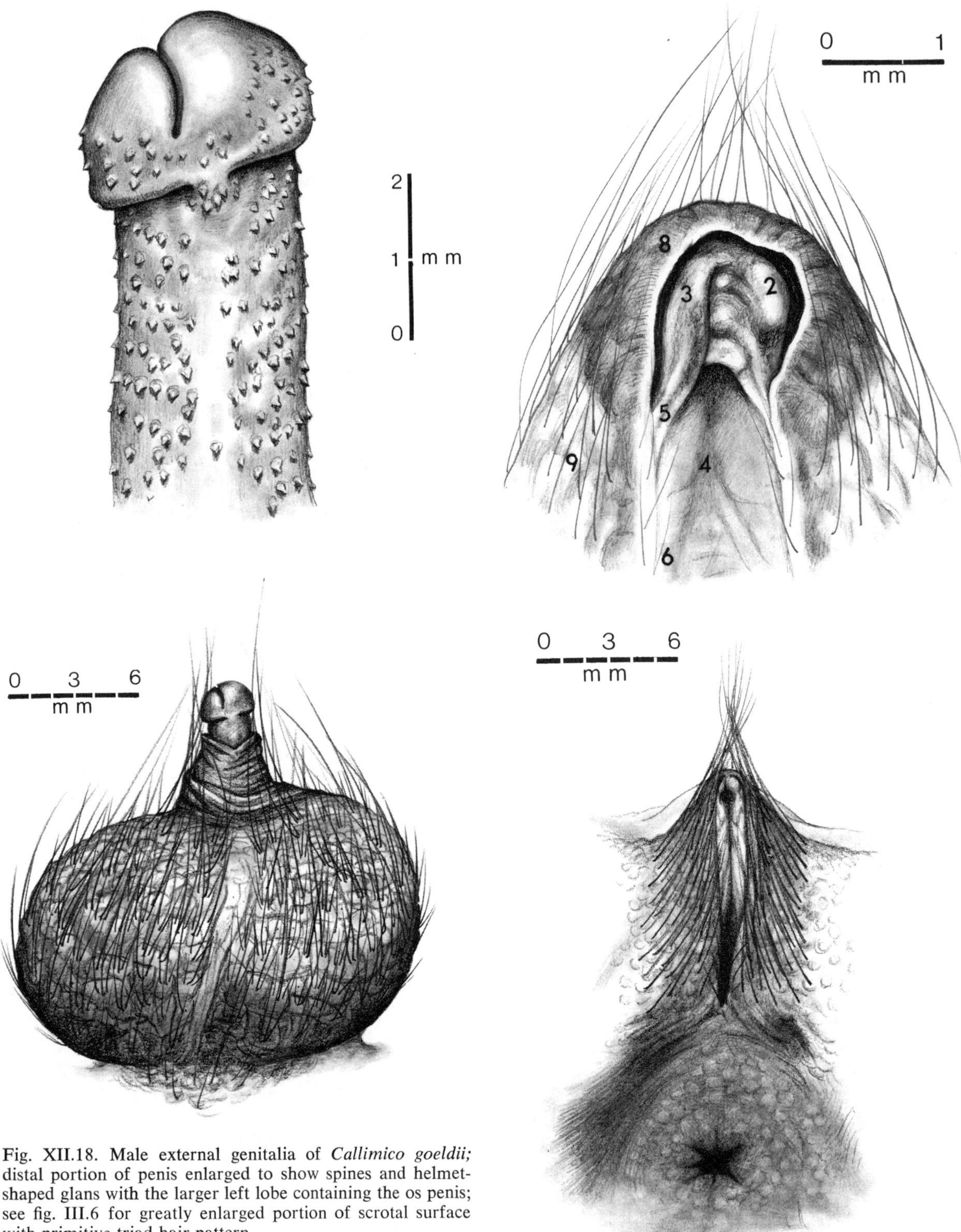

Fig. XII.18. Male external genitalia of *Callimico goeldii;* distal portion of penis enlarged to show spines and helmet-shaped glans with the larger left lobe containing the os penis; see fig. III.6 for greatly enlarged portion of scrotal surface with primitive triad hair pattern.

Fig. XII.19. Female external genitalia of *Callimico goeldii; upper figure,* enlargement of clitoris of different individual than one figured below (see pages 113–14 for explanation of symbols).

concave urethral groove well defined, urethral folds, or labia minora, merged with walls of vaginal vestibule; length of genital fissure about 11 mm; mons pubis small and angular; sexual skin pigmented but poorly developed in present material; perineal and anal regions lightly pigmented.

External genitalia of a second specimen (AMNH 183284) appear to have been aberrant in life and distorted in preservation. Its features are too vague for description here.

Remarks. The mature female external genitalia of *Callimico* are like those of an immature *Saguinus fuscicollis.* Superficial resemblance between *Callimico* and *Leontopithecus* in their genitalia is also striking, but those of the latter are more advanced in both sexes. It appears that the female genitalia of *Callimico* are more primitive, or generalized, and the male external genitalia more specialized than those of callitrichids.

Cytogenetics

Three karyotypes of *Callimico* have been demonstrated by Hsu and Hampton (1970). The first has the diploid number of 48, with XX/XY sex chromosomes; the second shows a translocated Y chromosome fused with an autosome; the third is like the second but with a portion of the translocated Y chromosome presumed lost. The sex determination system for types 2 and 3 is XX/XO (see also pp. 25, 434, 894).

Chu and Bender (1961, p. 1401), concluded that the chromosomal complement of *Callimico* was markedly different from that of callitrichids. Egozcue, Perkins, and Hagemenas (1968), however, find the karyotype of *Callimico* most like that of *Saguinus* but with one less biarmed pair and two more acrocentric pairs (table 48).

82 *Callimico goeldii* Thomas, Callimico, Goeldi's Monkey
1. History, Characters, and Evolution

Fig. XII.20. Callimico (*Callimico goeldii*)

Synonymic History

Midas (*Hapale*) *Weddellii,* Goeldi and Hagmann (not Deville), 1904, *Bol. Mus. Goeldi,* (*Mus. Paraense*) 4:54, footnote.

Hapale Gœldii Thomas, in Goeldi and Hagmann, 1904, *Bol. Mus. Goeldi* (*Mus. Paraense*) 4:54, footnote—description by Goeldi and Hagmann, name proposed by Thomas.

Midas Goeldii Thomas, 1904, *Ann. Mag. Nat. Hist.,* ser. 7, 14:189—name and description.

Callithrix goeldi [*sic*], Elliot, 1913, *A review of the Primates,* 1:224—description ex type.

Callimico goeldii, Thomas, 1913, *Ann. Mag. Nat. Hist.,* ser. 8, 11:131—*Callimico snethlageri* Miranda Ribeiro a synonym; species intermediate between Cebidae and Callitrichidae. Thomas, 1914, *Ann. Mag. Nat. Hist.,* ser. 8 13:345—BRAZIL: *Acre* (Rio Xapury, upper Rio Purús). Pocock, 1920, *Proc. Zool. Soc. London* 1920: 92, fig. 1 *b* (nostrils), fig. 3 *e* (ear), fig. 4 *a, b* (hand and foot), fig. 12 *g* (♂ genitalia)—"from the Ma River, Bolivia [= Rio Mú, Amazonas, Brazil]"; external characters; regarded as a primitive callitrichid. Thomas, 1928, *Ann. Mag. Nat. Hist.,* ser. 10, 2:255—PERU: *Loreto* (Cerro Azul, Contamana); a primitive callitrichid in agreement with Pocock; "Ma" River of Pocock probably Ina River, upper Rio Madeira, Bolivia. Miranda Ribeiro, 1940, *Mem. Inst. Oswaldo Cruz* 35:780, pl. 1 (skull), pl. 2 (skin)—BRAZIL: *Acre* (Rio Yaco); regarded as a cebid. Cruz Lima, 1945, *Mamíferos da Amazonia, Primates, Contr. Mus. Paraense,* p. 199, pl. 32 (animal)—BRAZIL: *Acre* (Rio Yaco; Rio Xapury); characters; variation; taxonomic history. Vieira, 1955, *Arq. Zool., São Paulo* 8:392—BRAZIL: *Acre;* Amazonas (extreme southeastern part). McClung, 1955, *Animal Kingdom* 58:29, fig. 15 (animal)—PERU: *Loreto* (near Iquitos?)—taxonomic history; color; vocalization. Osman Hill, 1957, *Primates,* 3:321, fig. 96 (ear), fig. 97 (dermatoglyphs of hand and foot), fig. 98 (♂ external genitalia), fig. 99 (dentition), fig. 100 (intestine), fig. 101 (distribution), fig. 102 (skull)—PERU: *Loreto* (Cerro Azul); BRAZIL: *Acre* (Rio Yaco; Rio Xapury); *Amazonas* (Mu River, upper Rio Juruá); characters; taxonomy; distribution. Cabrera, 1958, *Rev. Mus. Argentino Cienc. Nat. "Bernardino Rivadavia"* 4(1):184—BRAZIL: *Acre* (type locality restricted to Rio Xapury). Kuenzi, 1958, *Mitt. Naturf. Ges. Bern,* n.f., 16: xxxviii, pls. 1, 2 (animal)—habits in captivity. Osman Hill, 1959, *Trans. Amer. Philos. Soc.* n.s., 49(5):1–116, fig. 1 (animal), figs. 2, 3 (hair, photomicrograph), fig. 4 (palmar, plantar dermatoglyphs), figs. 5–7 (external genitalia), fig. 8 (body radiograph), figs. 9–12 (limb bones), figs. 13–19 (musculature), fig. 40 (oral region), figs. 41–76 (soft anatomy; larynx), fig. 77 (ear bones)—BRAZIL: "from Zoological Society of London,

April 1951, originally from Mu River, coll. F. D. Walker. Skin and skull"; PERU: *Loreto* (Cerro Azul, Contamana); type of *goeldii* and *snethlageri* in British Museum; comparative anatomy; taxonomic history; classification. Hershkovitz, 1958, *Fieldiana, Zool.* 36(6):614—Brazilian subregion; listed as cebid. Küenzi, 1960, *Mitt. Naturf. Ges., Bern,* n.f., 18:xxxv—habits of same animal [1958, supra cit.] in captivity. Osman Hill, 1960, *Primates,* 4:67—relative weight of brain. Küenzi, 1962, *Mitt. Naturf. Ges., Bern* 19:lxxxvi, pl. 3 (mounted animal)—death report of same [1958] animal. Chiarelli, 1963, *Folia Primat.* 1:91—taste sensitivity to phenylthiocarbamide. Hick, 1963, *Freunde Kölner Zoo.* 6(1):14, 7 text figs. (animal)—animal in Köln Zoo received 11 August 1959; characters; habits. Crandall, 1964, *Management of wild mammals in captivity,* p. 105—maintenance; color. Inglis and Cosgrove, 1965, *Parasitology* 55:734—captive individual infested with pinworm parasite, *Trypanoxyuris (Hapaloxyuris) goeldii.* Hernández and Barriga, 1966, *Caldasia* 9(44):365, figs. 1–3 (skull)—COLOMBIA: *Putumayo* (Quebrada del Hacha); *Amazonas* (La Chorrera; Río Igará Paraná); characters; review of literature. Lorenz, 1966, *Zool. Gart.* 32(5):248, figs. 1–3 (animals)—records of individuals held live in European and American zoos and laboratories. Lorenz, 1966, *Freunde das Kölner Zoo* 9(1):11, 6 text figs. (individuals, mother and young, leaping)—summary of records in captivity and births; distribution. Osman Hill, 1966, *Proc. Roy. Soc. Edinburgh,* ser. B 69:321, fig. 1 (hair tracts), pl. 1 (cheiridia), pls. 2–4 (4-day-old young)—external and skeletal characters of 4-day-old young. Lorenz and Heinemann, 1967, *Folia Primat.* 6:1, fig. 1 (animals), fig. 2 (ear), fig. 3 (adult male and young), fig. 4 (fetus), figs. 5, 8. 9 (animals)—reproduction, growth, development, external characters of young; dentition; pelage; color; size. Epple, 1967, *Folia Primat.* 7:37—comparative social and sexual behavior. Epple and Lorenz, 1967, *Folia Primat.* 7:98—sternal gland. Epple, 1968, *Folia Primat.* 8(1):32, figs. 42–44 (sonagrams)—vocalizations. Egozcue, Perkins, and Hagemenas, 1968, *Folia Primat.* 9:82, fig. 1 (animal)—karyotype ($2n = 48$). Lorenz, 1969, *Int. Zoo Yearb.* 9:150—behavior in captivity; feeding; care. Hsu and Hampton, 1970, *Folia Primat.* 13:183, figs. 4–7 (karyotypes)—karyotype (♀ $2n = 48$; ♂ $2n = 47$) xx/xo sex determination system. Travassos, Teixera de Freitas, Kohn, 1969, *Mem. Inst. Oswaldo Cruz* 67:146—trematode parasite, *Conspicuum conspicuum.* Hershkovitz, 1970, *Folia Primat.* 13:216 ff., figs. 2, 3 (endocranial cast)—PERU: *Madre de Dios* (Altamira, 400 m.); *Loreto* (Río Tapiche); cerebral fissural pattern; phylogeny. Hershkovitz, 1970, *Amer. J. Phys. Anthrop.* 32(3):380, pl. 3A (upper jaw)—supernumerary upper molar. Heinemann, 1970, *Int. Zoo Yearb.* 10:72, figs. 27, 28 (animal)—maintenance; breeding; behavior. Lorenz, 1970, *Int. Zoo News* 17:79—second-generation breeding; gestation period (150.5 days). Lorenz, 1970, *Int. Zoo News* 17:130—longevity record (nearly 9 years). Lorenz, 1970, *Lab. Primat. Newsl.* 9(2):11—individuals and institutions holding callimicos for study or exhibition; announcement of studbook project. Lorenz, 1971, *Folia Primat.* 15:133—food (amphibians, reptiles, including snakes). Hampton, Parmelee, and Rider, 1971, in *Med. Primat. 1970,* ed. Goldsmith and Moor-Jankowski, p. 245—plasma histaminase and diamine oxidase values. Hershkovitz, 1971, in *Dental morphology and evolution,* ed. A. Dahlberg, p. 104, fig. 5 (upper molar pattern), fig. 16 (upper and lower tooth rows)—dental homologies. Orihel and Seibold, 1971, *J. Parasit.* 57(6):1367—captive infected with spirurid, *Trichospirurosis leptostoma.* Porter, 1972, *Lab. Animal Sci.* 22(4):503—endoparasites. Hampton, Hampton, and Levy, 1972. *Saving the Lion Marmoset* (Bridgewater, ed), Proc. Wild Animal Propagation Trust Golden Lion Marmoset Conference, p. 70—breeding in captivity. Seibold, Lorenz, and Wolf, 1972, *Vet. Path.* 9:230—giant cell aortitis in captive male. Heltne, Turner, and Wolhandler, 1973, *Amer. J. Phys. Anthrop.* 38:355—relative duration of time spent in maternal and paternal care of young. P. Napier, 1976, *Catalogue of Primates in the British Museum* (Natural History), pt. 1:33—BRAZIL ("R. Mu. 7–8°S, 72°W; type of *c. snethlageri,* PERU: *Loreto* (Cerro Azul, 2 specimens); NO DATA (two specimens).

Callimico goeldi [*sic*], Carvalho, 1957, *Bol. Mus. Paraense, Emilio Goeldi, n.s., Zool.,* no. 6, p. 5—BRAZIL: *Acre* (Seringal Oriente, upper Rio Juruá). James, 1960, *Jaws and teeth of Primates* (London: Pitman), p. 152, figs. 34a, 34b, 34c (jaws and teeth of type of *Callimico snethlageri.* Anonymous, 1964, *Zoonooz* 37(11): cover (two animals), p. 2 (caption)—zoo records. Pournelle, 1965, *Zoonooz* 38(2):4, fig. (animal)—in San Diego Zoo. C. A. Hill, 1966, *Zoonooz* 39(10):14, figs. pp. 15, 16 (newborn and parents)—first zoo-born, 23 April 1966, infant-parent relations; characters; sternal glands; carpal vibrissae.

Callimico gœldii, Osman Hill, 1966, *Proc. Roy. Soc. Edinburgh,* ser. B, 69(3/4):321, fig. 1 (hair tracts), pl. 1 (hand, foot), pls. 2, 3 (4-day-old ♀, preserved), pl. 4 (radiograph of 4-day-old ♀)—external and skeletal features of 4-day-old ♀.

Callimico snethlageri Miranda Ribeiro, 1912, *Brasilianische Rundschau* (1911), 2:22, fig. (head)—BRAZIL: (precise locality unknown, purchased in Pará); original description based on the living animal in the zoological garden of Belém de Pará; type, female, skin and skull, British Museum (Natural History) no. 12.11.4.2. Thomas, 1913, *Proc. Zool. Soc. London* 1914:3—regarded as a cebid intermediate between Cebidae and Callitrichidae.

Callimidas [*sic*] *snethlageri,* Miranda Ribeiro, 1912, *Brasilianische Rundschau* (1911), 2:23—generic name lapsus for *Callimico.*

Callimico suethlageri [*sic*], Cabrera, 1958, *Rev. Mus. Argentino Cienc. Nat. "Bernardino Rivadavia"* 4 (1):184—misprint in synonymy of *Callimico goeldii* Thomas.

Callimico [sp.] Cosgrove, 1966, *Lab. Animal Care* 16 (1):29, 36—trematode parasites (*Platynosomum* [= *Conspicuum*] sp. on p. 36 but inadvertently listed under *Leipertrema* on p. 29).

Type. Male, skin only, British Museum (Natural History) no. 0.2.22.1; received 1904 from the Pará Museum.

Type Locality. Type brought alive to Pará, Brazil, where it was purchased for the Pará Museum; restricted to Río Yaco (211), Acre, southeastern Brazil, by Vieira (1955, *Arq. Zool.* 8:392 [cf. Miranda Ribeiro, 1941, p. 783, pl. 2]). Vieira's action supersedes restriction of type locality to Rio Xapury by Cabrera (1958, Rev. Mus. argentino "Bernardino Rivadavia," 4 [1]:184).

Distribution (fig. XII.1)

Upper Amazonian rain forests, hypothetically between the Río Madre de Dios–Río Madeira on the south, the Caquetá-Japurá on the north, and the Andean foothills on the west; actually recorded from the Río Madre de Dios basin in Bolivia and Peru, the upper Purús and Juruá in Brazil and Peru, the lower Marañon basin in Peru, and the Río Putumayo and lower Río Caquetá basins in Colombia; not recorded from Ecuador, where the species certainly occurs; altitudinal range between 75 and 500 meters.

Sight records of callimicos in the Iquitos area reported to Mr. Pekka Soini of Iquitos, Peru, and transmitted to me in a letter dated 28 June 1970 include lower Río Nanay; Quebrada Tocón (94b) above Mishana (94b) Río Nanay, and below mouth of Río Pintoyacu (94a); near Chiriara (94b) below Mishana; Río Pintoyacu, left bank; lower Río Tigre (95); Río Manití (89), right bank tributary of Marañon below Iquitos; Río Samiria (96), between Río Ucayali and Río Huallaga; Río Curaray (80), right tributary of Río Napo.

Dr. Medem of Villavicencio, Colombia, in a letter dated 1 November 1968, included photographs of a callimico taken at Puerto Arturo (58b), Río Caquetá, a settlement above Araracuara where the rapids begin. In another letter, dated 1 February 1969, he states that in Colombia, *Callimico* is known only from Araracuara (Puerto Arturo) down to the Río Cahuinari in the lower Río Caquetá basin, and in the areas of Igará-Paraná (La Chorrera [58a] and Cara-Paraná [58b] in the lower Río Putumayo basin. The animal, however, was also seen near Puerto Umbría (57a) on the Río Guinéo at the head of the Río Putumayo by Dr. Martin H. Moynihan, director of the Smithsonian Tropical Research Institute (in litt., 11 March 1970).

During the course of my survey of mammals in the upper Río Catatumbo, Norte de Santander, northern Colombia, near the Venezuelan border, I was informed by several hunters of the existence in the region of a black tamarinlike monkey. I was guided by one hunter to several sites along an abandoned and overgrown power line route where he had seen the animals on more than one occasion. I saw no primates there. Callitrichids do not occur naturally in the Río Catatumbo–Lake Maracaibo basin, but perhaps *Callimico* does.

Taxonomy

The authorship of the original description of *Callimico goeldii* is equivocal. The first and correctly proposed specific name, *Hapale Goeldii,* appeared in a footnote on page 54 of a catalog of the mammals of the Museu Goeldi de Historia Natural e Ethnographia (Museu Paraense), published by Goeldi and Hagmann (1904). The Portuguese note is here rendered in English.

> "Some years ago, the Zoological Garden of the Museum accessioned a small Amazonian monkey which, despite some difference in color (white patches on head and lumbar region), seemed to be an old individual of *Midas* (*Hapale*) *Weddelli* Deville [= *Saguinus fuscicollis weddelli*]. The appearance of the animal must have changed as a result of its long life in captivity. The white lumbar patch may be the effect of the leash tied to the animal. We have seen many similar white patches on the backs of saddle horses. New pelage on healed skin of injuries caused by hard or poorly fitted saddles is often white. This monkey was shown to Oldfield Thomas of the British Museum. He first regarded it as a new species for which the name *Hapale Goeldii* O. Thomas was proposed, the detailed description being reserved for later publication. Recently, the distinguished specialist wrote us that he was now inclined to accept our identification of the animal and that he no longer entertained the intention of describing the species."

It seems that Thomas (1904, p. 190) changed his mind and published the detailed description of *Midas goeldii* based on the specimen in question. He also observed,

> "as may be seen by the note [see above] in Dr. Goeldi's [and Hagmann's] Catalogue of Pará mammals, this marmoset has been a puzzle for some time, but was provisionally assigned to *M. Weddelli,* Deville. Now, however, that I have had the opportunity of studying the members of the group more closely, I am convinced that it is a form hitherto undescribed, and I am pleased to apply to it the name of its donor, to whom our knowledge of the Pará fauna is so largely due. I still consider, as stated above, that the white patches on the head and loins are abnormal; but apart from these it cannot be referred to *M. Weddelli* as that species has a white muzzle, marbled back, and rufous thighs, while the uniform hoary-washed blackish of *M. Goeldii* is quite unique."

Perhaps priority demands that Goeldi and Hagmann, not Thomas, be recognized as authors of the new species. Thomas, however, is both the intellectual authority for the new concept and the coiner of the name for it.

Callimico snethlageri Miranda Ribeiro was first described from a live animal seen in the Pará Zoological Garden. Its size was compared with that of *Midas ursulus* [= *Saguinus midas niger*] and its headdress with that of *Hapale rosalia* [*Leontopithecus rosalia*]. A sketch of the head of the new form is included in the description. No basis was offered for erection of a new genus of Primates, but the systematic position of the new species was given as between *Callicebus* and *Mico.* After death, the type was prepared as a study skin and skull and sent to the British Museum for examination by Oldfield Thomas (1913, p. 130) who readily identified *C. snethlageri* with the marmoset he had previously described as *Midas goeldii* on the basis of the skin alone.

The new material led Thomas to reexamine the systematics of New World primates. *Callimico* was made type of a new cebid subfamily, the Callimiconinae,

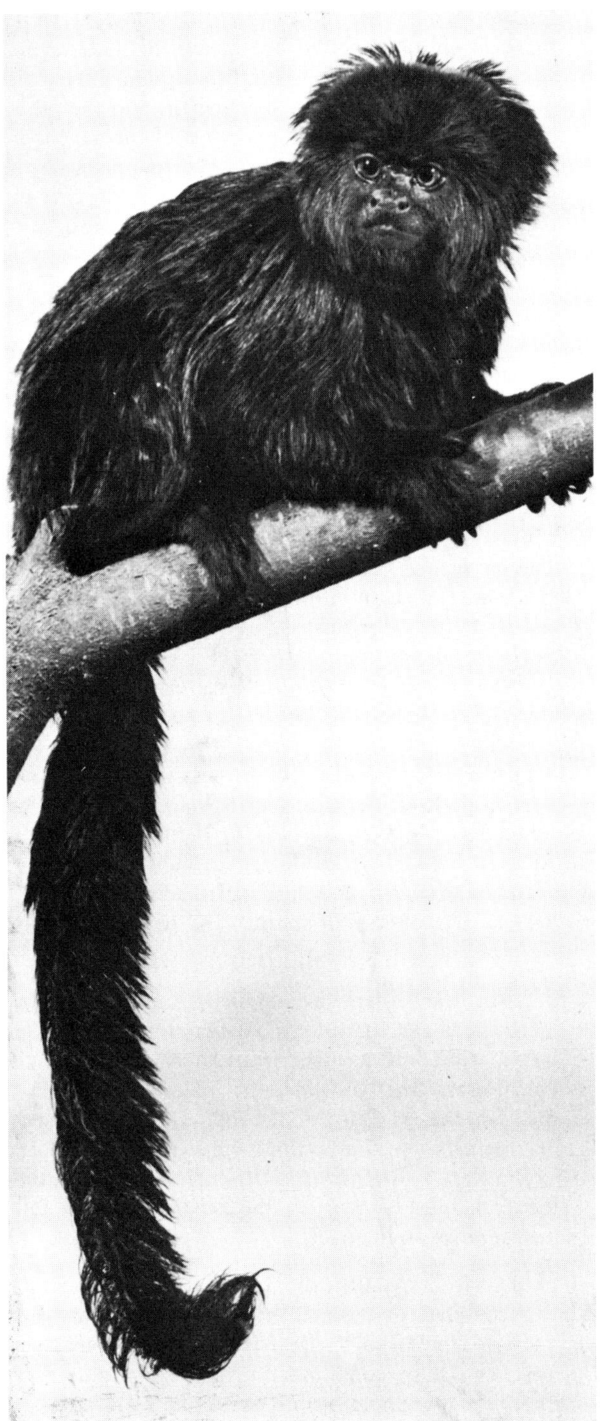

Fig. XII.21. Callimico (*Callimico goeldii*) adult. (Photo courtesy of San Diego Zoo.)

said to be intermediate between the Cebidae and Callitrichidae.

Characters

Diagnostic. Generally blackish or blackish brown throughout, but head, loins, and basal third of tail sometimes variegated with reddish drab, silvery brown, or white; peculiar bobbed mane with pompadour in forepart of head, tiered pair of lateral tufts on back of crown partly concealing ears and extending over nape; thick side whiskers extending below jaws, hairs of interramia and neck forming forwardly directed median crest.

Integument (figs. III.6, 13; XII.2, 20, 21). Facial skin pigmented; short black hairs covering upper lips extending around nostrils and cresting on midline of muzzle; pelage of crown and cheeks combining to form a blackish or brownish mane, the hairs blackish or dark brown, often tipped with drab or grayish, sometimes with reddish; side whiskers or muttonchops extending downward below jaws and concealing sides of throat; preauricular tufts partly concealing ears, hairs of front of crown radiating from midfrontal line upward, forward, and back to form a pompadour terminating in a point between ears, hairs behind longer and arranged in two lateral tufts forming a tiered cape spread over ears and nape; pinna with rim usually blackish, the remainder varying from unpigmented or flesh-colored to blackish, outer (medial) surface nearly bare, inner thinly haired; hairs of interramia and throat blackish, forming median crest directed forward; remainder of body blackish or dark brown with hair tips becoming brown, reddish, drab, or gray, mostly on lower back, thighs, and base of tail, the tipping sometimes arranged in striae or randomly distributed as patches; external genitalia pigmented; hands and feet blackish.

Skin. According to Perkins (1969*b*), the skin is histologically similar to that of *Saguinus*. However, nothing in the skin of *Saguinus* has been shown to be distinctive of the genus, the family, or of platyrrhines generally. Pigmentation of the adult face, genitalia, and newborn body is shown, respectively, in figs. XII.2, 18–20, and XII.22–24.

Vibrissae (figs. III.8; XII.2). Supraorbitals, mystacials, rhinarials, and mentals present and well developed; interramals absent, genals not distinguishable; 3 to 6 ulnar carpals present and well defined on each arm of two of four fluid-preserved specimens; gular and pectoral spines absent.

Young. See page 899 for chronology of growth and development.

Comparisons

The tamarinlike *Callimico* is distinguished from *Leontopithecus* by hands, feet, and digits of normal length and breadth, generally blackish color throughout, and the tiered and pompadoured mane; blackish tamarins of the genus *Saguinus* lack the mane present in *Callimico;* the darkest tamarin, *S. inustus,* is mottled or barefaced, and tamarins of the *S. mystax* and *S. nigricollis* groups are characterized by a white circumlabial band or mustache absent in *Callimico.*

Variation

Individual. Most striking deviations from the generally blackish brown color pattern are irregular markings of reddish, gray, or white spotting on the head, lower back, and basal third of tail and, less usually, limbs and underparts. The type of *Callimico goeldii,* [cf. Goeldi and Hagmann (1904, p. 54, footnote); Thomas (1904, p. 190)], is variegated, with white on sides of head and loins. An adult male from Rio Yaco, Acre, recorded and figured by Miranda Ribeiro (1941, p. 783, pl. 2) and described and illustrated in color by Cruz Lima (1945,

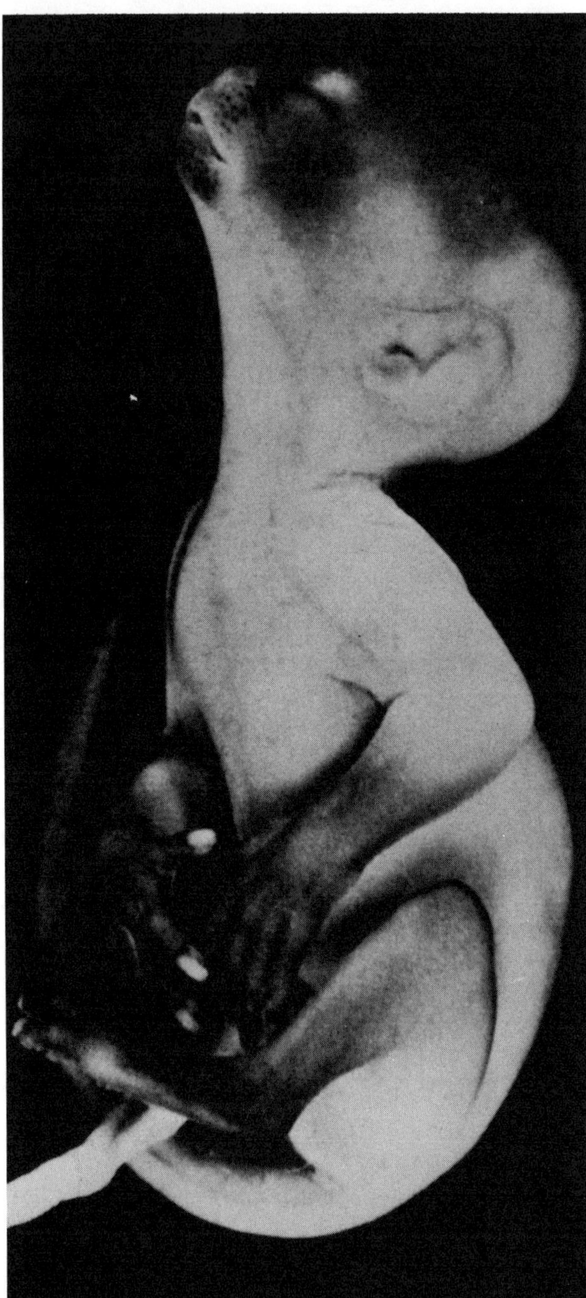

Fig. XII.22. Female fetus (Max Planck Institut für Hirnforschung, Primatologie [Frankfurt am Main]), "Kopf-Rumpflange" 75 mm; weight in utero 36 g (without uterus, 26.5 g) or about ⅗ term weight; notable characters include pigmentation pattern, well developed vibrissal fields (supraorbital, ciliary, rhinarial, mystacial, and mental), fingers III–IV united by web and projecting 1 mm beyond adjacent fingers; ungues cebidlike; deciduous teeth unerupted, but upper incisors and lower central incisor erupted from aveoli but not gingivae. (From Lorenz and Heinemann 1967, *Folia. Primat.*, vol. 6, fig. 4.)

p. 200, pl. 32) is unusual. According to the latter, "above the nape one finds a double stripe, tawny blond and white, slightly tinged with rufous. Above the ears there are pale-tipped hairs, present also on the nape, on the loins and, to a greater extent, on the tail, where this color appears in two or three rings on the upper third. The remainder of the body . . . [is] black." A second adult male in the Pará Museum collection from "alto Amazonas," is described by Cruz Lima (1945, p. 201) as follows:

"Front of the head from the forehead to the vertex [has] an entirely spotted aspect due to the irregular mixture of white, brownish and rufous hairs, the white ones being uniform in all their extent and the others black at the base. On the upper part of the nape there is a small dark chestnut patch. The few hairs on the face are white contrasting with the black skin; feet and hands entirely yellowish white, this color also being found on the inner side of the limbs and on the belly up to the chest. The tips of the hairs on the loins are rusty blond, while all the black hairs are blondish tipped. One also finds, as in the specimen described by Goeldi and on which Thomas based his first identification, tufts of white hairs irregularly placed along the body. In the specimen now described these white spots are found on the right forearm (outer side) on the left elbow, on the left leg and on the upper surface of the apical half of the tail."

The variegated condition was attributed to injury by Goeldi and Hagmann (1904) and Thomas (1904). Cruz Lima (1945, p. 201) insisted the cause was natural, perhaps the result of aging. Osman Hill (1966*b*:332) believed that "traces of the juvenile pattern, especially the white areas on the tail [fig. XII.23] are sometimes retained in the adult."

All explanation may be more or less valid. In the case of the first two, the old dark pelage must be lost whether through injury, disease, or natural molt, before or as it is replaced by unpigmented hair. Osman Hill's explanation excludes molt in the affected areas. Crandall (1964, p. 106) offers still another and perhaps the most likely explanation in the form of an analogous case.

"A male and a female [callimico] received here [New York Zoological Gardens] on April 6, 1955, were black, with only a slight infusion of brown on the dorsal area. One year later the male had the hair of the face, the last third of the tail, and irregular spots on the body and limbs white, while the forehead and crown were brown mixed with white. At the same time the female had white on the face only, with faint brown areas on the back."

Evidently, Crandall's callimicos had undergone a partial or complete unseasonal molt induced by change in climate or conditions in captivity. Old pigmented hairs of parts of skin preconditioned by disease or injury were then replaced by unpigmented hairs. The variegated type specimen of *Callimico goeldii* and the male described and figured by Cruz Lima (1945, p. 200, pl. 32, three views of same) both from Belém zoological gardens, were also long-time captives.

A piebald treeshrew (*Tupia glis*) described and figured by Elliot and Wong (1973) is an example of an analogous condition. The treeshrew, kept in a dark laboratory, lost patches of hair from all parts of its body. After exposure to sunlight the hair that regrew was white.

Geographic. Nothing in the character of 19 skins, skulls, or spirit-preserved specimens examined, or the score or more callimicos seen in captivity, suggests geographic variation of any kind. The callimicos described or figured in the literature, excluding the variegated individuals mentioned above, apparently agree in all respects with specimens at hand. Possibly fresh specimens in sufficient numbers from new localities may reveal characters not seen or not fully appreciated in present material collected from all parts of the known geographic range of the species.

Geographic variation in terms of cryptic characters, that is, those not apparent in the phenotype, may occur. A karyological study of samples of *Callimico goeldii* of unknown provenance, conducted by Hsu and Hampton (1970), revealed three distinct karyotypes. Type 1, based on previously published analyses of 2 males and 2 females from stock in the Oregon Regional Primate Research Center, represents the classic XX/XY sex-determination system. The diploid number was determined as 48. Type 2, found in 3 males housed in the Oak Ridge Institute of Nuclear Studies, is distinguished by a Y-chromosome translocation and autosome fusion, resulting in an XO male determination system. The male diploid chromosome number in this case is 47. Type 3, discovered in 7 males maintained in the University of Texas Dental Institute, Houston, is like type 2, but with a portion of the translocated Y-chromosomes presumed lost. The female diploid number is 48 in all cases.

Geographic distribution of the three cytological types of callimico can be determined only by field sampling. Cross-breeding in the laboratory may throw more light on the evolution and relative stability of the three karyotypes.

Bleaching, Depilation, Hypertrichy and Depigmentation

Callimico goeldii is more saturate than any callitrichid except *Saguinus inustus.* The coat is generally blackish brown to brown throughout with terminal portions of the hairs on certain parts of the body, usually head, nape, rump, limbs, and chest, bleaching to reddish brown, drab, and silvery brown or grayish. Bleaching is always more advanced on dorsal than on ventral surface of body. The primitive agouti pattern persists only on the dorsal surface in the newborn pelage. The black to reddish, orange, yellow to cream or white succession characteristic of *Leontopithecus rosalia* and other brightly colored callitrichids is absent in *Callimico.*

In some long-term captive zoo, laboratory, or household individuals the coat is variegated with whitish or gray, and the basal portion of the tail may be broadly annulated with whitish. Variegation in these samples appears to have been developed after an out-of-phase or abnormal molt precipitated by abnormal living conditions in captivity. This change of pelage color is ontogenetic or teratogenetic; it is not evolutionary bleaching.

The overall trend in evolution of the pelage pattern has been toward decrease in length and possibly loss of hairs on underparts and increase in length, with corresponding bushiness on dorsal surface, most notably cheeks, crown, nape, shoulders, and rump. The erectile, pompadoured headdress of *Callimico* is unique.

Skin of face, ears, hands, feet, and genitalia are more or less pigmented in consonance with the dark pelage.

Specimens Examined

Total:

19. PERU—*Loreto:* Río Pisqui, 1 (AMNH); Río Tapiche, 1 (AMNH); Cerro Azul, Contamana 2 (BM); Mishana, Río Nanay, 1 (FMNH); *Madre de Dios:* Altamira, Río Manú, 1 (FMNH); COLOMBIA—*Putumayo:* Quebrada El Hacha, 1 (ICN); *Amazonas:* La Chorrera, 1 (ICN). BRAZIL—*Amazonas:* Rio Mu, 1 (BM); UNKNOWN LOCALITY —10 (AMNH, 4, in spirits; BM, type of *goeldii,* type of *snethlageri;* FMNH, 2; USNM, 2).

83 *Callimico goeldii*
2. *Biology of Callimico*

REPRODUCTION

Information compiled from publications by Lorenz and Heinemann (1967), Heinemann (1970), and Lorenz (1972) is quoted, paraphrased, or abstracted under the following subject headings:

Estrus	Pregnancy
Courtship and Mating	Gestation
Copulation	Births
	Hour of Birth

Estrus

Lorenz 1972, p. 105

"The total duration of estrus was determinable in 19 cases involving three females. Mean duration of estrus was seven days with a range of 5–12 days. In one instance, a female was receptive over a period of 19 days; for two single days out of these 19 days, no receptivity was observed. This long receptive period occurred after introduction of a new male. The likelihood is that the male's presence altered the female's regular behavior. This value was not used for calculation.

"Intensity of estrus varied from day to day. There was usually a peak day with the female being extremely attracted to the male, showing maximum reactions, and preferring the mate to food. The position of this peak day was recorded 11 times in one female; (mean—4th day, range—3rd–6th day). If an estrus was very long the intensity during the first days was rather low and the peak tended to occur later than the fourth day. The lengths of 13 estrus cycles were recorded for one female. Mean cycle length from peak to peak was 22 days with a range of 21–24 days.

"So far we have been unable to detect physical changes of the genitalia associated with estrus; however, it would be interesting to study vaginal cytology."

[There is a postpartum estrus, since copulation often takes place the same day as parturition—P. H.]

Courtship and Mating

Lorenz 1972, p. 103

The male *Callimico* regularly "checks" his female's reproductive status. The male often smells, licks, and tastes urine deposited and carried by the female. The sternal gland secretion is another likely source of information. Also, he pulls on the female's tail or one hind limb to sniff or lick a sample of urine (the female commonly carries a droplet at the ventral tip of the labia minora, see also Klein and Klein 1971) or the secretion of the genital scent glands. If the male perceives that the female is in estrus he follows her closely all day, attempts mounting, and frequently updates his sensory impression. At that stage, no restlessness of the female, no harsh vocalization by her nor rude nipping with her teeth can discourage him for long. However insistent the male is, the female has means to avoid or interrupt copulation; quite often she does not stand still and drags the clinging male behind, or she turns sideways. As the female's readiness for physical contact builds up, the social distance between the partners decreases. Mutual grooming lasts longer and appears more intensive. If the check turns out contrary, the male creates a sharp smacking noise with his teeth (or tongue) which is commonly associated with situations of dissatisfaction (Lorenz 1969). Relations between male and female remain unchanged until another estrus begins.

Copulation

Lorenz 1972, p. 105

"Initially the male and then the female embraces the partner's head or body either from in front or from behind. The male licks the vagina and the female responds with rapid lateral movements of her hindquarters. She 'freezes' in the present location and when touched in the lumbar region shows lordosis, lateral movement of the tail, straightened arms and a staring view ahead. Now the male mounts while the female awaits intromission still staring and sometimes moving the lower jaw. The male but not the female sometimes shows tongue flicking during copulation. The female frequently looks back at the male and reaches with one hand for the male's head or shoulder. The male sits behind the female and performs 20–40 pelvic thrusts in fast sequence; every 5th–8th thrust has a greater amplitude. Moment of ejaculation is difficult to discern; however, after the male dismounts a slight vaginal opening and ejaculate are recognizable."

Lorenz 1972, p. 104

"Sexual activity is especially frequent at first meetings of strange heterosexual adults and at estrus periods. At such times, many copulations can be observed in one day. With the end of estrus the copulations come to a sudden stop."

Lorenz 1972, p. 106

"Copulation has been observed only once during pregnancy."

Pregnancy

Lorenz and Heinemann 1967, p. 4

First signs of pregnancy were changes in behavior of the mating pair. The belly of the female soon becomes prominent, her activity more restrained. Near term she becomes somewhat listless and looks for support in moving about. Some weeks before term breasts and nipples enlarge. The areola becomes pink at first then turn to a waxy yellow color. The nipples of multiparous females are cylindrical, those of primiparous females are smaller and conical.

Heinemann 1970, p. 76

In Blackie's first pregnancy, which terminated in miscarriage, abdominal swelling was noticed in early December; later, urination was more frequent and her bowels became loose. The fetus was aborted 1 January. Blackie and Devil mated again 3 January. Abdominal swelling was palpated late March, nipples remained large from previous pregnancy, but bowel movements were normal and the amount of urine was not more than usual. About 1 week before delivery, the usually smooth skin between vagina and anus appeared thicker and furrowed.

Lorenz 1972, p. 106

"Within the first two weeks of pregnancy, the behaviors of male and female change; for example, the female is allowed to groom certain areas of the male which she was not permitted to groom before. The male yields more privileges to the female in general (*e.g.,* taking food from him); this is the time when the female seems to dominate the male in some respects.

"Following these behavioral changes the appetite increases. Some time later, the female has loose stools and constantly loses drops of urine. When the abdominal swelling can be seen, the female's locomotion and general activity begin to decrease but this is quite variable according to the individual female and to her condition during individual pregnancy. The mammary glands and the nipples enlarge. During the last days preceding birth, the female loses so much urine that part of her tail is constantly wet. Sometimes even the hindlimbs are wet. Her appetite may fall off two days before delivery and during the last few days before birth the vagina swells and opens slightly."

Gestation

Lorenz and Heinemann 1967, p. 7;
Heinemann (pers. comm.)

Intervals in days between the 5 births produced by Blackie (p. 903) are, in chronological order, 165, 169, 167, and 169, birth dates included. The rather uniform duration of the intervals suggests that copulation may take place immediately after parturition. Indeed, mating observed between Blackie and Devil 2 days after the 1 January 1964 stillbirth, and between Happy and Goeldy 12 days after parturition, indicates a postpartum estrus. Nevertheless, Lorenz and Heinemann (1967, p. 7) postulate a delay of 4 weeks between parturition and a conception and estimate a gestation period of about 4½ months, or 135 days.

Lorenz 1970*a,* p. 79

On the basis of the duration of two second-generation pregnancies calculated at 152 and 149 days, the average of 150.5 days was suggested as being the normal gestation period.

Lorenz 1972, p. 106

"Due to knowledge of estrus, peak of estrus, and birth date, it was possible to estimate the gestation period to be five months. After the first estimate the date of delivery could be predicted. The prediction was close in every case and sometimes accurate to two days.

"The mean of seven pregnancies from three females yielded 154 days from the peak of the last estrus until delivery. The range was 151–159 days. An eighth pregnancy of our fourth female presented no contrary evidence. Previously, the upper limit for the length of gestation was established at 165 days (Lorenz and Heinemann 1967) as this was the shortest interval from birth to birth. Last year we established the minimum at 149 days as the male had been separated that many days before delivery and ten days following the previous birth. Since the female was in estrus before separation, we estimated the resulting new pregnancy at 153 days with the maximum possible being 159 days if conception occurred at the day of birth. All the various observations appear in perfect agreement and have a high probability of accuracy."

Fig. XII.23. Four-day-old callimico born 15 March 1965 in the laboratory of Dr. Leo Rane, School of Medicine, University of Miami (Florida); notable newborn characters include undeveloped mane, the ears full exposed, tegulae of front and hind digits; bare underparts, whitish hairs on upper surface of cheiridia, and tail whitish except at base. (Photograph from W. C. Osman Hill, 1966, *Proc. Roy. Soc., Edinburgh,* vol. 99, ser. B, pl. III).

Births

More than a score of pregnancies have been recorded and references have been made to many more. Most of the pregnancies terminated in live births, and all but one were of a single young. C. A. Hill (1966) recorded the first zoo-born callimico, a singleton in the San Diego Zoo. Heinemann (1970) recorded 5 pregnancies, each terminating in one offspring. Lorenz and Heinemann (1967, pp. 2, 3) listed the foregoing cases, 2 unrelated fetuses in the Max-Planck-Institüt für Hirnforschung in Frankfurt and stillbirths of singletons in the San Diego and Frankfurt zoos. Lorenz (1970*a*) added two more single births of captive-born parents, and Hampton, Hampton, and Levy (1971) likewise noted only one young in each of 11 pregnancies. The lone exception to the single birth rule is said to have been twins born 15 March 1965 in the monkey colony of Dr. Leo Rane of the School of Medicine, University of Miami. The information given Osman Hill (1966*b*, p. 321), who studied the survivor, was that "the other twin was macerated at birth. The placenta was not recovered."

Lorenz 1972, p. 107

"Highest number of term births occurring during one calendar year was three. Highest number of pregnancies recorded for one female is 12 (Hampton, pers. comm.); another female had six pregnancies while five and four are rather common."

Heinemann; Lorenz and Heinemann

The following 5 births were produced by Blackie and Devil, the callimico pair owned and maintained by Mrs. Heike Heinemann. The first birth occurred in Bloomington, Indiana, the others in Wiesbaden, Germany. Most of the information given here was communicated to me by Mrs. Heinemann in correspondence. A full account of the births and superficial anatomy and development of the young was published later by Lorenz and Heinemann (1967). Heinemann (1970) followed with another paper on the births and on the behavior of young and parents.

1. *Stillborn,* unsexed, premature, 1 January 1964.
2. Mating between Blackie and Devil observed 3 January 1964; abdominal swelling and slightly enlarged nipples noted end of March; perineum appeared thickened and furrowed, first week June 1964.
   Ebony (♀) born 13 June 1964.
3. Blackie: abdominal swelling noted September 1964.
   Fury (♂) born 27 November 1964.
4. Devil sniffed Blackie's genitalia a few times daily about 1 month after Fury's birth, then showed no sexual interest in following months.
   Goeldy (♂) born 13 May 1965.
5. *Happy* (♀) born 29 October 1965.

The following second-generation births were produced by offspring of Blackie and Devil.

Female, stillborn 16 October 1968.
Produced by Happy mated with father Devil or, more likely, brother Goeldy.
Happy and Goeldy seen mating again, 27 October 1968 (Heinemann 1970).

Female, born 17 January 1969.
Produced by Ebony mated with Fury in the Max Planck Institute for Brain Research, Frankfurt; duration of gestation calculated 152 days; young died 4 February 1969 (Lorenz 1970*a*).

Effy, female, born 21 July 1969.
Produced by Ebony mated with Fury as above, but birth took place in the Delta Primate Research Center, Covington, Louisiana; calculated gestation period, 149 days (Lorenz 1970*a*).

Hour of Birth

About 12 recorded births took place at night. Other births have been recorded by date but not by hour. Presumably, actual birth was not observed because it may have occurred in the nest box or at night. I find no published records of daytime births.

GROWTH AND DEVELOPMENT

Topics treated are:

Chronology of Growth and Development
Weights and Measurements
Longevity

Chronology of Growth and Development

Newborn and Juvenal

Physical Growth
Chronological increase in body weight, size of head and body, tail, hind foot, and ear of Ebony (no. 21) and brothers Fury (no. 11) and Goeldy (no. 12) is shown in table 111 (p. 902) (data from Lorenz and Heinemann 1967).

External Characters
1st day—Eyes open, color cloudy blue; face naked, the skin brownish; exposed parts of body (head, back, extremities) covered with short blackish hair, neck, chest, belly, innerside of arms and legs, superior surface of hands and lower arms naked; forehead pelage adpressed, hairs of mane hardly longer than hairs of back (data from Lorenz and Heinemann 1967, p. 11), based on ♂ no. 11 born 28 November 1964, and ♀ no. 21 born 13 June 1964, both in Weisbaden, Germany.

4th day (fig. XII.23)—Pelage and color of dorsal surface essentially as in adults except hairs of scapular region with single reddish subterminal band, the pheomelanic bands becoming wider and increasing to two per hair toward rump; underparts virtually bare; upper surface of hands and feet sparsely covered with white hairs; tail base white, terminal portions of hairs becoming black toward distal two-thirds of tail and entirely black on terminal third; ungues long, more nearly tegulate than falcate; tips of deciduous incisors $\frac{1}{1,2}$ exposed (data from Osman Hill 1966*b*, p. 321).

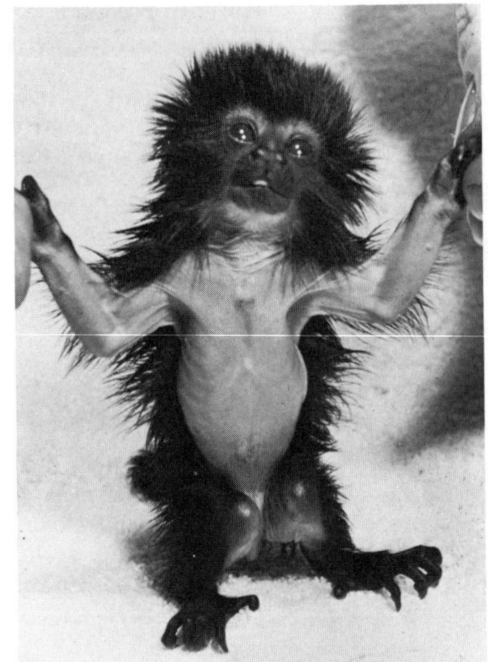

Fig. XII.24. Infant callimico (*Callimico goeldii*), 10 days old; sternal and ulnar glands exposed on virtually naked underparts. Matted condition of fur caused by oily secretions from maternal sternal gland. (Photos courtesy of San Diego Zoo.)

6th day—Ebony diagnosed as female (Heinemann 1970, p. 77).

10th day—(fig. XII.24) Skin of face, forearms, and outer and front sides of legs pigmented; face bare except for vibrissae and long blackish hairs of cheeks and forehead; pelage of crown, upper surface of hands, feet, and tail blackish; inner surface of limbs and ventral surface of throat, neck, chest, belly, and basal portion of tail bare, the navel, sternal gland, and vibrissal field of ulnar gland fully exposed to view; pelage pattern apparently like that of adult (data from C. A. Hill 1966, based on individual born 23 April 1966 in the San Diego Zoo).

13th day—Hairs of mane 12 mm, of back 9 mm (Lorenz and Heinemann 1967).

30th day—Fully furred; Fury's sex determined as male, the penis being so small "that one has to look for the presence or absence of a vagina" (Heinemann 1970, p. 77).

48th day—Pelage and color of exposed upper and outer sides as in adults (Lorenz and Heinemann 1967, p. 6, fig. 3).

54th day—Pelage and color as in adults (Cruz Lima 1945, p. 201).

60th day—Underparts of body, innersides of arms, legs, and superior surface of lower arms and hands more or less hairy as in adults (Lorenz and Heinemann 1967).

Activity

The following chronology of events is based on an account by Lorenz and Heinemann (1967) of no. 21 (Ebony), born in Wiesbaden, Germany, and observations by Heltne, Turner, and Wolhander (1973) of dependence measured in percentage of time of a pair of captive-born young on their parents in a Baltimore facility.

Abstracts from Lorenz and Heinemann (1967) are identified by the initials L and H; those from Heltne, Turner, and Wolhandler (1973) are designated H, T, and W.

Newborn—Opens eyes, climbs mother's back to nape, becoming hidden in mane; one arm grabs mother's neck, the other held in armpit, one leg anchored in fur of back, the other clutching hair of belly, tail rolled under mother's belly and pressing firmly with each of her movements (Lorenz and Heinemann 1967, data based on ♀ no. 21 described above).

2–3 days—Becomes interested in surroundings (L and H).

1st week—♀ young carried by mother exclusively; 40% of time spent in ventral position while suckling, sleeping, and being transported (H, T, and W).

2d week—♀ young carried by mother exclusively; 21% of time spent in nursing position (H, T, and W).

3d week—Ebony resists mother's attempt to remove her by rubbing against wall and rolling on back; father responds to wailing and permits young to climb onto his back; thereafter young not tolerated by mother except for suckling (L and H).

3d week—Time spent by ♀ young on mother drops from 100% to 13%, mostly for suckling; 87% of time mounted on father (H, T, and W).

4th week—Ebony eats solid food; sits beside parents when undisturbed (L and H).

4th week—♀ young, 12% of time on mother, half of which in nursing position; 87% of time on father; less than 1% near a parent (H, T, and W).

5th week—♀ young, 3.4% on mother; 96% on father; less than 1 % near a parent (H, T, and W).

6th week—Walks from one parent to the other; makes short leaps (L and H).

6th week—Partially independent of parents; ♀ and ♂ young, 3%/32% on mother; 82%/52% on father; 14%/6% near a parent; less than 1%/2% far from both parents (H, T, and W) [the ♂ juvenal time budget totals only 87% P. H.].

7th week—Increasingly independent of parents; eat solid food; ♀ and ♂ young, 11%/18% on mother; 71%/72% on father; 15%/6% near a parent; 3%/3% far from parents (H, T, and W).

8th week—Climbs around cage and exercises on hanging rope; more or less independent of parents (L and H).

8th week—♀ and ♂ young, 9%/9% on mother; 77%/70% on father; 7%/11% near a parent; 7%/10% far from both parents (H, T, and W).

9th week—♀ young, 7% on mother; 75% on father; 7% near parent; 11% far from parents.

10th week—Ebony weaned, too heavy for father to carry; mounts only when frightened, but he dislodges her by biting her tail.

10th week—♀ and ♂ young, 1%/4% on mother; 53%/48% on father; 18%/39% near a parent; 28%/9% far from both parents.

11th week—♀ young, 4% on mother (96% of the time in nursing position); 66% on father; 11% near a parent; 18% far from both parents.

3d month—Not permitted to take food from parents' hand (L and H).

Adolescence

Pelage brownish, fine, slightly curly, and less glossy than adult pelage; *cutaneous glands* developed and beginning to secrete. In adolescent female, *labia majora* large, olive in color, glandular cells prominent, sternal *glandular* area elevated. In adolescent male, *testes* descended and adult size; *scrotal skin* glandular, ducts elevated, secretions dark; spontaneous *penile* erections without visible external stimuli; adolescent copulatory attempts made without penile erection.

Contact with dominant male may retard maturation rate of adolescent male but separation accelerates compensatory development (data from Lorenz 1972, age of subject not given).

4th month—Hair pattern adult (Lorenz and Heinemann 1967).

Maturation

Female

7th–9th month—Adult weight attained (Lorenz 1972).

8th–9th month—Copulates with unrelated, strange wild-born male (Lorenz 1972).

10th month—"Second set of teeth erupted" (Heinemann 1970, p. 77).

11th–12th month—1st pregnancy of above female, probably at 5th estrus (Lorenz 1972).

15th month—Pelage of forehead raised in front as in adults (Lorenz and Heinemann 1967, but see 4th month above).

Weights and Measurements (table 111)

Lorenz 1969, p. 151

A male that weighed 645 g in 1966 when it became an office pet in Frankfurt, Germany, attained 680 g later in the year, and 805 g in 1967.

Lorenz 1972, p. 99

The same male, the offspring of captive-born parents, was transported to Covington, Louisiana, where it attained 860 g, the greatest weight known for the species. He sired four young.

The abnormally great weight from excessive feeding may have been correlated with a diseased aorta discovered during necropsy (Seibold, Lorenz, and Wolf 1972; [weights and reproductive figures in the work cited do not tally with those given in the preceding accounts, P. H.,]).

Osman Hill 1966, p. 322

The 31 bodily measurements of a fluid-preserved 4-day-old "neonate" are larger than the corresponding ones tabulated for fluid-preserved "neonates" each of *Callithrix jacchus, C. argentata, Saguinus fuscicollis illigeri,* and *Cebuella pygmaea.* However, Osman Hill fails to give the age, history, or condition of preservation of the callitrichids with which comparisons were made. The dimensions themselves do not suggest that the specimens are strictly comparable in age or that most of them are better than rough approximations. In any case, adult callimicos average larger than comparably aged adults of the larger callitrichids except *Leontopithecus rosalia.* It is not surprising, therefore, that the same size relationship should hold for newborn.

The weight of the 4-day-old *Callimico* measured by Osman Hill (1966, p. 321) "after transfer [from 10% formalin] to alcohol and subsequent drying to the stage at which the pelage had fluffed out, was 44 g." Live weight given for the San Diego Zoo newborn by C. A. Hill (1966, p. 14) is 59.8 g. Using this last figure and others extrapolated or taken directly from table 111 (p. 902) appendix table 2, and comparative data from table 54 (p. 445), the mean weights and linear measurements of *Callimico* relative to those of adults are as follows:

Newborn weight : *adult weight* = 12%, or greater than that of all callitrichids except *Cebuella,* with a mean of 12%.

Newborn head and body length : *adult head and body length* = 49% or greater than that of callitrichids but nearly equaled by *Cebuella* with a mean of 48%.

Newborn tail length : *adult tail length* = 33%, or shorter relative to adult length than the mean of all callitrichids except *Callithrix* with 27%, and equal to that of *Leontopithecus* with 33%. The mean proportional length in *Saguinus* is 36% and in *Cebuella,* 44%.

Newborn tail length/newborn head and body length : *adult tail length/head and body length* = 67%, or shorter than in callitrichids. The mean proportional tail length (relative to proportional length in adults) is extremely high in *Cebuella* with 93%. *Saguinus* follows with 84%, *Leontopithecus* with 71%, and *Callithrix* with 69%. Mean adult tail length relative to head and body length is also less in *Callimico* (135%) than in callitrichids. Osman Hill (1966, p. 323) had commented on the relatively shorter tail of *Callimico.*

Longevity

The male breeder Devil, bought by Mrs. Heinemann (1970) on 14 May 1963, was still alive in 1970. As estimated by Lorenz (1970*b*), the animal was probably not less than 2 years old when purchased, hence at least 9 years old up to the time.

BEHAVIOR

Almost nothing is known of the behavior of *Callimico goeldii* in the wild and very little is known of its comportment in captivity. Callimicos never gained favor as laboratory animals, and study of their behavior in scien-

Table. 111. Chronology of Growth of Three Callimicos (*Callimico goeldii*)

	Head and Trunk (H & T)[1]			*Tail*			*Hind Foot*			*Ear*			*Weight*		
Days	♀ *21*	♂ *11*	♂ *12*	♀ *21*	♂ *11*	♂ *12*	♀ *21*	♂ *11*	♂ *12*	♀ *21*	♂ *11*	♂ *12*	♀ *21*	♂ *11*	♂ *12*
1	—	150	—	—	120	—	—	—	—	—	10	—	—	—	—
6	—	—	120	—	—	110	—	—	30	—	—	—	—	—	—
12	—	—	—	—	—	120	—	—	—	—	—	—	—	—	—
18	—	—	—	—	—	—	—	—	—	—	20	—	—	—	—
23	—	—	—	155	—	—	—	—	40	—	—	—	—	—	—
24	—	—	—	—	—	—	—	—	—	—	—	—	—	—	110
27	—	—	130	—	180	140	—	—	—	—	—	—	—	100	—
29	—	—	—	—	—	—	—	—	—	—	—	—	55	—	—
34	—	—	140	—	—	150	—	—	—	—	—	—	—	—	—
45	—	—	—	—	190	—	—	—	—	—	—	—	—	—	—
46	—	—	—	—	—	—	—	—	—	—	—	—	—	—	150
50	—	—	—	—	—	190	—	—	44	—	—	—	—	—	—
55	—	—	—	210	—	—	—	—	—	—	—	—	—	—	—
57	—	—	—	—	—	—	—	—	—	—	—	—	127	—	—
64	—	—	—	—	250	—	—	—	—	—	20	—	—	—	—
65	—	—	—	—	—	—	—	—	—	—	—	—	155	—	—
71	—	—	—	—	—	—	—	—	—	—	—	—	190	—	—
75	—	—	—	240	—	—	—	—	—	20	—	—	—	—	200
84	—	—	—	—	—	—	—	—	—	—	—	—	—	280	—
93	—	—	—	—	—	—	—	—	—	—	—	—	220	—	—
95	200	—	—	280	—	—	—	60	—	22	25*	—	—	—	—
100	—	—	—	—	270	—	—	—	—	—	—	—	—	—	—
102	—	—	—	—	—	—	—	—	—	—	—	—	—	—	230
113	—	—	215	—	—	280	—	—	60	—	—	—	—	—	—
116	—	—	—	—	—	—	—	—	—	—	—	—	—	315	—
122	—	—	—	—	—	—	—	—	—	—	—	—	—	—	290
125	210	220	—	290	290*	—	—	—	—	—	—	—	265	—	—
143	—	—	—	—	—	—	—	—	—	—	—	—	—	360	—
146	—	230	—	—	—	—	—	—	—	—	—	—	—	—	—
160	220	—	—	—	—	—	—	63*	—	25	—	—	345	—	—
163	—	—	—	—	—	—	—	—	—	—	—	—	—	—	335
174	—	—	—	—	—	—	—	—	—	—	—	—	—	395	—
200	—	250	—	—	290	—	—	—	—	—	25	—	—	—	—
205	—	—	—	—	—	—	—	—	—	—	—	—	—	425	—
239	—	—	—	—	—	—	—	—	—	—	—	—	—	500	—
269	—	—	—	—	—	—	—	—	—	—	—	—	—	540	—
283	—	—	—	—	—	—	—	—	—	—	—	—	475	—	—
288	—	—	—	—	—	—	—	—	—	—	—	—	—	555	—
294	270	—	—	—	—	—	63	—	—	—	—	—	—	—	—
311	—	—	—	—	—	—	—	—	—	—	—	—	500	—	—
329	—	—	—	—	—	—	—	—	—	—	—	—	—	635	—
341	—	—	—	—	—	—	—	—	—	—	—	—	525	—	—
353	270*	—	—	290	—	—	63	—	—	—	—	—	—	—	—
373	—	—	—	—	—	—	—	—	—	—	—	—	540	—	—
407	—	—	—	—	—	—	—	—	—	—	—	—	555	—	—
436	—	—	—	—	—	—	—	—	—	—	—	—	575	—	—
456	—	—	—	—	—	—	—	—	—	—	—	—	560	—	—
497	—	—	—	—	—	—	—	—	—	—	—	—	570	—	—
Adults	278(250–310)6[1, 2]			300(287–317)6[2]			72(68–74)6[2, 6]			24(20–26)6[2]			481(400–555)11[8]		
	221(210–230)6[3]			—			—			—			—		
	224(210–234)18[4, 5]			302(255–324)18[4]			74(68–78)19[5, 7]			23(20–26)15[5]			445(393–670)40[9]		

Source: Data from Lorenz and Heinemann (1967, pp. 14, 18).

Note: Measurements given by Lorenz and Heinemann are not described. H. & T. is *Kopf-Rumpf*, or head and trunk combined and not equivalent to the standard combined head and body length measurement (see 1 below). Measurements for tail and ear lengths for young adults appear to be strictly comparable to those used in this work. Adult foot measurements were evidently taken from heel to tip of longest (middle) digit, without claw, or approximately 3 mm less than with claw. Maximum hind-foot length of 63 mm for young, however, is not comparable. The hind feet of newborn are disproportionately large and attain full size in the subadult stage.

* Indicates earliest age (in days) of attainment of adult size.

1. *Kopf-Rumpf* (= Head and trunk or H & T).

tific institutions was incidental or supplemental to investigations of the more abundant and prolific callitrichids used in biomedical research. The topics dealt with here are:

Dramatis Simiae	Food
Habitat	Drinking
Spatial Orientation	Foraging
Numbers and Visibility	Movements
Social Organization	Repose
Hierarchy	Display
Daily Rhythm	Temperament
Associations	Aggression
Care of Young	Fear
Sexual and Social Relations	Marking
Masturbation	Vocalization
Grooming	Thermoregulation

Dramatis Simiae

Blackie, an adult female, was purchased 27 November 1961 in Miami, Florida, by Mrs. Heike Heinemann (1970) and taken to Bloomington, Indiana. A mate, Devil, was acquired 14 May 1963, and both animals were taken to Germany "31 April, 1964." Blackie's sexual and social relations with Devil and other behavioral traits are related under appropriate headings. The history of her offspring has been given in the preceding sections.

Pepita, a young female callimico, was one of a pair espied by an Indian in April 1970, in a guava tree (*Inga edulis,* cultivated but not in fruit) near his hut on the banks of the Río Nanay, about 50 km southwest of Iquitos, Peru. The female was knocked out of the tree with a long rod, but her mate escaped into the forest. The captured animal was presented to Pekka Soini, a Finnish naturalist, and was kept in his home in Iquitos, where she had free run. Pepita died June 1970 from a bite inflicted on her chest and head by a tame short-eared fox (*Atelocynus microtis*). The skull, sent to the Field Museum along with the skin, bore signs of serious injuries. The right mandibular ramus was separated into two partially healed, abscessed fragments. The fracture may have been caused by a blow from the pole that felled Pepita from the guava tree. A second wound, a nearly closed puncture of the frontal bone below the left orbit, must have been inflicted much earlier, possibly by the fang of another callimico. A third abnormality is a deep depression with a puncture (or foramen?) of the ventral surface of the right tympanic bulla. I am unable to suggest a reason for the condition. A fourth set of fresh lesions, caused by the fox's bite, includes a broken left cheek bone and a fracture with perforation of the frontal bone at the angle of the frontoparietal sutures. Certain aspects of Pepita's behavior related to me by Mr. Soini (in litt., 28 June 1970) may have been more or less skewed or radically altered because of the earlier injuries.

The young male callimico observed by Küenzi (1958, p. xxxviii; 1960, p. xxxv) was kept as a household pet in Bern, Switzerland. He was acquired 17 January 1958 in good condition, with combined head and body length 220 mm; tail 300 mm, and weight, 7 February, 380 gm. The photographs (Küenzi 1958, pls. 1, 2) show what appears to be a three-quarter-grown individual.

Habitat

Nothing can be said of the habitat of *Callimico goeldii* in terms of niche, home range, or territory except that it lies within the tropical selva of the upper Amazonian region. Judging by the rarity of encounters, individuals seen in second-growth woods along roads, streams, clearings, or near houses are probably wanderers from the interior forests. During his travels in southeastern Colombia, Dr. Martin H. Moynihan (in litt., 11 March 1970) "saw a fair number of callimicos near Puerto Umbría, approximately half-way between Mocoa and Puerto Asis. They were in second growth mixed with abandoned plantations and imported Asiatic bamboos. The natives assured me that this species can also be found in mature forest."

Spatial Orientation

The young female callimico kept in Iquitos as a pet by Pekka Soini had opportunities for exercising on the same terrain and under conditions little modified from those where the species occurs naturally. Soini (in litt., 28 June 1970) observed that she always kept to the lower branches of the trees and descended frequently seeming to be more at home on the ground than other monkeys. She even descended to drink from a pool on the ground instead of licking moisture from the leaves as related callitrichids ordinarily do.

The Colombian naturalist, Dr. Jorge Hernández Camacho, also informed me that according to the Cofanes Indians of the Río Guamues, upper Río Putumayo, callimicos were often seen on the ground.

Lorenz 1972, pp. 94–95

"Normally *Callimico* will not spend much time on the ground. Goeldi's monkeys search there for food in the

2. Measurements from Lorenz and Heinemann (1967, p. 21).
3. *Scheitel-Steiss* (= crown-rump) equivalent to the standard combined head and body length used in my Tables of Measurements.
4. Head and Body (from Table of Measurements, p. 945), data compiled from specimens I examined.
5. From Table of Measurements, p. 945.
6. Hind Foot (HF) from back to heel to tip of middle digit, without claw.
7. Hind Foot (HF) to tip of claw.
8. Measurements from Lorenz and Heinemann (1967, p. 15).
9. Measurements from Lorenz and Heinemann (1967, pp. 16, 17) are means and extremes of 40 weight records of a breeding female taken from 12 January 1962 to 20 May 1965. Five births were given in the period; minimum weight followed a stillbirth 1 January 1964, maximum weight was registered 27 August 1968.

afternoon or early in the morning if their dishes are empty or if the food in the dish is spoiled; also infants descend regularly to the ground in exploratory behavior. In overheated cages the monkeys may sit on the floor. . . .

"The general avoidance of the ground by *Callimico* and the undesirability of having food near fecal materials caused us to place the food higher up in the cage (also see Hampton, *et al.,* 1965). We selected a small self-draining platform with ample sitting space. . . .

"Escaped *Callimico* in Louisiana invariably slept on heavy branches near the trunk of pine trees in 10–15 m (35–50 feet) height."

Numbers and Visibility

The geographic range of *Callimico goeldii* probably coincides with that of *Saguinus fuscicollis,* one of the best known, most widespread, and ubiquitous species of callitrichids. *Callimico,* in contrast, is one of the least known and most cryptic of platyrrhines. Until the last few years, none of the many trained naturalists and collectors of scientific specimens who explored the upper Amazonian region encountered a callimico, and none mentioned reports of its existence. Few native woodsmen and hunters who regularly stalk monkeys for food or trade have seen or known this animal. The Finnish naturalist Pekka Soini, a resident of Iquitos and a most valued correspondent, often saw the monkey brought to Iquitos by the Río Ucayali Indians, but, he informed me (in litt., 18 February 1970), the animal was unknown to the Indians of the Iquitos area and the Río Napo basin. After his discovery of callimicos along the Río Nanay near Iquitos, Soini wrote (in litt., 30 April 1970):

"During the last three years I spent many days and nights with my native Indian friend don Ramón on his hunting-grounds in the middle Río Nanay, west of Iquitos, but neither he nor his neighbors ever saw these monkeys before. Don Ramón who lived all his 36 years in the area recalled hearing rumors of the existence of a rarely-seen blackish monkey called *supai pichico* (devil tamarin). The description given him fitted the animal he had just captured alive."

The herpetologist Dr. Federico Medem, director of the Centro de Investigaciones Biológicas, Villavicencio, Colombia and an experienced Amazonian explorer, informed me (in litt., 1 November 1968) that the callimico he saw in the house of don Aniceto Fajardo of Araracuara, southeastern Colombia, was a novelty. "Sr. Fajardo himself and all others of the region including Indians from the Río Cahuinarí, the Río Mirití-Paraná and the lower Pirá-Paraná had either not seen this monkey before, or ever." Dr. Medem added that Sr. Novoa of Villavicencio, who spent 10 years crisscrossing the lower Caquetá region and its tributaries from La Tagua downstream, in search of jaguars and otters, never saw the monkey.

In my eleven years of fieldwork in South America, much of it in the upper Amazonian region of Colombia, Ecuador, and Peru, where *Callimico goeldii* might be present, I found no sign or heard no rumor of its existence. All other monkey species were common, well-known to everyone, and adequately represented in my collections.

The few callimicos seen in the Iquitos area and their very small representation among the thousands of primates annually shipped alive from Peru indicate a low population and a thin or scattered distribution, at least in Peru, Colombia, and no doubt Ecuador and Bolivia.

Some reasons may be adduced for the scarcity or low visibility of callimicos. *Callimico* produces only one young compared with the usual twinning of the numerous and highly visible callitrichids, and its gestation period is slightly longer. The animals evidently travel in small groups, perhaps only in pairs or small family units consisting of parents and one young. Their dark, shadowy figures, comparatively silent movements, infrequent vocalizations, cryptic habits, and less aggressive, more retiring nature—as compared with sympatric tamarins and squirrel monkeys—render them unobtrusive. The possibility that *Callimico* may be crepuscular or partially nocturnal, except perhaps in times of stress, and its very predaceous habits, must also be considered in accounting for its low visibility.

In sharp contrast to everything said above, F. C. Novaes and M. M. Moreira, who collected the two callimicos in the Territoria del Acre, extreme southwestern Brazil, recorded by Carvalho (1957, p. 5), report seeing "noisy bands of 30–40 individuals in the middle forest stratum about 4 meters above ground." Perhaps they exaggerated their count by a factor of 2 or more and mistook *Saguinus fuscicollis weddelli* for *Callimico goeldii.* The two have been confused before.

Social Organization

Lorenz 1972, pp. 97, 98

"The adult pair is the nucleus of a *Callimico* group, male and female having about equal rank; at least, there is no clear dominance of one sex. We have already mentioned that female and infant enjoy temporary privileges in gathering food. However, there are behavioral differences depending on sex. . . .

"*Callimico* has lived most peacefully and reproduced best if kept in pairs or families. Families have grown to five and six members. These large groups tended to show nervousness, higher than normal locomotor activity and aggression, developed digestive problems, failed to reproduce, and eventually collapsed. It was quite apparent that the oldest young challenged the parent of identical sex. The recommendation is to keep strictly not more than two offspring with the parents. Separation of the oldest can be delayed until the infant (third young) is weaned. Separation should occur in any case before the twentieth month of age. On the other hand, it appears desirable to let the juvenile experience delivery and infant care since studies of other species document the significance of such exposure. . . .

"In marmosets, owl monkeys (*Aotus*), and titi monkeys (*Callicebus*), there is no good evidence that not more than one female and male per group are *breeding* and *rearing.* Most groups composed of more unrelated adults than one male and one female finally broke apart when the first birth took place. It should be obvious that nothing can be gained if more adults than one heterosexual pair are kept together. . . .

"*Callimico* integrate familiar human beings in their social system; any change of attending personnel is a disturbance."

Hierarchy

Lorenz 1972, pp. 97, 98

"The high-ranking female initiates sexual behavior; it does address only to the high-ranking male. If the female considers the keeper the high-ranking male, she will address herself only to him whereas her con-specific male is disregarded and must feel suppressed. If the keeper is a girl, the male will be automatically high-ranking. Since the female keeper does not show any behavior typical of the high-ranking female (*e. g.*, permanent presence, high scent marking activity, initiation of sexual behavior or interference at copulations), there cannot be a severe effect on the female monkey.

"In one case, a second unrelated mature female lived with the breeding pair. After delivery, both adult females fought and the second female had to be separated. It was successfully reintroduced a little later. In another case, a second unrelated mature male lived with the breeding pair. The three adults lived in a large compound, and the second male was clearly peripheral to the pair."

Daily Rhythm

Soini's pet callimico, Pepita, awoke at daybreak, or slightly before 6:00 A.M. in the equatorial latitude of Iquitos. His other monkey pets (*Cebuella, Saguinus, Saimiri, Callicebus, Pithecia*) arose about the same time. All enjoyed complete freedom or were tied to long leashes. None was caged. Pepita spent the first 2 or 3 hours foraging, but the other monkeys continued active until 11:00 A.M. or later. Pepita resumed her activities toward nightfall about 6:00 P.M. and continued hunting and eating insects until 9:00 or 10:00 P.M., long after the other monkeys had retired for the night. Soini got the impression that Pepita could see well in nearly complete darkness, but he made no tests except to note that the callimico's eyes did not reflect torchlight in the dark. The eyes of the true night monkey, *Aotus trivirgatus,* also lack reflectance. In sum, the callimico was said to be more active during the night and less active during the day than all other members of Soini's monkey menage.

Blackie, Mrs. Heinemann's (1970) original callimico, began her day at 10:00 A.M. when she quit her sleeping box for a pair of bamboo poles held between two floor-to-ceiling metal rods by a window side.

Blackie's first toilet consisted of urinating, defecating, and grooming. A high-pitched, keening call was uttered during the morning, and only faint chirping noises were made at times during the rest of the day. Blackie napped at noon and spent many hours of the day sitting in her sleeping box. She returned for the night about 22:00 hours.

During a holiday, Blackie was taken by Mrs. Heinemann to a summer cottage with a screened-in porch. After a few days Mrs. Heinemann discovered to her surprise that Blackie was in the habit of escaping to the porch at night by climbing through the open window of her room. She never did this during the day.

The large eyes of *Callimico goeldii* do indeed suggest crepuscular or nocturnal habits, but my observations of laboratory callimicos do not bear this out. Crepuscular mammals, however, readily adjust in captivity to regimens imposed by their keepers. The night monkey (*Aotus trivirgatus*) in captivity as a pet, and often in zoos, becomes of necessity diurnal. In contrast to *Callimico,* the little night monkey is well known to natives wherever it occurs.

Küenzi's (1958, p. xxxviii) callimico, a young male, was differently but nevertheless concordantly attuned to his cultural surroundings. He was strictly diurnal, somewhat apathetic in the early morning, but very active between noon and late afternoon, when he received most attention.

Associations

According to Dr. Jorge Hernández Camacho, callimicos in the upper Río Putumayo region were seen in association with *Saguinus fuscicollis fuscus.* During my survey of the mammals between the upper Ríos Caquetá and Putumayo, I met many bands of *Saguinus fuscicollis fuscus* but saw no callimicos.

Care of Young

Heinemann 1970, p. 76

"During the first few days Blackie [the mother] moved carefully with her burden. Whenever Ebony wanted to nurse or just shift position, Blackie sat down and assisted the baby's movements with her arms. She sometimes twisted her head to give Ebony a short lick and groomed the infant daily, while Devil [the father] groomed them both. . . .

"During the third week Blackie tried to get the baby off her back. She rubbed herself against the walls of the cage and attempted to roll on her back. This caused Ebony to wail. Immediately, Devil went over and stood over them in semi-erect posture, licking Ebony, until finally the baby climbed on his back. From that day on Blackie tolerated the baby for nursing only. . . ."

"Devil was a good father. He licked Ebony occasionally on the cheek and permitted her to take tidbits from his hands. Often he offered her food by holding his hand out while whistling through his teeth."

At ten weeks of age Ebony "had been weaned and was apparently becoming too heavy for Devil. . . . Though he still permitted her to take her naps clinging to him and to jump on his back whenever she was frightened he now grabbed her tail and bit it to get her off his back.

Lorenz 1972, p. 98

"We had one breeding male who became so protective after carrying the baby that he would attack mother, caretaker, and scientist. After losing the first baby to starvation, he was separated for the following three births 24 hours after the baby was seen exclusively on his back. The male was kept in a small cage, 1 x 0.5 x 0.5 m (40 x 40 x 20 inches) within the breeding cage and released as soon as the infant began traveling independently and eating solid food. Although the mother, following the separation, was initially reluctant, she carried and cared well for the infant. From the second baby on the older juvenile assumed part of the parental duties.

"On another occasion, the breeding male died when the female was pregnant with delivery only one month away. Birth and rearing took place without complication. At the peak of the fourth estrus following delivery, a new adult male was introduced. The two offspring in the cage strongly rejected this male. The older one even bit the male's hands, when the baby once approached him, but quickly returned to the mother upon recognizing its misake. The male, however, did not respond to this but focused his attention on the female. Likewise, the female was interested in him, but tried to protect the young whenever the male came close. The same afternoon the female maneuvered both young in one corner and went over to the male. Repeated copulations were observed which resulted in a new pregnancy. After several days the male was fully accepted and cared excellently for the young. . . .

"Pregnant and infant-carrying females are allowed first choice and take food away from the male, the same is true for infants as long as they are carried and casually later on."

Hershkovitz (Notes)

It has been established that the mother alone cares for the baby during the first two to four weeks of life (C. A. Hill 1966; Heinemann 1970; Lorenz 1970*a*; Heltne, Turner, and Wolhandler 1973). Thereafter the father, or other adult or older sibling, takes over and carries the offspring except when it is nursed by the mother. Evidently, the mother is capable of coping with a single young until its weight, increasing activity, and greater diversity of movement impel her to seek relief. The callitrichid mother, as a rule, does little more than give birth and nurse the young while the father takes care of the babies from the day of birth, often assisting in the parturition and cleaning of the newborn.

The difference in the number of young produced at a birth by callimicos and callitrichids does not explain the difference in parental behavior. A large proportion of callitrichid litters are of singletons. Body mass is no factor either. Callimicos average slightly larger than most tamarins and smaller than lion-tamarins. It may be significant that in the single case where the father began carrying a 2-week-old callimico (Lorenz 1970*a*), the latter died of starvation because the former did not surrender the infant to its mother for nursing.

More on infant-parent relations is given in the section Growth and Development (p. 899).

Sexual and Social Relations

The first encounter between Blackie and her mate Devil is described by Mrs. Heinemann (1970, pp. 73, 74).

"The moment the two monkeys saw each other their hair stood on end and they uttered calls of excitement. Blackie circled the cage often and did not groom herself as usual that morning. In the afternoon I took her out for some time and when we returned she immediately jumped on to the cage. There she stood rigid, her back arched, her hair erected and her tail hanging down, the upper part of it pulled tight against her feet. Devil, too, was very excited and tried to get into mating position, but I took Blackie away as the male had not been checked for parasites."

After a separation while Devil was being cured of worms and an eye infection, the two callimicos were again brought together. "At the beginning, everytime Blackie looked in Devil's direction she pulled down her forehead and flicking her tongue rapidly over her nose, with her mouth nearly closed. (The female Goeldi marmoset in Frankfurt Zoo did the same thing when I watched her for a short while after she had been put in a cage with a newly-acquired male). As Blackie could enter Devil's cage at will after the worming she joined him a few times daily and offered herself for mating. But as he was so weak he usually did not respond and once I saw her bite him as a result. He immediately pulled down his forehead and flicked his tongue while Blackie froze in the mating position. This behaviour seems to be their reaction to differences of opinion. At first it occurred daily but as the weeks went by we saw it less and less often. Very often, after leaving Devil's cage, Blackie went to the mirror and pulled down her forehead."

"When I wanted to comb [Devil], Blackie tried to shield his body with hers and even attempted to bite me."

When Blackie became pregnant, Devil was more attentive. He let her groom herself longer and demanded less attention for himself. He checked Blackie's fur daily, cleaned her slightly swollen teats, and let her take tidbits from his hands.

Epple (1967*b*) compared the sexual behavior of 2 ♂♂/1 ♀ callimicos in the Frankfurt am Main and the Cologne Zoos and 3/3 in Mrs. Heike Heinemann's collection. She noted that, as in *Callithrix jacchus*, the female curled her tail, saturated it with urine and secretions from her circumgenital glands, while the male sniffed tail, genitalia, and face of his mate.

Masturbation

A subadult female I observed in the Brookfield Zoo in 1965 was attracted by the warmth of a photographic floodlamp placed near her cage. The animal cuddled up to the fixture as near as the bars permitted and, judging by her nearly limp body and glazed, half-closed eyes, derived intense pleasure from the warmth of the lamp. After a few minutes of exposure, she retired to her perch in the farthest corner of the cage and sat there kittenlike on her haunches, with tail hanging straight down. Moments later she coiled her tail while bringing it upward and forward between her legs and then brushed the coil vigorously against her belly and perineal region for a few seconds. The action was repeated at irregular intervals varying from about 25 seconds to 3 minutes. The entire operation lasted about 10 minutes. The stroke of the coiled tail was forward and backward against the lower ventral surface of the body. The number of strokes was usually three or four. Between frications, the tail remained either coiled ventrally or hanging freely distally.

Apparently, the warmth of the lamp and perhaps the stimulating effect of a playback of a recording of her own voice induced masturbation with the coiled tail. Titillation of the external genitalia and sexual skin with the coiled tail has been observed in callitrichids, but not with the orgiastic pleasure evinced by this callimico.

Grooming

Self- and social grooming seen in callimicos is practiced by monkeys generally. The habit of using the feet to scratch all parts of the body within reach is likewise common to all monkeys and to most clawed mammals.

Soini (in litt.) mentions that he did not see Pepita grooming. This is not to say that the callimico did not groom herself.

Lorenz (1972, p. 105) notes that "copulation was regularly followed by intensive self grooming in both sexes; the partners sit near each other."

Food

Pepita was extremely thin and suffered from diarrhea when Soini (in litt., 30 April 1970) brought her to Iquitos from the Río Nanay. At first she ate crickets, dragonflies, cockroaches, and other insects but refused or reluctantly ate bananas, bread, and cooked meat. Later, she accepted small pieces of boiled or fried meat and chicken, bananas, juicy fruits, milk, cereals, and bread. She ignored nuts and palm fruits, and caught no ants of any kind, although a pet saki (*Pithecia monacha*), with whom she got along well, ate the large black arboreal ants daily.

The Araracuara callimico seen in Señor Fajardo's house by Medem (in litt., 1 November 1968) "lived under the thatched roof eating insects, mostly spiders." He also ate table scraps and lapped water from a bowl (fig. XII.25).

Fig. XII.25. Callimico (*Callimico goeldii*), domesticated in region of capture near Puerto Arturo, Río Caquetá, Colombia; eating and drinking catlike without use of hands. (Photo courtesy of Frederick Medem.)

Küenzi's (1958) callimico used both hands for seizing food. Liquids were lapped cat-fashion, the rim of the bowl held with both hands. After eating, the callimico cleaned his nose on some rough object such as bark and then sneezed lightly.

A wild-caught pair of callimicos studied by Lorenz (1971) in the Delta Regional Primate Research Center immediately attacked and devoured between them an eastern ribbon snake (*Thamnophis sauritus*) introduced into their cage. Other wild-born callimicos noticed snakes placed in their cage but evinced little interest. Laboratory-bred and wild-caught callimicos in the same colony preyed regularly on anoles, ground skinks, and five-lined skinks. Frogs up to about 4.5 cm in length, representing all local species, were likewise devoured head first, as usual.

Blackie, Mrs. Heinemann's (1970) first female breeder, was fed bananas, apples, grapes, raisins, bread, raw egg yolk, and up to 50 mealworms daily. Later, ground beef, mice, and lizards were given.

An individual kept by Lorenz (1969) in his office, where it had free run, was maintained on a diet of which more than 50% was protein. Locusts, grasshoppers, minced meat, young mice, and chicks were mainstays. Heads, wings, and legs of the insects were discarded, the rest eaten. Live mice were devoured whole, beginning with the snout and working down to the tail. Freshly killed chicks were also eaten beak first, but often the head alone satisfied the callimico. The monkey caught and ate flies and crickets by himself. Coccinellid imagos were distasteful and were rejected after the first bite, which caused profuse salivation. A butterfly (*Vanessa io*) was gripped, sniffed, and thrown away. He also ignored or rejected the offering of a snail (*Arianta*), slug (*Arion*), and millipede. Fruits, vegetables, and bread were also fed to the animal. It lapped up water in copious quantities, and vitamin D_3 was administered in large doses to facilitate calcium absorption.

Lorenz (1969, p. 151) notes particularly that "once a lizard was killed by a bite in the neck, but it was afterwards thrown away." He concludes that "*Callimico* learns to eat lizards by imitating wild-caught specimens. Lizards, of course, are a favorite food of wild *Callimico*."

Possibly his overfed, overly fat [cf. p. 00] callimico was sated and killed wantonly. In any case, in the sentences immediately following the above quotation, Lorenz (1969, p. 151) avers that "a female exotic finch that was offered was caught, killed by bites into the brain, and only the head eaten. *This was the first time that our male Callimico had encountered an adult bird dead or alive* [italics mine]."

Lorenz 1969, p. 152

"Two pieces of tomato [eaten by my pet male *Callimico* produced regurgitation."

Lorenz 1972, p. 99

"I have fed pieces of tomato repeatedly without observing consequent regurgitation (Lorenz 1969)."

Lorenz 1972, p. 97

"Both cockroaches, the large *Periplaneta americana* and the small *Blatta germanica,* have caused sudden collapse or shock after *Callimico* and *Callicebus* have taken a mouthful. The animal commonly cries, falls to the ground, regurgitates, seems to suffocate and lacks all motor control. Recovery occurred always within minutes and no lasting consequences seemed to result. Both species also take in long-legged spiders (Opilionidae) and we cannot exclude the possibility that massive ingestion has a similar effect."

Lorenz 1972, p. 99

"We now tend to believe that almost any food can be digested if the animal is psychologically balanced."

Drinking

Lorenz 1969, p. 153

"Normally, *Callimico* drinks by lapping clear water. . . . The water is changed daily and is available throughout the day. Despite this, our male on one occasion licked all the drops of condensation from the windows for about 3 m; and it likes to drink water from the humidity cans. Because the slot in the can is so narrow, it inserts one hand through the slot and licks the water from its hand. Milk and lemonade are also taken, but only very small amounts are offered."

Foraging

Lorenz 1969, p. 154

"*Callimico* is very interested in dark slits, crevices, holes and the undersides of tins, papers and boxes. It always tries to look underneath or behind the object and to achieve this it sometimes has to turn its head and shoulders through 180° so that they lie on the table or floor, while the hind legs rest quite normally, the tail being pressed against the ground. Because of this the hairs on the crown of the head are often dusty. The behaviour seems to be innate stemming from searching activities for insect prey. As far as I can judge, *Callimico* depends primarily on its ears when hunting. Having heard a sound, it then tries to locate the source with its eyes. When it is chasing its prey it relies mainly on its eyes."

"In proportion to its size, *Callimico* transports large quantities of food (for example, eight mealworms, six morsels of breakfast cereal or four cubes of banana from one place to a more convenient one, feeding there on one piece of food at a time. The food is carried either in the mouth or in one hand. *Callimico* is able to put the medial aspect of the fist and the arm together, thus forming a small platform on which the food is placed."

Movements

I had the opportunity to observe a caged subadult female in the Brookfield Zoo shortly after she had been acquired in November 1965 from a dealer in Florida.

Her mien was alert, her movements quick. She ran, bounded, and maneuvered with the ease, agility, and grace of a kitten. The head, nevertheless, made the jerky movements characteristic of callitrichids and could be turned nearly 180° in either direction, for looking over the shoulder. The thumbs were not used in any special manner but simply reinforced the function of the other fingers of the hand. The tail usually hung limp when the animal rested but was swung about as a balancing organ in leaping.

Other callimicos I observed were restrained in their movements because of the small cages in which they were kept. Compared with callitrichids in the same kinds of cages in the same rooms, callimico limb movements appeared to be more deliberate and fluid, less jerky or springy.

Pepita's movements were described by Soini as very tamarinlike but less agile and less abrupt, with less jumping. She seemed to be more at home on the ground than any of the other monkeys observed and often spent long periods exploring the underbrush and basking on the ground. She always kept to the lower parts of trees and descended to drink from a pool instead of licking moisture from leaves.

At first, Küenzi's callimico climbed with caution in his new quarters, testing the strength of each branch or crosspiece with his teeth. The thinnest branches were avoided. Once oriented, however, he jumped confidently from branch to branch. His greatest leap measured 120 cm across and 26 cm high.

Unlike Soini's Pepita, Küenzi's callimico was uncomfortable on the ground, and his movements there compared with those of a hare or kangaroo.

Repose

As told by Soini (in litt., 28 June 1970), Pepita enjoyed sun basking and sometimes relaxed completely by letting arms and legs dangle from her perch.

Soini complained that he could not induce his callimico to play.

Lorenz 1972, p. 95

"Sprawling in a prone position as reported in *Callicebus* was not observed."

Hershkovitz (Notes)

A solitary callimico I observed asleep was in a sitting or crouched posture with tail coiled and drawn between the legs and pressed against the belly. A family group I saw in the outdoor monkey colony of the San Diego Zoo slept with young atop mother, and father covered both with his body. Mrs. Heinemann's house-kept callimicos slept inside the nest box. The San Diego callimicos slept outside the nest box in their outdoor cage.

Sprawling in a prone position is often used during the siesta hour. It is also a comfortable position for being groomed (fig. XII.26).

Fig. XII.26. *Callimico goeldii* resting. (Photo courtesy of Gisela Epple.)

Display

Erectibility of head, trunk, and tail hairs is highly developed in *Callimico,* more so than I observed in other monkeys. Judging from reports, piloerection is an expression of aggression or excitement correlated with fear, threat, or courtship.

Ear twitching, or laying back of the ears, was not seen in *Callimico.*

Brow beetling is variously interpreted as an expression of threat, perplexity, or curiosity. Callimicos use this facial expression for almost anything holding their attention and with much greater frequency than callitrichids, with which direct comparisons were made under identical conditions. In the Houston colony, a callimico beetled its brow with the frequency and facility of a cebid whereas a cotton-top tamarin in the same cage did not lower its brow once during the hour I watched both animals.

Tongue flicking, the rhythmic protrusion and retraction of the tongue between the lips performed by many kinds of monkeys to express a low-keyed response to conspecifics or familiar animals or people, may differ slightly in function and meaning from species to species. Mrs. Heinemann observed the frequent tongue flicking by her callimicos in social, sexual, and other contact situations. Lorenz (1972) regards it as an invitation to copulation, mainly by females and as a signal of appeasement in situations where direct eye contact alone implies aggression. The usual display of tongue flicking, according to Lorenz (1972), consists of bursts of 5 to 8 protrusions at a rate of 3 to 4 per second.

Temperament

Hershkovitz (Notes)

Callimico tames readily and appears to be one of the most docile, trusting, and inquisitive of platyrrhines. This is my impression of the score or more callimicos I have seen in zoos and laboratories, and the consensus of other observers.

My first entrance into a roomful of mixed species of caged callitrichids and callimicos always caused great excitement among the former but comparatively little disturbance to the latter. If anything, it seemed that the callimicos were more confused by the agitated chattering and movements of their relatives than alarmed by the intrusion.

Aggression

Lorenz 1972, p. 104

"During estrus, the male protects its home range and the female more strongly than usual. Aggression is directed towards keeper and scientist. The male always tends to be between the female and the source of competition or disturbance. If the female gets closer, he jumps right across her. This hopping over each other is quite characteristic of defensive behavior and not limited to estrus. The female may "drum" with her hands on his back which magnifies his emotion, or keep jumping over him until he becomes impatient and either slaps or bites her, thus causing her withdrawal. However, such action is rare and commonly the female retreats after being sure the male is on guard."

Fear

Pepita reacted to curious dogs or cats by erecting the hair of her head, body, and tail, arching her back, and jumping stiff-legged toward the intruder. If this approach failed to intimidate the adversary, Pepita turned tail and ran for the nearest tree.

Mrs. Heinemann's Blackie was excited by children, cats, and dogs seen through the window. Her hair stood on end and she uttered *chuck, chuck, chuck* calls. Devil, the mate acquired later, was the more aggressive of the two and in threat situations took up a protective position in front of the female.

The callimico observed by Küenzi was not afraid of people, including strangers, but the sight of a cat or dog made him utter a shrill cry. Even a dog seen from afar frightened him. Excitement usually provoked diarrhea in the callimico.

Lorenz 1969, p. 151

"On the few occasions that live chicks were offered [for food], the [pet] male *Callimico* [free-living in my office] showed an interest and tried to bite the chick, but each time the chicks' chirping produced a fear reaction, causing it to rush into its sleeping box."

Marking

The sternal gland is well developed and extensive in both sexes of adults and young. It plays a particular role in territorial marking, according to Epple and Lorenz (1967). As C. A. Hill (1966, p. 16) demonstrated, the entire body of the newborn callimico may be anointed by the odoriferous secretions of the mother's sternal gland. Heinemann (1970) does not mention the gland involved, but after she separated her callimicos into two colonies, they used secretions of the sternal gland "to cover all the porches and poles [for perching and climbing] heavily with a light brown smear which [Mrs. Heinemann] had to remove every few days since it made the cage look dirty."

Lorenz (1969) noted the strong body odor of his pet callimico and the animal's use of urine for marking.

Vocalization

Vocalization by the lone subadult female callimico I observed in the Brookfield Zoo was quite like that of callitrichids. Most of the sounds were uttered with mouth closed. The call usually consisted of an irregular series of high, evenly pitched and sustained notes, now and then interrupted by a more highly pitched note or call or a long trill, this time with mouth open. When excited by unusual noises, the animal responded with a lower-pitched and throaty call resembling a bark. This sound was uttered with mouth closed. The playing back of a tape recording of the callimico's own sounds created considerable excitement. The animal first jumped and ran frantically about her cage, evidently in search of the source of the call. She then sat on her perch and with head tilted back, mouth agape, responded with a series of piercing calls. The wide repertory of sounds emitted by the callimico with closed mouth may include many pitched at frequencies unperceived and unsuspected by the observer or possible predators.

The callitrichidlike twitters uttered by callimicos kept in the colony of the University of Texas Dental Branch in Houston were answered by two tamarins (*Saguinus fuscicollis nigrifrons* and *S. oedipus oedipus*) caged together about 40 feet away at the time I visited the establishment.

Küenzi (1958) mentioned the birdlike twitterings of satisfaction or shrill cries of distress sounded by his callimicos.

Epple (1968) attempted to analyze the vocal repertory of the callimicos of Mrs. Heike Heinemann's colony. The recordings were unsatisfactory because of resonance and background noises, and the living arrangements of the animals impeded all but a few tests. As a result, the fruits of the investigations were not strictly comparable to those obtained from callitrichids.

The callimico vocal repertory, sound qualities, pitch, and rhythms were described as much more varied than those of the callitrichids studied. The calls were said to be less specific with reference to particular situations and their social significance obscure. Very likely, the closely knit, insulated, and thoroughly Heinemann-conditioned callimicos studied by Epple required little in the way of special calls to signal their acts, needs, and intentions. Many of the calls heard may have been simple exercises of no social significance whatsoever, and others may have been uttered for solace or self-assurance.

Epple (1968, p. 33) was impressed with a *tschog* sound given in excitement and uttered with greater frequency as the excitement increased. "No call of similar phonetical character was ever heard in the other species studied here." A second peculiarity noted was absence of the series of *tsik* calls (cf. p. 564) characteristic of callitrichids. Rhythmic calls given in isolation were similar to those of *Leontopithecus rosalia,* and long series of trills emitted in high excitement resembled those made by *Saguinus oedipus.*

Andrew (1963, p. 46) recorded and analized the peculiar "chatters." These "consisted of bouts of five or more calls (1/0.10–0.12 sec[onds]) (F[undamental]: 4–4.5 Kc. to 6 Kc. (0.02 sec.) and then equally steep descent. N[oise]: horizontal prolongation of inflection (0.10 sec. E[nergy distribution]: 8–12 Kc. more marked than F]. The inflection point usually had the same pitch throughout the bout, but occasionally it descended and then rose.

"Chatters were given in defense with a slight opening of the mouth. They clearly correspond to twitter bouts, differing only in the presence of noise."

Thermoregulation

Lorenz 1972, p. 94

"*Callimico* slept alone or in a cluster on a board at temperatures as low as 0° C (32° F) and remained in excellent health. It is necessary that this place be dry and protected from draft. On one occasion, a *Callimico* was found immobilized at −6° C (21° F) with the time of exposure being unknown. It quickly revived at 25° C (77° F) room temperature and being placed on a heating pad without any resulting sickness. . . .

"Although we have no physiological data (except frequency of respiration) our observations suggest that metabolism is reduced during sleep. One can easily approach the monkeys at night. If awakened they are disoriented and require seconds to regain their normal reaction."

Lorenz 1972, p. 96

"If a preferable ambient temperature cannot be found, *Callimico* shows distinct behavioral reactions. In temperatures above 28° C (82° F), the general activity decreases and the animals sprawl, often with their limbs hanging loosely on either side of the branch (see also Hampton, *et al.,* 1966). In temperatures between 35° C (95° F) and 38° C (101° F), *Callimico* becomes lethargic. In temperatures lower than 21° C (70° F) the monkeys move as high as possible and eventually enter the nest box. If this proves insufficient, they sit with the tail pulled between the legs and arms and curled closing the gap between arms and chest. This behavior retains the warmth that is otherwise lost from the thinly haired underside of the body and inner aspect of the limbs. Often two or more monkeys huddle side by side (see also Hampton, *et al.,* 1966). At this temperature, *Callimico*'s activity is diminished. The narrow range of ambient temperatures comfortable for a tropical animal of this body size and this high a metabolism must be expected."

Küenzi (1960) mentions that his pet callimico became accustomed to low temperatures in the house and withstood night temperature of 14° C with no discomfort.

Gazetteer

Callitrichid and Callimiconid
Collecting Localities

Collecting localities of callitrichids and callimiconids recorded in the literature and on labels of museum specimens I examined are listed below in alphabetical order, each with its key number. These numbers refer to the same localities plotted on the master map (fig. XIII.2), three regional maps (figs. XIII.3–5), and in the gazetteer that follows. The same numbers are used to identify the localities plotted on the distribution maps in the text. Compare the plotted distribution of the Callitrichidae and Callimiconidae (fig. XIII.2) with the general distribution of living New World monkeys (fig. XIII.1).

The locality names are those provided by the collector on the original specimen labels. Most of the names agree with those found in official gazetteers and maps. The animals, however, were actually taken in near or distant forests. The official spelling of place names is used here, but other spellings or misspellings recorded in the scientific literature are also given with pertinent cross references.

The geographic coordinates shown for collecting localities are in most cases those given in the gazetteers of the United States Board on Geographic Names, prepared by the Office of Geography, Department of the Interior, Washington, D.C. Places no longer extant or place names no longer in use have been located on old, usually obsolete maps or determined from itineraries or reports of collectors or from various other reliable sources or clues. The Millionth Map of the American Geographical Society has been particularly useful for locating or plotting defunct place names. A number of modern large-scale official maps of Latin American countries have also been consulted. Apparent discrepancies between geographic coordinates given here and the points they define on current reference maps may be due to differences between the relative accuracy of maps used for plotting localities or to the distance between the actual geographic coordinates of a town or site given in an official gazetteer used for reference and the actual place or area where the animal was probably collected.

Fig. XIII.1. Distribution of living monkeys of the families Callitrichidae, Callimiconidae, and Cebidae (infraorder Platyrrhini). Only cebids occur in the northern and southern extremes of the range of the infraorder. The range of the Callimiconidae is also occupied by cebids and callitrichids. The distribution of the Callitrichidae is interrupted in Venezuela and northeastern Colombia.

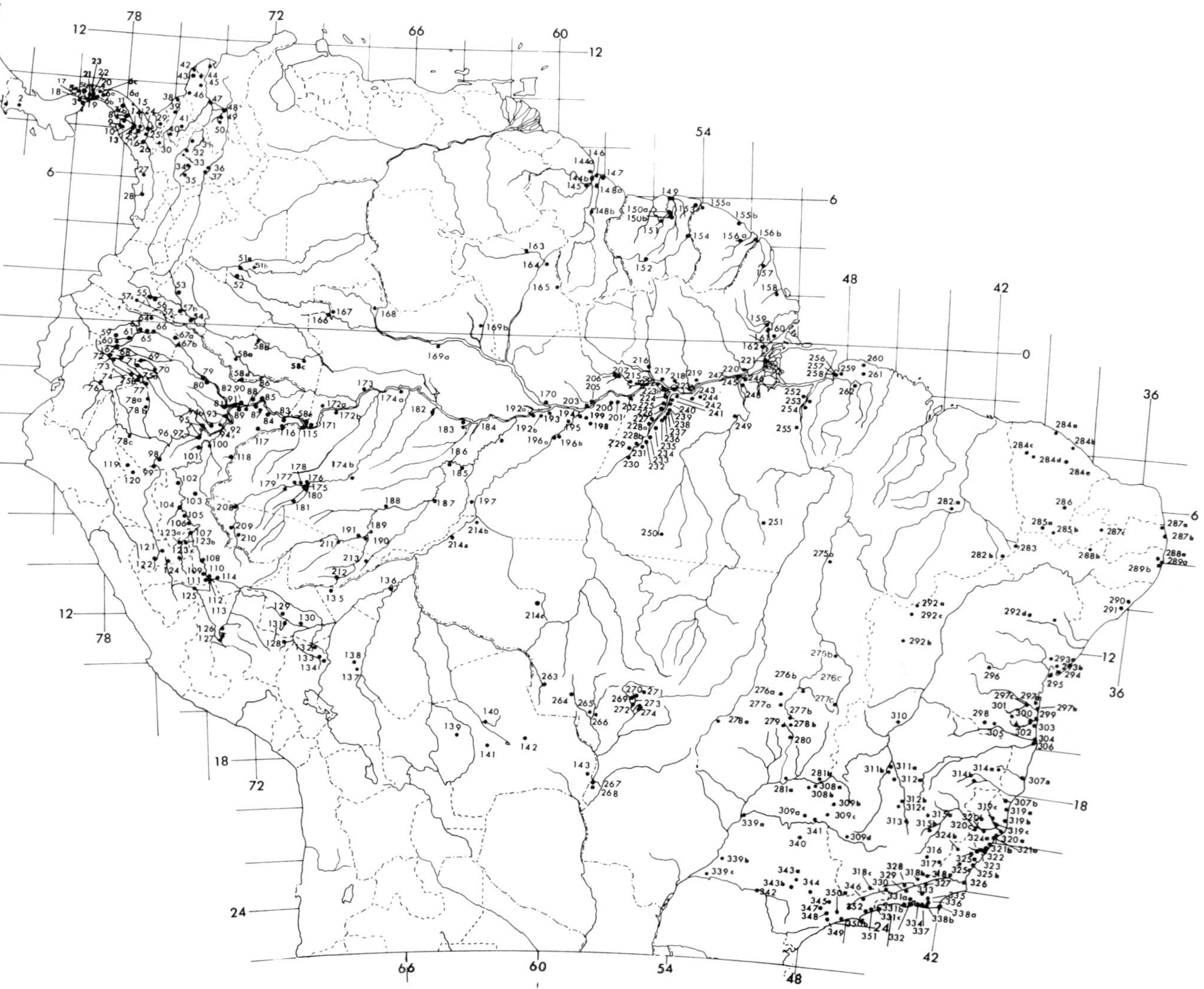

Fig. XIII.2. Callitrichid and callimico collecting and sight localities in South and Central America. The numbers with locality names, geographic coordinates, and collecting data are listed in the gazetteer (p. 924); see also fig. XIII.3 for the localities in Panamá and adjacent parts of Colombia, fig. XIII.4 for localities in upper Amazonia, and fig. XIII.5 for those of the lower Rio Tapajóz, Pará, Brazil.

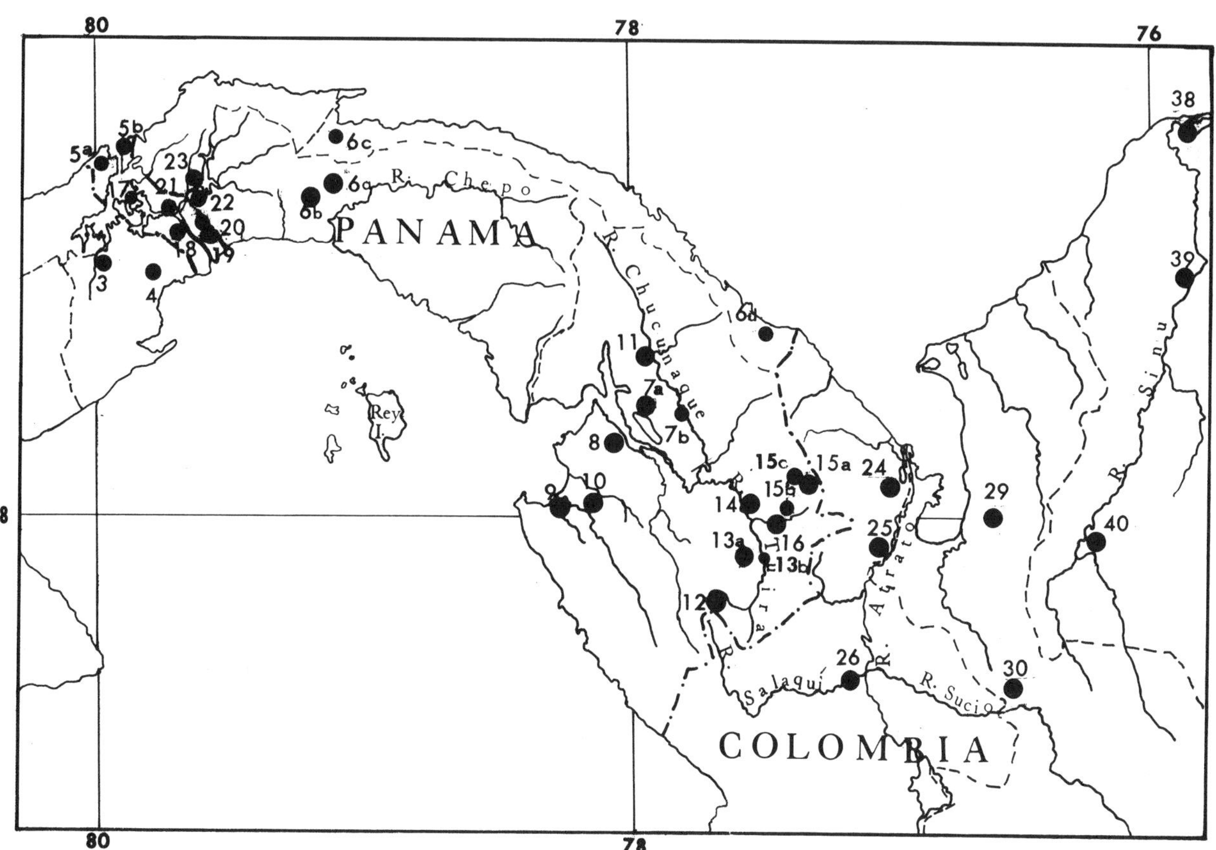

Fig. XIII.3. Collecting localities in Panamá and bordering parts of Colombia; for locality names and data see corresponding numbers in gazetteer (p. 924).

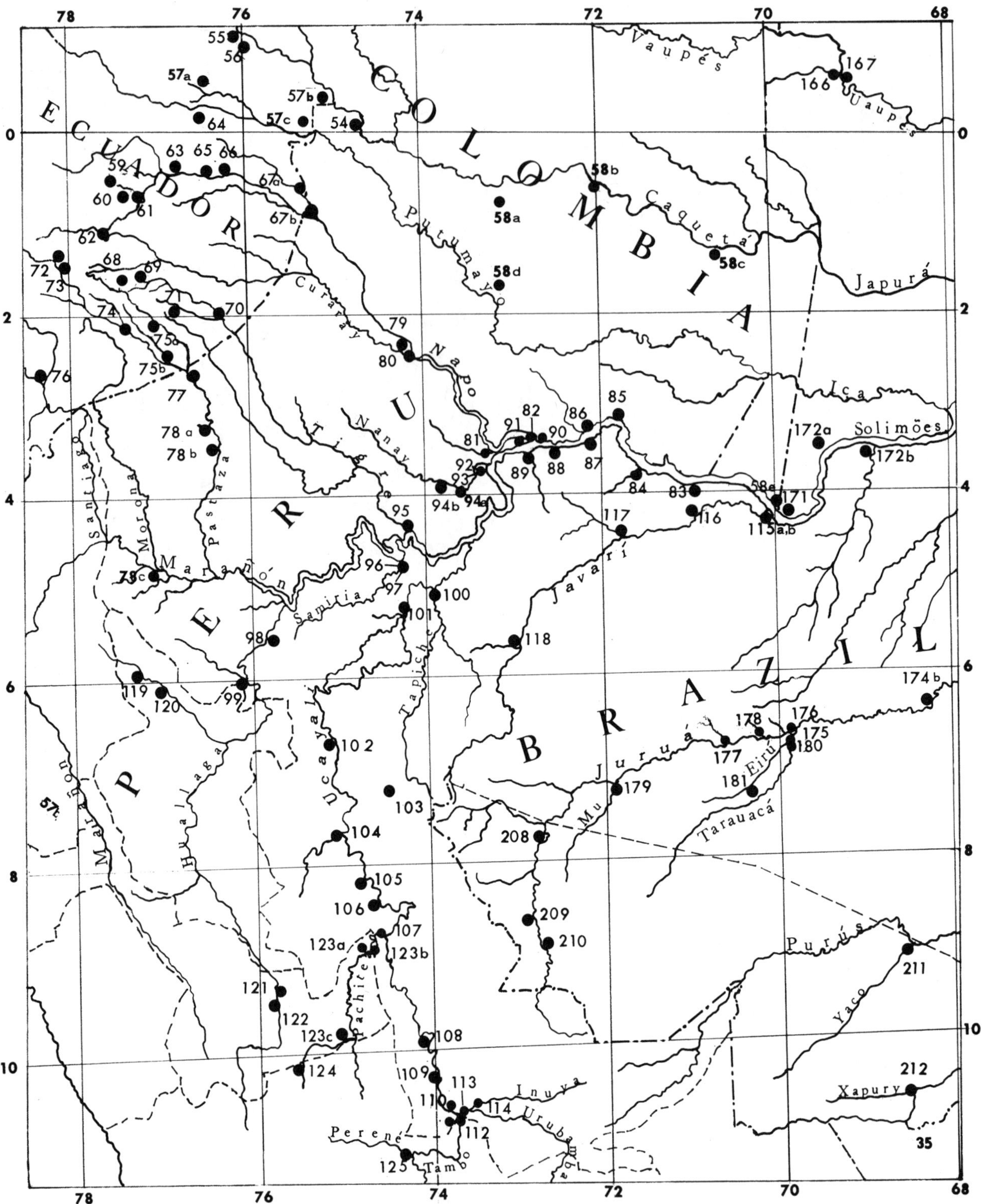

Fig. XIII.4. Collecting localities in upper Amazonian region of Ecuador, parts of Colombia, Peru and Brazil; for locality names and data see corresponding numbers in gazetteer (p. 924).

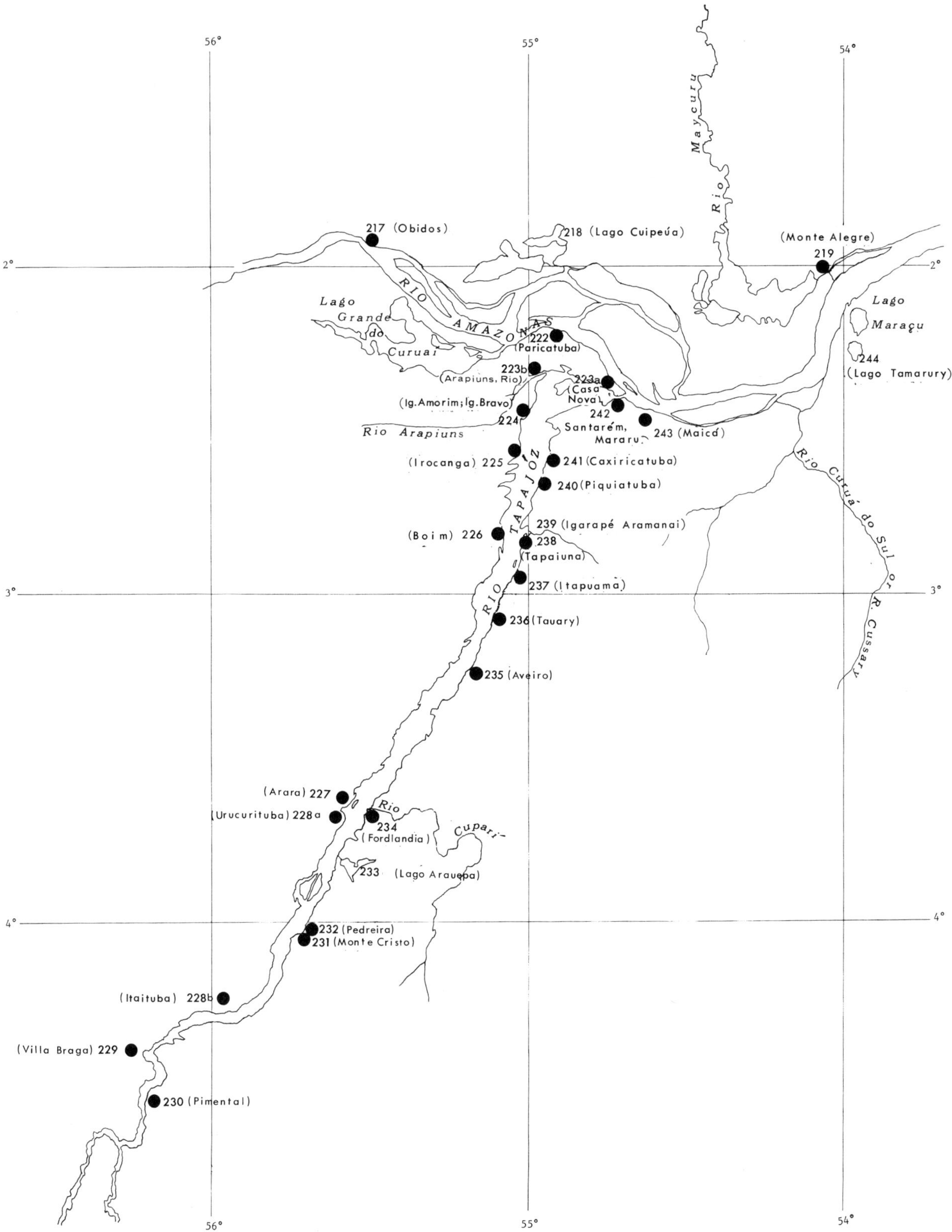

Fig. XIII.5. Collecting localities along the lower Rio Tapajóz, Pará, Brazil; for locality names and data see corresponding numbers in gazetteer (p. 924).

Key to Collecting Localities

(See Gazetteer, p. 924, for geographic coordinates and collector's data. Species and collection data for indefinite or undetermined localities are given below.)

Acre (Rio), Rio Purús; Amazonas, Brazil (190).
Açu (Igarapé); Pará, Brazil (260).
Agua Blanca; Canal Zone; Panamá (21).
Agua Caliente, Río Pachitéa; Huánuco, Peru (123a).
Água Limpa; Minas Gerais, Brazil (318a).
Água Suja (Romaria); Minas Gerais, Brazil (309c).
Água Viva; Minas Gerais, Brazil (318a).
Aguarico (Río); Loreto, Peru (67b).
Aguarico (Río); Napo-Pastaza, Ecuador (67b).
Aguas Buenas; Canal Zone, Panamá (21).
Alajuela; Canal Zone, Panamá (23).
Albrook Air Force Base; Canal Zone, Panamá (19).
Aldeia Velha (Rio); Rio de Janeiro, Brazil (336).
Alegre; Espírito Santo, Brazil (325c).
Além Paraiba; Minas Gerais, Brazil (318a).
Alfredo Chavez; Espírito Santo, Brazil (325a).
Almada (Fazenda); Bahia, Brazil (299).
Almas (Rio das); Goiás, Brazil (276b).
Alpayacu, Río Pastaza; Napo-Pastaza, Ecuador (72).
Altamira, Río Manú; Madre de Dios, Peru (129).
Altamira, Rio Xingu; Pará, Brazil (249).
Alto Caño Itilla, upper Río Vaupés; Vaupés, Colombia (52).
Alto da Serra; São Paulo, Brazil (350).
Amapá; Amapá, Brazil (158).
Amapari (Rio), Macapá; Amapá, Brazil (159).
Amarin (Igarapé), Rio Tapajóz; Pará, Brazil (224).
Amazonas (Rio); Pará, Brazil.
Saguinus midas niger
F. Lima; E. Heller, May 1923.
Amorin; Pará, Brazil (224).
Ananindeua, Belém; Pará, Brazil (259).
Anápolis; Goiás, Brazil (278b).
Anchieta; Espírito Santo, Brazil (325a).
Andirá (Lago), Rio Andirá; Amazonas, Brazil (200).
Andirá (Rio); Amazonas, Brazil (201).
Andoas, Río Pastaza; Loreto, Peru (77).
Apaga (Rio); Loreto, Peru (78c).
Apayacu (Río); Loreto, Peru (86).
Apolobamba; La Paz, Bolivia (137).
Aracruz; Espírito Santo, Brazil (320b).
Araçatiba, Rio Espírito Santo; Espírito Santo, Brazil (324a).
Araçauí; Minas Gerais, Brazil (314a).
Aragarças, Rio Araguaia; Goiás, Brazil (278a).
Araguaia (Rio); Goías, Brazil
Enters Tocantins from southeast at 5° 21′ S, 48° 41′ W; precise collecting locality unknown.
Callithrix jacchus penicillata
G. A. Baer Collection, August 1906, at 550 meters.
Araguari, Rio Jordão; Minas Gerais, Brazil (308b).
Araipe; Pará, Brazil (233).
Aramanai, Rio Tapajóz; Pará, Brazil (239).
Aramanay; Pará, Brazil (239).
Aran-tau, Rupununi District, Guyana (not located).
Saguinus midas midas
Arara; Piaui, Brazil (282).
Arara, Rio Tapajóz; Pará, Brazil (227).
Araracuara; Amazonas, Colombia (58b).
Arapiuns, Rio; Amazonas, Brazil (223b).
Arauepá, Rio Tapajóz; Pará, Brazil (233).
Aricá (Fazenda); Mato Grosso, Brazil (273).
Armila; San Blas, Panamá (6d).
Arraiján; Panamá, Panamá (18).
Arumatéua, Rio Tocantins; Pará, Brazil (255).
Araruama; Rio de Janeiro, Brazil (336).
Assú (Igarapé); Pará, Brazil (260).
Auara (Igarapé); Amazonas, Brazil (196a).
Aveiro, Rio Tapajóz; Pará, Brazil (235).
Ávila, Napo-Pastaza, Ecuador (60).
Ayapuá (Lago), Rio Purús; Amazonas, Brazil (184).
Bahia; Bahia, Brazil (294).
Baía; Bahia, Brazil (294).
Baião, Rio Tocantins; Pará, Brazil (254).
Baptista (Lago do), Rio Madeira; Amazonas, Brazil (199).
Barrachudo Caeau (Fazenda); Bahia, Brazil (299).
Barra da Vareda, Rio Pardo; Bahia, Brazil (305).
Barra do Itapemirim; Espírito Santo, Brazil (325b).
Barra do Paraopeba; Minas Gerais, Brazil (312c).
Barra do Rio Negro; Amazonas, Brazil (170).
Barra Sêca (Rio); Espírito Santo, Brazil (319b).
Barreiras; Bahia, Brazil (292b).
Barreirinha; Amazonas, Brazil (201).
Barretos, Rio Grande; São Paulo, Brazil (340).
Barro Alto, Rio São Francisco; (not located but may be in Bahia (11° 46′ S, 41° 54′ W)
Callithrix jacchus penicillata
J. Blaser, November 1931.
Barro Branco; Rio de Janeiro, Brazil (336).
Barro Colorado; Canal Zone, Panamá (17).
Baturité; Ceará, Brazil (284e).
Baudó (Río, upper); Chocó, Colombia (27).
Bauru; São Paulo, Brazil (343b).
Belém, Rio Guama; Pará, Brazil (256).
Belém de Pará; Pará, Brazil (256).
Bellavista, Río Porce; Antioquia, Colombia (34).
Belmonte (Rio); Bahia, Brazil (306).
Bem Posta, Rio Parahyba; Rio de Janeiro, Brazil (329).
Benevides, Belém; Pará, Brazil (259).
Blanco, Río (= Tapiche, Río); Loreto, Peru (100).
Boca de Cupe; Darién, Panamá (14).
Boca de Paya; Darién, Panamá (13b).
Boim, Rio Tapajóz; Pará, Brazil (226).
Bom Lugar, Rio Purús; Amazonas, Brazil (189).
Bonasica River; Guyana (146).
Boracéia; São Paulo, Brazil (343a).
Borba, Rio Madeira; Amazonas, Brazil (196b).
Borrachudo (Fazenda); Bahia, Brazil (299).
Botucatu; São Paulo, Brazil (344).
Bravo (Igarapé), Rio Tapajóz; Pará, Brazil (224).
Buenopolis; Minas Gerais, Brazil (312a).
Buerarema; Bahia, Brazil (299).
Buerema; Bahia, Brazil (299).
Cabo Frio; Rio de Janeiro, Brazil (338a).
Cabral, Rio Aricá-Assú; Mato Grosso, Brazil (270).
Cáceres, São Luis de, Mato Grosso, Brazil (266).
Cachoeiro do Itapemirim; Espírito Santo, Brazil (325c).
Cachoeiras; Rio de Janeiro, Brazil (336).
Cahuinari (Río), tributary of lower Río Caquetá; Amazonas, Colombia (58c).
Caiçara, Rio Paraguay; Mato Grosso, Brazil (265).
Calçado; Espírito Santo, Brazil (325c).

Camamu; Bahia, Brazil (297a).
Cametá, Rio Tocantins; Pará, Brazil (252).
Camp I; Suriname (not located).
Saguinus midas midas
I. T. Sanderson, July 1938.
Campinas; Rio de Janeiro, Brazil (335).
Campos Salles, Manaus, Rio Negro; Amazonas, Brazil (170).
Cana; Darién, Panamá (12).
Canabuoca; Amazonas, Brazil (192a).
Canabrava, Rio Tocantins; Goiás, Brazil (275).
Cana Brava; Goiás, Brazil (275).
Canaçari (Lago do), Rio Amazonas; Amazonas, Brazil (205).
Candamo, Río Huacamayo; Puno, Peru (132).
Caño Grande, upper Río Inírida; Vaupés, Colombia (51b).
Cantareira; São Paulo, Brazil (350a).
Capihuara (Río), Río Pastaza; Napo-Pastaza, Ecuador (75b).
Carabouca, Paraná de Jacaré; Amazonas, Brazil (192a).
Cara-Paraná (Río); Amazonas, Colombia (58d).
Carcado (= Cercado); Santa Cruz, Bolivia (141).
Carolinakreek; Suriname, Suriname (150b).
Cartagena; Bolívar, Colombia (42).
Casa Nova, Rio Arapium; Pará, Brazil (223a).
Casimiro de Abreu; Rio de Janeiro, Brazil (336).
Casita Camp; Darién, Panamá (15b).
Castanhal, Rio Nhamundá; Amazonas, Brazil (206).
Castanho or Castanhas (= Rio Roosevelt), foz de (= mouth of); Amazonas, Brazil (197b).
Catalão, Rio Jordão; Goiás, Brazil (281b).
Catival, upper Río San Jorge; Córdoba, Colombia (41).
Caupolicán; La Paz, Bolivia (137).
Caxiricatuba, Rio Tapajóz; Pará, Brazil (241).
Cayenne; French Guiana (155b).
Cercado; Santa Cruz, Bolivia (141).
Cerro Azul, Contamana, Río Ucayali; Loreto, Peru (103).
Chapada (Serra de); Mato Grosso, Brazil (271).
Chapada do Araripe; Ceará, Brazil (285).
Chepigana; Darién, Panamá (8).
Chepo; Panamá, Panamá (6a).
Chiatí (Río); Darién, Panamá (11).
Chicosa, Alto Río Ucayali; Loreto, Peru (109).
Chimbote, Río Marañón; Loreto, Peru (83).
Chinchavita, Río Huallaga; Huánuco, Peru (122).
Chiquitos; Santa Cruz, Bolivia (142).
Chiriara, Río Nanay; Loreto, Peru (94b).
Chiriquí, Panamá—no specific locality (2).
Saguinus oedipus geoffroyi
C. M. Keenan, July 1953.
Chiva Chiva; Canal Zone, Panamá (20).
Chorrera, (La); Panamá, Panamá (4).
Chucunaque (Río); Darién, Panamá (7b).
Cianate (Río); Darién, Panamá (11).
Cipo (Serra do) Minas Gerais, Brazil (315a).
Cituro; Darién, Panamá (13a).
Cobija, Río Madeira; Pando, Bolivia (135).
Cochiquinas (Río); Loreto, Peru (84).
Coco Plantation; Canal Zone, Panamá (not located).
Saguinus oedipus geoffroyi
C. M. Keenan, August 1955.
Cocoli; Canal Zone, Panamá (18).
Colaroo, Demerara River; Guyana (not located).
Saguinus midas midas
S. B. Warren, October 1905, at 9 meters.
Colatina, Rio Doce; Espírito Santo, Brazil (320a).
Colón; Panamá, Panamá (5b).
Colonia do Veado, Obidos; Pará, Brazil (217).
Conambo, upper Río Tigre; Napo-Pastaza, Ecuador (71).
Conceição da Barra; Espírito Santo, Brazil (319a).
Conceição de Macabu; Rio de Janeiro, Brazil (336).
Conceição do Mato Dentro; Minas Gerais, Brazil (315a).
Conceição, Rio Mojú; Pará, Brazil (262).
Condamo (= Candamo); Puno, Peru (132).
Copataza (Río = Río Copotaza); Napo-Pastaza, Ecuador (74).
Copotaza (Río), Río Pastaza; Napo-Pastaza, Ecuador (74).
Coremas; Paraíba, Brazil (287c).
Coroaba (Fazenda), Rio Espírito Santo; Espírito Santo, Brazil (324a).
Córrego do Cabral; Mato Grosso, Brazil (270).
Correntezas; Rio de Janeiro, Brazil (336).
Corumbá, Rio Paraguay; Mato Grosso, Brazil (267).
Corupeba, Recôncavo; Bahia, Brazil (294).
Cosireni (Río); Cusco, Peru (126).
Coto Region; Puntarenas, Costa Rica (1).
Crato; Ceará, Brazil (285b).
Cruzeiro do Sul, upper Rio Juruá; Acre, Brazil (208).
Cuiabá, Rio Cuiabá; Mato Grosso, Brazil (269).
Cuieras (Igarapé or Rio), Rio Demina; Amazonas, Brazil (169b).
Cuipeúa (Lago); Pará, Brazil (218).
Cuitêua (Lago); Pará, Brazil (218).
Cumaría; Loreto, Peru (108).
Cumería (= Cumaría); Loreto, Peru (108).
Cuminá (Rio, or Rio Erepecurú, q.v.); Pará, Brazil (216).
Cunambo; Napo-Pastaza, Ecuador (71).
Curaray (Río); Loreto, Peru (80).
Curupeba, Recôncavo; Bahia, Brazil (294).
Curulao (Río); Antioquia, Colombia (29).
Curvelo; Minas Gerais, Brazil (312b).
Cuyabá; Mato Grosso, Brazil (269).
Darién; Antioquia, Colombia
Name generally applied to region of lower Río Atrato basin and the Serranía del Darién.
Demerara River; Demerara, Guyana (147).
Deserto; Piaui, Brazil (283).
Destacamento, Río Marañon; Loreto, Peru (91).
Doce (Rio); Espírito Santo, Brazil (320a).
Doce (Rio); Minas Gerais, Brazil (315b).
Dois Irmãos; Pernambuco, Brazil (289b).
Domingos Martins; Espírito Santo, Brazil (322).
Dunoon, Demerara River; Guyana (148a).
Duque de Caxias; Rio de Janeiro, Brazil (336).
Ega; Amazonas, Brazil (182).
Eirunepé; Amazonas, Brazil (176).
Engenheiro Reeve; Espírito Santo, Brazil (325c).
Engenho do São Benjamin, Belém de Pará; Pará, Brazil (257).
Erepecurú (Rio); Pará, Brazil (216).
Esnape (Río); Darién, Panamá (10).
Espelho (Serra do), Rio Nhamundá; Amazonas, Brazil (207).
Esperanza (Fazenda), Rio Uruhu (or Rio Uru); Goiás, Brazil (277a).

Esperanza (Fazenda); São José da Lagôa; Minas Gerais, Brazil (315b).
Esperanza (Quebrada); Loreto, Peru (117).
Espírito Santo; Espírito Santo, Brazil (323).
Espírito Santo (Rio); Espírito Santo, Brazil (323).
Essequibo (River); Guyana (144b).
Estação da Mata do Cacau, Ribeirão do Fortuna; Bahia, Brazil (299).
Estanislau; Rio de Janeiro, Brazil (336).
Estrella (Puerto); Bolívar, Colombia (48).
Farfan; Canal Zone, Panamá (18).
Faro, Rio Nhamundá; Pará, Brazil (215).
Feira da Santana; Bahia, Brazil (293a).
Flores, suburb of Manaus; Amazonas, Brazil (170).
Floresta Estadual do Morro do Diabo; São Paulo, Brazil (339c).
Fonteboa; Amazonas, Brazil (174a).
Fordlandia, Rio Tapajóz; Pará, Brazil (234).
Fort Gulick; Canal Zone, Panamá (5b).
Fort Kobbe; Canal Zone, Panamá (18).
Forte do Rio Branco; Roraima, Brazil (164).
Fortuna; Bahia, Brazil (299).
Fundão; Pernambuco, Brazil (289b).
Gamboa; Canal Zone, Panamá (21).
Ganzo Azul Airport; Huánuco, Peru (123a).
Gaviões; Rio de Janeiro, Brazil (336).
Georgetown; Guyana (147).
Gi-Paraná; Rondônia, Brazil (214b).
Gordão (Igarapé do), Rio Juruá; Amazonas, Brazil (178).
Goiabeiras; Goiás, Brazil (not located).
Callithrix jacchus penicillata
Recorded by Vieira 1955.
Goiânia; Goiás, Brazil (280).
Gongogi (Rio); Bahia, Brazil (297c).
Gradaús, Rio Fresco; Pará, Brazil (251).
Grande (Igarapé), Rio Juruá; Amazonas, Brazil (177).
Grande (Lago), Rio Juruá; Amazonas, Brazil (175).
Grande (Rio); São Paulo, Brazil (339a).
Grungogy (Rio); Bahia, Brazil (297c).
Guaçí; Espírito Santo, Brazil (325c).
Guamués (Río); Putumayo, Colombia (57a).
Guapé; Rio de Janeiro, Brazil (336).
Gurupina (Fazenda), Lagôa Gurupina; Rio de Janeiro, Brazil (337).
Hacienda Cadena, Río Marcapata; Cusco, Peru (128).
Hacha, Quebrada del; Putumayo, Colombia (57c).
Haute Carterenne (or Carsevenne?); French Guiana (not located).
Saguinus midas midas
M. Geay 1898.
Huachi, Río Pastaza; Loreto, Peru (78b).
Huallaga (Río); Loreto, Peru (see also Santa Cruz and Yurimaguas).
Enters Marañon from south at 5° 10′ S, 75° 30′ W
Saguinus mystax mystax
H. Bassler, November 1927, at about 150 meters.
Saguinus fuscicollis leucogenys
E. Bartlett, between 1865 and 1869.
Humaitá, Rio Madeira; Amazonas, Brazil (197a).
Humaytha; Amazonas, Brazil (197a).
Humuyacu, Río Napo; Napo-Pastaza, Ecuador (63).
Ibiapaba (Serra do); Ceará, Brazil (284).
Ibiraçú; Espírito Santo, Brazil (320b).
Icarai-Mosquito; Ceará, Brazil (284a).
Iconha; Espírito Santo, Brazil (325a).
Igarapé Assu, see Açu; Igarapé (260).
Iguapé (Rio); Rio de Janeiro, Brazil (336).
Iguatu; Ceará, Brazil (286).
Ilha Madre de Deus; Bahia, Brazil (294).
Ilhéos; Bahia, Brazil (299).
Ilhéus; Bahia, Brazil (299).
Indiana (Puerto); Loreto, Peru (90).
Indillama, Río Napo; Napo-Pastaza, Ecuador (65).
Indio (Río); Canal Zone, Panamá (5a).
Inhumas; Goiás, Brazil (279).
Inõa (Serra de); Rio de Janeiro, Brazil (334).
Intillama, Río Napo; Napo-Pastaza, Ecuador (65).
Inuá (Serra de); Rio de Janeiro, Brazil (334).
Inuya (Río); Loreto, Peru (114).
Ipanema; São Paulo, Brazil (347).
Ipê Arcado; Goiás, Brazil (not located).
Callithrix jacchus penicillata
Dreher, April 1904.
Ipixuna (Lago do), Rio Solimões; Amazonas, Brazil (183).
Ipoucin; French Guiana (156a).
Ipoussin; French Guiana (156a).
Ipoxona (Lago do); Amazonas, Brazil (183).
Ipú, Serra do Ibiapaba; Ceará, Brazil (284).
Iquiri, Rio Iquirí; Acre, Brazil (213).
Iquitos, Río Marañón; Loreto, Peru (92).
Irocanga, Rio Tapajóz; Pará, Brazil (225).
"Islands region between Marajó Island and the mainlnad." Pará, Brazil (221).
Itaborai; Rio de Janeiro, Brazil (336).
Itabuna, Rio Ilhéus; Bahia, Brazil (299).
Itacoatiara, Rio Amazonas; Amazonas, Brazil (203).
Itaguaí, Rio; Rio de Janeiro, Brazil (336).
Itahuania, Río Alto Madre de Dios; Madre de Dios, Peru (131).
Itaituba, Rio Tapajóz; Pará, Brazil (228b).
Itaparica (Ilha de); Bahia, Brazil (295).
Itapemirim; Espírito Santo, Brazil (325b).
Itapoamá; Pará, Brazil (237).
Itapuamá, Rio Tapajóz; Pará, Brazil (237).
Itaquatiara; Amazonas, Brazil (203).
Itatiaya, Rio Parahyba; Rio de Janeiro, Brazil (330).
Itatiba; São Paulo, Brazil (345).
Itingo; Pará, Brazil (258).
Itumbiara, Goiás, Brazil (281a).
Itaúnas (Rio), Espírito Santo, Brazil (319a).
Ituxi (= Rio Iquirí); Acre, Brazil (213).
Jaburú, Rio Purús; Amazonas, Brazil (186).
Jacú (Rio); Espírito Santo, Brazil (323).
Jamundá (Rio); Amazonas, Brazil (see Nhamundá, Rio).
Janauacá (Lago do); Amazonas, Brazil (193).
Januária, Rio São Francisco; Minas Gerais, Brazil (310).
Jaraguá, Rio das Almas; Goiás, Brazil (277b).
Jaraquiél, Río Sinú; Córdoba, Colombia (39).
Jari (Rio), Rio Amazonas; Pará, Brazil (220).
Jary (Rio), Rio Amazonas; Pará, Brazil (220).
Jauanari, Rio Negro; Amazonas, Brazil (169a).
Jaurú (Rio); Mato Grosso, Brazil (264).
Javanari; Amazonas, Brazil (169a).
Javarí (Rio); Amazonas, Brazil (115b).
Jesucito (Río); Darién, Panamá (9).
Jiparaná, (Rio); Rondônia, Brazil (214b).
Joanacan (Lago do); Amazonas, Brazil (193).

João Pessõa, upper Rio Juruá; Amazonas, Brazil (176).
Jordão (Rio); Minas Gerais, Brazil (308a).
Juá; Ceará, Brazil (286).
Juárez (Río); Madre de Dios, Peru (129).
Jucú (Rio); Espírito Santo, Brazil (323).
Jucuruçú (Rio); Bahia, Brazil (307).
Jucururu (Rio); Bahia, Brazil (307).
Jucurussú (Rio); Bahia, Brazil (307).
Juruá (Rio); Amazonas, Brazil (174b).
Juturnaíba (Rio); Rio de Janeiro, Brazil (336).
Kaiserberg Airstrip, Zuid River; Nickerie, Suriname (152).
Kartabo, Cuyuni River; Guyana (145).
Kitayama (Fazenda), Presidente Wenceslau; São Paulo, Brazil (339b).
Labrea, Rio Purús; Amazonas, Brazil (187).
La Chorrera; Panamá, Panamá (4).
La Chorrera; Amazonas, Colombia (58a).
La Coca, Río Napo; Napo-Pastaza, Ecuador (63).
La Estrella, Río Magdalena; Bolívar, Colombia (48).
Lagarto, Right bank Alto Río Ucayali; Loreto, Peru (110).
Lagarto Cocha; Napo-Pastaza, Ecuador (67a).
Lagôa Juparaná; Espírito Santo, Brazil (320b).
Lagoa Santa, Rio das Velhas; Minas Gerais, Brazil (313).
Laguna Camp; Darién, Panamá (15c).
Laguna de la Pita; Darién, Panamá (7).
Lamarão, upper Rio Itapicurú; Bahia, Brazil (292d).
La Rastra, Río Orteguaza; Caquetá, Colombia (53).
Las Campanas, Colosó; Bolívar, Colombia (46).
Las Cascadas; Canal Zone, Panamá (18).
Lassance; Minas Gerais, Brazil (312a).
La Vaca (Río); Puntarenas, Costa Rica (1).
Leticia, Rio Solimões; Amazonas, Colombia (58e).
Libertade (Rio do); Amazonas, Brazil (179).
Linhares; Espírito Santo, Brazil (319c).
Lipuno (Río), Río Villano, upper Río Curaray; Napo-Pastaza, Ecuador (68).
Loksie Hattie, Saramacca River; Brokopondo, Suriname (151).
Luiz; Amazonas, Brazil (193).
Macaco Secco; Bahia, Brazil (296).
Macaé (Serra de); Rio de Janeiro, Brazil (336).
Macahé (Serra de); Rio de Janeiro, Brazil (336).
Macapá, Macapá; Amapá, Brazil (161).
Maceió; Alagoas, Brazil (290).
Machacales; Minas Gerais, Brazil (314a).
Madden Dam; Canal Zone, Panamá (22).
Madden Forest; Canal Zone, Panamá (22).
Madden Road; Canal Zone, Panamá (22).
Madeira (Rio); Amazonas, Brazil (194).
Madre de Deus (Ilha); Bahia, Brazil (294).
Magé; Rio de Janeiro, Brazil (336).
Mahaienbally (Creek), Demerara River; Guyana (may be Mahaikabally, misspelled).
Saguinus midas midas
S. B. Warren, October 1905, at 5 meters.
Mahaikabally (Creek); Guyana (148b).
Mahates (Canal de), Rio Magdalena; Bolívar, Colombia (44).
Maicá, Rio Amazonas; Pará, Brazil (243).
Mainas (see Maynas); Loreto, Peru.
Mairo (Puerto); Huánuco, Peru (123c).
Malena; Antioquia, Colombia (37).
Malhada; Bahia, Brazil (296).
Maloca, Rio Curuá; Pará, Brazil (250).
Mamaguape, Paraíba, Brazil (287a).
Mamoriá; Amazonas, Brazil (188).
Manaquiri, Rio Solimões; Amazonas, Brazil (192b).
Manarica Creek, Essequibo River; Guyana (not located).
Saguinus midas midas
Cozier (through F. V. McConnell).
Manaos, Rio Negro; Amazonas, Brazil (170).
Manaus, Rio Negro; Amazonas, Brazil (170).
Mandinga; San Blas, Panamá (6c).
Mangabeiras; Alagoas, Brazil (291).
Mangaratiba; Rio de Janeiro, Brazil (336).
Manití (Río); Loreto, Peru (89).
Mapaiso (Río), Santa Cruz, Bolivia (141).
Mapixi (Lago do), Rio Purús; Amazonas, Brazil (185).
Mararú, Rio Tapajóz; Pará, Brazil (242).
"Mararuni, Rio" (misprint for Mazaruni River); Guyana (145).
Marataízes, Espírito Santo, Brazil (325b).
Maraú; Bahia, Brazil (297b).
Maraú; Pará, Brazil (242).
Mar de Espanha; Minas Gerais, Brazil (318b).
Maricá; Rio de Janeiro, Brazil (336).
Maripa, Bonasica River; Guyana (146).
Maruá, Fazenda (= Mararú); Pará, Brazil (242).
Maruanum (Rio), Macapá; Amapá, Brazil (160).
Marupa, Río Marañon; Loreto, Peru (88).
Matodentro; São Paulo, Brazil (346).
Matogrosso; Mato Grosso, Brazil (263).
Mattodentro; São Paulo, Brazil (346).
Maxon Ranch, Río Trinidad; Panamá, Panamá (3).
Maycury (Rio); Pará, Brazil (219).
Maynas; Loreto, Peru (general region between lower Ríos Huallaga and Ucayali).
Saguinus "labiatus" (= *Saguinus* sp. ?).
Mazán (Río); Loreto, Peru (81).
Mazaruni (River); Guyana (145).
Mecaya (Río), Río Caquetá; Putumayo, Colombia (57b).
Medellín; Antioquia, Colombia (35).
Mendez, upper Río Santiago; Santiago-Zamora, Ecuador (76).
Miguel (Lago do); Amazonas, Brazil (195).
Mishana, Río Nanay; Loreto, Peru (94b).
Mocajuba, Rio Tocantins; Pará, Brazil (253).
Mocoa; Putumayo, Colombia (55).
Moengo Tapoe, Marowijne River; Marowijne, Suriname (153).
Mondubim; Ceará, Brazil (284b).
Monduby; Ceará, Brazil (284b).
Montalvo; Napo-Pastaza, Ecuador (75a).
Monte Alegre, Rio Gurupatuba; Pará, Brazil (219).
Monte Cristo, Rio Tapajóz; Pará, Brazil (231).
Monte Verde, upper Rio Purús; Amazonas, Brazil (191).
Morro das Pedras (Fazenda), Ilheus; Bahia, Brazil (299).
Moon Mountains; Roraima, Brazil (165).
Morro do Diabo; São Paulo, Brazil (339c).
Moyobamba, Río Mayo; San Martín, Peru (120).
Mu (Rio), Rio Juruá; Amazonas, Brazil (179).
Mulungu; Ceará, Brazil (284e).
Mundo Novo, Rio Pardo; Bahia, Brazil (298).
Murutucu; Pará, Brazil (not located).
Saguinus midas niger
E. Heller, February 1923.

Nanay (Río) (see Mishana).
Nanay (Río); Loreto, Peru (94b).
Mutum, Rio; Espírito Santo, Brazil (320c).
Napo (Puerto); Napo-Pastaza, Ecuador (62).
Napo (Río) (no precise locality); Napo-Pastaza, Ecuador
Saguinus fuscicollis tripartitus
P. Pozzi, before 1882; Olalla Bros., January 1924.
Napo (Río); Loreto, Peru (82).
Negro (Rio); Amazonas, Brazil (170).
Nhamundá (Rio); Amazonas, Brazil (see Faro and other localities on river).
Nilópolis; Rio de Janeiro, Brazil (336).
Niterói; Rio de Janeiro, Brazil (336).
Norosí; Bolívar, Colombia (49).
Nossa Senhora de Penha; Paraíba, Brazil (287b).
Nova Friburgo; Rio de Janeiro, Brazil (335).
Nova-Iguaçu; Rio de Janeiro, Brazil (336).
Novo Horizonte; Pará, Brazil (251).
Nuevo Emperador; Panamá, Panamá (18).
Óbidos, Rio Amazonas; Pará, Brazil (217).
Orgãos (Serra do); Rio de Janeiro, Brazil (333).
Oriente; Acre, Brazil (210).
Orosa, Río Marañon; Loreto, Peru (87).
Ouanary (River); French Guiana (156b).
Pac; Canal Zone, Panamá (not located).
Saguinus oedipus geoffroyi
C. M. Keenan, October 1953.
Pacaya (Río); opposite Sapote; Loreto, Peru (101).
Pachitea (Río); Loreto, Peru (107).
Pacoti; Ceará, Brazil (284e).
Palma; Goiás, Brazil (275b).
Palmares; Loreto, Peru (not located).
Saguinus fuscicollis
Palmarito, Santa Cruz, Bolivia (140).
Palmeiras; Mato Grosso, Brazil (274).
Pampa Chica; Loreto, Peru (93).
Pampa Grande, Río Tambopata; Puno, Peru (133).
Papuri (Rio); Rio Uaupés; Amazonas, Brazil (166).
Pará; Pará, Brazil (256).
Parahybado Sul (Rio); Rio de Janeiro, Brazil (326).
Paraíso; Canal Zone, Panamá (20).
Paramaribo; Suriname, Suriname (149).
Paraná (Rio); São Paulo, Brazil (339a).
Paranapanema (Rio); São Paulo, Brazil (342).
Paratucu (Rio); Amazonas, Brazil (207).
Pardo (Rio); Bahia, Brazil (304).
Paricatuba, Rio Tapajóz; Pará, Brazil (222).
Parintins; Amazonas, Brazil (202).
Parintins (Serra de); Amazonas, Brazil (202).
Paru de Oeste (Rio); Pará, Brazil (216).
Pau Gigante; Espírito Santo, Brazil (320b).
Paya (Boca de Río); Darién, Panamá (13b).
Pebas, Rio Marañon; Loreto, Peru (85).
Pedra Branca (Parati); Rio de Janeiro, Brazil (331c).
Pedra Marietta Antoinetta; Brazil (not located)
Callithrix jacchus jacchus
Wagner, 1902.
Pedra Preta, upper Rio Juruá; Acre, Brazil (209).
Pedreira (= Pedreiras), Rio Tapajóz, Brazil (232).
Pedreiras, Rio Tapajóz; Pará, Brazil (232).
Pedro Miguel; Canal Zone, Panamá (20).
Peixe-boi, Belém; Pará, Brazil (261).
Penha; Paraíba, Brazil (287b).
Perené (Río); Junín, Peru (125).
Pernambuco (= Recife); Pernambuco, Brazil (289).
Pernambuquinho; Ceará, Brazil (284e).
Petrópolis; Rio de Janeiro, Brazil (331a).
Pico do Calçado; Espírito Santo, Brazil (324b).
Pilar; Goiás, Brazil (276a).
Pimental, Rio Tapajóz; Pará, Brazil (230).
Pindo Yacu (Río) (Río Pinto Yacu); Napo-Pastaza, Ecuador (70).
Pinto Yacu (Río); Loreto, Peru (94a).
Piquiatuba, Rio Tapajóz; Pará, Brazil (240).
Piracicaba, Rio Doce; Minas Gerais, Brazil (315b).
Pirapora; Minas Gerais, Brazil (311).
Pirataquissé (Fazenda); Bahia, Brazil (299).
Piratucu (Rio), Nhamundá; Amazonas, Brazil (207).
Pisquí (Río); Loreto, Peru (104).
"Plaines de Mocoa"; Putumayo, Colombia (55).
Planaltina; Goiás, Brazil (277c).
Poço d'Anta; Rio de Janeiro, Brazil (336).
Poções; Bahia, Brazil (301).
Ponta Negra; Rio de Janeiro, Brazil (338b).
Ponte do Paranaíba; Goiás, Brazil (281a).
Ponte Ipê Arcado; Goiás, Brazil
Callithrix jacchus penicillata
Pôrto das Flores, Rio Parahyba; Rio de Janeiro, Brazil (328).
Pôrto de Moz, Rio Xingu; Pará, Brazil (248).
Pôrto do Rio Grande; São Paulo, Brazil (341).
Pôrto do Rio Paraná; São Paulo, Brazil (341).
Pôrto Velho, upper Rio Madeira; Rondônia, Brazil (214).
Pozuzo; Huánuco, Peru (124).
Prado (Rio); Bahia, Brazil (307).
Presidente; Rio de Janeiro, Brazil (336).
Presidente Epitácio; São Paulo, Brazil (339b).
Presidente Venceslau; São Paulo, Brazil (339b).
Presidente Wenceslau; São Paulo, Brazil (339b).
Pucallpa; Loreto, Peru (106).
Puerto Arturo; Amazonas, Colombia (58b).
Puerto Berrío, Río Magdalena; Antioquia, Colombia (36).
Puerto Estrella, opposite, Río Magdalena; Bolívar, Colombia (48).
Puerto Indiana, Río Marañon; Loreto, Peru (90).
Puerto Mairo; Huánuco, Peru (123c).
Puerto Napo, Río Napo; Napo-Pastaza, Ecuador (62).
Puerto Suarez, Río Paraguay; Santa Cruz, Bolivia (143).
Puerto Umbría; Río Guinéo; Putumayo, Colombia (57a).
Puerto Valdivia, Río Cauca; Antioquia, Colombia (32).
Purí; Antioquia, Colombia (31).
Purús (Rio); Amazonas, Brazil (see specific localities on Rio Purús).
Saguinus labiatus labiatus
Saguinus mystax pileatus
Callimico goeldii
Purús (Rio, upper); Amazonas, Brazil
Saguinus fuscicollis cruzlimae
Quebrada del Hacha; Putumayo, Colombia (57c).
Quebrada Esperanza; Loreto, Peru (117).
Quebrada Tocón; Loreto, Peru (94b).
Quebrada Venado (see Armila); San Blas, Panamá (6d).
Quebrangulo; Alagoas, Brazil (290).
Quiser (Río); Santa Cruz, Bolivia (140).
Radio Station Hill; Canal Zone, Panamá (22).
Recife; Pernambuco, Brazil (289b).
Recreio, Rio Majary; Pará, Brazil (not located).

Saguinus midas niger
A. M. Olalla, September 1931.
Callithrix argentata argentata
A. M. Olalla, September 1931.
Reis Magos (Rio), Espírito Santo, Brazil (321a).
Riachão das Neves; Bahia, Brazil (292c).
Ribeirão da Minhocas, Rio Ilhéus; Bahia, Brazil (302).
Rio Bonito; Rio de Janeiro, Brazil (336).
Rio de Janeiro; Guanabara, Brazil (332).
Río La Vaca; Puntarenas, Costa Rica (1).
Río Mecaya; Putumayo, Colombia (57b).
Rio Piracicaba; Minas Gerais, Brazil (315b).
Rive, Alegre; Espírito Santo, Brazil (325c).
Romaria; Minas Gerais, Brazil (309b).
Rosarhino, Rio Madeira; Amazonas, Brazil (195).
Rozarinho; Amazonas, Brazil (195).
Salaquí (Río), Río Atrato; Chocó, Colombia (26).
Salvador; Bahia, Brazil (294).
Samiria (Río); Loreto, Peru (96).
San Antonio; Huánuco, Peru (123b).
Sandia, Río Tambopata; Puno, Peru (133).
Sandó, (Río); Chocó, Colombia (28).
San Fernando; Loreto, Peru (116).
San Francisco, Río Napo; Napo-Pastaza, Ecuador (66).
San Ignacio; Puno, Peru (134).
San Jorge (Río); Bolívar, Colombia (47).
San José, Rio Nhamundá; Pará, Brazil (215).
San José Bajo, Río Suno; Napo-Pastaza, Ecuador (59).
San José de Chiquitos; Santa Cruz, Bolivia (142).
San José del Guaviare; Vaupés, Colombia (51a).
San José do Calçado; Espírito Santo, Brazil (325c).
San Juan Nepomuceno; Bolívar, Colombia (45).
San Miguel (Río); Cusco, Peru (127).
San Pedro (Río); Bolívar, Colombia (50).
Santa Ana de Chapada; Mato Grosso, Brazil (271).
Santa Cecilia, Río Manití; Loreto, Peru (89).
Santa Cruz, Rio Eirú; Amazonas, Brazil (181).
Santa Cruz, Río Huallaga; Loreto, Peru (98).
Santa Cruz de la Sierra; Santa Cruz, Bolivia (139).
Santa Elena, Río Samiria; Loreto, Peru (97).
Santa Leopoldina; Espírito Santo, Brazil (322).
Santarém, Rio Tapajóz, Pará, Brazil (242).
Santa Rita, Río Nanay; Loreto, Peru (94b).
Santa Rita, Rio Solimões; Amazonas, Brazil (172a).
Santa Rita da Floresta, Rio de Janeiro, Brazil (327).
Santa Rita de Cássia; Bahia, Brazil (292a).
Santa Rosa, Alto Río Ucayali; Loreto, Peru (111).
Santa Rosa de Sucumbíos; Napo-Pastaza, Ecuador (64).
Santa Teresa; Espírito Santo, Brazil (320b).
Santa Tereza, Espírito Santo; Brazil (320b).
Santo Amaro; Bahia, Brazil (293b).
Santo Antônio, Rio Eirú; Amazonas, Brazil (180).
Santo Antônio do Leverger; Mato Grosso, Brazil (272).
São Benedito; Ceará, Brazil (284c).
São Felipe; Amazonas, Brazil (176).
São Francisco (Rio), between 44°–45° W.; Minas Gerais, Brazil.
Callithrix jacchus penicillata
São Gonçalo; Rio de Janeiro, Brazil (336).
São João; São Paulo, Brazil (348).
São João Batista do Gloria; Minas Gerais, Brazil (309d).
São João da Barra; Rio de Janeiro, Brazil (336).
São João de Meriti; Rio de Janeiro, Brazil (336).
São João (Rio); Rio de Janeiro, Brazil (336).
São João do Gloria; Minas Gerais, Brazil (309d).
São João dos Patos; Maranhão; Brazil (282a).
São Joaquim, Rio Branco; Roraima, Brazil (164).
São José (Fazenda); Bahia, Brazil (299).
São José de Lagôa, Rio Doce; Minas Gerais, Brazil (315b).
São José do Calçado; Espírito Santo, Brazil (325c).
São Lourenço; Pernambuco, Brazil (289a).
São Luis de Cáçeres; Mato Grosso, Brazil (266).
São Luis de Mamoriá, Rio Purús; Amazonas, Brazil (188).
São Mateus; Espírito Santo, Brazil (319a).
São Miguel; Alagoas, Brazil (290).
São Paulo; São Paulo, Brazil (352).
São Paulo de Olivença, Rio Solimões; Amazonas, Brazil (172b).
São Pedro d'Aldeia; Rio de Janeiro, Brazil (336).
Sapatiba; Rio de Janeiro, Brazil (331b).
Saquarema; Rio de Janeiro, Brazil (336).
Sarayacu, Río Bobonaza; Napo-Pastaza, Ecuador (68).
Sarayacu, Río Ucayali; Loreto, Peru (102).
Sautatá, Río Atrato; Chocó, Colombia (25).
Saut Macaque, Mission River; French Guiana (not located).
Saguinus midas midas
Chauvancy 1962
Sepetiba; Rio de Janeiro, Brazil (331b).
Seringal Oriente, upper Rio Juruá; Acre, Brazil (210).
Serpa; Amazonas, Brazil (203).
Serra de Guaramiranga; Ceará, Brazil (284e).
Serra da Lua; Roraima, Brazil (165).
Serra do Castelo; Ceará, Brazil.
Callithrix jacchus jacchus
Serra do Espelho, Brazil (207).
Serra do Itatiaiá; Minas Gerais, Brazil (318c).
Serra do Mar; São Paulo, Brazil (351).
Serra Grande; Ceará, Brazil (284).
Sertam d'Ilhéus; Bahia, Brazil (299).
Sertão d'Ilhéus; Bahia, Brazil (299).
Sertão do Taquara, Serra da Bocaina, São Paulo, Brazil (346).
Seteganti (Río); Darién, Panamá (12).
Shahuía, opposite Cumaría, Río Ucayali; Loreto, Peru (108).
Shell Mera, Río Pastaza; Napo-Pastaza, Ecuador (73).
Siguín (= Sihuín), Río Pastaza; Loreto, Peru (78a).
Silva Jardim; Rio de Janeiro, Brazil (336).
Silveira Lobos; Minas Gerais, Brazil (317).
Sinú (Río); Córdoba, Colombia (38).
Socorré, Río Sinú; Córdoba, Colombia (40).
Solita, Río Caquetá, below Puerto Limón; Putumayo, Colombia (56).
St. Laurent, Maroni River; French Guiana (155a).
Suarez (Puerto); Santa Cruz, Bolivia (143).
Sumaco; Napo-Pastaza, Ecuador (59).
Summit Road; Canal Zone, Panamá (22).
Suno (Río); Napo-Pastaza, Ecuador (61).
Supinaam (River); Guyana (144a).
Tabatinga, Rio Solimões; Amazonas, Brazil (171).
Tabocal, Rio Negro; Amazonas, Brazil (168).
Tabucal, Rio Negro; Amazonas, Brazil (168).
Tacarcuna; Darién, Panamá (15a).
Tacarcuna Village; Darién, Panamá (15a).
Tahuapunta; Amazonas, Brazil (167).
Tahuapunta; opposite; Vaupés, Colombia (167). (see Tahuapunta; Amazonas, Brazil)

Talmapunta; Amazonas, Brazil (167).
Tamacury; Pará, Brazil (244).
Tamarury; Pará, Brazil (244).
Tambo (Río); Loreto, Peru (112).
Tapaiuna, Rio Tapajóz; Pará, Brazil (238).
Tapaiuna (Lago), Rio Madeira; Amazonas, Brazil (198).
Tapajós (Rio), Rio Amazonas; Pará, Brazil. (mouth at 2° 24′ S, 54° 41′ W)
See individual localities along river.
Tapajóz, Rio, also Tapajós, Rio (q.v.)
Tapalisa; Darién, Panamá (16).
Tapanahoni (River); Marowijne, Suriname (154).
Tapará, Rio Xingú; Pará, Brazil (247).
Tapera, Pernambuco, Brazil (288a).
Tapiche (Río) (= Río Blanco); Loreto, Peru (100).
Tarapoto, Río Napo; Loreto, Peru (79).
Tauari, Rio Tapajóz; Pará, Brazil (236).
Taubaté; São Paulo, Brazil (346).
Tefé (Lago de); Amazonas, Brazil (182).
Teffé (Lago de); Amazonas, Brazil (182).
Teófilo Otoni; Minas Gerais, Brazil (314b).
Teresópolis; Rio de Janeiro, Brazil (333).
Theófilo Ottoni; Minas Gerais, Brazil (314)
Therezópolis; Rio de Janeiro, Brazil (333).
Tietê (Rio); São Paulo, Brazil (350a).
Tigre (Río); Loreto, Peru (95).
Tigre (Río); Napo-Pastaza, Ecuador.
Saguinus fuscicollis lagonotus
Von Baumann-Roosevelt Expedition, July 1936.
Tijuca, Parque Nacional da; Guanabara, Brazil (332).
Tingo María; Huánuco, Peru (121).
Tocantins (Rio); Pará, Brazil
Saguinus midas niger
A. M. Olalla; Sieber
Tocoumé; Panamá (may be Tocumén, misspelled).
Saguinus oedipus geoffroyi
E. André, March 1899
Tocumén; Panamá (6b).
Tonantins (Rio); Amazonas, Brazil (173).
Tres Troncos, Río Caquetá; Caquetá, Colombia (54).
Triunfo; Pernambuco, Brazil (288b).
Tumapasa (Tumupasa), Río Beni; La Paz, Bolivia (138).
Turbaco; Bolívar, Colombia (43).
Tupinambarana, Rio; Amazonas, Brazil (202).
Uapoamá, Rio Tapajóz; Pará, Brazil (237).
Uaupés (Rio), (opposite Tahuapunta); Amazonas, Brazil (167).
Ubatuba; São Paulo, Brazil (351).
Uberaba; Minas Gerais, Brazil (309c).
Ucayali (Río); Loreto, Peru
Saguinus imperator
H. Bassler
Umbría (Puerto); Putumayo, Colombia (57a).
Una; Bahia, Brazil (303).
Unguía; Chocó, Colombia (24).
Urabá; Antioquia, Colombia (see Curulao, Río).
Uru (Rio); Goiás, Brazil (see Uruhu).
Urubamba (Río); Loreto, Peru (113).
Uruçuca; Bahia, Brazil (299).
Urucum, Rio Paraguay; Mato Grosso, Brazil (268).
Urucum de Corumbá; Mato Grosso, Brazil (268).
Urucurituba, Rio Tapajóz; Pará, Brazil (228a).
Urucutuca; Bahia, Brazil (299).
Uruhu (Rio); Goiás, Brazil (277a).
Urupá, Rio; Rondónia, Brazil (214c).
Utinga, Belém; Pará, Brazil (258).
Uvini, Río Cosireni; Cusco, Peru (see Yuvini).
Vaicajá (Fazenda), Rio Tocantins; Pará, Brazil (252).
Valdivia; Antioquia, Colombia (33).
Valdivia (Puerto); Antioquia, Colombia (32).
Varge Grande; São Paulo, Brazil (349).
Vargem Grande; São Paulo, Brazil (349).
Veadeiros; Goiás, Brazil (276c).
Velhas (Rio das); Minas Gerais, Brazil (313).
Veríssimo; Minas Gerais, Brazil (309a).
Vermilho (Fazenda); Rio de Janeiro, Brazil (336).
Victoria, Río Beni; Pando, Bolivia (136).
Victoria; São Paulo, Brazil (344).
Vila Braga, Rio Tapajóz; Pará, Brazil (229).
Vila (or Villa) Bela da Santissima Trinidade, Rio Guaporé; Mato Grosso, Brazil (263).
Vila Nova; Bahia, Brazil (300).
Vila Nova (Rio), Mazagão; Amapá, Brazil (162).
Vilarinho do Monte, Rio Xingu; Pará, Brazil (246).
Vila Velha do Cassiporé, Oiapoque; Amapá, Brazil (157).
Vila Velha do Espírito Santo; Espírito Santo, Brazil (322).
Villa Arteaga; Antioquia, Colombia (30).
Villa Bella Imperatriz; Amazonas, Brazil (200).
Villarinho do Monte; Pará, Brazil (246).
Villa Vittoria; Espírito Santo, Brazil (321b).
Village Camp, Darién, Panamá (15c).
Visconde do Rio Branco; Minas Gerais, Brazil (316).
Vitória; Espírito Santo, Brazil (321b).
Vitória; São Paulo, Brazil (344).
Xapury (Rio), upper Rio Purús; Acre, Brazil (212).
Xingu (Rio); Pará, Brazil (245).
Yaco (Rio); Acre, Brazil (211).
Yaguas; Loreto, Peru (85).
Yahuas; Loreto, Peru (see Yaguas).
Yamunda (Rio); Amazonas, Brazil (see Rio Nhamundá).
Yana Rumi (Río); Napo-Pastaza, Ecuador (69).
Yaquerana (Río); Loreto, Peru (118).
Yaracana, Rio Nhamundá; Pará, Brazil (215).
Yarinacocha, Río Ucayali; Loreto, Peru (105).
Yauanari; Amazonas, Brazil (169a).
Yavarí (Río); Loreto, Peru (115a).
Yavarí Mirim (Rio); Loreto, Peru (see Quebrada Esperanza, 117).
Ypanema; São Paulo, Brazil (347).
Yurac Yacu; San Martín, Peru (119).
Yurimaguas, Río Huallaga; Loreto, Peru (99).
Yuvini, Río Cosireni; Cusco, Peru (126).
Zanderij (Airfield); Suriname, Suriname (150a).
Zona Boca Amigo; Madre de Dios, Peru (130).

Gazetteer of Collecting Localities (Map, fig. XIII.2)

COSTA RICA—*Saguinus oedipus geoffroyi*
Puntarenas
1. Coto Region, 8° 35′ N, 83° 05′ W.
C. R. Carpenter, June 1932, February–March 1933.
1. Río La Vaca, Coto—see Coto Region.

PANAMA—*Saguinus oedipus geoffroyi*
Chiriquí
2. No specific locality, arbitrarily indicated on map, fig. XIII.3.
Collector unknown.

Panamá

3. Maxon Ranch (Río Trinidad), 8° 57′ N, 80° W.
   William B. Richardson, March 1914.
4. La Chorrera, 8° 53′ N, 79° 47′ W.
   J. Zetek; C. M. Keenan, July 1953.

5a. Río Indio, 9° 15′N, 79° 59′ W.

5b. Colón, 9° 22′ N, 79° 55′ W.

5b. Fort Gulick, 9° 19′ N, 79° 52′ W.
   C. M. Keenan, October 1953.

6a. Chepo, 9° 10′ N, 79° 06′ W.
   E. A. Goldman, March 1911; E. Arcé, between 1865 and 1870.

6b. Tocumén, 9° 04′ N, 79° 24′ W.

San Blas

6c. Mandinga, 9° 27′ N, 79° 04′ W.
   C. O. Handley, Jr., May 1957.

6d. Armila, Quebrada Venado, 8° 40′ N, 77° 28′ W.
   C. O. Handley, Jr., February–March 1963.

Darién

7a. Laguna de la Pita, 8° 20′ N, 77° 56′ W.
   Enrico Festa, *ca.* 1895.

7b. Río Chucunaque, near El Real, 8° 09′ N, 77° 44′ W.
   C. O. Handley, Jr., February 1958.

8. Chepigana, 8° 18′ N, 78° 03′ W.
   William B. Richardson, November–December 1914.

9. Río Jesucito, 8° 01′ N, 78° 16′ W (near sea level).
   O. Bangs and W. S. Brooks, 1922.

10. Río Esnape, 8° 02′ N, 78° 12′ W.
   O. Bangs and W. S. Brooks, 1922.

11. Río Cianata (see Río Chiatí)

11. Río Chiatí, 8° 38′ N, 77° 56′ W.
   Enrico Festa, *ca.* 1895.

12. Cana, 7° 49′ N, 77° 43′ W, 600 meters.
   E. A. Goldman, February–June 1912.

12. Río Seteganti, 7° 46′ N, 77° 38′ W.
   C. O. Handley, Jr., February 1961.

13a. Cituro, 7° 57′ N, 77° 33′ W.
   William B. Richardson, May 1915.

13b. Boca de Paya (= Boca del Río Paya), 7° 57′ N, 77° 31′ W.
   C. O. Handley, Jr., February–March 1958.

14. Boca de Cupe (= Boca del Río Cupe), 8° 03′ N, 77° 35′ W.
   William B. Richardson, April–May 1915.

15a. Tacarcuna, 8° 05′ N, 77° 17′ W, 812 meters.
   H. E. Anthony, February–March 1915.

15a. Tacarcuna Village, 8° 05′ N, 77° 17′ W.

15b. Casita Camp, 8° 01′ N, 77° 22′ W.
   C. O. Handley, Jr., January 1959.

15c. Laguna Camp, Tacarcuna, 8° 04′ N, 77° 19′ W, 3,200 feet
   C. O. Handley, Jr., March 1959.

15c. Village Camp, Tacarcuna, 8° 05′ N, 77° 17′ W, 1,800–3,000 feet.
   C. O. Handley, Jr., February 1959.

16. Tapalisa, 8° 01′ N, 77° 26′ W.
   H. E. Anthony, February–March 1915.

CANAL ZONE—*Saguinus oedipus geoffroyi*

17. Barro Colorado, 9° 10′ N, 79° 50′ W.
   R. K. Enders, July 1929.
18. Las Cascadas, 9° 05′ N, 79° 41′ W.
   R. K. Enders, June 1932.
18. Nuevo Emperador, 9° N, 79° 45′ W.
   C. O. Handley, Jr., November 1955.
18. Arraiján, 8° 57′ N, 79° 41′ W.
   C. O. Handley, Jr., October 1955.
18. Fort Kobbe, 8° 55′ N, 79° 35′ W.
   C. M. Keenan, April 1953; C. Yunker, July 1961.
18. Farfan, 8° 56′ N, 79° 35′ W.
   C. O. Handley, Jr., July 1955.
18. Cocoli, 8° 59′ N, 79° 35′ W.
   C. O. Handley, Jr., August–September 1955.
19. Albrook Air Force Base, 8° 59′ N, 79° 33′ W.
   V. J. Tipton, 29 September 1959.
20. Chiva Chiva, 9° 02′ N, 79° 35′ W.
   C. O. Handley, Jr., June 1955.
20. Pedro Miguel, 9° 01′ N, 79° 36′ W.
   C. O. Handley, Jr., May, July 1955.
20. Paraíso, 9° 01′ N, 79° 37′ W.
   C. O. Handley, Jr., May 1955.
21. Gamboa, 9° 07′ N, 79° 42′ W.
   C. M. Keenan, April–May, July, October 1955.
21. Aguas Buenas, 9° 07′ N, 79° 36′ W.
   R. K. Enders, May 1932.
21. Agua Blanca (= Aguas Buenas).
   E. A. Goldman, February 1911.
22. Madden Dam, 9° 13′ N, 79° 37′ W.
   C. O. Handley, Jr., August, October, November, 1955.
22. Madden Forest, 9° 06′ N, 79° 37′ W.
   V. J. Tipton, August 1959.
22. Madden Road, 9° 06′ N, 79° 37′ W.
22. Summit Road, 9° 04′ N, 79° 39′ W.
   C. O. Handley, Jr., November 1955.
22. Radio Station Hill, 9° 03′ N, 79° 40′ W.
   C. O. Handley, Jr., November 1955.
23. Alajuela, 9° 13′ N, 79° 38′ W.
   R. K. Enders, June 1932.

COLOMBIA

Chocó—Saguinus oedipus geoffroyi

24. Unguía, 8° 01′ N, 77° 07′ W.
   P. Hershkovitz, March 1950, near sea level.
25. Sautatá, Río Atrato, 7° 50′ N, 77° 05′ W.
   M. A. Carriker, Jr., January 1918.
26. Río Salaquí, Río Atrato, 7° 25′ N, 77° 06′ W, 100–400 meters.
   Mrs. E. L. Kerr, 1912.
27. Baudó (Río), upper, 6° N, 77° 08′ W.
   Mrs. E. L. Kerr, 1912.
28. Río Sandó, 5° 13′ N, 77° 05′ W.
   K. von Sneidern, October 1958, at 160 meters.

Antioquia.—Saguinus oedipus oedipus

29. Río Curulao, 8° N, 76° 44′ W.
   P. Hershkovitz, May 1950 at 50 meters.
30. Villa Arteaga, 7° 20′ N, 76° 26′ W, 135 meters.
   P. Hershkovitz, January 1950 at 120–130 meters.

Antioquia—Saguinus leucopus

31. Purí, 7° 24′ N, 75° 20′ W.
   P. Hershkovitz, July 1950 at 140–200 meters.

32. Puerto Valdivia, Río Cauca, 7° 14′ N, 75° 26′ W.
    H. S. Boyle, December 1914 at 112 meters.
33. Valdivia, 7° 10′ N, 75° 26′ W.
    P. Hershkovitz, July 1950 at 1,000 meters; A. E. Pratt, April 1897 at 1,150 meters.
34. Bellavista, Río Porce, 6° 26′ N, 75° 20′ W.
    P. Hershkovitz, February 1950, 1,200 meters.
35. Medellín, 6° 12′ N, 75° 35′ W, 1,540 meters.
    T. K. Salmon, *ca.* 1875; Frank (dealer), 1877.
36. Puerto Berrío, Río Magdalena, 6° 28′ N, 74° 25′ W, 130 meters.
    L. A. Fuertes, January 1913.
37. Malena, 6° 25′ N, 74° 31′ W, 150 meters.
    L. E. Miller, March 1915.

Córdoba—Saguinus oedipus oedipus

38. Río Sinú, mouth, 9° 25′ N, 75° 45′ W.
    A. Humboldt, *ca.* 1801.
39. Jaraquiél, Río Sinú, 8° 41′ N, 75° 57′ W, about 20 meters.
    M. A. Carriker, Jr., March 1916.
40. Socorré, Río Sinú, 7° 51′ N, 76° 17′ W.
    P. Hershkovitz, March–April 1949, at 100–150 meters.
41. Catival, upper Río San Jorge, 8° 17′ N, 75° 41′ W.
    P. Hershkovitz, July 1949 at 120 meters.

Bolívar—Saguinus oedipus oedipus

42. Cartagena, 10° 25′ N, 75° 30′ W, sea level.
    A. Humboldt, *ca.* 1801.
43. Turbaco, 10° 17′ N, 75° 24′ W, 200 meters.
    A. Humboldt, *ca.* 1801.
44. Mahates, Canal de (Río Magdalena), 10° 15′ N, 75° 12′ W, near sea level.
    A. Humboldt, *ca.* 1801.
45. San Juan Nepomuceno, 9° 58′ N, 75° 04′ W.
    P. Hershkovitz, January 1949, at 167 meters.
46. Las Campanas, Colosó, 9° 30′ N, 75° 21′ W.
    P. Hershkovitz, May 1949 at 175–350 meters.
47. Río San Jorge, mouth, 9° 08′ N, 74° 43′ W.
    Mrs. E. L. Kerr, December 1911.

Bolívar—Saguinus leucopus

48. La Estrella, Rio Magdalena (see Puerto Estrella).
48. Puerto Estrella, opposite, Río Magdalena, 8° 58′ N, 73° 56′ W, 36 meters.
    H. M. Curran, May 1916.
49. Norosí, 8° 40′ N, 74° 02′ W, 120 meters.
    P. Hershkovitz, May–June 1943.
50. Río San Pedro, 8° 38′ N, 74° 04′ W, 180 meters.
    P. Hershkovitz, June 1943.

Vaupés—Saguinus inustus

51a. San José del Guaviare, 2° 34′ N, 72° 39′ W.
    L. L. Klein 1969.
51b. Caño Grande, upper Río Inírida, 2° 10′ N, 72° 20′ W, 280 meters.
    F. Medem, February 1957.
52. Alto Caño Itilla, upper Río Vaupés, 2° N, 72° 47′ W, about 300 meters.
    F. Medem, March 1958.

Caquetá

53. La Rastra, Río Orteguaza, 1° 24′ N, 75° 28′ W.
    Saguinus fuscicollis fuscus
    Hermano Nicéforo María, July 1951.
54. Tres Troncos, Río Caquetá, 0° 08′ N, 74° 41′ W.
    Cebuella pygmaea
    P. Hershkovitz, January–February 1952 at 150 meters. (sight records).
    Saguinus fuscicollis fuscus
    P. Hershkovitz, February 1952, at 150 meters.

Putumayo

55. "Plaines de Mocoa" (see Mocoa).
55. Mocoa, 1° 08′ N, 76° 38′ W, 580 meters.
    Saguinus fuscicollis fuscus
    A. Humboldt, *ca.* 1801.
56. Solita, Río Caquetá, below Puerto Limón, 1° 05′ N, 76° 0′ W.
    Saguinus fuscicollis fuscus
    G. E. Erikson, July 1949.
57a. Puerto Umbría, Río Guinéo, upper Río Putumayo, approx. 0° 54′ N, 76° 35′ W.
    Callimico goeldii
    M. H. Moynihan, ? January–February 1970 (sight record).
57a. Guamués (Río), 0° 28′ N, 76° 40′ W.
    Callimico goeldii
    Jorge Hernández Camacho (personal communication).
57b. Río Mecaya, Río Caquetá, 0° 28′ N, 75° 20′ W.
    Cebuella pygmaea
    P. Hershkovitz, February–March 1952, at 185 meters (sight records only).
    Saguinus fuscicollis fuscus
    P. Hershkovitz, February–May 1952, at 185 meters.
57c. Hacha, Quebrada del, left bank, upper Río Putumayo, approx. 0° 01′ S, 75° 30′ W, 200 meters.
    Callimico goeldii
    H. Granados and H. Arévalo, January 1960.

Amazonas

58a. La Chorrera, Río Igará-Paraná, 0° 55′ S, 73° 02′ W, 180 meters.
    Callimico goeldii
    H. Granados and F. Medem.
58b. Puerto Arturo (see Araracuara).
58b. Araracuara, above mouth Río Yari, approx. 0° 30′ S, 72° W.
    Callimico goeldii
    Pet in house of Señor Aniseto Fajardo, where it was photographed by F. Medem, July 1968
58c. Cahuinari (Río), enters lower Río Caquetá from right, approx. 1° 20′ S, 70° 45′ W.
    Callimico goeldii
    F. Medem, 1968 (sight record).
58d. Cara-Paraná, enters Río Putumayo from north at approx. 73° 15′ W.
    Callimico goeldii
    F. Medem, 1968 (sight record near headwaters).

58e. Leticia, Río Solimões, 4° 15′ S, 69° 56′ W, 100 meters.
Saguinus nigricollis nigricollis
J. N. Layne, February 1956.
Cebuella pygmaea
P. Hershkovitz, June 1952.

ECUADOR

Napo-Pastaza

59. San José Bajo [= below San José], Río Suno, 0° 31′ S, 77° 25′ W, 500 meters.
Saguinus nigricollis graellsi
Olalla Bros., 1924.

59. Sumaco = San José Bajo = San José de Sumaco, 0° 34′ S, 77° 38′ W.
(cf. Chapman, 1926, *Bull. Amer. Mus. Nat. Hist.* 55:719).
Saguinus nigricollis graellsi
Olalla Bros., 1924.

60. Avila, 0° 38′ S, 77° 25′ W, 600 meters.
Saguinus nigricollis graellsi
W. Clarke-McIntyre, May 1937; A. Olalla, September 1938.

61. Suno (Río), 0° 42′ S, 77° 08′ W.
Saguinus nigricollis graellsi
Olalla Bros., 1923, March 1924; February 1929.

62. Puerto Napo, Río Napo, 1° 03′ S, 77° 47′ W, 468 meters.
Saguinus fuscicollis lagonotus
G. Osculati, 1847.

63. La Coca, Río Napo, 0° 28′ S, 76° 58′ W, 258 meters.
Saguinus fuscicollis lagonotus
Jiménez de la Espada, June–July 1865; Olalla Bros.
Cebuella pygmaea
Jiménez de la Espada, 1865.

63. Humuyacu, Río Napo, 0° 27′ S, 76° 51′ W.
Saguinus fuscicollis lagonotus
Jiménez de la Espada, 1862–65.

64. Santa Rosa de Sucumbios, 0° 15′ N, 76° 27′ W.
Saguinus nigricollis graellsi
Olalla, November 1931.

65. Intillama (Indillama), Río Napo, left bank, 0° 27′ S, 76° 31′ W.
Cebuella pygmaea
P. Hershkovitz, June 1936 at 250 meters.

66. San Francisco, Río Napo, left bank, 0° 30′ S, 76° 22′ W.
Saguinus fuscicollis tripartitus
P. Hershkovitz, February–March 1936, on left bank at 200 meters.
Saguinus nigricollis graellsi
P. Hershkovitz, February–March 1936, on right bank at 200 meters.

67a. Lagarto Cocha, mouth, 0° 39′ S, 75° 16′ W (190 m).
Saguinus nigricollis graellsi
Olalla Bros., January 1926.
Saguinus fuscicollis tripartitus
Olalla Bros., January 1926.

67b. Aguarico (Río), 0° 59′ S, 75° 11′ N.
Saguinus fuscicollis tripartitus
Olalla Bros., January 1924; December 1925.

68. Lipuno (Río), Río Villano, 1° 31′ S, 77° 21′ W. Upper Río Curaray.
Cebuella pygmaea
E. E. Loch, 1935–36.

68. Sarayacu, Río Bobonaza, 1° 44′ S, 77° 29′ W. Upper Río Pastaza.
Saguinus fuscicollis lagonotus
Olalla, March 1931.

69. Yana Rumi (Río), 1° 38′ S, 76° 59′ W.
Saguinus nigricollis graellsi
R. Olalla, December 1934, February 1935.

70. Pindo Yacu (Río), (Río Pinto Yacu), 2° 08′ S, 76° 04′ W, 250 meters.
Saguinus nigricollis graellsi
R. Olalla, October 1934.
Saguinus fuscicollis lagonotus
R. Olalla, March 1931.

71. Conambo (Cunambo), upper Río Tigre, 1° 52′ S, 76° 47′ W, 240 meters.
Saguinus fuscicollis lagonotus
E. E. Loch, 1935–36.

72. Alpayacu, Río Pastaza, 1° 28′ S, 78° 07′ W.
Saguinus fuscicollis lagonotus

73. Shell Mera, Río Pastaza, 1° 30′ S, 78° 03′ W, 1,160 meters.
Saguinus fuscicollis lagonotus
R. Olalla, February 1959; H. R. French, April 1958.

74. Copotaza (Río), Río Pastaza, 2° 07′ S, 77° 27′ W (419 m).
Saguinus fuscicollis lagonotus
C. Buckley, December 1877; February 1878; R. Olalla, April 1939 at 750 meters; G. H. Tate, 1924.
Cebuella pygmaea
R. Olalla, April 1939 at 450 meters; C. Buckley, 1877–78.

75a. Montalvo, Río Bobonaza, Río Pastaza, 2° 04′ S, 76° 58′ W, 314 meters.
Saguinus fuscicollis lagonotus
R. Olalla, February 1932.
Cebuella pygmaea
R. Olalla, February 1932.

75b. Capihuara (Río), Río Pastaza, 2° 31′ S, 76° 51′ W, 300 meters.
Saguinus nigricollis graellsi
R. Olalla, November 1934.

Santiago-Zamora

76. Méndez, upper Río Santiago, 2° 43′ S, 78° 19′ W.
Saguinus fuscicollis lagonotus
C. Olalla and Bros., July 1934.

PERU

Loreto

77. Andoas, Río Pastaza, 2° 13′ S, 76° 51′ W, 250 meters.
Cebuella pygmaea
R. Olalla, February 1946.

78a. Siguín (= Sihuín), Río Pastaza, 3° 07′ S, 76° 25′ W.
Saguinus fuscicollis lagonotus
C. Olalla, "Mission Flornoy," 1936.

78b. Huachi, Río Pastaza, 3° 25′ S, 76° 20′ W, 207 meters.

Cebuella pygmaea
E. J. Brundage, November 1937, presumably on left bank.

78c. Apaga (Río), enters Río Putumayo from south at approximately 4° 42′ S, 77° 10′ W.
Callimico goeldii
P. Soini, April 1970, sight record.

79. Tarapoto, Río Napo, 2° 15′ S, 74° 06′ W.
Saguinus nigricollis graellsi
Jiménez de la Espada, June–July 1865.
Saguinus fuscicollis lagonotus
Jiménez de la Espada, June–July 1865.

80. Curaray (Río) (mouth), 2° 22′ S, 74° 05′ W, 140 meters.
Cebuella pygmaea
Olalla Bros., October–December 1925, March 1926.
Saguinus fuscicollis lagonotus
Olalla Bros., May 1926.
Saguinus nigricollis graellsi
Olalla Bros., 1925.
Saguinus fuscicollis tripartitus
Olalla Bros., October–December 1925.
Callimico goeldii
P. Soini, sight record.

81. Mazán (Río), 3° 28′ S, 73° 02′ W, 100 meters.
Saguinus fuscicollis lagonotus
Mendo B., November 1930.

82. Napo (Río), mouth at 3° 22′ S, 72° 40′ W.
Cebuella pygmaea
H. Bassler, 1926–27.
Saguinus mystax mystax
Jiménez de la Espada, 1865 (opposite mouth).
Saguinus fuscicollis lagonotus
H. Bassler, between 1926 and 1927; Jiménez de la Espada, 1865.

83. Chimbote, Río Marañon, 3° 49′ S, 70° 41′ W. This locality is given for the following species by Cruz Lima (1945). The first two listed could have originated in the general region of Chimbote on the southern bank of the Marañon, the third, *S. nigricollis*, is from the opposite shore. The last two (*midas, bicolor*) do not occur here.
Cebuella pygmaea
Saguinus mystax mystax
Saguinus nigricollis
[*Saguinus tamarin* (= *S. midas niger*)]
[*Saguinus bicolor bicolor*]

84. Cochiquinas (Río), mouth, 3° 39′ S, 71° 33′ W.
Cebuella pygmaea
Jiménez de la Espada, 1865.

85. Pebas, Río Marañon, 3° 10′ S, 71° 48′ W.
Cebuella pygmaea
R. W. Hendee, January–February 1928, at 100 meters; J. J. Mounsey, July 1913.
Saguinus nigricollis
Castelnau and Deville, 1847; Olalla Bros., October 1926; R. W. Hendee, January 1928 at 91 meters; J. J. Mounsey, August 1913.
[*Saguinus bicolor bicolor*]
Incorrect locality for this species recorded by I. Geoffroy, 1851, 1855.
Saguinus fuscicollis nigrifrons
R. W. Hendee, February 1928 at 91 meters; E. Heller, June 1923; Castelnau and Deville, 1847.

85. Yaguas Territory, near Pebas (q.v.).
Saguinus nigricollis
J. J. Mounsey, August 1913 at 150 meters.
Cebuella pygmaea
J. J. Mounsey, July 1913, at 150 meters.

86. Apayacu (Río), 3° 21′ S, 72° 07′ W, about 100 meters.
Cebuella pygmaea
Olalla Bros., December 1926.
Saguinus nigricollis
Olalla Bros., May, December 1926, January 1927.

87. Orosa, Río Marañon, 3° 23′ S, 72° 07′ W.
Cebuella pygmaea
Olalla Bros., September, November, December 1926.
Saguinus mystax mystax
Olalla Bros., September–December 1926.
Saguinus fuscicollis nigrifrons
Olalla Bros., September–December 1926.

88. Marupa, Río Marañon, 3° 25′ S, 72° 33′ W.
Saguinus mystax mystax
H. Bassler, May 1926.
Saguinus fuscicollis lagonotus
Olalla Bros., May 1926, May 1927; H. Bassler, 1926.

89. Santa Cecilia, Río Manití, 3° 26′ S, 72° 46′ W.
Cebuella pygmaea
C. Kalinowski, January 1957 at 110 meters.
Saguinus mystax mystax
C. Kalinowski, December 1956, January 1957 at 110 meters.
Saguinus fuscicollis nigrifrons
C. Kalinowski, January 1957 at 110 meters.
Callimico goeldii
P. Soini, 1970 (sight record).

90. Puerto Indiana, Río Marañon, north bank, 3° 20′ S, 72° 40′ W, 100 meters.
Saguinus fuscicollis tripartitus
Olalla Bros., May, June, July 1926.
Saguinus fuscicollis lagonotus
Olalla Bros., August 1926.

91. Destacamento, Río Marañon, 3° 21′ S, 72° 45′ W.
Saguinus nigricollis graellsi
Jiménez de la Espada, 1865.
Saguinus fuscicollis lagonotus
Jiménez de la Espada, 1865.

92. Iquitos, Río Marañon, 3° 45′ S, 73° 12′ W, 106 meters.
Cebuella pygmaea
J. M. Schunke, January 1929; H. Bassler, January 1920, September 1925.
Saguinus mystax mystax
H. Bassler, June 1927 (opposite Iquitos).

Saguinus fuscicollis tripartitus
J. M. Schunke, January 1927; C. Arrevalos, February 1929.
This tamarin does not occur here naturally.
Saguinus fuscicollis lagonotus
J. M. Schunke, November–December 1926, July 1928 at 150 meters; H. Bassler, July 1924, 1927; R. W. Hendee, 1928 at 120 meters.

93. Pampa Chica, ca. 3° 45′ S, 73° 12′ W.
Saguinus fuscicollis lagonotus
C. Kalinowski, August 1956.

94a. Pinto Yacu (Río), enters Río Nanay from north, 3° 45′ S, 73° 20′ W.
Callimico goeldii
P. Soini, 1970 (sight record).

94b. Chiriara, below Mishana, Río Nanay, 3° 45′ S, 73° 35′ W.
Callimico goeldii
P. Soini, 1970 (sight record).

94b. Quebrada Tocón above Mishana, 3° 45′ S, 73° 35′ W.
Callimico goeldii
P. Soini, 1970 (sight record).

94b. Mishana, Río Nanay, 3° 45′ S, 73° 35′ W.
Cebuella pygmaea
W. G. Kinzey, A. L. Rosenberger and M. Ramírez, July–September, 1974.
Callimico goeldii
P. Soini, March 1970.

94b. Santa Rita, Río Nanay, 3° 46′ S, 73° 31′ W.
Saguinus fuscicollis lagonotus
C. Kalinowski, September 1956.

95. Tigre (Río), 4° 27′ S, 74° 05′ W.
Saguinus fuscicollis lagonotus
Von Bauman, July 1936.
Callimico goeldii
P. Soini, 1970 (sight record).

96. Samiria (Río), (mouth, 4° 42′ S, 74° 12′ W).
Saguinus mystax mystax
H. Bluntschli, 1912.
Saguinus fuscicollis illigeri
H. Bluntschli, 1912.
Callimico goeldii
P. Soini, 1970, sight record.

97. Santa Elena, Río Samiria, 4° 42′ S, 74° 12′ W, 130 meters.
Saguinus fuscicollis illigeri
C. Kalinowski, December 1956.

98. Santa Cruz, Río Huallaga, 5° 34′ S, 75° 47′ W.
Cebuella pygmaea
E. Bartlett, May 1868.

99. Yurimaguas, Río Huallaga, 5° 54′ S, 76° 05′ W, 180 meters.
Some specimens labeled "Río Huallaga" may have been collected here.

100. Tapiche (Río) (= Río Blanco), 5° 00′ S, 73° 52′ W.
Callimico goeldii
H. Bassler, September, November 1926.

101. Río Pacaya, opposite Sapote, 5° 14′ S, 74° 10′ W.
Saguinus fuscicollis illigeri
J. J. Mounsey, July 1912, 78 meters [!].

102. Sarayacu, Río Ucayali, 6° 44′ S, 75° 07′ W.
Cebuella pygmaea
Olalla Bros., July, March, April 1927; Castelnau and Deville, 1847, presumably on right bank.
Saguinus mystax mystax
Olalla Bros., March, April 1927.
Saguinus fuscicollis illigeri (left bank Río Ucayali)
Olalla Bros., March, April, May 1927; Castelnau and Deville, 1847.
Saguinus fuscicollis nigrifrons (right bank, Río Ucayali).
Olalla Bros., March, April, August 1927.

103. Cerro Azul, Contamana, east bank, Río Ucayali, 7° 14′ S, 74° 34′ W, about 625 meters.
Saguinus mystax mystax
R. W. Hendee, November 1927.
Saguinus fuscicollis nigrifrons
R. W. Hendee, November 1927.
Callimico goeldii
R. W. Hendee, October–November 1927.

104. Pisquí (Río), 7° 41′ S, 75° 03′ W, about 150 meters.
Callimico goeldii
H. Bassler, November 1926.

105. Yarinacocha, Río Ucayali, 8° 15′ S, 74° 43′ W, 160 meters.
Saguinus fuscicollis leucogenys
J. M. Schunke, 31 May 1946.

106. Pucallpa, 8° 28′ S, 74° 36′ W, 180 meters.
Saguinus fuscicollis leucogenys
J. M. Schunke, July 1947.

107. Pachitea (Río), near mouth, 8° 45′ S, 74° 32′ W, 150 meters.
Saguinus fuscicollis leucogenys
O. Garlepp, November 1903, at 150 meters; E. Heller, March 1923.

108. Cumeria (*sic,* see Shahuía, opposite Cumaría).

108. Shahuía, opposite Cumaría, Río Ucayali, 9° 52′ S, 74° 01′ W, 300 meters.
"The locality listed as Cumeria refers to a post or hacienda at the mouth of the Quebrada of Shahuia. As this appears on no maps and cannot be considered a permanent name, I have given only the name 'Cumeria,' although the locality and quebrada of that name are on the opposite side of the Ucayali, at about 10° S. The region is typical of tropical forest country." R. W. Hendee, in Thomas, 1928, *Ann. Mag. Nat. Hist.* 10 (2):251.
Saguinus fuscicollis leucogenys
R. W. Hendee, July–August 1927.

109. Chicosa, Alto Río Ucayali, 10° 21′ S, 74° 00′ W, about 350 meters.
Saguinus fuscicollis weddelli
R. W. Hendee, September 1927 on right bank of Río Ucayali opposite Chicosa.

110. Lagarto, right bank Alto Río Ucayali, 10° 41′ S, 73° 48′ W, about 250 meters.
Saguinus fuscicollis weddelli
Olalla Bros., January, March 1928.
Saguinus mystax mystax
Olalla Bros., January, February 1928.

111. Santa Rosa, Alto Río Ucayali, 10° 43′ S, 73° 53′ W, about 250 meters.
Saguinus fuscicollis leucogenys
Olalla Bros., January 1928.

112. Tambo (Río), 10° 42′ S, 73° 47′ W, about 250 meters.
Saguinus imperator
H. Bassler, March 1929. L. Raul de los Ríos.

113. Urubamba (Río) mouth, 10° 42′ S, 73° 42′ W, about 250 meters .
Saguinus fuscicollis weddelli
Olalla Bros., September–November 1927.
Saguinus imperator
Olalla Bros., 1927.

114. Inuya (Río), 10° 40′ S, 73° 37′ W, 288 meters.
Saguinus fuscicollis weddelli
Olalla Bros., September 1927.
Saguinus imperator
Olalla Bros., September 1927.

115a. Yavarí (Río), 4° 21′ S, 70° 02′ W.
Cebuella pygmaea
Frank, 1858.
Saguinus fuscicollis nigrifrons

115b. Javarí (Rio), Amazonas, Brazil (See also Río Yavarí, Peru).
Saguinus fuscicollis fuscicollis
Frank, 1858.
Bates, 1856.

116. San Fernando, 4° 11′ S, 70° 52′ W.
Saguinus fuscicollis nigrifrons
C. Kalinowski, July 1957, at 100 meters.

117. Quebrada Esperanza, Rio Yavarí Mirim, 200 meters, 4° 21′ S, 71° 58′ W.
Saguinus mystax mystax
C. Kalinowski, September 1957.
Saguinus fuscicollis nigrifrons
C. Kalinowski, September 1957.

118. Yaquerana (Río), mouth, left bank, 5° 43′ S, 72° 58′ W.
Cebuella pygmaea
C. Kalinowski, August 1957 at 210 meters.

San Martín—Saguinus fuscicollis leucogenys

119. Yurac Yacu, 5° 52′ S, 77° 14′ W, 800 meters.
R. W. Hendee, July 1926, at 760 meters.

120. Moyobamba, Río Mayo, 6° 03′ S, 76° 58′ W, 820 meters.
R. W. Hendee, 1926; L. Rutter, February 1924 at 820 meters.

Huánuco—Saguinus fuscicollis leucogenys

121. Tingo María, 9° 08′ S, 75° 57′ W, 700 meters.
E. Heller, October 1922; R. W. Hendee, January–February 1927 at 600 meters.

122. Chinchavita, Río Huallaga, 9° 30′ S, 75° 52′ W.
R. W. Hendee, December 1926.

123a. Ganso Azul Airport (see Agua Caliente).

123a. Agua Caliente, Río Pachitea, 8° 49′ S, 74° 40′ W.
C. C. Sanborn, April 1946.

123b. San Antonio, right bank Río Pachitea, 9° 15′ S, 74° 57′ W.
L. Rutter, July 1923.

123c. Mairo (Puerto Mayro), 9° 55′ S, 75° 05′ W.
L. Rutter at 460 meters.

124. Pozuzo, 10° 05′ S, 75° 35′ W, 752 meters.
E. Heller, February 1923.

Junín—Saguinus fuscicollis leucogenys

125. Perené (Río), 11° 09′ S, 74° 19′ W (mouth).
Precise collecting locality unknown.
P. O. Simons, March 1899 at 700 meters.

Cusco—Saguinus fuscicollis weddelli

126. Cosireni (Río) (See Yuvini).

126. Yuvini, Río Cosireni, 12° 33′ S, 73° 04′ W.
E. Heller, September 1915 at 915 meters.

127. San Miguel (Río), 13° S, 73° 10′ W.
E. Heller, October 1915 at 1400 meters.

128. Hacienda Cadena, Río Marcapata, 13° 20′ S, 70° 46′ W.
C. Kalinowski, January 1948 at 890 meters.

Madre de Dios

129. Juárez (Río), mouth, 12° 25′ S, 71° 06′ W.
Saguinus imperator
C. Kalinowski, September 1961 at 400 meters.

129. Altamira, Río Manú (opposite mouth Río Juárez), 12° 12′ S, 71° 08′ W.
Saguinus imperator
C. Kalinowski, March 1963 at 400 meters.
Callimico goeldii
C. Kalinowski, March 1963 at 400 meters.

130. Zona Boca Amigo, 12° 36′ S, 70° 06′ W, 260 meters.
Saguinus imperator
C. Kalinowski, November 1954.

131. Itahuania, Río Alto Madre de Dios, 12° 40′ S, 71° 10′ W.
Saguinus fuscicollis weddelli
C. Kalinowski, October 1954.

Puno—Saguinus fuscicollis weddelli

132. Candamo, Río Huacamayo, 13° 29′ S, 69° 42′ W.
C. C. Sanborn, October 1941.

133. Pampa Grande, Sandia, Río Tambopata, 13° 59′ S, 68° 59′ W.
Hilda Heller, October, December 1951 at about 915 meters.

134. San Ignacio, 14° 01′ S, 68° 58′ W.
Hilda Heller, May 1951 at about 915 meters.

BOLIVIA

Pando

135. Cobija, Río Madeira, 11° 1′ S, 68° 44′ W.
Saguinus imperator

136. Victoria, Río Beni, 10° 59′ S, 66° 10′ W.
Saguinus fuscicollis weddelli
A. M. Olalla, 1937.

La Paz

137. Apolobamba (= Caupolicán), 14° 30′ S, 68° 20′ W.
Saguinus fuscicollis weddelli
H. A. Weddell, 1848.

138. Tumapasa (Tumupasa), Río Beni, 14° 08′ S, 67° 54′ W.
Saguinus fuscicollis weddelli
W. Mann, April, May, December 1922.

Santa Cruz

139. Santa Cruz de la Sierra, 17° 50′ S, 63° 10′ W. [*Callithrix argentata melanura,* collected by A. d'Orbigny, 1834 and recorded by I. Geoffroy (1851, p. 60) but was taken elsewhere in the department of Santa Cruz].

140. Palmarito, Río San Julián (San Miguel), 16° 45′ S, 62° 35′ W.
Callithrix argentata melanura
J. Steinbach, May 1918 at 400 meters.

140. Quiser (Río), 16° 30′ S, 62° 30′ W.
Callithrix argentata melanura
J. Steinbach, May–June 1918 at 700 meters.

141. Carcado (see Cercado).

141. Cercado, 17° 45′ S, 63° 15′ W.
Callithrix argentata melanura
J. Steinbach, June 1937.

141. Mapaiso Río Grande, 17° 52′ S, 63° 17′ W.
Callithrix argentata melanura
J. Steinbach, August 1909 at 400 meters.

142. Chiquitos (see San José de Chiquitos).

142. San José de Chiquitos, 17° 50′ S, 61° W.
Callithrix argentata melanura
H. Kreig, September–October 1926.

143. Puerto Suárez, Río Paraguay, 18° 58′ S, 57° 47′ W.
Callithrix argentata melanura
H. Kreig, November 1926.

GUYANA—*Saguinus midas midas*

144a. Supinaam River (enters Essequibo from west), 6° 58′ N, 58° 31′ W.
F. V. McConnell (dealer).

144b. Essequibo River, mouth at 6° 55′ N, 58° 25′ W.
E. R. Blake, March 1937.

145. Kartabo, Cuyuni River, right bank, 6° 23′ N, 58° 41′ W.
W. Beebe, July 1922, January 1924.

145. "Rio Mararuni" (misprint for Mazaruni River).

145. Mazaruni River
Joins with Cuyuni River at Kartabo before entering the lower Essequibo at Bartica (6° 24′ N, 58° 36′ W).

146. Bonasica River (Bonasika River), see Maripa.

146. Maripa, Bonasica River, 6° 45′ N, 58° 30′ W.
F. V. McConnell (dealer).

147. Georgetown, 6° 48′ N, 58° 10′ W, sea level.
J. Rodway (specimen accessioned November 1909).

147. Demerara River, Demerara, north side, 6° 48′ N, 58° 11′ W.
Frank (dealer), 1877.

148a. Dunoon, Demerara River, left bank, 6° 25′ N, 58° 18′ W.

148b. Mahaikabally, Demerara River, between 5° and 6° N.

SURINAME—*Saguinus midas midas*

Suriname

149. Paramaribo, 5° 50′ N, 55° 13′ W.
Dieperink; A. Kappler; I. T. Sanderson, April 1948.

150a. Zanderij (Airfield), 5° 21′ N, 55° 19′ W.
I. T. Sanderson, August–September 1938.

150b. Carolinakreek, 5° 23′ N, 55° 10′ W.
P. Hershkovitz, November–December 1961.

Brokopondo

151. Loksie Hattie, Saramacca River, left bank, 5° 10′ N, 55° 28′ W.
P. Hershkovitz, December 1961.

Nickerie

152. Kaiserberg Airstrip, Zuid River, 3° 10′ N, 56° 15′ W.
H. A. Beatty, October–December 1960, at 275 meters.

Marowijne

153. Moengo Tapoe, Marowijne River, 5° 35′ N, 54° 17′ W.
D. C. Geijskes, October 1948.

154. Tapanahoni River, 4° 22′ N, 54° 27′ W.
H. A. Beatty, May 1961.

FRENCH GUIANA—*Saguinus midas midas*

155a. Laurent, Maroni River, 5° 30′ N, 54° 04′ W.
Dr. Arimont, 1909.

155b. Cayenne, 4° 56′ N, 52° 19′ W.
M. Poiteau, 1822; M. Loustau, 1898; S. N. Klages, January 1917.

156a. Ipoucin (See Ipoussin).

156a. Ipoussin, 4° 10′ N, 52° 24′ W.
Cherrie and Gault, December 1900.

156b. Ouanary River, 4° 12′ N, 51° 40′ W.
Geay, 1900.

BRAZIL

Amapá—*Saguinus midas midas*

157. Vila Velha do Cassiporé, Oiapoque (= Oyapock), 3° 13′ N, 51° 13′ W.
M. M. Moreira, April 1952.

158. Amapá, Amapá, 2° 03′ N, 50° 48′ W.
J. Hidasi, May 1958.

159. Amapari (Rio), Macapá, 1° 40′ N, 51° 23′ W.
M. M. Moreira, November 1952.

160. Maruanum (Rio), Macapá, 0° 40′ N, 51° 10′ W.
M. M. Moreira, August 1952.

161. Macapá, Macapá, 0° 02′ N, 51° 03′ W.
M. M. Moreira, June 1953.

162. Vila Nova (Rio), Mazagão, 0° 04′ S, 51° 13′ W.
M. Lasso, April–May 1936.

Roraima

163. Deleted.

164. Forte do Rio Branco (see São Joaquim).

164. São Joaquim, Rio Branco, left bank, 3° 01′ N, 60° 29′ W.
Saguinus midas midas
J. Natterer, March, April 1832.

165. Moon Mountains (see Serra da Lua).

165. Serra da Lua, 2° 15′ N, 60° 45′ W.
Saguinus midas midas
R. H. Becker and M. P. Anderson, March 1913; F. V. McConnell (dealer).

Amazonas

166. Papuri (Rio), mouth, Rio Uaupés, 0° 36′ N, 69° 13′ W, 82 meters.
Saguinus inustus
Olalla Bros., July 1929.

167. Uaupés (Rio), opposite Tahuapunta, 82 meters, 0° 36′ N, 69° 11′ W.
Saguinus inustus
Olalla Bros., July 1926.
167. Talmapunta (see Rio Uaupés).
167. Tahuapunta (see Rio Uaupés).
168. Tabocal, Rio Negro (see Tabucal).
168. Tabucal, right bank, Rio Negro, 0° 48′ N, 67° 14 W.
Saguinus inustus
Olalla Bros., September 1929.
169a. Javanari (see Jauanari).
169a. Yauanari (see Jauanari).
169a. Jauanari, Rio Negro, right bank, 0° 32′ S, 64° 49′ W.
Saguinus inustus
Olalla Brothers, September 1929.
169b. Cuieras (Igarapé or Rio), Rio Demina, 0° 27′ N, 62° 43′ W.
Saguinus midas midas
170. Campos Salles, Manaus, Rio Negro, 3° 07′ S, 60° 02′ W.
Saguinus bicolor bicolor
A. M. Olalla, August 1928.
170. Barra do Rio Negro (see Manaus).
170. Manaus (Manaos), Rio Negro, left bank, 21 meters. 3° 08′ S, 60° 01′ W.
Saguinus bicolor bicolor
J. de Spix and Martius.
J. Natterer, February, June, September, October 1830.
Conte de Castelnau and E. Deville.
R. H. Becker, April 1913.
G. E. Erikson, September 1966.
170. Negro (Rio) mouth, (see Manaus).
170. Flores, suburb of Manaus (q.v.).
Saguinus bicolor bicolor
171. Tabatinga, Rio Solimões, 4° 16′ S, 69° 56′ W.
Cebuella pygmaea
J. de Spix and Martius Expedition.
172a. Santa Rita, north bank Rio Solimões, 3° 30′ S, 69° 20′ W.
Saguinus nigricollis nigricollis
W. K. Ehrhardt, September 1926.
Cebuella pygmaea
W. K. Ehrhardt, September 1926.
172b. São Paulo de Olivença, Rio Solimões, 3° 27′ S, 68° 48′ W.
Cebuella pygmaea
H. W. Bates, 1855.
Saguinus mystax mystax
J. de Spix and Martius Expedition; Castelnau and Deville, 1847.
Saguinus nigricollis nigricollis
J. de Spix and Martius Expedition. (opposite, on north bank of the Solimões).
Saguinus fuscicollis fuscicollis
J. de Spix and Martius Expedition; Frank, 1864 (right bank).
173. Tonantins (Rio), 2° 48′ S, 67° 46′ W.
Saguinus labiatus thomasi
W. Bates, November 1856; W. Ehrhardt, September–October 1926.
Saguinus fuscicollis fuscus
Lako and Salache, June 1930.
174a. Fonteboa, Rio Amazonas, 2° 28′ S, 66° 01′ W.
Saguinus mystax mystax
W. Ehrhardt, July, August 1926; K. Lako, August 1927; Lako and Salache, July 1930.
174b. Juruá (Rio), Amazonas, 7° S.
Saguinus mystax pileatus
E. Garbe, April 1902.
175. Lago Grande, Rio Juruá, 6° 41′ S, 69° 53′ W.
Saguinus fuscicollis melanoleucus
A. M. Olalla, September 1936.
176. Eirunepé (see Joáo Pessõa).
176. São Felipe (see João Pessõa).
176. João Pessõa (formerly São Felipe, now Eirunepé), upper Rio Juruá, 6° 40′ S, 69° 52′ W.
Cebuella pygmaea
A. M. Olalla, July 1936; December 1936–January 1937.
Saguinus mystax mystax
A. M. Olalla, August–September, 1936.
Saguinus fuscicollis fuscicollis
A. M. Olalla, July–September 1936. E. Garbe, November 1901–January 1902.
177. Igarapé Grande, Rio Juruá, 6° 43′ S, 70° 26′ W, about 150 meters.
Saguinus fuscicollis melanoleucus
A. M. Olalla, September–November, 1936 (right bank Rio Juruá).
Saguinus mystax mystax
A. M. Olalla, August 1936; December 1936–January 1937.
Saguinus fuscicollis fuscicollis
A. M. Olalla, August–September 1936.
178. Igarapé do Gordão, Rio Juruá, 6° 43′ S, 70° 08′ W.
Saguinus fuscicollis fuscicollis
A. M. Olalla, August 1936.
179. Libertade (Rio do), Rio Juruá, 7° 18′ S, 71° 50′ W.
Callimico goeldii
(London Zoological Society)
179. Mu (Rio) (see Rio do Libertade).
180. Santo Antonio, Rio Eirú, 6° 43′ S, 69° 52′ W.
Saguinus imperator
A. M. Olalla, September, October 1936.
Saguinus fuscicollis melanoleucus
A. M. Olalla, September–November 1936.
181. Santa Cruz, Rio Eirú, 7° 23′ S, 70° 47′ W.
Saguinus imperator
A. M. Olalla, September–November 1936.
Saguinus fuscicollis melanoleucus
A. M. Olalla, September–November 1936.
182. Ega (see Tefé).
182. Tefé (Lago de), 3° 27′ S, 64° 47′ W, near sea level.
Cebuella pygmaea
Castelnau
Saguinus mystax pileatus
Olalla Brothers, July 1928.
Saguinus fuscicollis avilapiresi
Olalla Brothers, July 1928.
182. Teffé (Lago de) (= Tefé [Lago de]).

183. Ipixuna (Lago do), Rio Solimões, 3° 52′ S, 63° 52′ W.
Saguinus mystax pileatus
João Bezerra de Souza, before 1940.
Cebuella pygmaea
João Bezerra de Souza, before 1940.

183. Ipoxona (Lago do) (see Ipixuna [Lago do]).

184. Ayapuá (Lago), Rio Purús, 4° 27′ S, 62° 08′ W.
Saguinus fuscicollis avilapiresi
W. Ehrhardt, March 1927.
Saguinus mystax pluto
C. Lako, October 1925; W. Ehrhardt, September–October 1925, March 1927, July 1930.

185. Mapixi (Lago do), Rio Purús, 5° 40′ S, 63° 53′ W.
Saguinus labiatus labiatus
C. Lako, June 1931 (right bank of Purús).
Saguinus mystax pluto
C. Lako, June 1931 (left bank of Purús).
Saguinus fuscicollis weddelli
C. Lako, June 1931.

186. Jaburú, Rio Purús, 5° 36′ S, 64° 03′ W, about 25 meters.
Saguinus mystax pluto
A. M. Olalla, December 1935 (opposite, on right bank).

187. Labrea, Rio Purús, 7° 16′ S, 64° 47′ W.
Saguinus labiatus labiatus
A. M. Olalla, January 1936.

188. Mamoriá (see São Luís de Mamoriá).

188. São Luís de Mamoriá, Rio Purús, 7° 33′ S, 66° 25′ W.
Saguinus mystax pileatus
Collector unknown.

189. Bom Lugar, Rio Purús, 8° 43′ S, 67° 23′ W.
Saguinus imperator
J. de Sá, April–May 1904.
Saguinus labiatus labiatus
J. Schönmann, July–August 1903; Lohse, July 1903.

190. Acre, Rio, Rio Purús, 8° 56′ S, 67° 23′ W.
Saguinus imperator
J. de Sá, April–May 1904.
Saguinus labiatus labiatus

191. Monte Verde, upper Rio Purús, 8° 47′ S, 67° 25′ W.
Saguinus imperator
J. de Sá, April–May 1904.

192a. Carabouca, Paraná do Jacaré (See Canabuoca).

192a. Canabuoca, Rio Solimões, 3° 30′ S, 60° 41′ W.
Saguinus labiatus labiatus
W. K. Ehrhardt, November, 1925. (See Lönnberg 1938, *Ark Zool., Stockholm* 30(18):7, for locality data).

192b. Manaquiri, Rio Solimões, right bank, 3° 19′ S, 60° 21′ W.
[*Saguinus midas niger*]
J. Natterer, August 1832. *Note:* Incorrect locality for the species. According to Pelzeln, who recorded it as *Midas ursulus,* the specimen was received in exchange from Estanislão do Santos, a collector or dealer.

192b. Manaquery (See Manaquiri).

193. Janauaca (Lago do), 3° 28′ S, 60° 17′ W.
Saguinus labiatus labiatus
J. Natterer, January 1833.

193. Luiz (see Lago do Janauaca).

193. Joanacan (Lago do) (see Janauacá [Lago do]).

194. Madeira (Rio) (mouth), 3° 22′ S, 58° 45′ W.
Callithrix humeralifer chrysoleuca
J. Natterer; J. B. Steere.

195. Miguel (Lago do) (see Rosarinho).

195. Rosarinho, Rio Madeira, 3° 43′ S, 59° 08′ W.
Saguinus labiatus labiatus
Olalla Brothers, May, June 1930.

195. Rozarhino (see Rosarinho).

196a. Auara (Igarapé), flows from Lago Auará into Rio Madeira, from right, 4° 22′ S, 59° 43′ W.
Callithrix humeralifer chrysoleuca
A. M. Olalla, February–March 1930.

196b. Borba, Rio Madeira, 4° 24′ S, 59° 35′ W.
Callithrix humeralifer chrysoleuca
J. Natterer, January, June, December 1830; Olalla Bros., February, April 1930.

197a. Humaitá (Humaytha), Rio Madeira, 7° 31′ S, 63° 02′ W.
Saguinus labiatus labiatus
H. Hoffmanns, September 1906.

197b. Castanho, Rio Castanhas (= Rio Roosevelt), 7° 25′ S, 60° 20′ W.
Callithrix argentata melanura
Collector not recorded. G. K. Cherrie was here 15–26 April 1914.

198. Tapaiuna (Lago), Rio Madeira, 3° 23′ S, 58° 16′ W.
Callithrix humeralifer chrysoleuca
A. M. Olalla, April–May 1936.

199. Baptista (Lago do), Rio Madeira, 3° 18′ S, 58° 15′ W.
Callithrix humeralifer chrysoleuca
A. M. Olalla, January–April, July–November 1936, January 1937.

200. Villa Bella Imperatriz (see Lago Andirá).

200. Andirá (Lago), Rio Andirá, 2° 50′ S, 56° 55′ W.
Callithrix humeralifer humeralifer
A. M. Olalla, October 1930.

201. Andirá (Rio) (mouth), enters Furo de Ramos at Barreirinha, 2° 45′ S, 56° 49′ W.
Callithrix humeralifer humeralifer
A. M. Olalla, October 1930.

202. Parintins, 2° 36′ S, 56° 44′ W.
Town on south bank Rio Amazonas.
Callithrix humeralifer humeralifer

202. Tupinambarana, (Rio), 2° 42′ S, 56° 44′ W.
Callithrix humeralifer humeralifer

203. Itaquatiara (see Itacoatiara).

203. Itacoatiara (= Serpa), Rio Amazonas, north bank, 3° 08′ S, 58° 25′ W.
Saguinus midas midas
A. M. Olalla, November 1935, August 1936.

Saguinus midas niger
incorrectly reported here by Cruz Lima.
203. Serpa (see Itacoatiara)
204. Deleted.
205. Lago do Canacari, Rio Amazonas, north bank, 2° 57′ S, 58° 15′ W.
Saguinus midas midas
A. M. Olalla, August 1936, November 1935, January 1936, March 1936.
206. Castanhal (= Serra Castanhal), right bank Rio Nhamundá, 1° 50′ S, 56° 58′ W.
Saguinus bicolor ochraceus
A. M. Olalla, January 1931.
207. Serra do Espelho, Rio Nhamundá (see Rio Piratucu).
Saguinus bicolor ochraceus
Olalla Bros.
207. Paratucu (Rio) (see Rio Piratucu).
207. Piratucu (Rio), Rio Nhamundá, 1° 52′ S, 56° 55′ W.
Saguinus bicolor ochraceus
Olalla Bros., December 1930.

Acre

208. Cruzeiro do Sul, upper Rio Juruá, 7° 37′ S, 72° 36′ W.
Saguinus fuscicollis melanoleucus
M. Moreira, July 1956 (right bank).
209. Pedra Preta, upper Rio Juruá, 8° 48′ S, 72° 49′ W.
Saguinus imperator
M. Moreira, July 1956 (right bank).
Saguinus fuscicollis acrensis
M. Moreira, July 1956.
210. Oriente (See Seringal Oriente).
210. Seringal Oriente, upper Rio Juruá, 8° 48′ S, 72° 46′ W.
Cebuella pygmaea
M. Moreira, August 1956.
Saguinus fuscicollis acrensis
M. Moreira, July 1956.
Saguinus mystax mystax
M. Moreira, July–August 1956 (left bank).
Saguinus imperator
M. Moreira, July 1956 (right bank).
Callimico goeldii
M. Moreira, August 1956.
211. Yaco, Rio, 9° 03′ S, 68° 33′ W.
Callimico goeldii
212. Xapury, Rio, upper Rio Purús, 10° 39′ S, 68° 30′ W.
Saguinus fuscicollis weddelli
Callimico goeldii
213. Iquiri, Rio Iquiri (Ituxi), 10° 11′ S, 67° 33′ W.
Saguinus labiatus labiatus
P. E. Vanzolini, November 1951.
Saguinus fuscicollis weddelli
P. E. Vanzolini, November 1951.

Rondônia

214a. Pôrto Velho, upper Rio Madeira, 8° 46′ S, 63° 54′ W.
Saguinus fuscicollis weddelli
R. H. Becker, April 1915.
214b. Gi-Paraná, Rio (see Rio Jiparaná).
214b. Rio Jiparaná, upper Rio Madeira, mouth, 8° 03′ S, 62° 52′ W.
Callithrix argentata melanura
A. Machado and Pereira, before 1960, precise locality not specified.
214c. Urupá, Rio Jiparaná, 10° 54′ S, 61° 51′ W.
Callithrix argentata melanura

Pará

215. Faro, Rio Nhamundá, 2° 11′ S, 56° 44′ W.
Saguinus bicolor martinsi
O. Martins, 1911.
A. M. Olalla, December 1930, January 1931.
Museu Goeldi, January, February 1912.
E. Snethlage, January 1912.
215. San José, Rio Nhamundá (see Faro).
Saguinus bicolor martinsi
Olalla Bros., January 1931.
215. Yaracana, Rio Nhamundá (see Faro).
Saguinus bicolor martinsi
Olalla Bros., February 1931.
216. Erepecurú (Rio) (or Rio Cuminá), tributary of Rio Paru de Oeste, 1° 30′ S, 56° W.
Saguinus bicolor martinsi
M. Lasso.
217. Óbidos, Rio Amazonas, north bank, 1° 55′ S, 55° 31′ W.
Saguinus midas midas
H. W. Bates, October–November 1849; E. Snethlage, February 1912.
217. Colonia do Veado, Óbidos, 1° 55′ S, 55° 31′ W.
Saguinus midas midas
F. Lima and E. Snethlage, February 1912.
218. Lago Cuitêua (see Lago Cuipeua).
218. Lago Cuipeua, 1° 53′ S, 54° 53′ W.
Saguinus midas midas
A. M. Olalla, November 1934.
219. Maycury (Rio) (See Monte Alegre).
219. Monte Alegre, Rio Gurupatuba, left bank, 10 meters, 2° 01′ S, 54° 04′ W.
Saguinus midas midas
[Locality record for *Callithrix argentata argentata* by Goeldi and Hagmann (1904, p. 52) is based on living animal in zoo; the species is not found here naturally but does occur on the opposite or south side of the Amazon].
220. Jary (Rio) (or Rio Jari), Rio Amazonas, north bank, 1° 10′ S, 52° W.
Saguinus midas midas
Schultz Kampfhenkel.
221. "Islands region between Marajó Island and the mainland"
Saguinus midas midas
Cruz Lima, 1945, *Mammals of Amazonia; Primates*, p. 219.
222. Paricatuba, Rio Amazonas, near mouth of Rio Tapajóz, 2° 12′ S, 54° 54′ W.
Callithrix humeralifer humeralifer
Schultz.
223a. Casa Nova, Rio Arapiuns, 2° 18′ S, 54° 39′ W.
Callithrix humeralifer humeralifer
A. M. Olalla, July 1934.

223b. Arapiuns (Rio), 2° 10′ S, 55° 00′ W.
Callithrix humeralifer humeralifer

224. Amorin (see Amarim).

224. Amarim (Igarapé), Rio Tapajóz, 2° 26′ S, 55° W.
Callithrix humeralifer humeralifer
A. M. Olalla, June 1931.

224. Bravo (Igarapé) (see Amarim [Igarapé])
Callithrix humeralifer humeralifer
A. M. Olalla, June 1931.

225. Irocanga, Rio Tapajóz, 2° 34′ S, 55° 02′ W.
Callithrix humeralifer humeralifer
A. M. Olalla, April 1934.

226. Boim, Rio Tapajóz, 2° 49′ S, 55° 10′ W.
Callithrix humeralifer humeralifer
E. Snethlage, Museu Goeldi, September 1911; J. Lima, December 1924.

227. Arara, Rio Tapajóz, 3° 39′ S, 55° 36′ W.
Callithrix humeralifer humeralifer
A. M. Olalla, January 1959.

228a. Urucurituba, Rio Tapajóz, 3° 41′ S, 55° 37′ W.
Callithrix humeralifer humeralifer
A. M. Olalla, April, June 1958, January 1959.

228b. Itaituba, Rio Tapajóz, 4° 17′ S, 55° 59′ W.
Callithrix humeralifer humeralifer
E. Snethlage, January 1906.

229. Vila Braga, Rio Tapajóz, 4° 25′ S, 56° 17′ W.
Callithrix humeralifer humeralifer
E. Snethlage, November 1908.

230. Pimental, Rio Tapajóz, 4° 34′ S, 56° 12′ W.
Callithrix argentata leucippe
E. Snethlage, November 1908.

231. Monte Cristo, Rio Tapajóz, 4° 04′ S, 55° 38′ W.
Callithrix argentata leucippe
E. Garbe, 1920.

232. Pedreira (see Pedreiras).

232. Pedreiras, Rio Tapajóz, 4° 03′ S, 55° 37′ W.
Callithrix argentata leucippe
A. M. Olalla.

233. Araipe (see Arauepá).

233. Arauepá, Rio Tapajóz, 3° 50′ S, 55° 37′ W.
Callithrix argentata leucippe
A. M. Olalla.

234. Fordlandia, Rio Tapajóz, 3° 40′ S, 55° 30′ W.
Callithrix argentata leucippe
A. M. Olalla, June 1959; R. M. Gilmore, February, March 1938.

235. Aveiros(Ssee Aveiro).

235. Aveiro, Rio Tapajóz, 3° 15′ S, 55° 10′ W.
Callithrix argentata argentata
A. M. Olalla, June 1934.

236. Tauari, Rio Tapajóz, 3° 05′ S, 55° 06′ W.
Callithrix argentata argentata
A. M. Olalla, April 1931.

237. Itapoamá (See Itapuamá).

237. Itapuamá, Rio Tapajóz, 2° 57′ S, 55° 02′ W.
Callithrix argentata argentata
A. M. Olalla, March–April 1934.

237. Uapoamá, Rio Tapajóz (= Itapuamá misspelled).

238. Tapaiuna, Rio Tapajóz, 2° 54′ S, 55° 05′ W.
Callithrix argentata argentata
A. M. Olalla, July, August 1959.

239. Aramanay (See Aramanai).

239. Aramanai, Rio Tapajóz, 2° 45′ S, 54° 59′ W.
Callithrix argentata argentata
A. M. Olalla, March 1931.

240. Piquiatuba, Rio Tapajóz, 2° 40′ S, 54° 58′ W.
Callithrix argentata argentata
A. M. Olalla, May 1931; May–June 1936.

241. Caxiricatuba, Rio Tapajóz, 2° 36′ S, 54° 56′ W.
Callithrix argentata argentata
A. M. Olalla, May 1931, March 1936.

242. Mararú, Rio Tapajóz (see Santarém).
Callithrix argentata argentata
E. Snethlage, September 1911.

242. Maraú (= Mararú misspelled).

242. Marua (= Maraú = Mararú).

242. Santarém, Rio Tapajóz, 2° 26′ S, 54° 42′ W.
Callithrix argentata argentata
A. M. Olalla, June 1934.
Callithrix argentata leucippe

243. Maicá, Rio Amazonas, 2° 33′ S, 54° 24′ W.
Callithrix argentata argentata
C. R. Aschmeir, June 1923.

244. Tamacury (see Tamarury).

244. Tamarury, 2° 25′ S, 53° 52′ W.
Callithrix argentata argentata
E. Snethlage (O. Martins), August 1912.

245. Xingu (Rio) mouth, 1° 30′ S, 51° 53′ W.
Saguinus midas niger.

246. Villarinho do Monte (see Vilarhino do Monte).

246. Vilarinho do Monte, Rio Xingu (right bank), 1° 37′ S, 52° 01′ W.
Saguinus midas niger
A. M. Olalla, 20–26 September 1931.
Callithrix argentata argentata
A. M. Olalla, 21, 29 September 1931.

— Recreio, Rio Majary (not located).
Saguinus midas niger
A. M. Olalla, 6–8 September 1931.
Callithrix argentata argentata
A. M. Olalla, 7, 8 September 1931.

247. Tapará, Rio Xingu, 1° 38′ S, 52° 05′ W.
Saguinus midas niger
A. M. Olalla, 26 August 1931.
Callithrix argentata argentata
A. M. Olalla, 23, 30 August 1931.

248. Pôrto de Moz, Rio Xingu, right bank, mouth, 1° 45′ S, 52° 14′ W.
Saguinus midas niger
A. M. Olalla, 4 September 1931.

249. Altamira, Rio Xingu, 3° 12′ S, 52° 12′ W.
Callithrix argentata argentata

250. Maloca, Rio Curuá, 7° 55′ S, 54° 50′ W.
Callithrix argentata argentata
E. Snethlage, November 1914.

251. Gradaús (= Novo Horizonte), Rio Fresco, right bank, 252 meters, 7° 43′ S, 51° 11′ W.
Saguinus midas niger
C. T. de Carvalho, July–October 1957.

— Tocantins (Rio)
Saguinus midas niger
A. M. Olalla.
Sieber.

252. Vaicajá (Fazenda), Rio Tocantins (see Cametá).
Callithrix argentata argentata
252. Cametá, Rio Tocantins, left bank, 2° 15′ S, 49° 29′ W.
Saguinus midas niger
E. Snethlage, January 1911.
A. M. Olalla, October–November 1931; July 1930.
Museu Goeldi, January 1901.
Callithrix argentata argentata
Sieber.
E. Snethlage, January–February 1911.
A. M. Olalla, October–November 1931; July 1934, October 1936.
253. Mocajuba, Rio Tocantins, right bank, 2° 35′ S, 49° 30′ W.
Saguinus midas niger
A. M. Olalla, November 1931.
254. Baião, Rio Tocantins, right bank, 2° 41′ S, 49° 41′ W.
Saguinus midas niger
A. M. Olalla, November–December 1931.
255. Arumatéua, Rio Tocantins, left bank, 3° 54′ S, 49° 41′ W.
Saguinus midas niger
F. Lima, October 1912.
256. Pará (see Belém or Belém de Pará).
256. Belém, Rio Guama, right bank, 1° 27′ S, 48° 29′ W.
Saguinus midas niger
Sieber; J. Natterer, October–December 1834, January 1835; W. H. Bates, 1848.
257. Engenho do São Benjamin, Belém de Pará, 1° 27′ S, 48° 29′ W.
Saguinus midas niger
J. Natterer, October 1834.
258. Itingo (see Utinga).
258. Utinga, Belém, 1° 27′ S, 48° 29′ W.
Saguinus midas niger
F. Lima; E. Heller, May 1923.
259. Ananindeua, Belém, 1° 22′ S, 48° 23′ W.
Saguinus midas niger
E. Snethlage, May 1912.
259. Benevides, Belém, 1° 22′ S, 48° 15′ W.
Saguinus midas niger
E. Snethlage, July 1911.
260. Igarapé Assú (see Açu [Igarapé]).
260. Açu (Igarapé), 1° 32′ S, 47° 03′ W.
Saguinus midas niger
A. Robert, January–April 1904 at 50 meters.
261. Peixe-boi, Belém 1° 12′ S, 47° 18′ W.
Saguinus midas niger
E. Snethlage, February, 1908.
Museum Goeldi, May 1908.
262. Conceiçao, Rio Mojú, left bank (*sic* = Rio Guamá), 1° 38′ S, 47° 31′ W.
Saguinus midas niger

Mato Grosso—Callithrix argentata melanura

263. Matogrosso (see Vila Bella de Santissima Trinidade).
263. Vila [or Villa] Bella da Santissima Trinidade, Rio Guaporé, 15° S, 59° 57′ W, 250 meters.
J. Natterer, September–November 1824.
264. Jaurú (Rio), 15° 30′ S, 58° 33′ W.
A. Miranda Ribeiro, 1909–10.
265. Caiçara, Rio Paraguay, 16° 03′ S, 57° 43′ W, 152 meters.
J. Natterer, October, December 1824.
266. Cáceres (see São Luis de Cáceres)
266. São Luis de Cáceres, 16° 04′ S, 57° 41′ W, 152 meters.
A. Miranda-Ribeiro, 1909–10.
267. Corumbá, Rio Paraguay, 19° 01′ S, 57° 39′ W.
E. Garbe, 1917.
268. Urucum de Corumbá (see Urucum).
268. Urucum, Rio Paraguay, 19° 13′ S, 57° 33′ W.
L. E. Miller, November 1913 at 125 meters; C. Taylor (C. C. Sanborn), August 1926.
269. Cuyaba (= Cuiabá).
269. Cuiabá, Rio Cuiabá, 15° 35′ S, 56° 05′ W, 219 meters.
J. Natterer, July, October 1824; J. Lima, September 1937.
270. Córrego do Cabral (see Cabral).
270. Cabral, Rio Aricá-Assú, 15° 30′ S, 55° 48′ W.
F. C. Hoehne, 1911.
271. Santa Ana de Chapada, 15° 26′ S, 55° 45′ W, 643 meters.
A. Robert, September 1902.
271. Serra de Chapada (see Santa Ana de Chapada)
272. Santo Antônio do Leverger, 15° 52′ S, 56° 05′ W.
J. Lima, September 1937.
273. Aricá (Fazenda), 15° 40′ S, 55° 49′ W, 203 meters.
A. M. Olalla, June 1944.
274. Palmeiras, 16° 03′ S, 55° 30′ W.
A. M. Olalla, June 1944.

Goiás—Callithrix jacchus penicillata

275a. Cana Brava (see Canabrava).
275a. Canabrava, Rio Tocantins, 9° 14′ S, 48° 12′ W.
275b. Palma, 12° 33′ S, 47° 42′ W.
276a. Pilar, 14° 41′ S, 49° 27′ W.
276b. Almas, Rio das, 14° 35′ S, 49° 02′ W.
J. Lima, 1934.
276c. Veadeiros, Rio Corumbá, 14° 07′ S, 47° 31′ W.
277a. Esperanza, Fazenda, Rio Uruhu (see Uruhu, Rio).
277a. Uruhu (Uru), Rio, 15° 27′ S, 49° 44′ W.
G. A. Baer Collection, December 1905 at 700 meters.
277b. Jaragua, Rio das Almas, 15° 45′ S, 49° 20′ W.
277c. Planaltina, 15° 37′ S, 47° 40′ W.
278a. Aragarças, Rio Araguaia, 15° 55′ S, 52° 15′ W.
278b. Anápolis, 16° 20′ S, 48° 58′ W, 1,000 meters.
R. M. Gilmore, January–July, September–December 1936.
279. Inhumas, 16° 22′ S, 49° 30′ W.
280. Goiânia, 16° 23′ S, 49° 19′ W.
E. Dente and W. Bokermann (Expedicião

Cientifica do Instituto Butantã), August 1949.
281a. Ponte do Paranaíba (see Itumbiara).
281a. Itumbiara, Rio Paranaíba, 18° 25′ S, 49° 13′ W.
281b. Catalão, Rio Jordão, 18° 10′ S, 47° 57′ W, 844 meters.
Dreher, May 1904.
Maranhão—Callithrix jacchus jacchus
282a. São João dos Patos, 6° 30′ S, 43° 42′ W, 200 meters.
Emil Kaempfer, 26 July–8 August 1926.
Piauí—Callithrix jacchus jacchus
282b. Arara, 8° 39′ S, 41° 35′ W, 68 meters.
H. Snethlage, January 1925.
283. Deserto, 8° 06′ S, 40° 42′ W.
H. Snethlage, April 1925.
Ceará—Callithrix jacchus jacchus
284a. Icarai—Mosquito, 3° 03′ S, 39° 38′ W.
284b. Monduby (see Mondubim).
284b. Mondubim, 3° 48′ S, 38° 35′ W, near Fortaleza.
284c. São Benedito, 4° 03′ S, 40° 53′ W.
284d. Ipu, Serra do Ibiapaba, 4° 20′ S, 40° 42′ W, 300 meters.
E. Snethlage, May 1910.
284d. Serra da Ibiapaba (= Serra Grande, see Ipu).
284e. Pacoti, 4° 13′ S, 38° 56′ W.
284e. Pernambuquinho, 4° 14′ S, 38° 57′ W.
284e. Serra de Guaramiranga, 4° 14′ S, 38° 56′ W.
284e. Mulungu, 4° 18′ S, 39° 00′ W.
284e. Baturité, 4° 20′ S, 38° 53′ W.
285a. Chapada do Araripe, 7° 20′ S, 40° W.
Leitão de Carvalho, 1936.
285b. Crato, 7° 14′ S, 39° 23′ W.
286. Juá (see Iguatu).
286. Iguatu, 6° 22′ S, 39° 18′ W, 215 meters.
R. H. Becker, August 1913.
Paraíba—Callithrix jacchus jacchus
287a. Mamaguape, 6° 50′ S, 35° 07′ W.
287b. Penha (= Nossa Senhora de Penha), 7° 10′ S, 34° 48′ W.
P. Schirch and E. Bresslau, June 1914.
287c. Coremas, 7° 01′ S, 37° 58′ W.
Pernambuco—Callithrix jacchus jacchus
288a. Tapera, 8° 24′ S, 38° 05′ W.
288b. Triunfo, 7° 50′ S, 38° 07′ W.
289a. São Lourenço, 8° 00′ S, 35° 03′ W.
A. Robert, July–August 1903, at 28–60 meters.
289b. Dois Irmãos (small village NW Recife, see Recife).
P. Schirch and E. Bresslau, June 1914.
289b. Recife, 8° 03′ S, 34° 54′ W, sea level.
P. Schirch and E. Bresslau, May 1914.
289b. Fundão, suburb of Recife.
P. Schirch and E. Bresslau, June 1914.
289b. Pernambuco = Recife.
G. Marcgrave (16th–17th century).
Alagoas—Callithrix jacchus jacchus
290. Quebrangulo, 9° 20′ S, 36° 29′ W.
290. São Miguel, 9° 47′ S, 36° 05′ W.
O. Pinto and C. C. Andrade, October 1951; Dos Campos.
290. Maceió, 9° 40′ S, 35° 43′ W.
A. F. Coimbra-Filho, 1970.
291. Mangabeiras, 9° 57′ S, 36° 08′ W.
O. Pinto and C. C. Andrade, October 1952.
Bahia
292a. Santa Rita de Cássia, 11° 00′ S, 44° 32′ W, 434 meters.
Callithrix jacchus jacchus
292b. Barreires, 12° 08′ S, 45° 00′ W.
Callithrix jacchus penicillata
292c. Riachao das Neves, 11° 48′ S, 44° 44′ W.
Callithrix jacchus penicillata
292d. Lamarão, upper Rio Itapicurú, 10° 46′ S, 40° 21′ W, 490 meters.
Callithrix jacchus penicillata
A. Robert, May–June 1903, at 300 meters.
293a. Feira de Santana, 12° 15′ S, 38° 57′ W.
293b. Santo Amaro, 12° 32′ S, 38° 43′ W, 270 meters.
Callithrix jacchus jacchus
(= *C. j. jacchus* × *C. j. penicillata*)
R. H. Becker, October 1913.
294. Baia (= Salvador, see Bahia)
294. Bahia (= Salvador), 12° 59′ S, 38° 31′ W.
Callithrix jacchus penicillata
H. Sellow (early 19th century).
Schneider, 1875.
Verday, 1874.
Callithrix jacchus jacchus
Wied-Neuwied, 1815–17.
Spix and Martius Expedition (early 19th century).
294. Madre de Deus (Ilha), 12° 44′ S, 38° 37′ W.
Callithrix jacchus jacchus
294. Curupeba, Recôncavo, 12° 43′ S, 38° 36′ W.
Callithrix jacchus jacchus
294. Corupeba, Recôncavo (see Curupeba, Recôncavo).
295. Itaparica, Ilha de, 13° S, 38° 42′ W.
Callithrix jacchus jacchus
M. J. Nicoll, December 1905.
296. Macaco Secco, 12° 59′ S, 41° 07′ W, 480 meters.
Callithrix jacchus penicillata
R. H. Becker, November 1913.
296. Malhada, not precisely located.
Several localities named Malhada are in Bahia within the range of *"Callithrix penicillata jordani,"* to which the Malhada marmoset is referred by Avila Pires (1969, p. 60).
297a. Maraú, 14° 06′ S, 39° 00′ W.
[*Leontopithecus rosalia chrysomelas*]
Coimbra-Filho (1970*a*, p. 258) "believed" it might occur here, but locality is outside recognized range of *chrysomelas.*
297b. Camamu, 13° 57′ S, 39° 07′ W.
[*Leontopithecus rosalia chrysomelas*]
Coimbra-Filho (1970*a*, p. 258) "believed" it might occur here, but locality is outside recognized range of *chrysomelas.*
297c. Grungogy, Rio (see Gongogi, Rio).
297c. Gongogi, Rio, 14° 12′ S, 39° 38′ W.
[*Leontopithecus rosalia chrysomelas*]
O. M. O. Pinto (cf. Coimbra-Filho 1970*a*, p. 257).

298. Mundo Novo, Rio Pardo, 15° 16′ S, 40° 58′ W.
Callithrix jacchus penicillata
Wied-Neuwied 1815–17.

299. Almada (Fazenda), Rio Almada, 14° 38′ S, 39° 12′ W.
Callithrix jacchus penicillata
Serviço do Estudos e Pesquisa sôbre a Febra Amarela (SEPSFA).
Leontopithecus rosalia chrysomelas
Serviço do Estudos e Pesquisa sôbre a Febra Amarela (SEPSFA).

299. Buerarema, Ribeirão da Fortuna, Estação da Mata do Cacau, 14° 57′ S, 39° 19′ W.
Callithrix jacchus penicillata
Serviço do Estudos e Pesquisa sôbre a Febra Amarela (SEPSFA); 17 October 1944.
Leontopithecus rosalia chrysomelas
Serviço do Estudos e Pesquisa sôbre a Febra Amarela (SEPSFA); 17 October 1944.

299. Buerarema, Highway km 5, 14° 57′ S, 39° 19′ W.
Leontopithecus rosalia chrysomelas
Serviço do Estudos e Pesquisa sôbre a Febra Amarela (SEPSFA); 21 January 1945.

299. Fortuna (Fazenda), Buerarema, 14° 57′ S, 39° 19′ W.
Callithrix jacchus penicillata
Serviço do Estudos e Pesquisa sôbre a Febra Amarela (SEPSFA).
Leontopithecus rosalia chrysomelas
Serviço do Estudos e Pesquisa sôbre a Febra Amarela (SEPSFA).

299. Ilheos (see Ilhéus)

299. Ilhéus, 14° 49′ S, 39° 02′ W, sea level.
Callithrix jacchus penicillata
(= *C. j. penicillata* × *C. j. geoffroyi*)
Wied-Neuwied, 1815–1817.
Serviço do Estudos e Pesquisa sôbre a Febra Amarela (SEPSFA); September 1944.
E. Garbe, August 1919.
Leontopithecus rosalia chrysomelas
Wied-Neuwied 1815–17.
Coimbra-Filho (1970*a*, p. 258).

299. Morro das Pedras (Fazenda), Ilhéus, 14° 49′ S, 39° 02′ W.
Callithrix jacchus penicillata
(= *C. j. penicillata* × *C. j. geoffroyi*)
Serviço do Estudos e Pesquisa sôbre a Febra Amarela (SEPSFA); September 1944.

299. Estação da Mata do Cacau, Ribeirão do Fortuna (See Buerarema).

299. São José (Fazenda) Rio do Braco, Pontal, 14° 39′ S, 39° 01′ W.
Leontopithecus rosalia chrysomelas
Serviço do Estudos e Pesquisa sôbre a Febra Amarela (SEPSFA); 29 November 1944, 1 December 1944, 29 January 1945.

299. Sertam (= Sertao) d'Ilhéus, 14° 49′ S, 39° 02′ W.
Leontopithecus rosalia chrysomelas
Wied-Neuwied 1815–17.

299. Uruçuca, 14° 35′ S, 39° 16′ W.
Leontopithecus rosalia chrysomelas
Coimbra-Filho (1970*a*, p. 258).

299. Urucutuca, 14° 39′ S, 39° 03′ W.
Callithrix jacchus penicillata
Serviço do Estudos e Pesquisa sôbre a Febra Amarela (SEPSFA).
Leontopithecus rosalia chrysomelas
Serviço do Estudos e Pesquisa sôbre a Febra Amarela (SEPSFA).

299. Pirataquissé (Fazenda), 14° 50′ S, 39° 05′ W.
Callithrix jacchus penicillata
(*C. j. penicillata* × *C. j. geoffroyi*)
Serviço do Estudos e Pesquisa sôbre a Febra Amarela (SEPSFA).
Leontopithecus rosalia chrysomelas
Serviço do Estudos e Pesquisa sôbre a Febra Amarela (SEPSFA).

300. Borrachudo (Fazenda), Itabuna, 14° 48′ S, 39° 16′ W.
Leontopithecus rosalia chrysomelas
Serviço do Estudos e Pesquisa sôbre a Febra Amarela (SEPSFA); April 1945.

300. Itabuna, Rio Ilhéus, 14° 48′ S, 39° 16′ W, 55 meters.
Callithrix jacchus penicillata
Leontopithecus rosalia chrysomelas
Coimbra-Filho (1970*a*, p. 258).

301. Poções, 14° 31′ S, 40° 21′ W.
Leontopithecus rosalia chrysomelas
Vergilio de Oliveira, March 1944.

302. Ribeirão da Minhocas, Rio Ilhéus, 15° 12′ S, 39° 57′ W.
Leontopithecus rosalia chrysomelas
Wied-Neuwied, 1815–17.

303. Una, 15° 18′ S, 39° 04′ W.
Leontopithecus rosalia chrysomelas

304. Pardo (Rio), 15° 39′ S, 38° 57′ W.
Leontopithecus rosalia chrysomelas
Wied-Neuwied, 1815–17.
Callithrix jacchus penicillata
Wied-Neuwied, 1815–17.

305. Barra da Vareda, Rio Pardo, 15° 15′ S, 40° 39′ W.
Leontopithecus rosalia chrysomelas
Wied-Neuwied, 1815–17.

306. Belmonte, Rio, (cf. Rio Jequitinhonha) 15° 45′ S, 38° 53′ W.
Callithrix jacchus penicillata
(= *C. j. penicillata* × *C. j. geoffroyi*)
Wied-Neuwied, 1815–17.

307a. Jacurussú, Rio (see Jucurucú, Rio)

307a. Jucururu, Rio (see Jucurucú, Rio)

307a. Jucurucu, Rio, 17° 21′ S, 39° 13′ W.
Callithrix jacchus penicillata

307a. Prado, Rio (see Jucurucú, Rio)

307b. Mucuri, Rio, 15 km from coast, 18° 05′ S, 39° 34′ W.
[*Leontopithecus rosalia chrysomelas*]
A. Ruschi in Coimbra-Filho and Mittermeier (1973, p. 50); locality record not authentic.

Minas Gerais

308a. Jordão, Rio, 18° 26′ S, 48° 06′ W.
Callithrix jacchus penicillata
A. Robert, May–June 1901, at 800 meters.

308b. Araguari, 18° 38′ S, 48° 11′ W.

309a. Veríssimo, 19° 42′ C, 48° 18′ W.
Callithrix jacchus penicillata
J. Natterer, June 1823.

309b. Água Suja (Romaria), 18° 53′ S, 47° 38′ W.
Callithrix jacchus penicillata
O. Alver de Carvalho, 1910, 1932.

309c. Uberaba, 19° 45′ S, 47° 55′ W.
Callithrix jacchus penicillata
A second Uberaba, Minas Gerais, at 16° 27′ S, 40° 35′ W, also falls within the range of *C. j. penicillata.*

309d. São João do Glória (see São João Batista do Glória)

309d. São João Batista do Glória, 20° 38′ S, 46° 30′ W.
Callithrix jacchus penicillata

310. Januária, Rio São Francisco, 15° 30′ S, 44° 21′ W, 454 meters.
Callithrix jacchus penicillata
April 1935.

311. Pirapora, 17° 21′ S, 44° 56′ W, 488 meters.
Callithrix jacchus penicillata

312a. Lassance, 17° 54′ S, 44° 34′ W, 530 meters.
Callithrix jacchus penicillata
R. R. Gordon Harris, November 1910.

312a. Buenopolis, 17° 54′ S, 44° 11′ W, 674 meters.
Callithrix jacchus penicillata
A. Machado.

312b. Curvelo, 18° 45′ S, 44° 25′ W.
Callithrix jacchus penicillata

312c. Barra do Paraopeba, 18° 50′ S, 45° 11′ W.
Callithrix jacchus penicillata

313. Velhas (Rio das) (see Lagôa Santa).

313. Lagoa Santa, Rio das Velhas, 19° 40′ S, 43° 58′ W, 760 meters.
Callithrix jacchus penicillata
R. H. Becker, January 1914; P. W. Lund.

314a Araçauí, upper Rio Jequitinhonha, 16° 52′ S, 42° 04′ W.
Callithrix jacchus geoffroyi

314a. Machacalis, upper Rio Stanhem, 17° 05′ S, 40° 45′ W.
Callithrix jacchus geoffroyi
A. Machado and Pereira

314b. Teófilo Otoni (see Theófilo Ottoni).

314b. Theófilo Ottoni, 17° 51′ S, 41° 30′ W, 334 meters.
Callithrix jacchus geoffroyi

315a. Conceição do Mato Dentro, 19° 01′ S, 43° 25′ W.
Callithrix jacchus geoffroyi

315a. Serra do Cipo, near Conçeicão do Mato Dentro (q.v.).
Callithrix jacchus geoffroyi
A. Machado and G. E. Erikson.

315b. Esperanza (Fazenda) São José da Lagôa (see São José da Lagôa).

315b. São José da Lagôa, Rio Doce (on upper Rio Piracicaba), 19° 45′ S, 43° 03′ W.
Callithrix jacchus geoffroyi

315b. Doce (Rio), flows north to join the Rio Piracicaba at 19° 30′ S, 42° 31′ W.
Callithrix jacchus geoffroyi

315b. Piracicaba (Rio), 19° 55′ S, 43° 10′ W, on upper Rio Piracicaba.
Callithrix jacchus geoffroyi

316. Visconde do Rio Branco, 21° 01′ S, 42° 50′ W.
Callithrix jacchus geoffroyi

317. Silveira Lôbo, 21° 18′ S, 42° 16′ W.
Callithrix jacchus aurita
Pinto Peixota, 1922.

318a. Água Viva (see Água Limpa).

318a. Água Limpa, Além Paraíba, 21° 41′ S, 42° 33′ W.
Callithrix jacchus aurita
J. Moojen.

318b. Mar de Espanha, 21° 52′ S, 43° 00′ W.
Callithrix jacchus aurita

318c. Serra do Itatiaiá, 22° 23′ S, 44° 38′ W.
Callithrix jacchus penicillata
(cf. addendum p. 1013)

Espírito Santo

319a. São Mateus (Rio), 18° 38′ S, 39° 40′ W.
Not a specific collecting locality.
Callithrix jacchus geoffroyi unverified
(= ?*C. j. penicillata* × *C. j. geoffroyi*)
A. Ruschi.

319a. Conceição da Barra, 18° 35′ S, 39° 45′ W.
Not a specific collecting locality.
Callithrix jacchus penicillata unverified
(= ?*C. j. penicillata* × *C. j. geoffroyi*)
A. Ruschi.

319a. Itaúnas (Rio), 18° 00′ S, 40° 28′ W.
Not a specific collecting locality.
Callithrix jacchus geoffroyi unverified

319b. Barra Seca (Rio), 19° 09′ S, 39° 47′ W.
Not a specific collecting locality.
Callithrix jacchus geoffroyi
(= ?*C. j. penicillata* × *C. j. geoffroyi*)
A. Ruschi.

319c. Linhares, 19° 25′ S, 40° 04′ W.
Callithrix jacchus geoffroyi
A. Ruschi.

319c. Lagôa Juparana, 19° 20′ S, 40° 04′ W.
Callithrix jacchus geoffroyi

320a. Doce (Rio), 19° 37′ S, 39° 49′ W.
Not a specific collecting locality (see Colatina).
Callithrix jacchus geoffroyi
E. Garbe, 1906.

320b. Colatina, Rio Doce, 19° 32′ S, 40° 37′ W.
Callithrix jacchus geoffroyi

320b. Aracruz, 19° 49′ S, 40° 16′ W.
Callithrix jacchus flaviceps unverified
A. Ruschi.

320b. Pau Gigante, 19° 50′ S, 40° 22′ W.
Callithrix jacchus geoffroyi

320b. Ibiraçú, 19° 50′ S, 40° 22′ W.
Callithrix jacchus flaviceps (unverified)
A. Ruschi.

320b. Santa Teresa, 19° 55′ S, 40° 36′ W, 659 meters.
Callithrix jacchus geoffroyi
Below 500 meters.

Callithrix jacchus flaviceps
A. Ruschi, above 500 meters.
Callithrix jacchus penicillata
(= ? *flaviceps* × *geoffroyi*)
Recorded by Avila Pires (1969) and see pp. 505, **1015**.

320c. Mutum (Rio), 19° 30′, S, 40° 53′ W.
Callithrix jacchus geoffroyi

321a. Reis Magos (Rio), 20° 03′ S, 40° 12′ W.
Not a specific collecting locality.
Callithrix jacchus geoffroyi unverified.
A. Ruschi.

321b. Villa Vittória (see Vitória).

321b. Vitória, 20° 19′ S, 40° 21′ W, sea level.
Callithrix jacchus geoffroyi
Wied-Neuwied, 1815–17; Sellow.

321b. Vila Velha do Espírito Santo (see Espírito Santo).

321b. Espírito Santo, 20° 20′ S, 40° 17′ W.
Callithrix jacchus geoffroyi
Wied-Neuwied, 1815–17.

322. Santa Leopoldina, 20° 06′ S, 40° 32′ W.
Callithrix jacchus flaviceps unverified.
A. Ruschi.

322. Domingos Martins, 20° 22′ S, 40° 40′ W.
Callithrix jacchus flaviceps (unverified).
A. Ruschi.

323. Espírito Santo (Rio = Rio Jacú).

323. Jacú Rio, 20° 24′ S, 40° 20′ W.
Callithrix jacchus geoffroyi
Wied-Neuwied, 1815–17.

323. Júcú (Rio = Rio Jacú).

324a. Coroaba (Fazenda), Rio Espírito Santo, near Araçatiba (q.v.).
Callithrix jacchus geoffroyi
Wied-Neuwied, 1815–17.

324a. Araçatiba, Rio Espírito Santo, 20° 28′ S, 40° 30′ W.
Callithrix jacchus geoffroyi
Wied-Neuwied, 1815–17.

325a. Anchieta, 20° 48′ S, 40° 39′ W.
Leontopithecus rosalia rosalia (unverified)
A. Ruschi, 1964.

325a. Iconha, 20° 48′ S, 40° 48′ W.
Leontopithecus rosalia rosalia (unverified)
A. Ruschi, 1964.

325a. Alfredo Chaves, 20° 38′ S, 40° 45′ W.
Callithrix jacchus flaviceps (unverified)
A. Ruschi.

325b. Itapemirim, 21° 01′ S, 40° 50′ W.
Leontopithecus rosalia rosalia
Ruschi, 1964.

325b. Barra do Itapemirim, 21° 01′ S, 40° 48′ W.
Callithrix jacchus penicillata (unverified and improbable)
A. Ruschi.

325b. Marataízes, 21° 02′ S, 40° 50′ W.
Callithrix jacchus aurita (unverified)
A. Ruschi.

325c. Engenheiro Reeve (now Rive), Municipio de Alegre, 20° 46′ S, 41° 28′ W, 500 meters.
Callithrix jacchus flaviceps
A. Robert, February–April 1903, 400–600 meters.

325c. Alegre, 20° 46′ S, 41° 32′ W.
Callithrix jacchus flaviceps
A. Ruschi.

325c. Guaçuí, 20° 46′ S, 41° 41′ W.
Callithrix jacchus flaviceps
A. Ruschi.

325c. Cachoeira do Itapemirim, 20° 01′ S, 40° 50′ W.
Callithrix jacchus flaviceps
A. Ruschi.

325c. Calçado (see São José do Calçado).

325c. Sao José do Calçado, 21° 02′ S, 41° 40′ W.
Callithrix jacchus flaviceps (unverified)
A. Ruschi.

326. Parahyba do Sul (entered under Rio de Janeiro State).

Rio de Janeiro and *Guanabara*

326. Parahyba do Sul (Rio), 21° 37′ S, 41° 04′ W.
Leontopithecus rosalia rosalia
Lidth de Jeude; Schneider, 1876.

327. Santa Rita da Floresta, 21° 55′ S, 42° 26′ W.
Callithrix jacchus aurita

328. Pôrto das Flores, Rio Preto, 22° 06′ S, 43° 34′ W.
Callithrix jacchus aurita

329. Bem Posta, Rio Parahyba, 22° 09′ S, 43° 07′ W.
Callithrix jacchus aurita

330. Itatiaya, Rio Parahyba, 22° 30′ S, 44° 34′ W.
Callithrix jacchus aurita
Rudolf Pfrimer.

331a. Petropolis, 22° 31′ S, 43° 10′ W. Lowlands on road to Rio de Janeiro.
Leontopithecus rosalia rosalia

331b. Sepetiba (see Sapitiba).

331b. Sapitiba, 22° 58′ S, 43° 42′ W.
Leontopithecus rosalia rosalia
J. Natterer and Pohl, April–May (?), August 1818.

331c. Parati, 23° 13′ S, 44° 43′ W.
Callithrix jacchus aurita

331c. Pedra Branca (see Parati).

332. Rio de Janeiro (Guanabara), 22° 54′ S, 43° 14′ W.
Callithrix jacchus aurita

332. Tijuca, Parque Nacional da (Guanabara), 22° 58′ S, 43° 17′ W.
Leontopithecus rosalia rosalia

332. São João (Rio), 22° 36′ S, 42° 00′ W.
Leontopithecus rosalia rosalia

333. Órgãos, Serra do (see Teresópolis), 22° 22′ S, 42° 45′ W.

333. Therezópolis (see Teresópolis).

333. Teresópolis, Serra dos Órgãos, 22° 27′ S, 42° 57′ W, 951 meters.
Callithrix jacchus aurita
A. Miranda Ribeiro; Bresslau, April 1914.

334. Inuá (Serra de) (see Inõa [Serra de]).

334. Inõa (Serra de), 22° 53′ S, 42° 55′ W.
Leontopithecus rosalia rosalia
Wied-Neuwied, 1815–17.

335. Nova Friburgo, 22° 16′ S, 42° 32′ W.
Callithrix jacchus aurita
(captive believed to have originated in the Sierra de Macahé, cf. Burmeister 1854, p. 35).
Leontopithecus rosalia rosalia

336. Campinas, 22° 10′ S, 42° 41′ W.
Callithrix jacchus aurita

336. São João (Rio), 22° 36′ S, 41° 59′ W.
Leontopithecus rosalia rosalia
Seen (Coimbra-Filho 1969, p. 39).

336. Araruama, 22° 53′ S, 42° 20′ W.
Leontopithecus rosalia rosalia
Formerly present (Coimbra-Filho 1969, p. 38).

336. Silva Jardim, 22° 39′ S, 42° 23′ W.
Leontopithecus rosalia rosalia
Exterminated by 1964 (Coimbra-Filho 1969, p. 38).

336. São Pedro d'Aldeia, 22° 51′ S, 42° 06′ W.
Leontopithecus rosalia rosalia
Formerly present (Coimbra-Filho 1969, p. 38).

336. Casimiro de Abreu, 22° 29′ S, 42° 12′ W.
Leontopithecus rosalia rosalia
Formerly present (Coimbra-Filho 1969, p. 38).

336. Mangaratiba, 22° 57′ S, 44° 02′ W.
Leontopithecus rosalia rosalia
Formerly present (Coimbra-Filho 1969, p. 38).

336. Itaguaí, 22° 52′ S, 43° 47′ W.
Leontopithecus rosalia rosalia
Formerly present (Coimbra-Filho 1969, p. 38).

336. Nova Iguaçu, 22° 45′ S, 43° 27′ W.
Leontopithecus rosalia rosalia
Formerly present (Coimbra-Filho 1969, p. 38).

336. Nilópolis, 22° 49′ S, 43° 25′ W.
Leontopithecus rosalia rosalia
Formerly present (Coimbra-Filho 1969, p. 38).

336. Juturnaíba, 22° 38′ S, 42° 18′ W.
Leontopithecus rosalia rosalia
Formerly abundant (Coimbra-Filho 1969, p. 38).

336. Poço d'Anta, Rio Iguapé, 22° 35′ S, 42° 17′ W.
Leontopithecus rosalia rosalia
Seen (Coimbra-Filho 1969, p. 39).

336. Iguapé (Rio), near Poço d'Anta, 22° 35′ S, 42° 14′ W.
Leontopithecus rosalia rosalia
Over 300 individuals captured in six months by one hunter (Coimbra-Filho 1969, p. 39).

336. Gaviões, 22° 34′ S, 42° 33′ W.
Leontopithecus rosalia rosalia
Seen (Coimbra-Filho 1969, p. 39).

336. Correntezas, 22° 30′ S, 42° 31′ W.
Leontopithecus rosalia rosalia
Seen (Coimbra-Filho 1969, p. 39).

336. Aldeia Velha (Rio), southern part, 22° 47′ S, 42° 55′ W.
Leontopithecus rosalia rosalia
Seen (Coimbra-Filho 1969, p. 39).

336. Rio Bonito, 22° 43′ S, 42° 37′ W.
Leontopithecus rosalia rosalia
Formerly present (Coimbra-Filho 1969, p. 38).

336. Cachoeiras de Macacu, 22° 28′ S, 42° 39′ W.
Leontopithecus rosalia rosalia
Formerly present (Coimbra-Filho 1969, p. 38).

336. São João de Meriti, 22° 48′ S, 43° 22′ W.
Leontopithecus rosalia rosalia
Formerly present (Coimbra-Filho 1969, p. 38).

336. Duque de Caxias, 22° 47′ S, 43° 18′ W.
Leontopithecus rosalia rosalia
Formerly present (Coimbra-Filho 1969, p. 38).

336. Magé, 22° 39′ S, 43° 02′ W.
Leontopithecus rosalia rosalia
Formerly present (Coimbra-Filho 1969, p. 38).

336. São Goncalo, 22° 51′ S, 43° 04′ W.
Leontopitnecus rosalia rosalia
Formerly present (Coimbra-Filho 1969, p. 38).

336. Niterói, 22° 53′ S, 43° 07′ W.
Leontopithecus rosalia rosalia
Formerly present (Coimbra-Filho 1969, p. 38).

336. Itaborai, 22° 45′ S, 42° 52′ W.
Leontopithecus rosalia rosalia
Formerly present (Coimbra-Filho 1969, p. 38).

336. Maricá, 22° 55′ S, 42° 49′ W.
Leontopithecus rosalia rosalia
Rio de Janeiro Museum, 1940 (Coimbra-Filho 1969, p. 38).

336. Saquarema, 22° 56′ S, 42° 30′ W.
Leontopithecus rosalia rosalia
Formerly present (Coimbra-Filho 1969, p. 38).

336. Barro Branco, 22° 23′ S, 44° 30′ W.
Leontopithecus rosalia rosalia
Formerly present (Coimbra-Filho 1969, p. 38).

336. Fazenda Vermilho, Rio Alto Bacaxa, Rio Bonito, 22° 44′ S, 42° 21′ W.
Leontopithecus rosalia rosalia
Seen before 1968 (Coimbra-Filho 1969, p. 38).

336. Conceição de Macabu, 22° 04′ S, 41° 52′ W.
Leontopithecus rosalia rosalia
Formerly present (Coimbra-Filho 1969, p. 38).

336. Guapí, Lago Juturnaíba (*q.v.*).
Leontopithecus rosalia rosalia
Seen September 1967 (Coimbra-Filho 1969, p 38).

336. Macaé, 22° 23′ S, 41° 47′ W (see also Macaé, Serra de [336]).
Leontopithecus rosalia rosalia
Formerly present (Coimbra-Filho 1969, p. 38).

336. Macaé (Serra de), 22° 19′ S, 42° 20′ W.
Leontopithecus rosalia rosalia
H. Burmeister (recorded 1854).
Callithrix jacchus aurita
H. Burmeister (1854, p. 35, under *Hapale chrysopyga*).

336. Macahé, Serra de (see Macaé, Serra de).

336. Estanislau, Silva Jardim.
Leontopithecus rosalia rosalia
See note under Presidente.
336. Presidente, Silva Jardim.
Leontopithecus rosalia rosalia
Exterminated by collectors. In about 5 years more than 200 individuals were captured live in the vicinity of Estanislau and Presidente by a single collector. (Coimbra-Filho 1969, p. 38).
336. São João da Barra, 21° 38′ S, 41° 03′ W.
Leontopithecus rosalia rosalia
Wied-Neuwied, 1815–17.
337. Gurupina (Fazenda), Lagôa Gurupina, 22° 55′ S, 42° 42′ W.
Leontopithecus rosalia rosalia
Wied-Neuwied, 1815–17.
338a. Cabo Frio, 22° 53′ S, 42° 01′ W.
Leontopithecus rosalia rosalia
Wied-Neuwied, 1815–17.
H. Burmeister (recorded 1854).
Seen by Coimbra-Filho (1969, p. 38).
338b. Ponta Negra, 22° 58′ S, 42° 42′ W.
Leontopithecus rosalia rosalia
Wied-Neuwied, 1815–17.

São Paulo

339a. Paraná (Rio) (see Grande [Rio]).
339a. Grande (Rio), 20° 07′ S, 51° 04′ W.
Callithrix jacchus penicillata
E. Garbe, 1904.
339b. Presidente Epitácio, 21° 46′ S, 52° 06′ W.
Leontopithecus rosalia chrysopygus
339b. Kitayama (Fazenda), Presidente Wenceslau, 21° 52′ S, 51° 50′ W.
Leontopithecus rosalia chrysopygus
339b. Presidente Wenceslao (see Kitayama, Fazenda).
339b. Presidente Venceslau (see Kitayama, Fazenda).
339c. Florestal Estadual do Morro do Diabo, 22° 31′ S, 52° 10′ W.
Leontopithecus rosalia chrysopygus
340. Barretos, Rio Grande, 20° 33′ S, 48° 33′ W.
Callithrix jacchus penicillata
341. Pôrto do Rio Paraná (= Pôrto do Rio Grande), 19° 59′ S, 47° 48′ W.
Callithrix jacchus penicillata
J. Natterer, April 1823.
342. Paranapanema (Rio), 23° 00′ S, 49° 47′ W.
Numbered at confluence of Rio Itararé with which it forms boundary between the states of São Paulo (north) and Paraná.
Leontopithecus rosalia chrysopygus
on north bank.
343a. Boraçéia, upper Rio Tietê, 22° 10′ S, 48° 45′ W.
Callithrix jacchus aurita
Travassos, March 1958.
343b. Bauru, 22° 19′ S, 49° 04′ W.
Leontopithecus rosalia chrysopygus
O. Humel, 1905.
344. Vitória (or Victoria), Botucatu, 22° 47′ S, 48° 24′ W.
Leontopithecus rosalia chrysopygus
E. Garbe, July 1902.
344. Botucatu (see Vitória).
345. Campinas, 22° 54′ S, 47° 05′ W, 734 meters.
Callithrix jacchus aurita
345. Itatiba, 23° 00′ S, 46° 51′ W.
Callithrix jacchus aurita
Lima, 1926.
346. Mattodentro (see Matodentro).
346. Matodentro (5 leagues from Taubaté), 22° 54′ S, 44° 55′ W.
Callithrix jacchus aurita
J .Natterer, December 1818.
346. Sertão do Taquara, Serra da Bocaina.
Not located, the Serra da Bocaina is centered at approximately 22° 45′ S, 44° 45′ W.
Callithrix jacchus aurita
347. Ypanema (see Ipanema).
347. Ipanema, 23 ° 26′ S, 47° 36′ W, 600 meters.
Now known as Varnhagen or Bacaetava.
Leontopithecus rosalia chrysopygus
J. Natterer, March–September 1822.
348. São João, 23° 33′ S, 47° 01′ W.
Callithrix jacchus aurita
Bakkenist, 1929.
349. Varge Grande (see Vargem Grande).
349. Vargem Grande, 23° 39′ S, 47° W.
Leontopithecus rosalia chrysopygus
J. Natterer, January 1822.
350a. Cantareira, upper Rio Tietê, 23° 25′ S, 46° 39′ W.
Callithrix jacchus aurita
350b. Alto da Serra, 23° 47′ S, 46° 19′ W, 1,375 meters.
Callithrix jacchus aurita
351. Serra do Mar, 23° 25′ S, 45° 05′ W.
Callithrix jacchus aurita
H. Krieg.
351. Ubatuba, 23° 26′ S, 45° 04′ W.
Callithrix jacchus aurita
E. Garbe, June 1904.
352. São Paulo, 23° 30′ S, 46° 30′ W.
Callithrix jacchus aurita
H. Krieg.

Appendix: Tables of Measurements

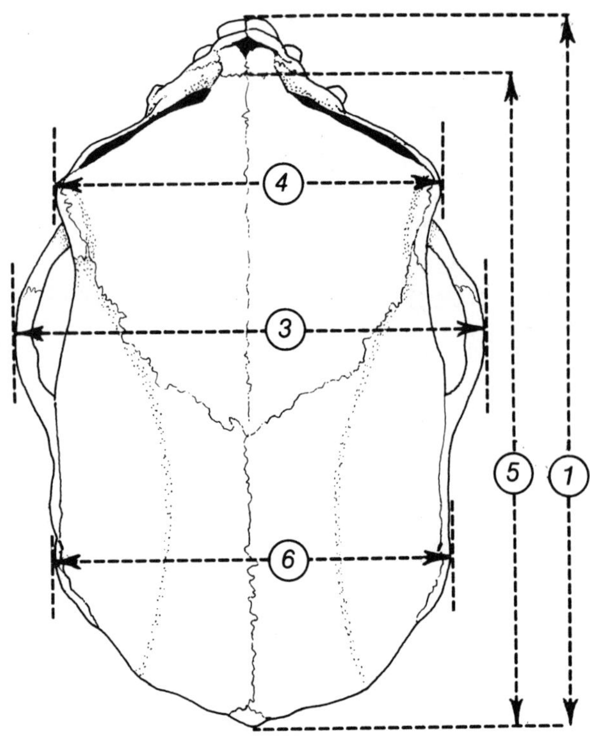

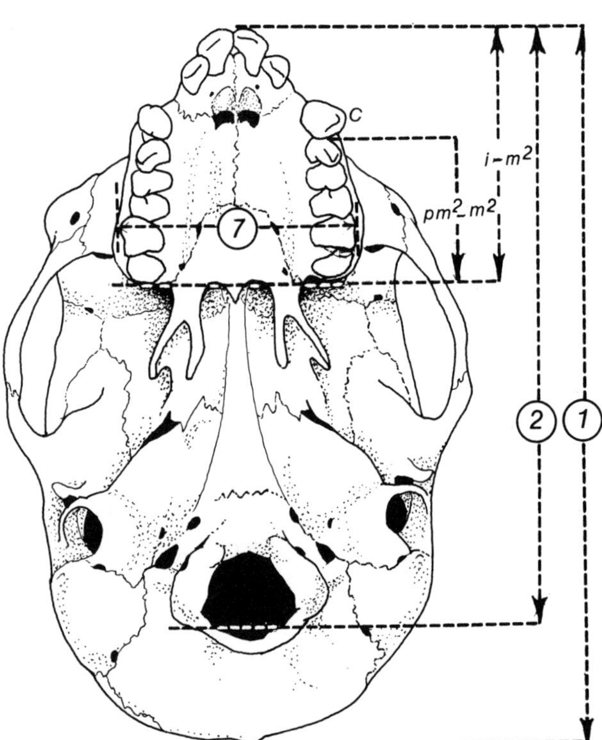

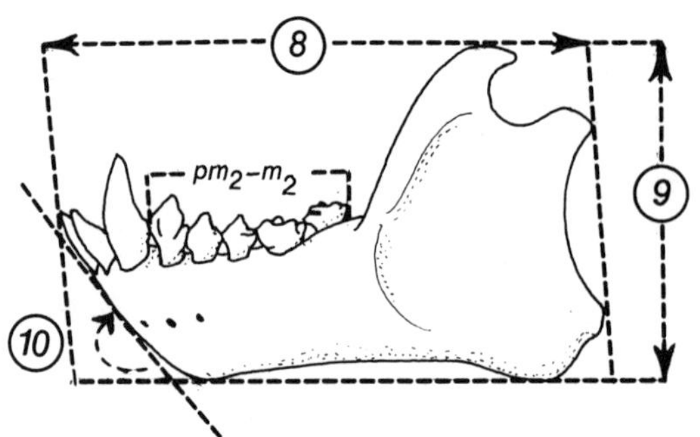

Fig. XIV.1. Explanation of cranial and dental measurements:

1. *Total length.* Greatest sagittal length (opisthocranium to incisor point or to tip of nasal spine, whichever is anteriormost).
2. *Condylobasal length.* Occipital condylion to incisor point.
3. *Zygomatic breadth.* Greatest width across outer margins of zygomatic arches (zygion to zygion).
4. *Orbital breadth.* Greatest width across outer margins of bony orbits (cyclosion to cyclosion).
5. *Braincase length.* Frontonasal suture (nasion) to opisthocranium.
6. *Braincase width.* Greatest width (euryon to euryon).
7. *Across molars* (M-M). Greatest distance between buccal (outer) surfaces.
8. *Mandibular length.* Greatest length, from incisor point to plane of gonion-condylion.
9. *Coronoidal height.* Greatest height, from basal plane of mandible to coronion.
10. *Symphyseal angle.* Angle at intersection of symphyseal and basal mandibular planes.
11. *Individual teeth.* Greatest length, width, and height at crown, unless otherwise specified.
12. *Individual or combined dental fields* (e.g., Pm2–4; Pm2–M3; I1–M3) measured along buccal (outer) surface.

Appendix Table 1. Comparative Measurements of the Species of Callitrichidae and Callimiconidae

Species	*Head and Body*	*Tail Length*	% *Tail* / *H & B*	*Hind Foot*	% *H.F.* / *H & B*	*Ear*	% *Ear* / *H & B*	*Greatest Skull Length*	% *GSL* / *H & B*	*Zygomatic Breadth*
Cebuella pygmaea	136(117–152)48	202(172–229)49	149	42(36–46)49	31	18(15–22)47	13	35.8(33.7–38.0)61	26	22.2(19.8–24.4)57
Callithrix jacchus	220(190–248)20	307(270–350)20	140	60(52–68)20	27	26(21–31)20	11	47.1(44.1–51.8)23	21	28.9(26.2–31.1)24
Callithrix argentata	217(180–280)64	330(265–380)64	152	64(52–72)64	29	31(25–31)12	14	47.1(41.1–49.4)51	22	29.0(25.5–32.0)49
Callithrix humeralifer	221(198–300)49	346(298–398)49	157	66(53–75)49	30	29(28–30)3	13	48.1(46.1–50.8)45	22	30.6(27.7–33.6)42
Saguinus fuscicollis	222(175–270)96	322(250–383)95	145	66(55–77)94	29	32(21–35)62	14	48.1(44.3–52.1)166	22	31.4(26.8–34.9)156
Saguinus nigricollis	223(210–251)8	338(308–361)9	152	68(63–72)6	30	28(26–29)7	13	49.8(46.4–52.5)71	22	31.5(27.7–35.1)68
Saguinus midas	234(206–282)101	379(316–440)101	162	69(57–80)104	29	32(28–40)15	14	50.8(45.9–55.7)108	22	32.3(30.1–35.5)103
Saguinus labiatus	261(234–300)8	387(345–410)8	148	73(69–78)9	28	—	—	50.8(49.5–52.3)9	19	33.1(31.9–34.8)7
Saguinus imperator	248(230–258)7	370(350–415)7	149	70(68–72)7	28	28(28–28)5	11	52.3(50.7–53.6)7	21	34.1(32.0–35.5)7
Saguinus mystax	257(235–280)22	390(365–435)22	152	73(66–79)22	28	29(26–31)20	11	54.0(51.1–55.7)46	21	34.7(30.6–36.9)45
Saguinus leucopus	240(223–263)31	383(347–417)30	159	74(68–80)30	31	27(24–30)32	11	51.0(46.5–54.6)30	21	34.2(31.6–37.6)30
Saguinus oedipus	237(200–287)149	368(307–423)147	155	72(60–82)151	30	23(20–31)139	10	51.8(47.8–56.4)152	22	34.6(27.6–39.8)148
Saguinus bicolor	237(208–283)28	380(335–420)28	160	72(62–83)28	30	29(25–31)4	12	52.2(50.5–54.1)25	22	34.7(29.8–37.2)25
Saguinus inustus	233(208–259)11	366(330–410)11	157	72(70–75)10	31	—	—	52.1(50.0–54.5)12	22	35.4(32.4–36.9)12
Leontopithecus rosalia	261(200–336)17	370(315–400)16	142	77(71–86)14	30	25(24–26)6	10	56.5(53.6–59.8)13	22	34.8(32.5–36.6)12
Callimico goeldii	224(210–234)18	302(255–324)18	135	74(68–78)19	33	23(20–26)15	10	53.3(50.5–55.5)10	24	34.5(32.8–35.1)9

Species	% *Zygo* / *Skull*	*Braincase Width*	% *B W* / *Skull*	*Braincase Length*	% *B W* / *B L*	% *B L* / *Skull*	*Mandible Length*	% *M L* / *Skull*	*Mandible Height*	% *M H* / *M L*	*Symphyseal Angle*
Cebuella pygmaea	62	21.1(20.0–22.9)61	59	30.9(28.3–32.8)62	68	86	20.8(18.7–22.0)53	58	9.4(7.9–11.5)54	45	28(19–40)53
Callithrix jacchus	61	25.6(24.3–28.5)24	54	40.5(36.4–45.5)23	63	86	28.1(26.4–30.7)25	59	15.7(13.6–17.4)25	56	36(30–43)23
Callithrix argentata	62	25.7(23.9–29.9)45	55	39.6(37.6–40.9)45	65	84	28.8(26.5–30.8)36	61	15.5(13.4–17.0)35	54	35(28–41)32
Callithrix humeralifer	64	25.7(24.6–27.0)44	53	40.0(38.2–41.8)46	64	83	29.9(28.0–31.2)28	62	16.9(15.2–18.8)26	57	37(31–45)27
Saguinus fuscicollis	65	26.1(24.0–27.8)164	54	42.1(38.2–42.3)161	62	88	29.2(25.9–31.8)90	61	17.9(15.3–20.8)92	61	50(42–58)85
Saguinus nigricollis	63	26.5(24.7–28.2)70	53	43.5(40.7–46.0)69	61	87	30.3(29.2–31.9)24	61	18.8(16.9–20.5)25	62	51(45–60)25
Saguinus midas	64	27.6(25.4–29.1)107	54	44.4(39.2–49.3)107	62	87	31.5(28.7–34.0)28	62	19.9(17.7–22.0)28	63	48(41–55)28
Saguinus labiatus	65	27.8(26.9–28.9)8	55	44.5(43.9–46.5)8	62	88	31.0(29.7–32.2)7	61	18.6(17.6–19.4)8	60	52(47–57)7
Saguinus imperator	65	27.9(27.1–28.6)7	53	44.1(43.1–45.3)7	63	84	32.4(31.4–33.7)7	62	19.5(18.2–21.0)8	60	51(48–57)7
Saguinus mystax	64	28.7(27.1–30.1)28	53	45.6(43.1–47.4)28	63	84	32.5(31.0–33.7)22	60	19.4(18.3–20.9)22	60	49(42–54)22
Saguinus leucopus	67	27.9(27.1–29.4)30	55	44.9(43.7–46.2)6	62	88	32.4(31.5–33.5)6	64	19.3(17.8–21.0)6	60	51(49–54)6
Saguinus oedipus	67	27.7(25.5–29.6)147	53	44.0(40.7–47.3)140	63	85	31.4(28.0–35.0)137	61	18.9(15.7–22.4)140	60	50(44–57)76
Saguinus bicolor	64	27.3(25.8–29.7)27	52	44.8(42.2–47.0)25	61	86	31.5(28.6–33.3)24	60	20.1(18.6–21.9)26	64	44(40–51)26
Saguinus inustus	68	27.5(26.4–28.1)12	53	45.5(43.3–46.8)12	60	87	31.3(30.4–33.3)12	60	19.5(18.3–20.6)12	62	45(42–48)11
Leontopithecus rosalia	62	28.4(27.5–29.3)13	50	47.3(46.3–49.4)10	60	84	35.4(32.3–37.0)13	63	23.3(21.9–25.2)11	60	42(36–51)11
Callimico goeldii	64	29.8(29.0–32.2)10	56	45.8(44.6–49.8)11	65	86	32.3(31.0–35.8)8	60	20.6(18.8–21.9)10	63	55(49–63)10

Appendix Table 2. Standard Measurements of Callitrichidae and Callimiconidae Arranged by Species or Subspecies and Locality

Name Locality	Head and Body	Tail	Hind Foot	Ear	Greatest Skull Length	Condylobasal Length	Zygomatic Width	Orbital Breadth	Braincase Width
Cebuella									
BRAZIL									
Tabatinga♂♂	134(123–44)13	202(185–219)13	42(39–45)13	18.5(17–21)13	35.9(34.7–37.0)14	27.7(26.4–28.8)14	22.0(20.4–23.1)14	20.6(19.7–21.9)14	20.9(20.3–21.5)14
Tabatinga♀♀	137(120–52)21	206(184–229)22	43(39–46)22	18(15–22)22	35.8(33.9–38.0)22	27.8(26.0–29.6)20	22.3(19.8–24.4)20	20.6(19.0–22.0)22	21.1(20.0–22.9)22
PERU									
Apayacu	—	—	—	—	36.3(35.3–37.1)9	28.2(27.3–29.0)9	21.8(20.7–23.6)8	20.9(19.6–21.8)10	21.4(20.3–22.3)9
Curaray	—	—	—	—	35.5(34.7–36.6)5	—	21.8(20.9–22.5)5	—	20.8(20.3–21.6)5
Santa Cecilia	141; 142; 150	172; 172; 160	40; 41; 43	19; 20; 19	34.6; 34.8; 35.5	27.5; 27.2; 28.4	21.8; 21.9; 23.0	20.9; 20.8; 21.1	20.7; 21.0; 21.3
Sarayacu	—	—	—	—	35.7; 35.9; 36.7	—	23.1; 22.6; 24.0	—	21.1; 21.1; 22.3
Yaquerana	147; 147	190; 208	43; 43	18; 20	36.1; 36.3	27.7; 28.6	21.4; 23.3	–; 21.0	21.2; 21.0
Pebas	130(117–39)6	200(190–204)6	39(36–43)6	18(16–20)6	—	—	—	—	—
ECUADOR									
Intillama	123	192	41	—	33.7	25.4	—	19.8	20.2
Montalvo	142	205	43	18	36.4	28.5	22.3	20.4	21.1
Río Copataza	145	220	46	—	36.7	28.5	23.8	20.3	22.7
jacchus									
Arara	189	312	58	31	46.2	36.5	28.9	24.8	25.0
Deserto	203, 206	298; 317	57; 57	29; 31	–; 46.7	–; 36.1	–; 28.1	–; 24.6	–; 24.4
Ipú	223	298	59	27	45.9	36.8	28.2	24.5	24.3
Juá	188; 209; 217	304; 349; 333	58; 59; 61	—	44.4; 46.3; 47.2	34.9; 37.7; 38.6	26.2; 29.6; 29.5	23.1; 24.9; 25.2	24.4; 24.7; –
Santo Amaro	196	295	52	—	45.6	33.9	28.4	24.7	25.4
penicillata									
Ilhéus	225; 220	335; 315	60; 60	24; 25	48.8; 50.4	39.4; 39.0	29.2; 30.4	24.7; 25.9	26.2; 27.6
Anápolis	202(190–210)5	282(270–90)5	60(55–65)5	—	45.4(44.1–46.1)6	35.6(34.6–36.7)6	27.9(26.2–29.1)6	24.3(23.7–24.9)6	24.9(24.4–25.6)6
Lassance	–; 213	–; 299	–; 62	—	45.8; 48.0	35.3; 38.8	27.5; 30.3	23.7; 25.3	25.7; 25.5
Velhas (Rio das)	209; –; –	304; –; –	54; –; –	—	46.9; 47.2; 49.3	36.3; 36.9; 38.5	29.5; 29.8; 30.6	25.5; 26.0; 26.9	25.1; 25.6; 25.3
flaviceps									
Eng. Reeve	222; 225; 248[a]	350; 320; 298[b]	65; 68; 65	21; 24; 23	48.6; 51.8; 51.5	—	29.1; 30.2; 31.1	25.5; 25.5; 23.1	26.2; 27.8; 28.6
aurita									
Itatiba	—	—	—	—	49.6	—	—	26.4	28.5
geoffroyi									
Rio Doce	—	—	—	—	50.4	—	30.5	25.5	26.0
argentata									
Cametá	215(191–240)10	341(308–380)10	64(55–72)10	27.5(27.0–28.0)3	46.2(45.9–46.5)7	—	29.3(28.1–30.5)6	—	25.1(24.6–25.6)6
Vilarinho	204(183–220)7	322(310–339)7	63(60–67)7	—	—	—	—	—	—
Tapara	209(201–19)6	325(316–335)6	61(57–64)6	—	46.3(45.2–47.6)5	36.7(34.4–38.5)5	29.4(28.6–30.1)5	25.1(24.8–25.5)	24.9(23.9–25.5)5
Tamarury	200	346	67	28	47.5	37.9	29.8	26.0	24.9
Maicá	—	—	—	—	46.5(45.1–47.9)5	36.6(35.7–37.9)5	28.0(25.5–29.5)5	25.2(24.2–26.1)5	25.1(24.9–25.5)5
Caxiricatuba	210; 215; 235	315; 350; 325	63; 66; 65	—	–; –; 48.4	–; –; 38.5	–; –; 31.2	–; –; 26.3	–; –; 25.7
Piquiatuba	180; 215	296; 335	62; 62	—	47.9; –	37.1; –	30.2; –	26.2; –	26.1; –
Aramanai	191; 200; 207; 205	310; 330; 356; 346	61; 66; 67; 69	—	45.2; 47.0; 47.5; 47.6	—	27.1; 29.1; 27.9; 30.2	—	—
Tapaiuna	220; 280; 240; 265	320; 340; 370; 340	65; 60; 65; 69	—	47.9; 48.2; 48.6; 48.8	37.5; 37.1; 38.0; 39.0	29.9; 28.4; 29.4; 31.1	25.4; 25.0; 25.7; 25.8	25.0; 26.0; 26.2; 25.6
Tauari	210(195–230)7	336(320–361)7	65(59–68)7	—	47.9(46.8–49.4)6	—	29.7(27.0–31.0)6	—	26.4(25.0–29.9)6
Recreio	227; 228; 231	313; 315; 324	61; 60; 65	—	—	—	—	—	—
Maloca[c]	199	308	61	29	44.0	35.0	29.0	25.5	—
leucippe									
Pimental[d]	235; 230	342; 330	64; 65	30; 29	48.5; 49.4	–; 38.9	–; 30.7	–; 26.2	26.2; 26.1
Fordlandia	232(205–80)6	320(265–370)6	65(60–70)6	—	46.9(45.7–49.0)6	37.3(36.5–38.4)6	30.7(29.8–31.8)6	26.4(26.0–27.1)6	25.8(25.1–26.2)6

[a] Third measurement in each column of series is of type.
[b] Probably collector's *lapsus* for 398.
[c] Of type of *emiliae* from original description, evidently a subadult.
[d] First measurement in each column of type from original description.

Name Locality	Braincase Length	$I–M^2$	$C–M^2$	Across Molars	Mandible Length	Coronoidal Height	$Pm–M_2$	Symphyseal Angle
Cebuella								
BRAZIL								
Tabatinga ♂♂	30.7(29.4–32.8)14	11.0(10.7–11.6)13	8.7(8.4–8.9)14	10.8(10.3–11.5)14	20.8(19.6–21.6)14	9.4(8.7–10.4)14	7.8(7.6–8.2)12	24(19–33)14
Tabatinga ♀♀	30.9(28.3–32.6)22	11.2(10.7–11.7)22	8.6(7.9–9.0)22	10.9(10.4–11.3)22	20.9(19.3–22.0)21	9.4(8.0–11.5)22	7.8(7.1–8.2)21	28(20–37)21
PERU								
Apayacu	31.3(30.1–31.8)10	11.2(10.7–11.5)10	8.8(8.5–9.0)10	10.7(10.3–11.1)10	20.5(18.7–21.8)10	9.3(8.2–10.0)10	8.0(7.7–8.3)9	31(21–40)10
Curaray	30.6(30.1–31.2)5	11.0(10.7–11.4)5	—	10.7(10.5–11.1)5	—	—	—	—
Santa Cecilia	30.1; 29.9; 31.2	10.9; 11.1; 11.2	8.4; 8.7; 8.9	10.7; 10.9; 11.4	20.8; 21.3; 21.7	9.4; 8.8; 10.3	7.8; 8.0; 7.9	30; 34; 31
Sarayacu	30.7; 31.0; 31.9	11.0; 11.0; 11.5	—	10.5; 11.2; 11.2	—	—	—	—
Yaquerana	31.0; 31.0	11.6; 11.3	9.1; 8.9	11.6; 11.3	20.9; 21.8	9.4; 9.8	8.0; 8.0	29; 31
Pebas	—	—	—	—	—	—	—	—
ECUADOR								
Intillama	29.4	11.1	8.5	10.6	19.1	7.9	7.9	37
Montalvo	31.2	11.1	8.6	11.2	21.0	10.1	7.6	35
Río Copataza	31.7	10.8	8.7	11.3	21.1	10.4	7.8	32
iacchus								
Arara	38.4	15.0	11.0	14.6	27.9	16.2	10.0	34
Deserto	–; 38.6	–; 15.0	–; 10.8	–; 14.1	–; 27.7	–; 16.4	–; 9.8	36
Ipú	37.3	15.5	11.1	13.6	28.0	15.6	10.2	34
Juá	36.4; 37.9; –	14.6; 16.1; 16.0	10.4; 11.7; 11.1	13.5; 13.8; 15.0	26.7; 29.5; 30.4	14.0; 17.0; 17.4	9.5; –; 10.5	36; –; 30
Santo Amaro	37.1	14.5	10.5	14.4	27.6	15.6	9.4	37
penicillata								
Ilhéus	39.3; 42.6	15.6; 15.6	11.8; 11.9	15.3; 15.1	31.3; 29.9	16.6; 15.8	10.8; 10.9	32; 34
Anápolis	37.7(36.6–38.4)5	14.7(14.2–15.1)6	10.7(10.4–10.9)6	13.6(12.8–14.3)6	27.4(26.4–28.6)6	15.1(13.9–15.8)6	9.5(9.0–9.8)6	36(29–42)6
Lassance	38.4; 40.5	14.5; 15.5	10.5; 10.7	13.9; 15.0	26.7; 30.3	13.6; 15.7	9.3; 10.0	42; 37
Velhas (Rio das)	39.3; 39.8; 41.5	14.8; 15.2; 15.4	10.8; 10.8; 11.0	14.2; 14.6; 15.1	28.2; 28.7; 29.4	15.3; 16.0; 17.2	9.5; 9.8; 10.0	45; 37; 29
flaviceps								
Eng. Reeve	39.8; 42.7; 45.5	15.2; 16.6; 15.1	11.6; 12.4; 12.2	—	29.1; 29.9; 30.7	15.5; 16.3; 16.1	11.0; 11.6; 11.4	37; 36; –
aurita								
Itatiba	41.9	14.4	10.5	—	28.5	16.9	10.1	36
geoffroyi								
Rio Doce	41.1	16.3	12.4	—	30.4	16.0	11.1	43
argentata								
Cametá	38.5(37.6–38.6)7	15.1(14.9–15.5)6	11.2; 10.9	14.8(14.4–15.2)7	27.2; 28.3	15.3; 14.5	10.0; 9.9	35; 33
Vilarinho	—	—	—	—	—	—	—	—
Tapara	38.8(38.2–39.5)5	15.3(15.0–15.9)5	11.1(10.9–11.3)5	14.9(14.6–15.2)5	28.0(27.4–28.6)6	15.8(15.5–16.2)6	10.3(10.1–10.4)6	37(34–41)6
Tamarury	39.4	15.2	11.3	14.1	30.0	15.8	9.9	35
Maicá	38.5(37.6–39.5)5	15.5(15.2–15.9)5	11.4(11.0–11.6)5	14.5(14.0–15.0)5	27.8(26.5–29.4)5	14.7(13.4–15.7)5	10.1(9.9–10.4)5	33(28–35)5
Caxiricatuba	–; –; 40.9	–; –; 15.7	–; –; 11.6	–; –; 15.0	–; –; 30.1	–; –; 16.0	–; –; 10.3	–; –; 35
Piquiatuba	40.0; –	15.5; –	11.5; –	15.7; –	29.4; –	17.3; –	10.6; –	35; –
Aramanai	—	—	—	—	—	—	—	—
Tapaiuna	40.3; 40.5; 40.8; 40.4	15.7; 15.7; 15.8; 15.6	11.5; 11.7; 11.3; 11.0	15.0; 15.0; 14.8; 15.7	29.2; 28.2; 29.3; 30.1	16.5; 16.2; 16.7; 17.2	10.4; 10.9; 10.5; 10.4	31; 36; 32; 34
Tauari	40.1(38.9–41.6)6	15.3(14.8–15.9)5	—	15.1(14.6–15.7)6	—	—	—	—
Recreio	—	—	—	—	—	—	—	—
Maloca[c]	—	—	—	—	—	—	—	—
leucippe								
Pimental[d]	–; 40.5	–; 15.8	–; 11.5	–; 15.0	–; 30.8	–; 16.4	–; 10.5	–; 35
Fordlandia	39.9(38.8–40.9)6	15.5(15.2–16.3)6	11.4(11.1–11.6)6	15.4(15.0–16.1)6	29.3(28.3–30.2)5	16.4(15.7–17.0)6	10.3(9.6–10.7)6	36(35–38)5

Appendix Table 2—*Continued*

Name Locality	Head and Body	Tail	Hind Foot	Ear	Greatest Skull Length	Condylobasal Length	Zygomatic Width	Orbital Breadth	Braincase Width
melanura									
BRAZIL									
Urucum	–; 240; 225; 220	–; 340; 340; 340	–; 70; 70; 68	—	46.6; 47.9; 48.0; 49.0	38.1; 38.5; 38.8; 39.0	28.9; 30.3; 29.9; 30.7	25.7; 26.6; 26.5; 26.1	24.7; 26.2; 26.0; 26.5
BOLIVIA									
Río Quiser	235; 240; 220; 225	315; 340; 305; 330	65; 62; 64; 62	27; 28; 28; 27	47.8; 47.2; 47.7; –	38.0; 37.8; 38.5; –	29.3; 29.9; 29.1; –	25.9; 25.9; 25.8; –	25.9; 26.3; 25.6; –
Cercado	220	320	65	25	48.8	38.9	32.0	26.7	26.8
chrysoleuca									
Lago Baptista♂♂	227(190–265)6	346(315–60)6	63(53–70)6	—	48.0(47.3–48.6)7	38.8(37.7–39.6)5	31.3(30.4–32.8)6	26.9(26.3–27.2)6	25.5(25.2–25.8)6
Lago Baptista♀♀	237(220–300)4	329(298–355)4	66(55–69)5	—	48.3(47.2–49.7)5	38.9(37.9–41.3)5	31.3(30.4–33.2)5	27.1(26.0–27.9)5	25.6(24.6–26.0)5
Ig. Auará	205, 220, 225, 236	325, 325, 310, 324	65, 68, 74, 72	—	47.0, 47.7, 48.5, 49.4	38.4, 38.0, 38.6, 39.5	31.1, 30.6, 33.6, 31.8	–, 26.9, 27.9, 26.8	24.7, 25.5, 26.8, 25.9
Borba	220, 219, 235, 220	340, 335, 355, 355	74, 73, 70, 75	—	48.4, 49.2, 49.3, 50.8	38.8, 38.7, 39.9, 41.0	30.9, 31.4, 31.8, 32.3	26.6, 27.1, 27.3, 27.6	26.4, 26.5, 26.4, 25.9
Tapaiuna	200	450	70	—	48.0	37.9	32.2	26.7	26.1
humeralifer									
Andirá	222, 228, 236	346, 336, 335	68, 70, 70	—	47.6, –, –	—	29.3	—	25.9, –, –
Boim	213	361	64	28	48.8	—	31.0	—	25.1
Vila Braga	230	348	—	29	49.1	38.7	29.6	26.8	26.1
Arará	204, 210, 220, 210	350, 360, 330, 340	67, 65, 61, 66	—	45.6, 46.1, 46.9, 48.6	36.8, 38.5, 37.2, 37.3	29.0, 29.3, 28.5, 28.5	27.1, 25.8, 25.6, 25.2	25.4, 25.0, 24.6, 25.9
Urucurituba	209(200–230)5	359(350–70)5	63(61–65)5	—	45.8, 46.9, 47.5, 48.8	36.9, 36.0, 36.2, 38.8	29.6, 28.4, 29.0, 30.3	27.3, 25.8, 27.0, 27.0	25.9, 25.2, 28.2, 26.8
Parintins	226(203–68)6	345(315–70)6	65(60–70)6	—	47.1, 47.5, 49.5, 50.7	—	27.7, 29.9, –, 31.4	—	25.7, –, 24.8, 25.5
Ig. Bravo	215(198–239)11	355(320–98)	66(60–73)11	—	48.0(46.8–50.5)10	—	30.6(28.9–32.6)8	—	25.8(24.9–27.0)10
graellsi									
PERU									
Curaray♂♂	—	—	—	—	49.5(48.0–51.8)8	—	31.7(29.5–34.2)8	—	26.2(25.3–26.9)7
Curaray♀♀	—	—	—	—	49.2(47.3–50.6)6	—	30.5(27.7–31.9)7	—	26.2(24.8–27.6)6
ECUADOR									
San José	—	—	—	—	49.9(46.4–51.1)14	—	31.5(28.3–32.6)11	—	26.3(25.2–27.3)14
Sumaco	—	—	—	—	48.0; 50.3; 50.6	—	29.2; 30.8; 32.7	—	26.1; 27.5; 26.8
Suno♂♂	—	—	—	—	50.2(48.5–51.9)6	38.0; 41.3	31.3(28.9–33.9)6	25.3; 27.6	26.5(25.7–27.1)6
Suno♀♀	—	—	—	—	49.4(47.1–51.1)10	—	30.5(28.0–33.4)10	—	26.3(24.7–28.3)10
S. Francisco	222; 251	308; 356	—	—	47.3; 49.1	37.5; 38.7	31.1; –	26.3; 26.5	25.4; 27.0
Pindo Yacu	224; 175[?]	330; 335	72[e]; 66[e]	28; 28	50.9; 50.9	39.0; 39.6	32.7; 34.2	27.7; 27.8	26.9; 26.5
Yana Rumi	215; 215	320; 340	71[e]	28; 28	50.4; 50.5	39.4; 38.3	31.5; 32.7	26.7; 27.3	28.1; 27.4
Capihuara	210	350	72[e]	28	49.9	38.4	31.5	26.1	26.8
nigricollis									
PERU									
Pebas	220; 226	356; 361	66; 63	29; 26	48.2; 49.9	38.1; 38.8	32.0; 31.5	26.6; 26.8	26.6; 26.3
Apayacu♂♂	—	—	—	—	50.7(49.2–52.5)6	39.9(38.2–41.9)6	32.2(31.6–33.3)6	26.6(26.1–27.1)6	27.2(26.6–27.9)6
Apayacu♀♀	—	—	—	—	50.4(48.9–51.6)9	39.8(38.1–41.2)9	32.4(30.4–35.1)9	26.9(25.3–28.6)9	26.4(25.6–28.2)9
fuscus									
COLOMBIA									
Caquetá♂♂	229(225–234)7	346(296–383)7	72(69–77)7	29(27–31)7	48.7(47.1–50.6)7	39.2(37.7–41.1)7	31.8(29.8–32.4)7	25.9(24.8–26.7)7	25.9(25.0–26.3)7
Caquetá♀♀	223(212–234)9	350(337–362)8	70(64–72)9	28(26–30)9	48.0(46.1–49.1)9	38.0(36.1–39.3)9	31.1(28.7–32.8)9	25.7(24.5–26.5)9	26.1(25.2–27.5)9
nigrifrons									
PERU									
Pebas[j]	211(190–219)5	323(305–333)5	63(59–64)5	28(27–28)5	47.9[k]	—	33.5	24.4	26.8
Sarayacu[l]	—	—	67.6(65–71)15[m]	—	47.3(45.1–49.2)13	—	30.5(27.3–32.4)13	—	25.8(24.8–27.0)13
Orosa	—	—	—	—	48.3(46.5–50.4)12	—	31.7(29.8–34.9)11	—	26.3(25.4–26.9)12
Sta. Cecilia	215; 210; 229	335; 346; 346	69; 73; 74	29; 33; 29	47.8; 47.9; 48.9	37.6; 37.8; 38.5	29.0; 31.2; 32.0	24.6; 26.9; 27.2	26.5; 25.4; 26.4
San Fernando	236	300	72	32	48	38.0	30.8	26.4	25.9
Esperanza	232	325	71	28	49.2	39.2	32.3	26.3	26.8

[e] Dry.
[j] External measurements include those of type of *pebilis*.
[k] Cranial measurements of type of *pebilis*.
[l] Right bank of Río Ucayali.
[m] Dry.

Name Locality	Braincase Length	I–M²	C–M²	Across Molars	Mandible Length	Coronoidal Height	$Pm–M_2$	Symphyseal Angle
melanura								
BRAZIL								
Urucum	39.0; 41.1; 39.9; 41.5	15.3; 15.0; 15.5; 15.5	11.3; 11.4; 11.2; 11.2	15.0; 15.5; 15.0; 15.8	28.6; 29.3; 29.6; 29.0	15.5; 16.1; 15.8; 16.1	10.5; 10.3; 10.1; 10.4	31; 35; 32; 37
BOLIVIA								
Río Quiser	40.1; 40.3; 40.1; –	15.1; 14.9; 14.9; 15.6	11.1; 10.9; 10.9; 11.9	14.1; 15.9; 15.8; 15.9	29.0; 29.4; 29.5; 29.5	16.3; 15.0; 15.6; 15.9	9.7; 10.8; 10.2; 10.9	32; –; –; –
Cercado	41.3	15.5	11.1	15.5	30.0	16.7	10.4	35
chrysoleuca								
Lago Baptista♂♂	40.0(38.7–40.8)7	15.8(15.3–16.1)7	11.8(11.5–12.3)7	15.6(15.1–16.1)7	30.0(29.3–30.6)6	17.1(16.1–18.0)6	10.8(10.6–11.0)7	36.6(34–41)5
Lago Baptista♀♀	40.1(39.6–40.8)5	15.9(15.1–16.8)5	11.7(11.2–12.3)5	15.7(15.2–16.0)5	30.3(28.8–31.9)5	17.6(17.3–17.8)3	11.0(10.8–11.3)5	33(29–38)5
Ig. Auará	39.2, 38.6, 40.3, 41.3	15.0, 15.9, 15.9, 17.1	10.7, 11.7, 11.5, 11.7	15.0, 15.2, 16.6, 16.5	30.0, 29.6, 30.4, 30.8	16.7, 15.9, 17.3, 16.5	9.9, 10.3, 10.4, 10.4	34, 40, 32, 34
Borba	39.9, 40.7, 41.8, 42.4	16.3, 16.7, 16.1, 16.3	11.3, 12.0, 11.8, 12.2	15.6, 15.9, 15.8, 16.9	31.0, 30.7, 31.2, 32.1	17.2, 17.0, 17.0, 18.8	11.1, 11.0, 10.8, 11.4	31, 32, 32, 35
Tapaiuna	39.9	15.7	11.7	15.7	29.2	16.0	10.7	43
humeralifer								
Andirá	39.8, –, –	15.4, –, –	—	16.1, –, –	—	—	—	—
Boim	41.4	16.0	—	14.9	—	—	—	—
Vila Braga	40.0	15.9	12.2	15.5	—	—	—	—
Arará	38.4, 38.9, 38.2, 39.3	14.9, 15.3, 15.6, 15.9	10.9, 11.7, 11.5, 11.5	15.1, 15.7, 15.0, 15.1	28.7, 29.1, 28.6, 29.0	16.6, 16.8, 15.2, 16.1	9.8, 10.2, 9.2, 10.3	35, 43, 31, 41
Urucurituba	39.4, 38.5, 39.3, 41.4	14.5, 14.7, 15.1, 15.5	11.0, 10.9, 11.3, 11.0	15.6, 15.8, 15.5, 15.7	28.0, 29.5, 28.4, 29.5	17.5, 15.6, 16.0, 16.7	9.7, 9.5, 9.7, 10.1	45, 44, 40, 45
Parintins	39.9, 38.7, 40.8, 41.0	15.3, 15.5, 15.6, 15.6	—	16.2, 15.7, 15.6, 16.2	—	—	—	—
Ig. Bravo	39.9(38.4–42.2)10	15.4(15.0–16.0)9	—	15.7(15.1–16.7)9	—	—	—	—
graellsi								
PERU								
Curaray♂♂	43.6(42.5–45.2)8	15.5(15.0–16.0)8	—	15.5(14.7–16.5)8	—	—	—	—
Curaray♀♀	43.1(41.5–44.0)6	15.4(14.9–16.3)7	—	15.2(14.6–16.4)7	—	—	—	—
ECUADOR								
San José	43.0(40.7–43.9)14	15.8(15.1–16.3)13	—	15.6(14.6–16.5)13	—	—	—	—
Sumaco	42.6; 43.2; 41.9	15.2; 16.1; 16.5	—	15.9; 15.6; 15.6	—	—	—	—
Suno♂♂	43.3(42.4–44.9)4	15.6(15.1–16.0)6	—	15.7(15.2–16.3)6	—	—	—	—
Suno♀♀	43.2(41.9–44.9)10	15.5(14.8–16.1)10	—	—	—	—	—	—
S. Francisco	41.6; 43.8	15.3; 15.7; 15.8	11.1; 10.8; 11.0	14.5; 15.4; 15.4	29.4; –; 30.0	18.2; 16.9; 18.6	9.7; 10.2; 10.2	52; 54; 52
Pindo Yacu	45.1; 44.5	16.1; 15.7	11.6; 11.7	15.9; 16.5	29.5; 31.3	19.3; 19.8	10.9; 10.6	45; 57
Yana Rumi	44.4; 44.9	16.2; 15.5	11.7; 11.3	15.9; 15.5	29.4; 29.3	18.6; 18.6	10.6; 10.4	52; 54
Capihuara	43.6	15.5	11.3	16.5	29.2	18.6	10.8	53
nigricollis								
PERU								
Pebas	41.5; 43.7	16.3; 16.5	11.6; 11.7	16.7; 17.0	30.1; 30.5	17.9; 20.5	10.7; 10.6	50; 44
Apayacu♂♂	44.5(43.9–46.0)6	16.5(15.9–17.3)6	12.0(11.4–12.7)6	16.4(15.6–17.1)6	30.7(29.3–31.9)6	18.5(17.7–19.2)6	10.8(10.0–11.2)6	49.5(46–52)6
Apayacu♀♀	44.3(42.7–45.2)9	16.0(15.0–16.8)9	11.5(10.2–12.1)9	16.4(15.8–16.9)9	30.7(29.4–31.7)9	19.1(17.8–20.5)9	10.6(10.1–10.9)9	51.6(46–60)9
fuscus								
COLOMBIA								
Caquetá♂♂	42.3(41.4–43.3)7	15.7(14.8–16.2)7	11.0(10.9–11.2)7	15.9(15.0–16.7)7	30.2(28.8–31.8)7	18.6(18.0–20.0)7	10.5(10.3–10.7)7	51(45–56)7
Caquetá♀♀	41.6(40.8–42.7)9	15.3(14.6–15.8)9	11.0(10.8–11.5)9	15.8(15.1–16.5)9	29.0(27.4–30.6)9	17.4(15.7–19.4)9	10.2(9.6–10.7)9	49(45–52)8
nigrifrons								
PERU								
Pebas[j]	40.9	15.1	11.2	—	29.1	18.1	10.3	—
Sarayacu[l]	41.3(39.4–42.6)13	15.3(14.7–16.0)13	—	15.7(15.1–16.6)13	—	—	—	—
Orosa	42.1(41.0–43.9)12	15.8(15.3–16.5)10	—	16.2(15.7–17.0)11	—	—	—	—
Sta. Cecilia	41.0; 42.0; 42.7	14.8; 15.5; 15.9	11.1; 11.3; 11.5	15.8; 15.9; 15.6	28.4; 29.3; 29.9	16.5; 17.6; 18.7	10.2; 10.2; 10.5	57; 55; 53
San Fernando	42.4	16.5	11.3	15.5	29.8	17.8	10.7	55
Esperanza	43.2	15.9	11.2	16.6	29.7	17.3	10.2	48

Appendix Table 2—*Continued*

Name Locality	Head and Body	Tail	Hind Foot	Ear	Greatest Skull Length	Condylobasal Length	Zygomatic Width	Orbital Breadth	Braincase Width
illigeri									
PERU									
Pacaya, Río[n]	175	300	55	24	—	—	—	24.0	24.5
Sarayacu[o]	—	—	63.5(59–69)17	—	47.4(45.5–49.9)13	—	29.6(27.0–31.7)13	—	25.5(24.3–26.2)13
Santa Elena	205	305	—	28	47.0	37.8	30.5	24.8	25.4
leucogenys									
PERU									
Moyobamba	217; 216	250; 310	67; 69	34; 35	46.1; –	–; –	30.9; –	24.9; –	25.3; –
Pucallpa	210; 220	310; 330	—	28; –	47.4; 48.6	37.0; 37.7	29.9; 31.1	24.7; 25.7	26.0; 26.2
Tingo María	208(185–221)12	305(285–330)12	61(57–68)12	28(27–31)9	46.9; 48.6; 47.7; 48.0	36.9; 38.6; 38.3; 39.0	30.6(29.8–31.1)5	25.1; 25.0; 24.9; 24.8	26.5; 26.1; 25.9; 25.0
Santa Rosa	—	—	—	—	44.3; 47.2; 47.6	34.4; 37.0; 37.3	26.8; 29.2; 29.9	23.5; 25.0; 25.2	25.1; 26.1; 26.0
Perené	205	312	62	25	—	—	—	—	—
Cumería	211(205–218)7	329(310–344)7	62(59–65)7	26(25–27)7	—	—	—	—	—
Mairo	225; 230	305; 330	67; 72	28; 25	—	—	—	—	—
San Antonio	215	320	70	27	—	—	—	—	—
Yurac Yacu	210; 202; 210; 211[p]	315; 289; 321; 299	61; 59; 65; 62	26; 27; 25; 26	47.5; –; –; 47.3	36.5; –; –; 37.5	29.2; –; –; –	24.6; –; –; 25.3	26.1; –; –; 25.7
Yarinacocha	230; 230	290; 320	—	27; 30	45.5; 47.6	35.8; 37.5	30.4; 32.0	25.7; 25.8	26.3; 26.2
lagonotus									
ECUADOR									
Copataza[q]	240(220–70)5	301(275–330)5	61(55–68)5	—	50.3; 49.2; 45.9	39.3; –; –	35.5; 34.3; 31.0	27.7; 27.6; 25.8	26.5; 26.9; 25.9
Montalvo	225, 220, 220	310, 325, 335	72[r], –, 68[r]	—	—	—	—	—	—
PERU									
Curaray♂♂	—	—	—	—	49.3(46.5–50.6)7	39.3(36.2–40.8)7	32.9(30.3–34.3)5	26.5(24.5–27.4)7	26.5(25.5–27.4)7
Curaray♀♀	—	—	—	—	48.5(46.4–49.8)5	38.6(37.1–39.9)5	30.7, 32.4	25.7(25.0–26.4)5	26.0(25.5–26.5)5
Pto. Indiana	—	—	—	—	49.8(48.4–51.4)15	—	32.9(31.2–34.8)15	—	26.5(25.8–27.1)15
Marupa	—	—	—	—	47.5, 48.2	37.7, 38.4	30.9, 31.8	26.1, 26.0	24.7, 25.5
Pampa Chica	229	311	—	28	48.4	38.2	31.5	25.7	26.4
Sta. Rita	234, 223	350, 302	72, 70	28; –	48.2, 48.3	39.5, 37.8	33.0, 33.5	27.7, 27.7	26.4, 26.5
tripartitus									
ECUADOR									
S. Francisco	218,240	316, 341	—	32, 31	51.2, –	41.3, –	33.7, –	27.4, 26.6	27.7, 27.4
Curaray[s]	—	—	—	—	49.8	39.9	33.1	27.1	26.5
Curaray[s]	—	—	—	—	49.0(46.2–52.1)12	—	31.6(27.9–33.5)11	—	26.4(24.9–27.5)12
Lagarto	—	—	—	—	47.2	—	30.4	—	25.2
Pto Indiana	—	—	—	—	48.7(46.7–50.2)7	—	31.5(30.5–33.1)7	—	26.3(25.0–27.3)7
crandalli[f]									
no locality	221	257	61[i]	—	48.5	38.1	31.8	26.1	25.7
acrensis									
BRAZIL									
Pedra Preta[g]	226	325	60	29	46	31.4[!]	33.2	27	25.8
melanoleucus									
BRAZIL									
Santo António[h]	250	380	55[!]	—	47	—	34	—	24.0
Santo António	—	—	69[i]	—	48.3	39.0	31.8	26.9	26.6

[n] Type of *Leontocebus mounseyi*.
[o] Left bank of Río Ucayali.
[p] Fourth measurement of series is of type of *Mystax devillei micans*.
[q] Includes two adults of original series of *apiculatus* (third and fourth sets of cranial measurements).
[r] Dry.
[s] Opposite mouth on Río Napo.
[f] Measurements of type.
[g] Of type of *acrensis* from original description.
[h] Type of *hololeucus*, measurements from original description.
[i] Dry.

Name Locality	Braincase Length	I–M^2	C–M^2	Across Molars	Mandible Length	Coronoidal Height	Pm–M_2	Symphyseal Angle
illigeri								
PERU								
Pacáya, Río[n]	40.9	15.0	10.9	—	28.2	17.8	10.1	—
Sarayacu[o]	41.2(39.8–43.9)13	14.9(14.1-16.5)13	—	15.4(15.0–16.5)13	—	—	—	—
Santa Elena	40.7	14.7	10.3	15.5	28.4	18.1	10.1	54
leucogenys								
PERU								
Moyobamba	40.5; –	14.7; –	10.9; –	–;–	28.1 ;–	18.7; –	10.3; –	–; –
Pucallpa	40.7; 42.9	14.7; 14.9	10.0; 10.6	15.7; 15.4	28.2; 28.7	17.6; 18.5	9.5; 9.9	50; 53
Tingo María	40.7; 41.5; 42.3; 42.6	15.2(14.8–15.5)5	10.6(10.3–10.8)5	—	28.4(27.8–29.0)5	18.0(17.2–18.6)5	9.9(9.7–10.1)5	50(43–58)5
Santa Rosa	38.2; 41.2; 40.9	14.2; 15.0; –	10.6; 11.1; 10.9	14.9; 15.1; 15.0	25.9; 28.0; 28.3	15.4; 16.3; 17.1	10.1; 10.2; 10.5	55; 50; 55
Perené	—	—	—	—	—	—	—	—
Cumería	—	—	—	—	—	—	—	—
Mairo	—	—	—	—	—	—	—	—
San Antoino	—	—	—	—	—	—	—	—
Yurac Yacu	42.7; –; –; –	14.2; –; –; 13.8	10.3; –; –; 9.5	–; –; –; –	27.5; –; –; 28.5	16.4; –; –; –	9.8; –; –; 10.2	47; –; –; –
Yarinacocha	41.0; 42.1	13.8; 14.6	10.7; 10.9	14.6; 15.7	28.7; 29.2	18.5; 18.2	9.9; 10.1	56; 55
lagonotus								
ECUADOR								
Copataza[q]	45.2; 43.8; 40.7	15.9; 15.2; 14.5	11.9; 10.8; 9.9	16.6; –; –	30.3; 29.8; 27.7	19.2; 19.5; 17.4	10.7; 10.8; 9.3	49; 47; 55
Montalvo	—	16.1, 15.4, 16.6	11.6, 11.3, 11.3	15.5, 16.1, 16.5	29.7, –, 30.0	17.9, 17.8, 18.0	10.5, 10.3, 10.7	50, 52, 50
PERU								
Curaray♂♂	43.2(40.6–44.7)7	15.9(15.3–16.7)7	11.6(11.3–12.3)7	16.3(15.2–17.1)7	29.8(27.9–30.7)7	18.9(16.8–20.8)7	10.9(10.2–11.9)7	48(46–51)7
Curaray♀♀	42.2(40.3–43.3)5	15.5(15.1–15.9)5	11.5(11.0–11.9)5	15.8(15.4–16.1)5	29.5(28.0–30.3)5	18.2(16.7–19.2)5	10.3(10.0–10.5)5	48(42–50)5
Pto Indiana	43.4(41.2–44.9)15	16.0(15.0–16.9)15	—	16.1(15.1–17.1)15	—	—	—	—
Marupa	40.2, 41.4	15.5, 15.5	11.4, 11.3	15.7, 16.0	28.3, 28.4	17.7, 17.7	10.4, 10.3	48, 46
Pampa Chica	42.2	15.5	11.5	16.0	29.1	18.2	10.5	50
Sta. Rita	43.0, 43.3	16.0, 15.6	11.5, 11.6	15.0, 16.1	29.8, 29.0	18.5, 18.0	10.8, 10.4	47, 45
tripartitus								
ECUADOR								
S. Francisco	45.5, 49.9	15.5, 16.0	11.3, 11.8	15.8, 15.4	–, 30.4	19.1, 17.9	10.9, 10.9	54, –
Curaray[s]	43.9	15.9	11.3	16.9	30.9	18.9	10.7	51
Curaray[s]	42.8(39.9–45.6)12	15.4(14.6–16.6)12	—	16.1(15.3–17.3)12	—	—	—	—
Lagarto	40.8	14.6, 16.5	—	15.7, 16.5	—	—	—	—
Pto Indiana	42.5(40.5–43.8)7	15.1(14.1–15.9)7	—	16.1(15.8–16.4)7	—	—	—	—
crandalli[f]								
no locality	42.0	14.7	11.0	15.3	29.9	16.1	9.8	53
acrensis								
BRAZIL								
Pedra Preta[g]	—	—	10.6	—	—	—	—	—
melanoleucus								
BRAZIL								
Santo António[h]	—	—	—	—	31.0	—	—	—
Santo António	41.8	15.5	11.0	16.0	29.9	18.3	9.8	52

Appendix Table 2—*Continued*

Name Locality	Head and Body	Tail	Hind Foot	Ear	Greatest Skull Length	Condylobasal Length	Zygomatic Width	Orbital Breadth	Braincase Width
fuscicollis									
BRAZIL									
João Pessõa	—	—	—	—	45.7, 46.3	36.4, 36.6	30.8, 29.8	25.5, 26.2	25.5, 24.9
Jordão	—	—	—	—	47.5	38.5	32.2	25.6	25.8
weddelli									
BOLIVIA									
Tumapasa	–; 221	–; 319	–; 69	–; –	45.8; 47.8	38.1; 35.8	28.4; 29.0	25.3; 25.8	25.9; 25.2
BRAZIL									
Mapixi	260; 270; 270; 260	330; 350; 330; 340	62; 68; 68; 68	–; –; 22; 21	47.7; –; –; –	37.3; –	29.9; 32.0	26.1; 26.2	25.3; 26.2
PERU									
Itahuania	222; 238; 245	296; 327; 308	57; 60; 57	26; 27; 28	47.5; 49.0; 49.6	37.0; 39.4; 38.9	31.5; 32.1; 33.6	26.8; 26.3; 27.2	27.1; 26.8; 27.2
San Ignacio	—	—	—	—	47.6; 47.9	36.9; 36.1	32.0; –	26.1; 26.2	27.3; 27.3
Pampa Grande	215(205–23)5	332(310–44)5	71(65–75)5	—	47.7(46.2–48.4)5	37.0(35.9–37.5)5	32.2(30.8–32.5)5	25.6(24.9–26.7)5	27.4(26.8–27.6)5
Candamo	—	—	—	—	48.4	38.0	31.8	25.8	27.0
Cadena	225; 225	315; 315	67[t]; 69[t]	28; 30	48.9; 49.2	37.6; 37.4	31.7; 32.9	26.1; 27.0	26.8; 26.1
Yuvini	215; 210; 210	345; 352; 340	70; 70; 70	25; 26; 25	48.6; 49.1; 49.5	38.2; 39.3; 38.9	32.4; 34.2; 33.1	25.6; 26.9; 25.3	26.9; 27.8; 26.7
avilapiresi									
BRAZIL									
Tefé, Lago[u]	–; 250[u]; –	–; 295(+ ?)[u]; –	–; 65[u]; –	–; –; –	46.3; 46.6[u]; 47.5	36.7; 37.6[u]; 38.2	27.7; 30.4[u]; 29.9	24.7; 25.2[u]; 25.2	25.8; 24.3[u]; 24.5
Ayapuá	240	320	—	—	46.8	36.3	29.0	25.1	25.1
mystax									
PERU									
Cerro Azul	250(235–75)7	398(377–435)7	70(66–77)7	28(26–30)7	—	—	—	—	—
Sta. Cecilia♂♂	258(248–72)9	386(372–423)9	75(72–79)9	30(28–31)9	54.1(53.2–55.7)9	42.0(40.6–43.9)9	35.2(34.0–36.9)9	29.5(28.9–30.2)9	29.0(28.3–30.1)9
Sta. Cecilia♀♀	256(245–65)4	378(365–92)4	74(70–77)4	28(26–30)4	53.4(52.7–54.4)4	41.9(40.4–42.8)4	33.5(31.7–35.3)4	29.1(28.7–29.6)4	28.2(27.1–29.6)4
Orosa	—	—	—	—	54.7(53.5–55.2)8	—	35.4(34.0–36.6)8	—	—
Sarayacu	—	—	—	—	53.8(52.1–55.2)10	—	34.2(30.6–35.8)9	—	—
Lagarto	—	—	—	—	54.1(52.3–54.9)6	—	35.0(33.9–36.4)6	—	29.0(28.5–29.9)6
BRAZIL									
Igarapé Grande	—	—	70[y]; 72[y]	—	53.7; 55.0	42.8, 43.4	35.1, 35.2	28.7, 28.4	28.6, 28.9
João Pessõa	—	—	74[y]; 75[y]	—	54.2; 55.2	44.0, 44.0	34.6, 35.6	28.7, 29.2	28.2, 28.6
pileatus									
BRAZIL									
Tefé	—	—	—	—	51.6; 52.9; 53.7	40.0, 41.0, 41.9	34.4, 33.5, 33.0	29.6, 28.4, 29.3	28.1, 27.6, 28.9
pluto									
BRAZIL									
Mapixi	280; 270	400; 410	72; 73	—	51.1; 54.5	40.6, 42.3	34.8, 35.4	29.4, 30.3	28.3, 28.6
labiatus									
No locality[v]	—	—	68.6[w]	—	50.4	40.1	34.2	28.2	27.8
BRAZIL									
Rosarinho	255; 234; 280; 246	345; 377; 405; 385	70; 70; 75; 75	—	49.5; 50.7; 50.7; 50.9	39.2, 39.8, 41.1, 40.4	32.2, 31.9, –, 33.6	27.0, 26.7, 27.9, 27.2	27.7, 26.9, 27.4, 27.5
Miguel, Lago	235; 236	385; 382	70; 72	—	49.5; 51.3	38.4, 38.9	32.9, 32.6	27.9, 27.7	27.4, 28.4
Mapixi	300; 300	410; 410	78; 75	—	52.0; 52.3	41.7, 42.0	34.8, 33.5	28.0, 27.7	28.9, 28.3
thomasi									
Rio Tonanfins[x]	–; 270, 290	–; 370	–; 68	–; 32	52.2; 52.6	–; 41.6	32; 33.3	27.2; 27.7	27.3; 27.9

[t] Dry.
[u] Type.
[y] Dry.
[v] Type of *elegantulus* Slack.
[w] Dry.
[x] First measurement is of type with broken skull.

Name Locality	Braincase Length	$I–M^2$	$C–M^2$	Across Molars	Mandible Length	Coronoidal Height	$Pm–M_2$	Symphyseal Angle
fuscicollis								
BRAZIL								
João Pessõa	40.2, 41.2	14.5, 14.6	10.5, 10.2	15.7, 15.4	28.2, 27.8	15.9, 16.2	9.7, 9.7	–, 51
Jordão	39.2	15.3	11.0	15.6	29.4	19.1	10.2	54
weddelli								
BOLIVIA								
Tumapasa	40.4; 41.3	14.6; 14.6	11.2; 10.6;	15.3; 15.4	28.5; 27.3	15.5; 15.3	10.4; 9.8	51; 52
BRAZIL								
Mapixi	41.5; 40.8	–; –	10.6; 11.0	15.4; 15.3	28.4; 28.0	18.0; 18.5	9.4; 10.0	52; 51
PERU								
Itahuania	41.9; 42.6; 43.0	15.3; 15.3; 15.7	11.0; 10.7; 10.8	15.8; 15.7; 15.9	28.4; 29.9; 30.6	17.5; 18.0; 18.5	9.6; 9.7; 9.9	46; 49; 47
San Ignacio	41.3; 42.1	15.2; 14.9	11.0; 10.9	15.8; 14.8	29.5; 29.3;	17.5; 16.5	10.0; 9.6	48; –
Pampa Grande	41.7(41.1–42.8)5	15.1(14.2–15.5)5	10.9(10.9–11.0)5	15.3(14.5–15.5)5	29.3(28.5–30.0)5	17.4(17.3–17.5)5	9.9(9.6–10.3)5	51(42–56)5
Candamo	42.6	15.8	11.4	15.7	29.7	16.3	10.2	48
Cadena	42.5; 42.5	15.2; 15.7	10.8; 11.3	15.2; 15.7	28.6; 29.1	16.8; 18.0	9.9; 10.2	50; 47
Yuvini	41.8; 42.5; 43.0	15.1; 15.8; 15.8	11.3; 11.3; 11.4	15.9; –; 15.4	29.0; –; 30.0	18.8; 19.1; 19.9	10.3; 9.9; 10.4	48; 45; 48
avilapiresi								
BRAZIL								
Tefé, lago[u]	39.3; 40.1[u]; 41.1	15.0; 14.8[u]; 15.3	10.2; 10.4[u]; 10.8	14.7; 15.4[u]; 15.2	–; 29.0[u]; 29.3	15.7; 18.5[u]; 18.2	9.4; 9.6[u]; 9.7	–; 49[u]; 42
Ayapuá	40.5	14.7	10.9	15.7	28.4	17.5	10.5	43
mytax								
PERU								
Cerro Azul	—	—	—	—	—	—	—	—
Sta. Cecilia ♂♂	45.9(44.8–47.4)9	18.0(17.2–18.5)9	12.8(12.3–13.4)9	17.4(16.5–18.1)8	32.4(31.1–33.5)9	19.2(18.3–20.9)9	11.4(11.0–12.0)9	48(42–54)9
Sta. Cecilia ♀♀	44.8(43.6–45.9)4	17.9(17.5–18.2)4	12.6(12.3–13.0)4	17.5(17.1–17.8)4	32.5(31.7–33.4)4	19.7(19.0–20.8)4	11.4(11.0–11.7)4	50.5(50–51)4
Orosa	—	17.2 17.4, 18.4	—	16.6, 17.9, 17.9	—	—	—	—
Sarayacu	—	—	—	—	—	—	—	—
Lagarto	45.6(44.2–46.4)6	18.0(17.6–18.4)6	—	17.3(16.9–17.6)6	—	—	—	—
BRAZIL								
Igarapé Grande	46.1, 47.2	17.1, 17.6	12.3, 12.9	16.7, 17.9	32.9, 33.3	19.2, 19.4	11.1, 11.3	50, 47
João Pessõa	45.6, 47.3	18.1, 18.6	13.0, 12.9	–, 17.8.	32.8, 33.7	19.0, 20.7	11.5, 11.9	47, 50
pileatus								
BRAZIL								
Tefé	44.9, 44.6, 45.7	16.8, 17.7, 18.6	12.0, 12.5, 12.8	17.2, 16.5, –	31.0, 31.9, 32.4	19, 18.7, 19.3	10.9, 11.2, 11.6	49, 51, 45
pluto								
BRAZIL								
Mapixi	43.1, 46.4	19.9, 17.4	12.3, 12.1	17.6, 17.8	31.9, 32.5	20.4, 19.8	11.5, 11.3	45, 47
labiatus								
No locality[v]	44.1	16.7	11.7	—	30.9	19.3	11.2	—
BRAZIL								
Rosarinho	44.4, 43.9, 44.4, 44.1	15.0, 16.7, 16.0, 16.7	11.2, 11.6, 11.8, 11.5	16.4, 16.9, 16.8, 16.1	–, 30.6, 32.0, 31.0	18.2, 17.6, 18.3, 18.1	10.2, 10.7, 11.4, 10.4	–, 54, 47, 50
Miguel, Lago	44.0, 44.6	15.7, 16.5	11.5, 12.3	16.4, 17.3	29.7, 30.3	19.4, 18.0	10.7, 10.9	53, 55
Mapixi	44.4, 46.5	16.5, 17.1	12.3, 12.0	17.1, 16.5	31.5, 32.2	19.0, 20.0	9.7, 10.6	57, 51
thomasi								
Rio Tonantins[x]	45.3; 45.8	16.8; 17.0	12.5, 12.6	16.1; 16.3	31.2; 31.7	18.4; 19.7	11.0, 11.0	53; 46

Appendix Table 2—*Continued*

Name Locality	Head and Body	Tail	Hind Foot	Ear	Greatest Skull Length	Condylobasal Length	Zygomatic Width	Orbital Breadth	Braincase Width
imperator									
BRAZIL									
San Antonio	255; –; 230	415; –; 390	70; –; 70	—	52.5; 52.5; 53.6	43.4, 42.2, 42.4	34.6, 34.0, 34.2	27.9, 27.8, 26.7	28.0, 27.1, 27.2
PERU									
Boca Amigo	245; 246; 242	350; 360; 356	70; 68; 68	28; 28; 28	–; 50.8; 53.5	–, 41.1, 41.8	–, 34.7, 35.5	–, 27.8, 27.5	–, 28.6, 28.3
Altamira	258; 257	360; 358	72; 72	28; 28	50.7; 52.6	41.0, 40.1	32.0, 33.6	27.0, 27.7	28.4, 28.2
midas									
GUYANA									
Mahaienbally Creek	230; 227	350; 397	60; 70	28; 30	—	—	—	—	—
Dunoon	—	—	—	—	53.0, 54.4	41.2, 43.1	32.7, 34.9	28.2, 28.6	26.9, 27.8
Georgetown	—	—	69[z]	—	52.5	41.0	32.4	28.2	26.9
Essequibo	—	—	—	—	52.5, 53.2, 54.1, 54.4	39.3, 40.0, 40.9, –	31.5, 33.0, 34.8, 34.4	28.0, 27.9, 29.1, 28.4	27.5, 28.8, 29.0, 28.6
SURINAME									
Loksie Hattie	223	393	68	32	52.1	39.6	31.1	26.0	27.6
Tapahoni	—	—	—	—	54.9	43.6	33.3	29.0	28.3
Kaiserberg	240, 278	440, 410	68, 80	35, 38	52,6, 55.1	40.5, 42.9	31.5, 35.5	27.7, 29.4	27.5, 29.0
Carolinakreek[aa]	234, 254	384, 392	67, 71	36,30	50.1, 51.4	38.9, 41.3	31.0, 35.5	27.2, 27.0	27.0, 25.9
FRENCH GUIANA									
Cayenne	258, 238	418, 414	74, 70	33, 34	54.0, 55.7	41.0, 43.0	33.5, 32.5	28.6, 28.7	29.3, 29.0
BRAZIL									
Obidos	230; 229[bb]	330; 384	65[z]; 69	30; 40	50.8; 50.4	38.9; 37.4	32.9; 31.8	27.5; 27.6	27.0; 28.3
Serra da Lua	217	363	59[z]	—	47.9	36.4	30.3	25.2	26.7
Canacari	—	—	71[z]	—	51.4	39.3	31.5	28.1	27.5
Itacoatiara	—	—	73[z]	—	52.1	42.0	33.4	28.3	27.7
niger									
BRAZIL									
Cametá♂♂	235(210–82)33	376(330–414)33	69(58–76)33	—	49.1(45.9–53.3)30	40.1(38.3–43.3)29	31.4(30.1–34.2)28	27.9(25.9–29.4)30	27.4(26.2–28.4)30
Cametá♀♀	228(206–55)15	378(324–400)15	69(57–75)15	—	50.5(48.8–51.9)13	39.8(38.2–41.7)11	32.6(30.7–34.1)12	27.6(26.8–28.9)11	27.3(25.4–28.4)13
Cametá	—	—	64[cc], 72[cc], 65[cc]	28	49.5, 51.0, 51.1	38.9, 40.9, 40.4	–, 31.7, 32.3	27.2, 28.1, 27.4	27.2, 26.8, 27.0
Benevides	220	370	—	30	51.8	41.7	33.9	29.0	28.6
Peixe-boi	250	370	—	30	49.7	39.4	32.3	27.2	27.5
Ananindeua	220	370	—	30	50.5	40.9	34.1	28.0	28.5
Itingo	—	—	—	—	52.0	41.5	33.1	28.3	28.3
Amazonas, Rio	—	—	—	—	51.8, 52.7	–, 42.1	32.5, 34.8	28.2, 28.4	28.4, 28.4
Vilarinho	241(207–56)10	387(359–439)10	69(66–74)10	—	51.6(50.4–53.3)10	40.7(39.4–42.3)10	32.7(31.9–34.6)9	28.1(27.3–28.8)10	27.3(26.1–28.4)10
Recreio	234(221–50)6	393(345–425)6	71(70–75)6	—	51.9(50.4–53.7)6	40.4(38.8–42.6)6	32.6(31.2–33.6)5	28.3(26.8–30.0)6	28.3(28.0–28.6)6
Mocajuba	234(211–50)8	371(316–97)8	69(65–72)8	—	50.3(48.1–52.5)7	39.4(37.6–42.5)6	32.9(31.6–34.2)7	28.1(27.2–28.9)7	27.5(26.9–28.4)7
Baião	228(214–42)14	376(345–97)14	68(64–74)14	—	51.1(49.1–53.2)13	40.4(38.3–42.4)12	32.3(31.3–34.8)14	27.8(27.1–28.6)14	27.8(26.7–29.1)13
inustus									
BRAZIL									
Tabacal	208, 245, 235, 215	330, 365, 380, 370	70, 75, 70, 74		50.0, 51.7, 51.8, 52.1	39.8, 41.9, 40.7, 41.9	32.4, 36.3, 36.3, 35.7	27.2, 29.4, 29.3, 28.9	26.4, 27.7, 27.4, 27.7
Jauanari	230, 230, 245	355, 370, 380	72, 71, 74		50.6, 52.4, 53.2	39.8, 41.1, 42.0	35.2, 36.0, 36.9	28.1, 29.3, 29.4	27.2, 27.7, 28.1
Papuri	246	410	72		54.5	43.1	34.8	27.9	27.9
Tahuapunta	259, 220	375, 345	71, 70		50.5, 52.3	39.8, –	36.0, 34.5	28.2, 28.0	27.7, 27.6
COLOMBIA									
Caño Grande	225	345	—		52.6	41.6	35.7	28.6	27.0
Itilla	—	—	—	—	53.1	41.6	34.7	28.7	27.7

[z] Dry.
[aa] Subadults.
[bb] Second set is of type of *Midas egans* Thomas.
[cc] Dry

Name Locality	Braincase Length	$I–M^2$	$C–M^2$	Across Molars	Mandible Length	Coronoidal Height	$Pm–M_2$	Symphyseal Angle
imperator								
BRAZIL								
San Antonio	43.2, 43.1, 45.3	17.2, 18.1, 17.4	13.5, 12.8, 12.5	17.5, 17.3, 17.4	33.7, 33.5, 32.5	20.6, 21.0, 19.5	13.1, 12.3, 11.9	49, 50, 56
PERU								
Boca Amigo	–, 43.5, 45.2	–, 16, 8, 16.6	–, 12.5, 11.8	–, 17.2, 17.2	–, 31.4, 32.3	19.5, 20.3, 18.0	12.2, 11.5, 11.4	–, 57, 48
Altamira	44.3, 44.2	16.7, 17.2	12.5, 12.7	16.9, 15.6	32.0, 31.8	18.7, 18.2	11.6, 11.5	48, 52
midas								
GUYANA								
Mahaienbally Creek	—	—	—	—	—	—	—	—
Dunoon	45.7, 46.7	17.2, 17.4	12.5, 12.8	17.2, 18.6	32.7, 34.0	20.1, 20.4	11.5, 12.3	47, 49
Georgetown	45.1	16.8	11.7	16.5	32.4	20.0	11.1	46
Essequibo	44.7, 46.2, 47.6, 46.6	16.2, 16.5, 17.2, 16.8	12.2, 12.4, 12.5, 11.9	17.0, 18.0, 17.6, 18.2	31.5, 30.5, 32.4, 32.5	19.0, 20.2, 21.6, 20.4	11.0, 11.4, 11.4, 11.6	50, 52, 50, 48
SURINAME								
Loksie Hattie	46.1	17.2	13.0	17.6	30.9	18.2	11.6	44
Tapahoni	47.6	17.0	12.4	17.9	33.4	21.4	11.0	48
Kaiserberg	47.1, 49.0	16.5, 17.6	11.6, 12.0	17.4, 17.8	30.9, 32.5	19.0, 20.0	10.9, 11.8	49, 47
Carolinakreek[aa]	44.0, 44.4	15.6, 16.0	11.6, 11.8	17.4, 17.2	29.5, 31.1	17.7, 18.5	11.1, 11.0	49, 52
FRENCH GUIANA								
Cayenne	47.4, 49.3	17.0, 17.5	12.6, 13.0	18.2, 17.6	32.2, 33.2	21.7, 21.4	11.9, 12.2	53, 52
BRAZIL								
Obidos	44.7; 43.9	16.5; 15.0	12.3; 12.0	16.5; 16.1	30.0; 29.4	19.1; 20.2	11.6; 11.2	41; –
Serra da Lua	41.3	15.5	11.8	15.9	28.7	17.9	11.0	43
Canacari	43.6	16.7	11.9	17.4	30.0	20.0	11.4	47
Itacoatiara	44.0	17.0	12.3	17.3	32.5	22.0	11.1	46
niger								
BRAZIL								
Cametá ♂♂	44.2(39.2–47.5)31	16.1(15.0–17.3)29	—	16.6(15.9–17.7)30	—	—	—	—
Cametá ♀♀	43.9(42.3–45.8)12	16.4(15.6–17.3)12	—	16.9(16.3–17.4)11	—	—	—	—
Cametá	43.0, 44.4, 43.9	16.0, 17.1, 17.1	11.9, 12.3, 12.2	16.3, 16.3, 16.9	30.2, 32.3, 31.9	18.4, 19.8, 19.4	10.9, 11.3, 11.4	55, 44, 46
Benevides	44.5	16.5	12.0	17.1	32.1	20.5	10.6	44
Peixe-boi	43.1	15.9	11.8	16.1	30.0	19.2	10.8	50
Ananindeua	43.2	16.7	12.5	17.7	30.5	19.6	11.1	45
Itingo	43.4	16.8	12.3	17.0	31.8	20.4	11.0	47
Amazonas, Rio	43.8, –	16.7, 16.3	12.5, 12.0	17.4, –	30.5, 32.0	19.5, 21.2	10.8, 11.4	44, 52
Vilarinho	44.1(42.9–46.2)10	16.8(16.0–17.3)10	—	16.8(15.8–17.8)10	—	—	—	—
Recreio	44.9(43.4–45.5)6	16.8(15.9–17.7)6	—	16.9(16.4–17.7)6	—	—	—	—
Mocajuba	44.3(43.2–45.3)7	16.0(14.7–16.8)7	—	16.5(15.7–17.3)7	—	—	—	—
Bajão	44.0(42.1–45.9)14	16.5(15.9–17.5)12	—	17.2(16.6–17.9)13	—	—	—	—
inustus								
BRAZIL								
Tabacal	43.3, 45.8, 45.9, 45.2	16.6, 16.4, 16.2, 16.8	12.1, 12.4, 11.9, 12.2	16.2, 17.1, 16.7, 16.8	30.6, 31.2, 30.9, 31.5	18.3, 19.7, 19.6, 19.2	10.7, 10.9, 10.9, 10.8	46, –, 42, 43
Jauanari	44.7, 46.2, 46.8	16.2, 16.2, 16.7	11.7, 11.4, 11.7	16.7, 17.3, 16.9	30.4, 31.5, 32.0	19.6, 19.9, 20.6	10.3, 10.7, 10.9	44, 48, 47
Papuri	46.5	18.0	12.7	17.9	33.3	19.4,	11.6	46
Tahuapunta	44.9, 45.2	16.7, –	12.4, 12.8	17.7, –	31.0, 30.5	19.0, 19.3	11.8, 10.7	48, 48
COLOMBIA								
Caño Grande	45.4	17.4	12.5	16.3	31.8	19.9	11.3	44
Itilla	46.2	17.7	12.4	16.9	31.7	19.0	11.4	45

Appendix Table 2—*Continued*

Name Locality	Head and Body	Tail	Hind Foot	Ear	Greatest Skull Length	Condylobasal Length	Zygomatic Width	Orbital Breadth	Braincase Width
leucopus									
COLOMBIA									
Norosí♂♂	241(232–50)11	375(347–405)10	73(69–79)12	27(25–30)12	49.9(46.5–51.7)10	39.6(37.6–41.2)10	34.1(32.6-34.9)10	27.7(26.8–29.2)10	27.9(27.1–29.2)10
Norosí♀♀	244(224–63)14	389(360–417)14	74(68–80)14	27(24–30)14	51.0(48.6–53.3)14	40.2(38.5–42.2)14	33.8(31.6–35.8)14	27.7(26.1–28.9)14	27.5(27.1–28.9)14
Bellavista	251, 239, 233	391, 411, 396	74, 76, 73	30, 27, 29	54.4, 53.7, 53.0	43.0, 43.2, –	35.0, 34.9, 32.1	29.6, 29.3, 27.4	29.7, 28.9, 28.1
Valdivia	230	353	74	27	51.6	40.8	35.1	28.9	29.1
Puri	232(223–39)5	390(383–94)5	74(74–74)3	28(27–29)5	53.4(52.7–54.6)5	42.1(41.8–42.6)5	35.6(34.2–37.6)5	28.4(27.5–29.0)5	28.7(28.5–29.4)5
bicolor									
BRAZIL[dd]									
Manaos[ee]	–, 229	–, 335	–, 70	—	50.5, 51.1	38.2, 40.0	29.8, 33.2	25.9, 28.0	27.7, 27.4
Manaos[ff]	240	350	—		46.5	36.5	31.5	—	26.5
ochraceus									
BRAZIL									
Paratucú	214(231–375)11	386(345–420)11	74(65–83)1	—	52.7(51.2–54.1)9	41.2(38.9–42.6)9	35.1(33.5–36.2)9	28.2(27.3–29.0)9	27.2(25.9–28.2)9
Paratucú[gg]	247	395	74	—	53.2	42.6	35.0	28.9	27.0
Espelho	235, 248	403, 404	74, 75	—	–, 51.9	–, 41.0	35.2, 35.4	28.4, 28.1	28.3, 27.8
Castanhal	240, 250, 237, 214	397, 380, 375	76, 78, 75, 79	—	52.1, 52.4, 53.4, 54.1	41.2, 41.4, 41.9, 41.7	34.6, 36.7, 37.2, 35.1	27.6, 29.5, 29.7, 29.1	26.9, 27.5, 29.7, 29.1
martinsi									
BRAZIL									
Faro[hh]	208	366	61	31	51.8	41.0	35.1	28.4	26.5
Faro	228(210–83)5	366(349–80)5	68(62–70)5	25, 30, 31	51.2(51.1–51.4)5	40.7(40.4–41.2)5	34.6(33.6–35.9)3	28.3(27.8–29.0)3	26.4(25.8–27.1)5
Yaracana	235	380	74	—	51.2	40.1	34.0	27.4	26.8
S. José	258	399	74	—	52.2	40.4	36.4	28.9	27.9
geoffroyi									
PANAMA									
Barro Colorado	276	355	—	23	53.7	43.0	36.9	28.8	28.6
Madden	—	—	73[ii]; 71[ii]; 70[ii]	—	51.8; 51.8; 53.1	40.1; 40.4; 41.4	34.0; 35.3; 35.4	28.9; 29.0; 29.5	28.9; 28.2; 29.1
Albrook	—	—	—	—	52.8; 53.1; 53.5	41.2; 41.1; 41.2	36.8; 36.5; 34.4	29.1; 28.9; 28.0	28.2; 28.4; 29.6
Tacarcuna	235(200–63)13	345(315–96)13	70(64–76)13	26(23–31)13	52.9(51.3–55.5)13	41.4(39.6–44.2)13	36.1(33.0–39.8)12	29.0(27.4–30.3)12	28.1(26.5–29.4)12
Madden Dam	242(225–55)8	369(360–86)7	72(65–75)8	27(23–30)8	52.8(51.5–54.3)8	41.4(39.2–42.9)8	35.7(32.3–37.2)8	29.0(27.2–30.6)8	27.9(26.6–29.1)8
Gamboa	240(225–64)8	358(335–70)8	71(70–75)8	25(22–27)8	52.5(51.5–53.5)8	41.3(39.7–43.5)8	34.6(31.4–36.0)8	28.5(27.4–28.9)7	28.3(28.0–28.8)8
Armila	242(220–55)10	386(350–415)10	71(69–73)10	27(25–29)10	53.0(51.9–54.8)9	41.7(40.4–43.2)9	36.6(35.5–37.6)8	29.0(28.2–30.3)9	28.1(27.4–29.6)9
Chiva Chiva	241(231–65)4	364(351–90)4	70(65–75)4	23(20–25)4	52.9(52.1–54.1)4	41.2(40.2–42.5)4	35.2(33.3–36.6)4	28.5(27.5–29.4)4	28.5(28.0–29.0)4
Cocoli	230(220–40)10	363(328–90)10	68(60–72)10	25(22–27)10	52.6(50.6–53.8)9	40.9(39.6–41.3)9	35.2(33.4–36.8)9	28.6(27.4–30.4)9	28.1(27.6–28.6)9
Mandinga	240(230–50)6	379(370–90)6	74(70–76)6	28(25–30)6	54.3(53.0–56.4)6	42.8(41.3–44.7)6	36.3(34.9–37.4)6	29.1(27.9–30.2)6	28.1(27.1–28.6)6
Paya	234(225–40)4	367(365–70)4	73(70–76)4	29(29–30)4	52.3(51.2–53.3)6	41.0(40.3–42.3)6	35.7(33.1–37.0)5	28.7(26.9–30.1)6	27.6(26.3–28.8)6
COLOMBIA									
Unguía♂♂	248(224–87)12	373(347–402)12	75(69–82)12	28(26–31)12	53.0(51.2–55.1)10	41.5(39.9–44.5)10	35.7(32.2–37.3)9	28.5(27.2–30.0)10	28.2(27.4–28.9)10
Unguía♀♀	244(221–64)8	392(375–423)8	75(72–81)8	27(26–30)8	52.8(49.3–55.3)8	41.0(38.3–43.0)8	35.0(32.6–37.1)8	28.4(26.9–29.6)8	28.1(27.2–28.4)8
Sautatá	241(232–50)5	373(360–86)5	73(71–74)5	—	51.2(49.2–52.5)5	40.8(40.0–41.8)5	34.7(32.9–36.3)5	28.1(27.2–29.5)5	27.8(27.4–28.4)5
Salaquí	—	—	—	—	54.0	42.8	36.2	29.5	27.6
Saudó	266; 256; 287; 265	381; 367; 312; 375	72; 72; 76; 76	26; 27; 28; 27	54.0; 54.0; 54.1; 55.5	41.6; –; 41.6; 43.6	37.6; 36.9; 37.7; 36.9	30.1; 29.4; 29.9; 29.7	27.5; 28.5; 28.7; 29.1

[dd] Measurements given by Cruz Lima (**1945**, p. 205), "head and body 320 mm, tail 410 mm" taken "on the mounted" skin of a specimen in the Pará Museum, are not comparable and are out of line with those taken on the freshly killed animal.

[ee] First specimen a subadult.

[ff] Measurements of a subadult from Lonnberg (**1940**, p. 15).

[gg] Of type of *ochraceus*.

[hh] Of type of *martinsi*.

[ii] Dry.

Name Locality	Braincase Length	$I–M^2$	$C–M^2$	Across Molars	Mandible Length	Coronoidal Height	$Pm–M_2$	Symphyseal Angle
leucopus								
COLOMBIA								
Norosí♂♂	—	—	—	—	—	—	—	—
Norosi♀♀	—	—	—	—	—	—	—	—
Bellavista	44.1, 44.1, 44.4	17.6, 18.6, 17.4	12.5, 13.4, 12.8	16.9, 17.0, 16.1	33.8, 33.4, 31.9	18.5, 20.0, 7.5	11.4, 12.0, 11.8	46, 50, 47
Valdivia	43.7	16.8	13.0	17.4	32.3	20.1	11.5	48
Purí	45.1(44.0–46.2)5	17.2(16.8–17.4)5	12.5(12.1–12.8)5	16.8(16.6–17.3)5	32.4(31.5–33.5)5	19.2(17.8–21.0)5	11.4(11.1–11.5)5	52(49–54)5
bicolor								
BRAZIL[dd]								
Manaos[ee]	43.4, 43.3	16.4, 16.8	11.6, 12.2	16.9, 17.0	28.6, 30.9	21.4, 21.0	11.3, 11.2	51, 43
Manaos[ff]	—	—	—	—	—	—	11.5	—
ochraceus								
BRAZIL								
Paratucú	45.0(43.5–46.8)9	17.3(16.5–17.9)9	12.8(12.0–13.2)9	17.7(17.1–18.5)9	31.8(30.5–33.3)10	20.1(18.6–21.7)10	11.9(11.1–12.3)10	44(40–49)10
Paratucú[gg]	45.9	17.9	12.9	17.3	32.9	19.5	11.8	40
Espelho	45.5, 45.0	17.2, 17.1	13.0, 12.9	17.9, 17.5	31.4 ,31.8	19.5, 19.4	12.2, 11.7	43, 50
Castanhal	44.5, 46.5, 46.4, 47.0	17.5, 17.7, 17.1, 17.6	13.0, 12.4, 12.8, 12.4	18.7, 17.6, 18.5, 18.5	31.4, 31.5, 32.1, 32	20.2, 21.7, 20.5, 20.7	9.5, 11.8, 11.3, 11.9	47, 40, 44, 40
martinsi								
BRAZIL								
Faro[hh]	44.1	17.4	12.4	17.0	32.1	20.2	11.0	—
Faro	43.3(42.2–44.3)5	17.0(16.8–17.4)4	12.2(12.0–12.7)5	16.9(16.7–17.2)4	31.3(31.0–31.7)3	19.8(19.1–20.7)5	11.2(10.9–11.5)5	45(40–47)5
Yaracana	44.1	16.5	12.0	17.0	30.7	20.2	11.8	41
S. José	45.8	16.9	12.5	17.5	31.9	21.9	11.4	44
geoffroyi								
PANAMA								
Barro Colorado	45.3	17.1	12.4	17.0	32.8	20.0	11.8	50
Madden	44.2; 43.6; 45.2	16.0; 17.0; 17.2	12.0; 13.1; 12.5	16.8; 17.0; 17.2	30.5; 30.7; 31.7	17.5; 18.5; 17.6	11.2; 12.1; 11.2	55; 52; 47
Albrook	45.2; 44.5; 45.3	16.6; 17.2; 17.3	12.2; 13.0; 12.5	17.5; 18.0; 17.2	32.6; 32.6; 31.3	19.6; 18.3; 19.0	11.8; 12.1; 11.7	45; 52; 46
Tacarcuna	45.0(43.5–46.2)12	17.4(16.3–18.1)13	12.8(12.1–13.5)13	17.5(16.7–18.4)11	31.3(30.0–33.3)12	19.1(17.3–22.4)13	12.0(11.3–12.6)12	—
Madden Dam	45.1(42.8–47.3)8	17.2(16.8–17.9)8	12.5(11.8–13.0)8	17.3(16.8–17.7)8	31.7(30.4–33.3)8	18.9(17.8–20.3)8	11.8(11.6–12.1)	—
Gamboa	44.1(42.9–45.7)8	17.3(16.7–18.1)8	12.7(12.0–13.4)8	17.2(16.6–17.6)8	31.5(30.6–32.4)8	18.5(15.8–21.0)8	12.1(11.6–12.6)8	—
Armila	44.9(42.9–45.9)9	17.5(16.7–18.5)9	12.9(11.9–14.4)9	17.1(16.6–17.5)9	32.4(31.3–34.0)9	19.8(17.8–21.0)9	11.9(11.3–13.0)9	—
Chiva Chiva	45.0(44.2–46.2)4	17.1(16.8–17.5)4	12.7(12.5–13.0)4	16.9(16.4–17.4)4	31.1(30.5–32.2)4	18.9(16.9–20.0)4	11.6(11.3–12.0)4	—
Cocoli	44.6(43.6–46.0)8	16.8(15.8–17.6)9	12.7(12.0–13.1)9	17.2(16.5–17.9)9	31.7(30.9–32.5)9	19.4(17.1–20.7)9	11.9(11.1–12.3)9	—
Mandinga	45.3(44.4–46.7)6	17.7(17.2–18.3)6	12.8(12.5–13.2)6	17.5(17.1–17.9)6	32.6(31.8–34.1)6	18.7(17.6–19.1)6	12.0(11.5–12.3)6	—
Paya	44.7(43.1–45.7)6	17.6(16.9–18.0)6	12.8(12.2–13.3)6	17.3(16.2–18.3)5	31.8(30.4–32.4)4	19.9(18.0–22.2)5	12.0(11.6–12.3)5	—
COLOMBIA								
Unguía♂♂	44.5(42.6–46.8)10	17.2(16.3–18.1)10	12.7(12.4–13.2)10	17.7)17.1–18.2)10	32.4(31.2–34.4)10	19.1(18.1–21.1)10	11.9(11.2–12.5)10	48(44–54)10
Unguía♀♀	44.7(42.2–46.5)8	17.1(16.1–17.7)8	12.8(12.6–13.0)8	17.5)15.9–18.2)8	31.8(30.1–33.3)7	18.9(17.1–21.1)8	11.8(11.3–12.1)8	49(45–54)7
Sautatá	—	—	—	—	—	—	—	—
Salaquí	—	—	—	—	—	—	—	—
Saudó	45.1; 45.2; 45.4; 46.1	18.2; –; 18.1; 18.3	13.1; –; 13.2; 13.5	18.0; 18.2; 17.8; 18.9	33.0; 35.0; 33.8; 34.1	20.9; 20.1; 20.0; 20.6	12.5; 12.8; 12.0; 12.9	54; –; 51; 49

Appendix Table 2—*Continued*

Name Locality	*Head and Body*	*Tail*	*Hind Foot*	*Ear*	*Greatest Skull Length*	*Condylobasal Length*	*Zygomatic Width*	*Orbital Breadth*	*Braincase Width*
oedipus									
COLOMBIA									
Socorré♂♂	224(205–36)8	367(349–87)8	70(66–74)8	22(20–24)8	51.8(49.9–53.1)8	40.4(39.1–41.5)8	33.4(27.6–34.8)8	27.9(25.9–28.6)8	27.0(25.7–27.9)8
Socorré♀♀	233(222–47)5	381(369–404)5	72(70–74)5	22(21–23)5	52.3(50.9–53.8)5	41.0(39.5–42.5)5	34.0(33.4–34.9)5	28.1(27.5–28.5)4	27.3(26.9–27.9)5
Jaraquiel	225, 224, 226, 245	370, 380, 380, 382	71, 72, 73, 70	—	47.8, 49.4, 50.4, 51.5	37.6, 39.0, 39.5, 41.8	30.8, 31.9, 30.9, 32.6	—	26.0, 26.0, 26.1, 26.8
San Juan♂♂	235(219–48)6	375(356–91)5	70(66–75)6	21(20–21)6	50.9(49.2–53.3)6	40.0(38.0–42.4)6	32.8(31.7–33.8)6	27.9(27.6–28.6)6	26.2(25.9–26.7)6
San Juan♀♀	237(231–55)5	395(381–411)5	74(69–78)5	21(20–21)5	50.6(50.0–51.9)4	39.7(39.4–40.2)4	31.7(31.0–32.9)4	26.6)26.0–27.3)4	26.1(26.1–26.3)4
Colosó	230(224–46)7	379(343–400)7	72(70–75)12	21(20–21)7	50.1(48.6–51.5)7	39.1(37.6–41.1)7	32.3(30.4–33.0)7	27.7(26.8–29.2)7	26.1(25.5–27.4)7
Catival	232(206–43)12	372(333–402)12	72(70–75)12	21(20–22)12	51.0(49.1–52.3)12	40.0(37.4–42.0)12	32.8(28.2–35.1)12	27.7(25.8–28.4)12	27.4(26.0–28.2)12
Villa Arteaga	230, 209, 223	348, 363, 357	72, 71, 72	21, 22, 21	49.1, 50.9, 50.9	38.2, 38.6, 39.5	32.7, 29.0, 32.7	28.2, 26.3, 27.1	27.0, 26.5, 26.6
Currulao	224(221–28)6	337(307–47)6	70(68–73)6	22(21–24)6	51.1(49.8–52.6)5	39.6(38.7–41.0)5	32.6(31.6–34.0)5	27.5(26.7–29.1)5	27.5(26.8–28.1)5
Leontopithecus									
BRAZIL									
rosalia									
Rio de Janeiro	229(200–250)5	335(315–68)4	76(72–81)5	25(24–26)4	56.5(53.6–59.8)13	45.9(42.5–48.5)13	34.8(32.5–36.6)12	28.8(27.5–30.6)12	28.4(27.5–29.3)13
Rio de Janeiro[jj]	254 (17 specimens)	334 (17 specimens)							
chrysomelas									
Bahia[kk]	257(240–90)7	376(360–400)7	78(71–86)7	—	—	—	—	—	—
chrysopygus									
São Paulo	—	—	—	—	—	—	—	—	—
Ipanema[ll]	273	366	—	—	—	—	—	—	—
Ipanema[mm]	305, 317	368, 387	—	—	—	—	—	—	—
Vargem Grande[mm]	317	381	—	—	—	—	—	—	—
Kitayama[nn]	330, 300	390, 380	90, 80	—	—	—	—	—	—
Vitória[oo]	290	330	70	—	56	—	35	—	29
Vitória[pp]	255, 255	400, 385	75, 75	25, 25	—	—	—	—	—

Callimico	Head & Body	Tail	Hind Foot	Ear	Greatest Skull Length	Condylo-basal Length	Zygomatic Width	Orbital Breadth	Braincase Width	Braincase Length	I–M³
goeldii[qq]	225(213–34)12	303(270–324)12	75(70–78)13	23(20–26)9	53.3(50.5–55.5)10	39.7(38.1–44.3)9	34.5(32.8–35.1)9	30.7(29.8–32.6)11	29.8(29.0–32.2)10	45.8(44.6–49.8)11	18.1(17.3–19.0)10[tt]
type[rr]	190	255	66	—	—	—	—	—	—	—	—
_[ss]	221(210–30)6	300(287–317)6	72(68–74)6	24(20-26)6	—	—	—	—	—	—	—

[jj] From Coimbra-Filho 1969, p. 36

[kk] From Coimbra-Filho 1970, p. 258

[ll] Type, from original description

[mm] From Pelzeln 1883, p. 26; old Austrian measurements converted to millimeters, in same order as above, total length, 2′ 2½″, 2′ 2¾″; tail, 14½″, 15¼″; total length, 2′ 3½″ (subtract tail length from total length for head and body length given above); original measurements evidently followed body curves in system used by taxidermists.

[nn] From Coimbra-Filho 1970, p. 612; taken from dry mounted skins with torsos probably stretched.

[oo] From Vieira 1944, p. 4, of male no. 2140, Departamento de Zoologia, São Paulo.

[pp] From Coimbra-Filho 1970, p. 262; first specimen said to be same male no. 2140 recorded by Vieira as given above; second specimen, a female no. 2141, also recorded by Vieira but without measurements.

[qq] Includes type of *snethlageri*.

[rr] From original description of "a skin, which has been stuffed and then dismounted." These measurements, if accurate, are not of an adult.

[ss] Captive, unknown locality, from Lorenz and Heinemann (**1967**:21).

[tt] Includes USNM 303322 with supernumerary molar (m^4).

Name Locality	Braincase Length	I–M²	C–M²	Across Molars	Mandible Length	Coronoidal Height	Pm–M₂	Symphyseal Angle
oedipus								
COLOMBIA								
Socorré♂♂	42.6(40.8–44.9)8	17.0(16.7–17.4)8	12.5(11.9–12.9)8	16.2(15.5–16.8)8	30.7(28.4–31.8)8	18.7(15.7–20.9)8	11.7(11.1–12.0)8	51(49–52)8
Socorré♀♀	43.4(42.2–45.2)5	16.8(16.0–17.2)5	12.6(12.3–12.9)5	17.2(16.6–17.5)5	31.3(30.5–32.5)5	19.6(18.6–20.5)5	11.5(11.2–12.0)5	49(46–54)5
Jaraquiel	—	—	—	—	—	—	—	—
San Juan♂♂	42.7(41.9–44.0)6	16.5(16.0–17.2)6	12.2(11.9–12.5)6	15.9(15.7–16.2)5	30.8(30.2–31.9)5	19.0(17.6–20.2)6	11.3(11.1–11.6)6	50(49–51)5
San Juan♀♀	41.9(40.7–42.6)5	16.5(16.1–16.8)4	12.3(12.0–12.5)4	16.1(15.7–16.5)4	30.5(29.8–30.5)4	18.2(17.3–18.8)4	11.4(11.1–12.0)5	52(51–54)4
Colosó	42.1(41.0–42.9)7	16.5(16.3–17.3)7	12.1(11.8–12.5)7	15.4(14.9–16.4)7	29.7(28.5–31.2)7	18.0(16.4–18.6)7	11.2(11.0–11.7)7	51(48–56)7
Catival	42.9(41.5–43.6)11	16.4(16.0–17.4)12	12.2(11.9–12.8)12	16.1(15.5–16.8)12	30.3(28.0–31.2)12	18.5(17.2–20.4)12	11.2(10.9–11.7)12	51(46–55)12
Villa Arteaga	43.7, 42.0, 42.3	16.0, 16.8, 16.7	12.0, 12.8, 12.0	15.9, 15.7, 15.2	29.5, 29.5, 29.8	–, 19.0, 17.4	10.9, 11.0, 11.0	48, 53, 54
Currulao	42.8(42.1–43.6)5	16.8(16.3–17.4)5	12.3(11.9–12.4)5	16.1(15.7–16.4)5	30.5(29.1–31.7)5	19.1(18.2–19.6)5	10.9(10.9–11.0)5	52(47–57)5
Leontopithecus								
BRAZIL								
rosalia								
Rio de Janeiro	47.3(46.3–49.4)10	20.6(18.6–21.8)12	15.1(14.7–15.9)12	19.6(18.1–20.4)10	35.4(32.3–37.0)13	23.3(21.9–25.2)11	13.7(13.3–14.4)12	42(36–51)11
Rie de Janeiro[jj]	—	—	—	—	—	—	—	—
chrysomelas								
Bahia[kk]	—	—	—	—	—	—	—	—
chrysopygus								
São Paulo	—	—	—	—	—	—	—	—
Ipanema[ll]	—	—	—	—	—	—	—	—
Ipanema[mm]	—	—	—	—	—	—	—	—
Vargem Grande[mm]	—	—	—	—	—	—	—	—
Kitayama[nn]	—	—	—	—	—	—	—	—
Vitória[oo]	—	—	—	—	—	—	—	—
Vitória[pp]	—	—	—	—	—	—	—	—

Callimico	I—M²	C—M³	C—M²	Across Molars	Mandible Length	Coronoidal Height	Pm—M₃	Pm—M₂	Symphyseal Angle
goeldii[qq]	16.6(15.2–17.9)10	15.2(14.7–16.8)10	14.0(13.4–15.5)10	18.5(17.5–19.8)11	32.3(31.0–35.8)8	20.6(18.8–21.9)10	14.2(13.5–15.3)9	12.1(11.3–13.3)10	55(49–63)10
type[rr]	—	—	—	—	—	—	—	—	—
_[ss]	—	—	—	—	—	—	—	—	—

Literature Cited

Ablashi, D. V.; Chopra, H. C.; and Armstrong, G. R. 1972. A cytomegalovirus isolated from an owl monkey. *Lab. Anim. Sci.* 22:190–95, 3 figs.

Adey, W. R. 1970. Higher olfactory centres. In *Taste and smell in vertebrates,* ed. G. Wolstenholme and J. Knight. Symp. Ciba Foundation, London, pp. 357–78, 9 figs.

Agassiz, Louis. 1868. *A journey to Brazil.* 2d ed. Boston: Tucknor and Fields. xix, 549 pp., illus.

Albuquerque, Rosa Domingues Ribeiro, and Barreto, Mauro Pereira. 1970. Estudos sobre reservatórios e vectores silvestres do *Trypanosoma cruzi.* XL—Infecção natural do símio, *Callithrix argentata melanura* (Geoffroy, 1812) pelo *T. cruzi. Rev. Inst. Med. Trop. São Paulo* 12(2):121–28, 33 figs.

Al-Doory, Y. 1972. Superficial mycoses. Intermediate mycoses. Systemic mycoses. In *Pathology of simian primates,* ed. R. N. T.-W. Fiennes, 2:206–13; 214–23, 3 figs.; 224–42. Basel: S. Karger.

Alexandersen, V. 1963. Double-rooted human lower canine teeth. In *Dental anthropology,* ed. D. R. Brothwell. 5:235–44. Symposium of the Society for the Study of Human Biology, 4 figs.

Allen, Glover M. 1931. Type specimens of mammals in the Museum of Comparative Zoology. *Bull. Mus. Comp. Zool.* 71(4):227–89.

Allen, Glover M., and Barbour, Thomas. 1923. Mammals from Darien. *Bull. Mus. Comp. Zool.* 65(8): 259–74.

Allen, Joel A. 1916. Mammals collected on the Roosevelt Brazilian Expedition, with field notes by Leo E. Miller. *Bull. Amer. Mus. Nat. History* 35(30):559–610.

Allyn, Georges. 1974. Mammalian socialization and the problem of imprinting. *Terre et Vie* 28 (2):209–71.

Altmann-Schönberner, Dagmar. 1965. Beobachtungen über Aufzucht und Entwicklung des Verhaltens beim Grossen Löwenäffschen, *Leontocebus rosalia. Zool. Gart.* 31(5):227–39.

Altner, G. 1971. Histologische und vergleichendanatomische Untersuchungen zur Ontogenie und Phylogenie des Handskeletts von *Tupaia glis* (Diard 1820) und *Microcebus murinus* (J. F. Miller 1777). *Folia Primat.* 14(suppl.):1–106, 24 pls.

Ammons, William F.; Schectman, Larry R.; and Page, Roy C. 1972. Host tissue response in chronic periodontal disease. 1. The normal periodontium and clinical manifestations of dental and periodontal disease in the marmoset. *J. Periodont. Res.* 7:131–43, 11 figs.

Amoroso, E. C. 1969. Physiological mechanisms in reproduction. *J. Reprod. Fert.,* suppl. 6:5–18.

Anderson, C. R., Aitken, T. H. G.; Spence, L. P.; and Downs, W. G. 1960. Kairi virus, a new virus from Trinidadian forest mosquitos. *Amer. J. Trop. Med. Hyg.* 9:70–72.

Anderson, C. R.; Spence, L. P.; Downs, W. G.; and Aitken, T. H. G. 1960. Manzanilla virus: A new virus isolated from the blood of the howler monkey in Trinidad, W. I. *Amer. J. Trop. Med. Hyg.* 9:78–80.

———. 1961. Aropouche virus: A new human disease agent from Trinidad, West Indies. *Amer. J. Trop. Med. Hyg.* 10:574–78.

Anderson, Earl T.; Lewis, Jerry P.; Passovoy, Mitchell; and Trobaugh, Frank E., Jr. 1967. The hematology of laboratory kept marmosets. *Lab. Animal Care* 17(1): 30–40, 2 figs.

Andrew, R. J. 1963. The origin and evolution of the calls and facial expressions of Primates. *Behaviour* 20:1–109, 35 figs.

Ankel, Friderun. 1962. Vergleichende Untersuchungen über die Skelettmorphologie des Greifschwanzes südamerikanischer Affen (Platyrrhina). *Z. Morph. Ökol. Tiere* 52:131–70.

———. 1963. Zur Morphologie des Griefschwanzes bei südamerikanischer Affen. *Z. Morph. Anthrop.* 53: 12–18.

———. 1967. Morphologie von Wirbelsäule und Brustkorb. *Primatologia* 4(4):120 pp., 69 figs.

Anson, Barry J., and Bast, Theodore H. 1946. The development of the auditory ossicles and associated structures in man. *Ann Otol., Rhinol., Laryng.* 55 (3): 467–94.

Anthony, Jean. 1942. L'évolution du lobe pariétal du cerveau chez les singes américains. *Comptes Rendu Acad. Sci., Paris* 215:589–90, 1 fig.

———. 1946*a*. Morphologie externe du cerveau des singes platyrrhiniens. *Ann. Sci. Nat., Zool.,* ser. 11, 8: 1–149, 55 figs.

———. 1946*b*. Le trou malaire des Atelidae et son interet dans la classification des singes platyrrhiniens. *Mammalia* 10(2):69–77, 5 figs.

———. 1947. Clef analytique pour la détermination

générique des singes américains par les caractères de la tête osseuse. *Bull. Mus. Nat. Hist. Nat., Paris* (2), 19 (1):47–50, 2 figs.

Anthony, R. 1912. Contribution a l'étude morphologique générale des caractères d'adaptation a la vie arboricole chez les vertébrés. *Ann. Sci. Nat.*, ser. 9, 15:101–342, 73 figs.

Antonius, O. 1939. Über die Schlangenfurcht der Affen. *Z. Tierpsychol.* 2:293–96.

Asdell, S. A. 1964. *Patterns of mammalian reproduction.* 2d ed. Ithaca, N.Y.: Cornell University Press, ix + 670 pp., 1 fig. (U.S., edition 2).

———. 1965. *Patterns of mammalian reproduction.* 2d ed. London: Constable, viii [+6], 670 pp. (England, edition 2).

Ashley-Montagu, M. F. 1935. The premaxilla in the Primates. *Quart. Rev. Biol.* 10:32–59; 181–208, 11 figs.

Ashton, E. H.; Healy, J. R.; Oxnard, Charles E.; and Spence, T. F. 1965. The combination of locomotor features of the primate shoulder girdle by canonical analysis. *J. Zool.* 147:408–29.

Ashton, E. H., and Oxnard, Charles E. 1961. Musculature variation in the primate shoulder girdle. *J. Anat.* (London) 95:618 (abstract).

———. 1963. The musculature of the primate shoulder. *Trans. Zool. Soc. London* 29(7):553–650, 10 pls.

———. 1964*a*. Locomotor patterns in primates. *Proc. Zool. Soc. London* 142:1–28, 5 figs.

———1964*b*. Functional adaptations in the primate shoulder girdle. *Proc. Zool. Soc. London* 142:49–66, 5 figs.

Ashton, E. H., and Zuckerman, S. 1956. Cranial crests in the Anthropoidea. *Proc. Zool. Soc. London* 126: 581–634, 11 pls.

Aubert, E. 1929. Essai d'ostéologie comparée. Etude des sinus chez les singes. *Ann. Mus. Hist. Nat. Marseilles* 22:1–30, 12 figs.

Audebert, Jean Baptiste. 1797. *Histoire naturelle des singes et des makis.* Paris, livr. 1, pp. iii + 24 and 61 articles, each with separate pagination, + 39 + 44 pp.; livr. 2, 61 pls. Paris.

Aulerich, Richard J., and Swindler, Daris R. 1968. The dentition of the mink (Mustela vison). *J. Mammal.* 49(3):488–94, 2 figs.

Avila Pires, Fernando Dias de. 1958. Mamíferos colecionados nos arredores de Belém do Pará. *Bol. Mus. Paraense Emilio Goeldi, Zool.*, no. 19, pp. 1–19.

———. 1959. Notas sôbre Primates. *Atas Soc. Biol., Rio de Janeiro* 3(4):2–3.

———. 1965. The type specimens of Brazilian mammals collected by Prince Maxilian zu Wied. *Amer. Mus. Novit.*, no. 2209, pp. 1–21.

———. 1968. Tipos de mamíferos recentes no Museu Nacional, Rio de Janeiro. *Arq. Mus. Nac.* 53:161–91.

———. 1969. Taxonomia e zoogeografia do género *"Callithrix"* Erxleben, 1777 (Primates, Callithricidae). *Rev. Bras. Biol.* 29:49–64.

Avis, Virginia. 1961. The significance of the angle of the mandible: An experimental and comparative study. *Amer. J. Phys. Anthrop.* 19:55–61, 6 figs.

Ayala, Stephan C.; D'Alessandro, Antonio; MacKensie, Ronald; and Angel, Darío. 1973. Hemoparasite infections in 830 wild animals from the eastern llanos of Colombia. *J. Parasit.* 59(1):52–57, 31 figs.

Azzali, Giacomo, and Di Dio, Liberato J. A. 1965. The lymphatic system of *Bradypus tridactylus. Anat. Rec.* 153(2):149–60, 8 figs.

Backhouse, K. 1959. Testicular descent and ascent in mammals. *Proc. 15th Int. Zool. Cong., London, 1958,* pp. 413–15.

Badoux, Dick M. 1974. An introduction to biomechanical principles in primate locomotion and structure. In *Primate locomotion,* ed. F. A. Jenkins, Jr., pp. 1–43. New York: Academic Press, 35 figs.

Baerg. David C. 1971. A naturally acquired infection of *Plasmodium brasilianum* in the marmoset, *Saguinus geoffroyi. J. Parasit.* 57(1):8.

Baerg, David C.; Porter, James A., Jr.; and Young, Martin D. 1969. Sporozoite transmission of *Plasmodium vivax* to Panamanian primates. *Amer. J. Trop. Med. Hyg.* 18:346–50.

Bafort, J. M., and P. Kageruka. 1974. Parasitological and zoonotic findings in South American monkeys. In *Parasitic zoonoses: Clinical and experimental studies,* ed. E. J. L. Soulsby, pp. 109–15. New York: Academic Press. 3 figs.

Baker, J. R. 1972. Protozoa of tissues and blood (other than the Haemosporina). In *Pathology of simian primates,* ed. R. N. T.-W. Fiennes, 2:29–56, 5 figs. Basel: S. Karger.

Barahona H.; García, F. G.; Meléndez, L. V.; and Hunt, P. D. 1975. A procedure for the isolation of *Herpesvirus saimiri* lymphocyte-associated viruses and blood parasites from monkeys living in the wild. *J. Med. Primat.* 3 (6), pp. 370–76.

Barahona, H. H.; Garcia F. G.; Melendez, L. V.; King, N. W.; Daniel, M. D.; and Ingalls, J. K. 1976. A new foamy virus isolated from uakari monkey (*Cacajao Rubicundus*) lymphocytes (abstract). *J. Med. Primat.* (1975) 4(6):344.

Barahona, Horacio H.; Meléndez, Luis V.; King, N. W.; Daniel, M. D.; Fraser, C. E. O.; and Preville, A. C. 1972. Isolation and characterization of a new herpesvirus from owl monkeys (*Aotus trivirgatus*). A preliminary report. In *Medical primatology 1972,* ed. Goldsmith and Moor-Jankowski, part III, pp. 22–30, 4 figs.

———. 1973. *Herpesvirus aotus* Type 2: A new viral agent from owl monkeys (*Aotus trivirgatus*). *J. Inf. Diseases* 127(2):171–78, 6 figs.

Barahona, Horacio; Meléndez, Luis V.; and Melnick, Joseph L. 1974. A compendium of herpesviruses isolated from non-human primates. *Intervirology* 3: 175–92.

Barker, M. J. M., and Herbert, R. T. 1972. Diseases of the skeleton. In *Pathology of simian primates,* ed. R. N. T.-W. Fiennes, 1:433–519, 29 figs. Basel: S. Karger.

Barnicot, N. A. 1957. Human pigmentation. *Man* 57 (144):114–20, 4 figs.

———. 1963. Characters of genetical interest in primates. In *The primates,* ed. J. Napier and N. A. Barnicot, Symp. Zool. Soc. London, no. 10(3), pp. 211–85.

Barrère, Pierre. 1741. *Essai sur l'histoire naturelle de la France équinoxiale,* Paris, xxvi + 215 + 8 unnumbered.

Bartels, Paul. 1905. Über die Nebenräume der Kehlkopfhöhle. *Z. Morph. Anthrop.* 8:11–61, 2 figs., 1 pl.

Bartlett, Edward. 1871. Notes on the monkeys of eastern Peru (communicated with notes by P. L. Sclater). *Proc. Zool. Soc. London* 1871:217–20, pl. 13.

Bates, H. W. 1863. *The naturalist on the river Amazons.* 1st ed. London: Murray, 1:viii + 351 pp., 18 figs., 1 fold map; 2:vi + 423 pp., 24 figs.

———. 1864. *The naturalist on the river Amazons.* 2d ed. London: Murray, xii + 462 pp., 39 figs.

Bauchot, R., and Stephan, H. 1964. Le poids encéphalique chez les insectivores malgaches. *Acta Zool.* 45:63–75.

———. 1966. Données nouvelles sur l'encéphalisation des insectivores et des prosimiens. *Mammalia* 30:160–96.

———. 1969. Encéphalisation et le niveau évolutif chez les simiens. *Mammalia* 33(2):225–75.

Beach, Frank A. 1942. Analysis of stimuli adequate to elicit mating behavior in the sexually inexperienced male rat. *J. Comp. Psychol.* 33:163–226.

———. 1965. *Sex and Behavior.* New York: John Wiley, xvi + 592 pp., illus.

Beattie, J. 1927. The anatomy of the common marmoset (*Hapale jacchus* Kuhl). *Proc. Zool. Soc. London* 1927:593–718, 39 figs., 2 pls.

Beddard, Frank E. 1901. On ectrain points in the anatomy of *Callithrix torquata. Novit. Zool.* 8:362–66, pl. 11.

———. 1902. Observations upon the carpal vibrissae in mammals. *Proc. Zool. Soc. London* 1902:127–36, figs. 17–21.

Beecher, William J. 1969. Possible motion detection in the vertebrate middle ear. *Bull. Chicago Acad. Sci.* 11(6):155–210.

Bender, Michael A., and Chu, E. H. Y. 1963. The chomosomes of primates. In *Evolutionary and genetic biology of primates,* ed. J. Buettner-Janusch, 1:261–310, 13 figs. New York: Academic Press.

Bender, Michael A., and Mettler, Lawrence E. 1958. Chromosome studies of primates. *Science* 128:186–90.

———. 1960. Chromosome studies of primates. II. *Callithrix, Leontocebus,* and *Callimico. Cytologia* (Tokyo) 25:400–404.

Benirschke, Kurt. 1969. Discussion paper: Cytogenetic contributions to primatology. *Ann. N.Y. Acad. Sci.* 162:217–24, 2 figs.

———, ed. 1969. *Comparative mammalian cytogenetics.* New York: Springer Verlag, xxi + 473 pp.

Benirschke, Kurt; Anderson, J. M.; and Brownhill, L. E. 1962. Marrow chimerism in marmosets. *Science* 138: 513–15, 2 figs.

Benirschke, Kurt, and Brownhill, Lydia E. 1962. Further observations on marrow chimerism in marmosets. *Cytogenetics* 1:245–57, 4 figs.

———. 1963. Heterosexual cells in testes of chimeric marmoset monkeys. *Cytogenetics* 2:331–41, 7 figs.

Benirschke, Kurt, and Layton, W. 1969. An early twin blastocyst of the golden lion marmoset, *Leontocebus rosalia. Folia Primat.* 10:131–38, 1 fig.

Benirschke, Kurt, and Richart, Ralph. 1963. The establishment of a marmoset breeding colony and its pregnancies. *Lab. Animal Care* (13(2):70–83, 2 figs.

Bennejeant, Ch. 1936. *Anomalies et variations dentaires chez les primates.* Imprimerie Pane Valadier, 258 pp.

Bensley, B. A. 1906. The homologies of the stylar cusps of the upper molars of the Didelphidae. *University of Toronto Studies, Biol.,* ser. 5:1–13, 6 figs.

Berger, H. 1969. The chin problem from an orthodonist's point of view. *Amer. J. Orth.* 56(5):516–22.

Berkson, Gershon. 1968. Weight and tooth development during the first year in *Macaca irus. Lab. Animal Care* 18(3):352–55, 3 figs.

Bernick, Sol, and Levy, Barnet M. 1968*a*. Studies on the biology of the periodontium of marmosets: I. Development of bifurcation in multirooted teeth in marmosets (*Callithrix jacchus*). *J. Dental Res.* 47(1):21–26.

———. 1968*b*. Studies on the biology of the periodontium of marmosets: IV. Innervation of the periodontal ligament. *J. Dental Res.* 47(6):1158–65.

Bernick, Sol; Levy, Barnet M.; and Patek, Paul R. 1969. Studies on the biology of the periodontium of marmosets. VI. Arteriosclerotic changes in the blood vessels of the periodontium. *J. Periodontol.-Periodont.* 40: 49/355–52/358, 11 figs.

Bernstein, Herschel. 1923. Über das Stimmorgan der Primaten. *Abh. Senckenberg Naturf. Ges.* 38:105–28, pls. 13, 14.

Bernstein, Irwin S. 1970. "Paternal" behavior in nonhuman primates. *Amer. Zool.* 10(4):480 (abstract).

Berry, D. L., and Baker, R. J. 1971. Apparent convergence of karyotypes in two species of pocket gophers of the genus *Thomomys* (Mammalia, Rodentia). *Cytogenetics* 10:1–9, 5 figs.

Berry, R. J., and Southern, H. N. 1970. Variation in mammalian populations. *Symp. Zool. Soc. London,* no. 26, xvi + 403 pp.

Bertram, D. S. 1962. Rickettsial infections and ticks. In *Aspects of disease transmission by ticks,* ed. R. Arthur. Symposia Zool. Soc. London no. 6, pp. 179–97.

Bhatnagar, Kunwar P., and Kallen, F. C. 1974. Cribriform plate of ethmoid, olfactory bulb and olfactory acuity in forty species of bats. *J. Morph.* 142:71–90, 3 plates, 6 figs.

Biegert, Josef. 1961. Volerhaut der Hände und Füsse. *Primatologia* 2(1, 3):3 + 326 pp., 100 figs.

———. 1963. The evaluation of characteristics of the skull, hands, and feet for primate taxonomy. In *Classification and human evolution,* ed. S. L. Washburn, pp. 116–45. Viking Fund. Publ. Anthrop., no. 37, 9 figs.

Bigalke, R. 1936. [Nachrichten aus Zoologischen Garten]. Pretoria. *Zool. Gart.* (n.f.), 8:169–70.

Billingham, R. E., and Silvers, W. K. 1960. The melanocytes of mammals. *Quart. Rev. Biol.* 35(1):1–40, 7 figs.

Bischoff, T. 1879. Vergleichend anatomische Untersuchungen über die äusseren weiblichen Geschlechts- und Begattungsorgane des Menschen und der Affen, insbesondere der Anthropoiden. *Abh. K. bayr. Akad. Wiss., Munchen,* II Cl., 13(2):207–73.

Bishop, Alison, 1964. Use of the hand in lower primates. In *Evolutionary and genetic biology of primates,* ed. J. Buettner-Janusch, 2:133–225, 25 figs. (chapter 12). New York: Academic Press.

Bissonnette, Thomas Hume. 1935. Relation of hair cycles in ferrets to changes in the anterior hypophysis and to light cycles. *Anat. Rec.* 63:159–68.

Bissonnette, Thomas Hume, and Bailey, Earl Elmore. 1944. Experimental modification and control of molts and changes in coat-color in weasels by controlling lighting. *Ann. N.Y. Acad. Sci.* 45(6):221–60, fig. 1, pl. 7.

Bissonnette, Thomas Hume, and Wilson E. 1939. Shortening daylight periods between May 15 and September 12 and the pelt cycle of the mink. *Science* 89:418–19.

Black, Eugenie Scott. 1970. Sexual dimorphism in the ischium and pubis of three species of South American monkeys. *J. Mammal.* 51(4):794–96.

Blackwell, K. 1969. Rearing and breeding Demidoff's galago (*Galago demidovii*). *Int. Zoo Yearb.* 9:74–76.

Blainville, H. M. Ducrotay de. 1839. *Ostéographie ou description iconographique comparée du squelette et du système dentaire des mammifères récents et fossiles pour servir de base à la zoologie et à la geologie. 1. Primatès—secundaté fascicle Sapajou* (Cebus), 31 pp., 9 pls.

Blair, W. Frank, and Howard, Walter E. 1944. Experimental evidence of sexual isolation between three forms of the cenospecies *Peromyscus maniculatus. Contrib. Lab. Vert. Biol., Univ. Mich.*, no. 26; 19 pp.

Blum, Harold F. 1961. Does the melanin pigment of human skin have adaptive value? An essay in human ecology and the evolution of race. *Quart. Rev. Biol.* 36:50–63, 2 figs.

Boas, J. E. V. 1912. *Ohrknorpel und äusseres Ohr der Säugetiere. Eine vergleichend-anatomische Untersuchung.* Copenhagen, 228 pp., 25 pls.

Boddaert, P. 1784. *Elenchus animalium. I. Sistens quadrupedia. . . .* Rotterdam, vi + 174 pp.

Boer, Leobert E. M., de. 1973*a*. Cytotaxonomy of the Lorisoidea (Primates: Prosimia). I. Chromosome studies and karyological relationships in the Galagidae. *Genetica* 44:155–93, 9 figs., 8 pls.

———. 1973*b*. Cytotaxonomy of the Lorisoidea (Primates Prosimii). II. Chromosome studies in the Lorisidae and karyological relationships within the superfamily. *Genetica* 44:330–67, 5 figs.

———. 1974. Cytotaxonomy of the Platyrrhini (Primates). *Genen Pnaenen* 17 (1):1–115, 29 figs.

Bolk, Louis. 1907. Beiträge zur Affen anatomie. VI. Zur Entwicklung und vergleichenden Anatomie des Tractus urethro-vaginalis der Primaten. *Z. Morph. Anthrop.* 10:251–316, 33 figs.

———. 1916. Problems of human dentition. *Amer. J. Anat.* 19(1):91–148, 28 fig.

Booth, A. H. 1957. Observations on the natural history of the olive colobus monkey, *Procolobus verus* (Van Beneden). *Proc. Zool. Soc. London* 129:421–30.

Boulay, G. H. du, and Crawford, M. A. 1968. Nutritional bone disease in captive primates. *Symp. Zool. Soc. London,* no. 21, pp. 223–36.

Bown, T. M., and Gingerich, P. D. 1973. The Paleocene primate *Plesiolestes* and the origin of Microsyopidae. *Fol. Primat.* 19:1–8, 3 figs.

Box, Hilary O. 1975. Quantitative studies of behaviour within captive groups of marmoset monkeys (*Callithrix jacchus*). *Primates* 16 (2):155–74.

Boyde, A. 1971. Comparative histology of mammalian teeth. In *Dental morphology and evolution,* ed. A. A. Dahlberg, pp. 81–94, 12 figs. Chicago: University of Chicago Press.

Brabant, H. 1960. Contribution à l'étude des parties organiques de l'émail dentaire humain et de leurs rapports avec la carie et le métabolisme de la dent. *Mém. Acad. Roy. Med. Belgique,* ser. 11, 4:137–86.

Brabant, H., and Klees, L. 1957. Contribution histologique à l'étude des craquelures de l'émail dentaire humain. *Actual. Odont. Stomat.* 8:359–96.

Brack, Manfred; Boncyk, L. H.; and Kalter, S. S. 1974. *Filaroides cebus* (Gebauer, 1933): Parasitism and respiratory infections in *Cebus apella. J. Med. Primat.* 3:164–73, 4 figs.

Brack, Manfred; Myers, Betty June; and Kuntz, Robert E. 1973. Pathogenic properties of *Molineus torulosus* in capuchin monkeys, *Cebus apella. Lab. Animal Sci.* 23 (3):360–65, 4 figs.

Bradley, D. W.; Krushak, D. H.; and Maynard, J. E. 1974. Viroids and viral hepatitis in marmosets. *Nature* 248:172.

Brand, D. J. 1963. Records of mammals bred in the National Zoological Gardens of South Africa during the period 1908 to 1960. *Proc. Zool. Soc. London* 140:617–59.

Brandes, G. 1938. Das Singen der alten Orangmänner. *Zool. Gart.* 10:31–33.

Brandes, R. 1932. Über den Kehlkopf des Orang-Utan in verschiedenen Altersstadien mit beconderer Berücksichtigung der Kehlsackfrage. *Morph. Jahrb.* 69: 1–61.

Breed, Robert S.; Murray, E. G. D.; and Hitchens, A. Parker. 1948. *Bergey's Manual of Determinative Bacteriology.* 6th ed. Baltimore: Williams and Wilkins Co., xvi + 1529 pp. illustrations.

Brennan, James M., and Reed, Jack T. 1975. A list of Venezuela chiggers, particularly of small mammalian hosts (Acarina: Trombiculidae). *Brigham Young Univ. Sci. Bull., Biol. Ser.* 20 (1):45–75.

Brennan, James M., and Yunker, Conrad E. 1966. The chiggers of Panamá (Acarina: Trombiculidae). In *The ectoparasites of Panamá,* ed. Rupert L. Wenzel and Vernon J. Tipton, pp. 221–66, figs. 12–30. Chicago: Field Museum of Natural History.

Breslau, E. 1927. Ergebnisse einer zoologischen Forschungsreise in Brasilien 1913–1914. *Abh. Senckenberg Naturf. Fes.* 40:181–235, 2 pls.

Bridgewater, Donald D. (ed.) 1972. *Saving the lion marmoset.* Proc. Wild Animal Propagation Trust Conference on the Golden Marmoset held at National Zoological Park, Washington, D.C., February 15–17, 1972. Wheeling W. Va.: Wild Animal Propagation Trust, ix + 223 pp.

Brisson, Mathurin J. 1756. *Regnum animale.* Paris, viii + 382 pp.

Brodman, Korbinian. 1909. Vergleichende Lokalisationslehre der Grosshirnrinde. Leipzig Barth, x + 324 pp., 150 figs.

Bronson, F. H., and Clarke, S. H. 1966. Adrenalectomy and coat color in deer mice. *Science* 154:1349–50, 1 fig.

Brown, Arthur Erwin. 1909. The tuberculin test in monkeys: With notes on the temperatures of mammals. *Proc. Zool. Soc. London* 1909: 81–90.

Brown, R. J.; Hinkle, D. K.; Trevethan, W. P.; Kupper, J. L.; and McKee, A. E. 1973. Nosematosis in a squirrel monkey (*Saimiri sciureus*). *J. Med. Primat.,* 2:114–23, 8 figs.

Brown, W. L., Jr., and Wilson, E. O. 1956. Character displacement. *Syst. Zool.* 5:49–64, 6 figs.

Buffon, George Louis Leclerc, Comte de. 1767. *Histoire naturelle générale et particulière avec description du cabinet du roi* [with supplement by M. Daubenton]. Paris, 15:[6] + 207 + cccxxiv pp., 18 pls.

———. 1789. *Histoire naturelle générale et particulière servant de suite à l'histoire des animaux quadrupèdes.* Paris. Suppl. 7. xx + 364 pp., 81 pls.

Bugge, Jørgen. 1972. The cephalic arterial system in the insectivores and the primates with special reference to the Macroscelidoidea and Tupaioidea and the insectivore-primate boundary. *Z. Anat. Entwickl.-Gesch.* 135:279–300, 6(10) figs.

———. 1974. The cephalic arterial system in insectivores, primates, rodents and lagomorphs, with special reference to the systematic classification. *Acta Anat.* 87 (suppl. 62):1–127, 15 figs., 7 plates, 15 tables.

Bull, J. W. D. 1969. Tentorium cerebelli. *Proc. Roy. Soc. Med.* 62(12):1301–10, 22 figs.

Bullock, B. C., and Bowen, J. A. 1966. Rickets and osteomalacia in squirrel monkeys (*Saimiri sciureus*). *Fed. Proc.* 25:533.

Bullock, B. C.; Lehner, N. D. M.; and Clarkson, T. B. 1969. New World monkeys. In *Primates in medicine,* ed. W. I. B. Beveridge, 2:62–74. Basel: S. Karger.

Burmeister, Hermann. 1846. *Beiträge zur nähreren Kenntniss der Gattung Tarsius.* Berlin, x + 149 pp., 7 pls.

———. 1854. *Systematische Uebersicht der Thiere Brasilien . . . Säugerthiere.* Vol. 1, x + 342. Berlin.

Burrows, R. B. 1972. Protozoa of the intestinal tract. In *Pathology of simian primates,* ed. R. N. T.-W. Fiennes, 2:2–28, 7 figs. Basel: S. Karger.

Burton, Maurice. 1962. The smallest of the true monkeys: The rare pygmy marmoset as a pet. *Illustr. London News* 241(6427):523 (6 October 1962), 4 figs.

———. 1963. Breeding pygmy monkeys: Nursery life of world's smallest monkeys. *Illustr. London News* 242 (6450): 393 (16 March 1963), 5 figs.

Busnel, Rene Guy, ed. 1963. *Acoustic behaviour of animals.* Amsterdam: Elsevier Publ. Co., xx + 933 pp., 383 figs.

Buss, David H. 1971. Mammary glands and lactation. In *Comparative reproduction of nonhuman primates,* ed. E. S. E. Hafez, pp. 315–33. Springfield, Ill.: C. C. Thomas.

———. 1975. Composition of milk from a golden lion marmoset. *Lab. Primate Newsl.* 14 (L):17–18.

Butler, H. 1974. Evolutionary trends in primate sex cycles. *Contrib. Primatol.,* 3:2–35, 8 figs.

Butler, Percy M. 1937. Studies on the mammalian dentition I. The teeth of Centetes ecaudatus and its allies. *Proc. Zool. Soc. London,* ser. B, 107:103.

———. 1939*a*. 1. Studies of the mammalian dentition: Differentiation of the postcanine dentition. *Proc. Zool. Soc. London,* ser. B, 109:1–36, 28 figs.

———. 1939*b*. The teeth of the Jurassic mammals. *Proc. Zool. Soc. London,* ser. B, 109:329–56.

———. 1941. A theory of the evolution of mammalian molar teeth. *Amer. J. Sci.* 239:421–50.

———. 1956. The ontogeny of molar pattern. *Biol. Rev.* 31:30–70, 12 figs.

———. 1963. Tooth morphology and primate evolution. In *Dental anthropology,* ed. D. R. Brothwell, pp. 1–13, 5 figs. Long Island City, N.Y.: Pergamon Press.

———. 1967. Dental merism and tooth development. *J. Dental Res.* 46(5, suppl.): 845–50, 3 figs.

———. 1972. Some functional aspects of molar evolution. *Evolution* 26:474–83, 6 figs.

———. 1973. Molar wear facets of early Tertiary North American Primates. In *Symp. 4th Inter. Cong. Primat.,* ed. W. Montagna, 3:1–27, 12 figs.

Büttikofer, J. 1917. Die Kurzschwanzaffen von Celebes. *Zool. Med., R. Mus. Nat. Hist., Leiden* 3(1):1–86, 10 figs., 12 pls.

Cabrera, Angel. 1900. Estudios sobre una colección de monos americanos. *Anal. Soc. Española Hist. Nat., Madrid,* ser. 2, 9:65–93, 3 figs., 1 pl.

———. 1912. Catálogo metódico de las colecciones de mamíferos del Museo de Ciencias Naturales de Madrid. *Trab. Mus. Cienc. Nat., Inst. Nac. Cienc. Fis.-Nat.,* no. 11, pp. 1–147, 4 pls.

———. 1917. Mamíferos del viaje al Pacífico verificado de 1862 a 1865 por una comisión de naturalistas enviada por el gobierno español. *Trab. Mus. Nac. Cienc. Nat., Madrid, Ser. Zool.,* no. 31, pp. 1–62.

———. 1940. Los nombres científicos de algunos monos americanos. *Ciencia, México* 1(9):402–5.

———. 1956. Sobre la identificación de *Simia leonina* Humboldt (Mammalia, Primates). *Neotrópica* 2(8): 49–53.

———. 1958. Catálogo de los mamíferos de America del sur. *Rev. Mus. Argentino Cienc. Nat., "Bernardino Rivadavia"* 4(1):iv + 307 pp.

Cameron, T. W. M. 1929. The species of *Enterobius* Leach, in Primates. *J. Helminth.* 7(3):161–82, 27 figs.

Campbell, Bernard, ed. 1972. *Sexual selection and the descent of man, 1871–1971.* Chicago: Aldine, 378 pp.

Campbell, C. B. G. 1966. The relationships of the tree shrews: The evidence of the nervous system. *Evolution* 20(3):276–81.

———. 1974. On the phyletic relationships of the tree shrews. *Mammal. Rev.* 4(4):125–43.

Carini, A., and Marcel, J. 1917. Sobre algunas microfilarias de mamíferos do Brasil. *Primera Conf. S. Amer. Hig. Microbiol. Patol. Buenos Aires,* p. 729.

Carpenter, Clarence Ray. 1934. A field study of the behavior and social relations of howling monkeys. *Comp. Psychol. Mong.* 10(2):1–168, 2 figs., 16 pls.

———. 1964. A field study in Siam of the behavior and social relations of the gibbon (*Hylobates lar*). Reprinted in *Naturalistic behavior of nonhuman primates.* University Park: Pennsylvania State University Press, pp. 145–271.

Carter, J. Thornton. 1922. On the structure of the enamel in the Primates and some other mammals. *Proc. Zool. Soc. London* 1922:599–608, 7 pls.

Cartmill, Matt. 1972. Arboreal adaptations and the origin of the order Primates. In The functional and evolutionary biology of Primates, ed. R. Tuttle, pp. 97–122. Chicago: Aldine-Atherton.

———. 1974*a*. Rethinking primate origins. *Science* 184: 436–43, 4 figs.

———. 1974*b*. Pads and claws in arboreal locomotion. In *Primate locomotion,* ed. F. A. Jenkins, Jr., pp. 45–83. New York: Academic Press, 7 figs.

Carvalho, Cory T. de. 1957. Alguns mamíferos do Acre Occidental. *Bol. Mus. Paraense Emilio Goeldi, Zool.,* no. 6, pp. 1–26, 1 fig.

———. 1959. Sobre a validez de *Callithrix leucippe* (Thos.) (Callithricidae, Primates). *Pap. Avulsos, Dept. Zool. Secretario Agric., São Paulo* 13(27):317–20.

———. 1965. Comentários sôbre os mamiféros descritos e figurados por Alexandre Rodrigues Ferreira em 1790. *Arq. Zool.* 12:7–70.

Carvalho, Jose C. de Melo. 1971. Three marmosets of the genus *Leontideus* in Brazil. *Biol. Cons.* 4(1):66.

Castellanos, Hector, and McCombs, H. Louis. 1968.

The reproductive cycle of the New World monkey. *Fertility and Sterility* 19:213–27, 9 figs.

Causey, O. R.; Causey, C. E.; Maroja, O. M.; and Macedo, D. G. 1961. The isolation of arthropod-borne viruses, including members of two hitherto undescribed serological groups, in the Amazon region of Brazil. *Amer. J. Trop. Med. Hyg.* 10:227–49, 7 figs.

Cave, A. J. E. 1967. Observations on the platyrrhine nasal fossa. *Amer. J. Phys. Anthrop.* 26(3):277–88, 8 figs.

Cave, A. J. E., and Haines, R. Wheeler. 1940. The paranasal sinuses of the anthropoid apes. *J. Anat.* 74:493–523, 21 figs.

Chaffee, R. R. J.; Allen, J. R.; Brewer, M.; Horvath, S. M.; Mason, C.; and Smith, R. E. 1966. Cellular physiology of cold and heat exposed squirrel monkeys (*Saimiri sciurea*). *J. Appl. Physiol.* 21(1):151–57.

Chalifoux, Laura V.; Hunt, Ronald D.; García, Felix G.; Sehgal, P. K.; and Comiskey, Janet R. 1973. Filariasis in New World monkeys: Histochemical differentiation of circulating microfilariae. *Lab. Animal Sci.* 23(2): 211–20, 12 figs.

Chapman, Frank A. 1929. *My tropical aircastle.* New York: Appleton, 416 pp.

Charles-Dominique, Pierre. 1971. Eco-ethologie des prosimiens du Gabon. *Biol. Gabonica* 7(2):121–28, 57 figs.

———. 1972. Ecologie et vie sociale de *Galago demidovii* (Fischer 1808; Prosimii). *Fortsch. Verhaltensf.* (*Zeit. Tierps.*, suppl.), 9:7–41, 24 figs.

Charles-Dominique, Pierre, and Hladik, C. M. 1971. Le *Lepilemur* du sud de Madagascar: Ecologie, alimentation et vie sociale. *Terre et Vie* 1:3–66, 35 figs.

Chartin, J., and Petter, F. 1960. Reproduction et élèvage en captivité du ouistiti. *Mammalia* 24(1):153–55.

Chase, John E., and Cooper, Robert W. 1968. Dental deposits and their control: An important aspect of the preventative medical program for laboratory primates. *Lab. Animal Care* 18(2):186–91, 3 figs.

———. 1969. *Saguinus nigricollis*: Physical growth and dental eruption in a small population of captive-born individuals. *Amer. J. Phys. Anthrop.* 30(1):111–16, 2 figs.

Chian, Lucia T. Y., and Wilgram, G. F. 1967. Tyrosinase inhibition: Its role in suntanning and in albinism. *Science* 155:198–200, 4 figs.

Chitwood, M. B. 1969. The systematics and Biology of some parasitic nematodes. In *Chem. Zool.*, ed. M. Florkin and B. T. Scheer, 3:223–44.

Chivers, D. J. 1969. On the daily behaviour and spacing of howling monkey groups. *Folia Primat.* 10:48–102, 12 figs.

Chopra, S. R. K. 1957. The cranial suture closure in monkeys. *Proc. Zool. Soc. London* 128:67–112, 8 figs.

Christen, Anita. 1968. Haltung und Brutbiologie von *Cebuella. Folia Primat.* 8:41–49.

———. 1974. Fortpflanzungsbiologie und Verhalten bei *Cebuella pygmaea* und *Tamarin tamarin.* Adv. in Ethology, suppl. *J. Comp. Ethol.* no. 14, pp. 1–79, 50 figs and cover pl.

Christensen, Howard A., and Herrer, Aristides. 1973. Attractiveness of sentinel animals to vectors of Leishmaniasis in Panama. *American J. Trop. Med. Hyg.* 22 (5):578–84, 2 figs.

Chu, E. H. Y., and Bender, M. A. 1961. Chromosome cytology and evolution in primates. *Science* 133:1399–1405, 2 figs.

Clark, Herbert C. 1952. Endemic yellow fever in Panama and neighboring areas. *Amer. J. Trop. Med. Hyg.* 1:78–86, 2 figs.

Clark, Herbert C.; Dunn, Lawrence H.; and Benavides, Joaquin. 1931. Experimental transmission to man of a relapsing fever spirochete in a wild monkey of Panama —*Leontocebus geoffroyi* (Pucheran). *Amer. J. Trop. Med.* 11(4):243–57.

Clark, Nigel A. 1974. A preliminary investigation into the diet of marmosets and tamarins Callithricidae (Thomas, 1903) at the Jersey Zoological Park. *Tenth Ann. Report, 1973, Jersey Wildl. Preserv. Trust.*

Clark, W. E. Le Gros. 1924. Notes on the living tarsier (*Tarsius spectrum*). *Proc. Zool. Soc. London* 1924: 217–23, 1 pl.

———. 1926. On the anatomy of the pen-tailed treeshrew (*Ptilocercus lowii*). *Proc. Zool. Soc. London* 1926:1179–1309, 62 figs., 5 pls.

———. 1936. The problem of the claw in primates. *Proc. Zool. Soc. London* 1936:1–24, 13 figs., 1 pl.

———. 1959. *The antecedents of man.* Edinburgh: Edinburgh University Press.

Clemens, William A. 1974. Purgatorius, an early Paromomyid primate (Mammalia). *Science* 184:903–5, 2 figs.

Coatney, G. Robert; Collins, William E.; Warren, McWilson; and Contacos, Peter G. 1971. *The primate malarias.* Washington, D.C.: U.S. Department of Health, Education, and Welfare, National Institute of Allergy and Infectious Diseases. x + 366 pp., 73 figs., 54 pls.

Cockerell, T. D. A.; Miller, Lewis I.; and Printz, Morris. 1914. The auditory ossicles of American rodents. *Bull. Amer. Mus. Nat. Hist.* 23:347–80, 124 figs.

Coimbra-Filho, Adelmar F. 1965. Breeding lion marmosets, *Leontideus rosalia,* at Rio de Janeiro Zoo. *Int. Zoo Yearb.* 5:109–10.

———. 1969. Mico-leão, *Leontideus rosalia* (Linnaeus, 1766), situação atual da espécie no Brasil (Callithricidae–Primates). *An. Acad. Brasil. Cienc.* 41 (suppl.): 29–52, 8 figs.

———. 1970*a*. Considerações gerais e situação atual dos micos leões escuros, *Leontideus chrysomelas* (Kuhl, 1820) e *Leontideus chrysopygus* (Mikan, 1823) (Callithricidae, Primates). *Rev. Brasil. Biol.* 30:249–68, 13 figs.

———. 1970*b*. Acêrca da redescoberta de *Leontideus chrysopygus* (Mikan, 1823), e apontamentos sôbre sua ecologia (Callithricidae, Primates). *Rev. Brasil. Biol.* 30:609–15, 6 figs.

———. 1970*c*. Acêrca de um caso de hibridismo entre *Callithrix jacchus* (L. 1758) × *C. geoffroyi* (Humboldt, 1812) (Callithricidae, Primates). *Rev. Brasil. Biol.* 30(4):507–17, 3 figs.

———. 1971. Os sagüis do gênero *Callithrix* da região oriental Brasileira e um caso de duplo-hibridismo entre três de suas formas (Callithricidae, Primates). *Rev. Brasil. Biol.* 31(3):377–88, 7 figs.

———. 1972*a*. Conservation and use of South American Primates. *Int. Zoo Yearb.* 12:14–15.

———. 1972*b*. Aspectos inéditos do comportamento de sagüis do gênero *Callithrix* (Callithricidae, Primates). *Rev. Brasil. Biol.* 32(4):505–12, 8 figs.

———. 1973. Novo aspecto de duplo-hibridismo em

Callithrix (Callithricidae, Primates). *Rev. Brasil. Biol.* 33(1):31–38, 6 figs.

Coimbra-Filho, Adelmar F., and Aldrighi, Antonio D. 1971. A restauração da fauna do Parque Nacional da Tijuca Estado da Guanabara, Brasil. *Publ. Avulsos Mus. Nac.*, no. 57, pp. 1–30, 11 figs., 2 pls. (color).

Coimbra-Filho, Adelmar F., and Magnanini, Alceo. 1972. On the present status of *Leontopithecus* and some data about new behavioural aspects and management of *L. rosalia rosalia*. In *Saving the lion marmoset,* ed. D. D. Bridgewater, pp. 56–69, 4 figs. Proc. Wild Animal Propagation Trust Conference on the Golden Marmoset held at National Zoological Park, Washington, D.C., February 15–17, 1972. Wheeling, W.Va.: Wild Animal Propagation Trust.

Coimbra-Filho, Aldemar F., and Mittermeier, Russell A. 1972. Taxonomy of the genus *Leontopithecus* Lesson, 1840. In *Saving the lion marmoset,* ed. D. D. Bridgewater, pp. 7–22, 9 figs. Proc. Wild Animal Propagation Trust Conference on the Golden Marmoset held at National Zoological Park, Washington, D.C., February 15–17, 1972. Wheeling, W.Va.: Wild Animal Propagation Trust.

———. 1973. Distribution and ecology of the genus *Leontopithecus* Lesson, 1840 in Brazil. *Primates* 14 (1):47–66, 11 figs. (1 color).

———. 1974. New data on the taxonomy of the Brazilian marmosets of the genus *Callithrix* Erxleben, 1777. *Folia Primat.* 20 (1973): 241–64, 6 figs.

Collins, W. E.; Contacos, P. G.; Guinn, E. G.; and Skinner, J. C. 1973. *Plasmodium simium* in the *Aotus trivirgatus* monkey. *J. Parasit.* 59(1):49–51.

Colyer, Frank. 1936. *Variations and diseases of the teeth of animals.* London, viii + 750 pp., 1,007 figs.

Connolly, Cornelius J. 1950. *External morphology of the primate brain.* Springfield, Ill.: Charles C. Thomas, xiii + 378 pp., 337 figs.

Contacos, Peter F., and Collins, William E. 1969. *Plasmodium malariae* transmission from monkey to man by mosquito bite. *Science* 165:918–19.

Cook, Norman. 1939. Notes on captive *Tarsius carbonarius. J. Mammal.* 20:173–78.

Cooke, H. B. S. 1972. The fossil mammal fauna of Africa. In *Evolution, mammals, and southern continents,* ed. A. Keast, F. C. Erk, and B. Glass, pp. 89–139, 17 figs. Albany: State University of New York Press.

Cooley, R. A., and Kohls, Glen M. 1944. *The Argasidae of North America, Central America, and Cuba.* Amer. Midl. Nat. Monog. no. 1, i + 152 pp., 57 figs., 14 pls.

———. 1945. *The genus* Ixodes *in North America.* Nat. Inst. Hlth. Bull. no. 184.

Cooper, Robert W. 1963–69. Experimental breeding of subhuman primates. Quarterly and Annual Reports of the Primate Colony, Zoological Society of San Diego, (contract no. PH43-63-56, Cancer Institute, National Institutes of Health). Unpublished.

Cooper, Sybil. 1960. Muscle spindles and other muscle receptors. In *The structure and function of muscle,* ed. G. H. Bourne, 1:381–420, 9 figs. New York: Academic Press.

Cope, Edward Drinkwater. 1883. Note on the trituberculate type of superior molar and the origin of the quadrituberculate. *Amer. Nat.* 17:407–8.

———. 1884. The Creodonta. *Amer. Nat.* 18:255–67, 11 figs.

———. 1887. *The origin of the fittest: Essay on evolution.* New York: Appleton, xix + 467 pp., 81 figs., 18 pls.

———. 1896. *The primary factors of organic evolution.* Chicago: Open Court, xvi + 547 pp.

Cosgrove, G. E. 1966. The trematodes of laboratory primates. *Lab. Animal Care* 16(1):23–39.

Cosgrove, G. E.; Humason, Gretchen; and Lushbaugh, C. C. 1970. *Trichospirura leptostoma,* a nematode of the pancreatic ducts of marmosets (*Saguinus* spp.). *J. Amer. Vet. Med. Assoc.* 157(5):696–98, 3 figs.

Cosgrove, G .E.; Nelson, Bill M.; and Gengozian, N. 1968. Helminth parasites of the tamarin, *Saguinus fuscicollis. Lab. Animal Care* 18(6):654–56.

Cosgrove, G. E.; Nelson, Bill M.; and Jones, A .W. 1963. *Spirura tamarini* sp. n. (Nematoda: Spiruridae), from an Amazonian primate, *Tamarinus nigricollis. J. Parasit.* 49(6):1010–13, 7 figs.

Cosgrove, G. E.; Nelson, Bill M.; and Self, J. T. 1970. The pathology of pentastomid infections in primates. *Lab. Animal Care* 20(2[2]):354–60, 16 figs.

Costa Lima, A. da, and Hathaway, C. R. 1946. *Pulgas. Bibliografia, catalogo e hospedadores.* Monog. Inst. Oswaldo Cruz, no. 4, 522 pp.

Cott, Hugh B. 1940. *Adaptive coloration in animals.* London: Methuen, 508 pp., 48 pls., 83 figs.

Cowles, Raymond B. 1945. Heat-induced sterility and its possible bearing on evolution. *Amer. Nat.* 79:160–75.

———. 1958. The evolutionary significance of the scrotum. *Evolution* 12(3):417–18.

Crandall, Lee S. 1951. Those "forest sprites" called marmosets. *Animal Kingdom* 54(6):178–84, 16 photos.

———. 1964. *The management of wild animals in captivity.* Chicago: University of Chicago Press, xv + 761 pp., 8 photos.

Crescitelli, F., and Pollack, J. D. 1965. Color vision in the antelope ground squirrel. *Science* 150:1316–18.

Crompton, A. W., and Jenkins, Jr., F. A. 1968. Molar occlusion in late Triassic mammals. *Biol. Rev.* 43:427–58, 10 figs., 3 pls.

Crotty, Michael J. 1975. Golden marmoset weaned at six weeks of age. *Amer. Ass. Zool. Parks, Aquariums* 16:11.

Cruz Lima, Eladio de. 1945. *Mammals of Amazonia. 1. General Introduction and Primates.* Contrib. Mus. Paraense Emilio Goeldi Hist. Nat., Etnogr., Belém do Pará, Rio de Janeiro, 274 pp., 42 col. pls.

Cullen, J. M. 1963. Allo-, auto-, and hetero-preening. *Ibis* 105:121.

Cuming, H. 1838. Memoranda on *Tarsius spectrum. Proc. Zool. Soc. London* 1838:67–68.

Cummins, Harold, and Midlo, Charles. 1961. *Finger prints, palms and soles: An introduction to dermatoglyphics.* New York: Dover Publication, xi, 319 pp., 149 figs. (Reprint of 1943 edition, with supplementary chapter, Identification in Action.)

Curtis, R. F.; Ballantine, J. A.; Keverne, E. G.; Bosnell, R. W.; and Michael, R. P. 1971. Identification of primate sexual pheromones and the properties of synthetic attractants. *Nature* 232(5310):396–98.

Cuvier, Frédéric. 1819. L'ouistiti et ses petits. In *Histoire naturelle des mammifères, avec des figures originales, coloriées, dessinées d'après des animaux vivans; publiée sous l'autorité de l'administration du Muséum d'His-*

toire Naturelle [Paris], ed. E. Geoffroy St.-Hilaire and F. Cuvier, 1819–24, vol. 1, livr. 8 (July 1819), 1 pl.

———. 1829. Pinche Mâle. In *Histoire naturelle des mammifères, avex des figures originales, coloriées, dessinées d'après des animaux vivans; publiée sous l'autorité de l'administration du Muséum d'Histoire Naturelle,* [Paris] ed. F. Curier and E. Geoffroy St. Hilaire, 1824–29, vol. 5, livr. 59, plates.

Cuvier, Georges. 1798. *Tableau élémentaire de l'Histoire naturelle des animaux.* Paris: Baudouin, xvi + 710 pp., 14 pls.

———. 1805. *Leçons d'anatomie comparée.* vol. 4, xii + 539 pp.

———. 1817. *La régne animal distribué d'près son organisation, pour servir de base a l'histoire naturelle des animaux et d'introduction a l'anatomie comparée.* Paris: Déterville, xxxvii + 540 pp.

Danforth, G. H. 1925. Hair and its relation to questions of homology and phylogeny. *Amer. J. Anat.* 36:47–68, 1 fig.

Daniel, M. D.; Meléndez, L. V.; King, N. W.; Barahona, H. H.; Fraser, C. E. O.; García, F. G.; and Silva, D. 1973. Isolation and characterization of a new virus from owl monkeys: *Herpesvirus aotus* Type 3. *Amer. J. Phys. Anthrop.* 38(2):497–500, 1 fig.

Daniels, Farrington Jr.; Post, Peter W.; and Johnson, Brian E. 1972. Theories of the role of pigments in the evolution of human races. In Pigmentation: Its genesis and biologic control, ed. Vernon Riley, pp. 13–22. New York: Appleton-Century-Crofts.

Dankmeijer, J. 1938. Zur biologischen Anatomie der Hautleisten bei den Beuteltieren. *Gegenbaur's Morph. Jahrb.* 82:293–312, 16 figs.

Darwin, Charles. 1899 [1874]. *The descent of man, and selection in relation to sex.* 2d ed., revised and augmented. London: John Murray, xvi + 693 pp., 78 figs.

Davis, D. Dwight. 1962. Mammals of the lowland rainforest of North Borneo. *Bull. Singapore Nat. Mus.,* no. 31, 129 pp., 20 figs., 23 pls.

Davis, Malcolm. 1960. Galago born in captivity. *J. Mammal.* 41(3):401–2.

Day, M. H., and Napier, John. 1963. The functional significance of the deep head of flexor pollicis brevis in primates. *Folia Primat.* 1:122–34, 3 figs.

Deane, Leonidas M. 1969. Plasmodia of monkeys and malaria eradication in Brazil. *Rev. Latino-americana Microbiol. Parasit.* 11:69–73.

———. 1972. Plasmodia of monkeys and malaria eradication in Brazil. *Int. Zoo Yearb.* 12:56–60. (Reprint of 1969 article.)

Deane, Leonidas M.; D'Andretta, Carlos, Jr.; and Kameyama, Issao. 1970. Malaria simiana no Brasil central: Encontro do *Plasmodium brasilianum* em guariba do Estado de Mato Grosso. *Rev. Inst. Med. Trop. São Paulo* 12(2):144–48.

Deane, Leonidas M.; Deane, Maria Paumgarten; and Ferreira Neto, Joaquin A. 1966. Studies on transmission of simian malaria and on a natural infection of man with *Plasmodium simium* in Brazil. *Bull. World Hlth. Org.* 35 (1965):805–8.

Deane, Leonidas M.; Deane, Maria Paumgarten; Ferreira Neto, Joaquin A.; and Barbosa de Almeida, Flavio. 1971. On the transmission of simian malaria in Brazil. *Rev. Inst. Med. Trop. São Paulo* 13(5):311–19, 1 fig. (map).

Deane, Leonidas M., and Ferreira Neto, Joaquin A. 1969. Encontro do *Plasmodium brasilianum* en macacos do Territorio Federal do Amapa, Brasil. *Rev. Inst. Med. Trop. São Paulo* 11(3):199–202.

Deane, L. M.; Ferreira Neto, Joaquin A.; Deane, Maria Paumgarten; and Silveira, I. P. S. 1970. *Anopheles (Kerteszia) cruzi,* a natural vector of the monkey malaria parasites, *Plasmodium simium* and *Plasmodium brasilianum. Trans. Roy. Soc. Trop. Med. Hyg.* 64:647.

Deane, Leonidas M.; Ferreira Neto, Joaquin A.; Kumura, M. O.; and Ferreira, M. O. 1969. Malaria parasites of Brazilian monkeys. *Rev. Ints. Med. Trop. São Paulo* 11(2):71–86.

Deane, Leonidas M.; Silva, J. E.; and Loures, L., Filho. 1974. Nycthemeral variation in the parasitaemia of *Trypanosoma minasense* in naturally infected marmosets of the genus *Callithrix* (Primates, Callithricidae). *Rev. Inst. Med. Trop. São Paulo* 16(1):1–6, 1 fig.

De Beaux, Oscar. 1917. Osservazione e considerazioni pulle vibrisse carpali e facciali degli Artopiteci. *Gion. Morf. dell'Uomo e dei Primati* 1:89–108.

Decker, Richard Lee, and Szalay, Frederick S. 1974. Origins and function of the pes in the Eocene Adapidae (Lemuriformes, Primates). In *Primate locomotion,* ed. F. A. Jenkins, Jr., pp. 261–91, 11 figs. N.Y.: Academic Press.

Deinhardt, Friedrich. 1966. Neoplasm induced by Rous sarcoma virus in New World monkeys. *Nature* 210 (5034):443.

———. 1967. Rous sarcoma virus-induced neoplasms in New World non-human Primates. In *Perspectives in virology,* 5:183–97, 12 figs. New York: Academic Press.

———. 1970*a*. Hepatitis in subhuman primates and the hazards to man. In *Infections and immuno-suppression in subhuman primates,* ed. H. Balner and W. I. Beveridge, pp. 55–63. Copenhagen.

———. 1970*b*. Nutritional requirements of marmosets. In *Feeding and nutrition of nonhuman primates,* ed. R. S. Harris, pp. 175–82, 2 figs. New York: Academic Press.

———. 1973. *Herpesvirus saimiri.* In *The herpesviruses,* ed. Albert S. Kaplan, pp. 595–625, 10 figs. New York: Academic Press.

Deinhardt, Friedrich, and Deinhardt, Jean. 1966. The use of platyrrhine monkeys in medical research. *Symp. Zool. Soc. London,* no. 17, pp. 127–52, 7 figs.

Deinhardt, Friedrich; Falk, Lawrence; Marczynska, Barbara; Shramek, Grace; and Wolfe, Lauren. 1972. *Herpesvirus saimiri*: A simian counterpart of Epstein-Barr virus of man? In *Comparative leukemia research* 1971, ed. R. M. Dutcher, pp. 416–27. Basel: S. Karger.

Deinhardt, Friedrich; Falk, Lawrence A.; and Wolfe, Lauren G. 1973. Simian herpesviruses. *Cancer Res.* 33:1424–26.

———. 1974. Transformation of nonhuman primate lymphocytes by Epstein Barr virus. *Cancer Res.* 34: 1241–44.

Deinhardt, Friedrich, and Holmes, Albert W. 1966. Epidemiology and etiology of viral hepatitis. In *Progress in liver diseases,* ed. H. Popper and F. Schaffner, pp. 373–94. New York: Grune and Stratton.

Deinhardt, Friedrich; Holmes, Albert W.; Capps, R. B.;

and Popper, H. 1967. Studies on the transmission of human viral hepatitis to marmoset monkeys. I. Transmission of disease, serial passages, and description of liver lesion. *J. Exp. Med.* 126:673–88.

Deinhardt, Friedrich; Holmes, Albert W.; Devine, James; and Deinhardt, Jean. 1967. Marmosets as laboratory animals. IV. The microbiology of laboratory kept marmosets. *Lab. Animal Care* 17(1):48–70.

Deinhardt, Friedrich; Holmes, Albert W.; Wolfe, Lauren; and Junge, D. 1970. Transmission of viral hepatitis to nonhuman primates. *Vox Sang.* 19:261–69.

Deinhardt, Friedrich; Wolfe, Lauren G.; Northrop, Robert L.; Marczynska, Barbara; Ogden, John; McDonald, Ruth; Falk, Lawrence; Shramek, Grace; Smith, Roger; and Deinhardt, Jean. 1972. Induction of neoplasms by viruses in marmoset monkeys. *J. Med. Primat.* 1 (1): 29–50.

Deinhardt, Friedrich; Wolfe, Lauren G.; Theilen, Gordon H.; and Snyder, Stanley P. 1970. ST-Feline fibrosarcoma virus: Induction of tumors in marmoset monkeys. *Science* 167:881, 1 fig.

De la Borde, M. 1789. Le tamarin negre. In *Histoire naturelle generale et particuliere servant de suite a l'histoire des animaux quadrupedes,* ed. George Louis Leclerc, Comte de Buffon, suppl. 7:116–17. Paris: L'Imprimérie royale.

Della Santa, Edouard. 1956. Revision du genre *Oochoristica* Luhe (Cestodes). *Rev. Suisse Zool.* 63(1):1–113, 1 fig.

Della Serra, Octavio. 1951. Divisão do gênero *Leontocebus* (Macacos Platyrrhina) em dos subgêneros sob bases de caracteres dento-morfológicos. *Pap. Avulsos, São Paulo,* 10(8):147–54.

———. 1952. *A seqüênçia eruptiva dos dentes definitivos nos símios Platyrrhina e seca interpretação filogenética.* São Paulo (privately published), 99 pages.

De Meijere, J. C. H. 1894. Ueber Haare der Säugetiere, besonders über ihre Anordnung. *Morph. Jahrb.* 21: 312–421.

Denniston, R. H. 1964. Notes on the vaginal cornification cycle of captive squirrel monkeys. *J. Mammal.* 45(3):471.

De Reuck, A. V. S., and Knight, Julie, eds. 1965. *Colour vision: Physiology and experimental psychology.* Ciba Foundation Symposia. xiii + 382 pp.

Desmarest, Anselme Gaetan. 1804. Tableau methodique des mammifères. *Nouv. Dict. Hist. Nat.* 24(6):5–58.

———. 1818. Article "Ouistitì, *Jacchus* et *Midas.*" *Nouv. Dict. Hist. Nat. Paris* 24:237–44.

———. 1820. *Mammalogie ou description des espèces de mammifères,* Paris, pt. 1, viii + 276 pp.

———. 1827. Article "Sagoin." *Dict. Sci. Nat.,* Paris, 47:9–24.

———. 1828. Article "Ouistiti." *Nouv. Dict. Hist. Nat.* 24:237–44.

De Valois, Russel L. 1966. Analysis and coding of color vision in the primate visual system. *Cold Spr. Harb. Symp. Quant. Biol.* 30:567–79, 11 figs.

De Valois, Russel, L., and Jacobs, Gerald H. 1968. Primate color vision. *Science* 162:533–40, 6 figs.

Díaz-Ungría, C. 1965. Nematodes de primates venezolanos. *Bol. Soc. Venezolana Cienc. Nat.* 25 (108):393–98, 1 fig.

Dietz, Robert S., and Holden, John C. 1970. Reconstruction of Pangaea: Breakup and dispersion of continents, Permian to Present. *J. Geoph. Res.* 75(26): 4939–56, 8 figs.

Dios, R. L.; Zuccarini, J. A.; and Werngren, E. T. 1925. Existence de *Trypanosoma minasense* et le microfilaria sp. chez singes. *Soc. Arg. Biol. (Paris)* 93:1458–59.

Disney, R. H. L. 1968. Observations on a zoonoses: Leishmaniasis in British Honduras. *J. Appl. Ecology* 5:1–59, 16 figs.

Ditmars, Raymond L. 1933. Development of the silky marmoset. *Bull. N.Y. Zool. Soc.* 36:175–76.

Dodd, Roger Y. 1974. Transmissible disease and blood transfusion. *Science* 186:1138–40.

Dollman, Guy. 1937. Exhibition and remarks upon a series of skins of marmosets and tamarins. *Proc. Zool. Soc. London,* ser. C, 107:64–65.

Doran, Alban H. G. 1878. Morphology of the mammalian ossicula auditus. *Trans. Linn. Soc. London, Zool.* 7(2):371–497, pls. 58–64.

Dos Santos, Agnaldo José; Miraglia, Tulio; and Costa Guedes, María Lucía. 1974. Histochemical data on the sebaceous glands in the lips of the marmoset (*Callithrix jacchus*). *Acta Anat.,* 89, pp. 314–20, 1 fig.

Doty, Robert William; Glickstein, Mitchell; and Calvin, William Howard. 1966. Lamination of the lateral geniculate nucleus in the squirrel monkey *Saimiri sciureus. J. Comp. Neurol.* 127(3):335–40, 11 figs.

Downs, W. G.; Spence, L.; Aitken, T. H. G.; and Whitman, L. 1961. Cache Valley virus, isolated from a trinidadian mosquito, *Aedes scapularis. West Indian Med. J.,* 10(13):13–15.

Doyle, G. A.; Pelletier, Annette; and Bekker, T. 1967. Courtship, mating and parturition in the lesser bushbaby (*Galago senegalensis moholi*) under seminatural conditions. *Folia Primat.* 7:169–97, 3 figs.

Dreizen, Samuel B.; Levy, Barnet M.; and Bernick, Sol. 1970*a.* Studies on the biology of the periodontium of marmosets. VII. The effect of vitamin C deficiency on the marmoset periodontium. *J. Periodont. Res.* 4: 274–80, 1969. Abstract: *Biol. Abstr.,* 51:#60560, 1970.

———. 1970*b.* Studies on the biology of the periodontium of marmosets. VIII. The effect of folic acid deficiency on the marmoset oral mucosa. *J. Dental Res.* 49(3):616–20, 6 figs.

Dreizen, Samuel; Levy, Barnet M.; Bernick, Sol; Hampton, John K., Jr., and Krantz, L. 1967. Studies on the biology of the periodontium of marmosets. III. Periodontal bone changes in marmosets with osteomalacia and hyperparathyroidism. *Israel J. Med. Sci.* 3:731–38.

Du Brul, E. Lloyd. 1965. The skull of the lion marmoset *Leontideus rosalia* Linnaeus. *Amer. J. Phys. Anthrop.* 23:261–76, 9 figs.

Du Brul, E. Lloyd, and Sicher, Harry. 1954. *The adaptive chin.* Springfield, Ill.: Charles C. Thomas, viii + 97 pp., 47 figs.

Dücker, Gerti. 1965. Colour-vision in mammals. *J. Bombay Nat. Hist. Soc.* 61(3):572–86, 6 figs.

Dummette, Clifton O., and Barens, Gaida. 1972. Oral pigmentation of marmosets. *Amer. J. Vet. Res.* 33 (10):2051–58, 10 figs.

DuMond, Frank V. 1967. Semi-free-ranging colonies of monkeys at Goulds Monkey Jungle. *Int. Zoo Yearb.* 7:202–7.

———. 1968. The squirrel monkey in a semi-natural environment. In *The squirrel monkey,* ed. L. A. Rosenblum and R. W. Cooper, pp. 87–145, 14 figs. New York: Academic Press.

———. 1972. Recommendations for a basic husbandry program for lion marmosets. In *Saving the lion marmoset,* ed. D. D. Bridgewater, pp. 120–36. Proc. Wild Animal Propogation Trust Conference on the Golden Marmoset held at National Zoological Park, Washington, D.C., February 15–17, 1972. Wheeling, W.Va.: Wild Animal Propagation Trust, Oglebay Park.

Dun, R. B. 1958. Growth of the mouse coat: VI. Distribution and number of vibrissae in the house mouse. *Austr. J. Biol. Sci.* 11:95–105, 5 figs.

———. 1959. The development and growth of vibrissae in the house mouse with particular reference to the time of action of the Tabby (Ta) and Ragged (Ra) genes. *Austr. J. Biol. Sci.* 12:312–30, 6 figs.

Dun, R. B., and Fraser, A. S. 1958. Selection for an invariant character—"vibrissae number"—in the house mouse. *Nature* 181:1018–19.

———. 1959. Selection for an invariant character, vibrissae number, in the house mouse. *Austr. J. Biol. Sci.* 12:506–23, 7 figs.

Dunn, Frederick L. 1961. *Molineus vexillarius* sp. n. (Nematoda: Trichostrongylidae) from a Peruvian primate, *Tamarinus nigricollis* (Spix, 1823). *J. Parasit.* 47:953–56.

———. 1963. Acanthocephalans and cestodes of South American monkeys and marmosets. *J. Parasit.* 49: 717–22.

———. 1965. On the antiquity of malaria in the western hemisphere. *Human Biol.* 37(4):385–93.

———. 1968. The parasites of *Saimiri*: In the context of platyrrhine parasitism. In *The squirrel monkey,* ed. L. H. Rosenblum and R. W. Cooper, pp. 31–68. New York: Academic Press.

———. 1970. Natural infection in primates: Helminths and problems in primatephylogeny, ecology, and behavior. *Symposium, Non-human primate parasites* 20 (2), part II of two parts. Reprinted in *Lab. Animal Care* 1970.

Dunn, Frederick L., and Lambrecht, F. L. 1963*a*. On some filarial parasites of South American primates, with a description of *Tetrapetalonema tamarinae* n. sp., from the Peruvian tamarin marmoset, *Tamarinus nigricollis* (Spix, 1823). *J. Helminth.* 37:261–86, 16 figs.

———. 1963*b*. The hosts of *Plasmodium brasilianum* Gonder and Von Berenberg-Gossler, 1908. *J. Parasit.* 49:316–19.

Dunn, F. L.; Lambrecht, F. L.; and Plessis, R. du. 1963. Trypanosomes of South American monkeys and marmosets. *Amer. J. Trop. Med. Hyg.* 12:524–34.

Dunn, Lawrence H., and Clark, Herbert C. 1933. Notes on relapsing fever in Panama with special reference to animal hosts. *Amer. J. Trop. Med.* 3:201–9.

Durward, A., and Rudall, K. M. 1949. Studies in hair growth in the rat. *J. Anat.* 83:325–35.

Duszynski, Donald W., File, Sharon K. 1974. Structure of the oocyst and excystation of sporoziotes of *Isospora endocallimici* n. sp. from the marmoset *Callimico goeldi. Trans. Amer. Microscop. Soc.* 93 (3): 403–8, 9 figs.

Du Toit, Alexander L. 1937. *Our wandering continents: An hypothesis of continental drifting.* London: Owen and Boyd, 366 pp., 48 figs.

———. 1944. Tertiary mammals and continental drift. A rejoinder to George G. Simpson. *Amer. J. Sci.* 242 (3):145–63.

Easter, Robert Q., and Nichols, Daryl G. 1951. The role of albedo in color discrimination of spider monkeys. *Proc. Iowa Acad. Sci.* 58:321–31, 4 figs.

Ebling, F. J. 1965. Systemic factors affecting the periodicity of hair follicles. In *Biology of the skin and hair growth,* ed. A. G. Lyne and B. F. Short, pp. 507–24, 8 figs. Sydney: Angus and Robeston.

Ebling, F. J., and Johnson, Elizabeth. 1964. The control of hair growth. *Symp. Zool. Soc. London,* no. 12, pp. 97–130, 17 figs., 1 pl.

Edinger, Lilly, and Kitts, David B. 1954. The foramen ovale. *Evolution* 8(4):389–404, 4 figs.

Edwards, George. [1743]–1751. *A natural history of uncommon birds, and . . . quadrupeds, . . .* London, 4 vols., col. plates.

———. 1758–64. *Gleanings of natural history. London,* 3 vols., 153 pls.

Egozcue, José. 1969. Primates. In *Comparative mammalian cytogenetics,* ed. Kurt Benirschke, pp. 357–89, 18 figs. New York: Springer Verlag.

Egozcue, José; Chiarelli, Bruno; and Sarti-Chiarelli, M. 1968. The somatic and meiotic chromosomes of *Cebuella pygmaea* (Spix, 1823), with special reference to the behavior of the sex chromosomes during spermatogenesis. *Folia Primat.* 8(1):50–57, 4 figs.

Egozcue, José; Perkins, Edwin M.; and Hagemenas, F. 1968. Chromosomal evolution in marmosets, tamarins, and pinches. *Folia Primat.* 9:81–94, 11 figs.

———. 1969. The chromosomes of *Saguinus fuscicollis illigeri* (Pucheran, 1845) and *Aotus trivirgatus* (Humboldt, 1811). *Folia Primat.* 10:154–59, 5 figs.

Ehara, Akiyoshi. 1969. Zur phylogenese und function der Orbitaseitenrandes der Primaten. *Z. Morph. Anthrop.* 60(3):263–71, 2 figs.

Ehara, Akiyoshi, and Seiler, Rolf. 1970. Die Strukturen der überaugen Region bei den Primaten, Deutungen und Definitionen. *Z. Morph. Anthrop.* 62(1):1–29, 7 figs.

Ehrlich, Annette, and Calvin, William H. 1967. Visual discrimination behavior in galago and owl monkey. *Psychon. Sci.* 9 (9):509–10.

Eichler, Wolfdietrich. 1949. Phthirapterorum nova genera. *Boll. Soc. Entomol. Italiana* 79(1–2):11–13.

Eisentraut, Martin. 1960. Heat regulation in primitive mammals and in tropical species. *Bull. Mus. Comp. Zool.* 124:31–44.

Elias, Hans, and Bortner, Seymour. 1957. On the phylogeny of hair. *Amer. Mus. Novit.,* no. 1820, p. 15, 31 figs.

Elias, H., and Schwartz, D. 1971. Cerebro-cortical surface areas, volumes, lengths of gyri and their interdependence in mammals, including man. *Z. Säugetierk.* 36 (3):147–63, 10 figs.

Elliot, Daniel Giraud. 1905. A checklist of mammals of the North American continent, the West Indies, and the neighboring Seas. *Field Columbian Mus., Zool. Ser.,* 6:1–768, 1 pl.

———. 1907. Descriptions of apparently new species and subspecies of mammals belonging to the families Lemuridae, Cebidae, Callitrichidae, and Cercopithecidae in the collection of the Natural History Museum. *Ann. Mag. Nat. Hist.,* ser. 7, 20:185–96.

———. 1911. The generic name *Cercopithecus*. *Bull. Amer. Mus. Nat. Hist.* 30:341–42.

———. 1912. New species of monkeys of the genera *Seniocebus, Alouatta,* and *Aotus. Bull. Amer. Mus. Nat. Hist.* 31:31–33.

———. 1913*a*. *A review of the Primates,* 1, cxxvii + 316 + xxxvii pp., 23 photos., 11 colored pls. + frontispiece.

———. 1913*b*. Descriptions of new species of monkeys of genera *Seniocebus* and *Aotus* from Colombia, South America. *Bull. Amer. Mus. Nat. Hist.* 32:251–53.

———. 1914. The genera *Œdipomidas* and *Seniocebus*. *Bull. Amer. Mus. Nat. Hist.* 33:643–45.

Elliot, O., and Wong, M. 1973. Piebaldism in tree shrews. *Primates* 14(2/3):309–14, 2 figs.

Emerson, K. C., and Price, Roger D. 1975. Mallophaga of Venezuelan mammals. *Sci. Bull. Brigham Young Univ., Biol. Ser.* 20(3):1–77, 218 figs.

Enders, Robert K. 1935. Mammalian life histories from Barro Colorado Island, Panama. *Bull. Mus. Comp. Zool.* 78(4):387–502, 5 pls.

———. 1939. Changes observed in the mammal fauna of Barro Colorado Island, 1929–1937. *Ecology* 20(1): 104–6.

English, W. L. 1932. Exhibition of living hybrid marmosets. *Proc. Zool. Soc. London* 1932:1079.

———. 1934. Notes on the breeding of a douroucouli (*Aotus trivirgatus*) in captivity. *Proc. Zool. Soc. London* 1934(1):143–44, 1 pl.

Epple, Gisela (Epple-Hosbacher). 1967*a*. Soziale Kommunikation bei *Callithrix jacchus* Erxleben, 1777. In *Progress in primatology,* ed. D. Starck, R. Schneider, and H. J. Kuhn, pp. 247–54, Stuttgart: Gustav Fischer.

———. 1967*b*. Vergleichende Untersuchungen über sexual- und socialverhalten der Krallenaffen (Hapalidae). *Folia Primat.* 7:37–65, 11 figs.

———. 1968. Comparative studies on vocalization in marmoset monkeys (Hapalidae). *Folia Primat.* 8:1–40, 44 figs.

———. 1970*a*. Maintenance, breeding and development of marmoset monkeys (Callithricidae) in captivity. *Folia Primat.* 12:56–76, 2 figs.

———. 1970*b*. Quantitive studies on scent marking in the marmoset (*Callithrix jacchus*). *Folia Primat.* 13: 48–62.

———. 1971. Discrimination of the odor of males and females by the marmoset *Saguinus fuscicollis ssp., Proc. 3rd Int. Congr. Primat., Zürich, 1970* 3:166–71.

———. 1972. Social communication by olfactory signal in marmosets. *Int. Zoo Yearb.,* 12:36–42.

———. 1973. The role of pheromones in the social communications of marmoset monkeys (Callithricidae). *J. Reprod. Fert.,* suppl., 19:447–54.

———. 1974*a*. Primate pheromones. In *Pheromones,* ed. M. C. Birch, pp. 366–85. Amsterdam: Elsevier.

———. 1974*b*. Olfactory communication in South American primates. *Ann. N.Y. Acad. Sci.* 237:261–78.

———. 1975*a*. Pheromones in primate reproduction and social behavior. In *Reproductive behavior,* ed. W. Montagna, pp. 131–55. New York: Plenum.

———. 1975*b*. The behavior of marmoset monkeys (Callithricidae). *Primate Behavior* 4:195–239, 3 figs.

———. 1975*c*. Parental behavior in *Saguinus fuscicollis* spp. (Callithricidae). *Folia Primat.* 24:221–38, 4 figs.

Epple, Gisela, and Lorenz, Rainer. 1967. Vorkommen, Morphologie und Function der Sternaldrüse bei den Platyrrhini. *Folia Primat.* 7:98–126, 14 figs.

Erickson, D. G.; Lichtenberg, F. van; Sadun, E. H.; Lucia, H. L.; and Hickman, R. L. 1971. Comparison of *Schistosoma haematobium, S. mansoni,* and *S. japonicum* infections in the owl monkey, *Aotus trivirgatus. J. Parasit.* 57(3):543–58, 10 figs.

Erikson, George E. 1963. Brachiation in New World monkeys and in anthropoid apes. *Symp. Zool. Soc. London,* no. 10, pp. 135–64, 5 figs., 3 pls.

Erxleben, Christian P. 1777. *Systema regni animalis per classes, ordines, genera, species, varietates cum synonymia et historia animalium.* Leipzig, xlviii + 636 + 62 (unnumbered index pages).

Esslinger, J. H. 1966. *Dipetalonema obtusa* (McCoy, 1936) comb. n. (Filarioidea: Onchocertidae) in Colombian primates with a description of the adult. *J. Parasit.* 52(3):498–502.

Esslinger, J. H., and Gardiner, C. H. 1974. *Dipetalonema barbascalensis* sp. n. (Nematoda: Filarioidea) from the owl monkey, *Aotus trivirgatus,* with a consideration of the status of *Parlitomosa zakii* Nagaty, 1935, *J. Parasit.* 60(60):1001–5, 10 figs.

Estes, Richard D. 1972. The role of the vomeronasal organ in mammalian reproduction. *Mammalia* 36(3): 315–41, 2 figs., 3 pls.

Evans, C. S., and Goy, R. W. 1968. Social behaviour and reproductive cycles in captive ring-tailed lemurs (*Lemur* catta). *J. Zool. London* 156:181–97, 3 figs, 3 pls.

Ewing, H. E. 1938. The sucking lice of American monkeys. *J. Parasit.* 24:13–33, 6 figs.

Ewing, S. A.; Helland, D. R.; Anthony, H. D.; and Leipold, H. W. 1968. Occurence of *Athesmia* sp. in the cinnamon ringtail monkey. *Cebus albifrons. Lab. Animal Care* 18(4):488–92, 4 figs.

Fain, A. 1959. Deux nouveau acariens nasicoles chez un singe platyrrhinien *Saimiri sciurea* (L.). *Bull. Soc. Roy. Anvers* 12:3–12.

———. 1963*a*. Nouveaux acariens, psoriques parasites de marsupiaux et des singes sud-américains (Psoralgidae: Sarcoptiformes). *Bull. Ann. Soc. Ent. Belg.* 99:322–32, 5 figs.

———. 1963*b*. Les acariens producteurs de gale chez les lemuriens et les singes avec une étude des Psoroptidae (Sarcoptiformes). *Bull. Inst. Sci. Nat. Belg.* 39(32): 1–125, 79 figs.

———. 1964*a*. Le developpment postembryonnaire chez les Acaridae, parasites cutanes des mamifères et des oiseaux (Acarina: Sarcoptiformes). *Bull. Acad. Belg. Cl. Sci.,* ser. 5, 50:19–34, 4 figs.

———. 1964*b*. Les Lemurnyssidae parasites nasicoles des Lorisidae africains et des Cebidae sud-américains. Descriptions d'une espèce nouvelle (Acarina: Sarcoptiformes). *Ann. Soc. Belge Med. Trop.* 44(3):453–58, 1 fig.

———. 1965. A review of the family Rhyncoptidae parasitic on porcupines and monkeys (Acarina: Sarcoptiformes). In *Advances in acarology,* ed. J. A. Naegele, 2:135–56, pls. 14–25. Ithaca, N.Y.: Comstock.

———. 1966. Les acariens producteurs gale chez les lemuriens et les singes. II. Nouvelles observations avec description d'une espèce nouvelle. *Acarologia* 8:94–114.

———. 1967. Diagnoses d'acariens nouveaux parasites

de rongeurs ou de singes (Sarcoptiformes). *Rev. Zool.-Bot. Afr.* 76:280–84.

———. 1968*a*. Notes sur trois acariens remarquables (Sarcoptiformes). *Acarologia* 10(2):276–91, 30 figs.

———. 1968*b*. Etude de la variabilité de *Sarcoptes scabiei* avec une revision des Sarcoptidae. *Acta Zool. Pathol. Antverpiensia,* no. 47, pp. 1–96, 209 figs.

Fairchild, Graham B.; Kohls, Glen M.; and Tipton, Vernon J. 1966. The ticks of Panama (Acarina: Ixodoidea). In *The ectoparasites of Panama,* ed. R. L. Wenzel and V. J. Tipton, pp. 167–219. Chicago: Field Museum of Natural History.

Falk, Lawrence A. 1974. Oncogenic DNA viruses of nonhuman primates: A review. *Lab. Animal Sci.* 24 (1, pt. 2):182–92.

Falk, Lawrence A.; Nigida, Stephen M.; Deinhardt, Friedrich; Wolfe, Lauren G.; Cooper, Robert W.; and Hernandez-Camacho, Jorge I. 1974. *Herpesvirus ateles*: Properties of an oncogenic herpesvirus isolated from circulating lymphocytes of spider monkeys (*Ateles* sp.). *Int. J. Cancer* 14:473–82, 1 fig.

Falk, Lawrence A.; Wolfe, Lauren G.; and Deinhardt, Friedrich A. 1973. *Herpesvirus saimiri:* Experimental infection of squirrel monkeys (*Saimiri sciureus*). *J. Nat. Cancer Inst.* 51:165–70.

Falk, Lawrence A.; Wolfe, Lauren G.; Deinhardt, Friedrich; Paciga, June; Dombos, Laszlo; Klein, George; Henle, Werner; and Henle, Gertrude. 1974. Epstein-Barr virus: Transformation of non-human primate lymphocytes in *vitro. Int. J. Cancer* 13:363–76, 2 figs.

Faust, Ernest Carrol, and Russell, Paul Farr. 1965. *Craig and Faust's Clinical parasitology,* 7th ed. Philadelphia: Lea and Febiger. 1099 pp., 352 figs.

Felsenfeld, A. D. 1972. The arboviruses. In *Pathology of simian primates,* ed. R. N. T.-W. Fiennes 2:523–36. Basel: S. Karger.

Fenart, Robert, and Anthony, Jean. 1967. La mandibule des singes platyrrhiniens. Donnèes ostéométriques et orientation vestibulaire. *Ann Paleo (Vert.)* 53(2): 201–33, 8 figs.

Ferreira Neto, J. A., and Deane, Leonidas M. 1973. New simian hosts of *Plasmodium brasilianum* in the State of Acre, Brazil. *Rev. Inst. Med. Trop., São Paulo* 15:112–15.

Ferreira Neto, Joaquin A.; Deane, Leonidas M.; and Almeida, F. B. 1972. Simian malaria in the State of Acre, Brazil: the finding of titi monkeys, *Callicebus moloch cupreus,* infected with *Plasmodium brasilianum. Rev. Inst. Med. Trop. São Paulo.* 14:231–34.

Ferris, Gordon Floyd. 1935. Contribution toward a monograph of the sucking lice. Part VIII. *Stanford U. Publ. Univ. Ser. Biol. Sci.* 2(8):529–620, figs. 306–38.

Ferris, Gordon Floyd, and Stojanovich, Chester J. 1951. The sucking lice. *Mem. Pacific Coast Entomol. Soc.,* vol. 1, 320 + ix pp., 124 figs.

Fiedler, Walter. 1956. Übersicht über das system der primates. *Primatologia* 1:1–266, 81 figs.

Fiennes, R. N. T.-W. 1967. *Zoonoses of primates: The epidemiology and ecology of simian diseases in relation to man.* Ithaca, N.Y.: Cornell University Press, 190 pp.

———. 1972*a*. Ectoparasites and vectors. In *Pathology of simian primates,* ed. R. N. T.-W. Fiennes 2:158–76. Basel: S. Karger.

———. 1972*b*. Rabies. In *Pathology of simian primates,* ed. R. N. T.-W. Fiennes 2:646–62. Basel: S. Karger.

———. 1972*c*. Tuberculosis. In *Pathology of simian primates,* ed. R. N. T.-W. Fiennes, 2:314–34. Basel: S. Karger.

Fischer, Gotthelf. 1803. *Das Nationalmuseum der Naturgeschichte zu Paris.* Frankfurt am Main: Esslinger, 2:vii(unnumbered) + 424 pp., 1 pl., 1 map.

Fischer, John Baptist. 1829. *Synopsis mammalium.* Stuttgart, xlii + 752 pp.

Fitch, Coy D. 1970. *Plasmodium falciparum* in owl monkeys: Drug resistence and chloroquinine binding capacity. *Science* 169:289–90.

Fitzgerald, Alice. 1935. Rearing marmosets in captivity. *J. Mammal.* 16:181–88.

Fitzpatrick, Thomas B.; Brunet, Peter; and Kukita, Atsushi. 1958. The nature of hair pigment. In *The biology of hair growth,* ed. W. Montagna and R. A. Ellis, pp. 255–303, 22 figs. New York: Academic Press.

Flatt, R. E. 1969. A mite infestation in squirrel monkeys (*Saimiri sciureus*). *J. Amer. Vet. Med. Assoc.* 155 (7): 1233–35, 2 figs.

Fleagle, John. 1974. Dynamics of a brachiating siamang [*Hylobates* (*Symphalangus*) *syndactylus*]. *Nature* 248 (5445):259–60, 1 fig.

Fleming, Theodore H. 1973. The reproductive cycles of three species of opossums and other mammals in the Panama Canal Zone. *J. Mammal.* 54 (2):439–55.

Flower, Stanley S. 1929. *List of the vertebrated animals exhibited in the gardens of the Zoological Society of London, 1828–1927.* Vol. 1. *Mammals.* London: London Zoological Society, pp. ix + 419.

———. 1931. Contributions to our knowledge of the duration of life in vertebrate animals. *Proc. Zool. Soc. London* 1931 (1):145–234.

Flower, William H. 1864. On the brain of the red howling monkey (*Mycetes seniculus* Linn.). *Proc. Zool. Soc. London* 1864:335–38.

Flynn, Robert J. 1973. *Parasites of laboratory animals.* Ames: Iowa State University Press. xvi + 884 pp., illus.

Fonseca, F. da. 1951. Plasmodio de primates do Brasil. *Mem. Inst. Oswaldo Crus.* 49:543–51, 12 figs.

Fooden, Jack. 1961. Urinary amino acids of non-human primates. *Zoologica* 46(3):167–80, 3 pls., 2 figs.

———. 1963. A revision of the woolly monkeys (genus *Lagothrix*). *J. Mammal.* 44(2):213–47, 1 fig., 5 pls.

———. 1965. Stomach contents and gastro-intestinal proportions in wild-shot Guianan monkeys. *Amer. J. Phys. Anthrop.* 22(2):227–32.

———. 1969*a*. Taxonomy and evolution of the monkeys of Celebes (Primates: Cercopithecidae). *Bibl. Primat.,* no. 10, pp. 1–148, 38 figs.

———. 1969*b*. Color-phase in gibbons. *Evolution* 23 (4):627–44, 3 figs.

———. 1971. Female genitalia and taxonomic relationships of *Macaca assamensis. Primates* 12(1):63–73, 5 figs.

Forbes, Henry Ogg. 1894. *A handbook to the Primates.* Vol. 1. Allen's Nat. Lib., 286 pp., 22 pls.

———. 1896–97. *A handbook to the Primates.* London: Lloyd Ltd., 2 vol., col. pls., maps.

Fox, Denis L. 1953. *Animal biochromes and structural colours; Physical, chemical, distributional and physio-*

logical features of coloured bodies in the animal world. Cambridge, xiii + 379 pp., 3 pls., 37 figs.

Fox, Herbert. 1925. *Diseases in captive wild mammals and birds.* Philadelphia: V. B. Lippincott Company, pp. [6] + 665, 87 figs.

Fox, H. Munro, and Vevers, Gynne. 1960. *The nature of animal colours.* London: Sidgewick and Jackson, 5 + 246 pp., 17 figs., 8 pls.

Fox, J. G.; Diaz, J. R.; and Barth, R. A. 1972. Nymphal *Porocephalus clavatus* in the brain of a squirrel monkey, *Saimiri sciureus. Lab. Animal Sci.* 22(6):908–10.

Fraenkel-Conrat, Heinz, and Wagner, Robert R., eds. 1974. *Comprehensive virology.* Vol. 1. *Descriptive catalogue of viruses.* New York: Plenum Press, pp. xii–191, 21 pls.

Frakes, Laurence A., and Kemp, Elizabeth M. 1972. Influence of continental positions on early Tertiary climates. *Nature* 240:97–100, 2 figs.

Frantz, Joaquim. 1963. Beobachtungen bei einer Löwenaffschen-Aufzucht. *Zool. Gart.* 28:115–20, 5 figs.

Fraser, A. S.; Nay, T.; and Kindred, B. 1959. Variation in vibrissa number in the mouse. *Austr. J. Biol. Sci.* 12:331–39.

Frederic, J. 1905. Untersuchungen über die sinus Haare der Affen, nebst Bemerkungen über die Augen brauen und den Schnurrbart des Menschen *Z. Morph. Anthrop.* 8:239–75, 1 fig., pl. 17.

Freidman, H. 1967. Colour vision in the Virginia opossum. *Nature* 213:835–36.

Friedman, L. A.; Levy, B. M.; and Ennever, J. 1972. Epidemiology of gingivitis and calculus in a marmoset colony. *J. Dental Res.* 51:803–6.

Gabis, R. V. 1960. Les os des mémbres des singes cynomorphs. *Mammalia* 24(4):577–607, 8 figs.

Galbraith, Donald B. 1964. The agouti pigment pattern of the mouse: A quantitative and experimental study. *J. Exp. Zool.* 155(1):71–89, 7 figs.

Galindo, Pedro. 1973. Monkeys and yellow fever. In *Nonhuman primates and medical research,* ed. G. H. Bourne, pp. 1–15. New York: Academic Press.

Garn, Stanley Marion. 1951. Types and distribution of the hair in man. *Ann. N.Y. Acad. Sci.* 53(3):498–507, 1 fig.

Garn, Stanley Marion, and Koski, Kalevi. 1957. Tooth eruption sequence in fossil and recent man. *Nature* 180:442–43.

Garn, Stanley Marion, and Lewis, Arthur B. 1963. Phylogenetic and intra-specific variation in tooth sequence polymorphism. In *Dental anthropology,* ed. D. R. Brothwell, 5:53–73, Symposia of the Society for the Study of Human Biology, 4 figs.

Garner, Edward; Hemrick, Frank; and Rudiger, Harry. 1967. Multiple helminth infections in cinnamon-ringtail monkeys (*Cebus albifrons*). *Lab. Animal Care* 17 (3):310–15, 4 figs.

Garnham, P. C. C. 1973. Distribution of malaria parasites in primates, insectivores and bats. *Symp. Zool. Soc. London,* no. 33, pp. 377–404.

Gaunt, W. A. 1955. The development of the molar pattern of the mouse (*Mus musculus*). *Acta Anat.* 24 (3–4):249–67.

———. 1959. The development of the deciduous teeth of the cat. *Acta Anat.* 38:187–212.

———. 1961. The development of the molar pattern of the golden hamster (*Mesocricetus auratus* W.) together with a re-assessment of the molar pattern of the mouse (*Mus musculus*). *Acta Anat.* 45:219–51.

Gautier, Jean-Pierre. 1971. Etude morphologique et fonctionelle des annexes extra-laryngées des Cercopithecinae. Liaison avec les cris d'espacement. *Biol. Gabonica* 7(2):229–67, 10 figs.

Gautier-Hion, A. 1971. Répertoire comportemental du talapoin (*Miopithecus talapoin*). *Biol. Gabon.* 7 (3): 295–391, 44 figs.

Gautier-Hion, A., and Gautier, Jean-Pierre. 1971. La nage chez les cercopithèques arboricoles du Gabon. *Terre et Vie* 1:67–76, 3 figs.

Gavan, J. A. 1967. Eruption of primate deciduous dentition: A comparative study. *J. Dental Res.* 46(5): 984–88.

Gebauer, O. 1933. Beitrag zur Kenntnis von Nematoden aus Aftenlungen. *Z. Parasitenk.* 5:724–34, 9 figs.

Geijskes, Derek C. 1957. Cited in A. M. Husson, Notes on Primates of Suriname. *Studies on the fauna of Suriname and other Guyanas* 1(2):13–40, 8 pls., 1 fig.

Gengozian, N. 1969. Marmosets: Their potential in experimental medicine. *Ann. N.Y. Acad. Sci.* 162(1): 336–62, 11 figs.

———. 1971. Male and female cell populations in the chimeric marmoset. In *Medical primatology, 1970,* ed. E. I. Goldsmith and J. Moor-Jankowski, pp. 926–38. Basel: S. Karger.

———. 1972*a*. Inter -and intrasubspecies red cell immunizations in the marmoset, *Saguinus fuscicollis* ssp. *J. Med. Primat.* 1:172–92, 5 figs.

———. 1972*b*. A blood factor in the marmoset, *Saguinus fuscicollis*: Its detection, mode of inheritance, and species specificity. *J. Med. Primat.* 1(5):272–86.

Gengozian, N., and Batson, J. S. 1975. Single-born marmosets without hemopoietic chimerism: Naturally occurring and induced. *J. Med. Primat.* 4:252–61.

Gengozian, N.; Batson, J. S.; and Eide, P. 1964. Hematologic and cytogenetic evidence for hematopoietic chimerism in the marmoset. *Cytogenetics* 3:384–93, 2 figs.

Gengozian, N.; Batson, J. S.; Greene, C. T.; and Gosslee, D. G. 1969. Hemopoietic chimerism in imported and laboratory bred marmosets. *Transplantation* 8: 633–52, 2 figs.

Gengozian, N., and Merrit, C. B. 1970. Effect of unilateral ovariectomy on twinning frequency in marmosets. *J. Reprod. Fertil.* 23:509–12.

Gengozian, N., and Patton, Mary L. 1972. Identification of three blood factors in the marmoset, *Saguinus fuscicollis* ssp. *Med. Primat. 1972* (Lyon), 1:349–60, 2 figs.

Gengozian, N., and Porter, R. P. 1971. Transplantation immunology in the marmoset. In *Medical primatology, 1970,* ed. E. I. Goldsmith and J. Moor-Jankowski, pp. 165–75, 3 figs.

Gengozian, N.; Smith, T. A.; and Gosslee, D. G. 1974. External uterine palpation to identify stages of pregnancy in the marmoset *Saguinus fuscicollis* ssp. *J. Med. Primat.* 3 (4):236–43, 2 figs.

Geoffroy, St. Hilaire Etienne. 1803. *Catalogue des mammifères du Museum National d'Histoire Naturelle.* Paris, 272 pp.

———. 1812. Tableau des quadrumanes, ou des animaux composant le premier ordre de la classe des mammifères. *Ann. Mus. Hist. Nat., Paris* 19:85–122.

Geoffroy Saint-Hilaire, Isidore. 1827. Article "ouistiti-*Jacchus*," *Dict. Class. Hist. Nat.*, 12:512–20.

———. 1851. *Catalogue méthodique de la collection de mammifères, de la collection des oiseaux et des collections annexes. Part. 1—mammifères. Introduction et catalogue des Primates.* Paris: Mus. Hist., xv + vii + 96 pp.

———. 1852. Descriptions des mammifères nouveaux ou imparfaitement connus de la collection du musèum national d'histoire naturelle et remarques sur la classification et les caracteres des mammifères. Troisième memoire. Famille des singes; supplement. *Arch. Mus. Hist. Nat. Paris* 5:529–84, pls. 26–31.

———. 1855. Primates. In *Animaux nouveaux ou rares recueillis pendant l'expédition dans les parties centrales de l'Amèrique du Sud . . . sous la direction du Comte Francis de Castelnau. Part. 7, Zoologie, mammifères* (by Paul Gervais), pp. 1–24, pls. 1–6 only.

Gerhardt, Ulrich. 1909. Ueber das Vorkommen eines Penis- und Clitorisknochen bei Hylobatiden. *Anat. Anz.* 35:353–58.

Gesner, Conrad. 1620. *Historia animalium. Liber primus. De quadrupedibus viviparis.* Frankfurt, 40 unnumbered + 967 pp., 130 figs. (first ed. published 1551, not seen).

Gidley, James William. 1906. Evidence bearing on tooth-cusp development. *Proc. Wash. Acad. Sci.* 8:91–110, pls. 4–5.

Gingerich, P. D. 1974. Anatomy of the temporal bone in the Oligocene anthropoid *Apidium* and the origin of Anthropoidea. *Folia Primat.* 19(1973):329–37.

Girgis, M. 1970. The rhinencephalon. *Acta Anat.* 76: 157–99, 12 figs.

Glaser, Dieter. 1968. Geschmacks schwellenwerte bei Callithricidae (Platyrrhini). *Folia Primat.* 9:246–57.

———. 1970*a*. Über Feschmacksleistungen bei Primaten. *Z. Morph. Anthrop.* 62(3):285–89.

———. 1970*b*. Geschmacks schwellenwerte von verschiedenen Zuckerarten bei Callithricidae (Platyrrhina). *Folia Primat.* 13:40–47.

———. 1972. Vergleichende Untersuchungen über den Geschmackssinn der Primates. *Folia Primat.* 17: 267–74.

Glass, R. L., and Jenness, R. 1971. Comparative biochemical studies of milks. VI. Constituent fatty acids of milk fats of additional species. *Comp. Biochem. Phys.* 38:353–59.

Glasstone, Shirley. 1967. Development of teeth in tissue culture. *J. Dental Res.* 46:858–61.

Glickstein, Mitchell. 1967. Laminar structure of the dorsal lateral geniculate nucleus in the tree shrew (*Tupaia glis*). *J. Com. Neurol.* 131(2):93–102, 6 pls.

———. 1969. Organization of the visual pathways. *Science* 164:917–26, 8 figs.

Glickstein, M.; Calvin, W.; and Doty, R. W. 1966. Laminar structure of the dorsal lateral geniculate body of *Saimiri* and *Tupaia. Anat. Rec.* 154:348.

Goeldi, Emil A. 1905. *Compte rendu des seances, sixième congrès international de zoologie, Berne* 1904:542–49.

———. 1907. On some new and insufficiently known species of marmoset monkeys from the Amazonian region. *Proc. Zool. Soc. London* 1907:88–99, figs. 20–23.

Goeldi, Emil A., and Hagmann, G. 1904. Prodromo de um catálogo crítico, commentado da collecção de mammíferos no museu do Pará (1894–1903). *Bol. Mus. Goeldi Hist. Nat. Ethn.* 4(1):35–106.

Goldman, Edward A. 1920. Mammals of Panama. *Smithsonian Misc. Coll.* 60(5):309 pp., 39 pls., 1 folding map.

Goodall, Jane M. 1962. Nest building behavior in the free ranging chimpanzee. *Ann. N.Y. Acad. Sci.* 102 (2):455–67, 6 figs.

———. 1963. Feeding behavior of wild chimpanzees. *Symp. Zool. Soc. London* 10:39–48.

———. 1965. Chimpanzees of the Gombe Stream Reserve. In *Primate behavior: Field studies of monkeys and apes,* ed. Irven DeVore, pp. 425–73. New York: Rinehart and Winston.

Graetz, Erich. 1968. Studien über das mittelamerikanische Krallenaffchen *Oedipomidas spixi. Sitzungsb. Ges. Naturf. Freunde* 8(1):29–40, 3 figs.

Grand, Theodore I. 1967. The functional anatomy of the ankle and foot of the slow loris (*Nycticebus coucang*). *Amer. J. Phys. Anthrop.* 26(2):205–18, 8 figs.

———. 1968*a*. The functional anatomy of the lower limb of the howler monkey (*Alouatta caraya*). *Amer. J. Phys. Anthrop.* 28:163–82, 8 figs.

———. 1968*b*. Functional anatomy of the upper limb. *Bibl. Primat.* 7:104–25, 9 figs.

Grand, Theodore I., and Lorenz, Rainer. 1968. Functional analysis of the hip joint in *Tarsius bancanus* (Horsfield, 1821) and *Tarsius syrichta* (Linnaeus, 1758). *Folia Primat.* 9:161–81, 3 figs.

Grant, Philip G. 1973. Lateral pterygoid: Two muscles? *Amer. J. Anat.* 138(1):1–9, 4 figs.

Gray, John Edward. 1821. *On the natural arrangement of vertebrose animals. London Med. Repos., Monthly J., and Rev.* 15:296–311.

———. 1825. An outline of an attempt at the disposition of Mammalia into tribes and families, with a list of the genera apparently appertaining to each tribe. *Ann. Philos.*, n.s., 10(v. 26 of series):337–44.

———. 1843. *List of the specimens of mammalia in the collection of the British Museum.* London, xxviii + 216 pp.

———. 1866. Notice of the new species of marmoset monkeys (*Hapale* and *Midas*). *Proc. Zool. Soc London* 1865:733–35.

———. 1870. *Catalogue of the monkeys, lemurs and fruit-eating bats in the collection of the British Museum.* London: British Museum (Natural History), viii + 137 pp., 21 figs.

———. 1875. Mammalia. *The Zoology of the Voyage of H.M.S.* Erebus *and* Terror, ed. John Richardson and John Edward Gray, 1:1–53, 37 pls. London: E. W. Jarison.

Gregory, William King. 1916. Studies on the evolution of primates. *Bull. Amer. Mus. Nat. Hist.* 35:239–55.

———. 1920. Studies in comparative myology and osteology; no. iv. A review of the evolution of the lacrymal bone in vertebrates with special reference to that of mammals. *Bull. Amer. Mus. Nat. Hist.* 42:95–263, 196 figs., pl. 17.

———. 1922. *The origin and evolution of the human dentition.* Baltimore: Williams and Wilkins, xviii + 548 pp., 353 figs.

———. 1934. A half century of trituberculy: The Cope-Osborn theory of dental evolution, with a revised summary of molar evolution from fish to man. *Proc. Amer. Philos. Soc.* 78:169–317.

Grieder, H. 1938. Filariden, Filariosis und Microfilarions bei verschieden Säugetieren. *Schweiz Arch. Tierheilk.* 80:485–90.

Griffith, Edward. 1821. *General and particular descriptions of the vertebrated animals, arranged conformably to the modern discoveries and improvements in zoology. . . . Order Quadrumana.* London: Baldwin, Cradock, and Joy, . . . and Rodwell and Martin, . . . 34 pls.

Grimwood, I. R. 1968. *Recommendations on the conservation of wild life and the establishment of national parks and reserves in Peru. Appendix III. Notes on the distribution and status of some Peruvian mammals.* British Ministry of Overseas Development, 100 pp., 11 maps.

Grosse, Ulrich. 1893. Ueber das Foramen pterygospinosum Civinini und das Foramen crotaphiticobuccinatorium *Hyrtl. Anat. Anz.* 8:321–47.

Groves, Colin P. 1970. The forgotten leaf-eaters, and the phylogeny of the Colobinae. In *Old World monkeys: Evolution, systematics, and behavior,* ed. J. R. Napier and P. H. Napier, pp. 557–87, 3 figs. New York: Academic Press.

———. 1972. Systematics and phylogeny of gibbons. *Gibbon and Siamang* 1:1–89, 22 figs.

Grüner, Manfred, and Krause, Pia. 1963. Biologische Beobachtungen an Weisspinseläffschen, *Hapale jacchus* (L., 1758) in Berliner Tierpark. *Zool. Gart.,* n.f., 28 (2/3): 108–14, 4 figs.

Guenther, Konrad. 1931. *A naturalist in Brazil.* Translated by Bernard Miall. Boston: Houghton Mifflin Co., 400 pp., 32 pls., 40 figs.

Guimarães, J. H. 1967. *A catalogue of the Diptera of the Americas south of the United States.* no. 105:1–11. São Paulo: Dept. Zoologia, Secretaria da Agricultura.

———. 1971 (1972 abs.). Notes on the hosts of neotropical Cuterebrini (Diptera, Cuterebridae), with new records from Brazil. *Pap. Avulsos, Dept. Zool. São Paulo* 25(10):89–94, 2 figs.

Haffer, Jurgen. 1969. Speciation in Amazonian forest birds. *Science* 165:131–37, 6 figs.

Hagler, Ernest. 1975. Einige Notizen zur Zucht und Haltung von zwei Paar Löwenäffchen (*Leontopithecus rosalia rosalia*). *Z. Kolner Zoo* 18(4):126–27, 4 figs.

Haines, R. Wheeler. 1958. Arboreal or terrestrial ancestry of placental mammals. *Quart. Rev. Biol.* 33(1): 1–23, 16 figs.

Hall, K. R. L.; Boelkins, R. C.; and Goswell, M. J. 1965. Behaviour of patas monkeys, *Erythrocebus patas,* in captivity, with notes on the natural habitat. *Folia Primat.* 3:22–49.

Hall-Craggs, E. C. B. 1965. An osteometric study of the hind limb of the Galagidae. *J. Anat.* (London) 99(1): 119–26, 1 fig., 1 pl.

———. 1966. Rotational movements in the foot of the *Galago senegalensis. Anat. Rec.* 154(2):287–94, 8 figs.

Hamasaki, D. I. 1967. An anatomical and electrophysiological study of the retina of the owl monkey, *Aotes trivirgatus. J. Comp. Neurol.* 130(2):163–69, 21 figs.

Hamilton, J. B., ed. 1951. The growth, replacement, and types of hair. *Ann. N.Y. Acad. Sci.* 53(3):461–752, illus.

Hamlett, G. W. D., and Wislocki, George B. 1934. A proposed classification for types of twins in mammals. *Anat. Rec.* 61:81–96.

Hampton, John K., Jr. 1964. Laboratory requirements and observations of *Oedipomidas oedipus. Amer. J. Phys. Anthrop.* 22(2):239–44.

———. 1973. Diurnal heart rate and body temperature in marmosets. *Amer. J. Phys. Anthrop.* 38(2):337–42, 1 fig.

Hampton, John K., Jr., and Hampton, Suzanne H. 1965. Marmosets (Hapalidae): Breeding seasons, twinning, and sex of offspring. *Science* 150:915–17.

Hampton, J. K., Jr.; Hampton, Suzanne H.; and Landwehr, Barbara T. 1966. Observations on a successful breeding colony of the marmoset *Oedipomidas oedipus. Folia Primat.* 4:265–87.

Hampton, John K., Jr.; Hampton, S. H.; and Levy, B. M. 1971. Reproductive physiology and pregnancy in marmosets. In *Medical primatology, 1970,* ed. E. I. Goldsmith and J. Moor-Jankowski, pp. 527–35. Basel: S. Karger.

Hampton, J. K., Jr.; Levy, Barnet M.; and Sweet, Pauline M. 1969. Chorionic gonadotropin excretion during pregnancy in the marmoset. *Endocrinology* 85(1): 171–74, 5 figs.

Hampton, John K., Jr., and Parmelee, Marian L. 1969. Plasma diamine oxidase activity in humans and marmosets. *Comp. Biochem. Physiol.* 30:367–73, 3 figs.

Hampton, J. K., Jr.; Parmelee, M. L.; and Rider, L. J. 1971. The comparative biology of histaminase and diamine oxidase among New and Old World primates. In *Medical primatology 1970,* ed. E. I. Goldsmith, and J. Moor-Jankowski, pp. 245–50. Basel: S. Karger.

Hampton, Suzanne H. 1972. Golden lion marmosets conference. *Science* 177:86–87.

———. 1973. Germ cell chimerism in male marmosets. *Amer. J. Phys. Anthrop.* 38(2):265–68, 3 figs.

———. 1975. Placental development in the marmoset. *Contemporary Primatology. 5th Intern. Congr. Primat., Nagoya 1974,* pp. 106–14.

Hampton, Suzanne H., and Hampton, John K., Jr. 1967. Rearing marmosets from birth by artificial laboratory techniques. *Lab. Animal Care* 17(1):1–10, 2 photos.

Hampton, Suzanne H., and Taylor, A. C. 1971. Gonadal development in marmosets. *Proc. 3rd Int. Cong. Primat. Zurich, 1970* 1:246–59, 30 figs.

Hanson, Jerome R., and Anson, Barry J. 1962. Development of the malleus of the human ear. *Quart. Bull. Northw. Univ. Med. Sch.* 33:119–37, 17 figs.

Hanson, Jerome R.; Anson, Barry J.; and Bast, Theodore H. 1959. The early embryology of the auditory ossicle in man. *Quart. Bull. Northw. Univ. Med. Sch.* 33: 358–79, 20 figs.

Hardy, Margaret H. 1951. The development of pelage hairs and vibrissae from skin in tissue culture. *Ann. N.Y. Acad. Sci.* 53(3):546–61, 3 figs., 4 pls.

Hardy, N. R.; Lewis, Linda; Little, Valerie; and Swyer, G. I. M. 1970. Use of a spot test for chloride in cervical mucus for self detection of the fertile phase in women. *J. Reprod. Fert.* 21:143–52, 9 figs., 2 pls.

Harper, Lawrence V. 1970. Ontogenetic and phylogenetic functions of the parent-offspring relationship in mammals. In *Advances in the study of behavior,* ed. Daniel S. Lehrman, Robert A. Hinde, and Evelyn Shaw, 2:75–117. New York: Academic Press.

Harrison, G. A.; Weiner, J. S.; Tanner, J. M.; and Barnicot, N. A. 1964. *Human biology: An introduction to human evolution, variation, and growth.* London: Oxford University Press, xvi + 536 pp., illus.

Harrisson, Barbara. 1963. Trying to breed *Tarsius. Malayan Nature J.* 17:218–31.

Hassler, R. 1966. Comparative anatomy of the central visual system in day and night active primates. In *Evolution of the forebrain,* ed. R. Hassler and H. Stephan, pp. 419–33. New York: Plenum Pub.

Hatt, Robert Torrens. 1932. The vertebral columns of richochetal rodents. *Bull. Amer. Mus. Nat. Hist.* 63 (6):599–737, 27 figs., pl. 11–20.

Hawking, Frank. 1973. The responses to various stimuli of microfilariae of *Dirofilaria corynodes* of *Dipetalonema marmosetae* and of unidentified species of filariae in *Saimiri sciureus* and Cacajao monkeys. *Int. J. Parasit.* 3:433–39.

Hayama, Sugio. 1970. The Saccus laryngis in primates. *J. Anthrop. Soc. Nippon* 78(4):274–98, 10 figs.

Hayman, R. H. 1964. Exercise of mating preference by a Merino ram. *Nature* 203:160–62.

Hearn, J. P., and Renfree, Marilyn B. 1975. Prealbumins in the vaginal flushings of the marmoset, *Callithrix jacchus. J. Reprod. Fert.* 43:159–61, 1 fig.

Heatherington, C. M.; Cooper, J. E.; and Dawson, P. 1975. A case of syndactyly in the white-lipped *Saguinus nigricollis. Folia Primat.* 24:24–28, 5 figs.

Heberling, R. L. 1972. The simian reoviruses. In *Pathology of simian primates,* ed. R. N. T.-W. Fiennes, 2:516–22. Basel: S. Karger.

Heberling, R. L., and Kalter, S. S. 1971. Recent development in nonhuman primate virology: A review. In *Medical Primatology, 1970,* ed. E. I. Goldsmith and J. Moor-Jankowski, pp. 648–659. Basel: S. Karger.

Hegner, Robert. 1935. Intestinal protozoa from Panama monkeys. *J. Parasit.* 21:60–61.

Heinemann, Heike. 1970. The breeding and maintenance of captive Goeldi's monkey, *Callimico goeldii. Int. Zoo Yearb.* 10:72–78, pls. 27, 28.

Heltne, Paul G.; Turner, Dennis C.; and Wolhandler, Jill. 1973. Maternal and paternal periods in the development of infant *Callimico goeldii. Amer. J. Phys. Anthrop.* 38:555–60.

Hemmer, H. 1971. Beitrag zur Erfassung der progressionen Cephalisation bei Primaten. *Proc. 3rd Int. Cong. Primat. Zurich, 1970* 2:99–107.

Henderson, J. D., and Bullock, B. C. 1968. A summary of lesions seen at necropsy in eight spontaneous woolly monkey (*Lagothrix* spp.) deaths. Abstr. 31, 19th Ann. Meet. Amer. Ass. Lab. Animal Sci. Las Vegas.

Hendricks, L. D. 1974. A redescription of *Isospora arctopitheci* Rodhain 1933 (Protozoa: Eimeriidae) from primates of Panama. *Proc. Helminth. Soc. Washington* 41:229–33.

Henson, O'Dell W., Jr. 1961. Some morphological and functional aspects of certain structures of the middle ear in bats and insectivores. *Sci. Bull. Univ. Kansas* 42(3):151–255, 37 figs.

Herrer, Aristides; Christensen, Howard A.; and Beumer, Ronald J. 1973. Reservoir hosts of cutaneous Leishmaniasis among Panamanian forest mammals. *Amer. J. Trop. Med. Hyg.* 22(5):585–91, 4 figs.

Hershkovitz, Philip. 1947. Mammals of northern Colombia. Preliminary Report no. 1: Squirrels (Sciuridae). *Proc. U.S. Nat. Mus.* 97(3208):1–46.

———. 1949. Mammals of northern Colombia. Preliminary report no. 4: Monkeys (Primates), with taxonomic revisions of some forms. *Proc. U.S. Nat. Mus.* 98:323–427, figs. 52–59, pls. 15–17.

———. 1957. The systematic position of the marmoset, *Simia leonina* Humboldt (Primates). *Proc. Biol. Soc. Wash.* 70:17–20.

———. 1958. Type localities and nomenclature of some American primates with remarks on secondary homonyms. *Proc. Biol. Soc. Wash.* 71:53–56.

———. 1962. Evolution of neotropical cricetine rodents (Muridae), with special reference to the phyllotine group. *Fieldiana: Zool.* 46:3–524, 123 figs.

———. 1963*a*. A systematic and zoogeographic account of the monkeys of the genus *Callicebus* (Cebidae) of the Amazonas and Orinoco River Basins. *Mammalia* 27(1):1–80, 11 pls., 3 figs.

———. 1963*b*. [Review] Primates: Comparative anatomy and taxonomy, [volume] V, *Cebidae,* part B, *A Monograph,* by W. C. Osman Hill. Edinburgh University Press. 1962, xxix 537 pp., 34 pls. 94 figs., 3 maps. A critical review with a summary of the volumes on New World Primates. *Amer. J. Phys. Anthrop.* 21(3): 391–98.

———. 1966*a*. On the identification of some marmosets, family Callithricidae (Primates). *Mammalia* 30(2): 327–32.

———. 1966*b*. Taxonomic notes on tamarins, genus *Saguinus* (Callithricidae, Primates) with descriptions of four new forms. *Folia Primat.* 4(5):381–95, 4 figs.

———. 1968. Metachromism or the principle of evolutionary change in mammalian tegumentary colors. *Evolution* 22(3):556–75, 13 figs.

———. 1969. The evolution of mammals on southern continents. VI. The recent mammals of the neotropical region: A zoogeographic and ecological review. *Quart. Rev. Biol.* 44(1):1–70, 16 figs.

———. 1970*a*. Notes on Tertiary platyrrhine monkeys and description of a new genus from the late Miocene of Colombia. *Folia Primat.* 12(1):1–37, 4 figs., 12 pls.

———. 1970*b*. Cerebral fissural patterns in platyrrhine monkeys. *Folia Primat.* 13:213–40, 8 figs.

———. 1970*c*. Dental and periodontal diseases and abnormalities in wild-caught marmosets (Primates–Callithricidae). *Amer. J. Phys. Anthrop.* 32(3):377–94, 5 pls.

———. 1970*d*. The decorative chin. *Bull. Field Mus. Nat. Hist.* 41(5):6–10, illus.

———. 1970*e*. Metachromism like it is. *Evolution* 24 (3):644–48.

———. 1971*a*. Basic crown patterns and cusp homologies of mammalian teeth. In *Dental morphology and evolution,* ed. A. Dahlberg, pp. 95–150, 17 figs. Chicago: University of Chicago Press.

———. 1971*b*. Stapedial processes in tympanic cavities of capuchin monkeys (*Cebus*). *J. Mammal.* 52(3): 607–9, 1 fig.

———. 1972. The recent mammals of the neotropical region: A zoogeographic and ecological review. In *Evolution, mammals, and southern continents,* ed. A. Keast, F. C. Erk, and B. Glass, pp. 311–431, 16 figs. Albany: State University of New York.

———. 1974. A new genus of Late Oligocene monkey (Cebidae, Platyrrhini) with notes on postorbital closure and Platyrrhine evolution. *Folia Primat.* 21(1):1–35, 14 figs., 2 pls.

———. 1975*a*. The ectotympanic bone and origin of higher primates. *Folia Primat.* 22(4)(1974):237–42, 5 figs.

———. 1975*b*. Comments on taxonomy of Brazilian marmosets (Callithrix, Callitrichidae). *Folia Primat.* 24:137–72, 14 figs.

Herter, Konrad. 1958. Über den Haarwechsel eines Hermelins. *Zool. Beitr. Bull.* 4(1):135–41, 4 figs.

Hess, Eckard H. 1973. *Imprinting: Early experience and developmental psychobiology of attachment.* Behavioral Science Series. New York: Van Nostrand Reinhold, xv + 472 pp., illustr.

Heusser, H. 1968. Ein frei gealtener Krallenaffe (*Callithrix jacchus*) erkennt Bilder. *Z. Tierpsychol.* 25(6): 710–18.

Hewson, Raymond. 1963. Moults and pelages in the brown hare, *Lepus europaeus occidentalis* de Winton. *Proc. Zool. Soc. London* 141(4):677–87.

Hick, Uta. 1961. "Stupps." *Fr. Kölner Zoo* 4(3):63, 1 fig.

Hiiemäe, Karen, and Crompton, A. W. 1971. A cinefluorographic study of feeding in the American opposum, *Didelphis marsupialis.* In *Dental morphology and evolution,* ed. A. A. Dahlberg, pp. 299–334. Chicago: University of Chicago Press, 13 figs.

Hiiemäe, Karen, and Kay, R. F. 1972. Trends in the evolution of primate mastication. *Nature* 240:486–87.

———. 1973. Evolutionary trends in the dynamics of primate mastication. In *Symp. 4th Int. Congr. Primatol.,* ed. W. Montagna, 3:28–64, 11 figs.

Hildebrand, Milton. 1967. Symmetrical gaits of primates. *Amer. J. Phys. Anthrop.* 26:119–30, 9 figs.

Hill, Clyde A. 1966. A callimico is born. *Zoonooz* 39 (10):14–15, 3 figs.

———. 1970. The last of the golden marmosets. *Lab. Primate Newsl.* 9(2):4–7.

Hill, J. P. 1926. Demonstration of the embryologia varia (Development of *Hapale jacchus*). *J. Anat.* 60:486–87.

———. 1932. II. Croonian Lecture. The developmental history of the Primates. *Philos. Trans. Roy. Soc. London,* ser. B, 221:45–178, 17 figs., 21 pls.

Hill, W. C. Osman. 1952. Exhibition of a rare marmoset. *Proc. Zool. Soc. London* 121:918.

———. 1953. Caudal cutaneous specializations in *Tarsius. Proc. Zool. Soc. London* 123:17–26, 1 fig., 3 pls.

———. 1955. Primates in the Royal Scottish Museum, part 2, Platyrrhini. *Proc. Roy. Phys. Soc. Edinburgh* 24:49–62.

———. 1957. *Primates. Comparative anatomy and Taxonomy. III. Pithecoidea: Platyrrhini (families Hapalidae and Callimiconidae).* New York: Wiley-Inter science, xix + 354, 27 pls., 102 figs.

———. 1958. External genitalia. *Primatologia* 3(1): 630–704, 36 figs.

———. 1959. The anatomy of *Callimico goeldii* (Thomas). A primitive American primate. *Trans. Amer. Philos. Soc.,* n.s., 49(5)1–116.

———. 1960. *Primates. Comparative anatomy and taxonomy. IV. Cebidae, Part A.* New York: Wiley-Interscience, vii + 523 pp., 36 plates, 90 figs.

———. 1961. Hybridization in marmosets. *Proc. Zool. Soc. London* 137(2):321–22.

———. 1962. *Primates. Comparative anatomy and taxonomy. V. Cebidae, Part B.* New York: Wiley-Interscience, vii + 537, 31 pls., 94 figs.

———. 1966*a*. *Primates. Comparative anatomy and taxonomy. VI. Catarrhini. Cercopithecoidea. Cercopithecinae.* New York: Wiley-Interscience, 757 pp., 50 pls. (2 color), 106 figs., 19 maps.

———. 1966*b*. On the neonatus of *Callimico goeldii* (Thomas). *Proc. Roy. Soc. Edinburgh,* ser. B, 69 (3/4):321–33.

———. 1970. *Primates. Comparative anatomy and taxonomy. VIII. Cynopithecinae,* Papio, Mandrillus, Theropithecus. New York: Wiley-Interscience, vii + 680 pp., 36 pls., 117 figs.

Hill, W. C. Osman. 1974. *Primates: Comparative anatomy and taxonomy.* VII. *Cynopithecinae:* Cercocebus, Macaca, Cynopithecus. *A monograph.* New York: John Wiley and Sons. xxi + 934 pp., 48 pls., 138 figs., 13 maps.

Hill, W. C. Osman, and Booth, A. H. 1957. Voice and larynx in African and Asiatic Colobidae. *J. Bombay Nat. Hist. Soc.* 54:309–21.

Hilloowala, R. A. 1975. Comparative anatomical study of the hyoid apparatus in selected primates. *Amer. J. Anat.* 142:367–84, 15 figs.

Hinde, Robert A. 1970. Animal behavior: A synthesis of ethology and comparative psychology. New York: McGraw Hill, xvi + 876 pp., illus.

Hladik, Annette, and Hladik, C. M. 1969. Rapports trophiques entre végétation et primates dans le forêt de Barro Colorado (Panama). *Terre et Vie,* no. 1–1969, pp. 25–117.

Hladik, C. M.; Hladik, A.; Bousset, J.; Valdebouze, P.; Viroben, G.; and Delort-Laval, J. 1971. La régime alimentaire des Primates de l'île de Barro-Colorado (Panama). Resultats des analyses quantitatives. *Folia Primat.,* 16:85–122, 3 figs.

Hoare, Cecil A. 1972. *The trypanosomes of mammals: A zoological monograph.* Oxford: Blackwell, xii + 749 pp., 108 figs.

Hochstetter, Ferdinand. 1946. Über die harte Hirnhaut und ihre Fortsatze bei den Säugetieren. Nebst Angeben über die Lageveziehung der Einzelnen Hirnteile dieser Tiere zu einander, zu den Fortsätzen der harten Hirnhaut und zur Schadelkapsel. *Denkschrift. Akad. Wiss. Univ., Math.-Kl.* 106(2):1–114, 4 figs., 11 pls.

Hofer, Helmuth O. 1955. Über die Falx cerebri der Affen, nebst einigen Bemerkungen über Hirn und Schädel der Primaten. *Gegenbauer's Morph. Jahrb.* 94:275–334, 7 figs.

———. 1957*a*. Die Evolution der Gehirnes des Primaten und die Interpretation der Schädelform des Menschen. *Ann. Soc. Roy Zool. Belg.* 94(1):97–115.

———. 1957*b*. Über die Bedeutung und die Afgaben der Primatologie. *Nachrichten Giessner Hochschulgesellschaft* 26:121–40, 3 fig.

———. 1965. Die morphologische Analyse des Schädels des Menschen. In *Menschliche abstammungslehre,* ed. G. Heberer, pp. 145–226, 23 figs. Stuttgart: Fischer.

———. 1969*a*. On the evolution of the craniocerebral topography in primates. *Ann. N.Y. Acad. Sci.* 162(1): 15–24, 4 figs.

———. 1969*b*. On the organon sublinguale in *Callicebus*

(Primates, Platyrrhini). *Folia Primat.* 11(4):268–88, 6 figs.

———. 1971. Comparative studies on the sublingual organ in primates: The sublingua in *Perodicticus potto* (Primates, Prosimiae, Lorisiformes). *Proc. 3rd Int. Cong. Primat., Zurich, 1970* 1:198–202, 2 figs.

Hofer, H. O., and Spatz, W. B. 1963. Studien zum Problem des Gestaltwandels des Schädels der Säugetiere, insbesondere der Primaten. II. Über die kyphosen fetales und neonater Primaten. *Z. Morph. Anthrop.* 53(1/2):29–52, 9 figs.

Hoffmannsegg, Graf von. 1807. Beschreibung Vier affenartiger Thiere aus Brasilian. *Mag. Gesellsch. Naturf. Fr., Berlin* 1:83–104.

Hoffstetter, Robert. 1969. Un primate de l'Oligocène. infèrieur sud-americain: *Branisella boliviana,* gen. et sp. nov. *C. R. Acad. Sci. Paris* 269:434–37, 1 fig., 1 pl.

———. 1972. Relationships, origins, and history of the ceboid monkeys and caviomorph rodents: A modern reinterpretation. In *Evolutionary biology,* ed. T. Dobzhansky, M. K. Hecht, and W. C. Steere, 6:323–47, 6 figs. New York: Appleton-Century-Crofts.

Holmes, A. W.; Caldwell, Richard G.; Dedmon, Robert E.; and Deinhardt, Friedrich. 1964. Isolation and characterization of a new herpes virus. *J. Immunol.* 92(4): 602–10.

Holmes, A. W.; Capps, R. B.; and Deinhardt, F. 1965. Results of inoculation of serum from patients with viral hepatitis into a subhuman primate. *Proc. 38th Ann. Mtg., J. Lab. Clin. Med.* 66(5):879–80.

Holmes, A. W.; Dedmon, Robert E.; and Deinhardt, Friedrich. 1963. Isolation of a new herpes-like virus from South American marmosets. *Fed. Proc.* 22(2): abstract.

Holmes, A. W., and Deinhardt, Friedrich. 1965. Results of inoculation of serum from patients with viral hepatitis into a subhuman primate. *J. Lab. Clin. Med.* 66 (5):879–80.

Holmes, A. W.; Devine, James A.; Nowakowski, Edward; and Deinhardt, Friedrich. 1966. The epidemiology of a herpes virus infection of New World monkeys. *J. Immunol.* 90(4):668–71.

Holmes, A. W.; Wolfe, Lauren; and Deinhardt, F. 1972. Infectious hepatitis in marmosets. In *Pathology of simian primates,* ed. R. N. T.-W. Fiennes, 2:684–701. Basel: S. Karger.

Holmes, A. W.; Wolfe, L.; Rosenblate, H.; and Deinhardt, F. 1969. Hepatitis in marmosets: Induction of disease with coded specimens from a human volunteer study. *Science* 165:816–17.

Hoogstraal, Harry. 1956. *African Ixodoidea. 1. Ticks of the Sudan.* Res. Rept. NM 005 050.29.07, U.S. Navy, Bureau of Medicine and Surgery, 1101 pp., 372 figs., 103 pls.

Hooks, John J.; Gibbs, Jr., C. J.; Chou, S.; Howk, R.; Lewis, M.; and Gajdusek, D. C. 1973. Isolation of a new simian foamy virus from a spider monkey brain culture. *Inf. Immun.,* Nov. 1973, pp. 804–13.

Hooper, Emmet T. 1968. Anatomy of middle ear walls and cavities in nine species of microtine rodents. *Occ. Pap. Mus. Zool. Univ. Michigan,* no. 657, 28 pp., 6 figs.

Hooten, Earnest, 1942. *Man's poor relations.* New York, xli + 412 pp., 11 text figs., 74 pls.

Hopkins, G. H. E. 1949. The host-associations of the lice of mammals. *Proc. Zool. Soc. London* 119:387–604.

———. 1957. The distribution of Phthiraptera on mammals. Inst. Zool. Univ. Neuchatel, 1st Symp. on host specificity among parasites of vertebrates, pp. 88–119.

Hopkins, G. H. E., and Rothschild, Miriam. 1953–56. *An illustrated catalogue of the Rothschild collection of fleas (Siphonaptera) in the British Museum (Natural History).* London, xv + 361 pp., map, 45 pls.

Hopson, James A. 1966. The organ of the mammalian middle ear. *Amer. Zool.* 6(3):437–50, 11 figs.

———. 1973. Endothermy, small size and the origin of mammalian reproduction. *Amer. Nat.* 107(955): 446–52.

Hornung, Victor. 1896. Der Pinselaffe (*Hapale penicillata*). Zool. Gart. 37:273–77.

———. 1899. Weitere Mitteilungen über den Pinselaffen (*Hapale penicillata*). *Zool. Gart.* 40:208–9.

Howell, A. Brazier. 1944. *Speed in animals. Their specialization for running and leaping.* Chicago: University of Chicago Press, xii + 270 pp., 55 figs.

Hrdlička, Ales. 1925. Weight of the brain and of the internal organs in American monkeys. *Amer. J. Phys. Anthrop.* 8:201–11.

Hsiung, G.-D. 1969. Recent advances in the study of simian viruses. *Ann. N.Y. Acad. Sci.* 162(1):483–98, 6 figs.

Hsiung, G.-D.; Black, F. L.; and Henderson, J. R. 1964. Susceptibility of primates to viruses in relation to taxonomic classification. In *Evolutionary and genetic biology of primates,* ed. J. Buettner-Janusch, 2:1–23.

Hsiung, G.-D., and Swack, N. S. 1972. *Myxovirus* and *Pseudomyxovirus* Groups. In *Pathology of simian primates,* ed. R. N. T.-W. Fiennes, 2:537–71, 9 figs. Basel: S. Karger.

Hsu, T. C., and Benirschke, Kurt 1967–71. *An atlas of mammalian chromosomes.* New York: Springer Verlag, vols. 1–6 (loose leaf folios).

Hsu, T. C., Hampton, Suzanne H. 1970. Chromosomes of Callitrichidae with special reference to an XX/'XO' sex chromosome system in Goeldi's marmoset (*Callimico goeldii* Thomas, 1904). *Folia Primat.* 13:183–95, 9 figs.

Huber, Ernst. 1930. Evolution of facial musculature. *Quart. Rev. Biol.* 5:133–88, 26 figs.

———. 1931. *Evolution of facial musculature and facial expression.* Baltimore: Johns Hopkins Press, 184 pp., 28 figs.

Hückinghaus, Folkhart. 1965*a*. Präbasiale und prämaxillare kyphose bein wild- und Hauskaninchen. *Z. Wiss. Zool.* 17(1/2):169–82, 2 figs.

———. 1965*b*. Craniometrische Untersuchung an verwilderten Hauskaninchen von den Kerguelen. *Z. Wiss. Zool.* 171(1/2):182–96, 8 figs.

Hugghins, E. J. 1969. Spirurid and oxyurid nematodes from a red howler monkey in Colombia. *J. Parasit.* 55:680.

Hull, R. N. 1968. *The simian viruses.* Virology Monographs, no. 2. N.Y.: Springer Verlag, 66 pp., 4 figs.

Hull, R. N.; Dwyer, A. C.; Holmes, A. W.; Nowakowski, E.; Deinhardt, F.; Lennette, E. H.; and Emmons, R. W. 1972. Recovery and characterization of a new simian herpes-virus from a fatally infected spider monkey. *J. Nat. Cancer Inst.* 49(1):225–31, 1 fig.

Hull, William B. 1970. Respiratory mite parasites in non-human primates. *Lab. Animal Care* 20(2[2]):402–6.

Hulse, Frederick S. 1974. Skin color and climate in Europe. *Amer. J. Phys. Anthrop.* 40(1):140 (abstr.).

Humboldt, Alexandre de. 1805. Première mémoire, sur l'os hyoide et le larynx des oiseaux, des singes, et du crocodile. *Recueil d'observations de zoologie et d'anatomie comparée; faites dans l'ocean atlantique, dans l'interieur du nouveau continent et dans la mer du sud, pendant les années 1799, 1800, 1801, 1802 et 1803.* Paris, pp. 1–31.

———. 1811–12. In *Recueil d'observations de zoologie et d'anatomie comparée, faites dans l'ocean atlantique dans l'interieur du nouveau continent et dans la mer du sud pendant les années 1799, 1800, 1801, 1802 et 1803,* ed. A. de Humboldt and A. Bonpland, pt. 2, vol. 1, Paris, viii + 368 pp., 40 pls.

Hunt, Ronald D.; García, Felix G.; and Hegsted, D. Mark. 1966*a*. Vitamin D requirement of New World monkeys. *Fed. Proc.* 21:715–17.

———. 1966*b*. Vitamin D deficiency in New World monkeys. *Lab. Primate Neurol.* 5(3):12–13.

———. 1967. A comparison of Vitamin D_2 and D_3 in New World primates. I. Production and regression of osteodystrophia fibrosa. *Lab. Animal Care* 17(2):222–34, 7 figs.

Hunt, Ronald D.; García, F. G.; Hegsted, D. Mark; and Kaplinsky, Noemi. 1967. Vitamins D_2 and D_3 in New World primates: Influence on calcium absorption. *Science* 157:943–45, 1 fig.

Hunt, Ronald D., and Meléndez, Luis V. 1966. Spontaneous herpes-T infection in the owl monkey (*Aotus trivirgatus*). *Path. Vet.* 3:1–26.

———. 1969. Herpes virus infections of non-human primates. *Lab. Anim. Care* 19(2):221–34, 12 figs.

Hunt, Ronald D.; Meléndez, Luis V.; King, N. W.; and García, Felix G. 1972. *Herpesvirus saimiri* malignant lymphoma in spider monkeys: A new susceptible host. *J. Med. Primat.* 1:114–28, 13 figs.

Hurme, V. O., and Wagenen, G. van. 1953. Basic data on the emergence of deciduous teeth in the monkey (*Macaca mulatta*). *Proc. Amer. Philos. Soc.* 97(3): 291–315, 10 figs.

———. 1961. Basic data on the emergence of permanent teeth in the rhesus monkey (*Macaca mulatta*). *Proc. Amer. Philos. Soc.* 105(1):105–40.

Hürzeler, Johannes. 1948. Zur stammesgeschichte der Necrolemuriden. *Schweiz. Paleo. Abh.* 66:1–46.

Huxley, Thomas H. 1872. *A manual of the anatomy of vertebrated animals.* New York: D. Appleton, 431 pp., illus.

Illiger, Carol. 1811. *Prodromus systematis mammalium et avium.* Berlin, xviii + 301 pp.

Ilse, D. R. 1955. Olfactory marking of territory in two young male loris, *Loris tardigradus lydekkerianus,* kept in captivity in Poona. *Brit. J. Anim. Behav.* 3:118–24, 1 pl.

Immelmann, Klaus. 1972. Sexual and other long-term aspects of imprinting in birds and other species. In *Advances in the study of behavior,* ed. Daniel S. Lehrman, Robert A. Hinde, and Evelyn Shaw, 4:147–74. New York: Academic Press.

Immendorf, Magret. 1961. Über die Aufzucht eines Krallenäffchen-Bastards aus dem Kölner Zoo. Mutter Roth-and-tamarin, *Leontocebus* (*Tamarin*) *midas* (Linne, 1758); Vater manteläffchen, *L.* (*Marikina*) *bicolor* (Spix, 1833 [*sic*]). *Säugetierk. Mitteil.* 9(4):145–51, pl., 6 figs.

Inglis, William G. 1958. The comparative anatomy of the subulurid head (Nematoda): With a consideration of its systematic importance. *Proc. Zool. Soc. London* 130:577–604, 33 figs. 21 + 934 pp., 138 figs., 13 maps, 48 pls.

———. 1961. The oxyurid parasites (Nematoda) of primates. *Proc. Zool. Soc. London* 136:103–22.

Inglis, William G., and Cosgrove, G. E. 1965. The pinworm parasites (Nematoda: Oxyuridae) of the Hapalidae (Mammalia: Primates). *Parasitology* 55:731–37, 6 figs.

Inglis, William G., and Díaz-Ungría, Carlos. 1959. Una revisión del género *Trypanoxyuris* (Ascaridina: Oxyuridae). *Mem. Soc. Cienc. La Salle* (Caracas) 19: 176–212, 38 figs.

———. 1960. Nematodes de Venezuela. V. Sobre una colección del Distrito Mara (Zulia). *Acta Biol. Venezuelica* 3(4):67–81, 13 figs.

Inglis, William G., and Dunn, Frederick L. 1964. Some oxyurids (Nematoda) from neotropical primates. *Z. Parasitenkunde* 24:83–87, 4 figs.

Inke, G. 1962. Quantitative anatomie der Innenfläche des Unterkiefers beim Menschen und bei den Simiae. I. die innere Fläche der Kinngegend (Spina retromentalis, Foramina retromentalia). *Gegenbauer's Morph. Jahrb.* 102(4):459–507, 17 figs.

Innes, J. R. M., and Hull, W. B. 1972. Endoparasites: Lung mites. In *Pathology of simian primates,* ed. R. N. T.-W. Fiennes, 2:177–93, 7 figs. Basel: S. Karger.

International Code of Zoological Nomenclature. 1961. (Revised 1964). Published for the International Commission on Zoological Nomenclature by the International Trust for Zoological Nomenclature, London. xx + 176 pp. Editors: N. R. Stoll (Chairman), R. Ph. Dollfus, J. Forest, N. D. Riley, C. W. Sabrowsky, C. W. Wright, R. V. Melville (Secretary).

International Commission on Zoological Nomenclature. 1925. *Opinion 90.* Smithsonian Misc. Coll. 73(3): 34–39.

Ismael, M. M. 1960. Possible function of the tiger's whiskers. *J. Bombay Nat. Hist. Soc.* 57:213.

Izawa, Kosei. 1975. Foods and feeding behavior of monkeys in the upper Amazon basin. *Primates* 16, (3): 295–316, 8 figs.

Jacobs, G. H. 1963. Spectral sensitivity and color vision of the squirrel monkey. *J. Comp. Physiol. Psychol.* 56:616–21.

Jane, J. A.; Campbell, C. B. G.; and Yashon, D. 1965. Pyramidal tract: A comparison of two prosimian primates. *Neurol. Surg. Anat.* 147(3654):153–55.

Jarvis, Caroline, and Morris, Desmond, eds. 1960. Longevity survey: Length of life of mammals in captivity at the London Zoo and Whipsnade Park. *Int. Zoo Yearb.* 2:288–99.

———. 1961. The breeding seasons of mammals in captivity. *Int. Zoo Yearb.* 3:292–301.

Jay, Phyllis. 1965. Field studies. In *Behavior of non-human primates: Modern research trends,* ed. Allan M. Schrier, Harry F. Harlow, and Fred Stollnitz, 2:525–95, 18 figs. New York: Academic Press.

Jenkins, Farish A., Jr. 1969. Occlusion in *Docodon*. *Postilla,* no. 139, 24 pp., 15 figs.

———. 1970. Anatomy and function of expanded ribs in certain edentates and primates. *J. Mamm.* 51(2): 288–301.

———. 1974*a*. The movement of the shoulder in claviculate and aclaviculate mammals. *J. Morph.* 144(1): 71–83, 7 figs.

———, ed. 1974*b*. *Primate locomotion.* New York: Academic Press. xii + 390 pp., illustr.

Job, Thesle T. 1918. Lymphatico-venous communication in the common rat and their significance. *Amer. J. Anat.* 24:467–85, 3 pls.

Johnson, Elizabeth. 1965. Inherent rhythms of activity in the hair follicle and their control. In *Biology of the skin and hair growth,* ed. A. G. Lyne and B. F. Short, pp. 491–505, 10 figs. New York: American Elsevier Pub. Co.

Johnson, P. T. 1957. A classification of the Siphonaptera of South America with descriptions of new species. *Mem. Ent. Soc. Wash.,* no. 5, pp. 1–299, pls. 1–114.

Johnston, G. W.; Dreizen, S.; and Levy, B. M. 1970. Dental development in the cotton ear marmoset (*Callithrix jacchus*). *Amer. J. Phys. Anthrop.* 33:41–38, 3 figs.

Johnston, P. B. 1969. Isolation and properties of simian foamy viruses provisionally designated as type 4 and type 5. Second Conference on experimental medicine and surgery in primates, Sept. 12, 1969. (unpublished in work cited, reference from Hsiung and Swack 1972, p. 565, q.v. above).

Joleaud, L. 1923. Essai sur l'évolution des milieux géophysiques et biogéographiques (à propos de la théorie de Wegener sur l'origine des continents). *Bull. Soc. Geol. France,* ser. 4, 23:205–57.

Jollie, William P. 1973. Fine structural changes in the placental membrane of the marmoset with increasing gestational age. *Anat. Rec.* 176:307–20, 3 pls.

Jolly, Alison. 1966*a*. *Lemur behavior: A Madagascar field study*. Chicago: University of Chicago Press, xiv + 187 pp., 7 figs.

———. 1966*b*. Lemur social behavior and primate intelligence. *Science* 153:501–6.

———. 1972. Hour of birth in primates and man. *Folia Primat.* 18:108–21, 3 figs.

Jones, Arthur E. 1965. The retinal structure of (*Aotes trivirgatus*) the owl monkey. *J. Comp. Neurol.* 125: 19–28, 3 pls.

———. 1966. The lateral geniculate complex of the owl monkey *Aotes trivirgatus. J. Comp. Neurol.* 126: 171–80, 4 pls.

Jones, E. K.; Clifford, Carleton M.; Keirans, J. E.; and Kohls, G. M. 1972. The ticks of Venezuela (Acarina: Ixodoidea) with a key to the species of Amblyomma in the western hemisphere. *Brigham Young Univ. Sci. Bull., Biol. Ser.* 17(4):1–40.

Jones, Frederic Wood. 1916 [1964]. Arboreal man. Reprint (3d impression) of 1926 edition. New York: Hafner, x + 230 pp., 81 figs.

———. 1929. *Man's place among the mammals.* London: Edward Arnold, v + 371 pp., 160 figs.

———. 1942. *The principle of anatomy as seen in the hand.* 2d ed. Baltimore, Williams and Wilkins, x + 418 pp., 144 figs.

Jones, Frederic Wood., and Lambert, V. F. 1939. The occurrence of the lemurine form of the ectotympanic in a primitive marsupial. *J. Anat.* (London) 74:72–75, 6 figs.

Jones, Marvin L. 1962. Mammals in captivity: Primate longevity. *Lab. Primate Newsl.* (mimeo.), 1(3):3–14.

Jouffroy, F. K., and Gasc, J. P. 1974. A cineradiographical analysis of leaping in an African prosimian (*Galago alleni*). In *Primate locomotion,* ed. F. A. Jenkins, Jr., pp. 117–142, 10 figs. New York: Academic Press.

Jouffroy, F. K., and Lessertisseur, J. 1960. Les spécialisations anatomiques de la main chez les singes à progression suspendu. *Mammalia* 24(1):93–151.

Kalin, J. 1962. Über *Moeripithecus marcgrafi* Schlosser und die phyletischen Vorstuffen der Bilophodontie der Cercopithecoidea. *Bibl. Primat.* 1:32–42.

Kalter, S. S. 1972*a*. Identification and study of viruses. In *Pathology of simian primates,* ed. R. N. T.-W. Fiennes, 2:382–468, 7 figs. Basel: S. Karger.

———. 1972*b*. Serologic surveys. In *Pathology of simian primates,* ed. R. N. T.-W. Fiennes, 2:469–96. Basel: S. Karger.

———. 1973. Virus research. In *Nonhuman primates and medical research,* ed. G. H. Bourne, pp. 61–165. New York: Academic Press.

Kalter, S. S., and Heberling, R. L. 1972. Serologic evidence of viral infection in South American monkeys. *J. Nat. Cancer Inst.* 49(1):251–59.

Kalter, S. S.; Heberling, R. L.; and Cooper, R. W. 1974. Serologic testing of various primate species maintained in a single outdoor breeding colony. *Lab. Animal Sci.* 24(4):636–45.

Kaplan, Joel. 1973. Responses of mother squirrel monkeys to dead infants. *Primates* 14(1):89–91.

Kaplan, William. 1959. The occurrence of black piedra in primate pelts. *Trop. Geog. Med.* 11(2):115–26, 8 figs.

Kaplan, William; Georg, Lucille K.; and Ajello, Libero. 1958. Recent developments in animal ringworm and their public implications. *Ann. N.Y. Acad. Sci.* 70(3): 636–49.

Karlson, Alfred G.; Seibold, Herman R.; and Wolf, Robert H. 1970. *Mycobacterium abscessum* infection in owl monkey (*Aotus trivirgatus*). *Path. Vet.* 7:448–54, 2 figs.

Karr, Stephen L., Jr., and Wong, Ming M. 1975. A survey of *Sarcocystis* in nonhuman primates. *Lab. Animal Sci.* 25(5):641–45, 4 figs.

Kawakami, T. G.; Buckley, Patricia; Huff, Sally; McKain, Deedra; and Fielding, Hazel. 1973. A comparative study *in vitro* of a simian virus isolated from spontaneous wooly monkey fiibrosarcoma and of a known feline fibrosarcoma virus. In R. M. Dutcher and L. Chieco-Bianchi, eds., Unifying concepts of leukemia, *Bibl. Haemat.,* no. 39, pp. 236–43.

Kay, Richard F. 1975. The functional adaptations of primate molar teeth. *Amer. J. Phys. Anthrop.* 43, (2): 195–216, 6 figs.

Kay, Richard F., and Hiiemäe, Karen M. 1974. Jaw movement and tooth use in recent and fossil primates. *Amer. J. Phys. Anthrop.* 40:227–56, 18 figs.

Kelemen, G. 1969. Anatomy of the larynx and the anatomical basis of vocal performance. In *Anatomy, behavior, and diseases of chimpanzees,* ed. G. H. Bourne, 1:165–87, 19 figs. Baltimore: University Park Press.

Kermack, D. M.; Kermack, K. A.; and Mussett, F. 1968.

The Welsh pantothere *Kuehneotherium praecursorius. J. Linn. Soc., (Zool.)* 47:407–23.

Kerr, Robert. 1792. *The animal kingdom or zoological system of the celebrated Sir Charles Linnaeus. Class I. Mammalia: . . . being a translation of that part of the Systema Naturae . . . by Professor Gmelin . . .* Edinburgh, A. Strahan and T. Cadell . . . 1792. xii + 400 pp.

Kessel, J. F. 1928. Intestinal protozoa of monkeys. *Univ. Calif. Publ. Zool.* 31:275–306.

Kidd, Walter A. 1903. *The direction of hair in animals and man.* London, 154 pp., illus.

———. 1907. *The sense of touch in mammals and birds with special reference to the papillary ridges.* London: Adam and Charles Black, viii + 176 pp., 174 figs.

King, James E.; Fobes, Jaqueline T.; and Fobes, James L. 1974. Development of early behavior in neonatal squirrel monkeys and cotton-top tamarins. *Develop. Psychbiol.* 7(2):97–109, 2 figs.

Kingston, N., and Cosgrove, G. E. 1967. Two new species of *Platynosomum* (Trematoda: Dicrocoeliidae) from South American monkeys. *Proc. Helm. Soc. Wash.* 34(2):147–51.

Kinzey, Warren G. 1971. Evolution of the human canine tooth. *Amer. Anthrop.* 73(3):680–94.

———. 1973. Reduction of the cingulum in Ceboidea. In *Symp. 4th Intern. Cong. Primat. Karger, Basel,* ed. Montagna, 3:101–27, 7 figs.

———. 1974. Ceboid models for the evolution of hominoid dentition. *J. Human Evol.* 3:193–203, 1 fig., 11 pls.

Kinzey, Warren G.; Rosenberger, A. L.; Ramírez, Marleni. 1975. Vertical clinging and leaping in a neotropical anthropoid. *Nature* 225(5506):327–28, 1 fig.

Kirikae, Ichiro. 1960. *The structure and function of the middle ear.* Tokyo: University of Tokyo Press, vi + 157 pp.

Klaatsch, H. 1892. Über embryonale Anlagen des Scrotums und der Labia Majora bei Arctopitheken. *Gegenbauer's Morph. Jahrb.* 18:383.

Kleiman, Devra G. 1972. Recommendations on research priorities for the lion marmoset. In *Saving the lion marmoset,* ed. D. D. Bridgewater, pp. 137–39. Proc. Wild Animal Propagation Trust Conference on the Golden Marmoset held at National Zoological Park, Washington, D.C., February 15–17, 1972. Wheeling, W.Va.: Wild Animal Propagation Trust.

———. 1976. International studbook: Golden Lion Tamarin, *Leontopithecus rosalia rosalia.* National Zoological Park, Smithsonian Institution, Washington, D.C. (circular).

Klein, L., and Klein, D. 1971. Aspects of social behaviour in a colony of spider monkeys. *Int. Zoo Yearb.* 11: 175–81.

Klintworth, Gordon K. 1968. The comparative anatomy and phylogeny of the tentorium cerebelli. *Anat. Rec.* 160:635–42, 12 figs.

Knussmann, Rainer, 1967. Humerus, Ulna, und Radius der Simiae. *Bibl. Primat.* 5:1–399, 228 figs.

Koprowski, Hilary, and Hughes, Thomas P. 1946. The virus of Ilhéus encephalitis. *J. Immunol.* 54:371–85.

Kraft, Helmuth. 1957. Lethargie-zustand einer Weiss Pinseläffchen, *Callithrix jacchus* (Linné, 1776). *Säugetierk. Mitt.* 5(4):175.

Kraus, Bertram S. 1963. Morphogenesis of deciduous molar pattern in man. In *Dental Anthropology: Symposia of the Society for the Study of Human Biology,* ed. D. R. Brothwell, 5:87–104.

Kraus, Bertram S., and Hampton, John K., Jr. 1969. Sequence of ossification of the foot in marmosets (*Saguinus oedipus*). *Amer. J. Phys. Anthrop.* 30:393–96, 3 figs.

Kraus, Bertram S., and Jordan, R. E. 1965. *The human dentition before birth.* Philadelphia: Lea and Febiger, 218 pp., 128 figs.

Kreiner, Jerzy. 1968. Homologies of the fissural and gyral patterns of the hemispheres of the dog and monkey. *Acta Anat.* 70:137–67, 5 figs.

Kreis, H. A. 1932. A new pathogenic nematode of the family Oxyuroidea (*Oxyuronema atelophora*), n. g., n. sp., in the red spider monkey (*Ateles geoffroyi*). *J. Parasit.* 18(4):295–302.

Krieg, Hans. 1930. Biologische Reisestudien in Südamerika. xvi. Die Affen des Gran Chaco und seiner Grenzgebiete. *Z. Morph. Okol. Tiere* 18:760–85, 14 figs.

———. 1948. *Zwischen Anden und Atlantik: Reisen eines Biologen in Südamerika.* Munich: Carl Hanser Verlag, 492 pp., 414 figs., 4 pls.

Krishnamurti, A. 1968. The cerebral arteries of *Nycticebus coucang coucang. Folia Primat.* 8:159–68, 4 figs.

Kubota, Kinziro, and Hayama, Sugio. 1964. Comparative anatomical and neurohistological observations on the tongues of pygmy and common marmosets. *Anat. Rec.* 150(4):473–86, 19 figs.

Küenzi, W. 1958. Ein lebender Springtamarin (*Callimico goeldii* Thos.) in der Schweiz. *Mitt. Naturf. Gesellsch., Bern,* n.f., 16:xxxviii–xl, 2 pls.

———. 1960. Zweiter Bericht über das Gefangenschaftsleben unseres Springtamarins (*Callimico goeldii* Thos.) *Mitt. Naturf. Gesellsch., Bern,* n.f., 17:xxxv–xxxvi.

Kugi, Guti, and Sawada, Isamu. 1970. *Mathevotaenia brasiliensis,* n. sp., a tapeworm from the squirrel monkey, *Saimiri sciureus. Jap. J. Parasit.* 19(5):467–70, 7 pls.

Kuhl, Heinrich. 1820. Beiträge zur Zoologie und vergleichenden Anatomie, Frankfurt am Main. *Erste Abth.,* pp. 1–152 + 8 unnumbered pages.

Kuhn, Hans-Jurg. 1968. Parasites and phylogeny of the catarrhine primates. In *Taxonomy and phylogeny of Old World primates . . . ,* ed. B. Chiarelli, pp. 187–95. Turin.

Kummer, Benno. 1965. Das mechanische Problem der Aufrichtung auf die Hinterextremität im Hinblick auf die Evolution der Bipedie des Menschen. In *Menschliche Abstammungslehre: Fortschritte der "Anthropogenie," 1863–1964,* ed. G. Heberer, pp. 226–48, 18 figs. Stuttgart: Gustav Fischer.

Kuntz, Robert E. 1972. Trematodes of the intestinal tract and biliary passages. In *Pathology of simian primates,* ed. R. N. T.-W. Fiennes, 2:104–23, 5 figs. Basel: S. Karger.

Kuntz, Robert E., and Myers, Betty June. 1972. Parasites of South American primates. *Int. Zoo Yearb.* 12: 61–68.

Kuntz, Robert E.; Myers, Betty June; Huang, T. C.; and Moore, J. A. 1971. Use of nonhuman primates in experimental Schistosomiasis haematobia. *Proc. 3rd Int. Cong. Primat. Zurich, 1970* 2:162–72.

Kurtén, Björn. 1968. *Pleistocene mammals of Europe.* Chicago: Aldine, viii + 317 pp., 110 figs.

La Condamine, M. de. [1745]. *Relation abregée d'un voyage fait dans l'intérieur de l'Amérique Méridionale depuis la cote de la mer du sud, jusqu'aux cotes du Brésil et de la Guyane, en déscendant la Riviere des Amazones* . . . New edition, Maestrict, 1778, p. xvi + 379 pp., frontispiece, fold. map [original edition cited, not seen].

Laemmert, H. W., Jr.; Castro Ferreira, Leoberto de; and Taylor, R. M. 1946. An epidemiological study of jungle yellow fever in an endemic area in Brazil. Part II—Investigations of vertebrate hosts and arthropod vectors. *American J. Trop. Med.* 26(6):23–60, 3 figs., 1 map.

Lam, H. Y. Peter; Schoes, H. K.; and De Luca, H. F. 1974. 1α-Hydroxy-vitamin D_2: A potent synthetic analog of vitamin D_2. *Science,* 186:1038–40, 2 figs.

Lambrecht, Frank L. 1965. An unusual trypanosome in *Cebus griseus* F. Cuvier, 1819, from Colombia, South America. *Rev. Inst. Med. Trop. São Paulo* 7(2):89–98, 2 figs.

Lampert, Heinrich. 1926. Zur Kenntniss das Platyrrhinen-Kehlkopfes. *Gegenbaur's Morph. Jahrb.* 55: 607–54, 28 figs.

Lancaster, J. B., and Lee, R. B. 1965. The annual reproductive cycle in monkeys and apes. In *Primate behavior: Field studies of monkeys and apes,* ed. Irven DeVore, pp. 486–513, 5 figs. New York: Holt, Rinehardt and Winston.

Lang, C. Max. 1967. The estrous cycle of the squirrel monkey (*Saimiri sciureus*). *Lab. Animal Care* 17(5): 442–51, 9 figs.

Lang, Ernst M. 1966. Austritt der Milchzähne beim Gorillakind. *Zool. Gart.* 32(5):219–21.

Langford, J. B. 1963. Breeding behaviour of *Hapale jacchus* (common marmoset). *S. Afr. J. Sci.* 59:299.

Lasinski, Wieslaw. 1960. Ausseres ohr. *Primatologia* vol. 2, part 1, Lf. 5, pp. 41–74, 17 figs.

Latreille, Pierre André. 1803. Exposition methodique des quadrupèdes. In *Histoire naturelle générale et particulière,* ed. Georges Louis Leclerc, Comte de Buffon, 34:257–324. Paris: Sonnini.

Lavigne, D. M., and Øritsland, N. A. 1974. Black polar bears. *Nature* 251:218–19, 1 fig.

Lavoipierre, M. M. J. 1964*a*. A new family of acarines belonging to the suborder Sarcoptiformes parasitic in the hair follicles of primates. *Ann. Natal Mus.* 16: 1–18.

———. 1964*b*. A note on the family Psoralgidae (Acari: Sarcoptiformes) together with a description of two new genera and two new species parasitic on primates. *Acarologia* 6:342–52, 3 figs.

Lawick-Goodall, Jane van. 1968. The behaviour of free-living chimpanzees in the Gombe Stream Reserve. *Anim. Behav. Monog.* 1(3):161–311, 12 pls., 42 figs.

Lawrence, Barbara. 1933. Howler monkeys of the *palliata* group. *Bull. Mus. Comp. Zool.* 75(8):315–54.

Lay, Douglas M. 1972. The anatomy, physiology, functional significance and evolution of specialized hearing organs of gerbilline rodents. *J. Morph.* 138(1):41–120, 56 figs.

Lebel, Robert Roger, and Nutting, William B. 1973. Demodectic mites of subhuman primates I: *Demodex saimiri* sp. n. (Acari: Demodicidae) from the squirrel monkey, *Saimiri sciureus. J. Parasit.* 59(4):719–22, 10 figs.

Ledoux, Luiz Jorge. 1963. Contribução ão estudo da lingua do sagüi. Doctoral diss., Univ. Bahia, Salvador, Bahia, Brazil, 26 pp., 15 figs.

———. 1964. A lingua do sagüi (*Callithrix jacchus*). *Folia Clin. Biol.* (Bahia) 33:23–31, 9 figs.

Ledoux, Luiz Jorge; Dos Santos, Agnaldo José; and Santana Moura, Cleide. 1967. O palato do sagüi (*Callithrix jacchus*). *Arq. Centro Est. Fac. Odontol., Univ. Fed. Minas Gerais* 4(1):73–85, 5 figs.

Leger, M. 1918. Microfilaires animales en Guyane française. *Bull. Soc. Path. Exot.* 11:392.

Le Gros Clark. *See* Clark, W. E. Le Gros

Lehner, N. D. M.; Bullock, B. C.; Clarkson, T. B.; and Lofland, H. B. 1966. Biological activity of vitamin D_2 and D_3 fed to squirrel monkeys. *Fed. Proc.* 25:533.

Lennette, E. H. 1968. Workshop on viral diseases which impede colonization of nonhuman primates. Nat. Center Primate Biol., Univ. Calif., Davis, May 22–24.

Leopold, Aldo S. 1959. *Wildlife of Mexico: The game birds and mammals.* Berkeley: University of California Press, pp. 568, 194 figs.

Lessertisseur, J., and Jouffroy, F. K. 1974. Tendances locomotrices des primates traduites par les proportions du pied. *Folia Primat.* 20:125–60 (1973), 12 figs.

Lesson, Réné-Primeverre. 1840. *Species des mammifères: Bimanes et quadrumanes; suivi d'un mémoire sur les Oryctéropes.* Paris, xiii + 291 pp.

Leutenegger, Walter. 1970*a*. Das Becken der rezenten Primates. *Morph. Jahrb.* 115(1):1–101.

———. 1970*b*. Das Becken der Primaten und seine Beziehungen zur Lokomotion. *Z. Morph. Anthrop.* 62 (3):328–33, 2 figs.

———. 1970*c*. Beziehungen zwischen der Neugeborenengrosse und dem Sexualdimorphismus am Becken bei simischen Primaten. *Folia Primat.* 12:224–35.

———. 1973. Sexual dimorphism in the pelves of African lorises. *Amer. J. Phys. Anthrop.* 38(2):251–54.

———. 1974. Maternal-fetal weight relationships in primates. *Folia Primat.* 20(4):280–94(1973).

Levine, Louis. 1958. Studies on sexual selection in mice. I. Reproductive competition between albino and black-agouti males. *Amer. Nat.* 92:21–26.

Levine, Norman D. 1970. Protozoan parasites of nonhuman primates as zoonotic agents. *Lab. Animal Care* 20(2):377–82.

Levy, Barnet M. 1971. Nonhuman primates as an analogus for study for periodontal disease. *J. Dental Res.* 50:246–53, 8 figs.

Levy, Barnet M., and Bernick, Sol. 1968*a*. Studies on the biology of the periodontium of marmosets. II. Development and organization of the periodontal ligament of deciduous teeth in marmosets (*Callithrix jacchus*). *J. Dental Res.* 47(1):27–33.

———. 1968*b*. Studies on the biology of the periodontium of marmosets: V. Lymphatic vessels of the periodontal ligament. *J. Dental Res.* 47:1166–70.

Levy, Barnet M.; Dreizen, S.; and Bernick, S. 1972. *The marmoset periodontium in health and disease.* Monographs in Oral Science. Basel: S. Karger, 1[4]+89 pp. 79 figs.

Levy, Barnet M.; Dreizen, S.; Bernick, S.; and Hampton, J. K. Jr. 1970. Studies on the biology of the periodontium of marmosets. IX. Effects of parathyroid hormone on the alveolar bone of marmosets, pretreated with fluoridated and nonflouridated drinking water. *J. Dental Res.* 49(4):816–21, 6 figs.

Levy, Barnet M.; Dreizen, S.; Hampton, J. K. Jr.; Taylor, A. C.; and Hampton, S. H. 1971. Primates in dental research. In *Medical primatology 1970,* ed. E. I. Goldsmith and J. Moor-Jankowski, pp. 859–69. Basel: S. Karger.

Levy, Barnet M.; Hampton, S. H.; and Hampton, J. K. Jr. 1972. Some aspects of marmoset biology. *Int. Zoo Yearb.* 12:51–55.

Levy, Barnet M., and Mirkovic, Radmila R. 1971. An epizootic of measles in a marmoset colony. *Lab. Animal Sci.* 21(1):33–39, 5 figs.

Levy, Barnet M.; Taylor, A. C.; Hampton, S. H.; and Thoma, G. W. 1969. Tumors of marmoset produced by Rous sarcoma virus. *Cancer Res.* 29:2237–48, 23 figs.

Lewis, M. A.; Frye, L. D.; Gibbs, C. J. Jr.; Chou, S. M.; Cutchins, E. C.; and Gajdusek, D. J. 1974. Isolation and characterization of two unrelated Herpesviruses from capuchin monkeys. *Abstr. Ann. Mtg. Amer. Soc. Microbiol., 1974,* p. 256.

Lewis, O. J. 1974. The wrist articulations of the Anthropoidea. In *Primate locomotion,* ed. F. A. Jenkins, Jr., pp. 143–69, 10 figs. New York: Academic Press.

Lim, Boo Liat. 1967. Note on the food habits of *Ptilocercus lowi* Gray (Pentail tree-shrew) and *Echinosorex gymnurus* (Raffles) (Moonrat) in Malaya with remarks on "ecological labelling" by parasite patterns. *J. Zool. Soc. London* 152:375–79, 2 pls.

Linnaeus, Carolus. 1758. *Systema Naturae. . . . Tomus I. Regnum Animalium.* 10th ed., reformed. Holm, 823 pp.

———. 1766. *Systema Naturae. . . . Tomus I. Regnum Animalium.* 12th ed., reformed. Holm, 532 pp.

———. 1771. *Mantissa plantarum altera generum editionis VI & specierum editionis II.* Holm, 588 pp. [Regni Animalis appendix. Mammalia, pp. 521–23.]

Little, M. D. 1966. Comparative morphology of six species of *Strongyloides* (Nematoda) and redefinition of the genera. *J. Parasit.* 52:69–84.

Liu, Si-Kwang. 1965. *Filaroides cebuellae* sp. n. (Nematoda: Metastrongyloidea) from the lung of a pygmy marmoset, *Cebuella pygmaea* (Spix, 1823). *J. Helminth.* 39(2/3):225–28, 2 figs., 1 pl.

Long, James O., and Cooper, Robert W. 1968. Physical growth and dental eruption in captive-bred squirrel monkeys *Saimiri sciureus* (Leticia, Colombia). In *The squirrel monkey,* ed. L. H. Rosenblum and R. W. Cooper, pp. 193–205, 4 figs. New York: Academic Press.

Lönnberg, Einar. 1940. Notes on marmosets. *Ark. Zool. Stockholm* 32A(10):1–22.

Loo, S. K. 1973. A comparative study of the nasal fossa of four nonhuman primates. *Folia Primat.* 20:410–22, 18 figs.

Loomis, W. Farnsworth. 1967. Skin-pigment regulation of Vitamin-D synthesis in man. *Science* 157:501–6, 5 figs.

Lorenz, Konrad Z. 1973. The fashionable fallacy of dispensing with description. *Naturwissenschaften* 60(1): 1–9.

Lorenz, Rainer. 1969. Notes on the care, diet and feeding habits of Goeldi's monkey. *Int. Zoo Yearb.* 9:150–55.

———. 1970*a*. Second generation bred in Goeldi's monkeys, *Callimico goeldii,* Callimiconidae, Primates. *Int. Zoo News* 17:79–80.

———. 1970*b*. Studbook of the Goeldi's monkey. *Int. Zoo News* 17:130.

———. 1971. Goeldi's monkey *Callimico goeldii* Thomas 1904 preying on snakes. *Folia Primat.* 15:133–42.

———. 1972. Management and reproduction of the Goeldi's monkey *Callimico goeldii* (Thomas, 1904), Callimiconidae, Primates. In *Saving the Lion Marmoset,* ed. D. D. Bridgewater, Proc. Wild Animal Propagation Trust Golden Lion Marmoset Conference, pp. 92–109.

———. 1974. On the thumb of the Hylobatidae. *Gibbon and Siamang* 3:157–75, 6 figs.

Lorenz, Rainer, and Heinemann, H. 1967. Beitrag zur Morphologie und Körperlichen Jungendentwicklung des Springtamarin (*Callimico goeldii*) (Thomas, 1904). *Folia Primat.* 6:1–27.

Low, R. J., and Benirschke, K. 1968. Chromosome study of a marmoset hybrid. *Folia Primat.* 8:180–91, 8 figs.

Loy, James. 1975. Changes in facial color associated with pregnancy in patas monkeys. *Folia Primat.* 22(1974): 251–57.

Lucas, N. S.; Hume, Margaret E.; and Henderson-Smith, H. 1927. On the breeding of the common marmoset (*Hapale jacchus* Linn.) in captivity when irradiated with ultra-violet rays. *Proc. Zool. Soc. London* 1927: 447–51, 2 pls.

———. 1937. On the breeding of the common marmoset (*Hapale jacchus* Linn.) II. A ten year's family history. *Proc. Zool. Soc. London,* ser. A, 107:205–11.

Luckett, W. P. 1974. Comparative development and evolution of the placenta in primates. *Contrib. Primatol.* 3:142–234, 56 figs.

Lund, P. W. 1839. Coup-d'oeil sur les espèces éteints de mammifères du Brésil. *Ann. Sci. Nat., Paris,* ser. 1, 11:214–34.

Lyman, C. P. 1943. Control of coat color in the varying hare *Lepus americanus* Erxleben. *Bull. Mus. Comp. Zool.* 93:391–461.

Lyne, A. G. 1959. The systematic and adaptive significance of the vibrissae in the Marsupialia. *Proc. Zool. Soc. London* 133:79–133, 26 figs., 5 pls.

Lyne, A. G., and Short, B. F., eds. 1965. *Biology of the skin and hair growth.* Sydney: Angers and Robertson, xi + 806 pp., illus.

Maccagno, Luis. 1932. Los auchénidos peruanos. Ministerio Fomento, Divisíon de Agricultura y Ganadería (Lima, Peru), Vol. 1:161–224 (separate, pp. 1–64), (1913).

McCoy, O. R. 1936. Filarial parasites of the monkeys of Panama. *Amer. J. Trop. Med.* 16(4):383–403, 2 pls.

Macdonald, Julie. 1965. *Almost human. The Baboons; wild and tame—in fact and legend.* Philadelphia: Chilton Books, xi + 161 pp., illustr.

McDowell, Samuel Booker, Jr. 1958. The greater Antillean insectivores. *Bull. Amer. Mus. Nat. Hist.* 115: 113–214, 46 figs.

Machado Filho, D. A. 1950. Revisão do género *Prosthenorchis* Travassos, 1915 (Acanthocephala). *Mem. Inst. Oswaldo Cruz* 48:493–544, 104 figs.

Machida, Haruo, and Perkins, Edwin M., Jr. 1967. The distribution of melanotic melanocytes in the skin of subhuman primates. In *Advances in biology of skin,*

Vol. 8. *The Pigmentary System,* ed. W. Montagna and Funan Hu, pp. 41–58, New York: Pergamon Press. 20 figs.

Machida, Haruo; Perkins, Edwin M.; and Giacometti, L. 1967. The anatomical and histochemical properties of the tongue of primates. *Folia Primat.* 5:264–79, 11 figs.

McKenna, Malcolm C. 1966. Paleontology and the origin of the primates. *Folia Primat.* 4(1):1–25, 10 figs.

———. 1969. The origin and early differentiation of therian mammals. *Ann. N.Y. Acad. Sci.* 167(1): 217–40.

McNab, Brian K. 1971. On the ecological significance of Bergmann's rule. *Ecology* 52(5):845–54, 8 figs.

McNamara, J. A., Jr. 1973. The independent functions of two heads of the lateral pterygoid muscle. *Amer. J. Anat.* 138:197–206, 6 figs.

Magnanini, Alceo, and Coimbra-Filho, Adelmar F. 1972. The establishment of a captive feeding program and a wildlife research center for the lion marmoset *Leontopithecus* in Brazil. In *Saving the lion marmoset,* ed. D. D. Bridgewater, pp. 110–19. Proc. Wild Animal Propagation Trust Conference on the Golden Marmoset held at National Zoological Park, Washington, D.C., February 15–17, 1972. Wheeling, W.Va.: Wild Animal Propagation Trust.

Magnanini, Alceo; Coimbra-Filho, Adelmar F.; Mittermeier, Russell A.; and Aldrighi, A. 1975. The Tijuca bank of lion marmosets *Leontopithecus rosalia:* A progress report. *Int. Zoo. Yearb.* 15:284–87, figs. 22, 23.

Mahoney, C. J. 1970. A study of the menstrual cycle in *Macaca irus* with special reference to the detection of ovulation. *J. Reprod. Fert.* 21:153–63.

———. 1972. A method for obtaining dated pregnancies in *Macaca irus. J. Anat.* 111:506 (abstract only).

Mahouy, G. B. 1972. The marmoset—a tool for the study of transplantation immunity mechanisms. In *Med. Primat., 1972,* ed. E. I. Goldsmith and J. Moor-Jankowski, pt. 2, pp. 117–24, 2 figs.

Mainardi, Danilo. 1963. Speciazioni nel topo. Fattori etologici determinanti barriere reproductive tra *Mus musculus domesticus* e *M. m. bactrianus. Rend. Sci. Inst. Lombardo,* ser. B, 97:135–42.

Mainardi, Danilo; Marson, Mario; and Pasquali, Antonio. 1965. Causation of sexual preferences of house mice: The behaviour of mice reared by parents whose odour was artificially altered. *Atti Soc. Italiana, Mus. Civico Stor. Nat. Milano* 104(3):325–38.

Mainardi, Danilo; Scudo, Francesco M.; and Barbieri, Daniele. 1965. Assortative mating based on early learning: Population genetics. *L'Ateneo Parmense* 36:581–605, 4 figs.

Major, C. I. Forsyth. 1899. Exhibitions of, and remarks upon, some skulls of foetal Malagasy lemurs. *Proc. Zool. Soc. London* 1899:987–88.

———. 1901. On some characters of the skull in the lemurs and monkeys. *Proc. Zool. Soc. London* 1901: 129–53, figs. 24–46, pls. 11–13.

Malinow, M. R.; Pope, B. L.; Depaoli, J. R.; and Katz, S. 1968. Laboratory observations on living howlers. *Bibl. Primat.* 7:224–30.

Mallinson, Jeremy J. C. 1965. Notes on the nutrition, social behaviour and reproduction of Hapalidae in captivity. *Int. Zoo Yearb.* 5:137–40.

———. 1968. Lemurs in captivity. *Oryx* 9(5):335–36.

———. 1969. Observations on a breeding group of black and white colobus monkeys. *Int. Zoo Yearb.* 9:79–81.

———. 1971. The breeding and maintenance of marmosets at Jersey Zoo. *Jersey Wildl. Pres. Trust, 6th Annual Rep., 1969,* pp. 5–10.

———. 1972. Observations on the breeding of red-handed tamarins, *Saguinus* (= *Tamarin*) *midas* (Linnaeus, 1758), with comparative notes on other species of Callithricidae (= Hapalidae) breeding in captivity. *8th Ann. Rep. Jersey Wildl. Pres. Trust,* pp. 19–31.

Manley, G. H. 1966. Reproduction in lorisoid primates. *Symp. Zool. Soc. London,* no. 15, pp. 493–509, 4 figs.

———. 1967. Gestation periods in the Lorisidae. *Int. Zoo Yearb.* 7:80–81.

Marback, Roberto L., and Costa, Alvaro R., Jr. 1962. Alguns dados relativos a estructura da retina do sägui (*Callithrix jacchus*). *Folia Clinica Biol.* 31:10–18, 6 figs.

Marcgraf, Georg. 1648. . . . Historiae rerum naturalium Brasiliae, libri . . . sextus de quadrupedibus et serpentibus. . . . Leiden and Amsterdam. 293 pp.

Marczynska, Barbara; Treu-Sarnat, Gabriela; and Deinhardt, Friedrich. 1970. Characteristics of long-term marmoset cell cultures spontaneously altered or transformed by Rous sarcoma virus. *J. Nat. Cancer Inst.* 44:545–72, 12 figs.

Marik, Margarethe. 1931. Beobachtungen zur Fortpflanzungsbiologie der Uistiti (*Callithrix jacchus*). *Zool. Gart.* n.f. 4(10–12):347–49.

Marinkelle, C. J. 1966. Observations on human, monkey and bat trypanosomes and their vectors in Colombia. *Trans. Roy. Soc. Trop. Med. Hyg.* 60:109–16.

———. 1969. *"Isospora cebi"* sp. n. aislada de un mico de Colombia (*"Cebus albifrons"*). *Rev. Bras. Biol.* 29:35–40.

Marinkelle, C. J., and Grose, E. S. 1968. *Plasmodium brasilianum* in Colombian monkeys. *Trop. Geog. Med.* 20(1968):276–80.

Marler, Peter. 1965. Communication in monkeys and apes. In *Primate Behavior: Field studies of monkeys and apes,* ed. Irven De Vore, pp. 544–84. New York: Holt, Rinehart and Winston.

Martin, Robert D. 1968. Reproduction and ontogeny in tree shrews (*Tupaia belangeri*) with reference to their general behaviour and taxonomic relationship. *Z. Tierpsychol.* 25(4):409–504, cont'd 25(5):505–32, 32 figs.

———. 1969. The evolution of reproductive mechanisms in primates. *J. Reprod. Fert.,* suppl., 6:49–66, 2 figs., 2 pls.

———. 1972*a*. A preliminary field-study of the lesser mouse lemur (*Microcebus murinus* J. F. Müller 1777). *Fortschr. Verhaltensf. (Zeit. Tierps., suppl.)* 9:42–89, 23 figs.

———. 1972*b*. Adaptive radiation and behaviour of the malagasy lemurs. *Phil. Trans. Roy. Soc. London,* ser. B, 264:295–352, 16 figs.

Mason, William A. 1966. Social organization of the South American monkey *Callicebus moloch;* a preliminary report. *Tulane Studies in Zool.* 13:23–28, 1 fig.

———. 1971. Field and laboratory studies of social organization in *Saimiri* and *Callicebus.* In *Primate behavior,* ed. L. A. Rosenblum, 2:107–37. New York: Academic Press.

Massengale, O. N., and Nussmeier, Mildred. 1930. The action of activated ergosterol in the chicken. II. The prevention of leg weakness. *J. Biol. Chem.* 87:423–26.

Matthew, William Diller. 1915. Climate and evolution. *Ann. N.Y. Acad. Sci.* 24:171–318.

Matthews, L. Harrison. 1952. Report of additions to the Society's Menagerie during the month of October, 1951. *Proc. Zool. Soc. London* 121:91.

Mayr, Ernst. 1963. *Animal species and evolution.* Cambridge, Mass.: Harvard University Press, 797 pp., illustr.

Mazur, Allan, and Baldwin, J. 1968. Social behavior of semi-free ranging white lipped tamarins. *Psychol. Repts.* 22(2):441–42.

Mazza, S. 1930. Doble parasitismo por filárias en monos *Cebus* del norte. *5ą Reunión Soc. Argent., Path. Reg. N., 1929,* p. 1140.

Melargno, Helen P., and Montagna, William. 1953. The tactile hair follicles in the mouse. *Anat. Rec.* 115(2): 129–42, 1 fig., 3 pls.

Meléndez, Luis V.; Castellanos, H.; Barahona, H. H.; Daniel, M. D.; Hunt, Ronald D.; Fraser, C. E. O.; García, Felix G.; and King, N. W. 1972. Two new herpesviruses from spider monkeys (*Ateles geoffroyi*). *J. Nat. Cancer Inst.* 49(1):233–37.

Meléndez, Luis V., and Daniel, M. D. 1971. Herpesviruses from South American monkeys. In *Medical primatology 1970,* ed. E. I. Goldsmith and J. Moor-Jankowski, pp. 686–93.

Meléndez, Luis V.; Daniel, M. D.; Barahona, H. H.; Fraser, C. E. O.; Hunt, Ronald D.; and García, Felix G. 1971. New herpesviruses from South American monkeys: Preliminary report. *Lab. Animal Sci.* 21(6), pt. 2, pp. 1051–54.

Meléndez, Luis V.; Daniel, M. D.; and Fraser, C. E. O. 1969. *Cebus* isolate (C. I.), and adeno-like virus from *Cebus apella. Fed. Proc.* 28:820 (abstr.).

Meléndez, Luis V.; Daniel, M. D.; García, Felix G.; Fraser, C. E. O.; Hunt, Ronald D.; and King, N. W. 1969. *Herpesvirus saimiri.* I. Further characterization studies of a new virus from the squirrel monkey. *Lab. Animal Care* 19(3):372–77, 1 fig.

Meléndez, Luis B.; Daniel, M. D.; Hunt, R. D.; and García, Felix G. 1968. An apparently new herpesvirus from primary kidney cultures of the squirrel monkey (*Saimiri sciureus*). *Lab. Animal Care* 18(3):374–81.

Meléndez, Luis V.; Daniel, M. D.; Hunt, R. D.; García, F. C.; Fraser, C. E. O.; Jones, T. C.; and Mitus, J. 1971. DNA viruses from South American monkeys: Their significance in the establishment of primate colonies for biomedical research. In: *Defining the laboratory animal.* IV Symposium, International Committee on Laboratory Animals. Washington, D.C.: National Academy of Science.

Meléndez, Luis V.; España, Carlos; Hunt, Ronald D.; Daniel, M. D.; and García, Felix G. 1969. Natural *Herpes simplex* infection in the owl monkey (*Aotus trivirgatus*). *Lab. Animal Care* 19(1):38–45, 5 figs.

Meléndez, Luis V.; Hunt, Ronald D.; Daniel, M. D.; Fraser, C. E. O.; Barahona, H. H.; King, N. W.; and García, Felix G. 1972. *Herpesvirus saimiri* and *ateles*: Their role in malignant lymphomas of monkeys. *Fed. Proc.* 31(6):1643–50.

Meléndez, Luis V.; Hunt, Ronald D.; Daniel, M. D.; García, Felix G.; and Fraser, C. E. O. 1969. *Herpesvirus saimiri.* II. Experimentally induced malignant lymphoma in primates. *Lab. Animal Care* 19(3):378–86, 6 figs.

Meléndez, Luis V.; Hunt, Ronald D.; García, Felix G.; and Trum, Bernard F. 1966. A latent herpes-T infection in *Saimiri sciureus* (squirrel monkey). *Symp. Zool. Soc. London,* no. 17, pp. 393–97, 3 figs.

Melnick, Joseph L. 1973. Classification and nomenclature of viruses. In *Ultrastructure of animal viruses and bacteriophages: An atlas,* ed. A. J. Dalton and F. Haguenau, pp. 1–20. New York: Academic Press.

Melnick, Joseph L.; Midulla, Mario; Wimberly, Ira; Barrera Oro, Julio G.; and Levy, Barnet M. 1964. A new member of the herpesvirus groups isolated from South American marmosets. *J. Immunol.* 92:596–601.

Melnick, Joseph L., Parks, Wade P. 1969. Hepatitis in marmosets: Reply to Deinhardt, Holmes, and Wolfe. *J. Infect. Diseases* 121(3):353–54.

———. 1970. Correspondence: Hepatitis in marmosets. *J. Infect. Diseases* 121(3):353–54.

Menschel, E., and Stroh, R. 1963. Helminthologische Untersuchungen bei pinche Äffchen (*Oedipomidas oedipus*). *Z. Parasitk.* 23:376–83, 7 figs.

Mervis, R. F. 1974. Evidence of color vision in a diurnal prosimian, *Lemur catta. Animal Learn. Behav.* 2:238–40.

Michael, C. R. 1966. Receptive fields of opponent color units in the optic nerve of the ground squirrel. *Science* 152:1095–97.

Michael, Richard P., and Keverne, E. B. 1968. Pheromones in the communication of sexual status in Primates. *Nature* 218:746–49.

———. 1970. Primate sex pheromones of vaginal origin. *Nature* 225:84–85.

Michael, Richard P.; Keverne, E. B.; and Bonsall, R. W. 1971. Pheromones: Isolation of male sex attractants from a female primate. *Science* 172:964–66.

Michael, Richard P.; Wilson, Margo; and Plant, T. M. 1973. Sexual behavior of male primates and the role of testosterone. In *Comparative ecology and behavior of primates.* ed. R. P. Michael and J. H. Crook, pp. 235–313. New York: Academic Press.

Midlo, Charles, and Cummins, Harold. 1942. Palmar and plantar dermatoglyphics in Primates. *Amer. Anat. Mem.,* no. 20, 198 pp., 602 figs.

Mikan, Johann Christian. 1823. *Delectus florae et faunae Brasiliensis.* Vienna: Anthony Strauss, 1820–25. 24 pls., 24 pp. (unnumbered).

Miles, A. E. W., ed. 1967. *Structural and chemical organization of teeth.* Vol. 1. New York: Academic Press, xiv + 525 pp.

Miles, Raymond C. 1957*a*. Delayed-response learning in the marmoset and the macaque. *J. Comp. Phys., Psychol.* 50:352–55, 4 figs.

———. 1957*b*. Learning-set formation in the squirrel monkey. *J. Comp. Phys. Psychol.* 50(4):356–57, 1 fig.

———. 1958*a*. Color vision in the marmoset. *J. Comp. Phys. Psychol.* 51:152–54, 1 fig.

———. 1958*b*. Color vision in the squirrel monkey. *J. Comp. Phys. Psychol.* 51:328–31.

Miles, Raymond C., and Meyer, Donald R. 1956. Learning sets in marmosets. *J. Comp. Phys. Psychol.* 49(3): 219–22, 2 figs.

Miller, Gerrit S., Jr. 1912. *List of North American land mammals. Bull. U.S. Nat. Mus.,* vol. 79; xiv + 455 pp.

———. 1929. Mammals eaten by Indians, owls and Spaniards in the coast region of the Dominican Republic. *Smithsonian Misc. Coll.* 66(13):1–3.

Miller, Leo E. 1916. Field notes. In J. A. Allen, Mammals collected in the Roosevelt Brazilian Expedition, with field notes by Leo F. Miller. *Bull. Amer. Mus. Nat. Hist.* 35:589–610.

Minette, Henri P. 1966. Leptospirosis in primates other than man. *Amer. J. Trop. Med. Hyg.* 15:190–98.

Miraglia, Tulio, and Teixeira, Augusto M. C. 1958. Dados sobre a morfologia, dimensões e relações da hipófise do sagüi (*Callithrix jacchus*). *Univ. da Bahia.* Publ., 7(2), pp. 5–21, 7 figs.

———. 1960. Appunti sulla structura e sulla vascolarizzazione dell'ipofisi del "sagüi" (*Callithrix jacchus*). *Biol. Latina* (Milano), 13:199–218 [not seen].

Miranda Ribeiro, Alipio de. 1912 (1911). Zwei neue Affen unserer Fauna. *Brasilianische Rundschau* 2(1): 21–23, 1 fig.

———. 1924. Alguns factos e mais dois simios novos da nossa fauna. *Bol. Mus. Nac. Rio de Janeiro,* no. 3, pp. 211–15.

———. 1941. Commentaries on South American Primates. *Mem. Inst. Oswaldo Cruz* 35(4):779–851, 18 pls.

Mitchell, Edward. 1970. Pigmentation pattern evolution in delphinid cetaceans: An essay in adaptive coloration. *Canadian J. Zool.* 48(4):717–40, 17 figs.

Mitchell, P. C. 1911. On longevity and relative viability in mammals and birds with a note on the theory of longevity. *Proc. Zool. Soc. London* 1911:425–548.

Mitchell, Sandra J., and Jones, S. M. 1975. Diagnosis of pregnancy in marmosets (*Callithrix jacchus*). *Lab. Animals* 9:49–56, 4 figs.

Mittermeier, Russel A., and Douglass, J. F. 1973. The plight of the lion marmosets. *Lab. Primate Newsl.* 12 (3):12–13.

Mivart, St. George. 1865. Contributions towards a more complete knowledge of the axial skeleton in the primates. *Proc. Zool. Soc. London* 1865:545–92, 13 figs.

———. 1873. On *Lepilemur* and *Cheirogaleus,* and on the zoological rank of the Lemuroidea. *Proc. Zool. Soc. London* 1873:484–510, 18 figs., pl. 43.

———. 1874. *Man and apes.* New York: Appleton, vii + 200 pp., 61 figs., frontispiece.

Molin, R. 1858. Versuch einer Monographie der Filarien. Sitzungsber. Akad. Wiss., Wien, Math.-Nat. Cl., 28: 365–461.

Mollison, Theodore, 1911. Die Körperproportionen der Primaten. *Gegenbaurs Morph. Jahrb.* 42:79–304, 91 figs.

Montagna, William. 1962. *The structure and function of skin.* New York: Academic Press, xi + 454, illus.

———. 1972. The skin of nonhuman primates. *Amer. Zool.* 12, pp. 109–24, 24 figs.

Montagna, William, and Ellis, Richard A. 1958*a*. *The biology of hair growth.* New York: Academic Press, xvii + 520 pp. illus.

———. 1958*b*. The vascularity and innervation of human hair follicles. In *The biology of hair growth,* ed. W. Montagna and R. A. Ellis, pp. 219–27, 10 figs. New York: Academic Press.

Montagna, William, and H. Machida. 1966. The skin of primates. XXXII. The Philippine tarsier (*Tarsius syrichta*). *Amer. J. Phys. Anthrop.* 25(1):71–84, 4 pls.

Moojen, João. 1950. Sobre *"Callithrix Aurita"* (E. Geoffroy, 1812) (Callithricidae, Primates). *Rev. Brasil. Biol.* 10(4):501–2.

Moore, Carl R. 1924. Properties of the gonads as controllers of somatic and psychical characteristics. VIII. Heat application and testicular degeneration: The function of the scrotum. *Amer. J. Anat.* 35:337–58, 5 figs.

———. 1926. The biology of the mammalian testis and scrotum. *Quart. Rev. Biol.* 1:4–50, 8 figs.

Moore, Carl R., and Chase, H. D. 1923. Heat applications and testicular degeneration. *Anat. Rec.* 26: 344–45.

Moore, Carl R., and Oslund, Robert. 1923. Experimental studies on sheep testes. *Anat. Rec.* 26:343–44.

Moore Carl R., and Quick, Wm. J. 1923. A comparison of scrotal and peritoneal temperatures. *Anat. Rec.* 26: 344.

Moreland, Alvin F. 1970. Tuberculosis in New World primates. *Lab. Animal Care* 20(2[pt. 1]):262–68.

Morrison, Peter, and Middleton, Elizabeth H. 1967. Body temperature and metabolism in the pygmy marmoset. *Folia Primat.* 6:70–82.

Morrison, Peter, and Simões, J., Jr. 1962. Body temperatures in two Brazilian primates. *Bol. Fac. Fil. Cien. Letr. Univ. São Paulo, no. 261, Zool.* no. 24, pp. 167–78.

Morton, Dudley J. 1924. Evolution of the human foot. *Amer. J. Phys. Anthrop.* 7(1):1–52, 25 figs.

———. 1935. *The human foot: Its evolution, physiology and functional disorders.* New York: Columbia University Press, xii + 244 pp., 100 figs.

———. 1952. *Human locomotion and body form.* Baltimore: Williams and Wilkins, xii + 285 pp., 82 figs.

Moss, Melvin L. 1968. Functional cranial analysis of mammalian mandibular ramal morphology. *Acta Anat.* 71(3):423–47.

Moss, Melvin L., and Young, Richard W. 1960. A functional approach to craniology. *Amer. J. Phys. Anthrop.* 18:281–92.

Mott, F.; Schuster, W. E.; and Halliburton, W. D. 1909. Cortical lamination and localization in the brain of the marmoset. *Proc. Roy. Soc. London,* ser. B, 82:124–33, 17 figs., pls. 6, 7.

Moynihan, M. 1964. Some behavior patterns of platyrrhine monkeys. I. The night monkey (*Aotus trivirgatus*). *Smithsonian Misc. Coll.,* 146(5):iv +84 pp., 22 figs.

———. 1970. Some behavior patterns of Platyrhhine monkeys. II. *Saguinus geoffroyi* and some other tamarins. Smith. Contr. Zool., no. 28, iv, 1–77 pp., figs.

Mullin, S. W., and Orihel, T. C. 1972. *Tetrapetalonema dunni* sp. nov. (Nematoda: Filarioidea) from Malaysian tree shrews. *J. Parasit.* 58(6):1047–51, 6 figs.

Murphy, B. L.; Maynard, J. E.; Krushak, D. H.; and Berquist, K. R. 1972. Microbial flora of imported marmosets: Viruses and enteric bacteria. *Lab. Animal Sci.* 22(3):339–43.

Murray, Raymond G.; Jones, Arthur E.; and Murray, Assia. 1973. Fine structure of photoreceptors in the owl monkey. *Anat. Rec.* 175(4):673–78, 8 pls.

Muybridge, Eadweard. 1887. *Animal locomotion: An electro-photographic investigation of consecutive phases of animal progressive movements.* x + 264 pp., 95 pls. Philadelphia: J. B. Lippincott Co.; London: Chapman and Hall (3d impression, 1907).

Myers, Betty J. 1972. Ectrinococcosis, coenurosis, cysticercosis, sparganosis, etc. In *Pathology of simian primates,* ed. R. N. T.-W. Fiennes, 2:124–43, 5 figs. Basel: S. Karger.

Napier, John R. 1960. Studies of the hands of living primates. *Proc. Zool. Soc. London* 134:647–57, 3 figs. 3 pls.

———. 1961. Prehensibility and opposability in the hands of Primates. *Symp. Zool. Soc. London,* no. 5, pp. 115–32, 7 figs., 1 pl.

———. 1963. Brachiation and brachiators. *Symp. Zool. Soc. London,* no. 10, pp. 183–95, 3 figs.

———. 1967. Evolutionary aspects of primate locomotion. *Amer. J. Phys. Anthrop.* 37:333–42, 4 figs.

Napier, John R., and Napier, P. H. 1967. *A handbook of living primates.* New York: Academic Press, xiv + 456 pp., 10 figs., 114 pls.

Napier, John R., and Walker, A. C. 1967*a*. Vertical clinging and leaping: A newly recognized category of locomotor behaviour of primates. *Folia Primat.* 6(3/4): 204–19, 4 figs.

———. 1967*b*. Vertical clinging and leaping in fossil primates. In *Progress in Primatology,* ed. D. Starck, R. Schneider, and H.-J. Kuhn, pp. 66–69, 2 figs., 1 pl. Stuttgart: Gustav Fischer.

Naumberg, Elsie M. B. 1935. Gazetteer and maps showing stations visited by Emil Kaempfer in eastern Brazil and Paraguay. *Bull. Amer. Mus. Nat. Hist.* 68:449–70, 26 pls., 2 maps.

Negus, V. E. 1949. *The comparative anatomy and physiology of the larynx.* New York: Grune and Stratton, xix + 230 pp., 191 figs.

Neill, P. 1829. Art. III. Account of the habits of a specimen of the *Simia jacchus,* Lin., or *Jacchus vulgaris,* Geoff., now in the possession of Gavin Milroy, Esq., Edinburgh, Communicated by Neill, Esq., etc., *Mag. Nat. Hist., J. Zool., Bot., Mineral., Geol., Meterol.* 1:18–20.

Nelson, Bill.; Cosgrove, G. E.; and Gengozian, N. 1966. Diseases of an imported primate *Tamarinus nigricollis. Lab. Animal Care* 16(3):255–75.

Nelson, T. W. 1975. Quantitative observations on feeding behavior *Saguinus geoffroyi* (Callithricidae, Primates). *Primates* 16(2):223–26.

Nery-Guimarães, F.; Franken, A. J.; and Chagas, W. A. 1971. Toxoplasmose em Primatas não humanos I. Infecção naturais em *Macaca mulatta* e *Cebus apella. Mem. Inst. Oswaldo Cruz (Rio de Janeiro)* 6(2):77–96.

Niemitz, Carsten. 1974. A contribution to the postnatal behavioral development of *Tarsius bancanus,* Horsfield, 1821, studied in two cases. *Folia Primat.* 21, (3/4):250–76, 9 figs.

Nissen, Henry W., and Riesen, A. H. 1964. The eruption of the permanent dentition of the chimpanzee. *Amer. J. Phys. Anthrop.* 22(3):285–94.

Noback, Charles R. 1951. Morphology and phylogeny of hair. *Ann. N.Y. Acad. Sci.* 53(3):476–92, 24 figs.

———. 1959. The heritage of the human brain. *James Arthur Lecture on the evolution of the human brain, 1959. Amer. Mus. Nat. Hist.,* 30 pp., 6 figs.

Noback, Charles R., and Moskowitz, N. 1962. Structural and functional correlates of "encephalization" in the primate brain. *Ann. N.Y. Acad. Sci.* 102:210–18.

———. 1963. The primate nervous system: Functional and structural aspects in phylogeny. In *Evolutionary and genetic biology of primates,* ed. John Buettner-Janusch, 1:131–77, 12 figs. New York: Academic Press.

Noback, Charles R., and Shriver, J. E. 1966. Phylogenetic and ontogenetic aspects of the lemniscal systems and pyramidal system. In *Evolution of the forebrain,* ed. R. Hassler and H. Stephan, pp. 316–25, 2 figs. New York: Plenum Press.

Nouvel, J. 1954. Spirochetoses des animaux sauvages. *Mammalia* 18(1):112–23.

Nuttall, George H. F.; Warburton, Cecil; Cooper, W. F. and Robinson, L. E. 1908–15. *Ticks: A monograph of the Ixodoidea.* Vol. 1. 550 pp., 450 figs., 13 pls. New York: Cambridge University Press.

Nuttall, George H. F.; Warburton, C.; and Robinson, L. E. 1911–26. *Ticks: A monograph of the Ixodoidea.* Vol. 2. 302 + 62 + 30 pp., 130 figs., 7 pls. New York: Cambridge University Press.

Olivier, Georges; Libersa, Claude; and Fenart, Raphaël. 1955. Le crâne du Semnopitheque. *Mammalia* 19(1): 1–292, 161 figs., 1 plate.

Ordy, J. M., and Keefe, J. R. 1965. Visual acuity and retinal specialization in primates: A comparison of the transitional primate tree shrew with the clinical rhesus monkey. *Anat. Rec.* 151:394.

Orihel, Thomas C., and Seibold, Herman R. 1971. Trichospirurosis in South American monkeys. *J. Parasit.* 57(6):1366–68, 1 fig.

———. 1972. Nematodes of the bowel and tissues. In *Pathology of simian primates,* ed. R. N. T.-W. Fiennes, 2:76–103. Basel: S. Karger.

Osborn, Henry Fairfield. 1888*a*. The evolution of mammalian molars to and from the tritubercular type. *Amer. Nat.* 22:1067–79, 1 fig.

———. 1888*b*. The nomenclature of the mammalian molar cusps. *Amer. Nat.* 22:926–28.

———. 1888*c*. On the structure and classification of the Mesozoic Mammalia. *J. Acad. Nat. Sci. Philadelphia* 9:186–265.

———. 1893. Recent researches upon the succession of teeth in mammals. *Amer. Nat.* 27:493–508.

———. 1895. The history of the cusps of the human molar teeth. *Int. Dental J.* 1895:1–26, 1 pl.

———. 1897. Trituberculy: A review dedicated to the late Professor Cope. *Amer. Nat.* 31:993–1016.

———. 1907. *Evolution of mammalian molar teeth to and from the triangular type.* Ed. W. K. Gregory. New York: Macmillan Co., ix + 250 pp., 215 figs.

Osborn, Rosalie M. 1963. Observations on the behaviour of the mountain gorilla. *Symp. Zool. Soc. London,* no. 10, pp. 29–37.

Osman Hill. *See* Hill, W. C. Osman

Ottaviani, G.; Di Dio, L. J. A.; and Manfredonia, M. 1958. Primeiras cbservaçoes bio-anatômicas sôbre o sistema linfático de alguns símios. *Anais Fac. Med. Univ. Minas Gerais* 18:173–78.

———. 1959. Prime osservazioni bioanatomiche sul sistema linfatico di alcune Scimmie. *L'Anteneo Parmense* 30(6):843–47.

Owen, R. 1859. On the orang, chimpanzee and gorilla. Appendix B, pp. 64–103. In *On the classification and geographical distribution of the Mammalia.* Cambridge University Press (Reade Lecture, Cambridge, May 1859). London: Parker.

Oxnard, Charles E. 1957. The maxillary nerve in the Ceboidea. *Proc. Zool. Soc. London* 128:113–17.

———. 1963. Locomotor adaptation in the primitive forelimb. *Symp. Zool. Soc. London,* no. 10:165–82, 12 figs.

———. 1967*a*. Aspects of the mechanical efficiency of the scapula in some primates. *Anat. Rec.* 157:296.

———. 1967*b*. The functional morphology of the primate shoulder as revealed by comparative anatomical, osteometric, and discriminant function techniques. *Amer. J. Phys. Anthrop.* 26:219–40, 9 figs.

———. 1968*a*. The architecture of the shoulder in some mammals. *J. Morph.* 126:249–90, 13 figs.

———. 1968*b*. Primate evolution: A method of investigations. *Amer. J. Phys. Anthrop.* 78:289–302.

———. 1969. Evolution of the human shoulder: Some possible pathways. *Amer. J. Phys. Anthrop.* 30(3): 319–32, 3 figs.

Oxnard, Charles E., and Neely, Peter M. 1969. The descriptive use of neighborhood limited classification in functional morphology: An analysis of the shoulder in primates. *J. Morph.* 129(2):127–48, 6 figs.

Pallas, P. S. 1781. Nachricht über ein Paar americanische Sagoinchen (*Simia Iacchus*) welche in St. Petersburg ihr Geschlecht fortgepflanzt haben. *Neue Nordische Beyträge* 2:41–47.

Papez, James W. 1929. *Comparative neurology.* New York: Thomas Y. Crowell Co., xxv + 518 pp., 315 figs.

Pařizek, J., and Varačka, M. 1967. Geherknöchelchen bei Makaken. *Z. Morph. Anthrop.* 58(2):190–98.

Parks, Wade P., and Melnick, Joseph L. 1969. Attempted isolation of hepatitis virus in marmosets. *J. Infect. Diseases* 120:539–47.

Parks, Wade P.; Melnick, Joseph L.; Voss, William R.; Singer, Don B.; Rosenberg, Harvey S.; Alcott, Judith; and Casazza, Anna M. 1969. Characterization of marmoset hepatitis virus. *J. Infect. Diseases* 120(5): 548–59.

Patterson, Bryan. 1956. Early Cretaceous mammals and the evolution of mammalian molar teeth. *Fieldiana: Geol.* 13:1–107, 17 illus.

Patterson, Bryan, and Pascual, Rosendo. 1972. The fossil mammal fauna of South America. In *Evolution, mammals, and southern continents,* ed. A. Keast, F. C. Erk, and B. Glass, pp. 247–309, 13 figs. Albany: State University of New York Press.

Paulli, Simon. 1899–1900. Über die Pneumaticitat des Schädels bei den Säugethieren. *Gegenbauer's Morph. Jahrb.* vol. 28, pt. I, pp. 147–78, 16 figs., pl. 7; pt. II, pp. 179–251, 44 figs., pls. 8–14; pt. III, pp. 483–564, 36 figs., pls. 27–29.

Pearson, Oliver P. 1962. Survival value of vibrissae. *J. Mammal.* 43(1):105–6.

Peden, James K., and Bonin, Gerhardt von. 1947. The neocortex of *Hapale. J. Comp. Neurol.* 86(1):37–93, 15 figs.

Pehrsen, Torsten. 1914. Beiträge zur Kenntnis der äusseren weiblichen Genitalien bei Affen, Halbaffen und Insectivoren. *Anat. Anz.* 46:161–79, 14 figs.

Pelzeln, August von. 1883. Brasilische Säugethiere: Resultate von Johann Natterer's Reisen in den Jahren 1817 bis 1835. *Verh. K. K. Zool.-bot. Gesellsch., Beih.* 33:1–140.

Peralta, P. H., and Shelokov, A. 1966. Isolation and characterization of arboviruses from Almirante, Republic of Panama. *Amer. J. Trop. Med. Hyg.* 15:369–78.

Perkins, Edwin M., Jr. 1966. The skin of primates. XXXI. The skin of the black-collared tamarin (*Tamarinus nigricollis*). *Amer. J. Phys. Anthrop.*, n.s., 25(1): 41–69, 20 figs.

———. 1968. The skin of primates. XXXVI. The skin of the pygmy marmoset—*Callithrix* (= *Cebuella*) *pygmaea. Amer. J. Phys. Anthrop.* 29(3):349–64, 11 figs.

———. 1969*a*. The skin of primates. XL. The skin of the cottontop pinché *Saguinus* (= *Oedipomidas*) *oedipus. Amer. J. Phys. Anthrop.* 30(1):13–28, 5 pls.

———. 1969*b*. The skin of primates. XXIV. The skin of Goeldi's marmoset (*Callimico goeldii*). *Amer. J. Phys. Anthrop.* 30:231–50.

———. 1969*c*. The skin of primates. XLI. The skin of the silver marmoset—*Callithrix* (= *Mico*) *argentata. Amer. J. Phys. Anthrop.* 30:361–88.

Perrin, William F. 1970. Color patterns of the eastern Pacific spotted porpoise (*Stenella graffmani* Lönnberg) (Cetacea, Delphinidae). *Zoologica* 54(4):135–41, 3 figs. 7 pls.

———. 1972. Color patterns of spinner porpoises (*Stenella* cf. *S. longirostris*) of the eastern Pacific and Hawaii with comments on delphinid pigmentation. *Fishery Bull.* 70(3):983–1003, 27 figs.

Perry, John. 1971. The golden lion marmoset. *Oryx* 11: 22–24, pl.

Petter, Jean Jacques. 1962. Recherches sur l'écologie et l'éthologie des lémuriens malgaches. *Mém. Mus. Nat. Hist. Nat. (A) Zool.* 27(1):1–146, 26 pls., 10 figs.

———. 1965. The lemurs of Madagascar. In *Primate behavior: Field studies of monkeys and apes,* ed. Irvin Devore. pp. 292–319, 9 figs. New York, Holt, Rinehart, and Winston.

Petter, Jean Jacques, and Peyrieras, A. 1970*a*. Nouvelle contribution ou l'étude d'un lemurien malgache, le ayeaye (*Daubentonia madagascariensis* E. Geoffroy). *Mammalia* 34(2):167–93, 5 figs.

———. 1970*b*. Observatiôns eco-ethologiques sur les lemuriens malgaches du genre *Hapalemur. Terre et Vie* 117(3):356–82.

Petter-Rousseaux, A. 1962. Recherches sur la biologie de la reproduction des primates inférieurs. *Mammalia* 26 (suppl. 1):1–88, 27 figs., 7 pls.

———. 1964. Reproductive physiology and behaviour of the Lemuroidea. In *Evolutionary and genetic biology of primates,* ed. J. Buettner-Janusch. 2:91–132, 17 figs. New York: Academic Press.

Phillips, I. R. 1975. Macaque and marmoset monkeys as animal models for the study of birth defects. Breeding simians for developmental biology. *Lab. Animal Handbook* 6:293–302, 4 figs.

Pinkerton, Mary. 1972. *Spirocheta, Spirillum, Leptospira.* In *Pathology of simian primates,* ed. R. N. T.-W. Fiennes, 2:243–54. Basel: S. Karger.

Pinkus, Hermann. 1958. Embryology of hair. In *The biology of hair growth,* ed. William Montagna and Richard A. Ellis, pp. 1–32, 50 figs. New York: Academic Press.

Pinto, R. Magalhaes. 1970. Ocorrencia de *Subulura jacchi* (Marcel, 1857) Railliet & Henry, 1913 (Nematoda, Subuluroidea) em novo hospedeiro: *Callithrix aurita coelestis* (M. Ribeiro, 1924). *Atas. Soc. Biol. Rio de Janeiro* 13(3/4):143–45, 6 figs.

Pirie, Antoinette. 1959. Crystals of riboflavin making up the tapetum lucidum in the eye of a lemur. *Nature* 183 (4666):985–86, 3 figs.

Plimmer, H. 1912. On certain blood parasites. *J. Roy. Micr. Soc.*, ser. 2, 2:133–50.

Po-Chedley, D. S., and Shadle, A. R. 1955. Pelage of the porcupine *Erethizon dorsatum dorsatum*. *J. Mammal.* 36:84–94, 1 fig.

Pocock, Reginald I. 1911. On the palatability of some British insects, with notes on the significance of mimetic resemblances. *Proc. Zool. Soc. London* 1911:809–64.

———. 1914*a*. On the facial vibrissae of mammalia. *Proc. Zool. Soc. London* 1914:889–912, 13 figs.

———. 1914*b*. On the feet and other external features of the Canidae and Ursidae. *Proc. Zool. Soc. London* 1914:913–41, 13 figs.

———. 1917. The genera of Hapalidae (Marmosets). *Ann. Mag. Nat. Hist.*, ser. 8, 20:247–58, 2 figs.

———. 1918. On the external characters of the lemurs and of *Tarsius*. *Proc. Zool. Soc. London* 1918:19–53, 16 figs.

———. 1920. On the external characters of the South American monkeys. *Proc. Zool. Soc. London* 1920: 91–113.

———. 1921*a*. The external characters and classification of the Procyonidae. *Proc. Zool. Soc. London* 1921: 389–422, 13 figs.

———. 1921*b*. On the external characters and classification of the Mustelidae. *Proc. Zool. Soc. London* 1921: 803–37, figs. 27–39.

———. 1922*a*. On the external characters of some hystrichomorph rodents. *Proc. Zool. Soc. London* 1922: 365–427, 28 figs.

———. 1922*b*. On the external characters of the beaver (Castoridae) and of some squirrels (Sciuridae). *Proc. Zool. Soc. London* 1922:1171–1212, figs. 38–60.

———. 1923*a*. On the external characters of *Elaphurus, Hydropotes, Pudu,* and other Cervidae. *Proc. Zool. Soc. London* 1923:181–207, figs. 2–17.

———. 1923*b*. The external characters of the pygmy hippopotamus (*Choeropsis liberiensis*) and of the Suidae and Camelidae. *Proc. Zool. Soc. London* 1923: 531–49, figs. 30–46.

———. 1924. The external characters of the South American edentates. *Proc. Zool. Soc. London* 1924: 983–1031, figs. 14–37.

———. 1925*a*. Additional notes on the external characters of some platyrrhine monkeys. *Proc. Zool. Soc. London* 1925:27–47, 12 figs.

———. 1925*b*. The external characters of the lagomorph rodents. *Proc. Zool. Soc. London* 1925:669–700, 18 figs.

———. 1925*c*. The external characters of the catarrhine monkeys and apes. *Proc. Zool. Soc. London* 1925: 1479–1579, 81 figs.

———. 1926*a*. The external characters of the Jamaican hutia (*Capromys brownii*). *Proc. Zool. Soc. London* 1926:413–18, figs. 13–15.

———. 1926*b*. The external characters of *Thylacinus, Sarcophilus,* and some related marsupials. *Proc. Zool. Soc. London* 1926:1037–1084, figs. 24–49.

———. 1926*c*. The external characters of the Patagonian weasel (*Lyncodon patagonicus*). *Proc. Zool. Soc. London* 1926:1085–94, 5 figs.

———. 1927. The external characters of a bush dog (*Speothos venaticus*) and of a maned wolf (*Chrysocyon brachyurus*), exhibited in the Society's Gardens. *Proc. Zool. Soc. London* 1927:307–21, 10 figs.

Poeppig, Edward. 1832. Naturhistorische Reiseberichte. *Froriep Not. Gebiete Nat.-Heilk.* 33(711):97–106.

Pohle, Hermann. 1927. Über die von Prof. Bresslau in Brasilian gessammelten Säugetiere (ausser den Nagetieren). *Avh. Senckenb. Naturf. Gesellsch.* 40:239–47.

Pola, Yvonne B., and Snowdon, Charles T. 1975. The vocalizations of pygmy marmosets (*Cebuella pygmaea*). *Animal Behaviour* 23(4):826–42, 27 figs.

Polyak, S. 1957. *The vertebrate visual system.* Chicago: University of Chicago Press, v + 1300 pp., 546 figs.

Pook, A. George. 1974. The hand-rearing and reintroduction to its parents of a saddleback tamarin. *Jersey Wildl. Preserv. Trust, 11th Ann. Rep. (1974),* pp. 35–39.

Poole, D. F. G. 1967. Phylogeny of tooth tissues: Enameloid and enamel in recent vertebrates, with a note on the history of cementum. In *Structural and chemical organization of teeth,* ed. A. E. W. Miles, 1:111–49, 40 figs. New York: Academic Press.

Pope, Betty Locker. 1966. Some parasites of the howler monkey of northern Argentina. *J. Parasit.* 52:166–68.

Porter, James A., Jr. 1972. Parasites of marmosets. *Lab. Animal Sci.* 22(4):503–6.

Porter, James A., Jr.; Johnson, Carl M.; and Sousa, L. de. 1966. Prevalence of malaria in Panamanian primates. *J. Parasit.* 52(4):669–70.

Porter, James A., Jr., and Young, M. D. 1967. The transfer of *Plasmodium falciparum* from man to the marmoset, *Saguinus geoffroyi, J. Parasit.* 53(4):845–46.

———. 1970. *Plasmodium vivax* infections in the spider monkeys, *Ateles fusciceps* and *A. geoffroyi. J. Parasit.* 56:426–30.

Porter, R. P., and Gengozian, N. 1969. Immunological tolerance and rejection of skin allografts in the marmoset. *Transplantation* 8(5):653–65.

———. 1973. Marmoset bone marrow. In *Tissue culture,* ed. P. K. Krause and M. K. Patterson, chapt. 13, pp. 93–97. New York: Academic Press.

Portmann, Adolph. 1952. *Animal forms and patterns: A study of the appearance of animals.* London: Faber and Faber, 254 pp., illus. (Reprinted; New York: Schocken Books, 1967.)

Poswillo, D. E.; Hamilton, W. J.; and Sopher, D. 1972. The marmoset as an animal model for teratological research. *Nature* 239:460–62, 3 figs.

Powers, J. Bradley, and Winans, Sarah H. 1975. Vomeronasal organ: Critical role in mediating sexual behavior of the male hamster. *Science* 187:961–63.

Premvati. 1959. Studies on *Strongyloides* of primates. V. Synonymy of the species in monkeys and apes. *Canadian J. Zool.* 37(1):75–82.

Preslock, James P.; Hampton, Suzanne H., and Hampton, John K., Jr. 1973. Cyclic variation of serum progestins and immunerative estrogen in marmoets. *Endocrinology* 92(4) 1096–1101, 3 figs.

Prost, J. H. 1965. The methodology of gait analysis and gaits of monkeys. *Amer. J. Phys. Anthrop.* 23(3):215–40, 6 figs.

———. 1967. Bipedalism of man and gibbon compared using estimates of joint motion. *Amer. J. Phys. Anthrop.* 26(2):135–48.

Prota, Giuseppe. 1972. Structure and biogenesis of phaeomelanins. In *Pigmentation: Its genesis and biologic control,* ed. Vernon Riley, pp. 615–30. New York: Appleton-Century-Crofts.

Prota, Giuseppe, and Nicolaus, Rodolfo Alessandro. 1967. On the biogenesis of phaeomelanins. In *Biology of skin.* Vol. 8. *The pigmentary system,* ed. W. Montagna and Funan Hu, pp. 323–28, 2 figs. New York: Pergamon Press.

Rabb, George, and Rowell, James E. 1960. Notes on reproduction in captive marmosets. *J. Mammal.* 41:401.

Rabin, Harvey. 1971. Assay and pathogenesis of oncogenic viruses in nonhuman primates. *Lab. Animal Sci.* 21(6 [pt. 2]):1032–49.

———. (ed.). 1974. Studies on experimental lymphomas induced by *Herpesvirus saimiri* in nonhuman primates. *J. Med. Primat.* 3(1):1–88.

Radinsky, Leonard B. 1968. Evolution of somatic sensory specialization in otter brains. *J. Comp. Neurol.* 134(4): 495–506, 6 figs.

———. 1972. Endocasts and studies of primate brain evolution. In *The functional and evolutionary biology of Primates,* ed. R. Tuttle, pp. 175–84, 3 figs. Chicago: Aldine-Atherton.

Rahaman, H., and Parthasarathy, M. D. 1969. Studies on the social behaviour of bonnet monkeys. *Primates* 10: 149–62.

Rand, Austin L. 1935. On the habits of some Madagascar mammals. *J. Mammal* 16(2):89–104.

———. 1937. Some original observations on the habits of *Dactylopsila trivirgatus* Gray. *Amer. Mus. Novit.,* no. 957, pp. 1–7.

Ray, John. 1693. *Synopsis methodica animalium quadrupedum et serpentini generis.* London, 336 pp.

Regan, C. Tate. 1930. The evolution of the primates. *Ann. Mag. Nat. Hist., ser.* 10, 6:383–92.

Reichenbach, H. G. Ludwig. 1862. *Die vollständigste Naturgeschichte der Affen.* Dresden and Leipzig, 204 pp., 495 figs.

Remane, Adolph. 1956. Paläontologie und Evolution der Primaten. In *Primatologie,* ed. H. Hofer, A. H. Schultz, and D. Starck, 1:267–378, 69 figs. Basel: S. Karger.

———. 1960. Zähne und Gebiss. In *Primatologie,* ed. H. Hofer, A. H. Schultz, and D. Starck, 3(2):637–846, 142 figs. Basel: S. Karger.

———. 1961. Probleme der Systematik der Primaten. *Z. Wiss. Zool.* 165(1/2):1–34, 6 figs.

Renjifo, Santiago; Sanmartín, Carlos; and Zulueta, Julián de. 1952. A survey of the blood parasites of vertebrates in eastern Columbia [*sic*]. *Acta Tropica* 9(2):151–69, 25 figs.

Reynolds, Vernon, and Reynolds, Frances. 1965. Chimpanzees of the Budongo forest. In *Primate behavior: Field studies of monkeys and apes,* ed. Irven DeVore, pp. 368–424, 11 figs. New York: Holt, Rinehart and Winston.

Riesenfeld, Alphonse. 1969. The adaptive mandible: An experimental study. *Acta Anat.* 72(2):246–62.

———. 1970. Body posture and litter size. *Acta Anat.* 76:90–101.

Ripley, Suzanne. 1967. The leaping of langurs: A problem in the study of locomotor adaptation. *Amer. J. Phys. Anthrop.* 26(2):149–70, 12 figs.

Roberts, David. 1974. Structure and function of the primate scapula. In *Primate locomotion,* ed. F. A. Jenkins, Jr., pp. 171–200, 15 figs. New York: Academic Press.

Robinson, M. H. 1966. Anti-predator adaptations in stick- and leaf-mimicking insects. *Animal Behav.* 14(4): 587–88 (abstr.)

Rode, Paul. 1938. Catalogue des types de mammifères du Muséum National d'Histoire Naturelle. I. Ordre des Primates. A. - Sous-ordre des simiens. *Bull. Mus. Nat. Hist. Nat., Paris, ser.* 2 10(3):202–51.

Rode, Paul, and Hershkovitz, Philip. 1945. Designation d'un lectotype de *Callithrix penicillatus* [sic] (E. Geoffrey). *Bull. Mus. Nat. Hist. Nat., Paris,* ser. 2, 17(3): 221–22.

Rodríguez López-Neyra, Carlos. 1956. Revisión de la superfamilia Filarioidea (Weinland, 1858). *Rev. Iberica Parasit,* 16(1–2):3–212, 41 figs.

———. 1957. Revisión de la superfamilia Filarioidea. *Rev. Iberica Parasit.* 17(3):169–276.

Rohen, J. W. 1962. Sehorgan. *Primatologia* 2(1), Lief. 6, pp. 1–210, 69 figs.

Rohen, J. W., and Castenholz, A. 1967 (1966). Über die centralisation der Retina bei Primaten. *Folia Primat.* 5:92–147, 10 figs.

Rolle, (Lady). 1835. Note on the rearing of a jacchus monkey (*Jacchus penicillatus* Geoff.). *Proc. Zool. Soc. London* 1835:21.

Romaña, C. 1932. Hemoparásitos hallados en el sur del Chaco en monos caraya (*Alouatta caraya* Humb.). *7me Reunión Soc. Argent. Path. Reg. N.,* p. 1008 [work not seen, cited from Yamashita, 1963, *Primates,* 4: 41–2].

Romer, A. S. 1966. *Vertebrate paleontology,* 3d ed. Chicago: University of Chicago Press. viii+468 pp., 443 figs.

Roney, Ernest E., Jr. 1975. Golden lion marmosets at San Antonio Zoo. *Amer. Assoc. Zool. Parks, Aquariums* 16(4):15.

Röse, C. 1892. Über die Entstehung un Formataenderungen der menschlichen Molaren. *Anat. Anz.* 7:392–421.

Rose, M. D. 1974*a*. Postural adaptations in New and Old World monkeys. *Primate Locomotion,* ed. F. A. Jenkins, Jr., pp. 201–22. New York: Academic Press.

———. 1974*b*. Ischial tuberosities and ischial callosities. *Amer. J. Phys. Anthrop.* 40:375–84, 3 figs.

Rosenblum, Leonard A. 1972. Mother-infant relations and early behavioral development in the squirrel monkey. In *The squirrel monkey,* ed. L. H. Rosenblum and R. W. Cooper, pp. 207–33, 19 figs. New York: Academic Press.

Rosenblum, L. A.; Nathan, T.; Nelson, J.; and Kaufman, I. C. 1967. Vaginal cornification in the squirrel monkey (*Saimiri sciurea*). *Folia Primat.* 6:83–91. 3 figs.

Roth, Harold H. 1960. Beobachtungen an *Tamarin* sp. *Zool. Gart.* 25(4):166–82, 7 figs. (1–3 in 2 col. pls.).

Rothe, Hartmut. 1971. Some remarks on the spontaneous use of the hand in the common marmoset (*Callithrix jacchus*). *Proc. 3rd Int. Congr. Primat., Zürich* (1970) 3:136–41. Basel: S. Karger.

———. 1972. Beobachtungen zum Bewegungsverhalten des Weissbüscheläffschens *Callithrix jacchus* Erxleben, 1777, mit besonderer Berücksichtigung der Handfunktion. *Z. Morph. Anthrop.* 64(1):90–101, 6 figs.

———. 1973*a*. Handedness in the common marmoset (*Callithrix jacchus*). *Amer. J. Phys. Anthrop.* 38(2): 561–66.

———. 1973*b*. Beobachtungen zur Geburt beim Weissbüscheläffschen (*Callithrix jacchus* Erxleben, 1777). *Folia Primat.* 19:257–85, 5 figs.

———. 1974*a*. Further observations on the delivery behaviour of the common marmoset. *Zeitschr. Säuget* 39: 135–42, 7 figs.

———. 1974*b*. Allogrooming by adult *Callithrix jacchus* in relation to postpartum oestrus. *J. Human Evolution* 3:535–40.

———. 1975*a*. Some aspects of sexuality and reproduction in groups of captive marmosets (*Callithrix jacchus*). *Zeitschr. Tierpsychol.* 37:255–73.

———. 1975*b*. Influence of newborn marmosets' (*Callithrix jacchus*) behaviour on expression and efficiency of maternal and paternal care. *5th Int. Congr. Primat., Nagoya 1974,* pp. 315–20, 1 fig.

———. 1975*c*. Beobachtungen, Analysen und Experimente zum Handgebrauch von *Callithrix jacchus* Erxleben, 1777. *Gegenbaurs Morph Jahrb.* 121(3):310–39, figs. 1–9; (4):353–88, figs. 10–19.

Rothschild, M. 1944. Pelage change of the stoat, *Mustela erminea* L. *Nature* 154:180–81.

Rothschild, M., and Lane, C. 1957. Note on change of pelage in the stoat (*Mustela erminea*). *Proc. Zool. Soc. London* 128:602.

Ruch, Theodore C. 1959. *Diseases of laboratory primates.* W. B. Saunders Co. Philadelphia, xxi + 600 pp., illus.

Ruge, Georg. 1887. *Untersuchungen über die Gesichtsmuskulatur der Primaten.* Leipzig, 130 pp., 8 pls.

Ruibal, Rodolfo. 1957. The evolution of the scrotum. *Evolution* 11(3):376–78.

Ruschi, Augusto, 1964. Macacos do Estado do Espírito Santo. *Bol. Mus. Biol. "Prof. Mello Leitao"* (Santa Teresa, Brazil), *Zool.,* no. 23A; 23 pp.

———. 1965. Lista dos mamíferos do Estado do Espírito Santo. *Bol. Mus. Biol. "Prof. Mello-Leitão," Zool.* 24*a*: 1–48.

Russell, A. E., and Zuckerman, Solly. 1935. A "sexual skin" in a marmoset. *J. Anat.* 69:356–62, 2 figs. 1 pl.

Ryan, K. J.; Benirschke, K.; and Smith, O. W. 1961. Conversion of androsenedione-4-C to estrone by the marmoset placenta. *Endocrinology* 69(3):613–18.

Saban, Roger. 1952. L'os temporal des singes anthropomorphs. *Ann. Sci. Nat. Zool.* 14(1952):25–76.

———. 1956–57. Les affinités du genre *Tupaia* Raffles 1821, d'après les caractères morphologiques de la tête osseuse. *Ann. Paleo.* 42:169–224; 43:1–44, 41 figs.

———. 1963. Contribution à l'étude de l'os temporal des Primates. Description chez l'homme et les prosimiens. Anatomie comparée et phylogénie. *Mem. Mus. Nat. Hist. Nat.,* ser. A, *Zool.,* 29:378 pp., 84 figs., 30 pl.

———. 1964. Sur la pneumatization de l'os temporal des primates adultes et sur development ontogenique chez le gênre *Alouatta* (Platyrrhini). *Morph. Jahrb.* 106 (4):569–93, 3 figs., 5 pls.

Saban, Roger; Khunson, X.; and Chawaf, R. 1967. La musculature intrinsèque de la langue chez les primates. In *Progress in primatology,* ed. D. Starck, R. Schneider, and H. J. Kuhn, pp. 90–107, 22 figs. Basel: S. Karger.

Sadleir, R. M. F. S. 1969. *The ecology of reproduction in wild and domestic mammals.* London: Methuen, xii + 321 pp., 56 figs.

Salcedo, S. R. 1950. Contribuciones a la parasitología Colombiana. II. Hemoparásitos de aves y otros vertebrados de los llanos orientales. *Rev. Acad. Colombianos* 7:539.

Sanborn, C. C. 1949. Mammals from the Río Ucayali, Peru. *J. Mammal* 30(3):277–88, 1 fig.

Sanderson, Ivan T. 1949. A brief review of the mammals of Suriname (Dutch Guiana), based upon a collection made in 1938. *Proc. Zool. Soc. London* 119(2):755–89, 1 map, 8 pls.

———. 1950. Marmosets, nature's imps. *Zoo Life, Zool. Soc. London* 5(2):34–39, 6 figs.

———. 1956. *Living mammals of the world.* Garden City, N.Y.: Hanover House, 303 pp., illus., 190 col. pls.

Sandosham, A. A. 1950. On *Enterobius vermicularis* (Linnaeus, 1758) and some related species from primates and rodents. *J. Helminth.* 24:171–204.

Sauer, Carl O. 1950. Geography of South America. In *Handbook of South American Indians,* ed. J. H. Steward, part 6, pp. 319–44, maps 7–9, pls. 28–35. Bull. no. 143, Bur. Amer. Ethnol., Smithsonian Institution, Washington, D.C.

Sauer, E. G. F. 1967*a*. Mother-infant relationship in galagos and the oral child-transport among primates. *Folia Primat.* 7:127–49.

———. 1967*b*. *Galago crassicaudatus* (Galagidae). Transport of the young by the mother. *Psychol. Cinema Reg.* 131:1–5.

Savoury, B., Cited in J. Roth. 1960. Marmosets (*Midas ursulus*) breed in captivity. *J. Brit. Guiana Mus.,* no. 26, pp. 54–5.

Sawaya, Paulo de. 1936. Alguns aspectos da biologia dos "saguis." *Bol. Biol., São Paulo, Brasil* n.s. 4; 2:141–49, 3 figs.

Sawin, Paul B. 1932. II. Albino allelomorphs of the rabbit with special reference to blue-eyed chinchilla and its variations. In *contributions to the genetics of the domestic rabbit,* ed. W. E. Castle and P. B. Sawin, pp. 15–50, 6 pls. Carnegie Inst. Publ., no. 427.

Schaller, George B. 1961. The orang-utan in Sarawak. *Zoologica* 46(2):73–82.

———. 1963. *The mountain gorilla: Ecology and behavior.* Chicago: University of Chicago Press, xvii + 431 pp., 69 figs., 35 pls.

———. 1965. Behavioral comparisons of the apes. In *Primate behavior: Field studies of monkeys and apes,* ed. Irven DeVore, pp. 474–81, 10 figs. New York: Holt, Rinehart and Winston.

Schäuffelen, Otmar. 1958. Über die naturungserwerb von pinche-äffchen *Marikina oedipus* (Linne, 1758). *Säugetierk. Mitt.* 6(4):159–60.

Schlegel, Hermann. 1876. Monographie des singes. Les Singes. Simiae. *Mus. Hist. Nat. Pays-Bas,* vol. 7, monog. 40, 356 pp.

Schmidt, Fritz. 1954. Beobachtungen bei der Aufzucht von Hermelinen. *Säugetierk. Mitt.* 2:166–74, 3 figs.

Schmidt, G. D. 1972. Acanthocephala of captive primates. In *Pathology of simian primates,* ed. R. N. T.-W. Fiennes, 2:144–56, 11 figs. Basel: S. Karger.

Schneider, Rolf. 1958. Zunge und weicher Gaumen. *Primatologia* 3(1):61–126, 36 figs.

Schön, Miguel A. 1968. The muscular system of the red howling monkey. *U.S. Nat. Mus. Bull.* 273:1–182, 48 figs.

Schreber, Johann C. D. 1774. *Die Säugtiere in Abbildungen nach der Natur mit Beschreibungen.* Erster Theil.

Der Mensch. Der Affe. . . . Erlangen: Wolfgang Walther.

Schreiber, G. R. 1968. A note on keeping and breeding the Philippine tarsier at Brookfield Zoo, Chicago. *Int. Zoo Yearb.* 8:114–15.

Schreiber, Hans. 1928. Die Gesichtsmuskulatur der Platyrrhinen. *Gegenbauer's Morph. Jahrb.* 60:179–295, 59 figs.

Schultz, Adolph H. 1926. Studies on the variability of platyrrhine monkeys. *J. Mammal.* 7:286–304, 9 figs.

———. 1930. The skeleton of the trunk and limbs of higher primates. *Human Biol.* 2:303–438, 23 figs.

———. 1935. Eruption and decay of the permanent teeth in primates. *Amer. J. Phys. Anthrop.* 19(4):489–581, 21 figs.

———. 1936. Characters common to higher primates and characters specific for man. *Quart. Rev. Biol.* 11(3):259–83, 425–55, 21 figs.

———. 1938. The relative weight of the testes in primates. *Anat. Rec.* 72:387–94.

———. 1940. The size of the orbit and of the eye in primates. *Amer. J. Phys. Anthrop.* 26:389–408, 3 figs.

———. 1941*a*. The relative size of the cranial capacity in primates. *Amer. J. Phys. Anthrop.* 28:273–87, 3 figs.

———. 1941*b*. Growth and development of the orangutan. Carnegie Inst. Washington Publ. 525, *Contributions to Embryology* 29(82):57–110, 14 figs., 1 pl.

———. 1948. The number of young at a birth and the number of nipples in primates. *Amer. J. Phys. Anthrop.*, n.s., 6(1):1–23.

———. 1949*a*. The palatine ridges of primates. Carnegie Inst. Washington Publ. 583, *Contributions to Embryology* 33:43–66, 7 figs.

———. 1949*b*. Sex differences in the pelves of primates. *Amer. J. Phys. Anthrop.* 7(3):401–23, 3 figs.

———. 1954. Die foramina infraorbitalia der primaten. *Z. Morph. Anthrop.* 46(3):404–7.

———. 1955. The position of the occipital condyles and of the face relative to the skull base in primates. *Amer. J. Phys. Anthrop.*, n.s., 13:97–120, 3 figs.

———. 1956. Postembryonic age changes. *Primatologia* 1:887–964, 27 figs.

———. 1958. Palatine ridges. *Primatologia* 3(1):127–38, 3 figs.

———. 1961. Vertebral column and thorax. *Primatologia* 4(5):1–66, 28 figs.

———. 1962. Metric age changes and sex differences in primate skulls. *Z. Morph. Anthrop.* 52:239–55, 2 figs.

———. 1963*a*. Age changes, sex differences, and variability as factors in the classification of primates. In *Classification and human evolution,* ed. Sherwood L. Washburn, pp. 85–115, 13 figs. Chicago: Aldine.

———. 1963*b*. Relations between the lengths of the main parts of the foot skeleton in primates. *Folia Primat.* 1(3/4):150–71, 7 figs.

Schultz, Adolph H., and Straus, William L., Jr. 1945. The number of vertebrae in primates. *Proc. Amer. Philos. Soc.* 89:601–26, 4 figs.

Schwalbe, G. 1916. Beiträge zur Kenntnis der ausseren Ohres der Primaten. *Z. Morph. Anthrop.* 19:545–668, 64 figs., 1 pl.

Schwartz, Jeffrey H. 1974. Observations on the dentition of the Indriidae. *Amer. J. Phys. Anthrop.* 41:107–14, 5 figs.

Schwarz, Ernst. 1930. Der fehlende Schneidezahn der Primaten. *Zool. Anz.* 89(1/2):36–38, 1 fig.

Sclater, P. L. 1876. On several rare and little-known mammals now or lately living in the Society's collection. *Proc. Zool. Soc. London* 1875:17, pls. 47–51.

Scott, William Berryman. 1893. The evolution of the premolar teeth in the mammals. *Proc. Acad. Nat. Sci. Phila.* 1892:405–44, 8 figs.

Searle, A. G. 1968. *Comparative genetics of coat colour in mammals.* London: Logos Press, Academic Press, xii + 308 pp., 35 figs., 11 pls.

Segall, Walter. 1969. The auditory ossicles (malleus, incus) and their relationships to the tympanic: in marsupials, *Acta Anat.* 73:176–91, 9 figs.

———. 1970. Morphological parallelisms of the bulla and auditory ossicles in some insectivores and marsupials. *Fieldiana: Zool.* 51(15):169–205, 25 figs.

———. 1971. The auditory region (ossicles, sinuses) in gliding mammals and selected representatives of non-gliding genera. *Fieldiana: Zool.* 58(5):27–59, 14 figs.

Seibold, H. R.; Lorenz, Rainer; and Wolf, R. H. 1972. Giant cell aortitis in a South American monkey (*Callimico goeldii*). *Vet. Path.*, 9:230–237, 5 figs.

Seibold, H. R., and Wolf, R. H. 1971. Toxoplasmosis in *Aotus trivirgatus* and *Callicebus moloch. Lab. Animal Sci.* 21:118–20, 2 figs.

Self, J. Teague, and Cosgrove, G. E. 1972. Pentastomida. In *Pathology of simian primates,* ed. R. N. T.-W. Fiennes, 2:194–204, 6 figs. Basel: S. Karger.

Seydel, Otto. 1891. Über die Nasenhöhle der höheren Säugethiere und des Menschen. *Gegenbauer's Morph. Jahrb.* 17:44–99, 3 figs., pls. 4–6.

Shackleton, C. H. L. 1974. Progesterone and oestrogen metabolism in the pregnant marmoset (*Callithrix jacchus*). *J. Steroid Biochem.* 5:597–600, 2 figs.

Shadle, Albert R.; Mirand, Edwin A.; and Grace, James T., Jr. 1965. Breeding responses in tamarins. *Lab. Animal Care* 15(1):1–10).

Shannon, R. C., and Greene, C. T. 1925. A bot-fly parasitic in monkeys. *Zoopathologica* 1(7):285–90, figs. 152–53.

Shaw, George. 1800. *General zoology or systematic natural history. Mammalia* 1(1):ix + 248 pp., 68 pls.

Shaw, James H., and Auskaps, A. M. 1954. Studies in the dentition of the marmoset. *Oral Surg., Oral Med., Oral Path.* 7(6):671–77, 14 figs.

Shope, Robert E.; Causey, Calista E.; and Causey, Ottis R. 1961. Itaqui virus, a new member of arthropod-borne Group C. *Amer. J. Trop. Med. Hyg.* 10:264–65.

Shope, Robert E.; Causey, Ottis R.; Homobono Paes de Andrade, Amelia; and Theiler, Max. 1964. The Venezuelan equine encephalomyelitis complex of Group A arthropod-borne viruses, including Mucambo and Pixuna from the Amazon region of Brazil. *Amer. J. Trop. Med. Hyg.* 13:723–27.

Shriver, J. E. and Noback, C. R. 1967. Color vision in the tree shrew (*Tupaia glis*). *Folia Primat.* 6:161–69.

Shriver, Joyce, and Matzke, H. A. 1965. Corticobulbar and corticospinal tracts in the marmoset monkey (*Oedipomidas oedipus*). *Anat. Rec.* 151:416 (abstract).

Silvers, Willys K. 1965. Agouti locus: Homology of its method of operation in rats and mice. *Science* 149: 651–52.

Silvester, C. F. 1912. On the presence of permanent communication between the lymphatic and the venous system at the level of the renal veins in adult South American monkeys. *Amer. J. Anat.* 12:447–72, 2 figs., 10 pls.

Simons, Elwyn L. 1962. Fossil evidence relating to the early evolution of primate behavior. *Ann. N.Y. Acad. Sci.* 102(2):282–95. 3 figs.

———. 1967. Fossil primates and the evolution of some primate locomotor systems. *Amer. J. Phys. Anthrop.* 26:241–53.

———. 1969. Origin and radiation of primates. *Ann. N.Y. Acad. Sci.* 167 (Art.1):319–31, 8 figs.

———. 1971. A current review of the interrelationships of Oligocene and Miocene Catarrhini. In *Dental morphology and evolution,* ed. A. Dahlberg, pp. 193–208, 8 figs. Chicago: University of Chicago Press.

———. 1972. *Primate evolution: An introduction to man's place in nature.* The Macmillan series in physical anthropology. New York: Macmillan Co. xii + 322 pp., 112 figs.

Simons, Elwyn L., and Ettel, Peter C. 1970. *Gigantopithecus. Scientific American* 222(1):76–85, 10 figs.

Simons, Elwyn L., and Russell, Donald E. 1960. Notes on the cranial anatomy of Necrolemur. *Breviora,* no. 127; 14 pp., 3 figs.

Simpson, D. I. H. 1969. Arboviruses and free-living wild animals. *Symp. Zool. Soc. London,* no. 24, pp. 13–28.

Simpson, George Gaylord, 1928. *A catalogue of the Mesozoic Mammalia in the geological department of the British Museum.* London: British Museum (Natural History).

———. 1929. American Mesozoic mammalia. *Mem. Peabody Mus. Yale Univ.* 3:1–71, 35 pls., 64 figs.

———. 1933. Critique of a new theory of mammalian dental evolution. *J. Dental Res.* 13(4):261–72.

———. 1936. Studies of the earliest mammalian dentitions. *Dent. Cosmos.* (Aug.–Sept.), pp. 2–24.

———. 1945. The principles of classification and a classification of mammals. *Bull. Amer. Mus. Nat. Hist.,* vol. 85; xvi + 350 pp.

———. 1950. History of the fauna of Latin America. *Amer. Scientist* 38(3):361–89, 10 figs.

———. 1955. The Phenacolemuridae, new family of early primates. *Bull. Amer. Mus. Nat. Hist.* 105:411–42.

———. 1967. The Tertiary lorisiform primates of Africa. *Bull. Mus. Comp. Zool. Harvard Coll.* 136(3):39–61, 2 pls.

———. 1969. South American mammals. In *Biogeography and ecology,* ed. E. J. Fittkau, J. Illies, H. Klinge, G. H. Schwabe, and H. Sioli, pp. 879–909, 3 figs. The Hague.

Siret, M. 1778. Observations sur l'ouistiti, espèce de sagouin. *J. Phys.* (Paris), 12(2):453–54.

Sisson, Septimus, 1910. *A text book of veterinary anatomy.* Philadelphia, 826 pp., 588 figs.

Slaughter, Bob H. 1965. A therian from the lower Cretaceous (Albian) of Texas. *Postilla,* no. 93; 18 pp., 6 figs.

Slee, J. 1965. Seasonal patterns of moulting in Wiltshire horn sheep. In *Biology of the skin and hair growth,* ed. A. G. Lyne and B. F. Short, pp. 545–63, 8 figs. New York: American Elsevier Pub. Co.

Slijper, E. J. 1962. *Whales* (Translated from the original Dutch by A. J. Pomerans). London, 475 pp., 229 figs.

Sluckin, W. 1965. *Imprinting and early learning.* Chicago: Aldine, x + 147 pp.

Smith, G. Elliot. 1902. Brain of mammalia. In *Descriptive and illustrated catalogue of the physiological series of comparative anatomy contained in the museum of the Royal College of Surgeons of England,* 2 ed. 2:138–518, figs. 34–253.

———. 1924. *Evolution of man: Essays.* London, viii + 159 pp., 19 figs.

Smith, W. N., and Chitwood, May Bell. 1967. *Trichospirura leptostoma* gen. et sp. n. (Nematoda: Thelazioidea) from the pancreatic ducts of the white-eared marmoset *Callithrix jacchus. J. Parasitol.* 53:1270–72, 12 figs.

Snell, Christian A. R. D. 1968. Bipedalism in primates. *Acta Morph. Neerlando-Scand.* (Utrecht) 7:95 (abstr.).

Snell, Christian A. R. D., and Donhuysen, H. W. A. 1968. The pelvis in the bipedalism of primates. *Amer. J. Phys. Anthrop.* 28:239–46.

Snyder, Patricia A. 1972. Behavior of *Leontopithecus rosalia* (the golden lion marmoset) and related species: A review. In *Saving the lion marmoset,* ed. D. D. Bridgewater, pp. 23–46. Proc. Wild Animal Propagation Trust Conference on the Golden Marmoset held at National Zoological Park, Washington, D.C., February 15–17, 1972. Wheeling, W.Va.: Wild Animal Propagation Trust.

Snyder, Richard C. 1962. The adaptations for bipedal locomotion of lizards. *Amer. Zool.* 2:191–203, 8 figs.

———. 1967. Adaptive values of bipedalism. *Amer. J. Phys. Anthrop.* 26:131–34.

Sobel, Harry; Mondon, Carl; and Means, Charles V. 1960. Pygmy marmoset as an experimental animal. *Science* 132(3424):415–16, 1 fig.

Soini, Pekka. 1972. The capture and commerce of live monkeys in the Amazonian region of Peru. *Int. Zoo Yearb.* 12:26–42.

Solange de Castro Faria, Marcia, and Miraglia, T. 1971. The eccrine sweat glands of the palms and soles of the common marmoset (*Callithrix jacchus*). *Acta Anat.* 79(4):466–80.

Sonntag, Charles F. 1920. The comparative anatomy of the tongues of the Mammalia. I. General description of the tongue. *Proc. Zool. Soc. London* 1920:115–29, fig. 6–17.

———. 1921*a*. The comparative anatomy of the tongue of the Mammalia. II. Family 1. Simiidae. *Proc. Zool. Soc. London* 1921:1–29, figs. 1–9.

———. 1921*b*. The comparative anatomy of the tongues of the mammalia. III. Family 2. Cercopithecidae: With notes on the comparative physiology of the tongues and stomachs of the langurs. *Proc. Zool. Soc. London* 1921:277–322, figs. 16–36.

———. 1921*c*. The comparative anatomy of the tongues of the Mammalia. IV. Families 3 and 4. Cebidae and Hapalidae. *Proc. Zool. Soc. London* 1921:497–524, figs. 37–52.

———. 1925. The comparative anatomy of the tongues of the Mammalia. XII. Summary, classification and phylogeny. *Proc. Zool. Soc. London* 1925:701–62, figs. 31–45.

Sorenson, M. W., and Conaway, C. H. 1966. Observations on the social behavior of tree shrews in captivity. *Folia Primat.* 4:124–45.

Sousa, Octavio E.; Rossan, Richard N.; and Baerg, David C. 1974. The prevalence of trypanosomes and microfilariae in Panamanian monkeys. *Amer. J. Trop. Med. Hyg.* 23(5):862–68.

Southwick, Margaret D. 1952. The natural history, endoparasites and pseudoparasites of the tarsier (*Tarsius carbonarius*) recently living in the Society's menagerie. In article by W. C. Osman Hill, Anna Porter, and M. D. Southwick, *Proc. Zool. Soc. London* 122:79–119.

Souza, Maria Madalena de; Teixeira, Augusto M. C.; and Miraglia, Tulio. 1962. Dados sobre a vascularizaçâo do encephalo do sagui (*Callithrix jacchus*). *Folia Clin. Biol.* 31:104–14.

Sparks, John. 1967. Allogrooming in primates: A review. In *Primate ethology,* ed. Desmond Morris, pp. 148–75. London: Weidenfeld and Nicholson.

Spatz, W. B. 1966 (1965). Zur Ontogenese der Bulla tympanica von *Tupaia glis* Diard 1820 (Prosimiae, Tupaiiformes). *Folia Primat.* 4:26–50, 12 figs.

Spatz, W. B., and Tigges, Johannes. 1972. Species difference between Old World and New World monkeys in the organization of the striate and striate-prestriate association. *Brain Res.* 43:591–94, 2 figs.

Spix, Jean de. 1823. *Simiarum et vespertiliarum brasiliensis species novae; ou, Histoire naturelle des espèces nouvelles de singes et de chauve-souris observées et recueillies pendant le voyage dans l'intérieur du Bresil.* Monaco. viii + 72 pp., 38 pls.

Sprankel, Heinrich. 1965. Untersuchungen an *Tarsius.* 1. Morphologie des Schwanzes nebst ethologischen Bemerkungen. *Folia Primat.* 3:153–88, 8 figs.

———. 1971. Zur vergleichenden Histologie von Hautdrüsenorganen in Lippenbereich bei *Tarsius bancanus borneanus* Horsfield 1821 und *Tarsius syrichta carbonarius* Linnaeus 1758. *Proc. 3rd Intern. Congr. Primat. (1970)* 1:189–97, 2 figs.

Srihongse, Sunthorn. 1969. Vesicular stomatitis virus infections in Panamanian primates and other vertebrates. *Amer. J. Epidemiol.* 90(1):69–76, 1 fig.

Stadie, R. 1931. Biologische Aufzeichnungen über ein Gefangenschaft gehaltene Affen und Halbaffen. *Zool. Gart.* 4:132–40.

Stanley, Steven M. 1973. An explanation for Cope's Rule. *Evolution* 27(1):1–26, 8 figs.

Starck, Dietrich. 1967. Le crane des mammifères. In *Traité de Zoologie,* ed. Pierre P. Grassé, 16(1):404–549, Paris: Masson et Cie, figs. 207–80.

———. 1969. The circumgenital gland organs of *Callithrix* (*Cebuella*) *pygmaea* (Spix, 1823). *Zool. Gart.* 36:312–26, 7 figs.

Starck, Dietrich, and Schneider, Rolf. 1960. Larynx. *Primatologia* 3(2):423–587, 75 figs.

Stare, F. J.; Andrus, S. B.; and Portman, O. W. 1963. Primates in medical research with special reference to New World monkeys. In *Proceedings of a conference on research with primates,* ed. Donald E. Pickering, pp. 59–66. Beaverton, Oregon: Tektronix Foundation.

Steggerda, Morris. 1950. The pigmentation and hair of South American Indians. In *Handbook of South American Indians,* ed. J. H. Steward, 6:85–90. Smith. Inst. Bur. Amer. Ethnol. Bull. no. 143.

Stehlin, H. G. 1916. Die Säugetiere des schweizerishern Eocaens: Critisches Catalog der Materialen Siebenter Teil, Zweite Halfte. *Abh. Schweiz. Paläont. Gesellsch.* 41:1299–1552, 82 figs., 2 pls.

Steiner, H. 1966. Atavismen bei Artbastarden und ihre Bedentung zur Festellung von Verwandstschaftsbeziehugen. Kreuzungoergebnisse innerhalb der Singvogelfamilie der Spermestidae. *Rev. Suisse* 73:321–37.

Stellar, Eliot. 1960. The marmoset as a laboratory animal: maintenance, general observation of behavior and simple learning. *J. Comp. Phys. Psychol.* 53(1):1–10.

Stephan, Heinz. 1965. Der Bulbus olfactorius accessorius bei Insectivoren und Primaten. *Acta Anat.* 62: 215–53.

———. 1966. Grossenanderungen im olfactorischen und limbuschen System wahrend der phylogenetischen Entwicklung der Primaten. In *Evolution of the forebrain,* ed. R. Hassler and H. Stephan, pp. 377–88, 5 figs. New York: Plenum Pub.

———. 1967*a*. Quantitative Vergleiche zur phylogenetischen Entwicklung der Gehirns der Primaten mit Hilfe von Progressionsindices. *Mitt. Max-Planck-Gesellsch.* 2:63–86, 28 figs.

———. 1967*b*. Zur Entwicklungshohe der Primaten nach Merkmalen des Gehirns. In *Progress in primatology,* ed. D. Starck, R. Schneider, and H.-J. Kuhn, pp. 108–19, 7 figs. Basel: S. Karger.

Stephan, Heinz, and Andy, Orlando J. 1964. Quantitative comparisons of brain structures from insectivores to primates. *Amer. Zool.* 4:59–74, 21 figs.

———. 1969. Quantitative comparative neuroanatomy of primates: An attempt at a phylogenetic interpretation. *Ann. N.Y. Acad. Sci.* 167(1):370–87, 12 figs.

Stern, Jack T., Jr. 1971. Functional myology of the hip and thigh of cebid monkeys and its implications for the evolution of erect posture. *Bibl. Primat.* 14:1–318, 25 figs.

Stern, Jack T., Jr., and Charles F. Oxnard. 1973. Primate locomotion: Some links with evolution and morphology. *Primatologia* 4(11):1–93, 19 figs.

Stiles, C. W., and Hassall, Albert. 1929. Key-catalogue of parasites reported for primates (monkeys and lemurs) with their possible public health importance. *U.S. Treas. Dept. Publ. Hlth. Serv., Hyg. Lab., Bull.,* no. 152, pp. 409–99, index, pp. 581–601.

Stiles, C. W. and Nolan, Mabelle Orleman. 1929. Key-catalogue of primates for which parasites are reported. *U.S. Treas. Dept. Publ. Hlth Serv., Hyg. Lab. Bull.,* no. 152, pp. 499–601.

Stirton, Ruben A. 1951. Ceboid monkeys from the Miocene of Colombia. *Bull. Univ. Calif. Publ. Geol. Sci.* 28(11):315–56, 14 pls.

Straile, William E. 1960. Sensory hair follicles in mammalian skin: The tylotrich follicle. *Amer. J. Anat., Philadelphia* 106:133–47, 1 fig., 3 pls.

Straus, William L., Jr. 1935. The structure of the primate kidney. *J. Anat.* 69:93–108, 5 figs.

———. 1949. The riddle of man's ancestry. *Quart. Rev. Biol.* 24:200–223.

———. 1962*a*. Fossil evidence of the evolution of the erect, bipedal posture. *Clin. Ortho.,* no. 25, pp. 9–19, 3 figs.

———. 1962*b*. The mylohyoid groove in primates. *Bibl. Primat.* 1:197–216, 1 fig.

Straus, William L., Jr., and Arcadi, John A. 1958. Urinary system. *Primatologia* 3(1):507–41, 11 figs.

Straus, William L., Jr., and Cave, A. J. E. 1957. III. Pathology and the posture of Neanderthal man. *Quart. Rev. Biol.* 32(4):348–63, 7 figs.

Streeter, George L. 1920. Embryological significance of the crus helicis. *Anat. Rec.* 18:263.

———. 1922. Some uniform characteristics of the primate auricle. *Anat. Rec.* 23:335–41, 14 figs.

Stunkard, H. W. 1965*a*. *Paratriotaenia oedipomidatis* gen. et sp. n. (Cestoda) from a marmoset. *J. Parasit.* 51:545–51.

———. 1965*b*. New intermediate hosts in the life cycle of *Prosthenorchis elegans* (Diessing, 1851), an acanthocephalan parasite of primates. *J. Parasit.* 51:645–49.

Susman, Randall L. 1974. Facultative terrestrial hand postures in an orang-utan (*Pongo pygmaeus*) and pongid evolution. *Amer. J. Phys. Anthrop.* 40(1):27–37, 3 figs.

Swainson, William. 1835. The cabinet cyclopedia . . . *On the natural history and classification of quadrupeds.* London: Longman, etc., vii + 397 pp., illus.

Swindler, D. R., and McCoy, H. A. 1964. Calcification of deciduous teeth in rhesus monkeys. *Science* 144: 1243–49

———. 1965. Primate odontogenesis. *J. Dental Res.* 44:283–95.

Szalay, Frederick S. 1968. The Picrodontidae, a family of early primates. *Amer. Mus. Novit.*, no. 2329, pp. 1–55, 34 figs.

———. 1969*a*. Mixodectidae, Microsyopidae, and the insectivore-primate transition. *Bull. Amer. Mus. Nat. Hist.* 140:193–330.

———. 1969*b*. Uintasoricinae, a new subfamily of Early Tertiary Mammals (? Primates). *Amer. Mus. Novit.*, no. 2363, pp. 1–36, 21 figs.

———. 1972*a*. Cranial morphology of the Early Tertiary *Phenacolemur* and its bearing on Primate phylogeny. *Amer. J. Phys. Anthrop.* 36(1):59–76, 16 figs.

———. 1972*b*. Paleobiology of the earliest primates. In *The functional and evolutionary biology of Primates,* ed. R. Tuttle, pp. 3–35, 9 figs., 9 pls. Chicago: Aldine-Atherton.

———. 1973. New Paleocene primates and a diagnosis of the suborder Paromomyiformes. *Folia Primat.* 19:73–87, 8 figs.

Szalay, Frederick S., and Decker, Richard Lee. 1974. Origins, evolution, and function of the tarsus in Late Cretaceous Eutheria and Paleocene primates. In *Primate locomotion,* ed. F. A. Jenkins, Jr., pp. 223–59, 14 figs. New York: Academic Press.

Taliaferro, W. H., and Taliaferro, L. G. 1934. Morphology, periodicity, and course of infection of *Plasmodium brasilianum* in Panamanian monkeys. *Amer. J. Hyg.* 20:1–49.

Tate, George H. H. 1939. The mammals of the Guiana region. *Bull. Amer. Mus. Nat. Hist.* 76:151–229.

Tattersall, Ian, and Schwartz, Jeffrey H. 1974. Craniodental morphology and the systematics of the Malagasy lemurs (Primates, Prosimii). *Anthrop. Pap., Amer. Mus. Nat. Hist.* 52(3):139–92, 24 figs.

Taylor, R. M. and Jose Fonseca da Cunha. 1946. An epidemiological study of jungle yellow fever in an endemic area in Brazil. Part I—Epidemiology of human infections. *American J. Trop. Med.*, 26(6):1–32, 1 fig. 4 maps.

Tembrock, G. 1963. Acoustic behaviour of mammals. In *Acoustic behaviour of animals,* ed. R. G. Busnel, pp. 751–86, figs. 403–15. Amsterdam; Elsevier.

Tesh, Robert B.; Chaniotis, Byron N.; and Johnson, Karl M. 1970. Vesicular stomatitis virus, Indiana serotype: Multiplication in and transmission by experimentally infected phlebotomine sand flies (*Lutzomyia trapidoi*). *Amer. J. Epidemiol.* 93(6):491–95.

———. 1972. Vesicular stomatitis virus (Indiana serotype): Transovarial transmission by phlebotomine sand flies. *Science* 175:1477–79.

Tesh, Robert B.; Peralta, Pauline H.; and Johnson, Karl M. 1969. Ecologic studies of vesicular stomatitis virus 1. Prevalence of infection among animals and humans living in an area of endemic VSV activity. *Amer. J. Epidemiol.* 90(3):255–61, 1 fig.

———. 1970. Ecologic studies of vesicular stomatitis virus. II. Results of experimental infection in Panamanian wild animals. *Amer. J. Epidemiol.* 91(2):216–24.

Thatcher, Vernon E., and Porter, James K., Jr. 1968. Some helminth parasites of Panamanian primates. *Trans. Amer. Micros. Soc.* 87(2):186–96.

Theilen, G. H.; Gould, D.; Fowler, M.; Dungworth, D. L. 1971. C-type virus in tumor tissue of a wooly monkey (*Lagothrix* spp.) with fibrosarcoma. *J. Nat. Cancer Inst.* 47:881–89.

Theilen, G. H.; Wolfe, L. G.; Rabin, H.; Deinhardt, F.; Dungworth, D. L.; Fowler, H. E.; Gould, D.; and Cooper, R. 1973. Biological studies in four species of nonhuman primates with simian sarcoma virus (*Lagothrix*). *Bibl. Haemat.*, no. 39, pp. 251–57, 1 fig.

Theiler, Max, and Downs, W. G. 1973. The arthropod-borne viruses of vertebrates. New Haven: Yale University Press. xxviii + 578 pp.

Thomas, Oldfield. 1880. On mammals from Ecuador. *Proc. Zool. Soc. London* 1880:393–402.

———. 1903. Notes on South American monkeys, bats, carnivores, and rodents, with descriptions of new species. *Ann. Mag. Nat. Hist.*, ser. 7, 12:455–64.

———. 1904. New *Callithrix, Midas, Felis, Rhipidomys,* and *Proechimys* from Brazil and Ecuador. *Ann. Mag. Nat. Hist.*, ser. 7, 14:188–95.

———. 1910. On mammals collected in Ceará, N.E. Brazil, by Fraulein Dr. Snethlage. *Ann. Mag. Nat. Hist.*, ser. 8, 6:500–503.

———. 1911. The mammals of the Tenth Edition of Linnaeus: An attempt to fix the types of the genera and the exact bases and localities of the species. *Proc. Zool. Soc. London* 1911:120–57.

———. 1912. On small mammals from the lower Amazon. *Ann. Mag. Nat. Hist.* ser. 8, 9:84–90.

———. 1913. On some rare Amazonian mammals from the collection of the Para Museum. *Ann. Mag. Nat. Hist.*, ser. 8, 11:130–36.

———. 1914. Nomina conservanda in Mammalia. *Zool. Anz.* 44(6):284–86.

———. 1920. Report on the Mammalia collected by Mr. Edmund Heller during the Peruvian Expedition of 1915 under the auspices of Yale University and the National Geographic Society. *Proc. U.S. Nat. Mus.* 58: 217–49, pls. 14–15.

———. 1922. On the systematic arrangement of the marmosets. *Ann. Mag. Nat. Hist.*, ser. 9, 9:196–99.

———. 1927*a*. The Godman-Thomas expedition to Peru. V. On mammals collected by Mr. R. W. Hendee in the province of San Martín, N. Peru, mostly at Yurac Yacu. *Ann. Mag. Nat. Hist.*, ser. 9, 19:361–75.

———. 1927*b*. The Godman-Thomas expedition to Peru. VI. On mammals from the upper Huallaga and neighbouring highlands. *Ann. Mag. Nat. Hist.*, ser. 9, 20: 594–608.

———. 1928*a*. The Godman-Thomas expedition to Peru. VII. The mammals of the Río Ucayali. *Ann. Mag. Nat. Hist.*, ser. 10, 2:249–65.

———. 1928*b*. The Godman-Thomas expedition to Peru. VIII. On mammals obtained by Mr. Hendee at Pebas and Iquitos, upper Amazons. *Ann. Mag. Nat. Hist.*, ser. 10, 2:285–94.

Thorington, Richard W. 1968*a*. Observations of the tamarin *Saguinus midas*. *Folia Primat.* 9:95–98.

———. 1968*b*. Observations of squirrel monkeys in a Colombian forest. In *The squirrel monkey,* ed. L. A. Rosenblum and R. W. Cooper, pp. 69–85. New York: Academic Press.

———. 1972. Importation, breeding, and mortality of New World primates in the United States. *Int. Zoo. Yearb.* 12:18–23.

Thunberg, Carl Peter. 1819. Beskrifning på *Simia albifrons*. *Kongl. Vetenskaps Stockholm, Akad. Handl.* 1819:65–68, pl. 3, 4.

Tigges, Johannes. 1963. On color vision in gibbon and orangutan. *Folia Primat.* 1:188–98, 6 figs.

Tiken, William S. 1970. *Tetrapetalonema marmosetae* in cotton-topped marmosets, *Saguinus oedipus,* from the region of San Marcos, Colombia. *Lab. Animal Care* 20(4):758–62.

Tims, H. W. M. 1896. On the tooth-genesis in the Canidae. *J. Linn. Soc.* (*Zool.*) 25:445–80, 8 figs.

Tipton, Vernon J., and Machado-Allison, Carlos E. 1972. Fleas of Venezuela. *Sci. Bull. Brigham Young Univ.*, Biol. Ser., 17(6):1–115 pp., 91 figs.

Tomes, Charles S. 1914. *A manual of dental anatomy.* 7th ed., edited by H. W. Marett Tims and A. Hopewell-Smith. Philadelphia: Blakiston, vii + 616 pp., 300 figs.

Travassos, Lauro. 1925. Nematodes (Oxyuroidea-Oxyuridæ) Revisão do género *Enterobius* Leach, 1853. *Fauna Brasil. Mus. Nac. Rio de Janeiro,* n.s. ,no. 2; 11 pp., 15 figs.

Travassos, Lauro; Teixeira de Freitas, J. F.; and Kohn, A. 1969. Trematódeos do Brasil. *Mem. Inst. Oswaldo Cruz* 67(1):1–886, 557 figs., 1 pl.

Travis, J. C., and Holmes, W. N. 1974. Some physiological and behavioral changes associated with oestrus and pregnancy in the squirrel monkey. *J. Zool.* 173(4):41–66, 6 figs.

Trouessart, E. L. 1882. Catalogue des mammifères vivants et fossiles. *Rev. Mag. Zool.* ser. 3, 6(1878):108–40.

———. 1897. *Catalogus mammalium tam viventium quam fossilium.* Fasc. 1; v + 218 pp., Berlin (Friedlander).

Tschudi, J. J. von. 1844. *Untersuchungen über die Fauna Peruana. Pt. 1* (*Therologie*). pp. xxx + 262. St. Gallen: Scheitlin and Zollipofer.

Turnbull, William D. 1970. Mammalian masticatory apparatus. *Fieldiana: Geol.* 18(2):151–356, 48 figs.

———. 1971. The Trinity therians: Their bearing on evolution in marsupials and other therians. In *Dental morphology and evolution,* ed. A. A. Dahlberg, pp. 151–79, 6 figs. Chicago: University of Chicago Press.

Tuttle, Russel H. 1967. Knuckle-walking and the evolution of hominoid hands. *Amer. J. Phys. Anthrop.* 26(2):171–206, 12 figs.

———. 1969*a*. Terrestrial trends in the hands of the Anthropoidea. *Proc. 2d Int. Cong. Primat.* 2:192–200, 1 fig.

———. 1969*b*. Quantitative and functional studies on the hands of the Anthropoidea, I. The Hominoidea. *J. Morph.* 128(3):309–64, 29 figs.

———. 1969*c*. Knuckle-walking and the problem of human origins. *Science* 166:953–61, 8 figs.

———. 1970. Postural, propulsive, and prehensile capabilities in the cheiridia of chimpanzees and other great apes. In *The chimpanzee,* ed. G. H. Bourne, 2:167–253, 39 figs. White Plains, N.Y.: Albert J. Phiebig.

———. 1972. Functional and evolutionary biology of hylobatid hands and feet. *Gibbon and Siamang* 1:136–206, 43 figs.

———. 1974. Knuckle walking and knuckle-walkers. *Amer. J. Phys. Anthrop.* 40(1):154 (abstr.).

Tuttle, Russel H., and Rogers, C. M. 1966. Genetic and selective factors in reduction of the hallux in *Pongo pygmaeus*. *Amer. J. Phys. Anthrop.* 24(2):191–98.

Uhlmann, K. 1969. Über Anzeichen der brachiatorischen und semibrachiatorischen Lokomotionsweise an der Huft- und Oberschenkelmusculatur der Affen. *Verh. Anat. Ges.* 126:451–58.

Ulberg, L. C. 1958. Influence of high temperature on reproduction. *J. Hered.* 49:62–64.

Ulmer, Frederick A. 1961. Gestation period of the lion marmoset. *J. Mammal.* 42:253–54.

———. 1963. Observations on the tarsier in captivity. *Zool. Gart.* n.f., 27(1–3):106–21, 6 pls.

Uno, H.; Adachi, K.; Allegra, F.; and Montagna, W. 1968. Studies of common baldness of the stumptailed macaque. II. Enzyme activities of carbohydrate metabolism in the hair follicles. *J. Invest. Dermat.* 51(1): 11–18.

Urbain, Achile; Dechambre, E.; and Rode, Paul. 1941. Observations faites sur un jeune orang-utan né à la ménagerie du Jardin des Plantes. *Mammalia* 5:82–85, 1 pl.

Urbain, Achile, and Rode, Paul. 1940. Un chimpanzé pygmée (*Pan satyrus paniscus*), au parc zoologique du Bois du Vincennes. *Mammalia* 4:12–14, 1 pl.

Ushijima, Richard N.; Gardner, C. E.; and Cate, Eddie. 1966. Transformation of renal cells from a prosimian by simian virus 40 (SV40). *Proc. Soc. Exper. Biol. Med.* 122:676–79.

Ushijima, Richard; Shininger, F. S.; and Gardner, Charles E. 1966. Susceptibility of cultural renal cells from different species of subhuman primates to simian virus 40 (31223). *Proc. Soc. Exper. Biol. Med.* 122: 673–75.

Ushijima, Richard N.; Shininger, F. Stuart; and Grand, Theodore I. 1964. Chromosome complements of two species of primates: *Cynopithecus niger* and *Presbytis entellus*. *Science* 146:78–79.

Vandebroek, G. 1960–61. The comparative anatomy of the teeth of lower and non-specialized mammals. *Inter. Colloq. on the evolution of lower and non-specialized mammals. Kon. VI.* Brussels: Acad. Wetensch. Lett. Sch. Kunsten van België, part 1, pp. 215–320 (1961); part 2, 44 pls. (1960).

———. 1967. Origin of the cusps and crests of the tribosphenic molar. *J. Dental Morph.* 46(suppl. 5):796–804, 7 figs.

Van Kampen, P. N. 1905. Die Tympanalgegend des Säugetierschädels. *Gegenbauer's Morph Jahrb.* 130:22–720, 96 figs.

Van Tienhoven, Ari. 1968. *Reproductive physiology of vertebrates.* Philadelphia: W. B. Saunders Co., pp. xii + 498.

Van Uden, N.; Barros Machado, A. de; and Castelo Branco, R. 1963. On black piedra in central African mammals caused by the ascomycete *Piedraia quintanilhae* nov. spec. *Rev. Biol. (Rev. Brasil. Portug. Biol. Geral)*, 3(2–4):271–76, pls. 12–16.

Van Valen, Leigh. 1965. Treeshrews, primates and fossils. *Evolution* 19(2):137–51, 1 fig.

———. 1966. Deltatheridia: A new order of mammals. *Bull. Amer. Mus. Nat. Hist.* 132:1–126.

———. 1967. New Paleocene insectivores and insectivore classification. *Bull. Amer. Mus. Nat. Hist.* 135: 217–84.

———. 1969. A classification of the Primates. *Amer. J. Phys. Anthrop.* 30(2):295–96.

Van Valen, Leigh; and Sloan, Robert E. 1965. The earliest primates. *Science* 150:743–45, 1 fig.

Vargas-Méndez, Oscar, and Elton, Norman W. 1953. Naturally acquired yellow fever in wild monkeys of Costa Rica. *Amer. J. Trop. Med. Hyg.* 2:850–63, 9 figs.

Veloso, Henrique P. 1946. A vegetação no municipio de Ilhéus, Estado da Bahia. *Mem. Inst. Oswaldo Cruz (Rio de Janeiro)* 44:13–103, 34 figs.; pp. 221–93; 323–41, 1 fig.

Verhaart, W. J. C. 1966. The pyramidal tract of *Tupaia,* compared to that in other primates. *J. Comp. Neurol.* 126(1):43–50.

Vickers, James H. 1969. Diseases of primates affecting the choice of species for toxicologic studies. *Ann. N.Y. Acad. Sci.* 162(1):659–72, 9 figs.

Vieira, Carlos O. da Cunha. 1944. Os simios do estado de Saõ Paulo. *Pap. Avulsos, Dept. Zool., Sec. Agric., Saõ Paulo* 4(1):1–31.

———. 1951. Notas sôbre os mamíferos obtenidos pela expedição do Instituto Butantan ão Rio das Mortes e Serra do Roncador. *Pap. Avulsos, Dept. Zool., São Paulo* 10(4):105–25.

———. 1952. Resultados de una expedição cientifico ão territorio do Acre: Mamíferos. *Pap. Avulsos, Dept. Zool. São Paulo* 11(2):21–32.

———. 1953. Sôbre una coleção de mamíferos do estado de Alagoas. *Arq. Zool., São Paulo* 8(7):209–21.

Vieira, Carlos O. da Cunha. 1955. Lista remissiva dos mamiferos do Brasil. *Arq. Zool., São Paulo* 8(11): 341–474.

Vincent, Francois. 1971. Les cycles sexuels et reproducteurs des prosimiens africains de forêt: Eléments de comparaison entre le Congo-Brazzaville et le Cameroun, *Proc. 3rd Int. Congr. Primat., Zurich, 1970* 1:260–78, 6 figs.

Vincent, S. B. 1913. The tactile hair of the white rat. *J. Comp. Neurol.* 23:1–34.

Vogel, Christian. 1963. Die Spina nasalis anterior und vergleichbare Strukturen bei rezenten Simien. *Zool. Anz.* 171:273–90, 10 figs.

———. 1966. Morphologische Studien an Gesichtschädel catarrhiner Primaten. *Bibl. Primat.* 4:1–226, 43 figs.

———. 1968. The phylogenetical evaluation of some characters and some morphological trends in the evolution of the skull in catarrhine primates. In *Taxonomy and phylogeny of Old World primates with references to the origin of man,* ed. Brunetto Chiarelli, pp. 21–55, 17 figs. Turin.

———. 1969. Funktionelle und phylogenetische Aspekte der Morphologie des Schädels hoherer Primaten einschliesslich der Hominiden. *Z. Morph. Anthrop.* 60 (3):242–62, 6 figs.

Vorez, C. 1970. Origine des dents bilophodonts des Cercopithecoidea. *Mammalia* 34:269–93.

Wagner, Johann Andres. 1833. Critische Revision der brasilian Affenarten. *Isis von Oken* 10(2):988–100.

———. 1837. Beiträge zur Kenntniss der warmblutigen Wirbelthiere Amerikas. *Abh. Akad. Wiss. München, Math.-Phys. Cl.* 2:417–510, 4 pls.

———. 1840. Die Säugthiere in Abbildungen nach des Natur mit Beschreibungen von Dr. Johann Christian Daniel von Schreber. Suppl., vol. 1: xiv + 551 pp. Erlangen.

———. 1848. Bieträge zur Kenntniss des Säugthiere Amerikas. Dritte Abteilung. Vierte Ordnung. *Affen, Abh. Akad. Wiss. München* 5:405–80, 1 pl.

———. 1855. Die Säugthiere in Abbildungen nach der Natur mit beschreibungen von Dr. Johann Christian Daniel von Schreber, Suppl., vol. 5:xxvi + 810 pp., 5 pls, Leipzig.

Walker, Alan. 1974. Locomotor adaptations in past and present prosimian primates. In *Primate locomotion,* ed. F. A. Jenkins, Jr., pp. 349–81. New York: Academic Press.

Walker, Ernest P. 1968. *Mammals of the world.* 2d ed., revised by John L. Paradiso. Baltimore: Johns Hopkins Press, 644 pp., illus.

Wallace, Alfred R. 1854. On the monkeys of the Amazon. *Proc. Zool. Soc. London* 1852:107–10.

Walls, Gordon Lynn. 1942. *The vertebrate eye and its adaptive radiation.* Cranbrook Inst. Sci., Bull. 19, 785 pp., 197 figs.

Warren, Kenneth S., and Simões, Jose. 1966. The marmoset: A primate resistent to *Schistosoma mansoni* infection. *Amer. J. Trop. Med. Hyg.* 15(2):153–55.

Warren, McWilson. 1970. Simian and anthropoid malarias: Their role in human disease. *Lab. Animal Care* 20(2): pt. 2, pp. 368–76.

Washburn, Sherwood L. 1948. Sex differences in the pubic bone. *Amer. J. Phys. Anthrop.* 6(2):199–207, 1 fig.

———. 1957. Ischial callosities as sleeping adaptations. *Amer. J. Phys. Anthrop.* 15(2):269–76, 2 figs.

Wassif, Kamal. 1957. The development of auditory ossicles and tympanic bones in mammals with special reference to the part played by the anterior process in the ossification of the malleus. *Ain Shams Sci. Bull.,* no. 2, pp. 259–89, 2 pls., 17 figs.

Watson, Adam. 1963. The effect of climate on the colour changes of mountain hares in Scotland. *Proc. Zool. Soc. London* 141(4):823–35.

Webber, Winfrith A. F., and Hawking, Frank. 1955. The filarial worms *Dipetalonema digitatum* and *D. gracile* in monkeys. *Parasitology* 45:401–8, 7 figs.

Weber, M. W. C. 1927–28. *Die Säugetiere einfuhrung in die Anatomie und Systematik der recenten und fos-*

silen Mammalia. . . . Jena; Gustax Fischer. Vol. 1, xiv + 898 pp., 573 figs.

Webster, Douglas B. 1966. Ear structure and function in modern mammals. *Amer. Zool.* 6:451–66, 10 figs.

Webster, W. A. 1968. *Molineus vexillarius* Dunn 1961 from South American primates. *Can. J. Zool.* 46:287.

Wegener, Alfred. 1966. *The origin of continents and oceans* [new English translation of 1962 printing of 4th rev. ed. of *Die Entstehung der Kontinente und Ozeane*, published in 1929 by Friedrich Vieweg & Sohn] New York: Dover, 246 pp., 63 figs.

Weinert, Hans. 1926. Die Ausbildung der Stirnhohlen als stammesgeschichtliches Merkmal. Eine vergleichend-anatomische Studie mit einem Atlas der Stirnhöhlen und einem neuen Messzirkel zur Ermittelung der inneren Schädelmasse. *Z. Morph. Anthrop.* 35:243–357, 365–418, 159 figs.

Wellde, B. T.; Johnson, A. J.; Williams, J .S.; Langbehn, H. R.; and Sadun, E. H. 1971. Hematologic, biochemical, and parasitological parameters of the night monkey (*Aotus trivirgatus*). *Lab. Animal Sci.* 21:575–80.

Wendt, Herbert. 1964. Erfolgreiche Zucht des Baum Wollkopschen oder Pinche-äffchen, *Leontocebus* (*Oedipomidas*) *oedipus* (Linne, 1758), in Gefangenschaft. *Säuget. Mitteil.* 12(2/3):49–52.

Wenzel, Rupert L., and Johnson, Phyllis T. 1966. Checklist of the sucking lice of Panama (Anoplura). In *Ectoparasites of Panama*, ed. R. L. Wenzel and Vernon J. Tipton, pp. 273–79. Chicago: Field Museum of Natural History.

Werneck, Fabio Leoni. 1935. Nova especie do gênero *Gliricola* (Mallophaga: Byropidae). *Mem. Inst. Oswaldo Cruz* 30:373–77, 6 figs.

———. 1948. *Os malófagos de mamíferos. Parte 1: Amblycera e Ischnocera (Philopteridae e parte Trichodectidae)*. Published by *Rev. Brasil. Biol.*, 243 pp., 431 figs.

———. 1950. *Os malófagos de mamíferos. Parte II. Ischnocera (continuação de Trichodectidae) e Rhynophthirinae.* Published by Instituto Oswaldo Cruz, 5 + 207 pp., 312 figs.

Werner, Clements Fritz. 1960*a*. *Das Gehörorgan der Wirbeltiere und des Menschen*. Leipzig, xii + 310 pp., 150 figs.

———. 1960*b*. Das Ohr: A. Mittel- und innen Ohr. *Primatologia* 1(5):1–74, 17 figs.

Wettstein, Erich B. 1963. Variabilität, Geschlechtsunterschiede und Altersvanderungen bei *Callithrix jacchus* L. *Morph. Jahrb.* 104(2):185–270, 19 fig.

Wever, Ernest Glen, and Vernon, Jack A. 1961. Cochlear potentials in the marmoset. *Proc. Nat. Acad. Sci.* 47 (1):739–41, 2 figs.

Wheeler, Russell C. 1968. *A textbook of dental anatomy and physiology*. 4th ed. Philadelphia: W. B. Saunders, xviii + 441 pp., 450 figs.

Whipple, I. L. 1904. The ventral surface of the mammalian chiridium. *Z. Morph.* (*Anthrop.*) 7:261–368, pls. 5 and 6.

Wied-Neuwied, Maximilian Prinz zu. 1821. *Reise nach Brasilien in den Jahren 1815 bis 1817*. Vol. 2. 543 pp., 8 pls.

———. 1826. *Beiträge zur Naturgeschichte von Brasilien*, Vol. 2. 620 pp., 5 pls.

Williams, Ernest E., and Koopman, Karl F. 1952. West Indian fossil monkeys. *Amer. Mus. Novit.* 1546: 1–16, 4 figs.

Willig, Axel, and Wendt, Sabine. 1970. Aufzucht und Verhalten des Geoffroyi-peruckenaffchens, *Oedipomidas geoffroyi* Pucheran, 1845. Mit 2 Abbildungen. *Säugetierk. Mitt.* 18(2):117–22, 2 figs.

Wilner, Burton I. 1969. *A classification of the major groups of human and other animal viruses*. 4th ed. Minneapolis: Burgess Publ. Co., 250 pp.

Wilson, Donald R. 1972. Tail reduction in *Macaca*. In *The functional and evolutionary biology of primates*, ed. R. H. Tuttle, pp. 241–61. Chicago: Aldine-Atherton.

Winans, Sarah H., and Scalia, Frank. 1970. Amygdaloid nucleus: New afferent input from the vomeronasal organ. *Science* 170:330–32.

Winge, Herluf. 1883. Om Pattedyrenes Tandskifte især med Hensyn til Tændernes Former. *Vid. Medd. fra Dansk Naturhist. Foren., Copenhagen* 1882.15–19.

———. 1895. Jordfundne og nulevende aber (primates) fra Lagôa Santa, Minas Geraes, Brasilien. *E Mus. Lundii* (*Copenhagen*) 2(3):45 pp., 2 pls.

———. 1941. *The interrelationships of the mammalian genera*, translated from the Danish by E. Deichmann and G. M. Allen; . . . Copenhagen: C. A. Reitzel, 2:1–376.

Winkelman, R. K. 1959. The innervation of a hair follicle. *Ann. N.Y. Acad. Sci.* 83(3):400–407, 7 figs.

———. 1963. Nerve endings in the skin of primates. In *Evolutionary and genetic biology of primates*, ed. John Buettner-Janusch, 1:229–59, 14 figs. New York: Academic Press.

———. 1965. Innervation of the skin: Notes on a comparison of primate and marsupial nerve endings. In *Biology of the skin and hair growth*, ed. A. G. Lynne and B. F. Short, pp. 71–182, 8 figs. New York: American Elsevier Pub. Co.

Wislocki, George B., 1930. A study of scent glands in the marmoset, especially *Oedipomidas geoffroyi*. *J. Mammal.* 11:475–82, pls. 22–24.

———. 1932. Placentation in the marmoset (*Oedipomidas geoffroyi*) with remarks on twinning in monkeys. *Anat. Rec.* 52(4):381–92, 3 pls.

———. 1933*a*. Location of the testes and body temperature in mammals. *Quart. Rev. Biol.* 8(4):385–96.

———. 1933*b*. The reproductive systems. In *The anatomy of the rhesus monkey* (Macaca mulatta), ed. Carl C. Hartmann, pp. 231–47. Baltimore.

———. 1936. The external genitalia of the simian primates. *Human Biol.* 8:309–47, 34 figs.

———. 1939. Observations on twinning in marmosets. *Amer. J. Anat.* 64:445–83, 5 figs., 5 pls.

Wislocki, George B., and Schultz, Adolph H. 1925. On the nature of modifications of the skin in the sternal region of certain primates. *J. Mammal.* 6:236–44, pl. 22.

Wohnus, J. F., and Benirschke, K. 1966. Chromosome analysis of four species of marmoset (*Callithrix jacchus, Tamarinus mystax, Tamarinus nigricollis, Cebuella pygmaea*). *Cytogenetics* 5(1–2):94–105, 1 fig.

Wolfe, H. Glenn, and Coleman, Douglas L. 1966. Pigmentation. In *Biology of the laboratory mouse*, ed. Earl L. Green, pp. 405–25, 2 pls., 2 figs. New York: McGraw-Hill.

Wolfe, Lauren G., and Deinhardt, Friedrich. 1972. Oncornaviruses associated with spontaneous and experimentally induced neoplasia in nonhuman primates: A review. In *Medical primatology 1973,* ed. E. I. Goldsmith and J. Moor-Jankowski, 3:76–196. Basel: S. Karger.

Wolfe, Lauren G.; Deinhardt, Friedrich; Ogden, James D.; Adams, Michael R.; and Fisher, Lester E. 1975. Reproduction of wild-caught and laboratory-born marmoset species used in biomedical research (*Saguinus* sp.; *Callithrix jacchus*). *Lab. Animal Sci.* 25 (6): 802–13.

Wolfe, Lauren G.; Deinhardt, Friedrich; Theilen, Gordon H.; Rabin, Harry; Kawakami, Tom; and Bustad, Leo K. 1971. Induction of tumors in marmoset monkeys by simian sarcoma virus, type 1 (*Lagothrix*): A preliminary report. *J. Nat. Cancer Inst.* 47:1115–20, 6 figs.

Wolfe, Lauren G.; McDonald, Ruth; and Deinhardt, Friedrich. 1970. Transmission of feline fibrosarcoma virus to marmoset monkeys. *Fed. Proc.* 29:371.

Wolfe, Lauren G.; Marczynska, Barbara; Rabin, Harry; Smith, Roger; Tischendorf, Peter; Gavitt, Francis; and Deinhardt, Friedrich. 1971. Viral oncogenesis in nonhuman primates. In *Medical primatology, 1970,* ed. E. I. Goldsmith and J. Moor-Jankowski, pp. 671–82, 1 fig. Basel: S. Karger.

Wolfe, Lauren G.; Ogden, J. D.; Deinhardt, J. B.; Fisher, L.; and Deinhardt, F. 1972. Breeding and hand-rearing marmosets for viral oncogenesis studies. In *Breeding primates,* ed. W. I. B. Beveridge, pp. 145–57. Basel: S. Karger.

Wolfe, Lauren G.; Smith, Roger D.; Hoekstra, John; Marczynska, Barbara; Smith, Richard K.; McDonald, Ruth; Northrop, Robert L.; and Deinhardt, Friedrich. 1972. Oncogenicity of feline fibrosarcoma viruses in marmoset monkeys: Pathologic, virologic, and immunologic findings. *J. Nat. Cancer Inst.* 47:519–39, 23 figs.

Wolin, Lee R., and Massopust, L. C., Jr. 1967. Characteristics of the ocular fundus in primates. *J. Anat.* 101(4): 693–99, 16 figs.

Wood, Albert E. 1962. The early Tertiary rodents of the family Paramyidae. *Trans. Amer. Philos. Soc.,* n.s., 52 (1): 1–261, 91 figs.

———. 1972. An Eocene hystricognathous rodent from Texas: Its significance in interpretation of continental drift. *Science* 715:1250–51, 1 fig.

———. 1973. Eocene rodents, Pruett Formation, Southwest Texas: Their pertinence to the origin of the South American Caviomorpha. *Texas Mem. Mus. Pearce-Sellards,* ser. no. 20; 40 pp., 8 figs.

Wood, Corinne Shear. 1975. New evidence for a late introduction of malaria into the New World. *Current Anthrop.* 16(1):93–6.

Wood, Jones. *See* Jones, Frederick Wood.

Woodward, M. F. 1896. Contribution to the study of mammalian dentition. Part II. On the teeth of certain insectivora. *Proc. Zool. Soc. London* 1896:557–94, 2 figs., pls. 23–26.

Woollard, H. H. 1925. The anatomy of *Tarsius spectrum. Proc. Zool. Soc. London* 1925:1071–84, 53 figs.

———. 1926. Notes on the retina and lateral geniculate body in *Tupaia, Tarsius, Nycticebus,* and *Hapale. Brain J. Neurol.* 49:77–104, 13 figs.

Workshop-Symposium. 1972. *Proceedings of the Workshop-Symposium on Venezuelan encephalitis virus.* PanAmerican Health Organization Sci. Publ. no. 243 (Washington, D.C.), xiii + 416 pp.

Wortman, J. L. 1902. Studies of Eocene mammalia in the Marsh collection, Peabody Museum. *Amer. J. Sci.* 13:39–46.

———. 1903. Studies of Eocene mammalia in the Marsh collection, Peabody Museum. *Amer. J. Sci.* 16:345–68.

———. 1921. Evolution of molar cusps in mammals. *Amer. J. Phys. Anthrop.* 45:177–88.

Wright, Sewall. 1917*a*. Color inheritance in mammals. *J. Heredity* 8(5):224–35, 2 figs.

———.· 1917*b*. Color inheritance in mammals. The guinea pig. *J. Heredity* 8(10):476–80.

Wynn, Ralph M. 1968. Morphology of the placenta. In *Biology of gestation. Vol. 1. The maternal organism,* ed. N. S. Assali, pp. 93–184, 55 figs. New York: Academic Press.

Wynn, Ralph M.; Richards, Steven C.; and Harris, Jennifer A. 1975. Electron microscopy of the placenta and related structures of the marmoset. *Amer. J. Obstr. Gynecol.* 122(1):60–69, 10 figs.

Yablokov, A. V. 1963. On the types of colour of Cetacea. *Bull. Moscow Soc. Protection Nat.* (*Biology*) 68(6): 27–41, 7 figs.

Yamaguti, S. 1958–59. *Systema Helminthum. 1. The digenetic trematodes of vertebrates. Parts I and II.* New York: Interscience Publ., 1575 pp., 106 pls.

———. 1959. *Systema helminthum. The cestodes of vertebrates.* New York: Interscience Publ., 860 pp., 70 pl.

———. 1961. *Systema helminthum. The nematodes of vertebrates.* Part I, pp. 1–680; Part II, pp. 681–1261, 102 pls. New York: Interscience Publ.

———. 1963. *Systema helminthum. 5. Acanthocephala.* New York: Interscience Publ., 423 pp., 85 pls.

Yamashita, Jiro. 1963. Ecological relationships between parasites and primates. *Primates* 4(1):1–96.

Yeates, N. T. M. 1955. Observations on the role of nutrition in coat shedding in cattle. *Austr. J. Agric. Sci.* 150:110–12.

———. 1958. Photoperiodicity in cattle. I. Seasonal changes in coat characters and their importance in heat regulation. *Austr. J. Agric. Res.* 6:891–902, 2 figs., 3 pls.

Young, Martin D. 1970. Natural and induced malarias in western hemisphere monkeys. *Lab. Animal Care* 20 (2):361–67.

Zimmerman, E. A. W. von. 1780. *Geographische Geschichte des Menchen und der vierfüssigen Thiere. Zweiter Band....* Leipzig: Wendgandschen Buchhandlung, iv + 432 pp.

Zuckerman, Solly. 1931. The menstrual cycle of the Primates. 3. The alleged breeding season of primates, with special reference to the chacma baboon (*Papio porcarius*). *Proc. Zool. Soc. London* 1931:325–43.

Zuckerman, Solly; Ashton, E. H.; and Pearson, J. B. 1962. The styloid of the primate skull. *Bibl. Primat.* 1:217–28, 4 figs.

Zuckerman, Solly; van Wagenen, G.; and Gardiner, R. H. 1938. The sexual skin of the rhesus monkey. *Proc. Zool. Soc. London,* ser. A, 108:385–401, 6 pls.

Zukowsky, Ludwig. 1937. [Nachrichten aus zoologischen Garten], *Zool. Gart.* 9:59–64.

———. 1940. Zur Haltung und Pflege einiger New Welt Affenarten. *Zool. Gart.,* n.f., 12:92–110, 9 figs.

Addendum

This supplement includes excerpts from recent literature received too late to incorporate into the main text, as well as a report on the callitrichids and callimicos I examined in Brazilian museums from 26 July through 7 August 1976. The study material included representatives of two forms new to science described herein.

Much of the recent literature cited in the Addendum advances our knowledge of platyrrhine biology and callitrichid behavior in the wild. Recalling remarks in the preface, (p. x), it can be said that now something is known about callitrichid sleeping quarters.

The arrangement of subject matter headings, the style, and the order of presentation are essentially the same as in the body of the text. Page references after the subject headings refer to the same or equivalent headings in the main text.

Works cited in the Addendum only are identified by the sign A- preceding the years of publication, and complete bibliographic references are given under the heading "Literature Cited in the Addendum [p. 1039]" New locality records and data are inclded in the Gazetteer Supplement (pp. 1034–39).

The three indexes to this volume include the items in the Addendum. It is regretted that a few names and more than a few page references failed to meet the deadlines or could not be squeezed into set pages.

My short visit to the various museums and scientific institutions in South America could not have been successful without the cooperation and courtesies received from the authorities and without their permission to study the primate collections in their charge. I am particularly grateful to the following: The authorities of the Museu Nacional, Rio de Janeiro; Dr. Jorge Hernández Camacho, Asesor, División Parques Nacionales y Vida Silvestre, INDERENA, Bogotá; Dr. Adelmar F. Coimbra-Filho, Director de Divisão de Pesquisas, Instituto de Conservação de Natureza, Rio de Janeiro; Dr. Fernando da Costa Novaes, Head, Department of Zoology, Museu Paraense Emilio Goeldi, Belém; Dr. Paulo Emilio Vanzolini, Director, Museu de Zoologia, Universidad de São Paulo, São Paulo.

Addendum Subject Matter

Primate Classification

(p. 9)

Luckett A-1976, p. 245

"Cladistic analysis of the total ontogenetic pattern of the fetal membranes and placenta in all extant primate superfamilies provides clear evidence of a strepsirhine-haplorhine dichotomy in the order Primates. The suborder Prosimii appears to be a paraphyletic taxon, based on the retention of numerous primitive character states in tarsiers and strepsirhines. Fetal membrane evidence supports the sister group relationship of Tarsiiformes and Anthropoidea in the suborder Haplorhini, based on their possession of shared derived characters. Morphogenetic patterns of the fetal membranes and placenta in haplorhines are consistent with the concept of a monophyletic origin of Anthropoidea from an ancestral tarsiiform stock."

External Characters: Nose and Snout

(p. 16)

Hofer A-1976

Following is a summary of the results of studies of the gross anatomy of the external nose of platyrrhines *Saguinus, Callimico, Saimiri, Aotus, Callicebus, Alouatta, Cebus, Lagothrix,* and *Ateles,* catarrhines *Macaca, Erythrocebus, Chimpansee,* and *Pongo,* the strepsirhine lorisoid *Nycticebus coucang,* and the microscopic anatomy of *Alouatta, Aotus,* and *Nycticebus.*

"(1) The disposition of the nostrils is caused by the lateral expansion of the internarium, which consists of the alar cartilages, the tissue in the sulcus interalaris and the skin between the nostrils. The internarium is situated in front of the septum nasi, which is not involved in platyrrhinism. (2) The alar cartilages form to a variable extent the anterior wall of the cavum nasi, which is in contrast to the catarrhine condition. (3) There is a remarkable similarity in the microscopic structure of the internarium of the lorisiform prosimian *Nycticebus* and the platyrrhine monkeys. This does not indicate a phylogenetic relationship. (4) *Aotus* and *Alouatta* are definitely platyrrhines according to the presence of an internarium. There is no similarity whatsoever with the catarrhine condition. (5) The division of the higher primates into Platyrrhina and Catarrhina is regarded as justified. This may indicate a very early evolutionary separation of the Old World and the New World primates. (6) The internarium of the New World monkeys shows sinus hairs and is accordingly a sensorial area, at least of the sense of touch."

Platyrrhine Origins and Relationships

(p. 67)

Cronin and Sarich (A-1975) interpret platyrrhine origin, evolution, and classification on the basis of a comparative immunological study of albumin and transferrin rates of change. They (A-1975, p. 357) emphasize their typological method and circular reasoning with the clarification "that the analysis of immunological data is not dependent on non-molecular information or assumptions concerning rates of evolution, and that the analysis provides its own indications of interpretative problems." It is unfortunate that none of the analyzed data can be preserved for reexamination. Other protein samples or other analytical techniques may yield varying or contradictory results (cf. Cronin and Sarich [A-1975, pp. 361, 370]).

The order Primates, according to Cronin and Sarich (A-1975, p. 359), is a "monophyletic unit *vis-à-vis* other mammals." Their inclusion of *Tupaia* and *Cynocephalus* (Dermoptera) with lemuriforms, lorisiforms, catarrhines, and platyrrhines, however, converts the order into a polyphyletic "wastebasket." What is known of the morphology of *Tupaia* and *Cynocephalus,* particularly their entotympanic auditory bullae, attests that neither could have sprung from the placental stock that gave rise to pre-primates, not to mention the basic primate stock itself. In any event, it is not clear where Cronin and Sarich (cf. A-1975, p. 361) place *Tupaia* and *Cynocephalus* among primates.

The phylogenetic relationships among platyrrhines suggested by the albumin and transferrin immunological data (Cronin and Sarich A-1975, p. 370, fig. 4) agree for the most part with arrangements based on nonmolecular data. The close relationship indicated between *Alouatta* and *Ateles-Lagothrix* may emphasize the retention of many ancestral cebid characters rather than a primary dichotomy from a common ancestor. The morphological and zoogeographic contradition apparent in the indication of a nearer relationship between *Callithrix* and *Callimico* than between *Callithrix* and *Saguinus* throws doubt on the validity of the immunological method or the criteria used for measuring phyletic distances. Cronin and Sarich (A-1975, p. 370) do note, nevertheless, a striking difference in the rates of albumin and transferrin evolution among callitrichids, and they find it "difficult to decide if the callithricids and *Callimico* are of as recent a common ancestry as the transferrin data would suggest or if their adaptive radiation began as long ago as the albumins would indicate." Perhaps use of the albumin meter stick for *Callimico* and the transferrin scale for callitrichids would solve the dilemma.

Aotus adds another discordant note to interpretations of evolutionary rates of molecular evolution. The problem as seen by Cronin and Sarich (A-1975, p. 371) is "whether *Aotus* represents a lineage that is part of a single, relatively recent, New World monkey adaptive radiation (as the transferrin data would suggest) or whether it is a relict form stemming from original adaptive radiation which must have occurred soon after the ancestor of the platyrrhines arrived in South America (as the albumins would indicate)." The immunological responses to malarial infections (above, p. 381) support the dictum of the albumin.

The timetable for primate origin and divergence of

primary stems based on albumin and transferrin immunological distances constructed by Cronin and Sarich (A-1975, p. 366, fig. 1) finds little if any real support in the fossil record. Their arguments (A-1975, p. 372) favoring the hypothesis of an African derivation of platyrrhine monkeys depend entirely on nonmolecular information. Their predications that "except for *Aotus* . . . all the modern New World monkeys are a part of a single primary adaptive radiation that occurred some appreciable time after the catarrhine-platyrrhine divergence [and that] there then followed three secondary radiations which led to modern forms" is debatable. It has been demonstrated (above, p. 71; Hershkovitz 1974) that the three known Oligocene fossil primates were already highly specialized products of widely separated lineages with no common New World ancestor in our purview. None of these or the few known South American Miocene fossils, with doubtful exception of *Neosaimiri,* could have given rise to any living platyrrhine.

Notes on Individual Dental Elements

(pp. 287–93)

Trigon, Trigonid, "Trigonid," and Talonid

The classical trigon of Cope-Osbornian terminology (cf. fig. V.21, and p. 284, section C, type 1) is defined by cusps *1* (eocone or paracone), *2* (protocone), and *4* (metacone), with symbol α representing the enclosed trigon basin. In some molariform teeth, cusps *1, 2,* and *5* (hypocone) demarcate the trigon (cf. p. 284, section C, type 2).

The classical trigonid of the Cope-Osbornian system is defined by cusps *1, 2,* and *3* (paraconid), and its basin lies between cristae *I* and *II*. The paraconid of this trigonid is absent in many mammals, and it has no upper tooth homologue; at the same time, crista *I* may be poorly defined or absent.

The differences between upper and lower structures described above are fundamental. Nevertheless, I retain the Cope-Osbornian terms but use quotation marks for "trigonid" to indicate that there is no homology with the trigon. Curiously, the apparent upper molariform tooth homologue of the "trigonid" basin (ε) had not been named. It is here identified as the pretrigon basin or fossa (p. 301).

Paradoxically, the homologue of the Cope-Osbornian trigon is a part of the Cope-Osbornian talonid. This part, like the trigon, is defined by cusps *1* (eoconid or protoconid), *2* (metaconid), and either *4* (hypoconid) or *5* (ectoconid) as described on page 286, section D, illustrated in figure V.11D. The classical terms trigon and talonid, however, are too firmly established to be lightly discarded. To avoid the appearance of unconformity, quotation marks should be used for "talonid." Regretably, this was not done in the body of the text of this volume.

The talon and its lower crown homologue are defined by cusps *4, 5, e,* and *b* and crests *IV* and *VI*. The enclosed basin is labeled β. The basin, in turn, may be divided by crista *VII* in the upper molariform tooth and by crista *VIII* in the lower. The talon, as defined, cannot be confused with anything else. The truly homologous talonid, on the other hand, has been treated within the Cope-Osbornian system as an integral portion of the composite "talonid."

Nearly all components of upper and lower dental crown formations can be homologized. However, such Cope-Osbornian structures as trigon-trigonid and talon-talonid are merely analogous.

Dental Form and Function

(fig. III.5, pp. 75–76; 281, 302–4)

Rosenberger and Kinzey A-1976

The authors report that adaptations of the molar crown elements of *Callithrix, Alouatta, Pithecia,* and *Cebus* for processing preferred foods can be determined from the physical properties of these foods. Conversely, they attempt to show that the preferred physical properties of foods suggest which of the molar crown elements are specialized for processing those foods. These functional features of the molars, the authors discover, suggest that *Callithrix* is insectivorous, *Alouatta* folivorous, *Pithecia* frugivorous, and *Cebus* omnivorous. They (p. 296) conclude that "functional studies of the masticatory system can yield important information on the adaptive significance of evolutionary grades and important clues concerning the cladistic relations among fossil and living taxa."

Dental Succession in *Saimiri*

(pp. 317–21)

Long and Cooper 1968

The following table (table A-1), showing the sequence of dental eruption in the squirrel monkey *Saimiri sciureus,* was inadvertently omitted from chapter 35.

Table A-1. *Saimiri sciureus*: Chronological Sequence of Dental Eruption and Succession, Means, Extremes (in Parentheses) in Weeks, Followed by Sample Size for Each Tooth

	Lower		*Upper*
	Deciduous		
di_1	1.3 (0–3) 10	di^1	1.3 (1–3) 10
di_2	2.2 (1–3) 10	di^2	1.4 (1–3) 10
dc	3.4 (2–4) 10	dc	3.4 (3–4) 10
dp_2	4.9 (4–6) 10	dp^2	4.8 (4–6) 10
dp_3	6.1 (5–7) 10	dp^3	5.7 (5–7) 10
dp_4	8.9 (8–11) 10	dp^4	8.3 (7–9) 10
	Permanent		
m_1	5.5 (5–6)8	m^1	5.1 (5–6) 8
m_2	8.4 (7–9) 8	m^2	7.0 (7) 8
i_1	9.7 (8–12) 8	i^1	9.2 (8–11) 8
i_2	12.0 (10–14) 8	i^2	9.6 (8–11) 8
p_3	13.0 (12–15) 5	m^3	12.3 (11–14) 3
p_4	13.0 (12–15) 7	p^4	12.8 (12–15) 6
p_2	14.7 (14–15) 3	p^2	14.3 (12–16) 3
m_3	20.0 (19–22) 3	p^3	15.0 (15) 2
c	21.5 (21–22) 4	c	20.5 (19–21) 4

SOURCE: Data from Long and Cooper (1968, pp. 195–96)

It appears that premolars 3 and 4 erupt about the same time in *Saimiri,* whereas in *Callithrix* (p. 318) p^3 erupts later, on the average, than p^4. The same sequence is found in *Saguinus* but with less delay between the eruption of p^3 and p^4, or more nearly as in *Saimiri.*

Criteria for dental eruption in *Saguinus* used by Chase and Cooper (above, p. 317) are the same used by Long and Cooper (1968, p. 194) for *Saimiri*. Different criteria used by Johnston, Dreizen, and Levy (above, p. 317) for *Callithrix* may account for some of the apparent chronological difference in sequence of eruption between the marmoset and tamarin.

Parasites

Additions to the number of parasites in chapter 43 are listed here in the same systematic order. Bacterial and fungal parasites with no special relationship to their primate hosts were, with few exceptions, excluded from consideration. More exceptions are made here, however, because of the special biomedical interest in the host species.

Viruses

Adenovirus Group (p. 370)

Two adenoviruses isolated from *Aotus trivirgatus* and reported by Daniel, Fraser, Barahona, Hajema, and Melendez (A-1976) have not been formally described.

Paramyxovirus Group (p. 374)

Daniel, Fraser, Barahona, Hajema, and Melendez (A-1976) announce the isolation of an undescribed paramyxovirus from a spontaneously degenerating *Aotus* kidney cell culture 66 days old. The find may be the first of paramyxovirus from a platyrrhine.

Papovavirus Group (p. 369)

A virus morphologically resembling a papovavirus was isolated from *Aotus* by Daniel, Fraser, Barahona, Hajema, and Melendez (A-1976). Its formal description is in preparation. Viruses of the group have not been previously reported from New World monkeys.

Herpesvirus Group

Herpesvirus cebus, AP 18 (p. 371)
First noted in abstract form by Lewis et al. (1974); described in full by Lewis, Frye, Gibbs, Chou, Cutchins, Gajdusek, and Ward (A-1976). Host *Cebus apella* is the tufted capuchin monkey.

Herpesvirus cebus, AL 5 (p. 371)
First reported in abstract form by Lewis et al. (1974); described in full by Lewis, Frye, Gibbs, Chou, Cutchins, Gajdusek, and Ward (A-1976). Host *Cebus albifrons* I now regard as a race of *Cebus capucinus*. Subspecific determination, however, awaits a taxonomic revision of the brown and black white-fronted capuchins.

Oncornavirus Group (p. 375)

C-type virus particles, isolated from mandibular and mesenteric lymph nodes of a crested capuchin (*Cebus apella*) by Kalter, Kuntz, Heberling, Smith, Moore, and McCullough (A-1977).

Squirrel monkey retravirus (SMRV)
D-type virus isolated by Heberling, Barker, Kalter, Smith, and Helmke (A-1977) from lung tissue of a stillborn male *Saimiri sciureus*.

Retraviridae
A new family erected by Heberling, Barker, Kalter, Smith, and Helmke (A-1977) to include D-type, slow, and foamy viruses.

Hepatitis Viruses (p. 375)

Deinhardt, Wolfe, Peterson, Cross, and Holmes, A-1975, pp. 400–401

[The term "marmoset" as used in the cited work refers to the tamarin species *Saguinus oedipus, S. fuscicollis,* and *S. mystax*—P.H.]

"The immunological and experimental human volunteer and animal studies indicate that . . . at least 3 or 4 types of viral hepatitis may exist:

"1. Hepatitis A (MS-1 type) which does not cross-react with hepatitis B, is positive for HA particles and their corresponding antibodies, can be transmitted to marmosets [*sic*] and chimpanzees and which cross-reacts with fecal hepatitis A antigen.

"2. Hepatitis A (GB type) which does not cross-react with hepatitis B, is antigenically not identical with MS-1, . . . can be transmitted to marmosets [*sic*] (chimpanzees are being tested currently) and which cross-reacts with fecal hepatitis A antigen.

"3. 'Non-type B' post tranfusion hepatitis which does not cross-react with hepatitis B antigens or HA particles by immunoelectron microscopy. Materials from this type of hepatitis are being tested currently for infectivity in non-human primates. . . .

"4. Hepatitis B which . . . can be transmitted to chimpanzees and rhesus monkeys but not to marmosets [*sic*]."

[For use of *Saguinus mystax* as a model species for study of human hepatitis see Maynard, Krushak, Bradley, and Berquist (A-1975), and following.]

Krushak, Maynard, Bradley, and Hornbeck (A-1975)

Results of a 4-year laboratory study of tamarins as infective models for hepatitis A convinced the authors that *Saguinus mystax* was better than *S. nigricollis* or *S. oedipus* because of its larger size, general heartiness [*sic*] and ability to survive in captivity.

[No evidence is given and none is known that would support the claims of superiority, but see next entry.]

Hilleman, Provost, Villarejos, Buynak, Miller, Ittensohn, Wolanski, and McAleer (A-1976)

Tests of susceptibility of three species of *Saguinus* to hepatitis A strain CR 326, isolated from humans in Costa Rica, showed significant differences. *Saguinus mystax mystax* proved to be highly susceptible, *S. nigri-*

collis nigricollis moderately so, and *S. oedipus oedipus* hardly at all.

[The indicated differences reflect both the phylogenetic and geographic distances between the species.]

Bacteria

(p. 376)

Bacteria infesting *Aotus* have been compiled from Daniel, Fraser, Barahona, Hajema, and Melendez (A-1976). Those parasitic in *Callicebus* are from Seibold, Perrin, and Garner (A-1970). The source for other platyrrhine hosts listed is N. King (A-1976). Only generic names are used here for the bacteria.

Escherichia
 Aotus trivirgatus
 Callicebus moloch
 Saimiri sciureus
 Ateles paniscus
Shigella
 Aotus trivirgatus
 Callicebus moloch
 Saimiri sciureus
 Cebus sp.
 Lagothrix lagothricha
 Ateles paniscus
Proteus
 Aotus trivirgatus
 Saimiri sciureus
Klebsiella
 Aotus trivirgatus
 Callicebus moloch
Bordetella
 Callicebus moloch
 Callicebus torquatus
Enterobacter
 Aotus trivirgatus
Salmonella
 Aotus trivirgatus
 Callicebus moloch
Streptobacillus
 Aotus trivirgatus
Providencia
 Aotus trivirgatus
Arizona
 Aotus trivirgatus
Citrobacter
 Aotus trivirgatus
Alcaligenes
 Aotus trivirgatus
Pasteurella
 Aotus trivirgatus
Yersinia (cf. p. 512)
 Aotus trivirgatus
Pseudomonas
 Aotus trivirgatus
Acinotobacter
 Aotus trivirgatus
Hemophilus
 Aotus trivirgatus
Neisseria
 Aotus trivirgatus
Corynebacterium
 Aotus trivirgatus
Bacteroides
 Aotus trivirgatus
Streptococcus
 Aotus trivirgatus
Aerococcus
 Aotus trivirgatus
Staphylococcus
 Aotus trivirgatus
Bacillus
 Aotus trivirgatus

Fungi

(p. 377)

Host records are from N. King (A-1976)

Dermatophilus
 Aotus trivirgatus
 Lagothrix lagothricha
Microsporum
 Ateles paniscus
Cryptococcus
 Saguinus
Histoplasma
 Saimiri sciureus

Protozoa

Eimeriidae (p. 380)
 Isospora arctopitheci
(Panamanian monkeys found susceptible to experimental infection by Hendricks A-1977.)
  Saguinus oedipus geoffroyi
  Saimiri sciureus
  Aotus trivirgatus
  Alouatta palliata
  Cebus capucinus
  Ateles paniscus
 Isospora endocallimici
  Callimico goeldii
  (G. King A-1976*b*, p. 91)
Trypanosomatidae
 Leishmania (p. 378)

The parasite was unknown among wild platyrrhines until 1972, when Baker reported infection in an individual of *Saguinus oedipus geoffroyi*. The following year Herrer, Christensen, and Beumer (1973) found the disease in another specimen of *S. o. geoffroyi* and in one of *Aotus*. The addition of *Aotus* was noted in the discussion on page 369 (line 1) but inadvertently not in the summary on page 449.

Plasmodiidae (p. 381)
 Plasmodium brasilianum
 (Deane A-1976)
  Alouatta belzebul (includes *nigerrima* and *ululata*)
  Callicebus torquatus
  Chiropotes albinasa
  Pithecia monachus

Deane (A-1976) found *Plasmodium brasilianum* in 1 of 18 specimens of *Pithecia monachus* and none in 15 samples of *Pithecia pithecia*. Amazonian *Aotus* (12 specimens) proved negative. Four samples of *Cacajao melanocephalus* were also negative. *Ateles beelzebuth*, listed as negative, I regard as conspecific with other named forms of *Ateles*, most of which have been shown to be susceptible to infection. A total of 340 callitrichids representing 9 species tested negative. Their names and sample numbers, in parentheses, follow.

Cebuella pygmaea (1)
Callithrix jacchus (with subspecies *jacchus, penicillata, geoffroyi, aurita*) (237)
Callithrix humeralifer (2)
Saguinus fuscicollis (3)
Saguinus labiatus (includes *griseovertex*) (9)
Saguinus mystax (3)
Saguinus imperator (2)
Saguinus midas (includes *"tamarin"* = *niger*) (65)
Saguinus bicolor (12)

Plasmodium simium (p. 381)

Rossan, Baerg, and Young (A-1975) provide the documentation missing in the Annual (1973) Report of the Gorgas Memorial Laboratory for the experimental infection of Panamanian *Saguinus oedipus geoffroyi, Aotus trivirgatus, Alouatta palliata, Cebus capucinus,* and *Ateles paniscus* (including *fusciceps* and *geoffroyi*).

The accumulated evidence strengthens the indication that all cebids except *Aotus* are natural malarial parasite hosts. With the questioned exception of a single representative of *Saguinus oedipus geoffroyi* (cf. p. 381), 13 species of the family Callitrichidae tested for malarial infection proved negative. Callitrichids *Saguinus inustus* and *Leontopithecus rosalia* remain to be tested. Susceptibility of *Callimico* to natural or experimental malarial infection is still unknown.

Nematoda

Strongyloididae (p. 385)
Strongyloides sp.
Callimico goeldii
(G. King A-1976*b*, p. 91)
Note: This parasite species brings to 19 the total number known for *Callimico goeldii* (p. 870)

Trichostrongylidae (p. 385)
Trichostrongylus sp.
Saguinus midas
(G. King A-1976*b*, p. 91)
Molineus vexillarius
Saimiri sciureus
(Tantaleán A-1976)

Acarina

Demodicidae (p. 392)
Demodex sp.
Aotus trivirgatus
(N. King A-1976)

Trombiculidae (p. 392)
Eutrombicula tropica
Callicebus torquatus
(Brennan and Reed 1975)

Insecta

Trichodectidae (p. 393)
Cebidicola extrarius
Alouatta seniculus
(Emerson and Price 1975)

FAMILY CALLITRICHIDAE

Facial Musculature

(p. 416)
Seiler A-1976, p. 96

The meager information on callitrichid facial musculature is based on *Callithrix jacchus jacchus, C. j. penicillata, Saguinus nigricollis nigricollis, Saguinus mystax mystax,* and *Leontopithecus rosalia rosalia*. The muscles appear to be very similar in all callitrichids studied. Some recall those of prosimians and some are distinctive and serve to separate callitrichids from cebids. Other muscles appear to be absent. Should *m. sphincter colli* be present it would be united with *m. depressor helicis*. The *platysma myoides* and *m. zygomaticus* are widely separated with no *m. auriculolabialis* between. The *"orbicularis-oris* fiber system" connects with the upper but not the lower jaw. Other muscles not found are *m. nasalis, m. auriculus anterior, m. tragus, m. incisurae Santorini,* and *m. intercartilagineus. M. auricularis inferior,* if present, is represented as a fibrous ligament between mandible and tympanic bulla and/or external auditory meatus.

The comparatively simple callitrichid facial musculature is evidently nearest the primitive state among living platyrrhines.

Placenta

(p. 440)

Jollie, Haar, and Craig (A-1975) describe the ultrafine structures of the hemopoitic sinuses in the trabeculae of the placenta in *Saguinus oedipus oedipus*.

Duration of Gestation

(p. 441)
Hodgen, Wolfe, Ogden, Adams, Descalzi, and Hildebrand, A-1976

The hemagglutination inhibition test for urinary chorionic gonadotropin in pregnant macaques and baboons (Hodgen and Nieman A-1975) is also diagnostic of pregnancy between the 4th and 10th week after conception in *Callithrix jacchus, Saguinus nigricollis, S. fuscicollis,* and *S. oedipus*. Callitrichid pregnancy urine, the investigators (A-1976, p. 228) find, "contains detectable chorionic gonadotropin as early as the second week after the estimated time of fertilization, reaches zenith levels of the hormone between the 7th and 9th week after fertilization and lacks measurable levels of this hormone during the final 4 weeks of gestation. . . . The number of fetuses did not influence the excretion pattern and levels of urinary chorionic gonadotropin."

There appears to be substantial structural similarity between chorionic gonadotropin of New and Old World primates tested, but the pattern of excretion is distinctly different.

Litters

(pp. 440, 442, 538, 670)

It had been assumed that litters consisting of 3, 4, and 5 young are more likely to be phenomena of managed life in well-endowed breeding facilities than of life in the wild. The very high percentage (40.5%) of triplet litters produced by captive *Callithrix jacchus* (above, p. 538) suggests, nevertheless, that a goodly percentage of triplets may be born in nature as well. However, the constant care and carrying required by infants and the availability of only two teats for suckling make it appear unlikely that more than one or two young of a litter of three would survive in the wild. The sighting by Izawa (A-1976, p. 385; below, p. 1026) in the wild of *Saguinus fuscicollis* triplets carried on their mother's back is good evidence of the birth and viability of triplets in nature.

Longevity

(p. 445, add title)

The following callitrichid longevity records established at the Jersey Zoological Park (Mallinson A-1976, pp. 49–50) are compared with previously published records, shown in parentheses, with text page references. Sex given applies to the Jersey Zoo animals.

Cebuella pygmaea – (4 years, 11 months, 14 days, p. 470)
Callithrix jacchus jacchus ♂ 9/10/18 (12/6/?; 16/?/?, p. 544)
Callithrix jacchus penicillata ♀ 5/2/–
Callithrix j. penicillata × *C. j. jacchus* ♂ 7/3/12, still living
Callithrix humeralifer humeralifer ♂ 5/9/16, still living (12–13/–/–, p. 599)
Saguinus fuscicollis ♂ 9/10/15 (7/2/28, p. 678)
Saguinus imperator ♂ 14/6/21, still living (8/6/21, p. 704)
Saguinus midas midas ♀ 6/11/22, still living (7/6/?, p. 725)
Saguinus midas niger (13/–/–, cf. Hellenkant et al. A-1976)
Saguinus oedipus geoffroyi ♂ 13/0/25 (13/?/?, p. 783)
Saguinus oedipus oedipus (7/2/?, p. 783)

Nutrition

(p. 446, add title)

G. King A-1976*a*, p. 81

In a 14-day controlled experiment, food, nutrient, energy, and vitamin intakes were measured in 3 adult pairs of *Saguinus oedipus oedipus* and 2–1/2 pairs (5 individuals) of *Callithrix jacchus jacchus* fed standardized laboratory diets of fruit, vegetables, eggs, cereals, bread, peanuts, honey, mealworms, crickets, vitamins, and mineral supplements.

Solid and liquid food intakes were about the same in both species. The nutrient intakes were likewise similar because of the standardized diet. Daily energy intakes related to units of metabolic weight, defined as (body weight in kilograms)$^{0.75}$, or W3/4, were 124 Kcals/W3/4 for the tamarins, and 120 Kcals/W3/4 for the marmosets.

ADDITIONAL SPECIMENS EXAMINED

The specimens of callitrichids examined in the South American Museums in July and August 1976 are listed below by locality and institution. The museums visited and the symbols used for them are as follows:

Museu Nacional, Rio de Janeiro	MNRJ
Museu Paraense Emilio Goeldi, Belém	MPEG
Museu de Zoologia, Universidad de São Paulo	MZUSP
Instituto de Ciéncias Naturales, Bogotá	ICN
Instituto de Desarrollo de los Recursos Naturales Renovables, Bogotá	INDERENA

Cebuella pygmaea Spix

(p. 462)

Additional specimens examined, 24 (total 145). BRAZIL—*Acre:* Seringal Oriente, near Vila Taumaturgo, Rio Juruá (210), 1 (MPEG); *Amazonas:* Boca do Chandless, Rio Purus, 1 (MZUSP); Igarapé Tacana, Alto Solimões 1 (MNRJ); Pauini, 1 (MZUSP); Rio Solimões, 1 (MPEG); PERU—*Loreto:* "Iquitos" (92), 8 (MPEG, 7; MZUSP, 1), "Chimbote, Río Solimões" (83), 3 (MPEG); Palmares, Río Solimões, 2 (MPEG); Pebas (85), 11 (MNRJ); *Locality unrecorded:* 2 (MNRJ; MZUSP).

Remarks Significant differences between the populations represented by specimens examined were not noted.

Distribution

(p. 464)

Freese A-1975, p. 29

"*C. pygmaea* was reported along all the tributary rivers of the Amazon (does not include Pachitea) and Marañon which we surveyed. In addition, our guide at Moyobamba stated that *C. pygmaea,* which he accurately described, inhabits forest near Moyobamba [120], and John Terborgh (personal communication) reports sightings of this species at Cocha Cashu [Río Manú, Madre de Dios, Peru (129)]."

Neville, N. Castro, Mármol, and Revilla A-1976

The pygmy marmoset is said to occur in the lower Río Samiria and middle Río Pacaya basins, both systems in the divide between the lower Ríos Ucayali and Huallaga.

Comments

The Santa Cruz, Río Huallaga specimen and others from Sarayacu, Río Ucayali, and Huachi, Río Pastaza, mentioned on page 464, have been examined (p. 466), and I see no reason now for questioning the precision of the locality data. On the other hand, the report of the occurrence of *Cebuella* near Moyobamba (126) awaits confirmation.

The accumulated data establish the western and northern boundaries of *Cebuella* as drawn in figure VIII.1 (p.

451), and the Pauini and Rio Chandless records (above) prove the presence of *Cebuella* on the east at least to the left bank of the Rio Purus. The reputed presence of the animal in the upper Rio Madeira basin in Manú, southeastern Peru (Freese A-1975), and in Pando, northwestern Bolivia (Heltne, Freese, and Whitesides A-1976), indicates that the Rio Madeira, at least for its upper half, marks the eastern boundary.

Hernández Camacho and Cooper (A-1976, p. 37) mention a "captive specimen reportedly from Caño Morrocoy, on the south bank of the Guayabero River, about 2 km eastward from the town of El Refugio (also known as La Macarena)," as possible evidence for occurrence of the species north of the Río Caquetá, in Colombia. Klein and Klein (A-1976, *Neotropical Primate Field Studies and Conservation,* p. 70) saw none in the La Macarena region during a two-month survey. The Colombian naturalist Kjell von Sneidern, who collected the mammals of the region for the Field Museum, also failed to see any.

Courtship

(p. 467)

Fess A-1975*b*, p. 15

"Before breeding [mating] occurred, scent marking behavior similar to that described for *Oedipomidas oedipus* was observed in [captive] *C. pygmaea, C. jacchus* and *C. geoffroyi.* All four species exhibited great interest by smelling and licking the marked areas of the cage as well as their mates' genitalia.

"Preceding and during marking displays, the male pygmy exhibited tongue-flicking, lip smacking and walking with its back arched."

Mating

(p. 467)

Fess A-1975*b*, p. 15

C. pygmaea were observed mating in their natural habitat near Leticia (see below) around 10:30 A.M. and again at 3:15 P.M. on 14 February 1970.

Growth and Development

(pp. 469–70)

Fess A-1975*b*, pp. 15–17

1–2d day:	Eyes open second day in five sets of infants; at birth in another set; all vocalized 3–12 hours after birth
3d day:	Follow objects with eyes
13th day:	Take food from parent's hands
14–16 days:	Walked distance of 3–6 inches between parents
20th day:	Eat solids

Offspring with parents 150–200 days before separation, that were fed live foods including mice at least twice a week, tended to continue eating live foods after separation.

One captive-born attained adult size 185 days after birth; captive-born twins "reached their parents' size at 164 days and surpassed their parents' height and weight at 225 days."

Habitat and Home Range

(pp. 471, 473, and title)

Moynihan A-1976*a*, pp. 79–80

"I was able to observe several groups of pygmy marmosets in and around the localities called El Pepino and Rumiyaco, between the towns of Mocoa and Puerto Asís in the Putumayo region of Colombia, during four field trips (September 17–24, 1968; July 4–11, 1969; February 19–23, 1970; August 12–14 1970). . . .

"Under present conditions, the human population of the region is increasing; much of the forest has been cut down; and there is the beginning of a pollution problem, a by-product of the developing petroleum industry. . . .

"All or most of the local marmosets of El Pepino and Rumiyaco have become commensals of man. . . . They seem most abundant in 'hedges,' strips and clumps of degraded woods found between pastures and crop fields from which the most economically valuable (tallest) trees have been removed by selective cutting and from which many of the larger mammals have been driven by hunting. . . .

"Each group of pygmy marmosets has a well-defined and apparently persistent home range, often the whole of an isolated or semi-isolated hedge or patch of scrub, at times several hundred meters long."

Hernández Camacho and Cooper A-1976, p. 37

"In Colombia *Cebuella* is typically an inhabitant of mature, nonflooding forest. Its ecological association with the guarango tree (*Parkia* sp.) as a source of sap is one of the more striking dietary specializations known among neotropical primates."

Freese A-1975, p. 29

"In a well-surveyed forest along approximately 1.5 km of a small tributary stream of the Nanay only 2 *C. pygmaea* groups live, and these 2 groups are located in the only two sites where the resin-source trees occur in distinctly higher densities. One of these troops had 9, and later, 8 individuals. In the Nanay basin our extensive fieldwork and local reports show that *C. pygmaea* inhabits almost strictly stream-side, inundatable forest, but along the Ampiyacu we found *C. pygmaea* inhabiting non-inundatable forest and utilizing some different tree species for resin. This species' specialized feeding habit and its apparent dependence on a limited number of tree species in any one forest or area probably means that numbers of this monkey may be locally abundant but that overall it is not abundant."

Fess A-1975*b*, pp. 12–13

A group of 5 individuals observed February 1970, and a group of 4 observed April 1972, near Leticia, Río Amazonas, Colombia, ranged "over a humid area of stream overgrowth, approximately 30 yards in width and 120 yards long. Water 6″ to 3′ deep covered most of the ground area directly under the trees and bush habituated by *C. pygmaea.* The monkeys' resting, grooming, breeding, insect and lizard hunting behavior occurred between the 15′ and 35′ level."

R. Castro and Soini A-1977

"At the Aucayo [above Iquitos, Peru] site we located five troops of *Cebuella* living within and near the native community of Centro Union and found evidence of presence of several others along the banks of the river. Three of these inhabited vegetation of the inundatable edges of the Aucayo river, a fourth lived 180 m inland at the edge of the village clearing, and a fifth at the edge of an old banana field, a half-kilometer further inland. Their presence was hardly noticed by the villagers.

"Although the home ranges of at least two of the troops included a portion of edge vegetation on either side of the narrow (about 7 m wide) and sinuous water course, connected by one or two established branch bridges, the river curves formed clear-cut boundaries between adjacent home ranges. The core area of each troop included one or several sap source trees and at least one sleeping tree, and the linear distance between the adjacent troops' core areas was only a little over 100 m. The troop of ten had a home range of approximately 1.3 Ha and the others about 0.8 Ha and 3.4 Ha, including the water surface within the home ranges . . . indicating that *Cebuella* as a rule maintains small home ranges. . . .

"The fourth troop, consisting of five animals, was isolated from the other troops by the village clearing. Its core area consisted of one large emergent tree that could properly be termed a "home tree," surrounded by rather low, mixed secondary vegetation. The monkeys were seen foraging all day long in that tree and also spent the night there."

Hernández Camacho and Cooper A-1976, p. 37

"They are most often found on the trunk or major branches of a guarango tree and, if disturbed while low on the trunk, are known to run to the ground for escape. Their terrestrial route to and from guarangos is evident by their intermittent presence in such trees in clearings a short distance from undisturbed forest. As mature guarangos are usually emergent over the forest canopy and somewhat free of climbers, it appears that such terrestrial passage must be rather common."

Visibility

(p. 473, add title)

Hernández Camacho and Cooper A-1976, p. 37

"Pygmy marmosets are rather difficult to find due to their small size, the camouflage of their coat color, their squirrellike habit of moving to the opposite side of a trunk when disturbed, and their lack of any conspicuous physical or vocal display."

Troop Size

(p. 473, Social Organization)

Moynihan A-1976*a*, p. 80

"Three to six individuals comprised each of the six groups that I could follow closely. In thick vegetation the animals are very difficult to count precisely, since they tend to 'string out'; but settlers claim to have seen groups of approximately eight or nine individuals. This suggests that the basic social unit is the family, composed of an adult male and female with their young of the year, sometimes with older young of previous years with their own mates and offspring."

R. Castro and Soini A-1977

"Complete counts of individuals in all but one of the troops ranged from five to ten. The only troop of ten animals consisted of eight self-locomoting individuals and a pair of infants, born in May."

Hernández Camacho and Cooper A-1976, p. 37

"They have been observed in groups as large as 10 or 15 and are seldom, if ever, seen alone."

R. Castro and Soini A-1977

Complete counts of individuals in all but one of the troops ranged from five to ten. The only group of ten animals consisted of eight self-locomoting individuals and a pair of infants born in May.

Izawa A-1976, p. 386

"The monkeys inhabited only the left bank of the River Caquetá and southwards. An intensive survey on them has not yet been made. . . .

"The maximum number of monkeys counted in the five encounters was six. The next most was four in one encounter, three in two encounters and one in one encounter. In all these cases, the possibility of oversights involving one to several monkeys has to be considered. The information given by local inhabitants suggests that the group size of the pygmy marmosets was four to five monkeys at least, with a maximum of 20 monkeys."

Sleeping Site

(p. 471, add title)

Moynihan A-1976*a*, p. 81

"Like all the smaller New World primates except *Saimiri*, pygmy marmosets sleep in tree holes. Their sleeping holes are not in the same trees as their feeding holes."

Daily Rhythm

(p. 473)

Moynihan A-1976*a*, p. 81

"Pygmy marmosets are thoroughly diurnal. Like many diurnal and endothermic vertebrates in the tropics, they are more active in the cooler hours of the mornings and late afternoons than at midday. It seems that their periods of activity are more prolonged, on the average, than are those of their larger relatives. This is what would be expected of such tiny animals, with their high metabolic and food requirements."

"In their natural habitat, *C. pygmaea* have been observed engaging in social grooming in the morning and afternoon and the longest grooming session lasted approximately five minutes."

Defense

(p. 473)

Moynihan A-1976*a*, p. 82

"Pygmy marmosets do not show the spectacular 'mobbing' behavior of many tamarins. Instead, like squirrels they frequently dodge behind trunks and branches. . . . When individuals pass from one tree to another, they almost always prefer to take a low route rather than a high one, thus keeping as far away as possible from the canopy and minimizing exposure to flying birds of prey."

Temperament

(p. 473, add title)

Moynihan A-1976*a*, p. 81

"Although pygmy marmosets can become tame in special situations, they seem to be terrified of potential predators, more so than any of their relatives. One group living in a hedge at the side of a highway paid little attention to either human beings or passing traffic, not even the heaviest, noisiest, most brightly painted or illuminated trucks. However, other less-sophisticated individuals in less extremely aberrant circumstances were exceedingly shy and timid."

Interspecific Relations

(cf. pp. 471, 474 add title)

Moynihan A-1976*a*, p. 82

"In the artificial hedges, pygmy marmosets are largely segregated from other nonhuman primates. Although there were reports of groups of *Saguinus fuscicollis* traversing *Cebuella* ranges, I did not see any contacts between the two species, nor are they likely to be common."

Pygmy squirrels (*Microsciurus*) occur in the same localities as, and their home ranges or territories broadly overlap with, those of pygmy marmosets. However, direct encounters between individuals or groups of the two species were not seen, although both can visit the same sites the same day. Tree bark chewed and stripped by squirrels may also be pitted by the pygmy marmosets.

Grooming

(p. 474)

Fess A-1975*b*, p. 18

"Mutual grooming took place and after almost every instance of breeding under captive as well as feral conditions.

"In captivity, parents have been observed grooming their babies as early as three days after birth and as late as seven days. Infants attempted to groom their parents as early as 35 days, and engaged in auto-grooming as early as 46 days.

Food

(p. 475)

Hernández Camacho and Cooper A-1976, p. 37

"The stomach contents of specimens examined in March 1965 in the vicinity of Puerto Leguízamo, Comisaría of Putumayo, contained largely jellylike, dirty-whitish-colored guarango sap in addition to some finely crushed insects (mostly *Coleoptera*) and evidence of fruit pulp. The small sap-producing holes in the bark of the trunk or branches of guarango used by *Cebuella* appear to be produced largely, if not exclusively, by their procumbent lower incisors."

Moynihan A-1976*a*, pp. 80–81

"The El Pepino and Rumiyaco marmosets eat a variety of fruits, buds, and insects. Local people catch them by baiting traps with any convenient fruit, even those not native to the area, such as bananas and plantains. The animals also come down to the ground or cleared pasture to catch grasshoppers. To reach the latter, they have been seen running across asphalt highways. . . . A more distinctive habit of the pygmy marmosets is 'sap-sucking.'

"Every family or group of pygmy marmosets has one or more trees in its home range that are riddled with small holes, sometimes hundreds of them. The majority of the ones that I inspected were roughly circular, approximately 1–1.5 cm (0.4–6.6 in.) in diameter and half as deep. Some holes appeared to be quite new. In these, it was evident that the cut extended through the bark and just down to the next level, presumably the cambium, but no further. Other holes appeared to be old. They were partly filled in by secondary proliferation of new bark, a sort of scar tissue spreading inward from the sides of the cut.

"The marmosets visit the holes, at least the newer ones, very frequently and repeatedly. They spend hours going from hole to hole, usually staying no more than a few minutes or even seconds at each. When an individual reaches a hole, it puts its face or muzzle down into the cavity and follows this by slight but rapid movements of the head. A human observer watching from the back or side cannot analyze these movements in detail, but they seem to accompany vigorous action of the mouth and jaws, chewing, licking, or sucking. . . . They are feeding on the liquids, presumably sap, which can be seen to leak from the cut surfaces. Considering the time spent in visiting holes, sap would appear to be a major food source for the marmosets. . . .

"The fact that existing holes are used frequently and repeatedly indicates that the actual digging or cutting cannot be a very frequent procedure. I never saw a marmoset dig or cut a hole in a tree that was already riddled, but I did see one individual begin a hole in a previously untouched tree. It is conceivable that the marmosets may prefer to gnaw at sites where the bark has already been damaged by other animals, but their finished feeding holes cannot be confused with either the deeper excavations of woodpeckers or the more extensive 'stripping' operations of the local pygmy squirrel.

"I found marmoset feeding holes in several different species of trees, including an *Inga* (probably *I. spectabilis*), *Matisia cordata,* and a tree named *cedro* by the settlers (possibly *Cedrela odorata,* Pérez-Arbeláez, 1956). I did not find (or recognize) holes in trees of *Parkia* sp., which appear to be favored by *Cebuella* elsewhere (Hernández Camacho and Cooper, 1976) and which may be the original or 'natural' source of sap for many animals in less-disturbed conditions.

"All the holes that I saw were in trees of appreciable size, and presumably age, in trunks and large branches, from only a few centimeters to more than 12 m (40 ft) above ground. The lowest holes seemed older, while the higher holes looked progressively younger. The marmosets must begin drilling at the bottom and gradually work upward. I saw one tree that appeared to have been recently attacked. There were only a few holes in the trunk, all below 3 m (10 ft), in spite of the fact that the tree was moderately thick and tall, reaching a total height of approximately 10 m (30 ft). The marmosets also tend to go from bottom to top during single feeding visits.

"To my knowledge, *Cebuella* is the first primate to be found to perform such elaborate sap-sucking."

Fess A-1975*b*, p. 13

"The group of 5 observed February 1970 and the group of 4 watched April 1972, in their natural habitat near Leticia [see above, p. 1008], spent their time eating the following foods.

"Insects—pygmies were observed eating insects during all daylight hours and more often than any other food.

"Lizards—lizards of the anolis variety or related genera were killed by a bite to the head and partially eaten on three different occasions during observations in February 1970. On four other occasions the lizards escaped the pygmy's grip and the pygmies [*sic*] did not pursue their prey to great lengths after the first attempt had failed.

" 'Andaroba' Tree—between 7:30 A.M. and 1:00 A.M. in April 1972, the pygmies were observed making holes with their teeth in the bark of this tree. These holes were about 1″ in diameter and about ½″ deep, and located on the trunk three to four feet from the ground. The reason for these holes is unclear; possibly they were eating the sap."

R. Castro and Soini A-1977

"Their principal sap source consisted of aerial root, stem and branches of a large epiphytic shrub growing on the trunk of the home tree 12 m above ground. The only other sap source plant in use was a slender 'quillo-sisa' tree that grew 5 m off the home tree. Judging from the very few holes on it, it was used infrequently."

Comments on Bark Gouging and Exudate Feeding
(pp. 446, 475, 556)

Sap feeding by nonhuman primates has held a particular fascination for field observers, although man himself is an important consumer. Tree saps or resins are readily available, but the exudation through a wound in the bark is usually slow, in small volume, and clots quickly, sealing the outlet. Exudate feeding by nonhuman primates thus appears uneconomical except for small, busy animals that can find enough resin stuck to the bark or are endowed with an efficient apparatus for tapping trees and maintaining the flow without unduly exposing themselves to predators.

The pygmy marmoset is one such animal, and some observers regard it as particularly specialized for sap feeding. Moynihan (A-1976*a*, p. 83), for example, describes *Cebuella* as "one of the most specialized of New World primates." He mentions no particulars, but characters involved with sap feeding are implied. Elsewhere, Moynihan (A-1976*b*, p. 41) points to the "specialized procumbent lower incisors [of *Cebuella*] which may help in the [bark drilling] process." Hernández Camacho and Cooper (A-1976, p. 37) also note use of the "procumbent lower incisors" for excavating holes in bark. Kinzey, Rosenberger, and Ramírez (1975), however, describe the lower incisors as "semiprocumbent" and include the small body size and clawed digits as "parts of an adaptive complex especially related to feeding on sap while clinging to large vertical supports."

Callithrix jacchus, with more than twice the bulk of *Cebuella,* is similarly equipped and, like *Cebuella,* also gouges bark for feeding on the exudate. As related by Coimbra-Filho and Mittermeier (A-1976, p. 630), the marmoset bites through the bark by anchoring the upper incisors on the tree trunk and scraping with the lower. "In both *Cebuella* and *Callithrix,*" they add, "wear patterns on the occlusal surface of the upper incisors indicate that they are used to hone the tips of the lower incisors (personal communication from R. D. Martin)." They also refer to the oft-cited long lower incisors/short canine complex of marmosets (*Cebuella* and *Callithrix*), which distinguishes them from the short lower incisors/long canine complex of tamarins, and note that "*Leontopithecus* and *Saguinus* have never been observed gouging holes in wood, although they occasionally chew or strip off bark and feed on already exuded gums if they happen to come across them."

In sum, characters of *Cebuella* (and *Callithrix jacchus*) said to be parts of a bark-boring complex involved with feeding are small body size, clawed digits, long procumbent or semiprocumbent lower incisors, short lower canines, and honing upper incisors. Other characters worth mentioning are enamel structure of the front teeth, configuration of the mandibular arch and palatal vault, lips, and tongue. The components of the complex are discussed and compared below.

Small body size and clawed digits of *Cebuella* are relatively primitive characters (cf. pp. 404–13, 476) that endow the animal with capabilities for a diversity of activities including sap feeding while clinging, although clinging is not essential to bark gouging or sap feeding. Derived large-body forms with ungulate digits (p. 32) have lost the ability to cling while sap feeding. In no case, however, is sap feeding obligatory. The catholicity of pygmy and common marmoset diets (see above feeding accounts and p. 475) is sufficient evidence that these animals are opportunistic feeders. There is also clear evidence that they have a predilection for sap or other delectable food available in quantity at low energy cost. The same may be said of tamarins.

The inclination or slope of the lower incisors of marmosets (*Cebuella* and *Callithrix jacchus*) has been loosely categorized. The teeth are not procumbent relative to the symphyseal axis or basal mandibular plane (cf. figs. IV.83, 86–106) and are not at all comparable to the specialized procumbent lower incisors of strepsirhines. If classified as "semiprocumbent," the lower incisors of *Saguinus, Leontopithecus,* and some cebids, notably pithecines, are more forward-inclined than those of marmosets. The lower incisors of *Cebuella* and *Callithrix jacchus* can be described as recurved with bases directed forward, unworn tips pointing upward. They appear to be better adapted for insect snagging than for bark biting.

Elongation of the marmoset lower incisors is indicated, but the length appears exaggerated because of the relatively low canine and shallow symphysis. Elongate incisors used as scrapers and gougers wear longer than short incisors, but used for insect snagging or fruit biting they would suffer little wear. Truly specialized lower incisors, such as those of rodents or their functional equivalents in *Daubentonia,* are open-rooted and renewable. Marmoset incisors are not renewable or resistant (cf. pp. 331–35). Attrition caused by bark gouging ultimately reduces them to stumps, and the destruction is hastened by the cutting action of lower incisors against the horizontal occlusal groove on the lingual surface of the upper incisors. This occlusal groove, alluded to by Coimbra-Filho and Mittermeier, is present in all callitrichids and in *Callimico* (cf. pp. 457, 496, 575, 613, 812, 881).

Lower incisor form, not mentioned by marmoset watchers, is tridentate in pygmy (fig. V.1, p. 277, fig. XII.15, p. 884) and common marmosets, and hence more primitive and more adaptable than those of other living primates. Tamarin and cebid incisors with broad chisel-shaped, contacting crowns are specialized (cf. p. 306), their bark-boring capability greatly reduced or lost.

The seemingly "short" lower canine of marmosets is actually slightly enlarged compared with the canine of a primitive mammal or hypothetical ancestral primate. Lower canines of tamarins are greatly hypertrophied (or caninized) and correspondingly specialized in a direction that blocks effective bark drilling by the incisors. The teeth are more fully described on page 308 and in the generic or species accounts.

Enamel structure, as indicated by the absence of crazing on the labial surface of the lower incisors and canines of *Cebuella* and *Callithrix jacchus* (pp. 327, 329–30), is definitely related to dental use. Whether the enamel structure in this case is primitive is not clear, but enamel that tends to craze seems to be derived. Apparent absence of crazing on the lingual surface of marmoset front teeth indicates an early or rapid erosion of enamel. In contrast, labial and lingual surfaces of the specialized upper and lower front teeth of tamarins (fig. V.29) and *Callimico* are crazed. The *Callithrix argentata* group is intermediate in this (table 25, p. 330) and all other dental and cranial characters under discussion.

The pointed or V-shaped mandibular arch of marmosets is primitive for platyrrhines, and in combination with its narrow, pointed front teeth disposed in wedge formation, serves as an efficient drilling or gouging tool. This character complex is not viewed as a specialization for a particular function related to feeding. There is no indication that any of its capabilities for other mandibular or dental functions have been reduced, restrained, or diverted because of this use, or that options for specialization in other directions have been compromised or lost.

The derived tamarin mandible (figs. IV.75, VII.5) is more powerful than that of marmosets, and in combination with its chisel-shaped, nearly transversely aligned front teeth may be well suited for bark stripping; but the pointed tooth edge and mandibular leverage for bark drilling or gouging are not there. Nonetheless, tamarins are opportunistic exudate feeders. Izawa (1976, and p. 681 above), who was much impressed, almost circularly classifies *Saguinus fuscicollis* as a "resin eater because of resin characterizing its food habit."

According to observers, marmoset sap feeding involves licking and sucking (see above). Gross anatomy of lips and tongue (figs. III.19, 20, pp. 108–9) in available formalin-preserved specimens reveals nothing suggestive of a unique specialization for these functions. The marmoset lips may surround the cavity while the tongue is thrust into the well to lick, and possibly funnel the accumulated syrup by suction. The angular, highly vaulted palatal arch, extreme in *Cebuella* (figs. IV.50, p. 161; VII.8, p. 415), may be designed to increase the suction drainage force.

At the time I compared the palatal vault of *Cebuella* with that of the vampire bat *Desmodus* (p. 160), nothing was known of the sap-feeding behavior of *Cebuella.* Evidently there are interesting analogies in the feeding behavior of the two animals. *Desmodus,* however, is a blood sucker and lapper that can feed on nothing but liquids. Marmosets are equipped to feed and survive on all food types consumed by primates, even if resins are excluded.

Among the marmoset characters considered here, the enamel structure and distribution may be considered specialized for bark gouging and the peaked palatal vault for exudate feeding. Form and function of the tongue are probably specialized for sap feeding, but it may be difficult to prove that it is not equally specialized for a number of other functions (cf. p. 111). Nonetheless, soft parts and hard parts of the marmoset mouth perform within an essentially primative framework as a highly specialized and unique feeding apparatus.

Locomotion

(p. 477)

Moynihan A-1976*a*, p. 81

"They can run along horizontal or diagonal branches as if on the ground, with a galloping gait, yet may walk or pace when advancing slowly on a branch. They can make long and nearly horizontal leaps of a meter or more, but in many circumstances they are also 'vertical clingers and leapers.' Even when not visiting feeding holes, they spend much of their time moving up and down tree trunks. They prefer to rest sitting up or clinging to a trunk in a vertical position. . . .

"Sometimes they move exceedingly slowly, making the movements difficult to detect, as in the case of sloths [*sic*]. More often, they advance in spurts, lizardlike alternations of dashes and frozen immobility."

Display

(p. 478, add title)

Fess A-1975*b*, p. 17

"Visual displays indicating non-hostile intent have included lip-smacking, tongue flicking and walking with the back arched. . . . *C. pygmaea* have been noticed to bristle facial hair and head hair slightly.

"Displays of threat and hostility . . . included direct staring, scowling, hair bristling with and without arching the back. . . .

"Signs of submission were a rigid prostrate position, lip-smacking and tongue flicking. Hair held taut and tight over the head and body has been observed in *C. pygmaea* engaged in hide-and-peek behavior."

Capture

(p. 479, add title)

Hernández Camacho and Cooper A-1976, p. 37

"Pygmy marmosets, of course, are unlikely to be hunted for their meat, but are sometimes collected for commercial purposes. In some areas the centuries old method of ringing a guarango trunk with a sticky resin to capture pygmy marmosets as they enter or leave the tree is used with considerable success. It is likely that this means of trapping is as ancient as the practice of some upper Putumayo River Indians who keep captive *Cebuella* to pick lice from their hair. *Cebuella* is also captured on occasion in banana-baited traps (intended for *Saguinus* spp.) near ground level."

Callithrix jacchus penicillata E. Geoffroy

(p. 500)

Additional specimens examined, 267 (total, 357). BRAZIL—*Bahia:* Aritagua, 17 (MNRJ); Banco da Victoria, 8 (MNRJ); Barreiras (292b), 19 (MNRJ); Belmonte (306), 1 (MNRJ); Bom Jesus da Lapa, 1 (MNRJ); Buererema, Riberão da Fortuna, Ilhéus (299), 3 (MNRJ); Castelo Novo, 6, (MNRJ); Fazenda Pirataquissé, Ilhéus (299), 19 (MNRJ); Fazenda Pontal, 6 (MZUSP, 1; MNRJ, 5); Itabuna, Ilhéus (299), 1 (MZUSP); Japu, Repartimento, 1 (MNRJ); Malhada, Fazenda Belém (296), 11 (MNRJ); Riacho dos Neves (292c), 11 (MNRJ); Rio do Braço, Ilhéus, 26 (MNRJ, 25; MZUSP, 1); Rio Jucurucu (307), 4 (MZUSP); São Gonzalo (293a), 30 km SW Feira de Santana, 1 (MNRJ); Vila Nova (300), 2 (MZUSP); *Distrito Federal* (Goiás): Vaõa dos Angicos, Rio do Sal (trib. of Rio Maranhão), 2 (MNRJ); *Goiás:* Anapolis (278b), 4 (MNRJ); Aragarças (278a), 3 (MPEG), Caldas Novas, 1, (MNRJ); Cana Brava (275a), 1 (MZUSP); Catalão (281b), 1 (MZUSP); Fazenda Esperanza (277a), 2 (MZUSP); Goiania (280), 3 (MZUSP, 1; MPEG, 2); Jaraguá, Rio das Almas (277b), 3 (MZUSP); Linhares (antigo Goiabeiras), 3 (MZUSP); Miriti Mirantiao, 2 (MNRJ); Nerópolis, 3 (MZUSP); Palma (275b): 14 (MNRJ); Planaltina (277c), 3 (MNRJ); Ponta Paranahiba (281a), 1 (MZUSP); Porto Nacional, 1 (MNRJ); Ponte Ipé Arcado, 5 (MZUSP); Trinidade, 2 (MZUSP); Veadeiros (276c), 3 (MNRJ); *Minas Gerais:* Araguari (308b), 10 (MNRJ); Barra do Paraopeba (312c), 5 (MNRJ); Curvelo (312b), (MNRJ); João Pinheiro, Fazenda de Ademar Silveira, 1 (MNRJ); Lagoa Santa (313), 9 (MNRJ); Pirapora (311), 2 (MZUSP); Pompeía, 1 (MNRJ); São João do Gloria (309d), 9 (MNRJ); Uberaba, Capão do Cachorro (309c), 1 (MNRJ; São Paulo: Barretos, Rio Grande (340), 5 (MZUSP); *Locality unrecorded:* 22, (MPEG, 1; MNRJ, 21).

Remarks. The Minas Gerais and Goias populations are generally darker on dorsum than those from Bahia. The overall trend, however, is a gradation into the paler *jacchus* to the north and the pale-headed, saturate-backed *geoffroyi* to the east. Material from various localities in the Ilhéus, Bahia, region (299) varies in facial coloration from nearly like *geoffroyi* to typical *penicillata.* These, more than specimens previously studied (pp. 492, 503), emphasize the fully integrading character of the southeastern Bahia marmosets named *kuhlii* (p. 503) and the inutility of separating them as a distinct race.

The specimen in the Museu Nacional from São Gonzalo, 30 km SW of Feira de Santana, Bahia (293a), agrees with *penicillata* populations of the Ilhéus region in its pale brown frontal region, crown, nape, and shoulders.

The near or presumed contact between *Callithrix jacchus penicillata* and *C. j. aurita* in southeastern Minas Gerais plotted in figure IX.5 (no. 318c), is based on a Museu Nacional specimen (or specimens) from "Serra do Itatiaia" recorded as *Callithrix penicillata jordani* by Avila Pires (1969, p. 61). The only Itatiaia marmosets I find in the National Museum are *C. j. aurita* from the state of Rio de Janeiro (fig. IX.5., no. 330, and gazetteer, p. 940). Present data suggest that *penicillata* is unknown south of the Rio Grande in Minas Gerais or its tributaries in São Paulo (cf. fig. IX.5, nos. 309a, 309d, 339a, 340).

Ruschi (1964) includes coastal Espírito Santo from Conceição da Barra to Barra do Itapemirim within the range of *Callithrix jacchus penicillata* (his *Hapale penicillata penicillata*). This projection may have been based on Vieira (1955, p. 393), who gave the range of his *C. p. penicillata* as eastern Bahia, eastern Minas Gerais, and eastern Espírito Santo. Vieira cites actual locality records for Bahia but none for Minas Gerais or Espírito Santo. I find no Espírito Santo representatives of *penicillata* in the Brazilian museums.

The Santa Teresa, Espírito Santo individual in the Museu Nacional identified by Avila Pires (1969, p. 60) as *penicillata* is almost certainly a hybrid *Callithrix jacchus geoffroyi* × *C. j. flaviceps,* discussed under that heading below.

Linhares, a locality given for 3 specimens in the São Paulo museum, is, according to the skin tags, the "antigo Goiabéiras." Vieira (1955, p. 393) recorded the same specimens from Goiabeiras, Goiás. No Goiabeiras or Linhares, Goiás, is listed in the gazetteer for Brazil published by the United States Board of Geographic Names (1963, no. 71, Washington, D.C.). There is a Linhares in Espírito Santo, but *penicillata* is unknown in that state.

Three adults (MNRJ 3927, 3973, 3976) that had lived in the Brazilian laboratories of the Rockefeller Foundation International Health Division are labeled "capturado em Marica—Est. do Rio." Ear tufts of MNRJ 3927 are dark brown as in *penicillata,* but their shape is more nearly like those of *jacchus.* Tufts of 3973, on the other hand, are more nearly typical *penicillata* in form, but the hairs are mixed dark gray and brown. Those of 3976 are also mixed gray and brown, but the tufts are nearly like those of *jacchus* in form. Frontal blazes of 3976 and 3973 are indifferently like that of *penicillata* or *jacchus*. In 3927 the blaze is enlarged and the cheeks are nearly as bleached as those of *C. jacchus geoffroyi*. The specimens are labeled *penicillata* but may be hybrids or perhaps aberrant or inbred *jacchus*. Neither *penicillata* nor *jacchus* is native to Rio de Janeiro, and I have not listed the specimens among those examined.

Callithrix jacchus geoffroyi Humboldt
(p. 506)

Additional specimens examined, 90 (total 97). BRAZIL—*Espírito Santo:* Colatina (320b), 10 (MNRJ, 4; MZUSP, 6); Estrada Linhares–São Mateus, (kms 12, 13, 14, 18), 5 (MNRJ); Fazenda Jacaré, Mata Jacaré, Linhares (319c), 2 (MNRJ); Los Domingos, 1 (MNRJ); Mata Dez de Agosto, 1 (MNRJ); Morro da Argola, 20 (MNRJ); Pau Gigante (320b); 17 (MNRJ); Rio Doce (320a), 5 (MZUSP); Rio Mutum (320c), 11 (MNRJ); Serra da Mula, 1 (MNRJ); Vitória (321b), 300 m, 1 (MNRJ); *Minas Gerais:* Dom Joaquim, Conceição do Mato Dentro (315a), 4 (MNRJ); Fazenda Bõa Esperanza, São José da Lagôa (314b), 1 (MZUSP); Machacalis (314a), 1 (MZUSP); Rio Doce, left bank, below Piracicaba (315b), 1 (MZUSP); Rio Doce, below Suaçui, 3 (MZUSP); Teófilo Otoni (315b), 4 (MNRJ, 2; MZUSP), 2); *Locality unrecorded:* 2 (MNRJ).

Material in the Museu Nacional from various sites along the Linhares–São Mateus highway confirms occurrence of *geoffroyi* in northeastern Espírito Santo. The 17 specimens of *geoffroyi* from Pau Gigante (320b) in central Espírito Santo, previously identified by Avila Pires (1969, p. 57) and so recorded by me (pp. 506, 939), are incorrectly indicated as *C. j. flaviceps* in my figure IX.6 (p. 491).

Callithrix jacchus jacchus Linnaeus
(p. 510)

Additional specimens examined, 174 (total, 226). BRAZIL—*Alagoas:* Engenho Riachão, Quebrangulo (290), 1 (MZUSP); Usina Sinimbú, Mangabeiras (291), 27 (MPEG, 11; MZUSP, 16); São Miguel (290), 1 (MZUSP); *Bahia:* Corupeba (294), 2 (MPEG, MZUSP); Ilha Madre de Dios (294), 6 (MNRJ); Recôncavo (294), 2 (MPEG); Santa Rita de Cassia, Rio Pieta (292a), 3 (MZUSP); *Locality unrecorded,* 1 (MPEG); *Ceará:* Acudinho, Baturité (284e), 5 (MZUSP); Bom Jardin, São Benedito (284c), 2 (MNRJ); Crato (285b), 1 (MNRJ); Estrada de Ferro Baturité (284e), Ceará (= Fortaleza, 284b), 1 (MPEG); Icarai-Mosquito (284a), 4 (MZUSP); Ipú (284d), 2 (MPEG); Monduby, E.F.B. (284b), 1 (MPEG); Pacoti, Mulungu (284e), 17 (MNRJ); Pacoti, Pernambuquinho (284e), 3 (MNRJ); Pacoti, Sitio Uruguaiana, Serra de Guaramiranga (284e), 24 (MNRJ); *Locality unrecorded,* 4 (MPEG); *Paraiba:* Coremas (287c), 2 (MZUSP); Camaratuba, Mamaguape (287a), 3 (MZUSP); Uruba, Mamaguape (287a), 4 (MZUSP); Princesa Isabel, 4 (MNRJ); *Pernambuco:* Agua Azul, Vicencia, 3 (MZUSP); Agua Preta, 3 (MNRJ); Sitio Vertentes (Serra Vertentes), Caruarú, 1 (MZUSP); Tapera (288a), 2 (MZUSP); Vitória de Santo Antão, 1 (MZUSP); *Piaui:* Valencia, 3 (MZUSP); *Rio de Janeiro* (introductions): Campo Grande, 1 (MNRJ); Rio de Janeiro (332), 28 (MNRJ); Jacarepajua, 1 (MNRJ); Tijuca, Bom Retiro (332), 3 (MNRJ); *Locality unrecorded,* 8 (MNRJ).

Remarks. Specimens from Valencia, Piaui, document the presence of *Callithrix jacchus jacchus* in the Rio Poti drainage basin. This is considerably north of the range boundary previously drawn along the Rio Canindé.

Note: Extracts from the recent literature on *Callithrix jacchus jacchus* begin on page 1016 following the accounts of additional specimens examined.

Callithrix jacchus aurita E. Geoffroy
(p. 521)

Additional specimens examined, 40 (total, 49). BRAZIL—*Minas Gerais:* Além Paraiba (318a), 1 (MNRJ); Gaspar Lopes, Alfenas, 1 (MNRJ); Fazenda da Gruta, Mar de Espanha (318b), 1 (MNRJ); Fazenda Pombal, Vargem Grande, 1 (MNRJ); Rio Novo, 3 (MNRJ); Silveira Lobo (317), 2 (syntypes of *Hapale petronius* Miranda Ribeiro (MZUSP); *Rio de Janeiro:* Angra dos Reis, 2 (MNRJ); Bem Posta (329), 3 (MNRJ); Fazenda Alexandreta, Porto das Flores (328); 1 (MNRJ); Itatiaya (330), 3 (syntypes of *Hapale caelestis itatiayae* Avila Pires); Teresopolis (333), 8 (MNRJ); Serra Macahé (336), 1 (MZUSP); *São Paulo:* Cantareira (350a), 2 (MZUSP); Itatiba, 3 (MZUSP); São João (348), 2 (MZUSP); São João do Barreira, 1400 m, 1 (MNRJ); Sertão do Taquara, Serra da Bocaina (346), 1 (MNRJ); *Locality unrecorded:* 4 (syntypes of *Hapale caelestis* Miranda Ribeiro, MNRJ).

Remarks. Coloration of the Museu Nacional collection of *aurita* varies from agouti on dorsum, with basal half of hairs black and terminal half orange, to entirely black, of crown from agouti to either saturate eumelanin or saturate pheomelanin.

Minas gerais *aurita* are dominately eumelanic, whereas most Rio de Janeiro *aurita* retain the agouti pattern at least on saddle. Intergradation between the extremes, however, is complete, with some melanic individuals present in Rio de Janeiro and some dominately pheomelanic representatives inhabiting Minas Gerais. São Paulo *aurita* ranges from entirely black, exclusive of the pheomelanic blaze, tufts, and caudal annulations, as in Minas Gerais samples, to dominately agouti on upper parts. In all regions, palest pheomelanic representatives of *aurita* closely match darkest-hued representatives of *flaviceps*.

An important character of *Callithrix jacchus aurita* is the prominent wedge-shaped midcoronal brush, which originates immediately above the frontal blaze and extends back to between the ears. The brush is equally prominent in adult *flaviceps* and the single juvenal examined (see below). A less developed and inconspicuous midcoronal brush may be present in adults but not juvenals of *penicillata, geoffroyi,* and *jacchus*.

The lectotype of *caelestis* (MNRJ 2825), an unmade-up, distorted dry skin, is characterized by crown patch orange, cheeks and forehead ochraceous-buff, ear tufts buffy, chin whiskers whitish, nape blackish, back and sides of body banded orange and blackish, the pattern obscured by long black guard hairs; lateral fringe dominantly orange; tail distinctly banded blackish and orange; upper surface of arms with mixture of blackish and orange hairs, legs darker; neck, chest, and belly black.

Syntype (MNRJ 2822) is like lectotype but with more black on lower back. A second syntype (MNRJ 2815) is darker on back and limbs than the first.

A series of five topotypes of *caelestis,* all well made-up round skins, average brighter, with more orange on upper parts than the lectotype; the variation ranges from yellowish orange to bright orange on crown, predominately black or orange on nape and shoulders, blackish to mixed with orange on hands and feet; tail conspicuously annulated, the pheomelanic bands silvery-buff to orange, underparts black.

The lectotype of *petronius* (MNRJ 2816) is black except for the buffy frontal blaze and ear tufts, silvery buff annulations of the tail, and silvery hairs mixed with black on upper surface of hands and feet. A syntype (MNRJ 2824) is similar.

The specimen from Gaspar Lopez, Alfenas (21° 22′ S, 45° 56′ W), is from that part of the range of the species in Minas Gerais bordering on São Paulo which heretofore could not be confidently marked as inhabited by *penicillata* or *aurita.* Additional comments on the boundary between *aurita* and *penicillata* are given above (p. 1013).

A female from Serra Macaé, Rio de Janeiro (MZUSP 2803), in the São Paulo Museum, with chin, throat, and neck ochraceous-buff, agrees best with Rio de Janeiro *aurita.* Avila Pires (1969, p. 57) refers the sample to *flaviceps.*

Measurements of an adult female from Teresopolis follow: Head and body length, 209; tail, 363; hind foot, 69; ear, 28; greatest skull length, 50.2; condylobasal length, 38.8; zygomatic breadth, 30.2; orbital breadth, 25.6; braincase width, 27.4; braincase length, 42.8; i–m^2, 15.6; c–m^2, 11.3; across molars, 15.0; mandible length, 29.2; coronoidal height, 12.9.

Callithrix jacchus flaviceps Thomas
(p. 525)

Additional specimens examined, 5 (total, 8). BRAZIL—*Espírito Santo:* Santa Teresa, 5 (MNRJ).

Four of the five specimens examined were collected or presented by Augusto Ruschi. Three are dated 20 November 1940, and one is dated 3 January 1941. The fifth sample, without collector's name and probably mislabeled, is dated 5 November 1949.

Ear tufts of an adult male (MNRJ 5875) taken 20 November 1940 with the juvenal female (MNRJ 5879) described below appear dark gray because of the mosaic of long buffy and blackish hairs; the underparts show more black hairs than usual, those of the belly being entirely black.

The aberrantly dark ear tufts suggest hybridization between *flaviceps* and *geoffroyi* in the Santa Teresa contact area. The individual in question may be a product, once removed, of a backcross between *flaviceps* × (*geoffroyi* × *flaviceps*).

The juvenal (MNRJ 5879 ♀) mentioned above measured, at time of capture, 140 mm in head and body length, 215 mm in tail length. These dimensions suggest a 6–7-week-old individual (cf. p. 541). As compared with adults, the ear tufts are undeveloped, head not uniformally buffy or yellowish, midfrontal blaze dark brown, not contrastingly pale or whitish, midcoronal brush more saturate than in adults, the hairs ochraceous-orange terminally, black basally, as in adult *aurita,* long ochraceous-orange hairs of cheeks and sides of head directed posteriad and hiding ears; back uniformly agouti, not striated, the hairs annulated ochraceous-buff and blackish; tail with 20 ochraceous bands alternating with blackish bands; hands and feet covered with mixture of short buffy and blackish hairs; neck, chest, and belly with thin covering of long, fine ochraceous-orange hairs and closely adpressed blackish spines, the skin showing through. Ventral spines noted in juvenal are absent in adult *Callithrix jacchus* and in a juvenal *Callithrix jacchus jacchus* at hand.

Measurements of two adult males (MNRJ 5875, MNRJ 5877) are as follows: Head and body length —, 220; tail, — , 335; greatest skull length, 48.4, 49.0; condylobasal length, 37.5, 37.9; zygomatic breadth, 29.7, 31.0; orbital breadth, 25.2, 26.0; braincase width, 40.5, 41.7; braincase length, 40.5, 41.7; i–m^2, 15.6, 15.5; c–m^2, 12.2, 11.2; across molars, 14.9, 14.7; mandible length, 18.5, 19.7; coronoidal height, 14.9, 17.4; pm–m$_2$, 11.0, 13.0.

Callithrix jacchus geoffroyi × *C. j. flaviceps*
(pp. 508, 510, 525)

The specimen examined, an adult male (MNRJ 5878), skin only, collected 27 December 1940 by Augusto Ruschi, was recorded by Avila Pires (1969, p. 60) as *Callithrix penicillata penicillata.* It was particularly distinguished, however, by the uncharacteristic fine black-and-white punctulations on dorsal surface, including mantel and crown. The fine grayish-buffy (silvery) and blackish agouti pattern of the pelage is indeed noteworthy on head, nape, and forearms, but the back is striated as in the species generally.

Characters that distinguish the races of *Callithrix jacchus* are confined to the forequarters. The contrastingly pale or whitish frontal blaze, however, is common to all subspecies except *geoffroyi,* in which the entire forehead and much of the whole crown are entirely whitish. The pale frontal blaze is present in the presumed hybrid, but the agouti pattern of the remainder of forehead and crown, a condition found in no recognized race, could result from a cross between *flaviceps* or *aurita,* on the one hand, and *geoffroyi* on the other. A cross with black-crowned *penicillata* would likely result in a black-crowned offspring. Coloration of the upper surface of the forearm in the present specimen is intermediate between that of the grizzled blackish state in *geoffroyi* and *flaviceps* but not the ochraceous orange in the wholly more saturate *aurita.* The midcoronal brush, however, is the most indicative character. It is prominent in the presumed hybrid, as well as in *flaviceps* and *aurita,* but in no other kind of marmoset examined.

The detailed combination of characters and the fact that only *flaviceps* and *geoffroyi* may meet in the Santa Teresa region lead to the conclusion that the subject animal is a product of one such encounter. A suspicion remains, nevertheless, that the animal might be less the result of a chance meeting of *flaviceps* and *geoffroyi* in the wild than a hybrid produced with the helping hand of the naturalist Augusto Ruschi, who resides and works in

Santa Teresa (cf. pp. 526–27) and who prepared the animal as a museum specimen.

When I wrote the subspecies accounts of *Callithrix jacchus,* I questionably included the Avila Pires (1969) reference to the Espírito Santa *"penicillata"* in the synonymy of *geoffroyi* (above p. 508); and I further suggested (pp. 510, 525) that the actual specimen was probably a hybrid *geoffroyi* × *flaviceps*.

Gestation

(p. 532)

Stevenson and Poole A-1976

Estimated durations of 3 gestations, from postpartum estrus to birth, were 144, 145, and 144 days.

Stevenson A-1976

143.5 ± 2.5 days for 18 births from conception estimated at day 10 postpartum for mated females.

Pregnancy

(p. 534)

Stevenson A-1976

In 18 pregnancies, advanced swelling apparent between 4 and 8 weeks before parturition.

Parturition

(p. 534)

Stevenson A-1976

Female parturent does not withdraw from caged group to be alone. Birth may take place in nest box or outside with group members observing.

Bloody discharge varies from moderate to slight or undetectable.

Complete expulsion usually occurs within 11 seconds, maximum 25 seconds, without manual assistance by mother.

Mother licks neonate while cupping one or both hands under infant's head. Cupping helps orient infant in correct position for climbing toward nipple.

In all observed births, fetus was expelled in vertex occiput posterior position.

Fused placenta, expelled 10–24 minutes after birth, was eaten by mother or by all members of group except adult male; placentas of stillborn infants were never eaten.

Comment: Perhaps another adult male would have partaken of the placenta (cf. above, pp. 534–35).

Time of Birth

(p. 534)

Stevenson A-1976

All births occurred between 19:00 and 08:00, with the majority between 20:00 and 23:00.

Litters

(p. 537)

Stevenson A-1976

In 18 births, 10 sets of twins and 8 sets of triplets were produced. A higher litter survival rate for twins than triplets was attributed to a limitation of the female's rearing capability to two offspring.

Reproductive Performance

(p. 537, add title)

Stevenson A-1976

Only dominant females in each of the five family groups conceived.

Breeding Seasons

(p. 536)

Phillips A-1976*b*

The five-year (1966–70) breeding record of a closed colony of marmosets maintained in Downe, England, was distributed as follows, on a trimonthly or seasonal basis.

Jan., Feb., Mar.	30
Apr., May, June	16
July, Aug., Sept.	28
Oct., Nov., Dec.	18
Total	92

Phillips thinks there has been "little indication of a breeding season in captivity." He avers that although "early research on marmosets suggested a tendency for births to group towards spring and autumn . . . the figures of this colony do not support that conclusion." That is correct. The figures clearly prove that in Downe, England, births peak in summer and winter. Births in captivity do occur in all months of the year, but this may reflect to a certain extent the fact that wild-caught breeders of a colony are probably a mixed lot genetically and geographically, each animal with an internal clock responsive to the periodicity of its native habitat. Despite powerful pressures exerted by uniform, unnatural living conditions and artificially controlled matings, breeding seasonality among wild-born captives often persists for an impressively long time (cf. pp. 536–37).

Stevenson A-1976

In 5 family groups, 18 births occurred randomly throughout the two years between 22 June 1973 and 29 June 1975; successive births occurred at 5-month intervals.

Hybridization

Callithrix geoffroyi ♂ × *Callithrix jacchus,* (Coimbra-Filho and Maia, A-1976)

Artificial hand-rearing of offspring; maternal "recuperation" of young of second birth after abandonment of young of first pregnancy.

([*C. jacchus* × *C. geoffroyi*] × *C. penicillata jordani* ♀) × (*C. jacchus* × *C. geoffroyi* ♂) (Coimbra-Filho, Cruz Rocha, and Pissinatti, A-1976).

Quadruplets, of which one was born normally, the other three by cesarean section. The first survived 48 hours, the others were stillborn, one of them in a rudimentary state of development, apparently because it was enveloped by its own umbilical cord, with consequent reduction of maternal-fetal blood flow. The two placentas, each with two umbilical cords, anastomosed through three veins.

Coimbra-Filho consistently treats *C. jacchus, C. geoffroyi,* and *C. penicillata* as distinct species. These named forms, however, are completely intergrading in nature, and the so-called hybrids are intermediates comparable to natural intergrades.

The triple hybridization was first reported in an abstract by Coimbra-Filho (1974).

Chronology of Growth
(p. 540)
Box A-1975

Observations by Box (1975) on behavioral development of a pair of young *Callithrix jacchus* provide some additional information.

2d–3d week:	Self-grooming noted.
4th week:	Chew on branches for first time.
4th–5th week:	First circumgenital marking by ♂; individual play.
5th–7th week:	Development of intertwin play, facial expressions, threat display with narrowing eyes and flattening ears and tufts [ear tufts undeveloped until 11th week, cf. p. 541].
7th week:	Social grooming of low frequency.
8th week:	Circumgenital marking by ♀ observed.

Evidently Box had minimal contact with the published literature on the subject.

Skeletal Development
(pp. 40, 425–30, 540)
Phillips A-1976*a*

Marmoset skeletal development was studied radiographically from gestational age 91 days—or 59 days before birth—in 16 pregnant females, to 50 days after birth, a conceptual age of about 200 days. Also examined were 30 ex-utero fetuses obtained from 14 pregnancies at various stages of gestation, and 29 preserved young ranging in age from birth to 50 days. Ex-utero fetuses and juvenals were alizarin-stained and radiographed. Qualitative and quantitative measurements were performed on the skeletons of fetuses, newborn, and young. The sequence of skeletal changes was used to assess developmental status, and prenatal growth was compared with that of other primates. Results of the investigation are summarized (Phillips 1976, p. 332) as follows:

"The earliest age at which skeletal development could be detected radiographically in the marmoset was 106–115 days in fixed specimens, and approximately 111 days in utero." In the rhesus, "bones were first seen at 56–60 days (Van Wagenen and Asling, 1964 [*Amer. J. Anat.* 114; 107–25])."

"Comparison of the skeleton of the newborn, particularly the carpus [cf. above, p. 40] suggests that the degree of development . . . at birth is more akin to that of the great apes and man than to the macaque and other Old World primates. However, even allowing for these differences, it would appear that the marmoset has a much shorter foetal period than the macaque and achieves the greater percentage of its growth during the second half of gestation."

Karyology
(p. 487)
Perrotez A-1974

Individual chromosomes are identified by the R banding method which is described. A close resemblance between human and marmoset X chromosomes is noted.

Behavior
(p. 545)
Box A-1975

Box, to whom I refer on page 545, studied four separately caged family groups and scored their activities for marking, grooming, play, and huddling.

Marking occupied much of Box's attention, but nothing in his report has not already been covered in the literature. Minor differences between groups noted by Box are purely individual and group variables, and what they mean among animals in the wild can only be inferred.

The observation that marmosets groom themselves (autogrooming) or another (allogrooming) but not each other (mutual grooming) was already made by Rothe (1971, cf. p. 553). The same is probably characteristic of *Cebuella* (pp. 474–75). In contrast, mutual grooming is normal among tamarins, genus *Saguinus* (pp. 680, 790), lion-tamarins, genus *Leontopithecus* (p. 857), and probably *Callimico* (cf. p. 906). Evidently, marmosets are least advanced among platyrrhines with respect to social grooming. The author's observations on play agree with earlier reports (cf. pp. 478, 798). Young spend more time in rough-and-tumble play, including wrestling and biting, Box finds, than in hide-and-seek and chasing. The study also shows that differences between the sexes are not significant and that time spent in play decreases with increasing age. Parents abstain from their youngsters' play, but nevertheless are indulgent.

Given the artificial setting and enforced crowding of the individuals of each group, Box could only philosophize about huddling.

Daily Rhythm
(p. 546)
Stevenson and Poole A-1976

Activities of four separately caged adult pairs during an average 12-hour day were distributed as follows, in percentages.

Moving	26%
Allogrooming	7
Stationary	
In contact	11
Separated	10
Feeding	11
In nest box	8
Unaccounted	27
	100%

Facial Expression and Head Movements
(pp. 416, 549, add title)
Stevenson and Poole A-1976

Facial expressions controlled by facial musculature, particularly those of the lips, muzzle, around the eyes, forehead, crown, and ears, are limited and often combined with head or jaw movements and tongue flicking.

Facial expressions mentioned include "head-cock-stare," directed at objects such as food; "slit stare," or staring with eyelids half-closed, often combined with tuft flattening and teeth baring, shown at approach of aggressive individual, strange objects, or strange animals; "frown," or brow lowering, shown in aggressive encounters with strange situations and sometimes accompanied with tuft erection; "pout," or lip pursing, exhibited by young animals when approached by strangers or in aggressive encounters; "open mouth," with teeth visible but lips not retracted, usually associated with other behavioral types; "grin," with lips retracted and teeth partially shown; "bared-teeth gecker face," same as in grin but accompanied by the "gecker" vocalization, or scream, displayed on the approach of an aggressive vocalizing individual.

Interaction with Objects or Individuals
(p. 549, add title)
Stevenson and Poole A-1976

"Marmosets frequently bite and gnaw objects, particularly branches and wooden structures in their cages. The scent markings of other marmosets are also licked and muzzle rubbed. Infant marmosets investigate objects by handling, sniffing and gently biting and walking around them....

"Nuzzling, or rhythmic muzzle rubbing between individuals and licking are forms of social greeting. All group members lick infants."

Piloerection
(p. 549, add title)
Stevenson and Poole A-1976

Piloerection is used to impress extragroup individuals. This display is not a substitute for facial expressions in larger primates. *C. j. jacchus* shows both facial expressions and piloerection.

Erection and flattening of ear tufts is also described as response to strange animals or objects, chastisement, and aggressive individuals.

Care and Behavior of Young
(p. 551)
Stevenson A-1976

Neonates clutch abdominal fur and move up toward nipple, nuzzling and rooting, the rooting becoming more intensive in glabrous area of nipple. Tail hangs limp up to a minute after birth, then begins to coil close to mother's body.

Food
(p. 557)
Guenther 1931, p. 41

"In sweeping trajectories these graceful little creatures swing themselves from tree to tree, running along the boughs, or coming to a standstill on the trunk in order to nibble the rind of the [cashew] tree, which exudes a sort of gum."

Note. My abstract of Guenther's observations, on page 557, lacks reference to the cashew tree's exudate.

Predation
(p. 558)
Stevenson and Poole A-1976

"Locust catching behavior appeared to be learnt. On the first occasion that live locusts were introduced to the colony, only the wild-caught animals responded by catching and eating the prey. The laboratory-bred females in pairs 1 and 3 watched their respective wild-caught males feeding and then grabbed a locust and subsequently dropped it, but on the second attempt these females held on to the insect and began eating. . . . Captive-bred animals . . . began by eating other parts of the body rather than the head. By the time they had captured their third locust, however, they ate it in the same manner as the wild-caught animals. Pair 4, the captive pair, did not catch and eat an insect until their fourth attempt. This pair was in visual contact with the animals which had successfully captured and eaten insects but there is no evidence as to whether this factor influenced their behavior....

"Juveniles did not begin catching locusts for themselves until they were 3 to 4 months old."

Tail Movements
(p. 560)
Stevenson and Poole A-1976

"Marmosets bend and coil their tails to various extents, and all degrees of coiling have been seen in stationary passive animals. . . .

"Moynihan (1970 [cf. p 805]) has stated that 'tip coiling' is associated with alarms in *Saguinus geoffroyi* but there is no evidence for this in *C. j. jacchus* where the pattern is seen in both mildly stressful and in relaxed situations. . . . All the [Moynihan] described types of coiling have been observed in both sexes during copulation."

Play
(pp. 560–61)
Stevenson and Poole A-1976

During 720 hours of observation of four caged adult pairs, only seventeen social play encounters were recorded before the birth of young. After birth, play was not observed between adults except when the young were involved.

Callithrix argentata melanura E. Geoffroy
(p. 581)

Additional specimens examined, 31 (total, 56). BRAZIL—*Amazonas:* Rio Castanho, mouth (197b), 3 (MNRJ); *Mato Grosso:* Corumbá (267), 7 (MZUSP); Fazenda Maravilha, Villa Pto. Antônio, Cuiabá (269), 3 (MZUSP); Palmeiras (274), 2 (MZUSP); Rio Aricá (273), 7 (MNRJ, 2; MZUSP, 5); Rio Jaurú (264), 1 (MNRJ); São Luiz de Cáceres (266), 5 (MNRJ); Aripuanã, 1 (MNRJ).

Remarks. Besides the Aripuaña specimen recorded above, there are 7 others in the U.S. National Museum, according to Dr. Charles O. Handley, Jr. (personal communication).

Callithrix argentata argentata Linnaeus
(p. 584)

Additional specimens examined, 78 (total, 155). BRAZIL—*Pará:* Altamira, Rio Xingu (249), 1 (MPEG); Cametá (252), 6 (MNRJ, 2; MZUSP, 4); Caxiricatuba, Rio Tapajóz, east bank (241), 25 (MZUSP); Fazenda Murua, 7 (MZUSP); Fazenda Vaicajá, Cametá (252), 9 (MPEG); Maloca, alto Curuá (250), 1 (MPEG); Marsan, Santarém (242), 1 (MPEG); Piquiatuba (240), 8 (MNRJ, 1; MZUSP, 7); Pracupi, Portel, 1 (MPEG); Santarém (242), 13 (MPEG, 3 MNRJ, 8; MZUSP, 2); Tauari (236), 1 (MZUSP); *Locality unrecorded:* 5 (MNRJ, 4; MPEG, 1).

Callithrix argentata leucippe Thomas
(p. 588)

Additional specimens examined, 18 (total, 26). BRAZIL—*Pará*: Fazenda do Nova, Fordlandia (234), 2 (MZUSP); Fazenda Monte Cristo, Rio Tapajóz (231), 5 (MZUSP); Fordlandia, Rio Tapajóz (234), 7 (MNRJ, 1; MZUSP, 6); Lago Araija, Rio Tapajóz, right bank (233), 1 (MZUSP); Pedreira, Rio Tapajóz, right bank (232); 1 (MZUSP); Tavio, Rio Tapajóz, 2 (MZUSP).

Remarks. Vieira (1955, p. 394) recorded *"Callithrix chrysoleucos"* from Monte Cristo, "Rio Tapajóz," and "Santarém." I find no specimens of *Callithrix humeralifer chrysoleuca,* or *C. argentata leucippe* which had been confused with it, labeled "Rio Tapajóz" or "Santarém" in the Brazilian museums visited. The Monte Cristo specimens in the São Paulo museum are referable to *Callithrix argentata leucippe.*

Callithrix humeralifer
(p. 593)

Additional material representing new locality records and a new subspecies of *C. humeralifer* provides the data for bridging large gaps in our knowledge of geographic distribution and for fulfilling predictions regarding the direction of variation within the species. It was possible to add an allusion to the third race in proof of text page 593 and to modify figures IX.36 and 37 (pp. 569, 570) to accommodate the newly acquired information. The key to the subspecies of *C. humeralifer* on page 594, however, is replaced by the one below.

Key to the Subspecies of *Callithrix humeralifer*

1. Tail with alternating dark and pale bands; blackish of lower back conspicuous; dark coronal cap more or less defined 2

1′. Tail unbanded; golden to orange of lower back with little or no blackish; coronal cap not defined . . . . *chrysoleuca*

2. Lower back and legs dominantly to nearly entirely blackish; inner (lateral) surface of ears pigmented, thickly pilose, the hair bases dark; cheeks blackish . . . . *humeralifer*

2′. Lower back and legs dominantly orange; inner (lateral) surface of ears unpigmented, thinly covered, the hairs entirely whitish; cheeks whitish . . . . *intermedius*

Callithrix humeralifer humeralifer
(p. 595)

Additional specimens examined, 62 (total, 103). BRAZIL—*Pará:* Arara, east of Urucurituba (227), 1 (MZUSP); Barreira, Rio Tapajóz, 1 (MZUSP); Itaituba (228b), 8 (MZUSP); Paricatuba (222), 1 (MNRJ); Parintins (202), 1 (MZUSP); Rio Arapiuns, Santarém (223b), 2 (MPEG); Santa Rosa, east of Urucurituba (228a), 5 (MZUSP); Seringal, 1 (MNRJ); Sumauma, Rio Tapajóz, 7 (MZUSP); Boim, Rio Tapajóz (226), 2 (MPEG; MZUSP); Urucurituba, Rio Tapajóz, left bank (228a), 19 (MZUSP); Vila Braga, Rio Tapajóz (229), 6 (MNRJ, 2; MPEG, 4); *Locality unrecorded:* 8 (MNRJ, 2; MPEG, 5; MZUSP, 1).

Remarks. All specimens examined are from localities in the left bank drainage basin of the Rio Tapajóz, from the mouth of the river south to Vila Brava (4° 25′ S). In addition, Anthony Rylands, primatologist of the Brazilian Instituto Nacional de Pesquisas da Amazonia (INPA) based in Manaus, informs me (in litt., September 1976) of a male *Callithrix h. humeralifer* in his possession that came from Maués. This notice confirms my extrapolation of the range of *humeralifer* from the left bank of the Tapajóz to the eastern border of the rete of waterways at the lower end of the Rio Canumá. I also learned, through the kindness of Dr. Charles O. Handley, Jr., of a specimen in the U.S. National Museum taken at kilometer 211 on the highway between Itaituba and Jacaré-a-Canga. The specimen represents a population not too far removed from the postulated center of origin of the species. It is described by Dr. Handley (in litt.) as more blackish throughout than the animals from the lower Tapajóz.

The km 211 site, Dr. Handley writes, "is marked on our map of Pará by the Brazilian collectors at 5° 34′ S, 57° 13′ W. It is near Lajinha and about 30 Km NE of where the highway crosses the Igarapé do Centrinho."

The name of the workcamp at kilometer 211, adds Dr. Handley, is Flexal.

Callithrix humeralifer intermedius, new subspecies
(add, p. 597)

Holotype. Adult female, skin and skull, Museu Paraense Emilio Goeldi no. 8.156; collected 28 October 1975 by M. Moreira, original number 65836.

Paratype. Adult male, skin and skull, without registry number, U.S. National Museum; collected 20 August 1974 by the Instituto Evandro Chavas Transamazonia Project, original number HM 32, in Aripuanã, Mato Grosso, Brazil.

Paratype. Juvenal female, skin only, without registry number, U.S. National Museum; collected 20 August 1974 by the Instituto Evandro Chavas Transamazonia Project, original number HM 33, in Aripuanã, Mato Grosso, Brazil.

Holotype locality. Near mouth of the Rio Guariba, left bank Rio Aripuanã, southeastern Amazonas, Brazil.

Distribution (fig. IX.36). Between the upper Rio Aripuanã and its western tributary, the Rio Roosevelt, upper Rio Madeira basin in southeastern Amazonas and northwestern Mato Grosso. *Callithrix argentata melanura* occurs in the same region.

Diagnostic characters. Ears tasselated whitish on outer (medial) surface only, mantle silvery buff or drab, lower back mixed blackish and orange, hip patches orange, tail silvery buff to yellowish with grayish annulations or blackish streaks and patches.

Coloration. Face thinly haired silvery, the skin showing through, skin of muzzle lightly pigmented, the remainder of face and ears hardly or not pigmented; frontal region whitish with blackish superciliary vibrissae, poorly defined coronal cap drab mixed with silvery buff, remainder of head silvery; ears with skin little or not pigmented, silvery hairs of outer (medial), surface long but not dense, those of inner (lateral) surface short, not concealing skin; nape drab middorsally, grayish to silvery buff laterally, the basal portions of hairs silvery or gray to ochraceous buff; shoulders and anterior portion of back more buff or orange, posterior portion of back with hairs orange basally, blackish terminally, short, concealed black hairs scattered over back, usually in adpressed tufts; hip patches orange, thighs orange, the outer side more saturate than inner, legs tawny orange, the pale basal portions of the hairs showing through; hairs of upper surface of feet mixed brownish, orange, and silvery; arms ochraceous buff and markedly paler than legs; upper surface of hands silvery buff, palms and soles virtually unpigmented; throat, chest, and inner sides of upper arms whitish or buff; belly and inguinal region buffy to orange; tail chestnut to dark brown at base, becoming yellowish or silvery gray distally either with weakly defined but evenly distributed dark bands or with scattered dark blotches and blackish pencil.

Juvenal coloration is like that of adults, the pelage thinner and more lax.

Variation. The adult types seem to represent two well-marked populations separated by the Rio Guariba. They are distinguished mainly by tail coloration. The adult holotype tail retains the banding pattern of *C. h. humeralifer* but with the dark portions of the hairs reduced, the pale portions expanded. The ancestral tail of the adult paratype may have been modified agouti but is now mostly yellow, with base and pencil broadly blackish and a number of blackish patches and streaks distributed irregularly between. Tail base and pencil of the juvenal paratype are like those of the adult but silvery buff between, with the blackish streaks more evenly distributed.

Short, adpressed tufts of blackish hairs on the dorsum of both adults appear to be remnants of the dominantly blackish ancestral pelage. The hairs are absent in the juvenal.

Measurements (in mm, fig. XIV.1). Dimensions of the holotype are followed by those of the adult and juvenal paratypes: Head and body, 240, 200, 115; tail, 320, 300, 180; hind foot, 68, 60, 40; ear, 32, 27, 20; greatest length of skull, 49.0, 46.7; condylobasal length, 38.6, 36.8; zygomatic width, ca. 33.3, 30.0; orbital breadth, 27.2, 25.1; braincase width, 25.2, 25.2; braincase length, 40.1; 38.2; i–m^2, 15.8, 15.1; c–m^2, 11.8, 11.0; across molars, 15.7, 15.3; mandible length, 31.4, 30.7; coronoidal height, ca. 16.0, 15.1; pm–m_2, 10.5, 10.1; symphyseal angle, 41°, 39°.

Comparison. The color pattern is as well marked as in *C. h. humeralifer,* but head and mantle are dominantly whitish or silvery buff, not grizzled, arms buffy to orange, not blackish, dark coronal cap vestigial, hairs of back two-banded, the basal portion buffy to orange, terminal portion blackish to drab, not three-banded (modified agouti) as in *humeralifer;* hindquarters dominantly orange or chestnut, not blackish; tail dominantly silvery buff or yellowish with shadowy dark bands or patches; underparts buffy to orange except for whitish area from chest to chin and without grizzling or brown areas; in albinotic *chrysoleuca* underparts are nearly uniformly whitish or buffy and dark markings that define dorsal and caudal patterns of *humeralifer* and *intermedius* are lacking; facial, ear, and volar surface pigmentation is heavy in *humeralifer,* nearly to entirely absent in *intermedius,* and intermediate in *chrysoleuca;* external genitalia are unpigmented in all races.

Ears are densely furred on inner and outer surfaces in *humeralifer,* long but appreciably less densely hirsute in northern populations of *chrysoleuca,* with hair significantly thinner in the southern or Rio Aripuanã *chrysoleuca,* and approximating the thinly haired condition in *intermedius* on the opposite bank of the Aripuanã.

Remarks. In most respects, *Callithrix humeralifer intermedius* appears to be intermediate between *C. h. humeralifer* and *C. h. chrysoleuca,* but the races must have evolved independently. *C. h. humeralifer* is clearly the most primitive, particularly in the persistence of the modified agouti pelage on most of the dorsum, the banded tail, and the dominance of eumelanin pigmentation. In *intermedius,* eumelanin is largely replaced by pheomelanin, whereas in the albinotic *chrysoleuca,* eumelanin is absent except in a few wisps of hair, and pheomelanin remains more or less saturate only on limbs, rump, and tail. Although *chrysoleuca* may seem to be a bleached form of *intermedius,* the discrepancies, particularly in the coloration of tail and exposed skin, point to independent origins.

The geographic distribution of the three races indicates that each is a dead-end descendent of a form that must have lived higher up the Madeira and Tapajóz basins in Mato Grosso. As the diverging lines spread northward, ear tufts became longer and thicker, more so in the *humeralifer* line than in the others, body color paler from front to back but least in the *humeralifer* line, and tail paler, with the pheomelanin most affected in the *humeralifer* line, the eumelanin in the other two lines. Depigmentation of facial and aural skin was slight in the *humeralifer* line, significantly greater in the *chrysoleuca* line, and extreme in *intermedius;* plantar surfaces remained fully pigmented in the *humeralifer* line, became lightly pigmented in *chrysoleuca,* and colorless in *intermedius.* The updated figure IX.37 (p. 570) shows the primary divergence of the species with respect to aural hair patterns and the convergent evolution in color patterns.

Discovery of *intermedius* was predictable. The metachromic distance between *humeralifer* and *chrysoleuca* predicates the existence of at least one intermediate form. Parallel or coextensive metachromic series like *Callithrix argentata melanura–C. a. argentata–C. a. leucippe* and *Saguinus fuscicollis cruzlima–S. f. crandalli–S. f. acrensis–S. f. melanoleucus* are comparable examples of the predictable evolutionary direction of mammalian tegumentary colors.

An orbicular process was not evident in the undisturbed malleoli of the two available skulls of *Callithrix humeralifer intermedius.*

Observation. The holotype was encountered by Senhor Moreira about 10 meters above the ground between 11 and 12 A.M. It was one of 5 members of a troop.

Specimens examined. The holotype and 2 paratypes listed above.

Callithrix humeralifer chrysoleuca Wagner
(p. 597)

Additional specimens examined, 39 (total, 70). BRAZIL—*Amazonas:* Lago do Baptista (199), 32 (MNRJ, 7 MZUSP, 25); Prainha, Rio Aripuanã (right bank), 1 (MZUSP); *Locality unrecorded,* 6 (MNRJ, 3; MPEG, 2; MZUSP, 1).

Remarks. The Prainha, Rio Aripuanã, record extends the hitherto known range of *chrysoleuca* from Borba, Rio Madeira (196b), southward into the region between the Rios Aripuanã and upper Canumá. The two specimens are slightly more bleached with ears somewhat less densely hirsute than the average of available representatives of the northern populations.

Saguinus nigricollis graellsi Jiménez de la Espada
(p. 628)

Additional specimens examined, 3 (total, 87). COLOMBIA—*Putumayo: Localities unrecorded,* 3 (ICN).

Distribution
(p. 629)

According to Hernández Camacho and Cooper (1976, p. 39), *Saguinus graellsi* "is known in Colombia from the Comisaría of Putumayo on the basis of a preserved specimen (Universidad Nacional de Colombia, Bogotá), a number of reliable sightings (e.g., Moynihan, 1976), and captive specimens from the neighborhood of Puerto Asís eastward to the vicinity of Puerto Leguízamo. The northern limit is probably the southern bank of the Caquetá River."

The same authors add that "*S. graellsi* is undoubtedly sympatric with *S. fuscicollis fuscus* throughout its range as well as with the population of *S. nigricollis* in the region of Puerto Leguízamo."

Hernández Camacho has since informed me (in litt., October 1976) that reference to sympatry between *graellsi* and *nigricollis* was mistakenly based on a mislabeled specimen from Curiplaya (0° 16′ N, 74° 52′ W) on the north bank of the Río Caquetá.

Reports of the occurrence of *Saguinus nigricollis* north of the Río Putumayo require confirmation. I found only *Saguinus fuscicollis fuscus* in the Río Caquetá basin between Florencia, Río Orteguaza (1° 36′ N, 75° 36′ W), and La Tagua, Río Caquetá (0° 03′ S, 74° 40′ W). Izawa (1975, p. 296), during a 16-month study of the monkeys between the Ríos Caquetá and Caguán (0° 8′ S, 74° 18′ W), saw no tamarins other than those he identified as *Saguinus fuscicollis* (cf. pp. 608–81, 1007, 1026).

NOTE: *After correction of page proof, I received the pelt of a tamarin sent for identification by Dr. Tsuyoshi Watanabe of the Primate Research Institute, Inuyama, Japan. The animal, taken by Dr. Watanbe in the Río Peneya region, Caquetá (cf. p. 1038), represents those recorded by him and his colleague, Kosei Izawa (1975), as* Saguinus fuscicollis. *The pelt received, however, is of a form of* Saguinus nigricollis *intermediate between* S. n. nigricollis *and* S. n. graellsi *but nearer the latter. The datum confirms the occurrence of* Saguinus nigricollis *cf.* graellsi *in the area between the Río Caquetá-Caguán and Río Putumayo (cf. map p. 626), and its sympatry with* Saguinus fuscicollis fuscus *(map, p. 636).*

Local Name
Hernández Camacho and Cooper A-1976

"Bebeleche" is used in the Putumayo region. The name, meaning milk-drinker, is an allusion to the white muzzle, which appears to have been dipped in a bowl of milk.

Saguinus nigricollis nigricollis Spix
(p.630)

Additional specimens examined, 5 (total, 52). PERU—*Loreto:* "Chimbote" (83), 3 (MPEG); "Iquitos" (92), 1 (MPEG); COLOMBIA—*Amazonas:* Leticia, 1 (INDERENA).

Remarks. Specimens of *Saguinus nigricollis nigricollis* in the Belém musem, labeled "Iquitos" and "Chimbote," were living in the museum's zoological garden, their precise geographic origin unknown. The species does not occur naturally in the Iquitos region.

The skin from Leticia, Colombia, that I saw in the INDERENA collection is typical *S. nigricollis nigricollis.* Those from the Comisaría de Putumayo preserved in the Instituto de Ciencias Naturales, Universidad Nacional, Bogotá, recorded as *Saguinus nigricollis* by Hernández Camacho and Cooper (1976, p. 37), are referable to *S. n. graellsi.*

Habitat

(p. 678)

Hernández Camacho and Cooper A-1976, p. 39

"They seem to prefer a middle canopy level and are most often seen at about 8 or 10 m above the forest floor."

Troop Size

(p. 678)

Freese A-1975, pp. 24, 29

Along the Río Ampiyacu troops averaged about 6 individuals.

Hernández Camacho and Cooper A-1976, p. 39

"Seems to average between 5 and 10 individuals."

Visibility

Hernández Camacho and Cooper A-1976, p. 37

"*S. nigricollis* was the most frequently encountered primate species during a field survey conducted in March 1972 from Leticia to a point some 70 km upriver on the Colombian bank. Within a 1,000-km region fronting on the Amazon and extending 15 to 18 km from its north bank, this species was encountered 10 times in a total of 75 hours of foot travel in undisturbed rain forest. It seems to be a rather adaptive species, living both close to human habitation and plantations and deep within relatively undisturbed primary forest."

Food

(p. 680)

Hernández Camacho and Cooper A-1976, p. 39

"Stomach contents usually contain a mixture of fruits, berries, and insects."

Local Name

Hernández Camacho and Cooper A-1976

"Leoncito," or little lion monkey, is used in the Putumayo region, "bebeleche" in the Amazonian region. The first is also used for the pygmy marmoset, *Cebuella pygmaea,* the second for *Saguinus fuscicollis.*

Saguinus fuscicollis fuscicollis Spix

(p. 644)

Additional specimens examined, 19 (total, 33). BRAZIL—*Amazonas:* Estirão do Ecuador, Rio Javarí, 7 (MPEG): Igarapé do Gordão, Rio Juruá (178), 3 (MNRJ, 2; MZUSP, 1); Igarapé Grande, Rio Juruá (177), 4 (MNRJ, 1; MZUSP, 3); João Pessôa, Rio Juruá (176), 1 (MNRJ); Rio Juruá (174b), 1 (MZUSP); Seringal Bõa Vista, Gondino, Rio Quixito, Benjamin Constant, 3 (MNRJ).

Remarks. Specimens from Estirão do Ecuador and Seringal Bõa Vista, Rio Quixito, serve to confirm the presence of *Saguinus fuscicollis fuscicollis* on the right or Brazilian bank of the Rio Javarí. *S. f. nigrifrons* inhabits the left or Peruvian bank of the same river.

The 5 females and 2 males in the Belém museum from Estirão do Ecuador are much paler than samples from the Rio Juruá described elsewhere (p. 645). The forehead, particularly, is less pigmented, with suggestions of a small blaze. One individual (MPEG 1825 ♀) is marked by a pale patch on midback and on each flank and a scattering of whitish hairs on cheeks, nape, shoulders, arms, and legs. See also the account of *Saguinus mystax mystax* from the same locality (p. 1027).

Saguinus fuscicollis nigrifrons I. Geoffroy

(p. 645)

Additional specimens examined, 4 (total, 51). PERU—*Loreto:* opposite Estirão do Ecuador, Rio Javarí, Amazonas, Brazil, 1 (MPEG); "Iquitos" (92), 3 (MPEG).

Remarks. The Belém museum specimen collected March 1963 by J. Hidasi in "Estirão do Ecuador, Rio Javarí," must have been taken on the opposite or Peruvian side of the river.

The 3 specimens labeled "Iquitos" were living in the Belém zoo and lack precise locality data.

Saguinus fuscicollis illigeri Pucheran

(p. 647)

Additional specimens examined, 2 (total, 51). PERU—*Loreto:* "Chimbote" (83), 2 (MPEG).

Remarks. The samples are juvenals I could not positively identify for lack of comparative material. In any event, *illigeri* does not occur in the Chimbote area, and the specimens are not certainly *Saguinus fuscicollis nigrifrons,* which does.

Saguinus fuscicollis lagonotus Jiménez de la Espada

(p. 653)

Additional specimens examined, 3 (total, 99). PERU—*Loreto:* "Iquitos" (92), 2 (MPEG); "Palmares," 1 (MPEG).

Remarks. The skins are of zoo animals which could have originated in the Iquitos region. I have not been able to locate Palmares.

Saguinus fuscicollis primitivus, new subspecies

Holotype. Adult female, skin and skull, received in exchange from the Museu Nacional, Rio de Janeiro; captured live 17 April 1957 by C. Lako and exhibited in the Zoological Garden in Rio de Janeiro, then passed to the Museu Nacional for preservation after death.

Holotype locality. Rio Juruá, Amazonas, Brazil.

Paratypes. Subadult female, skin and skeleton, Museu de Zoologia, Universidad de São Paulo, São Paulo, Brazil, no. 74.0657–74.0658, collected in Pauini, Rio Purus, Amazonas, Brazil, 14 December 1974, by P. E. Vanzolini. Subadult male, skin and skeleton, Museu de Zoologia, Universidad de São Paulo, no. 74.0969–74.0670, collected in Pauini, Rio Purus, Amazonas, Brazil, 19 December 1974, by P. E. Vanzolini.

Distribution (fig. X.15). Known only from Pauini, Rio Purus, below mouth of Rio Pauini, and from the upper Rio Purus region, presumably the east bank. The data, including known distribution of other subspecies, suggest that the range of *primitivus* extends from the Rio Pauini on the south to the Rio Tapauá on the north, and from the Purús on the east to the Rio Juruá-Tarauacá on the west.

The extrapolated range of *primitivus* fills part of the enormous gap between the Rios Juruá and Purus in the species range. It also indicates that the geographic position of *crandalli* and *cruzlimai* provisionally relegated to the unexplored territory between the Juruá and Purus or lower Purus and Madeira, is no longer tenable (cf. fig. X.24).

Diagnostic characters. Crown, mantle, arms, legs, chest, belly agouti; forehead with a well-defined grayish crescentic transverse band, tail dominantly blackish.

Coloration. Forehead with well-defined gray superciliary band extending to above outer canthus of eye in paratypes, to front of ears in holotype, and separated from agouti crown by a blackish line or narrow band; sides of head black more or less ticked with reddish or entirely black; nape and mantle agouti, the basal portions of the hairs mostly gray in holotype, mixed gray and black in female paratype, entirely black in male paratype; saddle weakly defined, the cover hairs with 1 or 2 reddish bands in holotype, 2 or 3 in paratypes; lower back, rump, thighs, legs, arms agouti, upper surface of hands and feet dark agouti in paratypes, mixed brownish and silvery buff in holotype; chin gray, throat and neck dominantly blackish in paratypes, reddish brown in holotype, the pheomelanin bands of the agouti hairs wider; chest and belly agouti, hairs of circumperineal region reddish in holotype, not certainly evident in paratypes; tail of paratypes dominantly agouti for first 5–7 cm of base, becoming entirely blackish distally, of holotype with basal 2–3 cm agouti, remainder blackish lightly mixed with silvery buff, the basal portion of hairs mostly drab.

Variation. Holotype compared with Rio Juruá paratypes is more pheomelanic throughout, saddle better defined, tail less agouti, frontal band longer and expanded distally to front of ear, inferiorly to level of eye; blaze in paratypes much shorter and, as usual, broader in front than behind; nape and mantle hair bases black in young male, mixed black and gray in young female, dominantly gray in holotype. These and other minor differences between holotype and either paratype are clear but, except for shape of the frontal band, are fully intergrading.

Measurements (in mm, fig. XIV.1). Dimensions of adult holotype are followed by those of subadult male and female paratypes: Head and body, 280, 190, 230; tail, 315, 300, 310; hind foot, 65 (dry), 60, 60; ear, 14 (15), 25, 15; greatest length of skull, 47.1, 45.1, 46.1; condylobasal length, 37.8, 35.2, 36.9; zygomatic width, 30.3, 25.9, 29.6; orbital breadth, 24.2, 22.8, 23.5; braincase width, 27.7, 24.8, 25.8; braincase length, 40.9, 39.2, ca. 39.8; i–m^2, 14.8, 14.4, ca. 14.9; c–m^2, 11.4, 10.1, 10.3; across molars, 15.5, 14.8, ca. 15; mandible length, 28.4, ca. 26.9, 27.7; coronoidal height, 17.3, 15.0, 16.6; pm–m_2, 10.0, 9.8, 9.6; symphyseal angle, 45°, 48°, 44°.

Comparisons. Distinguished from *Saguinus fuscicollis avilapiresi* by the conspicuous gray frontal band, short circumbuccal hairs and brownish agouti, not blackish agouti, crown, mantle, back, arms, legs, chest, and belly; from *weddelli* by the brownish agouti, not blackish, crown, nape, mantle and arms; from *cruzlimai* by the agouti, not dominantly or wholly pheomelanin, nape, mantle, arms and legs, the upper surface of hands and feet dominantly blackish, not orange, saddle not sharply defined, sides of head, neck, and chest dominantly tawny to blackish, not orange.

S. f. primitivus and *S. nigricollis graellsi* are similar in their generally agouti coat color and the weakly differentiated saddle of the former. On the other hand, the boldly defined grayish frontal band of *primitivus* and the pale brown temporal patches of *graellsi* are distinctive of each.

Remarks. Variation among the three specimens at hand points to the main trends of differentiation within the species. The saddle of the young female is hardly differentiated and is near the primitive condition as in *Saguinus nigricollis graellsi.* The saddle is faintly marked in the young male and distinct in the holotype but is not as well defined as in most saddle-back tamarins. The holotype, with dominantly pheomelanic agouti body color and bases of nape and mantle hairs gray, stands at the foot of the pheomelanic–albinotic series composed of *cruzlimai, crandalli, acrensis,* and *melanoleucus,* in the order named. Color pattern of the young male, with bases of nape and mantle hairs black, cheeks and chest blackish, and with a well-defined black band separating frontal blaze from agouti crown, can evolve into that of the dominantly eumelanic *Saguinus fuscicollis weddelli.*

A hypothetical ancestral form of *primitivus* with forehead agouti, saddle undifferentiated, and basal portion of tail more extensively agouti could give rise to all known forms of saddle-back tamarins and would be near to if not identical with the prototype of the white-mouth *Saguinus nigricollis* group (cf. p. 606).

Specimens examined, 3. The holotype and 2 paratypes.

Saguinus fuscicollis cruzlimai Hershkovitz
(p. 661)

Additional specimens examined, none (total 0).

Remarks. The name *cruzlimai* is based on a representation in color by Cruz Lima (1945, pl. 38, fig. 3a) of a mounted specimen that was preserved in the Museu Paraense de Historia Natural Emilio Goeldi. The actual specimen, however, was not found in the museum during my visit to Belém in August 1976. In the opinion of Dr. Fernando Novaes, head of the zoology department, the specimen had been removed without record from the now closed and deteriorated exhibition hall.

All callitrichids figured in color by Cruz Lima can be readily identified with previously described forms except for the one representing the since-named *Saguinus fuscicollis cruzlimai.* My description of the type makes ample allowance for possible defects in color reproduction of the original artwork and the fact that Cruz Lima's broad brush strokes did not distinguish the multibanded or agouti color pattern of hairs from the uniformly colored ones.

As figured by Cruz Lima, *Saguinus fuscicollis cruzlimai* could have evolved directly from a dominantly agouti prototype not very different from *S. f. primitivus.* Differentiation from a black-mantled type like *weddelli,* as suggested on page 639, requires a switch from saturate eumelanin to saturate pheomelanin on forequarters, an unnecessary, and in the light of *primitivus,* unlikely operation. Progressive bleaching of *cruzlimai* would result in phenotypes like *crandalli, acrensis,* and *melanoleucus.*

Saguinus fuscicollis weddelli **Deville**

Additional specimens examined, 22 (total, 79). BRAZIL—*Acre:* Iquiri (213), 9 (MZUSP); Rio Branco, 2 (MPEG); *Amazonas:* Aripuanan, Rio Jamary, 9 (MNRJ); Lago do Mapixi, Rio Purus, 2 (MNRJ).

Remarks. The Rio Jamary is an east-bank tributary of the Madeira, but I find no Aripuanan (Aripuanã) along its course. Tamarins (*Saguinus*) are restricted to the west bank of the Rio Madeira–Mamoré, and it is reasonable to assume that the 9 samples of *Saguinus fuscicollis weddelli* in the Museu Nacional originated on the west bank of that river opposite the mouth of the Rio Jamary. The specimens were collected by the Commissão Rondon. The Mato Grosso town of Aripuanã, Rio Roosevelt, also visited by the Commissão Rondon, lies far beyond the eastern limits of the range of *Saguinus.*

Because of the race's wide geographic range and strategic position, it seemed likely that an earlier version of *S. f. weddelli,* very nearly like *leucogenys,* could have given rise to the southern subspecies group of *Saguinus fuscicollis.* Discovery of *S. f. primitivus* indicates that *weddelli* is a divergent race with eumelanic forequarters. All other known southern races are or were dominantly or entirely pheomelanic on forequarters. It is clear that each group (*weddelli,* and the four other southern races) must have diverged independently from a form such as *primitivus,* with agouti forequarters.

Saguinus fuscicollis acrensis **Carvalho**
(p. 644)

Additional specimens examined, 8 (total, 8). BRAZIL—*Acre:* Pedra Preta, near Vila Taumaturgo (209), 5 (MPEG, including type of *Leontocebus melanoleucus acrensis* Carvalho); Seringal Oriente, near Vila Taumaturgo (210), 3 (MNRJ, 2; MZUSP).

Remarks. The Pedra Preta series of *acrensis* consists of the adult male holotype, an adult female, and 2 juvenal paratypes. The material exhibits color stages that range from the well-defined saddle-back or trizonally pigmented body pattern to the nearly uniformly whitish condition of typical *melanoleucus.*

In the holotype, crown and mantle are buffy to creamy white, the individual hairs uniformly colored; hairs of saddle drab basally, ochraceous-buff terminally, becoming ochraceous-orange on rump and outer sides of thighs; whitish frontal blaze clearly defined, cheeks creamy buff, throat and chest more saturate; belly, inner sides of thighs, and tail orange basally, becoming bicolor terminally, the underside paler than the upper.

Female paratype paler than holotype but saddle still discernible; juvenals buffy to nearly white on forequarters, saddle pale brown or buffy. Tail brown above, paler beneath.

Two adults from Seringal Oriente are more heavily pigmented, the São Paulo museum sample nearly like *crandalli.*

Measurements (in mm) of holotype are as follows: Head and body length, 226; tail, 325; hind foot, 60; ear, 29; greatest length of skull, 46.9; condylobasal length, 36.9; zygomatic breadth, 33.1; orbital breadth, 27.0; braincase width, 26.2, length, 41.9; i–m^2, 15.0; c–m^2, 11.0; $m^{1\text{-}2}$, 3.7; mandible length, 28.6; coronoidal height, 15.8; pm–m_2, 10.2.

Saguinus fuscicollis melanoleucus **Mirando Ribeiro**
(p. 664)

Additional specimens examined, 30 (total, 34): BRAZIL—*Acre:* Cruzeiro do Sul, Rio Juruá (208), 3 (MPEG); *Amazonas:* Igarapé Grande, Rio Juruá (177), 1 (MZUSP); Lago Grande, Rio Juruá (175), 2 (MNRJ); Santo Antonio, Rio Eirú (180), 9 (MNRJ, 1; MZUSP, 8, including type of *Leontocebus hololeucus* Pinto); Santa Cruz, Rio Eirú, upper Rio Juruá (181), 13 (MZUSP); *Locality unrecorded*: 2 (MPEG; MZUSP).

Remarks. The albinotic *Saguinus fuscicollis melanoleucus* and *S. f. acrensis* are fully intergrading. Specimens from Cruzeiro do Sul (208), a locality on the right bank of the Rio Juruá between the cluster of *melanoleucus* localities to the north and those of *acrensis* to the south (fig. XIII.4), are morphologically intermediate but nearer *melanoleucus.* A specimen from Seringal Oriente (210), south of the type locality of *acrensis,* is more pigmented than the Cruzeiro do Sul samples but still nearer *melanoleucus* than to the type of *acrensis.*

Color variation and geographic distribution of present material suggest that *melanoleucus* occupies the basins between the upper Rio Juruá and Rio Taraucá from the junction of the rivers south to the latitude of Vila Taumaturgo. Should this prove true, *Saguinus fuscicollis acrensis,* if valid as a taxon, would be confined to the opposite or left bank of the Juruá from Vila Taumaturgo north perhaps to the Rio Ouro Preto. This proposition presupposes that specimens of *acrensis* ostensibly from the vicinity of the two known localities on the right bank of the Juruá were actually taken on the left bank.

The alternative adopted here is that both *acrensis* and *melanoleucus* inhabit the Juruá-Tarauacá basins (map, fig. X.24). In this setting, southern populations of *acrensis,* with a preponderance of moderately to well pigmented individuals with saddles more or less defined, are gradually replaced northward by populations of *melanoleucus* composed mainly of indistinctly patterned or albinotic individuals.

Saguinus fuscicollis

Saguinus fuscicollis primitivus, the newly described (p. 1022) fourteenth race of saddle-back tamarins, very nearly resembles the hypothetical model from which the other thirteen races can be derived. The extrapolated range of *S. f. primitivus* accounts for part of the largest gap in the distribution of the species and indicates a probable solution for the zoogeographic problems posed by subspecies *crandalli* and the enigmatic *cruzlimai,* both of unknown provenance. Some figures and parts of text must be revised to accommodate the new data.

The position of *Saguinus fuscicollis primitivus* in table 79 (p. 639) is to the left of the first column between black-mantled *weddelli* and red-mantled *cruzlimai,* to denote their divergence from an agouti-mantled type like *primitivus. Saguinus fuscicollis leucogenys* is no longer needed as a link between southern and central races. *Saguinus fuscicollis primitivus* not only provides the continuity, but its phenotypic precurser could have given rise to all modern subspecies groups of *S. fuscicollis.*

Figure X.15 (map, p. 622) was revised in page proof to show the approximate range of *S. f. primitivus.* The tentatively placed and now displaced *S. f. cruzlimai* (cf. fig. III.16, p. 97) is shunted into another dubious post on the north bank of the Rio Tapauá pending discovery of its true habitat. *S. f. crandalli,* temporarily relegated to an unclaimed area between the lower Rios Madeira and Purus, is now moved to a position just south of *S. f. acrensis,* where it almost certainly belongs (cf. p. 664). Time did not permit alterations to figures III.16; X.24 and the diagram of geographic metachromism in figure X.26. Needed changes in the latter are described below.

Saguinus fuscicollis primitivus takes its place in figure X.26 (p. 640) between the Rio Purus and the upper Rio Tapauá and Tarauacá. *C. f. cruzlimai* displaces *weddelli,* and the arrow connecting them is deleted. The arrow between *weddelli* and *crandalli* is also deleted, and the latter moves to a position between *cruzlimai* and *acrensis,* with connecting arrowheads to show the metachromic sequence *cruzlimai–crandalli–acrensis–melanoleucus.* The new place for *weddelli* is south of *primitivus,* and the arrow that linked it with the central races is deleted.

The modified design requires an arrow leading from *primitivus* to *weddelli,* another to *cruzlimai,* and a third to the branching between central and northern races. *S. f. avilapiresi* may have been derived from the same prototype that gave rise to *primitivus.* If true, the arrow between *avilapiresi* and *fuscus* would be reversed or deleted. The heavy arrow connecting *fuscus* with all other subspecies loses its dominant form and now merges with the stem that gives rise to northern and central races. The arrows indicate the probable direction of metachromic change and relationship between the races. It is virtually certain that none of the living races as now constituted gave rise to another.

Key to Subspecies
(p. 640)

Incorporation of *Saguinus fuscicollis primitivus* into the key may be accomplished by the following arrangement:

2. Crown white, grayish, yellowish, or drab; forehead with gray or whitish superciliary band (frontal blaze or "eyebrows"); tail white, yellowish, grayish, drab, or brown except sometimes at base 3

2′. Crown buffy or orange ticked with black (agouti) or dominantly to entirely black; superciliary band present or absent; tail black or blackish brown except at base 4

4. Crown agouti 5

4′. Crown entirely or dominantly blackish 8

5. Forehead with whitish superciliary band 14

5′. Forehead agouti, like crown, or blackish 6

14. Nape, mantle, arms, legs agouti; saddle not sharply defined; sides of head, neck, and chest dominantly tawny to blackish . . . . *S. f. primitivus* (p. 1022)

14′. Nape, mantle, arms, legs dominantly orange; saddle well defined; sides of head, neck and chest orange . . . . *S. f. cruzlimai* (p. 661)

Distribution
(pp. 622, 636)

Hernández Camacho and Cooper A-1976, p. 39

The Colombian distribution of *Saguinus fuscicollis* plotted by Hernández Camacho and Cooper (1976, pp. 40, 41) shows an extension north (as compared with my figs. X.15, 24) to the Río Guayabero-Guaviare and east to the Río Yari, which enters the Caquetá about midway between the mouths of the Río Caguán and Apaporis. Evidence for the range extension is vague or confusing. Hernández Camacho and Cooper (A-1976, p. 39) write:

"The populations of the Putumayo River, including [*sic,* perhaps 'and' was intended] one specimen from the right bank of the Guayabero River in Angostura near the southern tip of the Macarena Mountains, are referable to *S. fuscicollis fuscus* (Lesson, 1840). Unpreserved specimens from San José de Guaviare suggest that a presently undescribed subspecies inhabits this region. Live specimens recently examined in Leticia and reportedly from Puerto Narino on the Colombia bank of the Amazon are referable to *S. fuscicollis tripartitus* (Milne-Edwards, 1878). *S. fuscicollis* is not known in the immediate region of Leticia. Also no specimens are available for the region between the Guamués and the Succumbíos Rivers of the southwestern Comisaría of Putumayo."

Regarding the record from Puerto Narino [= Nariño?] on the Río Amazonas in Colombia, the range of *S. f. tripartitus* (cf. fig. X.24, p. 636) may well extend to that point and beyond to the mouth of the Putumayo-Içá. Authentication of the specific identity of tamarins said to occur in the Río Guaviare and Río Yari regions awaits examination of reliably labeled preserved specimens.

Breeding Periodicity
(p. 670)

R. Castro and Soini A-1977

"One semi-tame pair of *S. fuscicollis illigeri* living unconfined in a large backyard garden in Iquitos had five sets of twins over the course of the last three years, at approximately six-month intervals. Two last births took place in late November or early December 1974 and mid May 1975 . . . whether a twice-a-year reproduction rate is maintained in wild populations, with stable, normal infant loss rates, remains to be investigated."

Habitat
(p. 678)

Freese A-1975

"This species survives similarly well in virgin forest . . . and in heavily disturbed, largely secondary forest near large population centers such as Iquitos."

Areas investigated included those of Iquitos (92); Río Orosa (87); Río Samiria (96); Río Nanay (94); Panguana, near Pucallpa; and Cocha Cashu, Río Manú (129).

R. Castro and Soini A-1977

Inhabits both primary forest and secondary growth in the Río Aucayo and Río Tahuayo basins, two small affluents of the Río Amazonas opposite and above Iquitos.

Territory

(p. 678)

R. Castro and Soini A-1977

"At the Tahuayo study site we found four or five troops within the 1 km² survey area."

Troop Size

(p. 678)

Izawa A-1976, pp. 384–86

The author encountered 11 platyrrhine species in a study area centered along the Río Peneya, a small left bank tributary of the middle Río Caqueta in Amazonian Colombia. The area, about 100 km square, encompassed the village of La Tagua, the lower Río Caguán and the bend of the Río Putumayo at Puerto Leguízamo. His notes on the one species of tamarin known to occur in the Río Caquetá region, follow.

"The monkeys lived both in Pto. Japon and in Pto. Tokio [Río Peneya]. The number of encounters with the monkeys in Pto. Japon during the study period from November 1971 to January 1972 amounted to 46. In 23 (50%) of these encounters, a group which was estimated to comprise from 20 to more than 40 monkeys was observed.

"They often separated as much as 50 to 150 m² during the daytime, whereas when moving in the morning and the evening, they generally formed a compact group. For three days beginning January 1, 1972, the author succeeded in tracing one of the large groups, comprising about 40 individuals. This group moved about from the south to the north along the camp.

"According to the places where these large groups were encountered, their nomadism and the same day's observations, it was confirmed that at least five groups lived in A-area in Pto. Japon and the nomadic range of each group was estimated at 1 km².

"The remaining 23 encounters were concerned with small groups of about 10 monkeys. Of these, eight (17.6%) encounters were those in which it could not be known how many individuals were in the vicinity of the approximately 10 monkeys counted, since the author was concentrating on the woolly monkeys, the capuchins and the sakis who were staying near the tamarins. And in the remaining 15 (32.4%) encounters, no other tamarins were confirmed excepting those approximately 10 monkeys, although the vicinity was searched.

"Since it was hard to trace the movements of small groups, it could not be confirmed whether the latter small groups, moving singly at the time of the observation, were small temporary ones separated from the above-mentioned larger groups, or were groups which existed independently of the large ones.

"In the observation from September to October 1973 in Pto. Japon, the result was the same as the above.

"However, from November 1973 to February 1974, large groups comprising more than 20 individuals, and probably more than 40 by estimate, were never encountered. The maximum number of monkeys counted in 12 encounters during this period was seven, though a few oversights were possible in each encounter. A group of more than 10 monkeys could not be found.

"On the other hand, also in the survey in Pto. Tokio held during the same period from November 1973 to February 1974, large groups of about 40 monkeys that the author had encountered before in Pto. Japon could not be seen. The maximum number of the tamarins counted in 37 encounters in this area was 12, including triplet infants carried on their mother's back. The files were checked on their leaving, so any oversights were impossible. The maximum number of tamarins counted in NISHIMURA's encounters was eleven.

"The author obtained the data on the group size of the tamarins in the other areas particularly in the basin of the River Putumayo. All the groups encountered four times, at different places in the basin of the River Paya, a tributary of the River Putumayo, on September 4 and 5, 1971, were large, comprising 30 to 40 individuals. Once, on January 29, 1972, a group of 20 to 30 monkeys was encountered in the basin of the River Caucaya, a tributary on the left bank of the River Putumayo.

"From the above-mentioned observations on the tamarins, it is difficult to determine whether (1) the unit group of the tamarin is a large one of 30 to 40 monkeys, and small groups consisting of 5 to 12 monkeys or less are temporary ones separated from the large group, or (2) contrariwise, the small-sized group is the unit group of the tamarins, and the larger one is a temporary assembly of some small groups, or (3) seasonal factors, the mating seasons or the birth seasons, for example, could influence the group size of the tamarins. (It is unknown whether or not the tamarins have such seasons.) At present, the author thinks the last conjecture is most probable. It should also be added that during his first survey, it rained constantly and a distinctive dry season could not be confirmed, whereas from the end of November to the beginning of February in the second survey, the season was dry and no large-sized groups were ever observed during this dry season.

"Among the hunters giving information to the author, there were more of those who suggested that in general the tamarins lived in large groups than there were of those who had other suggestions."

Freese A-1975

Troops seen in Peru (see above) consisted of 6 to 8 individuals, but as many as 24 were reported.

R. Castro and Soini A-1977

"In about 25 troops that we have observed, the number of animals ranged from two to ten. However, most troops had two to six animals, and we suspect that some of the largest troops recorded may actually have consisted of two closely feeding or temporarily merged troops."

Interspecific Relations
(p. 680)
R. Castro and Soini A-1977

Three of the four or five troops seen in the Tahuayo area were associated with *S. mystax* troops [cf. the *Saguinus mystax* account below].

Food
(p. 680)
Moynihan A-1976*a*, p. 82

"I watched [*Saguinus*] *fuscicollis* . . . and another form of *Saguinus*, possibly *graellsi*, at some length [in the upper Río Putumayo region in Colombia] . . . without seeing a trace of sap-sucking."

R. Castro and Soini A-1977

"Occasionally raids fruit trees in unguarded native orchards."

Marking
(pp. 447, 478, 561–62, 681–82, 802–7)
Smith, Yarger, and Epple A-1976

Seventeen major volatile constituents of the scent material of *Saguinus fuscicollis* are analyzed and identified. The substances, which constitute 96% of the total volatile material, are common to males and females but variably present in any one individual. Identification of the more volatile minor components is promised for a later publication.

Vocalization
(p. 682)
Moody and Menzel A-1976

Vocalizations of the experimental group housed in a seminatural environment were studied. The group consisted of an adult pair, juvenal female, and 4 male and 1 female infants. The investigators recorded and analyzed 30 call types elicited by spontaneously arising situations. Correlated bodily activity of sender, and vocal and bodily response of recipient were also tabulated. Infant call repertories appeared to be similar, but those of older individuals differed from each other. Functionally, the calls were classified as spatial cohesion, alerting, aggression, infantile, and adult during infant calls. Structurally, calls formed only two sound complexes, denominated twitter-hook and squawk.

Local Name
Hernández Camacho and Cooper A-1976

The Spanish name "bebeleche," meaning milk-drinker, used in Amazonian Colombia for *Saguinus fuscicollis* is in allusion to the whitish muzzle, which appears to have been dipped in a bowl of milk.

Saguinus labiatus labiatus E. Geoffroy
(p. 691)

Additional specimens examined, 16 (total, 33). BRAZIL—*Acre:* Iquiri (213), 8 (MZUSP); Rio Branco, 4 (MPEG); *Amazonas:* Bom Lugar, Rio Purus (189), 1 (MPEG, lectotype of *Midas griseovertex* Goeldi); Lago do Mapixi (185), 2 (MNRJ); *Locality unrecorded:* 1 (MNRJ).

Distribution
(pp. 684, 962)
Heltne, Freese, and Whitesides A-1976

"We found *S. labiatus* common at least 30 km west of Cobija [135] in Bolivia, and reliable accounts place it on both sides of the [Río] Acre at least as far west as Peru. Hoffman (pers. comm.), who has traveled the Pando region searching for monkeys, claims that *S. labiatus* occurs at least as far south as the Tahuamanu River in the western half of Pando, and south of the Abuna River in the eastern half of Pando."

The above information indicates that the range of *S. labiatus,* as shown in figure X.37 (p. 684), should be extended southward into the lowlands of Pando, Bolivia, and Madre de Dios, Peru, between the upper Ríos Madre de Dios and Purus. Evidently, the southern boundaries of *S. l. labiatus* and *S. imperator* are collinear. Sympatry in Brazil between *S. l. labiatus* and *S. mystax pluto* is shown in figure X.37.

Troop Size
Heltne, Freese, and Whitesides A-1976

Average troop size in Pando, Bolivia, is reported as 6. One troop with 13 individuals was seen by the authors, and a troop with more than 15 was reported to them.

Saguinus mystax mystax Spix
(p. 696)

Additional specimens examined, 44 (total, 123). BRAZIL—*Acre:* Seringal Oriente, near Vila Taumaturgo, Rio Juruá (210), 4 (MPEG); *Amazonas:* Colonia Agrícola, Coari, 1 (MNRJ); Estirão do Ecuador, 8 (MPEG); Fonteboa (174a), 6 (MNRJ); Igarapé Grande (177), 5 (MNRJ, 2; MZUSP, 3); João Pessõa, Rio Juruá (176), (MNRJ, 3; MZUSP, 6); Rio Juruá (174b), 2 (MZUSP); Rio Taquirana, 1 (MPEG); *Locality unrecorded:* 3 (MNRJ); PERU—*Loreto:* "Chimbote" (83), 1 (MPEG); "Palmares," Rio Solimões, 4 (MPEG).

Remarks. One of the eight samples from Estirão do Ecuador (MPEG 1556) has conspicuous white patches on nape, shoulders, lateral fringe, arms, and thighs. Scars of botfly larva infestation are visible in the skin of some of the patches. Pelage of the midback of a second sample (MPEG 1822) from the same locality consist of wholly white hairs with a scattering of the usual blackish hairs with white bases. See also the account of *Saguinus fuscicollis fuscicollis* from the same locality (p. 1022).

Coari (4° 05′ S, 63° 08′ W), on the south bank of the Rio Solimões between the Rios Juruá and Purus, is within the geographic range of *Saguinus mystax pileatus*. If correctly assigned in my notes to *Saguinus m. mystax*, the lone specimen in the Museu Nacional, labeled Colonia Agrícola, Coari, is not native to the aforementioned Coari region.

Distribution

(pp. 684, 685, 698, 929)

Freese A-1975, p. 29

"Two areas surveyed within this species' distribution, as described by Hershkovitz (1968), the Orosa and Samiria river basins [Loreto, Peru], yielded no direct evidence of the occurrence of *S. mystax*. A guard and longtime resident of the Samiria fishing reserve reported that 2 kinds of *Saguinus* inhabit the basin, but his description of the one other than *S. fuscicollis* was insufficient for us to be sure that it was *S. mystax*. Earlier expeditions by Neville also failed to observe this species."

Specimens of *Saguinus mystax mystax* from Orosa, collected by the Olalla brothers in 1927, are preserved in the American Museum of Natural History (cf. pp. 698, 928).

A tamarin from the Río Samiria was identified by Lampert (1926, p. 608) as "Hapale Leontocebus Mystax Spix ♂ ad (= Mystax Bluntschlii Matschie)." The record is included in my synonymy of *Saguinus mystax mystax* (cf. p. 697, line 6). However, the original description of *bluntschlii*, based primarily on the skins and skulls of an adult male and female, clearly corresponds to that of *Saguinus fuscicollis illigeri* (cf. pp. 647, 648, 649). The animal recorded by Lampert and used in his work on the larynx, is the formalin-preserved male mentioned by Matschie in his description of *bluntschlii*. Ostensibly, Lampert believed it represented Spix's moustached tamarin or *Saguinus mystax mystax*. If Lampert is right, the original Río Samiria series of *bluntschlii* is composed of *Saguinus fuscicollis illigeri* and *S. mystax mystax*.

Habitat

(p. 704, add title)

R. Castro and Soini A-1977

Observations were made in the Río Aucayo and Río Tahuayo basins, Loreto, Peru. The moustached tamarin is "usually found in a fairly undisturbed primary forest habitat, but a few troops were also observed in old secondary forest. . . . A preliminary survey of a rectangular area of approximately 1 km² of primary forest at Tahuayo indicated that at least five to seven *S. mystax* troops had their home ranges entirely or partly within that area, suggesting a fairly good population density."

Home Range and Territory

(p. 704, add title)

R. Castro and Soini A-1977

"The daily path lengths for one troop on two consecutive days were 1209 m and 1100 m with corresponding travel distances of 580 m and 480 m."

They also "make sporadic invasions into unguarded fruit tree groves, particularly when the domesticated 'uvilla' tree (*Pourouma* sp.) is in fruit. . . .

"Once we observed what seemed to be an attempt to defend a territory, when a troop of five *S. mystax* approached an area where another troop of two animals were foraging and feeding. One of the two occupants advanced towards the approaching troop and perched, visibly excited, on a horizontal branch about 10 m in front of the arrivals, confronting them with sharp, clearly hostile vocalization. After a brief vocal battle the defender made a sudden, rapid retreat and was followed by the intruding troop, which, however, soon resumed travel and left the area."

Social Organization

(p. 704, add title)

R. Castro and Soini A-1977

"Live in parental family troops of two to six animals. The largest troops are composed of one adult pair, two sub-adults, and one pair of dorsally carried infants." The smallest "consisted invariably of one adult male and one adult female. . . . Most of the time the progression of the troop was led by the adult male, and the rear was brought up by the infant-carrying and suckling female. . . .

Two nearby troops sometimes merge incidental to feeding or fleeing.

Interspecific Relations

(p. 704, cf. Dominance and Aggression)

R. Castro and Soini A-1977

"The majority of *S. mystax* troops travelled in mixed groups with *S. fuscicollis* in apparently stable associations. The interspecific cohesion varied largely, but the speed and direction of travel was always set by *S. mystax* who also tended to forage at a slightly higher level in the trees than *S. fuscicollis*.

"The first time we followed the troop for an entire day, this association continued all day through, and both troops spent the night together among the fronds of a tall 'ungurahui' palm (*Jessenia batana*). On the following morning the troops continued foraging together for four hours and became separated at about 10:30, when the *S. fuscicollis* troop remained feeding in one spot while the *S. mystax* troop continued moving on. The *S. fuscicollis* troop was not seen again even though we followed the *S. mystax* troop through the remainder of the day to their sleeping tree."

Food

(pp. 704–5)

R. Castro and Soini A-1977

The animals were seen eating fruit, often hanging by the hind feet to extend their reach. They also clung vertically to large trunks, where they reached for insects or grubs in holes and knots or licked the sweet exudates from the trees.

Locomotion
(p. 705, add title)
R. Castro and Soini A-1977

"Locomotion consists of quadrupedal walking and running and horizontal or diagonal leaping. Postural behavior includes vertical clinging to large tree trunks and hanging from hindfeet. . . .

"Leaping from and/or to vertical supports, as described for *Cebuella* by Kinzey et al. (1975) and observed by us in *S. fuscicollis*, was not seen in *S. mystax*. The quadrupedal locomotion in *S. mystax* is distinctly less jerky, more feline, than in *S. fuscicollis*."

Defense
(p. 705, add title)
R. Castro and Soini A-1977

"At the Aucayo study site, where *S. mystax* at least occasionally is hunted for food, and where a number of them were live-trapped in October and November 1974, they have become quite wary and difficult to approach. At the Tahuayo site, where they are not hunted or commercially trapped, most of the troops could be followed at close range."

Saguinus mystax pileatus I. Geoffroy and Deville

Additional specimens examined, 12 (total, 20). BRAZIL—*Amazonas:* Oiti, Tefé (182), 1 (MNRJ); Patrimonio, Rio Tefé, 3 (MNRJ); Pauini, 2 (MZUSP); Rio Purus, 2 (MPEG); Rio Juruá (174b), 1 (MZUSP); São Luiz de Mamoria, Rio Purus (188), 1 (MPEG); *Locality unrecorded,* 2 (MNRJ).

Saguinus imperator Goeldi

Additional specimens examined, 23 (total, 52), BRAZIL—*Acre:* Alto Rio Juruá, 1 (MPEG); Alto Rio Purus (cf. 191), 1 (MPEG, lectotype of *Midas imperator* Goeldi); Manoel Urbana, 2 (MZUSP); Oriente near Vila Taumaturgo, Rio Juruá (210), 1 (MPEG); Pedra Preta, above Vila Taumaturgo (209), 1 (MZUSP); Rio Branco, 2 (MPEG); *Amazonas:* Santo Antônio, Rio Eirú (180), 5 (MNRJ, 2; MZUSP, 3); Santa Cruz, Rio Eirú (181), 9 (MZUSP); *Locality unrecorded:* 1 (MPEG).

Remarks. The faded lectotype, an adult female (MPEG 914), is a mounted specimen no longer on display. The upper lip whiskers remain about as originally described (p. 703); the chin whiskers appear to have been clipped, and the chin itself is painted black.

Upper lip whiskers of the mounted skin of a juvenal (MPEG 868 ♂) zoo specimen, which may have been about 2 months old when it died, are as well-developed for the size of the animal as those of adults. The chin whiskers are short, but this may be an artifact. Hairs of the back are modified agouti, whereas those of adults are multibanded.

Distribution
(pp. 684, 702)
Gardner A-1976

Saguinus imperator has been recorded by Gardner from Balta, Río Curanja, Loreto, Peru. Other specimens mentioned from Quebrada Juárez, Madre de Dios, in the Ceballos collection, and Río Amigos, Madre de Dios, in the "Javier Prado" museum in Lima, may have been part of the series collected by C. Kalinowski and sent to the Field Museum (see gazetteer nos. 129, 130, p. 930).

Saguinus imperator is the only callitrichid seen by Gardner in the Balta locality in the upper Río Purús region. It is possible, however, that *Saguinus fuscicollis weddelli* inhabits an unexplored part of the same region. This tamarin is known from the upper Rio Purus in Brazil (cf. gazetteer nos. 185, 212, 213) and the upper Ríos Ucayali and Madre de Dios regions in Peru, where *S. imperator* occurs (nos. 113, 114, 129–31, p. 930).

Saguinus midas midas Linnaeus

Additional specimens examined, 126 (total, 195). BRAZIL—*Amapá:* Amapá (158), 2 (MPEG); Foz do Rio Falcino, 1 (MPEG); Macapá (161), 1 (MNRJ); Porto Platou, 5 (MNRJ); Rio Amapari, Macapá (159), 1 (MZUSP); Rio Maruanum de Macapá (160), 1 (MNPEG); Rio Vila Nova, Mazagão, 5 (MPEG); Serra do Navio, 10 (MNRJ); Vila Velha do Oiapoque (157), 1 (MPEG); *Amazonas:* Anibá (Igarapé), 5 (MZUSP); Apuahy (= Apuaú), 1 (MNRJ); Itacoatiara (203), 6 (MZUSP, 5; MPEG, 1); Lago do Canaçary (205), 2 (MZUSP); Lago do Serpa (203), 2 (MNRJ, MZUSP); Silves, 1 (MZUSP); Urubu (Rio), 3 (MZUSP); *Pará:* Bravo, Rio Amazonas, 15 (MZUSP); Cachoeira do Tronco, Rio Erepecurú, 3 (MNRJ, 1; MPEG, 2); Caracol Grande, Rio Amazonas, 2 (MZUSP); Colonio do Veado, Obidos (217), 1 (MPEG); Baiussú, Rio Amazonas, 16 (MZUSP); Lago Cuiteua (218), 1 (MZUSP); Obidos, Rio Amazonas (217), 6 (MNRJ, 1; MZUSP, 5); Oriximini, 1 (MPEG); Taioca, Paru do Oeste, 1 (MNRJ); Tapera, Rio Paru do Oeste, 1 (MNRJ); Tirios, Rio Paru do Oeste, 1 (MNRJ).

Remarks. Color variation is not remarkable. The average differences between the larger series appear to be no greater than differences between the extremes of any one series.

The localities Apuaú, Lago do Canaçary, Igarapé Anibá, Itacoatiara, Serpa, Silves, and Rio Urubu where *Saguinus midas* has been taken are within the range of *Saguinus bicolor bicolor*. The two species, however, have yet to be recorded from the same site.

A juvenal in the Belém museum (MPEG 680 ♂) from Itaquatiara, evidently the same identified by Cruz Lima (1945, p. 216) as *Tamarin tamarin tamarin* (= *Saguinus midas niger*), proves to be a red-handed tamarin, *S. m. midas.* A specimen in the Museu Nacional (MNRJ 4799) labeled "Lago do Baptista" (199) is certainly misplaced.

Saguinus midas niger E. Geoffroy

Additional specimens examined, 103 (total, 240). BRAZIL—*Maranhão:* Cururupu, 1 (MNRJ); *Pará:* Arumatheuá, Rio Tocantins (255), 1 (MPEG); Belém (256), 4 (MPEG, 3; MZUSP, 1); Benevides (259), 1 (MNRJ); Boiuçú, Ilha Marajó, 2 (MNRJ); Cametá (252), 20 (MNRJ, 18; MZUSP, 2); Capanema, E. F. de Bragança, 3 (MPEG); Capim, km 93 Belém-Bahia, 14 (MZUSP); Curalinho, Ilha Marajó, 2 (MNRJ); Castanhal, 9 (MPEG); Conceição, Rio Majú (262), 1 (MPEG); Gradaus, Rio Fresca, Rio Xingu (251), 1 (MPEG); Igarapé, Rio Guama, 1 (MNRJ); Paragominas, Estrada Belém-Marabú, 3 (MNRJ); Peixe-boi (261), 2 (MPEG); Retiro de Nazaré, Benevides (259), 3 (MPEG); Rodovía Belém-Brasilia, km 36, 1 (MPEG); Rodovía Belém-Brasilia, km 75, 4 (MPEG); Rodovía Belém-Brasilia, km 86, 2 (MPEG), 2 (MPEG); Santa Bárbara, Benevides (259), 1 (MPEG); "Santarém" (242), 1 (MPEG); Tauaquara, 1 (MNRJ); Tomé Assú, Estrada Jamic, km 43, 1 (MPEG); Tomé Assú, Massaranduba, Rio Acará, 1 (MPEG); Utinga (258), 2 (MNRJ; MPEG); Vigia, Mata São Francisco, 1 (MPEG); *Locality unrecorded:* 20 (MNRJ, 18; MPEG, 2).

Specimens from Boiuçu and Curalinho may be the first recorded from Ilha de Marajó. Vieira (1955, p. 395) included Ilha de Marajó in the range of *Saguinus midas midas* (his *Marikina* [*Tamarin*] *midas midas*), but either he saw no specimens or, unlikely, misidentified those he saw. Cruz Lima (1945, p. 219) mentions samples of *midas* (his *Tamarin midas egans*) in the Belém museum, said to be from "the islands region between Marajó Island and the [northern] mainland."

In any case, present data authenticate the occurrence of a callitrichid along with the cebids *Saimiri, Aotus,* and *Alouatta* on Ilha de Marajó.

A specimen in the Belém musem (MPEG 2412), labeled Santarém, collected 2 August 1958 by J. Hidasi, could not be native to the lower Rio Tapajóz region.

Troop Size

(pp. 726–77)

Muckenhirn, Mortensen, Vessey, Fraser, and Singh A-1976

Mean and extremes of individuals counted in 5 groups of *Saguinus midas midas* encountered in Guyana are 4.8(2–6).

Taste

(p. 730, add title)

Hellekant, Glaser, Brouwer, van der Wel A-1976

A group of *Saguinus midas niger* (= *tamarin* of authors) used in experiments on taste ranged in age from 1 to 13 years. Monellin (0.02%) and thaumatin (0.02%) elicited little or no taste response in an electrophysiological test, whereas miraculin (0.5%) enhanced the response to a sour stimulus but not to other taste qualities. In a behavioral test, the animals discriminated poorly or not at all between water and thaumatin or monellin. The effect of miraculin was to change the strong rejection of 0.02 M citric acid in a choice between water and the acid to a strong preference for the acid.

Saguinus inustus Schwarz

Additional specimens examined, 1 (total, 14). BRAZIL —*Amazonas:* Provação Santa Cruz, Igarapé Turi, right bank Rio Papuri (Uaupés), 1 (MPEG).

Distribution and Local Names

(pp. 604, 622, 749, 752, add second title)

The geographic range delineated by Hernández Camacho and Cooper (A-1976, p. 39) lies within that given here (pp. 622, 732). Local names for the animal, according to the authors, are "mico diablo," "diablito," and "titi diablito," all meaning monkey devil or little monkey devil, in allusion to its nearly uniformly blackish color. Dr. Frederick Medem, who collected the Field Museum specimens of *Saguinus inustus,* noted the same common names.

Saguinus bicolor bicolor Spix

Additional specimens examined, 17 (total, 24), BRAZIL —*Amazonas:* Colonia Santo Antônio, 1 (MPEG); Estrada AM-1, km 190 Manaus-Amapá, 4 (MPEG); Porto Mauá, 7 (MPEG); *Locality unrecorded:* 5 (MNRJ).

Remarks. I have not located Colonia Santo Antônio and Porto Mauá. The record for km 190 on the Manaus-Amapá highway, however, indicates that the range of *Saguinus bicolor bicolor* extends from Manaus to the west bank of the Rio Natumã. Northern limits of distribution may be the Rio Jauaperi, which empties into the Rio Negro at 1° 26′ S, 61° 35′ W.

The range of *Saguinus midas midas* overlaps that of *S. bicolor bicolor,* but the two tamarins have not been recorded from the same site. The fragmentary data available, however, allow for no definite conclusions regarding interspecific relationships.

Saguinus bicolor martinsi Thomas

Additional specimens examined, 4 (total, 15). BRAZIL —*Pará:* Faro, Fazenda Paraiso (215), 1 (MPEG); Faro, Rio Jamundá (215), 2 (MNRJ; MPEG); Porteira, Rio Mapuera, 1 (MPEG).

Remarks. Porteira, on the east bank of the Rio Trombetas below the mouth of the Rio Mapuera, is well to the north of localities previously recorded for *Saguinus bicolor martinsi* (cf. fig. X.15; gazetteer nos. 215, 216, p. 934).

Saguinus leucopus

Distribution

(pp. 604, 622, 749)

Hernández Camacho and Cooper A-1976, p. 41

The Isla de Mompós, where the Ríos San Jorge, Cauca, and Magdalena join through a rete of canals, is included within the range of *leucopus.* The species is also said to occur southward into northern Tolima "at least as far south as the vicinity of Mariquita," Río Magdalena.

Territory

(p. 752, add title)

Bernstein, Balcaen, Dresdale, Gouzoules, Kavanagh, Patterson, and Neyman-Warner A-1976

In an isolated woodlot between the lower Ríos Cauca and Magdalena, northern Colombia, with an area of one hectare, "we located a group of six tamarins, although we suspected the presence of a seventh unconfirmed tamarin. No other primates were present and it proved impossible to drive these animals out of this small patch of forest, thus supporting our belief that it was unlikely that these, or any other tamarins, crossed open ground between forest patches." (Compare with my notes on p. 726.)

Troop Size

(p. 752, add title)

Bernstein, Balcaen, Dresdale, Gouzoules, Kavanagh, Patterson, and Neyman-Warner A-1976

"Area five was undergoing rapid destruction and within six weeks was reduced from three to one square kilometer. One group of five and a second group of two tamarins were located." A group of 6 or 7 was watched in a smaller woodlot (see above).

Saguinus oedipus oedipus

Distribution

(p. 765)

Scott, Struhsaker, Glander, and Chirivi A-1976

Saguinus oedipus oedipus was not seen in 8 areas surveyed east of the Río Magdalena in the departments of Magdalena, Cesar, and Guajira. Relying on reports from questionable sources, however, the surveyors speculated that "if it is true that *Saguinus oedipus* is or was present in northern Cesar, then the zoogeographic interpretations of the ranges must be changed. The apparent control of distribution by major rivers may be only an artifact of agricultural patterns that obscure the true former distribution. *Saguinus oedipus* may be characteristic of the drier forests of all of northernmost Colombia, while *S. leucopus* appears in the wetter southern forests."

Comments

It has been conclusively established by repeated surveys since the turn of the century that in Colombia *Saguinus oedipus* is confined to the region west of the Río Cauca-Magdalena. *S. leucopus* is found only on the opposite bank of the Cauca, and there is no detectable climatic difference between the two sides of the river. The region east and north of the Río Magdalena, where *Saguinus oedipus* does not occur because it never got there (cf. pp. 399, 753, fig. X.2), once supported a mixed evergreen and deciduous climax forest; but deforestation and cattle grazing within historical times have converted much of the land to palm-savanna, scrub forest, or semidesert.

Notwithstanding the ecological similarity between opposing banks, the Río Magdalena marks the limits of distribution, whether from the east or the west, of many terrestrial vertebrate species and subspecies.

The cited report by Scott et al. (A-1976) was distributed in preliminary form one year earlier under the author name combination Struhsaker, Glander, Chirivi, and Scott (A-1975).

Parturition

(p. 771)

Fess A-1975*a*, p. 5

"In a birth observed on January 17, 1971, the mother appeared to be having contractions periodically at one minute intervals one hour before birth of the infants. Between contractions she walked around the cage, occasionally laying [*sic*] down. While experiencing the contractions she stood quite still with legs slightly spread looking under her body at her genital area. Four hours before delivery, her vulva was dilated. Three minutes before birth, while standing she made very slight vocalizations barely audible and seemed to be straining. The father was always near by and attentive, occasionally licking the discharge off his mate's hair and vulva.

"During a heavy strain, the top of the baby's head started to emerge and at the same time the father licked the discharge off the mother and the emerging infant. After the head appeared the mother reached back to touch her hair and the head of the infant, then licked the fluid from her hand. The mother and father both pulled at the baby until the shoulders appeared. After delivery the father aided in cleaning the infants and both ate the placental material until about ¼" to ½" remained attached to the babies. The mother's loss of blood during this birth was very slight compared to previous births, notably the first when the blood loss seemed much greater."

Growth and Development

(p. 778)

Fess A-1975*a*, p. 6

Birth—All 25 neonates observed were born with eyes open
12th day—Scratch with hind legs
18th day—Take food from parents' hands
21st–28th day—Make frog-like leaps of about 4–6 inches
24th–28th day—Run to parents when called
27th–33d day—Chew on branches, shelves; sleep next to but not on parents
60–80 days—Weaned

Habitat

(p. 785)

Green A-1975, p. 85

The history and current ecological status of the parts of northern Colombia where monkeys occur are reported. The survey includes an account of monkey capture, trade, transport, care and maintenance in captivity, and the role of the state in control and conservation of the monkey fauna.

Nesting Site
(p. 785, add title)
Moynihan A-1976*b*, p. 37

"Both *Saguinus geoffroyi* and *fuscicollis* . . . usually or often sleep in holes in trees at night. . . . G. A. Dawson (personal communication) has also found groups of *geoffroyi* sleeping huddled together in the open at the ends of branches of large trees. . . . Dawson was struck by the fact that the huddles looked like large termite nests at a distance."

I assume Dawson's observation was made at night, but except for the analogy, particulars of the encounters are not given. Moynihan, however, hastens to label this display, attractive as it must have appeared in the eyes of Dawson or any natural predator, as an "apparent example of crypsis or protective mimicry."

Leontopithecus rosalia chrysopygus Mikan

Additional specimens examined, 3 (total, 9). BRAZIL—*São Paulo:* Bauru (343b), 1 (MZUSP); Victoria, near Botucatu (344), 2 (MZUSP).

Remarks. Measurements of the three adults in the collection of the Museu de Zoología, Universidad de São Paulo, follow. They agree in general with those of *Leontopithecus rosalia rosalia* except that the coronoidal height is significantly less.

Number	2140 ♂	2141 ♀	2063 ♂
Locality	Victoria	Victoria	Bauru
Head and Body	255	275	—
Tail	400	385	—
Hind foot	75	75	—
Ear	23	25	—
Greatest skull length	56.6	57.0	58.5
Condylobasal length	45.5	45.4	47.9
Zygomatic width	34.3	34.4	36.0
Orbital breadth	27.6	28.2	29.7
Braincase width	29.1	29.4	29.6
Braincase length	47.9	48.2	48.6
$i–m^2$	20.0	19.6	20.1
$c–m^2$	15.5	15.0	16.0
$pm^2–m^2$	12.8	12.1	12.5
$m^1–m^2$	5.4	5.5	5.3
Across molars	19.8	19.1	19.5
Mandible length	35.5	35.7	36.6
Coronoidal height	19.4	19.1	19.8
$c–m_2$	17.2	17.0	17.2
$pm_2–m_2$	14.0	13.9	14.0
$m_1–m_2$	6.0	6.0	6.0

In a letter dated 20 September 1976, Dr. Adelmar Coimbra-Filho informs me of the existence of a small population of perhaps 30 *saguis-pretos,* in a relict forest in the Municipio of Galia, São Paulo (22° 18′ S, 49° 34′ W). Coimbra-Filho adds that the 500-acre plot, situated a short distance from Bauru (343b), is now a state forest preserve.

Leontopithecus rosalia chrysomelas Kuhl

Additional specimens examined, 11 (total, 15). BRAZIL—*Bahia:* Ilhéus (299), 10 (MNRJ); Rio Gongogy (297c), 1 (MZUSP).

Leontopithecus rosalia rosalia Linnaeus

Additional specimens examined, 31 (total, 68). BRAZIL—*Rio de Janeiro:* Serra do Barro Branco, 1 (MNRJ); *Locality unrecorded:* 30 (MNRJ, 25; MPEG, 2; MZUSP, 3).

Remarks. The Museu Nacional specimen from Barro Blanco, Rio de Janeiro, was taken in 1955. Golden lion-tamarins have since disappeared from the region.

Litters
(p. 851)
Coimbra-Filho and Mittermeier A-1976

A wild-caught, captive-raised *Leontopithecus rosalia chrysomelas* female mated with a captive-born *L. r. rosalia* produced 2 litters of twins and a singleton, all full term and physically normal. None of the infants, however, survived more than one day. Coloration of the hybrids was roughtly intermediate between that of the parents, but no two individuals were alike. Lack of success in raising the offspring was attributed to the inexperience of the parents, both of which had been separated from their family group during infancy.

Chronology of Growth
(p. 851)
Coimbra-Filho and Mittermeier A-1976

Measurements of the neonates described above follow (length in milimeters, weight in grams)

Head and body	—	105	150	110	112
Tail	128	120	110	140	95
Head length	—	40	—	40	—
Hand length	26	26	—	—	—
Foot length	33	30	—	35	30
Weight without placenta	—	55	—	68	50
Weight with placenta	—	—	—	77	—

Means of the measurements are not significantly different from those shown in table 54 (p. 445).

Nesting Site
(p. 853, add title)
Coimbra-Filho (personal communication)

Two photographs of lion-tamarin nests were kindly sent to me by Dr. Adelmar Coimbra-Filho. The first, taken in Morro do Diabo, São Paulo, is of a tree trunk showing the hole of a woodpecker's nest that had been occupied by *Leontopithecus rosalia chrysopygus.* The diameter of the hole, measured by Dr. Coimbra-Filho, is 6 cm, and the diameter of the tree trunk appears to be about five times greater. The second photograph, taken in Silva Jardim, Rio de Janeiro, is of a segment of a hollow tree with a knothole entrance. The golden lion-tamarins (*L. r. rosalia*) that nested in the cavity were captured. My estimate of the trunk's diameter is 25 cm, and that of the knothole, about 10 cm.

Callimico goeldii Thomas

Additional specimens examined, 6 (total, 25). BRAZIL—*Acre:* Rio Yaco, 1 (MPEG); Seringal Oriente, Rio Juruá, 2 (MPEG; MZUSP); upper Rio Xapury, 1 (MPEG); *Locality unrecorded:* 2 (MNRJ; MZUSP).

Remarks. The adult male from Rio Yaco (MPEG 443) described and figured by Cruz Lima (MPEG 433) had lived in the Belém Zoo. The proximal portion of its tail has two pale rings, not three as depicted by Cruz Lima, and the pale coronal band that extends from ear to ear of the Rio Yaco individual does not appear in his painting. A second variegated *Callimico* described by Cruz Lima had also lived for some time in the Belém Zoo. The two Seringal Oriente individuals, like all other wild-caught callimicos examined, lack aberrant markings.

Distribution

(pp. 864–65)

Heltne, Freese, and Whitesides A-1976, p. 9

"We were told that *Callimico goeldii* are also common in some areas along the [Río] Acre. The captive *C. goeldii* which we observed were reported captured near Espírito Santo on the Bolivian side of the Acre," upper Rio Purus.

The indicated presence of callimicos in the Río Acre region of Bolivia justifies my extrapolated range of the species given on page 892. My reference at the time to a Bolivian record, however, is an error that harks back to the "Ma River, Bolivia" provenance given by Pocock (1920) for a poorly labeled specimen (cf. pp. 865, 890).

The survey party (1976, p. 14) got only negative reports to inquiries regarding the presence of *Callimico* in the Riberalta area on the Río Beni. The animal, however, is known from the upper Río Madre de Dios basin in Peru, and the distributional patterns of the monkeys of that region indicate that *Callimico goeldii* may also range east to the upper Madeira in Bolivia.

Gestation

(p. 897)

Heltne, Turner, and Scott A-1976, p. 18

The following data are from Heltne's personal breeding colony; the number of samples is not given.

Gestation, 150–70 days; age to maturity, about 1½–2 years; record longevity, 4 years, 9 months.

Pook A-1976, p. 19

"Female Pair 1 gave birth to a single offspring 144 days after pairing (147 days after arrival), while the female of Pair 2 also produced a single offspring 143 days after pairing (160 days after arrival)."

The duration of gestation is appreciably less than the range given by Heltne, Turner, and Scott (A-1976, p. 18) and less than the mean and extremes of 154 (151–59) for seven pregnancies, determined by Lorenz (p. 897). Pook observed that his 3 pairs were shipped to the zoo as a single group and maintained as an extended group for 3 to 14 days. He suggests that conception may have occurred before the pairs were segregated in the zoo.

Births

(p. 899)

Pook A-1976, p. 19

A few minutes after birth the infant was seen clinging to its mother's chest while she licked it clean, then pulled out the placenta and ate it, followed by the umbilical cord.

Hour of Birth

(p. 899)

Pook A-1976, p. 19

The first birth occurred early in the evening just before the lights were switched off; the second birth occurred at night.

Chronology of Growth and Development

(p. 899)

Pook A-1976, p. 19

The observations are based on the first born of two infants, except as noted.

Newborn—Eyes open; vocalizes within a few minutes of birth, making a soft "chirring" noise.
14th day—Both infants take interest in surroundings
16th–17th day—Squeals as resists mother's attempts to dislodge it.
21st day—First infant seen on father's back for first time, then carried mainly by male; second infant first observed on father's back when 25 days old, then carried about equally by father and mother.
35th day—Stands alone on branch for a few seconds.
44th day—Still rides parents almost constantly.

Habitat

(p. 903)

Moynihan A-1976*b*, p. 25

Callimico was observed on an island in the Río Guineo, a tributary of the Putumayo in southern Colombia. The land is largely under cultivation and pasture, but stands of dense second growth interspersed with a few tall relict trees shelter the monkeys.

Spatial Orientation

(p. 903)

Moynihan A-1976*b*, p. 27

The callimicos move through all levels of bush and trees, but seek the canopy when undisturbed and bolt to the ground when surprised by predators, including man. Natives take advantage of this behavior by running the creatures down with dogs. "Two pairs I surprised [on the ground] by an unexpected approach first stashed their infants in the most convenient low bush and then ran away through the trees."

Pook A-1976, p. 18

Three wild-caught pairs of *Callimico* housed in the

Jersey Zoo "were rarely seen on the floor of the cage, except to catch insects, such as crickets."

Numbers and Visibility

(p. 904)

Sr. M. M. Moreira, whom I met in July 1976 in the Museu Paraense Emilio Goeldi, informed me that in Acre he saw a band of about 70 individuals at about 9:00 A.M. and observed them until 2:00 P.M. They kept to the lower levels of the trees, from 1 to 10 meters above the ground. They were active all the time, he recalled. The next day, at about 3:00 P.M., he saw a band of about 25 individuals.

The information was supplied in reply to my query regarding Moreira's earlier notes cited on page 904.

Associations

(p. 905)

Moynihan A-1976*b*, p. 34

The saddle-back tamarin, *Saguinus fuscicollis fuscus,* also lives on the island (see above) and was seen moving through the same trees as *Callimico* and raiding the same plantations.

Food

(p. 907)

Moynihan A-1976*a*, p. 82

"I watched . . . *Callimico goeldii* [in the upper Río Putumayo region, Colombia] at some length . . . without seeing a trace of sap-sucking."

Moynihan A-1976*b*, p. 28

Feeding [in the upper Río Putumayo region] was not observed, but according to the natives *Callimico* consumes insects, berries, fruit of the *Inga* and *Couscarea,* cacao (*Theobroma*), and "caime" (Sapotaceae).

Movements

(p. 908)

Moynihan A-1976*b*, p. 28

Locomotion is similar to that of tamarins or squirrels, "but they also cling to tree trunks in a vertical position, and leap or hop from trunk to trunk with the body and head kept upright."

Repose

(p. 908)

Pook A-1976, p. 18

"None of the specimens [in the Jersey Zoo] were ever observed to sleep inside the nest boxes. Instead, they sleep either on top of the nest box, or amongst the thin branches provided in one of the top corners of the cage."

GAZETTEER SUPPLEMENT

Collecting or other specific localities mentioned in the Addendum without numbers are listed alphabetically by country, then by state, department, or province. Numbered localities entered here are the same as those in the principal gazetteer but with additions or corrections. They are also arranged by country and political subdivision but follow the unnumbered localities in numerical order.

BRAZIL

Acre

—Juruá (Rio), alto.
Saguinus imperator
C. Britto, May 1939.

—Manuel Urbano, Rio Purus, 8° 53′ S, 69° 18′ W.
Saguinus imperator
P. Vanzolini, September 1973.

—Rio Branco, Rio Acre, 9° 58′ S, 67° 48′ W, 160 m.
Saguinus fuscicollis weddelli
F. Almeida, January 1971.
Saguinus labiatus labiatus
F. Almeida, January 1971.
Saguinus imperator
F. Almeida, January 1971.

208. Cruziero do Sul.
[*Saguinus fuscicollis melanoleucus*]
M. Moreira and F. Novaes, June 1956.

211. Yaco (Rio).
[*Callimico goeldii*]
C. Britto, June 1933.

Amapá—Saguinus midas midas

—Falcino (Rio, mouth), 0° 56′ N, 51° 35′ W.
M. Moreira, August 1963.

—Porto Platon, Rio Araguari, 0° 42′ N, 51° 27′ W,

—Serra do Navio, 0° 59′ N, 52° 03′ W.

157. Vilha Velha.
M. Moreira, March 1952.

158. Amapá.
M. Moreira, May 1958.

160. Maruanum (Rio).
M. Moreira, September 1952.

Amazonas

—Aniba (Igarapé), 2° 43′ S, 58° 48′ W.
Saguinus midas midas

—Apuaú (Apuahy), Rio Negro, east bank, 2° 32′ S, 60° 48′ W.
Saguinus midas midas

—Chandless (Rio, mouth), upper Rio Purus, 9° 08′ S, 69° 51′ W.
Cebuella pygmaea

—Colonia Agrícola, Coari, not certainly located. The town of Coari, 4° 05′ S, 63° 08′ W, on S bank of Rio Solimõés, may not be the one of the Colonia Agrícola.
Saguinus mystax mystax (?)

—Colonia Santo Antônio, Estrada Manaus—Amapá (AM-1), not located.
Saguinus bicolor bicolor
Collector's measurements on skin tag suggest that the specimen is mislabeled.

—Estirão do Ecuador, Rio Javarí, approximately 4° 20′ S, 70° 50′ W.
Saguinus fusicollis fuscicollis
J. Hidasi, September, October 1959; November 1960.
Saguinus mystax mystax
J. Hidasi, March, October 1959, November 1960.
—Gondino, Seringal Bõa Vista, Rio Quivito, Benjamin Constant, 4° 33′ S, 70° 28′ W.
Saguinus fuscicollis fuscicollis
—Guariba (Rio), Rio Aripuanã, 7° 42′ S, 60° 18′ W.
Callithrix humeralifer intermedius
M. Moreira, October 1975.
—Km 190, Estrada Manaus-Amapá (AM-1) near Rio Utumã northeast of Manaus (170).
Saguinus bicolor bicolor
Mozarth, December 1966, July 1967.
—Maués, Rio Maués-Açu. 3° 24′ S, 57° 42′ W.
Callithrix humeralifer humeralifer
A. B. Rylands (in litt., Sept. 1976).
—Oito, Tefé, see Tefé, 3° 22′ S, 64° 42′ W.
Saguinus mystax pileatus
—Patrimonio, Rio Tefé, not located; see Tefé (above).
Saguinus mystax pileatus
—Pauini, Rio Purus, left bank, 7° 40′ S, 66° 58′ W.
Cebuella pygmaea
Saguinus fuscicollis primitivus
P. E. Vanzolini, December 1974.
Saguinus pileatus mystax
—Porto Mauá, Rio Negro, not located, see Manaus, 3° 08′ S, 60° 0′ W.
Saguinus bicolor bicolor
—Prainha, Rio Aripuanã, right bank, 7° 16′ S, 60° 23′ W.
Callithrix humeralifer chrysoleuca
J. L. da Silva
—Provação Santa Cruz, Igarapé Turi, right bank, Rio Papuri 0° 38′ N, 69° 22′ W.
Saguinus inustus
M. Moreira, 1971.
—Purus (Rio), right bank.
Saguinus mystax pileatus
—Silves, 2° 54′ N, 58° 27′ W.
Saguinus midas midas
—Tacana (Igarapé) alto Rio Solimõés, not located.
Cebuella pygmaea
—Taquirana (Rio), not located.
Saguinus mystax mystax
Mozarth, January 1961.
—Urubu (Rio), 2° 06′ S, 60° 02′ W.
Saguinus midas midas

174b. Juruá (Rio)
Cebuella pygmaea
Saguinus fuscicollis fuscicollis
Saguinus mystax mystax
E. Garbe, left bank.
190. Acre (Rio), Rio Purus, 8° 56′ S, 67° 23′ W.
202. Parintins
Callithrix humeralifer humeralifer
E. Garbe, 1920.

Bahia

—Aritagua, 14° 43′ S, 39° 06′ W.
Callithrix jacchus penicillata
Serviço do Estudos e Pesquisas sôbre a Febra Amarela (SEPSFA).
—Banco da Vitória, 14° 48′ S, 39° 06′ W.
Callithrix jacchus penicillata
Serviço do Estudos e Pesquisas sôbre a Febra Amarela (SEPSFA).
—Bom Jesus da Lapa, Rio São Francisco, 13° 15′ S, 43° 25′ W.
Callithrix jacchus penicillata.
—Castelo Novo, 14° 38′ S, 39° 12′ W.
Callithrix jacchus penicillata
—Japu, Reportimento, 14° 55′ S, 39° 12′ W.
Callithrix jacchus penicillata
—Pontal dos Ilhéus, 14° 50′ S, 39° 01′ W.
Callithrix jacchus penicillata
Serviço do Estudos e Pesquisas sôbre a Febra Amarela (SEPSFA).
—Rio do Braço, Ilhéus, 14° 39′ S, 39° 16′ W.
Callithrix jacchus penicillata
Serviço do Estudos e Pesquisas sôbre a Febra Amarela (SEPSFA).
292a. Santa Rita de Cassia.
[*Callithrix jacchus jacchus*]
E. Dente, April 1958.
293a. São Gonzalo, 30 km SW Feira de Santana.
Callithrix jacchus penicillata
J. A. White, August 1948.

Ceará—Callithrix jacchus jacchus
—Cerro do Castello, not located.
F. Lima, August 1915.
284c. Bom Jardin, São Benedito.
284e. Acudinho, Baturité.
284e. Estrada do Ferro Baturité—Ceará (= Fortaleza).
284e. Sitio Uruguaiana, Pacoti, Serra de Guaramiranga.

Distrito Federal—Callithrix jacchus penicillata
—Vaõa dos Angicos, Rio do Sal, upper Rio Maranhão. Not located. Ribeirão dos Angicos, Goiás, 15° 10′ S, 48° 28′ W, is in the upper Rio Maranhão basin on northern border of Distrito Federal.

Espírito Santo
—Dez de Agosto, not located.
Callithrix jacchus geoffroyi
—Kms 12, 13, 14, 18, Estrada Linhares (319c)—São Matheus (319a).
Callithrix jacchus geoffroyi
—Los Domingos, not located.
Callithrix jacchus geoffroyi
—Morra da Argola, 20° 20′ S, 40° 21′ W.
Callithrix jacchus geoffroyi
—Serra da Mula, not located.
Callithrix jacchus geoffroyi
319c. Jacaré (Fazenda) Linares.
Callithrix jacchus geoffroyi
320b. Colatina.
[*Callithrix jacchus geoffroyi*]
E. Garbe, May 1906.
320b. Santa Teresa.
Callithrix jacchus geoffroyi × *C. j. flaviceps*
A. Ruschi, December 1940.

Goiás—Callithrix jacchus penicillata
—Caldas Novas, 17° 45′ S, 48° 38′ W.
—Linhares, not located.
(formerly Goiabeiras, not located).

—Miriti Mirantião, not located.
—Neropolis, 16° 25′ S, 49° 14′ W.
—Ponte Ipê Arcado, not located (cf. p. 922).
—Porto Nacional, Rio Tocantins, 40° 42′ S, 48° 25′ W.
—Trinidade, 16° 40′ S, 49° 30′ W.

277b. Jaraguá, Rio das Almas.
J. Lima.
278a. Aragarças
M. S. Amaral, April-May 1958;
J. Hidasi, October 1958.
280. Goiânia.
J. Hidasi, August, October 1958.

Maranhão

—Cururupú, 1° 50′ S, 44° 52′ W.
Saguinus midas niger

Mato Grosso

—Aripuanã, Rio Roosevelt, 9° 10′ S, 60° 38′ W.
Callithrix argentata melanura
Commissão Rondon
Instituto Evandro Chavas
Callithrix humeralifer intermedius
Instituto Evandro Chavas
269. Fazenda Maravilla, Villa Porto Antônio, Cuiabá.
Callithrix argentata melanura
F. Lima, September 1937.

Minas Gerais

—Doce (Rio), below mouth Rio Suaçui, 18° 50′ S, 41° 46′ W.
Callithrix jacchus geoffroyi
—Gaspar Lopes, 21° 22′ S, 45° 56′ W.
Callithrix jacchus aurita
—João Pinheiro, 17° 45′ S, 46° 10′ W.
Callithrix jacchus penicillata
—Pompeia, 19° 12′ S, 44° 59′ W.
Callithrix jacchus penicillata
—Rio Novo, 21° 29′ S, 43° 08′ W.
Callithrix jacchus aurita

308b. Araguari.
Callithrix jacchus penicillata
315a. Dom Joaquim, Conceição do Mato Dentro.
Callithrix jacchus geoffroyi
315b. Bõa Esperanza (Fazenda) São José da Lagô (= Nova Era, 500 m.
Callithrix jacchus geoffroyi
318b. Fazenda da Gruta, Mar de Espanha.
Callithrix jacchus aurita

Pará

—Baiussú, Rio Amazonas, not located; apparently not the same as Boiuçu (or Buiuçu), Ilha de Marajó (below).
Saguinus midas midas
—Barreira, Rio Tapajóz, left bank, 4° 04′ S, 55° 53′ W.
Callithrix humeralifer humeralifer
—Belém-Pará (?)
Saguinus midas niger
J. Hidasi, December 1957, May 1961.
—Boiuçu, Ilha de Marajó, 1° 48′ S, 50° 17′ W.
Saguinus midas niger
—Bravo, Rio Amazonas, not located.
Saguinus midas midas
—Cacheoira do Tronco, upper Rio Paru do Oeste, 1° 04′ S, 56° 02′ W.
Saguinus midas midas
Lasso, March 1937.
—Capanema, 1° 12′ S, 47° 11′ W.
Saguinus midas niger
Lasso, February 1936.
—Capim, km 93, Belém-Brasilia, 1° 41′ S, 47° 47′ W.
Saguinus midas niger
—Caracol Grande, Rio Amazonas, not located.
Saguinus midas midas
—Castanhal, 1° 43′ S, 55° 26′ W.
Saguinus midas niger
Instituto Oswaldo Cruz, September-December 1957, January-February 1958.
—Curalinho, Ilha de Marajó, 1° 48′ S, 49° 47′ W.
Saguinus midas niger
—Fazenda Muruá, not located.
Callithrix argentata argentata
—Flexal. See Km 211.
—Igarapé, Rio Guamá, not precisely located; mouth of Rio Guamá is at Belém (1° 27′ S, 48° 29′ W).
Saguinus midas midas
—Km 36, Rodovia Belém-Brasilia, south of Belém (256).
Saguinus midas niger
J. Hidasi.
—Km 75, Rodovia Belém-Brasilia.
Saguinus midas niger
J. Hidasi, February 1959.
—Km 86, Rodovia Belém-Brasilia.
Saguinus midas niger
E. Dente, May 1960.
—Km 211, Rodovia Itaituba—Jacaré-a-Canga, 5° 45′ S, 57° 13′ W.
Callithrix humeralifer humeralifer
Instituto Evandro Chavas TransAmazonian Project.
—Massaranduba, Tomé Assu, Rio Acará, not certainly located, see Tomé Assu (Açu) below.
Saguinus midas niger
F. Novaes, September 1965.
—Oriximiná, Rio Trombetas, 1° 45′ S, 55° 52′ W.
Saguinus midas midas
Lasso, July 1937.
—Paragominas, Estrada Belém (1° 27′ S, 48° 29′ W)—Marabá (5° 21′ S, 49° 07′ W).
Saguinus midas niger
—Porteira, Rio Mapuera, 1° 05′ S, 57° 04′ W.
Saguinus bicolor martinsi
Lasso, June 1937
—Pracupi, Portel, Rio Pará, not precisely located; Portel is 1° 57′ S, 50° 49′ W; Rio Pracupi and Baía Pracupi are 70–75 km SW.
Callithrix argentata argentata
—Retiro de Nazaré, Benevides, not located; Benevides (259) is at 1° 22′ S, 48° 15′ W.
Saguinus midas niger
M. Moreira, May 1964.
—San Francisco, Vigia, 0° 48′ S, 48° 08′ W.
Saguinus midas niger
Instituto Oswaldo Cruz, January 1955.
—Santa Bárbara, Benevides, not located; see Benevides (259).
Saguinus midas niger
M. Moreira, June 1964.

—Santa Rosa, east of Urucurutuba (228a), not located.
Callithrix humeralifer humeralifer
—Seringal, not located.
Callithrix humeralifer humeralifer
—Sumanama, Rio Tapajóz, 5 km S and opposite Fordlandia (234).
Callithrix humeralifer humeralifer
—Taioca, Rio Paru de Oeste, not located (cf. 216).
Saguinus midas midas
—Tapera, Rio Paru de Oeste, not located (cf. 216).
Saguinus midas midas
—Tirios, Rio Paru de Oeste, not located (cf. 216).
Saguinus midas midas
—Tomé Assu, Rio Acará, 2° 25′ S, 48°09′ W.
Saguinus midas niger
M. Moreira, December 1964.
—Tauaquera, not located.
Saguinus midas niger (?)
Note: a Tauaquera, Amazonas (0° 23′ N, 64° 03′ W), lies within the range of *S. m. midas.*
—Tavio, Rio Tapajóz, 3° 28′ S, 55° 12′ W.
Callithrix argentata leucippe

215. Fazenda Paraiso, Faro.
[*Saguinus bicolor martinsi*]
E. Snethlage, April 1911.
223b. Rio Arapiuns, Santarém.
[*Callithrix humeralifer humeralifer*]
Lasso, May, November 1937.
228a. Santa Rosa east of Urucurutuba.
Callithrix humeralifer humeralifer
228b. Itaituba.
[*Callithrix humeralifer humeralifer*]
E. Garbe, 1920.
229. Vila Braga
[*Callithrix humeralifer humeralifer*]
F. Lima, July 1917.
234. Fazenda de Nova, Fordlandia.
[*Callithrix argentata leucippe*]
242. Santarém.
[*Callithrix argentata argentata*]
Eladio Lima Filho, April 1932; Lasso, November 1937; M. Moreira, May 1957.
Note: Inclusion of *C. a. leucippe* under Santarém (p. 935) is an error; see Addendum p. 1019.
252. Vaicajá (Fazenda), Cametá.
[*Callithrix argentata argentata*]
F. Lima, February 1916.
256. Belém.
[*Saguinus midas niger*]
J. Hidasi, December 1957.
258. Utinga.
[*Saguinus midas niger*]
M. Moreira, May 1956.
262. Conceição.
[*Saguinus midas niger*]
E. Snethlage, December 1915.

Paraíba—Callithrix jacchus jacchus

287a. Camaratuba, Mamaguape.
287a. Uruba, Mamaguape.

Pernambuco—Callithrix jacchus jacchus

—Agua Azul, Vicência, 7° 40′ S, 35° 20′ W.
—Agua Preta, 8° 42′ S, 35° 31′ W.
—Sitio Vertentes, Caruaru, not precisely located; a Vertentes is situated at 7° 54′ S, 35° 59′ W. and a Caruarú at 8° 17′ S, 35° 58′ W.
—Victória de Santo Antão, 8° 07′ S, 35° 18′ W.

Piaui—Callithrix jacchus jacchus

—Valencia, 6° 24′ S, 41° 45′ W.

Rio de Janeiro (resident Callithrix jacchus jacchus is not autochthonous)

—Angra dos Reis, 23° 00′ S, 46° 70′ W.
Callithrix jacchus aurita
—Campo Grande, 22° 54′ S, 43° 14′ W.
Callithrix jacchus jacchus
—Jacarapegua, about 23° S, 43° W.
Callithrix jacchus jacchus
328. Fazenda Alexandreta,
[*Callithrix jacchus aurita*]
J. C. N. Penido, 1934.
332. Bom Retiro, Tijuca,
Callithrix jacchus jacchus
333. Teresópolis,
[*Callithrix jacchus aurita*]
Galdina Pereira, July 1942;
C. Guinle, July 1942;
P. M. Britto, March, April, August 1943;
D. E. Davis, April 1943.
336. Macaé (Serra de).
[*Callithrix jacchus aurita*]
E. Garbe, October 1909.
336. Silva Jardim
Leontopithecus rosalia rosalia
A. Coimbra-Filho, 1976.

Rondônia

—"Aripuanan," Rio Jamary, not precisely located.
Saguinus fuscicollis weddelli
Commissão Rondon.
The Rio Jamary enters the Madeira from the right at 8° 27′ S, 63° 30′ W. I find no Aripuanan in the Rio Jamary basin (cf. p. 1024).

São Paulo

345. Itatiba.
[*Callithrix jacchus aurita*]
E. Garbe, June 1905.
—Gália (municipio), 22° 18′ S, 49° 34′ W.
Leontopithecus rosalia chrysopygus
A. Coimbra-Filho (in litt., September 1976).
—Pombal (Fazenda), Vargem Grande, 23° 52′ S, 47° 45′ W.
Callithrix jacchus aurita
Note: Coordinates given are for the town of Pombal, near Varge Grande (349); another Vargem Grande, at 22° 48′ S, 46° 37′ W, near Campinas (345), is also within the range of *aurita.*
—São João do Barreira, 1400 m, not located.
Callithrix jacchus aurita
Note: A São João do Barreira at 22° 38′ S, 44° 35′ W, lies within the range of *aurita.*

339c. Morro do Diabo, 22° 31′ S, 52° 10′ W.
Leontopithecus rosalia chrysopygus
A. Coimbra-Filho, 1976.

BOLIVIA

Pando

—Abuna (Río), 9° 41′ S, 65° 23′ W.
Saguinus labiatus labiatus
Hoffman (cf. P. Heltne, C. Freese, and G. Whitesides, 1976).
—Espírito Santo, Río Acre, 11° 00′ S, 68° 58′ W.
Callimico goeldii
P. Heltne, C. Freese, and G. Whitesides, July, August 1975.
—Tahuamanu (Río), 11° 06′ S, 67° 36′ W.
Saguinus labiatus
Hoffman (cf. P. Heltne, C. Freese, and G. Whitesides 1976).

135. Cobija, Río Acre, 11° 01′ S, 68° 44′ W.
Saguinus labiatus labiatus
P. Heltne, C. Freese, and G. Whitesides, July, August 1975 (seen 30 miles west of Cobija).

COLOMBIA

Amazonas

—Puerto Narino (=Nariño?). On Río Amazonas above Leticia (58e).
Saguinus fuscicollis tripartitus
(Cf. J. Hernández Camacho and R. Cooper, 1976.)
—Apaporis (Río), 1° 23′ S, 69° 25′ W (mouth).
Saguinus fuscicollis
(Cf. J. Hernández Camacho and R. Cooper, 1976.)

58e. Leticia, 4° 15′ S, 69° 56′ W.
Cebuella pygmaea
K. Fess, February 1970; April 1972.
Saguinus nigricollis nigricollis
J. Hernández Camacho, March 1972.

Bolívar

—Mompós, Isla, 9° 05′ N, 74° 30′ W.
Saguinus leucopus
(Cf. J. Hernández Camacho and R. Cooper 1976.)

Caquetá

—Caguán (Río), 0° 08′ S, 74° 18′ W (mouth).
Saguinus fuscicollis
(Cf. J. Hernández Camacho and R. Cooper 1976.)
—Caucaya (Río), 0° 09′ S, 74° 49′ W.
Saguinus fuscicollis fuscus
K. Izawa, January 1972.
—Peneya (Río), 0° 07′ S, 74° 22′ W (mouth).
K. Izawa, 1971–72, 1973–74
—Puerto Japón, Río Peneya, 0° 07′ N, 74° 24′ W.
Saguinus fuscicollis
K. Izawa, September 1973–February 1974.
—Puerto Tokio, Río Peneya, 0° 12′ N, 74° 23′ W.
Saguinus fuscicollis
K. Izawa, November 1973–February 1974.
—Yari (Río), 0° 23′ N, 72° 16′ W (mouth).
Saguinus fuscicollis
(Cf. J. Hernández Camacho and R. Cooper 1976.)

Meta

—Morrocoy (Caño), Río Guayabero, 2° 11′ N, 73° 51′ W.
Cebuella pygmaea
(Cf. J. Hernández Camacho and R. Cooper 1976.)

Putumayo

—El Pepino, 1° 03′ N, 76° 38′ W.
Cebuella pygmaea
M. Moynihan, September 1968; July 1969; February, August 1970.
—Guineo (Río), 0° 48′ N, 76° 35′ W.
Saguinus fuscicollis fuscus
M. Moynihan, September 1968; July 1969; February, August 1970
Callimico goeldii
M. Moynihan, September 1968; July 1969; February, August 1970
—Paya (Río), Río Putumayo, not located.
Saguinus fuscicollis fuscus
K. Izawa, September 1971.
—Puerto Leguízamo, 0° 12′ S, 74° 46′ W.
Cebuella pygmaea
J. Hernández Camacho, March 1965.
—Rumiyaco, not located, said to be between Mocoa (1° 09′ N, 76° 37′ W) and Puerto Asís (0° 30′ N, 76° 31′ W). Mouth of Río Rumiyaco is at 0° 21′ N, 77° 13′ W.
Cebuella pygmaea
M. Moynihan, September 1968; July 1969; February, August 1970.

Tolima

—Mariquita, 5° 12′ N, 74° 54′ W.
Saguinus leucopus
(Cf. J. Hernández Camacho, and R. Cooper 1976.)

Vaupés

—Angostura, 2° 18′ N, 73° 57′ W.
Saguinus fuscicollis
(Cf. J. Hernández Camacho and R. Cooper 1976.)
—San José de Guaviare, 2° 35′ N, 72° 38′ W.
Saguinus fuscicollis
(Cf. J. Hernández Camacho and R. Cooper 1976.)

PERU

Loreto

—Ampiyacu (Río), 3° 19′ S, 71° 51′ W.
Cebuella pygmaea
C. Freese, October, November 1974.
Saguinus nigricollis nigricollis
C. Freese, October, November 1974.
—Aucayo (Río), 3° 50′ S, 73° 05′ W.
Cebuella pygmaea
R. Castro and P. Soini, May–July 1975.
Saguinus fuscicollis nigrifrons
R. Castro and P. Soini, May–July 1975.
Saguinus mystax mystax
R. Castro and P. Soini, May–July 1975.
—Balta, 10° 08′ S, 71° 15′ W.
Saguinus imperator
A. Gardner, April 1971.
—Centro Unión, Río Aucayo. *See* Aucayo (Río)
Cebuella pygmaea
R. Castro and P. Soini, May–July 1975.
—Estirão do Ecuador (opposite), Río Yavarí, about 40° 20′ S, 70° 50′ W.
Saguinus fuscicollis nigrifrons
J. Hidasi, March 1963.

—Orosa (Río), 3° 26′ S, 72° 08′ W.
Saguinus fuscicollis nigrifrons
C. Freese, June, July 1974.
Saguinus mystax mystax
C. Freese, June, July 1974.
—Palmares, not located (see p. 922).
Cebuella pygmaea
Saguinus fuscicollis lagonotus
Saguinus mystax mystax
Note: The represenetative specimens were living in the Belém zoo. There are no authentic data for each, but *S. f. lagonotus* and *S. f. mystax* do not occur on the same side of the Marañón.
—Panguana (near Pucallpa), 7° 05′ S, 74° 06′ W.
Saguinus fuscicollis leucogenys
C. Freese, June, July 1974.
—Tahuayo (Río), 4° 15′ S, 73° 04′ W.
Saguinus fuscicollis nigrifrons
R. Castro and P. Soini, May–July 1975.
Saguinus mystax mystax
R. Castro and P. Soini, May–July 1975.
Cebuella pygmaea
R. Castro and P. Soini, May–July 1975.

83. Chimbote (a shipping or purchasing point).
Cebuella pygmaea
Saguinus nigricollis nigricollis
Saguinus fuscicollis illigeri
Saguinus mystax mystax
Note: All specimens in the Goeldi Museum were living in the Belém Zoo. *S. n. nigricollis* inhabits the north bank of the Marañón (Amazonas), *illigeri* and *mystax* occur on the south.

92. Iquitos, Río Marañón, 3° 45′ S, 73° 12′ W.
Cebuella pygmaea
Saguinus nigricollis nigricollis
Saguinus fuscicollis nigrifrons
Saguinus fuscicollis lagonotus
C. Freese, April–December 1974.
Note: All specimens in the Goeldi Museum labeled "Iquitos" were living in the Belém Zoo and likely collected near Iquitos (cf. map, fig. X. 15).

94b. Nanay (Río), 3° 45′ S, 73° 35′ W.
Cebuella pygmaea
C. Freese, April, May 1974.
Saguinus fuscicollis lagonotus
C. Freese, April, May 1974.

96. Samiria (Río), 4° 42′ S, 74° 12′ W.
Cebuella pygmaea
M. Neville, N. Castro, A. Mármol, and J. Revilla, October, November 1973; March 1974.
Saguinus fuscicollis illigeri
C. Freese, October 1974.

101. Pacaya (Río), 5° 14′ S, 74° 10′ W.
Cebuella pygmaea
M. Neville, N. Castro, A. Mármol, and J. Revilla, January, February 1974.

Madre de Dios

129. Cocha Cashu, Río Manú, see Altamira, Río Manú (129).
Cebuella pygmaea
J. Terborgh, 1975.
Saguinus fuscicollis weddelli
C. Freese, August, September 1974.

San Martín

120. Moyobamba, 6° 03′ S, 76° 58′ W.
(?) *Cebuella pygmaea*
(see C. Freese 1975, p. 29).

Literature Cited in the Addendum

Bernstein, Irwin S.; Balcaen, Peter; Dresdale, Lawrence; Gouzoules, Harold; Kavanagh, Michael; Patterson, Thomas; and Neyman-Warner, Patricia. 1976. Differential effects of forest degradation on primate populations. *Primates* 17 (3):401–11, 2 figs.

Box, H. O. 1975. A social developmental study of young monkeys (*Callithrix jacchus*) within a captive family group. *Primates* 16 (4):419–35.

Castro, Rogerio, and Soini, Pekka. 1977. Field studies on *Saguinus mystax* and other callitrichids in Amazonian Peru. Paper presented at the Conference on "The Biology and Conservation of the Callitrichidae," Front Royal, Virginia, 18–20 August 1975. Unpublished manuscript.

Coimbra-Filho, A. F. 1974. Triplo híbridismo em *Callithrix*. (Callithricidae, Primates) *An. Acad. Brasil Ciênc.* 46:708.

Coimbra-Filho, A. F.; Cruz Rocha, Newton da; and Pissinatti, Alcides. 1976. Gestação quadrupla de triplohíbridos em *Callithrix* duplo-híbrida (Callitrichidae, Primates). *Rev. Brasil. Biol.* 36 (3):675–81, 2 figs.

Coimbra-Filho, A., and Maia, Angela de A. 1976. Híbridismo de *Callithrix geoffroyi* (Humboldt, 1812) × *C. jacchus* (Linnaeus, 1758), e criação artificial de filhote híbrido (Callitrichidae, Primates). *Rev. Brasil. Biol.* 36 (3):665–73, 9 figs.

Coimbra-Filho, Adelmar F., and Mittermeier, Russell A. 1976. Hybridization in the genus *Leontopithecus, L. r. rosalia* (Linnaeus, 1766) × *L. r. chrysomelas* (Kuhl, 1820) (Callitrichidae, Primates). *Rev. Brasil. Biol.* 36 (1):129–27, 4 figs.

Cronin, John E., and Sarich, Vincent M. 1975. Molecular systematics of the New World monkeys. *J. Human Evolution* 4 (5):357–375, 4 figs.

Daniel, M. D.; Fraser, C. E. O.; Barahona, H. H.; Hajema, E. M.; and Melendez, L. V. 1976. Microbial agents of the owl monkey (*Aotus trivirgatus*). *Lab. Animal Sci.* 26 (6):1073–77.

Deane, Leonidas de Mello. 1976. Epidemiology of simian malaria in the American continent. First Interamerican Conference on Conservation and Utilization of American Nonhuman Primates in Biomedical Research. *Pan American Health Organization (Washington, D. C.), Sci. Publ.* 317:144–63, 1 fig.

Deinhardt, Fredrich; Wolfe, Lauren; Peterson, D.; Cross, G. F.; and Holmes, A. W. 1975. The mythology of

various hepatitis A virus isolates. Int. Symp. Viral Hepatitis, Milan (1974). *Develop. Biol. Standard* 30:390–404.

Fess, Kenneth J., 1975*a*. Observations on a breeding pair of cotton-top pinches (*Oedipomides oedipus*) and nine twin births and three triplet births. *J. Marmoset Breeding Farm* (1975), pp. 1–11, 8 figs.

———. 1975*b*. Observations of feral and captive *Cebuella pygmaea* with comparisons to *Callithrix geoffroyi* and *Oedipomidas oedipus*. *J. Marmoset Breeding Farm* (1975), pp. 12–21.

Freese, Curtis. 1975. A census of non-human primates in Peru. Primate Censusing Studies in Peru and Colombia. Report to the National Academy of Sciences on the Activities of Project AMRO-0719, March 1975, pp. 17–41. Unpublished.

Gardner, Alfred. 1976. The distributional status of some Peruvian mammals. *Occ. Papers Mus. Zool. Louisiana St. U.* 48:1–18.

Green, Ken M. 1976. The nonhuman primate trade in Colombia. In *Neotropical Primates: Field studies and conservation,* ed. R. W. Thorington, Jr., and P. G. Heltne, pp. 85–98, 3 figs. Washington, D.C. : National Academy of Sciences.

Heberling, R. L.; Barker, S. T.; Kalter, S. S.; Smith, G. C.; and Helmke, R. J. 1977. Oncornavirus: Isolation from a squirrel monkey (*Saimiri sciureus*), lung culture. *Science* 195:289–92, 1 fig.

Hellekant, G.; Glaser, D.; Brouwer, J. N.; and van der Wel, H. 1976. Gustatory effects of miraculin and thaumatin in the *Saguinus midas tamarin* monkey studied with electrophysiological and behavioural techniques. *Acta Physiol. Scand.* 97:241–50, 5 figs.

Heltne, Paul; Freese, Curtis; and Whitesides, George. 1976. A field survey of nonhuman primate populations in Bolivia. Pan American Health Organization (Washington, D.C.), about 38 pages, 1 fig. Unpublished.

Heltne, Paul G.; Turner, Dennis C.; and Scott, Norman J., Jr. 1976. Censusing *Alouatta palliata, Ateles geoffroyi,* and *Cebus capucinus* in the Costa Rica dry forest. *Neotropical Primates: Field studies and conservation,* ed. R. W. Thorington, Jr., and P. G. Heltne, pp. 4–19, 1 fig. Washington, D.C.: National Academy of Sciences.

Hendricks, Larry G. 1977. Host range characteristics of the primate coccidian, *Isospora arctopitheci* Rodhain 1933. (Protozoa: Eimeriidae). *J. Parasit.* 63 (1):32–35.

Hernández Camacho, Jorge, and Cooper, Robert W. 1976. The nonhuman primates of Colombia. In *Neotropical Primates: Field studies and conservation,* ed. R. W. Thorington, Jr., and P. G. Heltne, pp. 35–69, 13 figs. Washington, D. C.: National Academy of Sciences.

Hilleman, M. R.; Provost, P. J.; Villarejos, V. M.; Buynak, E. B.; Miller, W. J.; Ittensohn, O. L.; Wolanski, B. S.; and McAleer, W. J. 1976. Infectious hepatitis (hepatitis A): Research in nonhuman primates. First Inter-american Conference on Conservation and Utilization of American Nonhuman Primates in Biomedical Research. *Pan-American Health Organization (Washington, D. C.), Sci. Publ.* 317:110–24.

Hodgen, Gary D., and Nieman, Wendell H. 1975. Application of the subhuman pregnancy test kit to pregnancy diagnosis in baboons. *Lab. Animal Sci.* 25:757–59.

Hodgen, Gary D.; Wolfe, Lauren G.; Ogden, James D.; Adams, Michael R.; Descalzi, Charles, C.; and Hildebrand, David D. 1976. Diagnosis of pregnancy in marmosets: Hemagglutination inhibition test and radioimmunoassay for urinary chorionic gonadotropin. *Lab. Animal Sci.* 26 (2, pt. 1):224–29, 1 fig.

Hofer, Helmut O. 1976. Preliminary study of the comparative anatomy of the external nose of South Amercan monkeys. *Folia Primat.* 25 (2–3):193–214, 9 figs.

Izawa, Kosei. 1976. Group sizes and composition of monkeys in the upper Amazon basin. *Primates* 17 (3):367–99, 6 figs.

Jollie, W. P.; Haar, J. L.; and Craig, S. S. 1975. Fine structural observation on hemopoiesis in the chorioallentoic placenta of the marmoset. *Amer. J. Anat.* 144 (1):9–38.

Kalter, S. S.; Kuntz, Robert E.; Heberling, R. L.; Smith, G. Con; Moore, Jerry A.; and McCullough, Bruce. 1977. Type C oncornaviruses in a capuchin (*Cebus apella*) previously infected with *Schistosoma haematobium*. *Lab. Animal Sci.* 27 (1):122–24, 2 figs.

King, G. 1976*a*. Feeding and nutrition of the Callitrichidae at the Jersey Zoological Park. *Jersey Wildlife Preservation Trust, Twelfth Annual Report (1975),* pp. 81–90.

———. 1976*b*. Parasite and post-mortem reports. *Jersey Wildlife Preservation Trust, Twelfth Annual Report (1975),* pp. 91–94.

King, Norval W., Jr. 1976. Synopsis of the pathology of New World monkeys. First Inter-American Conference on Conservation and Utilization of American Nonhuman Primates in Biomedical Research. *Pan American Health Organization (Washington, D.C.) Sci. Publ.* 317:169–98, 31 figs.

Klein, Lewis L.,and Klein, Dorothy J. 1976. Neotropical primates: Aspects of habitat usage, population density, and regional distribution in La Macarena, Colombia. In *Neotropical Primates: Field studies and conservation,* ed. R. W. Thorington, Jr., and P. G. Heltne, pp. 70–78, 3 figs. Washington, D.C.: National Academy of Sciences.

Krushak, D. H.; Maynard, J. E.; Bradley, D. W.; and Hornbeck, C. L. 1975. Hepatitis A in marmosets. *J. Med.Primat.* 4 (6):341.

Lewis, M. A.; Frye, L. D.; Gibbs, Jr., C. J.; Chou, S. M.; Cutchins, E. C.; Gajdusek, D. C.; and Ward, G. 1976. Isolation and characterization of two new herpeslike viruses from capuchin monkeys. *Infect. Immun.* 14: 759–66.

Luckett, W. P. 1976. Cladistic relationships among primate higher categories: Evidence of the fetal membranes and placenta. *Folia Primat.* 25:245–76.

Mallinson, Jeremy, J. C. 1976. A preliminary record of mammalian longevity at the Jersey Zoological Park. *Jersey Wildlife Preservation Trust, Twelfth Annual Report (1975),* pp. 48–52.

Maynard, J. E.; Krushak, D. H.; Bradley, D. W.; and Berquist, K. R. 1975. Infectivity studies of hepatitis A and B in non-human primates. Develop. Biol. Standard. 30:229–35.

Moody, M. L., and Menzel, F. W. 1976. Vocalizations and their behavioral contexts in the tamarin *Saguinus fuscicollis*. *Folia Primat.* 25 (2–3):73–94, 3 figs.

Moynihan, Martin. 1976*a*. Notes on the ecology and behavior of the pygmy marmoset (*Cebuella pygmaea*) in

Amazonian Colombia. In *Neotropical Primates: Field studies and conservation,* ed. R. W. Thorington Jr. and P. G. Heltne, pp. 79–84. Washington D.C.: National Academy of Sciences.

———. 1976*b*. *The New World Primates.* Princeton University Press, xi+ 1–262, 47 figs.

Muckenhirn, Nancy A.; Mortensen, B. Kim; Vessey, Stephen; Fraser, C. E. O.; and Singh, Balram. 1976. Report on a primate survey in Guyana July–October, 1975. Pan American Health Organization (Washington, D.C.). iii + 49 pp., 3 figs. Unpublished.

Neville, Melvin; Castro, Napoleón N.; Mármol, Andrés; and Revilla, Juán. 1976. Censusing primate populations in the reserved area of the Pacaya and Samiria Rivers, Department of Loreto, Peru. *Primates* 17 (2):151–81, 5 figs.

Perrotez, Chantal. 1974. Etude du caryotype du marmoset (*Callithrix jacchus*) avec les bandes R. *Experiment. Animale* 7 (4):173–80, 4 figs.

Phillips, I. R. 1976*a*. Skeletal development in fetal and neonatal marmoset (*Callithrix jacchus*). *Lab. Anim.* 10:317–33, 10 figs.

———. 1976*b*. The reproductive potential of the common cotton-eared marmoset (*Callithrix jacchus*) in captivity. *J. Med. Primat.* 5:49–55.

Pook, A. G. 1976. Breeding Goeldi's monkey (*Callimico goeldii*) at the Jersey Zoological Park. *Jersey Wildlife Preservation Trust, Twelfth Annual Report (1975),* pp. 17–20.

Rosenberger, A. L., and Kinzey, W. G. 1976. Functional patterns of molar occlusion in platyrrhine primates. *Amer. J. Phys. Anthrop.* 45:281–97.

Rossan, Richard N.; Baerg, David C.; and Young, Martin D. 1975. Five species of Panamanian monkeys as new experimental hosts for *Plasmodium simium. J. Parasit.* 61 (4):768–69.

Scott, N. J.; Struhsaker, T. T.; Glander, K.; and Chirivi, H. 1976. Primates and their habitats in northern Colombia with recommendations for future management and research. First Inter-American Conference on Conservation and Utilization of American Nonhuman Primates in Biomedical Research. *Pan American Health Organization (Washington, D.C.), Sci. Publ.* 317:30–50, 2 figs.

Seibold, H. R.; Perrin, Jr., E. A.; and Garner, Anna C. 1970. Pneumonia associated with *Bordella bronchoseptica* in *Callicebus* species Primates. *Lab. Animal Care* 20 (3):456–61, 4 figs.

Seiler, Rolf. 1976. Die Gesichtmuskeln. *Primatologia* 4 (6):i–vii+1–252, 148 figs.

Smith, Amos B.; Yarger, Ronald G.; and Epple, Gisella. 1976. The major volatile constituents of the marmoset (*Saguinus fuscicollis*) scent mark. *Tetrahedron Letters,* no. 13, pp. 983–86.

Stevenson, Miranda F. 1976. Birth and perinatal behaviour in family groups of the common marmoset (*Callithrix jacchus jacchus*), compared to other primates. *J. Human Evol.* 5:365–81, 3 figs.

Stevenson, Miranda F., and Poole, Trevor B. 1976. An ethogram of the common marmoset (*Callithrix jacchus jacchus*): General behavioural repertoire. *Animal Behav.* 24 (2):428–51, 7 figs., 6 pls.

Struhsaker, Thomas T.; Glander, Kenneth; Chirivi, Hernando; and Scott, Norman J. 1975. A survey of primates and their habitats in northern Colombia. May–August 1974. Primate Censusing Studies in Peru and Colombia. Report to the National Academy of Sciences on the Activities of Project AMRU-0719. Pan American Health Organization (Washington, D.C.), pp. 43–78, 2 maps. Unpublished.

Tantaleán, Manuel. 1976. Contribución al conocimiento de los helmintos de vertebrados del Peru. *Biota.* 10: 437–43.

Index

Index of Biotic Names

Subject Index

DATE DUE
GAYLORD